**Standard & Poor's
500 Guide**

D1288422

Standard & Poor's 500 Guide

2008 Edition

Standard & Poor's

Mc Graw Hill

New York   Chicago   San Francisco
Lisbon   London   Madrid   Mexico City
Milan   New Delhi   San Juan   Seoul
Singapore   Sydney   Toronto

FOR STANDARD & POOR'S
Vice President, Index Products & Services: Robert Barriera
Publisher: Frank LoVaglio

The **McGraw·Hill** Companies

1 2 3 4 5 6 7 8 9 0   CUS/CUS   0 9 8

ISBN-   978-0-07-159945-0
MHID-   0-07-159945-2

This book is printed on acid-free paper.

This publication is designed to provide accurate and authoritative
information in regard to the subject matter covered. It is sold with
the understanding that the publisher is not engaged in rendering
legal, accounting, or other professional service. If legal advice or
other expert assistance is required, the services of a competent professional person should be sought.
   —*From a declaration of principles jointly adopted by a committee of the American Bar Association and a committee of
   publishers*

The companies contained in this handbook represented the components of the
S&P 500 Index as of November 26, 2007.
Additions to or deletions from the Index will cause its composition to change
over time. Company additions and company deletions from the Standard &
Poor's equity indexes do not in any way reflect an opinion on the investment mer-
its of the company.

ABOUT THE AUTHOR

Standard & Poor's, a division of The McGraw-Hill Companies, Inc., is the nation's leading securities information company. It provides a broad range of financial services, including the respected Standard & Poor's ratings and stock rankings, advisory services, data guides, and the most closely watched and widely reported gauges of stock market activity—the S&P 500, S&P MidCap 400, S&P SmallCap 600, and the S&P Composite 1500 stock price indexes. Standard & Poor's products are marketed around the world and used extensively by financial professionals and individual investors.

Introduction

by Alan J. Miller, C.F.A.

While he was getting dressed one morning, Art Jones heard a news report on the radio saying that the Dow Jones Industrial Average had risen nine points on the previous day. Later he read in his morning newspaper that more stocks had declined than advanced. "How could that be?" he wondered. "Had the market gone up or down?"

Jenny Martin had been interviewing investment advisors to find someone to manage her stock portfolio and it seemed that everyone she spoke to claimed to have outperformed the market. That struck her as hard to believe and, in fact, all the managers she spoke to did seem to be comparing their results to different benchmarks. How could she tell how well those managers really had done?

"I think the market is really going to take off," Mark Johnson thought, "and I'd like to participate. But I'm afraid that even if I'm right, I could end up buying the wrong stocks and the ones I buy could go down while everything else goes up. I can't afford to diversify by buying 1,000 different companies. I just wish there were some way I could buy the whole market. Is there anything I can do?"

Mary Carter had a question for her accountant. "I'd like to invest in a few high-quality, well-established companies that are selling at reasonable prices," she said. "But with thousands and thousands of different companies around—including many that I just wouldn't be interested in because they're too new or too small—I just wouldn't know where to begin. Is there some way I could cut that number down to manageable size and know that the universe I'm looking at consists only of large capitalization, established companies?"

Andrew Perez is the marketing manager for a nationwide computer company whose products and services are used by many of the largest corporations in the country—and he's always on the lookout for even more customers. What he's really looking for are established companies that are in good financial shape and growing, so that they'll be responsive to his suggestions for upgrading their hardware, purchasing additional software, or engaging in more sophisticated networking—and will have the funds to carry out those plans if he convinces them of their value. But where can he find the names of those companies and the information about them which he requires?

Sally Kennedy is the founder and president of a small company in an industry dominated by a dozen or so major competitors. She'd really like to find out how well those larger companies in her industry are doing. Where can she look?

Six different questions, all leading to the same answer: Turn to the Standard & Poor's 500 Index.

What Is the S&P 500?

For sheer longevity, no other stock market indicators compare with the Dow Jones Industrial Average, which was first published in 1896, and the Standard & Poor's 500 Composite Stock Price Index, which was first introduced in 1923. Over the decades, both indicators have been consistently and widely cited as benchmarks of market performance.

Historically, the two indicators were viewed as complementary measures—but in recent years, the key differences between the DJIA and the S&P 500 Index have come into sharper focus. Today, sophisticated investors realize that the DJIA and the S&P 500 Index cannot be used interchangeably: based on different universes and methodologies, they provide very different pictures of market activity.

The DJIA tracks the stock performance of 30 "blue chip" companies, allowing equal weight to a one point move in each stock, notwithstanding substantial differences in stock prices and company capitalizations. As a result, a 5% move, say, in a $200 stock would have ten times the weight of a 5% move in a $20 stock and companies with larger equity capitalizations would not necessarily be weighted any more heavily than companies with smaller capitalizations. Despite these methodological shortcomings, the DJIA has generally been accepted as a reasonable indicator for the "blue chip" market but, because it contains nothing but "blue chip" stocks, by no stretch of the imagination could it be considered representative of the *overall* market.

The S&P 500, on the other hand, covers a far larger and more varied universe of companies, and hence is a more accurate barometer of the overall stock market.

Standard & Poor's 500 composite stock-price index is widely regarded as the most accurate proxy for the stock market and is used by virtually all professional consultants as the benchmark against which to measure money managers' performance. The index contains a representative sample of common stocks that trade on the New York Stock Exchange as well as on the Nasdaq Stock Market (those issues that are part of the Nasdaq National Market). Moreover, because the companies chosen for inclusion in the S&P 500 tend to be top companies in the United States, the S&P 500 Index became a component of the U.S. Department of Commerce's Index of Leading Economic Indicators in 1968. Now published by the Conference Board, a private research organization, that widely followed measure is used to signal potential turning points in the U.S. economy. Also, more than $1.3 trillion in passive index funds are currently indexed to the S&P 500.

As the name indicates, the S&P 500 consists of 500 U.S. companies, which represent about 77% of the total market value of American stocks. Although these are not necessarily the 500 largest companies in the United States, most of the largest companies are included. All of these stocks are widely held and the total market value of the "500" is over $13 trillion.

Approximately 85% (424 issues representing 86% of the market value) of the issues in the index are listed on the New York Stock Exchange. The remaining 15% (76 issues accounting for about 14% of the market value) are traded on the Nasdaq Stock Market.

But let's take another look at the half-dozen questions raised at the beginning of this introduction.

The Six Questions...Answered

1. Art Jones

If the Dow Jones Industrial Average rose nine points but more stocks declined than advanced, had the market really gone up or down?

In a sense, there really is no one answer to that question because it all depends on how you choose to define "the market." But in another sense, it is probably fair to say that the S&P 500 Index provides as good a picture of what the market "really" does as any index around. It is, after all, an average of 500 companies, not just 30, which makes it a better proxy for the overall market than the DJIA. And since, unlike advance-decline indices, the 500 stocks are *capitalization* weighted, it wouldn't be distorted by declines in a large number of small companies which might actually have been more than offset (in terms of total dollars gained or lost by investors) by increases in a smaller number of large companies. So if Art wants to know how the market "really" did, he ought to take a look at the S&P 500.

2. Jenny Martin

If all the investment advisors she talks to claim to have outperformed the market (by comparing their results to different benchmarks), how can she tell how well they've truly done?

Now this question turns out to be somewhat easier than it appeared to be at first blush. For if the S&P 500 really is the best proxy for the overall stock market, then an investment advisor who invests in common stocks can reasonably be measured by comparing his performance to that index. Of course, if the advisor invests only in international stocks, or small capitalization stocks, or long-term bonds, or some other mix of assets, a different benchmark would have to be developed to measure his performance fairly. But for the typical common stock manager, the best benchmark probably is the S&P 500.

3. Mark Johnson

How can he invest in the overall market without taking the risk of investing in the stocks of individual companies?

Consider the alternatives. First, Mark might just invest in an actively managed common stock mutual fund which is broadly diversified among hundreds of companies. If the diversification is broad enough, and if the securities owned are selected at random, the law of averages would suggest that the fund's results would approximate those of the overall market (as measured by the S&P 500).

Unfortunately, however, most funds *aren't* that diversified. They might own a couple of hundred stocks, but probably not 500. And for that reason alone, this approach might not work.

But there is another even more important reason why this approach would not work. It is because the portfolios of *actively managed* funds, by definition, are *not* randomized, but rather are consciously structured by their managers to reflect those managers' best judgments regarding the relative attractiveness of alternative investment vehicles. Thus, those managers *intentionally* overweight some companies (which the fund managers expect to be stellar performers) and underweight others (which they expect to fare relatively poorly).

Now, if the fund managers' judgments turn out to be right, terrific. But suppose they're not? In that case, the fund, despite its being broadly diversified, still may perform substantially worse than the market (as measured by the S&P 500). And remember, that risk—the chance of performing poorly as a result of picking the wrong stocks, even though the market on average did well—is precisely the risk that Mark is seeking to avoid.

No, selecting an *actively* managed fund *wouldn't* solve Mark's problem. But suppose Mark could invest in a *passively* managed fund—one whose managers simply tried to replicate the performance of the market as a whole, without trying to add value (and thereby running the risk of subtracting value instead) through individual stock selection. Would that satisfy Mark's need?

In fact, it would. And, fortunately for Mark, *passively* managed mutual funds which merely seek to replicate the performance of the S&P 500 Index (commonly known as index funds) abound. Indeed, these funds have grown in popularity (in large part because, strange as it may seem, stock market indices actually have tended to *outperform* a majority of mutual funds and pension plans actively managed by professionals). For those investors seeking intraday trading flexibility, exchange-traded funds (ETFs), such as Standard & Poor's Depository Receipts (SPDRs) and iShares, are listed securities representing a basket of equities that mirror the underlying index's performance.

But passively managed index funds and ETFs are not the only options open to Mark. He may make an even more direct bet on the direction of the market by investing in "stock index futures" themselves—or, if he is even more speculatively inclined, in *options* on stock index futures.

Stock index futures are, in effect, futures contracts on the value of the theoretical basket of securities which comprise a stock index. Indices on which futures contracts may be written include the New York Stock Exchange Composite Index (traded on the New York Futures Exchange), the Value Line Composite Index (traded on the Kansas City Board of Trade), and, of course, the Standard & Poor's 500 Index and Standard & Poor's MidCap 400 Index (both traded on the Chicago Mercantile Exchange). Since investors in such indices obviously can't deliver an index of stocks to a futures buyer, settlement of such contracts is in cash.

The Chicago Mercantile Exchange also trades options on Standard & Poor's 500 and MidCap 400 futures contracts. Exercise of one of those options establishes a position in the underlying futures contract. Options on the Standard & Poor's 500 Index are traded on the Chicago Board Options Exchange, and options on the Standard & Poor's MidCap 400 Index are traded on the American Stock Exchange. Unlike options on futures contracts, options on stock indices are settled in cash.

Of course, if Mark thought that the market was likely to decline rather than advance, but didn't want to incur the risk of going short the wrong stocks (those that might turn out to rise even in a falling market), trading in Standard & Poor's 500 Index futures contracts and options on those contracts could serve his purposes too. In that event, he would sell short futures contracts or call options on futures contracts or buy put options on futures contracts, rather than buying futures contracts or call options.

Finally, if Mark discovered a stock which he believed would outperform the market substantially but thought that the overall market itself was just as likely to decline as to rise, the futures contracts and options markets could help him too. In that event, he could buy the stock and short the market (by shorting futures contracts or calls on futures contracts on the S&P 500 Composite Index). If he turned out to be right and the stock did substantially outperform the market, he would do well whether the stock market itself rose or fell: if the stock market rose, the stock would rise even more (on a percentage basis), so he'd make more money on his long position in the stock than he would lose on his short positions in the futures or options markets. On the other hand, if the stock market declined, the stock would decline less (or maybe even rise) and he'd make more money on his short positions in futures contracts or options than he'd lose on the stock itself (or maybe, if he got really lucky, even make money on both).

4. Mary Carter

How can she find individual high-quality, well-established companies from which to select, for investment purposes, those that are selling at reasonable prices?

The components of the S&P 500 Composite Index are just what Mary is looking for. Indeed, the "average" S&P 500 company boasts a market value of $26.2 billion.

What Mary should do is to turn to the pages of this book, which include extensive data on all 500 companies in the S&P 500 Composite Index. But before doing so, she should be sure to read the final sections of this introduction—"What You'll Find in This Book" and "How to Use This Book to Select Investments"—in order to learn just how to extract the most value from that data.

5. Andrew Perez

How can Andrew find established companies that are in good financial shape, growing, and have the funds to acquire the hardware or software he'll be recommending to them?

The companies in the S&P 500 Composite Index should be Andrew's starting point, too, and the pages of this book are where he'll find the information on those companies which he requires. But before thumbing through these pages, Andrew, like Mary, would be well advised to refer first to the section titled "What You'll Find in This Book," which appears below.

6. Sally Kennedy

How can Sally find out how her major competitors, the larger companies in her industry, are doing?

You guessed it: A good place for Sally to start would be with the companies in this book. If Sally's industry is dominated by a number of large competitors, there is little doubt that most, if not all, will show up here. And here's where she's likely to find a lot of the information on those companies too.

But we're at the point now where we really must try to provide Mary, Andrew, and Sally with more guidance. Art, Jenny, and Mark, you will recall, were primarily concerned with using the Standard & Poor's 500

Composite Index in the aggregate, in order to find out how the market's "really" doing (Art), to measure investment managers' performance (Jenny), or to invest in the market as a whole or hedge individual stock positions (Mark). And we've explained all that.

Mary, Andrew, and Sally, however, are primarily interested in the *components* of the S&P 500, in their quest for companies which might represent good individual investments (Mary), or companies which could turn out to be good potential clients (Andrew), or companies which are important business competitors (Sally). And it is those individual companies which most of this book is about. So it's time to show Mary, Andrew, Sally—and you. . . .

What You'll Find in This Book

In the pages that follow you will find an array of text and statistical data on 500 different companies spanning 147 sub-industries. This information, dealing with everything from the nature of these companies' basic businesses, recent corporate developments, current outlooks, and select financial information relating to revenues, earnings, dividends, margins, capitalization, and so forth, might initially seem overwhelming. However, it's not that difficult. Just take a few moments to familiarize yourself with what you'll find on these pages.

Following is a glossary of terms and definitions used throughout this book. Please refer to this section as you encounter terms which need further clarification.

Glossary

S&P STARS -Since January 1, 1987, Standard & Poor's Equity Research Services has ranked a universe of common stocks based on a given stock's potential for future performance. Under proprietary STARS (STock Appreciation Ranking System), S&P equity analysts rank stocks according to their individual forecast of a stock's future total return potential versus the expected total return of a relevant benchmark (e.g., a regional index (S&P Asia 50 Index, S&P Europe 350 Index or S&P 500 Index)), based on a 12-month time horizon. STARS was designed to meet the needs of investors looking to put their investment decisions in perspective.

S&P 12-Month Target Price -The S&P equity analyst's projection of the market price a given security will command 12 months hence, based on a combination of intrinsic, relative, and private market valuation metrics.

Investment Style Classification - Characterizes the stock as either a growth- or value-oriented investment, and, indicates the market value (size) of the company as large-cap, mid-cap or small-cap. Growth stocks typically have a higher price-to-earnings and price-to-cash flow ratio, that represents the premium that is being paid for the expected higher growth. Value stocks typically have higher dividends and more moderate price-to-earnings ratios consistent with their current return policies.

Qualitative Risk Assessment - The S&P equity analyst's view of a given company's operational risk, or the risk of a firm's ability to continue as an ongoing concern. The Qualitative Risk Assessment is a relative ranking to the S&P U.S. STARS universe, and should be reflective of risk factors related to a company's operations, as opposed to risk and volatility measures associated with share prices.

Quantitative Evaluations - In contrast to our qualitative STARS recommendations, which are assigned by S&P analysts, the quantitative evaluations described below are derived from proprietary arithmetic models. These computer-driven evaluations may at times contradict an analyst's qualitative assessment of a stock. One primary reason for this is that different measures are used to determine each. For instance, when designating STARS, S&P analysts assess many factors that cannot be reflected in a model, such as risks and opportunities, management changes, recent competitive shifts, patent expiration, litigation risk, etc.

S&P Quality Rankings (also known as **S&P Earnings & Dividend Rankings**) - Growth and stability of earnings and dividends are deemed key elements in establishing S&P's Quality Rankings for common stocks, which are designed to capsulize the nature of this record in a single symbol. It should be noted, however, that the process also takes into consideration certain adjustments and modifications deemed desirable in establishing such rankings. The final score for each stock is measured against a scoring matrix determined by analysis of the scores of a large and representative sample of stocks. The range of scores in the array of this sample has been aligned with the following ladder of rankings:

A+	Highest	B-	Lower
A	High	C	Lowest
A-	Above Average	D	In Reorganization
B+	Average	NR	Not Ranked
B	Below Average		

S&P Fair Value Rank - Using S&P's exclusive proprietary quantitative model, stocks are ranked in one of five groups, ranging from Group 5, listing the most undervalued stocks, to Group 1, the most overvalued issues. Group 5 stocks are expected to generally outperform all others. A positive (+) or negative (-) Timing Index is placed next to the Fair Value ranking to further aid the selection process. A stock with a (+) added to the Fair Value Rank simply means that this stock has a somewhat better chance to outperform other stocks with the same Fair Value Rank. A stock with a (-) has a somewhat lesser chance to outperform other stocks with the same Fair Value Rank. The Fair Value rankings imply the following: 5-Stock is significantly undervalued; 4-Stock is moderately undervalued; 3-Stock is fairly valued; 2-Stock is modestly overvalued; 1-Stock is significantly overvalued.

S&P Fair Value Calculation - The price at which a stock should trade at, according to S&P's proprietary quantitative model that incorporates both actual and estimated variables (as opposed to only actual variables in the case of S&P Quality Ranking). Relying heavily on a company's actual return on equity, the S&P Fair Value model places a value on a security based on placing a formula-derived price-to-book multiple on a company's consensus earnings per share estimate.

Insider Activity - Gives an insight as to insider sentiment by showing whether directors, officers and key employees who have proprietary information not available to the general public, are buying or selling the company's stock during the most recent six months.

Investability Quotient (IQ) - The IQ is a measure of investment desirability. It serves as an indicator of potential medium-to-long term return and as a caution against downside risk. The measure takes into account variables such as technical indicators, earnings estimates, liquidity, financial ratios and selected S&P proprietary measures.

Volatility - Rates the volatility of the stock's price over the past year.

Technical Evaluation - In researching the past market history of prices and trading volume for each company, S&P's computer models apply special technical methods and formulas to identify and project price trends for the stock.

Relative Strength Rank - Shows, on a scale of 1 to 99, how the stock has performed versus all other companies in S&P's universe on a rolling 13-week basis.

Global Industry Classification Standard (GICS) - An industry classification standard, developed by Standard & Poor's in collaboration with Morgan Stanley Capital International (MSCI). GICS is currently comprised of 10 Sectors, 24 Industry Groups, 67 Industries, and 147 Sub-Industries.

S&P Core Earnings - Standard & Poor's Core Earnings is a uniform methodology for adjusting operating earnings by focusing on a company's after-tax earnings generated from its principal businesses. Included in the Standard & Poor's definition are employee stock option grant expenses, pension costs, restructuring charges from ongoing operations, write-downs of depreciable or amortizable operating assets, purchased research and development, M&A related expenses and unrealized gains/losses from hedging activities. Excluded from the definition are pension gains, impairment of goodwill charges, gains or losses from asset sales, reversal of prior-year charges and provision from litigation or insurance settlements.

S&P Issuer Credit Rating - A Standard & Poor's Issuer Credit Rating is a current opinion of an obligor's overall financial capacity (its creditworthiness) to pay its financial obligations. This opinion focuses on the obligor's capacity and willingness to meet its financial commitments as they come due. It does not apply to any specific financial obligation, as it does not take into account the nature of and provisions of the obligation, its standing in bankruptcy or liquidation, statutory preferences, or the legality and enforceability of the obligation. In addition, it does not take into account the creditworthiness of the guarantors, insurers, or other forms of credit enhancement on the obligation. The Issuer Credit Rating is not a recommendation to purchase, sell, or hold a financial obligation issued by an obligor, as it does not comment on market price or suitability for a particular investor. Issuer Credit Ratings are based on current information furnished by obligors or obtained by Standard & Poor's from other sources it considers reliable. Standard & Poor's does not perform an audit in connection with any Issuer Credit Rating and may, on occasion, rely on unaudited financial information. Issuer Credit Ratings may be changed, suspended, or withdrawn as a result of changes in, or unavailability of, such information, or based on other circumstances.

S&P Equity Research Services - Standard & Poor's Equity Research Services U.S. includes Standard & Poor's Investment Advisory Services LLC; Standard & Poor's Equity Research Services Europe includes Standard & Poor's LLC- London and Standard & Poor's AB (Sweden); Standard & Poor's Equity Research Services Asia includes Standard & Poor's LLC's offices in Hong Kong, Singapore and Tokyo, Standard & Poor's Malaysia Sdn Bhd, and Standard & Poor's Information Services (Australia) Pty Ltd.

Required Disclosures

S&P Global STARS Distribution
In the U.S.:
As of September 30, 2007, research analysts at Standard & Poor's Equity Research Services U.S. recommended 34.1% of issuers with buy recommendations, 57.6% with hold recommendations and 8.3% with sell recommendations.

In Europe:
As of September 30, 2007, research analysts at Standard & Poor's Equity Research Services Europe recommended 44.8% of issuers with buy recommendations, 36.0% with hold recommendations and 19.2% with sell recommendations.

In Asia:
As of September 30, 2007, research analysts at Standard & Poor's Equity Research Services Asia recommended 45.5% of issuers with buy recommendations, 46.8% with hold recommendations and 7.7% with sell recommendations.

Globally:
As of September 30, 2007, research analysts at Standard & Poor's Equity Research Services globally recommended 36.5% of issuers with buy recommendations, 53.7% with hold recommendations and 9.8% with sell recommendations.

5-STARS (**Strong Buy**): Total return is expected to outperform the total return of a relevant benchmark, by a wide margin over the coming 12 months, with shares rising in price on an absolute basis.

4-STARS (**Buy**): Total return is expected to outperform the total return of a relevant benchmark over the coming 12 months, with shares rising in price on an absolute basis.

3-STARS (Hold): Total return is expected to closely approximate the total return of a relevant benchmark over the coming 12 months, with shares generally rising in price on an absolute basis.

2-STARS (Sell): Total return is expected to underperform the total return of a relevant benchmark over the coming 12 months, and the share price not anticipated to show a gain.

1-STAR (Strong Sell): Total return is expected to underperform the total return of a relevant benchmark by a wide margin over the coming 12 months, with shares falling in price on an absolute basis.

Relevant benchmarks: In the U.S. the relevant benchmark is the S&P 500 Index, in Europe and in Asia, the relevant benchmarks are generally the S&P Europe 350 Index and the S&P Asia 50 Index.

For All Regions:
All of the views expressed in this research report accurately reflect the research analyst's personal views regarding any and all of the subject securities or issuers. No part of analyst compensation was, is, or will be directly or indirectly, related to the specific recommendations or views expressed in this research report.

Additional information is available upon request.

Other Disclosures

This report has been prepared and issued by Standard & Poor's and/or one of its affiliates. In the United States, research reports are prepared by Standard & Poor's Investment Advisory Services LLC ("SPIAS"). In the United States, research reports are issued by Standard & Poor's ("S&P"); in the United Kingdom by Standard & Poor's LLC ("S&P LLC"), which is authorized and regulated by the Financial Services Authority; in Hong Kong by Standard & Poor's LLC, which is regulated by the Hong Kong Securities Futures Commission; in Singapore by Standard & Poor's LLC, which is regulated by the Monetary Authority of Singapore; in Japan by Standard & Poor's LLC, which is regulated by the Kanto Financial Bureau; in Sweden by Standard & Poor's AB ("S&P AB"); in Malaysia by Standard & Poor's Malaysia Sdn Bhd ("S&PM"), which is regulated by the Securities Commission; in Australia by Standard & Poor's Information Services (Australia) Pty Ltd ("SPIS"), which is regulated by the Australian Securities & Investments Commission; and in Korea by SPIAS, which is also registered in Korea as a cross-border investment advisory company.

The research and analytical services performed by SPIAS, S&P LLC, S&P AB, S&PM, and SPIS are each conducted separately from any other analytical activity of Standard & Poor's.

Standard & Poor's or an affiliate may license certain intellectual property or provide pricing or other services to, or otherwise have a financial interest in, certain issuers of securities, including exchange-traded investments whose investment objective is to substantially replicate the returns of a proprietary Standard & Poor's index, such as the S&P 500. In cases where Standard & Poor's or an affiliate is paid fees that are tied to the amount of assets that are invested in the fund or the volume of trading activity in the fund, investment in the fund will generally result in Standard & Poor's or an affiliate earning compensation in addition to the subscription fees or other compensation for services rendered by Standard & Poor's. A reference to a particular investment or security by Standard & Poor's and/or one of its affiliates is not a recommendation to buy, sell, or hold such investment or security, nor is it considered to be investment advice.

Standard & Poor's and its affiliates provide a wide range of services to, or relating to, many organizations, including issuers of securities, investment advisers, broker-dealers, investment banks, other financial institutions and financial intermediaries, and accordingly may receive fees or other economic benefits from those organizations, including organizations whose securities or services they may recommend, rate, include in model portfolios, evaluate or otherwise address.

For a list of companies mentioned in this report with whom Standard & Poor's and/or one of its affiliates has had business relationships within the past year, please go to: http://www2.standardandpoors.com/portal/site/sp/en/us/page. article/2,5,1,0,1145719622102.html

Disclaimers

This material is based upon information that we consider to be reliable, but neither S&P nor its affiliates warrant its completeness, accuracy or adequacy and it should not be relied upon as such. With respect to reports issued by S&P LLC-Japan and in the case of inconsistencies between the English and Japanese version of a report, the English version prevails. Neither S&P LLC nor S&P guarantees the accuracy of the translation. Assumptions, opinions and estimates constitute our judgment as of the date of this material and are subject to change without notice. Neither S&P nor its affiliates are responsible for any errors or omissions or for results obtained from the use of this information. Past performance is not necessarily indicative of future results. This material is not intended as an offer or solicitation for the purchase or sale of any security or other financial instrument. Securities, financial instruments or strategies mentioned herein may not be suitable for all investors. Any opinions expressed herein are given in good faith, are subject to change without notice, and are only correct as of the stated date of their issue. Prices, values, or income from any securities or investments mentioned in this report may fall against the interests of the investor and the investor may get back less than the amount invested. Where an investment is described as being likely to yield income, please note that the amount of income that the investor will receive from such an investment may fluctuate. Where an investment or security is denominated in a different currency to the investor's currency of reference, changes in rates of exchange may have an adverse effect on the value, price or income of or from that investment to the investor. The information contained in this report does not constitute advice on the tax consequences of making any particular investment decision. This material is not intended for any specific investor and does not take into account your particular investment objectives, financial situations or needs and is not intended as a recommendation of particular securities, financial instruments or strategies to you. Before acting on any recommendation in this material, you should consider whether it is suitable for your particular circumstances and, if necessary, seek professional advice.

For residents of the U.K. - this report is only directed at and should only be relied on by persons outside of the United Kingdom or persons who are inside the United Kingdom and who have professional experience in matters relating to investments or who are high net worth persons, as defined in Article 19(5) or Article 49(2) (a) to (d) of the Financial Services and Markets Act 2000 (Financial Promotion) Order 2005, respectively.

For residents of Malaysia, all queries in relation to this report should be referred to Alexander Chia, Desmond Ch'ng, or Ching Wah Tam.

This investment analysis was prepared from the following sources: S&P MarketScope, S&P Compustat, S&P Industry Reports, I/B/E/S International, Inc.; Standard & Poor's, 55 Water St., New York, NY 10041.

Key Stock Statistics

Market Cap.—The stock price multiplied by number of shares outstanding, based on market value calculated at the issue level.

Institutional Holdings—Shows the percent of total common shares held by financial institutions. This information covers some 2,500 institutions and is compiled by Vickers Stock Research Corporation, 226 New York Avenue, Huntington, N.Y. 11743

Value of $10,000 Invested 5 years ago—The value today of a $10,000 investment in the stock made 5 years ago, assuming year-end reinvestment of dividends.

Beta—The beta coefficient is a measure of the volatility of a stock's price relative to the S&P 500 Index (a proxy for the overall market). An issue with a beta of 1.5 for example, tends to move 50% more than the overall market, in the same direction. An issue with a beta of 0.5 tends to move 50% less. If a stock moved exactly as the market moved, it would have a beta of 1.0. A stock with a negative beta tends to move in a direction opposite to that of the overall market.

Per Share Data ($) Tables

Cash Flow—Net income plus depreciation, depletion, and amortization, divided by shares used to calculate earnings per common share. (See also: "Cash Flow" under Industrial Companies.)

Earnings—The amount a company reports as having been earned for the year on its common stock based on generally accepted accounting standards. Earnings per share are presented on a *"diluted"* basis pursuant to FASB 128, which became effective December 15, 1997, and are generally reported from continuing operations, before extraordinary items. This reflects a change from previously reported *primary earnings per share.* Insurance companies report *operating earnings* before gains/losses on security transactions and *earnings* after such transactions.

Dividends—Generally total cash payments per share based on the ex-dividend dates over a 12-month period. May also be reported on a declared basis where this has been established to be a company's payout policy.

Net Asset Value—Appears on investment company reports and reflects the market value of stocks, bonds, and net cash divided by outstanding shares. The % difference indicates the percentage premium or discount of the market price over the net asset value.

Payout Ratio—Indicates the percentage of earnings paid out in dividends. It is calculated by dividing the annual dividend by the earnings. For insurance companies, *earnings* after gains/losses on security transactions are used.

P/E Ratio High/Low—The ratio of market price to earnings—essentially indicates the valuation investors place on a company's earnings. Obtained by dividing the annual earnings into the high and low market price for the year. For insurance companies, *operating earnings* before gains/losses on security transactions are used.

Portfolio Turnover—Appears on investment company reports and indicates percentage of total security purchases and sales for the year to overall investment assets. Primarily mirrors trading aggressiveness.

Prices High/Low—Shows the calendar year high and low of a stock's market price.

Tangible Book Value; Book Value (See also: "Common Equity" under Industrial Companies)—Indicates the theoretical dollar amount per common share one might expect to receive from a company's tangible "book" assets should liquidation take place. Generally, book value is determined by adding the stated value of the common stock, paid-in capital and retained earnings and then subtracting intangible assets (excess cost over equity of acquired companies, goodwill, and patents), preferred stock at liquidating value and unamortized debt discount. Divide that amount by the outstanding shares to get book value per common share.

Income/Balance Sheet Data Tables

Banks

Cash—Mainly vault cash, interest-bearing deposits placed with banks, reserves required by the Federal Reserve, and items in the process of collection—generally referred to as float.

Commercial Loans—Commercial, industrial, financial, agricultural loans and leases, gross.

Common Equity—Includes common/capital surplus, undivided profits, reserve for contingencies and other capital reserves.

Deposits—Primarily classified as either *demand* (payable at any time upon demand of depositor) or *time* (not payable within 30 days).

Deposits/Capital Funds—Average deposits divided by average capital funds. Capital funds include capital notes/debentures, other long-term debt, capital stock, surplus, and undivided profits. May be used as a "leverage" measure.

Earning Assets—Assets on which interest is earned.

Effective Tax Rate—Actual income tax expense divided by net before taxes.

Gains/Losses on Securities Transactions—Realized losses on sales of securities, usually bonds.

Government Securities—Includes United States Treasury securities and securities of other U.S. government agencies at book or carrying value. A bank's major "liquid asset."

Investment Securities—Federal, state, and local government bonds and other securities.

Loan Loss Provision—Amount charged to operating expenses to provide an adequate reserve to cover anticipated losses in the loan portfolio.

Loans—All domestic and foreign loans (excluding leases), less unearned discount and reserve for possible losses. Generally considered a bank's principal asset.

Long-Term Debt—Total borrowings for terms beyond one year including notes payable, mortgages, debentures, term loans, and capitalized lease obligations.

Money Market Assets—Interest-bearing interbank deposits, federal funds sold, trading account securities.

Net Before Taxes—Amount remaining after operating expenses are deducted from income, including gains or losses on security transactions.

Net Income—The final profit before dividends (common/preferred) from all sources after deduction of expenses, taxes, and fixed charges, but before any discontinued operations or extraordinary items.

Net Interest Income—Interest and dividend income, minus interest expense.

Net Interest Margin—A percentage computed by dividing net interest income, on a taxable equivalent basis, by average earning assets. Used as an analytical tool to measure profit margins from providing credit services.

Noninterest Income—Service fees, trading, and other income, excluding gains/losses on securities transactions.

Other Loans—Gross consumer, real estate and foreign loans.

% Equity to Assets—Average common equity divided by average total assets. Used as a measure of capital adequacy.

% Equity to Loans—Average common equity divided by average loans. Reflects the degree of equity coverage to loans outstanding.

% Expenses/Op. Revenues—Noninterest expense as a percentage of taxable equivalent net interest income plus noninterest income (before securities gains/losses). A measure of cost control.

% Loan Loss Reserve—Contra-account to loan assets, built through provisions for loan losses, which serves as a cushion for possible future loan charge-offs.

% Loans/Deposits—Proportion of loans funded by deposits. A measure of liquidity and an indication of bank's ability to write more loans.

% Return on Assets—Net income divided by average total assets. An analytical measure of asset-use efficiency and industry comparison.

% Return on Equity—Net income (minus preferred dividend requirements) divided by average common equity. Generally used to measure performance.

% Return on Revenues—Net income divided by gross revenues.

State and Municipal Securities—State and municipal securities owned at book value.

Taxable Equivalent Adjustment—Increase to render income from tax-exempt loans and securities comparable to fully taxed income.

Total Assets—Includes interest-earning financial instruments—principally commercial, real estate, consumer loans and leases; investment securities/ trading accounts; cash/money market investments; other owned assets.

Industrial Companies

Following data is based on Form 10K Annual Report data as filed with SEC.

Capital Expenditures—The sum of additions at cost to property, plant and equipment, and leaseholds, generally excluding amounts arising from acquisitions.

Cash—Includes all cash and government and other marketable securities.

Cash Flow—Net income (before extraordinary items and discontinued operations, and after preferred dividends) plus depreciation, depletion, and amortization.

Common Equity [See also "Tangible Book Value" under Per Share Data($) Tables]—Common stock plus capital surplus and retained earnings, less any difference between the carrying value and liquidating value of preferred stock.

Current Assets—Those assets expected to be realized in cash or used up in the production of revenue within one year.

Current Liabilities—Generally includes all debts/obligations falling due within one year.

Current Ratio—Current assets divided by current liabilities. A measure of liquidity.

Depreciation—Includes noncash charges for obsolescence, wear on property, current portion of capitalized expenses (intangibles), and depletion charges.

Effective Tax Rate—Actual income tax charges divided by net before taxes.

Interest Expense—Includes all interest expense on short/long-term debt, amortization of debt discount/premium, and deferred expenses (e.g., financing costs).

Long-Term Debt—Debts/obligations due after one year. Includes bonds, notes payable, mortgages, lease obligations, and industrial revenue bonds. Other long-term debt, when reported as a separate account, is excluded. This account generally includes pension and retirement benefits.

Net Before Taxes—Includes operating and nonoperating revenues (including extraordinary items not net of taxes), less all operating and nonoperating expenses, except income taxes and minority interest, but including equity in nonconsolidated subsidiaries.

Net Income—Profits derived from all sources after deduction of expenses, taxes, and fixed charges, but before any discontinued operations, extraordinary items, and dividends (preferred/common).

Operating Income—Net sales and operating revenues less cost of goods sold and operating expenses (including research and development, profit sharing, exploration and bad debt, but excluding depreciation and amortization).

% Long-Term Debt of Invested Capital—Long-term debt divided by total invested capital. Indicates how highly "leveraged" a business might be.

% Operating Income of Revenues—Net sales and operating revenues divided into operating income. Used as a measure of operating profitability.

% Net Income of Revenues—Net income divided by sales/operating revenues.

% Return on Assets—Net income divided by average total assets on a per common share basis. Used in industry analysis and as a measure of asset-use efficiency.

% Return on Equity—Net income less preferred dividend requirements divided by average common shareholders' equity on a per common share basis. Generally used to measure performance and industry comparisons.

Revenues—Net sales and other operating revenues. Includes franchise/leased department income for retailers, and royalties for publishers and oil and mining companies. Excludes excise taxes for tobacco, liquor, and oil companies.

Total Assets—Current assets plus net plant and other noncurrent assets (intangibles and deferred items).

Total Invested Capital—The sum of stockholders' equity plus long-term debt, capital lease obligations, deferred income taxes, investment credits, and minority interest.

Utilities

Capital Expenditures—Represents the amounts spent on capital improvements to plant and funds for construction programs.

Capitalization Ratios—Reflect the percentage of each type of debt/equity issues outstanding to total capitalization. % DEBT is obtained by dividing total debt by the sum of debt, preferred, common, paid-in capital and retained earnings. % PREFERRED is obtained by dividing the preferred stocks outstanding by total capitalization. % COMMON, divide the sum of common stocks, paid-in capital and retained earnings by total capitalization.

Construction Credits—Credits for interest charged to the cost of constructing new plant. A combination of allowance for equity funds used during construction and allowance for borrowed funds used during construction—credit.

Depreciation—Amounts charged to income to compensate for the decline in useful value of plant and equipment.

Effective Tax Rate—Actual income tax expense divided by the total of net income and actual income tax expense.

Fixed Charges Coverage—The number of times income before interest charges (operating income plus other income) after taxes covers total interest charges and preferred dividend requirements.

Gross Property—Includes utility plant at cost, plant work in progress, and nuclear fuel.

Long-Term Debt—Debt obligations due beyond one year from balance sheet date.

Maintenance—Amounts spent to keep plants in good operating condition.

Net Income—Amount of earnings for the year which is available for preferred and common dividend payments.

Net Property—Includes items in gross property less provision for depreciation.

Operating Revenues—Represents the amount billed to customers by the utility.

Operating Ratio—Ratio of operating costs to operating revenues or the proportion of revenues absorbed by expenses. Obtained by dividing operating expenses including depreciation, maintenance, and taxes by revenues.

% Earned on Net Property—Percentage obtained by dividing operating income by average net property for the year. A measure of plant efficiency.

% Return on Common Equity—Percentage obtained by dividing income available for common stock (net income less preferred dividend requirements) by average common equity.

% Return on Invested Capital—Percentage obtained by dividing income available for fixed charges by average total invested capital.

% Return on Revenues—Obtained by dividing net income for the year by revenues.

Total Capitalization—Combined sum of total common equity, preferred stock and long-term debt.

Total Invested Capital—Sum of total capitalization (common-preferred-debt), accumulated deferred income taxes, accumulated investment tax credits, minority interest, contingency reserves, and contributions in aid of construction.

Finally, at the very bottom of the right-hand page, you'll find general information about the company: its address and telephone number, the names of its senior executive officers and directors (usually including the name of the investor contact), and the state in which the company is incorporated.

How to Use This Book to Select Investments

And so, at last, we come to the $64,000 question: Given this vast array of data, how might a businesswoman seeking to find out about her competition, the marketing manager looking for clients, a job seeker, and the investor use it to best serve their respective purposes?

If you are like one of the first three of these individuals—a businesswoman, the marketing manager, or the job seeker—your task will be arduous, to be sure, but this book will provide you with an excellent starting point and your payoff can make it all worthwhile. You will have to go through this book page by page, looking for those companies that are in the industries in which you are interested, that are of the size and financial strength that appeal to you, that are located geographically in your territory or where you're willing to relocate, that have been profitable and growing, and so forth. And then you will have to read about just what's going on at those companies by referring to the appropriate "Highlights" and "Business Summary" comments in these reports.

Of course, this book won't do it *all* for you. It is, after all, just a starting point, not a conclusive summary of everything you might need to know. It is designed to educate, not to render advice or provide recommendations. But it will get you pointed in the right direction.

Finally, what about the investor who wants to use this book to find good individual investments from among the 500 stocks in the S&P 500 Index? If you fall into that category, what should you do?

Well, you can approach your quest the same way that the businesswoman looking for information about her competitors, the marketing manager, and the job seeker approached theirs—by thumbing through this book page by page, looking for companies with high historic growth rates, generous dividend payout policies, wide profit margins, A+ Standard & Poor's Quality Rankings, or whatever other characteristics you consider desirable in stocks in which you might invest. In this case, however, we have made your job just a little bit easier.

We have already prescreened the 500 companies in this book for several of the stock characteristics in which investors generally are most interested, including Standard & Poor's Quality Rankings, growth records, and dividend payment histories, and we're pleased to present on the next several pages lists of those companies which score highest on the bases of these criteria. So if you, like most investors, find these characteristics important in potential investments, you might want to turn first to the companies on these lists in your search for attractive investments.

Good luck and happy investment returns!

Companies With Five Consecutive Years of Earnings Increases

This table, compiled from a computer screen of the stocks in this handbook, shows companies that have recorded rising per-share earnings for five consecutive years, have a minimum 10% five-year EPS growth rate based on trailing 12-month earnings, have estimated 2007 EPS at least 10% above those reported for 2006, pay dividends, and have Standard & Poor's Quality Rankings of A– or better.

Company	Business	Fiscal Year End	5 Yr. EPS Growth Rate %	EPS $ 2006 Act.	EPS $ 2007 Est.	S&P Quality Rank	Price	P/E on 2007 Est.	% Yield
Amer Express	Travel & invest sv,insur,bk'g	Dec	10.46	2.99	3.50	A–	58.67	16.8	1.0
Amer Intl Group	Major int'l insur hldg co	Dec	19.75	5.35	6.35	A+	56.44	8.9	1.4
Dover Corp	Elevators:petrol eq:ind'l pr	Dec	26.90	2.74	3.18	A–	46.28	14.6	1.7
Franklin Resources	Mut'l fd inv advisory & svcs	Sep#	34.35	4.86	7.03	A–	118.95	16.9	0.5
Genl Dynamics	Armored/space launch vehicles	Dec	17.20	4.56	5.07	A+	89.75	17.7	1.2
Harman Intl	Audio video sys components	Jun#	24.11	3.75	4.72	A–	73.67	15.6	0.0
Illinois Tool Works	Fasteners,tools, plastic items	Dec	18.02	3.01	3.37	A+	54.45	16.2	2.0
Johnson & Johnson	Health care products	Dec	12.12	3.73	4.14	A+	67.75	16.4	2.4
Johnson Controls	Auto interior sys/bldg ctrls	Sep#	14.15	1.75	2.09	A+	38.11	18.2	1.3
L-3 Communications Hldgs	Communication systems/pds	Dec	19.16	4.22	5.90	A–	111.50	18.9	0.8
Nordstrom, Inc	Dept stores:upscale apparel	Jan+	46.43	2.55	2.85	A–	32.51	11.4	1.6
Northrop Grumman	Aerospace: aircraft:missile	Dec	21.54	4.37	5.11	A–	80.45	15.7	1.8
Omnicom Group	Major int'l advertising co	Dec	10.72	2.50	2.97	A+	47.00	15.8	1.2
Parker-Hannifin	Fluid pwr systems & comp	Jun#	33.24	3.71	4.67	A–	78.37	16.8	1.0
Sherwin-Williams	Large paint & varnish mfr	Dec	19.09	4.19	4.72	A	61.61	13.1	2.0
United Technologies	Aerospace,climate ctrl sys	Dec	13.82	3.71	4.24	A+	74.30	17.5	1.7
UnitedHealth Group	Manages health maint svcs	Dec	25.80	2.97	3.50	A+	53.42	15.3	0.0
Wal-Mart Stores	Operates discount stores	Jan+	10.64	2.71	3.16	A+	46.34	14.7	1.8
Walgreen Co	Major retail drug chain	Aug#	15.24	1.72	2.03	A+	39.97	19.7	0.9

+ Actual 2007 EPS & estimated 2008 EPS; P/E based on estimated 2008 EPS. #Actual 2007 EPS; P/E based on actual 2007 EPS.
Chart based on November 16, 2007 prices and data.
NOTE: All earnings estimates are Standard & Poor's projections.

S&P 500 STOCK SCREENS

Stocks With A+ Rankings

Based on the issues in this handbook, this screen shows stocks of all companies with Standard & Poor's Quality Rankings of A+.

Company	Business	Company	Business
Altria Group	Cigarettes,food prod,brew'g	Illinois Tool Works	Fasteners,tools, plastic items
Ambac Financial Group	Muni bond insurance co	Johnson & Johnson	Health care products
Amer Intl Group	Major int'l insur hldg co	Johnson Controls	Auto interior sys/bldg ctrls
Anheuser-Busch Cos	Largest U.S. brewer:baking	Kimco Realty	Real estate investment trust
Archer-Daniels-Midland	Process soybeans:flour mill'r	Lowe's Cos	Dstr bldg mtls: consum'r gds
Automatic Data Proc	Computer services	M&T Bank	Comm'l bkg,Buffalo,New York
Bear Stearns Cos	Investment bank'g,brokerage	McCormick & Co	Spices, flavoring, tea, mixes
C.H. Robinson Worldwide	Motor freight transportat'n	NIKE, Inc'B'	Athletic footwear
Capital One Financial	Bank card issuer/svcs	Omnicom Group	Major int'l advertising co
Cardinal Health	Wholesale dstr drug,hlth prod	Paychex Inc	Computer payroll acctg svcs
Carnival Corp	Cruise ships,hotel,casino	PepsiCo Inc	Soft drink:snack foods
Centex Corp	Home bldg,constr'n prd,S & L	Procter & Gamble	Hshld,personal care,food prod
Cintas Corp	Sales & rental of uniforms	Pulte Homes	Homebuilding/fin'l services
Citigroup Inc	Diversified financial svcs	Sigma-Aldrich	Specialty chem prod
Colgate-Palmolive	Household & personal care	SunTrust Banks	Comm'l bkg,Georgia,FL,Tenn
Commerce Bancorp	Commercial banking, New Jersey	Synovus Financial	Commercial bkg,Georgia
D.R.Horton	Single-family home constr'n	Sysco Corp	Food distr & service systems
Danaher Corp	Mfr hand tools,auto parts	TJX Companies	Off-price specialty stores
Expeditors Intl,Wash	Int'l air freight forward'g	Target Corp	Depart/disc/spec stores
Family Dollar Stores	Self-service retail stores	United Technologies	Aerospace,climate ctrl sys
First Horizon Natl	Comm'l bkg,Tennessee	UnitedHealth Group	Manages health maint svcs
Genl Dynamics	Armored/space launch vehicles	Wal-Mart Stores	Operates discount stores
Genl Electric	Consumer/ind'l prod,broad'cst	Walgreen Co	Major retail drug chain
Harley-Davidson	Manufactures motorcycles	Wrigley, (Wm) Jr	Major chewing gum producer
Home Depot	Bldg mtls,home improv strs		

Table based on November 16, 2007 prices and data.

S&P 500 STOCK SCREENS

Rapid Growth Stocks

The stocks listed below have shown strong and consistent earnings growth. Issues of rapidly growing companies tend to carry high price-earnings ratios and offer potential for substantial appreciation. At the same time, though, the stocks are subject to strong selling pressures should growth in earnings slow. Five-year earnings growth rates have been calculated for fiscal years 2002 through 2006 and the most current 12-month earnings.

Company	Business	S&P Quality Ranking	Fiscal Year End	— EPS $ — 2006 Act.	2007 Est.	5 Yr. EPS% Growth	Price	P/E on 2007 Est.	% Yield
Abercrombie & Fitch Co'A'	Retail casual apparel	B+	Jan+	4.59	5.30	23.49	75.01	14.2	0.9
Best Buy	Electronic/appliance stores	B+	Feb+	2.79	3.13	42.10	46.84	15.0	1.1
C.H. Robinson Worldwide	Motor freight transportat'n	A+	Dec	1.53	1.85	28.06	46.62	25.2	1.8
Cognizant Tech Solutions'	Computer software & svcs	B+	Dec	0.78	1.14	52.52	31.40	27.5	0.0
Coventry Health Care	Hlth benefit svcs/oper HMO's	B+	Dec	3.47	4.00	27.44	59.56	14.9	0.0
Disney (Walt) Co	Amusement parks: films, TV	B+	Sep	1.64	1.92	30.45	32.53	16.9	0.9
Express Scripts	Health care management svcs	B+	Dec	1.67	2.32	28.07	65.38	28.2	0.0
Franklin Resources	Mut'l fd inv advisory & svcs	A-	Sep#	4.86	7.03	34.35	118.95	16.9	0.5
Grainger (W.W.)	Natl dstr indus/comm'l prod	A-	Dec	4.24	4.98	15.63	88.39	17.7	1.5
Illinois Tool Works	Fasteners,tools, plastic items	A+	Dec	3.01	3.37	18.02	54.45	16.2	2.0
Johnson Controls	Auto interior sys/bldg ctrls	A+	Sep#	1.75	2.09	14.15	38.11	18.2	1.3
Laboratory Corp Amer Hldg	Clinical lab svcs in U.S.	B	Dec	3.24	4.15	15.36	69.72	16.8	0.0
Manitowoc Company	Mfr heavy-lift cranes:shipyd	B	Dec	1.33	2.50	101.77	39.82	15.9	0.2
Natl Oilwell Varco	Oil & gas ind equip/repair svc	B	Dec	1.94	3.77	53.05	64.44	17.1	0.0
Nordstrom, Inc	Dept stores:upscale apparel	A-	Jan+	2.55	2.85	46.43	32.51	11.4	1.6
Northern Trust	Comm'l bkg,Chicago, Ill.	A-	Dec	3.00	3.53	13.71	76.32	21.6	1.4
NVIDIA Corp	Computer software svcs	B	Jan+	0.77	1.30	51.07	32.45	25.0	0.0
T.Rowe Price Group	Advisor to mutual funds,dstr	A	Dec	1.90	2.34	25.48	64.70	27.6	1.0
Rockwell Collins	Aviation/communic elec tr'ns	NR	Sep#	2.73	3.45	22.74	72.10	20.9	0.8
Smith Intl	Varied line drill,boring eq	B+	Dec	2.49	3.20	49.81	62.05	19.4	0.6
Starbucks Corp	Retails high-quality coffees	B+	Sep#	0.73	0.87	27.06	23.17	26.6	0.0
Stryker Corp	Specialty medical devices	A	Dec	1.89	2.41	22.14	69.87	29.0	0.3
United Technologies	Aerospace,climate ctrl sys	A+	Dec	3.71	4.24	13.82	74.30	17.5	1.7
UnitedHealth Group	Manages health maint svcs	A+	Dec	2.97	3.50	25.80	53.42	15.3	0.0
Walgreen Co	Major retail drug chain	A+	Aug#	1.72	2.03	15.24	39.97	19.7	0.9
WellPoint Inc	Operate HMO svcs	NR	Dec	4.82	5.55	19.62	81.63	14.7	0.0
Zimmer Holdings	Dvlp reconstruction implants	NR	Dec	3.40	3.91	23.48	65.38	16.7	0.0

+ Actual 2007 EPS & estimated 2008 EPS; P/E based on estimated 2008 EPS. #Actual 2007 EPS; P/E based on actual 2007 EPS.
Chart based on November 16, 2007 prices and data.
NOTE: All earnings estimates are Standard & Poor's projections.

S&P 500 STOCK SCREENS

Fast-Rising Dividends

Based on the issues in this handbook, the companies below were chosen on the basis of their five-year annual growth rate in dividends from 2000 to the current 12-month indicated rate. All have increased their dividend payments each calendar year from 2002 to their current 12-month indicated rate.

Company	-- $ Divd. -- Paid 2002	Paid 2006	†Ind. Divd. Rate	* Divd. Growth Rate %	Price	% Yield
Ingersoll-Rand'A'	0.34	0.68	0.72	18.42	48.80	1.5
AFLAC Inc	0.23	0.55	0.82	26.84	60.66	1.4
Ambac Financial Group	0.38	0.66	0.84	16.95	27.46	3.1
Amer Intl Group	0.18	0.63	0.80	38.07	56.44	1.4
Apache Corp	0.19	0.45	0.60	26.99	99.40	0.6
Archer-Daniels-Midland	0.22	0.40	0.46	16.50	37.89	1.2
Automatic Data Proc	0.46	0.74	1.16	18.79	47.16	2.5
Bank of America	1.22	2.12	2.56	15.28	44.37	5.8
Bear Stearns Cos	0.62	1.12	1.28	15.46	99.07	1.3
Becton, Dickinson	0.39	0.86	0.98	22.44	83.48	1.2
Black & Decker Corp	0.48	1.52	1.68	31.16	84.55	2.0
Burlington Northn Santa Fe	0.48	0.85	1.28	20.66	85.82	1.5
C.H. Robinson Worldwide	0.12	0.38	0.88	44.07	46.62	1.9
Cardinal Health	0.10	0.30	0.48	37.94	58.54	0.8
Carnival Corp	0.42	1.03	1.60	31.73	44.91	3.6
Caterpillar Inc	0.70	1.10	1.44	15.60	69.44	2.1
Citigroup Inc	0.70	1.96	2.16	23.76	34.00	6.4
ConocoPhillips	0.74	1.44	1.64	18.57	78.93	2.1
Countrywide Financial	0.12	0.60	0.60	44.73	12.07	5.0
D.R.Horton	0.11	0.50	0.60	43.51	12.16	4.9
Danaher Corp	0.04	0.08	0.12	21.18	82.50	0.1
EOG Resources	0.08	0.22	0.36	34.86	85.28	0.4
Eaton Corp	0.88	1.48	1.72	15.08	87.38	2.0
Expeditors Intl,Wash	0.06	0.22	0.28	37.11	44.47	0.6
Federal Home Loan	0.88	1.91	2.00	19.26	40.72	4.9
Federated Investors 'B'	0.22	0.69	0.84	31.65	39.43	2.1
Harley-Davidson	0.14	0.81	1.20	56.29	47.88	2.5
Home Depot	0.21	0.68	0.90	34.39	29.07	3.1
Hudson City Bancorp	0.11	0.30	0.34	24.98	15.13	2.2
Illinois Tool Works	0.45	0.71	1.12	18.77	54.45	2.1
Intl Bus. Machines	0.59	1.10	1.60	21.33	104.79	1.5
Johnson & Johnson	0.80	1.46	1.66	15.99	67.75	2.5
Legg Mason Inc	0.27	0.75	0.96	29.97	71.73	1.3
Lehman Br Holdings	0.18	0.48	0.60	26.84	62.38	1.0
Lennar Corp'A'	0.03	0.64	0.64	81.20	19.24	3.3
Linear Technology Corp	0.19	0.60	0.72	32.16	31.33	2.3
Lockheed Martin	0.44	1.25	1.68	29.86	111.37	1.5
Lowe's Cos	0.04	0.16	0.32	49.58	25.01	1.3
M&T Bank	1.05	2.25	2.80	21.72	89.40	3.1
MBIA Inc	0.66	1.21	1.36	15.79	37.19	3.7

Company	-- $ Divd. -- Paid 2002	Paid 2006	†Ind. Divd. Rate	* Divd. Growth Rate %	Price	% Yield
Marathon Oil	0.46	0.77	0.96	16.17	57.51	1.7
Marriott Intl'A'	0.14	0.23	0.30	17.18	35.64	0.8
Mattel, Inc	0.05	0.65	0.75	53.95	19.86	3.8
McDonald's Corp	0.24	1.00	1.50	41.76	58.13	2.6
Medtronic, Inc	0.24	0.41	0.50	15.63	45.77	1.1
MetLife Inc	0.21	0.59	0.74	30.24	63.97	1.2
Monsanto Co	0.24	0.40	0.70	22.05	94.28	0.7
NIKE, Inc'B'	0.24	0.62	0.92	30.54	62.64	1.5
Noble Energy	0.08	0.28	0.48	44.51	71.73	0.7
Nordstrom, Inc	0.19	0.42	0.54	24.47	32.51	1.7
Norfolk Southern	0.26	0.68	1.04	30.92	50.44	2.1
Occidental Petroleum	0.50	0.76	1.00	15.25	68.50	1.5
Paychex Inc	0.44	0.69	1.20	20.11	39.98	3.0
Peabody Energy	0.10	0.24	0.24	21.82	52.41	0.5
PepsiCo Inc	0.59	1.12	1.50	20.99	74.15	2.0
Pfizer, Inc	0.52	0.96	1.16	17.13	23.39	5.0
Praxair Inc	0.38	1.00	1.20	26.68	82.41	1.5
T.Rowe Price Group	0.32	0.56	0.68	16.87	64.70	1.1
SLM Corp	0.28	0.97	1.00	25.39	39.05	2.6
Schwab(Charles)Corp	0.04	0.14	0.20	35.90	23.58	0.8
Sherwin-Williams	0.60	1.00	1.26	16.45	61.61	2.0
Sigma-Aldrich	0.17	0.42	0.46	19.20	51.02	0.9
Stryker Corp	0.05	0.11	0.22	31.10	69.87	0.3
Sunoco Inc	0.50	0.95	1.10	18.90	71.49	1.5
Sysco Corp	0.36	0.68	0.88	18.42	33.19	2.7
TJX Companies	0.11	0.27	0.36	26.31	29.34	1.2
Target Corp	0.24	0.44	0.56	18.69	53.88	1.0
Tiffany & Co	0.16	0.36	0.60	29.06	47.12	1.3
U.S. Bancorp	0.77	1.32	1.60	16.45	31.43	5.1
United Parcel'B'	0.76	1.47	1.68	17.78	72.01	2.3
United Technologies	0.49	1.02	1.28	21.35	74.30	1.7
VF Corp	0.97	1.94	2.32	19.94	76.97	3.0
Valero Energy	0.10	0.30	0.48	37.96	67.66	0.7
Wachovia Corp	1.00	2.14	2.56	20.30	39.14	6.5
Wal-Mart Stores	0.30	0.65	0.88	24.13	46.34	1.9
Walgreen Co	0.15	0.29	0.38	21.07	39.97	1.0
Washington Mutual	1.06	2.06	2.24	15.32	19.94	11.2
Wells Fargo	0.55	1.08	1.24	16.12	31.14	4.0
XTO Energy	0.02	0.30	0.60	113.02	63.58	0.9
Zions Bancorp	0.80	1.47	1.72	15.55	51.95	3.3

†12-month indicated rate.   *Five-year annual compounded growth rate.   Chart based on November 16, 2007 prices and data.

S&P 500 STOCK SCREENS

Stock Reports

In using the Stock Reports in this handbook, please pay particular attention to the dates attached to each evaluation, recommendation, or analysis section. Opinions rendered are as of that date and may change often. It is strongly suggested that before investing in any security you should obtain the current analysis on that issue.

To order the latest Standard & Poor's Stock Report on a company, for as little as $3.00 per report, please call:

S&P Reports On-Demand at 1-800-292-0808.

Abbott Laboratories

STANDARD &POOR'S

S&P Recommendation	**BUY** ★★★★☆	Price $55.49 (as of Nov 23, 2007)	12-Mo. Target Price $65.00	Investment Style Large-Cap Growth

GICS Sector Health Care
Sub-Industry Pharmaceuticals

Summary This diversified life science company is a leading maker of drugs, nutritional products, diabetes monitoring devices, and diagnostics.

Key Stock Statistics (Source S&P, Vickers, company reports)

52-Wk Range	$59.50– 46.22	S&P Oper. EPS 2007**E**	2.83	Market Capitalization(B)	$85.747	Beta	0.56
Trailing 12-Month EPS	$1.23	S&P Oper. EPS 2008**E**	3.28	Yield (%)	2.34	S&P 3-Yr. Proj. EPS CAGR(%)	15.00
Trailing 12-Month P/E	45.1	P/E on S&P Oper. EPS 2007**E**	19.6	Dividend Rate/Share	$1.30	S&P Credit Rating	AA
$10K Invested 5 Yrs Ago	NA	Common Shares Outstg. (M)	1,545.3	Institutional Ownership (%)	69		

Price Performance

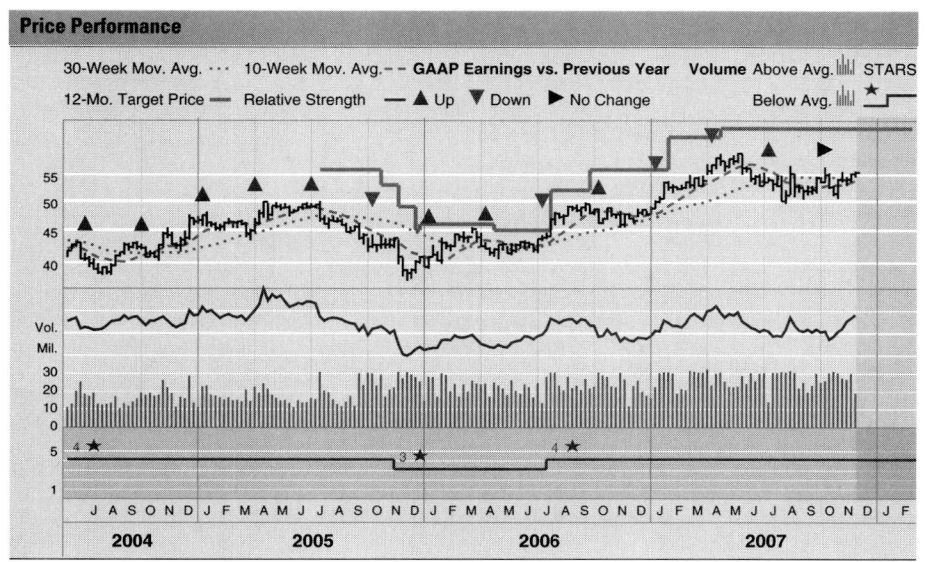

30-Week Mov. Avg. ··· 10-Week Mov. Avg. - - **GAAP Earnings vs. Previous Year** Volume Above Avg. STARS
12-Mo. Target Price — Relative Strength — ▲ Up ▼ Down ▶ No Change Below Avg.

Options: ASE, CBOE, P, Ph

Analysis prepared by **Robert M. Gold** on October 31, 2007, when the stock traded at **$ 54.64**.

Highlights

➤ We look for 2008 revenues of about $27 billion, up from a projected $25.4 billion in 2007, driven by continued strong demand for Humira in the treatment of autoimmune disorders, contributions from cholesterol-lowering pharmaceuticals, modest growth in diagnostics, and sharply higher sales in the vascular category on an expected U.S. launch of the Xience coronary stent.

➤ In July 2007, discussions to sell the majority of Abbott's in vitro diagnostics unit to General Electric (GE: buy, $40) were ended as the two parties could not come to a formal agreement over terms and conditions. However, we think ABT will continue to pursue a sale of this business, which generated 2006 revenues of $2.7 billion and operating profits of $205 million.

➤ We anticipate that gross and operating margins will continue to expand in 2008 and 2009 as the company realizes cost efficiencies resulting from the integration of recent acquisitions, and new products begin to contribute. We look for R&D spending to consume 9.5% to 10.0% of sales through 2009. Our operating EPS estimate for 2008 is $3.28, up from an estimated $2.83 in 2007.

Investment Rationale/Risk

➤ In our opinion, the shares are attractive at current levels, and we see potential catalysts on the horizon. We remain positive on both the short-term and long-term prospects for Humira, and we consider the drug to have an advantage over Enbrel in the dermatology space. During 2006, sales of Humira rose nearly 38% in the U.S., and 58% overseas (on a constant-currency basis). We think revenue growth in 2007 and 2008 will benefit further from increased sales in the vascular intervention area and expanded labeling for Humira, particularly in the treatment of Crohn's Disease and psoriasis.

➤ Risks to our recommendation and target price include lower than expected product sales (notably for Humira), new generic competition to Synthroid and Biaxin, and pipeline disappointments.

➤ We think ABT can generate annual EPS growth of 15% over the coming three years. Assuming ABT shares trade at a modest P/E to earnings growth premium to drug and device peers, which we believe is warranted by growth opportunities in the drug and interventional cardiology areas, our 12-month target price is $65.

Qualitative Risk Assessment

LOW	**MEDIUM**	HIGH

Our risk assessment reflects Abbott's operations in competitive markets and its exposure to the potential for generic competition. However, we believe the company has a relatively strong new product pipeline, with possible significant launches in both the medical device and pharmaceutical areas. In our opinion, the company is financially sound, with a strong balance sheet.

Quantitative Evaluations

S&P Quality Ranking   A-

D	C	B-	B	B+	**A-**	A	A+

Relative Strength Rank   STRONG

87

LOWEST = 1   HIGHEST = 99

Revenue/Earnings Data

Revenue (Million $)

	1Q	2Q	3Q	4Q	Year
2007	5,290	6,371	6,377	--	--
2006	5,183	5,501	5,574	6,218	22,476
2005	5,383	5,524	5,384	6,047	22,338
2004	4,641	4,703	4,682	5,654	19,680
2003	4,580	4,724	4,846	5,531	19,681
2002	4,189	4,315	4,342	4,839	17,685

Earnings Per Share ($)

2007	0.41	0.63	0.46	E0.92	E2.83
2006	0.56	0.40	0.46	-0.31	1.12
2005	0.53	0.56	0.44	0.63	2.16
2004	0.52	0.40	0.51	0.62	2.02
2003	0.51	0.16	0.48	0.60	1.75
2002	0.54	0.38	0.46	0.40	1.78

Fiscal year ended Dec. 31. Next earnings report expected: Late January. EPS Estimates based on S&P Operating Earnings; historical GAAP earnings are as reported.

Dividend Data (Dates: mm/dd Payment Date: mm/dd/yy)

Amount ($)	Date Decl.	Ex-Div. Date	Stk. of Record	Payment Date
0.295	12/08	01/10	01/12	02/15/07
0.325	02/16	04/11	04/13	05/15/07
0.325	06/14	07/11	07/13	08/15/07
0.325	09/14	10/11	10/15	11/15/07

Dividends have been paid since 1926. Source: Company reports.

Abbott Laboratories

STANDARD
&POOR'S

Business Summary October 31, 2007

CORPORATE OVERVIEW. Abbott Laboratories (ABT) is a leading player in several growing health care markets. Through acquisitions, product diversification and R&D programs, ABT offers a wide range of prescription pharmaceuticals, infant and adult nutritionals, diagnostics, and medical devices.

During 2006, pharmaceuticals accounted for 57% of operating revenues and 75% of operating profits. Nutritionals represented 20% of both sales and operating profits, while diagnostics contributed 18% and 7%, respectively. The vascular segment represented 5% of operating revenues and incurred an operating loss of $115 million during 2006.

ABT's Pharmaceutical Products Group markets a wide array of human therapeutics. Major products include: Humira to treat rheumatoid arthritis and psoriatic arthritis ($2.0 billion in 2006 sales, up 46% from 2005); Biaxin ($816 million, down 23%), a major class of a broad-spectrum antibiotic used for a wide variety of infections, including h-pylori (associated with duodenal ulcers); Depakote ($1.3 billion, up 19%), a leading antiepileptic and bipolar disorder drug; Kaletra, an antiHIV medication ($1.1 billion, up 13%); and cholesterol treatment TriCor ($1.0 billion, up 13%). In May 2005, the FDA approved oral Zemplar for secondary hyperparathyroidism in predialysis patients.

Nutritionals fall under U.S.-based Ross Products and Abbott Nutrition International. Products include leading infant formulas sold under the Similac and Isomil names, as well as adult nutritionals, such as Ensure and ProSure for patients with special dietary needs, including cancer and diabetes patients. ABT also markets enteral feeding items.

Abbott Diabetes Care markets the Precision and FreeStyle lines of hand-held glucose monitors for diabetes patients. This division also markets data management and point-of-care systems, insulin pumps and syringes, and Glucerna shakes and nutrition bars tailored for diabetics.

Abbott Vascular markets coronary and carotid stents, catheters and guide wires, and products used for surgical closure. In April 2006, Abbott acquired Guidant's vascular business from Boston Scientific for approximately $4.1 billion. Boston Scientific is also entitled to milestones if the Xience V stent is approved in the U.S. or Japan.

Company Financials Fiscal Year Ended Dec. 31

Per Share Data ($)	2006	2005	2004	2003	2002	2001	2000	1999	1998	1997
Tangible Book Value	NM	2.89	2.22	2.90	1.93	1.14	4.54	3.78	2.88	2.55
Cash Flow	2.13	3.02	2.84	2.56	2.52	1.74	2.31	2.10	2.02	1.81
Earnings	1.12	2.16	2.02	1.75	1.78	0.99	1.78	1.57	1.51	1.34
S&P Core Earnings	1.16	2.01	1.90	1.95	1.62	0.77	NA	NA	NA	NA
Dividends	1.16	1.09	1.03	0.97	0.92	0.82	0.74	0.66	0.58	0.52
Payout Ratio	104%	50%	51%	55%	51%	83%	42%	42%	39%	39%
Prices:High	49.87	50.00	47.63	47.15	58.00	57.17	56.25	53.31	50.06	34.88
Prices:Low	39.18	37.50	38.26	33.75	29.80	42.00	29.38	33.00	32.53	24.88
P/E Ratio:High	45	23	24	27	33	58	32	34	33	26
P/E Ratio:Low	35	17	19	19	17	42	16	21	22	19

Income Statement Analysis (Million $)										
Revenue	22,476	22,338	19,680	19,681	17,685	16,285	13,746	13,178	12,478	11,883
Operating Income	6,419	5,738	5,187	4,597	4,815	3,062	4,228	3,977	3,902	3,578
Depreciation	1,559	1,359	1,289	1,274	1,177	1,168	827	828	784	728
Interest Expense	416	241	200	146	239	307	114	81.8	160	135
Pretax Income	2,276	4,620	4,126	3,734	3,673	1,883	3,816	3,397	3,241	2,949
Effective Tax Rate	24.6%	27.0%	23.0%	26.3%	23.9%	17.7%	27.0%	28.0%	28.0%	29.0%
Net Income	1,717	3,372	3,176	2,753	2,794	1,550	2,786	2,446	2,333	2,094
S&P Core Earnings	1,787	3,158	2,972	2,971	2,561	1,233	NA	NA	NA	NA

Balance Sheet & Other Financial Data (Million $)										
Cash	521	2,894	1,226	995	704	657	914	608	383	230
Current Assets	11,282	11,386	10,734	10,290	9,122	8,419	7,376	6,420	5,553	5,038
Total Assets	36,178	29,141	28,767	26,715	24,259	23,296	15,283	14,471	13,216	12,061
Current Liabilities	11,951	7,416	6,826	7,640	7,002	7,927	4,298	4,517	4,962	5,034
Long Term Debt	7,010	4,572	4,788	3,452	4,274	4,335	1,076	1,337	1,340	938
Common Equity	14,054	14,415	14,326	13,072	10,665	9,059	8,571	7,428	5,714	4,999
Total Capital	21,064	19,570	19,334	16,525	14,939	13,395	9,647	9,046	7,163	6,074
Capital Expenditures	1,338	1,207	1,292	1,247	1,296	1,164	1,036	217	991	1,007
Cash Flow	3,276	4,731	4,465	4,027	3,971	2,718	3,613	3,274	3,117	2,822
Current Ratio	0.9	1.5	1.6	1.3	1.3	1.1	1.7	1.4	1.1	1.0
% Long Term Debt of Capitalization	33.3	23.4	24.8	20.9	28.6	32.4	11.2	14.8	18.7	15.4
% Net Income of Revenue	7.6	15.1	16.1	14.0	15.8	9.5	20.3	18.6	18.7	17.6
% Return on Assets	5.3	11.6	11.6	10.8	11.7	8.0	18.7	17.6	18.5	18.1
% Return on Equity	12.1	23.5	23.2	23.2	28.3	17.6	34.8	37.2	43.6	42.7

Data as orig reptd.; bef. results of disc opers/spec. items. Per share data adj. for stk. divs.; EPS diluted. E-Estimated. NA-Not Available. NM-Not Meaningful. NR-Not Ranked. UR-Under Review.

Office: 100 Abbott Park Road, Abbott Park, IL 60064-6400.
Telephone: 847-937-6100.
Website: http://www.abbott.com
Chrmn & CEO: M.D. White

Pres & COO: R.A. Gonzalez
EVP & CFO: T.C. Freyman
SVP, Secy & General Counsel: L.J. Schumacher
VP & Cntlr: G. Linder

Board Members: R. S. Austin, W. Daley, W. J. Farrell, H. L. Fuller, R. A. Gonzalez, J. M. Greenberg, D. Owen, B. Powell, Jr., W. A. Reynolds, R. S. Roberts, W. D. Smithburg, M. D. White
Founded: 1888
Domicile: Illinois
Employees: 66,663

The McGraw-Hill Companies

Abercrombie & Fitch Co.

STANDARD &POOR'S

S&P Recommendation	STRONG BUY ★★★★★	Price $76.06 (as of Nov 26, 2007)	12-Mo. Target Price $95.00	Investment Style Large-Cap Growth

GICS Sector Consumer Discretionary
Sub-Industry Apparel Retail

Summary This apparel retailer, which specializes in lifestyle branding, operates about 1000 retail apparel stores across four brands.

Key Stock Statistics (Source S&P, Vickers, company reports)

52-Wk Range	$85.77– 65.75	S&P Oper. EPS 2008E	5.20	Market Capitalization(B)	$6.592	Beta	0.94
Trailing 12-Month EPS	$4.97	S&P Oper. EPS 2009E	6.05	Yield (%)	0.92	S&P 3-Yr. Proj. EPS CAGR(%)	15.00
Trailing 12-Month P/E	15.3	P/E on S&P Oper. EPS 2008E	14.6	Dividend Rate/Share	$0.70	S&P Credit Rating	NA
$10K Invested 5 Yrs Ago	$33,857	Common Shares Outstg. (M)	86.7	Institutional Ownership (%)	97		

Price Performance

30-Week Mov. Avg. · · · 10-Week Mov. Avg. - - - **GAAP Earnings vs. Previous Year** Volume Above Avg. STARS
12-Mo. Target Price — Relative Strength — ▲ Up ▼ Down ► No Change Below Avg. ★

Options: ASE, CBOE, P, Ph

Analysis prepared by **Marie Driscoll, CFA** on November 26, 2007, when the stock traded at **$ 76.06**.

Highlights

➤ We see low single-digit same-store sales gains (comps) for FY 08 (Jan.), versus a 2% comp increase in FY 07 and a 26% gain in FY 06, driven by a modest increase in transactions per store and favorable pricing. Combined with an approximate 10% gain in square footage, we forecast sales growth of 15% for FY 08 and 13% in FY 09. Comps for the first nine months of FY 08 declined 1%, while direct sales rose 51%, to $150 million.

➤ We estimate a 20 basis point gross margin contraction, to 66.4%, in FY 08, with a modestly higher markdown in tandem with higher initial markups. We see store and distribution expense up 50 basis points, to 36.3% of sales, in tandem with a higher minimum wage, offset by a 90 basis point reduction in marketing, general and administrative expenses. We look for an operating margin expansion of 20 basis points in FY 08, followed by an other 10 basis point rise in FY 09.

➤ We estimate FY 08 and FY 09 operating EPS of $5.20 and $6.05, respectively.

Investment Rationale/Risk

➤ We see Hollister as ANF's major growth driver for boosting sales growth (up 36% in FY 07), although the "tween" abercrombie business produced a superior FY 07 same-store sales gain (10% versus 5%) and continues to achieve solid results. A fourth retail concept, RUEHL, targeting an older demographic, is in the early rollout phase, with about 15 stores, and a fifth concept is scheduled for an early 2008 introduction with seven stores. We see international expansion providing an incremental $1 billion opportunity.

➤ Risks to our recommendation and target price include negative same-store sales trends, and fashion and inventory risk. In terms of corporate governance, we are concerned about the presence of affiliated outsiders on the board.

➤ Our 12-month target price of $95 applies a 10% premium to the peer forward P/E of 14.2X to our FY 09 EPS estimate. The shares traded recently at about 13X our FY 09 EPS estimate, a 10% discount to the level of peers and a 5% discount to the S&P 500. We believe that as investors focus on ANF's brand-building strategies, superior operating metrics, and management acumen, the multiple will expand.

Qualitative Risk Assessment

LOW	MEDIUM	HIGH

Our risk assessment reflects our view of ANF's debt-free balance sheet and strong cash flow, offset by a consumer base whose tastes change constantly.

Quantitative Evaluations

S&P Quality Ranking B+

D	C	B-	B	B+	A-	A	A+

Relative Strength Rank STRONG

74

LOWEST = 1   HIGHEST = 99

Revenue/Earnings Data

Revenue (Million $)

	1Q	2Q	3Q	4Q	Year
2008	742.4	804.5	973.9	--	--
2007	657.3	658.7	863.5	1,139	3,318
2006	546.8	571.6	704.9	961.4	2,785
2005	411.9	401.4	520.7	687.3	2,021
2004	346.7	355.7	445.0	560.4	1,708
2003	312.8	329.2	419.3	534.5	1,596

Earnings Per Share ($)

	1Q	2Q	3Q	4Q	Year
2008	0.65	0.88	1.29	E2.40	E5.20
2007	0.62	0.72	1.11	2.14	4.59
2006	0.45	0.63	0.79	1.80	3.66
2005	0.30	0.44	0.42	1.15	2.28
2004	0.26	0.35	0.51	0.96	2.06
2003	0.23	0.31	0.48	0.93	1.94

Fiscal year ended Jan. 31. Next earnings report expected: Late February. EPS Estimates based on S&P Operating Earnings; historical GAAP earnings are as reported.

Dividend Data (Dates: mm/dd Payment Date: mm/dd/yy)

Amount ($)	Date Decl.	Ex-Div. Date	Stk. of Record	Payment Date
0.175	02/23	03/02	03/06	03/27/07
0.175	05/25	06/01	06/05	06/26/07
0.175	08/24	08/30	09/04	09/25/07
0.175	11/21	11/30	12/04	12/18/07

Dividends have been paid since 2004. Source: Company reports.

Abercrombie & Fitch Co.

Business Summary November 26, 2007

CORPORATE OVERVIEW. Abercrombie & Fitch, established in 1892, operates four branded retail concepts: Abercrombie & Fitch (360 stores as of February 2007), abercrombie (177), Hollister (393) and RUEHL (14), and e-commerce sites for the three larger retail concepts. Each targets a different age demographic and all employ casual luxury positioning. Hollister targets 14 to 17 year old high school boys and girls at lower price points than traditional A&F stores, thereby minimizing cannibalization between brands.

MARKET PROFILE. The company participates in the specialty apparel retail market targeted at youth, spanning the tween to young adult demographic. While the U.S. apparel market is considered mature, with demand mirroring population growth and a modicum related to fashion, the youth marketplace is generally considered attractive based on its spending clout. According to NPD consumer data, collectively, this group accounts for approximately 35% of total apparel spending, with the "sweet spot" being teenagers, who represent about 20%.

COMPETITIVE LANDSCAPE. The retail landscape is consolidating, with share accruing to the mass merchants and specialty chains while the traditional department store is losing ground. Specialty chains compete on customer

knowledge garnered from daily interactions, focus groups and marketing intelligence, and this knowledge is often combined with high customer service levels to result in an attractive price/value equation for the consumer. ANF's target demographic is attracted to strong brands, as well as fashion and value, when determining apparel selections. While the specialty channel holds the largest share of the apparel market, S&P estimates that the sub-segment serving the youth demographic represents about 3% of total retail sales. With barriers to entry minimal (capital investment in merchandise, rent and labor expense) and potential returns on investment high and quick (four wall return on investment exceed 40% in 12 months for many specialty retailers), there is a steady flow of new industry participants. In addition to competing with other apparel retailers, regardless of channel, for the youth's discretionary spending, ANF competes with merchandise and services, especially consumer electronics and entertainment services.

Company Financials Fiscal Year Ended Jan. 31

Per Share Data ($)	2007	2006	2005	2004	2003	2002	2001	2000	1999	1998
Tangible Book Value	19.17	11.34	7.78	9.21	7.71	6.02	4.28	3.05	1.83	0.58
Cash Flow	6.18	5.02	3.39	2.73	2.50	2.05	1.85	1.65	1.16	0.63
Earnings	4.59	3.66	2.28	2.06	1.94	1.65	1.55	1.39	0.96	0.47
S&P Core Earnings	4.59	3.38	2.32	1.81	1.70	1.45	1.35	NA	NA	NA
Dividends	0.60	0.50	0.50	Nil	Nil	Nil	Nil	Nil	Nil	Nil
Payout Ratio	13%	14%	22%	Nil	Nil	Nil	Nil	Nil	Nil	Nil
Calendar Year	2006	2005	2004	2003	2002	2001	2000	1999	1998	1997
Prices:High	79.42	74.10	47.45	33.65	33.85	47.50	31.31	50.75	36.13	18.06
Prices:Low	49.98	44.17	23.07	20.65	14.97	16.21	8.00	21.00	14.44	6.25
P/E Ratio:High	17	20	21	16	17	29	20	37	38	38
P/E Ratio:Low	11	12	10	10	8	10	5	15	15	13

Income Statement Analysis (Million $)	2007	2006	2005	2004	2003	2002	2001	2000	1999	1998
Revenue	3,318	2,785	2,021	1,708	1,596	1,365	1,238	1,042	816	522
Operating Income	794	661	453	398	370	313	284	270	188	100
Depreciation	146	124	106	66.6	56.9	41.2	30.7	27.7	20.9	16.3
Interest Expense	Nil	Nil	Nil	Nil	Nil	Nil	Nil	Nil	Nil	3.58
Pretax Income	672	549	353	335	316	277	261	249	170	80.5
Effective Tax Rate	37.2%	39.2%	38.7%	38.8%	38.4%	39.0%	39.5%	40.0%	40.0%	40.0%
Net Income	422	334	216	205	195	169	158	150	102	48.3
S&P Core Earnings	422	312	220	180	170	148	138	NA	NA	NA

Balance Sheet & Other Financial Data (Million $)	2007	2006	2005	2004	2003	2002	2001	2000	1999	1998
Cash	530	462	350	521	401	239	138	194	164	42.7
Current Assets	1,092	947	652	753	601	405	304	300	218	109
Total Assets	2,248	1,790	1,348	1,199	995	771	588	458	319	183
Current Liabilities	511	492	414	280	211	164	155	138	122	67.0
Long Term Debt	Nil	Nil	Nil	Nil	Nil	Nil	Nil	Nil	Nil	50.0
Common Equity	1,405	995	669	871	750	595	423	311	186	58.8
Total Capital	1,436	1,034	725	891	770	597	423	311	186	109
Capital Expenditures	403	256	185	99.1	93.0	127	153	83.8	41.9	29.5
Cash Flow	568	458	322	272	252	210	189	177	123	64.7
Current Ratio	2.1	1.9	1.6	2.7	2.8	2.5	2.0	2.2	1.8	1.6
% Long Term Debt of Capitalization	Nil	Nil	Nil	Nil	Nil	Nil	Nil	Nil	Nil	46.0
% Net Income of Revenue	12.7	12.0	10.7	12.0	12.2	12.4	12.8	14.4	12.5	9.3
% Return on Assets	20.9	21.0	15.8	18.5	22.1	24.8	30.2	38.5	40.6	33.4
% Return on Equity	35.2	40.1	28.3	25.3	29.0	33.1	43.1	60.2	83.4	138.0

Data as orig reptd.; bef. results of disc opers/spec. items. Per share data adj. for stk. divs.; EPS diluted. E-Estimated. NA-Not Available. NM-Not Meaningful. NR-Not Ranked. UR-Under Review.

Office: 6301 Fitch Path, New Albany, OH 43054.
Telephone: 614-283-6500.
Email: investor_relations@abercrombie.com
Website: http://www.abercrombie.com

Chrmn & CEO: M.S. Jeffries
EVP & CFO: M.W. Kramer
Investor Contact: T.D. Lennox (614-283-6751)

Board Members: J. B. Bachmann, D. J. Brestle, L. J. Brisky, R. M. Gertmenian, J. A. Golden, A. M. Griffin, M. S. Jeffries, J. W. Kessler, E. F. Limato, A. A. Tuttle

Founded: 1892
Domicile: Delaware
Employees: 86,400

ACE Ltd

STANDARD &POOR'S

S&P Recommendation BUY ★★★★☆

Price	12-Mo. Target Price	Investment Style
$58.78 (as of Nov 23, 2007)	$70.00	Large-Cap Blend

GICS Sector Financials
Sub-Industry Property & Casualty Insurance

Summary This Bermuda-based Cayman Islands company provides commercial insurance and reinsurance for a diverse group of international clients.

Key Stock Statistics (Source S&P, Vickers, company reports)

52-Wk Range	$64.32– 52.79	S&P Oper. EPS 2007E	7.75	Market Capitalization(B)	$19.339	Beta	1.31
Trailing 12-Month EPS	$7.96	S&P Oper. EPS 2008E	7.40	Yield (%)	1.84	S&P 3-Yr. Proj. EPS CAGR(%)	NA
Trailing 12-Month P/E	7.4	P/E on S&P Oper. EPS 2007E	7.6	Dividend Rate/Share	$1.08	S&P Credit Rating	BBB+
$10K Invested 5 Yrs Ago	$19,058	Common Shares Outstg. (M)	329.0	Institutional Ownership (%)	92		

Price Performance

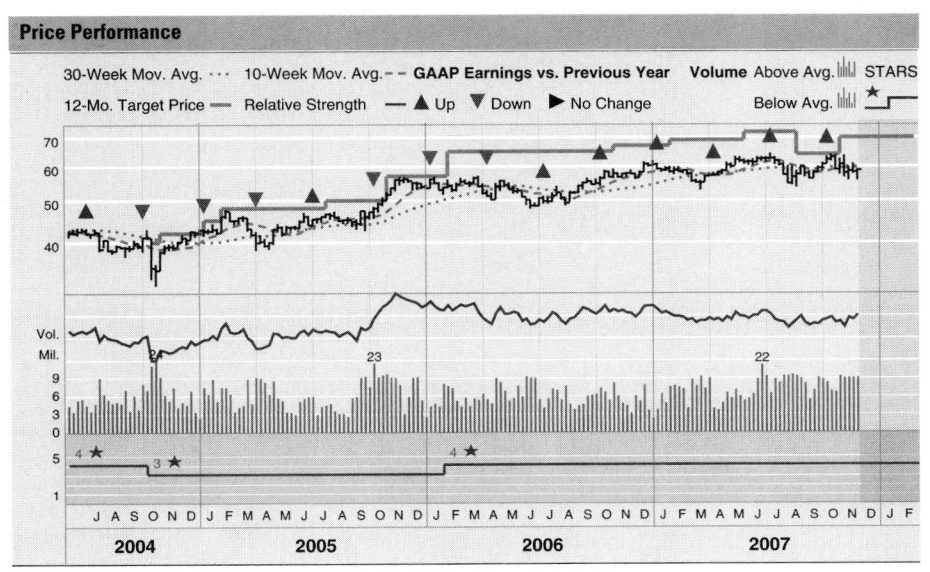

30-Week Mov. Avg. ···   10-Week Mov. Avg. - - -   **GAAP Earnings vs. Previous Year**   Volume Above Avg.▮▮▮ STARS
12-Mo. Target Price —   Relative Strength —   ▲ Up ▼ Down ► No Change   Below Avg.▮▮▮ ★▁

Options: ASE, CBOE, P, Ph

Analysis prepared by **Cathy A. Seifert** on November 13, 2007, when the stock traded at **$ 59.21**.

Highlights

➤ We estimate earned premium growth of less than 2% in 2008, versus growth of 4% to 6% we forecast for 2007. Competitive pricing pressures are being partly offset by the impact of a weaker U.S. dollar (versus most foreign currencies) on business written outside the U.S. Net written premiums were down fractionally, year to year, in the first nine months of 2007, as a 6% rise in business written overseas was offset by fractionally lower U.S. insurance premiums and a 21% drop in reinsurance premiums.

➤ We expect underwriting margins in 2008 to contract slightly from 2007 levels, amid a projected lower level of favorable loss development. Underwriting margins in the first nine months of 2007 benefited from favorable prior-year loss development, partly offset by higher catastrophe claims. As a result, the combined loss/expense ratio totaled 87.8% in the 2007 period, versus 88.1% in the 2006 interim.

➤ We anticipate a decline in operating EPS in 2008, to $7.40, from the $7.75 of operating EPS we forecast for 2007. Our forecast assumes underwriting results deteriorate slightly amid competitive pricing pressures and less favorable claim trends.

Investment Rationale/Risk

➤ Our buy recommendation reflects our view that the shares are undervalued versus peers, both on a price/book and price/earnings basis. Our view is tempered somewhat by a competitive pricing environment for casualty insurance. However, we believe ACE is well positioned to exploit opportunities for growth in certain specialty lines of coverage. We also note that ACE's subprime mortgage investment exposure is $272 million (less than 1% of the investment portfolio at September 30, 2007).

➤ Risks to our opinion and target price include a deterioration in claim trends and reserve levels; a deterioration in the credit quality of ACE's investment portfolio; and disclosure of any new developments or ACE's possibly greater-than-expected involvement in certain regulatory investigations.

➤ Our 12-month target price of $70 assumes the shares will trade at a P/E multiple of 9.5X our 2008 operating EPS estimate, a discount of about 15% to the property-casualty peer group average. Our target price also assumes the shares will trade at nearly 1.8X estimated 2008 tangible book value, about in line with the peer group average.

Qualitative Risk Assessment

LOW	MEDIUM	HIGH

Our risk assessment reflects our view of ACE as an opportunistic underwriter, offset by the company's exposure to catastrophe claims and concerns we have over reserve levels in certain lines of business and over the potential that credit quality in ACE's fixed income investment portfolio could deteriorate.

Quantitative Evaluations

S&P Quality Ranking   B

D	C	B-	B	B+	A-	A	A+

Relative Strength Rank   STRONG

73

LOWEST = 1   HIGHEST = 99

Revenue/Earnings Data

Revenue (Million $)

	1Q	2Q	3Q	4Q	Year
2007	3,549	3,468	3,642	--	--
2006	3,181	3,289	3,389	3,469	13,328
2005	3,148	3,258	3,494	3,188	13,088
2004	2,887	3,067	3,073	3,293	12,320
2003	2,256	2,710	2,690	3,236	10,892
2002	--	--	--	--	7,227

Earnings Per Share ($)

2007	2.10	1.93	1.95	E1.73	E7.75
2006	1.45	1.72	1.73	1.99	6.90
2005	1.48	1.58	-0.43	0.69	3.31
2004	1.53	1.44	-0.03	0.93	3.88
2003	0.96	1.42	1.21	1.61	5.25
2002	--	--	--	--	0.27

Fiscal year ended Dec. 31. Next earnings report expected: Late January. EPS Estimates based on S&P Operating Earnings; historical GAAP earnings are as reported.

Dividend Data (Dates: mm/dd Payment Date: mm/dd/yy)

Amount ($)	Date Decl.	Ex-Div. Date	Stk. of Record	Payment Date
0.250	02/28	03/28	03/30	04/13/07
0.270	05/17	06/27	06/29	07/13/07
0.270	08/17	09/26	09/30	10/12/07
0.270	11/16	12/27	12/31	01/11/08

Dividends have been paid since 1993. Source: Company reports.

ACE Ltd

STANDARD &POOR'S

Business Summary November 13, 2007

ACE Ltd. underwrites an array of insurance and reinsurance; and also provides funds to support underwriting capacity for Lloyd's syndicates managed by Lloyd's managing agencies. Net earned premiums totaled $11.8 billion in 2006 (up fractionally from $11.7 billion in 2005), with North American Insurance operations accounting for 48%, Overseas General Insurance for 37%, Global Reinsurance for 13%, and Financial Services and Life Insurance and Reinsurance for 2%. Underwriting results improved in 2006 amid a decline in catastrophe claims, and the combined ratio ended 2006 at 88.1%, versus 99.5% in 2005. The driver of these improved results was the loss ratio, which improved to 61.2% in 2006 from 74.5% in 2005. The expense ratio inched upward in 2006, to 26.9% from 25.0% in 2005.

Insurance - North America provides property and casualty insurance and reinsurance coverage, including excess liability, professional lines, satellite, excess property and political risk, to a diverse group of industrial, commercial and other enterprises.

Insurance - Overseas General includes the operations of ACE International, which provides property and casualty insurance, accident and health insurance and consumer-oriented products to individuals, mid-sized firms and large commercial clients. It also provides customized and comprehensive insurance policies and services to multinational companies and their cross-border subsidiaries. In addition, the segment includes the insurance operations of ACE Global Markets, which mainly encompasses operations in the Lloyd's market.

Global Reinsurance includes the operations of ACE Tempest Re and several other subsidiaries that mainly provide property catastrophe reinsurance worldwide to insurers of commercial and personal property.

Life Insurance and Reinsurance includes the operations of ACE Tempest Re and ACE International Life. This unit offers traditional life reinsurance products, and an array of other reinsurance products aimed at helping life insurance companies manage their mortality, morbidity, lapse, and/or capital market risks. ACE International Life offers individual life insurance and savings products in Thailand, Vietnam, Taiwan, China and Egypt. On April 28, 2004, ACE sold approximately 65% of Assured Guaranty Ltd. in an initial public offering that netted ACE about $835 million.

Company Financials Fiscal Year Ended Dec. 31

Per Share Data ($)	2006	2005	2004	2003	2002	2001	2000	1999	1998	1997
Tangible Book Value	35.37	28.17	25.11	21.52	13.20	12.13	10.35	7.49	16.40	14.60
Operating Earnings	NA	NA	NA	NA	NA	NA	NA	1.63	1.96	1.93
Earnings	6.90	3.31	3.88	5.25	0.27	-0.88	2.19	1.85	2.96	2.67
Dividends	0.98	0.90	0.82	0.74	0.66	0.58	0.48	0.40	0.50	0.27
Payout Ratio	14%	27%	21%	14%	NM	NM	22%	22%	17%	10%
Prices:High	61.90	56.85	45.98	42.80	44.98	43.19	43.94	35.25	43.00	33.69
Prices:Low	47.81	38.36	31.80	23.59	22.01	18.10	14.06	15.50	24.38	18.71
P/E Ratio:High	9	17	NM	NM	NM	NM	NM	19	15	13
P/E Ratio:Low	7	12	NM	NM	NM	NM	NM	8	8	7

Income Statement Analysis (Million $)										
Premium Income	11,825	11,748	11,110	9,727	6,905	6,039	4,539	2,486	894	645
Net Investment Income	1,601	1,264	1,013	901	812	803	781	493	325	238
Other Revenue	-98.0	76.0	198	265	-489	-58.0	-39.0	38.0	188	128
Total Revenue	13,328	13,088	12,320	10,892	7,227	6,784	5,281	3,017	1,407	1,011
Pretax Income	2,831	1,317	1,439	1,794	-11.7	-247	598	394	580	NA
Net Operating Income	NA	NA	NA	NA	NA	NA	NA	323	372	333
Net Income	2,301	1,028	1,153	1,482	100	-158	517	365	560	461

Balance Sheet & Other Financial Data (Million $)										
Cash & Equivalent	4,267	850	807	817	NA	NA	NA	771	318	147
Premiums Due	14,580	3,343	3,255	2,823	2,654	NA	NA	2,019	377	136
Investment Assets:Bonds	31,587	27,361	22,891	19,312	NA	NA	NA	9,850	5,057	3,290
Investment Assets:Stocks	1,713	1,507	1,266	562	NA	NA	NA	933	190	635
Investment Assets:Loans	Nil	Nil	Nil	Nil	NA	NA	NA	Nil	Nil	Nil
Investment Assets:Total	39,561	34,521	26,925	22,555	17,555	15,197	13,064	12,276	5,883	4,475
Deferred Policy Costs	1,077	930	944	1,005	832	679	573	514	76.4	NA
Total Assets	67,135	62,440	56,183	49,317	43,874	37,186	31,837	30,123	8,789	5,002
Debt	2,447	2,120	2,261	1,824	2,224	2,224	2,299	1,999	250	Nil
Common Equity	14,276	11,810	9,843	8,821	6,269	6,010	5,358	4,450	3,714	2,619
Property & Casualty:Loss Ratio	52.3	74.5	70.6	64.6	73.7	83.9	65.6	66.0	57.8	60.4
Property & Casualty:Expense Ratio	33.9	25.1	25.8	26.4	27.5	28.5	30.8	33.5	30.4	19.0
Property & Casualty Combined Ratio	86.2	99.6	96.4	91.0	101.2	112.4	96.4	99.5	88.2	79.4
% Return on Revenue	17.3	7.9	9.4	13.6	1.4	NM	9.8	12.1	39.8	45.6
% Return on Equity	17.6	9.5	11.9	19.2	1.2	NM	NA	8.7	17.7	19.0

Data as orig reptd.; bef. results of disc opers/spec. items. Per share data adj. for stk. divs.; EPS diluted. 2004-2000 data restated based on 2004 SEC Form 10-K/A. E-Estimated. NA-Not Available. NM-Not Meaningful. NR-Not Ranked. UR-Under Review.

Office: 17 Woodbourne Avenue, Hamilton, Bermuda HM 08.
Telephone: 441-295-5200.
Email: investorrelations@ace.bm
Website: http://www.acelimited.com

Chrmn, Pres & CEO: E.G. Greenberg
CFO: P.V. Bancroft
Chief Acctg Officer: P. Medini
Secy & General Counsel: R.F. Cusumano

Investor Contact: H.M. Wilson (441-299-9283)
Board Members: M. G. Atieh, M. A. Cirillo, B. L. Crockett, B. Duperreault, E. G. Greenberg, R. M. Hernandez, J. A. Krol, P. Menikoff, T. J. Neff, R. Ripp, D. F. Smurfit, G. M. Stuart

Founded: 1985
Domicile: Cayman Islands
Employees: 10,000

Adobe Systems Inc

STANDARD &POOR'S

S&P Recommendation **BUY** ★★★★☆	Price $41.91 (as of Nov 23, 2007)	12-Mo. Target Price $51.00	Investment Style Large-Cap Growth

GICS Sector Information Technology
Sub-Industry Application Software

Summary This company provides software for multimedia content creation, distribution and management.

Key Stock Statistics (Source S&P, Vickers, company reports)

52-Wk Range	$48.47– 37.20	S&P Oper. EPS 2007E	1.44	Market Capitalization(B)	$24.047	Beta	1.78
Trailing 12-Month EPS	$1.13	S&P Oper. EPS 2008E	1.66	Yield (%)	Nil	S&P 3-Yr. Proj. EPS CAGR(%)	15.00
Trailing 12-Month P/E	37.1	P/E on S&P Oper. EPS 2007E	29.1	Dividend Rate/Share	Nil	S&P Credit Rating	NA
$10K Invested 5 Yrs Ago	$28,204	Common Shares Outstg. (M)	573.8	Institutional Ownership (%)	88		

Price Performance

30-Week Mov. Avg. · · · 10-Week Mov. Avg. - - GAAP Earnings vs. Previous Year Volume Above Avg. STARS
12-Mo. Target Price — Relative Strength — ▲ Up ▼ Down ► No Change Below Avg. ★

2-for-1
105

J A S O N D J F M A M J J A S O N D J F M A M J J A S O N D J F M A M J J A S O N D J F
2004 / 2005 / 2006 / 2007

Options: ASE, CBOE, P, Ph

Analysis prepared by **Zaineb Bokhari** on November 14, 2007, when the stock traded at **$ 41.36**.

Highlights

➤ We expect total revenue in FY 07 (Nov.) to increase 22%, after the 31% advance in FY 06. We believe a major revenue growth driver will be Creative Suite 3 (CS3), certain versions of which began shipping in April 2007. CS3 includes the latest version of Adobe Photoshop and products acquired in the 2005 Macromedia acquisition. We anticipate that a native CS3 version for the Intel-based Macintosh will we received well, and we see continued strength in Acrobat products and the small but growing mobile and devices business segment. We see 12% revenue growth in FY 08.

➤ We believe gross margins in FY 07 will remain stable at about 88.8%, versus 88.6% in FY 06, despite a slight mix shift toward services and support revenues as services and support gross margins widen from a year ago. We see the FY 07 non-GAAP operating margin widening to 38.5%, from 37.1% in FY 06, due to better operating efficiency through economies of scale. We expect fairly stable operating margins in FY 08.

➤ Our estimates for operating EPS are $1.44 for FY 07 and $1.66 for FY 08, compared to operating EPS of $1.12 in FY 06.

Investment Rationale/Risk

➤ We believe ADBE is well positioned to benefit from the continuing growth and usage of the Internet, particularly as related to graphics and video creation and document processing. We also think the recently introduced CS3 reflects the enhancements to ADBE's technology and products following its acquisition of Macromedia. Near term, we expect the share price to be closely linked to the upgrade cycle for CS3, for which the pace of upgrades has been strong. We think this will moderate in FY 08.

➤ Risks to our recommendation and target price include weaker demand than we expect for ADBE's CS3 and increased competition for the Acrobat franchise from lower-cost PDF creation software.

➤ Our 12-month target price of $51 is based on a blend of our discounted cash flow (DCF) and P/E analyses. Our DCF model assumes a 10.3% weighted average cost of capital, 15% revenue growth for 10 years, and 4% terminal growth, yielding an intrinsic value of $52. For our P/E analysis, we value the shares at $50, based on 2.0X P/E to growth, above the industry's average of 1.8X due to ADBE's leadership position, or about 30X our FY 08 operating EPS estimate.

Qualitative Risk Assessment

LOW	MEDIUM	HIGH

Our risk assessment reflects our view of ADBE's size and market leadership, consistent operating history, and strong balance sheet. This is offset by the regularly changing nature of the software industry.

Quantitative Evaluations

S&P Quality Ranking B+

D	C	B-	B	B+	A-	A	A+

Relative Strength Rank MODERATE

55

LOWEST = 1   HIGHEST = 99

Revenue/Earnings Data

Revenue (Million $)

	1Q	2Q	3Q	4Q	Year
2007	649.4	745.6	851.7	--	--
2006	655.5	635.5	602.2	682.2	2,575
2005	472.9	496.0	487.0	510.4	1,966
2004	423.3	410.1	403.7	429.5	1,667
2003	296.9	320.2	319.1	358.6	1,295
2002	267.9	317.4	284.9	294.7	1,165

Earnings Per Share ($)

2007	0.24	0.25	0.34	E0.43	E1.44
2006	0.17	0.20	0.16	0.30	0.83
2005	0.30	0.29	0.29	0.31	1.19
2004	0.25	0.22	0.21	0.23	0.91
2003	0.12	0.14	0.14	0.17	0.55
2002	0.10	0.11	0.10	0.09	0.40

Fiscal year ended Nov. 30. Next earnings report expected: Mid December. EPS Estimates based on S&P Operating Earnings; historical GAAP earnings are as reported.

Dividend Data

No cash dividends have been paid since 2005.

Adobe Systems Inc

Business Summary November 14, 2007

CORPORATE OVERVIEW. Adobe Systems is one of the world's largest software companies. It offers creative, business, and mobile software and services used by consumers, artistic professionals, designers, knowledge workers, original equipment manufacturers, developers, and enterprises for producing, managing, delivering and experiencing content across multiple operating systems, devices and media. Its cornerstone products include Acrobat (for document creation, distribution and management), Illustrator (to make graphic artwork), and Photoshop (for photo design, enhancement, and editing). In December 2005, ADBE acquired Macromedia, a leading developer of software that enables the creation and consumption of digital content, for $4.3 billion in stock. We believe this was an extremely important transaction for the company. Macromedia's significant products include Dreamweaver (for Web development) and Flash (which provides an environment to produce dynamic digital content).

CORPORATE STRATEGY. ADBE's indicated strategy is to address the needs of a variety of customers with offerings that support industry standards and can be deployed in a variety of contexts. We believe ADBE is focused on leveraging its market leading software franchises with bundles and enhancements. Selling multiple products together has enabled ADBE to gain market share, increase penetration with existing customers, and expand its overall customer base, in our view. The Creative Suite is the company's flagship bundled offering. Macromedia was acquired to further this strategy, and bundles of legacy Adobe and Macromedia software were released just days after their combination was completed.

We believe the purchase of Macromedia was an excellent strategic move for ADBE because it contributed technologies and products that have achieved notable adoption in the areas of dynamic digital content creation, and mobile platforms. In our opinion, ADBE's offerings in these segments were previously somewhat lacking, and Macromedia should bolster these businesses.

Company Financials Fiscal Year Ended Nov. 30

Per Share Data ($)	2006	2005	2004	2003	2002	2001	2000	1999	1998	1997
Tangible Book Value	4.25	3.54	2.68	2.08	1.24	1.23	1.45	1.01	1.03	1.35
Cash Flow	1.33	1.31	1.03	0.65	0.52	0.53	0.65	0.56	0.30	0.41
Earnings	0.83	1.19	0.91	0.55	0.40	0.42	0.57	0.46	0.19	0.32
S&P Core Earnings	0.76	1.01	0.69	0.18	0.05	0.11	NA	NA	NA	NA
Dividends	Nil	0.01	0.03	0.03	0.03	0.03	0.03	0.03	0.03	0.03
Payout Ratio	Nil	1%	3%	5%	6%	6%	6%	5%	13%	8%
Prices:High	43.22	39.48	32.24	23.19	21.66	30.81	43.66	19.75	6.48	6.64
Prices:Low	25.98	25.80	17.15	12.29	8.25	11.10	13.36	4.71	2.95	4.06
P/E Ratio:High	52	33	35	42	55	74	77	43	33	21
P/E Ratio:Low	31	22	19	22	21	27	24	10	15	13

Income Statement Analysis (Million $)										
Revenue	2,575	1,966	1,667	1,295	1,165	1,230	1,266	1,015	895	912
Operating Income	870	793	653	428	368	447	457	337	220	296
Depreciation	308	64.3	60.8	49.0	63.5	56.6	43.3	50.8	56.3	59.4
Interest Expense	Nil	Nil	Nil	Nil	Nil	Nil	Nil	Nil	Nil	Nil
Pretax Income	680	766	609	380	285	307	444	374	168	296
Effective Tax Rate	25.6%	21.3%	26.0%	30.0%	32.8%	33.0%	35.1%	36.5%	37.3%	36.9%
Net Income	506	603	450	266	191	206	288	238	105	187
S&P Core Earnings	466	515	343	86.7	20.6	51.7	NA	NA	NA	NA

Balance Sheet & Other Financial Data (Million $)										
Cash	772	421	376	190	184	219	237	171	111	268
Current Assets	2,884	2,009	1,551	1,329	814	767	878	623	456	679
Total Assets	5,963	2,440	1,959	1,555	1,052	931	1,069	804	767	940
Current Liabilities	677	480	451	437	377	314	315	268	251	225
Long Term Debt	Nil	Nil	Nil	Nil	Nil	Nil	Nil	Nil	Nil	Nil
Common Equity	5,152	1,864	1,423	1,101	674	617	753	512	516	715
Total Capital	5,223	1,943	1,502	1,119	674	617	755	536	516	715
Capital Expenditures	83.3	48.9	63.2	39.5	31.6	46.6	29.8	42.2	59.7	33.9
Cash Flow	814	667	511	315	255	262	331	289	161	246
Current Ratio	4.3	4.2	3.4	3.0	2.2	2.4	2.8	2.3	1.8	3.0
% Long Term Debt of Capitalization	Nil	Nil	Nil	Nil	Nil	Nil	Nil	Nil	Nil	Nil
% Net Income of Revenue	19.6	30.7	27.0	20.6	16.4	16.7	22.7	23.4	11.8	20.5
% Return on Assets	12.0	27.4	25.6	20.4	19.3	20.6	30.7	30.3	12.3	19.1
% Return on Equity	14.4	36.7	35.7	30.0	29.6	30.0	45.5	46.2	17.1	26.3

Data as orig reptd.; bef. results of disc opers/spec. items. Per share data adj. for stk. divs.; EPS diluted. E-Estimated. NA-Not Available. NM-Not Meaningful. NR-Not Ranked. UR-Under Review.

Office: 345 Park Avenue, San Jose, CA, USA 95110-2704.
Telephone: 408-536-6000.
Email: ir@adobe.com
Website: http://www.adobe.com

Co-Chrmn: J.E. Warnock
Co-Chrmn: C.M. Geschke
Pres & COO: S. Narayen
CEO: B.R. Chizen

EVP & CFO: M. Garrett
Auditor: KPMG, Mountain View, CA
Board Members: E. W. Barnholt, R. Burgess, M. Cannon, B. R. Chizen, J. Daley, C. M. Geschke, C. Mills, C. M. Pouliot, R. Sedgewick, J. E. Warnock, D. W. Yocam

Founded: 1983
Domicile: Delaware
Employees: 6,068

Advanced Micro Devices Inc.

STANDARD & POOR'S

S&P Recommendation	HOLD ★★★☆☆	Price $10.78 (as of Nov 23, 2007)	12-Mo. Target Price $17.00	Investment Style Large-Cap Value

GICS Sector Information Technology
Sub-Industry Semiconductors

Summary This company is a leading producer of semiconductors that are used principally by the computer and telecommunications industries.

Key Stock Statistics (Source S&P, Vickers, company reports)

52-Wk Range	$23.00– 10.52	S&P Oper. EPS 2007**E**	-2.56	Market Capitalization(B)	$5.978	Beta	3.21
Trailing 12-Month EPS	$-4.08	S&P Oper. EPS 2008**E**	-1.41	Yield (%)	Nil	S&P 3-Yr. Proj. EPS CAGR(%)	NM
Trailing 12-Month P/E	NM	P/E on S&P Oper. EPS 2007**E**	NM	Dividend Rate/Share	Nil	S&P Credit Rating	B
$10K Invested 5 Yrs Ago	$15,714	Common Shares Outstg. (M)	554.6	Institutional Ownership (%)	90		

Price Performance

30-Week Mov. Avg. ···· 10-Week Mov. Avg. – – **GAAP Earnings vs. Previous Year** Volume Above Avg. |||| STARS
12-Mo. Target Price — Relative Strength — ▲ Up ▼ Down ► No Change Below Avg. |||| ★

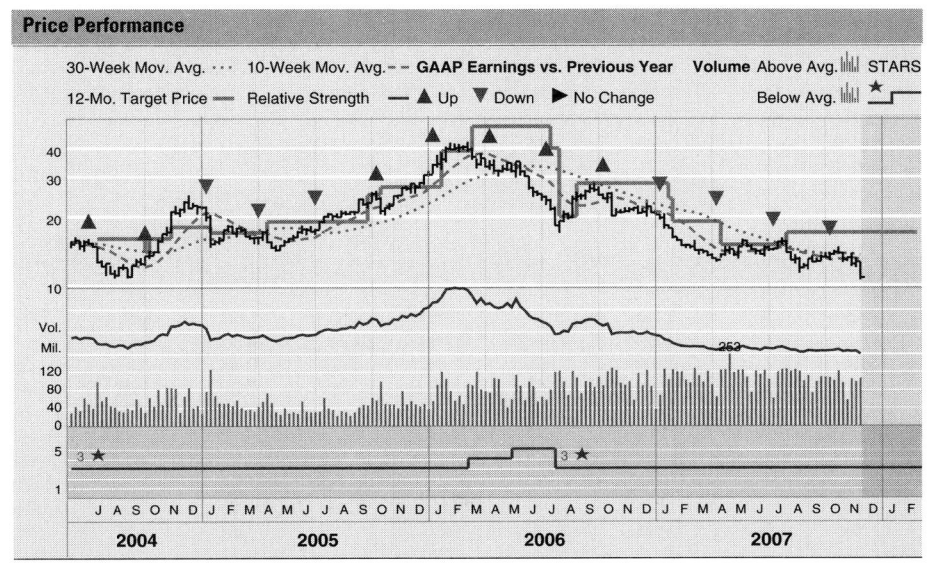

Options: ASE, CBOE, P, Ph

Analysis prepared by **Clyde Montevirgen** on October 19, 2007, when the stock traded at **$ 13.88**.

Highlights

➤ We expect a sales increase of 6% in 2007, as sales accretion from recently acquired ATI is partially offset by the negative impact from market share losses to Intel and deteriorating average selling prices (ASPs). In 2008, we anticipate 17% sales growth, supported by new chip offerings that should garner market share for higher-end products. However, we believe that sales growth for its graphics chips will slow as a result of expected market share gains by competitor NVIDIA Corp.

➤ We see gross margins in the high-30% area in 2007 due to competitive pricing earlier in the year, but we believe that gross margins will likely widen for the remainder of the year and throughout 2008 as production shifts to smaller linewidths, unit shipments increase, and new chip offerings gain traction. We project 2008 gross margins in the low-40% area. AMD recently reduced head count, but we think operating expenses will likely rise to support more advanced manufacturing processes in coming quarters.

➤ We project an operating loss per share of $2.56 for 2007 and a $1.41 loss per share for 2008.

Investment Rationale/Risk

➤ Although we think the acquisition of ATI will improve AMD's product offerings in the long term, we remain cautious due to expected market share losses, competitive pricing, and our view of a weak balance sheet. We believe that AMD has lost its technological edge and has become more vulnerable to market share losses for its core chip business. However, we expect that AMD's new line of quad-core chips, nicknamed Barcelona, will make it competitive against Intel's comparable offerings, and contribute to higher margins in 2008. We also expect rising PC demand to aid results. Although the shares appear to be inexpensive on a relative basis, we would not add to positions, based on our risk view.

➤ Risks to our recommendation and target price include demand for computers and semiconductors turning lower than we project, greater market share losses, and AMD's inability to pay off debt.

➤ Our 12-month target price of $17 is derived by applying a price-to-sales ratio of about 1.4X, at the mid-point of AMD's historical range and below peers, to our forward 12-month sales per share estimate.

Qualitative Risk Assessment

LOW	MEDIUM	HIGH

AMD is subject to the cyclical swings of the semiconductor industry, demand fluctuations for computer end-products, vacillation in average selling prices for chips, and strong competition from Intel, which is a much larger rival in microprocessors.

Quantitative Evaluations

S&P Quality Ranking B-

D	C	B-	B	B+	A-	A	A+

Relative Strength Rank WEAK

18

LOWEST = 1   HIGHEST = 99

Revenue/Earnings Data

Revenue (Million $)

	1Q	2Q	3Q	4Q	Year
2007	1,233	1,378	1,632	--	--
2006	1,332	1,216	1,328	1,773	5,649
2005	1,227	1,260	1,523	1,838	5,848
2004	1,236	1,262	1,239	1,264	5,001
2003	714.6	645.3	953.8	1,206	3,519
2002	902.1	600.3	508.2	686.4	2,697

Earnings Per Share ($)

2007	-1.11	-1.09	-0.71	E-0.39	E-2.56
2006	0.38	0.18	0.27	-1.08	-0.34
2005	-0.04	0.03	0.18	0.21	0.40
2004	0.12	0.09	0.12	-0.08	0.25
2003	-0.42	-0.40	-0.09	0.12	-0.79
2002	-0.03	-0.54	-0.74	-2.49	-3.81

Fiscal year ended Dec. 31. Next earnings report expected: Late January. EPS Estimates based on S&P Operating Earnings; historical GAAP earnings are as reported.

Dividend Data

Except for a special payment of $0.01 a share in 1995, no cash dividends have been paid.

The **McGraw-Hill** Companies

Advanced Micro Devices Inc.

STANDARD
&POOR'S

Business Summary October 19, 2007

CORPORATE OVERVIEW. Advanced Micro Devices makes digital integrated circuits, including microprocessors for computers, embedded microprocessors for personal connectivity devices and, as a result of the company's acquisition of ATI Technologies in October 2006, 3D graphics and chipsets for various computing and embedded products. It is the prime competitor of dominant player Intel Corp. in the PC microprocessor market, and leading graphic chipmaker NVIDIA (NVDA: hold, $45).

The company has four reportable segments: Computation Products, Embedded Products, Graphics and Chipsets, and Consumer Electronics. The largest portion of the company's revenues (90% in 2006, 65% in 2005) comes from the Computation Products Group, while the remaining segments comprised approximately 10% in 2006. AMD's processor brands for desktop PCs consist of the Athlon 64, the Athlon 64 FX, and Sempron processors. In 2003, the company introduced its Athlon 64 microprocessor, the first Windows-compatible, x86 architecture-based 64-bit PC processor. Athlon 64 processors, which allow the simultaneous use of both 32-bit and 64-bit software applications, are designed for enterprises and sophisticated PC users that seek to access large amounts of data and memory. Simultaneously with the introduction of the

Athlon 64, AMD introduced the Athlon 64 FX processor, designed specifically for gamers, PC enthusiasts, and digital content creators that require products that can perform graphic-intensive tasks. Sempron processors, introduced in July 2004, are designed for value-conscious consumers of desktop and notebook PCs.

AMD's microprocessors for the mobile computing market include AMD Turion 64 mobile technology, introduced in March 2005, and AMD Athlon 64 processors and mobile AMD Sempron processors. The company's x86 processors for servers and workstations consist mainly of the AMD Opteron processors. Like the Athlon 64 processors, Opteron processors are based on AMD 64 technology, and are designed to allow simultaneous 32-bit and 64-bit computing. The Opteron was first introduced in 2003. In April 2005, dual-core Opteron processors were introduced, offering improved multitasking capabilities and better performance per watt, which can save power costs for customers.

Company Financials Fiscal Year Ended Dec. 31

Per Share Data ($)	2006	2005	2004	2003	2002	2001	2000	1999	1998	1997
Tangible Book Value	2.49	7.70	7.68	6.96	7.16	10.64	10.09	6.66	6.89	7.14
Cash Flow	1.36	3.14	3.54	2.08	-1.60	1.69	4.53	1.45	1.27	1.33
Earnings	-0.34	0.40	0.25	-0.79	-3.81	-0.18	2.95	-0.30	-0.36	-0.08
S&P Core Earnings	-0.35	0.38	-0.19	-1.08	-4.24	-0.49	NA	NA	NA	NA
Dividends	Nil	Nil	Nil	Nil	Nil	Nil	Nil	Nil	Nil	Nil
Payout Ratio	Nil	Nil	Nil	Nil	Nil	Nil	Nil	Nil	Nil	Nil
Prices:High	42.70	31.84	24.95	18.50	20.60	34.65	48.50	16.50	16.38	24.25
Prices:Low	16.90	14.08	10.76	4.78	3.10	7.69	13.56	7.28	6.38	8.56
P/E Ratio:High	NM	80	NM	NM	NM	NM	16	NM	NM	NM
P/E Ratio:Low	NM	35	NM	NM	NM	NM	5	NM	NM	NM

Income Statement Analysis (Million $)	2006	2005	2004	2003	2002	2001	2000	1999	1998	1997
Revenue	5,649	5,848	5,001	3,519	2,697	3,892	4,644	2,858	2,542	2,356
Operating Income	1,238	1,451	1,452	748	-139	654	1,468	233	304	304
Depreciation	837	1,219	1,224	996	756	623	579	516	468	394
Interest Expense	126	105	112	110	71.3	61.4	60.0	69.3	66.5	45.3
Pretax Income	-115	33.7	116	-316	-1,258	-75.0	1,263	78.4	-196	-76.2
Effective Tax Rate	NM	NM	5.05%	NM	NM	NM	20.3%	NM	NM	NM
Net Income	-166	165	91.2	-274	-1,303	-60.6	1,006	-88.9	-104	-21.1
S&P Core Earnings	-170	155	-68.2	-373	-1,450	-161	NA	NA	NA	NA

Balance Sheet & Other Financial Data (Million $)	2006	2005	2004	2003	2002	2001	2000	1999	1998	1997
Cash	1,380	633	918	968	429	427	591	294	362	241
Current Assets	3,963	3,559	3,228	2,900	2,020	2,353	2,658	1,410	1,562	1,175
Total Assets	13,147	7,288	7,844	7,094	5,619	5,647	5,768	4,378	4,253	3,515
Current Liabilities	2,852	1,822	1,846	1,452	1,372	1,314	1,224	911	841	727
Long Term Debt	3,672	1,327	1,628	1,900	1,780	673	1,168	1,427	1,372	663
Common Equity	5,785	3,352	3,010	2,438	2,467	3,555	3,172	1,979	2,005	2,030
Total Capital	9,778	5,006	5,583	5,213	4,247	4,333	4,544	3,467	3,412	2,789
Capital Expenditures	1,857	1,513	1,440	570	705	679	805	620	996	685
Cash Flow	671	1,385	1,315	721	-547	562	1,585	427	364	373
Current Ratio	1.4	2.0	1.7	2.0	1.5	1.8	2.2	1.5	1.9	1.6
% Long Term Debt of Capitalization	37.6	26.5	29.2	36.4	41.9	15.5	25.7	41.2	40.2	23.8
% Net Income of Revenue	NM	2.8	1.8	NM	NM	NM	21.7	NM	NM	NM
% Return on Assets	NM	2.2	1.2	NM	NM	NM	19.8	NM	NM	NM
% Return on Equity	NM	5.2	3.3	NM	NM	NM	39.1	NM	NM	NM

Data as orig reptd.; bef. results of disc opers/spec. items. Per share data adj. for stk. divs.; EPS diluted. E-Estimated. NA-Not Available. NM-Not Meaningful. NR-Not Ranked. UR-Under Review.

Office: One AMD Place, Sunnyvale, CA 94088-3453.
Telephone: 408-749-4000.
Email: investor.relations@amd.com
Website: http://www.amd.com

Chrmn & CEO: H.d. Ruiz
Pres & COO: D.R. Meyer
EVP & CFO: R.J. Rivet
EVP & Chief Admin Officer: T.M. McCoy

SVP & CTO: P. Hester
Board Members: W. M. Barnes, J. E. Caldwell, B. Claflin, F. Clegg, H. P. Eberhart, R. B. Palmer, H. d. Ruiz, M. L. Topfer

Founded: 1969
Domicile: Delaware
Employees: 16,500

The McGraw-Hill Companies

AES Corporation (The)

STANDARD & POOR'S

S&P Recommendation	HOLD ★★★☆☆	Price	12-Mo. Target Price	Investment Style
		$21.65 (as of Nov 29, 2007)	$26.00	Large-Cap Growth

GICS Sector Utilities
Sub-Industry Independent Power Producers & Energy Traders

Summary The world's largest independent power producer, AES produces and distributes electricity in international and domestic markets.

Key Stock Statistics (Source S&P, Vickers, company reports)

52-Wk Range	$24.24–16.69	S&P Oper. EPS 2007E	1.00	Market Capitalization(B)	$14.475	Beta	0.79
Trailing 12-Month EPS	$-0.06	S&P Oper. EPS 2008E	1.16	Yield (%)	Nil	S&P 3-Yr. Proj. EPS CAGR(%)	12.00
Trailing 12-Month P/E	NM	P/E on S&P Oper. EPS 2007E	21.7	Dividend Rate/Share	Nil	S&P Credit Rating	BB-
$10K Invested 5 Yrs Ago	$119,548	Common Shares Outstg. (M)	668.6	Institutional Ownership (%)	86		

Price Performance

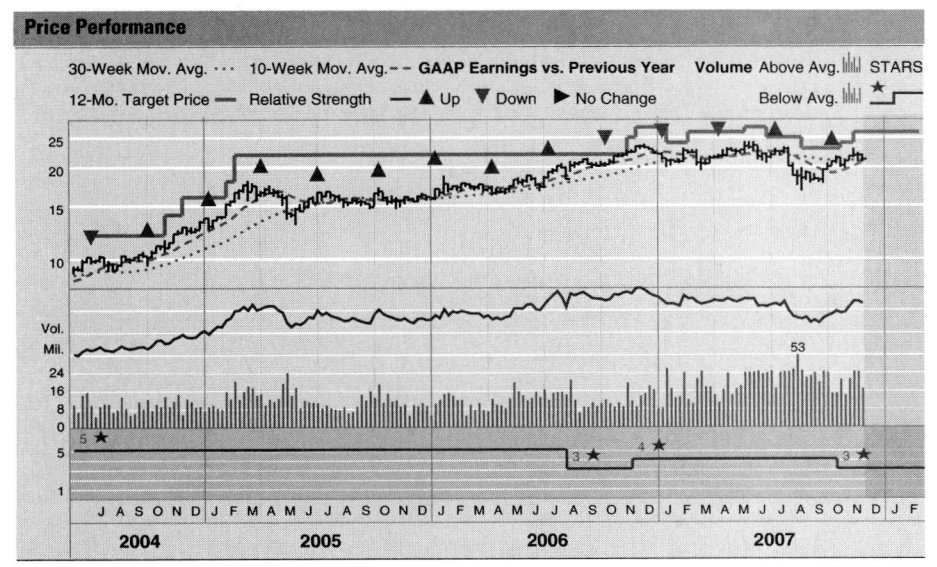

30-Week Mov. Avg. ···   10-Week Mov. Avg.- -   **GAAP Earnings vs. Previous Year**   Volume Above Avg. STARS
12-Mo. Target Price —   Relative Strength —   ▲ Up   ▼ Down   ► No Change   Below Avg.

2004   2005   2006   2007

Options: ASE, CBOE, P, Ph

Analysis prepared by **Christopher B. Muir** on November 29, 2007, when the stock traded at **$ 21.64**.

Highlights

➤ We see revenues rising 7.5% in 2007 and 9.5% in 2008. We project strong revenue growth in unregulated operations, supported by what we expect to be continued increases in demand for contract generation and strength in Latin American generation. We also see a rise in regulated revenues, aided by growth in customer demand overseas, partly offset by the absence of Venezuelan revenues.

➤ Our 2007 operating margin forecast is 23.2%, down from 27.0% in 2006. We expect the consolidation of Itabo and favorable volumes for contract generation and distribution to be offset by higher maintenance and administrative costs. We see a partial recovery in 2008, to 24.3%, on expense control. Our pretax margin forecasts for 2008 and 2007 are 16.2% and 15.4%, respectively, up from 14.6% for 2006. We think that lower net interest expense and higher non-operating income will help increase pretax earnings.

➤ Assuming an effective tax rate of 32.3% and a slight increase in shares outstanding, we estimate 2007 operating EPS of $1.00, down 6.5% from 2006. Our 2008 EPS forecast is $1.16, a 16% increase.

Investment Rationale/Risk

➤ We believe AES is a superior independent power producer. We think it should see above-average earnings growth and an improving balance sheet over the next couple of years, partly due to stronger economic growth in emerging markets. Results could also be helped by cost control and strategic growth initiatives. Recent financial restatements are relatively small and should not materially impact future results, and the forced sale of its Venezuelan assets should not have a negative impact on EPS growth, in our view. We think AES can use the proceeds of the sale to reduce debt or invest in other projects.

➤ Risks to our recommendation and target price include financial statement revisions, currency fluctuations, political and regulatory uncertainty regarding utility rates and U.S. power margins, and counterparty default risk.

➤ The stock recently traded at about 18.5X our 2008 EPS estimate, or about even with its independent power producer peers. Our 12-month target price of $26 is 22.5X our 2008 EPS estimate, or a small premium to our peer target, due to our view of AES's solid operations, partially offset by financial reporting difficulties.

Qualitative Risk Assessment

LOW	MEDIUM	HIGH

Our risk assessment reflects the company's relatively large capitalization and mix of lower risk regulated utility businesses in North America, offset by higher risk merchant power operations and utility operations in emerging markets in South America, Eastern Europe, Central America and Asia.

Quantitative Evaluations

S&P Quality Ranking   B-

D	C	B-	B	B+	A-	A	A+

Relative Strength Rank   STRONG

86

LOWEST = 1   HIGHEST = 99

Revenue/Earnings Data

Revenue (Million $)

	1Q	2Q	3Q	4Q	Year
2007	3,121	3,344	3,471	--	--
2006	2,973	3,044	3,135	3,147	12,299
2005	2,663	2,668	2,782	2,973	11,086
2004	2,257	2,263	2,423	2,543	9,486
2003	1,911	1,992	2,231	2,281	8,415
2002	2,228	2,080	2,110	2,214	8,632

Earnings Per Share ($)

2007	0.18	0.41	0.14	E0.17	E1.00
2006	0.53	0.33	-0.51	0.07	0.43
2005	0.19	0.13	0.37	0.27	0.95
2004	0.12	0.10	0.20	0.14	0.57
2003	0.23	0.24	0.10	0.01	0.56
2002	0.33	-0.19	-0.40	-4.50	-4.81

Fiscal year ended Dec. 31. Next earnings report expected: NA. EPS Estimates based on S&P Operating Earnings; historical GAAP earnings are as reported.

Dividend Data

No cash dividends have been paid.

AES Corporation (The)

Business Summary November 29, 2007

CORPORATE OVERVIEW. AES Corporation (AES) owns and operates a portfolio of electricity generation and distribution business in 28 countries through its subsidiaries and affiliates. The company has two principal businesses: the generation business and the regulated utilities business.

The generation business provides power for sale to utilities and other wholesale customers while the regulated utilities business distributes power to retail, commercial, industrial, and governmental customers. In 2006, the generation unit contributed 44% of total revenues. It primarily sells electricity to utilities or other wholesale customers under power purchase agreements that are generally for five years or longer. We are positive on AES usually retaining 75% or more of a given customer's total capacity needs. The generation business also sells electricity to wholesale customers through competitive markets.

The remaining 56% of total revenues in 2006 comes from the regulated utilities business. It markets electricity to residential, business, and government customers through integrated transmission and distribution systems.

The company also reports results geographically by segment. Latin American operations accounted for 64% of revenues, North American operations for

24%, European and African operations for 12%, Middle Eastern and Asian operations for 7% and corporate activities for -6%.

CORPORATE STRATEGY. AES pursues both a global and a local growth strategy to increase its business. The global strategy focuses on large-scale projects and pursues strategic initiatives. It concentrates on mergers and acquisitions, exploring opportunities in the climate change business such as the production of greenhouse gas reduction activities and related industries that involve environmental issues.

AES has stated its interest in pursuing the renewable energy and alternative energy markets. Its Wind Energy Ltd. acquisition is part of the company's alternative energy business. On the local growth level, AES focuses on expansion plans to fuel its organic growth. The company intends to identify opportunities to expand value through strategic platform expansions such as its 120 megawatts (MW) expansion project in Chile.

Company Financials Fiscal Year Ended Dec. 31

Per Share Data ($)	2006	2005	2004	2003	2002	2001	2000	1999	1998	1997
Tangible Book Value	1.97	NM	NM	NM	NM	2.87	5.21	3.88	4.79	4.17
Earnings	0.43	0.95	0.57	0.56	-4.81	0.87	1.42	0.63	0.84	0.56
S&P Core Earnings	0.78	1.04	0.51	0.94	-3.66	0.74	NA	NA	NA	NA
Dividends	Nil	Nil	Nil	Nil	Nil	Nil	Nil	Nil	Nil	Nil
Payout Ratio	Nil	Nil	Nil	Nil	Nil	Nil	Nil	Nil	Nil	Nil
Prices:High	23.85	18.13	13.71	9.50	17.92	60.15	72.81	38.19	29.00	24.81
Prices:Low	15.63	12.53	7.56	2.63	0.92	11.60	34.25	16.41	11.50	11.19
P/E Ratio:High	55	19	24	17	NM	69	51	61	35	45
P/E Ratio:Low	36	13	13	5	NM	13	24	26	14	20

Income Statement Analysis (Million $)

	2006	2005	2004	2003	2002	2001	2000	1999	1998	1997
Revenue	12,299	11,086	9,486	8,415	8,632	9,327	6,691	3,253	2,398	1,411
Depreciation	933	889	841	781	837	859	582	278	196	114
Maintenance	NA	NA	NA	NA	NA	NA	NA	NA	NA	NA
Fixed Charges Coverage	1.94	1.73	1.30	1.38	0.34	1.42	1.80	NA	NA	NA
Construction Credits	NA	NA	NA	NA	NA	NA	NA	NA	NA	NA
Effective Tax Rate	31.0%	31.9%	28.2%	30.3%	NM	28.7%	24.7%	26.4%	26.6%	21.3%
Net Income	286	632	366	336	-2,590	467	648	245	307	188
S&P Core Earnings	526	693	332	564	-1,970	394	NA	NA	NA	NA

Balance Sheet & Other Financial Data (Million $)

	2006	2005	2004	2003	2002	2001	2000	1999	1998	1997
Gross Property	26,053	24,741	24,141	23,098	23,050	26,748	19,150	NA	NA	NA
Capital Expenditures	1,460	1,143	892	1,228	2,116	3,173	2,150	NA	NA	NA
Net Property	19,074	18,654	18,788	18,505	18,846	23,434	17,846	NA	NA	NA
Capitalization:Long Term Debt	14,892	36,674	16,823	16,792	17,684	20,564	16,927	NA	NA	NA
Capitalization:% Long Term Debt	83.1	95.7	91.1	96.3	102.0	78.8	77.9	NA	NA	NA
Capitalization:Preferred	Nil	Nil	Nil	Nil	Nil	Nil	NA	NA	NA	NA
Capitalization:% Preferred	Nil	Nil	Nil	Nil	Nil	Nil	NA	NA	NA	NA
Capitalization:Common	3,036	1,649	1,645	645	-341	5,539	4,811	NA	NA	NA
Capitalization:% Common	16.9	4.30	8.91	3.70	-1.97	21.2	22.1	NA	NA	NA
Total Capital	21,818	40,655	20,758	19,293	19,142	29,537	24,752	17,708	8,585	7,414
% Operating Ratio	83.8	85.5	84.2	84.5	88.5	89.7	88.3	NA	NA	NA
% Earned on Net Property	23.0	20.9	18.5	17.0	14.3	13.6	14.0	NA	NA	NA
% Return on Revenue	2.3	5.7	3.9	4.0	NM	5.0	9.7	NA	NA	NA
% Return on Invested Capital	16.3	7.0	13.6	13.6	21.6	7.3	9.8	NA	NA	NA
% Return on Common Equity	12.3	48.5	33.4	221.1	NM	8.4	17.4	NA	NA	NA

Data as orig reptd.; bef. results of disc opers/spec. items. Per share data adj. for stk. divs.; EPS diluted. E-Estimated. NA-Not Available. NM-Not Meaningful. NR-Not Ranked. UR-Under Review.

Office: 4300 Wilson Blvd., Arlington, VA 22203-4167.
Telephone: 703-522-1315.
Email: invest@aes.com
Website: http://www.aes.com

Chrmn: R. Darman
Pres & CEO: P.T. Hanrahan
COO & EVP: A. Gluski
EVP & CFO: V. Harker

EVP, Secy & General Counsel: B. Miller
Investor Contact: A. Pasha (703-682-6552)
Board Members: R. Darman, P. T. Hanrahan, K. Johnson, J. A. Koskinen, P. Lader, J. H. McArthur, S. O. Moose, P. A. Odeen, C. O. Rossotti, S. Sandstrom

Founded: 1981
Domicile: Delaware
Employees: 32,000

STANDARD &POOR'S

Aetna Inc.

S&P Recommendation	**STRONG BUY** ★★★★★	Price $54.14 (as of Nov 23, 2007)	12-Mo. Target Price $68.00	Investment Style Large-Cap Blend

GICS Sector Health Care
Sub-Industry Managed Health Care

Summary This company is a leading U.S. provider of health care, dental, pharmacy, group life, disability and long-term care benefits.

Key Stock Statistics (Source S&P, Vickers, company reports)

52-Wk Range	$58.00– 39.02	S&P Oper. EPS 2007**E**	3.48	Market Capitalization(B)	$27.092	Beta	0.31
Trailing 12-Month EPS	$3.41	S&P Oper. EPS 2008**E**	4.00	Yield (%)	0.07	S&P 3-Yr. Proj. EPS CAGR(%)	15.00
Trailing 12-Month P/E	15.9	P/E on S&P Oper. EPS 2007**E**	15.6	Dividend Rate/Share	$0.04	S&P Credit Rating	A-
$10K Invested 5 Yrs Ago	$54,124	Common Shares Outstg. (M)	500.4	Institutional Ownership (%)	91		

Price Performance

30-Week Mov. Avg. ···· 10-Week Mov. Avg. – – **GAAP Earnings vs. Previous Year** Volume Above Avg. STARS
12-Mo. Target Price — Relative Strength — ▲ Up ▼ Down ► No Change Below Avg.

Options: ASE, CBOE, P, Ph

Analysis prepared by **Phillip M. Seligman** on October 31, 2007, when the stock traded at **$ 55.75**.

Highlights

➤ We expect health care segment revenues to increase by almost 17% in 2008, to over $28.7 billion, from the $24.6 billion we see in 2007. Drivers include AET's view of organic net membership growth in 2008 of at least 650,000 and the full-year benefit of the net new members it garnered throughout 2007 and retained, aided by new products and expansion into new markets. Additional contributors we see are the full-year benefit of the August 2007 acquisition of Schaller Anderson and the October 2007 acquisition of Goodhealth Worldwide.

➤ Assuming AET's medical cost trends remain at 7% to 8%, we expect the 2008 commercial risk medical cost ratio (MCR) to be even with that of 2007. However, we expect the firmwide MCR to edge up on the company's anticipated above-average growth of its Medicare business. Meanwhile, we look for a lower SG&A cost ratio, on revenue leverage and G&A cost controls.

➤ We project operating EPS of $3.48 in 2007 and $4.00 in 2008, compared to 2006's $2.82. We see share buybacks, supported by plans for taking on additional debt, contributing to EPS growth.

Investment Rationale/Risk

➤ We view the company's new products and geographies as opening growth opportunities and diversifying its revenue and earnings streams. For example, we see the acquisition of Schaller Anderson enabling AET to further penetrate Medicaid markets, while its acquisition of Goodhealth Worldwide expands its international private medical insurance business. AET also plans to bid for the Department of Defense's TRICARE health plan. Hence, we believe that it will attain its enrollment growth target of 3% to 5% per year for the longer term. While we have been concerned that it may underprice to achieve such growth and note it is targeting higher-cost markets due, we think, to limited growth opportunities elsewhere, we are encouraged by the pricing discipline and medical and SG&A cost controls we see.

➤ Risks to our recommendation and target price include intensified competition, enrollment declines, and spikes in medical costs.

➤ We apply a forward P/E of 17X to our 2008 EPS estimate to derive our 12-month target price of $68. This multiple is at the high end of the historical peer average of 15X to 17X, on our view of good management execution.

Qualitative Risk Assessment

LOW	**MEDIUM**	HIGH

Our risk assessment reflects AET's leadership in the highly fragmented managed care market. We see competition intensifying in the managed care sub-industry, as consolidation has led the largest companies, AET included, to bump up against one another in more market sectors and geographies. However, we believe AET's expanding product, market and geographic diversity will permit stable operational performance over the longer term.

Quantitative Evaluations

S&P Quality Ranking NR

D	C	B-	B	B+	A-	A	A+

Relative Strength Rank STRONG

84

LOWEST = 1 HIGHEST = 99

Revenue/Earnings Data

Revenue (Million $)

	1Q	2Q	3Q	4Q	Year
2007	6,700	6,794	6,961	--	--
2006	6,235	6,252	6,300	6,360	25,146
2005	5,427	5,497	5,701	5,867	22,492
2004	4,821	4,875	5,040	5,168	19,904
2003	4,467	4,466	4,469	4,575	17,976
2002	5,265	5,064	4,832	4,718	19,879

Earnings Per Share ($)

2007	0.81	0.85	0.95	E0.87	E3.48
2006	0.65	0.67	0.85	0.80	2.96
2005	0.70	0.68	0.63	0.71	2.70
2004	0.51	0.45	0.48	0.49	1.94
2003	0.53	0.22	0.34	0.39	1.48
2002	0.15	0.18	0.16	0.16	0.64

Fiscal year ended Dec. 31. Next earnings report expected: Early February. EPS Estimates based on S&P Operating Earnings; historical GAAP earnings are as reported.

Dividend Data (Dates: mm/dd Payment Date: mm/dd/yy)

Amount ($)	Date Decl.	Ex-Div. Date	Stk. of Record	Payment Date
0.040	09/29	11/13	11/15	11/30/06
0.040	09/28	11/13	11/15	11/30/07

Dividends have been paid since 2001. Source: Company reports.

Aetna Inc.

STANDARD &POOR'S

Business Summary October 31, 2007

CORPORATE OVERVIEW. In December 2000, Aetna sold its financial services and international operations for $5 billion ($35.33 a share, not adjusted) and the assumption of $2.7 billion of debt. AET shareholders received $35.33 a share in cash, plus one share of a new health care company named Aetna. Revenue contributions (excluding net investment and other income) from the company's business operations in 2006 were: Health Care 89%; Group Insurance 8%; and Large Case Pensions 3%.

The Health Care segment offers health maintenance organization (HMO), point-of-service (POS), preferred provider organization (PPO) and indemnity benefit products. The company had total health care enrollment of 16,613,000 lives at September 30, 2007, up from 15,433,000 at December 31, 2006. Commercial risk enrollment was 5,339,000 lives, versus 5,088,000, while commercial administrative services (for self-funded accounts) was 10,321,000 lives, versus 10,053,000. Medicare enrollment was 206,000 lives, versus 140,000, while Medicaid enrollment was 747,000 lives, versus 152,000. The company al-

so provided dental benefits to 13,264,000 members, versus 13,472,000.

Group Insurance provides group life, disability and long-term care products; membership was 15,087,000 at December 31, 2006, up from 13,618,000 at December 31, 2005.

Large Case Pensions manages various retirement products, including pension and annuity products, for defined benefit and defined contribution plans. Aetna has not marketed its Large Case Pension products since 1993, but continues to manage the run-off of existing business. At December 31, 2006, assets under management totaled $24.0 billion, up from $21.0 billion at December 31, 2005.

Company Financials Fiscal Year Ended Dec. 31

Per Share Data ($)	2006	2005	2004	2003	2002	2001	2000	1999	1998	1997
Tangible Book Value	7.46	8.57	8.42	6.15	4.69	4.51	4.25	NA	NA	NA
Cash Flow	2.96	3.04	2.22	1.79	1.14	0.54	0.82	NA	NA	NA
Earnings	2.96	2.70	1.94	1.48	0.64	-0.51	-0.23	0.84	NA	NA
S&P Core Earnings	2.96	2.55	1.71	1.51	0.19	-1.12	NA	NA	NA	NA
Dividends	0.04	0.02	0.01	0.01	0.01	0.01	Nil	NA	NA	NA
Payout Ratio	1%	NM	NM	1%	2%	NM	Nil	NA	NA	NA
Prices:High	52.48	49.68	31.89	17.56	12.98	10.67	10.59	NA	NA	NA
Prices:Low	30.94	29.93	16.41	9.98	7.48	5.75	8.23	NA	NA	NA
P/E Ratio:High	18	18	16	12	20	NM	NM	NA	NA	NA
P/E Ratio:Low	10	11	8	7	12	NM	NM	NA	NA	NA

Income Statement Analysis (Million $)										
Revenue	25,146	22,492	19,904	17,976	19,879	25,191	26,819	NA	NA	NA
Operating Income	2,983	2,807	2,184	1,596	1,119	460	1,104	NA	NA	NA
Depreciation	270	204	182	200	302	598	588	NA	NA	NA
Interest Expense	148	123	105	103	120	143	248	NA	NA	NA
Pretax Income	2,587	2,547	1,899	1,442	545	-379	-39.0	NA	NA	NA
Effective Tax Rate	34.8%	35.8%	36.0%	35.2%	27.8%	NM	NM	NA	NA	NA
Net Income	1,686	1,635	1,215	934	393	-292	-127	NA	NA	NA
S&P Core Earnings	1,682	1,542	1,072	957	140	-639	NA	NA	NA	NA

Balance Sheet & Other Financial Data (Million $)										
Cash	880	1,378	1,595	1,655	2,017	1,631	2,204	NA	NA	NA
Current Assets	18,304	18,235	19,516	19,557	19,349	18,751	19,768	NA	NA	NA
Total Assets	47,626	44,365	42,134	40,950	40,048	43,255	47,446	NA	NA	NA
Current Liabilities	7,103	7,617	7,011	7,368	7,719	8,139	10,003	NA	NA	NA
Long Term Debt	2,442	1,156	1,610	1,614	1,633	1,591	Nil	NA	NA	NA
Common Equity	11,009	12,167	9,081	7,924	6,980	9,890	10,127	NA	NA	NA
Total Capital	11,587	13,338	10,691	9,538	8,613	11,481	10,127	NA	NA	NA
Capital Expenditures	291	272	190	211	156	143	36.9	NA	NA	NA
Cash Flow	1,686	1,839	1,397	1,133	695	306	461	NA	NA	NA
Current Ratio	2.6	2.4	2.8	2.7	2.5	2.3	2.0	NA	NA	NA
% Long Term Debt of Capitalization	18.2	8.7	15.1	16.9	19.0	13.9	Nil	NA	NA	NA
% Net Income of Revenue	6.7	7.6	6.4	5.2	2.0	NM	NM	NA	NA	NA
% Return on Assets	3.7	3.8	2.9	2.3	0.9	NM	NM	NA	NA	NA
% Return on Equity	14.5	14.0	14.3	12.5	4.7	NM	NM	NA	NA	NA

Data as orig reptd.; bef. results of disc opers/spec. items. Per share data adj. for stk. divs.; EPS diluted. E-Estimated. NA-Not Available. NM-Not Meaningful. NR-Not Ranked. UR-Under Review.

Office: 151 Farmington Avenue, Hartford, CT 06156-0002.
Telephone: 860-273-0123.
Email: investorrelations@aetna.com
Website: http://www.aetna.com

Chrmn, Pres & CEO: R.A. Williams
SVP & CFO: A.M. Bennett
SVP & General Counsel: W.J. Casazza
Investor Contact: D.W. Entrekin (860-273-7830)

Board Members: F. M. Clark, B. Z. Cohen, M. J. Coye, B. H. Franklin, J. E. Garten, E. G. Graves, G. Greenwald, E. M. Hancock, M. H. Jordan, E. J. Ludwig, J. P. Newhouse, R. A. Williams
Founded: 1982
Domicile: Pennsylvania
Employees: 30,000

Affiliated Computer Services Inc.

STANDARD &POOR'S

S&P Recommendation	**HOLD** ★★★☆☆	Price $41.43 (as of Nov 23, 2007)	12-Mo. Target Price $51.00	Investment Style Large-Cap Growth

GICS Sector Information Technology
Sub-Industry Data Processing & Outsourced Services

Summary This company provides a full range of information technology services, including technology outsourcing, business process outsourcing, and professional services.

Key Stock Statistics (Source S&P, Vickers, company reports)

52-Wk Range	$61.67– 39.46	S&P Oper. EPS 2008**E**	3.50	Market Capitalization(B)	$3.890
Trailing 12-Month EPS	$2.55	S&P Oper. EPS 2009**E**	3.85	Yield (%)	Nil
Trailing 12-Month P/E	16.3	P/E on S&P Oper. EPS 2008**E**	11.8	Dividend Rate/Share	Nil
$10K Invested 5 Yrs Ago	$8,455	Common Shares Outstg. (M)	100.5	Institutional Ownership (%)	85

Beta	0.75
S&P 3-Yr. Proj. EPS CAGR(%)	10.00
S&P Credit Rating	BB

Price Performance

30-Week Mov. Avg. ··· 10-Week Mov. Avg. – – GAAP Earnings vs. Previous Year Volume Above Avg. STARS
12-Mo. Target Price — Relative Strength — ▲ Up ▼ Down ▶ No Change Below Avg.

Options: ASE, CBOE, P, Ph

Analysis prepared by **Dylan Cathers** on November 07, 2007, when the stock traded at **$ 44.13**.

Highlights

➤ The proposed buyout of ACS by Chairman Darwin Deason and partner Cerberus Capital Management, L.P. has been withdrawn, with Cerberus citing the poor conditions in the debt market. Subsequently, Deason called for ACS's independent directors to resign, which, after at first balking at the request, they did.

➤ We expect revenues to grow 7% in FY 08 (Jun.) and 6% in FY 09, with most of the gains coming from the Government segment, which we see increasing about 10%. The Commercial segment remains weak, with internal growth in the low single digits. We see operating margins widening modestly in FY 08, as higher revenues, cost savings from a recently completed restructuring, and improved contract terms offset start-up costs from recently signed contracts, expenses relating to the internal stock option probe and ongoing shareholder lawsuits, and increased investment in sales personnel.

➤ Our FY 08 operating EPS estimate is $3.50. For FY 09, we look for EPS of $3.85.

Investment Rationale/Risk

➤ We recently lowered our opinion on the shares to hold from buy. We have concerns about ongoing expenses related to shareholder lawsuits and restructuring charges, delays in recent contract signings, and our view of weak internal growth in the Commercial segment. These concerns are offset by the improvement in the government business, with its wider margins.

➤ Risks to our recommendation and target price include competition in the IT services marketplace, particularly the business process outsourcing arena, which could cause pricing pressures, and ongoing expenses related to shareholder lawsuits. We also have corporate governance concerns, including a non-shareholder approved "poison pill" and an ongoing investigation of ACS's historical stock option pricing practices.

➤ Our 12-month target price of $51 is based on a peer-average P/E of 14X our calendar 2008 estimate of $3.64, in line with more traditional outsourcers.

Qualitative Risk Assessment

LOW	MEDIUM	**HIGH**

Our risk assessment reflects what we see as the highly competitive nature of the IT outsourcing and business process outsourcing markets, the company's recently increased debt load, and the SEC's informal investigation surrounding the timing of ACS's stock options.

Quantitative Evaluations

S&P Quality Ranking   B+

D	C	B-	B	**B+**	A-	A	A+

Relative Strength Rank   WEAK

23

LOWEST = 1   HIGHEST = 99

Revenue/Earnings Data

Revenue (Million $)

	1Q	2Q	3Q	4Q	Year
2008	1,493	--	--	--	--
2007	1,385	1,427	1,441	1,520	5,772
2006	1,311	1,348	1,314	1,381	5,354
2005	1,046	1,027	1,063	1,214	4,351
2004	1,037	997.9	1,009	1,062	4,106
2003	822.6	908.8	981.6	1,014	3,787

Earnings Per Share ($)

	1Q	2Q	3Q	4Q	Year
2008	0.65	E0.85	E0.91	E0.96	E3.50
2007	0.59	0.72	0.82	0.37	2.49
2006	0.73	0.81	0.61	0.73	2.87
2005	0.72	0.73	0.88	0.87	3.19
2004	0.62	1.80	0.72	0.68	3.83
2003	0.50	0.53	0.57	0.60	2.20

Fiscal year ended Jun. 30. Next earnings report expected: Mid February. EPS Estimates based on S&P Operating Earnings; historical GAAP earnings are as reported.

Dividend Data

No cash dividends have been paid.

Affiliated Computer Services Inc.

STANDARD & POOR'S

Business Summary November 07, 2007

CORPORATE OVERVIEW. ACS provides business process and information technology outsourcing solutions to commercial and government clients. In the commercial sector, the company provides business outsourcing, systems integration services and technology outsourcing to a variety of clients. The business process outsourcing division provides services such as claims processing, finance and accounting, and loan processing. The technology outsourcing division offers the delivery of information processing services on a remote basis from host data centers that provide processing capacity, network management, and desktop support. The systems integration services unit offers application development and implementation, applications outsourcing, technical support and training, network design and installation.

In the federal government sector, ACS offers business process outsourcing and systems integration services. The business process outsourcing unit consists primarily of loan servicing and human resource services for federal agencies. Within the state and local governments sector, ACS designs, implements and operates large scale health and human services programs and the

supporting information technology solutions. ACS also provides child support and payment processing with high volume remittance processing and service center operations.

CORPORATE STRATEGY. Key elements of the company's business strategy include developing long-term relationships with new clients, expanding existing customer relationships, building recurring revenue streams, investing in technology, and completing strategic and tactical acquisitions. ACS provides a full range of information technology services to clients with time critical, transaction intensive business and information processing needs. Its services are designed to enable businesses and government agencies to focus on core operations, respond to rapidly changing technologies, and reduce expenses.

Company Financials Fiscal Year Ended Jun. 30

Per Share Data ($)	2007	2006	2005	2004	2003	2002	2001	2000	1999	1998
Tangible Book Value	NM	NM	0.30	2.64	1.94	0.11	0.90	0.44	NM	0.86
Cash Flow	5.90	5.19	4.98	5.11	3.20	2.47	1.96	1.74	1.37	1.01
Earnings	2.49	2.87	3.19	3.83	2.20	1.76	1.23	1.04	0.83	0.56
S&P Core Earnings	2.45	2.70	3.03	2.48	2.11	1.73	1.11	NA	NA	NA
Dividends	Nil	Nil	Nil	Nil	Nil	Nil	Nil	Nil	Nil	Nil
Payout Ratio	Nil	Nil	Nil	Nil	Nil	Nil	Nil	Nil	Nil	Nil
Prices:High	61.67	63.66	61.16	61.23	56.56	57.05	53.63	31.31	26.50	22.50
Prices:Low	39.46	46.50	45.81	46.01	40.01	32.70	26.81	15.50	15.88	11.19
P/E Ratio:High	25	22	19	16	26	32	44	30	32	41
P/E Ratio:Low	16	16	14	12	18	19	22	15	19	20

Income Statement Analysis (Million $)

	2007	2006	2005	2004	2003	2002	2001	2000	1999	1998
Revenue	5,772	5,354	4,351	4,106	3,787	3,063	2,064	1,963	1,642	1,189
Operating Income	960	926	887	742	671	511	317	265	225	159
Depreciation	346	290	233	184	152	110	93.6	84.8	66.7	47.5
Interest Expense	183	68.4	18.6	17.0	25.2	30.6	23.7	24.0	17.6	12.1
Pretax Income	383	558	641	829	491	360	221	195	146	94.1
Effective Tax Rate	34.0%	35.7%	35.1%	36.1%	37.5%	36.3%	39.3%	44.0%	40.8%	42.2%
Net Income	253	359	416	530	307	230	134	109	86.2	54.4
S&P Core Earnings	249	337	393	339	291	225	119	NA	NA	NA

Balance Sheet & Other Financial Data (Million $)

	2007	2006	2005	2004	2003	2002	2001	2000	1999	1998
Cash	307	101	62.7	76.9	51.2	33.8	242	44.5	32.8	84.0
Current Assets	1,811	1,529	1,244	1,044	979	874	810	772	416	365
Total Assets	5,982	5,502	4,851	3,907	3,699	3,404	1,892	1,656	1,224	950
Current Liabilities	971	825	838	638	557	486	281	358	222	167
Long Term Debt	2,342	1,614	750	372	498	708	649	526	382	235
Common Equity	2,066	2,456	2,838	2,590	2,429	2,095	886	711	607	504
Total Capital	4,776	4,402	3,829	3,197	3,104	2,899	1,590	1,272	989	763
Capital Expenditures	317	394	253	225	206	144	99.1	71.5	61.1	43.8
Cash Flow	599	649	649	714	459	340	228	194	153	102
Current Ratio	1.9	1.9	1.5	1.6	1.8	1.8	2.9	2.2	1.9	2.2
% Long Term Debt of Capitalization	49.0	36.7	19.6	11.6	16.1	24.4	40.8	41.3	38.6	30.8
% Net Income of Revenue	4.4	6.7	9.6	12.9	8.1	7.5	6.5	5.6	5.3	4.6
% Return on Assets	4.4	6.9	9.5	13.9	8.6	8.7	7.6	7.6	7.9	7.1
% Return on Equity	11.2	13.6	15.3	21.1	13.6	15.4	16.8	16.6	15.5	12.8

Data as orig reptd.; bef. results of disc opers/spec. items. Per share data adj. for stk. divs.; EPS diluted. E-Estimated. NA-Not Available. NM-Not Meaningful. NR-Not Ranked. UR-Under Review.

Office: 2828 North Haskell Avenue, Dallas, TX 75204-2988.
Telephone: 214-841-6111.
Email: info@acs-inc.com
Website: http://www.acs-inc.com

Chrmn: D. Deason
Pres & CEO: L. Blodgett
COO & EVP: T. Burlin
EVP & CFO: J. Rexford

EVP, Secy & General Counsel: W.L. Deckelman, Jr.
Board Members: L. R. Blodgett, D. Deason, R. B. Holland, III, J. L. Kosberg, D. McCuistion, J. P. O'Neill, J. Rexford, F. A. Rossi

Founded: 1971
Domicile: Pennsylvania
Employees: 60,000

AFLAC Inc

STANDARD &POOR'S

S&P Recommendation STRONG BUY ★★★★★	**Price** $61.91 (as of Nov 29, 2007)	**12-Mo. Target Price** $75.00	**Investment Style** Large-Cap Growth

GICS Sector Financials
Sub-Industry Life & Health Insurance

Summary This company provides supplemental health and life insurance in the U.S. and Japan.

Key Stock Statistics (Source S&P, Vickers, company reports)

52-Wk Range	$63.25– 43.34	S&P Oper. EPS 2007**E**	3.29	Market Capitalization(B)	$30.242	Beta	0.45
Trailing 12-Month EPS	$3.19	S&P Oper. EPS 2008**E**	3.82	Yield (%)	1.32	S&P 3-Yr. Proj. EPS CAGR(%)	13.00
Trailing 12-Month P/E	19.4	P/E on S&P Oper. EPS 2007**E**	18.8	Dividend Rate/Share	$0.82	S&P Credit Rating	A
$10K Invested 5 Yrs Ago	$20,616	Common Shares Outstg. (M)	488.5	Institutional Ownership (%)	66		

Price Performance

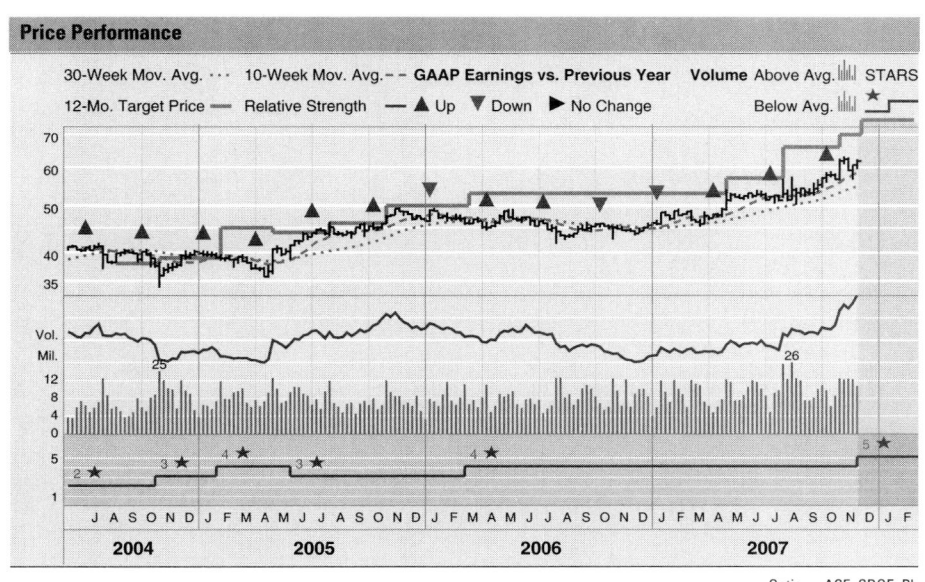

30-Week Mov. Avg. ··· 10-Week Mov. Avg. – – **GAAP Earnings vs. Previous Year** Volume Above Avg. STARS
12-Mo. Target Price — Relative Strength — ▲ Up ▼ Down ▶ No Change Below Avg. ★

Options: ASE, CBOE, Ph

Analysis prepared by **Tanjila Shafi** on November 29, 2007, when the stock traded at **$ 61.91**.

Highlights

➤ We expect total revenues to rise in the single-digit range in 2008, driven by growth in premiums. We believe AFL's focus on training and distribution in Japan should improve sales results for 2008. Sales of cancer life and the new WAYS life insurance product should remain strong, by our analysis. We believe increased ad spending and a solid distribution network will help AFL remain competitive, particularly in Japan. We expect the benefit ratio in Japan to improve, as new sales of products such as EVER have a lower average benefit ratio.

➤ We believe that the company's U.S. operations will maintain its sales momentum, based on improving marketing efforts. We see the combined ratio remaining relatively flat for Aflac U.S., with increased ad spending limiting further improvements in the ratio.

➤ We forecast operating EPS growth of more than 15% in 2007, to $3.29, from $2.85 in 2006. Our 2008 operating EPS estimate is $3.82.

Investment Rationale/Risk

➤ We believe Aflac will improve its Japanese sales in 2008, as it focuses on strengthening its regional sales force and builds its market-leading position. We expect that the company's recent distribution partnership with Japan Post Network Co. will improve sales in 2008. Furthermore, we believe that the company's investment portfolio which does not contain any sub-prime holdings, is more conservative than its peers, which we view favorably. We are encouraged by what we see as AFL's strong financial position and management's commitment to share repurchases and dividend increases.

➤ Risks to our opinion and target price include unfavorable movements in the yen/dollar exchange rate, less organic premium growth than we expect, particularly on new product sales and changes in distribution in Japan, higher-than-projected underwriting and marketing expenses, agent recruiting difficulties, and lower-than-forecast share repurchases.

➤ Our 12-month target price is $75, 19.6X our '08 operating EPS estimate, and in line with its historical multiples.

Qualitative Risk Assessment

LOW	MEDIUM	HIGH

Our risk assessment for Aflac reflects its strong market share position and high risk-based capital ratio, and management's consistent track record for share repurchases and dividend increases. This is offset by AFL's earnings variability stemming from currency exposure to the Japanese yen, from which 75% of AFL's earnings are derived.

Quantitative Evaluations

S&P Quality Ranking A

D	C	B-	B	B+	A-	A	A+

Relative Strength Rank STRONG

90

LOWEST = 1   HIGHEST = 99

Revenue/Earnings Data

Revenue (Million $)

	1Q	2Q	3Q	4Q	Year
2007	3,751	3,764	3,861	--	--
2006	3,559	3,697	3,672	3,687	14,616
2005	3,559	3,567	3,669	3,567	14,363
2004	3,280	3,233	3,321	3,448	13,281
2003	2,807	2,861	2,931	2,847	11,447
2002	2,371	2,513	2,707	2,666	10,257

Earnings Per Share ($)

2007	0.84	0.84	0.85	E0.83	E3.29
2006	0.74	0.81	0.73	0.67	2.95
2005	0.64	0.66	0.90	0.72	2.92
2004	0.61	0.51	0.58	0.81	2.52
2003	0.45	0.48	0.45	0.14	1.52
2002	0.34	0.40	0.45	0.35	1.55

Fiscal year ended Dec. 31. Next earnings report expected: Late January. EPS Estimates based on S&P Operating Earnings; historical GAAP earnings are as reported.

Dividend Data (Dates: mm/dd Payment Date: mm/dd/yy)

Amount ($)	Date Decl.	Ex-Div. Date	Stk. of Record	Payment Date
0.185	10/24	02/14	02/16	03/01/07
0.205	04/24	05/16	05/18	06/01/07
0.205	07/26	08/15	08/17	09/04/07
0.205	10/23	11/14	11/16	12/03/07

Dividends have been paid since 1973. Source: Company reports.

AFLAC Inc

**STANDARD
&POOR'S**

Business Summary November 29, 2007

CORPORATE OVERVIEW. Aflac provides supplemental health and life insurance in the U.S. and Japan. Most of Aflac's policies are individually underwritten and marketed at work sites through independent agents, with premiums paid by the employee. As of March 2007, Aflac believed it was the world's leading underwriter of individually issued policies marketed at work sites.

In 2006, Aflac Japan accounted for 72% of total revenues, compared to 74% in 2005. At December 31, 2006, Aflac Japan accounted for 82% of total company assets, the same as a year earlier. As of year-end 2005, Aflac Japan ranked first in terms of individual insurance policies in force, surpassing Nippon Life in March 2003.

Aflac Japan's insurance products are designed to help pay for costs that are not reimbursed under Japan's national health insurance system. Products include cancer life plans (28% of total sales in 2006; 26% in 2005); Rider MAX (10%; 11%), a rider for cancer life policies that provides accident and medical/sickness benefits; and EVER (33%; 37%), a stand-alone whole life medical plan. Aflac Japan also offers ordinary life products (23%; 18%) and other products such as living benefit life plans and care products.

Under a marketing alliance established in 2001, Dai-ichi Mutual Life Insurance Co. sold roughly 276,900 AFL cancer life policies in 2006, compared to 277,700 cancer life policies in 2005. During 2006, the number of licensed sales associates rose 10.4% to approximately 90,226, compared with 81,751 at December 31, 2005. The growth in licensed sales associates resulted primarily from individual agency recruitment.

Aflac U.S. sells cancer plans (17% of total sales in 2006; 19% in 2005) and various types of health insurance, including accident and disability (52%; 51%), fixed-benefit dental (6%; 8%), and hospital indemnity (12%; 11%). Other products include long-term care, short-term disability, and ordinary life policies.

Company Financials Fiscal Year Ended Dec. 31

Per Share Data ($)	2006	2005	2004	2003	2002	2001	2000	1999	1998	1997
Tangible Book Value	25.32	15.89	15.03	13.03	12.41	10.39	8.87	7.28	7.10	6.44
Operating Earnings	NA	NA	NA	NA	1.56	1.34	1.21	1.00	0.78	0.67
Earnings	2.95	2.92	2.52	1.52	1.55	1.28	1.26	1.04	0.88	1.04
S&P Core Earnings	2.86	2.60	2.47	1.85	1.49	1.25	NA	NA	NA	NA
Dividends	0.55	0.44	0.38	0.30	0.23	0.19	0.17	0.15	0.13	0.11
Payout Ratio	19%	15%	15%	20%	15%	15%	13%	14%	14%	11%
Prices:High	49.40	49.65	42.60	36.91	33.45	36.09	37.47	28.38	22.66	14.47
Prices:Low	41.63	35.50	33.85	28.00	23.10	23.00	16.78	19.50	11.34	9.38
P/E Ratio:High	17	17	17	24	22	28	30	27	26	14
P/E Ratio:Low	14	12	13	18	15	18	13	19	13	9

Income Statement Analysis (Million $)										
Life Insurance in Force	NA	80,610	80,496	69,582	56,680	46,610	51,496	44,993	28,182	19,310
Premium Income:Life	NA	1,139	1,031	876	761	697	716	625	508	474
Premium Income:A & H	NA	10,851	10,271	9,052	7,839	7,366	7,523	6,639	5,435	5,400
Net Investment Income	2,171	2,071	1,957	1,787	1,614	1,550	1,550	1,369	1,138	1,078
Total Revenue	14,616	14,363	13,281	11,447	10,257	9,598	9,720	8,640	7,104	6,983
Pretax Income	2,264	2,226	1,807	1,225	1,259	1,081	1,012	778	551	865
Net Operating Income	NA	NA	NA	NA	825	720	657	550	429	374
Net Income	1,483	1,483	1,299	795	821	687	687	571	487	585
S&P Core Earnings	1,438	1,321	1,274	962	791	670	NA	NA	NA	NA

Balance Sheet & Other Financial Data (Million $)										
Cash & Equivalent	2,036	1,781	4,308	1,508	1,793	1,233	989	985	690	265
Premiums Due	535	479	417	547	435	347	301	270	229	216
Investment Assets:Bonds	50,686	47,551	48,024	42,893	37,483	31,677	31,305	31,175	26,424	22,584
Investment Assets:Stocks	25.0	84.0	77.0	73.0	258	245	236	215	177	146
Investment Assets:Loans	Nil	Nil	Nil	Nil	Nil	Nil	Nil	Nil	9.00	Nil
Investment Assets:Total	50,769	47,692	48,142	42,999	37,768	31,941	31,558	31,408	26,620	22,644
Deferred Policy Costs	6,025	5,590	5,595	5,044	4,277	3,645	3,685	3,692	3,067	2,582
Total Assets	59,805	56,361	59,326	50,964	45,058	37,860	37,232	37,041	31,183	29,454
Debt	1,420	1,050	1,141	1,409	1,312	1,000	956	931	596	523
Common Equity	8,341	7,927	7,573	6,646	6,394	5,425	4,694	3,868	3,770	3,430
% Return on Revenue	10.1	10.4	9.8	6.9	8.0	7.2	7.1	6.6	6.9	8.4
% Return on Assets	2.6	2.6	2.4	1.7	2.0	1.8	1.8	1.7	1.6	2.1
% Return on Equity	18.2	19.1	18.3	12.2	13.9	13.6	16.0	15.0	13.5	21.1
% Investment Yield	4.4	4.3	4.3	4.4	4.6	4.9	4.9	4.7	4.6	4.9

Data as orig reptd.; bef. results of disc opers/spec. items. Per share data adj. for stk. divs.; EPS diluted. E-Estimated. NA-Not Available. NM-Not Meaningful. NR-Not Ranked. UR-Under Review.

Office: 1932 Wynnton Road, Columbus, GA 31999.
Telephone: 706-323-3431.
Email: ir@aflac.com
Website: http://www.aflac.com

Chrmn & CEO: D.P. Amos
Pres, CFO & Treas: K. Cloninger, III
EVP, Secy & General Counsel: J.M. Loudermilk
SVP & Chief Acctg Officer: R.A. Rogers, Jr.

Investor Contact: K.S. Janke, Jr. (706-596-3264)
Board Members: D. P. Amos, J. S. Amos, II, M. H. Armacost, K. Cloninger, III, J. F. Harris, E. J. Hudson, K. S. Janke, Sr., D. W. Johnson, R. B. Johnson, C. B. Knapp, H. Matsui, E. S. Purdom, B. K. Rimer, M. R. Schuster, D. G. Thompson, R. L. Wright

Founded: 1973
Domicile: Georgia
Employees: 7,411

The McGraw-Hill Companies

Agilent Technologies Inc.

STANDARD & POOR'S

S&P Recommendation	HOLD ★★★☆☆	Price	12-Mo. Target Price	Investment Style
		$36.91 (as of Nov 23, 2007)	$38.00	Large-Cap Blend

GICS Sector Information Technology
Sub-Industry Electronic Equipment Manufacturers

Summary This Hewlett-Packard (HPQ) spinoff is a diversified global manufacturer of test and measurement instruments, and life sciences and chemical analysis instruments.

Key Stock Statistics (Source S&P, Vickers, company reports)

52-Wk Range	$40.42– 30.26	S&P Oper. EPS 2008E	1.90	Market Capitalization(B)	$14.267	Beta	2.40
Trailing 12-Month EPS	$1.57	S&P Oper. EPS 2009E	NA	Yield (%)	Nil	S&P 3-Yr. Proj. EPS CAGR(%)	14.00
Trailing 12-Month P/E	23.5	P/E on S&P Oper. EPS 2008E	19.4	Dividend Rate/Share	Nil	S&P Credit Rating	BBB-
$10K Invested 5 Yrs Ago	NA	Common Shares Outstg. (M)	386.5	Institutional Ownership (%)	73		

Price Performance

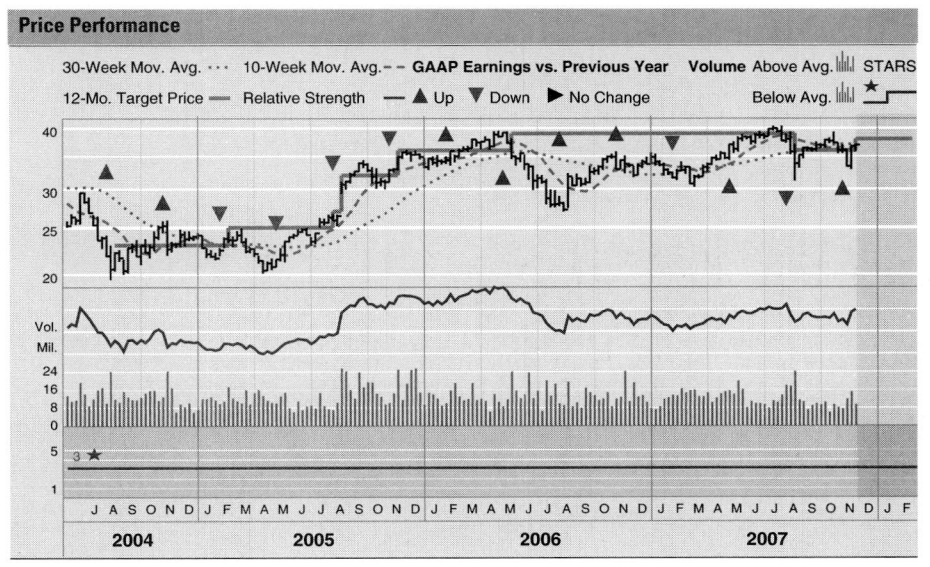

30-Week Mov. Avg. ··· 10-Week Mov. Avg. -- GAAP Earnings vs. Previous Year Volume Above Avg. ▐▌ STARS
12-Mo. Target Price — Relative Strength — ▲ Up ▼ Down ► No Change Below Avg. ▐▌ ★

Options: ASE, CBOE, P, Ph

Analysis prepared by **Angelo Zino** on November 16, 2007, when the stock traded at **$ 36.19**.

Highlights

➤ Following a 2% decline in revenues in FY 07 (Oct.), we expect revenues to increase 9% in FY 08, reflecting our projection of strong demand and higher market share in both the chemical analysis and life science end markets. We see recent product introductions, including the liquid chromatograph, mass spectroscopy and gas chromatograph platforms, gaining traction over the next several quarters. We anticipate mixed results for the electronic measurement unit in FY 08, but we see opportunities in the higher growth aerospace and defense and wireless R&D segments.

➤ We project annual gross margin in FY 08 between 54% and 56%, relatively flat versus a gross margin of 55% in FY 07. We expect the annual operating margin to widen in FY 08, reflecting cost savings from Agilent's multi-year restructuring efforts, which we expect to be completed in the first half of FY 08.

➤ Directors recently authorized a $2 billion share buyback program, and we expect Agilent to repurchase some shares in FY 08 and FY 09. Following EPS of $1.50 in FY 07, we see FY 08 EPS of $1.90.

Investment Rationale/Risk

➤ We expect Agilent to expand aggressively by introducing new products in high growth industries such as aerospace and defense and wireless R&D, complemented by opportunistic acquisitions in the company's core markets. We see the potential for Agilent to increase market share in both the electronic measurement and bio-analytical markets during FY 08. Agilent has made several divestitures over the past few years, which we believe has reduced the volatility of its quarterly results and improved the company's focus and predictability of results.

➤ Risks to our recommendation and target price include a weaker than expected global economy, narrower margins than we project, and a difficult transition to a new business model.

➤ Our 12-month target price of $38 is based on a blend of our three-year historical price-to-sales and price-to-book value analyses. We derive a value of $41 by applying a P/S multiple of 2.7X to our FY 08 sales per share estimate of $15.20, and we obtain a $35 value by using a P/B ratio of 3.9X our book value per share estimate of $9. Both employ a slight premium based on Agilent's potential market share gain.

Qualitative Risk Assessment

LOW	MEDIUM	HIGH

Our risk assessment reflects the variability of Agilent's results in the past, offset by recent efforts to streamline its businesses and divest parts of its portfolio that contributed to this variability.

Quantitative Evaluations

S&P Quality Ranking   **B-**

D	C	B-	B	B+	A-	A	A+

Relative Strength Rank   **STRONG**

84

LOWEST = 1   HIGHEST = 99

Revenue/Earnings Data

Revenue (Million $)

	1Q	2Q	3Q	4Q	Year
2007	1,280	1,320	1,374	1,446	5,420
2006	1,167	1,239	1,239	1,328	4,973
2005	1,212	1,688	1,242	1,407	5,139
2004	1,643	1,831	1,885	1,822	7,181
2003	1,412	1,467	1,502	1,675	6,056
2002	1,426	1,457	1,391	1,736	6,010

Earnings Per Share ($)

2007	0.36	0.30	0.45	0.46	1.57
2006	2.03	0.28	0.51	0.31	3.26
2005	0.10	0.11	0.10	-0.03	0.28
2004	0.14	0.21	0.20	0.15	0.71
2003	-0.24	-0.31	-3.25	0.03	-3.78
2002	-0.68	-0.54	-0.48	-0.51	-2.20

Fiscal year ended Oct. 31. Next earnings report expected: Early February. EPS Estimates based on S&P Operating Earnings; historical GAAP earnings are as reported.

Dividend Data

No cash dividends have been paid.

Agilent Technologies Inc.

STANDARD &POOR'S

Business Summary November 16, 2007

CORPORATE OVERVIEW. Agilent Technologies, which was spun off from Hewlett Packard (HPQ) in 1999, provides investors with exposure to the communications, electronics, life sciences and chemical analysis industries. The company had consisted of HPQ's heralded test and measurement business, its automated test equipment business, its semiconductor products, and its life sciences and chemical analysis businesses. However, in August 2005, Agilent announced the sale of its semiconductor products business (to Avago Technologies Ltd. for $2.66 billion), and separately announced that it would spin off its SOC and memory test business in 2006. Based on Agilent's new reporting segments, following restructuring efforts, segment contributions in FY 06 (Oct.) were: Bio-Analytical Measurement, 31% of sales; and Electronic Measurement, 69%.

A's test and measurement business was HPQ's founding technology, dating back to the late 1930s. The company is a global leader in electronic measurement. Its products are used by communications network equipment manufacturers and service providers, as well by its general purpose test customers. A also sells electronic test equipment products that are used for electronics manufacturing testing, parametric testing, and flat panel display (FPD) markets.

Agilent's bio-analytical measurement business products include microarrays, microfluidics, gas chromatography, liquid chromatography, mass spectrometry, software and informatics, and related consumables and services used in pharmaceutical analysis, the proteomics and gene expression markets, as well as the petrochemical and environmental markets, among others. Applications include measuring octane levels in gasoline, and analyzing pesticide levels in drinking water. Customers span the hydrocarbon-processing, environmental, pharmaceutical and bioscience markets. In the pharmaceutical and biopharmaceutical markets, A's instruments help lower the cost of discovering and developing new drugs.

Company Financials Fiscal Year Ended Oct. 31

Per Share Data ($)	2007	2006	2005	2004	2003	2002	2001	2000	1999	1998
Tangible Book Value	NA	7.79	7.39	6.42	5.09	8.44	9.95	10.37	8.90	NM
Cash Flow	NA	3.64	0.65	1.31	-3.02	-0.62	0.72	2.75	2.60	1.93
Earnings	1.57	3.26	0.28	0.71	-3.78	-2.20	-0.89	1.66	1.35	0.56
S&P Core Earnings	NA	1.59	-0.11	0.27	-5.70	-3.10	-2.63	NA	NA	NA
Dividends	Nil	Nil	Nil	Nil	Nil	Nil	Nil	Nil	Nil	NA
Payout Ratio	Nil	Nil	Nil	Nil	Nil	Nil	Nil	Nil	Nil	NA
Prices:High	40.42	39.54	36.10	38.80	29.42	38.00	68.00	162.00	80.00	NA
Prices:Low	30.26	26.96	20.11	19.51	18.35	10.50	18.00	38.06	30.00	NA
P/E Ratio:High	26	12	NM	55	NM	NM	NM	98	59	NA
P/E Ratio:Low	19	8	NM	27	NM	NM	NM	23	22	NA

Income Statement Analysis (Million $)										
Revenue	NA	4,973	5,139	7,181	6,056	6,010	8,396	10,773	8,331	7,952
Operating Income	NA	680	367	678	-363	-872	-44.0	1,548	1,216	919
Depreciation	NA	170	186	292	362	735	734	495	475	477
Interest Expense	NA	69.0	27.0	36.0	Nil	Nil	Nil	Nil	Nil	Nil
Pretax Income	NA	1,528	306	440	-690	-1,547	-477	1,164	787	396
Effective Tax Rate	NA	5.96%	50.7%	20.7%	NM	NM	NM	35.0%	34.9%	35.1%
Net Income	NA	1,437	141	349	-1,790	-1,022	-406	757	512	257
S&P Core Earnings	NA	701	-55.1	137	-2,695	-1,438	-1,202	NA	NA	NA

Balance Sheet & Other Financial Data (Million $)										
Cash	NA	2,262	2,251	2,315	1,607	1,844	1,170	996	Nil	Nil
Current Assets	NA	3,958	4,447	4,577	3,889	4,880	4,799	5,655	3,538	3,075
Total Assets	NA	7,369	6,751	7,056	6,297	8,203	7,986	8,425	5,444	4,987
Current Liabilities	NA	1,538	1,936	1,871	1,906	2,181	2,002	2,758	1,681	1,599
Long Term Debt	NA	1,500	Nil	1,150	1,150	1,150	Nil	Nil	Nil	Nil
Common Equity	NA	3,648	4,081	3,569	2,824	4,627	5,659	5,265	3,382	3,022
Total Capital	NA	5,341	4,081	4,719	3,974	5,777	5,659	5,265	3,382	3,022
Capital Expenditures	NA	185	139	118	205	301	881	824	434	410
Cash Flow	NA	1,607	327	641	-1,428	-287	328	1,252	987	734
Current Ratio	NA	2.6	2.3	2.4	2.0	2.2	2.4	2.1	2.1	1.9
% Long Term Debt of Capitalization	NA	29.1	Nil	24.4	28.9	19.9	Nil	Nil	Nil	Nil
% Net Income of Revenue	NA	28.9	2.7	4.9	NM	NM	NM	7.0	6.1	3.2
% Return on Assets	NA	20.4	2.0	5.2	NM	NM	NM	10.9	9.8	5.1
% Return on Equity	NA	37.2	3.7	10.9	NM	NM	NM	17.5	16.0	8.4

Data as orig reptd.; bef. results of disc opers/spec. items. Per share data adj. for stk. divs.; EPS diluted. E-Estimated. NA-Not Available. NM-Not Meaningful. NR-Not Ranked. UR-Under Review.

Office: 5301 Stevens Creek Blvd, Santa Clara, CA 95051-7201.
Telephone: 408-553-7777.
Email: investor_relations@agilent.com
Website: http://www.agilent.com

Chrmn: J.G. Cullen
Pres & CEO: W.P. Sullivan
EVP & CFO: A.T. Dillon
SVP, Secy & General Counsel: D.C. Nordlund

VP & Treas: H. Terry
Investor Contact: R. Gonsalves
Board Members: P. N. Clark, J. G. Cullen, R. J. Herbold, K. B. Hwee, R. L. Joss, H. Kunz, D. M. Lawrence, A. B. Rand, W. P. Sullivan

Founded: 1999
Domicile: Delaware
Employees: 18,700

Air Products and Chemicals Inc.

STANDARD &POOR'S

S&P Recommendation	HOLD ★★★☆☆	Price	12-Mo. Target Price	Investment Style
		$93.43 (as of Nov 23, 2007)	$100.00	Large-Cap Blend

GICS Sector Materials
Sub-Industry Industrial Gases

Summary This major producer of industrial gases and specialty and intermediate chemicals also has interests in environmental and energy-related businesses.

Key Stock Statistics (Source S&P, Vickers, company reports)

52-Wk Range	$101.16– 68.58	S&P Oper. EPS 2008E	4.90	Market Capitalization(B)	$20.188	Beta	0.61
Trailing 12-Month EPS	$4.64	S&P Oper. EPS 2009E	NA	Yield (%)	1.63	S&P 3-Yr. Proj. EPS CAGR(%)	10.00
Trailing 12-Month P/E	20.1	P/E on S&P Oper. EPS 2008E	19.1	Dividend Rate/Share	$1.52	S&P Credit Rating	A
$10K Invested 5 Yrs Ago	$24,463	Common Shares Outstg. (M)	216.1	Institutional Ownership (%)	88		

Price Performance

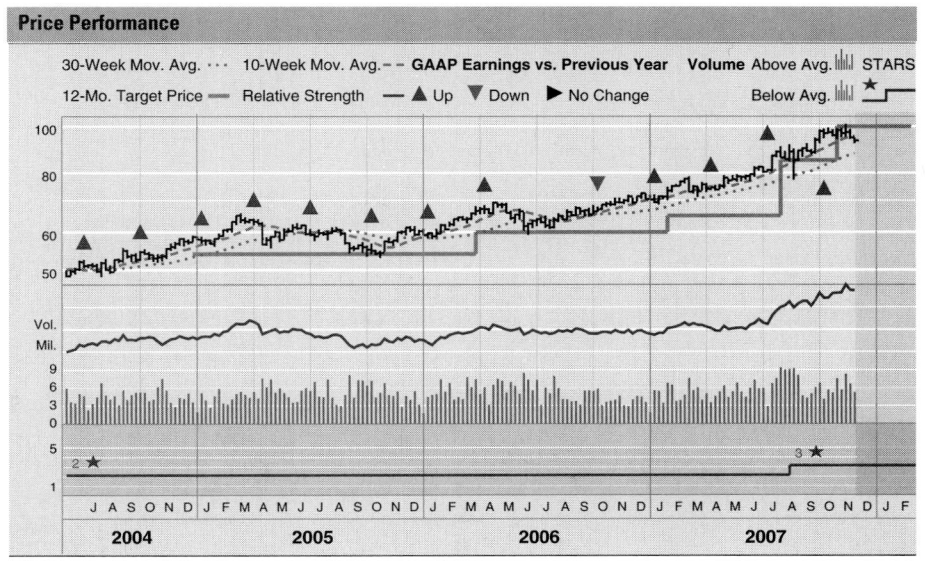

30-Week Mov. Avg. · · · 10-Week Mov. Avg. — **GAAP Earnings vs. Previous Year** Volume Above Avg. STARS
12-Mo. Target Price — Relative Strength — ▲ Up ▼ Down ▶ No Change Below Avg. ★—

Options: CBOE, P, Ph

Analysis prepared by **Richard O'Reilly, CFA** on November 13, 2007, when the stock traded at **$ 97.13**.

Highlights

➤ We expect sales to increase nearly 10% in FY 08 (Sep.) and operating EPS to rise about 12%, to $4.90, from $4.37 in FY 07. We believe sales comparisons for industrial gases will remain upbeat, on continued favorable volume growth for many key products. We expect continued good volume comparisons for tonnage gases, driven by six new domestic hydrogen facilities that started up during FY 06.

➤ U.S. merchant gases volumes should show low single digit percentage growth as APD operates at high rates while achieving continued good price hikes. Asian volumes will likely continue to increase at a double digit rate. We see continuing favorable volume growth for electronics and performance materials. We expect that the health care business will continue to struggle in the U.S., resulting in modest profitability.

➤ We expect equipment unit profits to decline sharply in FY 08, due to a lower LNG backlog. We see interest expense staying at about $160 million, and we forecast a tax rate of 27.5%, up from FY 07's 26.4%. Reported EPS for FY 07 included several one-time items that added $0.30.

Investment Rationale/Risk

➤ The shares recently traded at a P/E of about 19.5X our calendar 2008 EPS estimate, above the level of the S&P 500 (16X). We think overall fundamentals remain sound, as APD holds strong positions in several growth products and markets for industrial gases and specialty chemicals. However, we expect the equipment business to have sharply lower profits in FY 08, and believe APD will soon sell its polymer emulsions business.

➤ Risks to our recommendation and target price include weaker-than-expected growth in U.S. industrial activity and in the global electronics materials industry, and higher-than-forecast raw material and energy prices.

➤ The dividend was raised in 2007 for the 25th consecutive year, a record that we expect to be extended. We expect the company to continue to repurchase common stock at a $500 million annual rate. Based on a P/E of about 20X -- similar to that of APD's industrial gases peer group -- applied to our FY 08 EPS estimate, our 12-month target price is $100.

Qualitative Risk Assessment

LOW	MEDIUM	HIGH

Our risk assessment reflects the stable growth of the industrial gases industry versus commodity chemicals, and what we see as the company's relatively strong balance sheet, offset by volatile raw material cost exposure in the chemical segment.

Quantitative Evaluations

S&P Quality Ranking A

D	C	B-	B	B+	A-	A	A+

Relative Strength Rank STRONG

75

LOWEST = 1   HIGHEST = 99

Revenue/Earnings Data

Revenue (Million $)

	1Q	2Q	3Q	4Q	Year
2007	2,433	2,473	2,595	2,603	10,038
2006	2,016	2,230	2,246	2,359	8,850
2005	1,991	2,003	2,078	2,071	8,144
2004	1,685	1,857	1,893	1,978	7,411
2003	1,447	1,578	1,630	1,642	6,297
2002	1,317	1,313	1,374	1,398	5,401

Earnings Per Share ($)

2007	1.03	1.02	1.28	1.35	4.67
2006	0.80	0.89	E0.88	0.73	3.29
2005	0.72	0.75	0.82	0.79	3.08
2004	0.58	0.62	0.71	0.73	2.64
2003	0.58	0.51	0.12	0.58	1.79
2002	0.52	0.57	0.63	0.65	2.36

Fiscal year ended Sep. 30. Next earnings report expected: Late January. EPS Estimates based on S&P Operating Earnings; historical GAAP earnings are as reported.

Dividend Data (Dates: mm/dd Payment Date: mm/dd/yy)

Amount ($)	Date Decl.	Ex-Div. Date	Stk. of Record	Payment Date
0.380	03/15	03/29	04/02	05/14/07
0.380	05/17	06/28	07/02	08/13/07
0.380	09/20	09/27	10/01	11/12/07
0.380	11/15	12/28	01/02	02/11/08

Dividends have been paid since 1954. Source: Company reports.

Air Products and Chemicals Inc.

Business Summary November 13, 2007

CORPORATE OVERVIEW. Air Products & Chemicals is one of the largest global producers of industrial gases, and has a large specialty chemicals business. APD focuses on several areas for growth in industrial gases, including electronics, hydrogen for petroleum refining, health care, and Asia. International operations accounted for 44% of FY 06 (Sep.) sales.

The industrial gases businesses consists of nitrogen, oxygen, argon, hydrogen, helium, carbon monoxide, synthesis gas, and fluorine compounds for both merchant (32% of sales and 41% of profits in FY 07) and on-site tonnage (26%, 27%) customers. Sales of atmospheric gases (oxygen, nitrogen and argon) accounted for 18% of the total in FY 06. APD is the world's leading supplier of hydrogen (14% of total sales) and carbon monoxide products (HYCO) and helium.

The health care (6%, 2%) business provides respiratory therapies, home medical equipment, and infusion services to over 500,000 patients in 15 countries. APD is the market leader in Spain, Portugal, the U.K., and Mexico. In October 2002, the company entered the U.S. home health care market by purchasing American Homecare Supply (AHS) for $166 million. AHS had annual revenues of $110 million, and was one of the 10 largest home care providers of respiratory therapy and medical equipment. APD has since made a series of small

U.S. home care acquisitions, including four in FY 05.

The electronics and performance materials segment (21%,16%) supplies specialty gases (nitrogen trifluoride, silane, phosphine), specialty and bulk chemicals, services and equipment to makers of silicone and semiconductors, displays and photovoltaic devices. Performance materials include epoxy and polyurethane additives, specialty amines, and surfactants for coatings, adhesives, personal care and cleaning products, and polyurethanes.

Equipment and energy (6%, 5%) includes cryogenic and process equipment for air separation, gas processing, natural gas liquefaction (LNG), and hydrogen purification. The segment also includes 50%-owned ventures in power cogeneration and flue gas desulfurization facilities.

Chemicals (9%, 9%) include water-based polymers emulsions and polyurethane intermediates used for adhesives, fabric binders, coatings, paper, furniture, and automotive markets.

Company Financials Fiscal Year Ended Sep. 30

Per Share Data ($)	2007	2006	2005	2004	2003	2002	2001	2000	1999	1998
Tangible Book Value	NA	17.59	16.03	15.45	12.99	13.33	10.79	10.78	11.39	10.17
Cash Flow	NA	6.64	6.22	5.76	4.65	4.97	4.95	3.24	4.53	4.78
Earnings	4.67	3.29	3.08	2.64	1.79	2.36	2.12	0.57	2.09	2.48
S&P Core Earnings	NA	2.94	3.01	2.63	1.66	1.67	1.70	NA	NA	NA
Dividends	1.48	1.34	1.25	1.04	0.88	0.82	0.78	0.74	0.70	0.64
Payout Ratio	32%	41%	41%	39%	49%	35%	37%	130%	33%	26%
Prices:High	101.16	72.45	65.81	59.18	53.07	53.52	49.00	42.25	49.25	45.34
Prices:Low	68.58	58.01	53.00	46.71	36.97	40.00	32.25	23.00	25.69	29.00
P/E Ratio:High	22	22	21	22	30	23	23	74	24	18
P/E Ratio:Low	15	18	17	18	21	17	15	40	12	12

Income Statement Analysis (Million $)

	2007	2006	2005	2004	2003	2002	2001	2000	1999	1998
Revenue	NA	8,850	8,144	7,411	6,297	5,401	5,717	5,496	5,020	4,919
Operating Income	NA	1,777	1,700	1,567	1,218	1,319	1,313	1,407	725	1,320
Depreciation	NA	763	728	715	640	581	573	576	527	506
Interest Expense	NA	119	110	121	124	122	191	197	159	163
Pretax Income	NA	1,049	998	851	565	784	737	118	669	824
Effective Tax Rate	NA	25.8%	26.4%	26.6%	26.0%	30.7%	29.7%	NM	30.4%	33.6%
Net Income	NA	748	712	604	400	525	513	124	451	547
S&P Core Earnings	NA	670	695	601	369	369	370	NA	NA	NA

Balance Sheet & Other Financial Data (Million $)

	2007	2006	2005	2004	2003	2002	2001	2000	1999	1998
Cash	NA	35.2	55.8	146	76.2	254	66.2	94.1	61.6	61.5
Current Assets	NA	2,613	2,415	2,417	2,068	1,909	1,685	1,805	1,782	1,642
Total Assets	NA	11,181	10,409	10,040	9,432	8,495	8,084	8,271	8,236	7,490
Current Liabilities	NA	2,323	1,943	1,706	1,581	1,256	1,352	1,375	1,858	1,266
Long Term Debt	NA	2,280	2,053	Nil	2,169	2,041	2,028	2,616	1,962	2,279
Common Equity	NA	4,924	4,576	4,444	3,783	3,460	3,106	2,821	2,962	2,667
Total Capital	NA	8,215	7,644	5,401	6,845	6,411	6,030	6,334	5,782	5,649
Capital Expenditures	NA	1,261	930	706	613	628	708	768	889	771
Cash Flow	NA	1,511	1,440	1,319	1,040	1,106	1,086	700	978	1,053
Current Ratio	NA	1.1	1.2	1.4	1.3	1.5	1.2	1.3	1.0	1.3
% Long Term Debt of Capitalization	NA	27.8	26.9	Nil	31.7	31.8	33.6	41.3	33.9	40.3
% Net Income of Revenue	NA	8.5	8.7	8.2	6.4	9.7	9.0	2.3	9.0	11.1
% Return on Assets	NA	6.9	7.0	6.2	4.5	6.3	6.3	1.5	5.7	7.4
% Return on Equity	NA	15.8	15.8	14.7	11.1	16.0	17.3	4.3	16.0	20.6

Data as orig reptd.; bef. results of disc opers/spec. items. Per share data adj. for stk. divs.; EPS diluted. E-Estimated. NA-Not Available. NM-Not Meaningful. NR-Not Ranked. UR-Under Review.

Office: 7201 Hamilton Boulevard, Allentown, PA 18195-1501.
Telephone: 610-481-4911.
Website: http://www.airproducts.com
Chrmn & CEO: J.P. Jones, III

Pres & COO: J.E. McGlade
VP & CFO: P.E. Huck
VP & CTO: M. Alger
VP, Secy & General Counsel: W.D. Brown

Investor Contact: N. Squires (610-481-7461)
Board Members: M. Baeza, W. Davis, III, M. J. Donahue, U. F. Fairbairn, W. D. Ford, E. E. Hagenlocker, E. Henkes, J. P. Jones, III, J. E. McGlade, M. G. McGlynn, C. Noski, L. S. Smith

Founded: 1940
Domicile: Delaware
Employees: 20,700

STANDARD &POOR'S

Akamai Technologies Inc

S&P Recommendation **SELL** ★ ★ ☆ ☆ ☆	Price $36.35 (as of Nov 23, 2007)	12-Mo. Target Price $28.00	Investment Style Large-Cap Growth

GICS Sector Information Technology
Sub-Industry Internet Software & Services

Summary This company develops and deploys solutions designed to accelerate and improve the delivery of Internet content and applications.

Key Stock Statistics (Source S&P, Vickers, company reports)

52-Wk Range	$59.69– 27.75	S&P Oper. EPS 2007**E**	0.49	Market Capitalization(B)	$6.020	Beta	4.55
Trailing 12-Month EPS	$0.48	S&P Oper. EPS 2008**E**	0.65	Yield (%)	Nil	S&P 3-Yr. Proj. EPS CAGR(%)	35.00
Trailing 12-Month P/E	75.7	P/E on S&P Oper. EPS 2007**E**	74.2	Dividend Rate/Share	Nil	S&P Credit Rating	NR
$10K Invested 5 Yrs Ago	$165,227	Common Shares Outstg. (M)	165.6	Institutional Ownership (%)	88		

Price Performance

30-Week Mov. Avg. ··· 10-Week Mov. Avg. — **GAAP Earnings vs. Previous Year** Volume Above Avg.|||| STARS
12-Mo. Target Price — Relative Strength — ▲ Up ▼ Down ► No Change Below Avg.|||| ★

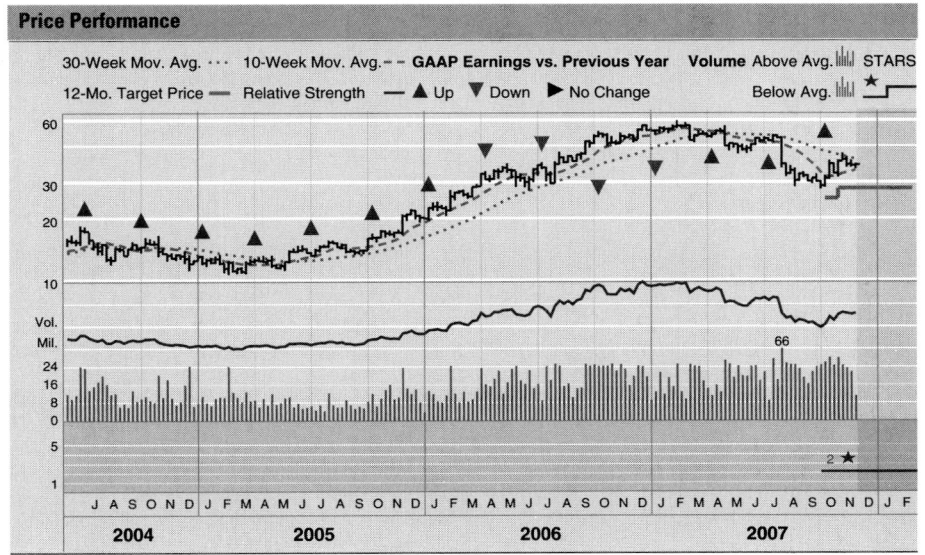

Options: ASE, CBOE, P, Ph

Analysis prepared by **Scott H. Kessler** on October 29, 2007, when the stock traded at **$ 39.05.**

Highlights

➤ We project that revenues will rise 46% in 2007 and 30% in 2008, reflecting healthy domestic and international demand, driven by the increasing use and importance of the Internet to distribute content and applications.

➤ We foresee annual gross margins declining through 2009, reflecting higher bandwidth costs and modest pricing pressures. But we believe yearly operating and net margins will widen in 2007 and 2008, owing largely to economies of scale.

➤ AKAM has made some $335 million in technology-focused acquisitions since late 2006, enhancing its capabilities regarding content and application transmission speeds, rich-media distribution, and peer-to-peer networks. In December 2006, it purchased Nine Systems for some $158 million in cash and stock. In March 2007, AKAM bought Netli for $162 million in stock. In April 2007, the company acquired Red Swoosh for $15 million in stock. As of September 2007, AKAM had some $366 million in net cash and equivalents, including about $200 million in convertible debt.

Investment Rationale/Risk

➤ AKAM is a pioneer in content and application distribution. However, we believe that even though this area will continue to grow rapidly, AKAM faces challenges from companies providing less sophisticated offerings. Despite what we expect will be largely successful efforts to broaden and enhance its products and services, we see the stock as overvalued.

➤ Risks to our recommendation and target price include stronger demand for AKAM's solutions than we expect, less significant competition, and better corporate execution than we foresee.

➤ Our P/E analysis relative to the S&P 500 Internet Software & Services sub-industry, allowing for a premium reflecting AKAM's market leadership and intellectual property, results in a value of $25. Similar P/E-to-growth considerations yield a price of $30. Our DCF analysis, with assumptions including a WACC of 13.9%, free cash flow growth averaging 45% from 2007 to 2011, and a terminal growth rate of 3%, leads to an intrinsic value calculation of $21. Weighting these evaluations results in our 12-month target price of $28.

Qualitative Risk Assessment

LOW	MEDIUM	**HIGH**

Our risk assessment reflects what we view as notable and increasing competition, considerable recent acquisition activity, some $200 million in convertible debt, and a history through 2003 of substantial net losses.

Quantitative Evaluations

S&P Quality Ranking NR

D	C	B-	B	B+	A-	A	A+

Relative Strength Rank **STRONG**

84

LOWEST = 1   HIGHEST = 99

Revenue/Earnings Data

Revenue (Million $)

	1Q	2Q	3Q	4Q	Year
2007	139.3	152.7	161.2	--	--
2006	90.83	100.7	111.5	125.7	428.7
2005	60.10	64.65	75.71	82.66	283.1
2004	48.37	50.79	53.29	57.58	210.0
2003	36.56	37.76	41.77	45.17	161.3
2002	37.93	36.32	35.38	35.35	145.0

Earnings Per Share ($)

2007	0.11	0.12	0.13	E0.14	E0.49
2006	0.07	0.07	0.08	0.12	0.34
2005	0.10	0.11	1.71	0.16	2.11
2004	0.02	0.05	0.08	0.10	0.25
2003	-0.07	-0.13	-0.03	-0.02	-0.25
2002	-0.54	-0.38	-0.42	-0.47	-1.81

Fiscal year ended Dec. 31. Next earnings report expected: Mid February. EPS Estimates based on S&P Operating Earnings; historical GAAP earnings are as reported.

Dividend Data

No cash dividends have been paid.

The McGraw-Hill Companies

Akamai Technologies Inc

Business Summary October 29, 2007

CORPORATE OVERVIEW. The Internet plays a crucial role in the way entities conduct business; however, it was not originally intended to accommodate the volume or complexity of today's demands. As a result, online information is often delayed or lost.

Akamai has developed solutions to accelerate and improve the delivery of Internet content and applications. Its solutions are designed to help customers enhance their revenues and reduce costs by maximizing the performance of their online businesses. Advancing website performance and reliability enable AKAM's customers to improve end-user experiences and promote more effective operations. Specifically, AKAM seeks to address issues related to performance, scalability and security. The company offers solutions focused on digital media distribution and storage, content and application delivery, application performance, on-demand managed services, and website intelligence.

CORPORATE STRATEGY. AKAM believes it has deployed the world's largest globally distributed computing platform, which includes more than 28,000 servers around the world. The company employs its proprietary solutions and

specialized technologies such as advanced routing, load balancing, and data collection and monitoring to deliver customer content and applications. We perceive this platform and the related intellectual property as a notable competitive advantage the company will continue to leverage.

Although competition in this area has increased notably over the past few years, AKAM's focus on both dynamic (i.e., back and forth) distribution and segments beyond media and entertainment help insulate the company from substantial pricing pressures, in our view. Nonetheless, we believe lower-end business is more at risk given additional players entering the market.

We believe recent acquisitions have bolstered the company's base and breadth of technologies related to streaming rich media, enhancing distribution speeds, and peer-to-peer networks. We expect AKAM to continue pursuing transactions that are not transformational in nature.

Company Financials Fiscal Year Ended Dec. 31

Per Share Data ($)	2006	2005	2004	2003	2002	2001	2000	1999	1998	1997
Tangible Book Value	4.10	3.19	NM	NM	NM	NM	2.02	3.04	NA	NA
Cash Flow	0.58	2.25	0.37	0.17	-1.01	-20.40	-1.98	-1.75	NA	NA
Earnings	0.34	2.11	0.25	-0.25	-1.81	-23.59	-10.07	-1.87	NA	NA
S&P Core Earnings	0.34	1.93	-0.16	-0.64	-2.05	-12.47	NA	NA	NA	NA
Dividends	Nil	Nil	Nil	Nil	Nil	Nil	Nil	Nil	NA	NA
Payout Ratio	Nil	Nil	Nil	Nil	Nil	Nil	Nil	Nil	NA	NA
Prices:High	56.80	22.25	18.47	14.20	6.34	37.44	345.50	344.87	NA	NA
Prices:Low	19.57	10.64	10.74	1.18	0.56	2.52	18.06	26.00	NA	NA
P/E Ratio:High	NM	11	74	NM	NM	NM	NM	NM	NA	NA
P/E Ratio:Low	NM	5	43	NM	NM	NM	NM	NM	NA	NA

Income Statement Analysis (Million $)

	2006	2005	2004	2003	2002	2001	2000	1999	1998	1997
Revenue	429	283	210	161	145	163	89.8	3.99	NA	NA
Operating Income	124	98.5	69.2	30.1	-46.3	-131	-187	-53.0	NA	NA
Depreciation	45.6	25.2	20.2	49.7	90.4	330	712	3.43	NA	NA
Interest Expense	3.17	5.33	10.2	18.3	18.4	18.9	8.93	2.15	NA	NA
Pretax Income	98.5	70.4	35.1	-28.7	-204	-2,434	-886	-54.2	NA	NA
Effective Tax Rate	41.7%	NM	2.20%	NM	NM	NM	NM	NM	NA	NA
Net Income	57.4	328	34.4	-29.3	-204	-2,436	-886	-54.2	NA	NA
S&P Core Earnings	57.2	300	-19.9	-75.6	-231	-1,286	NA	NA	NA	NA

Balance Sheet & Other Financial Data (Million $)

	2006	2005	2004	2003	2002	2001	2000	1999	1998	1997
Cash	270	292	70.6	165	115	211	310	270	NA	NA
Current Assets	375	355	109	202	142	228	355	274	NA	NA
Total Assets	1,248	891	183	279	230	421	2,791	301	NA	NA
Current Liabilities	89.3	61.9	46.8	62.7	81.1	91.3	84.9	18.6	NA	NA
Long Term Debt	200	200	257	386	301	300	300	0.73	NA	NA
Common Equity	955	624	-126	-175	-168	17.2	2,404	281	NA	NA
Total Capital	1,155	824	131	211	133	317	2,705	285	NA	NA
Capital Expenditures	56.8	26.9	12.3	1.42	7.25	64.5	132	25.7	NA	NA
Cash Flow	103	353	54.6	20.5	-114	-2,106	-174	-53.0	NA	NA
Current Ratio	4.2	5.7	2.3	3.2	1.7	2.5	4.2	14.7	NA	NA
% Long Term Debt of Capitalization	17.3	24.3	196.4	183.2	226.5	94.6	11.1	0.3	NA	NA
% Net Income of Revenue	13.4	115.9	16.4	NM	NM	NM	NM	NM	NA	NA
% Return on Assets	5.4	61.1	14.9	NM	NM	NM	NM	NM	NA	NA
% Return on Equity	7.3	131.7	NM	NM	NM	NM	NM	NM	NA	NA

Data as orig reptd.; bef. results of disc opers/spec. items. Per share data adj. for stk. divs.; EPS diluted. E-Estimated. NA-Not Available. NM-Not Meaningful. NR-Not Ranked. UR-Under Review.

Office: 8 Cambridge Ctr, Cambridge, MA 02142-1413.
Telephone: 617-444-3000.
Email: ir@akamai.com
Website: http://www.akamai.com

Exec Chrmn: G.H. Conrades
Pres & CEO: P. Sagan
VP, Secy & General Counsel: M. Haratunian
CFO: J.D. Sherman

CSO: F.T. Leighton
Investor Contact: S. Smith (617-444-2804)
Board Members: G. H. Conrades, M. M. Coyne, II, R. L. Graham, D. W. Kenny, P. J. Kight, F. T. Leighton, G. Moore, P. Sagan, F. V. Salerno, N. O. Seligman

Founded: 1998
Domicile: Delaware
Employees: 1,261

Alcoa Inc.

STANDARD &POOR'S

S&P Recommendation HOLD ★★★☆☆	**Price** $35.15 (as of Nov 23, 2007)	**12-Mo. Target Price** $40.00	**Investment Style** Large-Cap Value

GICS Sector Materials
Sub-Industry Aluminum

Summary Alcoa is the second largest producer of aluminum and the world's largest producer of alumina.

Key Stock Statistics (Source S&P, Vickers, company reports)

52-Wk Range	$48.77– 28.09	S&P Oper. EPS 2007**E**	2.76	Market Capitalization(B)	$29.812	Beta	2.04
Trailing 12-Month EPS	$2.61	S&P Oper. EPS 2008**E**	2.85	Yield (%)	1.93	S&P 3-Yr. Proj. EPS CAGR(%)	3.00
Trailing 12-Month P/E	13.5	P/E on S&P Oper. EPS 2007**E**	12.7	Dividend Rate/Share	$0.68	S&P Credit Rating	BBB+
$10K Invested 5 Yrs Ago	$15,904	Common Shares Outstg. (M)	848.1	Institutional Ownership (%)	87		

Price Performance

30-Week Mov. Avg. ···· 10-Week Mov. Avg. ‑ ‑ **GAAP Earnings vs. Previous Year**   Volume Above Avg. ▮▮▮ STARS
12-Mo. Target Price — Relative Strength   — ▲ Up ▼ Down ► No Change   Below Avg. ▮▮▮ ★

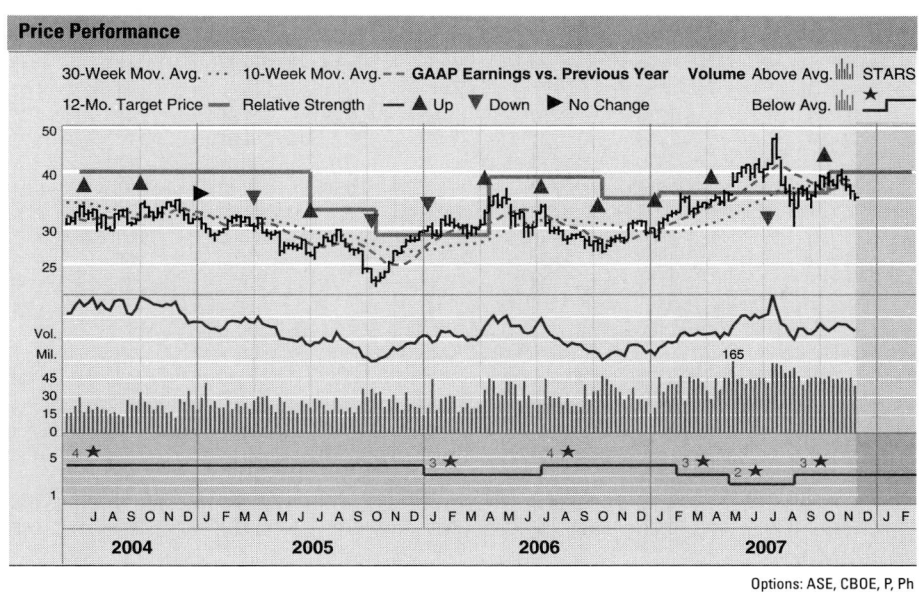

Analysis prepared by **Leo J. Larkin** on October 15, 2007, when the stock traded at **$ 38.13**.

Options: ASE, CBOE, P, Ph

Highlights

➤ Assuming 2.0% U.S. real GDP growth in 2008 versus estimated GDP growth of 2.0% in 2007, and slower growth in the global economy, we look for a 2% sales decline in 2008, versus 2007's estimated gain of 3%. In our view, less robust aerospace demand, continued weakness in residential construction and a flat auto market will depress volume. S&P estimates a 17% drop in housing starts in 2008, versus a projected drop of 25% in 2007 and total motor vehicle sales of 16.1 million units in 2008, unchanged from 2007. We estimate an average aluminum price of about $1.10 a pound in 2008, versus $1.15 estimated for 2007, as we believe that the market surplus which developed in 2007 will persist in 2008.

➤ Penalized by higher depreciation and a small decline in volume, we anticipate a decrease in operating profit. But, after flat interest expense, a lower tax rate, and fewer shares outstanding, we project an increase in EPS to $2.85 in 2008 from $2.76 estimated for 2007.

➤ Longer term, we think earnings will benefit from aluminum industry consolidation and a shift to lower cost aluminum plants.

Investment Rationale/Risk

➤ We believe that AA's long-term sales and EPS will benefit from ongoing consolidation of the aluminum industry and a generally higher aluminum price. In our view, consolidation will result in a more disciplined pricing environment and less volatility in sales and profits over the course of the business cycle. We believe aluminum hit a cyclical bottom in 2002 and will move higher through 2007. We look for a small pullback in the price in 2008. But, we believe the price of aluminum at the trough of the next cycle will be higher than the price in 2002 as a result of industry consolidation, in particular, consolidation of China's aluminum industry. In recent years, China's high level of exports has been a drag on the aluminum price.

➤ Risks to our recommendation and target price include a decline in the aluminum price in 2008 in excess of what we currently anticipate.

➤ Our 12-month target price of $40 is based on our view that the shares will trade at a P/E of 14X our 2008 EPS estimate, near the low end of AA's historical range, given our assumption that 2008 may represent a peak of cycle EPS, and that the shares would sell at a discount to its peers.

Qualitative Risk Assessment

LOW	MEDIUM	**HIGH**

Our risk assessment reflects our view that AA's sales and earnings are exposed to cyclical markets such as autos and the home building sector of the construction market. Partially offsetting this is what we view as the company's moderate balance sheet leverage and improving free cash flow.

Quantitative Evaluations

S&P Quality Ranking **B+**

D	C	B-	B	**B+**	A-	A	A+

Relative Strength Rank   **MODERATE**

48

LOWEST = 1   HIGHEST = 99

Revenue/Earnings Data

Revenue (Million $)

	1Q	2Q	3Q	4Q	Year
2007	7,908	8,066	7,387	--	--
2006	7,244	7,959	7,631	7,840	30,379
2005	6,226	6,698	6,566	6,669	26,159
2004	5,588	5,971	5,878	6,041	23,478
2003	5,140	5,497	5,335	5,532	21,504
2002	4,900	5,158	5,144	5,061	20,263

Earnings Per Share ($)

2007	0.77	0.81	0.64	E0.53	E2.76
2006	0.70	0.86	0.62	0.29	2.47
2005	0.30	0.53	0.33	0.24	1.40
2004	0.41	0.46	0.34	0.39	1.60
2003	0.23	0.26	0.33	0.39	1.20
2002	0.22	0.28	0.24	-0.15	0.58

Fiscal year ended Dec. 31. Next earnings report expected: Early January. EPS Estimates based on S&P Operating Earnings; historical GAAP earnings are as reported.

Dividend Data (Dates: mm/dd Payment Date: mm/dd/yy)

Amount ($)	Date Decl.	Ex-Div. Date	Stk. of Record	Payment Date
0.170	01/19	01/31	02/02	02/25/07
0.170	04/20	05/02	05/04	05/25/07
0.170	07/20	08/01	08/03	08/25/07
0.170	09/14	10/31	11/02	11/25/07

Dividends have been paid since 1939. Source: Company reports.

Alcoa Inc.

Business Summary October 15, 2007

CORPORATE OVERVIEW. Alcoa is the world's second largest producer of primary aluminum and is the world's largest supplier of alumina, an intermediate raw material used to make aluminum. In 2006 and 2005, primary aluminum production totaled 3.6 million metric tons.

MARKET PROFILE. The primary factor affecting demand for aluminum products is economic growth, in general, and growth in demand for durable goods, in particular. The three largest end markets for aluminum in North America are transportation, containers/packaging, and construction. In 2005 (latest

available), these markets accounted for 68.3% of revenues in North America. In terms of primary production, the size of the world market was 23.9 million metric tons in 2006. Alcoa's market share was 15.1%. From 1997 through 2006, global consumption rose at a compound annual growth rate (CAGR) of 5.2%.

Company Financials Fiscal Year Ended Dec. 31

Per Share Data ($)	2006	2005	2004	2003	2002	2001	2000	1999	1998	1997
Tangible Book Value	9.69	7.02	7.70	6.30	3.27	4.96	6.19	6.62	6.08	5.59
Cash Flow	3.96	2.85	2.98	2.61	3.20	2.49	3.29	2.61	2.42	2.24
Earnings	2.47	1.40	1.60	1.20	0.58	1.05	1.81	1.41	1.21	1.16
S&P Core Earnings	2.46	1.05	1.52	0.92	-0.17	0.17	NA	NA	NA	NA
Dividends	0.60	0.60	0.60	0.60	0.60	0.60	0.50	0.40	0.38	0.24
Payout Ratio	24%	43%	38%	50%	103%	57%	28%	29%	31%	21%
Prices:High	36.96	32.29	39.44	38.92	39.75	45.71	43.63	41.69	20.31	22.41
Prices:Low	26.39	22.28	28.51	18.45	17.62	27.36	23.13	17.97	14.50	16.06
P/E Ratio:High	15	23	25	32	69	44	24	30	17	19
P/E Ratio:Low	11	16	18	15	30	26	13	13	12	14

Income Statement Analysis (Million $)

	2006	2005	2004	2003	2002	2001	2000	1999	1998	1997
Revenue	30,379	26,159	23,478	21,504	20,263	22,859	22,936	16,323	15,340	13,482
Operating Income	5,410	3,398	3,397	2,885	2,663	3,523	4,304	2,821	2,509	2,238
Depreciation	1,280	1,267	1,212	1,202	2,224	1,253	1,219	901	856	754
Interest Expense	384	339	270	314	350	393	427	195	198	141
Pretax Income	3,432	1,933	2,204	1,669	925	1,641	2,812	1,849	1,605	1,602
Effective Tax Rate	24.3%	22.8%	25.3%	24.2%	31.6%	32.0%	33.5%	29.9%	32.0%	33.0%
Net Income	2,161	1,233	1,402	1,034	498	908	1,489	1,054	853	805
S&P Core Earnings	2,154	924	1,334	777	-143	146	NA	NA	NA	NA

Balance Sheet & Other Financial Data (Million $)

	2006	2005	2004	2003	2002	2001	2000	1999	1998	1997
Cash	506	762	457	576	344	512	315	237	342	801
Current Assets	9,157	8,790	7,493	6,740	6,313	6,792	7,578	4,800	5,025	4,417
Total Assets	37,183	33,696	32,609	31,711	29,810	28,355	31,691	17,066	17,463	13,071
Current Liabilities	7,281	7,368	6,298	5,084	4,461	5,003	7,954	3,003	3,268	2,453
Long Term Debt	5,910	5,279	5,346	6,692	8,365	6,388	4,987	2,657	2,877	1,457
Common Equity	14,576	13,318	13,245	12,020	9,872	10,614	11,366	6,262	6,000	4,363
Total Capital	23,103	20,892	20,852	20,911	20,087	18,927	18,892	10,870	10,767	6,140
Capital Expenditures	3,201	2,124	1,142	863	1,263	1,177	1,121	920	932	912
Cash Flow	3,441	2,498	2,612	2,234	2,720	2,159	2,706	1,953	1,707	1,557
Current Ratio	1.3	1.2	1.2	1.3	1.4	1.4	1.0	1.6	1.5	1.8
% Long Term Debt of Capitalization	25.6	25.3	25.6	32.0	41.6	33.8	26.4	24.4	26.7	23.7
% Net Income of Revenue	7.1	4.7	6.0	4.8	2.5	4.0	6.5	6.5	5.6	6.0
% Return on Assets	6.1	3.7	4.4	3.4	1.7	3.0	6.1	6.1	5.6	6.1
% Return on Equity	15.5	9.3	11.1	9.4	4.9	8.2	16.9	17.2	16.4	18.3

Data as orig reptd.; bef. results of disc opers/spec. items. Per share data adj. for stk. divs.; EPS diluted. E-Estimated. NA-Not Available. NM-Not Meaningful. NR-Not Ranked. UR-Under Review.

Office: 390 Park Ave, New York, NY 10022-4608.
Telephone: 212-836-2674.
Email: investor.relations@alcoa.com
Website: http://www.alcoa.com

Chrmn & CEO: A.J. Belda
EVP, General Counsel & CCO: L.R. Purtell
VP & CFO: C.D. McLane, Jr.
VP & Treas: P. Hong

VP & Cntlr: J.R. Lucot
Investor Contact: T. Thene (212-836-2674)
Board Members: A. J. Belda, K. S. Fuller, C. Ghosn, J. T. Gorman, J. M. Gueron, K. Kleinfeld, J. Owens, H. B. Schacht, R. N. Tata, F. A. Thomas, E. Zedillo

Founded: 1888
Domicile: Pennsylvania
Employees: 123,000

Allegheny Energy Inc.

STANDARD &POOR'S

S&P Recommendation	HOLD ★★★☆☆	Price	12-Mo. Target Price	Investment Style
		$58.69 (as of Nov 23, 2007)	$62.00	Large-Cap Blend

GICS Sector Utilities
Sub-Industry Electric Utilities

Summary This diversified energy company engages in electric generation and electric and natural gas delivery, and invests in and develops telecommunications and energy-related projects.

Key Stock Statistics (Source S&P, Vickers, company reports)

52-Wk Range	$60.95– 42.71	S&P Oper. EPS 2007**E**	2.24	Market Capitalization(B)	$9.756	Beta	0.12
Trailing 12-Month EPS	$2.16	S&P Oper. EPS 2008**E**	2.64	Yield (%)	NA	S&P 3-Yr. Proj. EPS CAGR(%)	18.00
Trailing 12-Month P/E	27.2	P/E on S&P Oper. EPS 2007**E**	26.2	Dividend Rate/Share	NA	S&P Credit Rating	BBB-
$10K Invested 5 Yrs Ago	$75,340	Common Shares Outstg. (M)	166.2	Institutional Ownership (%)	82		

Price Performance

30-Week Mov. Avg. ··· 10-Week Mov. Avg. - - GAAP Earnings vs. Previous Year   Volume Above Avg. STARS
12-Mo. Target Price — Relative Strength — ▲ Up ▼ Down ▶ No Change   Below Avg. ★

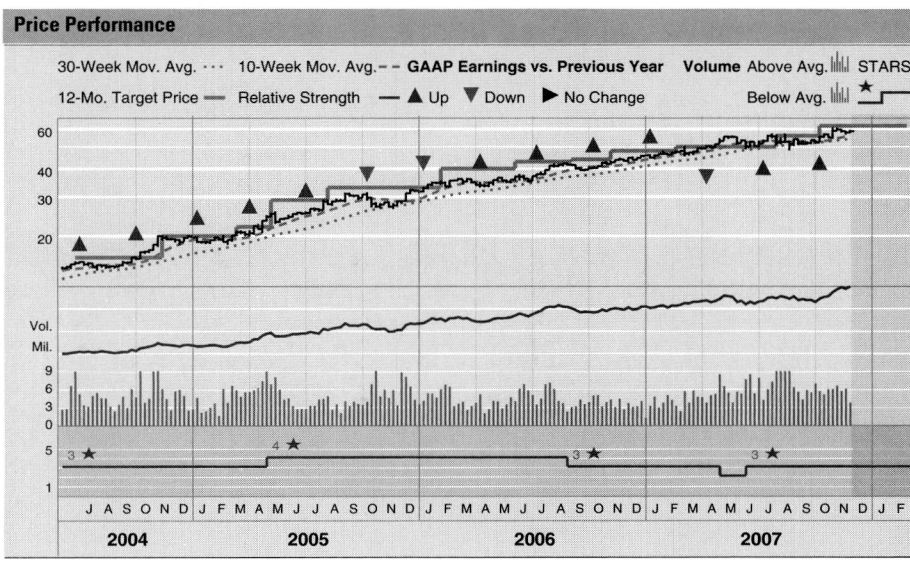

Options: ASE, CBOE, P

Analysis prepared by **Christopher B. Muir** on November 01, 2007, when the stock traded at **$60.07**.

Qualitative Risk Assessment

LOW	**MEDIUM**	HIGH

Our risk assessment reflects the company's mid-level capitalization and balanced sources of earnings, which include both low risk regulated electric utility and higher risk unregulated power generation operations.

Quantitative Evaluations

S&P Quality Ranking B

D	C	B-	**B**	B+	A-	A	A+

Relative Strength Rank STRONG

89

LOWEST = 1 HIGHEST = 99

Revenue/Earnings Data

Revenue (Million $)

	1Q	2Q	3Q	4Q	Year
2007	847.6	826.5	846.6	--	--
2006	845.6	722.2	816.6	737.0	3,121
2005	754.0	714.7	845.1	724.1	3,038
2004	735.4	608.9	723.3	688.5	2,756
2003	715.7	359.2	637.6	760.0	2,472
2002	1,005	784.6	537.1	661.7	2,988

Earnings Per Share ($)

2007	0.65	0.45	0.67	E0.46	E2.24
2006	0.68	0.19	0.65	0.37	1.89
2005	0.24	-0.04	0.26	0.02	0.47
2004	0.23	-0.26	0.37	0.53	0.99
2003	-0.30	-1.82	-0.40	-0.11	-2.64
2002	0.61	-0.27	-2.09	-2.23	-4.00

Fiscal year ended Dec. 31. Next earnings report expected: Early February. EPS Estimates based on S&P Operating Earnings; historical GAAP earnings are as reported.

Highlights

➤ We see 2007 and 2008 revenues increasing 5.3% and 7.1%, respectively, aided by regulated operations. We expect regulated utility revenues to benefit from more normal weather and customer growth. We expect non-regulated revenues to rise due to higher power prices increased generation capacity factors, more normal weather, rate increases for providers of last resort service in Pennsylvania, and the transitioning of some Virginia customers to market-based rates.

➤ We think operating profit margins will expand to 25.2% in 2007, from 23.5% in 2006. We look for operations and maintenance expense control to be a driving factor, partly offset by higher fuel costs. We expect operating margins in 2008 to rise to 26.2%, helped by improvements in all operating expense categories. We see pretax profit margins increasing to 18.9% in 2007 and 20.5% in 2008, from 15.9% in 2006, as we expect lower interest expense.

➤ Assuming an effective tax rate of 37.5%, we forecast 2007 operating EPS of $2.24, up 25% from $1.79 in 2006. Our 2008 EPS estimate is $2.64, an additional 18% increase.

Investment Rationale/Risk

➤ We believe continued debt reduction and strong cash flow from core operations will further reduce AYE's borrowing costs. AYE reduced debt by $825 million in 2005 and $517 million in 2006. Operationally, we like AYE's focus on improving plant performance and controlling operational expenses. We also expect the ending of distribution rate caps in Pennsylvania in 2007 and residential generation caps in Maryland in 2008. The shares recently traded at 22.8X our 2008 EPS estimate, or a 38% premium to its electric utility peers, which we view as appropriate given the high EPS growth rate.

➤ Risks to our recommendation and target price include lower than expected cash flows, and a weaker than projected economy.

➤ Our 12-month target price of $62 values the stock at a P/E multiple of 23.5X our 2008 EPS estimate, a 34% premium valuation to its peer target. We see this as merited by what we view as AYE's prospects for a continued recovery from near bankruptcy, which leads us to forecast double-digit earnings growth, significant strengthening of its balance sheet and above peer average dividend growth.

Dividend Data (Dates: mm/dd Payment Date: mm/dd/yy)

Amount ($)	Date Decl.	Ex-Div. Date	Stk. of Record	Payment Date
0.150	10/04	11/29	12/03	12/17/07

Dividends have been paid since 2007. Source: Company reports.

Please read the Required Disclosures and Analyst Certification on the last page of this report.

The McGraw-Hill Companies

Allegheny Energy Inc.

Business Summary November 01, 2007

CORPORATE OVERVIEW. AYE is an integrated electric distribution and generation company operating in the Mid-Atlantic region. Its three distribution businesses operate under the trade name Allegheny Power. West Penn operates an electric transmission and distribution (T&D) system in southwestern, northern and south central Pennsylvania, serving approximately 702,800 customers. Potomac Edison operates an electric T&D system in portions of West Virginia, Maryland and Virginia. Potomac Edison serves approximately 454,400 electric customers. Monongahela conducts an electric T&D business that serves roughly 371,400 electric customers in northern West Virginia. In December 2005, AYE sold its Ohio service territory to American Electric Power for net cash proceeds of approximately $52 million. In September 2005, Monongahela sold its Mountaineer natural gas operations in West Virginia for $161 million with the assumption of $87 million of debt by the purchaser.

Allegheny Energy Supply, AYE's primary unregulated generating division, ended 2005 with 8,245 megawatts (MW) of capacity. The division's capacity grew from 1999 to 2001 through the transfer of regulated power plants in Pennsylvania, Maryland, Virginia and Ohio from AYE utilities, acquisition of existing plants, and construction activities. In July 2005, Allegheny Energy Supply was awarded contracts to meet Allegheny Power's 2009 and 2010 generation supply needs in Pennsylvania. In August 2005, Allegheny Energy Supply completed the sale of its Indiana-based Wheatland generating facility for approximately $100 million. The division has also placed its 526 MW natural gas-fired Gleason, TN, power plant for sale.

Monongahela owns or controls about 2,130 MW of generating capacity, most of which is delivered to AYE's electric utilities. Additionally, AYE owns a 40% interest (about 1,010 MW) in the Bath County pumped-storage hydroelectric power station.

As of December 31, 2005, about 75.5% of AYE's 10,375 MW of owned and controlled capacity was coal-fired, 13.4% was gas-fired, 10.3% was hydroelectric and 0.8% oil-fired.

Company Financials Fiscal Year Ended Dec. 31

Per Share Data ($)	2006	2005	2004	2003	2002	2001	2000	1999	1998	1997
Tangible Book Value	10.36	7.98	6.94	9.05	12.05	16.48	13.80	14.97	16.49	18.31
Earnings	1.89	0.47	0.99	-2.64	-4.00	3.73	2.84	2.45	2.15	2.30
S&P Core Earnings	1.90	0.45	0.56	-2.60	-4.22	3.24	NA	NA	NA	NA
Dividends	Nil	Nil	Nil	Nil	1.29	1.72	1.72	1.72	1.72	1.72
Payout Ratio	Nil	Nil	Nil	Nil	NM	46%	61%	77%	74%	75%
Prices:High	46.25	32.32	20.20	13.09	43.86	55.09	48.75	35.19	34.94	32.59
Prices:Low	31.33	18.25	11.75	4.70	2.95	32.99	23.63	26.19	26.63	25.50
P/E Ratio:High	24	69	20	NM	NM	15	17	14	15	14
P/E Ratio:Low	16	39	12	NM	NM	9	8	11	11	11

Income Statement Analysis (Million $)	2006	2005	2004	2003	2002	2001	2000	1999	1998	1997
Revenue	3,121	3,038	2,756	2,472	2,988	10,379	4,012	2,808	2,576	2,369
Depreciation	273	308	299	327	309	302	248	257	270	266
Maintenance	NA	NA	NA	NA	NA	288	230	224	218	231
Fixed Charges Coverage	2.80	1.39	1.28	-0.35	-1.21	3.38	3.11	3.25	3.25	3.24
Construction Credits	NA	NA	NA	NA	13.0	11.5	7.28	6.91	5.02	NA
Effective Tax Rate	35.0%	46.1%	NM	NM	NM	35.2%	37.1%	36.6%	39.0%	37.4%
Net Income	320	75.1	130	-334	-502	449	314	285	263	281
S&P Core Earnings	321	72.0	61.8	-329	-530	391	NA	NA	NA	NA

Balance Sheet & Other Financial Data (Million $)	2006	2005	2004	2003	2002	2001	2000	1999	1998	1997
Gross Property	11,150	10,786	10,644	11,831	11,357	11,087	9,507	8,840	8,630	8,451
Capital Expenditures	447	306	266	254	403	463	402	467	234	280
Net Property	6,513	6,277	6,303	7,453	6,883	6,853	5,539	5,207	5,234	5,296
Capitalization:Long Term Debt	3,434	3,665	4,639	5,234	229	3,274	2,634	2,328	2,349	2,193
Capitalization:% Long Term Debt	62.3	58.8	77.4	77.5	10.6	54.7	60.2	57.9	53.6	47.5
Capitalization:Preferred	Nil	Nil	Nil	Nil	Nil	Nil	Nil	Nil	Nil	170
Capitalization:% Preferred	Nil	Nil	Nil	Nil	Nil	Nil	Nil	Nil	Nil	3.70
Capitalization:Common	2,080	1,695	1,354	1,516	1,932	2,710	1,741	1,695	2,034	2,257
Capitalization:% Common	37.7	98.6	22.6	22.5	89.4	45.3	39.8	42.1	46.4	48.8
Total Capital	6,462	6,228	6,733	7,713	3,358	7,090	5,372	5,062	5,351	5,784
% Operating Ratio	82.3	83.5	82.1	99.3	101.9	93.1	86.6	83.1	82.9	80.9
% Earned on Net Property	11.5	8.5	11.5	NM	NM	11.5	10.0	9.3	8.3	8.5
% Return on Revenue	10.2	2.5	4.7	NM	NM	4.3	7.8	10.2	10.2	11.9
% Return on Invested Capital	9.3	23.3	7.4	2.6	4.2	11.9	10.5	9.2	11.9	8.1
% Return on Common Equity	16.9	4.9	9.0	NM	NM	20.2	18.3	15.3	12.3	12.7

Data as orig reptd.; bef. results of disc opers/spec. items. Per share data adj. for stk. divs.; EPS diluted. E-Estimated. NA-Not Available. NM-Not Meaningful. NR-Not Ranked. UR-Under Review.

Office: 800 Cabin Hill Dr, Greensburg, PA 15601-1650.
Telephone: 724-837-3000.
Email: investorinfo@alleghenypower.com
Website: http://www.alleghenyenergy.com

Chrmn, Pres & CEO: P.J. Evanson
COO: J.H. Richardson
SVP & CFO: P.L. Goulding
VP, Chief Acctg Officer, Cntlr & CIO: T.R. Gardner

VP & General Counsel: D.M. Feinberg
Investor Contact: M. Kuniansky (724-838-6895)
Board Members: H. F. Baldwin, E. Baum, P. J. Evanson, C. F. Freidheim, Jr., J. L. Johnson, T. J. Kleisner, S. H. Rice, G. E. Sarsten, M. H. Sutton

Founded: 1925
Domicile: Maryland
Employees: 4,362

Allegheny Technologies Inc

STANDARD &POOR'S

S&P Recommendation HOLD ★★★☆☆	**Price** $93.28 (as of Nov 23, 2007)	**12-Mo. Target Price** $106.00	**Investment Style** Large-Cap Blend

GICS Sector Materials
Sub-Industry Steel

Summary This company is a leading producer of specialty metals for a wide variety of end markets.

Key Stock Statistics (Source S&P, Vickers, company reports)

52-Wk Range	$119.70–80.00	S&P Oper. EPS 2007**E**	7.15	Market Capitalization(B)	$9.534	Beta	3.60
Trailing 12-Month EPS	$7.38	S&P Oper. EPS 2008**E**	7.60	Yield (%)	0.77	S&P 3-Yr. Proj. EPS CAGR(%)	13.20
Trailing 12-Month P/E	12.6	P/E on S&P Oper. EPS 2007**E**	13.0	Dividend Rate/Share	$0.72	S&P Credit Rating	BB+
$10K Invested 5 Yrs Ago	$153,305	Common Shares Outstg. (M)	102.2	Institutional Ownership (%)	78		

Price Performance

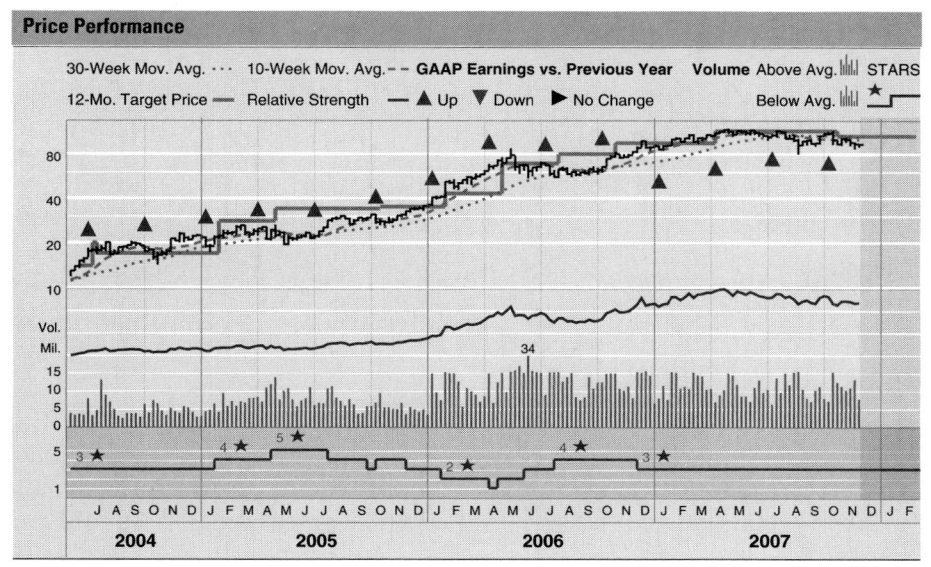

30-Week Mov. Avg. · · · 10-Week Mov. Avg. - - **GAAP Earnings vs. Previous Year** Volume Above Avg. STARS
12-Mo. Target Price — Relative Strength — ▲ Up ▼ Down ► No Change Below Avg. ★

Options: ASE, CBOE, P, Ph

Analysis prepared by **Leo J. Larkin** on October 19, 2007, when the stock traded at **$ 94.86**.

Highlights

➤ Following an estimated increase of almost 16% in 2007, we look for a 5.3% sales gain in 2008 on projected increases in the flat roll stainless steel and high performance metals segments. S&P forecasts GDP growth of 2.0% in 2008 versus projected GDP growth of 2.0% in 2007. We believe that slower demand from the aerospace market resulting from production delays by Boeing will limit gains in the high performance metals unit. Also, a projected drop of 16.6% in housing starts in 2008 will restrict the increase in sales of stainless steel flat roll products. Partly offsetting the lower housing starts will be the likelihood of some rebuilding of inventories by distributors and an improved product mix.

➤ Aided mostly by higher prices in the high performance metals unit, we look for margin expansion and a small rise in operating profit. After flat interest expense and an unchanged tax rate, we project EPS of $7.60 in 2008, versus EPS of $7.15 estimated for 2007.

➤ We think that consolidation in the stainless steel industry and continuation of the current upturn in aerospace will boost the long-term outlook for ATI's sales and EPS.

Investment Rationale/Risk

➤ We view ATI as a special situation turnaround story. After incurring losses from 2001 through 2003, the company returned to profitability in 2004 and posted large EPS gains in 2005 and 2006. We see continued growth in EPS through 2008. We foresee ATI benefiting from the consolidation in the stainless steel industry. We believe that the concentration of production in fewer hands will lead to better industry pricing discipline. Also, we see sales and EPS benefiting from increased demand from the aerospace/defense, electrical energy, chemical processing and medical products industries. However, with the shares recently trading with just modest upside to our target price, our recommendation is hold.

➤ Risks to our recommendation and target price include unexpected weakness in the aerospace and distributor markets.

➤ We apply a P/E of 13.9X to our 2008 EPS estimate, which is at the midpoint of ATI's P/E range for the past 10 years and slightly above its main peer. On that basis, our 12-month target price is $106 for these high beta shares.

Qualitative Risk Assessment

LOW	**MEDIUM**	HIGH

Our risk assessment reflects the exposure of ATI's sales and earnings to cyclical markets and our view of its comparatively high debt levels. Offsetting these factors are the company's improving free cash flow and its solid share of the markets it serves.

Quantitative Evaluations

S&P Quality Ranking **B-**

D	C	**B-**	B	B+	A-	A	A+

Relative Strength Rank **MODERATE**

49

LOWEST = 1   HIGHEST = 99

Revenue/Earnings Data

Revenue (Million $)

	1Q	2Q	3Q	4Q	Year
2007	1,373	1,471	1,335	--	--
2006	1,041	1,211	1,288	1,397	4,937
2005	879.6	904.2	861.7	894.4	3,540
2004	577.8	646.5	730.6	778.1	2,733
2003	480.5	489.9	482.6	484.4	1,937
2002	493.1	491.2	469.3	454.2	1,908

Earnings Per Share ($)

2007	1.92	2.00	1.88	E1.39	E7.15
2006	1.00	1.37	1.58	1.63	5.59
2005	0.61	0.91	0.87	1.19	3.59
2004	-0.63	0.31	0.09	0.35	0.22
2003	-0.32	-0.32	-0.36	-2.89	-3.87
2002	-0.14	-0.09	-0.09	-0.49	-0.82

Fiscal year ended Dec. 31. Next earnings report expected: Late January. EPS Estimates based on S&P Operating Earnings; historical GAAP earnings are as reported.

Dividend Data (Dates: mm/dd Payment Date: mm/dd/yy)

Amount ($)	Date Decl.	Ex-Div. Date	Stk. of Record	Payment Date
0.130	02/22	03/15	03/19	03/27/07
0.130	05/02	05/29	05/31	06/14/07
0.130	09/13	09/19	09/21	09/28/07
0.180	11/01	12/06	12/10	12/28/07

Dividends have been paid since 1996. Source: Company reports.

The McGraw-Hill Companies

Allegheny Technologies Inc

STANDARD &POOR'S

Business Summary October 19, 2007

In November 1999, Allegheny Technologies spun off all of the common stock of Teledyne Technologies Inc. (NYSE: TDY) and Water Pik Technologies, Inc. to ATI stockholders, and changed its name from Allegheny Teledyne Inc.

Following the spin-offs, ATI operates in three segments: Flat-Rolled Products, High Performance Metals, and Engineered Products. Markets for the three units include aerospace, oil and gas, transportation, food, chemical processing, consumer products, medical, and power generation.

The Flat-Rolled Products segment (54% of 2006 sales; 33% of operating profits) consists of Allegheny Ludlum Corp., Rodney Metals, the Allegheny Rodney Strip division of Allegheny Ludlum, and the company's interest in a Chinese

joint venture, Shanghai STAL Precision Stainless Steel Ltd. The companies in this segment produce, convert and distribute stainless steel sheet, strip and plate, precision rolled strip products, flat-rolled nickel-based alloys and titanium, silicon electrical steels and tool steels. Shipments totaled 695,815 tons in 2006, versus 574,369 tons in 2005. The average realized price per ton was $3,876 in 2006, versus $2,169 in 2005. Operating profits totaled $344.3 million, versus $149.9 million in 2005.

Company Financials Fiscal Year Ended Dec. 31

Per Share Data ($)	2006	2005	2004	2003	2002	2001	2000	1999	1998	1997
Tangible Book Value	12.71	6.11	2.30	NM	3.15	9.42	10.51	11.02	11.12	9.52
Cash Flow	6.48	4.47	1.00	-2.96	0.30	0.91	2.80	2.15	3.53	4.44
Earnings	5.59	3.59	0.22	-3.87	-0.82	-0.31	1.60	1.16	2.44	3.34
S&P Core Earnings	5.92	3.76	0.26	-3.19	-2.17	-2.09	NA	NA	NA	NA
Dividends	0.43	0.28	0.24	0.24	0.66	0.80	0.80	1.28	1.28	1.28
Payout Ratio	8%	8%	109%	NM	NM	NM	50%	110%	52%	38%
Prices:High	98.72	36.66	23.48	14.00	19.10	21.07	26.81	48.37	59.12	65.75
Prices:Low	35.47	17.30	8.64	2.10	5.21	12.50	12.50	20.25	28.00	42.00
P/E Ratio:High	18	10	NM	NM	NM	NM	17	42	24	20
P/E Ratio:Low	6	5	NM	NM	NM	NM	8	17	11	13

Income Statement Analysis (Million $)	2006	2005	2004	2003	2002	2001	2000	1999	1998	1997
Revenue	4,937	3,540	2,733	1,937	1,908	2,128	2,460	2,296	3,923	3,745
Operating Income	970	452	87.7	-110	65.0	166	358	284	579	531
Depreciation	84.2	77.3	76.1	74.6	90.0	98.6	99.7	95.3	109	98.5
Interest Expense	23.3	38.6	35.5	27.7	34.3	29.3	34.4	25.9	19.3	19.6
Pretax Income	869	307	19.8	-280	-104	-36.4	209	174	391	475
Effective Tax Rate	34.2%	NM	NM	NM	NM	NM	36.5%	36.3%	38.3%	37.4%
Net Income	572	362	19.8	-313	-65.8	-25.2	133	111	241	298
S&P Core Earnings	605	378	23.3	-258	-176	-168	NA	NA	NA	NA

Balance Sheet & Other Financial Data (Million $)	2006	2005	2004	2003	2002	2001	2000	1999	1998	1997
Cash	502	363	251	79.6	59.4	33.7	26.2	50.7	74.8	50.3
Current Assets	1,988	1,484	1,160	743	812	926	1,023	1,034	1,365	1,229
Total Assets	3,282	2,732	2,316	1,885	2,093	2,643	2,776	2,751	3,176	2,605
Current Liabilities	646	561	493	395	342	333	414	540	622	562
Long Term Debt	530	547	553	504	509	573	491	200	447	326
Common Equity	1,493	800	426	175	449	945	1,039	1,200	1,340	1,000
Total Capital	2,023	1,347	979	679	958	1,671	1,689	1,401	1,787	1,326
Capital Expenditures	235	90.1	49.9	74.4	48.7	104	60.2	74.1	173	96.3
Cash Flow	656	439	95.9	-239	24.2	73.4	232	206	350	396
Current Ratio	3.1	2.6	2.4	1.9	2.4	2.8	2.5	1.9	2.2	2.2
% Long Term Debt of Capitalization	26.2	40.6	56.5	74.3	53.2	34.3	29.1	14.3	25.0	24.6
% Net Income of Revenue	11.6	10.2	0.7	NM	NM	NM	5.4	4.8	6.1	7.9
% Return on Assets	19.0	14.3	0.9	NM	NM	NM	4.8	3.9	8.3	11.4
% Return on Equity	49.9	59.0	6.6	NM	NM	NM	11.8	8.7	20.6	31.8

Data as orig reptd.; bef. results of disc opers/spec. items. Per share data adj. for stk. divs.; EPS diluted. E-Estimated. NA-Not Available. NM-Not Meaningful. NR-Not Ranked. UR-Under Review.

Office: 1000 PPG Place, Pittsburgh, PA 15222-5479.
Telephone: 412-394-2800.
Website: http://www.alleghenytechnologies.com
Chrmn, Pres & CEO: L.P. Hassey

EVP & CFO: R.J. Harshman
EVP, Secy, Chief Lgl Officer & General Counsel: J.D. Walton
VP, Chief Acctg Officer, Treas & Cntlr: D.G. Reid
Investor Contact: D.L. Greenfield (412-394-3004)

Board Members: H. K. Bowen, R. P. Bozzone, D. C. Creel, J. C. Diggs, L. P. Hassey, M. J. Joyce, W. C. McClelland, J. E. Rohr, L. J. Thomas, J. D. Turner

Founded: 1960
Domicile: Delaware
Employees: 9,500

Allergan Inc.

**STANDARD
&POOR'S**

S&P Recommendation	HOLD ★ ★ ★ ☆ ☆	Price $62.61 (as of Nov 23, 2007)	12-Mo. Target Price $71.00	Investment Style Large-Cap Growth

GICS Sector Health Care
Sub-Industry Pharmaceuticals

Summary This technology-driven global health care company develops and commercializes products in the eye care, neuromodulator, skin care and other specialty markets.

Key Stock Statistics (Source S&P, Vickers, company reports)

52-Wk Range	$69.15– 52.50	S&P Oper. EPS 2007**E**	2.15	Market Capitalization(B)	$19.253	Beta	0.93
Trailing 12-Month EPS	$1.58	S&P Oper. EPS 2008**E**	2.60	Yield (%)	0.32	S&P 3-Yr. Proj. EPS CAGR(%)	17.00
Trailing 12-Month P/E	39.6	P/E on S&P Oper. EPS 2007**E**	29.1	Dividend Rate/Share	$0.20	S&P Credit Rating	A
$10K Invested 5 Yrs Ago	$21,856	Common Shares Outstg. (M)	307.5	Institutional Ownership (%)	96		

Price Performance

30-Week Mov. Avg. · · · 10-Week Mov. Avg. - - **GAAP Earnings vs. Previous Year** Volume Above Avg. STARS
12-Mo. Target Price — Relative Strength — ▲ Up ▼ Down ► No Change Below Avg.

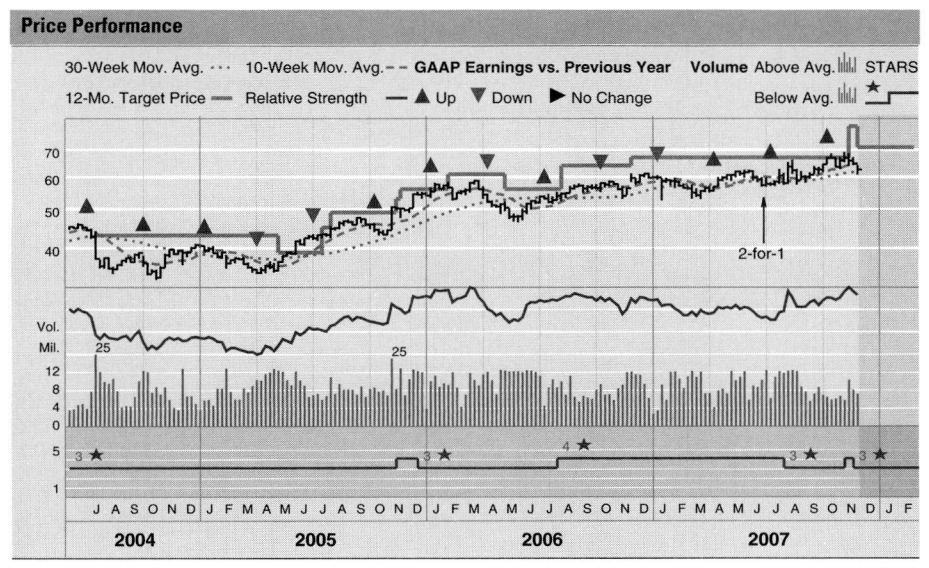

Options: ASE, CBOE, Ph

Analysis prepared by **Phillip M. Seligman** on November 16, 2007, when the stock traded at **$ 64.48**.

Highlights

➤ We forecast that net product sales will rise 15% in 2008 to slightly under $4.5 billion, from over $3.8 billion that we see in 2007. We view the deceleration from the 27% growth we see in 2007 as partly due to the Inamed Corp. acquisition in March 2006. Drivers include new drugs and geographic sales expansion of existing drugs, continued Botox growth, and continued sales of breast implants and Juvederm dermal fillers.

➤ We see gross margins in 2008 as flat to modestly below our 2007 estimate of 82.5%, partly on product and geographic mix. We also expect the R&D expense ratio to remain stable with the 17% we estimate for 2007. We look for the SG&A cost ratio to decline from the 42% we see in 2007, as revenue leverage outweighs increased sales and marketing investments. The latter includes sales force expansion and direct-to-consumer (DTC) campaigns for Botox, Juvederm, and the LAP-BAND gastric band.

➤ Our outlook for operating EPS is $2.15 in 2007 and $2.60 in 2008, compared to 2006's $1.83.

Investment Rationale/Risk

➤ We recently downgraded our opinion on AGN shares to hold, from buy, as we believe recession worries will continue to pressure the shares. In particular, we see concerns about tempered demand for AGN's premium-priced aesthetics products, including breast implants, Juvederm dermal filler, and Botox for cosmetic use. On the upside, we view its eye care drugs, Botox for therapeutic use, skin care drugs, and obesity intervention products, which we estimate accounted for 72% of aggregate net sales in 2007's first nine months, as reasonably recession-resistant because of medical need. We also remain encouraged by its eye care drugs' global market share gains, drugs and other products in the pipeline, and above-average R&D expense ratio.

➤ Risks to our recommendation and target price include clinical trial failures, FDA rejection or delay of a new drug or medical device, and increased competition.

➤ Our 12-month target price of $71 is derived by applying a modestly above-peer 1.6X target P/E-to-growth (PEG) ratio, assuming three-year growth of 17%, to our 2008 EPS estimate.

Qualitative Risk Assessment

LOW	MEDIUM	HIGH

Our risk assessment reflects AGN's increased diversification of aesthetic products and markets via the acquisition of Inamed, our view of its strong focus on R&D, its leading market position in several ophthalmic drugs, and continued strong demand for Botox. However, we view the eye care and aesthetics markets as competitive, and we are concerned that certain pipeline products may not be successful.

Quantitative Evaluations

S&P Quality Ranking B

D	C	B-	B	B+	A-	A	A+

Relative Strength Rank MODERATE

67

LOWEST = 1 HIGHEST = 99

Revenue/Earnings Data

Revenue (Million $)

	1Q	2Q	3Q	4Q	Year
2007	886.5	988.1	993.7	--	--
2006	625.7	801.7	806.8	829.1	3,063
2005	527.2	591.0	606.1	594.9	2,319
2004	472.4	506.2	510.8	556.2	2,046
2003	391.2	447.7	443.3	479.4	1,771
2002	327.7	346.7	360.0	390.9	1,425

Earnings Per Share ($)

2007	0.14	0.45	0.50	E0.57	E2.15
2006	-1.65	0.25	0.35	0.45	-0.43
2005	0.30	0.13	0.56	0.52	1.50
2004	0.31	0.35	0.35	0.43	1.41
2003	0.26	-0.42	0.29	-0.35	-0.20
2002	0.15	-0.01	-0.14	0.25	0.25

Fiscal year ended Dec. 31. Next earnings report expected: Late January. EPS Estimates based on S&P Operating Earnings; historical GAAP earnings are as reported.

Dividend Data (Dates: mm/dd Payment Date: mm/dd/yy)

Amount ($)	Date Decl.	Ex-Div. Date	Stk. of Record	Payment Date
0.100	05/03	05/16	05/18	06/08/07
2-for-1	05/02	06/25	06/11	06/22/07
0.050	08/01	08/15	08/17	09/07/07
0.050	11/06	11/07	11/09	11/30/07

Dividends have been paid since 1989. Source: Company reports.

Please read the Required Disclosures and Analyst Certification on the last page of this report.

Allergan Inc.

STANDARD &POOR'S

Business Summary November 16, 2007

CORPORATE OVERVIEW. Allergan is a leading producer of ophthalmic, neuromuscular and skin care pharmaceuticals, and, with its March 2006 acquisition of Inamed Corp., aesthetic products. Eye care drugs accounted for 51% of 2006 sales from continuing operations, Botox/neuromodulator 32%, skin care treatments 4%, breast implants 6%, devices for obesity treatment 5%, and dermal fillers 2%. About 33% of 2006 sales were derived from foreign markets.

Eye care drugs include prescription and nonprescription products to treat eye diseases and disorders, including glaucoma, inflammation, infection, allergy, and dry eye. Important products are Alphagan, Alphagan P, and Combigan (sales of $328 million in 2006, versus $268 million in 2005), Lumigan ($328 million versus $268 million) treatments, which are used to lower eye pressure in patients with open-angle glaucoma or ocular hypertension, and Restasis ($270 million, versus $191 million), for dry eye disease. Other eye care products include Acular, Alocril, and Elestat, for seasonal allergic conjunctivitis; and Zymar and Ocuflox, for bacterial conjunctivitis.

Originally used for ophthalmic movement disorders, AGN believes that Botox (botulinum toxin type A) is the widely accepted treatment for neuromuscular

disorders and related pain. More recently, Botox garnered a rapidly growing market as a facial cosmetic agent. In April 2002, the FDA approved the injectable drug for removing brow furrows and other facial wrinkles. About 52% of Botox sales in 2006 (57% in 2005) were for therapeutic indications, with cosmetic uses comprising the balance. Botox is being studied for treating excessive sweating, post-stroke spasticity, back spasms, and migraines.

Skin care products include Zorac/Tazorac receptor-selective retinoids for acne and psoriasis; Prevage for fine lines and wrinkles; and Avage for facial fine wrinkling and blotchy skin discoloration.

Aesthetic products include breast implants for aesthetic augmentation and reconstructive surgery following a mastectomy, a range of dermal products to correct facial wrinkles, and the LAP-BAND and Intragastric Balloon (BIB) systems for obesity treatment.

Company Financials Fiscal Year Ended Dec. 31

Per Share Data ($)	2006	2005	2004	2003	2002	2001	2000	1999	1998	1997
Tangible Book Value	0.88	5.34	3.99	2.47	3.02	3.24	2.82	1.87	1.99	2.41
Cash Flow	0.08	1.82	1.69	0.03	0.42	1.19	1.09	0.97	-0.05	0.75
Earnings	-0.44	1.51	1.41	-0.20	0.25	0.85	0.81	0.70	-0.35	0.49
S&P Core Earnings	-0.42	1.36	1.26	-0.33	0.45	0.70	NA	NA	NA	NA
Dividends	0.20	0.20	0.18	0.18	0.18	0.18	0.16	0.14	0.13	0.13
Payout Ratio	NM	13%	13%	NM	73%	21%	20%	20%	NM	27%
Prices:High	61.51	55.25	46.31	40.90	37.55	49.69	50.56	28.91	16.63	9.30
Prices:Low	46.29	34.51	33.39	35.83	24.53	29.50	22.25	15.84	7.94	6.47
P/E Ratio:High	NM	37	33	NM	NM	59	63	42	NM	19
P/E Ratio:Low	NM	23	24	NM	NM	35	28	23	NM	13

Income Statement Analysis (Million $)										
Revenue	3,063	2,319	2,046	1,771	1,425	1,746	1,626	1,452	1,296	1,138
Operating Income	854	694	603	39.1	349	404	372	326	294	207
Depreciation	152	78.9	68.3	59.6	45.0	85.5	77.7	73.8	76.5	68.8
Interest Expense	60.2	12.4	18.1	15.6	17.4	21.4	19.8	15.1	16.4	8.90
Pretax Income	-19.5	599	532	-29.5	89.8	336	304	269	-57.7	157
Effective Tax Rate	NM	32.1%	28.9%	NM	28.0%	32.4%	29.0%	30.0%	NM	18.5%
Net Income	-127	404	377	-52.5	64.0	227	215	188	-90.2	128
S&P Core Earnings	-123	363	339	-87.3	118	187	NA	NA	NA	NA

Balance Sheet & Other Financial Data (Million $)										
Cash	1,369	1,296	895	508	774	782	774	163	182	181
Current Assets	2,130	1,826	1,376	928	1,200	1,325	1,326	698	661	636
Total Assets	5,767	2,851	2,257	1,755	1,807	2,046	1,971	1,339	1,334	1,390
Current Liabilities	658	1,044	460	383	404	490	433	420	369	363
Long Term Debt	1,606	57.5	570	573	526	521	585	209	201	143
Common Equity	3,143	1,567	1,116	719	808	977	874	634	696	841
Total Capital	4,836	1,626	1,689	1,294	1,337	1,499	1,459	843	897	984
Capital Expenditures	131	78.5	96.4	110	78.8	89.9	66.9	63.3	50.6	64.4
Cash Flow	25.0	483	445	7.10	109	312	293	262	-13.7	197
Current Ratio	3.2	1.7	3.0	2.4	3.0	2.7	3.1	1.7	1.8	1.8
% Long Term Debt of Capitalization	33.2	3.5	33.8	44.3	39.4	34.7	40.1	24.8	22.4	14.5
% Net Income of Revenue	NM	17.4	18.4	NM	4.5	13.0	13.2	13.0	NM	11.3
% Return on Assets	NM	15.8	18.8	NM	3.3	11.3	13.0	14.1	NM	9.4
% Return on Equity	NM	30.1	41.1	NM	7.2	24.5	28.5	28.3	NM	16.1

Data as orig reptd.; bef. results of disc opers/spec. items. Per share data adj. for stk. divs.; EPS diluted. E-Estimated. NA-Not Available. NM-Not Meaningful. NR-Not Ranked. UR-Under Review.

Office: 2525 Dupont Drive, Irvine, CA 92612.
Telephone: 714-246-4500.
Email: corpinfo@allergan.com
Website: http://www.alergan.com

Chrmn, Pres & CEO: D.E. Pyott
Pres: F.M. Ball
EVP & CFO: J.L. Edwards
EVP, Chief Admin Officer, Secy & General Counsel: D.S. Ingram

SVP, Chief Acctg Officer & Cntlr: J.F. Barlow
Investor Contact: J. Hindman (714-246-4636)
Board Members: H. W. Boyer, D. Dunsire, H. E. Evans, M. R. Gallagher, R. A. Ingram, T. M. Jones, L. J. Lavigne, Jr., D. E. Pyott, R. T. Ray, S. J. Ryan, L. D. Shaeffer

Founded: 1948
Domicile: Delaware
Employees: 6,772

The McGraw-Hill Companies

Allied Waste Industries Inc.

STANDARD &POOR'S

S&P Recommendation HOLD ★★★☆☆	**Price** $11.02 (as of Nov 23, 2007)	**12-Mo. Target Price** $14.00	**Investment Style** Large-Cap Value

GICS Sector Industrials
Sub-Industry Environmental & Facilities Services

Summary This leading waste services company provides collection, recycling and disposal services to residential, commercial and industrial customers in the U.S.

Key Stock Statistics (Source S&P, Vickers, company reports)

52-Wk Range	$14.10–10.74	S&P Oper. EPS 2007**E**	0.75	Market Capitalization(B)	$4.074	Beta	1.91
Trailing 12-Month EPS	$0.35	S&P Oper. EPS 2008**E**	0.85	Yield (%)	Nil	S&P 3-Yr. Proj. EPS CAGR(%)	15.00
Trailing 12-Month P/E	31.5	P/E on S&P Oper. EPS 2007**E**	14.7	Dividend Rate/Share	Nil	S&P Credit Rating	BB
$10K Invested 5 Yrs Ago	$11,143	Common Shares Outstg. (M)	369.7	Institutional Ownership (%)	97	

Price Performance

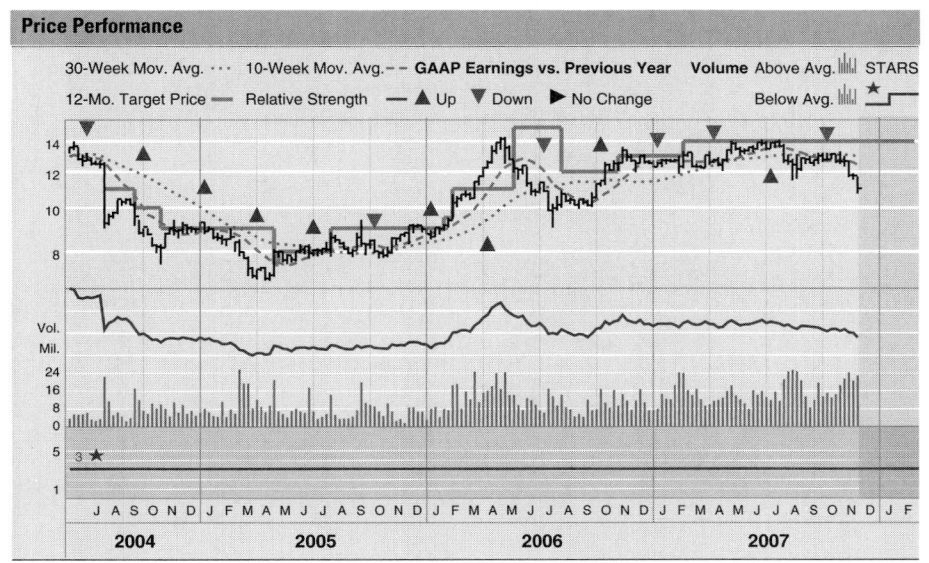

30-Week Mov. Avg. ··· 10-Week Mov. Avg. ─ ─ **GAAP Earnings vs. Previous Year** Volume Above Avg. STARS
12-Mo. Target Price ── Relative Strength ─ ▲ Up ▼ Down ► No Change Below Avg. ★

Options: ASE, CBOE, P, Ph

Analysis prepared by **Stewart Scharf** on November 13, 2007, when the stock traded at **$ 11.82**.

Highlights

➤ We project core organic revenue growth of over 2% for 2007, with a modest improvement seen for 2008, driven by price initiatives in both commercial collection and landfill operations, while volume will likely remain weak for roll-off, construction & demolition (C&D) and special waste. We expect AW to continue to sacrifice market share in favor of higher returns.

➤ Gross margins (before D&A) in 2007 should expand to near 37.5%, from 35.7% in 2006, with further expansion in 2008, based on price hikes and a better mix as AW rolls out a new national account. We believe EBITDA margins will widen by at least 75 basis points from nearly 26% in 2006, reflecting lower repair, maintenance, disposal and labor costs, and new employee safety programs. We see well controlled SG&A expense, with additional cost controls via supply chain and procurement initiatives aiding margins in 2008 as well.

➤ We project a lower effective tax rate in 2007, and we estimate EPS of $0.75 (before at least $0.17 of debt redemption, refinancing and other costs), rising 13%, to $0.85, in 2008.

Investment Rationale/Risk

➤ We maintain our hold recommendation, based primarily on our valuation models and modest volume outlook. Although AW's debt levels are still above peer averages, AW expects to save $5 million in interest a year by redeeming its $250 million in senior notes due 2012 in September 2007.

➤ Risks to our recommendation and target price include a weaker economy; an inability to implement sustainable price hikes; a significant market share loss based on price hikes; increased leverage; and a further significant rise in fuel costs. We have some corporate governance concerns, as the positions of chairman and CEO are held by the same person.

➤ Correlating our relative metrics, we apply a P/E of 16X our 2008 estimate, modestly below AW's closest peers, and we target a value of $13.50. Our DCF model suggests that the shares are at a 19% discount to their intrinsic value of $14.50, assuming a terminal growth rate of 3.5% and a weighted average cost of capital (WACC) of 8%. Blending these measures, our 12-month target price is $14.

Qualitative Risk Assessment

LOW	MEDIUM	HIGH

Our risk assessment reflects the cyclical nature of the business, volatile energy costs, landfill overcapacity, a high leverage ratio, and concerns related to corporate governance practices. This is offset by what we view as AW's positive cash generation and improving working capital.

Quantitative Evaluations

S&P Quality Ranking B-

D	C	B-	B	B+	A-	A	A+

Relative Strength Rank WEAK

28

LOWEST = 1   HIGHEST = 99

Revenue/Earnings Data

Revenue (Million $)

	1Q	2Q	3Q	4Q	Year
2007	1,457	1,560	1,556	--	--
2006	1,439	1,541	1,555	1,494	6,029
2005	1,341	1,449	1,477	1,468	5,735
2004	1,275	1,362	1,378	1,347	5,362
2003	1,231	1,343	1,362	1,313	5,248
2002	1,316	1,402	1,429	1,371	5,517

Earnings Per Share ($)

2007	0.07	0.21	0.15	E0.18	E0.75
2006	0.08	0.08	0.17	Nil	0.33
2005	0.05	0.12	0.10	0.15	0.43
2004	Nil	-0.05	0.13	0.04	0.11
2003	0.07	Nil	0.12	-2.29	-2.36
2002	0.17	0.18	0.23	0.19	0.76

Fiscal year ended Dec. 31. Next earnings report expected: Mid February. EPS Estimates based on S&P Operating Earnings; historical GAAP earnings are as reported.

Dividend Data

No cash dividends have been paid.

Please read the Required Disclosures and Analyst Certification on the last page of this report.

The McGraw-Hill Companies

**STANDARD
&POOR'S**

Allied Waste Industries Inc.

Business Summary November 13, 2007

CORPORATE OVERVIEW. Allied Waste Industries provides non-hazardous waste collection, transfer, recycling and disposal services to 10 million residential, municipal and commercial customers in 37 states and Puerto Rico. As of December 31, 2006, it had 304 collection companies, 161 transfer stations, 57 recycling facilities, and 168 active landfills. In 2006, revenues were derived from collection (70%), disposal (21%, including 7% from transfer), recycling-commodity (3.6%), and other (4.9%). Collection operations involve collecting and transporting nonhazardous waste from the point of generation to the transfer station or the site of disposal. A transfer station receives solid waste from third-party and company-owned collection vehicles and then compacts and transfers the waste to specially constructed trailers for transportation to disposal facilities. As of late 2007, the customer retention rate was above 92%, well above AW's historical rate, while the commercial churn rate (spread between the price of new work and the price of business lost) was positive for the fifth straight quarter.

We believe the company will continue to make progress with its strategic turnaround plan, divesting non-core assets and completing asset swaps with its closest competitors Waste Management and Republic Services. We think this plan will support AW's goal of improving margins, allocating capital more effectively, and improving return on invested capital (ROIC). In the third quarter of 2007, AW sold certain landfill and collection assets ($54 million in revenues) in Indiana, Illinois, Kentucky and Georgia for $90 million to Veolia ES Solid Waste. During 2006, AW divested assets accounting for $100 million of annualized revenues. In March 2007, AW sold its South Florida operations ($64 million in revenues) to Waste Services, and acquired Waste Services' Phoenix, AZ, operations ($20 million in revenues). The company is also implementing changes, including the temporary closing of certain landfills and the divestiture of low-density collection routes.

In the third quarter of 2007, AW incurred a landfill impairment pretax charge of nearly $25 million ($0.04 a share, after tax), and a $16 million loss ($0.03) on a divestiture. In the fourth quarter of 2006, AW incurred a $0.16 tax-related charge and a $0.01 charge for asset impairments.

Company Financials Fiscal Year Ended Dec. 31

Per Share Data ($)	2006	2005	2004	2003	2002	2001	2000	1999	1998	1997
Tangible Book Value	NM	NM	NM	NM	NM	NM	NM	NM	NM	NM
Cash Flow	1.91	2.11	1.86	2.76	3.33	3.57	3.89	0.13	0.45	1.78
Earnings	0.33	0.43	0.11	-2.36	0.76	0.01	0.36	-1.33	-0.54	0.57
S&P Core Earnings	0.33	0.37	0.07	-2.43	0.53	0.13	NA	NA	NA	NA
Dividends	Nil	Nil	Nil	Nil	Nil	Nil	Nil	Nil	Nil	Nil
Payout Ratio	Nil	Nil	Nil	Nil	Nil	Nil	Nil	Nil	Nil	Nil
Prices:High	14.38	9.46	14.44	14.05	14.55	19.90	14.75	24.06	31.63	24.38
Prices:Low	8.50	6.90	7.50	7.51	5.54	8.90	5.31	6.50	16.13	7.25
P/E Ratio:High	44	22	NM	NM	19	NM	41	NM	NM	43
P/E Ratio:Low	26	16	NM	NM	7	NM	15	NM	NM	13

Income Statement Analysis (Million $)										
Revenue	6,029	5,735	5,362	5,248	5,517	5,565	5,707	3,341	1,576	875
Operating Income	1,559	1,470	1,446	1,581	1,743	1,931	2,010	1,161	528	300
Depreciation	569	554	559	546	496	693	674	273	180	113
Interest Expense	568	588	588	707	774	854	882	443	88.4	94.0
Pretax Income	400	328	128	202	411	270	381	-227	-54.5	90.7
Effective Tax Rate	59.7%	40.9%	56.6%	44.0%	44.7%	70.7%	62.3%	NM	NM	40.9%
Net Income	161	194	58.0	111	225	75.5	138	-221	-98.3	53.6
S&P Core Earnings	116	120	26.9	-494	105	28.2	NA	NA	NA	NA

Balance Sheet & Other Financial Data (Million $)										
Cash	94.1	56.1	68.0	445	180	159	122	121	39.7	11.9
Current Assets	1,048	920	923	1,286	1,072	1,198	1,272	2,248	500	187
Total Assets	13,811	13,626	13,440	13,861	13,929	14,347	14,514	14,963	3,753	2,449
Current Liabilities	1,533	1,576	1,757	1,568	1,450	1,434	1,600	2,629	455	233
Long Term Debt	6,674	6,853	7,429	7,985	8,719	9,238	9,635	9,240	2,119	1,356
Common Equity	3,018	2,526	2,272	2,185	689	586	698	638	930	596
Total Capital	10,630	10,598	10,242	10,631	11,165	11,411	11,761	11,085	3,049	1,967
Capital Expenditures	669	696	583	492	542	501	390	339	302	120
Cash Flow	687	696	596	562	644	695	743	24.3	81.7	167
Current Ratio	0.7	0.6	0.5	0.8	0.7	0.8	0.8	0.9	1.1	0.8
% Long Term Debt of Capitalization	62.8	64.7	72.5	75.1	78.1	81.0	81.9	83.4	69.5	68.9
% Net Income of Revenue	2.7	3.4	1.1	2.1	4.1	1.4	2.4	NM	NM	6.1
% Return on Assets	1.2	1.4	0.4	0.8	1.6	0.5	0.9	NM	NM	2.2
% Return on Equity	4.3	5.9	1.6	1.1	23.1	0.4	10.4	NM	NM	12.2

Data as orig reptd.; bef. results of disc opers/spec. items. Per share data adj. for stk. divs.; EPS diluted. E-Estimated. NA-Not Available. NM-Not Meaningful. NR-Not Ranked. UR-Under Review.

Office: 18500 N Allied Way , Phoenix, AZ 85054.
Telephone: 480-627-2700.
Email: info@awin.com
Website: http://www.alliedwaste.com

Chrmn & CEO: J.J. Zillmer
Pres & COO: D.W. Slager
EVP & CFO: P.S. Hathaway
EVP, Secy & General Counsel: S.M. Helm

Investor Contact: M. Burnett (480-627-2785)
Board Members: R. M. Agate, C. H. Cotros, J. W. Crownover, S. Drescher, W. J. Flynn, D. I. Foley, J. J. Harris, D. R. Hendrix, N. Lehmann, L. J. Level, S. Martinez, J. A. Quella, J. M. Trani, J. J. Zillmer

Founded: 1987
Domicile: Delaware
Employees: 24,200

The McGraw-Hill Companies

Allstate Corp (The)

STANDARD &POOR'S

S&P Recommendation BUY ★★★★☆	**Price** $50.09 (as of Nov 23, 2007)	**12-Mo. Target Price** $65.00	**Investment Style** Large-Cap Blend

GICS Sector Financials
Sub-Industry Property & Casualty Insurance

Summary Allstate, the second largest U.S. personal lines property-casualty insurer, has expanded into the life insurance and retirement savings arena.

Key Stock Statistics (Source S&P, Vickers, company reports)

52-Wk Range	$66.14– 48.90	S&P Oper. EPS 2007**E**	7.08	Market Capitalization(B)	$29.453	Beta	1.01
Trailing 12-Month EPS	$8.34	S&P Oper. EPS 2008**E**	7.25	Yield (%)	3.03	S&P 3-Yr. Proj. EPS CAGR(%)	NA
Trailing 12-Month P/E	6.0	P/E on S&P Oper. EPS 2007**E**	7.1	Dividend Rate/Share	$1.52	S&P Credit Rating	A+
$10K Invested 5 Yrs Ago	$14,388	Common Shares Outstg. (M)	588.0	Institutional Ownership (%)	68		

Price Performance

30-Week Mov. Avg. · · · 10-Week Mov. Avg. - - **GAAP Earnings vs. Previous Year**   Volume Above Avg. STARS
12-Mo. Target Price — Relative Strength — ▲ Up ▼ Down ► No Change   Below Avg. ★—

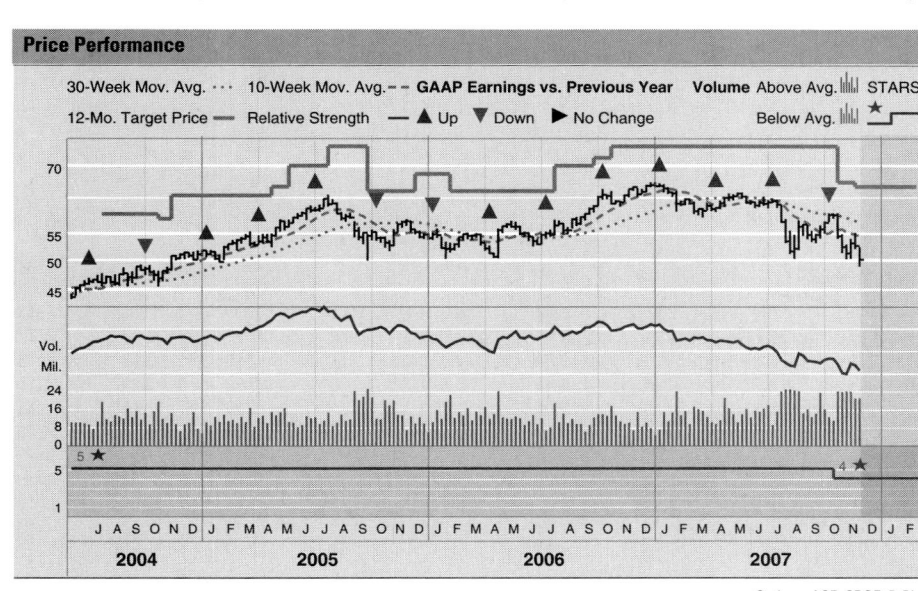

Options: ASE, CBOE, P, Ph

Analysis prepared by **Cathy A. Seifert** on November 14, 2007, when the stock traded at **$ 54.48**.

Highlights

➤ We expect operating revenue growth of 2% to 3% in 2008, reflecting a forecast of flat to slightly lower property-casualty earned premiums, flat to very little growth of financial services revenues, and a mid- single digit increase in net investment income. This compares with a forecast of operating revenue growth of about 5% in 2007.

➤ Barring a surge in catastrophe losses, we expect underwriting results to remain profitable in 2008, though we see underwriting margins contracting somewhat amid a deterioration in claim trends in a number of core lines. Underwriting results in the first nine months of 2007 deteriorated, and the combined loss/expense ratio increased to 87.7% in the 2007 period, from 82.9% in the 2006 period.

➤ We estimate 2007 operating EPS of $7.08 and 2008 operating EPS of $7.25, versus the $7.76 that ALL reported for 2006 and the $2.37 posted in 2005. Our operating EPS estimates assume a "normal" level of catastrophe losses and the absence of any significant reserve increases, and exclude any asset writedowns.

Investment Rationale/Risk

➤ Our buy recommendation reflects our view that the shares are undervalued versus many of ALL's peers. We are also encouraged by steps ALL has taken to refine its risk assessment and pricing capabilities and to reduce its exposure to catastrophe losses. But, our view of the shares is tempered by what we see as a heightened competitive environment for many lines of insurance, coupled with our belief that ALL has not made significant progress at leveraging opportunities for growth at Allstate Financial. Also, we note that as of September 30, 2007, 29% ALL's $121.1 billion investment portfolio included mortgage loans (9%), asset backed securities (8%), commercial mortgage-backed securities (7%), and mortgage-backed securities (5%).

➤ Risks to our opinion and target price include a sharp rise in loss costs and greatly increased premium price competition, and a deterioration in the credit quality of ALL's fixed income investment portfolio.

➤ Our 12-month target price of $65 assumes the shares trade at 9.2X our $7.08 operating EPS estimated for 2007 and at 9X our $7.25 operating EPS estimate for 2008. This valuation represents a discount to many of ALL's peers.

Qualitative Risk Assessment

LOW	MEDIUM	HIGH

Our risk assessment reflects our view of ALL as a solid underwriter with sound risk management and capital management practices and a diversified base of business, offset by our concern over the company's exposure to catastrophe losses and to write-downs in its fixed income investment portfolio.

Quantitative Evaluations

S&P Quality Ranking   B

D	C	B-	B	B+	A-	A	A+

Relative Strength Rank   MODERATE

40

LOWEST = 1   HIGHEST = 99

Revenue/Earnings Data

Revenue (Million $)

	1Q	2Q	3Q	4Q	Year
2007	9,331	9,455	8,992	--	--
2006	9,081	8,875	8,738	9,102	35,796
2005	8,705	8,791	8,942	8,945	35,383
2004	8,311	8,304	8,442	8,879	33,936
2003	7,861	7,899	8,127	8,262	32,149
2002	7,298	7,455	7,239	7,587	29,579

Earnings Per Share ($)

2007	2.41	2.30	1.70	E1.85	E7.08
2006	2.19	1.89	1.83	1.93	7.84
2005	1.64	1.71	-2.36	1.59	2.64
2004	1.59	1.47	0.09	1.64	4.79
2003	0.94	0.84	0.98	1.09	3.85
2002	0.60	0.48	0.35	0.63	1.13

Fiscal year ended Dec. 31. Next earnings report expected: Late January. EPS Estimates based on S&P Operating Earnings; historical GAAP earnings are as reported.

Dividend Data (Dates: mm/dd Payment Date: mm/dd/yy)

Amount ($)	Date Decl.	Ex-Div. Date	Stk. of Record	Payment Date
0.380	02/20	03/07	03/09	04/02/07
0.380	05/15	05/30	06/01	07/02/07
0.380	07/17	08/29	08/31	10/01/07
0.380	11/13	11/28	11/30	01/02/08

Dividends have been paid since 1993. Source: Company reports.

The **McGraw-Hill** Companies

Allstate Corp (The)

**STANDARD
&POOR'S**

Business Summary November 14, 2007

Established in 1931 by Sears, Roebuck & Co., Allstate is the second largest U.S. personal lines property-casualty insurer (based on earned premiums), and the 13th largest life insurer (based on life insurance in force). It writes business mainly through 12,500 exclusive agencies. ALL has also implemented a multi-access distribution model designed to allow customers to purchase company products through agents, over the Internet, via telephone, and through The Good Hands Network. ALL became an independent company in June 1995, when Sears, Roebuck & Co. spun off its 80% interest in the company.

The company's primary business is the sale of private passenger automobile and homeowners insurance, and it maintains national market shares of about 11% to 12% in each of these lines. ALL is licensed to write policies in all 50 states, the District of Columbia, Puerto Rico, and Canada. In 2006, property-liability net written premiums exceeded $27.5 billion, up from the $27.4 billion in net written premiums recorded in 2005. Of the 2006 total, standard automobile policies accounted for 61%, non-standard automobile policies 5%, homeowners' coverage 24%, and other lines 10%. Property-liability premiums earned in-

creased 1.5% in 2006, to $27.4 billion, from $27.0 billion. Underwriting results in 2006 improved amid a significant decline in catastrophe losses and continued improved automobile claim trends. As a result, the combined loss and expense ratio improved to 83.6% in 2006, from 102.4% in 2005.

Allstate Financial (formerly Allstate Life) offers an array of life insurance, annuity, savings and investment and pension products through Allstate agents, financial institutions, independent agents and brokers, and direct marketing. Total premiums and contract charges declined 4.4% in 2006, to $1.96 billion, from $2.05 billion in 2005. Of the 2006 total, traditional life insurance accounted for 14%, immediate annuities 14%, accident/health 17%, interest-sensitive life 44%, fixed annuities 4% and variable annuities 7%.

Company Financials Fiscal Year Ended Dec. 31

Per Share Data ($)	2006	2005	2004	2003	2002	2001	2000	1999	1998	1997
Tangible Book Value	33.80	29.97	30.74	27.89	23.52	22.35	22.26	21.09	21.08	18.37
Operating Earnings	NA	NA	NA	3.77	2.94	2.06	2.68	2.59	3.08	2.78
Earnings	7.84	2.64	4.79	3.85	1.13	1.61	2.95	3.38	3.94	3.56
S&P Core Earnings	7.91	2.21	4.33	3.82	2.64	1.66	NA	NA	NA	NA
Dividends	1.40	1.28	1.12	0.92	0.84	0.76	0.68	0.58	0.52	0.48
Relative Payout	18%	48%	23%	24%	74%	47%	23%	17%	13%	14%
Prices:High	66.14	63.22	51.99	43.27	41.95	45.90	44.75	41.00	52.38	47.19
Prices:Low	50.22	49.66	42.55	30.05	31.03	30.00	17.19	22.88	36.06	28.13
P/E Ratio:High	8	24	11	11	37	29	15	12	13	13
P/E Ratio:Low	6	19	9	8	27	19	6	7	9	8

Income Statement Analysis (Million $)										
Life Insurance in Force	NA	NA	NA	409,068	396,943	387,039	367,914	334,895	276,032	247,192
Premium Income:Life A & H	27,369	27,039	25,989	24,677	23,361	2,230	2,205	1,623	1,519	1,502
Premium Income:Casualty/Property.	1,964	2,049	2,072	2,304	2,293	22,197	21,871	20,112	19,307	18,604
Net Investment Income	6,177	5,746	5,284	4,972	4,854	4,796	4,633	4,112	3,890	3,861
Total Revenue	35,796	35,383	33,936	32,149	29,579	28,865	29,134	26,959	25,879	24,949
Pretax Income	7,178	2,088	4,586	3,566	868	1,240	3,006	3,868	4,716	4,429
Net Operating Income	NA	NA	NA	2,662	2,075	1,492	2,004	2,082	2,573	2,429
Net Income	4,993	1,765	3,356	2,720	803	1,167	2,211	2,720	3,294	3,105
S&P Core Earnings	5,040	1,487	3,028	2,692	1,879	1,201	NA	NA	NA	NA

Balance Sheet & Other Financial Data (Million $)										
Cash & Equivalent	4,935	1,387	1,428	1,434	1,408	1,146	1,164	1,066	1,009	220
Premiums Due	4,789	4,739	4,721	4,386	6,958	6,674	3,802	3,927	3,082	NA
Investment Assets:Bonds	98,320	98,065	95,715	87,741	77,152	65,720	60,758	55,286	53,560	50,860
Investment Assets:Stocks	7,777	6,164	5,895	5,288	3,683	5,245	6,086	6,738	6,421	6,765
Investment Assets:Loans	9,467	8,748	7,856	6,539	6,092	5,710	4,599	4,068	3,458	3,002
Investment Assets:Total	119,757	118,297	115,530	103,081	90,650	79,876	74,483	69,645	66,525	8,000
Deferred Policy Costs	5,332	5,802	4,968	4,842	4,385	4,421	4,309	4,119	3,096	2,826
Total Assets	157,554	156,072	149,725	134,142	117,426	109,175	104,808	98,119	87,691	80,918
Debt	4,620	4,887	5,291	5,073	4,161	3,894	3,862	3,150	2,103	2,446
Common Equity	21,846	20,186	21,823	20,565	34,128	17,196	17,451	16,601	17,240	15,610
Combined Loss-Expense Ratio	83.6	102.4	93.0	94.6	98.9	102.9	99.2	97.4	93.2	94.0
% Return on Revenue	13.9	5.0	9.9	8.5	2.7	4.0	7.6	10.1	12.7	12.4
% Return on Equity	23.8	8.4	15.8	14.3	2.4	6.7	13.0	16.1	20.1	21.4
% Investment Yield	5.2	4.9	4.8	5.1	5.7	6.2	6.4	6.0	10.4	6.4

Data as orig reptd.; bef. results of disc opers/spec. items. Per share data adj. for stk. divs.; EPS diluted. E-Estimated. NA-Not Available. NM-Not Meaningful. NR-Not Ranked. UR-Under Review.

Office: 2775 Sanders Road, Northbrook, IL 60062-6127.
Telephone: 800-574-3553.
Website: http://www.allstate.com
Pres & CEO: T.J. Wilson

SVP & CIO: C. Brune
Investor Contact: D.L. Hale (800-416-8803)
VP & CFO: D.L. Hale
VP & General Counsel: M.J. McCabe

Board Members: D. Ackerman, J. G. Andress, R. D. Beyer, E. A. Brennan, W. J. Farrell, J. M. Greenberg, R. T. LeMay, E. M. Liddy, J. C. Reyes, H. J. Riley, Jr., J. I. Smith, J. A. Sprieser, M. A. Taylor, T. J. Wilson

Founded: 1953
Domicile: Delaware
Employees: 37,900

The McGraw-Hill Companies

Altera Corp

STANDARD &POOR'S

S&P Recommendation	HOLD ★ ★ ★ ★ ★	Price $18.70 (as of Nov 23, 2007)	12-Mo. Target Price $23.00	Investment Style Large-Cap Growth

GICS Sector Information Technology
Sub-Industry Semiconductors

Summary ALTR is one of the largest makers of high-performance, high-density programmable logic devices (PLDs) and associated computer-aided engineering logic development tools.

Key Stock Statistics (Source S&P, Vickers, company reports)

52-Wk Range	$26.24–18.00	S&P Oper. EPS 2007E	0.80	Market Capitalization(B)	$6.659	Beta	1.84
Trailing 12-Month EPS	$0.90	S&P Oper. EPS 2008E	0.85	Yield (%)	0.86	S&P 3-Yr. Proj. EPS CAGR(%)	15.00
Trailing 12-Month P/E	20.8	P/E on S&P Oper. EPS 2007E	23.4	Dividend Rate/Share	$0.16	S&P Credit Rating	NA
$10K Invested 5 Yrs Ago	$13,546	Common Shares Outstg. (M)	356.1	Institutional Ownership (%)	92		

Price Performance

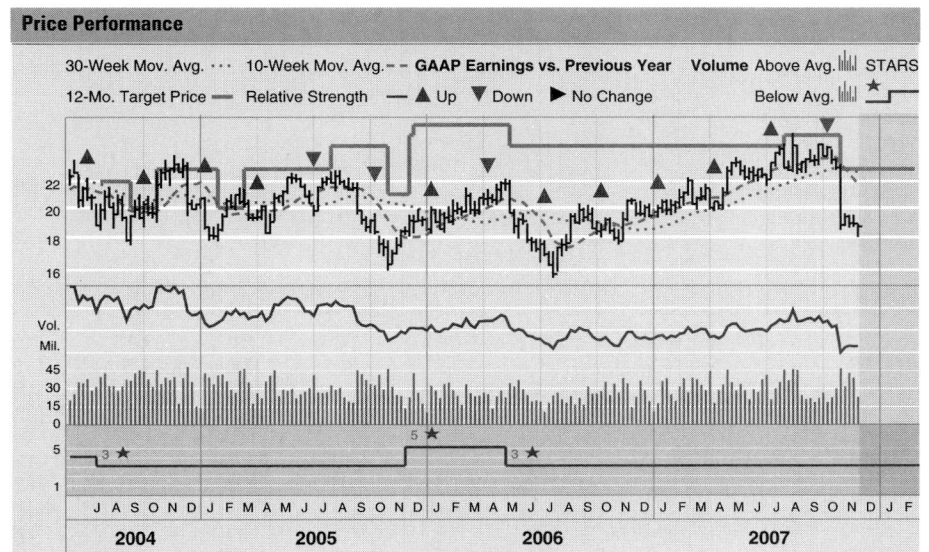

30-Week Mov. Avg. · · · 10-Week Mov. Avg. - - GAAP Earnings vs. Previous Year Volume Above Avg. STARS
12-Mo. Target Price — Relative Strength — ▲ Up ▼ Down ► No Change Below Avg. ★

Options: ASE, CBOE, P, Ph

Analysis prepared by **Clyde Montevirgen** on October 25, 2007, when the stock traded at **$ 18.93**.

Qualitative Risk Assessment

LOW	MEDIUM	HIGH

Our risk assessment reflects our view that Altera is subject to the sales swings of the semiconductor industry and competition from a larger rival. The shares have above-average price volatility, as indicated by a high beta. This is offset by participation in a high-growth niche market.

Quantitative Evaluations

S&P Quality Ranking   B

D	C	B-	B*	B+	A-	A	A+

Relative Strength Rank   WEAK

26

LOWEST = 1   HIGHEST = 99

Highlights

➤ We see essentially flat revenues in 2007. Although an industrywide inventory correction and negative seasonality limited first half sales, and see continued weakness for the rest of the year owing to soft demand of communications products, we expect growth to resume next year due to stronger sales for communications, computer, and industrial products. Consequently, we project sales growth of 5% in 2008. We think ALTR will gain market share in a few markets, but our optimism is tempered by technology advancements by its main competitor that we think is capable of reversing this trend with new offerings.

➤ We believe the company's new products will continue to drive growth in consumer, industrial and automotive markets, some of which represent new markets for Altera. In particular, we think that the Stratix and Cyclone products are attracting business from new customers. As the sales mix shifts to these newer and higher-margin products, we believe ALTR will exceed its long-term gross margin goal of 65% in 2008.

➤ We estimate operating EPS of $0.80 for 2007 and $0.85 for 2008.

Investment Rationale/Risk

➤ We believe Altera manages its business effectively, but we do not see sales exceeding seasonal averages due to our concerns for communications and industrial product demand. We expect a rebound in demand next year, but we see the rate of order growth slightly slower than previously expected as competition rises. Further, the lack of visibility in future quarters poses substantial risks to the turns-based business that ALTR needs to meet its guidance, in our opinion.

➤ Risks to our recommendation and target price include possible sudden downturns in demand for semiconductors, a reliance on chip foundry partners overseas for production, and stock option expense levels that we view as above that of most companies.

➤ Our 12-month target price of $23 is based on a blend of relative metrics. We apply a price-to-sales (P/S) ratio of about 7.3X, below ALTR's historical average, to our forward 12-month sales per share estimate, to derive a value of $26. We also use a P/E of 21X, above ALTR's peer average, to our 2008 EPS estimate, implying a value of $18.

Revenue/Earnings Data

Revenue (Million $)

	1Q	2Q	3Q	4Q	Year
2007	304.9	319.7	315.8	--	--
2006	292.8	334.1	341.2	317.4	1,286
2005	264.8	285.5	291.5	281.9	1,124
2004	242.9	269.0	264.6	239.9	1,016
2003	195.1	205.3	209.5	217.4	827.2
2002	172.0	178.9	180.1	180.7	711.7

Earnings Per Share ($)

	1Q	2Q	3Q	4Q	Year
2007	0.21	0.22	0.20	E0.17	E0.80
2006	0.16	0.21	0.24	0.27	0.88
2005	0.17	0.18	0.21	0.19	0.74
2004	0.15	0.20	0.22	0.15	0.72
2003	0.08	0.09	0.11	0.12	0.40
2002	0.05	0.06	0.06	0.07	0.23

Fiscal year ended Dec. 31. Next earnings report expected: Mid February. EPS Estimates based on S&P Operating Earnings; historical GAAP earnings are as reported.

Dividend Data (Dates: mm/dd Payment Date: mm/dd/yy)

Amount ($)	Date Decl.	Ex-Div. Date	Stk. of Record	Payment Date
0.040	03/28	05/08	05/10	06/01/07
0.040	07/23	08/08	08/10	09/04/07
0.040	10/23	11/07	11/12	12/03/07

Dividends have been paid since 2007. Source: Company reports.

Please read the Required Disclosures and Analyst Certification on the last page of this report.

Altera Corp

STANDARD
&POOR'S

Business Summary October 25, 2007

CORPORATE OVERVIEW. Altera Corp. is a worldwide supplier of programmable logic devices (PLDs), HardCopy brand structured application specific integrated circuits (ASICs), pre-defined design building blocks known as intellectual property cores, and associated software for logic development. PLDs are a high-growth category of semiconductors that address many applications in the communications, computer peripheral, consumer and industrial markets. PLDs offer high speed, high density, and low power characteristics. We believe competitive advantages offered to electronic system manufacturers by its products include enhanced design flexibility, shorter design cycles, lower up-front development costs, and the ability to get end-products to market faster, which can lead to significant cost savings for the customer. Drawbacks to PLDs compared to traditional ASICs include larger die size and higher cost per chip.

The company's PLDs are standard products, shipped blank for user programming. They are programmed at the customer's PC or workstation, using ALTR's proprietary software. Since the company's chips are programmed at a desktop and not at a foundry, product time to market is dramatically shortened. In addition, because ALTR's integrated circuits are standard products, inventory risks are minimized for both the company and customers. The HardCopy product line assists customers who use PLDs for prototyping ASIC chips

in converting the design for low cost production of non-programmable ASIC products.

Field Programmable Gate Arrays (FPGAs) include the Stratix lines, aimed at high performance applications, and the Cyclone product family, aimed at low-cost, high volume applications. General purpose Complex Programmable Logic Device (CPLD) product lines include the MAX family, which aims at low cost, high volume markets. Sales from FPGA, CPLD, and Other in 2006 were 71%, 19%, and 10%, respectively. By end market, sales were as follows: communications end markets 42% (42% in 2005), industrial 34% (32%), consumer 14% (16%), and computer and storage 10% (10%). International sales are significant, providing 76% of total sales in 2006, up from 75% in 2005 and 71% in 2004. About 93% of 2006 sales were handled by independent distributors, with about 47% by Arrow Electronics, and 15% by Altima Corp., which serves the Japan market. No single end customer accounted for over 10% of sales in 2006.

Company Financials Fiscal Year Ended Dec. 31

Per Share Data ($)	2006	2005	2004	2003	2002	2001	2000	1999	1998	1997
Tangible Book Value	4.46	3.52	3.42	2.93	2.95	2.89	3.21	2.82	2.26	1.49
Cash Flow	0.96	0.82	0.80	0.51	0.36	0.04	1.29	0.61	0.45	0.44
Earnings	0.88	0.74	0.72	0.40	0.23	-0.10	1.19	0.54	0.39	0.39
S&P Core Earnings	0.88	0.54	0.48	0.19	-0.02	-0.28	NA	NA	NA	NA
Dividends	Nil	Nil	Nil	Nil	Nil	Nil	Nil	Nil	Nil	Nil
Payout Ratio	Nil	Nil	Nil	Nil	Nil	Nil	Nil	Nil	Nil	Nil
Prices:High	22.29	22.99	26.82	25.64	26.18	34.69	67.13	34.28	15.47	16.44
Prices:Low	15.54	15.96	17.50	10.30	8.32	14.66	19.63	11.97	7.06	7.59
P/E Ratio:High	25	31	37	64	NM	NM	56	63	40	42
P/E Ratio:Low	18	22	24	26	NM	NM	16	22	18	20

Income Statement Analysis (Million $)										
Revenue	1,286	1,124	1,016	827	712	839	1,377	837	654	631
Operating Income	331	352	345	243	146	48.8	598	335	262	254
Depreciation	29.7	29.4	30.5	45.3	48.5	54.3	40.1	29.4	30.0	27.1
Interest Expense	Nil	Nil	Nil	Nil	Nil	Nil	Nil	Nil	6.36	11.7
Pretax Income	360	357	331	213	123	-13.0	744	335	234	230
Effective Tax Rate	10.1%	21.9%	16.8%	27.0%	26.0%	NM	33.2%	33.2%	34.0%	34.0%
Net Income	323	279	275	155	91.3	-39.8	497	224	154	152
S&P Core Earnings	323	204	182	70.7	-8.66	-106	NA	NA	NA	NA

Balance Sheet & Other Financial Data (Million $)										
Cash	738	788	580	259	255	145	496	164	131	22.8
Current Assets	1,735	1,495	1,537	1,270	1,176	1,129	1,769	1,107	800	616
Total Assets	2,215	1,823	1,747	1,488	1,372	1,361	2,004	1,440	1,093	953
Current Liabilities	598	555	468	385	241	247	756	322	212	186
Long Term Debt	1.30	3.87	Nil	Nil	Nil	Nil	Nil	Nil	Nil	230
Common Equity	1,608	1,326	1,279	1,102	1,131	1,115	1,248	1,118	882	537
Total Capital	1,609	1,330	1,279	1,102	1,131	1,115	1,248	1,118	882	767
Capital Expenditures	36.5	25.9	24.7	13.9	9.87	65.8	87.5	29.8	24.0	80.9
Cash Flow	353	308	306	200	140	14.5	537	253	184	179
Current Ratio	2.9	2.7	3.3	3.3	4.9	4.6	2.3	3.4	3.8	3.3
% Long Term Debt of Capitalization	0.1	0.3	Nil	Nil	Nil	Nil	Nil	Nil	Nil	30.0
% Net Income of Revenue	25.1	24.8	27.1	18.8	12.8	NM	36.1	26.8	23.6	24.0
% Return on Assets	16.0	15.5	17.1	10.9	6.7	NM	28.9	17.7	15.1	17.5
% Return on Equity	22.5	21.0	23.1	13.9	8.1	NM	42.0	22.4	21.8	33.4

Data as orig reptd.; bef. results of disc opers/spec. items. Per share data adj. for stk. divs.; EPS diluted. E-Estimated. NA-Not Available. NM-Not Meaningful. NR-Not Ranked. UR-Under Review.

Office: 101 Innovation Drive, San Jose, CA 95134.
Telephone: 408-544-7000.
Email: inv_rel@altera.com
Website: http://www.altera.com

Chrmn, Pres & CEO: J.P. Daane
Vice Chrmn: R.W. Reed
COO: D. Berlan
SVP & CFO: T.R. Morse

VP, Secy & General Counsel: K.E. Schuelke
Investor Contact: S. Wylie (408-544-6996)
Board Members: J. P. Daane, R. J. Finocchio, Jr., K. McGarity, R. W. Reed, J. Shoemaker, S. Wang

Founded: 1983
Domicile: Delaware
Employees: 2,654

The McGraw-Hill Companies

Altria Group Inc.

S&P Recommendation	STRONG BUY ★ ★ ★ ★ ★	Price $72.97 (as of Nov 23, 2007)	12-Mo. Target Price $85.00	Investment Style Large-Cap Blend

GICS Sector Consumer Staples
Sub-Industry Tobacco

Summary Altria Group (formerly Philip Morris Companies) is the world's largest cigarette producer. It recently spun off Kraft Foods, the largest U.S. food processor.

Key Stock Statistics (Source S&P, Vickers, company reports)

52-Wk Range	$90.50– 63.13	S&P Oper. EPS 2007 **E**	4.25	Market Capitalization(B)	$153.421	Beta	0.46
Trailing 12-Month EPS	$4.99	S&P Oper. EPS 2008 **E**	4.60	Yield (%)	4.11	S&P 3-Yr. Proj. EPS CAGR(%)	7.00
Trailing 12-Month P/E	14.6	P/E on S&P Oper. EPS 2007 **E**	17.2	Dividend Rate/Share	$3.00	S&P Credit Rating	BBB+
$10K Invested 5 Yrs Ago	NA	Common Shares Outstg. (M)	2,102.5	Institutional Ownership (%)	76		

Price Performance

30-Week Mov. Avg. · · · 10-Week Mov. Avg. - - **GAAP Earnings vs. Previous Year** Volume Above Avg. STARS
12-Mo. Target Price — Relative Strength — ▲ Up ▼ Down ► No Change Below Avg. ★

Options: ASE, CBOE, P, Ph

Analysis prepared by **Raymond Mathis** on October 01, 2007, when the stock traded at **$ 69.86**.

Highlights

➤ MO's Philip Morris International (PMI) subsidiary has filed a preliminary registration statement with the SEC in preparation for a spin-off from Altria. Earlier, MO announced it would optimize cigarette production by sourcing production for PMI from its overseas facilities and close a U.S. plant. MO previously spun off its 89% interest in Kraft Foods (KFT: hold, $35) as a stock dividend at the end of March 2007.

➤ We expect sales volume to grow, driven by brand investments, acquisitions, line extensions, and new product introductions. For PMI, we see revenues growing 8%, on acquisitions, currency benefits, and volume gains in most countries. We foresee higher prices, a positive mix shift, and improving volume trends supporting a 2% rise in Philip Morris USA's (PM USA) revenues. We expect MO's margins to widen as it begins to source PMI cigarettes overseas, saving an estimated $335 million annually.

➤ With a reduction of debt following the spin-off of KFT, we expect reduced interest expense. Excluding restructuring charges for plant closure, and with KFT reported as a discontinued operation, we see 2007 operating EPS of $4.25. For 2008, we see EPS of $4.60.

Investment Rationale/Risk

➤ We see domestic litigation pressures continuing to ease. Following the dismissal of the Price and Engle class action cases, a Supreme Court review of the Williams case did not cap punitive damages, but it did result in the case being remanded to the state court, with instructions to reduce the punitive damages award to a reasonable multiple of actual damages. We believe the rulings reduce Altria's cash flow risk considerably. We still await the appeal of the DOJ case, and a review of the Schwab class certification.

➤ Risks to our recommendation and target price include possible pressures on trading multiples, as investors remain cautious about court trials, and potential increases in excise taxes and smoking bans at the state and local level.

➤ Our 12-month target price of $85 is based on a blend of metrics. Using our sum-of-the parts analysis, applying peer P/E multiples of 24X to PMI's estimated 2007 EPS, and 16.5X PM USA's portion, we arrive at $90. Our intrinsic value estimate of $82 stems from our DCF analysis (assuming a WACC of 8.5% and a five-year growth rate of 4%). We derive an $87 value by applying a 13X EV/EBITDA multiple.

Qualitative Risk Assessment

LOW	MEDIUM	HIGH

MO is a large-cap company in an industry that is operationally very stable. However, the tobacco industry is beset by litigation. The company is subject to several ongoing legal actions, which could have a material impact on future cash flows.

Quantitative Evaluations

S&P Quality Ranking A+

D	C	B-	B	B+	A-	A	A+

Relative Strength Rank STRONG
86
LOWEST = 1   HIGHEST = 99

Revenue/Earnings Data

Revenue (Million $)

	1Q	2Q	3Q	4Q	Year
2007	17,556	18,809	19,207	--	--
2006	24,355	25,769	25,885	25,398	101,407
2005	23,618	24,784	24,962	24,490	97,854
2004	21,721	22,894	22,615	22,380	89,610
2003	19,371	20,831	20,939	20,691	81,832
2002	20,535	21,103	19,996	18,774	80,408

Earnings Per Share ($)

2007	1.01	1.05	1.24	E0.96	E4.25
2006	1.65	1.29	1.36	1.40	5.71
2005	1.24	1.40	1.38	1.09	5.10
2004	1.06	1.26	1.28	0.96	4.57
2003	1.07	1.20	1.22	1.02	4.52
2002	1.09	1.21	2.06	0.85	5.21

Fiscal year ended Dec. 31. Next earnings report expected: Late January. EPS Estimates based on S&P Operating Earnings; historical GAAP earnings are as reported.

Dividend Data (Dates: mm/dd Payment Date: mm/dd/yy)

Amount ($)	Date Decl.	Ex-Div. Date	Stk. of Record	Payment Date
0.860	02/28	03/13	03/15	04/10/07
Stk.	01/31	04/02	03/16	03/30/07
0.690	06/01	06/13	06/15	07/10/07
0.750	08/29	09/12	09/14	10/10/07

Dividends have been paid since 1928. Source: Company reports.

Please read the Required Disclosures and Analyst Certification on the last page of this report.

Altria Group Inc.

Business Summary October 01, 2007

CORPORATE OVERVIEW. Altria Group (formerly Philip Morris Cos., Inc.) is a holding company for wholly owned and majority owned subsidiaries that make and market various consumer products, now primarily including cigarettes, around the world. Prior to the March 30, 2007, spin-off of Kraft Foods, Altria Group's reportable segments were domestic tobacco, international tobacco, North American food, international food and financial services. International operations accounted for 58.6% of sales and 54.1% of operating profits in 2006.

Philip Morris U.S.A. (PM USA) is the largest U.S. tobacco company, with total U.S. cigarette shipments amounting to 183.4 billion units in 2006 (down 1.1% from 2005), accounting for 50.3% of total U.S. cigarette market shipments (up from 50.0% in 2005). PM USA contributed 18.2% of total company sales and 27.6% of operating profits in 2006. Focus brands include Marlboro (the largest selling brand in the U.S.), Virginia Slims and Parliament in the premium category, and Basic in the discount category. Philip Morris International's (PMI) total cigarette shipments rose 3.4% in 2006, to 831.4 billion units. PMI contributed 47.6% of total company sales and 48.6% of operating profits in 2006.

Kraft Foods is the largest packaged food company in North America and second largest in the world, accounting for 33.9% of total company sales and

27.1% of operating profits in 2006. Kraft Foods was spun off on March 30, 2007, to MO shareholders as a tax-free stock dividend. MO shareholders received approximately 0.68 of a KFT share per MO share owned as a stock dividend at the end of March 2007, and cash in lieu of fractional shares.

In July 2002, MO sold its Miller Brewing Co. subsidiary to South African Brewers, plc., receiving $3.38 billion worth of shares in the newly formed company, SABMiller. As of December 31, 2005, this stake represented a 28.7% economic interest and voting interest.

CORPORATE STRATEGY. MO has been looking at a number of restructuring alternatives, including the possibility of separating Altria Group, Inc. into two, or potentially three, independent entities. Following the spin-off of KFT, we believe the company may explore the possibility of selling its 28.7% stake in SABMiller, a large international brewer, and splitting the domestic and international tobacco businesses into separate entities.

Company Financials Fiscal Year Ended Dec. 31

Per Share Data ($)	2006	2005	2004	2003	2002	2001	2000	1999	1998	1997
Tangible Book Value	NM	NM	NM	NM	NM	NM	NM	NM	NM	NM
Cash Flow	6.57	5.92	5.35	5.22	6.10	4.93	4.50	3.90	2.89	3.28
Earnings	5.71	5.10	4.57	4.52	5.21	3.88	3.75	3.19	2.20	2.58
S&P Core Earnings	5.62	5.14	4.54	4.49	4.03	3.62	NA	NA	NA	NA
Dividends	3.32	3.06	2.82	2.64	2.44	2.22	2.02	1.80	1.64	1.60
Payout Ratio	58%	60%	62%	58%	47%	57%	54%	56%	75%	62%
Prices:High	86.56	78.68	61.88	55.03	57.79	53.88	45.94	55.56	59.50	48.13
Prices:Low	68.36	60.40	44.50	27.70	35.40	38.75	18.69	21.25	34.75	36.00
P/E Ratio:High	15	15	14	12	11	14	12	17	27	19
P/E Ratio:Low	12	12	10	6	7	10	5	7	16	14
Income Statement Analysis (Million $)										
Revenue	101,407	97,854	89,610	81,832	80,408	89,924	80,356	78,596	74,391	72,055
Operating Income	19,705	19,004	17,929	17,663	18,476	18,039	16,396	15,192	15,048	14,820
Depreciation	1,804	1,675	1,607	1,440	1,331	2,337	1,717	1,702	1,690	1,700
Interest Expense	877	1,556	1,417	1,367	1,327	1,659	1,078	1,100	1,144	1,185
Pretax Income	16,536	15,435	14,004	14,760	18,098	14,284	13,960	12,695	9,087	10,611
Effective Tax Rate	26.3%	29.9%	32.4%	34.9%	35.5%	37.9%	39.0%	39.5%	40.9%	40.5%
Net Income	12,022	10,668	9,420	9,204	11,102	8,566	8,510	7,675	5,372	6,310
S&P Core Earnings	11,818	10,766	9,348	9,145	8,593	7,959	NA	NA	NA	NA
Balance Sheet & Other Financial Data (Million $)										
Cash	5,020	6,258	5,744	3,777	565	453	937	5,100	4,081	2,282
Current Assets	26,152	25,781	25,901	21,382	17,441	17,275	17,238	20,895	20,230	17,440
Total Assets	104,270	107,949	101,648	96,175	87,540	84,968	79,067	61,381	59,920	55,947
Current Liabilities	25,427	26,158	23,574	21,393	19,082	20,141	25,949	18,017	16,379	15,071
Long Term Debt	14,498	17,868	18,683	21,163	21,355	18,651	19,154	12,226	12,615	12,430
Common Equity	39,619	35,707	30,714	25,077	19,478	19,620	15,005	15,305	16,197	14,920
Total Capital	68,496	71,945	67,714	64,110	56,832	52,768	40,824	33,211	33,892	32,116
Capital Expenditures	2,454	2,206	1,913	1,974	2,009	1,922	1,682	1,749	1,804	1,874
Cash Flow	13,826	12,343	11,027	10,644	12,433	10,903	10,227	9,377	7,062	8,010
Current Ratio	1.0	1.0	1.1	1.0	0.9	0.9	0.7	1.2	1.2	1.2
% Long Term Debt of Capitalization	21.2	24.8	27.6	33.0	37.6	35.3	46.9	36.8	37.2	38.7
% Net Income of Revenue	11.9	10.9	10.5	11.2	13.8	9.5	10.6	9.8	7.2	8.7
% Return on Assets	11.3	10.2	9.5	10.0	12.9	10.4	12.1	12.7	9.3	11.4
% Return on Equity	31.9	32.1	33.8	41.3	56.8	49.5	56.2	48.7	34.5	43.3

Data as orig reptd.; bef. results of disc opers/spec. items. Per share data adj. for stk. divs.; EPS diluted. E-Estimated. NA-Not Available. NM-Not Meaningful. NR-Not Ranked. UR-Under Review.

Office: 120 Park Avenue, New York, NY 10017-5577.
Telephone: 917-663-4000.
Website: http://www.altria.com
Chrmn & CEO: L.C. Camilleri

Investor Contact: D.S. Devitre (917-663-2200)
SVP & CFO: D.S. Devitre
SVP & General Counsel: C.R. Wall
SVP & CCO: D.I. Greenberg

Board Members: E. E. Bailey, H. Brown, M. Cabiallavetta, L. C. Camilleri, J. D. Fishburn, R. E. Huntley, T. W. Jones, G. Munoz, L. A. Noto, S. M. Wolf

Founded: 1919
Domicile: Virginia
Employees: 175,000

Amazon.com Inc

STANDARD &POOR'S

S&P Recommendation	SELL ★ ★ ★ ★ ★	Price $81.43 (as of Nov 23, 2007)	12-Mo. Target Price $70.00	Investment Style Large-Cap Growth

GICS Sector Consumer Discretionary
Sub-Industry Internet Retail

Summary This leading online retailer sells a broad range of items from books to consumer electronics to home and garden products.

Key Stock Statistics (Source S&P, Vickers, company reports)

52-Wk Range	$101.09–36.30	S&P Oper. EPS 2007**E**	1.13	Market Capitalization(B)	$33.808	Beta	2.68
Trailing 12-Month EPS	$0.87	S&P Oper. EPS 2008**E**	1.63	Yield (%)	Nil	S&P 3-Yr. Proj. EPS CAGR(%)	30.00
Trailing 12-Month P/E	93.6	P/E on S&P Oper. EPS 2007**E**	72.1	Dividend Rate/Share	Nil	S&P Credit Rating	BB
$10K Invested 5 Yrs Ago	$33,943	Common Shares Outstg. (M)	415.2	Institutional Ownership (%)	77		

Price Performance

30-Week Mov. Avg. ··· 10-Week Mov. Avg. - - **GAAP Earnings vs. Previous Year** Volume Above Avg. ▮▮▮ STARS

12-Mo. Target Price — Relative Strength — ▲ Up ▼ Down ► No Change Below Avg. ▮▮▮ ★

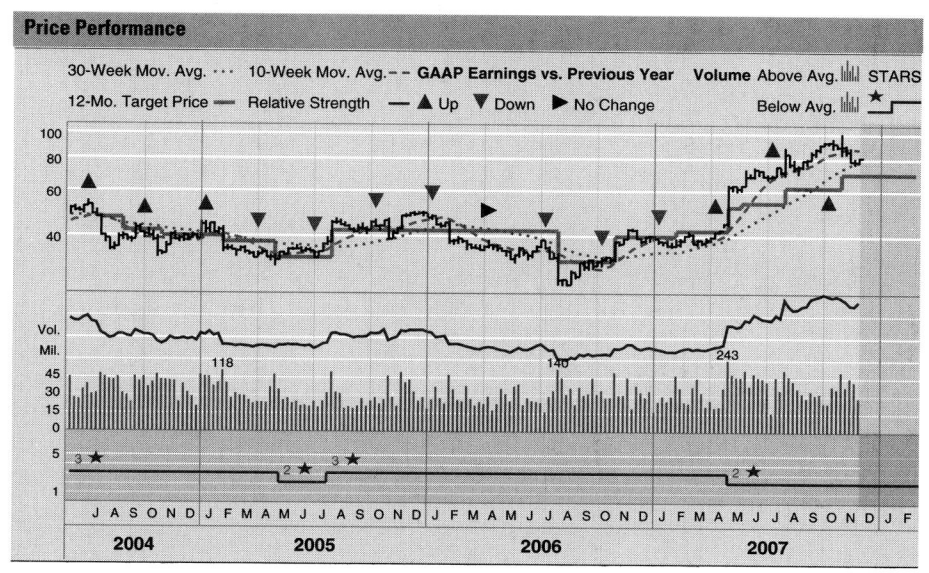

Options: ASE, CBOE, P, Ph

Analysis prepared by **Michael Souers** on October 30, 2007, when the stock traded at **$ 88.24.**

Highlights

► We believe that AMZN has become quite a formidable online marketplace in the U.S. We project net sales will rise 24%-25% in 2008, following a projected 35% advance in 2007. We expect this rapid growth to be driven by new products, low pricing, and international expansion. Shipping promotions, including the Amazon Prime membership program, which offers customers unlimited, express two-day shipping for an annual fee of $79, should also increase Web site traffic and conversion rates.

► Gross margins are likely to widen slightly in 2008 due to a continued increase in third party sellers and a shift in the product mix. This should be partially offset by the impact of free shipping offers, continued price reductions and other promotions. Due to slightly lower projected marketing, G&A and technology and content expenses, we look for operating margins to widen by 60 basis points in 2008.

► Factoring anticipated share buybacks under AMZN's $500 million authorization and a 29% effective tax rate, we expect 2008 EPS of $1.63, a 44% increase from the $1.13 we expect the company to earn in 2007.

Investment Rationale/Risk

► Although AMZN has reported better than expected earnings results thus far in 2007, we view the shares as overvalued, trading at about 55X our 2008 EPS estimate. While continued investments in long-term growth opportunities such as Amazon Prime, seller platforms and a digital music store should provide new sources of revenue over the next few years, we think margin gains will be limited by an intensely competitive environment. Longer term, we expect AMZN's initiatives to result in significant margin expansion, as it leverages its leading brand name and position as a leading Internet retailer.

► Risks to our recommendation and target price include the potential for higher than projected revenues due to greater than expected payoffs from AMZN's investments in growth initiatives, and an acceleration in consumer discretionary spending.

► Our 12-month target price of $70 is based on our discounted cash flow analysis, which assumes a weighted average cost of capital of 11.4% and a terminal growth rate of 4%.

Qualitative Risk Assessment

LOW	MEDIUM	HIGH

Our risk assessment reflects AMZN's large market capitalization and leading position in the e-commerce industry, offset by increasing competition and the stock's high beta.

Quantitative Evaluations

S&P Quality Ranking   B-

D	C	B-	B	B+	A-	A	A+

Relative Strength Rank   MODERATE

62

LOWEST = 1   HIGHEST = 99

Revenue/Earnings Data

Revenue (Million $)

	1Q	2Q	3Q	4Q	Year
2007	3,015	2,886	3,262	--	--
2006	2,279	2,139	2,307	3,986	10,711
2005	1,902	1,753	1,858	2,977	8,490
2004	1,530	1,387	1,462	2,541	6,921
2003	1,084	1,100	1,134	1,946	5,264
2002	847.4	805.6	851.3	1,429	3,933

Earnings Per Share ($)

2007	0.26	0.19	0.19	E0.49	E1.13
2006	0.12	0.05	0.05	0.23	0.45
2005	0.12	0.12	0.07	0.47	0.78
2004	0.26	0.18	0.13	0.82	1.39
2003	-0.03	-0.11	0.04	0.17	0.08
2002	-0.06	-0.25	-0.09	0.01	-0.40

Fiscal year ended Dec. 31. Next earnings report expected: Early February. EPS Estimates based on S&P Operating Earnings; historical GAAP earnings are as reported.

Dividend Data

No cash dividends have been paid.

Amazon.com Inc

Business Summary October 30, 2007

CORPORATE OVERVIEW. Since opening for business as "Earth's Biggest Bookstore" in July 1995, Amazon.com has expanded into a number of other product areas, such as apparel, shoes and accessories, electronics, computers, kitchen and housewares, music, DVDs, videos, cameras and photo items, office products, toys, baby items and baby registry, software, computer and video games, cell phones and service, tools and hardware, travel services, outdoor living items, and, most recently, jewelry.

AMZN has virtually unlimited online shelf space, and can offer customers a vast selection of products through an efficient search and retrieval interface. The company personalizes shopping by recommending items which, based on previous purchases, are likely to interest a particular customer. Key Web site features also include editorial and customer reviews, manufacturer product information, secure payment systems, wedding and baby registries, customer wish lists, and the ability to view selected interior pages and search the entire contents of many books (Look Inside the Book and Search Inside the Book).

The company operates the following retail Web sites: www.amazon.com (U.S.), www.amazon.co.uk (U.K.), www.amazon.de (Germany), www.amazon.fr (France), www.amazon.co.jp (Japan), www.amazon.ca (Canada), www.joyo.com, www.shopbop.com, and www.endless.com. AMZN also operates www.a9.com and www.alexa.com, which enable search and navigation, and www.imdb.com, a comprehensive movie database.

In addition to being the seller of record for a broad range of new products, AMZN allows other businesses and individuals to sell new, used and collectible products on its Web sites through its Merchant and Amazon Marketplace programs. The company earns fixed fees, sales commissions, and/or per-unit activity fees under these programs.

Starting in 2003, the company began reporting results for two core segments: North America (55% of 2006 net sales) and International (45%). In 2006, media products accounted for 66% of net sales, electronics and other general merchandise 31%, and other 3%.

Company Financials Fiscal Year Ended Dec. 31

Per Share Data ($)	2006	2005	2004	2003	2002	2001	2000	1999	1998	1997
Tangible Book Value	0.58	0.15	NM	NM	NM	NM	NM	NM	NM	0.10
Cash Flow	0.93	1.07	1.56	0.27	-0.16	-0.80	-2.86	-3.26	-0.23	-0.09
Earnings	0.45	0.78	1.39	0.08	-0.40	-1.53	-4.02	-2.20	-0.42	-0.11
S&P Core Earnings	0.48	0.83	1.27	0.02	-0.64	-2.49	NA	NA	NA	NA
Dividends	Nil	Nil	Nil	Nil	Nil	Nil	Nil	Nil	Nil	Nil
Payout Ratio	Nil	Nil	Nil	Nil	Nil	Nil	Nil	Nil	Nil	Nil
Prices:High	48.58	50.00	57.82	61.15	25.00	22.38	91.50	113.00	60.31	5.50
Prices:Low	25.76	30.60	33.00	18.55	9.03	5.51	14.88	41.00	4.15	1.31
P/E Ratio:High	NM	64	42	NM	NM	NM	NM	NM	NM	NM
P/E Ratio:Low	NM	39	24	NM	NM	NM	NM	NM	NM	NM

Income Statement Analysis (Million $)

	2006	2005	2004	2003	2002	2001	2000	1999	1998	1997
Revenue	10,711	8,490	6,921	5,264	3,933	3,122	2,762	1,640	610	148
Operating Income	629	553	508	349	193	35.1	-257	-346	-55.2	-25.8
Depreciation	205	121	75.7	78.3	87.8	266	406	253	56.8	3.39
Interest Expense	78.0	92.0	107	130	143	139	131	84.6	26.6	0.28
Pretax Income	377	428	356	35.3	-150	-557	-1,411	-720	-125	-27.6
Effective Tax Rate	49.6%	22.2%	NM	NM	NM	NM	NM	NM	NM	NM
Net Income	190	333	588	35.3	-150	-557	-1,411	-720	-125	-27.6
S&P Core Earnings	203	354	539	10.3	-242	-910	NA	NA	NA	NA

Balance Sheet & Other Financial Data (Million $)

	2006	2005	2004	2003	2002	2001	2000	1999	1998	1997
Cash	2,019	2,000	1,779	1,395	1,301	997	1,101	706	373	110
Current Assets	3,373	2,929	2,539	1,821	1,616	1,208	1,361	1,012	424	137
Total Assets	4,363	3,696	3,249	2,162	1,990	1,638	2,135	2,472	648	149
Current Liabilities	2,532	1,929	1,620	1,253	1,066	921	975	739	162	43.8
Long Term Debt	1,247	1,521	1,855	1,945	2,277	2,156	2,127	1,466	348	76.7
Common Equity	431	246	-227	-1,036	-1,353	-1,440	-967	266	139	28.5
Total Capital	1,678	1,767	1,628	909	924	716	1,160	1,733	487	105
Capital Expenditures	216	204	89.1	46.0	39.2	50.3	135	287	28.3	7.20
Cash Flow	395	454	664	114	-62.2	-291	-1,005	-1,015	-67.7	-24.2
Current Ratio	1.3	1.5	1.6	1.5	1.5	1.3	1.4	1.4	2.6	3.1
% Long Term Debt of Capitalization	74.3	86.1	113.9	213.9	246.3	301.1	183.4	84.6	71.5	72.9
% Net Income of Revenue	1.8	3.9	8.5	0.7	NM	NM	NM	NM	NM	NM
% Return on Assets	4.7	9.6	21.8	1.7	NM	NM	NM	NM	NM	NM
% Return on Equity	56.1	NM	NM	NM	NM	NM	NM	NM	NM	NM

Data as orig reptd.; bef. results of disc opers/spec. items. Per share data adj. for stk. divs.; EPS diluted. E-Estimated. NA-Not Available. NM-Not Meaningful. NR-Not Ranked. UR-Under Review.

Office: 1200 12th Avenue South, Seattle, WA 98144-2734.
Telephone: 206-266-1000.
Email: ir@amazon.com
Website: http://www.amazon.com

Chrmn, Pres & CEO: J.P. Bezos
SVP & CFO: T.J. Szkutak
SVP, Secy & General Counsel: L.M. Wilson
SVP & CIO: R.L. Dalzell

VP & Chief Acctg Officer: M.S. Peek
Board Members: T. A. Alberg, J. P. Bezos, J. S. Brown, L. J. Doerr, W. B. Gordon, M. S. Potter, T. O. Ryder, P. Q. Stonesifer

Founded: 1994
Domicile: Delaware
Employees: 13,900

Ambac Financial Group Inc.

STANDARD
&POOR'S

S&P Recommendation HOLD ★★★☆☆	**Price** $25.55 (as of Nov 23, 2007)	**12-Mo. Target Price** $29.00	**Investment Style** Large-Cap Blend

GICS Sector Financials
Sub-Industry Property & Casualty Insurance

Summary ABK, the second largest municipal bond insurer, has leveraged that strength and expanded into other types of financial guarantees.

Key Stock Statistics (Source S&P, Vickers, company reports)

52-Wk Range	$96.10– 20.55	S&P Oper. EPS 2007**E**	7.75	Market Capitalization(B)	$2.599	Beta	1.60
Trailing 12-Month EPS	$2.14	S&P Oper. EPS 2008**E**	8.45	Yield (%)	3.29	S&P 3-Yr. Proj. EPS CAGR(%)	NA
Trailing 12-Month P/E	11.9	P/E on S&P Oper. EPS 2007**E**	3.3	Dividend Rate/Share	$0.84	S&P Credit Rating	AA
$10K Invested 5 Yrs Ago	$4,357	Common Shares Outstg. (M)	101.7	Institutional Ownership (%)	NM		

Price Performance

30-Week Mov. Avg. ··· 10-Week Mov. Avg. ‑‑ **GAAP Earnings vs. Previous Year** Volume Above Avg. ⅢⅡ STARS
12-Mo. Target Price — Relative Strength — ▲ Up ▼ Down ▶ No Change Below Avg. ⅢⅡ ★

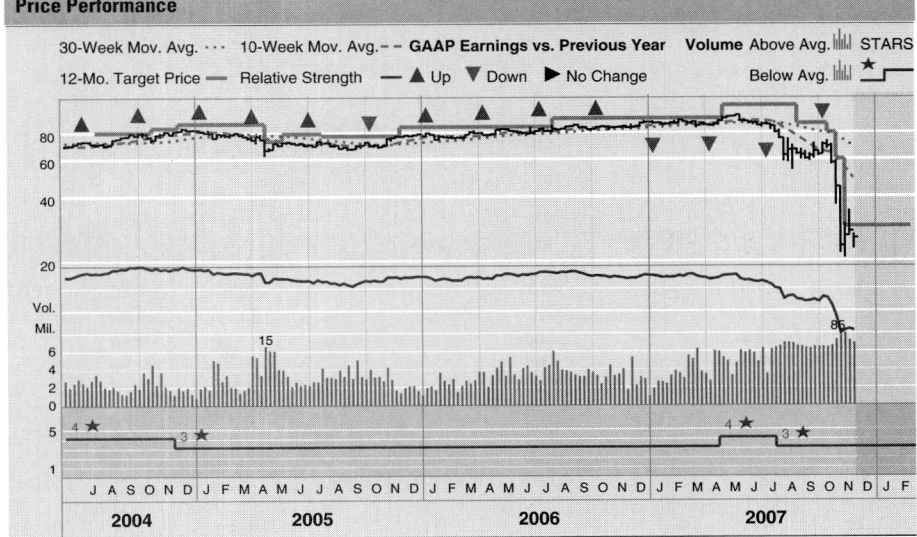

Options: ASE, CBOE, P, Ph

Analysis prepared by **Cathy A. Seifert** on November 19, 2007, when the stock traded at **$ 25.76**.

Highlights

➤ Earned premium growth in 2008 could approach double digits, reflecting heightened demand for credit enhancement products amid a widening of credit spreads. Credit enhancement production (CEP), which is defined as direct and assumed up-front premiums plus the present value of installment premiums on policies and structured credit derivatives, advanced 13%, year to year, during the first nine months of 2007. CEP, or "deal flow," advanced 19% in public finance, 5% in structured finance, and 17% in the international segment.

➤ We anticipate that ABK will incur claims to cover losses in its subprime RMBS (residential mortgage backed securities) portfolio, although we cannot yet quantify the extent of these losses or their timing. Loss and loss adjustment expenses equaled 7.5% of earned premiums in the first nine months of 2007.

➤ We estimate operating EPS of $7.75 in 2007, versus $7.71 of operating EPS reported for 2006. Our $8.45 operating EPS estimate for 2008 excludes mark-to-market adjustments and the potentially dilutive impact of any capital raising efforts ABK may have to undertake.

Investment Rationale/Risk

➤ Our hold recommendation reflects our view that while ABK's valuation is at a historically low level, the market turmoil, headline risk and likelihood of rising loss costs and mark-to-market writedowns stemming from the subprime mortgage market situation will keep the shares under pressure. However, a widening of credit spreads and reduced investor appetite for risk could actually increase demand for ABK's products over the longer term.

➤ Risks to our opinion and target price include a sharper than anticipated rise in interest rates, a significant deterioration in credit quality, and the need for ABK to raise additional capital.

➤ Our 12-month target price of $29 assumes that the shares will remain under pressure from concerns over the adequacy of ABK's capital base and its ability to retain its top-tier financial strength rating unless it raises additional capital. Although these valuation metrics are at unprecedented low levels relative to some of ABK's peers and its historical averages, we do not recommend adding to positions until a greater degree of clarity emerges regarding ABK's capital adequacy.

Qualitative Risk Assessment

LOW	MEDIUM	HIGH

Our risk assessment reflects the impact that alternative credit enhancements have had on the company's production, and by concerns over ABK's exposure to the subprime mortgage market and the potential impact claims there will have on ABK's capital base. This is only partially offset by our view of ABK as a sound underwriter with acceptable risk and capital management practices in place.

Quantitative Evaluations

S&P Quality Ranking A+

D	C	B-	B	B+	A-	A	A+

Relative Strength Rank WEAK

2

LOWEST = 1   HIGHEST = 99

Revenue/Earnings Data

Revenue (Million $)

	1Q	2Q	3Q	4Q	Year
2007	461.8	412.6	-301.0	--	--
2006	453.9	500.9	460.3	454.3	1,832
2005	390.8	406.4	438.3	429.8	1,662
2004	337.4	352.0	352.1	363.2	1,411
2003	290.7	321.6	321.7	338.1	1,272
2002	196.9	202.0	220.4	121.2	971.8

Earnings Per Share ($)

2007	2.02	1.67	-3.51	E1.94	E7.75
2006	2.06	2.22	1.98	1.88	8.15
2005	1.66	1.69	1.61	1.90	6.87
2004	1.55	1.63	1.65	1.69	6.54
2003	1.27	1.48	1.45	1.52	5.74
2002	1.07	1.09	1.21	0.59	3.97

Fiscal year ended Dec. 31. Next earnings report expected: Late January. EPS Estimates based on S&P Operating Earnings; historical GAAP earnings are as reported.

Dividend Data (Dates: mm/dd Payment Date: mm/dd/yy)

Amount ($)	Date Decl.	Ex-Div. Date	Stk. of Record	Payment Date
0.180	02/01	02/08	02/12	03/07/07
0.180	05/08	05/18	05/22	06/06/07
0.210	07/26	08/08	08/10	09/05/07
0.210	10/24	11/07	11/12	12/05/07

Dividends have been paid since 1991. Source: Company reports.

The McGraw-Hill Companies

Ambac Financial Group Inc.

STANDARD &POOR'S

Business Summary November 19, 2007

Ambac Financial Group is the second largest municipal bond insurer, and has leveraged that strength and market dominance into a diversification effort centered on other types of financial guarantees and investment management services. Gross premiums (which include up-front and installment premiums) totaled $996.7 million in 2006 (versus $1.1 billion in 2005) and were divided: public finance 38% ($375.7 million); structured finance 33% ($333.6 million); and international 29% ($287.4 million).

The company guarantees payment when due of principal and interest on the bond insured. Ambac primarily insures newly issued bonds, and the issuer normally pays a single premium to the company when the policy becomes effective. Premium rates are based on a percentage of the spread between a bond's intrinsic credit quality and an AAA-rated bond. At year-end 2006, 43% of the insured portfolio had an internal credit rating of A, 20% was rated AA, 20% was rated BBB, 16% was rated AAA, and 1% was rated below investment grade.

At December 31, 2006, the $282.3 billion public finance insured portfolio was comprised of lease and tax backed bonds (31%); general obligation bonds

(22%); utility revenue bonds (14%); health care revenue bonds (10%); transportation revenue bonds (9%); and other (14%).

The Specialized Finance division is a significant participant, in our opinion, in the structured, asset-backed and mortgage-backed finance markets in the U.S. and abroad. At the end of 2006, the $162.6 billion U.S. structured finance portfolio was comprised of mortgage-backed and home equity obligations (29%); pooled debt obligations (25%); asset-backed and conduits (21%); investor owned utilities (11%); student loan obligations (11%); and other (3%).

At December 31, 2006, ABK's $74.2 billion international portfolio was comprised of pooled debt obligations (27%); asset-backed and conduits (24%); mortgage-backed and home equity loans (16%); investor owned and public utilities (14%); and other international credits (19%).

Company Financials Fiscal Year Ended Dec. 31

Per Share Data ($)	2006	2005	2004	2003	2002	2001	2000	1999	1998	1997
Tangible Book Value	60.47	50.85	46.13	39.71	34.20	28.26	24.60	19.23	19.98	17.85
Operating Earnings	NA	NA	NA	NA	4.68	4.00	3.46	2.93	2.46	1.98
Earnings	8.15	6.87	6.54	5.74	3.97	3.97	3.41	2.87	2.37	2.09
S&P Core Earnings	7.74	6.82	6.27	5.41	4.39	3.87	NA	NA	NA	NA
Dividends	0.66	0.55	0.47	0.42	0.38	0.34	0.31	0.28	0.25	0.23
Payout Ratio	8%	8%	7%	7%	10%	9%	Nil	10%	11%	11%
Prices:High	90.75	82.92	84.73	72.21	71.25	64.00	58.31	42.00	43.96	31.71
Prices:Low	73.74	62.20	63.80	43.79	49.86	42.20	25.92	29.79	27.25	20.67
P/E Ratio:High	11	12	13	13	18	16	17	15	19	15
P/E Ratio:Low	9	9	10	8	13	11	8	10	11	10

Income Statement Analysis (Million $)										
Premium Income	812	816	717	620	472	379	311	383	311	154
Net Investment Income	435	429	363	321	297	268	241	209	186	160
Other Revenue	585	404	331	652	500	78.3	380	324	-40.0	25.8
Total Revenue	1,832	1,662	1,411	1,272	972	725	621	533	457	339
Pretax Income	1,210	1,023	977	850	564	569	482	405	329	286
Net Operating Income	NA	NA	NA	NA	510	436	372	313	263	212
Net Income	876	751	726	628	433	433	366	308	254	223
S&P Core Earnings	832	745	695	592	479	422	NA	NA	NA	NA

Balance Sheet & Other Financial Data (Million $)										
Cash & Equivalent	828	207	182	184	25.8	10.3	20.5	142	134	9.26
Premiums Due	3.90	3.70	16.8	3.03	4.84	2.26	1.09	15.4	16.2	106
Investment Assets:Bonds	17,107	15,495	14,243	13,521	12,141	9,871	8,065	8,738	8,622	6,774
Investment Assets:Stocks	Nil	Nil	Nil	Nil	Nil	Nil	Nil	Nil	Nil	Nil
Investment Assets:Loans	Nil	Nil	Nil	Nil	Nil	Nil	Nil	685	Nil	Nil
Investment Assets:Total	17,707	16,400	15,121	13,830	12,539	10,288	8,324	8,963	9,698	7,281
Deferred Policy Costs	252	202	185	175	174	163	153	135	121	106
Total Assets	20,268	19,725	18,585	16,747	15,356	12,268	10,120	11,345	11,212	8,250
Debt	992	2,234	1,866	792	617	1,044	424	424	424	224
Common Equity	6,184	5,372	5,024	4,444	3,797	3,136	2,729	2,018	2,096	1,872
Property & Casualty:Loss Ratio	NA	NA	NA	NA	NA	NA	NA	NA	NA	NA
Property & Casualty:Expense Ratio	NA	NA	NA	NA	NA	NA	NA	NA	NA	NA
Property & Casualty Combined Ratio	NA	NA	NA	NA	NA	NA	NA	NA	NA	NA
% Return on Revenue	47.8	45.5	51.4	49.4	44.5	59.7	58.9	57.7	62.2	65.8
% Return on Equity	15.1	14.4	15.6	15.2	12.5	14.8	15.0	15.0	12.8	12.8

Data as orig reptd.; bef. results of disc opers/spec. items. Per share data adj. for stk. divs.; EPS diluted. E-Estimated. NA-Not Available. NM-Not Meaningful. NR-Not Ranked. UR-Under Review.

Office: 1 State Street Plz, New York, NY 10004-1505.
Telephone: 212-668-0340.
Website: http://www.ambac.com
Chrmn, Pres & CEO: R.J. Genader

SVP & CFO: S.T. Leonard
SVP & General Counsel: K.J. Doyle
Investor Contact: P.R. Poillon (212-208-3333)

Board Members: M. A. Callen, J. M. Considine, R. J. Genader, W. G. Gregory, P. B. Lassiter, T. C. Theobald, L. S. Unger, H. D. Wallace

Founded: 1971
Domicile: Delaware
Employees: 359

The McGraw-Hill Companies

Ameren Corp

STANDARD &POOR'S

S&P Recommendation	HOLD ★★★☆☆	Price	12-Mo. Target Price	Investment Style
		$52.96 (as of Nov 26, 2007)	$55.00	Large-Cap Value

GICS Sector Utilities
Sub-Industry Multi-Utilities

Summary Ameren is the holding company for the largest electric utility in the state of Missouri, and several utilities in Illinois.

Key Stock Statistics (Source S&P, Vickers, company reports)

52-Wk Range	$55.08– 47.10	S&P Oper. EPS 2007**E**	3.30	Market Capitalization(B)	$10.995	Beta	0.49
Trailing 12-Month EPS	$2.75	S&P Oper. EPS 2008**E**	3.60	Yield (%)	4.80	S&P 3-Yr. Proj. EPS CAGR(%)	14.00
Trailing 12-Month P/E	19.3	P/E on S&P Oper. EPS 2007**E**	16.0	Dividend Rate/Share	$2.54	S&P Credit Rating	BBB-
$10K Invested 5 Yrs Ago	$16,948	Common Shares Outstg. (M)	207.6	Institutional Ownership (%)	61		

Price Performance

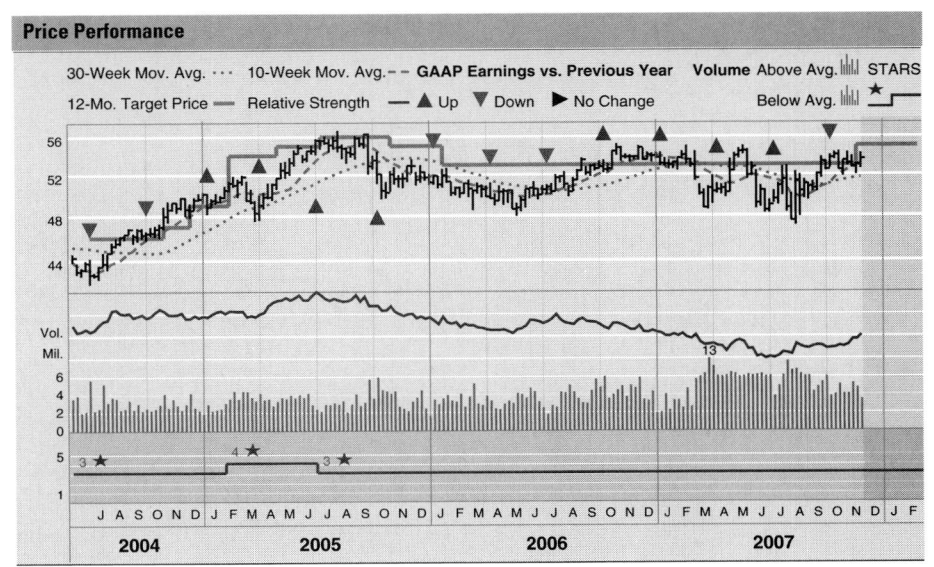

30-Week Mov. Avg. · · · 10-Week Mov. Avg. - - **GAAP Earnings vs. Previous Year** Volume Above Avg. STARS
12-Mo. Target Price — Relative Strength — ▲ Up ▼ Down ► No Change Below Avg.

Options: P, Ph

Analysis prepared by **Justin McCann** on November 26, 2007, when the stock traded at **$ 53.89**.

Highlights

➤ We expect operating EPS in 2007 to advance about 24% from 2006 operating EPS of $2.66, which was hurt by costs related to an unplanned nuclear outage, the absence of power from the Taum Sauk hydroelectric plant, and three severe storms. We see 2007 EPS being aided by rate increases, partially offset by rate relief and customer assistance and bad debt expenses related to the increases.

➤ For 2008, we expect operating EPS to rise about 9% from anticipated results in 2007. We believe earnings will benefit from the replacement of expiring below-market power supply agreements with higher market-based contracts for AEE's unregulated generation units in Illinois.

➤ On August 28, 2007, the governor of Illinois signed Senate Bill 1592, the electric rate compromise reached among state legislators, the Attorney General, the state's utilities, and power marketers. Under the terms of the agreement, Ameren will contribute $150 million to a $1 billion fund for rate relief programs aimed at mitigating the effect of the rate increases that went into effect on January 2, 2007. The compromise agreement was reached after months of intense public and political debate.

Investment Rationale/Risk

➤ With the Illinois governor's signing of Senate Bill 1592, the uncertainties surrounding the electric rate settlement agreement have been removed. Although Ameren's electric utility customers in Illinois will receive benefits of $488 million, AEE will only have to contribute about $150 million to the $1 billion rate relief fund. We see the shares being partially supported by a dividend yield (recently 4.7%) that is well above the industry average. With the current 15% federal tax rate on dividends (which Congress extended through the end of 2010), this would indicate an after-tax yield of 4.0%.

➤ Risks to our recommendation and target price include a sharp decline in power supply margins, unfavorable rulings related to Taum Sauk litigation, and a sharp drop in the average P/E ratio of AEE's peer group as a whole.

➤ While we do not expect Ameren's dividend to be increased (it has not been raised since 1997), we view it as stable, despite the above-average payout ratio of 77% of our EPS estimate for 2007. Our 12-month target price is $55, based on a projected discount-to-peers P/E of 15.3X our EPS estimate for 2008.

Qualitative Risk Assessment

LOW	MEDIUM	HIGH

Our risk assessment reflects our expectation of steady cash flow from the company's regulated utilities, which have the benefit of fuel costs that are well below the industry average. We believe that this, as well as the recent electric rate settlement agreement, should more than offset the increased level of purchased power needed due to the absence of power from the Taum Sauk hydroelectric plant.

Quantitative Evaluations

S&P Quality Ranking A-

D	C	B-	B	B+	A-	A	A+

Relative Strength Rank STRONG
83
LOWEST = 1   HIGHEST = 99

Revenue/Earnings Data

Revenue (Million $)

	1Q	2Q	3Q	4Q	Year
2007	2,019	1,723	1,997	--	--
2006	1,800	1,550	1,910	1,620	6,880
2005	1,626	1,590	1,868	1,701	6,780
2004	1,216	1,152	1,317	1,475	5,160
2003	1,108	1,088	1,350	1,047	4,593
2002	1,115	1,111	1,232	823.0	3,841

Earnings Per Share ($)

2007	0.59	0.69	1.18	E0.52	E3.30
2006	0.34	0.60	1.42	0.30	2.66
2005	0.62	0.93	1.37	0.21	3.13
2004	0.55	0.65	1.20	0.42	2.84
2003	0.52	0.68	1.70	0.24	3.14
2002	0.42	0.80	1.63	-0.20	2.60

Fiscal year ended Dec. 31. Next earnings report expected: Mid February. EPS Estimates based on S&P Operating Earnings; historical GAAP earnings are as reported.

Dividend Data (Dates: mm/dd Payment Date: mm/dd/yy)

Amount ($)	Date Decl.	Ex-Div. Date	Stk. of Record	Payment Date
0.635	02/09	03/05	03/07	03/30/07
0.635	04/24	06/04	06/06	06/29/07
0.635	08/10	09/04	09/06	09/28/07
0.635	10/12	12/03	12/05	12/31/07

Dividends have been paid since 1906. Source: Company reports.

Ameren Corp

STANDARD &POOR'S

Business Summary November 26, 2007

CORPORATE OVERVIEW. Ameren Corporation (AEE) is a holding company that operates regulated electric and natural gas utilities and non-regulated operations, including energy marketing, trading and consulting services, in Missouri and Illinois. AEE's Utility Operations segment is comprised of its electric generation and electric and gas transmission and distribution operations. The company's subsidiaries include Union Electric Company (UE), Central Illinois Public Service Company (CIPS), Ameren Energy Generating Company (Genco), CILCORP Inc., and Illinois Power Company (IP). In 2006, electric services contributed to 81.2% of total revenues while gas services contributed to the rest.

CORPORATE STRATEGY. AEE has undertaken a cost control initiative related to its strategic sourcing of purchases and the streamlining of all aspects of its business. This is partly in response to the lower coal inventory it faced in 2005

due to disruptions in coal deliveries. In case of future disruptions, AEE would pursue a strategy that could include reducing sales of power during low-margin periods or utilizing higher cost fuels to generate required electricity and purchasing power. To meet projected demand growth, the company has decided to expand its generating capacity through asset purchases. It has also entered into long-term supply agreements for ensuring its future gas supply. AEE is focused on realizing the integration synergies associated with the CILCORP and IP acquisitions, which include utilizing more economical fuels at CILCORP and reducing administrative and operating expenses at IP.

Company Financials Fiscal Year Ended Dec. 31

Per Share Data ($)	2006	2005	2004	2003	2002	2001	2000	1999	1998	1997
Tangible Book Value	26.80	25.08	24.92	23.19	24.95	24.26	23.34	22.55	22.27	21.92
Earnings	2.66	3.13	2.84	3.14	2.60	3.45	3.33	2.81	2.82	2.82
S&P Core Earnings	2.90	3.32	3.12	3.28	2.36	2.81	NA	NA	NA	NA
Dividends	2.54	2.54	2.54	2.54	2.54	2.54	2.54	2.54	2.54	2.54
Payout Ratio	95%	81%	89%	81%	98%	74%	76%	90%	90%	90%
Prices:High	55.24	56.77	50.36	46.50	45.25	46.00	46.94	42.94	44.31	43.75
Prices:Low	47.96	47.51	40.55	42.55	34.72	36.53	27.56	32.00	35.56	34.50
P/E Ratio:High	21	18	18	15	17	13	14	15	16	16
P/E Ratio:Low	18	15	14	14	13	11	8	11	13	12

Income Statement Analysis (Million $)	2006	2005	2004	2003	2002	2001	2000	1999	1998	1997
Revenue	6,880	6,780	5,160	4,593	3,841	4,506	3,856	3,524	3,318	3,327
Depreciation	661	632	557	519	431	406	382	351	348	346
Maintenance	NA	NA	NA	NA	NA	382	368	371	312	310
Fixed Charges Coverage	3.48	4.32	3.81	3.61	4.04	4.65	4.86	4.48	NA	4.08
Construction Credits	NA	NA	NA	4.00	11.0	20.8	14.0	14.0	12.0	12.7
Effective Tax Rate	32.7%	35.6%	34.7%	37.3%	38.3%	38.7%	39.7%	40.2%	40.9%	38.0%
Net Income	558	628	530	506	382	475	457	385	386	387
S&P Core Earnings	597	666	582	530	347	387	NA	NA	NA	NA

Balance Sheet & Other Financial Data (Million $)	2006	2005	2004	2003	2002	2001	2000	1999	1998	1997
Gross Property	22,013	20,800	20,291	17,511	15,745	14,962	13,910	13,056	12,531	12,273
Capital Expenditures	992	947	806	682	787	1,103	929	571	325	381
Net Property	14,286	13,572	13,297	10,917	8,914	8,427	7,706	7,165	6,928	6,987
Capitalization:Long Term Debt	5,498	5,568	5,236	4,273	3,626	3,071	2,980	2,683	2,525	2,506
Capitalization:% Long Term Debt	45.5	46.7	47.4	49.5	48.6	47.8	48.3	46.5	45.2	43.5
Capitalization:Preferred	Nil	Nil	Nil	Nil	Nil	Nil	Nil	Nil	NA	235
Capitalization:% Preferred	Nil	Nil	Nil	Nil	Nil	Nil	Nil	Nil	NA	4.10
Capitalization:Common	6,583	6,364	5,800	4,354	3,842	3,349	3,196	3,089	3,056	3,019
Capitalization:% Common	54.5	53.3	52.6	50.5	51.4	52.2	51.7	53.5	54.8	52.4
Total Capital	14,241	14,047	13,075	10,653	9,339	8,144	7,884	7,441	7,285	7,507
% Operating Ratio	87.1	86.3	84.6	83.9	81.0	85.2	83.4	84.1	82.8	82.5
% Earned on Net Property	8.4	9.6	8.9	10.7	7.2	8.2	8.6	8.0	8.2	8.4
% Return on Revenue	8.0	9.3	10.3	11.0	9.9	10.6	11.9	10.9	11.6	11.6
% Return on Invested Capital	6.6	7.0	6.9	7.4	8.1	8.6	8.5	7.7	11.3	7.7
% Return on Common Equity	8.4	10.3	10.4	12.3	10.6	14.5	14.5	12.5	12.7	12.8

Data as orig reptd.; bef. results of disc opers/spec. items. Per share data adj. for stk. divs.; EPS diluted. E-Estimated. NA-Not Available. NM-Not Meaningful. NR-Not Ranked. UR-Under Review.

Office: 1901 Chouteau Avenue, St. Louis, MO 63103.
Telephone: 314-621-3222.
Email: invest@ameren.com
Website: http://www.ameren.com

Chrmn, Pres & CEO: G.L. Rainwater
COO & EVP: T.R. Voss
EVP & CFO: W.L. Baxter
SVP, Secy & General Counsel: S.R. Sullivan

VP & Treas: J.E. Birdsong
Investor Contact: B. Steinke (314-554-2574)
Board Members: S. F. Brauer, S. S. Elliott, G. P. Jackson, J. C. Johnson, R. A. Liddy, G. R. Lohman, C. W. Mueller, D. R. Oberhelman, G. L. Rainwater, H. Saligman, P. T. Stokes, J. D. Woodard

Founded: 1881
Domicile: Missouri
Employees: 8,988

STANDARD &POOR'S

American Capital Strategies Ltd

S&P Recommendation	STRONG BUY ★★★★★	Price $37.79 (as of Nov 23, 2007)	12-Mo. Target Price $51.00	Investment Style Large-Cap Growth

GICS Sector Financials
Sub-Industry Asset Management & Custody Banks

Summary This buyout and mezzanine fund provides investment capital to middle market companies.

Key Stock Statistics (Source S&P, Vickers, company reports)

52-Wk Range	$49.96– 35.00	S&P Oper. EPS 2007E	3.24	Market Capitalization(B)	$7.102	Beta	0.94
Trailing 12-Month EPS	$7.66	S&P Oper. EPS 2008E	3.84	Yield (%)	9.29	S&P 3-Yr. Proj. EPS CAGR(%)	7.00
Trailing 12-Month P/E	4.9	P/E on S&P Oper. EPS 2007E	11.7	Dividend Rate/Share	$3.51	S&P Credit Rating	NA
$10K Invested 5 Yrs Ago	$29,828	Common Shares Outstg. (M)	187.9	Institutional Ownership (%)	46		

Price Performance

Options: ASE, CBOE, P, Ph

Analysis prepared by **Matthew Albrecht** on November 12, 2007, when the stock traded at **$ 39.62**.

Highlights

➤ We expect ACAS, with a current portfolio of more than $17 billion, to increase its assets under management to about $18 billion in 2007, from $11 billion at the end of 2006. We expect the company to continue its transition to an alternative asset manager by introducing new funds utilizing capital of its own and from outside investors, flowing into both permanent capital funds and finite-life investment vehicles, which may total about $6 billion by year-end. We anticipate that this will have a positive effect on both ACAS's asset management and fee income and dividend income. We look for this rapid portfolio growth to help operating income grow more than 40% in 2007, followed by a 36% increase in 2008.

➤ We believe the company's transition to a third-party asset manager and geographic expansion may put upward pressure on its compensation ratios in the near term, with compensation and benefits approximating 20% of operating income in each year. Combined with other costs, these increases will likely result in operating margin compression as well.

➤ We forecast net operating earnings of $3.24 for 2007 and $3.84 for 2008.

Investment Rationale/Risk

➤ We view favorably ACAS's market share in the middle market, relationships with private equity sponsors, and an impressive track record of returning capital to shareholders. We have a positive view of the company's plan to grow its external asset management business, given predictable management fee income and net profit participation, and we believe the size of its investment portfolio and origination platform will allow it to create and structure favorable external asset management transactions. Our recommendation is strong buy, based on our total return expectations.

➤ Risks to our recommendation and target price include potential credit deterioration, increased competition for new investments, the illiquid nature of ACAS's investments, and difficulty accurately valuing these investments.

➤ Our 12-month target price of $51 is equal to 1.3X our 2008 projected NAV. A recent dividend policy change allows ACAS to utilize retained long-term capital gains for distribution, lending additional security to its payout, in our view. We believe the firm's forecasted dividend of $4.19 for 2008 adds to the stock's attractive total return potential.

Qualitative Risk Assessment

LOW	MEDIUM	HIGH

Our risk assessment for ACAS reflects our view of the illiquid nature of many of the company's investments, the difficulty in placing an accurate value on these investments, and the uncertain timing around realized investment gains. We think this is offset by ACAS's diversified portfolio and track record of consistent dividend growth.

Quantitative Evaluations

S&P Quality Ranking   **B**

D	C	B-	B	B+	A-	A	A+

Relative Strength Rank   **MODERATE**

39

LOWEST = 1   HIGHEST = 99

Revenue/Earnings Data

Revenue (Million $)

	1Q	2Q	3Q	4Q	Year
2007	250.0	326.0	310.0	--	--
2006	173.0	212.0	231.0	244.0	1,033
2005	100.9	131.7	148.8	173.2	554.5
2004	66.53	75.58	82.27	111.7	336.1
2003	43.06	43.21	53.32	66.69	206.3
2002	32.64	34.18	39.28	40.93	147.0

Earnings Per Share ($)

2007	0.86	4.68	0.11	E0.79	E3.24
2006	1.33	2.16	0.92	2.10	6.55
2005	1.22	0.82	0.90	0.71	3.60
2004	0.51	1.22	0.74	1.11	3.63
2003	-0.02	0.48	0.48	1.07	2.15
2002	0.09	0.32	-0.29	0.37	0.50

Fiscal year ended Dec. 31. Next earnings report expected: Early March. EPS Estimates based on S&P Operating Earnings; historical GAAP earnings are as reported.

Dividend Data (Dates: mm/dd Payment Date: mm/dd/yy)

Amount ($)	Date Decl.	Ex-Div. Date	Stk. of Record	Payment Date
0.890	02/13	02/28	03/02	04/02/07
0.910	05/01	06/07	06/11	07/02/07
0.920	07/31	09/05	09/07	10/01/07
1.000	10/30	12/05	12/07	01/16/08

Dividends have been paid since 1997. Source: Company reports.

Please read the Required Disclosures and Analyst Certification on the last page of this report.

The McGraw-Hill Companies

American Capital Strategies Ltd

Business Summary November 12, 2007

CORPORATE OVERVIEW. American Capital Strategies Ltd. is a publicly traded buyout and mezzanine fund that provides investment capital to middle-market companies. American Capital is an equity partner in management and employee buyouts; provides mezzanine and senior debt financing for buyouts led by private equity firms; and supplies capital to private and small public companies to fund growth, acquisitions, and recapitalizations. ACAS's wholly owned operating subsidiary, American Capital Financial Services, Inc. (ACFS), provides financial advisory services to portfolio companies.

ACAS completed its IPO in August 1997, becoming a non-diversified, closed end investment company; it elected to be regulated as a business development company, or BDC. ACAS began operations in October 1997 in order to qualify to be taxed as a regulated investment company (RIC). It is not subject to federal income tax on the portion of its taxable income and capital gains that it distributes to its stockholders.

Since its August 1997 IPO, ACAS has invested over $13 billion in debt and equity securities in middle market companies. The company's portfolio includes services, transportation, construction, wholesale, retail, health care, and industrial, consumer, chemical and food products. At the end of 2006, ACAS's

portfolio consisted of investments in 223 companies with an average investment size of $43 million. ACAS's largest concentration of investments was in the commercial services industry, representing 15% of its portfolio at fair value, with only its stake in diversified financial services concerns also representing more than 10% of its portfolio. At the end of 2006, the company had about 484 employees, with 182 investment professionals actively engaged in the origination and approval process of its investing activities.

CORPORATE STRATEGY. ACAS generally focuses on middle market companies that have been in business over 10 years, have positive cash flow, and have a significant market share in their products or services. As of December 31, 2006, the company's current portfolio had an average age of 33 years, with 2006 sales of $132 million and EBITDA of $24 million. ACAS generally invests between $10 million and $500 million in its North American targets and 10 million euros and 200 million euros in its European targets.

Company Financials Fiscal Year Ended Dec. 31

Per Share Data ($)	2006	2005	2004	2003	2002	2001	2000	1999	1998	1997
Tangible Book Value	29.42	24.37	21.11	17.83	15.82	16.84	15.90	17.08	13.78	13.61
Cash Flow	6.54	3.60	3.63	2.15	0.50	0.58	-0.19	5.33	1.53	0.53
Earnings	6.55	3.60	3.63	2.15	0.50	0.58	-0.19	6.80	1.48	0.52
S&P Core Earnings	6.55	3.59	3.59	1.65	0.88	0.04	NA	NA	NA	NA
Dividends	3.33	3.05	2.85	2.79	2.57	2.30	2.17	1.74	1.34	0.21
Payout Ratio	51%	85%	79%	130%	NM	NM	NM	27%	88%	40%
Prices:High	46.45	39.61	34.91	30.00	32.98	29.89	27.75	23.13	24.63	20.75
Prices:Low	29.65	29.51	24.70	20.75	15.17	21.88	19.81	14.00	9.19	15.00
P/E Ratio:High	7	11	10	14	66	52	NM	3	17	40
P/E Ratio:Low	5	8	7	10	30	38	NM	2	6	29

Income Statement Analysis (Million $)										
Loan Fees	191	129	64.9	47.0	25.0	15.6	11.3	2.57	2.55	3.02
Interest Income	669	426	271	159	122	88.3	58.0	30.8	14.4	2.68
Total Revenue	1,033	591	336	206	147	104	70.0	33.4	17.0	5.70
Interest Expense	190	101	36.9	18.5	14.3	10.3	9.69	4.72	0.06	0.06
% Expense/Operating Revenue	41.0%	38.6%	33.9%	28.7%	35.2%	31.3%	22.8%	21.7%	10.1%	56.2%
Pretax Income	906	377	284	118	20.1	18.6	-4.37	97.2	16.9	8.01
Effective Tax Rate	1.21%	3.31%	0.75%	NM	NM	NM	NM	NM	NM	26.6%
Net Income	895	365	281	118	20.1	18.6	-4.37	97.2	16.9	5.88
S&P Core Earnings	895	364	279	90.5	35.0	1.40	NA	NA	NA	NA

Balance Sheet & Other Financial Data (Million $)										
Net Property	Nil	Nil	Nil	Nil	Nil	Nil	Nil	Nil	Nil	Nil
Cash & Securities	77.0	5,216	3,280	1,920	1,262	877	594	384	96.1	122
Loans	Nil	Nil	Nil	Nil	Nil	Nil	Nil	Nil	Nil	Nil
Total Assets	8,609	5,449	3,491	2,042	1,319	904	615	395	270	151
Capitalization:Debt	3,573	2,286	1,430	772	323	103	87.2	Nil	Nil	Nil
Capitalization:Equity	4,342	2,957	1,872	1,176	688	640	445	312	153	151
Capitalization:Total	7,915	5,243	3,303	1,948	1,011	744	532	312	153	151
Price Times Book Value:High	1.6	1.6	1.7	1.7	2.1	1.8	1.7	1.4	1.8	2.9
Price Times Book Value:Low	1.0	1.2	1.2	1.2	1.0	1.3	1.2	0.8	0.7	1.5
Cash Flow	895	365	281	118	20.1	18.6	-4.37	97.2	16.9	5.91
% Return on Revenue	86.6	61.8	83.7	57.3	15.9	17.8	NM	291.0	99.6	NM
% Return on Assets	12.7	8.2	10.1	7.0	1.8	2.5	NM	29.2	8.0	NM
% Return on Equity	24.7	15.0	18.5	12.6	3.0	3.4	NM	41.9	11.2	NM

Data as orig reptd.; bef. results of disc opers/spec. items. Per share data adj. for stk. divs.; EPS diluted. E-Estimated. NA-Not Available. NM-Not Meaningful. NR-Not Ranked. UR-Under Review.

Office: 2 Bethesda Metro Ctr 14th Floor, Bethesda, MD 20814-6319.
Telephone: 301-951-6122.
Email: info@American-Capital.com
Website: http://www.AmericanCapital.com

Chrmn, Pres & CEO: M. Wilkus
COO & EVP: I. Wagner
EVP, CFO & Secy: J.R. Erickson
EVP, Secy, General Counsel & CCO: S.A. Flax

Investor Contact: A. Ladd Cuthbertson (301-951-6122)
Board Members: M. C. Baskin, N. M. Hahl, P. Harper, J. A. Koskinen, S. Lundine, K. D. Peterson, Jr., A. Puryear, M. Wilkus
Founded: 1986
Domicile: Delaware
Employees: 484

American Electric Power

S&P Recommendation	**BUY** ★★★★☆	Price	12-Mo. Target Price	Investment Style
		$46.45 (as of Nov 23, 2007)	$55.00	Large-Cap Value

GICS Sector Utilities
Sub-Industry Electric Utilities

Summary This Ohio-based electric utility holding company has subsidiaries operating in 11 states in the U.S.

Key Stock Statistics (Source S&P, Vickers, company reports)

52-Wk Range	$51.24– 40.95	S&P Oper. EPS 2007**E**	3.00	Market Capitalization(B)	$18.543	Beta		1.00
Trailing 12-Month EPS	$2.60	S&P Oper. EPS 2008**E**	3.20	Yield (%)	3.53	S&P 3-Yr. Proj. EPS CAGR(%)		6.00
Trailing 12-Month P/E	17.9	P/E on S&P Oper. EPS 2007**E**	15.5	Dividend Rate/Share	$1.64	S&P Credit Rating		BBB
$10K Invested 5 Yrs Ago	$20,325	Common Shares Outstg. (M)	399.2	Institutional Ownership (%)	71			

Price Performance

30-Week Mov. Avg. · · · 10-Week Mov. Avg. - - **GAAP Earnings vs. Previous Year** Volume Above Avg. |ıl| **STARS**
12-Mo. Target Price — Relative Strength — ▲ Up ▼ Down ▶ No Change Below Avg. |ıl| ★

Options: ASE, CBOE, P, Ph

Analysis prepared by **Justin McCann** on October 25, 2007, when the stock traded at **$ 46.97**.

Qualitative Risk Assessment

LOW	MEDIUM	HIGH

Our risk assessment reflects our view of the steady cash flow expected from the regulated utilities, with their low-cost fuel sources and generally supportive regulatory environments. The proceeds from the divestiture of most of AEP's high-risk unregulated energy businesses were used to enhance its balance sheet and financial strength.

Quantitative Evaluations

S&P Quality Ranking B

D	C	B-	B	B+	A-	A	A+

Relative Strength Rank STRONG

76

LOWEST = 1   HIGHEST = 99

Highlights

➤ We expect 2007 operating EPS to grow about 8% from 2006 operating EPS of $2.77. This will reflect, in our view, a full year of rate increases, more normal weather, higher off-system sales, increased generating and marketing income, and growth in power demand. This should more than offset a projected decline in earnings from the MEMCO barge operation, a decrease in net transmission revenues, and higher operating, depreciation and interest expense. Results in the first three quarters of 2007 benefited from a lower effective tax rate.

➤ For 2008, we expect operating EPS to increase about 6% from anticipated results in 2007, reflecting additional rate increases, higher off-system sales and net transmission revenues, and a modest decline in operation and maintenance expenses. We believe this will be partially offset by a higher level of interest expense.

➤ We project AEP's longer-term annual EPS growth rate to range between 5% and 9%, with results driven by rate base investments in the company's generation and transmission operations. AEP plans to reduce its greenhouse gas emissions to 6% below a baseline average of 1998 to 2001 emission levels by 2010.

Investment Rationale/Risk

➤ We believe AEP stock, which has moderately outperformed the company's electric utility peers year to date, remains attractive for above-average total return. While the shares may be restricted by concern over the potential impact of probable greenhouse gas legislation, we do not expect any significant impact until after the 2015-2020 period, and we believe AEP's substantial environmental investments will smooth the transition.

➤ Risks to our recommendation and target price include the potential for weaker than anticipated results from the wholesale operations, and a sharp decline in the average P/E multiple of the group as a whole.

➤ Reflecting the company's improved financial profile, AEP recently declared an increase of $0.02 a share (5.1%) in its quarterly dividend, effective with the December 2007 payment. This has helped to lift the current yield (recently at 3.5%) closer to the recent average for AEP's electric utility peers (3.7%). We expect the shares to trade at a modest premium-to-peers P/E of about 17X our EPS estimate for 2008. Our 12-month target price is $55.

Revenue/Earnings Data

Revenue (Million $)

	1Q	2Q	3Q	4Q	Year
2007	3,169	3,146	3,800	--	--
2006	3,108	2,936	3,594	2,984	12,622
2005	3,065	2,819	3,328	2,899	12,111
2004	3,364	3,408	3,780	3,505	14,057
2003	3,834	3,451	3,940	3,320	14,545
2002	3,169	3,575	3,870	3,941	14,555

Earnings Per Share ($)

2007	0.68	0.64	1.02	E0.50	E3.00
2006	0.95	0.43	0.67	0.44	2.50
2005	0.90	0.57	0.94	0.23	2.63
2004	0.73	0.38	1.04	0.69	2.85
2003	0.83	0.47	0.75	-0.65	1.35
2002	0.49	0.49	1.14	-2.01	0.06

Fiscal year ended Dec. 31. Next earnings report expected: NA. EPS Estimates based on S&P Operating Earnings; historical GAAP earnings are as reported.

Dividend Data (Dates: mm/dd Payment Date: mm/dd/yy)

Amount ($)	Date Decl.	Ex-Div. Date	Stk. of Record	Payment Date
0.390	01/24	02/07	02/09	03/09/07
0.390	04/24	05/08	05/10	06/08/07
0.390	07/24	08/08	08/10	09/10/07
0.410	10/23	11/07	11/09	12/10/07

Dividends have been paid since 1909. Source: Company reports.

Please read the Required Disclosures and Analyst Certification on the last page of this report.

American Electric Power

**STANDARD
&POOR'S**

Business Summary October 25, 2007

CORPORATE OVERVIEW. AEP is a holding company that primarily operates electric utility services through its regulated subsidiaries. The utility services include the generation, transmission and distribution of electricity for sale to retail and wholesale customers in the U.S. AEP's non-regulated operations include the MEMCO Barge Line subsidiary, which is engaged in the transportation of coal and dry bulk commodities, mainly on the Ohio, Illinois and lower Mississippi rivers. In 2006, the utility segment accounted for 95.6% of total revenues.

CORPORATE STRATEGY. AEP's strategy is to focus on its core utility operations and to deliver low-cost electric power to the communities served. The company plans to improve its efficiency and to maximize the power that is delivered from its generation facilities. In order to provide safe and reliable pow-

er, AEP is making investments to upgrade its transmission and distribution infrastructure, as well as to be in compliance with the appropriate environmental standards. In January 2007, AEP signed a participation agreement with MidAmerican Energy Holdings to form a joint venture company, Electric Transmission Texas (ETT), to fund, own and operate electric transmission assets in Texas. Subject to necessary approvals, ETT (which would be 50%-owned by both AEP and MidAmerican) is expected to begin operations by the end of 2007.

Company Financials Fiscal Year Ended Dec. 31

Per Share Data ($)	2006	2005	2004	2003	2002	2001	2000	1999	1998	1997
Tangible Book Value	24.88	22.87	21.31	19.74	19.67	20.92	20.72	25.80	25.21	24.62
Earnings	2.50	2.63	2.85	1.35	0.06	3.11	0.94	2.69	2.81	3.28
S&P Core Earnings	2.35	2.26	2.58	1.47	0.07	2.17	NA	NA	NA	NA
Dividends	1.50	1.42	1.40	1.65	2.40	2.40	2.40	2.40	2.40	2.40
Payout Ratio	60%	54%	49%	NM	NM	77%	255%	89%	85%	73%
Prices:High	43.13	40.80	35.53	31.51	48.80	51.20	48.94	48.19	53.31	52.00
Prices:Low	32.27	32.25	28.50	19.01	15.10	39.25	25.94	30.56	42.06	39.13
P/E Ratio:High	17	16	12	23	NM	16	52	18	19	16
P/E Ratio:Low	13	12	10	14	NM	13	28	11	15	12

Income Statement Analysis (Million $)										
Revenue	12,622	12,111	14,057	14,545	14,555	61,257	13,694	6,916	6,346	6,161
Depreciation	1,467	1,318	1,300	1,299	1,377	1,383	1,062	600	580	591
Maintenance	NA	NA	NA	NA	NA	NA	NA	NA	543	483
Fixed Charges Coverage	2.96	2.80	2.60	2.97	2.84	2.64	1.95	2.44	2.98	3.27
Construction Credits	30.0	21.0	NA	NA	NA	NA	NA	NA	NA	NA
Effective Tax Rate	32.7%	29.4%	33.7%	39.8%	79.3%	35.9%	66.4%	33.3%	37.1%	35.5%
Net Income	995	1,029	1,127	522	21.0	1,003	302	520	536	620
S&P Core Earnings	934	883	1,021	573	21.1	698	NA	NA	NA	NA

Balance Sheet & Other Financial Data (Million $)										
Gross Property	42,021	39,121	37,286	36,033	37,857	40,709	38,088	22,205	20,146	19,596
Capital Expenditures	3,528	2,404	1,693	1,358	1,722	1,832	1,773	867	792	760
Net Property	26,781	24,284	22,801	22,029	21,684	24,543	22,393	13,055	11,730	11,633
Capitalization:Long Term Debt	12,490	11,073	11,069	12,459	9,329	10,230	10,097	6,500	6,974	5,304
Capitalization:% Long Term Debt	57.0	54.9	56.5	61.3	56.9	55.4	55.6	56.5	59.0	53.1
Capitalization:Preferred	Nil	Nil	Nil	Nil	Nil	Nil	Nil	Nil	Nil	Nil
Capitalization:% Preferred	Nil	Nil	Nil	Nil	Nil	Nil	Nil	Nil	Nil	Nil
Capitalization:Common	9,412	9,088	8,515	7,874	7,064	8,229	8,054	5,006	4,841	4,677
Capitalization:% Common	43.0	45.1	43.5	38.7	43.1	44.6	44.4	43.5	41.0	46.9
Total Capital	26,802	25,032	24,403	24,290	21,523	24,523	23,554	14,577	14,767	12,918
% Operating Ratio	87.2	84.1	85.8	88.8	91.3	96.1	85.2	81.1	84.9	84.0
% Earned on Net Property	7.7	8.2	8.9	7.7	5.8	10.2	9.2	10.1	8.2	8.5
% Return on Revenue	7.9	8.5	8.0	3.6	0.1	1.6	2.2	7.5	8.4	10.1
% Return on Invested Capital	7.5	6.2	6.1	9.4	8.8	8.4	6.8	7.2	7.0	8.1
% Return on Common Equity	10.7	11.7	13.8	7.0	0.3	12.3	3.6	10.6	11.3	13.4

Data as orig reptd.; bef. results of disc opers/spec. items. Per share data adj. for stk. divs.; EPS diluted. E-Estimated. NA-Not Available. NM-Not Meaningful. NR-Not Ranked. UR-Under Review.

Office: 1 Riverside Plz , Columbus , OH 43215-2373.
Telephone: 614-716-1000.
Email: corpcomm@aep.com
Website: http://www.aep.com

Chrmn, Pres & CEO: M.G. Morris
EVP & CFO: H. Koeppel
SVP, Secy & General Counsel: J.B. Keane
Investor Contact: J. Sloat (614-716-2885)

Board Members: E. R. Brooks, D. M. Carlton, R. D. Crosby, Jr., J. P. DesBarres, R. W. Fri, L. A. Goodspeed, W. R. Howell, L. A. Hudson, Jr., M. G. Morris, L. L. Nowell, III, R. L. Sandor, D. G. Smith, K. D. Sullivan

Founded: 1906
Domicile: New York
Employees: 20,442

The McGraw·Hill Companies

American Express Co

STANDARD &POOR'S

S&P Recommendation BUY ★★★★☆	**Price** $55.63 (as of Nov 23, 2007)	**12-Mo. Target Price** $73.00	**Investment Style** Large-Cap Growth

GICS Sector Financials
Sub-Industry Consumer Finance

Summary American Express is a leading global payments, network, and travel company.

Key Stock Statistics (Source S&P, Vickers, company reports)

52-Wk Range	$65.89– 53.91	S&P Oper. EPS 2007**E**	3.50	Market Capitalization(B)	$65.055	Beta	1.36
Trailing 12-Month EPS	$3.40	S&P Oper. EPS 2008**E**	3.90	Yield (%)	1.29	S&P 3-Yr. Proj. EPS CAGR(%)	12.00
Trailing 12-Month P/E	16.4	P/E on S&P Oper. EPS 2007**E**	15.9	Dividend Rate/Share	$0.72	S&P Credit Rating	A+
$10K Invested 5 Yrs Ago	NA	Common Shares Outstg. (M)	1,169.4	Institutional Ownership (%)	82		

Price Performance

30-Week Mov. Avg. · · · 10-Week Mov. Avg. - - **GAAP Earnings vs. Previous Year** **Volume** Above Avg. ▮▮▮ STARS
12-Mo. Target Price — Relative Strength — ▲ Up ▼ Down ► No Change Below Avg. ▮▮▮ ★

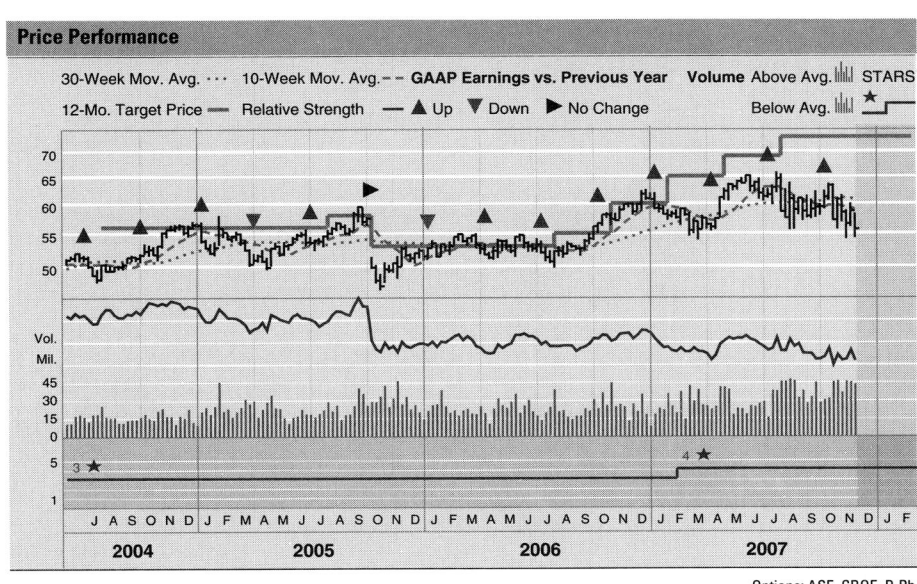

Options: ASE, CBOE, P, Ph

Analysis prepared by **Frank Braden, CFA** on October 23, 2007, when the stock traded at **$ 58.66**.

Highlights

➤ We expect 2008 revenue growth of 11% at AXP, exceeding its long-term growth target of 8%, mainly due to strong cardmember average spending and growth in cards in force. We also see U.S. consumer travel sales and solid loan growth helping to boost revenues. We anticipate that higher marketing and promotional expenses in 2008 will be focused on cardmember acquisition outside the U.S. We think an increase in reward costs will be partially offset by AXP driving cardmembers to lower-costs points.

➤ Despite relatively solid credit quality, we forecast an increase in the provision for losses, largely due to higher global loan volumes and rising write-off and delinquency rates. We believe AXP's flexible spending structure will allow company to trim marketing spend to help offset provision expense during the near term. We see the issuance of American Express cards through partnerships with various large banking players having a slightly negative impact on proprietary cardmember growth, but a positive long-term impact on total billed business for AXP's merchant network.

➤ We see EPS of $3.50 in 2007 and $3.90 in 2008.

Investment Rationale/Risk

➤ We view positively AXP's strong brand name, customer loyalty, and growth prospects. We believe the Ameriprise spinoff has helped focus the company, and we view AXP as having above peer credit and solid growth prospects. The company's closed loop network helps increase AXP's value to its merchant partners, in our view. While we see difficult credit conditions and competition continuing to increase, we view AXP as the market leader, and we look for it to continue to innovate.

➤ Risks to our recommendation and target price include a possible deterioration in consumer confidence that would have an impact on domestic consumer spending, a slowdown in business spending, and a rise in unemployment that would pressure credit quality.

➤ Our 12-month target price of $73 values the stock at about 18.7X our 2008 EPS estimate, in line with its historical P/E. We think this is an appropriate valuation multiple based on our view of the company's less capital intensive structure and growth prospects.

Qualitative Risk Assessment

LOW	MEDIUM	HIGH

Our risk assessment reflects what we see as solid business fundamentals and a strong customer base. We view AXP as able to withstand a major global or U.S. economic downturn, and we consider its credit quality to be solid.

Quantitative Evaluations

S&P Quality Ranking A-

D	C	B-	B	B+	A-	A	A+

Relative Strength Rank MODERATE

50

LOWEST = 1   HIGHEST = 99

Revenue/Earnings Data

Revenue (Million $)

	1Q	2Q	3Q	4Q	Year
2007	7,631	8,199	7,953	--	--
2006	6,319	6,850	6,759	7,208	27,136
2005	5,672	6,090	6,068	6,437	24,267
2004	6,910	7,232	7,202	7,771	29,115
2003	6,023	6,356	6,419	7,068	25,866
2002	5,759	5,945	5,907	6,196	23,807

Earnings Per Share ($)

2007	0.88	0.88	0.90	E0.88	E3.50
2006	0.70	0.78	0.78	0.76	3.01
2005	0.59	0.69	0.69	0.60	2.56
2004	0.66	0.68	0.69	0.71	2.74
2003	0.53	0.59	0.59	0.60	2.31
2002	0.46	0.51	0.52	0.52	2.01

Fiscal year ended Dec. 31. Next earnings report expected: Late January. EPS Estimates based on S&P Operating Earnings; historical GAAP earnings are as reported.

Dividend Data (Dates: mm/dd Payment Date: mm/dd/yy)

Amount ($)	Date Decl.	Ex-Div. Date	Stk. of Record	Payment Date
0.150	03/26	04/03	04/05	05/10/07
0.150	05/21	07/03	07/06	08/10/07
0.150	09/25	10/03	10/05	11/09/07
0.180	11/19	01/02	01/04	02/08/08

Dividends have been paid since 1870. Source: Company reports.

Please read the Required Disclosures and Analyst Certification on the last page of this report.

The McGraw-Hill Companies

American Express Co

Business Summary October 23, 2007

CORPORATE PROFILE. AXP is a leading global payments, network, and travel company that is principally engaged in businesses comprising three operating segments: U.S. Card Services; International Card & Global Commercial Services; and Global Network & Merchant Services.

U.S. Card Services includes the U.S. proprietary consumer card business, OPEN from American Express, the global Travelers Cheques and Prepaid Services business, and the American Express U.S. Consumer Travel Network.

International Card & Global Commercial Services provides proprietary consumer cards and small business cards outside the U.S. This division also offers global corporate products and services, including the corporate card, issued to individuals through a corporate account established by their employer; business travel, which helps businesses manage their travel expenses through a variety of travel-related products and services; and corporate purchasing solutions, addressing a business need to pay for everyday expenses such as office and computer supplies. International Card & Global Commer-

cial Services also includes international banking operations that provide financial products and services to retail customers and wealthy individuals outside the U.S. and financial institutions around the world.

Global Network & Merchant Services consists of the merchant services businesses and global network services. Global Network Services develops and manages relationships with third parties that issue American Express branded cards. The Global Merchant Services businesses develop and manage relationships with merchants that accept American Express branded cards; authorize and record transactions; pay merchants; and provide a variety of value-added point of sale and back office services. In addition, in particular emerging markets, issuance of certain proprietary cards is managed within the Global Network Services business.

Company Financials Fiscal Year Ended Dec. 31

Per Share Data ($)	2006	2005	2004	2003	2002	2001	2000	1999	1998	1997
Tangible Book Value	7.52	8.50	12.83	11.93	10.62	9.04	8.81	7.53	7.18	6.84
Earnings	3.01	2.56	2.74	2.31	2.01	0.98	2.07	1.81	1.54	1.38
S&P Core Earnings	2.85	2.49	2.53	2.09	1.68	0.73	NA	NA	NA	NA
Dividends	0.54	0.48	0.32	0.38	0.32	0.32	0.32	0.30	0.30	0.30
Payout Ratio	18%	19%	12%	16%	16%	33%	15%	17%	19%	22%
Prices:High	62.50	59.50	57.05	49.11	44.91	57.06	63.00	56.29	39.54	30.50
Prices:Low	49.73	46.59	47.32	30.90	26.55	24.20	39.83	31.63	22.33	17.88
P/E Ratio:High	21	23	21	21	22	58	30	31	26	22
P/E Ratio:Low	17	18	17	13	13	25	19	18	14	13
Income Statement Analysis (Million $)										
Cards in Force	NA	71.0	65.4	60.5	57.3	55.2	51.7	46.0	42.7	42.7
Card Charge Volume	NA	484,400	416,100	352,200	311,400	298,000	296,700	254,100	227,500	209,200
Premium Income	Nil	Nil	1,525	1,366	802	674	575	517	469	424
Commissions	4,333	4,236	4,079	3,484	3,521	3,969	4,165	3,626	3,304	4,386
Interest & Dividends	4,535	3,635	3,118	3,063	2,991	3,049	4,277	4,679	4,631	2,750
Total Revenue	28,710	24,267	29,115	25,866	23,807	22,582	23,675	16,599	14,501	17,760
Net Before Taxes	5,328	4,248	4,951	4,247	3,727	1,596	3,908	3,438	2,925	2,750
Net Income	3,729	3,221	3,516	3,000	2,671	1,311	2,810	2,475	2,141	1,991
S&P Core Earnings	3,531	3,144	3,244	2,723	2,245	986	NA	NA	NA	NA
Balance Sheet & Other Financial Data (Million $)										
Total Assets	127,853	113,960	192,638	175,001	157,253	151,100	154,423	148,517	126,933	120,003
Cash Items	11,270	7,126	9,907	5,726	10,288	7,222	8,487	7,471	4,092	4,179
Investment Assets:Bonds	Nil	Nil	Nil	Nil	Nil	Nil	Nil	Nil	Nil	Nil
Investment Assets:Stocks	Nil	Nil	Nil	Nil	Nil	Nil	Nil	Nil	Nil	Nil
Investment Assets:Loans	50,248	40,801	35,942	33,421	29,003	27,401	26,884	24,332	21,861	20,816
Investment Assets:Total	61,518	62,135	60,809	57,067	53,638	46,488	43,747	43,052	41,299	59,757
Accounts Receivable	89,099	35,497	34,650	31,269	29,087	29,498	30,543	26,467	22,224	21,774
Customer Deposits	24,656	24,579	21,091	21,250	18,317	14,557	13,870	12,197	10,398	9,444
Travel Cheques Outstanding	7,215	7,175	7,287	6,819	6,623	6,190	6,127	6,213	5,823	5,634
Debt	57,909	30,781	33,061	30,809	16,819	8,288	5,211	6,495	7,519	7,873
Common Equity	10,511	10,549	16,020	15,323	13,861	12,037	11,684	10,095	9,698	9,574
% Return on Assets	3.1	2.1	1.9	1.8	1.7	0.9	1.9	1.8	1.7	1.7
% Return on Equity	35.4	24.2	22.4	20.6	20.6	11.1	25.8	25.0	22.2	22.0

Data as orig reptd.; bef. results of disc opers/spec. items. Per share data adj. for stk. divs.; EPS diluted. E-Estimated. NA-Not Available. NM-Not Meaningful. NR-Not Ranked. UR-Under Review.

Office: World Financial Ctr, 200 Vesey Street, New York, NY 10285-4814.
Telephone: 212-640-2000.
Website: http://www.americanexpress.com
Chrmn & CEO: K.I. Chenault

EVP & CFO: D.T. Henry
EVP & General Counsel: L.M. Parent
EVP & CIO: S. Squeri
Secy: S.P. Norman

Investor Contact: R. Stovall (212-640-5574)
Board Members: D. F. Akerson, C. Barshefsky, U. M. Burns, K. I. Chenault, P. Chernin, V. E. Jordan, Jr., J. Leschly, R. C. Levin, R. A. McGinn, E. D. Miller, F. P. Popoff, S. S. Reinemund, R. D. Walter, R. A. Williams

Auditor: PricewaterhouseCoopers
Founded: 1868
Domicile: New York
Employees: 65,400

American International Group Inc

STANDARD &POOR'S

S&P Recommendation BUY ★★★★☆	**Price** $53.03 (as of Nov 23, 2007)	**12-Mo. Target Price** $66.00

GICS Sector Financials
Sub-Industry Multi-line Insurance

Summary One of the world's leading insurance organizations, AIG provides property, casualty and life insurance, as well as other financial services, in 130 countries and territories.

Key Stock Statistics (Source S&P, Vickers, company reports)

52-Wk Range	$72.97–50.86	S&P Oper. EPS 2007**E**	6.35	Market Capitalization(B)	$136.818	Beta	1.54
Trailing 12-Month EPS	$5.71	S&P Oper. EPS 2008**E**	7.05	Yield (%)	1.51	S&P 3-Yr. Proj. EPS CAGR(%)	11.00
Trailing 12-Month P/E	9.3	P/E on S&P Oper. EPS 2007**E**	8.4	Dividend Rate/Share	$0.80	S&P Credit Rating	AA
$10K Invested 5 Yrs Ago	$8,385	Common Shares Outstg. (M)	2,580.0	Institutional Ownership (%)	70		

Price Performance

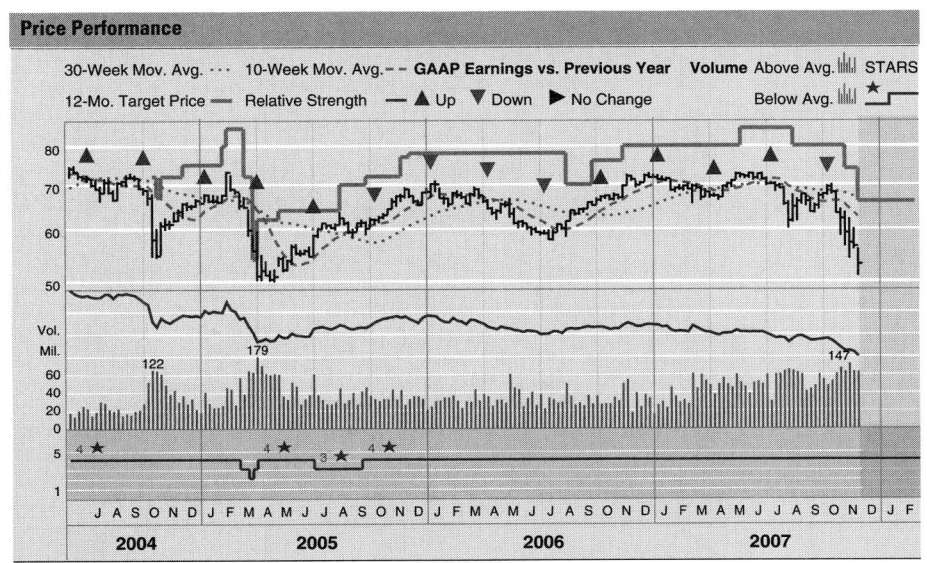

- 30-Week Mov. Avg. ··· 10-Week Mov. Avg. -- GAAP Earnings vs. Previous Year Volume Above Avg. STARS
- 12-Mo. Target Price — Relative Strength — ▲ Up ▼ Down ► No Change Below Avg. ★

Options: ASE, CBOE, P, Ph

Analysis prepared by **Cathy A.** Seifert on November 20, 2007, when the stock traded at **$ 54.11**.

Highlights

➤ We forecast property-casualty earned premium growth of 6% to 7% in 2008, versus growth of 5% to 6% that we expect for 2007. Both of these growth rates are above our estimate for the broader property-casualty insurance market, reflecting the impact of AIG's broad overseas network, partly offset by what we view as heightened competitive pressures.

➤ We think AIG's significant overseas life insurance franchise will continue to be a core contributor to operating profits. The company is well positioned, in our view, to exploit growth opportunities that exist in a number of Asian and developing economies. Offsetting this is what we perceive to be some challenges with AIG's U.S.-based life insurance segment.

➤ We forecast operating EPS of $6.35 for 2007 and $7.05 for 2008, versus operating EPS of $5.88 in 2006. Our EPS estimates assume that underwriting results reflect the impact of a more "normalized" level of catastrophe losses, and that AIG does not have to materially add to loss reserves or incur any large, one-time charges or write-downs.

Investment Rationale/Risk

➤ Our buy recommendation reflects our view that the shares are undervalued, on both a historical and relative basis. Our favorable outlook is tempered by concerns that AIG could have additional internal control issues that may need to be addressed, and that the company has an outsized (relative to peers) exposure to the mortgage market. But, we also believe that AIG has a number of competitive advantages, including its low property-casualty expense ratio and its global franchise (particularly in Asia).

➤ Risks to our recommendation and target price include a deterioration in loss reserve levels, the possibility of additional significant disclosures related to internal control and/or regulatory issues, and a significant deterioration in AIG's mortgage-related units and investments.

➤ Our sum-of-the-parts valuation supports our 12-month target price of $66, or 9.4X our 2008 operating EPS estimate, a slight discount to some of AIG's peers. We view this discount as warranted, in light of what we view as AIG's above-average (versus peers), multi-faceted exposure to the mortgage market.

Qualitative Risk Assessment

LOW	MEDIUM	**HIGH**

Our risk assessment reflects our view of the company as a leading underwriter with an unmatched global franchise. This is offset by our concern that AIG has an outsized exposure (versus its peers in the insurance industry) to the mortgage industry as a provider of mortgages, an insurer of mortgages and as an investor in mortgage-backed securities.

Quantitative Evaluations

S&P Quality Ranking A+

D	C	B-	B	B+	A-	A	**A+**

Relative Strength Rank WEAK

21

LOWEST = 1   HIGHEST = 99

Revenue/Earnings Data

Revenue (Million $)

	1Q	2Q	3Q	4Q	Year
2007	30,645	31,150	30,900	--	--
2006	27,259	26,743	29,199	29,993	113,194
2005	27,202	27,903	26,408	27,392	108,905
2004	23,637	23,809	25,411	25,760	97,987
2003	18,927	19,891	20,306	22,179	81,303
2002	16,137	16,662	17,150	17,533	67,482

Earnings Per Share ($)

	1Q	2Q	3Q	4Q	Year
2007	1.58	1.64	1.19	E1.70	E6.35
2006	1.21	1.21	1.61	1.31	5.35
2005	1.45	1.71	0.66	0.17	3.99
2004	1.08	1.09	0.95	1.15	3.75
2003	0.74	0.87	0.89	1.03	3.53
2002	0.75	0.68	0.70	-0.03	2.10

Fiscal year ended Dec. 31. Next earnings report expected: Early March. EPS Estimates based on S&P Operating Earnings; historical GAAP earnings are as reported.

Dividend Data (Dates: mm/dd Payment Date: mm/dd/yy)

Amount ($)	Date Decl.	Ex-Div. Date	Stk. of Record	Payment Date
0.165	03/14	05/30	06/01	06/15/07
0.200	05/16	09/05	09/07	09/21/07
0.200	09/04	12/05	12/07	12/21/07
0.200	11/14	03/05	03/07	03/21/08

Dividends have been paid since 1969. Source: Company reports.

Please read the Required Disclosures and Analyst Certification on the last page of this report.

The McGraw-Hill Companies

American International Group Inc

STANDARD &POOR'S

Business Summary November 20, 2007

One of the world's leading insurance organizations, American International Group provides property, casualty and life insurance, as well as other financial services, in 130 countries and territories.

Investigations by the New York Attorney General and the SEC into AIG's use of non-traditional insurance products and certain assumed reinsurance transactions (sometimes referred to as finite reinsurance) culminated in a number of events, including a management shake-up that led to: the resignation of AIG's long-time CEO, Maurice Greenberg; a write-down to earnings from 2000-2004 totaling nearly $4 billion; and a write-down of shareholders' equity of $2.26 billion. During 2005, AIG also incurred after-tax charges totaling $1.15 billion to settle its numerous regulatory issues and $1.19 billion to boost loss reserves. Having put many of these issues behind them, AIG's new management team has focused on regaining some of the company's lost momentum.

Revenues totaled $113.2 billion in 2006 (versus $108.9 billion in 2005), with domestic general insurance accounting for 33%, foreign life and retirement services for 29%, domestic life and retirement services for 14%, foreign general

insurance for 10%, financial services for 9%, and asset management for 5%. During 2006, activities in the United States and Canada accounted for 51% of revenues, while those in other foreign countries accounted for the remaining 49% of revenues.

General Insurance net written premiums totaled $44.9 billion in 2006 (versus $41.9 billion in 2005), of which the Domestic Brokerage Group accounted for 54%, Foreign General 25%, Domestic Personal Lines 10%, Reinsurance 9%, and Mortgage Guaranty 2%. The Domestic Brokerage Group underwrites an array of standard and specialty lines of commercial coverage. AIG maintains a majority ownership in Transatlantic Holdings (TRH), through which it underwrites reinsurance. The Foreign General division conducts AIG's international property-casualty operations.

Company Financials Fiscal Year Ended Dec. 31

Per Share Data ($)	2006	2005	2004	2003	2002	2001	2000	1999	1998	1997
Tangible Book Value	37.96	30.13	27.73	24.39	20.32	19.94	16.98	14.33	13.78	12.20
Operating Earnings	NA	NA	NA	NA	NA	NA	2.45	2.13	1.87	1.64
Earnings	5.35	3.99	3.75	3.53	2.10	2.07	2.41	2.15	1.91	1.68
S&P Core Earnings	5.36	4.35	3.77	3.89	2.63	2.06	NA	NA	NA	NA
Dividends	0.63	0.55	0.28	0.22	0.18	0.16	0.14	0.13	0.11	0.10
Relative Payout	12%	14%	7%	6%	8%	8%	6%	6%	6%	6%
Prices:High	72.97	73.46	77.36	66.35	80.00	98.31	103.75	75.25	54.73	40.02
Prices:Low	57.52	49.91	54.28	42.92	47.61	66.00	52.38	51.00	34.60	25.24
P/E Ratio:High	14	18	21	19	38	47	43	35	29	24
P/E Ratio:Low	11	13	14	12	23	32	22	24	18	15

Income Statement Analysis (Million $)										
Life Insurance in Force	2,070,600	1,852,833	1,858,094	1,596,626	1,324,451	1,228,501	583,059	584,959	499,167	436,573
Premium Income:Life A & H	74,083	29,400	28,082	22,879	20,320	19,243	13,610	11,942	10,247	9,926
Premium Income:Casualty/Property.	44,866	41,872	40,607	31,734	24,269	19,365	17,407	15,544	14,098	12,421
Net Investment Income	25,292	22,165	18,434	16,662	15,034	14,628	9,824	8,723	5,424	4,750
Total Revenue	113,489	108,905	97,987	81,303	67,482	52,852	40,717	36,356	29,939	27,246
Pretax Income	21,687	15,213	14,950	13,908	8,142	8,139	8,349	7,512	5,529	4,731
Net Operating Income	NA	105	NA	NA	NA	NA	5,737	4,999	3,689	49,662
Net Income	14,014	10,477	9,875	9,265	5,519	5,499	5,636	5,055	3,766	3,332
S&P Core Earnings	14,018	11,396	9,928	10,208	6,931	5,476	NA	NA	NA	NA

Balance Sheet & Other Financial Data (Million $)										
Cash & Equivalent	74,870	7,624	7,597	5,881	1,165	698	256	132	1,874	87.0
Premiums Due	17,789	15,333	15,137	14,166	13,088	11,647	11,832	12,737	11,679	10,283
Investment Assets:Bonds	417,865	385,680	365,677	309,254	243,366	200,616	102,010	90,144	61,906	51,566
Investment Assets:Stocks	30,222	23,588	17,851	9,584	7,066	7,937	7,181	6,714	5,893	5,209
Investment Assets:Loans	28,418	24,909	22,463	21,249	19,928	18,092	12,243	12,134	8,247	7,920
Investment Assets:Total	719,685	614,759	494,592	449,657	339,320	357,602	140,910	185,882	141,923	116,221
Deferred Policy Costs	37,235	33,248	29,736	26,398	22,256	17,443	10,189	9,624	7,647	6,593
Total Assets	979,414	853,370	798,660	678,346	561,229	492,982	306,577	268,238	194,398	163,971
Debt	186,866	78,625	66,850	57,877	50,076	34,503	5,801	23,795	31,093	25,260
Common Equity	101,677	86,317	80,607	71,253	59,103	52,150	39,619	33,306	27,131	24,002
Combined Loss-Expense Ratio	89.1	104.7	100.1	92.4	106.0	100.7	96.7	96.4	96.4	96.2
% Return on Revenue	12.4	9.6	10.1	11.4	8.2	10.5	13.8	13.9	12.6	14.8
% Return on Equity	14.9	12.6	13.1	14.2	9.9	11.0	15.5	15.9	14.7	14.5
% Investment Yield	3.8	3.7	3.9	4.1	4.8	4.5	7.4	4.9	4.9	4.3

Data as orig reptd.; bef. results of disc opers/spec. items. Per share data adj. for stk. divs.; EPS diluted. E-Estimated. NA-Not Available. NM-Not Meaningful. NR-Not Ranked. UR-Under Review.

Office: 70 Pine Street, New York, NY 10270-0094.
Telephone: 212-770-7000.
Website: http://www.aigcorporate.com
Chrmn: R.B. Willumstad

Pres & CEO: M.J. Sullivan
Vice Chrmn: E.S. Tse
Vice Chrmn: J.A. Frenkel
Vice Chrmn: F.G. Wisner

Investor Contact: S.J. Bensinger (212-770-6580)
Board Members: M. A. Cohen, M. S. Feldstein, E. V. Futter, S. L. Hammerman, R. C. Holbrooke, F. H. Langhammer, G. L. Miles, Jr., M. W. Offit, J. F. Orr, III, V. M. Rometty, M. J. Sullivan, M. H. Sutton, E. S. Tse, R. B. Willumstad, F. G. Zarb

Founded: 1967
Domicile: Delaware
Employees: 106,000

American Tower Corp

STANDARD &POOR'S

S&P Recommendation **BUY** ★★★★☆	Price $44.13 (as of Nov 23, 2007)	12-Mo. Target Price $54.00	Investment Style Large-Cap Blend

GICS Sector Telecommunication Services
Sub-Industry Wireless Telecommunication Services

Summary This company operates the largest independent portfolio of wireless communications and broadcast towers in North America.

Key Stock Statistics (Source S&P, Vickers, company reports)

52-Wk Range	$46.53–35.99	S&P Oper. EPS 2007**E**	0.26	Market Capitalization(B)	$18.129	Beta	2.68
Trailing 12-Month EPS	$0.19	S&P Oper. EPS 2008**E**	0.43	Yield (%)	Nil	S&P 3-Yr. Proj. EPS CAGR(%)	15.00
Trailing 12-Month P/E	NM	P/E on S&P Oper. EPS 2007**E**	NM	Dividend Rate/Share	Nil	S&P Credit Rating	BB+
$10K Invested 5 Yrs Ago	$124,310	Common Shares Outstg. (M)	410.8	Institutional Ownership (%)	100		

Price Performance

30-Week Mov. Avg. ···   10-Week Mov. Avg. - -   **GAAP Earnings vs. Previous Year**   **Volume** Above Avg. ▮▮▮ STARS
12-Mo. Target Price —   Relative Strength —   ▲ Up ▼ Down ▶ No Change   Below Avg. ▮▮▮ ★

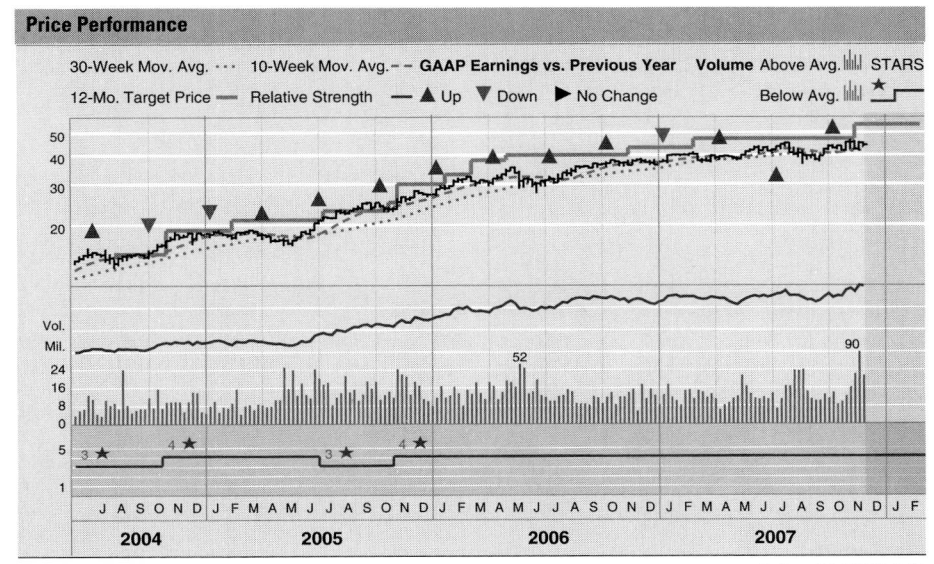

Options: ASE, CBOE, P, Ph

Analysis prepared by **James Moorman** on November 09, 2007, when the stock traded at **$ 42.50**.

Highlights

➤ Following a 39% revenue increase in 2006, which includes a full year of the SpectraSite properties acquired in 2005, we estimate 10% revenue growth in 2007 and 7% in 2008, reflecting increased lease activity per active tower and more new towers. We believe AMT will benefit from favorable tower industry trends such as wireless carriers' demand to improve their network quality and coverage both in the U.S. and internationally.

➤ We are positive on AMT's operating discipline, and look for operating expenses as a percentage of sales to decline markedly in 2007. Driven by higher tower utilization, we forecast EBITDA margins widening by roughly 300 basis points, to 67%, in 2007, from 64% in 2006, and then to 68% in 2008, a level that is well above the peer average.

➤ We estimate operating EPS of $0.26 for 2007 and $0.43 for 2008, including projected stock option expense of $0.14 per share in 2007 and $0.13 in 2008. The company plans to continue buying back shares, and we expect it to complete its current $1.5 billion repurchase program by February 2008.

Investment Rationale/Risk

➤ As the market leader in the wireless tower industry, we believe AMT's August 2005 acquisition of SpectraSite will enable it to continue to achieve greater economies of scale into 2008. We also expect AMT to continue to expand internationally in Mexico and Brazil, with a future entry into India. We think the internal review of stock option practices will not impair AMT's customer relationships or its cash flow outlook. We consider the shares attractive.

➤ Risks to our recommendation and target price include slower demand for the tower lease business; a negative outcome from the current internal review of past stock option granting practices; and an inability to meet $3.5 billion in total debt obligations.

➤ Our 12-month target price of $54 is largely based on 31X our free cash flow estimate for 2008, in line with the peer mean. The target price also represents an enterprise value of 25X our 2008 EBITDA estimate, slightly above the industry average. We believe this premium is warranted by our view of AMT's ability to increase cash flow generation faster than its peers.

Qualitative Risk Assessment

LOW	MEDIUM	HIGH

Our risk assessment reflects a possible negative outcome of the internal review of stock option practices. Despite the company's high 54% total debt to total capitalization, we believe AMT has steady cash flow and sufficient cash and investments to meet its working capital, capital expenditure and debt requirements.

Quantitative Evaluations

S&P Quality Ranking NR

D	C	B-	B	B+	A-	A	A+

Relative Strength Rank STRONG

87

LOWEST = 1   HIGHEST = 99

Revenue/Earnings Data

Revenue (Million $)

	1Q	2Q	3Q	4Q	Year
2007	352.5	358.4	367.6	--	--
2006	320.4	325.9	333.5	337.7	1,317
2005	184.4	188.1	264.8	307.6	944.8
2004	168.8	172.3	180.9	184.7	706.7
2003	161.5	175.3	186.9	191.5	715.1
2002	270.4	257.4	266.6	208.1	788.4

Earnings Per Share ($)

2007	0.05	0.03	0.14	E0.08	E0.26
2006	-0.01	0.02	0.01	0.04	0.06
2005	-0.14	-0.14	-0.06	0.13	-0.44
2004	-0.19	-0.27	-0.25	-0.30	-1.07
2003	-0.41	-0.40	-0.18	-0.20	-1.17
2002	-0.36	-0.43	-1.80	-0.27	-1.61

Fiscal year ended Dec. 31. Next earnings report expected: Mid February. EPS Estimates based on S&P Operating Earnings; historical GAAP earnings are as reported.

Dividend Data

No cash dividends have been paid.

The McGraw-Hill Companies

American Tower Corp

STANDARD &POOR'S

Business Summary November 09, 2007

CORPORATE OVERVIEW. American Tower Corp. operates the largest independent portfolio of wireless communications and broadcast towers in North America, based on the number of towers and revenue. The company's primary business is leasing antenna space on multi-tenant communications towers to wireless service providers and radio and television broadcast companies. The tower portfolio provides AMT with a recurring base of leased revenues from its customers and growth potential to add more tenants and equipment to these towers from its unused capacity. The company also continues to expand its operations in Mexico and Brazil, and we believe it is beginning to put together a team to start operations in India.

IMPACT OF MAJOR DEVELOPMENTS. In August 2005, AMT issued approximately 181 million shares valued at $3.1 billion in a merger with SpectraSite. The transaction resulted in the combined company having a portfolio of 22,600 communications sites.

In May 2006, AMT announced it was conducting an internal review of its historical stock option granting practices. A securities class action lawsuit was filed in U.S. District Court (MA) against the company and its officers related to this matter. AMT said it plans to vigorously defend itself in the lawsuit.

PRIMARY BUSINESS DYNAMICS. Rental and management of the antenna sites is AMT's principal business, operating a tower portfolio of about 22,405 multi-user sites in the U.S., Mexico and Brazil, as of December 31, 2006. Competition includes other national tower companies like Crown Castle International and SBA Communications, wireless carriers that own towers and lease antenna space to other carriers, and site development companies that can manage alternative site structures (e.g., building rooftops, billboards and utility poles).

The wireless industries that the company serves include a wide range of wireless services. AMT is well positioned, we think, to be a preferred partner to major wireless carriers in leasing tower space and new tower development projects because of the national scope of the company's tower portfolio and services.

Company Financials Fiscal Year Ended Dec. 31

Per Share Data ($)	2006	2005	2004	2003	2002	2001	2000	1999	1998	1997
Tangible Book Value	0.88	0.74	NM	0.28	NM	1.94	2.06	13.78	10.08	3.81
Cash Flow	1.28	0.92	0.40	0.34	0.01	-0.05	0.55	0.53	0.13	0.39
Earnings	0.06	-0.44	-1.07	-1.17	-1.61	-2.35	-1.13	-0.33	-0.48	-0.14
S&P Core Earnings	0.05	-0.50	-1.17	-1.35	-1.60	-2.50	NA	NA	NA	NA
Dividends	Nil	Nil	Nil	Nil	Nil	Nil	Nil	Nil	Nil	NA
Payout Ratio	Nil	Nil	Nil	Nil	Nil	Nil	Nil	Nil	Nil	NA
Prices:High	38.74	28.33	18.75	12.00	10.40	41.50	55.50	33.25	29.63	NA
Prices:Low	26.66	16.28	9.89	3.55	0.60	5.25	27.63	17.13	13.25	NA
P/E Ratio:High	NM	NM	NM	NM	NM	NM	NM	NM	NM	NA
P/E Ratio:Low	NM	NM	NM	NM	NM	NM	NM	NM	NM	NA

Income Statement Analysis (Million $)										
Revenue	1,317	945	707	715	788	1,134	735	258	104	94.9
Operating Income	803	589	423	377	312	251	196	91.5	36.7	40.2
Depreciation	528	411	329	313	317	440	283	133	52.1	54.9
Interest Expense	217	224	264	280	257	309	186	27.5	24.6	3.50
Pretax Income	70.9	-130	-317	-305	-248	-567	-250	-49.0	-42.2	-14.9
Effective Tax Rate	58.9%	NM	NM	NM	NM	NM	NM	NM	NM	NM
Net Income	28.3	-134	-239	-242	-315	-450	-190	-49.4	-38.0	-14.3
S&P Core Earnings	24.6	-154	-261	-281	-313	-480	NA	NA	NA	NA

Balance Sheet & Other Financial Data (Million $)										
Cash	281	113	216	105	127	130	128	25.2	186	97.5
Current Assets	486	226	309	412	536	522	471	139	208	NA
Total Assets	8,613	8,768	5,086	5,332	5,662	6,830	5,661	3,019	1,502	1,139
Current Liabilities	570	453	332	295	670	343	298	125	116	NA
Long Term Debt	3,289	3,451	3,155	3,284	3,195	3,549	2,457	736	279	1.65
Common Equity	4,382	4,527	1,464	1,706	1,740	2,869	2,877	2,145	1,092	1,000
Total Capital	7,678	7,988	4,626	5,008	4,950	6,433	5,350	2,890	1,385	1,002
Capital Expenditures	127	88.6	42.2	61.6	180	568	549	294	126	NA
Cash Flow	556	277	90.2	71.0	2.11	-9.72	93.1	83.2	14.1	40.6
Current Ratio	0.9	0.5	0.9	1.4	0.8	1.5	1.6	1.1	1.8	NA
% Long Term Debt of Capitalization	42.9	43.2	68.2	65.6	64.5	55.2	45.9	25.5	20.2	0.2
% Net Income of Revenue	2.2	NM	NM	NM	NM	NM	NM	NM	NM	NM
% Return on Assets	0.3	NM	NM	NM	NM	NM	NM	NM	NM	NM
% Return on Equity	0.6	NM	NM	NM	NM	NM	NM	NM	NM	NM

Data as orig reptd.; bef. results of disc opers/spec. items. Per share data adj. for stk. divs.; EPS diluted. E-Estimated. NA-Not Available. NM-Not Meaningful. NR-Not Ranked. UR-Under Review.

Office: 116 Huntington Avenue, Boston, MA 02116.
Telephone: 617-375-7500.
Email: ir@americantower.com
Website: http://www.americantower.com

Chrmn, Pres & CEO: J.D. Taiclet, Jr.
EVP, Chief Admin Officer & General Counsel: E. DiSanto
EVP & Cntlr: J.A. Bua
CFO & Treas: B.E. Singer

Investor Contact: M. Powell (617-375-7500)
Board Members: G. L. Cantu, R. P. Dolan, R. M. Dykes, C. F. Katz, J. A. Reed, P. D. Reeve, D. E. Sharbutt, J. D. Taiclet, Jr., S. Thompson

Founded: 1995
Domicile: Delaware
Employees: 995

The McGraw-Hill Companies

Ameriprise Financial Inc

| S&P Recommendation | **BUY** ★ ★ ★ ★ ☆ | Price $57.98 (as of Nov 23, 2007) | 12-Mo. Target Price $75.00 | Investment Style Large-Cap Growth |

GICS Sector Financials
Sub-Industry Asset Management & Custody Banks

Summary This Minneapolis-based diversified financial services company, spun off from American Express in September 2005, provides insurance, brokerage and asset management services.

Key Stock Statistics (Source S&P, Vickers, company reports)

52-Wk Range	$69.25– 51.31	S&P Oper. EPS 2007**E**	3.92	Market Capitalization(B)	$13.445	Beta	NA
Trailing 12-Month EPS	$3.01	S&P Oper. EPS 2008**E**	4.44	Yield (%)	1.03	S&P 3-Yr. Proj. EPS CAGR(%)	9.00
Trailing 12-Month P/E	19.3	P/E on S&P Oper. EPS 2007**E**	14.8	Dividend Rate/Share	$0.60	S&P Credit Rating	NA
$10K Invested 5 Yrs Ago	NA	Common Shares Outstg. (M)	231.9	Institutional Ownership (%)	85		

Price Performance

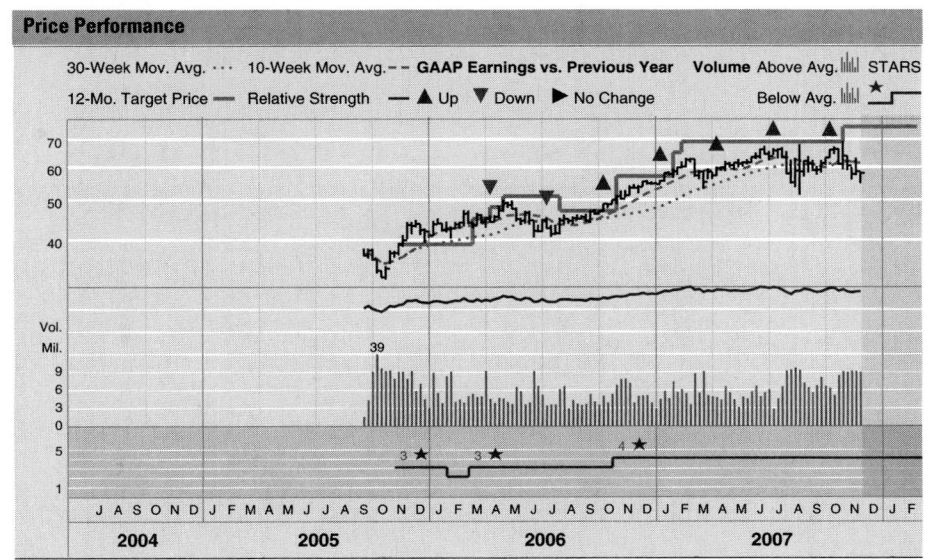

30-Week Mov. Avg. ··· 10-Week Mov. Avg.-- GAAP Earnings vs. Previous Year Volume Above Avg.|||| STARS
12-Mo. Target Price — Relative Strength — ▲ Up ▼ Down ▶ No Change Below Avg.|||| ★

Options: ASE, CBOE, P, Ph

Analysis prepared by **Matthew Albrecht** on November 05, 2007, when the stock traded at **$ 57.90**.

Highlights

➤ Nearing the completion of its transition to a standalone company, Ameriprise continues to grow its client asset base. We anticipate current initiatives underway will improve the productivity of its employee advisor network to aid profitability. We also expect improving performance in the RiverSource and Threadneedle funds, combined with further strength in sales of variable annuities and insurance products, to help revenues rise about 7% in 2007, followed by 8% growth in 2008.

➤ We believe compensation will increase more than 200 basis points as a percentage of revenues in 2007, to about 40.5% for the year, before leveling off in 2008, based on higher gross dealer concessions, as well as incentives based on Threadneedle performance. Cost savings elsewhere, due primarily to finalizing its separation from American Express, may not be enough to increase pretax margins in 2007, but we look for that ratio to improve in 2008.

➤ We see EPS, adjusted to exclude separation costs and discontinued operations, of $3.92 in 2007 and $4.44 in 2008.

Investment Rationale/Risk

➤ We think AMP has significant franchise value but will need to execute successfully as an independent company. We expect the company to improve its return on equity through capital redeployment, aided by common share repurchases. Although we believe AMP's stronger focus on insurance products merits a lower valuation than other asset managers, we believe that recent sales momentum and growing brand awareness and rising income should move the stock higher over the coming year, which is the basis for our buy opinion.

➤ Risks to our recommendation and target price include potential market depreciation in client assets, and various regulatory issues. We are somewhat concerned about potential selling by American Express shareholders, who received AMP shares as a result of the spinoff.

➤ AMP recently traded at 15.4X our adjusted 2007 EPS estimate, a substantial discount to its peer group, which trades at about 19X, primarily due, we think, to its revenue mix, with more reliance on insurance and annuity products. Our 12-month target price of $75 is equal to about 16.9X our adjusted 2008 EPS estimate.

Qualitative Risk Assessment

| LOW | **MEDIUM** | HIGH |

Our risk assessment reflects our view of the company's significant franchise value, offset by our concerns that the loss of the highly recognized American Express name could negatively affect AMP's ability to raise and retain client assets.

Quantitative Evaluations

S&P Quality Ranking NR

| D | C | B- | B | B+ | A- | A | A+ |

Relative Strength Rank MODERATE

| 53 |

LOWEST = 1   HIGHEST = 99

Revenue/Earnings Data

Revenue (Million $)

	1Q	2Q	3Q	4Q	Year
2007	2,063	2,182	2,202	--	--
2006	1,949	2,053	1,977	2,161	8,140
2005	1,847	1,895	1,873	1,869	7,484
2004	--	--	--	--	6,770
2003	--	--	--	--	--
2002	--	--	--	--	--

Earnings Per Share ($)

2007	0.68	0.81	0.83	E1.04	E3.92
2006	0.57	0.57	0.71	0.69	2.54
2005	0.71	0.61	0.50	0.44	2.26
2004	--	--	--	--	2.80
2003	--	--	--	--	--
2002	--	--	--	--	--

Fiscal year ended Dec. 31. Next earnings report expected: Late January. EPS Estimates based on S&P Operating Earnings; historical GAAP earnings are as reported.

Dividend Data (Dates: mm/dd Payment Date: mm/dd/yy)

Amount ($)	Date Decl.	Ex-Div. Date	Stk. of Record	Payment Date
0.110	01/25	02/01	02/05	02/16/07
0.150	03/15	05/02	05/04	05/18/07
0.150	07/25	08/02	08/06	08/17/07
0.150	10/24	11/01	11/05	11/16/07

Dividends have been paid since 2005. Source: Company reports.

Ameriprise Financial Inc

Business Summary November 05, 2007

CORPORATE OVERVIEW. Ameriprise Financial completed its spinoff from American Express on September 30, 2005, and began trading on the New York Stock Exchange on October 3 under the symbol AMP. As of December 31, 2006, Ameriprise owned, managed and administered over $466 billion of client assets, had about 2.8 million clients, and operated a network of over 12,500 financial advisers. Ameriprise offers a broad assortment of products, including mutual funds, annuities and life insurance products. Ameriprise was originally named Investors Diversified Services before it was acquired by American Express in 1984. We think AMP will need to prove that it can grow and prosper without the benefits of its previous owner, American Express, which spun off the company in 2005. We believe the spinoff and new marketing campaign have raised AMP's visibility among prospective clients and may also help attract and retain financial advisers. In terms of corporate governance, we view favorably the high proportion of independent directors on the board, but would prefer that the company split the roles of chairman and CEO.

Ameriprise has two operating segments. Asset Accumulation and Income ac-

counted for about 70% of pretax earnings in 2006, and Protection accounted for about 30%. The Asset Accumulation and Income segment offers mutual funds and annuities to retail clients through its adviser network. This operating segment also serves institutional clients in the separately managed account, sub-advisory and 401(k) markets. We estimate that nearly 50% of the earnings within the Asset Accumulation and Income segment are derived from fixed and variable annuities, which typically combine insurance and investment features. Through its Protection segment, AMP offers various life insurance, disability income and long-term care insurance products through its adviser network. AMP also offers personal auto and home insurance products on a direct basis to retail clients principally through strategic marketing alliances, which include Costco Wholesale, Delta Air Lines, Marriott Vacation Club International, and eWomen Network.

Company Financials Fiscal Year Ended Dec. 31

Per Share Data ($)	2006	2005	2004	2003	2002	2001	2000	1999	1998	1997
Tangible Book Value	31.10	30.75	6.45	NA	NA	NA	NA	NA	NA	NA
Cash Flow	3.21	2.26	NA	NA	NA	NA	NA	NA	NA	NA
Earnings	2.54	2.26	2.80	NA	NA	NA	NA	NA	NA	NA
S&P Core Earnings	2.41	2.37	3.02	2.46	NA	NA	NA	NA	NA	NA
Dividends	0.44	0.11	NA	NA	NA	NA	NA	NA	NA	NA
Payout Ratio	17%	5%	NA	NA	NA	NA	NA	NA	NA	NA
Prices:High	55.79	44.78	NA	NA	NA	NA	NA	NA	NA	NA
Prices:Low	40.30	32.00	NA	NA	NA	NA	NA	NA	NA	NA
P/E Ratio:High	22	20	NA	NA	NA	NA	NA	NA	NA	NA
P/E Ratio:Low	16	14	NA	NA	NA	NA	NA	NA	NA	NA

Income Statement Analysis (Million $)

	2006	2005	2004	2003	2002	2001	2000	1999	1998	1997
Income Interest	2,204	2,241	2,125	NA	NA	NA	NA	NA	NA	NA
Income Other	5,936	5,243	4,645	NA	NA	NA	NA	NA	NA	NA
Total Income	8,140	7,484	6,770	NA	NA	NA	NA	NA	NA	NA
General Expenses	7,343	6,739	5,756	NA	NA	NA	NA	NA	NA	NA
Interest Expense	116	73.0	78.0	NA	NA	NA	NA	NA	NA	NA
Depreciation	166	164	NA	NA	NA	NA	NA	NA	NA	NA
Net Income	631	556	708	NA	NA	NA	NA	NA	NA	NA
S&P Core Earnings	599	588	762	622	NA	NA	NA	NA	NA	NA

Balance Sheet & Other Financial Data (Million $)

	2006	2005	2004	2003	2002	2001	2000	1999	1998	1997
Cash	4,775	2,474	3,319	NA	NA	NA	NA	NA	NA	NA
Receivables	6,668	2,172	2,526	NA	NA	NA	NA	NA	NA	NA
Cost of Investments	35,553	39,100	40,157	NA	NA	NA	NA	NA	NA	NA
Total Assets	104,172	93,121	90,934	NA	NA	NA	NA	NA	NA	NA
Loss Reserve	Nil	Nil	Nil	NA	NA	NA	NA	NA	NA	NA
Short Term Debt	Nil	Nil	Nil	NA	NA	NA	NA	NA	NA	NA
Capitalization:Debt	2,225	1,833	1,878	NA	NA	NA	NA	NA	NA	NA
Capitalization:Equity	7,925	7,687	8,058	NA	NA	NA	NA	NA	NA	NA
Capitalization:Total	10,150	9,520	9,936	NA	NA	NA	NA	NA	NA	NA
Price Times Book Value:High	1.7	1.5	NA	NA	NA	NA	NA	NA	NA	NA
Price Times Book Value:Low	1.2	1.0	NA	NA	NA	NA	NA	NA	NA	NA
Cash Flow	759	556	NA	NA	NA	NA	NA	NA	NA	NA
% Expense/Operating Revenue	90.2	90.0	86.2	NA	NA	NA	NA	NA	NA	NA
% Earnings & Depreciation/Assets	0.1	0.1	NA	NA	NA	NA	NA	NA	NA	NA

Data as orig reptd.; bef. results of disc opers/spec. items. Per share data adj. for stk. divs.; EPS diluted. E-Estimated. NA-Not Available. NM-Not Meaningful. NR-Not Ranked. UR-Under Review.

Office: 55 Ameriprise Financial Ctr, Minneapolis, MN 55474-9900.
Telephone: 612-671-3131.
Website: http://www.ameriprise.com
Chrmn & CEO: J.M. Cracchiolo

Investor Contact: W.S. Berman (612-671-3131)
EVP & CFO: W.S. Berman
EVP & General Counsel: J. Junek
VP & Cntlr: D.K. Stewart

Board Members: J. M. Cracchiolo, I. D. Hall, W. D. Knowlton, W. W. Lewis, S. S. Marshall, J. Noddle, R. F. Powers, III, H. J. Sarles, R. F. Sharpe, Jr., W. H. Turner

Founded: 1983
Domicile: Delaware
Employees: 11,858

AmerisourceBergen Corp

STANDARD &POOR'S

S&P Recommendation `HOLD` ★★★☆☆

Price $43.89 (as of Nov 23, 2007)	**12-Mo. Target Price** $52.00	**Investment Style** Large-Cap Blend

GICS Sector Health Care
Sub-Industry Health Care Distributors

Summary This distributor of pharmaceutical products and related health care services was formed via the August 2001 merger of Amerisource Health Corp. and Bergen Brunswig Corp.

Key Stock Statistics (Source S&P, Vickers, company reports)

52-Wk Range	$56.56– 42.35	S&P Oper. EPS 2008**E**	2.88	Market Capitalization(B)	$7.908	Beta	0.34
Trailing 12-Month EPS	$2.50	S&P Oper. EPS 2009**E**	3.30	Yield (%)	0.68	S&P 3-Yr. Proj. EPS CAGR(%)	14.00
Trailing 12-Month P/E	17.6	P/E on S&P Oper. EPS 2008**E**	15.2	Dividend Rate/Share	$0.30	S&P Credit Rating	BBB-
$10K Invested 5 Yrs Ago	NA	Common Shares Outstg. (M)	180.2	Institutional Ownership (%)	95		

Price Performance

30-Week Mov. Avg. ··· 10-Week Mov. Avg. -- **GAAP Earnings vs. Previous Year** Volume Above Avg. STARS
12-Mo. Target Price — Relative Strength — ▲ Up ▼ Down ▶ No Change Below Avg.

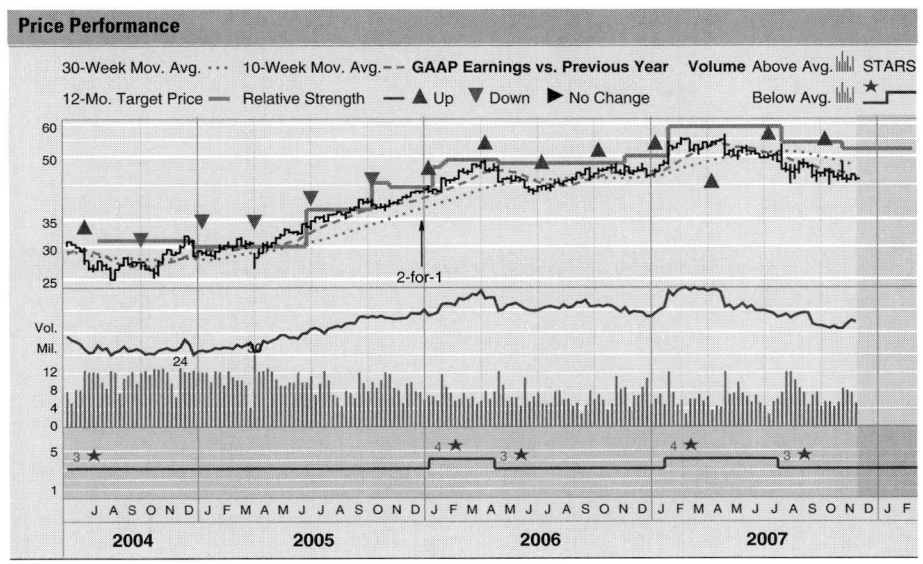

Options: ASE, CBOE, P

Analysis prepared by **Phillip M. Seligman** on November 08, 2007, when the stock traded at **$ 43.83**.

Highlights

➤ We look for FY 08 (Sep.) operating revenue, which excludes bulk deliveries to customers' warehouses, to rise 6% to about $65.5 billion, from FY 07's $61.7 billion. Growth drivers we see include the October 2007 acquisition of Bellco Health, a $2 billion distributor with nationwide footprints in generics and the dialysis market, and mid-single-digit organic drug distribution revenue growth, in line with the market and incorporating branded drug price hikes and fast-growing generic drug volumes. However, we see these gains partly offset by lower prices of generic drugs and up to 5% lower specialty drug revenue due to lower utilization of EPO drugs (for anemia) and the loss of a major client of these and other dialysis drugs to a competitor. In addition, the PharMerica segment's long-term care unit was spun off on July 31.

➤ We forecast drug distribution operating margins to be up in the low-single-digit basis-point range, as sell-side pricing pressure is outweighed by generic drug penetration and cost reduction initiatives.

➤ We look for FY 08 operating EPS of $2.88, versus FY 07's $2.63 ($2.55 excluding the spinoff), and see $3.30 in FY 09, aided by share buybacks.

Investment Rationale/Risk

➤ The company's June-quarter operating EPS of $0.63 matched our estimate. But revenues were less than we expected, despite strong performance by the specialty group, and we expect lower specialty sales in FY 08. Moreover, we do not see any near-term catalysts. We view the drug distribution group's long-term fundamentals, supported by demographic trends and new specialty and generic drugs, as favorable. We expect specialty drug revenues to return to mid-teens growth levels in FY 09 with the lapping of FY 08's lower anemia drug sales. Meanwhile, we see FY 08 sales benefiting from branded drug price hikes in July. We believe ABC's strong cash flow provides financial flexibility and the spinoff of the underperforming business allowed ABC to focus more on its core drug distribution business and PharMerica's workers' comp unit, which it kept.

➤ Risks to our opinion and target price include intensified competition and a major client loss.

➤ Our 12-month target price is $52, based on our calendar 2008 EPS estimate of $2.97 and P/E target multiple of 17.5X, below peers, since it is less diversified.

Qualitative Risk Assessment

LOW	MEDIUM	HIGH

Our risk assessment reflects what we view as ABC's improving financial performance, ability to attract new accounts to more than compensate for account losses, and healthy operating cash flow. However, the drug distribution arena is highly competitive, and ABC is less diversified than many of its large health care distribution peers.

Quantitative Evaluations

S&P Quality Ranking A-

D	C	B-	B	B+	A-	A	A+

Relative Strength Rank MODERATE
64
LOWEST = 1   HIGHEST = 99

Revenue/Earnings Data

Revenue (Million $)

	1Q	2Q	3Q	4Q	Year
2007	16,725	16,513	16,446	16,390	66,074
2006	14,653	15,221	15,686	15,643	61,203
2005	13,639	13,192	13,832	13,918	54,577
2004	13,355	13,364	13,072	13,389	53,179
2003	12,435	12,163	12,421	12,640	49,657
2002	11,069	10,944	11,621	11,601	45,235

Earnings Per Share ($)

2007	0.63	0.68	0.69	0.63	2.63
2006	0.47	0.61	0.58	0.61	2.26
2005	0.33	0.46	0.48	0.10	1.37
2004	0.47	0.62	0.55	0.41	2.03
2003	0.42	0.52	0.50	0.52	1.95
2002	0.32	0.42	0.41	0.43	1.58

Fiscal year ended Sep. 30. Next earnings report expected: Late January. EPS Estimates based on S&P Operating Earnings; historical GAAP earnings are as reported.

Dividend Data (Dates: mm/dd Payment Date: mm/dd/yy)

Amount ($)	Date Decl.	Ex-Div. Date	Stk. of Record	Payment Date
0.050	05/09	05/17	05/21	06/04/07
Stk.	07/13	08/01	07/20	07/31/07
0.050	08/09	08/16	08/20	09/04/07
0.075	11/08	11/15	11/19	12/03/07

Dividends have been paid since 2001. Source: Company reports.

AmerisourceBergen Corp

STANDARD &POOR'S

Business Summary November 08, 2007

CORPORATE OVERVIEW. AmerisourceBergen Corp., one of the largest U.S. pharmaceutical distributors, began operation in August 2001, following the merger of Amerisource Health Corp. and Bergen Brunswig Corp. ABC accounted for the merger as an acquisition by Amerisource of Bergen.

The pharmaceutical distribution segment includes the AmerisourceBergen Drug Corporation (ABDC), AmerisourceBergen Specialty Group (ABSG) and the AmerisourceBergen Packaging Group (ABPG). ABDC distributes branded and generic pharmaceuticals, over-the-counter health care products, and home health care supplies and equipment to hospitals, pharmacies, mail order facilities, clinics, and alternate site facilities. ABSG ($9.9 billion of operating revenue) supplies goods and services to physicians and alternate care providers that specialize in disease states, such as oncology. The ABPG repackages drugs from bulk to unit dose, unit of use, blister pack and standard bottle sizes.

National and retail drugstore chains, independent community drugstores, and pharmacy departments of supermarkets and mass merchandisers account for its retail market segment (42% of FY 06 (Sep.) operating revenues), while the hospital/acute care, mail order and specialty pharmaceuticals markets together comprise its institutional market segment (58%). Its top 10 customers represented approximately 36% of FY 06 operating revenue. Revenues generated from sales to pharmacy benefit manager Medco Health Solutions accounted for 98% of bulk deliveries to customer warehouses and 7% of operating revenue in FY 06.

On July 31, 2007, ABC spun off the PharMerica segment's long-term care business, a leading national dispenser of pharmaceutical products and services to patients in long-term care facilities. The company retained PharMerica's workers' compensation-related business, which provides mail order and on-line pharmacy services to chronically and catastrophically ill patients under workers' comp programs, and provides pharmaceutical claims administration services for payors.

Company Financials Fiscal Year Ended Sep. 30

Per Share Data ($)	2007	2006	2005	2004	2003	2002	2001	2000	1999	1998
Tangible Book Value	NA	7.91	7.38	8.62	7.21	5.22	1.80	2.41	1.44	0.75
Cash Flow	NA	2.72	1.73	2.36	2.21	1.81	1.16	1.11	0.86	0.67
Earnings	2.63	2.26	1.37	2.03	1.95	1.58	1.05	0.95	0.69	0.52
S&P Core Earnings	NA	2.07	1.24	1.55	1.86	1.53	0.85	NA	NA	NA
Dividends	0.20	0.10	0.05	0.05	0.05	0.05	Nil	Nil	Nil	Nil
Payout Ratio	8%	4%	4%	2%	3%	3%	Nil	Nil	Nil	Nil
Prices:High	56.56	48.96	42.18	32.01	36.72	41.43	36.00	26.84	20.69	20.19
Prices:Low	42.35	40.15	26.48	24.87	22.83	25.10	20.06	6.00	5.50	11.12
P/E Ratio:High	22	22	31	16	19	26	34	28	30	39
P/E Ratio:Low	16	18	19	12	12	16	19	6	8	21

Income Statement Analysis (Million $)										
Revenue	NA	61,203	54,577	53,179	49,657	45,235	16,191	11,645	9,760	8,575
Operating Income	NA	814	723	978	963	804	302	217	191	166
Depreciation	NA	96.9	81.2	87.1	71.0	61.2	21.6	16.1	17.4	14.8
Interest Expense	NA	12.5	57.2	113	145	141	45.7	41.9	39.0	42.1
Pretax Income	NA	741	469	760	726	572	202	160	119	82.8
Effective Tax Rate	NA	36.8%	37.7%	38.4%	39.2%	39.7%	38.6%	38.0%	40.6%	39.0%
Net Income	NA	468	292	468	441	345	124	99.0	70.9	50.5
S&P Core Earnings	NA	429	264	356	421	333	99.8	NA	NA	NA

Balance Sheet & Other Financial Data (Million $)										
Cash	NA	1,261	1,316	871	800	663	298	121	59.5	85.5
Current Assets	NA	9,210	7,988	8,295	8,859	8,350	7,513	2,321	1,920	1,418
Total Assets	NA	12,784	11,381	11,654	12,040	11,213	10,291	2,459	2,061	1,552
Current Liabilities	NA	7,459	6,052	6,104	6,256	6,100	5,532	1,751	1,327	1,015
Long Term Debt	NA	1,094	951	1,157	1,723	1,756	1,872	413	559	454
Common Equity	NA	4,141	4,280	4,339	4,005	3,316	5,677	565	166	75.3
Total Capital	NA	5,235	5,232	5,496	5,728	5,073	7,549	978	725	529
Capital Expenditures	NA	113	203	189	90.6	64.2	23.4	16.6	15.8	10.4
Cash Flow	NA	565	373	555	512	406	145	115	88.3	65.3
Current Ratio	NA	1.2	1.3	1.4	1.4	1.4	1.4	1.3	1.4	1.4
% Long Term Debt of Capitalization	NA	20.9	18.2	21.1	30.1	34.6	24.8	42.3	77.1	85.8
% Net Income of Revenue	NA	0.8	0.5	0.9	0.9	0.8	0.8	0.9	0.7	0.6
% Return on Assets	NA	3.9	2.5	4.0	3.8	3.2	1.9	4.4	3.9	3.1
% Return on Equity	NA	11.1	6.8	11.2	12.1	11.2	4.0	22.1	58.8	112.7

Data as orig reptd.; bef. results of disc opers/spec. items. Per share data adj. for stk. divs.; EPS diluted. E-Estimated. NA-Not Available. NM-Not Meaningful. NR-Not Ranked. UR-Under Review.

Office: 1300 Morris Drive, Chesterbrook, PA 19087-5594.
Telephone: 610-727-7000.
Email: investorrelations@amerisourcebergen.com
Website: http://www.amerisourcebergen.com

Chrmn: R.C. Gozon
Pres & COO: K.J. Hilzinger
CEO: R.D. Yost
EVP & CFO: M.D. DiCandilo

Investor Contact: M.N. Kilpatric (610-727-7118)
Board Members: R. H. Brady, C. H. Cotros, R. C. Gozon, E. E. Hagenlocker, J. E. Henney, K. J. Hilzinger, M. J. Long, H. W. McGee, J. L. Wilson, R. D. Yost

Founded: 1985
Domicile: Delaware
Employees: 14,700

The McGraw-Hill Companies

Amgen Inc

STANDARD
&POOR'S

S&P Recommendation	BUY ★★★★☆	Price	12-Mo. Target Price	Investment Style
		$53.76 (as of Nov 23, 2007)	$64.00	Large-Cap Growth

GICS Sector Health Care
Sub-Industry Biotechnology

Summary Amgen, the world's leading biotech company, has major treatments for anemia, neutropenia, rheumatoid arthritis, psoriatic arthritis, psoriasis and cancer.

Key Stock Statistics (Source S&P, Vickers, company reports)

52-Wk Range	$76.95–48.30	S&P Oper. EPS 2007**E**	4.10	Market Capitalization(B)	$58.545	Beta	0.91
Trailing 12-Month EPS	$2.77	S&P Oper. EPS 2008**E**	4.29	Yield (%)	Nil	S&P 3-Yr. Proj. EPS CAGR(%)	12.00
Trailing 12-Month P/E	19.4	P/E on S&P Oper. EPS 2007**E**	13.1	Dividend Rate/Share	Nil	S&P Credit Rating	A+
$10K Invested 5 Yrs Ago	$11,330	Common Shares Outstg. (M)	1,089.0	Institutional Ownership (%)	76		

Price Performance

30-Week Mov. Avg. ···· 10-Week Mov. Avg. – – GAAP Earnings vs. Previous Year Volume Above Avg. ▮▮▮ STARS
12-Mo. Target Price — Relative Strength — ▲ Up ▼ Down ► No Change Below Avg. ▮▮▮ ★

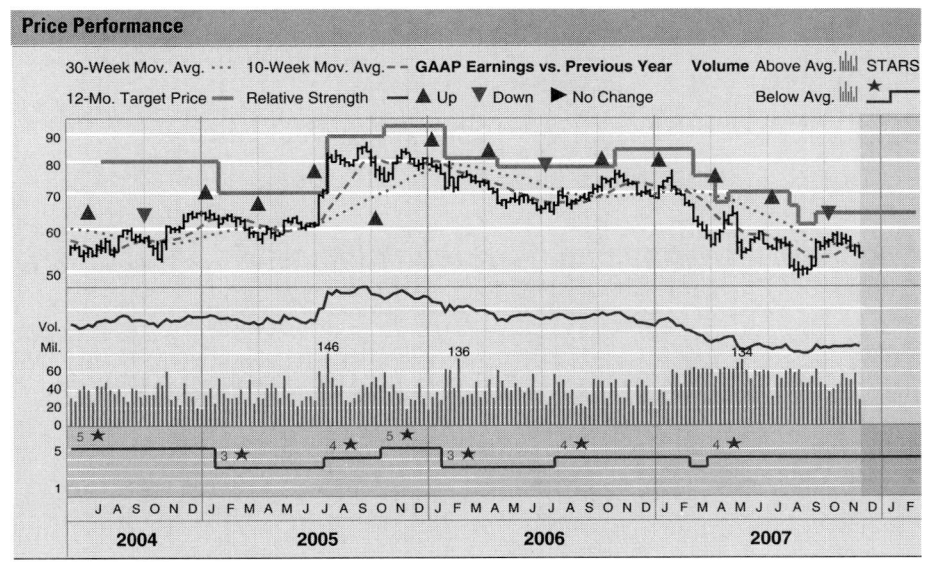

Analysis prepared by **Steven Silver** on October 29, 2007, when the stock traded at **$ 56.86**.

Options: ASE, CBOE, P, Ph

Qualitative Risk Assessment

LOW	MEDIUM	HIGH

Our risk assessment reflects that the company's products are sold in highly competitive markets and are subject to government regulation. Changes to government reimbursement policies could significantly affect AMGN's revenues and profitability. We believe that generics for Epogen could be a threat in Europe though we note slightly reduced risk due to favorable trial ruling against Roche's Mircera.

Quantitative Evaluations

S&P Quality Ranking B+

D	C	B-	B	B+	A-	A	A+

Relative Strength Rank MODERATE

63

LOWEST = 1   HIGHEST = 99

Revenue/Earnings Data

Revenue (Million $)

	1Q	2Q	3Q	4Q	Year
2007	3,687	3,728	3,611	--	--
2006	3,217	3,491	3,503	3,737	14,268
2005	2,833	3,172	3,154	3,271	12,430
2004	2,343	2,585	2,713	2,909	10,550
2003	1,761	2,041	2,207	2,346	8,356
2002	1,009	1,249	1,499	1,766	5,523

Earnings Per Share ($)

2007	0.94	0.90	0.18	E0.92	E4.10
2006	0.82	0.01	0.94	0.71	2.48
2005	0.67	0.82	0.77	0.66	2.93
2004	0.52	0.57	0.18	0.53	1.81
2003	0.37	0.45	0.46	0.41	1.69
2002	0.32	0.38	2.10	0.34	-1.21

Fiscal year ended Dec. 31. Next earnings report expected: Late January. EPS Estimates based on S&P Operating Earnings; historical GAAP earnings are as reported.

Dividend Data

No cash dividends have been paid.

Highlights

➤ Third quarter worldwide product sales were even with last year's period, as 16% higher Enbrel sales and 10% higher Neulasta/Neupogen sales offset 36% lower U.S. Aranesp sales, related to regulatory and reimbursement limits. While Medicare may reconsider proposed reimbursement limits on EPO drugs due to Congressional intervention, we see it as more likely that Medicare's proposal could go into effect at year-end. We see a recent FDA panel ruling to not impose a dosing cap on Epogen supporting a more favorable sales outlook for that drug.

➤ Gross margins have been impacted, as Enbrel comprises a larger percentage of sales, given cost obligations to partner Wyeth. We see 2007 and 2008 gross margins of 83-84%, down from prior 85% range. Third quarter R&D expense declined 16% over the 2006 period, and we see 2008 R&D expenses declining in absolute terms but comprising 21-22% of sales. In August 2007, AMGN announced a corporate restructuring, reducing staff by 12%-14%, and cutting $1.9 billion in capital expenses by the end of 2008.

➤ Our 2007 EPS estimate is $4.10 and we forecast 2008 EPS of $4.29.

Investment Rationale/Risk

➤ In our view, AMGN is managing expenses well during a period of uncertainty, cutting operating expenses and aggressively buying back shares to aid EPS results. We believe AMGN's fundamentals remain solid, and we see late-stage candidate denosumab in osteoporosis, which should reach the market in 2009/2010, boosting sales and diversifying AMGN's revenues. In the third quarter, AMGN filed romiplostim (AMG 531) in ITP with the FDA and expects international filings by the end of 2007. We expect continued volatility due to ongoing regulatory issues, but see recent positive patent rulings over Roche's CERA, an FDA decision against limiting dosing on Epogen, and a positive Vectibix opinion in Europe, stabilizing the shares.

➤ Risks to our recommendation and target price include further FDA and Medicare restrictions to anemia drug sales, negative clinical trial results, competition to existing products, and challenges to AMGN's product patents.

➤ Our 12-month target price of $64 applies a 15X multiple to our 2008 EPS estimate, in line with our projected three-year growth rate.

Please read the Required Disclosures and Analyst Certification on the last page of this report.

The McGraw-Hill Companies

Amgen Inc

STANDARD
&POOR'S

Business Summary October 29, 2007

CORPORATE OVERVIEW. Amgen, the world's largest biotech company, makes and markets five of the world's best-selling biotech drugs.

Epogen is a genetically engineered version of human erythropoietin (EPO), a hormone that stimulates red blood cell production in bone marrow. Its primary market is dialysis patients suffering from chronic anemia. Epogen sales were $2.51 billion in 2006 ($2.46 billion in 2005). Aranesp, a recombinant protein that stimulates the production of red blood cells in pre-dialysis and dialysis patients, is approved to treat anemia associated with chronic renal failure and cancer patients with chemotherapy-induced anemia (CIA). Aranesp sales were $4.12 billion in 2006 ($3.27 billion). AMGN is developing AMG 114, a next-generation EPO drug. In early 2007, Phase III trial data showed a higher rate of death when using Aranesp in treating anemia-of cancer (AoC) not associated with chemotherapy, an off-label prescribed indication. Medicare removed AoC as a reimbursable use for Aranesp. In April 2007, Phase III data in lung cancer patients undergoing chemotherapy showed no death rate rise when using Aranesp versus placebo.

Neupogen stimulates neutrophils (white blood cells that defend against bac-

terial infection) production in cancer patients whose natural neutrophils were destroyed by chemotherapy. In 2002, the FDA approved Neulasta, a long-acting white blood cell stimulant protecting chemo patients from infection. Total Neupogen and Neulasta 2006 sales were $3.92 billion ($3.50 billion in 2005).

Enbrel, acquired through the purchase of Immunex, had 2006 sales of $2.88 billion ($2.57 billion in 2005) and is approved to treat rheumatoid arthritis (RA), juvenile RA, and psoriatic arthritis, as well as the spinal condition ankylosing spondylitis and to treat adults with moderate to severe chronic plaque psoriasis.

In 2004, Sensipar was approved to treat secondary hyperparathyroidism in patients on dialysis, and hypercalcemia in patients with parathyroid carcinoma and is marketed in Europe as Mimpara.

Company Financials Fiscal Year Ended Dec. 31

Per Share Data ($)	2006	2005	2004	2003	2002	2001	2000	1999	1998	1997
Tangible Book Value	3.36	5.08	4.08	4.06	2.80	4.99	4.16	2.97	2.52	2.07
Cash Flow	3.29	3.59	2.35	2.19	-0.82	1.28	1.24	1.18	0.95	0.69
Earnings	2.48	2.93	1.81	1.69	-1.21	1.03	1.05	1.02	0.82	0.59
S&P Core Earnings	2.48	2.77	1.58	1.50	-1.46	0.87	NA	NA	NA	NA
Dividends	Nil	Nil	Nil	Nil	Nil	Nil	Nil	Nil	Nil	0.00
Payout Ratio	Nil	Nil	Nil	Nil	Nil	Nil	Nil	Nil	Nil	NM
Prices:High	81.24	86.92	66.88	72.37	62.94	75.06	80.44	66.44	27.25	17.34
Prices:Low	63.52	56.19	52.00	48.09	30.57	45.44	50.00	25.69	11.66	11.22
P/E Ratio:High	33	30	37	43	NM	73	77	65	33	30
P/E Ratio:Low	26	19	29	28	NM	44	48	25	14	19

Income Statement Analysis (Million $)										
Revenue	14,268	12,430	10,550	8,356	5,523	4,016	3,629	3,340	2,718	2,401
Operating Income	6,022	5,689	4,636	3,758	2,501	2,003	1,761	1,638	1,338	1,103
Depreciation	963	841	734	686	447	266	212	177	144	117
Interest Expense	129	99.0	38.0	31.5	44.2	13.6	15.9	15.2	10.0	3.70
Pretax Income	4,020	4,868	3,395	3,173	-684	1,686	1,674	1,566	1,224	861
Effective Tax Rate	26.6%	24.5%	30.4%	28.8%	NM	33.6%	32.0%	30.0%	29.5%	25.2%
Net Income	2,950	3,674	2,363	2,260	-1,392	1,120	1,139	1,096	863	644
S&P Core Earnings	2,951	3,470	2,074	2,006	-1,683	936	NA	NA	NA	NA

Balance Sheet & Other Financial Data (Million $)										
Cash	6,277	5,255	5,808	5,123	4,664	2,662	2,028	1,333	1,276	1,027
Current Assets	11,712	9,235	9,170	7,402	6,404	3,859	2,937	2,065	1,863	1,544
Total Assets	33,788	29,297	29,221	26,177	24,456	6,443	5,400	4,078	3,672	3,110
Current Liabilities	7,022	3,595	4,157	2,246	1,529	1,003	862	831	887	742
Long Term Debt	7,134	3,957	3,937	3,080	3,048	223	223	223	223	229
Common Equity	18,964	20,451	19,705	19,389	18,286	5,217	4,315	3,024	2,562	2,139
Total Capital	26,465	25,571	24,936	23,930	22,927	5,440	4,538	3,247	2,785	2,368
Capital Expenditures	1,218	867	1,336	1,357	658	442	438	304	408	388
Cash Flow	3,913	4,515	3,097	2,946	-945	1,386	1,350	1,273	1,007	761
Current Ratio	1.7	2.6	2.2	3.3	4.2	3.8	3.4	2.5	2.1	2.1
% Long Term Debt of Capitalization	27.0	15.5	15.8	12.9	13.3	4.1	4.9	6.9	8.0	9.7
% Net Income of Revenue	20.7	29.6	22.4	27.0	NM	27.9	31.4	32.8	31.8	26.8
% Return on Assets	9.4	12.6	8.5	8.9	NM	18.9	24.0	28.3	25.5	21.9
% Return on Equity	15.0	18.3	12.1	12.0	NM	23.5	31.0	39.3	36.7	30.7

Data as orig reptd.; bef. results of disc opers/spec. items. Per share data adj. for stk. divs.; EPS diluted. E-Estimated. NA-Not Available. NM-Not Meaningful. NR-Not Ranked. UR-Under Review.

Office: One Amgen Center Drive, Thousand Oaks, CA 91320-1799.
Telephone: 805-447-1000.
Email: investor.relations@amgen.com
Website: http://www.amgen.com

Chrmn, Pres & CEO: K.W. Sharer
Investor Contact: R. Bradway
EVP & CFO: R. Bradway
SVP, Secy & General Counsel: D.J. Scott

SVP & CIO: T.J. Flanagan
Board Members: D. Baltimore, F. J. Biondi, Jr., J. D. Choate, F. W. Gluck, F. C. Herringer, G. S. Omenn, J. C. Pelham, J. P. Reason, L. D. Schaeffer, K. W. Sharer

Founded: 1980
Domicile: Delaware
Employees: 20,100

The McGraw·Hill Companies

STANDARD &POOR'S

Anadarko Petroleum Corp

S&P Recommendation	HOLD ★★★☆☆	Price $57.42 (as of Nov 23, 2007)	12-Mo. Target Price $66.00	Investment Style Large-Cap Blend

GICS Sector Energy
Sub-Industry Oil & Gas Exploration & Production

Summary This international oil and natural gas exploration and production company has associated businesses in marketing and trading and minerals.

Key Stock Statistics (Source S&P, Vickers, company reports)

52-Wk Range	$61.22– 38.40	S&P Oper. EPS 2007**E**	3.61	Market Capitalization(B)	$26.637	Beta		0.67
Trailing 12-Month EPS	$12.13	S&P Oper. EPS 2008**E**	3.74	Yield (%)	0.63	S&P 3-Yr. Proj. EPS CAGR(%)		19.00
Trailing 12-Month P/E	4.7	P/E on S&P Oper. EPS 2007**E**	15.9	Dividend Rate/Share	$0.36	S&P Credit Rating		BBB-
$10K Invested 5 Yrs Ago	$26,337	Common Shares Outstg. (M)	463.9	Institutional Ownership (%)	86			

Price Performance

30-Week Mov. Avg. ··· 10-Week Mov. Avg. – – **GAAP Earnings vs. Previous Year** Volume Above Avg. STARS
12-Mo. Target Price — Relative Strength — ▲ Up ▼ Down ► No Change Below Avg.

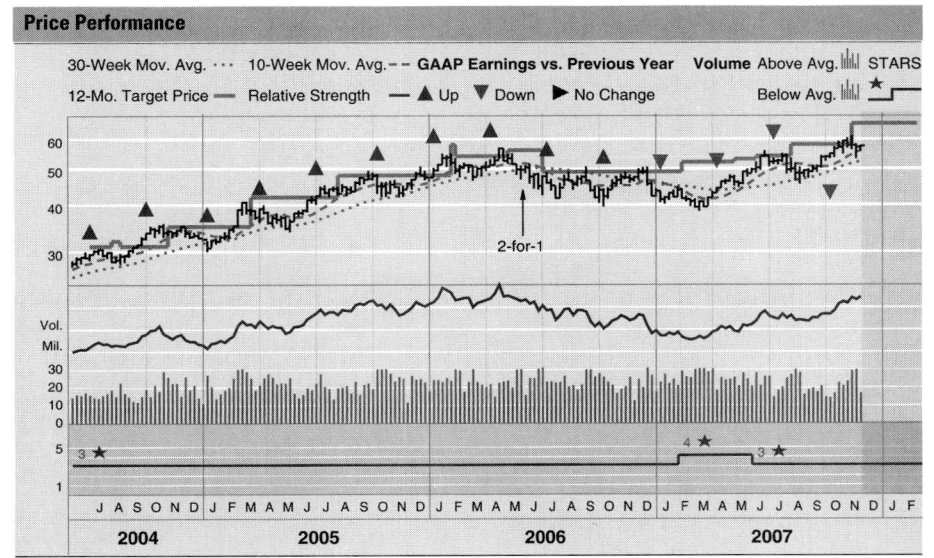

2-for-1

Options: ASE, CBOE, P, Ph

Analysis prepared by **Tina J. Vital** on November 20, 2007, when the stock traded at **$ 56.68**.

Highlights

➤ Third-quarter oil and gas production declined 3.8% to 510,000 boe/d, reflecting asset sales, but was slightly above our expectations, driven by strong offshore production. Using updated guidance from APC (includes the impact from gas disruptions in the Rocky Mountains, which are expected to last through mid-November), we expect fourth-quarter volumes to average 538,500 boe/d with volume growth of over 13% in 2007 and over 9% in 2008. The Independence Hub Project is currently producing about 850 MMcf/d and APC expects a steady ramp-up to the Hub's capacity of 1 Bcf/d by year-end.

➤ We believe APC's purchase of Kerr-McGee and Western Gas Resources has increased its costs, but we are hopeful that ongoing restructurings will significantly reduce costs by year-end 2008. In August, APC formed a master limited partnership (MLP), called Western Gas Partners, LP, to own certain of the company's midstream assets.

➤ We project after-tax operating earnings will drop over 40% in 2007, before rising over 4% in 2008 on improved production.

Investment Rationale/Risk

➤ We believe APC is in the process of digesting its August 2006 acquisitions of Kerr-McGee and Western Gas Resources for about $22.5 billion. While these acquisitions made APC a much larger company with a business focus shifted toward natural gas, this transformation has weakened its balance sheet and led to increased costs. As a result, APC has raised cash through asset sales to repay a large amount of debt incurred for its recent acquisitions. By year-end 2007, the company expects its net debt will be reduced to about $12 billion.

➤ Risks to our recommendation and target price include changes to economic, industrial or operating conditions, such as rising costs or difficulty in replacing reserves.

➤ A blend of our discounted cash flow ($55; assuming a WACC of 6.5%, and terminal growth of 3%) and our relative valuations leads to our 12-month target price of $66 per share. This represents an expected enterprise value of 6X our 2008 EBITDA estimate, a slight discount to peers.

Qualitative Risk Assessment

LOW	MEDIUM	HIGH

Our risk assessment reflects APC's solid business risk profile, as evidenced by its large undeveloped land base and significant long-life production assets, offset by an aggressive financial policy, as reflected in its two recent relatively high-priced leveraged acquisitions.

Quantitative Evaluations

S&P Quality Ranking   B+

D	C	B-	B	B+	A-	A	A+

Relative Strength Rank   **STRONG**

89

LOWEST = 1   HIGHEST = 99

Revenue/Earnings Data

Revenue (Million $)

	1Q	2Q	3Q	4Q	Year
2007	2,683	3,313	3,030	--	--
2006	1,701	1,809	3,498	3,179	10,187
2005	1,526	1,592	1,737	2,245	7,100
2004	1,460	1,443	1,562	1,602	6,067
2003	1,255	1,249	1,340	1,278	5,122
2002	790.0	1,002	951.0	1,117	3,860

Earnings Per Share ($)

2007	0.17	1.38	1.10	E0.61	E3.61
2006	1.22	1.43	2.98	0.40	6.02
2005	1.03	1.06	1.26	1.87	5.20
2004	0.78	0.80	0.79	0.82	3.18
2003	0.73	0.60	0.55	0.58	2.46
2002	0.17	0.47	0.37	0.61	1.61

Fiscal year ended Dec. 31. Next earnings report expected: Early February. EPS Estimates based on S&P Operating Earnings; historical GAAP earnings are as reported.

Dividend Data (Dates: mm/dd Payment Date: mm/dd/yy)

Amount ($)	Date Decl.	Ex-Div. Date	Stk. of Record	Payment Date
0.090	02/13	03/12	03/14	03/28/07
0.090	05/16	06/11	06/13	06/27/07
0.090	08/07	09/10	09/12	09/26/07
0.090	11/07	12/10	12/12	12/26/07

Dividends have been paid since 1986. Source: Company reports.

Please read the Required Disclosures and Analyst Certification on the last page of this report.

The McGraw-Hill Companies

Anadarko Petroleum Corp

STANDARD &POOR'S

Business Summary November 20, 2007

CORPORATE OVERVIEW. Anadarko Petroleum (APC) is an oil and gas exploration and production company, with operations in Texas, Louisiana, the mid-continent region, the Rockies, the deepwater Gulf of Mexico, and Algeria. The company also has production in Venezuela and Qatar, and has exploration programs in several other countries.

APC's oil and gas reserves have grown about 20% from year-end 2003 to year-end 2006, reflecting acquisitions and successful exploration and development drilling in North America. This was partially offset by the implementation of a refocused strategy announced in June 2004, which resulted in APC divesting what it deemed non-core properties in a series of unrelated transactions for over $3 billion in pretax proceeds, representing about 11% of 2003 reserves and about 20% of 2004 oil and gas production. Proved oil and gas reserves climbed 23% to 3.011 billion barrel oil equivalent (boe; 89% liquids, 66% developed, 89% located in the U.S.), at year-end 2006. Oil and gas production rose 29% to an average 178 million boe during 2006 (52% natural gas, 83% located in the U.S.).

MARKET PROFILE. For a super large exploration and production company, APC has a particularly narrow regional focus given the dominance of its North American assets on its portfolio. We believe North America is a relatively mature supply source for hydrocarbons, with natural gas production changing little over the past five years. We think the realignment that APC implemented in 2004 allowed the company to monetize non-core properties at attractive prices and to redeploy its energies into higher-margin projects, while using the sale proceeds to strengthen its balance sheet. The company was able to simultaneously continue the development of its emerging deepwater Gulf of Mexico projects, which are currently ramping up.

The combination of substantial long-lived onshore natural gas properties, with prolific deepwater properties, is unique among large capitalization independent oil and gas exploration and production companies. The capital intensity and high-risk nature of deepwater developments and the accelerating pace of service cost inflation require superior execution for companies engaged in these projects. We believe APC needs a longer history of demonstrable success to attract more investors.

Company Financials Fiscal Year Ended Dec. 31

Per Share Data ($)	2006	2005	2004	2003	2002	2001	2000	1999	1998	1997
Tangible Book Value	21.95	21.06	16.45	13.97	11.01	9.59	10.50	5.15	4.32	12.55
Cash Flow	10.28	8.04	6.05	5.01	3.74	2.09	3.64	1.00	0.65	1.28
Earnings	6.02	5.20	3.18	2.46	1.61	-0.37	2.13	0.13	-0.21	0.45
S&P Core Earnings	6.09	5.22	3.27	2.47	1.53	-0.49	NA	NA	NA	NA
Dividends	0.36	0.36	0.28	0.22	0.16	0.11	0.10	0.10	0.09	0.08
Payout Ratio	6%	7%	9%	9%	10%	NM	5%	80%	NM	17%
Prices:High	56.98	50.71	35.78	25.86	29.28	36.99	37.97	21.38	22.44	19.19
Prices:Low	39.51	30.01	24.00	20.14	18.39	21.50	13.78	13.13	12.38	12.69
P/E Ratio:High	9	10	11	11	18	NM	18	NM	NM	43
P/E Ratio:Low	7	6	8	8	11	NM	6	NM	NM	29

Income Statement Analysis (Million $)										
Revenue	10,187	7,100	6,067	5,122	3,860	8,369	5,686	701	560	673
Operating Income	6,945	5,436	4,400	3,648	2,585	3,702	2,190	421	267	402
Depreciation, Depletion and Amortization	1,976	1,343	1,447	1,297	1,121	1,227	593	218	204	199
Interest Expense	655	201	352	253	203	92.0	Nil	74.1	57.7	41.0
Pretax Income	4,238	3,895	2,477	1,974	1,207	-390	1,426	105	-65.1	164
Effective Tax Rate	34.0%	36.6%	35.2%	36.9%	31.2%	NM	42.2%	59.4%	NM	34.7%
Net Income	2,796	2,471	1,606	1,245	831	-176	824	42.6	-42.2	107
S&P Core Earnings	2,826	2,478	1,646	1,248	785	-243	NA	NA	NA	NA

Balance Sheet & Other Financial Data (Million $)										
Cash	491	739	874	62.0	34.0	37.0	199	44.8	17.0	8.91
Current Assets	4,614	2,916	2,502	1,324	1,280	1,201	1,894	356	230	219
Total Assets	58,844	22,588	20,192	20,546	18,248	16,771	16,590	4,098	3,633	2,992
Current Liabilities	16,758	2,403	1,993	1,715	1,861	1,801	1,676	387	289	252
Long Term Debt	11,520	3,555	3,671	5,058	5,171	4,638	3,984	1,443	1,425	956
Common Equity	15,201	10,967	9,219	8,510	6,673	6,262	6,586	1,335	1,059	1,117
Total Capital	39,673	19,330	17,393	17,909	15,578	14,454	10,770	3,555	3,208	2,620
Capital Expenditures	1,086	3,408	3,064	2,772	2,388	3,316	1,708	680	917	686
Cash Flow	4,769	3,809	3,048	2,537	1,946	1,044	1,406	250	155	306
Current Ratio	0.3	1.2	1.3	0.8	0.7	0.7	1.1	0.9	0.8	0.9
% Long Term Debt of Capitalization	28.8	18.4	21.1	28.2	33.2	32.1	37.0	40.6	44.4	36.5
% Return on Assets	6.9	11.5	7.9	6.4	4.7	NM	8.0	1.1	NM	3.8
% Return on Equity	21.3	24.4	17.9	16.1	12.8	NM	20.5	2.6	NM	10.1

Data as orig reptd.; bef. results of disc opers/spec. items. Per share data adj. for stk. divs.; EPS diluted. E-Estimated. NA-Not Available. NM-Not Meaningful. NR-Not Ranked. UR-Under Review.

Office: 1201 Lake Robbins Drive, The Woodlands, TX 77380-1124.
Telephone: 832-636-1000.
Website: http://www.anadarko.com
Chrmn, Pres & CEO: J.T. Hackett

COO: K. Kurz
SVP & CFO: R.A. Walker
VP & Chief Acctg Officer: B.W. Busmire
VP & Treas: R.G. Gwin

Investor Contact: J. Colglazier (832-636-2306)
Board Members: R. J. Allison, Jr., L. Barcus, J. L. Bryan, J. R. Butler, Jr., L. R. Corbett, H. P. Eberhart, J. R. Gordon, J. T. Hackett, J. W. Poduska, Sr.

Founded: 1985
Domicile: Delaware
Employees: 4,400

Analog Devices Inc.

STANDARD &POOR'S

| S&P Recommendation | HOLD ★★★★★ | Price $31.39 (as of Nov 29, 2007) | 12-Mo. Target Price $34.00 | Investment Style Large-Cap Growth |

GICS Sector Information Technology
Sub-Industry Semiconductors

Summary This Massachusetts company manufactures high-performance integrated circuits (ICs) used in analog and digital signal processing applications.

Key Stock Statistics (Source S&P, Vickers, company reports)

52-Wk Range	$41.10– 30.19	S&P Oper. EPS 2008**E**	1.87	Market Capitalization(B)	$9.768	Beta	2.20
Trailing 12-Month EPS	$1.50	S&P Oper. EPS 2009**E**	NA	Yield (%)	2.29	S&P 3-Yr. Proj. EPS CAGR(%)	24.00
Trailing 12-Month P/E	20.9	P/E on S&P Oper. EPS 2008**E**	16.8	Dividend Rate/Share	$0.72	S&P Credit Rating	BBB+
$10K Invested 5 Yrs Ago	$11,028	Common Shares Outstg. (M)	311.2	Institutional Ownership (%)	85		

Price Performance

30-Week Mov. Avg. ··· 10-Week Mov. Avg. - - **GAAP Earnings vs. Previous Year** Volume Above Avg. STARS
12-Mo. Target Price — Relative Strength — ▲ Up ▼ Down ▶ No Change Below Avg. ★

Options: ASE, CBOE, P, Ph

Qualitative Risk Assessment

| LOW | MEDIUM | HIGH |

Our risk assessment reflects that ADI is subject to the sales cycles of the semiconductor industry, offset by our view of relatively stable chip pricing owing to high proprietary design content, broad end-markets, a leading market share in key converter and amplifier product categories and what we consider a lack of debt.

Quantitative Evaluations

S&P Quality Ranking B

| D | C | B- | B | B+ | A- | A | A+ |

Relative Strength Rank MODERATE

35

LOWEST = 1 HIGHEST = 99

Revenue/Earnings Data

Revenue (Million $)

	1Q	2Q	3Q	4Q	Year
2007	691.6	669.1	680.3	648.5	2,546
2006	621.3	643.9	663.7	644.3	2,573
2005	580.5	603.7	582.4	622.1	2,389
2004	605.4	678.5	717.8	632.1	2,634
2003	467.4	501.9	520.5	557.5	2,047
2002	393.0	413.4	445.5	455.7	1,708

Earnings Per Share ($)

2007	0.44	0.37	0.37	0.31	1.51
2006	0.32	0.39	0.39	0.39	1.48
2005	0.28	0.31	0.32	0.18	1.08
2004	0.30	0.39	0.43	0.34	1.45
2003	0.16	0.19	0.21	0.38	0.78
2002	0.06	0.04	0.08	0.09	0.28

Fiscal year ended Oct. 31. Next earnings report expected: Late February. EPS Estimates based on S&P Operating Earnings; historical GAAP earnings are as reported.

Highlights

▸ The 12-month target price for ADI has recently been changed to $34.00 from $32.00. The Highlights section of this Stock Report will be updated accordingly.

Investment Rationale/Risk

▸ The Investment Rationale/Risk section of this Stock Report will be updated shortly. For the latest News story on ADI from MarketScope, see below.

▸ 11/28/07 09:04 am EST... S&P REITERATES HOLD OPINION ON SHARES OF ANALOG DEVICES (ADI 31.22***): ADI posts adjusted Oct-Q EPS of $0.39 vs. $0.35, before charges and discontinued operations, in line with our estimate. Adjusted revenues rose 2% on sales of consumer and computer products. Adjusted gross margin narrowed on a less favorable sales mix. Share buybacks aided EPS growth. We are concerned about future sales of industrial and consumer chips, but we see divestitures and better cost containment supporting higher margins ahead. We are lifting our FY 08 (Oct.) EPS estimate by $0.08 to $1.87, and raising our 12-month target price by $2 to $34, based on relative analysis. / C.Montevirgen

Dividend Data (Dates: mm/dd Payment Date: mm/dd/yy)

Amount ($)	Date Decl.	Ex-Div. Date	Stk. of Record	Payment Date
0.180	02/21	03/07	03/09	03/28/07
0.180	05/22	05/30	06/01	06/20/07
0.180	08/23	08/29	08/31	09/19/07
0.180	11/26	12/05	12/07	12/26/07

Dividends have been paid since 2003. Source: Company reports.

Please read the Required Disclosures and Analyst Certification on the last page of this report.

The McGraw-Hill Companies

Analog Devices Inc.

STANDARD &POOR'S

Business Summary November 21, 2007

CORPORATE OVERVIEW. Analog Devices designs, manufactures, and markets a broad line of high-performance analog, mixed-signal and digital signal processing (DSP) integrated circuits (ICs) that address a wide range of real-world signal processing applications. Real-world phenomena that these applications are designed for include temperature, pressure, sound, images, speed, acceleration, position and rotation. These phenomena are specifically analog in nature, consisting of continuously varying information. The expansion of broadband and wireless communications applications helps drive demand for analog and DSP chips. ADI's products are built into data and digital subscriber lines (DSL) modems, wireless telephones, base station equipment, and remote access servers. The company's analog products are typically general purpose in nature and are used in a wide variety of equipment and systems. The company's chips are increasingly sold to PC and digital entertainment markets, as consumer equipment to handle voice, video and images becomes increasingly complex and sells to a wider audience. ADI's products are sold both to OEMs and to customers building their own equipment. Key

markets are industrial, which accounted for approximately 42% of sales in FY 06 (39% of FY 05 sales), communications 29% (31%), computers 12% (14%), and consumer 17% (16%).

The customer base is fairly broad: the 20 largest customers, excluding distributors, accounted for about 29% of sales in FY 06 (29% of sales in FY 05), and the largest customer, excluding distributors, accounted for approximately 3% (4%). Broken down geographically, North America was responsible for 25% of FY 06 sales (25% of FY 05 sales), and the remainder came from Europe 22% (23%), Japan 19% (19%), China 13% (11%), and other markets in Asia 21% (22%). About 51% of FY 06 sales (49% of FY 05 sales) were derived from sales made through distributors.

Company Financials Fiscal Year Ended Oct. 31

Per Share Data ($)	2007	2006	2005	2004	2003	2002	2001	2000	1999	1998
Tangible Book Value	NA	9.17	9.61	9.66	8.42	7.50	7.20	5.90	4.54	3.47
Cash Flow	NA	1.95	1.49	1.84	1.22	0.90	1.48	2.00	0.94	0.69
Earnings	1.51	1.48	1.08	1.45	0.78	0.28	0.93	1.59	0.55	0.36
S&P Core Earnings	NA	1.46	0.29	0.91	0.20	-0.32	0.44	NA	NA	NA
Dividends	0.70	0.56	0.32	0.20	Nil	Nil	Nil	Nil	Nil	Nil
Payout Ratio	46%	38%	30%	14%	Nil	Nil	Nil	Nil	Nil	Nil
Prices:High	41.10	41.48	41.40	52.37	50.35	48.84	64.00	103.00	47.25	19.81
Prices:Low	30.19	26.07	31.71	31.36	22.58	17.88	29.00	41.31	12.19	6.00
P/E Ratio:High	27	28	38	36	65	NM	69	65	86	56
P/E Ratio:Low	20	18	29	22	29	NM	31	26	22	17

Income Statement Analysis (Million $)										
Revenue	NA	2,573	2,389	2,634	2,047	1,708	2,277	2,578	1,450	1,231
Operating Income	NA	771	703	852	552	405	675	924	391	289
Depreciation	NA	172	156	153	168	238	210	157	143	128
Interest Expense	NA	0.05	0.03	0.22	32.2	44.5	62.5	5.84	8.07	11.2
Pretax Income	NA	664	588	733	382	140	507	866	258	150
Effective Tax Rate	NA	17.1%	29.4%	22.1%	21.9%	25.0%	29.7%	29.9%	23.6%	20.6%
Net Income	NA	549	415	571	298	105	356	607	197	119
S&P Core Earnings	NA	542	113	364	74.2	-118	170	NA	NA	NA

Balance Sheet & Other Financial Data (Million $)										
Cash	NA	344	628	519	518	1,614	1,365	1,736	356	263
Current Assets	NA	3,011	3,732	3,529	2,886	3,624	3,435	3,168	1,379	904
Total Assets	NA	3,987	4,583	4,720	4,093	4,980	4,885	4,411	2,218	1,862
Current Liabilities	NA	491	819	567	463	484	528	650	479	321
Long Term Debt	NA	Nil	Nil	Nil	Nil	1,274	1,206	1,213	16.2	341
Common Equity	NA	3,436	3,692	3,800	3,288	2,900	2,843	2,304	1,616	1,128
Total Capital	NA	3,439	3,692	3,810	3,305	4,197	4,100	3,568	1,672	1,501
Capital Expenditures	NA	129	85.5	146	67.7	57.4	297	275	77.5	167
Cash Flow	NA	722	570	723	467	343	567	764	339	247
Current Ratio	NA	6.1	4.6	6.2	6.2	7.5	6.5	4.9	2.9	2.8
% Long Term Debt of Capitalization	NA	Nil	Nil	Nil	Nil	30.4	29.4	34.0	1.0	22.7
% Net Income of Revenue	NA	21.4	17.4	21.7	14.6	6.2	15.7	23.6	13.6	9.7
% Return on Assets	NA	12.8	8.9	13.0	6.6	2.1	7.7	18.3	9.6	6.6
% Return on Equity	NA	15.4	11.1	16.1	9.6	3.7	13.8	31.0	14.3	10.5

Data as orig reptd.; bef. results of disc opers/spec. items. Per share data adj. for stk. divs.; EPS diluted. E-Estimated. NA-Not Available. NM-Not Meaningful. NR-Not Ranked. UR-Under Review.

Office: One Technology Way, Norwood, MA 02062-9106.
Telephone: 800-262-5643.
Email: investor.relations@analog.com
Website: http://www.analog.com

Chrmn: R. Stata
Pres & CEO: J.G. Fishman
VP & CFO: J.E. McDonough
VP, Secy & General Counsel: M.K. Seif

Treas: W.A. Martin
Investor Contact: M. Tagliaferro (781-461-3282)
Board Members: J. Champy, J. L. Doyle, J. G. Fishman, J. C. Hodgson, C. King, F. G. Saviers, P. J. Severino, K. Sicchitano, R. Stata, L. C. Thurow

Founded: 1965
Domicile: Massachusetts
Employees: 9,800

The McGraw-Hill Companies

Anheuser-Busch Companies Inc.

STANDARD & POOR'S

S&P Recommendation BUY ★★★★☆

Price	12-Mo. Target Price	Investment Style
$49.54 (as of Nov 26, 2007)	$59.00	Large-Cap Growth

GICS Sector Consumer Staples
Sub-Industry Brewers

Summary BUD, the parent company of the world's largest brewer, also has interests in packaging and in entertainment operations.

Key Stock Statistics (Source S&P, Vickers, company reports)

52-Wk Range	$55.19–46.05	S&P Oper. EPS 2007**E**	2.80	Market Capitalization(B)	$37.134	Beta	0.46
Trailing 12-Month EPS	$2.74	S&P Oper. EPS 2008**E**	3.10	Yield (%)	2.66	S&P 3-Yr. Proj. EPS CAGR(%)	9.00
Trailing 12-Month P/E	18.1	P/E on S&P Oper. EPS 2007**E**	17.7	Dividend Rate/Share	$1.32	S&P Credit Rating	A
$10K Invested 5 Yrs Ago	$10,931	Common Shares Outstg. (M)	749.6	Institutional Ownership (%)	64		

Price Performance

30-Week Mov. Avg. ···   10-Week Mov. Avg.- -   **GAAP Earnings vs. Previous Year**   Volume Above Avg. STARS
12-Mo. Target Price —   Relative Strength —   ▲ Up ▼ Down ▶ No Change   Below Avg. ★

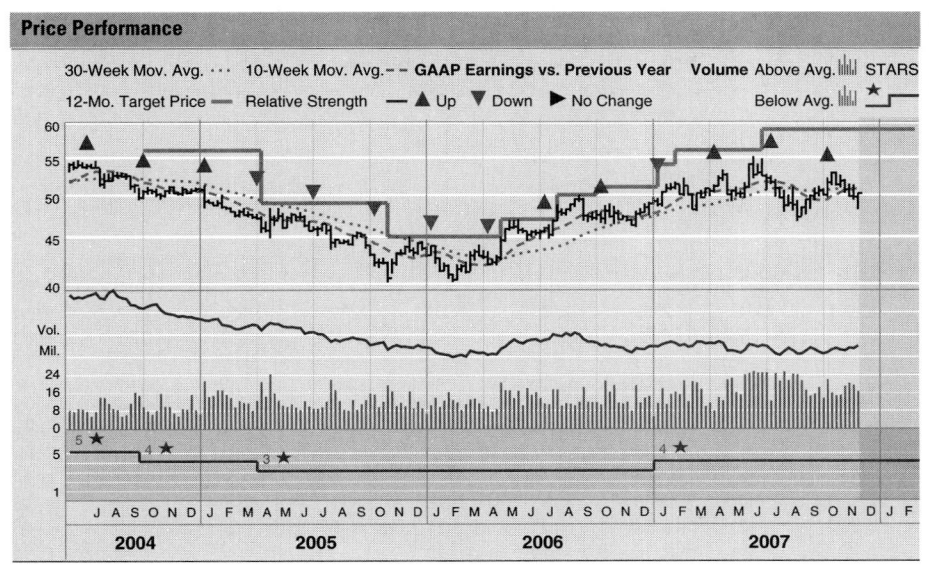

Options: ASE, CBOE, P, Ph

Analysis prepared by **Esther Y. Kwon, CFA** on November 26, 2007, when the stock traded at **$ 50.31**.

Highlights

➤ We see net sales (after excise taxes) continuing to rise at a low single digit pace, on improving domestic volume trends and strength in international sales. Pricing trends should also strengthen, and we expect net revenue per barrel to increase 1.0% to 1.5%. We look for worldwide shipment volumes to expand in the low single digits, reflecting acquisitions and growth in China and Canada.

➤ We foresee operating margins widening slightly, as relatively high packaging and energy costs, increased marketing efforts, and rising commodity costs are offset by price increases, efficiency improvement, and volume gains. We expect mid-single digit increases in general and administrative expense. In our view, growth in equity income from BUD's 50% interest in Grupo Modelo will be the main earnings driver over the near term, particularly in light of Modelo's new distribution partnership with Constellation Brands (STZ: hold, $27).

➤ We see flat interest expense, but possibly a higher effective tax rate in 2007. We look for a rise in 2007 operating EPS to $2.80, from $2.52 in 2006, aided by share repurchases. For 2008, we see EPS rising further to $3.10.

Investment Rationale/Risk

➤ We expect domestic beer pricing to remain favorable through 2008 as BUD implements another price increase early in the year. We think volume growth should continue on increased investments in U.S. sales personnel and marketing for its trademark brands. In addition, we see increased equity income from BUD's stake in Modelo. Longer term, we believe the company's deal to import and distribute InBev brands will benefit the bottom line, as should joint ventures to brew beer overseas. We expect BUD to use free cash flow for share repurchases.

➤ Risks to our recommendation and target price include potential market share declines due to aggressive marketing by competitors, particularly in the wine and spirits categories, for first-time drinkers. Also, greater than expected increases in energy and commodity costs could hurt margins.

➤ Our 12-month target price of $59 is supported by our DCF and P/E analyses. Our DCF model calculates an intrinsic value of $58, assuming an 8.5% cost of capital, a 3.5% five-year growth rate, and a terminal growth rate of 2.5%. Applying a historical average P/E of 21X to our 2007 EPS estimate, we arrive at a $59 value.

Qualitative Risk Assessment

LOW	MEDIUM	HIGH

BUD is a large cap company, and has the biggest market share in an industry that has historically demonstrated stable revenue streams. Shareholders recently approved an amendment to eliminate staggered board elections by 2009.

Quantitative Evaluations

S&P Quality Ranking   A+

D	C	B-	B	B+	A-	A	A+

Relative Strength Rank   STRONG

72

LOWEST = 1   HIGHEST = 99

Revenue/Earnings Data

Revenue (Million $)

	1Q	2Q	3Q	4Q	Year
2007	3,858	4,515	4,618	--	--
2006	3,756	4,256	4,281	3,425	15,717
2005	3,564	4,018	4,089	3,365	15,036
2004	3,477	4,010	4,080	3,367	14,934
2003	3,281	3,770	3,881	3,215	14,147
2002	3,137	3,626	3,706	3,098	13,566

Earnings Per Share ($)

2007	0.67	0.88	0.95	E0.37	E2.80
2006	0.64	0.82	0.82	0.25	2.53
2005	0.65	0.78	0.66	0.26	2.35
2004	0.67	0.83	0.85	0.42	2.77
2003	0.57	0.75	0.80	0.36	2.48
2002	0.51	0.66	0.71	0.32	2.20

Fiscal year ended Dec. 31. Next earnings report expected: Early February. EPS Estimates based on S&P Operating Earnings; historical GAAP earnings are as reported.

Dividend Data (Dates: mm/dd Payment Date: mm/dd/yy)

Amount ($)	Date Decl.	Ex-Div. Date	Stk. of Record	Payment Date
0.295	01/11	02/07	02/09	03/09/07
0.295	04/25	05/07	05/09	06/11/07
0.330	07/25	08/07	08/09	09/10/07
0.330	10/24	11/07	11/09	12/10/07

Dividends have been paid since 1932. Source: Company reports.

Please read the Required Disclosures and Analyst Certification on the last page of this report.

The McGraw-Hill Companies

Anheuser-Busch Companies Inc.

STANDARD &POOR'S

Business Summary November 26, 2007

CORPORATE OVERVIEW. Anheuser-Busch Cos. is the holding company parent of the largest U.S. brewer, Anheuser-Busch, Inc. (ABI)--which dates back to 1875, as Anheuser-Busch International, Inc. (ABII)--and other subsidiaries that conduct various business operations.

BUD's beer products are sold in more than 80 countries and U.S. territories. Worldwide sales of the company's beer brands in 2006 totaled 156.6 million barrels (up from 148.3 million barrels in 2005). BUD operates 12 breweries, strategically located across the U.S., to serve its distribution system economically. U.S. sales totaled 102.3 million barrels in 2006 (up 1.2% from 2005), or about 48.4% of U.S. industry sales. International beer volume was 22.7 million barrels (up 9.3%), while equity investees produced 31.6 million barrels (up 19.7%). In 2005, domestic beer contributed 72.5% of net sales, and international beer 6.4%.

Major beer brands include Budweiser, Bud Light, Budweiser Select, Michelob, Busch, Natural Light, King Cobra, Hurricane Malt Liquor, and in 2006, the company acquired Rolling Rock. BUD also imports and distributes Kirin, Tsingtao, Grolsch, Stella Artois, Beck's and Bass. Non-beer offerings include Bac-

ardi branded malt beverages, Tilt, PEELS, and Tequiza. Non-alcoholic malt beverages include O'Doul's, and 180 energy drink.

Through various subsidiaries, the company is involved in a number of beer-related operations that help to insulate it from occasional rises in packaging and ingredient costs. These operations include can manufacturing, metalized paper printing, and barley malting. Packaging operations accounted for 10.6% of total net sales in 2006, excluding the nearly 1/3 of segment sales that were internal.

Through Busch Entertainment Corp., the company operates nine theme parks, including Busch Gardens in Florida and Virginia; Sea World parks in Florida, Texas and California; water parks in Florida and Virginia; and an educational play park in Pennsylvania. Busch Entertainment contributed 7.4% of total net sales in 2006.

Company Financials Fiscal Year Ended Dec. 31

Per Share Data ($)	2006	2005	2004	2003	2002	2001	2000	1999	1998	1997
Tangible Book Value	3.36	2.71	1.88	2.74	3.61	4.15	4.11	3.80	3.96	3.69
Cash Flow	3.80	3.60	4.04	3.53	3.16	2.82	2.56	1.47	2.02	1.86
Earnings	2.53	2.35	2.77	2.48	2.20	1.89	1.69	1.47	1.27	1.18
S&P Core Earnings	2.60	2.38	2.61	2.33	1.96	1.67	NA	NA	NA	NA
Dividends	1.13	1.03	0.93	0.83	0.75	0.69	0.63	0.58	0.54	0.50
Payout Ratio	45%	44%	34%	33%	34%	37%	37%	39%	43%	42%
Prices:High	50.00	51.32	54.74	53.84	55.00	46.95	49.88	42.00	34.13	24.13
Prices:Low	40.17	40.15	49.42	45.30	43.65	36.75	27.31	32.22	21.47	19.25
P/E Ratio:High	20	22	20	22	25	25	30	29	27	20
P/E Ratio:Low	16	17	18	18	20	19	16	22	17	16

Income Statement Analysis (Million $)										
Revenue	15,717	15,036	14,934	14,147	13,566	12,911	12,262	11,704	11,245	11,066
Operating Income	3,708	3,705	4,294	4,077	3,827	3,540	3,299	3,080	2,862	2,737
Depreciation	989	979	933	877	847	834	804	777	738	684
Interest Expense	434	435	405	377	351	334	315	290	265	219
Pretax Income	2,866	2,690	2,999	3,169	2,975	2,618	2,380	2,165	1,937	1,883
Effective Tax Rate	31.4%	31.6%	38.7%	34.5%	35.0%	34.9%	34.8%	35.2%	36.3%	37.4%
Net Income	1,965	1,839	2,240	2,076	1,934	1,705	1,552	1,402	1,233	1,179
S&P Core Earnings	2,022	1,860	2,111	1,952	1,722	1,507	NA	NA	NA	NA

Balance Sheet & Other Financial Data (Million $)										
Cash	219	226	228	191	189	163	160	152	225	147
Current Assets	1,830	1,759	1,818	1,630	1,505	1,550	1,548	1,601	1,640	1,584
Total Assets	16,377	16,555	16,173	14,690	14,120	13,862	13,085	12,640	12,484	11,727
Current Liabilities	2,246	1,983	1,969	1,857	1,788	1,732	1,676	1,987	1,730	1,501
Long Term Debt	7,654	1,682	8,279	7,285	6,603	5,984	5,375	4,881	4,719	4,366
Common Equity	3,939	3,343	2,668	2,712	3,052	4,062	4,128	3,921	4,216	4,042
Total Capital	12,787	6,708	12,674	11,459	11,962	11,334	10,876	10,147	10,238	9,701
Capital Expenditures	812	1,137	1,090	993	835	1,022	1,075	856	818	1,199
Cash Flow	2,954	2,818	3,173	2,953	2,781	2,539	2,356	1,402	1,971	1,863
Current Ratio	0.8	0.9	0.9	0.9	0.8	0.9	0.9	0.8	0.9	1.1
% Long Term Debt of Capitalization	59.9	25.1	65.3	63.6	55.2	52.8	49.4	48.1	46.1	45.0
% Net Income of Revenue	12.5	12.2	15.0	14.7	14.3	13.2	12.7	12.0	11.0	10.7
% Return on Assets	11.9	11.2	14.5	14.4	13.8	12.7	12.1	11.2	10.2	10.6
% Return on Equity	51.6	61.2	83.3	72.0	45.3	41.6	38.6	34.5	29.9	29.2

Data as orig reptd.; bef. results of disc opers/spec. items. Per share data adj. for stk. divs.; EPS diluted. E-Estimated. NA-Not Available. NM-Not Meaningful. NR-Not Ranked. UR-Under Review.

Office: 1 Busch Place , St. Louis, MO 63118.
Telephone: 314-577-2000.
Website: http://www.anheuser-busch.com
Chrmn: P. Stokes

Pres & CEO: A.A. Busch IV
VP & CFO: W.R. Baker
VP & Cntlr: J. Kelly
VP & CIO: J. Castellano

Board Members: A. A. Busch IV, A. A. Busch, III, C. G. Fernandez, J. J. Forese, J. E. Jacob, J. R. Jones, C. F. Knight, V. R. Loucks, Jr., V. S. Martinez, W. P. Payne, J. M. Roche, H. H. Shelton, P. T. Stokes, A. C. Taylor, D. A. Warner, III, E. E. Whitacre, Jr.

Founded: 1852
Domicile: Delaware
Employees: 30,183

The McGraw-Hill Companies

Aon Corp.

STANDARD &POOR'S

S&P Recommendation HOLD ★★★☆☆	**Price** $48.15 (as of Nov 23, 2007)	**12-Mo. Target Price** $53.00	**Investment Style** Large-Cap Blend

GICS Sector Financials
Sub-Industry Insurance Brokers

Summary This Chicago-based holding company is comprised of a family of insurance brokerage, consulting and insurance underwriting subsidiaries.

Key Stock Statistics (Source S&P, Vickers, company reports)

52-Wk Range	$48.50–34.30	S&P Oper. EPS 2007**E**	2.95	Market Capitalization(B)	$14.137	Beta	0.99
Trailing 12-Month EPS	$2.72	S&P Oper. EPS 2008**E**	3.20	Yield (%)	1.25	S&P 3-Yr. Proj. EPS CAGR(%)	17.00
Trailing 12-Month P/E	17.7	P/E on S&P Oper. EPS 2007**E**	16.3	Dividend Rate/Share	$0.60	S&P Credit Rating	BBB+
$10K Invested 5 Yrs Ago	$28,359	Common Shares Outstg. (M)	293.6	Institutional Ownership (%)	94		

Price Performance

- 30-Week Mov. Avg. ··· 10-Week Mov. Avg. — **GAAP Earnings vs. Previous Year**   Volume Above Avg. STARS
- 12-Mo. Target Price — Relative Strength — ▲ Up ▼ Down ► No Change   Below Avg. ★

Options: ASE, CBOE, P, Ph

Analysis prepared by **Tanjila Shafi** on November 12, 2007, when the stock traded at **$ 45.78**.

Highlights

➤ We expect single-digit revenue growth for the company's risk and insurance brokerage services segment in 2008 as we see improved topline gains in the Americas reflecting growth in its U.S. retail sub-segment's middle market and large corporate accounts. We anticipate the Asia-Pacific region will continue to experience solid new business growth and effective renewal book management. By our analysis, the pretax margin for risk and insurance brokerage will range between 18%-19%. We believe that the company's ongoing restructuring program should result in cost savings of approximately $60 million to $70 million in 2008.

➤ We see single-digit revenue growth for the company's consulting segment in 2008, aided by the restructuring program and operational enhancements. We expect the increase in consulting revenues to come from the services sub-segment. In addition, we anticipate pretax income for the consulting segment to improve.

➤ We estimate 2007 operating EPS of $2.95, compared to 2006 operating EPS of $2.12. Our EPS estimate for 2008 is $3.20.

Investment Rationale/Risk

➤ We believe that the company is capturing market share from its competitors, given industry trends. AOC is making strides in gaining new businesses while maintaining its retention rate. In addition, we view positively the company's focus on its core businesses and its willingness to shed low-margin, non-core segments as evidenced by its recent announcement of its interest in selling its Combined Insurance business. We see further opportunities for AOC to reduce operating costs and expand overall operating margins in 2008.

➤ Risks to our recommendation and target price include continuing pressure on operating results from the elimination of contingent commissions and from a soft property and casualty market; possible client defections following legal/regulatory settlements; currency risks; and potential additional contingent commission probes by international authorities.

➤ Our 12-month target price is $53, 16.6X our 2007 EPS from continuing operations, in line with historical multiples.

Qualitative Risk Assessment

LOW	MEDIUM	HIGH

Our risk assessment reflects what see as the well-diversified operations of the company and a solid balance sheet with low debt, offset by the impact of the loss of contingent commissions and business restructuring.

Quantitative Evaluations

S&P Quality Ranking B+

D	C	B-	B	B+	A-	A	A+

Relative Strength Rank STRONG

92

LOWEST = 1   HIGHEST = 99

Revenue/Earnings Data

Revenue (Million $)

	1Q	2Q	3Q	4Q	Year
2007	2,381	2,488	2,407	--	--
2006	2,165	2,208	2,168	2,413	8,954
2005	2,464	2,456	2,387	2,530	9,837
2004	2,564	2,544	2,402	2,662	10,172
2003	2,384	2,434	2,391	2,601	9,810
2002	2,088	2,122	2,246	2,366	8,822

Earnings Per Share ($)

2007	0.66	0.74	0.59	E0.81	E2.95
2006	0.57	0.53	0.27	0.57	1.86
2005	0.58	0.54	0.35	0.42	1.89
2004	0.58	0.54	0.36	0.25	1.72
2003	0.49	0.48	0.44	0.67	2.08
2002	0.57	Nil	0.46	0.59	1.64

Fiscal year ended Dec. 31. Next earnings report expected: Mid February. EPS Estimates based on S&P Operating Earnings; historical GAAP earnings are as reported.

Dividend Data (Dates: mm/dd Payment Date: mm/dd/yy)

Amount ($)	Date Decl.	Ex-Div. Date	Stk. of Record	Payment Date
0.150	01/19	01/30	02/01	02/14/07
0.150	04/13	04/27	05/01	05/14/07
0.150	07/20	07/30	08/01	08/14/07
0.150	10/11	10/30	11/01	11/14/07

Dividends have been paid since 1950. Source: Company reports.

Please read the Required Disclosures and Analyst Certification on the last page of this report.

The McGraw·Hill Companies

Aon Corp.

STANDARD
&POOR'S

Business Summary November 12, 2007

CORPORATE OVERVIEW. Aon Corp. is a global provider of insurance broker-age services, insurance products, and risk and insurance advice, as well as other consulting services, conducting business in more than 120 countries and sovereignties. As of December 31, 2006, the company was the world's largest insurance broker based on pure brokerage operations, the largest reinsurance broker, and the leading manager of captive insurance companies worldwide, based on surveys by Business Insurance.

AOC classifies its businesses into three operating segments: risk and insur-ance brokerage, consulting, and insurance underwriting. The risk and insur-ance brokerage segment accounted for 63% of total revenue from continuing operations in 2006, the consulting segment 14%, and the insurance underwrit-ing segment 23%.

LEGAL/REGULATORY ISSUES. In March 2005, AOC reached a settlement with the New York, Illinois and Connecticut attorneys general and other regulators resolving all issues related to investigations conducted by these agencies. Under the settlement, AOC agreed to institute certain business reforms and pay $190 million into a fund to be distributed to eligible U.S. clients where AOC received certain related contingent commissions, with no portion of the pay-ments considered a fine or penalty.

CORPORATE STRATEGY. Due to the regulatory scrutiny regarding contingent commissions, AOC announced in October 2004 that it was terminating its con-tingent commission arrangements with underwriters. We believe replacing this lost income will be a challenge for AOC, which earned about $132 million in contingent commission revenue in 2004, versus $169 million in 2003.

The company recently announced a new a new restructuring program that it believes will improve its expense discipline. This program is expected to re-sult in $360 million of charges and $50 million-$70 million of savings in 2008, $175 million-$200 million in 2009, and $240 million of cumulative annualized savings by 2010, before any potential reinvestment of savings.

Company Financials Fiscal Year Ended Dec. 31

Per Share Data ($)	2006	2005	2004	2003	2002	2001	2000	1999	1998	1997
Tangible Book Value	2.14	2.48	0.76	NM	NM	NM	NM	NM	NM	NM
Operating Earnings	NA	NA	NA	NA	NA	NA	NA	NA	NA	1.53
Earnings	1.86	1.89	1.72	2.08	1.64	0.73	1.82	1.33	2.07	1.12
S&P Core Earnings	2.03	2.10	2.29	2.05	1.00	-0.06	NA	NA	NA	NA
Dividends	0.75	0.60	0.60	0.60	0.83	0.90	0.87	0.81	0.73	0.68
Relative Payout	40%	32%	35%	29%	50%	123%	48%	61%	35%	61%
Prices:High	42.76	37.14	29.44	26.79	39.63	44.80	42.75	46.67	50.37	39.25
Prices:Low	31.01	20.64	18.15	17.41	13.30	29.75	20.69	26.06	32.17	26.78
P/E Ratio:High	23	20	17	13	24	61	23	35	24	35
P/E Ratio:Low	17	11	11	8	8	41	11	20	16	24

Income Statement Analysis (Million $)										
Life Insurance in Force	9,385	17,182	20,529	26,784	28,136	31,454	28,170	22,011	16,163	19,262
Premium Income:Life A & H	NA	NA	1,620	1,680	1,628	1,350	1,233	1,137	1,084	1,081
Premium Income:Casualty/Property.	NA	NA	1,168	869	732	672	673	671	589	528
Net Investment Income	NA	343	324	317	252	213	508	577	590	494
Total Revenue	8,954	9,837	10,172	9,810	8,822	7,676	7,375	7,070	6,493	5,751
Pretax Income	920	965	880	1,110	793	399	854	635	931	542
Net Operating Income	NA	NA	NA	NA	NA	NA	NA	NA	NA	402
Net Income	626	642	577	663	466	203	481	352	541	299
S&P Core Earnings	683	709	765	652	281	-19.4	NA	NA	NA	NA

Balance Sheet & Other Financial Data (Million $)										
Cash & Equivalent	4,726	476	570	540	506	439	1,118	837	786	1,085
Premiums Due	9,032	9,697	1,645	1,504	1,213	953	1,278	1,116	1,120	863
Investment Assets:Bonds	2,790	4,218	3,482	2,751	2,089	2,149	2,337	2,497	3,103	4,841
Investment Assets:Stocks	62.0	40.0	40.0	42.0	62.0	382	492	574	768	806
Investment Assets:Loans	Nil	Nil	Nil	Nil	Nil	Nil	Nil	NA	Nil	Nil
Investment Assets:Total	7,575	9,064	13,720	7,324	6,587	6,146	6,019	6,184	6,452	5,922
Deferred Policy Costs	541	1,186	1,137	1,021	882	704	656	636	573	549
Total Assets	24,318	27,818	28,329	27,027	25,334	22,386	22,251	21,132	19,688	18,691
Debt	2,285	2,105	2,117	2,095	1,721	2,494	1,848	1,811	1,380	2,201
Common Equity	5,218	5,303	5,103	4,498	3,895	3,521	3,388	3,051	3,017	2,822
Combined Loss-Expense Ratio	NA	NA	NA	NA	NA	NA	NA	NA	NA	NA
% Return on Revenue	7.0	6.5	5.7	6.8	5.3	2.6	6.5	5.0	8.3	5.2
% Return on Equity	11.9	12.3	12.0	15.7	12.6	5.8	14.8	11.5	18.4	10.1
% Investment Yield	5.1	4.6	4.4	4.6	4.0	3.5	8.3	9.1	9.5	8.9

Data as orig reptd.; bef. results of disc opers/spec. items. Per share data adj. for stk. divs.; EPS diluted. E-Estimated. NA-Not Available. NM-Not Meaningful. NR-Not Ranked. UR-Under Review.

Office: 200 East Randoph Street, Chicago, IL 60601-6436.
Telephone: 312-381-1000.
Website: http://www.aon.com
Exec Chrmn: P.G. Ryan

Pres & CEO: G.C. Case
Sr EVP: M.D. O'Halleran
EVP & General Counsel: D.C. Findlay
SVP & Treas: D.M. Aigotti

Investor Contact: S. Malchow (312-381-3983)
Board Members: G. C. Case, E. D. Jannotta, P. J. Kalff, L. B. Knight, J. M. Losh, R. E. Martin, A. J. McKenna, R. S. Morrison, R. B. Myers, R. B. Myers, R. C. Notebaert, J. W. Rogers, Jr., P. G. Ryan, G. Santona, C. Y. Woo

Founded: 1919
Domicile: Delaware
Employees: 43,100

Apache Corp

STANDARD &POOR'S

S&P Recommendation BUY ★★★★☆	**Price** $101.60 (as of Nov 23, 2007)	**12-Mo. Target Price** $113.00	**Investment Style** Large-Cap Blend

GICS Sector Energy
Sub-Industry Oil & Gas Exploration & Production

Summary This international independent exploration and production company explores for, develops and produces natural gas, crude oil and natural gas liquids.

Key Stock Statistics (Source S&P, Vickers, company reports)

52-Wk Range	**$107.73– 63.01**	S&P Oper. EPS 2007**E**	7.53	Market Capitalization(B)	**$33.646**	Beta	0.20
Trailing 12-Month EPS	**$6.75**	S&P Oper. EPS 2008**E**	9.84	Yield (%)	0.59	S&P 3-Yr. Proj. EPS CAGR(%)	15.80
Trailing 12-Month P/E	**15.1**	P/E on S&P Oper. EPS 2007**E**	13.5	Dividend Rate/Share	$0.60	S&P Credit Rating	A-
$10K Invested 5 Yrs Ago	**$42,029**	Common Shares Outstg. (M)	331.2	Institutional Ownership (%)	86		

Price Performance

- 30-Week Mov. Avg. ···· 10-Week Mov. Avg. –– **GAAP Earnings vs. Previous Year** Volume Above Avg. STARS
- 12-Mo. Target Price — Relative Strength — ▲ Up ▼ Down ► No Change Below Avg. ★

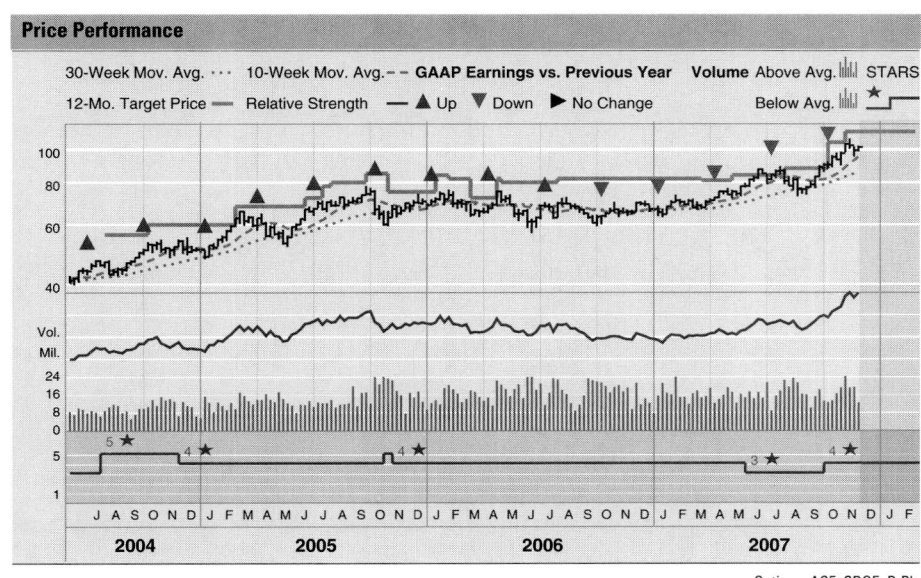

Options: ASE, CBOE, P, Ph

Analysis prepared by **Tina J. Vital** on November 06, 2007, when the stock traded at **$ 104.25**.

Highlights

➤ Third quarter oil and gas production rose 9.4%, but was below our expectations, reflecting planned turnarounds in the North Sea. With 108,000 boe/d of new production from six large projects coming on line over the next three years (2008-10), we project that APA's oil and gas volumes will increase over 11% in 2007 and over 6% in 2008. APA believes it can generate double-digit production growth for the next decade.

➤ The company plans to drill nine wells in Canada this winter at its British Columbia oil shale play. The government of Alberta hiked oil and gas royalties on October 25 (oil sands by 57%-66%, conventional oil by about 5%, and natural gas by about 2%); we believe APA's capital spending in this region could rise as a result.

➤ We project that after-tax operating earnings will decline by 1.1% in 2007, before rising around 30% in 2008 on improved pricing amid continued solid production growth.

Investment Rationale/Risk

➤ We believe APA will continue to achieve consistent growth through internal investment and external acquisitions. While acquisitions had been the primary source of reserve growth for the company, we believe APA will derive significant future growth from its development and exploitation of mature assets and exploration for new resources. With several exploration discoveries entering the development stage, driving near-term growth, we like APA, given its oil leverage (about half of its 2007 production is oil, which generated about 66% of revenues in the 2007 third quarter), strong organic growth projected through 2011, and attractive production plays in the U.S., Australia, Canada and Egypt.

➤ Risks to our recommendation and target price include changes to economic, industrial and operating conditions, such as difficulty in replacing reserves and geopolitical risk.

➤ A blend of our discounted cash flow (WACC of 5.2% and terminal growth of 3%) and relative valuations lead to our 12-month target price of $113, which represents an expected enterprise value of 4.6X our 2008 EBITDA estimate, a discount to peers.

Qualitative Risk Assessment

LOW	MEDIUM	HIGH

Our risk assessment for APA reflects our view of its position as a super-large exploration and production company diversified across major producing regions, focused on exploiting North American reserves and growing capital internationally. This is offset by moderate financial risk as the company uses its balance sheet to fund what we consider its aggressive acquisition strategy.

Quantitative Evaluations

S&P Quality Ranking   B+

D	C	B-	B	B+	A-	A	A+

Relative Strength Rank   **STRONG**

94

LOWEST = 1   HIGHEST = 99

Revenue/Earnings Data

Revenue (Million $)

	1Q	2Q	3Q	4Q	Year
2007	1,997	2,468	2,499	--	--
2006	1,999	2,062	2,261	1,967	8,289
2005	1,662	1,759	2,061	2,102	7,584
2004	1,150	1,241	1,407	1,535	5,333
2003	966.6	1,054	1,105	1,065	4,190
2002	528.0	656.3	645.2	730.4	2,560

Earnings Per Share ($)

2007	1.47	1.89	1.83	E2.34	E7.53
2006	1.97	2.17	1.94	1.56	7.64
2005	1.67	1.76	2.05	2.35	7.84
2004	1.05	1.16	1.30	1.53	5.04
2003	0.97	0.75	0.85	0.80	3.35
2002	0.26	0.48	0.48	0.59	1.80

Fiscal year ended Dec. 31. Next earnings report expected: Early February. EPS Estimates based on S&P Operating Earnings; historical GAAP earnings are as reported.

Dividend Data (Dates: mm/dd Payment Date: mm/dd/yy)

Amount ($)	Date Decl.	Ex-Div. Date	Stk. of Record	Payment Date
0.150	12/29	01/18	01/22	02/22/07
0.150	02/14	04/19	04/23	05/22/07
0.150	05/16	07/19	07/23	08/22/07
0.150	10/05	10/18	10/22	11/23/07

Dividends have been paid since 1965. Source: Company reports.

Apache Corp

Business Summary November 06, 2007

CORPORATE OVERVIEW. A large independent exploration and production (E&P) company, Apache Corp. (APA) explores for, develops and produces natural gas, crude oil and natural gas liquids (NGLs).

APA's strategy is built on a portfolio of assets that provide opportunities to grow through grassroots drilling and acquisition activities. As of year-end 2006, the company operations were focused in six core regions: the U.S., Canada, Egypt, the U.K. sector of the North Sea, Australia, and the newest core region, Argentina. In North America, interests were focused in the Gulf of Mexico, the Gulf Coast, East Texas, the Permian Basin, the Anadarko Basin, and the Western Sedimentary Basin of Canada.

APA's oil and gas production rose 10% in 2006, to 182.9 million barrels of oil

equivalent per day (boe), with the U.S. accounting for 37%, Canada 18%, Egypt 19%, Australia 9%, the U.K. 12%, Argentina 5%, and China less than 1%). We estimate that proved oil and gas reserves rose 9.2% in 2006, to 2,313.2 million boe (U.S. 41%, Canada 25%, Egypt 12%, Australia 9%, North Sea 9%, Argentina 5%), representing a reserve life of 12.6 years. Using data from John S. Herold, we estimate APA's three-year (2004-2006) organic reserve replacement at 233%, and its three-year finding and development costs at $12.90 per boe.

Company Financials Fiscal Year Ended Dec. 31

Per Share Data ($)	2006	2005	2004	2003	2002	2001	2000	1999	1998	1997
Tangible Book Value	39.30	31.06	24.18	19.25	15.33	14.69	12.07	8.97	7.54	8.02
Cash Flow	13.19	12.22	8.81	6.67	4.55	5.30	4.46	2.51	2.20	2.37
Earnings	7.64	7.84	5.04	3.35	1.80	2.37	2.48	0.74	-0.58	0.72
S&P Core Earnings	7.30	7.60	5.19	3.29	1.73	2.28	NA	NA	NA	NA
Dividends	0.60	0.34	0.32	0.21	0.19	0.12	0.09	0.12	0.12	0.12
Payout Ratio	8%	4%	6%	6%	11%	5%	4%	16%	NM	17%
Prices:High	76.25	78.15	55.16	41.68	28.88	31.55	32.12	21.62	16.77	19.51
Prices:Low	56.50	47.45	36.79	26.26	21.12	16.56	13.91	7.63	9.12	13.04
P/E Ratio:High	10	10	11	12	16	13	13	29	NM	27
P/E Ratio:Low	7	6	7	8	12	7	6	10	NM	18

Income Statement Analysis (Million $)	2006	2005	2004	2003	2002	2001	2000	1999	1998	1997
Revenue	8,289	7,584	5,333	4,190	2,560	2,777	2,284	1,300	876	1,176
Operating Income	5,753	5,792	4,119	3,241	1,048	2,146	1,310	870	509	712
Depreciation, Depletion and Amortization	1,816	1,416	1,222	1,073	844	821	584	443	630	388
Interest Expense	158	122	120	127	133	132	109	84.6	70.4	68.7
Pretax Income	4,010	4,206	2,663	1,922	899	1,199	1,204	345	-188	259
Effective Tax Rate	36.3%	37.6%	37.3%	43.0%	38.3%	39.7%	40.1%	41.7%	NM	40.1%
Net Income	2,552	2,624	1,670	1,095	554	723	721	201	-129	155
S&P Core Earnings	2,434	2,539	1,713	1,069	524	681	NA	NA	NA	NA

Balance Sheet & Other Financial Data (Million $)	2006	2005	2004	2003	2002	2001	2000	1999	1998	1997
Cash	141	229	111	33.5	51.9	35.6	37.2	13.2	14.5	9.69
Current Assets	2,490	2,162	1,349	899	767	698	630	343	227	348
Total Assets	24,308	19,272	15,502	12,416	9,460	8,934	7,482	5,503	3,996	4,139
Current Liabilities	3,812	2,187	1,283	820	532	522	553	337	306	344
Long Term Debt	2,020	2,192	2,588	2,327	2,159	2,244	2,193	1,880	1,343	150
Common Equity	13,093	10,443	8,106	6,434	4,826	4,112	3,448	2,361	1,703	1,729
Total Capital	18,830	12,733	10,793	8,860	7,083	7,655	5,948	4,549	3,416	3,586
Capital Expenditures	3,892	3,716	2,456	1,595	1,037	1,525	1,011	591	700	732
Cash Flow	4,363	4,034	2,887	2,163	1,387	1,525	1,284	629	499	543
Current Ratio	0.7	1.0	1.1	1.1	1.4	1.3	1.1	1.0	0.7	1.0
% Long Term Debt of Capitalization	13.3	17.2	24.0	26.3	30.5	29.3	36.9	41.3	39.3	41.9
% Return on Assets	11.7	15.1	12.0	10.0	6.0	8.8	11.1	4.2	NM	4.1
% Return on Equity	21.6	28.2	22.9	19.4	12.2	18.6	24.1	9.2	NM	9.5

Data as orig reptd.; bef. results of disc opers/spec. items. Per share data adj. for stk. divs.; EPS diluted. E-Estimated. NA-Not Available. NM-Not Meaningful. NR-Not Ranked. UR-Under Review.

Office: 2000 Post Oak Blvd Ste 100, Houston, TX 77056-4400.
Telephone: 713-296-6000.
Website: http://www.apachecorp.com
Chrmn: R. Plank

Pres, CEO & COO: G.S. Farris
EVP & CFO: R.B. Plank
SVP & General Counsel: A. Lannie
VP & Treas: M.W. Dundrea

Investor Contact: R.J. Dye (713-296-6662)
Board Members: F. M. Bohen, G. S. Farris, R. M. Ferlic, E. C. Fiedorek, A. D. Frazier, Jr., P. A. Graham, J. A. Kocur, G. D. Lawrence, F. H. Merelli, R. D. Patton, C. J. Pitman, R. Plank, J. A. Precourt

Founded: 1954
Domicile: Delaware
Employees: 3,150

Apartment Investment and Management Co

STANDARD &POOR'S

S&P Recommendation **HOLD** ★★★☆☆	Price $38.53 (as of Nov 23, 2007)	12-Mo. Target Price $46.00	Investment Style Large-Cap Value

GICS Sector Financials
Sub-Industry Residential REITS

Summary This real estate investment trust is one of the largest U.S. owners and managers of multifamily apartment properties.

Key Stock Statistics (Source S&P, Vickers, company reports)

52-Wk Range	**$65.79– 36.17**	S&P FFO/Sh. 2007**E**	**3.40**	Market Capitalization(B)	**$3.727**
Trailing 12-Month FFO/Share	**NA**	S&P FFO/Sh. 2008**E**	**3.55**	Yield (%)	**6.23**
Trailing 12-Month P/FFO	**NA**	P/FFO on S&P FFO/Sh. 2007**E**	**11.3**	Dividend Rate/Share	**$2.40**
$10K Invested 5 Yrs Ago	**$13,857**	Common Shares Outstg. (M)	**96.7**	Institutional Ownership (%)	**NM**

Beta	**0.79**
S&P 3-Yr. FFO/Sh. Proj. CAGR(%)	**6.00**
S&P Credit Rating	**BB+**

Price Performance

30-Week Mov. Avg. ···· 10-Week Mov. Avg.– – **GAAP Earnings vs. Previous Year** Volume Above Avg. STARS
12-Mo. Target Price — Relative Strength — ▲ Up ▼ Down ► No Change Below Avg.

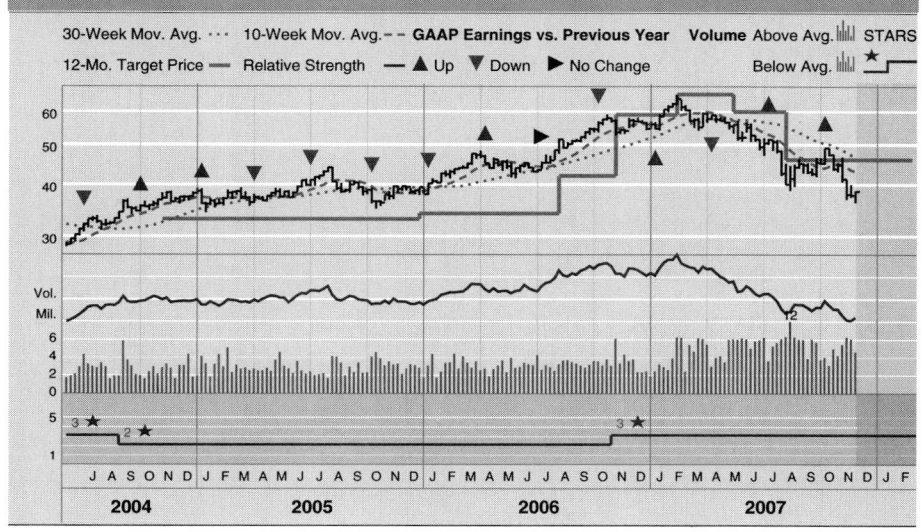

Options: CBOE, P, Ph

Analysis prepared by **Royal F. Shepard, CFA** on November 07, 2007, when the stock traded at **$ 37.80**.

Highlights

➤ We think rent growth for AIV's diversified portfolio, oriented largely toward middle income renters, is slowing along with many residential peers. For 2008, we forecast same-property revenues will increase about 3%, down from about 4% in 2007. The trust's Florida market, about 13% of segment earnings, is of particular concern to us as condominiums come back on the market as rental units. AIV also holds significant positions in what we view as less attractive mid-continent markets, such as Chicago and Indianapolis.

➤ AIV is sacrificing some near-term earnings growth, in our opinion, to re-develop existing properties. We expect total investment of about $300 million in 2007, increasing to $350 million in 2008. Dilution from portfolio re-balancing, including asset sales, is also affecting reported EPS. Our 2008 EPS forecast is a loss of $1.40, wider than the $1.18 loss we see in 2007.

➤ We project 2008 FFO of $3.55, up from the $3.40 we see in 2007. AIV's 2007 cash flow, after capital expenditures, will, we think, modestly cover the $2.40 annual dividend. Based on our current projections, we think AIV will provide a small increase in the dividend payout during 2008.

Investment Rationale/Risk

➤ AIV holds a large and diversified portfolio of conventional and affordable residential properties, in our view. In 2006, improved industry fundamentals and an active redevelopment program assisted the trust in its ongoing effort to increase average unit rent. We think moderating economic growth and greater supply have made 2007 more difficult, and we expect slowing revenue gains through 2008. Redevelopment efforts, though, should eventually add to net asset value, in our opinion. In view of our forecast of positive dividend coverage and a possible small hike in the payout, we would hold the shares.

➤ Risks to our recommendation and target price include the possibility of slower than expected employment growth limiting the ability to raise rents, and lower interest rates, which could increase the rate of home ownership.

➤ Our 12-month target price of $46 is based on a multiple of about 13X our 2008 FFO estimate, a discount to peers based on AIV's below average financial position. Our dividend discount model uses a 9.6% discount rate and a perpetual growth rate of 3.0%, and arrives at a value of $48.

Qualitative Risk Assessment

LOW	MEDIUM	HIGH

Our risk assessment of AIV reflects its large, diversified operations and low stock volatility, offset by our view of a recent weak operating performance and only modest coverage of the current common dividend.

Quantitative Evaluations

S&P Quality Ranking **B-**

D	C	B-	B	B+	A-	A	A+

Relative Strength Rank **MODERATE**

31

LOWEST = 1   HIGHEST = 99

Revenue/FFO Data

Revenue (Million $)

	1Q	2Q	3Q	4Q	Year
2007	430.8	438.3	431.2	--	--
2006	408.5	420.0	423.9	438.6	1,691
2005	361.6	372.3	386.8	400.9	1,522
2004	376.4	380.2	334.1	384.4	1,469
2003	397.5	378.4	377.4	381.9	1,516
2002	340.9	373.4	380.4	411.5	1,506

FFO Per Share ($)

2007	0.74	0.88	0.83	E0.94	E3.40
2006	0.68	0.73	0.74	0.91	3.07
2005	0.63	0.67	0.58	0.60	2.48
2004	0.67	0.63	0.78	0.72	2.79
2003	0.90	0.86	0.80	0.72	3.23
2002	1.30	1.20	1.09	1.05	4.64

Fiscal year ended Dec. 31. Next earnings report expected: Early February. FFO Estimates based on S&P Funds From Operations Est..

Dividend Data (Dates: mm/dd Payment Date: mm/dd/yy)

Amount ($)	Date Decl.	Ex-Div. Date	Stk. of Record	Payment Date
0.600	12/20	12/27	12/31	01/31/07
0.600	05/02	05/16	05/18	05/31/07
0.600	08/01	08/15	08/17	08/31/07
0.600	10/30	11/14	11/16	11/30/07

Dividends have been paid since 1994. Source: Company reports.

Apartment Investment and Management Co

STANDARD &POOR'S

Business Summary November 07, 2007

CORPORATE OVERVIEW. Apartment Investment and Management Co. is one of the largest U.S. multifamily residential REITs in terms of units. At September 30, 2007, it owned, held an equity interest in, or managed a geographically diversified portfolio of 1,194 properties, including about 206,217 apartment units, located in 47 states, the District of Columbia and Puerto Rico.

The trust conducts substantially all its business, and owns all its assets, through AIMCO Properties, L.P., of which AIV owns approximately a 90% interest. AIV operates in two segments: the ownership, operation and management of apartment properties; and the management of apartment properties for third parties and affiliates.

MARKET PROFILE. The U.S. housing market is highly fragmented, and is characterized broadly by two types of housing units -- multifamily and single-family. At the end of 2005, the U.S. Census Bureau estimated that there were 123.93 million housing units in the country, an increase of 1.4% from 2004. Partially due to the high fragmentation since residents have the option of either being owners or tenants (renters), the housing market can be highly competitive. Main demand drivers for apartments are household formation and em-

ployment growth. We expect 1.3 million new households to be formed in 2007, lower than the estimated 1.5 million in 2006. Supply is created by new housing unit construction, which could consist of single-family homes, or multifamily apartment buildings or condominiums. We forecast 1.36 million total housing unit starts in 2007, down about 25% from 2006. Multifamily starts are anticipated to fall somewhat less, declining approximately 15%.

With apartment tenants on relatively short leases compared to those of commercial and industrial properties, apartment REITs are generally more sensitive to changes in market conditions than REITs in other property categories. Results could be hurt by new construction that adds new space in excess of actual demand. Trends in home price affordability also affect both rent levels and the level of new construction, since the relative price attractiveness of owning versus renting is an important factor in consumer decision making.

Company Financials Fiscal Year Ended Dec. 31

Per Share Data ($)	2006	2005	2004	2003	2002	2001	2000	1999	1998	1997
Tangible Book Value	NA	NA	NA	NA	NA	18.90	23.33	24.27	20.26	19.02
Earnings	NA	NA	NA	NA	NA	0.23	0.52	0.38	0.80	1.08
S&P Core Earnings	-1.29	-1.25	-0.39	-0.32	0.89	0.19	NA	NA	NA	NA
Dividends	NA	NA	NA	NA	NA	3.12	2.80	2.50	2.25	1.85
Payout Ratio	NM	NM	NM	NM	NM	NM	NM	NM	NM	171%
Prices:High	59.17	44.14	39.25	42.05	51.46	50.13	50.06	44.13	41.00	38.00
Prices:Low	37.76	34.17	26.45	33.00	33.90	39.25	36.31	34.06	30.00	25.50
P/E Ratio:High	NM	NM	NM	NM	55	NM	96	NM	51	35
P/E Ratio:Low	NM	NM	NM	NM	36	NM	70	NM	37	24

Income Statement Analysis (Million $)										
Rental Income	1,630	1,460	1,402	1,446	1,292	1,298	1,051	534	377	193
Mortgage Income	Nil	Nil	Nil	Nil	Nil	Nil	Nil	43.5	Nil	Nil
Total Income	1,691	1,522	1,469	1,516	1,506	1,464	1,101	577	377	193
General Expenses	874	816	768	729	664	652	485	406	190	88.2
Interest Expense	408	368	367	373	340	316	270	140	89.4	51.4
Provision for Losses	Nil	Nil	Nil	Nil	Nil	Nil	Nil	Nil	Nil	Nil
Depreciation	471	412	369	328	289	364	330	151	93.4	37.7
Net Income	-42.7	-27.9	55.7	70.7	175	107	99.2	83.7	64.5	28.9
S&P Core Earnings	-124	-117	-35.5	-29.2	77.1	13.8	NA	NA	NA	NA

Balance Sheet & Other Financial Data (Million $)										
Cash	230	330	293	98.0	97.0	820	1,068	1,123	127	37.1
Total Assets	10,290	10,017	10,072	10,113	10,317	8,323	7,700	5,685	4,268	2,101
Real Estate Investment	11,982	10,990	10,800	10,601	10,227	8,416	7,012	4,509	2,803	1,657
Loss Reserve	Nil	Nil	Nil	Nil	Nil	Nil	Nil	Nil	Nil	Nil
Net Investment	9,081	8,752	8,785	8,753	8,616	6,796	6,099	4,092	2,574	1,504
Short Term Debt	Nil	Nil	Nil	Nil	Nil	214	329	630	460	53.0
Capitalization:Debt	6,873	6,284	5,734	6,198	5,529	4,670	4,031	2,525	1,350	755
Capitalization:Equity	1,516	1,706	1,967	2,005	2,218	1,592	1,664	1,622	1,110	910
Capitalization:Total	9,165	9,436	9,246	9,580	9,180	7,904	7,037	5,181	2,795	1,948
% Earnings & Depreciation/Assets	4.2	3.8	4.2	3.9	5.0	5.9	1.5	4.7	4.7	4.6
Price Times Book Value:High	4.0	2.5	1.9	2.0	2.3	2.7	2.1	1.8	2.0	2.0
Price Times Book Value:Low	2.5	1.9	1.3	1.6	1.5	2.1	1.6	1.4	1.5	1.3

Data as orig reptd.; bef. results of disc opers/spec. items. Per share data adj. for stk. divs.; EPS diluted. E-Estimated. NA-Not Available. NM-Not Meaningful. NR-Not Ranked. UR-Under Review.

Office: 4582 S Ulster St Pkwy Ste 1100, Denver, CO 80237-2662.
Telephone: 303-757-8101.
Email: investor@aimco.com
Website: http://www.aimco.com

Chrmn, Pres & CEO: T. Considine
EVP & CFO: T.M. Herzog
EVP & Treas: P.K. Fielding
EVP, Secy & General Counsel: M. Cortez

SVP & Chief Acctg Officer: S.W. Fordham
Investor Contact: J. Martin (303-691-4440)
Trustees: J. N. Bailey, T. Considine, R. S. Ellwood, T. L. Keltner, J. L. Martin, R. A. Miller, T. L. Rhodes, M. A. Stein

Founded: 1994
Domicile: Maryland
Employees: 6,000

The McGraw-Hill Companies

Apollo Group Inc

STANDARD &POOR'S

S&P Recommendation BUY ★★★★☆	**Price** $71.10 (as of Nov 23, 2007)	**12-Mo. Target Price** $88.00	**Investment Style** Large-Cap Growth

GICS Sector Consumer Discretionary
Sub-Industry Education Services

Summary This leading provider of higher education programs for working adults offers educational programs and services at a total of some 260 campuses and learning centers.

Key Stock Statistics (Source S&P, Vickers, company reports)

52-Wk Range	$80.75– 35.85	S&P Oper. EPS 2008**E**	2.85	Market Capitalization(B)	$12.280	Beta	-0.01
Trailing 12-Month EPS	$2.35	S&P Oper. EPS 2009**E**	3.25	Yield (%)	Nil	S&P 3-Yr. Proj. EPS CAGR(%)	15.00
Trailing 12-Month P/E	30.3	P/E on S&P Oper. EPS 2008**E**	24.9	Dividend Rate/Share	Nil	S&P Credit Rating	NA
$10K Invested 5 Yrs Ago	$16,233	Common Shares Outstg. (M)	173.3	Institutional Ownership (%)	83		

Price Performance

30-Week Mov. Avg. · · · 10-Week Mov. Avg. – – **GAAP Earnings vs. Previous Year** **Volume** Above Avg. STARS
12-Mo. Target Price — Relative Strength — ▲ Up ▼ Down ▶ No Change Below Avg. ★

Options: ASE, CBOE, P, Ph

Analysis prepared by **Michael W. Jaffe** on November 19, 2007, when the stock traded at **$ 73.47**.

Highlights

➤ We see a 10% revenue gain in FY 08 (Aug.), on our outlook for greater student counts, particularly in associate degree programs at Axia. We also see revenues being lifted by the 10% price hike implemented in APOL's associate degree programs in May 2007, as well as certain select price increases that we expect in other programs. We foresee these factors being partly offset by our belief that associate degree studies, which have lower tuition rates than more advanced degrees at Apollo, will account for a larger proportion of APOL's program mix.

➤ We expect somewhat wider net margins in FY 08. We see profits being aided by the larger student base that we forecast, and some likely benefits from APOL's recent initiatives, including efforts to raise advertising efficiency and to improve productivity among the enrollment staff. We look for these factors to be partly offset by the shift in the student mix that we see toward associate degree seekers, and a likely ongoing high level of advertising spending.

➤ Our positive growth outlook for APOL's student base partly stems from what we view as strong gains in new students throughout FY 07.

Investment Rationale/Risk

➤ After enrollment growth at Apollo decelerated sharply for a two-year period, it has revived since FY 06's fourth quarter. In addition, after going through a period of considerable uncertainty following the discovery of stock option backdating in late 2006, APOL completed its required restatement of results in May 2007 (for the period from 1994 through 2006), and can now focus on actions to rejuvenate its business. Based on these factors and our valuation model, we find the shares undervalued.

➤ Risks to our recommendation and target price include a resumption of the major downturn in enrollment growth, and an inability to improve margins through recent initiatives.

➤ APOL traded recently at about 26X our calendar 2008 EPS forecast of $2.93, or the low end of its historical range prior to its period of operating problems. Given our positive view of the early results of APOL's actions to place greater focus on its Axia associates degree programs, and its steps to improve student retention and advertising efficiency, we think a higher multiple is merited. Applying a multiple of 30X to our calendar 2008 forecast, we arrive at our 12-month target price of $88.

Qualitative Risk Assessment

LOW	MEDIUM	HIGH

Our risk assessment reflects a less vital for-profit education market, APOL's current transformation of its business model and recent executive changeover. In the corporate governance area, we have a negative view of the near 100% voting control held by insiders through separate voting shares. We believe these factors are offset by what we view as APOL's consistently solid levels of cash flow and a healthy balance sheet.

Quantitative Evaluations

S&P Quality Ranking B+

D	C	B-	B	B+	A-	A	A+

Relative Strength Rank STRONG

90

LOWEST = 1 HIGHEST = 99

Revenue/Earnings Data

Revenue (Million $)

	1Q	2Q	3Q	4Q	Year
2007	668.3	608.7	733.4	713.9	--
2006	628.9	569.6	653.6	624.2	2,478
2005	534.9	505.7	619.0	591.8	2,251
2004	411.8	396.9	497.0	492.8	1,798
2003	308.9	295.2	364.2	371.3	1,340
2002	228.2	222.6	276.4	282.3	1,009

Earnings Per Share ($)

2007	0.66	0.35	0.75	0.60	2.35
2006	0.73	0.46	0.77	0.54	2.35
2005	0.58	0.47	0.77	0.58	2.39
2004	0.44	0.35	0.56	-0.59	0.77
2003	0.30	0.24	0.39	0.37	1.30
2002	0.18	0.15	0.27	0.26	0.87

Fiscal year ended Aug. 31. Next earnings report expected: Early February. EPS Estimates based on S&P Operating Earnings; historical GAAP earnings are as reported.

Dividend Data

No cash dividends have been paid.

Apollo Group Inc

STANDARD
&POOR'S

Business Summary November 19, 2007

CORPORATE OVERVIEW. Historically, Apollo Group has derived most of its revenues through the provision of higher education programs for working adults. It has several school units, but the large majority of its students have taken education programs at its University of Phoenix (UOP) unit. UOP offers its education programs at campuses, as well as through online programs. They consist mostly of associates, bachelors and masters degree programs in business, education, information technology, criminal justice and nursing. As of August 31, 2007, APOL offered programs and services at 102 campuses and 157 learning centers in 40 states, the District of Columbia, Puerto Rico, Canada, the Netherlands and Mexico. Enrollment at UOP (including the Axia associates degree program, which became part of UOP in mid-calendar 2006) totaled 313,700 at August 31, 2007, up 11% from 282,300 at year-end FY 06 (Aug.) The company no longer gives breakdowns of students at campuses versus those in online programs. However, online started to account for a slight majority of APOL's student base in FY 05's third quarter, and has since accounted for most of its enrollment growth.

CORPORATE STRATEGY. The level of Apollo's enrollment growth fell from 27.7% in FY 04's fourth quarter (under the old definition of enrollments), to 3.3% in FY 06's third quarter (under the new definition; it now reports only UOP and Axia), with sequential growth levels declining in all but one quarter. How-

ever, growth has since revived, and stood at 15.4% in the fourth quarter of FY 07; after moving as high as 25.3% in the first. We attribute the initial downturn to changing demographic trends, greater competition, more regulatory scrutiny and the law of big numbers. Until very recently, APOL focused almost entirely on students who were older than the traditional 18-to-22 year-old college student, particularly baby boomers. Yet, with the youngest baby boomers now over the age of 40, APOL has started to seek students in other demographic categories. As a result, it began to place much more concentration on its Axia College program, which offers associate degrees and targets younger students. We believe early results of its shift in focus have been very encouraging.

In October 2007, the company formed a $1 billion joint venture with the Carlyle Group, a private equity firm, to make a range of investments in the international education services sector. APOL committed up to $801 million, and will own 80.1% of the venture. We view this as an important step for APOL in preparing to expand its global footprint.

Company Financials Fiscal Year Ended Aug. 31

Per Share Data ($)	2007	2006	2005	2004	2003	2002	2001	2000	1999	1998
Tangible Book Value	NA	3.40	3.73	4.89	5.23	3.60	2.47	1.39	1.10	0.91
Cash Flow	NA	2.74	2.68	1.79	1.62	1.12	0.81	0.57	0.45	0.33
Earnings	2.35	2.35	2.39	0.77	1.30	0.87	0.60	0.41	0.33	0.26
S&P Core Earnings	2.35	2.42	2.30	0.72	1.22	0.79	0.52	NA	NA	NA
Dividends	Nil	Nil	Nil	Nil	Nil	Nil	Nil	Nil	Nil	Nil
Payout Ratio	Nil	Nil	Nil	Nil	Nil	Nil	Nil	Nil	Nil	Nil
Prices:High	80.75	63.26	84.20	98.01	73.09	46.15	33.31	22.64	15.22	19.22
Prices:Low	39.02	33.33	57.40	62.55	40.72	28.13	19.33	8.17	7.81	9.11
P/E Ratio:High	34	25	35	NM	56	53	56	55	46	73
P/E Ratio:Low	17	13	24	NM	31	32	32	20	23	35

Income Statement Analysis (Million $)										
Revenue	NA	2,478	2,251	1,798	1,340	1,009	769	610	499	385
Operating Income	NA	738	767	481	428	293	194	141	113	82.9
Depreciation	NA	67.3	54.5	43.2	40.3	35.2	32.7	27.4	20.6	12.8
Interest Expense	NA	Nil	Nil	Nil	Nil	Nil	Nil	Nil	Nil	Nil
Pretax Income	NA	668	730	456	402	266	175	120	98.0	76.3
Effective Tax Rate	NA	37.9%	39.1%	39.1%	38.5%	39.4%	38.4%	40.8%	39.8%	39.3%
Net Income	NA	415	445	278	247	161	108	71.2	59.0	46.3
S&P Core Earnings	409	428	427	131	218	140	90.1	NA	NA	NA

Balance Sheet & Other Financial Data (Million $)										
Cash	NA	355	595	677	800	610	375	154	108	103
Current Assets	NA	803	835	855	950	730	487	247	198	174
Total Assets	NA	1,283	1,303	1,452	1,378	980	680	405	348	305
Current Liabilities	NA	596	518	465	335	264	182	131	109	95.6
Long Term Debt	NA	Nil	Nil	Nil	Nil	15.5	14.8	9.97	4.22	3.80
Common Equity	NA	604	707	957	1,027	699	482	261	231	200
Total Capital	NA	604	707	957	1,027	715	497	272	237	205
Capital Expenditures	NA	44.6	104	80.3	55.8	36.7	44.4	34.8	44.7	30.9
Cash Flow	NA	482	499	321	287	196	141	98.6	79.6	59.1
Current Ratio	NA	1.3	1.6	1.8	2.8	2.8	2.7	1.9	1.8	1.8
% Long Term Debt of Capitalization	NA	Nil	Nil	Nil	Nil	2.2	3.0	3.7	1.8	1.9
% Net Income of Revenue	NA	16.7	19.8	15.4	18.4	16.0	14.0	11.7	11.8	12.0
% Return on Assets	NA	32.4	31.8	19.6	20.9	19.4	19.9	18.9	18.1	18.5
% Return on Equity	NA	67.0	53.5	28.0	28.6	29.3	29.0	28.9	27.4	28.6

Data as orig reptd.; bef. results of disc opers/spec. items. Per share data adj. for stk. divs.; EPS diluted. E-Estimated. NA-Not Available. NM-Not Meaningful. NR-Not Ranked. UR-Under Review.

Office: 4615 East Elwood Street, Phoenix, AZ 85040-1958.
Telephone: 480-966-5394.
Website: http://www.apollogrp.edu
Exec Chrmn: J.G. Sperling

Pres: B.E. Mueller
EVP & CFO: J.L. D'Amico
SVP & Chief Acctg Officer: B.L. Swartz
SVP, Treas & Secy: P. Sperling

Investor Contact: J. Pasinski (800-990-2765)
Board Members: G. W. Cappelli, D. J. DeConcini, R. A. Herberger, Jr., A. Kirshner, B. E. Mueller, K. S. Redman, J. R. Reis, J. G. Sperling, P. V. Sperling, G. A. Zimmer

Founded: 1981
Domicile: Arizona
Employees: 36,418

The McGraw-Hill Companies

Apple Inc

STANDARD &POOR'S

S&P Recommendation **BUY** ★★★★☆	Price $171.54 (as of Nov 23, 2007)	12-Mo. Target Price $207.00	Investment Style Large-Cap Growth

GICS Sector Information Technology
Sub-Industry Computer Hardware

Summary This company is a leading provider of hardware and software, including the Macintosh (Mac) computer, the iPod digital media player, and the iPhone.

Key Stock Statistics (Source S&P, Vickers, company reports)

52-Wk Range	$192.68– 76.77	S&P Oper. EPS 2008**E**	4.70	Market Capitalization(B)	$150.190	Beta	1.33
Trailing 12-Month EPS	$3.93	S&P Oper. EPS 2009**E**	5.70	Yield (%)	Nil	S&P 3-Yr. Proj. EPS CAGR(%)	26.00
Trailing 12-Month P/E	43.7	P/E on S&P Oper. EPS 2008**E**	36.5	Dividend Rate/Share	Nil	S&P Credit Rating	NR
$10K Invested 5 Yrs Ago	$214,291	Common Shares Outstg. (M)	875.5	Institutional Ownership (%)	69		

Price Performance

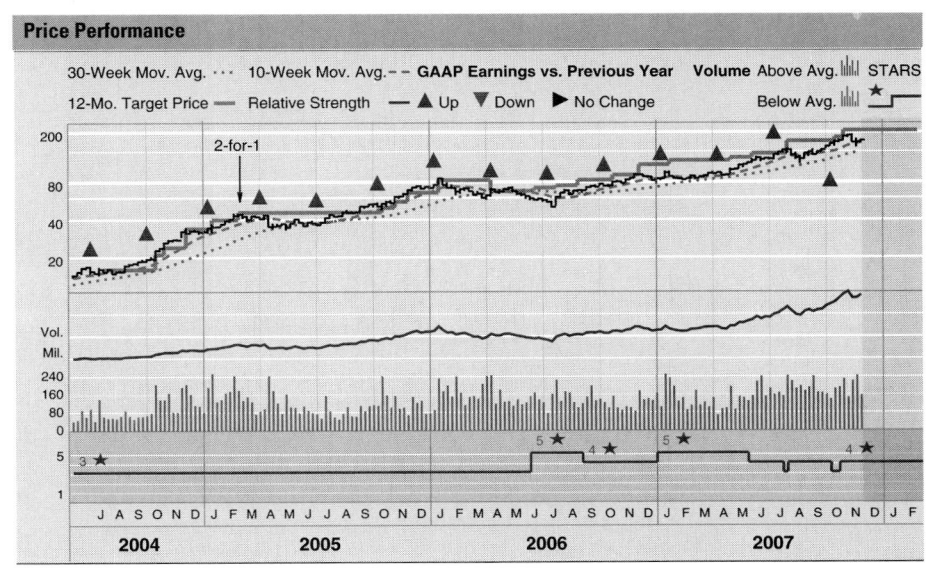

30-Week Mov. Avg. ··· 10-Week Mov. Avg. - - **GAAP Earnings vs. Previous Year** Volume Above Avg. ▨▨ STARS
12-Mo. Target Price — Relative Strength — ▲ Up ▼ Down ▶ No Change Below Avg. ▨▨ ★

2004 2005 2006 2007

Options: ASE, CBOE, P, Ph

Analysis prepared by **Thomas W. Smith, CFA** on October 23, 2007, when the stock traded at **$ 187.27**.

Highlights

➤ We project revenue growth of 33% for FY 08 (Sep.) and 24% for FY 09, driven by market share gains we project for desktop and note-book computers, and sustained digital-media leadership from iPod and iTunes. We also be-lieve that the iPhone, a new operating system (called Leopard), and new iPods will contribute more meaningfully in FY 08. Revenues for the sale of an iPhone are recognized ratably over the 24 months following the transaction.

➤ We believe that gross and operating margins will narrow in FY 08, reflecting expenses asso-ciated with new product launches, including the iPhone's introduction in several European countries, and a likely uptick in component costs. Higher volumes should partially offset the downward pressure on margins. We model a higher effective tax rate of 32% for FY 08, ver-sus 30.2% for FY 07.

➤ We expect results to be aided by what we con-sider a healthy balance sheet, consisting of $15.4 billion in net cash and investments as of September 2007, and amounting to roughly $17.17 per share. We see the potential for no-table share repurchases at some point in the future.

Investment Rationale/Risk

➤ We believe AAPL continues to benefit from its strategy of providing simple, superior and dif-ferentiated offerings. Its computer sales are outpacing the industry's, in our opinion, while also enjoying materially higher average selling prices. Moreover, we think the iPhone will be notably accretive to earnings, reflecting solid initial sales and considerable associated cus-tomer traffic.

➤ Risks to our recommendation and target price include possible delays in the introduction of anticipated major products, competitive threats to AAPL's digital media offerings, and the po-tential for the ongoing stock option backdating investigation implicating Steve Jobs.

➤ AAPL recently traded at a P/E of 47X its trailing EPS of $3.93 for FY 07, which is near the high end of a recent historical range for AAPL, re-flecting a period of strong growth based on new product introductions. We foresee EPS growth slowing over the next 12 months and employ a slightly lower target P/E of 44X, ap-plied to our FY 08 EPS estimate of $4.70 to arrive at our 12-month target price of $207.

Qualitative Risk Assessment

LOW	MEDIUM	HIGH

Our risk assessment reflects our view of a seemingly ever-evolving market for consumer-oriented technology products, potential challenges associated with the company's growing size and offerings, and the critical importance to the company of founder and CEO Steve Jobs.

Quantitative Evaluations

S&P Quality Ranking B

D	C	B-	B	B+	A-	A	A+

Relative Strength Rank STRONG

91

LOWEST = 1 HIGHEST = 99

Revenue/Earnings Data

Revenue (Million $)

	1Q	2Q	3Q	4Q	Year
2007	7,115	5,264	5,410	6,217	24,006
2006	5,749	4,359	4,370	4,837	19,315
2005	3,490	3,243	3,520	3,678	13,931
2004	2,006	1,909	2,014	2,350	8,279
2003	1,472	1,475	1,545	1,715	6,207
2002	1,375	1,495	1,429	1,443	5,742

Earnings Per Share ($)

	1Q	2Q	3Q	4Q	Year
2007	1.14	0.87	0.92	1.01	3.93
2006	0.65	0.47	0.54	0.62	2.27
2005	0.35	0.34	0.37	0.50	1.56
2004	0.09	0.06	0.08	0.13	0.36
2003	-0.01	0.02	0.03	0.06	0.10
2002	0.06	0.06	0.05	-0.07	0.09

Fiscal year ended Sep. 30. Next earnings report expected: Mid January. EPS Estimates based on S&P Operating Earnings; historical GAAP earnings are as reported.

Dividend Data

No cash dividends have been paid since 1996.

Apple Inc

STANDARD &POOR'S

Business Summary October 23, 2007

CORPORATE OVERVIEW. Apple Inc. may have a relatively small share of the worldwide market for computers (according to market research firm IDC), but in the rapidly growing digital media player market, it has dominated with the success of the iPod. We believe the iPod has contributed to greater demand for AAPL computers. In fact, AAPL's share of the U.S. computer market has risen from about 3% to roughly 5% in recent years.

In August 2006, as a result of an internal stock option investigation, AAPL announced it would likely need to restate its historical financial statements to record non-cash charges. In December 2006, AAPL confirmed that it was restating results for prior periods and recording non-cash charges totaling $84 million on an after-tax basis. While we view the news as disappointing, we believe it does not change AAPL's fundamental operating model. In April 2007, the SEC indicated it is not pursuing actions against AAPL or any of its current employees, including founder and CEO Steve Jobs.

COMPETITIVE LANDSCAPE. In our opinion, AAPL derives a competitive advantage from its focus on, and success with, innovation. We believe the iPod is a clear example of this strategy's success. AAPL entered the consumer de-

vice market with the iPod in 2001, and in FY 06 (Sep.), it accounted for 40% of total revenues. In mid-2007, AAPL introduced the iPhone, and it expects to sell at least 10 million units in 2008.

In addition, AAPL's computers are based on its own operating system, enabling an additional area upon which to innovate, in our view. AAPL's computers are based on the Mac OS (versus the ubiquitous Windows operating system from Microsoft). AAPL believes that the Mac OS embodies graphical sophistication and ease of use.

Similarly, AAPL differentiated the iPod from other digital media players by creating the iTunes digital music download service (launched in 2003, with primarily television video content added as of October 2005 and movies in September 2006).

Company Financials Fiscal Year Ended Sep. 30

Per Share Data ($)	2007	2006	2005	2004	2003	2002	2001	2000	1999	1998
Tangible Book Value	16.27	11.47	8.83	6.36	5.61	5.54	5.59	6.00	4.59	2.76
Cash Flow	4.29	2.52	1.77	0.55	0.50	0.25	0.09	1.21	0.99	0.63
Earnings	3.93	2.27	1.56	0.36	0.10	0.09	-0.06	1.09	0.90	0.52
S&P Core Earnings	3.93	2.27	1.47	0.22	-0.17	-0.19	-0.72	NA	NA	NA
Dividends	Nil	Nil	Nil	Nil	Nil	Nil	Nil	Nil	Nil	Nil
Payout Ratio	Nil	Nil	Nil	Nil	Nil	Nil	Nil	Nil	Nil	Nil
Prices:High	192.68	93.16	75.46	34.79	12.51	13.09	13.56	37.59	29.50	10.94
Prices:Low	81.90	50.16	31.30	10.59	6.36	6.68	7.22	6.81	8.00	3.38
P/E Ratio:High	49	41	48	98	NM	NM	NM	34	33	21
P/E Ratio:Low	21	22	20	30	NM	NM	NM	6	9	6

Income Statement Analysis (Million $)										
Revenue	24,006	19,315	13,931	8,279	6,207	5,742	5,363	7,983	6,134	5,941
Operating Income	4,726	2,645	1,829	499	138	164	-231	704	471	379
Depreciation	317	225	179	150	113	118	102	84.0	85.0	111
Interest Expense	Nil	Nil	Nil	3.00	8.00	11.0	16.0	21.0	47.0	62.0
Pretax Income	5,008	2,818	1,815	383	92.0	87.0	-52.0	1,092	676	329
Effective Tax Rate	30.2%	29.4%	26.4%	27.9%	26.1%	25.3%	NM	28.0%	11.1%	6.10%
Net Income	3,496	1,989	1,335	276	68.0	65.0	-37.0	786	601	309
S&P Core Earnings	3,496	1,989	1,259	164	-119	-137	-465	NA	NA	NA

Balance Sheet & Other Financial Data (Million $)										
Cash	9,352	6,392	3,491	2,969	3,396	2,252	2,310	1,191	1,326	1,481
Current Assets	21,956	14,509	10,300	7,055	5,887	5,388	5,143	5,427	4,285	3,698
Total Assets	25,347	17,205	11,551	8,050	6,815	6,298	6,021	6,803	5,161	4,289
Current Liabilities	9,299	6,471	3,484	2,680	2,357	1,658	1,518	1,933	1,549	1,520
Long Term Debt	Nil	Nil	Nil	Nil	Nil	316	317	300	300	954
Common Equity	14,532	9,984	7,466	5,076	4,223	4,095	3,920	4,031	2,954	1,492
Total Capital	15,151	10,365	7,466	5,076	4,223	4,640	4,503	4,870	3,612	2,769
Capital Expenditures	NA	657	260	176	164	174	735	107	47.0	46.0
Cash Flow	3,813	2,214	1,514	426	181	183	65.0	870	686	420
Current Ratio	2.4	2.2	3.0	2.6	2.5	3.2	3.4	2.8	2.8	2.4
% Long Term Debt of Capitalization	Nil	Nil	Nil	Nil	Nil	6.8	7.0	6.2	8.3	34.5
% Net Income of Revenue	14.6	10.3	9.6	3.3	1.1	1.1	NM	9.8	9.8	5.2
% Return on Assets	16.4	13.9	13.6	3.7	1.0	1.1	NM	13.1	12.7	7.3
% Return on Equity	28.5	22.8	21.3	5.9	1.6	1.6	NM	22.5	27.0	24.3

Data as orig reptd.; bef. results of disc opers/spec. items. Per share data adj. for stk. divs.; EPS diluted. E-Estimated. NA-Not Available. NM-Not Meaningful. NR-Not Ranked. UR-Under Review.

Office: 1 Infinite Loop, Cupertino, CA 95014.
Telephone: 408-996-1010.
Email: investor_relations@apple.com
Website: http://www.apple.com

CEO: S.P. Jobs
COO: T.D. Cook
Investor Contact: P. Oppenheimer (408-974-3123)
SVP & CFO: P. Oppenheimer

SVP, Secy & General Counsel: D. Cooperman
Board Members: W. V. Campbell, M. S. Drexler, A. Gore, Jr., S. P. Jobs, A. D. Levinson, E. Schmidt, J. B. York

Founded: 1977
Domicile: California
Employees: 23,700

The McGraw-Hill Companies

Applera Corp-Applied Biosystems Group

STANDARD &POOR'S

S&P Recommendation **BUY** ★★★★☆	Price $33.14 (as of Nov 23, 2007)	12-Mo. Target Price $40.00	Investment Style Large-Cap Growth

GICS Sector Health Care
Sub-Industry Life Sciences Tools & Services

Summary This company supplies instrument systems, reagents, software and related services for life science research applications.

Key Stock Statistics (Source S&P, Vickers, company reports)

52-Wk Range	$38.31–27.79	S&P Oper. EPS 2008**E**	1.58	Market Capitalization(B)	$6.077	Beta	1.29
Trailing 12-Month EPS	$1.58	S&P Oper. EPS 2009**E**	1.79	Yield (%)	0.51	S&P 3-Yr. Proj. EPS CAGR(%)	13.00
Trailing 12-Month P/E	21.0	P/E on S&P Oper. EPS 2008**E**	21.0	Dividend Rate/Share	$0.17	S&P Credit Rating	NA
$10K Invested 5 Yrs Ago	$15,148	Common Shares Outstg. (M)	183.4	Institutional Ownership (%)	86		

Price Performance

30-Week Mov. Avg. ··· 10-Week Mov. Avg. –– GAAP Earnings vs. Previous Year Volume Above Avg. ||||| STARS
12-Mo. Target Price — Relative Strength — ▲ Up ▼ Down ▶ No Change Below Avg. ||||| ★

Options: ASE, CBOE, P

Analysis prepared by **Jeffrey Loo, CFA** on October 29, 2007, when the stock traded at **$ 36.04**.

Highlights

➤ In August, the board of Applera Corporation retained Morgan Stanley to explore alternatives to its current tracking stock structure for ABI and Celera Group, including the possibility of creating two independently traded public companies. The board also doubled ABI's stock buyback program to $1.2 billion, representing about 20% of its common stock at current prices. Subsequently, ABI executed an accelerated stock buyback transaction with Morgan Stanley for 16 million shares or about 8.7% of its outstanding shares.

➤ We see sales increasing 7% in FY 08 (Jun.), to $2.25 billion, on mixed performances in ABI's five business units and contributions from recent acquisitions. We see low double digit growth in Mass Spectrometry and in Real-time PCR/Other Applied Genomics, aided by licensing agreements, and low single digit growth in DNA Sequencing, partly offset by declines in Core DNA & PCR and in Other product lines. We see gross margins improving 40 basis points and operating margins improving 70 basis points, as leverage is partially offset by increased R&D costs.

➤ Our FY 08 EPS estimate is $1.58.

Investment Rationale/Risk

➤ We view the potential corporate restructuring and increased stock buyback favorably. With a cash balance of $277.2 million as of September 30, 2007, our expectation of strong cash flow generation, and access to a credit facility, we believe ABI has sufficient funds for its buyback program. We view positively an improvement in sales, and we think ABI is well positioned to benefit from its years-long restructuring and product portfolio rebalancing. We believe ABI's focus on expanding consumable sales will aid margin expansion. However, we remain slightly cautious due to ABI's heavy dependence on academic clients that rely on government funding, as we continue to see pressure on government funding in the U.S. and Europe.

➤ Risks to our recommendation and target price include lower than expected sales, an inability to increase its commercial client base, and limited market acceptance of new products.

➤ Our 12-month target price of $40 is based on our DCF analysis (a WACC of 9.7% and terminal growth of 3%) and our P/E to growth (PEG) analysis, applying a 1.6X PEG ratio to our FY 08 EPS estimate, slightly above peers. We see ABI's stock buyback aiding EPS growth.

Qualitative Risk Assessment

LOW	MEDIUM	HIGH

Our risk assessment reflects ABI's diverse product portfolio and broad geographic client base, offset by its heavy dependence on academic clients that rely on government funding and the highly competitive industry in which it competes.

Quantitative Evaluations

S&P Quality Ranking B+

D	C	B-	B	B+	A-	A	A+

Relative Strength Rank MODERATE

63

LOWEST = 1   HIGHEST = 99

Revenue/Earnings Data

Revenue (Million $)

	1Q	2Q	3Q	4Q	Year
2008	501.2	--			--
2007	476.3	530.0	530.0	557.3	2,093
2006	415.5	481.9	490.7	523.1	1,911
2005	390.3	463.4	454.8	478.6	1,787
2004	382.7	458.4	439.6	460.4	1,741
2003	395.9	444.7	409.4	432.9	1,683

Earnings Per Share ($)

	1Q	2Q	3Q	4Q	Year
2008	0.32	E0.39	E0.42	E0.45	E1.58
2007	-0.32	0.39	0.39	0.42	0.90
2006	0.21	0.17	0.65	0.41	1.43
2005	0.18	0.37	0.28	0.35	1.19
2004	0.16	0.25	0.22	0.20	0.83
2003	0.16	0.14	0.19	0.46	0.95

Fiscal year ended Jun. 30. Next earnings report expected: Late January. EPS Estimates based on S&P Operating Earnings; historical GAAP earnings are as reported.

Dividend Data (Dates: mm/dd Payment Date: mm/dd/yy)

Amount ($)	Date Decl.	Ex-Div. Date	Stk. of Record	Payment Date
0.043	01/18	02/27	03/01	04/02/07
0.043	03/26	05/30	06/01	07/02/07
0.043	08/16	08/30	09/04	10/01/07
0.043	11/15	11/29	12/03	01/02/08

Dividends have been paid since 1971. Source: Company reports.

Please read the Required Disclosures and Analyst Certification on the last page of this report.

The McGraw-Hill Companies

Applera Corp-Applied Biosystems Group

STANDARD
&POOR'S

Business Summary October 29, 2007

Applera Corp.-Applied Biosystems Group was formed in 1999 via a reorganization of Applera Corp. that created Applied Biosystems Group (ABI) and Celera Genomics Group (CRA). ABI serves the life science and research industry by developing and manufacturing instrument-based systems, consumables and reagents, software, and related services. Its instruments and tools are used in genomics to analyze nucleic acids (DNA and RNA), small molecule analysis and development, and proteomics to make scientific discoveries and develop new pharmaceuticals, and to conduct standardized testing.

ABI has developed technologies and products to support applications in genomics research such as sequencing, genotyping, and gene expression studies. Customers in the genomics market use ABI's instrument-based systems for the analysis of nucleic acids for basic research, pharmaceutical and diagnostic discovery and development, biosecurity, food and environmental testing, analysis of infectious diseases, and human identification and forensic analysis.

In the field of proteomics, the company has developed products for the identification, characterization, and measurement of expression of proteins and peptides. Gene codes for proteins in biological organisms and proteins are the key biological molecules that function in all aspects of living things such as

growth, development and reproduction. The proteomics research market uses the company's products for the analysis of proteins and peptides for the discovery of drug targets, protein therapeutics and diagnostics.

Products such as mass spectrometers are used by researchers to analyze small molecules (generally smaller than peptides), including metabolites, other small biological molecules found naturally in the body such as hormones, and trace contaminants in food, beverages, or environmental applications.

ABI also develops and manufactures informatics software and services used to integrate and automate life sciences research, development, and manufacturing laboratories, with the goal of increasing efficiency and effectiveness. Users are typically involved in gene mapping, drug discovery, drug development, and drug manufacturing. The company also offers software products for laboratory information management systems, to facilitate sample tracking, data collection, data analysis, and data mining to assist researchers in transforming data into useful information.

Company Financials Fiscal Year Ended Jun. 30

Per Share Data ($)	2007	2006	2005	2004	2003	2002	2001	2000	1999	1998
Tangible Book Value	NA	6.40	7.68	6.36	6.63	5.38	NM	NM	NM	2.86
Cash Flow	NA	1.83	1.61	1.29	1.45	1.16	1.27	1.11	0.93	0.55
Earnings	0.90	1.43	1.19	0.83	0.95	0.78	0.96	0.86	0.72	0.28
S&P Core Earnings	0.89	1.46	0.36	0.30	0.31	0.34	0.32	NA	NA	NA
Dividends	0.17	0.17	0.17	0.17	0.17	0.17	0.17	0.17	0.17	0.17
Payout Ratio	19%	12%	14%	20%	18%	22%	18%	20%	24%	61%
Prices:High	37.67	39.49	28.17	24.44	24.00	39.28	94.25	160.00	62.94	25.17
Prices:Low	27.79	26.13	19.20	17.76	14.90	13.00	18.49	42.81	21.97	13.63
P/E Ratio:High	42	28	24	29	25	50	98	NM	87	90
P/E Ratio:Low	31	18	16	21	16	17	19	NM	31	49

Income Statement Analysis (Million $)										
Revenue	NA	1,911	1,787	1,741	1,683	1,604	1,619	1,388	1,222	1,531
Operating Income	NA	-388	357	330	324	318	347	270	234	220
Depreciation	NA	77.2	82.9	96.8	106	81.2	66.8	54.5	44.3	53.1
Interest Expense	NA	Nil	Nil	Nil	Nil	0.89	1.30	8.13	4.50	4.91
Pretax Income	NA	317	297	240	239	238	304	276	192	101
Effective Tax Rate	NA	13.3%	20.3%	28.2%	19.6%	29.1%	30.2%	32.5%	15.9%	38.4%
Net Income	NA	275	237	172	200	168	212	186	148	56.4
S&P Core Earnings	169	282	72.7	63.8	63.3	72.9	71.7	NA	NA	NA

Balance Sheet & Other Financial Data (Million $)										
Cash	NA	374	756	505	602	441	392	395	237	82.9
Current Assets	NA	1,013	1,391	1,110	1,232	1,072	1,014	998	918	796
Total Assets	NA	2,246	2,290	1,948	2,127	1,819	1,678	1,698	1,348	1,334
Current Liabilities	NA	573	547	518	541	522	508	603	644	508
Long Term Debt	NA	Nil	Nil	Nil	Nil	Nil	Nil	36.1	31.5	33.7
Common Equity	NA	1,477	1,523	1,244	1,388	1,125	1,041	934	534	564
Total Capital	NA	1,477	1,523	1,244	1,388	1,125	1,041	970	566	642
Capital Expenditures	NA	41.5	84.6	60.4	132	88.3	144	94.4	82.5	101
Cash Flow	NA	352	320	269	306	250	279	241	193	110
Current Ratio	NA	1.8	2.5	2.1	2.3	2.1	2.0	1.7	1.4	1.6
% Long Term Debt of Capitalization	NA	Nil	Nil	Nil	Nil	Nil	Nil	3.7	5.6	Nil
% Net Income of Revenue	NA	14.4	13.3	9.9	11.9	10.5	13.1	13.4	12.1	3.7
% Return on Assets	NA	12.1	11.2	8.5	10.1	9.6	12.6	12.2	12.0	4.6
% Return on Equity	NA	18.3	17.1	13.1	15.9	15.5	21.5	25.4	27.0	11.3

Data as orig reptd.; bef. results of disc opers/spec. items. Per share data adj. for stk. divs.; EPS diluted. E-Estimated. NA-Not Available. NM-Not Meaningful. NR-Not Ranked. UR-Under Review.

Office: 301 Merritt 7, Norwalk, CT 06856-5435.
Telephone: 203-840-2000.
Website: http://www.appliedbiosystems.com
Chrmn, Pres & CEO: T.L. White

VP & CSO: D. Gilbert
Investor Contact: P. Dworkin (650-554-2479)

Board Members: R. H. Ayers, J. Belingard, R. H. Hayes, A. J. Levine, W. H. Longfield, T. E. Martin, C. W. Slayman, O. R. Smith, J. R. Tobin, T. L. White

Founded: 1937
Domicile: Delaware
Employees: 5,000

The McGraw-Hill Companies

Applied Materials Inc

STANDARD &POOR'S

S&P Recommendation HOLD ★★★☆☆	Price $18.33 (as of Nov 23, 2007)	12-Mo. Target Price $21.00	Investment Style Large-Cap Blend

GICS Sector Information Technology
Sub-Industry Semiconductor Equipment

Summary This company is the world's largest manufacturer of wafer fabrication equipment for the semiconductor industry.

Key Stock Statistics (Source S&P, Vickers, company reports)

52-Wk Range	$23.00–17.35	S&P Oper. EPS 2008**E**	1.13	Market Capitalization(B)	$25.261
Trailing 12-Month EPS	$1.20	S&P Oper. EPS 2009**E**	**NA**	Yield (%)	1.31
Trailing 12-Month P/E	15.3	P/E on S&P Oper. EPS 2008**E**	16.2	Dividend Rate/Share	$0.24
$10K Invested 5 Yrs Ago	$11,179	Common Shares Outstg. (M)	1,378.1	Institutional Ownership (%)	83

Beta	2.03
S&P 3-Yr. Proj. EPS CAGR(%)	10.00
S&P Credit Rating	A-

Price Performance

30-Week Mov. Avg. ··· 10-Week Mov. Avg. -- **GAAP Earnings vs. Previous Year** Volume Above Avg. ▍▍▍ STARS

12-Mo. Target Price — Relative Strength — ▲ Up ▼ Down ▶ No Change   Below Avg. ▍▍▍ ★

Options: ASE, CBOE, P, Ph

Analysis prepared by **Angelo Zino** on November 15, 2007, when the stock traded at **$ 18.80.**

Highlights

➤ Following a 6% increase in FY 07 (Oct.), we project revenues will decline 7% in FY 08 as we expect demand for semiconductor equipment to decrease over the next several quarters. Although we think potential market share gains and the NAND memory end-market will continue to support sales, we believe that overcapacity and pricing pressure for DRAM may lead to reduced spending for equipment. We also remain cautious of sales from foundry customers, as we expect foundries to cut back on spending. We anticipate sales from AMAT's solar and flat panel display businesses to be its most significant growth drivers in FY 08.

➤ By our analysis, the annual gross margin in FY 08 should range between 45% and 47%, compared with 46.1% in FY 07. We expect margins to be challenged by lower average selling prices, weaker volume from DRAM customers, and an increase in spending related to the company's solar business expansion.

➤ We expect AMAT to continue using excess cash flow to aggressively repurchase shares, with an authorized buyback of $5 billion in place through March 2009. Following EPS of $1.20 in FY 07, we project EPS of $1.13 for FY 08.

Investment Rationale/Risk

➤ We believe the semiconductor equipment industry will experience some softness in the first half of calendar year 2008, followed by moderate growth in the second half of the year. However, considering our view of AMAT's diversified offerings, market share gains, and growth opportunities from new businesses, we think the company will fare better than most peers. Nevertheless, we are becoming increasingly concerned about near-term growth as DRAM chipmakers digest capacity, and as foundry production remains lower than our expectation. Given our risk and reward analysis, we see the stock as fairly valued.

➤ Risks to our recommendation and target price include a greater-than-expected slowdown in the global economy, which could weaken demand for chips and increase pricing pressure.

➤ Our 12-month target price of $21 is based on a blend of our relative price-to-earnings multiple and three-year historical average price-to-sales ratio. We derive a value of $21 via both methodologies, applying a peer average P/E multiple of 18.7X our FY 08 EPS forecast, and a P/S multiple of 3.0X, using our FY 08 sales per share estimate of $6.85.

Qualitative Risk Assessment

LOW	MEDIUM	HIGH

Our risk assessment reflects the historical cyclicality of the semiconductor equipment industry, the lack of visibility in the intermediate term, the dynamic nature of the change in semiconductor technology, and intense competition. This is offset by AMAT's market leadership, size, and what we consider its solid balance sheet.

Quantitative Evaluations

S&P Quality Ranking   **B**

D	C	B-	B	B+	A-	A	A+

Relative Strength Rank   **MODERATE**

44

LOWEST = 1   HIGHEST = 99

Revenue/Earnings Data

Revenue (Million $)

	1Q	2Q	3Q	4Q	Year
2007	2,277	2,530	2,561	2,367	9,735
2006	1,858	2,248	2,543	2,518	9,167
2005	1,781	1,861	1,632	1,718	6,992
2004	1,555	2,018	2,236	2,203	8,013
2003	1,054	1,107	1,095	1,221	4,477
2002	1,000	1,156	1,460	1,446	5,062

Earnings Per Share ($)

2007	0.29	0.29	0.34	0.30	1.20
2006	0.09	0.26	0.33	0.30	0.97
2005	0.17	0.18	0.23	0.15	0.73
2004	0.05	0.22	0.26	0.27	0.78
2003	-0.04	-0.04	-0.02	0.01	-0.09
2002	-0.03	0.03	0.07	0.09	0.16

Fiscal year ended Oct. 31. Next earnings report expected: Mid February. EPS Estimates based on S&P Operating Earnings; historical GAAP earnings are as reported.

Dividend Data (Dates: mm/dd Payment Date: mm/dd/yy)

Amount ($)	Date Decl.	Ex-Div. Date	Stk. of Record	Payment Date
0.050	12/14	02/13	02/15	03/08/07
0.060	03/14	05/15	05/17	06/07/07
0.060	06/19	08/14	08/16	09/06/07
0.060	09/12	11/13	11/15	12/06/07

Dividends have been paid since 2005. Source: Company reports.

The McGraw-Hill Companies

Applied Materials Inc

STANDARD &POOR'S

Business Summary November 15, 2007

CORPORATE OVERVIEW. AMAT leads the semiconductor capital equipment market, with FY 06 (Oct.) sales nearly twice those of its nearest competitor, Tokyo Electron. AMAT divides its business into four segments. The silicon segment, which accounted for 65% of FY 06 sales, is focused on developing and selling equipment for use in the front end of the semiconductor fabrication process. The Fab Solutions segment, which accounted for 24% of FY 06 sales, provides solutions to optimize and increase productivity at customers fabs (semiconductor fabrication facilities). The Display segment, which accounted for 10% of FY 06 sales, develops equipment for the fabrication of flat panel displays. The Adjacent Technology Segment, which is a new area for AMAT, accounted for less than 1% of sales in FY 06, and involves products targeting the solar PV cell market and energy efficient glass. We expect rapid growth in the solar business, following AMAT's acquisition of Applied Films in July 2006.

AMAT's equipment in the silicon segment address most of the primary steps in chip fabrication. AMAT's deposition products are used to plant thin films of conductive or insulating material to form an integrated circuit (IC). AMAT deposition equipment use various technologies, including ALD (atomic layer de-

position), CVD (chemical vapor deposition), PVD (physical vapor deposition), and ECP (Electrochemical plating). AMAT's etch products selectively remove thin films of three different types of materials: metal, silicon, and dielectric thin films. Chemical-mechanical polishing products are used to smooth the surface of a wafer following deposition in order to facilitate subsequent processing steps. Metrology and inspection tools are used to measure critical parameters and find and classify defects.

Sales by geographic region in FY 06 were as follows: Taiwan 23%, North America 19%, Korea 18%, Japan 16%, Asia-Pacific 13%, and Europe 11%. While 70% of sales were derived from Asia, the output of Asian chip manufacturers are exported widely across the globe, limiting the risk of economic weakness in that region. During FY 06, Samsung was the only customer to account for more than 10% of sales.

Company Financials Fiscal Year Ended Oct. 31

Per Share Data ($)	2007	2006	2005	2004	2003	2002	2001	2000	1999	1998
Tangible Book Value	NA	5.80	5.30	5.33	4.62	4.67	4.51	4.20	2.59	2.05
Cash Flow	NA	1.14	0.91	0.99	0.14	0.39	0.69	1.41	0.63	0.38
Earnings	1.20	0.97	0.73	0.78	-0.09	0.16	0.46	1.20	0.46	0.19
S&P Core Earnings	NA	0.97	0.54	0.59	-0.33	-0.04	0.33	NA	NA	NA
Dividends	0.22	0.16	0.06	Nil	Nil	Nil	Nil	Nil	Nil	Nil
Payout Ratio	18%	16%	8%	Nil	Nil	Nil	Nil	Nil	Nil	Nil
Prices:High	23.00	21.06	19.47	24.75	25.94	27.95	29.55	57.50	32.25	11.75
Prices:Low	17.35	14.39	14.33	15.36	11.25	10.26	13.30	17.06	10.72	5.39
P/E Ratio:High	19	22	27	32	NM	NM	65	48	70	77
P/E Ratio:Low	14	15	20	20	NM	NM	29	14	23	35

Income Statement Analysis (Million $)										
Revenue	NA	9,167	6,992	8,013	4,477	5,062	7,343	9,564	4,859	4,042
Operating Income	NA	2,517	1,748	2,313	440	683	1,538	3,149	1,257	910
Depreciation	NA	270	300	356	382	388	387	362	275	285
Interest Expense	NA	36.1	37.8	52.9	46.9	49.4	47.6	51.4	47.1	45.3
Pretax Income	NA	2,167	1,582	1,829	-212	341	1,104	2,948	1,056	438
Effective Tax Rate	NA	30.0%	23.5%	26.1%	NM	21.0%	29.8%	30.0%	31.3%	34.0%
Net Income	NA	1,517	1,210	1,351	-149	269	775	2,064	726	289
S&P Core Earnings	NA	1,511	905	1,017	-562	-65.2	558	NA	NA	NA

Balance Sheet & Other Financial Data (Million $)										
Cash	NA	861	990	2,282	1,365	1,285	1,356	1,648	823	575
Current Assets	NA	6,081	9,449	10,282	8,371	8,073	7,782	8,839	5,060	3,519
Total Assets	NA	9,481	11,269	12,093	10,312	10,225	9,829	10,546	6,707	4,930
Current Liabilities	NA	2,436	1,765	2,288	1,641	1,501	1,533	2,760	1,669	1,118
Long Term Debt	NA	205	407	410	456	574	565	573	584	617
Common Equity	NA	6,651	8,929	9,262	8,068	8,020	7,607	7,104	4,337	3,121
Total Capital	NA	6,856	9,336	9,672	8,524	8,594	8,172	7,677	4,954	3,749
Capital Expenditures	NA	179	200	191	265	417	711	383	204	449
Cash Flow	NA	1,787	1,510	1,707	233	657	1,162	2,426	1,001	573
Current Ratio	NA	2.5	5.4	4.5	5.1	5.4	5.1	3.2	3.0	3.1
% Long Term Debt of Capitalization	NA	3.0	4.4	4.2	5.4	6.7	6.9	7.5	11.8	16.4
% Net Income of Revenue	NA	16.5	17.3	16.9	NM	5.3	10.5	21.6	14.9	7.1
% Return on Assets	NA	14.6	10.4	12.1	NM	2.7	7.6	23.5	12.5	5.8
% Return on Equity	NA	19.5	13.3	15.6	NM	3.4	10.5	35.3	19.5	9.5

Data as orig reptd.; bef. results of disc opers/spec. items. Per share data adj. for stk. divs.; EPS diluted. E-Estimated. NA-Not Available. NM-Not Meaningful. NR-Not Ranked. UR-Under Review.

Office: 3050 Bowers Avenue, Santa Clara, CA, United States 95054-3298.
Telephone: 408-727-5555.
Email: investor_relations@appliedmaterials.com
Website: http://www.appliedmaterials.com

Chrmn: J.C. Morgan
Pres & CEO: M. Splinter
SVP & CFO: G.S. Davis
SVP, Secy & General Counsel: J.J. Sweeney

VP & Cntlr: Y. Weatherford
Board Members: M. H. Armacost, R. H. Brust, D. A. Coleman, P. V. Gerdine, T. Iannotti, C. Y. Liu, J. C. Morgan, G. Parker, W. P. Roelandts, M. R. Splinter

Founded: 1967
Domicile: Delaware
Employees: 14,072

The McGraw-Hill Companies

Archer-Daniels-Midland Co

STANDARD
&POOR'S

S&P Recommendation BUY ★★★★☆	**Price** $35.59 (as of Nov 23, 2007)	**12-Mo. Target Price** $41.00	**Investment Style** Large-Cap Blend

GICS Sector Consumer Staples
Sub-Industry Agricultural Products

Summary This company is a major processor and merchandiser of agricultural commodities, including oilseeds, corn and wheat.

Key Stock Statistics (Source S&P, Vickers, company reports)

52-Wk Range	$39.65– 30.20	S&P Oper. EPS 2008**E**	2.83	Market Capitalization(B)	$22.905	Beta	0.75
Trailing 12-Month EPS	$3.37	S&P Oper. EPS 2009**E**	3.03	Yield (%)	1.29	S&P 3-Yr. Proj. EPS CAGR(%)	12.00
Trailing 12-Month P/E	10.6	P/E on S&P Oper. EPS 2008**E**	12.6	Dividend Rate/Share	$0.46	S&P Credit Rating	A
$10K Invested 5 Yrs Ago	$28,537	Common Shares Outstg. (M)	643.6	Institutional Ownership (%)	64		

Price Performance

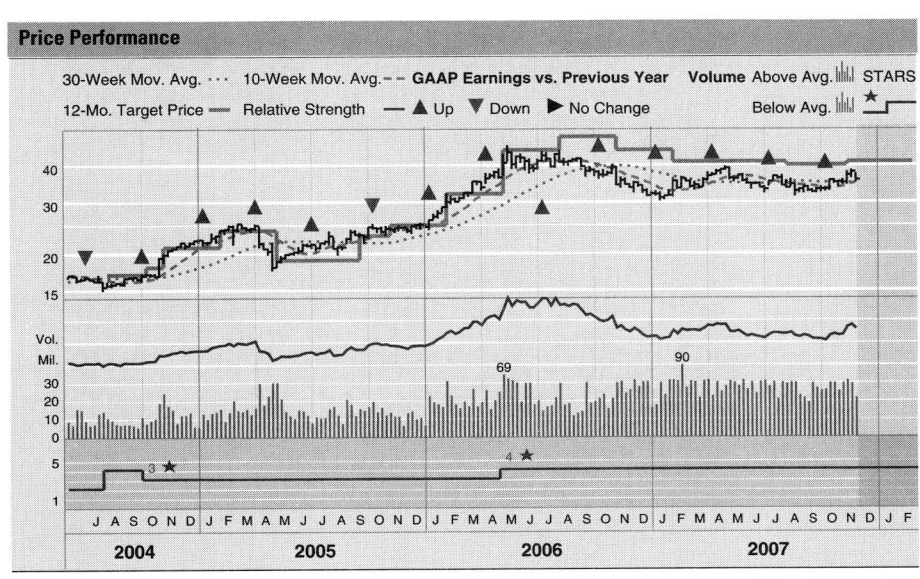

30-Week Mov. Avg. · · · 10-Week Mov. Avg. — **GAAP Earnings vs. Previous Year** Volume Above Avg. STARS
12-Mo. Target Price — Relative Strength — ▲ Up ▼ Down ▶ No Change Below Avg.

Options: ASE, CBOE, P, Ph

Analysis prepared by **Stephen Ham, CFA** on November 14, 2007, when the stock traded at **$ 38.34**.

Highlights

➤ We expect ADM to increase revenues 23% in FY 2008 (Jun.) and 10% in FY 2009. Our forecast reflects improved grains in merchandising results from more volatile and higher grain prices and better oilseed processing results from stronger demand for soybean, partially offset by reduced corn processing results from lower ethanol sales volumes, despite better corn sweetener pricing.

➤ We look for soybean margins to widen in FY 2008 due to improving capacity utilization rates in the U.S. and South America, partially offset by lower European margins. We expect lower ethanol sales prices from the supply/demand imbalance for biofuels along with higher corn prices from increased ethanol production to pressure margins. Agricultural services should benefit as increased worldwide demand and large crop supplies in the U.S. lead to increased demand and higher crop pricing. We project improving cost controls expanding operating margins to 4.7% in FY 08 from 4.6% in FY 07.

➤ We estimate FY 08 operating EPS of $2.83, up 16% from $2.43 in FY 07, with a further gain to $3.03 in FY 09. We expect shares outstanding to decrease 1% in FY 2008.

Investment Rationale/Risk

➤ We believe ADM will experience accelerating earnings growth through the end of FY 08 due to the strong pricing levels in soybean, corn sweetener and wheat commodities worldwide, resulting from strong demand. We believe the company is well positioned to benefit when bio-fuel supply/demand is back in balance and we continue to project that the company's diversified business model can help it to withstand weakness in parts of its business such as ADM's recent ethanol results.

➤ Risks to our recommendation and target price include the possibility of losses resulting from fluctuations in worldwide commodity supply and demand levels and gasoline prices, and rising raw material prices. The company tries to mitigate commodity risks through the use of hedging contracts, which can result in losses.

➤ Based on our expectations for strengthening demand, we think the shares should trade at the high end of their historical relative P/E range and at a forward 12-month P/E multiple in line with peers. On that basis, our 12-month target price is $41, applying a P/E of 14X to our 12-month forward EPS projection.

Qualitative Risk Assessment

LOW	MEDIUM	**HIGH**

Our risk assessment reflects the company's cyclical operations, which are significantly affected by exposure to crop and meat commodity markets, as well as high political risks.

Quantitative Evaluations

S&P Quality Ranking A+

D	C	B-	B	B+	A-	A	**A+**

Relative Strength Rank STRONG

84

LOWEST = 1   HIGHEST = 99

Revenue/Earnings Data

Revenue (Million $)

	1Q	2Q	3Q	4Q	Year
2008	12,828	--	--	--	--
2007	9,447	10,976	11,381	12,214	44,018
2006	8,627	9,299	9,123	9,547	36,596
2005	8,972	9,064	8,484	9,424	35,944
2004	7,968	9,189	9,309	9,686	36,151
2003	6,944	7,807	7,909	8,048	30,708

Earnings Per Share ($)

2008	0.68	E0.68	E0.74	E0.72	E2.83
2007	0.61	0.67	0.56	1.47	3.30
2006	0.29	0.56	0.53	0.62	2.00
2005	0.41	0.48	0.41	0.30	1.59
2004	0.23	0.34	0.35	-0.16	0.76
2003	0.17	0.20	0.18	0.15	0.70

Fiscal year ended Jun. 30. Next earnings report expected: Early February. EPS Estimates based on S&P Operating Earnings; historical GAAP earnings are as reported.

Dividend Data (Dates: mm/dd Payment Date: mm/dd/yy)

Amount ($)	Date Decl.	Ex-Div. Date	Stk. of Record	Payment Date
0.115	02/06	02/14	02/16	03/09/07
0.115	05/03	05/15	05/17	06/07/07
0.115	08/01	08/13	08/15	09/05/07
0.115	11/08	11/20	11/23	12/06/07

Dividends have been paid since 1927. Source: Company reports.

Archer-Daniels-Midland Co

STANDARD
&POOR'S

Business Summary November 14, 2007

CORPORATE OVERVIEW. Archer-Daniels-Midland (ADM) calls itself "super-market to the world." The company is principally engaged in procuring, transporting, storing, processing and merchandising agricultural commodities and products. Within a network of more than 235 domestic and international plants, cereal grains and oilseeds are processed into a multitude of products used in food, beverage, nutraceutical, industrial and animal feed markets worldwide.

Most of the company's business involves converting raw soybeans, corn and wheat into further-processed ingredients for the food manufacturing industry in the U.S. and abroad. ADM's operations are classified into three primary business segments: Corn Processing, Oilseeds Processing and Agricultural Services. The company's remaining operations are classified as Other. In FY 06 (Jun.), Corn Processing contributed 43% of segment operating profits (34% in FY 05); Oilseeds Processing 29% (22%); Agricultural Services 13% (17%); and Other 15% (27%).

ADM is the world's largest corn processor. The corn processing segment is involved in corn wet and dry milling operations. Wet milling products include syrup, starch, glucose, dextrose, crystalline dextrose, high-fructose sweeteners, crystalline fructose, corn gluten feed and ethyl alcohol. Dry milled products include ethanol, distilled grains, meal and grits. In gasoline, ethanol in-

creases octane and is used as an extender and oxygenate.

The company is one of the world's largest processors of oilseeds (soybeans, cottonseed, sunflower seeds, canola, peanuts, flaxseed and corn germ), which are processed to provide vegetable oils and meals principally for the food and feed industries. Crude vegetable oil is sold to others or refined and hydrogenated to produce oils for margarine, shortening, salad oils and other food products. Oilseed meals supply more than one-half of the high protein ingredients used in the manufacture of commercial livestock and poultry feeds.

ADM is vertically integrated, with its agricultural services segment utilizing grain elevators and transportation networks to buy, store, clean and transport agricultural commodities such as oilseeds, corn, wheat, milo, oats and barley. In addition to supplying its processing operations, these commodities are resold primarily as food or feed ingredients. ADM owns 80% of A.C. Toepfer International, one of the world's largest trading companies specializing in agricultural commodities and processed products.

Company Financials Fiscal Year Ended Jun. 30

Per Share Data ($)	2007	2006	2005	2004	2003	2002	2001	2000	1999	1998
Tangible Book Value	17.01	14.47	12.47	11.31	10.43	10.39	9.56	9.21	9.23	9.48
Cash Flow	4.36	3.00	2.60	1.82	1.69	1.64	1.44	1.35	1.26	1.36
Earnings	3.30	2.00	1.59	0.76	0.70	0.78	0.58	0.46	0.41	0.60
S&P Core Earnings	2.31	2.02	1.53	1.14	0.61	0.55	0.58	NA	NA	NA
Dividends	0.43	0.37	0.32	0.27	0.24	0.20	0.19	0.14	0.13	0.17
Payout Ratio	13%	19%	20%	36%	34%	25%	32%	30%	32%	29%
Prices:High	39.65	46.71	25.55	22.55	15.24	14.85	15.80	14.46	14.74	19.44
Prices:Low	30.20	24.05	17.50	14.90	10.50	10.00	10.24	7.80	10.37	12.80
P/E Ratio:High	12	23	16	30	22	19	27	32	35	33
P/E Ratio:Low	9	12	11	20	15	13	18	17	25	21

Income Statement Analysis (Million $)										
Revenue	44,018	36,596	35,944	36,151	30,708	23,454	20,051	12,877	14,283	16,146
Operating Income	2,743	2,450	2,015	1,432	1,423	1,424	1,272	1,094	1,116	1,247
Depreciation	701	657	665	686	644	567	572	604	585	527
Interest Expense	Nil	365	Nil	Nil	Nil	356	397	377	326	293
Pretax Income	3,154	1,855	1,516	718	631	719	522	353	420	610
Effective Tax Rate	31.5%	29.3%	31.1%	31.1%	28.5%	28.9%	26.6%	14.7%	33.1%	33.8%
Net Income	2,162	1,312	1,044	495	451	511	383	301	281	404
S&P Core Earnings	1,508	1,322	1,001	739	397	363	382	NA	NA	NA

Balance Sheet & Other Financial Data (Million $)										
Cash	2,087	2,334	1,430	1,412	765	844	676	477	1,461	346
Current Assets	15,122	11,826	9,711	10,339	8,422	7,363	6,150	6,162	5,790	5,452
Total Assets	25,118	21,269	18,598	19,369	17,183	15,416	14,340	14,423	14,030	13,834
Current Liabilities	7,868	6,165	5,367	6,750	5,147	4,719	3,867	4,333	3,840	3,717
Long Term Debt	4,752	4,050	3,530	3,740	3,872	3,111	3,351	3,277	3,192	2,847
Common Equity	11,253	9,807	8,433	7,698	7,069	6,755	6,332	6,110	6,241	6,505
Total Capital	16,537	14,614	12,743	12,092	11,485	10,498	10,327	9,948	10,053	9,985
Capital Expenditures	1,198	762	624	509	420	350	273	429	671	703
Cash Flow	2,863	1,969	1,709	1,180	1,095	1,078	955	905	866	931
Current Ratio	1.9	1.9	1.8	1.5	1.6	1.6	1.6	1.4	1.5	1.5
% Long Term Debt of Capitalization	28.7	27.7	27.7	30.9	33.7	29.6	32.4	32.9	31.8	28.5
% Net Income of Revenue	4.9	3.6	2.9	1.4	1.5	2.2	1.9	2.3	2.0	2.5
% Return on Assets	9.3	6.6	5.5	2.7	2.8	3.4	2.7	2.1	2.0	3.2
% Return on Equity	20.5	14.4	12.9	6.7	6.5	7.8	6.2	4.9	4.4	6.4

Data as orig reptd.; bef. results of disc opers/spec. items. Per share data adj. for stk. divs.; EPS diluted. E-Estimated. NA-Not Available. NM-Not Meaningful. NR-Not Ranked. UR-Under Review.

Office: 4666 Faries Parkway, Decatur, IL 62525.
Telephone: 217-424-5200.
Website: http://www.admworld.com
Chrmn, Pres & CEO: P.A. Woertz

EVP, Secy & General Counsel: D.J. Smith
SVP & CFO: D.J. Schmalz
VP & Treas: V. Luthar
VP & Cntlr: J. Stott

Investor Contact: D. Grimestad (217-424-4586)
Board Members: A. L. Boeckmann, M. H. Carter, R. S. Joslin, A. Maciel Neto, P. J. Moore, M. B. Mulroney, T. F. O'Neill, O. G. Webb, K. R. Westbrook, P. A. Woertz

Founded: 1898
Domicile: Delaware
Employees: 27,300

The McGraw-Hill Companies

Ashland Inc

STANDARD &POOR'S

S&P Recommendation BUY ★★★★☆	**Price** $48.15 (as of Nov 23, 2007)	**12-Mo. Target Price** $65.00	**Investment Style** Large-Cap Blend

GICS Sector Materials
Sub-Industry Diversified Chemicals

Summary This diversified chemical company has operations in more than 100 countries worldwide.

Key Stock Statistics (Source S&P, Vickers, company reports)

52-Wk Range	$71.04– 47.40	S&P Oper. EPS 2008**E**	3.65	Market Capitalization(B)	$3.023	Beta	0.57
Trailing 12-Month EPS	$3.60	S&P Oper. EPS 2009**E**	4.38	Yield (%)	2.28	S&P 3-Yr. Proj. EPS CAGR(%)	20.00
Trailing 12-Month P/E	13.4	P/E on S&P Oper. EPS 2008**E**	13.2	Dividend Rate/Share	$1.10	S&P Credit Rating	BBB
$10K Invested 5 Yrs Ago	$27,565	Common Shares Outstg. (M)	62.8	Institutional Ownership (%)	80		

Price Performance

30-Week Mov. Avg. ···   10-Week Mov. Avg. - -   **GAAP Earnings vs. Previous Year**   Volume Above Avg. STARS
12-Mo. Target Price —   Relative Strength —   ▲ Up   ▼ Down   ▶ No Change   Below Avg.

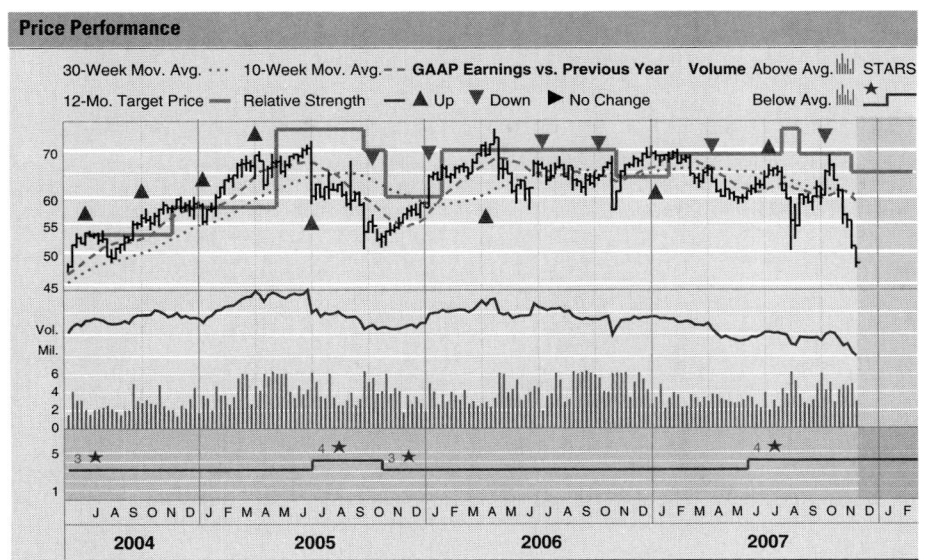

Options: ASE, CBOE, P, Ph

Analysis prepared by **Pearl Wang** on November 13, 2007, when the stock traded at **$ 52.74**.

Highlights

➤ We expect revenues to increase about 3% in FY 08 (Sep.), led by growth in the Water Technologies and Valvoline segments. For FY 08, we see these divisions driving high single digit sales growth. We believe the Distribution segment will experience substantial headwinds due to the loss of the Dow Chemical contract, as well as potentially slowing industrial production. We think the Performance Materials division will also encounter softer sales growth in FY 08, as housing and auto markets in North America remain weak.

➤ We believe operating margins will expand in FY 08 as the Valvoline segment benefits from improved pricing and stable base oil costs, and as the Water Technologies segment benefits from cost reduction efforts with a business model redesign. We expect further restructuring benefits and international expansion to help lower costs.

➤ We forecast operating EPS of $3.65 in FY 08.

Investment Rationale/Risk

➤ We believe ASH will see better sales growth and operating margin expansion now that it is solely focused on diversified chemicals. This reflects restructuring benefits, cost reduction efforts, price increases and stable commodity supply costs and volume. While we think the stock discounts the headwinds ASH is encountering, such as the loss of a major contract and weak housing and auto markets, we do not believe its valuation reflects the improving outlook in other parts of its business. We view the shares' valuation as attractive.

➤ Risks to our recommendation and target price include weaker than expected global economic growth, the risk of higher feedstock and utility costs, and lower than expected margins.

➤ Our 12-month target price of $65 is based on a blend of valuation methods. Our discounted cash flow model, which assumes a 3% perpetual growth rate and a 9% discount rate, implies an intrinsic value of $65. On a relative valuation basis, we apply a P/E of around 18X, roughly in line with peers and ASH's 10-year historical median, to our FY 08 EPS estimate, suggesting a $66 value.

Qualitative Risk Assessment

LOW	MEDIUM	HIGH

Our risk assessment reflects the highly cyclical nature of the company's end markets, offset by what we view as a strong balance sheet with a relatively low amount of debt. As of September 2007, the company had net cash and short-term investments in excess of $1 billion.

Quantitative Evaluations

S&P Quality Ranking   B

D	C	B-	**B**	B+	A-	A	A+

Relative Strength Rank   WEAK

18

LOWEST = 1   HIGHEST = 99

Revenue/Earnings Data

Revenue (Million $)

	1Q	2Q	3Q	4Q	Year
2007	1,813	1,915	1,983	2,104	7,834
2006	1,686	1,786	1,853	1,908	7,233
2005	2,177	2,062	2,492	2,538	9,270
2004	1,974	1,812	2,425	2,334	8,301
2003	1,846	1,736	2,125	2,130	7,865
2002	1,812	1,598	2,047	2,086	7,543

Earnings Per Share ($)

2007	0.81	0.49	1.35	0.51	3.15
2006	0.48	0.68	0.59	0.79	2.53
2005	1.28	0.44	23.65	1.49	26.86
2004	0.56	-0.16	2.35	2.81	5.59
2003	0.04	-0.50	1.03	0.89	1.37
2002	0.55	-0.31	0.93	0.68	1.83

Fiscal year ended Sep. 30. Next earnings report expected: Late January. EPS Estimates based on S&P Operating Earnings; historical GAAP earnings are as reported.

Dividend Data (Dates: mm/dd Payment Date: mm/dd/yy)

Amount ($)	Date Decl.	Ex-Div. Date	Stk. of Record	Payment Date
0.275	01/24	02/14	02/19	03/15/07
0.275	05/17	05/24	05/29	06/15/07
0.275	07/19	08/16	08/20	09/15/07
0.275	11/15	11/21	11/26	12/15/07

Dividends have been paid since 1936. Source: Company reports.

Please read the Required Disclosures and Analyst Certification on the last page of this report.

The McGraw·Hill Companies

Ashland Inc

STANDARD
&POOR'S

Business Summary November 13, 2007

Founded in 1936, Ashland (ASH) operates as a global, diversified chemical company with four business segments: Ashland Performance Materials (20% of FY 06 (Sep.) revenues; 66% of FY 06 operating income); Ashland Distribution (56%; 70%); Valvoline (20%, -12); and Ashland Water Technologies (7%; 8%).

The Ashland Performance Materials segment focuses on providing composite polymers and casting solutions on a worldwide basis, manufacturing thermosetting resins and gelcoats, metal-casting consumables and adhesives. This division makes specialty chemicals for the transportation, building and construction, foundry, marine, paint, paper, ink, and flexible packaging industries. The segment owns and operates 29 manufacturing facilities, and participates in 10 manufacturing joint ventures in 15 countries.

Through Ashland Distribution, the company distributes chemicals, plastics, reinforcements and resins, and fine ingredients in North America, and plastics in Europe. Ashland Distribution specializes in providing mixed truckloads and less-than-truckload quantities to customers in a wide range of industries. Deliveries are performed through a network of owned or leased facilities, including 68 locations in North America. Distribution of thermoplastic resins in Europe is conducted through 17 third-party warehouses in 13 foreign countries.

Company Financials Fiscal Year Ended Sep. 30

Per Share Data ($)	2007	2006	2005	2004	2003	2002	2001	2000	1999	1998
Tangible Book Value	NA	41.58	42.32	30.46	25.44	24.29	24.61	20.40	27.50	25.40
Cash Flow	NA	4.39	30.11	8.32	4.32	4.99	9.37	7.45	6.91	4.99
Earnings	3.15	2.53	26.86	5.59	1.37	1.83	5.77	4.10	3.89	2.63
S&P Core Earnings	NA	2.27	15.98	5.69	1.73	1.45	5.25	NA	NA	NA
Dividends	1.10	1.10	1.10	1.10	1.10	1.10	1.10	1.10	1.10	1.10
Payout Ratio	35%	43%	4%	20%	80%	60%	19%	27%	28%	42%
Prices:High	70.20	75.17	72.20	60.17	44.55	46.98	46.54	37.19	50.63	57.94
Prices:Low	47.40	57.25	50.45	43.73	25.91	23.60	34.39	28.63	30.31	42.25
P/E Ratio:High	22	30	3	11	33	26	8	9	13	22
P/E Ratio:Low	15	23	2	8	19	13	6	7	8	16

Income Statement Analysis (Million $)										
Revenue	NA	7,233	9,270	8,301	7,865	7,543	7,719	7,961	6,801	6,534
Operating Income	NA	237	349	375	123	309	273	433	400	229
Depreciation, Depletion and Amortization	NA	111	193	193	204	220	250	237	228	181
Interest Expense	NA	12.0	82.0	114	128	138	170	188	140	130
Pretax Income	NA	212	1,803	548	138	58.0	681	483	482	317
Effective Tax Rate	NA	13.7%	NM	27.4%	31.9%	NM	40.4%	39.5%	39.8%	36.0%
Net Income	NA	183	2,005	398	94.0	129	406	292	290	203
S&P Core Earnings	NA	164	1,189	405	120	103	371	NA	NA	NA

Balance Sheet & Other Financial Data (Million $)										
Cash	NA	1,820	985	243	223	90.0	236	67.0	110	34.0
Current Assets	NA	4,250	3,757	2,302	2,085	1,925	2,213	2,131	2,059	1,828
Total Assets	NA	6,590	6,815	7,502	7,006	6,725	6,945	6,771	6,424	6,082
Current Liabilities	NA	2,041	1,545	1,815	1,484	1,511	1,497	1,699	1,396	1,361
Long Term Debt	NA	70.0	82.0	1,109	1,512	1,606	1,786	1,899	1,927	1,507
Common Equity	NA	3,096	3,739	2,706	2,253	2,339	2,399	1,965	2,200	2,137
Total Capital	NA	3,166	3,821	4,182	4,056	4,201	4,625	4,152	4,353	3,644
Capital Expenditures	NA	175	380	210	110	185	205	232	248	274
Cash Flow	NA	294	2,198	591	298	349	656	529	518	384
Current Ratio	NA	2.1	2.4	1.3	1.4	1.3	1.5	1.3	1.5	1.3
% Long Term Debt of Capitalization	NA	2.2	2.1	26.5	37.3	38.2	38.6	45.7	44.3	41.4
% Return on Assets	NA	2.7	28.0	5.5	1.4	1.9	5.9	4.4	4.6	2.9
% Return on Equity	NA	5.4	62.2	16.1	4.2	5.4	17.9	14.0	13.4	9.8

Data as orig reptd.; bef. results of disc opers/spec. items. Per share data adj. for stk. divs.; EPS diluted. E-Estimated. NA-Not Available. NM-Not Meaningful. NR-Not Ranked. UR-Under Review.

Office: 50 E Rivercenter Blvd, Covington, KY 41011-1683.
Telephone: 859-815-3333.
Email: investor_relations@ashland.com
Website: http://www.ashland.com

Chrmn & CEO: J.J. O'Brien
Investor Contact: J.M. Quin
SVP & CFO: J.M. Quin
SVP, Secy & General Counsel: D.L. Hausrath

VP & Cntlr: L.M. Chambers
Board Members: E. H. Drew, R. W. Hale, B. P. Healy, M. L. Jackson, K. Ligocki, P. F. Noonan, J. J. O'Brien, B. W. Perry, G. A. Schaefer, Jr., T. M. Solso, M. J. Ward

Founded: 1918
Domicile: Kentucky
Employees: 11,700

The McGraw-Hill Companies

Assurant Inc.

STANDARD &POOR'S

S&P Recommendation **HOLD** ★★★☆☆	Price $66.11 (as of Nov 23, 2007)	12-Mo. Target Price $65.00	Investment Style Large-Cap Value

GICS Sector Financials
Sub-Industry Multi-line Insurance

Summary This company, 18.6%-owned by Fortis N.V., pursues a differentiated strategy of building leading positions in niche insurance markets.

Key Stock Statistics (Source S&P, Vickers, company reports)

52-Wk Range	$67.17–45.27	S&P Oper. EPS 2007**E**	5.71	Market Capitalization(B)	$7.875	Beta	1.50
Trailing 12-Month EPS	$6.35	S&P Oper. EPS 2008**E**	6.00	Yield (%)	0.73	S&P 3-Yr. Proj. EPS CAGR(%)	9.80
Trailing 12-Month P/E	10.4	P/E on S&P Oper. EPS 2007**E**	11.6	Dividend Rate/Share	$0.48	S&P Credit Rating	NA
$10K Invested 5 Yrs Ago	NA	Common Shares Outstg. (M)	119.1	Institutional Ownership (%)	95		

Price Performance

30-Week Mov. Avg. · · · 10-Week Mov. Avg. – – GAAP Earnings vs. Previous Year   Volume Above Avg. STARS

12-Mo. Target Price — Relative Strength — ▲ Up ▼ Down ► No Change   Below Avg.

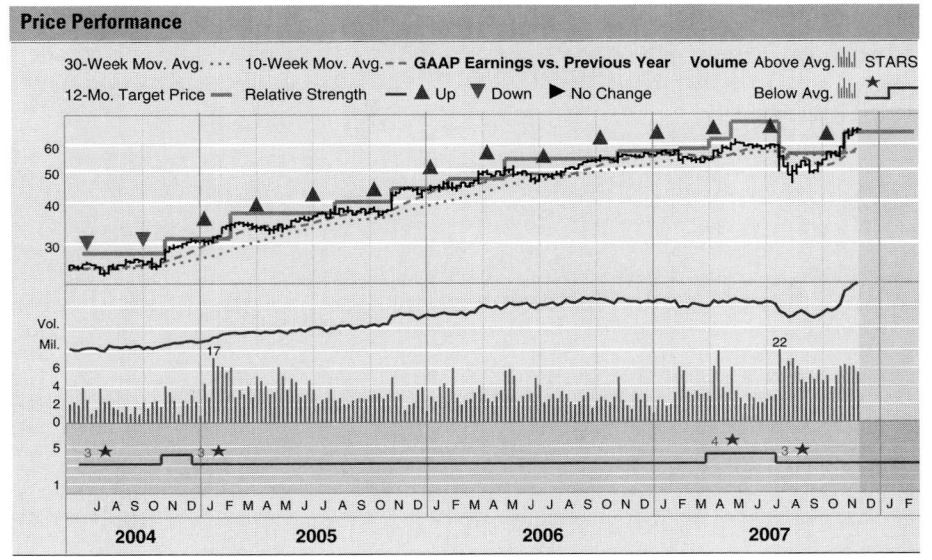

Options: ASE, CBOE, P, Ph

Analysis prepared by **Tanjila Shafi** on November 13, 2007, when the stock traded at **$ 64.68**.

Highlights

➤ We expect high single digit to low double digit growth in operating income for Assurant Solutions in 2008, benefiting from increased growth in its credit and extended service contracts sub-segments. We also anticipate solid growth in its pre-need business, enhanced by the acquisition of Mayflower National Life. We believe that international earnings will act as a major contributor to the Solutions business as the company plans to step up its efforts in China. However, we anticipate that profitability will be hampered by earnings from Assurant Health as the segment will continue to experience competitive pressures and losses in small group membership.

➤ We expect double digit growth in operating income in 2008 for the Specialty Property segment, driven by gains in creditor-placed homeowners insurance, acquisitions, and an improving combined ratio. We forecast solid growth in operating earnings in 2008 for Assurant Employee Benefits, helped by disciplined underwriting, a lower loss ratio, and growth in investment income.

➤ We forecast 2007 operating EPS of $5.71. Our EPS estimate for 2008 is $6.00.

Investment Rationale/Risk

➤ We believe that AIZ's underwriting remains strong, the company has a high level of expertise in the specialized lines it markets, and it faces limited competition. The company's strategic alignment with industry leaders will enhance its marketing abilities, in our opinion. In addition, we forecast that the company has substantial growth opportunities in its Specialty Property segment as we think that its creditor-placed homeowners business will benefit from the woes in the sub-prime mortgage market.

➤ Risks to our recommendation and target price include competitive pricing in the individual medical market, catastrophe risks, risks associated with further SEC subpoenas related to loss mitigation insurance products, and the possibility that demand for homeowners coverage could slow. We are also concerned about uncertainty resulting from recent management changes.

➤ Our 12-month target price is $65, 10.8X our 2008 operating EPS estimate, in line with its historical valuation.

Qualitative Risk Assessment

LOW	MEDIUM	HIGH

Our risk assessment for Assurant reflects our view of its disciplined capital management, solid excess capital, and low debt to capital ratio. In its short history as a public company, AIZ has shown a willingness to use excess capital for share buybacks and dividends.

Quantitative Evaluations

S&P Quality Ranking   NR

D	C	B-	B	B+	A-	A	A+

Relative Strength Rank   STRONG

96

LOWEST = 1   HIGHEST = 99

Revenue/Earnings Data

Revenue (Million $)

	1Q	2Q	3Q	4Q	Year
2007	2,057	2,065	2,148	--	--
2006	1,930	1,949	1,984	2,208	8,071
2005	1,862	1,874	1,879	1,882	7,498
2004	1,858	1,837	1,832	1,877	7,403
2003	1,732	1,723	1,776	1,836	7,066
2002	1,613	1,612	1,625	1,682	6,532

Earnings Per Share ($)

2007	1.45	1.36	1.56	E1.29	E5.71
2006	1.22	1.16	1.18	2.01	5.56
2005	0.82	0.92	0.74	1.03	3.50
2004	0.73	0.67	0.53	0.61	2.53
2003	0.67	0.83	0.91	-0.71	1.70
2002	--	--	--	--	--

Fiscal year ended Dec. 31. Next earnings report expected: Early February. EPS Estimates based on S&P Operating Earnings; historical GAAP earnings are as reported.

Dividend Data (Dates: mm/dd Payment Date: mm/dd/yy)

Amount ($)	Date Decl.	Ex-Div. Date	Stk. of Record	Payment Date
0.100	02/15	02/22	02/26	03/12/07
0.120	05/18	05/24	05/29	06/12/07
0.120	08/14	08/23	08/27	09/11/07
0.120	11/09	11/21	11/26	12/10/07

Dividends have been paid since 2004. Source: Company reports.

Assurant Inc.

STANDARD &POOR'S

Business Summary November 13, 2007

CORPORATE OVERVIEW. Assurant Inc. provides specialized insurance products in North America and other selected markets. The company was indirectly wholly owned by Fortis N.V. until February 2004, when Fortis sold about 65% of its stake via an IPO. In January 2005, Fortis sold 27.2 million shares of AIZ in a secondary public offering at $30.60 per share. In conjunction with the offering, Fortis issued $774 million of 7.75% bonds that are mandatorily exchangeable for up to 23.0 million shares of AIZ, or the cash value thereof, by January 2008. As of February 16, 2007, Fortis retained almost 23 million shares, for an approximate 18.6% stake in AIZ.

As of March 31, 2006, AIZ believed it was a leader or was aligned with clients who were leaders in creditor-placed homeowners insurance (based on servicing volume), manufactured housing homeowners insurance (based on the number of homes built), debt protection administration (based on credit card balances outstanding), group dental plans sponsored by employers (based on the number of subscribers and master contracts in force), and pre-funded funeral insurance (based on the face amount of new policies sold).

On April 1, 2006, the company separated its Assurant Solutions unit into two

business segments: Assurant Solutions and Assurant Specialty Property. In addition, with the creation of the new Assurant Solutions and Assurant Specialty Property segments, the company realigned the PreNeed segment under the new Assurant Solutions segment. In total, AIZ operates through four decentralized business segments: Assurant Solutions (35% of net earned premiums and other consideration, as of year-end 2006); Assurant Specialty Property (18%); Assurant Health (31%); and Assurant Employee (17%). AIZ also reports a fifth segment, Corporate and Other, which includes the activities of the holding company, financing expenses, net realized gains and losses on investments, interest income from short-term investments, amortization of deferred gains related to sales of operations sold through reinsurance agreements, and, prior to 2004, interest income from excess surplus of insurance subsidiaries not allocated to other segments.

Company Financials Fiscal Year Ended Dec. 31

Per Share Data ($)	2006	2005	2004	2003	2002	2001	2000	1999	1998	1997
Tangible Book Value	28.46	21.01	18.90	14.76	NA	NA	NA	NA	NA	NA
Operating Earnings	NA	NA	NA	NA	NA	NA	NA	NA	NA	NA
Earnings	5.56	3.50	2.53	1.70	NA	NA	NA	NA	NA	NA
S&P Core Earnings	4.77	3.49	2.50	1.72	38.61	15.43	NA	NA	NA	NA
Dividends	0.38	0.31	0.21	NA	NA	NA	NA	NA	NA	NA
Relative Payout	7%	9%	8%	NA	NA	NA	NA	NA	NA	NA
Prices:High	56.78	44.68	31.29	NA	NA	NA	NA	NA	NA	NA
Prices:Low	42.72	29.70	22.00	NA	NA	NA	NA	NA	NA	NA
P/E Ratio:High	10	13	12	NA	NA	NA	NA	NA	NA	NA
P/E Ratio:Low	8	8	9	NA	NA	NA	NA	NA	NA	NA

Income Statement Analysis (Million $)										
Life Insurance in Force	99,645	111,186	166,452	169,787	192,984	203,660	NA	NA	NA	NA
Premium Income:Life A & H	4,203	4,595	4,789	4,565	4,385	4,215	NA	NA	NA	NA
Premium Income:Casualty/Property.	2,641	1,926	1,694	1,591	1,297	1,027	NA	NA	NA	NA
Net Investment Income	737	687	635	607	632	712	691	NA	NA	NA
Total Revenue	7,963	7,498	7,403	7,066	6,532	6,187	6,212	NA	NA	NA
Pretax Income	1,096	656	536	259	370	206	194	NA	NA	NA
Net Operating Income	NA	NA	NA	NA	NA	NA	NA	NA	NA	NA
Net Income	716	479	351	186	260	98.1	89.7	NA	NA	NA
S&P Core Earnings	613	477	345	187	320	128	NA	NA	NA	NA

Balance Sheet & Other Financial Data (Million $)										
Cash & Equivalent	1,561	984	935	1,093	NA	NA	NA	NA	NA	NA
Premiums Due	612	455	435	368	NA	NA	NA	NA	NA	NA
Investment Assets:Bonds	9,118	8,962	9,178	8,729	NA	NA	NA	NA	NA	NA
Investment Assets:Stocks	742	693	527	456	NA	NA	NA	NA	NA	NA
Investment Assets:Loans	1,325	1,273	1,119	1,001	NA	NA	NA	NA	NA	NA
Investment Assets:Total	12,429	12,516	13,472	10,924	NA	NA	NA	NA	NA	NA
Deferred Policy Costs	2,398	2,022	1,648	1,394	NA	NA	NA	NA	NA	NA
Total Assets	25,165	25,365	24,504	23,728	22,924	NA	NA	NA	NA	NA
Debt	972	972	972	1,946	975	NA	NA	NA	NA	NA
Common Equity	3,833	3,778	3,768	2,832	3,346	NA	NA	NA	NA	NA
Combined Loss-Expense Ratio	91.4	90.8	92.4	93.3	NA	NA	NA	NA	NA	NA
% Return on Revenue	9.3	6.4	4.9	2.6	4.0	1.6	1.4	NA	NA	NA
% Return on Equity	18.7	12.8	10.6	6.7	NA	NA	NA	NA	NA	NA
% Investment Yield	5.7	5.2	5.2	5.8	NA	NA	NA	NA	NA	NA

Data as orig reptd.; bef. results of disc opers/spec. items. Per share data adj. for stk. divs.; EPS diluted. E-Estimated. NA-Not Available. NM-Not Meaningful. NR-Not Ranked. UR-Under Review.

Office: One Chase Manhattan Plaza, New York, NY 10005.
Telephone: 212-859-7000.
Website: http://www.assurant.com
Chrmn: J.M. Palms

Pres & CEO: R.B. Pollock
Vice Chrmn: J.K. Clayton
EVP & CFO: P.B. Camacho
EVP & CCO: J.A. Atkinson

Investor Contact: M. Kivett (212-859-7029)
Board Members: M. Baise, R. J. Blendon, B. L. Bronner, H. L. Carver, J. N. Cento, A. R. Freedman, D. B. Kelso, C. J. Koch, H. C. Mackin, M. C. Mayes, J. M. Palms, R. B. Pollock

Auditor: PricewaterhouseCoopers
Founded: 1969
Domicile: Delaware
Employees: 13,400

The McGraw-Hill Companies

AT&T Inc

STANDARD &POOR'S

S&P Recommendation STRONG BUY ★★★★★	**Price** $37.63 (as of Nov 23, 2007)	**12-Mo. Target Price** $44.00

Investment Style Large-Cap Value

GICS Sector Telecommunication Services
Sub-Industry Integrated Telecommunication Services

Summary AT&T Inc. (formerly SBC Communications) provides telephone and broadband service, and the company holds full ownership of AT&T Mobility (formerly Cingular Wireless). AT&T Corp. was acquired in late 2005 and BellSouth in late 2006.

Key Stock Statistics (Source S&P, Vickers, company reports)

52-Wk Range	$42.97– 31.94	S&P Oper. EPS 2007E	2.78	Market Capitalization(B)	$232.742	Beta	1.23
Trailing 12-Month EPS	$1.92	S&P Oper. EPS 2008E	3.13	Yield (%)	3.77	S&P 3-Yr. Proj. EPS CAGR(%)	9.00
Trailing 12-Month P/E	19.6	P/E on S&P Oper. EPS 2007E	13.5	Dividend Rate/Share	$1.42	S&P Credit Rating	A
$10K Invested 5 Yrs Ago	$17,413	Common Shares Outstg. (M)	6,185.0	Institutional Ownership (%)	61		

Price Performance

30-Week Mov. Avg. · · · 10-Week Mov. Avg. - - GAAP Earnings vs. Previous Year   Volume Above Avg. STARS
12-Mo. Target Price — Relative Strength   ▲ Up ▼ Down ▶ No Change   Below Avg.

Options: ASE, CBOE, P, Ph

Analysis prepared by **Todd Rosenbluth** on November 12, 2007, when the stock traded at **$ 39.30**.

Highlights

➤ We expect revenues of $123 billion in 2008, up from a projected $119 billion in 2007, including full ownership of wireless and the acquired BellSouth (BLS) wireline assets. We see wireless revenue growth of 11% in 2008 from customer additions and wireless data service, and smaller gains in wireline data and regional business, helping offset competition in consumer voice and enterprise operations.

➤ We believe that wireline operating margins will be helped by workforce reductions and network integrations. On the wireless side, a margin improvement should stem from improved customer retention and higher revenue per user. We see an operating margin of 23.8% in 2007 and 24.8% in 2008, up from 18.5% in 2006. The addition of higher margin BLS assets are a large contributor.

➤ For 2008, we estimate operating EPS of $3.13, up from an expected $2.78 for 2007, before one-time integration and amortization adjustments and reduced share count from buybacks. Reported results in 2006 included $0.45 of one-time charges related to merger activities.

Investment Rationale/Risk

➤ We believe that through wireline cost reductions and growth stemming from wireless, T will generate strong free cash flow in 2008 to support capex and a dividend increase. We contend that as competitors face operational challenges, T will gain market share in wireless and broadband. We expect the shares to be driven by operating margin expansion from improvements in its fiber offering and supported by its dividend and share repurchases. Despite increased competition, we view the high quality shares as undervalued.

➤ Risks to our recommendation and target price include a change in regulations for the telecom segment, increased competition from cable carriers, weaker than projected wireless services execution, the integration of BLS, and the rollout of its fiber-based video services.

➤ Our 12-month target price of $44 is based on our relative analysis, which assumes a P/E of 14X our 2008 EPS estimate and an enterprise value/EBITDA multiple of 6.5X, in line with peers. T's total return potential is bolstered by its dividend yield, which was recently 3.6%.

Qualitative Risk Assessment

LOW	MEDIUM	HIGH

Our risk assessment reflects our view of the company's strong balance sheet and T's power over its suppliers, offset by the competitive nature of the telecom landscape and the integration challenges of its numerous acquisitions.

Quantitative Evaluations

S&P Quality Ranking   B+

D	C	B-	B	B+	A-	A	A+

Relative Strength Rank   MODERATE
46
LOWEST = 1   HIGHEST = 99

Revenue/Earnings Data

Revenue (Million $)

	1Q	2Q	3Q	4Q	Year
2007	28,969	29,478	30,132	--	--
2006	15,756	15,770	15,638	15,891	63,055
2005	10,248	10,328	10,320	12,966	43,862
2004	10,128	10,314	10,292	10,287	40,787
2003	10,333	10,204	10,239	10,067	40,843
2002	10,522	10,843	10,556	11,217	43,138

Earnings Per Share ($)

	1Q	2Q	3Q	4Q	Year
2007	0.45	0.47	0.50	E0.71	E2.78
2006	0.37	0.46	0.56	0.50	1.89
2005	0.27	0.30	0.38	0.46	1.42
2004	0.59	0.35	0.38	0.21	1.50
2003	0.74	0.42	0.37	0.28	1.80
2002	0.48	0.53	0.51	0.71	2.23

Fiscal year ended Dec. 31. Next earnings report expected: Late January. EPS Estimates based on S&P Operating Earnings; historical GAAP earnings are as reported.

Dividend Data (Dates: mm/dd Payment Date: mm/dd/yy)

Amount ($)	Date Decl.	Ex-Div. Date	Stk. of Record	Payment Date
0.355	12/15	01/08	01/10	02/01/07
0.355	03/30	04/05	04/10	05/01/07
0.355	06/29	07/06	07/10	08/01/07
0.355	09/28	10/05	10/10	11/01/07

Dividends have been paid since 1984. Source: Company reports.

AT&T Inc

Business Summary November 12, 2007

CORPORATE OVERVIEW. AT&T Inc. combined SBC Communications with the acquired assets of AT&T Corp. following an acquisition completed in November 2005. At the end of 2006, T closed on its acquisition of BellSouth (BLS) for $86 billion in stock, creating the largest U.S. telecom carrier. As of September 2007, the combined company had 63 million in-region local phone lines (down 6.9% from a year earlier) and 13.8 million broadband customers. With the acquisition of BLS, T took full control of Cingular Wireless (35% of projected 2007 T revenues), the nation's largest wireless provider with 65.7 million subscribers, and expanded its wireline presence into the Southeastern U.S. In early 2007, Cingular was renamed AT&T Mobility.

The inclusion of AT&T Corp. added voice, data, IP, and hosting services for enterprise customers as well as a national network. SBC expanded through a number of mergers of fellow Bell companies over the past 10 years. Meanwhile, Cingular Wireless began operations through the merger of the wireless operations of SBC Communications and BellSouth. Reported results in 2006 largely exclude BLS operations, including its 40% stake in Cingular. Pro forma revenues for the entity in 2006 were $117 billion.

COMPETITIVE LANDSCAPE. In 2007, wireline operations have been facing technology substitution effects, primarily from wireless and cable telephony. In 2006, AT&T Inc lost 6.3% of its access lines and BellSouth lost 6.4%. As of September 2007, T was partnering with satellite providers to offer video services to 2 million customers, including a customized offering, Homezone. Loyalty is also a challenge for wireless carriers, in our opinion. We believe AT&T Mobility has differentiated itself by focusing on increasing data services usage (18% of wireless service revenues) and using initially exclusive wireless handsets from suppliers. T's post-paid churn rate of 1.3% is below the industry average. We estimate that AT&T has about a 28% share of the U.S. wireless market, aided by third quarter net additions of 2.0 million subscribers (1.2 million retail postpaid).

On the enterprise side, consolidation and migration to IP services has moderately reduced competitive pressure, helping T to sign longer-term deals with corporate customers than in the past.

Company Financials Fiscal Year Ended Dec. 31

Per Share Data ($)	2006	2005	2004	2003	2002	2001	2000	1999	1998	1997
Tangible Book Value	NM	8.29	11.77	11.09	9.51	8.62	7.38	5.87	4.95	3.60
Cash Flow	2.77	3.68	3.80	4.16	4.79	2.25	5.16	4.37	4.66	3.47
Earnings	1.89	1.42	1.50	1.80	2.23	2.14	2.32	1.90	2.05	0.80
S&P Core Earnings	1.82	1.24	1.22	1.50	1.21	1.39	NA	NA	NA	NA
Dividends	1.33	1.29	1.25	1.37	1.07	1.02	1.01	0.97	0.93	0.89
Payout Ratio	70%	91%	83%	76%	48%	48%	43%	51%	45%	111%
Prices:High	36.21	25.98	27.73	31.65	40.99	53.06	59.00	59.94	54.88	38.06
Prices:Low	24.24	21.75	22.98	18.85	19.57	36.50	34.81	44.06	35.00	24.63
P/E Ratio:High	19	18	18	18	18	25	25	32	27	48
P/E Ratio:Low	13	15	15	10	9	17	15	23	17	31

Income Statement Analysis (Million $)	2006	2005	2004	2003	2002	2001	2000	1999	1998	1997
Revenue	63,055	43,862	40,787	40,843	43,138	45,908	51,476	49,489	28,777	24,856
Depreciation	9,907	7,643	7,564	7,870	8,578	9,077	9,748	8,553	5,177	4,922
Maintenance	NA	NA	NA	NA	NA	NA	NA	NA	NA	NA
Construction Credits	73.0	36.0	31.0	37.0	58.0	119	81.0	81.0	59.0	120
Effective Tax Rate	32.4%	16.3%	30.5%	32.9%	28.5%	36.1%	38.2%	39.4%	36.2%	36.9%
Net Income	7,356	4,786	4,979	5,971	7,473	7,260	7,967	6,573	4,068	1,474
S&P Core Earnings	7,080	4,189	4,031	5,000	4,048	4,717	NA	NA	NA	NA

Balance Sheet & Other Financial Data (Million $)	2006	2005	2004	2003	2002	2001	2000	1999	1998	1997
Gross Property	202,149	149,238	136,177	133,923	131,755	127,524	119,753	116,332	73,466	65,286
Net Property	94,596	58,727	50,046	52,128	48,490	49,827	47,195	46,571	29,920	27,339
Capital Expenditures	8,320	5,576	5,099	5,219	6,808	11,189	13,124	10,304	5,927	5,766
Total Capital	193,009	96,727	77,544	69,607	62,705	58,476	54,079	50,411	27,741	24,967
Fixed Charges Coverage	5.8	4.4	6.9	7.0	6.9	6.6	8.0	7.5	6.8	2.1
Capitalization:Long Term Debt	50,063	26,115	21,231	16,060	18,536	17,133	16,492	18,415	12,612	13,019
Capitalization:Preferred	Nil	Nil	Nil	Nil	Nil	Nil	Nil	Nil	Nil	Nil
Capitalization:Common	115,540	54,690	40,504	38,248	33,199	32,491	30,463	26,726	12,780	9,892
% Return on Revenue	11.7	10.9	12.2	14.6	17.3	15.8	15.5	13.3	14.1	5.9
% Return on Invested Capital	4.9	6.5	7.0	9.0	11.4	12.9	16.6	15.0	17.7	12.0
% Return on Common Equity	8.6	10.1	12.6	16.7	22.6	23.1	27.9	26.6	34.9	15.1
% Earned on Net Property	13.4	11.3	11.6	12.9	17.5	22.4	22.9	25.6	23.3	11.9
% Long Term Debt of Capitalization	30.3	32.3	34.4	29.6	35.8	34.5	35.1	40.9	49.7	56.8
Capital % Preferred	Nil	Nil	Nil	Nil	Nil	Nil	Nil	Nil	Nil	Nil
Capitalization:% Common	67.8	67.7	65.6	70.4	64.2	65.5	64.9	59.1	50.3	43.2

Data as orig reptd.; bef. results of disc opers/spec. items. Per share data adj. for stk. divs.; EPS diluted. E-Estimated. NA-Not Available. NM-Not Meaningful. NR-Not Ranked. UR-Under Review.

Office: 175 East Houston, San Antonio, TX 78205-2255.
Telephone: 210-821-4105.
Website: http://www.att.com
Chrmn & CEO: R.L. Stephenson

Sr EVP: K. Jennings
Sr EVP: J.W. Callaway
Sr EVP: J. Kahan
Sr EVP: J.W. Cicconi

Investor Contact: D. Cessac (210-351-2058)
Board Members: W. F. Aldinger, III, G. F. Amelio, R. V. Anderson, J. H. Blanchard, A. A. Busch, III, J. A. Henderson, J. P. Kelly, J. P. Kelly, C. F. Knight, J. C. Madonna, L. M. Martin, J. B. McCoy, M. S. Metz, T. Rembe, S. D. Ritchey, J. M. Roche, R. L. Stephenson, L. D. Tyson, P. P. Upton, E. E. Whitacre, Jr.

Founded: 1983
Domicile: Delaware
Employees: 302,770

Autodesk Inc

STANDARD
&POOR'S

S&P Recommendation **HOLD** ★★★☆☆	Price $45.79 (as of Nov 23, 2007)	12-Mo. Target Price $53.00	Investment Style Large-Cap Growth

GICS Sector Information Technology
Sub-Industry Application Software

Summary The company develops, markets and supports computer-aided design and drafting (CAD) software for use on desktop computers and workstations.

Key Stock Statistics (Source S&P, Vickers, company reports)

52-Wk Range	$51.32–36.74	S&P Oper. EPS 2008**E**	1.54	Market Capitalization(B)	$10.532	Beta	1.28
Trailing 12-Month EPS	$1.46	S&P Oper. EPS 2009**E**	1.90	Yield (%)	Nil	S&P 3-Yr. Proj. EPS CAGR(%)	15.00
Trailing 12-Month P/E	31.4	P/E on S&P Oper. EPS 2008**E**	29.7	Dividend Rate/Share	Nil	S&P Credit Rating	NA
$10K Invested 5 Yrs Ago	$62,410	Common Shares Outstg. (M)	230.0	Institutional Ownership (%)	95		

Price Performance

30-Week Mov. Avg. ⋯	10-Week Mov. Avg. - -	**GAAP Earnings vs. Previous Year**	Volume Above Avg. STARS
12-Mo. Target Price —	Relative Strength —	▲ Up ▼ Down ► No Change	Below Avg.

2-for-1

J A S O N D | J F M A M J J A S O N D | J F M A M J J A S O N D | J F M A M J J A S O N D | J F
2004 · 2005 · 2006 · 2007

Options: ASE, CBOE, P, Ph

Analysis prepared by **Jim Yin** on November 17, 2007, when the stock traded at **$ 46.41**.

Highlights

➤ We project total revenue will grow 17% and 14% in FY 08 (Jan.) and FY 09, respectively. We believe revenue growth will be led by sales of 3D products, which we think are in the early stages of a long upgrade cycle. We see stronger growth in international markets, reflecting expectations for higher GDP growth rates, increased manufacturing and construction activities, and lower market penetration.

➤ We project gross margins in FY 09 will widen to 91%, from 90% seen in FY 08, due to a favorable revenue mix. We expect total operating expenses to increase modestly due to higher headcount and higher stock option expense, but should decline as a percentage of revenue. We estimate that non-GAAP operating margins will widen to 29% in FY 09, from 27% seen in FY 08, as a result of higher revenues and better operating efficiency through economies of scale.

➤ Our estimates for operating EPS are $1.54 and $1.90 for FY 08 and FY 09, respectively, compared to $1.28 in FY 07. The increase reflects higher revenues, higher operating margins, and fewer shares outstanding due to ADSK's stock repurchase program.

Investment Rationale/Risk

➤ We believe ADSK is in the early stages of a long product cycle, as customers upgrade to 3D versions of its products. We think the company will benefit from solid GDP growth in emerging markets and the Asia-Pacific region excluding Japan. In addition, management has been focusing on controlling costs, and we estimate that the operating margin will widen by 2% in FY 09. Despite these positives, we view the shares as fairly valued at recent levels.

➤ Risks to our opinion and target price include a loss of market share to competitors, poor sales execution, and a slowdown in the global economy that could cause a reduction in information technology spending.

➤ Our 12-month target price of $53 is based on a blend of our discounted cash flow (DCF) and P/E analyses. Our DCF model assumes a 12% weighted average cost of capital and 3% terminal growth, yielding an intrinsic value of $55. For our P/E analysis, we derive a value of $51 based on an industry average P/E-to-growth ratio of 1.8X, or 26.8X our FY 09 operating EPS estimate of $1.90.

Qualitative Risk Assessment

LOW	MEDIUM	HIGH

Our risk assessment reflects ADSK's exposure to cyclical business spending and intense competition, partially offset by our view of the company's strong market position and size.

Quantitative Evaluations

S&P Quality Ranking B

D	C	B-	**B**	B+	A-	A	A+

Relative Strength Rank MODERATE
62
LOWEST = 1 · HIGHEST = 99

Revenue/Earnings Data

Revenue (Million $)

	1Q	2Q	3Q	4Q	Year
2008	508.6	525.9	538.4	--	--
2007	436.0	449.6	456.8	497.4	1,840
2006	355.1	373.0	378.3	416.8	1,523
2005	297.9	279.6	300.2	356.2	1,234
2004	210.8	211.7	233.9	295.3	951.6
2003	229.3	211.4	188.7	195.5	825.0

Earnings Per Share ($)

	1Q	2Q	3Q	4Q	Year
2008	0.34	0.38	0.35	E0.43	E1.54
2007	0.20	0.36	0.24	0.40	1.19
2006	0.31	0.30	0.38	0.33	1.33
2005	0.18	0.16	0.30	0.26	0.90
2004	0.04	0.15	0.10	0.24	0.52
2003	0.08	0.05	-0.02	0.03	0.14

Fiscal year ended Jan. 31. Next earnings report expected: NA. EPS Estimates based on S&P Operating Earnings; historical GAAP earnings are as reported.

Dividend Data

Quarterly cash dividends were discontinued after April 2005.

Please read the Required Disclosures and Analyst Certification on the last page of this report.

The McGraw-Hill Companies

Autodesk Inc

STANDARD
&POOR'S

Business Summary November 17, 2007

CORPORATE OVERVIEW. ADSK develops software solutions that enable customers in land development, manufacturing, infrastructure, media and entertainment markets to create, manage and share their data and designs digitally. The company is organized into two reportable operating segments: the Design Solutions segment, which accounted for 87% of net revenue in FY 07 (Jan.), and the Media and Entertainment segment, which accounted for 13% of net revenue in FY 07.

The Design Solutions segment sells design software for professionals and consumers who design, build and manage building and other infrastructure projects for both public and private users. The segment is comprised of four divisions: Platform Technology and Other, which accounted for 51% of the segment's revenues in FY 07; Manufacturing Solutions, 21%; Infrastructure Solutions, 15%; and Infrastructure Solutions Division, 13%.

Principal products sold by the Design Solutions segment include AutoCAD, a general-purpose computer aided design (CAD) tool for design, modeling, drafting, mapping, rendering and facility management tasks, AutoCAD LT, a low-cost CAD package with 2D and basic 3D drafting capabilities, and Au-

todesk Buzzsaw, an online collaboration service that allows users to store, manage and share project documents from any Internet connection. Other products include Autodesk Mechanical Desktop, Autodesk Civil 3D, and Autodesk Revit products. The Design Solutions segment also offers a range of services including consulting, support and training.

The Media and Entertainment segment develops digital systems and software for creating 3D animation, color grading, visual effects compositing, editing and finishing. Its products are used for PC and console game development, animation, film, television, and design visualization. Products include Autodesk 3ds Max, a 3D modeling and animation software package; Discreet Flame, a digital system used by professionals to create and edit special visual effects in real-time; and Discreet Inferno, which provides all the features of flame with film tools, and increased image resolution and color control for digital film work.

Company Financials Fiscal Year Ended Jan. 31

Per Share Data ($)	2007	2006	2005	2004	2003	2002	2001	2000	1999	1998
Tangible Book Value	3.07	2.06	2.07	2.07	1.84	2.20	1.85	2.22	2.06	1.57
Cash Flow	1.37	1.51	1.11	0.74	0.35	0.68	0.69	0.36	0.79	0.30
Earnings	1.19	1.33	0.90	0.52	0.14	0.40	0.40	0.04	0.46	0.08
S&P Core Earnings	1.19	1.05	0.67	0.33	-0.07	0.09	0.17	NA	NA	NA
Dividends	0.02	0.06	0.06	0.06	0.06	0.06	0.06	0.06	0.06	0.06
Payout Ratio	1%	5%	7%	12%	43%	15%	15%	150%	13%	77%
Calendar Year	2006	2005	2004	2003	2002	2001	2000	1999	1998	1997
Prices:High	44.75	48.27	38.98	12.45	11.84	10.55	14.02	12.36	12.52	12.78
Prices:Low	29.56	26.20	12.10	6.41	5.09	6.05	4.86	4.25	5.41	7.00
P/E Ratio:High	38	36	43	24	85	26	35	NM	27	NM
P/E Ratio:Low	25	20	13	12	36	15	12	NM	12	NM

Income Statement Analysis (Million $)										
Revenue	1,840	1,523	1,234	952	825	947	936	820	740	632
Operating Income	440	414	314	0.16	99.7	195	208	115	200	147
Depreciation	43.9	43.7	51.9	50.3	48.8	62.9	68.8	79.7	63.2	43.9
Interest Expense	2.10	Nil	Nil	Nil	Nil	Nil	Nil	Nil	Nil	Nil
Pretax Income	367	383	246	117	38.5	55.1	41.7	23.9	147	55.0
Effective Tax Rate	21.0%	14.1%	10.1%	NM	17.1%	NM	NM	59.0%	38.2%	72.1%
Net Income	290	329	222	120	31.9	90.3	93.2	9.81	90.6	15.4
S&P Core Earnings	292	258	161	74.4	-16.2	19.5	38.5	NA	NA	NA

Balance Sheet & Other Financial Data (Million $)										
Cash	778	369	533	364	247	505	423	359	378	96.1
Current Assets	1,190	739	782	597	450	564	491	545	450	308
Total Assets	1,798	1,361	1,142	1,017	884	902	808	907	694	534
Current Liabilities	574	507	477	385	310	371	334	299	232	199
Long Term Debt	Nil	Nil	Nil	Nil	Nil	Nil	Nil	Nil	Nil	Nil
Common Equity	1,115	791	648	622	569	529	460	602	460	303
Total Capital	1,115	791	648	629	571	529	473	607	461	304
Capital Expenditures	35.3	20.5	40.8	25.9	36.1	45.1	32.4	14.9	30.4	15.0
Cash Flow	334	373	273	171	80.7	153	162	89.6	154	59.2
Current Ratio	2.1	1.5	1.6	1.6	1.5	1.5	1.5	1.8	1.9	1.5
% Long Term Debt of Capitalization	NA	Nil	Nil	Nil	Nil	Nil	Nil	Nil	Nil	Nil
% Net Income of Revenue	15.8	21.6	18.0	12.6	3.9	9.5	10.0	1.2	12.2	2.4
% Return on Assets	18.4	26.3	20.5	12.7	3.6	10.6	10.9	1.1	14.8	3.0
% Return on Equity	30.4	45.7	34.9	20.2	5.8	18.3	17.6	1.7	23.7	5.6

Data as orig reptd.; bef. results of disc opers/spec. items. Per share data adj. for stk. divs.; EPS diluted. E-Estimated. NA-Not Available. NM-Not Meaningful. NR-Not Ranked. UR-Under Review.

Office: 111 McInnis Parkway, San Rafael, CA 94903-2700.
Telephone: 415-507-5000.
Email: investor.relations@autodesk.com
Website: http://www.autodesk.com

Exec Chrmn: C.A. Bartz
Pres & CEO: C. Bass
SVP & CFO: A.J. Castino
SVP, Secy & General Counsel: P.W. Di Fronzo

Investor Contact: S. Pirri (415-507-6467)
Board Members: C. A. Bartz, C. Bass, M. A. Bertelsen, C. W. Beveridge, J. H. Dawson, M. Fister, P. Halvorsen, S. L. Scheid, M. A. Taylor, L. W. Wangberg

Founded: 1982
Domicile: Delaware
Employees: 5,169

Automatic Data Processing Inc.

STANDARD &POOR'S

S&P Recommendation **STRONG BUY** ★★★★★	Price $45.73 (as of Nov 23, 2007)	12-Mo. Target Price $56.00	Investment Style Large-Cap Growth

GICS Sector Information Technology
Sub-Industry Data Processing & Outsourced Services

Summary ADP, one of the world's largest independent computing services companies, provides a broad range of data processing services.

Key Stock Statistics (Source S&P, Vickers, company reports)

52-Wk Range	$51.50– 43.89	S&P Oper. EPS 2008**E**	2.16	Market Capitalization(B)	$24.285	Beta		1.05
Trailing 12-Month EPS	$2.13	S&P Oper. EPS 2009**E**	2.51	Yield (%)	2.54	S&P 3-Yr. Proj. EPS CAGR(%)		18.00
Trailing 12-Month P/E	21.5	P/E on S&P Oper. EPS 2008**E**	21.2	Dividend Rate/Share	$1.16	S&P Credit Rating		AAA
$10K Invested 5 Yrs Ago	NA	Common Shares Outstg. (M)	531.1	Institutional Ownership (%)	76			

Price Performance

30-Week Mov. Avg. · · · · 10-Week Mov. Avg. - · - GAAP Earnings vs. Previous Year   Volume Above Avg. STARS
12-Mo. Target Price — Relative Strength — ▲ Up ▼ Down ▶ No Change   Below Avg.

Options: ASE, CBOE, P, Ph

Analysis prepared by **Dylan Cathers** on November 01, 2007, when the stock traded at **$ 47.94**.

Qualitative Risk Assessment

LOW	MEDIUM	HIGH

Our risk assessment reflects what we see as the company's strong balance sheet, steady cash inflow, and recurring revenue stream, offset by intense competition in payroll processing and the threat of new entrants into the marketplace.

Quantitative Evaluations

S&P Quality Ranking   A+

D	C	B-	B	B+	A-	A	A+

Relative Strength Rank   MODERATE

63

LOWEST = 1   HIGHEST = 99

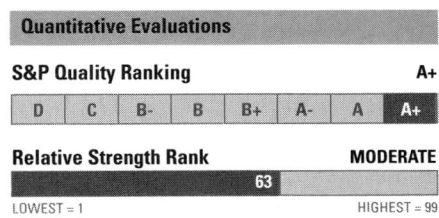

Revenue/Earnings Data

Revenue (Million $)

	1Q	2Q	3Q	4Q	Year
2008	1,992	--	--	--	--
2007	1,755	1,874	2,171	2,000	7,800
2006	1,922	2,047	2,439	2,474	8,882
2005	1,855	1,994	2,349	2,302	8,499
2004	1,720	1,927	2,121	2,086	7,755
2003	1,648	1,683	1,906	1,912	7,147

Earnings Per Share ($)

2008	0.45	E0.53	E0.74	E0.44	E2.16
2007	0.39	0.45	0.65	0.35	1.83
2006	0.36	0.44	0.61	0.44	1.85
2005	0.35	0.42	0.57	0.44	1.79
2004	0.32	0.38	0.50	0.36	1.56
2003	0.34	0.43	0.54	0.36	1.68

Fiscal year ended Jun. 30. Next earnings report expected: Early February. EPS Estimates based on S&P Operating Earnings; historical GAAP earnings are as reported.

Highlights

➤ We see revenues increasing 12% in FY 08 (June) and 8.0% in FY 09. We think revenue growth in the core traditional payroll and tax filing businesses will increase in the upper single digits, but we foresee additional services--such as beyond payroll--adding meaningfully to overall growth in the quarters to come. In addition, we think revenues will be aided by recent acquisitions, strong customer retention rates, higher levels of funds held for clients, and upward trending payroll data. We see revenues from the Professional Employer Organization segment increasing rapidly, albeit off of a small base. We expect Dealer Services revenue gains to stem from acquisitions and mid-single digit internal growth, reflecting healthy automobile sales outside of the U.S.

➤ We look for modestly wider operating margins in FY 08, reflecting rising sales of higher-margin services and increased leverage from greater sales volumes, partially offset by integration expenses from recent acquisitions.

➤ Our FY 08 EPS estimate is $2.16, and we look for EPS of $2.51 in FY 08, excluding potential share buyback activity.

Investment Rationale/Risk

➤ Our strong buy recommendation is based on valuation and what we see as an improvement in payroll employment. Despite a rise in the unemployment rate, an increase in payroll employment aided payroll providers in 2007, and we expect momentum to continue in 2008. We think the market for payroll outsourcing is relatively untapped, providing opportunities for future earnings growth. We view the company's balance sheet as strong, even as ADP repurchased 11 million shares in the September quarter alone.

➤ Risks to our recommendation and target price stem from competition in the business process outsourcing market, an area into which ADP is venturing, which could lead to downward pressure on pricing and profit margins; a decrease in payrolls due to a slower economy; and a failure of ADP to expand further into small- and mid-sized business and international markets.

➤ Our 12-month target price of $56 is based on our relative valuation analysis, using a peer-based P/E of about 24X our calendar 2008 EPS estimate of $2.31 and a P/E to growth ratio of around 1.35X, assuming a three-year growth rate of 18%.

Dividend Data (Dates: mm/dd Payment Date: mm/dd/yy)

Amount ($)	Date Decl.	Ex-Div. Date	Stk. of Record	Payment Date
0.230	01/26	03/07	03/09	04/01/07
0.230	04/25	06/13	06/15	07/01/07
0.230	08/09	09/12	09/14	10/01/07
0.290	11/13	12/12	12/14	01/01/08

Dividends have been paid since 1974. Source: Company reports.

Automatic Data Processing Inc.

**STANDARD
&POOR'S**

Business Summary November 01, 2007

CORPORATE OVERVIEW. ADP is the largest global provider of payroll outsourcing services based on revenue. The company also offers human resources outsourcing, tax filing, and benefits administration, with a broad range of data processing services in two business segments: employer and dealer.

Employer Services provides payroll, human resource, benefits administration, time and attendance, and tax filing and reporting services to more than 570,000 clients in North America, Europe, Australia, Asia and Brazil. Dealer Services provides transaction systems, data products and professional services to automobile and truck dealers and manufacturers worldwide.

MARKET PROFILE. The market for HR services, which is the largest segment of ADP's Employer Services division, totaled $88.7 billion worldwide in calen-

dar 2006, according to market researcher IDC. Between 2006 and 2011, IDC expects this area to expand at a compound annual growth rate (CAGR) of 8.3%, with the market in the U.S. increasing at a CAGR of 9.4%, from $44.9 billion in 2006. For the more narrow Processing services market, where we believe ADP is the dominant company, IDC sees a CAGR of 6.8% in the U.S. between 2006 and 2011. In contrast, in the market for business process outsourcing (BPO) services, an area in which we see ADP expanding further, IDC expects a CAGR of 13.7% over the same time frame.

Company Financials Fiscal Year Ended Jun. 30

Per Share Data ($)	2007	2006	2005	2004	2003	2002	2001	2000	1999	1998
Tangible Book Value	3.93	5.21	4.55	4.23	4.57	5.25	4.97	4.71	3.97	2.90
Cash Flow	2.35	5.35	2.30	2.07	2.13	2.19	1.93	1.74	1.52	1.37
Earnings	1.83	1.85	1.79	1.56	1.68	1.75	1.44	1.31	1.10	0.99
S&P Core Earnings	1.78	1.85	1.60	1.38	1.42	1.49	1.31	NA	NA	NA
Dividends	1.06	0.71	0.61	0.54	0.48	0.45	0.40	0.34	0.30	0.26
Payout Ratio	58%	38%	34%	35%	28%	26%	27%	26%	21%	26%
Prices:High	51.50	49.94	48.11	47.31	40.81	59.53	63.56	69.31	54.81	42.16
Prices:Low	43.89	42.50	40.37	38.60	27.24	31.15	41.00	40.00	36.25	28.78
P/E Ratio:High	28	27	27	30	24	34	44	53	50	43
P/E Ratio:Low	24	23	23	25	16	18	28	31	33	29
Income Statement Analysis (Million $)										
Revenue	7,800	8,882	8,499	7,755	7,147	7,004	7,018	6,288	5,540	4,798
Operating Income	1,795	1,967	1,948	1,745	1,793	1,952	1,938	1,904	1,376	1,153
Depreciation	289	289	304	307	275	279	321	284	273	245
Interest Expense	94.9	72.8	32.3	Nil	Nil	21.2	14.3	13.1	19.1	24.0
Pretax Income	1,624	3,486	1,678	1,495	1,645	1,787	1,525	1,290	1,085	884
Effective Tax Rate	37.1%	19.2%	37.1%	37.4%	38.1%	38.4%	39.4%	34.8%	35.7%	31.5%
Net Income	1,021	2,815	1,055	936	1,018	1,101	925	841	697	605
S&P Core Earnings	992	1,077	940	824	857	940	842	NA	NA	NA
Balance Sheet & Other Financial Data (Million $)										
Cash	1,817	2,269	1,671	1,129	2,344	2,750	1,791	1,824	1,092	752
Current Assets	3,364	4,760	4,441	2,762	3,676	2,817	3,083	3,064	2,194	1,829
Total Assets	26,649	27,490	27,615	21,121	19,834	18,277	17,889	16,851	5,825	5,175
Current Liabilities	1,791	2,593	2,801	1,768	1,999	1,411	1,336	1,297	1,286	1,221
Long Term Debt	43.5	74.3	75.8	76.2	84.7	90.6	110	132	146	192
Common Equity	5,148	6,012	5,784	5,418	5,371	5,114	4,701	4,583	4,062	3,406
Total Capital	5,319	6,210	6,150	5,778	5,777	5,442	5,019	4,866	4,346	3,745
Capital Expenditures	173	292	196	196	134	146	185	166	178	199
Cash Flow	1,310	3,104	1,360	1,242	1,293	1,380	1,246	1,125	970	850
Current Ratio	1.9	1.8	1.6	1.6	1.8	2.0	2.3	2.4	1.7	1.5
% Long Term Debt of Capitalization	0.8	1.2	1.2	1.3	1.5	1.7	2.2	2.7	3.4	5.1
% Net Income of Revenue	13.1	31.7	12.4	12.1	14.2	15.7	13.2	13.4	12.6	12.6
% Return on Assets	3.8	10.2	4.3	4.6	5.3	6.1	5.3	5.7	12.6	12.7
% Return on Equity	18.3	47.7	18.8	17.3	19.4	22.4	19.9	19.6	17.9	20.0

Data as orig reptd.; bef. results of disc opers/spec. items. Per share data adj. for stk. divs.; EPS diluted. E-Estimated. NA-Not Available. NM-Not Meaningful. NR-Not Ranked. UR-Under Review.

Office: 1 Adp Blvd, Roseland, NJ 07068-1728.
Telephone: 973-974-5000.
Website: http://www.adp.com
Chrmn: A.F. Weinbach

Pres & CEO: G.C. Bulter
COO: S.M. Martone
VP & Treas: R.L. Colotti
VP, Secy & General Counsel: J.B. Benson

Board Members: G. D. Brenneman, L. Brun, G. C. Butler, L. G. Cooperman, G. Hubbard, J. P. Jones, F. V. Malek, H. Taub, A. F. Weinbach

Founded: 1949
Domicile: Delaware
Employees: 46,000

The McGraw-Hill Companies

AutoNation Inc

STANDARD &POOR'S

S&P Recommendation **HOLD** ★★★☆☆	Price $16.37 (as of Nov 23, 2007)	12-Mo. Target Price $20.00	Investment Style Large-Cap Blend

GICS Sector Consumer Discretionary
Sub-Industry Automotive Retail

Summary AutoNation, the largest U.S. retail auto dealer, owns and operates about 325 new vehicle franchises in 16 states.

Key Stock Statistics (Source S&P, Vickers, company reports)

52-Wk Range	$23.19– 15.42	S&P Oper. EPS 2007 E	1.51	Market Capitalization(B)	$3.011
Trailing 12-Month EPS	$1.45	S&P Oper. EPS 2008 E	1.68	Yield (%)	Nil
Trailing 12-Month P/E	11.3	P/E on S&P Oper. EPS 2007 E	10.8	Dividend Rate/Share	Nil
$10K Invested 5 Yrs Ago	$14,052	Common Shares Outstg. (M)	184.0	Institutional Ownership (%)	NM

Beta	0.71
S&P 3-Yr. Proj. EPS CAGR(%)	9.00
S&P Credit Rating	BBB-

Price Performance

30-Week Mov. Avg. · · · 10-Week Mov. Avg. – – GAAP Earnings vs. Previous Year Volume Above Avg. ▍▍ STARS
12-Mo. Target Price — Relative Strength — ▲ Up ▼ Down ▶ No Change Below Avg. ▍▍ ★

Options: ASE, CBOE, P, Ph

Analysis prepared by **Efraim Levy, CFA** on November 16, 2007, when the stock traded at **$ 16.47**.

Highlights

➤ New vehicle sales in coming months should continue to be restrained by weaker housing markets, especially in AutoNation's key California and Florida markets, and by higher gas prices and the impact of the credit crunch. We expect revenues to be down nearly 7% in 2007. We believe same-store new vehicle sales will decrease, on weaker demand for domestic vehicle brands, amid a decline that we expect in the overall U.S. market. For 2008, we look for stable industry volume, at 16.0 million light vehicles, and for AN sales to advance 1% to 2%, aided by higher parts and services revenues.

➤ We foresee margins benefiting from continued cost cutting. However, we project that macroeconomic factors, such as pressures on car prices and intensifying competition, will continue to weigh on AN's profitability. We expect floor plan interest expense to rise in 2008.

➤ We see AutoNation's EPS rising via increased operating efficiencies and continued share buybacks, which should help comparisons. We foresee cash flow being used to expand the business internally and via acquisitions, and to repurchase shares.

Investment Rationale/Risk

➤ The stock recently traded at P/E and price to free cash flow multiples within its peer average. The company's net margins are above peers. Based on S&P's Core Earnings methodology, we view AN's earnings quality for 2007 as high, as we do not expect adjustments for stock option expense, and the company does not offer its employees a pension plan.

➤ Risks to our recommendation and target price include lower multiples for automotive retailers, and less-than-expected vehicle demand and pricing for new and used vehicles.

➤ Applying a P/E of 12.5X, reflecting peer and historical P/E comparisons, to our 2008 EPS estimate leads to a value of $21. Our discounted cash flow model, which assumes a weighted average cost of capital of 10.3%, a compound annual growth rate of 5.7% over the next 15 years, and a terminal growth rate of 3%, calculates intrinsic value of about $19. Based on a combination of our discounted cash flow and P/E multiple analyses, our 12-month target price is $20.

Qualitative Risk Assessment

LOW	MEDIUM	HIGH

Our risk assessment reflects the cyclical nature of the automotive retailing industry, which is affected by interest rates, consumer confidence and personal discretionary spending, offset by the company's highly variable cost structure.

Quantitative Evaluations

S&P Quality Ranking B

D	C	B-	**B**	B+	A-	A	A+

Relative Strength Rank MODERATE

41

LOWEST = 1 HIGHEST = 99

Revenue/Earnings Data

Revenue (Million $)

	1Q	2Q	3Q	4Q	Year
2007	4,395	4,559	4,602	--	--
2006	4,612	4,959	4,945	4,473	18,989
2005	4,561	5,019	5,188	4,485	19,253
2004	4,630	4,916	5,041	4,838	19,425
2003	4,459	5,069	5,257	4,596	19,381
2002	4,751	5,016	5,194	4,519	19,479

Earnings Per Share ($)

2007	0.39	0.38	0.39	E0.35	E1.51
2006	0.37	0.33	0.40	0.35	1.45
2005	0.33	0.40	0.45	0.30	1.48
2004	0.32	0.35	0.35	0.43	1.45
2003	0.72	0.37	0.38	0.28	1.76
2002	0.28	0.32	0.33	0.26	1.19

Fiscal year ended Dec. 31. Next earnings report expected: Early February. EPS Estimates based on S&P Operating Earnings; historical GAAP earnings are as reported.

Dividend Data

No cash dividends have been paid.

Please read the Required Disclosures and Analyst Certification on the last page of this report.

The McGraw·Hill Companies

AutoNation Inc

STANDARD
&POOR'S

Business Summary November 16, 2007

CORPORATE OVERVIEW. AutoNation's vehicle retailing unit segment operates in saturated markets, in our view; about 75% of total U.S. vehicle sales are to replace existing autos.

AN's new auto retailing operations (59% of 2006 revenues) consist of about 325 dealerships. Although the company is the largest U.S. auto retailer, it controls only about 2% of the $1 trillion U.S. new and used car market.

The sale of used vehicles accounted for nearly 24% of revenues in 2006. Fixed operations provided nearly 14% of sales, while finance and insurance and other accounted for the balance.

MARKET PROFILE. The automotive retailing industry is the largest retail trade sector in the United States. It generates approximately $1.0 trillion in annual sales. The industry is highly fragmented, with the 100 largest automotive retailers generating about 17% of industry revenues in 2004 (latest available).

Car retailing is a very competitive business. With razor-thin profit margins and highly leveraged inventories that depreciate rapidly, dealers must generate

high volume and fast turnover. However, auto demand itself is driven by volatile factors such as strength of the economy, interest rate levels, and consumer confidence. In addition, dealerships operate with high overhead costs, resulting in a high sales break-even point.

Consolidation is an important trend, as the number of franchised stores in the U.S. has declined in the past 20 years, from approximately 24,725 in 1983 to 21,761 in 2006. The large capital requirements necessary to operate and be competitive in today's retailing environment make it likely that consolidation will continue.

U.S. new vehicle sales totaled more than 16.5 million units in 2006; we expect a drop to 16.0 million in 2007 and for volume to approximate that level again in 2008.

Company Financials Fiscal Year Ended Dec. 31

Per Share Data ($)	2006	2005	2004	2003	2002	2001	2000	1999	1998	1997
Tangible Book Value	2.66	6.53	4.53	3.91	3.14	2.99	2.64	4.72	11.84	4.34
Cash Flow	1.81	1.78	1.78	2.01	1.40	1.18	1.28	0.07	2.94	2.72
Earnings	1.45	1.48	1.45	1.76	1.19	0.73	0.91	-0.07	0.71	0.46
S&P Core Earnings	1.45	1.44	1.41	1.69	1.12	0.57	NA	NA	NA	NA
Dividends	Nil	Nil	Nil	Nil	Nil	Nil	Nil	Nil	Nil	Nil
Payout Ratio	Nil	Nil	Nil	Nil	Nil	Nil	Nil	Nil	Nil	Nil
Prices:High	22.94	22.84	19.33	19.19	18.73	13.07	10.75	18.38	30.00	44.38
Prices:Low	18.95	17.91	15.01	11.61	9.05	4.94	4.63	7.50	10.00	19.00
P/E Ratio:High	16	15	13	11	16	18	12	NM	42	96
P/E Ratio:Low	13	12	10	7	8	7	5	NM	14	41

Income Statement Analysis (Million $)

	2006	2005	2004	2003	2002	2001	2000	1999	1998	1997
Revenue	18,989	19,253	19,425	19,381	19,479	19,989	20,610	20,112	16,118	10,306
Operating Income	879	888	861	805	786	667	855	461	1,588	1,350
Depreciation	82.9	80.7	89.7	71.0	69.7	152	134	60.0	1,052	971
Interest Expense	267	191	159	143	125	43.7	248	35.0	22.0	17.0
Pretax Income	542	623	607	591	618	401	525	-27.0	523	315
Effective Tax Rate	38.9%	36.5%	34.7%	14.4%	38.3%	38.9%	37.5%	NM	35.9%	36.5%
Net Income	331	396	396	506	382	245	328	-31.0	335	200
S&P Core Earnings	331	385	385	486	359	192	NA	NA	NA	NA

Balance Sheet & Other Financial Data (Million $)

	2006	2005	2004	2003	2002	2001	2000	1999	1998	1997
Cash	52.2	244	107	171	176	128	82.2	369	217	148
Current Assets	3,386	3,880	3,678	3,990	3,629	3,153	4,176	4,301	8,406	6,826
Total Assets	8,607	8,825	8,699	8,823	8,585	8,065	8,830	9,613	13,926	10,527
Current Liabilities	3,031	3,412	3,411	3,810	2,981	2,578	3,141	3,165	5,540	4,263
Long Term Debt	1,558	484	798	808	643	647	850	836	2,316	2,334
Common Equity	3,713	4,670	4,263	3,950	3,910	3,828	3,843	4,601	5,425	3,484
Total Capital	5,496	5,340	5,218	4,935	5,500	5,329	5,570	6,241	9,968	5,818
Capital Expenditures	170	132	133	133	183	164	148	242	438	460
Cash Flow	414	476	486	577	451	397	462	29.0	1,387	1,171
Current Ratio	1.1	1.1	1.1	1.0	1.2	1.2	1.3	1.4	1.5	1.6
% Long Term Debt of Capitalization	28.3	9.1	15.3	16.4	11.7	12.1	15.3	13.4	29.1	40.1
% Net Income of Revenue	1.7	2.1	2.0	2.6	2.0	1.2	1.6	NM	2.1	1.9
% Return on Assets	3.8	4.5	4.5	5.8	4.6	2.9	3.6	NM	2.8	2.8
% Return on Equity	7.9	8.9	9.7	12.9	9.9	6.4	7.8	NM	7.5	8.4

Data as orig reptd.; bef. results of disc opers/spec. items. Per share data adj. for stk. divs.; EPS diluted. E-Estimated. NA-Not Available. NM-Not Meaningful. NR-Not Ranked. UR-Under Review.

Office: 110 SE 6th St , Ft. Lauderdale, FL 33301-5012.
Telephone: 954-769-6000.
Website: http://www.autonation.com
Chrmn & CEO: M.J. Jackson

Pres & COO: M.E. Maroone
EVP & CFO: M.J. Short
SVP, Secy & General Counsel: J.P. Ferrando
VP & Cntlr: A. McAllister

Board Members: R. J. Brown, R. L. Burdick, W. C. Crowley, K. C. Goodman, R. R. Grusky, M. J. Jackson, E. S. Lampert, M. E. Maroone, C. A. Migoya, I. B. Rosenfeld

Founded: 1991
Domicile: Delaware
Employees: 26,000

AutoZone Inc

STANDARD &POOR'S

S&P Recommendation **HOLD** ★★★☆☆	Price $107.24 (as of Nov 23, 2007)	12-Mo. Target Price $135.00	Investment Style Large-Cap Growth

GICS Sector Consumer Discretionary
Sub-Industry Automotive Retail

Summary This retailer of automotive parts and accessories operates over 3,800 AutoZone stores throughout most of the U.S. and in Mexico.

Key Stock Statistics (Source S&P, Vickers, company reports)

52-Wk Range	**$140.29– 104.53**	S&P Oper. EPS 2008**E**	9.45	Market Capitalization(B)	**$6.961**	Beta	1.23
Trailing 12-Month EPS	**$8.53**	S&P Oper. EPS 2009**E**	10.30	Yield (%)	**Nil**	S&P 3-Yr. Proj. EPS CAGR(%)	10.00
Trailing 12-Month P/E	**12.6**	P/E on S&P Oper. EPS 2008**E**	11.3	Dividend Rate/Share	**Nil**	S&P Credit Rating	BBB+
$10K Invested 5 Yrs Ago	**$12,569**	Common Shares Outstg. (M)	64.9	Institutional Ownership (%)	**NM**		

Price Performance

30-Week Mov. Avg. · · · 10-Week Mov. Avg. - - GAAP Earnings vs. Previous Year Volume Above Avg. STARS
12-Mo. Target Price — Relative Strength — ▲ Up ▼ Down ► No Change Below Avg.

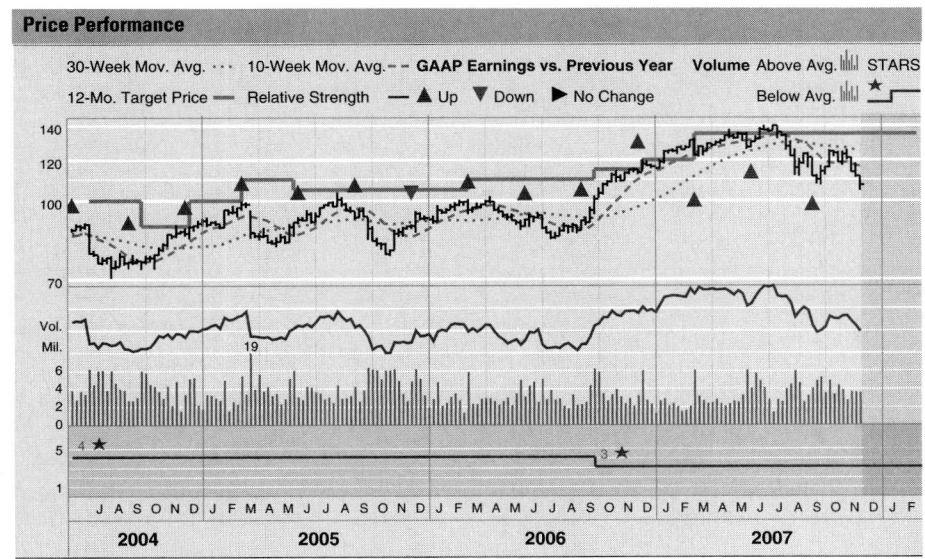

Options: ASE, CBOE, P, Ph

Analysis prepared by **Michael Souers** on September 26, 2007, when the stock traded at **$ 114.47**.

Highlights

➤ We see sales growth of between 4% and 5% in FY 08 (Aug.), following a 3.7% advance in FY 07. This reflects our projections of approximately 200 new stores and a low single digit rise in same-store sales, driven primarily by gains in commercial sales. We think rising gasoline prices are posing a financial burden on consumers, inducing them to delay preventative maintenance on their vehicles.

➤ We look for operating margins to widen slightly, as leverage from sales growth, well controlled store and payroll costs, and a greater share of wider margin private label products in the retail segment outweigh an expected increased proportion of lower margin commercial sales in the mix and projected higher advertising and marketing spending.

➤ After our estimates of slightly higher interest expense, effective taxes of 37.0%, and about 5% fewer shares, reflecting AZO's active share repurchase program, we forecast that FY 08 operating EPS will increase 11%, to $9.45, from the $8.53 earned in FY 07. We project FY 09 EPS of $10.30.

Investment Rationale/Risk

➤ At about 12X our FY 08 EPS estimate, the shares recently traded at slight discounts to both the S&P 500 and to peers. While the company maintains an industry leading sales to square foot ratio, and sports higher gross, operating, and net margins than any of its peers, its recent sales trends have been rather anemic, in our opinion. Despite what we view as a rational pricing environment, we think margins will continue to be pressured if same-store sales trends fail to improve from those in recent years. Longer term, we expect AZO to benefit from what we see as favorable vehicle demographic trends.

➤ Risks to our recommendation and target price include a slowdown in the U.S. economy; higher oil prices; a decrease in auto usage; technological changes that might reduce the need for auto parts; and execution risk for AZO as it tries to drive top line growth.

➤ Our 12-month target price of $135, based on our discounted cash flow (DCF) analysis, is equal to about 14X our FY 08 EPS estimate. Our DCF model assumes a weighted average cost of capital of 8.9% and a terminal growth rate of 3.0%.

Qualitative Risk Assessment

LOW	MEDIUM	HIGH

Our risk assessment for AutoZone reflects the cyclical and seasonal nature of the auto parts retailing industry, which is sensitive to various economic data points, offset by what we view as the company's strong financial metrics and margins.

Quantitative Evaluations

S&P Quality Ranking   B+

D	C	B-	B	B+	A-	A	A+

Relative Strength Rank   MODERATE

35

LOWEST = 1   HIGHEST = 99

Revenue/Earnings Data

Revenue (Million $)

	1Q	2Q	3Q	4Q	Year
2007	1,393	1,300	1,474	2,003	6,170
2006	1,338	1,254	1,417	1,939	5,948
2005	1,286	1,204	1,338	1,882	5,711
2004	1,282	1,159	1,360	1,836	5,637
2003	1,219	1,121	1,288	1,830	5,457
2002	1,176	1,081	1,225	1,843	5,326

Earnings Per Share ($)

2007	1.73	1.45	2.17	3.23	8.53
2006	1.48	1.25	1.89	2.92	7.50
2005	1.52	1.16	1.86	2.66	7.18
2004	1.35	1.04	1.68	2.53	6.56
2003	1.04	0.79	1.30	2.27	5.34
2002	0.76	0.58	0.96	1.73	4.00

Fiscal year ended Aug. 31. Next earnings report expected: Early December. EPS Estimates based on S&P Operating Earnings; historical GAAP earnings are as reported.

Dividend Data

No cash dividends have been paid.

AutoZone Inc

**STANDARD
&POOR'S**

Business Summary September 26, 2007

AutoZone is a leading specialty retailer of automotive parts, chemicals and accessories, focusing primarily on do-it-yourself (DIY) consumers. As of August 26, 2006, the company operated 3,771 U.S. AutoZone stores, in 48 states, the District of Columbia and Puerto Rico, and 100 stores in Mexico. AZO also sells automotive diagnostic equipment and repair software through ALLDATA, and diagnostic and repair information, along with and parts and accessories, online at autozone.com.

The company's 3,771 U.S. stores represented 24.7 million sq. ft., up from 3,592 stores and 22.8 million sq. ft. a year earlier.

Each store's product line includes new and remanufactured automotive hard parts, such as alternators, starters, water pumps, brake shoes and pads, carburetors, clutches and engines; maintenance items, such as oil, antifreeze, transmission, brake and power steering fluids, engine additives, protectants and waxes; and accessories, such as car stereos and floor mats. Parts are carried for domestic and foreign cars, sport utility vehicles, vans, and light trucks.

Stores, generally in high-visibility locations, range in size from about 4,000 sq.

ft. to 8,100 sq. ft., with new stores increasingly using a larger format. As of August 26, 2006, Autozone stores were principally in the following locations: 457 stores in Texas, 418 in California, 203 in Ohio, 180 in Illinois, 170 in Florida, 149 in Georgia, 138 in Tennessee, 136 in North Carolina, 132 in Michigan, 120 in Indiana, 111 in New York and 105 in Arizona, with the rest in other states.

AZO offers everyday low prices, and attempts to be the price leader in hard parts. Stores generally carry about 21,000 stock-keeping units. In addition to targeting the DIY customer, the company also has a commercial sales program in the U.S. (AZ Commercial), which provides commercial credit and delivery of parts and other products to local, regional and national repair garages, dealers and service stations. As of August 26, 2006, 2,134 stores had commercial sales programs. The hub stores provide fast replenishment of key merchandise to support the DIY and commercial sales businesses. AZO does not perform repairs or installations.

Company Financials Fiscal Year Ended Aug. 31

Per Share Data ($)	2007	2006	2005	2004	2003	2002	2001	2000	1999	1998
Tangible Book Value	1.52	2.35	1.15	NM	0.90	3.87	5.13	5.49	6.83	7.37
Cash Flow	10.82	9.34	8.92	7.79	6.47	5.10	2.70	2.88	2.44	2.10
Earnings	8.53	7.50	7.18	6.56	5.34	4.00	1.54	2.00	1.63	1.48
S&P Core Earnings	8.53	7.50	7.03	6.40	5.09	3.87	1.45	NA	NA	NA
Dividends	Nil	Nil	Nil	Nil	Nil	Nil	Nil	Nil	Nil	Nil
Payout Ratio	Nil	Nil	Nil	Nil	Nil	Nil	Nil	Nil	Nil	Nil
Prices:High	140.29	120.37	103.94	92.35	103.53	89.34	80.00	32.50	37.31	38.00
Prices:Low	104.53	83.81	77.76	70.35	58.21	59.20	24.37	21.00	22.56	20.50
P/E Ratio:High	16	16	14	14	19	22	52	16	23	26
P/E Ratio:Low	12	11	11	11	11	15	16	10	14	14

Income Statement Analysis (Million $)										
Revenue	6,170	5,948	5,711	5,637	5,457	5,326	4,818	4,483	4,116	3,243
Operating Income	1,215	1,239	1,114	1,106	1,028	889	646	630	555	478
Depreciation	159	139	138	107	110	118	131	118	122	95.5
Interest Expense	119	110	104	93.0	84.8	79.9	101	76.8	45.3	18.2
Pretax Income	936	902	873	906	833	691	287	435	388	364
Effective Tax Rate	36.4%	36.9%	34.6%	37.5%	37.9%	38.1%	38.8%	38.5%	36.9%	37.4%
Net Income	596	569	571	566	518	428	176	268	245	228
S&P Core Earnings	596	569	560	553	492	415	165	NA	NA	NA

Balance Sheet & Other Financial Data (Million $)										
Cash	86.7	91.6	74.8	76.9	6.74	6.50	7.29	6.97	5.92	6.63
Current Assets	2,270	2,119	1,929	1,756	1,585	1,450	1,329	1,187	1,225	1,117
Total Assets	4,805	4,526	4,245	3,913	3,680	3,478	3,433	3,333	3,285	2,748
Current Liabilities	2,286	2,055	1,811	1,818	1,676	1,534	1,267	1,035	1,001	860
Long Term Debt	1,936	1,857	1,862	1,869	1,547	1,195	1,225	1,250	888	545
Common Equity	403	470	391	171	374	1,378	866	997	1,324	1,302
Total Capital	2,339	2,327	2,253	2,046	1,921	2,573	2,092	2,247	2,212	1,302
Capital Expenditures	224	264	283	185	182	117	169	250	428	337
Cash Flow	755	709	709	673	627	546	307	386	367	323
Current Ratio	1.0	1.0	1.1	1.0	0.9	0.9	1.0	1.1	1.2	1.3
% Long Term Debt of Capitalization	82.8	79.8	82.6	91.3	80.5	46.4	58.6	55.6	40.2	29.5
% Net Income of Revenue	9.7	9.6	10.0	10.0	9.5	8.0	3.6	6.0	5.9	7.0
% Return on Assets	12.8	13.0	14.0	14.7	14.5	12.4	5.2	8.1	8.1	9.8
% Return on Equity	136.5	132.3	203.1	207.7	97.4	27.5	18.9	23.1	18.6	19.2

Data as orig reptd.; bef. results of disc opers/spec. items. Per share data adj. for stk. divs.; EPS diluted. E-Estimated. NA-Not Available. NM-Not Meaningful. NR-Not Ranked. UR-Under Review.

Office: 123 South Front Street, Memphis, TN 38103-3607.
Telephone: 901-495-6500.
Email: investor.relations@autozone.com
Website: http://www.autozone.com

Chrmn, Pres & CEO: W.C. Rhodes, III
Investor Contact: W.T. Giles (901-495-7185)
EVP, CFO & Treas: W.T. Giles
EVP, Secy & General Counsel: H.L. Goldsmith

VP & Cntlr: C. Pleas, III
Board Members: C. M. Elson, S. E. Gove, E. G. Graves, Jr., N. G. House, J. R. Hyde, III, W. A. McKenna, G. MrKonic, Jr., W. C. Rhodes, III, T. W. Ullyot

Founded: 1986
Domicile: Nevada
Employees: 55,000

AvalonBay Communities Inc.

STANDARD &POOR'S

S&P Recommendation HOLD ★★★☆☆	Price $99.33 (as of Nov 23, 2007)	12-Mo. Target Price $111.00	Investment Style Large-Cap Blend

GICS Sector Financials
Sub-Industry Residential REITS

Summary This real estate investment trust, formed via the 1998 merger of Bay Apartment Communities and Avalon Properties, specializes in upscale apartment communities.

Key Stock Statistics (Source S&P, Vickers, company reports)

52-Wk Range	**$149.94– 95.03**	S&P FFO/Sh. 2007**E**	**4.65**	Market Capitalization(B)	**$7.920**	Beta	**0.62**
Trailing 12-Month FFO/Share	**NA**	S&P FFO/Sh. 2008**E**	**5.05**	Yield (%)	**3.42**	S&P 3-Yr. FFO/Sh. Proj. CAGR(%)	**7.00**
Trailing 12-Month P/FFO	**NA**	P/FFO on S&P FFO/Sh. 2007**E**	**21.4**	Dividend Rate/Share	**$3.40**	S&P Credit Rating	**BBB+**
$10K Invested 5 Yrs Ago	**$30,854**	Common Shares Outstg. (M)	**79.7**	Institutional Ownership (%)	**NM**		

Price Performance

30-Week Mov. Avg. ··· 10-Week Mov. Avg. — **GAAP Earnings vs. Previous Year** Volume Above Avg. STARS
12-Mo. Target Price — Relative Strength — ▲ Up ▼ Down ▶ No Change Below Avg.

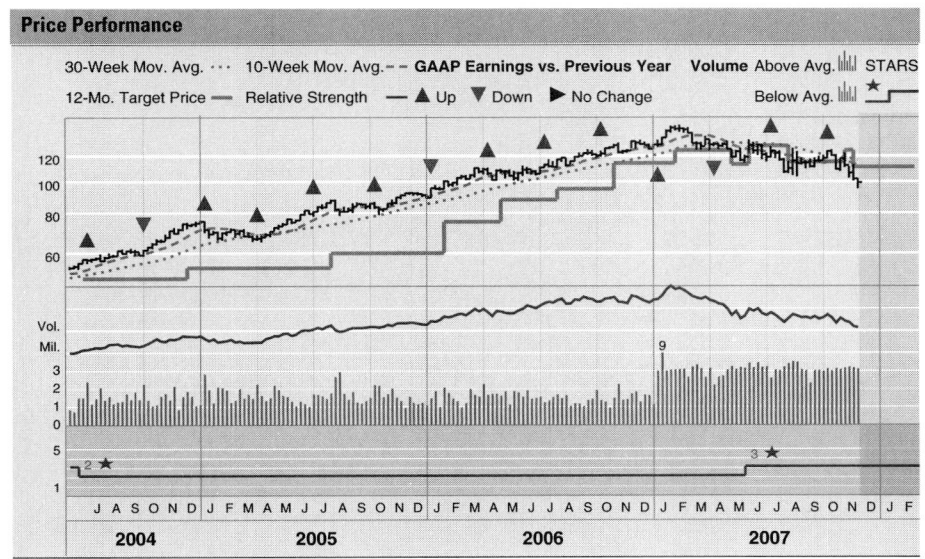

Options: ASE, CBOE, P

Analysis prepared by **Royal F. Shepard, CFA** on November 09, 2007, when the stock traded at **$ 105.85**.

Highlights

➤ We think rental rate increases will continue to moderate for the apartment sub-industry in 2008. AVB, in our view, is positioned to outperform most of its peers. We project 3%-4% average rent increases in 2008, following an estimated 5.5% average hike in 2007. The trust's position in relatively strong Northern California and Pacific Northwest markets is offsetting more negative trends in Boston and Washington, DC.

➤ The trust has a healthy pipeline of new development communities, in our view. As of September 30, 2007, it had 6,086 units in various stages of construction with a total capital cost of about $1.7 billion. We expect overall development activities to make an increasing contribution to revenues as 2008 progresses, leading to an overall revenue increase of 5%.

➤ Our 2008 FFO per share forecast of $5.05 represents an 8.6% increase from our 2007 estimate on higher revenues and effective cost control. We also think dividend coverage is adequate to increase the current annual payout of $3.40 by 5% - 10%.

Investment Rationale/Risk

➤ We think AVB is positioned in some of the best rental markets, particularly near coastal urban centers. It also has the largest pipeline of new development projects among our coverage universe. Near term, we believe moderating employment growth and increased rental supply will temper the trust's ability to hike rents. In addition, turmoil in the credit markets may reduce the value of income-oriented real estate properties, AVB's principal underlying asset. Recently selling at about 20.5X our 2008 FFO estimate, we think the shares fairly reflect growth prospects over the next 12 months.

➤ Risks to our recommendation and target price include the potential for slower than expected employment growth; higher than projected sales of single-family homes; and any reduction in the trust's dividend payout ratio.

➤ Our 12-month target price of $111 is based primarily on our net asset valuation calculation, using recent market transactions and a one-year cash yield of 4.5%. This implies a multiple of about 22X our 2008 FFO estimate, a premium to apartment peers.

Qualitative Risk Assessment

LOW	MEDIUM	HIGH

Our risk assessment reflects AVB's geographically diverse asset base, strong dividend coverage ratio and low stock price volatility.

Quantitative Evaluations

S&P Quality Ranking   A

D	C	B-	B	B+	A-	**A**	A+

Relative Strength Rank   WEAK

28

LOWEST = 1   HIGHEST = 99

Revenue/FFO Data

Revenue (Million $)

	1Q	2Q	3Q	4Q	Year
2007	196.7	201.9	208.1	--	--
2006	175.2	180.7	187.7	193.8	737.3
2005	161.3	165.6	170.8	173.1	670.7
2004	154.8	160.0	165.2	168.4	648.5
2003	149.7	151.0	153.2	155.8	609.7
2002	158.3	159.0	160.4	161.4	639.0

FFO Per Share ($)

2007	1.11	1.17	1.19	E1.18	E4.65
2006	1.15	1.03	1.11	1.09	4.38
2005	0.96	0.97	0.91	0.93	3.77
2004	0.79	0.83	0.86	0.88	3.36
2003	0.83	0.83	0.80	0.81	3.27
2002	0.99	0.95	0.87	0.85	3.65

Fiscal year ended Dec. 31. Next earnings report expected: NA. FFO Estimates based on S&P Funds From Operations Est..

Dividend Data (Dates: mm/dd Payment Date: mm/dd/yy)

Amount ($)	Date Decl.	Ex-Div. Date	Stk. of Record	Payment Date
0.780	12/11	12/27	12/29	01/16/07
0.850	01/30	03/29	04/02	04/16/07
0.850	06/14	06/27	06/29	07/16/07
0.850	09/12	09/26	09/28	10/15/07

Dividends have been paid since 1994. Source: Company reports.

AvalonBay Communities Inc.

**STANDARD
&POOR'S**

Business Summary November 09, 2007

CORPORATE OVERVIEW. AvalonBay Communities (AVB) is a real estate investment trust (REIT) specializing in the ownership of multi-family apartment communities. At September 30, 2007, AVB owned or held an interest in 182 apartment communities containing 51,898 apartment homes in 10 states and the District of Columbia, of which 19 communities were under construction and nine communities were under reconstruction. AVB also owned a direct or indirect ownership interest in rights to develop an additional 53 communities; if developed in the manner expected, these would contain an estimated 14,108 apartment homes.

MARKET PROFILE. The housing market is highly fragmented, and is characterized broadly by two types of housing units- multi-family and single-family. At the end 2005, the U.S. Census Bureau estimated that there were 123.93 million housing units in the country. Partly due to the high fragmentation and because residents have the option of either being owners or tenants (renters), the housing market can be highly competitive. Main demand drivers for apartments are household formation and employment growth. We expect 1.3 million new households to be formed in 2007, lower than an estimated 1.5 million

in 2006. Supply is created by new housing unit construction, which could consist of single-family homes, or multi-family apartment buildings or condominiums. We forecast 1.36 million total housing unit starts in 2007, down about 25% from 2006. Multi-family starts are expected to slip somewhat less, falling approximately 15%.

With apartment tenants on relatively short leases compared to those of commercial and industrial properties, we believe apartment REITs are generally more sensitive to changes in market conditions than REITs in other property categories. Results could be hurt by new construction that adds new space in excess of actual demand. Trends in home price affordability also affect both rent levels and the level of new construction, since the relative price attractiveness of owning versus renting is an important factor in consumer decision making.

Company Financials Fiscal Year Ended Dec. 31

Per Share Data ($)	2006	2005	2004	2003	2002	2001	2000	1999	1998	1997
Tangible Book Value	NA	NA	NA	NA	31.88	NA	29.31	36.04	36.42	29.94
Earnings	NA	NA	NA	NA	NA	3.12	2.53	2.00	1.37	1.40
S&P Core Earnings	2.27	1.34	1.09	1.27	1.22	3.07	NA	NA	NA	NA
Dividends	NA	NA	NA	NA	NA	2.56	2.24	2.05	1.86	1.66
Payout Ratio	137%	NM	NM	NM	188%	82%	89%	102%	136%	119%
Prices:High	134.60	92.99	75.93	49.71	52.65	51.90	50.63	37.00	39.25	40.63
Prices:Low	88.95	64.98	46.72	35.24	36.38	42.45	32.63	30.81	30.50	32.13
P/E Ratio:High	59	69	65	38	35	17	20	18	29	29
P/E Ratio:Low	39	48	40	27	24	14	13	15	22	23

Income Statement Analysis (Million $)										
Rental Income	731	666	648	Nil	Nil	637	572	503	352	122
Mortgage Income	Nil	Nil	Nil	Nil	Nil	Nil	Nil	Nil	Nil	4.16
Total Income	737	671	648	610	639	642	573	505	353	126
General Expenses	236	376	368	192	247	229	203	186	133	72.5
Interest Expense	111	127	131	135	121	103	83.6	74.7	54.0	21.1
Provision for Losses	Nil	Nil	Nil	Nil	Nil	Nil	Nil	Nil	Nil	Nil
Depreciation	163	159	152	151	144	130	123	110	78.4	27.0
Net Income	180	108	86.3	100	121	249	211	172	94.4	38.9
S&P Core Earnings	171	98.9	76.7	87.6	85.7	213	NA	NA	NA	NA

Balance Sheet & Other Financial Data (Million $)										
Cash	146	48.0	4,921	4,744	4,813	4,479	4,286	4,068	16.4	4.79
Total Assets	5,813	5,165	5,068	4,910	4,952	4,664	4,397	4,155	4,030	1,318
Real Estate Investment	5,662	5,874	NA	5,431	5,369	4,838	4,875	4,259	4,034	1,374
Loss Reserve	Nil	Nil	NA	Nil	Nil	Nil	Nil	Nil	Nil	Nil
Net Investment	4,562	4,946	4,919	4,736	4,800	4,391	4,212	4,052	3,891	1,294
Short Term Debt	Nil	Nil	Nil	Nil	165	101	14.1	3.60	4.50	2.02
Capitalization:Debt	2,705	2,177	2,335	2,337	2,307	1,983	1,716	1,411	1,480	485
Capitalization:Equity	2,631	2,542	2,385	2,311	2,194	2,314	2,442	2,370	2,339	793
Capitalization:Total	5,194	4,738	4,741	2,336	4,579	4,353	4,208	3,817	5.60	1,278
% Earnings & Depreciation/Assets	6.2	5.2	NA	5.1	5.5	8.4	7.8	6.8	6.5	6.5
Price Times Book Value:High	4.0	2.8	NA	1.5	1.7	1.6	1.7	1.0	1.1	1.4
Price Times Book Value:Low	2.7	2.0	NA	1.1	1.1	1.3	1.1	0.9	0.8	1.1

Data as orig reptd.; bef. results of disc opers/spec. items. Per share data adj. for stk. divs.; EPS diluted. E-Estimated. NA-Not Available. NM-Not Meaningful. NR-Not Ranked. UR-Under Review.

Avery Dennison Corp

STANDARD &POOR'S

S&P Recommendation BUY ★★★★☆	**Price** $50.50 (as of Nov 23, 2007)	**12-Mo. Target Price** $82.00	**Investment Style** Large-Cap Blend

GICS Sector Industrials
Sub-Industry Office Services & Supplies

Summary This company is a leading worldwide manufacturer of pressure-sensitive adhesives and materials, office products, labels, retail systems and specialty chemicals.

Key Stock Statistics (Source S&P, Vickers, company reports)

52-Wk Range	$71.35– 49.70	S&P Oper. EPS 2007**E**	3.80	Market Capitalization(B)	$5.377	Beta	0.66
Trailing 12-Month EPS	$3.27	S&P Oper. EPS 2008**E**	4.50	Yield (%)	3.25	S&P 3-Yr. Proj. EPS CAGR(%)	10.00
Trailing 12-Month P/E	15.4	P/E on S&P Oper. EPS 2007**E**	13.3	Dividend Rate/Share	$1.64	S&P Credit Rating	BBB+
$10K Invested 5 Yrs Ago	$8,870	Common Shares Outstg. (M)	106.5	Institutional Ownership (%)	86		

Price Performance

30-Week Mov. Avg. · · · 10-Week Mov. Avg. - - GAAP Earnings vs. Previous Year Volume Above Avg. STARS
12-Mo. Target Price — Relative Strength — ▲ Up ▼ Down ► No Change Below Avg.

Options: CBOE, P, Ph

Analysis prepared by **Richard O'Reilly, CFA** on August 13, 2007, when the stock traded at **$ 59.52**.

Qualitative Risk Assessment

LOW	MEDIUM	HIGH

Our risk assessment reflects the company's leading market shares in pressure-sensitive adhesives and office products, and our view of above-average growth rates in key end markets and a relatively strong balance sheet, offset by possible adverse legal issues. The stock's S&P Quality Ranking is A, the second highest possible, indicating a solid 10-year historical record of earnings and dividend growth.

Quantitative Evaluations

S&P Quality Ranking A

D	C	B-	B	B+	A-	A	A+

Relative Strength Rank MODERATE

31

LOWEST = 1   HIGHEST = 99

Revenue/Earnings Data

Revenue (Million $)

	1Q	2Q	3Q	4Q	Year
2007	1,390	1,524	1,680	--	--
2006	1,337	1,410	1,418	1,411	5,576
2005	1,346	1,419	1,363	1,364	5,474
2004	1,247	1,324	1,336	1,434	5,341
2003	1,135	1,192	1,204	1,231	4,763
2002	930.8	1,056	1,115	1,105	4,207

Earnings Per Share ($)

2007	0.80	0.87	0.59	E0.96	E3.80
2006	0.69	0.96	0.85	1.01	3.51
2005	0.58	0.89	0.86	0.57	2.90
2004	0.52	0.68	0.75	0.83	2.78
2003	0.71	0.70	0.65	0.40	2.43
2002	0.66	0.74	0.64	0.56	2.59

Fiscal year ended Dec. 31. Next earnings report expected: Late January. EPS Estimates based on S&P Operating Earnings; historical GAAP earnings are as reported.

Highlights

➤ We expect sales in 2007 to rise about 15%, largely reflecting the June 2007 purchase of Paxar Corp. We see ongoing businesses growing about 3% in 2007, assuming a rebound in volumes in the U.S. roll material business and continued good gains in Europe, Asia and Latin America.

➤ We expect a better back-to-school season on top of a good gain in 2006 for the office products and consumer unit, but economically sensitive products such as graphics and tapes will likely remain sluggish. The benefit of modestly favorable currency exchange rates should be partly offset by a negative impact from an overall lower price mix, especially in pressure-sensitive materials.

➤ We expect margins to be helped by volume growth and by annualized cost reductions doubling to almost $100 million, partly offset by higher marketing spending. We expect interest expense of about $105 million on higher debt, and a 21% effective tax rate, versus a 17% rate in 2006. Our estimates include modest EPS dilution expected from the purchase of Paxar but exclude merger-related costs, including $0.13 in the second quarter.

Investment Rationale/Risk

➤ While growth since 2005 was slower than we had expected, we see stronger comparisons for the rest of 2007 and into 2008. We believe fundamentals remain sound, with growth driven by the increasing use of non-impact printing systems for computers and for product tracking and information needs. We see a proliferation of high-quality graphics on packaging and consumer products spurring sales of pressure-sensitive labels. We view favorably the purchase of Paxar, a major competitor in the products identification industry, and expect significant cost savings over the next two years.

➤ Risks to our recommendation and target price include the potentially adverse impact of remaining antitrust investigations and related civil suits involving AVY, an inability to introduce new products or raise selling prices in response to changes in raw material costs, and risk related to integration of the Paxar acquisition.

➤ Our 12-month target price is $82. We value AVY shares using a P/E of 18X our 2008 EPS estimate, near their historical premium to the S&P 500 of almost 20% on a P/E basis.

Dividend Data (Dates: mm/dd Payment Date: mm/dd/yy)

Amount ($)	Date Decl.	Ex-Div. Date	Stk. of Record	Payment Date
0.400	01/25	03/05	03/07	03/21/07
0.400	04/26	06/04	06/06	06/20/07
0.400	07/25	08/31	09/05	09/19/07
0.410	10/30	12/03	12/05	12/19/07

Dividends have been paid since 1964. Source: Company reports.

Avery Dennison Corp

Business Summary August 13, 2007

CORPORATE OVERVIEW. Avery Dennison is the leading global manufacturer of pressure-sensitive technology and self-adhesive solutions for consumer products and label systems, including office products, product identification and control systems, and specialty tapes and chemicals.

Foreign operations accounted for 58% of sales in 2006.

The pressure-sensitive adhesives and materials group (58% of sales and 56% of operating profits in 2006) includes Fasson- and JAC-brand pressure sensitive, self-adhesive coated papers; plastic films and metal foils in roll and sheet form; graphic and decoration films and labels; and adhesives, protective coatings and electroconductive resins for industrial, automotive, aerospace, appliance, electronic, medical and consumer markets. The acquisition of Jackstadt in May 2002 was AVY's largest purchase in more than a decade, and, we believe, strengthened its business in many developing markets worldwide.

The office and consumer products group (19% and 33%) consists of consumer and office products such as pressure-sensitive labels; copier, laser and ink-jet print labels and template software; notebooks; presentation and organizing products (binders, sheet protectors, dividers); writing instruments; marking devices; security badge systems; and many other products sold under the Avery, National, and Hi-Liter brands for office, home, and school uses.

Retail information services (12% and 8%) sell a variety of price marking and brand identification products for retailers, apparel manufacturers, distributors and industrial customers. Products include woven and printed labels; heat transfers; graphic and barcode tags; patches; integrated tags; price tickets; customer hard and soft good packaging; barcode printers; software; plastics fastening; and applications devices for use in identification, tracking and control applications.

Other businesses (11% and 3%) consists of industrial and automotive decoration films and graphics sold primarily to original equipment manufacturers; self-adhesive postal stamps and on-battery testing labels; and specialty fastening and bonding tapes sold in roll form. The radio frequency identification (RFID) business (inlays and labels) has been reported in this segment beginning in 2005. The RFID business had a net loss of about $30 million in each of 2005 and 2006, but we expect the loss to decline modestly in 2007 followed by a further reduction in 2008.

Company Financials Fiscal Year Ended Dec. 31

Per Share Data ($)	2006	2005	2004	2003	2002	2001	2000	1999	1998	1997
Tangible Book Value	8.84	6.74	5.85	4.08	2.53	4.70	3.94	3.66	5.98	5.91
Cash Flow	5.50	4.95	4.66	4.22	4.12	4.05	4.41	3.61	3.37	3.03
Earnings	3.51	2.90	2.78	2.43	2.59	2.47	2.84	2.13	2.15	1.93
S&P Core Earnings	3.48	2.66	2.51	2.05	2.02	1.81	NA	NA	NA	NA
Dividends	1.57	1.53	1.49	1.45	1.35	1.23	1.11	0.99	0.87	0.72
Payout Ratio	45%	53%	54%	60%	52%	50%	39%	46%	40%	37%
Prices:High	69.31	63.58	66.60	63.75	69.70	60.50	78.50	73.00	62.06	45.75
Prices:Low	54.95	49.60	53.50	46.25	52.06	43.25	41.13	39.38	39.44	33.38
P/E Ratio:High	20	22	24	26	27	24	28	34	29	24
P/E Ratio:Low	16	17	19	19	20	18	14	18	18	17

Income Statement Analysis (Million $)										
Revenue	5,576	5,474	5,341	4,763	4,207	3,803	3,894	3,768	3,460	3,346
Operating Income	683	690	655	602	593	566	638	589	499	460
Depreciation	199	202	188	179	153	156	157	150	127	117
Interest Expense	55.5	57.9	58.5	57.7	43.7	50.2	54.6	43.4	34.6	31.7
Pretax Income	426	367	373	335	365	360	426	330	337	311
Effective Tax Rate	17.2%	20.4%	25.1%	27.5%	29.5%	32.4%	33.5%	34.8%	33.7%	34.2%
Net Income	353	292	280	243	257	243	284	215	223	205
S&P Core Earnings	348	269	251	205	201	179	NA	NA	NA	NA

Balance Sheet & Other Financial Data (Million $)										
Cash	58.5	98.5	84.8	29.5	22.8	19.1	11.4	6.90	18.5	3.30
Current Assets	1,655	1,558	1,542	1,441	1,216	982	982	956	802	794
Total Assets	4,294	4,204	4,399	4,105	3,652	2,819	2,699	2,593	2,143	2,047
Current Liabilities	1,699	1,526	1,387	1,496	1,296	951	801	850	664	630
Long Term Debt	502	723	1,007	888	837	627	773	701	466	404
Common Equity	1,681	1,512	1,549	1,319	1,056	929	828	810	833	838
Total Capital	2,261	2,235	2,647	2,274	1,968	1,647	1,695	1,610	1,363	1,292
Capital Expenditures	162	163	179	201	152	135	198	178	160	177
Cash Flow	552	493	468	422	410	399	440	366	351	322
Current Ratio	1.0	1.0	1.1	1.0	0.9	1.0	1.2	1.1	1.2	1.3
% Long Term Debt of Capitalization	22.2	32.4	38.1	39.0	42.5	38.0	45.6	43.5	34.2	31.3
% Net Income of Revenue	6.3	5.3	5.2	5.1	6.1	6.4	7.3	5.7	6.5	6.1
% Return on Assets	8.3	6.8	6.6	6.3	7.8	8.8	10.7	9.1	10.7	10.0
% Return on Equity	22.1	19.1	19.5	20.4	25.9	27.7	34.6	26.2	26.7	24.5

Data as orig reptd.; bef. results of disc opers/spec. items. Per share data adj. for stk. divs.; EPS diluted. E-Estimated. NA-Not Available. NM-Not Meaningful. NR-Not Ranked. UR-Under Review.

Office: 150 North Orange Grove Boulevard, Pasadena, CA 91103.
Telephone: 626-304-2000.
Email: investorcom@averydennison.com
Website: http://www.averydennison.com

Chrmn: K. Kresa
Pres & CEO: D.A. Scarborough
EVP & CFO: D.R. O'Bryant
EVP, Secy & Chief Lgl Officer: R.G. van Schoonenberg

VP, Chief Acctg Officer & Cntlr: M.R. Butier
Investor Contact: C.S. Guenther (626-304-2204)
Board Members: P. K. Barker, R. Borjesson, J. T. Cardis, R. M. Ferry, K. Kresa, P. W. Mullin, D. E. Pyott, D. A. Scarborough, P. Siewert, J. A. Stewart

Founded: 1935
Domicile: Delaware
Employees: 22,700

Avon Products Inc.

STANDARD &POOR'S

S&P Recommendation **HOLD** ★★★★★	Price $41.17 (as of Nov 23, 2007)	12-Mo. Target Price $43.00	Investment Style Large-Cap Growth

GICS Sector Consumer Staples
Sub-Industry Personal Products

Summary This company is the world's leading direct marketer of cosmetics, toiletries, fashion jewelry and fragrances, with more than 3 million sales representatives worldwide.

Key Stock Statistics (Source S&P, Vickers, company reports)

52-Wk Range	$42.51–31.95	S&P Oper. EPS 2007**E** 1.63	Market Capitalization(B) $17.812	Beta	0.15
Trailing 12-Month EPS	$1.33	S&P Oper. EPS 2008**E** 1.89	Yield (%) 1.80	S&P 3-Yr. Proj. EPS CAGR(%)	11.00
Trailing 12-Month P/E	31.0	P/E on S&P Oper. EPS 2007**E** 25.3	Dividend Rate/Share $0.74	S&P Credit Rating	A
$10K Invested 5 Yrs Ago	$17,179	Common Shares Outstg. (M) 432.6	Institutional Ownership (%) 88		

Price Performance

30-Week Mov. Avg. ···   10-Week Mov. Avg. - - GAAP Earnings vs. Previous Year   Volume Above Avg. STARS
12-Mo. Target Price —   Relative Strength — ▲ Up ▼ Down ▶ No Change   Below Avg.

Options: ASE, CBOE, P, Ph

Analysis prepared by **Loran Braverman, CFA** on October 31, 2007, when the stock traded at **$ 40.98**.

Highlights

➤ In late 2005, AVP announced a multi-year restructuring plan in an effort to drive revenue and profit growth. The plan entails reorganizing and downsizing the organization, implementing global manufacturing, and increasing supply chain efficiencies. AVP plans to reinvest the savings from this plan in marketing, R&D, and incentivizing its sales force.

➤ Year-to-year sales comparisons started to pick up in mid-2006. For 2007, we see sales rising 11%, reflecting favorable foreign currency, strong sales in Latin America and China, and stabilization in Asia-Pacific. We look for modest sales growth in the U.S. For 2008, we forecast sales growth of 6%, assuming neutral foreign currency effect, with the strongest growth expected in China and Central & Eastern Europe.

➤ In our opinion, the timing is getting pushed further out for the profit margin goals of the restructuring plan. We previously believed the operating margin would increase substantially in 2007, but we now look for little change, with a 140 basis point gain in 2008, following 2006's 280 bp decline. We project that operating EPS will increase to $1.63 in 2007 and $1.89 in 2008, from $1.38 in 2006.

Investment Rationale/Risk

➤ We are encouraged by signs of stabilization in the Asia Pacific region, a flattening to improvement in the active sales force base in North America following declines, and indications that the restructuring plan is helping to bring down costs. However, we are concerned that the company's path to consistent, sustainable growth through new products, heavy marketing support, investing more in the sales force, and continued restructuring may be both prolonged and uneven, and, thus, we would not add to positions.

➤ Risks to our recommendation and target price include renewed deterioration in the U.S. market, political and economic instability in international markets, competition from various sales channels, and unfavorable consumer reception of new products.

➤ Our 12-month target price of $43 is a blend of our historical and relative analyses. Our historical analysis suggests a P/E of 26X, close to the 10-year average, implying a value of $49 on our 2008 EPS estimate of $1.89. Given our concerns about consistency, we believe AVP should trade at only a slight premium to its peers, or at 19.7X, implying a value of $37.

Qualitative Risk Assessment

LOW	MEDIUM	HIGH

Our risk assessment reflects that demand for personal care products is usually static and not generally affected by changes in the economy or geopolitical factors. However, certain product categories such as fragrances are more susceptible to the aforementioned factors.

Quantitative Evaluations

S&P Quality Ranking A

D	C	B-	B	B+	A-	A	A+

Relative Strength Rank STRONG

93

LOWEST = 1   HIGHEST = 99

Revenue/Earnings Data

Revenue (Million $)

	1Q	2Q	3Q	4Q	Year
2007	2,185	2,329	2,349	--	--
2006	2,003	2,080	2,059	2,623	8,764
2005	1,881	1,984	1,886	2,398	8,150
2004	1,765	1,866	1,806	2,311	7,748
2003	1,481	1,656	1,629	2,109	6,876
2002	1,384	1,527	1,463	1,854	6,228

Earnings Per Share ($)

2007	0.34	0.26	0.32	E0.54	E1.63
2006	0.12	0.34	0.19	0.41	1.06
2005	0.36	0.69	0.35	0.40	1.81
2004	0.31	0.49	0.37	0.61	1.77
2003	0.21	0.36	0.28	0.55	1.39
2002	0.20	0.32	0.19	0.40	1.11

Fiscal year ended Dec. 31. Next earnings report expected: Early February. EPS Estimates based on S&P Operating Earnings; historical GAAP earnings are as reported.

Dividend Data (Dates: mm/dd Payment Date: mm/dd/yy)

Amount ($)	Date Decl.	Ex-Div. Date	Stk. of Record	Payment Date
0.185	02/01	02/13	02/15	03/01/07
0.185	05/03	05/16	05/18	06/01/07
0.185	08/02	08/15	08/17	09/03/07
0.185	11/02	11/13	11/15	12/03/07

Dividends have been paid since 1919. Source: Company reports.

Please read the Required Disclosures and Analyst Certification on the last page of this report.

The **McGraw-Hill** Companies

Avon Products Inc.

Business Summary October 31, 2007

CORPORATE OVERVIEW. Avon Products, which began operations in 1886, is a global manufacturer and marketer of beauty and related products. The company has three product categories: Beauty, Beauty Plus and Beyond Beauty. Beauty consists of cosmetics, fragrance and toiletries and accounted for 70% of sales in 2006. Beauty Plus (19%) consists of jewelry, watches and apparel and accessories. Beyond Beauty (11%) consists of home products, gift and decorative and candles. The company has operations in 62 countries, including the U.S., and its products are distributed in 51 additional countries, for coverage in 113 markets. Geographically, 29% of 2006 sales were derived from North America, while Latin America accounted for 32%, Western Europe, the Middle East & Africa 13%, Central & Eastern Europe 15%, Asia Pacific 9%, and China 2%. Operations outside North America accounted for 80% of operating profits in 2006. Sales are made to the ultimate customer mainly through a combination of direct selling and marketing by about 5.3 million independent Avon representatives, around 446,000 of whom are in the U.S.

CORPORATE STRATEGY. AVP embarked on a multi-year restructuring plan in November 2005 in an effort to drive revenue and profit growth. The plan entails reorganizing and downsizing the organization, implementing global manufacturing, and increasing supply chain efficiencies. AVP expects restructuring benefits will help fund an increase in consumer research, marketing, and product development to ultimately enhance sales beginning in 2007. In fact, we have seen an improvement in the quarterly year-to-year sales growth rate starting in mid-2006, but, so far, savings from the plan have not been large enough to offset increases in the expenses mentioned above. Also in 2005, Avon started to implement a global supply chain strategy, which includes the development of a new common systems platform, known as enterprise resource planning (ERP).

Company Financials Fiscal Year Ended Dec. 31

Per Share Data ($)	2006	2005	2004	2003	2002	2001	2000	1999	1998	1997
Tangible Book Value	1.79	1.68	2.02	0.79	NM	NM	NM	NM	0.55	0.54
Cash Flow	1.42	2.10	2.05	1.63	1.34	1.10	1.20	0.74	0.64	0.77
Earnings	1.06	1.81	1.77	1.39	1.11	0.90	1.01	0.58	0.51	0.64
S&P Core Earnings	1.16	1.80	1.80	1.37	0.95	0.77	NA	NA	NA	NA
Dividends	0.70	0.66	0.70	0.42	0.40	0.38	0.37	0.36	0.34	0.32
Payout Ratio	66%	36%	40%	30%	36%	42%	37%	62%	67%	50%
Prices:High	34.25	45.66	46.65	34.88	28.55	25.06	24.88	29.56	23.13	19.50
Prices:Low	26.16	24.33	30.81	24.47	21.75	17.78	12.63	11.66	12.50	12.66
P/E Ratio:High	32	25	26	25	26	28	25	51	45	31
P/E Ratio:Low	25	13	17	18	20	20	12	20	25	20

Income Statement Analysis (Million $)										
Revenue	8,764	8,150	7,748	6,876	6,228	5,995	5,715	5,289	5,213	5,079
Operating Income	1,146	1,289	1,361	1,162	1,029	951	886	762	706	616
Depreciation	160	140	135	124	125	109	97.1	83.0	72.0	72.1
Interest Expense	99.6	54.1	33.8	33.3	52.0	71.1	84.7	43.2	41.0	41.8
Pretax Income	704	1,124	1,188	994	836	666	691	507	456	535
Effective Tax Rate	31.8%	24.0%	27.8%	32.1%	35.0%	34.7%	29.2%	40.3%	41.9%	37.0%
Net Income	478	848	846	665	535	430	485	302	270	339
S&P Core Earnings	518	845	859	652	455	367	NA	NA	NA	NA

Balance Sheet & Other Financial Data (Million $)										
Cash	1,199	1,059	770	694	607	509	123	117	106	142
Current Assets	3,334	2,921	2,506	2,226	2,048	1,889	1,546	1,338	1,341	1,344
Total Assets	5,238	4,763	4,148	3,562	3,328	3,193	2,826	2,529	2,434	2,273
Current Liabilities	2,550	2,502	1,526	1,588	1,976	1,461	1,359	1,713	1,330	1,356
Long Term Debt	1,171	766	866	878	767	1,236	1,108	701	201	102
Common Equity	790	794	950	371	-128	-74.6	-216	-406	285	285
Total Capital	2,028	1,595	1,829	1,300	712	1,192	954	365	559	456
Capital Expenditures	175	207	250	163	127	155	194	203	190	169
Cash Flow	637	987	981	788	659	539	582	385	342	411
Current Ratio	1.3	1.2	1.6	1.4	1.0	1.3	1.3	0.8	1.0	1.0
% Long Term Debt of Capitalization	58.8	48.1	47.4	67.5	107.8	103.7	116.1	192.3	36.0	22.3
% Net Income of Revenue	5.4	10.4	10.9	9.7	8.6	7.2	8.5	5.7	5.2	6.7
% Return on Assets	9.6	19.0	21.9	19.3	16.4	14.3	18.1	12.2	11.5	15.1
% Return on Equity	60.3	97.2	128.0	545.8	NM	NM	NM	NM	94.7	128.7

Data as orig reptd.; bef. results of disc opers/spec. items. Per share data adj. for stk. divs.; EPS diluted. E-Estimated. NA-Not Available. NM-Not Meaningful. NR-Not Ranked. UR-Under Review.

Office: 1345 Avenue Of The Americas, New York, NY 10105-0196.
Telephone: 212-282-5000.
Email: individual.investor@avon.com
Website: http://www.avoninvestor.com

Chrmn & CEO: A. Jung
EVP & CFO: C. Cramb
SVP & General Counsel: G.L. Klemann, II
VP & Chief Acctg Officer: K. Byrne

VP & Secy: K.K. Azzarelli
Investor Contact: R. Johansen (212-282-5320)
Board Members: W. D. Cornwell, E. T. Fogarty, F. Hassan, A. Jung, M. E. Lagomasino, A. S. Moore, P. S. Pressler, G. M. Rodkin, P. Stern, L. A. Weinbach

Founded: 1886
Domicile: New York
Employees: 40,300

Baker Hughes Inc

STANDARD &POOR'S

S&P Recommendation **STRONG BUY** ★★★★★	Price $82.31 (as of Nov 23, 2007)	12-Mo. Target Price $113.00	Investment Style Large-Cap Growth

GICS Sector Energy
Sub-Industry Oil & Gas Equipment & Services

Summary This company is one of the world's largest oilfield services companies, providing products and services to the energy industry.

Key Stock Statistics (Source S&P, Vickers, company reports)

52-Wk Range	**$100.29– 62.26**	S&P Oper. EPS 2007**E**	**4.86**	Market Capitalization(B)	**$26.303**	Beta	**0.96**
Trailing 12-Month EPS	**$4.52**	S&P Oper. EPS 2008**E**	**6.28**	Yield (%)	**0.63**	S&P 3-Yr. Proj. EPS CAGR(%)	**20.00**
Trailing 12-Month P/E	**18.2**	P/E on S&P Oper. EPS 2007**E**	**16.9**	Dividend Rate/Share	**$0.52**	S&P Credit Rating	**A**
$10K Invested 5 Yrs Ago	**$27,487**	Common Shares Outstg. (M)	**319.6**	Institutional Ownership (%)	**95**		

Price Performance

30-Week Mov. Avg. · · ·   10-Week Mov. Avg. – – –   **GAAP Earnings vs. Previous Year**   Volume Above Avg. STARS
12-Mo. Target Price —   Relative Strength —   ▲ Up ▼ Down ▶ No Change   Below Avg.

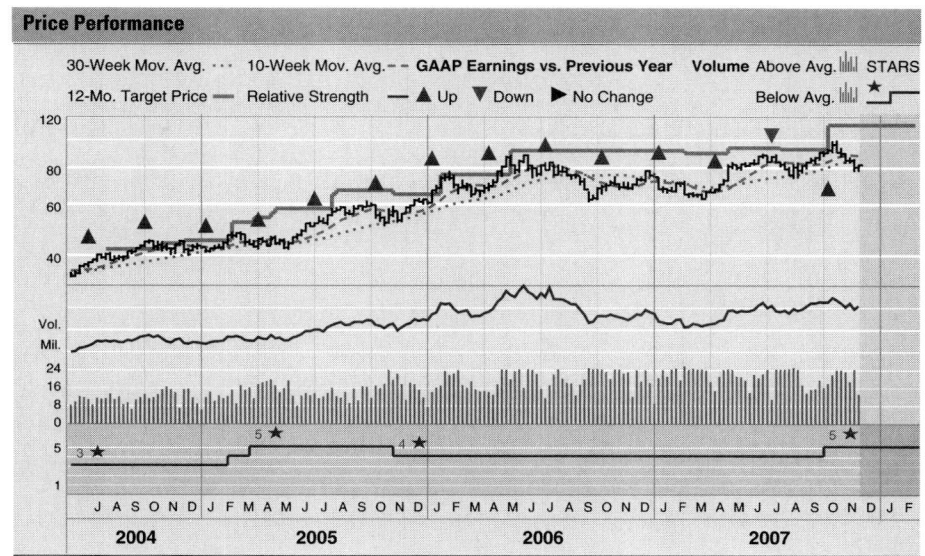

Options: ASE, CBOE, P, Ph

Analysis prepared by **Stewart Glickman, CFA** on November 16, 2007, when the stock traded at **$ 78.71**.

Highlights

➤ In the third quarter, BHI's North American business generated year over year incremental margins of 23%, an improvement from 17% in the second quarter, and worldwide year over year incremental margins reached 24% in the third quarter. We expect incremental margins to trend higher, albeit not to the 30% range in the near term, given current investments in infrastructure in the Eastern Hemisphere and pricing pressure in North America. However, we see strong growth opportunities in the Eastern Hemisphere and see this as a primary catalyst for BHI.

➤ In October, BHI said that Mexico and Venezuela could see strong oilfield activity in 2008, as well as Brazil, and Russia is expected to remain a strong source of activity growth.

➤ We expect total revenues to increase about 16% in 2007, with greater gains in international markets than in North America. We estimate that operating margins of the core oilfield segment will widen to about 25% in 2007, versus 24.3% in 2006. For 2008, we see revenue growth of about 16%, with further margin gains to the 27% range. We estimate 2007 EPS of $4.86, rising to $6.28 in 2008.

Investment Rationale/Risk

➤ With 48% of total oilfield revenues generated in the faster growing Eastern Hemisphere in the first nine months of 2007, we see strong growth prospects for BHI going forward. In addition, unlike most peers, BHI does not offer pressure pumping services, which is the one service offering we view as most likely to be at risk for pricing weakness in 2008 (relative to other oilfield services) given relatively large additions to market capacity.

➤ Risks to our recommendation and target price include lower prices for oil and natural gas; reduced drilling activity in international markets; and higher than expected cost inflation.

➤ Our discounted cash flow model, which assumes free cash flow growth of about 9% for 10 years, with 3% growth thereafter, discounted at a weighted average cost of capital of 9.1%, shows an intrinsic value of about $119 per share. Based on our view of above-average 2008 ROIC, we think a premium to peer valuation is warranted. Applying multiples of 11X to projected 2008 EBITDA and 13X to estimated 2008 cash flow (both premiums to peers), and blending with our DCF model, our 12-month target price is $113.

Qualitative Risk Assessment

LOW	**MEDIUM**	HIGH

Our risk assessment reflects BHI's exposure to volatile crude oil and natural gas prices, capital spending decisions by its exploration and production customers, and political risk associated with operating in frontier regions. Offsetting these risks is BHI's strong position in drilling and completion products.

Quantitative Evaluations

S&P Quality Ranking   **B**

D	C	B-	**B**	B+	A-	A	A+

Relative Strength Rank   **MODERATE**

56

LOWEST = 1   HIGHEST = 99

Revenue/Earnings Data

Revenue (Million $)

	1Q	2Q	3Q	4Q	Year
2007	2,473	2,538	2,678	--	--
2006	2,062	2,203	2,309	2,453	9,027
2005	1,643	1,768	1,785	1,989	7,186
2004	1,388	1,499	1,538	1,679	6,104
2003	1,200	1,315	1,338	1,440	5,293
2002	1,203	1,245	1,280	1,292	5,020

Earnings Per Share ($)

2007	1.17	1.09	1.22	E1.39	E4.86
2006	0.93	4.14	1.09	1.02	7.21
2005	0.53	0.64	0.64	0.76	2.56
2004	0.28	0.35	0.41	0.53	1.57
2003	0.15	0.24	-0.29	0.30	0.40
2002	0.21	0.21	0.19	-0.01	0.66

Fiscal year ended Dec. 31. Next earnings report expected: Mid February. EPS Estimates based on S&P Operating Earnings; historical GAAP earnings are as reported.

Dividend Data (Dates: mm/dd Payment Date: mm/dd/yy)

Amount ($)	Date Decl.	Ex-Div. Date	Stk. of Record	Payment Date
0.130	01/25	02/01	02/05	02/16/07
0.130	04/26	05/03	05/07	05/18/07
0.130	07/26	08/02	08/06	08/17/07
0.130	10/25	11/01	11/05	11/16/07

Dividends have been paid since 1987. Source: Company reports.

Please read the Required Disclosures and Analyst Certification on the last page of this report.

The McGraw-Hill Companies

Baker Hughes Inc

Business Summary November 16, 2007

CORPORATE OVERVIEW. Baker Hughes was formed through the 1987 merger of Baker International Corp. and Hughes Tool Co. In 1998, it acquired seismic and wireline logging company Western Atlas, creating the third largest oilfield services company. BHI has operations in over 90 countries. North America accounted for 44% of total revenues in 2006, followed by the Europe, CIS and Africa region (27%) and the Middle East and Asia-Pacific region (19%). In 2005, the company reorganized its seven product-line focused divisions into three operating segments: Drilling & Evaluation; Completion & Production; and Western Geco (which provides reservoir imaging, monitoring and development services). In April 2006, however, BHI sold its 30% minority stake in seismic company Western Geco to the majority joint venture partner, Schlumberger. We like the deal for BHI, as we think it should enable BHI to focus on its core oilfield operations of drilling, completion and production.

The Drilling & Evaluation segment (52% of 2006 total oilfield revenues and 57% of total oilfield segment income) consists of four operating divisions: Baker Hughes Drilling Fluids, Hughes Christensen, INTEQ, and Baker Atlas. The products and services in this segment are typically used in the drilling of crude oil and natural gas wells.

Baker Hughes Drilling Fluids provides drilling and completion fluids, and fluid

environmental services. Fluids are used in order to control downhole pressure, clean the bottom of the well, and to cool and lubricate the drill bit and drill string. Hughes Christensen manufactures drill bit products, primarily Tri-cone roller cone drill bits and polycrystalline diamond compact (PDC) fixed cutter bits. INTEQ supplies directional and horizontal drilling services, coring services, subsurface surveying, logging-while-drilling, and measurement-while-drilling services.

Baker Atlas provides formation evaluation and perforating services for oil and natural gas wells. Formation evaluation involves measuring and analyzing specific physical properties of the rock in the vicinity of the wellbore to determine a reservoir's boundaries, hydrocarbon volume, and ability to produce fluids to the surface. Perforating services involve puncturing a well's steel casing and cement sheath with explosive charges; this creates a fracture in the formation, and provides a path for the hydrocarbons in the formation to enter the wellbore.

Company Financials Fiscal Year Ended Dec. 31

Per Share Data ($)	2006	2005	2004	2003	2002	2001	2000	1999	1998	1997
Tangible Book Value	11.58	9.42	7.35	5.87	6.05	5.69	4.64	4.17	3.98	9.16
Cash Flow	8.85	3.68	2.69	1.59	1.56	2.32	2.14	2.52	1.43	1.93
Earnings	7.21	2.56	1.57	0.40	0.66	1.31	0.31	0.16	-0.92	0.71
S&P Core Earnings	4.24	2.47	1.50	0.62	0.55	1.17	NA	NA	NA	NA
Dividends	0.52	0.48	0.46	0.46	0.46	0.46	0.46	0.46	0.46	0.46
Payout Ratio	7%	19%	29%	115%	70%	35%	148%	NM	NM	65%
Prices:High	89.30	63.13	45.30	36.15	39.95	45.29	43.38	36.25	44.13	49.63
Prices:Low	60.60	40.73	31.56	26.90	22.60	25.76	19.63	15.00	15.00	32.63
P/E Ratio:High	12	25	29	90	61	35	NM	NM	NM	70
P/E Ratio:Low	8	16	20	67	34	20	NM	NM	NM	46

Income Statement Analysis (Million $)										
Revenue	9,027	7,186	6,104	5,293	5,020	5,382	5,234	4,547	6,312	3,685
Operating Income	2,417	1,616	1,195	957	856	1,077	1,076	992	1,058	616
Depreciation, Depletion and Amortization	434	382	374	349	302	345	612	778	758	186
Interest Expense	68.9	72.3	83.6	103	111	126	173	159	149	48.6
Pretax Income	3,737	1,279	780	328	380	662	236	85.0	-281	213
Effective Tax Rate	35.8%	31.6%	32.3%	45.1%	41.2%	33.7%	56.7%	37.6%	NM	48.8%
Net Income	2,399	874	528	180	224	439	102	53.0	-297	109
S&P Core Earnings	1,393	842	506	209	186	393	NA	NA	NA	NA

Balance Sheet & Other Financial Data (Million $)										
Cash	750	697	319	98.4	144	45.4	34.6	18.0	16.6	8.60
Current Assets	4,968	3,840	2,967	2,524	2,556	2,697	2,487	2,330	2,725	2,221
Total Assets	8,706	7,807	6,821	6,302	6,401	6,676	6,453	7,040	7,811	4,756
Current Liabilities	1,622	1,361	1,236	1,302	1,080	1,212	988	1,000	1,310	936
Long Term Debt	1,074	1,078	1,086	1,133	1,424	1,682	2,050	2,706	2,726	772
Common Equity	5,243	4,698	3,895	3,350	3,397	3,328	3,047	3,072	3,199	2,605
Total Capital	6,617	6,004	5,214	4,611	4,988	5,221	5,255	5,813	6,082	3,652
Capital Expenditures	922	478	348	405	317	319	599	634	1,318	343
Cash Flow	2,832	1,257	902	529	525	783	714	831	461	295
Current Ratio	3.1	2.8	2.4	1.9	2.4	2.2	2.5	2.3	2.1	2.4
% Long Term Debt of Capitalization	16.2	18.0	20.8	24.6	28.6	32.2	39.0	46.6	44.8	21.1
% Return on Assets	29.1	12.0	8.0	2.8	3.4	6.7	1.5	0.7	NM	2.7
% Return on Equity	48.3	20.4	14.6	5.3	6.7	13.8	3.3	1.7	NM	5.1

Data as orig reptd.; bef. results of disc opers/spec. items. Per share data adj. for stk. divs.; EPS diluted. E-Estimated. NA-Not Available. NM-Not Meaningful. NR-Not Ranked. UR-Under Review.

Office: 2929 Allen Pkwy Ste 2100, Houston, TX 77019-7104.
Telephone: 713-439-8600.
Website: http://www.bakerhughes.com
Chrmn & CEO: C.C. Deaton

Pres & COO: J.R. Clark
SVP & CFO: P.A. Ragauss
VP & General Counsel: A.R. Crain
VP & Cntlr: A.J. Keifer

Board Members: L. D. Brady, C. P. Cazalot, Jr., C. Deaton, E. Djerejian, A. G. Fernandes, C. W. Gargalli, P. H. Jungels, J. A. Lash, J. F. McCall, J. L. Nichols, H. J. Riley Jr., C. C. Watson

Founded: 1972
Domicile: Delaware
Employees: 34,600

Ball Corp

STANDARD &POOR'S

S&P Recommendation HOLD ★★★☆☆

Price	**12-Mo. Target Price**	**Investment Style**
$45.47 (as of Nov 23, 2007)	$55.00	Large-Cap Blend

GICS Sector Materials
Sub-Industry Metal & Glass Containers

Summary Ball, one of the largest producers of metal beverage cans in the world, derives about 10% of its revenues from sales of hi-tech equipment to the aerospace industry.

Key Stock Statistics (Source S&P, Vickers, company reports)

52-Wk Range	$56.05–41.03	S&P Oper. EPS 2007E	3.50	Market Capitalization(B)	$4.570	Beta	0.34
Trailing 12-Month EPS	$2.86	S&P Oper. EPS 2008E	3.90	Yield (%)	0.88	S&P 3-Yr. Proj. EPS CAGR(%)	19.00
Trailing 12-Month P/E	15.9	P/E on S&P Oper. EPS 2007E	13.0	Dividend Rate/Share	$0.40	S&P Credit Rating	BB+
$10K Invested 5 Yrs Ago	$19,662	Common Shares Outstg. (M)	100.5	Institutional Ownership (%)	78		

Price Performance

30-Week Mov. Avg. · · · 10-Week Mov. Avg. — **GAAP Earnings vs. Previous Year** Volume Above Avg. STARS
12-Mo. Target Price — Relative Strength — ▲ Up ▼ Down ► No Change Below Avg.

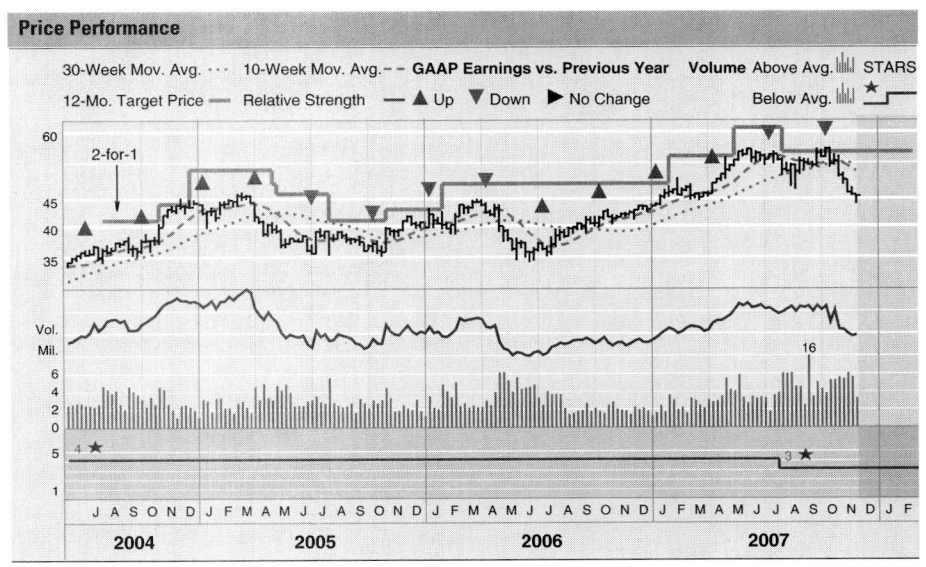

Options: ASE, CBOE, P, Ph

Analysis prepared by **Stewart Scharf** on November 01, 2007, when the stock traded at **$ 49.58**.

Highlights

➤ We project sales growth of at least 10% for 2007, with low- to mid-single digit organic growth likely through 2008, as demand for metal beverage cans, especially in Europe and China, and new aerospace and technologies contracts, are offset by soft beverage can volume in North America, and weaker plastic container, and metal food and household products volume. We see difficult comparisons, year to year, in the fourth quarter of 2007 and during the first half of 2008.

➤ We expect gross margins (before D&A) to widen somewhat into 2008, from 16.3% in 2006, as pricing initiatives should offset high freight, energy and raw material costs. North American beverage can margins should moderate as BLL works off inventories. We look for wider EBIT-DA margins (12% in 2006), on restructuring efforts in the metal food and household products segment, synergies from acquisitions, global production efficiencies, and a better product mix.

➤ We estimate 2007 EPS of $3.50 (before a $0.50 legal settlement charge and $0.25 restructuring charge), advancing to $3.90 for 2008.

Investment Rationale/Risk

➤ Our hold recommendation is based on valuation and our belief that trends for BLL's global beverage can markets will remain fairly positive. We also view favorably the company's earnings and dividend track record, and we believe BLL is well positioned to maintain its strong market share.

➤ Risks to our recommendation and target price include weak exchange rates, softening domestic beer sales in favor of wine and spirits, cost pressures in Europe and China, supply disruptions, integration problems, and a further steep rise in raw material costs.

➤ We attribute the stock's recent forward P/E of near 13X, a 10% discount to the S&P's Metal & Glass Containers group, to volatile commodities costs and the integration of new businesses. Based on our relative metrics, we value the stock at $52. Our DCF model, which assumes a 3.5% perpetual growth rate and a weighted average cost of capital of 8.3%, derives an intrinsic value of $57. We blend these valuations, and apply a below historical average P/E of 14X to our 2008 estimate, to arrive at our 12-month target price of $55.

Qualitative Risk Assessment

LOW	MEDIUM	HIGH

Our risk assessment reflects the seasonality inherent in the beverage can business, our view of BLL's high debt levels, our corporate governance concerns related to board and audit issues, and volatile raw material prices, which are offset by our expectations of lower interest expense due to debt refinancing and redemptions.

Quantitative Evaluations

S&P Quality Ranking B+

D	C	B-	B	B+	A-	A	A+

Relative Strength Rank MODERATE

35

LOWEST = 1 HIGHEST = 99

Revenue/Earnings Data

Revenue (Million $)

	1Q	2Q	3Q	4Q	Year
2007	1,694	2,033	1,907	--	--
2006	1,365	1,843	1,822	1,592	6,622
2005	1,324	1,552	1,584	1,291	5,751
2004	1,232	1,467	1,479	1,263	5,440
2003	1,071	1,353	1,359	1,194	4,977
2002	875.9	1,034	1,039	910.2	3,859

Earnings Per Share ($)

2007	0.78	1.03	0.59	E0.60	E3.50
2006	0.43	1.23	1.02	0.46	3.14
2005	0.51	0.71	0.73	0.42	2.38
2004	0.41	0.80	0.90	0.50	2.60
2003	0.28	0.65	0.61	0.49	2.01
2002	0.24	0.44	0.44	0.28	1.38

Fiscal year ended Dec. 31. Next earnings report expected: Late January. EPS Estimates based on S&P Operating Earnings; historical GAAP earnings are as reported.

Dividend Data (Dates: mm/dd Payment Date: mm/dd/yy)

Amount ($)	Date Decl.	Ex-Div. Date	Stk. of Record	Payment Date
0.100	01/24	02/27	03/01	03/15/07
0.100	04/25	05/30	06/01	06/15/07
0.100	07/25	08/30	09/04	09/18/07
0.100	10/24	11/29	12/03	12/17/07

Dividends have been paid since 1958. Source: Company reports.

Ball Corp

STANDARD &POOR'S

Business Summary November 01, 2007

CORPORATE OVERVIEW. Ball Corp. primarily manufactures rigid packaging products for beverages and foods. Two beverage companies account for a substantial part of its packaging sales: SABMiller plc and PepsiCo. BLL is comprised of five segments: Metal Beverage Packaging (Americas); Metal Beverage Packaging (Europe/Asia); Metal Food & Household Packaging (Americas); Plastic Packaging (Americas); and Aerospace and Technologies. The Aerospace and Technologies segment provides products and services to the defense and commercial markets, with U.S. government agencies accounting for more than 80% of the segment's sales.

The company's packaging products include aluminum and steel two-piece beverage cans, and two- and three-piece steel food cans. Metal Beverage Packaging (Americas) segment net sales represented 39% of the total in 2006 ($269 million in pretax earnings); Metal Beverage Packaging (Europe/Asia) 23% ($193 million); Metal Food and Household Packaging (Americas) 18% ($42 million); Plastic Packaging (Americas) 10% ($25 million); and Aerospace and Technologies 10% ($50 million). BLL entered the plastics business in 1995, when it began to make polyethylene terephthalate (PET) bottles. Sales volumes of metal food containers in North America tend to be highest from June

through October due to seasonal vegetable and salmon packs. BLL believes this accounts for more than 30% of all North American metal beverage can shipments.

In March 2006, the company acquired U.S. Can's Argentinean and U.S. operations for 444,677 BLL common shares and the assumption of $598 million of debt. Sales for the two divisions totaled about $600 million in 2005, with EBITDA near $80 million. The transaction makes BLL the largest supplier in the U.S. of aerosol cans, primarily for food and household products. Separately, the company completed the acquisition of certain North American plastic container assets of Alcan Packaging for $185 million. The operations had annual sales of $150 million.

2006 EPS of $3.14 includes a net gain of $0.24, reflecting insurance proceeds from a plant fire.

Company Financials Fiscal Year Ended Dec. 31

Per Share Data ($)	2006	2005	2004	2003	2002	2001	2000	1999	1998	1997
Tangible Book Value	NM	NM	NM	NM	NM	1.27	1.81	1.27	0.32	3.45
Cash Flow	5.55	4.30	4.49	3.81	2.68	0.44	1.81	2.03	1.41	1.34
Earnings	3.14	2.38	2.60	2.01	1.38	-0.93	0.54	0.79	0.23	0.44
S&P Core Earnings	2.30	2.54	2.67	2.12	1.10	-0.88	NA	NA	NA	NA
Dividends	0.40	0.40	0.35	0.24	0.18	0.15	0.15	0.15	0.15	0.15
Payout Ratio	13%	17%	13%	12%	13%	NM	28%	19%	66%	34%
Prices:High	45.00	46.45	45.20	29.88	27.25	18.03	11.98	14.78	12.23	9.75
Prices:Low	34.16	35.06	28.26	21.15	16.30	9.52	6.50	8.84	7.16	5.94
P/E Ratio:High	14	20	17	15	20	NM	22	19	54	22
P/E Ratio:Low	11	15	11	11	12	NM	12	11	31	14

Income Statement Analysis (Million $)										
Revenue	6,622	5,751	5,440	4,977	3,859	3,686	3,665	3,584	2,896	2,389
Operating Income	729	697	739	663	458	127	445	442	334	248
Depreciation	253	214	215	206	149	153	159	163	155	118
Interest Expense	134	116	104	126	75.6	88.3	95.2	108	78.6	53.5
Pretax Income	462	362	436	331	245	-110	110	171	32.9	85.2
Effective Tax Rate	28.5%	27.5%	31.9%	30.2%	34.3%	NM	38.9%	38.0%	26.7%	37.6%
Net Income	330	262	296	230	159	-99.2	68.2	104	32.0	58.3
S&P Core Earnings	242	280	304	242	127	-96.0	NA	NA	NA	NA

Balance Sheet & Other Financial Data (Million $)										
Cash	152	61.0	199	36.5	259	83.1	25.6	35.8	34.0	25.5
Current Assets	1,761	1,226	1,246	924	1,225	794	969	896	886	798
Total Assets	5,841	4,343	4,478	4,070	4,132	2,314	2,650	2,732	2,855	2,090
Current Liabilities	1,454	1,176	996	861	1,069	575	659	670	688	838
Long Term Debt	2,270	1,473	1,538	1,579	1,854	949	1,012	1,093	1,230	366
Common Equity	1,165	835	1,087	808	493	504	640	635	565	574
Total Capital	3,437	2,314	2,631	2,393	2,353	1,463	1,709	1,803	1,877	1,113
Capital Expenditures	280	292	196	137	158	68.5	98.7	107	84.2	97.7
Cash Flow	582	475	511	435	309	51.3	225	264	184	173
Current Ratio	1.2	1.0	1.3	1.1	1.1	1.4	1.5	1.3	1.3	1.0
% Long Term Debt of Capitalization	66.1	63.7	58.5	66.0	78.8	64.9	59.2	60.6	65.5	32.9
% Net Income of Revenue	5.0	4.5	5.4	4.6	4.1	NM	1.9	2.9	1.1	2.4
% Return on Assets	6.5	5.9	6.9	5.6	4.9	NM	2.5	3.7	1.3	3.1
% Return on Equity	32.7	27.2	31.2	35.4	32.0	NM	10.1	16.9	5.1	9.9

Data as orig reptd.; bef. results of disc opers/spec. items. Per share data adj. for stk. divs.; EPS diluted. E-Estimated. NA-Not Available. NM-Not Meaningful. NR-Not Ranked. UR-Under Review.

Office: 10 Longs Peak Dr, Broomfield, CO 80021-2510.
Telephone: 303-469-3131.
Website: http://www.ball.com
Chrmn, Pres & CEO: R.D. Hoover

COO & SVP: J.R. Friedery
SVP & CFO: R.J. Seabrook
SVP & Secy: D.A. Westerlund
VP & Treas: S. Morrison

Investor Contact: A.T. Scott (303-460-3537)
Board Members: H. M. Dean, H. C. Fiedler, R. D. Hoover, J. F. Lehman, G. R. Nelson, J. Nicholson, G. A. Sissel, G. M. Smart, T. M. Solso, S. A. Taylor, II, E. H. van der Kaay

Founded: 1880
Domicile: Indiana
Employees: 15,500

Bank of America Corp

STANDARD
&POOR'S

S&P Recommendation	STRONG BUY ★★★★★	Price $43.15 (as of Nov 23, 2007)	12-Mo. Target Price $57.00	Investment Style Large-Cap Blend

GICS Sector Financials
Sub-Industry Other Diversified Financial Services

Summary This banking company has offices in 30 states and in Washington, D.C., and provides international corporate financial services.

Key Stock Statistics (Source S&P, Vickers, company reports)

52-Wk Range	$55.00– 41.73	S&P Oper. EPS 2007E	4.06	Market Capitalization(B)	$191.454	Beta	0.52
Trailing 12-Month EPS	$4.40	S&P Oper. EPS 2008E	4.80	Yield (%)	5.93	S&P 3-Yr. Proj. EPS CAGR(%)	9.00
Trailing 12-Month P/E	9.8	P/E on S&P Oper. EPS 2007E	10.6	Dividend Rate/Share	$2.56	S&P Credit Rating	AA
$10K Invested 5 Yrs Ago	$14,869	Common Shares Outstg. (M)	4,436.9	Institutional Ownership (%)	60		

Price Performance

30-Week Mov. Avg. · · · 10-Week Mov. Avg. — **GAAP Earnings vs. Previous Year** Volume Above Avg. STARS
12-Mo. Target Price — Relative Strength — ▲ Up ▼ Down ▶ No Change Below Avg. ★

Options: ASE, CBOE, P, Ph

Analysis prepared by **Frank Braden, CFA** on October 26, 2007, when the stock traded at **$ 47.69**.

Highlights

➤ We forecast modest total revenue growth of around 7% in 2008, and expect positive operating leverage to be largely driven by organic growth and expense controls. Following the acquisition of LaSalle Bank, large U.S. acquisitions will be limited by the 10% cap on deposit market share, which may, in our view, lead to more international acquisitions. After reporting large losses and write-downs in its global corporate and investment bank in the third quarter, BAC announced restructurings that will eliminate 3,000 positions, shake up management, and cut its wholesale mortgage business, in an attempt to reduce earnings volatility.

➤ We continue to anticipate that non-mortgage consumer, large-market commercial lending and market-sensitive fee-based businesses will drive revenue growth in 2008. We think expenses will remain under tight control, and we see the company's efficiency ratio improving steadily in the quarters ahead.

➤ Excluding merger-related expense, we estimate operating EPS of $4.40 in 2007. We see EPS rising 14% in 2008, to $5.02.

Investment Rationale/Risk

➤ We believe BAC shares offer an attractive risk/reward ratio at current valuation levels, and an above-peer dividend yield. We see continued positive operating leverage driving the improvement in BAC's efficiency ratio, which has been helped by growth in its online business. We view the acquisition of U.S. Trust favorably, as BAC has been seeking to expand its more profitable private banking business. We also favor the acquisition of LaSalle Bank, which will add exposure to the higher-growth Chicago market, but we think exposure to the Southeast Michigan market will hamper near-term results.

➤ Risks to our recommendation and target price include merger integration difficulties, significant credit quality deterioration, a severe economic downturn, or a serious event that could affect domestic equity markets.

➤ Our 12-month target price of $57 equates to about 11.4X our 2008 operating EPS estimate, in line with BAC's historical average. Our valuation is based on our expectation of solid economic conditions, BAC's extensive geographic footprint, and our view of its balanced business model.

Qualitative Risk Assessment

LOW	MEDIUM	HIGH

Our risk assessment reflects what we see as strong business fundamentals and a robust customer base. We view BAC as having a diverse product line and geographic presence, which should enable it to withstand a major economic downturn.

Quantitative Evaluations

S&P Quality Ranking A

D	C	B-	B	B+	A-	A	A+

Relative Strength Rank MODERATE

35

LOWEST = 1   HIGHEST = 99

Revenue/Earnings Data

Revenue (Million $)

	1Q	2Q	3Q	4Q	Year
2007	30,385	32,409	--	--	--
2006	27,026	28,895	30,739	30,357	117,017
2005	19,168	21,222	21,621	22,280	83,980
2004	12,289	16,448	16,413	--	63,324
2003	11,410	12,250	12,294	12,111	48,065
2002	11,311	11,465	11,405	--	45,732

Earnings Per Share ($)

2007	1.16	1.28	0.82	E0.80	E4.06
2006	1.07	1.19	1.18	1.16	4.59
2005	1.07	1.17	0.95	0.88	4.04
2004	0.92	0.93	0.91	0.94	3.69
2003	0.80	0.90	0.96	0.92	3.57
2002	0.69	0.70	0.73	0.85	2.96

Fiscal year ended Dec. 31. Next earnings report expected: Late January. EPS Estimates based on S&P Operating Earnings; historical GAAP earnings are as reported.

Dividend Data (Dates: mm/dd Payment Date: mm/dd/yy)

Amount ($)	Date Decl.	Ex-Div. Date	Stk. of Record	Payment Date
0.560	01/24	02/28	03/02	03/23/07
0.560	04/25	05/30	06/01	06/22/07
0.640	07/25	09/05	09/07	09/28/07
0.640	10/24	12/05	12/07	12/28/07

Dividends have been paid since 1903. Source: Company reports.

Bank of America Corp

Business Summary October 26, 2007

CORPORATE OVERVIEW. Bank of America has operations in 30 states, the District of Columbia and 44 foreign countries. In the U.S., it has more than 5,700 retail banking centers and approximately 17,000 ATMs. BAC reports the results of its operations through four business segments: Global Consumer and Small Business Banking, Global Business and Financial Services, Global Capital Markets and Investment Banking, and Global Wealth and Investment Management.

Global Consumer and Small Business Banking provides a diversified range of products and services to individuals and small businesses through multiple delivery channels. Global Business and Financial Services serves domestic and international business clients providing financial services, specialized industry expertise and local delivery through a global team of client managers and a variety of businesses. Global Capital Markets and Investment Banking provides capital-raising solutions, advisory services, derivatives capabilities, equity and debt sales and trading for BAC's clients, as well as traditional bank deposit and loan products, and treasury management and payment services for large corporations and institutional clients. Global Wealth and Investment

Management offers investment services, estate management, financial planning services, fiduciary management, credit and banking expertise, and diversified asset management products to institutional clients as well as high-net-worth individuals.

IMPACT OF MAJOR DEVELOPMENTS. On October 1, 2007, BAC acquired LaSalle Bank from ABN AMRO for $21 billion in cash, with a $5 billion rebate of excess capital to BAC. The proposed deal is expected to be immediately accretive to EPS, and BAC sees $400 million in annual after-tax cost savings in 2008, and $800 million in 2009. We believe the deal will provide BAC with a strong presence in the attractive Chicago market, and we expect BAC's experience in similar transactions, such as the acquisition of Fleet Financial, will add to the likelihood of a successful integration.

Company Financials Fiscal Year Ended Dec. 31

Per Share Data ($)	2006	2005	2004	2003	2002	2001	2000	1999	1998	1997
Tangible Book Value	12.18	13.18	12.41	12.34	12.59	11.65	10.66	9.06	9.01	8.33
Earnings	4.59	4.04	3.69	3.57	2.96	2.09	2.26	2.24	1.45	2.09
S&P Core Earnings	4.47	4.06	3.75	3.54	2.70	1.96	NA	NA	NA	NA
Dividends	2.12	1.90	1.70	1.44	1.22	1.14	1.03	0.93	0.80	0.69
Payout Ratio	46%	47%	46%	40%	41%	55%	46%	41%	55%	33%
Prices:High	55.08	47.44	47.47	42.45	38.54	32.77	30.50	38.19	44.22	35.84
Prices:Low	40.93	41.13	38.51	32.13	26.98	22.50	18.16	23.81	22.00	24.00
P/E Ratio:High	12	12	13	12	13	16	13	17	30	17
P/E Ratio:Low	9	10	10	9	9	11	8	11	15	12

Income Statement Analysis (Million $)

	2006	2005	2004	2003	2002	2001	2000	1999	1998	1997
Net Interest Income	34,591	30,737	28,797	21,464	20,923	20,290	18,442	18,237	18,298	7,898
Tax Equivalent Adjustment	1,224	832	716	643	588	343	322	215	128	116
Non Interest Income	38,432	26,438	20,097	16,422	13,571	14,348	14,489	14,069	12,189	6,351
Loan Loss Provision	5,010	4,014	2,769	2,839	3,697	4,287	2,535	182	2,920	800
% Expense/Operating Revenue	47.9%	50.4%	54.5%	52.2%	63.1%	59.8%	63.7%	56.9%	67.4%	52.3%
Pretax Income	31,973	24,480	21,221	15,861	12,991	10,117	11,788	12,215	8,048	4,796
Effective Tax Rate	33.9%	32.7%	33.4%	31.8%	28.8%	32.9%	36.2%	35.5%	35.8%	35.8%
Net Income	21,133	16,465	14,143	10,810	9,249	6,792	7,517	7,882	5,165	3,077
% Net Interest Margin	2.82	2.84	3.26	3.36	3.75	3.68	3.22	3.47	3.69	3.79
S&P Core Earnings	20,568	16,499	14,308	10,708	8,452	6,384	NA	NA	NA	NA

Balance Sheet & Other Financial Data (Million $)

	2006	2005	2004	2003	2002	2001	2000	1999	1998	1997
Money Market Assets	302,482	294,292	197,308	153,090	115,687	81,384	76,544	81,226	73,498	36,095
Investment Securities	NA	221,603	195,073	68,240	69,148	85,499	65,838	83,069	80,587	47,203
Commercial Loans	240,785	218,334	193,930	131,304	145,170	163,898	203,542	195,779	196,130	71,442
Other Loans	465,705	355,457	327,907	240,159	197,585	165,255	188,651	174,883	161,198	69,568
Total Assets	1,459,737	1,291,803	1,110,457	736,445	660,458	621,764	642,191	632,574	617,679	264,562
Demand Deposits	184,808	186,736	169,899	121,530	124,359	113,934	100,645	95,469	94,336	34,674
Time Deposits	508,689	447,934	448,671	292,583	262,099	259,561	263,599	251,804	262,974	103,520
Long Term Debt	146,000	100,848	98,078	75,343	67,176	68,026	72,502	60,441	50,842	27,204
Common Equity	132,421	101,262	99,374	47,926	50,261	48,455	47,556	44,355	45,855	21,243
% Return on Assets	1.5	1.4	1.5	1.5	1.4	1.1	1.2	1.3	0.9	1.4
% Return on Equity	18.1	16.3	19.2	22.0	18.7	14.1	16.3	17.5	11.5	17.6
% Loan Loss Reserve	0.4	1.4	1.7	1.7	2.0	2.1	1.7	1.8	2.0	1.9
% Loans/Deposits	304.3	87.4	84.4	89.7	88.4	97.8	107.7	106.7	99.4	104.1
% Equity to Assets	8.5	8.4	8.0	7.0	7.7	7.6	7.2	7.2	7.6	7.7

Data as orig reptd.; bef. results of disc opers/spec. items. Per share data adj. for stk. divs.; EPS diluted. E-Estimated. NA-Not Available. NM-Not Meaningful. NR-Not Ranked. UR-Under Review.

Office: 100 N Tryon St, Charlotte, NC 28255.
Telephone: 704-386-8486.
Website: http://www.bankofamerica.com
Chrmn, Pres & CEO: K.D. Lewis

CFO: J.L. Price
Investor Contact: K. Stitt (704-386-5667)

Board Members: W. Barnet, III, F. P. Bramble, Sr., J. T. Collins, G. L. Countryman, T. R. Franks, P. Fulton, C. K. Gifford, W. S. Jones, K. D. Lewis, M. C. Lozano, W. E. Massey, T. J. May, P. E. Mitchell, T. M. Ryan, O. T. Sloan, Jr., M. R. Spangler, R. L. Tillman, J. M. Ward

Founded: 1874
Domicile: Delaware
Employees: 203,425

Bank of New York Mellon Corp (The)

STANDARD &POOR'S

S&P Recommendation **BUY** ★★★★☆	Price $45.41 (as of Nov 23, 2007)	12-Mo. Target Price $54.00	Investment Style Large-Cap Blend

GICS Sector Financials
Sub-Industry Asset Management & Custody Banks

Summary This company is a leader in securities processing, and also provides a complete range of banking, asset management and other financial services.

Key Stock Statistics (Source S&P, Vickers, company reports)

52-Wk Range	$49.00–37.24	S&P Oper. EPS 2007E	2.70	Market Capitalization(B)	$51.670	Beta	1.83
Trailing 12-Month EPS	$4.24	S&P Oper. EPS 2008E	3.00	Yield (%)	2.11	S&P 3-Yr. Proj. EPS CAGR(%)	11.00
Trailing 12-Month P/E	10.7	P/E on S&P Oper. EPS 2007E	16.8	Dividend Rate/Share	$0.96	S&P Credit Rating	A+
$10K Invested 5 Yrs Ago	$16,431	Common Shares Outstg. (M)	1,137.9	Institutional Ownership (%)	74		

Price Performance

30-Week Mov. Avg. · · · 10-Week Mov. Avg. - - **GAAP Earnings vs. Previous Year** Volume Above Avg. STARS
12-Mo. Target Price — Relative Strength — ▲ Up ▼ Down ▶ No Change Below Avg. ★

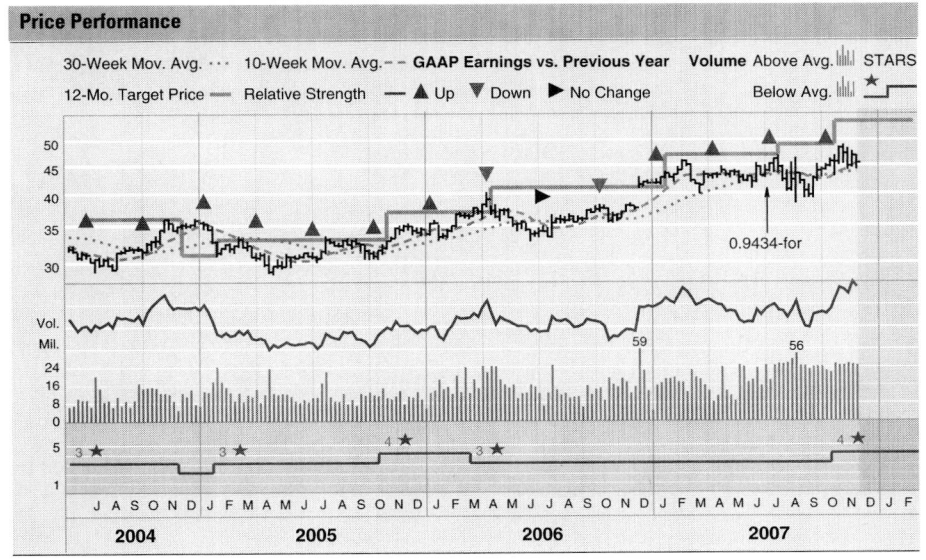

0.9434-for

Options: ASE, CBOE, P, Ph

Analysis prepared by **Frank Braden, CFA** on October 19, 2007, when the stock traded at **$46.14**.

Highlights

➤ Following the July 2 merger with Mellon Financial, management sees annual cost savings of $700 million, equivalent to 8.5% of pro forma 2006 expenses, but we expect the savings to be greater as the combined company benefits from its more scalable asset-servicing business. We expect much of the benefits of scale to help international growth. We see total revenue growth of 25% in 2008, based on our projection of healthy capital markets activity.

➤ Although we expect new business wins to be modestly disrupted during the merger process, BK has thus far been able to maintain new business trends. We look for foreign partnerships to help diversify the business mix, and we believe they will be an area of healthy growth in the future. We are encouraged by BK's business strategy and see continued expense discipline and expansion through smaller acquisitions and international alliances going forward.

➤ We forecast operating EPS of $2.70 in 2007 and $3.00 in 2008.

Investment Rationale/Risk

➤ We believe BK has taken the right steps to become a major global player in custody banking and corporate trust. We see execution and clearing services, foreign exchange and trading as areas for growth in 2008. We are encouraged by the strong performance of future growth drivers for BK, including new business wins, expense savings and international growth. In the longer term, we think a trend on the part of investment advisers and brokers toward outsourcing middle and back-office processing will support revenue growth.

➤ Risks to our recommendation and target price include a significant decline in capital markets activity, credit losses and/or loan loss reserve provisions that are greater than our expectations, and execution risks related to the Mellon merger.

➤ Our 12-month target price of $54 equates to a P/E of 18X our 2008 EPS estimate, in line with BK's peers.

Qualitative Risk Assessment

LOW	MEDIUM	HIGH

Our risk assessment reflects what we view as solid fundamentals and diverse business lines. BK has provided stable earnings over the long term and we believe it would be able to sustain a prolonged economic downturn.

Quantitative Evaluations

S&P Quality Ranking   A-

D	C	B-	B	B+	A-	A	A+

Relative Strength Rank   STRONG

80

LOWEST = 1   HIGHEST = 99

Revenue/Earnings Data

Revenue (Million $)

	1Q	2Q	3Q	4Q	Year
2007	2,496	2,893	3,600	--	--
2006	2,074	2,276	2,219	2,493	9,062
2005	1,917	2,077	2,126	2,230	8,312
2004	1,671	1,767	1,739	1,968	7,144
2003	1,420	1,591	1,638	1,686	6,336
2002	1,480	1,530	1,285	1,461	5,756

Earnings Per Share ($)

2007	0.60	0.59	0.56	E0.78	E2.70
2006	0.50	0.55	0.41	0.59	2.05
2005	0.52	0.55	0.54	0.56	2.15
2004	0.50	0.51	0.49	0.48	1.96
2003	0.43	0.41	0.36	0.42	1.61
2002	0.53	0.53	0.12	0.15	1.31

Fiscal year ended Dec. 31. Next earnings report expected: Mid January. EPS Estimates based on S&P Operating Earnings; historical GAAP earnings are as reported.

Dividend Data (Dates: mm/dd Payment Date: mm/dd/yy)

Amount ($)	Date Decl.	Ex-Div. Date	Stk. of Record	Payment Date
0.220	04/10	04/23	04/25	05/04/07
0.9434-for-1	--	07/02	--	07/02/07
0.240	07/10	07/23	07/25	08/03/07
0.240	10/09	10/22	10/24	11/02/07

Dividends have been paid since 1785. Source: Company reports.

Please read the Required Disclosures and Analyst Certification on the last page of this report.

The McGraw-Hill Companies

Bank of New York Mellon Corp (The)

STANDARD &POOR'S

Business Summary October 19, 2007

CORPORATE OVERVIEW. Bank of New York Mellon provides a comprehensive array of services that enable institutions and individuals to move and manage their financial assets in more than 100 markets worldwide. The company has several core competencies: institutional services, private banking, and asset management. Its global client base includes a broad range of leading financial institutions, corporations, government entities, endowments, and foundations.

Key products include advisory and asset management services to support the investment decision, trade execution, clearance and settlement capabilities, custody, securities lending, accounting, and administrative services for investment portfolios, sophisticated risk and performance measurement tools for analyzing portfolios, and services for issuers of both equity and debt securities.

CORPORATE STRATEGY. BK's strategy over the past decade has been to focus on scalable, fee-based securities servicing and fiduciary businesses, and it has achieved top three market share in most of its major product lines. The company attempts to distinguish itself competitively by offering products and services around the investment lifecycle.

By providing integrated solutions for clients' needs, BK strives to be the preferred partner in helping its clients succeed in the world's rapidly evolving financial markets. The company's key objectives include achieving positive operating leverage on an annual basis and sustaining top-line growth by expanding client relationships and winning new ones.

To achieve its top objectives, BK has grown both through internal reinvestments as well as the execution of strategic acquisitions to expand product offerings and increase market share in its scale businesses. Internal reinvestment occurs mainly through increased technology spending, staffing levels, marketing/branding initiatives, quality programs, and product development. The company invests in technology to improve the breadth and quality of its product offerings, and to increase economies of scale. BK has acquired over 90 businesses over the past 10 years, almost exclusively in its securities servicing and asset management areas.

Company Financials Fiscal Year Ended Dec. 31

Per Share Data ($)	2006	2005	2004	2003	2002	2001	2000	1999	1998	1997
Tangible Book Value	11.50	7.48	6.84	5.93	6.00	6.14	8.80	7.37	7.47	7.07
Earnings	2.05	2.15	1.96	1.61	1.31	1.92	2.04	2.41	1.62	1.44
S&P Core Earnings	2.01	2.11	1.83	1.55	1.07	1.65	NA	NA	NA	NA
Dividends	0.91	0.87	0.84	0.81	0.81	0.76	0.70	0.61	0.57	0.52
Payout Ratio	45%	40%	43%	50%	61%	40%	34%	26%	35%	36%
Prices:High	42.98	35.71	36.94	35.50	49.29	61.61	62.94	47.90	43.00	31.04
Prices:Low	32.66	28.55	28.88	20.40	22.10	31.53	31.53	33.72	25.44	17.36
P/E Ratio:High	21	17	19	22	37	32	31	20	27	22
P/E Ratio:Low	16	13	15	13	17	16	15	14	16	12

Income Statement Analysis (Million $)										
Net Interest Income	1,499	1,909	1,645	1,609	1,665	1,681	1,870	1,701	1,651	1,855
Tax Equivalent Adjustment	NA	29.0	30.0	35.0	49.0	60.0	54.0	44.0	58.0	35.0
Non Interest Income	8,771	4,888	4,613	3,971	3,261	3,386	2,959	3,294	2,108	2,001
Loan Loss Provision	20.0	15.0	15.0	155	685	375	105	135	20.0	280
% Expense/Operating Revenue	45.5%	65.7%	65.6%	65.9%	55.3%	54.4%	51.4%	44.0%	50.5%	48.6%
Pretax Income	2,170	2,367	2,199	1,762	1,372	2,058	2,251	2,840	1,891	1,773
Effective Tax Rate	32.0%	33.6%	34.5%	34.3%	34.3%	34.7%	36.5%	38.8%	37.0%	37.7%
Net Income	1,476	1,571	1,440	1,157	902	1,343	1,429	1,739	1,192	1,104
% Net Interest Margin	2.01	2.36	2.07	2.22	2.62	2.57	2.96	3.11	3.24	3.89
S&P Core Earnings	1,452	1,536	1,350	1,097	728	1,159	NA	NA	NA	NA

Balance Sheet & Other Financial Data (Million $)										
Money Market Assets	23,830	16,999	18,527	18,521	13,798	19,684	23,178	20,948	9,422	7,562
Investment Securities	21,106	27,326	23,802	22,903	18,300	12,862	7,401	6,899	6,415	6,628
Commercial Loans	5,925	13,252	12,624	13,646	20,335	19,034	21,327	17,851	16,407	14,429
Other Loans	31,868	27,474	23,157	21,637	11,004	16,713	14,934	21,251	21,979	20,698
Total Assets	103,370	102,074	94,529	92,397	77,564	81,025	77,114	74,756	63,503	59,961
Demand Deposits	19,554	18,236	17,442	14,789	13,301	12,635	13,255	12,162	11,480	12,561
Time Deposits	45,992	46,188	41,279	41,617	42,086	43,076	43,121	43,589	33,152	28,796
Long Term Debt	8,773	Nil	Nil	Nil	Nil	Nil	4,536	4,311	3,386	1,809
Common Equity	11,593	9,876	9,290	8,428	6,684	6,317	6,151	5,142	5,447	5,001
% Return on Assets	1.4	1.6	1.5	1.4	1.1	1.7	1.9	2.5	1.9	1.9
% Return on Equity	13.7	16.4	16.3	15.3	13.9	21.5	25.3	32.8	22.8	21.9
% Loan Loss Reserve	0.8	1.0	1.7	1.9	2.7	1.7	1.7	1.6	1.7	1.8
% Loans/Deposits	60.8	63.2	60.9	62.6	56.6	64.2	64.3	67.3	86.0	84.9
% Equity to Assets	10.5	9.7	9.5	8.9	8.2	7.9	7.4	7.7	8.5	8.7

Data as orig reptd.; bef. results of disc opers/spec. items. Per share data adj. for stk. divs.; EPS diluted. E-Estimated. NA-Not Available. NM-Not Meaningful. NR-Not Ranked. UR-Under Review.

Office: One Wall Street, New York, NY 10286.
Telephone: 212-495-1784.
Email: shareowner-svcs@bankofny.com
Website: http://www.bankofny.com

Chrmn & CEO: T.A. Renyi
Pres: G.L. Hassell
Vice Chrmn: B.W. Van Saun
Vice Chrmn & Chief Admin Officer: D.R. Monks

Vice Chrmn & General Counsel: J.M. Liftin
Board Members: F. J. Biondi, Jr., N. M. Donofrio, G. L. Hassell, R. J. Kogan, M. J. Kowalski, J. A. Luke, Jr., J. C. Malone, C. A. Rein, T. A. Renyi, W. C. Richardson, B. L. Roberts, S. C. Scott, III, R. C. Vaughan
Founded: 1784
Domicile: New York
Employees: 22,961

The McGraw-Hill Companies

Bard (C.R.) Inc

STANDARD &POOR'S

S&P Recommendation HOLD ★★★☆☆	**Price** $83.58 (as of Nov 23, 2007)	**12-Mo. Target Price** $90.00	**Investment Style** Large-Cap Growth

GICS Sector Health Care
Sub-Industry Health Care Equipment

Summary This diversified maker of therapeutic and diagnostic medical devices has exposure to the vascular, urology, oncology, and specialty surgical markets.

Key Stock Statistics (Source S&P, Vickers, company reports)

52-Wk Range	$89.96– 76.61	S&P Oper. EPS 2007**E**	3.79	Market Capitalization(B)	$8.517	Beta	0.46
Trailing 12-Month EPS	$3.04	S&P Oper. EPS 2008**E**	4.35	Yield (%)	0.72	S&P 3-Yr. Proj. EPS CAGR(%)	14.00
Trailing 12-Month P/E	27.5	P/E on S&P Oper. EPS 2007**E**	22.1	Dividend Rate/Share	$0.60	S&P Credit Rating	A
$10K Invested 5 Yrs Ago	$29,574	Common Shares Outstg. (M)	101.9	Institutional Ownership (%)	91		

Price Performance

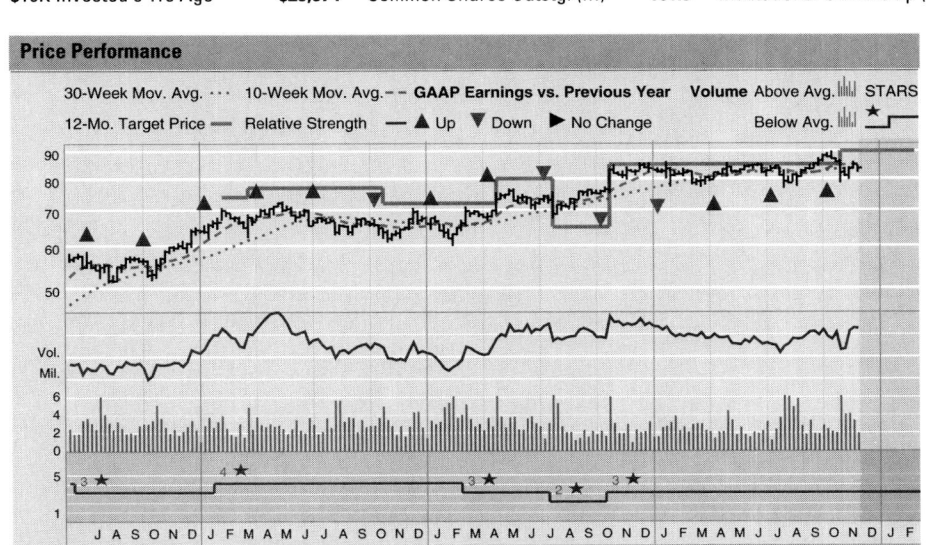

30-Week Mov. Avg. ··· 10-Week Mov. Avg.- - **GAAP Earnings vs. Previous Year** Volume Above Avg. �"⁣ STARS
12-Mo. Target Price — Relative Strength — ▲ Up ▼ Down ► No Change Below Avg. ⁣⁣

J A S O N D J F M A M J J A S O N D J F M A M J J A S O N D J F M A M J J A S O N D J F
2004   2005   2006   2007

Options: ASE, CBOE, P, Ph

Analysis prepared by **Robert M. Gold** on November 07, 2007, when the stock traded at **$ 80.85**.

Qualitative Risk Assessment

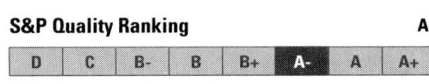
| LOW | **MEDIUM** | HIGH |

Our risk assessment reflects that BCR operates in a highly competitive environment. In addition, hospital customers generate a large portion of revenues from Medicare, and are therefore subject to reimbursement risks that could reduce prices paid to suppliers. However, we believe BCR's product line is largely focused on areas that have not been subject to intense pricing pressure, and we think management has a solid track record in terms of identifying and integrating acquisitions.

Quantitative Evaluations

S&P Quality Ranking   A-

| D | C | B- | B | B+ | **A-** | A | A+ |

Relative Strength Rank   **STRONG**

75

LOWEST = 1   HIGHEST = 99

Highlights

➤ We believe net sales in 2008 will approximate $2.4 billion, up from a projected $2.2 billion in 2007, as double-digit growth in the vascular and oncology segments joins with a high-single-digit gain in urology, flat performance in hernia repair and approximately 5% growth in other products. We think new product launches will provide incremental sales growth in coming quarters.

➤ It is our belief that gross margins in 2007 will decline, reflecting the adverse effect of some product recalls, although we expect some recovery in 2008 due to increased product manufacturing at a facility in Puerto Rico, possible new product introductions and a recovery in the hernia repair product category. We forecast that SG&A costs will remain at about 29% to 30% of sales through 2008, with R&D costs absorbing approximately 6.0%. We see an effective tax rate of 28.5% through 2008.

➤ Our 2008 EPS estimate is $4.35, up from a projected $3.79 in operating EPS from continuing operations in 2007, which includes our expectation of continued common share repurchases.

Investment Rationale/Risk

➤ We believe new products in the oncology, hernia repair, and urology segments, plus momentum in existing categories, will help drive low-double-digit constant currency sales growth over the coming three years. We view the stock's performance relative to medical device peers in 2007 as weak and largely due to concerns about reduced gross margins reported in the second and third quarters. Although we share some of these concerns, we think BCR has relatively easy gross margin comparisons in 2008 and believe the impact of product recalls will abate by the fourth quarter.

➤ Risks to our recommendation and target price include unfavorable patent litigation outcomes, adverse reimbursement changes, and a failure to commercialize new products in a timely fashion.

➤ Our projected long-term earnings growth rate for BCR is below peers. However, we think its revenue stream is less volatile than peers, and that a valuation in line with peers is appropriate. By applying a forward P/E to earnings ratio of 1.48X to our 2008 EPS estimate, and assuming three-year EPS growth of 14%, our 12-month target price is $90.

Revenue/Earnings Data

Revenue (Million $)

	1Q	2Q	3Q	4Q	Year
2007	528.2	545.7	544.8	--	--
2006	467.5	498.2	498.9	520.9	1,986
2005	428.6	447.4	443.3	452.0	1,771
2004	393.8	416.3	421.9	424.1	1,656
2003	335.9	354.2	361.8	381.2	1,433
2002	301.9	317.5	322.7	331.7	1,274

Earnings Per Share ($)

2007	0.95	0.91	0.96	E1.00	E3.79
2006	0.76	0.76	0.82	0.21	2.55
2005	0.75	0.79	0.83	0.75	3.12
2004	0.68	0.55	0.95	0.65	2.82
2003	0.45	0.47	0.49	0.20	1.60
2002	0.33	0.42	0.29	0.45	1.47

Fiscal year ended Dec. 31. Next earnings report expected: Late January. EPS Estimates based on S&P Operating Earnings; historical GAAP earnings are as reported.

Dividend Data (Dates: mm/dd Payment Date: mm/dd/yy)

Amount ($)	Date Decl.	Ex-Div. Date	Stk. of Record	Payment Date
0.140	12/13	01/18	01/22	02/02/07
0.140	04/18	04/26	04/30	05/11/07
0.150	06/13	07/19	07/23	08/03/07
0.150	10/10	10/18	10/22	11/02/07

Dividends have been paid since 1960. Source: Company reports.

Bard (C.R.) Inc

**STANDARD
&POOR'S**

Business Summary November 07, 2007

CORPORATE OVERVIEW. This company offers a range of medical, surgical, diagnostic and patient care devices. Sales in 2006 came from urology (30%), vascular (24%), oncology (24%), surgery (18%), and other (4%) products.

Bard's vascular products include percutaneous transluminal angioplasty catheters, guide wires, introducers and accessories, peripheral stents, vena cava filters and biopsy devices; electrophysiology products such as lab systems, and diagnostic therapeutic and temporary pacing electrode catheters; and fabrics, meshes and implantable vascular grafts.

Urological diagnosis and intervention products include Foley catheters, procedure kits and trays, and related urine monitoring and collection systems; urethral stents; and specialty devices for incontinence, endoscopic procedures, and stone removal. Newer products include the Infection Control Foley catheter that reduces the rate of urinary tract infections; a collagen implant and sling materials used to treat urinary incontinence; and brachytherapy services, devices, and radioactive seeds to treat prostate cancer.

Oncology products include specialty access catheters and ports; gastroen-

terological products (endoscopic accessories, percutaneous feeding devices and stents); biopsy devices; and a suturing system for gastroesophageal reflux disease.

Surgical specialties products include meshes for hernia and other soft tissue repairs; irrigation devices for orthopedic, laparoscopic and gynecological procedures; and topical hemostatic devices. In January 2003, Bard introduced the VentralexT hernia patch, a simplified intra-abdominal hernia repair technology characterized by minimal suturing, small incisions, and potentially shorter recovery times. To further expand its markets around the hernia repair call point, in June 2004, Bard acquired the Salute Fixation system and related technology from Onux Inc. The device is used to attach mesh to host tissue for laparoscopic hernia repair procedures.

Company Financials Fiscal Year Ended Dec. 31

Per Share Data ($)	2006	2005	2004	2003	2002	2001	2000	1999	1998	1997
Tangible Book Value	9.46	10.39	7.26	5.35	4.84	3.97	2.53	2.34	2.03	1.31
Cash Flow	3.25	3.71	3.33	2.03	1.87	1.89	1.53	1.61	2.78	1.13
Earnings	2.55	3.12	2.82	1.60	1.47	1.38	1.04	1.14	2.26	0.63
S&P Core Earnings	2.96	2.86	2.29	1.73	1.27	1.21	NA	NA	NA	NA
Dividends	0.54	0.50	0.47	0.45	0.43	0.42	0.41	0.39	0.37	0.35
Payout Ratio	21%	16%	17%	28%	29%	31%	39%	34%	16%	56%
Prices:High	85.72	72.79	65.13	40.80	31.97	32.47	27.47	29.94	25.13	19.50
Prices:Low	59.89	60.82	40.09	27.02	22.05	20.43	17.50	20.84	14.25	13.19
P/E Ratio:High	34	23	23	25	22	24	26	26	11	31
P/E Ratio:Low	23	19	14	17	15	15	17	18	6	21
Income Statement Analysis (Million $)										
Revenue	1,986	1,771	1,656	1,433	1,274	1,181	1,099	1,037	1,165	1,214
Operating Income	550	503	418	333	295	266	244	239	217	222
Depreciation	74.9	63.8	54.7	44.7	42.3	53.2	49.6	49.1	58.7	57.3
Interest Expense	16.9	12.2	12.7	12.5	12.6	14.2	19.3	19.3	26.4	32.9
Pretax Income	348	450	414	223	211	205	154	173	464	105
Effective Tax Rate	21.7%	25.0%	26.9%	24.5%	26.5%	30.1%	30.6%	31.9%	45.7%	31.1%
Net Income	272	337	303	169	155	143	107	118	252	72.3
S&P Core Earnings	317	309	244	182	134	126	NA	NA	NA	NA
Balance Sheet & Other Financial Data (Million $)										
Cash	416	754	541	417	23.1	30.8	21.3	17.3	25.6	8.00
Current Assets	1,134	1,264	1,054	875	758	647	527	529	489	564
Total Assets	2,277	2,266	2,009	1,692	1,417	1,231	1,089	1,126	1,080	1,279
Current Liabilities	296	641	390	422	317	235	225	353	303	311
Long Term Debt	151	0.80	151	152	152	156	204	158	160	341
Common Equity	1,698	1,536	1,360	1,046	880	789	614	574	568	573
Total Capital	1,871	1,544	1,534	1,197	1,033	945	818	733	728	914
Capital Expenditures	70.4	97.2	74.0	72.1	41.0	27.4	19.4	26.1	43.8	32.8
Cash Flow	347	401	358	213	197	196	157	167	311	130
Current Ratio	3.8	2.0	2.7	2.1	2.4	2.8	2.3	1.5	1.6	1.8
% Long Term Debt of Capitalization	8.1	0.1	9.9	12.7	14.7	16.5	25.0	21.6	22.0	37.3
% Net Income of Revenue	13.7	19.0	18.3	11.8	12.2	12.1	9.7	11.4	21.7	6.0
% Return on Assets	12.0	15.8	16.4	10.8	11.5	12.3	9.6	10.7	21.4	5.5
% Return on Equity	16.8	23.3	25.2	17.5	18.6	20.4	18.0	20.7	44.2	12.3

Data as orig reptd.; bef. results of disc opers/spec. items. Per share data adj. for stk. divs.; EPS diluted. E-Estimated. NA-Not Available. NM-Not Meaningful. NR-Not Ranked. UR-Under Review.

Office: 730 Central Avenue, Murray Hill, NJ 07974.
Telephone: 908-277-8000.
Website: http://www.crbard.com
Chrmn & CEO: T.M. Ring

Pres & COO: J.H. Weiland
SVP & CFO: T.C. Schermerhorn
VP, Secy & General Counsel: S.J. Long
Investor Contact: E.J. Shick (908-277-8413)

Board Members: M. C. Breslawsky, T. K. Dunnigan, H. L. Henkel, T. E. Martin, G. K. Naughton, T. M. Ring, T. G. Thompson, J. H. Weiland, A. Welters, T. L. White

Founded: 1907
Domicile: New Jersey
Employees: 9,400

The McGraw·Hill Companies

STANDARD &POOR'S

Barr Pharmaceuticals Inc

S&P Recommendation **BUY** ★★★★☆	Price	12-Mo. Target Price	Investment Style
	$52.10 (as of Nov 23, 2007)	$63.00	Large-Cap Growth

GICS Sector Health Care
Sub-Industry Pharmaceuticals

Summary This company (formerly Barr Laboratories) produces a wide range of generic drugs in varying strengths. BRL also offers its own line of branded drug products. In October 2006, BRL acquired Pliva, a Croatia-based drugmaker, for about $2.5 billion in cash.

Key Stock Statistics (Source S&P, Vickers, company reports)

52-Wk Range	$58.38–45.41	S&P Oper. EPS 2007**E**	3.10	Market Capitalization(B)	$5.586	Beta	0.16
Trailing 12-Month EPS	**NA**	S&P Oper. EPS 2008**E**	3.70	Yield (%)	**Nil**	S&P 3-Yr. Proj. EPS CAGR(%)	10.00
Trailing 12-Month P/E	**NM**	P/E on S&P Oper. EPS 2007**E**	16.8	Dividend Rate/Share	**Nil**	S&P Credit Rating	**NA**
$10K Invested 5 Yrs Ago	$19,347	Common Shares Outstg. (M)	107.2	Institutional Ownership (%)	88		

Price Performance

30-Week Mov. Avg. ··· 10-Week Mov. Avg. − − **GAAP Earnings vs. Previous Year** Volume Above Avg. STARS
12-Mo. Target Price — Relative Strength — ▲ Up ▼ Down ► No Change   Below Avg.

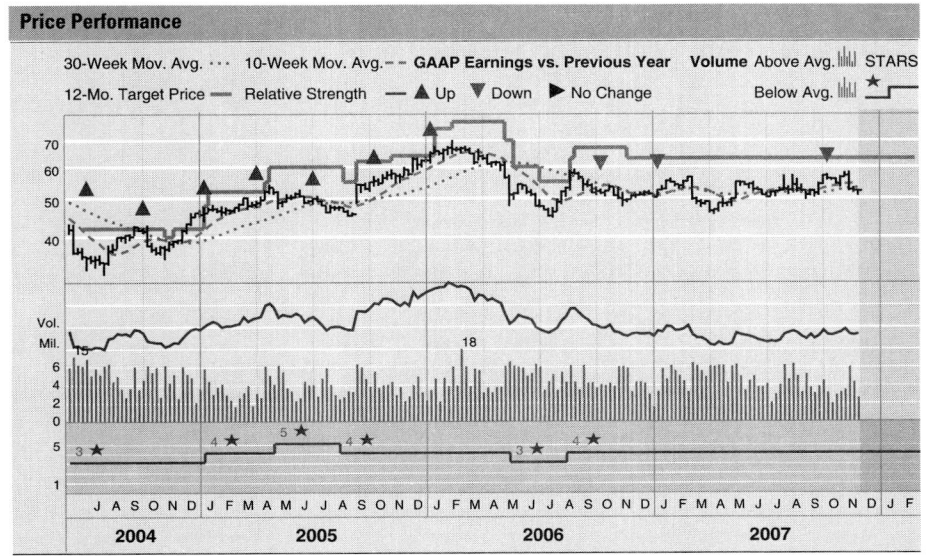

Options: ASE, CBOE, P, Ph

Analysis prepared by **Herman B. Saftlas** on November 20, 2007, when the stock traded at **$ 51.55**.

Highlights

➤ We expect revenues to rise about 12% in 2008 from the $2.5 billion that we forecast for 2007. Generics volume should be augmented by the anticipated launch of generic Fosamax, increased sales of injectables, and gains in Pliva's international sales. Projected strength in newer branded products such as Seasonique oral contraceptive, ParaGard IUD, and Plan B emergency OC should more than offset expected declines in older lines.

➤ We expect gross margins to expand on the projected higher volume and ongoing synergies accruing from the Pliva acquisition. As a percentage of total revenues, we expect SG&A and R&D spending to decline from indicated 2007 levels. Comparisons are also likely to benefit from lower interest expense and higher other income.

➤ We project calendar 2008 operating EPS of $3.70, up from the $3.10 that we estimate for 2007. Results include options expense, but exclude amortization of acquired products and merger-related costs.

Investment Rationale/Risk

➤ Benefiting from the development of what we consider innovative generic and specialty drugs, coupled with strategic acquisitions, Barr has shown solid growth in operating EPS in recent years, in our view. With the October 2006 acquisition of Pliva, Barr now ranks as the world's third largest generic drugmaker. Although initially dilutive, we think Pliva has afforded Barr many significant advantages, such as expansion in growing European markets, low-cost manufacturing, tax benefits, and entry into generic biologics. We expect aggregate pretax synergies from Pliva to total close to $200 million in the years 2007-2009.

➤ Risks to our recommendation and target price include stronger than expected competition in key generic and branded drug lines, and failure to successfully integrate Pliva.

➤ Our 12-month target price of $63 applies a peer level P/E of 17X to our EPS estimate for 2008. Our DCF model, which assumes a weighted average cost of capital of 8.2% and terminal growth of 2%, also supports an intrinsic valuation of $63.

Qualitative Risk Assessment

LOW	MEDIUM	HIGH

Our risk assessment reflects risks inherent in the generic pharmaceutical business, which include the ability to develop generic products and legally challenge branded patents. However, we believe Barr's proven expertise in developing novel generic and proprietary drugs, and successful litigation of patent challenges, together with anticipated long-term benefits from the recent acquisition of Pliva, are offsetting factors.

Quantitative Evaluations

S&P Quality Ranking   **B**

D	C	B-	**B**	B+	A-	A	A+

Relative Strength Rank   **MODERATE**

62

LOWEST = 1   HIGHEST = 99

Revenue/Earnings Data

Revenue (Million $)

	1Q	2Q	3Q	4Q	Year
2007	332.4	637.0	601.4	--	--
2006	--	--	332.4	548.0	916.4
2005	310.4	325.5	326.8	351.7	1,314
2004	244.5	257.4	265.0	280.5	1,047
2003	310.7	374.1	321.1	303.2	1,309
2002	220.4	209.0	171.9	301.5	902.9

Earnings Per Share ($)

	1Q	2Q	3Q	4Q	Year
2007	0.49	-0.42	0.41	E0.78	E3.10
2006	--	--	0.49	-3.67	-3.18
2005	0.78	0.88	0.70	0.76	3.12
2004	0.49	0.56	0.58	0.40	2.03
2003	0.37	0.33	0.33	0.13	1.15
2002	0.41	0.42	0.44	0.35	1.62

Fiscal year ended Dec. 31. Next earnings report expected: Early March. EPS Estimates based on S&P Operating Earnings; historical GAAP earnings are as reported.

Dividend Data

No cash dividends have been paid.

Barr Pharmaceuticals Inc

STANDARD
&POOR'S

Business Summary November 20, 2007

CORPORATE OVERVIEW. Founded in 1970, Barr Pharmaceuticals (formerly Barr Laboratories) is a leading developer, producer and marketer of generic pharmaceuticals. BRL also sells a number of proprietary products. Much of Barr's growth has come from acquisitions such as Duramed, a maker of women's health and hormone replacement products, and Enhance Pharmaceuticals, an R&D company developing vaginal ring drug delivery systems. Pliva, a Croatia-based pharmaceutical company, was purchased on October 24, 2006, for $2.5 billion in cash.

With the acquisition of Pliva, Barr now ranks as the world's third largest generic drugmaker, with projected annual sales of about $2.5 billion in 2007. We believe Pliva has brought a number of positives to Barr, including entry into growing European markets, low-cost manufacturing, tax benefits, and new opportunities in the lucrative field of generic biologics. Revenues in the first nine months of 2007 were divided as follows: generic drugs 76%, proprietary products 17%, and other revenues 7%. Oral contraceptives accounted for 31% of product sales in the first nine months of 2007, psychotherapeutics 12%, cardiovasculars 12%, antivirals and anti-infectives 10%, and all other 35%. Sales outside the U.S. represented 30% of product sales.

The company's generic division manufactures and distributes some 115 generic pharmaceuticals in the U.S. that are available in different dosage forms and strengths. The company's annual worldwide generic drug sales approximate $1.6 billion, including about $1 billion in the U.S. Barr is a leading supplier of oral contraceptives in the U.S., accounting for about 30% of the market. The company's oral contraceptives are sold under the Tri-Sprintec, Sprintec, Apri, Aviane, Kariva and other names. The company also sells generic versions of antidepressants Prozac and Remeron, Tamoxifen for breast cancer, anticoagulant Coumadin, and Adderall, a treatment for attention deficit hyperactivity disorder and other products.

Overseas, the company offers a portfolio of 550 generic and branded products that compete in Croatia, Poland, Germany, Spain, the U.K. and Russia. Barr also markets a large number of active pharmaceutical ingredients.

Company Financials Fiscal Year Ended Dec. 31

Per Share Data ($)	2006	2005	2004	2003	2002	2001	2000	1999	1998	1997
Tangible Book Value	NM	11.54	10.81	9.18	8.07	6.80	4.59	3.60	2.78	2.07
Cash Flow	-2.48	3.70	2.41	1.45	1.84	2.21	0.86	0.66	0.74	0.50
Earnings	-3.18	3.12	2.03	1.15	1.62	2.08	0.74	0.53	0.62	0.43
S&P Core Earnings	3.20	2.20	1.49	2.03	2.43	0.97	NA	NA	NA	NA
Dividends	Nil	Nil	Nil	Nil	Nil	Nil	Nil	Nil	Nil	Nil
Payout Ratio	Nil	Nil	Nil	Nil	Nil	Nil	Nil	Nil	Nil	Nil
Prices:High	70.25	70.25	63.60	53.99	56.91	35.56	40.27	35.61	14.39	14.74
Prices:Low	44.60	44.60	43.71	32.01	28.93	21.96	19.78	8.89	8.39	7.30
P/E Ratio:High	NM	23	31	47	35	17	55	67	23	34
P/E Ratio:Low	NM	14	22	28	18	11	27	17	14	17

Income Statement Analysis (Million $)										
Revenue	916	1,314	1,047	1,309	903	1,189	510	482	444	377
Operating Income	240	549	357	225	249	341	72.4	75.2	88.9	58.9
Depreciation	74.4	62.0	40.8	32.1	22.7	15.3	10.8	10.4	9.31	5.52
Interest Expense	32.4	0.49	1.46	2.64	1.47	3.53	1.86	2.41	2.70	0.86
Pretax Income	-303	524	330	194	263	338	101	67.8	8.13	54.7
Effective Tax Rate	NM	35.6%	34.8%	36.7%	36.2%	37.1%	38.2%	38.5%	NA	38.7%
Net Income	-338	336	215	123	168	212	62.5	42.3	49.3	33.5
S&P Core Earnings	345	233	159	141	166	55.3	NA	NA	NA	NA

Balance Sheet & Other Financial Data (Million $)										
Cash	906	602	643	452	412	331	222	156	103	73.0
Current Assets	2,088	1,109	993	878	848	638	437	315	248	217
Total Assets	4,962	1,921	1,483	1,333	1,181	889	543	424	348	311
Current Liabilities	1,212	187	213	208	275	177	152	113	101	122
Long Term Debt	1,937	7.43	15.5	32.4	34.0	42.6	24.9	28.1	30.0	32.2
Common Equity	1,465	1,691	1,234	1,042	868	667	366	282	214	156
Total Capital	3,665	1,698	1,249	1,074	902	709	391	311	246	189
Capital Expenditures	33.7	61.0	55.2	46.9	80.6	47.2	17.7	12.1	12.3	20.4
Cash Flow	264	398	256	155	190	226	73.3	52.8	58.6	39.0
Current Ratio	1.7	5.9	4.7	4.2	3.1	3.6	2.9	2.8	2.5	1.8
% Long Term Debt of Capitalization	52.9	0.4	1.2	3.0	3.8	6.0	6.4	9.0	12.2	17.0
% Net Income of Revenue	NM	25.6	20.5	9.4	18.6	17.9	12.3	8.8	11.1	8.9
% Return on Assets	NM	19.7	15.3	9.8	16.2	27.3	12.9	11.0	15.0	13.0
% Return on Equity	NM	23.0	18.9	12.9	21.8	38.8	19.3	17.1	26.6	26.0

Data as orig reptd.; bef. results of disc opers/spec. items. Per share data adj. for stk. divs.; EPS diluted. Prior to 2006 (six months), fiscal year ended Jun. 30 of the fol. cal. yr. E-Estimated. NA-Not Available. NM-Not Meaningful. NR-Not Ranked. UR-Under Review.

Office: 400 Chestnut Ridge Rd, Woodcliff Lake, NJ 07677-7604.
Telephone: 201-930-3300.
Email: ir@barrlabs.com
Website: http://www.barrlabs.com

Chrmn & CEO: B.L. Downey
Pres & COO: P.M. Bisaro
VP, CFO & Treas: W.T. McKee
VP, Secy & General Counsel: F.J. Killion

Board Members: P. M. Bisaro, H. N. Chefitz, B. L. Downey, R. R. Frankovic, J. S. Gilmore, III, P. R. Seaver, G. P. Stephan

Founded: 1970
Domicile: Delaware
Employees: 2,040

Baxter International Inc

STANDARD &POOR'S

S&P Recommendation **HOLD** ★★★☆☆	Price $57.89 (as of Nov 23, 2007)	12-Mo. Target Price $63.00	Investment Style Large-Cap Growth

GICS Sector Health Care
Sub-Industry Health Care Equipment

Summary This global medical products and services company provides critical therapies for people with life-threatening conditions.

Key Stock Statistics (Source S&P, Vickers, company reports)

52-Wk Range	$60.98– 43.38	S&P Oper. EPS 2007**E**	2.76	Market Capitalization(B)	$37.468	Beta	0.95
Trailing 12-Month EPS	$2.53	S&P Oper. EPS 2008**E**	3.00	Yield (%)	1.50	S&P 3-Yr. Proj. EPS CAGR(%)	12.00
Trailing 12-Month P/E	22.9	P/E on S&P Oper. EPS 2007**E**	21.0	Dividend Rate/Share	$0.87	S&P Credit Rating	A+
$10K Invested 5 Yrs Ago	$20,350	Common Shares Outstg. (M)	647.2	Institutional Ownership (%)	87		

Price Performance

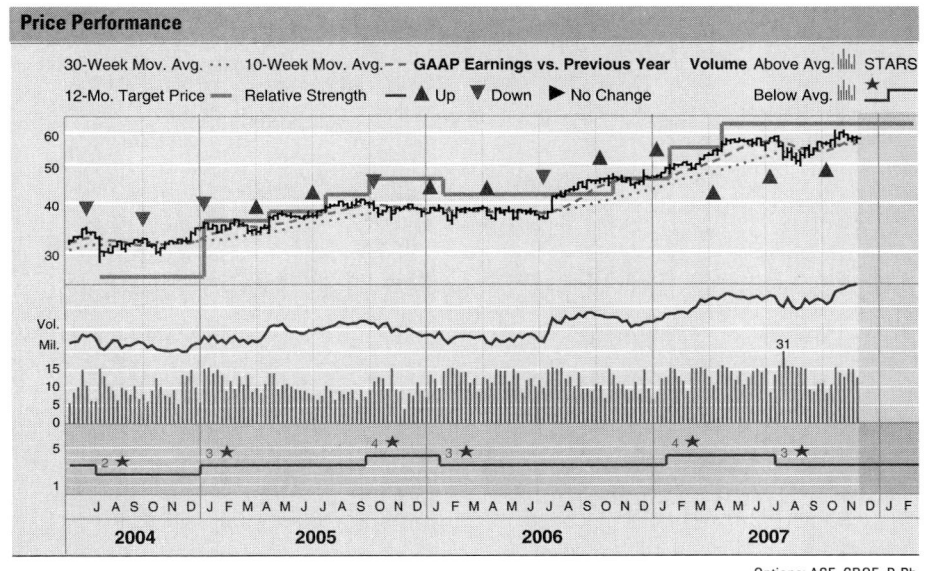

30-Week Mov. Avg. ··· 10-Week Mov. Avg.-- **GAAP Earnings vs. Previous Year** Volume Above Avg. STARS
12-Mo. Target Price — Relative Strength — ▲ Up ▼ Down ▶ No Change Below Avg.

Options: ASE, CBOE, P, Ph

Analysis prepared by **Herman B. Saftlas** on October 23, 2007, when the stock traded at **$ 59.02**.

Qualitative Risk Assessment

LOW	**MEDIUM**	HIGH

Our risk assessment reflects that BAX operates in a highly competitive business characterized by rapid technological change and new market entrants. In addition, the business entails regulatory and reimbursement risks, as well as liability risks from malfunctioning products. This is offset by our belief that health care products are immune to economic cycles, and that long-term demand should benefit from demographic growth in the elderly and a greater penetration of developing global markets.

Quantitative Evaluations

S&P Quality Ranking B+

D	C	B-	B	**B+**	A-	A	A+

Relative Strength Rank STRONG

84

LOWEST = 1 HIGHEST = 99

Highlights

➤ We project revenue growth of about 7% in 2008, from the $11.1 billion expected in 2007, reflecting growth in each of the company's principal business segments. BioSciences sales should reflect further growth in recombinants such as Advate factor VIII, plasma proteins, and antibody therapies. We expect sales of Advate to exceed $1.3 billion in 2008. Volume in the Medication Delivery division will likely benefit from gains in IV and infusion products, while Renal Care sales should be lifted by further growth in the peritoneal products business. The possible return of the Colleague infusion pump to the U.S. market would also augment volume.

➤ We see gross margins expanding to about 50%, from an estimated 49.1% in 2007, helped by stronger top-line growth, a more profitable sales mix and ongoing productivity enhancements. We also forecast good control over SG&A costs. However, we see R&D spending ramping up to fund new products. The tax rate should be comparable to the 20% estimated for 2007.

➤ We project EPS of $3.00 for 2008, up from the $2.76 we expect for 2007.

Investment Rationale/Risk

➤ We credit management with improving BAX's profitability by focusing on high-margin recombinants, plasma proteins, and antibody therapies, divesting low-margin businesses, and closing excess manufacturing capacity. We view BAX's recent divestiture of its Transfusion Therapies unit as in line with a strategy of moving away from commodity-type products toward higher-margin medical technology items. Despite recent problems with a Colleague product, we think the overall Colleague infusion pump line, off the U.S. market since 2005 because of quality control issues, may return to the market in 2008.

➤ Risks to our recommendation and target price include lower-than-expected Advate sales, adverse adjustments to Medicare reimbursement rates, and an inability to further streamline operating costs.

➤ Our 12-month target price of $63 assumes a peer-level P/E of 21.0X our 2008 EPS estimate. Our target price also matches our intrinsic value estimate for BAX, derived from our DCF model, which assumes a WACC of 8.4%, and a terminal growth rate of 2%.

Revenue/Earnings Data

Revenue (Million $)

	1Q	2Q	3Q	4Q	Year
2007	2,675	2,829	2,750	--	--
2006	2,409	2,649	2,557	2,763	10,378
2005	2,383	2,577	2,398	2,491	9,849
2004	2,209	2,379	2,320	2,601	9,509
2003	1,997	2,163	2,219	2,537	8,916
2002	1,875	1,945	2,029	2,261	8,110

Earnings Per Share ($)

	1Q	2Q	3Q	4Q	Year
2007	0.61	0.65	0.61	E0.76	E2.76
2006	0.43	0.47	0.57	0.66	2.13
2005	0.36	0.51	0.18	0.46	1.52
2004	0.30	-0.28	0.42	0.17	0.62
2003	0.36	0.08	0.47	0.62	1.52
2002	0.41	0.32	0.51	0.42	1.67

Fiscal year ended Dec. 31. Next earnings report expected: Late January. EPS Estimates based on S&P Operating Earnings; historical GAAP earnings are as reported.

Dividend Data (Dates: mm/dd Payment Date: mm/dd/yy)

Amount ($)	Date Decl.	Ex-Div. Date	Stk. of Record	Payment Date
0.168	02/13	03/07	03/10	04/02/07
0.168	05/01	06/06	06/10	07/02/07
0.168	07/31	09/06	09/10	10/01/07
0.218	11/13	12/06	12/10	01/03/08

Dividends have been paid since 1934. Source: Company reports.

Baxter International Inc

Business Summary October 23, 2007

CORPORATE OVERVIEW. Founded in 1931 as the first producer of commercially prepared intravenous (IV) solutions, Baxter International makes and distributes medical products and equipment, with a focus on the blood and circulatory system. In 2006, international sales accounted for 56% of the total. In March 2007, the company sold its Transfusion Therapies business to Texas Pacific Group and Maverick Capital for $540 million. Transfusion Therapies, a maker of manual and automated blood-collection products and storage equipment, had annual sales of about $500 million.

The BioSciences unit (42% of 2006 sales) produces plasma-based and recombinant clotting factors for hemophilia, as well as biopharmaceuticals for immune deficiencies, cancer, and other disorders. It also offers biosurgery products for hemostasis, tissue sealing and tissue regeneration, vaccines, and blood processing and storage systems used by hospitals, blood banks and others. In addition, BAX sells a meningitis C vaccine, and is developing cell culture-derived vaccines for influenza, smallpox, Severe Acute Respiratory Syndrome and other diseases. Its most important Biosciences product is Advate, a recombinant blood-clotting agent produced without adding human or animal proteins in the cell culture, purification or final formulation process.

The Medication Delivery unit (38%) makes IV solutions and various specialty products such as critical-care generic injectable drugs, anesthetic agents, and nutrition and oncology products. The products work with devices such as drug-reconstitution systems, IV infusion pumps, nutritional compounding equipment, and medication management systems to provide fluid replenishment, general anesthesia, parenteral nutrition, pain management, antibiotic therapy, and chemotherapy.

Renal Care products (20%) comprise dialysis equipment and other products and services provided for kidney failure patients. BAX sells products for peritoneal dialysis (PD), including solutions, container systems and automated machines that cleanse patients' blood overnight while they sleep. The company also makes dialyzers and instrumentation for hemodialysis (HD). Another renal care product is Extraneal (icodextrin) solution, which facilitates increased fluid removal from the bloodstream during dialysis.

Company Financials Fiscal Year Ended Dec. 31

Per Share Data ($)	2006	2005	2004	2003	2002	2001	2000	1999	1998	1997
Tangible Book Value	6.42	3.61	2.45	1.74	1.53	3.44	2.43	4.19	1.79	1.78
Cash Flow	3.01	2.45	1.59	2.42	2.38	1.81	1.91	1.95	1.28	1.24
Earnings	2.13	1.52	0.62	1.52	1.67	1.09	1.24	1.32	0.55	0.53
S&P Core Earnings	2.24	1.38	0.52	1.25	1.30	0.53	NA	NA	NA	NA
Dividends	0.58	0.58	0.58	0.58	0.58	0.58	0.15	0.58	0.58	0.57
Payout Ratio	27%	38%	94%	38%	35%	53%	12%	44%	107%	107%
Prices:High	48.54	41.07	34.84	31.32	59.90	55.90	45.13	38.00	33.00	30.13
Prices:Low	35.12	33.08	27.10	18.18	24.07	40.06	25.88	28.41	24.25	19.94
P/E Ratio:High	23	27	56	21	36	51	37	29	61	57
P/E Ratio:Low	16	22	44	12	14	37	21	22	44	38

Income Statement Analysis (Million $)										
Revenue	10,378	9,849	9,509	8,916	8,110	7,663	6,896	6,380	6,599	6,138
Operating Income	2,479	2,110	2,039	2,161	2,168	1,934	1,673	1,522	1,545	1,403
Depreciation	575	580	601	545	439	441	405	372	426	398
Interest Expense	101	166	99.0	118	71.0	108	124	152	193	198
Pretax Income	1,746	1,444	430	1,150	1,397	964	946	1,052	549	523
Effective Tax Rate	19.9%	33.7%	10.9%	19.8%	26.1%	31.1%	22.0%	26.0%	42.6%	42.6%
Net Income	1,398	958	383	922	1,033	664	738	779	315	300
S&P Core Earnings	1,467	864	323	756	794	313	NA	NA	NA	NA

Balance Sheet & Other Financial Data (Million $)										
Cash	2,485	841	1,109	927	1,169	582	579	606	709	465
Current Assets	6,970	5,116	6,019	5,437	5,160	3,977	3,651	3,819	4,651	3,870
Total Assets	14,686	12,727	14,147	13,779	12,478	10,343	8,733	9,644	10,085	8,707
Current Liabilities	3,610	4,165	4,286	3,819	3,851	3,294	3,372	2,700	2,988	2,557
Long Term Debt	2,567	2,414	3,933	4,421	4,398	2,486	1,726	2,601	3,096	2,635
Common Equity	6,272	4,299	3,705	3,323	2,939	3,757	2,659	3,348	2,839	2,619
Total Capital	8,839	6,713	7,638	7,744	7,366	6,461	4,545	6,260	6,440	5,570
Capital Expenditures	526	444	558	789	734	669	101	529	492	403
Cash Flow	1,973	1,538	984	1,467	1,472	1,105	1,143	1,151	741	698
Current Ratio	1.9	1.2	1.4	1.4	1.3	1.2	1.1	1.4	1.6	1.5
% Long Term Debt of Capitalization	29.0	36.0	51.5	57.1	59.7	38.5	38.0	41.5	48.1	47.3
% Net Income of Revenue	13.5	9.7	4.0	10.3	12.7	8.7	10.7	12.2	4.8	4.9
% Return on Assets	10.2	7.1	2.8	7.0	9.1	7.0	8.0	8.0	3.4	3.7
% Return on Equity	26.4	23.9	10.8	29.4	30.9	20.7	24.6	25.2	11.5	11.7

Data as orig reptd.; bef. results of disc opers/spec. items. Per share data adj. for stk. divs.; EPS diluted. E-Estimated. NA-Not Available. NM-Not Meaningful. NR-Not Ranked. UR-Under Review.

Office: One Baxter Parkway, Deerfield, IL 60015.
Telephone: 847-948-2000.
Website: http://www.baxter.com
Chrmn, Pres & CEO: R.L. Parkinson, Jr.

VP & CFO: R.M. Davis
VP & CSO: N.J. Riedel
VP & Treas: R.J. Hombach
VP & Secy: D.P. Scharf

Investor Contact: M. Ladone (847-948-3371)
Board Members: W. E. Boomer, B. E. Devitt, J. D. Forsyth, G. D. Fosler, J. R. Gavin, III, P. S. Hellman, J. B. Martin, R. L. Parkinson, Jr., C. U. Shapazian, T. T. Stallkamp, K. J. Storm, A. P. Stroucken

Founded: 1931
Domicile: Delaware
Employees: 48,000

BB&T Corp

STANDARD &POOR'S

S&P Recommendation	BUY ★★★★☆	Price $34.00 (as of Nov 23, 2007)	12-Mo. Target Price $45.00	Investment Style Large-Cap Blend

GICS Sector Financials
Sub-Industry Regional Banks

Summary This bank holding company has a large presence in its home state of North Carolina, as well as in Virginia, with additional offices in Georgia, South Carolina, the District of Columbia, and seven other states.

Key Stock Statistics (Source S&P, Vickers, company reports)

52-Wk Range	$44.74–32.10	S&P Oper. EPS 2007**E**	3.18	Market Capitalization(B)	$18.766	Beta	0.61
Trailing 12-Month EPS	$2.86	S&P Oper. EPS 2008**E**	3.42	Yield (%)	5.41	S&P 3-Yr. Proj. EPS CAGR(%)	12.30
Trailing 12-Month P/E	11.9	P/E on S&P Oper. EPS 2007**E**	10.7	Dividend Rate/Share	$1.84	S&P Credit Rating	A+
$10K Invested 5 Yrs Ago	$10,878	Common Shares Outstg. (M)	551.9	Institutional Ownership (%)	32		

Price Performance

- 30-Week Mov. Avg. · · · 10-Week Mov. Avg. - - **GAAP Earnings vs. Previous Year** Volume Above Avg. STARS
- 12-Mo. Target Price — Relative Strength — ▲ Up ▼ Down ▶ No Change Below Avg. ★

Options: ASE, CBOE, P, Ph

Analysis prepared by **Erik Oja** on October 23, 2007, when the stock traded at **$ 36.77**.

Highlights

➤ We expect earning asset growth of 7.6% in 2007 and 6.0% in 2008, driven by commercial and industrial lending, partly offset by a slowdown in residential construction lending and direct retail lending. For all of 2007, we expect funding costs to compress the net interest margin to 3.52%, from 3.74% in 2006. For 2008, we forecast a moderation in funding costs, and a nine basis point expansion of the net interest margin, to 3.61%. We see fee income growth of 8.6% in 2007 and 4.3% in 2008, despite competitive pressure in insurance commissions. We expect total revenue growth of 6.3% in 2007 and 7.1% in 2008.

➤ BBT's non-performing assets have increased to 0.42% of the total, from 0.33% at June 30 and 0.29% at December 31, well below industry averages. However, we expect additions (provisions) to the reserve to climb to about $385 million in 2007 and almost $480 million in 2008, from $240 million in 2006.

➤ We see 2007 operating EPS rising to $3.18, a 13% increase from $2.81 in 2006. EPS included various charges totaling $0.38 in 2006. Our 2008 operating EPS forecast is $3.42, up 7.5%.

Investment Rationale/Risk

➤ In a difficult operating environment, BBT has continued to grow commercial and industrial lending, while maintaining acceptable credit quality as well as funding growth. According to the latest FDIC data, BBT maintained or expanded deposit market share in every state it serves. Fee income, which we expect to be about 41% of total revenues in 2007, a level higher than most of BBT's peers, should grow at nearly 9% in 2007, by our estimates. Although the insurance business is facing steeper competition, we expect investment banking, brokerage and deposit fees to make up the difference.

➤ Risks to our opinion and target price include a flat or inverted yield curve that increases the cost of deposits, and an economic slowdown adversely affecting loan growth and credit quality.

➤ Our 12-month target price of $45 is equal to 13.3X our 2008 operating EPS estimate, in line with large-cap regional banking peers, which we think is appropriate, given our view of BBT's growth prospects and credit quality.

Qualitative Risk Assessment

LOW	MEDIUM	HIGH

Our risk assessment reflects the company's large-cap valuation, our view of the strong credit quality of its loan portfolio, and its history of profitability. While the company operates in a highly competitive and fragmented industry, the industry tends to produce relatively stable financial results.

Quantitative Evaluations

S&P Quality Ranking A-

D	C	B-	B	B+	A-	A	A+

Relative Strength Rank MODERATE

36

LOWEST = 1   HIGHEST = 99

Revenue/Earnings Data

Revenue (Million $)

	1Q	2Q	3Q	4Q	Year
2007	2,543	2,690	2,719	--	--
2006	2,165	2,319	2,463	2,468	9,414
2005	1,760	1,918	2,036	2,118	7,831
2004	1,559	1,693	1,698	1,736	6,666
2003	1,500	1,507	1,611	1,627	6,244
2002	1,456	1,526	1,549	1,629	6,127

Earnings Per Share ($)

2007	0.77	0.83	0.80	E0.77	E3.18
2006	0.79	0.79	0.77	0.46	2.81
2005	0.71	0.70	0.80	0.78	3.00
2004	0.60	0.72	0.74	0.75	2.80
2003	0.69	0.67	0.21	0.55	2.07
2002	0.64	0.68	0.68	0.70	2.70

Fiscal year ended Dec. 31. Next earnings report expected: Mid January. EPS Estimates based on S&P Operating Earnings; historical GAAP earnings are as reported.

Dividend Data (Dates: mm/dd Payment Date: mm/dd/yy)

Amount ($)	Date Decl.	Ex-Div. Date	Stk. of Record	Payment Date
0.420	12/12	01/10	01/12	02/01/07
0.420	02/20	04/11	04/13	05/01/07
0.460	06/26	07/11	07/13	08/01/07
0.460	08/21	10/10	10/12	11/01/07

Dividends have been paid since 1903. Source: Company reports.

Please read the Required Disclosures and Analyst Certification on the last page of this report.

The McGraw-Hill Companies

BB&T Corp

STANDARD &POOR'S

Business Summary October 23, 2007

CORPORATE OVERVIEW. BBT has bank operations providing loan, deposit and financial products primarily in the Southeast. BBT has seven reportable business segments: Banking Network, Mortgage Banking, Trust Services, Insurance Services, Investment Banking and Brokerage, Specialized Lending, and Treasury.

The Banking Network generated almost 66% of total revenues and almost 82% of segment net income in 2006. In addition to providing banking services, BBT's bank subsidiaries also offer brokerage, insurance and other financial services. The Specialized Lending segment generated 6.8% of revenues and 4.3% of segment net income, Financial Services generated 8.2% and 1.5% respectively, and Residential Mortgage Banking segment generated 5.3 and 6.0%, respectively. The remaining 14.1% of revenues and 6.6% of segment net income was generated by Insurance Services, Specialized Lending, Investment Banking, Trust, and Other.

MARKET PROFILE. As of June 30, 2006, which is the latest available FDIC branch-level data, BBT had 1,447 branches and $79.7 billion in deposits, with about 55% of its deposits and 52% of its branches concentrated in North Car-

olina and Virginia, by our calculations. The acquisition of Coastal Financial Corp, which closed May 1, 2007, added 22 branches and $1.1 billion in deposits to BBT, and are included, on a pro-forma basis, in the total of 1,447 branches. In North Carolina, BBT had 342 branches, $25.3 billion in deposits, and a deposit market share of about 12%, which ranks third. In Virginia, BBT had 397 branches, $19.4 billion in deposits, and a deposit market share of about 9%, which ranks fifth. In Georgia, BBT had 140 branches, $7.5 billion in deposits, and a deposit market share of about 4%, which ranks fifth. In South Carolina, BBT had 112 branches, $6.6 billion in deposits, and a deposit market share of about 10%, which ranks third. In Maryland, BBT had 124 branches, $5.8 billion in deposits, and a deposit market share of about 5%, which ranks seventh. In addition, BBT had a number one market ranking in West Virginia, is fourth in Kentucky, seventh in DC, sixth in Tennessee, and fifteenth in Florida. Finally, BBT had a small presence in Alabama and Indiana.

Company Financials Fiscal Year Ended Dec. 31

Per Share Data ($)	2006	2005	2004	2003	2002	2001	2000	1999	1998	1997
Tangible Book Value	11.04	11.76	12.26	11.66	12.04	13.50	11.91	9.66	9.95	8.23
Earnings	2.81	3.00	2.80	2.07	2.70	2.12	1.55	1.83	1.71	1.30
S&P Core Earnings	2.79	2.90	2.75	1.97	2.59	2.02	NA	NA	NA	NA
Dividends	1.60	1.46	1.34	1.22	1.10	0.98	0.86	0.75	0.66	0.58
Payout Ratio	57%	49%	48%	59%	41%	46%	55%	41%	39%	45%
Prices:High	44.74	43.92	43.25	39.69	39.47	38.84	38.25	40.63	40.75	32.50
Prices:Low	38.24	37.04	33.02	30.66	31.03	30.24	21.69	27.19	26.25	17.50
P/E Ratio:High	16	15	15	19	15	18	25	22	24	25
P/E Ratio:Low	14	12	12	15	11	14	14	15	15	13

Income Statement Analysis (Million $)

	2006	2005	2004	2003	2002	2001	2000	1999	1998	1997
Net Interest Income	3,708	3,525	3,348	3,082	2,747	2,434	2,018	1,582	1,247	1,100
Tax Equivalent Adjustment	NA	82.7	NA	21.2	151	19.1	130	86.7	64.8	52.9
Non Interest Income	2,594	2,326	2,113	1,782	1,522	1,256	996	639	520	473
Loan Loss Provision	240	217	249	248	264	224	127	92.1	80.3	89.9
% Expense/Operating Revenue	55.8%	53.4%	57.6%	63.6%	54.0%	60.1%	56.0%	58.4%	52.5%	59.6%
Pretax Income	2,473	2,467	2,322	1,617	1,791	1,360	906	904	734	547
Effective Tax Rate	38.2%	33.0%	32.9%	34.1%	27.8%	28.4%	30.8%	32.2%	31.6%	34.2%
Net Income	1,528	1,654	1,558	1,065	1,293	974	626	613	502	360
% Net Interest Margin	3.74	3.89	4.04	4.06	4.25	4.17	3.56	4.27	3.75	4.55
S&P Core Earnings	1,514	1,608	1,529	1,012	1,241	927	NA	NA	NA	NA

Balance Sheet & Other Financial Data (Million $)

	2006	2005	2004	2003	2002	2001	2000	1999	1998	1997
Money Market Assets	688	697	1,244	604	591	458	379	390	168	178
Investment Securities	22,868	20,489	19,173	16,317	17,655	16,662	13,851	10,579	8,099	6,629
Commercial Loans	41,300	37,655	34,321	12,429	7,061	6,551	5,894	4,593	3,444	3,018
Other Loans	41,611	36,739	33,228	49,151	44,079	38,985	33,561	24,320	19,932	16,499
Total Assets	121,351	109,170	100,509	90,467	80,217	70,870	59,340	43,481	34,427	29,178
Demand Deposits	14,726	13,477	12,246	11,098	7,864	6,940	5,064	3,908	3,247	2,829
Time Deposits	66,245	60,805	55,453	48,252	43,416	37,794	32,951	23,343	19,800	17,381
Long Term Debt	12,604	13,119	11,420	10,808	13,588	11,721	8,355	5,492	4,737	3,283
Common Equity	11,745	11,129	10,874	9,935	7,388	6,150	4,786	3,199	2,759	2,238
% Return on Assets	1.3	1.6	1.6	1.2	1.7	1.4	1.1	1.5	1.6	1.4
% Return on Equity	13.4	15.0	15.0	12.3	19.1	16.8	14.2	19.2	20.1	18.1
% Loan Loss Reserve	1.1	1.1	1.2	1.3	1.4	1.4	1.3	1.3	1.4	1.3
% Loans/Deposits	103.2	99.0	100.7	105.0	104.4	106.1	106.0	107.1	98.3	97.9
% Equity to Assets	9.9	10.5	10.9	10.1	9.0	8.4	7.9	7.7	7.9	7.9

Data as orig reptd.; bef. results of disc opers/spec. items. Per share data adj. for stk. divs.; EPS diluted. E-Estimated. NA-Not Available. NM-Not Meaningful. NR-Not Ranked. UR-Under Review.

Office: 200 West Second Street, Winston-Salem, NC 27101.
Telephone: 336-733-2000.
Website: http://www.bbandt.com
Chrmn & CEO: J.A. Allison, IV

COO: K.S. King
Sr EVP: C.L. Wilson, III
Sr EVP: W.K. Chalk
Sr EVP: R.E. Greene

Investor Contact: T. Gjesdal (336-733-3058)
Board Members: J. A. Allison, IV, J. S. Banner, A. R. Cablik, N. R. Chilton, R. E. Deal, T. D. Efird, B. J. Fitzpatrick, L. V. Hackley, J. P. Helm, J. P. Howe, III, J. H. Maynard, A. O. McCauley, J. H. Morrison, N. R. Qubein, E. R. Sasser

Founded: 1968
Domicile: North Carolina
Employees: 29,300

The McGraw-Hill Companies

Bear Stearns Companies Inc (The)

STANDARD &POOR'S

S&P Recommendation HOLD ★★★☆☆

Price	12-Mo. Target Price	Investment Style
$99.50 (as of Nov 28, 2007)	$120.00	Large-Cap Blend

GICS Sector Financials
Sub-Industry Investment Banking & Brokerage

Summary This company's Bear, Stearns & Co. unit is a leading investment bank and broker, and is ranked as one of the largest NYSE member firms.

Key Stock Statistics (Source S&P, Vickers, company reports)

52-Wk Range	$172.61– 89.55	S&P Oper. EPS 2007**E**	6.60	Market Capitalization(B)	$11.488	Beta	1.06
Trailing 12-Month EPS	$11.53	S&P Oper. EPS 2008**E**	9.60	Yield (%)	1.29	S&P 3-Yr. Proj. EPS CAGR(%)	8.00
Trailing 12-Month P/E	8.6	P/E on S&P Oper. EPS 2007**E**	15.1	Dividend Rate/Share	$1.28	S&P Credit Rating	A
$10K Invested 5 Yrs Ago	$15,107	Common Shares Outstg. (M)	115.5	Institutional Ownership (%)	77		

Price Performance

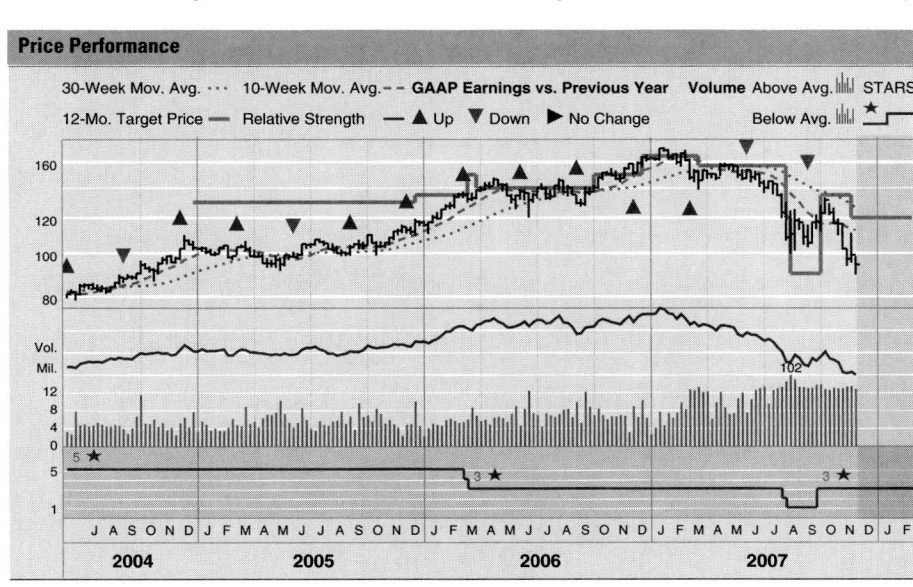

30-Week Mov. Avg. ··· 10-Week Mov. Avg. - - **GAAP Earnings vs. Previous Year** Volume Above Avg.▮▮▮ STARS
12-Mo. Target Price — Relative Strength — ▲ Up ▼ Down ► No Change Below Avg.▮▮▮ ★

Options: ASE, CBOE, P, Ph

Analysis prepared by **Matthew Albrecht** on November 16, 2007, when the stock traded at **$ 98.37**.

Highlights

➤ Recent results highlighted BSC's exposure to turmoil in the credit markets. Mortgage securities and leveraged loan commitments on its balance sheet have been written down, fixed income origination and trading volumes are down, and hedge fund troubles have hurt results. Problems in those markets have continued, and we expect additional write-downs related to CDO and sub-prime mortgage exposure. We anticipate a decline in overall investment banking volume in the fourth quarter and into FY 08 (Nov.) as deals backlogged from the first half of FY 07 are worked off and new deals may be smaller in size, but the business should remain profitable. We look for net revenues to decline sharply this fiscal year before a rebound in FY 08.

➤ The revenue decline we anticipate will likely lead to higher compensation ratios in FY 07, before a moderation in FY 08 to historic levels of about 48% of net revenues. Non-compensation costs will also likely rise in FY 07, before a decline on a percentage basis in FY 08, widening that margin.

➤ We forecast EPS of $6.60 in FY 07 and $9.60 in FY 08.

Investment Rationale/Risk

➤ We think BSC shares merit a lower valuation than larger peers given our view that the company is generally less diversified by business and region. Also, we think BSC has been slow to focus on faster growing areas. We have a hold recommendation on the stock, as we believe the share price appropriately discounts the current operating environment, and we no longer expect write-downs to book value.

➤ Risks to our recommendation and target price include potentially higher interest rates, widening credit spreads, trading losses, regulatory issues and slower global economic growth.

➤ The shares recently traded at 15.6X our FY 07 EPS estimate and 1.1X book value, discounts to the company's peer group in our coverage universe. Our 12-month target price of $120 is equal to 1.3X our 12-month projected book value. This multiple remains slightly below its historical average multiple due to an improving but uncertain operating environment, as well as recent troubles that may have caused some operational harm to BSC.

Qualitative Risk Assessment

LOW	MEDIUM	HIGH

Our risk assessment is based on our view that the company has a strong competitive position. However, we believe BSC is less diversified by business and by region relative to certain larger peers; we also note significant industry cyclicality.

Quantitative Evaluations

S&P Quality Ranking A+

D	C	B-	B	B+	A-	A	A+

Relative Strength Rank MODERATE

30

LOWEST = 1   HIGHEST = 99

Revenue/Earnings Data

Revenue (Million $)

	1Q	2Q	3Q	4Q	Year
2007	4,798	4,976	4,340	--	--
2006	3,638	4,304	4,136	4,474	16,551
2005	2,622	2,824	2,925	3,181	11,552
2004	2,081	2,064	1,894	2,382	8,422
2003	1,838	1,850	1,842	1,865	7,395
2002	1,718	2,070	1,581	1,521	6,891

Earnings Per Share ($)

	1Q	2Q	3Q	4Q	Year
2007	3.82	2.52	1.16	E-0.90	E6.60
2006	3.54	3.72	3.02	4.00	14.27
2005	2.64	2.09	2.69	2.90	10.31
2004	2.57	2.49	2.09	2.61	9.76
2003	2.00	2.05	2.30	2.19	8.52
2002	2.00	2.59	1.23	1.36	6.47

Fiscal year ended Nov. 30. Next earnings report expected: Mid December. EPS Estimates based on S&P Operating Earnings; historical GAAP earnings are as reported.

Dividend Data (Dates: mm/dd Payment Date: mm/dd/yy)

Amount ($)	Date Decl.	Ex-Div. Date	Stk. of Record	Payment Date
0.320	12/18	01/11	01/16	01/26/07
0.320	03/22	04/13	04/17	04/27/07
0.320	06/13	07/13	07/17	07/27/07
0.320	09/21	10/12	10/16	10/26/07

Dividends have been paid since 1986. Source: Company reports.

Please read the Required Disclosures and Analyst Certification on the last page of this report.

The McGraw-Hill Companies

Bear Stearns Companies Inc (The)

STANDARD
&POOR'S

Business Summary November 16, 2007

CORPORATE OVERVIEW. Bear Stearns is a leading investment banking, securities and derivatives trading, clearance and brokerage firm serving corporations governments, institutional and individual investors worldwide. The company is divided into three principal segments: Capital Markets, Global Clearing Services and Wealth Management.

The Capital Markets segment (79% of net revenues in FY 06) includes the institutional equities, fixed income and investment banking areas. It provides the sales, trading and origination efforts for various fixed income, equity and advisory products and services. Institutional equities includes sales, trading and research for domestic and international equities, block trading, convertible bonds, equity derivatives, and specialist and market-making activities. The fixed income business includes sales, trading, origination and research provided to institutional clients for products such as mortgage and asset-backed securities, corporate and government bonds, municipal bonds, high yield products, foreign exchange, interest rate, and credit derivatives. Investment banking provides services, including equity and debt underwriting, strategic advice, merger and acquisition advice, and merchant banking.

The Global Clearing Services segment (12%) provides execution, clearing and margin and securities lending to clients. Prime brokerage clients include hedge funds and clients of money managers, short sellers, arbitrageurs, and other professional investors. Correspondent broker-dealer clients engage in retail, institutional and money management activities on a fully disclosed basis.

The Wealth Management segment (9%) is comprised of the Private Client Services (PCS) and the asset management businesses. PCS provides high net worth investors with investment service through its network of account executives throughout the world. Asset management manages equity, fixed income and alternative assets for corporate pension plans, public systems, endowments, foundations, multi-employer plans, insurance companies, corporations, families and high net worth investors around the globe. It had $52.5 billion in assets under management at the end of FY 06.

Company Financials Fiscal Year Ended Nov. 30

Per Share Data ($)	2006	2005	2004	2003	2002	2001	2000	1999	1998	1997
Tangible Book Value	225.31	91.50	82.31	67.58	57.91	45.25	45.49	33.90	27.84	22.69
Cash Flow	13.68	9.75	9.06	7.76	5.75	3.85	4.89	4.64	4.47	4.16
Earnings	14.27	10.31	9.76	8.52	6.47	4.31	5.35	4.27	4.17	3.81
S&P Core Earnings	14.27	10.76	9.44	8.16	6.15	4.09	NA	NA	NA	NA
Dividends	1.12	1.00	0.85	0.74	0.62	0.60	0.55	0.55	0.54	0.53
Payout Ratio	8%	10%	9%	9%	10%	14%	10%	13%	13%	14%
Prices:High	166.20	119.40	109.85	83.12	67.55	64.45	72.50	50.48	58.05	43.99
Prices:Low	110.39	91.27	75.44	57.58	50.50	40.65	36.50	31.90	23.58	23.22
P/E Ratio:High	12	12	11	10	10	15	14	12	14	12
P/E Ratio:Low	8	9	8	7	8	9	7	7	6	6

Income Statement Analysis (Million $)										
Commissions	1,163	1,200	1,178	1,078	1,111	1,117	1,207	1,014	903	732
Interest Income	8,536	5,107	2,317	1,955	2,232	4,339	5,642	4,009	4,286	3,058
Total Revenue	16,551	11,552	8,422	7,395	6,891	8,701	10,277	7,882	7,980	6,077
Interest Expense	7,324	4,142	1,609	1,401	1,763	3,794	4,801	3,380	3,639	2,551
Pretax Income	3,147	2,207	2,022	1,772	1,311	934	1,172	1,064	1,063	1,014
Effective Tax Rate	34.7%	33.8%	33.5%	34.8%	33.0%	33.1%	34.0%	36.8%	37.9%	39.5%
Net Income	2,054	1,462	1,345	1,156	878	625	773	673	660	613
S&P Core Earnings	2,080	1,555	1,341	1,154	883	622	NA	NA	NA	NA

Balance Sheet & Other Financial Data (Million $)										
Total Assets	350,433	292,635	255,950	212,168	184,854	185,530	171,166	153,894	154,496	121,434
Cash Items	13,399	11,129	8,596	12,495	12,620	16,620	6,093	5,020	3,357	2,698
Receivables	136,517	37,233	35,364	23,645	19,762	23,702	19,305	18,065	90,537	79,258
Securities Owned	125,168	93,364	81,203	59,233	53,116	51,911	61,760	41,943	44,620	38,437
Securities Borrowed	11,451	10,104	10,719	6,648	58,879	63,794	69,036	64,819	59,960	53,848
Due Brokers & Customers	76,385	75,888	84,535	71,343	62,365	61,470	51,236	43,019	47,175	32,730
Other Liabilities	4,976	3,665	5,180	2,688	2,378	2,660	23,863	25,954	29,423	23,109
Capitalization:Debt	54,570	43,490	36,843	29,993	24,244	24,192	17,243	15,147	13,296	8,120
Capitalization:Equity	11,770	10,562	8,538	6,932	5,689	4,829	4,958	4,156	3,499	2,941
Capitalization:Total	60,215	54,424	45,829	37,463	30,626	29,820	22,898	20,103	17,938	11,746
% Return on Revenue	13.3	14.1	18.6	18.3	15.2	8.2	8.5	9.8	8.3	10.1
% Return on Assets	0.6	0.5	0.6	0.6	0.5	0.4	0.5	0.4	0.5	0.6
% Return on Equity	18.3	14.9	17.0	17.8	16.0	12.1	16.2	16.6	19.5	22.1

Data as orig reptd.; bef. results of disc opers/spec. items. Per share data adj. for stk. divs.; EPS diluted. E-Estimated. NA-Not Available. NM-Not Meaningful. NR-Not Ranked. UR-Under Review.

Office: 383 Madison Avenue, New York, NY 10179.
Telephone: 212-272-2000.
Email: ir@bear.com
Website: http://www.bearstearns.com

Chrmn & CEO: J.E. Cayne
COO & Co-Pres: A.D. Schwartz
COO & Co-Pres: W.J. Spector
EVP & CFO: S.L. Molinaro, Jr.

SVP, Chief Acctg Officer & Cntlr: J.M. Farber
Investor Contact: E. Ventura (212-272-9251)
Board Members: H. S. Bienen, J. E. Cayne, C. D. Glickman, M. Goldstein, A. C. Greenberg, D. J. Harrington, F. T. Nickell, P. A. Novelly, F. V. Salerno, A. D. Schwartz, W. J. Spector, V. Tese, W. S. Williams, Jr.

Founded: 1923
Domicile: Delaware
Employees: 13,566

Becton, Dickinson and Co

STANDARD
&POOR'S

S&P Recommendation **BUY** ★★★★☆	Price $83.52 (as of Nov 23, 2007)	12-Mo. Target Price $90.00	Investment Style Large-Cap Growth

GICS Sector Health Care
Sub-Industry Health Care Equipment

Summary BDX provides a wide range of medical devices and diagnostic products used in hospitals, doctors' offices, research labs, and other settings.

Key Stock Statistics (Source S&P, Vickers, company reports)

52-Wk Range	$85.89– 69.30	S&P Oper. EPS 2008**E**	4.30	Market Capitalization(B)	$20.328	Beta	0.53
Trailing 12-Month EPS	$3.46	S&P Oper. EPS 2009**E**	4.80	Yield (%)	1.36	S&P 3-Yr. Proj. EPS CAGR(%)	14.00
Trailing 12-Month P/E	24.1	P/E on S&P Oper. EPS 2008**E**	19.4	Dividend Rate/Share	$1.14	S&P Credit Rating	A+
$10K Invested 5 Yrs Ago	$29,624	Common Shares Outstg. (M)	243.4	Institutional Ownership (%)	83		

Price Performance

30-Week Mov. Avg. · · · 10-Week Mov. Avg. - - **GAAP Earnings vs. Previous Year** Volume Above Avg. STARS
12-Mo. Target Price — Relative Strength — ▲ Up ▼ Down ▶ No Change Below Avg. ★

Options: CBOE, P, Ph

Analysis prepared by **Robert M. Gold** on November 13, 2007, when the stock traded at **$82.85**.

Highlights

➤ We look for FY 08 (Sep.) revenues of $6.9 billion, with high single digit growth seen across the medical, diagnostics and biosciences divisions. In our opinion, the acquisition of Tripath Imaging and GeneOhm Sciences improved the company's position in the diagnostics markets, and we see significant growth opportunities in the detection of bacterial (including drug-resistant) infections and cervical cancer. Our FY 09 revenue forecast is $7.5 billion.

➤ In our view, gross margin expansion is likely to persist through FY 08, due to a more favorable sales mix and manufacturing efficiencies. We think R&D will absorb about 6% of sales through FY 10, while SG&A accounts for 24% to 25% of sales. With increased capital expenditures, we think FY 08 free cash flow will approximate $800 million, but believe a significant portion of this will be allocated to common share buybacks. Management recently said it intends to repurchase about $450 million of common stock in FY 08.

➤ Our FY 08 EPS estimate is $4.30, and we see FY 09 EPS rising 12%, to $4.80. In our view, the company remains well positioned to generate three-year EPS growth of about 14% a year.

Investment Rationale/Risk

➤ We think BDX will continue to benefit from recovering end user demand in the life sciences industry, momentum in the diagnostics and diabetes management areas, and exposure to cancer diagnostics following the December purchase of TriPath. With a recent dividend yield of 1.2%, BDX provides the highest yield in our medical equipment coverage universe, and the stock offers one of the highest S&P Quality Rankings in the health care sector, at A, reflecting its history of consistent growth in earnings and dividends.

➤ Risks to our recommendation and target price include a slower than expected recovery in key life science markets, adverse patent litigation, and unfavorable foreign currency fluctuations.

➤ At about 19X our FY 08 EPS forecast and 2.9X our FY 08 sales estimate, the shares were recently trading at a discount to our medical device coverage universe. In our opinion, a peer-average valuation is warranted by what we see as the company's strong underlying long-term fundamentals. Our 12-month target price of $90 is based on an absolute P/E and forward PEG valuation in line with peers.

Qualitative Risk Assessment

LOW	**MEDIUM**	HIGH

BDX's markets are competitive, and new product introductions by current and future competitors have the potential to significantly affect market dynamics. In addition, changes in domestic and foreign health care industry practices and regulations may result in increased pricing pressures and lower reimbursements for some of its products. However, we believe Becton's product line has more favorable demand and pricing characteristics than those in the medical equipment industry in general.

Quantitative Evaluations

S&P Quality Ranking A

D	C	B-	B	B+	A-	**A**	A+

Relative Strength Rank STRONG

86

LOWEST = 1 HIGHEST = 99

Revenue/Earnings Data

Revenue (Million $)

	1Q	2Q	3Q	4Q	Year
2007	1,502	1,576	1,631	1,651	6,360
2006	1,414	1,449	1,484	1,488	5,835
2005	1,288	1,366	1,381	1,379	5,415
2004	1,185	1,254	1,243	1,253	4,935
2003	1,052	1,134	1,165	1,177	4,528
2002	945.0	1,013	998.5	1,077	4,033

Earnings Per Share ($)

2007	0.51	0.92	0.95	0.98	3.36
2006	0.85	0.61	0.81	0.69	2.95
2005	0.74	0.71	0.73	0.47	2.66
2004	0.48	0.62	0.41	0.70	2.21
2003	0.43	0.54	0.49	0.61	2.07
2002	0.37	0.48	0.44	0.50	1.79

Fiscal year ended Sep. 30. Next earnings report expected: Late January. EPS Estimates based on S&P Operating Earnings; historical GAAP earnings are as reported.

Dividend Data (Dates: mm/dd Payment Date: mm/dd/yy)

Amount ($)	Date Decl.	Ex-Div. Date	Stk. of Record	Payment Date
0.245	01/30	03/07	03/09	03/30/07
0.245	05/22	06/06	06/08	06/29/07
0.245	07/24	09/05	09/07	09/28/07
0.285	11/20	12/10	12/12	01/02/08

Dividends have been paid since 1926. Source: Company reports.

Please read the Required Disclosures and Analyst Certification on the last page of this report.

The McGraw-Hill Companies

Becton, Dickinson and Co

STANDARD & POOR'S

Business Summary November 13, 2007

Becton, Dickinson traces its roots to a concern started by Maxwell Becton and Fairleigh Dickinson in 1897. One of the first companies to sell U.S.-made glass syringes, BDX was also a pioneer in the production of hypodermic needles. The company now manufactures and sells medical supplies, devices, lab equipment and diagnostic products used by health care institutions, life science researchers, clinical laboratories, industry and the general public. In FY 07 (Sep.), more than half of the company's sales were generated from non-U.S. markets.

Major products in the core medical systems division (54% of FY 07 revenues) include hypodermic syringes and needles for injection, insulin syringes and pen needles for diabetes care, infusion therapy devices, prefillable drug delivery systems, and surgical blades and scalpels. The segment also markets specialty blades and cannulas for ophthalmic surgery procedures, anesthesia needles, critical care systems, elastic support products, and thermometers. The company decided to exit the blood glucose monitoring and test strip markets in September 2006 and now classifies this unit as discontinued.

The diagnostics segment (30%) sells clinical and industrial microbiology products, sample collection products, specimen management systems, hematology instruments, and other diagnostic systems, including immunodiagnostic

test kits. The segment also includes consulting services and customized, automated bar-code systems for patient identification and point-of-care data capture.

The biosciences unit (16%) provides research tools and reagents to clinicians and medical researchers studying genes, proteins and cells in order to better understand disease, improve diagnosis and disease management, and facilitate the discovery and development of novel therapeutics. Products include instrument systems for cell sorting and analysis, monoclonal antibody reagents and kits for diagnostic and research use, tools to aid in drug discovery and vaccine development, molecular biology products, fluid handling, cell growth and screening products.

Research and development spending in FY 07 was $360 million, or 5.7% of revenues, compared with $302 million (5.3%) in FY 06, before acquired in-process R&D costs of $122 million and $53 million, respectively.

Company Financials Fiscal Year Ended Sep. 30

Per Share Data ($)	2007	2006	2005	2004	2003	2002	2001	2000	1999	1998
Tangible Book Value	NA	11.96	10.28	9.28	8.82	6.06	5.35	3.80	2.74	3.30
Cash Flow	NA	4.52	4.36	3.57	3.54	2.92	2.76	2.58	2.01	1.77
Earnings	3.36	2.95	2.66	2.21	2.07	1.79	1.63	1.49	1.04	0.90
S&P Core Earnings	NA	2.99	2.75	2.39	2.01	1.57	1.38	NA	NA	NA
Dividends	0.98	0.86	0.72	0.60	0.40	0.39	0.38	0.37	0.34	0.29
Payout Ratio	29%	29%	27%	27%	19%	22%	23%	25%	33%	32%
Prices:High	85.89	74.25	61.17	58.18	41.82	38.60	39.25	35.31	44.19	49.63
Prices:Low	69.30	58.08	49.71	40.90	28.82	24.70	29.96	23.75	22.38	24.38
P/E Ratio:High	26	25	23	26	20	22	24	24	42	55
P/E Ratio:Low	21	20	19	19	14	14	18	16	21	27

Income Statement Analysis (Million $)										
Revenue	NA	5,835	5,415	4,935	4,528	4,033	3,754	3,618	3,418	3,117
Operating Income	NA	1,456	1,419	1,244	1,094	1,002	952	861	780	714
Depreciation	NA	405	387	357	344	305	306	288	259	229
Interest Expense	NA	66.0	55.7	29.6	73.1	33.3	47.1	78.3	72.1	64.2
Pretax Income	NA	1,035	1,005	753	710	629	577	520	373	341
Effective Tax Rate	NA	27.0%	31.1%	22.6%	22.9%	23.6%	24.0%	24.4%	26.0%	30.6%
Net Income	NA	756	692	583	547	480	438	393	276	237
S&P Core Earnings	NA	766	714	628	523	417	364	NA	NA	NA

Balance Sheet & Other Financial Data (Million $)										
Cash	NA	1,000	1,043	719	520	243	82.1	49.2	59.9	83.3
Current Assets	NA	3,185	2,975	2,641	2,339	1,929	1,763	1,661	1,684	1,543
Total Assets	NA	6,825	6,072	5,753	5,572	5,040	4,802	4,505	4,437	3,846
Current Liabilities	NA	1,576	1,299	1,050	1,043	1,252	1,265	1,354	1,329	1,092
Long Term Debt	NA	957	1,061	1,172	1,184	803	1,902	780	954	765
Common Equity	NA	3,836	3,284	3,037	2,863	2,450	2,288	1,912	1,722	1,565
Total Capital	NA	4,793	4,345	4,328	4,200	3,396	4,321	2,823	2,764	2,428
Capital Expenditures	NA	459	318	266	261	260	371	376	312	181
Cash Flow	NA	1,161	1,080	940	889	783	742	679	532	463
Current Ratio	NA	2.0	2.3	2.5	2.2	1.5	1.4	1.2	1.3	1.4
% Long Term Debt of Capitalization	NA	20.0	24.4	27.1	28.2	23.6	44.0	27.6	34.5	31.5
% Net Income of Revenue	NA	12.9	12.8	11.8	12.1	11.9	11.7	10.9	8.1	7.6
% Return on Assets	NA	11.7	11.7	10.3	10.3	9.8	9.4	8.8	6.7	6.8
% Return on Equity	NA	21.2	21.9	19.7	20.5	20.2	20.8	21.5	16.6	16.1

Data as orig reptd.; bef. results of disc opers/spec. items. Per share data adj. for stk. divs.; EPS diluted. E-Estimated. NA-Not Available. NM-Not Meaningful. NR-Not Ranked. UR-Under Review.

Office: One Becton Drive, Franklin Lakes, NJ 07417-1880.
Telephone: 201-847-6800.
Email: investor_relations@bdhq.bd.com
Website: http://www.bd.com

Chrmn, Pres & CEO: E.J. Ludwig
EVP & CFO: J. Considine
VP & Secy: D. Paranicas
VP & General Counsel: J.S. Sherman

VP & Cntlr: W. Tozzi
Investor Contact: P.A. Spinella (201-847-5453)
Board Members: B. L. Anderson, H. P. Becton, Jr., E. F. DeGraan, C. M. Fraser-Liggett, E. J. Ludwig, A. A. Mahmoud, G. A. Mecklenburg, J. F. Orr, W. J. Overlock, Jr., J. E. Perrella, B. L. Scott, A. Sommer, M. af Ugglas

Founded: 1897
Domicile: New Jersey
Employees: 26,990

**STANDARD
&POOR'S**

Bed Bath & Beyond Inc

S&P Recommendation **BUY** ★★★★☆	Price $30.62 (as of Nov 23, 2007)	12-Mo. Target Price $44.00	Investment Style Large-Cap Growth

GICS Sector Consumer Discretionary
Sub-Industry Homefurnishing Retail

Summary BBBY operates a nationwide chain of more than 800 superstores selling better-quality domestics merchandise and home furnishings at prices below those offered by department stores.

Key Stock Statistics (Source S&P, Vickers, company reports)

52-Wk Range	$43.32– 29.68	S&P Oper. EPS 2008**E**	2.20	Market Capitalization(B)	$8.109	Beta	1.24
Trailing 12-Month EPS	$2.15	S&P Oper. EPS 2009**E**	2.52	Yield (%)	Nil	S&P 3-Yr. Proj. EPS CAGR(%)	14.00
Trailing 12-Month P/E	14.2	P/E on S&P Oper. EPS 2008**E**	13.9	Dividend Rate/Share	Nil	S&P Credit Rating	BBB
$10K Invested 5 Yrs Ago	$8,771	Common Shares Outstg. (M)	264.8	Institutional Ownership (%)	92		

Price Performance

30-Week Mov. Avg. ···· 10-Week Mov. Avg. – – **GAAP Earnings vs. Previous Year** Volume Above Avg. ▏▍▋ STARS
12-Mo. Target Price — Relative Strength — ▲ Up ▼ Down ▶ No Change Below Avg. ▏▍▋ ★

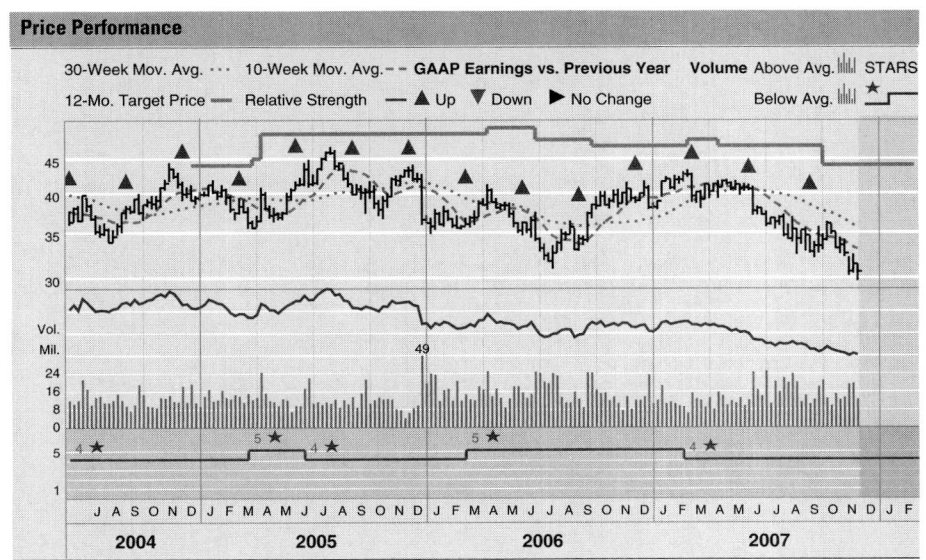

Options: ASE, CBOE, Ph

Analysis prepared by **Michael Souers** on October 02, 2007, when the stock traded at **$ 34.54**.

Highlights

➤ We expect sales to rise 9%-10% in FY 09 (Feb.), following our projection of an 8%-9% advance in FY 08. This reflects the forecast addition of about 70-75 new Bed Bath & Beyond stores, representing around 2.5 million square feet of store space, and a same-store sales increase of 3%. We also anticipate the opening of 10-15 new Christmas Tree Shops, as well as the opening of a handful of new Harmon Stores and buybuy BABY stores, a recent acquisition. We see same-store sales growth likely being driven by an increase in the average ticket.

➤ We forecast a slight widening in operating margins, as we expect promotional activity to wane following our expectations of a high level of discounting in FY 08. We expect that the leveraging of SG&A expenses caused by same-store-sales increases will be offset by higher advertising spending and a slight rise in store opening costs.

➤ After slightly lower projected interest income, an anticipated effective tax rate of 36.5%, and approximately 4% fewer shares, we estimate FY 09 EPS of $2.52, a 15% increase from the $2.20 we expect the company to earn in FY 08.

Investment Rationale/Risk

➤ BBBY recently traded at a P/E to earnings growth (PEG) ratio of under 1.0X, a discount to peers and to the S&P 500 (1.2X). In addition, BBBY's forward P/E of about 14X is low on an historical basis, as the company's average forward P/E has been approximately 25X over the past five years. The company has approved 1,100 domestic sites, and we believe that annual sales will rise at a compound annual growth rate (CAGR) of nearly 10% over the next five years. We expect that BBBY will continue to gain market share in home furnishings, with better merchandising and store level execution than peers.

➤ Risks to our recommendation and target price include a major slowdown in the U.S. economy, an unanticipated shift in consumer spending away from home-centered products, and possible miscues in BBBY's store expansion strategy.

➤ Our 12-month target price of $44, or about 17X our FY 09 EPS estimate, is based on our discounted cash flow analysis, which assumes a weighted average cost of capital of 10.8% and a terminal growth rate of 4.0%.

Qualitative Risk Assessment

LOW	**MEDIUM**	HIGH

Our risk assessment reflects the cyclical nature of the home furnishing retail industry, which relies heavily on consumer spending, and, to a lesser extent, housing turnover, offset by significant growth areas we see in major domestic metro markets and Canada, and an S&P Quality Ranking of A-, which reflects above-average historical earnings growth.

Quantitative Evaluations

S&P Quality Ranking A-

D	C	B-	B	B+	**A-**	A	A+

Relative Strength Rank MODERATE

39

LOWEST = 1   HIGHEST = 99

Revenue/Earnings Data

Revenue (Million $)

	1Q	2Q	3Q	4Q	Year
2008	1,553	1,768	--	--	--
2007	1,396	1,607	1,619	1,995	6,617
2006	1,244	1,431	1,449	1,685	5,810
2005	1,101	1,274	1,305	1,468	5,148
2004	893.9	1,111	1,175	1,298	4,478
2003	776.8	903.0	936.0	1,049	3,665

Earnings Per Share ($)

2008	0.38	0.55	E0.52	E0.76	E2.20
2007	0.35	0.51	0.50	0.72	2.09
2006	0.33	0.47	0.45	0.67	1.92
2005	0.27	0.39	0.40	0.59	1.65
2004	0.19	0.32	0.33	0.47	1.31
2003	0.15	0.25	0.25	0.35	1.00

Fiscal year ended Feb. 28. Next earnings report expected: Late December. EPS Estimates based on S&P Operating Earnings; historical GAAP earnings are as reported.

Dividend Data

No cash dividends have been paid.

Please read the Required Disclosures and Analyst Certification on the last page of this report.

The **McGraw·Hill** Companies

Bed Bath & Beyond Inc

Business Summary October 02, 2007

CORPORATE OVERVIEW. Bed Bath & Beyond operates one of the largest U.S. chains of superstores selling domestics merchandise and home furnishings. BBBY stores predominantly range in size from 20,000 sq. ft. to 50,000 sq. ft., with some encompassing 100,000 sq. ft. The company has grown rapidly, from 34 stores at the end of FY 93 (Feb.) to 815 Bed Bath and Beyond stores in 48 states and Puerto Rico at year-end FY 07. BBBY opened 74 Bed Bath and Beyond Stores stores in FY 07, after opening 83 stores in FY 06; it expected to open about 70 new stores in FY 08. During FY 07, total square footage of Bed Bath & Beyond stores grew 9%, to 27.8 million sq. ft., from 25.5 million sq. ft. Company stores are principally located in suburban areas of medium and large sized cities. These stores are situated in strip and power strip shopping centers, as well as in major off-price and conventional malls, and freestanding buildings.

In March 2002, the company acquired Harmon Stores, Inc., a health and beauty care retailer. The Harmon chain had 39 stores in three states at March 3, 2007, ranging in size from approximately 5,000 to 9,000 sq. ft. In June 2003, BBBY acquired Christmas Tree Shops, a retailer of home decor, giftware, housewares, food, paper goods and seasonal products, for approximately $194.4 million, net of cash acquired. The company operated 34 Christmas Tree Shops in eight states at year-end FY 07, ranging in size between 30,000 and 50,000 sq. ft.

BBBY believes that the breadth and depth of selection that it offers in most product categories exceeds what is generally available in department stores or other specialty retail stores, and that this enables it to offer customers the convenience of one-stop shopping for most household items. The company sells domestics merchandise such as bed linens, sheets, comforters, bedspreads, draperies, pillows and blankets. Bath accessories include towels, shower curtains, waste baskets, hampers and rugs. Kitchen textiles include tablecloths, placemats, napkins, and dish towels. BBBY stores also sell home furnishings such as kitchen and tabletop items, including cookware, cutlery, flatware and glassware; basic housewares, consisting of storage items and closet items; small electric appliances such as blenders, coffee makers, vacuum cleaners, toaster ovens and hair dryers; and miscellaneous gift items, consisting of picture frames, luggage, small toys and seasonal merchandise.

Company Financials Fiscal Year Ended Feb. 28

Per Share Data ($)	2007	2006	2005	2004	2003	2002	2001	2000	1999	1998
Tangible Book Value	9.56	8.05	6.99	6.14	4.93	3.75	2.84	1.99	1.48	1.07
Cash Flow	2.56	2.29	1.96	1.59	1.25	0.94	0.75	0.57	0.42	0.32
Earnings	2.09	1.92	1.65	1.31	1.00	0.74	0.59	0.46	0.34	0.26
S&P Core Earnings	2.09	1.87	1.55	1.23	0.92	0.67	0.53	NA	NA	NA
Dividends	Nil	Nil	Nil	Nil	Nil	Nil	Nil	Nil	Nil	Nil
Payout Ratio	Nil	Nil	Nil	Nil	Nil	Nil	Nil	Nil	Nil	Nil
Calendar Year	2006	2005	2004	2003	2002	2001	2000	1999	1998	1997
Prices:High	41.72	46.99	44.43	45.00	37.90	35.70	27.31	19.69	17.59	9.81
Prices:Low	30.92	35.50	33.88	30.18	26.70	18.70	11.00	12.75	8.56	5.72
P/E Ratio:High	20	24	27	34	38	48	46	43	52	38
P/E Ratio:Low	15	18	21	23	27	25	19	28	25	22

Income Statement Analysis (Million $)	2007	2006	2005	2004	2003	2002	2001	2000	1999	1998
Revenue	6,617	5,810	5,148	4,478	3,665	2,928	2,397	1,878	1,397	1,067
Operating Income	1,026	990	890	724	555	409	319	241	181	137
Depreciation	136	111	97.5	84.6	74.8	62.5	46.7	31.6	23.2	18.2
Interest Expense	Nil	Nil	Nil	Nil	Nil	Nil	Nil	Nil	Nil	Nil
Pretax Income	933	915	811	650	491	357	282	215	162	121
Effective Tax Rate	36.3%	37.4%	37.8%	38.5%	38.5%	38.5%	39.0%	39.0%	39.7%	39.8%
Net Income	594	573	505	399	302	220	172	131	97.3	73.1
S&P Core Earnings	594	557	470	370	277	200	155	NA	NA	NA

Balance Sheet & Other Financial Data (Million $)	2007	2006	2005	2004	2003	2002	2001	2000	1999	1998
Cash	988	652	851	867	617	429	239	144	90.4	53.3
Current Assets	2,699	2,072	2,097	1,969	1,594	1,227	886	647	455	326
Total Assets	3,959	3,382	3,200	2,865	2,189	1,648	1,196	866	633	458
Current Liabilities	1,145	990	874	770	680	511	353	287	206	150
Long Term Debt	Nil	Nil	Nil	Nil	Nil	Nil	Nil	Nil	Nil	Nil
Common Equity	2,649	2,262	2,204	1,991	1,452	1,094	817	559	411	295
Total Capital	2,649	2,262	2,204	1,991	1,452	1,094	817	559	411	295
Capital Expenditures	318	220	191	113	135	121	140	90.1	62.3	41.2
Cash Flow	731	684	602	484	377	282	219	163	121	91.4
Current Ratio	2.4	2.1	2.4	2.6	2.3	2.4	2.5	2.3	2.2	2.2
% Long Term Debt of Capitalization	Nil	Nil	Nil	Nil	Nil	Nil	Nil	Nil	Nil	Nil
% Net Income of Revenue	9.0	9.9	9.8	8.9	8.2	7.5	7.2	7.0	7.0	6.9
% Return on Assets	16.2	17.4	16.7	15.8	15.8	15.4	16.7	17.5	17.8	18.6
% Return on Equity	24.2	25.7	24.1	23.2	23.7	23.0	25.0	27.1	27.6	28.7

Data as orig reptd.; bef. results of disc opers/spec. items. Per share data adj. for stk. divs.; EPS diluted. E-Estimated. NA-Not Available. NM-Not Meaningful. NR-Not Ranked. UR-Under Review.

Office: 650 Liberty Ave , Union, NJ 07083-8135.
Telephone: 908-688-0888.
Website: http://www.bedbathandbeyond.com
Co-Chrmn: W. Eisenberg

Co-Chrmn: L. Feinstein
Pres: A. Stark
CEO: S.H. Temares
VP & General Counsel: A.N. Rauch

Board Members: D. S. Adler, S. F. Barshay, W. Eisenberg, K. Eppler, L. Feinstein, P. Gaston, J. Heller, R. S. Kaplan, V. A. Morrison, F. Stoller, S. H. Temares

Founded: 1971
Domicile: New York
Employees: 35,000

Bemis Co Inc

STANDARD &POOR'S

S&P Recommendation HOLD ★★★☆☆	**Price** $26.84 (as of Nov 23, 2007)	**12-Mo. Target Price** $30.00	**Investment Style** Large-Cap Blend

GICS Sector Materials
Sub-Industry Paper Packaging

Summary This company is a leading maker of a broad range of flexible packaging and pressure-sensitive materials.

Key Stock Statistics (Source S&P, Vickers, company reports)

52-Wk Range	$36.53–26.40	S&P Oper. EPS 2007**E**	1.70	Market Capitalization(B)	$2.805	Beta	0.92
Trailing 12-Month EPS	$1.71	S&P Oper. EPS 2008**E**	1.85	Yield (%)	3.13	S&P 3-Yr. Proj. EPS CAGR(%)	14.00
Trailing 12-Month P/E	15.7	P/E on S&P Oper. EPS 2007**E**	15.8	Dividend Rate/Share	$0.84	S&P Credit Rating	A
$10K Invested 5 Yrs Ago	$11,750	Common Shares Outstg. (M)	104.5	Institutional Ownership (%)	74		

Price Performance

30-Week Mov. Avg. ··· 10-Week Mov. Avg. - - GAAP Earnings vs. Previous Year Volume Above Avg. STARS
12-Mo. Target Price — Relative Strength — ▲ Up ▼ Down ► No Change Below Avg.

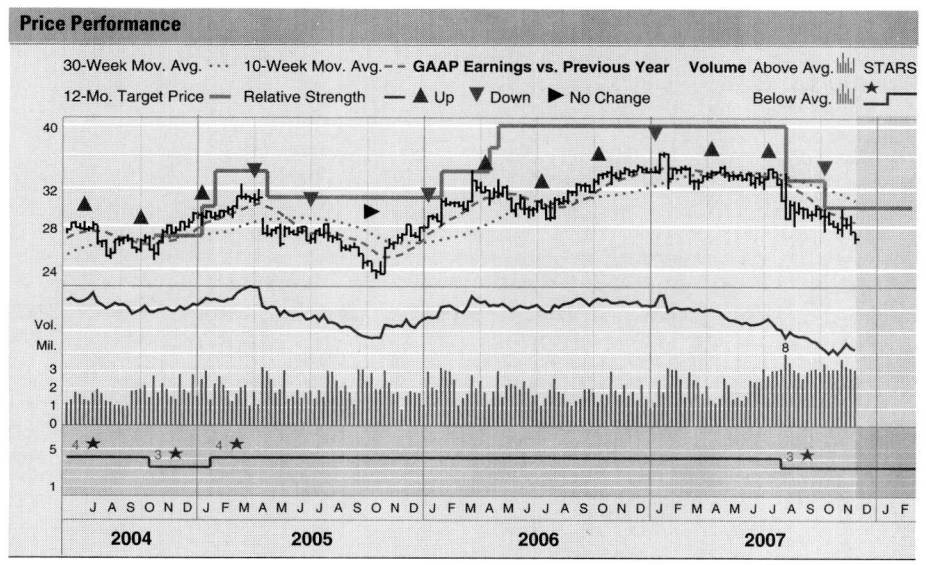

Options: ASE, CBOE, P

Analysis prepared by **Stewart Scharf** on November 12, 2007, when the stock traded at **$28.18.**

Highlights

➤ We project that net sales (before about a 3% positive foreign currency effect) will decline in the low single digits in 2007, with a return to growth, albeit modest, likely in 2008, based on soft demand for dry foods, meat and cheese products, confectionary items and industrial products. We see challenging market conditions based on weak customer demand for flexible packaging products in North America and softness in the European pressure-sensitive materials business.

➤ We think gross margins in 2007 will narrow to about 18.5%, from 2006's 19.2%, due to soft unit volume, a negative sales mix, rising polyethylene prices, and customer delays in ramping up new business. We expect further pricing initiatives, but gross margins should remain pressured in early 2008, while we see operating margins (EBITDA) widening sequentially based on work force reductions and other cost-cutting measures, new products, and efforts to increase market share.

➤ We project a lower tax rate near 37% in 2007, and EPS of $1.70 (after a $0.04 projected benefit from buybacks), advancing 8.8%, to $1.85, in 2008.

Investment Rationale/Risk

➤ Based on our valuation metrics, and our expectations of weak unit volume and volatile oil prices, we would not add to positions in the stock.

➤ Risks to our recommendation and target price include a change in customer order patterns due to a further rise in commodities prices, softer global demand, and negative foreign exchange rates. We have corporate governance concerns based on board and audit issues, including the CEO being a party to one or more related-party transactions.

➤ The shares recently traded on par with our projected 2008 P/E for S&P's Paper Packaging sub-industry group, and at a modest premium to our 14X projected multiple for the S&P 500. With a recent yield of about 2.9%, versus 1.9% for the S&P 500 Index, and a solid earnings track record, we apply a near five-year historical forward P/E to derive a value of $32. Based on our DCF analysis, the stock is slightly below its intrinsic value of $29, assuming a 3.5% terminal growth rate and an 8.3% weighted average cost of capital. Blending these valuations, we arrive at our 12-month target price of $30.

Qualitative Risk Assessment

LOW	MEDIUM	HIGH

Our risk assessment reflects the possibility of softer global economic conditions, higher raw material prices, and difficulty in integrating acquisitions. However, BMS has an S&P Quality Ranking of A, which indicates historically stable earnings and dividend growth.

Quantitative Evaluations

S&P Quality Ranking A

D	C	B-	B	B+	A-	**A**	A+

Relative Strength Rank MODERATE

45

LOWEST = 1   HIGHEST = 99

Revenue/Earnings Data

Revenue (Million $)

	1Q	2Q	3Q	4Q	Year
2007	909.1	921.8	905.7	--	--
2006	901.7	933.8	903.3	900.6	3,639
2005	831.9	879.9	870.1	892.1	3,474
2004	684.0	712.9	711.9	725.6	2,834
2003	638.6	670.2	662.0	664.3	2,635
2002	552.7	584.8	601.0	630.6	2,369

Earnings Per Share ($)

2007	0.45	0.47	0.40	E0.38	E1.70
2006	0.35	0.46	0.45	0.39	1.65
2005	0.30	0.38	0.41	0.42	1.51
2004	0.40	0.42	0.41	0.44	1.67
2003	0.33	0.36	0.32	0.35	1.37
2002	0.33	0.41	0.41	0.40	1.54

Fiscal year ended Dec. 31. Next earnings report expected: Late January. EPS Estimates based on S&P Operating Earnings; historical GAAP earnings are as reported.

Dividend Data (Dates: mm/dd Payment Date: mm/dd/yy)

Amount ($)	Date Decl.	Ex-Div. Date	Stk. of Record	Payment Date
0.210	02/01	02/13	02/15	03/01/07
0.210	05/03	05/16	05/18	06/01/07
0.210	08/02	08/15	08/17	09/04/07
0.210	11/01	11/14	11/16	12/03/07

Dividends have been paid since 1922. Source: Company reports.

Please read the Required Disclosures and Analyst Certification on the last page of this report.

The McGraw-Hill Companies

Bemis Co Inc

STANDARD &POOR'S

Business Summary November 12, 2007

CORPORATE OVERVIEW. Bemis Co., a leading North American producer of flexible packaging products, as well as pressure-sensitive materials, focuses primarily on the food industry (about 65% of sales). Markets also include the chemicals, agribusiness, pharmaceutical, personal care products, electronics, automotive and graphic industries. BMS has 55 manufacturing plants in 10 countries.

Although BMS focuses on marketing its products in the U.S. (66% of 2006 net sales), Europe (16%) and Canada (1.8%), it has broadened its reach to Southeast Asia, South America and Mexico, due to strong demand for barrier films to extend the shelf life of perishable foods. South America had sales of 14% while 2.4% came from other regions.

The Flexible Packaging Products segment (82% of net sales in 2006; $335 million of operating profits) produces a wide range of consumer and industrial packaging products, including high barrier, polyethylene and paper products. High barrier products, which comprise more than 50% of net sales, include flexible polymer film structures and barrier laminates for food, medical and personal care products.

The Pressure Sensitive Materials segment (18%; $50 million in operating profits) produces printing products, decorative and sheet products, and technical products.

Flexible packaging competitors include Alcan Packaging, Sealed Air, Sonoco Products, Smurfit-Stone Container and Intertape Polymer Group. Pressure-sensitive materials competitors include Avery Dennison, Minnesota Mining and Manufacturing (3M), Ricoh and Spinnaker Industries.

In January 2005, the company acquired majority ownership of Brazil-based Dixie Toga, a leading South American packaging company, for $250 million in cash (less than 6X Dixie's 2004 EBITDA). Dixie had annual sales of over $450 million in 2005. BMS controls 85% of Dixie's preferred shares.

Company Financials Fiscal Year Ended Dec. 31

Per Share Data ($)	2006	2005	2004	2003	2002	2001	2000	1999	1998	1997
Tangible Book Value	7.31	6.29	7.48	5.81	4.11	4.39	4.76	5.52	4.88	4.62
Cash Flow	3.08	2.98	2.88	2.56	2.65	2.49	2.24	2.02	1.88	1.73
Earnings	1.65	1.51	1.67	1.37	1.54	1.32	1.22	1.09	1.04	1.00
S&P Core Earnings	1.64	1.48	1.65	1.32	1.28	1.02	NA	NA	NA	NA
Dividends	0.76	0.72	0.64	0.56	0.52	0.50	0.48	0.46	0.44	0.40
Payout Ratio	46%	48%	38%	41%	34%	38%	39%	42%	42%	40%
Prices:High	34.99	32.50	29.49	25.58	29.12	26.24	19.66	20.19	23.47	23.97
Prices:Low	27.86	23.20	23.24	19.67	19.70	14.34	11.47	15.09	16.75	16.81
P/E Ratio:High	21	22	18	19	19	20	16	19	22	24
P/E Ratio:Low	17	15	14	14	13	11	9	14	16	17

Income Statement Analysis (Million $)

	2006	2005	2004	2003	2002	2001	2000	1999	1998	1997
Revenue	3,639	3,474	2,834	2,635	2,369	2,293	2,165	1,918	1,848	1,877
Operating Income	492	472	420	384	401	384	363	316	297	274
Depreciation	152	151	131	128	119	124	108	97.7	88.9	78.9
Interest Expense	49.3	38.7	15.5	12.6	15.4	30.3	31.6	21.2	21.9	18.9
Pretax Income	289	282	294	240	268	228	212	190	186	180
Effective Tax Rate	37.8%	40.3%	38.7%	38.4%	37.9%	38.2%	38.2%	37.4%	37.8%	37.4%
Net Income	176	163	180	147	166	140	131	115	111	108
S&P Core Earnings	176	160	179	142	137	108	NA	NA	NA	NA

Balance Sheet & Other Financial Data (Million $)

	2006	2005	2004	2003	2002	2001	2000	1999	1998	1997
Cash	112	91.1	93.9	76.5	56.4	35.1	28.9	18.2	23.7	13.8
Current Assets	1,094	988	874	752	722	587	640	584	518	516
Total Assets	3,039	2,965	2,487	2,293	2,257	1,923	1,889	1,532	1,453	1,363
Current Liabilities	555	474	375	316	326	238	495	253	243	251
Long Term Debt	722	790	534	583	718	595	438	372	371	317
Common Equity	1,472	1,349	1,308	1,139	959	886	799	726	671	640
Total Capital	2,358	2,336	2,019	1,878	1,788	1,606	1,342	1,227	1,156	1,055
Capital Expenditures	159	187	135	106	91.0	117	100	137	140	168
Cash Flow	329	313	311	275	285	264	239	212	200	186
Current Ratio	2.0	2.1	2.3	2.4	2.2	2.5	1.3	2.3	2.1	2.1
% Long Term Debt of Capitalization	30.6	33.8	26.4	31.1	40.2	37.1	32.6	30.3	32.1	30.0
% Net Income of Revenue	4.8	4.7	6.3	5.6	7.0	6.1	6.0	6.0	6.0	5.7
% Return on Assets	5.9	6.0	7.5	6.5	7.9	7.4	7.6	7.6	7.9	8.5
% Return on Equity	12.5	12.2	14.7	14.0	17.9	16.7	17.1	16.2	17.0	17.8

Data as orig reptd.; bef. results of disc opers/spec. items. Per share data adj. for stk. divs.; EPS diluted. E-Estimated. NA-Not Available. NM-Not Meaningful. NR-Not Ranked. UR-Under Review.

Office: 1 Neenah Ctr 4th Fl, Neenah, WI 54956-3087.
Telephone: 920-727-4100.
Website: http://www.bemis.com
Pres & CEO: J.H. Curler
COO & EVP: H.J. Theisen
VP, CFO & Treas: G.C. Wulf
VP, Secy & General Counsel: J.J. Seifert
Investor Contact: M.E. Miller (920-527-5045)
Board Members: W. J. Bolton, J. H. Curler, D. S. Haffner, B. L. Johnson, T. M. Manganello, N. P. McDonald, R. D. O'Shaughnessy, P. S. Peercy, E. N. Perry, W. J. Scholle, H. J. Theisen, P. Weaver, G. C. Wulf
Founded: 1858
Domicile: Missouri
Employees: 15,736

Best Buy Co. Inc.

STANDARD
&POOR'S

S&P Recommendation	STRONG BUY ★★★★★	Price $48.02 (as of Nov 23, 2007)	12-Mo. Target Price $63.00	Investment Style Large-Cap Growth

GICS Sector Consumer Discretionary
Sub-Industry Computer & Electronics Retail

Summary This leading retailer of consumer electronics and entertainment software operates more than 1,100 stores in the U.S., Canada, and China.

Key Stock Statistics (Source S&P, Vickers, company reports)

52-Wk Range	$56.69– 41.85	S&P Oper. EPS 2008 E	3.13	Market Capitalization(B)	$20.062	Beta	1.55
Trailing 12-Month EPS	$2.79	S&P Oper. EPS 2009 E	3.69	Yield (%)	1.08	S&P 3-Yr. Proj. EPS CAGR(%)	14.00
Trailing 12-Month P/E	17.2	P/E on S&P Oper. EPS 2008 E	15.3	Dividend Rate/Share	$0.52	S&P Credit Rating	BBB
$10K Invested 5 Yrs Ago	$29,360	Common Shares Outstg. (M)	417.8	Institutional Ownership (%)	85		

Price Performance

30-Week Mov. Avg. · · · 10-Week Mov. Avg. - - **GAAP Earnings vs. Previous Year** Volume Above Avg. STARS
12-Mo. Target Price — Relative Strength — ▲ Up ▼ Down ▶ No Change Below Avg. ★

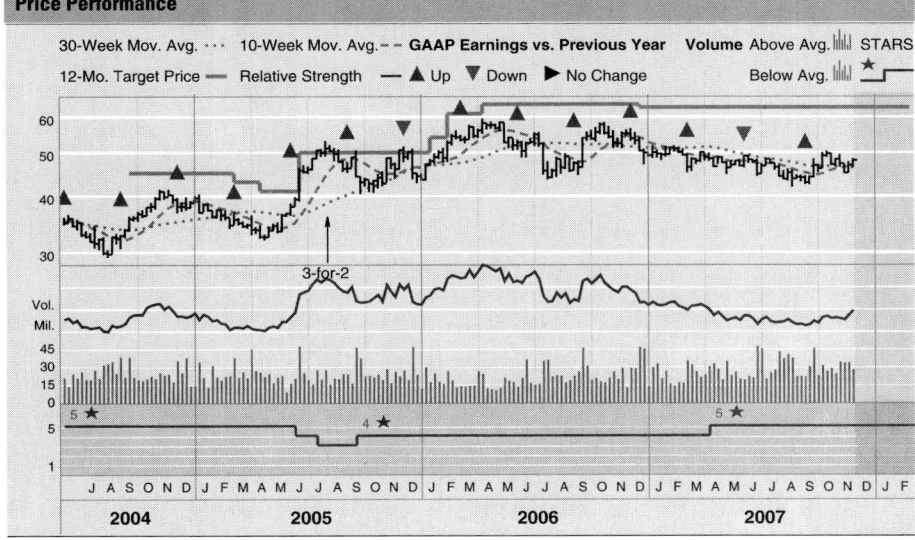

Options: ASE, CBOE, P, Ph

Analysis prepared by **Michael Souers** on September 25, 2007, when the stock traded at **$ 46.01**.

Highlights

➤ We view BBY as the best-of-class U.S. consumer electronics retailer, based on its digital product focus, knowledgeable sales staff, and effective advertising and marketing campaigns. We think BBY's focus on advanced TVs, laptops, and digital imaging products will support strong revenue growth near term. Declining average selling prices of digital TVs will ignite sales volume and be a key driver of BBY's growth, in our opinion.

➤ We project a 9%-10% increase in revenues for FY 09 (Feb.), following our projections of an 11% advance in FY 08. We expect this growth to be driven by approximately 150 net new stores worldwide and a projected 3%-4% comparable-store sales gain. We expect flat gross margins due to persistence in competitive pressures, but think operating margins will widen approximately 20 basis points, due to SG&A expense leverage.

➤ After significantly higher net interest expense and about 7% fewer shares outstanding due to BBY's aggressive share repurchase plan, we project FY 09 EPS of $3.69, an 18% increase from the $3.13 we expect the company to earn in FY 08.

Investment Rationale/Risk

➤ We continue to have confidence in Best Buy's ability to execute on its growth strategy. In addition to capitalizing on the strength of the current consumer electronics product cycle, we believe BBY is positioned to grow its market share through initiatives such as Best Buy for Business, Geek Squad, and Magnolia store-within-a-store offerings. Combined with BBY's customer focus, we think these initiatives will enable BBY to continue to differentiate itself in a competitive marketplace. Trading at under 13X our FY 09 EPS estimate, a significant discount to historical averages and peers, the shares are extremely attractive, in our view.

➤ Risks to our recommendation and target price include a sharp decline in the economic climate and consumer confidence, and the risk that BBY will be unable to successfully execute its strategic objectives and meet market expectations for sales growth and profitability.

➤ Our 12-month target price of $63, about 17X our FY 09 EPS estimate, is based on our DCF analysis. Our DCF model assumes a weighted average cost of capital of 11.1% and a terminal growth rate of 4.0%.

Qualitative Risk Assessment

LOW	MEDIUM	HIGH

Our risk assessment reflects what we view as BBY's strong balance sheet, sizable market share, numerous suppliers and buyers, and a history of profitability, offset by a highly competitive environment for consumer electronics retailing, with numerous rivals and strong price competition.

Quantitative Evaluations

S&P Quality Ranking B+

D	C	B-	B	B+	A-	A	A+

Relative Strength Rank STRONG

86

LOWEST = 1 HIGHEST = 99

Revenue/Earnings Data

Revenue (Million $)

	1Q	2Q	3Q	4Q	Year
2008	7,927	8,750	--	--	--
2007	6,959	7,603	8,473	12,899	35,934
2006	6,118	6,702	7,335	10,693	30,848
2005	5,479	6,080	6,647	9,227	27,433
2004	4,668	5,396	6,034	8,449	24,547
2003	4,202	4,624	5,131	6,989	20,946

Earnings Per Share ($)

2008	0.39	0.55	E0.42	E1.81	E3.13
2007	0.47	0.47	0.31	1.55	2.79
2006	0.34	0.37	0.28	1.29	2.27
2005	0.23	0.30	0.29	1.03	1.86
2004	0.14	0.28	0.25	0.95	1.63
2003	0.16	0.16	0.18	0.77	1.27

Fiscal year ended Feb. 28. Next earnings report expected: Mid December. EPS Estimates based on S&P Operating Earnings; historical GAAP earnings are as reported.

Dividend Data (Dates: mm/dd Payment Date: mm/dd/yy)

Amount ($)	Date Decl.	Ex-Div. Date	Stk. of Record	Payment Date
0.100	12/13	12/28	01/02	01/23/07
0.100	04/05	04/23	04/25	05/16/07
0.100	06/20	07/06	07/10	07/31/07
0.130	06/27	10/04	10/09	10/30/07

Dividends have been paid since 2003. Source: Company reports.

Please read the Required Disclosures and Analyst Certification on the last page of this report.

The McGraw-Hill Companies

Best Buy Co. Inc.

STANDARD &POOR'S

Business Summary September 25, 2007

CORPORATE OVERVIEW. This leading consumer electronics retailer operated, as of March 3, 2007, 869 Best Buy stores (822 in the U.S. and 47 in Canada), 20 Magnolia Audio Video stores, 14 Pacific Sales showrooms, and 12 Geek Squad stores in the U.S., 121 Future Shop stores in Canada, 135 Five Star stores in China, and one Best Buy China store.

CORPORATE STRATEGY. BBY's business strategy centers on meeting individual consumer electronics needs with end-to-end solutions, which involves greater employee involvement and increased services. Some 40% of U.S. Best Buy stores have been converted or opened with the customer-centric operating model, and BBY is committed to scaling BBY customer-centricity across the organization. In FY 08 (Feb.), BBY plans to open approximately 95 new stores in the U.S., 12-14 new stores in Canada and 20-25 new stores in China. In addition, BBY is expanding its relationship with Apple by offering Apple computers in 200 stores by the fall of 2007.

BBY sees an opportunity to expand to 1,200-1,400 superstores in North America. Based on our expectations for approximately 125-150 net new store openings per year, we believe BBY has about four years of organic growth potential from its core business. However, we expect the majority of new store openings to be in smaller 20,000 square foot locations, compared to BBY's average store square footage of 38,000. We look for new concepts, such as stand-alone Geek Squad stores, to provide incremental growth opportunities. In total, we project a five-year square footage compound annual growth rate (CAGR) in the mid- to high-single digits.

Company Financials Fiscal Year Ended Feb. 28

Per Share Data ($)	2007	2006	2005	2004	2003	2002	2001	2000	1999	1998
Tangible Book Value	10.82	9.60	7.91	5.97	4.70	3.65	3.07	2.44	2.32	1.39
Cash Flow	3.80	3.16	2.76	2.41	1.91	1.91	1.18	0.95	0.64	0.36
Earnings	2.79	2.27	1.86	1.63	1.27	1.18	0.83	0.72	0.48	0.23
S&P Core Earnings	2.76	2.27	1.77	1.45	1.11	1.08	0.76	NA	NA	NA
Dividends	0.36	0.31	0.50	0.27	Nil	Nil	Nil	Nil	Nil	Nil
Payout Ratio	13%	14%	38%	17%	Nil	Nil	Nil	Nil	Nil	Nil
Calendar Year	2006	2005	2004	2003	2002	2001	2000	1999	1998	1997
Prices:High	59.50	18.03	41.47	41.80	35.83	33.42	39.50	35.78	13.83	4.56
Prices:Low	43.32	14.84	29.25	15.77	11.33	12.36	9.33	13.72	4.00	0.88
P/E Ratio:High	21	14	22	26	28	28	48	49	29	20
P/E Ratio:Low	16	11	16	10	9	10	11	19	8	4

Income Statement Analysis (Million $)

	2007	2006	2005	2004	2003	2002	2001	2000	1999	1998
Revenue	35,934	30,848	27,433	24,547	20,946	19,597	15,327	12,494	10,078	8,358
Operating Income	2,508	2,100	1,901	1,699	1,320	1,246	772	649	443	255
Depreciation	509	456	459	385	310	309	167	110	78.4	68.3
Interest Expense	Nil	30.0	44.0	31.0	25.0	2.00	6.90	5.10	23.8	37.7
Pretax Income	2,130	1,721	1,443	1,296	1,014	936	642	563	365	154
Effective Tax Rate	35.3%	33.8%	35.3%	38.3%	38.7%	39.1%	38.3%	38.3%	38.5%	38.6%
Net Income	1,377	1,140	934	800	622	570	396	347	224	94.5
S&P Core Earnings	1,364	1,140	873	704	538	512	361	NA	NA	NA

Balance Sheet & Other Financial Data (Million $)

	2007	2006	2005	2004	2003	2002	2001	2000	1999	1998
Cash	1,205	681	470	2,600	1,914	1,855	747	751	786	520
Current Assets	9,081	7,985	6,903	5,724	4,867	4,611	2,929	2,238	2,063	1,710
Total Assets	13,570	11,864	10,294	8,652	7,663	7,375	4,840	2,995	2,512	2,056
Current Liabilities	6,301	6,056	4,959	4,501	3,793	3,730	2,715	1,785	1,387	1,034
Long Term Debt	590	178	528	482	828	813	181	14.9	30.5	490
Common Equity	6,201	5,257	4,449	3,422	2,730	2,521	1,822	1,096	1,064	558
Total Capital	6,826	5,435	4,977	3,904	3,558	3,334	2,003	1,111	1,095	1,005
Capital Expenditures	733	648	502	545	725	627	658	361	166	72.0
Cash Flow	1,886	1,596	1,393	1,185	932	925	563	457	303	163
Current Ratio	1.4	1.3	1.4	1.3	1.3	1.2	1.1	1.3	1.5	1.7
% Long Term Debt of Capitalization	8.6	3.3	10.6	12.3	23.3	24.4	9.0	1.4	2.8	48.8
% Net Income of Revenue	3.8	3.7	3.4	3.3	3.0	2.9	2.6	2.8	2.2	1.1
% Return on Assets	10.8	10.3	9.9	9.8	8.3	9.3	10.1	12.6	9.8	5.0
% Return on Equity	24.0	23.5	23.7	26.0	23.8	26.2	27.1	32.6	27.7	19.0

Data as orig reptd.; bef. results of disc opers/spec. items. Per share data adj. for stk. divs.; EPS diluted. E-Estimated. NA-Not Available. NM-Not Meaningful. NR-Not Ranked. UR-Under Review.

Office: 7075 Flying Cloud Drive, Eden Prairie, MN 55344-3538.
Telephone: 952-947-2000.
Email: moneytalk@bestbuy.com
Website: http://www.bestbuy.com

Chrmn: R.M. Schulze
Pres & COO: B.J. Dunn
Vice Chrmn: A.U. Lenzmeier
Vice Chrmn & CEO: B.H. Anderson

EVP & CFO: D.R. Jackson
Investor Contact: J. Driscoll (612-291-6110)
Board Members: B. H. Anderson, A. Bousbib, K. J. Higgins Victor, R. James, E. S. Kaplan, A. U. Lenzmeier, M. H. Paull, J. E. Press, R. M. Rebolledo, R. M. Schulze, M. A. Tolan, F. D. Trestman, H. A. Tyabji

Founded: 1966
Domicile: Minnesota
Employees: 140,000

The McGraw·Hill Companies

Big Lots Inc

STANDARD
&POOR'S

S&P Recommendation	**BUY** ★ ★ ★ ★ ☆	Price $20.87 (as of Nov 23, 2007)	12-Mo. Target Price $30.00	Investment Style Large-Cap Blend

GICS Sector Consumer Discretionary
Sub-Industry General Merchandise Stores

Summary This leading broadline closeout retailer, based in Ohio, has over 1,300 Big Lots stores in 47 states.

Key Stock Statistics (Source S&P, Vickers, company reports)

52-Wk Range	$36.15– 19.17	S&P Oper. EPS 2008E	1.47	Market Capitalization(B)	$2.124	Beta	0.82
Trailing 12-Month EPS	$1.43	S&P Oper. EPS 2009E	1.75	Yield (%)	Nil	S&P 3-Yr. Proj. EPS CAGR(%)	19.00
Trailing 12-Month P/E	14.6	P/E on S&P Oper. EPS 2008E	14.2	Dividend Rate/Share	Nil	S&P Credit Rating	NA
$10K Invested 5 Yrs Ago	$16,356	Common Shares Outstg. (M)	101.8	Institutional Ownership (%)	NM		

Price Performance

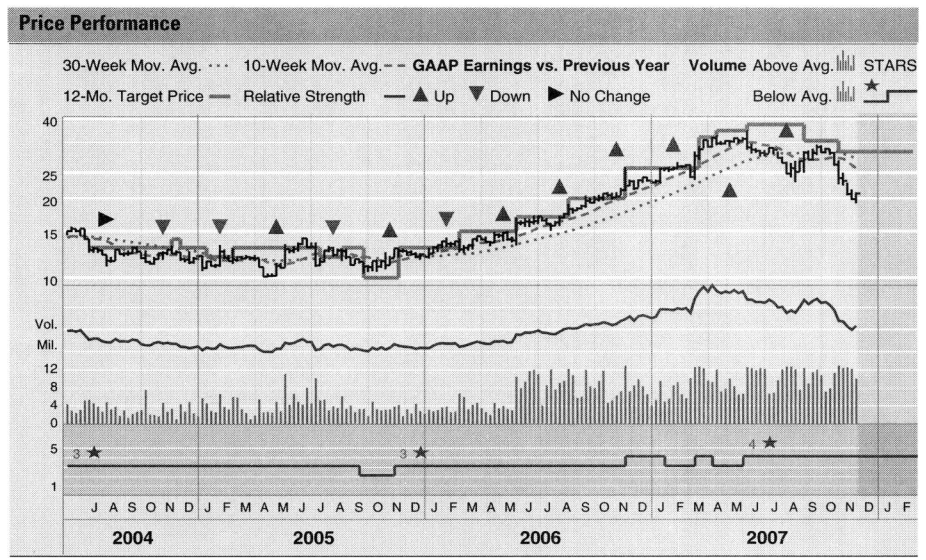

30-Week Mov. Avg. · · · 10-Week Mov. Avg. - - GAAP Earnings vs. Previous Year Volume Above Avg. STARS
12-Mo. Target Price — Relative Strength — ▲ Up ▼ Down ► No Change Below Avg.

Options: P, Ph

Analysis prepared by **Jason N. Asaeda** on October 26, 2007, when the stock traded at **$ 23.56**.

Highlights

➤ From a projected $4.6 billion in FY 08 (Jan.), we see net sales of $4.7 billion in FY 09. Annually, we anticipate an increased focus on traffic-driving brand-name closeouts and "treasure hunt" items, and improved product quality and in-stock levels. Balancing these positive factors against our expectation of a slowdown in consumer spending, we look for a 2% to 4% annual rise in same-store sales. Based on BIG's plans to close 45 to 50 underperforming units, we project about a 3% decline in selling square footage in FY 08. In FY 09, we believe the company will likely limit expansion to its most successful trade areas in an effort to achieve high sales productivity.

➤ Operating margins are likely to widen annually on: improving initial markups, supported, in part, by global sourcing; BIG's taking of markdowns more consistently in an effort to drive both same-store sales growth and higher inventory turns; a reduction in depreciation expense on disciplined capital allocation; and cost saving initiatives.

➤ Factoring in likely share buybacks under BIG's $600 million authorization, we see operating EPS of $1.47 in FY 08 rising to $1.75 in FY 09.

Investment Rationale/Risk

➤ Despite recent weakening in sales, we look for BIG to deliver strong earnings growth over the balance of FY 08 and into FY 09, supported by the company's efforts to raise sales productivity and lower its cost structure by: better aligning products with customer preferences; moving to a new store layout that brings more merchandise to the selling floor and allocates more square footage to key categories; and accelerating the closure of underperforming units. Given what we see as its strong price-value proposition and attractive mix of everyday necessities and more discretionary-purchase items, we see potential for BIG to gain incremental business over the next year from middle- and upper-income consumers trading down from national drugstore and supermarket chains and mass merchandisers.

➤ Risks to our recommendation and target price include sales shortfalls due to changes in consumer confidence and buying preferences, merchandise availability, and increased promotional activity by competitors.

➤ Our 12-month target price of $30 applies a 0.65X peer-median forward price to sales multiple to our $46 FY 09 forward sales per share estimate.

Qualitative Risk Assessment

LOW	MEDIUM	HIGH

Our risk assessment reflects our expectation of improving company fundamentals, supported by BIG's new merchandising and cost reduction initiatives, offset by what we see as a challenging retail environment that could hinder a turnaround.

Quantitative Evaluations

S&P Quality Ranking　　　　　　　B-

D	C	B-	B	B+	A-	A	A+

Relative Strength Rank　　　　　**WEAK**

17

LOWEST = 1　　　　　　　　　　HIGHEST = 99

Revenue/Earnings Data

Revenue (Million $)

	1Q	2Q	3Q	4Q	Year
2008	1,128	1,085	--	--	--
2007	1,092	1,057	1,050	1,545	4,743
2006	1,099	1,051	1,041	1,395	4,430
2005	1,019	995.0	980.0	1,381	4,375
2004	948.4	949.3	948.1	1,329	4,174
2003	904.1	879.3	868.2	1,217	3,869

Earnings Per Share ($)

	1Q	2Q	3Q	4Q	Year
2008	0.26	0.21	E0.12	E0.90	E1.47
2007	0.13	0.04	0.02	0.83	1.01
2006	0.07	-0.12	-0.17	0.33	0.14
2005	0.05	-0.07	-0.23	0.51	0.27
2004	0.08	-0.07	-0.05	0.80	0.77
2003	0.11	0.03	-0.04	0.57	0.65

Fiscal year ended Jan. 31. Next earnings report expected: NA. EPS Estimates based on S&P Operating Earnings; historical GAAP earnings are as reported.

Dividend Data

Proceeds from the sale of rights amounting to $0.01 a share were distributed in 2001.

Big Lots Inc

STANDARD &POOR'S

Business Summary October 26, 2007

CORPORATE OVERVIEW. BIG's strategy is to position itself as a preferred shopping destination for middle-income consumers seeking savings on brand-name closeouts and other value-priced merchandise. The company's product offerings range from everyday essentials such as food and other consumables, to more discretionary-purchase items, including furniture, holiday assortments, electronics, apparel, and small appliances. In our view, FY 07 (Jan.) was a transitional year for BIG, as the company slowed chain expansion in order to better focus on implementing operational changes to reverse a two-year trend of declining operating profits. Over the next few years, we look for BIG to apply successful merchandising and marketing strategies tested during FY 07 to further strengthen its financial performance.

CORPORATE STRATEGY. BIG's primary growth driver is expansion. The company seeks to build on its leadership position in broadline closeout retailing by expanding its market presence in both existing and new markets. From FY 00 through FY 05, the company increased its selling square footage at a compound annual growth rate (CAGR) of about 6% as it expanded its store count from 1,230 to 1,502. In FY 06, BIG continued to expand its store base, adding 73 new stores. However, the company also accelerated the closure of underperforming locations as part of its What's Important Now (WIN) turnaround strategy, which was announced in November 2005. BIG closed 174 stores in FY 06.

As a result, the company ended the fiscal year with 1,401 stores in 47 states, reflecting a 3.5% decline in selling square footage.

WIN is aimed at improving its financial performance via changes in the company's merchandising, cost structure, and real estate. As its first steps, BIG is attempting to raise productivity of its chain by closing low-volume stores located mainly in small, rural, or weaker performing markets, and by moving from an opportunistic real estate strategy to one focused on its most successful trade areas. These areas include California, Arizona, Washington, New York and New Jersey. During FY 07, the company scaled back new store openings to 11 and closed an additional 37 underperforming stores, ending the fiscal year with 1,375 stores. BIG anticipates a further reduction in its store base over the next three years, reflecting its more market focused real estate strategy and its view that commercial real estate is currently overpriced. The company plans to open 10 to 15 new stores and to close 45 to 50 locations during FY 08.

Company Financials Fiscal Year Ended Jan. 31

Per Share Data ($)	2007	2006	2005	2004	2003	2002	2001	2000	1999	1998
Tangible Book Value	11.10	9.47	9.54	9.51	8.83	8.11	8.28	11.71	10.79	9.60
Cash Flow	1.91	1.15	1.17	1.56	1.38	0.37	1.44	1.74	1.71	1.47
Earnings	1.01	0.14	0.27	0.77	0.65	-0.25	0.87	0.85	0.97	0.77
S&P Core Earnings	1.06	0.05	0.25	0.78	0.60	-0.32	0.83	NA	NA	NA
Dividends	Nil	Nil	Nil	Nil	Nil	Nil	Nil	Nil	Nil	Nil
Payout Ratio	Nil	Nil	Nil	Nil	Nil	Nil	Nil	Nil	Nil	Nil
Calendar Year	2006	2005	2004	2003	2002	2001	2000	1999	1998	1997
Prices:High	26.36	14.29	15.62	18.39	19.90	15.75	16.38	38.13	46.13	50.00
Prices:Low	11.83	10.06	11.05	9.92	9.75	7.15	8.25	13.69	15.50	24.50
P/E Ratio:High	26	NM	58	24	31	NM	19	45	48	65
P/E Ratio:Low	12	NM	41	13	15	NM	9	16	16	32

Income Statement Analysis (Million $)										
Revenue	4,743	4,430	4,375	4,174	3,869	3,433	3,277	4,700	4,194	4,055
Operating Income	276	141	172	222	231	43.4	249	271	288	268
Depreciation	101	115	104	93.7	85.7	72.0	64.5	100	84.0	79.2
Interest Expense	0.68	6.27	24.8	16.4	21.0	20.5	23.6	25.3	24.3	25.7
Pretax Income	170	20.9	43.3	113	125	-48.7	161	145	179	162
Effective Tax Rate	34.0%	24.8%	29.8%	20.6%	39.5%	NM	39.5%	39.5%	39.0%	47.0%
Net Income	113	15.7	30.4	89.9	75.7	-29.5	97.6	96.1	109	85.9
S&P Core Earnings	118	4.93	27.8	91.6	70.7	-36.7	92.6	NA	NA	NA

Balance Sheet & Other Financial Data (Million $)										
Cash	282	1.71	2.52	174	160	NA	NA	96.3	75.9	41.7
Current Assets	1,149	994	1,035	1,134	NA	NA	NA	1,420	1,335	1,107
Total Assets	1,721	1,625	1,734	1,801	1,656	1,470	1,528	2,187	2,043	1,746
Current Liabilities	474	437	413	416	NA	NA	NA	711	460	525
Long Term Debt	Nil	5.50	159	204	204	204	268	60.5	296	115
Common Equity	1,130	1,167	1,075	1,109	1,020	923	924	1,300	1,182	1,035
Total Capital	1,130	1,173	1,235	1,313	1,224	1,127	1,192	1,468	1,583	1,106
Capital Expenditures	35.9	68.5	135	170	110	NA	NA	147	167	146
Cash Flow	214	130	135	184	161	42.5	162	197	193	165
Current Ratio	2.4	2.3	2.5	2.7	NA	NA	NA	2.0	2.9	2.1
% Long Term Debt of Capitalization	NA	0.5	12.9	15.5	16.7	18.1	22.5	4.1	18.7	11.1
% Net Income of Revenue	2.4	0.4	0.7	2.2	2.0	NM	3.0	2.0	2.6	2.1
% Return on Assets	6.7	0.9	1.7	5.2	4.8	NM	5.3	4.5	5.8	5.6
% Return on Equity	10.2	1.4	2.8	8.4	7.8	NM	8.8	7.7	9.9	10.0

Data as orig reptd.; bef. results of disc opers/spec. items. Per share data adj. for stk. divs.; EPS diluted. E-Estimated. NA-Not Available. NM-Not Meaningful. NR-Not Ranked. UR-Under Review.

Office: 300 Phillipi Road, Columbus, OH 43228-1310.
Telephone: 614-278-6800.
Website: http://www.biglots.com
Chrmn, Pres & CEO: S.S. Fishman

SVP & CFO: J.R. Cooper
SVP, Secy & General Counsel: C.W. Haubiel, II
Investor Contact: T.A. Johnson (614-278-6622)
VP & Cntlr: P.A. Schroeder

Board Members: J. P. Berger, S. M. Berman, S. S. Fishman, D. T. Kollat, B. J. Lauderback, P. E. Mallott, R. Solt, J. R. Tener, D. B. Tishkoff

Founded: 1983
Domicile: Ohio
Employees: 38,738

The McGraw-Hill Companies

Biogen Idec Inc

STANDARD &POOR'S

S&P Recommendation BUY ★★★★☆	**Price** $69.51 (as of Nov 23, 2007)	**12-Mo. Target Price** $90.00	**Investment Style** Large-Cap Growth

GICS Sector Health Care
Sub-Industry Biotechnology

Summary This major biopharmaceutical firm develops and markets targeted therapies for the treatment of multiple sclerosis, non-Hodgkin's lymphoma, and rheumatoid arthritis.

Key Stock Statistics (Source S&P, Vickers, company reports)

52-Wk Range	$84.75– 42.86	S&P Oper. EPS 2007**E**	2.51	Market Capitalization(B)	$20.014	Beta	0.39
Trailing 12-Month EPS	$1.66	S&P Oper. EPS 2008**E**	3.14	Yield (%)	Nil	S&P 3-Yr. Proj. EPS CAGR(%)	15.00
Trailing 12-Month P/E	41.9	P/E on S&P Oper. EPS 2007**E**	27.7	Dividend Rate/Share	Nil	S&P Credit Rating	BB
$10K Invested 5 Yrs Ago	$17,656	Common Shares Outstg. (M)	287.9	Institutional Ownership (%)	NM		

Price Performance

30-Week Mov. Avg. · · · 10-Week Mov. Avg. – – **GAAP Earnings vs. Previous Year** Volume Above Avg. STARS
12-Mo. Target Price — Relative Strength — ▲ Up ▼ Down ► No Change Below Avg. ★

Options: ASE, CBOE, P, Ph

Analysis prepared by **Steven Silver** on November 16, 2007, when the stock traded at **$ 70.60**.

Highlights

➤ In the third quarter, Tysabri revenues rose 32% sequentially, to $63 million, continuing its Europe launch. BIIB maintained a goal of 100,000 Tysabri patients by year-end 2010, up from 17,000 recently, including clinical trials. Avonex sales were 2% higher, $17 million below our estimate, and Rituxan revenues increased 15%. We see revenues rising 16% in 2007, to $3.1 billion, and to $3.43 billion in 2008, which would represent 11% growth. BIIB set a goal of 15% annual revenue growth through 2010.

➤ Third quarter R&D costs were 35.7% of sales, up from 29.3% a year earlier, due to a $50 million payment to Cardiokine for its Lixivaptan license deal, without which the comparison would have been flat. SG&A costs of 23% of sales were consistent with the prior year. We see an easing of expenses in 2008, with revenue increases aiding margins. BIIB is appealing a negative EU opinion for Crohn's disease, and the U.S. FDA will review a favorable committee opinion into early 2008.

➤ Our 2007 and 2008 EPS estimates are $2.51 and $3.14, respectively. In September 2007, BIIB introduced a goal of 20% compound annual non-GAAP EPS growth from 2007 through 2010.

Investment Rationale/Risk

➤ In October 2007, BIIB began exploring a sale of the company; we believe the shares have reflected acquisition speculation since investor Carl Icahn took a stake in BIIB this summer. Despite recent share price declines, which we attribute to lengthy negotiations over complex change of control issues with Tysabri and Rituxan, we expect a sale to a large pharmaceutical company, for BIIB's manufacturing capabilities and its biologics platform and pipeline. We are skeptical on BIIB as a stand-alone entity, however, as we see few long-term catalysts outside the MS market. Despite investment in daclizumab and Rituxan to help protect its leading MS position, we see competing drugs on the horizon.

➤ Risks to our recommendation and target price include failure to complete a sale of the company, weakening Tysabri sales, unfavorable Rituxan arbitration outcomes, and increased MS market competition.

➤ Our 12-month target price of $90, which assumes a sale of the company, applies a 7.5X multiple to our 2008 sales estimate of $3.43 billion, a slight premium to large cap peers, on our assumption that the company will be sold.

Qualitative Risk Assessment

LOW	MEDIUM	**HIGH**

Biogen Idec sells products in competitive markets and must contend with the potential for generic threats, additional regulatory oversight, and changes in drug reimbursement. Also, the company is engaged in the development of new drugs, which is a risky endeavor.

Quantitative Evaluations

S&P Quality Ranking B

D	C	B-	**B**	B+	A-	A	A+

Relative Strength Rank STRONG

81

LOWEST = 1   HIGHEST = 99

Revenue/Earnings Data

Revenue (Million $)

	1Q	2Q	3Q	4Q	Year
2007	715.9	773.2	789.2	--	--
2006	611.2	660.0	703.5	708.3	2,683
2005	587.8	605.6	596.2	632.9	2,423
2004	541.7	538.8	543.3	587.8	2,212
2003	117.3	123.6	138.5	299.9	679.2
2002	79.74	97.13	103.7	123.7	404.2

Earnings Per Share ($)

2007	0.38	0.54	0.41	E0.71	E2.51
2006	0.35	-0.50	0.45	0.32	0.62
2005	0.12	0.10	0.08	0.16	0.47
2004	-0.12	Nil	0.10	0.08	0.07
2003	0.24	0.17	0.26	-4.03	-4.92
2002	0.17	0.20	0.22	0.26	0.85

Fiscal year ended Dec. 31. Next earnings report expected: Mid February. EPS Estimates based on S&P Operating Earnings; historical GAAP earnings are as reported.

Dividend Data

No cash dividends have been paid.

Please read the Required Disclosures and Analyst Certification on the last page of this report.

The McGraw-Hill Companies

Biogen Idec Inc

STANDARD
&POOR'S

Business Summary November 16, 2007

CORPORATE OVERVIEW. Biogen Idec researches, develops and markets therapeutics to treat cancer and autoimmune diseases, formed through the 2003 merger of IDEC Pharmaceuticals and Biogen.

BIIB's primary sources of revenue are Avonex and Rituxan. Avonex was approved by the FDA to treat relapsing forms of MS in 1996. European approval was granted in 1997. Avonex sales were $1.71 billion in 2006, up from 1.54 billion in 2005. The company estimates that more than 120,000 patients use Avonex worldwide.

Rituxan is a treatment for relapsed or refractory low-grade or follicular B-cell non-Hodgkin's lymphomas (NHL). There are over 300,000 U.S. patients with various forms of this disease. Rituxan is marketed and sold in the U.S. under a co-promotion agreement with Genentech; BIIB receives joint business revenues on a percentage of sales. Roche has marketing rights (under the name MabThera) outside the U.S., with BIIB receiving royalties. U.S. Rituxan generated revenues of $811 million for BIIB in 2006, 14% higher than 2005. Rituxan is also being developed for use in treating lupus and MS.

BIIB developed Tysabri with Elan Corp. Tysabri was approved for treating re-

lapsing MS in late 2004. However, three adverse events related to progressive multifocal leukoencephalopathy (PML)--a rare, fatal nervous system disorder--were reported in 2005, causing the drug to be removed from the market. Following safety evaluations and an analysis of additional data, the FDA approved U.S. re-launch in June 2006, contingent upon a restricted distribution program to limit risks. Tysabri is being launched across Europe in 2007 and 2008, with 15 EU countries expected by year-end. In October 2007, BIIB listed 17,000 patients on Tysabri worldwide.

Tysabri is also being developed for Crohn's disease, which afflicts nearly one million people worldwide. In July 2007, the European Medicines Agency (EMEA) issued a negative ruling that BIIB and Elan are appealing. A final ruling is expected in early 2008, while a U.S. FDA committee recommended the drug for moderate-to-severe Crohn's disease in July 2007. The FDA plans to rule on this indication in early 2008.

Company Financials Fiscal Year Ended Dec. 31

Per Share Data ($)	2006	2005	2004	2003	2002	2001	2000	1999	1998	1997
Tangible Book Value	9.60	8.38	7.08	6.85	7.25	6.22	4.63	1.11	0.88	0.53
Cash Flow	1.71	1.63	1.35	-4.57	0.88	0.62	0.39	0.31	0.18	-0.10
Earnings	0.62	0.47	0.07	-4.92	0.85	0.59	0.36	0.29	0.15	-0.14
S&P Core Earnings	0.69	0.16	-0.06	-5.13	0.54	0.34	NA	NA	NA	NA
Dividends	Nil	Nil	Nil	Nil	Nil	Nil	Nil	Nil	Nil	Nil
Payout Ratio	Nil	Nil	Nil	Nil	Nil	Nil	Nil	Nil	Nil	Nil
Prices:High	52.72	70.00	68.13	42.15	71.40	75.00	77.65	35.00	8.03	7.71
Prices:Low	40.24	33.18	36.60	27.80	20.76	32.63	18.54	6.60	2.88	2.63
P/E Ratio:High	85	NM	NM	NM	84	NM	NM	NM	52	NM
P/E Ratio:Low	65	NM	NM	NM	24	NM	NM	NM	19	NM

Income Statement Analysis (Million $)										
Revenue	2,683	2,423	2,212	679	404	273	155	118	87.0	44.6
Operating Income	1,117	756	483	14.6	285	137	60.6	45.8	23.2	-14.0
Depreciation	376	402	439	61.3	10.2	6.31	4.74	4.37	4.28	4.01
Interest Expense	Nil	Nil	18.9	15.2	16.1	7.30	7.05	6.06	0.63	0.92
Pretax Income	492	256	64.1	-881	232	162	69.3	45.6	21.9	-15.5
Effective Tax Rate	56.6%	37.3%	60.9%	NM	36.0%	37.1%	17.2%	5.37%	1.93%	NM
Net Income	214	161	25.1	-875	148	102	57.4	43.2	21.5	-15.5
S&P Core Earnings	237	56.6	-21.6	-914	93.4	61.4	NA	NA	NA	NA

Balance Sheet & Other Financial Data (Million $)										
Cash	2,315	851	1,058	836	373	426	401	61.4	73.5	34.8
Current Assets	1,713	1,618	1,931	1,839	978	700	631	279	101	79.2
Total Assets	8,553	8,367	9,166	9,504	2,060	1,141	856	307	125	106
Current Liabilities	583	583	1,261	405	56.2	35.3	23.0	15.6	14.5	19.4
Long Term Debt	96.7	43.4	102	887	866	136	129	123	2.10	2.02
Common Equity	7,150	6,906	6,826	7,053	1,110	956	695	160	106	80.7
Total Capital	7,890	7,712	7,850	9,049	1,976	1,092	824	283	109	84.4
Capital Expenditures	198	318	361	301	166	0.07	31.4	4.29	1.72	5.88
Cash Flow	590	563	465	-814	158	108	62.1	47.5	25.8	-11.5
Current Ratio	2.9	2.8	1.5	4.5	17.4	19.8	27.4	17.8	7.0	4.1
% Long Term Debt of Capitalization	1.2	0.6	1.3	9.8	43.8	12.4	15.7	43.4	1.9	2.4
% Net Income of Revenue	8.0	6.6	1.1	NM	36.6	37.3	37.1	36.6	24.7	NM
% Return on Assets	2.5	1.8	0.3	NM	9.3	10.2	9.9	20.0	18.6	NM
% Return on Equity	3.0	2.3	0.4	NM	14.3	12.3	13.4	32.4	23.0	NM

Data as orig reptd.; bef. results of disc opers/spec. items. Per share data adj. for stk. divs.; EPS diluted. E-Estimated. NA-Not Available. NM-Not Meaningful. NR-Not Ranked. UR-Under Review.

Office: 14 Cambridge Center, Cambridge, MA 02142.
Telephone: 617-679-2000.
Website: http://www.biogenidec.com
Chrmn: B.R. Ross

Pres & CEO: J.C. Mullen
EVP & CFO: P.N. Kellogg
EVP, Secy & General Counsel: S.H. Alexander
SVP & Chief Acctg Officer: M. MacLean

Investor Contact: R. Jacobson (617-679-3710)
Board Members: A. Belzer, L. C. Best, A. B. Glassberg, M. L. Good, T. F. Keller, J. C. Mullen, R. W. Pangia, C. Pickett, B. R. Ross, L. Schenk, P. A. Sharp, W. D. Young

Founded: 1985
Domicile: Delaware
Employees: 3,900

BJ Services Co

STANDARD &POOR'S

S&P Recommendation **HOLD** ★★★☆☆	Price $25.12 (as of Nov 23, 2007)	12-Mo. Target Price $29.00	Investment Style Large-Cap Growth

GICS Sector Energy
Sub-Industry Oil & Gas Equipment & Services

Summary This company provides pressure pumping and other oilfield services to the petroleum industry worldwide.

Key Stock Statistics (Source S&P, Vickers, company reports)

52-Wk Range	**$34.14– 23.48**	S&P Oper. EPS 2008**E**	2.51	Market Capitalization(B)	**$7.325**	Beta	0.97
Trailing 12-Month EPS	**$2.55**	S&P Oper. EPS 2009**E**	2.70	Yield (%)	0.80	S&P 3-Yr. Proj. EPS CAGR(%)	12.00
Trailing 12-Month P/E	9.9	P/E on S&P Oper. EPS 2008**E**	10.0	Dividend Rate/Share	$0.20	S&P Credit Rating	BBB+
$10K Invested 5 Yrs Ago	**$15,767**	Common Shares Outstg. (M)	291.6	Institutional Ownership (%)	91		

Price Performance

30-Week Mov. Avg. ···· 10-Week Mov. Avg. – – **GAAP Earnings vs. Previous Year** Volume Above Avg. ▥▥ STARS
12-Mo. Target Price — Relative Strength — ▲ Up ▼ Down ► No Change Below Avg. ▥▥ ★

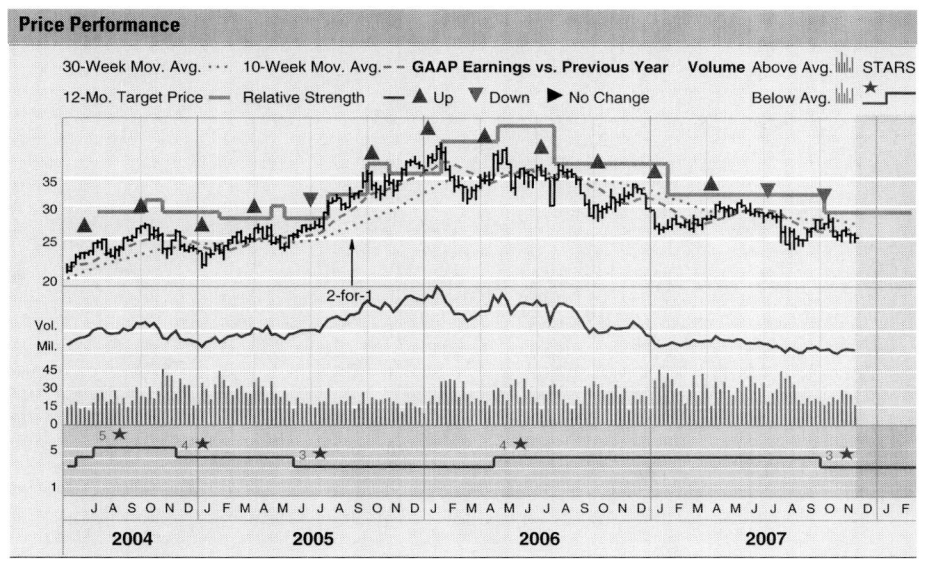

2-for-1

2004 2005 2006 2007

Options: ASE, CBOE, P, Ph

Analysis prepared by **Stewart Glickman, CFA** on November 16, 2007, when the stock traded at **$ 25.12**.

Highlights

➤ Although the main growth driver continues to be the U.S. market, which is relatively sensitive to natural gas price expectations, we see growing importance of overseas markets, which we view as less price sensitive. Based on data from Global Insight, we project natural gas prices of $8.11/MMBtu in 2008 (versus an estimated $6.96/MMBtu in 2007), and rising to $9.01 in 2009.

➤ While activity levels in the U.S./Mexico pressure pumping segment appeared flat in the September quarter (unlike Canada, which continues to show unusually pronounced year over year weakness), operating income dropped 22% on lower pricing and higher labor and materials costs. We see further near-term weakness in pricing due to industry capacity build, but think a rebound in FY 08 (Sep.) is likely, partly on expectation of improved natural gas prices. All told, we see total revenue growth of 3% and 8% in FY 08 and FY 09, respectively, with operating margins in the mid-20% area in both years.

➤ We project EPS of $2.51 in FY 08, rising to $2.70 in FY 09.

Investment Rationale/Risk

➤ We think that rising North American service cost inflation could induce some exploration and production companies to defer a portion of their near-term capital spending plans, which could hamper BJS's earnings visibility. Nonetheless, we think BJS's international demand should remain strong, and despite recent project delays, we see improving overseas growth.

➤ Risks to our recommendation and target price include reduced demand for pressure pumping services; higher than expected cost inflation; lower than projected natural gas and oil prices; and lower than anticipated returns from International operations.

➤ Our DCF model, which assumes free cash flow growth of about 11% for 10 years and 3% thereafter, discounted at a weighted average cost of capital of 11%, shows an intrinsic value of about $27. We think a modest discount to peers is warranted in light of relatively weaker earnings visibility. Applying peer-discount multiples of 7X our calendar 2008 EBITDA projection and 9X our 2008 cash flow estimate, blended with our DCF analysis, we arrive at our 12-month target price of $29.

Qualitative Risk Assessment

LOW	MEDIUM	**HIGH**

Our risk assessment for BJS reflects its exposure to volatile hydrocarbon prices, particularly natural gas, the company's leverage to the North American market, and concerns over capacity additions for pressure pumping. Partly offsetting these risks is the company's strong position in pressure pumping services.

Quantitative Evaluations

S&P Quality Ranking B+

D	C	B-	B	**B+**	A-	A	A+

Relative Strength Rank MODERATE

61

LOWEST = 1   HIGHEST = 99

Revenue/Earnings Data

Revenue (Million $)

	1Q	2Q	3Q	4Q	Year
2007	1,184	1,187	1,153	1,279	4,802
2006	956.2	1,079	1,117	1,216	4,368
2005	737.8	795.9	817.3	892.3	3,243
2004	600.8	647.1	658.7	694.5	2,601
2003	473.1	534.6	546.6	588.6	2,143
2002	510.1	442.4	439.7	473.7	1,866

Earnings Per Share ($)

2007	0.70	0.64	0.57	0.64	2.55
2006	0.48	0.62	0.67	0.76	2.52
2005	0.29	0.33	0.35	0.41	1.38
2004	0.19	0.23	0.40	0.29	1.11
2003	0.11	0.14	0.16	0.19	0.59
2002	0.21	0.12	0.09	0.11	0.52

Fiscal year ended Sep. 30. Next earnings report expected: Late January. EPS Estimates based on S&P Operating Earnings; historical GAAP earnings are as reported.

Dividend Data (Dates: mm/dd Payment Date: mm/dd/yy)

Amount ($)	Date Decl.	Ex-Div. Date	Stk. of Record	Payment Date
0.050	12/07	12/15	12/19	01/12/07
0.050	01/30	03/13	03/15	04/13/07
0.050	05/24	06/13	06/15	07/13/07
0.050	07/26	09/11	09/13	10/12/07

Dividends have been paid since 2004. Source: Company reports.

Please read the Required Disclosures and Analyst Certification on the last page of this report.

The McGraw-Hill Companies

BJ Services Co

Business Summary November 16, 2007

CORPORATE OVERVIEW. BJ Services is a leading provider of pressure pumping and other oilfield services to the petroleum industry worldwide. Demand for its services depends on the number of oil and natural gas wells being drilled, the depth and drilling conditions of the wells, the number of well completions, and the level of workover activity worldwide. BJS's principal customers consist of major and independent oil and natural gas producing companies. The company operates in 50 countries in the major international oil and natural gas producing areas of Canada, Latin America, Europe, Africa, Russia, Asia, the Middle East, Russia and China. In FY 06 (Sep.), 54% of revenues were generated by U.S./Mexico pressure pumping; 11% from Canada pressure pumping; 20% from International pressure pumping; and 15% other oilfield services. Other than Canada, the international market tends to be less volatile than the U.S. due to the size and complexity of investment, and projects tend to be managed with a longer-term perspective with regard to commodity prices. In addition, the international market is dominated by major oil and national oil companies, which tend to have different objectives and more operating stability than typical independent U.S. producers.

Pressure pumping services (85% of FY 06 revenues and 90% of segment operating profits) are used in the completion of oil and gas wells, both onshore and offshore. Customers are mainly served in the U.S. Stimulation services are designed to improve the flow of oil and natural gas from producing formations using fracturing, acidizing, sand control, nitrogen, coiled tubing and downhole tool services. Cementing is done between the casing pipe and the wellbore during the drilling and completion phase of a well. This is done to isolate fluids that could damage productivity, seal the casing from corrosive fluids, and provide structural support for the casing string. Cementing services are also used when recompleting wells from one producing zone to another, and when plugging and abandoning wells.

Company Financials Fiscal Year Ended Sep. 30

Per Share Data ($)	2007	2006	2005	2004	2003	2002	2001	2000	1999	1998
Tangible Book Value	NA	4.16	4.94	3.73	2.44	1.74	2.79	2.40	1.36	1.54
Cash Flow	NA	3.05	1.79	1.49	0.96	0.84	1.36	0.65	0.25	0.64
Earnings	2.55	2.52	1.38	1.11	0.59	0.52	1.04	0.35	-0.11	0.36
S&P Core Earnings	NA	2.52	1.35	0.90	0.54	0.45	0.97	NA	NA	NA
Dividends	0.20	0.20	0.12	0.04	Nil	Nil	Nil	Nil	Nil	Nil
Payout Ratio	8%	8%	9%	4%	Nil	Nil	Nil	Nil	Nil	Nil
Prices:High	31.26	42.85	39.78	27.33	21.20	19.75	21.55	19.19	10.86	10.95
Prices:Low	23.48	27.43	21.13	17.42	14.63	11.50	7.28	9.53	3.36	2.97
P/E Ratio:High	12	17	29	25	36	38	21	53	NM	30
P/E Ratio:Low	9	11	15	16	25	22	7	26	NM	8

Income Statement Analysis (Million $)										
Revenue	NA	4,368	3,243	2,601	2,143	1,866	2,234	1,555	1,131	1,527
Operating Income	NA	1,340	788	567	414	368	641	297	125	316
Depreciation, Depletion and Amortization	NA	167	137	126	120	105	105	102	99.8	91.0
Interest Expense	NA	14.6	11.0	16.4	31.9	8.98	13.3	20.0	31.4	26.0
Pretax Income	NA	1,172	653	521	276	253	529	175	-44.9	175
Effective Tax Rate	NA	31.4%	30.7%	30.7%	31.7%	34.1%	34.0%	32.7%	NM	31.1%
Net Income	NA	805	453	361	188	166	349	118	-29.7	117
S&P Core Earnings	NA	805	447	295	174	142	324	NA	NA	NA

Balance Sheet & Other Financial Data (Million $)										
Cash	NA	92.4	357	425	278	84.7	84.1	6.47	3.92	2.00
Current Assets	NA	1,459	1,334	1,424	942	649	733	506	439	452
Total Assets	NA	3,862	3,396	3,331	2,786	2,442	1,985	1,785	1,825	1,743
Current Liabilities	NA	948	684	910	471	356	390	337	445	513
Long Term Debt	NA	500	Nil	78.9	494	489	79.4	142	423	242
Common Equity	NA	2,147	2,484	2,094	1,651	1,419	1,370	1,170	877	900
Total Capital	NA	2,713	2,548	2,262	2,152	1,917	1,460	1,320	1,306	1,151
Capital Expenditures	NA	460	324	201	167	179	183	80.5	111	168
Cash Flow	NA	971	590	487	308	271	454	220	70.1	208
Current Ratio	NA	1.5	2.0	1.6	2.0	1.8	1.9	1.5	1.0	0.9
% Long Term Debt of Capitalization	NA	18.4	Nil	3.5	22.9	25.5	5.4	10.8	32.4	21.0
% Return on Assets	NA	22.1	13.5	11.8	7.2	7.5	18.5	6.5	NM	6.7
% Return on Equity	NA	34.7	19.8	19.3	12.3	11.9	27.5	11.5	NM	12.6

Data as orig reptd.; bef. results of disc opers/spec. items. Per share data adj. for stk. divs.; EPS diluted. E-Estimated. NA-Not Available. NM-Not Meaningful. NR-Not Ranked. UR-Under Review.

Office: 4601 Westway Park Blvd, Houston, TX 77041-2037.
Telephone: 713-462-4239.
Website: http://www.bjservices.com
Chrmn, Pres & CEO: J.W. Stewart

COO & EVP: D.D. Dunlap
VP & CFO: J.E. Smith
VP, Secy & General Counsel: M.B. Shannon
Treas: B. Wells

Board Members: L. W. Heiligbrodt, J. R. Huff, D. D. Jordan, M. E. Patrick, J. L. Payne, J. W. Stewart, W. H. White

Founded: 1872
Domicile: Delaware
Employees: 16,000

Black & Decker Corp (The)

STANDARD &POOR'S

S&P Recommendation	HOLD ★★★☆☆	Price	12-Mo. Target Price	Investment Style
		$82.11 (as of Nov 23, 2007)	$93.00	Large-Cap Blend

GICS Sector Consumer Discretionary
Sub-Industry Household Appliances

Summary This company is a leading global producer of power tools, hardware and home improvement products, and fastening systems.

Key Stock Statistics (Source S&P, Vickers, company reports)

52-Wk Range	$97.01– 76.85	S&P Oper. EPS 2007**E**	6.60	Market Capitalization(B)	$5.394	Beta	1.13
Trailing 12-Month EPS	$6.34	S&P Oper. EPS 2008**E**	7.15	Yield (%)	2.05	S&P 3-Yr. Proj. EPS CAGR(%)	7.00
Trailing 12-Month P/E	13.0	P/E on S&P Oper. EPS 2007**E**	12.4	Dividend Rate/Share	$1.68	S&P Credit Rating	BBB
$10K Invested 5 Yrs Ago	$20,261	Common Shares Outstg. (M)	65.7	Institutional Ownership (%)	95		

Price Performance

Options: CBOE, P, Ph

Analysis prepared by **Kenneth M. Leon, CPA** on October 25, 2007, when the stock traded at **$ 86.86**.

Highlights

➤ We forecast that revenues will increase 2% in 2007, excluding potential acquisitions, although we think BDK continues to seek bolt-on acquisitions. In March 2006, the company acquired Vector Products, which added about 2% to 2006 sales. We expect a U.S. housing market downturn to dampen results into 2008, especially in the Power Tools and Accessories business unit. We project that revenue will rise 2% in 2008. We think new products will aid sales growth.

➤ We see operating margins narrowing to 10.4% in both 2007 and 2008, compared to 12.4% in 2005, which we view as the cycle-top year for new home starts, and 11.5% in 2006. The company completed a major cost savings campaign in 2005, which should provide some offset to escalating raw material costs that we foresee. We expect BDK to continue to integrate acquisitions well.

➤ We project EPS of $6.60 in 2007, and $7.15 in 2008. BDK's strategy includes a consideration of share buybacks if it does not execute bolt-on acquisitions, which we assume in our EPS estimates.

Investment Rationale/Risk

➤ We believe recent progress in improving operating margins through restructurings and productivity initiatives is largely meeting the challenge of a slower sales environment and rising costs for raw materials. Despite a declining housing market, the company reported 2% sales growth for the first nine months of 2007. We anticipate 2.3% sales growth in the fourth quarter versus the prior-year period, with 2% to 3% sales growth in 2008. We believe about 20% of BDK's sales are tied to new housing starts.

➤ Risks to our recommendation and target price include any unexpected weakening in the company's major markets, any negative change in BDK's relationships with leading customers, lack of market acceptance of new products, and negative changes in currency exchange rates or raw material prices.

➤ Our 12-month target price of $93 represents a target P/E of 13X our 2007 EPS estimate, which is slightly above the middle of the historical range for BDK and is appropriate, we believe, given the moderate conditions we see in its markets.

Qualitative Risk Assessment

LOW	MEDIUM	HIGH

Our risk assessment reflects our view of BDK's strong brand name and solid cash flow, offset by cyclicality related to homebuilding sales.

Quantitative Evaluations

S&P Quality Ranking B+

D	C	B-	B	B+	A-	A	A+

Relative Strength Rank MODERATE

64

LOWEST = 1   HIGHEST = 99

Revenue/Earnings Data

Revenue (Million $)

	1Q	2Q	3Q	4Q	Year
2007	1,577	1,700	1,634	--	--
2006	1,529	1,697	1,610	1,611	6,447
2005	1,519	1,699	1,576	1,730	6,524
2004	1,093	1,298	1,283	1,725	5,398
2003	939.2	1,090	1,116	1,338	4,483
2002	951.7	1,125	1,085	1,232	4,394

Earnings Per Share ($)

2007	1.61	1.75	1.59	E1.64	E6.60
2006	1.45	1.98	1.74	1.38	6.55
2005	1.79	1.88	1.73	1.28	6.69
2004	0.93	1.50	1.35	1.60	5.40
2003	0.55	0.94	0.95	1.23	3.68
2002	0.41	0.81	0.68	0.94	2.84

Fiscal year ended Dec. 31. Next earnings report expected: Late January. EPS Estimates based on S&P Operating Earnings; historical GAAP earnings are as reported.

Dividend Data (Dates: mm/dd Payment Date: mm/dd/yy)

Amount ($)	Date Decl.	Ex-Div. Date	Stk. of Record	Payment Date
0.420	02/08	03/14	03/16	03/30/07
0.420	04/25	06/13	06/15	06/29/07
0.420	07/26	09/12	09/14	09/28/07
0.420	10/17	12/12	12/14	12/28/07

Dividends have been paid since 1937. Source: Company reports.

Please read the Required Disclosures and Analyst Certification on the last page of this report.

The McGraw-Hill Companies

Black & Decker Corp (The)

Business Summary October 25, 2007

Black & Decker, incorporated in 1910, is a global manufacturer and marketer of power tools and accessories, hardware and home improvement products, and technology-based fastening systems. Its products are sold under a number of well known brand names in more than 100 countries. The company has 44 manufacturing facilities, including 24 located outside the U.S. in 10 foreign countries.

Operations consist of three segments: Power Tools and Accessories (74% of 2006 sales), Hardware and Home Improvement (16%), and Fastening and Assembly Systems (10%). The U.S. accounted for 64% of sales in 2006, Europe 21%, and other countries 15%.

BDK is one of the world's leading producers of portable electric power tools and electric lawn and garden tools, as well as one of the largest suppliers of power tool accessories and specialized, engineered fastening and assembly systems in the markets it serves. Its plumbing products business is one of the largest North American faucet makers.

The Power Tools and Accessories segment manufactures and sells consumer and professional power tools (such as drills, screwdrivers and saws) and accessories, outdoor products (electric lawn and garden tools), cleaning and

lighting products and product services. Products are sold mainly to retailers, wholesalers, jobbers, and distributors, although some discontinued or reconditioned products are sold through company-operated service centers and factory outlets directly to end users. Principal materials used to manufacture products in this segment include plastics, aluminum, copper, steel, certain electronic components, and batteries.

The Hardware and Home Improvement segment (formerly building products) makes and sells security hardware (locksets and deadbolts) and plumbing products (faucets, shower heads and bath accessories). Products are sold primarily to retailers, wholesalers, distributors, and jobbers. Certain security hardware products are sold to commercial, institutional, and industrial customers. The principal materials used in the manufacture of products in this segment are plastics, aluminum, steel, brass, zamak (zinc alloy), and ceramics.

Company Financials Fiscal Year Ended Dec. 31

Per Share Data ($)	2006	2005	2004	2003	2002	2001	2000	1999	1998	1997
Tangible Book Value	NM	5.27	4.57	0.96	NM	NM	NM	0.66	NM	NM
Cash Flow	9.61	8.97	7.12	5.40	4.49	3.30	5.28	5.21	-6.52	4.55
Earnings	6.55	6.69	5.40	3.68	2.84	1.33	3.34	3.40	-8.22	2.35
S&P Core Earnings	6.79	6.22	4.93	3.23	1.56	0.11	NA	NA	NA	NA
Dividends	1.52	1.12	0.84	0.57	0.48	0.48	0.48	0.48	0.48	0.48
Payout Ratio	23%	17%	16%	15%	17%	36%	14%	14%	NM	20%
Prices:High	94.90	93.71	89.64	49.90	50.50	46.95	52.38	64.63	65.50	43.44
Prices:Low	66.04	75.70	48.07	33.20	35.00	28.26	27.56	41.00	37.94	29.63
P/E Ratio:High	14	14	17	14	18	35	16	19	NM	18
P/E Ratio:Low	10	11	9	9	12	21	8	12	NM	13

Income Statement Analysis (Million $)										
Revenue	6,447	6,524	5,398	4,483	4,394	4,333	4,561	4,521	4,560	4,940
Operating Income	894	964	772	594	549	407	686	696	639	703
Depreciation	155	151	143	133	128	159	163	160	155	214
Interest Expense	103	81.9	57.9	60.7	84.3	84.3	104	126	145	133
Pretax Income	664	819	604	391	307	155	405	441	-589	349
Effective Tax Rate	26.8%	33.6%	27.0%	26.5%	25.3%	30.5%	30.3%	32.0%	NM	35.0%
Net Income	486	544	441	287	230	108	282	300	-755	227
S&P Core Earnings	505	506	401	251	126	9.48	NA	NA	NA	NA

Balance Sheet & Other Financial Data (Million $)										
Cash	233	968	514	308	517	245	135	147	88.0	247
Current Assets	2,703	3,347	2,927	2,203	2,194	1,892	1,962	1,911	1,752	2,079
Total Assets	5,248	5,817	5,531	4,223	4,131	4,014	4,090	4,013	3,853	5,361
Current Liabilities	1,780	2,264	1,793	1,312	1,453	1,071	1,632	1,573	1,375	1,373
Long Term Debt	1,170	1,030	1,201	916	928	1,191	798	847	1,149	1,624
Common Equity	1,164	1,524	1,559	846	600	751	692	801	573	1,791
Total Capital	2,532	2,742	2,930	1,942	1,739	2,204	1,712	1,892	2,002	3,473
Capital Expenditures	105	111	118	103	96.6	135	200	171	146	203
Cash Flow	641	695	584	421	358	267	445	460	-600	441
Current Ratio	1.5	1.5	1.6	1.7	1.5	1.8	1.2	1.2	1.3	1.5
% Long Term Debt of Capitalization	46.2	37.6	41.0	47.1	53.4	54.1	46.6	44.8	57.4	46.8
% Net Income of Revenue	7.5	8.3	8.2	6.4	5.2	2.5	6.2	6.6	NM	4.6
% Return on Assets	8.8	9.6	9.0	6.9	5.6	2.7	7.0	7.6	NM	4.3
% Return on Equity	35.7	35.3	36.7	39.7	34.0	15.0	37.8	43.7	NM	13.3

Data as orig reptd.; bef. results of disc opers/spec. items. Per share data adj. for stk. divs.; EPS diluted. E-Estimated. NA-Not Available. NM-Not Meaningful. NR-Not Ranked. UR-Under Review.

Office: 701 East Joppa Road, Towson, MD 21286.
Telephone: 410-716-3900.
Email: investor.relations@bdk.com
Website: http://www.bdk.com

Chrmn, Pres & CEO: N.D. Archibald
SVP & CFO: M.D. Mangan
SVP & General Counsel: C.E. Fenton
Investor Contact: M.M. Rothleitner (410-716-3979)

VP & Treas: M.M. Rothleitner
Board Members: N. D. Archibald, N. R. Augustine, B. L. Bowles, G. W. Buckley, M. A. Burns, K. B. Clark, M. A. Fernandez, B. H. Griswold, IV, A. Luiso, R. L. Ryan, M. Willes

Founded: 1910
Domicile: Maryland
Employees: 25,500

The McGraw-Hill Companies

BMC Software Inc.

STANDARD
&POOR'S

S&P Recommendation	HOLD ★★★☆☆	Price $32.49 (as of Nov 23, 2007)	12-Mo. Target Price $39.00	Investment Style Large-Cap Blend

GICS Sector Information Technology
Sub-Industry Systems Software

Summary This Houston-based company provides systems management software that improves the availability, performance and recovery of applications and data.

Key Stock Statistics (Source S&P, Vickers, company reports)

52-Wk Range	$36.92– 24.77	S&P Oper. EPS 2008E	1.59	Market Capitalization(B)	$6.362	Beta	1.65
Trailing 12-Month EPS	$1.28	S&P Oper. EPS 2009E	1.79	Yield (%)	Nil	S&P 3-Yr. Proj. EPS CAGR(%)	14.00
Trailing 12-Month P/E	25.4	P/E on S&P Oper. EPS 2008E	20.4	Dividend Rate/Share	Nil	S&P Credit Rating	NA
$10K Invested 5 Yrs Ago	$18,513	Common Shares Outstg. (M)	195.8	Institutional Ownership (%)	97		

Price Performance

30-Week Mov. Avg. · · · 10-Week Mov. Avg. - - **GAAP Earnings vs. Previous Year** Volume Above Avg. STARS
12-Mo. Target Price — Relative Strength — ▲ Up ▼ Down ► No Change Below Avg.

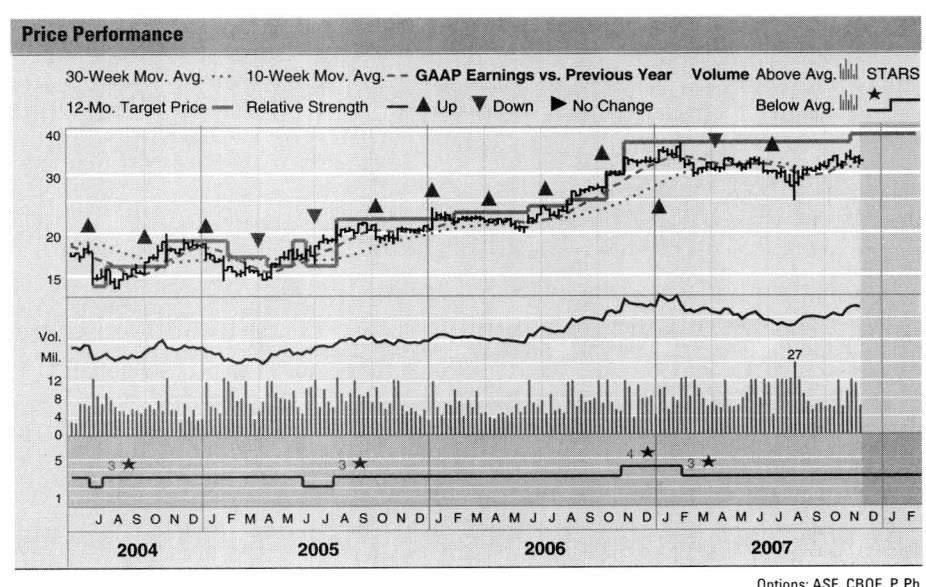

Options: ASE, CBOE, P, Ph

Analysis prepared by **Jim Yin** on November 14, 2007, when the stock traded at **$ 33.30.**

Highlights

➤ We expect revenues to increase 6.9% in FY 08 (Mar.), after a 5.5% advance in FY 07, as high single-digit growth in the Enterprise Service Management business segment is partly offset by flat growth in the Mainframe Service Management segment. We project that total bookings will increase about 10% in FY 08 with ratable revenue becoming 52% of total revenue, compared to 49% in FY 07.

➤ We forecast that FY 08 gross margins will widen to 78%, from 76% in FY 07, reflecting an expected improvement in maintenance revenue margins. We believe operating margins will widen to 27% in FY 08, from 22% in FY 07, due to recent cost-cutting efforts, which include headcount reductions and property sales.

➤ Our estimate of FY 08 operating EPS is $1.59, up from $1.29 in FY 07. We expect EPS to benefit from interest income earned on the $1.48 billion in cash and investments on BMC's balance sheet. We look for continued aggressive share repurchases in future periods. The company has about $1.0 billion remaining under its existing share repurchase program.

Investment Rationale/Risk

➤ We believe BMC is executing well demonstrated by revenue growth in the mid- to high single-digit range, slightly above the industry average. The company has widened its operating margins following a recent work force reduction. We expect BMC to utilize cash flows from operations to repurchase shares and seek growth via acquisitions, integrating companies that will be complementary to its newer service management business. On the negative side, we forecast flat growth for BMC's mainframe business. Overall, we view the shares as fairly valued at current levels.

➤ Risks to our recommendation and target price include increased competition from large platform vendors, a significant decline in corporate spending on information technology, and greater pricing pressures.

➤ We arrive at our 12-month target price of $39 by applying a 1.75X P/E-to-growth ratio to our FY 08 EPS estimate of $1.59, in line with the peer average. We believe that long-term earnings growth of 14% is achievable by the company.

Qualitative Risk Assessment

LOW	MEDIUM	HIGH

Our risk assessment for BMC Software reflects our concern that the company's legacy mainframe business remains vulnerable to competition from hardware vendors, notably IBM. Despite this competitive pressure, we see the company's newer product initiatives gaining traction in the marketplace and look for strong earnings gains supported by cost-cutting measures.

Quantitative Evaluations

S&P Quality Ranking   C

D	C	B-	B	B+	A-	A	A+

Relative Strength Rank   **STRONG**

83

LOWEST = 1   HIGHEST = 99

Revenue/Earnings Data

Revenue (Million $)

	1Q	2Q	3Q	4Q	Year
2008	385.0	420.7	--	--	--
2007	361.4	386.7	412.9	419.4	1,580
2006	348.3	361.8	380.3	407.9	1,498
2005	326.0	355.1	386.8	395.1	1,463
2004	309.9	333.8	374.8	400.2	1,419
2003	305.2	291.2	349.6	380.7	1,327

Earnings Per Share ($)

2008	0.28	E0.40	E0.45	E0.44	E1.59
2007	0.15	0.28	0.30	0.30	1.03
2006	-0.19	0.19	0.22	0.31	0.47
2005	0.05	0.06	0.16	0.07	0.34
2004	-0.03	-0.06	-0.20	0.16	-0.12
2003	0.02	0.04	0.05	0.09	0.20

Fiscal year ended Mar. 31. Next earnings report expected: Mid February. EPS Estimates based on S&P Operating Earnings; historical GAAP earnings are as reported.

Dividend Data

No cash dividends have been paid.

BMC Software Inc.

STANDARD &POOR'S

Business Summary November 14, 2007

CORPORATE OVERVIEW. BMC Software is a leading independent software vendor. The company's software, called Business Service Management (BSM), helps customers increase productivity and reduce costs by automating IT processes and improving how IT responds to business decisions and challenges. BMC focuses on eight areas of BSM: Incident and Problem Management, Asset Management and Discovery, Identity Management, Service Impact and Event Management, Service Level Management, Capacity Management and Provisioning, Infrastructure and Application Management and Change and Configuration Management. These solutions are supported by a family of enabling technologies called BMC Atrium that provide a shared view of how IT supports business priorities.

BMC sells its software directly through its sales force and indirectly through resellers, distributors and systems integrators. The company also provides maintenance and support, which give customers the right to receive product upgrades. Product license and maintenance revenues accounted for 94% of total revenues in FY 06 and FY 07. BMC also provides professional services, which include implementation, integration and education services and contributed 6% of total revenues in FY 06 and FY 07.

In FY 07, BMC reorganized its software business into two segments. The Enterprise Service Management (ESM) business segment targets non-mainframe computing and addresses broad categories of IT management issues including Application Management, Database Management, Security Management, and Transaction Management. ESM license revenue accounted for 58%, 54%, and 53% of total license revenue for FY 07, FY 06, and FY 05, respectively.

The Mainframe Service Management (MSM) segment includes automated tools that enhance the performance and availability of database management systems on mainframe platforms. This segment includes BMC's mainframe performance monitoring and management product line, MAINVIEW. It also includes the management and recovery of IBM's DB2 and IMS databases. MSM license revenue accounted for 42%, 46%, and 47% of total license revenue for FY 07, FY 06, and FY 05, respectively.

Company Financials Fiscal Year Ended Mar. 31

Per Share Data ($)	2007	2006	2005	2004	2003	2002	2001	2000	1999	1998
Tangible Book Value	1.66	2.31	2.60	3.11	3.70	5.49	5.67	5.67	5.64	3.68
Cash Flow	1.79	1.40	1.33	1.03	1.25	0.78	1.42	1.89	1.77	1.03
Earnings	1.03	0.47	0.34	-0.12	0.20	-0.75	0.17	0.96	1.47	0.76
S&P Core Earnings	1.00	0.29	-0.03	-0.56	-0.01	-0.94	-0.19	NA	NA	NA
Dividends	Nil	Nil	Nil	Nil	Nil	Nil	Nil	Nil	Nil	Nil
Payout Ratio	Nil	Nil	Nil	Nil	Nil	Nil	Nil	Nil	Nil	Nil
Calendar Year	2006	2005	2004	2003	2002	2001	2000	1999	1998	1997
Prices:High	33.67	21.68	21.87	19.84	23.00	33.00	86.63	84.06	60.25	35.63
Prices:Low	19.90	14.44	13.70	13.18	10.85	11.50	13.00	30.00	29.25	19.81
P/E Ratio:High	33	41	64	NM	NM	NM	NM	88	41	47
P/E Ratio:Low	19	27	40	NM	NM	NM	NM	31	20	26

Income Statement Analysis (Million $)										
Revenue	1,580	1,498	1,463	1,419	1,327	1,289	1,504	1,719	1,304	731
Operating Income	413	334	264	162	349	400	336	656	548	357
Depreciation	161	205	222	259	248	376	315	236	76.8	58.0
Interest Expense	1.50	1.70	2.00	1.10	Nil	0.40	11.3	23.4	Nil	Nil
Pretax Income	301	204	98.2	-29.4	69.3	-231	60.4	311	478	257
Effective Tax Rate	28.2%	50.0%	23.3%	NM	30.7%	NM	29.8%	22.1%	23.8%	35.4%
Net Income	216	102	75.3	-26.8	48.0	-184	42.4	243	364	166
S&P Core Earnings	211	63.9	-5.94	-128	-3.42	-232	-46.6	NA	NA	NA

Balance Sheet & Other Financial Data (Million $)										
Cash	1,296	1,063	929	909	1,015	546	146	152	1,205	72.1
Current Assets	1,790	1,506	1,440	1,425	1,098	997	903	896	873	374
Total Assets	3,260	3,211	3,298	3,045	2,846	2,676	3,034	2,962	2,283	1,248
Current Liabilities	1,233	1,202	1,085	987	839	681	829	884	651	336
Long Term Debt	Nil	Nil	Nil	Nil	Nil	Nil	Nil	Nil	Nil	Nil
Common Equity	1,049	1,099	1,262	1,215	1,383	1,507	1,815	1,781	1,334	759
Total Capital	1,049	1,099	1,262	1,215	1,383	1,507	1,815	1,781	1,334	803
Capital Expenditures	33.7	24.1	57.7	50.4	23.6	64.3	183	148	116	67.0
Cash Flow	377	307	297	233	296	192	357	478	441	224
Current Ratio	1.5	1.3	1.3	1.4	1.3	1.5	1.1	1.0	1.3	1.1
% Long Term Debt of Capitalization	Nil	Nil	Nil	Nil	Nil	Nil	Nil	Nil	Nil	Nil
% Net Income of Revenue	13.7	6.8	5.1	NM	3.6	NM	2.8	14.1	27.9	22.7
% Return on Assets	6.7	3.1	2.4	NM	1.7	NM	1.4	9.2	20.6	15.9
% Return on Equity	20.1	8.6	6.1	NM	3.3	NM	2.4	15.6	34.8	25.4

Data as orig reptd.; bef. results of disc opers/spec. items. Per share data adj. for stk. divs.; EPS diluted. E-Estimated. NA-Not Available. NM-Not Meaningful. NR-Not Ranked. UR-Under Review.

Office: 2101 Citywest Boulevard, Houston, TX 77042-2827.
Telephone: 713-918-8800.
Email: investor@bmc.com
Website: http://www.bmc.com

Chrmn: B.G. Cupp
Pres & CEO: R.E. Beauchamp
Investor Contact: S.B. Solcher (800-793-4262)
SVP, CFO & Treas: S.B. Solcher

SVP, Secy & General Counsel: D.M. Clolery
Board Members: J. E. Barfield, J. W. Barter, R. E. Beauchamp, B. G. Cupp, M. K. Gafner, L. W. Gray, P. T. Jenkins, K. A. O'Neill, G. F. Raymond, T. C. Tinsley

Founded: 1980
Domicile: Delaware
Employees: 6,000

The McGraw-Hill Companies

Boeing Co (The)

S&P Recommendation **BUY** ★★★★☆	Price $89.54 (as of Nov 23, 2007)	12-Mo. Target Price $118.00	Investment Style Large-Cap Growth

GICS Sector Industrials
Sub-Industry Aerospace & Defense

Summary This company is the world's second largest commercial jet and military weapons manufacturer.

Key Stock Statistics (Source S&P, Vickers, company reports)

52-Wk Range	$107.83–84.60	S&P Oper. EPS 2007**E**	5.11	Market Capitalization(B)	$69.399	Beta	1.20
Trailing 12-Month EPS	$5.20	S&P Oper. EPS 2008**E**	5.76	Yield (%)	1.56	S&P 3-Yr. Proj. EPS CAGR(%)	18.00
Trailing 12-Month P/E	17.2	P/E on S&P Oper. EPS 2007**E**	17.5	Dividend Rate/Share	$1.40	S&P Credit Rating	A+
$10K Invested 5 Yrs Ago	$28,613	Common Shares Outstg. (M)	775.1	Institutional Ownership (%)	71		

Price Performance

30-Week Mov. Avg. · · · 10-Week Mov. Avg. – – GAAP Earnings vs. Previous Year   Volume Above Avg. STARS
12-Mo. Target Price — Relative Strength — ▲ Up ▼ Down ► No Change   Below Avg.

Options: ASE, CBOE, P, Ph

Analysis prepared by **Richard Tortoriello** on October 30, 2007, when the stock traded at **$ 98.04**.

Qualitative Risk Assessment

LOW	MEDIUM	HIGH

Our risk assessment reflects BA's participation in highly cyclical, very competitive, and capital intensive businesses. This is offset by what we see as its strong cash position and strong free cash flow generation, along with a healthy and rising backlog of business.

Quantitative Evaluations

S&P Quality Ranking B+

D	C	B-	B	B+	A-	A	A+

Relative Strength Rank MODERATE

44

LOWEST = 1   HIGHEST = 99

Revenue/Earnings Data

Revenue (Million $)

	1Q	2Q	3Q	4Q	Year
2007	15,365	17,028	16,517	--	--
2006	14,264	14,986	14,739	17,541	61,530
2005	12,987	15,025	12,629	14,204	54,845
2004	12,903	13,088	13,152	13,314	52,457
2003	12,258	12,772	12,241	13,214	50,485
2002	13,821	13,857	12,690	13,701	54,069

Earnings Per Share ($)

	1Q	2Q	3Q	4Q	Year
2007	1.12	1.35	1.43	E1.29	E5.11
2006	0.88	-0.21	0.89	1.28	2.84
2005	0.64	0.70	1.26	0.59	3.19
2004	0.76	0.72	0.54	0.23	2.24
2003	-0.60	-0.24	0.32	1.40	0.89
2002	0.72	0.96	0.46	0.73	2.87

Fiscal year ended Dec. 31. Next earnings report expected: Late January. EPS Estimates based on S&P Operating Earnings; historical GAAP earnings are as reported.

Highlights

➤ We project a 9% sales increase in both 2007 and 2008, as BA expands aircraft production to meet customer demand. We believe BA will benefit both from increased aircraft production and easier year-to-year comparisons in its commercial airplanes segment in 2008, and will see a return to growth in integrated defense systems. We are encouraged by BA's continued backlog strength, as backlog as of September 2007 rose 46% for commercial aircraft and integrated defense systems backlog remained flat, resulting in a record total backlog of $295 billion, or 4.5X our 2007 sales forecast.

➤ We see operating margins rising to 8.6% in 2007 and 9.1% in 2008, from 4.9% in 2006, with an expected improvement in both commercial airplanes and integrated defense systems, based on our outlook for volume increases and greater efficiencies, as well as the absence of settlement charges.

➤ We estimate 2007 EPS of $5.11 and free cash flow (cash from operating activities less capital expenditures) of near $10.00 per share. We project EPS of $5.76 in 2008, with lower free cash flow per share than in 2007, due to delays in the 787.

Investment Rationale/Risk

➤ With a six-year commercial aircraft backlog and our view of strong order flow so far in 2007, we see BA posting healthy earnings and free cash flow growth for the next two to three years. In addition, we foresee the potential for long-term profit margin improvement. In October 2007, BA said that the first delivery of the 787 would be delayed from May 2008 to late November or December 2008. Although we do not believe a six-month delay will significantly affect profitability, we see increased risk in the possibility of further delays.

➤ Risks to our recommendation and target price include the potential for government cuts in defense programs, slowing global economic growth, and aircraft development and production problems.

➤ Our 12-month target price of $118 is based on our discounted cash flow (DCF) analysis. Our DCF model assumes a weighted average cost of capital of 8.8%, and 7% average growth in free cash flow in years one to 10, slowing to 3% growth thereafter. On a P/E basis, we view the shares as attractive relative to peers, with BA recently selling at about 16X our 2008 EPS estimate, versus a 17X peer average.

Dividend Data (Dates: mm/dd Payment Date: mm/dd/yy)

Amount ($)	Date Decl.	Ex-Div. Date	Stk. of Record	Payment Date
0.350	12/11	02/07	02/09	03/02/07
0.350	04/30	05/09	05/11	06/01/07
0.350	06/25	08/08	08/10	09/07/07
0.350	10/29	11/07	11/09	12/07/07

Dividends have been paid since 1942. Source: Company reports.

Please read the Required Disclosures and Analyst Certification on the last page of this report.

Boeing Co (The)

STANDARD
&POOR'S

Business Summary October 30, 2007

CORPORATE OVERVIEW. This $62 billion in revenues global aerospace and defense giant conducts business through three operating segments. Boeing Commercial Aircraft (BCA; 46% of revenues and 45% of operating profits in 2006) and EADS's 80%-owned Airbus division are the world's only makers of 100-plus seat passenger jets. Integrated Defense Systems (IDS; 52%, 50%) is the world's second largest military contractor behind Lockheed Martin Corp. Boeing Capital Corp. (2%, 5%) primarily finances commercial aircraft for airlines. In 2006, Boeing discontinued its money-losing Connexion by Boeing unit, which provided in-flight Internet services (not included in figures above).

BCA's commercial jet aircraft family includes the 737 Next-Generation narrow body model and the 747, 767, 777, and 787 wide body models. The 787 (Dreamliner) is Boeing's newest model, and is due for first delivery in May 2008. BCA also offers aviation support, aircraft modifications, spare parts, training, maintenance documents, and technical advice. In September 2006, BCA acquired Aviall, an independent provider of new aviation parts and services. A new, larger 747 model is also under development, the 747-8 Intercontinental, as is a freighter version of the 747-8. Boeing had a commercial aircraft backlog at year-end 2006 of $174 billion.

IDS designs, develops, and supports military aircraft, including fighters, transports, tankers, and helicopters; missiles; space systems; missile defense systems; satellites and satellite launch systems; and communication, information, and battle management systems. IDS's primary customer is the U.S. Department of Defense (84% of sales), but it also sells to NASA, international defense customers, civil markets, and commercial satellite markets. Major programs include the AH-64 Apache and CH-47 Chinook helicopters, the C-17 Globemaster military transport, F/A-18E/F Super Hornet fighter jets, as well as commercial and military satellites.

MARKET PROFILE. Based on total unit orders of 100-plus seat jetliners in 2006, BCA and Airbus control about 56% and 44%, respectively, of the global commercial jetliner market. Demand for jetliners is driven primarily by growth in the global 100-plus seat commercial aircraft fleet. Independent research firm Avitas, Inc. projects that the global fleet of 100-plus seat jetliners will grow at a 4.3% compound annual rate over the next 20 years, due to its projection of 5.9% compound annual growth in passenger traffic over the same period. We believe that given the economic development of many former third-world countries in Asia, Eastern Europe, and the Middle East, fleet growth should continue at an above-average rate for the foreseeable future.

Company Financials Fiscal Year Ended Dec. 31

Per Share Data ($)	2006	2005	2004	2003	2002	2001	2000	1999	1998	1997
Tangible Book Value	NM	10.33	10.08	6.17	4.53	5.23	6.63	10.14	10.25	10.56
Cash Flow	4.76	5.08	4.00	2.68	2.46	5.52	4.14	4.27	2.84	1.32
Earnings	2.84	3.19	2.24	0.89	2.87	3.41	2.44	2.49	1.15	-0.18
S&P Core Earnings	3.90	3.05	1.99	1.33	0.26	-0.06	NA	NA	NA	NA
Dividends	1.20	1.00	0.77	0.68	0.68	0.68	0.56	0.56	0.56	0.56
Payout Ratio	42%	31%	34%	76%	24%	20%	23%	22%	49%	NM
Prices:High	92.05	72.40	55.48	43.37	51.07	69.85	70.94	48.50	56.25	60.50
Prices:Low	65.90	49.52	38.04	24.73	28.53	27.60	32.00	32.56	29.00	43.00
P/E Ratio:High	32	23	25	49	18	20	29	19	49	NM
P/E Ratio:Low	23	16	17	28	10	8	13	13	25	NM

Income Statement Analysis (Million $)										
Revenue	61,530	54,845	52,457	50,485	54,069	58,198	51,321	57,993	56,154	45,800
Operating Income	5,176	3,707	3,405	3,198	5,447	6,467	4,996	4,724	3,189	2,503
Depreciation	1,545	1,503	1,509	1,450	1,497	1,750	1,479	1,645	1,622	1,458
Interest Expense	593	653	685	800	730	650	445	431	453	513
Pretax Income	1,218	2,819	1,960	550	1,353	3,565	2,999	3,324	1,397	-341
Effective Tax Rate	NM	9.12%	7.14%	NM	63.6%	20.7%	29.0%	30.5%	19.8%	NM
Net Income	2,206	2,562	1,820	718	492	2,827	2,128	2,309	1,120	-178
S&P Core Earnings	3,042	2,450	1,616	1,074	203	284	NA	NA	NA	NA

Balance Sheet & Other Financial Data (Million $)										
Cash	6,118	5,412	3,204	4,633	2,333	633	1,010	3,354	2,462	4,420
Current Assets	22,983	21,968	15,100	17,258	16,855	16,206	15,864	15,712	16,375	19,263
Total Assets	51,794	60,058	53,963	53,035	52,342	48,343	42,028	36,147	36,672	38,024
Current Liabilities	29,701	28,188	20,835	18,448	19,810	20,486	18,289	13,656	13,422	14,152
Long Term Debt	8,157	9,538	10,879	13,299	12,589	10,866	7,567	5,980	6,103	6,123
Common Equity	4,739	11,059	11,286	8,139	7,696	10,825	11,020	11,462	12,316	12,953
Total Capital	12,896	22,664	23,255	21,438	20,285	21,868	18,587	17,614	18,419	19,076
Capital Expenditures	1,681	1,547	978	741	1,001	1,068	932	1,236	1,584	1,391
Cash Flow	3,751	4,065	3,329	2,168	1,989	4,577	3,607	3,954	2,742	1,280
Current Ratio	0.8	0.8	0.7	0.9	0.9	0.8	0.9	1.2	1.2	1.4
% Long Term Debt of Capitalization	63.3	42.1	46.8	62.0	62.1	49.7	40.7	34.0	33.1	47.2
% Net Income of Revenue	3.6	4.7	3.5	1.4	0.9	4.9	4.1	4.0	2.0	NM
% Return on Assets	3.9	4.4	3.4	1.4	1.0	6.2	5.4	6.3	3.0	NM
% Return on Equity	27.9	22.9	18.7	9.1	5.3	25.9	18.9	19.4	8.9	NM

Data as orig reptd.; bef. results of disc opers/spec. items. Per share data adj. for stk. divs.; EPS diluted. E-Estimated. NA-Not Available. NM-Not Meaningful. NR-Not Ranked. UR-Under Review.

Office: 100 N. Riverside, Chicago, IL 60606.
Telephone: 312-544-2000 .
Website: http://www.boeing.com
Chrmn, Pres & CEO: W.J. McNerney, Jr.

EVP & CFO: J.A. Bell
SVP & General Counsel: D.G. Bain
Investor Contact: P. Kinscherff (312-544-2140)

Board Members: J. H. Biggs, J. E. Bryson, A. D. Collins Jr., L. Z. Cook, W. M. Daley, K. M. Duberstein, J. F. McDonnell, W. J. McNerney, Jr., R. L. Ridgway, M. S. Zafirovski

Founded: 1934
Domicile: Delaware
Employees: 154,000

Boston Properties Inc

STANDARD &POOR'S

S&P Recommendation	HOLD ★★★☆☆	Price	12-Mo. Target Price	Investment Style
		$93.25 (as of Nov 23, 2007)	$106.00	Large-Cap Blend

GICS Sector Financials
Sub-Industry Office REITS

Summary This real estate investment trust primarily owns office buildings in the Boston, Washington, DC, New York City, San Francisco and Princeton markets.

Key Stock Statistics (Source S&P, Vickers, company reports)

52-Wk Range	$133.02– 89.46	S&P Oper. EPS 2007**E**	2.65	Market Capitalization(B)	$11.100	Beta	0.57
Trailing 12-Month EPS	$10.56	S&P Oper. EPS 2008**E**	2.60	Yield (%)	2.92	S&P 3-Yr. Proj. EPS CAGR(%)	-29.00
Trailing 12-Month P/E	8.8	P/E on S&P Oper. EPS 2007**E**	35.2	Dividend Rate/Share	$2.72	S&P Credit Rating	A-
$10K Invested 5 Yrs Ago	$33,723	Common Shares Outstg. (M)	119.0	Institutional Ownership (%)	NM		

Price Performance

- 30-Week Mov. Avg. ···· 10-Week Mov. Avg. – – GAAP Earnings vs. Previous Year   Volume Above Avg. |lll| STARS
- 12-Mo. Target Price — Relative Strength   ▲ Up   ▼ Down   ► No Change   Below Avg. |lll| ★

Options: ASE, CBOE, P

Analysis prepared by **Royal F. Shepard, CFA** on October 29, 2007, when the stock traded at **$ 107.04**.

Highlights

➤ We think leasing activity will remain positive in all BXP's core markets during 2008. Boston and San Francisco portfolios are now mirroring strong trends previously seen in the New York and Washington, DC, regions. Operating at close to full capacity, however, we think it will take time for higher rents to work their way through BXP's portfolio. In 2008, only 5% of rentable space is subject to lease expiration.

➤ Investments in new development may pick up steam in 2008, as we expect groundbreaking on new towers in Boston and New York City. As of September 30, 2007, BXP's total pipeline of construction projects stood at $2.1 billion, including $910 million budgeted for office space on Manhattan's West Side. A meaningful contribution to earnings, though, is not likely until at least 2009. Our 2008 estimate of FFO is $4.70, up from $4.60 in 2007.

➤ BXP pays an annual base dividend of $2.72 per share. In addition, the trust expects to declare a year-end special dividend of over $5 a share, to distribute gains on 2007 asset sales.

Investment Rationale/Risk

➤ In early 2007, BXP took advantage of strong market conditions to sell non-strategic assets. Going forward, we view positively its strategy of re-investing capital in new development properties located in supply-constrained markets. Long-term leases and limited opportunities to raise rents in place are likely to restrain FFO growth in 2008, in our opinion. However, we believe new properties will be delivered to market as rents are still near record levels in 2009. In addition, we think a special dividend of $5 to $6 a share will add to total return over the next 12 months.

➤ Risks to our recommendation and target price include national employment growth lagging our expectations, and less than anticipated regional economic strength in BXP's core markets.

➤ Our 12-month target price of $106 is based on applying a multiple of 23X to our 2008 FFO estimate, comparable to REITs serving supply-constrained markets. Our dividend discount model, which assumes a $5.50 special dividend, a 9% discount rate, and a terminal growth rate of 4%, leads to intrinsic value of $102.

Qualitative Risk Assessment

LOW	MEDIUM	HIGH

Our risk assessment reflects what we see as BXP's large and diverse asset portfolio, relatively unleveraged balance sheet, consistent cash distribution, and low stock volatility as measured by its beta.

Quantitative Evaluations

S&P Quality Ranking A-

D	C	B-	B	B+	A-	A	A+

Relative Strength Rank MODERATE

37

LOWEST = 1   HIGHEST = 99

Revenue/Earnings Data

Revenue (Million $)

	1Q	2Q	3Q	4Q	Year
2007	363.7	392.4	371.5	--	--
2006	356.1	370.4	372.5	378.7	1,478
2005	356.2	360.6	361.8	366.3	1,438
2004	333.3	344.9	359.7	362.6	1,400
2003	319.7	323.4	331.2	336.2	1,310
2002	279.6	295.6	313.7	346.0	1,235

Earnings Per Share ($)

2007	5.64	0.74	1.99	E0.67	E2.65
2006	0.59	5.23	0.91	0.60	7.46
2005	0.55	1.36	0.50	1.00	3.46
2004	0.61	0.61	0.58	0.55	2.35
2003	1.13	0.64	0.57	0.61	2.94
2002	0.53	0.59	0.74	2.64	4.40

Fiscal year ended Dec. 31. Next earnings report expected: Late January. EPS Estimates based on S&P Operating Earnings; historical GAAP earnings are as reported.

Dividend Data (Dates: mm/dd Payment Date: mm/dd/yy)

Amount ($)	Date Decl.	Ex-Div. Date	Stk. of Record	Payment Date
5.4 Ext.	12/18	12/27	12/29	01/30/07
0.680	03/13	03/28	03/30	04/30/07
0.680	06/18	06/27	06/29	07/31/07
0.680	09/17	09/26	09/28	10/31/07

Dividends have been paid since 1997. Source: Company reports.

Boston Properties Inc

Business Summary October 29, 2007

CORPORATE OVERVIEW. Boston Properties, founded in 1970, is a real estate investment trust (REIT) that develops, acquires, manages, operates, and is one of the largest U.S. owners of, Class A office properties. BXP conducts substantially all of its business through its limited partnership, of which it is the sole general partner, and holds an 84% economic interest.

At December 31, 2006, the property portfolio consisted of 131 properties, totaling 33.4 million net rentable sq. ft. and structured parking facilities for vehicles containing approximately 10.0 million sq. ft. The properties included 127 office buildings, two hotels, and two retail properties. In addition, BXP had five properties under construction totaling 1.4 million sq. ft.

MARKET PROFILE The market for office leases is inherently cyclical. Local economic conditions, particularly the employment level, play an important role in determining competitive dynamics. Standard & Poor's estimates that nonfarm payrolls will increase 92,000 per month, on average, in 2008, compared to about 150,000 per month growth in 2007.

The U.S. office market tends to track the overall economy on a lagged basis. At the end of September 2007, we believe the national vacancy rate was

about 12.5%, reflecting an improvement since cyclical lows in 2002-2003. In our opinion, BXP's Washington, DC, and midtown Manhattan markets are among the nation's strongest. The metropolitan Boston, San Francisco and Princeton, NJ, markets have trailed the current recovery. In total, on September 30, 2007, BXP had an office vacancy rate of 5.1%, much better than the national averages. Leases will expire on only about 5.0% of existing office space in 2008, limiting opportunities for taking advantage of more favorable market rents. Moreover, only 252,000 square feet roll in the particularly strong midtown Manhattan market.

Competition for leasing real estate is high. In addition, we believe that competition for the acquisition of new properties is intensifying from other REITs, private real estate funds, financial institutions, insurance companies and others. As a result, we think BXP could have difficulty finding new assets at attractive prices.

Company Financials Fiscal Year Ended Dec. 31

Per Share Data ($)	2006	2005	2004	2003	2002	2001	2000	1999	1998	1997
Tangible Book Value	27.45	25.92	26.61	22.51	20.79	19.34	19.02	15.57	14.93	4.52
Earnings	7.46	3.46	2.35	2.94	4.40	2.26	2.01	1.71	1.61	0.70
S&P Core Earnings	7.46	3.46	2.34	2.88	4.37	2.20	NA	NA	NA	NA
Dividends	2.72	5.19	2.58	2.50	2.41	2.27	1.96	1.73	1.64	0.85
Payout Ratio	36%	150%	110%	85%	55%	100%	96%	101%	101%	121%
Prices:High	118.22	76.67	64.90	48.47	41.55	43.88	44.88	37.50	36.06	35.25
Prices:Low	72.98	56.66	42.99	34.80	32.95	34.00	29.00	27.25	23.44	25.00
P/E Ratio:High	16	22	28	16	9	19	22	22	22	NM
P/E Ratio:Low	10	16	18	12	7	15	14	16	14	NM

Income Statement Analysis (Million $)	2006	2005	2004	2003	2002	2001	2000	1999	1998	1997
Rental Income	1,344	1,339	1,293	1,219	1,174	1,008	859	765	488	140
Mortgage Income	Nil	Nil	Nil	Nil	Nil	Nil	Nil	Nil	Nil	Nil
Total Income	1,502	1,438	1,400	1,310	1,235	1,033	879	787	514	146
General Expenses	557	545	528	498	464	351	300	279	173	46.8
Interest Expense	298	308	306	299	272	223	217	205	125	38.3
Provision for Losses	Nil	Nil	Nil	Nil	Nil	Nil	Nil	Nil	Nil	Nil
Depreciation	277	267	252	210	186	150	133	120	75.4	21.7
Net Income	874	393	255	290	420	215	153	120	98.6	27.2
S&P Core Earnings	874	393	254	284	413	203	NA	NA	NA	NA

Balance Sheet & Other Financial Data (Million $)	2006	2005	2004	2003	2002	2001	2000	1999	1998	1997
Cash	752	377	345	133	199	201	378	88.7	78.0	34.9
Total Assets	9,695	8,902	9,063	8,551	8,427	7,254	6,226	5,435	5,235	1,673
Real Estate Investment	9,552	9,151	9,291	8,983	8,671	7,458	6,113	5,612	4,917	1,797
Loss Reserve	Nil	Nil	Nil	Nil	Nil	Nil	Nil	Nil	Nil	Nil
Net Investment	8,160	7,886	8,148	7,981	7,848	6,738	5,526	5,142	4,560	1,502
Short Term Debt	Nil	Nil	Nil	Nil	Nil	282	194	680	26.9	9.00
Capitalization:Debt	4,559	4,679	4,733	5,005	3,336	4,033	3,415	2,642	3,062	1,332
Capitalization:Equity	3,223	2,917	2,936	2,400	2,160	1,754	1,648	1,058	948	175
Capitalization:Total	8,406	8,335	8,455	8,235	6,340	6,732	6,040	4,582	5,089	1,498
% Earnings & Depreciation/Assets	12.3	7.3	5.8	5.9	7.7	5.4	4.9	4.5	5.0	NM
Price Times Book Value:High	4.3	3.0	2.4	2.1	2.0	2.3	2.4	2.4	2.4	7.8
Price Times Book Value:Low	2.7	2.2	1.6	1.5	1.6	1.8	1.5	1.8	1.6	5.5

Data as orig reptd.; bef. results of disc opers/spec. items. Per share data adj. for stk. divs.; EPS diluted. E-Estimated. NA-Not Available. NM-Not Meaningful. NR-Not Ranked. UR-Under Review.

Office: 111 Huntington Ave Ste 300, Boston, MA 02199-7627.
Telephone: 617-236-3300.
Email: investor_relations@bostonproperties.com
Website: http://www.bostonproperties.com

Chrmn: M.B. Zuckerman
Pres, CFO & Treas: D.T. Linde
CEO: E.H. Linde
SVP, Secy & General Counsel: F.D. Burt

Trustees: L. S. Bacow, Z. Baird, C. Einiger, E. H. Linde, A. J. Patricof, R. E. Salomon, M. Turchin, D. A. Twardock, M. B. Zuckerman

Founded: 1970
Domicile: Delaware
Employees: 650

Boston Scientific Corp

**STANDARD
&POOR'S**

S&P Recommendation **SELL** ★ ★ ☆ ☆ ☆	Price $12.51 (as of Nov 23, 2007)	12-Mo. Target Price $12.00	Investment Style Large-Cap Growth

GICS Sector Health Care
Sub-Industry Health Care Equipment

Summary This manufacturer of minimally invasive medical devices acquired device rival Guidant Corp. in April 2006 for $27 billion in cash and stock.

Key Stock Statistics (Source S&P, Vickers, company reports)

52-Wk Range	$18.69– 11.98	S&P Oper. EPS 2007**E**	0.37	Market Capitalization(B)	$18.650	Beta	1.40
Trailing 12-Month EPS	$0.36	S&P Oper. EPS 2008**E**	0.50	Yield (%)	Nil	S&P 3-Yr. Proj. EPS CAGR(%)	4.00
Trailing 12-Month P/E	34.8	P/E on S&P Oper. EPS 2007**E**	33.8	Dividend Rate/Share	Nil	S&P Credit Rating	BB+
$10K Invested 5 Yrs Ago	$6,261	Common Shares Outstg. (M)	1,490.8	Institutional Ownership (%)	72		

Price Performance

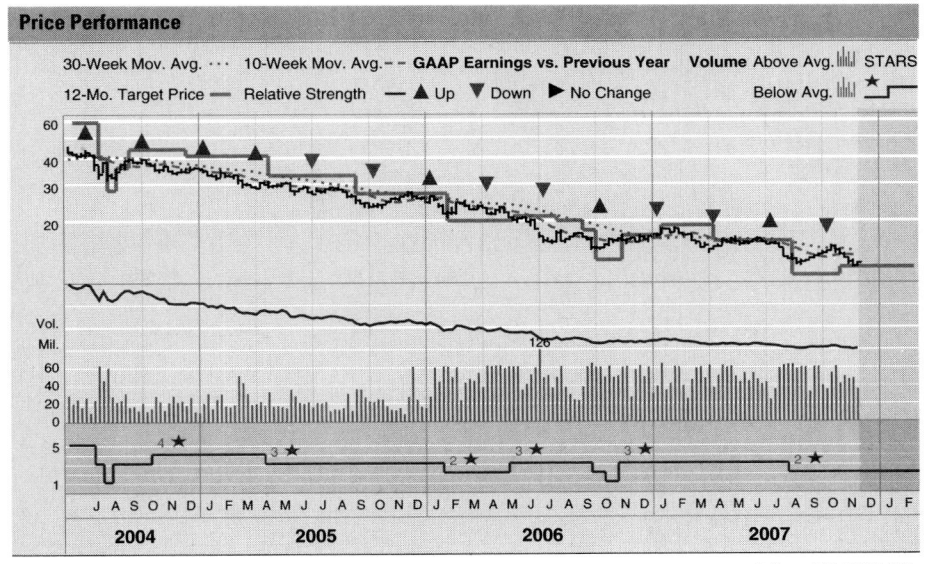

30-Week Mov. Avg. ···· 10-Week Mov. Avg. - - **GAAP Earnings vs. Previous Year** Volume Above Avg. STARS
12-Mo. Target Price — Relative Strength — ▲ Up ▼ Down ▶ No Change Below Avg. ★

Options: ASE, CBOE, P, Ph

Analysis prepared by **Robert M. Gold** on November 02, 2007, when the stock traded at **$ 13.34**.

Highlights

➤ We expect that difficult conditions in the defibrillator and stent markets will persist in 2008. Our 2008 sales forecast of $8.6 billion would represent growth of about 1.2% over our 2007 sales estimate of $8.4 billion. We see cardiac rhythm management revenues of $2.3 billion in 2008 (up from an estimated $2.1 billion in 2007), vascular of $4.1 billion ($4.3 billion), endosurgery of $1.6 billion ($1.5 billion), cardiac surgery of $200 million ($190 million) and neuromodulation of $460 million ($305 million).

➤ We believe the Guidant merger will be dilutive to EPS through at least 2009, and although we think asset sales and restructuring actions will help reduce debt and realign the operating cost structure and decelerate revenue growth, we continue to have concerns about BSX's ability to generate sufficient excess cash flow and believe it may be forced to divest some important product lines in order to raise capital.

➤ We estimate 2008 operating EPS of $0.50, up from a projected $0.37 in 2007 (before restructuring and purchased in-process R&D charges).

Investment Rationale/Risk

➤ We think the purchase of Guidant's cardiac rhythm management businesses can potentially fuel a higher long-term revenue growth rate for BSX. However, we are concerned about the dilution to shareholders, and believe BSX's ability to retire debt incurred in the deal will continue to be negatively affected by weakness in the cardiac stent and defibrillator markets. Amid less robust revenue growth, we think the company will continue to focus on cost reductions and asset sales in order to sustain profit margins and deleverage the balance sheet. Should a recovery in the CRM and stent business not materialize, however, we think BSX could be forced to sell important strategic assets.

➤ Risks to our recommendation and target price include favorable litigation outcomes, less competition in key markets, and successful commercialization of key products in the pipeline.

➤ Our 12-month target price is $12, or 24X our 2008 EPS estimate. Although a premium P/E to the S&P 500, our target is a discount to large-cap device peers, which we think is justified by low visibility on the ICD and cardiac stent businesses, and our concerns about what we see as a highly leveraged balance sheet.

Qualitative Risk Assessment

LOW	MEDIUM	**HIGH**

Our risk assessment reflects that the company operates within intensely competitive areas of the health care industry, and its ability to sustain growth largely depends on its ability to develop and commercialize new products. In addition, a large percentage of customers are reimbursed by the federal Medicare program, and we believe the government is likely to reduce the pace of expenditure growth by lowering reimbursement rates for expensive medical devices such as defibrillators and cardiac stents.

Quantitative Evaluations

S&P Quality Ranking B-

D	C	**B-**	B	B+	A-	A	A+

Relative Strength Rank MODERATE
43
LOWEST = 1 HIGHEST = 99

Revenue/Earnings Data

Revenue (Million $)

	1Q	2Q	3Q	4Q	Year
2007	2,086	2,071	2,048	--	--
2006	1,620	2,110	2,206	2,065	7,821
2005	1,615	1,617	1,511	1,540	6,283
2004	1,082	1,460	1,482	1,600	5,624
2003	807.0	854.0	876.0	939.0	3,476
2002	675.0	708.0	722.0	814.0	2,919

Earnings Per Share ($)

2007	0.08	0.08	-0.18	E0.09	E0.37
2006	0.40	-3.21	0.05	0.19	-2.81
2005	0.42	0.24	-0.33	0.40	0.75
2004	0.23	0.36	0.30	0.35	1.24
2003	0.12	0.14	0.15	0.16	0.56
2002	0.10	0.03	0.20	0.13	0.45

Fiscal year ended Dec. 31. Next earnings report expected: Early February. EPS Estimates based on S&P Operating Earnings; historical GAAP earnings are as reported.

Dividend Data

No cash dividends have been paid.

Boston Scientific Corp

STANDARD &POOR'S

Business Summary November 02, 2007

Boston Scientific develops and markets minimally invasive medical devices that are used in a broad range of interventional medical specialties, including interventional cardiology, cardiac rhythm management, peripheral intervention, electrophysiology, gastroenterology, gynecology, oncology, and urology.

Within the cardiovascular market, the company sells products used to treat coronary vessel disease known as arteriosclerosis. The majority of BSX's cardiovascular products are used in percutaneous transluminal coronary angioplasty (PTCA) and percutaneous transluminal coronary rotational atherectomy. These products include PTCA balloon catheters, rotational atherectomy systems, guide wires, guide catheters, diagnostic catheters, and, more recently, a cutting balloon catheter. Other products include thrombectomy catheters, peripheral vascular stents, embolic protection filters, blood clot filter systems, and electrophysiology products. In July 2007, the company said it was exploring the sale of a business that produces a range of products used to manage fluid and measure pressure during angiography and angioplasty procedures.

In addition, BSX markets balloon-expandable and self-expanding coronary stent systems. Stents are tiny mesh tubes that are used in the treatment of coronary artery disease. They are implanted in patients to prop open arteries and facilitate blood flow to the heart. In 2002, the company launched its Express 2 coronary stent system, featuring both the Express stent and the Maverick balloon dilation catheter. In early 2004, BSX launched Taxus, an Express stent coated with a polymer embedded with the anticancer compound paclitaxel. Clinical studies showed that this stent significantly reduced the rate of instent restenosis, or vessel reclosure, which occurs in about one-third of patients who undergo angioplasty and stenting. In January 2005, BSX launched its next-generation Taxus Liberte paclitaxel-eluting coronary stent in 18 Inter-Continental countries and in Europe.

Company Financials Fiscal Year Ended Dec. 31

Per Share Data ($)	2006	2005	2004	2003	2002	2001	2000	1999	1998	1997
Tangible Book Value	NM	0.67	0.82	0.49	0.12	NM	0.33	NM	NM	0.87
Cash Flow	-1.90	1.12	1.60	0.79	0.64	0.22	0.68	0.67	-0.18	0.31
Earnings	-2.81	0.75	1.24	0.56	0.45	-0.07	0.46	0.45	-0.34	0.20
S&P Core Earnings	-2.75	1.39	1.27	0.50	0.33	-0.10	NA	NA	NA	NA
Dividends	Nil	Nil	Nil	Nil	Nil	Nil	Nil	Nil	Nil	Nil
Payout Ratio	Nil	Nil	Nil	Nil	Nil	Nil	Nil	Nil	Nil	Nil
Prices:High	26.56	35.50	46.10	36.85	22.15	13.95	14.59	23.53	20.42	19.59
Prices:Low	14.43	22.80	31.25	19.10	10.24	6.63	6.09	8.78	10.06	10.25
P/E Ratio:High	NM	47	37	66	49	NM	32	52	NM	112
P/E Ratio:Low	NM	30	25	34	23	NM	13	20	NM	59

Income Statement Analysis (Million $)										
Revenue	7,821	6,283	5,624	3,476	2,919	2,673	2,664	2,842	2,234	1,872
Operating Income	-2,383	2,338	1,989	945	757	614	819	857	-93.8	502
Depreciation	781	314	275	196	161	232	181	178	129	86.7
Interest Expense	435	90.0	64.0	46.0	43.0	59.0	70.0	118	67.6	14.3
Pretax Income	-3,535	891	1,494	643	549	44.0	527	562	-274	259
Effective Tax Rate	NM	29.5%	28.9%	26.6%	32.1%	NM	29.2%	34.0%	NM	38.0%
Net Income	-3,577	628	1,062	472	373	-54.0	373	371	-263	160
S&P Core Earnings	-3,498	1,162	1,082	423	269	-77.0	NA	NA	NA	NA

Balance Sheet & Other Financial Data (Million $)										
Cash	1,688	848	1,640	671	277	180	54.0	64.0	70.3	58.0
Current Assets	4,901	2,631	3,289	1,880	1,208	1,106	992	1,055	1,267	1,064
Total Assets	31,096	8,196	8,170	5,699	4,450	3,974	3,427	3,572	3,893	1,968
Current Liabilities	2,630	1,479	2,605	1,393	923	831	819	1,055	1,620	808
Long Term Debt	8,895	1,864	1,139	1,172	847	973	562	678	1,364	46.3
Common Equity	15,298	4,282	4,025	2,862	2,467	2,015	1,935	1,724	821	986
Total Capital	26,977	6,408	5,423	4,185	3,414	2,988	2,497	2,402	2,185	1,091
Capital Expenditures	341	341	274	188	112	121	76.0	80.0	174	220
Cash Flow	-2,796	942	1,337	668	534	178	554	549	-135	247
Current Ratio	1.9	1.8	1.3	1.3	1.3	1.3	1.2	1.0	0.8	1.3
% Long Term Debt of Capitalization	33.0	29.1	21.0	28.0	24.8	32.6	22.5	28.2	62.4	4.2
% Net Income of Revenue	NM	10.0	18.9	13.6	12.8	NM	14.0	13.1	9.6	8.6
% Return on Assets	NM	7.7	15.3	9.3	8.9	NM	10.7	9.9	NM	9.2
% Return on Equity	NM	15.1	30.8	17.7	16.6	NM	20.4	29.2	NM	16.9

Data as orig reptd.; bef. results of disc opers/spec. items. Per share data adj. for stk. divs.; EPS diluted. E-Estimated. NA-Not Available. NM-Not Meaningful. NR-Not Ranked. UR-Under Review.

Office: One Boston Scientific Place, Natick, MA 01760-1537.
Telephone: 508-650-8000.
Email: investor_relations@bsci.com
Website: http://www.bostonscientific.com

Chrmn: P.M. Nicholas
Pres & CEO: J.R. Tobin
COO: P.A. LaViolette
EVP & CFO: S. Leno

EVP & CTO: F.A. Colen
Board Members: J. E. Abele, U. M. Burns, N. DeParle, J. L. Fleishman, M. Fox, R. J. Groves, K. M. Johnson, E. Mario, P. M. Nicholas, N. J. Nicholas, Jr., J. E. Pepper, U. E. Reinhardt, W. B. Rudman, J. R. Tobin

Founded: 1979
Domicile: Delaware
Employees: 28,600

Bristol-Myers Squibb Co

| S&P Recommendation **STRONG BUY** ★ ★ ★ ★ ★ | Price $28.08 (as of Nov 23, 2007) | 12-Mo. Target Price $38.00 | Investment Style Large-Cap Value |

GICS Sector Health Care
Sub-Industry Pharmaceuticals

Summary This leading global drugmaker is strong in both prescription and nonprescription products.

Key Stock Statistics (Source S&P, Vickers, company reports)

52-Wk Range	$32.35– 24.41	S&P Oper. EPS 2007**E** 1.45	Market Capitalization(B) $55.557	Beta	1.31
Trailing 12-Month EPS	$1.07	S&P Oper. EPS 2008**E** 1.70	Yield (%) 3.99	S&P 3-Yr. Proj. EPS CAGR(%)	14.00
Trailing 12-Month P/E	26.2	P/E on S&P Oper. EPS 2007**E** 19.4	Dividend Rate/Share $1.12	S&P Credit Rating	A+
$10K Invested 5 Yrs Ago	$13,203	Common Shares Outstg. (M) 1,978.5	Institutional Ownership (%) 78		

Price Performance

30-Week Mov. Avg. ··· 10-Week Mov. Avg. – – **GAAP Earnings vs. Previous Year** Volume Above Avg. STARS
12-Mo. Target Price — Relative Strength — ▲ Up ▼ Down ► No Change Below Avg.

Options: ASE, CBOE, P, Ph

Analysis prepared by **Herman B. Saftlas** on October 31, 2007, when the stock traded at **$ 29.99**.

Highlights

➤ We see revenue growth of 8% in 2008, following our forecast for a 10% gain in 2007. The 2008 gain should be led by a projected 18% rise in sales of Plavix blood thinning agent (estimated to account for 25% of total sales in 2007). We also see higher volume in Avapro antihypertensive, Abilify antipsychotic, and Reyataz and Sustiva HIV/AIDS therapies. In addition, contributions from new launches such as Orencia for rheumatoid arthritis and Sprycel for leukemia will likely augment volume. We look for these gains to more than offset lower sales of off-patent products. Sales of nutritional and other healthcare products should post modest gains.

➤ We see gross margins in 2008 expanding to 69%, from an estimated 68.6% in 07. Although R&D spending will probably climb 8%, we expect profitability to benefit from flat SG&A spending and higher other income. The tax rate, however, is expected to rise to 23%, from 20%.

➤ We forecast operating EPS of $1.70 in 08, up from an indicated $1.45 in 07, excluding gains from asset sales, milestone payments, restructuring charges and other specified items.

Investment Rationale/Risk

➤ In our opinion, the recent Plavix patent victory is a major positive for BMY, which markets Plavix for Sanofi in the U.S. We expect BMY to book Plavix sales of $4.7 billion in 2007, up from 2006's $3.2 billion, which was affected by temporary generic erosion. We look for BMY to now focus greater resources on its R&D pipeline, which includes new partnering deals with Pfizer, AstraZeneca and others. We view BMY as a potential takeover candidate. In our view, annual interest costs on a possible $80 billion takeout price (around $40 a share) could be financed via free cash flow, the elimination of cash dividends, and reductions in SG&A and R&D spending.

➤ Risks to our recommendation and target include a failure to attract takeover offers on favorable terms, greater competition in key lines, and possible pipeline setbacks.

➤ Our 12-month target price of $38 reflects our DCF-based valuation of BMY's present business of $32 (assuming a WACC of 7.5% and terminal growth of 1%) plus a $6 takeover premium. The dividend recently yielded 3.7%.

Qualitative Risk Assessment

| LOW | MEDIUM | **HIGH** |

In common with other large capitalization drugmakers, BMY is subject to the threat of generic challenges to its branded drugs, as well as risks associated with new drug development and regulatory approval. We believe BMY is more heavily reliant on the success of its R&D pipeline than many of its peers, given the large number of patent expirations of BMY drugs in recent years.

Quantitative Evaluations

S&P Quality Ranking B+

| D | C | B- | B | **B+** | A- | A | A+ |

Relative Strength Rank MODERATE

64

LOWEST = 1   HIGHEST = 99

Revenue/Earnings Data

Revenue (Million $)

	1Q	2Q	3Q	4Q	Year
2007	4,476	4,928	5,050	--	--
2006	4,676	4,871	4,154	4,213	17,914
2005	4,532	4,889	4,767	5,019	19,207
2004	4,626	4,819	4,778	5,157	19,380
2003	4,728	5,129	5,372	5,665	20,894
2002	4,661	4,127	4,537	4,794	18,119

Earnings Per Share ($)

2007	0.35	0.36	0.43	E0.34	E1.45
2006	0.36	0.34	0.17	-0.07	0.81
2005	0.27	0.50	0.49	0.26	1.52
2004	0.49	0.27	0.38	0.07	1.21
2003	0.41	0.46	0.47	0.26	1.59
2002	0.43	0.25	0.17	0.19	1.05

Fiscal year ended Dec. 31. Next earnings report expected: Late January. EPS Estimates based on S&P Operating Earnings; historical GAAP earnings are as reported.

Dividend Data (Dates: mm/dd Payment Date: mm/dd/yy)

Amount ($)	Date Decl.	Ex-Div. Date	Stk. of Record	Payment Date
0.280	12/05	01/03	01/05	02/01/07
0.280	03/06	04/03	04/06	05/01/07
0.280	06/12	07/03	07/06	08/01/07
0.280	09/11	10/03	10/05	11/01/07

Dividends have been paid since 1900. Source: Company reports.

Bristol-Myers Squibb Co

STANDARD &POOR'S

Business Summary October 31, 2007

CORPORATE OVERVIEW. Bristol-Myers Squibb is a major global drugmaker, offering a wide range of prescription drugs. In recent years, BMY divested non-core beauty care, orthopedic devices and cancer drug distribution businesses.

Prescription drugs accounted for 77% of sales in 2006, nutritionals 13%, and medical devices 10%. Foreign sales accounted for 46% of total sales in 2006. A relatively large portion of BMY's pharmaceutical portfolio is now off patent and subject to generic erosion. These products include: Taxol and Paraplatin, anticancer drugs; Glucophage and Glucovance, diabetes drugs; and Pravachol cholesterol agent.

The company's largest selling drug is Plavix (sales of $3.2 billion in 2006), a platelet aggregation inhibitor for the prevention of stroke, heart attack, and vascular disease. Plavix is produced through a joint venture with French drugmaker Sanofi-Aventis SA. Other cardiovasculars include Pravachol anticholesterol ($1.2 billion); Avapro/Avalide ($1.1 billion), an angiotensin II receptor blocker for hypertension; Coumadin blood thinning agent ($220 million);

and Monopril antihypertensive ($159 million). Principal anticancer drugs are Erbitux ($652 million), Taxol ($563 million), and Sprycel ($25 million).

The company's principal anti-infective drugs are HIV/AIDS treatments such as Reyataz ($931 million), Sustiva ($791 million), Zerit ($155 million), and Baraclude ($83 million). BMY also offers Cefzil, Tequin, Maxipime, and other antibiotics. Central nervous system agents include Abilify, an antipsychotic ($1.3 billion), Sinemet for Parkinson's disease, and various other drugs. Orencia, a new treatment for rheumatoid arthritis ($89 million), was approved in December 2005.

The Mead Johnson division offers nutritionals, consisting of infant formulas such as Enfamil and ProSobee, as well as vitamins and nutritional supplements. The Convatec unit offers ostomy and wound care products.

Company Financials Fiscal Year Ended Dec. 31

Per Share Data ($)	2006	2005	2004	2003	2002	2001	2000	1999	1998	1997
Tangible Book Value	1.68	2.28	1.76	1.62	0.88	1.70	3.96	3.61	3.01	2.82
Cash Flow	1.28	1.98	1.66	1.99	1.43	1.68	2.42	2.39	1.85	1.86
Earnings	0.81	1.52	1.21	1.59	1.05	1.29	2.36	2.06	1.55	1.57
S&P Core Earnings	0.88	1.43	1.24	1.57	1.07	0.67	NA	NA	NA	NA
Dividends	1.12	1.12	1.12	1.12	1.12	1.10	0.98	0.86	0.78	0.77
Payout Ratio	138%	74%	93%	70%	107%	85%	42%	42%	50%	49%
Prices:High	26.41	26.60	31.30	29.21	51.95	73.50	74.88	79.25	67.63	49.09
Prices:Low	20.08	20.70	22.22	21.00	19.49	48.50	42.44	57.25	44.16	26.63
P/E Ratio:High	33	17	26	18	49	57	32	38	44	31
P/E Ratio:Low	25	14	18	13	19	38	18	28	29	17

Income Statement Analysis (Million $)

	2006	2005	2004	2003	2002	2001	2000	1999	1998	1997
Revenue	17,914	19,207	19,380	20,894	18,119	19,423	18,216	20,222	18,284	16,701
Operating Income	3,483	4,880	5,373	5,726	4,851	7,034	6,732	6,531	5,746	5,029
Depreciation	927	929	909	779	735	781	746	678	625	591
Interest Expense	498	349	310	277	410	182	108	130	154	118
Pretax Income	2,635	4,516	4,418	4,694	2,647	2,986	5,478	5,767	4,268	4,482
Effective Tax Rate	23.1%	20.6%	34.4%	25.9%	16.4%	15.4%	25.2%	27.7%	26.4%	28.5%
Net Income	1,585	2,992	2,378	3,106	2,034	2,527	4,096	4,167	3,141	3,205
S&P Core Earnings	1,727	2,808	2,448	3,043	2,076	1,321	NA	NA	NA	NA

Balance Sheet & Other Financial Data (Million $)

	2006	2005	2004	2003	2002	2001	2000	1999	1998	1997
Cash	4,013	5,799	7,474	5,457	3,989	5,654	3,385	2,957	2,529	1,794
Current Assets	10,302	12,283	14,801	11,918	9,975	12,349	9,824	9,267	8,782	7,736
Total Assets	25,575	28,138	30,435	27,471	24,874	27,057	17,578	17,114	16,272	14,977
Current Liabilities	6,496	6,890	9,843	7,530	8,220	8,826	5,632	5,537	5,791	5,032
Long Term Debt	7,248	8,364	8,463	8,522	6,261	6,237	1,336	1,342	1,364	1,279
Common Equity	9,991	11,208	10,202	19,572	8,967	10,736	9,180	8,645	7,576	7,219
Total Capital	17,307	19,572	18,665	28,094	15,228	16,973	10,516	9,987	8,940	8,498
Capital Expenditures	762	738	676	937	997	1,023	589	709	788	767
Cash Flow	2,512	3,921	3,287	3,885	2,769	3,308	4,842	4,845	3,766	3,796
Current Ratio	1.6	1.8	1.5	1.6	1.2	1.4	1.7	1.7	1.5	1.5
% Long Term Debt of Capitalization	42.0	42.7	45.3	30.3	41.1	36.7	12.7	13.4	15.3	15.1
% Net Income of Revenue	8.8	15.6	12.3	14.9	11.2	13.0	22.5	20.6	17.2	19.2
% Return on Assets	5.9	10.2	8.2	11.8	7.7	11.3	23.6	25.0	20.1	21.6
% Return on Equity	15.0	27.9	23.8	16.8	22.5	25.4	46.0	51.4	42.5	46.5

Data as orig reptd.; bef. results of disc opers/spec. items. Per share data adj. for stk. divs.; EPS diluted. E-Estimated. NA-Not Available. NM-Not Meaningful. NR-Not Ranked. UR-Under Review.

Office: 345 Park Ave, New York, NY 10154-0004.
Telephone: 212-546-4000.
Website: http://www.bms.com
Chrmn: J.D. Robinson, III

CEO: J.M. Cornelius
EVP & CFO: A.R. Bonfield
EVP & CSO: E. Sigal
SVP, Secy & General Counsel: S. Leung

Investor Contact: J. Elicker (212-546-3775)
Board Members: R. E. Allen, L. B. Campbell, V. D. Coffman, J. M. Cornelius, P. R. Dolan, L. J. Freeh, L. H. Glimcher, M. Grobstein, L. Johansson, J. D. Robinson, III, V. L. Sato, R. S. Williams

Founded: 1887
Domicile: Delaware
Employees: 43,000

The McGraw-Hill Companies

Broadcom Corp

STANDARD &POOR'S

S&P Recommendation **BUY** ★★★★☆	Price $27.83 (as of Nov 23, 2007)	12-Mo. Target Price $40.00	Investment Style Large-Cap Blend

GICS Sector Information Technology
Sub-Industry Semiconductors

Summary This company provides semiconductors for broadband communications markets, including cable set-top boxes, cable modems, office networks and home networking.

Key Stock Statistics (Source S&P, Vickers, company reports)

52-Wk Range	$43.07– 26.45	S&P Oper. EPS 2007 E	0.43	Market Capitalization(B)	$13.097	Beta	3.53
Trailing 12-Month EPS	$0.28	S&P Oper. EPS 2008 E	0.53	Yield (%)	Nil	S&P 3-Yr. Proj. EPS CAGR(%)	11.00
Trailing 12-Month P/E	NM	P/E on S&P Oper. EPS 2007 E	64.7	Dividend Rate/Share	Nil	S&P Credit Rating	NA
$10K Invested 5 Yrs Ago	$20,225	Common Shares Outstg. (M)	540.8	Institutional Ownership (%)	86		

Price Performance

30-Week Mov. Avg. · · · 10-Week Mov. Avg. - - GAAP Earnings vs. Previous Year Volume Above Avg. STARS
12-Mo. Target Price — Relative Strength ▲ Up ▼ Down ► No Change Below Avg.

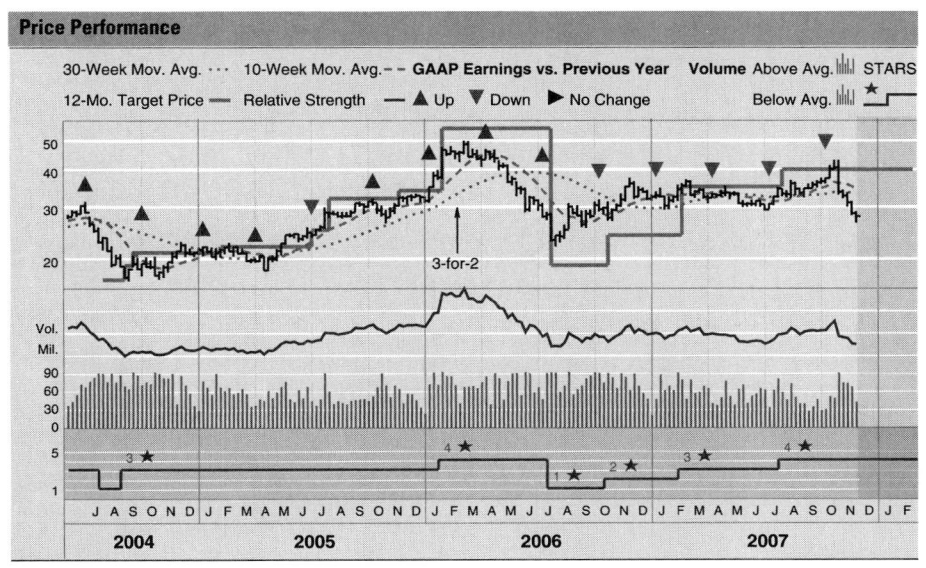

Options: ASE, CBOE, P, Ph

Analysis prepared by **Clyde Montevirgen** on October 24, 2007, when the stock traded at **$ 33.21**.

Qualitative Risk Assessment

LOW	MEDIUM	**HIGH**

Our risk assessment reflects Broadcom's exposure to the sales cycles of the semiconductor industry, a limited number of key customers, dependence on foundry partners for production, and greater reliance than most companies on stock-based compensation. This is partially offset by our view of a lack of debt and a broadening base of end users.

Quantitative Evaluations

S&P Quality Ranking B-

D	C	**B-**	B	B+	A-	A	A+

Relative Strength Rank WEAK

17

LOWEST = 1   HIGHEST = 99

Revenue/Earnings Data

Revenue (Million $)

	1Q	2Q	3Q	4Q	Year
2007	901.5	897.9	950.0	--	--
2006	900.7	941.1	902.6	923.5	3,668
2005	550.3	604.9	695.0	820.6	2,671
2004	573.4	641.3	646.5	539.4	2,401
2003	327.5	377.9	425.6	479.1	1,610
2002	238.8	258.2	290.0	296.0	1,083

Earnings Per Share ($)

2007	0.10	0.06	0.05	E0.11	E0.43
2006	0.20	0.18	0.19	0.08	0.64
2005	0.13	0.03	0.23	0.33	0.73
2004	0.08	0.12	0.09	0.13	0.42
2003	-0.17	-2.05	-0.01	0.01	-2.19
2002	-0.42	-0.33	-0.45	-4.27	-5.57

Fiscal year ended Dec. 31. Next earnings report expected: Early February. EPS Estimates based on S&P Operating Earnings; historical GAAP earnings are as reported.

Dividend Data

No cash dividends have been paid.

Highlights

► We project 1.9% and 14.5% sales advances for 2007 and 2008, respectively, reflecting robust sales for its well diversified communications offerings. Although we think first half revenues in 2007 were held back by inventory problems and negative seasonality, we see stronger sales ahead, supported by growth for DTV, Bluetooth, Wireless LAN, and FM products. We also believe that the company's mobile handset products and licensing revenues will provide notable growth longer-term, and we see a positive top-line impact starting in 2008. Our forecasts do not include revenues from BRCM's recent agreement with Verizon Wireless.

► We expect 2007 and 2008 gross margins to be unchanged from 52% in 2006, as the company's fabless production model should allow for some sales volatility without drastically affecting margins. However, we are projecting higher R&D expenses as the company aggressively moves to 65nm process technology and provides support for new projects. Consequently, we forecast operating margins in the mid-teens over the next few quarters.

► We estimate operating EPS of $0.43 in 2007 and $0.53 in 2008.

Investment Rationale/Risk

► We believe that new mobile and wireless products, as well as anticipated growth for certain broadband communications products, will provide notable growth in the long term. We view favorably BRCM's migration to 65nm, and we think new designs, such as its latest 3G chip offering, will lead to market share gains ahead. Although BRCM is heavily investing in future growth, limiting near-term operating margin expansion, we see the shares appreciating as BRCM gets closer to executing on its supply agreements with large handset providers Nokia and Samsung.

► Risks to our recommendation and target price include a sharp downturn in demand for semiconductors, slower customer acceptance of new products, and quickly rising operating expenses due to technology investments.

► Our 12-month target price of $40 is based on our price-to-sales (P/S) analyses. We use a P/S multiple of 6.3X --above the historical average- -our forward 12-month sales per share estimate to derive a value of $40. We believe that the higher multiple is justified given expected sales growth stemming from recent handset design wins and a licensing deal.

Broadcom Corp

STANDARD &POOR'S

Business Summary October 24, 2007

CORPORATE OVERVIEW. Founded in 1991, Broadcom designs, develops and supplies semiconductor products that address business and consumer demand for high-speed access to multimedia information and entertainment content consisting of voice, video and data. The company's integrated circuits (ICs) address all major broadband communications markets, including digital cable, direct broadcast satellite and Internet Protocol set-top boxes and media servers; cable and DSL modems; high definition television; high-speed transmission and switching for local, metropolitan, wide area and storage networking; wireless and personal area networking; wireless communications; Voice over Internet Protocol (VoIP) gateway and telephony systems; broadband network processors; and system I/O server solutions.

Broadband products mainly consist of high-performance digital signal processing ICs working with analog and mixed-signal ICs and often with radio-frequency ICs that are increasingly offered as system-on-a-chip solutions with related software. According to the company, BRCM aims to make highly integrated, comprehensive systems solutions on single chips or chipsets, reducing board space, simplifying the customer's manufacturing process, low-

ering the customer's system costs, and boosting performance.

In 2006, net revenue by major target market was 32% (40% in 2005) enterprise networking; 38% (34%) broadband communications; and 30% (26%) mobile and wireless. Net revenue from international sales has been increasing recently, and stood at 87% of 2006 total sales, 85% in 2005, and 79% in 2004.

Customers include leading communications equipment and computer companies such as Alcatel, Apple, 3Com, Cisco Systems, Echostar, Nortel Networks, IBM, Samsung, and Scientific-Atlanta. BRCM does most of its business with a small number of customers. In 2006, the five leading customers accounted for approximately 47% of total revenue, down from 49% of total revenue in 2005 and 53% in 2004.

Company Financials Fiscal Year Ended Dec. 31

Per Share Data ($)	2006	2005	2004	2003	2002	2001	2000	1999	1998	1997
Tangible Book Value	5.43	3.79	2.59	1.43	0.94	2.19	3.31	1.59	0.78	0.81
Cash Flow	0.73	0.85	0.59	-1.98	-5.20	-4.87	-1.59	0.28	0.16	0.02
Earnings	0.64	0.73	0.42	-2.19	-5.57	-7.19	-2.09	0.24	0.13	-0.01
S&P Core Earnings	0.64	-0.04	-0.70	-2.31	-5.07	-6.87	NA	NA	NA	NA
Dividends	Nil	Nil	Nil	Nil	Nil	Nil	Nil	Nil	Nil	NA
Payout Ratio	Nil	Nil	Nil	Nil	Nil	Nil	Nil	Nil	Nil	NA
Prices:High	50.00	33.28	31.37	25.10	35.57	93.00	183.17	96.33	22.50	NA
Prices:Low	21.98	18.25	16.83	7.91	6.35	12.27	49.83	15.42	4.00	NA
P/E Ratio:High	78	46	75	NM	NM	NM	NM	NM	NM	NA
P/E Ratio:Low	34	25	40	NM	NM	NM	NM	NM	NM	NA

Income Statement Analysis (Million $)										
Revenue	3,668	2,671	2,401	1,610	1,083	962	1,096	518	203	37.0
Operating Income	309	557	450	-30.4	-442	-573	-169	157	59.7	0.81
Depreciation	47.6	68.5	91.7	90.9	147	889	165	14.0	7.50	3.04
Interest Expense	Nil	Nil	Nil	Nil	3.60	5.00	0.33	0.55	0.47	0.26
Pretax Income	367	392	294	-935	-1,939	-2,799	-692	119	56.0	-1.95
Effective Tax Rate	NM	NM	25.7%	NM	NM	NM	NM	30.2%	35.0%	NM
Net Income	379	412	219	-960	-2,237	-2,742	-688	83.3	36.4	-1.17
S&P Core Earnings	379	-25.7	-330	-1,011	-2,039	-2,617	NA	NA	NA	NA

Balance Sheet & Other Financial Data (Million $)										
Cash	2,680	1,733	1,183	606	503	540	524	174	62.6	91.2
Current Assets	3,352	2,336	1,584	996	722	674	876	391	157	NA
Total Assets	4,877	3,752	2,886	2,018	2,216	3,623	4,678	585	237	114
Current Liabilities	679	595	497	504	534	412	203	86.1	27.1	NA
Long Term Debt	Nil	Nil	Nil	Nil	1.21	4.01	Nil	0.55	Nil	0.10
Common Equity	4,192	3,145	2,366	1,490	1,645	3,207	4,475	499	210	105
Total Capital	4,192	3,145	2,366	1,490	1,646	3,211	4,475	499	210	NA
Capital Expenditures	92.5	41.8	49.9	47.9	75.2	71.4	80.7	29.2	27.3	NA
Cash Flow	427	480	310	-869	-2,090	-1,853	-523	97.3	43.9	1.87
Current Ratio	4.9	3.9	3.2	2.0	1.4	1.6	4.3	4.5	5.8	NA
% Long Term Debt of Capitalization	Nil	Nil	Nil	Nil	0.1	0.1	Nil	0.1	Nil	NA
% Net Income of Revenue	10.3	15.4	9.1	NM	NM	NM	NM	16.1	17.9	NM
% Return on Assets	8.8	12.4	8.9	NM	NM	NM	NM	19.7	25.8	NM
% Return on Equity	10.3	14.9	11.3	NM	NM	NM	NM	23.3	33.8	NM

Data as orig reptd.; bef. results of disc opers/spec. items. Per share data adj. for stk. divs.; EPS diluted. E-Estimated. NA-Not Available. NM-Not Meaningful. NR-Not Ranked. UR-Under Review.

Office: 16215 Alton Parkway, Irvine, CA 92618-3616.
Telephone: 949-926-5000.
Email: investorinfo@broadcom.com
Website: http://www.broadcom.com

Chrmn: H. Samueli
Pres & CEO: S.A. McGregor
SVP & CFO: E.K. Brandt
SVP, Secy & General Counsel: D.A. Dull

SVP & CIO: K.E. Venner
Investor Contact: P. Andrew (949-926-5663)
Board Members: G. L. Farinsky, M. E. Grzelakowski, N. H. Handel, J. E. Major, S. A. McGregor, A. E. Ross, H. Samueli, R. E. Switz, W. F. Wolfen

Founded: 1991
Domicile: California
Employees: 5,233

Brown-Forman Corp

STANDARD &POOR'S

S&P Recommendation BUY ★★★★☆	**Price** $69.57 (as of Nov 29, 2007)	**12-Mo. Target Price** $79.00	**Investment Style** Large-Cap Growth

GICS Sector Consumer Staples
Sub-Industry Distillers & Vintners

Summary This leading distiller and importer of alcoholic beverages, based in Kentucky, markets such brands as Jack Daniel's, Southern Comfort, Finlandia, Korbel and Bolla.

Key Stock Statistics (Source S&P, Vickers, company reports)

52-Wk Range	$79.88– 63.17	S&P Oper. EPS 2008**E**	3.48	Market Capitalization(B)	$4.646	Beta	0.27
Trailing 12-Month EPS	$3.15	S&P Oper. EPS 2009**E**	3.90	Yield (%)	1.95	S&P 3-Yr. Proj. EPS CAGR(%)	10.00
Trailing 12-Month P/E	22.1	P/E on S&P Oper. EPS 2008**E**	20.0	Dividend Rate/Share	$1.36	S&P Credit Rating	A
$10K Invested 5 Yrs Ago	$22,497	Common Shares Outstg. (M)	123.5	Institutional Ownership (%)	89		

Price Performance

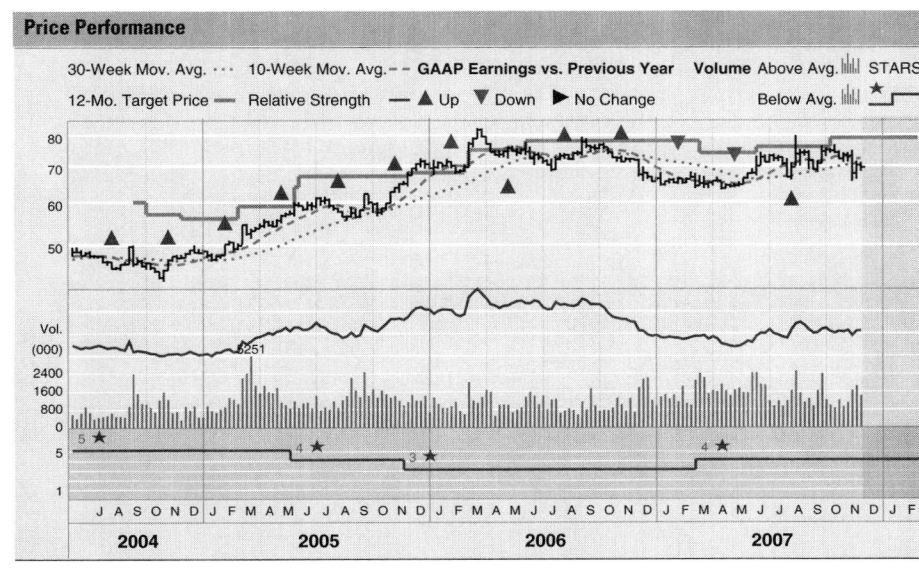

30-Week Mov. Avg. ··· 10-Week Mov. Avg.- - GAAP Earnings vs. Previous Year Volume Above Avg. STARS
12-Mo. Target Price — Relative Strength — ▲ Up ▼ Down ► No Change Below Avg. ★

Analysis prepared by **Raymond Mathis** on October 05, 2007, when the stock traded at **$ 74.68**.

Highlights

➤ We look for 7% to 8% wine and spirits sales growth in FY 08 (Apr.) on organic growth, international expansion, and development of the Casa Herradura brand. We also expect trade inventory reductions in late FY 07 to allow for better pricing power and a volume boost on possible inventory rebuilds. Along with price increases, our FY 08 growth projection reflects continued momentum in top spirits brands Jack Daniel's, Southern Comfort and Finlandia. In addition, we see beverage volumes benefiting further from strong advertising and marketing, plus recent acquisitions.

➤ We look for gross margin expansion as increased volumes better leverage fixed costs, likely improvement in the product mix, pricing power, and a declining dollar. Operating margins should benefit, in our view, from improvements in global distribution arrangements, partly offset by increased marketing support and higher SG&A costs related to the recent Chambord liqueur and Casa Herradura acquisitions.

➤ We expect greater net interest expense as the company funds acquisitions, and a higher effective tax rate. Excluding unusual items, we estimate FY 08 EPS of $3.60.

Investment Rationale/Risk

➤ Long term, we look for continued strength in the global market, and think that spirits will continue to make successful inroads in the 21- to 27-year old demographic. BF should continue to capitalize on what we see as positive industry trends with its strong portfolio of spirits and international reach, particularly with its Jack Daniel's brand. In addition, we believe BF's commitment to improving distribution and brand building will support outperformance.

➤ Risks to our recommendation and target price include an unexpected slowdown in the growth of top-performing brands. Also, BF's dual-class structure and the majority representation of insiders on its board of directors pose corporate governance concerns to us.

➤ Our 12-month target price of $79 is supported by our DCF and P/E analyses. Based on our discounted cash flow model, assuming an 8.5% cost of capital, we estimate intrinsic value of $76. We apply a P/E of about 23X, slightly above the stock's historical average high of 22X, to our FY 08 EPS estimate, which leads to a value of $83. With the stock's recent 1.6% dividend yield, we recommend the shares for their total return potential.

Qualitative Risk Assessment

LOW	MEDIUM	HIGH

Brown-Forman is a large-cap competitor in an industry that has historically demonstrated relative stability. However, we believe the company's dual-class structure and the majority representation of insiders on its board of directors pose corporate governance concerns.

Quantitative Evaluations

S&P Quality Ranking A

D	C	B-	B	B+	A-	A	A+

Relative Strength Rank MODERATE

58

LOWEST = 1   HIGHEST = 99

Revenue/Earnings Data

Revenue (Million $)

	1Q	2Q	3Q	4Q	Year
2008	739.1	--	--	--	--
2007	633.0	727.0	754.8	690.8	2,806
2006	547.0	666.0	637.0	594.0	2,444
2005	578.0	780.0	758.0	613.0	2,729
2004	532.6	725.2	697.0	625.0	2,577
2003	479.0	692.0	636.0	571.0	2,378

Earnings Per Share ($)

2008	0.77	E0.98	E0.98	E0.65	E3.48
2007	0.76	1.00	0.90	0.56	3.22
2006	0.71	0.91	0.98	0.61	3.20
2005	0.42	0.83	0.78	0.49	2.52
2004	0.26	0.73	0.66	0.47	2.11
2003	0.26	0.59	0.51	0.45	1.82

Fiscal year ended Apr. 30. Next earnings report expected: Mid December. EPS Estimates based on S&P Operating Earnings; historical GAAP earnings are as reported.

Dividend Data (Dates: mm/dd Payment Date: mm/dd/yy)

Amount ($)	Date Decl.	Ex-Div. Date	Stk. of Record	Payment Date
1.653	03/23	04/09	04/05	05/10/07
0.030	05/24	06/04	06/06	07/01/07
0.303	07/26	08/30	09/04	10/01/07
0.340	11/15	12/03	12/05	01/01/08

Dividends have been paid since 1960. Source: Company reports.

Brown-Forman Corp

Business Summary October 05, 2007

CORPORATE OVERVIEW. Brown-Forman Corp.'s origins date back to 1870. It is the world's fourth largest producer of distilled spirits. With a portfolio of well known brands, the company is best known for its popular Jack Daniel's Tennessee Whiskey, which continues to be its largest sales and profit producer. BF also manufactures and sells consumer durables, primarily under the Hartmann luggage brand.

Although many alcoholic beverage companies have moved in recent years to reduce their dependence on the highly mature brown spirits market, BF has remained whiskey-oriented. Its product line is stocked with well known whiskies, bourbons, vodkas, tequilas, rums, and liqueurs. Brands include Jack Daniel's, Southern Comfort, Canadian Mist, Woodford Reserve, and Early Times. Jack Daniel's volume growth in FY 06 (Apr.) was 8%, with the U.S. market accounting for 55% of sales. Statistics based on case sales rank Jack Daniel's as the largest selling American whiskey in the world, Canadian Mist as the second largest selling Canadian whiskey in the U.S. and third largest in the world, and Southern Comfort as the largest selling domestic proprietary liqueur in the U.S. Other major alcoholic beverage lines include Fetzer and Bolla wines, Finlandia vodka, Chambord liqueur, and Korbel Champagnes.

International sales, consisting principally of exports of wines and spirits, increased to over $1 billion in FY 06, accounting for 41% of total net revenues. Beverage growth in recent years has come primarily from international markets for the company's spirits brands. The key export markets for brands include the U.K., Poland, Germany, Australia, South Africa, Spain, Italy, Japan, China and France.

Until year-end FY 05, the consumer durables segment consisted of the Lenox Inc. subsidiary, which produced and marketed china, crystal and giftware under the Lenox and Gorham trademarks. The segment also included Dansk, a producer of tableware and giftware, Gorham, Kirk Steiff, and Hartmann Luggage. In July 2005, following a strategic review, the company agreed to sell Lenox to Department 56, Inc. for $190 million. On September 1, 2005, BF consummated the sale of substantially all of Lenox to Department 56 for $196 million. Consumer durables was eliminated as a segment, and in August 2006, BF said it would seek strategic alternatives for Hartmann as well.

Company Financials Fiscal Year Ended Apr. 30

Per Share Data ($)	2007	2006	2005	2004	2003	2002	2001	2000	1999	1998
Tangible Book Value	1.78	8.49	5.69	4.29	2.41	7.72	6.75	5.68	4.77	4.04
Cash Flow	3.61	3.60	2.98	2.29	2.21	2.05	2.15	2.03	1.87	1.70
Earnings	3.22	3.20	2.52	2.11	1.82	1.66	1.70	1.59	1.47	1.34
S&P Core Earnings	3.17	3.15	2.38	2.07	1.55	1.39	1.52	NA	NA	NA
Dividends	0.77	0.92	0.80	0.73	0.73	0.68	0.64	0.61	0.58	0.55
Payout Ratio	24%	29%	32%	34%	40%	41%	38%	38%	39%	41%
Calendar Year	2006	2005	2004	2003	2002	2001	2000	1999	1998	1997
Prices:High	82.55	72.40	50.09	47.56	40.27	36.00	34.63	38.63	38.44	27.69
Prices:Low	65.27	46.62	42.80	30.13	29.35	28.83	20.94	27.47	25.88	21.00
P/E Ratio:High	26	23	20	23	22	22	20	24	26	21
P/E Ratio:Low	20	15	17	14	16	17	12	17	18	16

Income Statement Analysis (Million $)										
Revenue	2,806	2,444	2,729	2,577	2,378	1,958	1,924	1,877	1,776	1,669
Operating Income	627	560	513	473	429	408	438	410	377	358
Depreciation	44.0	44.0	58.0	56.0	55.0	55.0	64.0	62.0	55.0	51.0
Interest Expense	34.0	18.0	21.0	21.0	8.00	8.00	16.0	15.0	10.0	14.0
Pretax Income	586	559	476	388	373	348	366	343	318	296
Effective Tax Rate	31.7%	29.3%	35.3%	33.5%	34.3%	34.5%	36.3%	36.4%	36.5%	37.5%
Net Income	400	395	308	258	245	228	233	218	202	185
S&P Core Earnings	393	389	289	252	209	190	208	NA	NA	NA

Balance Sheet & Other Financial Data (Million $)										
Cash	283	475	295	68.0	72.0	116	86.0	180	171	78.0
Current Assets	1,635	1,610	1,317	1,083	1,068	1,029	994	1,020	999	869
Total Assets	3,551	2,728	2,624	2,376	2,264	2,016	1,939	1,802	1,735	1,494
Current Liabilities	1,347	569	638	369	548	495	538	522	517	382
Long Term Debt	422	351	352	630	629	40.0	40.0	41.0	53.0	50.0
Common Equity	1,672	1,563	1,310	1,085	840	1,311	1,187	1,048	917	805
Total Capital	2,150	2,047	1,794	1,837	1,547	1,409	1,289	1,184	1,107	1,005
Capital Expenditures	58.0	52.0	49.0	56.0	119	71.0	96.0	78.0	46.0	44.0
Cash Flow	444	439	366	314	300	283	297	280	257	235
Current Ratio	1.2	2.8	2.1	2.9	1.9	2.1	1.8	2.0	1.9	2.3
% Long Term Debt of Capitalization	19.6	17.1	19.6	34.3	40.7	2.8	3.1	3.5	4.8	4.9
% Net Income of Revenue	14.3	16.2	11.3	10.0	10.3	11.6	12.1	11.6	11.4	11.1
% Return on Assets	12.7	14.7	12.3	11.1	11.4	11.5	12.5	12.3	12.3	12.7
% Return on Equity	24.7	27.5	25.6	26.8	22.8	18.3	20.9	22.2	23.5	24.3

Data as orig reptd.; bef. results of disc opers/spec. items. Per share data adj. for stk. divs.; EPS diluted. E-Estimated. NA-Not Available. NM-Not Meaningful. NR-Not Ranked. UR-Under Review.

Office: 850 Dixie Highway, Louisville, KY 40210-1091.
Telephone: 502-585-1100.
Website: http://www.brown-forman.com
Chrmn: O. Brown, II

Pres & CEO: P.C. Varga
Vice Chrmn: J.S. Welch, Jr.
Vice Chrmn, Secy & General Counsel: M.B. Crutcher
EVP & CFO: P.A. Wood

Investor Contact: T. Graven (502-774-7442)
Board Members: P. Bousquet-Chavanne, B. D. Bramley, O. Brown, II, G. Brown, IV, M. Brown, Jr., D. G. Calder, S. A. Frazier, R. P. Mayer, W. E. Mitchell, M. R. Simmons, W. M. Street, D. B. Stubbs, P. C. Varga, J. Welch, Jr.

Founded: 1870
Domicile: Delaware
Employees: 4,440

Brunswick Corp

STANDARD & POOR'S

S&P Recommendation HOLD ★★★☆☆	**Price** $19.26 (as of Nov 23, 2007)	**12-Mo. Target Price** $24.00	**Investment Style** Large-Cap Blend

GICS Sector Consumer Discretionary
Sub-Industry Leisure Products

Summary This leading manufacturer of marine engines and boats also has other recreational businesses.

Key Stock Statistics (Source S&P, Vickers, company reports)

52-Wk Range	$34.99–18.43	S&P Oper. EPS 2007E	0.86	Market Capitalization(B)	$1.712	Beta	1.34
Trailing 12-Month EPS	$0.61	S&P Oper. EPS 2008E	1.33	Yield (%)	3.12	S&P 3-Yr. Proj. EPS CAGR(%)	-7.00
Trailing 12-Month P/E	31.6	P/E on S&P Oper. EPS 2007E	22.4	Dividend Rate/Share	$0.60	S&P Credit Rating	BBB
$10K Invested 5 Yrs Ago	$10,213	Common Shares Outstg. (M)	88.9	Institutional Ownership (%)	94		

Price Performance

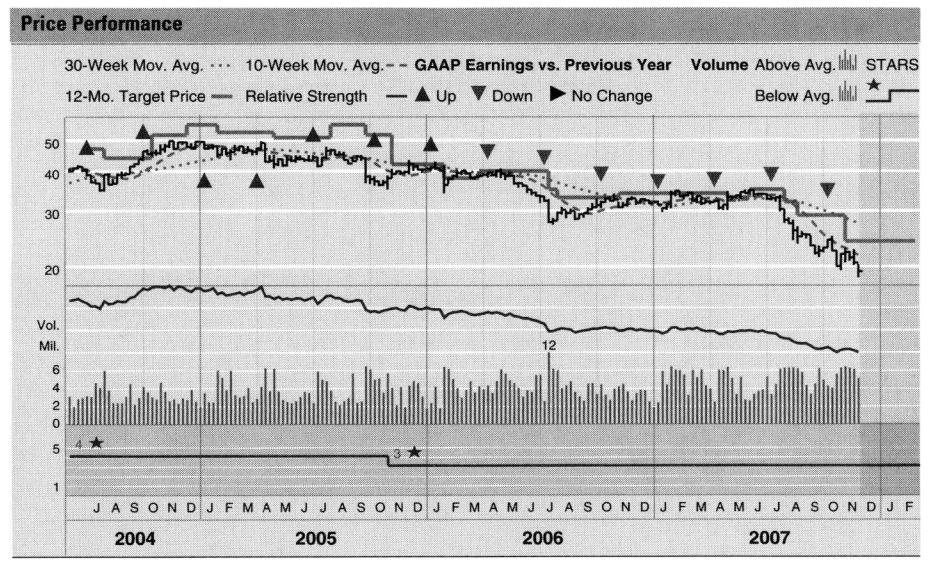

30-Week Mov. Avg. ···· 10-Week Mov. Avg. -- **GAAP Earnings vs. Previous Year** Volume Above Avg. STARS
12-Mo. Target Price — Relative Strength — ▲ Up ▼ Down ▶ No Change Below Avg. ★

2004   2005   2006   2007

Options: ASE, CBOE, P, Ph

Analysis prepared by **Erik Kolb** on November 01, 2007, when the stock traded at **$ 22.31**.

Highlights

➤ Following weak sales in the second half of 2006 and the first three quarters of 2007, we expect a high-single digit to low double-digit decline in marine retail demand this year as BC plans to reduce production through the next few quarters to lower pipeline inventories. For the full year 2007, we project an 10% decline in marine segment sales, a 4.9% increase in fitness, and a 3.5% increase in bowling & billiards, leading to a 2.5% decline in total company sales. We expect similar headwinds in 2008 to lead to a 1.1% decline in total sales.

➤ We see operating margins declining in 2007, to 4.1%, from 6.0% in 2006, with the marine and fitness segments showing lower margins as they reduce inventory, and the bowling & billiards segment nearly flat. We think margins will stabilize in 2008 at 3.9%

➤ We estimate operating EPS of $0.86 in 2007, which includes a $0.47 impairment charge. In 2006, the company had operating EPS of $2.70, excluding $0.25 of tax credits in the first three quarters and $1.04 of one-time charges in the fourth quarter. For 2008, we see an advance in EPS to $1.33.

Investment Rationale/Risk

➤ We think that the marine market will continue to be soft in the near term as consumers are feeling the increased pressures of higher energy costs, which, given recent mild income gains and low savings rates, are likely to lead to no more than moderate growth in discretionary spending. However, we continue to believe the company's production of fully integrated boats will bolster the reputation of its brands, especially on the high end, boosting long-term growth and pricing power. However, we see no near-term catalysts likely to lead to much higher stock valuations.

➤ Risks to our recommendation and target price include a prolonged weakening of the marine retail environment that could further dampen sales, and poor execution of key product, manufacturing, sourcing and service initiatives.

➤ Our 12-month target price of $24 is based on a blend of our DCF analysis and relative P/E valuation. Our DCF model assumes a WACC of 8.4% and terminal growth of 3.0%, yielding a value of $27. Our relative analysis leads us to apply a P/E of 16X, which is above the historical average given the increased clarity we see, to our 2008 operating EPS estimate, yielding a value of $21.

Qualitative Risk Assessment

LOW	MEDIUM	**HIGH**

Our risk assessment for Brunswick Corp. reflects the highly discretionary nature of its products and their significant unit prices, as well as the integration risks of BC's many acquisitions. This is only partially offset, in our view, by the company's corporate governance practices, which we consider more favorable than those of many peers.

Quantitative Evaluations

S&P Quality Ranking   B

D	C	B-	**B**	B+	A-	A	A+

Relative Strength Rank   WEAK

21

LOWEST = 1   HIGHEST = 99

Revenue/Earnings Data

Revenue (Million $)

	1Q	2Q	3Q	4Q	Year
2007	1,386	1,523	1,326	--	--
2006	1,413	1,543	1,338	1,371	5,665
2005	1,401	1,599	1,435	1,490	5,924
2004	1,200	1,423	1,273	1,334	5,229
2003	934.5	1,071	1,036	1,087	4,129
2002	866.7	1,017	900.0	928.0	3,712

Earnings Per Share ($)

	1Q	2Q	3Q	4Q	Year
2007	0.38	0.65	-0.27	E0.10	E0.86
2006	0.77	0.99	0.54	0.48	2.78
2005	0.96	1.15	0.89	0.90	3.90
2004	0.50	0.93	0.75	0.59	2.77
2003	0.04	0.59	0.41	0.43	1.47
2002	0.15	0.51	0.26	0.22	1.14

Fiscal year ended Dec. 31. Next earnings report expected: Late January. EPS Estimates based on S&P Operating Earnings; historical GAAP earnings are as reported.

Dividend Data (Dates: mm/dd Payment Date: mm/dd/yy)

Amount ($)	Date Decl.	Ex-Div. Date	Stk. of Record	Payment Date
0.600	10/25	11/22	11/27	12/15/06
0.600	10/24	11/19	11/21	12/14/07

Dividends have been paid since 1969. Source: Company reports.

Brunswick Corp

Business Summary November 01, 2007

CORPORATE OVERVIEW. Brunswick Corp. is a major marine products company that also sells fitness equipment as well as products related to bowling and billiards. In addition, the company operates Brunswick bowling centers in the U.S. and internationally and retail billiards stores in the U.S.

In 2006, the company's marine-related businesses accounted for 81% of net sales, or $4.6 billion (after eliminations); $2.3 billion was from the marine engine segment and $2.9 billion was from the boat segment. Operating profits totaled $194 million for the marine engine segment and $136 million for the boat segment. The marine engine group (Mercury Marine) manufactures and markets a full range of outboard, inboard and sterndrive engines; water-jet propulsion systems; and related parts and accessories. The boat segment designs, manufactures and markets fiberglass pleasure boats, high-performance boats, offshore fishing boats, and aluminum fishing, deck and pontoon boats.

The fitness segment includes cardiovascular fitness equipment (including treadmills, total body cross trainers, stair climbers, and stationary exercise bicycles) and strength-training equipment under the Life Fitness, Hammer Strength and ParaBody brands. In 2006, the company reported fitness seg-

ment sales of $593 million (10% of total net sales), and operating earnings of $58 million. Fitness segment sales are derived from commercial as well as high-end consumer markets.

In 2006, BC's bowling and billiards segment had net sales of $458 million (8%) and operating earnings of $22.1 million. The segment includes the production of bowling balls and bowling capital equipment; the operation of more than 100 bowling centers; and the marketing of billiards tables, cues and accessories.

In addition, BC owns 49% of Brunswick Acceptance Co. (BAC), a joint venture with GE Commercial Finance. BAC provides secured wholesale floor-plan financing to BC's boat and engine dealers and purchases and services a portion of Mercury Marine's domestic accounts receivables related to its boatbuilder and dealer customers. In 2006, BAC purchased $832.0 million of receivables from BC.

Company Financials Fiscal Year Ended Dec. 31

Per Share Data ($)	2006	2005	2004	2003	2002	2001	2000	1999	1998	1997
Tangible Book Value	9.75	9.99	7.85	6.77	5.90	5.78	6.41	6.98	5.34	4.75
Cash Flow	4.55	5.54	4.39	3.11	2.78	2.78	3.96	2.20	3.42	3.07
Earnings	2.78	3.90	2.77	1.47	1.14	0.96	2.28	0.41	1.80	1.51
S&P Core Earnings	2.76	3.58	2.78	1.77	0.69	0.42	NA	NA	NA	NA
Dividends	0.60	0.60	0.60	0.50	0.50	0.50	0.50	0.50	0.50	0.50
Payout Ratio	22%	15%	22%	34%	44%	52%	22%	122%	28%	33%
Prices:High	42.84	49.77	49.85	32.08	30.01	25.01	22.13	30.00	35.69	37.00
Prices:Low	27.08	35.00	31.25	16.35	18.30	14.03	14.75	18.06	12.00	23.13
P/E Ratio:High	15	13	18	22	26	26	10	73	20	25
P/E Ratio:Low	10	9	11	11	16	15	6	44	7	15

Income Statement Analysis (Million $)										
Revenue	5,665	5,924	5,229	4,129	3,712	3,371	3,812	4,284	3,945	3,657
Operating Income	526	641	558	397	345	352	601	544	560	526
Depreciation	167	162	158	151	148	160	149	166	160	157
Interest Expense	60.5	53.2	45.2	41.0	43.3	52.9	67.6	61.0	62.7	51.3
Pretax Income	310	496	379	201	162	132	323	55.0	284	236
Effective Tax Rate	15.0%	22.3%	28.7%	32.8%	36.0%	35.9%	37.5%	31.1%	37.1%	36.0%
Net Income	263	385	270	135	104	84.7	202	37.9	179	151
S&P Core Earnings	261	354	271	163	63.7	37.1	NA	NA	NA	NA

Balance Sheet & Other Financial Data (Million $)										
Cash	283	488	500	346	351	109	125	101	126	85.6
Current Assets	2,078	2,235	2,099	1,715	1,660	1,401	1,832	1,578	1,454	1,366
Total Assets	4,450	4,622	4,346	3,603	3,407	3,158	3,397	3,355	3,352	3,241
Current Liabilities	1,293	1,305	1,254	1,102	1,006	903	1,248	1,088	1,036	948
Long Term Debt	726	724	728	584	590	600	602	Nil	635	646
Common Equity	1,872	1,979	1,658	1,323	1,102	1,111	1,067	1,300	1,311	1,366
Total Capital	2,684	2,850	2,567	1,907	1,691	1,896	1,884	1,432	2,112	2,105
Capital Expenditures	205	234	171	160	113	111	156	198	198	191
Cash Flow	431	548	427	286	252	245	351	204	338	308
Current Ratio	1.6	1.7	1.7	1.6	1.7	1.6	1.5	1.5	1.4	1.4
% Long Term Debt of Capitalization	27.0	25.4	28.4	30.6	34.9	31.7	31.9	Nil	30.1	30.7
% Net Income of Revenue	4.6	6.5	5.2	3.3	2.8	2.5	5.3	0.9	4.5	4.1
% Return on Assets	5.8	8.6	6.8	3.9	3.2	2.7	6.1	1.1	5.4	5.0
% Return on Equity	13.7	20.9	18.6	11.2	9.4	7.8	17.1	2.9	13.3	11.7

Data as orig reptd.; bef. results of disc opers/spec. items. Per share data adj. for stk. divs.; EPS diluted. E-Estimated. NA-Not Available. NM-Not Meaningful. NR-Not Ranked. UR-Under Review.

Office: 1 North Field Court, Lake Forest, IL 60045-4811. **Telephone:** 847-735-4700. **Website:** http://www.brunswick.com **Chrmn & CEO:** D.E. McCoy

SVP & CFO: P.G. Leemputte **VP, Secy & General Counsel:** M.I. Smith **VP & Cntlr:** A.L. Lowe

Board Members: N. D. Archibald, J. L. Bleustein, M. J. Callahan, C. W. Dunaway, M. A. Fernandez, P. Harf, D. E. McCoy, G. H. Phillips, R. W. Schipke, R. C. Stayer, L. A. Zimmerman

Founded: 1844 **Domicile:** Delaware **Employees:** 28,000

Burlington Northern Santa Fe Corp

STANDARD &POOR'S

S&P Recommendation	HOLD ★★★☆☆	Price $82.45 (as of Nov 23, 2007)	12-Mo. Target Price $88.00	Investment Style Large-Cap Growth

GICS Sector Industrials
Sub-Industry Railroads

Summary Through BNSF Railway Co. (formerly The Burlington Northern and Santa Fe Railway Co.), BNI owns one of the largest railroad networks in the U.S.

Key Stock Statistics (Source S&P, Vickers, company reports)

52-Wk Range	**$95.47– 71.51**	S&P Oper. EPS 2007**E**	5.12	Market Capitalization(B)	$28.910	Beta	0.89
Trailing 12-Month EPS	**$5.05**	S&P Oper. EPS 2008**E**	6.36	Yield (%)	1.55	S&P 3-Yr. Proj. EPS CAGR(%)	11.00
Trailing 12-Month P/E	**16.3**	P/E on S&P Oper. EPS 2007**E**	16.1	Dividend Rate/Share	$1.28	S&P Credit Rating	BBB
$10K Invested 5 Yrs Ago	**$35,012**	Common Shares Outstg. (M)	350.6	Institutional Ownership (%)	73		

Price Performance

30-Week Mov. Avg. ··· 10-Week Mov. Avg. - - **GAAP Earnings vs. Previous Year** Volume Above Avg. STARS
12-Mo. Target Price — Relative Strength — ▲ Up ▼ Down ▶ No Change Below Avg.

Options: ASE, CBOE, P

Analysis prepared by **Kevin Kirkeby** on November 14, 2007, when the stock traded at **$ 85.49**.

Highlights

➤ We see revenue rising a little under 8% in 2008 on a nearly 3% rise in volumes and 5% yield gain (price and mix). The recovery in volumes, after being down an expected 2.5% in 2007, will be largely driven by coal and agricultural shipments, both non-cyclical segments, in our view. We anticipate that intermodal shipments will decline in the first half of 2008 on account of shifts in ocean carrier routes and the weak outlook provided by various retailers. However, we expect revenue per intermodal carload to improve due to contract repricings.

➤ We project an operating margin of about 24% in 2008, as we see the positive impact of higher pricing and asset utilization outweighing the impact of rising salaries and stepped up depreciation charges. We also consider 2007 to have had above normal incidences of severe weather that raised fuel and labor expenses.

➤ We forecast EPS of $6.36 in 2008, up from $5.12 expected in 2007, including $0.12 in special charges. Our EPS estimates factor in a 3% reduction in the average share count in 2007 and another 2% in 2008, based on BNI's buyback announcements.

Investment Rationale/Risk

➤ We think BNI will continue to generate above-average revenue growth, driven by its exposure to the intermodal transport, long-haul coal and grain markets. For the 2007-2012 period, we see a compound annual growth rate in revenue of 7%, down from 17% over the prior three years. With our view of slowing top-line growth and fewer opportunities for margin enhancement, but valuations near the 10-year average, we see the shares as fairly valued.

➤ Risks to our recommendation and target price include weaker than expected economic growth, rising customer resistance to price increases, a greater role by regulators in setting rates, and disruptions at ports or rails during contract negotiations.

➤ Our DCF model, which assumes an 8.3% weighted average cost of capital, 10% annual growth in free cash flow over the next five years, and 3.5% terminal growth, calculates an intrinsic value of $98. We believe an enterprise value to 12-month forward EBITDA ratio of about 6.7X, which is modestly above the 10-year average, is appropriate, leading to a value of $78. Combining these models, our 12-month target price is $88.

Qualitative Risk Assessment

LOW	MEDIUM	HIGH

Our risk assessment reflects what we believe is BNI's strong profitability, cash flow generation, and balance sheet, as well as a diverse customer base, offset somewhat by its exposure to economic cycles, freight demand, and regulations.

Quantitative Evaluations

S&P Quality Ranking A-

D	C	B-	B	B+	A-	A	A+

Relative Strength Rank MODERATE

68

LOWEST = 1   HIGHEST = 99

Revenue/Earnings Data

Revenue (Million $)

	1Q	2Q	3Q	4Q	Year
2007	3,645	3,843	4,069	--	--
2006	3,463	3,701	3,939	3,882	14,985
2005	2,982	3,138	3,317	3,550	12,987
2004	2,490	2,685	2,793	2,978	10,946
2003	2,232	2,294	2,395	2,492	9,413
2002	2,163	2,207	2,308	2,301	8,979

Earnings Per Share ($)

2007	0.96	1.20	1.48	E1.48	E5.12
2006	1.09	1.27	1.33	1.42	5.10
2005	0.83	0.96	1.09	1.13	4.01
2004	0.52	0.67	0.01	0.91	2.10
2003	0.40	0.54	0.55	0.61	2.09
2002	0.45	0.51	0.51	0.54	2.00

Fiscal year ended Dec. 31. Next earnings report expected: Late January. EPS Estimates based on S&P Operating Earnings; historical GAAP earnings are as reported.

Dividend Data (Dates: mm/dd Payment Date: mm/dd/yy)

Amount ($)	Date Decl.	Ex-Div. Date	Stk. of Record	Payment Date
0.250	10/19	12/08	12/12	01/02/07
0.250	02/14	03/08	03/12	04/02/07
0.250	04/23	06/07	06/11	07/02/07
0.320	07/19	09/06	09/10	10/01/07

Dividends have been paid since 1940. Source: Company reports.

Burlington Northern Santa Fe Corp

STANDARD &POOR'S

Business Summary November 14, 2007

CORPORATE OVERVIEW. Burlington Northern Santa Fe Corp., through its BNSF Railway Co. subsidiary, operates the second largest U.S. rail system, delivering about 45% of rail traffic in the West, and about 23% of U.S. rail traffic. BNSF operates a rail system of about 32,000 miles (24,000 owned, 8,000 trackage rights) that spans 28 western and midwestern states and two Canadian provinces.

MARKET PROFILE. We believe BNI's consumer/intermodal business, sensitive to U.S. import and consumption trends, is the industry volume leader, and is at the heart of its competitive strategy. Consumer freight provided 39% of freight revenues in 2006 and consisted primarily of intermodal service: international container traffic, services to United Parcel Service, less-than-truckload and truckload carriers, and automotive traffic. Industrial products, sensitive to U.S. GDP trends, provided 25% of freight revenues in 2006, and was comprised of construction and building products, chemicals, and petroleum. Coal, which we believe is BNI's most profitable segment, accounted for 20% of 2006 freight revenues. A major transporter of low-sulfur coal, 90% of BNI's coal traffic originates in the Powder River Basin of Wyoming and Montana, primar-

ily delivered to power utilities. Agricultural products, sensitive to annual crop volumes, accounted for 17% of 2006 freight revenues, including deliveries of grains, ethanol and fertilizer.

COMPETITIVE LANDSCAPE. The U.S. rail industry has an oligopoly-like structure, with over 80% of revenues generated by the four largest railroads: BNI and Union Pacific Corp. operating on the West Coast, and CSX Corp. and Norfolk Southern Corp. operating on the East Coast. Railroads simultaneously compete for customers while cooperating by sharing assets, interfacing systems, and cooperatively fulfilling customer transports. Key suppliers include locomotive and rail equipment manufacturers, fuel suppliers, and labor. BNI's employees, about 85% of whom are unionized, enjoy above national average compensation due to their significant bargaining power.

Company Financials Fiscal Year Ended Dec. 31

Per Share Data ($)	2006	2005	2004	2003	2002	2001	2000	1999	1998	1997
Tangible Book Value	29.04	25.57	24.71	22.84	21.10	20.33	19.08	17.96	16.53	14.53
Cash Flow	8.16	6.83	4.79	4.53	4.44	4.21	4.52	4.36	4.17	3.52
Earnings	5.10	4.01	2.10	2.09	2.00	1.89	2.36	2.45	2.43	1.88
S&P Core Earnings	5.13	4.10	2.03	2.01	1.75	1.73	NA	NA	NA	NA
Dividends	0.90	0.74	0.64	0.54	0.48	0.49	0.48	0.48	0.42	0.40
Payout Ratio	18%	18%	30%	26%	24%	26%	20%	20%	17%	21%
Prices:High	87.99	72.00	49.25	32.50	31.75	34.00	29.56	37.94	35.71	33.65
Prices:Low	63.80	44.58	29.52	23.29	23.18	22.40	19.06	22.88	26.88	23.42
P/E Ratio:High	17	18	23	16	16	18	13	15	15	18
P/E Ratio:Low	13	11	14	11	12	12	8	9	11	12

Income Statement Analysis (Million $)										
Revenue	14,985	12,987	10,946	9,413	8,979	9,208	9,205	9,100	8,941	8,413
Operating Income	4,625	3,997	2,698	2,575	2,587	2,664	3,003	3,096	2,990	2,630
Depreciation	1,130	1,075	1,012	910	931	909	895	897	832	773
Interest Expense	485	437	409	420	428	463	453	387	354	344
Pretax Income	2,992	2,448	1,273	1,231	1,216	1,182	1,585	1,819	1,849	1,404
Effective Tax Rate	36.9%	37.5%	37.9%	36.9%	37.5%	37.6%	38.2%	37.5%	37.5%	37.0%
Net Income	1,887	1,531	791	777	760	737	980	1,137	1,155	885
S&P Core Earnings	1,898	1,563	767	743	667	676	NA	NA	NA	NA

Balance Sheet & Other Financial Data (Million $)										
Cash	375	75.0	322	18.0	28.0	26.0	11.0	22.0	25.0	31.0
Current Assets	2,181	1,880	1,615	862	791	723	976	1,066	1,206	1,234
Total Assets	31,643	30,304	28,925	26,939	25,767	24,721	24,375	23,700	22,690	21,336
Current Liabilities	3,326	3,229	2,716	2,346	2,091	2,161	2,186	2,075	2,197	2,060
Long Term Debt	6,912	6,698	6,051	6,440	6,641	6,363	6,614	5,655	5,188	5,181
Common Equity	10,396	9,925	9,311	8,495	7,932	7,849	7,480	8,172	7,770	6,812
Total Capital	25,524	24,539	23,182	22,416	21,548	20,943	20,516	19,924	18,620	17,168
Capital Expenditures	2,014	1,750	1,527	1,726	1,358	1,459	1,399	1,788	2,147	2,182
Cash Flow	3,017	2,606	1,803	1,687	1,691	1,646	1,875	2,034	1,987	1,658
Current Ratio	0.7	0.6	0.6	0.4	0.4	0.3	0.4	0.5	0.5	0.6
% Long Term Debt of Capitalization	27.1	27.3	26.1	28.7	30.8	30.4	32.2	28.4	27.9	30.2
% Net Income of Revenue	12.6	11.8	7.2	8.3	8.5	8.0	10.6	12.5	12.9	10.5
% Return on Assets	6.1	5.2	2.8	2.9	3.0	3.0	4.1	4.9	5.2	4.3
% Return on Equity	18.9	15.6	8.9	9.5	9.6	9.6	12.5	14.3	15.8	13.8

Data as orig reptd.; bef. results of disc opers/spec. items. Per share data adj. for stk. divs.; EPS diluted. E-Estimated. NA-Not Available. NM-Not Meaningful. NR-Not Ranked. UR-Under Review.

Office: 2650 Lou Menk Dr, Fort Worth, TX 76131-2830.
Telephone: 800-795-2673.
Email: investor.relations@bnsf.com
Website: http://www.bnsf.com

Chrmn, Pres & CEO: M.K. Rose
EVP & CFO: T.N. Hund
EVP & Secy: R. Nober
Investor Contact: M. Bracker (817-352-4813)

Board Members: A. L. Boeckmann, D. G. Cook, V. S. Martinez, M. F. Racicot, R. S. Roberts, M. K. Rose, M. J. Shapiro, J. C. Watts, Jr., R. H. West, J. S. Whisler, E. E. Whitacre, Jr.
Founded: 1994
Domicile: Delaware
Employees: 41,000

The McGraw-Hill Companies

Campbell Soup Co

STANDARD & POOR'S

S&P Recommendation	HOLD ★★★☆☆	Price $35.06 (as of Nov 23, 2007)	12-Mo. Target Price $42.00	Investment Style Large-Cap Growth

GICS Sector Consumer Staples
Sub-Industry Packaged Foods & Meats

Summary Campbell Soup is a major producer of branded soups and other grocery food products.

Key Stock Statistics (Source S&P, Vickers, company reports)

52-Wk Range	$42.65–34.17	S&P Oper. EPS 2008**E**	2.07	Market Capitalization(B)	$13.467	Beta	0.42
Trailing 12-Month EPS	$2.14	S&P Oper. EPS 2009**E**	2.25	Yield (%)	2.51	S&P 3-Yr. Proj. EPS CAGR(%)	7.00
Trailing 12-Month P/E	16.4	P/E on S&P Oper. EPS 2008**E**	16.9	Dividend Rate/Share	$0.88	S&P Credit Rating	A
$10K Invested 5 Yrs Ago	$16,630	Common Shares Outstg. (M)	384.1	Institutional Ownership (%)	43		

Price Performance

30-Week Mov. Avg. · · · 10-Week Mov. Avg. - - - **GAAP Earnings vs. Previous Year** Volume Above Avg. STARS
12-Mo. Target Price — Relative Strength — ▲ Up ▼ Down ▶ No Change Below Avg.

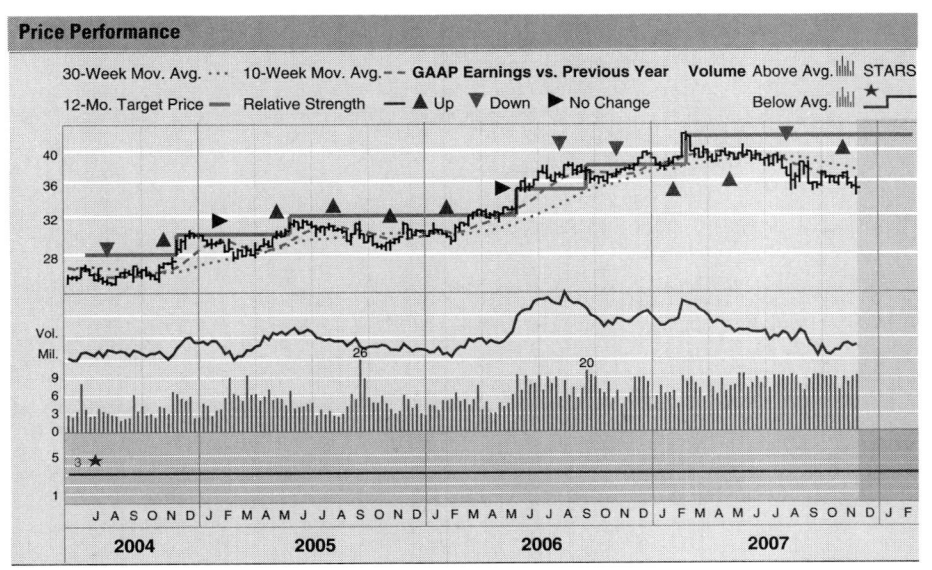

Options: ASE, CBOE, P, Ph

Analysis prepared by **Tom Graves, CFA** on November 19, 2007, when the stock traded at **$ 34.94**.

Highlights

➤ For the company as currently constituted, we look for FY 08 (Jul.) net sales from continuing operations to rise about 7% from the $7.9 billion reported for FY 07. We expect sales to benefit from new or enhanced products and from some expansions in packaging or distribution. Also, we expect FY 08 to include a 53rd week of sales. We believe that improved convenience and lower-salt products will help longer-term soup sales.

➤ We expect that CPB's profit margins will be face pressure in FY 08 from cost inflation, and that this will be at least partly offset by productivity gains and price increases. Excluding some year-ago special items, we expect the tax rate to be higher, and we estimate that net income, before special items, will total $786 million, up 2% from about $771 million in FY 07. In FY 08, we expect that there will be incremental costs related to CPB's expected entry into Russian and Chinese markets.

➤ With fewer shares outstanding, we look for FY 08 EPS of $2.07, up from FY 07's $1.95, which excluded a benefit of about $0.13 a share related to a reversal of legal reserves, a settlement, and an asset sale gain.

Investment Rationale/Risk

➤ We see the company bolstering growth prospects through new or enhanced products, increasingly portable packaging, and some expanded distribution, including overseas markets.

➤ Risks to our recommendation and target price include competitive pressures in CPB's businesses, consumer acceptance of new products, and the company's ability to achieve sales and earnings growth forecasts.

➤ The stock was recently trading at about 17.5X our calendar 2007 EPS estimate of $2.01, moderately below the valuation on average, by a peer group of packaged food stocks. Our 12-month target price of $42 is based on our expectation that the stock will trade closer to the peer average. Also, our discounted cash flow (DCF) model, which assumes average sales growth of about 5% during the next five years, a long-term blended WACC of 8.2%, and a perpetuity annual cash flow growth rate of 3%, shows an intrinsic value of about $43. The shares had a recent indicated dividend yield of 2.5%.

Qualitative Risk Assessment

LOW	MEDIUM	HIGH

Our risk assessment for Campbell Soup reflects the relatively stable nature of the company's end markets, our view that the company has strong cash flow, and corporate governance practices that we see as favorable relative to peers.

Quantitative Evaluations

S&P Quality Ranking   B+

D	C	B-	B	B+	A-	A	A+

Relative Strength Rank   MODERATE

63

LOWEST = 1   HIGHEST = 99

Revenue/Earnings Data

Revenue (Million $)

	1Q	2Q	3Q	4Q	Year
2008	2,298	--	--	--	--
2007	2,153	2,252	1,868	1,594	7,867
2006	2,002	2,159	1,728	1,454	7,343
2005	2,091	2,223	1,736	1,498	7,548
2004	1,909	2,100	1,667	1,433	7,109
2003	1,705	1,918	1,600	1,455	6,678

Earnings Per Share ($)

2008	0.70	E0.73	E0.43	E0.21	E2.07
2007	0.66	0.72	0.55	0.14	2.08
2006	0.69	0.58	0.35	0.20	1.82
2005	0.56	0.57	0.35	0.23	1.71
2004	0.51	0.57	0.34	0.14	1.57
2003	0.47	0.56	0.31	0.18	1.52

Fiscal year ended Jul. 31. Next earnings report expected: Mid February. EPS Estimates based on S&P Operating Earnings; historical GAAP earnings are as reported.

Dividend Data (Dates: mm/dd Payment Date: mm/dd/yy)

Amount ($)	Date Decl.	Ex-Div. Date	Stk. of Record	Payment Date
0.200	03/22	04/04	04/09	04/30/07
0.200	06/28	07/05	07/09	07/30/07
0.220	09/27	10/04	10/09	10/29/07
0.220	11/15	12/27	12/31	01/28/08

Dividends have been paid since 1902. Source: Company reports.

Please read the Required Disclosures and Analyst Certification on the last page of this report.

The McGraw-Hill Companies

Campbell Soup Co

Business Summary November 19, 2007

CORPORATE OVERVIEW. Probably known best for its ubiquitous red and white soup cans (elevated to icon status by Andy Warhol), Campbell Soup Co. is a major force in the U.S. packaged foods industry. The company, which traces its origins in the food business back to 1869, manufactures and markets a wide array of branded, prepared convenience food products worldwide.

In FY 06 (Jul.), operations outside the U.S. accounted for 30% of net sales and 20% of segment operating profits (before corporate expense), with much of the international sales and profits coming from Australia/Asia Pacific (13% of total net sales and 7% of segment profits) and Europe (9% and 4%).

The company reports results based on the following segments: U.S. Soup, Sauces and Beverages (44% of FY 07 sales, 62% of FY 07 segment profits); Baking and Snacking (24%, 17%), International Soup and Sauces (18%, 12%), and Other (14%, 9%).

Campbell's U.S. Soup, Sauces and Beverages segment includes major U.S. products such as both condensed and ready-to-serve soups (Campbell's, Home Cookin', Chunky, Healthy Request); broth (Swanson); chili (Campbell's Chunky); meal kits (Campbell's Supper Bakes); juices (Campbell's Tomato, V8,

V8 Splash); canned pasta, gravies and beans (Campbell's); spaghetti sauce (Prego); and Mexican sauces (Pace).

The company's Baking and Snacking division includes Pepperidge Farm cookies, crackers, breads and frozen products in the U.S.; Arnotts biscuits in Australia and Asia Pacific; and Arnotts salty snacks in Australia. The International Soup and Sauces segment includes the soup, sauces and beverage businesses outside of the United States, including Europe, Mexico, Latin America, the Asia Pacific region, and the retail business in Canada.

The balance of the portfolio reported in Other includes Godiva Chocolatier (worldwide) and the company's Away From Home operations, which represent the distribution of products such as soup, specialty entrees, beverage products, other prepared foods and Pepperidge Farm products through various foodservice channels in the U.S. and Canada.

Company Financials Fiscal Year Ended Jul. 31

Per Share Data ($)	2007	2006	2005	2004	2003	2002	2001	2000	1999	1998
Tangible Book Value	NM	NM	NM	NM	NM	NM	NM	NM	NM	NM
Cash Flow	2.79	2.52	2.39	2.20	2.11	2.05	2.19	2.23	2.20	2.07
Earnings	2.08	1.82	1.71	1.57	1.52	1.28	1.55	1.65	1.63	1.50
S&P Core Earnings	1.95	1.81	1.63	1.47	1.46	1.00	1.28	NA	NA	NA
Dividends	0.80	0.72	0.68	0.63	0.63	0.63	0.90	0.68	0.89	0.82
Payout Ratio	38%	40%	40%	40%	41%	49%	58%	41%	55%	55%
Prices:High	42.65	39.98	31.60	30.52	27.90	30.00	35.44	39.63	55.75	62.88
Prices:Low	34.17	28.88	27.35	25.03	19.95	19.65	25.52	23.75	37.44	46.69
P/E Ratio:High	21	22	18	19	18	23	23	24	34	42
P/E Ratio:Low	16	16	16	16	13	15	16	14	23	31

Income Statement Analysis (Million $)										
Revenue	7,867	7,343	7,548	7,109	6,678	6,133	6,664	6,267	6,424	6,696
Operating Income	1,541	1,445	1,483	1,394	1,376	1,442	1,470	1,516	1,625	1,782
Depreciation	23.0	289	279	260	243	319	266	251	255	261
Interest Expense	163	165	184	174	186	190	216	192	184	189
Pretax Income	1,149	1,001	1,030	947	924	798	987	1,077	1,097	1,079
Effective Tax Rate	28.4%	24.6%	31.4%	31.7%	32.3%	34.2%	34.2%	33.7%	34.0%	35.6%
Net Income	823	755	707	647	626	525	649	714	724	689
S&P Core Earnings	772	751	675	603	604	413	536	NA	NA	NA

Balance Sheet & Other Financial Data (Million $)										
Cash	71.0	657	40.0	32.0	32.0	21.0	24.0	27.0	6.00	16.0
Current Assets	1,578	2,112	1,512	1,481	1,290	1,199	1,221	1,168	1,294	1,440
Total Assets	6,445	7,870	6,776	6,675	6,205	5,721	5,927	5,196	5,522	5,633
Current Liabilities	2,030	2,962	2,002	2,339	2,783	2,678	3,120	3,032	3,146	2,803
Long Term Debt	2,074	2,116	2,542	2,543	2,249	2,449	2,243	1,218	1,330	1,169
Common Equity	1,295	1,768	1,270	874	387	-114	-247	137	275	874
Total Capital	3,369	3,884	3,812	3,417	2,636	2,335	1,996	1,355	1,564	2,293
Capital Expenditures	334	309	332	288	283	269	200	200	297	256
Cash Flow	1,106	1,044	986	907	869	844	915	965	979	950
Current Ratio	0.8	0.7	0.8	0.6	0.5	0.4	0.4	0.4	0.4	0.5
% Long Term Debt of Capitalization	61.6	54.5	66.7	74.4	85.3	104.9	112.4	89.9	85.0	51.0
% Net Income of Revenue	10.5	10.3	9.4	9.1	9.4	8.6	9.7	11.4	11.3	10.3
% Return on Assets	11.5	10.3	10.5	10.0	10.5	9.0	11.7	13.3	13.0	11.4
% Return on Equity	53.7	49.7	66.0	102.6	458.6	NA	NA	383.9	130.6	60.1

Data as orig reptd.; bef. results of disc opers/spec. items. Per share data adj. for stk. divs.; EPS diluted. E-Estimated. NA-Not Available. NM-Not Meaningful. NR-Not Ranked. UR-Under Review.

Office: 1 Campbell Pl, Camden, NJ 08103-1799.
Telephone: 856-342-4800.
Website: http://www.campbellsoup.com
Chrmn: H. Golub

Pres & CEO: D.R. Conant
SVP & CFO: R.A. Schiffner
SVP & CIO: D.A. Wright
Investor Contact: L.F. Griehs (856-342-6427)

Board Members: E. M. Carpenter, P. R. Charron, D. R. Conant, B. Dorrance, K. B. Foster, H. Golub, R. W. Larrimore, P. E. Lippincott, M. A. Malone, S. Mathew, D. C. Patterson, C. R. Perrin, A. B. Rand, G. Strawbridge, Jr., L. C. Vinney, C. C. Weber

Founded: 1869
Domicile: New Jersey
Employees: 22,500

CA Inc

STANDARD &POOR'S

S&P Recommendation   HOLD ★★★☆☆

Price	12-Mo. Target Price	Investment Style
$24.65 (as of Nov 23, 2007)	$30.00	Large-Cap Blend

GICS Sector Information Technology
Sub-Industry Systems Software

Summary This company (formerly Computer Associates International) develops systems software, database management systems, and applications software.

Key Stock Statistics (Source S&P, Vickers, company reports)

52-Wk Range	$28.46– 21.29	S&P Oper. EPS 2008**E**	1.07	Market Capitalization(B)	$12.605	Beta	2.23
Trailing 12-Month EPS	$0.56	S&P Oper. EPS 2009**E**	1.25	Yield (%)	0.65	S&P 3-Yr. Proj. EPS CAGR(%)	13.00
Trailing 12-Month P/E	44.0	P/E on S&P Oper. EPS 2008**E**	23.0	Dividend Rate/Share	$0.16	S&P Credit Rating	BB
$10K Invested 5 Yrs Ago	$16,827	Common Shares Outstg. (M)	511.4	Institutional Ownership (%)	77		

Price Performance

30-Week Mov. Avg. ···· 10-Week Mov. Avg. -- **GAAP Earnings vs. Previous Year**   Volume Above Avg. ⅡⅡⅡ STARS
12-Mo. Target Price — Relative Strength — ▲ Up ▼ Down ► No Change   Below Avg. ⅠⅡⅡ ★

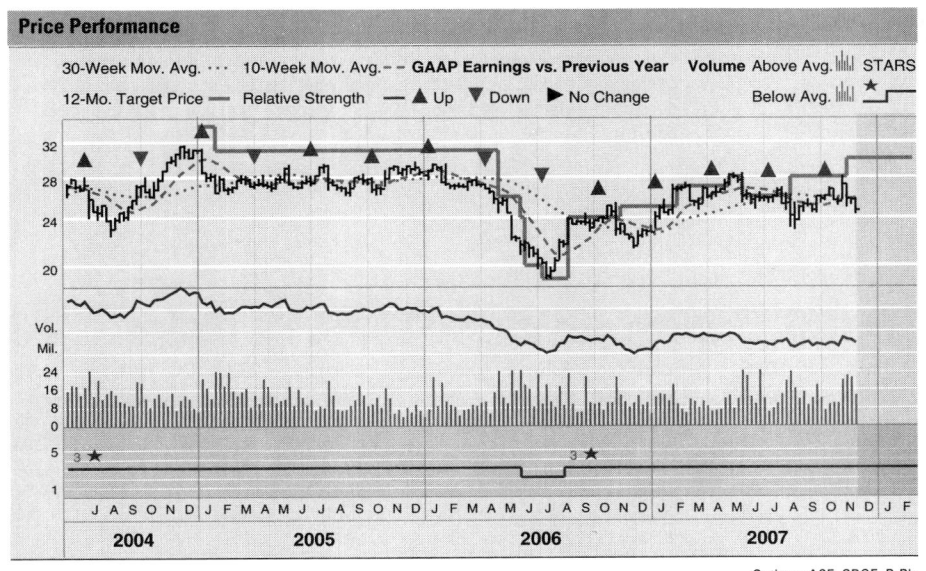

Options: ASE, CBOE, P, Ph

Analysis prepared by **Jim Yin** on November 05, 2007, when the stock traded at **$ 27.18.**

Highlights

➤ We estimate total revenues will increase 5.6% in FY 08 (Mar.), following a 4.6% increase in FY 07. We expect subscription revenue to rise 10% and to account for 81% of total revenue, as CA shifts to a ratable revenue recognition model. We believe CA will benefit from its sales force reorganization, a broader product portfolio, and a favorable currency exchange. We expect bookings to increase in the high teens in FY 08.

➤ We expect the gross margin in FY 08 to increase to 89%, from 83% in FY 07, due to a higher revenue contribution of subscription revenue and an improvement in professional service margins. We see operating expenses decreasing as a percentage of revenue to 62%, from 69% in FY 07, as CA reduces its employee headcount. We project that non-GAAP operating margins in FY 08 will widen to 27%, from 19%, on effective cost control.

➤ Our EPS estimate for FY 08 is $1.07 compared to EPS of $0.85 in FY 07. The projected increase in earnings is due to expected higher revenues and operating margins, partially offset by a higher effective tax rate of 35% compared to 21% in FY 07.

Investment Rationale/Risk

➤ We believe CA has improved its operations by restructuring its sales force and reducing employee headcount. In our opinion, the company has strengthened is product offerings in higher growth market segments by making acquisitions in recent quarters. We also think CA has benefited from a shift to a ratable revenue recognition model, which results in more predictable revenues. We believe these factors will offset our view for modest IT spending growth of 5%-8% and CA's dependence on its legacy mainframe software business, where we project flat growth.

➤ Risks to our opinion and target price include significant declines in corporate spending on enterprise software from current levels, pricing pressure from increased competition, and a slowdown in the global economy.

➤ We derive our 12-month target price of $30 by applying a 28X P/E multiple to our FY 08 EPS estimate, which is within the three-year average trading range of 34.7X-22.7X, and is in line with software peers.

Qualitative Risk Assessment

LOW	MEDIUM	**HIGH**

Our risk assessment for the company reflects our concerns regarding what we consider to be inconsistent execution, weak financial results and modest underlying growth.

Quantitative Evaluations

S&P Quality Ranking   **B-**

D	C	**B-**	B	B+	A-	A	A+

Relative Strength Rank   **MODERATE**

57

LOWEST = 1   HIGHEST = 99

Revenue/Earnings Data

Revenue (Million $)

	1Q	2Q	3Q	4Q	Year
2008	1,025	1,067	--	--	--
2007	949.0	987.0	1,002	1,005	3,943
2006	927.0	950.0	971.0	948.0	3,796
2005	850.0	858.0	910.0	912.0	3,530
2004	813.0	833.0	844.0	850.0	3,276
2003	765.0	772.0	778.0	801.0	3,116

Earnings Per Share ($)

2008	0.24	0.26	E0.28	E0.30	E1.07
2007	0.06	0.09	0.10	-0.04	0.22
2006	0.16	0.08	0.09	-0.07	0.26
2005	0.08	-0.16	0.06	0.04	0.02
2004	0.02	-0.15	0.04	0.05	-0.06
2003	-0.11	-0.09	-0.08	-0.18	-0.46

Fiscal year ended Mar. 31. Next earnings report expected: Early February. EPS Estimates based on S&P Operating Earnings; historical GAAP earnings are as reported.

Dividend Data (Dates: mm/dd Payment Date: mm/dd/yy)

Amount ($)	Date Decl.	Ex-Div. Date	Stk. of Record	Payment Date
0.040	11/21	12/13	12/15	12/29/06
0.040	02/23	03/13	03/15	03/30/07
0.040	06/12	06/20	06/22	06/29/07
0.040	08/22	09/10	09/12	09/26/07

Dividends have been paid since 1990. Source: Company reports.

Business Summary November 05, 2007

CORPORATE OVERVIEW. CA provides information technology (IT) management software, which helps customers better manage their IT infrastructure. The company has a broad portfolio of software products and services that span the areas of infrastructure management, security management, storage management and business service optimization.

In April 2007, CA announced a new strategy, Enterprise IT Management (EITM), for transforming the way companies manage their IT. The goal of EITM is to unify disparate elements of IT including hardware, processes, and people so customers can have better control and manage these resources rather than replace existing IT investments. For example, CA's Unicenter Advanced Systems Management provides centralized management for virtualized and clustered server environments, enabling customers to assess and optimize network resources.

Key parts of CA's EITM strategy include:

Internal Product Development - CA plans to ship new versions of every major product, including those products obtained through acquisitions. The company has added headcount in India and Czech Republic research centers.

Strengthening Partner Relationships - CA intends to strengthen its global distribution by recruiting and educating channel partners on CA products and services. The company formed a Mid-Market and Storage organization that targets enterprises with 500-5000 employees.

International Expansion - CA will invest in regions outside the U.S., especially in emerging markets such as China and India to increase the volume of enterprise sales. The company has also pursued small and medium-sized customers in the Europe, Middle East and Africa (EMEA) region. International revenue comprised nearly 46% of total sales in FY 07, down from about 47% in FY 06.

Strategic Acquisitions - CA has made several small acquisitions that the company considers strategic and complementary to its systems and security management offerings. In FY 07, the company completed the acquisitions of Cendura Corporation, XOsoft, Inc., MDY Group International, Inc. and Cybermation, Inc.

Company Financials Fiscal Year Ended Mar. 31

Per Share Data ($)	2007	2006	2005	2004	2003	2002	2001	2000	1999	1998
Tangible Book Value	NM	NM	0.50	8.09	NM	NM	0.66	1.71	2.06	2.53
Cash Flow	0.47	1.22	0.24	0.17	0.60	-0.01	0.89	2.32	1.69	2.68
Earnings	0.22	0.26	0.02	-0.06	-0.46	-1.91	-1.02	1.25	1.11	2.06
S&P Core Earnings	0.23	0.26	0.22	0.02	-0.53	-2.05	-1.18	NA	NA	NA
Dividends	0.16	0.08	0.08	0.08	0.08	0.08	0.08	0.08	0.08	0.07
Payout Ratio	73%	31%	NM	NM	NM	NM	NM	6%	7%	3%
Calendar Year	2006	2005	2004	2003	2002	2001	2000	1999	1998	1997
Prices:High	29.50	31.35	31.71	29.29	38.74	39.03	79.44	70.63	61.94	57.50
Prices:Low	18.97	26.04	22.37	12.39	7.47	18.31	18.13	32.13	26.00	24.83
P/E Ratio:High	NM	NM	NM	NM	NM	NM	NM	56	56	28
P/E Ratio:Low	NM	NM	NM	NM	NM	NM	NM	26	23	12

Income Statement Analysis (Million $)

	2007	2006	2005	2004	2003	2002	2001	2000	1999	1998
Revenue	3,943	3,796	3,530	3,276	3,116	2,964	4,198	6,766	5,253	4,719
Operating Income	560	836	504	417	421	-62.0	604	3,318	2,529	2,366
Depreciation	148	583	130	134	612	1,096	1,110	594	325	349
Interest Expense	126	41.0	106	Nil	172	227	344	339	154	147
Pretax Income	154	121	11.0	-54.0	-363	-1,385	-666	1,590	1,010	1,874
Effective Tax Rate	21.4%	NM	NM	NM	NM	NM	NM	56.2%	38.0%	37.6%
Net Income	121	156	13.0	-36.0	-267	-1,102	-591	696	626	1,169
S&P Core Earnings	122	155	136	7.10	-301	-1,185	-688	NA	NA	NA

Balance Sheet & Other Financial Data (Million $)

	2007	2006	2005	2004	2003	2002	2001	2000	1999	1998
Cash	2,280	1,865	3,125	1,902	1,512	1,180	850	1,387	536	251
Current Assets	3,101	2,648	3,954	3,358	3,565	3,061	2,643	3,992	2,631	2,255
Total Assets	10,585	10,438	11,082	10,679	11,054	12,226	14,143	17,493	8,070	6,706
Current Liabilities	3,714	3,377	3,664	2,455	2,974	2,321	2,286	3,004	1,863	1,876
Long Term Debt	2,572	1,810	1,810	2,298	2,298	3,334	3,639	4,527	2,032	1,027
Common Equity	3,690	4,680	4,840	4,718	4,363	4,617	5,780	7,037	2,729	2,481
Total Capital	6,282	6,536	6,822	7,634	7,525	9,218	11,319	13,929	5,795	4,460
Capital Expenditures	150	143	69.0	30.0	30.0	25.0	89.0	198	222	84.0
Cash Flow	269	739	143	98.0	345	-6.00	519	1,290	951	1,518
Current Ratio	0.8	0.8	1.1	1.4	1.2	1.3	1.2	1.3	1.4	1.2
% Long Term Debt of Capitalization	41.1	27.7	26.5	30.1	30.5	36.2	32.1	32.5	35.1	23.0
% Net Income of Revenue	3.1	4.1	0.4	NM	NM	NM	NM	10.2	11.9	24.8
% Return on Assets	1.2	1.4	0.1	NM	NM	NM	NM	5.4	8.5	18.3
% Return on Equity	2.9	3.2	0.3	NM	NM	NM	NM	14.3	24.0	58.7

Data as orig reptd.; bef. results of disc opers/spec. items. Per share data adj. for stk. divs.; EPS diluted. E-Estimated. NA-Not Available. NM-Not Meaningful. NR-Not Ranked. UR-Under Review.

Office: 1 Computer Associates Plz, Islandia, NY 11749-7000.
Telephone: 631-342-6000.
Email: cainvestor@ca.com
Website: http://www.ca.com

Chrmn: L.S. Ranieri
Pres & CEO: J.A. Swainson
COO & EVP: M.J. Christenson
EVP & CFO: N.E. Cooper

EVP & Chief Admin Officer: J.E. Bryant
Board Members: R. J. Bromark, A. M. D'Amato, G. J. Fernandes, R. E. La Blanc, C. B. Lofgren, J. W. Lorsch, W. E. McCracken, L. S. Ranieri, W. P. Schuetze, J. A. Swainson, L. S. Unger, R. Zambonini

Founded: 1974
Domicile: Delaware
Employees: 14,500

Capital One Financial Corp.

STANDARD &POOR'S

S&P Recommendation HOLD ★★★☆☆	**Price** $52.07 (as of Nov 23, 2007)	**12-Mo. Target Price** $70.00	**Investment Style** Large-Cap Blend

GICS Sector Financials
Sub-Industry Consumer Finance

Summary This diversified consumer finance company is one of the largest issuers of Visa and MasterCard credit cards in the world.

Key Stock Statistics (Source S&P, Vickers, company reports)

52-Wk Range	$83.84–48.83	S&P Oper. EPS 2007E	4.88	Market Capitalization(B)	$21.749	Beta	1.84
Trailing 12-Month EPS	$4.44	S&P Oper. EPS 2008E	7.32	Yield (%)	0.20	S&P 3-Yr. Proj. EPS CAGR(%)	12.00
Trailing 12-Month P/E	11.7	P/E on S&P Oper. EPS 2007E	10.7	Dividend Rate/Share	$0.11	S&P Credit Rating	BBB+
$10K Invested 5 Yrs Ago	$16,646	Common Shares Outstg. (M)	417.7	Institutional Ownership (%)	79		

Price Performance

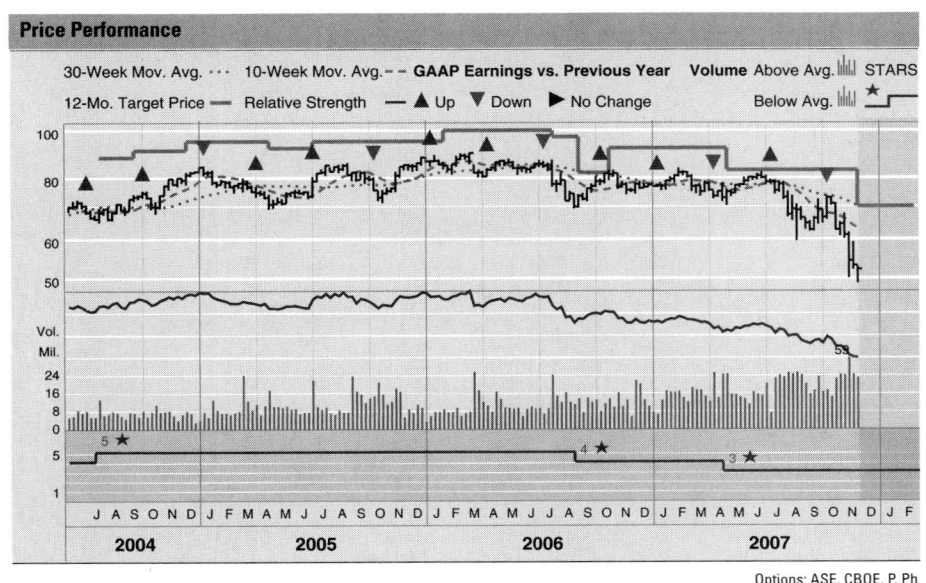

30-Week Mov. Avg. · · · 10-Week Mov. Avg. − − **GAAP Earnings vs. Previous Year** Volume Above Avg. ⅢⅢ STARS
12-Mo. Target Price — Relative Strength — ▲ Up ▼ Down ► No Change Below Avg. ⅢⅢ ★

Options: ASE, CBOE, P, Ph

Analysis prepared by **Frank Braden, CFA** on November 20, 2007, when the stock traded at **$ 50.31**.

Highlights

➤ We anticipate revenue growth of 20%, to $16.6 billion, in 2007, due largely to the recent acquisition of North Fork Bank, followed by a modest 4% rise in 2008. After continued weakness in COF's mortgage banking business from both gain-on-sale margin pressure and lower origination volumes primarily on Alt-A loans, COF decided to close its wholesale mortgage banking unit, GreenPoint Mortgage, in August. We see further pressure on COF's prime auto portfolio and credit card portfolio in 2008.

➤ While credit pressures in the U.K. business are showing signs of stabilizing, we see a gradual deterioration in consumer credit in the U.S. card business and expect further pressure on margins, as competition remains fierce. While we anticipate the continuation of solid expense management, we do not expect it to meaningfully offset credit pressures.

➤ Including charges related to the closure of GreenPoint Mortgages, our operating EPS estimate for 2007 is $4.88. Our estimate for 2008 is $7.32.

Investment Rationale/Risk

➤ We see progress in implementing Capital One's dual operating strategy of diversification and emphasis on lower loss rate products. We have concerns about intense competition and credit exposure in U.K. operations, as well as lower margins in COF's banking operations. We anticipate that cost-cutting initiatives and share repurchases will help support growth in earnings per share.

➤ Risks to our recommendation and target price include increased competition from larger credit card issuers; a decline in consumer confidence that could restrict consumer spending; integration risk; increased pressure on COF's remaining mortgage portfolio, and a rise in unemployment that could negatively affect credit quality.

➤ Our 12-month target price of $70 is equal to about 9.5X our 2008 EPS estimate. We believe this is an appropriate valuation multiple based on its discount to historical averages, justified, we believe, by increased integration and credit risk, and growth in lower-margin banking products.

Qualitative Risk Assessment

LOW	MEDIUM	HIGH

Our risk assessment reflects what we see as solid business fundamentals, diverse product offerings and a strong customer base. We view COF as well diversified and able to withstand a major economic downturn.

Quantitative Evaluations

S&P Quality Ranking **A+**

D	C	B-	B	B+	A-	A	A+

Relative Strength Rank **WEAK**

18

LOWEST = 1 HIGHEST = 99

Revenue/Earnings Data

Revenue (Million $)

	1Q	2Q	3Q	4Q	Year
2007	4,598	4,719	4,917	--	--
2006	3,737	3,607	2,826	4,021	15,191
2005	2,852	2,934	2,999	3,300	12,085
2004	2,608	2,548	2,768	2,771	10,695
2003	2,411	2,381	2,466	2,525	9,784
2002	2,133	2,369	2,628	2,434	9,648

Earnings Per Share ($)

2007	1.62	1.89	-2.09	E1.58	E4.88
2006	2.86	1.78	1.89	1.14	7.62
2005	1.99	2.03	1.81	0.97	6.73
2004	1.84	1.65	1.97	0.77	6.21
2003	1.35	1.23	1.23	1.11	4.92
2002	0.83	0.92	1.13	1.05	3.93

Fiscal year ended Dec. 31. Next earnings report expected: Mid January. EPS Estimates based on S&P Operating Earnings; historical GAAP earnings are as reported.

Dividend Data (Dates: mm/dd Payment Date: mm/dd/yy)

Amount ($)	Date Decl.	Ex-Div. Date	Stk. of Record	Payment Date
0.027	01/25	02/08	02/12	02/22/07
0.027	04/26	05/08	05/10	05/21/07
0.027	07/26	08/08	08/10	08/20/07
0.027	10/25	11/07	11/12	11/23/07

Dividends have been paid since 1995. Source: Company reports.

Capital One Financial Corp.

STANDARD &POOR'S

Business Summary November 20, 2007

CORPORATE OVERVIEW. COF is one of the world's largest financial services franchises. It is a diversified financial services corporation focused primarily on consumer lending and deposits. Its principal business segments are domestic credit card lending, automobile and other motor vehicle financing, global financial services and banking.

U.S. Card Segment. COF offers a wide variety of credit card products throughout the US. It customizes products to appeal to different consumer preferences and needs by combining different product features, including annual percentage rates, fees and credit limits, rewards programs and other special features. COF's pricing strategies are risk based; lower risk customers may likely be offered products with more favorable pricing and we expect these products to yield lower delinquencies and credit losses. On products offered to higher risk customers, however, COF is likely to experience higher delinquencies and losses, and it prices these products accordingly.

Auto Finance Segment. Through Capital One Auto Finance, Inc., the company

purchases retail installment contracts, secured by automobiles or other motor vehicles, through dealer networks throughout the U.S. In addition, COF utilizes direct marketing to offer automobile financing directly to consumers. Its direct marketed products include financing for the purchase of new and used vehicles, as well as refinancing of existing motor vehicle loans. As of December 31, 2006, COF was the third largest non-captive auto lender in the U.S. In January 2005, it acquired Onyx Acceptance Corporation, an auto finance company that provides financing to franchised and select independent dealerships throughout the U.S. The corporation also completed the acquisition of Key Bank's non-prime auto loan portfolio in 2005. Similar to its credit card strategy, COF customizes product features, such as interest rate, loan amount and loan terms, enabling it to lend to customers with a wide range of credit profiles.

Company Financials Fiscal Year Ended Dec. 31

Per Share Data ($)	2006	2005	2004	2003	2002	2001	2000	1999	1998	1997
Tangible Book Value	25.37	33.99	33.98	25.75	20.44	15.33	9.94	7.69	6.45	4.55
Earnings	7.62	6.73	6.21	4.92	3.93	2.91	2.24	1.72	1.32	0.93
S&P Core Earnings	7.61	6.61	5.72	4.41	3.37	2.55	NA	NA	NA	NA
Dividends	0.11	0.11	0.11	0.11	0.11	0.11	0.11	0.11	0.11	0.11
Payout Ratio	1%	2%	2%	2%	3%	4%	5%	6%	8%	11%
Prices:High	90.04	88.56	84.45	64.25	66.50	72.58	73.25	60.25	43.31	18.10
Prices:Low	69.30	69.09	60.04	24.91	24.05	36.40	32.06	35.81	16.85	10.17
P/E Ratio:High	12	13	14	13	17	25	33	35	33	19
P/E Ratio:Low	9	10	10	5	6	13	14	21	13	11

Income Statement Analysis (Million $)	2006	2005	2004	2003	2002	2001	2000	1999	1998	1997
Net Interest Income	5,100	3,680	3,003	2,785	2,719	1,663	1,589	1,053	695	383
Non Interest Income	6,997	6,358	5,900	5,416	5,467	4,420	3,034	2,372	1,488	1,069
Loan Loss Provision	1,476	1,491	1,221	1,517	2,149	990	718	383	267	263
Non Interest Expenses	6,967	5,718	5,322	4,857	4,586	4,058	3,148	2,465	1,472	884
% Expense/Operating Revenue	57.6%	57.0%	59.8%	59.2%	56.0%	66.7%	68.1%	72.0%	67.4%	60.9%
Pretax Income	3,653	2,829	2,360	1,827	1,451	1,035	757	577	444	305
Effective Tax Rate	33.9%	36.1%	34.6%	37.0%	38.0%	38.0%	38.0%	37.1%	38.0%	38.0%
Net Income	2,414	1,809	1,543	1,151	900	642	470	363	275	189
% Net Interest Margin	6.03	6.63	6.44	7.45	8.73	8.03	12.0	10.8	9.95	8.86
S&P Core Earnings	2,412	1,792	1,431	1,012	742	545	NA	NA	NA	NA

Balance Sheet & Other Financial Data (Million $)	2006	2005	2004	2003	2002	2001	2000	1999	1998	1997
Money Market Assets	1,843	2,049	1,084	1,598	641	352	162	112	284	174
Investment Securities	15,452	14,350	9,300	5,867	4,424	3,116	1,697	1,856	1,797	1,243
Earning Assets:Total Loans	106,947	59,848	38,216	32,850	27,854	20,921	14,059	9,914	6,157	4,862
Total Assets	149,739	88,701	53,747	46,284	37,382	28,184	18,889	13,336	9,419	7,078
Demand Deposits	NA	NA	NA	Nil	Nil	Nil	Nil	Nil	Nil	Nil
Time Deposits	74,123	43,092	NA	22,416	17,326	12,839	8,379	3,784	2,000	1,314
Long Term Debt	20,217	14,863	Nil	14,813	8,124	Nil	4,051	4,181	3,038	3,633
Common Equity	25,235	14,129	8,388	6,052	4,623	3,324	1,963	1,518	1,270	893
% Return on Assets	2.0	2.5	3.1	2.8	2.7	2.7	2.9	3.2	3.3	2.8
% Return on Equity	12.3	16.1	21.4	21.6	22.6	24.3	27.0	26.0	25.4	23.2
% Loan Loss Reserve	2.0	3.0	3.9	4.9	6.2	4.0	3.7	3.5	3.8	3.8
% Loans/Deposits	124.7	124.8	149.1	146.5	160.8	162.9	167.8	262.0	307.9	370.1
% Loans/Assets	70.0	68.8	71.0	71.9	74.4	74.3	72.3	70.6	66.8	68.0
% Equity to Assets	16.5	15.8	14.4	12.8	12.1	11.2	10.8	12.3	13.1	12.1

Data as orig reptd.; bef. results of disc opers/spec. items. Per share data adj. for stk. divs.; EPS diluted. E-Estimated. NA-Not Available. NM-Not Meaningful. NR-Not Ranked. UR-Under Review.

Office: 1680 Capital One Drive, McLean, VA 22102-3406.
Telephone: 703-720-1000.
Email: investor.relations@capitalone.com
Website: http://www.capitalone.com

Chrmn, Pres & CEO: R.D. Fairbank
EVP, CFO & Chief Acctg Officer: G.L. Perlin
EVP, Secy & General Counsel: J.G. Finneran, Jr.
EVP & CIO: R.M. Alexander

Investor Contact: M. Rowen (703-720-2455)
Board Members: E. R. Campbell, W. R. Dietz, R. D. Fairbank, P. W. Gross, A. F. Hackett, L. Hay, III, J. A. Kanas, P. E. Leroy, M. A. Shattuck, III, S. Westreich

Founded: 1993
Domicile: Delaware
Employees: 31,800

Cardinal Health Inc

STANDARD &POOR'S

S&P Recommendation **BUY** ★★★★☆	Price $56.98 (as of Nov 23, 2007)	12-Mo. Target Price $73.00	Investment Style Large-Cap Blend

GICS Sector Health Care
Sub-Industry Health Care Distributors

Summary This company is one of the leading wholesale distributors of pharmaceuticals, medical/surgical supplies and related products to a broad range of health care customers.

Key Stock Statistics (Source S&P, Vickers, company reports)

52-Wk Range	$76.15–56.41	S&P Oper. EPS 2008**E**	3.95	Market Capitalization(B)	$20.602	Beta	0.72
Trailing 12-Month EPS	$4.93	S&P Oper. EPS 2009**E**	4.65	Yield (%)	0.84	S&P 3-Yr. Proj. EPS CAGR(%)	15.00
Trailing 12-Month P/E	11.6	P/E on S&P Oper. EPS 2008**E**	14.4	Dividend Rate/Share	$0.48	S&P Credit Rating	BBB
$10K Invested 5 Yrs Ago	$9,310	Common Shares Outstg. (M)	361.6	Institutional Ownership (%)	86		

Price Performance

30-Week Mov. Avg. ··· 10-Week Mov. Avg. ─ ─ **GAAP Earnings vs. Previous Year** Volume Above Avg. ▮▮▮ STARS
12-Mo. Target Price ─ Relative Strength ─ ▲ Up ▼ Down ► No Change Below Avg. ▮▮▮ ★

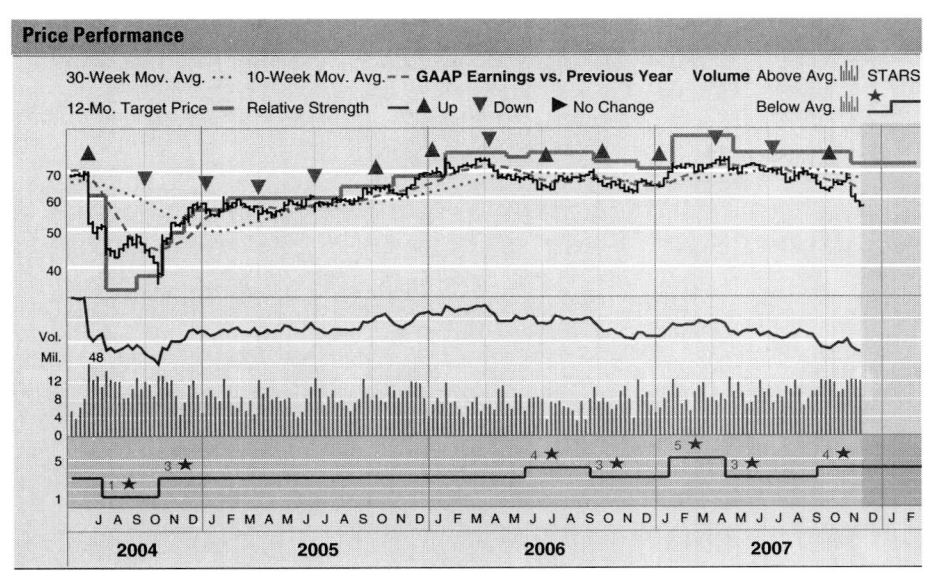

Options: ASE, CBOE, P, Ph

Analysis prepared by **Phillip M. Seligman** on November 13, 2007, when the stock traded at **$ 60.82**.

Highlights

➤ We project total revenue will rise by slightly over 6% in FY 08 (Jun.), to about $92.2 billion. We anticipate drug distribution revenue to grow more slowly than in FY 07, partly on customer losses and the lapping of large bulk sale increases. However, we now expect faster med-surg distribution (M/S) growth, despite the customer service transition. We also see medical product manufacturing (MPM) sales boosted by the recent acquisition of respiratory product maker Viasys, while the clinical technologies segment (CTS) benefits from acquisitions, new products, and overseas growth.

➤ We see narrower drug distribution profit margins, as the impact of retail contract repricing and competition in the nuclear pharmacy business outweigh improved operating leverage. We also expect the corporate cost reallocation to hurt med-surg distribution profit margins, while an improving sales mix aids those of MPM and CTS.

➤ We look for FY 08 operating EPS of $3.95, compared to FY 07's $3.42, and project $4.65 in FY 09. For FY 08, we expect the benefits to EPS from share buybacks to outweigh the dilutive impact that CAH sees from Viasys.

Investment Rationale/Risk

➤ Our buy opinion is based on valuation. CAH now sees its drug distribution segment's FY 08 revenue growth below its 7% to 10% target range, and we think that its growth is now level with the market's. But given intense competition and sell-side pricing pressure, we think the segment's profit margin will contract. On the positive side, we see sequential performance improvement in the second half on cost-reduction steps and the pending generic drug launches. We also think the launch of generic Cardiolite slated for FY 09 will relieve margin pressure on the nuclear pharmacy unit. Meanwhile, we are encouraged by CAH's intent to refocus marketing efforts on independent pharmacies and small chains, which offer wider margins than large chains.

➤ Risks to our recommendation and target price include the loss of major accounts and unfavorable changes in contracts with drugmakers and/or retailers.

➤ Our 12-month target price of $73 reflects a forward P/E of 18X applied to our calendar 2008 EPS estimate of $4.06. This multiple is below that of peers, given our view of below-average drug distribution performance characteristics.

Qualitative Risk Assessment

LOW	MEDIUM	HIGH

Our risk assessment reflects CAH's diversified products and services and what we believe are good growth prospects for its contract drugmaking and its drug dispensing systems. However, we also see intense competition in the drug distribution market and we believe that future drugmaker-distributor contract negotiations might be less favorable for distributors.

Quantitative Evaluations

S&P Quality Ranking A+

D	C	B-	B	B+	A-	A	A+

Relative Strength Rank MODERATE

31

LOWEST = 1   HIGHEST = 99

Revenue/Earnings Data

Revenue (Million $)

	1Q	2Q	3Q	4Q	Year
2008	21,973	--	--	--	--
2007	20,938	21,785	21,867	22,263	86,852
2006	19,237	19,781	20,638	21,708	81,364
2005	17,796	18,555	19,103	19,457	74,911
2004	15,388	16,351	16,392	16,923	65,054
2003	11,417	12,706	12,837	13,506	50,467

Earnings Per Share ($)

2008	0.82	E0.95	E1.00	E1.14	E3.95
2007	0.71	0.77	-0.01	0.61	2.07
2006	0.55	0.72	0.83	0.80	2.90
2005	0.50	0.47	0.84	0.59	2.40
2004	0.72	0.85	0.99	0.91	3.47
2003	0.64	0.82	0.74	0.82	3.12

Fiscal year ended Jun. 30. Next earnings report expected: Late January. EPS Estimates based on S&P Operating Earnings; historical GAAP earnings are as reported.

Dividend Data (Dates: mm/dd Payment Date: mm/dd/yy)

Amount ($)	Date Decl.	Ex-Div. Date	Stk. of Record	Payment Date
0.090	01/31	03/28	04/01	04/15/07
0.120	05/02	06/27	07/01	07/15/07
0.120	08/08	09/27	10/01	10/15/07
0.120	11/07	12/27	01/01	01/15/08

Dividends have been paid since 1983. Source: Company reports.

Please read the Required Disclosures and Analyst Certification on the last page of this report.

The McGraw-Hill Companies

Cardinal Health Inc

STANDARD &POOR'S

Business Summary November 13, 2007

CORPORATE OVERVIEW. As of FY 07 (Jun.), Cardinal Health's reportable segments were realigned into two main businesses comprised of four reportable segments:

Healthcare Supply Chain Services:

Healthcare Supply Chain Services - Pharmaceutical (SCSP; 86% of FY 07 operating revenue) distributes pharmaceutical and related health care products to independent and chain drug stores, hospitals, alternate care centers, and supermarket and mass merchandiser pharmacies. PDS operates a pharmaceutical repackaging and distribution program for retail and mail order customers. It is also a franchiser of retail pharmacies (Medicine Shoppe International, Inc. and Medicap Pharmacies Inc.).

Healthcare Supply Chain Services - Medical (SCSM; 9%) -- provides non-pharmaceutical health care products for hospitals and other health care providers.

Clinical and Medical Products:

Clinical Technologies and Services (CTS; 3%) provides automation and information products and services. One unit, Pyxis Corp., develops, manufactures

and markets point-of-use pharmacy systems that automate the distribution and management of medications and supplies in hospitals and other health care facilities.

Medical Products Manufacturing (MPM; 2%) -- manufactures sterile and non-sterile procedure kits, single-use surgical drapes, gowns and apparel, exam and surgical gloves, fluid suction and collection systems, respiratory therapy products, surgical instruments, special procedure products and other products.

CORPORATE STRATEGY. We believe it is CAH's intention to be viewed as a diversified health care services company, with a sizable drug distribution arm, rather than to be seen as a pharmaceutical distributor. We see this trend continuing as demand for CTS's higher-margin products and services increase. We expect that the bulk of the 25% of the operating cash flow CAH plans to reinvest into internal growth and the 25% it plans to use for acquisitions will be devoted to CTS and MPM.

Company Financials Fiscal Year Ended Jun. 30

Per Share Data ($)	2007	2006	2005	2004	2003	2002	2001	2000	1999	1998
Tangible Book Value	4.12	8.52	8.20	7.05	12.10	11.50	9.50	7.28	6.13	9.04
Cash Flow	2.87	3.82	3.34	4.15	3.70	2.98	2.50	2.17	1.65	1.86
Earnings	2.07	2.90	2.40	3.47	3.12	2.45	1.88	1.59	1.09	0.97
S&P Core Earnings	3.08	2.88	2.16	3.14	2.78	2.26	1.69	NA	NA	NA
Dividends	0.39	0.27	0.15	0.12	0.11	0.10	0.09	0.05	0.05	0.05
Payout Ratio	19%	9%	6%	3%	4%	4%	5%	3%	5%	5%
Prices:High	76.15	75.74	69.64	76.54	67.96	73.70	77.32	69.96	55.50	50.92
Prices:Low	56.41	61.15	52.85	36.08	50.00	46.60	56.67	24.67	24.67	30.97
P/E Ratio:High	37	26	29	22	22	30	41	44	51	53
P/E Ratio:Low	27	21	22	10	16	19	30	15	23	32

Income Statement Analysis (Million $)	2007	2006	2005	2004	2003	2002	2001	2000	1999	1998
Revenue	86,852	81,364	74,911	65,054	50,467	44,394	47,948	29,871	25,034	15,918
Operating Income	2,485	2,474	2,555	2,694	3,723	2,216	1,893	1,377	1,257	538
Depreciation	322	393	410	299	266	244	281	246	234	64.3
Interest Expense	121	132	134	98.9	115	133	155	117	99.4	23.0
Pretax Income	1,252	1,835	1,629	2,238	2,127	1,701	1,332	1,078	759	403
Effective Tax Rate	32.9%	32.2%	35.8%	31.9%	33.6%	33.8%	35.6%	36.9%	39.9%	38.6%
Net Income	840	1,245	1,047	1,525	1,412	1,126	857	680	456	247
S&P Core Earnings	1,247	1,236	936	1,369	1,266	1,045	771	NA	NA	NA

Balance Sheet & Other Financial Data (Million $)	2007	2006	2005	2004	2003	2002	2001	2000	1999	1998
Cash	1,309	1,321	1,412	1,096	1,724	1,382	934	505	165	305
Current Assets	14,545	14,777	13,443	13,058	13,250	11,907	10,716	6,871	5,147	3,229
Total Assets	23,154	23,374	22,059	21,369	18,521	16,438	14,642	10,265	8,289	3,961
Current Liabilities	11,460	11,373	10,105	9,369	7,314	6,810	6,575	4,262	2,959	1,844
Long Term Debt	3,457	2,600	2,320	2,835	2,472	2,207	1,871	1,486	1,224	273
Common Equity	7,377	8,491	8,593	7,976	7,758	6,393	5,437	3,981	3,463	1,625
Total Capital	10,834	11,090	10,913	12,000	11,207	8,600	7,308	5,467	5,208	1,898
Capital Expenditures	1,630	443	572	410	423	285	341	308	320	111
Cash Flow	1,162	1,637	1,456	1,824	1,678	1,370	1,138	926	690	311
Current Ratio	1.3	1.3	1.3	1.4	1.8	1.7	1.6	1.6	1.7	1.8
% Long Term Debt of Capitalization	31.9	23.4	21.3	23.6	22.1	25.7	25.6	27.2	23.5	14.4
% Net Income of Revenue	1.0	1.5	1.4	2.3	2.8	2.5	1.8	2.3	1.8	1.6
% Return on Assets	3.6	5.5	4.8	7.7	8.1	7.2	6.4	7.3	5.8	7.0
% Return on Equity	10.6	14.6	12.6	19.5	20.0	19.0	17.4	18.0	14.2	16.7

Data as orig reptd.; bef. results of disc opers/spec. items. Per share data adj. for stk. divs.; EPS diluted. E-Estimated. NA-Not Available. NM-Not Meaningful. NR-Not Ranked. UR-Under Review.

Office: 7000 Cardinal Place, Dublin, OH 43017.
Telephone: 614-757-5000.
Website: http://www.cardinal.com
Chrmn: R.D. Walter

Pres & CEO: R.K. Clark
EVP & CFO: J.W. Henderson
EVP & Cntlr: J. Hinrichs
VP & Chief Acctg Officer: S.G. Laws

Board Members: C. F. Arnold, R. K. Clark, G. H. Conrades, C. Darden, J. F. Finn, P. L. Francis, R. L. Gerbig, G. B. Kenny, J. M. Losh, J. B. McCoy, R. C. Notebaert, M. D. O'Halleran, D. Raisbeck, J. G. Spaulding, M. D. Walter, R. D. Walter

Founded: 1979
Domicile: Ohio
Employees: 43,500

The McGraw·Hill Companies

Carnival Corp

STANDARD &POOR'S

S&P Recommendation HOLD ★★★☆☆	**Price** $44.80 (as of Nov 28, 2007)	**12-Mo. Target Price** $52.00	**Investment Style** Large-Cap Blend

GICS Sector Consumer Discretionary **Sub-Industry** Hotels, Resorts & Cruise Lines	**Summary** Carnival Corp. and Carnival plc own businesses that operate more than 80 cruise ships.

Key Stock Statistics (Source S&P, Vickers, company reports)

52-Wk Range	$52.73– 41.70	S&P Oper. EPS 2007 **E**	2.94	Market Capitalization(B)	$27.926	Beta	1.80
Trailing 12-Month EPS	$3.03	S&P Oper. EPS 2008 **E**	3.24	Yield (%)	3.57	S&P 3-Yr. Proj. EPS CAGR(%)	10.00
Trailing 12-Month P/E	14.8	P/E on S&P Oper. EPS 2007 **E**	15.2	Dividend Rate/Share	$1.60	S&P Credit Rating	A-
$10K Invested 5 Yrs Ago	$16,418	Common Shares Outstg. (M)	623.4	Institutional Ownership (%)	75		

Price Performance

30-Week Mov. Avg. ··· 10-Week Mov. Avg. - - **GAAP Earnings vs. Previous Year** Volume Above Avg. STARS
12-Mo. Target Price — Relative Strength — ▲ Up ▼ Down ► No Change Below Avg. ★

2004 2005 2006 2007

Options: ASE, CBOE, P, Ph

Highlights

► The 12-month target price for CCL has recently been changed to $52.00 from $53.00. The Highlights section of this Stock Report will be updated accordingly.

Investment Rationale/Risk

► The Investment Rationale/Risk section of this Stock Report will be updated shortly. For the latest News story on CCL from MarketScope, see below.

► 11/27/07 03:28 pm EST... S&P REITERATES HOLD OPINION ON SHARES OF CARNIVAL CORP (CCL 43.22***): We look for five new Carnival ships to debut in FY 08 (Nov.), including the Queen Victoria in December. Also, two Iberocruceros ships have been added via a 75%-owned joint venture that closed in September '07. We are wary that a slower-growth U.S. economy may dampen cruiseship demand in FY 08. However, we expect that Carnival's plan to implement a fuel surcharge will help to ease pressure from higher fuel costs. We are lowering our FY 08 EPS estimate to $3.24 from $3.31, and our FY 07 estimate to $2.94 from $2.98, and reduce our 12-month target price to $52 from $53. / T.Graves-CFA

Qualitative Risk Assessment

LOW	MEDIUM	HIGH

We believe that Carnival has competitive advantages related to its industry leading position, and we view the company's financial condition as being relatively strong. However, Carnival's operations are subject to external factors, including economic conditions and hurricane activity.

Quantitative Evaluations

S&P Quality Ranking A+

D	C	B-	B	B+	A-	A	A+

Relative Strength Rank MODERATE

56

LOWEST = 1 HIGHEST = 99

Revenue/Earnings Data

Revenue (Million $)

	1Q	2Q	3Q	4Q	Year
2007	2,688	2,900	4,321	--	--
2006	2,463	2,662	3,905	2,809	11,839
2005	2,396	2,519	3,605	2,567	11,087
2004	1,980	2,256	3,245	2,243	9,727
2003	1,031	1,335	2,524	1,817	6,718
2002	905.8	989.2	1,438	1,036	4,368

Earnings Per Share ($)

2007	0.35	0.48	1.67	E0.44	E2.94
2006	0.31	0.46	1.49	0.51	2.77
2005	0.42	0.49	1.36	0.43	2.70
2004	0.25	0.41	1.23	0.36	2.24
2003	0.22	0.19	0.90	0.26	1.66
2002	0.22	0.33	0.85	0.33	1.73

Fiscal year ended Nov. 30. Next earnings report expected: Late December. EPS Estimates based on S&P Operating Earnings; historical GAAP earnings are as reported.

Dividend Data (Dates: mm/dd Payment Date: mm/dd/yy)

Amount ($)	Date Decl.	Ex-Div. Date	Stk. of Record	Payment Date
0.275	01/24	02/14	02/16	03/09/07
0.350	04/16	05/16	05/18	06/08/07
0.350	07/17	08/22	08/24	09/14/07
0.400	10/17	11/20	11/23	12/14/07

Dividends have been paid since 1988. Source: Company reports.

Carnival Corp

STANDARD &POOR'S

Business Summary September 28, 2007

CORPORATE OVERVIEW. Carnival Corp. is the world's largest cruise ship company, with about 45% of the global cruise market, and has grown significantly through both acquisitions and the addition of new ships. In 2003, Carnival merged with P&O Princess Cruises plc, which was renamed Carnival plc. As of mid-FY 07 (Nov.), the combined Carnival had 82 cruise ships with capacity for about 154,000 passengers. Also, Carnival has tour operations in Alaska and the Canadian Yukon.

With Carnival's dual listing company (DLC) format, there are separate stocks trading under the Carnival Corp. and Carnival plc names. Each company has retained its separate legal identity, but the two share a single senior executive management team, have identical boards of directors, and are run as if they were a single economic enterprise. In valuing CCL shares, we look at the combined financial results and equity base of the Carnival entities.

The cruise industry carried more than 15.7 million passengers in 2006, with about two-thirds of them coming from the North American market. Looking ahead, we expect demand for cruise ship vacations to grow. In the U.S., we believe that most people have never taken a multi-night cruise ship vacation, and we expect that an aging U.S. population will lead to more interest in cruises.

PRIMARY BUSINESS DYNAMICS. In FY 07, we look for average fuel costs per

metric ton above $350, or up about $20 from FY 06. Also, at least near term, we look for overall pricing for Caribbean and Mediterranean cruises to rise from the prior year level, and continue higher into FY 08.

MARKET PROFILE. Looking ahead, we expect demand for cruise ship vacations to grow. In the U.S., we believe that most people have never taken a multi-night cruise ship vacation, and we expect that an aging U.S. population will lead to more interest in cruises. Also, we believe that a continued industry emphasis on providing ships with more features and the addition of more local ports will bolster passenger demand.

COMPETITIVE LANDSCAPE. We see Carnival enhancing its competitive position through the addition of new ships, which should encourage both returning and new customers. As of August 2007, there were 17 new Carnival ships scheduled to enter service between April 2007 and June 2011, resulting in about a 25% increase in capacity. In terms of capacity, Carnival is about twice the size of its biggest competitor -- Royal Caribbean Cruises Ltd. (RCL) -- which recently operated 35 ships with over 71,000 berths.

Company Financials Fiscal Year Ended Nov. 30

Per Share Data ($)	2006	2005	2004	2003	2002	2001	2000	1999	1998	1997
Tangible Book Value	17.10	15.47	13.96	11.83	11.48	10.13	8.84	8.86	6.46	4.82
Cash Flow	3.89	3.91	3.13	2.46	2.38	2.21	2.08	2.06	1.73	1.40
Earnings	2.77	2.70	2.24	1.66	1.73	1.58	1.60	1.66	1.40	1.12
Dividends	1.03	0.80	0.52	0.44	0.42	0.42	0.42	0.38	0.32	0.24
Payout Ratio	37%	30%	23%	27%	24%	27%	26%	23%	22%	22%
Prices:High	56.14	58.98	58.75	39.84	34.64	34.94	51.25	53.50	48.50	27.94
Prices:Low	36.40	45.78	39.75	20.34	22.07	16.95	18.31	38.13	19.00	15.69
P/E Ratio:High	20	22	26	24	20	22	32	32	35	25
P/E Ratio:Low	13	17	18	12	13	11	11	23	14	14

Income Statement Analysis (Million $)										
Revenue	11,839	11,087	9,727	6,718	4,368	4,536	3,779	3,497	3,009	2,447
Operating Income	3,601	3,541	2,985	1,968	1,444	1,448	1,233	1,188	1,020	828
Depreciation	988	902	812	585	382	372	288	244	201	167
Interest Expense	312	330	284	195	111	121	41.4	47.0	57.8	55.9
Pretax Income	2,240	2,184	1,901	1,223	959	948	967	1,044	851	672
Effective Tax Rate	NM	NM	2.47%	2.37%	NM	2.34%	0.11%	0.27%	0.45%	0.93%
Net Income	2,279	2,257	1,854	1,194	1,016	926	965	1,027	836	666

Balance Sheet & Other Financial Data (Million $)										
Cash	1,163	1,178	643	1,070	667	1,421	189	522	137	140
Current Assets	1,995	2,215	1,728	2,132	1,132	1,959	549	792	370	336
Total Assets	30,552	28,432	27,636	24,491	12,335	11,564	9,831	8,286	7,179	5,427
Current Liabilities	5,415	5,192	5,034	3,315	1,620	1,480	1,715	1,405	1,135	786
Long Term Debt	6,355	5,727	6,291	6,918	3,012	2,955	2,099	868	1,563	1,015
Common Equity	18,210	16,972	15,760	13,793	7,418	6,591	5,871	5,931	4,285	3,605
Total Capital	24,565	22,699	22,051	20,711	10,430	9,546	7,970	6,799	5,981	4,620
Capital Expenditures	2,480	1,977	3,586	2,516	1,986	827	1,003	873	1,150	498
Cash Flow	3,267	3,159	2,666	1,779	1,398	1,298	1,253	1,271	1,037	833
Current Ratio	0.4	0.4	0.3	0.6	0.7	1.3	0.3	0.6	0.3	0.4
% Long Term Debt of Capitalization	25.9	25.2	28.5	33.4	28.9	31.0	26.3	12.8	26.1	22.0
% Net Income of Revenue	19.2	20.4	19.1	17.8	23.3	20.4	25.6	29.4	27.8	27.2
% Return on Assets	7.7	8.1	7.1	6.5	8.5	8.7	10.7	13.3	13.3	12.7
% Return on Equity	13.0	13.8	12.5	11.3	14.5	14.9	16.4	20.1	21.2	20.1

Data as orig reptd.; bef. results of disc opers/spec. items. Per share data adj. for stk. divs.; EPS diluted. E-Estimated. NA-Not Available. NM-Not Meaningful. NR-Not Ranked. UR-Under Review.

Office: 3655 NW 87th Avenue, Miami, FL 33178-2428.
Telephone: 305-599-2600.
Website: http://www.carnivalcorp.com
Chrmn & CEO: M. Arison

Vice Chrmn & COO: H.S. Frank
EVP, CFO & Chief Acctg Officer: G.R. Cahill
SVP, Secy & General Counsel: A. Perez
Investor Contact: B. Roberts (305-599-2600)

Board Members: M. Arison, R. G. Capen, Jr., R. H. Dickinson, A. W. Donald, P. L. Foschi, H. S. Frank, R. J. Glasier, B. Hogg, A. K. Lanterman, M. A. Maidique, J. Parker, P. Ratcliffe, S. S. Subotnick, L. Weil, U. Zucker

Founded: 1974
Domicile: Panama
Employees: 74,700

Caterpillar Inc

STANDARD &POOR'S

S&P Recommendation HOLD ★★★☆☆	Price $68.63 (as of Nov 23, 2007)	12-Mo. Target Price $82.00	Investment Style Large-Cap Blend

GICS Sector Industrials
Sub-Industry Construction & Farm Machinery & Heavy Trucks

Summary CAT, the world's largest producer of earthmoving equipment, is also a big maker of truck engines and power generators.

Key Stock Statistics (Source S&P, Vickers, company reports)

52-Wk Range	**$87.00– 57.98**	S&P Oper. EPS 2007**E**	**5.25**
Trailing 12-Month EPS	**$5.18**	S&P Oper. EPS 2008**E**	**5.55**
Trailing 12-Month P/E	**13.3**	P/E on S&P Oper. EPS 2007**E**	**13.1**
$10K Invested 5 Yrs Ago	**$31,131**	Common Shares Outstg. (M)	**640.4**

Market Capitalization(B)	**$43.950**	Beta	**1.47**
Yield (%)	**2.10**	S&P 3-Yr. Proj. EPS CAGR(%)	**6.00**
Dividend Rate/Share	**$1.44**	S&P Credit Rating	**A**
Institutional Ownership (%)	**66**		

Price Performance

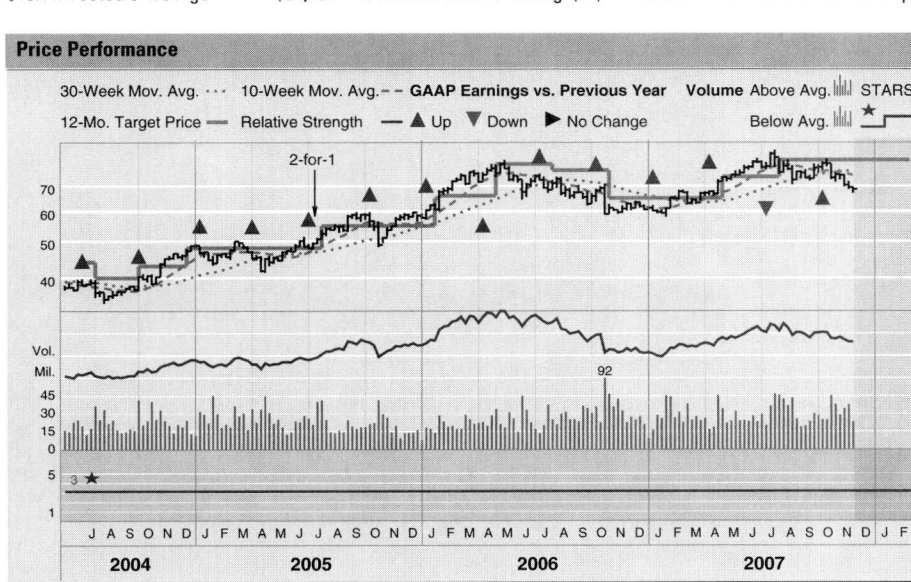

30-Week Mov. Avg. · · · 10-Week Mov. Avg. - - **GAAP Earnings vs. Previous Year** Volume Above Avg. STARS
12-Mo. Target Price — Relative Strength — ▲ Up ▼ Down ► No Change Below Avg.

2-for-1

| 2004 | 2005 | 2006 | 2007 |

Options: ASE, CBOE, P, Ph

Analysis prepared by **Pearl Wang** on November 20, 2007, when the stock traded at **$ 69.08**.

Highlights

➤ We expect sales of machinery and engines to rise 5% in 2007, followed by an additional 7% gain in 2008. We see strength outside of North America in all of CAT's major product categories and geographic end markets, and expect these estimated gains to outweigh a likely downturn in North American sales. Our positive outlook for CAT's foreign sales stem from our forecast of ongoing strength in global economies, as well as in nonresidential and infrastructure construction. The primary factors behind our soft North American sales forecast are the weak residential construction market and a big downturn in demand for on-highway engines, in light of prebuying before new emissions standards took place at the start of 2007.

➤ We expect narrower operating margins in 2007, on the likely lower absorption of overhead costs due to a projected decline in North American sales volumes, as well as our forecast of certain operating inefficiencies and still high materials costs. We see flat margins in 2008, when we expect U.S. sales trends to firm.

➤ We forecast EPS of $5.25 in 2007, rising to $5.55 in 2008.

Investment Rationale/Risk

➤ We expect conflicting geographic trends to limit CAT's operating performance through 2008, as we think its end markets will be quite strong internationally, but lackluster in North America. However, we expect the company's U.S. business to bottom over the next year, on our outlook for troughs in its construction and trucking end markets. Based on these factors and valuation considerations, we think Caterpillar stock is appropriately valued.

➤ Risks to our opinion and target price include slower than expected economic growth; a downturn in the infrastructure, non-residential construction and/or power markets; and continued escalation of raw material costs.

➤ The shares recently traded at 12X our 2008 EPS forecast, which is in line with Caterpillar's typical valuation during periods of muted earnings growth. We believe that the valuation is appropriate based on our outlook for various challenges to the company's North American businesses in coming periods (although we think they will finally trough over the next year). Applying a multiple of about 15X to our 2008 EPS forecast, we arrive at a value of $82, which is our 12-month target price.

Qualitative Risk Assessment

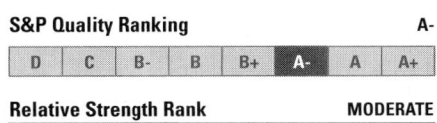

| LOW | MEDIUM | HIGH |

Our risk assessment for Caterpillar reflects its leading position in many of the end markets it serves and our positive outlook for continued strength in nonresidential construction activity, offset by the highly cyclical nature of the construction equipment and engine businesses.

Quantitative Evaluations

S&P Quality Ranking A-

| D | C | B- | B | B+ | A- | A | A+ |

Relative Strength Rank MODERATE

40

LOWEST = 1 HIGHEST = 99

Revenue/Earnings Data

Revenue (Million $)

	1Q	2Q	3Q	4Q	Year
2007	10,016	11,356	11,442	--	--
2006	9,392	10,605	10,517	11,003	41,517
2005	8,339	9,360	8,977	9,663	36,339
2004	6,467	7,564	7,649	8,571	30,251
2003	4,821	5,932	5,545	6,465	22,763
2002	4,409	5,291	5,075	5,377	20,152

Earnings Per Share ($)

2007	1.23	1.24	1.40	E1.38	E5.25
2006	1.20	1.52	1.14	1.32	5.17
2005	0.81	1.08	0.94	1.20	4.04
2004	0.60	0.80	0.71	0.78	2.88
2003	0.19	0.58	0.31	0.49	1.57
2002	0.12	0.29	0.31	0.44	1.15

Fiscal year ended Dec. 31. Next earnings report expected: Late January. EPS Estimates based on S&P Operating Earnings; historical GAAP earnings are as reported.

Dividend Data (Dates: mm/dd Payment Date: mm/dd/yy)

Amount ($)	Date Decl.	Ex-Div. Date	Stk. of Record	Payment Date
0.300	12/13	01/18	01/22	02/20/07
0.300	04/11	04/19	04/23	05/19/07
0.360	06/13	07/18	07/20	08/20/07
0.360	10/10	10/18	10/22	11/20/07

Dividends have been paid since 1914. Source: Company reports.

Caterpillar Inc

**STANDARD
&POOR'S**

Business Summary November 20, 2007

CORPORATE OVERVIEW. Caterpillar's distinctive yellow machines are in service in nearly every country in the world; roughly half of the company's revenues are derived from outside of North America. As of December 2006, about 58% of CAT's independent dealers were located outside the U.S.

CAT's largest operating segment, the Machinery unit (63% of revenues in 2006 and 12% operating margin), makes the company's well known earthmoving equipment. Machinery's end-markets include heavy construction, general construction, and mining quarry and aggregate, industrial, waste, forestry and agriculture. End markets are very cyclical and competitive; demand for CAT's earthmoving equipment is driven by many volatile factors, including the health of global economies, commodity prices, and interest rates, in our view. Principal competitors include Japan's Komatsu Ltd.; CNH Global NV (Case and NewHolland brands); Deere & Co.; and Sweden's Volvo.

For decades, the Engine segment (31% and 13%) made diesel engines solely for CAT's own earthmoving equipment. Currently, however, Engine derives the majority of its sales from third-party customers, such as Paccar, Inc., the maker of well known Kenworth and Peterbilt brand tractor/trailer trucks. Engine's

major end markets are electric power generation, on-highway truck, oil and gas, industrial/OEM and marine. In recent years, sales of on-highway engines have benefited from a replacement cycle that has historically averaged about three to five years. We expect industry sales of on-highway engines to peak in 2006 before falling sharply in 2007. CAT, Cummins Inc., and DaimlerChrysler's Detroit Diesel division each account for about 30% of the world diesel engine market.

The Financial Products segment (6% and 22%) primarily provides equipment financing to CAT dealers and customers. Financing plans include operating and finance leases, installment sales contracts, working capital loans and wholesale financing plans. At December 31, 2006, total long-term finance related receivables and long-term finance related debt stood at $12.2 billion and $14.0 billion, respectively.

Company Financials Fiscal Year Ended Dec. 31

Per Share Data ($)	2006	2005	2004	2003	2002	2001	2000	1999	1998	1997
Tangible Book Value	7.07	9.77	8.34	6.48	5.51	5.75	5.97	5.56	5.45	6.05
Cash Flow	7.52	6.14	4.85	3.48	2.91	2.85	2.97	2.63	3.23	3.16
Earnings	5.17	4.04	2.88	1.57	1.15	1.16	1.51	1.32	2.06	2.19
S&P Core Earnings	5.48	4.05	2.76	1.50	0.20	0.16	NA	NA	NA	NA
Dividends	1.10	0.91	0.78	0.71	0.70	0.69	0.67	0.63	0.55	0.45
Payout Ratio	21%	23%	27%	45%	61%	59%	44%	48%	27%	21%
Prices:High	82.03	59.88	49.36	42.48	30.00	28.42	27.56	33.22	30.38	30.81
Prices:Low	57.05	41.31	34.25	20.62	16.88	19.88	14.78	21.00	19.53	18.13
P/E Ratio:High	16	15	17	27	26	24	18	25	15	14
P/E Ratio:Low	11	10	12	13	15	17	10	16	10	8

Income Statement Analysis (Million $)										
Revenue	41,517	36,339	30,251	22,763	20,152	20,450	20,175	19,702	20,977	18,925
Operating Income	7,634	6,029	4,650	3,505	3,060	3,137	3,447	2,999	3,607	3,529
Depreciation	1,602	1,477	1,397	1,347	1,220	1,169	1,022	945	865	738
Interest Expense	1,297	1,028	750	716	800	942	980	829	753	580
Pretax Income	4,942	3,974	2,766	1,497	1,110	1,172	1,500	1,401	2,178	2,461
Effective Tax Rate	28.4%	28.2%	26.4%	26.6%	28.1%	31.3%	29.8%	32.5%	30.5%	32.3%
Net Income	3,537	2,854	2,035	1,099	798	805	1,053	946	1,513	1,665
S&P Core Earnings	3,748	2,860	1,951	1,052	133	98.7	NA	NA	NA	NA

Balance Sheet & Other Financial Data (Million $)										
Cash	530	1,108	445	342	309	400	334	548	360	292
Current Assets	23,093	22,790	20,856	16,791	14,628	13,400	12,521	11,734	11,459	9,814
Total Assets	50,879	47,069	43,091	36,465	32,851	30,657	28,464	26,635	25,128	20,756
Current Liabilities	19,252	19,092	16,210	12,621	11,344	10,276	8,568	8,178	7,945	6,379
Long Term Debt	17,680	15,677	15,837	14,078	11,596	11,291	11,334	9,928	9,404	6,942
Common Equity	6,859	8,432	7,467	6,078	5,472	5,611	5,600	5,465	5,131	4,679
Total Capital	24,539	24,109	23,304	20,156	17,068	16,902	16,934	15,393	14,535	11,621
Capital Expenditures	2,675	2,415	2,114	1,765	1,773	1,968	1,388	1,280	1,269	1,106
Cash Flow	5,139	4,331	3,432	2,446	2,018	1,974	2,075	1,891	2,378	2,403
Current Ratio	1.2	1.2	1.3	1.3	1.3	1.3	1.5	1.4	1.4	1.5
% Long Term Debt of Capitalization	72.0	65.0	68.0	69.8	67.9	66.8	66.9	64.5	64.7	59.7
% Net Income of Revenue	8.5	7.9	6.7	4.8	4.0	3.9	5.2	4.8	7.2	8.8
% Return on Assets	7.2	6.3	5.1	3.2	2.5	2.7	3.8	3.7	6.6	8.4
% Return on Equity	46.3	35.9	30.0	19.0	14.4	14.4	19.0	17.9	30.8	37.9

Data as orig reptd.; bef. results of disc opers/spec. items. Per share data adj. for stk. divs.; EPS diluted. E-Estimated. NA-Not Available. NM-Not Meaningful. NR-Not Ranked. UR-Under Review.

Office: 100 N.E. Adams Street, Peoria, IL 61629.
Telephone: 309-675-1000.
Email: catir@cat.com
Website: http://www.cat.com

Chrmn & CEO: J.W. Owens
VP & CFO: D.B. Burritt
VP, Secy & General Counsel: J.B. Buda
CTO: T.L. Utley

Treas: K.E. Colgan
Board Members: W. F. Blount, J. R. Brazil, D. M. Dickinson, J. T. Dillon, E. V. Fife, G. D. Fosler, J. Gallardo, D. R. Goode, P. A. Magowan, W. A. Osborn, J. W. Owens, C. D. Powell, E. B. Rust, Jr., J. I. Smith

Founded: 1925
Domicile: Delaware
Employees: 96,315

The McGraw-Hill Companies

CB Richard Ellis Group Inc

STANDARD &POOR'S

S&P Recommendation HOLD ★★★☆☆ | **Price** $19.80 (as of Nov 23, 2007) | **12-Mo. Target Price** $32.00 | **Investment Style** Large-Cap Growth

GICS Sector Financials
Sub-Industry Real Estate Management & Development

Summary CB Richard Ellis Group is a global commercial real estate services company.

Key Stock Statistics (Source S&P, Vickers, company reports)

52-Wk Range	$42.74– 17.49	S&P Oper. EPS 2007**E**	2.05	Market Capitalization(B)	$4.540	Beta	1.83
Trailing 12-Month EPS	$1.65	S&P Oper. EPS 2008**E**	2.48	Yield (%)	Nil	S&P 3-Yr. Proj. EPS CAGR(%)	22.00
Trailing 12-Month P/E	12.0	P/E on S&P Oper. EPS 2007**E**	9.7	Dividend Rate/Share	Nil	S&P Credit Rating	NA
$10K Invested 5 Yrs Ago	NA	Common Shares Outstg. (M)	229.3	Institutional Ownership (%)	NM		

Price Performance

30-Week Mov. Avg. · · · · 10-Week Mov. Avg. - - GAAP Earnings vs. Previous Year Volume Above Avg. STARS
12-Mo. Target Price — Relative Strength — ▲ Up ▼ Down ► No Change Below Avg.

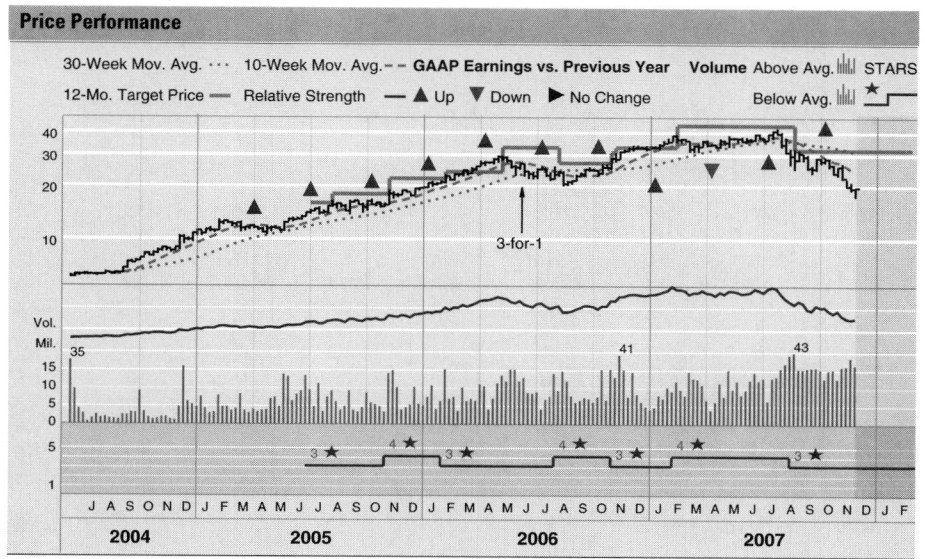

Options: ASE, CBOE, P, Ph

Analysis prepared by **Robert McMillan** on November 01, 2007, when the stock traded at **$23.08**.

Highlights

➤ We expect CBG to benefit from healthy world-wide GDP growth, which we see generating increased demand for its broad array of commercial real estate products and services. Ongoing acquisitions, especially overseas, should further enhance CBG's competitive position and help the company sustain its EPS growth of about 20%-25% in the intermediate term.

➤ After gaining 26% in 2006, we see revenue rising about 50% in 2007 and 30% in 2008, on continued organic growth as well as contributions from acquisitions. Although economic growth in the U.S. may slow, which could potentially dampen sales and leasing activity in the U.S. market, we think that growth in Europe and particularly Asia is poised to offset any weakness in the U.S. We also see CBG's investment management business benefiting from continued strong capital flows into commercial real estate. Further, we believe that CBG, which manages a portfolio of properties for various corporations, will continue to benefit from the increasing trend of corporations to outsource the management of real estate properties.

➤ We project EPS of $2.05 in 2007 and $2.48 in 2008.

Investment Rationale/Risk

➤ We see CBG benefiting from its large size and its broad array of products and services relative to peers. We think the global reach of CBG's operations helps generate economies of scale that few other real estate firms can match, helping create sustainable barriers to entry. However, we see the shares remaining volatile until the turmoil in the financial markets abates; we are concerned that CBG's commercial mortgage origination business (4% of 2006 revenues) may suffer a slowdown due to higher financing rates.

➤ Risks to our recommendation and target price include lower demand for office and industrial space, employee defections, increased competition, and a sharp rise in interest rates.

➤ The stock recently traded at a P/E of 9.8X our 2008 EPS estimate. Our 12-month target price of $32 is equal to about 13X our 2008 EPS estimate. The shares have dropped sharply on concerns of a slowdown in the commercial financing market, but we see the valuation multiple expanding over the next year, driven by easing interest rates, which should help the commercial real estate financing market, and continued robust growth overseas.

Qualitative Risk Assessment

LOW	MEDIUM	HIGH

Our risk assessment reflects CBG's position as one of the world's largest commercial real estate firms, with a diversified portfolio of operations and customers around the world.

Quantitative Evaluations

S&P Quality Ranking NR

D	C	B-	B	B+	A-	A	A+

Relative Strength Rank WEAK

14

LOWEST = 1   HIGHEST = 99

Revenue/Earnings Data

Revenue (Million $)

	1Q	2Q	3Q	4Q	Year
2007	1,214	1,490	1,493	--	--
2006	903.5	751.3	967.9	1,409	4,032
2005	538.3	672.2	744.2	956.0	2,911
2004	441.0	550.9	575.0	798.2	2,365
2003	--	--	--	--	1,949
2002	--	--	--	--	--

Earnings Per Share ($)

	1Q	2Q	3Q	4Q	Year
2007	0.05	0.59	0.48	E0.72	E2.05
2006	0.16	0.27	0.39	0.53	1.35
2005	0.06	0.22	0.25	0.41	0.95
2004	-0.09	0.01	0.05	0.29	0.30
2003	--	--	--	--	-0.11
2002	--	--	--	--	--

Fiscal year ended Dec. 31. Next earnings report expected: Early February. EPS Estimates based on S&P Operating Earnings; historical GAAP earnings are as reported.

Dividend Data

No cash dividends have been paid.

CB Richard Ellis Group Inc

STANDARD &POOR'S

Business Summary November 01, 2007

CB Richard Ellis Group, Inc. is one of the largest global commercial real estate services companies in the world. The company's business is focused on several service competencies, including strategic advice and execution assistance for property leasing and sales, forecasting, valuations, origination and servicing of commercial mortgage loans, facilities and project management and real estate investment management. The company generates revenues both on a per project or transaction basis and from annual management fees.

The company's primary business objective is to leverage its integrated global platform to garner an increasing share of industry revenues relative to competitors. CBG believes this will enable the company to maximize and sustain its long-term cash flow and increase long-term stockholder value. Management's strategy to achieve these business objectives consists of several elements: increasing revenues from large clients; capitalizing on cross-selling opportunities; continuing to grow the investment management business; ex-

panding through fill-in acquisitions; and focusing on improving operating efficiency.

CBG's Real Estate Services business offers a broad spectrum of services to occupiers/tenants and investors/owners. Real estate services include offering strategic advice and execution to owners, investors and occupiers of real estate in connection with leasing, disposition and the acquisition of property. During 2006, the company advised on over 25,000 lease transactions involving aggregate rents of approximately $38.7 billion and over 6,200 real estate sales transactions with an aggregate value of approximately $73.9 billion. This segment also provides investment sales property and valuation advice.

Company Financials Fiscal Year Ended Dec. 31

Per Share Data ($)	2006	2005	2004	2003	2002	2001	2000	1999	1998	1997
Tangible Book Value	NM	NM	NM	NM	NA	NA	NA	NA	NA	NA
Cash Flow	1.64	1.14	0.56	0.38	NA	NA	NA	NA	NA	NA
Earnings	1.35	0.95	0.30	-0.11	NA	NA	NA	NA	NA	NA
S&P Core Earnings	1.33	0.94	0.30	NA	NA	NA	NA	NA	NA	NA
Dividends	Nil	Nil	Nil	Nil	NA	NA	NA	NA	NA	NA
Payout Ratio	Nil	Nil	Nil	Nil	NA	NA	NA	NA	NA	NA
Prices:High	34.26	19.92	11.36	NA	NA	NA	NA	NA	NA	NA
Prices:Low	19.46	10.40	6.03	NA	NA	NA	NA	NA	NA	NA
P/E Ratio:High	25	21	37	NA	NA	NA	NA	NA	NA	NA
P/E Ratio:Low	14	11	20	NA	NA	NA	NA	NA	NA	NA

Income Statement Analysis (Million $)										
Commissions	Nil	Nil	Nil	Nil	NA	NA	NA	NA	NA	NA
Interest Income	9.80	9.30	4.30	6.00	NA	NA	NA	NA	NA	NA
Total Revenue	4,032	2,911	2,365	1,949	NA	NA	NA	NA	NA	NA
Interest Expense	45.0	54.3	65.4	71.3	NA	NA	NA	NA	NA	NA
Pretax Income	523	358	108	-41.0	NA	NA	NA	NA	NA	NA
Effective Tax Rate	37.9%	38.8%	40.2%	NM	NA	NA	NA	NA	NA	NA
Net Income	319	217	64.7	-34.7	NA	NA	NA	NA	NA	NA
S&P Core Earnings	314	216	64.0	NA	NA	NA	NA	NA	NA	NA

Balance Sheet & Other Financial Data (Million $)										
Total Assets	5,945	2,816	2,272	2,213	NA	NA	NA	NA	NA	NA
Cash Items	244	449	257	164	NA	NA	NA	NA	NA	NA
Receivables	985	739	532	553	NA	NA	NA	NA	NA	NA
Securities Owned	Nil	Nil	Nil	Nil	NA	NA	NA	NA	NA	NA
Securities Borrowed	Nil	Nil	Nil	Nil	NA	NA	NA	NA	NA	NA
Due Brokers & Customers	Nil	Nil	Nil	Nil	NA	NA	NA	NA	NA	NA
Other Liabilities	1,906	1,138	809	833	NA	NA	NA	NA	NA	NA
Capitalization:Debt	2,193	821	761	1,061	NA	NA	NA	NA	NA	NA
Capitalization:Equity	1,182	794	560	333	NA	NA	NA	NA	NA	NA
Capitalization:Total	3,573	1,622	1,321	1,394	NA	NA	NA	NA	NA	NA
% Return on Revenue	7.8	7.4	2.7	NM	NA	NA	NA	NA	NA	NA
% Return on Assets	7.2	8.5	2.8	NM	NA	NA	NA	NA	NA	NA
% Return on Equity	32.2	32.0	14.4	NM	NA	NA	NA	NA	NA	NA

Data as orig reptd.; bef. results of disc opers/spec. items. Per share data adj. for stk. divs.; EPS diluted. E-Estimated. NA-Not Available. NM-Not Meaningful. NR-Not Ranked. UR-Under Review.

Office: 100 N Sepulveda Blvd,00 Suite 1050, El Segundo, CA 90245-4359.
Telephone: 310-606-4700.
Website: http://www.cbre.com
Chrmn: R.C. Blum

Pres & CEO: B. White
Vice Chrmn: R. Wirta
Sr EVP: C.W. Frese, Jr.
Sr EVP & CFO: K.J. Kay

Investor Contact: S. Young (212-984-8359)
Board Members: R. C. Blum, P. M. Daniels, T. A. Daschle, C. F. Feeny, B. M. Freeman, M. Kantor, F. V. Malek, J. G. Nugent, J. Su, R. E. Sulentic, B. White, G. L. Wilson, R. Wirta

Founded: 2001
Domicile: Delaware
Employees: 24,000

CBS Corp

**STANDARD
&POOR'S**

S&P Recommendation **HOLD** ★★★☆☆	Price $26.58 (as of Nov 23, 2007)	12-Mo. Target Price $33.00	Investment Style Large-Cap Value

GICS Sector Consumer Discretionary
Sub-Industry Broadcasting & Cable TV

Summary This major operator of TV, radio and outdoor advertising properties is one of the two companies created after the separation of the "old" Viacom into two public entities.

Key Stock Statistics (Source S&P, Vickers, company reports)

52-Wk Range	$35.75– 25.57	S&P Oper. EPS 2007**E**	1.86	Market Capitalization(B)	$16.608	Beta	1.11
Trailing 12-Month EPS	$1.73	S&P Oper. EPS 2008**E**	2.06	Yield (%)	3.76	S&P 3-Yr. Proj. EPS CAGR(%)	9.00
Trailing 12-Month P/E	15.4	P/E on S&P Oper. EPS 2007**E**	14.3	Dividend Rate/Share	$1.00	S&P Credit Rating	BBB
$10K Invested 5 Yrs Ago	NA	Common Shares Outstg. (M)	684.9	Institutional Ownership (%)	90		

Price Performance

30-Week Mov. Avg. · · · 10-Week Mov. Avg. - - **GAAP Earnings vs. Previous Year**   **Volume** Above Avg.|||| STARS
12-Mo. Target Price — Relative Strength — ▲ Up ▼ Down ▶ No Change   Below Avg.|||| ★

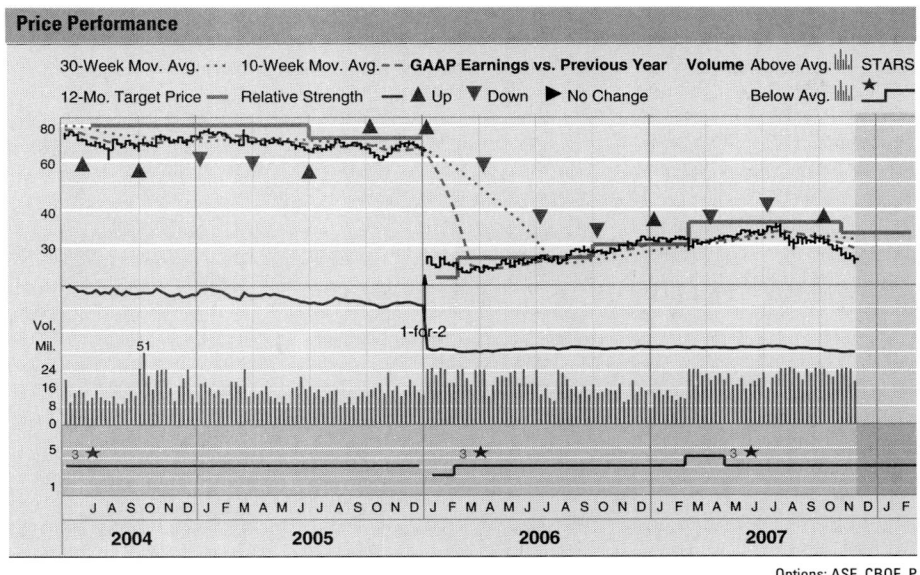

Options: ASE, CBOE, P

Analysis prepared by **Tuna N. Amobi, CFA, CPA** on November 06, 2007, when the stock traded at **$ 27.36**.

Highlights

➤ From a projected 1% decline in 2007, which reflects the UPN shutdown as well as certain TV and radio divestitures, we estimate that total revenues will advance under 4% in 2008, to about $14.7 billion, with likely strong contributions from TV political advertising. We see flat to modestly lower 2008 revenue at the radio division, after a sharp decline in 2007. We expect relatively modest growth at the outdoor division, which has benefited recently from steady pricing in North America and currency fluctuations at the international unit.

➤ We project little change in total 2007 EBITDA, at about $3.1 billion, reflecting the divestitures and higher stock compensation, followed by a modest advance to $3.3 billion in 2008, in the absence of certain unprofitable outdoor transit contracts and assuming modest margin improvement at the radio division.

➤ We forecast EPS of $1.86 and $2.06 for 2007 and 2008, respectively. In March 2007, CBS completed an accelerated $1.5 billion share buy-back program, and in April, it repurchased another 7.6 million of its shares via an exchange agreement.

Investment Rationale/Risk

➤ In early November 2007, CBS reported what we saw as somewhat encouraging results for the third quarter, which were nevertheless constrained by certain unusual and/or infrequent items. With the CBS network's 2007-08 upfront market relatively healthy, management said scatter pricing was up 35%, and was also upbeat on political spending for the upcoming presidential elections. Longer term, we see potential upside from continued deployment of digital billboards, cash payments for local TV retransmission consent, and growing revenues from various digital initiatives. We view the company's balance sheet as strong.

➤ Risks to our recommendation and target price include continued turnaround challenges for the radio division, a sharp advertising and/or macroeconomic slowdown, reduced operating leverage at the outdoor unit, and foreign currency exposure.

➤ Based on our 2008 estimates, our 12-month target price of $33 reflects a 9X enterprise value to EBITDA, or a P/E-to-growth (PEG) ratio of 1.9X, both above peers and the S&P 500. The stock currently offers a 3.6% dividend yield.

Qualitative Risk Assessment

LOW	MEDIUM	HIGH

Our risk assessment reflects CBS's leading TV and outdoor properties and our view of the company's strong balance sheet and free cash flow generation. This is offset by continued challenges in the radio business and a soft advertising market.

Quantitative Evaluations

S&P Quality Ranking   **B-**

D	C	B-	B	B+	A-	A	A+

Relative Strength Rank   **MODERATE**

36

LOWEST = 1   HIGHEST = 99

Revenue/Earnings Data

Revenue (Million $)

	1Q	2Q	3Q	4Q	Year
2007	3,658	3,375	3,281	--	--
2006	3,575	3,483	3,379	3,883	14,320
2005	5,577	5,876	5,943	3,828	14,536
2004	6,772	6,842	5,485	6,296	22,526
2003	6,051	6,418	6,600	7,516	26,585
2002	5,672	5,850	6,307	6,778	24,606

Earnings Per Share ($)

2007	0.28	0.55	0.48	E0.55	E1.86
2006	0.31	0.64	0.42	0.43	1.79
2005	0.72	0.94	0.94	-6.07	-5.27
2004	0.82	0.86	0.84	-20.42	-17.56
2003	0.52	0.74	0.80	-0.44	1.62
2002	0.42	0.62	0.72	0.72	2.48

Fiscal year ended Dec. 31. Next earnings report expected: NA. EPS Estimates based on S&P Operating Earnings; historical GAAP earnings are as reported.

Dividend Data (Dates: mm/dd Payment Date: mm/dd/yy)

Amount ($)	Date Decl.	Ex-Div. Date	Stk. of Record	Payment Date
0.220	02/27	03/05	03/07	04/01/07
0.220	05/25	05/31	06/04	07/01/07
0.250	09/04	09/12	09/14	10/01/07
0.250	11/01	11/28	11/30	01/01/08

Dividends have been paid since 2003. Source: Company reports.

Please read the Required Disclosures and Analyst Certification on the last page of this report.

The McGraw-Hill Companies

CBS Corp

STANDARD &POOR'S

Business Summary November 06, 2007

CORPORATE OVERVIEW. In its current form, the company is one of the two independent public entities created after the early 2006 separation of the "old" Viacom (which was renamed CBS Corp., while the other entity adopted the "Viacom" name). Pursuant to the separation, each Class A and B shareholder of the "old" Viacom received 0.5 of a share of corresponding A or B stock of each of the new entities. We believe that CBS Corp. was the lower-growth entity resulting from the separation, and that it was targeted to value-oriented investors. Nearly 70% of its revenues are generated from advertising-related businesses.

The television segment includes the CBS networks, CW network (a new joint venture with Time Warner's WB), 39 owned and operated (O&O) TV stations, Showtime cable networks and Paramount/King World TV production and syndication. The radio division, CBS Radio, operates 178 radio stations in 40 U.S. markets (and owns interests of 18% in Westwood One and 10% in Spanish Broadcasting). The outdoor unit, Viacom Outdoor, operates billboards and out-of-home displays in the U.S. and abroad. The Publishing segment mainly includes book publishers Simon & Schuster. In 2006, the company sold its

Paramount Parks for $1.24 billion in cash.

CORPORATE STRATEGY. As CBS leverages its TV (entertainment and news) franchises across both traditional and emerging platforms, it has struck deals with Internet, technology and cable companies to offer its content for on-demand and mobile users. In April 2007, the company unveiled plans for a new CBS Interactive Audience Network for online video syndication, with a host of initial online distribution partners such as AOL, Microsoft, CNET Networks, Comcast, Joost, Bebo, Brightcove, Netvibes, Sling Media and Veoh. CBS is focused on a turnaround of its radio division, recently divesting about 39 radio stations as well as 11 TV stations (mostly in smaller markets). In May 2007, CBS acquired Last.fm, a music-based social network with more than 15 million users across more than 200 countries, for $280 million in cash.

Company Financials Fiscal Year Ended Dec. 31

Per Share Data ($)	2006	2005	2004	2003	2002	2001	2000	1999	1998	1997
Tangible Book Value	NM	NM	NM	NM	NM	NM	NM	NM	NM	NM
Cash Flow	2.36	-9.91	-16.62	2.77	3.55	3.31	3.04	3.43	1.90	3.55
Earnings	1.79	-5.27	-17.56	1.62	2.48	-0.26	-0.60	1.02	-0.20	0.89
S&P Core Earnings	1.90	1.10	2.92	2.40	2.08	-0.76	NA	NA	NA	NA
Dividends	0.68	0.56	0.50	0.24	Nil	Nil	Nil	Nil	Nil	Nil
Payout Ratio	NM	NM	NM	15%	Nil	Nil	Nil	Nil	Nil	Nil
Prices:High	32.04	77.98	90.10	99.50	103.78	119.00	151.75	120.87	74.25	42.25
Prices:Low	23.85	59.86	60.18	66.22	59.50	56.50	88.63	70.75	40.50	25.25
P/E Ratio:High	18	NM	NM	61	42	NM	NM	NM	NM	47
P/E Ratio:Low	13	NM	NM	41	24	NM	NM	NM	NM	28

Income Statement Analysis (Million $)										
Revenue	14,320	14,536	22,526	26,585	24,606	23,223	20,044	12,859	12,096	13,206
Operating Income	3,135	3,165	5,838	5,957	5,542	4,667	4,243	2,162	1,529	1,696
Depreciation	440	499	810	1,000	946	3,087	2,224	845	777	943
Interest Expense	566	720	719	776	848	963	822	449	622	782
Pretax Income	2,036	-7,513	-13,676	2,861	3,695	656	436	783	96.0	1,060
Effective Tax Rate	32.0%	NM	NM	55.9%	39.2%	NM	NM	52.5%	145.0%	65.1%
Net Income	1,383	-8,322	-15,060	1,435	2,207	-220	-364	372	-44.0	375
S&P Core Earnings	1,468	871	2,497	2,087	1,845	-656	NA	NA	NA	NA

Balance Sheet & Other Financial Data (Million $)										
Cash	3,075	1,655	928	851	631	727	934	681	267	292
Current Assets	8,144	6,796	7,494	7,736	7,167	7,206	7,832	5,198	5,065	5,714
Total Assets	43,509	43,030	68,002	89,849	89,754	90,810	82,646	24,486	23,613	28,289
Current Liabilities	4,400	5,379	6,880	7,585	7,341	7,562	7,758	4,400	5,633	5,053
Long Term Debt	7,027	7,153	9,649	9,683	10,205	10,824	12,474	Nil	3,813	7,423
Common Equity	24,153	21,737	59,862	63,205	62,488	62,717	47,967	11,132	11,450	12,184
Total Capital	32,862	31,007	70,879	73,812	74,337	75,884	67,481	12,379	15,863	19,607
Capital Expenditures	394	376	415	534	537	515	659	706	604	530
Cash Flow	1,822	-7,823	-14,250	2,435	3,152	2,867	1,860	1,216	676	1,318
Current Ratio	1.9	1.3	1.1	1.0	1.0	1.0	1.0	1.2	0.9	1.1
% Long Term Debt of Capitalization	21.0	23.1	13.6	13.1	13.7	14.3	18.5	Nil	24.0	37.8
% Net Income of Revenue	9.7	NM	NM	5.4	9.0	NM	NM	2.9	NM	2.8
% Return on Assets	3.2	NM	NM	1.6	2.4	NM	NM	1.5	NM	1.3
% Return on Equity	5.9	NM	NM	2.3	3.5	NM	NM	3.3	NM	2.7

Data as orig reptd.; bef. results of disc opers/spec. items. Per share data adj. for stk. divs.; EPS diluted. Data as orig reptd., for "old" Viacom through third qtr. 2005. E-Estimated. NA-Not Available. NM-Not Meaningful. NR-Not Ranked. UR-Under Review.

Office: 51 W 52nd St , New York, NY 10019-6188.
Telephone: 212-975-4321.
Website: http://www.cbscorporation.com
Chrmn: S.M. Redstone

Pres & CEO: L. Moonves
EVP & CFO: F.G. Reynolds
EVP & General Counsel: L.J. Briskman
Investor Contact: M.M. Shea

Board Members: D. R. Andelman, J. A. Califano, Jr., W. S. Cohen, P. P. Dauman, C. K. Gifford, L. Goldberg, B. S. Gordon, L. Moonves, S. Redstone, S. M. Redstone, A. N. Reese, J. A. Sprieser, R. D. Walter

Founded: 1986
Domicile: Delaware
Employees: 23,654

The McGraw-Hill Companies

Celgene Corp

STANDARD &POOR'S

S&P Recommendation **BUY** ★★★★☆	Price $62.35 (as of Nov 23, 2007)	12-Mo. Target Price $76.00	Investment Style Large-Cap Growth

GICS Sector Health Care
Sub-Industry Biotechnology

Summary This company's primarily develops and commercializes small molecule drugs for the treatment of bloodborne and solid tumor cancers and inflammatory disease.

Key Stock Statistics (Source S&P, Vickers, company reports)

52-Wk Range	$75.44– 49.46	S&P Oper. EPS 2007**E**	0.94	Market Capitalization(B)	$23.863	Beta	0.86
Trailing 12-Month EPS	$0.42	S&P Oper. EPS 2008**E**	1.55	Yield (%)	Nil	S&P 3-Yr. Proj. EPS CAGR(%)	40.00
Trailing 12-Month P/E	NM	P/E on S&P Oper. EPS 2007**E**	66.3	Dividend Rate/Share	Nil	S&P Credit Rating	NR
$10K Invested 5 Yrs Ago	$99,760	Common Shares Outstg. (M)	382.7	Institutional Ownership (%)	89		

Price Performance

30-Week Mov. Avg. ···· 10-Week Mov. Avg. -- **GAAP Earnings vs. Previous Year** Volume Above Avg.||||| STARS
12-Mo. Target Price — Relative Strength — ▲ Up ▼ Down ▶ No Change Below Avg.||||| ★

Options: ASE, CBOE, P, Ph

Analysis prepared by **Steven Silver** on November 19, 2007, when the stock traded at **$ 64.00**.

Highlights

➤ Third quarter 2007 Revlimid sales of $199 million were $13 million below our estimate, but nearly double last year's $100 million. Management recently lowered its 2007 revenue guidance to $1.375 billion, from $1.4 billion. We have adjusted our model to $1.37 billion, from $1.39 billion, and we now expect 2007 Revlimid sales of $760 million, down from $800 million previously, and 84% growth in 2008, to $1.4 billion. Revlimid launched only in Germany during the quarter, and we expect further expansion and strong uptake through 2008.

➤ The gross margin in the third quarter was 90%, down from 92% in the prior quarter. We see long-term gross margins of 92%-93%, as CELG leverages its sales growth to maximize manufacturing efficiencies. We see opportunity for further operating margin expansion upon integration of the proposed Pharmion acquisition, as CELG would be able to sell Revlimid, Thalomid and Vidaza within the same sales infrastructure.

➤ We project 2007 and 2008 EPS of $0.94 and $1.55, respectively. Assuming a successful Pharmion acquisition, we would expect slightly diluted 2008 EPS, but accretion thereafter.

Investment Rationale/Risk

➤ We see continued Revlimid growth as the key catalyst for the shares. We are encouraged by market research suggesting that Revlimid should become the standard of care for first-line multiple myeloma despite recent positive data from competitor Velcade. We expect a front-line FDA filing in 2008, and approval in 2009, given data to date. We expect the European Revlimid rollout to be boosted by sales infrastructure to be acquired in the proposed Pharmion deal, expected in mid-2008. We see the proposed $2.9 billion deal, which would add lead compound Vidaza to the portfolio and return European rights to Thalomid, expanding CELG's global footprint. Further, we view favorably the acceleration of mid-stage candidate CC-10004, following release of positive Phase II data.

➤ Risks to our recommendation and target price include slower than expected Revlimid sales growth, and clinical failure of CELG's earlier-stage pipeline candidates.

➤ Our 12-month target price of $76 applies a 40X multiple to our 2009 EPS estimate of $2.18, discounted back one period at 15%, in line with our long-term growth rate for CELG.

Qualitative Risk Assessment

LOW	MEDIUM	**HIGH**

Our risk assessment reflects the strong competition we see in the blood cancer treatment markets. In addition, CELG receives royalties on sales of Ritalin-based products for attention deficit hyperactivity disorder (ADHD), which is also a very competitive market with several large players. The company currently depends on two products in the same markets for the majority of its revenues.

Quantitative Evaluations

S&P Quality Ranking B-

D	C	**B-**	B	B+	A-	A	A+

Relative Strength Rank MODERATE

51

LOWEST = 1 HIGHEST = 99

Revenue/Earnings Data

Revenue (Million $)

	1Q	2Q	3Q	4Q	Year
2007	293.4	347.9	349.9	--	--
2006	181.8	197.2	244.8	275.0	898.9
2005	112.4	145.7	129.5	149.3	536.9
2004	82.87	87.75	101.5	105.4	377.5
2003	49.09	67.29	74.33	80.77	271.5
2002	30.69	33.62	34.26	37.17	135.8

Earnings Per Share ($)

2007	0.14	0.13	0.09	E0.27	E0.94
2006	0.04	0.03	0.05	0.06	0.18
2005	0.13	0.03	Nil	0.01	0.18
2004	0.03	0.01	0.06	0.07	0.16
2003	Nil	Nil	0.01	0.01	0.04
2002	Nil	Nil	Nil	-0.31	-0.33

Fiscal year ended Dec. 31. Next earnings report expected: Early February. EPS Estimates based on S&P Operating Earnings; historical GAAP earnings are as reported.

Dividend Data

No cash dividends have been paid.

The **McGraw·Hill** Companies

Celgene Corp

STANDARD &POOR'S

Business Summary November 19, 2007

CORPORATE OVERVIEW. Celgene develops and markets pharmaceuticals to treat cancer, immunological disorders, and other diseases. Its research focuses on small molecule compounds that inhibit Tumor Necrosis Factor alpha (TNFa) production or aberrant estrogen production, or may regulate kinases and ligases (enzymes involved in gene function that may contribute to disease when their proper function is altered).

The company is using its small molecule technology to develop Immunomodulatory Drugs (IMiDs) and Selective Cytokine Inhibitory Drugs (SelCIDs), an array of potent, orally available agents to fight acute and chronic diseases. The company's primary focus to date has been treating multiple myeloma, the second most commonly diagnosed blood cancer. According to the International Myeloma Foundation, there are an estimated 750,000 people with MM worldwide. At any one time, there are more than 85,000 men and women in Europe undergoing treatment for multiple myeloma, and 25,000 people are expected to die from this blood cancer in 2007.

To date, Celgene's primary marketed products have been Thalomid and Revlimid. Thalomid is CELG's version of thalidomide, an antiangiogenic agent capable of inhibiting blood vessel growth and down-regulating TNFa. In 1998,

Thalomid was approved by the FDA to treat leprosy-related conditions. In February 2004, the company filed for FDA approval of Thalomid to treat multiple myeloma (MM). The FDA approved Thalomid in May 2006. Thalomid is also being studied in numerous clinical trials for the treatment of myelodysplastic syndrome (MDS), prostate cancer, renal cell carcinoma, and various other cancer types.

On December 28, 2005, CELG announced FDA approval of Revlimid (the company's primary IMiD) to treat MDS patients with a rare chromosomal deletion (5q minus). On a monthly basis, the company estimates the cost of therapy to be between $4,500 and $4,700 per patient. Revlimid has received FDA approval to be used in combination with dexamethasone for the treatment of relapsed or refractory MM and, in June 2007, was approved in Europe for the same indications. The drug is also being tested in a number of earlier stage trials including multiple myeloma in a first-line setting, amyloidosis, non-Hodgkin's lymphoma, and various solid tumor cancers.

Company Financials Fiscal Year Ended Dec. 31

Per Share Data ($)	2006	2005	2004	2003	2002	2001	2000	1999	1998	1997
Tangible Book Value	4.83	1.48	1.06	0.93	0.85	1.03	1.00	NM	0.02	0.06
Cash Flow	0.23	0.23	0.18	0.06	-0.31	0.01	-0.05	-0.31	-0.16	-0.17
Earnings	0.18	0.18	0.16	0.04	-0.33	-0.01	-0.06	-0.11	-0.17	-0.18
S&P Core Earnings	0.19	0.05	0.08	-0.04	-0.33	-0.09	NA	NA	NA	NA
Dividends	Nil	Nil	Nil	Nil	Nil	Nil	Nil	Nil	Nil	Nil
Payout Ratio	Nil	Nil	Nil	Nil	Nil	Nil	Nil	Nil	Nil	Nil
Prices:High	60.12	32.68	16.29	12.22	8.05	9.72	19.00	6.05	1.44	1.11
Prices:Low	31.51	12.35	9.37	5.04	2.83	3.60	4.58	0.94	0.34	0.41
P/E Ratio:High	NM	NM	NM	NM	NM	NM	NM	NM	NM	NM
P/E Ratio:Low	NM	NM	NM	NM	NM	NM	NM	NM	NM	NM

Income Statement Analysis (Million $)										
Revenue	899	537	378	271	136	114	84.2	26.2	3.80	NA
Operating Income	200	97.9	52.4	5.38	-31.0	-19.9	-23.9	-21.7	-31.7	-24.9
Depreciation	25.7	14.3	9.69	8.03	5.18	5.09	3.72	0.99	0.81	0.51
Interest Expense	9.42	9.50	9.55	5.67	0.03	0.08	2.08	2.84	0.26	NA
Pretax Income	203	84.2	63.2	12.0	-101	-4.14	-18.8	-24.8	-7.30	NA
Effective Tax Rate	66.0%	24.4%	16.5%	NM	NM	NM	NM	NM	NM	NM
Net Income	69.0	63.7	52.8	12.8	-101	-2.90	-17.0	-21.8	-32.0	NA
S&P Core Earnings	71.5	10.8	25.0	-13.0	-88.6	-26.5	NA	NA	NA	NA

Balance Sheet & Other Financial Data (Million $)										
Cash	1,982	724	749	667	261	310	161	15.3	5.12	13.6
Current Assets	2,311	973	850	730	296	336	332	27.8	9.59	15.9
Total Assets	2,736	1,247	1,107	791	327	354	347	32.3	11.9	18.2
Current Liabilities	240	136	141	71.8	44.3	30.0	33.8	9.30	7.12	2.44
Long Term Debt	400	400	400	400	0.04	11.8	12.3	38.5	8.55	0.35
Common Equity	1,976	636	477	310	277	310	296	-15.7	-3.73	11.4
Total Capital	2,376	1,036	877	710	277	322	308	22.8	4.81	15.8
Capital Expenditures	46.1	35.9	36.0	11.2	11.1	7.87	9.64	1.78	0.79	1.24
Cash Flow	94.7	77.9	62.4	20.8	-95.8	2.18	-13.3	-20.8	-31.2	-25.5
Current Ratio	9.6	7.2	6.0	10.2	6.7	11.2	9.8	3.0	1.3	6.5
% Long Term Debt of Capitalization	16.8	38.6	45.6	56.3	0.0	3.7	4.0	168.9	177.6	2.2
% Net Income of Revenue	7.7	11.9	14.0	4.7	NM	NM	NM	NM	NM	NM
% Return on Assets	3.5	5.4	5.5	2.3	NM	NM	NM	NM	NM	NM
% Return on Equity	5.3	11.4	13.0	4.3	NM	NM	NM	NM	NM	NM

Data as orig reptd.; bef. results of disc opers/spec. items. Per share data adj. for stk. divs.; EPS diluted. E-Estimated. NA-Not Available. NM-Not Meaningful. NR-Not Ranked. UR-Under Review.

Office: 86 Morris Ave, Summit, NJ 07901-3915.
Telephone: 908-673-9000.
Email: info@celgene.com
Website: http://www.celgene.com

Chrmn & CEO: S.J. Barer
Pres & COO: R.J. Hugin
CFO: D.W. Gryska
Chief Acctg Officer & Cntlr: J.R. Swenson

Investor Contact: B.P. Gill (908-673-9530)
Board Members: S. J. Barer, J. L. Bowman, M. D. Casey, R. L. Drake, A. H. Hayes, Jr., R. J. Hugin, J. W. Jackson, G. Kaplan, J. J. Loughlin, R. C. Morgan, W. L. Robb

Founded: 1986
Domicile: Delaware
Employees: 1,287

CenterPoint Energy Inc.

STANDARD &POOR'S

S&P Recommendation **HOLD** ★★★☆☆	Price **$17.49** (as of Nov 23, 2007)	12-Mo. Target Price **$18.00**	Investment Style Large-Cap Value

GICS Sector Utilities
Sub-Industry Multi-Utilities

Summary This Houston-based energy company (formerly Reliant Energy) is one of the largest electric and natural gas delivery companies in the U.S.

Key Stock Statistics (Source S&P, Vickers, company reports)

52-Wk Range	$20.20–14.70	S&P Oper. EPS 2007E	1.11	Market Capitalization(B)	$5.617	Beta	1.08
Trailing 12-Month EPS	$1.04	S&P Oper. EPS 2008E	1.20	Yield (%)	3.89	S&P 3-Yr. Proj. EPS CAGR(%)	3.00
Trailing 12-Month P/E	16.8	P/E on S&P Oper. EPS 2007E	15.8	Dividend Rate/Share	$0.68	S&P Credit Rating	BBB
$10K Invested 5 Yrs Ago	NA	Common Shares Outstg. (M)	321.2	Institutional Ownership (%)	83		

Price Performance

30-Week Mov. Avg. · · · 10-Week Mov. Avg. - - **GAAP Earnings vs. Previous Year** Volume Above Avg. STARS
12-Mo. Target Price — Relative Strength — ▲ Up ▼ Down ► No Change Below Avg. ★

Options: ASE, CBOE, P, Ph

Analysis prepared by **Justin McCann** on November 07, 2007, when the stock traded at **$ 18.04**.

Highlights

➤ We expect operating EPS in 2007 to remain relatively flat with 2006 operating EPS of $1.11. Operating EPS in the first nine months of 2007 benefited from gains in the natural gas distribution, interstate pipelines and field services segments. However, this was largely offset by a decline in the electric transmission and distribution segment, reflecting an electric rate base reduction in Texas.

➤ For 2008, we expect operating EPS to increase approximately 8% from anticipated results in 2007. We expect this increase to reflect customer growth at the utilities, continuing strong performances at the interstate pipelines and field services operations, and more improvement in the natural gas distribution business.

➤ In August 2007, CNP's gas transmission unit placed into service the expanded capacity of a pipeline from Carthage, TX to its Perryville hub in Northeast Louisiana. Earlier, on January 31, 2007, CNP agreed to discontinue the development of its proposed pipeline with Spectra Energy (the spun-off gas transmission unit of Duke Energy) due to market conditions. The proposed pipeline (announced on June 1, 2006) would have stretched from Texas to Pennsylvania.

Investment Rationale/Risk

➤ The shares have advanced approximately 10% year-to-date, and we consider them fairly valued relative to peers. We think the recent increase reflects the overall improvement in CNP's financial strength, while the earlier decline reflected a general investor shift away from electric and gas utilities as a group. We expect the stock to perform more closely in line with peers over the next 12 months.

➤ Risks to our recommendation and target price include the impact that would likely result from a potential weakening of CNP's financial strength, including a decreased ability to access capital markets on reasonable terms; as well as a sharp drop in the average P/E of the stock's industry peers.

➤ We expect CNP to use much of the proceeds from its "true-up" recovery to reduce its debt, which, at the end of 2006, was $7.8 billion. We expect CNP to emerge from this transitional period financially stronger. However, despite a recent above-peers dividend yield of around 3.7%, we see the stock trading at a modest discount-to-peers P/E of about 15X our 2008 EPS estimate. Our 12-month target price is $18.

Qualitative Risk Assessment

LOW	MEDIUM	HIGH

Our risk assessment reflects the strong and steady cash flow that we expect from the Houston electric operations, which have a growing service territory; a low commodity risk profile; a generally supportive regulatory environment; and the gas purchase adjustment clauses that reduce the commodity risks related to the company's more diversified gas distribution operations.

Quantitative Evaluations

S&P Quality Ranking   **B**

D	C	B-	B	B+	A-	A	A+

Relative Strength Rank   **STRONG**

86

LOWEST = 1   HIGHEST = 99

Revenue/Earnings Data

Revenue (Million $)

	1Q	2Q	3Q	4Q	Year
2007	3,106	2,033	1,882	--	--
2006	3,077	1,843	1,935	2,464	9,319
2005	2,762	1,932	2,073	3,212	9,722
2004	2,959	2,241	1,667	2,618	8,510
2003	2,900	2,090	2,250	2,519	9,760
2002	2,078	1,804	1,923	2,117	7,923

Earnings Per Share ($)

2007	0.38	0.20	0.27	E0.28	E1.11
2006	0.28	0.61	0.26	0.20	1.33
2005	0.20	0.09	0.15	0.25	0.67
2004	0.24	0.19	0.05	0.46	0.61
2003	0.27	0.27	0.60	0.23	1.37
2002	0.49	0.29	0.54	-0.03	1.29

Fiscal year ended Dec. 31. Next earnings report expected: Late February. EPS Estimates based on S&P Operating Earnings; historical GAAP earnings are as reported.

Dividend Data (Dates: mm/dd Payment Date: mm/dd/yy)

Amount ($)	Date Decl.	Ex-Div. Date	Stk. of Record	Payment Date
0.170	02/01	02/14	02/16	03/09/07
0.170	04/26	05/14	05/16	06/08/07
0.170	07/26	08/14	08/16	09/10/07
0.170	10/25	11/14	11/16	12/10/07

Dividends have been paid since 1922. Source: Company reports.

The **McGraw-Hill** Companies

CenterPoint Energy Inc.

STANDARD &POOR'S

Business Summary November 07, 2007

CORPORATE OVERVIEW. CenterPoint Energy (formerly Reliant Energy) is a Houston-based energy delivery company with operations that include electric transmission and distribution (55.0% of operating income in 2006), interstate pipelines (17.3%), natural gas distribution (11.8%), field services (8.5%), and competitive natural gas sales and services ((7.4%).

MARKET PROFILE. The CenterPoint Energy Houston Electric (CEHE) utility serves approximately 2 million customers in a 5,000 square mile territory that includes the cities of Houston and Galveston, TX, and (with the exception of Texas City), nearly all of the Houston/Galveston metropolitan area. Following the deregulation of the industry in Texas, wholesale and retail suppliers pay the company to deliver the electricity over its transmission lines. The natural gas subsidiary, CenterPoint Energy Resources Corp. (CERC), serves about 3.2 million residential, commercial and industrial customers in Arkansas, Louisiana, Minnesota, Mississippi, Oklahoma and Texas. In 2006, approxi-

mately 60% of total demand was accounted for by residential customers, and about 40% was from commercial and industrial customers.

CERC's interstate pipeline business owns and operates about 7,900 miles of gas transmission lines primarily located in Arkansas, Illinois, Louisiana, Missouri, Oklahoma and Texas. It also owns and operates six natural gas storage fields with a combined daily volume of about 1.2 billion cubic feet per day. CERC's field services business owns and operates around 3,700 miles of gathering pipelines and processing plants, and about 150 natural gas gathering systems in Arkansas, Oklahoma, Louisiana, and Texas.

Company Financials Fiscal Year Ended Dec. 31

Per Share Data ($)	2006	2005	2004	2003	2002	2001	2000	1999	1998	1997
Tangible Book Value	NM	NM	NM	NM	NM	13.05	8.11	7.69	6.77	9.01
Earnings	1.33	0.67	0.61	1.37	1.29	3.14	2.68	5.82	-0.50	1.66
S&P Core Earnings	1.18	0.75	0.65	1.28	2.17	3.00	NA	NA	NA	NA
Dividends	0.60	0.40	0.40	0.40	1.07	1.50	1.50	1.50	1.50	1.50
Payout Ratio	45%	60%	66%	29%	83%	48%	56%	26%	NM	90%
Prices:High	16.87	15.14	12.32	10.49	27.10	50.45	49.00	32.50	33.38	27.25
Prices:Low	11.62	10.55	9.66	4.35	4.24	23.27	19.75	22.75	25.00	18.88
P/E Ratio:High	13	23	20	8	21	16	18	6	NM	16
P/E Ratio:Low	9	16	16	3	3	7	7	4	NM	11

Income Statement Analysis (Million $)

	2006	2005	2004	2003	2002	2001	2000	1999	1998	1997
Revenue	9,319	9,722	8,510	9,760	7,923	46,226	29,339	15,303	11,488	6,873
Depreciation	599	541	490	625	616	911	906	911	857	652
Maintenance	NA	NA	NA	NA	NA	NA	NA	NA	NA	NA
Fixed Charges Coverage	1.80	1.35	1.15	1.37	1.80	3.33	2.60	2.32	1.64	2.56
Construction Credits	NA	NA	NA	NA	NA	NA	NA	Nil	4.00	3.00
Effective Tax Rate	12.6%	40.5%	NM	35.6%	35.0%	33.3%	32.9%	35.0%	NM	32.9%
Net Income	432	225	206	420	386	919	771	1,666	-141	421
S&P Core Earnings	384	254	224	390	642	868	NA	NA	NA	NA

Balance Sheet & Other Financial Data (Million $)

	2006	2005	2004	2003	2002	2001	2000	1999	1998	1997
Gross Property	12,567	11,558	10,963	11,812	11,409	24,214	15,260	20,133	17,030	16,039
Capital Expenditures	1,007	693	530	648	854	2,053	1,842	1,179	743	329
Net Property	9,204	8,492	8,186	11,812	11,409	15,857	15,260	13,267	11,531	11,269
Capitalization:Long Term Debt	7,802	8,568	7,193	10,783	9,194	6,448	5,701	5,666	7,153	5,218
Capitalization:% Long Term Debt	83.4	86.9	86.7	86.0	71.0	48.4	51.0	51.6	62.4	49.8
Capitalization:Preferred	Nil	Nil	Nil	Nil	Nil	Nil	10.0	10.0	10.0	10.0
Capitalization:% Preferred	Nil	Nil	Nil	Nil	Nil	Nil	0.09	0.09	0.01	0.10
Capitalization:Common	1,556	1,296	1,106	1,761	3,756	6,881	5,472	5,296	4,312	4,887
Capitalization:% Common	16.6	13.1	13.3	14.0	29.0	51.6	48.9	48.3	37.6	46.7
Total Capital	12,036	12,769	10,767	12,934	13,180	16,970	13,998	13,694	14,158	13,619
% Operating Ratio	15.9	15.0	88.2	85.8	85.8	96.6	94.9	97.8	86.9	87.5
% Earned on Net Property	11.8	11.3	10.6	21.8	17.2	12.8	13.2	10.0	13.0	10.6
% Return on Revenue	2.8	1.4	2.4	4.3	4.9	2.0	2.6	10.9	NM	6.1
% Return on Invested Capital	8.3	7.9	7.6	11.1	14.7	11.2	10.3	20.5	16.6	7.9
% Return on Common Equity	30.3	18.7	14.4	26.4	10.3	14.8	14.3	34.7	NM	9.7

Data as orig reptd.; bef. results of disc opers/spec. items. Per share data adj. for stk. divs.; EPS diluted. E-Estimated. NA-Not Available. NM-Not Meaningful. NR-Not Ranked. UR-Under Review.

Office: 1111 Louisiana Street, Houston, TX 77002-5230.
Telephone: 713-207-1111.
Email: info@reliantenergy.nl
Website: http://www.centerpointenergy.com

Chrmn: M. Carroll
Pres & CEO: D.M. McClanahan
EVP & CFO: G.L. Whitlock
EVP, Secy & General Counsel: S.E. Rozzell

SVP & Chief Acctg Officer: J.S. Brian
Investor Contact: M. Paulsen (713-207-6500)
Board Members: D. R. Campbell, M. Carroll, J. T. Cater, D. Cody, O. H. Crosswell, J. M. Longoria, T. F. Madison, D. M. McClanahan, R. T. O'Connell, M. E. Shannon, P. S. Wareing

Founded: 1882
Domicile: Texas
Employees: 8,623

The McGraw-Hill Companies

Centex Corp.

STANDARD &POOR'S

S&P Recommendation HOLD ★★★☆☆	**Price** $19.96 (as of Nov 23, 2007)	**12-Mo. Target Price** $25.00	**Investment Style** Large-Cap Blend

GICS Sector Consumer Discretionary
Sub-Industry Homebuilding

Summary This major U.S. homebuilder sells homes in 25 states and engages in mortgage banking and title insurance sales.

Key Stock Statistics (Source S&P, Vickers, company reports)

52-Wk Range	$58.42– 19.05	S&P Oper. EPS 2008**E**	-9.00	Market Capitalization(B)	$2.395	Beta	1.80
Trailing 12-Month EPS	$-6.48	S&P Oper. EPS 2009**E**	-0.95	Yield (%)	0.80	S&P 3-Yr. Proj. EPS CAGR(%)	5.00
Trailing 12-Month P/E	NM	P/E on S&P Oper. EPS 2008**E**	NM	Dividend Rate/Share	$0.16	S&P Credit Rating	BBB-
$10K Invested 5 Yrs Ago	NA	Common Shares Outstg. (M)	120.0	Institutional Ownership (%)	NM		

Price Performance

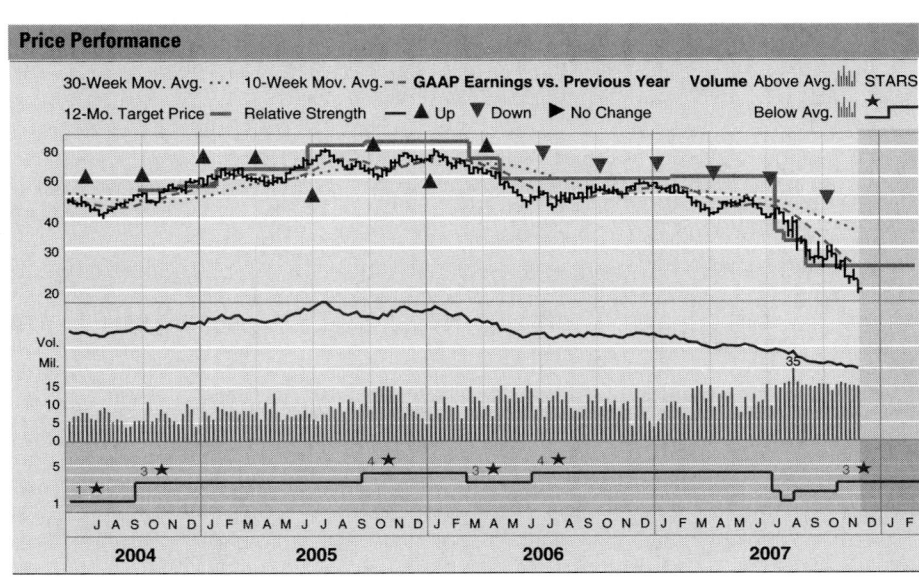

30-Week Mov. Avg. · · · 10-Week Mov. Avg. – – **GAAP Earnings vs. Previous Year** Volume Above Avg. STARS
12-Mo. Target Price — Relative Strength — ▲ Up ▼ Down ▶ No Change Below Avg.

Options: ASE, CBOE, P, Ph

Analysis prepared by **Kenneth M. Leon, CPA** on October 24, 2007, when the stock traded at **$ 24.65.**

Highlights

➤ We estimate that total revenue will decrease about 36% in FY 08 (Mar.) and be flat in FY 09, reflecting a U.S. housing industry downturn and the absence of divested operations. On April 2, 2007, Centex completed the sale of its commercial construction division for about $362 million. Revenues in the homebuilding segment, CTX's prime focus, were down 33% in the first half of FY 08, as home closings declined 23% and the average unit selling price decreased to the 6% level.

➤ We anticipate pressure on home prices and gross margins in FY 08. The company took writedowns in the September quarter of $983 million for impairments and other land charges, following writedowns of $193 million in the June quarter, and $202 million in the March quarter. We view these inventory charges as large but on par with peers during the current industry downturn.

➤ Acknowledging low earnings visibility, and given the potential we see for further inventory writedowns, we estimate a loss per share of $9.00 for FY 08, and a loss per share of $0.95 for FY 09.

Investment Rationale/Risk

➤ While we do not expect a housing recovery until mid-2008, we believe the rate of decline in the quarter-to-quarter fundamental trends such as cancellation rates, new contracts and net order backlog will begin to improve in early 2008. One measure that we see as weak into 2008 is average selling prices as homebuilders try to reduce homesite inventory. We would hold CTX shares based on our expectation of increasing cash and a smaller amount of home inventory and land writeoffs beyond the September quarter charges.

➤ Risks to our recommendation and target price include any significant increase in mortgage rates or a weakening of job growth. These factors are key demand inputs for the highly cyclical homebuilding industry.

➤ We arrive at our 12-month target price of $25 by applying just under a 0.8X target price-to-book ratio, toward the low end of CTX's historical range, to our estimated book value of $32. Despite a weak housing market, we are confident in management's ability to operate through the downturn and position the company to gain share when housing recovers, which we expect by mid-2008.

Qualitative Risk Assessment

LOW	MEDIUM	**HIGH**

Our high risk assessment reflects Centex's exposure to the sharp cyclicality of the housing industry and the company's liquidity should the current downturn extend beyond the first six months of 2008. Partly offsetting these concerns are the company's national scope of operations with geographic diversity and large scale to gain volume discounts on material costs.

Quantitative Evaluations

S&P Quality Ranking A+

D	C	B-	B	B+	A-	A	**A+**

Relative Strength Rank WEAK

10

LOWEST = 1 HIGHEST = 99

Revenue/Earnings Data

Revenue (Million $)

	1Q	2Q	3Q	4Q	Year
2008	1,941	2,221	--	--	--
2007	2,804	2,816	2,726	3,669	12,015
2006	3,222	3,630	3,738	4,550	14,400
2005	2,766	2,985	3,119	3,990	12,860
2004	2,173	2,428	2,570	3,193	10,363
2003	1,844	2,084	2,305	2,885	9,117

Earnings Per Share ($)

2008	-1.08	-5.26	E-1.89	E-0.77	E-9.00
2007	1.37	0.65	-2.02	-0.18	-0.10
2006	1.74	2.49	2.52	2.92	9.20
2005	1.35	1.61	1.91	2.75	7.64
2004	1.04	1.56	1.43	2.05	6.01
2003	0.69	0.92	1.25	1.56	4.41

Fiscal year ended Mar. 31. Next earnings report expected: Late January. EPS Estimates based on S&P Operating Earnings; historical GAAP earnings are as reported.

Dividend Data (Dates: mm/dd Payment Date: mm/dd/yy)

Amount ($)	Date Decl.	Ex-Div. Date	Stk. of Record	Payment Date
0.040	02/14	03/02	03/06	03/27/07
0.040	05/16	05/25	05/30	06/20/07
0.040	07/16	07/30	08/01	08/22/07
0.040	10/15	10/29	10/31	11/21/07

Dividends have been paid since 1973. Source: Company reports.

Please read the Required Disclosures and Analyst Certification on the last page of this report.

The McGraw-Hill Companies

Centex Corp.

Business Summary October 24, 2007

CORPORATE OVERVIEW. Centex Corp. constructs site-built homes in 79 markets in 25 states and the District of Columbia. CTX sells homes to first-time and move-up buyers, as well as active adult and second home buyers. It also has operations in real estate-related finance businesses. The company estimates that it accounted for about 3% of the new homes sold in the U.S. in FY 07 (Mar.).

To reduce exposure to local market volatility, the company built homes in an average of 687 neighborhoods in FY 07, up from 626 neighborhoods in FY 06. CTX delivered 35,785 homes in FY 07, down from 39,232 homes in FY 06, a dip that reflects a housing industry slowdown. Sales prices vary widely, with an average of about $307,810 for FY 07, up slightly from $303,850 in FY 06. In the past fiscal year, 80% of the homes closed were single-family detached homes, which includes homes from resort and second homes, as well as on-your-lot operations.

IMPACT OF MAJOR DEVELOPMENTS. Relative to peers, Centex has historically relied less on acquisitions for its expansion. Its most recent acquisition occurred in January 2003, with the purchase of The Jones Company. Since

that time, as the homebuilding upcycle entered its later stages, the company has become even more cautious about businesses that it considers non-core. As a result, Centex has been on the selling end of most strategic activity in the past few years.

In June 2003, CTX spun off its Cavco Industries manufactured home business to shareholders. Likewise, in January 2004, CTX spun off its 65% stake in Centex Construction Products, which was renamed Eagle Materials (EXP).

In September 2005, CTX sold Fairclough Homes, which operates in the U.K., generating cash proceeds of almost $320 million. In July 2006, the company sold its sub-prime lending operations for about $540 million, or a slight premium to the unit's book value. On April 2, 2007, the company sold its commercial construction operations for about $362 million.

Company Financials Fiscal Year Ended Mar. 31

Per Share Data ($)	2007	2006	2005	2004	2003	2002	2001	2000	1999	1998
Tangible Book Value	42.26	44.51	32.97	23.89	19.05	14.49	11.59	10.32	8.77	7.20
Cash Flow	0.40	9.67	8.08	6.79	5.31	3.75	2.65	2.51	2.17	1.39
Earnings	-0.10	9.20	7.64	6.01	4.41	3.06	2.33	2.11	1.88	1.18
S&P Core Earnings	-0.10	9.20	7.64	5.90	4.25	2.86	2.17	NA	NA	NA
Dividends	0.16	0.16	0.14	0.08	0.08	0.08	0.08	0.08	0.08	0.07
Payout Ratio	NM	2%	2%	1%	2%	3%	3%	4%	4%	6%
Calendar Year	2006	2005	2004	2003	2002	2001	2000	1999	1998	1997
Prices:High	79.40	79.66	59.98	56.54	31.55	29.40	20.00	22.88	22.88	16.50
Prices:Low	42.90	54.60	39.94	24.15	19.16	14.02	8.75	11.19	13.19	8.38
P/E Ratio:High	NM	9	8	9	7	10	9	11	12	14
P/E Ratio:Low	NM	6	5	4	4	5	4	5	7	7

Income Statement Analysis (Million $)

	2007	2006	2005	2004	2003	2002	2001	2000	1999	1998
Revenue	12,015	14,400	12,860	10,363	9,117	7,748	6,711	5,956	5,155	3,975
Operating Income	17.2	1,884	1,583	1,221	1,058	846	608	597	505	334
Depreciation	59.8	63.1	58.3	102	113	91.0	41.0	49.0	36.2	25.6
Interest Expense	Nil	12.1	22.2	39.9	120	116	99.0	67.0	41.6	33.3
Pretax Income	103	1,895	1,574	1,149	825	640	468	481	427	232
Effective Tax Rate	NM	35.6%	35.7%	32.4%	29.0%	37.0%	32.9%	33.1%	33.1%	37.5%
Net Income	-11.8	1,221	1,011	777	556	382	282	257	232	145
S&P Core Earnings	-11.8	1,221	1,011	765	536	358	264	NA	NA	NA

Balance Sheet & Other Financial Data (Million $)

	2007	2006	2005	2004	2003	2002	2001	2000	1999	1998
Cash	883	47.2	503	193	644	326	115	140	111	98.3
Current Assets	NA	NA	NA	NA	NA	NA	NA	NA	NA	NA
Total Assets	13,206	21,365	20,011	16,069	11,611	8,985	6,649	4,039	4,335	3,416
Current Liabilities	NA	NA	NA	NA	NA	NA	NA	NA	NA	NA
Long Term Debt	3,963	6,059	12,968	8,616	6,237	4,944	3,041	751	284	238
Common Equity	5,112	5,012	4,281	3,050	2,459	2,116	1,714	1,420	1,198	991
Total Capital	9,252	11,604	17,706	12,002	8,866	7,214	4,899	2,300	1,623	1,464
Capital Expenditures	40.6	92.2	43.3	53.8	63.0	60.0	52.0	88.0	52.5	36.9
Cash Flow	48.0	1,284	1,070	879	669	473	323	306	268	170
Current Ratio	NA	NA	NA	NA	NA	NA	NA	NA	NA	NA
% Long Term Debt of Capitalization	42.8	52.2	73.2	71.8	70.3	68.5	62.1	32.7	17.5	16.2
% Net Income of Revenue	NM	8.5	7.9	7.5	6.1	4.9	4.2	4.3	4.5	3.6
% Return on Assets	NM	5.9	5.6	5.6	5.4	4.9	5.3	6.1	6.0	4.8
% Return on Equity	NM	26.3	27.6	27.2	24.3	19.9	18.0	19.6	21.2	15.9

Data as orig reptd.; bef. results of disc opers/spec. items. Per share data adj. for stk. divs.; EPS diluted. E-Estimated. NA-Not Available. NM-Not Meaningful. NR-Not Ranked. UR-Under Review.

Office: 2728 N Harwood St., Dallas, TX, USA 75201-1516.
Telephone: 214-981-5000.
Email: ir@centex.com
Website: http://www.centex.com

Chrmn, Pres & CEO: T.R. Eller
EVP & CFO: C.R. Smith
SVP, Chief Lgl Officer & General Counsel: B.J. Woram
SVP & Cntlr: M.D. Kemp

Investor Contact: M.G. Moyer (214-981-5000)
Board Members: B. T. Alexander, J. L. Elek, T. R. Eller, U. Fairbairn, T. J. Falk, C. W. Murchison, III, F. M. Poses, J. J. Postl, D. W. Quinn, M. K. Rose, T. M. Schoewe

Founded: 1950
Domicile: Nevada
Employees: 11,418

CenturyTel Inc.

STANDARD &POOR'S

S&P Recommendation **BUY** ★★★★☆	Price $41.19 (as of Nov 26, 2007)	12-Mo. Target Price $48.00	Investment Style Large-Cap Blend

GICS Sector Telecommunication Services
Sub-Industry Integrated Telecommunication Services

Summary This holding company provides a range of telephone services in 25 states, with operations concentrated in Alabama, Arkansas, Louisiana, Missouri and Wisconsin.

Key Stock Statistics (Source S&P, Vickers, company reports)

52-Wk Range	$49.94– 40.90	S&P Oper. EPS 2007E	3.02	Market Capitalization(B)	$4.547	Beta	0.89
Trailing 12-Month EPS	$3.31	S&P Oper. EPS 2008E	2.87	Yield (%)	0.63	S&P 3-Yr. Proj. EPS CAGR(%)	5.00
Trailing 12-Month P/E	12.4	P/E on S&P Oper. EPS 2007E	13.6	Dividend Rate/Share	$0.26	S&P Credit Rating	BBB
$10K Invested 5 Yrs Ago	$14,188	Common Shares Outstg. (M)	110.4	Institutional Ownership (%)	91		

Price Performance

- 30-Week Mov. Avg. ···· 10-Week Mov. Avg. - - GAAP Earnings vs. Previous Year Volume Above Avg. STARS
- 12-Mo. Target Price — Relative Strength — ▲ Up ▼ Down ► No Change Below Avg.

Options: Cycle P, Ph

Analysis prepared by **Todd Rosenbluth** on November 26, 2007, when the stock traded at **$ 41.85**.

Highlights

- ➤ We see 2008 revenues of $2.63 billion, up slightly from a projected $2.61 billion in 2007, including a full year of benefits from the Madison River Communications (MRC) assets that CTL acquired in mid-2007. On an organic basis, we foresee growth in DSL services offsetting the impact of weakness in voice services due to fewer access lines. We look for video services to make modest contributions for CTL.

- ➤ Despite strong cost-cutting efforts, we look for EBITDA margins--near the industry's best--to narrow to 48% in 2008, from an expected 49% in 2007, as benefits from system integrations are counterbalanced by increased selling and marketing costs related to the rollout of new services in both legacy and acquired properties. We believe the 2007 EBITDA margin will be aided by a revenue settlement in the third quarter.

- ➤ Results in 2006 were aided by a 13% reduction in the share count. We expect a 7% reduction in 2007. We see EPS of $3.02 for 2007 and $2.87 in 2008. Third quarter 2007 results included a $0.23 gain for non-recurring revenue settlements.

Investment Rationale/Risk

- ➤ We believe this rural carrier faces similar competitive pressure from wireless and cable carriers as its small telecom peers. While we see some gains through broadband, overall growth is limited due to its dependence on voice service, in our view. We expect the Madison River acquisition to modestly help free cash flow, but add operational challenges. We view positively CTL's share buybacks and its relatively wide margins. Our buy recommendation is based on valuation, as we see the large discount to peers as unwarranted.

- ➤ Risks to our recommendation and target price include adjustments to the universal service fund or access charges, from which CTL receives revenues; a dilutive acquisition; and an increase in customer migration.

- ➤ The stock currently trades at an enterprise value/EBITDA multiple of 6X, below the 7X peer average. Despite its lower dividend payout ratio, given its successful share buyback efforts, we believe a more modest discount is warranted. Our 12-month target price of $48 values CTL at an enterprise value of 6.8X our 2008 EBITDA per share projection.

Qualitative Risk Assessment

LOW	MEDIUM	HIGH

Our risk assessment reflects what we see as CTL's strong balance sheet, the rural nature of most of the company's operations, and the less competitive nature of its markets relative to peers.

Quantitative Evaluations

S&P Quality Ranking   A

D	C	B-	B	B+	A-	A	A+

Relative Strength Rank   MODERATE

46

LOWEST = 1   HIGHEST = 99

Revenue/Earnings Data

Revenue (Million $)

	1Q	2Q	3Q	4Q	Year
2007	600.9	690.0	708.8	--	--
2006	611.3	608.9	619.8	607.7	2,448
2005	595.3	606.4	657.1	620.5	2,479
2004	593.7	603.6	603.9	606.2	2,407
2003	580.5	590.2	603.8	606.3	2,381
2002	422.9	438.7	524.5	585.9	1,972

Earnings Per Share ($)

2007	0.68	1.00	1.01	E0.70	E3.02
2006	0.55	1.26	0.64	0.62	3.07
2005	0.59	0.64	0.68	0.59	2.49
2004	0.58	0.60	0.63	0.62	2.41
2003	0.58	0.60	0.63	0.57	2.38
2002	0.30	0.28	0.45	0.30	1.33

Fiscal year ended Dec. 31. Next earnings report expected: Mid February. EPS Estimates based on S&P Operating Earnings; historical GAAP earnings are as reported.

Dividend Data (Dates: mm/dd Payment Date: mm/dd/yy)

Amount ($)	Date Decl.	Ex-Div. Date	Stk. of Record	Payment Date
0.065	02/27	03/08	03/12	03/23/07
0.065	05/22	05/31	06/04	06/15/07
0.065	08/21	08/30	09/04	09/17/07
0.065	11/14	11/23	11/27	12/10/07

Dividends have been paid since 1974. Source: Company reports.

Please read the Required Disclosures and Analyst Certification on the last page of this report.

The **McGraw-Hill** Companies

CenturyTel Inc.

Business Summary November 26, 2007

CORPORATE OVERVIEW. At September 2007, CTL operated 2.2 million telephone access lines, with about 85% penetration of households in its primarily rural and suburban markets. The company also generated revenues by providing long distance service to more than 60% of its customers, as well as by offering DSL broadband to 530,000 customers, and dial up Internet access to approximately 81,000 customers. In addition, the company partnered with Echostar Communications to offer wholesale satellite services in CTL's product bundles in late 2005. In the nine months ended September 2007, 69% of revenues were from voice and network access services.

COMPETITIVE LANDSCAPE. We believe CTL faces fewer challenges from technology substitution to cable telephony than metropolitan based carriers such as AT&T. The penetration of the necessary broadband connection is smaller in the Tier II and Tier III markets in which CTL operates; as of September 2007, more than 60% of its access line customers had the choice of cable broadband, and 35% had the choice for cable telephony from companies such as Charter and Comcast. Excluding acquisitions, CTL's local access lines declined 5.4% in the 12 months ended September 2007. CTL believes it has more than a 50% share of the broadband market in most territories.

CORPORATE STRATEGY. The company has made acquisitions to add assets in underserved incumbent local exchange carrier (ILEC) markets and expand its fiber network. In the second quarter of 2007, CTL completed its $800 million acquisition of Madison River Communications (MRC), adding 164,000 access lines and 57,000 broadband customers in four states and fiber assets. We expect MRC to contribute $128 million in revenues during 2007. In 2002, CTL acquired from Verizon approximately 675,000 access lines in Alabama and Missouri. In addition, CTL purchased metro fiber networks in 16 markets during 2005.

Organically, CTL looks to grow by finding cost efficiencies in its existing workforce, through call center segmentation and automation, and by adding enhanced service offerings to its voice service bundle. We view the company's broadband strategy as intended to retain access line customers and increase revenues per household with higher-speed offerings. In the middle of 2007, one third of CTL customers had access to 6 megabits of speed. and the company plans to expand that ratio to one half by the end of 2007.

Company Financials Fiscal Year Ended Dec. 31

Per Share Data ($)	2006	2005	2004	2003	2002	2001	2000	1999	1998	1997
Tangible Book Value	NM	1.41	NM	0.37	NM	NM	NM	1.39	NM	NM
Cash Flow	7.31	6.37	5.90	5.63	4.21	5.73	4.36	4.16	2.65	3.02
Earnings	3.07	2.49	2.41	2.38	1.33	2.41	1.63	1.70	1.63	1.87
S&P Core Earnings	2.52	2.30	2.36	2.35	1.08	1.21	NA	NA	NA	NA
Dividends	0.25	0.24	0.23	0.22	0.21	0.20	0.19	0.18	0.17	0.16
Payout Ratio	8%	10%	10%	9%	16%	8%	12%	5%	11%	9%
Prices:High	44.11	36.50	35.54	36.76	35.50	39.88	47.31	49.00	45.17	22.42
Prices:Low	32.54	29.55	26.20	25.25	21.13	25.45	24.44	35.19	21.56	12.67
P/E Ratio:High	14	15	15	15	27	17	29	29	28	12
P/E Ratio:Low	11	12	11	11	16	11	15	21	13	7

Income Statement Analysis (Million $)

	2006	2005	2004	2003	2002	2001	2000	1999	1998	1997
Revenue	2,448	2,479	2,407	2,381	1,972	2,117	1,846	1,677	1,577	902
Depreciation	524	532	501	471	412	473	388	349	329	159
Maintenance	NA	NA	NA	NA	NA	NA	NA	NA	NA	NA
Construction Credits	NA	NA	NA	NA	NA	NA	NA	NA	NA	NA
Effective Tax Rate	37.4%	37.8%	38.4%	35.2%	35.3%	37.2%	39.0%	41.5%	39.7%	36.8%
Net Income	370	334	337	345	190	343	231	240	229	256
S&P Core Earnings	302	307	330	339	153	171	NA	NA	NA	NA

Balance Sheet & Other Financial Data (Million $)

	2006	2005	2004	2003	2002	2001	2000	1999	1998	1997
Gross Property	7,894	7,801	7,431	3,455	6,668	5,839	5,915	4,194	4,290	3,845
Net Property	3,109	3,304	3,341	3,455	3,532	3,000	2,959	2,256	2,351	2,259
Capital Expenditures	314	415	385	378	386	507	450	390	311	181
Total Capital	5,604	5,993	6,172	6,588	6,666	4,425	5,082	3,926	4,471	4,237
Fixed Charges Coverage	4.4	3.6	3.6	3.4	2.3	3.4	3.2	3.4	2.9	5.3
Capitalization:Long Term Debt	2,413	2,376	2,762	3,109	3,578	2,088	3,050	2,078	2,558	2,610
Capitalization:Preferred	Nil	Nil	Nil	7.98	7.98	7.98	7.98	7.98	8.11	8.11
Capitalization:Common	3,191	3,617	3,410	3,471	3,080	2,329	2,024	1,840	1,523	1,292
% Return on Revenue	15.1	13.5	14.0	14.5	9.6	16.2	12.5	14.3	14.5	28.4
% Return on Invested Capital	9.8	8.8	8.6	8.6	7.4	12.2	9.4	10.4	14.1	15.8
% Return on Common Equity	10.9	9.5	9.8	10.5	7.0	15.7	12.0	14.2	16.2	22.1
% Earned on Net Property	37.1	38.2	36.9	35.0	31.5	34.6	35.0	37.2	35.1	25.1
% Long Term Debt of Capitalization	43.1	39.6	44.8	47.2	53.7	47.2	60.0	52.9	62.6	61.7
Capital % Preferred	Nil	Nil	Nil	0.1	0.1	0.2	0.2	0.2	0.2	1.9
Capitalization:% Common	56.9	60.4	55.2	52.7	46.2	52.6	39.8	46.9	37.3	30.5

Data as orig reptd.; bef. results of disc opers/spec. items. Per share data adj. for stk. divs.; EPS diluted. E-Estimated. NA-Not Available. NM-Not Meaningful. NR-Not Ranked. UR-Under Review.

Office: 100 Centurytel Dr, Monroe, LA 71203.
Telephone: 318-388-9000.
Website: http://www.centurytel.com
Chrmn & CEO: G.F. Post, III

Pres & COO: K.A. Puckett
EVP & CFO: R.S. Ewing, Jr.
SVP, Secy & General Counsel: S.W. Goff
SVP & CIO: M. Maslowski

Investor Contact: T. Davis (318-388-9525)
Board Members: W. R. Boles, Jr., V. Boulet, C. Czeschin, J. B. Gardner, W. B. Hanks, G. J. McCray, C. G. Melville, Jr., F. Nichols, H. P. Perry, G. F. Post, III, J. D. Reppond, J. Zimmel

Founded: 1968
Domicile: Louisiana
Employees: 6,400

Chesapeake Energy Corp

STANDARD &POOR'S

S&P Recommendation **BUY** ★★★★☆	Price $38.13 (as of Nov 23, 2007)	12-Mo. Target Price $47.00	Investment Style Large-Cap Blend

GICS Sector Energy
Sub-Industry Oil & Gas Exploration & Production

Summary As the third largest independent producer of natural gas in the U.S., CHK has operations in the Mid-Continent, Forth Worth Barnett Shale, Appalachian Basin, Fayetteville Shale, South Texas, Permian Basin, Delaware Basin, Ark-La-Tex and Texas Gulf Coast.

Key Stock Statistics (Source S&P, Vickers, company reports)

52-Wk Range	$41.19– 27.27	S&P Oper. EPS 2007**E**	3.28	Market Capitalization(B)	$17.568	Beta	0.61
Trailing 12-Month EPS	$3.18	S&P Oper. EPS 2008**E**	4.65	Yield (%)	0.71	S&P 3-Yr. Proj. EPS CAGR(%)	23.40
Trailing 12-Month P/E	12.0	P/E on S&P Oper. EPS 2007**E**	11.6	Dividend Rate/Share	$0.27	S&P Credit Rating	BB
$10K Invested 5 Yrs Ago	$55,079	Common Shares Outstg. (M)	473.9	Institutional Ownership (%)	78		

Price Performance

- 30-Week Mov. Avg. · · ·
- 10-Week Mov. Avg. - -
- **GAAP Earnings vs. Previous Year**
- Volume Above Avg. STARS
- 12-Mo. Target Price —
- Relative Strength - - -
- ▲ Up ▼ Down ▶ No Change
- Below Avg.

Options: ASE, CBOE, P, Ph

Analysis prepared by **Tina J. Vital** on November 15, 2007, when the stock traded at **$ 38.19.**

Highlights

➤ Despite the voluntary curtailment of about 3.0 Bcfe of production in September in response to a drop in natural gas prices, third quarter oil and gas production rose 27%, above our expectations. As a result of better-than-expected results from its drilling program, CHK has raised its prior guidance forecasts for 2007-09. As a result, we now expect over 22% volume growth in 2007, and over 20% in 2008.

➤ CHK is in process of monetizing certain producing assets in Kentucky and West Virginia (proceeds in excess of $1 billion are expected by year-end 2007); some of non-core exploration & production assets in the Rocky Mountains and southeastern Oklahoma Woodford Shale (proceeds of over $300 million expected by the 2008 first quarter); and its mid-stream MLP assets (proceeds of over $1 billion by the 2008 first quarter).

➤ We expect after-tax operating earnings will to decline about 16% in 2007 on lower natural gas prices and higher per unit operating costs, before climbing over 50% in 2008 on increased production and natural gas pricing.

Investment Rationale/Risk

➤ We view the business profile as solid, but view its historical acquisition strategy as aggressive. Since 1998, the company has spent more than $14 billion on acquisitions, focused on unconventional natural gas plays, and often paying market clearing prices. However, we believe its business profile may significantly improve due to CHK's recent strategic shift from "resource capture" to "resource conversion" (i.e. to developing its large inventory of drilling prospects).

➤ Risks to our recommendation and target price include changes in economic, industrial, and operating conditions, such as rising operating costs, difficulty in replacing reserves and overpaying for asset purchases.

➤ A blend of our discounted cash flow ($54; assuming a WACC of 7.7%, and terminal growth of 3%) and relative valuations leads us to our 12-month target price of $47, which represents an expected enterprise value of 4.6X our 2008 EBITDA estimate, a discount to peers.

Qualitative Risk Assessment

LOW	**MEDIUM**	HIGH

Our risk assessment reflects CHK's business profile in a volatile, cyclical, and capital intensive segment of the energy industry. We believe CHK's financial strategy is aggressive, as the company has been one of the most active acquirers in exploration and production, and one of the most active users of commodity hedges.

Quantitative Evaluations

S&P Quality Ranking   **B**

D	C	B-	**B**	B+	A-	A	A+

Relative Strength Rank   **STRONG**

86

LOWEST = 1   HIGHEST = 99

Revenue/Earnings Data

Revenue (Million $)

	1Q	2Q	3Q	4Q	Year
2007	1,580	2,105	2,027	--	--
2006	1,945	1,584	1,929	1,868	7,326
2005	783.5	1,048	1,083	1,751	4,665
2004	563.1	574.3	629.8	942.1	2,709
2003	374.4	429.6	454.6	456.7	1,717
2002	89.84	194.3	198.2	255.4	737.8

Earnings Per Share ($)

	1Q	2Q	3Q	4Q	Year
2007	0.50	1.01	0.72	E1.06	E3.28
2006	1.44	0.82	1.13	0.96	4.35
2005	0.36	0.52	0.43	1.11	2.51
2004	0.38	0.30	0.29	0.52	1.53
2003	0.31	0.31	0.33	0.25	1.20
2002	-0.18	0.13	0.08	0.13	0.17

Fiscal year ended Dec. 31. Next earnings report expected: Late February. EPS Estimates based on S&P Operating Earnings; historical GAAP earnings are as reported.

Dividend Data (Dates: mm/dd Payment Date: mm/dd/yy)

Amount ($)	Date Decl.	Ex-Div. Date	Stk. of Record	Payment Date
0.060	12/19	12/28	01/02	01/16/07
0.060	03/15	03/29	04/02	04/16/07
0.068	06/12	06/28	07/02	07/16/07
0.068	09/05	09/27	10/01	10/15/07

Dividends have been paid since 2002. Source: Company reports.

Chesapeake Energy Corp

STANDARD &POOR'S

Business Summary November 15, 2007

CORPORATE OVERVIEW. Chesapeake Energy Corp. (CHK) is engaged in exploratory and developmental drilling, as well as corporate and property acquisitions in the Mid-Continent, Forth Worth Barnett Shale, Appalachian Basin, Fayetteville Shale, South Texas, Permian Basin, Delaware Basin, Ark-La-Tex and Texas Gulf Coast regions of the U.S. The company estimates it is the third largest independent producer of natural gas in the U.S. and seventh largest overall, as of year-end 2006.

MARKET PROFILE. CHK believes one of the most distinctive characteristics is its ability to increase its reserves and production through the drillbit. As of year-end 2006, CHK utilized about 132 operated drilling rigs and about 90 non-operated drilling rigs to conduct what the company believed was the most active drilling program in the U.S. The company characterizes its drilling activity by one of four play types: conventional gas resource, unconventional gas resource, emerging unconventional gas resource, and Appalachian Basin gas resource.

CHK acquisition program has focused on purchases of natural gas that offer high quality, long-lived production and significant future potential. From January 1, 1998 through December 31, 2006, CHK purchased about 6.5 trillion cubic feet equivalent (Tcfe) of proved reserves for about $14.3 billion.

CHK has created value through acquisitions by employing "unconventional resource recovery techniques" which include basin-centered tight gas formations, coal-bed methane formations, and fractured shale formations. These techniques are characterized by a low proportion of exploration capital expenditures, resulting in relatively low risk resource acquisition capability. We believe the main driver of value of these resource plays is the development of drilling techniques that are repeatable in a particular basin; thereby, increasing organic growth and proved reserves.

Company Financials Fiscal Year Ended Dec. 31

Per Share Data ($)	2006	2005	2004	2003	2002	2001	2000	1999	1998	1997
Tangible Book Value	20.32	12.42	8.57	5.45	3.99	3.75	2.05	NM	NM	3.77
Cash Flow	7.36	5.05	3.56	2.61	1.54	2.52	3.67	1.30	-8.18	0.43
Earnings	4.35	2.51	1.53	1.20	0.17	1.51	3.01	0.16	-9.83	-0.45
S&P Core Earnings	4.19	2.48	1.50	1.19	0.17	1.36	NA	NA	NA	NA
Dividends	0.23	0.20	0.17	0.14	0.06	Nil	Nil	Nil	0.06	0.04
Payout Ratio	5%	8%	11%	11%	35%	Nil	Nil	Nil	NM	NM
Prices:High	35.57	40.20	18.31	14.00	8.55	11.06	10.50	4.13	7.75	31.75
Prices:Low	26.81	15.06	11.70	7.27	4.50	4.50	1.94	0.63	0.75	6.31
P/E Ratio:High	8	16	12	12	50	7	3	26	NM	NM
P/E Ratio:Low	6	6	8	6	26	3	1	4	NM	NM

Income Statement Analysis (Million $)										
Revenue	7,326	4,665	2,709	1,717	738	969	628	355	378	233
Operating Income	3,413	1,773	992	675	191	597	384	207	177	158
Depreciation, Depletion and Amortization	1,463	945	611	386	235	178	105	99.5	152	62.0
Interest Expense	301	220	167	154	111	98.3	86.3	81.1	68.2	29.8
Pretax Income	3,255	1,493	805	501	67.1	438	196	35.0	-921	-31.6
Effective Tax Rate	38.5%	36.5%	36.0%	38.0%	40.0%	39.9%	NM	5.04%	NM	Nil
Net Income	2,003	948	515	311	40.3	263	456	33.3	-921	-31.6
S&P Core Earnings	1,831	871	431	283	29.9	235	NA	NA	NA	NA

Balance Sheet & Other Financial Data (Million $)										
Cash	2.52	60.0	6.90	40.6	248	125	3.50	38.9	35.3	124
Current Assets	1,154	1,183	568	342	435	361	167	97.5	118	218
Total Assets	24,417	16,118	8,245	4,572	2,876	2,287	1,440	851	813	953
Current Liabilities	1,890	1,964	964	513	266	173	163	88.2	131	153
Long Term Debt	7,376	5,490	3,075	2,058	1,651	1,329	945	964	919	509
Common Equity	9,293	4,598	2,672	1,180	758	617	282	-447	-479	280
Total Capital	21,944	13,469	7,172	3,982	2,559	2,097	1,270	753	671	789
Capital Expenditures	986	484	127	71.5	33.6	24.9	78.9	49.9	271	217
Cash Flow	3,377	1,851	1,087	674	265	439	556	133	-776	30.5
Current Ratio	0.6	0.6	0.6	0.7	1.6	2.1	1.0	1.1	0.9	1.4
% Long Term Debt of Capitalization	33.6	40.8	42.9	51.7	64.5	63.4	74.4	128.0	137.1	NM
% Return on Assets	9.9	7.8	8.0	8.3	1.6	14.1	39.8	4.0	NM	NM
% Return on Equity	27.6	24.9	24.7	29.7	4.4	58.1	NM	NM	NM	NM

Data as orig reptd.; bef. results of disc opers/spec. items. Per share data adj. for stk. divs.; EPS diluted. E-Estimated. NA-Not Available. NM-Not Meaningful. NR-Not Ranked. UR-Under Review.

Office: 6100 North Western Avenue, Oklahoma City, OK 73118.
Telephone: 405-848-8000.
Website: http://www.chkenergy.com
Chrmn & CEO: A.K. McClendon

COO & EVP: S.C. Dixon
EVP & CFO: M.C. Rowland
SVP, Chief Acctg Officer & Cntlr: M.A. Johnson
SVP, Treas & Secy: J.M. Grigsby

Investor Contact: J.L. Mobley (405-767-4763)
Board Members: R. K. Davidson, F. Keating, B. M. Kerr, C. T. Maxwell, A. K. McClendon, M. A. Miller, Jr., D. Nickles, F. B. Whittemore

Founded: 1991
Domicile: Oklahoma
Employees: 4,900

Chevron Corp

S&P Recommendation **BUY** ★★★★☆	Price $86.67 (as of Nov 23, 2007)	12-Mo. Target Price $99.00	Investment Style Large-Cap Blend

GICS Sector Energy
Sub-Industry Integrated Oil & Gas

Summary This global integrated oil company (formerly ChevronTexaco) has interests in exploration, production, refining and marketing, and petrochemicals.

Key Stock Statistics (Source S&P, Vickers, company reports)

52-Wk Range	$95.50– 64.99	S&P Oper. EPS 2007E	7.72	Market Capitalization(B)	$182.999	Beta	0.69
Trailing 12-Month EPS	$8.19	S&P Oper. EPS 2008E	7.25	Yield (%)	2.68	S&P 3-Yr. Proj. EPS CAGR(%)	-0.43
Trailing 12-Month P/E	10.6	P/E on S&P Oper. EPS 2007E	11.2	Dividend Rate/Share	$2.32	S&P Credit Rating	AA
$10K Invested 5 Yrs Ago	$30,770	Common Shares Outstg. (M)	2,111.4	Institutional Ownership (%)	65		

Price Performance

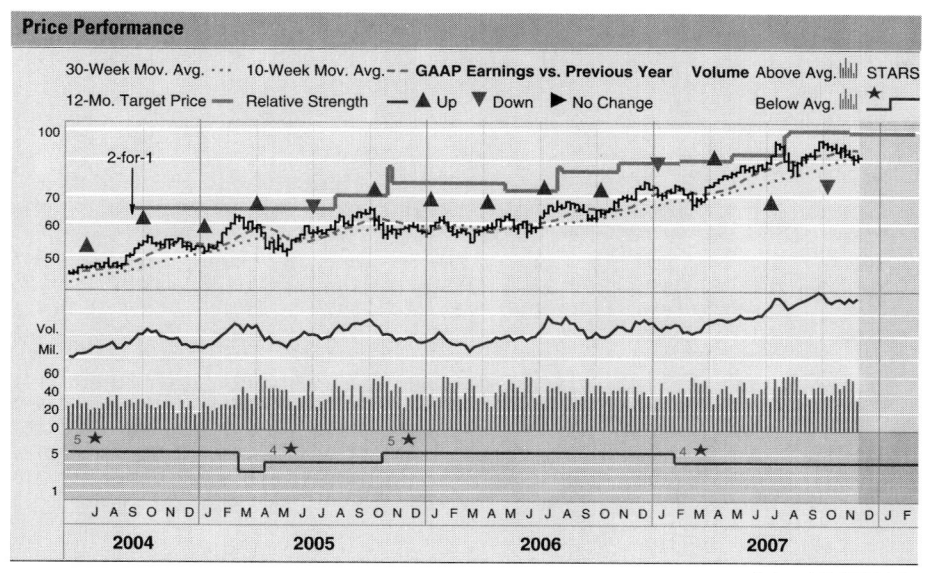

30-Week Mov. Avg. · · · 10-Week Mov. Avg. - - **GAAP Earnings vs. Previous Year** Volume Above Avg. STARS
12-Mo. Target Price — Relative Strength — ▲ Up ▼ Down ► No Change Below Avg. ★

2-for-1

Options: ASE, CBOE, P, Ph

Analysis prepared by **Tina J. Vital** on November 12, 2007, when the stock traded at **$ 84.86**.

Highlights

➤ Third quarter oil and gas production declined 4%, in line with our expectations, reflecting maintenance-related work in the U.K. North Sea and the absence of Venezuelan volumes. CVX expects its Tengiz SGI/SGP project to begin production the 2007 fourth quarter, its Blind Faith deepwater Gulf of Mexico (GOM) project to start up in the 2008 second quarter, its Agbami deepwater Nigerian project in the 2008 third quarter, and its Tahiti deepwater GOM project in the 2009 third quarter. We expect 2007 oil and gas production to decline more than 1%, before rising over 2% in 2008.

➤ Refining and marketing margins weakened in the 2007 second half, and we expect 2008 U.S. refining margins to narrow more than 30% from 2007 levels on continued high crude oil prices, but to remain relatively high compared to historical norms.

➤ We see after-tax operating earnings declining more than 5% in 2007 and in excess of 6% in 2008, before rising over 5% in 2009. In September, CVX initiated a new stock repurchase program of up to $15 billion over a period of up to three years.

Investment Rationale/Risk

➤ We have a positive outlook for CVX's upstream business, given its 2005 acquisition of Unocal and its ongoing international "Big Five" upstream development projects. We estimate CVX's three-year (2004-2006) organic reserve replacement rate at 103%, below the peer average, and its three-year finding and development costs at $29.49 per boe, above the peer average. Downstream, we think CVX will benefit from its considerable capacity to refine lower-cost, lower-quality crude oil feedstocks.

➤ Risks to our recommendation and target price include changes in economic, industry and operating conditions, such as CVX's ability to organically replace its reserves, and its increased exposure to geopolitical risks.

➤ Blending our discounted cash flow model (estimated value of $102; assuming a WACC of 8.0% and a terminal growth rate of 3%) and relative valuations leads to our 12-month target price of $99. This represents an expected enterprise value of 6.1X our 2008 EBITDA estimate, a discount to peers.

Qualitative Risk Assessment

LOW	MEDIUM	HIGH

Our risk assessment reflects Chevron's diversified and strong business profile in volatile, cyclical and capital intensive segments of the energy industry. With improved returns since the Texaco merger in 2001, we view its corporate governance practices as generally sound and its earnings stability as favorable.

Quantitative Evaluations

S&P Quality Ranking   A-

D	C	B-	B	B+	A-	A	A+

Relative Strength Rank   MODERATE

67
LOWEST = 1   HIGHEST = 99

Revenue/Earnings Data

Revenue (Million $)

	1Q	2Q	3Q	4Q	Year
2007	48,227	56,094	55,173	--	--
2006	54,624	53,536	54,212	47,746	210,118
2005	41,607	48,343	54,456	53,794	198,200
2004	33,063	36,579	39,611	41,612	155,300
2003	30,965	29,361	30,970	30,465	121,761
2002	21,155	25,333	25,503	27,058	99,049

Earnings Per Share ($)

	1Q	2Q	3Q	4Q	Year
2007	2.18	2.52	1.75	E2.27	E7.72
2006	1.80	1.97	2.29	1.74	7.80
2005	1.28	1.76	1.64	1.86	6.54
2004	1.20	1.93	1.38	1.63	6.14
2003	1.00	0.75	1.01	0.82	3.57
2002	0.34	0.20	-0.43	0.43	0.54

Fiscal year ended Dec. 31. Next earnings report expected: Early February. EPS Estimates based on S&P Operating Earnings; historical GAAP earnings are as reported.

Dividend Data (Dates: mm/dd Payment Date: mm/dd/yy)

Amount ($)	Date Decl.	Ex-Div. Date	Stk. of Record	Payment Date
0.520	01/31	02/14	02/16	03/12/07
0.580	04/25	05/16	05/18	06/11/07
0.580	07/25	08/15	08/17	09/10/07
0.580	10/31	11/14	11/16	12/10/07

Dividends have been paid since 1912. Source: Company reports.

Please read the Required Disclosures and Analyst Certification on the last page of this report.

The McGraw-Hill Companies

Chevron Corp

Business Summary November 12, 2007

CORPORATE OVERVIEW. In October 2001, Chevron Corp. (CHV) and Texaco Inc. (TX) merged, creating the second largest U.S.-based oil company, ChevronTexaco Corp. (CVX). In May 2005, the company changed its name to Chevron Corp.

CVX separately manages its exploration and production (26% of 2006 revenues; 74% of 2006 segment income); refining, marketing and transportation (73%; 23%); chemicals (less than 1%; 3%); and other businesses, including its 24% common equity interest in Dynegy, mining operations of coal and other minerals, power generation, and other businesses.

Using data from John S. Herold, we estimate CVX's three-year (2004-2006) organic reserve replacement rate at 103%, its three-year finding and development costs at $29.49 per barrel of oil equivalent (boe), and its three-year proved acquisition costs at $8.02 per boe. Net production of crude oil and natural gas liquids (excluding affiliates) improved 4.1%, to 1.554 million barrels per day (b/d), in 2006. Net production of natural gas rose 18%, to 4.75 billion

cubic feet (Bcf) per day, in 2006. Proved liquids reserves (excluding affiliates) fell 6.0%, to 5.294 billion barrels, as of year-end 2006, and proved natural gas reserves (excluding affiliates) fell by 3%, to 19.910 trillion cubic feet (Tcf). The average sales price for liquids was $57.53 per barrel in 2006, and $4.85 per thousand cubic feet (Mcf) for natural gas.

As of December 31, 2006, CVX owned 20 fuel refineries and an asphalt plant, for a total refining capacity of 2.221 million b/d (42% U.S., 15% Europe, 2% Canada, and 41% Asia Pacific and Africa). As of year-end 2006, it had a network of 20,493 retail sites in nearly 90 countries (47% U.S.). In April 2006, CVX agreed to buy a 5% stake (for $300 million) in Reliance Petroleum Limited, a company formed to own and operate a new export refinery in Jamnagar, India.

Company Financials Fiscal Year Ended Dec. 31

Per Share Data ($)	2006	2005	2004	2003	2002	2001	2000	1999	1998	1997
Tangible Book Value	29.71	25.99	21.47	16.98	14.80	15.92	15.54	13.53	13.05	13.32
Cash Flow	11.38	8.96	8.53	5.99	2.98	5.17	6.17	3.74	2.78	4.22
Earnings	7.80	6.54	6.14	3.57	0.54	1.85	3.99	1.57	1.02	2.47
S&P Core Earnings	7.88	6.62	5.88	3.50	1.22	1.66	NA	NA	NA	NA
Dividends	2.01	1.75	1.53	1.43	1.40	1.33	1.30	1.24	1.22	1.14
Payout Ratio	26%	27%	25%	40%	NM	72%	33%	79%	120%	46%
Prices:High	76.20	65.98	56.07	43.50	45.80	49.25	47.44	52.47	45.09	44.59
Prices:Low	53.76	49.81	42.00	30.66	32.71	39.22	34.97	36.56	33.88	30.88
P/E Ratio:High	10	10	9	12	86	27	12	33	44	18
P/E Ratio:Low	7	8	7	9	61	21	9	23	33	12

Income Statement Analysis (Million $)										
Revenue	204,892	193,641	150,865	120,032	98,691	104,409	50,592	35,448	29,943	40,583
Operating Income	35,748	27,129	21,542	49,336	28,848	16,031	15,834	5,848	3,945	6,747
Depreciation, Depletion and Amortization	7,506	5,913	4,935	5,384	5,231	7,059	2,848	2,866	2,320	2,300
Interest Expense	451	482	406	474	565	833	460	463	405	312
Pretax Income	32,046	25,293	20,636	12,850	4,213	8,412	9,270	3,648	1,834	5,502
Effective Tax Rate	46.3%	43.9%	36.4%	41.6%	71.8%	51.8%	44.1%	43.3%	27.0%	40.8%
Net Income	17,138	14,099	13,034	7,426	1,132	3,931	5,185	2,070	1,339	3,256
S&P Core Earnings	17,310	14,277	12,471	7,454	2,590	3,518	NA	NA	NA	NA

Balance Sheet & Other Financial Data (Million $)										
Cash	11,446	11,144	10,742	5,267	3,781	3,150	2,630	2,032	1,413	1,015
Current Assets	36,304	34,336	28,503	19,426	17,776	18,327	8,213	8,297	6,297	7,006
Total Assets	132,628	125,833	93,208	81,470	77,359	77,572	41,264	40,668	36,540	35,473
Current Liabilities	28,409	25,011	18,795	16,111	19,876	20,654	7,674	8,889	7,166	6,946
Long Term Debt	7,679	12,131	10,456	10,894	10,911	8,989	5,153	5,485	4,393	4,431
Common Equity	73,684	66,722	48,575	40,022	36,176	37,120	21,761	17,749	17,034	17,472
Total Capital	93,219	90,315	66,471	57,601	53,009	52,524	31,822	28,244	25,072	25,118
Capital Expenditures	13,813	8,701	6,310	5,625	7,597	9,713	3,657	4,366	3,880	3,899
Cash Flow	24,644	20,012	17,969	12,810	6,363	10,990	8,033	4,936	3,659	5,556
Current Ratio	1.3	1.4	1.5	1.2	0.9	0.9	1.1	0.9	0.9	1.0
% Long Term Debt of Capitalization	8.2	13.4	15.7	18.9	20.6	17.1	16.2	19.4	17.5	17.6
% Return on Assets	13.3	12.9	14.9	9.4	1.5	5.1	12.7	5.4	3.7	9.3
% Return on Equity	24.4	24.5	29.4	19.5	3.1	10.7	25.1	11.9	7.8	19.7

Data as orig reptd.; bef. results of disc opers/spec. items. Per share data adj. for stk. divs.; EPS diluted. Quarterly revs. incl. other inc. E-Estimated. NA-Not Available. NM-Not Meaningful. NR-Not Ranked. UR-Under Review.

Office: 6001 Bollinger Canyon Road, San Ramon, CA 94583-2324.
Telephone: 925-842-1000.
Email: invest@chevrontexaco.com
Website: http://www.chevrontexaco.com

Chrmn & CEO: D.J. O'Reilly
Vice Chrmn: P.J. Robertson
VP & CFO: S.J. Crowe
VP & Treas: P.E. Yarrington

VP & General Counsel: C.A. James
Board Members: S. H. Armacost, L. F. Deily, R. E. Denham, R. J. Eaton, S. Ginn, F. G. Jenifer, S. Nunn, D. J. O'Reilly, D. B. Rice, P. J. Robertson, K. W. Sharer, C. R. Shoemate, R. D. Sugar, C. Ware

Founded: 1901
Domicile: Delaware
Employees: 62,500

C.H. Robinson Worldwide Inc

STANDARD
&POOR'S

S&P Recommendation	HOLD ★★★☆☆	Price	12-Mo. Target Price	Investment Style
		$46.89 (as of Nov 23, 2007)	$58.00	Large-Cap Growth

GICS Sector Industrials
Sub-Industry Air Freight & Logistics

Summary This global provider of multimodal transportation services and logistics solutions has a network of over 200 offices in North America, South America, Europe and Asia.

Key Stock Statistics (Source S&P, Vickers, company reports)

52-Wk Range	$58.19–39.44	S&P Oper. EPS 2007**E**	1.85	Market Capitalization(B)	$8.093	Beta	0.94
Trailing 12-Month EPS	$1.79	S&P Oper. EPS 2008**E**	2.15	Yield (%)	1.88	S&P 3-Yr. Proj. EPS CAGR(%)	15.00
Trailing 12-Month P/E	26.2	P/E on S&P Oper. EPS 2007**E**	25.3	Dividend Rate/Share	$0.88	S&P Credit Rating	NA
$10K Invested 5 Yrs Ago	$32,877	Common Shares Outstg. (M)	172.6	Institutional Ownership (%)	79		

Price Performance

30-Week Mov. Avg. · · · 10-Week Mov. Avg. - - GAAP Earnings vs. Previous Year Volume Above Avg. STARS
12-Mo. Target Price — Relative Strength — ▲ Up ▼ Down ► No Change Below Avg.

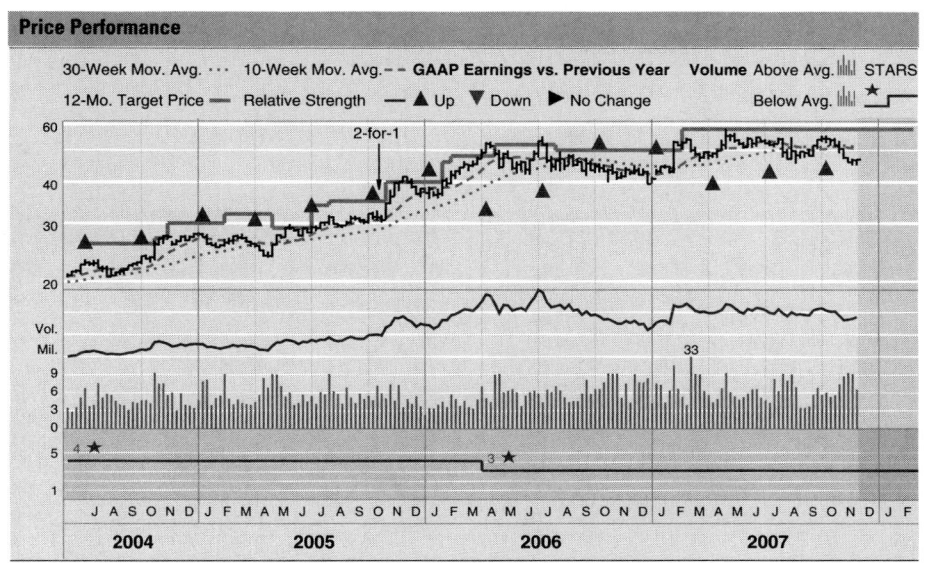

Options: ASE, CBOE, P, Ph

Analysis prepared by **Jim Corridore** on November 02, 2007, when the stock traded at **$ 47.44**.

Highlights

➤ We forecast 2008 gross revenue growth of about 8%, after an expected 10% rise in 2007. We believe CHRW will see decelerating growth in intermodal, ocean, and air shipping services in the first half of 2008 due to a slower U.S. economy. We expect price increases to be driven by a higher percentage of transactional versus contractual business, which should allow CHRW to take advantage of higher spot prices.

➤ We project the gross margin to widen, reflecting likely lower purchased transportation costs, as we expect an overcapacity of trucks to put pressure on transportation rates charged by the companies CHRW hires to fulfill its shipping services. Also, we believe operating margins will be aided by fixed cost leverage on a higher revenue base and restrained costs, more than offsetting the likely continued effect of an increased percentage of revenues from large customers, generally priced slightly below smaller customers.

➤ Our 2008 EPS estimate is $2.15, up 16% from the $1.85 we forecast for 2007. We believe the quality of reported earnings to be high relative to most other transportation companies we cover.

Investment Rationale/Risk

➤ Despite a valuation premium to the average of its peers, our recommendation is hold due to CHRW's history of posting what we view as strong returns on assets and equity relative to most other transportation companies. Also, CHRW has no long-term debt, has been a generator of cash over the past few years, and we think the quality of its reported earnings has been high relative to peers, since it has no defined benefit pension plan.

➤ Risks to our recommendation and target price include the possibility of an investor rotation out of transportation stocks, a potential weakening of transport volumes if the U.S. economy sharply slows down, and the possibility that tight industry capacity could lead to lost revenue opportunities, restricting earnings growth.

➤ Our 12-month target price of $58 values the stock at about 27X our 2008 EPS estimate of $2.15. Our valuation is above peer levels, but in the middle of CHRW's historical P/E range over the past five years of 20.1X-36.1X earnings.

Qualitative Risk Assessment

LOW	MEDIUM	HIGH

Our risk assessment reflects CHRW's lack of long-term debt, what we see as a high quality of earnings, and a non-asset based structure. However, as a transportation company, CHRW is exposed to a cyclical economic slowdown and also to rising transportation costs.

Quantitative Evaluations

S&P Quality Ranking A+

D	C	B-	B	B+	A-	A	A+

Relative Strength Rank MODERATE

50

LOWEST = 1   HIGHEST = 99

Revenue/Earnings Data

Revenue (Million $)

	1Q	2Q	3Q	4Q	Year
2007	1,619	1,880	1,865	--	--
2006	1,499	1,701	1,713	1,643	6,556
2005	1,215	1,405	1,485	1,584	5,689
2004	946.6	1,077	1,124	1,194	4,342
2003	816.7	935.2	919.3	942.4	3,614
2002	740.0	842.7	872.3	839.5	3,294

Earnings Per Share ($)

2007	0.42	0.47	0.48	E0.49	E1.85
2006	0.33	0.38	0.40	0.42	1.53
2005	0.24	0.29	0.31	0.33	1.16
2004	0.17	0.19	0.22	0.22	0.80
2003	0.16	0.17	0.17	0.17	0.67
2002	0.12	0.15	0.15	0.14	0.56

Fiscal year ended Dec. 31. Next earnings report expected: Late January. EPS Estimates based on S&P Operating Earnings; historical GAAP earnings are as reported.

Dividend Data (Dates: mm/dd Payment Date: mm/dd/yy)

Amount ($)	Date Decl.	Ex-Div. Date	Stk. of Record	Payment Date
0.180	02/16	12/06	12/08	01/02/07
0.180	02/15	03/07	03/09	04/02/07
0.220	05/17	12/05	12/07	01/02/08

Dividends have been paid since 1997. Source: Company reports.

Please read the Required Disclosures and Analyst Certification on the last page of this report.

The McGraw-Hill Companies

C.H. Robinson Worldwide Inc

STANDARD &POOR'S

Business Summary November 02, 2007

CORPORATE OVERVIEW. With 2006 revenues of about $6.6 billion, C.H. Robinson Worldwide is one of the largest third-party logistics companies in North America. At December 31, 2006, the company provided multimodal transportation services and logistics solutions through a network of 214 offices in North America, South America, Europe and Asia. In 2006, gross profits were divided as follows: 88% from transportation, 8% from sourcing, and 4% from information services. Within the transportation segment, CHRW offers several modes of service, including trucks (87% of gross profits in the transportation segment in 2006), intermodal (4%), ocean (4%), air (2%), and miscellaneous (3%).

Through contracts with about 45,000 transportation companies, including motor carriers, railroads, air freight and ocean carriers, the company maintains the largest network of motor carrier capacity in North America. One of the largest third-party providers of intermodal services in the U.S., it also provides air, ocean and customs services. In addition, CHRW operates value-added logistics services, including fresh produce sourcing, freight consolidation and cross-docking. In 2006, the company handled more than 5.2 million shipments

for more than 25,000 customers.

STRATEGY. CHRW has historically grown through internal growth, by expanding current offices, opening new branch offices and hiring additional salespeople. Growth has also been augmented through selective acquisitions. In February 2005, the company acquired three produce sourcing and marketing companies: FoodSource Inc., FoodSource Procurement, LLC, and Epic Roots, Inc. The three companies had about $270 million in gross revenues in 2004. In the third quarter of 2005, CHRW purchased two freight forwarding businesses: Hirdes Group Worldwide and Bussini Transport S.r.l., with combined gross revenues of about $52 million in 2004. In May 2006 CHRW acquired certain assets of Paine Lynch, and Associates, a third-party logistics company, for $30 million.

Company Financials Fiscal Year Ended Dec. 31

Per Share Data ($)	2006	2005	2004	2003	2002	2001	2000	1999	1998	1997
Tangible Book Value	3.86	3.11	2.60	2.09	1.59	1.23	0.85	0.55	0.95	0.80
Cash Flow	1.66	1.27	0.86	0.73	0.64	0.60	0.52	0.38	0.31	0.12
Earnings	1.53	1.16	0.80	0.67	0.56	0.49	0.42	0.32	0.26	0.07
S&P Core Earnings	1.53	1.16	0.79	0.63	0.56	0.47	NA	NA	NA	NA
Dividends	0.18	0.36	0.26	0.18	0.13	0.11	0.08	0.07	0.05	0.02
Payout Ratio	12%	31%	32%	27%	23%	21%	19%	22%	17%	21%
Prices:High	55.18	41.70	28.20	21.50	17.70	16.13	16.44	10.52	6.75	6.63
Prices:Low	35.55	23.60	18.30	13.50	12.92	11.41	8.58	6.00	3.59	4.50
P/E Ratio:High	36	36	35	32	32	33	40	33	26	95
P/E Ratio:Low	23	20	23	20	23	23	21	19	14	64

Income Statement Analysis (Million $)										
Revenue	6,556	5,689	4,342	3,614	3,294	3,090	2,882	2,261	2,038	1,791
Operating Income	439	345	235	195	171	153	134	94.0	77.0	65.4
Depreciation	23.9	18.5	11.8	11.0	14.0	19.1	17.3	10.1	8.52	8.68
Interest Expense	Nil	Nil	Nil	Nil	Nil	Nil	Nil	Nil	Nil	Nil
Pretax Income	430	333	226	186	158	138	118	88.5	71.3	35.0
Effective Tax Rate	37.9%	38.9%	39.3%	38.7%	39.0%	39.3%	39.5%	39.7%	39.7%	67.2%
Net Income	267	203	137	114	96.3	84.0	71.2	53.3	43.0	11.5
S&P Core Earnings	267	203	136	107	94.9	79.8	NA	NA	NA	NA

Balance Sheet & Other Financial Data (Million $)										
Cash	349	231	166	199	133	116	79.9	49.6	130	62.5
Current Assets	1,256	1,085	846	717	589	503	460	343	375	311
Total Assets	1,632	1,395	1,081	908	778	683	644	523	409	341
Current Liabilities	687	612	453	381	343	324	346	276	240	202
Long Term Debt	Nil	Nil	Nil	Nil	Nil	Nil	Nil	Nil	Nil	Nil
Common Equity	944	780	621	517	426	356	297	247	170	139
Total Capital	944	782	621	524	432	359	298	247	170	139
Capital Expenditures	43.2	21.8	34.7	8.57	17.3	17.1	15.5	9.43	5.07	6.31
Cash Flow	291	222	149	125	110	103	88.6	63.5	51.5	20.2
Current Ratio	1.8	1.8	1.9	1.9	1.7	1.6	1.3	1.2	1.6	1.5
% Long Term Debt of Capitalization	Nil	Nil	Nil	Nil	Nil	Nil	Nil	Nil	Nil	Nil
% Net Income of Revenue	4.1	3.6	3.2	3.2	2.9	2.7	2.5	2.4	2.1	0.6
% Return on Assets	17.6	16.4	13.8	13.5	13.2	12.7	12.2	11.5	11.5	3.5
% Return on Equity	31.0	29.0	24.1	24.2	24.6	25.7	26.2	25.6	27.9	7.8

Data as orig reptd.; bef. results of disc opers/spec. items. Per share data adj. for stk. divs.; EPS diluted. E-Estimated. NA-Not Available. NM-Not Meaningful. NR-Not Ranked. UR-Under Review.

Office: 8100 Mitchell Rd , Eden Prairie, MN 55344-2248.
Telephone: 952-937-8500.
Website: http://www.chrobinson.com
Chrmn, Pres & CEO: J.P. Wiehoff

VP & CFO: C.M. Lindbloom
VP, Secy & General Counsel: L.U. Feuss
Investor Contact: A. Freeman (952-937-7847)
Cntlr: T.K. Mahlke

Board Members: R. Ezrilov, W. M. Fortun, K. E. Keiser, R. K. Roloff, G. A. Schwalbach, B. P. Short, M. W. Wickham, J. P. Wiehoff

Founded: 1905
Domicile: Delaware
Employees: 6,768

The McGraw-Hill Companies

Chubb Corp (The)

STANDARD &POOR'S

S&P Recommendation **STRONG BUY** ★★★★★	Price $52.17 (as of Nov 23, 2007)	12-Mo. Target Price $65.00	Investment Style Large-Cap Blend

GICS Sector Financials
Sub-Industry Property & Casualty Insurance

Summary As one of the largest U.S. property-casualty insurers, Chubb has carved out a number of niches, including high-end personal lines and specialty liability lines coverage.

Key Stock Statistics (Source S&P, Vickers, company reports)

52-Wk Range	$55.99–45.65	S&P Oper. EPS 2007**E**	6.10	Market Capitalization(B)	$20.519	Beta	1.16
Trailing 12-Month EPS	$6.88	S&P Oper. EPS 2008**E**	6.40	Yield (%)	2.22	S&P 3-Yr. Proj. EPS CAGR(%)	NA
Trailing 12-Month P/E	7.6	P/E on S&P Oper. EPS 2007**E**	8.6	Dividend Rate/Share	$1.16	S&P Credit Rating	A
$10K Invested 5 Yrs Ago	$19,898	Common Shares Outstg. (M)	393.3	Institutional Ownership (%)	86		

Price Performance

| 30-Week Mov. Avg. · · · 10-Week Mov. Avg. - - GAAP Earnings vs. Previous Year   Volume Above Avg. STARS |
| 12-Mo. Target Price — Relative Strength — ▲ Up ▼ Down ▶ No Change   Below Avg. |

Options: CBOE, P, Ph

Analysis prepared by **Cathy A. Seifert** on November 13, 2007, when the stock traded at **$ 52.48**.

Highlights

➤ We expect earned premium growth from ongoing operations to decline fractionally in 2008, as strength in some core lines (such as homeowners and surety) is offset by a competitive pricing environment for certain casualty lines of coverage. We estimate a fractional decline in earned premiums in 2007. We anticipate that underwriting margins will be buoyed by continued favorable claim trends in a number of core lines, although year-to-year comparisons could be difficult in 2008. Barring a surge in catastrophe claims, we expect CB to post underwriting profits in 2007 and 2008.

➤ We see investment income rising 5% to 8% in 2008 and 7% to 9% in 2007, as still relatively low investment yields are being offset by continued favorable cash flow trends. EPS results will likely be aided by share buybacks, such as the 31.9 million shares repurchased in the first nine months of 2007 at a cost of $1.7 billion.

➤ Our operating EPS estimates of $6.40 for 2008 and $6.10 for 2007 assume Chubb does not incur any large one-time reserve boosts, such as those for asbestos, and that its exposure to catastrophe losses remains stable.

Investment Rationale/Risk

➤ We view the shares of this property-casualty insurer as undervalued on both a relative and a historical basis. We believe the stock deserves a premium-to-peers P/E and price/tangible book multiple, based on what we see as CB's superior personal lines franchise and its wider margin mix of business. Our outlook is tempered slightly by our concerns about the adequacy of loss reserves in certain lines of business, and the potential for ongoing price competition in CB's commercial casualty line of business.

➤ Risks to our recommendation and target price include a deterioration in claim trends and loss reserves, an escalation in premium price competition, and a significant terrorist attack or catastrophe in the U.S.

➤ Our 12-month target price of $65 assumes that the stock's forward P/E will increase to approximately 10.7X our operating EPS estimate for 2007, 10.2X our operating EPS estimate for 2008, and 1.8X estimated 2008 tangible book value. These multiples represent slight premiums to some of CB's peers.

Qualitative Risk Assessment

LOW	MEDIUM	HIGH

Our risk assessment reflects our view that CB is a superior underwriter with sound capital and risk management practices and an attractive mix of business. This is offset by our concerns about the adequacy of loss reserves in certain lines of business and by CB's exposure to catastrophe claims.

Quantitative Evaluations

S&P Quality Ranking   B+

D	C	B-	B	**B+**	A-	A	A+

Relative Strength Rank   STRONG

75

LOWEST = 1   HIGHEST = 99

Revenue/Earnings Data

Revenue (Million $)

	1Q	2Q	3Q	4Q	Year
2007	3,519	3,521	3,549	--	--
2006	3,506	3,445	3,451	3,601	14,003
2005	3,449	3,451	3,479	3,703	14,082
2004	3,178	3,206	3,345	3,448	13,177
2003	2,616	2,839	2,947	2,992	11,394
2002	2,105	2,224	2,364	2,447	9,140

Earnings Per Share ($)

	1Q	2Q	3Q	4Q	Year
2007	1.71	1.75	1.87	E1.29	E6.10
2006	1.58	1.41	1.43	1.56	5.98
2005	1.18	1.23	0.60	1.46	4.47
2004	0.94	0.93	0.94	1.20	4.01
2003	0.66	0.73	0.69	0.19	2.23
2002	0.58	0.60	-0.71	0.17	0.65

Fiscal year ended Dec. 31. Next earnings report expected: Late January. EPS Estimates based on S&P Operating Earnings; historical GAAP earnings are as reported.

Dividend Data (Dates: mm/dd Payment Date: mm/dd/yy)

Amount ($)	Date Decl.	Ex-Div. Date	Stk. of Record	Payment Date
0.290	03/02	03/14	03/16	04/03/07
0.290	03/02	03/14	03/16	04/03/07
0.290	06/08	06/20	06/22	07/10/07
0.290	09/06	09/19	09/21	10/09/07

Dividends have been paid since 1902. Source: Company reports.

Please read the Required Disclosures and Analyst Certification on the last page of this report.

The McGraw-Hill Companies

Chubb Corp (The)

Business Summary November 13, 2007

CORPORATE OVERVIEW. CB's property-casualty operations are divided into three strategic business units: Personal Lines (30% of net written insurance premiums in 2006); Commercial Insurance (44%); and Specialty Insurance (26%). Net written premiums approached $12 billion in 2006, down 2.4% from net written premiums of $12.3 billion recorded in 2005. During 2006, 80% of CB's written premiums originated in the United States, while 20% was derived overseas.

The Personal Insurance division offers primarily automobile and homeowners' insurance coverage. The company's products are typically targeted to individuals with upscale homes and automobiles, requiring more coverage choices and higher policy limits than are offered under standard insurance policies. Net written premiums totaled $3.5 billion in 2006 (up 6.1% from $3.3 billion in 2005), and were divided as follows: homeowners' 64%, automobile 19%, and other (mainly personal article coverage) 17%.

Chubb Commercial Insurance underwrites an array of commercial insurance policies, including those for multiple peril, casualty, workers' compensation,

and property and marine coverage. Net written premiums totaled $5.1 billion in 2006 (up 2.0% from $5.0 billion in 2005) and were divided as follows: commercial casualty 35%, commercial multi-peril 26%, property and marine 21%, and workers' compensation 18%.

Chubb Specialty Insurance offers a variety of specialized executive protection and professional liability products for privately and publicly owned companies, financial institutions, professional firms, and health care organizations. Net written premiums totaled $2.9 billion in 2006 (down 3.3% from $3.0 billion in 2005, which represents certain reclassifications), and were divided as follows: professional liability 90% and surety 10%. Reinsurance assumed totaled $390 million in 2006 (or about 3.3% of net written premiums), down from $904 million (7.4% of net written premiums) in 2005.

Company Financials Fiscal Year Ended Dec. 31

Per Share Data ($)	2006	2005	2004	2003	2002	2001	2000	1999	1998	1997
Tangible Book Value	32.57	28.56	25.06	21.50	18.67	17.81	18.58	16.42	17.42	16.74
Operating Earnings	NA	NA	NA	NA	0.58	0.31	1.91	1.67	1.83	2.00
Earnings	5.98	4.47	4.01	2.23	0.65	0.32	2.01	1.83	2.10	2.20
S&P Core Earnings	5.63	3.87	3.63	2.08	0.42	0.19	NA	NA	NA	NA
Dividends	1.00	1.08	0.78	0.72	0.70	0.68	0.66	0.64	0.61	0.58
Payout Ratio	17%	24%	19%	32%	109%	NM	33%	35%	29%	26%
Prices:High	54.73	49.73	38.73	34.65	39.32	43.31	45.13	38.19	44.41	39.25
Prices:Low	46.61	36.51	31.50	20.89	25.96	27.77	21.63	22.00	27.69	25.56
P/E Ratio:High	9	11	10	16	61	NM	23	21	21	18
P/E Ratio:Low	8	8	8	9	40	NM	11	12	13	12

Income Statement Analysis (Million $)	2006	2005	2004	2003	2002	2001	2000	1999	1998	1997
Premium Income	11,958	12,176	11,636	10,183	8,035	6,656	6,146	5,652	5,304	5,157
Net Investment Income	1,580	1,408	1,256	1,118	997	983	957	893	822	785
Other Revenue	2,045	12,675	286	93.2	57.7	115	6,294	184	224	721
Total Revenue	14,003	14,082	13,177	11,394	9,140	7,754	7,252	6,730	6,350	6,664
Pretax Income	3,525	2,447	2,068	934	168	-66.0	851	710	850	973
Net Operating Income	NA	NA	NA	NA	201	111	681	565	615	701
Net Income	2,528	1,826	1,548	809	223	112	715	621	707	770
S&P Core Earnings	2,378	1,578	1,402	754	146	65.2	NA	NA	NA	NA

Balance Sheet & Other Financial Data (Million $)	2006	2005	2004	2003	2002	2001	2000	1999	1998	1997
Cash & Equivalent	449	427	392	1,044	1,644	691	720	735	229	12.0
Premiums Due	2,314	2,319	2,336	2,188	6,112	6,198	3,263	1,235	1,199	1,144
Investment Assets:Bonds	31,966	30,523	28,009	22,412	18,263	16,117	15,564	14,519	13,319	12,454
Investment Assets:Stocks	1,957	2,212	1,841	1,514	795	710	831	769	1,092	871
Investment Assets:Loans	Nil	Nil	Nil	Nil	Nil	Nil	Nil	Nil	Nil	Nil
Investment Assets:Total	37,693	34,893	31,504	26,934	21,279	17,784	17,001	16,019	14,755	14,049
Deferred Policy Costs	1,480	1,445	1,435	1,343	1,150	929	842	780	729	677
Total Assets	50,277	48,061	44,260	38,361	34,114	29,449	25,027	23,537	20,746	19,616
Debt	1,791	2,467	2,814	2,814	1,959	2,901	754	759	608	399
Common Equity	13,863	12,407	10,126	8,522	6,859	6,525	6,982	6,272	5,644	5,657
Property & Casualty:Loss Ratio	55.2	64.3	63.1	67.6	75.4	80.8	67.5	70.3	66.3	64.5
Property & Casualty:Expense Ratio	29.0	28.0	29.2	30.4	31.3	32.6	32.9	32.5	33.5	32.4
Property & Casualty Combined Ratio	84.2	92.3	92.3	98.0	106.7	113.4	100.4	102.8	99.8	96.9
% Return on Revenue	18.1	13.0	11.8	7.1	2.4	1.4	9.9	9.2	11.1	11.6
% Return on Equity	19.2	16.2	16.6	10.5	3.3	1.7	10.8	10.4	12.5	13.8

Data as orig reptd.; bef. results of disc opers/spec. items. Per share data adj. for stk. divs.; EPS diluted. E-Estimated. NA-Not Available. NM-Not Meaningful. NR-Not Ranked. UR-Under Review.

Office: 15 Mountain View Road, Warren, NJ 07061-1615.
Telephone: 908-903-2000.
Email: info@chubb.com
Website: http://www.chubb.com

Chrmn, Pres & CEO: J.D. Finnegan
Vice Chrmn & COO: T.F. Motamed
Vice Chrmn & CFO: M. O'Reilly
Vice Chrmn & Chief Admin Officer: J.J. Degnan

SVP & Chief Acctg Officer: H.B. Schram
Investor Contact: G.A. Montgomery (908-903-2365)
Board Members: Z. Baird, S. P. Burke, J. I. Cash, Jr., J. J. Cohen, J. Finnegan, K. J. Mangold, M. O'Reilly, D. G. Scholey, R. G. Seitz, L. M. Small, D. E. Somers, K. H. Williams, A. W. Zollar

Founded: 1967
Domicile: New Jersey
Employees: 10,800

CIENA Corp

STANDARD &POOR'S

S&P Recommendation BUY ★★★★☆

Price	12-Mo. Target Price	Investment Style
$42.84 (as of Nov 29, 2007)	$52.00	Large-Cap Blend

GICS Sector Information Technology
Sub-Industry Communications Equipment

Summary This company manufactures telecommunications equipment used to increase the capacity of fiber optic networks.

Key Stock Statistics (Source S&P, Vickers, company reports)

52-Wk Range	$49.55– 24.39	S&P Oper. EPS 2007 **E**	1.17	Market Capitalization(B)	$3.683	Beta	2.84
Trailing 12-Month EPS	$0.73	S&P Oper. EPS 2008 **E**	1.75	Yield (%)	Nil	S&P 3-Yr. Proj. EPS CAGR(%)	20.00
Trailing 12-Month P/E	58.7	P/E on S&P Oper. EPS 2007 **E**	36.6	Dividend Rate/Share	Nil	S&P Credit Rating	B
$10K Invested 5 Yrs Ago	$10,679	Common Shares Outstg. (M)	86.0	Institutional Ownership (%)	NM		

Price Performance

30-Week Mov. Avg. · · · 10-Week Mov. Avg. - - GAAP Earnings vs. Previous Year   Volume Above Avg. STARS
12-Mo. Target Price — Relative Strength — ▲ Up ▼ Down ► No Change   Below Avg.

Options: ASE, CBOE, P, Ph

Analysis prepared by **Ari Bensinger** on November 29, 2007, when the stock traded at **$ 43.58.**

Highlights

➤ After an estimated 38% sales increase in FY 07 (Oct.), we see sales advancing 20% in FY 08, reflecting higher demand for optical transport and switching products. We look for CIEN to benefit from new product introductions and penetration into new large customer accounts. We think industry fundamentals are strong, as telecom operators accelerate capital expenditures on network infrastructure to support a material increase in bandwidth demand.

➤ Aided by the projected higher sales volume, as well as a more favorable product mix, we see FY 08 gross margins widening roughly 200 basis points from the prior year, to the 48% level. With major cost control initiatives in place, we look for FY 08 operating expense as a percentage of sales to decrease materially from FY 07.

➤ After minimal effective taxes due to loss carryovers and increased interest income on a higher cash balance, we forecast FY 08 EPS of $1.75, up sharply from the $1.17 that we estimate for FY 07.

Investment Rationale/Risk

➤ We acknowledge the sales lumpiness inherent in the company's business model as it depends on the uneven nature of telecom spending. Nevertheless, aided by strong industry fundamentals, new product traction, and aggressive cost-cutting initiatives, we view CIEN's growth profile as one of the best in the industry, as evidenced by our forecast for FY 08 sales and earnings to increase some 20% and 50%, respectively.

➤ Risks to our recommendation and target price include lower-than-expected sales growth for the company's core optical products, poor execution in realizing higher sales from several recent acquisitions, and the loss of a major customer.

➤ Our 12-month target price of $52 is largely based on 30X our FY 08 EPS estimate of $1.75, above peers. Combined with our three-year earnings growth estimate of 20%, the target price reflects a P/E to growth ratio of 1.5X, in line with the industry average. Our target price also represents 5X our FY 08 sales estimate and 4X book value, in line with the peer mean.

Qualitative Risk Assessment

LOW	MEDIUM	HIGH

Our risk assessment is tied to the company's intense competitive landscape and the increased buying power of customers. Competing against larger equipment companies, which have broader product offerings and larger service teams to meet customer needs, we believe CIEN's profitability runs the risk of being pressured.

Quantitative Evaluations

S&P Quality Ranking B-

D	C	B-	B	B+	A-	A	A+

Relative Strength Rank STRONG

76

LOWEST = 1   HIGHEST = 99

Revenue/Earnings Data

Revenue (Million $)

	1Q	2Q	3Q	4Q	Year
2007	165.1	193.5	205.0	--	--
2006	120.4	131.2	152.5	160.0	564.1
2005	94.75	103.9	110.5	118.2	427.3
2004	66.41	74.70	75.59	82.01	298.7
2003	70.47	73.54	68.48	70.64	283.1
2002	162.2	87.05	50.03	61.92	361.2

Earnings Per Share ($)

2007	0.12	0.15	0.29	E0.41	E1.17
2006	-0.08	-0.02	-0.05	0.14	0.01
2005	-0.70	-0.91	-0.63	-3.08	-5.32
2004	-1.12	-1.12	-1.75	-6.09	-10.57
2003	-1.75	-1.19	-1.40	-1.68	-6.09
2002	-1.54	-13.03	-2.94	-12.25	-30.60

Fiscal year ended Oct. 31. Next earnings report expected: Mid December. EPS Estimates based on S&P Operating Earnings; historical GAAP earnings are as reported.

Dividend Data

No cash dividends have been paid.

CIENA Corp

STANDARD &POOR'S

Business Summary November 29, 2007

CORPORATE OVERVIEW. Ciena Corp. supplies application-focused communications networking equipment, software and services to communications service providers, cable operators, governments and enterprises. The company specializes in transitioning legacy communications networks to converged, next-generation architectures, capable of efficiently delivering a broader mix of high-bandwidth services. Customers Sprint, Verizon, and AT&T accounted for 16%,12%, and 12% of FY 06 (Oct.) sales, respectively. Product revenue is reported in four segments: optical networking; broadband networking; data networking; and network and service management software.

PRIMARY BUSINESS DYNAMICS. Optical networking products account for the majority of company revenue (67% of FY 06 sales) and consist of metro and core transport and switching products, as well as multiservice optical access solutions. These products enable service providers to increase the efficiency and bandwidth of their communications networks, allowing them to service more customers, more cost effectively. Flagship offerings include the CoreDirector optical switch and the CN 4200 FlexSelect advanced services platform.

Broadband networking products (15%) allow telecommunications service providers to transition their legacy voice networks to support next-generation services such as Internet-based (IP) telephony, video services and DSL. These products facilitate broader service offerings to compete with cable operators.

Data networking products (6%) include multiservice edge switching and routing products. These products enable telecommunications service providers and multiservice operators to transition their communications networks from legacy technologies, such as ATM and Frame Relay, to next-generation technologies, such as Ethernet and IP/MPLS.

We believe CIEN continues to focus on cost reductions across all product lines. It relies on electronic manufacturing service (EMS) providers to perform the majority of the manufacturing operations for its products and components, and is increasingly utilizing overseas suppliers in Asia.

Company Financials Fiscal Year Ended Oct. 31

Per Share Data ($)	2006	2005	2004	2003	2002	2001	2000	1999	1998	1997
Tangible Book Value	5.19	0.66	6.58	13.10	20.24	40.62	19.54	26.19	15.55	12.82
Cash Flow	0.54	-4.41	-9.17	-4.59	-28.08	-33.96	3.39	2.44	2.81	4.13
Earnings	0.01	-5.32	-10.57	-6.09	-30.60	-40.27	1.89	-0.11	1.72	3.82
S&P Core Earnings	-0.09	-4.48	-7.70	-6.09	-23.52	-22.47	NA	NA	NA	NA
Dividends	Nil	Nil	Nil	Nil	Nil	Nil	Nil	Nil	Nil	Nil
Payout Ratio	Nil	Nil	Nil	Nil	Nil	Nil	Nil	Nil	Nil	Nil
Prices:High	39.36	24.02	57.00	54.20	121.15	756.30	1057	261.07	323.44	222.78
Prices:Low	20.38	11.51	11.69	29.35	16.88	64.43	158.88	47.71	28.45	77.91
P/E Ratio:High	NM	NM	NM	NM	NM	NM	NM	NM	NM	58
P/E Ratio:Low	NM	NM	NM	NM	NM	NM	NM	NM	NM	20

Income Statement Analysis (Million $)										
Revenue	564	427	299	283	361	1,603	859	482	508	374
Operating Income	15.1	-115	-185	-209	-569	324	163	43.5	157	187
Depreciation	45.5	76.0	107	93.7	131	283	63.6	50.4	33.3	10.2
Interest Expense	24.2	25.4	26.8	36.3	45.3	30.6	0.34	0.50	0.26	0.34
Pretax Income	1.98	-434	-788	-385	-1,487	-1,707	121	-5.99	93.4	184
Effective Tax Rate	69.9%	NM	NM	NM	NM	NM	32.5%	NM	43.1%	38.6%
Net Income	0.60	-436	-789	-387	-1,597	-1,794	81.4	-3.92	53.2	113
S&P Core Earnings	-7.67	-367	-573	-386	-1,225	-1,001	NA	NA	NA	NA

Balance Sheet & Other Financial Data (Million $)										
Cash	220	373	203	310	377	398	238	262	243	263
Current Assets	1,098	1,102	1,079	1,229	1,638	2,191	813	533	428	379
Total Assets	1,840	1,675	2,137	2,378	2,751	3,317	1,027	678	572	447
Current Liabilities	162	178	159	186	224	254	173	106	61.9	53.6
Long Term Debt	844	650	692	794	919	870	Nil	Nil	1.41	1.88
Common Equity	754	735	1,154	1,331	1,527	2,129	810	530	475	364
Total Capital	1,598	1,385	1,846	2,125	2,246	3,063	849	567	510	394
Capital Expenditures	33.0	11.3	33.0	29.5	66.3	239	124	46.8	86.4	66.6
Cash Flow	46.0	-360	-682	-293	-1,466	-1,511	145	46.5	86.5	123
Current Ratio	6.8	6.2	6.8	6.6	7.3	8.6	4.7	5.1	6.9	7.1
% Long Term Debt of Capitalization	52.8	46.9	37.5	37.4	37.6	28.4	Nil	Nil	2.8	0.5
% Net Income of Revenue	0.1	NM	NM	NM	NM	NM	9.5	NM	10.5	30.2
% Return on Assets	0.0	NM	NM	NM	NM	NM	9.5	NM	10.4	43.9
% Return on Equity	0.1	NM	NM	NM	NM	NM	12.1	NM	12.7	61.3

Data as orig reptd.; bef. results of disc opers/spec. items. Per share data adj. for stk. divs.; EPS diluted. E-Estimated. NA-Not Available. NM-Not Meaningful. NR-Not Ranked. UR-Under Review.

Office: 1201 Winterson Road, Linthicum, MD 21090-2205.
Telephone: 410-865-8500.
Email: ir@ciena.com
Website: http://www.ciena.com

Exec Chrmn: P.H. Nettles
Pres & CEO: G. Smith
COO: A. Smith
SVP & CFO: J.R. Chinnici

SVP & CTO: S.B. Alexander
Board Members: S. P. Bradley, H. B. Cash, B. L. Claflin, L. W. Fitt, P. H. Nettles, J. M. O'Brien, M. J. Rowny, G. B. Smith, G. H. Taylor

Founded: 1992
Domicile: Delaware
Employees: 1,485

The McGraw-Hill Companies

CIGNA Corp.

STANDARD &POOR'S

S&P Recommendation HOLD ★★★★☆

Price	$50.46 (as of Nov 27, 2007)
12-Mo. Target Price	$56.00
Investment Style	Large-Cap Growth

GICS Sector Health Care
Sub-Industry Managed Health Care

Summary CIGNA is one of the largest investor-owned employee benefits organizations in the U.S. Its subsidiaries are major providers of employee benefits offered through the workplace.

Key Stock Statistics (Source S&P, Vickers, company reports)

52-Wk Range	$57.61– 40.83	S&P Oper. EPS 2007**E**	4.00	Market Capitalization(B)	$14.273	Beta	0.53
Trailing 12-Month EPS	$3.71	S&P Oper. EPS 2008**E**	4.30	Yield (%)	0.08	S&P 3-Yr. Proj. EPS CAGR(%)	12.00
Trailing 12-Month P/E	13.6	P/E on S&P Oper. EPS 2007**E**	12.6	Dividend Rate/Share	$0.04	S&P Credit Rating	BBB+
$10K Invested 5 Yrs Ago	$36,996	Common Shares Outstg. (M)	282.9	Institutional Ownership (%)	82		

Price Performance

Legend: 30-Week Mov. Avg. · · · · 10-Week Mov. Avg. - - GAAP Earnings vs. Previous Year Volume Above Avg. STARS
12-Mo. Target Price — Relative Strength — ▲ Up ▼ Down ► No Change Below Avg.

Options: ASE, CBOE, P, Ph

Analysis prepared by **Phillip M. Seligman** on November 12, 2007, when the stock traded at **$ 49.74**.

Highlights

► We forecast health plan premium and fee revenue to grow about 5% in 2008, following our expectation of 9% growth in 2007. We believe that medical enrollment will rise organically 4% in 2008, aided by the launch of Medicare Advantage private-fee-for-service plans for employer groups. Such growth is below the 5.3% we expect in 2007, due to intensified competition. We also project continued strong revenue and earnings growth by CI's International segment given the attractiveness of its products to the growing Asian middle class.

► With pricing discipline and assuming medical cost trends remain at 6.5% to 7.5%, we think the guaranteed cost medical loss ratio can decline 100 basis points to 83% in 2008 before prior-year reserve development. Other Health Care segment earnings growth drivers we see are an improving market mix, with specialty-products and individual/small group membership accounting for a higher proportion of the total.

► We see operating EPS of $4.00 in 2007 and $4.30 in 2008, aided by share buybacks, versus $3.17 in 2006.

Investment Rationale/Risk

► We look favorably on CI's improved membership retention, and believe that even achieving its recently reduced 2007 enrollment growth target (now at 5% to 5.5%) places CI ahead of most peers. We view positively the Health Care segment's improved execution, and view its upgraded customer service and expanding product portfolio as competitive strengths. We think intensifying competition will slow enrollment growth in 2008, but believe CI's healthy cash flow gives it the financial ability to continue to make acquisitions. Elsewhere, we believe CI's small Medicare unit will be less impacted from proposed funding cuts than peers with much larger Medicare businesses.

► Risks to our recommendation and target price include intensified competition and higher-than-expected medical costs.

► Our 12-month target price of $56 assumes a P/E of 13X our 2008 EPS estimate. This multiple is below the high end of its recent historical range based on our view of intensifying competition.

Qualitative Risk Assessment

LOW	MEDIUM	HIGH

Our risk assessment reflects our view of CI's improving cost structure, account retention, significant provider network, and wide range of attractive product and service offerings. However, the managed care market is intensely competitive, and we believe CI's national peers have strengthened while CI had to focus on turning itself around.

Quantitative Evaluations

S&P Quality Ranking   B

D	C	B-	B	B+	A-	A	A+

Relative Strength Rank   STRONG

74

LOWEST = 1   HIGHEST = 99

Revenue/Earnings Data

Revenue (Million $)

	1Q	2Q	3Q	4Q	Year
2007	4,374	4,381	4,413	--	--
2006	4,107	4,098	4,137	4,205	16,547
2005	4,345	4,107	4,022	4,210	16,684
2004	4,722	4,633	4,479	4,342	18,176
2003	4,900	4,634	4,773	4,501	18,808
2002	4,690	4,877	5,083	4,748	19,348

Earnings Per Share ($)

	1Q	2Q	3Q	4Q	Year
2007	0.93	0.75	1.28	E0.96	E4.00
2006	0.96	0.78	0.93	0.76	3.44
2005	1.09	0.94	0.67	0.59	3.28
2004	0.49	1.20	0.75	1.39	3.81
2003	0.45	-0.13	0.46	0.69	1.47
2002	0.51	0.50	-2.09	0.11	-0.94

Fiscal year ended Dec. 31. Next earnings report expected: Early February. EPS Estimates based on S&P Operating Earnings; historical GAAP earnings are as reported.

Dividend Data (Dates: mm/dd Payment Date: mm/dd/yy)

Amount ($)	Date Decl.	Ex-Div. Date	Stk. of Record	Payment Date
3-for-1	04/25	06/05	05/21	06/04/07
0.010	04/25	06/08	06/12	07/10/07
0.010	07/25	09/10	09/12	10/10/07
0.010	10/24	12/11	12/13	01/10/08

Dividends have been paid since 1867. Source: Company reports.

CIGNA Corp.

STANDARD &POOR'S

Business Summary November 12, 2007

CORPORATE OVERVIEW. CIGNA Corp., one of the largest U.S. employee benefits organizations, provides health care products and services and group life, accident and disability insurance.

Health Care offers group medical, dental, behavioral health and pharmacy services products. Medical products include consumer directed health plans (CDHPs), HMOs, network only, point-of-service (POS) plans, preferred provider organizations (PPOs), and traditional indemnity coverage. The health care products and services are offered through guaranteed cost, retrospectively experience-rated, administrative services only (ASO) and minimum premium funding arrangements. Under ASO, the employer or other plan sponsor self-funds all of its claims and assumes the risk for claim costs incurred. CI's CDHPs offer a modular product portfolio that provides a choice of benefits network and various funding, medical management, consumerism and health advocacy options for employers and consumers.

Medical covered lives at September 30, 2007, totaled 10,223,000 (versus

9,389,000 as of December 31, 2006): 1,278,000 (1,326,000) guaranteed cost (commercial HMO, Medicare, and voluntary/limited benefits); 898,000 (935,000) experience-related indemnity; and 8,047,000 (7,128,000) ASO.

Disability and Life, which provides employer-paid and voluntary life, accident and disability products, held group life insurance policies covering 5.8 million lives at year-end 2006, even with the 5.8 million at year-end 2005. International operates in selected markets outside the U.S., providing individual and group life, accident and health, health care and pension products. CI's assets under management at year-end 2006 totaled $18.3 billion, versus $21.4 billion at year-end 2005.

Company Financials Fiscal Year Ended Dec. 31

Per Share Data ($)	2006	2005	2004	2003	2002	2001	2000	1999	1998	1997
Tangible Book Value	8.73	10.30	9.05	6.85	2.74	7.62	7.75	8.22	9.36	8.32
Operating Earnings	NA	NA	NA	NA	NA	2.45	2.02	1.17	1.54	1.57
Earnings	3.44	3.28	3.81	1.47	-0.94	2.20	2.03	1.18	2.02	1.63
S&P Core Earnings	3.34	2.80	2.62	1.21	-0.24	1.77	NA	NA	NA	NA
Dividends	0.03	0.03	0.14	0.44	0.44	0.43	0.41	0.40	0.38	0.37
Relative Payout	1%	1%	4%	30%	NM	19%	20%	34%	19%	23%
Prices:High	44.59	39.94	27.76	19.53	37.00	44.98	45.58	32.88	27.46	22.31
Prices:Low	29.35	26.04	17.63	13.03	11.38	23.29	20.25	21.15	18.67	14.90
P/E Ratio:High	13	12	7	13	NM	20	22	28	14	14
P/E Ratio:Low	9	8	5	9	NM	11	10	18	9	9

Income Statement Analysis (Million $)

	2006	2005	2004	2003	2002	2001	2000	1999	1998	1997
Life Insurance in Force	NA	NA	NA	459,995	516,661	609,970	647,464	662,693	670,667	695,272
Premium Income:Life A & H	13,641	13,695	14,236	15,441	15,737	15,367	16,328	15,079	13,913	12,251
Premium Income:Casualty/Property.	NA	Nil	Nil	Nil	Nil	Nil	Nil	Nil	2,500	2,684
Net Investment Income	1,195	1,359	1,643	2,594	2,716	2,843	2,942	2,959	3,705	4,245
Total Revenue	16,547	16,684	18,176	18,808	19,348	19,115	19,994	18,781	21,437	20,038
Pretax Income	1,731	1,793	2,375	903	-569	1,497	1,497	1,219	2,010	1,650
Net Operating Income	NA	NA	NA	NA	NA	1,101	983	695	1,190	971
Net Income	1,159	1,276	1,577	620	-397	989	987	699	1,292	1,086
S&P Core Earnings	1,127	1,090	1,082	509	-99.2	794	NA	NA	NA	NA

Balance Sheet & Other Financial Data (Million $)

	2006	2005	2004	2003	2002	2001	2000	1999	1998	1997
Cash & Equivalent	1,647	1,991	2,804	1,860	2,079	2,455	2,739	2,732	3,797	2,625
Premiums Due	9,501	8,616	16,223	9,421	9,981	2,832	2,814	2,475	4,469	4,265
Investment Assets:Bonds	12,155	14,947	16,136	17,121	27,803	23,401	24,776	22,944	32,634	36,358
Investment Assets:Stocks	131	135	33.0	11,300	295	404	569	585	1,043	854
Investment Assets:Loans	5,393	5,271	5,123	10,227	11,134	12,694	12,755	12,816	15,784	18,112
Investment Assets:Total	18,303	21,376	21,919	39,658	40,362	38,261	41,516	38,295	50,707	37,697
Deferred Policy Costs	707	618	544	580	494	448	1,052	927	1,069	1,542
Total Assets	42,399	44,863	81,059	90,953	88,950	91,589	95,088	95,333	114,612	108,199
Debt	1,294	1,338	1,438	1,500	1,500	1,627	1,163	1,359	1,431	2,155
Common Equity	4,330	5,360	5,203	4,465	3,665	5,055	5,634	6,149	8,277	7,932
Combined Loss-Expense Ratio	NA	NA	NA	NA	NA	NA	NA	NA	107.1	NA
% Return on Revenue	7.0	7.6	8.7	3.3	NM	5.2	4.9	3.7	6.0	5.4
% Return on Equity	23.9	24.2	32.2	15.3	NM	18.9	16.5	9.1	15.9	14.3
% Investment Yield	6.0	6.3	5.3	6.5	6.9	7.3	7.1	7.4	8.4	7.5

Data as orig reptd.; bef. results of disc opers/spec. items. Per share data adj. for stk. divs.; EPS diluted. E-Estimated. NA-Not Available. NM-Not Meaningful. NR-Not Ranked. UR-Under Review.

Office: 2 Liberty Pl, Philadelphia, PA 19192-0001.
Telephone: 215-761-1000.
Website: http://www.cigna.com
Chrmn, Pres & CEO: H.E. Hanway

EVP & CFO: M.W. Bell
EVP & General Counsel: C.A. Petren
Investor Contact: T. Detrick (215-761-1414)

Board Members: R. H. Campbell, H. E. Hanway, I. Harris, Jr., J. E. Henney, P. N. Larson, R. Martinez IV, H. A. Wagner, C. C. Wait, E. C. Wiseman, D. F. Zarcone, W. D. Zollars

Founded: 1792
Domicile: Delaware
Employees: 27,100

The McGraw-Hill Companies

Cincinnati Financial Corp

STANDARD &POOR'S

S&P Recommendation HOLD ★★★☆☆

Price	12-Mo. Target Price	Investment Style
$40.61 (as of Nov 23, 2007)	$45.00	Large-Cap Blend

GICS Sector Financials
Sub-Industry Property & Casualty Insurance

Summary This insurance holding company markets primarily property and casualty coverage; it also conducts life insurance and asset management operations.

Key Stock Statistics (Source S&P, Vickers, company reports)

52-Wk Range	$48.45– 36.00	S&P Oper. EPS 2007**E**	3.25	Market Capitalization(B)	$6.985	Beta	0.71
Trailing 12-Month EPS	$4.60	S&P Oper. EPS 2008**E**	3.20	Yield (%)	3.50	S&P 3-Yr. Proj. EPS CAGR(%)	NA
Trailing 12-Month P/E	8.8	P/E on S&P Oper. EPS 2007**E**	12.5	Dividend Rate/Share	$1.42	S&P Credit Rating	A
$10K Invested 5 Yrs Ago	$13,439	Common Shares Outstg. (M)	172.0	Institutional Ownership (%)	56		

Price Performance

30-Week Mov. Avg. · · · 10-Week Mov. Avg. - - **GAAP Earnings vs. Previous Year** Volume Above Avg. STARS
12-Mo. Target Price — Relative Strength — ▲ Up ▼ Down ▶ No Change Below Avg. ★

Options: ASE

Analysis prepared by **Cathy A. Seifert** on November 16, 2007, when the stock traded at **$ 40.27.**

Highlights

➤ We project property casualty earned premiums will decline by 1% to 3% in 2008, versus growth of less than 2% forecasted for 2007. We see the effects of CINF's expansion being offset by price competition, particularly in the commercial lines segment. We also believe that competition in many non-coastal regions (like those in which CINF operates) will remain intense. Underwriting margins are also expected to contract slightly in 2008, reflecting our expectation that the erosion in certain claim trends that emerged in 2007 continues into 2008.

➤ We estimate net investment income growth of 5% to 6% in 2008 and 6% in 2007. This rate of growth is below that of a number of CINF's peers and is partly due to a different asset mix. As of September 30, 2007, nearly 55% of CINF's invested assets were in equity securities, versus an industry average that we estimate is less than 15%.

➤ We expect tepid premium growth and narrower underwriting margins, partly offset by contributions from investment income, to produce operating EPS of $3.25 in 2007 and $3.20 in 2008, versus the $2.82 of operating EPS the company earned in 2006.

Investment Rationale/Risk

➤ We believe that CINF has done an admirable job of improving its underwriting and investment results and profitability. We also think that the company's lack of meaningful exposure to hurricane losses has resulted in superior results relative to many of its peers. However, we anticipate that CINF will face price competition in its core markets. We regard the shares' current valuation as fair. The stock's P/E multiple and P/E-to-growth (PEG) ratios were recently at premiums to peers. CINF also has among the lowest rates of return on equity in its peer group.

➤ Risks to our opinion and target price include a lower-than-expected premium growth rate and a sharp deterioration in underwriting results and profitability.

➤ Our 12-month target price of $45 assumes the shares will trade at approximately 14.1X our 2008 operating EPS estimate, a more than 20% premium to most peers. Our target price also assumes a forward price/book multiple of about 1.3X, a discount to peers.

Qualitative Risk Assessment

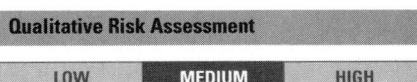

LOW	MEDIUM	HIGH

Our risk assessment reflects our view of the company as a fairly conservative underwriter with sound risk and capital management policies. However, CINF's investment allocation is more heavily weighted toward equity holdings than the company's peers.

Quantitative Evaluations

S&P Quality Ranking A

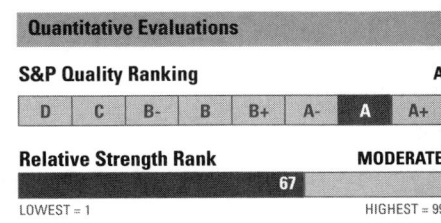

D	C	B-	B	B+	A-	A	A+

Relative Strength Rank MODERATE

67

LOWEST = 1 HIGHEST = 99

Revenue/Earnings Data

Revenue (Million $)

	1Q	2Q	3Q	4Q	Year
2007	1,031	1,270	982.0	--	--
2006	1,607	981.0	967.0	995.0	4,550
2005	916.0	940.0	944.0	967.0	3,767
2004	870.0	923.0	879.0	942.0	3,614
2003	707.0	798.0	836.0	840.0	3,181
2002	687.0	703.0	731.0	722.0	2,843

Earnings Per Share ($)

2007	1.11	2.02	0.72	E0.80	E3.25
2006	3.13	0.76	0.66	0.75	5.30
2005	0.81	0.89	0.66	1.03	3.40
2004	0.82	0.87	0.50	1.09	3.28
2003	0.31	0.48	0.58	0.72	2.10
2002	0.42	0.19	0.40	0.31	1.32

Fiscal year ended Dec. 31. Next earnings report expected: Early February. EPS Estimates based on S&P Operating Earnings; historical GAAP earnings are as reported.

Dividend Data (Dates: mm/dd Payment Date: mm/dd/yy)

Amount ($)	Date Decl.	Ex-Div. Date	Stk. of Record	Payment Date
0.355	02/02	03/21	03/23	04/16/07
0.355	05/25	06/20	06/22	07/16/07
0.355	08/16	09/19	09/21	10/15/07
0.355	11/19	12/19	12/21	01/15/08

Dividends have been paid since 1954. Source: Company reports.

Cincinnati Financial Corp

Business Summary November 16, 2007

Cincinnati Financial Corp. underwrites and sells property-casualty insurance primarily in the Midwest and Southeast, through a network of independent agents. Operations as of 2006 year-end were conducted in 32 states, through a network of 1,066 independent insurance agents, many of whom own stock in the company. The company is licensed in all 50 states, the District of Columbia, and Puerto Rico. An ongoing geographical expansion plan is being implemented.

Property-casualty net earned premiums totaled $3.2 billion in 2006, with commercial lines accounting for 76% and personal lines for 24%. Four lines of business (commercial multi-peril, workers compensation, commercial auto and other liability) accounted for 90% of commercial lines earned premiums in 2005 (latest available). Personal auto and homeowners coverage accounted for over 89% of personal lines earned premiums in 2005.

Underwriting results deteriorated in 2006, partly due to higher catastrophe losses. The loss ratio in 2006 equaled 63.5% (including 5.5 points of catastrophe losses), versus 59.2% (including 4.1 points of catastrophe losses). The expense ratio inched upward, to 30.3%, from 29.8%. The policyholder dividend

ratio increased to 0.5% in 2006, from 0.2% in 2005. Taken together, the GAAP combined ratio equaled 94.3% in 2006, a deterioration from 2005's combined ratio of 89.2%.

Life, accident and health insurance is marketed through property-casualty agents and independent life insurance agents. This unit has been expanding its work site marketing activities, introducing a new product line and exploring expansion opportunities. Term life insurance represents this unit's largest product line.

Total invested assets of nearly $13.8 billion at December 31, 2006, were divided as follows: fixed maturities 42%, equity securities 57%, and other investments 1%. CinFin Capital Management offers asset management services to institutions and high-net-worth individuals.

Company Financials Fiscal Year Ended Dec. 31

Per Share Data ($)	2006	2005	2004	2003	2002	2001	2000	1999	1998	1997
Tangible Book Value	39.38	34.88	35.60	35.10	31.42	33.62	33.80	30.35	30.58	25.71
Operating Earnings	2.82	3.02	2.93	NA	1.67	1.17	0.82	1.38	1.08	1.39
Earnings	5.30	3.40	3.28	2.10	1.32	1.08	0.66	1.38	1.28	1.61
S&P Core Earnings	2.78	3.10	2.87	2.09	1.55	1.06	NA	NA	NA	NA
Dividends	1.34	1.21	1.04	0.91	0.81	0.76	0.69	0.60	0.54	0.50
Relative Payout	25%	35%	32%	43%	61%	71%	104%	44%	42%	31%
Prices:High	49.19	45.95	43.52	38.01	42.90	38.94	39.29	38.55	42.55	42.78
Prices:Low	41.21	38.38	36.57	30.00	29.42	30.84	23.75	27.32	27.66	18.75
P/E Ratio:High	9	14	13	18	32	36	59	28	33	27
P/E Ratio:Low	8	11	11	14	22	29	36	20	22	12

Income Statement Analysis (Million $)

	2006	2005	2004	2003	2002	2001	2000	1999	1998	1997
Life Insurance in Force	56,971	51,493	44,921	48,492	32,486	27,534	23,525	17,890	13,048	10,845
Premium Income:Life A & H	115	106	101	95.0	87.0	81.0	79.3	75.0	70.1	62.9
Premium Income:Casualty/Property.	3,163	3,058	2,919	2,653	2,391	2,071	1,828	1,657	1,543	1,454
Net Investment Income	570	526	492	465	445	421	415	387	368	349
Total Revenue	4,550	3,767	3,614	3,181	2,843	2,561	2,331	2,128	2,054	1,942
Pretax Income	1,329	823	800	480	279	221	109	322	307	395
Net Operating Income	496	562	524	286	300	210	120	255	199	254
Net Income	930	602	584	374	238	193	118	255	242	299
S&P Core Earnings	487	549	512	372	279	189	NA	NA	NA	NA

Balance Sheet & Other Financial Data (Million $)

	2006	2005	2004	2003	2002	2001	2000	1999	1998	1997
Cash & Equivalent	202	119	306	91.0	112	93.0	60.3	420	135	80.2
Premiums Due	1,811	1,797	1,799	1,677	1,483	732	652	192	164	159
Investment Assets:Bonds	5,805	5,476	5,141	3,925	3,305	3,010	2,721	2,617	2,812	2,751
Investment Assets:Stocks	7,799	7,106	7,498	8,524	7,884	8,495	8,526	7,511	7,455	5,999
Investment Assets:Loans	Nil	Nil	Nil	Nil	Nil	Nil	Nil	Nil	Nil	Nil
Investment Assets:Total	13,759	12,702	12,677	12,527	11,257	11,571	11,316	10,194	10,325	8,797
Deferred Policy Costs	453	429	400	372	343	286	259	154	143	135
Total Assets	17,222	16,003	16,107	15,509	14,059	13,959	13,287	11,380	11,087	9,493
Debt	840	791	791	603	420	609	449	457	472	339
Common Equity	6,808	4,145	6,249	6,204	5,998	5,998	5,995	5,420	5,621	4,717
Combined Loss-Expense Ratio	94.3	89.2	89.8	94.7	98.4	104.9	112.5	100.0	103.6	97.7
% Return on Revenue	23.4	16.0	16.2	11.8	8.4	7.5	5.1	12.0	11.8	15.4
% Return on Equity	14.4	15.4	8.0	5.4	3.6	3.2	1.0	4.6	4.7	7.6
% Investment Yield	4.3	4.1	3.9	3.9	3.9	3.7	3.9	3.8	3.8	4.6

Data as orig reptd.; bef. results of disc opers/spec. items. Per share data adj. for stk. divs.; EPS diluted. E-Estimated. NA-Not Available. NM-Not Meaningful. NR-Not Ranked. UR-Under Review.

Office: 6200 South Gilmore Road, Fairfield, OH 45014-5141.
Telephone: 513-870-2000.
Email: investor_inquiries@cinfin.com
Website: http://www.cinfin.com

Chrmn & CEO: J.J. Schiff, Jr.
Pres, Vice Chrmn & COO: J.E. Benoski
EVP, CFO, Treas & Secy: K.W. Stecher
Investor Contact: H.J. Wietzel (513-870-2768)

Board Members: W. F. Bahl, J. E. Benoski, G. T. Bier, D. J. Debbink, K. C. Lichtendahl, W. R. McMullen, G. W. Price, T. R. Schiff, J. J. Schiff, Jr., D. S. Skidmore, J. Steele, Jr., L. R. Webb, E. A. Woods

Founded: 1968
Domicile: Ohio
Employees: 4,048

Cintas Corp

STANDARD &POOR'S

S&P Recommendation **BUY** ★★★★☆	Price $32.71 (as of Nov 23, 2007)	12-Mo. Target Price $45.00	Investment Style Large-Cap Growth

GICS Sector Industrials
Sub-Industry Diversified Commercial & Professional Services

Summary A leader in the corporate identity uniform business, Cintas also provides entrance mats, sanitation supplies, and first aid and safety products.

Key Stock Statistics (Source S&P, Vickers, company reports)

52-Wk Range	$43.24–31.88	S&P Oper. EPS 2008**E**	2.26	Market Capitalization(B)	$5.196	Beta	1.65
Trailing 12-Month EPS	$2.07	S&P Oper. EPS 2009**E**	2.43	Yield (%)	1.19	S&P 3-Yr. Proj. EPS CAGR(%)	8.00
Trailing 12-Month P/E	15.8	P/E on S&P Oper. EPS 2008**E**	14.5	Dividend Rate/Share	$0.39	S&P Credit Rating	A
$10K Invested 5 Yrs Ago	$6,638	Common Shares Outstg. (M)	158.9	Institutional Ownership (%)	66		

Price Performance

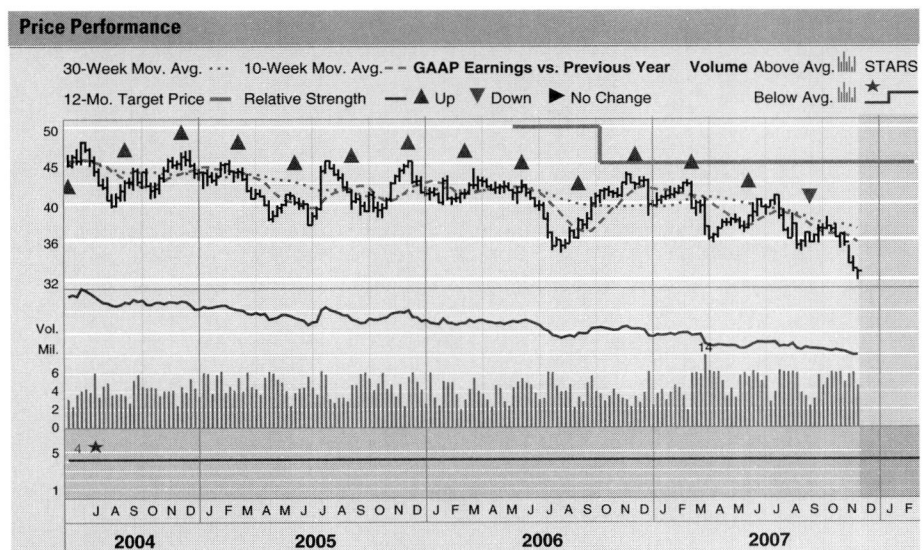

30-Week Mov. Avg. ··· 10-Week Mov. Avg. – – **GAAP Earnings vs. Previous Year**   Volume Above Avg. STARS
12-Mo. Target Price — Relative Strength — ▲ Up ▼ Down ▶ No Change   Below Avg. ★

Options: ASE, CBOE, P, Ph

Analysis prepared by **Kevin Kirkeby** on October 02, 2007, when the stock traded at **$ 37.72**.

Highlights

➤ Following a 9% revenue rise in FY 07 (May) aided in part by acquisitions, we forecast further growth of 6.5% in FY 08. The market for rental and facility services is likely to remain challenging as the impact of further plant closures flows through the auto and auto-related industries. Other services should show a 15% gain in FY 08, compared to 16% in FY 07. We believe CTAS has limited ability to increase prices beyond inflation in the current industrial economy.

➤ We see margins narrowing modestly in FY 08 as CTAS invests in labor and equipment for new businesses, like Sanis UltraClean. We also expect fuel costs to remain at a historically high 3.4% of revenues. However, as the expanded sales force gains proficiency and can focus on cross selling initiatives, we expect margin pressures will lessen over coming quarters.

➤ We estimate EPS will rise about 9% in FY 08 to $2.26. Relatively low debt levels and a stable cash flow should permit CTAS to pursue additional acquisitions, most likely in the growth areas of first aid and document services. The company had about $420 million remaining in its stock buyback authorization as of September 2007.

Investment Rationale/Risk

➤ CTAS has historically traded at a premium valuation to the S&P 500 and peers due to its consistent growth, in our view. We think it can achieve a 39th consecutive year of sales and profit growth in FY 08. However, as employment growth nationwide has slowed and a greater percentage of earnings gains have come from acquisitions and share buybacks, valuations have compressed to historical lows. As the newer service businesses achieve sufficient scale and demonstrate margin expansion, we expect valuations to expand modestly.

➤ Risks to our recommendation and target price include slower-than-expected growth in employment levels and uniform rentals, and potentially rising labor and material costs.

➤ The shares have traded in a range of 16X to 55X forward EPS over the past 10 years. Using an 18X multiple, near the low end of its historical range, applied to our four-quarter forward EPS estimate, we calculate a value of $42. Our DCF model yields an intrinsic value of $48, based on a 10.4% WACC, 8% annual free cash flow growth over the next 10 years, and 3.5% growth in perpetuity. Blending our valuation models results in our 12-month target price of $45.

Qualitative Risk Assessment

LOW	MEDIUM	HIGH

Our risk assessment reflects the company's leading position in its core business, other related services that we believe are showing good growth, and what we view as a relatively strong balance sheet and cash flow.

Quantitative Evaluations

S&P Quality Ranking **A+**

D	C	B-	B	B+	A-	A	A+

Relative Strength Rank **MODERATE**

39

LOWEST = 1   HIGHEST = 99

Revenue/Earnings Data

Revenue (Million $)

	1Q	2Q	3Q	4Q	Year
2008	969.1	--	--	--	--
2007	914.2	923.3	905.4	964.1	3,707
2006	823.5	835.8	836.4	907.9	3,404
2005	746.0	756.8	755.2	809.3	3,067
2004	677.7	701.3	696.9	738.2	2,814
2003	665.7	681.0	663.8	676.1	2,687

Earnings Per Share ($)

2008	0.51	E0.56	E0.56	E0.63	E2.26
2007	0.53	0.51	0.48	0.57	2.09
2006	0.47	0.46	0.46	0.55	1.94
2005	0.42	0.43	0.41	0.48	1.74
2004	0.37	0.40	0.39	0.42	1.58
2003	0.36	0.37	0.34	0.38	1.45

Fiscal year ended May 31. Next earnings report expected: Mid December. EPS Estimates based on S&P Operating Earnings; historical GAAP earnings are as reported.

Dividend Data (Dates: mm/dd Payment Date: mm/dd/yy)

Amount ($)	Date Decl.	Ex-Div. Date	Stk. of Record	Payment Date
0.390	01/16	02/02	02/06	03/13/07

Dividends have been paid since 1984. Source: Company reports.

Cintas Corp

Business Summary October 02, 2007

CORPORATE OVERVIEW. Cintas Corp. is North America's leading supplier of corporate uniforms, as well as a significant provider of related services. FY 07 (May) marked Cintas Corp.'s 38th consecutive year of sales and profit growth.

The Rental operating segment (74% of total revenues in FY 07 and 77% of gross profits, with a 44.6% margin) designs and manufactures corporate uniforms that it rents--together with other items--to its customers. Services provided to the rental markets by the company also include the cleaning of uniforms, as well as the provision of ongoing replacements as required by each customer. CTAS rents uniforms to a variety of industries, including hospitality, auto aftermarket, and food service. The company also offers ancillary products, including the rental or sale of entrance and special purpose mats, towels, mops, and linen products, as well as sanitation supplies and services and cleanroom supplies.

The Other Services segment (26%, 23%, and 37.2% margin) includes the design, manufacture and direct sale of uniforms to CTAS's national account customers. The company also provides on-site and off-site shredding of confiden-

tial documents. In FY 06, CTAS made several small acquisitions in the document storage business. Document management services are now available in 70 of the 100 largest markets in the U.S. and Canada. The company estimates the potential annual market is $8 billion. In addition, the company offers first aid, safety, and emergency care supplies and training. These services are available through local distributors in 42 major U.S. cities. The company has broadened its product line to include fire protection services, including the inspection, repair and recharging of portable fire extinguishers, fire suppression systems, and emergency and exit lights. In a short period of time, the company believes it has become the second-largest fire protection services company in the U.S., with capabilities in 23 of the top 50 cities. The company estimates the market size for first aid and fire protection services at a combined $4.5 billion a year.

Company Financials Fiscal Year Ended May 31

Per Share Data ($)	2007	2006	2005	2004	2003	2002	2001	2000	1999	1998
Tangible Book Value	4.73	4.73	6.15	6.32	5.42	4.39	6.42	5.42	4.54	3.71
Cash Flow	2.96	2.78	2.43	2.26	2.12	1.95	1.82	1.60	1.23	1.09
Earnings	2.09	1.94	1.74	1.58	1.45	1.36	1.30	1.14	0.82	0.79
S&P Core Earnings	2.09	1.92	1.69	1.54	1.43	1.33	1.27	NA	NA	NA
Dividends	0.35	0.32	0.32	0.29	0.27	0.25	0.22	0.19	0.15	0.12
Payout Ratio	17%	16%	18%	18%	19%	18%	17%	17%	18%	15%
Calendar Year	2006	2005	2004	2003	2002	2001	2000	1999	1998	1997
Prices:High	44.30	45.50	50.35	50.68	56.62	53.25	54.00	52.25	47.50	28.33
Prices:Low	34.57	37.51	39.51	30.60	39.15	33.75	23.17	26.00	26.00	17.00
P/E Ratio:High	21	23	29	32	42	39	42	46	58	36
P/E Ratio:Low	17	19	23	19	29	25	18	23	32	21

Income Statement Analysis (Million $)

	2007	2006	2005	2004	2003	2002	2001	2000	1999	1998
Revenue	3,707	3,404	3,067	2,814	2,687	2,271	2,161	1,902	1,752	1,198
Operating Income	713	674	614	602	539	478	459	423	338	258
Depreciation	135	127	120	117	115	101	90.2	78.5	68.8	45.8
Interest Expense	50.3	31.8	24.4	25.1	30.9	11.0	15.1	15.9	16.4	9.08
Pretax Income	534	522	477	432	396	372	356	312	224	179
Effective Tax Rate	37.3%	37.3%	37.0%	37.0%	37.0%	37.0%	37.6%	38.0%	38.0%	31.5%
Net Income	335	327	301	272	249	234	222	193	139	123
S&P Core Earnings	335	324	293	265	245	229	219	NA	NA	NA

Balance Sheet & Other Financial Data (Million $)

	2007	2006	2005	2004	2003	2002	2001	2000	1999	1998
Cash	155	241	309	254	57.7	85.1	110	110	88.1	12.7
Current Assets	1,157	1,178	1,167	1,034	878	853	820	721	634	509
Total Assets	3,570	3,425	3,060	2,810	2,583	2,519	1,752	1,581	1,408	1,018
Current Liabilities	403	412	356	326	305	313	251	235	212	159
Long Term Debt	877	794	465	474	535	703	221	254	284	180
Common Equity	2,168	2,088	2,104	1,888	1,646	1,424	1,231	1,043	871	654
Total Capital	3,167	3,013	2,703	2,485	2,278	2,207	1,501	1,346	1,196	858
Capital Expenditures	181	157	141	113	115	170	147	161	171	97.0
Cash Flow	470	454	420	389	365	335	313	272	208	169
Current Ratio	2.9	2.9	3.3	3.2	2.9	2.7	3.3	3.1	3.0	3.2
% Long Term Debt of Capitalization	27.7	26.4	17.2	19.1	23.5	31.9	14.7	18.9	23.7	21.0
% Net Income of Revenue	9.0	9.6	9.8	44.4	9.3	10.3	10.3	10.3	7.9	10.3
% Return on Assets	9.6	10.1	10.2	10.1	9.8	11.0	13.3	12.9	10.2	13.8
% Return on Equity	15.7	15.6	15.1	15.4	16.2	17.6	19.6	20.2	17.1	21.1

Data as orig reptd.; bef. results of disc opers/spec. items. Per share data adj. for stk. divs.; EPS diluted. E-Estimated. NA-Not Available. NM-Not Meaningful. NR-Not Ranked. UR-Under Review.

Office: 6800 Cintas Boulevard, Cincinnati, OH 45262-5737.
Telephone: 513-459-1200.
Website: http://www.cintas.com
Chrmn: R.T. Farmer

Pres & CEO: S.D. Farmer
Vice Chrmn: R.J. Kohlhepp
Investor Contact: W.C. Gale (513-459-1200)
SVP & CFO: W.C. Gale

Board Members: G. S. Adolph, P. R. Carter, G. V. Dirvin, R. T. Farmer, S. D. Farmer, J. Hergenhan, R. L. Howe, R. J. Kohlhepp, D. C. Phillips

Founded: 1968
Domicile: Washington
Employees: 34,000

Circuit City Stores Inc

STANDARD &POOR'S

S&P Recommendation	BUY ★★★★☆	Price $6.51 (as of Nov 23, 2007)	12-Mo. Target Price $13.00	Investment Style Large-Cap Value

GICS Sector Consumer Discretionary
Sub-Industry Computer & Electronics Retail

Summary Circuit City is a large retailer of brand-name consumer electronics, personal computers, and entertainment software.

Key Stock Statistics (Source S&P, Vickers, company reports)

52-Wk Range	$25.52– 5.35	S&P Oper. EPS 2008**E**	-0.31	Market Capitalization(B)	$1.097	Beta	0.55
Trailing 12-Month EPS	$-0.86	S&P Oper. EPS 2009**E**	0.40	Yield (%)	2.46	S&P 3-Yr. Proj. EPS CAGR(%)	21.00
Trailing 12-Month P/E	NM	P/E on S&P Oper. EPS 2008**E**	NM	Dividend Rate/Share	$0.16	S&P Credit Rating	NA
$10K Invested 5 Yrs Ago	$7,683	Common Shares Outstg. (M)	168.5	Institutional Ownership (%)	95		

Price Performance

30-Week Mov. Avg. ··· 10-Week Mov. Avg. - - **GAAP Earnings vs. Previous Year** Volume Above Avg. STARS
12-Mo. Target Price — Relative Strength — ▲ Up ▼ Down ► No Change Below Avg.

Options: ASE, CBOE, P

Analysis prepared by **Michael Souers** on October 01, 2007, when the stock traded at **$ 7.89**.

Highlights

➤ We see a 7%-8% sales gain in FY 09 (Feb.), following our projection of a 1%-2% decline in FY 08. We believe this forecast growth will be achieved through the opening of about 60 new and relocated stores, partially offset by a low single digit comparable store sales decline. CC is also exploring options for the sale of its Canadian retail stores, which operate under the InterTan name. We think consumer electronics retailers will continue to benefit from moderately strong demand for advanced TVs, as declines in average selling prices continue to make TVs more affordable.

➤ We see a slight widening in operating margins in FY 09 following a significant estimated decline in FY 08. We think a focus on cost containment, including wage reductions, will be partially offset by increased occupancy costs and a growing shift in the product mix to lower-margin flat panel TVs, notebook PCs and next-generation video game consoles.

➤ We see FY 09 EPS of $0.40, a significant improvement from the $0.31 net loss per share we expect the company to incur in FY 08.

Investment Rationale/Risk

➤ We think CC shares are currently undervalued, following a greater than 50% decline over the past four months. CC recently traded at a FY 07 price/sales ratio of about 0.1X, well below its five-year historical average and peers. In addition, we believe that what we see as CC's strong balance sheet, with over $2 of net cash per share and book value of about $10 per share, will limit downside risk. We expect weak results over the next quarter or two due to stiff competition and macroeconomic factors, but we think CC's valuation more than offsets our negative near-term outlook. We favor CC's commitment to cut costs in a challenging environment; however, reductions in service may result in further market share losses.

➤ Risks to our recommendation and target price include an adverse shift in the economic climate and consumer confidence, and the possibility that CC will fail to achieve its strategic objectives and will be unable to meet sales growth and profitability expectations.

➤ Our 12-month target price of $13 is based on our DCF model, which assumes a weighted average cost of capital of 11.4% and a terminal growth rate of 4.0%.

Qualitative Risk Assessment

LOW	MEDIUM	HIGH

Our risk assessment reflects our view of CC's strong balance sheet, with little debt, and improving financial trends, offset by intense rivalry in the consumer electronics industry.

Quantitative Evaluations

S&P Quality Ranking B-

D	C	B-	B	B+	A-	A	A+

Relative Strength Rank WEAK

11

LOWEST = 1   HIGHEST = 99

Revenue/Earnings Data

Revenue (Million $)

	1Q	2Q	3Q	4Q	Year
2008	2,486	2,644	--	--	--
2007	2,597	2,819	3,060	3,955	12,430
2006	2,228	2,562	2,906	3,911	11,598
2005	2,067	2,345	2,493	3,469	10,472
2004	1,933	2,156	2,407	3,249	9,745
2003	2,118	2,221	2,422	3,192	9,954

Earnings Per Share ($)

2008	-0.33	-0.38	E-0.30	E0.72	E-0.31
2007	0.03	0.07	-0.12	-0.04	-0.06
2006	-0.07	0.01	0.06	0.84	0.83
2005	-0.03	-0.06	-0.03	0.43	0.31
2004	-0.14	-0.19	-0.14	0.46	Nil
2003	-0.01	-0.05	-0.10	0.36	0.20

Fiscal year ended Feb. 28. Next earnings report expected: Mid December. EPS Estimates based on S&P Operating Earnings; historical GAAP earnings are as reported.

Dividend Data (Dates: mm/dd Payment Date: mm/dd/yy)

Amount ($)	Date Decl.	Ex-Div. Date	Stk. of Record	Payment Date
0.040	12/15	12/27	12/31	01/15/07
0.040	03/15	03/28	03/31	04/16/07
0.040	06/15	06/27	06/29	07/15/07
0.040	09/17	09/26	09/28	10/15/07

Dividends have been paid since 1979. Source: Company reports.

Please read the Required Disclosures and Analyst Certification on the last page of this report.

The **McGraw-Hill** Companies

Circuit City Stores Inc

Business Summary October 01, 2007

CORPORATE OVERVIEW. This large specialty retailer of consumer electronics goods has two reportable segments: domestic (95% of FY 07 (Feb.) revenues) and international (5%). Domestically, CC sells brand-name products through Circuit City Superstores (642 as of year-end FY 07), 12 other stores and its Web site. The international segment sells private-label and brand-name consumer electronics through 509 company-owned stores, 296 dealer outlets and one Battery Plus store.

Major merchandise categories are: video (41% of FY 07 sales); information technology (26%); audio (16%); entertainment (11%); and warranty, services and other (7%). CC's services offerings include extended warranty programs, revenues from computer-related services, mobile installations, home theater installations and product repairs, net financing and revenues received from third parties for services subscriptions. With our view of increasing price deflation and the commoditization of consumer electronic goods, we expect re-

tailers such as CC to increasingly focus on growing service revenues. In addition to generating a higher margin, we think services can help companies differentiate themselves in the marketplace, as well as build brand loyalty.

In May 2004, CC acquired Ontario-based consumer electronics retailer Inter-TAN for $14 a share in cash. Also in May, CC sold its private-label credit card operation to Bank One Corp. In November 2003, the company completed the sale of its bank card operation to FleetBoston Financial. In October 2002, the CarMax vehicle retail business was separated from CC, becoming a separately traded public company, CarMax, Inc. (KMX).

Company Financials Fiscal Year Ended Feb. 28

Per Share Data ($)	2007	2006	2005	2004	2003	2002	2001	2000	1999	1998
Tangible Book Value	9.67	9.73	9.78	10.91	11.15	11.13	10.13	9.33	7.69	7.12
Cash Flow	1.00	1.74	1.09	0.96	0.95	1.78	1.53	2.33	1.41	1.11
Earnings	-0.06	0.83	0.31	Nil	0.20	0.92	0.73	1.60	0.74	0.57
S&P Core Earnings	0.43	0.81	0.32	0.01	0.08	0.80	0.63	NA	NA	NA
Dividends	0.07	0.07	0.07	0.07	0.07	0.07	0.07	0.07	0.07	0.07
Payout Ratio	NM	9%	23%	NM	35%	8%	10%	4%	9%	8%
Calendar Year	2006	2005	2004	2003	2002	2001	2000	1999	1998	1997
Prices:High	31.54	23.12	17.87	13.21	31.40	26.65	65.19	53.88	27.25	22.75
Prices:Low	18.25	13.40	8.69	3.91	6.95	9.55	8.69	23.69	14.41	14.31
P/E Ratio:High	NM	28	60	NM	NM	29	89	34	37	33
P/E Ratio:Low	NM	16	29	NM	NM	10	12	15	19	21

Income Statement Analysis (Million $)

	2007	2006	2005	2004	2003	2002	2001	2000	1999	1998
Revenue	12,430	11,598	10,472	9,745	9,954	12,791	12,959	12,614	10,804	8,871
Operating Income	268	384	247	166	163	519	462	701	399	311
Depreciation	181	164	155	198	157	151	153	148	140	116
Interest Expense	1.52	3.14	2.07	1.80	1.09	5.84	19.4	24.2	28.3	36.5
Pretax Income	20.3	239	95.8	-1.24	67.0	353	259	529	231	168
Effective Tax Rate	NM	36.8%	37.5%	NM	38.0%	38.0%	38.0%	38.0%	38.0%	38.0%
Net Income	-10.2	151	59.9	-0.79	41.6	219	161	328	143	104
S&P Core Earnings	73.2	144	61.9	0.83	16.3	166	129	NA	NA	NA

Balance Sheet & Other Financial Data (Million $)

	2007	2006	2005	2004	2003	2002	2001	2000	1999	1998
Cash	141	316	880	783	885	1,252	446	644	266	117
Current Assets	2,884	2,833	2,686	2,919	3,103	3,653	2,847	2,943	2,395	2,146
Total Assets	4,007	4,069	3,789	3,633	3,799	4,539	3,871	3,955	3,445	3,232
Current Liabilities	1,714	1,622	12,164	1,177	1,280	1,641	1,292	1,406	964	906
Long Term Debt	50.5	52.0	11.5	22.7	11.3	14.1	116	249	427	424
Common Equity	1,791	1,955	2,087	2,224	2,342	2,734	2,356	2,142	1,905	1,730
Total Capital	1,842	2,007	2,099	2,247	2,353	2,749	2,488	2,419	2,369	2,181
Capital Expenditures	286	255	269	176	151	214	286	222	367	588
Cash Flow	171	315	215	197	199	370	314	476	283	221
Current Ratio	1.7	1.7	0.2	2.5	2.4	2.2	2.2	2.1	2.5	2.4
% Long Term Debt of Capitalization	2.7	2.6	0.5	1.0	0.5	0.5	4.7	10.3	18.0	24.5
% Net Income of Revenue	NM	1.3	0.6	NM	0.4	1.7	1.2	2.6	1.3	1.2
% Return on Assets	NM	3.8	1.6	NM	1.0	5.2	4.1	8.9	4.3	3.3
% Return on Equity	NM	7.5	2.8	NM	1.6	8.6	7.1	16.2	7.9	6.2

Data as orig reptd.; bef. results of disc opers/spec. items. Per share data adj. for stk. divs.; EPS diluted. E-Estimated. NA-Not Available. NM-Not Meaningful. NR-Not Ranked. UR-Under Review.

Office: 9950 Mayland Drive, Richmond, VA 23233-1464.
Telephone: 804-527-4000.
Website: http://www.circuitcity.com
Chrmn, Pres & CEO: P.J. Schoonover

EVP & CFO: M.E. Foss
SVP, Treas & Cntlr: P.J. Dunn
SVP, Secy & General Counsel: R.D. Hedgebeth
SVP & CIO: W.E. McCorey, Jr.

Investor Contact: C. Benjamin (804-527-4033)
Board Members: R. M. Brill, C. H. Byrd, U. O. Fairbairn, B. S. Feigin, M. E. Foss, J. F. Hardymon, A. Kane, A. B. King, M. Salovaara, P. J. Schoonover, J. P. Spainhour, C. Y. Woo

Founded: 1949
Domicile: Virginia
Employees: 46,082

Cisco Systems Inc

STANDARD
&POOR'S

S&P Recommendation	HOLD ★ ★ ★ ☆ ☆	Price	12-Mo. Target Price	Investment Style
		$28.69 (as of Nov 23, 2007)	$33.00	Large-Cap Growth

GICS Sector Information Technology
Sub-Industry Communications Equipment

Summary This company offers a complete line of routers and switching products that connect and manage communications among local and wide area computer networks employing a variety of protocols.

Key Stock Statistics (Source S&P, Vickers, company reports)

52-Wk Range	$34.24–24.82	S&P Oper. EPS 2008E	1.48	Market Capitalization(B)	$174.747	Beta	1.61
Trailing 12-Month EPS	$1.26	S&P Oper. EPS 2009E	1.65	Yield (%)	Nil	S&P 3-Yr. Proj. EPS CAGR(%)	13.00
Trailing 12-Month P/E	22.8	P/E on S&P Oper. EPS 2008E	19.4	Dividend Rate/Share	Nil	S&P Credit Rating	A+
$10K Invested 5 Yrs Ago	$19,268	Common Shares Outstg. (M)	6,090.9	Institutional Ownership (%)	71		

Price Performance

30-Week Mov. Avg. ··· 10-Week Mov. Avg.-- **GAAP Earnings vs. Previous Year** Volume Above Avg. STARS
12-Mo. Target Price — Relative Strength — ▲ Up ▼ Down ► No Change Below Avg. ★

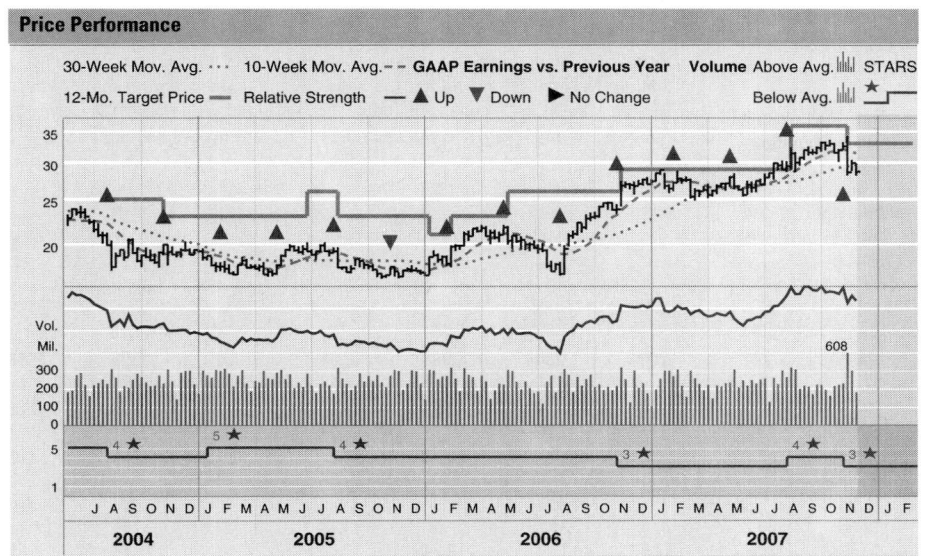

Options: ASE, CBOE, P, Ph

Analysis prepared by **Ari Bensinger** on November 12, 2007, when the stock traded at **$29.15.**

Highlights

➤ Following a 23% rise in FY 07 (Jul.), including a full fiscal year contribution from Scientific-Atlanta, which was acquired in February 2006, we project that revenues will advance 17% in FY 08. We expect the switching and routing divisions to post double digit growth. We believe the advanced technologies division could increase more than 25%, fueled by video systems and unified communications, which includes the May 2007 acquisition of WebEx.

➤ We look for the gross margin to narrow modestly, to about 65% in FY 08, primarily attributable to a less favorable sales mix that reflects strong advanced technology and emerging market growth, as well as the addition of WebEx products. Other factors affecting profitability include component costs, channel mix, and competitive pricing pressures.

➤ Reflecting anticipated higher sales volume, we see operating expenses as a percentage of sales declining moderately from the prior period. After higher interest income, we forecast FY 08 EPS of $1.48, versus the $1.25 posted in FY 07. We see $1.65 EPS in FY 09.

Investment Rationale/Risk

➤ In our view, CSCO is maintaining its dominant market position in the large network routing and switching markets, while successfully positioning itself in attractive subsegments. We view CSCO as well positioned to benefit from accelerating spend on communications infrastructure, as businesses and service providers upgrade network equipment to handle increased traffic loads.

➤ Risks to our recommendation and target price include potential market share losses as peers increasingly target CSCO's dominant share and narrowing margins due to intensifying pricing pressures.

➤ Our 12-month target price of $33 is based on a P/E of 22X our FY 08 operating EPS estimate, in line with the peer mean. Using our five-year earnings growth rate projection of 13%, our target price reflects a forward P/E-to-growth (PEG) ratio of 1.7X, in line with the industry average. Our discounted cash flow model, assuming a weighted average cost of capital of 11.9% and terminal growth of free cash flow of 3%, also indicates an intrinsic value slightly below $34.

Qualitative Risk Assessment

LOW	MEDIUM	HIGH

Our risk assessment for CSCO reflects the highly competitive nature of the industry in which it operates, balanced by our view of its strong financials, including roughly $23 billion in cash, and its dominant market position.

Quantitative Evaluations

S&P Quality Ranking B+

D	C	B-	B	B+	A-	A	A+

Relative Strength Rank MODERATE

41

LOWEST = 1   HIGHEST = 99

Revenue/Earnings Data

Revenue (Million $)

	1Q	2Q	3Q	4Q	Year
2008	9,554	--	--	--	--
2007	8,184	8,439	8,866	9,433	34,922
2006	6,550	6,628	7,322	7,984	28,484
2005	5,971	6,062	6,187	6,581	24,801
2004	5,101	5,398	5,620	5,926	22,045
2003	4,845	4,713	4,618	4,702	18,878

Earnings Per Share ($)

2008	0.35	E0.36	E0.36	E0.39	E1.48
2007	0.26	0.31	0.30	0.31	1.17
2006	0.20	0.22	0.22	0.25	0.89
2005	0.21	0.21	0.21	0.24	0.87
2004	0.15	0.18	0.17	0.20	0.70
2003	0.08	0.14	0.14	0.14	0.50

Fiscal year ended Jul. 31. Next earnings report expected: Early February. EPS Estimates based on S&P Operating Earnings; historical GAAP earnings are as reported.

Dividend Data

No cash dividends have been paid.

Cisco Systems Inc

STANDARD &POOR'S

Business Summary November 12, 2007

CORPORATE OVERVIEW. Cisco Systems, which supplies the majority of networking gear used for the Internet, is the world's largest supplier of high-performance computer internetworking systems. The company's sales strategy is primarily based on distribution channel partners, with over 40,000 reseller partner sales representatives around the world.

Product families are categorized into four segments: switches (42% of total FY 07 (Jul.) product sales), routers (23%), advanced technologies (27%), and other. There are currently eight primary advanced technology segments: home networking, unified communications, security, storage area networking, wireless technology, application networking services, hosted small business systems, and video systems (primarily digital set-top boxes and transport and access products via the acquisition of Scientific Atlanta). We estimate that the video systems, security, unified communications, home networking, and wireless sub-segments are all above or near the billion dollar level on an annual basis. Other products are comprised of primarily optical, access and network management software. The company also has a broad range of service offerings, including technical support services and advanced services.

In our view, the primary driver of company sales growth will be the advanced technologies segment. CSCO distinguishes its advanced technology sub-segments as industry segments with the potential to become billion dollar

businesses. We see the company continuing to identify additional advanced technology sub-segments.

MARKET PROFILE. With a dominant market share of approximately 70% of the overall Ethernet switching market, we believe CSCO has become the de facto choice for Ethernet switches. We view the company's large installed base as a significant competitive advantage over peers, especially in cases of modular switching solutions, where it is very difficult for competitors to displace the large modular chassis equipment. Because of its reputation and related large market share, in our opinion, Cisco products typically enjoy a price premium over the competition.

CSCO leads the overall routing market, with a more than 50% share. For core routers, which have speeds of more than 2.5 gigabits per second, CSCO and Juniper Networks dominate the market, with a combined market share of over 95%. In May 2004, Cisco introduced its new high-end core router, the Carrier Routing System-1 (CRS-1), with capacity for 1.2 terabits per second.

Company Financials Fiscal Year Ended Jul. 31

Per Share Data ($)	2007	2006	2005	2004	2003	2002	2001	2000	1999	1998
Tangible Book Value	2.76	2.07	2.74	3.16	3.35	3.33	3.07	3.14	3.57	1.14
Cash Flow	1.40	1.10	1.02	0.91	0.72	0.52	0.17	0.47	0.76	0.26
Earnings	1.17	0.89	0.87	0.70	0.50	0.25	-0.14	0.36	0.31	0.21
S&P Core Earnings	1.15	0.88	0.70	0.52	0.28	0.12	-0.37	NA	NA	NA
Dividends	Nil	Nil	Nil	Nil	Nil	Nil	Nil	Nil	Nil	Nil
Payout Ratio	Nil	Nil	Nil	Nil	Nil	Nil	Nil	Nil	Nil	Nil
Prices:High	34.24	27.96	20.25	29.39	24.60	21.84	44.50	82.00	53.59	24.44
Prices:Low	24.82	17.10	16.83	17.53	12.33	12.24	11.04	35.16	22.47	8.58
P/E Ratio:High	29	31	23	42	49	87	NM	NM	NM	NM
P/E Ratio:Low	21	19	19	25	25	49	NM	98	72	41

Income Statement Analysis (Million $)

	2007	2006	2005	2004	2003	2002	2001	2000	1999	1998
Revenue	34,922	28,484	24,801	22,045	18,878	18,915	22,293	18,928	12,154	8,459
Operating Income	10,034	8,380	8,451	7,738	6,477	4,941	2,257	4,098	3,470	2,432
Depreciation	1,413	1,293	1,009	1,443	1,591	1,957	2,236	863	486	327
Interest Expense	Nil	Nil	Nil	Nil	Nil	Nil	Nil	Nil	Nil	Nil
Pretax Income	9,461	7,633	8,036	6,992	5,013	2,710	-874	4,343	3,316	2,302
Effective Tax Rate	22.5%	26.9%	28.6%	28.9%	28.6%	30.1%	NM	38.6%	36.8%	41.4%
Net Income	7,333	5,580	5,741	4,968	3,578	1,893	-1,014	2,668	2,096	1,350
S&P Core Earnings	7,197	5,499	4,645	3,652	2,051	931	-2,641	NA	NA	NA

Balance Sheet & Other Financial Data (Million $)

	2007	2006	2005	2004	2003	2002	2001	2000	1999	1998
Cash	3,728	3,297	4,742	3,722	3,925	9,484	4,873	4,234	829	535
Current Assets	31,574	25,676	13,031	14,343	13,415	17,433	12,835	11,110	4,615	3,762
Total Assets	53,340	43,315	33,883	35,594	37,107	37,795	35,238	32,870	14,725	8,917
Current Liabilities	13,358	11,313	9,511	8,703	8,294	8,375	8,096	5,196	3,003	1,767
Long Term Debt	6,408	6,332	Nil	Nil	Nil	Nil	Nil	Nil	Nil	Nil
Common Equity	31,480	23,912	23,174	25,826	28,029	28,656	27,120	26,497	11,678	7,107
Total Capital	37,898	30,250	23,184	25,916	28,039	28,671	27,142	27,674	11,722	7,150
Capital Expenditures	1,251	772	692	613	717	2,641	2,271	1,086	584	415
Cash Flow	8,746	6,873	6,750	6,411	5,169	3,850	1,222	3,531	2,582	1,677
Current Ratio	2.4	2.3	1.4	1.6	1.6	2.1	1.6	2.1	1.5	2.1
% Long Term Debt of Capitalization	16.9	20.9	Nil	Nil	Nil	Nil	Nil	Nil	Nil	Nil
% Net Income of Revenue	21.0	19.6	23.1	22.5	19.0	10.0	NM	14.1	17.2	16.0
% Return on Assets	15.2	14.5	16.5	13.7	9.6	5.2	NM	11.2	17.7	18.8
% Return on Equity	26.5	23.7	23.4	18.4	12.6	6.8	NM	13.9	22.3	23.7

Data as orig reptd.; bef. results of disc opers/spec. items. Per share data adj. for stk. divs.; EPS diluted. E-Estimated. NA-Not Available. NM-Not Meaningful. NR-Not Ranked. UR-Under Review.

Office: 170 West Tasman Drive, San Jose, CA 95134-1706.
Telephone: 408-526-4000.
Email: investor-relations@cisco.com
Website: http://www.cisco.com

Chrmn & CEO: J.T. Chambers
EVP & CFO: D.D. Powell
SVP, Secy & General Counsel: M. Chandler
SVP & Cntlr: J. Chadwick

Investor Contact: L. Graves (408-526-6521)
Board Members: C. A. Bartz, M. M. Burns, M. D. Capellas, L. R. Carter, J. T. Chambers, B. L. Halla, J. L. Hennessy, R. M. Kovacevich, R. C. McGeary, M. K. Powell, S. M. West, J. Yang

Founded: 1984
Domicile: California
Employees: 61,535

The McGraw-Hill Companies

Citigroup Inc.

STANDARD &POOR'S

S&P Recommendation HOLD ★★★☆☆

Price
$30.32 (as of Nov 27, 2007)

12-Mo. Target Price
$43.00

Investment Style
Large-Cap Blend

GICS Sector Financials
Sub-Industry Other Diversified Financial Services

Summary This diversified financial services company provides a wide range of financial services to consumers and corporate customers in more than 100 countries and territories.

Key Stock Statistics (Source S&P, Vickers, company reports)

52-Wk Range	$57.00– 29.50	S&P Oper. EPS 2007E	2.39	Market Capitalization(B)	$151.028	Beta	0.99
Trailing 12-Month EPS	$3.72	S&P Oper. EPS 2008E	4.40	Yield (%)	7.12	S&P 3-Yr. Proj. EPS CAGR(%)	9.00
Trailing 12-Month P/E	8.2	P/E on S&P Oper. EPS 2007E	12.7	Dividend Rate/Share	$2.16	S&P Credit Rating	AA
$10K Invested 5 Yrs Ago	$9,889	Common Shares Outstg. (M)	4,981.1	Institutional Ownership (%)	66		

Price Performance

30-Week Mov. Avg. ···   10-Week Mov. Avg. - - GAAP Earnings vs. Previous Year   Volume Above Avg. STARS
12-Mo. Target Price — Relative Strength — ▲ Up ▼ Down ▶ No Change   Below Avg.

Options: ASE, CBOE, P, Ph

Analysis prepared by **Frank Braden, CFA** on November 06, 2007, when the stock traded at **$ 35.90**.

Highlights

➤ Despite the pretax writedowns of between $8 billion and $11 billion that C expects to take in the fourth quarter, its large exposure to sub-prime-related assets of about $55 billion leaves open the possibility of further writedowns if conditions worsen. While we believe the recent departure of CEO Charles Prince may placate some investors, we think uncertainty surrounding his replacement will continue to pressure the shares. We think near-term growth may suffer as C focuses on boosting capital levels instead of making acquisitions.

➤ We see revenue being bolstered by international growth and expansion in the global wealth management and transaction services businesses. We expect C's expense savings plan to remain on track, limiting growth in operating expenses in 2008.

➤ Our 2007 EPS estimate is $2.47, based on our expectation of approximately $6.5 billion of sub-prime-related writedowns, after tax, in the fourth quarter. Our 2008 EPS projection is $4.40.

Investment Rationale/Risk

➤ We see C's main focus for the rest of 2007 and the first half of 2008 on boosting capital levels and reaching its target Tier 1 capital ratio of 7.5% and tangible common equity to risk-weighted managed assets ratio of 6.5%, versus the September 30 levels of 7.3% and 5.9%, re-spectively. While we can not rule out the possi-bility of a dividend cut, especially if credit mar-kets worsen, we believe this would be a mea-sure of last resort, after the suspension of share repurchases and the sale of assets.

➤ Risks to our recommendation and target price include a severe downturn in global economic conditions, a significant rise in credit losses, failure to implement announced cost reduction initiatives, and a serious geopolitical event that could affect global capital markets.

➤ Our 12-month target price of $43 is equal to 9.8X our 2008 EPS estimate and is a discount to C's historical average, reflecting our view of a de-crease in investor confidence and uncertainty surrounding future writedowns and a new CEO.

Qualitative Risk Assessment

LOW	MEDIUM	HIGH

Our risk assessment reflects our view of C's large customer base, diversified business model, and a healthy global economy. We believe C's diversity in its geographic presence and product offerings provide protection from a local or regional downturn.

Quantitative Evaluations

S&P Quality Ranking   A+

D	C	B-	B	B+	A-	A	A+

Relative Strength Rank   WEAK

10

LOWEST = 1   HIGHEST = 99

Revenue/Earnings Data

Revenue (Million $)

	1Q	2Q	3Q	4Q	Year
2007	43,021	45,802	43,197	--	--
2006	34,290	35,899	36,323	40,046	146,558
2005	28,620	28,837	31,147	31,714	120,318
2004	25,976	27,287	26,408	28,605	108,276
2003	23,199	23,840	23,334	24,340	94,713
2002	22,654	23,601	23,505	22,796	92,556

Earnings Per Share ($)

2007	1.01	1.24	0.44	E-0.30	E2.39
2006	1.11	1.05	1.06	1.03	4.25
2005	0.98	0.91	0.97	0.98	3.82
2004	1.01	0.22	1.02	1.02	3.26
2003	0.79	0.83	0.90	0.91	3.42
2002	0.66	0.73	0.72	0.47	2.59

Fiscal year ended Dec. 31. Next earnings report expected: Late January. EPS Estimates based on S&P Operating Earnings; historical GAAP earnings are as reported.

Dividend Data (Dates: mm/dd Payment Date: mm/dd/yy)

Amount ($)	Date Decl.	Ex-Div. Date	Stk. of Record	Payment Date
0.540	01/19	02/01	02/05	02/23/07
0.540	04/16	05/03	05/07	05/25/07
0.540	07/16	08/02	08/06	08/24/07
0.540	10/15	11/01	11/05	11/21/07

Dividends have been paid since 1986. Source: Company reports.

Please read the Required Disclosures and Analyst Certification on the last page of this report.

The McGraw-Hill Companies

Citigroup Inc.

STANDARD &POOR'S

Business Summary November 06, 2007

CORPORATE OVERVIEW. Citigroup is organized into three major business groups: Global Consumer; Institutional Clients Group (comprised of Markets and Banking and Alternative Investments); and Global Wealth Management. The Citigroup Global Consumer business includes banking services, credit cards, loans and insurance. The Institutional Clients Group operates in about 100 countries and advises companies, governments and institutional investors on the best ways to realize their strategic objectives. The Global Wealth Management division at Citigroup is comprised of The Citigroup Private Bank, Smith Barney (private wealth management), and Citigroup Investment Research, and serves both private and institutional clients.

CORPORATE STRATEGY. Citigroup has five strategic initiatives: expand international distribution; increase U.S. distribution; transfer expertise; invest in technology and people; and allocate capital.

In our view, the large increase in international branches and consumer finance centers shows the growing importance C attaches to organic growth. Although we expect Citigroup to continue its international organic growth in 2007 and 2008, we anticipate that the pace will slow significantly from 2006. We believe the increased pressure on C to cut expenses will lead to lower investment spending internationally.

UPCOMING CATALYSTS. A key catalyst for C will, in our opinion, be the execution of expense savings resulting from the company's structural expense review. Former CEO Charles Prince put Robert Druskin in charge of researching strategic cost-cutting initiatives to allow C to generate positive operating leverage. The results of the cost savings plan, announced April 11, included projected expense savings of $2.1 billion in 2007, $3.7 billion in 2008, and $4.6 billion in 2009. The company took a pretax charge of $1.38 billion in the first quarter and plans to take $200 million in additional charges over the rest of 2007. Approximately $1.0 billion of the charge is related to severance packages for 17,000 job cuts. Most of the job eliminations are expected to come from back office, middle office and corporate functions, with approximately 57% from international operations. We believe management was careful not to hurt its ability to generate future revenue growth, and therefore limited the impact of the job cuts on client-facing functions.

Company Financials Fiscal Year Ended Dec. 31

Per Share Data ($)	2006	2005	2004	2003	2002	2001	2000	1999	1998	1997
Tangible Book Value	14.14	12.76	11.72	10.75	9.70	15.49	12.84	10.64	8.95	6.99
Earnings	4.25	3.82	3.26	3.42	2.59	2.75	2.62	2.12	1.22	1.27
S&P Core Earnings	4.09	3.69	4.02	3.35	2.33	2.51	NA	NA	NA	NA
Dividends	1.96	1.76	1.60	1.10	0.70	0.60	0.52	0.41	0.28	0.20
Payout Ratio	46%	46%	49%	32%	27%	22%	20%	19%	23%	16%
Prices:High	57.00	49.99	52.88	49.15	52.20	57.38	59.13	43.69	36.75	28.69
Prices:Low	44.81	42.91	42.10	30.25	24.48	34.51	35.34	24.50	14.25	14.58
P/E Ratio:High	13	13	16	14	20	21	23	21	30	23
P/E Ratio:Low	11	11	13	9	9	13	13	12	12	11

Income Statement Analysis (Million $)

	2006	2005	2004	2003	2002	2001	2000	1999	1998	1997
Premium Income	3,202	3,132	3,993	3,749	3,410	13,460	12,429	10,441	9,850	8,995
Investment Income	34,177	28,833	22,728	18,937	21,036	26,949	27,562	21,728	23,696	16,214
Other Revenue	46,925	88,353	81,555	72,027	68,110	71,613	71,835	49,836	42,885	12,400
Total Revenue	146,558	120,318	108,276	94,713	92,556	112,022	111,826	82,005	76,431	37,609
Interest Expense	56,943	36,676	22,086	17,271	21,248	31,965	36,638	24,768	27,495	11,443
% Expense/Operating Revenue	117.3%	75.5%	77.6%	72.2%	77.8%	80.5%	81.1%	80.6%	87.9%	86.7%
Pretax Income	29,639	29,433	24,182	26,333	20,537	21,897	21,143	15,948	9,269	5,012
Effective Tax Rate	27.3%	30.8%	28.6%	31.1%	34.1%	34.4%	35.6%	35.8%	34.9%	33.8%
Net Income	21,249	19,806	17,046	17,853	13,448	14,284	13,519	9,994	5,807	3,104
S&P Core Earnings	20,311	19,114	20,934	17,424	12,000	12,943	NA	NA	NA	NA

Balance Sheet & Other Financial Data (Million $)

	2006	2005	2004	2003	2002	2001	2000	1999	1998	1997
Receivables	44,445	42,823	44,056	31,053	29,714	47,528	36,237	32,677	30,905	30,939
Cash & Investment	300,105	208,970	236,799	204,041	186,839	179,352	134,743	127,284	117,509	65,867
Loans	679,192	583,503	548,829	478,006	447,805	391,933	367,022	244,206	221,958	10,816
Total Assets	1,884,318	1,494,037	1,484,101	1,264,032	1,097,190	1,051,450	902,210	716,937	668,641	386,555
Capitalization:Debt	288,494	217,499	207,910	168,759	133,079	128,756	116,698	52,012	52,991	30,597
Capitalization:Equity	118,783	111,412	108,166	96,889	85,318	79,722	64,461	47,761	40,395	19,443
Capitalization:Total	408,277	330,036	317,201	284,251	219,797	210,003	182,904	101,698	95,839	51,905
Price Times Book Value:High	4.0	3.9	4.5	4.6	5.4	3.7	4.6	4.1	4.1	4.1
Price Times Book Value:Low	3.2	3.4	3.5	2.8	2.5	2.2	2.7	2.3	1.6	2.1
% Return on Revenue	22.0	16.5	15.7	18.8	14.5	12.8	12.9	12.2	7.6	8.3
% Return on Assets	1.3	1.3	1.2	1.5	1.3	1.5	1.6	1.4	1.1	1.2
% Return on Equity	18.5	18.0	16.6	19.5	11.6	19.7	22.2	22.3	14.2	18.6
Loans/Equity	5.5	5.2	5.1	5.1	3.6	5.3	5.6	5.3	516.9	51.7

Data as orig reptd.; bef. results of disc opers/spec. items. Per share data adj. for stk. divs.; EPS diluted. E-Estimated. NA-Not Available. NM-Not Meaningful. NR-Not Ranked. UR-Under Review.

Office: 399 Park Avenue, New York, NY, USA 10043.
Telephone: 212-559-1000.
Website: http://www.citigroup.com
Chrmn: R.E. Rubin

Vice Chrmn: S.R. Volk
Vice Chrmn & Chief Admin Officer: L.B. Kaden
CEO: W. Bischoff
COO: R. Druskin

Board Members: C. M. Armstrong, A. J. Belda, G. David, K. T. Derr, J. M. Deutch, R. Hernandez Ramirez, A. N. Liveris, A. Mulcahy, R. D. Parsons, J. Rodin, R. E. Rubin, R. L. Ryan, F. A. Thomas

Founded: 1901
Domicile: Delaware
Employees: 337,000

STANDARD &POOR'S

Citizens Communications Co

S&P Recommendation	STRONG BUY ★★★★★	Price $12.64 (as of Nov 23, 2007)	12-Mo. Target Price $16.00	Investment Style Large-Cap Value

GICS Sector Telecommunication Services
Sub-Industry Integrated Telecommunication Services

Summary This company provides wireline communications services in rural areas and small and medium sized towns and cities. In March 2007, it acquired Commonwealth Telephone Enterprises, a fellow rural telecom carrier.

Key Stock Statistics (Source S&P, Vickers, company reports)

52-Wk Range	$16.05–12.42	S&P Oper. EPS 2007E	0.67	Market Capitalization(B)	$4.143	Beta	1.15
Trailing 12-Month EPS	$0.67	S&P Oper. EPS 2008E	0.69	Yield (%)	7.91	S&P 3-Yr. Proj. EPS CAGR(%)	4.00
Trailing 12-Month P/E	18.9	P/E on S&P Oper. EPS 2007E	18.9	Dividend Rate/Share	$1.00	S&P Credit Rating	BB+
$10K Invested 5 Yrs Ago	$17,172	Common Shares Outstg. (M)	327.8	Institutional Ownership (%)	73		

Price Performance

- 30-Week Mov. Avg. ···· 10-Week Mov. Avg. -- **GAAP Earnings vs. Previous Year** Volume Above Avg. STARS
- 12-Mo. Target Price — Relative Strength — ▲ Up ▼ Down ▶ No Change Below Avg.

Options: CBOE, P, Ph

Analysis prepared by **Todd Rosenbluth** on November 06, 2007, when the stock traded at **$13.12**.

Highlights

➤ We expect revenues of $2.32 billion in 2008, including $317 million from the recently acquired Commonwealth Telephone business, up from a projected $2.29 billion in 2007. On an organic basis, we project that revenues will be down 1% in 2008, as additional long-distance and DSL penetration is offset by a one-time revenue settlement in 2007 and lower access charges due to a decline in universal service support and access line weakness.

➤ We believe EBITDA margins will widen slightly -- to 56% -- in 2008, and will remain among the industry's best, as the integration of lower-margin Commonwealth commences. We see the company benefiting from work force cuts, its billing and call center conversion, and continued deployment of higher-margin calling services that should outweigh increased promotional activities.

➤ With higher depreciation and interest charges related to an acquisition, we see operating EPS of $0.67 in 2007 and $0.69 in 2008. First quarter 2007 results were helped by a one-time gain of $0.07, while there was a $0.02 one-time charge in the third quarter.

Investment Rationale/Risk

➤ CZN's relatively strong margins reflect what we see as its limited vulnerability to pricing pressures compared to national telecom peers, and its stringent cost-cutting measures. We believe that CZN can gain synergies from increasing enhanced services penetration in the CTCO region and lowering operating expenses to further support its dividend, which we view as well supported by free cash flow. We see the shares as undervalued versus peers.

➤ Risks to our recommendation and target price include a balance sheet that appears more leveraged than peers; difficulties integrating its recent acquisition; and changes to the universal service fund, from which CZN receives revenues.

➤ Our 12-month target price of $16 is based on an EV/EBITDA multiple of 7.5X, in line with rural peers. CZN's recent dividend yield of about 7.7% adds to total return potential. In the first nine months of 2007, 60% of free cash flow was paid out in dividends, a lower level than most small telecom peers, creating flexibility, in our view, to support share repurchase activity and internal investments.

Qualitative Risk Assessment

LOW	MEDIUM	HIGH

Our risk assessment for Citizens Communications reflects the rural, less competitive nature of its operations, and what we see as the strong and stable cash flow that supports its dividend policy.

Quantitative Evaluations

S&P Quality Ranking B-

D	C	B-	B	B+	A-	A	A+

Relative Strength Rank MODERATE

50

LOWEST = 1   HIGHEST = 99

Revenue/Earnings Data

Revenue (Million $)

	1Q	2Q	3Q	4Q	Year
2007	556.2	578.8	575.8	--	--
2006	506.9	506.9	507.2	504.4	2,025
2005	537.2	531.8	537.4	556.1	2,162
2004	558.5	544.1	545.4	545.0	2,193
2003	651.9	644.0	595.0	554.1	2,445
2002	679.3	662.4	668.8	658.7	2,669

Earnings Per Share ($)

	1Q	2Q	3Q	4Q	Year
2007	0.21	0.12	0.14	E0.17	E0.67
2006	0.13	0.29	0.16	0.20	0.78
2005	0.11	0.13	0.11	0.23	0.59
2004	0.15	0.08	-0.04	0.05	0.23
2003	0.22	0.12	0.04	0.05	0.42
2002	-0.16	-0.15	-2.49	-0.13	-2.93

Fiscal year ended Dec. 31. Next earnings report expected: Late February. EPS Estimates based on S&P Operating Earnings; historical GAAP earnings are as reported.

Dividend Data (Dates: mm/dd Payment Date: mm/dd/yy)

Amount ($)	Date Decl.	Ex-Div. Date	Stk. of Record	Payment Date
0.250	02/23	03/07	03/09	03/30/07
0.250	05/18	06/06	06/09	06/29/07
0.250	07/27	09/05	09/09	09/28/07
0.250	10/25	12/05	12/09	12/31/07

Dividends have been paid since 2004. Source: Company reports.

Citizens Communications Co

STANDARD &POOR'S

Business Summary November 06, 2007

CORPORATE OVERVIEW. Citizens Communications provides wireline services to rural areas and small and medium sized towns and cities in 24 states, including Arizona, California, New York and Pennsylvania, as an incumbent local exchange carrier (ILEC) for 2.5 million access lines as of September 2007, including about 400,000 acquired from Commonwealth Telephone (CTCO) in a largely cash deal in March 2007. The company also had 497,000 DSL subscribers. CZN has increased its revenues due to rising penetration of its bundle of services, including enhanced features such as caller ID, voicemail and DSL. Electric Lightwave (7% of 2005 revenues), which CZN operated to provide competitive local access services to business customers, was sold at the end of July 2006, for $247 million.

CORPORATE STRATEGY. In 2007, CZN has focused on expanding by providing rural local residential phone customers with enhanced services as well as long-distance and DSL. As of September 2007, CZN had DSL penetration of 30% of its residential access lines (20% of total lines) . In the first nine months of 2007, the company reduced operating expenses through the consolidation of call centers and by enabling some employees to work from home. In the fourth quarter of 2007, CZN plans in certain markets to offer a free computer to those who sign up for a two-year service bundle that includes broadband, in an effort to increase penetration and customer loyalty.

COMPETITIVE LANDSCAPE. We believe CZN faces challenges from cable telephony and wireless that led to its 5% access line erosion in the 12 months ended September 2007 (before acquisitions), as the lines lost were not fully offset by the organic DSL additions in the period. The company competes with cable providers such as Time Warner in its most competitive Rochester, NY, market, and Comcast in California, which began to offer telephony services in 2006, along with other cable providers in its smallest markets. At September 2007, approximately 57% of CZN's operating territory faced cable telephony competition, and this rate should increase in 2008. In 2005, CZN began a partnership with Echostar Communications to provide digital video services to CZN's wireline customers, and announced a wholesale arrangement with Verizon Wireless to allow wireline customers to receive wireless service on one phone number. We believe that in the third quarter of 2007, the average monthly revenue per access line declined 1%, to $77, due to lower penetration of broadband in the CTCO markets.

Company Financials Fiscal Year Ended Dec. 31

Per Share Data ($)	2006	2005	2004	2003	2002	2001	2000	1999	1998	1997
Tangible Book Value	NM	NM	NM	NM	NM	NM	4.09	7.36	7.27	6.93
Cash Flow	2.25	2.26	2.09	2.37	-0.24	2.08	1.30	1.45	1.22	NA
Earnings	0.78	0.59	0.23	0.42	-2.93	-0.28	-0.15	0.45	0.23	0.04
S&P Core Earnings	0.64	0.59	0.19	0.68	-2.89	-0.58	NA	NA	NA	NA
Dividends	1.00	1.00	0.50	Nil	Nil	Nil	Nil	Nil	Nil	Nil
Payout Ratio	128%	169%	NM	Nil	Nil	Nil	Nil	Nil	Nil	Nil
Prices:High	14.95	14.05	14.80	13.40	11.52	15.88	19.00	14.31	11.18	11.71
Prices:Low	11.97	12.08	11.37	8.81	2.51	8.20	12.50	7.25	6.89	7.61
P/E Ratio:High	19	24	62	32	NM	NM	NM	32	51	NM
P/E Ratio:Low	15	20	47	21	NM	NM	NM	16	31	NM

Income Statement Analysis (Million $)	2006	2005	2004	2003	2002	2001	2000	1999	1998	1997
Revenue	2,025	2,162	2,193	2,445	2,669	2,457	1,802	1,087	1,542	1,394
Operating Income	1,121	1,149	1,148	1,173	1,179	927	549	8.07	178	15.8
Depreciation	476	542	573	595	756	632	388	262	258	236
Interest Expense	336	339	379	423	478	386	194	93.2	112	114
Pretax Income	390	285	85.5	189	-1,238	-78.7	-44.0	158	73.9	23.5
Effective Tax Rate	35.0%	29.6%	15.6%	35.5%	NM	NM	NM	40.8%	25.4%	41.5%
Net Income	254	200	72.2	122	-823	-63.9	-40.1	117	59.6	16.3
S&P Core Earnings	206	201	57.7	198	-811	-164	NA	NA	NA	NA

Balance Sheet & Other Financial Data (Million $)	2006	2005	2004	2003	2002	2001	2000	1999	1998	1997
Cash	1,041	266	167	584	393	57.7	31.2	37.1	31.9	35.1
Current Assets	1,273	542	450	896	1,201	2,533	2,263	309	414	377
Total Assets	6,791	6,412	6,668	7,689	8,147	10,554	6,955	5,772	5,293	4,873
Current Liabilities	426	617	418	536	771	1,567	992	467	508	418
Long Term Debt	4,461	3,999	4,267	4,397	5,159	5,736	3,264	2,309	1,900	1,707
Common Equity	1,058	1,042	1,362	1,415	1,172	1,946	1,720	1,920	1,793	1,679
Total Capital	6,033	5,366	5,629	6,259	6,468	8,112	5,474	4,700	4,669	4,305
Capital Expenditures	269	268	276	278	469	531	537	485	483	531
Cash Flow	730	742	645	717	-67.5	568	348	380	318	252
Current Ratio	3.0	0.9	1.1	1.7	1.6	1.6	2.3	0.7	0.8	0.9
% Long Term Debt of Capitalization	73.9	74.5	75.8	70.2	79.8	70.7	59.6	49.1	52.0	50.0
% Net Income of Revenue	12.5	9.3	3.3	5.0	NM	NM	NM	10.8	3.9	1.2
% Return on Assets	3.8	3.1	1.0	1.5	NM	NM	NM	2.1	1.2	0.3
% Return on Equity	24.2	16.7	5.2	9.4	NM	NM	NM	6.5	3.4	3.4

Data as orig reptd.; bef. results of disc opers/spec. items. Per share data adj. for stk. divs.; EPS diluted. E-Estimated. NA-Not Available. NM-Not Meaningful. NR-Not Ranked. UR-Under Review.

Office: 3 High Ridge Park, Stamford, CT 06905-1337.
Telephone: 203-614-5600.
Email: citizens@cnz.com
Website: http://www.czn.net

Chrmn & CEO: M.A. Wilderrotter
COO & EVP: D.J. McCarthy
SVP & Chief Acctg Officer: R.J. Larson
SVP, Secy & General Counsel: H.E. Glassman

CFO: D.R. Shassian
Board Members: K. Q. Abernathy, L. T. Barnes, Jr., M. T. Dugan, J. B. Finard, L. Fitt, S. Harfenist, W. Kraus, H. L. Schrott, L. D. Segil, B. E. Singer, E. Tornberg, D. H. Ward, M. A. Wick, III, M. Wilderotter

Founded: 1927
Domicile: Delaware
Employees: 5,446

CIT Group Inc.

STANDARD
&POOR'S

S&P Recommendation	HOLD ★★★☆☆	Price	12-Mo. Target Price	Investment Style
		$28.46 (as of Nov 23, 2007)	$42.00	Large-Cap Value

GICS Sector Financials
Sub-Industry Specialized Finance

Summary This diversified finance company engages in vendor, equipment, commercial, consumer and structured financing as well as leasing activities.

Key Stock Statistics (Source S&P, Vickers, company reports)

52-Wk Range	$61.59– 23.05	S&P Oper. EPS 2007**E**	1.27	Market Capitalization(B)	$5.430	Beta	2.23
Trailing 12-Month EPS	$1.38	S&P Oper. EPS 2008**E**	5.75	Yield (%)	3.51	S&P 3-Yr. Proj. EPS CAGR(%)	10.00
Trailing 12-Month P/E	20.6	P/E on S&P Oper. EPS 2007**E**	22.4	Dividend Rate/Share	$1.00	S&P Credit Rating	A
$10K Invested 5 Yrs Ago	$14,640	Common Shares Outstg. (M)	190.8	Institutional Ownership (%)	91		

Price Performance

30-Week Mov. Avg. ···· 10-Week Mov. Avg.─── **GAAP Earnings vs. Previous Year** Volume Above Avg. |lil| STARS
12-Mo. Target Price── Relative Strength ─ ▲ Up ▼ Down ▶ No Change   Below Avg. |lil| ★

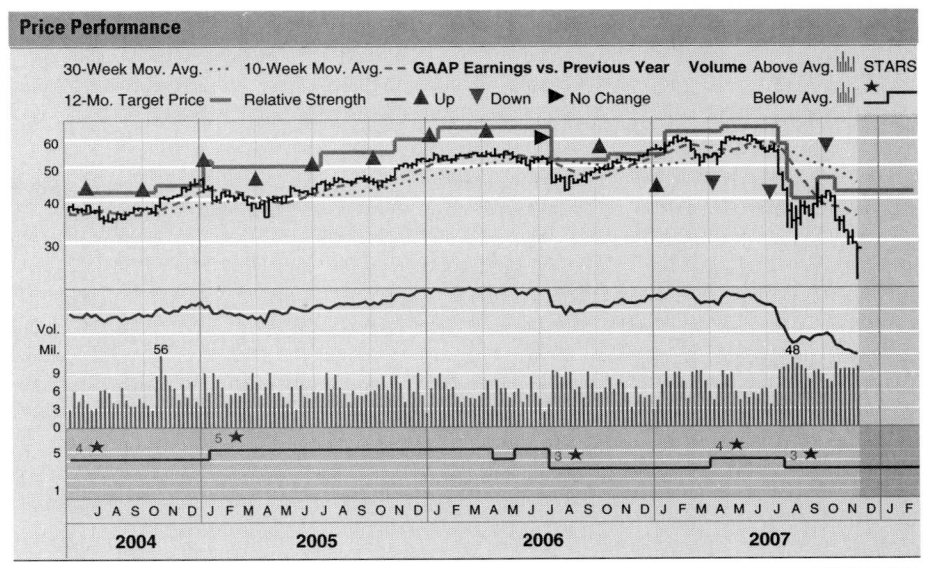

Options: ASE, CBOE, P, Ph

Analysis prepared by **Matthew Albrecht** on October 22, 2007, when the stock traded at **$ 34.44**.

Highlights

➤ CIT's managed asset base has continued to grow despite slowing origination volume, but syndication volume has declined as well, reducing some fee income. We expect the current environment to result in steady but slower growth in managed assets through 2008, but we also look for a compression of net finance revenue margins due to higher funding costs. We believe the company has done well to monetize some of its troubled mortgage portfolio, despite losses related to its writedown, and we expect long-term benefits from its decision to exit that business, which should improve its company-wide return on invested capital. We see non-spread revenues continuing to grow as a percentage of total revenues due to recent moves to expand its middle-market advisory platform through acquisitions.

➤ We expect salaries and general operating expenses to decline on a percentage basis as CIT streamlines its back office capabilities following recent acquisitions, but higher loss provisions will offset gains somewhat, and allow for only a modest pretax margin expansion in 2008.

➤ We forecast earnings of $1.27 in 2007 and $5.75 in 2008.

Investment Rationale/Risk

➤ We view CIT as well managed, with an established brand and disciplined risk management policies. Due to the recent deterioration of underlying economic indicators and growing competition in the middle-market lending space, we are increasingly concerned that future asset growth and net financing margins may be limited. We view favorably the company's efforts to exit underperforming businesses and redeploy capital in higher return businesses.

➤ Risks to our recommendation and target price include sharply higher interest rates and declining demand for commercial or consumer financing services. We think that a deterioration in credit quality in the company's target markets -- notably commercial aerospace -- represents an additional risk. Regarding corporate governance, we would prefer that CIT split the roles of chairman and CEO.

➤ The shares recently traded at about 1.2X current tangible book value, a discount to their peer average multiple. Our 12-month target price of $42 is based on a 1.5X multiple applied to 12-month projected tangible book value, a slight discount to the stock's historical average multiple.

Qualitative Risk Assessment

LOW	MEDIUM	HIGH

Our risk assessment reflects our view of the company's disciplined risk management policies and sound competitive position, offset by declining net interest margins and a deteriorating credit environment.

Quantitative Evaluations

S&P Quality Ranking   NR

D	C	B-	B	B+	A-	A	A+

Relative Strength Rank   WEAK

15

LOWEST = 1   HIGHEST = 99

Revenue/Earnings Data

Revenue (Million $)

	1Q	2Q	3Q	4Q	Year
2007	1,946	1,758	1,810	--	--
2006	1,555	1,379	1,472	500.4	6,928
2005	1,261	1,387	1,408	1,522	5,653
2004	1,134	1,149	1,180	1,219	4,676
2003	1,175	1,161	1,142	1,172	4,678
2002	1,199	1,107	1,022	--	5,275

Earnings Per Share ($)

	1Q	2Q	3Q	4Q	Year
2007	1.01	-0.70	-0.24	E1.20	E1.27
2006	1.12	1.16	1.44	1.28	5.00
2005	1.06	1.16	1.02	1.21	4.44
2004	0.88	0.82	0.86	0.95	3.50
2003	0.60	0.65	0.69	0.72	2.66
2002	0.87	-21.84	-11.33	0.64	-31.66

Fiscal year ended Dec. 31. Next earnings report expected: Mid January. EPS Estimates based on S&P Operating Earnings; historical GAAP earnings are as reported.

Dividend Data (Dates: mm/dd Payment Date: mm/dd/yy)

Amount ($)	Date Decl.	Ex-Div. Date	Stk. of Record	Payment Date
0.250	01/16	02/13	02/15	02/28/07
0.250	04/17	05/11	05/15	05/30/07
0.250	07/16	08/13	08/15	08/30/07
0.250	10/16	11/13	11/15	11/30/07

Dividends have been paid since 2002. Source: Company reports.

Please read the Required Disclosures and Analyst Certification on the last page of this report.

The *McGraw-Hill* Companies

CIT Group Inc.

STANDARD
&POOR'S

Business Summary October 22, 2007

CORPORATE OVERVIEW. CIT Group is a commercial and consumer finance company that has been providing financing and leasing products and services since 1908. The company seeks to mitigate losses and diversify risk by spreading its business around the globe, and it primarily focuses on firms in the middle-market. It concentrates its business on the manufacturing, transportation, retailing, wholesaling healthcare, communications, energy and various service-related industries, as well as the education and home mortgage lending markets.

The company sources its loans through direct marketing efforts through referral sources and other channels to borrowers, lessees, manufacturers, vendors, distributors and end users. It also buys and sells participations in syndications of finance receivables and lines of credit and may buy or sell finance receivables on a whole-loan basis. In addition, it provides collection and servicing operations. Revenue is primarily generated through interest income from loans on the balance sheet, rental fees from the equipment it leases, and

fee and other income for services. It may also syndicate and sell receivables and equipment to leverage its origination capabilities and manage its balance sheet.

CIT aims to meet customer needs through two groups of businesses, including five business segments. Its Commercial Finance Group includes corporate and transportation finance operations, and its Specialty Finance Group offers trade and vendor finance, as well as consumer and small business lending. At December 31, 2006, the company had managed assets of $74.2 billion, comprised of a loan and lease portfolio of $67.9 billion and a securitized portfolio of $6.3 billion. It also serviced more than $3 billion in third-party assets under fee-based contracts at year end.

Company Financials Fiscal Year Ended Dec. 31

Per Share Data ($)	2006	2005	2004	2003	2002	2001	2000	1999	1998	1997
Tangible Book Value	31.48	27.38	25.94	23.14	20.67	NA	NA	NA	NA	NA
Cash Flow	10.19	9.10	7.95	7.61	-25.75	NA	NA	NA	NA	NA
Earnings	5.00	4.44	3.50	2.66	-31.66	NA	NA	NA	NA	NA
S&P Core Earnings	5.00	3.80	3.42	2.58	-1.03	NA	NA	NA	NA	NA
Dividends	0.80	0.61	0.52	0.48	Nil	NA	NA	NA	NA	NA
Payout Ratio	16%	14%	15%	18%	Nil	NA	NA	NA	NA	NA
Prices:High	56.66	52.94	46.23	36.20	24.05	NA	NA	NA	NA	NA
Prices:Low	41.91	35.41	32.65	16.08	13.80	NA	NA	NA	NA	NA
P/E Ratio:High	11	12	13	14	NM	NA	NA	NA	NA	NA
P/E Ratio:Low	8	8	9	6	NM	NA	NA	NA	NA	NA

Income Statement Analysis (Million $)										
Revenue	6,928	5,653	4,676	4,678	5,275	4,548	NA	NA	NA	NA
Operating Income	4,089	3,410	3,481	3,270	2,299	2,394	NA	NA	NA	NA
Depreciation	1,024	1,001	956	1,053	1,241	1,037	NA	NA	NA	NA
Interest Expense	2,868	1,912	1,260	1,319	2,102	1,620	NA	NA	NA	NA
Pretax Income	1,412	1,417	1,237	937	-6,314	622	NA	NA	NA	NA
Effective Tax Rate	25.7%	32.8%	39.1%	38.9%	NM	45.0%	NA	NA	NA	NA
Net Income	1,046	949	754	567	-6,699	334	NA	NA	NA	NA
S&P Core Earnings	1,017	802	735	549	-200	379	NA	NA	NA	NA

Balance Sheet & Other Financial Data (Million $)										
Cash	4,458	4,811	3,438	1,974	2,274	808	NA	NA	NA	NA
Accounts Receivable	54,405	45,293	36,072	31,575	27,681	31,387	NA	NA	NA	NA
Accounts Payable	4,131	4,188	3,847	3,895	2,514	2,393	NA	NA	NA	NA
Total Assets	77,068	63,387	51,111	46,343	42,710	51,090	NA	NA	NA	NA
Long Term Debt	60,705	33,468	25,569	20,758	17,327	18,907	NA	NA	NA	NA
Lease Obligations	NA	NA	NA	NA	NA	NA	NA	NA	NA	NA
Common Equity	7,251	6,463	6,055	5,394	4,758	10,598	NA	NA	NA	NA
Total Capital	68,496	40,480	31,665	26,191	22,085	29,505	NA	NA	NA	NA
Capital Expenditures	2,860	2,359	1,489	2,096	1,877	1,451	NA	NA	NA	NA
Cash Flow	2,070	1,950	1,710	1,620	-5,458	1,371	NA	NA	NA	NA
% Long Term Debt of Capitalization	88.6	82.6	80.7	79.3	78.5	64.1	NA	NA	NA	NA
% Net Income of Revenue	18.3	16.7	16.1	12.1	NM	7.3	NA	NA	NA	NA
% Return on Assets	1.4	1.6	1.6	1.3	NM	NM	NA	NA	NA	NA
% Return on Equity	15.2	15.1	13.1	11.2	NM	NM	NA	NA	NA	NA

Data as orig reptd.; bef. results of disc opers/spec. items. Per share data adj. for stk. divs.; EPS diluted. E-Estimated. NA-Not Available. NM-Not Meaningful. NR-Not Ranked. UR-Under Review.

Office: 1 CIT Drive, Livingston, NJ 07039.
Telephone: 973-740-5000.
Email: investor.relations@cit.com
Website: http://www.citgroup.com

Chrmn & CEO: J.M. Peek
Vice Chrmn: T. Hallman
Vice Chrmn: L. Marsiello
Vice Chrmn & CFO: J.M. Leone

EVP, Chief Acctg Officer & Cntlr: W. Taylor
Investor Contact: S. Klimas (866-542-4847)
Board Members: G. C. Butler, W. M. Freeman, T. H. Kean, S. Lyne, M. M. Parrs, J. M. Peek, T. Ring, J. R. Ryan, S. Sternberg, P. J. Tobin, L. M. Van Deusen

Auditor: Pricewaterhousecoopers
Founded: 1908
Domicile: Delaware
Employees: 7,300

Citrix Systems Inc

STANDARD &POOR'S

S&P Recommendation	**STRONG BUY** ★ ★ ★ ★ ★	Price $36.69 (as of Nov 23, 2007)	12-Mo. Target Price $50.00	Investment Style Large-Cap Growth

GICS Sector Information Technology
Sub-Industry Application Software

Summary This company is a leading developer and supplier of access infrastructure software and services.

Key Stock Statistics (Source S&P, Vickers, company reports)

52-Wk Range	$43.90– 26.10	S&P Oper. EPS 2007E	1.35	Market Capitalization(B)	$6.960	Beta		2.12
Trailing 12-Month EPS	$1.10	S&P Oper. EPS 2008E	1.56	Yield (%)	Nil	S&P 3-Yr. Proj. EPS CAGR(%)		18.00
Trailing 12-Month P/E	33.4	P/E on S&P Oper. EPS 2007E	27.2	Dividend Rate/Share	Nil	S&P Credit Rating		NR
$10K Invested 5 Yrs Ago	$32,326	Common Shares Outstg. (M)	189.7	Institutional Ownership (%)	83			

Price Performance

30-Week Mov. Avg. · · · 10-Week Mov. Avg. — **GAAP Earnings vs. Previous Year** Volume Above Avg. STARS
12-Mo. Target Price — Relative Strength — ▲ Up ▼ Down ► No Change Below Avg.

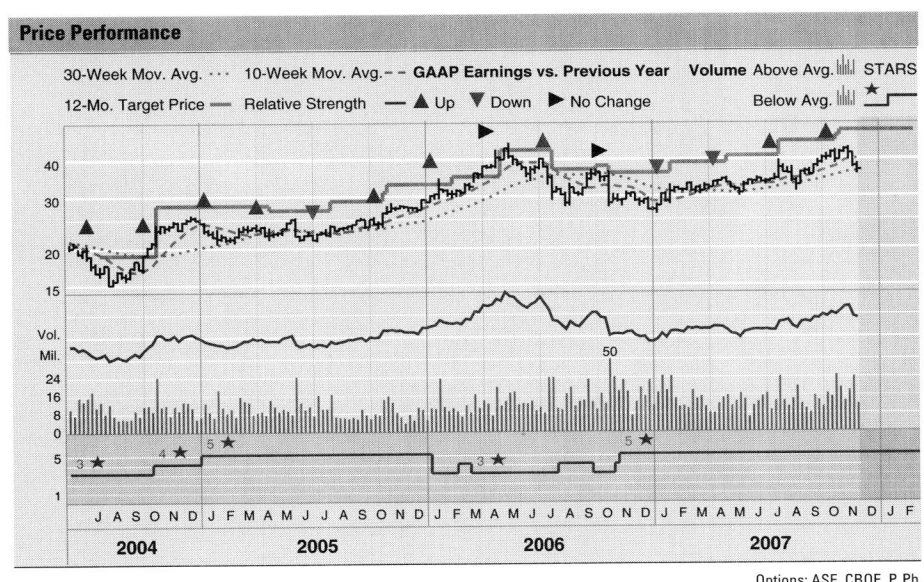

Options: ASE, CBOE, P, Ph

Analysis prepared by **Jim Yin** on October 23, 2007, when the stock traded at **$ 40.94**.

Highlights

➤ We estimate that total revenue will increase 19% in 2008, after projected 21% growth in 2007, led by online service revenue rising 27% and license update revenue climbing 19%. We see product license revenue increasing 17%, reflecting continued sales momentum of Platinum Edition of Presentation Server 4.5. We expect the acquisition of XenSource to add about $50 million of revenue in 2008.

➤ We believe the gross margin in 2008 will remain steady at 91%. We project that operating expenses will increase to 71% of revenue, from 66% in 2007, due to higher operating expenses associated with the acquisition of XenSource and higher R&D expenses. We expect non-GAAP operating margins in 2008 to decrease to 22%, from a projected 24% in 2007.

➤ Our operating EPS estimates for 2007 and 2008 are $1.35 and $1.56, respectively, compared to operating EPS of $1.15 in 2006. The projected increase in earnings reflects higher revenues, partially offset by the earnings dilution of the XenSource acquisition and increased spending in developing new products.

Investment Rationale/Risk

➤ Our strong buy recommendation reflects our view of CTXS's leadership position in the areas of computing mobility and virtualization. The company's main product enhances data security and reduces the costs of managing separate applications on every user's desktop. We also are positive on the acquisition of XenSource, which expands CTXS's growth opportunity to include the server virtualization market.

➤ Risks to our recommendation and target price include slowing demand for the company's offerings due to a slowdown in the global economy, and increased competition in the virtualization market.

➤ Our 12-month target price of $50 is based on a blend of our discounted cash flow (DCF) and P/E analyses. Our DCF model assumes a 12% weighted average cost of capital and 3% terminal growth, yielding an intrinsic value of $46. For our P/E analysis, we derive a value of $53, based on an industry average P/E-to-growth ratio of 1.8X, or 34X our 2008 EPS estimate of $1.56.

Qualitative Risk Assessment

LOW	**MEDIUM**	HIGH

Our risk assessment reflects the competitive nature of the enterprise software market, partially offset by the company's steady cash flow from operations and large cash position.

Quantitative Evaluations

S&P Quality Ranking B+

D	C	B-	B	**B+**	A-	A	A+

Relative Strength Rank MODERATE
45
LOWEST = 1   HIGHEST = 99

Revenue/Earnings Data

Revenue (Million $)

	1Q	2Q	3Q	4Q	Year
2007	308.1	334.4	349.9	--	--
2006	260.0	275.5	277.9	321.0	1,134
2005	201.9	211.2	227.0	268.7	908.7
2004	161.3	178.3	187.6	214.0	741.2
2003	143.5	143.1	144.3	157.7	588.6
2002	142.3	117.5	118.9	148.8	527.5

Earnings Per Share ($)

2007	0.20	0.29	0.33	E0.36	E1.35
2006	0.22	0.23	0.23	0.29	0.97
2005	0.22	0.16	0.23	0.32	0.93
2004	0.05	0.18	0.22	0.30	0.75
2003	0.18	0.17	0.18	0.21	0.74
2002	0.14	0.06	0.10	0.23	0.52

Fiscal year ended Dec. 31. Next earnings report expected: Late January. EPS Estimates based on S&P Operating Earnings; historical GAAP earnings are as reported.

Dividend Data

No cash dividends have been paid.

Please read the Required Disclosures and Analyst Certification on the last page of this report.

The McGraw-Hill Companies

Citrix Systems Inc

STANDARD &POOR'S

Business Summary October 23, 2007

CORPORATE OVERVIEW. Citrix Systems designs, develops and markets technology solutions that enable users to access applications and files on-demand with a higher performance and level of security. CTXS's solutions help people conduct business in remote and mobile locations as they move from location to location, use multiple devices, and connect with a wide range of heterogeneous applications over wired, wireless and Internet networks.

CTXS offers solutions for individual consumers and professionals, small businesses, and enterprises. Key products for the enterprises include: Presentation Server, an application virtualization solution that runs the business logic of applications on a central server and displays the video on the users' computers, and by keeping applications under a centralized control, improves data security and reduces the costs of managing many different applications on every user's desktop; and NetScaler applications, a suite of applications that optimize the performance of a network by balancing the load and providing firewall protection.

CTXS also provides Web-based access and collaboration software and ser-

vices that are targeted for individuals and small businesses. GoToMyPC allows users to remotely access PCs via the Internet. GoToMeeting enables online meetings, training sessions and collaborative gatherings. Small business offerings consist of Citrix Access Essentials, Citrix Access Gateway, and Citrix GoToMeeting Corporate. GoToAssist is an online solution that enables businesses to provide customer support over the Internet. GoToWebinar helps organizations conduct online events, such as large marketing events.

CTXS has a technology collaboration agreement with Microsoft to further enhance the overall functionality of Windows Terminal Server. As a result, CTXS and Microsoft entered into patent cross license and source code licensing agreements related to Microsoft's operating systems. The technology collaboration agreement expires in December 2009.

Company Financials Fiscal Year Ended Dec. 31

Per Share Data ($)	2006	2005	2004	2003	2002	2001	2000	1999	1998	1997
Tangible Book Value	NA	2.68	2.80	3.24	2.57	2.48	2.94	2.59	2.92	1.19
Cash Flow	NA	1.06	0.95	0.94	0.75	0.95	0.72	0.75	0.84	0.25
Earnings	0.97	0.93	0.75	0.74	0.52	0.54	0.47	0.61	0.34	0.24
S&P Core Earnings	0.97	0.74	0.48	0.23	-0.34	-0.19	NA	NA	NA	NA
Dividends	Nil	Nil	Nil	Nil	Nil	Nil	Nil	Nil	Nil	Nil
Payout Ratio	Nil	Nil	Nil	Nil	Nil	Nil	Nil	Nil	Nil	Nil
Prices:High	45.50	29.46	26.00	27.86	24.70	37.19	122.31	65.00	24.44	14.08
Prices:Low	26.62	20.70	15.02	10.48	4.70	16.88	14.25	13.25	9.09	1.63
P/E Ratio:High	47	32	35	38	47	69	NM	NM	73	59
P/E Ratio:Low	27	22	20	14	9	31	NM	NM	27	7

Income Statement Analysis (Million $)										
Revenue	NA	909	741	589	527	592	471	403	249	124
Operating Income	NA	233	212	189	145	216	172	201	119	60.4
Depreciation	NA	22.0	33.6	34.3	41.4	79.6	50.2	27.6	15.2	1.71
Interest Expense	NA	2.23	4.37	18.3	18.2	20.6	17.0	12.6	Nil	NA
Pretax Income	NA	226	164	161	113	153	135	183	95.5	64.6
Effective Tax Rate	NA	26.2%	20.0%	21.0%	17.0%	31.0%	30.0%	36.0%	36.0%	36.0%
Net Income	NA	166	132	127	93.9	105	94.5	117	61.1	41.4
S&P Core Earnings	183	131	83.5	39.3	-60.5	-36.2	NA	NA	NA	NA

Balance Sheet & Other Financial Data (Million $)										
Cash	NA	484	73.5	359	143	140	375	216	128	140
Current Assets	NA	726	427	809	375	346	587	570	244	258
Total Assets	NA	1,682	1,286	1,345	1,162	1,208	1,113	1,038	431	283
Current Liabilities	NA	426	342	626	189	193	159	137	85.1	35.4
Long Term Debt	NA	31.0	Nil	Nil	334	346	330	314	Nil	Nil
Common Equity	NA	1,203	925	707	622	647	593	533	297	197
Total Capital	NA	1,234	925	707	955	994	923	847	297	197
Capital Expenditures	NA	26.4	24.4	11.1	19.1	60.6	43.5	26.3	11.4	6.10
Cash Flow	NA	188	165	161	135	185	145	145	76.3	43.1
Current Ratio	NA	1.7	1.2	1.3	2.0	1.8	3.7	4.2	2.9	7.3
% Long Term Debt of Capitalization	NA	2.5	Nil	Nil	34.9	34.8	35.8	37.1	Nil	Nil
% Net Income of Revenue	NA	18.3	17.7	21.6	17.8	17.8	10.0	29.0	24.6	33.4
% Return on Assets	NA	11.2	10.0	10.1	7.9	9.1	8.8	15.9	17.1	19.1
% Return on Equity	NA	15.6	16.1	19.1	14.6	17.0	16.8	28.2	24.7	24.4

Data as orig reptd.; bef. results of disc opers/spec. items. Per share data adj. for stk. divs.; EPS diluted. E-Estimated. NA-Not Available. NM-Not Meaningful. NR-Not Ranked. UR-Under Review.

Office: 851 West Cypress Creek Road, Fort Lauderdale, FL 33309.
Telephone: 954-267-3000.
Email: investor@citrix.com
Website: http://www.citrix.com

Chrmn: T.F. Bogan
Pres & CEO: M.B. Templeton
SVP & CFO: D.J. Henshall
SVP, Secy & General Counsel: D.R. Friedman

Investor Contact: E. Fleites (954-267-3000)
Board Members: T. F. Bogan, M. J. Demo, S. M. Dow, A. Hirji, G. Morin, G. R. Sullivan, M. B. Templeton

Founded: 1989
Domicile: Delaware
Employees: 3,742

STANDARD &POOR'S

Clear Channel Communications Inc.

S&P Recommendation **HOLD** ★★★☆☆	Price $33.68 (as of Nov 23, 2007)	12-Mo. Target Price $40.00	Investment Style Large-Cap Blend

GICS Sector Consumer Discretionary
Sub-Industry Broadcasting & Cable TV

Summary This company, the largest U.S. radio operator, has agreed to be acquired by a private equity group for $39.20 a share in cash.

Key Stock Statistics (Source S&P, Vickers, company reports)

52-Wk Range	$38.58– 32.02	S&P Oper. EPS 2007**E**	1.54	Market Capitalization(B)	$16.770	Beta	1.30
Trailing 12-Month EPS	$1.68	S&P Oper. EPS 2008**E**	1.59	Yield (%)	2.23	S&P 3-Yr. Proj. EPS CAGR(%)	9.00
Trailing 12-Month P/E	20.1	P/E on S&P Oper. EPS 2007**E**	21.9	Dividend Rate/Share	$0.75	S&P Credit Rating	B+
$10K Invested 5 Yrs Ago	$9,137	Common Shares Outstg. (M)	497.9	Institutional Ownership (%)	79		

Price Performance

30-Week Mov. Avg. ··· 10-Week Mov. Avg. - - **GAAP Earnings vs. Previous Year** Volume Above Avg. STARS
12-Mo. Target Price — Relative Strength — ▲ Up ▼ Down ▶ No Change Below Avg. ★

[Chart spanning 2004–2007 with price and volume data]

Options: ASE, CBOE, P, Ph

Analysis prepared by **Tuna N. Amobi, CFA, CPA** on November 20, 2007, when the stock traded at **$ 33.90**.

Highlights

➤ Excluding certain discontinued TV and radio businesses, we see total revenues up about 6% in 2008, after a projected 5% growth in 2007, mainly driven by the 90%-owned Clear Channel Outdoor (CCU: hold; $27), where we see increased pricing for bulletins and airport displays at the domestic division, as well as increased pricing and occupancies for billboards, street furniture and transit at the international unit (on constant currency). We project radio revenues essentially flat to down slightly, as modest gains in rates are offset by reduced minutes sold.

➤ We see overall margins benefiting from a continued strong operating leverage at the outdoor division. Consistent with management's long-term target, we project radio expense growth of 3.0%-3.5% per year (including spending on new media initiatives).

➤ From a projected $2.3 billion in 2007, we see consolidated EBITDA rising to over $2.5 billion in 2008. After interest expense, we see EPS of $1.54 in 2007 and $1.59 in 2008. Pending a private buyout, CCU had suspended share repurchases under a $1 billion program.

Investment Rationale/Risk

➤ In late September, CCU shareholders voted for a pending private buyout at $39.20 a share in cash, in a deal under which unaffiliated holders may swap some of their stake on 1-for-1 basis for stub equity in the new company. With the vote removing a potential major hurdle, we believe the transaction will be consummated by the end of the first quarter of 2008, subject to regulatory approvals. Meanwhile, in early November, CCU reported what we saw as in-line third quarter results, paced by the outdoor business, which the company said was trending up 9% for the fourth quarter, with the radio division down 5%.

➤ Risks to our recommendation and target price include uncertainties with the pending buyout due to a tightened credit market, a sluggish radio advertising environment, and a sharp slowdown in outdoor advertising.

➤ Our 12-month target price of $40 reflects the terms of the pending buyout, with a modest premium to peers on relative enterprise value to EBITDA. We note the deal would trigger additional per share consideration if the closing occurs later than December 31, 2007.

Qualitative Risk Assessment

LOW	**MEDIUM**	HIGH

Amid a pending private buyout of the company, our risk assessment reflects continued challenges with the radio advertising environment, offset by the company's leading radio market share, a rebounding outdoor business, and our view of ample financial flexibility.

Quantitative Evaluations

S&P Quality Ranking B

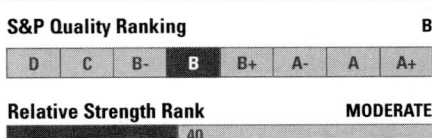

D	C	B-	**B**	B+	A-	A	A+

Relative Strength Rank MODERATE

40

LOWEST = 1 HIGHEST = 99

Revenue/Earnings Data

Revenue (Million $)

	1Q	2Q	3Q	4Q	Year
2007	1,608	1,778	1,727	--	--
2006	1,497	1,842	1,787	1,941	7,067
2005	1,448	1,723	1,683	1,757	6,610
2004	1,970	2,485	2,649	2,315	9,419
2003	1,779	2,317	2,544	2,290	8,931
2002	1,698	2,173	2,340	2,210	8,421

Earnings Per Share ($)

	1Q	2Q	3Q	4Q	Year
2007	0.20	0.42	0.52	E0.43	E1.54
2006	0.19	0.39	0.38	0.43	1.37
2005	0.12	0.39	0.32	0.34	1.16
2004	0.19	0.41	0.44	0.37	1.41
2003	0.12	0.41	1.03	0.30	1.85
2002	0.15	0.39	0.34	0.30	1.18

Fiscal year ended Dec. 31. Next earnings report expected: Early January. EPS Estimates based on S&P Operating Earnings; historical GAAP earnings are as reported.

Dividend Data (Dates: mm/dd Payment Date: mm/dd/yy)

Amount ($)	Date Decl.	Ex-Div. Date	Stk. of Record	Payment Date
0.188	10/25	12/27	12/31	01/15/07
0.188	02/21	03/28	03/31	04/15/07
0.188	04/19	06/27	06/30	07/15/07
0.188	07/27	09/26	09/30	10/15/07

Dividends have been paid since 2003. Source: Company reports.

Please read the Required Disclosures and Analyst Certification on the last page of this report.

The **McGraw-Hill** Companies

Clear Channel Communications Inc.

STANDARD &POOR'S

Business Summary November 20, 2007

CORPORATE OVERVIEW. Clear Channel Communications is the nation's leading radio operator, with nearly 1,200 radio stations (many in the top markets) and a national radio network. The company also owns 90% of Clear Channel Outdoor (CCO: hold, $27), a leading global outdoor advertising company with nearly 900,000 displays worldwide. Its other interests include 41 TV stations and Katz Media, a media representation firm. In November 2005, CCU completed an IPO of 10% of its outdoor business, and in December 2005, spun off its live entertainment assets to create Live Nation (LYV: sell, $16.

CORPORATE STRATEGY. In December 2004, in a move to stimulate demand and improve inventory pricing, CCU's radio division launched a major compa-

nywide initiative dubbed Less Is More (LIM). The program entailed a lower ceiling on commercial minutes played per hour, and another ceiling on the length and number of units in any given commercial break (with some variations by station, format and time of day). LIM has resulted in a 20% reduction in commercial and promotional minutes, as local managers sell fewer of the traditional 60-second spot lengths, and more of the newly created 30s, 15s, and premium spots.

Company Financials Fiscal Year Ended Dec. 31

Per Share Data ($)	2006	2005	2004	2003	2002	2001	2000	1999	1998	1997
Tangible Book Value	NM	NM	NM	NM	NM	NM	NM	NM	0.35	NM
Cash Flow	2.68	2.35	2.57	2.93	2.19	2.40	2.82	2.49	1.44	0.97
Earnings	1.37	1.16	1.41	1.85	1.18	-1.93	0.57	0.26	0.22	0.34
S&P Core Earnings	1.27	1.06	1.21	1.06	1.04	-2.00	NA	NA	NA	NA
Dividends	0.75	0.69	0.45	0.20	Nil	Nil	Nil	Nil	Nil	Nil
Payout Ratio	55%	59%	32%	11%	Nil	Nil	Nil	Nil	Nil	Nil
Prices:High	35.88	35.07	47.76	47.48	54.90	68.08	95.50	91.50	62.31	39.94
Prices:Low	27.17	28.75	29.96	31.00	20.00	35.20	43.87	52.00	31.00	16.81
P/E Ratio:High	26	30	34	26	47	NM	NM	NM	NM	NM
P/E Ratio:Low	20	25	21	17	17	NM	NM	NM	NM	NM

Income Statement Analysis (Million $)

	2006	2005	2004	2003	2002	2001	2000	1999	1998	1997
Revenue	7,067	6,610	9,419	8,931	8,421	7,970	5,345	2,678	1,351	697
Operating Income	2,246	2,053	2,368	2,263	2,186	1,899	1,722	976	546	282
Depreciation	634	630	694	671	621	2,562	1,401	722	305	114
Interest Expense	484	443	368	388	433	560	383	192	136	75.1
Pretax Income	1,222	1,079	1,364	1,925	1,218	-1,249	714	236	126	111
Effective Tax Rate	41.0%	39.5%	38.0%	40.5%	40.5%	NM	65.1%	63.8%	57.2%	42.6%
Net Income	689	635	846	1,146	725	-1,144	249	85.7	54.0	63.6
S&P Core Earnings	636	581	724	653	635	-1,181	NA	NA	NA	NA

Balance Sheet & Other Financial Data (Million $)

	2006	2005	2004	2003	2002	2001	2000	1999	1998	1997
Cash	114	82.8	210	123	170	159	825	81.1	36.5	24.7
Current Assets	2,206	2,248	2,270	2,186	2,123	1,941	2,343	925	410	199
Total Assets	18,890	18,703	19,928	28,353	27,672	47,603	50,056	16,822	7,540	3,456
Current Liabilities	1,664	2,107	2,185	1,893	3,011	2,960	2,129	686	258	86.9
Long Term Debt	7,395	6,275	6,963	7,075	7,382	7,968	1,597	4,584	2,324	1,540
Common Equity	8,042	8,826	9,488	15,554	14,210	29,736	30,347	10,084	4,483	1,747
Total Capital	16,528	15,920	16,756	25,736	24,109	44,269	38,777	15,987	7,206	3,318
Capital Expenditures	350	328	357	378	549	598	496	239	142	31.0
Cash Flow	1,323	1,266	1,540	1,817	1,346	1,418	1,650	808	359	178
Current Ratio	1.3	1.1	1.0	1.2	0.7	0.7	1.1	1.3	1.6	2.3
% Long Term Debt of Capitalization	44.7	39.4	41.6	27.5	30.6	18.0	4.1	28.7	32.2	46.4
% Net Income of Revenue	9.7	9.6	9.0	12.8	8.6	NM	4.7	3.2	4.0	9.1
% Return on Assets	3.7	3.3	3.5	4.1	1.9	NM	0.7	0.7	1.0	2.7
% Return on Equity	8.2	6.9	6.8	7.7	3.3	NM	1.2	1.2	1.7	5.6

Data as orig reptd.; bef. results of disc opers/spec. items. Per share data adj. for stk. divs.; EPS diluted. E-Estimated. NA-Not Available. NM-Not Meaningful. NR-Not Ranked. UR-Under Review.

Office: 200 East Basse Road, San Antonio, TX 78209-8328.
Telephone: 210-822-2828.
Website: http://www.clearchannel.com
Chrmn: L.L. Mays

Pres & CFO: R.T. Mays
CEO: M.P. Mays
EVP, Secy & Chief Lgl Officer: A. Levin
SVP & Chief Acctg Officer: H.W. Hill, Jr.

Investor Contact: R. Palmer (210-822-2828)
Board Members: A. D. Feld, P. J. Lewis, L. L. Mays, M. P. Mays, R. T. Mays, B. J. McCombs, P. Riggins, T. H. Strauss, J. C. Watts, J. H. Williams, J. B. Zachry

Founded: 1974
Domicile: Texas
Employees: 30,900

The McGraw-Hill Companies

Clorox Co (The)

STANDARD &POOR'S

S&P Recommendation	HOLD ★★★☆☆	Price	12-Mo. Target Price	Investment Style
		$65.17 (as of Nov 23, 2007)	$68.00	Large-Cap Growth

GICS Sector Consumer Staples
Sub-Industry Household Products

Summary This company is a diversified producer of household cleaning, grocery, and specialty food products.

Key Stock Statistics (Source S&P, Vickers, company reports)

52-Wk Range	$69.36–56.22	S&P Oper. EPS 2008E	3.41	Market Capitalization(B)	$9.018	Beta	0.25
Trailing 12-Month EPS	$3.29	S&P Oper. EPS 2009E	NA	Yield (%)	2.46	S&P 3-Yr. Proj. EPS CAGR(%)	9.00
Trailing 12-Month P/E	19.8	P/E on S&P Oper. EPS 2008E	19.1	Dividend Rate/Share	$1.60	S&P Credit Rating	BBB+
$10K Invested 5 Yrs Ago	$16,097	Common Shares Outstg. (M)	138.4	Institutional Ownership (%)	77		

Price Performance

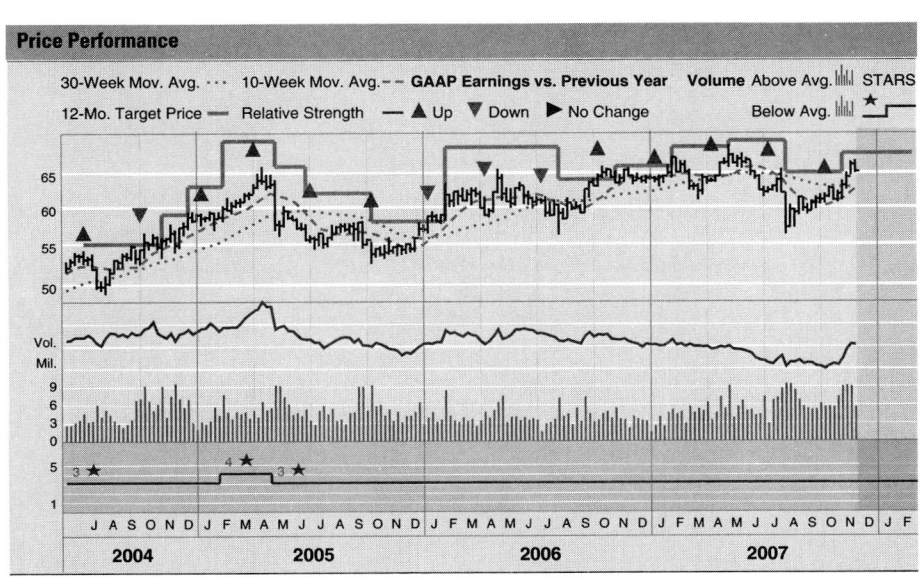

30-Week Mov. Avg. · · · 10-Week Mov. Avg. – – GAAP Earnings vs. Previous Year   Volume Above Avg. ▮▮▮ STARS
12-Mo. Target Price — Relative Strength — ▲ Up ▼ Down ► No Change   Below Avg. ▮▮▮ ★

Options: ASE, CBOE, P, Ph

Analysis prepared by **Loran Braverman, CFA** on November 01, 2007, when the stock traded at **$ 62.57**.

Highlights

➤ We expect sales to increase 4.5% in FY 08 (Jun.), reflecting modest volume growth driven by new product introductions across most business segments, price increases, and the acquisition of bleach businesses in Canada and five Latin American countries. Our estimates include no contribution or effect from the potential acquisition of Burt's Bees, a natural personal care products company, which management expects to close (subject to approvals) by the end of calendar 2007.

➤ We believe operating margins will widen to 18.5% in FY 08, from 17.9% in FY 07, with price hikes and cost saving programs more than offsetting higher commodity costs. Management expects higher than previously anticipated pressure in FY 08 from agricultural commodities and resin. We see increases of 70 basis points (bps) in restructuring charges and 40 bps in interest expense as a percentage of sales.

➤ We see FY 08 EPS increasing to $3.41, from FY 07's $3.23. Our FY 08 estimate includes $0.24 for consolidation and write-down charges versus FY 07's $0.09 from transitional and restructuring costs associated with CLX's information technology services outsourcing agreement.

Investment Rationale/Risk

➤ In recent years, CLX's performance has been positive but erratic, in our view, due to the seasonal nature of some businesses and the diverse categories in which the company operates. We also believe the timing of new product introductions adds to volatility. However, we think the level of CLX's product innovation is respectable and bolsters the company's pricing power and competitive stance. We view the potential acquisition of Burt's Bees positively and estimate that it could be accretive to EPS starting in FY 09, excluding one-time costs.

➤ Risks to our recommendation and target price include increased competition and promotional activity that would affect profitability, low consumer acceptance of new products, unfavorable foreign exchange, and potential challenges in the implementation of new enterprise resource planning system software.

➤ Our 12-month target price of $68 is a blend of our historical and relative analyses. Our historical analysis uses a modest discount to the 10-year historical median P/E applied to our calendar 2008 EPS estimate of $3.67, implying a $71 value. Our relative analysis uses an average peer P/E multiple to arrive at a value of $66.

Qualitative Risk Assessment

LOW	MEDIUM	HIGH

Our risk assessment reflects our view of stable demand for household and personal care products, which is generally not affected by changes in the economy or by geopolitical factors.

Quantitative Evaluations

S&P Quality Ranking A

D	C	B-	B	B+	A-	A	A+

Relative Strength Rank STRONG

88

LOWEST = 1   HIGHEST = 99

Revenue/Earnings Data

Revenue (Million $)

	1Q	2Q	3Q	4Q	Year
2008	1,239	--	--	--	--
2007	1,161	1,101	1,241	1,344	4,847
2006	1,104	1,064	1,157	1,319	4,644
2005	1,048	1,000	1,086	1,254	4,388
2004	1,048	947.0	1,086	1,243	4,324
2003	1,047	926.0	1,019	1,152	4,144

Earnings Per Share ($)

2008	0.76	E0.58	E0.91	E1.16	E3.41
2007	0.73	0.59	0.84	1.07	3.23
2006	0.70	0.55	0.72	0.92	2.89
2005	0.50	0.72	0.75	1.00	2.88
2004	0.60	0.52	0.59	0.83	2.55
2003	0.71	0.39	0.51	0.72	2.33

Fiscal year ended Jun. 30. Next earnings report expected: Early February. EPS Estimates based on S&P Operating Earnings; historical GAAP earnings are as reported.

Dividend Data (Dates: mm/dd Payment Date: mm/dd/yy)

Amount ($)	Date Decl.	Ex-Div. Date	Stk. of Record	Payment Date
0.310	02/06	04/25	04/27	05/15/07
0.400	05/24	07/25	07/27	08/15/07
0.400	09/19	10/29	10/31	11/15/07
0.400	11/13	01/24	01/28	02/15/08

Dividends have been paid since 1968. Source: Company reports.

The McGraw-Hill Companies

Clorox Co (The)

**STANDARD
&POOR'S**

Business Summary November 01, 2007

CORPORATE OVERVIEW. Following its divestiture from The Procter & Gamble Company in 1969 through its January 1999 acquisition of First Brands, Clorox has grown into a company with approximately $4.8 billion in annual sales, by focusing on building big-share brands in mid-sized categories. In November 2004, CLX completed the exchange of its ownership interest in a subsidiary for approximately 61.4 million of its shares held by Henkel KGaA, which represented about 29% of CLX's outstanding common stock prior to the exchange. The subsidiary transferred to Henkel contained CLX's existing insecticides and Soft Scrub cleaner businesses, its 20% interest in the Henkel Iberica, S.A. joint venture, and approximately $2.1 billion in cash.

Clorox has three segments for reporting purposes: the Household Group - North America (44% of FY 07 (Jun.) sales and 50% of segmental profits); Specialty Group (41% and 40%); and International (15% and 10%). In FY 07, Wal-Mart Stores and its affiliated companies accounted for 26% of consolidated net sales.

The company's Household Group - North America segment includes bleach

and cleaning products, water filtration systems and filters, professional cleaning products for institutional, janitorial, healthcare and food-service markets, and auto-care products. The Specialty Group segment includes plastic bags, wraps and containers under the Glad brand, cat litter products, dressings and sauces, and charcoal products. Its International segment includes operations in the Asia-Pacific and Latin America regions, selling similar products as those in North America. CLX's major brands include: Clorox, Formula 409, Liquid-Plumr, Pine-Sol, Tilex, S.O.S., Brita, Hidden Valley Ranch, Glad, Kingsford, Armor All, and STP. In FY 07, Clorox liquid bleach represented 12% of sales and Glad trash bags 14%.

CLX owns and operates 24 manufacturing facilities in the U.S. The company also owns and operates 22 manufacturing facilities internationally. CLX leases seven distribution centers located in the U.S. and Canada.

Company Financials Fiscal Year Ended Jun. 30

Per Share Data ($)	2007	2006	2005	2004	2003	2002	2001	2000	1999	1998
Tangible Book Value	NM	NM	NM	0.77	NM	0.24	1.38	1.10	0.31	NM
Cash Flow	4.47	4.12	3.95	3.47	3.19	2.18	2.30	2.48	1.87	2.27
Earnings	3.23	2.89	2.88	2.55	2.33	1.37	1.36	1.64	1.03	1.41
S&P Core Earnings	3.26	2.94	2.73	2.43	2.26	1.63	1.11	NA	NA	NA
Dividends	1.20	1.14	1.10	1.08	0.88	0.84	0.84	0.61	0.76	0.64
Payout Ratio	37%	39%	38%	42%	38%	61%	62%	37%	74%	45%
Prices:High	69.36	66.00	66.04	59.45	49.16	47.95	40.85	56.38	66.47	58.75
Prices:Low	56.22	56.17	52.50	46.50	37.40	31.92	29.95	28.38	37.50	37.19
P/E Ratio:High	21	23	23	23	21	35	30	34	65	42
P/E Ratio:Low	17	19	18	18	16	23	22	17	36	26

Income Statement Analysis (Million $)

	2007	2006	2005	2004	2003	2002	2001	2000	1999	1998
Revenue	4,847	4,644	4,388	4,324	4,144	4,061	3,903	4,083	4,003	2,741
Operating Income	1,059	967	1,011	1,069	1,046	942	895	981	933	676
Depreciation	192	188	190	197	191	190	225	201	202	137
Interest Expense	113	127	79.0	30.0	28.0	39.0	88.0	98.0	97.0	69.7
Pretax Income	743	653	731	840	802	498	487	622	430	472
Effective Tax Rate	33.2%	32.2%	29.3%	35.0%	35.9%	35.3%	33.3%	36.7%	42.8%	36.9%
Net Income	496	443	517	546	514	322	325	394	246	298
S&P Core Earnings	501	450	489	521	496	383	266	NA	NA	NA

Balance Sheet & Other Financial Data (Million $)

	2007	2006	2005	2004	2003	2002	2001	2000	1999	1998
Cash	182	192	293	232	172	177	251	245	132	89.7
Current Assets	1,032	1,007	1,090	1,043	951	1,002	1,103	1,454	1,116	799
Total Assets	3,666	3,616	3,617	3,834	3,652	3,630	3,995	4,353	4,132	3,030
Current Liabilities	1,427	1,130	1,348	1,268	1,451	1,225	1,069	1,541	1,368	1,225
Long Term Debt	1,462	1,966	2,122	475	495	678	685	590	702	316
Common Equity	171	-156	-553	1,540	1,215	1,354	1,900	1,794	1,178	1,085
Total Capital	1,723	1,939	1,651	2,189	1,825	2,174	2,732	2,608	2,117	1,401
Capital Expenditures	147	180	151	172	205	177	192	158	176	99.0
Cash Flow	688	631	707	743	705	512	550	595	448	480
Current Ratio	0.7	0.9	0.8	0.8	0.7	0.8	1.0	0.9	0.8	0.7
% Long Term Debt of Capitalization	84.9	101.4	128.5	21.7	27.1	31.2	25.1	22.6	33.2	22.6
% Net Income of Revenue	10.2	9.5	11.8	12.6	12.4	7.9	8.3	9.6	6.1	10.9
% Return on Assets	13.6	12.2	13.9	14.6	14.3	8.4	7.8	9.3	6.0	10.3
% Return on Equity	6613.3	NM	104.8	39.6	39.8	19.8	17.6	23.4	19.6	28.1

Data as orig reptd.; bef. results of disc opers/spec. items. Per share data adj. for stk. divs.; EPS diluted. E-Estimated. NA-Not Available. NM-Not Meaningful. NR-Not Ranked. UR-Under Review.

Office: 1221 Broadway , Oakland, CA, USA 94612.
Telephone: 510-271-7000.
Email: investor_relations@clorox.com
Website: http://www.thecloroxcompany.com

Chrmn & CEO: D.R. Knauss
SVP & CFO: D.J. Heinrich
SVP, Secy & General Counsel: L. Stein
Investor Contact: S. Austenfeld

Board Members: D. Boggan, Jr., R. H. Carmona, T. M. Friedman, G. Harad, D. K. Knauss, R. W. Matschullat, G. Michael, E. A. Mueller, J. L. Murley, M. E. Shannon, P. Thomas-Graham, C. M. Ticknor
Founded: 1913
Domicile: Delaware
Employees: 7,800

CME Group Inc

STANDARD &POOR'S

S&P Recommendation HOLD ★★★☆☆

Price	12-Mo. Target Price	Investment Style
$638.75 (as of Nov 23, 2007)	$700.00	Large-Cap Growth

GICS Sector Financials
Sub-Industry Specialized Finance

Summary The CME Group is a combination of the Chicago Mercantile Exchange and CBOT Holdings and is the world's largest futures exchange.

Key Stock Statistics (Source S&P, Vickers, company reports)

52-Wk Range	$693.00– 497.00	S&P Oper. EPS 2007**E**	15.24	Market Capitalization(B)	$34.981	Beta	1.02
Trailing 12-Month EPS	$14.10	S&P Oper. EPS 2008**E**	19.20	Yield (%)	0.54	S&P 3-Yr. Proj. EPS CAGR(%)	35.00
Trailing 12-Month P/E	45.3	P/E on S&P Oper. EPS 2007**E**	41.9	Dividend Rate/Share	$3.44	S&P Credit Rating	NA
$10K Invested 5 Yrs Ago	NA	Common Shares Outstg. (M)	54.8	Institutional Ownership (%)	59		

Price Performance

30-Week Mov. Avg. · · · 10-Week Mov. Avg. - - - GAAP Earnings vs. Previous Year Volume Above Avg. STARS
12-Mo. Target Price — Relative Strength — ▲ Up ▼ Down ▶ No Change Below Avg. ★

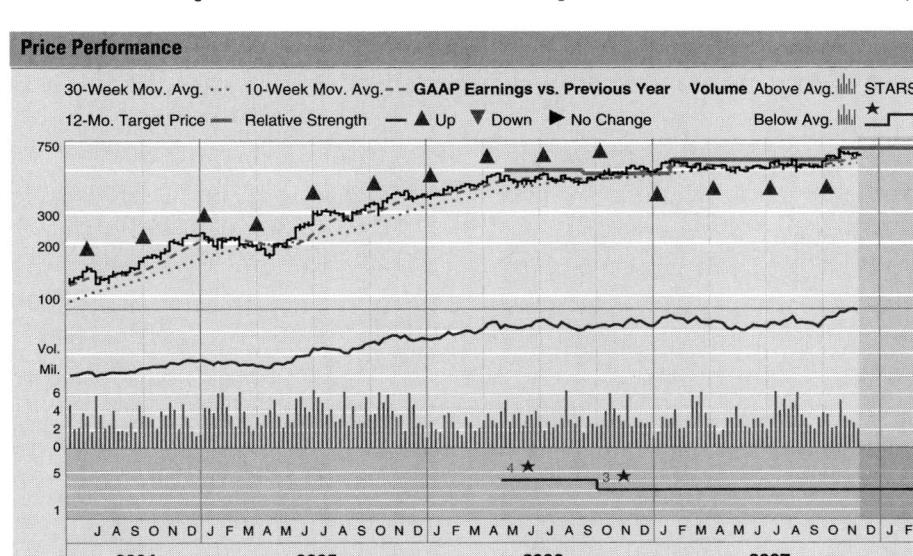

Options: ASE, CBOE, P, Ph

Analysis prepared by **Jason Willey** on October 26, 2007, when the stock traded at **$ 663.00**.

Highlights

➤ We believe CME's trading volumes will continue to benefit from increased investor sophistication, more active investment strategies, and growing demand for alternative investments. We view CME's market leading position in key interest rate, agriculture, and equity index futures as highly defensible, and we see ongoing uncertainty in interest rates, energy costs, and equity markets benefiting CME's trading volumes.

➤ Third quarter results benefited, in our view, from strong volatility across a number of financial markets, which drove record volumes in a number of product categories. CME's operating margin of 61% was a record, as incremental margins in excess of 90% drove upside in this key statistic. We expect the operating margin to continue expanding in 2008 as CME integrates CBOT Holdings and benefits from higher volumes over its primarily fixed cost infrastructure.

➤ Driven by growth in the ADV, and the expansion of newer initiatives in foreign exchange and energy, we forecast EPS of $15.24 for 2007 and $19.20 in 2008. We expect free cash flow per share to closely mirror EPS growth.

Investment Rationale/Risk

➤ Following its recent combination with CBOT Holdings, we believe CME holds a dominant position in the futures markets for interest rates, agriculture, and equities, and is expanding its presence in foreign exchange and energy. In 2008, we expect to see an increasing contribution from CME's technology relationship with the New York Mercantile Exchange (NMX: $130) and its growing international partnerships. With what we see as broad product exposure, highly defensible positioning, and a low variable cost model, we see CME delivering sustained revenue and margin growth.

➤ Risks to our recommendation and target price include a decrease in trading volumes, a faster than expected mix shift to lower margin member trading, stronger regulatory scrutiny, and integration risk concerning its combination with CBOT Holdings.

➤ Our 12-month target price of $700 is based on a P/E of 36.5X our 2008 EPS estimate, which is a premium to the current peer group multiple of 32X. We believe this valuation premium fairly reflects our positive operational outlook and CME's dominant market position in a number of key derivatives markets.

Qualitative Risk Assessment

LOW	MEDIUM	HIGH

Our risk assessment reflects potential volatility in results due to changes in futures trading volumes, recent acquisition activity in the sector, and a changing regulatory environment.

Quantitative Evaluations

S&P Quality Ranking   NR

D	C	B-	B	B+	A-	A	A+

Relative Strength Rank   STRONG
88
LOWEST = 1   HIGHEST = 99

Revenue/Earnings Data

Revenue (Million $)

	1Q	2Q	3Q	4Q	Year
2007	332.3	329.0	565.2	--	--
2006	251.7	282.2	274.7	281.3	1,090
2005	223.9	252.2	249.6	251.6	977.3
2004	169.6	190.5	192.4	196.0	752.8
2003	128.6	142.4	135.0	134.6	544.8
2002	453.2	107.5	125.2	119.4	469.1

Earnings Per Share ($)

2007	3.69	3.57	3.87	E3.98	E15.24
2006	2.61	3.12	2.95	2.91	11.60
2005	2.04	2.36	2.22	2.18	8.81
2004	1.35	1.66	1.72	1.64	6.38
2003	0.77	1.03	0.93	0.87	3.60
2002	0.63	0.71	0.77	1.02	3.13

Fiscal year ended Dec. 31. Next earnings report expected: Late January. EPS Estimates based on S&P Operating Earnings; historical GAAP earnings are as reported.

Dividend Data (Dates: mm/dd Payment Date: mm/dd/yy)

Amount ($)	Date Decl.	Ex-Div. Date	Stk. of Record	Payment Date
0.860	01/31	03/07	03/09	03/26/07
0.860	04/26	06/06	06/08	06/25/07
0.860	08/08	09/06	09/10	09/25/07
0.860	11/07	12/06	12/10	12/26/07

Dividends have been paid since 2003. Source: Company reports.

The **McGraw·Hill** Companies

CME Group Inc

STANDARD &POOR'S

Business Summary October 26, 2007

CORPORATE OVERVIEW. The CME Group is the largest futures exchange in the world and was formed in July 2007 from the merger of the Chicago Mercantile Exchange and CBOT Holdings. CME serves the risk management needs of clients worldwide through a diverse range of futures and options-on-futures products on its CME Globex electronic trading platform and on its trading floors. CME offers futures and options on futures primarily in four product areas: interest rates, stock indexes, foreign exchange, and commodities. CME is the leading exchange for trading Eurodollar futures, the world's most actively traded futures contract and a benchmark for measuring the relative value of U.S. dollar denominated short-term fixed income securities.

CME operates its own clearing house, which clears, settles and guarantees every contract traded through its exchange. We view CME's internal clearing capabilities as a key competitive advantage as CME is able to capture the revenue associated with both the trading and clearing of its products. We expect CME to expand its clearing business by partnering with other exchanges, both domestically and abroad, and clearing over-the-counter (OTC) transactions.

In 2006, CME derived almost 80% of its revenue from fees associated with trading and clearing its products. These fees include per contract charges for trade execution, clearing and CME Globex fees. Fees are charged at various rates based on the product traded, the method of trade, and the exchange trading privileges of the customer making the trade. Generally, members are charged lower fees than non-members. Certain customers benefit from volume discounts and limits on fees as part of an effort to encourage increased liquidity.

The remainder of CME's revenue is derived from a number of sources, including processing services (8% of 2006 revenue), quotation and data fees (7%), Globex access fees (2%), communication fees (1%), and other (2%). Of these secondary revenue sources, we view processing services--which are generated through clearing and transaction processing agreements with other exchanges--as the most likely area of growth. Moving forward, we expect the majority of CME's processing revenue will be from its clearing agreements with the New York Mercantile Exchange (NYMEX).

Company Financials Fiscal Year Ended Dec. 31

Per Share Data ($)	2006	2005	2004	2003	2002	2001	2000	1999	1998	1997
Tangible Book Value	42.91	32.38	23.83	17.10	13.71	12.39	NA	NA	NA	NA
Cash Flow	13.67	10.71	7.93	5.16	4.76	3.61	NA	NA	NA	NA
Earnings	11.60	8.81	6.38	3.60	3.13	2.33	NA	NA	NA	NA
S&P Core Earnings	11.59	8.80	6.37	3.61	3.23	NA	NA	NA	NA	NA
Dividends	2.52	1.84	1.04	0.63	Nil	NA	NA	NA	NA	NA
Payout Ratio	22%	21%	16%	18%	Nil	NA	NA	NA	NA	NA
Prices:High	557.97	396.90	229.80	79.30	45.50	NA	NA	NA	NA	NA
Prices:Low	354.50	163.80	72.50	41.35	35.00	NA	NA	NA	NA	NA
P/E Ratio:High	48	45	36	22	15	NA	NA	NA	NA	NA
P/E Ratio:Low	31	19	11	11	11	NA	NA	NA	NA	NA

Income Statement Analysis (Million $)										
Revenue	1,240	977	753	545	469	397	NA	NA	NA	NA
Operating Income	751	631	464	290	NA	NA	NA	NA	NA	NA
Depreciation	72.8	66.0	53.0	53.0	48.5	37.6	NA	NA	NA	NA
Interest Expense	92.1	57.0	19.0	8.74	15.9	9.48	NA	NA	NA	NA
Pretax Income	672	508	368	206	154	114	NA	NA	NA	NA
Effective Tax Rate	39.4%	39.6%	40.2%	40.7%	39.0%	40.3%	NA	NA	NA	NA
Net Income	407	307	220	122	94.1	68.3	NA	NA	NA	NA
S&P Core Earnings	407	307	219	123	97.2	NA	NA	NA	NA	NA

Balance Sheet & Other Financial Data (Million $)										
Cash	3,872	904	660	442	339	292	NA	NA	NA	NA
Current Assets	4,030	3,783	2,695	4,723	3,215	2,818	NA	NA	NA	NA
Total Assets	4,307	3,969	2,857	4,873	3,355	2,958	NA	NA	NA	NA
Current Liabilities	2,755	2,830	2,026	4,288	2,889	2,544	NA	NA	NA	NA
Long Term Debt	Nil	Nil	Nil	Nil	2.33	8.22	NA	NA	NA	NA
Common Equity	1,519	1,119	813	563	446	394	NA	NA	NA	NA
Total Capital	1,519	1,119	813	563	448	402	NA	NA	NA	NA
Capital Expenditures	87.8	85.6	67.0	63.0	56.3	NA	NA	NA	NA	NA
Cash Flow	480	373	273	175	143	106	NA	NA	NA	NA
Current Ratio	1.5	1.3	1.3	1.1	1.1	1.1	NA	NA	NA	NA
% Long Term Debt of Capitalization	Nil	Nil	Nil	Nil	0.5	2.0	NA	NA	NA	NA
% Net Income of Revenue	32.9	31.4	29.2	22.5	20.1	17.2	NA	NA	NA	NA
% Return on Assets	9.8	8.9	5.6	3.0	3.5	NA	NA	NA	NA	NA
% Return on Equity	30.9	31.7	31.9	24.2	27.1	NA	NA	NA	NA	NA

Data as orig reptd.; bef. results of disc opers/spec. items. Per share data adj. for stk. divs.; EPS diluted. E-Estimated. NA-Not Available. NM-Not Meaningful. NR-Not Ranked. UR-Under Review.

Office: 20 S Wacker Dr, Chicago, IL 60606-7408.
Telephone: 312-930-1000.
Email: info@cme.com
Website: http://www.cme.com

Chrmn: T.A. Duffy
Pres & COO: P. Gill
Vice Chrmn: J.E. Oliff
Vice Chrmn: W.R. Shepard

CEO: C.S. Donohue
Investor Contact: J. Perschier (312-930-8491)
Board Members: D. H. Chookaszian, C. S. Donohue, T. A. Duffy, M. J. Gepsman, D. R. Glickman, E. Harrington, B. F. Johnson, G. M. Katler, P. B. Lynch, L. Melamed, W. P. Miller, II, J. E. Oliff, A. J. Pollock, W. G. Salatich, Jr., J. F. Sandner, T. L. Savage, M. S. Scholes, W. R. Shepard, H. J. Siegel, D. J. Wescott

Founded: 2001
Domicile: Delaware
Employees: 1,430

CMS Energy Corp

STANDARD &POOR'S

S&P Recommendation HOLD ★★★☆☆

Price	12-Mo. Target Price	Investment Style
$17.17 (as of Nov 23, 2007)	$19.00	Large-Cap Value

GICS Sector Utilities
Sub-Industry Multi-Utilities

Summary This energy holding company's principal subsidiary is Consumers Energy, the largest utility in Michigan and the sixth largest gas and 13th largest electric utility in the U.S.

Key Stock Statistics (Source S&P, Vickers, company reports)

52-Wk Range	$19.55– 14.94	S&P Oper. EPS 2007**E**	0.81	Market Capitalization(B)	$3.856	Beta	2.38
Trailing 12-Month EPS	$-1.12	S&P Oper. EPS 2008**E**	1.20	Yield (%)	1.16	S&P 3-Yr. Proj. EPS CAGR(%)	8.00
Trailing 12-Month P/E	NM	P/E on S&P Oper. EPS 2007**E**	21.2	Dividend Rate/Share	$0.20	S&P Credit Rating	BBB-
$10K Invested 5 Yrs Ago	$17,116	Common Shares Outstg. (M)	224.6	Institutional Ownership (%)	NM		

Price Performance

30-Week Mov. Avg. · · · 10-Week Mov. Avg. - - **GAAP Earnings vs. Previous Year** Volume Above Avg. STARS
12-Mo. Target Price — Relative Strength — ▲ Up ▼ Down ► No Change Below Avg.

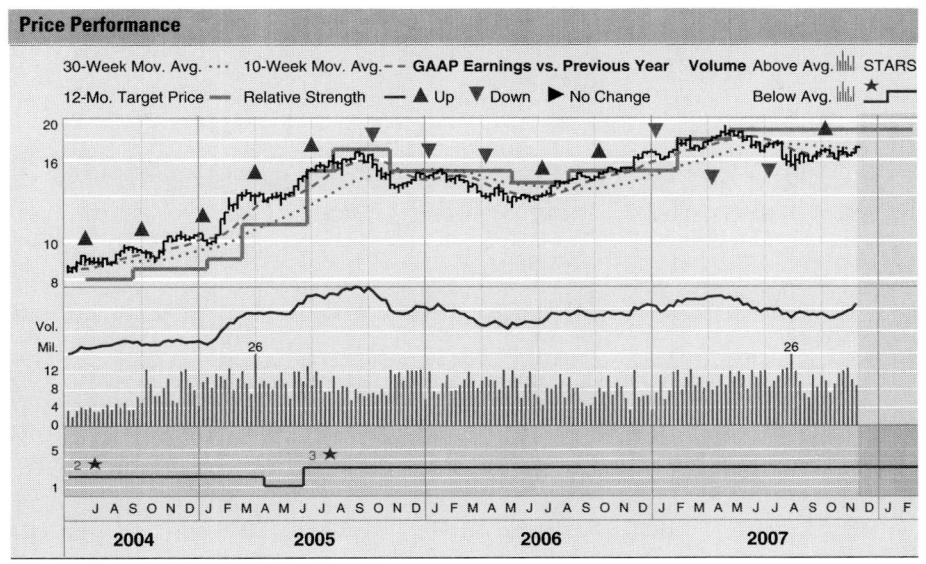

Options: ASE, CBOE, P, Ph

Analysis prepared by **Justin McCann** on November 20, 2007, when the stock traded at **$ 17.02**.

Highlights

➤ After an anticipated decline of about 25% in 2007 (from 2006 operating EPS of $1.08), we expect operating EPS to advance around 48% in 2008. The decline in 2007 will reflect the absence of earnings from CMS's divested international businesses and non-utility gas assets in Michigan. The sharp rebound we project for 2008 reflects our expectation that the use of the proceeds from the asset sales for debt reduction and new investments will result in lower interest expense and increased earnings.

➤ On August 1, 2007, CMS announced that it had closed on the sale of its interests in the GasAtacama natural gas pipeline and power plant in South America for $80 million. Earlier, on May 2, 2007, it completed the sale of its business interests in the Middle East, Africa and India for $900 million. We expect the company to use the proceeds from both sales for debt reduction and investment in the utility operations.

➤ On May 25, 2007, Consumers Energy agreed to acquire a 946 megawatt natural gas-fired power plant in Zeeland, MI, for about $517 million. Subject to approval from the Michigan Public Service Commission, the transaction is expected to close in 2008.

Investment Rationale/Risk

➤ CMS stock is little changed year to date and has continued to underperform electric and gas utility peers. However, we expect the shares to recover over the next 12 months, as investors focus more on the company's improved liquidity profile and the positive earnings outlook we project for 2008. While the company still has a below investment grade credit rating, it has greatly reduced its debt. We are also encouraged by the recent restoration of the dividend, which had been suspended since January 2003.

➤ Risks to our recommendation and target price include CMS making slower than anticipated progress in the strengthening of its balance sheet, as well as a sharp decrease in the average P/E of the group as a whole.

➤ While the recently restored dividend is yielding just 1.2%, we believe it is a signal of the company's financial recovery. Given the modest level of the dividend, we do not expect it to have a significant impact on CMS's financial flexibility. Our 12-month target price is $19, a discount-to-peers P/E of about 16X our 2008 EPS estimate of $1.20.

Qualitative Risk Assessment

LOW	MEDIUM	HIGH

Our risk assessment reflects a balance between the steady cash flow from the regulated electric and gas utility businesses, which operate within a generally supportive regulatory environment, and an improved but still weak financial risk profile, reflecting a high level of debt and a well above average cost of capital due to the company's below investment grade credit rating.

Quantitative Evaluations

S&P Quality Ranking **C**

D	C	B-	B	B+	A-	A	A+

Relative Strength Rank **STRONG**

88

LOWEST = 1   HIGHEST = 99

Revenue/Earnings Data

Revenue (Million $)

	1Q	2Q	3Q	4Q	Year
2007	2,237	1,319	1,282	--	--
2006	2,032	1,396	1,462	1,920	6,810
2005	1,845	1,230	1,307	1,906	6,288
2004	1,754	1,093	1,063	1,562	5,472
2003	1,968	1,126	1,047	1,372	5,513
2002	2,263	2,137	2,579	1,708	8,687

Earnings Per Share ($)

	1Q	2Q	3Q	4Q	Year
2007	-0.16	-0.26	0.34	E0.18	E0.81
2006	-0.13	0.30	-0.47	-0.16	-0.44
2005	0.74	0.12	-1.21	-0.09	-0.51
2004	-0.06	0.10	0.29	0.29	0.67
2003	0.47	-0.08	-0.47	-0.22	-0.30
2002	0.70	0.27	0.07	-3.78	-2.99

Fiscal year ended Dec. 31. Next earnings report expected: NA. EPS Estimates based on S&P Operating Earnings; historical GAAP earnings are as reported.

Dividend Data (Dates: mm/dd Payment Date: mm/dd/yy)

Amount ($)	Date Decl.	Ex-Div. Date	Stk. of Record	Payment Date
0.050	01/26	02/05	02/07	02/28/07
0.050	04/24	05/08	05/10	05/31/07
0.050	07/20	08/08	08/10	08/31/07
0.050	10/26	11/07	11/09	11/30/07

Dividends have been paid since 2007. Source: Company reports.

CMS Energy Corp

Business Summary November 20, 2007

CORPORATE OVERVIEW. CMS Energy (CMS) is the energy holding company for Consumers Energy (formerly Consumers Power Co.), a regulated electric and gas utility serving Michigan's Lower Peninsula, and CMS Enterprises, which is engaged in U.S. and international energy-related businesses. CMS operates in three business segments: electric utility, gas utility, and enterprises. CMS's electric utility operations include generation, purchase, distribution and sale of electricity. CMS's gas utility purchases, transports, stores, distributes and sells natural gas. The enterprises segment, through its various subsidiaries and equity investments, is engaged in diversified energy businesses, including independent power production, electric distribution, and natural gas transmission, storage and processing.

MARKET PROFILE. CMS's electric utility provides electricity to approximately 1.8 million customers in 60 of the 68 counties in the lower peninsula of Michigan. In 2006, the electric utility had total electric deliveries of 38 billion kWh.

Consumers' electric utility customer base includes a mix of residential, commercial and diversified industrial customers, the largest segment of which is the automotive industry. The automotive industry accounted for about 5% of total electric revenues in 2006. CMS's gas utility serves some 1.7 million customers in 47 of the 68 counties in Michigan's lower peninsula. The gas utility also owned 1,671 miles of transmission lines at the end of 2006, and 15 gas storage fields in Michigan, with a storage capacity of 308 bcf. The electric utility segment accounted for 48.5% of consolidated revenues in 2006; the gas utility segment, 34.8%; and Enterprises, 16.7%. The automotive industry accounted for about 5% of consolidated CMS revenues in 2006.

Company Financials Fiscal Year Ended Dec. 31

Per Share Data ($)	2006	2005	2004	2003	2002	2001	2000	1999	1998	1997
Tangible Book Value	9.90	10.53	10.51	9.69	7.47	8.11	12.15	13.23	20.30	19.49
Earnings	-0.44	-0.51	0.67	-0.30	-2.99	-2.53	0.36	2.17	2.22	2.61
S&P Core Earnings	-0.16	-0.44	0.36	0.25	-3.75	-3.29	NA	NA	NA	NA
Dividends	Nil	Nil	Nil	Nil	1.09	1.46	1.46	1.39	1.26	1.14
Payout Ratio	Nil	Nil	Nil	Nil	NM	NM	NM	64%	57%	44%
Prices:High	17.00	16.80	10.65	10.74	24.80	31.80	32.25	48.44	50.13	44.06
Prices:Low	12.09	9.70	7.81	3.41	5.45	19.49	16.06	30.31	38.75	31.13
P/E Ratio:High	NM	NM	16	NM	NM	NM	NM	22	23	17
P/E Ratio:Low	NM	NM	12	NM	NM	NM	NM	14	17	12

Income Statement Analysis (Million $)	2006	2005	2004	2003	2002	2001	2000	1999	1998	1997
Revenue	6,810	6,288	5,472	5,513	8,687	9,597	8,998	6,103	5,141	4,787
Depreciation	576	525	431	428	403	530	637	595	484	477
Maintenance	326	249	256	226	211	263	298	216	176	174
Fixed Charges Coverage	1.18	-0.56	1.01	1.23	0.12	1.26	1.63	1.73	1.75	2.28
Construction Credits	NA	NA	NA	NA	NA	NA	NA	Nil	Nil	16.0
Effective Tax Rate	NM	NM	NM	NM	NM	NM	57.7%	18.8%	29.2%	30.4%
Net Income	-85.0	-98.0	127	-43.0	-416	-331	41.0	277	242	268
S&P Core Earnings	-31.0	-93.1	63.4	40.6	-522	-431	NA	NA	NA	NA

Balance Sheet & Other Financial Data (Million $)	2006	2005	2004	2003	2002	2001	2000	1999	1998	1997
Gross Property	13,293	12,448	14,751	11,790	11,344	15,195	14,087	14,278	11,253	10,705
Capital Expenditures	670	593	525	535	747	1,262	1,032	1,124	1,295	711
Net Property	7,976	7,325	8,636	6,944	5,234	8,362	7,835	8,121	6,040	5,435
Capitalization:Long Term Debt	6,466	7,286	7,307	8,652	6,399	6,983	7,913	7,075	5,486	3,347
Capitalization:% Long Term Debt	72.2	73.8	75.8	84.5	85.0	78.7	77.0	74.2	71.2	60.1
Capitalization:Preferred	261	261	261	Nil	Nil	Nil	Nil	Nil	Nil	238
Capitalization:% Preferred	2.91	2.64	2.71	Nil	Nil	Nil	Nil	Nil	Nil	4.28
Capitalization:Common	2,234	2,322	2,072	1,585	1,133	1,890	2,361	2,456	2,216	1,977
Capitalization:% Common	24.9	23.5	21.5	15.5	15.0	21.3	23.0	25.8	28.8	35.5
Total Capital	9,234	10,566	11,123	11,010	8,058	9,834	11,221	10,359	8,486	6,456
% Operating Ratio	92.8	84.8	88.2	91.5	92.1	89.6	88.9	84.7	86.9	86.9
% Earned on Net Property	NM	NM	7.6	8.1	1.8	3.7	9.1	12.9	13.5	13.9
% Return on Revenue	NM	NM	2.3	NM	NM	NM	0.5	4.5	4.7	5.6
% Return on Invested Capital	8.1	11.0	9.5	6.7	7.9	9.4	9.5	10.0	12.0	9.9
% Return on Common Equity	NM	NM	6.3	NM	NM	NM	1.7	11.9	11.5	14.6

Data as orig reptd.; bef. results of disc opers/spec. items. Per share data adj. for stk. divs.; EPS diluted. E-Estimated. NA-Not Available. NM-Not Meaningful. NR-Not Ranked. UR-Under Review.

Office: One Energy Plaza Dr, Jackson, MI 49201-2357.
Telephone: 517-788-0550.
Email: invest@cmsenergy.com
Website: http://www.cmsenergy.com

Chrmn & CEO: K. Whipple
Pres & CEO: D.W. Joos
Vice Chrmn & Chief Lgl Officer: S.K. Smith, Jr.
EVP & CFO: T.J. Webb

SVP & General Counsel: J.E. Brunner
Investor Contact: L.L. Mountcastle (517-788-2590)
Board Members: M. S. Ayres, J. E. Barfield, R. M. Gabrys, D. W. Joos, P. R. Lochner, Jr., M. T. Monahan, J. F. Paquette, Jr., P. A. Pierre, K. L. Way, K. Whipple, J. B. Yasinsky

Founded: 1987
Domicile: Michigan
Employees: 8,640

Coach Inc.

STANDARD &POOR'S

S&P Recommendation	STRONG BUY ★★★★★	Price $35.91 (as of Nov 23, 2007)	12-Mo. Target Price $53.00	Investment Style Large-Cap Growth

GICS Sector Consumer Discretionary
Sub-Industry Apparel, Accessories & Luxury Goods

Summary COH designs, makes and markets fine accessories for women and men, including handbags, weekend and travel accessories, outerwear, footwear and business cases.

Key Stock Statistics (Source S&P, Vickers, company reports)

52-Wk Range	$54.00–30.52	S&P Oper. EPS 2008E	2.10	Market Capitalization(B)	$13.398	Beta	1.61
Trailing 12-Month EPS	$1.83	S&P Oper. EPS 2009E	2.50	Yield (%)	Nil	S&P 3-Yr. Proj. EPS CAGR(%)	25.00
Trailing 12-Month P/E	19.6	P/E on S&P Oper. EPS 2008E	17.1	Dividend Rate/Share	Nil	S&P Credit Rating	NA
$10K Invested 5 Yrs Ago	$43,980	Common Shares Outstg. (M)	373.1	Institutional Ownership (%)	86		

Price Performance

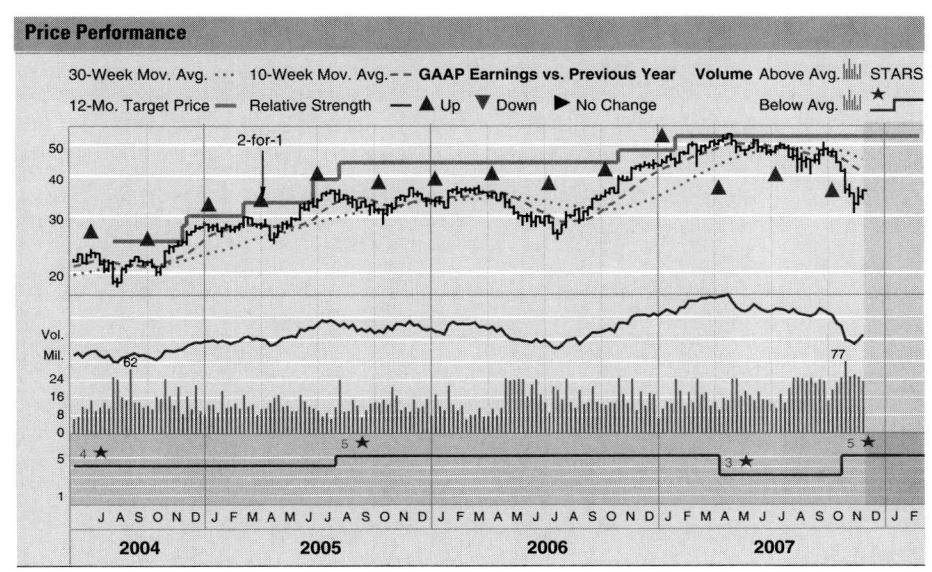

30-Week Mov. Avg. ··· 10-Week Mov. Avg. – – GAAP Earnings vs. Previous Year Volume Above Avg. STARS
12-Mo. Target Price — Relative Strength — ▲ Up ▼ Down ► No Change Below Avg.

Options: ASE, CBOE, P, Ph

Analysis prepared by **Marie Driscoll, CFA** on October 26, 2007, when the stock traded at **$ 36.20**.

Highlights

➤ We continue to see ample opportunities for COH as it further penetrates the estimated $7 billion U.S. market for luxury handbags and small leather goods and as it benefits from the category's strong momentum, up an estimated 20% in 2006 and in the first half of 2007. Japan provides significant growth potential as well; we expect COH to double its market share there to 15% by 2010.

➤ We project 20% sales growth in FY 08 (Jun.), to $3.2 billion, driven by store expansion, a low double digit increase in same-store sales for U.S. retail locations, about $550 million in Japan-based sales, and a 10% gain in the indirect channel.

➤ We look for a modest 20 basis point gross margin contraction to 77.2% of sales, and see the earnings before interest and taxes (EBIT) margin widening 30 basis points to 38.5% of sales, driven by scale economies and the leveraging of SG&A expenses and fixed costs and positive same-store sales gains. COH entered FY 08 in strong financial condition, in our view, with $1.2 billion in cash; we expect interest income to nearly double, to about $70 million.

Investment Rationale/Risk

➤ We see favorable long-term sales and earnings prospects for COH. We look for FY 08 same-store sales growth of about 10%; first quarter comps were 19% -- 11% in full-price retail locations and 27% in factory stores. Productivity and profitability metrics are more than double those of COH's specialty apparel peers, at $2,280 trailing 12-months sales per square foot and 38% EBIT margin. We see the steady flow of new products, elevated service levels and successful brand extensions driving increased store traffic and supporting a three-year EPS CAGR of 25%. Strong initial response to jewelry and fragrance launches could generate 4.5% of FY 08 sales.

➤ Risks to our recommendation and target price include changes in consumer spending patterns, and risks associated with sourcing, fashion and inventory.

➤ The stock traded recently at about 15X our calendar 2008 EPS estimate of $2.40, in line with specialty apparel retail peers. Our 12-month target price of $53 represents 25X our FY 08 EPS estimate, a modest discount to COH's historical five-year average forward P/E multiple of 28X.

Qualitative Risk Assessment

LOW	MEDIUM	HIGH

Our risk assessment reflects our view of COH's strong brand equity and growing cash flow, offset by a highly competitive market amid retail consolidation.

Quantitative Evaluations

S&P Quality Ranking NR

D	C	B-	B	B+	A-	A	A+

Relative Strength Rank MODERATE

32

LOWEST = 1   HIGHEST = 99

Revenue/Earnings Data

Revenue (Million $)

	1Q	2Q	3Q	4Q	Year
2008	676.7	--	--	--	--
2007	529.4	805.6	625.3	652.1	2,612
2006	449.0	650.3	497.9	514.4	2,112
2005	344.1	531.8	415.9	418.7	1,710
2004	258.4	411.5	313.1	338.2	1,321
2003	192.8	308.5	220.4	231.5	953.2

Earnings Per Share ($)

2008	0.41	E0.70	E0.47	E0.50	E2.10
2007	0.31	0.57	0.39	0.42	1.69
2006	0.24	0.45	0.28	0.31	1.27
2005	0.17	0.34	0.23	0.25	1.00
2004	0.11	0.25	0.15	0.17	0.68
2003	0.06	0.17	0.09	0.08	0.40

Fiscal year ended Jun. 30. Next earnings report expected: Late January. EPS Estimates based on S&P Operating Earnings; historical GAAP earnings are as reported.

Dividend Data

No cash dividends have been paid.

Please read the Required Disclosures and Analyst Certification on the last page of this report.

The McGraw-Hill Companies

Coach Inc.

STANDARD & POOR'S

Business Summary October 26, 2007

CORPORATE OVERVIEW. Coach is a leading U.S. designer and marketer of high quality accessories. Founded in 1941, over the past several years, COH has transformed the Coach brand, building on its popular core categories by introducing new products in a broader array of materials, styles and categories. The company has also implemented a flexible sourcing and manufacturing model, which, it believes, enables it to bring a broader range of products to market more rapidly and efficiently.

MARKET PROFILE. Coach is the number one luxury accessories brand in the U.S., with an estimated 20% share of this $7 billion market ($100 handbags). This sub-segment of the handbag/accessories market grew at an estimated

20% pace in 2006 and 17% in 2005, following a 30% year-over-year gain in 2004, and 23% in 2003. COH was able to outpace industry growth and add an estimated five market share points in the 2002-2006 period, as it executed its five pronged multi-channel growth strategy. The Japanese consumer makes up about 40% of the global luxury handbag market. COH estimates that it currently has 8% of the domestic Japanese market and aims to increase its share to 15% over the next five years by opening new stores.

Company Financials Fiscal Year Ended Jun. 30

Per Share Data ($)	2007	2006	2005	2004	2003	2002	2001	2000	1999	1998
Tangible Book Value	4.52	2.57	2.07	2.00	1.11	0.67	0.43	0.15	NA	NA
Cash Flow	1.90	1.44	1.14	0.79	0.48	0.31	0.24	0.17	NA	NA
Earnings	1.69	1.27	1.00	0.68	0.40	0.24	0.19	0.10	NA	NA
S&P Core Earnings	1.69	1.26	0.91	0.61	0.35	0.21	0.17	NA	NA	NA
Dividends	Nil	Nil	Nil	Nil	Nil	Nil	Nil	NA	NA	NA
Payout Ratio	Nil	Nil	Nil	Nil	Nil	Nil	Nil	NA	NA	NA
Prices:High	54.00	44.99	36.84	28.85	20.42	8.93	5.34	3.67	NA	NA
Prices:Low	30.52	25.18	24.51	16.88	7.26	4.30	2.50	2.00	NA	NA
P/E Ratio:High	32	35	37	42	52	38	28	NM	NA	NA
P/E Ratio:Low	18	20	25	25	18	18	13	NM	NA	NA

Income Statement Analysis (Million $)	2007	2006	2005	2004	2003	2002	2001	2000	1999	1998
Revenue	2,612	2,112	1,710	1,321	953	719	616	549	NA	NA
Operating Income	1,074	830	679	487	274	163	130	78.5	NA	NA
Depreciation	80.9	65.1	57.0	42.9	30.2	25.5	24.1	22.6	NA	NA
Interest Expense	Nil	Nil	1.22	0.81	0.70	1.12	2.26	6.60	NA	NA
Pretax Income	1,035	797	638	448	245	133	99.4	51.1	NA	NA
Effective Tax Rate	38.5%	38.0%	36.9%	37.5%	37.0%	35.5%	35.6%	30.6%	NA	NA
Net Income	637	494	389	262	147	85.8	64.0	35.4	NA	NA
S&P Core Earnings	637	492	356	236	129	74.9	58.3	NA	NA	NA

Balance Sheet & Other Financial Data (Million $)	2007	2006	2005	2004	2003	2002	2001	2000	1999	1998
Cash	557	143	155	263	229	94.0	3.69	NA	NA	NA
Current Assets	1,740	974	709	706	449	288	152	134	NA	NA
Total Assets	2,450	1,627	1,347	1,029	618	441	259	233	NA	NA
Current Liabilities	408	342	266	182	161	159	104	79.6	NA	NA
Long Term Debt	2.87	3.10	3.27	3.42	3.54	3.62	3.69	87.8	NA	NA
Common Equity	1,910	1,189	1,033	782	427	260	148	65.0	NA	NA
Total Capital	1,950	1,223	1,041	842	453	279	152	153	NA	NA
Capital Expenditures	141	134	94.6	67.7	57.1	42.8	31.9	NA	NA	NA
Cash Flow	717	559	446	305	177	111	88.2	58.0	NA	NA
Current Ratio	4.3	2.9	2.7	3.9	2.8	1.8	1.5	1.7	NA	NA
% Long Term Debt of Capitalization	0.1	0.3	0.3	0.4	0.8	1.3	2.4	57.4	NA	NA
% Net Income of Revenue	24.4	23.4	22.7	19.8	15.4	11.9	10.4	6.4	NA	NA
% Return on Assets	31.2	33.0	32.5	31.8	27.7	24.5	23.1	NA	NA	NA
% Return on Equity	41.1	44.0	42.8	43.3	42.7	42.0	35.5	NA	NA	NA

Data as orig reptd.; bef. results of disc opers/spec. items. Per share data adj. for stk. divs.; EPS diluted. E-Estimated. NA-Not Available. NM-Not Meaningful. NR-Not Ranked. UR-Under Review.

Office: 516 W 34th St , New York, NY 10001-1394.
Telephone: 212-594-1850.
Email: info@coach.com
Website: http://www.coach.com

Chrmn & CEO: L. Frankfort
Pres & COO: K. Monda
Investor Contact: M. Devine (212-594-1850)
SVP, CFO & Chief Acctg Officer: M. Devine

SVP, Secy & General Counsel: C. Sadler
Board Members: L. Frankfort, S. J. Kropf, G. Loveman, I. Menezes, I. Miller, K. Monda, M. Murphy, J. Zeitlin

Founded: 1941
Domicile: Maryland
Employees: 10,100

The **McGraw·Hill** Companies

Coca-Cola Co (The)

STANDARD &POOR'S

S&P Recommendation **BUY** ★★★★☆	Price $62.30 (as of Nov 23, 2007)	12-Mo. Target Price $67.00	Investment Style Large-Cap Growth

GICS Sector Consumer Staples
Sub-Industry Soft Drinks

Summary The world's largest soft drink company, KO also has a sizable fruit juice business. Its bottling interests include a 36% stake in NYSE-listed Coca-Cola Enterprises (CCE).

Key Stock Statistics (Source S&P, Vickers, company reports)

52-Wk Range	$63.45– 45.56	S&P Oper. EPS 2007E	2.64	Market Capitalization(B)	$143.974	Beta	0.63
Trailing 12-Month EPS	$2.34	S&P Oper. EPS 2008E	2.95	Yield (%)	2.18	S&P 3-Yr. Proj. EPS CAGR(%)	9.00
Trailing 12-Month P/E	26.6	P/E on S&P Oper. EPS 2007E	23.6	Dividend Rate/Share	$1.36	S&P Credit Rating	A+
$10K Invested 5 Yrs Ago	$15,475	Common Shares Outstg. (M)	2,311.0	Institutional Ownership (%)	66		

Price Performance

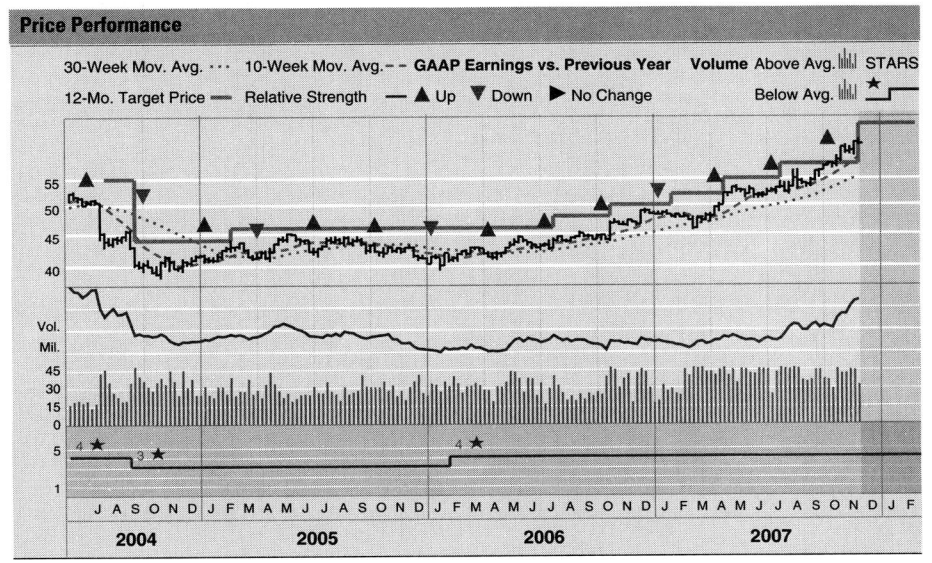

30-Week Mov. Avg. ··· 10-Week Mov. Avg. – – **GAAP Earnings vs. Previous Year** Volume Above Avg. STARS
12-Mo. Target Price — Relative Strength — ▲ Up ▼ Down ▶ No Change Below Avg.

Options: ASE, CBOE, P, Ph

Analysis prepared by **Esther Y. Kwon, CFA** on November 19, 2007, when the stock traded at **$ 62.23**.

Highlights

➤ KO recently acquired Energy Brands (known as glaceau), maker of Vitamin Water, for $4.1 billion. We expect the deal to be slightly dilutive to EPS in 2007, but become accretive in 2008 and beyond. KO's longer-term financial objectives include 3% to 4% annual volume growth, 6% to 8% operating income growth, and EPS growth in the high single digits.

➤ We see net sales up about 18% in 2007, reflecting 5% to 6% higher worldwide volumes and increased net prices, in addition to acquisitions, and the benefit from the introduction of Coke Zero in international markets. In 2008, we project sales growth of about 9% on higher prices and as distribution for Energy Brands' products is expanded. We expect operating profits to advance at a mid-single digit rate for both years, as a more favorable product mix and improved leverage are partially offset by higher commodity costs, particularly for orange juice and high fructose corn syrup, and increased marketing spending.

➤ Based on our expectation for a 1% to 2% reduction in KO's shares outstanding, we expect EPS of $2.64 in 2007, up 11.4% from operating EPS of $2.37 for 2006, and $2.95 for 2008.

Investment Rationale/Risk

➤ Our buy recommendation reflects what we see as improving volume trends for the company's businesses and our expectation that the company can generate sustainable volume and earnings growth longer term. We view KO's long-term growth targets as reasonable, particularly in light of its high exposure to international markets and its potential to expand distribution of its recent non-carb acquisitions. We also view positively KO's strong free cash flow generation.

➤ Risks to our recommendation and target price include a rise in competitive pressures for KO's beverage businesses, an inability to meet growth targets, and unfavorable weather conditions in the company's markets. With regard to corporate governance, we would favor the separation of the chairman and CEO roles.

➤ Our DCF model, which assumes 9% weighted average cost of capital and 4% terminal growth, calculates intrinsic value at $67. Our relative valuation model is derived from an analysis of comparative peer P/E and EV/EBITDA multiples and indicates a value of $67. Our 12-month target price is $67.

Qualitative Risk Assessment

LOW	MEDIUM	HIGH

Our risk assessment for the Coca-Cola Company reflects the relatively stable nature of the company's end markets, its dominant market share positions around the world, and our view of its strong balance sheet and cash flow.

Quantitative Evaluations

S&P Quality Ranking A-

D	C	B-	B	B+	A-	A	A+

Relative Strength Rank **STRONG**

91

LOWEST = 1   HIGHEST = 99

Revenue/Earnings Data

Revenue (Million $)

	1Q	2Q	3Q	4Q	Year
2007	6,103	7,733	7,690	--	--
2006	5,226	6,476	6,454	5,932	24,088
2005	5,206	6,310	6,037	5,551	23,104
2004	5,078	5,965	5,662	5,257	21,962
2003	4,502	5,695	5,671	5,176	21,044
2002	4,079	5,368	5,322	4,795	19,564

Earnings Per Share ($)

2007	0.54	0.80	0.71	E0.48	E2.64
2006	0.47	0.78	0.62	0.29	2.16
2005	0.42	0.72	0.54	0.36	2.04
2004	0.46	0.65	0.39	0.50	2.00
2003	0.34	0.55	0.50	0.38	1.77
2002	0.71	0.49	0.44	0.38	1.60

Fiscal year ended Dec. 31. Next earnings report expected: Mid February. EPS Estimates based on S&P Operating Earnings; historical GAAP earnings are as reported.

Dividend Data (Dates: mm/dd Payment Date: mm/dd/yy)

Amount ($)	Date Decl.	Ex-Div. Date	Stk. of Record	Payment Date
0.340	02/15	03/13	03/15	04/01/07
0.340	04/19	06/13	06/15	07/01/07
0.340	07/19	09/12	09/15	10/01/07
0.340	10/18	11/28	12/01	12/15/07

Dividends have been paid since 1893. Source: Company reports.

Coca-Cola Co (The)

**STANDARD
&POOR'S**

Business Summary November 19, 2007

The Coca-Cola Company is the world's largest producer of soft drink concentrates and syrups, as well as the world's biggest producer of juice and juice-related products. Finished soft drink products bearing the company's trademarks have been sold in the U.S. since 1886, and are now sold in more than 200 countries. Sales and operating profits in 2006 by geographic region were derived as follows: North America (29% of revenues, 27% of segment operating profits); European Union (15%, 36%); North Asia, Eurasia and Middle East (17%, 25%); Latin America (10%, 23%); East and South Asia and Pacific Rim (3.3%, 5.7%); and Africa (4.6%, 6.7%). Intercompany sales and corporate overhead accounted for the remaining 16% of revenue and -22% of operating profit.

The company's business, which is extremely focused, in our view, encompasses the production and sale of soft drink and non-carbonated beverage concentrates and syrups. These products are sold to the company's authorized independent and company-owned bottling/canning operations, and fountain wholesalers. These customers then either combine the syrup with carbonated water, or combine the concentrate with sweetener, water and carbonated water to produce finished soft drinks. The finished soft drinks are packaged in containers bearing the company's well-known trademarks,

which include Coca-Cola Classic (the best-selling soft drink in the world), caffeine free Coca-Cola, diet Coke (sold as Coke light in many markets outside the U.S.), Cherry Coke, Vanilla Coke, Coke Zero, Fanta, Full Throttle, Sprite, diet Sprite/Sprite Zero, Barq's, Surge, Mr. PiBB, Mello Yello, TAB, Fresca, Hi-C, Fruitopia, and other products developed for specific markets. The company also markets the Schweppes and Canada Dry mixer (such as tonic water, club soda and ginger ale), Crush and Dr. Pepper brands in more than 160 countries outside of the U.S. In 2006, concentrates and syrups for beverages bearing the trademark "Coca-Cola" or including the trademark "Coke" accounted for approximately 55% of the company's total gallon sales.

In 2006, gallon sales in the U.S. represented approximately 26% of KO's worldwide sales. About 54% of gallon sales were beverage concentrates and syrups to 76 authorized bottlers in 393 licensed territories, 24% were fountain syrups sold to fountain retailers and 507 wholesalers, and the remaining 12% were sales by the company of finished products.

Company Financials Fiscal Year Ended Dec. 31

Per Share Data ($)	2006	2005	2004	2003	2002	2001	2000	1999	1998	1997
Tangible Book Value	5.08	5.29	5.02	4.14	3.34	3.53	2.98	3.06	3.19	2.67
Cash Flow	2.56	2.43	2.36	2.11	1.93	1.92	1.19	1.30	1.67	1.89
Earnings	2.16	2.04	2.00	1.77	1.60	1.60	0.88	0.98	1.42	1.64
S&P Core Earnings	2.04	2.03	2.08	1.77	1.62	1.46	NA	NA	NA	NA
Dividends	1.24	1.12	1.00	0.88	0.80	0.72	0.68	0.64	0.60	0.56
Payout Ratio	57%	55%	50%	50%	50%	45%	77%	65%	42%	34%
Prices:High	49.35	45.26	53.50	50.90	57.91	62.19	66.88	70.88	88.94	72.63
Prices:Low	39.36	40.31	38.30	37.01	42.90	42.37	42.88	47.31	53.63	51.13
P/E Ratio:High	23	22	27	29	36	39	76	72	63	44
P/E Ratio:Low	18	20	19	21	27	26	49	48	38	31

Income Statement Analysis (Million $)	2006	2005	2004	2003	2002	2001	2000	1999	1998	1997
Revenue	24,088	23,104	21,962	21,044	19,564	20,092	20,458	19,805	18,813	18,868
Operating Income	7,246	7,017	6,591	6,071	6,264	6,155	4,464	4,774	5,612	5,627
Depreciation	938	932	893	850	806	803	773	792	645	626
Interest Expense	220	240	196	178	199	289	447	337	277	258
Pretax Income	6,578	6,690	6,222	5,495	5,499	5,670	3,399	3,819	5,198	6,055
Effective Tax Rate	22.8%	27.2%	22.1%	20.9%	27.7%	29.8%	36.0%	36.3%	32.0%	31.8%
Net Income	5,080	4,872	4,847	4,347	3,976	3,979	2,177	2,431	3,533	4,129
S&P Core Earnings	4,797	4,854	5,063	4,350	4,021	3,654	NA	NA	NA	NA

Balance Sheet & Other Financial Data (Million $)	2006	2005	2004	2003	2002	2001	2000	1999	1998	1997
Cash	2,590	4,767	6,768	3,482	2,345	1,934	1,892	1,812	1,807	1,737
Current Assets	8,441	10,250	12,094	8,396	7,352	7,171	6,620	6,480	6,380	5,969
Total Assets	29,963	29,427	31,327	27,342	24,501	22,417	20,834	21,623	19,145	16,940
Current Liabilities	8,890	9,836	10,971	7,886	7,341	8,429	9,321	9,856	8,640	7,379
Long Term Debt	1,314	1,154	1,157	2,517	2,701	1,219	835	854	687	801
Common Equity	16,920	16,355	15,935	14,090	11,800	11,366	9,316	9,513	8,403	7,311
Total Capital	18,842	17,861	17,542	16,944	14,900	13,027	10,509	10,865	9,514	8,560
Capital Expenditures	1,407	899	755	812	851	769	733	1,069	863	1,093
Cash Flow	6,018	5,804	5,740	5,197	4,782	4,782	2,950	3,223	4,178	4,755
Current Ratio	0.9	1.0	1.1	1.1	1.0	0.9	0.7	0.7	0.7	0.8
% Long Term Debt of Capitalization	7.0	6.5	6.6	14.9	18.1	9.4	7.9	7.9	7.2	9.4
% Net Income of Revenue	21.1	21.1	22.1	20.7	20.3	19.8	10.6	12.3	18.8	21.9
% Return on Assets	17.1	16.0	16.5	16.8	16.9	18.4	10.3	11.9	19.6	24.9
% Return on Equity	30.5	30.2	32.3	33.6	34.3	38.5	23.1	27.1	45.0	61.3

Data as orig reptd.; bef. results of disc opers/spec. items. Per share data adj. for stk. divs.; EPS diluted. E-Estimated. NA-Not Available. NM-Not Meaningful. NR-Not Ranked. UR-Under Review.

Office: 1 Coca Cola Plz , Atlanta, GA 30313-2499.
Telephone: 404-676-2121.
Website: http://www.coca-cola.com
Chrmn & CEO: E.N. Isdell

Pres & COO: M. Kent
Investor Contact: G.P. Fayard (404-676-2121)
EVP & CFO: G.P. Fayard
SVP & General Counsel: G.J. Kelly

Board Members: H. A. Allen, R. W. Allen, C. P. Black, B. Diller, E. N. Isdell, D. R. Keough, D. F. McHenry, S. Nunn, J. D. Robinson, III, P. V. Ueberroth, J. B. Williams
Founded: 1886
Domicile: Delaware
Employees: 71,000

The McGraw·Hill Companies

Coca-Cola Enterprises Inc.

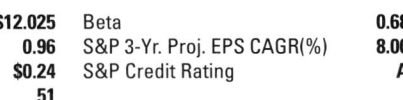

S&P Recommendation **HOLD** ★★★☆☆	Price $24.89 (as of Nov 26, 2007)	12-Mo. Target Price $25.00	Investment Style Large-Cap Blend

GICS Sector Consumer Staples
Sub-Industry Soft Drinks

Summary This company is the world's largest bottler of Coca-Cola beverage products, distributing to about 78% of the North American market. Coca-Cola Co. holds 36% of CCE's common stock.

Key Stock Statistics (Source S&P, Vickers, company reports)

52-Wk Range	**$26.28– 19.78**	S&P Oper. EPS 2007**E**	1.30	Market Capitalization(B)	**$12.025**	Beta	0.68
Trailing 12-Month EPS	**$-2.45**	S&P Oper. EPS 2008**E**	1.40	Yield (%)	0.96	S&P 3-Yr. Proj. EPS CAGR(%)	8.00
Trailing 12-Month P/E	**NM**	P/E on S&P Oper. EPS 2007**E**	19.1	Dividend Rate/Share	$0.24	S&P Credit Rating	A
$10K Invested 5 Yrs Ago	**$12,330**	Common Shares Outstg. (M)	483.1	Institutional Ownership (%)	51		

Price Performance

- 30-Week Mov. Avg. ···· 10-Week Mov. Avg. – – GAAP Earnings vs. Previous Year   Volume Above Avg. ▏▍▊ STARS
- 12-Mo. Target Price — Relative Strength — ▲ Up ▼ Down ▶ No Change   Below Avg. ▏▍▊ ★

[Price performance chart showing years 2004, 2005, 2006, 2007. Options: ASE, CBOE, P, Ph]

Analysis prepared by **Esther Y. Kwon, CFA** on November 26, 2007, when the stock traded at **$ 25.25**.

Highlights

➤ Over the next 12 months, we expect net revenues to advance overall 4% to 5%, reflecting weak consolidated bottle and can unit case volume, offset by an increase of 4% in net revenues per case, and a modest positive impact from foreign currency translations. We project that North American volumes will decline due to higher pricing and continued weakness in carbonated soft drinks (CSDs).

➤ We see gross margins coming under pressure, as benefits from a product mix shift toward cold channel sales and higher pricing are offset by rising sweetener, energy and packaging costs. We think SG&A expenses will decrease modestly as a percentage of sales, but we expect productivity savings to come at a cost of $300 million in restructuring expenses through 2008.

➤ Following a modest decrease in shares outstanding, we estimate 2007 operating EPS of $1.30, flat compared to the prior year. However, for 2008, we see EPS rising to $1.40. For the longer term, we expect annual EPS growth of 7% to 9%.

Investment Rationale/Risk

➤ Our hold recommendation reflects our expectation of a challenging operating environment for the company. We see results benefiting from pricing gains, but we expect commodity cost inflation, high energy prices, and sluggish CSD trends to be offsets. In light of these factors, we believe appreciation potential is limited, as we wait for signs of an improvement in volume and earnings growth trends. We look for recent acquisitions by Coca-Cola (KO: buy, $62) to potentially stabilize domestic volumes in 2008.

➤ Risks to our recommendation and target price include more rapid commodity cost inflation than expected, potential consumer reluctance to accept new product introductions, and CCE's ability to achieve sales and earnings growth forecasts. In terms of corporate governance, the board is controlled by a majority of insiders and affiliated outsiders, which we view unfavorably.

➤ Our 12-month target price of $25 is based on our analysis of peer P/E and enterprise value to EBITDA multiples, and our DCF model, which assumes a weighted average cost of capital of 9% and a terminal growth rate of 3%.

Qualitative Risk Assessment

LOW	MEDIUM	HIGH

Our risk assessment for Coca-Cola Enterprises reflects our view of the relatively stable nature of the company's end markets, strong cash flow, and its relationship with corporate partner Coca-Cola Company.

Quantitative Evaluations

S&P Quality Ranking B

D	C	B-	**B**	B+	A-	A	A+

Relative Strength Rank STRONG
84
LOWEST = 1   HIGHEST = 99

Revenue/Earnings Data

Revenue (Million $)

	1Q	2Q	3Q	4Q	Year
2007	4,567	5,665	5,405	--	--
2006	4,333	5,467	5,218	4,786	19,804
2005	4,196	5,128	4,895	4,487	18,706
2004	4,240	4,844	4,670	4,404	18,158
2003	3,667	4,617	4,734	4,312	17,330
2002	3,642	4,448	4,549	4,249	16,889

Earnings Per Share ($)

2007	0.03	0.56	0.55	E0.17	E1.30
2006	0.03	0.71	0.44	-3.59	-2.41
2005	0.10	0.70	0.40	-0.12	1.08
2004	0.22	0.43	0.44	0.17	1.26
2003	0.06	0.56	0.56	0.28	1.48
2002	0.02	0.47	0.42	0.17	1.07

Fiscal year ended Dec. 31. Next earnings report expected: Mid February. EPS Estimates based on S&P Operating Earnings; historical GAAP earnings are as reported.

Dividend Data (Dates: mm/dd Payment Date: mm/dd/yy)

Amount ($)	Date Decl.	Ex-Div. Date	Stk. of Record	Payment Date
0.060	02/09	03/14	03/16	03/29/07
0.060	04/24	06/13	06/15	06/28/07
0.060	07/23	09/12	09/14	09/27/07
0.060	10/24	11/28	11/30	12/13/07

Dividends have been paid since 1986. Source: Company reports.

Please read the Required Disclosures and Analyst Certification on the last page of this report.

The McGraw-Hill Companies

Coca-Cola Enterprises Inc.

STANDARD &POOR'S

Business Summary November 26, 2007

Coca-Cola Enterprises is the world's largest bottler of Coca-Cola beverage products, distributing about 79% of all bottle/can volumes of carbonated soft-drink products of The Coca-Cola Co. (KO) in North America. KO owns about 35% of the company's common stock. CCE's product line also includes other nonalcoholic beverages, such as still and sparkling waters, juices, isotonics and teas. In 2006, the company sold approximately 42 billion bottles and cans throughout its territories, representing about 19% of The Coca-Cola Company's worldwide volume. About 93% of this volume consisted of beverages produced and sold under licenses from The Coca-Cola Company. CCE also distributes Dr. Pepper and several other beverage brands.

Based on net operating revenues in 2006, North America accounted for 72% of total revenues, and Europe for 28%. CCE operates in parts of 46 states in the U.S., the District of Columbia, the U.S. Virgin Islands, all 10 Canadian provinces, and portions of Europe that include Belgium, France, the U.K., Luxembourg, Monaco, and the Netherlands. At December 31, 2006, CCE's bottling territories encompassed an aggregate population of 412 million people. The company's five leading brands in North America in 2006 were Coca-Cola classic, Diet Coke, Sprite, Dasani, and caffeine POWERade, while the five leading

brands in Europe were Coca-Cola, diet Coke/Coke light, Fanta, Schweppes and Sprite.

The soft drink industry is mature, and highly concentrated. CCE conducts its business primarily under bottle contracts with KO. It has the exclusive right to produce and market Coca-Cola soft drinks in authorized containers in specified territories; KO has the ability, at its sole discretion, to set prices for concentrates and syrups. CCE's competitors include the local bottlers of competing products and manufacturers of private label products. It competes with bottlers of products of PepsiCo, Inc. (PEP) and its largest bottler Pepsi Americas (PAS), Cadbury Schweppes plc (CSG), Nestle S.A. (NSRGY), Groupe Danone, Kraft Foods Inc. (KFT), and private label products, including those of some of its customers. In some territories, CCE sells products it competes against in other territories.

Company Financials Fiscal Year Ended Dec. 31

Per Share Data ($)	2006	2005	2004	2003	2002	2001	2000	1999	1998	1997
Tangible Book Value	NM	NM	NM	NM	NM	6.25	6.67	6.83	6.08	4.61
Cash Flow	-0.28	3.27	3.52	3.88	3.35	3.08	3.48	3.22	3.11	2.82
Earnings	-2.41	1.08	1.26	1.48	1.07	-0.05	0.54	0.13	0.35	0.43
S&P Core Earnings	-2.34	1.01	1.19	1.22	0.78	-0.34	NA	NA	NA	NA
Dividends	0.24	0.16	0.16	0.16	0.16	0.12	0.16	0.16	0.15	0.08
Payout Ratio	NM	15%	13%	11%	15%	NM	30%	123%	41%	19%
Prices:High	22.49	23.92	29.34	23.30	24.50	23.90	30.25	37.50	41.56	36.00
Prices:Low	18.83	18.52	18.45	16.85	15.94	13.46	14.00	16.81	22.88	15.71
P/E Ratio:High	NM	22	23	16	23	NM	56	NM	NM	84
P/E Ratio:Low	NM	17	15	11	15	NM	26	NM	NM	37

Income Statement Analysis (Million $)										
Revenue	19,804	18,706	18,158	17,330	16,889	15,700	14,750	14,406	13,414	11,278
Operating Income	2,439	2,475	2,504	2,674	2,409	1,954	2,387	2,187	1,989	1,666
Depreciation	1,012	1,044	1,068	1,097	1,045	1,353	1,261	1,348	1,120	946
Interest Expense	633	633	619	607	662	753	791	751	703	538
Pretax Income	-2,118	790	818	972	705	-150	333	88.0	169	178
Effective Tax Rate	NM	34.9%	27.1%	30.5%	29.9%	NM	29.1%	33.0%	16.0%	3.90%
Net Income	-1,143	514	596	676	494	-19.0	236	59.0	142	171
S&P Core Earnings	-1,110	478	563	563	356	-147	NA	NA	NA	NA

Balance Sheet & Other Financial Data (Million $)										
Cash	184	107	155	80.0	68.0	284	294	141	68.0	45.0
Current Assets	3,691	3,395	3,264	3,000	2,844	2,876	2,631	2,581	2,285	1,813
Total Assets	23,225	25,357	26,354	25,700	24,375	23,719	22,162	22,730	21,132	17,487
Current Liabilities	3,818	3,846	3,431	3,941	3,455	4,522	3,094	3,614	3,397	3,032
Long Term Debt	9,218	9,165	10,523	10,552	11,236	10,365	10,348	10,153	9,605	7,760
Common Equity	4,526	5,643	5,378	4,365	3,310	2,783	2,790	2,877	2,389	1,782
Total Capital	17,801	19,914	21,139	19,882	19,122	17,521	17,956	18,028	16,758	13,538
Capital Expenditures	882	914	946	1,099	1,029	972	1,181	1,480	1,551	967
Cash Flow	-131	1,558	1,664	1,771	1,536	1,331	1,494	1,404	1,262	1,115
Current Ratio	1.0	0.9	1.0	0.8	0.8	0.6	0.9	0.7	0.7	0.6
% Long Term Debt of Capitalization	51.8	46.0	49.8	53.1	58.8	59.2	57.6	56.3	57.3	57.3
% Net Income of Revenue	NM	2.7	3.3	3.9	2.9	NM	1.6	0.4	1.1	1.5
% Return on Assets	NM	2.0	2.3	2.7	2.1	NM	1.1	0.3	0.7	1.2
% Return on Equity	NM	9.3	12.2	17.6	16.1	NM	8.2	2.1	6.8	10.6

Data as orig reptd.; bef. results of disc opers/spec. items. Per share data adj. for stk. divs.; EPS diluted. E-Estimated. NA-Not Available. NM-Not Meaningful. NR-Not Ranked. UR-Under Review.

Office: 2500 Windy Ridge Pkwy , Atlanta, GA 30339.
Telephone: 770-989-3000.
Website: http://www.cokecce.com
Chrmn: L.F. Kline

Pres & CEO: J.F. Brock
EVP & General Counsel: J.J. Culhane
SVP & CFO: W.W. Douglas, III
VP, Chief Acctg Officer & Cntlr: C. Lischer   .

Board Members: F. Aguirre, J. Brock, J. E. Copeland, Jr., C. Darden, J. T. Eyton, G. P. Fayard, I. Finan, M. J. Herb, L. P. Humann, D. A. James, T. H. Johnson, S. K. Johnston, III, L. F. Kline, P. R. Reynolds, C. R. Welling

Founded: 1944
Domicile: Delaware
Employees: 74,000

The McGraw-Hill Companies

Cognizant Technology Solutions Corp

STANDARD &POOR'S

S&P Recommendation **STRONG BUY** ★★★★★	**Price** $30.46 (as of Nov 23, 2007)	**12-Mo. Target Price** $40.00	**Investment Style** Large-Cap Growth

GICS Sector Information Technology
Sub-Industry IT Consulting & Other Services

Summary This company offers full life-cycle solutions to complex software development and maintenance problems.

Key Stock Statistics (Source S&P, Vickers, company reports)

52-Wk Range	$47.78– 29.44	S&P Oper. EPS 2007E	1.14	Market Capitalization(B)	$8.844	Beta	0.97
Trailing 12-Month EPS	$1.07	S&P Oper. EPS 2008E	1.48	Yield (%)	Nil	S&P 3-Yr. Proj. EPS CAGR(%)	26.00
Trailing 12-Month P/E	28.5	P/E on S&P Oper. EPS 2007E	26.7	Dividend Rate/Share	Nil	S&P Credit Rating	NA
$10K Invested 5 Yrs Ago	$50,202	Common Shares Outstg. (M)	290.4	Institutional Ownership (%)	95		

Price Performance

30-Week Mov. Avg. ···· 10-Week Mov. Avg. - - GAAP Earnings vs. Previous Year Volume Above Avg. STARS
12-Mo. Target Price — Relative Strength — ▲ Up ▼ Down ► No Change Below Avg.

Options: ASE, CBOE, P, Ph

Analysis prepared by **Dylan Cathers** on November 08, 2007, when the stock traded at **$ 33.19**.

Qualitative Risk Assessment

LOW	MEDIUM	HIGH

Our risk assessment reflects what we see as CTSH's strong balance sheet, steady cash inflows, and rapid revenue growth, offset by intense competition in the IT services peer group from both companies domiciled in India as well as multinationals.

Quantitative Evaluations

S&P Quality Ranking B+

D	C	B-	B	B+	A-	A	A+

Relative Strength Rank WEAK

17

LOWEST = 1   HIGHEST = 99

Revenue/Earnings Data

Revenue (Million $)

	1Q	2Q	3Q	4Q	Year
2007	460.3	516.5	558.8	--	--
2006	285.5	336.8	377.5	424.4	1,424
2005	181.7	211.7	235.5	256.9	885.8
2004	119.7	138.7	155.4	172.8	586.7
2003	74.52	87.45	98.11	108.2	368.2
2002	46.48	54.36	61.23	67.01	229.1

Earnings Per Share ($)

2007	0.25	0.27	0.32	E0.31	E1.14
2006	0.16	0.19	0.20	0.23	0.78
2005	0.11	0.13	0.14	0.20	0.57
2004	0.07	0.09	0.09	0.11	0.35
2003	0.04	0.05	0.06	0.06	0.21
2002	0.03	0.03	0.04	0.04	0.14

Fiscal year ended Dec. 31. Next earnings report expected: Early February. EPS Estimates based on S&P Operating Earnings; historical GAAP earnings are as reported.

Highlights

➤ We see revenue growth of 50% in 2007, but we expect growth to be lower than is typical for CTSH in the fourth quarter, reflecting a difficult comparison and what management is reporting as a lack of a normal "budget flush," which is when companies spend whatever is left of their 2007 budgets. Looking to 2008, we have lowered our growth expectation to 30%, from 38%, as we are concerned about the 2008 IT spending budgets of companies, particularly within the financial vertical. Typically, CTSH has excellent revenue visibility, in our view, due to the long-term nature of its contracts.

➤ We expect operating margins to be down slightly in 2007, versus 2006, and flat in 2008, including projected stock option expense. We think increased utilization, cost controls, revenue growth, and an improved mix of offshore/on-site workers will be offset by CTSH's investments in the business, rising wages for workers in India, elevated levels of employee attrition, and the continuing appreciation of the rupee.

➤ We estimate EPS of $1.14 in 2007, rising to $1.48 in 2008.

Investment Rationale/Risk

➤ Our strong buy recommendation is based on valuation and our favorable projections for top-line growth. Although we think there is less visibility going into next year than normal, we still think that CTSH's revenue growth will be faster than its peers. Further, we believe the company has done a good job moving into high-growth verticals, such as media, new technology, and telecommunications and maintaining its margins despite strong headwinds.

➤ Risks to our recommendation and target price include increasing competition in offshore outsourcing, with consequent margin pressures; rising wages of Indian employees; the continuing appreciation of the rupee; and immigration restrictions that could affect personnel. Our corporate governance concerns center around a classified board of directors and the "poison pill" in place.

➤ We use a peer-average P/E to growth (PEG) ratio of 1.04X our 2008 EPS estimate, assuming an expected three year growth rate of 26%, to arrive at our 12-month target price of $40. At that level, the stock's P/E would be 27X our 2008 EPS estimate.

Dividend Data (Dates: mm/dd Payment Date: mm/dd/yy)

Amount ($)	Date Decl.	Ex-Div. Date	Stk. of Record	Payment Date
2-for-1	09/17	10/17	10/01	10/16/07

Source: Company reports.

Cognizant Technology Solutions Corp

STANDARD
&POOR'S

Business Summary November 08, 2007

CORPORATE OVERVIEW. Cognizant Technology Solutions began operations in 1994 as an in-house technology development center for Dun & Bradstreet Corp. and its operating units. In its June 1998 IPO, 2,917,000 common shares were sold at $10 each.

The company's objective is to be a leading provider of full life-cycle e-business and application development projects, take full responsibility for on-going management of a client's software systems, and help clients move legacy transformation projects through to completion. The company's solutions include application development and integration, application management, and re-engineering services.

Applications development services are provided using a full life-cycle application development approach in which the company assumes total start to finish responsibility and accountability for analysis, design, implementation, testing and integration of systems, or through cooperative development, in which CTSH employees work with the customer's in-house IT personnel. In either case, the company's on-site team members work closely with end users

of the application to develop specifications and define requirements.

CTSH applications management services seeks to ensure that a customer's core operational systems are free of defects and responsive to end-users' changing needs. The company is often able to introduce product and process enhancements and improve service levels.

Through its re-engineering services, the company works with customers to migrate systems based on legacy computing environments to newer, open systems-based platforms and client/server architectures, often in response to the more stringent demands of e-business. CTSH's re-engineering tools automate many processes required to implement advanced client/server technologies.

Company Financials Fiscal Year Ended Dec. 31

Per Share Data ($)	2006	2005	2004	2003	2002	2001	2000	1999	1998	1997
Tangible Book Value	3.60	2.44	1.61	0.98	0.62	0.42	0.29	0.20	0.14	0.01
Cash Flow	0.89	0.64	0.41	0.26	0.17	0.12	0.07	0.12	0.04	0.02
Earnings	0.78	0.57	0.35	0.21	0.14	0.09	0.07	0.05	0.03	0.01
S&P Core Earnings	0.78	0.51	0.30	0.16	0.09	0.07	NA	NA	NA	NA
Dividends	Nil	Nil	Nil	Nil	Nil	Nil	Nil	Nil	Nil	Nil
Payout Ratio	Nil	Nil	Nil	Nil	Nil	Nil	Nil	Nil	Nil	Nil
Prices:High	41.25	26.24	21.47	12.40	6.38	4.48	6.01	5.04	1.40	NA
Prices:Low	24.26	17.79	9.80	4.28	2.70	1.48	2.02	0.80	0.29	NA
P/E Ratio:High	53	46	61	59	47	49	83	NM	46	NA
P/E Ratio:Low	31	31	28	20	20	16	28	NM	10	NA

Income Statement Analysis (Million $)										
Revenue	1,424	886	587	368	229	178	137	88.9	58.6	24.7
Operating Income	293	199	134	84.2	106	42.0	30.6	19.7	11.1	3.49
Depreciation	34.2	21.4	16.4	11.9	7.84	6.37	4.51	3.04	2.22	1.36
Interest Expense	Nil	Nil	Nil	Nil	Nil	Nil	Nil	Nil	Nil	Nil
Pretax Income	278	185	122	72.2	45.1	35.4	28.2	17.9	9.64	2.15
Effective Tax Rate	16.2%	10.3%	17.9%	20.6%	23.4%	37.4%	37.4%	37.4%	37.4%	27.0%
Net Income	233	166	100	57.4	34.6	22.2	17.7	11.2	6.03	1.03
S&P Core Earnings	233	148	85.1	42.4	23.0	16.3	NA	NA	NA	NA

Balance Sheet & Other Financial Data (Million $)										
Cash	266	197	293	194	126	85.0	62.0	42.6	28.4	2.72
Current Assets	1,040	663	454	278	176	117	88.2	56.7	42.4	10.9
Total Assets	1,326	870	573	361	231	145	110	69.0	51.7	18.3
Current Liabilities	250	156	115	62.6	41.5	21.7	26.7	13.2	13.0	5.20
Long Term Debt	Nil	Nil	Nil	Nil	Nil	Nil	Nil	Nil	Nil	Nil
Common Equity	1,073	714	454	274	165	98.8	66.1	45.5	32.6	3.86
Total Capital	1,073	714	458	298	190	123	82.8	55.8	38.7	6.50
Capital Expenditures	105	71.8	46.6	30.0	22.3	15.0	10.7	5.92	3.74	3.00
Cash Flow	267	188	117	69.3	42.4	28.5	17.7	14.3	8.26	2.39
Current Ratio	4.2	4.3	3.9	4.4	4.2	5.4	3.3	4.3	3.3	2.1
% Long Term Debt of Capitalization	Nil	Nil	Nil	Nil	Nil	Nil	Nil	Nil	Nil	Nil
% Net Income of Revenue	16.3	18.8	17.1	15.6	15.1	12.5	12.9	12.6	10.3	4.2
% Return on Assets	21.2	23.1	21.4	19.4	18.4	17.4	19.8	18.6	17.2	7.8
% Return on Equity	26.0	28.5	27.6	26.1	26.2	26.9	31.7	28.8	33.1	30.4

Data as orig reptd.; bef. results of disc opers/spec. items. Per share data adj. for stk. divs.; EPS diluted. E-Estimated. NA-Not Available. NM-Not Meaningful. NR-Not Ranked. UR-Under Review.

Office: 500 Glenpointe Ctr W Ste, Teaneck, NJ 07666-6821.
Telephone: 201-801-0233.
Website: http://www.cognizant.com
Chrmn: J.E. Klein

Pres & CEO: F. D'Souza
Vice Chrmn: L. Narayanan
COO, CFO, Treas & Secy: G. Coburn

Board Members: F. D'Souza, R. W. Howe, J. E. Klein, L. Narayanan, R. W. Weissman, T. M. Wendel

Founded: 1988
Domicile: Delaware
Employees: 38,800

Colgate-Palmolive Co

STANDARD &POOR'S

S&P Recommendation	STRONG BUY ★ ★ ★ ★ ★	Price $79.00 (as of Nov 23, 2007)	12-Mo. Target Price $87.00	Investment Style Large-Cap Growth

GICS Sector Consumer Staples
Sub-Industry Household Products

Summary This major consumer products company markets oral, personal and household care, and pet nutrition products in more than 200 countries and territories.

Key Stock Statistics (Source S&P, Vickers, company reports)

52-Wk Range	$79.93–63.75	S&P Oper. EPS 2007**E**	3.34	Market Capitalization(B)	$40.286	Beta	0.29
Trailing 12-Month EPS	$3.16	S&P Oper. EPS 2008**E**	3.80	Yield (%)	1.82	S&P 3-Yr. Proj. EPS CAGR(%)	11.00
Trailing 12-Month P/E	25.0	P/E on S&P Oper. EPS 2007**E**	23.7	Dividend Rate/Share	$1.44	S&P Credit Rating	AA-
$10K Invested 5 Yrs Ago	$16,896	Common Shares Outstg. (M)	509.9	Institutional Ownership (%)	73		

Price Performance

- 30-Week Mov. Avg. ···
- 10-Week Mov. Avg. - -
- **GAAP Earnings vs. Previous Year**
- Volume Above Avg. ▮▮▮ STARS
- 12-Mo. Target Price —
- Relative Strength —
- ▲ Up ▼ Down ► No Change
- Below Avg. ▮▮▮ ★

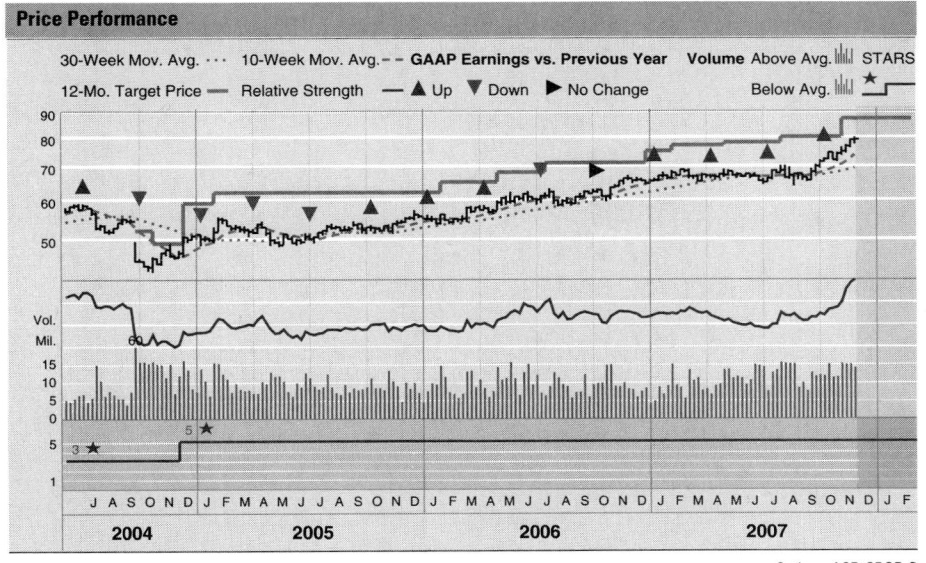

Options: ASE, CBOE, P

Analysis prepared by **Loran Braverman, CFA** on October 31, 2007, when the stock traded at **$ 76.01**.

Highlights

➤ In December 2004, CL embarked on a four-year restructuring program that involves a 12% work force reduction, the closing of a third of CL's factories, an increased focus on faster growing markets, new product innovation, and more efficient spending on marketing.

➤ For 2007, we expect sales to rise 11%, due to solid volume growth, led by the Latin America and Greater Asia/Africa regions and, to a lesser extent, foreign currency and price increases. We project an operating margin increase of 40 basis points (bps), with the benefits of the restructuring program and price increases offsetting higher material costs and marketing expenses. For 2008, we project a 6% sales gain (assuming no foreign exchange effect) and a 100 bp improvement in the operating margin, with the same factors affecting the margin in 2007 continuing. All of the expense ratios exclude one-time and restructuring charges.

➤ With our assumption of slightly higher interest expense, a 32% effective tax rate and 1% fewer shares as a result of share repurchases in both years, we expect EPS to increase to $3.34 in 2007 and to $3.80 in 2008, from 2006's $2.91. All years exclude restructuring charges.

Investment Rationale/Risk

➤ Our strong buy opinion reflects our view that CL's restructuring plans are likely to drive EPS growth in the low double digits from 2006 onward for at least several years. We expect savings derived from the restructuring program to be reinvested in R&D and marketing, with more resources to be allocated to faster growing markets. We also expect a smooth CEO transition, from Reuben Mark, CEO since 1984, to Ian Cook, formerly COO and himself a long-time CL employee, who became CEO on July 1.

➤ Risks to our recommendation and target price include intensified competition in the global oral care market, unfavorable currency translations, and low consumer acceptance of new products.

➤ Our 12-month target price of $87 is a blend of our three valuation models. Our DCF model assumes a WACC of 8.5% and a terminal growth rate of 3% to arrive at a value of $83. Given the stable and improving outlook that we see for CL, we believe the shares should trade at a premium to peers, which suggests a 21X P/E applied to our 2008 EPS estimate, or $78. Our historical analysis suggests a value of $100, using a P/E close to the 10-year average of 28X.

Qualitative Risk Assessment

LOW	MEDIUM	HIGH

Our risk assessment reflects that demand for household and personal care products is generally static, and not affected by changes in the economy or geopolitical factors. This is partially offset by the mature and competitive nature of these industries.

Quantitative Evaluations

S&P Quality Ranking   A+

D	C	B-	B	B+	A-	A	A+

Relative Strength Rank   STRONG

93

LOWEST = 1   HIGHEST = 99

Revenue/Earnings Data

Revenue (Million $)

	1Q	2Q	3Q	4Q	Year
2007	3,214	3,405	3,528	--	--
2006	2,871	3,014	3,144	3,209	12,238
2005	2,743	2,838	2,912	2,905	11,397
2004	2,514	2,572	2,696	2,803	10,584
2003	2,348	2,459	2,524	2,573	9,903
2002	2,195	2,297	2,382	2,420	9,294

Earnings Per Share ($)

2007	0.89	0.76	0.77	E0.87	E3.34
2006	0.59	0.51	0.63	0.73	2.46
2005	0.53	0.62	0.63	0.65	2.43
2004	0.59	0.66	0.58	0.50	2.33
2003	0.56	0.62	0.63	0.65	2.46
2002	0.49	0.55	0.57	0.59	2.19

Fiscal year ended Dec. 31. Next earnings report expected: Late January. EPS Estimates based on S&P Operating Earnings; historical GAAP earnings are as reported.

Dividend Data (Dates: mm/dd Payment Date: mm/dd/yy)

Amount ($)	Date Decl.	Ex-Div. Date	Stk. of Record	Payment Date
0.320	01/11	01/24	01/26	02/15/07
0.360	03/08	04/20	04/24	05/15/07
0.360	07/12	07/19	07/23	08/15/07
0.360	10/04	10/24	10/26	11/15/07

Dividends have been paid since 1895. Source: Company reports.

Please read the Required Disclosures and Analyst Certification on the last page of this report.

The McGraw-Hill Companies

Colgate-Palmolive Co

STANDARD &POOR'S

Business Summary October 31, 2007

CORPORATE OVERVIEW. Colgate-Palmolive Co. is a leading global consumer products company that operates in the oral, personal, and household care, and pet food markets. Its products are marketed in more than 200 countries and territories worldwide. Sales of oral, personal, and home care products accounted for 86% of total worldwide sales in 2006. The balance of revenues was derived from the sale of pet foods. The company's oral care products include toothbrushes, toothpaste and pharmaceutical products for oral health professionals. CL's personal care products include bar and liquid soaps, shampoos, conditioners, deodorants antiperspirants, and shave products. The home care division produces major brands such as Palmolive and Ajax soaps. Oral, personal and home care sales outside of North America accounted for 65% of total sales in 2006. Sales in Latin America, Europe/South Pacific and Greater Asia/Africa accounted for 29%, 28% and 19% of total oral, personal and home care sales segment sales, respectively.

MARKET PROFILE. CL is a dominant player in its categories. According to the company, in 2006, CL expanded upon its number one position in the U.S. tooth-

paste market to a record 37.3%. Furthermore, the company says, over the past decade, CL's global toothpaste market share has increased almost eight percentage points, and CL is now the market leader in 53 of the 71 largest toothpaste markets worldwide. While volume growth for CL's categories in developed countries has been modest, in our view, growth in the developing and emerging markets is projected to rise at a rate two to three times that of developed markets in the near term. Colgate has the advantage of having operated in these markets for an extended period of time (several decades) and this is evident in the leading market shares that the company enjoys. With plans to increase consumer awareness and product innovation, coupled with growing economies, we believe Colgate is well situated to benefit from this market growth.

Company Financials Fiscal Year Ended Dec. 31

Per Share Data ($)	2006	2005	2004	2003	2002	2001	2000	1999	1998	1997
Tangible Book Value	NM	NM	NM	NM	NM	NM	NM	NM	NM	NM
Cash Flow	3.06	2.97	2.86	3.15	2.65	2.40	2.32	1.96	1.69	1.60
Earnings	2.46	2.43	2.33	2.46	2.19	1.89	1.70	1.47	1.31	1.14
S&P Core Earnings	2.42	2.21	2.26	2.31	2.00	1.71	NA	NA	NA	NA
Dividends	1.25	1.11	0.96	0.90	0.72	0.68	0.63	0.59	0.55	0.53
Payout Ratio	51%	46%	41%	37%	33%	36%	37%	40%	42%	47%
Prices:High	67.08	57.15	59.04	60.99	58.86	64.75	66.75	65.00	49.44	39.34
Prices:Low	53.41	48.25	42.89	48.56	44.05	48.50	40.50	36.56	32.53	22.50
P/E Ratio:High	27	24	25	25	27	34	39	44	38	35
P/E Ratio:Low	22	20	18	20	20	26	24	25	25	20

Income Statement Analysis (Million $)										
Revenue	12,238	11,397	10,584	9,903	9,294	9,428	9,358	9,118	8,972	9,057
Operating Income	2,674	2,613	2,540	2,467	2,333	2,198	2,132	1,904	1,733	1,591
Depreciation	329	329	328	316	297	336	410	340	330	320
Interest Expense	159	143	124	124	151	192	200	212	205	232
Pretax Income	2,002	2,134	2,050	2,042	1,870	1,709	1,600	1,425	1,278	1,131
Effective Tax Rate	32.4%	34.1%	32.9%	30.4%	31.1%	30.6%	31.4%	32.1%	31.4%	32.0%
Net Income	1,353	1,351	1,327	1,421	1,288	1,147	1,064	937	849	740
S&P Core Earnings	1,306	1,207	1,262	1,309	1,152	1,011	NA	NA	NA	NA

Balance Sheet & Other Financial Data (Million $)										
Cash	490	341	320	265	168	173	213	235	182	183
Current Assets	3,301	2,757	2,740	2,497	2,228	2,203	2,347	2,355	2,245	2,196
Total Assets	9,138	8,507	8,673	7,479	7,087	6,985	7,252	7,423	7,685	7,539
Current Liabilities	3,469	2,743	2,731	2,445	2,149	2,124	2,244	2,274	2,114	1,959
Long Term Debt	2,720	2,918	3,090	2,685	3,211	2,812	2,537	2,243	2,301	2,341
Common Equity	1,188	1,380	971	594	27.3	505	1,115	1,467	1,709	1,793
Total Capital	4,441	5,106	4,845	4,028	4,050	4,139	4,453	4,701	4,834	4,805
Capital Expenditures	476	389	348	302	344	340	367	373	390	479
Cash Flow	1,682	1,653	1,629	1,736	1,563	1,461	1,453	1,255	1,158	1,039
Current Ratio	1.0	1.0	1.0	1.0	1.0	1.0	1.0	1.0	1.1	1.1
% Long Term Debt of Capitalization	61.3	57.1	63.8	66.7	79.3	67.9	57.0	47.7	47.6	48.7
% Net Income of Revenue	11.1	11.9	12.5	14.4	13.9	12.2	11.4	10.3	9.5	8.2
% Return on Assets	15.3	15.7	16.4	19.5	18.3	16.1	14.5	12.4	11.2	9.6
% Return on Equity	118.5	99.5	166.2	457.2	475.7	139.0	80.8	57.6	47.3	41.9

Data as orig reptd.; bef. results of disc opers/spec. items. Per share data adj. for stk. divs.; EPS diluted. E-Estimated. NA-Not Available. NM-Not Meaningful. NR-Not Ranked. UR-Under Review.

Office: 300 Park Avenue, New York, NY 10022.
Telephone: 212-310-2000.
Email: investor_relations@colpal.com
Website: http://www.colgate.com

Chrmn & CEO: R. Mark
Pres & COO: I.M. Cook
Vice Chrmn: J.G. Teruel
SVP, Secy & General Counsel: A.D. Hendry

VP & Treas: E.J. Filusch
Board Members: J. T. Cahill, J. K. Conway, E. M. Hancock, D. W. Johnson, R. J. Kogan, D. E. Lewis, R. Mark, J. P. Reinhard, H. B. Wentz, Jr.

Founded: 1806
Domicile: Delaware
Employees: 34,700

The McGraw-Hill Companies

Comcast Corp

**STANDARD
&POOR'S**

S&P Recommendation SELL ★ ★ ☆ ☆ ☆

Price	12-Mo. Target Price	Investment Style
$20.31 (as of Nov 29, 2007)	$20.00	Large-Cap Blend

GICS Sector Consumer Discretionary
Sub-Industry Broadcasting & Cable TV

Summary With over 24.1 million subscribers, this company is the largest U.S. cable multiple system operator (MSO), as well as a provider of cable programming content.

Key Stock Statistics (Source S&P, Vickers, company reports)

52-Wk Range	$30.18– 18.83	S&P Oper. EPS 2007**E**	0.77	Market Capitalization(B)	$42.201	Beta	0.55
Trailing 12-Month EPS	$0.75	S&P Oper. EPS 2008**E**	1.03	Yield (%)	Nil	S&P 3-Yr. Proj. EPS CAGR(%)	20.00
Trailing 12-Month P/E	27.1	P/E on S&P Oper. EPS 2007**E**	26.4	Dividend Rate/Share	Nil	S&P Credit Rating	BBB
$10K Invested 5 Yrs Ago	$11,273	Common Shares Outstg. (M)	3,073.2	Institutional Ownership (%)	77		

Price Performance

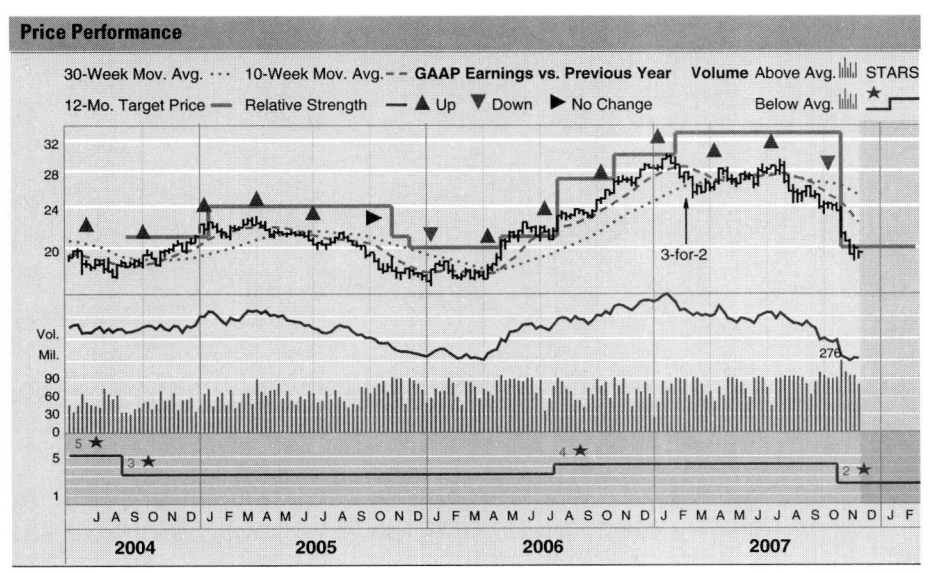

30-Week Mov. Avg. · · · 10-Week Mov. Avg. - - **GAAP Earnings vs. Previous Year** Volume Above Avg. STARS
12-Mo. Target Price — Relative Strength — ▲ Up ▼ Down ▶ No Change Below Avg. ★

Options: ASE, CBOE, P, Ph

Analysis prepared by **Tuna N. Amobi, CFA, CPA** on October 26, 2007, when the stock traded at **$ 20.98**.

Qualitative Risk Assessment

LOW	MEDIUM	HIGH

Our risk assessment reflects intensifying competition from satellite operators and telcos, partly offset by economies of scale and what we view as a relatively sound financial condition.

Quantitative Evaluations

S&P Quality Ranking B-

D	C	B-	B	B+	A-	A	A+

Relative Strength Rank MODERATE

34

LOWEST = 1 HIGHEST = 99

Revenue/Earnings Data

Revenue (Million $)

	1Q	2Q	3Q	4Q	Year
2007	7,388	7,712	7,781	--	--
2006	5,595	5,908	6,432	7,031	24,966
2005	5,363	5,598	5,578	5,716	22,255
2004	4,908	5,066	5,098	5,235	20,307
2003	4,466	4,594	4,546	4,742	18,348
2002	2,672	2,709	2,705	4,374	12,460

Earnings Per Share ($)

2007	0.26	0.19	0.18	E0.24	E0.77
2006	0.15	0.13	0.31	0.14	0.70
2005	0.04	0.13	0.07	0.04	0.28
2004	0.02	0.08	0.07	0.13	0.29
2003	-0.11	Nil	-0.05	0.11	-0.07
2002	-0.06	-0.15	0.05	-0.02	-0.17

Fiscal year ended Dec. 31. Next earnings report expected: Early February. EPS Estimates based on S&P Operating Earnings; historical GAAP earnings are as reported.

Dividend Data (Dates: mm/dd Payment Date: mm/dd/yy)

Amount ($)	Date Decl.	Ex-Div. Date	Stk. of Record	Payment Date
3-for-2 Stk.	02/01	02/22	02/14	02/21/07

Source: Company reports.

Highlights

➤ We forecast that consolidated pro forma revenues will increase nearly 14% in 2007 (from about $27.6 billion in 2006 -- including certain acquisitions and dispositions from the beginning of that year), and 12% in 2008, to reach about $35.4 billion. While we see the company as on track for its 2007 target of about 6.5 million revenue-generating unit (RGU) net adds, we think stiffening competition could weigh on RGU growth starting in 2008. We see continued strong growth in the content businesses, and relatively modest gains in ad revenues.

➤ Despite potential margin upside with the integration of new acquisitions, results could be adversely affected by price discounting, as well as further investments in content, technology and wireless initiatives. From about $10.4 billion in 2006, we project consolidated pro forma EBITDA of about $12.0 billion and $13.7 billion for the next two years.

➤ After higher D&A charges on the newly acquired systems, we estimate EPS of $0.77 and $1.03 for 2007 and 2008, respectively. The company recently had about $8.2 billion available under its buyback authorization.

Investment Rationale/Risk

➤ Our recent downgrade of the shares to sell, from buy, partly reflects stiffer competition. In late October, the shares sold off sharply after what we consider lackluster third quarter results, with basic subscriber losses for the second consecutive quarter, and digital/data net adds shy of our projections. Despite potential benefits of digital phone deployment in the years ahead, such gains increasingly could be muted by decelerating RGU growth. We think management could respond with more aggressive discounting of the triple-play bundle, as DBS providers bulk up on high-def offerings, and the telcos make forays with fiber-based offerings. We doubt sustained share buybacks could otherwise offer support.

➤ Risks to our recommendation and target price include potential upside with digital phone and, longer term, the commercial market; a strong balance sheet; and favorable regulatory developments.

➤ Our 12-month target price of $20 implies nearly 7X cable-only enterprise value to projected 2008 EBITDA, nearly $3,800 per subscriber, which we view as in line with cable peers.

Comcast Corp

STANDARD &POOR'S

Business Summary October 26, 2007

CORPORATE OVERVIEW. Comcast Corp. became the largest U.S. cable multiple system operator (MSO) after its acquisition of the former AT&T Broadband (ATTB) in November 2002. As of September 30, 2007, the company counted about 24.1 million subscribers to its basic service, about 14.7 million for digital video, 12.9 million for high-speed Internet service, and 4.1 million for telephone (3.8 million digital phone and 304,000 for circuit-switched phone). The company's content assets include cable networks E! Entertainment Television, The Golf Channel, Outdoor Life Network and G4, among other programming investments.

COMPETITIVE LANDSCAPE. In a typical market, Comcast faces competition from direct broadcast satellite (DBS) providers DirecTV Group and EchoStar Communications, and from incumbent phone companies such as Verizon Communications and AT&T (formerly SBC Communications). In addition, the company competes in several markets that are served by overbuilders that also provide video, voice and data services to residential, and in some cases, enterprise customers.

We expect this competition to intensify in the years ahead, as both DBS companies launch new satellites to drive advanced video offerings, while the telcos accelerate their own deployment of fiber-based video and broadband offerings. A possible national franchising bill could also help the new entrants attain a much quicker time-to-market in head-to-head competition with cable operators. With DSL discounts already aggressive in several markets, we believe the pending AT&T acquisition of BellSouth could create a stronger competitor that could further drive increased promotional activity.

However, we think Comcast has thus far successfully resisted price competition, focusing instead on product differentiation through newer offerings such as VOD, and enhanced features such as higher data speeds and a broadband portal. We expect cable operators to increasingly experiment with package discounts, as the rapidly changing competitive landscape continues to evolve.

Company Financials Fiscal Year Ended Dec. 31

Per Share Data ($)	2006	2005	2004	2003	2002	2001	2000	1999	1998	1997
Tangible Book Value	NM	NM	NM	NM	NM	NM	NM	NM	NM	NM
Cash Flow	2.22	1.79	1.69	0.24	1.05	0.99	3.27	1.60	1.59	0.70
Earnings	0.70	0.28	0.29	-0.07	-0.17	-0.89	1.44	0.63	0.83	-0.22
S&P Core Earnings	0.48	0.33	0.14	-0.30	0.47	-1.03	NA	NA	NA	NA
Dividends	Nil	Nil	Nil	Nil	Nil	Nil	Nil	0.01	0.03	0.03
Payout Ratio	Nil	Nil	Nil	Nil	Nil	Nil	Nil	1%	4%	NM
Prices:High	28.94	23.00	24.33	23.23	25.03	30.54	34.91	36.42	19.67	11.04
Prices:Low	16.90	17.20	17.50	15.61	11.37	21.23	18.62	18.71	9.83	4.79
P/E Ratio:High	41	82	85	NM	NM	NM	24	57	24	NM
P/E Ratio:Low	24	61	61	NM	NM	NM	13	30	12	NM

Income Statement Analysis (Million $)										
Revenue	24,966	22,255	20,307	18,348	12,460	19,697	8,219	6,209	5,145	4,913
Operating Income	9,442	8,493	7,531	6,392	3,691	1,576	2,470	1,880	1,497	1,469
Depreciation	4,823	4,803	4,623	4,438	2,032	6,345	2,631	1,216	940	936
Interest Expense	2,064	1,796	1,876	2,018	884	2,341	691	538	467	565
Pretax Income	3,594	1,880	1,810	-137	70.0	-5,927	3,602	1,500	1,557	-229
Effective Tax Rate	37.5%	49.6%	45.6%	NM	NM	NM	40.0%	48.2%	38.1%	NM
Net Income	2,235	928	970	-218	-276	-3,021	2,045	781	1,008	-209
S&P Core Earnings	1,541	1,090	465	-979	792	-1,482	NA	NA	NA	NA

Balance Sheet & Other Financial Data (Million $)										
Cash	1,239	693	452	1,550	781	558	652	922	871	414
Current Assets	5,202	2,594	3,535	5,403	7,076	4,944	5,144	9,759	5,624	1,560
Total Assets	110,405	103,146	104,694	109,159	113,105	109,319	35,745	28,686	14,817	12,804
Current Liabilities	7,440	6,269	8,635	9,654	15,383	12,489	4,042	5,527	3,093	1,418
Long Term Debt	27,992	21,682	20,093	23,835	27,957	27,528	10,517	8,707	5,464	6,559
Common Equity	41,167	40,219	41,422	41,662	38,329	38,451	28,113	9,772	3,243	1,101
Total Capital	96,489	89,928	88,798	91,689	92,070	94,758	45,734	23,159	10,780	10,317
Capital Expenditures	4,395	3,621	3,660	4,161	1,975	NA	1,637	894	899	926
Cash Flow	7,058	5,731	5,593	4,220	1,756	3,324	4,653	1,967	1,918	713
Current Ratio	0.7	0.4	0.4	0.6	0.5	0.4	1.3	1.8	1.8	1.1
% Long Term Debt of Capitalization	29.0	24.1	22.6	26.0	30.4	29.1	23.0	37.6	50.7	63.6
% Net Income of Revenue	9.0	4.2	4.8	NM	NM	NM	24.9	12.6	19.6	NM
% Return on Assets	2.1	0.9	0.9	NM	NM	NM	6.3	3.6	7.3	NM
% Return on Equity	5.5	2.3	2.3	NM	NM	NM	8.4	11.5	45.1	NM

Data as orig reptd.; bef. results of disc opers/spec. items. Per share data adj. for stk. divs.; EPS diluted. E-Estimated. NA-Not Available. NM-Not Meaningful. NR-Not Ranked. UR-Under Review.

Office: 1500 Market St , Philadelphia, PA 19102-2148.
Telephone: 215-665-1700.
Website: http://www.comcast.com
Chrmn, Pres & CEO: B.L. Roberts

COO & EVP: S. Burke
EVP & CFO: M.J. Angelakis
EVP, CFO & Treas: J.R. Alchin
SVP, Chief Acctg Officer & Cntlr: L.J. Salva

Investor Contact: M. Dooner (866-281-2100)
Board Members: S. D. Anstrom, K. J. Bacon, S. M. Bonovitz, E. D. Breen, J. A. Brodsky, J. J. Collins, J. M. Cook, J. A. Honickman, B. L. Roberts, R. J. Roberts, J. Rodin, M. I. Sovern

Founded: 1969
Domicile: Pennsylvania
Employees: 90,000

Comerica Inc

STANDARD &POOR'S

S&P Recommendation	STRONG SELL ★☆☆☆☆	Price	12-Mo. Target Price	Investment Style
		$43.09 (as of Nov 23, 2007)	$39.00	Large-Cap Value

GICS Sector Financials
Sub-Industry Diversified Banks

Summary This bank holding company operates banking affiliates mainly in Michigan, Texas, California, Arizona and Florida.

Key Stock Statistics (Source S&P, Vickers, company reports)

52-Wk Range	$63.89–41.34	S&P Oper. EPS 2007**E**	4.71	Market Capitalization(B)	$6.507	Beta	0.80
Trailing 12-Month EPS	$5.48	S&P Oper. EPS 2008**E**	4.60	Yield (%)	5.94	S&P 3-Yr. Proj. EPS CAGR(%)	7.00
Trailing 12-Month P/E	7.9	P/E on S&P Oper. EPS 2007**E**	9.1	Dividend Rate/Share	$2.56	S&P Credit Rating	A
$10K Invested 5 Yrs Ago	$11,111	Common Shares Outstg. (M)	151.0	Institutional Ownership (%)	71		

Price Performance

30-Week Mov. Avg. · · · 10-Week Mov. Avg. - - GAAP Earnings vs. Previous Year Volume Above Avg. STARS
12-Mo. Target Price — Relative Strength — ▲ Up ▼ Down ► No Change Below Avg. ★

Options: ASE, CBOE, P, Ph

Analysis prepared by **Frank Braden, CFA** on November 21, 2007, when the stock traded at **$ 41.69**.

Highlights

➤ We see rising pressure on CMA's commercial real estate portfolio, given its exposure to the California and Michigan markets. In the third quarter, nonperforming real estate construction loans rose to $59 million from $4 million and total net charge-offs rose to 32 bps from 2 bps. We expect the net interest margin to decline to 3.6% in 2008, as competitive deposit pricing should more than offset any expected steepening of the yield curve. We believe intense competition in the Midwest will continue to affect both deposit growth and earnings over the next several quarters.

➤ We remain favorable on CMA's de novo branch building strategy and look for additional new branches in higher-growth Texas markets during 2008. However, we believe CMA's home equity, auto and real estate exposure will pressure results. We believe prudent expense management will be of critical importance in 2008, given the company's expectation of margin pressure and new branch expenses.

➤ We estimate 2007 operating EPS of $4.71, down from $4.81 in 2006, on a modest decrease in share count and a projected 31.5% effective tax rate. Our EPS projection for 2008 is $4.60.

Investment Rationale/Risk

➤ While we believe CMA has done a good job geographically diversifying its loan portfolio, the company's exposure still predominantly lies in the struggling markets of Florida, California and Michigan. We remain cautious as we see the interest rate environment and competition remaining fierce for the long term in CMA's primary Midwest market. We believe CMA will continue to take provisions in the quarters ahead due to the challenging commercial real estate, home equity, and auto markets. We expect CMA to continue to emphasize growth in its markets in the West and Texas.

➤ Risks to our recommendation and target price include a pickup in the economy, a recovery of the real estate market, and an improvement in business spending.

➤ Our 12-month target price of $39 equates to approximately 8.5X our 2008 operating EPS estimate, a discount to the stock's average historical valuation multiple, given the lack of near-term earnings visibility.

Qualitative Risk Assessment

LOW	MEDIUM	HIGH

Our risk assessment reflects what we see as solid business fundamentals and a strong customer base. We view CMA as well diversified and able to withstand a major regional or U.S. economic downturn.

Quantitative Evaluations

S&P Quality Ranking A

D	C	B-	B	B+	A-	A	A+

Relative Strength Rank WEAK

26

LOWEST = 1 HIGHEST = 99

Revenue/Earnings Data

Revenue (Million $)

	1Q	2Q	3Q	4Q	Year
2007	1,104	1,158	1,182	--	--
2006	967.0	1,048	1,088	1,174	4,277
2005	817.0	874.0	951.0	1,026	3,668
2004	763.0	773.0	764.0	794.0	3,094
2003	866.0	853.0	800.0	780.0	3,299
2002	920.0	927.0	910.0	940.0	3,697

Earnings Per Share ($)

2007	1.19	1.25	1.17	E1.10	E4.71
2006	1.26	1.19	1.20	1.16	4.81
2005	1.16	1.28	1.41	1.25	5.11
2004	0.92	1.10	1.13	1.21	4.36
2003	1.00	0.97	0.89	0.89	3.75
2002	1.20	0.88	0.14	1.18	3.40

Fiscal year ended Dec. 31. Next earnings report expected: Mid January. EPS Estimates based on S&P Operating Earnings; historical GAAP earnings are as reported.

Dividend Data (Dates: mm/dd Payment Date: mm/dd/yy)

Amount ($)	Date Decl.	Ex-Div. Date	Stk. of Record	Payment Date
0.640	01/23	03/13	03/15	04/01/07
0.640	05/15	06/13	06/15	07/01/07
0.640	07/24	09/12	09/15	10/01/07
0.640	11/13	12/12	12/15	01/01/08

Dividends have been paid since 1936. Source: Company reports.

Please read the Required Disclosures and Analyst Certification on the last page of this report.

The **McGraw·Hill** Companies

Comerica Inc

STANDARD &POOR'S

Business Summary November 21, 2007

CORPORATE OVERVIEW. The owner of one of Michigan's oldest banks, Comerica is a Detroit-based bank holding company that operates banking units mainly in Michigan, California, Texas, Arizona and Florida. It also has banking subsidiaries in Canada and Mexico.

Operations are divided into three major lines of business: the Business Bank, the Retail Bank (formerly known as Small Business and Personal Financial Services), and Wealth & Institutional Management. The Business Bank is primarily comprised of middle market, commercial real estate, national dealer services, global finance, large corporate, leasing, financial services, and technology and life sciences. This business segment offers various products and services, including commercial loans and lines of credit, deposits, cash management, capital market products, international trade finance, letters of credit, foreign exchange management services and loan syndication services.

The Retail Bank includes small business banking (entities with annual sales under $10 million) and personal financial services, consisting of consumer

lending, consumer deposit gathering and mortgage loan origination. In addition to a full range of financial services provided to small businesses and their owners, this business segment offers a variety of consumer products, including deposit accounts, installment loans, credit and debit cards, student loans, home equity loans and lines of credit, and residential mortgage loans.

Wealth & Institutional Management offers products and services consisting of personal trust, which is designed to meet the personal financial needs of the affluent, private banking, institutional trust, retirement services, investment management and advisory services, investment banking, and discount securities brokerage services. This business segment also offers the sale of mutual funds and annuity products, as well as life, disability and long-term care insurance products.

Company Financials Fiscal Year Ended Dec. 31

Per Share Data ($)	2006	2005	2004	2003	2002	2001	2000	1999	1998	1997
Tangible Book Value	32.82	33.01	29.85	29.20	28.31	27.15	23.94	20.60	17.94	16.02
Earnings	4.81	5.11	4.36	3.75	3.40	3.88	4.63	4.14	3.72	3.19
S&P Core Earnings	4.71	4.90	4.27	3.72	3.30	3.27	NA	NA	NA	NA
Dividends	2.36	2.20	2.08	2.00	1.92	1.76	1.60	1.40	1.25	1.15
Payout Ratio	49%	43%	48%	53%	56%	45%	35%	34%	34%	36%
Prices:High	60.10	63.38	63.80	56.34	66.09	65.15	61.13	70.00	73.00	61.87
Prices:Low	50.12	53.17	50.45	37.10	35.20	44.02	32.94	44.00	46.50	34.17
P/E Ratio:High	12	12	15	15	19	17	13	17	20	19
P/E Ratio:Low	10	10	12	10	10	11	7	11	12	11

Income Statement Analysis (Million $)										
Net Interest Income	1,983	1,956	1,810	1,926	2,132	2,102	1,659	1,547	1,461	1,443
Tax Equivalent Adjustment	NA	4.00	3.00	3.00	4.00	4.00	4.00	5.00	7.00	9.00
Non Interest Income	855	942	857	837	819	784	827	711	597	522
Loan Loss Provision	37.0	-47.0	64.0	377	635	236	145	114	113	146
% Expense/Operating Revenue	59.0%	57.4%	55.9%	53.6%	51.3%	53.9%	53.6%	49.3%	49.4%	51.3%
Pretax Income	1,127	1,279	1,110	953	882	1,111	1,151	1,033	931	817
Effective Tax Rate	30.6%	32.7%	31.8%	30.6%	31.9%	36.1%	34.9%	34.9%	34.8%	35.0%
Net Income	782	861	757	661	601	710	749	673	607	530
% Net Interest Margin	3.79	4.06	3.86	3.95	4.55	4.61	4.54	4.55	4.57	4.53
S&P Core Earnings	766	826	744	657	584	587	NA	NA	NA	NA

Balance Sheet & Other Financial Data (Million $)										
Money Market Assets	2,632	1,159	3,230	4,013	2,446	1,079	165	613	110	203
Investment Securities	3,989	5,399	7,173	8,502	5,499	5,370	2,843	2,739	2,822	4,006
Commercial Loans	35,924	33,707	31,540	32,153	33,732	32,660	28,001	25,429	23,266	16,323
Other Loans	11,507	9,540	9,303	7,274	8,549	8,536	8,060	7,265	7,339	12,572
Total Assets	58,001	53,013	51,766	52,592	53,301	50,732	41,985	38,653	36,601	36,292
Demand Deposits	29,151	15,666	15,164	14,104	16,335	12,596	6,815	6,136	6,999	6,761
Time Deposits	15,776	26,765	25,772	27,359	25,440	24,974	20,353	17,155	17,314	15,825
Long Term Debt	5,949	3,961	4,286	4,801	5,216	5,503	8,089	8,580	5,282	7,286
Common Equity	5,153	5,068	5,105	5,110	4,947	4,807	3,757	3,225	2,797	2,512
% Return on Assets	1.4	1.6	1.5	1.2	1.2	1.4	1.9	1.8	1.7	1.5
% Return on Equity	15.3	16.9	14.8	13.1	12.3	15.4	21.0	21.8	22.2	21.1
% Loan Loss Reserve	1.0	1.2	-1.6	2.0	1.9	-1.6	1.5	1.5	1.5	1.5
% Loans/Deposits	105.6	101.9	99.8	99.3	101.2	109.7	132.7	140.4	125.9	127.9
% Equity to Assets	9.2	9.7	9.8	9.5	9.4	9.0	8.7	8.0	7.3	6.9

Data as orig reptd.; bef. results of disc opers/spec. items. Per share data adj. for stk. divs.; EPS diluted. E-Estimated. NA-Not Available. NM-Not Meaningful. NR-Not Ranked. UR-Under Review.

Office: 1717 Main St, Dallas, TX 75201-4612.
Telephone: 214-969-6476.
Website: http://www.comerica.com
Chrmn, Pres & CEO: R.W. Babb, Jr.

Vice Chrmn: J.J. Buttigieg, III
EVP & CFO: E.S. Acton
SVP & Treas: P.E. Burdiss
Investor Contact: J.S. Love (313-222-2840)

Board Members: R. W. Babb, Jr., L. Bauder, J. J. Buttigieg, III, J. F. Cordes, R. A. Cregg, P. D. Cummings, T. K. DeNicola, A. F. Earley, Jr., A. A. Piergallini, R. S. Taubman, R. M. Turner, Jr., W. P. Vititoe, K. L. Way

Founded: 1849
Domicile: Delaware
Employees: 11,270

Commerce Bancorp Inc.

STANDARD &POOR'S

S&P Recommendation	HOLD ★★★☆☆	Price $36.70 (as of Nov 27, 2007)	12-Mo. Target Price $37.00	Investment Style Large-Cap Growth

GICS Sector Financials
Sub-Industry Regional Banks

Summary This multibank holding company, based in New Jersey, has agreed to be acquired by Canada's TD Bank Financial Group for cash and stock.

Key Stock Statistics (Source S&P, Vickers, company reports)

52-Wk Range	$41.00–30.45	S&P Oper. EPS 2007**E**	1.51	Market Capitalization(B)	$7.055	Beta	0.77
Trailing 12-Month EPS	$0.86	S&P Oper. EPS 2008**E**	1.70	Yield (%)	1.42	S&P 3-Yr. Proj. EPS CAGR(%)	5.10
Trailing 12-Month P/E	42.7	P/E on S&P Oper. EPS 2007**E**	24.3	Dividend Rate/Share	$0.52	S&P Credit Rating	BBB+
$10K Invested 5 Yrs Ago	$17,107	Common Shares Outstg. (M)	192.2	Institutional Ownership (%)	96		

Price Performance

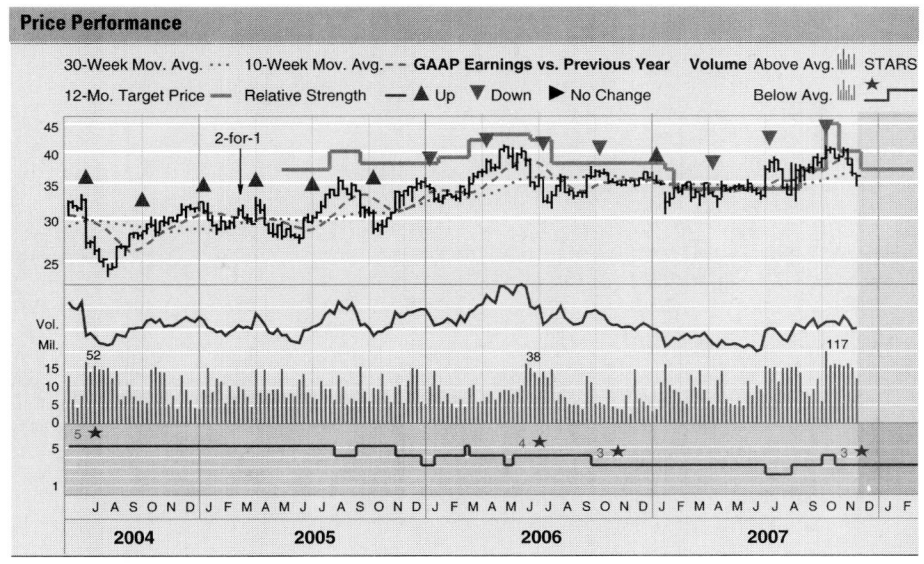

30-Week Mov. Avg. ··· 10-Week Mov. Avg. - - **GAAP Earnings vs. Previous Year** Volume Above Avg. STARS
12-Mo. Target Price — Relative Strength ▲ Up ▼ Down ► No Change Below Avg.

Options: ASE, CBOE, P, Ph

Analysis prepared by **Erik Oja** on November 27, 2007, when the stock traded at **$ 36.16**.

Highlights

➤ CBH opened only 14 branches in the first two quarters of 2007, partly due to a pair of regulatory inquiries, which were settled in early July. CBH added 15 branches in the third quarter and plans to add 21 more in the fourth, bringing the total for the year to 50 new branches, which would raise CBH's total to 478 branches. Deposit growth in the third quarter rebounded to 19.3%, annualized, in line with the 10.1% to 27.5% annualized rates of the previous 12 quarters through March 31. We estimate a 15% rate for 2007, and 9.0% in 2008.

➤ We expect CBH's non-interest expenses to remain high relative to peers, as a result of its branch expansion plans and legal and severance costs associated with the recent regulatory settlements. Credit deteriorated in the third quarter, in our view, with 0.58% of loans rated non-performing; we expect this to lead to loan loss provisions of about $75 million in 2007 and $81 million in 2008, up from $33.7 million in 2006.

➤ We see operating EPS of $1.51 in 2007, a 2.6% decrease from 2006's $1.55. Our 2008 EPS estimate is $1.70, a 12.6% increase.

Investment Rationale/Risk

➤ CBH has agreed to be acquired by TD Bank Financial Group (TD: $65), in a deal worth $8.34 billion at the time of the announcement, but $7.61 billion currently. Under the agreement, CBH shareholders will receive 0.4142 of a TD share and US$10.50 in cash in exchange for each common share of CBH, a transaction that is currently worth $37.40 per share. The merger agreement, subject to shareholder and regulatory approval, is expected to close by April 2008.

➤ Risks to our recommendation and target price include lower than expected operational performance, and the possibility that the merger agreement is not consummated.

➤ CBH's current market value is 0.15X total September 30 deposits, below similarly sized banks. Our 12-month target price of $37 is equal to 0.16X total September 30 deposits, still below most other banks, and equal to about 22X our 2008 EPS estimate of $1.70, a premium to peers that we think reflects CBH's industry-leading deposit growth rates.

Qualitative Risk Assessment

LOW	MEDIUM	HIGH

Our risk assessment reflects our view of the strong credit quality of the company's loan portfolio, and its history of profitability. While the company operates in a highly competitive and fragmented industry, the industry tends to produce relatively stable financial results.

Quantitative Evaluations

S&P Quality Ranking A+

D	C	B-	B	B+	A-	A	A+

Relative Strength Rank MODERATE

66

LOWEST = 1 HIGHEST = 99

Revenue/Earnings Data

Revenue (Million $)

	1Q	2Q	3Q	4Q	Year
2007	791.3	833.7	685.0	--	--
2006	641.5	705.1	748.0	775.7	2,870
2005	474.2	513.3	548.6	571.9	2,108
2004	358.3	384.3	420.9	449.9	1,613
2003	282.9	302.1	319.1	344.0	1,248
2002	224.1	250.1	220.2	272.2	1,013

Earnings Per Share ($)

2007	0.40	0.39	-0.24	E0.43	E1.51
2006	0.41	0.41	0.41	0.32	1.55
2005	0.45	0.46	0.45	0.26	1.61
2004	0.38	0.40	0.42	0.44	1.63
2003	0.30	0.32	0.34	0.36	1.31
2002	0.23	0.25	0.26	0.29	1.02

Fiscal year ended Dec. 31. Next earnings report expected: Mid January. EPS Estimates based on S&P Operating Earnings; historical GAAP earnings are as reported.

Dividend Data (Dates: mm/dd Payment Date: mm/dd/yy)

Amount ($)	Date Decl.	Ex-Div. Date	Stk. of Record	Payment Date
0.130	12/20	01/03	01/05	01/19/07
0.130	03/20	04/03	04/05	04/20/07
0.130	06/27	07/05	07/09	07/20/07
0.130	09/19	10/02	10/04	10/18/07

Dividends have been paid since 1984. Source: Company reports.

Please read the Required Disclosures and Analyst Certification on the last page of this report.

The **McGraw·Hill** Companies

Commerce Bancorp Inc.

STANDARD &POOR'S

Business Summary November 27, 2007

CORPORATE OVERVIEW. Commerce Bancorp, Inc. owns three nationally chartered bank subsidiaries and one New Jersey chartered bank subsidiary. At the end of 2006, the company had assets of $45.3 billion and a market capitalization of $6.3 billion. The company operates two reportable segments: Community Banks and Parent/Other.

The Community Banks segment offers a relatively standard group of banking services, which include: free minimum balance checking accounts, savings programs, money market accounts, negotiable orders of withdrawal (NOW) accounts, certificates of deposit (CDs), safe deposit facilities, free coin counting, consumer installment loan programs (such as home improvement or automobile loans), home equity and revolving lines of credit, overdraft checking, construction loans, and home mortgages. The segment also provides corporate trust services.

The Parent/Other segment includes Commerce Insurance, Commerce Capital Markets (CCMI), and the holding company. Commerce Insurance operates an insurance brokerage agency concentrating on commercial property, casualty and surety, as well as personal lines of insurance and employee benefits for clients, primarily in Delaware, New Jersey, New York and Pennsylvania. CCMI engages in various securities, investment banking and brokerage activities.

MARKET PROFILE. As of June 30, 2007, which is the latest available FDIC branch-level data, CBH had 444 branches and $44.6 billion in deposits. About 50% of deposits and 47% of branches were concentrated in New Jersey, according to Highline Data. In New Jersey, CBH had 207 branches, $22.3 billion in deposits, and a deposit market share of about 9.7%, ranking third, behind Bank of America (BAC: strong buy, $43), and Wachovia (WB: buy, $40). In New York, CBH had 104 branches, $12.0 billion in deposits, and a deposit market share of about 1.6%, ranking 15th. In Pennsylvania, CBH had 85 branches, $8.4 billion in deposits, and a deposit market share of about 3.0%, ranking sixth. In Connecticut, the District of Columbia, Delaware, Florida, Maryland, and Virginia, CBH had a total of 48 branches and $1.8 billion in deposits.

Company Financials Fiscal Year Ended Dec. 31

Per Share Data ($)	2006	2005	2004	2003	2002	2001	2000	1999	1998	1997
Tangible Book Value	14.11	12.33	10.42	8.35	6.77	4.84	3.89	2.99	2.98	2.69
Earnings	1.55	1.61	1.63	1.31	1.02	0.76	0.63	0.54	0.47	0.41
S&P Core Earnings	1.55	1.30	1.56	1.24	0.97	0.70	NA	NA	NA	NA
Dividends	0.48	0.44	0.38	0.33	0.30	0.28	0.24	0.21	0.22	0.15
Payout Ratio	29%	27%	23%	25%	29%	36%	39%	38%	46%	34%
Prices:High	41.20	35.98	33.83	26.74	25.25	19.80	17.70	11.90	12.02	8.97
Prices:Low	31.20	26.87	23.35	18.12	18.05	13.00	7.72	9.23	7.53	4.51
P/E Ratio:High	25	22	21	20	25	26	28	22	25	21
P/E Ratio:Low	19	17	14	14	18	17	12	17	16	11

Income Statement Analysis (Million $)										
Net Interest Income	1,275	1,154	1,018	756	573	401	297	244	174	147
Tax Equivalent Adjustment	NA	19.7	18.4	15.6	13.1	11.4	9.22	5.19	2.37	1.36
Non Interest Income	588	457	372	329	257	196	148	112	86.0	55.1
Loan Loss Provision	33.7	19.2	39.2	31.9	33.2	26.4	13.9	9.18	5.87	4.67
% Expense/Operating Revenue	72.8%	70.3%	66.6%	69.4%	68.7%	69.0%	69.5%	69.8%	69.4%	68.2%
Pretax Income	476	431	415	293	218	152	118	97.3	74.8	61.9
Effective Tax Rate	37.1%	34.3%	34.1%	33.7%	33.5%	32.1%	32.4%	32.2%	34.1%	34.9%
Net Income	299	283	273	194	145	103	80.0	66.0	49.3	40.3
% Net Interest Margin	3.35	3.77	4.28	4.36	4.69	4.76	4.62	4.65	4.38	4.55
S&P Core Earnings	299	227	262	184	136	94.9	NA	NA	NA	NA

Balance Sheet & Other Financial Data (Million $)										
Money Market Assets	9.30	156	169	170	326	283	161	123	85.4	168
Investment Securities	25,983	22,524	18,508	13,141	8,570	5,285	3,535	2,866	2,411	2,197
Commercial Loans	7,143	5,591	4,115	3,298	3,859	3,034	2,440	1,766	367	254
Other Loans	8,465	7,068	5,340	4,143	1,963	1,549	1,247	1,195	1,564	1,157
Total Assets	45,272	38,466	30,502	22,712	16,404	11,364	8,297	6,636	4,894	3,939
Demand Deposits	24,435	30,793	18,011	13,149	3,243	6,012	1,789	1,421	1,037	763
Time Deposits	16,853	3,933	9,648	7,552	11,306	4,173	5,598	4,188	3,398	2,607
Long Term Debt	Nil	Nil	200	200	200	80.5	80.5	80.5	80.5	23.0
Common Equity	2,801	2,309	1,666	1,277	918	640	492	358	302	248
% Return on Assets	0.7	0.8	1.0	1.0	1.0	1.0	1.1	1.1	1.1	1.2
% Return on Equity	11.7	14.2	18.6	17.7	18.6	18.1	18.9	19.3	17.9	18.6
% Loan Loss Reserve	1.0	1.1	1.4	1.5	1.5	1.4	1.3	1.3	1.4	1.5
% Loans/Deposits	37.9	36.5	34.3	36.1	40.7	45.7	50.5	52.9	43.5	39.9
% Equity to Assets	6.1	5.8	5.5	5.6	5.6	5.8	5.7	5.7	6.2	6.3

Data as orig reptd.; bef. results of disc opers/spec. items. Per share data adj. for stk. divs.; EPS diluted. E-Estimated. NA-Not Available. NM-Not Meaningful. NR-Not Ranked. UR-Under Review.

Office: 1701 Route 70 , Cherry Hill, NJ 08003-2335.
Telephone: 856-751-9000.
Website: http://www.commerceonline.com
Chrmn, Pres, CEO & Secy: V.W. Hill, II

EVP & CFO: D.J. Pauls
EVP & Treas: P.M. Musumeci, Jr.
Investor Contact: C.E. Jordan, Jr. (856-751-7502)

Board Members: J. R. Bershad, J. E. Buckelew, D. T. DiFrancesco, V. W. Hill, II, M. N. Kerr, S. M. Lewis, J. K. Lloyd, G. E. Norcross, III, III, D. J. Ragone, W. A. Schwartz, Jr., J. T. Tarquini, Jr., J. S. Vassalluzzo

Founded: 1982
Domicile: New Jersey
Employees: 11,800

Computer Sciences Corp

STANDARD &POOR'S

S&P Recommendation **HOLD** ★★★☆☆	Price $52.21 (as of Nov 28, 2007)	12-Mo. Target Price $60.00	Investment Style Large-Cap Blend

GICS Sector Information Technology
Sub-Industry Data Processing & Outsourced Services

Summary This leading computer services company provides consulting, systems integration, and outsourcing services.

Key Stock Statistics (Source S&P, Vickers, company reports)

52-Wk Range	$63.76– 46.95	S&P Oper. EPS 2008**E**	4.13	Market Capitalization(B)	$9.084	Beta		1.12
Trailing 12-Month EPS	$2.16	S&P Oper. EPS 2009**E**	4.50	Yield (%)	Nil	S&P 3-Yr. Proj. EPS CAGR(%)		13.00
Trailing 12-Month P/E	24.2	P/E on S&P Oper. EPS 2008**E**	12.6	Dividend Rate/Share	Nil	S&P Credit Rating		A-
$10K Invested 5 Yrs Ago	$14,613	Common Shares Outstg. (M)	174.0	Institutional Ownership (%)	90			

Price Performance

30-Week Mov. Avg. · · · 10-Week Mov. Avg. - - **GAAP Earnings vs. Previous Year** Volume Above Avg. STARS
12-Mo. Target Price — Relative Strength — ▲ Up ▼ Down ► No Change Below Avg. ★

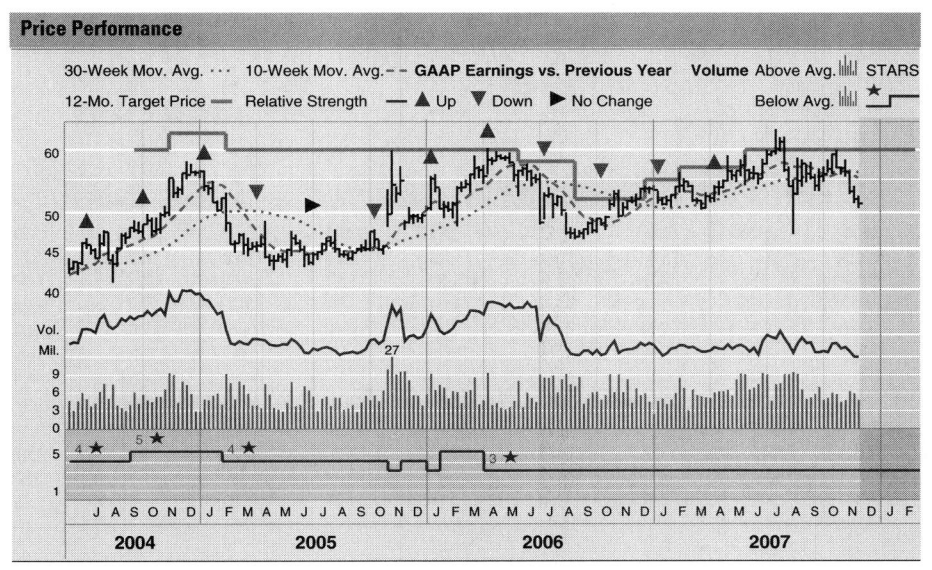

Options: ASE, CBOE, P, Ph

Analysis prepared by **Dylan Cathers** on November 28, 2007, when the stock traded at **$ 51.71**.

Highlights

➤ CSC will restate its FY 07 (Mar.) 10-K, as it found accounting errors related to FASB #48 regarding accounting for income taxes and the effect of foreign currency exchange rate movements over the past 10 years. After the company releases its amended FY 07 10-K, it intends to file its June quarter results.

➤ We see revenues from operations increasing 6% in FY 08 (Mar.); however, much of the increase we expect stems from a weak dollar and recent acquisitions. Within the U.S. federal government segment, we look for revenues to rise at a mid-single digit pace. CSC sees its addressable federal market pipeline of opportunities consisting of $44 billion in awards that are projected to be allocated over the next 22 months. We expect CSC's commercial operations to remain weak, with softness in selected areas in Europe and declines in the U.S. partially offset by strength in Asia and Australia. We think that CSC's margins will widen slightly in FY 08, improving as the year progresses due to restructuring activities.

➤ We forecast FY 08 EPS of $4.13, versus operating EPS of $3.72 in FY 07, and we see $4.50 for FY 09.

Investment Rationale/Risk

➤ We believe the shares are appropriately valued. We think increased levels of U.S. federal government outsourcing, cost-cutting and revenue growth initiatives from restructuring programs, as well as a continued upward momentum in outsourcing in general in calendar years 2006 and 2007, are likely sources of future revenue and profit gains. In July 2006, management announced that it intends to repurchase up to $2 billion (about 19%) of CSC shares.

➤ Risks to our recommendation and target price stem from increased competition for large long-term contracts in the IT infrastructure and outsourcing arena, further terminations of contracts in the commercial segment, and ongoing shareholder litigation against CSC. We also have concerns regarding corporate governance, including a combination of the president and CEO roles.

➤ Our 12-month target price of $60 is based on a peer discount P/E of about 14.7X and a P/E to growth (PEG) ratio of 1.15X, using our calendar 2007 EPS estimate of $4.07 and an assumed three-year growth rate of 13%.

Qualitative Risk Assessment

LOW	**MEDIUM**	HIGH

Our risk assessment reflects the highly competitive nature of the IT consulting and outsourcing market, offset by our view of CSC's strong balance sheet and the stability afforded the company by the numerous long-term contracts that it has signed with customers.

Quantitative Evaluations

S&P Quality Ranking B+

D	C	B-	B	**B+**	A-	A	A+

Relative Strength Rank MODERATE

47

LOWEST = 1 HIGHEST = 99

Revenue/Earnings Data

Revenue (Million $)

	1Q	2Q	3Q	4Q	Year
2007	3,561	3,609	3,641	4,046	14,857
2006	3,583	3,573	3,577	3,884	14,616
2005	3,736	3,935	3,517	3,879	14,059
2004	3,555	3,591	3,621	4,000	14,768
2003	2,754	2,720	2,794	3,079	11,347
2002	2,714	2,765	2,901	3,046	11,426

Earnings Per Share ($)

2007	-0.31	0.51	0.62	1.42	2.16
2006	0.58	0.53	0.88	1.08	3.07
2005	0.58	0.68	0.69	0.86	2.59
2004	0.49	0.57	0.68	1.01	2.75
2003	0.46	0.54	0.61	0.93	2.54
2002	0.28	0.40	0.51	0.82	2.01

Fiscal year ended Mar. 31. Next earnings report expected: NA.
EPS Estimates based on S&P Operating Earnings; historical GAAP earnings are as reported.

Dividend Data

No cash dividends have been paid since 1998.

Please read the Required Disclosures and Analyst Certification on the last page of this report.

The McGraw-Hill Companies

Computer Sciences Corp

STANDARD &POOR'S

Business Summary November 28, 2007

CORPORATE OVERVIEW. Computer Sciences offers what it believes is a broad array of services to clients in the global commercial and government markets. The company specializes in the application of complex information technology (IT) to achieve the strategic objectives of its customers. Offerings include IT and business process outsourcing, and IT and professional services.

Outsourcing involves operating all or a portion of a customer's technology infrastructure, including systems analysis, applications development, network operations, desktop computing, and data center management. CSC also provides business process outsourcing, which involves managing key functions for clients such as claims processing, credit checking, logistics, and customer call centers.

IT and professional services includes systems integration, consulting, and professional services. Systems integration encompasses designing, developing, implementing, and integrating complete information systems. Consulting

and professional services includes advising clients on the strategic acquisition and utilization of IT, and on business strategy, security, modeling, engineering, and business process re-engineering. CSC also licenses sophisticated software systems for healthcare and financial services markets, and provides a broad array of end-to-end e-business solutions to meet the needs of large commercial and government clients.

The company provides services to clients in global commercial industries and to the U.S. federal government. In the global commercial segment, offerings are marketed to clients in a wide variety of industries. In the U.S. federal government market, CSC provides traditional systems integration and outsourcing for complex project management and technical services.

Company Financials Fiscal Year Ended Mar. 31

Per Share Data ($)	2007	2006	2005	2004	2003	2002	2001	2000	1999	1998
Tangible Book Value	19.51	23.85	21.71	15.44	11.78	11.58	9.26	12.78	10.98	9.32
Cash Flow	8.95	9.42	8.56	8.29	6.95	7.02	5.17	5.59	4.85	4.08
Earnings	2.16	3.07	2.59	2.75	2.54	2.01	1.37	2.37	2.11	1.64
S&P Core Earnings	2.13	3.00	2.59	2.68	1.84	1.48	0.80	NA	NA	NA
Dividends	NA	Nil	Nil	Nil	Nil	Nil	Nil	Nil	Nil	Nil
Payout Ratio	NA	Nil	Nil	Nil	Nil	Nil	Nil	Nil	Nil	Nil
Calendar Year	2006	2005	2004	2003	2002	2001	2000	1999	1998	1997
Prices:High	NA	59.90	58.00	44.99	53.47	66.71	99.88	94.63	74.88	43.88
Prices:Low	NA	42.31	38.07	26.52	24.30	28.99	58.25	52.38	39.97	28.94
P/E Ratio:High	NA	20	22	16	21	33	73	40	35	27
P/E Ratio:Low	NA	14	15	10	10	14	43	22	19	18

Income Statement Analysis (Million $)

	2007	2006	2005	2004	2003	2002	2001	2000	1999	1998
Revenue	14,857	14,616	14,059	14,768	11,347	11,426	10,524	9,371	7,660	6,601
Operating Income	2,211	2,149	1,845	1,968	1,609	1,497	1,302	1,239	990	849
Depreciation	1,162	1,188	1,146	1,038	858	858	649	546	445	387
Interest Expense	175	104	157	170	143	155	106	58.1	48.5	51.0
Pretax Income	607	821	715	747	612	497	330	611	511	191
Effective Tax Rate	35.9%	29.7%	30.6%	30.5%	28.0%	30.7%	29.4%	34.1%	33.3%	NM
Net Income	389	577	496	519	440	344	233	403	341	260
S&P Core Earnings	384	565	495	507	319	254	137	NA	NA	NA

Balance Sheet & Other Financial Data (Million $)

	2007	2006	2005	2004	2003	2002	2001	2000	1999	1998
Cash	1,050	1,291	1,010	610	300	149	185	260	603	275
Current Assets	6,706	6,306	5,690	4,867	4,088	3,304	3,204	2,766	2,669	1,983
Total Assets	13,731	12,943	12,634	11,804	10,433	8,611	8,175	5,874	5,008	4,047
Current Liabilities	5,260	4,141	3,878	3,253	2,987	2,708	3,589	1,984	2,081	1,215
Long Term Debt	1,412	1,377	1,303	2,306	2,205	1,873	1,029	652	398	736
Common Equity	5,886	6,772	6,495	5,504	4,606	3,624	3,215	3,044	2,400	2,001
Total Capital	7,298	8,149	7,798	7,810	6,811	5,497	4,245	3,780	2,798	2,737
Capital Expenditures	686	827	855	725	638	672	897	586	426	349
Cash Flow	1,551	1,765	1,642	1,558	1,298	1,202	882	949	786	647
Current Ratio	1.3	1.5	1.5	1.5	1.4	1.2	0.9	1.4	1.3	1.6
% Long Term Debt of Capitalization	19.4	16.9	16.7	29.5	32.4	34.1	24.3	17.3	14.2	26.9
% Net Income of Revenue	2.6	3.9	3.5	3.5	3.9	3.0	2.2	4.3	4.5	3.9
% Return on Assets	2.9	4.5	4.1	4.7	4.6	4.1	3.3	7.2	7.5	6.8
% Return on Equity	6.3	8.7	8.3	10.3	10.7	10.1	7.5	14.3	15.5	14.2

Data as orig reptd.; bef. results of disc opers/spec. items. Per share data adj. for stk. divs.; EPS diluted. E-Estimated. NA-Not Available. NM-Not Meaningful. NR-Not Ranked. UR-Under Review.

Office: 2100 East Grand Avenue, El Segundo, CA 90245.
Telephone: 310-615-0311.
Email: investorrelations@csc.com
Website: http://www.csc.com

Chrmn: V.B. Honeycutt
Pres & CEO: M.W. Laphen
VP & CFO: M.E. Keane
VP & Treas: T.R. Irvin

VP, Secy & General Counsel: H.D. Fisk
Investor Contact: B. Lackey (310-615-1700)
Board Members: I. W. Bailey, II, D. J. Barram, S. L. Baum, R. F. Chase, V. B. Honeycutt, M. W. Laphen, F. W. McFarlan, T. H. Patrick

Founded: 1959
Domicile: Nevada
Employees: 79,000

The McGraw-Hill Companies

STANDARD &POOR'S

Compuware Corp

S&P Recommendation **HOLD** ★★★☆☆	Price $8.46 (as of Nov 23, 2007)	12-Mo. Target Price $9.50	Investment Style Large-Cap Blend

GICS Sector Information Technology
Sub-Industry Application Software

Summary This company provides software products and professional services designed to increase the productivity of information systems departments.

Key Stock Statistics (Source S&P, Vickers, company reports)

52-Wk Range	$12.56– 7.32	S&P Oper. EPS 2008**E**	0.52	Market Capitalization(B)	$2.421	Beta	3.37
Trailing 12-Month EPS	$0.43	S&P Oper. EPS 2009**E**	0.63	Yield (%)	Nil	S&P 3-Yr. Proj. EPS CAGR(%)	11.00
Trailing 12-Month P/E	19.7	P/E on S&P Oper. EPS 2008**E**	16.3	Dividend Rate/Share	Nil	S&P Credit Rating	NR
$10K Invested 5 Yrs Ago	$17,301	Common Shares Outstg. (M)	286.2	Institutional Ownership (%)	82		

Price Performance

30-Week Mov. Avg. ···· 10-Week Mov. Avg. - - **GAAP Earnings vs. Previous Year**   **Volume** Above Avg. ▮▮▮ STARS
12-Mo. Target Price — Relative Strength   — ▲ Up ▼ Down ► No Change   Below Avg. ▮▮▮ ★

Options: CBOE, P

Analysis prepared by **Jim Yin** on October 30, 2007, when the stock traded at **$ 9.87**.

Highlights

➤ We estimate total revenue will rise 1.1% in FY 08 (Mar.), after a 0.6% increase in FY 07. We expect a modest decline in software license fees and single digit growth for maintenance revenues and professional services fees. Our outlook is based on lower demand for the mainframe business, but an improving sales execution and a higher maintenance renewal rate.

➤ We forecast that gross margins will decline to 60% in FY 08 from 61% in FY 07. We anticipate that operating margins will widen to 15.6% in FY 08 from 10.9% in FY 07, reflecting a cost saving initiative aimed at a $90 million to $100 million reduction in operating expenses, including a decrease in headcount.

➤ Our FY 08 EPS forecast is $0.52, up from $0.45 for FY 07. The expected increase in EPS can be attributed to a higher operating margin and fewer shares outstanding partially offset by restructuring charges, lower interest income, and a higher effective tax rate. CPWR has been actively repurchasing its shares, spending about $800 million for its shares in the past two years.

Investment Rationale/Risk

➤ We remain concerned about slower demand for CPWR's mainframe business and lower software license revenue. Although the company plans to reduce annual operating expenses by $90 million to $100 million, we believe restructuring and cost saving initiatives could cause further sales disruption. In addition, we do not believe these initiatives address CPWR's main problem of declining growth in its core business. However, we view the shares as fairly valued.

➤ Risks to our opinion and target price include a slowdown in the global economy, lower-than-expected corporate IT spending, and lower-than-expected cost savings from restructuring.

➤ Our 12-month target price of $9.50 is based on a blend of our discounted cash flow (DCF) and P/E analyses. Our DCF model assumes a weighted average cost of capital (WACC) of 11.5% and a terminal growth rate of 3%, yielding an intrinsic value of $9. For our P/E analysis, we derive a value of $10, based on an industry P/E-to-growth ratio of 1.8X, or 19.2X our FY 08 operating EPS estimate of $0.52.

Qualitative Risk Assessment

LOW	MEDIUM	**HIGH**

Our risk assessment reflects our concern over CPWR's ability to generate future revenue growth, as newer initiatives have been slow to bear fruit, in our opinion. Absent a meaningful pickup in revenue growth, we expect ongoing cost reduction and interest income to drive future earnings growth.

Quantitative Evaluations

S&P Quality Ranking NR

D	C	B-	B	B+	A-	A	A+

Relative Strength Rank MODERATE

50

LOWEST = 1   HIGHEST = 99

Revenue/Earnings Data

Revenue (Million $)

	1Q	2Q	3Q	4Q	Year
2008	279.4	302.0	--	--	--
2007	296.3	288.5	315.2	313.0	1,213
2006	297.3	292.7	305.9	309.5	1,205
2005	287.1	295.5	330.5	318.8	1,232
2004	306.0	302.8	318.2	337.7	1,265
2003	346.6	358.0	333.1	337.6	1,375

Earnings Per Share ($)

2008	Nil	0.13	E0.15	E0.16	E0.52
2007	0.08	0.07	0.11	0.21	0.45
2006	0.06	0.06	0.10	0.15	0.37
2005	Nil	0.02	0.11	0.07	0.20
2004	0.01	-0.02	0.06	0.09	0.13
2003	0.06	0.09	0.07	0.06	0.27

Fiscal year ended Mar. 31. Next earnings report expected: Late January. EPS Estimates based on S&P Operating Earnings; historical GAAP earnings are as reported.

Dividend Data

No cash dividends have been paid.

Compuware Corp

Business Summary October 30, 2007

CORPORATE OVERVIEW. Originally founded as a professional services company, Compuware provides software, maintenance and professional services intended to increase the productivity of the information technology (IT) departments of businesses. CPWR offers mainframe software for testing, debugging and system maintenance of IBM and IBM-compatible mainframes. The company's distributed products support requirements management (Changepoint), application development (Uniface, Optimal, and DevPartner), testing (QA Center and File-AID/CS), and application performance analysis (Vantage).

LEGAL/REGULATORY ISSUES. On March 21, 2005, Compuware settled all pending litigation with IBM (originally filed in March 2002). Pursuant to the terms of the settlement agreement, IBM also entered into a four-year license and maintenance arrangement with Compuware, worth $140 million, and offered to purchase $260 million of the company's services over a four-year period extending from March 2005 through March 2009. In late 2005, this settlement agreement was amended to extend the period over which IBM could purchase $140 million of Compuware's software and maintenance to five

years (ending March 31, 2010). In addition, according to this amendment, IBM will offer Compuware the opportunity to bid on a minimum of $260 million of IBM-sourced services over a four-and-a-half year period. We do not see the resolution of CPWR's lawsuit against IBM having a meaningful impact on the competitive environment.

FINANCIAL TRENDS. Like those of many of its enterprise software peers, and, in particular, those with sizable mainframe-related revenues, CPWR's revenues peaked in FY 00 (Mar.), driven by Y2K-related spending. Revenues declined annually from FY 00 to FY 06, despite a number of acquisitions., but rose slightly in FY 07. Operating income has followed a similar pattern, although it seems to us to have bottomed in FY 04 due to ongoing expense reductions.

Company Financials Fiscal Year Ended Mar. 31

Per Share Data ($)	2007	2006	2005	2004	2003	2002	2001	2000	1999	1998
Tangible Book Value	2.57	3.33	3.15	3.11	2.93	2.60	2.02	1.51	2.70	1.81
Cash Flow	0.70	0.51	0.34	0.27	0.41	-0.40	0.60	1.10	0.97	0.59
Earnings	0.45	0.37	0.20	0.13	0.27	-0.66	0.32	0.91	0.87	0.50
S&P Core Earnings	0.41	0.33	0.12	0.03	0.14	-0.15	0.17	NA	NA	NA
Dividends	Nil	Nil	Nil	Nil	Nil	Nil	Nil	Nil	Nil	Nil
Payout Ratio	Nil	Nil	Nil	Nil	Nil	Nil	Nil	Nil	Nil	Nil
Calendar Year	2006	2005	2004	2003	2002	2001	2000	1999	1998	1997
Prices:High	9.55	9.99	8.95	6.52	14.00	14.50	37.81	40.00	39.91	19.75
Prices:Low	6.02	5.51	4.35	3.22	2.35	6.25	5.63	16.38	15.56	6.03
P/E Ratio:High	NM	27	45	50	52	NM	NM	44	46	39
P/E Ratio:Low	NM	15	22	25	9	NM	NM	18	18	12

Income Statement Analysis (Million $)										
Revenue	1,213	1,205	1,232	1,265	1,375	1,729	2,010	2,231	1,638	1,139
Operating Income	188	198	143	90.5	188	264	296	641	547	317
Depreciation	55.0	50.2	56.4	55.2	53.8	98.2	104	71.5	41.5	36.5
Interest Expense	Nil	Nil	Nil	Nil	6.10	7.43	31.3	24.5	Nil	Nil
Pretax Income	193	191	106	56.0	156	-245	192	562	530	291
Effective Tax Rate	18.1%	25.3%	28.0%	11.0%	34.0%	NM	38.0%	37.3%	34.0%	33.3%
Net Income	158	143	76.5	49.8	103	-245	119	352	350	194
S&P Core Earnings	143	126	46.1	9.72	51.2	-55.3	62.2	NA	NA	NA

Balance Sheet & Other Financial Data (Million $)										
Cash	261	612	498	455	319	233	53.3	30.5	193	206
Current Assets	921	1,445	1,358	1,143	1,050	1,063	1,004	988	1,072	676
Total Assets	2,029	2,511	2,478	2,234	2,123	1,994	2,279	2,416	1,677	1,073
Current Liabilities	529	545	578	493	469	556	569	596	522	314
Long Term Debt	Nil	Nil	Nil	Nil	Nil	Nil	140	450	Nil	6.96
Common Equity	1,132	1,579	1,516	1,414	1,332	1,170	1,377	1,204	1,080	708
Total Capital	1,167	1,605	1,516	1,418	1,332	1,170	1,538	1,667	1,080	715
Capital Expenditures	18.6	14.5	134	74.6	225	90.4	39.8	34.9	26.4	28.0
Cash Flow	213	193	133	105	157	-147	223	423	391	230
Current Ratio	1.7	2.6	2.3	2.3	2.2	1.9	1.8	1.7	2.1	2.2
% Long Term Debt of Capitalization	Nil	Nil	Nil	Nil	Nil	Nil	9.1	27.0	Nil	1.0
% Net Income of Revenue	13.0	11.9	6.2	3.9	7.5	NM	5.9	15.8	21.4	17.0
% Return on Assets	7.0	5.7	3.2	2.3	5.0	NM	5.1	17.2	25.5	21.2
% Return on Equity	11.7	9.2	5.2	3.6	8.2	NM	9.2	30.8	39.1	33.6

Data as orig reptd.; bef. results of disc opers/spec. items. Per share data adj. for stk. divs.; EPS diluted. E-Estimated. NA-Not Available. NM-Not Meaningful. NR-Not Ranked. UR-Under Review.

Office: 1 Campus Martius, Detroit, MI 48226-5099.
Telephone: 313-227-7300.
Email: investor.relations@compuware.com
Website: http://www.compuware.com

Chrmn, Pres & CEO: P. Karmanos, Jr.
SVP, CFO & Treas: L.L. Fournier
SVP, Secy & General Counsel: T. Costello, Jr.
Investor Contact: L. Elkin (248-737-7345)

Board Members: D. W. Archer, G. S. Bedi, W. O. Grabe, W. R. Halling, P. Karmanos, Jr., F. A. Nelson, G. D. Price, W. J. Prowse, G. S. Romney

Founded: 1973
Domicile: Michigan
Employees: 7,539

ConAgra Foods Inc.

STANDARD &POOR'S

S&P Recommendation HOLD ★★★☆☆

Price	12-Mo. Target Price	Investment Style
$23.82 (as of Nov 23, 2007)	$28.00	Large-Cap Value

GICS Sector Consumer Staples
Sub-Industry Packaged Foods & Meats

Summary This company is one of the largest U.S. packaged food processors.

Key Stock Statistics (Source S&P, Vickers, company reports)

52-Wk Range	$28.35– 22.81	S&P Oper. EPS 2008E	1.48	Market Capitalization(B)	$11.606	Beta	0.57
Trailing 12-Month EPS	$1.54	S&P Oper. EPS 2009E	NA	Yield (%)	3.19	S&P 3-Yr. Proj. EPS CAGR(%)	9.00
Trailing 12-Month P/E	15.5	P/E on S&P Oper. EPS 2008E	16.1	Dividend Rate/Share	$0.76	S&P Credit Rating	BBB+
$10K Invested 5 Yrs Ago	$11,668	Common Shares Outstg. (M)	487.3	Institutional Ownership (%)	71		

Price Performance

30-Week Mov. Avg. ··· 10-Week Mov. Avg. --- **GAAP Earnings vs. Previous Year** **Volume** Above Avg. ▓ **STARS**
12-Mo. Target Price — Relative Strength ▲ Up ▼ Down ▶ No Change Below Avg. ▓ ★

Options: ASE, CBOE, P

Analysis prepared by **Tom Graves, CFA** on July 19, 2007, when the stock traded at **$ 26.73**.

Highlights

➤ In FY 08 (May), we look for sales to increase modestly from the $12.0 billion reported for FY 07. We estimate EPS from continuing operations of $1.48, up from $1.35 in FY 07, which included a variety of special items, including restructuring charges and an asset sale gain. Also, in FY 07, we believe that CAG's profit from its trading and merchandising business was unusually large, and we do not look for it to be repeated in FY 08. CAG's FY 07 also included $0.08 of costs related to a recall of peanut butter products.

➤ CAG is making efforts to streamline manufacturing operations, including some plant closures. In January 2007, CAG said that by FY 09, it expects total plant rationalization efforts to result in a $100 million reduction in annual fixed costs.

➤ In FY 07, CAG sold its refrigerated packaged meats business, its cheese business, its refrigerated pizza business, and an oat milling business for net proceeds of about $707 million. Also, in FY 07, CAG repurchased about 24.3 million of its common shares for about $615 million. At the end of FY 07, CAG had $88 million of a remaining repurchase authorization.

Investment Rationale/Risk

➤ Our hold recommendation reflects our view that CAG has been a company in transition, including asset sales since 2003 that have generated total pretax proceeds of more than $2 billion. We expect operational improvements from the company, including cost benefits from the streamlining of manufacturing operations. CAG's reported earnings have included a variety of special items, including asset sale gains, restructuring charges, and impairment charges.

➤ Risks to our recommendation and target price include competitive pressures in CAG's businesses, the potential for increased commodity cost inflation, and the company's ability to achieve cost savings and efficiency targets.

➤ Our 12-month target price of $28 is based on our view that the stock should trade at a valuation that is about 10% below the average P/E (based on estimated calendar 2007 EPS) that we expect from a peer group of packaged food companies. This is partly because we view some of CAG's recent earnings from its trading and merchandising segment as unusually large. The dividend was reduced in FY 06, but the stock still had a recent indicated dividend yield of 2.7%.

Qualitative Risk Assessment

LOW	MEDIUM	HIGH

Our risk assessment reflects the relatively stable nature of the company's end markets, and what we view as relatively strong expected cash flows.

Quantitative Evaluations

S&P Quality Ranking A-

D	C	B-	B	B+	A-	A	A+

Relative Strength Rank **MODERATE**

66

LOWEST = 1   HIGHEST = 99

Revenue/Earnings Data

Revenue (Million $)

	1Q	2Q	3Q	4Q	Year
2008	2,956	--	--	--	--
2007	2,689	3,089	2,918	3,333	12,028
2006	2,700	3,026	2,879	2,975	11,579
2005	3,496	4,116	3,570	3,706	14,567
2004	4,394	3,873	3,598	3,962	14,522
2003	6,529	5,438	3,963	3,910	19,839

Earnings Per Share ($)

2008	0.36	E0.42	E0.42	E0.34	E1.48
2007	0.21	0.39	0.37	0.38	1.35
2006	0.63	0.24	0.18	0.10	1.15
2005	0.26	0.47	0.32	0.20	1.27
2004	0.38	0.45	0.36	0.37	1.50
2003	0.42	0.44	0.30	0.42	1.58

Fiscal year ended May 31. Next earnings report expected: Late December. EPS Estimates based on S&P Operating Earnings; historical GAAP earnings are as reported.

Dividend Data (Dates: mm/dd Payment Date: mm/dd/yy)

Amount ($)	Date Decl.	Ex-Div. Date	Stk. of Record	Payment Date
0.180	12/07	01/25	01/29	03/01/07
0.180	04/03	04/27	05/01	06/01/07
0.180	07/18	07/31	08/02	09/04/07
0.190	09/27	10/31	11/02	12/03/07

Dividends have been paid since 1976. Source: Company reports.

Please read the Required Disclosures and Analyst Certification on the last page of this report.

The McGraw-Hill Companies

ConAgra Foods Inc.

STANDARD &POOR'S

Business Summary July 19, 2007

CORPORATE OVERVIEW. ConAgra Foods is one of the largest food companies in North America. The company's businesses are divided into four reporting segments: consumer foods, which provided 54% of total sales in FY 07 (May); foods and ingredients (29%); trading and merchandising (12%); and international foods (5%).

The consumer foods segment consists of branded shelf-stable, frozen and re-frigerated food products Major shelf-stable brands include Hunt's, Healthy Choice, Chef Boyardee, Wesson, Orville Redenbacher, Slim Jim, ACT II, Peter Pan, Gulden's, Swiss Miss, Knott's Berry Farm, La Choy, Pemmican, and Penrose. Major frozen grocery brands include Healthy Choice, Banquet, Marie Callender's, Kid Cuisine, Morton, Chun King, La Choy and Wolfgang Puck. Refrigerated products include brands such as Armour, Butterball, Cook's, Brown 'N Serve, Healthy Choice, Hebrew National, Parkay, Blue Bonnet, Fleischmann's, Egg Beaters, and Reddi-wip.

CAG's foods and ingredients segment includes meals, entrees, prepared potatoes, a variety of custom-manufactured products for sale to foodservice establishments, and branded and commodity food ingredients. CAG's trading

and merchandising segment includes the sourcing, marketing and distribution of agricultural and energy commodities. International foods includes branded food products.

In FY 06, CAG's largest customer, Wal-Mart Stores, Inc. and its affiliates, accounted for about 12% of net sales.

CORPORATE STRATEGY. In recent years, CAG has been pursuing an acquisition and divestiture strategy to shift its focus toward its core branded and value-added food products, while exiting commodity-related businesses.

Also, ConAgra has been implementing operational improvement initiatives that are intended to generate profitable sales growth, improve profit margins, and expand returns on capital over time.

Company Financials Fiscal Year Ended May 31

Per Share Data ($)	2007	2006	2005	2004	2003	2002	2001	2000	1999	1998
Tangible Book Value	0.73	0.79	0.47	0.41	NM	NM	NM	1.22	1.02	0.81
Cash Flow	2.10	1.74	1.95	2.16	2.30	2.39	2.30	1.98	1.80	2.33
Earnings	1.35	1.15	1.27	1.50	1.58	1.47	1.33	0.86	0.75	1.36
S&P Core Earnings	1.29	0.91	1.14	1.39	1.42	1.27	1.20	NA	NA	NA
Dividends	1.00	1.08	1.03	0.98	NA	0.88	0.79	0.74	0.65	0.60
Payout Ratio	74%	94%	81%	65%	NA	60%	59%	86%	86%	44%
Calendar Year	2006	2005	2004	2003	2002	2001	2000	1999	1998	1997
Prices:High	28.35	30.24	29.65	26.41	27.65	26.00	26.19	34.38	33.63	38.75
Prices:Low	18.85	19.99	25.38	17.75	20.90	17.50	15.06	20.63	22.56	24.50
P/E Ratio:High	21	26	23	18	18	18	20	40	45	28
P/E Ratio:Low	14	17	20	12	14	12	11	24	30	18

Income Statement Analysis (Million $)										
Revenue	12,028	11,579	14,567	14,522	19,839	27,630	27,194	25,386	24,594	23,841
Operating Income	1,577	1,184	1,618	1,735	1,123	2,144	2,026	1,828	1,940	1,767
Depreciation	346	311	351	352	392	474	499	537	500	446
Interest Expense	226	307	341	275	276	402	423	303	354	338
Pretax Income	1,050	906	1,133	1,151	1,276	1,268	1,104	666	682	1,021
Effective Tax Rate	34.8%	34.2%	41.5%	30.9%	34.2%	38.1%	38.2%	38.0%	47.5%	38.5%
Net Income	684	596	663	796	840	785	682	413	358	628
S&P Core Earnings	657	470	589	740	750	668	612	NA	NA	NA

Balance Sheet & Other Financial Data (Million $)										
Cash	735	332	208	589	629	158	198	158	62.8	95.0
Current Assets	5,006	4,790	4,524	5,145	6,060	6,434	7,363	5,967	5,656	5,487
Total Assets	11,836	11,970	12,792	14,230	15,071	15,496	16,481	12,296	12,146	11,703
Current Liabilities	2,681	2,965	2,389	3,002	3,803	4,313	6,936	5,489	5,386	5,070
Long Term Debt	3,420	3,155	4,349	5,281	5,570	5,919	4,635	3,092	3,068	3,028
Common Equity	4,583	4,650	4,859	4,840	4,622	4,308	3,983	2,964	2,909	2,780
Total Capital	8,003	7,805	9,209	10,120	10,192	10,227	8,618	6,056	5,977	5,808
Capital Expenditures	425	263	453	352	390	531	560	539	662	569
Cash Flow	1,030	907	1,014	1,148	1,232	1,259	1,181	950	858	1,074
Current Ratio	1.9	1.6	1.9	1.7	1.6	1.5	1.1	1.1	1.1	1.1
% Long Term Debt of Capitalization	42.7	40.4	47.2	52.2	54.7	57.9	53.8	51.1	51.3	52.1
% Net Income of Revenue	5.7	5.1	4.6	5.5	4.2	2.8	2.5	1.6	1.5	2.6
% Return on Assets	5.7	4.8	4.9	5.4	5.5	4.9	4.8	3.4	3.0	5.5
% Return on Equity	14.8	12.5	13.7	16.8	18.8	18.9	19.9	14.1	12.5	23.9

Data as orig reptd.; bef. results of disc opers/spec. items. Per share data adj. for stk. divs.; EPS diluted. E-Estimated. NA-Not Available. NM-Not Meaningful. NR-Not Ranked. UR-Under Review.

Office: One Conagra Dr, Omaha, NE 68102-5001.
Telephone: 402-595-4000.
Website: http://www.conagra.com
Chrmn: S.F. Goldstone

Pres & CEO: G.M. Rodkin
EVP & CFO: A.J. Hawaux
EVP & Chief Admin Officer: O.C. Johnson
EVP & Secy: R.F. Sharpe Jr.

Investor Contact: C.W. Klinefelter (402-595-4154)
Board Members: M. C. Bay, S. G. Butler, J. T. Chain, Jr., S. F. Goldstone, A. B. Hayes, W. G. Jurgensen, R. Marshall, M. H. Rauenhorst, C. E. Reichardt, G. M. Rodkin, R. W. Roskens, A. J. Schindler, K. E. Stinson

Founded: 1919
Domicile: Delaware
Employees: 24,500

The McGraw·Hill Companies

ConocoPhillips

STANDARD &POOR'S

S&P Recommendation **BUY** ★★★★☆	Price $79.12 (as of Nov 23, 2007)	12-Mo. Target Price $97.00	Investment Style Large-Cap Blend

GICS Sector Energy
Sub-Industry Integrated Oil & Gas

Summary This integrated oil and gas company (formerly Phillips Petroleum), the second largest U.S. refiner, acquired Tosco Corp. in 2001, and merged with Conoco Inc. in 2002.

Key Stock Statistics (Source S&P, Vickers, company reports)

52-Wk Range	$90.84– 61.59	S&P Oper. EPS 2007**E**	9.15	Market Capitalization(B)	$126.557	Beta	0.35
Trailing 12-Month EPS	$6.42	S&P Oper. EPS 2008**E**	8.88	Yield (%)	2.07	S&P 3-Yr. Proj. EPS CAGR(%)	-0.02
Trailing 12-Month P/E	12.3	P/E on S&P Oper. EPS 2007**E**	8.6	Dividend Rate/Share	$1.64	S&P Credit Rating	A
$10K Invested 5 Yrs Ago	$36,774	Common Shares Outstg. (M)	1,599.6	Institutional Ownership (%)	80		

Price Performance

30-Week Mov. Avg. · · · 10-Week Mov. Avg. - - GAAP Earnings vs. Previous Year Volume Above Avg. STARS
12-Mo. Target Price — Relative Strength — ▲ Up ▼ Down ▶ No Change   Below Avg.

Options: ASE, CBOE, P, Ph

Analysis prepared by **Tina J. Vital** on October 31, 2007, when the stock traded at **$ 84.58**.

Highlights

➤ Third quarter oil and gas production fell about 10%, year to year, in line with our expectations, reflecting asset sales and exits from Venezuela and Dubai. Given the loss of its Venezuelan production, we believe COP's 3% annual growth target may be difficult to achieve. COP sees fourth quarter volumes rising by an estimated 60,000 b/d.

➤ In late October, COP said it remained in negotiations with Venezuela over potential compensation for its nationalized oil ventures in the Orinoco belt, and expects to file for arbitration within a few weeks. COP took a $4.5 billion writedown of its Venezuelan assets in the second quarter.

➤ Refining margins weakened in the 2007 second half, and we project 2008 refining margins will narrow more than 30% from 2007 levels, as refined product prices have failed to keep pace with a sharp increase in crude oil prices. We expect after-tax operating earnings to decline about 8% in 2007 and approximately 4% in 2008, reflecting weakened refining margins and volume growth, partially offset by strong oil and gas price realizations.

Investment Rationale/Risk

➤ COP has been reshaping its upstream portfolio to focus on higher growth assets. In March 2006, COP acquired Burlington Resources. We like the deal, and we see its premium justified by Burlington Resources' relatively low cost and its strong organic growth focused on North American natural gas. As of year-end 2006, COP bought 20% of Lukoil shares, which should boost reserves and production by over 10%, and we estimate its re-entry into Libya will raise its oil production at an attractive cost.

➤ Risks to our recommendation and target price include changes in economic, industrial and operating conditions, including COP's ability to replace its oil and gas reserves; geopolitical risk associated with COP's international operations; and operational risk from large development projects.

➤ A blend of our discounted cash flow (assuming a WACC of 6.3% and a terminal growth rate of 3%) and relative valuations leads to our 12-month target price of $97. This represents an expected enterprise value of about 11X our 2008 EBITDA estimate, a premium to supermajor peers.

Qualitative Risk Assessment

LOW	MEDIUM	HIGH

Our risk assessment reflects the company's diversified and strong business profile in volatile, cyclical and capital intensive segments of the energy industry. While COP has a history of aggressive acquisition activity, we believe that its earnings stability is good and that its corporate governance practices are sound.

Quantitative Evaluations

S&P Quality Ranking   B+

D	C	B-	B	B+	A-	A	A+

Relative Strength Rank   MODERATE

57

LOWEST = 1   HIGHEST = 99

Revenue/Earnings Data

Revenue (Million $)

	1Q	2Q	3Q	4Q	Year
2007	42,867	47,400	47,933	--	--
2006	47,927	48,476	49,585	42,535	188,523
2005	38,918	42,614	49,659	51,258	183,364
2004	29,800	31,886	34,741	40,100	136,916
2003	27,077	25,347	26,493	25,830	105,097
2002	8,431	10,414	14,557	23,346	57,224

Earnings Per Share ($)

2007	2.12	0.18	2.23	E2.20	E9.15
2006	2.34	3.09	2.31	1.91	9.66
2005	2.06	2.21	2.68	2.69	9.63
2004	1.16	1.44	1.44	1.76	5.79
2003	0.93	0.79	0.91	0.74	3.53
2002	-0.14	0.48	-0.06	0.43	0.74

Fiscal year ended Dec. 31. Next earnings report expected: Late January. EPS Estimates based on S&P Operating Earnings; historical GAAP earnings are as reported.

Dividend Data (Dates: mm/dd Payment Date: mm/dd/yy)

Amount ($)	Date Decl.	Ex-Div. Date	Stk. of Record	Payment Date
0.410	10/04	10/29	10/31	12/03/07

Dividends have been paid since 1934. Source: Company reports.

Please read the Required Disclosures and Analyst Certification on the last page of this report.

The McGraw-Hill Companies

ConocoPhillips

STANDARD &POOR'S

Business Summary October 31, 2007

CORPORATE OVERVIEW. On August 30, 2002, Phillips Petroleum and Conoco merged, creating ConocoPhillips (COP), the third largest oil company in the U.S. COP operates in six operating segments: exploration and production (E&P; 27% of 2006 sales, 63% of 2006 net income); refining and marketing (R&M; 71%, 29%); midstream (2%, 3%); Lukoil Investment; chemicals; and emerging businesses.

In January 2007, COP estimated its five-year (2002-2006) organic reserve replacement at 65%. Proved crude oil reserves (excluding equity affiliates) fell 4.1%, to 3.200 billion barrels (76% developed) in 2006. Proved natural gas reserves (excluding equity affiliates) rose 42%, to 23.446 trillion cubic feet (Tcf; 85% developed) in 2006. Crude oil production (excluding equity affiliates) rose to 856,000 barrels per day (b/d) in 2006, from 786,000 b/d in 2005. Natural gas liquids (NGL) production increased to 136,000 b/d in 2006, from 91,000 b/d in 2005. Natural gas production (excluding equity affiliates) rose to 4.961 billion cubic feet (Bcf) per day in 2006, from 3.263 Bcf per day in 2005. The average worldwide sales price for crude oil was $62.39 per barrel in 2006, and $6.20

per thousand cubic feet (Mcf) for natural gas. Three-year (2004-2006) production costs averaged $4.59 per barrel oil equivalent (boe).

As of December 31, 2006, COP owned or had interests in 12 U.S. refineries, five European refineries, and one refinery in Malaysia, with a capacity of 2.90 million b/d. In April 2005, COP unveiled a five year $3 billion program to expand its ability to refine heavy-sour crude oils. At year-end 2006, gasoline and distillates were sold through approximately 10,600 branded outlets in the U.S. (under Phillips 66, Conoco and 76 brands), Europe and Asia Pacific (under the JET and ProJET brands). In December 2006, COP reached an agreement to sell 376 of its fueling stations in European countries to Lukoil; the transaction is expected to close in the second quarter of 2007.

Company Financials Fiscal Year Ended Dec. 31

Per Share Data ($)	2006	2005	2004	2003	2002	2001	2000	1999	1998	1997
Tangible Book Value	29.69	25.49	18.53	12.85	9.91	14.07	10.77	8.06	7.51	8.25
Cash Flow	14.19	12.63	8.49	5.90	5.31	5.14	5.94	2.97	2.96	3.44
Earnings	9.66	9.63	5.79	3.53	0.74	2.79	3.63	1.20	0.46	1.81
S&P Core Earnings	9.59	9.72	5.88	3.43	0.64	2.60	NA	NA	NA	NA
Dividends	1.44	1.18	0.90	0.82	0.74	0.70	0.68	0.68	0.68	0.67
Payout Ratio	15%	12%	15%	23%	101%	25%	19%	57%	149%	37%
Prices:High	74.89	71.48	45.61	33.02	32.05	34.00	35.00	28.63	26.63	26.13
Prices:Low	54.90	41.40	32.15	26.80	22.02	25.00	17.97	18.84	20.09	18.69
P/E Ratio:High	8	7	8	9	44	12	10	24	59	14
P/E Ratio:Low	6	4	6	8	30	9	5	16	44	10

Income Statement Analysis (Million $)										
Revenue	183,650	183,364	135,076	104,196	56,748	26,868	21,113	13,751	11,545	15,210
Operating Income	37,433	24,077	17,033	11,866	4,571	8,393	5,528	2,452	1,630	2,748
Depreciation, Depletion and Amortization	7,284	4,253	3,798	3,485	4,446	1,391	1,179	902	1,302	863
Interest Expense	1,087	497	546	864	614	391	422	332	253	280
Pretax Income	28,409	23,580	14,401	8,337	2,164	3,302	3,769	1,185	421	1,900
Effective Tax Rate	45.0%	42.0%	43.5%	44.9%	67.0%	50.2%	50.6%	48.6%	43.7%	49.5%
Net Income	15,550	13,640	8,107	4,593	714	1,643	1,862	609	237	959
S&P Core Earnings	15,442	13,753	8,241	4,697	618	1,533	NA	NA	NA	NA

Balance Sheet & Other Financial Data (Million $)										
Cash	817	2,214	1,387	490	307	142	149	138	97.0	163
Current Assets	25,066	19,612	15,021	11,192	10,903	4,363	2,606	2,773	2,349	2,648
Total Assets	164,781	106,999	92,861	82,455	76,836	35,217	20,509	15,201	14,216	13,860
Current Liabilities	26,431	21,359	15,586	14,011	12,816	4,542	3,492	2,520	2,132	2,445
Long Term Debt	23,091	10,758	14,370	16,340	19,267	9,295	7,272	4,921	4,756	2,775
Common Equity	82,646	52,731	42,723	34,366	29,517	14,340	6,093	4,549	4,219	4,814
Total Capital	106,939	76,137	68,583	60,113	57,796	27,650	15,259	10,950	10,292	9,497
Capital Expenditures	15,596	11,620	9,496	6,169	4,388	3,085	2,022	1,690	2,052	2,043
Cash Flow	22,834	17,893	11,905	8,078	5,160	3,034	3,041	1,511	1,539	1,822
Current Ratio	0.9	0.9	1.0	0.8	0.9	1.0	0.7	1.1	1.1	1.1
% Long Term Debt of Capitalization	21.6	14.1	21.0	27.2	33.3	33.6	47.7	44.9	46.2	29.2
% Return on Assets	11.4	13.6	9.2	5.8	1.3	5.9	10.4	4.1	1.7	7.0
% Return on Equity	23.0	28.6	21.0	14.4	3.3	16.1	35.0	13.9	5.2	21.2

Data as orig reptd.; bef. results of disc opers/spec. items. Per share data adj. for stk. divs.; EPS diluted. E-Estimated. NA-Not Available. NM-Not Meaningful. NR-Not Ranked. UR-Under Review.

Office: 600 N Dairy Ashford St, Houston, TX 77079-1175.
Telephone: 281-293-1000.
Website: http://www.conocophillips.com
Chrmn, Pres & CEO: J.J. Mulva

EVP & CFO: J.A. Carrig
SVP & General Counsel: S.F. Gates
VP & Cntlr: R.C. Berney
Investor Contact: G. Russell (212-207-1996)

Board Members: R. L. Armitage, R. H. Auchinleck, N. R. Augustine, J. E. Copeland, Jr., K. M. Duberstein, R. R. Harkin, C. C. Krulak, H. W. McGraw, III, J. J. Mulva, H. J. Norvik, W. K. Reilly, W. R. Rhodes, J. S. Roy, B. S. Shackouls, V. J. Tschinkel, K. C. Turner, W. E. Wade, Jr.

Founded: 1917
Domicile: Delaware
Employees: 38,400

The McGraw-Hill Companies

Consolidated Edison Inc.

STANDARD &POOR'S

S&P Recommendation **HOLD** ★★★☆☆	Price $48.56 (as of Nov 29, 2007)	12-Mo. Target Price $48.00	Investment Style Large-Cap Value

GICS Sector Utilities
Sub-Industry Multi-Utilities

Summary This electric and gas utility holding company serves parts of New York, New Jersey and Pennsylvania.

Key Stock Statistics (Source S&P, Vickers, company reports)

52-Wk Range	$52.90– 43.10	S&P Oper. EPS 2007**E**	3.30	Market Capitalization(B)	$13.185	Beta	0.18
Trailing 12-Month EPS	$3.51	S&P Oper. EPS 2008**E**	3.35	Yield (%)	4.78	S&P 3-Yr. Proj. EPS CAGR(%)	4.00
Trailing 12-Month P/E	13.8	P/E on S&P Oper. EPS 2007**E**	14.7	Dividend Rate/Share	$2.32	S&P Credit Rating	A
$10K Invested 5 Yrs Ago	$15,431	Common Shares Outstg. (M)	271.5	Institutional Ownership (%)	54		

Price Performance

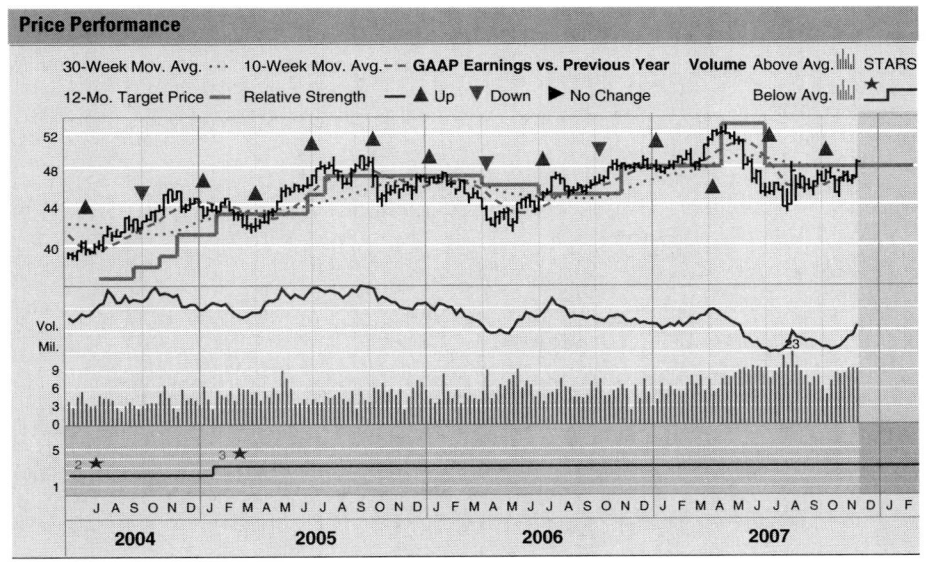

Options: ASE, CBOE, P, Ph

Analysis prepared by **Justin McCann** on November 29, 2007, when the stock traded at **$ 48.56**.

Highlights

➤ We expect EPS to rise nearly 12% in 2007 from 2006 EPS of $2.95. EPS in the first nine months of 2007 rose from $2.17 in the year-earlier period to $2.73, with the gain driven by rate increases, more favorable weather, and a sharp drop in operating costs. On April 1, 2007, electric rates for Con Edison of New York were increased by $220.4 million. The increase was authorized by the New York Public Service Commission (PSC) in the three-year electric rate plan that it approved in April 2005.

➤ We see EPS in 2008 growing less than 2% from expected results in 2007. The modest gain would reflect the favorable impact of rate increases being restricted by more shares outstanding, higher interest expense, and a potential slowdown in the local New York economy.

➤ On May 4, 2007, Con Edison of New York filed a three-year electric rate increase proposal with the New York PSC. The filing requested a nearly $1.23 billion increase (11.6%) that would take effect on April 1, 2008, a second increase of $335 million (3.2%) and a third year increase of $390 million (3.7%). We expect the PSC to issue a final ruling on the proposal in March 2008.

Investment Rationale/Risk

➤ After a 3.8% increase in 2006, the stock is up less than 2% year to date. ED's underperformance to its electric and gas utility peers has largely reflected, in our view, the dilutive impact of new equity issuances on EPS growth, and the uncertain political and regulatory environment that has resulted in a critical regulatory report on its performance during an extended power outage in the summer of 2006. We expect modest price appreciation over the next 12 months, and for the dividend to increase at an annual rate of around 1%.

➤ Risks to our recommendation and target price include a significant weakening of the economy in the utility's service territory, the emergence of an unfavorable regulatory environment, and a sharp decline in the average P/E multiple of the peer group as a whole.

➤ We believe the shares will be supported by a dividend yield (recently 4.8%) that is well above the industry average (3.5%). However, given the political and regulatory uncertainties confronting the company, we expect the shares to trade at a discount-to-peers P/E multiple of about 14.3X our EPS estimate for 2008. Our 12-month target price is $48.

Qualitative Risk Assessment

LOW	MEDIUM	HIGH

Our risk assessment reflects our view of the company's: strong and steady cash flows from regulated electric and gas utility operations, its solid balance sheet and B+ credit rating, a healthy economy in its service territory, and a supportive regulatory environment historically.

Quantitative Evaluations

S&P Quality Ranking B+

D	C	B-	B	B+	A-	A	A+

Relative Strength Rank STRONG **86**
LOWEST = 1   HIGHEST = 99

Revenue/Earnings Data

Revenue (Million $)

	1Q	2Q	3Q	4Q	Year
2007	3,418	3,029	3,643	--	--
2006	3,317	2,555	3,441	2,824	12,137
2005	2,801	2,406	3,375	3,108	11,690
2004	2,679	2,164	2,734	2,182	9,758
2003	2,570	2,175	2,801	2,279	9,827
2002	2,099	1,900	2,539	2,057	8,482

Earnings Per Share ($)

	1Q	2Q	3Q	4Q	Year
2007	0.99	0.58	1.15	E0.60	E3.30
2006	0.74	0.51	0.92	0.78	2.95
2005	0.75	0.48	1.17	0.59	2.99
2004	0.69	0.38	1.03	0.22	2.32
2003	0.72	0.29	1.16	0.19	2.36
2002	0.78	0.46	1.33	0.56	3.13

Fiscal year ended Dec. 31. Next earnings report expected: Late January. EPS Estimates based on S&P Operating Earnings; historical GAAP earnings are as reported.

Dividend Data (Dates: mm/dd Payment Date: mm/dd/yy)

Amount ($)	Date Decl.	Ex-Div. Date	Stk. of Record	Payment Date
0.580	01/19	02/12	02/14	03/15/07
0.580	04/19	05/14	05/16	06/15/07
0.580	07/23	08/13	08/15	09/15/07
0.580	10/18	11/09	11/14	12/15/07

Dividends have been paid since 1885. Source: Company reports.

Consolidated Edison Inc.

STANDARD &POOR'S

Business Summary November 29, 2007

CORPORATE OVERVIEW. Consolidated Edison is a holding company with electric and gas utilities serving a territory that includes New York City (except part of Queens), most of Westchester County, southeastern New York state, northern New Jersey, and northeastern Pennsylvania. Although the company also has some competitive subsidiaries that participate in energy-related businesses, we expect the two regulated utilities to provide substantially all of ED's earnings over the next few years.

MARKET PROFILE. The company's principal business operations are Con Edison of New York's regulated electric, gas and steam utility operations, and Orange and Rockland Utilities' (O&R)regulated electric and gas utility operations. In 2006, electric revenues accounted for 62.9% of consolidated sales (64.8% in 2005); gas revenues 15.2% (16.0%); non-utility revenues 16.7% (13.6%); and steam revenues 5.1% (5.6%). At December 31, 2006, the distribution system of Consolidated Edison Company of New York had about 36,240 miles of overhead distribution lines and around 93,297 miles of underground distribution lines. The distribution system of O&R had about 3,643 miles of overhead distribution lines, and 1,532 miles of underground distribution lines.

The company's Con Edison of New York (CENY) unit provides electric service (75.9% of CENY's operating revenues in 2006) to about 3.2 million customers and gas service (17.4%) to around 1.1 million customers in New York City and Westchester County. It also provides steam service (6.7%) in parts of Manhattan to around 2,000 customers (mostly large office buildings, apartment houses and hospitals). Most of the electricity sold by CENY in 2005 was purchased under firm power contracts (primarily with non-utility generators) or through the wholesale electricity market administered by the New York Independent System Operator (NYISO). We expect this to continue for the foreseeable future.

The company's O&R unit provides electric and gas service in southeastern New York and adjacent areas of eastern Pennsylvania, and electric service in areas of New Jersey adjacent to its New York service territory. In 2006, electric sales accounted for 71.1% of its operating revenues and gas sales, 28.9%.

Company Financials Fiscal Year Ended Dec. 31

Per Share Data ($)	2006	2005	2004	2003	2002	2001	2000	1999	1998	1997
Tangible Book Value	32.13	30.69	29.86	29.09	25.40	24.23	23.50	22.41	25.19	24.52
Earnings	2.95	2.99	2.32	2.36	3.13	3.21	2.74	3.13	3.04	2.95
S&P Core Earnings	2.54	2.54	1.78	1.66	0.50	0.66	NA	NA	NA	NA
Dividends	2.30	2.28	2.26	2.24	2.22	2.20	2.18	2.14	2.12	2.10
Payout Ratio	78%	76%	97%	95%	71%	69%	80%	68%	70%	71%
Prices:High	49.28	49.29	45.59	46.02	45.40	43.37	39.50	53.44	56.13	41.50
Prices:Low	41.17	41.10	37.23	36.55	32.65	31.44	26.19	33.56	39.06	27.00
P/E Ratio:High	17	16	20	20	15	14	14	17	18	14
P/E Ratio:Low	14	14	16	15	10	10	10	11	13	9

Income Statement Analysis (Million $)										
Revenue	12,137	11,690	9,758	9,827	8,482	9,634	9,431	7,491	7,093	7,121
Depreciation	621	584	551	529	495	526	586	526	519	503
Maintenance	NA	NA	NA	353	387	430	458	438	477	475
Fixed Charges Coverage	2.97	3.19	2.64	3.13	3.25	3.46	3.06	4.03	4.24	4.05
Construction Credits	12.0	16.0	43.0	27.0	14.0	9.00	8.00	6.00	4.00	7.00
Effective Tax Rate	34.6%	34.6%	33.1%	37.5%	35.6%	38.9%	34.0%	34.3%	35.7%	34.8%
Net Income	738	732	549	525	680	696	596	715	730	713
S&P Core Earnings	635	621	421	370	106	141	NA	NA	NA	NA

Balance Sheet & Other Financial Data (Million $)										
Gross Property	23,028	21,467	20,394	19,294	18,000	16,630	17,021	16,088	16,132	15,659
Capital Expenditures	1,847	1,617	1,359	1,292	1,216	1,104	986	695	626	669
Net Property	18,445	17,112	16,106	15,225	13,330	12,136	11,786	11,354	11,406	11,267
Capitalization:Long Term Debt	8,511	7,641	6,807	6,769	6,206	5,542	5,447	4,560	4,087	4,229
Capitalization:% Long Term Debt	51.1	50.5	48.5	51.3	50.3	48.3	48.8	44.5	39.4	40.4
Capitalization:Preferred	Nil	Nil	Nil	Nil	Nil	250	250	250	250	233
Capitalization:% Preferred	Nil	Nil	Nil	Nil	Nil	2.18	2.24	2.44	2.41	3.00
Capitalization:Common	8,159	7,477	7,234	6,423	5,921	5,690	5,471	5,448	6,026	5,930
Capitalization:% Common	48.9	49.5	51.5	48.7	48.0	49.6	49.0	53.1	58.1	56.6
Total Capital	20,806	18,804	17,806	16,406	15,037	13,835	13,602	12,666	12,911	12,949
% Operating Ratio	89.5	90.3	90.3	88.8	74.1	88.1	117.8	86.0	85.1	85.3
% Earned on Net Property	7.1	7.0	5.9	6.4	8.3	9.4	8.8	9.0	9.3	9.4
% Return on Revenue	6.1	6.3	5.6	5.3	8.0	7.2	6.3	9.5	10.3	10.0
% Return on Invested Capital	6.7	6.7	5.9	7.3	7.8	8.3	7.7	8.2	11.1	8.1
% Return on Common Equity	9.4	10.0	7.9	8.5	11.5	12.2	10.7	12.2	11.9	11.9

Data as orig reptd.; bef. results of disc opers/spec. items. Per share data adj. for stk. divs.; EPS diluted. E-Estimated. NA-Not Available. NM-Not Meaningful. NR-Not Ranked. UR-Under Review.

Office: 4 Irving Place, New York, NY 10003.
Telephone: 212-460-4600.
Email: corpcom@coned.com
Website: http://www.coned.com

Chrmn, Pres & CEO: K. Burke
SVP & CFO: R.N. Hoglund
VP & Treas: J.P. Oates
VP & Cntlr: E.J. Rasmussen

General Counsel: C.E. McTiernan, Jr.
Board Members: K. Burke, V. A. Calarco, G. Campbell, Jr., G. J. Davis, M. J. Del Giudice, E. V. Futter, S. Hernandez, P. W. Likins, E. R. McGrath, L. F. Sutherland, S. R. Volk

Founded: 1884
Domicile: New York
Employees: 14,795

The McGraw·Hill Companies

CONSOL Energy Inc.

STANDARD &POOR'S

S&P Recommendation **BUY** ★★★★☆	Price $54.95 (as of Nov 23, 2007)	12-Mo. Target Price $64.00	Investment Style Large-Cap Blend

GICS Sector Energy
Sub-Industry Coal & Consumable Fuels

Summary This company is a major producer of high-bituminous coal and coalbed methane gas. We estimate CNX is the second largest U.S. coal producer by annual production and its coal reserves of 4.3 billion tons.

Key Stock Statistics (Source S&P, Vickers, company reports)

52-Wk Range	$58.49– 29.15	S&P Oper. EPS 2007**E**	2.08	Market Capitalization(B)	$10.019	Beta	1.41
Trailing 12-Month EPS	$2.03	S&P Oper. EPS 2008**E**	3.27	Yield (%)	0.73	S&P 3-Yr. Proj. EPS CAGR(%)	27.00
Trailing 12-Month P/E	27.1	P/E on S&P Oper. EPS 2007**E**	26.4	Dividend Rate/Share	$0.40	S&P Credit Rating	BB
$10K Invested 5 Yrs Ago	$90,965	Common Shares Outstg. (M)	182.3	Institutional Ownership (%)	NM		

Price Performance

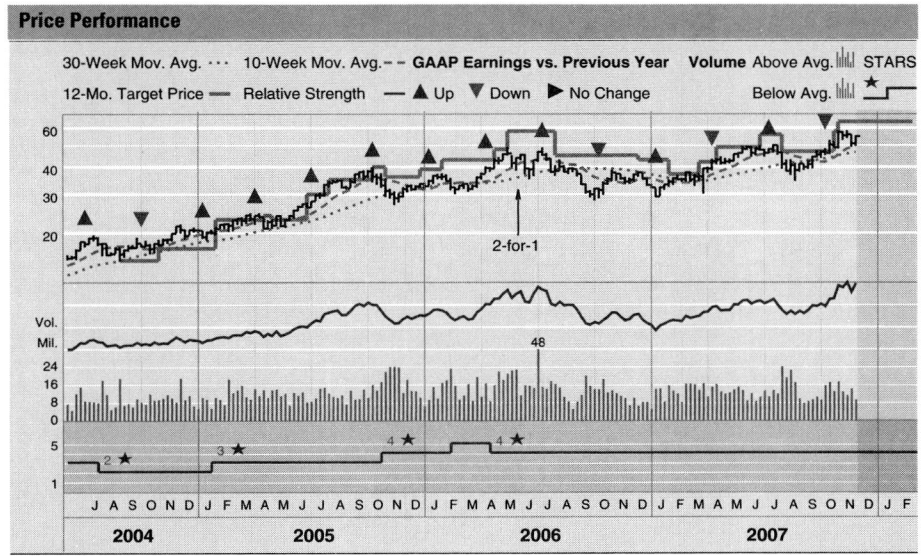

30-Week Mov. Avg. ··· 10-Week Mov. Avg.- - **GAAP Earnings vs. Previous Year** Volume Above Avg. STARS
12-Mo. Target Price — Relative Strength ▲ Up ▼ Down ▶ No Change Below Avg.

2-for-1

Options: ASE, CBOE, P, Ph

Analysis prepared by **Christopher Lippincott** on October 31, 2007, when the stock traded at **$ 56.71**.

Highlights

➤ We expect revenues to be flat in 2007 and rise 12% in 2008, led mostly by strong growth in produced tons sold in 2008 and rising average realized prices. We project that the acquisition of AMVEST, which closed on August 1, will enable CNX to add over 4 million tons of annual production to its volume for 2008. We calculate that per-ton prices will rise in the low single digits in 2008, as contracts for 2008 may lock in recent spot prices, while demand shifts to Western Region coal.

➤ We think 2007 EBIT margins will decline slightly, but expand to 19% in 2008 due to higher productivity and cost reduction efforts, especially considering our forecast of declining labor costs as employee turnover decreases, in addition to operating leverage from higher volume. We forecast that average cash cost per ton will rise 2% in 2007 but decrease 8% in 2008.

➤ We project operating EPS of $2.08 in 2007 and we estimate operating EPS of $3.27 in 2008.

Investment Rationale/Risk

➤ We believe CNX will benefit from stable volume and improving pricing for northern Appalachia coal through its long-term supply contracts that are beginning to display premiums. We think the AMVEST acquisition will boost CNX's volume and pricing, and signals that industry consolidation may ramp up. We expect industry supply and demand to substantially improve in 2008, supporting higher prices. We view positively CNX's financial flexibility due to its 27% average debt-to-capital and 0.6X average debt-to-EBITDA ratios for 2006.

➤ Risks to our recommendation and target price include lower than expected prices for steam and metallurgical grade coal, less productivity, increased supply costs, and slower than forecast U.S. economic activity.

➤ Our 12-month target price of $64 is a blend of two metrics. Our discounted cash flow model, which assumes a 3% perpetual growth rate and a 10.6% discount rate, indicates an intrinsic value of $65. On a relative valuation basis, we apply an EV/EBITDA multiple of about 11X our 2008 EBITDA estimate, in line with its largest global peers, suggesting a value of $64.

Qualitative Risk Assessment

LOW	MEDIUM	HIGH

Our risk assessment reflects the cyclical nature of the coal market, our view of unfavorable corporate governance practices concerning takeover defenses, and the heavily regulated nature of the industry and its utilities' end market, notwithstanding expected benefits from the pricing cycle and a rising market share.

Quantitative Evaluations

S&P Quality Ranking NR

D	C	B-	B	B+	A-	A	A+

Relative Strength Rank STRONG
95
LOWEST = 1   HIGHEST = 99

Revenue/Earnings Data

Revenue (Million $)

	1Q	2Q	3Q	4Q	Year
2007	915.2	1,060	868.4	--	--
2006	985.9	932.3	843.4	953.7	3,715
2005	817.0	817.2	879.9	969.1	3,483
2004	650.9	674.6	659.9	791.4	2,777
2003	559.8	556.5	552.2	554.0	2,222
2002	552.0	536.3	546.4	554.6	2,184

Earnings Per Share ($)

2007	0.61	0.83	-0.03	E0.54	E2.08
2006	0.67	0.57	0.27	0.69	2.20
2005	0.41	0.22	2.02	0.47	3.13
2004	0.18	0.15	-0.07	0.37	0.64
2003	0.02	0.07	-0.04	-0.14	-0.05
2002	0.04	0.06	-0.05	0.03	0.08

Fiscal year ended Dec. 31. Next earnings report expected: Late January. EPS Estimates based on S&P Operating Earnings; historical GAAP earnings are as reported.

Dividend Data (Dates: mm/dd Payment Date: mm/dd/yy)

Amount ($)	Date Decl.	Ex-Div. Date	Stk. of Record	Payment Date
0.070	01/26	02/06	02/08	02/23/07
0.070	04/27	05/04	05/08	05/29/07
0.070	07/27	08/07	08/09	08/27/07
0.100	10/26	11/05	11/07	11/23/07

Dividends have been paid since 1999. Source: Company reports.

CONSOL Energy Inc.

STANDARD &POOR'S

Business Summary October 31, 2007

CORPORATE OVERVIEW. Through expansion and acquisitions, CONSOL Energy has grown from a single fuel mining company formed in 1860 into a multi-energy producer of coal and gas. CNX produces high Btu coal and gas, two fuels that collectively generate two thirds of all U.S. electric power, from reserves located mainly east of the Mississippi River.

The coal segment (CNX Coal) has 17 mining complexes in the U.S., and sells steam coal to power generators and metallurgical coal to metal and coke producers. The company had an estimated 4.3 billion tons of proven and probable coal reserves at the end of 2006, nearly all of which was located in underground mines. About 64% of CNX's reserves are found in Northern Appalachia, with 17% in the Midwest, 10% in Central Appalachia, 6% in the western U.S., and 3% in western Canada. The company is a major fuel supplier to the electric power industry in the northeast quadrant of the U.S. Coal produced at CNX's mines is transported to customers via railroad cars, barges, trucks and conveyor belts, or by a combination of such methods. In 2006, the company sold 67.4 million produced tons of coal, down from 69.1 million tons in 2005. Approximately 90% of coal produced in 2006 was sold under contracts

with terms of one year or more. The average sales price per produced ton sold in 2006 was $38.99, versus $35.61 in 2005. In 2006, one customer, Allegheny Energy, accounted for 10% of total company revenue.

CONSOL Energy owns 81.5% of CNX Gas Corporation, which is one of the largest U.S. producers of coalbed methane (CBM), with daily gas production of 161 MMcf. CBM produces pipeline quality gas that is found in coal seams, usually in formations at depths of less than 2,500 feet versus conventional natural gas fields with depths of up to 15,000 feet. At the end of 2006, CNX Gas had 1.3 Tcf of proved CBM reserves, of which approximately 48% was developed, and more than 2,000 active wells connected to over 1,000 miles of gathering lines. In 2006, the company sold 56.1 Bcf of gas at an average price of $7.04, versus 48.4 Bcf of $5.90 in 2005.

Company Financials Fiscal Year Ended Dec. 31

Per Share Data ($)	2006	2005	2004	2003	2002	2001	2000	1999	1998	1997
Tangible Book Value	5.84	5.54	2.59	NM	1.03	2.23	1.62	1.59	NA	NA
Cash Flow	3.80	4.54	2.17	1.40	1.74	2.71	2.24	1.24	NA	NA
Earnings	2.20	3.13	0.64	-0.05	0.08	1.17	0.68	0.31	NA	NA
S&P Core Earnings	1.88	2.05	0.69	0.04	0.03	0.98	NA	NA	NA	NA
Dividends	0.28	0.28	0.28	0.28	0.42	0.56	0.56	Nil	NA	NA
Payout Ratio	13%	9%	44%	NM	NM	48%	83%	Nil	NA	NA
Prices:High	49.09	39.91	21.95	13.40	14.16	21.24	14.00	8.00	NA	NA
Prices:Low	28.07	18.58	10.12	7.28	4.90	9.15	4.97	4.81	NA	NA
P/E Ratio:High	22	13	35	NM	NM	18	21	NM	NA	NA
P/E Ratio:Low	13	6	16	NM	NM	8	7	NM	NA	NA

Income Statement Analysis (Million $)	2006	2005	2004	2003	2002	2001	2000	1999	1998	1997
Revenue	3,715	3,483	2,777	2,222	2,184	2,368	2,159	1,110	NA	NA
Operating Income	701	617	308	246	268	418	599	409	NA	NA
Depreciation	296	262	280	242	263	243	250	121	NA	NA
Interest Expense	25.1	27.3	31.4	34.5	46.2	57.6	55.0	30.5	NA	NA
Pretax Income	551	655	82.6	-33.5	-40.4	240	107	40.2	NA	NA
Effective Tax Rate	20.4%	9.83%	NM	NM	NM	23.6%	NM	0.30%	NA	NA
Net Income	409	581	115	-12.6	11.7	184	107	40.0	NA	NA
S&P Core Earnings	349	381	125	6.95	3.70	154	NA	NA	NA	NA

Balance Sheet & Other Financial Data (Million $)	2006	2005	2004	2003	2002	2001	2000	1999	1998	1997
Cash	224	341	6.42	6.51	11.5	16.6	8.20	23.6	NA	NA
Current Assets	914	998	470	471	623	566	578	623	NA	NA
Total Assets	5,663	5,088	4,196	4,319	4,293	3,895	3,866	3,875	NA	NA
Current Liabilities	740	804	705	825	814	934	953	884	NA	NA
Long Term Debt	493	438	426	442	488	231	301	313	NA	NA
Common Equity	984	1,025	469	291	162	352	254	255	NA	NA
Total Capital	1,612	1,557	895	733	650	583	555	567	NA	NA
Capital Expenditures	659	523	411	291	295	214	143	105	NA	NA
Cash Flow	705	843	396	230	275	427	357	161	NA	NA
Current Ratio	1.2	1.2	0.7	0.6	0.8	0.6	0.6	0.7	NA	NA
% Long Term Debt of Capitalization	30.6	28.2	47.6	60.3	75.1	39.6	54.1	55.1	NA	NA
% Net Income of Revenue	11.5	17.2	4.1	NM	NM	7.8	4.9	3.6	NA	NA
% Return on Assets	7.6	12.5	2.7	NM	NM	4.7	2.7	NM	NA	NA
% Return on Equity	40.7	77.7	30.3	NM	NM	60.6	42.0	NM	NA	NA

Data as orig reptd.; bef. results of disc opers/spec. items. Per share data adj. for stk. divs.; EPS diluted. E-Estimated. NA-Not Available. NM-Not Meaningful. NR-Not Ranked. UR-Under Review.

Office: 1800 Washington Road, Pittsburgh, PA 15241.
Telephone: 412-831-4000.
Website: http://www.consolenergy.com
Chrmn: J.L. Whitmire

Pres & CEO: J.B. Harvey
COO: B.J. Hyita
Investor Contact: W.J. Lyons (412-831-4000)
EVP & CFO: W.J. Lyons

Board Members: J. Altmeyer, Sr., W. E. Davis, R. K. Gupta, P. A. Hammick, D. C. Hardesty, Jr., J. B. Harvey, J. T. Mills, W. P. Powell, J. L. Whitmire, J. T. Williams

Founded: 1991
Domicile: Delaware
Employees: 7,253

The McGraw-Hill Companies

Constellation Brands Inc.

STANDARD &POOR'S

S&P Recommendation **HOLD** ★★★☆☆	Price $23.51 (as of Nov 23, 2007)	12-Mo. Target Price $27.00	Investment Style Large-Cap Growth

GICS Sector Consumer Staples
Sub-Industry Distillers & Vintners

Summary This leading international producer and marketer of alcoholic beverages has a broad portfolio of wine, imported beer and distilled spirits brands.

Key Stock Statistics (Source S&P, Vickers, company reports)

52-Wk Range	$29.17– 18.83	S&P Oper. EPS 2008**E**	1.35	Market Capitalization(B)	$4.505	Beta	0.52
Trailing 12-Month EPS	$1.19	S&P Oper. EPS 2009**E**	1.70	Yield (%)	Nil	S&P 3-Yr. Proj. EPS CAGR(%)	11.00
Trailing 12-Month P/E	19.8	P/E on S&P Oper. EPS 2008**E**	17.4	Dividend Rate/Share	Nil	S&P Credit Rating	BB-
$10K Invested 5 Yrs Ago	$19,326	Common Shares Outstg. (M)	215.4	Institutional Ownership (%)	92		

Price Performance

30-Week Mov. Avg. ··· 10-Week Mov. Avg. - - **GAAP Earnings vs. Previous Year** Volume Above Avg. STARS
12-Mo. Target Price — Relative Strength — ▲ Up ▼ Down ► No Change Below Avg.

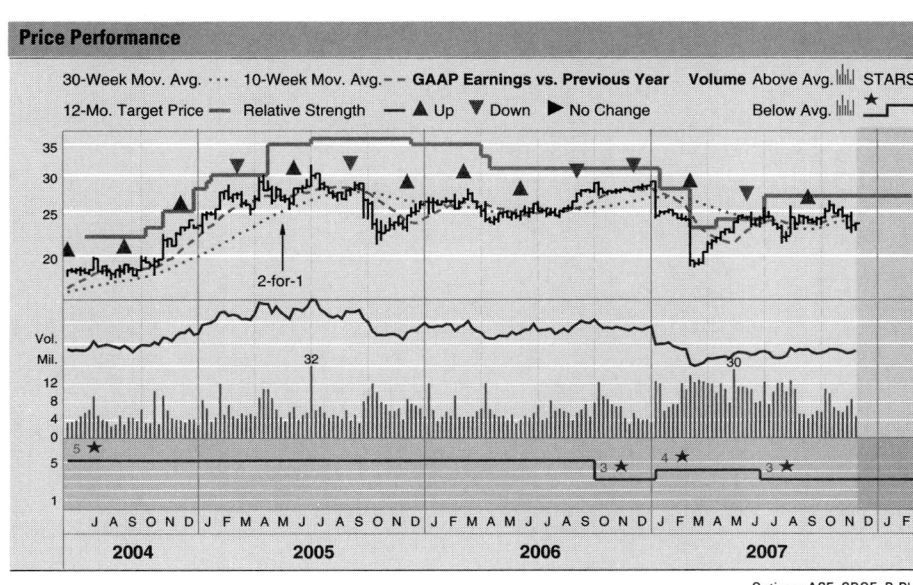

Options: ASE, CBOE, P, Ph

Analysis prepared by **Esther Y. Kwon, CFA** on November 19, 2007, when the stock traded at **$ 22.93.**

Highlights

➤ STZ recently entered into a 50/50 joint venture with Grupo Modelo SA to import and distribute beers, primarily top import brand Corona. This will cause STZ's beer sales to be deconsolidated, with the entity accounted for on an equity basis. The company also sold half of its Matthew Clark wholesale business to a joint venture with Punch Taverns plc.

➤ We expect FY 08 (Feb.) net revenues to fall 30%, as benefits from a stronger portfolio following the purchase of Vincor and SVEDKA vodka are offset by the deconsolidation of beer sales. We see heavy competition in the U.K. market continuing, but expect competitive pressures due to oversupply conditions in the Australian market to begin to wane in 2008. We expect a contraction in the operating margin in early FY 08, as likely distribution and sourcing synergies are offset by dilution from acquisitions. In FY 09, we estimate sales growth of 5%.

➤ With expectations of higher interest expense due to acquisition financing, and an effective tax rate of 39%, offset by a lower share count, we project a rise in FY 08 operating EPS to $1.35, excluding restructuring charges and integration costs. For FY 09, we see EPS of $1.70.

Investment Rationale/Risk

➤ We believe the Mondavi and Vincor acquisitions will support strong growth over the longer term, as STZ's distribution provides significant reach for the major acquired brands. In November, STZ agreed to buy Fortune Brands' U.S. wine business, which should give STZ a stronger presence in the faster growing super-premium and above segment. We see healthy global demand for premium wines continuing, and U.S. wine exports benefiting from a relatively weak U.S. dollar. We look for a turnaround in grape supply issues in 2008, and we believe U.S. and U.K. competitive pressures will ease over the longer term.

➤ Risks to our recommendation and target price include continued pricing pressures in the U.K. wine market, resistance to further beer price increases, and integration risks.

➤ Our 12-month target price of $27 is based on a P/E multiple of 16X our FY 09 EPS estimate of $1.70. We think a mix shift to faster growing segments and an expected rebound from oversupply in FY 09 merits at least this mid-range multiple. On an EV/EBITDA basis, we use 10X, slightly below the middle of the recent range, to also derive a $27 value.

Qualitative Risk Assessment

LOW	**MEDIUM**	HIGH

STZ operates in an industry that we believe has demonstrated stable revenue streams. This is offset by our corporate governance concerns relating to STZ's dual class stock structure with unequal voting rights.

Quantitative Evaluations

S&P Quality Ranking B+

D	C	B-	B	**B+**	A-	A	A+

Relative Strength Rank MODERATE

68

LOWEST = 1   HIGHEST = 99

Revenue/Earnings Data

Revenue (Million $)

	1Q	2Q	3Q	4Q	Year
2008	901.2	1,168	--	--	--
2007	1,156	1,418	1,501	1,142	5,216
2006	1,097	1,192	1,267	1,048	4,603
2005	927.3	1,037	1,086	1,038	4,088
2004	772.8	911.1	987.3	881.3	3,552
2003	650.4	689.8	738.4	653.0	2,732

Earnings Per Share ($)

2008	0.13	0.34	E0.55	E0.34	E1.35
2007	0.36	0.28	0.45	0.29	1.38
2006	0.32	0.34	0.46	0.24	1.36
2005	0.23	0.35	0.42	0.20	1.19
2004	0.21	0.17	0.37	0.28	1.03
2003	0.20	0.26	0.35	0.28	1.10

Fiscal year ended Feb. 28. Next earnings report expected: Early January. EPS Estimates based on S&P Operating Earnings; historical GAAP earnings are as reported.

Dividend Data

No cash dividends have been paid.

Please read the Required Disclosures and Analyst Certification on the last page of this report.

The McGraw-Hill Companies

Constellation Brands Inc.

STANDARD &POOR'S

Business Summary November 19, 2007

CORPORATE OVERVIEW. Through an aggressive acquisition program over the past few years, Constellation Brands (formerly Canandaigua Brands) has become a leading international producer and marketer of alcoholic beverages in North America, Europe and Australia. STZ recently restructured into three divisions, Constellation Wines, Constellation Spirits, and Crown Imports.

Constellation Wines produces and markets table wines, dessert wines and sparkling wines. It is the second largest producer and marketer in the U.S., the largest producer in Canada and Australia, and the largest marketer in the U.K. The company sells wines in the popular, premium, super-premium and ultra-premium categories. The higher category wines are supported by vineyard holdings in California, Canada, Australia, New Zealand and Chile. At the end of FY 07 (Feb.), the company operated 21 wineries in the U.S., 12 in Australia, eight in Canada, and four in New Zealand.

STZ has developed a premium wine portfolio through acquisitions, selling 24 of the top 100 U.S. table wines in 2007. Leading wine brands include Almaden, Arbor Mist, Vendange, Woodbridge, Robert Mondavi, Inniskillin, Kim Crawford, Hardys, Nobilo, Alice White, Ruffino, Blackstone, Ravenswood, Estancia, Franciscan Oakville Estate, Simi, Estancia, and Toasted Head.

The former Constellation Beers has been contributed to the Crown Imports joint venture. It imports and markets a diversified line of beer. The company is the largest marketer of imported beer in 25 mostly western states. It distributes six of the top 20 imported beer brands in the U.S.: Corona Extra, the best selling imported beer, Modelo Especial, Corona Light, Pacifico, St. Pauli Girl, and Negra Modelo. It also imports the top-selling Chinese beer, Tsingtao.

Constellation Spirits operates seven facilities where it produces and bottles, imports and markets a diversified line of distilled spirits. Distilled spirits brands are marketed primarily in the value and mid-premium priced category. Principal brands include Black Velvet, Barton, Skol, Fleischmann's Canadian LTD, Montezuma, Ten High, Chi-Chi's, Mr. Boston, Inver House, and Monte Alban. STZ also sells bulk spirits and other related products and services. The company moved to improve its mix of premium brands with the 2007 acquisition of SVEDKA vodka.

Company Financials Fiscal Year Ended Feb. 28

Per Share Data ($)	2007	2006	2005	2004	2003	2002	2001	2000	1999	1998
Tangible Book Value	NM	NM	NM	NM	0.39	NM	NM	NM	NM	1.16
Cash Flow	1.95	1.86	1.59	1.39	1.42	1.08	0.95	0.80	0.67	0.55
Earnings	1.38	1.36	1.19	1.03	1.10	0.79	0.65	0.52	0.41	0.33
S&P Core Earnings	1.41	1.24	1.02	0.96	0.97	0.66	0.54	NA	NA	NA
Dividends	Nil	Nil	Nil	Nil	Nil	Nil	Nil	Nil	Nil	Nil
Payout Ratio	Nil	Nil	Nil	Nil	Nil	Nil	Nil	Nil	Nil	Nil
Calendar Year	2006	2005	2004	2003	2002	2001	2000	1999	1998	1997
Prices:High	29.14	31.60	23.91	17.33	16.00	11.63	7.38	7.69	7.47	7.20
Prices:Low	23.32	21.15	14.65	10.95	10.53	6.63	5.05	5.36	4.41	2.73
P/E Ratio:High	22	23	20	17	15	15	11	15	18	22
P/E Ratio:Low	18	16	12	11	10	8	8	10	11	8

Income Statement Analysis (Million $)

	2007	2006	2005	2004	2003	2002	2001	2000	1999	1998
Revenue	5,216	4,603	4,088	3,552	2,732	2,821	2,397	2,340	1,497	1,213
Operating Income	895	840	689	601	470	394	315	281	187	150
Depreciation	140	128	104	82.0	60.1	51.9	44.6	40.9	38.6	33.2
Interest Expense	269	190	138	145	105	114	109	106	41.5	32.2
Pretax Income	535	477	432	344	335	230	162	129	104	84.9
Effective Tax Rate	38.0%	31.8%	36.0%	36.0%	39.3%	40.0%	40.0%	40.0%	59.3%	41.0%
Net Income	332	325	276	220	203	138	97.3	77.4	61.9	50.1
S&P Core Earnings	334	288	230	199	181	115	80.7	NA	NA	NA

Balance Sheet & Other Financial Data (Million $)

	2007	2006	2005	2004	2003	2002	2001	2000	1999	1998
Cash	33.5	10.9	17.6	37.1	13.8	8.96	146	34.3	27.6	1.20
Current Assets	3,023	2,701	2,734	2,071	1,330	1,231	1,191	996	856	564
Total Assets	9,438	7,401	7,804	5,559	3,196	3,069	2,512	2,349	1,794	1,073
Current Liabilities	1,591	1,298	1,138	1,030	585	595	427	438	832	283
Long Term Debt	3,715	2,516	3,205	1,779	1,192	1,293	1,307	1,237	415	309
Common Equity	3,418	2,975	2,780	2,378	1,207	956	616	521	435	415
Total Capital	7,607	5,862	6,375	4,344	2,544	2,412	2,056	1,874	1,355	783
Capital Expenditures	192	132	120	105	71.6	71.1	68.2	57.7	49.9	31.2
Cash Flow	467	444	370	297	263	190	142	118	101	83.2
Current Ratio	1.9	2.1	2.4	2.0	2.3	2.1	2.8	2.3	1.0	2.0
% Long Term Debt of Capitalization	48.8	42.9	50.3	41.0	46.8	53.6	63.6	66.0	30.6	39.5
% Net Income of Revenue	6.4	7.1	6.8	6.2	7.4	4.9	4.1	3.3	4.1	4.1
% Return on Assets	3.9	4.3	4.1	5.0	6.5	4.9	4.0	3.7	4.3	4.8
% Return on Equity	10.2	11.0	10.3	12.1	18.5	17.5	17.1	16.2	14.6	12.8

Data as orig reptd.; bef. results of disc opers/spec. items. Per share data adj. for stk. divs.; EPS diluted. E-Estimated. NA-Not Available. NM-Not Meaningful. NR-Not Ranked. UR-Under Review.

Office: 370 Woodcliff Dr., Suite 300, Fairport, NY 14450-4238.
Telephone: 585-218-3600.
Website: http://www.cbrands.com
Chrmn: R. Sands

CEO: R.S. Sands
EVP & CFO: R.P. Ryder
EVP & General Counsel: T.J. Mullin
Chief Admin Officer: K. Wilson

Investor Contact: P. Yahn-Urlaub (585-218-3838)
Board Members: B. A. Fromberg, J. K. Hauswald, J. A. Locke, III, T. C. McDermott, R. Sands, R. S. Sands, P. L. Smith, P. H. Soderberg

Founded: 1972
Domicile: Delaware
Employees: 9,200

Constellation Energy Group Inc.

STANDARD &POOR'S

S&P Recommendation **BUY** ★★★★☆	Price $99.53 (as of Nov 23, 2007)	12-Mo. Target Price $110.00	Investment Style Large-Cap Blend

GICS Sector Utilities
Sub-Industry Independent Power Producers & Energy Traders

Summary This company is the largest wholesale power supplier in the U.S. and the parent of Baltimore Gas and Electric.

Key Stock Statistics (Source S&P, Vickers, company reports)

52-Wk Range	$101.24– 66.70	S&P Oper. EPS 2007**E**	4.56	Market Capitalization(B)	$17.965	Beta	0.40
Trailing 12-Month EPS	$5.30	S&P Oper. EPS 2008**E**	5.65	Yield (%)	1.75	S&P 3-Yr. Proj. EPS CAGR(%)	19.00
Trailing 12-Month P/E	18.8	P/E on S&P Oper. EPS 2007**E**	21.8	Dividend Rate/Share	$1.74	S&P Credit Rating	BBB+
$10K Invested 5 Yrs Ago	$42,313	Common Shares Outstg. (M)	180.5	Institutional Ownership (%)	72		

Price Performance

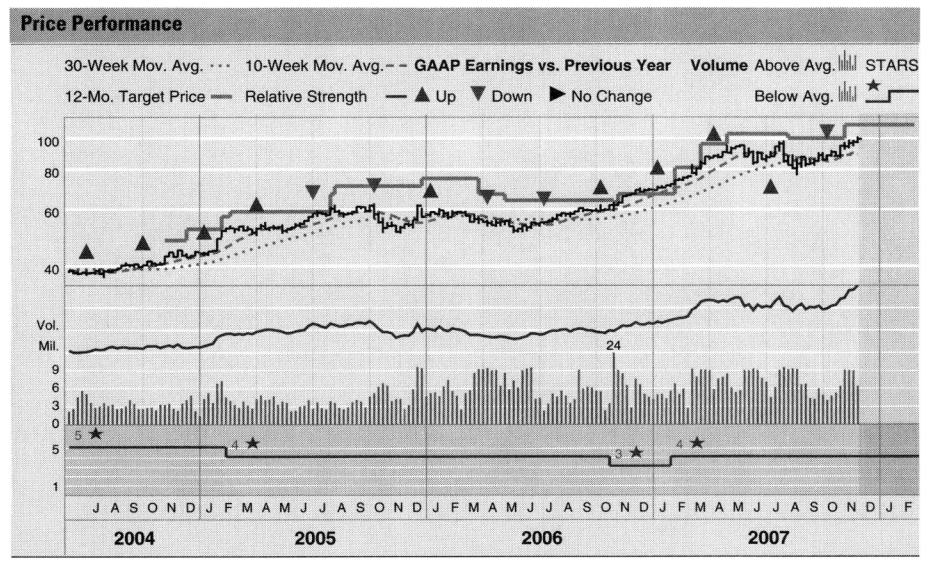

30-Week Mov. Avg. · · · 10-Week Mov. Avg. – – **GAAP Earnings vs. Previous Year** Volume Above Avg. STARS
12-Mo. Target Price — Relative Strength — ▲ Up ▼ Down ► No Change Below Avg.

Options: ASE, CBOE, P, Ph

Analysis prepared by **Justin McCann** on November 07, 2007, when the stock traded at **$ 96.18**.

Highlights

➤ We expect 2007 EPS to grow about 26% from 2006 EPS from continuing operations of $3.61. We believe the merchant business will earn about $3.76 in 2007 (up around 40% from $2.68 in 2006), as the expiring below-market contracts of the Mid-Atlantic operations are replaced by higher-priced contracts. We think this will be partially offset by a further decline at BG&E (to about $0.73, from $0.87 in 2006), as a result of higher operating costs. Operating EPS for the first nine months of 2007 was up 23% from the year-earlier period, driven by a sharp rise in the merchant business and a return to profitability in its operations in the Mid-Atlantic.

➤ Driven by the company's merchant energy operations and its recently announced share repurchase program, we expect EPS growth of approximately 24% in 2008 and around 10% in 2009. This largely reflects the replacement of expiring below market contracts by higher-margin, market-based contracts.

➤ On October 31, 2007, CEG announced that its board had approved a $1 billion share repurchase program over the next two years and was repurchasing $250 million of the program on an accelerated basis.

Investment Rationale/Risk

➤ Although the shares are up around 40% year to date, we believe the stock is still attractive for above-average return. The shares have fully recovered from the recent decline that had resulted, in our view, from speculation that private equity interest in certain utilities had been deferred due to the recent credit tightening. Given CEG's position as the nation's largest wholesale power seller and competitive electricity supplier, and the strong EPS outlook we see for the next three years, we believe the shares merit an above-peers P/E.

➤ Risks to our recommendation and target price include trading related risks for contracted electric load obligations, and increased competition in wholesale power and competitive commercial and industrial markets.

➤ CEG increased its dividend by 15% with the April 2007 payment, which raised the recent yield to 1.8%. While this yield is now slightly below the average yield of other utility holding companies whose earnings are driven by their high-growth non-regulated operations, it is still competitive. Our 12-month target price of $110 is based on a premium-to-peers P/E of about 19.5X our EPS estimate for 2008.

Qualitative Risk Assessment

LOW	**MEDIUM**	HIGH

Our risk assessment reflects a balance between stable and steady earnings provided by CEG's regulated electric and gas utility operations and cyclical and volatile earnings from the unregulated merchant energy business, including power generation, energy and energy-related marketing and trading.

Quantitative Evaluations

S&P Quality Ranking   B+

D	C	B-	B	**B+**	A-	A	A+

Relative Strength Rank   **STRONG**

94

LOWEST = 1   HIGHEST = 99

Revenue/Earnings Data

Revenue (Million $)

	1Q	2Q	3Q	4Q	Year
2007	5,056	4,820	5,761	--	--
2006	4,859	4,379	5,393	4,644	19,285
2005	3,630	3,549	4,922	5,159	17,132
2004	3,037	2,793	3,435	3,286	12,550
2003	2,330	2,271	2,604	2,498	9,703
2002	1,046	1,021	1,270	1,372	4,703

Earnings Per Share ($)

	1Q	2Q	3Q	4Q	Year
2007	1.08	0.64	1.37	E1.35	E4.56
2006	0.56	0.41	1.69	1.46	4.12
2005	0.67	0.66	1.02	1.04	3.38
2004	0.66	0.77	1.19	0.76	3.40
2003	0.40	0.58	1.15	0.71	2.85
2002	1.40	0.50	0.92	0.39	3.20

Fiscal year ended Dec. 31. Next earnings report expected: Late January. EPS Estimates based on S&P Operating Earnings; historical GAAP earnings are as reported.

Dividend Data (Dates: mm/dd Payment Date: mm/dd/yy)

Amount ($)	Date Decl.	Ex-Div. Date	Stk. of Record	Payment Date
0.435	03/05	03/08	03/12	04/02/07
0.435	05/18	06/07	06/11	07/02/07
0.435	07/20	09/06	09/10	10/01/07
0.435	10/18	12/06	12/10	01/02/08

Dividends have been paid since 1910. Source: Company reports.

Constellation Energy Group Inc.

STANDARD &POOR'S

Business Summary November 07, 2007

CORPORATE OVERVIEW. Constellation Energy is the largest U.S. wholesale power seller and biggest competitive supplier of electricity to large commercial and industrial customers. It is also the holding company for Baltimore Gas & Electric Company, a regulated utility.

MARKET PROFILE. CEG's Merchant Energy operations (which accounted for 77.5% of income from continuing operations in 2006) include wholesale power generation, energy marketing and risk management services for wholesale customers, competitive retail supply services for commercial and industrial customers, and consulting services. Merchant Energy also houses energy marketing and risk management operations, which are conducted by NewEnergy, serving the commercial and industrial (C&I) market, and Constellation Commodities Group, serving the wholesale market. The company's regulated electric (16.1%) and gas (4.9%) utility operations are performed by Baltimore Gas and Electric (BGE), which serves around 1.2 million electric customers and approximately 620,000 gas customers in a service territory that covers the city of Baltimore and all or part of 10 counties in central Maryland. CEG's oth-

er non-regulated operations accounted for 1.5% of 2006's income from continuing operations.

IMPACT OF MAJOR DEVELOPMENTS. On October 25, 2006, CEG and FPL Group (FPL) announced the termination of the merger agreement that had been announced on December 19, 2005. If the merger had been completed, the shareholders of FPL, the holding company for Florida Power & Light Company and FPL Energy (an independent power supplier), would have had an approximate 60% interest in the new company, and CEG shareholders a 40% interest. The combined entity would have been one of the largest electric companies in the U.S. Although we were disappointed that the merger was terminated, we believe the regulatory and judicial uncertainties surrounding the approval process in Maryland justified the decision.

Company Financials Fiscal Year Ended Dec. 31

Per Share Data ($)	2006	2005	2004	2003	2002	2001	2000	1999	1998	1997
Tangible Book Value	24.66	26.76	25.99	23.81	22.71	23.44	20.88	19.95	19.98	19.44
Earnings	4.12	3.38	3.40	2.85	3.20	0.52	2.30	2.18	2.06	1.72
S&P Core Earnings	3.93	3.31	3.33	2.66	1.75	0.34	NA	NA	NA	NA
Dividends	1.51	1.34	1.14	1.04	0.96	0.48	1.68	1.68	1.66	1.63
Payout Ratio	37%	40%	34%	36%	30%	92%	73%	77%	81%	95%
Prices:High	70.20	62.60	44.90	39.61	32.38	50.14	52.06	31.50	35.25	34.31
Prices:Low	50.55	43.01	35.89	25.17	19.30	20.90	27.06	24.69	29.25	24.75
P/E Ratio:High	17	19	13	14	10	96	23	14	17	20
P/E Ratio:Low	12	13	11	9	6	40	12	11	14	14

Income Statement Analysis (Million $)	2006	2005	2004	2003	2002	2001	2000	1999	1998	1997
Revenue	19,285	17,132	12,550	9,703	4,703	3,928	3,879	3,787	3,358	3,308
Depreciation	524	542	526	479	481	419	470	450	377	343
Maintenance	NA	NA	NA	NA	NA	NA	NA	186	178	179
Fixed Charges Coverage	4.01	3.50	3.40	3.12	2.90	3.01	3.12	2.98	2.81	2.92
Construction Credits	NA	NA	NA	NA	NA	NA	NA	NA	9.70	5.30
Effective Tax Rate	31.9%	25.2%	22.6%	36.2%	37.1%	31.5%	40.0%	36.3%	35.2%	35.8%
Net Income	749	607	589	476	526	82.4	345	326	328	283
S&P Core Earnings	714	594	578	444	290	54.9	NA	NA	NA	NA

Balance Sheet & Other Financial Data (Million $)	2006	2005	2004	2003	2002	2001	2000	1999	1998	1997
Gross Property	13,680	14,403	14,315	13,580	12,354	11,862	10,442	8,989	8,744	8,495
Capital Expenditures	963	760	704	658	850	1,318	1,079	436	339	373
Net Property	9,222	10,067	10,087	9,602	7,957	7,700	6,644	5,523	5,657	5,652
Capitalization:Long Term Debt	4,222	4,559	5,003	5,229	4,804	2,903	3,349	2,765	3,128	2,989
Capitalization:% Long Term Debt	47.8	48.1	51.4	55.8	55.4	43.0	51.5	48.0	51.3	48.5
Capitalization:Preferred	Nil	Nil	Nil	Nil	Nil	Nil	Nil	Nil	-7.00	23.0
Capitalization:% Preferred	Nil	Nil	Nil	Nil	Nil	Nil	Nil	Nil	NM	4.87
Capitalization:Common	4,609	4,916	4,727	4,141	3,862	3,844	3,153	2,993	2,982	2,870
Capitalization:% Common	52.2	51.9	48.6	44.2	44.6	57.0	48.5	52.0	48.9	46.6
Total Capital	10,419	10,720	11,105	10,833	10,083	8,271	7,943	7,157	7,727	7,432
% Operating Ratio	94.7	94.5	92.2	91.6	87.2	78.3	84.3	84.8	82.5	75.4
% Earned on Net Property	13.1	10.5	17.0	17.1	17.8	5.0	13.3	13.6	13.1	11.9
% Return on Revenue	3.9	3.5	4.7	4.9	11.2	2.1	8.9	8.6	9.8	8.6
% Return on Invested Capital	11.4	9.2	9.0	8.2	9.8	10.5	8.2	7.8	11.0	8.6
% Return on Common Equity	15.7	12.6	13.3	11.9	13.6	2.3	11.2	10.9	10.5	8.9

Data as orig reptd.; bef. results of disc opers/spec. items. Per share data adj. for stk. divs.; EPS diluted. E-Estimated. NA-Not Available. NM-Not Meaningful. NR-Not Ranked. UR-Under Review.

Office: 750 E Pratt St, Baltimore, MD 21202-3142.
Telephone: 410-783-2800.
Website: http://www.constellationenergy.com
Chrmn, Pres & CEO: M.A. Shattuck III

Vice Chrmn & EVP: T.V. Brooks
EVP, CFO & Chief Admin Officer: E.F. Smith
EVP & General Counsel: I.B. Yoskowitz
SVP & CIO: B.S. Perlman

Investor Contact: K. Hadlock (410-864-6440)
Board Members: D. L. Becker, J. T. Brady, F. P. Bramble, Sr., E. A. Crooke, J. R. Curtiss, F. J. Dawson, F. A. Hrabowski, III, N. Lampton, R. J. Lawless, L. M. Martin, M. A. Shattuck, III, M. D. Sullivan, Y. C. de Balmann

Founded: 1906
Domicile: Maryland
Employees: 9,645

The McGraw-Hill Companies

Convergys Corp

STANDARD &POOR'S

S&P Recommendation **HOLD** ★★★★★	Price $17.05 (as of Nov 23, 2007)	12-Mo. Target Price $20.00	Investment Style Large-Cap Growth

GICS Sector Information Technology
Sub-Industry Data Processing & Outsourced Services

Summary This company is a provider of outsourced billing and customer management solutions for communications companies and state governments.

Key Stock Statistics (Source S&P, Vickers, company reports)

52-Wk Range	$27.26–14.67	S&P Oper. EPS 2007E	1.23	Market Capitalization(B)	$2.312	Beta	1.70
Trailing 12-Month EPS	$1.20	S&P Oper. EPS 2008E	1.28	Yield (%)	Nil	S&P 3-Yr. Proj. EPS CAGR(%)	8.00
Trailing 12-Month P/E	14.2	P/E on S&P Oper. EPS 2007E	13.9	Dividend Rate/Share	Nil	S&P Credit Rating	BBB
$10K Invested 5 Yrs Ago	$10,107	Common Shares Outstg. (M)	135.6	Institutional Ownership (%)	86		

Price Performance

30-Week Mov. Avg. ··· 10-Week Mov. Avg. - - GAAP Earnings vs. Previous Year Volume Above Avg. STARS
12-Mo. Target Price — Relative Strength — ▲ Up ▼ Down ► No Change Below Avg.

Options: CBOE, P, Ph

Analysis prepared by **James Moorman** on October 30, 2007, when the stock traded at **$18.15**.

Highlights

➤ We expect revenues to rise 3.7% in 2007 and 5% in 2008, as gains at the larger customer care group (CCG) are likely to be somewhat offset by declines in the information management group (IMG). However, we think growth at CCG operations will be somewhat restricted by delayed contract signings. Employee care should continue to exhibit growth, despite a slow start in the first half of 2007. We see CVG being hurt as key customers AT&T and Sprint Nextel migrate off of CVG's systems.

➤ We see operating margins narrowing to 8.8% in 2007, before recovering to 9.3% in 2008. We believe that many of the growth and cost-cutting initiatives that we expect to weigh on margins in 2007 will begin to show benefits in 2008. The cost-cutting initiatives have started to show some results, but have been largely outweighed by an increase in hiring that should bolster revenue growth in 2008.

➤ We estimate EPS of $1.23 in 2007 and $1.28 in 2008. We believe that strength in CVG's cellular partnership contributed $0.06 of after-tax non-operating income in 2006 and will add $0.07 in 2007.

Investment Rationale/Risk

➤ We believe recent restructuring efforts and the buildout of the small employee care segment are designed to offset the sizable challenges we see related to customer migration and competition. However, we think CVG will have difficulty increasing earnings at a pace similar to peers, given slow revenue growth and low margins. With a sharp decline in CVG shares thus far in 2007, we believe the stock's valuation reflects the challenges we see for growth.

➤ Risks to our recommendation and target price include reduced business with large customers, below-average growth in demand from non-communications companies, ongoing operating losses in employee care, and currency losses from international operations.

➤ We believe CVG deserves its P/E-to-growth discount to peers given our view of sizable customer migration risk, narrower margins, and sluggish top-line growth. Our 12-month target price is $20, based on a P/E-to-growth ratio of 1.7X, or a P/E of 16X applied to our 2008 EPS estimate. We believe CVG's cash balance provides some support for the shares.

Qualitative Risk Assessment

LOW	**MEDIUM**	HIGH

Our risk assessment for Convergys reflects the competitive nature of serving the communications industry, and the concentration of its customer base, with approximately 30% of its revenues coming from three companies. This is offset by the company's use of long-term contracts.

Quantitative Evaluations

S&P Quality Ranking B

D	C	B-	**B**	B+	A-	A	A+

Relative Strength Rank MODERATE

55

LOWEST = 1   HIGHEST = 99

Revenue/Earnings Data

Revenue (Million $)

	1Q	2Q	3Q	4Q	Year
2007	719.9	707.0	703.7	--	--
2006	675.3	691.8	702.7	720.0	2,790
2005	637.3	630.4	644.8	669.6	2,582
2004	573.9	601.7	639.9	672.2	2,488
2003	560.4	563.2	570.7	594.5	2,289
2002	587.5	572.7	561.2	564.8	2,286

Earnings Per Share ($)

2007	0.31	0.28	0.30	E0.31	E1.23
2006	0.26	0.28	0.32	0.32	1.17
2005	0.22	0.18	0.30	0.16	0.86
2004	0.22	0.20	0.21	0.14	0.77
2003	0.22	0.29	0.31	0.33	1.15
2002	0.35	0.35	0.34	-0.18	0.88

Fiscal year ended Dec. 31. Next earnings report expected: Late January. EPS Estimates based on S&P Operating Earnings; historical GAAP earnings are as reported.

Dividend Data

No cash dividends have been paid.

Please read the Required Disclosures and Analyst Certification on the last page of this report.

The **McGraw-Hill** Companies

Convergys Corp

Business Summary October 30, 2007

CORPORATE OVERVIEW. Convergys Corp. is a provider of outsourced, integrated billing, and employee and customer care software and services. The information management group, known as IMG (26% of revenues and 18% operating margin in the first nine months of 2007), serves clients principally by providing and managing complex billing and information software that addresses all segments of the communications industry. The customer care group, known as CCG (65% and 10%), provides outsourced customer management services for clients, utilizing its advanced information systems capabilities and industry experience through call centers and Web-based assistance programs.

Communications customers contributed 53% of CCG revenues in 2006. Noncommunications clients include technology companies and a number of financial institutions. The employee care segment (9%and operating losses) helps clients with the administration of benefits, human resources, recruiting, and payroll services using a single point of contact system. The company has a 45% limited partnership interest in the Cellular Partnership, which operates a cellular telecommunications business in central and southwestern Ohio and northern Kentucky.

COMPETITIVE LANDSCAPE. Convergys's chief competitor for communications business is Amdocs (DOX), which serves the customer care and billing needs of telecom providers such as Sprint Nextel and wireline and wireless operations at AT&T Inc., as well as a number of cable providers. We expect DOX to compete aggressively to capture additional customers given the rollout of triple-play packages of voice, video and data services by telecom and cable providers. In January 2006, Sprint Nextel announced an eight-year agreement with Amdocs to provide a single billing and customer care platform, allowing the wireless phone company to migrate off of Convergys's system. CVG said it expects billing revenue from Sprint to have an accelerated decline in the second half of 2007. The customer loss follows the migration of Cingular customers off of CVG's billing system that was largely completed in first quarter of 2007. The employee care and non-communications customer care businesses compete with companies such as Accenture, Automatic Data Processing and Hewitt Associates.

Company Financials Fiscal Year Ended Dec. 31

Per Share Data ($)	2006	2005	2004	2003	2002	2001	2000	1999	1998	1997
Tangible Book Value	3.85	3.13	2.62	2.60	2.54	3.08	2.41	1.13	0.29	NM
Cash Flow	2.18	1.89	1.74	1.99	1.70	1.81	2.25	1.73	1.28	1.07
Earnings	1.17	0.86	0.77	1.15	0.88	0.80	1.23	0.89	0.57	0.54
S&P Core Earnings	1.12	0.81	0.60	0.91	0.54	0.51	NA	NA	NA	NA
Dividends	Nil	Nil	Nil	Nil	Nil	Nil	Nil	Nil	Nil	NA
Payout Ratio	Nil	Nil	Nil	Nil	Nil	Nil	Nil	Nil	Nil	NA
Prices:High	24.93	17.90	19.96	20.80	37.98	50.25	55.44	31.75	23.75	NA
Prices:Low	15.43	12.57	12.30	11.30	12.50	24.46	26.63	14.50	9.63	NA
P/E Ratio:High	21	21	26	18	43	63	45	36	42	NA
P/E Ratio:Low	13	15	16	10	14	31	22	16	17	NA

Income Statement Analysis (Million $)	2006	2005	2004	2003	2002	2001	2000	1999	1998	1997
Revenue	2,790	2,582	2,488	2,289	2,286	2,321	2,163	1,763	1,447	988
Operating Income	408	392	327	415	498	543	489	388	313	220
Depreciation	143	147	141	124	137	176	161	130	101	61.0
Interest Expense	22.8	21.2	10.3	6.90	11.0	20.0	32.9	32.5	33.9	5.40
Pretax Income	245	213	173	272	244	255	317	223	131	131
Effective Tax Rate	32.1%	42.5%	35.7%	36.8%	40.3%	45.5%	38.6%	38.4%	38.0%	33.7%
Net Income	166	123	112	172	146	139	195	137	81.0	86.6
S&P Core Earnings	160	117	87.6	133	88.9	91.3	NA	NA	NA	NA

Balance Sheet & Other Financial Data (Million $)	2006	2005	2004	2003	2002	2001	2000	1999	1998	1997
Cash	236	196	58.4	37.2	12.2	41.1	28.2	30.8	3.80	2.10
Current Assets	930	849	593	420	418	523	481	298	361	266
Total Assets	2,540	2,411	2,208	1,810	1,620	1,743	1,780	1,580	1,451	654
Current Liabilities	596	618	577	543	462	492	359	387	698	217
Long Term Debt	260	298	302	58.8	4.60	3.60	291	250	Nil	430
Common Equity	1,455	1,355	1,285	1,144	1,126	1,227	1,113	927	732	431
Total Capital	1,759	1,697	1,588	1,202	1,131	1,230	1,403	1,178	732	NA
Capital Expenditures	105	131	156	174	90.8	114	175	155	93.5	NA
Cash Flow	309	270	253	296	283	315	356	267	182	148
Current Ratio	1.6	1.4	1.0	0.8	0.9	1.1	1.3	0.8	0.5	1.2
% Long Term Debt of Capitalization	14.8	17.5	19.0	4.9	0.4	0.3	20.7	21.3	Nil	NA
% Net Income of Revenue	6.0	4.7	4.5	7.5	6.4	6.0	9.0	7.8	5.6	8.8
% Return on Assets	6.7	5.3	5.5	10.0	8.7	7.8	11.6	9.0	7.7	NA
% Return on Equity	11.8	9.3	9.2	15.1	12.4	11.8	19.1	16.5	13.9	NA

Data as orig reptd.; bef. results of disc opers/spec. items. Per share data adj. for stk. divs.; EPS diluted. E-Estimated. NA-Not Available. NM-Not Meaningful. NR-Not Ranked. UR-Under Review.

Office: 201 E 4th St, Cincinnati, OH 45202-4206.
Telephone: 513-723-7000.
Email: investor@convergys.com
Website: http://www.convergys.com

Chrmn: J.F. Orr
Pres & CEO: D.F. Dougherty
SVP, Secy & General Counsel: W.H. Hawkins, II
SVP & Cntlr: T.M. Wesolowski

CFO: E.C. Shanks
Board Members: Z. Baird, J. F. Barrett, D. B. Dillon, D. F. Dougherty, E. C. Fast, J. E. Gibbs, S. C. Mason, P. A. Odeen, J. F. Orr, S. A. Ribeau, D. R. Whitwam

Founded: 1998
Domicile: Ohio
Employees: 75,000

Cooper Industries Ltd.

STANDARD &POOR'S

S&P Recommendation STRONG BUY ★★★★★

Price	12-Mo. Target Price	Investment Style
$47.53 (as of Nov 23, 2007)	$63.00	Large-Cap Growth

GICS Sector Industrials
Sub-Industry Electrical Components & Equipment

Summary This company is a diversified worldwide manufacturer of electrical products, tools and hardware.

Key Stock Statistics (Source S&P, Vickers, company reports)

52-Wk Range	$59.05–40.00	S&P Oper. EPS 2007E	3.12	Market Capitalization(B)	$8.559	Beta	1.02
Trailing 12-Month EPS	$3.45	S&P Oper. EPS 2008E	3.58	Yield (%)	1.77	S&P 3-Yr. Proj. EPS CAGR(%)	14.00
Trailing 12-Month P/E	13.8	P/E on S&P Oper. EPS 2007E	15.2	Dividend Rate/Share	$0.84	S&P Credit Rating	NA
$10K Invested 5 Yrs Ago	$29,912	Common Shares Outstg. (M)	180.1	Institutional Ownership (%)	83		

Price Performance

30-Week Mov. Avg. · · · 10-Week Mov. Avg. - - GAAP Earnings vs. Previous Year   Volume Above Avg. STARS
12-Mo. Target Price — Relative Strength — ▲ Up ▼ Down ► No Change   Below Avg.

2-for-1

Options: ASE, CBOE, P, Ph

Analysis prepared by **Efraim Levy, CFA** on October 24, 2007, when the stock traded at **$53.10**.

Highlights

➤ Based on our expectation of continued favorable economic conditions in the U.S. and abroad, we look for sales growth of 9% to 10% in 2008, following the 13% increase we see for 2007. We also anticipate margin improvement from restructuring. Our EPS estimates for CBE reflect the relatively low tax rates the company enjoys as a Bermuda corporation; however, we think the effective tax rate will rise to around 28% in 2008, from 25.2% in 2006.

➤ Our 2008 EPS estimate of $3.58 is 15% above our 2007 EPS forecast of $3.12. Both estimates exclude any residual income that may be received from Belden Inc.

➤ We forecast that free cash flow (net income before depreciation but after capital expenditures) will exceed net income in 2007 and 2008. We think that a focus on cash generation will help boost cash flow and allow for share repurchases and acquisitions. Long-term debt, including current maturities, amounted to 29% of total capitalization at the end of 2006, and we expect a reduction by year-end 2007, assuming no major acquisitions.

Investment Rationale/Risk

➤ Cooper's P/E and price-to-free cash flow multiples are toward the low end of peer group ranges, while its projected P/E-to-growth ratio and net margin of 10% are within the peer ranges. CBE's dividend recently yielded about 1.6%. Possible exposure to asbestos liabilities stemming from the 2001 Federal-Mogul (FMO) bankruptcy filing remains a concern to us, but to a lesser degree than in the past. FMO has said it may not fulfill an agreement to indemnify CBE for asbestos claims stemming from Pneumo-Abex product lines that it bought from CBE. However, CBE may find a judicial resolution.

➤ Risks to our recommendation and target price include weaker than expected industrial and economic demand.

➤ Our use of a P/E multiple of 18X applied to our 2008 EPS estimate reflects peer and historical P/E multiple comparisons and implies a $64 value. Our discounted cash flow model, which assumes a weighted average cost of capital of 10.4%, a compound annual growth rate of 6.0% over the next 15 years, and a terminal growth rate of 3.6%, calculates intrinsic value of nearly $62. Based on a combination of our P/E and DCF analyses, our 12-month target price is $63.

Qualitative Risk Assessment

LOW	MEDIUM	HIGH

Our risk assessment reflects favorable growth prospects in the markets CBE serves, and what we consider good corporate governance and a healthy balance sheet, offset by the company's vulnerability to a slowdown in real GDP growth in the U.S. or abroad.

Quantitative Evaluations

S&P Quality Ranking B+

D	C	B-	B	B+	A-	A	A+

Relative Strength Rank MODERATE

36

LOWEST = 1   HIGHEST = 99

Revenue/Earnings Data

Revenue (Million $)

	1Q	2Q	3Q	4Q	Year
2007	1,394	1,464	1,501	--	--
2006	1,241	1,288	1,315	1,341	5,185
2005	1,145	1,189	1,210	1,186	4,730
2004	1,065	1,109	1,140	1,149	4,463
2003	957.8	1,011	1,049	1,044	4,061
2002	975.0	1,001	999.3	985.0	3,961

Earnings Per Share ($)

2007	0.71	1.12	0.93	E0.81	E3.12
2006	0.57	0.64	0.69	0.69	2.58
2005	0.46	0.51	0.54	0.55	2.06
2004	0.41	0.45	0.48	0.47	1.79
2003	0.31	0.39	0.38	0.39	1.46
2002	0.26	0.39	0.34	0.15	1.14

Fiscal year ended Dec. 31. Next earnings report expected: Late January. EPS Estimates based on S&P Operating Earnings; historical GAAP earnings are as reported.

Dividend Data (Dates: mm/dd Payment Date: mm/dd/yy)

Amount ($)	Date Decl.	Ex-Div. Date	Stk. of Record	Payment Date
0.210	02/14	02/26	02/28	04/02/07
0.210	04/24	05/29	05/31	07/02/07
0.210	08/07	08/29	08/31	10/01/07
0.210	11/06	11/28	11/30	01/02/08

Dividends have been paid since 1947. Source: Company reports.

Cooper Industries Ltd.

**STANDARD
&POOR'S**

Business Summary October 24, 2007

CORPORATE OVERVIEW. Cooper Industries, a diversified, worldwide manufacturer of electrical products, tools and hardware, focuses on leveraging its strong brand name recognition by broadening its product line; strengthening its manufacturing and distribution systems to lower costs and improve customer service; expanding globally via acquisitions and joint ventures to participate in growing economies; and improving working capital efficiency and increasing cash flow to fuel future growth.

Electrical products contributed nearly 85% of revenues in 2006 and tools and hardware provided more than 15%.

About 27% of sales in 2006 were outside the U.S.

The countries that generate the most international revenues for CBE are Canada, Germany, Mexico and the U.K. The company has several small joint ventures with operations in China.

Cash flow from operations in 2006 was $601 million, up from 2005's 574 million and 2004's $474 million.

CORPORATE STRATEGY. In the four years through 2000, CBE completed 33 ac-

quisitions: 23 in the electrical products group and 10 in the tools and hardware segment. Six acquisitions in 2000 cost about $578 million. The company did not make any acquisitions in 2001 through 2003, but concluded two acquisitions at an aggregate cost of nearly $49 million in 2004. The company did not complete any acquisitions in 2005. The company's acquisition program resumed in 2006, with four acquisitions for approximately $280 million.

Reflecting slowing demand, the company reduced 2001 capital spending to $115 million, from 2000's $175 million. A further reduction was seen in 2002, to $74 million. Capital spending in 2003 totaled $80 million, but such expenditures increased to $103 million in 2004, as CBE invested in new products, new business systems, and cost reduction programs. However, capital expenditures declined again in both 2005 and 2006, to $97 million and $85 million, respectively. For 2007 and 2008, we expect capital spending to exceed $100 million per year.

Company Financials Fiscal Year Ended Dec. 31

Per Share Data ($)	2006	2005	2004	2003	2002	2001	2000	1999	1998	1997
Tangible Book Value	0.76	0.66	0.77	0.33	0.04	0.63	NM	0.02	0.46	0.80
Cash Flow	3.27	2.74	2.40	2.11	1.79	2.36	2.84	2.53	2.10	2.63
Earnings	2.58	2.06	1.79	1.46	1.14	1.38	1.90	1.75	1.47	1.63
Dividends	0.74	0.74	0.70	0.70	0.70	0.70	0.70	0.66	0.66	0.66
Payout Ratio	29%	36%	39%	48%	61%	51%	37%	38%	45%	40%
Prices:High	48.06	37.88	34.22	29.43	23.51	30.23	23.50	28.38	35.19	29.31
Prices:Low	36.02	31.04	25.67	16.93	13.57	15.81	14.69	19.81	18.44	20.00
P/E Ratio:High	19	18	19	20	21	22	12	16	24	18
P/E Ratio:Low	14	15	14	12	12	11	8	11	13	12

Income Statement Analysis (Million $)	2006	2005	2004	2003	2002	2001	2000	1999	1998	1997
Revenue	5,185	4,730	4,463	4,061	3,961	4,210	4,460	3,869	3,651	5,289
Operating Income	811	671	614	516	516	662	825	725	683	939
Depreciation	112	111	118	121	122	186	174	148	138	220
Interest Expense	51.5	64.8	68.1	74.1	74.5	84.7	100	55.2	102	90.0
Pretax Income	648	495	429	347	280	316	550	519	524	627
Effective Tax Rate	25.2%	21.0%	20.7%	20.8%	23.7%	17.4%	35.0%	36.0%	35.9%	37.0%
Net Income	484	391	340	274	214	261	357	332	336	395

Balance Sheet & Other Financial Data (Million $)	2006	2005	2004	2003	2002	2001	2000	1999	1998	1997
Cash	424	453	653	464	302	11.5	26.4	26.9	21.0	30.0
Current Assets	2,194	2,131	2,219	1,961	1,689	1,651	1,735	1,467	1,417	2,137
Total Assets	5,375	5,215	5,341	4,965	4,688	4,611	4,789	4,143	3,779	6,053
Current Liabilities	1,499	1,161	1,828	1,022	960	1,106	1,174	1,086	971	1,385
Long Term Debt	703	1,003	699	1,337	1,281	1,107	1,301	894	775	1,272
Common Equity	2,475	2,205	2,287	2,118	2,002	2,023	1,904	1,743	1,563	2,577
Total Capital	3,178	3,208	2,985	3,455	3,283	3,130	3,205	2,638	2,338	3,849
Capital Expenditures	85.3	96.7	103	79.9	73.8	115	175	166	142	196
Cash Flow	596	502	457	396	335	448	532	480	474	615
Current Ratio	1.5	1.8	1.2	1.9	1.8	1.5	1.5	1.4	1.5	1.5
% Long Term Debt of Capitalization	22.1	31.3	23.4	38.7	39.0	35.4	40.6	33.9	33.1	33.0
% Net Income of Revenue	9.3	8.3	7.6	6.8	5.4	6.2	8.0	8.6	9.2	7.5
% Return on Assets	9.1	7.4	6.6	5.7	4.6	5.6	8.0	8.4	6.8	6.6
% Return on Equity	20.7	17.4	15.4	13.3	10.6	13.3	19.6	20.1	16.2	17.7

Data as orig reptd.; bef. results of disc opers/spec. items. Per share data adj. for stk. divs.; EPS diluted. E-Estimated. NA-Not Available. NM-Not Meaningful. NR-Not Ranked. UR-Under Review.

Office: 600 Travis, Houston, TX 77002-1001.
Telephone: 713-209-8400.
Email: info@cooperindustries.com
Website: http://www.cooperindustries.com

Chrmn, Pres & CEO: K.S. Hachigian
SVP & CFO: T.A. Klebe
SVP & General Counsel: K.M. McDonald
Secy: T.V. Helz

Investor Contact: J. Safran (713-209-8610)
Board Members: S. G. Butler, R. M. Devlin, I. J. Evans, K. S. Hachigian, L. A. Hill, L. D. Kingsley, J. J. Postl, D. F. Smith, G. B. Smith, M. S. Thompson, J. R. Wilson

Founded: 1833
Domicile: Bermuda
Employees: 30,561

The McGraw-Hill Companies

Corning Inc

STANDARD &POOR'S

S&P Recommendation	**STRONG BUY** ★★★★★	Price $24.05 (as of Nov 28, 2007)	12-Mo. Target Price $31.00	Investment Style Large-Cap Blend

GICS Sector Information Technology
Sub-Industry Communications Equipment

Summary GLW, once an old-line housewares company, is now a leading maker of fiber optics and semiconductor components for the telecommunications and electronics industries.

Key Stock Statistics (Source S&P, Vickers, company reports)

52-Wk Range	$27.25–18.12	S&P Oper. EPS 2007**E**	1.37	Market Capitalization(B)	$37.831	Beta	2.67
Trailing 12-Month EPS	$1.29	S&P Oper. EPS 2008**E**	1.53	Yield (%)	0.83	S&P 3-Yr. Proj. EPS CAGR(%)	12.00
Trailing 12-Month P/E	18.6	P/E on S&P Oper. EPS 2007**E**	17.6	Dividend Rate/Share	$0.20	S&P Credit Rating	BBB+
$10K Invested 5 Yrs Ago	$56,272	Common Shares Outstg. (M)	1,573.0	Institutional Ownership (%)	77		

Price Performance

30-Week Mov. Avg. ··· 10-Week Mov. Avg. - - GAAP Earnings vs. Previous Year   Volume Above Avg. STARS
12-Mo. Target Price — Relative Strength — ▲ Up ▼ Down ► No Change   Below Avg.

Options: ASE, CBOE, P, Ph

Analysis prepared by **Todd Rosenbluth** on November 14, 2007, when the stock traded at **$ 23.75**.

Highlights

➤ Following a projected 13% sales advance in 2007, we see an acceleration to 16% in 2008, due to higher demand for liquid crystal display (LCD) glass substrates, a recovery in the telecom unit as a result of new fiber business, and emerging sales in the diesel engine unit. Our sales forecast for the LCD market assumes more stable pricing tight glass supply in 2008. We believe end user demand for LCD products will remain robust.

➤ We believe GLW's top customers in flat panel television--Samsung, Sharp and Sony--will continue to gain market share and demand larger size glass from their vendors. GLW has invested in more plant capacity for large size glass than any of its competitors. We expect gross margins to widen from 47% in 2007 to 47.5% in 2008, and we see operating margin expansion stemming from well controlled SG&A expenses.

➤ With a 14% effective tax rate, modest share buybacks, and increased equity earnings that we expect from Dow Corning and Samsung Corning, we project operating EPS of $1.37 in 2007 and $1.53 in 2008, aided by a weak U.S. dollar.

Investment Rationale/Risk

➤ We expect GLW's markets for LCD glass panels will remain strong (as shown in its mid-quarter update in November), due to continued investment in facilities and relationships with the market leaders. We think that demand will improve into 2008, even though there is some risk that consumer spending will deteriorate. We forecast that telecom fiber optic sales will strengthen, as we see increased demand and more stable pricing from large carrier customers. While we believe sales will be volatile, we are encouraged by GLW's expense control.

➤ Risks to our recommendation and target price include soft demand for flat panel displays, unstable pricing on display technologies products, and weaker demand with narrower margins in the telecom unit.

➤ Our 12-month target price of $31 is largely based on a P/E of 20X our 2008 EPS estimate, slightly above the peer average, but supported, we believe, by GLW's EPS growth rate. With the strong demand we see, and the shares well below our target price at a below average 15X multiple, we view GLW as compelling.

Qualitative Risk Assessment

LOW	**MEDIUM**	HIGH

Our risk assessment reflects Corning's exposure to intense competition in its major businesses, offset by its market leadership and what we consider its positive cash flow and strong balance sheet.

Quantitative Evaluations

S&P Quality Ranking   **C**

D	**C**	B-	B	B+	A-	A	A+

Relative Strength Rank   **STRONG**

76

LOWEST = 1   HIGHEST = 99

Revenue/Earnings Data

Revenue (Million $)

	1Q	2Q	3Q	4Q	Year
2007	1,307	1,418	1,553	--	--
2006	1,262	1,261	1,282	1,369	5,174
2005	1,050	1,141	1,188	1,200	4,579
2004	844.0	971.0	1,006	1,033	3,854
2003	746.0	752.0	772.0	820.0	3,090
2002	839.0	827.0	762.0	736.0	3,164

Earnings Per Share ($)

2007	0.20	0.30	0.38	E0.39	E1.37
2006	0.16	0.32	0.27	0.41	1.16
2005	0.17	0.11	0.13	-0.02	0.38
2004	0.04	0.07	-1.79	0.11	-1.57
2003	-0.17	-0.02	0.02	-0.02	-0.18
2002	-0.10	-0.41	-0.27	-0.96	-1.85

Fiscal year ended Dec. 31. Next earnings report expected: Late January. EPS Estimates based on S&P Operating Earnings; historical GAAP earnings are as reported.

Dividend Data (Dates: mm/dd Payment Date: mm/dd/yy)

Amount ($)	Date Decl.	Ex-Div. Date	Stk. of Record	Payment Date
0.050	07/18	08/27	08/29	09/28/07
0.050	10/03	11/13	11/15	12/14/07

Dividends have been paid since 2007. Source: Company reports.

Corning Inc

Business Summary November 14, 2007

CORPORATE OVERVIEW. Corning (GLW) has completed a transformation from an old-line, slow-growing housewares company into a leading maker of high technology fiber optics and high performance glass components for the global telecommunications and personal computer industries. Results are reported in the following primary business segments: display technologies (43% of sales in the first nine months of 2007), telecommunications (32%), environmental technologies (13%), life sciences (5%) and other (7%). GLW's 10 largest customers account for about 50% of its sales, but no individual customer accounted for more than 10% of consolidated sales in its 2006 results.

PRIMARY BUSINESS DYNAMICS. The display technologies segment manufactures glass substrates for active matrix liquid crystal displays (LCDs), which are used primarily in notebook computers, flat panel desktop monitors, and LCD televisions. In October 2007, GLW said it expects the LCD glass market, measured in square feet of glass, to increase 37% to 38% in 2007. The company's LCD glass volume is expected to expand at a faster pace than the market in 2007, given the higher growth rates of larger sized glass substrates. GLW believes that the market for Generation 5.5 to Generation 8.0 glass substrates will rise faster in 2007. While desktop monitors and notebooks accounted for the majority of demand in 2006, in our opinion, LCD TVs should ac-

count for almost half of all LCD glass produced in 2007 and 2008.

The telecommunications segment produces optical fiber and cable, and hardware and equipment products for the worldwide telecommunications industry. A significant portion of GLW's optical fiber is sold to its own subsidiaries. GLW's hardware and equipment products include cable assemblies, fiber optic hardware, fiber optic connectors, optical components and couplers, and other equipment. We believe fiber-to-the-premise (FTTP) products will benefit from increased demand and more stable pricing from large carriers in their fiber deployment spending. In July 2007, GLW said it added a new European FTTP customer. Corning also announced a new optical fiber technology in July, which allows cable equipment to bend around tight corners with almost no signal loss, and, in our view, could help Corning to support FTTP telecom customers target multi-dwelling units in the U.S. Increased use of the Internet has fueled demand for broadband access technologies such as digital subscriber line (DSL), cable modem and fiber optic cable.

Company Financials Fiscal Year Ended Dec. 31

Per Share Data ($)	2006	2005	2004	2003	2002	2001	2000	1999	1998	1997
Tangible Book Value	4.43	3.43	2.38	2.65	2.14	3.39	3.56	2.60	1.72	1.28
Cash Flow	1.56	0.71	-1.20	0.23	-1.04	-4.74	1.34	1.15	0.85	1.03
Earnings	1.16	0.38	-1.57	-0.18	-1.85	-5.89	0.46	0.65	0.46	0.62
S&P Core Earnings	1.17	0.48	-1.01	-0.16	-1.89	-3.11	NA	NA	NA	NA
Dividends	Nil	Nil	Nil	Nil	Nil	0.12	0.24	0.24	0.24	0.24
Payout Ratio	Nil	Nil	Nil	Nil	Nil	NM	52%	37%	52%	39%
Prices:High	29.61	21.95	13.89	12.34	11.15	72.19	113.29	43.02	15.23	21.71
Prices:Low	17.50	10.61	9.29	3.34	1.10	6.92	34.33	14.92	7.63	11.25
P/E Ratio:High	26	58	NM	NM	NM	NM	NM	66	33	35
P/E Ratio:Low	15	28	NM	NM	NM	NM	NM	23	16	18

Income Statement Analysis (Million $)										
Revenue	5,174	4,579	3,854	3,090	3,164	6,272	7,127	4,297	3,484	4,090
Operating Income	1,489	1,284	892	386	21.0	805	1,929	1,053	847	1,083
Depreciation	591	512	523	517	661	1,080	765	381	298	322
Interest Expense	76.0	116	141	154	179	153	107	79.9	56.7	85.0
Pretax Income	2,421	1,170	-1,137	-550	-2,604	-5,963	840	735	535	757
Effective Tax Rate	22.9%	49.4%	NM	NM	NM	NM	48.4%	25.7%	24.8%	30.0%
Net Income	1,855	585	-2,185	-223	-1,780	-5,498	410	477	328	440
S&P Core Earnings	1,863	738	-1,420	-200	-1,947	-2,908	NA	NA	NA	NA

Balance Sheet & Other Financial Data (Million $)										
Cash	1,157	1,342	1,009	833	1,471	1,037	138	116	12.2	65.3
Current Assets	4,798	3,860	3,281	2,694	3,825	4,107	4,634	1,783	1,310	1,424
Total Assets	13,065	11,175	9,710	10,752	11,548	12,793	17,526	6,012	4,982	4,811
Current Liabilities	2,319	2,216	2,336	1,553	1,680	1,994	1,949	1,488	1,075	1,017
Long Term Debt	1,696	1,789	2,214	2,668	3,963	4,461	3,966	1,289	1,364	1,499
Common Equity	7,246	5,609	3,752	5,379	4,536	5,414	10,633	2,227	1,506	1,246
Total Capital	8,987	7,441	6,059	8,168	8,713	10,001	14,808	3,814	3,233	3,116
Capital Expenditures	1,182	1,553	857	366	357	1,800	1,525	733	714	775
Cash Flow	2,446	1,097	-1,662	294	-1,247	-4,418	1,175	858	626	761
Current Ratio	2.1	1.7	1.4	1.7	2.3	2.1	2.4	1.2	1.2	1.4
% Long Term Debt of Capitalization	18.9	24.0	36.5	32.7	45.5	44.6	26.8	33.8	42.2	32.6
% Net Income of Revenue	35.9	12.8	NM	NM	NM	NM	5.7	11.1	9.4	10.8
% Return on Assets	15.3	5.6	NM	NM	NM	NM	3.4	8.7	6.7	9.6
% Return on Equity	29.1	12.5	NM	NM	NM	NM	6.2	25.5	23.7	39.7

Data as orig reptd.; bef. results of disc opers/spec. items. Per share data adj. for stk. divs.; EPS diluted. E-Estimated. NA-Not Available. NM-Not Meaningful. NR-Not Ranked. UR-Under Review.

Office: One Riverfront Plaza, Corning, NY 14831-0001.
Telephone: 607-974-9000.
Email: info@corning.com
Website: http://www.corning.com

Chrmn: J.R. Houghton
Pres & CEO: W.P. Weeks
Vice Chrmn & CFO: J.B. Flaws
COO: P.F. Volanakis

EVP & Chief Admin Officer: K.P. Gregg
Investor Contact: M.S. Rogus (888-267-6464)
Board Members: J. S. Brown, R. F. Cummings, Jr., J. B. Flaws, G. Gund, J. M. Hennessy, J. R. Houghton, J. Knowles, K. M. Landgraf, J. J. O'Connor, D. D. Rieman, H. O. Ruding, W. D. Smithburg, H. E. Tookes II, P. F. Volanakis, P. Warrior, W. P. Weeks

Founded: 1851
Domicile: New York
Employees: 24,500

Costco Wholesale Corp

STANDARD &POOR'S

S&P Recommendation HOLD ★★★☆☆

Price $66.97 (as of Nov 23, 2007)	**12-Mo. Target Price** $75.00	**Investment Style** Large-Cap Blend

GICS Sector Consumer Staples
Sub-Industry Hypermarkets & Super Centers

Summary This company operates about 520 membership warehouses in the U.S., Puerto Rico, Canada, the U.K., Taiwan, Japan, Korea, and Mexico.

Key Stock Statistics (Source S&P, Vickers, company reports)

52-Wk Range	$70.55– 51.52	S&P Oper. EPS 2008E	3.00	Market Capitalization(B)	$29.071	Beta	0.86
Trailing 12-Month EPS	$2.37	S&P Oper. EPS 2009E	3.40	Yield (%)	0.87	S&P 3-Yr. Proj. EPS CAGR(%)	13.00
Trailing 12-Month P/E	28.3	P/E on S&P Oper. EPS 2008E	22.3	Dividend Rate/Share	$0.58	S&P Credit Rating	A
$10K Invested 5 Yrs Ago	$21,947	Common Shares Outstg. (M)	434.1	Institutional Ownership (%)	82		

Price Performance

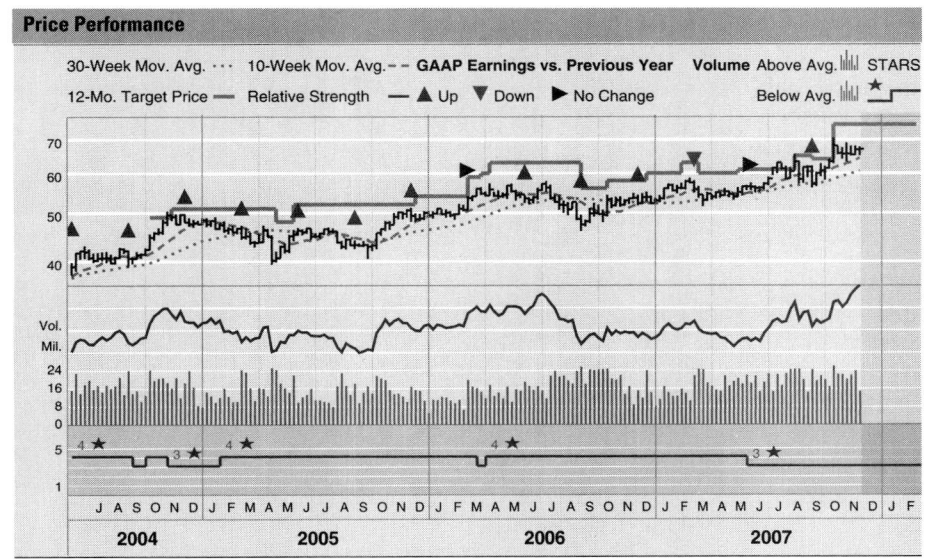

30-Week Mov. Avg. · · · 10-Week Mov. Avg. - - GAAP Earnings vs. Previous Year Volume Above Avg. STARS
12-Mo. Target Price — Relative Strength — ▲ Up ▼ Down ▶ No Change Below Avg.

Options: ASE, CBOE, P, Ph

Analysis prepared by **Joseph Agnese** on October 17, 2007, when the stock traded at **$ 66.25**.

Highlights

➤ We see net sales advancing to almost $70 billion in FY 08 (Aug.), from $64 billion in FY 07, reflecting a same-store sales increase of about 4% and about 7% square footage growth. We look for membership fees to equal 2.2% of sales, benefiting from rising membership and retention rates and growing conversions to higher priced executive memberships.

➤ We project that margins will widen due to the benefits from increased sales leverage, a shift in mix toward expanded margin categories such as food and sundries, soft and hard lines, and fresh foods, which are likely to offset narrower ancillary business margins, the impact of a 2% reward on executive memberships, and higher employee compensation. We see increased pre-opening expenses, reflecting new club openings and higher interest income due to what we see as strong cash positions.

➤ After an estimated modest reduction in the share count, as we believe the company will become more active at repurchasing shares, we estimate that FY 08 operating EPS will increase 14%, to $3.00, from operating EPS of $2.63 for FY 07.

Investment Rationale/Risk

➤ We expect COST to maintain or increase its market share, reflecting what we view as a strong value proposition and a relatively upscale product mix that appeals to a more affluent customer base. We see category strength in fresh foods and electronics with additional growth provided by expansion of ancillary businesses. We think the company is well positioned to generate future earnings growth due to improved labor cost controls and an acceleration of new store expansion.

➤ Risks to our recommendation and target price include a slowdown in sales due to weakness in the economy, increased pricing competition in an intensely competitive environment, more difficult foreign currency comparisons or increased cannibalization from new store expansion.

➤ We believe the stock's valuation will benefit as the company implements a new return policy on electronics and as fresh food margins benefit from reduced shrink. We apply a P/E of 24X to our calendar year 2008 EPS estimate of $3.12, above its three year historical average of about 22X, to arrive at our 12-month target price of $75.

Qualitative Risk Assessment

LOW	MEDIUM	HIGH

Our risk assessment for Costco Wholesale incorporates our view of a strong balance sheet, its market leadership position, and our expectation that consistent earnings and dividend growth will continue.

Quantitative Evaluations

S&P Quality Ranking A-

D	C	B-	B	B+	A-	A	A+

Relative Strength Rank STRONG
89
LOWEST = 1   HIGHEST = 99

Revenue/Earnings Data

Revenue (Million $)

	1Q	2Q	3Q	4Q	Year
2007	14,152	15,112	14,659	20,477	64,400
2006	12,933	14,059	13,284	19,875	60,151
2005	11,578	12,658	11,997	16,702	52,935
2004	10,521	11,549	10,897	15,139	48,107
2003	9,199	10,114	9,543	13,690	42,546
2002	8,467	9,383	8,617	12,296	38,763

Earnings Per Share ($)

2007	0.51	0.54	0.49	0.83	2.37
2006	0.45	0.62	0.49	0.75	2.30
2005	0.40	0.62	0.43	0.73	2.18
2004	0.34	0.48	0.42	0.62	1.85
2003	0.31	0.39	0.33	0.51	1.53
2002	0.28	0.41	0.28	0.52	1.48

Fiscal year ended Aug. 31. Next earnings report expected: NA. EPS Estimates based on S&P Operating Earnings; historical GAAP earnings are as reported.

Dividend Data (Dates: mm/dd Payment Date: mm/dd/yy)

Amount ($)	Date Decl.	Ex-Div. Date	Stk. of Record	Payment Date
0.130	02/01	02/12	02/14	02/28/07
0.145	04/10	04/25	04/27	05/18/07
0.145	07/09	07/25	07/27	08/24/07
0.145	11/13	11/28	11/30	12/14/07

Dividends have been paid since 2004. Source: Company reports.

Costco Wholesale Corp

STANDARD &POOR'S

Business Summary October 17, 2007

Costco Wholesale (formerly Costco Companies, Inc., and prior to that, Price/ Costco, Inc.) began the pioneering "I can get it for you wholesale" membership warehouse concept in 1976, in San Diego, CA. The company operated 520 warehouses worldwide as of October 2007, mainly in the U.S. and Canada (including 30 stores operated through a joint venture in Mexico). COST also operates an e-commerce Web site, costco.com.

The company believes that low prices on a limited selection of national brand merchandise and selected private-label products in a wide range of merchandise categories produce high sales volume and rapid inventory turnover. According to COST, high levels of turnover, combined with operating efficiencies achieved by volume purchasing in a no-frills, self-service warehouse facility enable the company to operate profitably at significantly narrower gross margins than traditional retailers and even discounters and supermarkets. COST buys virtually all of its merchandise directly from manufacturers, for shipment either directly to warehouse clubs or to a consolidation point (depot), at which

shipments are combined in order to minimize freight and handling costs. The company generally receives cash from the sale of a substantial portion of its inventory at mature warehouse operations before it is required to pay vendors, even though COST often pays early to obtain payment discounts.

COST has two primary types of memberships: Gold Star (individual) and Business members. Individual memberships are available to employees of federal, state and local governments; financial institutions; corporations; utility and transportation companies; public and private educational institutions; and other organizations. Gold Star membership is $50 annually. There were 18.6 million Gold Star memberships as of September 2007, up from 17.3 million as of September 2006.

Company Financials Fiscal Year Ended Aug. 31

Per Share Data ($)	2007	2006	2005	2004	2003	2002	2001	2000	1999	1998
Tangible Book Value	19.73	19.78	18.80	16.48	14.33	12.51	10.71	9.37	7.98	6.71
Cash Flow	3.60	3.37	3.13	2.74	2.32	2.17	1.90	1.86	1.57	1.41
Earnings	2.37	2.30	2.18	1.85	1.53	1.48	1.29	1.35	1.12	1.02
S&P Core Earnings	2.37	2.30	2.12	1.76	1.40	1.32	1.12	NA	NA	NA
Dividends	0.55	0.49	0.43	0.20	Nil	Nil	Nil	Nil	Nil	Nil
Payout Ratio	23%	21%	20%	11%	Nil	Nil	Nil	Nil	Nil	Nil
Prices:High	70.55	57.94	51.21	50.46	39.02	46.90	46.38	60.50	49.38	38.06
Prices:Low	51.52	46.00	39.48	35.05	27.00	27.09	29.83	25.94	32.69	20.63
P/E Ratio:High	30	25	23	27	26	32	36	45	44	38
P/E Ratio:Low	22	20	18	19	18	18	23	19	29	20

Income Statement Analysis (Million $)

	2007	2006	2005	2004	2003	2002	2001	2000	1999	1998
Revenue	64,400	60,151	52,935	48,107	42,546	38,763	34,797	32,164	27,456	24,270
Operating Income	2,189	2,146	1,969	1,827	1,567	1,494	1,312	1,299	1,141	989
Depreciation	566	515	478	441	391	342	301	254	225	196
Interest Expense	64.1	12.6	34.4	36.7	36.9	29.1	32.0	39.3	45.5	48.0
Pretax Income	1,710	1,751	1,549	1,401	1,158	1,138	1,003	1,052	859	766
Effective Tax Rate	36.7%	37.0%	31.4%	37.0%	37.8%	38.5%	40.0%	40.0%	40.0%	39.9%
Net Income	1,083	1,103	1,063	882	721	700	602	631	515	460
S&P Core Earnings	1,082	1,104	1,044	837	660	624	525	NA	NA	NA

Balance Sheet & Other Financial Data (Million $)

	2007	2006	2005	2004	2003	2002	2001	2000	1999	1998
Cash	2,780	1,511	2,063	2,823	1,545	806	603	525	441	362
Current Assets	9,324	8,232	8,086	7,269	5,712	4,631	3,882	3,470	3,316	2,628
Total Assets	19,607	17,495	16,514	15,093	13,192	11,620	10,090	8,634	7,505	6,260
Current Liabilities	8,582	7,819	6,609	6,171	5,011	4,450	4,112	3,404	2,866	2,197
Long Term Debt	2,108	215	711	994	1,290	1,211	859	790	919	930
Common Equity	8,623	9,143	8,881	7,625	6,555	5,694	4,883	4,240	3,532	2,966
Total Capital	10,801	9,422	9,650	8,922	8,181	7,025	5,858	5,139	4,572	3,896
Capital Expenditures	1,386	1,213	995	706	811	1,039	1,448	1,228	788	572
Cash Flow	1,649	1,619	1,541	1,323	1,112	1,042	903	886	740	656
Current Ratio	1.1	1.1	1.2	1.2	1.1	1.0	0.9	1.0	1.2	1.2
% Long Term Debt of Capitalization	19.5	2.3	7.4	11.1	15.8	17.2	14.7	15.4	20.1	23.9
% Net Income of Revenue	1.7	1.8	2.0	1.8	1.7	1.8	1.7	2.0	1.9	1.9
% Return on Assets	5.8	6.5	6.7	6.2	5.8	6.4	6.4	7.8	7.5	7.8
% Return on Equity	12.2	12.2	12.9	12.4	11.8	13.2	13.2	16.2	15.9	16.9

Data as orig reptd.; bef. results of disc opers/spec. items. Per share data adj. for stk. divs.; EPS diluted. E-Estimated. NA-Not Available. NM-Not Meaningful. NR-Not Ranked. UR-Under Review.

Office: 999 Lake Dr Ste, Issaquah, WA 98027.
Telephone: 425-313-8100.
Email: investor@costco.com
Website: http://www.costco.com

Chrmn: J.H. Brotman
Pres & CEO: J.D. Sinegal
COO & Sr EVP: R.D. DiCerchio
Investor Contact: R.A. Galanti (425-313-8203)

EVP & CFO: R.A. Galanti
Board Members: J. H. Brotman, B. S. Carson, Sr., S. Decker, R. D. DiCerchio, D. J. Evans, R. A. Galanti, W. H. Gates, II, H. E. James, R. M. Libenson, J. W. Meisenbach, C. T. Munger, J. S. Ruckelshaus, J. D. Sinegal

Auditor: KPMG
Founded: 1976
Domicile: Washington
Employees: 136,000

Countrywide Financial Corp

STANDARD &POOR'S

S&P Recommendation HOLD ★★★☆☆	Price $8.64 (as of Nov 26, 2007)	12-Mo. Target Price $11.00	Investment Style Large-Cap Blend

GICS Sector Financials
Sub-Industry Thrifts & Mortgage Finance

Summary This financial services company originates, purchases, securitizes, sells and services mortgages, and offers loan closing, banking and insurance services.

Key Stock Statistics (Source S&P, Vickers, company reports)

52-Wk Range	$45.26– 8.21	S&P Oper. EPS 2007**E**	-1.54	Market Capitalization(B)	$5.000	Beta	1.18
Trailing 12-Month EPS	$-0.23	S&P Oper. EPS 2008**E**	1.60	Yield (%)	6.94	S&P 3-Yr. Proj. EPS CAGR(%)	NA
Trailing 12-Month P/E	NM	P/E on S&P Oper. EPS 2007**E**	NM	Dividend Rate/Share	$0.60	S&P Credit Rating	BBB+
$10K Invested 5 Yrs Ago	$8,086	Common Shares Outstg. (M)	578.7	Institutional Ownership (%)	96		

Price Performance

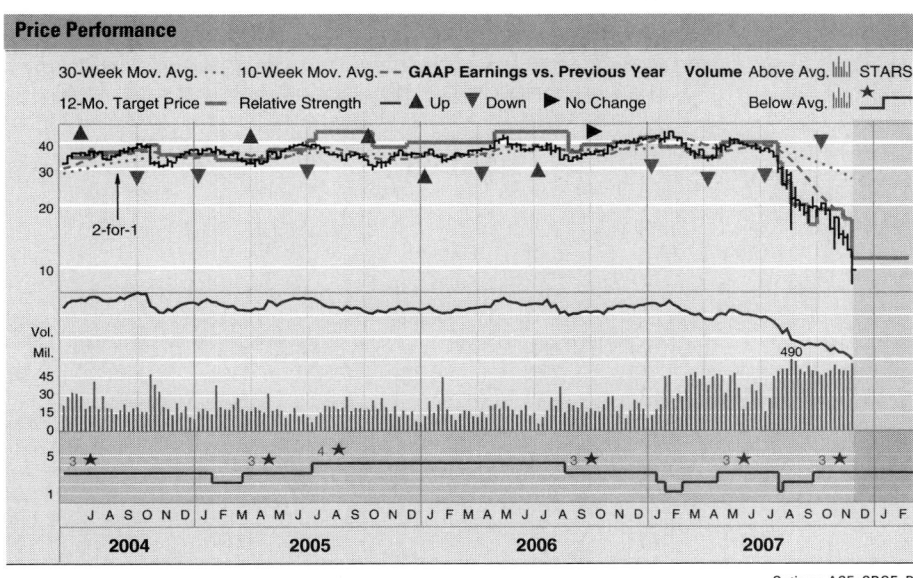

30-Week Mov. Avg. ··· 10-Week Mov. Avg.-- **GAAP Earnings vs. Previous Year** Volume Above Avg.|||| STARS
12-Mo. Target Price — Relative Strength — ▲ Up ▼ Down ► No Change Below Avg.|||| ★

Options: ASE, CBOE, P

Analysis prepared by **Stuart Plesser** on November 26, 2007, when the stock traded at **$ 8.77**.

Highlights

➤ We expect CFC's mortgage originations to be down roughly 30% in 2008, largely due to loan restrictions, capital restraints and continued weakness in the housing market. Given the illiquidity in the secondary markets and CFC's more conservative loan origination policies, we look for CFC gain-on-sale margins to be lower than historical levels in 2008 but for margins to improve as the year progresses. We see an increase in net interest income, as CFC will likely add loans to its thrift's balance sheet until pricing in the secondary market improves.

➤ Based on our expectation for continued growth in CFC's servicing portfolio, a recovery in mortgage servicing rights due to lower prepayment levels, and our view of its successful hedging strategy, we forecast double digit growth in net loan servicing fees in 2008. Based on declining home prices, we look for provisions of $1.4 billion in 2008, versus a projected $1.6 billion in 2007. Given CFC's expense and head count initiatives, we see expenses declining modestly in 2008.

➤ We forecast an operating loss of $1.54 per share in 2007, versus 2006's income of $4.30. In 2008, we look for EPS of $1.60.

Investment Rationale/Risk

➤ The majority of CFC's loans are now being originated through its thrift, enabling the company to tap deposits and FHLB loans. However, with the GSEs facing capital restraints of their own, CFC may have to scale down originations due to further compression of the secondary market. From an operations standpoint, CFC's earnings will likely come under pressure versus historical levels due to lower originations, net interest margin pressure and lower gain-on-sale margins. Also, based on declining home prices and the resetting of loans, we believe CFC's provisions will continue to run high and that residual securities will need to be further written down. We are also concerned that pay-option ARMs, which comprise roughly 35% of CFC's loans held, will begin to default. We think the stock price, at a recent 6.3X our 2008 EPS estimate, adequately reflects our concerns.

➤ Risks to our recommendation and target price include greater-than-expected credit deterioration and possible liquidity issues.

➤ Our 12-month target price of $11 applies a 0.4X multiple to recent book value of $26.46, a discount to historical levels that we think is justified by the likelihood of further writedowns.

Qualitative Risk Assessment

LOW	MEDIUM	HIGH

Our risk assessment reflects that as a leader in mortgage originations, CFC is exposed to the mortgage cycle. The company is experiencing rising default rates due largely to declining home prices. If default rates rise above our expectations, this may lead to liquidity issues.

Quantitative Evaluations

S&P Quality Ranking   A-

D	C	B-	B	B+	A-	A	A+

Relative Strength Rank   WEAK

2

LOWEST = 1   HIGHEST = 99

Revenue/Earnings Data

Revenue (Million $)

	1Q	2Q	3Q	4Q	Year
2007	2,406	2,548	-49.97	--	--
2006	2,836	3,000	2,823	2,785	11,417
2005	2,405	2,308	2,712	2,592	10,017
2004	1,965	2,475	2,110	2,017	8,567
2003	1,451	1,636	2,934	2,006	8,027
2002	913.8	998.3	1,211	1,397	4,519

Earnings Per Share ($)

2007	0.72	0.81	-2.85	E-0.09	E-1.54
2006	1.10	1.15	1.03	1.01	4.30
2005	1.13	0.92	1.03	1.03	4.11
2004	0.90	1.29	0.81	0.61	3.63
2003	0.61	0.68	1.93	0.91	4.15
2002	0.33	0.37	0.44	0.49	1.62

Fiscal year ended Dec. 31. Next earnings report expected: Late January. EPS Estimates based on S&P Operating Earnings; historical GAAP earnings are as reported.

Dividend Data (Dates: mm/dd Payment Date: mm/dd/yy)

Amount ($)	Date Decl.	Ex-Div. Date	Stk. of Record	Payment Date
0.150	01/30	02/07	02/09	02/28/07
0.150	04/27	05/10	05/14	05/31/07
0.150	07/25	08/13	08/15	08/31/07
0.150	10/26	11/08	11/13	11/30/07

Dividends have been paid since 1979. Source: Company reports.

Countrywide Financial Corp

STANDARD
&POOR'S

Business Summary November 26, 2007

CORPORATE OVERVIEW. Countrywide Financial Corporation is a financial holding company primarily engaged in residential mortgage banking and related businesses. It has five operating segments: Mortgage Banking, 47% of pre-tax earnings in 2006 (59% in 2005), Banking, 32% (25%), Capital Markets, 13% (11%), Insurance, 7% (4%) and Global Operations, 1% (1%). In 2007, the company will likely continue to focus on diversification in an attempt to leverage its core Mortgage Banking business and provide earnings that are less cyclical.

The Mortgage Banking segment produces loans through four divisions of Countrywide Home Loans: its primary subsidiary, Consumer Markets, which originates loans directly with consumers as well as through real estate agents, builders, relocation companies and other entities; Wholesale Lending, which originates mortgages through mortgage brokers and other financial intermediaries; Correspondent Lending, which purchases loans from other lenders; and Full Spectrum Lending, which originates non-prime loans. Nearly all mortgage loans produced in this segment are sold in the secondary market in the form of mortgage-backed securities, but CFC generally retains mortgage servicing rights (MSRs), or the rights to service these loans, as well as other residual interests related to these loans. As the value of MSRs and other retained interests typically decline when mortgage rates decline, CFC main-

tains a portfolio of financial instruments called the Servicing Hedge, which tend to increase in value when interest rates decline.

The Banking segment consists of: Treasury Bank, which originates and invests in mortgage loans and home equity lines of credit while funding its operations with retail and commercial deposits, borrowings and repurchase agreements; and Countrywide Warehouse Lending, which provides lines of credit to mortgage bankers to finance their mortgage loan inventories, or warehouse. Properties securing mortgage loans held in CFC's portfolio are mainly concentrated in California (46%).

The Capital Markets segment consists of: Countrywide Securities, a broker-dealer specializing in underwriting and trading mortgage securities; Countrywide Asset Management, which acquires and disposes of loans from third parties as well as CFC's Mortgage Banking segment; and Countrywide Commercial Real Estate Finance, which originates and holds commercial mortgages for sale or securitization.

Company Financials Fiscal Year Ended Dec. 31

Per Share Data ($)	2006	2005	2004	2003	2002	2001	2000	1999	1998	1997
Tangible Book Value	24.47	22.03	17.73	14.61	10.20	8.33	7.56	6.36	5.59	4.78
Cash Flow	4.57	4.35	3.63	4.15	1.62	3.42	2.08	0.88	0.93	0.88
Earnings	4.30	4.11	3.63	4.15	1.62	0.97	0.79	0.88	0.82	0.77
S&P Core Earnings	4.31	3.94	3.58	4.12	1.59	0.93	NA	NA	NA	NA
Dividends	0.60	0.59	0.37	0.15	0.11	0.10	0.10	0.10	0.08	0.08
Payout Ratio	14%	14%	10%	4%	7%	10%	13%	11%	10%	10%
Prices:High	43.67	40.31	39.93	27.27	13.75	13.00	12.63	12.86	14.06	10.81
Prices:Low	31.86	29.34	23.01	12.62	9.40	9.35	5.58	6.16	7.16	6.09
P/E Ratio:High	10	10	11	7	8	13	16	15	17	14
P/E Ratio:Low	7	7	6	3	6	10	7	7	9	8

Income Statement Analysis (Million $)										
Loan Fees	NA	NA	NA	2,804	2,029	2,048	1,600	1,599	1,647	1,209
Interest Income	12,056	7,970	4,630	3,342	2,253	1,822	1,341	999	999	440
Total Revenue	1,621	13,675	9,421	10,430	10,663	5,331	4,022	3,394	3,676	2,495
Interest Expense	9,134	5,616	2,608	1,940	1,461	1,475	1,348	930	984	424
% Expense/Operating Revenue	4221.7%	108.3%	110.2%	78.5%	58.5%	70.1%	82.6%	131.6%	205.3%	119.4%
Pretax Income	4,334	4,148	3,596	3,846	1,343	789	586	631	632	566
Effective Tax Rate	38.3%	39.0%	38.9%	38.3%	37.3%	38.4%	36.2%	35.0%	39.0%	39.0%
Net Income	2,675	2,528	2,198	2,373	842	486	374	410	385	345
S&P Core Earnings	2,680	2,430	2,166	2,351	826	462	NA	NA	NA	NA

Balance Sheet & Other Financial Data (Million $)										
Net Property	1,625	1,280	985	755	577	447	397	411	312	226
Cash & Securities	42,912	73,291	73,229	58,962	41,388	9,876	8,337	2,044	1,519	5,303
Loans	109,619	70,260	37,350	24,104	15,026	10,369	1,964	2,653	6,231	5,292
Total Assets	199,946	175,085	128,496	97,950	58,031	37,217	22,956	15,822	15,648	12,219
Capitalization:Debt	61,863	40,553	66,614	20,104	14,117	11,309	8,144	7,753	6,453	7,975
Capitalization:Equity	14,318	12,816	10,310	8,085	5,161	4,088	3,559	2,888	2,519	2,088
Capitalization:Total	76,180	53,369	76,924	28,188	19,278	17,212	13,273	10,641	8,972	6,284
Price Times Book Value:High	1.8	1.8	2.3	1.9	1.3	1.6	1.7	2.0	2.5	2.3
Price Times Book Value:Low	1.3	1.3	1.3	0.9	0.9	1.1	0.7	1.0	1.3	1.3
Cash Flow	2,675	2,528	2,198	2,373	842	1,706	991	476	435	390
% Return on Revenue	595.6	19.9	25.4	22.8	8.3	9.1	9.3	12.1	10.5	13.8
% Return on Assets	1.4	1.7	1.9	3.0	1.8	1.6	1.9	2.6	2.9	3.4
% Return on Equity	19.7	21.9	23.9	35.8	18.2	12.7	11.6	14.2	16.7	18.7

Data as orig reptd.; bef. results of disc opers/spec. items. Per share data adj. for stk. divs.; EPS diluted. E-Estimated. NA-Not Available. NM-Not Meaningful. NR-Not Ranked. UR-Under Review.

Office: 4500 Park Granada, Calabasas, CA 91302-7137.
Telephone: 818-225-3000.
Email: ir@countrywide.com
Website: http://www.countrywide.com

Chrmn & CEO: A.R. Mozilo
Pres & COO: D. Sambol
CFO: E.P. Sieracki
Chief Acctg Officer: L. Milleman

Investor Contact: D. Bigelow (818-225-3550)
Board Members: H. G. Cisneros, J. M. Cunningham, R. J. Donato, M. R. Melone, A. R. Mozilo, R. T. Parry, O. P. Robertson, K. P. Russell, H. W. Snyder

Founded: 1969
Domicile: Delaware
Employees: 54,655

The McGraw-Hill Companies

Coventry Health Care Inc.

S&P Recommendation **HOLD** ★★★☆☆	Price $56.58 (as of Nov 23, 2007)	12-Mo. Target Price $64.00	Investment Style Large-Cap Growth

GICS Sector Health Care
Sub-Industry Managed Health Care

Summary This national managed health care company operates health plans, insurance companies, network rental/managed care services companies, and workers' compensation services companies.

Key Stock Statistics (Source S&P, Vickers, company reports)

52-Wk Range	**$64.00– 45.70**	S&P Oper. EPS 2007**E**	**4.00**	Market Capitalization(B)	**$8.763**	Beta	**0.46**
Trailing 12-Month EPS	**$3.77**	S&P Oper. EPS 2008**E**	**4.58**	Yield (%)	**Nil**	S&P 3-Yr. Proj. EPS CAGR(%)	**13.00**
Trailing 12-Month P/E	**15.0**	P/E on S&P Oper. EPS 2007**E**	**14.1**	Dividend Rate/Share	**Nil**	S&P Credit Rating	**BBB**
$10K Invested 5 Yrs Ago	**$42,648**	Common Shares Outstg. (M)	**154.9**	Institutional Ownership (%)	**94**		

Price Performance

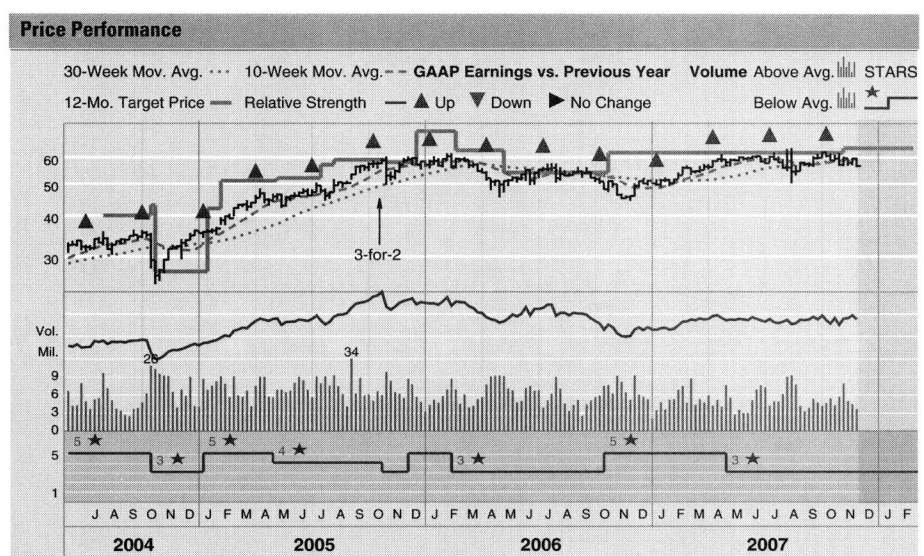

30-Week Mov. Avg. ··· 10-Week Mov. Avg.- - **GAAP Earnings vs. Previous Year** Volume Above Avg. STARS
12-Mo. Target Price — Relative Strength — ▲ Up ▼ Down ▶ No Change Below Avg.

3-for-2

Options: ASE, CBOE, P, Ph

Analysis prepared by **Phillip M. Seligman** on November 01, 2007, when the stock traded at **$ 60.00**.

Highlights

➤ We project that revenues will rise 32% in 2008, to $12.9 billion, from the $9.8 billion we forecast for 2007. Drivers we see include the full-year benefit of the September 2007 acquisition of Vista Healthplans, the July 2007 acquisition of the Mutual of Omaha health plans, and the April 2007 acquisition of the Concentra workers' compensation unit. We estimate 100,000 additional Medicare Advantage (MA) members and over 30,000 additional Medicare prescription drug program members. We also see gains in the individual market and geographic expansion, but expect fee revenue from the federal employee account to decline by $50 million.

➤ We expect the consolidated medical loss ratio (MLR) to rise by up to 80 basis points (bps) in 2008, on increased MA and Medicaid revenue in the mix. We look for a 110 bps decline in the SG&A cost ratio, on consolidation and other operating improvements. We see cost of sales more than doubling, reflecting the Concentra acquisition.

➤ We see operating EPS of $4.00 in 2007 and $4.58 in 2008, versus $3.48 in 2006. Our model excludes future potential acquisitions.

Investment Rationale/Risk

➤ We believe CVH's growing diversification can limit the earnings impact from weakness in any one business or geography. We expect more member attrition in the legacy First Health group business, but see this trend outweighed partly by expansions into new geographies. We also look for organic gains in the individual, MA and Medicaid markets, while the recent acquisition of Mutual of Omaha added 215,000 members and the Vista Healthplans acquisition added 295,000 and provided entry into Florida. Elsewhere, we see the highly profitable workers' comp service business benefiting from the recent Concentra acquisition. We view cash flow as healthy, and expect additional acquisitions and/or new ventures, such as bringing the behavioral health service in-house or entering the life insurance business.

➤ Risks to our recommendation and target price include a potential government probe of the managed care industry, higher than expected medical costs, and a weakened job market.

➤ Our 12-month target price of $64 is based on a peer-level 1.1X PEG ratio, 12.7% three-year EPS growth, and our 2008 EPS estimate.

Qualitative Risk Assessment

LOW	MEDIUM	HIGH

Our risk assessment reflects CVH's industry-leading operating margins and its January 2005 acquisition of First Health, which we think provides good growth prospects. Even so, the company faces intense competition, which has limited enrollment growth, and we do not see an opportunity for membership to grow more strongly until CVH can successfully reduce more of First Health's costs.

Quantitative Evaluations

S&P Quality Ranking   B+

D	C	B-	B	B+	A-	A	A+

Relative Strength Rank   MODERATE

59

LOWEST = 1   HIGHEST = 99

Revenue/Earnings Data

Revenue (Million $)

	1Q	2Q	3Q	4Q	Year
2007	2,237	2,332	2,523	--	--
2006	1,939	1,945	1,909	1,941	7,734
2005	1,565	1,653	1,674	1,719	6,611
2004	1,288	1,310	1,330	1,384	5,312
2003	1,065	1,096	1,150	1,223	4,535
2002	848.6	890.1	892.0	946.3	3,577

Earnings Per Share ($)

2007	0.76	0.96	1.08	E1.18	E4.00
2006	0.74	0.84	0.92	0.97	3.47
2005	0.73	0.79	0.81	0.77	3.10
2004	0.55	0.62	0.64	0.67	2.48
2003	0.37	0.47	0.49	0.51	1.83
2002	0.20	0.27	0.29	0.30	1.06

Fiscal year ended Dec. 31. Next earnings report expected: Early February. EPS Estimates based on S&P Operating Earnings; historical GAAP earnings are as reported.

Dividend Data

No cash dividends have been paid.

Please read the Required Disclosures and Analyst Certification on the last page of this report.

Coventry Health Care Inc.

Business Summary November 01, 2007

CORPORATE OVERVIEW. Coventry Health Care is a diversified national managed care company. It traditionally offered individual and employer groups a full range of commercial risk products, including health maintenance organization (HMO), preferred provider organization (PPO) and point-of service (POS) products. Through its January 2005 acquisition of First Health Group (FH), it gained a nationwide provider network and high-margin, fee-based service businesses, such as network rental, clinical programs, workers' compensation administration, Medicaid health care management services, and pharmacy benefit management. CVH also gained additional PPO members, including the Federal Employee Health Benefit program, the largest employer-sponsored group health program in the U.S., and an administrative services only (ASO, or non-risk) product for large employers with locations in several states that self-insure. Starting in 2007, CVH combined the enrollment of its existing business with that of FH.

As of September 30, 2007, the company had a total of 3,949,000 members (versus 3,420,000 at December 31, 2006), excluding standalone Medicare prescription drug program members, divided into two operating segments -- the Commercial division and the Individual/Government division.

The Commercial division is comprised of Commercial Group Risk members

(1,572,000, versus 1,457,000), Health Plan ASO (737,000, versus 621,000), and Other ASO (792,000, versus 866,000). Commercial Group Risk membership includes the health plan commercial group business and a small group PPO insurance block that was previously embedded within FH. It excludes the Individual business (under 65 years of age). In the ASO businesses, CVH offers management services and access to its provider networks to employers that self-insure their employee health benefits. The Other ASO membership includes active National Accounts and Federal Employees Health Benefits Plan (FEHBP) administrative services business.

The Individual/Government division consists of Medicare Advantage (286,000, versus 80,000), Medicaid Risk (478,000, versus 373,000) and Individual Risk (84,000, versus 23,000) plans. Medicare Advantage includes Medicare Advantage HMO, Medicare Advantage PPO, and Medicare Advantage PFFS (Private Fee-For-Service). Medicare Part D (Prescription Drug Program) had 717,000 members (versus 687,000).

Company Financials Fiscal Year Ended Dec. 31

Per Share Data ($)	2006	2005	2004	2003	2002	2001	2000	1999	1998	1997
Tangible Book Value	5.92	3.21	6.60	4.57	2.85	2.89	2.31	1.60	1.06	0.12
Cash Flow	4.17	3.63	2.61	1.97	1.24	0.72	0.60	0.50	0.12	0.32
Earnings	3.47	3.10	2.48	1.83	1.06	0.55	0.41	0.31	-0.10	0.16
S&P Core Earnings	3.47	3.01	2.41	1.80	1.03	0.52	NA	NA	NA	NA
Dividends	Nil	Nil	Nil	Nil	Nil	Nil	Nil	Nil	Nil	Nil
Payout Ratio	Nil	Nil	Nil	Nil	Nil	Nil	Nil	Nil	Nil	Nil
Prices:High	61.88	60.31	36.20	29.46	16.89	12.22	13.31	6.81	8.56	8.94
Prices:Low	44.33	34.21	24.66	10.80	8.67	5.78	3.06	2.22	1.72	2.94
P/E Ratio:High	18	19	15	16	16	22	32	22	NM	56
P/E Ratio:Low	13	11	10	6	8	11	7	7	NM	18

Income Statement Analysis (Million $)										
Revenue	7,734	6,611	5,312	4,535	3,577	3,147	2,605	2,162	2,110	1,228
Operating Income	954	878	514	384	220	117	81.1	71.8	51.1	18.5
Depreciation	113	86.2	17.6	18.2	18.9	25.9	27.0	28.2	25.8	12.7
Interest Expense	52.4	58.4	14.3	15.1	13.4	Nil	Nil	Nil	8.57	10.3
Pretax Income	896	799	527	393	226	135	102	76.0	-17.5	20.3
Effective Tax Rate	37.5%	37.3%	36.0%	36.4%	35.5%	38.0%	39.9%	42.8%	NM	41.4%
Net Income	560	502	337	250	146	83.5	61.3	43.4	-11.7	11.9
S&P Core Earnings	560	485	328	245	143	78.5	NA	NA	NA	NA

Balance Sheet & Other Financial Data (Million $)										
Cash	1,371	392	418	253	187	312	256	240	409	154
Current Assets	2,134	1,326	973	534	424	579	507	483	591	237
Total Assets	5,665	4,895	2,341	1,982	1,643	1,451	1,239	1,082	1,091	469
Current Liabilities	1,652	1,270	932	855	801	752	632	523	566	261
Long Term Debt	750	760	171	171	175	Nil	Nil	Nil	46.4	85.7
Common Equity	2,953	2,555	1,212	929	646	689	662	480	437	118
Total Capital	3,704	3,315	1,383	1,099	821	689	662	527	483	204
Capital Expenditures	72.6	71.4	15.0	13.4	13.0	11.9	16.0	14.7	3.24	7.20
Cash Flow	673	588	355	268	164	109	88.4	71.6	14.1	24.6
Current Ratio	1.3	1.0	1.0	0.6	0.5	0.8	0.8	0.9	1.0	0.9
% Long Term Debt of Capitalization	20.3	22.9	12.3	15.5	21.3	Nil	Nil	Nil	9.6	42.1
% Net Income of Revenue	7.2	7.6	6.3	5.5	4.1	2.7	2.4	2.0	NM	1.0
% Return on Assets	10.6	13.9	15.6	13.8	9.4	6.2	5.3	4.0	NM	2.6
% Return on Equity	20.3	26.6	31.5	31.8	21.8	13.0	10.7	9.5	NM	10.9

Data as orig reptd.; bef. results of disc opers/spec. items. Per share data adj. for stk. divs.; EPS diluted. E-Estimated. NA-Not Available. NM-Not Meaningful. NR-Not Ranked. UR-Under Review.

Office: 6705 Rockledge Drive, Bethesda, MD 20817.
Telephone: 301-581-0600.
Email: investor-relations@cvty.com
Website: http://www.coventryhealth.com

Chrmn: A.F. Wise
Pres: T.P. McDonough
CEO: D.B. Wolf
EVP, CFO & Treas: S.M. Guertin

EVP & CIO: H.C. DeMovick, Jr.
Board Members: J. Ackerman, J. H. Austin, L. D. Crandall, E. D. Farley, Jr., L. N. Kugelman, D. N. Mendelson, R. W. Moorhead, III, R. W. Morey, E. E. Tallett, T. T. Weglicki, A. F. Wise, D. B. Wolf

Founded: 1986
Domicile: Delaware
Employees: 10,250

Covidien Ltd

STANDARD &POOR'S

S&P Recommendation SELL ★ ★ ★ ★ ★

Price	12-Mo. Target Price	Investment Style
$38.35 (as of Nov 23, 2007)	$34.00	Large-Cap Growth

GICS Sector Health Care
Sub-Industry Health Care Equipment

Summary Formerly a wholly owned division of Tyco International, Covidien develops, manufactures and distributes medical devices and supplies, diagnostic imaging agents, pharmaceuticals and other health care products used in both clinical and home settings.

Key Stock Statistics (Source S&P, Vickers, company reports)

52-Wk Range	$49.70–36.90	S&P Oper. EPS 2007E	2.70	Market Capitalization(B)	$18.986	Beta	NA
Trailing 12-Month EPS	$0.17	S&P Oper. EPS 2008E	2.50	Yield (%)	1.67	S&P 3-Yr. Proj. EPS CAGR(%)	NM
Trailing 12-Month P/E	NM	P/E on S&P Oper. EPS 2007E	14.2	Dividend Rate/Share	$0.64	S&P Credit Rating	NA
$10K Invested 5 Yrs Ago	NA	Common Shares Outstg. (M)	495.1	Institutional Ownership (%)	50		

Price Performance

- 30-Week Mov. Avg. · · · 10-Week Mov. Avg. - - **GAAP Earnings vs. Previous Year** Volume Above Avg. ▫▫▫ STARS
- 12-Mo. Target Price — Relative Strength — ▲ Up ▼ Down ▶ No Change Below Avg. ▫▫▫ ★—

Options: ASE, CBOE, P

Analysis prepared by **Robert M. Gold** on November 19, 2007, when the stock traded at **$ 39.56**.

Highlights

➤ We believe sales in FY 08 (Sep.) will reach $10.5 billion, up modestly from the $10.2 billion we estimate for FY 07. In our opinion, the company's current product lines can support a sustained revenue growth rate of 3% to 4%, excluding the impact of foreign currency. We estimate that sales outside of the U.S. will represent nearly 40% of total sales in both FY 07 and FY 08, which places some risk on our revenue assumption should the dollar strengthen against some of the major overseas currencies.

➤ In our view, the company will report stable gross profit margins in coming quarters, on an increased proportion of medical device and pharmaceutical product revenues and improved sales force efficiencies. However, we anticipate that as a standalone entity, COV will sharply increase spending on both R&D and sales, and we think interest costs will rise as a result of the spinoff from Tyco.

➤ We look for FY 07 operating EPS of $2.70, and see FY 08 EPS declining to $2.50, as higher sales are outweighed by reduced operating margins, a higher effective tax rate and an increased common share count.

Investment Rationale/Risk

➤ We believe the company will generate sales and earnings growth well below comparable large cap medical equipment and supply peers, reflecting its relatively mature product lines, competitive pressures and higher operating costs as it reinvests in its operations following the spinoff from Tyco. While we think management is pursuing appropriate steps to improve operating margins, we do not anticipate that sales or earnings will rise materially over the coming three years.

➤ Risks to our recommendation and target price include a faster-than-expected sales recovery in the imaging and consumer products categories, reduced competitive pricing pressures, and a material decline in the value of the U.S. dollar relative to major overseas currencies.

➤ Our 12-month target price of $34 is based on an FY 08 P/E of 14X and an FY 08 price/sales multiple of 1.7X, both below medical device and supply peers in our coverage universe and the S&P 500. In our opinion, a discounted valuation is warranted by the relatively weak revenue and earnings growth outlook we see over the coming two years.

Qualitative Risk Assessment

LOW	MEDIUM	HIGH

COV operates in a highly competitive industry subject to pricing pressures, a loss of sales due to patent expirations and the introduction of new and potentially disruptive technologies or products that can adversely impact sales. The newly independent COV generates a significant portion of revenues outside the U.S. and is implementing a new global management structure that could disrupt near-term operations. However, we believe COV is a global leader in many areas of the health care products and supplies markets and has competitive advantages afforded larger players in the industry.

Quantitative Evaluations

S&P Quality Ranking NR

D	C	B-	B	B+	A-	A	A+

Relative Strength Rank MODERATE

50

LOWEST = 1   HIGHEST = 99

Revenue/Earnings Data

Revenue (Million $)

	1Q	2Q	3Q	4Q	Year
2007	--	--	2,579	--	--
2006	--	--	--	--	9,647
2005	--	--	--	--	--
2004	--	--	--	--	--
2003	--	--	--	--	--
2002	--	--	--	--	--

Earnings Per Share ($)

	1Q	2Q	3Q	4Q	Year
2007	--	--	-2.23	E0.60	E2.70
2006	--	--	--	--	2.57
2005	--	--	--	--	--
2004	--	--	--	--	--
2003	--	--	--	--	--
2002	--	--	--	--	--

Fiscal year ended Sep. 30. Next earnings report expected: NA. EPS Estimates based on S&P Operating Earnings; historical GAAP earnings are as reported.

Dividend Data (Dates: mm/dd Payment Date: mm/dd/yy)

Amount ($)	Date Decl.	Ex-Div. Date	Stk. of Record	Payment Date
0.160	09/28	10/04	10/09	11/09/07

Dividends have been paid since 2007. Source: Company reports.

Please read the Required Disclosures and Analyst Certification on the last page of this report.

The McGraw-Hill Companies

Covidien Ltd

Business Summary November 19, 2007

CORPORATE OVERVIEW. Covidien (COV) is a global leader in the development, manufacture and sale of medical products and supplies, diagnostic imaging agents, pharmaceuticals and other health care products used in both clinical and home settings. During FY 06 (Sep.), about 36% of sales were generated in non-U.S. markets. The company was separated from parent Tyco International on July 2, 2007, and NYSE trading commenced under the ticker COV.

The medical devices division (59% of FY 06 sales) develops, makes and sells surgical instruments and devices, respiratory and monitoring products and other products. COV offers a complete line of surgical stapling and laparoscopic instrumentation, and expanded its offerings of surgical mesh for hernia repair through the purchase of a controlling interest in Floreane Medical Implants S.A. during FY 06. Through its Valleylab franchise, COV offers electrosurgery products such as tissue fusing, vessel sealing systems and a radiofrequency ablation system.

The medical device division is also developing and marketing a broad line of innovative biosurgery solutions, including internal sealants, topical adhesives and anti-adhesion products that have potential applications in many types of surgical procedures. It also sells an extensive line of products used to moni-

tor, diagnose and treat respiratory disease and sleep disorders, vascular compression devices, needles and syringes, sharps collection systems, enteral feeding pumps and accessories, tympanic and electronic thermometers, advanced wound care products, urology products and dialysis catheters.

The imaging solutions segment (9%) develops, manufactures and markets contrast agents, contrast delivery systems and radiopharmaceuticals. Its imaging products are used to enhance the quality of images obtained through CT, X-ray, MRI and nuclear medicine procedures. Some of the key products include Optiray non-ionic X-ray contrast agent, OptiMark magnetic resonance imaging agent, OptiVantage contrast delivery system and OctreoScan nuclear medicine imaging agent for cancer. COV also operates its own network of 37 radiopharmacies. In November 2007, the company signed an agreement to supply X-ray contrast imaging agents to customers of MedAssets Supply Chain Systems, a St. Louis-based group purchasing organization.

Company Financials Fiscal Year Ended Sep. 30

Per Share Data ($)	2006	2005	2004	2003	2002	2001	2000	1999	1998	1997
Tangible Book Value	NM	NA	NA	NA	NA	NA	NA	NA	NA	NA
Cash Flow	3.23	NA	NA	NA	NA	NA	NA	NA	NA	NA
Earnings	2.57	NA	NA	NA	NA	NA	NA	NA	NA	NA
Dividends	NA	NA	NA	NA	NA	NA	NA	NA	NA	NA
Payout Ratio	NA	NA	NA	NA	NA	NA	NA	NA	NA	NA
Prices:High	NA	NA	NA	NA	NA	NA	NA	NA	NA	NA
Prices:Low	NA	NA	NA	NA	NA	NA	NA	NA	NA	NA
P/E Ratio:High	NA	NA	NA	NA	NA	NA	NA	NA	NA	NA
P/E Ratio:Low	NA	NA	NA	NA	NA	NA	NA	NA	NA	NA

Income Statement Analysis (Million $)	2006	2005	2004	2003	2002	2001	2000	1999	1998	1997
Revenue	9,647	NA	NA	NA	NA	NA	NA	NA	NA	NA
Operating Income	2,476	NA	NA	NA	NA	NA	NA	NA	NA	NA
Depreciation	333	NA	NA	NA	NA	NA	NA	NA	NA	NA
Interest Expense	NA	NA	NA	NA	NA	NA	NA	NA	NA	NA
Pretax Income	1,858	NA	NA	NA	NA	NA	NA	NA	NA	NA
Effective Tax Rate	29.8%	NA	NA	NA	NA	NA	NA	NA	NA	NA
Net Income	1,304	NA	NA	NA	NA	NA	NA	NA	NA	NA

Balance Sheet & Other Financial Data (Million $)	2006	2005	2004	2003	2002	2001	2000	1999	1998	1997
Cash	800	NA	NA	NA	NA	NA	NA	NA	NA	NA
Current Assets	7,308	NA	NA	NA	NA	NA	NA	NA	NA	NA
Total Assets	17,895	NA	NA	NA	NA	NA	NA	NA	NA	NA
Current Liabilities	8,740	NA	NA	NA	NA	NA	NA	NA	NA	NA
Long Term Debt	148	NA	NA	NA	NA	NA	NA	NA	NA	NA
Common Equity	6,803	NA	NA	NA	NA	NA	NA	NA	NA	NA
Total Capital	6,951	NA	NA	NA	NA	NA	NA	NA	NA	NA
Capital Expenditures	NA	NA	NA	NA	NA	NA	NA	NA	NA	NA
Cash Flow	1,637	NA	NA	NA	NA	NA	NA	NA	NA	NA
Current Ratio	0.8	NA	NA	NA	NA	NA	NA	NA	NA	NA
% Long Term Debt of Capitalization	2.1	NA	NA	NA	NA	NA	NA	NA	NA	NA
% Net Income of Revenue	13.5	NA	NA	NA	NA	NA	NA	NA	NA	NA
% Return on Assets	NA	NA	NA	NA	NA	NA	NA	NA	NA	NA
% Return on Equity	NA	NA	NA	NA	NA	NA	NA	NA	NA	NA

Data as orig reptd.; bef. results of disc opers/spec. items. Per share data adj. for stk. divs.; EPS diluted. Pro forma data in 2006, bal. sheet & book val. as of March 30, 2007. E-Estimated. NA-Not Available. NM-Not Meaningful. NR-Not Ranked. UR-Under Review.

Office: 90 Pitts Bay Road, Pembroke, Bermuda HM 08.
Telephone: 441-292-8674.
Website: http://www.covidien.com
Chrmn: D.H. Reilley

Pres & CEO: R.J. Meelia
EVP & CFO: C.J. Dockendorff
SVP & General Counsel: J.H. Masterson
VP, Chief Acctg Officer & Cntlr: R.G. Brown, Jr.

Investor Contact: C.N. Lannum (508-452-4343)
Board Members: C. Arnold, R. H. Brust, J. M. Connors, Jr., C. J. Coughlin, T. M. Donahue, K. J. Herbert, R. J. Hogan, III, R. J. Meelia, D. H. Reilley, T. Yamada, J. A. Zaccagnino

Founded: 2000
Domicile: Bermuda
Employees: 43,300

CSX Corp

STANDARD &POOR'S

S&P Recommendation BUY ★★★★☆	**Price** $41.31 (as of Nov 23, 2007)	**12-Mo. Target Price** $52.00	**Investment Style** Large-Cap Value

GICS Sector Industrials
Sub-Industry Railroads

Summary This company operates a major U.S. rail network, and provides intermodal and U.S. container shipping services.

Key Stock Statistics (Source S&P, Vickers, company reports)

52-Wk Range	$51.88– 33.50	S&P Oper. EPS 2007**E**	2.58	Market Capitalization(B)	$18.136	Beta	0.82
Trailing 12-Month EPS	$2.88	S&P Oper. EPS 2008**E**	3.03	Yield (%)	1.45	S&P 3-Yr. Proj. EPS CAGR(%)	12.00
Trailing 12-Month P/E	14.3	P/E on S&P Oper. EPS 2007**E**	16.0	Dividend Rate/Share	$0.60	S&P Credit Rating	BBB-
$10K Invested 5 Yrs Ago	$31,801	Common Shares Outstg. (M)	439.0	Institutional Ownership (%)	68		

Price Performance

30-Week Mov. Avg. · · · 10-Week Mov. Avg. – – **GAAP Earnings vs. Previous Year**   **Volume** Above Avg. ▮▮▮ STARS
12-Mo. Target Price — Relative Strength — ▲ Up ▼ Down ▶ No Change   Below Avg. ▮▮▮

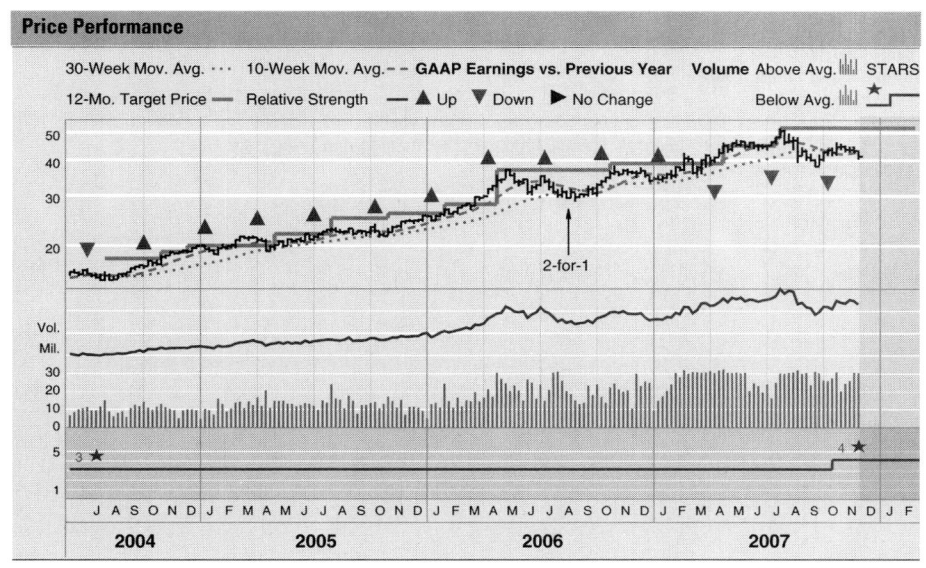

Options: ASE, CBOE, P, Ph

Analysis prepared by **Kevin Kirkeby** on October 22, 2007, when the stock traded at **$ 44.55**.

Highlights

➤ We see revenues rising 4.6% in 2007, with gains in yield (freight rates and mix) more than offsetting volume declines. Challenges in the building materials and automotive markets, in our view, will extend into 2008, but should lessen as the year progresses. We anticipate a 2% rise in volumes and 5% increase in average per unit pricing contributing to an overall revenue gain of 7.4% in 2008. We see relatively flat coal shipments, while intermodal volumes are expected to improve modestly on service additions.

➤ We expect margins to improve in 2008 due mostly to contract repricings and improved asset utilization. Numerous capacity expansion projects completed in 2006 and 2007 should improve network dwell time and velocity. After rising sharply in 2007 as its hedges rolled off, we see only moderate increases in fuel costs for 2008, tied to a rise in gross ton-miles.

➤ We see 2007 EPS of $2.58, up about 15% from the $2.25, before special items reported in 2006. For 2008, we forecast an EPS increase of about 17%, to $3.03. Our estimates incorporate share reduction of more than 7%, representing partial completion of the $3 billion expanded stock buyback CSX announced in May 2007.

Investment Rationale/Risk

➤ We believe that recent improvements in operating efficiency, despite the near-term impact of volume weakness, are sustainable over the medium-term. Further, we see additional improvement in coming quarters as CSX strives to narrow the gap between its performance and that of peers on metrics like velocity and dwell time. We consider the shares attractively priced following recent declines, and believe they already discount the potential for continued economic weakness.

➤ Risks to our opinion and target price include a further weakening in economic growth, a softening in shipments of export coal, increased regulatory oversight, unusually severe weather, and rapid changes in diesel prices.

➤ Our DCF model derives an intrinsic value of $53, assuming a weighted average cost of capital of 9% and a 3.5% terminal growth rate. Applying an enterprise value to EBITDA multiple of 8.6X, which we calculate at a modest premium to the historical 10-year average of 8.2X, to our 12-month forward EBITDA estimate, we derive a value of $51. Blending these models, we arrive at our 12-month target price of $52.

Qualitative Risk Assessment

LOW	**MEDIUM**	HIGH

Our risk assessment reflects what we believe is CSX's exposure to economic cycles, freight demand and pricing and fuel prices, offset by its consistently positive cash flow generation, moderate debt levels and diverse customer base.

Quantitative Evaluations

S&P Quality Ranking   B

D	C	B-	**B**	B+	A-	A	A+

Relative Strength Rank   MODERATE

55

LOWEST = 1   HIGHEST = 99

Revenue/Earnings Data

Revenue (Million $)

	1Q	2Q	3Q	4Q	Year
2007	2,422	2,530	2,501	--	--
2006	2,331	2,421	2,418	2,396	9,566
2005	2,108	2,166	2,125	2,219	8,618
2004	1,915	1,995	1,938	2,172	8,020
2003	2,016	1,942	1,882	1,953	7,793
2002	1,964	2,073	2,055	2,060	8,152

Earnings Per Share ($)

2007	0.52	0.71	0.67	E0.74	E2.58
2006	0.53	0.83	0.71	0.75	2.82
2005	0.34	0.37	0.36	0.52	1.59
2004	0.06	0.26	0.26	0.36	0.94
2003	0.10	0.29	-0.24	0.29	0.44
2002	0.16	0.32	0.30	0.32	1.10

Fiscal year ended Dec. 31. Next earnings report expected: Late January. EPS Estimates based on S&P Operating Earnings; historical GAAP earnings are as reported.

Dividend Data (Dates: mm/dd Payment Date: mm/dd/yy)

Amount ($)	Date Decl.	Ex-Div. Date	Stk. of Record	Payment Date
0.120	02/14	02/27	03/01	03/15/07
0.120	05/02	05/30	06/01	06/15/07
0.150	05/08	08/29	08/31	09/14/07
0.150	09/12	11/28	11/30	12/14/07

Dividends have been paid since 1922. Source: Company reports.

CSX Corp

Business Summary October 22, 2007

CORPORATE OVERVIEW. CSX operates the largest rail network in the eastern U.S., with a 22,000-mile rail network linking commercial markets in 23 states and two Canadian provinces, and owns companies providing intermodal and rail-to-truck transload services. In 1997, the company purchased a 42% stake in Conrail, bringing CSX's system into New York City, Boston, Philadelphia and Buffalo; in 2004, CSX gained direct ownership and control of Conrail's New York Central Lines. With these routes, the company was able to offer shippers broader geographic coverage, access more ports, and expand its share of north-south traffic. In 2003, CSX saw a decline in certain performance measures, including personal injury frequency, train accident frequency, train velocity, train recrews, and on-time originations and arrivals. CSX experienced continuing operational difficulties in 2004, with train velocity and on-time performance worsening. In the third quarter of 2004, CSX initiated a major initiative to improve network performance called the "One Plan," which we believe is leading to improving safety, efficiency and service quality.

MARKET PROFILE. We consider railroads to be a mature industry, and expect 2.3% annualized U.S. rail tonnage growth between 2006 and 2020. We believe CSX's growth opportunities are at the industry average, as we see above average future growth in intermodal traffic being offset by expected slow coal traffic growth. Over the past 5 years, as the US economy recovered from a sharp economic slowdown, CSX's intermodal volumes have grown at a compound annual rate of 8.3%, and total carloads have grown 4.9%, compared to 6.6% and 0.1% respectively, for the overall industry.

We believe growth in CSX's intermodal business, representing 15% of 2006 revenue, will be driven by rising international trade and its cost savings over trucks for long-distance container movements, although we see CSX's service quality as lagging its primary competitor. Coal accounted for 25% of 2006 revenues. Most of this traffic originates from the Appalachian coal fields and is primarily delivered to power utilities. We expect CSX's coal tonnage to experience below average growth as its customers look for ways to limit the amount of high sulfur content coal they utilize. CSX's merchandise freight provided 50% of freight revenues in 2006, and includes chemical, forest products, metals, and agricultural products. We believe this business is sensitive to U.S. GDP trends, and faces average long-term volume growth prospects. We believe automotive freight, at 9% of revenues in 2006, has a weak volume growth outlook, due to slowing domestic manufacturing trends.

Company Financials Fiscal Year Ended Dec. 31

Per Share Data ($)	2006	2005	2004	2003	2002	2001	2000	1999	1998	1997
Tangible Book Value	20.42	18.25	15.77	15.01	14.52	14.32	14.13	13.20	13.55	13.23
Cash Flow	4.67	3.41	2.55	1.94	2.62	2.16	2.76	1.46	2.73	3.36
Earnings	2.82	1.59	0.94	0.44	1.10	0.69	0.44	0.12	1.26	1.81
S&P Core Earnings	2.57	1.60	0.90	0.66	0.85	0.59	NA	NA	NA	NA
Dividends	0.63	0.22	0.20	0.20	0.20	0.40	0.60	0.60	0.60	0.54
Payout Ratio	22%	14%	21%	45%	18%	58%	136%	NM	48%	30%
Prices:High	38.30	25.80	20.23	18.15	20.70	20.65	16.72	26.97	30.38	31.22
Prices:Low	24.29	18.45	14.40	12.75	12.55	12.41	9.75	14.41	18.25	20.63
P/E Ratio:High	14	16	22	41	19	30	38	NM	24	17
P/E Ratio:Low	9	12	15	29	11	18	22	NM	15	11

Income Statement Analysis (Million $)

	2006	2005	2004	2003	2002	2001	2000	1999	1998	1997
Revenue	9,566	8,618	8,020	7,793	8,152	8,110	8,191	10,811	9,898	10,621
Operating Income	2,837	2,345	1,730	1,269	1,776	1,579	1,405	1,685	1,790	2,271
Depreciation	867	833	730	643	649	622	600	621	630	688
Interest Expense	392	423	435	418	445	518	543	521	506	451
Pretax Income	1,841	1,036	637	265	723	448	656	130	808	1,224
Effective Tax Rate	28.8%	30.5%	34.4%	28.7%	35.4%	34.6%	13.9%	67.7%	29.2%	31.4%
Net Income	1,310	720	418	189	467	293	565	51.0	537	799
S&P Core Earnings	1,194	729	405	280	363	249	NA	NA	NA	NA

Balance Sheet & Other Financial Data (Million $)

	2006	2005	2004	2003	2002	2001	2000	1999	1998	1997
Cash	461	309	859	368	264	618	684	974	533	690
Current Assets	2,672	2,372	2,987	1,903	1,789	2,074	2,046	2,563	1,984	2,175
Total Assets	25,129	24,232	24,581	21,760	20,951	20,801	20,491	20,720	20,427	19,957
Current Liabilities	2,522	2,979	3,317	2,210	2,454	3,303	3,280	3,473	2,600	2,707
Long Term Debt	5,362	5,093	6,234	6,886	6,519	5,839	5,810	6,196	6,432	6,416
Common Equity	9,863	8,918	7,858	7,569	7,091	7,060	6,017	5,756	5,880	5,766
Total Capital	21,335	20,093	20,071	18,207	17,177	16,520	15,211	15,179	15,485	15,121
Capital Expenditures	1,639	1,136	1,030	1,059	1,080	930	913	1,517	1,479	1,125
Cash Flow	2,177	1,553	1,148	832	1,116	915	1,165	623	1,167	1,487
Current Ratio	1.1	0.8	0.9	0.9	0.7	0.6	0.6	0.7	0.8	0.8
% Long Term Debt of Capitalization	25.1	25.3	31.1	37.8	38.0	35.3	38.2	40.8	41.5	42.4
% Net Income of Revenue	13.7	8.4	5.2	2.4	5.7	3.6	6.9	0.5	5.4	7.5
% Return on Assets	5.3	2.9	1.8	0.9	2.2	1.4	2.7	0.2	2.7	4.3
% Return on Equity	14.0	8.6	5.4	2.6	6.6	4.2	9.6	0.9	9.2	14.8

Data as orig reptd.; bef. results of disc opers/spec. items. Per share data adj. for stk. divs.; EPS diluted. E-Estimated. NA-Not Available. NM-Not Meaningful. NR-Not Ranked. UR-Under Review.

Office: 500 Water Street , Jacksonville , FL 32202.
Telephone: 904-359-3200.
Website: http://www.csx.com
Chrmn, Pres & CEO: M.J. Ward

EVP & CFO: O. Munoz
VP & Cntlr: C.T. Sizemore
Investor Contact: D. Baggs (904-359-4812)

Board Members: D. M. Alvarado, E. E. Bailey, J. B. Breaux, S. T. Halverson, E. J. Kelly, R. D. Kunisch, S. J. Morcott, D. M. Ratcliffe, W. C. Richardson, F. S. Royal, D. J. Shepard, M. J. Ward

Founded: 1978
Domicile: Virginia
Employees: 36,005

Cummins Inc.

STANDARD &POOR'S

S&P Recommendation **BUY** ★★★★☆	Price $106.32 (as of Nov 23, 2007)	12-Mo. Target Price $140.00	Investment Style Large-Cap Value

GICS Sector Industrials
Sub-Industry Construction & Farm Machinery & Heavy Trucks

Summary This leading manufacturer of truck engines also makes stand-by power equipment and industrial filters.

Key Stock Statistics (Source S&P, Vickers, company reports)

52-Wk Range	$143.45– 56.32	S&P Oper. EPS 2007**E**	7.53	Market Capitalization(B)	$10.653	Beta	1.52
Trailing 12-Month EPS	$7.27	S&P Oper. EPS 2008**E**	9.20	Yield (%)	0.94	S&P 3-Yr. Proj. EPS CAGR(%)	10.00
Trailing 12-Month P/E	14.6	P/E on S&P Oper. EPS 2007**E**	14.1	Dividend Rate/Share	$1.00	S&P Credit Rating	BBB-
$10K Invested 5 Yrs Ago	$80,336	Common Shares Outstg. (M)	100.2	Institutional Ownership (%)	94		

Price Performance

30-Week Mov. Avg. ··· 10-Week Mov. Avg. — **GAAP Earnings vs. Previous Year** Volume Above Avg. STARS
12-Mo. Target Price — Relative Strength — ▲ Up ▼ Down ▶ No Change Below Avg. ★

Options: ASE, CBOE, P, Ph

Analysis prepared by **Pearl Wang** on November 12, 2007, when the stock traded at **$ 113.68.**

Highlights

➤ We expect revenues to increase about 9% in 2007, following a 15% advance in 2006. We expect near 30% growth each in the power generation and components businesses to be complemented by 7% growth in the distribution business and 5% in the engines business. We expect weakness in heavy-duty engines, due to stockpiling that occurred in 2006 prior to new emission standards, to be offset by strong small and medium-duty and bus engine sales. We also see sales benefiting from expected strength in power generation end markets, due to a global economic expansion that has increased demand for power generation. For 2008, we project a 7% sales rise.

➤ We expect operating margins to narrow to 8.1% in 2007, from 8.7% in 2006, based on our outlook for lower heavy-duty engine volumes, partly offset by expected benefits from cost reduction actions implemented over the past few years. For 2008, we project an increase to 9.3%.

➤ We estimate that EPS will rise 6% in 2007, to $7.53, and project a 22% advance in 2008, to $9.15.

Investment Rationale/Risk

➤ With over 50% of its sales outside the U.S., we expect CMI to benefit from global demand for transportation equipment, as well as demand for power generation equipment. We believe that CMI has the technological expertise to gain market share, amid strong demand in international markets. We also note that strong free cash flow generation enabled CMI to reduce long-term debt by 47% in 2006, and should permit the company to achieve its plans to fully fund its pension plan by year end.

➤ Risks to our recommendation and target price include weaker than projected demand in the truck manufacturing and/or power generation markets; slower than anticipated economic growth and/or industrial production; and lower than estimated savings from expense reduction initiatives.

➤ Our 12-month target price of $140 is based on a multiple of 15.2X our 2008 EPS estimate. This is above the 10-year average forward P/E ratio of 11.6X for CMI. We believe the premium is warranted based on our view of CMI's international growth opportunities.

Qualitative Risk Assessment

LOW	MEDIUM	HIGH

Our risk assessment reflects the highly cyclical nature of the North America medium (class 5-7) and heavy-duty (class 8) truck markets and significant pension and post-retirement benefit obligations, offset by a geographically diverse mix of business.

Quantitative Evaluations

S&P Quality Ranking B

D	C	B-	**B**	B+	A-	A	A+

Relative Strength Rank WEAK

27

LOWEST = 1 HIGHEST = 99

Revenue/Earnings Data

Revenue (Million $)

	1Q	2Q	3Q	4Q	Year
2007	2,817	3,343	3,372	--	--
2006	2,678	2,842	2,809	3,033	11,362
2005	2,208	2,490	2,467	2,753	9,918
2004	1,771	2,124	2,194	2,349	8,438
2003	1,387	1,539	1,634	1,736	6,296
2002	1,333	1,458	1,648	1,414	5,853

Earnings Per Share ($)

	1Q	2Q	3Q	4Q	Year
2007	1.42	2.13	1.84	E2.14	E7.53
2006	1.35	2.19	1.69	1.88	7.11
2005	0.98	1.42	1.45	1.66	5.51
2004	0.38	0.88	1.20	1.21	3.70
2003	-0.40	0.17	0.30	0.54	0.68
2002	-0.35	0.20	0.53	0.55	1.03

Fiscal year ended Dec. 31. Next earnings report expected: Late January. EPS Estimates based on S&P Operating Earnings; historical GAAP earnings are as reported.

Dividend Data (Dates: mm/dd Payment Date: mm/dd/yy)

Amount ($)	Date Decl.	Ex-Div. Date	Stk. of Record	Payment Date
2-for-1	03/08	04/10	03/26	04/09/07
0.180	05/08	05/16	05/18	06/01/07
0.250	07/10	08/15	08/17	08/31/07
0.250	10/09	11/14	11/16	11/30/07

Dividends have been paid since 1948. Source: Company reports.

Please read the Required Disclosures and Analyst Certification on the last page of this report.

The McGraw-Hill Companies

Cummins Inc.

STANDARD &POOR'S

Business Summary November 12, 2007

Truck engine makers such as Cummins continue to contend with price wars, highly cyclical markets, and an overabundance of global engine-making capacity. In addition, engine makers are constantly plowing back profits into engine development and plant and machinery just to maintain market share. Over the past 10 years, research and development expenses and capital spending averaged 4.1% and 3.8% of revenues, respectively.

Strong, consistent earnings growth and return on equity (ROE) have been hard to achieve in the truck engine-making business. Over the past 10 years, earnings have been very erratic. During this period, CMI reported EPS as high as $11.01, and losses per share of as much as $2.66. ROE over the past 10 years averaged 12%, versus an estimated 14% for the S&P 500.

In an effort to reduce earnings cyclicality and enter markets with better long-term growth potential, the company has been expanding into the power generation equipment and industrial filter arenas. As a result, these segments have been accounting for an increasing proportion of CMI's total sales and profits.

CMI's diesel engine making segment (67% and 47% of sales and operating profits in 2006) consists of heavy, medium and small truck/bus engines, and machinery engines. Major competitors include Caterpillar's truck engine operations and DaimlerChrysler's Detroit Diesel subsidiary.

The power generation segment (20% and 25%) primarily makes backup power generators for homes, offices and hospitals. Increasing unreliability of power utility authorities, improving technology, and the need to prevent computer and Internet systems from power outages are driving consumer and institutional demand for the company's stand-by power generators. Primary competitors include Caterpillar, Emerson Electric, Ingersoll Rand and Honeywell International.

Company Financials Fiscal Year Ended Dec. 31

Per Share Data ($)	2006	2005	2004	2003	2002	2001	2000	1999	1998	1997
Tangible Book Value	22.25	15.12	10.36	5.58	4.83	8.12	10.10	12.83	6.63	14.79
Cash Flow	9.91	9.09	6.76	3.51	3.58	1.70	3.25	5.04	2.28	4.74
Earnings	7.11	5.51	3.70	0.68	1.03	-1.33	-0.10	2.07	-0.28	2.74
S&P Core Earnings	7.25	5.70	4.01	0.80	-0.78	-2.88	NA	NA	NA	NA
Dividends	0.66	0.60	0.60	0.60	0.60	0.60	0.60	0.56	0.55	0.54
Payout Ratio	9%	11%	16%	88%	58%	NM	NM	27%	NM	20%
Prices:High	69.60	46.94	42.34	26.16	25.15	22.75	25.00	32.84	31.38	41.50
Prices:Low	44.35	31.80	24.06	10.86	9.80	14.00	13.53	17.28	14.16	22.13
P/E Ratio:High	10	9	11	38	24	NM	NM	16	NM	15
P/E Ratio:Low	6	6	7	16	10	NM	NM	8	NM	8

Income Statement Analysis (Million $)										
Revenue	11,362	9,918	8,438	6,296	5,853	5,681	6,597	6,639	6,266	5,625
Operating Income	1,287	1,058	696	316	327	304	479	625	498	434
Depreciation	296	295	272	223	219	231	240	233	199	158
Interest Expense	96.0	109	113	101	82.0	87.0	86.0	75.0	71.0	26.0
Pretax Income	1,083	798	432	80.0	57.0	-129	3.00	221	-6.00	286
Effective Tax Rate	29.9%	27.1%	13.0%	15.0%	NM	NM	NM	24.9%	NM	25.9%
Net Income	715	550	350	54.0	79.0	-102	8.00	160	-21.0	212
S&P Core Earnings	729	570	380	62.8	-61.4	-221	NA	NA	NA	NA

Balance Sheet & Other Financial Data (Million $)										
Cash	935	840	690	195	298	92.0	62.0	74.0	38.0	49.0
Current Assets	4,488	3,916	3,273	2,130	1,982	1,635	1,830	2,180	1,876	1,710
Total Assets	7,465	6,885	6,527	5,126	4,837	4,335	4,500	4,697	4,542	3,765
Current Liabilities	2,399	2,218	2,197	1,391	1,329	970	1,223	1,314	1,071	1,055
Long Term Debt	647	1,213	1,299	1,380	1,290	1,206	1,032	1,092	1,137	522
Common Equity	2,802	1,864	2,802	949	841	1,025	1,336	1,429	1,272	1,422
Total Capital	3,703	3,302	4,309	2,452	2,223	2,314	2,440	2,595	2,471	1,997
Capital Expenditures	249	186	151	111	90.0	206	228	215	271	405
Cash Flow	1,011	845	622	277	298	129	248	393	178	370
Current Ratio	1.9	1.8	1.5	1.5	1.5	1.7	1.5	1.7	1.8	1.6
% Long Term Debt of Capitalization	17.5	36.7	30.1	56.3	58.0	52.1	42.3	42.1	46.0	26.1
% Net Income of Revenue	6.3	5.5	4.1	0.9	1.3	NM	0.1	2.4	NM	3.8
% Return on Assets	10.0	8.2	6.0	1.1	1.7	NM	0.2	3.5	NM	5.9
% Return on Equity	30.6	33.7	14.9	6.0	8.7	NM	0.6	11.8	NM	15.5

Data as orig reptd.; bef. results of disc opers/spec. items. Per share data adj. for stk. divs.; EPS diluted. E-Estimated. NA-Not Available. NM-Not Meaningful. NR-Not Ranked. UR-Under Review.

Office: 500 Jackson Street, Columbus, IN 47202-3005.
Telephone: 812-377-5000.
Email: investor_relations@cummins.com
Website: http://www.cummins.com

Chrmn & CEO: T.M. Solso
Pres & COO: F.J. Loughrey
EVP & CFO: J.S. Blackwell
VP & Treas: R.E. Harris

VP, Secy & General Counsel: M.M. Rose
Investor Contact: D. Cantrell (812-377-0162)
Board Members: R. J. Darnall, J. M. Deutch, A. M. Herman, F. J. Loughrey, W. I. Miller, G. R. Nelson, T. M. Solso, C. Ware, J. L. Wilson

Founded: 1919
Domicile: Indiana
Employees: 34,600

The McGraw-Hill Companies

STANDARD &POOR'S

CVS Caremark Corp

S&P Recommendation	STRONG BUY ★★★★★	Price $41.94 (as of Nov 23, 2007)	12-Mo. Target Price $48.00	Investment Style Large-Cap Blend

GICS Sector Consumer Staples
Sub-Industry Drug Retail

Summary This company is one of the largest U.S. drug store operators, with about 6,200 stores.

Key Stock Statistics (Source S&P, Vickers, company reports)

52-Wk Range	$42.60– 27.09	S&P Oper. EPS 2007E	1.91	Market Capitalization(B)	$61.647	Beta	0.93
Trailing 12-Month EPS	$1.85	S&P Oper. EPS 2008E	2.30	Yield (%)	0.57	S&P 3-Yr. Proj. EPS CAGR(%)	17.00
Trailing 12-Month P/E	22.7	P/E on S&P Oper. EPS 2007E	22.0	Dividend Rate/Share	$0.24	S&P Credit Rating	BBB+
$10K Invested 5 Yrs Ago	$33,230	Common Shares Outstg. (M)	1,469.9	Institutional Ownership (%)	88		

Price Performance

- 30-Week Mov. Avg. ··· 10-Week Mov. Avg. - GAAP Earnings vs. Previous Year Volume Above Avg. STARS
- 12-Mo. Target Price — Relative Strength — ▲ Up ▼ Down ▶ No Change Below Avg.

Options: ASE, CBOE, P, Ph

Analysis prepared by **Joseph Agnese** on November 12, 2007, when the stock traded at **$ 41.79**.

Highlights

➤ We expect total sales to increase about 15%, to $87 billion, in 2008 from our estimate of $76 billion in 2007, reflecting the integration of Caremark Rx in March and the continued turnaround of acquired drugstores. Our estimate also assumes 3.0% organic retail square footage growth and same-store sales growth of approximately 6%.

➤ We see margins widening in 2007 and 2008, reflecting synergies from prior acquisitions that include increased sales leverage and improved purchasing power, partially offset by a rise in the mix of lower margin pharmacy sales, higher employee benefit costs and costs associated with adding health care clinics to existing stores. Margin benefits we foresee also include an increased proportion of pharmacy sales coming from wider margin generic drugs and improved cost management, due to inventory and pharmacy efficiency programs. We expect interest expense to rise significantly in 2007 due to higher debt levels.

➤ We estimate 2008 operating EPS of $2.30, up 20% from our estimate of $1.91 in 2007.

Investment Rationale/Risk

➤ We believe the March 2007 acquisition of Caremark will provide an opportunity for accelerated earnings growth not only through overhead savings, but also from new customer wins as the company leverages retail offerings to gain new clients. Additionally, we anticipate earnings benefits from the integration of 700 drugstores acquired from Albertson's in June 2006.

➤ Risks to our recommendation and target price include potential problems that may arise in implementing and managing the acquisition of Albertson's drug stores, as well as risk from other acquisitions.

➤ Due to benefits we see stemming from the acquisition of Caremark RX, as well as synergies from the integration of recently acquired retail drugstores, we believe the shares should trade at a premium P/E to growth compared to the S&P 500. Assuming that the shares trade at 1.25X our projected long-term growth rate of 17%, compared to 1.1X for the S&P 500, and applying that to our forward 12-month EPS estimate of $2.24, we arrive at our 12-month target price of $48.

Qualitative Risk Assessment

LOW	MEDIUM	HIGH

Our risk assessment reflects our view of the company's leadership position, and strong market share position, in a relatively stable U.S. retail drug industry, offset by the potential for acquisition integration risk and growth of non-traditional competitors.

Quantitative Evaluations

S&P Quality Ranking A-

D	C	B-	B	B+	A-	A	A+

Relative Strength Rank STRONG

90

LOWEST = 1   HIGHEST = 99

Revenue/Earnings Data

Revenue (Million $)

	1Q	2Q	3Q	4Q	Year
2007	13,185	20,703	20,495	--	--
2006	9,979	10,561	11,207	12,066	43,814
2005	9,182	9,122	8,970	9,732	37,006
2004	6,819	6,943	7,909	8,923	30,594
2003	6,313	6,445	6,378	7,452	26,588
2002	5,971	5,990	5,876	6,345	24,182

Earnings Per Share ($)

2007	0.43	0.47	0.45	E0.55	E1.91
2006	0.39	0.40	0.33	0.49	1.60
2005	0.35	0.33	0.30	0.48	1.45
2004	0.29	0.28	0.22	0.31	1.10
2003	0.24	0.25	0.23	0.32	1.03
2002	0.22	0.22	0.20	0.25	0.88

Fiscal year ended Dec. 31. Next earnings report expected: Early February. EPS Estimates based on S&P Operating Earnings; historical GAAP earnings are as reported.

Dividend Data (Dates: mm/dd Payment Date: mm/dd/yy)

Amount ($)	Date Decl.	Ex-Div. Date	Stk. of Record	Payment Date
0.049	01/10	01/18	01/22	02/02/07
0.060	03/29	04/20	04/24	05/04/07
0.060	07/11	07/19	07/23	08/03/07
0.060	09/26	10/18	10/22	11/02/07

Dividends have been paid since 1916. Source: Company reports.

The **McGraw·Hill** Companies

CVS Caremark Corp

Business Summary November 12, 2007

CORPORATE OVERVIEW. CVS Corp. operates one of the largest drug store chains in the U.S., based on revenues, net income and store count. The company offers prescription drugs and a wide assortment of general merchandise, including OTC drugs, beauty products and cosmetics, film and photo finishing services, seasonal merchandise, greeting cards and convenience foods. As of December 2006, net selling space in retail and specialty drugstores was 55.5 million sq. ft., with about half of its store base opened or significantly remodeled within the past five years. Most new stores being built range in size between 10,000 sq. ft. and 13,000 sq. ft. and typically include a drive-thru pharmacy.

MARKET PROFILE. CVS is the largest U.S. drug store chain, based on store count, with about 6,200 stores as of December 2006, in 43 states and the District of Columbia. The company has stores in 77 of the top 100 U.S. drug store markets, holding the number one or number two market share in 58 of these

markets, and 75% of all markets in which it operates. It filled more than 513 million prescriptions in 2006, accounting for about 16% of the U.S. retail pharmacy market. Pharmacy operations are critical to CVS's success, in our view, accounting for 70% of sales in 2006. Payments by third party managed care providers under prescription drug plans accounted for 95% of total pharmacy sales in 2006. Sales to Medicaid plans were approximately 7% of pharmacy sales in 2006. CVS's pharmacy benefit management (PBM) business generated $3.7 billion in sales in 2006 and covered over 30 million lives as of January 2006, ranking as the fourth largest full service PBM in the U.S., based on lives covered.

Company Financials Fiscal Year Ended Dec. 31

Per Share Data ($)	2006	2005	2004	2003	2002	2001	2000	1999	1998	1997
Tangible Book Value	6.29	6.77	4.98	5.98	5.05	4.45	4.11	3.44	2.70	1.99
Cash Flow	2.45	2.14	1.69	1.46	1.25	0.88	1.26	1.10	0.78	0.36
Earnings	1.60	1.45	1.10	1.03	0.88	0.50	0.92	0.78	0.49	0.04
S&P Core Earnings	1.61	1.41	1.06	0.98	0.80	0.41	NA	NA	NA	NA
Dividends	0.16	0.15	0.13	0.12	0.12	0.12	0.12	0.12	0.14	0.11
Payout Ratio	10%	10%	12%	11%	13%	23%	13%	15%	29%	NM
Prices:High	36.14	31.60	23.67	18.78	17.85	31.88	30.22	29.19	28.00	17.50
Prices:Low	26.06	22.02	16.87	10.92	11.52	11.45	13.88	15.00	15.22	9.75
P/E Ratio:High	23	22	22	18	20	64	33	38	57	NM
P/E Ratio:Low	16	15	15	11	13	23	15	19	31	NM

Income Statement Analysis (Million $)										
Revenue	43,814	37,006	30,594	26,588	24,182	22,241	20,088	18,098	15,274	12,738
Operating Income	3,175	2,609	1,952	1,765	1,517	1,091	1,619	1,413	1,181	864
Depreciation	733	589	497	342	310	321	297	278	250	222
Interest Expense	216	111	58.3	48.0	50.4	61.0	79.3	59.1	61.0	45.0
Pretax Income	2,226	1,909	1,396	1,376	1,156	710	1,243	1,076	711	155
Effective Tax Rate	38.5%	35.8%	34.2%	38.4%	38.0%	41.8%	40.0%	41.0%	44.3%	76.1%
Net Income	1,369	1,225	919	847	717	413	746	635	396	37.0
S&P Core Earnings	1,365	1,171	869	785	635	323	NA	NA	NA	NA

Balance Sheet & Other Financial Data (Million $)										
Cash	531	513	392	843	700	236	337	230	181	169
Current Assets	10,392	8,393	7,920	6,497	5,982	5,454	4,937	4,608	4,349	3,685
Total Assets	20,570	15,283	14,547	10,543	9,645	8,628	7,950	7,275	6,736	5,637
Current Liabilities	7,001	4,584	4,859	3,489	3,106	3,066	2,964	2,890	3,183	2,855
Long Term Debt	2,870	1,594	1,926	753	1,076	810	537	558	276	273
Common Equity	9,704	8,109	6,759	6,022	4,991	4,306	4,037	3,404	2,830	2,077
Total Capital	12,788	9,925	8,913	6,817	6,318	12,706	4,869	4,265	3,386	2,634
Capital Expenditures	1,769	1,495	1,348	1,122	1,109	714	695	494	502	312
Cash Flow	2,088	1,800	1,401	1,189	1,012	719	1,028	898	632	245
Current Ratio	1.5	1.8	1.6	1.9	1.9	1.8	1.7	1.6	1.4	1.3
% Long Term Debt of Capitalization	22.4	16.1	21.6	11.0	17.0	63.8	11.0	13.1	8.2	10.4
% Net Income of Revenue	3.1	3.3	3.0	3.2	3.0	1.9	3.7	3.5	2.6	0.3
% Return on Assets	7.6	8.2	7.3	8.4	7.8	5.0	9.8	9.1	6.4	0.9
% Return on Equity	15.2	16.3	14.4	15.4	15.1	9.6	19.7	19.9	15.6	1.5

Data as orig reptd.; bef. results of disc opers/spec. items. Per share data adj. for stk. divs.; EPS diluted. E-Estimated. NA-Not Available. NM-Not Meaningful. NR-Not Ranked. UR-Under Review.

Office: One CVS Drive, Woonsocket, RI 02895-6184.
Telephone: 401-765-1500.
Email: investorinfo@cvs.com
Website: http://www.cvs.com

Chrmn: E.M. Crawford
Pres & CEO: T.M. Ryan
EVP, CFO & Chief Admin Officer: D.B. Rickard
SVP & Cntlr: P.A. Price

Investor Contact: N.R. Christal (914-722-4704)
Auditor: KPMG, Providence
Board Members: E. M. Banks, C. D. Brown II, E. M. Crawford, D. W. Dorman, K. E. Gibney Williams, R. L. Headrick, M. L. Heard, W. H. Joyce, J. Millon, T. Murray, C. L. Piccolo, S. Z. Rosenberg, T. M. Ryan, R. J. Swift

Founded: 1892
Domicile: Delaware
Employees: 176,000

STANDARD & POOR'S

Danaher Corp

S&P Recommendation	STRONG BUY ★ ★ ★ ★ ★	Price	12-Mo. Target Price	Investment Style
		$81.15 (as of Nov 23, 2007)	$94.00	Large-Cap Growth

GICS Sector Industrials
Sub-Industry Industrial Machinery

Summary This company is a leading maker of tools, including Sears Craftsman hand tools, and of process/environmental controls and telecommunications equipment.

Key Stock Statistics (Source S&P, Vickers, company reports)

52-Wk Range	$86.01– 69.11	S&P Oper. EPS 2007E	3.88	Market Capitalization(B)	$25.681	Beta	0.72
Trailing 12-Month EPS	$4.22	S&P Oper. EPS 2008E	4.44	Yield (%)	0.15	S&P 3-Yr. Proj. EPS CAGR(%)	17.00
Trailing 12-Month P/E	19.2	P/E on S&P Oper. EPS 2007E	20.9	Dividend Rate/Share	$0.12	S&P Credit Rating	A+
$10K Invested 5 Yrs Ago	$26,035	Common Shares Outstg. (M)	316.5	Institutional Ownership (%)	73		

Price Performance

30-Week Mov. Avg. ···   10-Week Mov. Avg. - -   **GAAP Earnings vs. Previous Year**   Volume Above Avg. ⅊⅊⅊   STARS
12-Mo. Target Price —   Relative Strength —   ▲ Up   ▼ Down   ► No Change   Below Avg. ⅊⅊⅊   ★

Options: ASE, CBOE, P, Ph

Analysis prepared by **Efraim Levy, CFA** on October 19, 2007, when the stock traded at **$81.24**.

Highlights

➤ We expect revenue growth of 15% in 2007 and 16% in 2008, driven by a combination of U.S. and foreign economic growth, and acquisitions. We project organic sales growth from all four operating segments.

➤ We see margins benefiting from streamlining activities, partly offset by narrower margins at some acquired businesses. In October, DHR said it expects EPS for 2007 of between $3.80 and $3.85; this excludes about $0.02 from favorable discrete tax items and $0.02 from indemnification proceeds. Our EPS estimate for 2007 is $3.88 and includes the tax benefit but excludes the indemnification proceeds. We expect a 15% increase, to $4.44, in 2008.

➤ For the longer term, we look for sales increases to be driven by internal growth, supplemented by acquisitions. We anticipate that a steady flow of new and enhanced products, as well as greater sales of traditional tool lines, will aid comparisons. We expect margins to widen over time, as DR consolidates acquisitions and likely benefits from higher capacity utilization, productivity gains, and cost-cutting efforts. DHR has authorized a 10 million share buyback program that we view positively.

Investment Rationale/Risk

➤ We view the balance sheet as strong. Based on several valuation measures, the stock is at a premium to that of some peers. We believe this reflects DHR's wider net margins and faster growth. Its quality of earnings appears high to us, as we expect free cash flow in both 2007 and 2008 to exceed net income, and we think that S&P Core EPS adjustments will be less than 1% in both 2007 and 2008.

➤ Risks to our recommendation and target price include slowing demand for DHR's products, and unfavorable changes in foreign exchange rates. Also, we are concerned about some of Danaher's corporate governance practices, particularly its classified board of directors with its staggered terms, which may allow certain policies to be entrenched longer despite shareholders' possible desire to change them.

➤ Given what we see as a sound balance sheet and strong cash flow growth that we expect in coming years, we think the company could raise its $0.12 annual cash dividend in 2008. Our 12-month target price of $94 is derived by applying a P/E of about 21X to our 2008 EPS estimate, reflecting relative peer and historical P/E multiples.

Qualitative Risk Assessment

LOW	MEDIUM	HIGH

Our risk assessment reflects our view of favorable growth prospects in most of its markets, good corporate leadership, and a solid balance sheet, offset by corporate governance issues.

Quantitative Evaluations

S&P Quality Ranking   A+

D	C	B-	B	B+	A-	A	A+

Relative Strength Rank   STRONG

78

LOWEST = 1   HIGHEST = 99

Revenue/Earnings Data

Revenue (Million $)

	1Q	2Q	3Q	4Q	Year
2007	2,556	2,671	2,731	--	--
2006	2,144	2,350	2,443	2,660	9,596
2005	1,826	1,929	1,966	2,264	7,985
2004	1,543	1,621	1,745	1,980	6,889
2003	1,196	1,299	1,309	1,489	5,294
2002	1,004	1,146	1,152	1,275	4,577

Earnings Per Share ($)

	1Q	2Q	3Q	4Q	Year
2007	0.78	0.96	1.03	E1.14	E3.88
2006	0.67	0.98	0.83	1.00	3.48
2005	0.58	0.70	0.70	0.78	2.76
2004	0.45	0.56	0.62	0.67	2.30
2003	0.33	0.40	0.44	0.53	1.69
2002	0.28	0.33	0.37	0.52	1.49

Fiscal year ended Dec. 31. Next earnings report expected: Late January. EPS Estimates based on S&P Operating Earnings; historical GAAP earnings are as reported.

Dividend Data (Dates: mm/dd Payment Date: mm/dd/yy)

Amount ($)	Date Decl.	Ex-Div. Date	Stk. of Record	Payment Date
0.020	12/05	12/27	12/29	01/26/07
0.020	03/13	03/28	03/30	04/27/07
0.030	05/24	06/27	06/29	07/27/07
0.030	09/14	09/26	09/28	10/26/07

Dividends have been paid since 1993. Source: Company reports.

Danaher Corp

Business Summary October 19, 2007

CORPORATE OVERVIEW. Danaher Corp. is a leading maker of hand tools and process and environmental controls. Following the end of 2006, the company has four reporting segments: professional instrumentation (30% of 2006 sales), industrial technologies (almost 33%), tools and components (14%), and medical technologies, formerly included in professional instrumentation (23%).

The professional instrumentation segment offers professional and technical customers various products and services that are used in connection with the performance of their work.

The industrial technologies segment manufactures products and sub-systems that are typically incorporated by original equipment manufacturers (OEMs) into various end-products and systems, as well as by customers and systems integrators into production and packaging lines.

The tools and components segment encompasses one strategic line of business--mechanics' hand tools--and four focused niche businesses--Delta Consolidated Industries, Hennessy Industries, Jacobs Chuck Manufacturing Company, and Jacobs Vehicle Systems.

Sales in 2006 by geographic destination were: U.S. 51%, Europe 30%, Asia 12%, and other regions 7%.

CORPORATE STRATEGY. The company's strategy is to expand revenues through a combination of internal growth and acquisitions. We expect the company to continue its tradition of successful acquisition integrations.

In May 2006, as part of its acquisition strategy, the company purchased Sybron Dental Specialties Inc. for $47 per share. The total transaction, including the assumption of debt, was valued at about $2 billion. Sybron manufactures a broad range of equipment for the dental industry and had about $650 million in revenues in its fiscal year ended September 30, 2005.

In October 2007, the company agreed to purchase Tektronix Inc. for $38 per share, or about $2.8 billion including debt, subject to necessary approvals. We expect the planned transaction to close in the 2007 fourth quarter. Tektronix is a supplier of test, measurement and monitoring products, with about $1.1 billion in annual sales.

Company Financials Fiscal Year Ended Dec. 31

Per Share Data ($)	2006	2005	2004	2003	2002	2001	2000	1999	1998	1997
Tangible Book Value	NM	NM	NM	0.99	0.01	NM	0.28	1.46	0.25	0.27
Cash Flow	4.12	3.28	2.75	2.07	1.87	1.57	1.63	1.33	1.05	0.96
Earnings	3.48	2.76	2.30	1.69	1.49	1.01	1.12	0.90	0.66	0.64
S&P Core Earnings	3.47	2.70	2.20	1.55	1.20	0.85	NA	NA	NA	NA
Dividends	0.08	0.06	0.06	0.06	0.05	0.04	0.04	0.03	0.03	0.03
Payout Ratio	2%	2%	2%	4%	3%	4%	3%	3%	4%	4%
Prices:High	75.28	58.40	58.90	46.18	37.73	34.34	34.91	34.50	27.63	16.00
Prices:Low	54.04	48.32	43.83	29.78	26.30	21.95	18.22	21.38	14.00	9.75
P/E Ratio:High	22	21	26	27	25	34	31	39	42	25
P/E Ratio:Low	16	18	19	18	18	22	16	24	21	15

Income Statement Analysis (Million $)										
Revenue	9,596	7,985	6,889	5,294	4,577	3,782	3,778	3,197	2,910	2,051
Operating Income	1,719	1,446	1,253	957	824	750	702	584	475	343
Depreciation	217	177	156	133	130	178	150	126	109	76.1
Interest Expense	79.8	44.9	55.0	59.0	43.7	25.7	29.2	16.7	24.9	13.1
Pretax Income	1,446	1,234	1,058	797	657	476	523	430	301	254
Effective Tax Rate	22.4%	27.3%	29.5%	32.6%	29.4%	37.5%	38.0%	39.1%	39.2%	39.0%
Net Income	1,122	898	746	537	464	298	324	262	183	155
S&P Core Earnings	1,121	876	715	491	373	249	NA	NA	NA	NA

Balance Sheet & Other Financial Data (Million $)										
Cash	318	316	609	1,230	810	707	177	260	41.9	33.3
Current Assets	3,395	2,945	2,919	2,942	2,387	1,875	1,474	1,202	887	618
Total Assets	12,864	9,163	8,494	6,890	6,029	4,820	4,032	3,047	2,739	1,880
Current Liabilities	2,460	2,269	2,202	1,380	1,265	1,017	1,019	709	689	524
Long Term Debt	2,423	858	926	1,284	1,197	1,119	714	341	413	163
Common Equity	6,645	5,080	4,620	3,647	3,010	2,229	1,942	1,709	1,352	917
Total Capital	9,068	5,938	5,545	4,931	4,207	3,348	2,656	2,050	1,765	1,080
Capital Expenditures	138	121	116	80.3	65.4	80.6	88.5	88.9	90.3	62.8
Cash Flow	1,339	1,075	902	670	594	476	474	388	292	231
Current Ratio	1.4	1.3	1.3	2.1	1.9	1.8	1.4	1.7	1.3	1.2
% Long Term Debt of Capitalization	26.7	14.4	16.7	26.0	28.5	33.4	26.9	16.6	23.4	15.1
% Net Income of Revenue	11.7	11.2	10.8	10.1	10.1	7.9	8.6	8.2	6.3	7.5
% Return on Assets	10.2	10.2	9.7	8.3	8.6	6.7	9.2	8.9	7.4	8.5
% Return on Equity	19.1	18.5	18.0	16.1	17.7	14.3	17.8	16.8	14.7	18.0

Data as orig reptd.; bef. results of disc opers/spec. items. Per share data adj. for stk. divs.; EPS diluted. E-Estimated. NA-Not Available. NM-Not Meaningful. NR-Not Ranked. UR-Under Review.

Office: 2099 Pennsylvania Ave NW Fl 12, Washington, DC 20006-6807.
Telephone: 202-828-0850.
Email: ir@danaher.com
Website: http://www.danaher.com

Chrmn: S.M. Rales
Pres & CEO: H.L. Culp, Jr.
EVP & CFO: D.L. Comas
SVP & General Counsel: J.P. Graham

VP & Chief Acctg Officer: R.S. Lutz
Board Members: M. M. Caplin, H. L. Culp, Jr., D. J. Ehrlich, L. P. Hefner, W. G. Lohr, Jr., M. P. Rales, S. M. Rales, J. T. Schwieters, A. G. Spoon, A. E. Stephenson, Jr.

Founded: 1969
Domicile: Delaware
Employees: 45,000

Darden Restaurants Inc.

STANDARD & POOR'S

S&P Recommendation HOLD ★★★☆☆	

Price	**12-Mo. Target Price**	**Investment Style**
$39.40 (as of Nov 23, 2007)	$49.00	Large-Cap Growth

GICS Sector Consumer Discretionary
Sub-Industry Restaurants

Summary This restaurant company operates the Red Lobster, Olive Garden, Bahama Breeze and Seasons 52 chains. It recently agreed to acquire RARE Hospitality International, operator of the Longhorn Steakhouse and Capital Grille chains.

Key Stock Statistics (Source S&P, Vickers, company reports)

52-Wk Range	$47.60–38.11	S&P Oper. EPS 2008E	2.80	Market Capitalization(B)	$5.591	Beta	0.96
Trailing 12-Month EPS	$1.48	S&P Oper. EPS 2009E	3.05	Yield (%)	1.83	S&P 3-Yr. Proj. EPS CAGR(%)	4.00
Trailing 12-Month P/E	26.6	P/E on S&P Oper. EPS 2008E	14.1	Dividend Rate/Share	$0.72	S&P Credit Rating	BBB+
$10K Invested 5 Yrs Ago	$19,210	Common Shares Outstg. (M)	141.9	Institutional Ownership (%)	81		

Price Performance

- 30-Week Mov. Avg.
- 10-Week Mov. Avg.
- GAAP Earnings vs. Previous Year
- Volume Above Avg. STARS
- 12-Mo. Target Price
- Relative Strength
- ▲ Up ▼ Down ► No Change
- Below Avg.

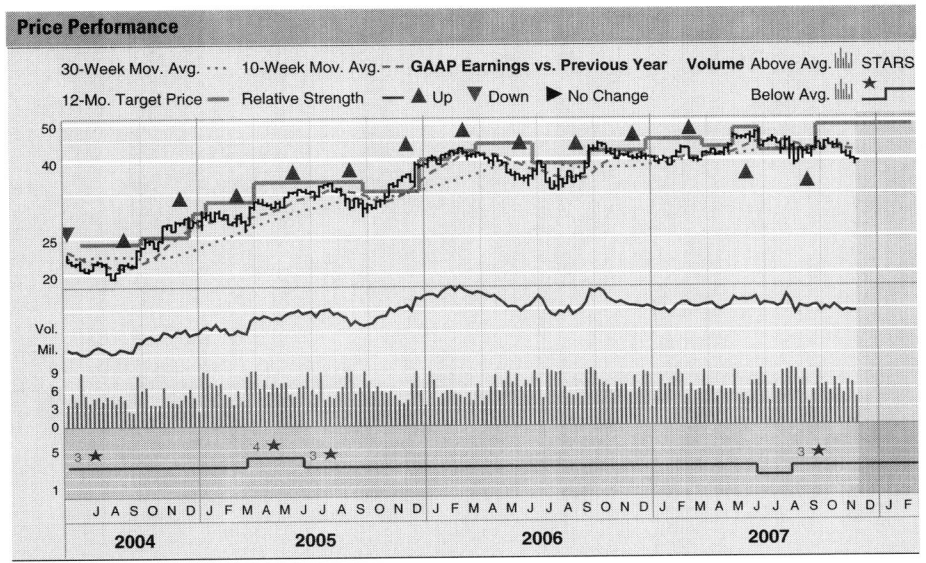

Options: ASE, CBOE, P, Ph

Analysis prepared by **Mark S. Basham** on September 26, 2007, when the stock traded at **$ 42.92**.

Qualitative Risk Assessment

LOW	MEDIUM	HIGH

DRI competes in the stable casual dining industry, and we believe that its Red Lobster and Olive Garden concepts have among the strongest brand name recognition in the industry. The casual dining segment over-expanded in recent years, in our opinion, and has begun a necessary consolidation, a part of which includes DRI's plans to dispose of its Smokey Bones Barbeque & Grill chain.

Quantitative Evaluations

S&P Quality Ranking   **A**

D	C	B-	B	B+	A-	A	A+

Relative Strength Rank   **MODERATE**

49

LOWEST = 1   HIGHEST = 99

Revenue/Earnings Data

Revenue (Million $)

	1Q	2Q	3Q	4Q	Year
2008	1,468	--	--	--	--
2007	1,360	1,298	1,450	1,460	5,567
2006	1,409	1,325	1,474	1,414	5,721
2005	1,279	1,229	1,376	1,394	5,278
2004	1,260	1,143	1,242	1,359	5,003
2003	1,175	1,143	1,181	1,227	4,655

Earnings Per Share ($)

	1Q	2Q	3Q	4Q	Year
2008	0.73	E0.50	E0.85	E0.72	E2.80
2007	0.62	0.45	0.79	0.67	2.53
2006	0.53	0.35	0.67	0.62	2.16
2005	0.44	0.26	0.56	0.52	1.78
2004	0.40	0.18	0.46	0.32	1.36
2003	0.40	0.18	0.35	0.35	1.31

Fiscal year ended May 31. Next earnings report expected: Mid December. EPS Estimates based on S&P Operating Earnings; historical GAAP earnings are as reported.

Dividend Data (Dates: mm/dd Payment Date: mm/dd/yy)

Amount ($)	Date Decl.	Ex-Div. Date	Stk. of Record	Payment Date
0.230	03/20	04/05	04/10	05/01/07
0.180	06/21	07/06	07/10	08/01/07
0.180	09/18	10/05	10/10	11/01/07

Dividends have been paid since 1995. Source: Company reports.

Highlights

➤ We expect comparable-store sales to be up about 3% in FY 08 (May) at Darden, versus company expectations of 2% to 4% growth. This reflects an approximate 3% price increase combined with marginally higher traffic. We expect 3% unit growth, with a rise in total revenues of about 6%.

➤ We forecast that restaurant operating margins will narrow slightly compared to FY 07, as higher food and labor costs are largely offset by efficiencies elsewhere. We estimate EPS will rise 11% in FY 08 to $2.80 from $2.53 from continuing operations in FY 07. Continuing operations exclude DRI's Smokey Bones chain; on May 5, 2007, DRI closed 54 restaurants and said it intends to sell the remaining 73 locations.

➤ On August 16, 2007, DRI agreed to acquire RARE Hospitality International (RARE: hold, $38), in a cash tender offer for all RARE common shares at $38.15 per share. The offer commenced on August 31 and the acquisition is expected to close during October, subject to the tender of a majority of RARE shares, as well as regulatory approval and other customary conditions.

Investment Rationale/Risk

➤ While the company achieved better results than we expected in the first quarter of FY 08, we remain mindful of weak fundamentals within the casual dining sector. DRI will update its expectations on the earnings impact of the proposed RARE deal when it release its fiscal second quarter results in December. Initially, DRI said it expects to achieve modest earnings accretion in FY 08 on the planned deal.

➤ Risks to our recommendation and target price include an unexpected acceleration in food cost inflation. Also, consumers may be more price sensitive than we expect, suggesting weaker traffic in response to recent price increases.

➤ Our 12-month target price of $49 is based on our discounted cash flow model, which assumes 5% to 6% annual revenue growth excluding acquisitions and divestitures, and a weighted average cost of equity of 9.1%. At $49, the shares would trade at about 17X our calendar 2008 EPS estimate of $2.95, a multiple that is in line with DRI's peer group.

Please read the Required Disclosures and Analyst Certification on the last page of this report.

The McGraw-Hill Companies

Darden Restaurants Inc.

STANDARD
&POOR'S

Business Summary September 26, 2007

CORPORATE OVERVIEW. With systemwide sales from continuing operations of more than $5.5 billion in FY 07 (May), Darden Restaurants is the world's largest publicly held casual dining restaurant company. As of May 2007, it operated over 1,300 restaurants in the U.S. and Canada, including 680 Red Lobster units, 614 Olive Garden units, 23 Bahama Breeze restaurants, and seven Seasons 52 locations.

Olive Garden is the U.S. market share leader among casual dining Italian food restaurants. FY 07 systemwide sales grew 6.6%, to $2.8 billion. Same-restaurant sales growth slowed to 2.7%, after rising 5.5% in FY 06 and 7.2% in FY 05, and average restaurant sales were $4.7 million. The average check per person was $15 to $16 in FY 07.

Red Lobster, founded by William Darden in 1968, is the largest U.S. casual dining seafood-specialty restaurant operator. System sales totaled $2.6 billion in

FY 07, up 0.9% from FY 06. Average restaurant sales were $3.8 million in FY 07, unchanged from FY 06. Same-store sales rose 0.2% in FY 07, following a 4.9% increase in FY 06 and a 0.9% rise in FY 05. The average check per person was $18.00 to $19.00.

The company's other concepts, Bahama Breeze and Seasons 52, are relatively new and have not yet gained enough scale to contribute meaningfully to profits. Bahama Breeze, first opened in 1996, is a Caribbean-themed restaurant that offers a distinctive island dining experience. It is currently experimenting with a new prototype for the Bahama Breeze chain in an attempt to closely match its cost structure with expected revenues.

Company Financials Fiscal Year Ended May 31

Per Share Data ($)	2007	2006	2005	2004	2003	2002	2001	2000	1999	1998
Tangible Book Value	7.57	8.20	8.25	7.86	7.03	6.56	5.66	5.09	4.81	4.69
Cash Flow	3.88	3.57	3.08	2.60	2.43	2.20	1.85	1.55	1.34	1.00
Earnings	2.53	2.16	1.78	1.36	1.31	1.30	1.06	0.89	0.66	0.45
S&P Core Earnings	2.52	2.10	1.68	1.27	1.18	1.16	0.97	NA	NA	NA
Dividends	0.40	0.08	0.08	0.08	0.05	0.05	0.05	0.05	0.05	0.05
Payout Ratio	16%	4%	4%	6%	4%	4%	5%	6%	8%	12%
Calendar Year	2006	2005	2004	2003	2002	2001	2000	1999	1998	1997
Prices:High	44.43	39.53	28.54	23.01	29.76	24.98	18.00	15.58	12.62	8.33
Prices:Low	32.91	25.78	18.48	16.50	18.00	12.67	8.29	10.42	7.83	4.50
P/E Ratio:High	18	18	16	17	23	19	17	17	19	19
P/E Ratio:Low	13	12	10	12	14	10	8	12	12	10

Income Statement Analysis (Million $)										
Revenue	5,567	5,721	5,278	5,003	4,655	4,369	4,021	3,701	3,458	3,287
Operating Income	774	757	685	636	588	563	479	421	352	300
Depreciation	200	221	213	210	198	166	147	130	125	126
Interest Expense	40.7	43.1	43.1	43.7	44.1	37.8	31.5	23.1	40.6	20.5
Pretax Income	531	483	424	340	348	363	301	274	216	154
Effective Tax Rate	29.0%	29.9%	31.4%	31.9%	33.2%	34.5%	34.6%	35.5%	34.9%	33.8%
Net Income	377	338	291	231	232	238	197	177	141	102
S&P Core Earnings	376	330	274	214	208	212	181	NA	NA	NA

Balance Sheet & Other Financial Data (Million $)										
Cash	30.2	42.3	42.8	36.7	48.6	153	61.8	26.1	41.0	33.5
Current Assets	545	378	407	346	326	450	328	290	328	398
Total Assets	2,881	3,010	2,938	2,780	2,665	2,530	2,218	1,971	1,906	1,985
Current Liabilities	1,074	1,026	1,045	683	640	601	554	607	534	559
Long Term Debt	492	495	350	653	658	663	518	304	314	311
Common Equity	1,115	1,230	1,273	1,246	1,196	1,129	1,035	960	964	1,020
Total Capital	1,633	1,815	1,738	2,075	2,005	1,909	1,644	1,344	1,350	1,408
Capital Expenditures	345	338	329	354	423	318	355	269	124	112
Cash Flow	578	560	504	441	430	404	344	307	266	228
Current Ratio	0.5	0.4	0.4	0.5	0.5	0.7	0.6	0.5	0.6	0.7
% Long Term Debt of Capitalization	30.1	27.3	20.2	31.5	32.8	34.7	31.5	22.6	23.3	22.0
% Net Income of Revenue	6.8	5.9	5.5	4.6	5.0	5.4	4.9	4.8	4.1	3.1
% Return on Assets	12.8	11.4	10.2	8.5	8.9	10.0	9.4	9.2	7.2	5.2
% Return on Equity	31.6	27.0	23.7	19.0	20.0	22.0	19.7	18.4	14.2	9.7

Data as orig reptd.; bef. results of disc opers/spec. items. Per share data adj. for stk. divs.; EPS diluted. E-Estimated. NA-Not Available. NM-Not Meaningful. NR-Not Ranked. UR-Under Review.

Office: 5900 Lake Ellenor Drive, Orlando, FL 32809-4634.
Telephone: 407-245-4000.
Email: irinfo@darden.com
Website: http://www.darden.com

Chrmn & CEO: C. Otis, Jr.
Pres & COO: A.H. Madsen
SVP, Secy & General Counsel: P.J. Shives
SVP & Cntlr: C.B. Richmond

Board Members: L. L. Berry, O. C. Donald, D. H. Hughes, C. A. Ledsinger, Jr., W. M. Lewis, Jr., A. H. Madsen, C. McGillicuddy, III, C. Otis, Jr., M. D. Rose, M. A. Sastre, J. A. Smith, R. P. Wilson

Founded: 1968
Domicile: Florida
Employees: 156,500

Dean Foods Co

STANDARD &POOR'S

S&P Recommendation HOLD ★★★☆☆	Price $24.71 (as of Nov 23, 2007)	12-Mo. Target Price $27.00	Investment Style Large-Cap Blend

GICS Sector Consumer Staples
Sub-Industry Packaged Foods & Meats

Summary This leading U.S. dairy processor and distributor was formed in December 2001 when Suiza Foods acquired Dean Foods.

Key Stock Statistics (Source S&P, Vickers, company reports)

52-Wk Range	$50.50– 24.11	S&P Oper. EPS 2007**E**	1.23	Market Capitalization(B)	$3.252	Beta	-0.01
Trailing 12-Month EPS	$1.24	S&P Oper. EPS 2008**E**	1.30	Yield (%)	Nil	S&P 3-Yr. Proj. EPS CAGR(%)	-10.00
Trailing 12-Month P/E	19.9	P/E on S&P Oper. EPS 2007**E**	20.1	Dividend Rate/Share	Nil	S&P Credit Rating	BB-
$10K Invested 5 Yrs Ago	NA	Common Shares Outstg. (M)	131.6	Institutional Ownership (%)	89		

Price Performance

30-Week Mov. Avg. · · · 10-Week Mov. Avg. - - **GAAP Earnings vs. Previous Year**   Volume Above Avg. STARS
12-Mo. Target Price — Relative Strength — ▲ Up ▼ Down ► No Change   Below Avg.

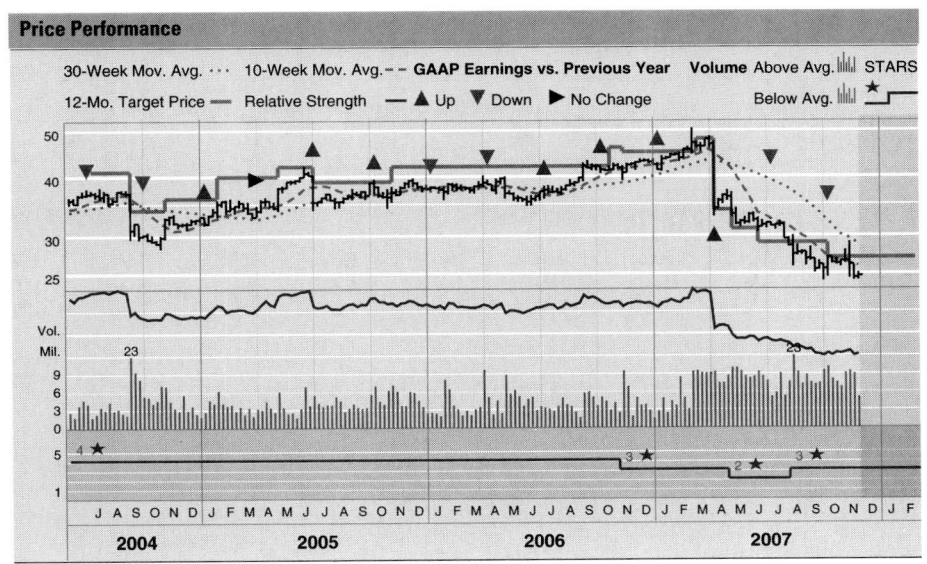

Analysis prepared by **Tom Graves, CFA** on October 04, 2007, when the stock traded at **$ 26.13**.

Options: CBOE, P, Ph

Highlights

➤ In April 2007, DF paid a $15 per share special dividend. With about 130 million common shares outstanding, this resulted in a payment totaling $1.9 billion. We believe that the dividend reflects a strategic shift for the company, with acquisitions likely to be less of a focus in the future.

➤ In 2008, we look for net sales to increase no more than modestly from the $11.6 billion projected for 2007. We anticipate that in 2008, costs and prices for conventional milk will have receded from 2007's peak levels. We estimate that DF's operating profits in 2008 will increase to $678 million, up 14% from what we project for 2007 before some special items. We expect interest expense to be up in 2008, largely due to financing for 2007's special dividend. We look for net income in 2008 to increase about 18%, to $1.40, from the $1.20 we project for 2007, which excludes such special items as an expected restructuring charge in 2007's third quarter.

➤ As a result of a recent recapitalization and what we view as a one-time special dividend, we do not expect additional near-term stock repurchases.

Investment Rationale/Risk

➤ We expect near-term weakness from DF's conventional milk business to be more extensive and deeper than previously anticipated, with pressure from commodity costs and private label competition. We look for near-term EPS negatives to also include recapitalization-related interest expense and increased supply of organic milk. However, we see the company deriving long-term benefits from improved operational efficiency and growth in the organic milk business. During the next few years, possibly starting in 2008, we look for DF to use expected free cash flow (after capital expenditures) largely for debt reduction. This would follow, in 2007, the payment of a large special dividend and the completion of an acquisition.

➤ Risks to our recommendation and target price include the possibility that consumer spending on dairy products, competitive conditions, milk prices, and commodity costs will be less favorable than we anticipate.

➤ Our 12-month target price of $27 reflects our view that the stock should sell at a similar P/E (based on estimated 2008 EPS) to the peer group average that we expect.

Qualitative Risk Assessment

LOW	MEDIUM	HIGH

Our risk assessment for Dean Foods reflects our view of its leading position in the U.S. milk market, and our expectation of future free cash flow. However, milk prices can be volatile and some products are likely to have stronger demand and growth than others. Also, following a recent special dividend, DF's debt level has increased sharply.

Quantitative Evaluations

S&P Quality Ranking   B+

D	C	B-	B	B+	A-	A	A+

Relative Strength Rank   MODERATE
44
LOWEST = 1   HIGHEST = 99

Revenue/Earnings Data

Revenue (Million $)

	1Q	2Q	3Q	4Q	Year
2007	2,630	2,844	3,117	--	--
2006	2,509	2,478	2,518	2,594	10,099
2005	2,562	2,603	2,647	2,695	10,506
2004	2,452	2,807	2,773	2,791	10,822
2003	2,145	2,223	2,307	2,510	9,185
2002	2,226	2,295	2,230	2,240	8,991

Earnings Per Share ($)

2007	0.47	0.21	0.05	E0.29	E1.23
2006	0.37	0.53	0.54	0.56	2.01
2005	0.43	0.52	0.43	0.49	1.78
2004	0.43	0.47	0.25	0.64	1.78
2003	0.43	0.54	0.76	0.54	2.27
2002	0.37	0.48	0.45	0.47	1.77

Fiscal year ended Dec. 31. Next earnings report expected: Early February. EPS Estimates based on S&P Operating Earnings; historical GAAP earnings are as reported.

Dividend Data (Dates: mm/dd Payment Date: mm/dd/yy)

Amount ($)	Date Decl.	Ex-Div. Date	Stk. of Record	Payment Date
15 Spl.	03/02	04/03	03/27	04/02/07

Dividends have been paid since 2007. Source: Company reports.

Dean Foods Co

STANDARD &POOR'S

Business Summary October 04, 2007

CORPORATE OVERVIEW. Dean Foods Co. is a leading U.S. processor and distributor of milk and other dairy products. In December 2001, Suiza Foods Corp., the largest U.S. dairy, acquired Dean Foods Co. Suiza subsequently changed its name to Dean Foods Co. The company has grown partly through an acquisition strategy and by realizing regional economies of scale and operating efficiencies by consolidating manufacturing and distribution operations.

The company's Dairy Group had about $8.82 billion of net sales in 2006, or about 87% of DF's total net sales. Segment operating profit, before special items, totaled $678 million, up 5.5% from that of the prior year. Fluid milk accounted for 64% of the Dairy Group's 2006 net sales, and ice-cream-related products accounted for 10%. Within the Dairy Group, 63% of sales carried company brands and 37% were private label. In 2006, Wal-Mart (including subsidiaries such as Sam's Club) was the Dairy Group's largest customer, accounting for about 18.2% of the Dairy Group's sales. As of early 2007, the Dairy Group operated 98 manufacturing facilities in 34 states.

The company's WhiteWave Foods business, which had about $1.28 billion of sales in 2006, develops, manufactures and sells a variety of nationally branded soy, dairy, and dairy-related products, such as Silk soy milk and cultured soy products, Horizon Organic dairy products, International Delight coffee creamers, LAND O'LAKES creamers and fluid dairy products, and Rachel's Organic Dairy products. The company licenses the LAND O'LAKES and Hershey's names from third parties. In 2006, combined sales of Horizon organic (including The Organic Cow dairy products) and Silk products represented about 53% of WhiteWave's total. Wal-Mart accounted for about 14.3% of WhiteWave's sales in 2006. Before special items, WhiteWave's segment operating profit in 2006 totaled $139 million, up 21% from the year-ago level.

Company Financials Fiscal Year Ended Dec. 31

Per Share Data ($)	2006	2005	2004	2003	2002	2001	2000	1999	1998	1997
Tangible Book Value	NM	NM	NM	NM	NM	NM	NM	NM	NM	NM
Cash Flow	3.63	3.22	1.58	3.41	2.71	2.44	2.35	2.05	1.55	0.95
Earnings	2.01	1.78	1.78	2.27	1.77	1.23	1.27	1.04	0.97	0.42
S&P Core Earnings	2.00	1.66	1.58	1.85	1.57	0.91	NA	NA	NA	NA
Dividends	Nil	Nil	Nil	Nil	Nil	Nil	Nil	Nil	Nil	Nil
Payout Ratio	Nil	Nil	Nil	Nil	Nil	Nil	Nil	Nil	Nil	Nil
Prices:High	43.55	42.10	38.00	33.75	27.03	24.16	17.48	16.75	22.33	20.83
Prices:Low	34.66	31.60	28.25	24.60	18.05	14.00	12.00	9.88	8.56	6.42
P/E Ratio:High	22	24	21	15	15	20	14	16	23	49
P/E Ratio:Low	17	18	16	11	10	11	9	10	9	15

Income Statement Analysis (Million $)

	2006	2005	2004	2003	2002	2001	2000	1999	1998	1997
Revenue	10,099	10,506	10,822	9,185	8,991	6,230	5,756	4,482	3,321	1,795
Operating Income	903	867	919	889	856	542	524	406	334	177
Depreciation	228	221	224	192	174	155	145	155	91.8	44.6
Interest Expense	195	169	205	195	231	135	147	87.8	82.3	36.7
Pretax Income	456	439	462	574	421	231	234	193	164	82.7
Effective Tax Rate	38.5%	37.9%	38.3%	38.0%	36.4%	36.3%	38.4%	39.1%	36.4%	52.4%
Net Income	280	272	285	356	268	116	114	109	103	39.3
S&P Core Earnings	278	254	253	288	236	79.2	NA	NA	NA	NA

Balance Sheet & Other Financial Data (Million $)

	2006	2005	2004	2003	2002	2001	2000	1999	1998	1997
Cash	31.1	25.1	27.6	47.1	45.9	78.3	31.0	25.2	54.9	24.4
Current Assets	1,379	1,477	1,596	1,401	1,311	1,482	818	639	814	396
Total Assets	6,770	7,051	7,756	6,993	6,582	6,732	3,780	2,659	3,014	1,403
Current Liabilities	1,337	1,137	1,106	1,170	1,268	1,175	700	479	559	233
Long Term Debt	2,872	3,329	3,116	2,611	3,140	3,556	1,809	1,373	1,576	778
Common Equity	1,809	1,872	2,661	2,543	1,643	1,476	599	584	656	356
Total Capital	5,186	5,688	6,308	5,542	5,077	5,313	3,047	2,145	2,390	1,157
Capital Expenditures	237	307	356	292	242	137	137	188	177	62.1
Cash Flow	508	494	509	548	442	270	259	264	195	83.9
Current Ratio	1.0	1.3	1.4	1.2	1.0	1.3	1.2	1.3	1.5	1.7
% Long Term Debt of Capitalization	55.4	58.5	49.4	47.1	61.8	66.9	59.3	64.0	65.9	67.2
% Net Income of Revenue	2.8	2.6	2.6	3.9	3.0	1.9	1.9	2.4	3.1	2.2
% Return on Assets	4.1	3.7	3.9	5.2	4.0	2.2	3.5	3.8	4.7	4.4
% Return on Equity	15.1	12.0	11.0	17.0	17.2	11.1	19.2	17.6	20.3	17.5

Data as orig reptd.; bef. results of disc opers/spec. items. Per share data adj. for stk. divs.; EPS diluted. E-Estimated. NA-Not Available. NM-Not Meaningful. NR-Not Ranked. UR-Under Review.

Office: 2515 McKinney Avenue, Dallas, TX 75201.
Telephone: 214-303-3400.
Website: http://www.deanfoods.com
Chrmn & CEO: G.L. Engles

EVP & CFO: J.F. Callahan, Jr.
EVP, Chief Admin Officer, Secy & General Counsel: M.P. Goolsby
SVP & Chief Acctg Officer: R.L. McCrummen
Investor Contact: B. Sievert (214-303-3437)

Board Members: A. J. Bernon, L. M. Collens, T. Davis, G. L. Engles, S. L. Green, J. S. Hardin, Jr., J. Hill, R. Kirk, J. R. Muse, H. M. Nevares, P. Schenkel, J. L. Turner

Founded: 1925
Domicile: Delaware
Employees: 26,348

The McGraw-Hill Companies

Deere & Co

STANDARD &POOR'S

S&P Recommendation	HOLD ★★★☆☆	Price $156.64 (as of Nov 23, 2007)	12-Mo. Target Price $149.00	Investment Style Large-Cap Blend

GICS Sector Industrials
Sub-Industry Construction & Farm Machinery & Heavy Trucks

Summary DE, the world's largest producer of farm equipment, is also a large maker of construction machinery and lawn and garden equipment.

Key Stock Statistics (Source S&P, Vickers, company reports)

52-Wk Range	$160.49–90.23	S&P Oper. EPS 2007**E**	7.50	Market Capitalization(B)	$34.755	Beta	1.77
Trailing 12-Month EPS	$7.34	S&P Oper. EPS 2008**E**	9.30	Yield (%)	1.28	S&P 3-Yr. Proj. EPS CAGR(%)	19.00
Trailing 12-Month P/E	21.3	P/E on S&P Oper. EPS 2007**E**	20.9	Dividend Rate/Share	$2.00	S&P Credit Rating	B+
$10K Invested 5 Yrs Ago	$34,447	Common Shares Outstg. (M)	221.9	Institutional Ownership (%)	83		

Price Performance

30-Week Mov. Avg. ··· 10-Week Mov. Avg. – – GAAP Earnings vs. Previous Year Volume Above Avg. ▕▏STARS
12-Mo. Target Price — Relative Strength — ▲ Up ▼ Down ► No Change Below Avg. ▕▏★

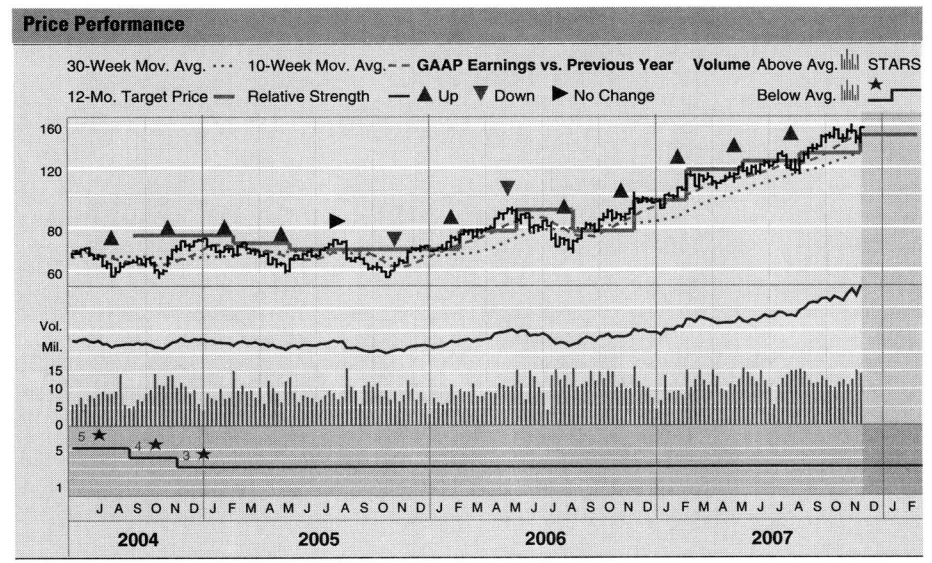

Options: ASE, CBOE, Ph

Analysis prepared by **Pearl Wang** on November 21, 2007, when the stock traded at **$ 153.65**.

Highlights

➤ We expect revenue growth of 12% in FY 08 (Oct.), driven mostly by ongoing strength in global farm markets, based on our outlook for continued growth in the global economy, relatively high commodity prices and increasing use of renewable fuels. We also see DE's top line being lifted by the full-year inclusion of LESCO (purchased in May 2007) and higher average prices. We foresee these factors outweighing what we expect to be ongoing soft demand for construction and forestry equipment, based on our outlook for relatively slow domestic homebuilding markets over the coming year.

➤ We expect wider margins in FY 08, based on our outlook for improved prices in the farm equipment and commercial and consumer equipment businesses, and higher farm equipment sales volume. We see these factors outweighing the soft margins that we forecast in the construction and forestry area, along with the high raw material costs.

➤ We expect Deere to continue to benefit from what we view as solid business strategies. We project FY 08 (Oct.) EPS of $9.30.

Investment Rationale/Risk

➤ We expect conditions in the various markets that Deere serves to continue to be mixed in coming quarters, but we see its agricultural equipment business, particularly in international markets, remaining strong enough to drive what we view as solid EPS growth. We also believe that DE is well managed. However, our relative valuation models shows the stock to be appropriately valued.

➤ Risks to our recommendation and target price include a slowdown in global economies; the potential for lower crop prices to negatively affect spending on farm equipment; continued raw material cost escalation; and an unexpected slowdown in end markets.

➤ The shares recently traded at about 16X our FY 08 EPS forecast, which falls about in line with the company's traditional valuation in the middle of positive earnings cycles. Based on our belief that favorable global farm markets will allow Deere to post earnings growth for at least a couple of more years, we think DE stock is fairly valued. We have a 12-month target price of $149, or 16X our 2008 EPS estimate.

Qualitative Risk Assessment

LOW	MEDIUM	HIGH

Our risk assessment for Deere & Co. reflects its leading position in many of the markets it serves, and our view of a strong equipment operations balance sheet with large cash balances, offset by its significant post retirement benefit obligations and the highly cyclical nature of the company's business.

Quantitative Evaluations

S&P Quality Ranking B+

D	C	B-	B	B+	A-	A	A+

Relative Strength Rank STRONG
94
LOWEST = 1   HIGHEST = 99

Revenue/Earnings Data

Revenue (Million $)

	1Q	2Q	3Q	4Q	Year
2007	4,425	6,883	6,634	--	--
2006	4,202	6,562	6,267	5,118	22,148
2005	4,127	6,621	6,005	5,177	21,931
2004	2,912	5,877	5,418	5,207	19,986
2003	2,794	4,400	4,402	3,939	15,535
2002	2,522	3,987	3,969	3,469	13,947

Earnings Per Share ($)

2007	1.04	2.72	2.37	E1.38	E7.50
2006	0.94	2.17	1.85	1.20	6.16
2005	0.89	2.43	1.58	0.96	5.87
2004	0.68	1.88	1.58	1.41	5.56
2003	0.28	1.07	1.02	0.27	2.64
2002	-0.16	0.59	0.61	0.28	1.33

Fiscal year ended Oct. 31. Next earnings report expected: Late November. EPS Estimates based on S&P Operating Earnings; historical GAAP earnings are as reported.

Dividend Data (Dates: mm/dd Payment Date: mm/dd/yy)

Amount ($)	Date Decl.	Ex-Div. Date	Stk. of Record	Payment Date
0.440	02/28	03/28	03/31	05/01/07
0.440	05/30	06/27	06/30	08/01/07
0.500	08/29	09/26	09/28	11/01/07
2-for-1	08/29	12/04	11/26	12/03/07

Dividends have been paid since 1937. Source: Company reports.

Deere & Co

STANDARD &POOR'S

Business Summary November 21, 2007

CORPORATE OVERVIEW. Deere & Co. is the world's largest maker of farm tractors and combines, and a leading producer of construction equipment. Its largest competitors include construction equipment behemoth Caterpillar Inc.; Netherlands-based CNH Global N.V., a worldwide maker of both farm and construction equipment; and AGCO Corp., the world's third largest global farm equipment maker.

The farm equipment segment (50% of FY 07 (Oct.) revenues; 12% operating margin) primarily makes tractors; combine, cotton and sugar cane harvesters; tillage, seeding and soil preparation machinery; hay and forage equipment; material handling equipment; and integrated agricultural management systems technology for the global farming industry. Over the past five years, segment margins averaged about 8.0%.

The commercial and consumer equipment segment (C&CE; 18%; 7.0%) manufactures and distributes equipment and service parts for commercial uses. Products include small tractors for lawn, garden, commercial and utility purposes; riding and walk-behind mowers; golf course equipment; utility vehicles; landscape and irrigation equipment; and other outdoor products. In addition, this division also includes John Deere Landscapes, Inc., a distributor of irrigation equipment, nursery products and landscape products. The company expanded its C&CE division in May 2007, through its $150 million acquisition of

LESCO, which supplies consumable lawn care, landscape, golf course and pest control products. Over the past five years, C&CE segment margins averaged 5.5%.

The construction and forestry segment (21%; 11%) manufactures and distributes a broad range of machines and service parts used in construction, earthmoving, material handling and timber harvesting. Products include backhoe loaders; crawler dozers and loaders; four-wheel-drive loaders; excavators; motor graders; articulated dump trucks; landscape loaders; skid-steer loaders; and log skidders, feller bunchers, harvesters and related attachments. Over the past five years, margins for this segment averaged 8.6%.

The credit segment finances sales and leases by John Deere dealers of new and used agricultural, commercial and consumer, and construction and forestry equipment. In addition, this division provides wholesale financing to dealers, provides operating loans, and finances retail revolving charge accounts. Credit operations had receivables under management of $14.0 billion at October 31, 2006.

Company Financials Fiscal Year Ended Oct. 31

Per Share Data ($)	2006	2005	2004	2003	2002	2001	2000	1999	1998	1997
Tangible Book Value	27.84	24.25	21.86	11.82	9.49	13.14	15.56	16.24	16.65	15.96
Cash Flow	9.10	8.46	8.01	5.24	4.34	2.78	4.80	3.21	5.85	5.30
Earnings	6.16	5.87	5.56	2.64	1.33	-0.27	2.06	1.02	4.16	3.78
S&P Core Earnings	6.49	6.04	5.67	3.07	-0.38	-1.63	NA	NA	NA	NA
Dividends	1.56	1.21	1.06	0.88	0.88	0.88	0.88	0.88	0.88	0.80
Payout Ratio	22%	21%	19%	33%	66%	NM	43%	86%	21%	21%
Prices:High	101.40	74.41	74.93	67.41	51.60	46.13	49.63	45.94	64.13	60.50
Prices:Low	66.90	56.99	56.72	37.56	37.50	33.50	30.31	31.56	28.38	39.88
P/E Ratio:High	14	13	13	26	39	NM	24	45	15	16
P/E Ratio:Low	9	10	10	14	28	NM	15	31	7	11

Income Statement Analysis (Million $)										
Revenue	22,148	21,931	19,986	15,535	13,947	13,293	13,137	11,751	13,749	12,791
Operating Income	3,883	3,553	2,976	2,231	1,696	1,274	2,102	1,435	2,497	2,295
Depreciation	691	636	621	631	725	718	648	513	418	366
Interest Expense	1,018	761	592	1,257	637	766	676	557	519	422
Pretax Income	2,195	2,162	2,115	980	578	-46.3	779	374	1,575	1,511
Effective Tax Rate	33.8%	33.1%	33.5%	34.4%	44.7%	NM	37.7%	36.1%	35.2%	36.5%
Net Income	1,453	1,447	1,406	643	319	-64.0	486	239	1,021	960
S&P Core Earnings	1,531	1,483	1,430	743	-94.8	-385	NA	NA	NA	NA

Balance Sheet & Other Financial Data (Million $)										
Cash	3,504	4,708	3,428	4,616	3,004	1,206	419	612	1,177	330
Current Assets	NA	NA	NA	NA	NA	NA	NA	NA	NA	NA
Total Assets	34,720	33,637	28,754	26,258	23,768	22,663	20,469	17,578	18,002	16,320
Current Liabilities	NA	NA	NA	NA	NA	NA	NA	NA	NA	NA
Long Term Debt	11,584	11,739	11,090	10,404	8,950	6,561	4,764	3,806	2,792	2,623
Common Equity	7,565	6,825	6,350	2,834	1,797	3,992	4,302	4,094	4,080	4,148
Total Capital	19,214	18,564	17,441	13,238	10,772	10,566	9,141	7,963	6,892	6,792
Capital Expenditures	766	513	364	310	359	491	427	316	435	485
Cash Flow	2,145	2,083	2,027	1,275	1,045	654	1,133	752	1,439	1,326
Current Ratio	NA	NA	NA	NA	NA	NA	NA	NA	NA	NA
% Long Term Debt of Capitalization	60.3	63.2	63.6	78.6	83.1	62.1	52.1	47.8	40.5	38.6
% Net Income of Revenue	6.6	6.6	7.0	4.2	2.4	NM	3.8	2.0	7.4	7.5
% Return on Assets	4.3	4.6	5.1	2.6	1.4	NM	2.6	1.3	5.9	6.2
% Return on Equity	20.2	22.0	30.6	27.8	11.8	NM	11.6	5.8	24.8	24.9

Data as orig reptd.; bef. results of disc opers/spec. items. Per share data adj. for stk. divs.; EPS diluted. E-Estimated. NA-Not Available. NM-Not Meaningful. NR-Not Ranked. UR-Under Review.

Office: One John Deere Place, Moline, IL 61265.
Telephone: 309-765-8000.
Email: stockholder@deere.com
Website: http://www.deere.com

Chrmn, Pres & CEO: R.W. Lane
SVP & CFO: M.J. Mack, Jr.
SVP & General Counsel: J.R. Jenkins
Investor Contact: M. Ziegler (309-765-4491)

Secy: M.H. Howze
Board Members: C. C. Bowles, V. D. Coffman, T. K. Dunnigan, C. O. Holliday, Jr., D. C. Jain, A. L. Kelly, R. W. Lane, A. Madero, J. Milberg, R. B. Myers, T. H. Patrick, A. L. Peters

Founded: 1837
Domicile: Delaware
Employees: 46,549

Dell Inc

STANDARD &POOR'S

S&P Recommendation	HOLD ★★★☆☆		Price	12-Mo. Target Price	Investment Style
			$26.13 (as of Nov 23, 2007)	$31.00	Large-Cap Growth

GICS Sector Information Technology
Sub-Industry Computer Hardware

Summary This company (formerly Dell Computer Corp.) is the leading direct marketer and one of the world's 10 leading manufacturers of PCs compatible with industry standards established by IBM.

Key Stock Statistics (Source S&P, Vickers, company reports)

52-Wk Range	$30.77– 21.61	S&P Oper. EPS 2008**E**	1.36	Market Capitalization(B)	$58.423	Beta	1.21
Trailing 12-Month EPS	$1.25	S&P Oper. EPS 2009**E**	1.60	Yield (%)	Nil	S&P 3-Yr. Proj. EPS CAGR(%)	13.00
Trailing 12-Month P/E	20.9	P/E on S&P Oper. EPS 2008**E**	19.2	Dividend Rate/Share	Nil	S&P Credit Rating	A-
$10K Invested 5 Yrs Ago	$9,133	Common Shares Outstg. (M)	2,235.9	Institutional Ownership (%)	72		

Price Performance

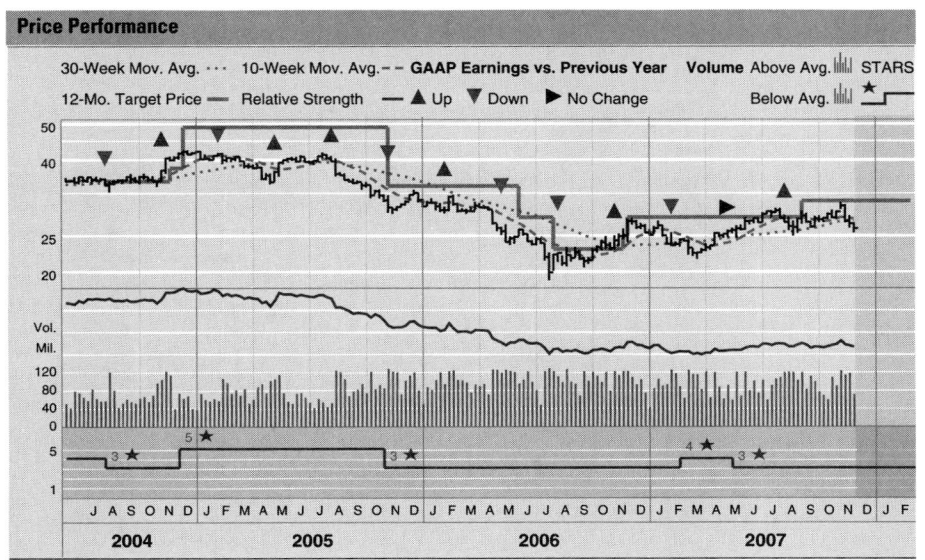

30-Week Mov. Avg. ···· 10-Week Mov. Avg. – – **GAAP Earnings vs. Previous Year** Volume Above Avg. STARS
12-Mo. Target Price — Relative Strength — ▲ Up ▼ Down ▶ No Change Below Avg. ★

Options: ASE, CBOE, P, Ph

Analysis prepared by **Thomas W. Smith, CFA** on September 04, 2007, when the stock traded at **$ 28.51**.

Highlights

➤ We forecast revenue to increase 4% for FY 08 (Jan.) and 4% for FY 09, compared with an estimated rise of 2% for FY 07. We believe results will be positively affected by new corporate strategy changes, such as introducing new products for consumers and small businesses, and by broadening distribution through the retail channels. Also, we think sales will be aided somewhat by increased adoption of Vista operating software, especially when enterprises upgrade from prior versions of Windows.

➤ We see gross margins widening to about 19.5% in FY 08, from 17% expected in FY 07, on improving supply chain management, lower component costs, and a favorable product mix. We estimate that FY 08 SG&A expenses will increase as a percentage of revenue, as new investments related to customer service are likely to be completed, partially offset by head count reductions in other areas.

➤ We project FY 08 EPS of $1.36 and $1.60 for FY 09, up from our FY 07 estimate of $1.15. We believe that additional share repurchases are unlikely, pending the resolution of a formal SEC probe.

Investment Rationale/Risk

➤ Our hold opinion reflects uncertainty related to Dell's change in management and strategy. While we view new products and attempts to expand in retail channels as pluses, we believe Dell faces challenges in the PC market. We see faster industry growth coming from consumers and the retail stores, where Dell is not as well positioned as some competitors. We expect further market share erosion due to stronger growth in international markets, whereas Dell's strength has been in the U.S.

➤ Risks to our recommendation and target price include market share losses, a slowdown in technology spending, and slower adoption of Windows Vista than we project. Although an Audit Committee investigation into accounting matters was completed on August 16, 2007, indicating what we view as small amounts of EPS ($0.02 to $0.07) to be restated for past periods, a formal SEC investigation is ongoing and could produce additional findings.

➤ Applying a target P/E multiple of 21X, toward the low end of the historical range, to our 12-month forward EPS estimate of $1.48, we arrive at our 12-month target price of $31.

Qualitative Risk Assessment

LOW	MEDIUM	HIGH

Our risk assessment reflects our view of Dell's solid balance sheet and strong execution in asset management, offset by what we see as heightened competitive pressures from peers over the past year.

Quantitative Evaluations

S&P Quality Ranking B+

D	C	B-	B	B+	A-	A	A+

Relative Strength Rank MODERATE

47

LOWEST = 1 HIGHEST = 99

Revenue/Earnings Data

Revenue (Million $)

	1Q	2Q	3Q	4Q	Year
2008	14,722	14,776	--	--	--
2007	14,320	14,211	14,419	14,470	57,420
2006	13,386	13,428	13,911	15,183	55,908
2005	11,540	11,706	12,502	13,457	49,205
2004	9,532	9,778	10,622	11,512	41,444
2003	8,066	8,459	9,144	9,735	35,404

Earnings Per Share ($)

2008	0.34	0.33	E0.35	E0.35	E1.36
2007	0.34	0.21	0.27	0.32	1.14
2006	0.37	0.41	0.25	0.43	1.46
2005	0.28	0.31	0.33	0.26	1.18
2004	0.23	0.34	0.26	0.29	1.01
2003	0.17	0.19	0.21	0.23	0.80

Fiscal year ended Jan. 31. Next earnings report expected: NA. EPS Estimates based on S&P Operating Earnings; historical GAAP earnings are as reported.

Dividend Data

No cash dividends have been paid.

Please read the Required Disclosures and Analyst Certification on the last page of this report.

The McGraw-Hill Companies

Dell Inc

STANDARD &POOR'S

Business Summary September 04, 2007

CORPORATE OVERVIEW. We view Dell as a key player in the global market for information technology (IT). According to data from IDC, a market researcher based in Framingham, MA, IT spending growth is slowing to a five-year compound annual rate (CAGR) of about 6%, from double digit rates last decade, partly reflecting the law of large numbers, but also due to intense pricing pressure in many key categories, especially computer hardware.

Computer hardware comprises about 40% of total IT spending, according to IDC, with PCs accounting for approximately 70% of this category. While leading computer hardware manufacturers have been grappling with plunging PC prices over the past decade, Dell has been leading this charge, in our opinion, and we think it has emerged as a key force with which all computer hardware vendors have had to reckon.

Dell's share of the global PC market, recently at 17.1%, is up dramatically from 10.5% earlier in the decade, but below 2005's 18.2%. In servers, Dell commands the number three spot (based on global system revenues). The majority of Dell's sales are from PCs (61%), but other categories are increasingly important to sales, such as servers (9%), services (10%), storage (4%), and software and peripherals (16%).

IMPACT OF MAJOR DEVELOPMENTS. In January 2007, Michael Dell reassumed his role as CEO, while retaining his duties as chairman of the board. We are encouraged by this development, as we think it will reinvigorate the corporate culture and streamline the decision-making process. In August 2006, the company announced a recall of up to 4.1 million battery packs manufactured by Sony Corp. (SNE). While it is difficult to calculate the total amount, we believe that SNE is likely to be responsible for the majority of the relevant expenses.

Company Financials Fiscal Year Ended Jan. 31

Per Share Data ($)	2007	2006	2005	2004	2003	2002	2001	2000	1999	1998
Tangible Book Value	1.60	1.77	2.61	2.46	1.89	1.80	2.16	2.06	0.91	0.50
Cash Flow	1.34	1.62	1.32	1.11	0.88	0.54	0.90	0.67	0.56	0.34
Earnings	1.14	1.46	1.18	1.01	0.80	0.46	0.81	0.61	0.53	0.32
S&P Core Earnings	1.13	1.03	0.88	0.68	0.49	0.28	0.58	NA	NA	NA
Dividends	Nil	Nil	Nil	Nil	Nil	Nil	Nil	Nil	Nil	Nil
Payout Ratio	Nil	Nil	Nil	Nil	Nil	Nil	Nil	Nil	Nil	Nil
Calendar Year	2006	2005	2004	2003	2002	2001	2000	1999	1998	1997
Prices:High	30.77	42.30	42.57	37.18	31.06	31.32	59.69	55.00	37.91	12.98
Prices:Low	21.61	28.62	31.14	22.59	21.90	16.01	16.25	31.37	9.92	3.12
P/E Ratio:High	27	29	36	37	39	68	74	90	73	41
P/E Ratio:Low	19	20	26	22	27	35	20	51	19	10

Income Statement Analysis (Million $)										
Revenue	55,472	55,908	49,205	41,444	35,404	31,168	31,888	25,265	18,243	12,327
Operating Income	3,541	4,740	4,588	3,807	3,055	2,510	3,008	2,613	2,149	1,383
Depreciation	471	393	334	263	211	239	240	156	103	67.0
Interest Expense	45.0	28.0	16.0	14.0	17.0	29.0	47.0	34.0	Nil	3.00
Pretax Income	3,345	4,574	4,445	3,724	3,027	1,731	3,194	2,451	2,084	1,368
Effective Tax Rate	22.8%	21.9%	31.5%	29.0%	29.9%	28.0%	30.0%	32.0%	29.9%	31.0%
Net Income	2,583	3,572	3,043	2,645	2,122	1,246	2,236	1,666	1,460	944
S&P Core Earnings	2,563	2,494	2,227	1,806	1,356	781	1,602	NA	NA	NA

Balance Sheet & Other Financial Data (Million $)										
Cash	9,546	7,042	4,747	4,317	4,232	3,641	4,910	3,809	3,181	1,844
Current Assets	19,939	17,706	16,897	10,633	8,924	7,877	9,491	7,681	6,339	3,912
Total Assets	25,635	23,109	23,215	19,311	15,470	13,535	13,435	11,471	6,877	4,268
Current Liabilities	17,791	15,927	14,136	10,896	8,933	7,519	6,543	5,192	3,695	2,697
Long Term Debt	569	504	505	505	506	520	509	508	512	17.0
Common Equity	4,328	4,129	6,485	6,280	4,873	4,694	5,622	5,308	2,321	1,293
Total Capital	5,008	4,633	6,990	6,785	5,379	5,214	6,131	5,816	2,833	1,310
Capital Expenditures	896	728	525	329	305	303	482	397	296	187
Cash Flow	3,054	3,965	3,377	2,908	2,333	1,485	2,476	1,822	1,563	1,011
Current Ratio	1.1	1.1	1.2	1.0	1.0	1.0	1.5	1.5	1.7	1.5
% Long Term Debt of Capitalization	11.4	10.9	7.2	7.4	9.4	10.0	8.3	8.7	18.1	1.3
% Net Income of Revenue	4.5	6.4	6.2	6.4	6.0	4.0	7.0	6.6	8.0	7.7
% Return on Assets	10.6	15.4	14.3	15.2	14.6	9.2	18.0	18.2	26.2	26.0
% Return on Equity	61.1	67.3	47.7	47.4	44.4	24.2	40.9	43.7	80.8	89.9

Data as orig reptd.; bef. results of disc opers/spec. items. Per share data adj. for stk. divs.; EPS diluted. E-Estimated. NA-Not Available. NM-Not Meaningful. NR-Not Ranked. UR-Under Review.

Office: One Dell Way, Round Rock, TX 78682.
Telephone: 512-338-4400.
Email: investor_relations_fulfillment@dell.com
Website: http://www.dell.com

Chrmn & CEO: M.S. Dell
Vice Chrmn & CFO: D.J. Carty
SVP & General Counsel: L. Tu
Investor Contact: L.A. Tyson (512-723-1130)

Board Members: D. J. Carty, M. S. Dell, W. H. Gray, III, S. L. Krawcheck, A. Lafley, J. C. Lewent, T. W. Luce, III, K. S. Luft, A. J. Mandl, M. A. Miles, S. A. Nunn, Jr.

Founded: 1984
Domicile: Delaware
Employees: 90,500

Developers Diversified Realty Corp

STANDARD &POOR'S

S&P Recommendation	**BUY** ★★★★☆	Price $43.10 (as of Nov 23, 2007)	12-Mo. Target Price $57.00	Investment Style Large-Cap Blend

GICS Sector Financials
Sub-Industry Retail REITS

Summary This self-administered and self-managed real estate investment trust acquires, develops, leases and manages shopping centers across the U.S.

Key Stock Statistics (Source S&P, Vickers, company reports)

52-Wk Range	$72.33–42.15	S&P FFO/Sh. 2007E	3.83	Market Capitalization(B)	$5.295	Beta	0.72
Trailing 12-Month FFO/Share	NA	S&P FFO/Sh. 2008E	4.05	Yield (%)	6.13	S&P 3-Yr. FFO/Sh. Proj. CAGR(%)	6.00
Trailing 12-Month P/FFO	NA	P/FFO on S&P FFO/Sh. 2007E	11.3	Dividend Rate/Share	$2.64	S&P Credit Rating	BBB
$10K Invested 5 Yrs Ago	$24,604	Common Shares Outstg. (M)	122.9	Institutional Ownership (%)	88		

Price Performance

30-Week Mov. Avg. ···· 10-Week Mov. Avg. ── **GAAP Earnings vs. Previous Year** Volume Above Avg. ▮▮▮ STARS
12-Mo. Target Price ── Relative Strength ── ▲ Up ▼ Down ► No Change Below Avg. ▮▮▮ ★

Options: P

Analysis prepared by **Robert McMillan** on October 31, 2007, when the stock traded at **$ 50.22**.

Highlights

➤ We expect DDR to continue to benefit from its strategy of operating shopping centers. We look for total revenues, after rising 24% in 2006, to advance about 18% in 2007 and 6% in 2008, driven by acquisitions and organic growth.

➤ We believe that moderate retail sales growth and continuing retailer expansion will bolster results. We see occupancy rates remaining at healthy levels. The core portfolio was 95.9% leased as of September 30, 2007, down slightly from 96.1% last year. We expect strong demand for space to enable the trust to continue to achieve moderate rent increases on new leases and renewals of expiring leases. During the September quarter, rental rates on new leases and renewal leases increased 11.3%. We look for DDR's increasing international expansion to contribute to the long-term growth and diversity of the portfolio.

➤ We estimate operating EPS of $1.10 for 2007 and $1.80 for 2008. Our FFO projections are $3.83 per share for 2007 and $4.05 for 2008. We see fourth-quarter 2007 FFO of $0.85.

Investment Rationale/Risk

➤ We think investors in DDR will benefit from the company's position as one of the largest owners and managers of shopping centers in the U.S., and from the company's established relationships with numerous retailers, which should allow it to continue to generate robust growth. We also view DDR's success in acquiring and integrating new shopping centers and re-developing existing sites as a positive to our valuation of the shares.

➤ Risks to our recommendation and target price include slower-than-expected growth in retailer expansion, a large increase in shopping center supply, and sharply higher interest rates.

➤ The shares recently traded at 13.5X DDR's trailing 12-month FFO. The stock and the multiple fell sharply between May and August, but have rebounded recently, in our opinion, on easing interest rate concerns. Our 12-month target price of $57 is 14.7X our forward 12-month FFO estimate of $3.88. We think that continued improvements in operating trends and a gradual easing of concerns about the residential property market will allow the multiple to expand modestly to a level still considerably below its historical peak.

Qualitative Risk Assessment

LOW	MEDIUM	HIGH

Our risk assessment for DDR reflects its position as one of the largest owners of shopping centers in the U.S., its broad customer and geographic base, and our view of its strong financial condition.

Quantitative Evaluations

S&P Quality Ranking A-

D	C	B-	B	B+	A-	A	A+

Relative Strength Rank WEAK
20
LOWEST = 1   HIGHEST = 99

Revenue/FFO Data

Revenue (Million $)

	1Q	2Q	3Q	4Q	Year
2007	230.4	279.5	234.1	--	--
2006	200.6	198.3	204.8	214.4	818.1
2005	171.9	176.3	180.5	198.5	727.2
2004	123.2	146.9	164.0	164.8	598.9
2003	102.6	123.2	123.9	126.4	476.1
2002	85.42	85.25	92.09	94.49	357.2

FFO Per Share ($)

	1Q	2Q	3Q	4Q	Year
2007	0.91	0.89	0.80	E0.85	E3.83
2006	0.78	0.99	0.83	0.82	1.81
2005	0.90	0.84	0.74	0.74	2.08
2004	0.71	0.84	0.72	0.69	2.95
2003	0.61	0.64	0.59	0.68	2.51
2002	0.64	0.62	0.61	0.64	2.50

Fiscal year ended Dec. 31. Next earnings report expected: NA. FFO Estimates based on S&P Funds From Operations Est..

Dividend Data (Dates: mm/dd Payment Date: mm/dd/yy)

Amount ($)	Date Decl.	Ex-Div. Date	Stk. of Record	Payment Date
0.660	02/16	03/21	03/23	04/09/07
0.660	05/21	06/18	06/20	07/03/07
0.660	08/17	09/20	09/24	10/02/07
0.660	11/19	12/19	12/21	01/08/08

Dividends have been paid since 1993. Source: Company reports.

Developers Diversified Realty Corp

STANDARD
&POOR'S

Business Summary October 31, 2007

CORPORATE OVERVIEW. Developers Diversified Realty Corp., a self-administered and self-managed REIT, acquires, develops, redevelops, owns, leases and manages shopping centers and business centers. At December 31, 2006, the trust's portfolio consisted of 467 shopping centers (167 of which are owned through joint ventures) and seven business centers The shopping centers consist of 446 community shopping centers, 17 enclosed mini-malls and four lifestyle centers. The company also owned over 1,170 undeveloped acres primarily located adjacent to some of the shopping centers.

The trust's shopping centers are designed to attract local area customers, and are typically anchored by one or more discount department stores .They often include a supermarket, drug store, junior department store and/or other major discount retailer as additional anchors. The shopping centers are typically anchored by two or more strong national tenant anchors such as Wal-Mart, Kohl's, Target, Home Depot or Lowe's Home Improvement and two or more medium-sized national big-box tenants such as Best Buy, Bed Bath & Beyond, TJ Maxx or Michaels.

CORPORATE STRATEGY. For DDR, location and the financial health and growth of its retail tenants are among the most important factors affecting the success of its portfolio, in our view. Further, we believe the companies in this industry enjoy relatively high barriers to entry, since developing new shopping centers requires large amounts of capital as well as time-consuming regulatory approval, which has been difficult to obtain in the recent past amid concerns about traffic and pollution. We expect DDR to continue to derive numerous growth opportunities from being large and having a well-located and varied array of shopping center formats and relationships with a broad array of retailers, which should allow DDR to cross-promote its properties and generate growth from the introduction of new retail concepts.

Company Financials Fiscal Year Ended Dec. 31

Per Share Data ($)	2006	2005	2004	2003	2002	2001	2000	1999	1998	1997
Tangible Book Value	16.44	17.12	23.42	12.35	9.63	8.92	8.64	9.15	9.69	9.30
Earnings	1.69	1.91	2.17	2.28	1.14	1.17	1.31	0.95	1.00	1.03
S&P Core Earnings	1.69	1.92	2.17	2.27	1.09	1.15	NA	NA	NA	NA
Dividends	2.36	2.16	1.94	1.69	1.52	1.48	1.44	1.38	0.98	1.26
Payout Ratio	140%	113%	89%	74%	133%	126%	110%	145%	98%	123%
Prices:High	66.36	49.49	45.85	33.90	23.65	19.38	16.25	18.50	21.47	20.63
Prices:Low	46.96	38.74	30.80	21.22	17.25	12.88	11.00	12.31	15.88	17.13
P/E Ratio:High	39	26	21	15	21	17	12	19	21	20
P/E Ratio:Low	28	20	14	9	15	11	8	13	16	17

Income Statement Analysis (Million $)										
Rental Income	753	523	439	348	330	291	261	242	214	159
Mortgage Income	Nil	Nil	Nil	Nil	Nil	Nil	Nil	Nil	Nil	Nil
Total Income	818	727	599	476	357	322	286	264	228	10.3
General Expenses	174	153	119	105	73.1	59.3	47.5	69.7	33.0	27.0
Interest Expense	222	182	130	89.7	76.8	81.8	77.0	68.0	57.2	35.6
Provision for Losses	Nil	Nil	Nil	Nil	Nil	Nil	Nil	Nil	Nil	NA
Depreciation	192	165	132	94.4	77.7	64.5	54.2	52.0	43.2	32.3
Net Income	168	176	262	167	101	92.4	101	87.0	78.8	67.5
S&P Core Earnings	184	210	212	189	71.2	64.4	NA	NA	NA	NA

Balance Sheet & Other Financial Data (Million $)										
Cash	28.4	30.7	49.9	11.7	16.4	19.1	4.24	6.00	2.30	Nil
Total Assets	7,180	6,863	5,584	3,941	2,777	2,497	2,332	2,321	2,127	1,392
Real Estate Investment	7,442	7,029	5,603	3,885	2,804	2,494	2,162	2,068	1,897	1,398
Loss Reserve	Nil	Nil	Nil	Nil	Nil	Nil	Nil	Nil	Nil	Nil
Net Investment	6,581	6,337	5,035	3,427	2,395	2,142	1,865	1,818	2,041	NA
Short Term Debt	429	Nil	Nil	Nil	207	158	261	183	81.1	4.60
Capitalization:Debt	3,820	3,832	2,478	2,083	1,292	1,151	967	969	919	669
Capitalization:Equity	1,791	1,865	1,849	1,079	642	530	480	852	599	519
Capitalization:Total	6,438	6,533	5,088	3,745	2,452	2,235	1,986	2,037	1,963	1,333
% Earnings & Depreciation/Assets	5.1	5.4	8.3	7.8	6.8	6.5	6.7	6.3	5.7	8.4
Price Times Book Value:High	4.0	2.9	1.9	2.7	2.5	2.2	1.9	2.0	2.2	2.2
Price Times Book Value:Low	2.9	2.3	1.3	1.7	1.8	1.4	1.3	1.4	1.6	1.8

Data as orig reptd.; bef. results of disc opers/spec. items. Per share data adj. for stk. divs.; EPS diluted. E-Estimated. NA-Not Available. NM-Not Meaningful. NR-Not Ranked. UR-Under Review.

Office: 3300 Enterprise Parkway, Beachwood, OH 44122.
Telephone: 216-755-5500.
Email: ir@ddrc.com
Website: http://www.ddr.com

Chrmn & CEO: S.A. Wolstein
Pres & COO: D.M. Jacobstein
Sr EVP: D.B. Hurwitz
EVP & CFO: W.H. Schafer

SVP & Chief Acctg Officer: C.A. Vesy
Trustees: D. S. Adler, T. R. Ahern, R. H. Gidel, V. B. MacFarlane, C. Macnab, S. D. Roulston, B. A. Sholem, W. B. Summers, Jr., S. A. Wolstein

Founded: 1965
Domicile: Ohio
Employees: 641

Devon Energy Corp

STANDARD &POOR'S

S&P Recommendation	HOLD ★★★☆☆	Price	12-Mo. Target Price	Investment Style
		$85.34 (as of Nov 23, 2007)	$97.00	Large-Cap Blend

GICS Sector Energy
Sub-Industry Oil & Gas Exploration & Production

Summary This independent oil and gas exploration and production company has grown through its acquisitions of Ocean Energy, Mitchell Energy, Anderson Exploration and Chief Holdings.

Key Stock Statistics (Source S&P, Vickers, company reports)

52-Wk Range	$94.75– 62.80	S&P Oper. EPS 2007**E**	6.30	Market Capitalization(B)	$37.973	Beta	0.53
Trailing 12-Month EPS	$6.36	S&P Oper. EPS 2008**E**	8.51	Yield (%)	0.66	S&P 3-Yr. Proj. EPS CAGR(%)	28.30
Trailing 12-Month P/E	13.4	P/E on S&P Oper. EPS 2007**E**	13.5	Dividend Rate/Share	$0.56	S&P Credit Rating	BBB
$10K Invested 5 Yrs Ago	$38,888	Common Shares Outstg. (M)	445.0	Institutional Ownership (%)	83		

Price Performance

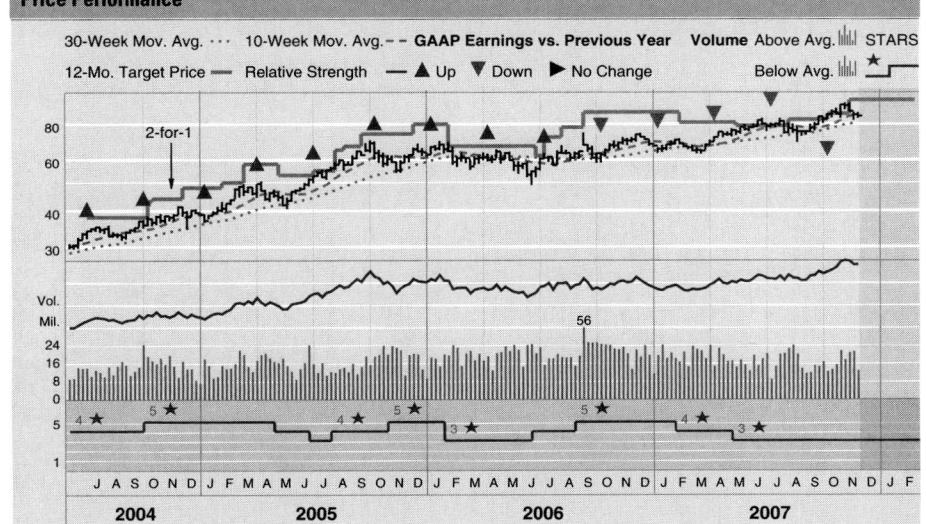

Options: ASE, CBOE, P

Analysis prepared by **Tina J. Vital** on November 20, 2007, when the stock traded at **$ 86.81**.

Highlights

➤ Third quarter oil and gas production rose 9.6%, to 56.8 million boe, above our expectations, reflecting organic growth and the June 2006 Chief Holdings LLC acquisition. Based on upwardly revised guidance from DVN, we project volume growth of about 4% in 2007 and over 9% in 2008, reflecting strong prospects in the Gulf of Mexico and the Barnett Shale. In reaction to recent royalty hikes in western Canada by the government of Alberta, DVN is reviewing its options and may shift certain of its operations elsewhere in Canada or the U.S.

➤ DVN is selling international assets with lower growth prospects. In October, DVN completed the sale of its Egyptian operations for $375 million, and is in the process of divesting its operations in West Africa. In November, DVN decided not to proceed with its plans to form a publicly traded master limited partnership (MLP), due to changing financial market conditions.

➤ We expect after-tax operating earnings to increase more than 6% in 2007 and over 30% in 2008, reflecting improved production.

Investment Rationale/Risk

➤ We believe recent discoveries have shifted DVN's focus to organic production growth, from restructuring of historical acquisitions. We estimate that the successful production test of the deepwater Jack #2 well (DVN has a 25% working interest) in the Gulf of Mexico's Lower Tertiary Trend in 2006, and its Miocene-age discovery on the Mission Deep prospect (50%) in the Gulf of Mexico, have raised the company's production growth prospects through 2015, while its Chief Holdings acquisition has increased its presence and production outlook in the Barnett Shale.

➤ Risks to our recommendation and target price include changes in economic, industry and operating conditions, such as rising costs and difficulty in organically replacing reserves.

➤ A blend of our discounted cash flow ($100; assuming a WACC of 8.0% and a terminal growth rate of 3%) and relative valuations leads us to our 12-month target of $97. This represents an expected enterprise value of 5.4X our 2008 EBITDA estimate, a discount to peers.

Qualitative Risk Assessment

LOW	MEDIUM	HIGH

Our risk assessment for DVN reflects our view of its position as a large independent exploration and production company focused on stable, lower risk assets located in North America, offset by exposure to economic, commodity price and operational risk.

Quantitative Evaluations

S&P Quality Ranking   A-

D	C	B-	B	B+	A-	A	A+

Relative Strength Rank   STRONG

79

LOWEST = 1   HIGHEST = 99

Revenue/Earnings Data

Revenue (Million $)

	1Q	2Q	3Q	4Q	Year
2007	2,473	2,929	2,763	--	--
2006	2,684	2,589	2,696	2,609	10,578
2005	2,351	2,468	2,704	3,218	10,741
2004	2,238	2,219	2,267	2,465	9,189
2003	1,671	1,813	1,948	1,921	7,352
2002	903.0	1,149	1,031	1,233	4,316

Earnings Per Share ($)

2007	1.27	1.82	1.43	E1.95	E6.30
2006	1.56	1.92	1.57	1.26	6.29
2005	1.14	1.38	1.63	2.14	6.26
2004	1.00	1.01	1.04	1.35	4.38
2003	1.29	0.81	0.86	1.13	4.00
2002	0.20	-0.65	0.35	0.25	0.16

Fiscal year ended Dec. 31. Next earnings report expected: Early February. EPS Estimates based on S&P Operating Earnings; historical GAAP earnings are as reported.

Dividend Data (Dates: mm/dd Payment Date: mm/dd/yy)

Amount ($)	Date Decl.	Ex-Div. Date	Stk. of Record	Payment Date
0.113	12/04	12/13	12/15	12/29/06
0.140	03/07	03/13	03/15	03/30/07
0.140	06/01	06/13	06/15	06/29/07
0.140	09/04	09/12	09/14	09/28/07

Dividends have been paid since 1993. Source: Company reports.

Devon Energy Corp

STANDARD
&POOR'S

Business Summary November 20, 2007

CORPORATE OVERVIEW. Devon Energy Corp. (DVN) is an independent exploration and production company primarily engaged in the exploration, development and production of oil and natural gas; the acquisition of producing properties; the transportation of oil, natural gas and natural gas liquids (NGLs); and the processing of natural gas. The company began operations as a private company in 1971, and its common stock began trading publicly in 1988.

The company operates oil and gas properties in the U.S. (61% of 2006 earnings from continuing operations before income taxes), Canada (19%), and internationally (20%). U.S. operations focus on fields in the Barnett Shale in north central Texas, Carthage in east Texas, the Permian Basin in west Texas and southeast New Mexico, Washakie in southern Wyoming, Groesbeck in east Texas, and offshore the deepwater Gulf of Mexico. Canadian operations focus on developments such as the thermal heavy oil Jackfish project in the nonconventional oil sands of east central Alberta, the Deep Basin in west central Alberta and east central British Columbia, Lloydminster in eastern Alberta and western Saskatchewan, Peace River Arch in west central Alberta, and other projects in northeastern British Columbia and northwestern Alberta. Opera-

tions outside North America include Azerbaijan, Brazil and China.

Proved oil and gas reserves rose 13% in 2006, to 2.376 billion boe (59% natural gas; 90% North America; 70% developed). However, total oil and gas production declined 4.5%, to 214 million boe (64% natural gas) in 2006, reflecting the sale of non-core assets in the 2005 first half.

MARKET PROFILE. DVN was one of the first independent oil and gas exploration and production companies to successfully implement an "acquire and exploit" strategy via aggressive implementation of repeatable development drilling techniques. The company has since modified this strategy to include different geologic formations and geographic locations. However, the core goal of establishing a repeatable drilling program in each basin remains.

Company Financials Fiscal Year Ended Dec. 31

Per Share Data ($)	2006	2005	2004	2003	2002	2001	2000	1999	1998	1997
Tangible Book Value	26.09	20.31	16.30	11.50	3.20	4.32	11.03	16.03	5.40	8.41
Cash Flow	11.73	10.87	8.95	8.10	4.04	3.54	5.37	2.65	0.66	2.49
Earnings	6.29	6.26	4.38	4.00	0.16	0.17	2.75	0.73	-0.63	1.09
S&P Core Earnings	6.29	6.01	4.30	3.99	0.47	0.09	NA	NA	NA	NA
Dividends	0.45	0.30	0.20	0.10	0.10	0.10	0.10	0.10	0.10	0.10
Payout Ratio	7%	5%	5%	3%	63%	59%	4%	14%	NM	9%
Prices:High	74.75	70.35	41.64	29.40	26.55	33.38	32.37	22.47	20.56	24.56
Prices:Low	48.94	36.48	25.90	21.23	16.94	15.28	15.69	10.06	13.06	13.69
P/E Ratio:High	12	11	10	7	NM	NM	12	31	NM	23
P/E Ratio:Low	8	6	6	5	NM	NM	6	14	NM	13

Income Statement Analysis (Million $)										
Revenue	10,578	10,741	9,189	7,352	4,316	3,075	2,784	734	388	306
Operating Income	6,938	7,290	6,038	4,589	2,403	2,350	2,094	491	237	209
Depreciation, Depletion and Amortization	2,442	2,191	2,290	1,793	1,211	876	693	254	124	85.3
Interest Expense	421	533	475	504	533	220	154	66.9	22.6	0.27
Pretax Income	4,012	4,552	3,293	2,245	-134	84.0	1,142	160	-75.8	121
Effective Tax Rate	29.6%	35.6%	33.6%	22.9%	NM	35.7%	36.0%	40.8%	NM	38.0%
Net Income	2,823	2,930	2,186	1,731	59.0	54.0	730	94.6	-60.3	75.3
S&P Core Earnings	2,815	2,801	2,136	1,715	147	22.9	NA	NA	NA	NA

Balance Sheet & Other Financial Data (Million $)										
Cash	739	1,606	2,119	1,273	292	193	228	167	19.2	42.1
Current Assets	3,212	4,206	3,583	2,364	1,064	1,081	934	417	111	93.2
Total Assets	35,063	30,273	29,736	27,162	16,225	13,184	6,860	4,623	1,226	846
Current Liabilities	4,645	2,934	3,100	2,071	1,042	919	629	227	80.7	30.8
Long Term Debt	5,568	5,957	7,031	8,635	7,562	6,589	2,049	1,787	555	Nil
Common Equity	17,441	14,999	13,673	11,055	4,652	3,258	3,276	2,024	523	544
Total Capital	28,660	26,362	25,505	24,061	14,842	11,990	5,953	4,204	1,111	795
Capital Expenditures	7,551	4,090	3,103	2,587	3,426	5,326	1,280	315	376	130
Cash Flow	5,255	5,111	4,466	3,514	1,260	920	1,414	345	63.6	161
Current Ratio	0.7	1.4	1.2	1.1	1.0	1.2	1.5	1.8	1.4	3.0
% Long Term Debt of Capitalization	19.4	22.6	27.6	35.9	51.0	55.0	34.4	42.5	49.9	Nil
% Return on Assets	8.6	9.7	7.7	8.0	NM	0.5	11.3	3.2	NM	9.5
% Return on Equity	17.4	20.3	17.6	21.9	NM	1.3	24.9	7.1	NM	14.8

Data as orig reptd.; bef. results of disc opers/spec. items. Per share data adj. for stk. divs.; EPS diluted. E-Estimated. NA-Not Available. NM-Not Meaningful. NR-Not Ranked. UR-Under Review.

Office: 20 N Broadway, Oklahoma City, OK 73102-8260.
Telephone: 405-235-3611.
Website: http://www.devonenergy.com
Chrmn & CEO: J.L. Nichols

Pres: J. Richels
SVP & General Counsel: L.C. Taylor
VP & Chief Acctg Officer: D.J. Heatly
VP & Cntlr: R.A. Marcum

Investor Contact: V. White (405-552-4526)
Board Members: T. F. Ferguson, D. M. Gavrin, J. A. Hill, R. L. Howard, W. J. Johnson, M. M. Kanovsky, J. T. Mitchell, J. L. Nichols, J. Richels

Founded: 1988
Domicile: Delaware
Employees: 4,600

The McGraw-Hill Companies

Dillard's Inc.

STANDARD &POOR'S

| **S&P Recommendation** HOLD ★★★☆☆ | **Price** $17.46 (as of Nov 26, 2007) | **12-Mo. Target Price** $19.00 | **Investment Style** Large-Cap Value |

GICS Sector Consumer Discretionary
Sub-Industry Department Stores

Summary Dillard's operates about 331 department stores, located primarily in the South and the Midwest.

Key Stock Statistics (Source S&P, Vickers, company reports)

52-Wk Range	$40.56– 15.52	S&P Oper. EPS 2008E	0.65	Market Capitalization(B)	$1.328	Beta	1.35
Trailing 12-Month EPS	$2.00	S&P Oper. EPS 2009E	0.75	Yield (%)	0.92	S&P 3-Yr. Proj. EPS CAGR(%)	11.00
Trailing 12-Month P/E	8.7	P/E on S&P Oper. EPS 2008E	26.9	Dividend Rate/Share	$0.16	S&P Credit Rating	BB
$10K Invested 5 Yrs Ago	$10,888	Common Shares Outstg. (M)	80.1	Institutional Ownership (%)	95		

Price Performance

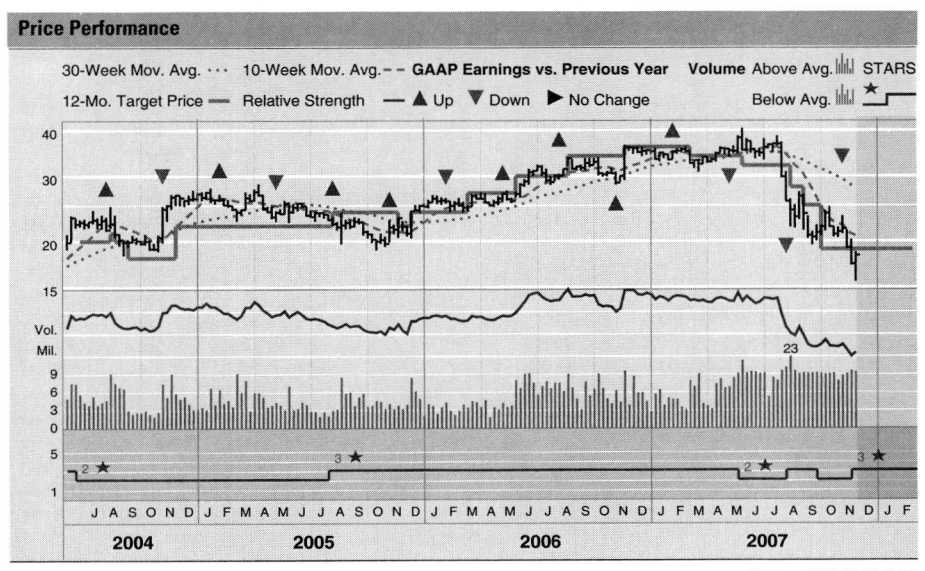

30-Week Mov. Avg. ··· 10-Week Mov. Avg. -- **GAAP Earnings vs. Previous Year** Volume Above Avg. STARS
12-Mo. Target Price — Relative Strength — ▲ Up ▼ Down ► No Change Below Avg.

Options: ASE, CBOE, P, Ph

Analysis prepared by **Jason N. Asaeda** on November 26, 2007, when the stock traded at **$ 17.60**.

Highlights

► Balancing our view of a challenging retail environment against DDS's ongoing efforts to increase differentiation in its assortments by offering more upscale and contemporary choices, we see low to mid-single digit same-store sales declines in both FY 08 (Jan.) and FY 09. In FY 08, we anticipate flat net square footage growth as DDS plans to open nine stores, including one replacement unit, expand one existing location, and close 11 stores. Our expectation is for a modest increase in square footage during FY 09. Taking into account these factors, we project net sales of $7.2 billion in FY 08 and $7.1 billion in FY 09.

► We expect increased sales penetration of higher margin exclusive brand merchandise, and we look for the company to exercise more disciplined inventory planning and management. However, we also see DDS taking higher markdowns in response to competitive pressures, and we anticipate limited expense leverage on weak same-store sales.

► Factoring in likely share buybacks, we see operating EPS of $0.65 in FY 08 and $0.75 in FY 09.

Investment Rationale/Risk

► This fiscal year, we look for DDS to begin leveraging systems investments to align merchandise assortments closer to local market preferences, and to better plan store level inventory and expense. However, we do not expect the company's market positioning to improve, due to perceived ongoing execution risk in merchandising; heightened promotional activity by Macy's Inc. (M: hold, $29) and other competitors; and its concentration of stores in the Midwest and Southeast, including about 45 of its 331 stores in Florida, where we believe retail conditions are particularly challenging.

► Risks to our recommendation and target price include sales shortfalls due to changes in consumer confidence and increased promotional activity by competitors. With regard to DDS's corporate governance practices, we are concerned about a non-shareholder approved "poison pill" and the non-disclosure of specific performance criteria and hurdle rates for equity incentive awards.

► Our 12-month target price of $19 is based on our discounted cash flow analysis, which assumes a weighted average cost of capital of 9.3% and a terminal growth rate of 2.5%.

Qualitative Risk Assessment

| LOW | MEDIUM | HIGH |

Our risk assessment reflects our view of DDS's improving sales and profit margins, driven by successful turnaround initiatives, offset by its history of what we consider inconsistent results under the Dillard's family's management.

Quantitative Evaluations

S&P Quality Ranking   B+

| D | C | B- | B | B+ | A- | A | A+ |

Relative Strength Rank   WEAK

16

LOWEST = 1   HIGHEST = 99

Revenue/Earnings Data

Revenue (Million $)

	1Q	2Q	3Q	4Q	Year
2008	1,799	1,649	1,674	--	--
2007	1,837	1,688	1,722	2,459	7,810
2006	1,803	1,692	1,727	2,338	7,560
2005	1,854	1,671	1,699	2,304	7,529
2004	1,814	1,721	1,764	2,299	7,599
2003	1,911	1,818	1,794	2,388	7,911

Earnings Per Share ($)

	1Q	2Q	3Q	4Q	Year
2008	0.53	-0.31	-0.15	E0.67	E0.65
2007	0.77	0.20	0.17	1.90	3.05
2006	0.46	-0.15	-0.03	1.24	1.49
2005	0.64	-0.31	-0.23	1.30	1.41
2004	0.29	-0.60	-0.19	0.61	0.11
2003	0.68	0.15	-0.07	0.85	1.60

Fiscal year ended Jan. 31. Next earnings report expected: Late February. EPS Estimates based on S&P Operating Earnings; historical GAAP earnings are as reported.

Dividend Data (Dates: mm/dd Payment Date: mm/dd/yy)

Amount ($)	Date Decl.	Ex-Div. Date	Stk. of Record	Payment Date
0.040	03/06	03/28	03/30	05/01/07
0.040	05/30	06/27	06/29	08/01/07
0.040	09/04	09/26	09/28	11/01/07
0.040	11/21	12/27	12/31	02/04/08

Dividends have been paid since 1969. Source: Company reports.

Please read the Required Disclosures and Analyst Certification on the last page of this report.

The McGraw-Hill Companies

Dillard's Inc.

STANDARD &POOR'S

Business Summary November 26, 2007

Dillard's is an outgrowth of a department store originally founded in 1938 by William Dillard. As of November 3, 2007, the company operated 331 traditional department stores offering fashion apparel and home furnishings in 29 states. The heaviest concentrations of stores are in the Southwest, the Southeast and the Midwest.

Given a highly competitive retail environment, DDS has adopted a number of strategies intended to improve its profitability. In FY 06 (Jan.), the company began to increase its emphasis on nationally known contemporary and better lines, and to expand its exclusive brand lines such as Antonio Melani, Gianni Bini, and Daniel Cremieux.

DDS continues to focus on improving its merchandise mix, eliminating and replacing underperforming products from both national and exclusive sources with more promising brands, and tailoring its assortments to local demographics. Exclusive brand merchandise accounted for 23.8% of sales in FY 07, down slightly from 24.0% in FY 06.

Company Financials Fiscal Year Ended Jan. 31

Per Share Data ($)	2007	2006	2005	2004	2003	2002	2001	2000	1999	1998
Tangible Book Value	63.72	29.08	27.51	26.35	26.25	25.02	25.06	22.68	20.39	25.76
Cash Flow	6.80	5.37	5.01	3.67	5.21	4.49	4.40	4.31	3.47	4.09
Earnings	3.05	1.49	1.41	0.11	1.60	0.35	1.06	1.55	1.26	2.31
S&P Core Earnings	3.06	1.23	0.72	-0.03	1.01	0.71	0.92	NA	NA	NA
Dividends	0.16	0.16	0.16	0.16	0.16	0.16	0.16	0.16	0.16	0.16
Payout Ratio	5%	11%	11%	145%	10%	46%	15%	10%	13%	7%
Calendar Year	2006	2005	2004	2003	2002	2001	2000	1999	1998	1997
Prices:High	36.47	28.60	27.50	17.80	31.20	22.50	20.81	37.44	44.50	44.75
Prices:Low	23.94	18.91	15.21	12.32	12.94	11.44	9.43	17.75	26.50	28.00
P/E Ratio:High	12	19	20	NM	20	64	20	24	35	19
P/E Ratio:Low	8	13	11	NM	8	33	9	11	21	12

Income Statement Analysis (Million $)	2007	2006	2005	2004	2003	2002	2001	2000	1999	1998
Revenue	7,810	7,560	7,529	7,599	7,911	8,155	8,567	8,921	7,797	6,632
Operating Income	641	604	645	538	429	386	469	640	441	554
Depreciation	301	304	302	297	306	314	303	293	240	200
Interest Expense	112	106	139	181	183	190	224	237	197	129
Pretax Income	266	136	185	16.0	211	112	141	284	219	410
Effective Tax Rate	7.73%	10.5%	36.2%	41.6%	35.4%	41.0%	31.2%	42.3%	38.4%	37.1%
Net Income	246	121	118	9.34	136	65.8	97.0	164	135	258
S&P Core Earnings	246	100	60.6	-2.90	85.8	60.1	83.8	NA	NA	NA

Balance Sheet & Other Financial Data (Million $)	2007	2006	2005	2004	2003	2002	2001	2000	1999	1998
Cash	194	300	498	161	142	153	194	199	72.0	42.0
Current Assets	2,048	2,150	2,293	3,024	3,130	2,815	2,843	3,424	3,438	2,998
Total Assets	5,408	5,517	5,692	6,411	6,676	7,075	7,199	7,918	8,178	5,592
Current Liabilities	977	1,147	1,045	1,336	886	928	877	811	1,094	1,099
Long Term Debt	1,185	1,291	1,543	2,073	2,743	2,677	2,906	3,452	3,562	1,378
Common Equity	2,587	2,341	2,325	2,237	2,264	2,668	2,630	2,832	2,840	2,807
Total Capital	4,225	4,110	4,377	4,927	5,007	5,989	6,175	6,986	7,084	4,493
Capital Expenditures	321	456	285	227	233	271	226	247	248	509
Cash Flow	547	426	420	307	442	379	400	457	375	458
Current Ratio	2.1	1.9	2.2	2.3	3.5	3.0	3.2	4.2	3.1	2.7
% Long Term Debt of Capitalization	31.4	31.4	35.3	42.1	54.8	44.7	47.1	49.4	50.3	30.6
% Net Income of Revenue	3.2	1.6	1.6	0.1	1.7	0.8	1.1	1.9	1.7	3.9
% Return on Assets	4.5	2.2	1.9	0.1	2.0	0.9	1.3	2.0	2.0	4.8
% Return on Equity	10.0	5.2	5.2	0.4	5.5	2.5	3.6	5.8	4.8	9.3

Data as orig reptd.; bef. results of disc opers/spec. items. Per share data adj. for stk. divs.; EPS diluted. E-Estimated. NA-Not Available. NM-Not Meaningful. NR-Not Ranked. UR-Under Review.

Office: 1600 Cantrell Rd, Little Rock, AR 72201-1145.
Telephone: 501-376-5200.
Website: http://www.dillards.com
Chrmn & CEO: W. Dillard, II

Pres: A. Dillard
Investor Contact: J.I. Freeman
SVP & CFO: J.I. Freeman
VP, Secy & General Counsel: P.J. Schroeder, Jr.

Board Members: R. C. Connor, D. Corbusier, W. D. Davis, A. Dillard, M. J. Dillard, W. Dillard, II, J. I. Freeman, J. P. Hammerschmidt, P. R. Johnson, W. A. Stephens, W. H. Sutton, J. C. Watts, Jr.

Founded: 1938
Domicile: Delaware
Employees: 51,385

The McGraw-Hill Companies

DIRECTV Group Inc (The)

STANDARD &POOR'S

S&P Recommendation	HOLD ★★★★★	Price	12-Mo. Target Price	Investment Style
		$23.68 (as of Nov 29, 2007)	$30.00	Large-Cap Blend

GICS Sector Consumer Discretionary
Sub-Industry Broadcasting & Cable TV

Summary This company is the larger of the two major U.S. providers of direct broadcast satellite (DBS) television service, with over 16.5 million subscribers across the U.S., and nearly 3.1 million in Latin America.

Key Stock Statistics (Source S&P, Vickers, company reports)

52-Wk Range	$27.73– 20.73	S&P Oper. EPS 2007**E**	1.19	Market Capitalization(B)	$27.419	Beta	0.89
Trailing 12-Month EPS	$1.20	S&P Oper. EPS 2008**E**	1.46	Yield (%)	Nil	S&P 3-Yr. Proj. EPS CAGR(%)	16.00
Trailing 12-Month P/E	19.7	P/E on S&P Oper. EPS 2007**E**	19.9	Dividend Rate/Share	Nil	S&P Credit Rating	BBB
$10K Invested 5 Yrs Ago	$28,618	Common Shares Outstg. (M)	1,157.9	Institutional Ownership (%)	55		

Price Performance

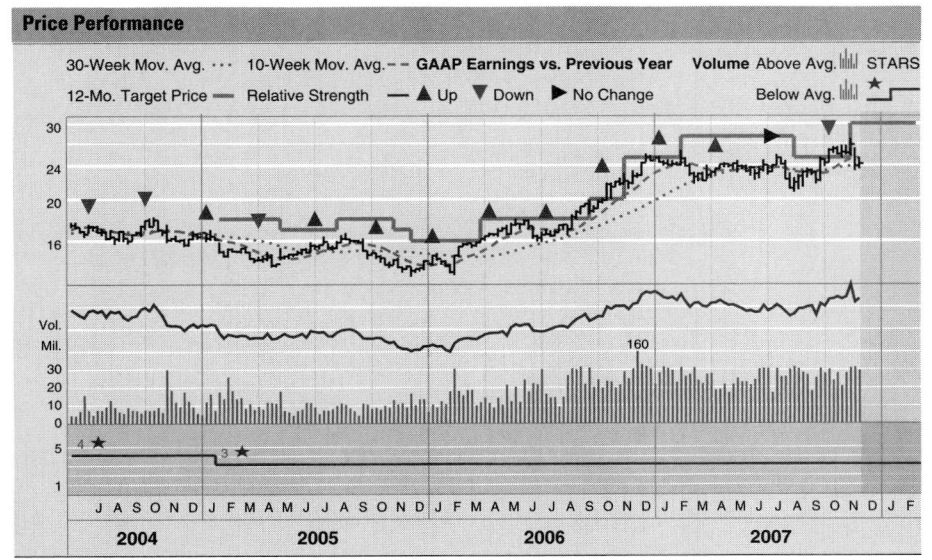

Options: ASE, CBOE, P, Ph

Analysis prepared by **Tuna N. Amobi, CFA, CPA** on November 29, 2007, when the stock traded at **$ 23.70**.

Highlights

► After a projected 3.9 million in 2007, we see DTV U.S. gross adds of nearly 4.2 million in 2008. With improved average monthly churn on a credit tightening, we expect net adds of about 900,000 and 1 billion in the respective years, reaching about 17.8 million U.S. subscribers by the end of 2008, with the strongest gains in the direct sales channel. Aided by advanced services, we project nearly 6% annual growth in average revenue per U.S. subscriber. Including growing ad revenues and relatively modest contributions from DTV Latin America, we forecast about 17% and 12% total revenue growth in 2007 and 2008, respectively.

► We see higher programming costs on the NFL Sunday Ticket, as well as further increases in subscriber acquisition costs (SAC) and retention/upgrade expenses, with a continued penetration of advanced HD and DVR boxes.

► Including the benefit from an accounting change under a new lease program, we project total EBITDA of about $4.2 billion in 2007 and nearly $4.8 billion in 2008. With significantly higher D&A expense on new satellites, we forecast EPS of $1.19 in 2007 and $1.46 in 2008.

Investment Rationale/Risk

► In early November, DTV posted what we saw as notable all-around improvements in key operating metrics for the 2007 third quarter. It said more than half of over 1 million gross adds in the quarter took advanced offerings, likely aided by a continued aggressive rollout of HD channels. We also saw what we view as the most remarkable operating turnaround strides yet at DTV Latin America. Separately, a pending transfer of a 38.4% DTV controlling stake to Liberty Media (LINTA: $20) (LCAPA: $111) from News Corp (NWS: buy, $21; NWS.A: buy, $20) could close in 2007, subject to regulatory approvals. We view DTV as highly underleveraged, providing significant financial flexibility.

► Risks to our recommendation and target price include uncertainties with the proposed change of control, increased competition from cable's bundled offerings, and higher-than-projected SAC and upgrade/retention expenses.

► Our 12-month target price is $30, based on enterprise value per subscriber relative to DBS peer Echostar (DISH: sell, $43). We see accelerating free cash flow starting in 2008, as DTV wraps its satellite expansion program.

Qualitative Risk Assessment

LOW	MEDIUM	HIGH

Our risk assessment reflects what we view as ample financial flexibility, and a projected acceleration of free cash flow, offset by increased competition from cable operators' bundled offerings, and uncertainties with a planned change in control.

Quantitative Evaluations

S&P Quality Ranking B-

D	C	B-	B	B+	A-	A	A+

Relative Strength Rank MODERATE

52

LOWEST = 1   HIGHEST = 99

Revenue/Earnings Data

Revenue (Million $)

	1Q	2Q	3Q	4Q	Year
2007	3,908	4,135	4,327	--	--
2006	3,386	3,520	3,667	4,183	14,756
2005	3,148	3,188	3,233	3,596	13,165
2004	2,493	2,643	2,862	3,362	11,360
2003	2,227	2,371	2,570	2,953	9,372
2002	2,038	2,210	2,214	2,473	8,935

Earnings Per Share ($)

	1Q	2Q	3Q	4Q	Year
2007	0.27	0.36	0.27	E0.31	E1.19
2006	0.17	0.36	0.30	0.29	1.12
2005	-0.03	0.10	0.07	0.09	0.22
2004	0.13	-0.01	-0.67	-0.20	-0.77
2003	-0.04	0.02	0.04	-0.22	-0.27
2002	-0.14	-0.14	-0.01	0.06	-0.21

Fiscal year ended Dec. 31. Next earnings report expected: Early February. EPS Estimates based on S&P Operating Earnings; historical GAAP earnings are as reported.

Dividend Data

No cash dividends have been paid since 1997.

Please read the Required Disclosures and Analyst Certification on the last page of this report.

The McGraw-Hill Companies

DIRECTV Group Inc (The)

STANDARD &POOR'S

Business Summary November 29, 2007

CORPORATE OVERVIEW. The DIRECTV Group (formerly Hughes Electronics) is a leading provider of direct broadcast satellite (DBS) television service, providing hundreds of digital video and audio channels to over 16.5 million monthly subscribers in the U.S., and a selection of local and international programming to nearly 3.1 million subscribers in Latin America (mostly in Brazil, Argentina, Venezuela and Puerto Rico). DTV distributes its services mainly through direct sales and retail channels, and through co-branding partnerships with three of the four RBOCs. In November 2006, Liberty Media (LINTA: $20, NR) (LCAPA: $111, NR) agreed to acquire News Corp.'s (NWS: buy, $21; NWS.A: buy, $20) 38.4% controlling stake in the company, as a key part of a nearly $12 billion asset swap expected to close by the end of 2007, subject to necessary approvals.

CORPORATE STRATEGY. We see several key strategic initiatives to launch enhanced features and services. These include an aggressive expansion of local and national high-definition (HD) offerings, and a transition from MPEG-2 to MPEG-4 HD and DVR receivers. After the launch of the DIRECTV 10 satellite in June 2007, and a planned launch of DIRECTV 11 in 2008, we see ample capacity to offer a wide breadth of HD programming. Other recent initiatives include expanded availability of on-demand programming from TV networks, broadband video, games, enhanced program guides, home networked DVRs, and portable devices. Already with a contract extension through the NFL's 2010 season, we view DTV's exclusive NFL Sunday Ticket as the epicenter of its sports programming package.

In June 2007, DTV and DBS peer Echostar simultaneously unveiled distribution pacts to offer WiMax-based wireless high-speed broadband service from Clearwire (CLWR: $12, NR), which in turn will offer their DBS video services. Expected to launch in 2007, the deal contemplates each company offering data, video and voice services in CLWR's current and future markets. Earlier, in 2004, the company divested assets such as Hughes Networks Systems and PanAmSat, and separately DTV Latin America emerged from a bankruptcy reorganization.

Company Financials Fiscal Year Ended Dec. 31

Per Share Data ($)	2006	2005	2004	2003	2002	2001	2000	1999	1998	1997
Tangible Book Value	1.10	2.17	1.61	4.36	2.76	NM	4.20	6.78	15.16	17.10
Cash Flow	1.93	0.83	-0.16	0.27	0.88	0.50	0.73	0.55	0.61	0.58
Earnings	1.12	0.22	-0.77	-0.27	-0.21	-0.55	-0.34	-0.35	0.23	0.36
S&P Core Earnings	1.05	0.20	-0.96	-0.32	-0.78	-0.86	NA	NA	NA	NA
Dividends	Nil	Nil	Nil	Nil	Nil	Nil	Nil	Nil	Nil	0.33
Payout Ratio	Nil	Nil	Nil	Nil	Nil	Nil	Nil	Nil	Nil	93%
Prices:High	25.57	17.01	18.81	16.91	17.55	28.00	46.67	32.54	19.29	22.98
Prices:Low	13.28	13.17	14.70	9.40	8.00	11.50	21.33	12.83	10.13	11.92
P/E Ratio:High	23	77	NM	NM	NM	NM	NM	NM	85	64
P/E Ratio:Low	12	60	NM	NM	NM	NM	NM	NM	45	33

Income Statement Analysis (Million $)										
Revenue	14,756	13,165	11,360	9,372	8,935	8,262	7,288	5,560	5,964	5,128
Operating Income	3,274	1,441	-1,281	617	668	390	594	219	683	582
Depreciation	1,034	853	838	755	1,067	1,148	948	647	434	296
Interest Expense	246	238	132	156	336	196	218	123	112	33.1
Pretax Income	542	480	-1,734	-478	-140	-990	-816	-660	191	618
Effective Tax Rate	NM	36.1%	NM	NM	NM	NM	NM	NM	23.4%	38.3%
Net Income	1,420	305	-1,056	-375	-213	-614	-355	-391	260	470
S&P Core Earnings	1,336	279	-1,312	-439	-862	-923	NA	NA	NA	NA

Balance Sheet & Other Financial Data (Million $)										
Cash	2,499	3,701	2,830	1,720	1,129	700	1,508	238	1,342	2,784
Current Assets	4,556	6,096	4,771	10,356	3,656	3,341	4,154	3,858	3,846	4,806
Total Assets	15,141	15,630	14,324	18,978	17,885	19,210	19,279	18,597	13,435	12,764
Current Liabilities	3,323	2,828	2,695	5,840	3,203	4,407	2,691	2,642	2,010	1,483
Long Term Debt	3,395	3,405	2,410	2,435	2,390	989	1,292	1,586	779	638
Common Equity	6,681	7,940	7,507	9,631	9,063	9,574	10,830	10,194	8,382	8,312
Total Capital	10,138	11,395	9,965	12,305	12,590	13,339	14,941	14,501	10,286	10,128
Capital Expenditures	1,754	889	1,023	444	566	799	939	472	344	251
Cash Flow	2,455	1,158	-218	380	808	438	496	205	694	766
Current Ratio	1.4	2.2	1.8	1.8	1.1	0.8	1.5	1.5	1.9	3.2
% Long Term Debt of Capitalization	33.5	29.9	24.2	19.8	19.0	7.4	8.6	10.9	7.6	6.3
% Net Income of Revenue	9.6	2.3	NM	NM	NM	NM	NM	NM	4.4	9.2
% Return on Assets	9.2	2.0	NM	NM	NM	NM	NM	NM	2.0	5.5
% Return on Equity	19.4	3.9	NM	NM	NM	NM	NM	NM	3.1	8.7

Data as orig reptd.; bef. results of disc opers/spec. items. Per share data adj. for stk. divs.; EPS diluted. E-Estimated. NA-Not Available. NM-Not Meaningful. NR-Not Ranked. UR-Under Review.

Office: 2230 E Imperial Hwy, El Segundo, CA 90245-3531.
Telephone: 310-964-5000.
Website: http://www.directv.com
Chrmn: K.R. Murdoch

Pres & CEO: C. Carey
EVP & CFO: M.W. Palkovic
SVP, Chief Acctg Officer, Treas & Cntlr: P.T. Doyle
Investor Contact: J. Rubin (212-462-5200)

Board Members: N. R. Austrian, R. F. Boyd, Jr., C. Carey, P. Chernin, J. M. Cornelius, D. F. DeVoe, C. R. Lee, P. A. Lund, K. R. Murdoch, N. Newcomb, H. Saban

Founded: 1977
Domicile: Delaware
Employees: 11,200

Discover Financial Services Inc

STANDARD &POOR'S

S&P Recommendation HOLD ★★★☆☆	**Price** $16.68 (as of Nov 23, 2007)	**12-Mo. Target Price** $26.00	**Investment Style** Large-Cap Growth

GICS Sector Financials
Sub-Industry Consumer Finance

Summary Discover Financial Services is the fourth-largest network and sixth-largest card issuer in the U.S. The company offers credit and prepaid cards and provides payment processing services to merchants and financial institutions.

Key Stock Statistics (Source S&P, Vickers, company reports)

52-Wk Range	$32.17– 15.72	S&P Oper. EPS 2007**E**	1.63	Market Capitalization(B)	$7.966	Beta	**NA**
Trailing 12-Month EPS	**NA**	S&P Oper. EPS 2008**E**	1.78	Yield (%)	**NA**	S&P 3-Yr. Proj. EPS CAGR(%)	**NA**
Trailing 12-Month P/E	**NM**	P/E on S&P Oper. EPS 2007**E**	10.2	Dividend Rate/Share	**NA**	S&P Credit Rating	**NA**
$10K Invested 5 Yrs Ago	**NA**	Common Shares Outstg. (M)	477.6	Institutional Ownership (%)	37		

Price Performance

- 30-Week Mov. Avg. ···
- 10-Week Mov. Avg. ‒ ‒
- **GAAP Earnings vs. Previous Year**
- Volume Above Avg. ▐░▐ STARS
- 12-Mo. Target Price ‒
- Relative Strength ‒
- ▲ Up ▼ Down ▶ No Change
- Below Avg. ▐▐ ★

Options: ASE, CBOE, P

Analysis prepared by **Frank Braden, CFA** on October 11, 2007, when the stock traded at **$ 22.63**.

Highlights

➤ We expect receivables growth of around 5% in FY 08 (Nov.), at the low end of management's guidance of 4% to 8%, reflecting an uncertain credit environment. In light of the difficult credit environment and liquidity issues surrounding its securitizations, DFS has strengthened is balance sheet, raising its short-term liquidity position from $5 billion at the end of June to $8 billion at the end of August.

➤ We forecast moderate growth in U.S. charge-offs, but believe DFS has taken steps in anticipation of the turn in the credit environment and continues to focus on lending to the prime credit segment and strengthening its collection abilities. Although the U.K. economy is showing some signs of moderation in bankruptcy, the country is still struggling with high consumer debt and a weak housing market. We expect cost reduction efforts and modifications to its rewards program will help offset some of the earnings pressure from its U.K. business.

➤ We estimate EPS of $1.63 in FY 07 and $1.78 in FY 08.

Investment Rationale/Risk

➤ Recent deals with Chase Paymentech Solutions, Wells Fargo Merchant Services and Bank of America Merchant Services will give DFS acquiring agreements with firms representing over 90% of the U.S. industry's sales volume. We expect the weak environment in the U.K. to be a drag on earnings in the near term, and view the lack of global diversification as both a risk and potential growth opportunity for DFS going forward. Over the long term, we expect DFS to benefit from the continuing migration of purchasers from cash payment to debit and credit cards.

➤ Risks to our recommendation and target price include possible deterioration in U.S. consumer confidence that would have an impact on consumer spending, further credit issues in the U.K., and a rise in unemployment that would pressure credit quality.

➤ Our 12-month target price of $26 values the stock at 14.6X our FY 08 EPS estimate. This multiple represents a discount to peers, reflecting what we see as DFS's conservative managed loan growth and its U.S. and U.K. credit exposure.

Qualitative Risk Assessment

LOW	MEDIUM	HIGH

Our risk assessment reflects what we see as solid business fundamentals and a growing merchant base. Our view is tempered by DFS's exposure to consumer spending habits and the U.S. economy.

Quantitative Evaluations

S&P Quality Ranking NR

D	C	B-	B	B+	A-	A	A+

Relative Strength Rank WEAK

17

LOWEST = 1   HIGHEST = 99

Revenue/Earnings Data

Revenue (Million $)

	1Q	2Q	3Q	4Q	Year
2007	1,541	1,575	1,601	--	--
2006	--	--	--	--	6,211
2005	--	--	--	--	--
2004	--	--	--	--	--
2003	--	--	--	--	--
2002	--	--	--	--	--

Earnings Per Share ($)

	1Q	2Q	3Q	4Q	Year
2007	0.42	0.44	0.42	E0.32	E1.63
2006	--	--	--	--	1.89
2005	--	--	--	--	--
2004	--	--	--	--	--
2003	--	--	--	--	--
2002	--	--	--	--	--

Fiscal year ended Nov. 30. Next earnings report expected: NA. EPS Estimates based on S&P Operating Earnings; historical GAAP earnings are as reported.

Dividend Data (Dates: mm/dd Payment Date: mm/dd/yy)

Amount ($)	Date Decl.	Ex-Div. Date	Stk. of Record	Payment Date
0.060	09/25	10/03	10/05	10/23/07

Dividends have been paid since 2007. Source: Company reports.

Please read the Required Disclosures and Analyst Certification on the last page of this report.

The **McGraw-Hill** Companies

Discover Financial Services Inc

**STANDARD
&POOR'S**

Business Summary October 11, 2007

CORPORATE OVERVIEW. Discover Financial Services (DFS), formerly a business segment of Morgan Stanley, is a credit card issuer and electronic payment services company. DFS offers credit and prepaid cards and other financial products and services to qualified customers in the United States and United Kingdom, and provides payment processing and related services to merchants and financial institutions in the United States. DFS manages its operations through three business segments: U.S. Card, International Card, and Third-Party Payments. The U.S. Card segment is the major contributor to the company, in terms of income before income taxes. The International Card segment contributes a marginal percentage to the total, while the Third-Party Payments segment has been unprofitable since the company's inception.

The U.S. Card segment offers Discover Card-branded credit cards issued to more than 50 million individuals and small businesses over the Discover Network, which is the company's proprietary credit card network in the United States. The segment also includes DFS's other consumer products and services businesses, including prepaid and other consumer lending and deposit products offered primarily through the company's Discover Bank subsidiary.

The company entered the debit card business in 2006, allowing banks to offer Discover-branded debit cards.

The International Card segment offers consumer finance products and services in the United Kingdom. The products include Morgan Stanley-branded, Goldfish-branded and various affinity-branded credit cards issued on the MasterCard and Visa networks. The company also has reciprocity alliances with card issuers in Japan (JCB) and China (China Union Pay).

The Third-Party Payments segment includes PULSE and the company's third-party payments business. PULSE, an automated teller machine (ATM), debit and electronic funds transfer network, serves more than 4,400 financial institutions and includes nearly 260,000 ATMs, as well as point-of-sale terminals nationwide.

Company Financials Fiscal Year Ended Nov. 30

Per Share Data ($)	2006	2005	2004	2003	2002	2001	2000	1999	1998	1997
Tangible Book Value	NA	NA	NA	NA	NA	NA	NA	NA	NA	NA
Earnings	1.89	NA	NA	NA	NA	NA	NA	NA	NA	NA
S&P Core Earnings	2.26	1.21	NA	NA	NA	NA	NA	NA	NA	NA
Dividends	Nil	NA	NA	NA	NA	NA	NA	NA	NA	NA
Payout Ratio	NA	NA	NA	NA	NA	NA	NA	NA	NA	NA
Prices:High	NA	NA	NA	NA	NA	NA	NA	NA	NA	NA
Prices:Low	NA	NA	NA	NA	NA	NA	NA	NA	NA	NA
P/E Ratio:High	NA	NA	NA	NA	NA	NA	NA	NA	NA	NA
P/E Ratio:Low	NA	NA	NA	NA	NA	NA	NA	NA	NA	NA

Income Statement Analysis (Million $)										
Net Interest Income	1,459	NA	NA	NA	NA	NA	NA	NA	NA	NA
Tax Equivalent Adjustment	NA	NA	NA	NA	NA	NA	NA	NA	NA	NA
Non Interest Income	3,539	NA	NA	NA	NA	NA	NA	NA	NA	NA
Loan Loss Provision	756	NA	NA	NA	NA	NA	NA	NA	NA	NA
% Expense/Operating Revenue	55.5%	NA	NA	NA	NA	NA	NA	NA	NA	NA
Pretax Income	1,467	NA	NA	NA	NA	NA	NA	NA	NA	NA
Effective Tax Rate	31.8%	NA	NA	NA	NA	NA	NA	NA	NA	NA
Net Income	1,001	NA	NA	NA	NA	NA	NA	NA	NA	NA
% Net Interest Margin	NA	NA	NA	NA	NA	NA	NA	NA	NA	NA
S&P Core Earnings	1,078	578	NA	NA	NA	NA	NA	NA	NA	NA

Balance Sheet & Other Financial Data (Million $)										
Money Market Assets	Nil	NA	NA	NA	NA	NA	NA	NA	NA	NA
Investment Securities	86.0	NA	NA	NA	NA	NA	NA	NA	NA	NA
Commercial Loans	111	NA	NA	NA	NA	NA	NA	NA	NA	NA
Other Loans	21,707	NA	NA	NA	NA	NA	NA	NA	NA	NA
Total Assets	32,403	NA	NA	NA	NA	NA	NA	NA	NA	NA
Demand Deposits	86.0	NA	NA	NA	NA	NA	NA	NA	NA	NA
Time Deposits	21,042	NA	NA	NA	NA	NA	NA	NA	NA	NA
Long Term Debt	1,706	NA	NA	NA	NA	NA	NA	NA	NA	NA
Common Equity	5,425	NA	NA	NA	NA	NA	NA	NA	NA	NA
% Return on Assets	NM	NA	NA	NA	NA	NA	NA	NA	NA	NA
% Return on Equity	NM	NA	NA	NA	NA	NA	NA	NA	NA	NA
% Loan Loss Reserve	3.5	NA	NA	NA	NA	NA	NA	NA	NA	NA
% Loans/Deposits	NM	NA	NA	NA	NA	NA	NA	NA	NA	NA
% Equity to Assets	NM	NA	NA	NA	NA	NA	NA	NA	NA	NA

Data as orig reptd.; bef. results of disc opers/spec. items. Per share data adj. for stk. divs.; EPS diluted. 2006 data pro forma; bal. sheet as of Feb. 28 '07. E-Estimated. NA-Not Available. NM-Not Meaningful. NR-Not Ranked. UR-Under Review.

Office: 2500 Lake Cook Road, Riverwoods, IL 60015.
Telephone: 224-405-0900.
Website: http://www.discoverfinancial.com
Chrmn: D.D. Dammerman

Pres & COO: R.C. Hochschild
CEO: D.W. Nelms
EVP & CFO: R.A. Guthrie
EVP & CTO: D.E. Offereins

Investor Contact: C. Streem (224-405-4555)
Board Members: J. S. Aronin, M. K. Bush, D. D. Dammerman, R. W. Devlin, D. H. Komansky, P. A. Laskawy, D. W. Nelms, M. L. Rankowitz, L. A. Weinbach

Founded: 1960
Domicile: Delaware
Employees: 14,000

The McGraw-Hill Companies

Walt Disney Co (The)

STANDARD &POOR'S

S&P Recommendation	**STRONG BUY** ★★★★★	Price $32.69 (as of Nov 28, 2007)	12-Mo. Target Price $45.00	Investment Style Large-Cap Growth

GICS Sector Consumer Discretionary
Sub-Industry Movies & Entertainment

Summary This media and entertainment conglomerate has diversified global operations in theme parks, motion pictures, and television broadcasting and merchandise licensing.

Key Stock Statistics (Source S&P, Vickers, company reports)

52-Wk Range	$36.79–30.68	S&P Oper. EPS 2008E	2.21	Market Capitalization(B)	$62.225	Beta	1.31
Trailing 12-Month EPS	$2.25	S&P Oper. EPS 2009E	2.50	Yield (%)	1.07	S&P 3-Yr. Proj. EPS CAGR(%)	13.00
Trailing 12-Month P/E	14.5	P/E on S&P Oper. EPS 2008E	14.8	Dividend Rate/Share	$0.35	S&P Credit Rating	A
$10K Invested 5 Yrs Ago	NA	Common Shares Outstg. (M)	1,903.5	Institutional Ownership (%)	65		

Price Performance

30-Week Mov. Avg. ··· 10-Week Mov. Avg. -- **GAAP Earnings vs. Previous Year** Volume Above Avg. STARS
12-Mo. Target Price — Relative Strength — ▲ Up ▼ Down ▶ No Change Below Avg. ★

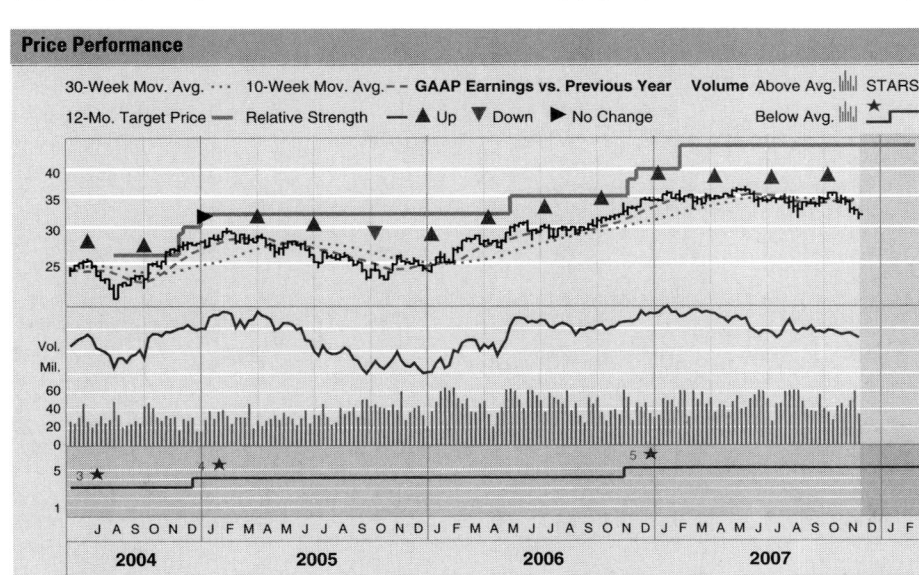

Options: ASE, CBOE, P, Ph

Analysis prepared by **Tuna N. Amobi, CFA, CPA** on November 28, 2007, when the stock traded at **$ 32.69**.

Highlights

➤ Reflecting the divestiture of ABC Radio in June 2007, we project DIS's consolidated revenues will increase 6.0% in FY 08 (Sep.), and 5.5% in FY 09, and reach about $39.7 billion, mainly driven by continued ad and affiliate revenue gains at the media networks, and relatively healthy traffic at the worldwide theme parks. Also, we see further gains in worldwide merchandise licensing revenues, with continued difficult film comparisons expected to ease by FY 09. DIS should also benefit from solid growth in Internet revenues, which likely topped $700 million in FY 07.

➤ We assume relatively modest margin expansion through FY 09, as reduced cost pressures at the parks, improved results at ABC, and cost savings at the film studio are partly offset by higher NFL sports programming costs, and further investments in new media initiatives and development of video games.

➤ From about $7.3 billion in FY 07, we estimate total operating income will climb to $7.9 billion and $8.3 billion in FY 08, respectively. With ample capacity for continued share buybacks, we forecast EPS of $2.21 in FY 08 and $2.50 in FY 09.

Investment Rationale/Risk

➤ In early November, DIS reported what we saw as encouraging FY 07 results which, despite difficult film comparisons and some non-recurring costs, showed healthy underlying trends in several key businesses. Extended park promotions could help to sustain current attendance levels. Key franchises should contribute strongly to the holiday season and beyond, including Pirates, High School Musical and Ratatouille. We see a continued healthy TV ad market, reflecting the upfront and scatter markets. With ample financial flexibility, we view DIS's balance as among the strongest in its peer group.

➤ Risks to our recommendation and target price include the potential adverse impact of a sharp slowdown in consumer discretionary spending (for advertising and park attendance); uncertainties with an ongoing entertainment writers' strike; an inherent film volatility; and heightened geopolitical anxieties.

➤ Our 12-month target price of $45 is derived from our sum-of-the parts valuation analysis, which reflects relative enterprise values for the various business segments. The stock offers a modest 1.0% dividend yield.

Qualitative Risk Assessment

LOW	**MEDIUM**	HIGH

Our risk assessment reflects the strength of the company's content-oriented media and entertainment brands, counterbalanced by a relatively high exposure to cyclical advertising-related and theme park businesses.

Quantitative Evaluations

S&P Quality Ranking A-

D	C	B-	B	B+	**A-**	A	A+

Relative Strength Rank MODERATE

59

LOWEST = 1 HIGHEST = 99

Revenue/Earnings Data

Revenue (Million $)

	1Q	2Q	3Q	4Q	Year
2007	9,581	7,954	9,045	8,930	35,510
2006	8,854	8,027	8,620	8,784	34,285
2005	8,666	7,829	7,715	7,734	31,944
2004	8,549	7,189	7,471	7,543	30,752
2003	7,170	6,500	6,377	7,014	27,061
2002	7,016	5,856	5,795	6,662	25,329

Earnings Per Share ($)

2007	0.79	0.43	0.58	0.44	2.33
2006	0.37	0.37	0.53	0.36	1.64
2005	0.33	0.31	0.39	0.20	1.24
2004	0.33	0.26	0.29	0.25	1.12
2003	0.06	0.15	0.24	0.20	0.65
2002	0.21	0.13	0.18	0.09	0.60

Fiscal year ended Sep. 30. Next earnings report expected: Early February. EPS Estimates based on S&P Operating Earnings; historical GAAP earnings are as reported.

Dividend Data (Dates: mm/dd Payment Date: mm/dd/yy)

Amount ($)	Date Decl.	Ex-Div. Date	Stk. of Record	Payment Date
0.310	11/28	12/13	12/15	01/12/07
Stk.	05/29	06/13	06/06	06/12/07
0.350	11/28	12/05	12/07	01/11/08

Dividends have been paid since 1957. Source: Company reports.

Walt Disney Co (The)

STANDARD &POOR'S

Business Summary November 28, 2007

CORPORATE OVERVIEW. The Walt Disney Co. is a leading media conglomerate with key operations in theme parks, television, filmed entertainment and merchandise licensing. Theme Parks and Resorts (30% of FY 07 (Sep.) revenues) includes the company's best known assets: Disney World and Disneyland parks in Orlando, FL, and Anaheim, CA, respectively; the Disney Cruise Line; Euro Disney, Paris (39%-owned); and Hong Kong Disneyland (43%-owned).

Media Networks (42% of revenues) includes the ABC broadcast network; 10 television stations; and cable networks ESPN (80%-owned), The Disney Channel, ABC Family and Lifetime (50%). In November 2006, DIS sold its 39.5% stake in the E! cable network to Comcast for $1.23 billion. Studio entertainment (21% of revenues) includes the film, television and home video businesses under the Walt Disney, Touchstone and Miramax brands. Consumer products (6% of revenues) includes merchandise licensing, children's book publishing, video game development, and 104 retail stores mainly in Europe (the 315-store U.S. chain is operated by specialty retailer Children's Place under a licensing deal).

CORPORATE STRATEGY. As a content-oriented company, DIS's top strategic

priorities include creativity and innovation, international expansion, and leveraging new technology applications. Under CEO Robert Iger, we see senior management aggressively exploring new avenues to offer its branded content, characters and entertainment franchises across emerging digital platforms such as broadband and wireless, while making further investments in other areas such as video games. Recent initiatives include: a deal to provide content from its ABC networks and the film studios on Apple's video iPod, the launch of Disney Mobile cellular phone service, and an ad-supported streaming of ABC's shows.

In July 2006, DIS unveiled a restructuring of its studio division, with more focus on Disney-branded films, and a sharp reduction in its annual slate (to 10 live-action/animation films plus two to three Touchstone titles). It has aggressively expanded its Disney Channel in the past few years, and in September 2005, opened Hong Kong Disneyland.

Company Financials Fiscal Year Ended Sep. 30

Per Share Data ($)	2007	2006	2005	2004	2003	2002	2001	2000	1999	1998
Tangible Book Value	3.15	3.10	3.24	3.15	2.01	1.78	3.99	2.24	2.59	1.75
Cash Flow	3.08	2.40	1.93	1.69	1.17	1.11	0.89	1.48	2.22	2.70
Earnings	2.33	1.64	1.24	1.12	0.65	0.60	0.11	0.57	0.62	0.89
S&P Core Earnings	NA	1.69	1.27	1.04	0.49	0.29	0.21	NA	NA	NA
Dividends	0.31	0.27	0.24	0.21	0.21	0.21	0.21	0.21	0.21	0.19
Payout Ratio	13%	16%	19%	19%	32%	35%	191%	37%	34%	21%
Prices:High	36.79	34.89	29.99	28.41	23.80	25.17	34.80	43.88	38.69	42.79
Prices:Low	30.68	23.77	22.89	20.88	14.84	13.48	15.50	26.00	23.38	22.50
P/E Ratio:High	16	21	24	25	37	42	NM	77	62	48
P/E Ratio:Low	13	14	18	19	23	22	NM	46	38	25

Income Statement Analysis (Million $)										
Revenue	35,510	34,285	31,944	30,752	27,061	25,329	25,269	25,402	23,402	22,976
Operating Income	8,272	6,914	5,446	5,258	3,790	3,426	4,586	5,043	7,010	7,533
Depreciation	1,491	1,436	1,339	1,210	1,077	1,042	1,754	2,195	3,323	3,754
Interest Expense	593	592	605	629	666	453	417	558	717	685
Pretax Income	7,725	5,447	3,987	3,739	2,254	2,190	1,283	2,633	2,314	3,157
Effective Tax Rate	37.2%	34.7%	31.1%	32.0%	35.0%	38.9%	82.5%	61.0%	43.8%	41.4%
Net Income	4,674	3,374	2,569	2,345	1,338	1,236	120	920	1,300	1,850
S&P Core Earnings	NA	3,479	2,635	2,201	1,006	606	458	NA	NA	NA

Balance Sheet & Other Financial Data (Million $)										
Cash	3,670	2,411	1,723	2,042	1,583	1,239	618	842	414	127
Current Assets	11,314	9,562	8,845	9,369	8,314	7,849	7,029	10,007	10,200	9,375
Total Assets	60,928	59,998	53,158	53,902	49,988	50,045	43,699	45,027	43,679	41,378
Current Liabilities	11,391	10,210	9,168	11,059	8,669	7,819	6,219	8,402	7,707	7,525
Long Term Debt	11,892	10,843	10,157	9,395	10,643	12,467	8,940	6,959	9,278	9,562
Common Equity	30,753	31,820	26,210	26,081	23,791	23,445	22,672	24,100	20,975	19,388
Total Capital	45,218	46,657	40,045	39,224	37,574	38,943	34,724	34,248	32,913	31,438
Capital Expenditures	1,566	1,299	1,823	1,427	1,049	1,086	1,795	2,013	2,134	2,314
Cash Flow	6,165	4,810	3,908	3,555	2,415	2,278	1,874	3,115	4,623	5,604
Current Ratio	1.0	0.9	1.0	0.8	1.0	1.0	1.1	1.2	1.3	1.2
% Long Term Debt of Capitalization	26.2	23.2	25.4	24.0	28.3	32.0	25.7	20.3	28.2	30.4
% Net Income of Revenue	13.1	9.8	8.0	7.6	4.9	4.9	0.5	3.6	5.6	8.1
% Return on Assets	7.7	6.0	4.8	4.5	2.7	2.6	0.3	2.1	3.1	4.7
% Return on Equity	14.9	11.6	9.8	9.4	5.7	5.4	0.5	4.1	6.4	10.1

Data as orig reptd.; bef. results of disc opers/spec. items. Per share data adj. for stk. divs.; EPS diluted. E-Estimated. NA-Not Available. NM-Not Meaningful. NR-Not Ranked. UR-Under Review.

Office: 500 South Buena Vista Street, Burbank, CA 91521.
Telephone: 818-560-1000.
Website: http://www.disney.com
Chrmn: J.E. Pepper, Jr.

Pres & CEO: R.A. Iger
Sr EVP & CFO: T.O. Staggs
Sr EVP, Secy & General Counsel: A. Braverman
Investor Contact: L. Singer

Board Members: S. E. Arnold, J. E. Bryson, J. S. Chen, J. L. Estrin, R. A. Iger, S. P. Jobs, F. H. Langhammer, A. B. Lewis, M. C. Lozano, R. W. Matschullat, J. E. Pepper, Jr., O. C. Smith

Founded: 1936
Domicile: Delaware
Employees: 133,000

Dominion Resources Inc.

STANDARD &POOR'S

S&P Recommendation	BUY ★★★★☆	Price $45.71 (as of Nov 23, 2007)	12-Mo. Target Price $51.00	Investment Style Large-Cap Blend

GICS Sector Utilities
Sub-Industry Multi-Utilities

Summary This energy holding company's principal subsidiaries are Virginia Electric & Power Co. and Consolidated Natural Gas.

Key Stock Statistics (Source S&P, Vickers, company reports)

52-Wk Range	$46.99–39.84	S&P Oper. EPS 2007**E**	2.75	Market Capitalization(B)	$26.733	Beta	0.21
Trailing 12-Month EPS	$3.57	S&P Oper. EPS 2008**E**	3.10	Yield (%)	3.46	S&P 3-Yr. Proj. EPS CAGR(%)	5.00
Trailing 12-Month P/E	12.8	P/E on S&P Oper. EPS 2007**E**	16.6	Dividend Rate/Share	$1.58	S&P Credit Rating	BBB
$10K Invested 5 Yrs Ago	$21,280	Common Shares Outstg. (M)	584.8	Institutional Ownership (%)	69		

Price Performance

30-Week Mov. Avg. · · · 10-Week Mov. Avg. - - **GAAP Earnings vs. Previous Year** Volume Above Avg. STARS
12-Mo. Target Price — Relative Strength — ▲ Up ▼ Down ▶ No Change Below Avg. ★

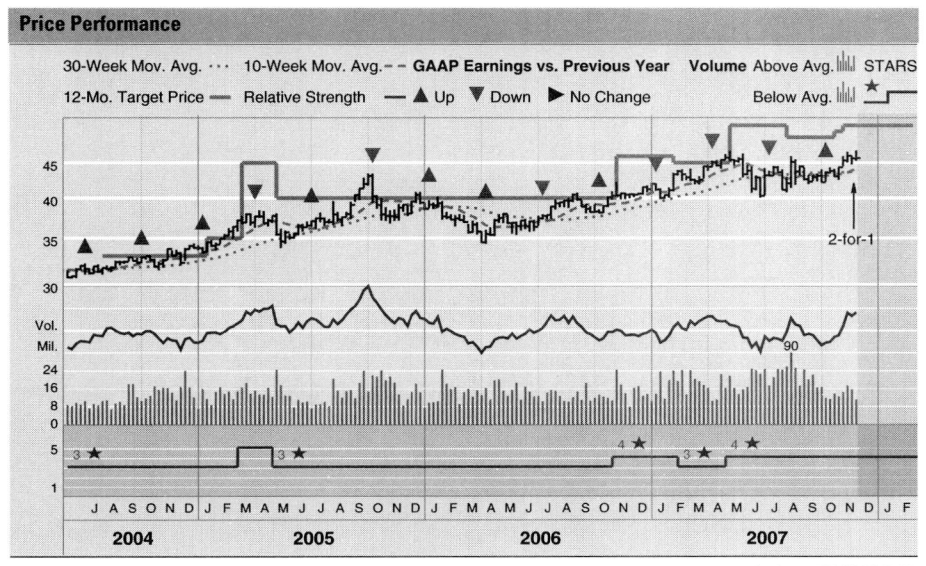

Options: ASE, CBOE, P, Ph

Analysis prepared by **Christopher B. Muir** on November 06, 2007, when the stock traded at **$ 91.23**.

Highlights

➤ D has completed transformational transactions by selling a vast majority of its exploration and production (E&P) assets for $14 billion, which will allow the company to focus on its core business of delivering electricity and natural gas. The asset sales have already funded substantial share repurchases, debt reductions and an announced increase in the dividend. We believe that continued share repurchases are likely over the coming year.

➤ We think utility revenues will increase 3.8% in 2007 and 2.4% in 2008, helped by a return to more normal weather in the utility service territories, a mid-year adjustment to Virginia fuel recoveries in 2007, and customer growth in both years. We expect operating margins to remain close to year-ago levels in both years. We look for interest costs to decline in both years as D reduces debt with cash from the asset sales.

➤ Assuming an effective tax rate of 38.3% and the successful completion of a $5.3 billion share tender offer, our 2007 operating EPS estimate is $5.50, up about 7.4% from 2006's $5.12. Our 2008 operating EPS forecast is $6.19, up an additional 12.5%.

Investment Rationale/Risk

➤ We think D's strategy of acquiring or building power plants that serve its utilities will reduce purchased power costs and provide greater operational flexibility. The reset of rates in Virginia in 2007 should help offset the impact of high fuel costs. We view the completed sale transactions of the E&P assets as positive in the current environment. We think D's announced target of a 55% payout ratio by 2010 will support double digit dividend increases over the next two years. We also view positively D's commitment to sell its international energy-related operations.

➤ Risks to our recommendation and target price include potential delays or cost overruns related to development projects; a sharp decline in natural gas prices; sharply higher interest rates; and a weaker economy.

➤ The shares recently traded at about 14.8X our 2008 EPS estimate, about even with multi-utility peers. Our 12-month target price of $101 is 16.3X our 2008 EPS estimate, a 20% premium to peer valuations, as we see above peer average EPS and dividend growth and the potential to benefit from substantial share repurchases beyond those already completed.

Qualitative Risk Assessment

LOW	MEDIUM	HIGH

Our risk assessment reflects our view of Dominion's relatively large capitalization and balanced sources of earnings, which include low-risk regulated electric and gas distribution and pipeline operations, offset by higher risk exploration and production and energy marketing businesses.

Quantitative Evaluations

S&P Quality Ranking B+

D	C	B-	B	B+	A-	A	A+

Relative Strength Rank STRONG

87

LOWEST = 1 HIGHEST = 99

Revenue/Earnings Data

Revenue (Million $)

	1Q	2Q	3Q	4Q	Year
2007	4,712	3,730	3,589	--	--
2006	4,951	3,548	4,016	3,967	16,482
2005	4,736	3,646	4,564	5,095	18,041
2004	3,879	3,040	3,292	3,761	13,972
2003	3,579	2,630	2,853	3,016	12,078
2002	2,634	2,332	2,545	2,707	10,218

Earnings Per Share ($)

2007	0.69	-0.57	3.63	E0.64	E2.75
2006	0.78	0.24	0.93	0.28	2.23
2005	0.63	0.49	0.02	0.38	1.50
2004	0.68	0.40	0.51	0.34	1.91
2003	0.66	0.39	0.51	-0.05	1.49
2002	0.60	0.49	0.77	0.56	2.41

Fiscal year ended Dec. 31. Next earnings report expected: Late January. EPS Estimates based on S&P Operating Earnings; historical GAAP earnings are as reported.

Dividend Data (Dates: mm/dd Payment Date: mm/dd/yy)

Amount ($)	Date Decl.	Ex-Div. Date	Stk. of Record	Payment Date
0.710	04/27	05/30	06/01	06/20/07
0.710	08/08	08/29	08/31	09/20/07
2-for-1 Stk.	10/29	11/20	11/09	11/19/07
0.395	10/29	11/28	11/30	12/20/07

Dividends have been paid since 1925. Source: Company reports.

Please read the Required Disclosures and Analyst Certification on the last page of this report.

The **McGraw·Hill** Companies

Dominion Resources Inc.

**STANDARD
&POOR'S**

Business Summary November 06, 2007

CORPORATE OVERVIEW. D is a fully integrated gas and electric holding company. The company operates in four primary segments: Delivery, Energy, Generation, and Exploration and Production (E&P). The Delivery segment (25.6% of 2006 external revenue) operates regulated electric and gas distribution businesses as well as non-regulated retail energy marketing. The Energy segment (8.3%) operates in tariff-based electric transmission, natural gas transmission and storage businesses, and the Cove Point LNG facility. The Generation segment (41.4%) is involved in generation for the electric utility and merchant power along with energy marketing and risk management activities. The Exploration and Production segment (18.4%) explores for and produces gas only in the Appalachian region of the U.S., having sold a significant portion of its U.S. and Canadian assets in 2007.

CORPORATE STRATEGY. D focuses its efforts mainly on the Northeast, Mid-Atlantic and Midwest regions of the U.S. As part of a strategy to concentrate on expanding its core businesses in the above-mentioned markets, D is committed to divesting all of its energy-related operations outside the U.S. D believes that focusing on its core businesses will reduce earnings volatility and help to grow EPS 4% to 5% per year. It has a proactive risk management strategy, and has entered into commodity derivative agreements to hedge against commodity price risks.

MARKET PROFILE. As of December 31, 2006, D had total power generation capacity of 27,992 MW. The Delivery segment served a total of 2.35 million electric and 1.70 million gas utility customers in five states. The Energy segment has approximately 6,000 miles of electric transmission lines in North Carolina, Virginia and West Virginia, and about 7,800 miles of gas transmission, gathering and storage pipelines located in Maryland, New York, Ohio, Pennsylvania, Virginia and West Virginia. D's underground natural gas storage system had a capacity of 776 billion cubic feet (Bcf). The division also operates a liquefied natural gas (LNG) terminal at Cove Point, MD.

Company Financials Fiscal Year Ended Dec. 31

Per Share Data ($)	2006	2005	2004	2003	2002	2001	2000	1999	1998	1997
Tangible Book Value	11.45	8.79	16.37	9.60	9.09	7.85	7.10	12.40	13.28	8.27
Earnings	2.22	1.50	1.91	1.49	2.41	1.08	0.88	1.41	1.38	1.08
S&P Core Earnings	2.21	1.47	1.90	1.58	1.92	0.66	NA	NA	NA	NA
Dividends	0.35	1.34	1.30	1.29	1.29	1.29	1.29	1.29	1.29	1.29
Payout Ratio	16%	89%	68%	87%	54%	120%	147%	92%	94%	120%
Prices:High	42.22	43.49	34.43	32.97	33.53	35.00	33.97	24.69	24.47	21.44
Prices:Low	34.36	33.26	30.39	25.87	17.70	27.57	17.41	18.28	18.91	16.63
P/E Ratio:High	19	29	18	22	14	33	39	18	18	20
P/E Ratio:Low	15	22	16	17	7	26	20	13	14	15

Income Statement Analysis (Million $)										
Revenue	16,482	18,041	13,972	12,078	10,218	10,558	9,260	5,520	6,086	7,678
Depreciation	1,606	1,412	1,305	1,216	1,258	1,245	1,176	716	734	819
Maintenance	NA	NA	NA	NA	NA	NA	NA	NA	NA	NA
Fixed Charges Coverage	3.42	2.63	3.09	2.63	3.15	2.02	1.99	2.44	1.83	2.38
Construction Credits	Nil	Nil	Nil	Nil	Nil	Nil	Nil	Nil	Nil	Nil
Effective Tax Rate	37.0%	36.0%	35.6%	38.6%	33.3%	40.5%	30.5%	31.3%	35.2%	34.3%
Net Income	1,563	1,034	1,264	949	1,362	544	415	551	536	399
S&P Core Earnings	1,555	1,010	1,254	1,004	1,088	331	NA	NA	NA	NA

Balance Sheet & Other Financial Data (Million $)										
Gross Property	43,575	42,063	38,663	37,107	32,631	33,105	31,011	18,646	18,106	19,520
Capital Expenditures	4,052	1,683	1,451	2,138	2,828	1,224	1,385	737	755	649
Net Property	29,382	28,940	26,716	25,850	20,257	18,681	14,849	10,764	10,637	12,533
Capitalization:Long Term Debt	15,048	14,910	15,764	16,033	13,714	12,119	10,486	7,321	5,071	7,196
Capitalization:% Long Term Debt	53.8	58.9	58.0	60.3	57.3	58.1	58.3	58.2	44.2	49.1
Capitalization:Preferred	Nil	Nil	Nil	Nil	Nil	Nil	509	509	1,074	1,074
Capitalization:% Preferred	Nil	Nil	Nil	Nil	Nil	Nil	2.83	4.05	9.40	7.30
Capitalization:Common	12,913	10,397	11,426	10,538	10,213	8,368	6,992	4,752	5,315	5,040
Capitalization:% Common	46.2	41.1	42.0	39.7	42.7	40.1	38.9	37.8	46.4	34.4
Total Capital	33,842	30,291	32,689	31,134	28,136	24,811	20,955	14,427	13,475	14,658
% Operating Ratio	85.3	89.7	85.6	83.7	78.5	85.6	80.5	80.9	64.4	83.6
% Earned on Net Property	11.5	8.8	10.3	10.6	21.4	10.6	11.9	9.7	9.4	13.0
% Return on Revenue	9.5	5.7	9.0	7.9	13.3	5.2	4.5	10.0	8.8	5.2
% Return on Invested Capital	8.1	6.4	6.5	6.5	8.5	7.2	10.7	7.9	8.4	7.6
% Return on Common Equity	13.4	9.5	11.5	9.1	14.7	7.1	7.1	10.9	10.4	8.0

Data as orig reptd.; bef. results of disc opers/spec. items. Per share data adj. for stk. divs.; EPS diluted. E-Estimated. NA-Not Available. NM-Not Meaningful. NR-Not Ranked. UR-Under Review.

Office: 120 Tredegar Street, Richmond, VA 23219.
Telephone: 804-819-2000.
Email: investor_relations@domres.com
Website: http://www.dom.com

Chrmn, Pres & CEO: T.F. Farrell II
EVP & CFO: T.N. Chewning
SVP & Chief Admin Officer: M.C. Doswell
SVP & Treas: G.S. Hetzer

SVP & General Counsel: J.F. Stutts
Investor Contact: J. O'Hare (804-819-2156)
Board Members: P. W. Brown, G. A. Davidson, Jr., T. F. Farrell II, J. W. Harris, R. S. Jepson, Jr., M. J. Kington, B. J. Lambert, III, M. A. McKenna, F. S. Royal, D. A. Wollard

Founded: 1909
Domicile: Virginia
Employees: 17,500

R.R. Donnelley & Sons Co

STANDARD &POOR'S

S&P Recommendation	BUY ★★★★☆	Price	12-Mo. Target Price	Investment Style
		$35.27 (as of Nov 27, 2007)	$50.00	Large-Cap Value

GICS Sector Industrials
Sub-Industry Commercial Printing

Summary R.R. Donnelley, the largest U.S. commercial printer, specializes in the production of catalogs, inserts, magazines, books, directories, and financial and computer documentation.

Key Stock Statistics (Source S&P, Vickers, company reports)

52-Wk Range	$45.25– 32.59	S&P Oper. EPS 2007E	2.80	Market Capitalization(B)	$7.833	Beta	1.24
Trailing 12-Month EPS	$2.14	S&P Oper. EPS 2008E	3.10	Yield (%)	2.95	S&P 3-Yr. Proj. EPS CAGR(%)	14.00
Trailing 12-Month P/E	16.5	P/E on S&P Oper. EPS 2007E	12.6	Dividend Rate/Share	$1.04	S&P Credit Rating	BBB+
$10K Invested 5 Yrs Ago	$20,507	Common Shares Outstg. (M)	222.1	Institutional Ownership (%)	86		

Price Performance

30-Week Mov. Avg. · · · 10-Week Mov. Avg. — **GAAP Earnings vs. Previous Year** Volume Above Avg. STARS
12-Mo. Target Price — Relative Strength — ▲ Up ▼ Down ► No Change Below Avg.

Options: CBOE, P, Ph

Analysis prepared by **Pearl Wang** on November 27, 2007, when the stock traded at **$ 35.13**.

Highlights

➤ For 2008, we forecast revenue growth in the mid- to high single digits, including contributions from the 2007 acquisitions of Banta, Perry-Judd's and Von Hoffman. We see organic revenue growth of about 3%, driven by new business wins and a greater share from existing customers. We also foresee more favorable foreign exchange comparisons boosting growth, partly offset by continued pricing pressures.

➤ We expect that a likely rise in stock option expense, pricing pressure, and higher energy and paper costs will be more than offset by operating leverage from revenue growth as well as continued productivity advances and cost synergies as RRD integrates its 2007 acquisitions. We forecast a modest improvement in RRD's operating margin before restructuring, impairment and acquisition integration charges.

➤ After higher expected interest payments and a likely increase in the effective tax rate, we see 2007 operating EPS (excluding $342 million of pretax asset impairment and restructuring charges) rising to $2.88. Our 2008 EPS estimate is $3.10.

Investment Rationale/Risk

➤ We expect RRD to continue to gain market share by leveraging its geographic and product breadth and through its low cost structure. We believe the company will continue to be able to improve operating margins through fixed cost leverage and productivity increases. While we think that the softening of the U.S. economy warrants a valuation toward the low end of historical levels on a P/E basis, we believe the shares still look attractive based on that view. We think the company will continue to pursue selective acquisitions as RRD aims to expand its global reach and further increase its operating leverage.

➤ Risks to our recommendation and target price include acquisition integration problems, substantially higher input costs, and greater than expected growth of information disseminated electronically.

➤ Our 12-month target price of $50 values the shares at about 16X our 2008 EPS estimate of $3.10, toward the low end of RRD's five-year historical P/E range of 11.0X-60.7X EPS.

Qualitative Risk Assessment

LOW	MEDIUM	HIGH

Our risk assessment reflects economies of scale that the company realizes as the largest U.S. commercial printer in a fragmented print industry, offset by industry pricing pressure and the increasingly electronic nature of communication.

Quantitative Evaluations

S&P Quality Ranking B

D	C	B-	B	B+	A-	A	A+

Relative Strength Rank MODERATE

47

LOWEST = 1 HIGHEST = 99

Revenue/Earnings Data

Revenue (Million $)

	1Q	2Q	3Q	4Q	Year
2007	2,793	2,796	2,910	--	--
2006	2,267	2,274	2,309	2,467	9,317
2005	1,927	1,932	2,184	2,388	8,430
2004	1,289	1,843	1,913	2,112	7,156
2003	1,074	1,142	1,194	1,377	4,787
2002	1,094	1,149	1,177	1,335	4,755

Earnings Per Share ($)

2007	0.63	-0.32	0.80	E0.73	E2.80
2006	0.52	0.57	0.75	-0.01	1.84
2005	0.50	0.44	0.59	-1.09	0.44
2004	-0.35	-0.06	0.52	0.61	0.88
2003	0.05	0.17	0.47	0.85	1.54
2002	0.20	0.22	0.42	0.42	1.24

Fiscal year ended Dec. 31. Next earnings report expected: Late February. EPS Estimates based on S&P Operating Earnings; historical GAAP earnings are as reported.

Dividend Data (Dates: mm/dd Payment Date: mm/dd/yy)

Amount ($)	Date Decl.	Ex-Div. Date	Stk. of Record	Payment Date
0.260	01/11	01/24	01/26	03/01/07
0.260	04/27	05/09	05/11	06/01/07
0.260	07/25	08/07	08/09	09/04/07
0.260	10/24	11/06	11/08	12/03/07

Dividends have been paid since 1911. Source: Company reports.

R.R. Donnelley & Sons Co

STANDARD &POOR'S

Business Summary November 27, 2007

RRD is the largest printing company in North America, serving customers in the publishing, health care, advertising, retail, telecommunications, technology, financial services and other industries. The company provides solutions in long- and short-run commercial printing, direct mail, financial printing, print fulfillment, forms and labels, logistics, digital printing, call centers, transactional print-and-mail, print management, online services, digital photography, color services, and content and database management. Geographically, the company derives the majority of its revenues from the U.S. (77% of 2006 revenues), with Europe accounting for 12% and the rest of the world 11%. In 2006, no customer accounted for 10% or more of the company's sales.

The company was reorganized in 2006 into two reportable segments: Global Print Solutions, and Global Services. This was the second time in two years that RRD reorganized the way it classified its business segments. RRD said this was done to reflect changes in the management reporting structure of the organization.

The Global Print Solutions segment (61% of revenues in 2006) consists of the

following businesses: magazine, catalog and retail, which includes print services to consumer magazine and catalog publishers as well as retailers; book, which serves the consumer, religious, educational and specialty book and telecommunications sectors; directories, which serves the global printing needs of yellow and white pages directory publishers; logistics, which delivers company and third party printed products as well as performs the distribution of time-sensitive and secure material, warehousing and fulfillment services; direct mail, which offers content creation, database management, printing, personalization finishing and distribution services to direct marketing companies; and short-run commercial print, which provides print and print related services to a diversified customer bases. The segment also includes results from Asia and Europe.

Company Financials Fiscal Year Ended Dec. 31

Per Share Data ($)	2006	2005	2004	2003	2002	2001	2000	1999	1998	1997
Tangible Book Value	0.54	NM	3.81	5.14	4.51	3.92	5.89	6.01	6.85	8.31
Cash Flow	3.96	2.40	5.07	4.43	4.32	3.41	5.34	5.29	4.66	3.91
Earnings	1.84	0.44	0.88	1.54	1.24	0.21	2.17	2.40	2.08	1.40
S&P Core Earnings	1.97	1.27	1.20	1.18	0.18	-0.65	NA	NA	NA	NA
Dividends	1.04	1.04	1.04	1.02	0.98	0.94	0.90	0.86	0.82	0.78
Payout Ratio	57%	NM	118%	66%	79%	NM	41%	36%	39%	56%
Prices:High	36.00	38.27	35.37	30.15	32.10	31.90	27.50	44.75	48.00	41.75
Prices:Low	28.50	29.54	27.62	16.94	18.50	24.30	19.00	21.50	33.75	29.50
P/E Ratio:High	20	87	40	20	26	NM	13	19	23	30
P/E Ratio:Low	15	67	31	11	15	NM	9	9	16	21

Income Statement Analysis (Million $)

	2006	2005	2004	2003	2002	2001	2000	1999	1998	1997
Revenue	9,317	8,430	7,156	4,787	4,755	5,298	5,764	5,183	5,018	4,850
Operating Income	1,420	1,295	952	617	686	722	891	905	856	811
Depreciation	463	425	771	329	352	379	390	374	367	371
Interest Expense	139	111	85.9	50.4	62.8	71.2	89.6	88.2	78.0	91.0
Pretax Income	601	332	357	208	176	74.9	434	507	510	304
Effective Tax Rate	32.6%	71.5%	26.0%	15.3%	19.1%	66.6%	38.5%	38.5%	42.2%	31.9%
Net Income	403	95.6	265	177	142	25.0	267	312	295	207
S&P Core Earnings	430	275	243	136	21.3	-78.3	NA	NA	NA	NA

Balance Sheet & Other Financial Data (Million $)

	2006	2005	2004	2003	2002	2001	2000	1999	1998	1997
Cash	211	367	642	60.8	60.5	48.6	60.9	41.9	66.0	48.0
Current Assets	2,517	2,622	2,601	1,000	866	940	1,206	1,230	1,145	1,147
Total Assets	9,636	9,374	8,554	3,189	3,152	3,400	3,914	3,853	3,788	4,134
Current Liabilities	1,612	1,814	1,487	884	955	984	1,191	1,203	898	813
Long Term Debt	2,359	2,365	1,581	752	753	881	739	748	999	1,153
Common Equity	4,125	3,724	3,987	983	915	888	1,233	1,138	1,301	1,592
Total Capital	7,087	6,686	6,144	1,970	1,882	1,982	2,205	2,140	2,585	2,974
Capital Expenditures	374	471	265	203	242	273	237	276	225	360
Cash Flow	866	521	1,036	506	495	404	657	686	662	578
Current Ratio	1.6	1.4	1.7	1.1	0.9	1.0	1.0	1.0	1.3	1.4
% Long Term Debt of Capitalization	33.3	35.4	25.7	38.2	40.0	44.5	33.5	35.0	38.6	38.8
% Net Income of Revenue	4.3	1.1	3.7	3.7	3.0	0.5	4.6	6.0	5.9	4.3
% Return on Assets	4.2	1.1	4.5	5.5	4.4	0.7	6.9	8.1	7.4	4.6
% Return on Equity	10.3	2.5	10.7	18.6	15.8	2.4	22.5	25.5	20.4	12.8

Data as orig reptd.; bef. results of disc opers/spec. items. Per share data adj. for stk. divs.; EPS diluted. E-Estimated. NA-Not Available. NM-Not Meaningful. NR-Not Ranked. UR-Under Review.

Office: 111 W Wacker Dr, Chicago, IL 60606.
Telephone: 312-326-8000.
Email: investor.info@rrd.com
Website: http://www.rrdonnelley.com

Chrmn: S.M. Wolf
Pres & CEO: T.J. Quinlan, III
COO: J.R. Paloian
EVP, Secy, General Counsel & CCO: S.S. Bettman

SVP, Chief Acctg Officer & Cntlr: M.W. McHugh
Investor Contact: D.N. Leib (312-326-7710)
Board Members: R. F. Cummings, Jr., J. H. Hamilton, T. S. Johnson, J. C. Pope, T. J. Quinlan III, M. T. Riordan, L. H. Schipper, O. R. Sockwell, B. L. Thomas, N. Wesley, S. M. Wolf

Founded: 1864
Domicile: Delaware
Employees: 53,000

The McGraw-Hill Companies

Dover Corp

STANDARD &POOR'S

S&P Recommendation	HOLD ★★★☆☆	Price $45.74 (as of Nov 23, 2007)	12-Mo. Target Price $52.00	Investment Style Large-Cap Growth

GICS Sector Industrials
Sub-Industry Industrial Machinery

Summary This company manufactures a broad range of specialized industrial products and sophisticated manufacturing equipment.

Key Stock Statistics (Source S&P, Vickers, company reports)

52-Wk Range	$54.59– 44.34	S&P Oper. EPS 2007**E** 3.18	Market Capitalization(B) $9.089	Beta	1.41
Trailing 12-Month EPS	$2.90	S&P Oper. EPS 2008**E** 3.35	Yield (%) 1.75	S&P 3-Yr. Proj. EPS CAGR(%)	17.00
Trailing 12-Month P/E	15.8	P/E on S&P Oper. EPS 2007**E** 14.4	Dividend Rate/Share $0.80	S&P Credit Rating	A
$10K Invested 5 Yrs Ago	$16,121	Common Shares Outstg. (M) 198.7	Institutional Ownership (%) 87		

Price Performance

30-Week Mov. Avg. · · ·   10-Week Mov. Avg. – –   **GAAP Earnings vs. Previous Year**   Volume Above Avg. ▮▮▮ STARS
12-Mo. Target Price —   Relative Strength —   ▲ Up   ▼ Down   ► No Change   Below Avg. ▮▮▮ ★

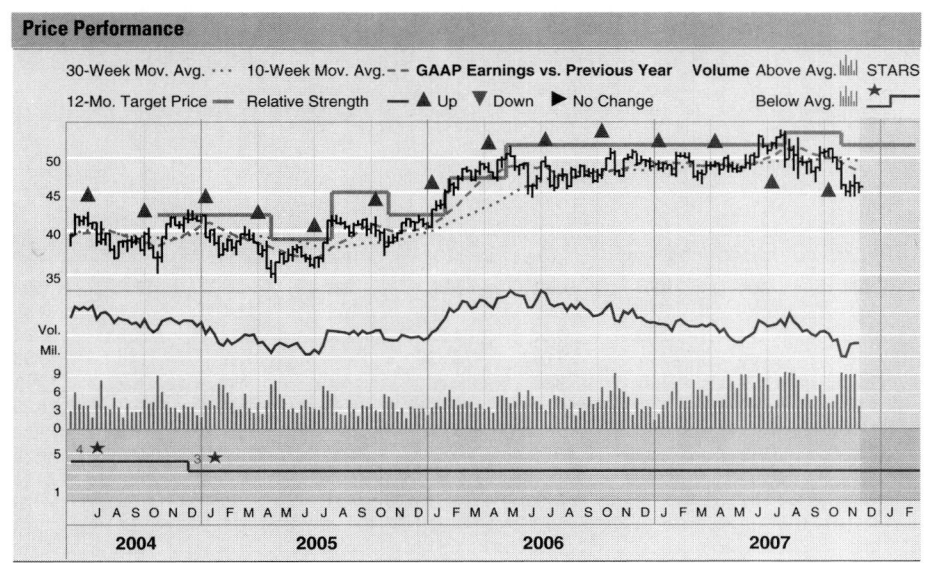

Options: P, Ph

Analysis prepared by **Christopher Lippincott** on October 24, 2007, when the stock traded at **$ 46.78**.

Highlights

► We believe revenues will increase approximately 13% in 2007 and 6% in 2008. We expect over 4% organic growth in 2007, with the balance from recent acquisition contributions. Price increases and currency translation should also help drive sales growth, while acquisitions may provide additional growth. We expect strength in the oil & gas, mobile equipment and industrial markets, partly offset by weak electronics and ATM end-markets. Strong demand from international markets should represent the greatest driver of organic revenue growth in 2008, in our view, as domestic industrial and residential construction markets should exhibit softness.

► In our opinion, greater operating leverage, capacity utilization and business mix should help expand gross margins in 2007 and 2008, although we expect raw material price inflation to restrict margin expansion in 2007. Lower SG&A expenses as a percentage of sales should drive operating margin expansion through 2008.

► On a modestly lower tax rate, we project operating EPS of $3.18 in 2007 and $3.35 in 2008.

Investment Rationale/Risk

► We believe DOV continues to improve its ability to generate strong free cash flow as it improves the quality of business within its portfolio. As a result of discontinuing 20 low-margin, capital-intensive and volatile businesses over the past two years, and replacing them with 17 new steady-growth, high-margin units, we expect that DOV will continue to drive both top and bottom line growth, translating into steady free cash flow, solid dividend payments and shareholder value. Nevertheless, we believe these attractive qualities are already reflected in the share price.

► Risks to our recommendation and target price include weaker than expected global economic growth, softer industrial, energy and electronics markets, and potential value-diminishing acquisitions.

► Our 12-month target price of $52 represents a combination of two valuation metrics. Our discounted cash flow model, which assumes a 3% perpetual growth rate and an 11.6% discount rate, indicates an intrinsic value of $52. For our relative valuation, we apply an EV/EBITDA multiple of 9.3X, slightly below peers, to our 2008 EBITDA estimate, also implying a value of $52.

Qualitative Risk Assessment

LOW	MEDIUM	HIGH

Our risk assessment reflects the company's acquisition strategy, its model of operating numerous different businesses as stand-alone entities, and its exposure to several cyclical end markets.

Quantitative Evaluations

S&P Quality Ranking   A-

D	C	B-	B	B+	A-	A	A+

Relative Strength Rank   MODERATE

56

LOWEST = 1   HIGHEST = 99

Revenue/Earnings Data

Revenue (Million $)

	1Q	2Q	3Q	4Q	Year
2007	1,780	1,859	1,844	--	--
2006	1,500	1,650	1,647	1,715	6,512
2005	1,383	1,525	1,556	1,614	6,078
2004	1,242	1,380	1,444	1,421	5,488
2003	1,028	1,124	1,154	1,198	4,413
2002	994.6	1,082	1,062	1,045	4,184

Earnings Per Share ($)

2007	0.67	0.85	0.88	E0.82	E3.18
2006	0.64	0.77	0.77	0.76	2.94
2005	0.47	0.59	0.65	0.61	2.32
2004	0.41	0.53	0.58	0.48	2.00
2003	0.29	0.36	0.37	0.39	1.40
2002	0.22	0.31	0.29	0.19	1.04

Fiscal year ended Dec. 31. Next earnings report expected: Early February. EPS Estimates based on S&P Operating Earnings; historical GAAP earnings are as reported.

Dividend Data (Dates: mm/dd Payment Date: mm/dd/yy)

Amount ($)	Date Decl.	Ex-Div. Date	Stk. of Record	Payment Date
0.185	02/08	02/26	02/28	03/15/07
0.185	05/03	05/29	05/31	06/15/07
0.200	08/02	08/29	08/31	09/15/07
0.200	11/08	11/28	11/30	12/15/07

Dividends have been paid since 1947. Source: Company reports.

Please read the Required Disclosures and Analyst Certification on the last page of this report.

Dover Corp

STANDARD
&POOR'S

Business Summary October 24, 2007

CORPORATE OVERVIEW. Dover Corporation is a diversified manufacturer of a broad range of specialized industrial products and manufacturing equipment. The company has evolved largely through acquisitions, with 75 acquisitions costing approximately $4 billion completed between January 2000 and December 2006. There are four operating segments: Industrial Products, Engineered Systems, Fluid Management and Electronic Technologies.

Industrial Products (30% of 2006 sales, with 13% operating margin) manufactures a diverse mix of equipment and components for use in the waste handling, bulk transport and automotive service industries. Its two sub-units are Material Handling and Mobile Equipment. Major units include Paladin, PDQ Manufacturing, Heil Environmental, Rotary Lift, Heil Trailer International, Chief Automotive, and Marathon Equipment.

Engineered Systems (26%, 14%) manufactures food equipment (refrigeration systems, display cases, walk-in coolers, etc.) and packaging machinery. It is composed of two primary sub-groups -- Product Identification and Engineered Products. The food equipment businesses (Hill Phoenix and Unified Brands)

sell to the institutional and commercial foodservice markets. The packaging machinery businesses sell to the beverage and food processing industries.

Fluid Management (21%, 20%) manufactures products primarily for the oil and gas, automotive fueling, fluid handling, engineered components, material handling and chemical equipment industries. This segment consists of two primary sub-units -- Energy and Fluid Solutions.

Electronic Technologies (22%, 15%) manufactures an array of specialized electronic, electromechanical and plastic components for OEMs in multiple end markets, including hearing aids, telecom, defense and aerospace electronics, and life sciences. It also supplies ATM hardware and software for retail applications and financial institutions, and chemical proportioning and dispensing systems for janitorial/sanitation applications.

Company Financials Fiscal Year Ended Dec. 31

Per Share Data ($)	2006	2005	2004	2003	2002	2001	2000	1999	1998	1997
Tangible Book Value	NM	NM	2.16	2.71	2.66	1.97	1.79	1.08	2.11	2.81
Cash Flow	3.92	3.18	2.78	2.14	1.83	1.89	3.60	2.79	2.20	2.54
Earnings	2.94	2.32	2.00	1.40	1.04	0.82	2.61	1.92	1.45	1.79
S&P Core Earnings	2.98	2.25	1.92	1.31	0.90	0.68	NA	NA	NA	NA
Dividends	0.71	0.66	0.62	0.57	0.54	0.52	0.48	0.44	0.40	0.36
Payout Ratio	24%	28%	31%	41%	52%	63%	18%	23%	28%	20%
Prices:High	51.92	42.11	44.13	40.45	43.55	43.55	54.38	47.94	39.94	36.69
Prices:Low	40.30	34.11	35.12	22.85	23.54	26.40	34.13	29.31	25.50	24.13
P/E Ratio:High	18	18	22	29	42	53	21	25	28	20
P/E Ratio:Low	14	15	18	16	23	32	13	15	18	13

Income Statement Analysis (Million $)										
Revenue	6,512	6,078	5,488	4,413	4,184	4,460	5,401	4,446	3,978	4,548
Operating Income	1,113	876	773	595	503	518	1,047	819	700	783
Depreciation	202	176	161	151	161	219	203	183	168	171
Interest Expense	77.0	72.2	61.3	62.2	70.0	91.2	97.5	53.4	60.7	46.9
Pretax Income	823	644	552	372	270	238	772	615	489	617
Effective Tax Rate	26.7%	26.3%	25.9%	23.3%	21.7%	30.0%	31.0%	34.1%	33.2%	34.3%
Net Income	603	474	409	285	211	167	533	405	326	405
S&P Core Earnings	613	460	392	267	182	138	NA	NA	NA	NA

Balance Sheet & Other Financial Data (Million $)										
Cash	374	191	358	370	295	177	187	138	96.8	125
Current Assets	2,272	1,976	2,150	1,850	1,658	1,655	1,975	1,612	1,305	1,591
Total Assets	7,627	6,573	5,792	5,134	4,437	4,602	4,892	4,132	3,627	3,278
Current Liabilities	1,434	1,207	1,356	911	697	819	1,605	1,345	990	1,197
Long Term Debt	1,480	1,344	753	1,004	1,030	1,033	632	608	610	263
Common Equity	3,811	3,330	3,119	2,743	2,395	2,520	2,442	2,039	1,911	1,778
Total Capital	5,656	5,046	4,168	3,980	3,561	3,656	3,141	2,689	2,571	2,007
Capital Expenditures	195	152	107	96.4	102	167	198	130	126	146
Cash Flow	805	650	570	437	372	386	737	588	494	576
Current Ratio	1.6	1.6	1.6	2.0	2.4	2.0	1.2	1.2	1.3	1.3
% Long Term Debt of Capitalization	26.2	26.6	18.1	25.2	28.9	28.3	20.1	22.6	23.7	13.1
% Net Income of Revenue	9.3	7.8	7.5	6.5	5.0	3.7	9.9	9.1	8.2	8.9
% Return on Assets	8.5	7.7	7.5	6.0	4.7	3.5	11.8	10.4	9.5	12.9
% Return on Equity	16.9	14.7	14.0	11.1	8.6	6.7	23.8	20.5	17.7	24.4

Data as orig reptd.; bef. results of disc opers/spec. items. Per share data adj. for stk. divs.; EPS diluted. E-Estimated. NA-Not Available. NM-Not Meaningful. NR-Not Ranked. UR-Under Review.

Office: 280 Park Ave Rm, New York, NY 10017-1215.
Telephone: 212-922-1640.
Website: http://www.dovercorporation.com
Chrmn: T.L. Reece

Pres, CEO & COO: R.L. Hoffman
VP & CFO: R.G. Kuhbach
VP, Secy & General Counsel: J.W. Schmidt
VP & Cntlr: R.T. McKay, Jr.

Investor Contact: P.E. Goldberg (212-922-1640)
Board Members: D. H. Benson, R. W. Cremin, J. M. Ergas, K. C. Graham, R. L. Hoffman, J. L. Koley, R. K. Lochridge, T. L. Reece, B. G. Rethore, M. B. Stubbs, M. A. Winston

Founded: 1947
Domicile: Delaware
Employees: 33,000

Dow Chemical Co (The)

STANDARD
&POOR'S

S&P Recommendation	**HOLD** ★★★☆☆	Price	12-Mo. Target Price	Investment Style
		$40.15 (as of Nov 23, 2007)	$50.00	Large-Cap Blend

GICS Sector Materials
Sub-Industry Diversified Chemicals

Summary Dow, the largest U.S. chemical company, provides chemical, plastic and agricultural products and services to many consumer markets.

Key Stock Statistics (Source S&P, Vickers, company reports)

52-Wk Range	$47.96–38.89	S&P Oper. EPS 2007**E**	3.75	Market Capitalization(B)	$37.918	Beta	1.19
Trailing 12-Month EPS	$3.49	S&P Oper. EPS 2008**E**	4.25	Yield (%)	4.18	S&P 3-Yr. Proj. EPS CAGR(%)	10.00
Trailing 12-Month P/E	11.5	P/E on S&P Oper. EPS 2007**E**	10.7	Dividend Rate/Share	$1.68	S&P Credit Rating	A-
$10K Invested 5 Yrs Ago	$16,539	Common Shares Outstg. (M)	944.4	Institutional Ownership (%)	68		

Price Performance

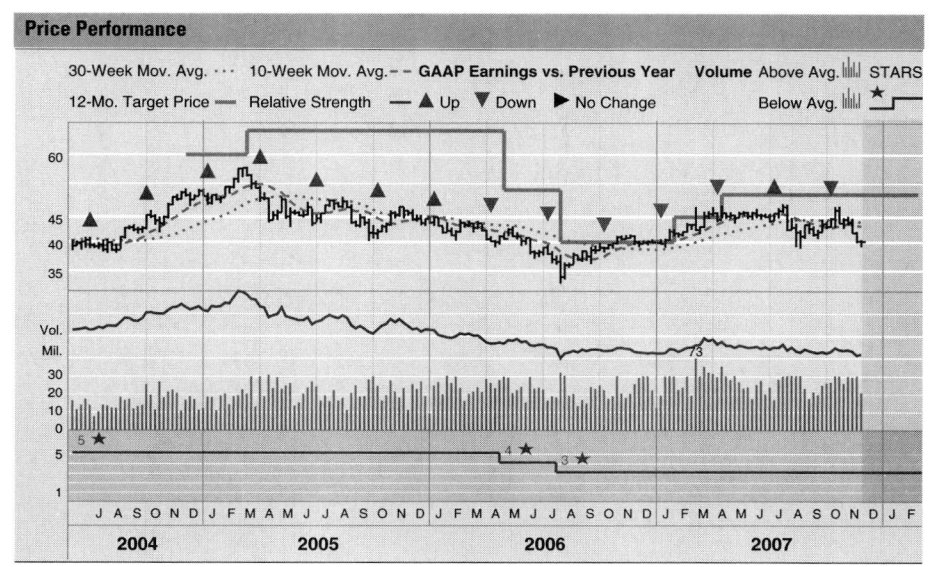

30-Week Mov. Avg. · · · · 10-Week Mov. Avg. - - GAAP Earnings vs. Previous Year Volume Above Avg. STARS
12-Mo. Target Price — Relative Strength — ▲ Up ▼ Down ► No Change Below Avg.

Options: ASE, CBOE, P, Ph

Analysis prepared by **Richard O'Reilly, CFA** on September 14, 2007, when the stock traded at **$ 41.98**.

Highlights

➤ We expect the company to post operating EPS of $4.25 in 2008, modestly above what we expect for 2007 and similar to 2006's $4.25, as we anticipate somewhat favorable industry fundamentals on healthy global economic growth offset by continued volatility in feedstock costs.

➤ We look for sales to increase in 2007 as volume growth continues. Prices for many basic plastics and chemicals should remain volatile; resin prices have strengthened since early in the second quarter in response to stronger demand and higher feedstock costs, although we think chlor-alkali has a softer fundamental outlook. The specialty segments will likely be squeezed as price hikes lag higher costs. We see joint ventures in low-cost feedstock locations such as Kuwait performing well, and we expect the agricultural segment to have normal seasonal losses in the second half.

➤ We see lower interest expense due to a further reduction of debt in 2006. We expect the effective tax rate for 2007 to be about 25%, before a possible one-time charge in the third quarter. We think EPS comparisons will benefit from fewer shares outstanding as a result of a stock buyback program.

Investment Rationale/Risk

➤ We believe the commodity chemical industry's supply/demand fundamentals will show cyclical stability over the next two years, but we think historically high and volatile feedstock costs will limit margin improvements. DOW plans to control overhead costs and continue to focus on capital discipline, as capital spending in 2007 should again remain below depreciation. We expect the company to continue to repurchase its common stock.

➤ Risks to our recommendation and target price include a larger than expected softening of the U.S. economy, sharply higher energy costs, and unplanned production outages and interruptions. We remain somewhat concerned about possible additional asbestos liabilities for DOW, largely related to its Union Carbide unit.

➤ We dismissed speculation early this year about DOW being subject to a possible buyout by a private group. Our 12-month target price of $50 is based on an historical mid-cycle P/E of about 12X and an annualized earnings rate of about $4.25 that we believe DOW should achieve in 2008.

Qualitative Risk Assessment

LOW	MEDIUM	HIGH

Our risk assessment reflects the diverse business and geographic sales mix and manufacturing integration of this company, offset by the cyclical nature of the commodity chemical industry and the volatility of raw material costs.

Quantitative Evaluations

S&P Quality Ranking B

D	C	B-	**B**	B+	A-	A	A+

Relative Strength Rank MODERATE

45

LOWEST = 1   HIGHEST = 99

Revenue/Earnings Data

Revenue (Million $)

	1Q	2Q	3Q	4Q	Year
2007	12,432	13,265	13,589	--	--
2006	12,020	12,509	12,359	12,236	49,124
2005	11,679	11,450	11,261	11,917	46,307
2004	9,309	9,844	10,072	10,936	40,161
2003	8,081	8,242	7,977	8,332	32,632
2002	6,305	7,259	7,084	6,961	27,609

Earnings Per Share ($)

2007	1.00	1.07	0.24	E0.85	E3.75
2006	1.24	1.05	0.53	1.00	3.82
2005	1.39	1.30	0.82	1.14	4.64
2004	0.50	0.72	0.65	1.06	2.93
2003	0.09	0.43	0.36	0.99	1.88
2002	0.04	0.26	0.14	-0.89	-0.44

Fiscal year ended Dec. 31. Next earnings report expected: Late January. EPS Estimates based on S&P Operating Earnings; historical GAAP earnings are as reported.

Dividend Data (Dates: mm/dd Payment Date: mm/dd/yy)

Amount ($)	Date Decl.	Ex-Div. Date	Stk. of Record	Payment Date
0.375	12/14	12/27	12/29	01/30/07
0.375	02/15	03/28	03/30	04/30/07
0.420	05/10	06/27	06/29	07/30/07
0.420	09/13	09/26	09/28	10/30/07

Dividends have been paid since 1911. Source: Company reports.

Please read the Required Disclosures and Analyst Certification on the last page of this report.

The McGraw-Hill Companies

Dow Chemical Co (The)

**STANDARD
&POOR'S**

Business Summary September 14, 2007

CORPORATE OVERVIEW. The 2001 purchase of Union Carbide Corp., a leading producer of polyethylene, ethylene glycol, solvents and specialty chemicals, made DOW the largest U.S. chemical company. Foreign operations accounted for 63% of 2006 sales.

Chemicals (11% of sales and 11% of profits in 2006) include inorganics (chlorine, caustic soda, chlorinated solvents, calcium chlorides, ethylene dichloride and vinyl chloride), ethylene oxide/glycol, and vinyl acetate monomer, used primarily as raw materials in the manufacture of customer products. Performance chemicals (16%, 21%) consist of latex (including styrene-butadiene) coatings and binders, acrylics, water-based emulsions (acrylic latexes), water soluble polymers, cellulose ethers and resins, ion exchange resins, membranes, biocides, custom manufacturing, fine chemicals, glycine, glycols, amines, surfactants, heat transfer and deicing fluids, coolants, and lubricants and solvents. The segment also includes results of the Dow Corning joint venture.

Dow AgroSciences (7%, 7%) is a leading global maker of herbicides (Clincher, Starane), insecticides (Lorsban, Sentricon termite colony elimination system, Tracer) and fungicides for crop protection and industrial/commercial pest control. It is also building a plant genetics and biotechnology business in crop seeds (Mycogen, Nexera), traits (Herculex) and value-added grains.

The company, a major producer of plastics (24%, 34%), is the world's largest producer of polyethylene and polystyrene resins, which are used in a broad variety of applications. It also makes polypropylene and has a joint venture for PET polyester plastics. Performance plastics (29%, 27%) consist of engineering plastics (polycarbonates, ABS), elastomers, synthetic rubbers, adhesives and sealants, polyolefins for wire and cable insulation, Saran resins and films, specialty films, polyurethanes (systems, sealants and adhesives, polyols, isocyanates, propylene oxide/glycol), epoxy resins and intermediates (phenol and acetone), fabricated building products (foams and films, STYROFOAM insulation products, weather barrier products), and technology licensing (UNIPOL for polyethylene and polypropylene, Meteor for ethylene oxide/glycol). The hydrocarbons and energy business (13%, nil) procures fuels and raw materials and produces ethylene, propylene, aromatics, styrene, and power and steam.

Company Financials Fiscal Year Ended Dec. 31

Per Share Data ($)	2006	2005	2004	2003	2002	2001	2000	1999	1998	1997
Tangible Book Value	14.50	12.14	9.01	5.79	4.19	7.59	10.78	9.59	8.77	8.69
Cash Flow	5.83	6.83	5.12	3.93	4.57	1.55	4.14	3.91	3.83	4.46
Earnings	3.82	4.64	2.93	1.88	-0.44	-0.46	2.22	1.98	1.91	2.57
S&P Core Earnings	3.73	4.04	2.34	1.58	-1.41	-1.43	NA	NA	NA	NA
Dividends	1.50	1.34	1.34	1.34	1.34	1.30	1.16	1.16	1.16	1.12
Payout Ratio	39%	29%	46%	71%	NM	NM	52%	59%	61%	44%
Prices:High	45.15	56.75	51.34	42.00	37.00	39.67	47.17	46.00	33.81	34.21
Prices:Low	33.00	40.18	36.35	24.83	23.66	25.06	23.00	28.50	24.90	25.46
P/E Ratio:High	12	12	18	22	NM	NM	21	23	18	13
P/E Ratio:Low	9	9	12	13	NM	NM	10	14	13	10

Income Statement Analysis (Million $)

	2006	2005	2004	2003	2002	2001	2000	1999	1998	1997
Revenue	49,124	46,307	40,161	32,632	27,609	27,805	23,008	18,929	18,441	20,018
Operating Income	6,675	7,437	5,466	3,922	2,925	2,953	3,462	3,407	3,498	4,013
Depreciation	1,954	2,134	2,088	1,903	1,825	1,815	1,315	1,301	1,305	1,287
Interest Expense	689	702	747	828	774	733	460	431	493	471
Pretax Income	4,972	6,399	3,796	1,751	-622	-613	2,401	2,166	2,012	2,948
Effective Tax Rate	23.2%	27.8%	23.1%	NM	NM	NM	34.3%	35.4%	34.0%	35.3%
Net Income	3,724	4,535	2,797	1,739	-405	-417	1,513	1,331	1,310	1,808
S&P Core Earnings	3,638	3,956	2,236	1,462	-1,295	-1,303	NA	NA	NA	NA

Balance Sheet & Other Financial Data (Million $)

	2006	2005	2004	2003	2002	2001	2000	1999	1998	1997
Cash	2,910	3,838	3,192	2,434	1,573	264	304	1,212	390	235
Current Assets	17,209	17,404	15,890	13,002	11,681	10,308	9,260	8,847	8,040	8,640
Total Assets	45,581	45,934	45,885	41,891	39,562	35,515	27,645	25,499	23,830	24,040
Current Liabilities	10,601	10,663	10,506	9,534	8,856	8,125	7,873	6,295	6,842	7,340
Long Term Debt	8,036	10,186	12,629	12,763	12,659	10,266	5,365	5,022	4,051	4,196
Common Equity	17,065	15,324	12,270	9,175	7,626	9,993	9,186	8,323	7,429	7,626
Total Capital	27,465	27,241	26,649	23,438	21,645	21,376	15,848	14,642	12,802	13,196
Capital Expenditures	1,775	1,597	1,333	1,100	1,623	1,587	1,349	1,412	1,546	1,198
Cash Flow	5,678	6,669	4,885	3,642	1,420	1,398	2,828	2,627	2,609	3,089
Current Ratio	1.6	1.6	1.5	1.4	1.3	1.3	1.2	1.4	1.2	1.2
% Long Term Debt of Capitalization	30.4	37.4	47.4	54.5	58.5	48.0	33.9	34.3	31.6	31.7
% Net Income of Revenue	7.6	9.8	7.0	5.3	NM	NM	6.6	7.0	7.1	9.0
% Return on Assets	8.1	9.9	6.4	4.3	NM	NM	5.7	5.4	5.5	7.4
% Return on Equity	23.0	32.9	26.1	20.7	NM	NM	17.3	16.8	17.3	23.1

Data as orig reptd.; bef. results of disc opers/spec. items. Per share data adj. for stk. divs.; EPS diluted. E-Estimated. NA-Not Available. NM-Not Meaningful. NR-Not Ranked. UR-Under Review.

Office: 2030 Dow Center, Midland, MI 48674-0001.
Telephone: 989-636-1000.
Website: http://www.dow.com
Chrmn, Pres & CEO: A.N. Liveris

EVP & CFO: G.E. Merszei
SVP & CIO: D.E. Kepler
VP & CTO: W.F. Banholzer
VP & Treas: F. Ruiz

Investor Contact: T. McNeill (989-636-0626)
Board Members: A. A. Allemang, J. K. Barton, J. A. Bell, J. M. Fettig, B. H. Franklin, J. B. Hess, A. N. Liveris, G. E. Merszei, J. M. Ringler, R. G. Shaw, P. G. Stern

Founded: 1897
Domicile: Delaware
Employees: 42,578

Dow Jones and Co Inc.

STANDARD &POOR'S

S&P Recommendation HOLD ★★★☆☆	**Price** $59.90 (as of Nov 23, 2007)	**12-Mo. Target Price** $60.00	**Investment Style** Large-Cap Blend

GICS Sector Consumer Discretionary
Sub-Industry Publishing

Summary Dow Jones publishes The Wall Street Journal and Barron's, provides newswire, news retrieval and financial information services, and publishes general circulation newspapers. The company has agreed to be acquired for $60 per share.

Key Stock Statistics (Source S&P, Vickers, company reports)

52-Wk Range	$61.76– 33.67	S&P Oper. EPS 2007**E**	1.53	Market Capitalization(B)	$4.001	Beta	1.08
Trailing 12-Month EPS	$2.95	S&P Oper. EPS 2008**E**	2.00	Yield (%)	1.67	S&P 3-Yr. Proj. EPS CAGR(%)	34.00
Trailing 12-Month P/E	20.3	P/E on S&P Oper. EPS 2007**E**	39.2	Dividend Rate/Share	$1.00	S&P Credit Rating	BBB
$10K Invested 5 Yrs Ago	$15,832	Common Shares Outstg. (M)	86.2	Institutional Ownership (%)	84		

Price Performance

30-Week Mov. Avg. · · · 10-Week Mov. Avg. – – **GAAP Earnings vs. Previous Year** Volume Above Avg. STARS
12-Mo. Target Price — Relative Strength — ▲ Up ▼ Down ▶ No Change Below Avg. ★

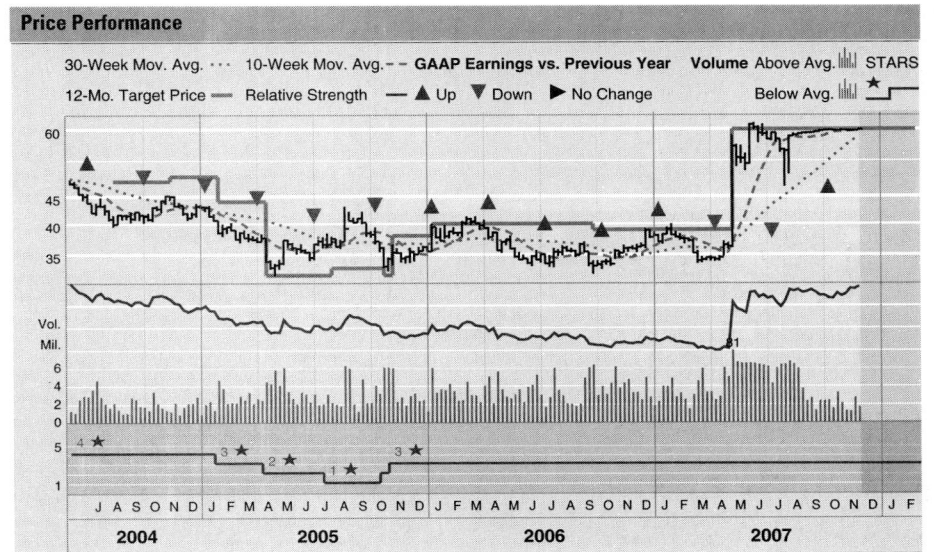

Options: ASE, P, Ph

Analysis prepared by **James Peters, CFA** on October 19, 2007, when the stock traded at **$ 59.69**.

Highlights

➤ We see revenue growth of about 4.0% in 2008, following a rise of 17% we see for 2007. Our 2007 estimate reflects about $300 million of incremental revenues from the Factiva acquisition, and a decline of around $48 million to incorporate the sale of six community newspapers. While we expect a difficult print advertising environment to persist in 2008, we see continued online revenue growth boosting results. We note that DJ is well ahead of peers with about 50% of revenue from online sources.

➤ We forecast operating margin expansion to 13.8% in 2008, up from our projection of 10.8% for 2007. We see cost savings generated from various efficiency initiatives started over the past few years, including a web width reduction project DJ began in 2007 that we expect to further reduce newsprint expense in 2008.

➤ After lower projected interest expense, we see EPS rising to $2.00 in 2008, up from our forecast of $1.53 in 2007. EPS in 2007 excludes $0.26 of one-time charges mostly associated with the planned acquisition of DJ. Our 2008 EPS forecast is for DJ as a stand-alone entity.

Investment Rationale/Risk

➤ On August 1, News Corporation (NWS: buy, $23) agreed to acquire DJ for $60 per share in cash. The agreement allows DJ's shareholders to convert up to 10% of outstanding company shares into a newly formed subsidiary of NWS. The board of directors for both companies approved the deal, and members of the Bancroft family agreed to vote about 37% of all shares in favor of the transaction. We see shareholders in aggregate approving the deal, as it reflects a 65% premium to DJ's closing price the day before the deal was first announced. In October, DJ said the deal is expected to close in December, subject to shareholder and regulatory approval and other customary closing conditions.

➤ Risks to our recommendation and target price include the forecast deal to purchase DJ not being consummated, a rapid decline in advertising, and the possibility that DJ will not achieve savings from cost-cutting actions.

➤ Our 12-month target price of $60 reflects our belief that the announced deal to purchase DJ will be consummated.

Qualitative Risk Assessment

LOW	**MEDIUM**	HIGH

Our risk assessment reflects the cyclical nature of technology and financial advertising, significant competition from various media for advertising, and the possibility that the deal to purchase DJ is not consummated, offset by what we view as the company's superior-to-peers ability to monetize its reputation via sales of Web-based content and other products.

Quantitative Evaluations

S&P Quality Ranking B

D	C	B-	**B**	B+	A-	A	A+

Relative Strength Rank STRONG

83

LOWEST = 1 HIGHEST = 99

Revenue/Earnings Data

Revenue (Million $)

	1Q	2Q	3Q	4Q	Year
2007	507.2	529.7	493.3	--	--
2006	430.1	456.0	412.4	485.4	1,784
2005	412.1	454.2	421.2	482.2	1,770
2004	401.6	437.8	394.9	437.2	1,671
2003	358.2	393.6	376.0	420.7	1,548
2002	392.9	417.0	352.4	396.9	1,559

Earnings Per Share ($)

2007	0.27	0.25	0.16	E0.60	E1.53
2006	0.74	0.34	0.15	0.70	1.83
2005	0.10	0.01	0.12	0.49	0.73
2004	0.22	0.41	0.15	0.43	1.21
2003	0.82	0.38	0.35	0.54	2.08
2002	1.53	0.64	0.03	0.18	2.40

Fiscal year ended Dec. 31. Next earnings report expected: NA. EPS Estimates based on S&P Operating Earnings; historical GAAP earnings are as reported.

Dividend Data (Dates: mm/dd Payment Date: mm/dd/yy)

Amount ($)	Date Decl.	Ex-Div. Date	Stk. of Record	Payment Date
0.250	01/17	01/30	02/01	03/01/07
0.250	04/18	04/27	05/01	06/01/07
0.250	06/20	07/30	08/01	09/04/07
0.250	09/19	10/30	11/01	12/03/07

Dividends have been paid since 1906. Source: Company reports.

Please read the Required Disclosures and Analyst Certification on the last page of this report.

The McGraw-Hill Companies

Dow Jones and Co Inc.

STANDARD
&POOR'S

Business Summary October 19, 2007

CORPORATE OVERVIEW. Dow Jones & Co., a global provider of financial news and information, is the parent of The Wall Street Journal and Barron's. In February 2006, DJ was realigned into consumer, enterprise and community media segments in order to reflect its markets and customers, rather than its media distribution methods.

The Consumer Media Group (about 62% of 2006 revenues) includes the Wall Street Journal Franchise (including domestic and international print, online, television and radio), the Barron's Franchise (print, online and conferences), and the MarketWatch Franchise (online, newsletters, television and radio). The Enterprise Media Group (23%) includes Factiva, Dow Jones Newswires, Dow Jones Licensing Services, Dow Jones Indexes, Dow Jones Financial Information Services, and Dow Jones Reprints and Permissions. The Community Media Group (15%) includes the Ottaway Community newspaper properties.

COMPETITIVE LANDSCAPE. The Wall Street Journal (WSJ) is one of only three national newspapers, along with the New York Times and Gannett's

USA Today. Because of wide national distribution of the paper, WSJ's advertiser base is skewed more toward national advertisers than most newspaper publishers. In turn, this makes WSJ's advertising levels more volatile than most newspaper publishers since there is a greater level of competition for national advertiser spending, in our view. DJ's advertiser base is also more skewed toward B2B advertising than that of most newspaper publishers, with a reliance on technology and financial advertising that has hurt revenue results in recent years, in our opinion, as those advertising categories have struggled. In September 2005, DJ launched the Weekend Edition of the WSJ on Saturdays in an attempt to diversify its advertising base by incorporating more consumer-based advertising.

Company Financials Fiscal Year Ended Dec. 31

Per Share Data ($)	2006	2005	2004	2003	2002	2001	2000	1999	1998	1997
Tangible Book Value	NM	NM	NM	NM	NM	NM	0.98	5.24	4.60	4.07
Cash Flow	2.99	2.03	2.48	3.38	3.71	2.36	-0.13	4.13	1.56	-5.74
Earnings	1.83	0.73	1.21	2.08	2.40	1.14	-1.35	2.99	0.09	-8.36
S&P Core Earnings	1.09	0.89	0.88	0.91	0.16	1.09	NA	NA	NA	NA
Dividends	1.00	1.00	1.00	1.00	1.00	1.00	1.00	0.96	0.96	0.96
Payout Ratio	55%	137%	83%	48%	42%	88%	NM	32%	NM	NM
Prices:High	41.39	43.35	52.74	53.62	60.20	64.30	77.31	71.38	59.00	55.88
Prices:Low	32.16	31.94	39.50	33.25	29.50	43.05	51.38	43.63	41.56	33.38
P/E Ratio:High	23	59	44	26	25	56	NM	24	NM	NM
P/E Ratio:Low	18	44	33	16	12	38	NM	15	NM	NM

Income Statement Analysis (Million $)

	2006	2005	2004	2003	2002	2001	2000	1999	1998	1997
Revenue	1,784	1,770	1,671	1,548	1,559	1,773	2,203	2,002	2,158	2,573
Operating Income	245	241	271	231	209	289	606	496	437	510
Depreciation	97.5	108	105	106	110	106	108	104	142	251
Interest Expense	30.2	19.3	3.74	2.83	3.08	0.50	2.04	5.27	7.19	19.4
Pretax Income	161	104	156	221	258	99.7	76.4	418	71.7	-764
Effective Tax Rate	4.95%	41.7%	37.5%	23.4%	24.8%	98.5%	NM	34.8%	88.0%	NM
Net Income	153	60.4	99.5	171	202	98.2	-119	272	8.36	-802
S&P Core Earnings	91.3	74.5	72.0	74.9	12.3	93.2	NA	NA	NA	NA

Balance Sheet & Other Financial Data (Million $)

	2006	2005	2004	2003	2002	2001	2000	1999	1998	1997
Cash	13.2	10.6	17.2	23.5	39.3	21.0	49.3	86.4	143	23.8
Current Assets	314	284	254	246	251	246	368	456	442	507
Total Assets	1,956	1,782	1,380	1,304	1,208	1,298	1,362	1,531	1,491	1,920
Current Liabilities	828	1,018	717	614	622	602	587	579	600	672
Long Term Debt	225	225	136	153	92.9	174	151	150	150	229
Common Equity	2,198	1,905	151	130	40.6	41.8	159	553	509	781
Total Capital	2,422	2,130	290	289	134	220	318	703	659	1,010
Capital Expenditures	91.3	65.3	76.0	55.9	77.7	129	187	191	226	348
Cash Flow	251	169	204	277	311	204	-11.1	376	151	-551
Current Ratio	0.4	0.3	0.4	0.4	0.4	0.4	0.6	0.8	0.7	0.8
% Long Term Debt of Capitalization	9.3	10.6	46.7	52.9	69.3	79.2	47.4	21.3	22.7	22.7
% Net Income of Revenue	8.6	3.4	6.0	11.0	12.9	5.5	NM	13.6	0.4	NM
% Return on Assets	8.2	3.8	7.4	13.6	16.1	7.4	NM	18.1	0.5	NM
% Return on Equity	7.5	3.1	5.0	7.7	489.5	98.0	NM	51.3	1.3	NM

Data as orig reptd.; bef. results of disc opers/spec. items. Per share data adj. for stk. divs.; EPS diluted. E-Estimated. NA-Not Available. NM-Not Meaningful. NR-Not Ranked. UR-Under Review.

Office: 200 Liberty St, New York, NY 10281.
Telephone: 212-416-2000.
Email: investorrelations@dowjones.com
Website: http://www.dowjones.com

Chrmn: M.R. McPherson
CEO: R.F. Zannino
VP, Secy & General Counsel: J.A. Stern
CFO: W.B. Plummer

Investor Contact: M. Donohue (609-520-5660)
Board Members: C. Bancroft, J. E. Barfield, J. F. Brock, L. B. Campbell, E. Castro-Wright, M. B. Elefante, J. M. Engler, H. Golub, L. Hill, I. O. Hockaday, Jr., V. E. Jordan, Jr., D. K. Li, M. P. McPherson, F. N. Newman, J. H. Ottaway, Jr., P. Sagan, E. Steele, W. C. Steere, Jr., R. F. Zannino, D. von Holtzbrinck

Founded: 1882
Domicile: Delaware
Employees: 7,400

D.R. Horton Inc.

STANDARD &POOR'S

S&P Recommendation BUY ★★★★☆

Price	12-Mo. Target Price	Investment Style
$11.38 (as of Nov 23, 2007)	$18.00	Large-Cap Blend

GICS Sector Consumer Discretionary
Sub-Industry Homebuilding

Summary DHI is the largest homebuilder in the U.S., based on the number of homes sold.

Key Stock Statistics (Source S&P, Vickers, company reports)

52-Wk Range	**$31.13– 10.46**	S&P Oper. EPS 2008**E**	**1.00**	Market Capitalization(B)	**$3.574**	Beta	**2.10**
Trailing 12-Month EPS	**$-2.27**	S&P Oper. EPS 2009**E**	**2.00**	Yield (%)	**5.27**	S&P 3-Yr. Proj. EPS CAGR(%)	**30.00**
Trailing 12-Month P/E	**NM**	P/E on S&P Oper. EPS 2008**E**	**11.4**	Dividend Rate/Share	**$0.60**	S&P Credit Rating	**BB+**
$10K Invested 5 Yrs Ago	**$13,258**	Common Shares Outstg. (M)	**314.1**	Institutional Ownership (%)	**86**		

Price Performance

30-Week Mov. Avg. ··· 10-Week Mov. Avg. — **GAAP Earnings vs. Previous Year** Volume Above Avg. STARS
12-Mo. Target Price — Relative Strength — ▲ Up ▼ Down ▶ No Change Below Avg.

Options: ASE, CBOE, P, Ph

Analysis prepared by **Kenneth M. Leon, CPA** on November 21, 2007, when the stock traded at **$ 11.18**.

Highlights

➤ After a 25% sales decline in FY 07 (Sep.), we are forecasting mid-single digit sales growth in FY 08 and FY 09, as a multi-year slowdown in the housing industry plays out. Net sales orders fell 35% in units and 41% in dollar value in FY 07 compared to a year earlier. We believe housing market conditions may begin to stabilize in the second half of 2008 as lower mortgage interest rates should increase affordability for DHI's target market of first-time buyers and first-time move-up buyers.

➤ We estimate DHI's homebuilding gross margin will remain near 20% in FY 08 and FY 09 in line with FY 07. DHI realized a peak gross margin of 24% in FY 06. Asset impairment charges, which were $1.3 billion in FY 07, should continue, in our view, and we are forecasting $400 million in FY 08.

➤ By our analysis, pretax margins should widen in FY 08 with DHI's strong focus on lowering SG&A costs to the low 10% level as a percentage of total revenues, one of the best levels in the industry. With strong cost controls, we estimate EPS of $1.00 in FY 08 and $2.00 in FY 09.

Investment Rationale/Risk

➤ As DHI is the largest U.S. homebuilder, we see reduced interest rates raising affordability in its target markets. Less than 5% of DHI's pending contracts are subprime borrowers. We view DHI as one of the best managed homebuilders, with strong SG&A cost controls and the drive to lower labor costs with subcontractors and material costs. We believe a housing recovery in the second half of 2008 should benefit DHI with a return to more stable home prices and an improved pace to complete its communities.

➤ Risks to our recommendation and target price include the possibility of higher mortgage rates and weakening housing affordability. We see the potential for further writedowns of inventory and joint venture investments above our target, which would be detrimental to our FY 08 EPS estimate and book value.

➤ Our 12-month target price of $18 reflects a target price-to-book multiple of 1X applied to our estimated forward book value, near the low end of the historical range for DHI but still a premium to its peers, reflecting its strong balance sheet, operating scale advantages and cost-control efforts.

Qualitative Risk Assessment

LOW	**MEDIUM**	HIGH

Our medium risk assessment reflects DHI's exposure to an extended downturn in the housing market, offset by DHI's focus on reducing debt with free cash flow from operations. As the largest U.S. homebuilder, DHI has scale advantages to reduce subcontractor labor costs and material costs, but weak demand may delay profitability.

Quantitative Evaluations

S&P Quality Ranking   **A**

D	C	B-	B	B+	A-	**A**	A+

Relative Strength Rank   **WEAK**

19

LOWEST = 1   HIGHEST = 99

Revenue/Earnings Data

Revenue (Million $)

	1Q	2Q	3Q	4Q	Year
2007	2,868	2,616	2,548	3,123	11,089
2006	2,903	3,598	3,668	4,883	15,051
2005	2,520	2,877	3,370	5,097	13,864
2004	2,205	2,335	2,790	3,511	10,841
2003	1,745	1,909	2,212	2,862	8,728
2002	1,160	1,600	1,808	2,170	6,739

Earnings Per Share ($)

2007	0.35	0.16	-2.62	-0.16	-2.27
2006	0.98	1.11	0.93	0.88	3.90
2005	0.76	0.92	1.17	1.77	4.62
2004	0.58	0.60	0.80	1.10	3.08
2003	0.38	0.43	0.50	0.73	2.05
2002	0.31	0.32	0.34	0.46	1.44

Fiscal year ended Sep. 30. Next earnings report expected: Late January. EPS Estimates based on S&P Operating Earnings; historical GAAP earnings are as reported.

Dividend Data (Dates: mm/dd Payment Date: mm/dd/yy)

Amount ($)	Date Decl.	Ex-Div. Date	Stk. of Record	Payment Date
0.150	01/11	01/24	01/26	02/09/07
0.150	04/24	05/02	05/04	05/18/07
0.150	08/02	08/15	08/17	08/27/07
0.150	10/24	11/01	11/05	11/16/07

Dividends have been paid since 1997. Source: Company reports.

D.R. Horton Inc.

STANDARD &POOR'S

Business Summary November 21, 2007

CORPORATE OVERVIEW. D.R. Horton was founded in 1978 by Donald Horton, now chairman. In 1992, it went public in order to gain broader access to capital markets, which has helped fuel its subsequent growth beyond its base in the Dallas/Fort Worth area. With operating divisions in 27 states and 84 markets, D.R. Horton is the largest domestic homebuilder by number of homes closed in FY 06 (Sept.) and the most geographically diversified.

The company was the first U.S. builder to sell 50,000 homes in a single year (FY 05 (Sept.)) and it aims to be the first to eclipse the 100,000 unit mark (by FY 10). By emphasizing entry level and first-time move-up buyers, it targets the broadest segments of the population. With an average selling price at $253,000 in FY 07 and $273,900 in FY 06, DHI's homes are among the most affordable of all public builders. Detached homes accounted for 80% of home sales revenue in FY 06.

CORPORATE STRATEGY. Most of D.R. Horton's growth in the past 15 to 20 years has been the result of organic initiatives, in our opinion. Generally, the company has established satellite operations in new markets located in rela-

tively close proximity to existing markets. We think the company has been successful at quickly ramping up volumes in these satellite operations--often at the expense of smaller competitors -- aided by materials purchasing agreements struck at the regional level and relatively favorable access to capital markets.

Complementing this organic growth has been an aggressive takeover program, with close to 20 acquisitions since DHI went public. Most of these deals have occurred in new markets in an effort to either create a platform for future growth in a locale or to expand an existing satellite operation there. The majority of these acquisitions have been focused on a single market and have been asset-based transactions, rather than purchases of companies. However, in 2002, DHI bought Schuler Homes for about $1.8 billion, in a deal that we believe increased its revenue base about 25%.

Company Financials Fiscal Year Ended Sep. 30

Per Share Data ($)	2007	2006	2005	2004	2003	2002	2001	2000	1999	1998
Tangible Book Value	NA	18.75	15.28	10.87	7.93	5.77	4.83	3.81	3.01	2.43
Cash Flow	NA	4.10	4.87	3.24	2.16	1.54	1.24	0.94	0.78	0.46
Earnings	-2.27	3.90	4.62	3.08	2.05	1.44	1.10	0.84	0.69	0.43
S&P Core Earnings	NA	3.90	4.61	3.07	2.04	1.44	1.16	NA	NA	NA
Dividends	0.60	0.44	0.31	0.22	0.14	0.10	0.06	0.05	0.03	0.02
Payout Ratio	NM	11%	7%	7%	7%	7%	5%	5%	5%	6%
Prices:High	31.13	41.66	42.82	31.41	22.69	14.58	11.17	7.81	6.34	6.87
Prices:Low	10.46	19.52	26.83	18.47	8.48	8.02	5.83	3.00	2.76	2.93
P/E Ratio:High	NM	11	9	10	11	10	10	9	9	16
P/E Ratio:Low	NM	5	6	6	4	6	5	4	4	7

Income Statement Analysis (Million $)										
Revenue	NA	15,051	13,864	10,841	8,728	6,739	4,456	3,654	3,156	2,177
Operating Income	NA	2,036	2,402	1,430	1,049	693	480	339	273	189
Depreciation	NA	61.7	52.8	49.6	41.8	32.8	31.2	22.0	20.8	9.83
Interest Expense	NA	55.0	21.2	9.30	12.6	11.5	14.1	15.8	16.5	16.2
Pretax Income	NA	1,987	2,379	1,583	1,008	648	408	309	264	159
Effective Tax Rate	NA	37.9%	38.2%	38.4%	37.9%	37.5%	37.5%	38.0%	39.4%	41.3%
Net Income	NA	1,233	1,471	975	626	405	255	192	160	93.4
S&P Core Earnings	NA	1,233	1,463	969	622	406	267	NA	NA	NA

Balance Sheet & Other Financial Data (Million $)										
Cash	NA	588	1,150	518	583	104	239	72.5	129	76.8
Current Assets	NA	NA	NA	NA	NA	NA	NA	NA	NA	NA
Total Assets	NA	14,821	12,515	8,985	7,279	6,018	3,652	2,695	2,362	1,668
Current Liabilities	NA	NA	NA	NA	NA	NA	NA	NA	NA	NA
Long Term Debt	NA	4,861	3,660	3,032	2,665	2,636	1,884	1,344	1,191	855
Common Equity	NA	6,453	5,360	3,961	3,031	2,270	1,250	970	798	549
Total Capital	NA	11,419	9,224	7,159	5,832	4,927	3,143	2,319	1,993	1,407
Capital Expenditures	NA	83.3	68.2	55.2	48.7	39.8	33.4	19.6	17.3	11.6
Cash Flow	NA	1,295	1,523	1,025	668	437	286	214	181	103
Current Ratio	NA	NA	NA	NA	NA	NA	NA	NA	NA	NA
% Long Term Debt of Capitalization	NA	42.6	39.7	42.4	45.7	53.5	59.9	58.0	59.7	60.8
% Net Income of Revenue	NA	8.2	10.6	8.9	7.2	6.0	5.7	5.2	5.1	4.3
% Return on Assets	NA	9.0	13.7	12.0	9.4	8.4	8.0	7.6	7.9	7.8
% Return on Equity	NA	20.9	31.5	27.9	23.6	23.0	23.0	21.7	23.7	23.0

Data as orig reptd.; bef. results of disc opers/spec. items. Per share data adj. for stk. divs.; EPS diluted. E-Estimated. NA-Not Available. NM-Not Meaningful. NR-Not Ranked. UR-Under Review.

Office: 301 Commerce St Ste 500, Fort Worth, TX 76102-4178.
Telephone: 817-390-8200.
Website: http://www.drhorton.com
Chrmn: D.R. Horton

Pres, Vice Chrmn & CEO: D.J. Tomnitz
Sr EVP: S.R. Fuller
EVP & CFO: B. Wheat
Investor Contact: S.H. Dwyer (817-390-8200)

Board Members: B. S. Anderson, M. R. Buchanan, R. I. Galland, M. W. Hewatt, D. R. Horton, D. J. Tomnitz, B. Wheat

Founded: 1991
Domicile: Delaware
Employees: 8,772

The McGraw·Hill Companies

DTE Energy Co

STANDARD &POOR'S

| S&P Recommendation **HOLD** ★★★☆☆ | Price $48.76 (as of Nov 23, 2007) | 12-Mo. Target Price $51.00 |

GICS Sector Utilities
Sub-Industry Multi-Utilities

Summary This Detroit-based diversified energy company is involved in the development and management of energy-related businesses and services nationwide.

Key Stock Statistics (Source S&P, Vickers, company reports)

52-Wk Range	$54.74– 45.14	S&P Oper. EPS 2007E	2.60	Market Capitalization(B)	$7.983	Beta	0.57
Trailing 12-Month EPS	$4.92	S&P Oper. EPS 2008E	3.30	Yield (%)	4.35	S&P 3-Yr. Proj. EPS CAGR(%)	4.00
Trailing 12-Month P/E	9.9	P/E on S&P Oper. EPS 2007E	18.8	Dividend Rate/Share	$2.12	S&P Credit Rating	BBB
$10K Invested 5 Yrs Ago	$13,635	Common Shares Outstg. (M)	163.7	Institutional Ownership (%)	63		

Price Performance

30-Week Mov. Avg. · · · 10-Week Mov. Avg. - - GAAP Earnings vs. Previous Year Volume Above Avg. STARS
12-Mo. Target Price — Relative Strength — ▲ Up ▼ Down ▶ No Change Below Avg.

Options: ASE, Ph

Analysis prepared by **Justin McCann** on November 12, 2007, when the stock traded at **$ 47.84**.

Highlights

➤ Excluding the impact of synfuel-related tax credits, we expect operating EPS in 2007 to decrease 10% from 2006 EPS from continuing operations of $2.89. We believe the projected ex-synfuel decline will reflect lower earnings from energy trading and Detroit Edison. We think synfuel EPS in 2007 could range between $0.60 and $1.25. However, we expect synfuel related hedges and tax credit carryforwards on the business to contribute about $900 million in cash between 2007 and the end of 2009.

➤ We expect EPS in 2008 to increase more than 25% from anticipated ex-synfuel results in 2007, largely driven by DTE's plan to use the after-tax proceeds of its asset sales for debt reduction and share buybacks. Following the agreed to sale of its Antrim gas assets, DTE hopes to realize at least $1.25 billion in after-tax proceeds from the sale of some of its non-utility business.

➤ On April 13, 2007, Detroit Edison filed a general rate case with the Michigan Public Service Commission (MPSC). If approved as filed, it would result in a 2.9% average rate increase in 2008, and an authorized ROE of 11.25% (up from 11.0%). We expect the MPSC to issue a ruling on the request during the first half of 2008.

Investment Rationale/Risk

➤ We believe the shares are fairly valued relative to the company's electric and gas utility peers, and we expect the stock to perform in line with the group over the next 12 months. After rising about 13% through early May, the stock has declined around 8% from its year-to-date high. While it is uncertain what DTE will receive in tax credits (set to expire at the end of 2007), we believe that the uncertainty related to synfuel tax credits and earnings will be mitigated by the $900 million in cash produced from synfuel related hedges through 2009.

➤ Risks to our recommendation and target price include a sharp decline in the average P/E of the peer group, as well as inadequate reform of the electric choice program, which has led to a loss of industrial and commercial customers.

➤ The shares recently yielded about 4.4% on what we consider a secure dividend, well above the recent industry average of 3.5%. As we expect the above peer yield to provide some support to the shares, we believe the stock will trade at a modest discount-to-peers' P/E of approximately 15.5X our EPS estimate for 2008. Our 12-month target price is $51.

Qualitative Risk Assessment

| LOW | **MEDIUM** | HIGH |

Our risk assessment reflects a balance between the steady cash flow that we expect from both the regulated utilities, which operate within a generally supportive regulatory environment, and most of the unregulated operations, which we project will contribute approximately one-third of DTE's consolidated cash flow. This is offset by the higher risk and far less predictable contribution we see from the synthetic fuel operations.

Quantitative Evaluations

S&P Quality Ranking B

| D | C | B- | **B** | B+ | A- | A | A+ |

Relative Strength Rank STRONG
79
LOWEST = 1   HIGHEST = 99

Revenue/Earnings Data

Revenue (Million $)

	1Q	2Q	3Q	4Q	Year
2007	2,730	1,954	2,417	--	--
2006	2,635	1,895	2,196	2,296	9,022
2005	2,309	1,941	2,060	2,712	9,022
2004	2,093	1,501	1,594	1,926	7,114
2003	2,095	1,600	1,654	1,692	7,041
2002	1,896	1,478	1,636	1,739	6,749

Earnings Per Share ($)

2007	0.76	2.20	1.19	E0.80	E2.60
2006	0.76	-0.18	1.07	0.81	2.45
2005	0.72	0.19	0.17	2.18	3.27
2004	1.15	0.20	0.54	0.68	2.55
2003	0.64	-0.22	1.06	1.36	2.85
2002	1.24	0.42	0.96	1.21	3.83

Fiscal year ended Dec. 31. Next earnings report expected: Late February. EPS Estimates based on S&P Operating Earnings; historical GAAP earnings are as reported.

Dividend Data (Dates: mm/dd Payment Date: mm/dd/yy)

Amount ($)	Date Decl.	Ex-Div. Date	Stk. of Record	Payment Date
0.530	12/07	12/14	12/18	01/15/07
0.530	03/08	03/15	03/19	04/15/07
0.530	06/01	06/14	06/18	07/15/07
0.530	08/31	09/17	09/19	10/15/07

Dividends have been paid since 1909. Source: Company reports.

Please read the Required Disclosures and Analyst Certification on the last page of this report.

The McGraw-Hill Companies

DTE Energy Co

STANDARD
&POOR'S

Business Summary November 12, 2007

CORPORATE OVERVIEW. DTE Energy, formed on January 1, 1996, is the holding company for The Detroit Edison Company and Michigan Consolidated Gas (MichCon), regulated electric and gas utilities serving customers within the state of Michigan, and three non-utility operations engaged in a variety of energy-related businesses in various portions of the United States. In 2006, the regulated utility operations accounted for 73.0% of consolidated revenues and 85.8% of income from continuing operations, and the non-utility operations 27.0% and 14.2%, respectively.

MARKET PROFILE. Detroit Edison is a regulated electric utility serving approximately 2.2 million customers in southeastern Michigan. In 2006, residential customers accounted for 36.6% of the utility's revenues; commercial customers 35.1%; industrial customers 18.3%; other 7.4%; and wholesale 2.4%. With its high percentage of commercial and industrial customers, the utility has been hurt by the state's Customer Choice program, losing about 6% of retail sales in 2006,12% in 2005, 18% in 2004, and 12% in 2003. However, the loss of customers also had the effect of reducing the need for purchased power, and allowed it to sell excess power into the wholesale market when conditions were favorable. The utility's generating capability is heavily dependent

on the availability of coal, which accounts for approximately 70% of its fuel requirements. The majority of the utility's coal needs are obtained through long-term contracts, with the remainder purchased through short-term agreements or purchases in the spot market.

MichCon is a regulated natural gas utility serving about 1.3 million residential, commercial, and industrial customers in the state of Michigan. It also has subsidiaries involved in the gathering and transmission of natural gas in northern Michigan, and operates one of the largest natural gas distribution and transmission systems in the U.S., with connections to interstate pipelines providing access to most of the major natural gas producing regions in the Gulf Coast, Mid-Continent and Canadian regions. The company purchases its natural gas supplies on the open market through a diversified portfolio of supply contracts, and given its storage capacity, should be able to meet its supply requirements.

Company Financials Fiscal Year Ended Dec. 31

Per Share Data ($)	2006	2005	2004	2003	2002	2001	2000	1999	1998	1997
Tangible Book Value	21.02	20.88	20.01	19.05	14.61	16.06	28.15	26.96	25.49	24.55
Earnings	2.45	3.27	2.55	2.85	3.83	2.14	3.27	3.33	3.05	2.88
S&P Core Earnings	2.88	2.13	1.97	3.22	2.80	2.09	NA	NA	NA	NA
Dividends	2.08	2.06	2.06	2.06	2.06	2.06	2.06	2.06	2.06	2.06
Payout Ratio	85%	63%	81%	72%	54%	96%	63%	62%	68%	72%
Prices:High	49.24	48.31	45.49	49.50	47.70	47.13	41.31	44.69	49.25	34.75
Prices:Low	38.77	41.39	37.88	34.00	33.05	33.13	28.44	31.06	33.44	26.13
P/E Ratio:High	20	15	18	17	12	22	13	13	16	12
P/E Ratio:Low	16	13	15	12	9	15	9	9	11	9

Income Statement Analysis (Million $)	2006	2005	2004	2003	2002	2001	2000	1999	1998	1997
Revenue	9,022	9,022	7,114	7,041	6,749	7,849	5,597	4,728	4,221	3,764
Depreciation	1,014	869	744	687	759	795	758	735	661	660
Maintenance	NA	NA	NA	NA	NA	NA	NA	NA	NA	NA
Fixed Charges Coverage	1.82	1.21	1.35	1.49	2.00	2.04	2.42	2.60	2.84	3.21
Construction Credits	NA	NA	NA	NA	NA	NA	NA	NA	Nil	Nil
Effective Tax Rate	NM	NM	NM	24.0%	NM	NM	1.89%	11.0%	25.8%	38.1%
Net Income	437	576	443	480	632	329	468	483	443	417
S&P Core Earnings	512	374	344	542	463	322	NA	NA	NA	NA

Balance Sheet & Other Financial Data (Million $)	2006	2005	2004	2003	2002	2001	2000	1999	1998	1997
Gross Property	19,224	18,660	18,011	17,679	17,862	17,067	13,162	12,746	12,178	14,495
Capital Expenditures	1,403	1,065	904	751	984	1,096	749	739	555	456
Net Property	11,451	10,830	10,491	10,324	9,813	9,543	7,387	7,148	6,943	8,934
Capitalization:Long Term Debt	7,474	7,080	7,606	7,669	7,785	7,928	4,062	4,052	4,323	3,914
Capitalization:% Long Term Debt	56.1	55.1	57.8	59.2	63.0	63.0	50.3	50.9	53.9	51.3
Capitalization:Preferred	Nil	Nil	Nil	Nil	Nil	Nil	Nil	Nil	Nil	144
Capitalization:% Preferred	Nil	Nil	Nil	Nil	Nil	Nil	Nil	Nil	Nil	1.80
Capitalization:Common	5,849	5,769	5,548	5,287	4,565	4,657	4,015	3,909	3,698	3,562
Capitalization:% Common	43.9	44.9	42.2	40.8	37.0	37.0	49.7	49.1	46.1	46.7
Total Capital	14,950	14,468	13,429	14,256	13,434	14,063	9,878	9,886	9,909	9,904
% Operating Ratio	91.2	96.1	93.4	91.1	82.8	86.3	85.3	82.2	81.4	80.2
% Earned on Net Property	7.4	8.9	8.1	7.2	11.4	8.2	11.4	12.8	11.8	8.4
% Return on Revenue	4.8	6.4	6.2	6.8	9.4	4.2	8.4	10.2	10.5	11.1
% Return on Invested Capital	5.4	6.0	6.1	7.5	9.1	8.9	8.1	8.3	6.2	9.9
% Return on Common Equity	7.5	10.2	8.2	9.7	13.8	7.6	11.8	12.7	12.2	11.9

Data as orig reptd.; bef. results of disc opers/spec. items. Per share data adj. for stk. divs.; EPS diluted. E-Estimated. NA-Not Available. NM-Not Meaningful. NR-Not Ranked. UR-Under Review.

Office: 2000 2nd Ave, Detroit, MI 48226-1279.
Telephone: 313-235-4000.
Email: shareholdersvcs@dteenergy.com
Website: http://www.dteenergy.com

Chrmn & CEO: A.F. Earley, Jr.
Pres & COO: G.M. Anderson
Vice Chrmn: S. Ewing
EVP & CFO: D.E. Meador

SVP & General Counsel: B.D. Peterson
Investor Contact: D. McClung (313-235-8030)
Board Members: L. Bauder, A. F. Earley, Jr., A. D. Gilmour, A. R. Glancy, III, F. M. Hennessey, J. E. Lobbia, G. J. McGovern, E. A. Miller, C. W. Pryor, Jr., J. Robles, Jr., H. F. Sims, J. H. Vandenberghe

Founded: 1995
Domicile: Michigan
Employees: 0

Duke Energy Corp

S&P Recommendation **BUY** ★★★★☆	Price $19.91 (as of Nov 23, 2007)	12-Mo. Target Price $21.00	Investment Style Large-Cap Value

GICS Sector Utilities
Sub-Industry Electric Utilities

Summary DUK provides service to about 3.9 million electric customers in North Carolina, South Carolina, Indiana, Ohio and Kentucky, and 500,000 gas customers in Kentucky and Ohio.

Key Stock Statistics (Source S&P, Vickers, company reports)

52-Wk Range	$34.50–16.91	S&P Oper. EPS 2007**E**	1.24	Market Capitalization(B)	$25.091	Beta	0.86
Trailing 12-Month EPS	$1.29	S&P Oper. EPS 2008**E**	1.26	Yield (%)	4.22	S&P 3-Yr. Proj. EPS CAGR(%)	5.00
Trailing 12-Month P/E	15.4	P/E on S&P Oper. EPS 2007**E**	16.1	Dividend Rate/Share	$0.84	S&P Credit Rating	BBB
$10K Invested 5 Yrs Ago	NA	Common Shares Outstg. (M)	1,260.2	Institutional Ownership (%)	62		

Price Performance

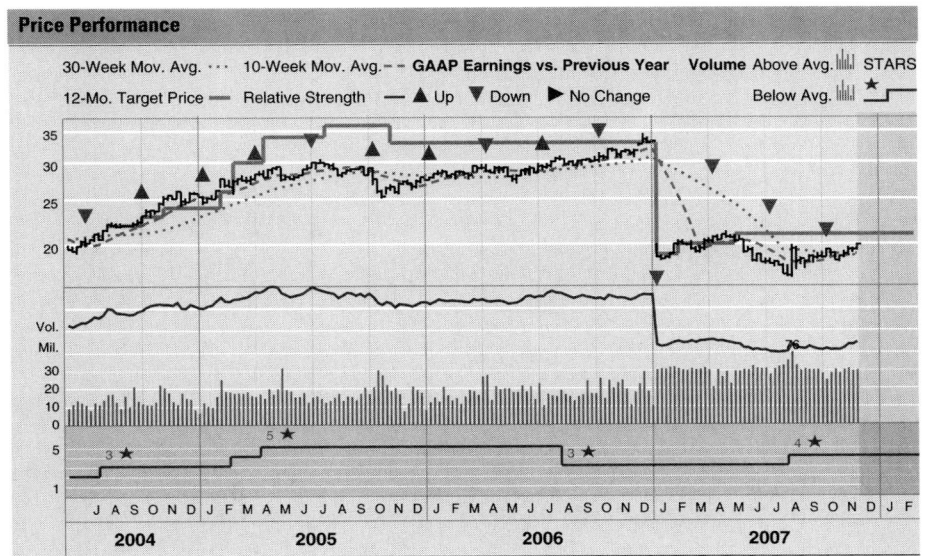

30-Week Mov. Avg. · · · 10-Week Mov. Avg. – – **GAAP Earnings vs. Previous Year** Volume Above Avg. STARS
12-Mo. Target Price — Relative Strength — ▲ Up ▼ Down ▶ No Change Below Avg. ★

Options: ASE, CBOE, P, Ph

Analysis prepared by **Christopher B. Muir** on November 19, 2007, when the stock traded at **$ 19.44**.

Highlights

➤ We look for 2007 revenues to fall by 11.9% as DUK spun-off its Field Services unit, Spectra Energy (SE; hold, $25) on January 1, 2007, partly offset by a full year of revenues from Cinergy, which was acquired in March 2006. We expect 2008 revenues to increase by 6%, helped by customer growth at the utility and growth at the unregulated power generation unit.

➤ Operating margins in 2007 should fall to 18.4% from 20.0% in 2006 due to the spin-off of Field Services. In 2008, we see it recovering to 18.6% due to merger savings and cost control efforts, partly offset by higher depreciation related to the company's heightened capital spending program. In 2007, we expect pretax margin to fall even more due to lower non-operating income, partly offset by higher interest expense. We see 2008 pretax margins rebounding slightly on higher non-operating income.

➤ Assuming an effective tax rate of 27.2% and no share repurchases, we estimate 2007 recurring EPS of $1.24, down 32% from 2006's $1.82 due to the spin-off of Spectra Energy. We see 2008 EPS rising 1.6%, to $1.26.

Investment Rationale/Risk

➤ We believe DUK's exit from several higher risk businesses will be beneficial to the company. We also see the company's underutilized Midwest gas-fired plants benefiting from sales to Cinergy's electric utilities. We think DUK has an improved profile, with our forecast of more than 80% operating income from the company's core utility and merchant electric businesses. We also like DUK's higher growth Carolina service territories and the prospect for increasing the company's rate base through 2012.

➤ Risks to our recommendation and target price include lower electric margins, a higher than expected rise in interest rates, and unfavorable commodity price trends.

➤ The stock recently traded at 15.3X our 2008 EPS estimate, a 7% discount to its electric utility peers. Our 12-month target price of $21 is 16.6X our 2008 EPS estimate, a 7% discount to our peer target. We think this is warranted by what we see as earnings growth that is even with, or slightly less than, peers, and a strong balance sheet. We view positively recent developments at the company, and believe the shares are undervalued.

Qualitative Risk Assessment

LOW	MEDIUM	HIGH

Our risk assessment reflects DUK's large market capitalization and a balanced portfolio of businesses that include lower risk regulated electric and gas utility, partly offset by a higher risk unregulated businesses, though they make up less than 25% of the company's earnings.

Quantitative Evaluations

S&P Quality Ranking B

D	C	B-	**B**	B+	A-	A	A+

Relative Strength Rank STRONG

89

LOWEST = 1 HIGHEST = 99

Revenue/Earnings Data

Revenue (Million $)

	1Q	2Q	3Q	4Q	Year
2007	3,087	3,044	3,818	--	--
2006	3,106	3,865	4,143	4,070	15,184
2005	5,328	5,274	3,028	3,116	16,746
2004	5,635	5,318	5,504	6,046	22,503
2003	6,228	5,235	5,609	5,457	22,529
2002	3,227	3,698	3,982	4,756	15,663

Earnings Per Share ($)

2007	0.27	0.24	0.48	E0.24	E1.24
2006	0.50	0.34	0.60	0.31	1.70
2005	0.88	0.32	0.96	0.43	2.61
2004	0.07	0.43	0.42	0.36	1.27
2003	0.43	0.46	0.05	-1.99	-1.13
2002	0.48	0.56	0.27	-0.06	1.22

Fiscal year ended Dec. 31. Next earnings report expected: Early February. EPS Estimates based on S&P Operating Earnings; historical GAAP earnings are as reported.

Dividend Data (Dates: mm/dd Payment Date: mm/dd/yy)

Amount ($)	Date Decl.	Ex-Div. Date	Stk. of Record	Payment Date
0.210	01/05	02/14	02/16	03/15/07
0.210	04/04	05/09	05/11	06/18/07
0.220	06/26	08/15	08/17	09/17/07
0.220	10/25	11/14	11/16	12/17/07

Dividends have been paid since 1926. Source: Company reports.

Please read the Required Disclosures and Analyst Certification on the last page of this report.

The **McGraw·Hill** Companies

Duke Energy Corp

STANDARD
&POOR'S

Business Summary November 19, 2007

CORPORATE OVERVIEW. Duke provides electric and gas utility services, sells wholesale power, has investments in various South American generation plants, and owns 50% of a real estate joint venture. Operating segments include Franchised Electric and Gas, Commercial Power, Duke Energy International, and Crescent Resources.

MARKET PROFILE. Franchised Electric and Gas serves about 3.9 million electric customers in North Carolina, South Carolina, Indiana, Ohio and Kentucky and about 500,000 gas customers in Kentucky and Ohio, and owns about 28,000 MW of power (net) as of December 2006. The company's service territory now covers 47,000 square miles. We expect that electricity sales in MWh will be broken down into the following categories, after accounting for the inclusion of Cinergy's sales: 31% residential, 27% commercial, 33% industrial and 9% other. We believe the combination with Cinergy effectively reduces the impact that the slowing textile industry in the Carolinas will have on the company's overall sales going forward.

The Commercial Power segment consists of 8,737 net MW, mostly supporting regulated operations in Ohio. There are 5,965 net MW located in Ohio, 640 net MW in Illinois, 620 net MW in Pennsylvania, 552 net MW in Mississippi, and

480 net MW each in Indiana and Tennessee. DEI primarily consists of power generation (4,241 net MW) in Central and South America. In April 2004, the company sold its Australian pipeline assets for $1.24 billion (including $900 million of assumed debt). Crescent Resources develops and manages commercial, residential and multi-family real estate projects in the Southeast and Southwest, and manages legacy land holdings in North and South Carolina.

CORPORATE STRATEGY. We believe DUK has become an electric company focused on regulated operations and electric sales to regulated businesses. In September 2005, Duke began disposing a portion of its former wholesale power generation and marketing unit assets (9,860 net MW of generation capacity at 2004 year end) and contracts outside the Midwest. In March 2006, DUK purchased a Cincinnati-based electric distribution company; in September 2006, DUK sold 51% of Crescent Resources to Morgan Stanley; and in January 2007, the company spun off its natural gas businesses to shareholders.

Company Financials Fiscal Year Ended Dec. 31

Per Share Data ($)	2006	2005	2004	2003	2002	2001	2000	1999	1998	1997
Tangible Book Value	13.54	13.65	12.54	10.74	12.51	14.11	11.21	10.69	10.09	9.36
Earnings	1.70	2.61	1.27	-1.13	1.22	2.56	2.38	1.13	1.71	1.25
S&P Core Earnings	1.80	1.29	1.24	-1.10	1.01	2.29	NA	NA	NA	NA
Dividends	0.95	1.17	1.10	1.10	1.10	1.10	1.10	1.10	1.10	1.08
Payout Ratio	56%	45%	87%	NM	90%	43%	46%	98%	64%	86%
Prices:High	34.50	30.55	26.16	21.57	40.00	47.74	45.22	32.66	35.50	28.28
Prices:Low	26.94	24.37	18.85	12.21	16.42	32.22	22.88	23.38	26.56	20.94
P/E Ratio:High	20	12	21	NM	33	19	19	29	21	23
P/E Ratio:Low	16	9	15	NM	13	13	10	21	16	17

Income Statement Analysis (Million $)										
Revenue	15,184	16,746	22,503	22,529	15,663	59,503	49,318	21,742	17,610	16,309
Depreciation	2,049	1,728	1,851	1,803	1,571	1,336	1,167	968	909	841
Maintenance	NA	NA	NA	NA	NA	NA	NA	NA	NA	NA
Fixed Charges Coverage	2.77	2.91	2.40	1.96	2.46	5.33	4.25	3.16	4.78	3.67
Construction Credits	NA	NA	NA	NA	NA	53.0	63.0	82.0	88.0	109
Effective Tax Rate	28.8%	29.5%	27.5%	NM	35.1%	33.1%	32.9%	31.4%	36.4%	39.1%
Net Income	2,019	2,533	1,232	-1,005	1,034	1,994	1,776	847	1,260	974
S&P Core Earnings	2,131	1,249	1,199	-994	908	1,777	NA	NA	NA	NA

Balance Sheet & Other Financial Data (Million $)										
Gross Property	58,330	40,574	46,806	47,157	48,677	39,464	34,615	30,436	27,128	25,448
Capital Expenditures	322	2,309	2,055	2,470	4,924	5,930	5,634	NA	2,159	1,323
Net Property	41,447	29,200	33,506	34,986	36,219	28,415	24,469	20,995	16,875	15,736
Capitalization:Long Term Debt	18,118	14,547	16,932	20,622	21,629	13,728	12,425	10,087	7,191	6,530
Capitalization:% Long Term Debt	41.0	46.9	50.5	59.8	58.9	51.5	54.7	52.0	45.9	44.8
Capitalization:Preferred	Nil	Nil	134	134	157	234	247	313	313	489
Capitalization:% Preferred	Nil	Nil	0.40	0.39	0.43	0.88	1.09	1.61	2.00	3.40
Capitalization:Common	26,102	16,439	16,441	13,748	14,944	12,689	10,056	8,998	8,150	7,540
Capitalization:% Common	59.0	53.1	49.1	39.8	40.7	47.6	44.2	46.4	52.1	51.8
Total Capital	52,203	36,988	40,375	40,490	43,644	33,393	29,225	24,225	19,882	18,673
% Operating Ratio	87.6	89.6	88.6	85.4	87.1	95.0	94.3	93.8	90.6	91.8
% Earned on Net Property	9.0	11.5	8.9	NM	7.6	15.5	16.8	9.5	14.9	15.4
% Return on Revenue	13.3	15.1	5.5	NM	6.6	3.4	3.6	3.9	7.2	6.0
% Return on Invested Capital	7.5	11.1	7.0	8.7	6.3	10.5	11.2	7.6	13.2	11.2
% Return on Common Equity	9.5	15.3	8.1	NM	7.4	17.4	18.4	9.6	15.5	14.1

Data as orig reptd.; bef. results of disc opers/spec. items. Per share data adj. for stk. divs.; EPS diluted. E-Estimated. NA-Not Available. NM-Not Meaningful. NR-Not Ranked. UR-Under Review.

Office: 526 South Church Street, Charlotte, NC 28202-1904.
Telephone: 704-594-6200.
Website: http://www.duke-energy.com
Chrmn, Pres & CEO: J.E. Rogers

SVP & Treas: L.J. Good
SVP & Cntlr: S.K. Young
VP & CFO: D. Hauser
Chief Admin Officer: C.C. Rolfe

Board Members: W. Barnet III, G. A. Bernhardt, Sr., M. G. Browning, P. R. Cox, A. M. Gray, J. H. Hance, Jr., J. T. Rhodes, J. E. Rogers, M. L. Schapiro, D. S. Taft
Founded: 1916
Domicile: North Carolina
Employees: 25,600

The McGraw-Hill Companies

E. I. du Pont de Nemours and Co

S&P Recommendation **HOLD** ★★★☆☆	Price $44.69 (as of Nov 23, 2007)	12-Mo. Target Price $52.00	Investment Style Large-Cap Value

GICS Sector Materials
Sub-Industry Diversified Chemicals

Summary This broadly diversified company is the second largest U.S. chemicals manufacturer.

Key Stock Statistics (Source S&P, Vickers, company reports)

52-Wk Range	$53.90– 43.79	S&P Oper. EPS 2007**E**	3.18	Market Capitalization(B)	$40.178	Beta	1.18
Trailing 12-Month EPS	$3.55	S&P Oper. EPS 2008**E**	3.40	Yield (%)	3.67	S&P 3-Yr. Proj. EPS CAGR(%)	10.00
Trailing 12-Month P/E	12.6	P/E on S&P Oper. EPS 2007**E**	14.1	Dividend Rate/Share	$1.64	S&P Credit Rating	A
$10K Invested 5 Yrs Ago	$12,224	Common Shares Outstg. (M)	899.0	Institutional Ownership (%)	70		

Price Performance

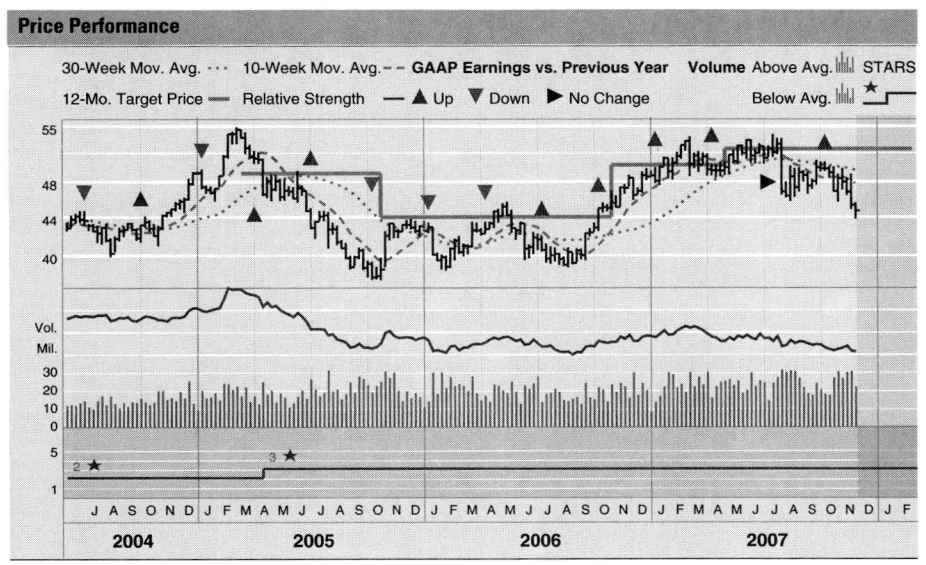

30-Week Mov. Avg. ··· 10-Week Mov. Avg. – – GAAP Earnings vs. Previous Year Volume Above Avg. ▮▮▮ STARS
12-Mo. Target Price — Relative Strength — ▲ Up ▼ Down ► No Change Below Avg. ▮▮▮ ★

Options: ASE, CBOE, P, Ph

Analysis prepared by **Richard O'Reilly, CFA** on August 17, 2007, when the stock traded at **$ 48.00**.

Highlights

➤ We expect sales in 2007 to grow about 6% and operating EPS to rise almost 10% from the $2.88 of 2006. We see DD achieving modest volume growth for the rest of 2007 in its chemicals operations, helped by global economic growth despite softness in key U.S. markets. We believe that selling prices--aided by growth of newer products--will continue to advance. We expect raw material costs to remain moderately higher after the significant increases of the past several years.

➤ We think the agriculture segment's profits for 2007 will recover somewhat from 2006's reduced level, helped by sales of new seed products. While DD's U.S. corn seed sales this year have risen over 20%, in part due to increased acreage, we believe that its market share has continued to decline. Soybean seed sales dropped as U.S. acreage fell about 15%. After increased first half profits for pharmaceuticals as a result of increased sales of Cozaar/Hyzaar, we see second half earnings similar to 2006.

➤ We look for an effective tax rate of about 27% for 2007, versus 2006's 21.5%, which would reduce EPS by about $0.20, mostly in the second half.

Investment Rationale/Risk

➤ While we expect the company to achieve increased profits on global volume gains and better agricultural markets, we look for it to face headwinds in the form of slowdowns in the U.S. housing and auto markets. Historically, high raw material costs pressure chemicals margins. We believe the company lost additional market share in 2007 in the important domestic corn seed market.

➤ Risks to our recommendation and target price include weaker than expected global industrial activity, higher raw material costs than we assume, adverse weather conditions reducing demand for agricultural products, and an inability to successfully develop and launch new products.

➤ The stock recently traded at a P/E in line with that of the S&P 500, at about 15X our 2007 EPS estimate of $3.15, and below our intrinsic value calculation, which assumes average annual free cash flow growth of 10% over 10 years and a discount rate of 9.1%. Using a blend of our relative P/E and DCF metrics, our 12-month target price is $52. DD's recent dividend yield was about 1.6X that of the S&P 500.

Qualitative Risk Assessment

LOW	**MEDIUM**	HIGH

Our risk assessment reflects the company's diverse business and geographic sales mix and its leadership positions in key products, offset by the cyclical nature of the chemical industry and the volatility of raw material costs.

Quantitative Evaluations

S&P Quality Ranking B

D	C	B-	**B**	B+	A-	A	A+

Relative Strength Rank MODERATE

46

LOWEST = 1 HIGHEST = 99

Revenue/Earnings Data

Revenue (Million $)

	1Q	2Q	3Q	4Q	Year
2007	8,161	7,875	6,675	--	--
2006	7,394	7,442	6,309	6,276	27,421
2005	7,431	7,511	5,870	5,827	26,639
2004	8,073	7,527	5,740	6,000	27,340
2003	7,008	7,369	6,142	6,477	26,996
2002	6,142	6,700	5,482	5,682	24,006

Earnings Per Share ($)

2007	1.01	1.04	0.56	E0.48	E3.18
2006	0.88	1.04	0.52	0.94	3.38
2005	0.96	1.01	-0.09	0.16	2.07
2004	0.66	0.50	0.33	0.28	1.77
2003	0.56	0.67	-0.88	0.63	0.99
2002	0.48	0.54	0.47	0.35	1.84

Fiscal year ended Dec. 31. Next earnings report expected: Late January. EPS Estimates based on S&P Operating Earnings; historical GAAP earnings are as reported.

Dividend Data (Dates: mm/dd Payment Date: mm/dd/yy)

Amount ($)	Date Decl.	Ex-Div. Date	Stk. of Record	Payment Date
0.370	01/25	02/13	02/15	03/14/07
0.370	04/25	05/11	05/15	06/12/07
0.370	07/25	08/13	08/15	09/12/07
0.410	10/23	11/13	11/15	12/14/07

Dividends have been paid since 1904. Source: Company reports.

The *McGraw-Hill* Companies

E. I. du Pont de Nemours and Co

STANDARD &POOR'S

Business Summary August 17, 2007

E.I. du Pont de Nemours and Company, the second largest domestic chemicals producer, has made several major changes in recent years, including expanding its life sciences businesses (now crop pesticides and nutrition). In April 2004, it sold the Textile and Interiors unit (consisting of nylon, polyester and Lycra fibers, with total annual sales of $6.3 billion) for $4.2 billion; proceeds were largely used to repay debt. The sale of the fiber businesses reduced DD's exposure to raw material cost changes by about 55%.

Foreign sales accounted for 59% of the total in 2006.

The Agricultural and Nutrition segment (23% of sales in 2006, and 12% of pre-tax operating income) consists of Pioneer Hi-Bred (46% of segment sales in 2006), the world's largest seed company, including corn (70% of sales) and soybeans; DuPont is also a major global supplier of crop protection chemicals (35%). Pioneer estimates that its U.S. corn market share declined slightly in 2006--partly due to a limited supply of certain biotech traits--but that its share in soybeans increased. The segment also includes nutrition and health (including the Solae soy business and food packaging products) and microbial diagnostic testing products. Segment sales declined 1% in 2006 and profits fell 41%, partly due to, in our opinion, a restructuring charge.

The Coatings and Color Technologies unit (23%, 18%) is one of the largest global auto paint suppliers (including OEM and refinish markets) and the largest maker of titanium pigments (35% of segment sales). During 2006, DD restarted its largest pigment plant that suffered extensive hurricane damage in 2005 and said it regained market share lost during the outage in 2005. The segment also includes industrial and powder coatings, and inks for digital printing.

The Electronic and Communication Technologies segment (12%, 14%) includes electronic and advanced display materials and products (photoresins, slurries, films, laminants), and flexographic printing and proofing systems. DD is the world's largest maker of fluorochemicals (refrigerants, blowing agents, aerosols) and fluoropolymers (Teflon resins and coatings).

Performance Materials (22%, 15%) includes engineering polymers for auto, electrical, consumer and industrial uses; packaging and industrial polymers; polyester films; and elastomers.

Company Financials Fiscal Year Ended Dec. 31

Per Share Data ($)	2006	2005	2004	2003	2002	2001	2000	1999	1998	1997
Tangible Book Value	4.56	4.24	6.25	4.63	4.54	7.30	4.50	3.72	9.78	8.66
Cash Flow	4.49	3.45	3.11	2.58	3.35	5.83	3.96	1.73	2.70	4.16
Earnings	3.38	2.07	1.77	0.99	1.84	4.15	2.19	0.19	1.43	2.08
S&P Core Earnings	2.98	1.98	2.00	1.14	0.40	-1.04	NA	NA	NA	NA
Dividends	1.48	1.46	1.40	1.40	1.40	1.40	1.40	1.40	1.37	1.23
Payout Ratio	44%	71%	79%	141%	76%	34%	64%	NM	96%	59%
Prices:High	49.68	54.90	49.39	46.00	49.80	49.88	74.00	75.19	84.44	69.75
Prices:Low	38.52	37.60	39.88	38.60	35.02	32.64	38.19	50.06	51.69	46.38
P/E Ratio:High	15	27	28	46	27	12	34	NM	59	34
P/E Ratio:Low	11	18	23	39	19	8	17	NM	36	22

Income Statement Analysis (Million $)										
Revenue	27,421	26,639	27,340	26,996	24,006	24,726	28,268	26,918	24,767	45,079
Operating Income	3,612	3,507	3,574	3,176	4,263	4,130	5,244	5,469	5,680	8,118
Depreciation	1,384	1,358	1,347	1,584	1,515	1,754	1,860	1,690	1,452	2,385
Interest Expense	460	518	362	347	359	590	810	535	640	642
Pretax Income	3,329	3,558	1,442	143	2,124	6,844	3,447	1,690	2,613	4,680
Effective Tax Rate	5.89%	41.3%	NM	NM	8.71%	36.0%	31.1%	83.4%	36.0%	48.6%
Net Income	3,148	2,053	1,780	1,002	1,841	4,328	2,314	219	1,648	2,405
S&P Core Earnings	2,768	1,965	2,008	1,132	398	-1,087	NA	NA	NA	NA

Balance Sheet & Other Financial Data (Million $)										
Cash	1,893	1,851	3,536	3,298	4,143	5,848	1,617	1,582	1,069	1,146
Current Assets	12,870	12,422	15,211	18,462	13,459	14,801	11,656	12,653	9,236	11,874
Total Assets	31,777	33,250	35,632	37,039	34,621	40,319	39,426	40,777	38,536	42,942
Current Liabilities	7,940	7,463	7,939	13,043	7,096	8,067	9,255	11,228	11,610	14,070
Long Term Debt	6,013	6,783	5,548	4,301	5,647	5,350	6,658	6,625	4,495	5,929
Common Equity	9,185	8,670	11,140	9,544	8,826	14,215	13,062	12,638	13,717	11,033
Total Capital	16,145	17,346	19,001	15,087	18,755	24,916	22,442	21,677	19,286	19,953
Capital Expenditures	1,532	1,340	1,232	1,713	1,280	1,494	1,925	2,055	2,240	4,768
Cash Flow	4,532	3,411	3,117	2,576	3,346	6,072	4,164	1,899	3,090	4,780
Current Ratio	1.6	1.7	1.9	1.4	1.9	1.8	1.3	1.1	0.8	0.8
% Long Term Debt of Capitalization	37.2	39.1	29.2	28.5	30.1	21.5	29.7	30.6	23.3	29.7
% Net Income of Revenue	11.5	7.7	6.5	3.7	7.7	17.5	8.2	0.8	6.7	5.3
% Return on Assets	9.7	6.0	4.9	2.8	4.9	10.9	5.8	0.6	4.4	5.9
% Return on Equity	35.2	20.6	17.1	10.8	15.9	31.7	17.9	1.6	13.3	22.3

Data as orig reptd.; bef. results of disc opers/spec. items. Per share data adj. for stk. divs.; EPS diluted. E-Estimated. NA-Not Available. NM-Not Meaningful. NR-Not Ranked. UR-Under Review.

Office: 1007 Market Street, Wilmington, DE 19898.
Telephone: 302-774-1000.
Email: info@dupont.com
Website: http://www.dupont.com

Chrmn & CEO: C.O. Holliday, Jr.
COO & EVP: R.R. Goodmanson
EVP & CFO: J.L. Keefer
SVP, Chief Admin Officer & General Counsel: S.J. Mobley

SVP & CTO: U. Chowdhry
Investor Contact: C.J. Lukach (800-441-7515)
Board Members: R. H. Brown, R. A. Brown, B. P. Collomb, C. J. Crawford, J. T. Dillon, L. C. Duemling, C. O. Holliday, Jr., L. D. Juliber, M. Naitoh, S. O'Keefe, W. K. Reilly, H. Sharp, III, T. du Pont

Founded: 1802
Domicile: Delaware
Employees: 59,000

The McGraw-Hill Companies

Dynegy Inc.

STANDARD &POOR'S

S&P Recommendation **BUY** ★★★★☆	Price $7.36 (as of Nov 23, 2007)	12-Mo. Target Price $11.00	Investment Style Large-Cap Value

GICS Sector Utilities
Sub-Industry Independent Power Producers & Energy Traders

Summary This company generates and sells wholesale power from plants located primarily in the U.S. Midwest, Northeast and South.

Key Stock Statistics (Source S&P, Vickers, company reports)

52-Wk Range	$10.95– 6.02	S&P Oper. EPS 2007**E**	0.25	Market Capitalization(B)	$3.680	Beta	1.36
Trailing 12-Month EPS	$0.32	S&P Oper. EPS 2008**E**	0.46	Yield (%)	Nil	S&P 3-Yr. Proj. EPS CAGR(%)	34.00
Trailing 12-Month P/E	23.0	P/E on S&P Oper. EPS 2007**E**	29.4	Dividend Rate/Share	Nil	S&P Credit Rating	NA
$10K Invested 5 Yrs Ago	$66,306	Common Shares Outstg. (M)	840.0	Institutional Ownership (%)	80		

Price Performance

30-Week Mov. Avg. · · · 10-Week Mov. Avg. - - GAAP Earnings vs. Previous Year Volume Above Avg. STARS
12-Mo. Target Price — Relative Strength — ▲ Up ▼ Down ▶ No Change Below Avg.

Options: ASE, CBOE, P, Ph

Analysis prepared by **Christopher B. Muir** on November 16, 2007, when the stock traded at **$ 8.11**.

Highlights

➤ We expect revenues to increase about 51% in 2007 as a result of the second quarter purchase of LS Power's generation assets. Revenues in 2008 should climb an additional 20%, in our view, helped by the acquisition and our expectations for higher natural gas prices. We also expect DYN revenues to see a longer term benefit from capacity auctions in various regions.

➤ We forecast gross margins to increase significantly in both 2007 and 2008, due to the acquisition and expected stronger power prices, partly offset by higher per-revenue fuel costs in 2007. In addition, we look for operating margins to be aided by lower per-revenue general and administrative expenses in both years. We forecast that interest expense will increase considerably on higher acquisition related debt levels in 2007, but that 2008 interest expense will decline slightly.

➤ Assuming an effective tax rate of 34.8%, we project 2007 operating EPS of $0.25, compared to an operating loss of $0.14 in 2006. Our 2008 EPS estimate is $0.46, an increase of about 84%.

Investment Rationale/Risk

➤ In April 2007, DYN purchased LS Power's generation portfolio. We expect the acquisition to be immediately accretive to cash flow and earnings. We expect further benefits as we see DYN using its free cash flows to rapidly deleverage its balance sheet. We like the company's efforts to reduce balance sheet debt and that it acquired LS Power's assets using mostly stock. We also think DYN will benefit from merger savings.

➤ Risks to our recommendation and target price include higher coal transportation costs and lower electricity demand. The variability of sales volumes, fuel and commodity prices, and operational activities leads to less earnings visibility, in our opinion.

➤ The shares recently traded at 17.7X our 2008 estimate, or a 6% discount to its peers. Our 12-month target price of $11 is 23.7X our 2008 EPS estimate, a 9% premium to peers. We believe this premium valuation is warranted by DYN's potential for rapid debt reduction, which we think will lead to swift EPS growth in the next few years, and by our perception that the LS Power assets enhance DYN's current power plant portfolio and will add to its earnings.

Qualitative Risk Assessment

LOW	MEDIUM	**HIGH**

Our risk assessment is based on Dynegy's significant exposure to cyclical power markets and volatile commodity markets for fuels that it uses to generate power.

Quantitative Evaluations

S&P Quality Ranking C

D	**C**	B-	B	B+	A-	A	A+

Relative Strength Rank WEAK

20

LOWEST = 1   HIGHEST = 99

Revenue/Earnings Data

Revenue (Million $)

	1Q	2Q	3Q	4Q	Year
2007	573.0	6.75	1,046	--	--
2006	600.0	439.0	581.0	397.0	2,017
2005	462.0	459.0	770.0	622.0	2,313
2004	1,657	1,440	1,650	1,406	6,153
2003	1,879	1,067	1,385	1,456	5,787
2002	1,444	1,380	1,407	1,322	5,553

Earnings Per Share ($)

	1Q	2Q	3Q	4Q	Year
2007	0.03	Nil	0.11	E0.03	E0.25
2006	-0.01	-0.48	-0.14	-0.12	-0.80
2005	-0.71	-0.30	-0.05	-0.98	-2.13
2004	0.14	Nil	0.16	-0.47	-0.09
2003	-0.03	-0.99	2.65	-0.54	1.30
2002	-0.26	-1.76	-4.71	-0.98	-6.24

Fiscal year ended Dec. 31. Next earnings report expected: Late February. EPS Estimates based on S&P Operating Earnings; historical GAAP earnings are as reported.

Dividend Data

No cash dividends have been paid since 2002.

Dynegy Inc.

**STANDARD
&POOR'S**

Business Summary November 16, 2007

CORPORATE OVERVIEW. At the end of 2006, DYN owned or leased 10,675 net Megawatts (MW) of generating capacity. The company provides energy, capacity and ancillary services primarily through bilateral negotiated contracts with third parties and into regional central markets. The power generation business consists of three segments--the Midwest (7,450 MW), the Northeast (1,678 MW), and the South (1,547 MW). About 65% of DYN's generation capacity is gas-fired, 33% is coal-fired, and 2% is oil fired. About 17% of its capacity can be switched to alternate fuels, including gas or oil. In terms of dispatch type, about 39% is base load generation, 11% is intermediate, and 50% is peaking.

By 2006, DYN had completed the fuel conversion of all its Midwest coal generation facilities to exclusively burn Powder River Basin (PRB) coal. PRB coal is a cleaner-burning coal with lower sulfur content, making it more economic to burn while emitting lower amounts of sulfur dioxide. DYN believes the conversion to PRB coal and attendant upgrades to new equipment and technologies will allow its units to improve operating margins and reliability.

CORPORATE STRATEGY. Dynegy has sought to strengthen its balance sheet, in our opinion, in the wake of credit, accounting, regulatory, and operating dif-

ficulties that negatively affected the energy merchant industry in 2002 and 2003. The company raised $389 million in cash from the sale or exchange of businesses and investments in 2006, versus $2.4 billion in 2005, $246 million in 2004, $72 million in 2003, and $1.58 billion in 2002. However in recent years, we believe the company has gained the financial flexibility to make acquisitions, including Sithe Energies in 2005 and the mostly for stock acquisition of LS Power's generation portfolio.

IMPACT OF MAJOR DEVELOPMENTS. In January 2005, DYN completed the acquisition of Sithe Energies for $135 million in cash and the assumption of $919 million of project debt. The acquisition included the 1,021 MW Independence power generation facility located near Scriba, NY, four natural gas-fired merchant facilities in New York, and four hydroelectric generation facilities in Pennsylvania. In addition, Dynegy acquired a 750 MW firm capacity sales agreement with Con Edison, which runs through 2014, and provides annual cash receipts of $100 million.

Company Financials Fiscal Year Ended Dec. 31

Per Share Data ($)	2006	2005	2004	2003	2002	2001	2000	1999	1998	1997
Tangible Book Value	3.86	5.58	4.87	5.04	4.57	8.85	6.49	4.03	3.15	4.52
Cash Flow	-0.20	-1.06	0.64	-0.05	-4.00	3.23	2.71	1.22	0.93	1.41
Earnings	-0.80	-2.13	-0.09	1.30	-6.24	1.89	1.48	0.65	0.48	-0.42
S&P Core Earnings	-0.68	-0.71	0.06	1.76	-1.96	0.73	NA	NA	NA	NA
Dividends	Nil	Nil	Nil	Nil	0.15	0.30	0.32	0.04	0.04	0.04
Payout Ratio	Nil	Nil	Nil	Nil	NM	16%	22%	5%	8%	NM
Prices:High	7.32	5.70	6.09	5.43	32.19	59.00	59.88	17.93	12.68	17.48
Prices:Low	4.50	3.21	3.40	1.13	0.49	20.00	17.12	7.34	6.79	10.67
P/E Ratio:High	NM	NM	NM	4	NM	31	40	27	27	NM
P/E Ratio:Low	NM	NM	NM	1	NM	11	12	11	14	NM

Income Statement Analysis (Million $)										
Revenue	2,017	2,313	6,153	5,787	5,553	42,242	29,445	15,430	14,258	13,378
Operating Income	469	507	620	367	327	1,424	1,130	343	225	490
Depreciation	265	284	356	454	613	454	389	129	103	379
Interest Expense	382	389	480	509	374	259	251	78.2	75.0	63.5
Pretax Income	-526	-1,199	-74.0	-675	-2,546	977	791	243	175	-140
Effective Tax Rate	NM	NM	NM	NM	NM	27.5%	33.0%	30.7%	28.7%	NM
Net Income	-358	-804	-10.0	-474	-1,955	646	501	152	108	-87.7
S&P Core Earnings	-310	-274	27.6	734	-711	246	NA	NA	NA	NA

Balance Sheet & Other Financial Data (Million $)										
Cash	371	1,549	628	496	774	218	86.0	45.2	28.4	23.0
Current Assets	2,082	3,706	2,752	3,030	7,586	9,507	10,150	2,805	2,117	2,019
Total Assets	7,630	10,126	9,852	13,293	20,030	24,874	21,406	6,525	5,264	4,517
Current Liabilities	1,259	2,116	1,802	2,576	6,748	8,555	9,405	2,539	2,026	1,753
Long Term Debt	3,190	4,228	4,332	5,893	5,666	3,854	3,174	1,499	1,247	1,202
Common Equity	2,267	2,153	1,867	2,045	2,087	4,719	3,613	1,234	1,053	944
Total Capital	5,926	7,326	7,302	9,221	10,062	12,694	8,214	3,144	2,692	2,475
Capital Expenditures	155	195	311	333	947	1,845	769	365	299	220
Cash Flow	-102	-542	324	-20.0	-1,672	1,097	855	281	211	291
Current Ratio	1.7	1.8	1.5	1.2	1.1	1.1	1.1	1.1	1.0	1.2
% Long Term Debt of Capitalization	53.8	57.7	59.3	63.9	56.3	30.4	38.6	47.7	46.3	40.5
% Net Income of Revenue	NM	NM	NM	NM	NM	1.5	1.7	1.0	0.8	NM
% Return on Assets	NM	NM	NM	NM	NM	2.8	3.6	2.6	2.2	NM
% Return on Equity	NM	NM	NM	NM	NM	15.5	19.2	13.2	10.8	NM

Data as orig reptd.; bef. results of disc opers/spec. items. Per share data adj. for stk. divs.; EPS diluted. E-Estimated. NA-Not Available. NM-Not Meaningful. NR-Not Ranked. UR-Under Review.

Office: 1000 Louisiana Street, Houston, TX 77002-5050.
Telephone: 713-507-6400.
Email: ir@dynegy.com
Website: http://www.dynegy.com

Chrmn & CEO: B.A. Williamson
Pres & COO: S.A. Furbacher
EVP & CFO: H.C. Nichols
EVP, Secy & General Counsel: J.K. Blodgett

SVP & Cntlr: C.J. Stone
Investor Contact: N. Grossman (713-507-6466)
Board Members: D. W. Biegler, T. D. Clark, Jr., V. E. Grijalva, P. A. Hammick, G. L. Mazanec, R. C. Oelkers, R. Roberts, H. B. Sheppard, W. L. Trubeck, B. A. Williamson

Founded: 1985
Domicile: Illinois
Employees: 1,339

Eastman Chemical Co

STANDARD &POOR'S

S&P Recommendation **BUY** ★★★★☆	Price $60.41 (as of Nov 23, 2007)	12-Mo. Target Price $80.00	Investment Style Large-Cap Value

GICS Sector Materials
Sub-Industry Diversified Chemicals

Summary This global company manufactures and markets more than 1,200 chemicals, fibers and polyester plastics products.

Key Stock Statistics (Source S&P, Vickers, company reports)

52-Wk Range	$72.44– 57.54	S&P Oper. EPS 2007**E**	4.80	Market Capitalization(B)	$4.895	Beta	0.79
Trailing 12-Month EPS	$3.50	S&P Oper. EPS 2008**E**	5.00	Yield (%)	2.91	S&P 3-Yr. Proj. EPS CAGR(%)	10.00
Trailing 12-Month P/E	17.3	P/E on S&P Oper. EPS 2007**E**	12.6	Dividend Rate/Share	$1.76	S&P Credit Rating	BBB
$10K Invested 5 Yrs Ago	$19,750	Common Shares Outstg. (M)	81.0	Institutional Ownership (%)	93		

Price Performance

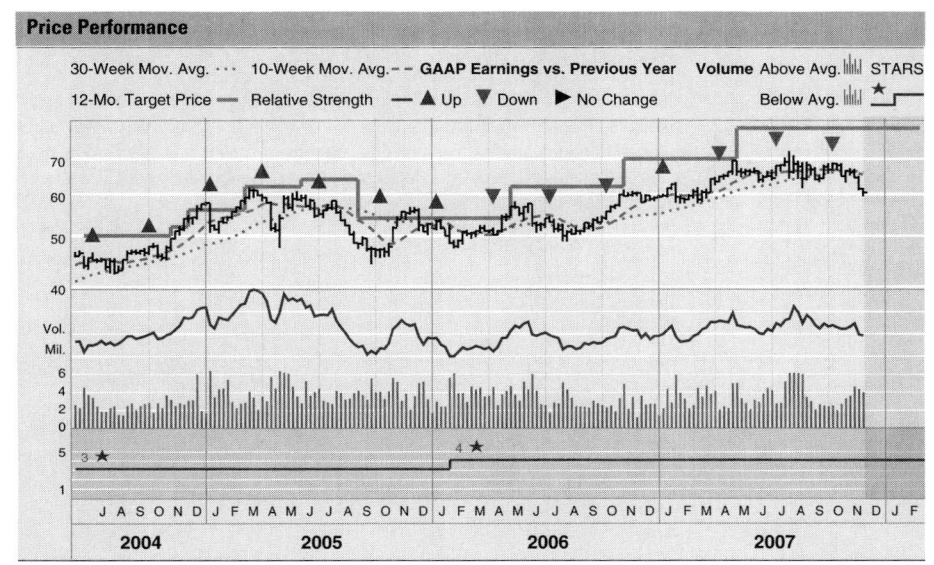

- 30-Week Mov. Avg. ···
- 10-Week Mov. Avg. ──
- **GAAP Earnings vs. Previous Year**
- Volume Above Avg. ▮▮ STARS
- 12-Mo. Target Price ──
- Relative Strength ──
- ▲ Up ▼ Down ▶ No Change
- Below Avg. ▮▮ ★──

Options: ASE, CBOE, P, Ph

Analysis prepared by **Richard O'Reilly, CFA** on November 07, 2007, when the stock traded at **$ 65.88**.

Highlights

➤ We expect sales in 2008 to decline slightly, assuming the sale of the unprofitable Latin American polyester resin business by 2008 and the European facilities in 2008. The chemicals segments should continue to expand, with volumes boosted by overall healthy global economies and an improving product mix. We believe fibers profits in 2008 will again be modestly higher, reflecting growing Asian filter tow demand and healthy industry fundamentals.

➤ We expect polyester resins to turn profitable during 2008 as EMN completes the shut down of additional high-cost domestic capacity and sells or closes the unprofitable non-U.S. facilities. The business had a loss of $36 million in the first nine months, including start-up costs for a new U.S. plant using new technology. We believe that overall raw material trends will remain volatile into 2008.

➤ We expect interest expense in 2007 will decrease to about $68 million. We assume that the absence of the profitable polyethylene resin business will be dilutive to EPS by up to $0.30 in 2007. Our EPS estimate for 2007 excludes projected restructuring charges totaling almost $1.50 a share.

Investment Rationale/Risk

➤ Based on our 2007 EPS estimate, the shares were recently trading at what we view as an excessive P/E discount to those of other major diversified chemical company equities and the S&P 500. We expect the coatings, specialty plastics and fibers segments (over 75% of annual profits) in total to grow in 2008 and think the challenging polyester resins business will turn profitable from the sales of the non-U.S. operations and reduced costs at the domestic operations.

➤ Risks to our recommendation and target price include the cyclical character of polyester resins, unplanned production outages and interruptions, possible greater-than-estimated asbestos liabilities, and higher-than-expected raw material costs.

➤ Applying a P/E of about 16X, closer to the P/Es of diversified chemicals peers in our coverage universe, to our 2008 EPS estimate of $5.00, results in our 12-month target price of $80. We believe the dividend, which recently provided an above-average yield of about 2.7%, is secure.

Qualitative Risk Assessment

LOW	**MEDIUM**	HIGH

Our risk assessment reflects the diverse business and geographic sales mix of the company, offset by the cyclical nature of the chemicals industry and the volatility of raw material costs.

Quantitative Evaluations

S&P Quality Ranking   **B-**

D	C	**B-**	B	B+	A-	A	A+

Relative Strength Rank   **MODERATE**

43

LOWEST = 1   HIGHEST = 99

Revenue/Earnings Data

Revenue (Million $)

	1Q	2Q	3Q	4Q	Year
2007	1,795	1,895	1,813	--	--
2006	1,803	1,929	1,966	1,752	7,450
2005	1,762	1,752	1,816	1,729	7,059
2004	1,597	1,676	1,649	1,658	6,580
2003	1,441	1,481	1,444	1,434	5,800
2002	1,236	1,395	1,374	1,315	5,320

Earnings Per Share ($)

2007	0.91	1.22	0.24	E1.00	E4.80
2006	1.27	1.37	1.15	1.12	4.91
2005	2.00	2.51	1.50	0.81	6.81
2004	-0.07	1.07	0.49	0.68	2.18
2003	0.23	0.46	-4.35	0.13	-3.54
2002	0.30	0.58	0.31	-0.16	1.02

Fiscal year ended Dec. 31. Next earnings report expected: Late January. EPS Estimates based on S&P Operating Earnings; historical GAAP earnings are as reported.

Dividend Data (Dates: mm/dd Payment Date: mm/dd/yy)

Amount ($)	Date Decl.	Ex-Div. Date	Stk. of Record	Payment Date
.01 Spl.	12/08	12/14	12/18	01/02/07
0.440	02/20	03/13	03/15	04/02/07
0.440	05/03	06/13	06/15	07/02/07
0.440	08/02	09/13	09/17	10/01/07

Dividends have been paid since 1994. Source: Company reports.

Eastman Chemical Co

STANDARD
&POOR'S

Business Summary November 07, 2007

CORPORATE OVERVIEW. Eastman Chemical Co. is a large global maker of a broad range of chemicals, plastics and fibers. International operations accounted for 46% of sales in 2006.

The Chemicals and Fibers group consists of three segments. The coatings, adhesive, specialty polymers and inks segment (19% of 2006 sales, operating profits of $229 million) is a leading supplier of alcohols and solvents used in coatings (60% of segment sales) and resins, dispersions and specialty polymers used in adhesives. In August 2004, EMN sold certain product lines acquired in the late 1990s with annual sales of about $600 million, for $215 million. Performance chemicals and intermediates (22%, $132 million) includes oxo chemicals, acetyls, plasticizers, and glycols used for polymers, photographic and home care products, agricultural chemicals, and pharmaceutical intermediates; and additives for food and beverage ingredients. In the fibers business (12%, $226 million), EMN is one of the world's two largest suppliers of acetate cigarette filter tow and the leader in acetate yarn. The company projects global growth in demand for filter tow of 3% annually through 2010, with Asia and Eastern Europe having the fastest growth rates. The business also includes acetyl chemicals (acetate flake, acetic anhydride).

The Polyester group consists of polymers (36%, $54 million) and specialty plastics (11%, $46 million). EMN is the world's largest producer of polyester plastics (sales of $2.0 billion and operating loss of $29 million), consisting of

polyethylene terephthalate (PET), used for packaging applications and beverage containers such as soft-drink bottles; the company sold its polyethylene resin business in December 2006 (sales of $635 million in 2006 and profits of $136 million, including a $75 million gain on the sale). The company had annual PET capacity of 3.3 billion lbs. at year-end 2006. In early 2007, EMN completed the start-up of a new U.S. plant with annual capacity of 770 million lbs. using new IntegRex technology. EMN plans to expand the new plant by 50% by late 2008, and to close up to 770 million lbs. of higher-cost domestic capacity. IntegRex would then account for over 60% of EMN's U.S. PET capacity. The company is evaluating a second facility using refinements to the new technology. EMN has decided to close or sell its unprofitable polyester production sites outside the U.S.; in April 2007, it sold its plant in Spain and in September agreed to sell its two facilities in Latin America (sales of nearly $500 million in 2006 and a loss of $14 million). The polyester business had an operating loss of $29 million in 2006, which included losses in the non-U.S. operations and much reduced domestic profits. The polyethylene business was a U.S.-based business, and had a relatively small market share, accounting for about 25% of annual polymers segment sales.

Company Financials Fiscal Year Ended Dec. 31

Per Share Data ($)	2006	2005	2004	2003	2002	2001	2000	1999	1998	1997
Tangible Book Value	20.42	15.85	10.70	9.00	9.06	9.92	15.64	16.81	24.45	22.40
Cash Flow	8.64	10.50	6.23	1.22	6.18	3.33	9.36	5.46	7.59	7.86
Earnings	4.91	6.81	2.18	-3.54	1.02	-2.33	3.94	0.61	3.13	3.63
S&P Core Earnings	4.42	5.63	2.23	-3.45	0.26	-3.06	NA	NA	NA	NA
Dividends	1.76	1.76	1.76	1.76	1.76	1.76	1.76	1.76	1.76	1.76
Payout Ratio	36%	26%	81%	NM	173%	NM	45%	NM	56%	48%
Prices:High	61.29	61.80	58.17	39.57	49.55	55.65	54.75	60.31	72.94	65.38
Prices:Low	47.30	44.10	38.00	27.56	34.53	29.03	33.63	36.00	43.50	50.75
P/E Ratio:High	12	9	27	NM	49	NM	14	99	23	18
P/E Ratio:Low	10	6	17	NM	34	NM	9	59	14	14

Income Statement Analysis (Million $)										
Revenue	7,450	7,059	6,580	5,800	5,320	5,384	5,292	4,590	4,481	4,678
Operating Income	981	1,092	696	590	610	755	989	663	785	895
Depreciation	308	304	322	367	397	435	418	383	351	327
Interest Expense	80.0	100	115	124	128	140	135	126	96.0	87.0
Pretax Income	576	783	64.0	-381	84.0	-297	452	72.0	360	446
Effective Tax Rate	29.0%	28.9%	NM	NM	5.95%	NM	33.0%	33.3%	30.8%	35.9%
Net Income	409	557	170	-273	79.0	-179	303	48.0	249	286
S&P Core Earnings	368	459	173	-266	20.4	-236	NA	NA	NA	NA

Balance Sheet & Other Financial Data (Million $)										
Cash	939	524	325	558	77.0	66.0	101	186	29.0	29.0
Current Assets	2,422	1,924	1,768	2,010	1,529	1,458	1,523	1,489	1,415	1,490
Total Assets	6,173	5,773	5,872	6,230	6,273	6,086	6,550	6,303	5,876	5,778
Current Liabilities	1,059	1,051	1,099	1,477	1,224	958	1,258	1,608	985	954
Long Term Debt	1,589	1,621	2,061	2,089	2,054	2,143	1,914	1,506	1,649	1,714
Common Equity	2,029	1,612	1,184	1,913	1,271	1,378	1,812	2,521	1,934	1,753
Total Capital	3,618	3,550	3,455	4,318	3,809	3,973	4,333	4,512	3,998	3,864
Capital Expenditures	389	343	248	230	427	234	226	292	500	749
Cash Flow	717	861	492	94.0	476	256	721	431	600	613
Current Ratio	2.3	1.8	1.6	1.4	1.2	1.5	1.2	0.9	1.4	1.6
% Long Term Debt of Capitalization	43.9	45.7	59.7	48.4	53.9	53.9	44.2	33.4	41.2	44.4
% Net Income of Revenue	5.5	7.9	2.6	NM	1.5	NM	5.7	1.0	5.6	6.1
% Return on Assets	6.8	9.6	2.8	NM	1.3	NM	4.7	0.8	4.3	5.6
% Return on Equity	22.5	39.8	15.3	NM	6.0	NM	17.0	1.9	13.5	16.9

Data as orig reptd.; bef. results of disc opers/spec. items. Per share data adj. for stk. divs.; EPS diluted. E-Estimated. NA-Not Available. NM-Not Meaningful. NR-Not Ranked. UR-Under Review.

Office: 200 S Wilcox Dr, Kingsport, TN, USA 37660-5147.
Telephone: 423-229-2000.
Website: http://www.eastman.com
Chrmn & CEO: J.B. Ferguson

SVP & CFO: R.A. Lorraine
SVP & CTO: R.C. Lindsay
SVP, Secy & General Counsel: T.K. Lee
VP & Cntlr: C.E. Espeland

Investor Contact: G. Riddle (423-229-8692)
Board Members: M. P. Connors, S. R. Demeritt, J. B. Ferguson, D. W. Griffin, R. M. Hernandez, R. J. Hornbaker, L. M. Kling, H. L. Lance, T. H. McLain, D. W. Raisbeck, P. M. Wood

Founded: 1993
Domicile: Delaware
Employees: 11,000

Eastman Kodak Co

STANDARD &POOR'S

S&P Recommendation	HOLD ★★★☆☆	Price	12-Mo. Target Price	Investment Style
		$23.15 (as of Nov 23, 2007)	$29.00	Large-Cap Value

GICS Sector Consumer Discretionary
Sub-Industry Photographic Products

Summary This multinational company has a large presence in consumer, professional and health imaging.

Key Stock Statistics (Source S&P, Vickers, company reports)

52-Wk Range	$30.20–22.19	S&P Oper. EPS 2007E	-0.52	Market Capitalization(B)	$6.644	Beta	1.81
Trailing 12-Month EPS	$1.66	S&P Oper. EPS 2008E	0.75	Yield (%)	2.16	S&P 3-Yr. Proj. EPS CAGR(%)	31.00
Trailing 12-Month P/E	14.0	P/E on S&P Oper. EPS 2007E	NM	Dividend Rate/Share	$0.50	S&P Credit Rating	B+
$10K Invested 5 Yrs Ago	$6,997	Common Shares Outstg. (M)	287.0	Institutional Ownership (%)	NM		

Price Performance

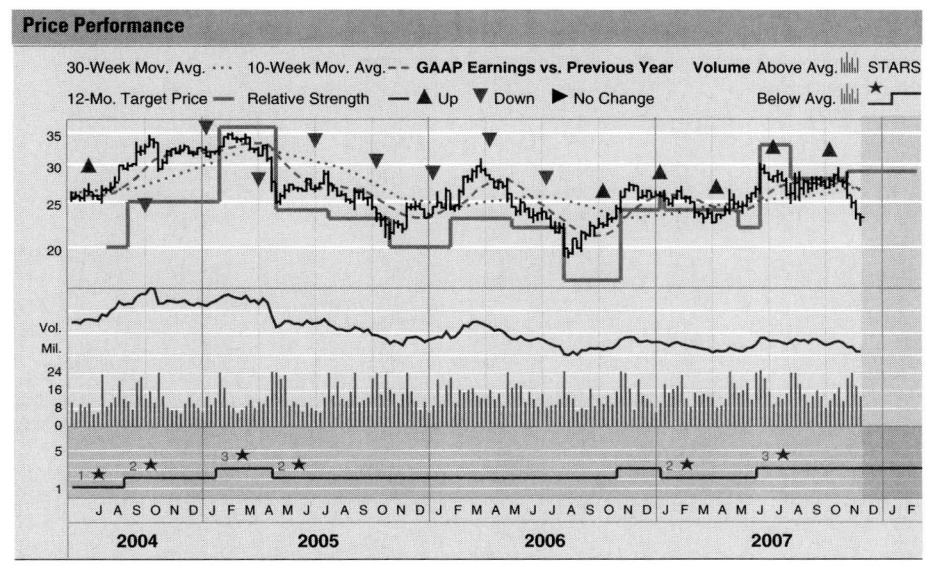

30-Week Mov. Avg. · · · 10-Week Mov. Avg. - - GAAP Earnings vs. Previous Year Volume Above Avg. STARS
12-Mo. Target Price — Relative Strength — ▲ Up ▼ Down ► No Change Below Avg.

Options: ASE, CBOE, P, Ph

Analysis prepared by **Erik Kolb** on November 07, 2007, when the stock traded at **$ 25.62**.

Highlights

➤ We estimate 2007 revenue of $10.2 billion, compared to $13.3 billion in 2006, but we note that 2006's results included $2.5 billion from the Health Group, which was recently sold to Onex Corp. for $2.35 billion. We project a sizable decline in EK's traditional film market being at least largely offset by growth elsewhere, including a mid-single digit increase in digital revenue. In 2008, we expect double-digit growth in digital businesses as recent restructuring efforts take hold, but further declines in traditional revenues, leading to about a 1% decline in total revenues, to $10.1 billion.

➤ In 2007, we see further challenges in EK's consumer digital imaging business, although we look for overall profitability to benefit from restructuring efforts. We are uncertain if the $50 million increase in inkjet printer spending will benefit the new product segment in the near term. Sizable labor reductions should help improve margins a bit in both 2007 and 2008.

➤ Before special items and assuming a 35% tax rate, we estimate a 2007 loss of $0.52 a share, compared to a loss of $2.09 in 2006. For 2008, we estimate EPS of $0.75.

Investment Rationale/Risk

➤ We believe EK has made modest progress in its shift toward a more digitally focused product line. However, we think the ultimate outcome of the transition remains in question.

➤ Risks to our recommendation and target price include a faster than anticipated decline in demand for traditional film product offerings, more than forecast pricing pressure for digital products, and decreases in market share.

➤ In our view, a shifting product mix is creating both opportunities and significant risk regarding profits. We are disappointed by the recent sale price for EK's Health Group of up to $2.55 billion, which is 8.5X our estimate of 2007 Health Group operating profits. The divestiture will likely be dilutive to 2007 EPS. Looking ahead, we expect EK to have a narrower focus, including a larger profit dependence on consumer digital imaging and graphic communications. Our 12-month target price of $29 reflects a blend of our DCF and relative valuations. Our DCF model assumes a WACC of 8.5% and long-term growth of 3.0%. Our relative model uses an EBITDA multiple below EK's historical average, reflecting the heightened risk we see.

Qualitative Risk Assessment

LOW	MEDIUM	HIGH

Our risk assessment is based on the company's ongoing shift toward digital photography. While we think EK has made progress in this endeavor, we are concerned about competitive threats and margin declines in this space.

Quantitative Evaluations

S&P Quality Ranking B-

D	C	B-	B	B+	A-	A	A+

Relative Strength Rank WEAK

27

LOWEST = 1 HIGHEST = 99

Revenue/Earnings Data

Revenue (Million $)

	1Q	2Q	3Q	4Q	Year
2007	2,119	2,510	2,581	--	--
2006	2,889	3,360	3,204	3,821	13,274
2005	2,832	3,686	3,553	4,197	14,268
2004	2,919	3,469	3,364	3,765	13,517
2003	2,740	3,352	3,447	3,778	13,317
2002	2,707	3,339	3,354	3,441	12,835

Earnings Per Share ($)

	1Q	2Q	3Q	4Q	Year
2007	-0.61	-0.47	0.12	E0.44	E-0.52
2006	-1.04	-0.98	-0.13	0.06	-2.09
2005	-0.49	-0.49	-3.62	-0.47	-5.05
2004	0.06	0.50	0.16	-0.06	0.28
2003	-0.01	0.39	0.42	0.03	0.83
2002	0.13	0.97	1.15	0.39	2.72

Fiscal year ended Dec. 31. Next earnings report expected: Late January. EPS Estimates based on S&P Operating Earnings; historical GAAP earnings are as reported.

Dividend Data (Dates: mm/dd Payment Date: mm/dd/yy)

Amount ($)	Date Decl.	Ex-Div. Date	Stk. of Record	Payment Date
0.250	10/17	10/30	11/01	12/14/06
0.250	05/09	05/30	06/01	07/16/07
0.250	10/16	10/30	11/01	12/14/07

Dividends have been paid since 1902. Source: Company reports.

Please read the Required Disclosures and Analyst Certification on the last page of this report.

The McGraw-Hill Companies

Eastman Kodak Co

STANDARD &POOR'S

Business Summary November 07, 2007

CORPORATE OVERVIEW. Eastman Kodak offers products in the photographic, graphic communications and health care markets. In 2006, the Film & Photofinishing System Group accounted for 31% of revenue, while the Consumer Digital area represented 22%, the Graphic Communications Group 27%, the Health Group 19%, and other activities 1%.

The company has sought to increase its presence in the digital photography market, but according to market research firm IDC, in 2006, it had a market share of 10% within the global digital camera shipments category, a decline from 14% in 2005.

CORPORATE STRATEGY. In April 2007, EK sold it Health Group for $2.35 billion, with the possibility of an additional $200 million depending on the group's future performance. EK said that the move would sharpen its strategic focus on consumer and professional imaging and the graphic communications industry.

As consumers continue to migrate away from film (U.S. consumer film volumes declined by 25% in 2005, latest available), EK has implemented a number of restructuring initiatives. In January 2004, the company introduced a cost reduction program that was expected to result in charges of $1.3 billion to $1.7 billion and 12,000 to 15,000 layoffs by the end of 2006. However, in July 2005, EK extended its original forecast to accelerate its shift toward digital businesses and to respond to a faster than expected decline in consumer film sales. In August 2006 (prior to announcing the agreed-upon sale of the Health Group), EK estimated that the total restructuring program would result in an employee headcount reduction of 25,000 to 27,000 positions and a total cost of $3.0 billion to $3.4 billion, with the program to be essentially completed in 2007. Through March 31, 2007, EK recorded charges of $2.1 billion, including $985 billion for severance, $608 million for accelerated depreciation, $272 million for long-lived asset impairments, $205 million for exit costs, and $57 million for inventory.

Company Financials Fiscal Year Ended Dec. 31

Per Share Data ($)	2006	2005	2004	2003	2002	2001	2000	1999	1998	1997
Tangible Book Value	NM	NM	6.57	5.53	6.27	6.71	8.56	9.45	8.54	8.09
Cash Flow	2.55	-0.18	3.88	3.72	5.52	3.42	7.48	7.19	6.84	2.51
Earnings	-2.09	-5.05	0.28	0.83	2.72	0.26	4.59	4.33	4.24	0.01
S&P Core Earnings	-2.65	-4.93	-0.42	0.53	0.44	-1.86	NA	NA	NA	NA
Dividends	0.50	0.50	0.50	1.15	1.80	1.77	1.76	1.76	1.76	1.76
Payout Ratio	NM	NM	179%	139%	68%	NM	38%	41%	42%	NM
Prices:High	30.91	35.19	34.74	41.08	38.48	49.95	67.50	80.38	88.94	94.75
Prices:Low	18.93	20.77	24.25	20.39	25.58	24.40	35.31	56.63	57.94	53.31
P/E Ratio:High	NM	NM	NM	49	15	19	15	19	21	NM
P/E Ratio:Low	NM	NM	NM	25	10	9	8	13	14	NM

Income Statement Analysis (Million $)	2006	2005	2004	2003	2002	2001	2000	1999	1998	1997
Revenue	13,274	14,268	13,517	13,317	12,835	13,234	13,994	14,089	13,406	14,538
Operating Income	1,600	1,493	1,638	1,685	2,898	1,923	3,103	2,908	2,783	2,431
Depreciation	1,331	1,402	1,030	830	818	919	889	918	853	828
Interest Expense	262	211	168	148	173	219	178	142	110	98.0
Pretax Income	-346	-762	-92.0	196	946	97.0	2,132	2,109	2,106	53.0
Effective Tax Rate	NM	NM	NM	NM	16.1%	33.0%	34.0%	34.0%	34.0%	90.6%
Net Income	-600	-1,455	81.0	238	793	76.0	1,407	1,392	1,390	5.00
S&P Core Earnings	-757	-1,419	-119	149	127	-541	NA	NA	NA	NA

Balance Sheet & Other Financial Data (Million $)	2006	2005	2004	2003	2002	2001	2000	1999	1998	1997
Cash	1,469	1,665	1,255	1,250	569	448	251	393	500	728
Current Assets	5,557	5,781	5,648	5,455	4,534	4,683	5,491	5,444	5,599	5,475
Total Assets	14,320	14,921	14,737	14,818	13,369	13,362	14,212	14,370	14,733	13,145
Current Liabilities	4,971	5,489	4,990	5,307	5,377	5,354	6,215	5,769	6,178	5,177
Long Term Debt	2,714	2,764	1,852	2,302	1,164	1,666	1,166	Nil	504	585
Common Equity	1,388	1,967	3,811	3,264	2,777	2,894	3,428	3,912	3,988	3,161
Total Capital	4,102	4,731	5,663	5,566	3,941	4,560	4,655	3,971	1,108	3,746
Capital Expenditures	379	472	460	506	577	743	945	1,127	4,561	1,485
Cash Flow	731	-53.0	1,111	1,068	1,611	995	2,296	2,310	2,243	833
Current Ratio	1.1	1.1	1.1	1.0	0.8	0.9	0.9	0.9	0.9	1.1
% Long Term Debt of Capitalization	66.2	58.4	32.7	41.4	29.5	36.5	25.0	Nil	11.1	15.6
% Net Income of Revenue	NM	NM	NM	1.8	6.2	0.6	10.1	9.9	10.4	0.0
% Return on Assets	NM	NM	NM	1.7	5.9	0.6	9.8	9.6	10.0	0.0
% Return on Equity	NM	NM	NM	7.9	27.9	2.4	38.3	35.2	38.9	0.1

Data as orig reptd.; bef. results of disc opers/spec. items. Per share data adj. for stk. divs.; EPS diluted. E-Estimated. NA-Not Available. NM-Not Meaningful. NR-Not Ranked. UR-Under Review.

Office: 343 State Street, Rochester, NY 14650.
Telephone: 585-724-4000.
Website: http://www.kodak.com
Chrmn & CEO: A.M. Perez

EVP & CFO: F.S. Sklarsky
SVP & General Counsel: J.P. Haag
Chief Acctg Officer & Cntlr: D.E. Wilfong
Investor Contact: A.P. McCorvey

Board Members: R. S. Braddock, M. L. Collins, L. D'Andrea Tyson, T. M. Donahue, M. Hawley, W. H. Hernandez, D. I. Jager, D. L. Lee, D. E. Lewis, A. M. Perez, H. de J. Ruiz

Founded: 1880
Domicile: New Jersey
Employees: 40,900

Eaton Corp

STANDARD &POOR'S

S&P Recommendation **BUY** ★★★★☆	Price $87.96 (as of Nov 23, 2007)	12-Mo. Target Price $110.00	Investment Style Large-Cap Blend

GICS Sector Industrials
Sub-Industry Industrial Machinery

Summary This diversified industrial manufacturer's products include electrical systems and components for power management; truck transmissions; and fluid power systems and services for industrial, mobile and aircraft equipment.

Key Stock Statistics (Source S&P, Vickers, company reports)

52-Wk Range	$104.12– 71.91	S&P Oper. EPS 2007E	6.75	Market Capitalization(B)	$12.886	Beta	1.36
Trailing 12-Month EPS	$6.51	S&P Oper. EPS 2008E	7.70	Yield (%)	1.96	S&P 3-Yr. Proj. EPS CAGR(%)	14.00
Trailing 12-Month P/E	13.5	P/E on S&P Oper. EPS 2007E	13.0	Dividend Rate/Share	$1.72	S&P Credit Rating	A
$10K Invested 5 Yrs Ago	$25,769	Common Shares Outstg. (M)	146.5	Institutional Ownership (%)	81		

Price Performance

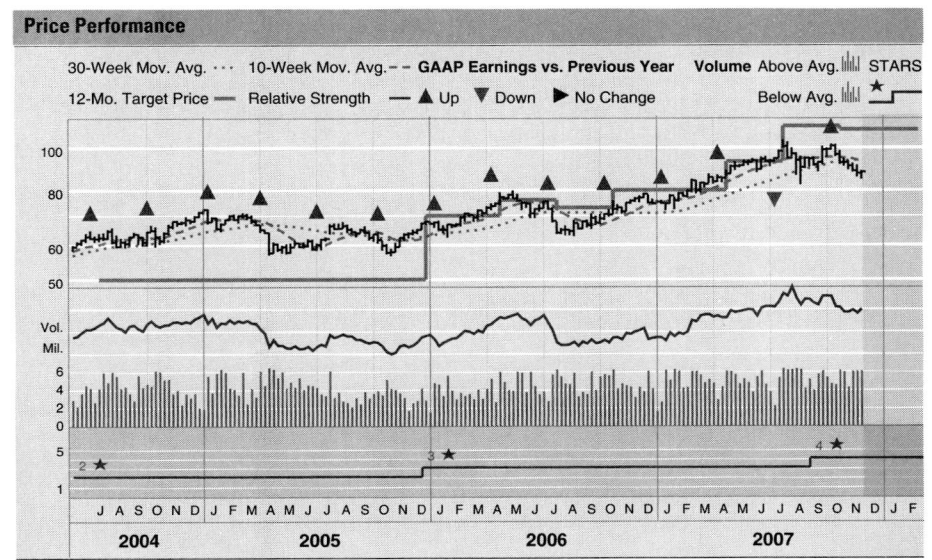

30-Week Mov. Avg. ··· 10-Week Mov. Avg. -- **GAAP Earnings vs. Previous Year** Volume Above Avg. STARS
12-Mo. Target Price — Relative Strength — ▲ Up ▼ Down ▶ No Change Below Avg.

Options: CBOE, P, Ph

Analysis prepared by **Christopher Lippincott** on October 16, 2007, when the stock traded at **$ 93.04**.

Highlights

➤ We expect revenues to increase 5% in 2007 and 8% in 2008, led by contributions from recent acquisitions and growth in the Electrical and Fluid Power segments. We project a 16% drop in the Truck components business in 2007, largely reflecting an anticipated decline in the medium- and heavy-duty truck markets. Our forecast calls for NAFTA Class 8 truck volume to decrease by over 44% from 2006 levels, to approximately 210,000 units.

➤ We look for operating margins to expand modestly in 2007 and 2008, driven primarily by increased profitability in the electrical, fluid power, and automotive components segments, partly offset by moderating profitability in the truck segment. We see benefits coming primarily from greater operating leverage and recent cost reduction efforts, partly offset by raw material cost inflation and lower truck profitability.

➤ We project operating EPS of $6.75 in 2007 and $7.70 in 2008, representing expected EPS growth of 14% in 2008, with steady interest expenses and tax rates.

Investment Rationale/Risk

➤ We believe ETN's business prospects over the next two years are favorable, weighted primarily toward 2008. We think end markets will grow nearly 5% next year, in addition to market share gains and continued acquisitions. We are positive about ETN's efforts to improve its balance of businesses toward a portfolio of businesses that is less cyclical and capital intensive, but generates strong returns and cash flow.

➤ Risks to our recommendation and target price include weaker than expected global economic growth and a greater than forecast downturn in heavy-duty truck markets.

➤ Our 12-month target price of $110 represents a blend of our three valuation metrics. Our discounted cash flow model, which assumes a 3% perpetuity growth rate and an 11.7% discount rate, indicates an intrinsic value of $111. Our sum-of-the-parts analysis, assuming low- to mid-teens EV/EBITDA valuations for each segment, indicates a $109 value. Regarding relative valuation, we apply a multiple of about 10X--in line with peers--to our 2008 EBITDA estimate, implying a $112 valuation.

Qualitative Risk Assessment

LOW	**MEDIUM**	HIGH

Our risk assessment reflects our view that ETN has good geographic and product diversification, offset by the highly cyclical nature of the company's various end markets, and significant pension and other post-retirement benefit obligations.

Quantitative Evaluations

S&P Quality Ranking B+

D	C	B-	B	**B+**	A-	A	A+

Relative Strength Rank MODERATE

54

LOWEST = 1   HIGHEST = 99

Revenue/Earnings Data

Revenue (Million $)

	1Q	2Q	3Q	4Q	Year
2007	3,153	3,248	3,298	--	--
2006	2,991	3,162	3,115	3,102	12,370
2005	2,654	2,834	2,789	2,838	11,115
2004	2,238	2,403	2,543	2,633	9,817
2003	1,925	2,027	2,026	2,083	8,061
2002	1,723	1,881	1,830	1,775	7,209

Earnings Per Share ($)

2007	1.56	1.60	1.59	E1.73	E6.75
2006	1.35	1.63	1.39	1.59	5.97
2005	1.19	1.37	1.30	1.38	5.23
2004	0.85	1.03	1.09	1.16	4.13
2003	0.50	0.64	0.70	0.72	2.56
2002	0.24	0.61	0.65	0.47	1.96

Fiscal year ended Dec. 31. Next earnings report expected: Late January. EPS Estimates based on S&P Operating Earnings; historical GAAP earnings are as reported.

Dividend Data (Dates: mm/dd Payment Date: mm/dd/yy)

Amount ($)	Date Decl.	Ex-Div. Date	Stk. of Record	Payment Date
0.430	01/22	02/01	02/05	02/23/07
0.430	04/25	05/03	05/07	05/25/07
0.430	07/25	08/02	08/06	08/24/07
0.430	10/24	11/01	11/05	11/23/07

Dividends have been paid since 1923. Source: Company reports.

The **McGraw-Hill** Companies

Eaton Corp

STANDARD
&POOR'S

Business Summary October 16, 2007

Eaton Corp., a diversified industrial equipment and parts manufacturer, conducts business through four business segments with $12.4 billion in revenues in 2006.

ETN's Electrical segment (34% of 2006 revenues with 11.5% operating margins excluding one-time items) makes a wide range of power distribution and control equipment, such as switchboards, circuit boards, circuit breakers, starters, AC and DC Uninterruptible Power Systems (UPS) and power management software. The segment also produces electronic sensors that control industrial machinery, as well as electricity quality-monitoring systems. The unit's primary competitors include GE, Germany-based Siemens and Schneider Electric. Demand for ETN's electrical equipment and components mainly reflects the health of the non-residential (35% of segment sales), power quality (30%), industrial (18%), residential construction (12%) and telecom (5%) industries.

The Fluid Power segment (32%; 11%) makes hydraulic pumps, motors, valves cylinders and power steering for everything from jet planes to farm tractors. The segment also sells hydraulic and electromechanical equipment such as actuators, pumps, steering systems cockpit controls and pneumatic systems. It sells primarily to three market channels: mobile (primarily earthmovers and farm tractors; about 40% of sales); stationary (primarily machine tools; 23%);

and aerospace (mainly commercial and military aircraft; 37%).

Parker-Hannifin, the world's largest hydraulics equipment maker, Eaton (the second largest), Germany-based Sauer Danfoss (the third), and Germany-based Mannesmann (fourth) account for about 40% of the $50 billion in revenue global hydraulics equipment industry. The 60% balance is comprised of hundreds of smaller hydraulics equipment makers.

With about 85% of the global truck transmission market (such as drive trains, clutches, gearboxes and shafts), ETN's Truck Component unit (20%; 18%) is the world's largest maker of medium and heavy duty truck transmissions. The segment's primary competitor is Germany-based ZedF. ETN is also a major manufacturer of brake clutches. The segment's primary competitor in this segment is Wabco. Other truck transmission and clutch makers include European truck manufacturers, which primarily make transmissions and clutches for their own trucks. Demand for ETN's truck components is mainly driven by the health of the medium and heavy duty truck market.

Company Financials Fiscal Year Ended Dec. 31

Per Share Data ($)	2006	2005	2004	2003	2002	2001	2000	1999	1998	1997
Tangible Book Value	2.30	0.09	3.46	3.14	NM	0.29	NM	0.64	7.17	7.37
Cash Flow	8.80	8.08	6.67	5.18	4.49	3.78	5.05	7.25	4.66	5.17
Earnings	5.97	5.23	4.13	2.56	1.96	1.20	2.50	4.18	2.40	2.97
S&P Core Earnings	6.45	5.40	4.15	2.43	0.99	-0.18	NA	NA	NA	NA
Dividends	1.48	1.24	1.08	0.92	0.88	0.88	0.88	0.88	0.88	0.86
Payout Ratio	24%	24%	26%	36%	45%	74%	35%	21%	37%	29%
Prices:High	79.98	72.69	72.64	54.70	44.34	40.72	43.28	51.75	49.81	51.69
Prices:Low	62.37	56.65	52.74	33.01	29.55	27.56	28.75	31.00	28.75	33.63
P/E Ratio:High	13	14	18	21	23	34	17	12	21	17
P/E Ratio:Low	10	11	13	13	15	23	11	7	12	11

Income Statement Analysis (Million $)										
Revenue	12,370	11,115	9,817	8,061	7,209	7,299	8,309	8,402	6,625	7,563
Operating Income	1,487	1,468	1,287	984	870	703	1,013	1,170	813	1,042
Depreciation	434	409	400	394	353	355	364	441	331	342
Interest Expense	104	90.0	78.0	87.0	104	142	177	152	88.0	86.0
Pretax Income	989	996	781	508	399	278	552	963	485	668
Effective Tax Rate	7.79%	19.2%	17.0%	24.0%	29.6%	39.2%	34.2%	35.9%	28.0%	30.5%
Net Income	912	805	648	386	281	169	363	617	349	464
S&P Core Earnings	985	832	651	367	141	-25.0	NA	NA	NA	NA

Balance Sheet & Other Financial Data (Million $)										
Cash	114	110	85.0	61.0	75.0	112	82.0	81.0	80.0	53.0
Current Assets	4,408	3,578	3,182	3,093	2,457	2,387	2,571	2,782	1,982	2,055
Total Assets	11,417	10,218	9,075	8,223	7,138	7,646	8,180	8,437	5,665	5,465
Current Liabilities	3,407	2,968	2,262	2,126	1,734	1,669	2,107	2,649	1,516	1,357
Long Term Debt	1,774	1,830	Nil	1,651	1,887	2,252	2,447	1,915	1,191	1,272
Common Equity	4,106	3,778	3,606	3,117	2,302	2,475	2,410	2,624	2,057	2,071
Total Capital	5,880	5,608	3,606	4,768	4,752	5,307	4,857	4,539	3,248	3,343
Capital Expenditures	360	363	330	2,733	228	295	386	496	483	438
Cash Flow	1,346	1,214	1,048	780	634	524	727	1,058	680	806
Current Ratio	1.3	1.2	1.4	1.5	1.4	1.4	1.2	1.1	1.3	1.5
% Long Term Debt of Capitalization	30.2	32.6	Nil	34.6	39.7	42.4	50.4	42.2	36.7	38.0
% Net Income of Revenue	7.4	7.2	6.6	4.8	3.9	2.3	4.4	7.3	5.3	6.1
% Return on Assets	8.4	8.3	7.5	5.0	3.8	2.1	4.4	8.8	6.3	8.6
% Return on Equity	23.1	21.8	19.3	14.2	11.8	6.9	14.4	26.4	16.9	21.9

Data as orig reptd.; bef. results of disc opers/spec. items. Per share data adj. for stk. divs.; EPS diluted. E-Estimated. NA-Not Available. NM-Not Meaningful. NR-Not Ranked. UR-Under Review.

Office: Eaton Center, Cleveland, OH 44114-2584.
Telephone: 216-523-5000.
Website: http://www.eaton.com
Chrmn, Pres & CEO: A.M. Cutler

EVP & CFO: R.H. Fearon
VP & CTO: Y. Tsavalas
VP & Treas: R.E. Parmenter
VP & Secy: E.R. Franklin

Investor Contact: B. Hartman (216-523-4501)
Board Members: C. M. Connor, M. J. Critelli, A. M. Cutler, C. E. Golden, E. Green, N. C. Lautenbach, D. L. McCoy, J. R. Miller, G. R. Page, V. A. Pelson, G. L. Tooker

Founded: 1916
Domicile: Ohio
Employees: 60,000

The McGraw-Hill Companies

eBay Inc

STANDARD &POOR'S

S&P Recommendation STRONG BUY ★★★★★	**Price** $31.94 (as of Nov 23, 2007)	**12-Mo. Target Price** $50.00	**Investment Style** Large-Cap Growth

GICS Sector Information Technology
Sub-Industry Internet Software & Services

Summary EBAY owns one of the world's most popular e-commerce destinations, which bears its name, as well as PayPal, an online payments company, and Skype, an Internet telephony business.

Key Stock Statistics (Source S&P, Vickers, company reports)

52-Wk Range	$40.73–28.60	S&P Oper. EPS 2007**E**	1.34	Market Capitalization(B)	$43.232	Beta	1.98
Trailing 12-Month EPS	$0.12	S&P Oper. EPS 2008**E**	1.77	Yield (%)	Nil	S&P 3-Yr. Proj. EPS CAGR(%)	33.00
Trailing 12-Month P/E	NM	P/E on S&P Oper. EPS 2007**E**	23.8	Dividend Rate/Share	Nil	S&P Credit Rating	NA
$10K Invested 5 Yrs Ago	$18,228	Common Shares Outstg. (M)	1,353.5	Institutional Ownership (%)	72		

Price Performance

30-Week Mov. Avg. ··· 10-Week Mov. Avg. – – **GAAP Earnings vs. Previous Year** Volume Above Avg. ▌▌▌ STARS
12-Mo. Target Price — Relative Strength — ▲ Up ▼ Down ► No Change Below Avg. ▌▌▌ ★

Options: ASE, CBOE, P, Ph

Analysis prepared by **Scott H. Kessler** on October 22, 2007, when the stock traded at **$ 36.72**.

Highlights

► We expect net revenues to rise 29% in 2007 and 25% in 2008, aided by a relatively weak dollar versus other currencies. For 2008, we foresee 21% growth in marketplaces (including EBAY), 28% in payments (PayPal), and 53% in communications (Skype). We expect the communications business acquired in 2005 to account for 6% of revenues in 2008.

► EBAY's non-GAAP operating margin narrowed in 2006, following major acquisitions, and significant investments in international operations (especially in China) and technology. This margin stabilized in 2007, and we expect it to be sustained through 2009, reflecting a less favorable overall revenue mix and substantial new development and expansion efforts.

► In February 2007, EBAY acquired online ticket marketplace StubHub for $307 million, including $21 million in cash. In October 2005, EBAY acquired Skype Technologies, a provider of Internet communications offerings, in a transaction valued at $2.5 billion in cash and stock. EBAY announced a $2.0 billion share buyback in January 2007.

Investment Rationale/Risk

► We see EBAY as the clear leader in online auctions, a mainstream Internet retail destination, a major facilitator of large transactions involving cars and real estate, a growing international presence, and the owner of the world's leading purely online payment platform. We are optimistic about its international and payment segments.

► Risks to our recommendation and target price include a sharp weakening of consumer sentiment and/or spending, potentially greater related regulation and taxation, and significant and increasing international competition. We also believe the Skype purchase was not very strategic and was excessively priced.

► Comparing EBAY to certain large-cap Internet peers based on 2008 P/E and P/E to growth (PEG) rates results in a price of $75. Our DCF model, with assumptions that include a weighted average cost of capital of 10.9% and projected average annual free cash flow growth of 20% over the next five years, yields an intrinsic value of $40. A weighting of these methodologies results in our 12-month target price of $50.

Qualitative Risk Assessment

LOW	MEDIUM	HIGH

Our risk assessment reflects our view that EBAY is a well established leader in the Internet segment, operates a business model that we see as attractive, and has a strong balance sheet. However, the company operates in fast-changing areas and faces notable competition. Over the past couple of years, we have viewed EBAY's quarterly results, financial outlook, strategic decisions and management changes as disappointing at times. We believe this has contributed to stock volatility that is greater than that of the S&P 500.

Quantitative Evaluations

S&P Quality Ranking B

D	C	B-	B	B+	A-	A	A+

Relative Strength Rank MODERATE

35

LOWEST = 1   HIGHEST = 99

Revenue/Earnings Data

Revenue (Million $)

	1Q	2Q	3Q	4Q	Year
2007	1,768	1,418	1,889	--	--
2006	1,390	1,411	1,449	1,720	5,970
2005	1,032	1,086	1,106	1,329	4,552
2004	756.2	773.4	805.9	935.8	3,271
2003	476.5	509.3	530.9	648.4	2,165
2002	245.1	266.3	288.8	413.9	1,214

Earnings Per Share ($)

2007	0.27	0.27	-0.69	E0.40	E1.34
2006	0.17	0.17	0.20	0.25	0.79
2005	0.19	0.21	0.18	0.20	0.78
2004	0.15	0.14	0.13	0.15	0.57
2003	0.08	0.07	0.08	0.11	0.34
2002	0.04	0.05	0.05	0.07	0.21

Fiscal year ended Dec. 31. Next earnings report expected: Late January. EPS Estimates based on S&P Operating Earnings; historical GAAP earnings are as reported.

Dividend Data

No cash dividends have been paid.

eBay Inc

STANDARD &POOR'S

Business Summary October 22, 2007

CORPORATE OVERVIEW. eBay operates the world's largest online trading community. As of September 2007, eBay had 247.6 million confirmed registered users (up from 211.9 million a year earlier) and 83.0 million active users (79.8 million), which accounted for 473.2 million non-store listings (488.3 million) and 82.4 million store listings (95.4 million). Following acquisitions in recent years, the company also owns Half.com (fixed price retail sales), PayPal (online payments), Rent.com (apartment and home rentals), Shopping.com (comparison shopping), Skype (Internet calling), and StubHub (online ticket sales).

The company and its affiliates have Web sites directed toward the following geographies: Argentina, Australia, Austria, Belgium, Brazil, Canada, China, France, Germany, Hong Kong, India, Ireland, Italy, Malaysia, Mexico, the Netherlands, New Zealand, the Philippines, Poland, Singapore, South Korea, Spain, Sweden, Switzerland, Taiwan, Turkey and the U.K. eBay discontinued its Web site in Japan in early 2002. In December 2006, EBAY announced it would contribute its China operations to a joint venture with Internet portal and wireless services company TOM Online. EBAY owns a 49% stake in the venture, which was created in February 2007.

CORPORATE STRATEGY. The company's stated goal is to become the world's most efficient and abundant marketplace by expanding its community of users, delivering value to buyers and sellers, creating a global marketplace, and providing a faster, easier and safer trading experience. EBAY has increasingly employed acquisitions to fulfill the aforementioned goal, with a focus on international expansion and offering more choices and services to its buyers and sellers. In our view, PayPal was an extremely successful acquisition because it dramatically enhanced the user experience. Moreover, the combination accelerated the benefits the companies already derived from the Network Effect (whereby a product/service becomes more valuable to its users as its number of users increases), in our opinion. Although we are skeptical as to whether the October 2005 purchase of Skype will yield comparable results, and this opinion is underscored by the company taking a related impairment charge of $1.4 billion, we have grown modestly more optimistic about Skype's longer term potential as a stand-alone business, and we also see synergies with PayPal.

Company Financials Fiscal Year Ended Dec. 31

Per Share Data ($)	2006	2005	2004	2003	2002	2001	2000	1999	1998	1997
Tangible Book Value	2.69	2.21	2.73	2.23	1.46	1.11	0.93	0.81	0.09	0.07
Cash Flow	1.17	1.05	0.75	0.46	0.28	0.16	0.08	0.03	0.01	NA
Earnings	0.79	0.78	0.57	0.34	0.21	0.08	0.04	0.01	Nil	Nil
S&P Core Earnings	0.79	0.61	0.43	0.21	0.04	-0.00	NA	NA	NA	NA
Dividends	Nil	Nil	Nil	Nil	Nil	Nil	Nil	Nil	Nil	NA
Payout Ratio	Nil	Nil	Nil	Nil	Nil	Nil	NM	Nil	Nil	NA
Prices:High	47.86	58.89	59.21	32.40	17.71	18.19	31.88	29.25	12.97	NA
Prices:Low	22.83	30.78	31.30	16.88	12.21	7.11	6.69	6.92	0.75	NA
P/E Ratio:High	61	75	NM	95	83	NM	NM	NM	NM	NA
P/E Ratio:Low	29	39	NM	50	57	NM	NM	NM	NM	NA

Income Statement Analysis (Million $)										
Revenue	5,970	4,552	3,271	2,165	1,214	749	431	225	47.4	5.76
Operating Income	1,968	1,820	1,313	828	431	227	74.6	23.8	8.88	NA
Depreciation	545	378	254	159	76.6	86.6	38.1	20.7	2.79	NA
Interest Expense	5.92	3.48	8.88	4.31	1.49	2.85	3.37	1.94	0.04	Nil
Pretax Income	1,547	1,549	1,128	662	398	163	78.0	20.5	7.03	-1.98
Effective Tax Rate	27.2%	30.2%	30.5%	31.3%	36.7%	49.1%	42.0%	45.8%	65.9%	NM
Net Income	1,126	1,082	778	447	250	90.4	48.3	10.8	2.40	-1.91
S&P Core Earnings	1,126	853	589	270	52.2	-4.04	NA	NA	NA	NA

Balance Sheet & Other Financial Data (Million $)										
Cash	2,663	1,314	1,330	1,382	1,109	524	202	220	31.8	67.7
Current Assets	4,971	3,183	2,911	2,146	1,468	884	675	460	83.4	NA
Total Assets	13,494	11,789	7,991	5,820	4,124	1,679	1,182	964	92.5	76.8
Current Liabilities	2,518	1,485	1,085	647	386	180	137	88.8	8.04	NA
Long Term Debt	Nil	Nil	0.08	124	13.8	12.0	11.4	15.0	Nil	0.01
Common Equity	10,905	10,048	6,728	4,896	3,556	1,429	1,014	852	84.4	71.1
Total Capital	10,905	10,264	6,868	5,139	3,715	1,479	1,038	867	84.4	71.1
Capital Expenditures	515	338	293	365	139	57.4	49.8	141	8.86	NA
Cash Flow	1,670	1,460	1,032	606	326	177	86.3	31.5	5.19	NA
Current Ratio	2.0	2.1	2.7	3.3	3.8	4.9	4.9	5.2	10.4	NA
% Long Term Debt of Capitalization	Nil	Nil	NM	2.4	0.4	0.8	1.1	1.7	Nil	6.9
% Net Income of Revenue	18.9	23.8	23.8	20.7	20.6	12.1	11.2	4.8	5.1	NM
% Return on Assets	8.9	10.9	11.3	9.1	8.6	6.3	4.5	1.9	4.9	NM
% Return on Equity	10.7	12.9	13.4	10.6	10.0	7.4	5.2	2.3	5.6	NM

Data as orig reptd.; bef. results of disc opers/spec. items. Per share data adj. for stk. divs.; EPS diluted. E-Estimated. NA-Not Available. NM-Not Meaningful. NR-Not Ranked. UR-Under Review.

Office: 2145 Hamilton Ave, San Jose, CA 95125-5905.
Telephone: 408-376-7400.
Email: investor_relations@ebay.com
Website: http://www.ebay.com

Chrmn: P.M. Omidyar
Pres & CEO: M.C. Whitman
Investor Contact: R.H. Swan (866-696-3229)
SVP & CFO: R.H. Swan

SVP, Secy & General Counsel: M.R. Jacobson
Board Members: F. D. Anderson, E. Barnholt, P. Bourguignon, S. D. Cook, W. C. Ford, Jr., R. C. Kagle, D. G. Lepore, P. M. Omidyar, R. T. Schlosberg, III, T. J. Tierney, M. C. Whitman

Founded: 1995
Domicile: Delaware
Employees: 13,200

The McGraw-Hill Companies

Ecolab Inc.

STANDARD &POOR'S

S&P Recommendation **BUY** ★★★★☆	Price $45.87 (as of Nov 23, 2007)	12-Mo. Target Price $53.00	Investment Style Large-Cap Growth

GICS Sector Materials
Sub-Industry Specialty Chemicals

Summary This company is the leading worldwide marketer of cleaning, sanitizing and maintenance products and services for the hospitality, institutional and industrial markets.

Key Stock Statistics (Source S&P, Vickers, company reports)

52-Wk Range	$48.37– 37.01	S&P Oper. EPS 2007**E**	1.66	Market Capitalization(B)	$11.252	Beta	0.61
Trailing 12-Month EPS	$1.59	S&P Oper. EPS 2008**E**	1.88	Yield (%)	1.00	S&P 3-Yr. Proj. EPS CAGR(%)	13.00
Trailing 12-Month P/E	28.9	P/E on S&P Oper. EPS 2007**E**	27.6	Dividend Rate/Share	$0.46	S&P Credit Rating	A
$10K Invested 5 Yrs Ago	$19,375	Common Shares Outstg. (M)	245.3	Institutional Ownership (%)	56		

Price Performance

30-Week Mov. Avg. · · · 10-Week Mov. Avg. - - **GAAP Earnings vs. Previous Year**   Volume Above Avg. STARS
12-Mo. Target Price — Relative Strength — ▲ Up ▼ Down ▶ No Change   Below Avg.

Options: P, Ph

Analysis prepared by **Richard O'Reilly, CFA** on October 23, 2007, when the stock traded at **$ 46.49.**

Highlights

➤ We expect sales for 2008 to rise close to a 10% rate, assuming favorable currency rates. We see organic sales growth from existing businesses rising at about 7%, aided by expected healthy conditions in key domestic markets, continued benefits from new products and customers, a forecast price increase of 2%, and a 4%-5% annual expansion in the salesforce over the past two years.

➤ We look for the domestic institutional, Kay, food & beverage, health care, and pest elimination units to continue to expand. We believe international sales will increase in most parts of the world, including stronger comparisons in Europe. We project that operating margins in 2008 will remain stable on our estimated sales gain and possible higher raw material costs. We expect the loss from the GCS kitchen repair unit to narrow in late 2007 and into 2008 as costs associated with new systems' implementation decline.

➤ Interest expense may be about $60 million in 2008, up from 2007, reflecting a pending acquisition, and we assume an effective tax rate of 34.5%, up from 2007, which is expected to include one-time benefits.

Investment Rationale/Risk

➤ We expect ECL to post ongoing solid sales and EPS gains in coming periods, based on our belief that conditions will remain healthy in the global industries that it serves.

➤ Risks to our recommendation and target price include unexpected slowdowns in the hospitality, travel, and foodservice industries, an inability to continue to successfully introduce new products and services, and higher than projected raw material costs.

➤ The shares recently traded at about 28X our 2007 EPS forecast, a large premium to the S&P 500 but at the midpoint of ECL's annual P/E for the past decade. We believe that a steady grower such as ECL will be sought by investors as the economic recovery matures, and we think the shares offer solid upside potential. Our 12-month target price is $53, which is about 25X our 2008 EPS forecast and a P/E to growth (PEG) multiple of 1.6X the 15% EPS gains that we see for the next few years. The dividend rate has been raised for 15 consecutive years.

Qualitative Risk Assessment

LOW	MEDIUM	HIGH

Our risk assessment reflects the company's leading share positions in its core businesses, the stable nature of its end markets and customers, and our view of its strong balance sheet and cash generation. The stock's S&P Quality Ranking is A, the second highest possible, indicating a solid 10-year historical record of earnings and dividend growth.

Quantitative Evaluations

S&P Quality Ranking   A

D	C	B-	B	B+	A-	**A**	A+

Relative Strength Rank   **STRONG**

82

LOWEST = 1   HIGHEST = 99

Revenue/Earnings Data

Revenue (Million $)

	1Q	2Q	3Q	4Q	Year
2007	1,254	1,362	1,413	--	--
2006	1,120	1,226	1,279	1,271	4,896
2005	1,070	1,159	1,165	1,142	4,535
2004	979.4	1,043	1,090	1,073	4,185
2003	875.9	946.7	982.8	956.5	3,762
2002	786.1	839.2	894.9	883.4	3,404

Earnings Per Share ($)

	1Q	2Q	3Q	4Q	Year
2007	0.35	0.44	0.46	E0.40	E1.66
2006	0.30	0.36	0.43	0.34	1.43
2005	0.27	0.31	0.38	0.27	1.23
2004	0.25	0.30	0.36	0.27	1.19
2003	0.21	0.25	0.33	0.26	1.06
2002	0.14	0.20	0.28	0.20	0.81

Fiscal year ended Dec. 31. Next earnings report expected: Mid February. EPS Estimates based on S&P Operating Earnings; historical GAAP earnings are as reported.

Dividend Data (Dates: mm/dd Payment Date: mm/dd/yy)

Amount ($)	Date Decl.	Ex-Div. Date	Stk. of Record	Payment Date
0.115	12/07	12/15	12/19	01/16/07
0.115	02/23	03/16	03/20	04/16/07
0.115	05/04	06/15	06/19	07/16/07
0.115	08/03	09/14	09/18	10/15/07

Dividends have been paid since 1936. Source: Company reports.

Ecolab Inc.

Business Summary October 23, 2007

CORPORATE OVERVIEW. Ecolab is a global supplier of cleaning, sanitizing, and maintenance products and services for hospitality, institutional, and industrial markets. In the U.S. cleaning and sanitizing business (44% of 2006 sales, 54% of profits), the institutional division (27% of 2006 total sales) is the leading provider of cleaners and sanitizers for warewashing, on-premise laundry, kitchen cleaning and general housekeeping, product dispensing equipment and dishwashing racks and related kitchen sundries to the food-service, lodging and health care industries. It also provides pool and spa treatment products. In addition, the division includes professional janitorial products (detergents, floor care, disinfectants, odor control) sold under the Airkem brand name.

The Kay division (5%) is the largest supplier of cleaning and sanitizing products (surface cleaners, degreasers, sanitizers and hand care products) for the quick-service restaurant, convenience store and food retail markets. The Food and Beverage division (8%) offers cleaning and sanitizing products and services to farms, dairy plants, food and beverage processors, and pharmaceutical plants.

ECL also sells health care products (skin care, disinfectants and sterilants; 1%) under the Huntington name; textile care products (1%) for large institu-

tional and commercial laundries; vehicle care products (soaps, polishes, wheel treatments) for rental, fleet and retail car washes (1%); and water treatment products (1%) to institutional, laundry and food and beverage, and processing markets for boilers, cooling and waste treatment systems.

Other U.S. services (9%, 6%) include institutional and commercial pest elimination and prevention services (6%) and GCS Services, a provider of commercial kitchen equipment repair and maintenance services (3%). ECL bought GCS Service in 1998, and has added to this business through small acquisitions; this business had operating losses for the four years through 2006.

The International business (47%, 40%) provides services similar to those offered in the U.S. to Canada (3%) and about 70 countries in Europe (32%), Latin America (4%), the Asia/Pacific region (7%), and other (1%). The institutional and food & beverage businesses constitute a larger portion of the international business compared to the U.S.

Company Financials Fiscal Year Ended Dec. 31

Per Share Data ($)	2006	2005	2004	2003	2002	2001	2000	1999	1998	1997
Tangible Book Value	1.67	2.00	1.33	1.14	0.83	0.41	1.77	1.98	1.76	1.30
Cash Flow	2.48	2.22	2.13	1.93	1.67	1.35	1.35	1.15	1.03	0.88
Earnings	1.43	1.23	1.19	1.06	0.81	0.73	0.79	0.66	0.58	0.50
S&P Core Earnings	1.46	1.24	1.10	0.98	0.64	0.61	NA	NA	NA	NA
Dividends	0.42	0.36	0.33	0.30	0.28	0.26	0.25	0.21	0.19	0.17
Payout Ratio	29%	29%	28%	28%	34%	36%	31%	32%	33%	34%
Prices:High	46.40	37.15	35.59	27.92	25.20	22.09	22.84	22.22	19.00	14.00
Prices:Low	33.64	30.68	26.12	23.08	18.27	14.25	14.00	15.84	13.06	9.06
P/E Ratio:High	32	30	30	26	31	30	29	34	33	28
P/E Ratio:Low	24	25	22	22	23	20	18	24	23	18

Income Statement Analysis (Million $)										
Revenue	4,896	4,535	4,185	3,762	3,404	2,355	2,264	2,080	1,888	1,640
Operating Income	880	799	786	713	656	482	471	714	384	319
Depreciation	269	257	247	230	223	163	148	135	122	101
Interest Expense	51.3	49.8	45.3	45.3	43.9	28.4	24.6	22.7	25.0	12.6
Pretax Income	567	498	489	448	354	306	338	286	256	219
Effective Tax Rate	35.0%	35.9%	36.5%	38.1%	39.6%	38.4%	38.3%	38.4%	39.7%	38.9%
Net Income	369	319	310	277	214	188	209	176	155	134
S&P Core Earnings	376	322	283	260	167	157	NA	NA	NA	NA

Balance Sheet & Other Financial Data (Million $)										
Cash	484	104	71.2	85.6	49.2	41.8	44.0	47.7	28.4	61.2
Current Assets	1,854	1,422	1,279	1,150	1,016	930	601	577	504	510
Total Assets	4,419	3,797	3,716	3,229	2,878	2,525	1,714	1,586	1,471	1,416
Current Liabilities	1,503	1,119	940	851	866	828	532	471	400	404
Long Term Debt	557	519	Nil	604	540	512	234	169	227	259
Common Equity	1,680	1,649	1,563	1,295	1,100	880	757	929	691	552
Total Capital	2,237	2,169	1,563	1,900	1,639	1,393	991	1,098	918	811
Capital Expenditures	288	269	276	212	213	158	150	146	148	122
Cash Flow	637	576	558	507	437	351	357	310	276	235
Current Ratio	1.2	1.3	1.4	1.4	1.2	1.1	1.1	1.2	1.3	1.3
% Long Term Debt of Capitalization	24.9	23.9	Nil	31.8	32.9	36.8	23.6	15.4	24.7	31.9
% Net Income of Revenue	7.5	7.0	7.4	7.4	6.3	8.0	9.2	8.5	8.2	8.2
% Return on Assets	9.0	8.5	8.9	9.1	7.9	8.9	12.6	11.5	10.7	10.2
% Return on Equity	22.1	19.7	21.7	23.2	21.6	23.0	27.5	18.9	24.9	25.0

Data as orig reptd.; bef. results of disc opers/spec. items. Per share data adj. for stk. divs.; EPS diluted. E-Estimated. NA-Not Available. NM-Not Meaningful. NR-Not Ranked. UR-Under Review.

Office: 370 North Wabasha Street, Saint Paul, MN 55102-1390.
Telephone: 651-293-2233.
Email: investor.info@ecolab.com
Website: http://www.ecolab.com

Chrmn, Pres & CEO: D.M. Baker, Jr.
EVP & CFO: S.L. Fritze
SVP, Secy & General Counsel: L.T. Bell
SVP & Cntlr: D.J. Schmechel

VP & CIO: R.P. Tabb
Investor Contact: M.J. Monahan (651-293-2809)
Board Members: D. M. Baker, Jr., L. S. Biller, R. U. De Schutter, J. A. Grundhofer, S. Hamelmann, J. W. Johnson, J. W. Levin, R. L. Lumpkins, B. M. Pritchard, K. Rorsted, H. Van Bylen, J. J. Zillmer

Founded: 1924
Domicile: Delaware
Employees: 23,130

Edison International

STANDARD &POOR'S

S&P Recommendation	**BUY** ★★★★☆	Price $54.53 (as of Nov 23, 2007)	12-Mo. Target Price $66.00	Investment Style Large-Cap Blend

GICS Sector Utilities
Sub-Industry Electric Utilities

Summary EIX is the holding company for Southern California Edison. Other businesses include electric power generation, financial investments, and real estate development.

Key Stock Statistics (Source S&P, Vickers, company reports)

52-Wk Range	$60.26– 42.76	S&P Oper. EPS 2007**E**	3.55	Market Capitalization(B)	$17.766	Beta	0.41
Trailing 12-Month EPS	$3.53	S&P Oper. EPS 2008**E**	3.75	Yield (%)	2.13	S&P 3-Yr. Proj. EPS CAGR(%)	6.00
Trailing 12-Month P/E	15.5	P/E on S&P Oper. EPS 2007**E**	15.4	Dividend Rate/Share	$1.16	S&P Credit Rating	BBB-
$10K Invested 5 Yrs Ago	$51,456	Common Shares Outstg. (M)	325.8	Institutional Ownership (%)	76		

Price Performance

30-Week Mov. Avg. ··· **10-Week Mov. Avg.** - - **GAAP Earnings vs. Previous Year** **Volume** Above Avg. STARS
12-Mo. Target Price — **Relative Strength** — ▲ Up ▼ Down ▶ No Change Below Avg.

(chart: 2004, 2005, 2006, 2007 — months J A S O N D ...)

Options: ASE, CBOE, P

Analysis prepared by **Justin McCann** on November 16, 2007, when the stock traded at **$ 54.56**.

Highlights

➤ We expect 2007 operating EPS to grow about 16% from 2006 EPS from ongoing operations of $3.07. Operating EPS in the first nine months of 2007 grew 25% to $3.04, aided $0.18 by the delayed recording of the retroactive rate increase for the first four months of 2006. We expect Southern California Edison (SCE) to earn about $2.03 a share in 2007 (up from $1.89 in 2006), and Edison Mission Energy (EME) $1.65 ($1.30). We project a per-share loss of about $0.13 (a loss of $0.12) from the parent company.

➤ For 2008, we expect operating EPS to increase by nearly 6% from anticipated results in 2007, reflecting the returns from an enhanced rate base at SCE, and continuing strength at EME.

➤ We expect EPS growth to be driven by SCE's five-year, $17 billion infrastructure development plan. This has resulted--and should continue to result--in an enhanced rate base. The California Public Utility Commission (CPUC) approved a 7.3% increase in SCE's rate base, to $11.7 billion in 2007 and an 8.5% increase in 2008, to $12.7 billion. SCE is currently seeking additional rate base hikes of 14.2%, to $14.5 billion in 2009, 21.4%, to $17.6 billion in 2010, and 15.9%, to $20.4 billion in 2011.

Investment Rationale/Risk

➤ Although EIX shares are up approximately 20% year-to-date, we believe they are significantly undervalued trading at a recent discount-to-peers P/E of less than 15X our EPS estimate for 2008. Given our solid EPS outlook for the next couple of years, we continue to recommend the shares for above-average total return. We expect earnings to be aided by the rate increases granted to SCE and by higher wholesale power margins for Edison Mission Energy.

➤ Risks to our recommendation and target price include the potential for unfavorable regulatory or legislative acts, a sharp decline in the gas/coal price spread, and a significant market-related change in the P/E of the electric utility group as a whole.

➤ Given our favorable outlook for SCE and EME, we expect the stock to trade at a premium-to-peers P/E of about 17.6X our 2008 EPS estimate. After a recent decrease in peer valuations, we believe the stock, despite its below-peers dividend yield (recently 2.1%), has above-peers total return potential over the next 12 months. Our 12-month target price is $66.

Qualitative Risk Assessment

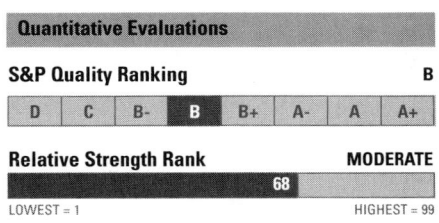

| LOW | MEDIUM | HIGH |

Our risk assessment reflects our view of the strong and steady earnings and cash flow that we expect from the regulated Southern California Edison utility, with its large and rapidly growing service territory and a generally supportive regulatory environment.

Quantitative Evaluations

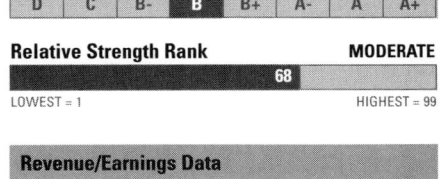

S&P Quality Ranking   B

| D | C | B- | **B** | B+ | A- | A | A+ |

Relative Strength Rank   MODERATE

68

LOWEST = 1   HIGHEST = 99

Revenue/Earnings Data

Revenue (Million $)

	1Q	2Q	3Q	4Q	Year
2007	2,912	3,047	3,942	--	--
2006	2,751	3,001	3,802	3,067	12,622
2005	2,446	2,649	3,783	2,975	11,852
2004	2,116	2,565	3,188	2,327	10,199
2003	2,523	3,125	3,833	2,654	12,135
2002	2,488	2,824	3,707	2,469	11,488

Earnings Per Share ($)

2007	1.00	0.28	1.40	E0.56	E3.55
2006	0.56	0.53	1.39	0.80	3.28
2005	0.59	0.55	1.31	0.90	3.34
2004	0.16	-1.21	0.95	0.78	0.68
2003	0.19	0.07	1.52	0.59	2.37
2002	0.24	1.99	1.05	0.17	3.46

Fiscal year ended Dec. 31. Next earnings report expected: Late February. EPS Estimates based on S&P Operating Earnings; historical GAAP earnings are as reported.

Dividend Data (Dates: mm/dd Payment Date: mm/dd/yy)

Amount ($)	Date Decl.	Ex-Div. Date	Stk. of Record	Payment Date
0.290	12/14	12/27	12/29	01/31/07
0.290	02/22	03/28	03/30	04/30/07
0.290	04/26	06/27	06/29	07/31/07
0.290	09/06	09/26	09/28	10/31/07

Dividends have been paid since 2004. Source: Company reports.

Please read the Required Disclosures and Analyst Certification on the last page of this report.

The **McGraw-Hill** Companies

Edison International

STANDARD &POOR'S

Business Summary November 16, 2007

CORPORATE OVERVIEW. Edison International (EIX) is the holding company of the regulated Southern California Edison (SCE) utility and several non-regulated subsidiaries. The principal non-utility companies are Edison Mission Energy (EME), an independent power producer that also conducts price risk management and energy trading activities, and Edison Capital, which holds equity investments in energy and infrastructure projects. In 2006, SCE accounted for 81.7% of EIX's consolidated revenues, the non-utility power generation business 17.7%, and financial servicers and other operations 0.6%. The utility's retail operations are regulated by the purview of the California Public Utilities Commission (CPUC), while its wholesale operations fall under the oversight of the Federal Energy Regulatory Commission (FERC).

CORPORATE STRATEGY. In 2005, EIX's strategic plan established a balanced approach for growth, dividends, and balance sheet strength. To implement this strategy, the company initiated efforts to reduce administration expenses in the non-utility companies and a multi-year productivity effort at the utility. EIX has taken steps to rebalance its capital structure in order to further reduce debt, and has worked to enhance liquidity through strong cash flow generation. SCE is working on new projects that should expand its transmission and distribution systems, and intends to implement a comprehensive software system to support the majority of its critical business processes. We also expect to see EIX further strengthen the independent power business, expand investment in renewable energy, and evaluate prospects for growth in the non-utility sector.

Company Financials Fiscal Year Ended Dec. 31

Per Share Data ($)	2006	2005	2004	2003	2002	2001	2000	1999	1998	1997
Tangible Book Value	23.65	20.30	18.56	13.86	11.59	8.10	7.43	14.03	13.55	13.75
Earnings	3.28	3.34	0.68	2.37	3.46	7.36	-5.84	1.79	1.84	1.73
S&P Core Earnings	3.28	3.35	0.60	2.45	2.81	6.78	NA	NA	NA	NA
Dividends	1.10	1.02	1.05	Nil	Nil	Nil	1.11	1.07	1.04	1.00
Payout Ratio	34%	31%	154%	Nil	Nil	Nil	NM	60%	56%	58%
Prices:High	47.15	49.16	32.52	22.07	19.60	16.12	30.00	29.63	31.00	27.81
Prices:Low	37.90	30.43	21.24	10.57	7.80	6.25	14.13	21.63	25.13	19.38
P/E Ratio:High	14	15	48	9	6	2	NM	17	17	16
P/E Ratio:Low	12	9	31	4	2	1	NM	12	14	11

Income Statement Analysis (Million $)										
Revenue	12,622	11,852	10,199	12,135	11,488	11,436	11,717	9,670	10,208	9,235
Depreciation	1,181	1,061	1,022	1,184	1,030	973	1,933	1,794	1,662	1,362
Maintenance	NA	NA	NA	NA	NA	NA	NA	NA	411	406
Fixed Charges Coverage	3.18	3.28	2.20	1.73	1.91	3.38	-0.98	1.96	1.71	2.27
Construction Credits	NA	NA	NA	NA	NA	NA	NA	Nil	12.0	17.0
Effective Tax Rate	32.3%	26.4%	NM	21.5%	25.6%	40.7%	NM	32.0%	40.4%	40.3%
Net Income	1,083	1,108	226	779	1,135	2,402	-1,943	623	668	700
S&P Core Earnings	1,082	1,111	199	808	921	2,211	NA	NA	NA	NA

Balance Sheet & Other Financial Data (Million $)										
Gross Property	25,090	24,775	23,214	24,674	23,264	22,396	25,737	27,203	17,223	24,661
Capital Expenditures	2,536	1,868	1,733	1,288	1,590	933	1,488	1,231	963	783
Net Property	20,269	18,588	17,397	20,288	15,170	14,427	17,903	19,683	10,326	14,117
Capitalization:Long Term Debt	10,016	9,552	9,807	12,221	12,915	14,007	13,660	15,050	8,543	8,871
Capitalization:% Long Term Debt	56.5	59.1	61.3	69.4	74.4	81.1	85.0	74.3	62.6	59.1
Capitalization:Preferred	Nil	Nil	Nil	9.00	Nil	Nil	Nil	Nil	Nil	609
Capitalization:% Preferred	Nil	Nil	Nil	0.05	Nil	Nil	Nil	Nil	Nil	4.05
Capitalization:Common	7,709	6,615	6,049	5,383	4,437	3,272	2,420	5,211	5,099	5,527
Capitalization:% Common	43.5	40.9	37.8	30.6	25.6	18.9	15.0	25.7	37.4	36.8
Total Capital	23,415	21,854	21,688	24,246	23,786	24,163	21,609	26,252	18,520	19,452
% Operating Ratio	84.7	80.7	80.6	75.2	82.8	93.2	86.4	92.9	96.9	87.8
% Earned on Net Property	12.8	6.9	6.6	9.1	16.0	36.9	NM	11.6	6.4	10.2
% Return on Revenue	8.6	9.3	2.2	6.4	9.9	21.0	NM	6.4	6.5	7.6
% Return on Invested Capital	10.2	12.2	10.4	14.9	10.9	4.8	7.8	3.6	7.9	10.5
% Return on Common Equity	15.1	17.1	3.8	15.9	29.4	84.4	NM	12.1	12.6	11.7

Data as orig reptd.; bef. results of disc opers/spec. items. Per share data adj. for stk. divs.; EPS diluted. E-Estimated. NA-Not Available. NM-Not Meaningful. NR-Not Ranked. UR-Under Review.

Office: 2244 Walnut Grove Avenue, Rosemead, CA 91770-3714.
Telephone: 877-379-9515.
Website: http://www.edison.com
Chrmn, Pres & CEO: J.E. Bryson

EVP, CFO & Treas: T.R. McDaniel
EVP & General Counsel: J.A. Bouknight, Jr.
Investor Contact: S. Cunningham
VP & Cntlr: L.G. Sullivan

Board Members: J. E. Bryson, V. C. Chang, F. A. Cordova, C. B. Curtis, B. M. Freeman, L. G. Nogales, R. L. Olson, J. M. Rosser, R. T. Schlosberg, III, R. H. Smith, T. C. Sutton

Founded: 1886
Domicile: California
Employees: 16,139

The McGraw-Hill Companies

Electronic Arts Inc

S&P Recommendation **SELL** ★★☆☆☆	Price	12-Mo. Target Price	Investment Style
	$54.29 (as of Nov 23, 2007)	$53.00	Large-Cap Growth

GICS Sector Information Technology
Sub-Industry Home Entertainment Software

Summary This company produces entertainment software for PCs, home video game consoles, and mobile gaming devices.

Key Stock Statistics (Source S&P, Vickers, company reports)

52-Wk Range	$61.62– 46.27	S&P Oper. EPS 2008**E**	0.90	Market Capitalization(B)	$17.100	Beta	1.27
Trailing 12-Month EPS	$-0.62	S&P Oper. EPS 2009**E**	1.07	Yield (%)	Nil	S&P 3-Yr. Proj. EPS CAGR(%)	20.00
Trailing 12-Month P/E	NM	P/E on S&P Oper. EPS 2008**E**	60.3	Dividend Rate/Share	Nil	S&P Credit Rating	NA
$10K Invested 5 Yrs Ago	$16,163	Common Shares Outstg. (M)	315.0	Institutional Ownership (%)	92		

Price Performance

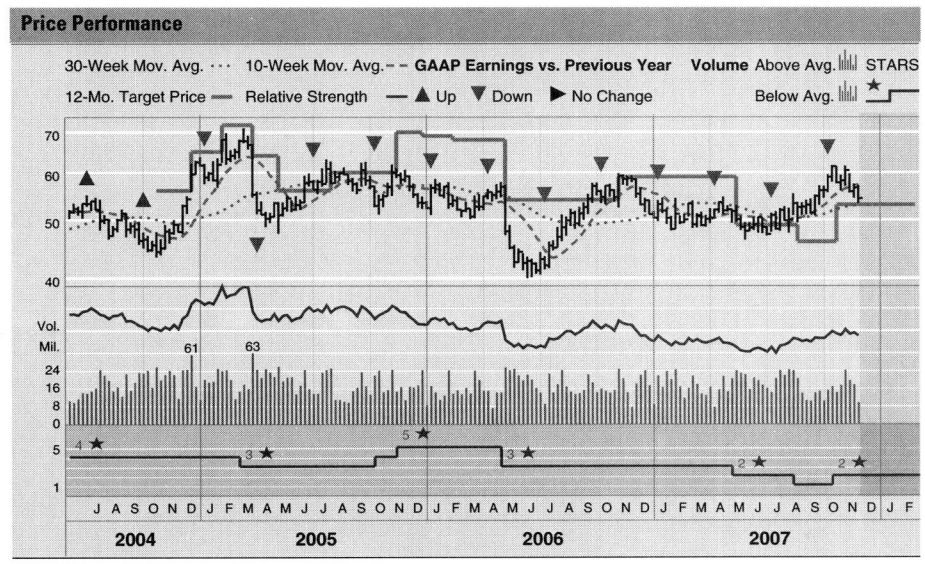

30-Week Mov. Avg. ···   10-Week Mov. Avg. --   **GAAP Earnings vs. Previous Year**   Volume Above Avg. STARS
12-Mo. Target Price —   Relative Strength —   ▲ Up   ▼ Down   ► No Change   Below Avg.

Options: ASE, CBOE, P, Ph

Analysis prepared by **Jim Yin** on November 06, 2007, when the stock traded at **$ 58.28**.

Highlights

➤ We see non-GAAP revenue, which includes about $433 million of deferred revenue, rising 27% in FY 08 (Mar.), following 4.7% growth in FY 07. We believe the revenue growth rate will accelerate due to continued strong sales of Madden NFL, FIFA, and The Sims, increased adoption of next-generation game consoles, and higher average selling prices. However, we believe ERTS will lose market share, reflecting the increasing popularity of Wii, which appeals to players other than core video game players that have been ERTS's strength.

➤ We see non-GAAP gross margins decreasing to 56% in FY 08, from 61% in FY 07, due to a higher number of titles produced by ERTS's partners. We project that operating margins will increase to 10.7%, from 7.9%, reflecting effective control of development and marketing costs.

➤ Our operating EPS estimate for FY 08 is $0.90, compared to operating EPS of $0.51 in FY 07. The projected increase reflects higher revenues, expanding margins, and a lower tax rate. For FY 09, we see EPS of $1.07.

Investment Rationale/Risk

➤ We recently upgraded our opinion to sell, from strong sell, after ERTS announced that results for the September quarter would exceed expectations. We believe better-than-expected results were driven by strong sales of Madden NFL 08 and Skate. In addition, ERTS plans to release a list of new game titles for the Christmas season. Despite these positives, we still view the shares as overvalued, trading at a multiple of 65X our FY 08 operating EPS estimate, a premium to its peer average of 27X.

➤ Risks to our recommendation and target price include better-than-expected sales of game consoles as the next-generation hardware cycle begins to ramp up, an upturn in the U.S. economy, and top game titles releasing earlier than expected.

➤ Our 12-month target price of $53 is based on a blend of our discounted cash flow (DCF) and P/E analyses. Our DCF model assumes a 12.0% weighted average cost of capital and 4% terminal growth, yielding an intrinsic value of $51. For our P/E analysis, we derive a value of $54, based on a historical P/E-to-growth ratio of 3.0X, or a multiple of 60X our FY 08 operating EPS estimate of $0.90.

Qualitative Risk Assessment

LOW	MEDIUM	HIGH

Our risk assessment takes into account the volatile nature of the home entertainment software industry and the company's focus on the consumer market. These factors are offset, in our view, by ERTS's leading market share position and advantageous financial structure.

Quantitative Evaluations

S&P Quality Ranking   B+

D	C	B-	B	B+	A-	A	A+

Relative Strength Rank   MODERATE

62

LOWEST = 1   HIGHEST = 99

Revenue/Earnings Data

Revenue (Million $)

	1Q	2Q	3Q	4Q	Year
2008	395.0	640.0	--	--	--
2007	413.0	784.0	1,281	613.0	3,091
2006	365.0	675.0	1,270	641.0	2,951
2005	431.6	715.7	1,428	553.0	3,129
2004	353.4	530.0	1,475	598.4	2,957
2003	331.9	453.5	1,234	463.1	2,482

Earnings Per Share ($)

	1Q	2Q	3Q	4Q	Year
2008	-0.42	-0.62	E0.98	E-0.03	E0.90
2007	-0.26	0.07	0.50	-0.08	0.24
2006	-0.19	0.16	0.83	-0.05	0.75
2005	0.08	0.31	1.18	0.02	1.59
2004	0.06	0.25	1.26	0.29	1.87
2003	0.03	0.17	0.85	0.03	1.09

Fiscal year ended Mar. 31. Next earnings report expected: Early February. EPS Estimates based on S&P Operating Earnings; historical GAAP earnings are as reported.

Dividend Data

No cash dividends have been paid.

Electronic Arts Inc

STANDARD
&POOR'S

Business Summary November 06, 2007

CORPORATE OVERVIEW. Electronic Arts is one of the primary third-party video game publishers, garnering close to $3.1 billion in revenue in FY 07 (Mar.). ERTS owns many of today's most popular video game franchises, including Madden NFL, The Sims, and Need for Speed. The company organizes its business into four labels: EA SPORTS, EA Games, EA Casual Entertainment and The Sims. Each label operates with dedicated studio and marketing teams. ERTS markets, publishes and distribute games in over 30 countries throughout the world. International revenue accounted for $1.425 billion, or 46% of total revenue, in FY 07. The company also uses third parties to develop games at their own development and production studios.

CORPORATE STRATEGY. We believe that one of ERTS's main advantages is its ability to publish titles across all major platforms, including consoles (56% of FY 07 revenues), PCs (16%), and handheld gaming devices (18%). Within the console segment, ERTS's revenues are spread among the PlayStation 2 (29%), X-Box (5%), X-Box 360 (15%) and PlayStation 3 (3%), which we think reduces the risk ERTS faces that sales of any particular console will languish. We believe ERTS further diversified its revenue base with the February 2006 acquisition of cellular phone game developer JAMDAT Mobile. ERTS attempts to maintain diversity among genres and individual titles, in our view. During FY 07, ERTS published 32 EA Studio titles compared to 31 titles in FY 06. Four titles sold more than five million units in FY 07 -- Madden NFL 07, Need for Speed Carbon, FIFA 07, and The Sims 2 Pets. ERTS has also secured several exclusive licenses, including those for the NFL, ESPN, NCAA football, NASCAR, Tiger Woods and the PGA, which we believe will enable it to attain higher market shares in certain genres, offsetting the increased cost for exclusivity.

In October 2007, ERTS announced it has agreed to acquire BioWare Corp. and Pandemic Studios, two privately owned video game studios, for about $860 million in cash and stock, subject to customary approvals. The two game studios are known for creating role-playing action/adventure games and have ten franchises under development. ERTS expects the proposed deal to be mildly dilutive to FY 08 earnings.

Company Financials Fiscal Year Ended Mar. 31

Per Share Data ($)	2007	2006	2005	2004	2003	2002	2001	2000	1999	1998
Tangible Book Value	9.93	8.29	10.66	8.52	11.62	3.92	3.33	2.86	2.38	2.34
Cash Flow	0.70	1.05	1.82	2.12	2.79	0.74	0.22	0.62	0.47	0.41
Earnings	0.24	0.75	1.59	1.87	1.09	0.36	-0.04	0.44	0.29	0.30
S&P Core Earnings	0.24	0.49	1.35	1.59	0.82	0.10	-0.25	NA	NA	NA
Dividends	Nil	Nil	Nil	Nil	Nil	Nil	Nil	Nil	Nil	Nil
Payout Ratio	Nil	Nil	Nil	Nil	Nil	Nil	Nil	Nil	Nil	Nil
Calendar Year	2006	2005	2004	2003	2002	2001	2000	1999	1998	1997
Prices:High	59.85	71.16	63.71	52.89	36.22	33.46	28.97	31.11	14.28	10.06
Prices:Low	39.99	47.45	43.38	23.76	24.74	17.25	12.25	9.50	8.31	4.81
P/E Ratio:High	NM	95	40	28	33	94	NM	71	50	34
P/E Ratio:Low	NM	63	27	13	23	49	NM	22	29	16

Income Statement Analysis (Million $)										
Revenue	3,091	2,951	3,129	2,957	2,482	1,725	1,322	1,420	1,222	909
Operating Income	204	454	759	863	629	267	42.1	207	190	123
Depreciation	147	95.0	75.0	77.5	91.6	111	69.7	46.7	40.4	26.9
Interest Expense	Nil	Nil	Nil	Nil	Nil	Nil	Nil	Nil	Nil	Nil
Pretax Income	138	389	725	797	461	148	-13.4	170	118	108
Effective Tax Rate	47.8%	37.8%	30.5%	27.5%	30.9%	31.0%	NM	30.9%	38.3%	33.0%
Net Income	76.0	236	504	577	317	102	-11.1	117	72.9	72.6
S&P Core Earnings	76.0	153	425	482	239	28.0	-68.2	NA	NA	NA

Balance Sheet & Other Financial Data (Million $)										
Cash	1,712	1,402	1,410	2,151	951	804	477	340	318	378
Current Assets	3,597	3,012	3,706	2,911	1,911	1,153	819	705	569	590
Total Assets	5,146	4,386	4,370	3,401	2,360	1,699	1,379	1,192	902	746
Current Liabilities	1,026	869	828	722	571	453	340	265	236	182
Long Term Debt	Nil	Nil	Nil	Nil	Nil	Nil	Nil	Nil	Nil	Nil
Common Equity	4,032	3,408	3,498	2,678	1,785	1,243	1,034	923	663	564
Total Capital	4,040	3,449	3,509	2,678	1,789	1,246	1,039	927	666	564
Capital Expenditures	178	123	126	89.6	59.1	51.5	120	135	116	45.2
Cash Flow	223	331	579	655	409	212	58.6	163	119	99.5
Current Ratio	3.5	3.5	4.5	4.0	3.3	2.5	2.4	2.7	2.4	3.2
% Long Term Debt of Capitalization	Nil	Nil	Nil	Nil	Nil	Nil	Nil	Nil	Nil	Nil
% Net Income of Revenue	2.5	8.0	16.1	19.5	12.8	5.9	NM	8.2	6.0	8.0
% Return on Assets	1.6	5.4	12.9	20.0	15.6	6.6	NM	11.2	8.8	11.5
% Return on Equity	2.0	6.8	16.3	25.9	20.9	8.9	NM	14.7	11.9	15.2

Data as orig reptd.; bef. results of disc opers/spec. items. Per share data adj. for stk. divs.; EPS diluted. E-Estimated. NA-Not Available. NM-Not Meaningful. NR-Not Ranked. UR-Under Review.

Office: 209 Redwood Shores Parkway, Redwood City, CA 94065-1175.
Telephone: 650-628-1500.
Email: investorrelations@ea.com
Website: http://www.ea.com

Chrmn: L.F. Probst, III
Pres: V.P. Lee
CEO: J.S. Riccitiello
EVP, CFO & Chief Admin Officer: W.C. Jenson

SVP & Chief Acctg Officer: K.A. Barker
Investor Contact: J. Brown (650-628-7922)
Board Members: M. R. Asher, L. S. Coleman, G. M. Kusin, G. B. Maffei, T. Mott, V. Paul, L. F. Probst, III, J. S. Riccitiello, R. A. Simonson, L. J. Srere

Founded: 1982
Domicile: Delaware
Employees: 7,900

The McGraw-Hill Companies

Electronic Data Systems Corp

STANDARD &POOR'S

| **S&P Recommendation** SELL ★★☆☆☆ | **Price** $20.53 (as of Nov 23, 2007) | **12-Mo. Target Price** $20.00 | **Investment Style** Large-Cap Value |

GICS Sector Information Technology
Sub-Industry Data Processing & Outsourced Services

Summary This Texas-based company, which was split off from GM in 1996, is a leading provider of a full range of information technology (IT) services.

Key Stock Statistics (Source S&P, Vickers, company reports)

52-Wk Range	$29.95– 18.89	S&P Oper. EPS 2007E	1.58	Market Capitalization(B)	$10.513	Beta	1.17
Trailing 12-Month EPS	$1.41	S&P Oper. EPS 2008E	1.60	Yield (%)	0.97	S&P 3-Yr. Proj. EPS CAGR(%)	20.00
Trailing 12-Month P/E	14.6	P/E on S&P Oper. EPS 2007E	13.0	Dividend Rate/Share	$0.20	S&P Credit Rating	BBB-
$10K Invested 5 Yrs Ago	$13,293	Common Shares Outstg. (M)	512.1	Institutional Ownership (%)	87		

Price Performance

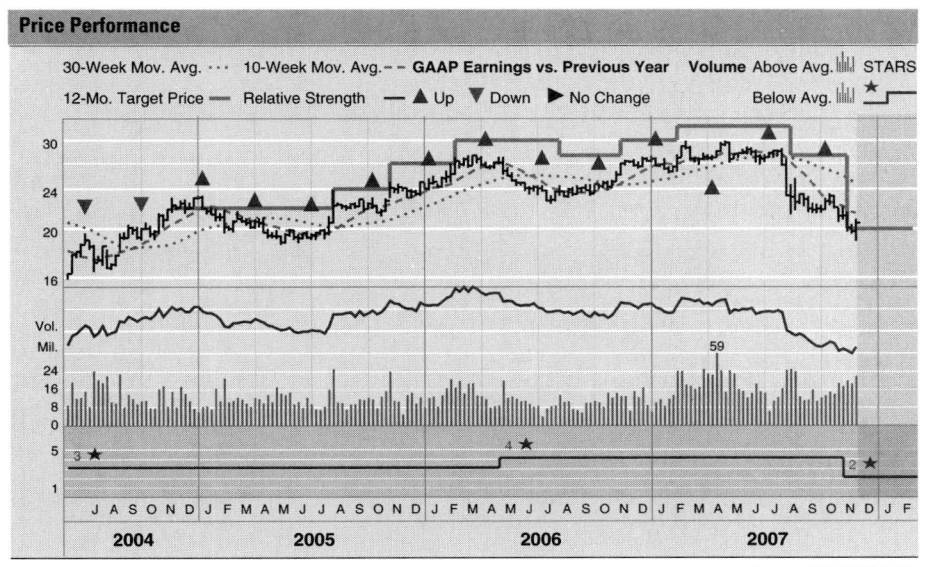

30-Week Mov. Avg. ···· 10-Week Mov. Avg. — **GAAP Earnings vs. Previous Year** Volume Above Avg. STARS
12-Mo. Target Price — Relative Strength — ▲ Up ▼ Down ▶ No Change Below Avg.

Options: ASE, CBOE, P, Ph

Analysis prepared by **Dylan Cathers** on November 06, 2007, when the stock traded at **$ 21.15**.

Highlights

➤ We expect revenue growth to be 5% in 2007. Total contract signings in the first nine months of the year were $13.3 billion, which was down notably from a year earlier. Although excluding 2006's GM and Navy megadeals, signings increased 17%. We still believe that the company's backlog of opportunities is healthy, and we expect revenue growth to be robust in the Government and Financial Services segments. Still, we think the loss of contracts and a major client (Verizon), will dampen revenue growth in 2008, which we believe will slow to 2%.

➤ We see operating margins widening to 6% this year, versus about 4% in 2006, due to benefits from restructuring efforts, rising usage of offshore workers, and a modest slowdown in investment spending. However, we don't see much improvement in 2008, as the company invests heavily in automation and standardization, absorbs increased costs as it cuts jobs and moves jobs overseas, and restructures processes.

➤ We forecast 2007 and 2008 EPS of $1.58 and $1.60, respectively.

Investment Rationale/Risk

➤ We recently lowered our opinion on the shares to sell, from buy. We believe the company will be unable to increase revenues or widen operating margins to any significant degree in 2008, as it works through another "transition" year. We think further efforts are needed as EDS faces challenges addressing intensifying competition and continues to invest in its business.

➤ Risks to our recommendation and target price include a decrease in competition in the outsourcing market, which could ease pricing pressures and positively affect profit margins. Other risks include decreased expenses related to the company's restructuring efforts, and a more-rapid shift towards offshore labor, with a faster ramp-up of EDS's global delivery platform.

➤ Our 12-month target price of $20 is based on a P/E-to-growth (PEG) ratio of 0.62X our 2008 EPS estimate, assuming a three-year growth rate of 20% (off a low base), and a P/E of 12.5X our estimate. Both valuations are a discount to Data Processing and Outsourcing peers that regularly compete in the marketplace with EDS.

Qualitative Risk Assessment

| LOW | MEDIUM | **HIGH** |

Our risk assessment reflects our view of the difficulties surrounding some of EDS's mega-deals and in implementing a global sourcing model, and the intense competition in the IT services and outsourcing industry.

Quantitative Evaluations

S&P Quality Ranking B

| D | C | B- | **B** | B+ | A- | A | A+ |

Relative Strength Rank MODERATE

47

LOWEST = 1   HIGHEST = 99

Revenue/Earnings Data

Revenue (Million $)

	1Q	2Q	3Q	4Q	Year
2007	5,224	5,449	5,629	--	--
2006	5,078	5,194	5,292	5,704	21,268
2005	4,737	5,000	4,874	5,146	19,757
2004	5,196	5,235	4,943	5,295	20,669
2003	5,221	5,273	5,220	5,762	21,476
2002	5,266	5,395	5,334	5,507	21,502

Earnings Per Share ($)

	1Q	2Q	3Q	4Q	Year
2007	0.31	0.27	0.42	E0.58	E1.58
2006	0.06	0.21	0.25	0.42	0.94
2005	0.03	0.06	0.22	0.24	0.54
2004	-0.07	-0.27	-0.33	0.08	-0.59
2003	0.01	0.19	Nil	-0.73	-0.53
2002	0.70	0.63	0.21	0.52	2.06

Fiscal year ended Dec. 31. Next earnings report expected: Early February. EPS Estimates based on S&P Operating Earnings; historical GAAP earnings are as reported.

Dividend Data (Dates: mm/dd Payment Date: mm/dd/yy)

Amount ($)	Date Decl.	Ex-Div. Date	Stk. of Record	Payment Date
0.050	02/06	02/15	02/20	03/09/07
0.050	04/17	05/11	05/15	06/11/07
0.050	07/17	08/13	08/15	09/10/07
0.050	10/16	11/13	11/15	12/10/07

Dividends have been paid since 1984. Source: Company reports.

Electronic Data Systems Corp

STANDARD
&POOR'S

Business Summary November 06, 2007

CORPORATE OVERVIEW. Electronic Data Systems is a leading provider of professional information technology (IT) services. The company was purchased by General Motors in 1984, and was a wholly owned subsidiary of the auto manufacturer until 1996, when GM spun it off.

EDS has three main segments. Infrastructure Services is the company's largest division, accounting for over half of EDS's revenues. It delivers hosting, workplace, store security and privacy and communications services to customers in an attempt to decrease costs and increase productivity. Applications Services assists its clients in planning, developing, and integrating and managing custom applications, packaged software and industry-specific solutions. The Business Process Outsourcing segment allows companies to outsource entire non-core segments of their business, such as human resources, finance and accounting, and supply-chain management

PRIMARY BUSINESS DYNAMICS. One of the prominent features of EDS's business model is its dependence on large contracts, in our opinion. For example, in October 2000, EDS was awarded a contract by the U.S. Navy and Marine Corps to provide end-to-end IT infrastructure on a seat management

basis. The contract had a base period of five years, extended in October 2002 to seven years, with a minimum aggregate order obligation of $6 billion. Since its inception, the contract has been problematic for EDS, in our view, as it took charges against long-term assets and recorded losses. In 2005, the company recorded revenues of $817 million, but booked an operating loss of $75 million. The deal, which was recently extended to 2010, has shown some signs of improvement for EDS, in our opinion, as it was cash flow positive last year. The company expects free cash flow to be about $2.4 billion between 2005 and 2010.

Another large contract of EDS's is with General Motors, its former parent company, which accounted for about 9% of total revenues in 2005. In February 2006, GM announced about half of its $15 billion worth of five-year contracts with IT outsourcers. EDS accounted for the majority of the awards, but with slightly less than under its previous contracts.

Company Financials Fiscal Year Ended Dec. 31

Per Share Data ($)	2006	2005	2004	2003	2002	2001	2000	1999	1998	1997
Tangible Book Value	5.41	5.62	5.58	NM	3.22	3.05	4.53	6.04	11.06	8.15
Cash Flow	3.57	3.33	3.25	4.73	5.01	5.93	5.40	3.73	4.31	3.95
Earnings	0.94	0.54	-0.59	-0.53	2.06	2.86	2.40	0.85	1.50	1.48
S&P Core Earnings	0.84	0.52	-0.93	-0.97	1.16	1.64	NA	NA	NA	NA
Dividends	0.20	0.20	0.40	0.60	0.60	0.60	0.60	0.60	0.60	0.60
Payout Ratio	21%	37%	NM	NM	29%	21%	25%	71%	40%	41%
Prices:High	28.09	24.82	25.44	25.03	68.55	72.45	76.69	70.00	51.31	49.63
Prices:Low	22.42	18.59	15.62	19.85	10.09	50.90	38.38	44.13	30.44	25.50
P/E Ratio:High	30	46	NM	NM	33	25	32	82	34	34
P/E Ratio:Low	24	34	NM	NM	5	18	16	52	20	17

Income Statement Analysis (Million $)										
Revenue	21,268	19,757	20,669	21,476	21,502	21,543	19,227	18,534	16,891	15,236
Operating Income	2,153	1,972	2,040	2,601	3,312	3,707	3,252	1,909	2,509	2,753
Depreciation	1,337	1,456	1,974	2,529	1,443	1,482	1,431	1,436	1,394	1,210
Interest Expense	239	241	321	266	258	247	210	150	131	176
Pretax Income	756	439	-388	-389	1,525	2,199	1,800	658	1,133	1,142
Effective Tax Rate	34.0%	34.9%	NM	NM	34.0%	36.9%	36.5%	36.0%	34.4%	36.0%
Net Income	499	286	-295	-252	1,007	1,387	1,143	421	743	731
S&P Core Earnings	446	275	-464	-461	560	795	NA	NA	NA	NA

Balance Sheet & Other Financial Data (Million $)										
Cash	3,017	3,220	3,592	2,313	1,890	839	693	729	1,312	677
Current Assets	8,257	8,502	8,479	6,823	9,385	7,374	6,167	5,878	5,633	5,169
Total Assets	17,954	17,087	17,744	18,280	18,880	16,353	12,700	12,522	11,526	11,174
Current Liabilities	5,234	5,048	5,256	7,473	6,129	4,367	4,318	4,996	3,657	3,258
Long Term Debt	2,965	2,939	3,168	3,488	4,148	4,692	2,586	2,391	1,184	1,791
Common Equity	7,896	7,512	7,440	5,714	7,022	6,446	5,139	4,535	5,917	5,310
Total Capital	11,316	10,866	10,608	9,686	11,221	11,986	8,382	7,194	7,869	7,575
Capital Expenditures	729	718	666	703	973	1,285	768	685	870	769
Cash Flow	1,836	1,742	1,679	2,277	2,450	2,869	2,575	1,857	2,137	1,941
Current Ratio	1.6	1.7	1.6	0.9	1.5	1.7	1.4	1.2	1.5	1.6
% Long Term Debt of Capitalization	26.2	27.0	29.9	36.0	37.0	39.1	30.8	33.2	15.0	23.6
% Net Income of Revenue	2.3	1.4	NM	NM	4.7	6.4	5.9	2.3	4.4	4.8
% Return on Assets	2.8	1.6	NM	NM	5.7	9.6	9.1	3.5	6.5	6.5
% Return on Equity	6.5	3.8	NM	NM	15.0	23.9	23.6	8.1	13.2	14.5

Data as orig reptd.; bef. results of disc opers/spec. items. Per share data adj. for stk. divs.; EPS diluted. E-Estimated. NA-Not Available. NM-Not Meaningful. NR-Not Ranked. UR-Under Review.

Office: 5400 Legacy Drive, Plano, TX 75024-3199.
Telephone: 972-605-6000.
Email: invest@eds.com
Website: http://www.eds.com

Chrmn & CEO: M.H. Jordan
Pres & COO: R. Rittenmeyer
Vice Chrmn: J.M. Heller
Sr EVP: C.S. Feld

EVP & CFO: R. Vargo
Investor Contact: D. Kost (972-605-6660)
Board Members: W. R. Dunbar, R. A. Enrico, M. C. Faga, S. M. Gillis, R. J. Groves, E. M. Hancock, J. M. Heller, R. L. Hunt, M. H. Jordan, E. A. Kangas, J. K. Sims, R. D. Yost

Founded: 1962
Domicile: Delaware
Employees: 131,000

El Paso Corp

STANDARD &POOR'S

S&P Recommendation **SELL** ★ ★ ☆ ☆ ☆	Price $16.18 (as of Nov 23, 2007)	12-Mo. Target Price $16.00	Investment Style Large-Cap Value

GICS Sector Energy
Sub-Industry Oil & Gas Storage & Transportation

Summary This provider of natural gas and related energy products owns North America's largest natural gas pipeline system and is one of its biggest independent natural gas producers.

Key Stock Statistics (Source S&P, Vickers, company reports)

52-Wk Range	$18.56–13.63	S&P Oper. EPS 2007**E**	0.97	Market Capitalization(B)	$11.335	Beta	1.30
Trailing 12-Month EPS	$1.08	S&P Oper. EPS 2008**E**	1.06	Yield (%)	0.99	S&P 3-Yr. Proj. EPS CAGR(%)	8.00
Trailing 12-Month P/E	15.0	P/E on S&P Oper. EPS 2007**E**	16.7	Dividend Rate/Share	$0.16	S&P Credit Rating	BB
$10K Invested 5 Yrs Ago	$15,925	Common Shares Outstg. (M)	700.6	Institutional Ownership (%)	78		

Price Performance

30-Week Mov. Avg. · · · 10-Week Mov. Avg. – – **GAAP Earnings vs. Previous Year** Volume Above Avg. ▍▍▍ STARS
12-Mo. Target Price — Relative Strength — ▲ Up ▼ Down ► No Change Below Avg. ▍▍▍ ★

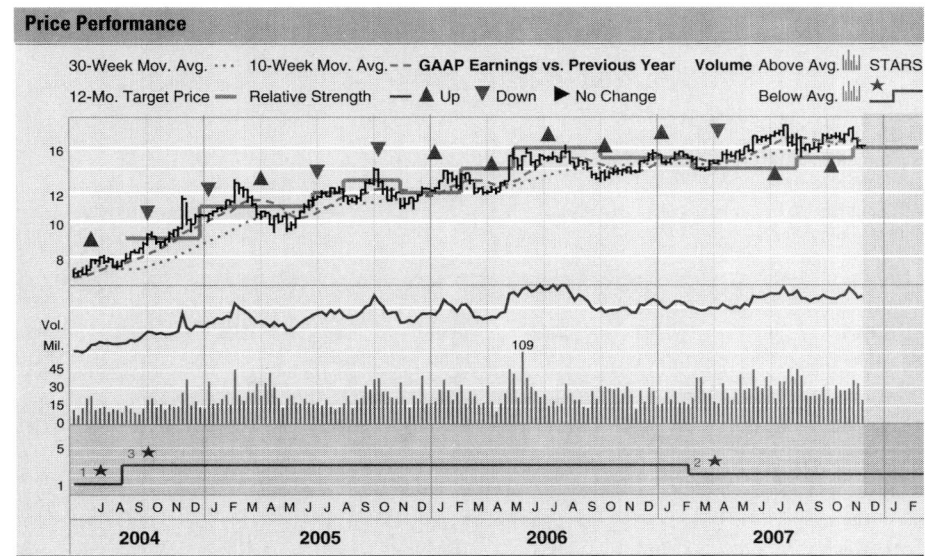

Options: ASE, CBOE, P

Analysis prepared by **Stephen Ham, CFA** on November 20, 2007, when the stock traded at **$ 16.08**.

Highlights

➤ We see 2007 production growth of 4% in the exploration and production (E&P) segment; however, third quarter volumes were up 5%, on acquisitions, recovery of hurricane shut-in volumes and successful drilling programs. The development of EP's Brazilian E&P assets will be crucial, in our view, to future segment growth. EP is progressing toward a fourth quarter $500 million IPO of a pipeline master limited partnership, which would own interests in several interstate pipelines.

➤ Pipelines have benefited from higher rates at El Paso Natural Gas (EPNG), and several new projects have been placed into service, including the completion of the Elba Island LNG terminal, the expansion of the Piceance pipeline, the Cheyenne Plains pipeline expansion, and the start-up of the Cypress Pipeline.

➤ The Pipeline segment should continue its solid growth. While we are skeptical of the E&P business, we view EP's lower risk onshore emphasis as positive. For 2007, we forecast a 3.2% increase in EBITDA, to $3.2 billion, and expect capital expenditures of $2.7 billion, of which $1.7 billion will be allocated toward E&P.

Investment Rationale/Risk

➤ EP recently closed on the sale of its ANR Pipeline, its Michigan storage assets, and its 50% interest in Great Lakes Transmission for $4.14 billion, including the assumption of $744 million in debt, to Transcanada Corp (TRP: hold, $40) and TC Pipelines LP (TCLP: hold, $37). With this sale and the recent E&P acquisition of Peoples Energy Production Company, we believe that EP's risk profile will increase, but that growth prospects will expand as EP's business becomes more concentrated on E&P. In an effort to upgrade its E&P portfolio, EP plans to sell several properties in the Gulf of Mexico and south Texas by the first quarter of 2008.

➤ Risks to our recommendation and target price include an increase in natural gas prices, strong economic growth, the successful integration of acquired E&P properties, and the unforeseen sale of assets.

➤ Although we like EP's premier gas pipeline franchise and its strong and diverse organic growth potential, we would prefer reserve additions through the drillbit rather than acquisitions. Our 12-month target price of $16 is based on an EV to estimated 2008 EBITDA ratio of 7X.

Qualitative Risk Assessment

LOW	MEDIUM	**HIGH**

Our risk assessment is based on our view of the struggling exploration and production (E&P) segment, which has proven to be very volatile. EP's balance sheet is highly leveraged, in our opinion, making it difficult to turn around the E&P segment. Partly offsetting these risks is EP's involvement in several different business lines, including regulated pipelines.

Quantitative Evaluations

S&P Quality Ranking B-

D	C	**B-**	B	B+	A-	A	A+

Relative Strength Rank MODERATE

59

LOWEST = 1 HIGHEST = 99

Revenue/Earnings Data

Revenue (Million $)

	1Q	2Q	3Q	4Q	Year
2007	1,022	1,198	1,166	--	--
2006	1,337	1,089	942.0	913.0	4,281
2005	1,108	1,184	768.0	957.0	4,017
2004	1,557	1,524	1,429	1,364	5,874
2003	1,844	1,574	1,724	1,569	6,711
2002	3,755	2,987	2,656	2,796	12,194

Earnings Per Share ($)

2007	-0.08	0.22	0.20	E0.27	E0.97
2006	0.42	0.19	0.15	-0.30	0.72
2005	0.18	-0.34	-0.51	-0.45	-1.13
2004	-0.15	0.07	-0.31	-0.86	-1.25
2003	-0.33	-0.53	0.12	-0.28	-1.03
2002	0.43	0.02	-0.06	-2.54	-2.30

Fiscal year ended Dec. 31. Next earnings report expected: Late February. EPS Estimates based on S&P Operating Earnings; historical GAAP earnings are as reported.

Dividend Data (Dates: mm/dd Payment Date: mm/dd/yy)

Amount ($)	Date Decl.	Ex-Div. Date	Stk. of Record	Payment Date
0.040	02/14	02/28	03/02	04/02/07
0.040	04/03	05/30	06/01	07/02/07
0.040	07/27	09/05	09/07	10/01/07
0.040	10/25	12/05	12/07	01/07/08

Dividends have been paid since 1992. Source: Company reports.

El Paso Corp

Business Summary November 20, 2007

CORPORATE OVERVIEW. Founded in 1928, El Paso originally served as a regional natural gas pipeline company that ultimately expanded geographically and into complimentary business lines. By 2001, its total assets exceeded $44 billion and included natural gas production, power generation, trading operations and its traditional natural gas pipeline businesses. In late 2001 through 2003, various industry and company-specific events led to a substantial decline in EP's fundamentals. In late 2003, EP announced a long-term business strategy principally focused on core pipeline and production businesses. During the past several years, EP has sold off non-core assets to reduce debt and improve liquidity.

Operations are conducted through three primary segments: Pipelines, Exploration and Production and Marketing. EP also has a Power segment that holds its remaining interests in international power plants in Brazil, Asia and Central America.

PRIMARY BUSINESS DYNAMICS. The Pipeline segment is the largest U.S. owner of interstate natural gas pipelines and owns or has interests in 55,000 miles of pipeline. The division also has 470 billion cubic feet (Bcf) of natural gas storage capacity, and a liquefied natural gas terminal at Elba Island, GA with 806 million cubic feet (Mmcf) of daily base load sendout capacity. Each

pipeline system and storage facility operates under Federal Energy Regulatory Commission (FERC) approved tariffs that establish rates, cost recovery mechanisms, and service terms and conditions. The established rates are a function of EP's costs of providing services, including a "reasonable" return on invested capital.

In February 2007, EP sold ANR Pipeline Company (ANR), its Michigan storage assets, and its 50% interest in Great Lakes Gas Transmission, which comprised approximately 12,600 miles of pipeline and 236 Bcf of storage capacity.

EP's strategy to create value in this segment is to: 1) Expand systems into new markets while leveraging existing assets; 2) recontract or contract available or expiring capacity and resolve open rate cases; 3) leverage its coast-to-coast scale economies; and 4) invest in maintenance and pipeline integrity projects to maintain the value and ensure the safety of its pipeline systems and assets.

Company Financials Fiscal Year Ended Dec. 31

Per Share Data ($)	2006	2005	2004	2003	2002	2001	2000	1999	1998	1997
Tangible Book Value	6.00	3.38	4.68	5.36	11.70	17.65	15.25	10.47	13.06	15.39
Cash Flow	2.09	0.61	0.45	0.99	0.21	2.76	4.82	1.61	3.92	3.60
Earnings	0.72	-1.13	-1.25	-1.03	-2.30	0.13	2.44	-1.06	1.85	1.59
S&P Core Earnings	0.69	-1.07	-0.84	-0.68	-1.95	-0.37	NA	NA	NA	NA
Dividends	0.16	0.16	0.16	0.16	0.87	0.85	0.82	0.79	0.76	0.73
Payout Ratio	22%	NM	NM	NM	NM	NM	34%	NM	41%	46%
Prices:High	16.39	14.16	11.85	10.30	46.89	75.30	74.25	43.44	38.94	33.75
Prices:Low	11.80	9.30	6.57	3.33	4.39	36.00	30.31	30.69	24.69	24.44
P/E Ratio:High	23	NM	NM	NM	NM	NM	30	NM	21	21
P/E Ratio:Low	16	NM	NM	NM	NM	NM	12	NM	13	15

Income Statement Analysis (Million $)										
Revenue	4,281	4,017	5,874	6,711	12,194	57,475	21,950	10,581	5,782	5,638
Operating Income	1,427	934	2,386	2,907	2,872	4,391	2,155	1,482	775	757
Depreciation	1,047	1,121	1,088	1,207	1,405	1,359	589	609	269	236
Interest Expense	1,228	1,389	1,632	1,839	1,400	1,155	538	453	267	238
Pretax Income	523	-991	-777	-1,200	-1,567	466	1,012	-287	377	340
Effective Tax Rate	NM	NM	NM	NM	NM	39.1%	28.3%	NM	33.7%	37.9%
Net Income	531	-702	-802	-616	-1,289	67.0	582	-242	225	186
S&P Core Earnings	471	-696	-531	-401	-1,096	-194	NA	NA	NA	NA

Balance Sheet & Other Financial Data (Million $)										
Cash	537	2,132	2,117	1,429	1,591	1,139	688	545	90.0	116
Current Assets	7,167	6,185	5,632	8,922	11,924	12,659	10,076	2,911	1,209	1,629
Total Assets	27,261	31,838	31,383	37,084	46,224	48,171	27,445	16,657	10,069	9,532
Current Liabilities	6,151	5,712	4,572	7,074	10,350	13,565	10,467	3,702	2,162	2,464
Long Term Debt	13,260	17,054	18,608	20,722	19,727	14,109	6,574	5,548	3,177	2,119
Common Equity	3,436	2,639	3,439	4,474	8,377	9,356	3,569	2,947	2,108	1,959
Total Capital	18,396	21,850	23,358	25,196	31,680	31,012	14,623	11,601	6,914	5,993
Capital Expenditures	2,164	1,718	1,782	2,452	3,716	4,079	1,336	1,086	406	293
Cash Flow	1,541	392	286	591	116	1,426	1,171	367	494	422
Current Ratio	1.2	1.1	1.2	1.3	1.2	0.9	1.0	0.8	0.6	0.7
% Long Term Debt of Capitalization	72.1	78.1	79.7	82.2	62.3	45.5	45.0	47.8	46.0	35.4
% Net Income of Revenue	12.4	NM	NM	NM	NM	0.1	2.7	NM	3.9	3.3
% Return on Assets	1.8	NM	NM	NM	NM	0.1	2.6	NM	2.3	2.0
% Return on Equity	16.3	NM	NM	NM	NM	0.8	17.9	NM	11.1	10.3

Data as orig reptd.; bef. results of disc opers/spec. items. Per share data adj. for stk. divs.; EPS diluted. E-Estimated. NA-Not Available. NM-Not Meaningful. NR-Not Ranked. UR-Under Review.

Office: El Paso Energy Building, Houston, TX 77002-5089.
Telephone: 713-420-2600.
Email: investorrelations@epenergy.com
Website: http://www.elpaso.com

Chrmn: R.L. Keuhn, Jr.
Pres & CEO: D.L. Foshee
EVP & CFO: D.M. Leland
EVP & General Counsel: R.W. Baker

Investor Contact: B. Connery (713-420-5855)
Board Members: J. C. Braniff, J. Dunlap, D. L. Foshee, R. W. Goldman, A. W. Hall, Jr., T. R. Hix, W. H. Joyce, R. L. Kuehn, Jr., F. P. McClean, S. J. Shapiro, M. Talbert, R. F. Vagt, J. L. Whitmire, J. B. Wyatt

Founded: 1928
Domicile: Delaware
Employees: 5,050

Embarq Corp

**STANDARD
&POOR'S**

S&P Recommendation HOLD ★ ★ ★ ☆ ☆

Price	**12-Mo. Target Price**	**Investment Style**
$50.67 (as of Nov 23, 2007)	$57.00	Large-Cap Value

GICS Sector Telecommunication Services
Sub-Industry Integrated Telecommunication Services

Summary Embarq, which provides wireline services to 6.6 million access lines, is the fifth-largest wireline provider in the U.S. The company was spun off from Sprint Nextel in May 2006.

Key Stock Statistics (Source S&P, Vickers, company reports)

52-Wk Range	$65.50– 48.99	S&P Oper. EPS 2007E	4.44	Market Capitalization(B)	$7.731	Beta	NA
Trailing 12-Month EPS	$4.49	S&P Oper. EPS 2008E	4.46	Yield (%)	4.93	S&P 3-Yr. Proj. EPS CAGR(%)	2.00
Trailing 12-Month P/E	11.3	P/E on S&P Oper. EPS 2007E	11.4	Dividend Rate/Share	$2.50	S&P Credit Rating	BBB-
$10K Invested 5 Yrs Ago	NA	Common Shares Outstg. (M)	152.6	Institutional Ownership (%)	90		

Price Performance

30-Week Mov. Avg. · · · 10-Week Mov. Avg. – – **GAAP Earnings vs. Previous Year** Volume Above Avg. ▮▮▮ STARS
12-Mo. Target Price — Relative Strength — ▲ Up ▼ Down ► No Change Below Avg. ▮▮▮ ★

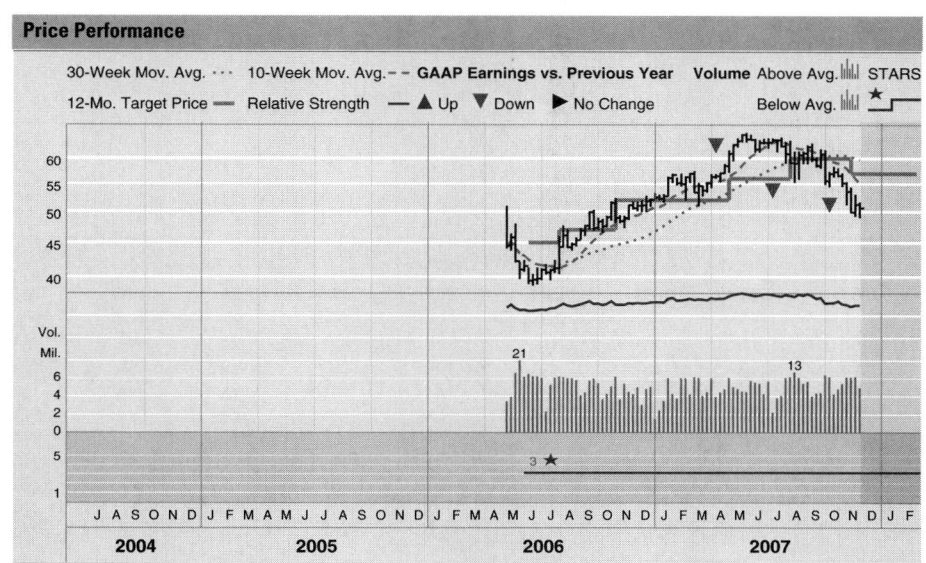

Options: ASE, CBOE, P, Ph

Analysis prepared by **Todd Rosenbluth** on November 02, 2007, when the stock traded at **$ 53.60**.

Highlights

➤ We see revenues declining to $6.22 billion in 2008, from a projected $6.36 billion in 2007, as the carrier faces increased competition from cable and wireless carriers in its urban markets and is hurt by slower housing demand. We expect access line losses of an additional 6% in 2008, with the rate of decline consistent with 2007, adding to pressure on voice services. We believe EQ will offset some of the customer losses with the expansion of its DSL services and the addition of wholesale wireless through its own service bundle.

➤ Despite pressure from revenue weakness in high margin services and a buildout of its wireless business, we look for EBITDA margins to remain within the range of 40% to 41% in 2007 and 2008, as we see benefits from work force reductions in its call center and additional savings from restructuring.

➤ Our EPS estimates are $4.44 for 2007 and $4.46 for 2008, below the pro forma $5.21 in 2006. We believe that fourth quarter 2006 EPS was aided by a $0.12 per share tax benefit.

Investment Rationale/Risk

➤ Despite the company's short operating history, we believe EQ has the flexibility to repurchase shares even after boosting its dividend in mid-2007. We think the company's wireline operations have greater exposure to cable telephony competition and a slowdown in housing markets in Florida and Nevada than peers. The key driver for EQ, in our view, will be the bundling of broadband services in an effort to keep customers loyal.

➤ Risks to our recommendation and target price include the independent operation of the company's new management team, greater-than-expected cable competition, higher capital spending by EQ, and higher customer migration from wireless substitution.

➤ EQ trades at an enterprise value/EBITDA multiple below that of rural peers. We believe a discount to rural peers is warranted given the company's short history and its less stable customer base. Our 12-month target price of $57 values EQ at an enterprise value/EBITDA multiple of 5.7X, in line with larger Bell carriers. With its dividend increase, EQ's yield is 4.8%.

Qualitative Risk Assessment

LOW	MEDIUM	HIGH

Our risk assessment reflects the competitive nature of the telecom industry and the company's short operating history, offset by our view of its steady operating cash flow that supports its dividend.

Quantitative Evaluations

S&P Quality Ranking NR

D	C	B-	B	B+	A-	A	A+

Relative Strength Rank MODERATE

38

LOWEST = 1   HIGHEST = 99

Revenue/Earnings Data

Revenue (Million $)

	1Q	2Q	3Q	4Q	Year
2007	1,589	1,605	1,594	--	--
2006	1,561	1,579	1,606	1,617	6,363
2005	--	--	--	--	6,701
2004	--	--	--	--	--
2003	--	--	--	--	--
2002	--	--	--	--	--

Earnings Per Share ($)

2007	1.05	1.15	1.01	E1.11	E4.44
2006	1.42	1.44	1.06	1.28	5.21
2005	--	--	--	--	4.96
2004	--	--	--	--	--
2003	--	--	--	--	--
2002	--	--	--	--	--

Fiscal year ended Dec. 31. Next earnings report expected: Early February. EPS Estimates based on S&P Operating Earnings; historical GAAP earnings are as reported.

Dividend Data (Dates: mm/dd Payment Date: mm/dd/yy)

Amount ($)	Date Decl.	Ex-Div. Date	Stk. of Record	Payment Date
0.500	02/22	03/07	03/09	03/31/07
0.625	04/25	06/06	06/08	06/30/07
0.625	08/16	09/05	09/07	09/30/07
0.625	10/15	12/06	12/10	12/31/07

Dividends have been paid since 2006. Source: Company reports.

Please read the Required Disclosures and Analyst Certification on the last page of this report.

The **McGraw-Hill** Companies

Embarq Corp

STANDARD & POOR'S

Business Summary November 02, 2007

CORPORATE OVERVIEW. In mid-May 2006, Sprint Nextel (S) spun off its local telephone business as a separate entity now known as Embarq Corp. (EQ). The corporate action was a tax-free distribution to Sprint's shareholders, who received one share of EQ for every 20 shares of S. As of September 2007, EQ provided local service to 6.56 million access lines in 18 states, down 6.2% from a year earlier. The majority of EQ's access lines are located in Florida, North Carolina, Nevada and Ohio. The company serves customers in Fort Myers, Las Vegas, Orlando and Raleigh-Durham, in addition to numerous smaller markets. The company's offerings include local and long distance voice and data services, including high-speed DSL Internet services, both for residential and corporate customers.

CORPORATE STRATEGY. EQ's business strategy is to bundle services to sell the commoditized wireline services with high-growth services such as broadband. It has launched an MVNO wireless service under the Embarq brand name to cash in on the growing wireless segment. The company also has an agency arrangement with EchoStar Communications for providing video services. As of September 2007, the company had 1.3 million DSL customers, up 30% from a year earlier, and 190,000 video customers. In late 2006, EQ in-

creased its focus on offering wireless service and signed up 108,000 subscribers by the end of September 2007, through a wholesale relationship with Sprint Nextel.

COMPETITIVE LANDSCAPE. We believe that to date, wireless substitution has been the greatest threat to EQ's access lines in 2007. Wireless coverage has improved over the past couple of years, and we believe that many of these customers have dropped their landlines and switched to Sprint Nextel, the former parent of EQ. However, with approximately 65% of EQ's access lines being covered by cable competition at the end of June 2007 and our expectation that this figure will grow to 70% by the end of 2007, the company should face higher cable telephony competition. The largest of the competitors in EQ's territory include Time Warner, Comcast, Charter and Cox. EQ has tried to offset the competition by bundling DSL and wireless services for households. As of September 2007, the monthly revenue per household was $54.38.

Company Financials Fiscal Year Ended Dec. 31

Per Share Data ($)	2006	2005	2004	2003	2002	2001	2000	1999	1998	1997
Tangible Book Value	NM	NM	NA	NA	NA	NA	NA	NA	NA	NA
Cash Flow	12.10	12.09	NA	NA	NA	NA	NA	NA	NA	NA
Earnings	5.21	4.96	NA	NA	NA	NA	NA	NA	NA	NA
S&P Core Earnings	4.94	5.91	6.04	NA	NA	NA	NA	NA	NA	NA
Dividends	1.00	Nil	NA	NA	NA	NA	NA	NA	NA	NA
Payout Ratio	19%	Nil	NA	NA	NA	NA	NA	NA	NA	NA
Prices:High	53.32	NA	NA	NA	NA	NA	NA	NA	NA	NA
Prices:Low	38.81	NA	NA	NA	NA	NA	NA	NA	NA	NA
P/E Ratio:High	10	NA	NA	NA	NA	NA	NA	NA	NA	NA
P/E Ratio:Low	7	NA	NA	NA	NA	NA	NA	NA	NA	NA

Income Statement Analysis (Million $)	2006	2005	2004	2003	2002	2001	2000	1999	1998	1997
Revenue	6,363	6,701	NA	NA	NA	NA	NA	NA	NA	NA
Operating Income	2,571	2,911	NA	NA	NA	NA	NA	NA	NA	NA
Depreciation	1,027	1,070	NA	NA	NA	NA	NA	NA	NA	NA
Interest Expense	324	520	NA	NA	NA	NA	NA	NA	NA	NA
Pretax Income	1,234	1,245	NA	NA	NA	NA	NA	NA	NA	NA
Effective Tax Rate	36.5%	40.2%	NA	NA	NA	NA	NA	NA	NA	NA
Net Income	784	744	NA	NA	NA	NA	NA	NA	NA	NA
S&P Core Earnings	745	887	907	NA	NA	NA	NA	NA	NA	NA

Balance Sheet & Other Financial Data (Million $)	2006	2005	2004	2003	2002	2001	2000	1999	1998	1997
Cash	53.0	200	NA	NA	NA	NA	NA	NA	NA	NA
Current Assets	1,023	1,194	NA	NA	NA	NA	NA	NA	NA	NA
Total Assets	9,091	9,473	NA	NA	NA	NA	NA	NA	NA	NA
Current Liabilities	1,264	1,157	NA	NA	NA	NA	NA	NA	NA	NA
Long Term Debt	6,421	7,248	NA	NA	NA	NA	NA	NA	NA	NA
Common Equity	-468	-1,071	NA	NA	NA	NA	NA	NA	NA	NA
Total Capital	6,992	7,268	NA	NA	NA	NA	NA	NA	NA	NA
Capital Expenditures	923	NA	NA	NA	NA	NA	NA	NA	NA	NA
Cash Flow	1,811	1,814	NA	NA	NA	NA	NA	NA	NA	NA
Current Ratio	0.8	1.0	NA	NA	NA	NA	NA	NA	NA	NA
% Long Term Debt of Capitalization	91.8	99.7	NA	NA	NA	NA	NA	NA	NA	NA
% Net Income of Revenue	12.3	11.1	NA	NA	NA	NA	NA	NA	NA	NA
% Return on Assets	8.4	NA	NA	NA	NA	NA	NA	NA	NA	NA
% Return on Equity	NM	NA	NA	NA	NA	NA	NA	NA	NA	NA

Data as orig reptd.; bef. results of disc opers/spec. items. Per share data adj. for stk. divs.; EPS diluted. E-Estimated. NA-Not Available. NM-Not Meaningful. NR-Not Ranked. UR-Under Review.

Office: 5454 W. 110th Street, Overland Park, KS 66211.
Telephone: 913-323-4637.
Website: http://www.embarq.com
Chrmn, Pres & CEO: D.R. Hesse

CFO: G.M. Betts
Treas: L.H. Meredith
General Counsel: T.A. Gerke
Cntlr: M.K. Coleman

Board Members: P. C. Brown, S. A. Davis, D. R. Hesse, J. P. Mullen, W. A. Owens, D. C. Paliwal, S. M. Shern, L. A. Siegel

Founded: 2005
Domicile: Delaware
Employees: 20,000

The McGraw-Hill Companies

EMC Corp

STANDARD &POOR'S

S&P Recommendation	BUY ★★★★☆	Price $18.19 (as of Nov 27, 2007)	12-Mo. Target Price $24.00	Investment Style Large-Cap Blend

GICS Sector Information Technology
Sub-Industry Computer Storage & Peripherals

Summary This company is the leading supplier of enterprise data storage systems and software.

Key Stock Statistics (Source S&P, Vickers, company reports)

52-Wk Range	$25.47– 12.74	S&P Oper. EPS 2007**E**	0.73	Market Capitalization(B)	$38.150	Beta	1.91
Trailing 12-Month EPS	$0.71	S&P Oper. EPS 2008**E**	0.94	Yield (%)	Nil	S&P 3-Yr. Proj. EPS CAGR(%)	24.70
Trailing 12-Month P/E	25.6	P/E on S&P Oper. EPS 2007**E**	24.9	Dividend Rate/Share	Nil	S&P Credit Rating	BBB+
$10K Invested 5 Yrs Ago	$28,828	Common Shares Outstg. (M)	2,097.3	Institutional Ownership (%)	79		

Price Performance

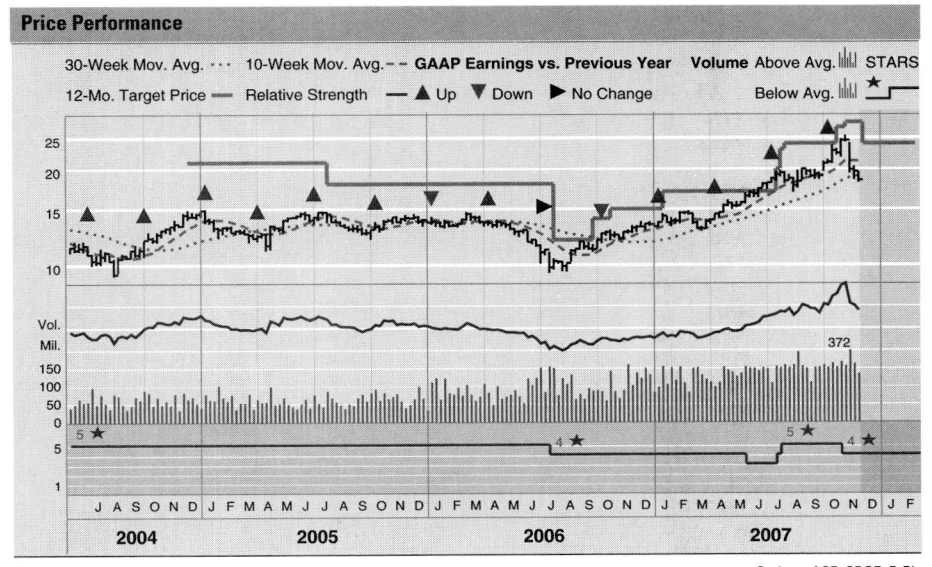

30-Week Mov. Avg. · · · 10-Week Mov. Avg. - - **GAAP Earnings vs. Previous Year** Volume Above Avg. STARS
12-Mo. Target Price — Relative Strength — ▲ Up ▼ Down ▶ No Change   Below Avg.

Options: ASE, CBOE, P, Ph

Analysis prepared by **Jawahar Hingorani** on November 27, 2007, when the stock traded at **$ 18.17**.

Highlights

➤ We see revenues rising about 17% in 2007, followed by a 14% increase in 2008, as a result of acquisitions, the completion of major product transitions, market share gains, and international expansion. We believe data storage and management remain high priorities for IT managers despite weakness in the U.S. market, and we see EMC benefiting from an increase in implementation of virtualization and storage security. In our view, the perceived downturn in financial services will not have a major impact on EMC's revenues.

➤ We see gross margins rising from an expected 53.6% in 2007 to above 54% in 2008. We expect operating expenses to decline as a percentage of revenues due to efficiency improvements. Results should also benefit from ongoing share repurchases, albeit at a slower pace than in 2006. EMC has almost $1 billion remaining toward this endeavor, which it intends to deploy by March 2008.

➤ We forecast 2007 EPS of $0.73, a 35% increase from 2006's $0.54, which included almost $0.09 in restructuring and other charges. Our 2007 EPS estimate is negligibly affected by restructuring charges. We see 2008 EPS of $0.94.

Investment Rationale/Risk

➤ Our buy opinion is based on our belief that the recent market pullback provides investors an excellent opportunity to invest in EMC, which continues to be undervalued relative to peers. In our view, valuing the assets of EMC (other than VMware, which has a public market value) in line with peers along with its remaining stake in VMW, provides a 20% premium to current prices. We think increases in software revenues will improve margins. We are encouraged by strong cash flow generation.

➤ Risks to our recommendation and target price include component shortages, an elongated sales cycle, and greater than anticipated pricing declines. Regarding corporate governance practices, we are somewhat concerned that the roles of chairman and CEO are held by the same individual.

➤ Our 12-month target price of $24 combines our P/E and discounted cash flow (DCF) metrics. At 22.8X our 2008 EPS estimate, a slight premium to peers, we value EMC at $21. Our DCF analysis assumes a weighted average cost of capital of 8.5% and a terminal growth rate of 3%, and leads to an intrinsic value of $26.50.

Qualitative Risk Assessment

LOW	MEDIUM	HIGH

Our risk assessment reflects our view that EMC has an industry leading market share position, consistent free cash flow generation, and a strong balance sheet with no long-term debt. However, we see the data storage industry as cyclical, highly competitive, and prone to precipitous declines in selling prices.

Quantitative Evaluations

S&P Quality Ranking — B

D	C	B-	**B**	B+	A-	A	A+

Relative Strength Rank — MODERATE

30

LOWEST = 1   HIGHEST = 99

Revenue/Earnings Data

Revenue (Million $)

	1Q	2Q	3Q	4Q	Year
2007	2,975	3,125	3,300	--	--
2006	2,551	2,575	2,815	3,215	11,155
2005	2,243	2,345	2,366	2,710	9,664
2004	1,872	1,971	2,029	2,358	8,229
2003	1,384	1,479	1,511	1,863	6,237
2002	1,302	1,388	1,259	1,489	5,438

Earnings Per Share ($)

	1Q	2Q	3Q	4Q	Year
2007	0.15	0.16	0.23	E0.22	E0.73
2006	0.12	0.12	0.13	0.18	0.54
2005	0.11	0.12	0.17	0.06	0.47
2004	0.06	0.08	0.09	0.13	0.36
2003	0.02	0.04	0.07	0.09	0.22
2002	-0.03	Nil	0.01	-0.03	-0.05

Fiscal year ended Dec. 31. Next earnings report expected: Late January. EPS Estimates based on S&P Operating Earnings; historical GAAP earnings are as reported.

Dividend Data

No cash dividends have been paid.

EMC Corp

STANDARD &POOR'S

Business Summary November 27, 2007

CORPORATE OVERVIEW. EMC offers a wide range of information storage systems, software and services designed to meet the specific needs of its customers in terms of performance, functionality, scalability, data availability, and cost. Customers are located worldwide and represent a cross section of industries and government agencies. The company's products and services are used in conjunction with a variety of computing platforms that support key business processes, including transaction processing, data warehousing, electronic commerce, and content management. In 2006, revenues reached a record level of $11.16 billion.

Revenues outside of the United States accounted for 43% of EMC's total in 2006, flat compared to 2005. Moreover, all of EMC's markets expanded at a double digit rate during the year, with Latin America growing the fastest at 22%.

CORPORATE STRATEGY. EMC's strategy focuses on the concept of information lifecycle management (ILM). This idea centers on the management of information across its entire life, from creation and use to archive and disposal.

Through its utilization, ILM simultaneously lowers the cost and reduces the risk of managing data, in our view, regardless of what format it is in (documents, images or e-mail). ILM also provides for cost effective business continuity and more efficient compliance with government and industry regulations.

As part of this plan, EMC has engaged in a number of acquisitions over the past two years. One of its more successful deals, in our view, was the purchase of VMware, Inc., a virtual infrastructure software company, which is operated as an independent subsidiary. VMware's software is designed to enable customers to achieve much higher utilization of the server, storage, and network resources deployed within their operations, while dramatically simplifying how the workloads that are run on those systems are operated and managed. In 2006, VMware's revenues rose 83%.

Company Financials Fiscal Year Ended Dec. 31

Per Share Data ($)	2006	2005	2004	2003	2002	2001	2000	1999	1998	1997
Tangible Book Value	4.39	3.20	3.22	3.19	3.05	3.31	3.72	2.38	1.60	1.19
Cash Flow	0.87	0.73	0.61	0.45	0.24	0.07	1.02	0.66	0.46	0.32
Earnings	0.54	0.47	0.36	0.22	-0.05	-0.23	0.79	0.46	0.37	0.26
S&P Core Earnings	0.55	0.35	0.21	0.04	-0.23	-0.33	NA	NA	NA	NA
Dividends	Nil	Nil	Nil	Nil	Nil	Nil	Nil	Nil	Nil	Nil
Payout Ratio	Nil	Nil	Nil	Nil	Nil	Nil	Nil	Nil	Nil	Nil
Prices:High	14.75	15.09	15.80	14.66	17.97	82.00	104.94	55.50	21.66	8.14
Prices:Low	9.44	11.10	9.24	5.98	3.67	10.01	47.50	21.00	6.00	3.97
P/E Ratio:High	27	32	44	67	NM	NM	NM	NM	58	31
P/E Ratio:Low	17	24	26	27	NM	NM	NM	NM	16	15

Income Statement Analysis (Million $)	2006	2005	2004	2003	2002	2001	2000	1999	1998	1997
Revenue	11,155	9,664	8,229	6,237	5,438	7,091	8,873	6,716	3,974	2,938
Operating Income	2,170	2,222	1,716	988	310	355	2,774	1,897	1,185	798
Depreciation	764	640	616	521	654	655	517	447	203	136
Interest Expense	34.1	7.99	7.52	3.03	11.4	11.3	14.6	33.5	20.2	15.5
Pretax Income	1,390	1,652	1,185	571	-296	-577	2,441	1,357	1,058	718
Effective Tax Rate	11.7%	31.4%	26.5%	13.1%	NM	NM	27.0%	25.5%	25.0%	25.0%
Net Income	1,227	1,133	871	496	-119	-508	1,782	1,011	793	539
S&P Core Earnings	1,241	839	504	84.2	-477	-720	NA	NA	NA	NA

Balance Sheet & Other Financial Data (Million $)	2006	2005	2004	2003	2002	2001	2000	1999	1998	1997
Cash	1,828	2,322	1,477	1,869	1,687	2,129	1,983	1,109	705	955
Current Assets	6,521	6,574	4,831	4,687	4,217	4,923	6,100	4,320	3,105	2,627
Total Assets	18,566	16,790	15,423	14,093	9,590	9,890	10,628	7,173	4,569	3,490
Current Liabilities	3,881	3,674	2,949	2,547	2,042	2,179	2,114	1,398	653	506
Long Term Debt	3,450	127	128	130	Nil	Nil	14.5	687	539	559
Common Equity	10,326	12,065	11,523	10,885	7,226	7,601	8,177	4,952	3,324	2,376
Total Capital	13,776	12,368	11,793	11,015	7,226	7,601	8,494	5,764	3,914	2,980
Capital Expenditures	718	601	371	369	391	889	858	524	373	211
Cash Flow	1,992	1,773	1,488	1,017	535	147	2,299	1,458	997	675
Current Ratio	1.7	1.8	1.6	1.8	2.1	2.3	2.9	3.1	4.8	5.2
% Long Term Debt of Capitalization	25.0	1.0	1.1	1.2	Nil	Nil	0.2	11.9	13.8	18.8
% Net Income of Revenue	11.0	11.7	10.6	8.0	NM	NM	20.1	15.0	20.0	18.3
% Return on Assets	6.9	7.0	5.9	4.2	NM	NM	20.0	15.8	19.7	18.6
% Return on Equity	11.0	9.6	7.8	5.5	NM	NM	27.1	34.4	27.8	26.8

Data as orig reptd.; bef. results of disc opers/spec. items. Per share data adj. for stk. divs.; EPS diluted. E-Estimated. NA-Not Available. NM-Not Meaningful. NR-Not Ranked. UR-Under Review.

Office: 176 South Street, Hopkinton, MA 01748-2230.
Telephone: 508-435-1000.
Email: emc_ir@emc.com
Website: http://www.emc.com

Chrmn, Pres & CEO: J.M. Tucci
Vice Chrmn: W.J. Teuber, Jr.
EVP & CFO: D.I. Goulden
EVP & General Counsel: P.T. Dacier

SVP & CTO: J.M. Nick
Board Members: M. W. Brown, M. J. Cronin, G. Deegan, J. R. Egan, W. P. Fitzgerald, O. Kallasvuo, W. B. Priem, D. N. Strohm, J. M. Tucci, A. M. Zeien

Founded: 1979
Domicile: Massachusetts
Employees: 31,100

The **McGraw-Hill** Companies

Emerson Electric Co.

STANDARD &POOR'S

S&P Recommendation BUY ★★★★☆	Price $54.68 (as of Nov 23, 2007)	12-Mo. Target Price $64.00	Investment Style Large-Cap Blend

GICS Sector Industrials
Sub-Industry Electrical Components & Equipment

Summary This company primarily makes backup power equipment for telecom and Internet providers and users, climate control components, and electric motors.

Key Stock Statistics (Source S&P, Vickers, company reports)

52-Wk Range	$56.70– 41.26	S&P Oper. EPS 2008**E**	3.00	Market Capitalization(B)	$43.046	Beta	1.26
Trailing 12-Month EPS	$2.66	S&P Oper. EPS 2009**E**	3.24	Yield (%)	2.19	S&P 3-Yr. Proj. EPS CAGR(%)	13.00
Trailing 12-Month P/E	20.6	P/E on S&P Oper. EPS 2008**E**	18.2	Dividend Rate/Share	$1.20	S&P Credit Rating	A
$10K Invested 5 Yrs Ago	$23,867	Common Shares Outstg. (M)	787.2	Institutional Ownership (%)	75		

Price Performance

30-Week Mov. Avg. ···   10-Week Mov. Avg.--   GAAP Earnings vs. Previous Year   Volume Above Avg. STARS
12-Mo. Target Price —   Relative Strength —   ▲ Up ▼ Down ► No Change   Below Avg.

2-for-1

Options: ASE, CBOE, P, Ph

Analysis prepared by **Christopher Lippincott** on November 16, 2007, when the stock traded at **$ 54.70**.

Highlights

➤ We expect that revenues will increase 8% in FY 08 (Sep.) and FY 09, led by growth in the network power and industrial automation segments. We look for EMR to benefit from increasing power demand from emerging markets, investments in power infrastructures in industrialized countries, increasing telecom spending, and corporate spending on efficiency improvements. We forecast 6% organic growth, with currency translation and acquisitions helping drive the balance.

➤ We think operating margins will expand modestly in FY 08 and FY 09. We see benefits from better capacity utilization, an improved global supply chain, greater operating leverage, increased efficiencies, and cost controls, partly offset by raw material cost inflation and ramp-up costs from product transitions and plant realignments.

➤ We project operating EPS of $3.00 in FY 08 and $3.24 in FY 09, representing 13% EPS growth in FY 08.

Investment Rationale/Risk

➤ We believe EMR's business prospects over the next two years remain strong, as the company gains continued organic revenue growth from international sales, globally valued brand platforms, and new product introductions in key business segments, as well as opportunistic bolt-on acquisitions and favorable currency translation. We forecast that EMR's business efficiency and operating metrics will improve, enabling the company to further strengthen its free cash flow growth, providing more cash for acquisitions and share repurchases.

➤ Risks to our recommendation and target price include weaker than expected global economic growth, softer industrial, energy and electronics markets, and potential value-diminishing acquisitions.

➤ Our 12-month target price of $64 represents a blend of three valuation metrics. Our discounted cash flow model, which assumes a 3.5% perpetual growth rate and a 10.2% discount rate, indicates an intrinsic value of $64. Our sum-of-the-parts analysis indicates a $65 value. Our relative valuation applies an 11.7X multiple, a slight premium to peers, to our 2008 EBITDA estimate, indicating a $64 value.

Qualitative Risk Assessment

LOW	MEDIUM	HIGH

Our risk assessment reflects the cyclical nature of several of the company's major end markets, its acquisition strategy, and corporate governance practices that we view as unfavorable versus peers. This is offset by our view of its strong competitive position in its major product categories and an S&P Quality Ranking of A, which indicates above-average growth of earnings and dividends.

Quantitative Evaluations

S&P Quality Ranking   A

D	C	B-	B	B+	A-	A	A+

Relative Strength Rank   STRONG

90

LOWEST = 1   HIGHEST = 99

Revenue/Earnings Data

Revenue (Million $)

	1Q	2Q	3Q	4Q	Year
2007	5,051	5,513	5,874	6,134	22,572
2006	4,548	4,852	5,217	5,516	20,133
2005	3,970	4,227	4,465	4,643	17,305
2004	3,600	3,859	4,036	4,120	15,615
2003	3,226	3,465	3,573	3,694	13,958
2002	3,295	3,421	3,571	3,538	13,824

Earnings Per Share ($)

2007	0.55	0.61	0.72	0.78	2.66
2006	0.48	0.52	0.59	0.65	2.24
2005	0.35	0.42	0.43	0.51	1.70
2004	0.29	0.38	0.41	0.42	1.49
2003	0.26	0.28	0.33	0.33	1.21
2002	0.31	0.33	0.34	0.29	1.26

Fiscal year ended Sep. 30. Next earnings report expected: Early February. EPS Estimates based on S&P Operating Earnings; historical GAAP earnings are as reported.

Dividend Data (Dates: mm/dd Payment Date: mm/dd/yy)

Amount ($)	Date Decl.	Ex-Div. Date	Stk. of Record	Payment Date
0.263	02/06	02/14	02/16	03/09/07
0.263	05/01	05/09	05/11	06/11/07
0.263	08/07	08/15	08/17	09/10/07
0.300	11/06	11/14	11/16	12/10/07

Dividends have been paid since 1947. Source: Company reports.

Emerson Electric Co.

STANDARD
&POOR'S

Business Summary November 16, 2007

CORPORATE OVERVIEW. Emerson is an industrial conglomerate operating more than 60 diverse businesses in five primary business segments: Process Management, Industrial Automation, Network Power, Climate Technologies, and Appliance and Tools.

The company's Process Management segment, which accounted for 24% of FY 06 (Sep.) total revenues and 29% of operating profits, and had 18% margins, produces process management software and systems, analytical instrumentation, valves, control systems for measurement and control of fluid flow, and integrated solutions for process and industrial applications. The Industrial Automation segment (19%, 19%, 15%) primarily makes industrial motors and drives, transmissions, alternators, controls and equipment for automated equipment. The Network Power segment (22%, 16%, 11%) mainly makes pow-

er systems and precision cooling products used in computer, telecommunications and Internet infrastructure. The Climate Technologies segment (17%, 17%, 15%) mostly makes home and building thermostats and compressors. Compressors are cooling components used in air conditioning units and refrigerators. The Appliance and Tools segment (21%, 18%, 13%) mainly makes various household appliances, electric motors and controls for appliances, hand-held tools, and storage solutions. In terms of geography, total sales in FY 06 broke down as follows: United States 53%, Europe 22%, Asia 14%, and other regions 11%.

Company Financials Fiscal Year Ended Sep. 30

Per Share Data ($)	2007	2006	2005	2004	2003	2002	2001	2000	1999	1998
Tangible Book Value	2.99	2.67	2.34	2.36	1.81	0.99	1.11	1.27	2.21	2.40
Cash Flow	3.47	3.04	2.41	4.37	1.84	1.90	2.07	2.44	2.23	2.02
Earnings	2.66	2.24	1.70	1.49	1.21	1.26	1.20	1.65	1.50	1.39
S&P Core Earnings	NA	2.24	1.70	1.49	1.13	0.94	0.88	NA	NA	NA
Dividends	1.05	0.89	0.83	0.80	0.79	0.78	0.77	0.72	0.65	0.63
Payout Ratio	39%	40%	49%	54%	65%	62%	64%	44%	43%	45%
Prices:High	56.70	45.21	38.92	35.44	32.50	33.04	39.63	39.88	35.72	33.72
Prices:Low	41.26	36.78	30.35	28.11	21.89	20.87	22.02	20.25	25.72	27.25
P/E Ratio:High	21	20	23	24	27	26	33	24	24	24
P/E Ratio:Low	16	16	18	19	18	17	18	12	17	20

Income Statement Analysis (Million $)										
Revenue	22,572	20,133	17,305	15,615	13,958	13,824	15,480	15,545	14,270	13,447
Operating Income	4,174	3,676	3,150	2,842	2,497	2,443	2,988	3,219	2,943	2,738
Depreciation	656	607	562	557	534	541	708	678	638	563
Interest Expense	261	225	243	234	246	250	304	288	190	152
Pretax Income	3,107	2,684	2,149	3,704	1,414	1,565	1,589	2,178	2,021	1,924
Effective Tax Rate	31.3%	31.3%	33.8%	16.1%	28.4%	32.3%	35.0%	34.7%	35.0%	36.1%
Net Income	2,136	1,845	1,422	3,109	1,013	1,060	1,032	1,422	1,314	1,229
S&P Core Earnings	NA	1,846	1,424	1,250	951	784	753	NA	NA	NA

Balance Sheet & Other Financial Data (Million $)										
Cash	1,008	810	1,233	1,346	696	381	356	281	266	210
Current Assets	8,065	7,330	6,837	6,416	5,500	4,961	5,320	5,483	5,124	5,001
Total Assets	19,680	18,672	17,227	16,361	15,194	14,545	15,046	15,164	13,624	12,660
Current Liabilities	5,546	5,374	4,931	4,339	3,417	4,400	5,379	5,219	4,590	4,022
Long Term Debt	3,372	3,128	3,128	3,136	3,733	2,990	2,256	2,248	1,317	1,057
Common Equity	8,772	7,848	7,400	12,266	6,460	5,741	6,114	10,248	6,181	5,803
Total Capital	12,144	10,976	10,528	15,402	10,193	8,731	8,370	12,496	7,498	6,860
Capital Expenditures	681	601	518	400	337	384	554	692	592	603
Cash Flow	2,792	2,452	1,984	3,666	1,547	1,601	1,740	2,101	1,951	1,792
Current Ratio	1.5	1.4	1.4	1.5	1.6	1.1	1.0	1.1	1.1	1.2
% Long Term Debt of Capitalization	27.8	28.5	29.7	20.4	36.6	34.2	26.9	18.0	17.6	15.4
% Net Income of Revenue	9.5	9.2	8.2	19.9	7.3	7.7	6.7	9.2	9.2	9.1
% Return on Assets	11.1	10.3	8.5	19.7	6.8	7.2	6.8	9.9	10.0	10.2
% Return on Equity	25.7	24.1	19.4	26.1	16.6	17.9	16.5	14.5	21.9	21.9

Data as orig reptd.; bef. results of disc opers/spec. items. Per share data adj. for stk. divs.; EPS diluted. E-Estimated. NA-Not Available. NM-Not Meaningful. NR-Not Ranked. UR-Under Review.

Office: 8000 W Florissant Ave, Saint Louis, MO 63136.
Telephone: 314-553-2000.
Website: http://www.gotoemerson.com
Chrmn, Pres & CEO: D.N. Farr

COO: E.L. Monser
Sr EVP: C.A. Peters
Sr EVP & CFO: W.J. Galvin
SVP, Secy & General Counsel: F.L. Steeves

Investor Contact: C. Tucker (314-553-2197)
Board Members: A. A. Busch, III, D. N. Farr, D. C. Farrell, C. G. Fernandez, W. J. Galvin, A. F. Golden, R. B. Horton, V. R. Loucks, Jr., J. B. Menzer, C. A. Peters, J. W. Prueher, R. L. Ridgway, R. L. Stephenson

Founded: 1890
Domicile: Missouri
Employees: 127,800

The **McGraw·Hill** Companies

ENSCO International Inc.

STANDARD &POOR'S

S&P Recommendation	BUY ★★★★☆	Price $54.29 (as of Nov 23, 2007)	12-Mo. Target Price $76.00	Investment Style Large-Cap Growth

GICS Sector Energy
Sub-Industry Oil & Gas Drilling

Summary This company provides offshore contract drilling services to the oil and gas industry worldwide.

Key Stock Statistics (Source S&P, Vickers, company reports)

52-Wk Range	$67.61– 45.00	S&P Oper. EPS 2007E	7.09	Market Capitalization(B)	$7.865	Beta	0.89
Trailing 12-Month EPS	$6.49	S&P Oper. EPS 2008E	8.62	Yield (%)	0.18	S&P 3-Yr. Proj. EPS CAGR(%)	25.00
Trailing 12-Month P/E	8.4	P/E on S&P Oper. EPS 2007E	7.7	Dividend Rate/Share	$0.10	S&P Credit Rating	BBB+
$10K Invested 5 Yrs Ago	$19,840	Common Shares Outstg. (M)	144.9	Institutional Ownership (%)	95		

Price Performance

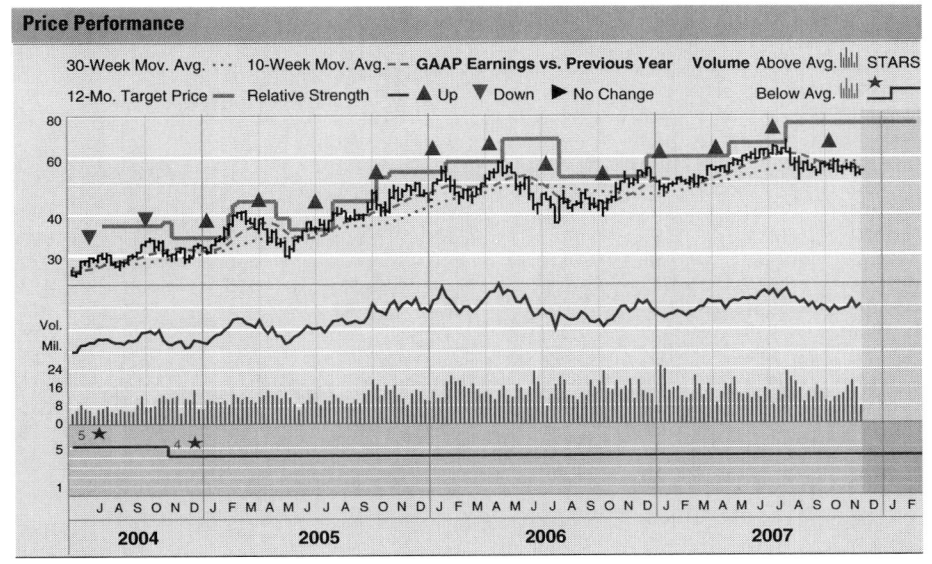

- 30-Week Mov. Avg. · · · 10-Week Mov. Avg. - - **GAAP Earnings vs. Previous Year** Volume Above Avg. STARS
- 12-Mo. Target Price — Relative Strength — ▲ Up ▼ Down ► No Change Below Avg.

Options: ASE, CBOE, P

Analysis prepared by **Stewart Glickman, CFA** on November 19, 2007, when the stock traded at **$ 52.91**.

Highlights

➤ We forecast the utilization of ESV's Europe/Africa jackup fleet at 92% in 2007, rising to 94% in 2008. With a projected marketed deficit of rigs in this operating segment, we think ESV will generate an average dayrate of $194,000 in this region in 2007, rising to $229,000 in 2008. Third quarter utilization for ESV's North American fleet dropped modestly to about 87%, from 89% in the second quarter, and despite the exodus of a high number of rigs from the region, we expect utilization in this region to remain relatively low given weaker demand visibility.

➤ Although jackup capacity during 2008 and 2009 is expected to rise by virtue of new rig deliveries (a total of 85 new jackups are being built through 2010 industry-wide), we believe there is sufficient growth in demand to enable such rigs to be absorbed without dayrate degradation, at least outside of the Pacific Rim, where we see potential for a modest reduction. In the Middle East alone, where ESV maintains seven jackups, we see potential for significant new demand.

➤ We estimate total revenue growth of 22% in 2007 and 15% in 2008. We expect EPS of $7.09 in 2007, rising to $8.62 in 2008.

Investment Rationale/Risk

➤ We believe ESV's premium jackup fleet is well positioned in the North Sea, India and Middle East markets, which we think will face ongoing supply deficits into 2009. By contrast, in the Pacific Rim, a region where ESV operates nine of its 44 jackups, we see a possible surplus of marketed jackups by late 2008 (largely due, in our view, to new rig deliveries) which we believe will lead to modest dayrate cuts in that region. ESV's newbuild program includes four more ultra-deepwater floaters, which should significantly improve the balance between jackup- and floater-derived revenues by 2010.

➤ Risks to our recommendation and target price include lower dayrates and utilization; lower crude oil and natural gas prices; and delays in newbuild deliveries.

➤ Our net asset value model, assuming terminal growth of 3% and a WACC of 11.1%, indicates the shares have an intrinsic value of about $75. Assuming a 6X multiple applied to our 2008 EBITDA estimate and a 7.5X multiple applied to our 2008 cash flow projection (a discount to peers, owing to perceived higher jackup-related risk in the near term), our 12-month target price is $76.

Qualitative Risk Assessment

LOW	MEDIUM	HIGH

Our risk assessment reflects ESV's exposure to volatile crude oil and natural gas prices, capital spending decisions made by its oil and gas producing customers, and political risk associated with operating in frontier regions. Offsetting these risks is the company's relatively large fleet of premium jackup equipment.

Quantitative Evaluations

S&P Quality Ranking   B

D	C	B-	B	B+	A-	A	A+

Relative Strength Rank   MODERATE

69

LOWEST = 1   HIGHEST = 99

Revenue/Earnings Data

Revenue (Million $)

	1Q	2Q	3Q	4Q	Year
2007	514.1	548.6	551.9	--	--
2006	381.6	475.2	486.1	470.6	1,814
2005	210.6	246.3	275.1	314.9	1,047
2004	186.5	181.4	190.9	209.2	768.0
2003	195.1	196.9	199.6	199.2	790.8
2002	142.3	157.2	191.8	206.8	698.1

Earnings Per Share ($)

2007	1.54	1.72	1.82	E2.02	E7.09
2006	0.94	1.26	1.40	1.36	4.96
2005	0.27	0.39	0.52	0.67	1.86
2004	0.14	0.12	0.17	0.26	0.69
2003	0.17	0.18	0.18	0.18	0.71
2002	0.12	0.17	0.21	-0.07	0.42

Fiscal year ended Dec. 31. Next earnings report expected: Late February. EPS Estimates based on S&P Operating Earnings; historical GAAP earnings are as reported.

Dividend Data (Dates: mm/dd Payment Date: mm/dd/yy)

Amount ($)	Date Decl.	Ex-Div. Date	Stk. of Record	Payment Date
0.025	02/28	03/08	03/12	03/23/07
0.025	05/22	06/07	06/11	06/22/07
0.025	08/29	09/06	09/10	09/21/07
0.025	11/06	12/06	12/10	12/21/07

Dividends have been paid since 1997. Source: Company reports.

ENSCO International Inc.

Business Summary November 19, 2007

CORPORATE OVERVIEW. ENSCO International is an international offshore oil and gas contract drilling company. As of December 2006, ESV's offshore drilling fleet was comprised of 43 active jackup rigs, and one newbuild jackup under construction; one active semisubmersible rig (and three more under construction); and one barge rig. The company is one of the leading international providers of offshore contract drilling services, operating in North and South America, Europe/Africa, and the Asia/Pacific Rim regions. As of February 2007, the total backlog of contract drilling work was approximately $3.2 billion, of which approximately 35% is derived from semisubmersibles, with the remaining 65% largely derived from jackups.

As of February 2007, ESV had 19 of its 45 active rigs in Asia and the Pacific Rim, 16 rigs in the Gulf of Mexico (GOM), nine rigs in Europe/Africa, and one rig in Venezuela. Of the four rigs currently under construction, the lone jackup, the Ensco 108, is expected to be delivered in the second quarter of 2007. The

first of the three ultra-deepwater semisubmersible rigs currently under construction (the Ensco 8500) is slated for delivery in the second quarter of 2008; the Ensco 8501 is due in the first quarter of 2009; and the Ensco 8502, announced in September at a projected capital cost of $385 million, is due in the fourth quarter of 2009.

The company's 2006 jackup rig utilization rate was 95%, up from 87% in 2005; dayrates increased to $114,587 from $71,694, in 2005. Barge rig utilization was flat at 98%; dayrates rose to $57,168 from $52,684. Semisubmersible rig utilization was 87%, versus 86% in 2005, and the average dayrate was $191,163, versus $161,527 in 2005.

Company Financials Fiscal Year Ended Dec. 31

Per Share Data ($)	2006	2005	2004	2003	2002	2001	2000	1999	1998	1997
Tangible Book Value	18.97	14.32	12.14	11.55	10.85	10.70	9.59	9.05	8.25	6.75
Cash Flow	6.11	2.92	1.69	1.61	1.29	2.41	1.32	0.76	2.40	2.41
Earnings	4.96	1.86	0.69	0.71	0.42	1.50	0.61	-0.05	1.81	1.64
S&P Core Earnings	4.96	1.79	0.64	0.64	0.30	1.34	NA	NA	NA	NA
Dividends	0.10	0.10	0.10	0.10	0.10	0.10	0.10	0.10	0.10	0.05
Payout Ratio	2%	5%	14%	14%	24%	7%	16%	NM	6%	3%
Prices:High	58.75	50.34	34.15	31.10	35.50	44.49	43.13	25.00	33.56	47.00
Prices:Low	37.36	29.25	24.95	23.58	20.87	12.81	20.25	8.75	8.69	20.25
P/E Ratio:High	12	27	49	44	85	30	71	NM	19	29
P/E Ratio:Low	8	16	36	33	50	9	33	NM	5	12

Income Statement Analysis (Million $)										
Revenue	1,814	1,047	768	791	698	817	534	364	813	815
Operating Income	1,192	573	323	316	290	442	230	102	469	494
Depreciation, Depletion and Amortization	175	161	150	135	124	124	98.7	98.2	83.5	105
Interest Expense	16.5	28.8	36.6	36.7	31.1	32.8	13.4	19.3	26.2	21.4
Pretax Income	1,011	391	140	149	87.1	292	125	5.20	383	376
Effective Tax Rate	25.0%	27.4%	25.8%	28.2%	31.9%	29.0%	31.8%	NM	32.4%	36.7%
Net Income	759	284	104	107	59.3	207	85.4	6.70	254	235
S&P Core Earnings	759	273	94.8	96.1	42.5	182	NA	NA	NA	NA

Balance Sheet & Other Financial Data (Million $)										
Cash	566	269	267	354	147	279	107	165	330	262
Current Assets	987	578	494	543	388	461	289	273	476	447
Total Assets	4,334	3,618	3,322	3,183	3,062	2,324	2,108	1,978	1,993	1,772
Current Liabilities	385	231	216	187	198	149	117	135	159	131
Long Term Debt	309	475	527	550	548	462	422	371	376	401
Common Equity	3,216	2,533	2,182	2,081	1,967	1,440	1,329	1,241	1,245	1,077
Total Capital	3,881	3,354	3,084	2,977	2,847	2,162	1,981	1,829	1,817	1,478
Capital Expenditures	529	478	305	187	227	145	256	248	331	282
Cash Flow	934	445	254	242	183	332	184	105	337	340
Current Ratio	2.6	2.5	2.3	2.9	2.0	3.1	2.5	2.0	3.0	3.4
% Long Term Debt of Capitalization	7.9	14.2	17.1	18.5	19.2	21.4	21.3	20.3	20.7	27.4
% Return on Assets	19.1	8.2	3.2	3.4	2.2	9.4	4.2	0.3	13.5	15.2
% Return on Equity	26.4	12.0	4.9	5.3	3.5	15.0	6.7	0.5	21.9	24.4

Data as orig reptd.; bef. results of disc opers/spec. items. Per share data adj. for stk. divs.; EPS diluted. E-Estimated. NA-Not Available. NM-Not Meaningful. NR-Not Ranked. UR-Under Review.

Office: 500 North Akard Street, Dallas, TX, USA 75201-3331.
Telephone: 214-397-3000.
Email: hrstaff@enscous.com
Website: http://www.enscous.com

Chrmn, Pres & CEO: D.W. Rabun
COO & EVP: W.S. Chadwick
SVP & CFO: J.W. Swent
VP, Secy & General Counsel: C.A. Moomjian

Investor Contact: R.A. LeBlanc (214-397-3000)
Board Members: D. M. Carmichael, G. W. Haddock, T. L. Kelly, II, M. H. Meyerson, D. W. Rabun, R. M. Rodriguez, P. E. Rowsey, III, J. V. Staff, C. F. Thorne

Founded: 1978
Domicile: Delaware
Employees: 3,900

Entergy Corp.

STANDARD &POOR'S

S&P Recommendation	**BUY** ★★★★☆	Price	12-Mo. Target Price	Investment Style
		$115.13 (as of Nov 23, 2007)	$137.00	Large-Cap Blend

GICS Sector Utilities
Sub-Industry Electric Utilities

Summary This electric utility holding company serves 2.6 million customers in Arkansas, Louisiana, Mississippi and Texas.

Key Stock Statistics (Source S&P, Vickers, company reports)

52-Wk Range	$125.00– 88.56	S&P Oper. EPS 2007**E**	5.68	Market Capitalization(B)	$22.529	Beta	0.28
Trailing 12-Month EPS	$5.91	S&P Oper. EPS 2008**E**	6.90	Yield (%)	2.61	S&P 3-Yr. Proj. EPS CAGR(%)	14.00
Trailing 12-Month P/E	19.5	P/E on S&P Oper. EPS 2007**E**	20.3	Dividend Rate/Share	$3.00	S&P Credit Rating	BBB
$10K Invested 5 Yrs Ago	$30,299	Common Shares Outstg. (M)	195.7	Institutional Ownership (%)	80		

Price Performance

| 30-Week Mov. Avg. ··· 10-Week Mov. Avg.- - **GAAP Earnings vs. Previous Year** Volume Above Avg.▐▐ STARS |
| 12-Mo. Target Price — Relative Strength — ▲ Up ▼ Down ► No Change Below Avg.▐▐ ★ ─┌─ |

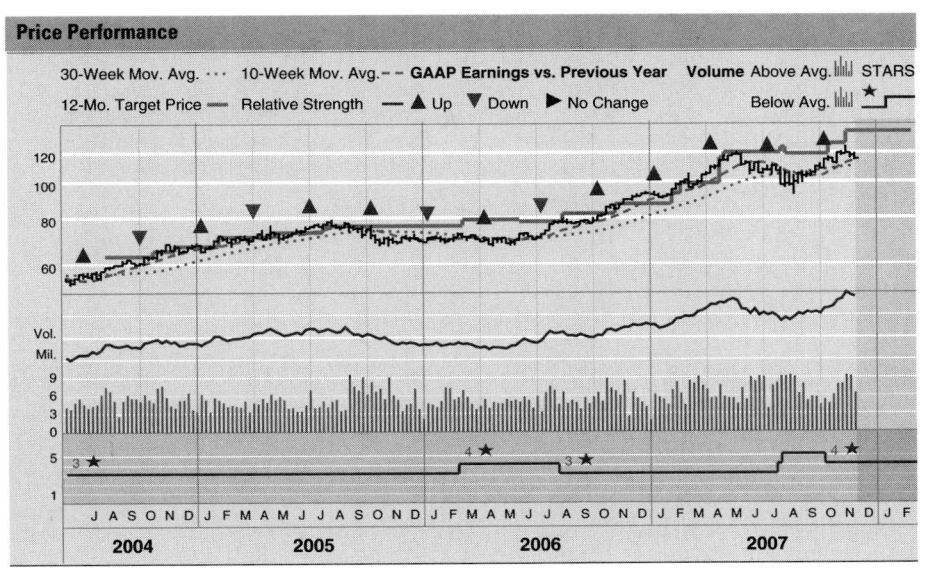

Options: ASE, CBOE, P, Ph

Analysis prepared by **Justin McCann** on November 21, 2007, when the stock traded at **$ 115.31**.

Highlights

➤ We expect the company's planned tax-free spin-off of its non-utility nuclear assets, as well as the equally owned joint venture to be formed with the spun-off company, to be completed, pending required approvals, during the third quarter of 2008.

➤ We expect operating EPS in 2007 to increase about 20% from 2006's operating EPS of $4.72. This will include results from Entergy New Orleans, which emerged from bankruptcy on May 8, 2007. We see 2007 EPS benefiting from rate hikes and increased earnings from the nuclear operations, as rising operating costs and interest expense should be more than offset by higher-margin contracts.

➤ We believe combined operating EPS in 2008 will expand about 21% from anticipated results in 2007. In addition to continued margin expansion at the nuclear operations, we expect the projected sharp rise to be driven by fewer shares outstanding, reflecting the company's two-year, $1.5 billion share repurchase program. We see these factors resulting in a strong combined double-digit EPS growth though the remainder of the decade.

Investment Rationale/Risk

➤ We believe Entergy's plan to spin off its non-utility nuclear operations would enable the yet-to-be-named company to realize higher growth and P/E multiples than ETR would as a single combined entity. We would also expect the retained regulated utilites to achieve shareholder value with a targeted 70% to 75% dividend payout, the capacity for a new $2.5 billion share repurchase program following the spin-off, and annual EPS growth of 6% to 8%.

➤ Risks to our recommendation and target price include a sharp drop in the margins of ETR's non-regulated operations, unanticipated problems with its nuclear facilities, and a decline in the average P/E of the group as a whole.

➤ The yield from the dividend (increased 39% with the September payment) was recently around 2.6%. While this is below the peer average (3.6%), we think it is acceptable for a growth-oriented utility holding company. We believe the stock could benefit from ETR's planned spin-off of its non-utility nuclear assets, and we expect the shares to trade at a premium-to-peers P/E of our 19.9X our $6.90 EPS estimate for 2008. Our 12-month target price is $137.

Qualitative Risk Assessment

LOW	**MEDIUM**	HIGH

Our risk assessment reflects the steady cash flow we expect from most of the regulated utilities and the nuclear operations, offset by uncertainties related to the recovery of the utility operations in New Orleans.

Quantitative Evaluations

S&P Quality Ranking A-

D	C	B-	B	B+	**A-**	A	A+

Relative Strength Rank STRONG

| 83 |

LOWEST = 1 HIGHEST = 99

Revenue/Earnings Data

Revenue (Million $)

	1Q	2Q	3Q	4Q	Year
2007	2,600	2,769	3,289	--	--
2006	2,568	2,629	3,255	2,481	10,932
2005	2,323	2,710	3,130	2,652	10,106
2004	2,252	2,485	2,964	2,424	10,124
2003	2,038	2,354	2,700	2,103	9,195
2002	1,861	2,097	2,469	1,879	8,305

Earnings Per Share ($)

2007	1.03	1.32	2.30	E1.06	E5.68
2006	0.93	1.27	1.83	1.32	5.36
2005	0.79	1.33	1.65	0.59	4.40
2004	0.88	1.14	1.22	0.68	3.93
2003	1.10	0.89	1.57	-0.14	3.42
2002	-0.36	1.06	1.59	0.35	2.64

Fiscal year ended Dec. 31. Next earnings report expected: Late January. EPS Estimates based on S&P Operating Earnings; historical GAAP earnings are as reported.

Dividend Data (Dates: mm/dd Payment Date: mm/dd/yy)

Amount ($)	Date Decl.	Ex-Div. Date	Stk. of Record	Payment Date
0.540	01/26	02/07	02/09	03/01/07
0.540	04/04	05/08	05/10	06/01/07
0.750	07/31	08/08	08/10	09/01/07
0.750	10/26	11/07	11/09	12/01/07

Dividends have been paid since 1988. Source: Company reports.

Please read the Required Disclosures and Analyst Certification on the last page of this report.

Entergy Corp.

Business Summary November 21, 2007

CORPORATE OVERVIEW. Entergy is an integrated energy company primarily engaged in electric power production and retail electric distribution operations. It owns and operates power plants with about 30,000 megawatts (MW) of electric generating capacity, and is the second largest nuclear power generator in the U.S. As the holding company for Entergy Arkansas, Entergy Gulf States, Entergy Louisiana, Entergy Mississippi, and Entergy New Orleans, Entergy Corp. provides electricity to 2.6 million U.S. retail customers. ETR also owns System Energy Resources, which has a 90% interest in the Grand Gulf 1 nuclear plant. The non-utility nuclear business owns and operates five nuclear plants in the northeastern U.S., selling mainly to wholesale customers.

IMPACT OF MAJOR DEVELOPMENTS. On November 5, 2007, Entergy announced that it planned to spin off to shareholders the company's non-utility nuclear business. It also intends to form an equally owned joint venture with the yet-to-be-named spun-off company, that will be involved in the operation of the new company's nuclear assets and which will offer ancillary nuclear services to third parties. The company has targeted, pending required approvals, the third quarter of 2008 for the spin-off and joint venture transactions to be completed. The transaction is expected to be tax-free for both the company and the shareholders.

Hurricanes Katrina and Rita in 2005 caused catastrophic damage to large portions of ETR's service territories in Louisiana, Mississippi and Texas, including

the effect of extensive flooding in and around greater New Orleans. Through December 31, 2006, Entergy reported total restoration costs of $1.48 billion. It is seeking to recover these costs through a combination of insurance reimbursements, federal and state assistance, and rate mechanisms. ETR estimates that the impact of lost customers will result in lost net revenues of about $194 million for Entergy New Orleans in 2007.

On July 19, 2007, the Federal Energy Regulatory Commission approved ETR's plan to split its Gulf States utility into two separate companies and jurisdictions, one in Louisiana and one in Texas. The plan still needs to be approved by the Nuclear Regulatory Commission.

On May 8, 2007, Entergy New Orleans emerged from Chapter 11 bankruptcy. This followed the approval of the company's plan of reorganization by the U.S Bankruptcy Court for the Eastern District of Louisiana. The utility had filed for Chapter 11 reorganization in September 2005, soon after the devastation caused by Hurricane Katrina. Under the reorganization plan, all creditors would be fully compensated.

Company Financials Fiscal Year Ended Dec. 31

Per Share Data ($)	2006	2005	2004	2003	2002	2001	2000	1999	1998	1997
Tangible Book Value	38.59	35.49	36.43	36.38	33.61	33.74	31.83	29.71	28.82	19.72
Earnings	5.36	4.40	3.93	3.42	2.64	3.13	2.97	2.25	3.00	1.03
S&P Core Earnings	5.54	4.49	3.99	3.70	2.14	2.21	NA	NA	NA	NA
Dividends	2.16	2.16	1.89	1.60	1.34	1.28	1.22	1.20	1.50	1.80
Payout Ratio	40%	49%	48%	47%	51%	41%	41%	53%	50%	175%
Prices:High	94.03	79.22	68.67	57.24	46.85	44.67	43.88	33.50	32.44	30.25
Prices:Low	66.78	64.48	50.64	42.26	32.12	32.56	15.94	23.69	23.25	22.38
P/E Ratio:High	18	18	17	17	18	14	15	15	11	29
P/E Ratio:Low	12	15	13	12	12	10	5	11	8	22

Income Statement Analysis (Million $)										
Revenue	10,932	10,106	10,124	9,195	8,305	9,621	10,016	8,773	11,495	9,562
Depreciation	888	856	896	851	839	721	785	745	985	980
Maintenance	NA	NA	NA	NA	NA	NA	NA	NA	NA	NA
Fixed Charges Coverage	3.36	3.69	3.54	2.66	2.23	2.25	2.83	2.34	1.91	1.87
Construction Credits	63.8	75.1	65.3	75.9	57.0	48.0	56.0	52.0	23.0	18.0
Effective Tax Rate	28.1%	36.6%	28.2%	37.6%	32.1%	38.5%	40.3%	37.5%	24.4%	59.4%
Net Income	1,133	969	933	813	623	727	711	595	786	301
S&P Core Earnings	1,171	961	922	856	487	495	NA	NA	NA	NA

Balance Sheet & Other Financial Data (Million $)										
Gross Property	33,366	32,437	32,055	31,181	32,964	32,403	29,865	28,178	26,892	29,102
Capital Expenditures	1,586	1,458	1,411	1,569	1,580	1,380	1,494	1,196	1,144	847
Net Property	19,651	19,426	18,915	18,561	20,657	20,597	18,501	17,279	16,816	19,517
Capitalization:Long Term Debt	8,809	8,838	7,034	7,498	7,458	7,536	8,014	7,253	7,349	9,304
Capitalization:% Long Term Debt	50.8	53.2	44.5	45.2	47.6	49.1	52.2	49.3	49.7	54.7
Capitalization:Preferred	345	Nil	365	334	359	361	335	338	338	1,003
Capitalization:% Preferred	1.99	Nil	2.31	2.01	2.29	2.35	2.18	2.30	2.28	5.80
Capitalization:Common	8,198	7,761	8,400	8,773	7,839	7,456	7,003	7,118	7,107	6,693
Capitalization:% Common	47.2	46.8	53.2	52.8	50.1	48.6	45.6	48.4	48.0	39.3
Total Capital	23,531	22,399	21,266	21,805	20,355	19,399	19,095	18,539	18,942	22,156
% Operating Ratio	88.7	63.3	87.6	89.4	85.8	88.6	89.0	88.3	86.8	81.3
% Earned on Net Property	9.2	9.3	8.8	8.1	5.8	8.1	8.6	7.3	8.3	10.1
% Return on Revenue	10.4	9.6	9.2	8.8	7.5	7.6	7.1	6.8	6.8	3.1
% Return on Invested Capital	7.0	6.6	6.5	2.4	7.7	7.6	7.1	7.0	14.8	7.7
% Return on Common Equity	14.2	11.7	10.6	9.5	7.8	9.7	9.6	7.8	10.7	3.7

Data as orig reptd.; bef. results of disc opers/spec. items. Per share data adj. for stk. divs.; EPS diluted. E-Estimated. NA-Not Available. NM-Not Meaningful. NR-Not Ranked. UR-Under Review.

Office: 639 Loyola Ave, New Orleans, LA 70113-3125.
Telephone: 504-576-4000.
Website: http://www.entergy.com
Chrmn & CEO: J.W. Leonard

Pres & COO: R.J. Smith
EVP & CFO: L. Denault
EVP & General Counsel: R.D. Sloan
Investor Contact: N. Morovich (504-576-5506)

Board Members: M. S. Bateman, W. F. Blount, G. Edwards, A. M. Herman, D. C. Hintz, J. W. Leonard, S. L. Levenick, J. R. Nichols, W. A. Percy, II, W. J. Tauzin, S. V. Wilkinson, S. D. deBree
Founded: 1989
Domicile: Delaware
Employees: 13,814

The McGraw-Hill Companies

EOG Resources Inc.

STANDARD &POOR'S

S&P Recommendation	HOLD ★★★☆☆	Price $83.64 (as of Nov 23, 2007)	12-Mo. Target Price $89.00	Investment Style Large-Cap Growth

GICS Sector Energy
Sub-Industry Oil & Gas Exploration & Production

Summary This company explores for, develops, produces and markets natural gas and crude oil in the U.S., Trinidad and Canada.

Key Stock Statistics (Source S&P, Vickers, company reports)

52-Wk Range	$90.73– 59.21	S&P Oper. EPS 2007**E**	3.91	Market Capitalization(B)	$20.575	Beta	0.50
Trailing 12-Month EPS	$3.89	S&P Oper. EPS 2008**E**	5.16	Yield (%)	0.43	S&P 3-Yr. Proj. EPS CAGR(%)	28.90
Trailing 12-Month P/E	21.5	P/E on S&P Oper. EPS 2007**E**	21.4	Dividend Rate/Share	$0.36	S&P Credit Rating	A-
$10K Invested 5 Yrs Ago	$44,437	Common Shares Outstg. (M)	246.0	Institutional Ownership (%)	94		

Price Performance

30-Week Mov. Avg. · · · 10-Week Mov. Avg. – – **GAAP Earnings vs. Previous Year** **Volume** Above Avg. ▥▥ **STARS**
12-Mo. Target Price — Relative Strength — ▲ Up ▼ Down ▶ No Change Below Avg. ▥▥ ★

Options: ASE, CBOE, P, Ph

Analysis prepared by **Tina J. Vital** on October 31, 2007, when the stock traded at **$ 85.95**.

Highlights

➤ We expect EOG's oil and gas production will increase over 11% in 2007 and 17% in 2008, driven by its Fort Worth Basin Barnett Shale natural gas and North Dakota Bakken crude oil plays. EOG expects its liquids production will average 10% in 2007 and 33% in 2008, and has targeted its overall oil and gas production targets during 2009E-2010E at 10%. EOG plans to sell shallow natural gas assets in Appalachia, which are low decline and low risk assets. It also intends to build its own midstream infrastructure in the Barnett and Bakken plays.

➤ While industry costs have been rising, we believe EOG has kept these increases low relative to peers, reflecting what we view as its efficient operations in North America and low cost operations in Trinidad. EOG believes its North Dakota Bakken, Fort Worth Barnett Shale and Uinta Basin plays offer very high relative returns.

➤ We expect weaker natural gas prices and increased service costs will lead after-tax operating earnings to a decline of 18% in 2007, before rising about 34% in 2008 on production increases and higher oil and natural gas price realizations.

Investment Rationale/Risk

➤ We believe EOG's onshore U.S. drilling prospects should enable strong near-term organic production growth. As a result, EOG believes there is little chance of merger activity in 2008. However, production from Canada, Trinidad and the U.K. North Sea in 2008 is expected to be flat with 2007 levels. EOG has hedged about 18% of its 2008 North American gas production at a price of near $8.6 per MMBtu, and is likely to add to positions as the market permits; this is a positive, in our view, given EOG's presence in the Rocky Mountains where difficult natural gas price differentials exist. EOG has no 2008 oil hedges in place.

➤ Risks to our recommendation and target price include negative changes to economic, industrial and operating conditions, including difficulty in replacing reserves, and increased geopolitical risk.

➤ Blending our discounted cash flow analysis (assuming a WACC of 7.94%, and terminal growth of 3%) and relative valuations, leads us to our 12-month target price of $89, representing an expected enterprise value of 6.5X our 2008 EBITDA estimate.

Qualitative Risk Assessment

LOW	**MEDIUM**	HIGH

Our risk assessment for EOG reflects our view of its solid business and financial risk profile, reflecting its significant net acreage position, active drilling program and history of relatively low operating costs, offset by its participation in a very competitive, capital intensive and cyclical industry.

Quantitative Evaluations

S&P Quality Ranking B+

D	C	B-	B	**B+**	A-	A	A+

Relative Strength Rank STRONG

90

LOWEST = 1   HIGHEST = 99

Revenue/Earnings Data

Revenue (Million $)

	1Q	2Q	3Q	4Q	Year
2007	875.2	1,055	990.5	--	--
2006	1,085	919.1	968.3	932.5	3,904
2005	688.2	783.9	934.5	1,214	3,620
2004	464.3	519.0	594.2	693.7	2,271
2003	464.7	424.8	458.7	396.5	1,745
2002	186.5	290.5	279.9	338.2	1,095

Earnings Per Share ($)

2007	0.88	1.24	0.82	E0.97	E3.91
2006	1.73	1.34	1.21	0.96	5.24
2005	0.83	1.02	1.40	1.88	5.13
2004	0.42	0.60	0.71	0.85	2.58
2003	0.58	0.46	0.50	0.31	1.83
2002	-0.12	0.15	0.11	0.18	0.33

Fiscal year ended Dec. 31. Next earnings report expected: Early February. EPS Estimates based on S&P Operating Earnings; historical GAAP earnings are as reported.

Dividend Data (Dates: mm/dd Payment Date: mm/dd/yy)

Amount ($)	Date Decl.	Ex-Div. Date	Stk. of Record	Payment Date
0.060	12/04	01/12	01/17	01/31/07
0.090	02/01	04/12	04/16	04/30/07
0.090	04/24	07/13	07/17	07/31/07
0.090	09/06	10/15	10/17	10/31/07

Dividends have been paid since 1990. Source: Company reports.

Please read the Required Disclosures and Analyst Certification on the last page of this report.

The McGraw-Hill Companies

EOG Resources Inc.

Business Summary October 31, 2007

CORPORATE OVERVIEW. EOG Resources, Inc. (EOG), a Delaware corporation organized in 1985, together with its subsidiaries, explores for, develops, produces and markets natural gas and crude oil primarily in major producing basins in the U.S., Canada, offshore Trinidad, and the U.K. North Sea.

At December 31, 2006, EOG's total estimated net proved reserves were 6.8 trillion cubic feet equivalent (Tcfe), of which 6.09 Tcf were natural gas reserves and 118 million barrels (MMbbl), or 708 Bcfe, were crude oil and hydrocarbon liquids reserves. About 60% of EOG's reserves were in the U.S., 20% Trinidad, 20% Canada and less than 1% the North Sea. This compares to year-end 2005 total estimated net proved reserves of 6.19 Tcfe, of which 5.56 Tcf were natural gas reserves and 106 million barrels (MMBbl), or 637 Bcfe, were crude oil and hydrocarbon liquids reserves. About 56% of EOG's reserves were in the U.S., 21% Trinidad, 22% Canada and 1% the North Sea.

MARKET PROFILE. EOG's addressable markets include North American operations, where about 80% of its reserve base is located, with the remainder in Trinidad. As a large onshore primarily natural gas producer, EOG competes in a fragmented market that is beginning to rationalize with several large onshore players such as Devon Energy (DVN: hold, $84) and XTO Energy (XTO: hold, $62). We believe North America is a relatively mature supply source for

hydrocarbons, and natural gas production has been little changed in North America over the past five years. We think EOG has overcome this situation by astutely purchasing land in attractive regions such as the Barnett Shale, East Texas, and the Rocky Mountains, and employing unconventional drilling and production techniques to successfully boost production volumes. Such unconventional resource plays include basin-centered tight gas formations, coal-bed methane formations, and fractured shale formations, which are characterized by a low proportion of exploration capital expenditures, resulting in relatively low risk resource acquisition capability. In our view, the main driver of value in these resource plays is the development of drilling techniques--in a basin--that are repeatable, increasing productivity organically and moving reserves characterized as probable and possible to the proven category.

The company also has producing operations in offshore Trinidad (253 MMcf, 4.3 MBbl per day). EOG sells natural gas to Trinidad under five separate take-or-pay contracts, with terminations ranging from 2015 to 2025.

Company Financials Fiscal Year Ended Dec. 31

Per Share Data ($)	2006	2005	2004	2003	2002	2001	2000	1999	1998	1997
Tangible Book Value	22.76	17.21	11.97	8.95	6.64	6.47	5.27	4.11	4.17	4.13
Cash Flow	8.56	7.81	4.69	3.73	2.02	3.32	3.17	3.61	1.20	1.27
Earnings	5.24	5.13	2.58	1.83	0.33	1.65	1.12	2.00	0.18	0.39
S&P Core Earnings	5.21	5.08	2.54	1.77	0.26	1.60	NA	NA	NA	NA
Dividends	0.22	0.15	0.12	0.09	0.08	0.08	0.07	0.06	0.06	0.06
Payout Ratio	4%	3%	5%	5%	25%	5%	6%	3%	33%	15%
Prices:High	86.91	82.00	38.25	23.76	22.08	27.75	28.34	12.69	12.25	13.50
Prices:Low	56.31	32.05	21.23	17.85	15.01	12.90	6.84	7.19	5.88	8.75
P/E Ratio:High	17	16	15	13	68	17	25	6	68	35
P/E Ratio:Low	11	6	8	10	46	8	6	4	33	22

Income Statement Analysis (Million $)

	2006	2005	2004	2003	2002	2001	2000	1999	1998	1997
Revenue	3,904	3,620	2,271	1,745	1,095	1,655	1,490	801	769	774
Operating Income	1,895	1,992	979	697	648	1,181	697	18.2	114	193
Depreciation, Depletion and Amortization	817	654	504	442	398	392	370	460	315	278
Interest Expense	43.2	62.5	63.1	58.7	59.7	45.1	61.0	61.8	48.6	27.7
Pretax Income	1,913	1,965	926	654	120	631	634	568	60.3	163
Effective Tax Rate	32.0%	35.9%	32.5%	33.1%	27.2%	36.9%	37.3%	NM	6.82%	25.4%
Net Income	1,300	1,260	625	437	87.2	399	397	569	56.2	122
S&P Core Earnings	1,281	1,238	605	412	62.4	376	NA	NA	NA	NA

Balance Sheet & Other Financial Data (Million $)

	2006	2005	2004	2003	2002	2001	2000	1999	1998	1997
Cash	218	644	21.0	4.44	9.85	2.51	20.2	24.8	6.30	9.33
Current Assets	1,350	1,563	587	396	395	272	394	201	246	282
Total Assets	9,402	7,753	5,799	4,749	3,814	3,414	3,001	2,611	3,018	2,723
Current Liabilities	1,255	1,172	632	477	276	311	370	219	263	291
Long Term Debt	733	859	1,078	1,109	1,145	856	859	990	1,143	741
Common Equity	5,547	4,217	2,847	2,098	1,524	1,495	1,234	982	1,280	1,281
Total Capital	7,846	6,298	4,925	4,125	3,478	3,050	2,580	2,346	2,683	2,310
Capital Expenditures	2,819	1,725	1,417	1,204	714	974	603	403	690	626
Cash Flow	2,106	1,906	1,118	868	474	780	756	1,028	371	400
Current Ratio	1.1	1.3	0.9	0.8	1.4	0.9	1.1	0.9	0.9	1.0
% Long Term Debt of Capitalization	9.3	13.6	21.9	26.9	32.9	28.1	33.3	42.2	42.6	32.1
% Return on Assets	15.2	18.6	11.8	10.2	2.4	12.4	14.1	20.2	2.0	4.7
% Return on Equity	26.4	35.5	24.9	23.4	5.0	28.4	34.8	50.3	4.4	9.6

Data as orig reptd.; bef. results of disc opers/spec. items. Per share data adj. for stk. divs.; EPS diluted. E-Estimated. NA-Not Available. NM-Not Meaningful. NR-Not Ranked. UR-Under Review.

Office: 333 Clay Street, Houston, TX 77002-4006.
Telephone: 877-363-3647.
Email: ir@eogresources.com
Website: http://www.eogresources.com

Chrmn & CEO: M.G. Papa
Sr EVP: E.P. Segner, III
Sr EVP: G.L. Thomas
Sr EVP: L.M. Leiker

SVP & General Counsel: F.J. Plaeger, II
Investor Contact: M.A. Baldwin (713-651-6364)
Board Members: G. A. Alcorn, C. R. Crisp, M. G. Papa, E. P. Segner, III, W. Stevens, H. L. Steward, D. F. Textor, F. G. Wisner

Founded: 1985
Domicile: Delaware
Employees: 1,570

STANDARD & POOR'S

E TRADE Financial Corporation

S&P Recommendation	HOLD ★★★☆☆	Price $4.82 (as of Nov 29, 2007)	12-Mo. Target Price $6.00	Investment Style Large-Cap Growth

GICS Sector Financials
Sub-Industry Investment Banking & Brokerage

Summary This company provides online discount brokerage, mortgage and banking services, primarily to retail customers.

Key Stock Statistics (Source S&P, Vickers, company reports)

52-Wk Range	$26.08– 3.46	S&P Oper. EPS 2007E	0.73	Market Capitalization(B)	$2.042	Beta	2.37
Trailing 12-Month EPS	$1.03	S&P Oper. EPS 2008E	1.27	Yield (%)	Nil	S&P 3-Yr. Proj. EPS CAGR(%)	7.50
Trailing 12-Month P/E	4.7	P/E on S&P Oper. EPS 2007E	6.6	Dividend Rate/Share	Nil	S&P Credit Rating	B
$10K Invested 5 Yrs Ago	$9,158	Common Shares Outstg. (M)	423.8	Institutional Ownership (%)	87		

Price Performance

30-Week Mov. Avg. · · · 10-Week Mov. Avg. – – GAAP Earnings vs. Previous Year Volume Above Avg. STARS
12-Mo. Target Price — Relative Strength — ▲ Up ▼ Down ► No Change Below Avg. ★

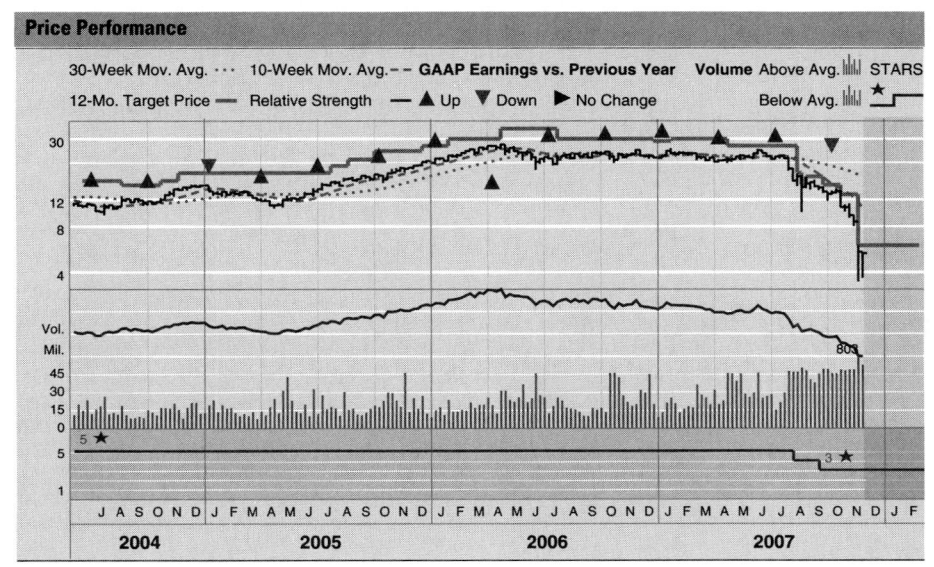

Options: ASE, CBOE, P, Ph

Analysis prepared by **Jason Willey** on November 16, 2007, when the stock traded at **$ 5.21**.

Highlights

➤ ETFC has begun restructuring its operations and balance sheet to focus on its retail clients and reduce its exposure to consumer lending and securities investments. Prime first-lien mortgages and margin debt will make up 80% to 85% of interest-earning assets following the change, up from about 40% at the end of August. Liabilities will also be shifted away from wholesale borrowings to customer cash and deposits. We believe loan provisions and securities impairments will dampen earnings into 2008, but we view the restructuring as a long-term positive for earnings and the shares.

➤ Despite the noise around its mortgage and security investments, ETFC's core retail operations posted strong results for the third quarter, with daily average revenue trades (DARTs) up 44%, year to year, and solid growth in customer accounts and assets. We expect ongoing market volatility to drive strong retail revenue, but we see provisions and asset impairments pressuring pretax margins in the fourth quarter and into 2008.

➤ We project EPS of $0.73 in 2007, growing to $1.27 in 2008, as we expect lower loan loss provisions as 2008 progresses.

Investment Rationale/Risk

➤ ETFC's recent reliance on wholesale operations to build its balance sheet, and its recent restructuring of these operations, should hurt results in coming quarters, but we believe the recent moves to realign operations to focus on its core retail customers will pay off over the next few years. Still, a hangover from mortgage operations will likely outweigh the near-term positives we have seen in its retail business. While ETFC expects further writedowns in its securities investment portfolio and has withdrawn formal financial guidance for the fourth quarter, we believe it remains well capitalized and can sustain further depreciation of its investment portfolio.

➤ Risks to our recommendation and target price include increased price competition, various regulatory issues, potential equity market depreciation, notably in the Nasdaq, and further writedowns in its securities investment portfolio.

➤ We arrive at our 12-month target price of $6 by applying a multiple of 0.6X to our estimate of ETFC's book value, a discount to online broker peers. We believe this discount is warranted by ETFC's mortgage and securities exposure.

Qualitative Risk Assessment

LOW	MEDIUM	HIGH

Our risk assessment reflects our concerns about significant industry volatility and ETFC's exposure to asset-backed securities, partially offset by our view of its strong client relationships.

Quantitative Evaluations

S&P Quality Ranking B-

D	C	B-	B	B+	A-	A	A+

Relative Strength Rank WEAK

2

LOWEST = 1   HIGHEST = 99

Revenue/Earnings Data

Revenue (Million $)

	1Q	2Q	3Q	4Q	Year
2007	1,105	1,185	1,042	--	--
2006	598.4	611.4	581.8	628.9	2,420
2005	417.4	387.7	419.8	478.9	1,704
2004	400.5	380.9	337.1	409.5	1,947
2003	322.2	381.1	397.7	382.8	1,719
2002	554.6	531.2	468.6	484.7	2,302

Earnings Per Share ($)

2007	0.39	0.37	-0.14	E0.12	E0.73
2006	0.33	0.36	0.34	0.40	1.44
2005	0.27	0.29	0.29	0.31	1.16
2004	0.23	0.24	0.21	0.24	0.92
2003	0.06	0.03	0.17	0.27	0.55
2002	0.05	0.09	0.06	0.08	0.30

Fiscal year ended Dec. 31. Next earnings report expected: Mid January. EPS Estimates based on S&P Operating Earnings; historical GAAP earnings are as reported.

Dividend Data

No cash dividends have been paid.

E TRADE Financial Corporation

STANDARD
&POOR'S

Business Summary November 16, 2007

CORPORATE OVERVIEW. E Trade Financial Corporation is one of the industry's leading online financial services concerns. The company provides online discount brokerage and banking services, primarily to retail customers. Although most of the company's business is done over the Internet, ETFC also serves customers through branches, automated and live telephone service, and Internet-enabled wireless devices. Retail customers can move money electronically between brokerage, banking and lending accounts. As of December 31, 2006, ETFC had about 3.6 million brokerage accounts and around 821,000 banking accounts. We expect the company, which had 24 branch locations at the end of 2006, to open about 12 branches over the next two years, bringing its total to approximately 36, and to continue to shed non-core businesses.

Through its Brokerage segment, ETFC's customers can buy and sell stocks, bonds, options, futures, and over 6,000 non-proprietary mutual funds. Customers can also obtain streaming quotes and charts, access real-time market commentary and research reports, and perform personalized portfolio tracking. Brokerage customers can obtain margin loans collateralized by their securities. The company uses sophisticated proprietary transaction-enabling technology to automate traditionally labor-intensive transactions. The brokerage business continues to be the primary point of introduction for the majority of ETFC's customers, which are typically self-directed investors.

Through its Banking segment, the company has historically offered residential mortgage products, home equity loans and home equity lines of credit (HELOC). The segment also offers credit card, automobile, recreational vehicle (RV), marine, and other consumer loans. In late 2003, the Banking segment began sweeping Brokerage customer money market balances into an FDIC-insured Sweep Deposit Account (SDA) product, which lowered its cost of funds. At the end of 2006, ETFC had $10.8 billion in the SDA product, up from $4.3 billion at the end of 2003. We estimate that nearly half of the bank's customers are also brokerage customers. ETFC's loan portfolio consists of first mortgages, the majority of which are adjustable-rate, home equity lines of credit (HELOC), second mortgage loan products, and consumer loans for RVs, marine, automobile, and credit card loans. Going forward, we expect the asset composition of this segment to change significantly as ETFC completes its restructuring plan announced in September 2007 and realigns its focus on its core retail business.

Company Financials Fiscal Year Ended Dec. 31

Per Share Data ($)	2006	2005	2004	2003	2002	2001	2000	1999	1998	1997
Tangible Book Value	3.87	2.07	4.58	3.73	2.68	2.54	4.43	3.81	3.14	1.82
Cash Flow	1.61	1.36	1.07	0.55	1.20	-0.28	0.37	-0.09	0.07	0.13
Earnings	1.44	1.16	0.92	0.55	0.30	-0.81	-0.06	-0.23	-0.01	0.10
S&P Core Earnings	1.33	0.88	0.66	0.27	0.27	-0.86	NA	NA	NA	NA
Dividends	Nil	Nil	Nil	Nil	Nil	Nil	Nil	Nil	Nil	Nil
Payout Ratio	Nil	Nil	Nil	Nil	Nil	Nil	Nil	Nil	Nil	Nil
Prices:High	27.76	21.71	15.40	12.91	12.64	15.38	34.25	72.25	16.25	11.97
Prices:Low	18.81	10.53	9.51	3.65	2.81	4.07	6.66	12.74	2.50	2.75
P/E Ratio:High	19	19	17	23	42	NM	NM	NM	NM	119
P/E Ratio:Low	13	9	10	7	9	NM	NM	NM	NM	27

Income Statement Analysis (Million $)	2006	2005	2004	2003	2002	2001	2000	1999	1998	1997
Commissions	625	459	350	337	302	407	739	356	162	110
Interest Income	2,775	1,650	1,146	893	946	1,160	960	196	95.7	40.2
Total Revenue	3,840	2,537	2,077	2,009	1,903	2,062	1,973	695	285	158
Interest Expense	1,527	853	558	532	609	832	630	73.4	39.7	14.9
Pretax Income	929	676	514	310	194	-310	104	-91.5	-1.67	23.3
Effective Tax Rate	32.5%	34.0%	31.6%	36.2%	43.9%	NM	81.8%	NM	NM	40.4%
Net Income	627	446	351	203	107	-271	19.2	-54.4	-0.71	13.9
S&P Core Earnings	580	339	247	101	96.1	-291	NA	NA	NA	NA

Balance Sheet & Other Financial Data (Million $)	2006	2005	2004	2003	2002	2001	2000	1999	1998	1997
Total Assets	53,739	44,568	31,033	26,049	21,534	18,172	17,317	3,927	1,969	990
Cash Items	1,212	844	940	921	2,223	1,601	301	189	26.8	36.8
Receivables	7,636	7,174	3,035	2,298	1,500	2,139	6,543	2,913	1,310	728
Securities Owned	13,922	12,565	12,589	9,876	8,702	4,726	985	189	503	191
Securities Borrowed	Nil	Nil	Nil	Nil	Nil	Nil	NA	NA	NA	NA
Due Brokers & Customers	7,825	7,316	3,619	3,696	2,792	2,700	6,056	2,824	1,185	681
Other Liabilities	34.6	38.1	52.2	79.3	775	818	471	189	73.8	18.1
Capitalization:Debt	7,166	6,189	586	695	907	605	3,336	Nil	Nil	9.40
Capitalization:Equity	4,196	3,400	2,228	1,918	1,506	1,571	1,857	914	710	281
Capitalization:Total	11,363	9,589	2,814	2,614	2,412	2,175	5,192	914	710	291
% Return on Revenue	20.7	68.4	18.0	11.8	5.4	NM	1.6	NM	NM	8.8
% Return on Assets	1.3	1.2	1.2	0.9	0.5	NM	0.2	NM	NM	2.2
% Return on Equity	16.5	15.9	16.9	11.9	7.0	NM	1.2	NM	NM	7.9

Data as orig reptd.; bef. results of disc opers/spec. items. Per share data adj. for stk. divs.; EPS diluted. E-Estimated. NA-Not Available. NM-Not Meaningful. NR-Not Ranked. UR-Under Review.

Office: 135 E 57th St, New York, NY 10022-2050.
Telephone: 646-521-4300.
Email: ir@etrade.com
Website: http://www.etrade.com

Chrmn: G. Hayter
Pres & COO: R.J. Lilien
CEO: M. Caplan
CFO: R.J. Simmons

Chief Admin Officer: A.W. Gelbard
Board Members: D. Brewster, M. H. Caplan, R. D. Fisher, G. Hayter, R. J. Lilien, M. K. Parks, C. C. Raffaeli, L. E. Randall, D. L. Weaver, S. H. Willard

Founded: 1982
Domicile: Delaware
Employees: 4,126

Equifax Inc.

STANDARD &POOR'S

S&P Recommendation HOLD ★★★☆☆	**Price** $37.17 (as of Nov 23, 2007)	**12-Mo. Target Price** $43.00	**Investment Style** Large-Cap Growth

GICS Sector Industrials
Sub-Industry Diversified Commercial & Professional Services

Summary This company is a leading worldwide source of consumer and commercial credit information.

Key Stock Statistics (Source S&P, Vickers, company reports)

52-Wk Range	$46.30– 35.22	S&P Oper. EPS 2007**E**	2.30	Market Capitalization(B)	$4.900	Beta	1.37
Trailing 12-Month EPS	$2.03	S&P Oper. EPS 2008**E**	2.55	Yield (%)	0.43	S&P 3-Yr. Proj. EPS CAGR(%)	12.00
Trailing 12-Month P/E	18.3	P/E on S&P Oper. EPS 2007**E**	16.2	Dividend Rate/Share	$0.16	S&P Credit Rating	BBB+
$10K Invested 5 Yrs Ago	$15,126	Common Shares Outstg. (M)	131.8	Institutional Ownership (%)	87		

Price Performance

30-Week Mov. Avg. ··· 10-Week Mov. Avg. -- **GAAP Earnings vs. Previous Year** **Volume** Above Avg. STARS
12-Mo. Target Price — Relative Strength — ▲ Up ▼ Down ▶ No Change Below Avg. ★

Options: ASE, P, Ph

Analysis prepared by **Zaineb Bokhari** on October 24, 2007, when the stock traded at **$37.40.**

Highlights

➤ We expect revenues to rise 19% in 2007, to about $1.84 billion, aided by the recent acquisition of TALX (May 2007), organic growth, and geographic expansion. We expect EFX to pursue additional strategic acquisitions to broaden its geographic reach and expand its existing markets. We project 2008 revenue growth of approximately 13%.

➤ EFX recently realigned and flattened its organizational structure, and while we expect these changes to yield cost savings, we see operating margins narrowing to about 26% in 2007, from 28% in 2006, affected by the acquisition of TALX. We expect operating margins to widen modestly in 2008 as the company continues to invest in future growth opportunities to achieve its stated 7%-10% (organic) revenue growth targets through 2010.

➤ After higher interest expense following issuance/assumption of debt related to the acquisition of TALX, and a higher share count, we estimate operating EPS of $2.30 in 2007 (before amortization of acquisition-related intangibles), up from $2.12 reported for 2006; we estimate EPS of $2.55 in 2008.

Investment Rationale/Risk

➤ We believe that rising consumer awareness of identity theft and the importance of protecting credit information will benefit the company. International markets should offer attractive avenues for growth, in our view, particularly in the U.K. and Latin America. Nevertheless, EFX's slowest growing segment, U.S. Consumer Information Solutions, remains the largest contributor to total revenues (50% in the September 2007 quarter), and retains the highest operating margins. We look for a rising revenue contribution in 2007 and 2008 from acquisitions, including TALX, but expect this to hurt operating margins near term. We are optimistic about new products, including VantageScore.

➤ Risks to our recommendation and target price include increasing competition from the other major credit bureaus and data providers. We are also concerned about a further slowdown in the company's North American mortgage reporting and direct and credit marketing segments.

➤ Our 12-month target price of $43 is derived by applying a 17X P/E to our 2008 EPS estimate, within the average historical range for EFX of 13.3X to 18.0X.

Qualitative Risk Assessment

LOW	MEDIUM	HIGH

Our risk assessment reflects our view that the majority of the company's domestic operations are relatively mature, offset by our positive outlook for its European and Latin American operations, which we see growing faster than its domestic operations.

Quantitative Evaluations

S&P Quality Ranking B+

D	C	B-	B	B+	A-	A	A+

Relative Strength Rank MODERATE

64

LOWEST = 1   HIGHEST = 99

Revenue/Earnings Data

Revenue (Million $)

	1Q	2Q	3Q	4Q	Year
2007	405.1	454.5	492.5	--	--
2006	374.0	387.7	394.6	390.0	1,546
2005	343.4	363.4	375.3	361.3	1,443
2004	309.9	315.4	319.9	327.6	1,273
2003	301.6	317.0	309.8	297.0	1,225
2002	259.0	268.0	289.7	292.6	1,109

Earnings Per Share ($)

2007	0.54	0.51	0.48	E0.61	E2.30
2006	0.48	0.53	0.61	0.50	2.12
2005	0.44	0.47	0.47	0.48	1.86
2004	0.38	0.58	0.40	0.42	1.78
2003	0.33	0.36	0.39	0.23	1.31
2002	0.30	0.34	0.36	0.38	1.39

Fiscal year ended Dec. 31. Next earnings report expected: Early February. EPS Estimates based on S&P Operating Earnings; historical GAAP earnings are as reported.

Dividend Data (Dates: mm/dd Payment Date: mm/dd/yy)

Amount ($)	Date Decl.	Ex-Div. Date	Stk. of Record	Payment Date
0.040	02/07	02/20	02/22	03/15/07
0.040	05/04	05/10	05/14	06/15/07
0.040	08/08	08/22	08/24	09/14/07
0.040	11/07	11/20	11/23	12/14/07

Dividends have been paid since 1914. Source: Company reports.

The McGraw-Hill Companies

Equifax Inc.

Business Summary October 24, 2007

CORPORATE OVERVIEW. Equifax is one of three global providers of consumer and commercial credit information. Equifax collects, organizes and manages credit, financial, demographic and marketing information regarding individuals and businesses, which the company collects from various sources. These sources include financial or credit granting institutions (which provide accounts receivable information), government organizations and consumers. The company maintains information in proprietary databases regarding approximately 400 million consumers and businesses worldwide. EFX amasses and processes this data using proprietary systems, and makes the data available to customers in various formats.

Products and services include consumer credit information, information database management, marketing information, business credit information, decisioning and analytical tools, and identity verification services that enable businesses to make informed decisions about extending credit or providing services, managing portfolio risk, and developing marketing strategies. According to the company, EFX allows consumers to manage and protect their financial affairs through products that the company sells directly to individuals using the Internet. Geographically, the company is becoming increasingly diverse; in 2006, it operated 14 countries.

Equifax derived 80% of operating revenue from North America in 2006, down from 81% in 2005 and 82% in 2004. The company's largest segment, U.S. Consumer Information Services (63% of revenues in 2006, down from 65% in 2005), includes Consumer Information Services (credit information regarding individuals, 40% of 2006 revenues, down from 41%), Mortgage Reporting Solutions (credit loan origination information, 7%, 7%) Credit Marketing Services (11%, 10%) and Direct Marketing Services (7%, 7%). Other North American operating segments include Personal Solutions (credit information sales to consumers, 8%, 8%) and Commercial Solutions (credit information concerning businesses 3%, 3%). EFX's Canadian consumer business contributed 6% of total revenues in 2006 and 2005.

Company Financials Fiscal Year Ended Dec. 31

Per Share Data ($)	2006	2005	2004	2003	2002	2001	2000	1999	1998	1997
Tangible Book Value	NM	NM	NM	NM	NM	NM	NM	NM	NM	NM
Cash Flow	2.76	2.49	2.39	2.00	1.96	1.61	2.77	2.44	2.06	1.78
Earnings	2.12	1.86	1.78	1.31	1.39	0.84	1.68	1.55	1.34	1.25
S&P Core Earnings	2.07	1.88	1.59	1.18	1.04	0.52	NA	NA	NA	NA
Dividends	0.16	0.15	0.11	0.08	0.08	0.25	0.37	0.36	0.35	0.35
Payout Ratio	8%	8%	6%	6%	6%	29%	22%	23%	26%	28%
Prices:High	41.64	39.00	28.46	27.59	31.30	38.76	36.50	39.88	45.00	37.19
Prices:Low	30.15	26.97	22.60	17.84	18.95	18.60	19.88	20.13	29.75	26.50
P/E Ratio:High	20	21	16	21	23	46	22	26	34	30
P/E Ratio:Low	14	14	13	14	14	22	12	13	22	21

Income Statement Analysis (Million $)										
Revenue	1,546	1,443	1,273	1,225	1,109	1,139	1,966	1,773	1,621	1,366
Operating Income	519	504	459	438	432	420	604	540	469	401
Depreciation	82.8	82.2	81.1	95.3	80.5	106	149	125	104	77.1
Interest Expense	31.9	35.6	34.9	39.6	41.2	47.8	76.0	61.0	42.7	20.8
Pretax Income	420	396	388	286	317	205	385	366	327	323
Effective Tax Rate	33.6%	36.5%	38.1%	36.5%	39.0%	41.7%	40.8%	41.0%	40.9%	42.6%
Net Income	275	247	237	179	191	117	228	216	193	186
S&P Core Earnings	268	248	211	162	146	73.6	NA	NA	NA	NA

Balance Sheet & Other Financial Data (Million $)										
Cash	67.8	37.5	52.1	39.3	30.5	33.2	89.4	137	90.6	52.3
Current Assets	345	280	300	286	286	358	605	609	520	401
Total Assets	1,791	1,832	1,557	1,553	1,507	1,423	2,070	1,840	1,829	1,177
Current Liabilities	582	295	457	355	428	276	426	505	419	328
Long Term Debt	174	464	399	663	691	694	994	934	869	339
Common Equity	838	820	524	372	221	244	384	393	366	349
Total Capital	1,083	1,410	961	1,079	938	1,026	1,467	1,400	1,286	688
Capital Expenditures	52.0	17.2	16.5	14.6	12.8	13.0	37.1	39.0	44.9	34.5
Cash Flow	357	329	318	274	272	224	377	341	297	263
Current Ratio	0.6	1.0	0.7	0.8	0.7	1.3	1.4	1.2	1.2	1.2
% Long Term Debt of Capitalization	16.1	32.9	41.5	61.5	73.7	67.6	67.7	66.7	67.6	49.2
% Net Income of Revenue	17.8	17.1	18.6	14.6	17.2	10.3	11.6	12.2	11.9	13.6
% Return on Assets	15.2	14.5	15.3	11.7	13.1	7.1	11.7	11.8	12.9	15.0
% Return on Equity	33.1	36.7	53.0	60.3	82.4	37.4	76.1	49.7	54.0	47.9

Data as orig reptd.; bef. results of disc opers/spec. items. Per share data adj. for stk. divs.; EPS diluted. E-Estimated. NA-Not Available. NM-Not Meaningful. NR-Not Ranked. UR-Under Review.

Office: 1550 Peachtree St NW, Atlanta, GA 30309.
Telephone: 404-885-8000.
Email: investor@equifax.com
Website: http://www.equifax.com

Chrmn & CEO: R.F. Smith
SVP & Cntlr: N.M. King
VP & CFO: L. Adrean
VP & Chief Admin Officer: C.M. Rushing

VP & General Counsel: K.E. Mast
Board Members: J. L. Clendenin, J. E. Copeland, Jr., A. W. Dahlberg, R. D. Daleo, M. A. Feidler, L. P. Humann, L. A. Kennedy, S. S. Marshall, L. L. Prince, R. F. Smith, J. M. Ward

Founded: 1913
Domicile: Georgia
Employees: 4,960

Equity Residential

STANDARD &POOR'S

S&P Recommendation **SELL** ★★	Price $36.92 (as of Nov 23, 2007)	12-Mo. Target Price $36.00	Investment Style Large-Cap Value

GICS Sector Financials
Sub-Industry Residential REITs

Summary This equity real estate investment trust (formerly Equity Residential Properties Trust) owns and operates a nationally diversified portfolio of apartment properties.

Key Stock Statistics (Source S&P, Vickers, company reports)

52-Wk Range	$56.46–35.00	S&P FFO/Sh. 2007E	2.30	Market Capitalization(B)	$10.008	Beta	0.97
Trailing 12-Month FFO/Share	NA	S&P FFO/Sh. 2008E	2.45	Yield (%)	5.01	S&P 3-Yr. FFO/Sh. Proj. CAGR(%)	3.00
Trailing 12-Month P/FFO	NA	P/FFO on S&P FFO/Sh. 2007E	16.1	Dividend Rate/Share	$1.85	S&P Credit Rating	A-
$10K Invested 5 Yrs Ago	$18,094	Common Shares Outstg. (M)	271.1	Institutional Ownership (%)	97		

Price Performance

Options: ASE, CBOE, Ph

Analysis prepared by **Royal F. Shepard, CFA** on November 05, 2007, when the stock traded at **$ 38.54**.

Highlights

➤ We think EQR is facing increased competitive supply in several markets, including Florida, Phoenix, and Washington, DC, which are digesting higher supply from the reversion of condo units and single-family home inventories. Third quarter rental growth slowed to 3.7%, year to year, down from 4.6% in the first half of 2007. In our view, this moderating trend will continue into 2008. We estimate property level operating income growth of 3.5%-4.0% in 2008, down from an estimated 4.25% in 2007.

➤ EQR is on track to dispose of $1.75 billion of properties in 2007, with a focus on selling mid-continent properties in less attractive markets such as Texas and Minnesota. We see softer demand for these assets in 2008, in view of tightened credit market conditions. To date, a portion of proceeds has gone toward share repurchases, including $1.1 billion through the first nine months of 2007.

➤ Incorporating some dilution from dispositions, we estimate 2008 FFO of $2.45, up about 6.5% from the $2.30 we estimate for 2007. Based on our outlook for limited cash flow expansion, we do not foresee an increase in EQR's current annual dividend of $1.85 over the next 12 months.

Investment Rationale/Risk

➤ We think rental growth at EQR's established rental properties has begun to slow in the second half of 2007, as new supply from condo reversions has entered some of the trust's markets. We also anticipate a minimum contribution from EQR's own condo conversion program and ongoing dilution from recent asset sales. We think it will take at least another year for EQR to complete its re-positioning toward higher growth coastal markets. Recently trading at about 16X our 2008 FFO estimate, EQR sells about in line with residential peers. We believe a discount is warranted.

➤ Risks to our recommendation and target price include a sharper than expected increase in interest rates contributing to lower single-family home sales, and faster than projected job growth and new household formation.

➤ Our 12-month target price of $36 is based partly on applying a multiple of 15X our 2008 FFO estimate ($37 value), about a 10% discount to peers. We also blend in our dividend discount model, which assumes a 9.5% discount rate and a 4% terminal growth rate, and arrives at intrinsic value of $35.

Qualitative Risk Assessment

LOW	MEDIUM	HIGH

Our risk assessment of EQR reflects our view that it is one of the largest, most diversified residential REITs and has below average financial leverage and moderate stock price volatility.

Quantitative Evaluations

S&P Quality Ranking B+

| D | C | B- | B | B+ | A- | A | A+ |

Relative Strength Rank MODERATE
39
LOWEST = 1   HIGHEST = 99

Revenue/FFO Data

Revenue (Million $)

	1Q	2Q	3Q	4Q	Year
2007	526.2	531.8	527.5	--	--
2006	470.5	490.6	511.5	517.9	1,990
2005	461.6	478.9	495.5	518.9	1,955
2004	443.9	474.7	483.5	487.4	1,890
2003	448.5	455.9	459.4	459.5	1,823
2002	498.8	502.7	499.6	492.9	1,994

FFO Per Share ($)

2007	0.55	0.60	0.58	E0.57	E2.30
2006	0.56	0.61	0.62	0.49	2.27
2005	0.74	0.56	0.56	0.66	2.52
2004	0.52	0.56	0.50	0.56	2.14
2003	0.57	0.57	0.56	0.45	2.15
2002	0.64	0.63	0.54	0.59	2.46

Fiscal year ended Dec. 31. Next earnings report expected: Early February. FFO Estimates based on S&P Funds From Operations Est..

Dividend Data (Dates: mm/dd Payment Date: mm/dd/yy)

Amount ($)	Date Decl.	Ex-Div. Date	Stk. of Record	Payment Date
0.463	12/12	12/20	12/22	01/12/07
0.463	02/16	03/15	03/19	04/13/07
0.463	05/24	06/14	06/18	07/13/07
0.463	08/17	09/13	09/17	10/12/07

Dividends have been paid since 1993. Source: Company reports.

Equity Residential

Business Summary November 05, 2007

CORPORATE OVERVIEW. Equity Residential is one of the largest publicly held owners of multi-family properties. Structured as a real estate investment trust (REIT), it owns, manages and operates properties through its 93.4% interest in its operating limited partnership. At September 30, 2007, EQR owned or had interests in 584 multi-family properties with 154,152 units in 24 states. The trust adopted its current name in May 2002.

During 2006, EQR sold a majority of its ranch style properties, leaving a focus on garden and mid-rise/high-rise assets. Garden-style properties have two or three floors, while mid-rise/high-rise properties have more than three floors. At the end of September 2007, the trust's largest geographic markets as measured by net operating income were the New York Metro Area (9.9%), South Florida (8.8%), Washington DC/N. Virginia (7.3%), Los Angeles (7.8%) and Seattle/Tacoma (7.0%). Average occupancy during the third quarter of 2007 was 94.6%, even with the same period in 2006.

MARKET PROFILE. The housing market is highly fragmented, and is characterized broadly by two types of housing units -- multi-family and single-family. At the end of 2005, the U.S. Census Bureau estimated that there were 123.93 million housing units in the country. Partly due to the high fragmentation, and the fact that residents have the option of either being owners or tenants (renters),

the housing market can be highly competitive, in our view. Main demand drivers for apartments are household formation and employment growth. S&P expects 1.3 million new households to be formed in 2007, lower than the estimated 1.5 million in 2006. Supply is created by new housing unit construction, which could consist of single-family homes, or multi-family apartment buildings or condominiums. We forecast 1.36 million total housing unit starts in 2007, down about 25% from 2006. We expect multi-family starts to fall somewhat less, declining approximately 15%.

With apartment tenants on relatively short leases compared to those of commercial and industrial properties, we believe apartment REITs are generally more sensitive to changes in market conditions than REITs in other property categories. Results could be hurt by new construction that adds new space in excess of actual demand. Trends in home price affordability also affect both rent levels and the level of new construction, since the relative price attractiveness of owning versus renting is an important factor in consumer decision making.

Company Financials Fiscal Year Ended Dec. 31

Per Share Data ($)	2006	2005	2004	2003	2002	2001	2000	1999	1998	1997
Tangible Book Value	18.58	16.65	15.28	15.43	15.57	16.20	20.82	16.33	16.46	14.74
Earnings	0.20	0.51	0.37	0.43	0.78	1.36	1.67	1.15	0.82	0.88
S&P Core Earnings	0.20	0.51	0.34	0.41	0.72	1.38	NA	NA	NA	NA
Dividends	1.79	1.74	1.73	1.73	1.73	1.68	1.58	1.47	1.36	1.27
Payout Ratio	NM	NM	NM	NM	222%	124%	94%	128%	167%	145%
Prices:High	61.50	42.17	36.75	30.30	30.96	30.45	28.63	24.19	26.28	27.50
Prices:Low	38.84	30.70	26.65	23.12	21.55	24.80	19.34	19.06	17.34	19.88
P/E Ratio:High	NM	83	99	70	40	22	17	21	32	31
P/E Ratio:Low	NM	60	72	54	28	18	12	17	21	23

Income Statement Analysis (Million $)										
Rental Income	1,981	1,944	1,878	1,809	1,970	2,075	1,960	1,712	1,296	708
Mortgage Income	Nil	Nil	Nil	Nil	Nil	8.79	11.2	12.6	18.6	20.4
Total Income	1,990	1,955	1,890	1,823	1,994	2,171	2,030	1,753	1,337	747
General Expenses	881	925	870	802	841	924	812	673	833	291
Interest Expense	436	391	349	333	343	361	388	341	249	124
Provision for Losses	Nil	Nil	Nil	Nil	Nil	Nil	Nil	Nil	Nil	Nil
Depreciation	563	508	484	444	462	457	450	409	302	157
Net Income	101	152	135	212	302	474	555	394	258	177
S&P Core Earnings	59.5	98.5	74.5	86.4	194	374	NA	NA	NA	NA

Balance Sheet & Other Financial Data (Million $)										
Cash	14,477	13,798	83.5	49.6	540	449	417	114	4.00	209
Total Assets	15,062	14,099	12,645	11,467	11,811	12,236	12,264	11,716	10,700	7,095
Real Estate Investment	17,235	16,597	14,864	12,874	13,046	13,016	12,591	12,239	10,942	7,121
Loss Reserve	Nil	Nil	Nil	Nil	Nil	Nil	Nil	Nil	Nil	Nil
Net Investment	14,217	13,709	12,264	10,578	10,934	11,297	11,239	11,168	10,224	6,677
Short Term Debt	Nil	Nil	Nil	Nil	334	699	Nil	250	151	61.1
Capitalization:Debt	7,136	7,032	5,642	4,836	5,050	5,044	5,706	5,224	4,530	2,887
Capitalization:Equity	5,498	4,891	4,436	4,345	4,251	4,447	4,436	4,195	5,330	3,690
Capitalization:Total	13,432	12,850	10,714	10,452	10,858	11,094	11,938	11,186	9,860	6,851
% Earnings & Depreciation/Assets	4.5	4.9	5.1	5.6	6.4	7.6	8.3	7.2	6.3	6.6
Price Times Book Value:High	3.3	2.5	2.4	2.0	2.0	1.9	1.4	1.5	1.6	1.9
Price Times Book Value:Low	2.1	1.8	1.7	1.5	1.4	1.5	0.9	1.2	1.1	1.3

Data as orig reptd.; bef. results of disc opers/spec. items. Per share data adj. for stk. divs.; EPS diluted. E-Estimated. NA-Not Available. NM-Not Meaningful. NR-Not Ranked. UR-Under Review.

Exelon Corp

S&P Recommendation BUY ★★★★☆

Price	12-Mo. Target Price	Investment Style
$80.64 (as of Nov 23, 2007)	$90.00	Large-Cap Blend

GICS Sector Utilities
Sub-Industry Electric Utilities

Summary This holding company for Philadelphia-based PECO Energy and Chicago-based ComEd terminated its merger agreement with New Jersey-based Public Service Enterprise Group in September 2006.

Key Stock Statistics (Source S&P, Vickers, company reports)

52-Wk Range	$84.92–58.74	S&P Oper. EPS 2007E	4.30	Market Capitalization(B)	$54.365	Beta	0.27
Trailing 12-Month EPS	$4.07	S&P Oper. EPS 2008E	4.70	Yield (%)	2.18	S&P 3-Yr. Proj. EPS CAGR(%)	16.00
Trailing 12-Month P/E	19.8	P/E on S&P Oper. EPS 2007E	18.8	Dividend Rate/Share	$1.76	S&P Credit Rating	BBB+
$10K Invested 5 Yrs Ago	$37,532	Common Shares Outstg. (M)	674.2	Institutional Ownership (%)	69		

Price Performance

30-Week Mov. Avg. · · · 10-Week Mov. Avg. – – **GAAP Earnings vs. Previous Year**   Volume Above Avg. STARS
12-Mo. Target Price — Relative Strength — ▲ Up ▼ Down ► No Change   Below Avg.

Options: ASE, CBOE, P, Ph

Analysis prepared by **Justin McCann** on November 20, 2007, when the stock traded at **$ 81.16**.

Highlights

➤ We expect EPS in 2007 to advance more than 33% from 2006 operating EPS of $3.22. We project that the non-regulated Generation segment will contribute about $3.67, PECO Energy around $0.63, and ComEd roughly $0.10. This should be partially offset by a projected loss of about $0.10 from the holding company.

➤ For 2008, we expect operating EPS to increase approximately 9% from anticipated results in 2007, driven by expected continued margin expansion at the nuclear operations.

➤ On August 28, 2007, the governor of Illinois signed Senate Bill 1592, which outlined the electric rate compromise reached among state legislators, the attorney general, the state's utilities and power marketers. Under the terms of the agreement, Exelon will contribute $800 million to a $1 billion fund for rate relief programs aimed at mitigating the effect of the rate increases that went into effect on January 2, 2007. The compromise agreement was reached after months of intense public and political pressure aimed at rolling back the increased rates to 2006 levels, and then freezing them for a three-year period.

Investment Rationale/Risk

➤ With the Illinois governor's signing of Senate Bill 1592, the uncertainties that surrounded the electric rate settlement agreement were removed. Although Exelon will have to provide $800 million in rate credits over the next few years, this was clearly preferable, we believe, to the electric rate rollback and freeze legislation the governor and the state attorney general had been strongly fighting for. We expect the stock to continue to benefit from the strength of its non-regulated operations.

➤ Risks to our recommendation and target price include the possibility of an economic recession, sharply reduced wholesale power margins, and a sharp decline in the average P/E of the group as a whole.

➤ Although the dividend yield (recently about 2.2%) is well below the peer average for electric and gas utilities, it is roughly in line with utility holding companies that have non-regulated operations with above-peers' consolidated earnings growth. We think this growth should enable the shares to trade at a premium-to-peers' P/E of about 19X our EPS estimate for 2008. Our 12-month target price is $90.

Qualitative Risk Assessment

LOW	MEDIUM	HIGH

Our risk assessment reflects our view of Exelon's strong and steady cash flow from the regulated PECO Energy and ComEd utilities, as well as the healthy earnings and cash flow from very profitable but higher-risk power generating and energy marketing operations.

Quantitative Evaluations

S&P Quality Ranking   B+

D	C	B-	B	B+	A-	A	A+

Relative Strength Rank   STRONG
88
LOWEST = 1   HIGHEST = 99

Revenue/Earnings Data

Revenue (Million $)

	1Q	2Q	3Q	4Q	Year
2007	4,829	4,501	5,032	--	--
2006	3,861	3,697	4,401	3,696	15,655
2005	3,561	3,484	4,473	3,838	15,357
2004	3,722	3,550	3,865	3,378	14,515
2003	4,074	3,721	4,441	3,577	15,812
2002	3,357	3,519	4,370	3,709	14,955

Earnings Per Share ($)

	1Q	2Q	3Q	4Q	Year
2007	1.01	1.03	1.15	E1.03	E4.30
2006	0.59	0.95	-0.07	0.87	2.35
2005	0.77	0.76	1.07	-1.19	1.40
2004	0.57	0.78	0.86	0.54	2.75
2003	0.39	0.57	-0.16	0.42	1.20
2002	0.37	0.75	0.75	0.61	2.58

Fiscal year ended Dec. 31. Next earnings report expected: Late January. EPS Estimates based on S&P Operating Earnings; historical GAAP earnings are as reported.

Dividend Data (Dates: mm/dd Payment Date: mm/dd/yy)

Amount ($)	Date Decl.	Ex-Div. Date	Stk. of Record	Payment Date
0.440	12/14	02/13	02/15	03/10/07
0.440	02/27	05/11	05/15	06/11/07
0.440	07/24	08/13	08/15	09/10/07
0.440	10/23	11/13	11/15	12/10/07

Dividends have been paid since 1902. Source: Company reports.

Please read the Required Disclosures and Analyst Certification on the last page of this report.

The McGraw-Hill Companies

Exelon Corp

STANDARD
&POOR'S

Business Summary November 20, 2007

CORPORATE OVERVIEW. Exelon Corp. was formed in October 2000 through the acquisition by Philadelphia-based PECO Energy of Chicago-based Unicom Corp. The company, along with its subsidiaries, is engaged in the energy delivery, generation and other businesses. Exelon operates in three business segments: ComEd (Commonwealth Edison), PECO, and Generation. Segment contributions to 2006 net income were: ComEd, after a goodwill impairment charge of $776 million, a loss of $112 million (compared to a loss of $676 million in 2005, on a goodwill impairment charge of $1,207 million); PECO, $441 million ($520 million); Generation, $1,403 million ($1,109 million); and other, a loss of $142 million (a loss of $2 million).

IMPACT OF MAJOR DEVELOPMENTS. On September 14, 2006, the company and Public Service Enterprise Group (PEG) announced the termination of the merger agreement that had been announced on December 20, 2004. If the

merger had been completed, the combined company would have been the largest electric utility, the seventh biggest gas utility, and one of the largest power generators in the U.S. With the expiration of Exelon's nuclear services contract with PEG set to expire in January 2007, PEG hired the senior leaders from the Exelon team, and, effective January 1, 2007, resumed the direct management of its nuclear plants. Although we were disappointed that a settlement could not be reached with the New Jersey Board of Public Utilities (BPU), we believe the rate concessions and additional power plant divestitures demanded by the BPU would have significantly diluted many of the benefits of the proposed transaction.

Company Financials Fiscal Year Ended Dec. 31

Per Share Data ($)	2006	2005	2004	2003	2002	2001	2000	1999	1998	1997
Tangible Book Value	11.08	8.48	7.10	5.77	4.26	4.51	3.18	4.57	6.81	6.13
Earnings	2.35	1.40	2.75	1.20	2.58	2.20	1.44	1.58	1.16	0.72
S&P Core Earnings	3.49	3.01	2.79	1.74	1.64	1.49	NA	NA	NA	NA
Dividends	2.00	1.60	1.53	0.96	0.88	0.91	0.46	0.50	0.50	0.90
Payout Ratio	85%	114%	56%	80%	34%	41%	32%	32%	43%	125%
Prices:High	63.62	57.46	44.90	33.31	28.50	35.13	35.50	25.25	21.09	13.19
Prices:Low	51.13	41.77	30.92	23.04	18.92	19.38	16.50	15.38	9.44	9.38
P/E Ratio:High	27	41	16	28	11	16	25	16	18	18
P/E Ratio:Low	22	30	11	19	7	9	11	10	8	13

Income Statement Analysis (Million $)										
Revenue	15,655	15,357	14,515	15,812	14,955	15,140	7,499	5,437	5,210	4,618
Depreciation	1,487	1,334	1,305	1,126	1,340	1,449	458	237	643	581
Maintenance	NA	NA	NA	NA	NA	NA	NA	NA	NA	NA
Fixed Charges Coverage	5.19	4.88	3.94	2.19	3.56	2.98	2.94	3.24	3.52	2.41
Construction Credits	NA	NA	NA	NA	NA	NA	Nil	4.00	3.52	21.8
Effective Tax Rate	43.1%	49.8%	27.5%	29.4%	37.4%	39.7%	27.3%	36.6%	37.5%	46.5%
Net Income	1,590	951	1,841	793	1,670	1,416	907	619	532	337
S&P Core Earnings	2,358	2,035	1,865	1,142	1,062	962	NA	NA	NA	NA

Balance Sheet & Other Financial Data (Million $)										
Gross Property	30,025	29,853	28,711	27,578	25,904	21,526	19,886	9,412	7,228	6,574
Capital Expenditures	2,418	2,165	1,921	1,954	2,150	2,041	752	491	415	490
Net Property	22,775	21,981	21,482	20,630	17,134	13,742	12,936	5,045	4,337	3,884
Capitalization:Long Term Debt	11,998	11,760	12,235	13,576	14,580	13,492	14,398	6,098	3,269	4,325
Capitalization:% Long Term Debt	54.6	56.3	56.5	61.5	65.3	62.1	66.6	75.6	49.9	59.4
Capitalization:Preferred	Nil	Nil	Nil	Nil	Nil	Nil	Nil	193	230	230
Capitalization:% Preferred	Nil	Nil	Nil	Nil	Nil	Nil	Nil	2.39	3.51	3.20
Capitalization:Common	9,973	9,125	9,423	8,503	7,742	8,230	7,215	1,773	3,057	3,079
Capitalization:% Common	45.4	43.7	43.5	38.5	34.7	37.9	33.4	22.0	46.6	37.4
Total Capital	27,395	25,964	26,463	26,724	26,325	26,341	26,352	10,760	9,233	9,897
% Operating Ratio	80.3	80.5	81.1	82.2	73.1	83.9	80.5	80.7	81.5	84.6
% Earned on Net Property	15.7	12.5	16.3	11.4	21.3	25.2	17.0	28.6	31.2	14.4
% Return on Revenue	10.2	6.2	12.7	5.0	11.2	9.4	12.1	11.4	10.2	7.3
% Return on Invested Capital	12.1	11.4	10.3	10.2	10.2	9.8	9.8	10.3	14.3	6.3
% Return on Common Equity	16.7	10.2	20.5	9.8	21.1	18.3	20.2	25.1	16.9	8.0

Data as orig reptd.; bef. results of disc opers/spec. items. Per share data adj. for stk. divs.; EPS diluted. E-Estimated. NA-Not Available. NM-Not Meaningful. NR-Not Ranked. UR-Under Review.

Office: 10 S Dearborn St, Chicago, IL 60603-2300.
Telephone: 312-394-7398.
Website: http://www.exeloncorp.com
Chrmn, Pres & CEO: J.W. Rowe

Investor Contact: J.F. Young (866-530-8108)
EVP & CFO: J.F. Young
EVP, Chief Admin Officer & Chief Lgl Officer: R.E. Mehrberg
SVP & Treas: M. Metzner

Board Members: E. A. Brennan, M. W. D'Alessio, N. DeBenedictis, B. DeMars, N. A. Diaz, S. L. Gin, R. B. Greco, E. D. Jannotta, J. M. Palms, W. Richardson, T. Ridge, J. W. Rogers, Jr., R. Rubin, S. D. Steinour, R. L. Thomas, D. Thompson

Founded: 1887
Domicile: Pennsylvania
Employees: 17,200

The McGraw-Hill Companies

Expedia Inc

STANDARD &POOR'S

S&P Recommendation HOLD ★★★☆☆	**Price** $29.35 (as of Nov 23, 2007)	**12-Mo. Target Price** $32.00	**Investment Style** Large-Cap Blend

GICS Sector Consumer Discretionary
Sub-Industry Internet Retail

Summary Expedia is one of the world's largest online travel-services companies. Businesses include Expedia, Hotels.com, Hotwire and TripAdvisor.

Key Stock Statistics (Source S&P, Vickers, company reports)

52-Wk Range	$35.28– 17.98	S&P Oper. EPS 2007**E**	1.01	Market Capitalization(B)	$7.599	Beta	2.92
Trailing 12-Month EPS	$0.92	S&P Oper. EPS 2008**E**	1.29	Yield (%)	Nil	S&P 3-Yr. Proj. EPS CAGR(%)	20.00
Trailing 12-Month P/E	31.9	P/E on S&P Oper. EPS 2007**E**	29.1	Dividend Rate/Share	Nil	S&P Credit Rating	BB
$10K Invested 5 Yrs Ago	NA	Common Shares Outstg. (M)	284.5	Institutional Ownership (%)	88		

Price Performance

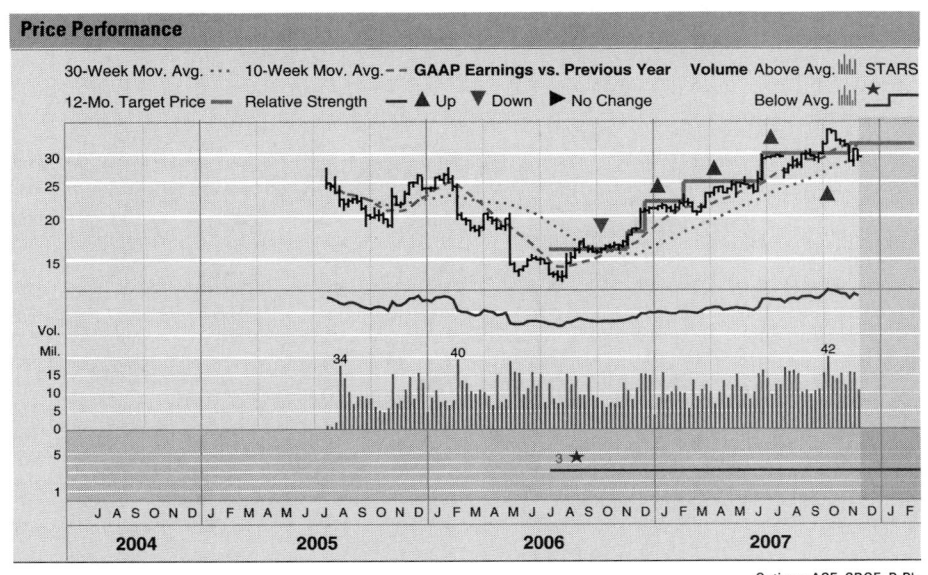

30-Week Mov. Avg. ···   10-Week Mov. Avg.- -   **GAAP Earnings vs. Previous Year**   Volume Above Avg. STARS
12-Mo. Target Price —   Relative Strength —   ▲ Up   ▼ Down   ▶ No Change   Below Avg.   ★

Options: ASE, CBOE, P, Ph

Analysis prepared by **Scott H. Kessler** on November 15, 2007, when the stock traded at **$ 29.04.**

Highlights

➤ We believe EXPE is among the worldwide leaders in the Internet travel segment and will benefit from the continuing migration of associated purchases online. We forecast revenue growth of 15% in 2007 and 13% in 2008, reflecting notable international success, a healthy domestic business, and competition from other online travel agencies, travel suppliers, and emerging market participants.

➤ We estimate that annual operating income before amortization (OIBA) and net margins bottomed in 2006, partly due to considerable sales and marketing expenses and technology investments, which we expect to yield benefits in 2007 and 2008. We are forecasting improvements in these margins in 2007 and 2008.

➤ In June 2007, EXPE announced a tender offer to repurchase up to 117 million shares from $27.50 to $30. However, credit-market uncertainties caused EXPE to reduce the size of this potential repurchase to up 25 million shares (8% of the shares outstanding as of June 2007). EXPE had $446 million in net cash and investments as of September 2007, including $500 million in long-term debt.

Investment Rationale/Risk

➤ We believe that EXPE has some of the Internet's best known travel franchises, strong international operations, and a healthy domestic business. We also think it has done a good job over the last few quarters at seizing upon opportunities and executing. However, we believe the company faces many challenges, including a maturing online travel market in the U.S. and significant competition. We see the stock as fairly valued.

➤ Risks to our recommendation and target price include a notable weakening of global or domestic consumer sentiment or spending, and increasing competitive or pricing pressures.

➤ EXPE's P/E and P/E-to-growth multiples were recently higher than those of other publicly traded online travel companies, and such comparisons lead to a value of about $23. Our discounted cash flow assumptions include a WACC of 14.2%, annual free cash flow growth averaging 13% over the next five years, and a perpetuity growth rate of 3%, and leads to an intrinsic value of $38. Weighting these methodologies results in our 12-month target price of $32.

Qualitative Risk Assessment

LOW	MEDIUM	HIGH

Our risk assessment reflects what we believe is a maturing online travel market in the U.S., an intensely competitive landscape, and relatively low barriers to entry.

Quantitative Evaluations

S&P Quality Ranking   NR

D	C	B-	B	B+	A-	A	A+

Relative Strength Rank   MODERATE

57

LOWEST = 1   HIGHEST = 99

Revenue/Earnings Data

Revenue (Million $)

	1Q	2Q	3Q	4Q	Year
2007	550.5	689.9	759.6	--	--
2006	493.9	598.5	613.9	531.3	2,238
2005	485.1	555.0	584.1	494.8	2,119
2004	413.3	487.0	503.8	439.0	1,843
2003	--	--	--	--	--
2002	--	--	--	--	--

Earnings Per Share ($)

2007	0.11	0.30	0.32	E0.23	E1.01
2006	0.06	0.27	0.17	0.20	0.70
2005	--	--	0.23	0.07	0.65
2004	--	--	--	--	0.37
2003	--	--	--	--	--
2002	--	--	--	--	--

Fiscal year ended Dec. 31. Next earnings report expected: Mid February. EPS Estimates based on S&P Operating Earnings; historical GAAP earnings are as reported.

Dividend Data

No cash dividends have been paid.

Please read the Required Disclosures and Analyst Certification on the last page of this report.

The *McGraw-Hill* Companies

Expedia Inc

Business Summary November 15, 2007

CORPORATE OVERVIEW. Expedia, Inc. leverages its portfolio of brands to target a broad range of travelers interested in different travel options. EXPE provides a wide selection of travel products and services, from simple discounted travel, to more complex luxury trips. The company's offerings primarily include airline tickets, hotel reservations, car rentals, cruise arrangements, and destination services.

The company's localized Expedia-branded Web sites (focused on the U.S., as well as Australia, Canada, France, Germany, Italy, the Netherlands, and the U.K.) offer a large variety of travel products and services. Expedia Web sites also serve as the travel channel on MSN.com. Expedia Corporate Travel is a full-service travel management firm available to corporate travelers in the U.S., Canada, and Europe. Hotels.com provides a multitude of lodging options to travelers, from traditional hotels, to vacation rentals. Part of Hotels.com's strategy is to position itself as a hotel expert offering premium content about

lodging properties. These businesses are planning to provide other travel products and services. Hotwire.com is a discount travel Web site that offers deals to travelers willing to make purchases without knowing certain itinerary details such as brand, time of departure, and hotel address. TripAdvisor is an online travel content destination, with search and directory features, guidebook reviews, and user opinions.

In December 2004, IAC/InterActiveCorp (IACI) announced a plan to spin off what became EXPE. In August 2005, EXPE was spun off as a separate publicly traded company.

Company Financials Fiscal Year Ended Dec. 31

Per Share Data ($)	2006	2005	2004	2003	2002	2001	2000	1999	1998	1997
Tangible Book Value	NM	NM	NA	NA	NA	NA	NA	NA	NA	NA
Cash Flow	1.40	1.82	NA	NA	NA	NA	NA	NA	NA	NA
Earnings	0.70	0.65	0.37	NA	NA	NA	NA	NA	NA	NA
S&P Core Earnings	0.79	0.69	0.48	0.27	0.26	-1.04	NA	NA	NA	NA
Dividends	Nil	Nil	NA	NA	NA	NA	NA	NA	NA	NA
Payout Ratio	Nil	Nil	NA	NA	NA	NA	NA	NA	NA	NA
Prices:High	27.55	27.50	NA	NA	NA	NA	NA	NA	NA	NA
Prices:Low	12.87	18.49	NA	NA	NA	NA	NA	NA	NA	NA
P/E Ratio:High	39	42	NA	NA	NA	NA	NA	NA	NA	NA
P/E Ratio:Low	18	28	NA	NA	NA	NA	NA	NA	NA	NA

Income Statement Analysis (Million $)	2006	2005	2004	2003	2002	2001	2000	1999	1998	1997
Revenue	2,238	2,119	1,843	NA	NA	NA	NA	NA	NA	NA
Operating Income	648	678	NA	NA	NA	NA	NA	NA	NA	NA
Depreciation	249	407	NA	NA	NA	NA	NA	NA	NA	NA
Interest Expense	17.3	Nil	7.45	NA	NA	NA	NA	NA	NA	NA
Pretax Income	385	414	219	NA	NA	NA	NA	NA	NA	NA
Effective Tax Rate	36.2%	44.9%	40.0%	NA	NA	NA	NA	NA	NA	NA
Net Income	245	229	131	NA	NA	NA	NA	NA	NA	NA
S&P Core Earnings	275	244	163	92.3	34.2	-98.1	NA	NA	NA	NA

Balance Sheet & Other Financial Data (Million $)	2006	2005	2004	2003	2002	2001	2000	1999	1998	1997
Cash	853	297	232	NA	NA	NA	NA	NA	NA	NA
Current Assets	1,183	590	569	NA	NA	NA	NA	NA	NA	NA
Total Assets	8,269	7,757	7,803	NA	NA	NA	NA	NA	NA	NA
Current Liabilities	1,400	1,438	1,515	NA	NA	NA	NA	NA	NA	NA
Long Term Debt	500	Nil	NA	NA	NA	NA	NA	NA	NA	NA
Common Equity	5,904	5,734	5,820	NA	NA	NA	NA	NA	NA	NA
Total Capital	6,835	6,174	NA	NA	NA	NA	NA	NA	NA	NA
Capital Expenditures	92.6	52.3	NA	NA	NA	NA	NA	NA	NA	NA
Cash Flow	494	636	NA	NA	NA	NA	NA	NA	NA	NA
Current Ratio	0.8	0.4	0.4	NA	NA	NA	NA	NA	NA	NA
% Long Term Debt of Capitalization	7.3	Nil	NA	NA	NA	NA	NA	NA	NA	NA
% Net Income of Revenue	10.9	10.8	7.1	NA	NA	NA	NA	NA	NA	NA
% Return on Assets	3.1	2.6	NA	NA	NA	NA	NA	NA	NA	NA
% Return on Equity	4.2	3.3	NA	NA	NA	NA	NA	NA	NA	NA

Data as orig reptd.; bef. results of disc opers/spec. items. Per share data adj. for stk. divs.; EPS diluted. E-Estimated. NA-Not Available. NM-Not Meaningful. NR-Not Ranked. UR-Under Review.

Office: 3150 139th Avenue SE, Bellevue, WA 98005-4046.
Telephone: 425-679-7200.
Website: http://www.expedia.com
Chrmn: B. Diller

Vice Chrmn: V.A. Kaufman
CEO: D. Khosrowshahi
SVP, Chief Acctg Officer & Cntlr: P. Zuccotti
SVP & General Counsel: K. Conder

Investor Contact: S. Haas (425-679-7852)
Board Members: A. G. Battle, B. Diller, J. Dolgen, W. R. Fitzgerald, D. Goldhill, V. A. Kaufman, P. Kern, D. Khosrowshahi, J. C. Malone

Founded: 1996
Domicile: Delaware
Employees: 6,600

Expeditors International of Washington Inc

STANDARD &POOR'S

S&P Recommendation **BUY** ★★★★☆	Price $42.72 (as of Nov 26, 2007)	12-Mo. Target Price $60.00	Investment Style Large-Cap Growth

GICS Sector Industrials
Sub-Industry Air Freight & Logistics

Summary This company is a global air and ocean freight forwarder and customs broker.

Key Stock Statistics (Source S&P, Vickers, company reports)

52-Wk Range	$54.46– 38.31	S&P Oper. EPS 2007**E**	1.28	Market Capitalization(B)	$9.104	Beta	0.51
Trailing 12-Month EPS	$1.18	S&P Oper. EPS 2008**E**	1.50	Yield (%)	0.66	S&P 3-Yr. Proj. EPS CAGR(%)	17.00
Trailing 12-Month P/E	36.2	P/E on S&P Oper. EPS 2007**E**	33.4	Dividend Rate/Share	$0.28	S&P Credit Rating	NA
$10K Invested 5 Yrs Ago	$27,700	Common Shares Outstg. (M)	213.1	Institutional Ownership (%)	94		

Price Performance

30-Week Mov. Avg. · · ·   10-Week Mov. Avg. – –   **GAAP Earnings vs. Previous Year**   Volume Above Avg. ▮▮▮ STARS
12-Mo. Target Price —   Relative Strength —   ▲ Up   ▼ Down   ► No Change   Below Avg. ▮▮▮ ★

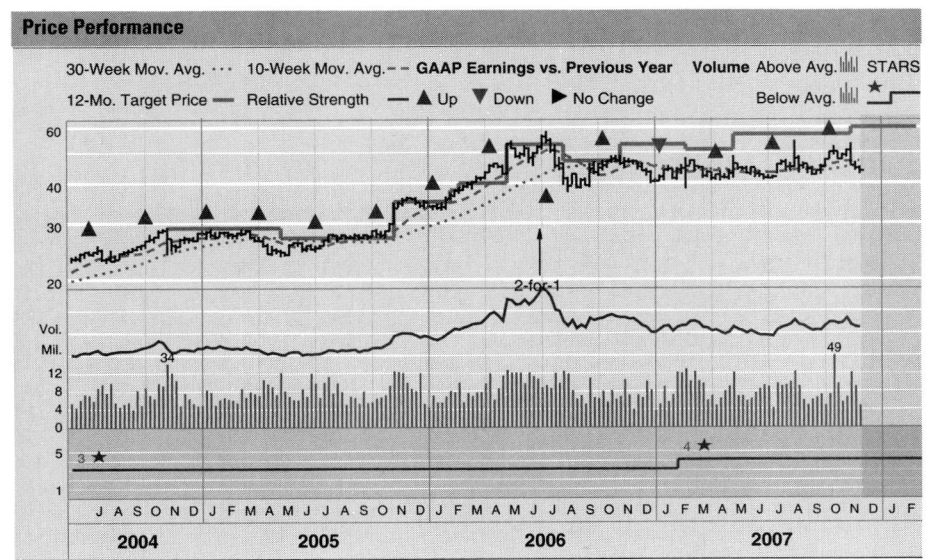

Options: ASE, CBOE, P, Ph

Analysis prepared by **Jim Corridore** on November 26, 2007, when the stock traded at **$ 43.28.**

Highlights

➤ We expect 2008 net revenues to advance about 12%, following our forecast of 13% growth in 2007. Revenue growth in both periods should be led by higher volumes in air and ocean freight. We expect EXPD to continue to experience strong demand in Europe and Asia, reflecting strengthening economies in these regions, and robust shipping activity in the U.S. We project that airfreight and ocean freight customs revenues will rise about 9% in 2008 and 14% in 2007, and we see customs brokerage revenues increasing about 12% and 15%, respectively.

➤ We expect margins to benefit from the leveraging of a higher revenue base to decrease payroll, rents and selling costs as a percentage of revenues. We think that new ocean freight capacity, which has come on line in the past year, could drive ocean freight transportation costs lower, which we think could allow for additional margin expansion opportunities in 2008

➤ Including estimated stock option expense of $0.20, we forecast 2008 operating EPS of $1.50, which would represent about 17% growth over our 2007 EPS estimate of $1.28.

Investment Rationale/Risk

➤ EXPD's stock has come down from its 52-week high and was recently trading well below our 12-month target price. We think the shares will benefit from stronger than industry average net revenue growth that we expect. While the logistics sector would likely suffer if the U.S. economy slows versus current expectations, we think EXPD's strong international revenue base will allow it to outperform peers. A debt-free balance sheet and what we view as strong projected long-term earnings and cash flow growth are additional positives.

➤ Risks to our recommendation and target price include the potential impact of a sharp economic slowdown. We also see management's communication style, in which it mainly answers questions through 8-K filings, as a risk, in that it may not allow investors to react fast enough to potentially important news.

➤ The shares recently traded at about 29X our 2008 EPS estimate. Our 12-month target price of $60 values the stock at 40X our 2008 EPS estimate of $1.50, in the middle of EXPD's five-year historical P/E range of 24.1X-54.5X EPS.

Qualitative Risk Assessment

LOW	MEDIUM	HIGH

Our risk assessment reflects that EXPD operates in a highly cyclical industry and is exposed to currency and global economic risk. We see its communication style as an additional risk. However, we think EXPD has a diversified stream of air, ocean, and customs businesses, and we also believe the balance sheet is strong, with no debt and a relatively large amount of cash.

Quantitative Evaluations

S&P Quality Ranking   **A+**

D	C	B-	B	B+	A-	A	A+

Relative Strength Rank   **MODERATE**

42

LOWEST = 1   HIGHEST = 99

Revenue/Earnings Data

Revenue (Million $)

	1Q	2Q	3Q	4Q	Year
2007	1,119	1,259	1,411	--	--
2006	1,025	1,129	1,230	1,242	4,626
2005	825.2	928.0	1,046	1,102	3,902
2004	686.9	798.7	897.2	934.8	3,318
2003	556.4	625.7	711.5	731.4	2,625
2002	449.5	535.8	620.4	691.2	2,297

Earnings Per Share ($)

2007	0.27	0.30	0.34	E0.36	E1.28
2006	0.24	0.25	0.29	0.28	1.06
2005	0.17	0.20	0.25	0.36	0.98
2004	0.15	0.17	0.20	0.20	0.71
2003	0.12	0.13	0.15	0.17	0.56
2002	0.10	0.11	0.14	0.17	0.52

Fiscal year ended Dec. 31. Next earnings report expected: Mid February. EPS Estimates based on S&P Operating Earnings; historical GAAP earnings are as reported.

Dividend Data (Dates: mm/dd Payment Date: mm/dd/yy)

Amount ($)	Date Decl.	Ex-Div. Date	Stk. of Record	Payment Date
0.110	11/08	11/29	12/01	12/15/06
0.140	05/03	05/30	06/01	06/15/07
0.140	11/13	11/29	12/03	12/17/07

Dividends have been paid since 1993. Source: Company reports.

Expeditors International of Washington Inc

STANDARD & POOR'S

Business Summary November 26, 2007

With an international network supporting the movement and strategic positioning of goods, Expeditors International of Washington is engaged in the business of providing global logistics services to customers diversified in terms of industry specialization and geographic location. In each of its U.S. offices, and in many international offices, the company acts as a customs broker, and also provides additional services, including distribution management, vendor consolidation, cargo insurance, purchase order management, and customized logistics information. EXPD does not compete for domestic freight, overnight courier, or small parcel business, and does not own aircraft or steamships. The company has historically pursued a strategy emphasizing organic growth supplemented by strategic acquisitions. As of May 2007, EXPD had a network of 172 full-service offices, 60 satellite locations and five international service centers located on six continents.

Shipments of computer components, other electronic equipment, housewares, sporting goods, machine parts and toys comprise a significant percentage of the company's business. Import customers include computer re-

tailers and distributors of consumer electronics, department store chains, clothing and shoe wholesalers. Historically, no single customer has accounted for over 5% of revenues.

Air freight services accounted for 48% of net revenues in 2006, and 47% in 2005. EXPD typically acts either as a freight consolidator (purchasing cargo space on airlines and reselling it to customers at lower rates than the airline would charge customers directly), or as an agent for the airlines (receiving shipments from suppliers, and consolidating and forwarding them to the airlines). Shipments are usually characterized by a high value-to-weight ratio, a need for rapid delivery, or both. The company estimates that its average air freight consolidation weighs 3,500 lbs. to 4,500 lbs.

Company Financials Fiscal Year Ended Dec. 31

Per Share Data ($)	2006	2005	2004	2003	2002	2001	2000	1999	1998	1997
Tangible Book Value	4.95	4.21	3.70	2.98	2.49	2.01	1.76	1.40	1.10	0.87
Cash Flow	1.27	1.12	0.82	0.67	0.62	0.55	0.48	0.37	0.30	0.24
Earnings	1.06	0.98	0.71	0.56	0.52	0.45	0.38	0.28	0.22	0.18
S&P Core Earnings	1.06	0.85	0.59	0.46	0.44	0.39	NA	NA	NA	NA
Dividends	0.22	0.15	0.11	0.08	0.06	0.04	0.04	0.03	0.02	0.01
Payout Ratio	21%	15%	16%	14%	12%	10%	9%	9%	8%	7%
Prices:High	58.32	36.37	29.20	20.42	17.22	16.48	15.03	11.59	6.03	6.09
Prices:Low	32.83	23.59	17.85	14.81	12.47	10.49	8.16	5.08	3.11	2.58
P/E Ratio:High	55	37	41	36	33	37	40	42	27	33
P/E Ratio:Low	31	24	25	26	24	24	21	18	14	14

Income Statement Analysis (Million $)	2006	2005	2004	2003	2002	2001	2000	1999	1998	1997
Revenue	4,626	3,902	3,318	2,625	2,297	1,653	1,695	1,445	1,064	954
Operating Income	411	337	268	211	194	170	150	114	88.9	71.1
Depreciation	35.4	32.3	26.7	24.4	22.7	23.5	22.5	20.8	15.5	11.2
Interest Expense	0.20	0.31	0.04	0.19	0.18	0.52	0.43	1.07	0.49	0.36
Pretax Income	396	320	250	196	178	154	133	94.6	75.6	62.6
Effective Tax Rate	40.6%	29.6%	35.4%	36.4%	36.8%	37.0%	37.7%	37.5%	37.4%	38.6%
Net Income	235	219	156	122	113	97.2	83.0	59.2	47.3	38.4
S&P Core Earnings	235	187	130	98.4	92.7	83.8	NA	NA	NA	NA

Balance Sheet & Other Financial Data (Million $)	2006	2005	2004	2003	2002	2001	2000	1999	1998	1997
Cash	511	464	409	296	212	219	169	71.2	49.4	42.1
Current Assets	1,342	1,202	1,046	762	605	511	523	382	284	260
Total Assets	1,822	1,566	1,364	1,041	880	688	662	512	407	342
Current Liabilities	709	613	524	392	356	274	230	229	189	172
Long Term Debt	Nil	Nil	Nil	Nil	Nil	Nil	Nil	Nil	Nil	Nil
Common Equity	1,070	914	807	646	524	415	362	282	217	170
Total Capital	1,113	954	840	649	524	415	362	282	217	170
Capital Expenditures	141	90.8	66.2	20.7	81.4	37.4	25.6	26.6	52.5	36.0
Cash Flow	271	251	183	146	135	121	106	80.0	62.8	49.6
Current Ratio	1.9	2.0	2.0	1.9	1.7	1.9	2.3	1.7	1.5	1.5
% Long Term Debt of Capitalization	Nil	Nil	Nil	Nil	Nil	Nil	Nil	Nil	Nil	Nil
% Net Income of Revenue	5.1	5.6	4.7	4.6	4.9	5.9	4.9	4.1	4.4	4.0
% Return on Assets	13.9	14.9	13.0	12.7	14.3	14.4	13.9	12.9	12.6	12.5
% Return on Equity	23.6	25.4	21.5	20.9	24.0	25.0	25.8	23.7	24.4	24.8

Data as orig reptd.; bef. results of disc opers/spec. items. Per share data adj. for stk. divs.; EPS diluted. E-Estimated. NA-Not Available. NM-Not Meaningful. NR-Not Ranked. UR-Under Review.

Office: 1015 Third Avenue, Seattle, WA 98104-1190.
Telephone: 206-674-3400.
Website: http://www.expeditors.com
Chrmn & CEO: P.J. Rose

Pres & COO: G.M. Alger
Investor Contact: R.J. Gates (206-674-3400)
EVP, CFO & Treas: R.J. Gates
SVP & Cntlr: C.J. Lynch

Board Members: J. J. Casey, R. J. Gates, D. P. Kourkoumelis, M. J. Malone, J. W. Meisenbach, P. J. Rose, J. L. Wang

Founded: 1979
Domicile: Washington
Employees: 11,600

The McGraw-Hill Companies

Express Scripts Inc

STANDARD &POOR'S

S&P Recommendation **BUY** ★★★★☆	Price $68.26 (as of Nov 29, 2007)	12-Mo. Target Price $75.00	Investment Style Large-Cap Growth

GICS Sector Health Care
Sub-Industry Health Care Services

Summary This company offers prescription benefits and disease state management services.

Key Stock Statistics (Source S&P, Vickers, company reports)

52-Wk Range	$69.62– 32.32	S&P Oper. EPS 2007E	2.32	Market Capitalization(B)	$17.205	Beta	0.22
Trailing 12-Month EPS	$2.14	S&P Oper. EPS 2008E	2.85	Yield (%)	Nil	S&P 3-Yr. Proj. EPS CAGR(%)	22.00
Trailing 12-Month P/E	31.9	P/E on S&P Oper. EPS 2007E	29.4	Dividend Rate/Share	Nil	S&P Credit Rating	BBB
$10K Invested 5 Yrs Ago	$50,353	Common Shares Outstg. (M)	252.0	Institutional Ownership (%)	NM		

Price Performance

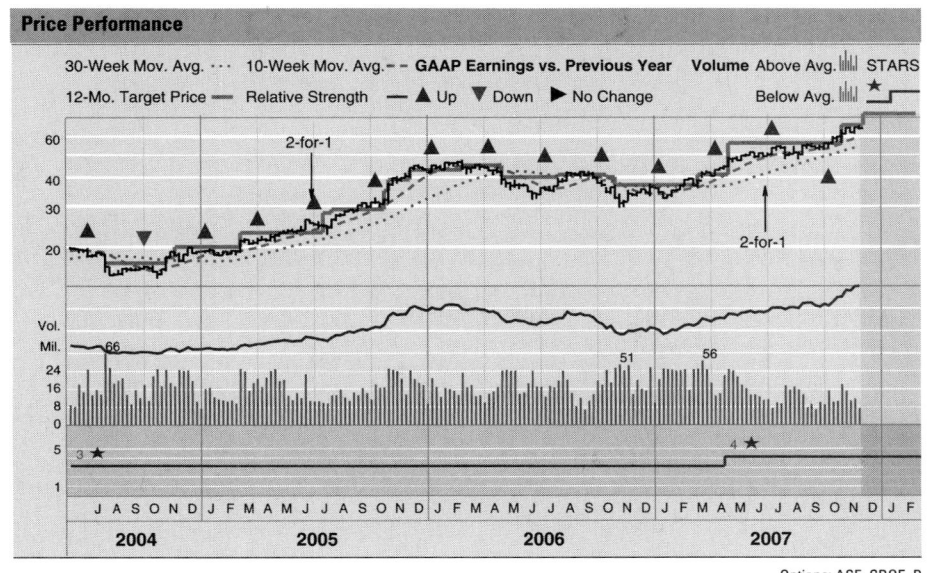

30-Week Mov. Avg. · · · 10-Week Mov. Avg. – – **GAAP Earnings vs. Previous Year** Volume Above Avg. STARS
12-Mo. Target Price — Relative Strength — ▲ Up ▼ Down ▶ No Change Below Avg. ★

Options: ASE, CBOE, P

Analysis prepared by **Phillip M. Seligman** on November 29, 2007, when the stock traded at **$ 68.26**.

Highlights

➤ We expect revenues to increase about 6% in 2008, to $19.4 billion, from the $18.3 billion we estimate for 2007. Drivers we see include a 2% to 3% increase in total adjusted scripts and higher generic drug penetration, partly offset by the generic drugs' low prices.

➤ We look for EBITDA per adjusted script to rise in excess of 10% on generic drug, specialty drug, and mail penetration, as well as lower drug purchasing costs and productivity gains. Regarding the first factor, the third quarter generic drug penetration rate rose 390 basis points from a year earlier, to a record 62.2%. Looking ahead, we see this rate expanding up to 300 bps from year-end 2007 levels as more branded drugs convert to generic status.

➤ Our 2007 and 2008 operating EPS estimates are $2.32 and $2.85, respectively, versus 2006's $1.65. We see EPS growth also aided by a $1 billion share repurchase authorization. Our model also assumes that the implementation of the AWP (average wholesale price -- the branded drug reference price) litigation settlement has been delayed until 2008.

Investment Rationale/Risk

➤ We are encouraged that ESRX has been experiencing strong underlying trends in its business, including winning a lot of new business, albeit small and medium sized accounts, increasing generic drug penetration and lowering drug purchasing costs. Indeed, while our current estimate for 2008 growth of EBITDA per adjusted script is below 2006 and 2007 levels, partly on the cost of integrating the many new accounts, we think it may be conservative assuming certain blockbuster drugs go generic in 2008, before their patent expiration dates. Moreover, given what we consider its successful track record in helping clients manage drug spending, we think ESRX can hold its own against its larger peers. But we also expect it to increasingly use its strong cash flow for acquisitions to aid its competitive position.

➤ Risks to our recommendation and target price include increased government oversight and a potential loss of key clients. We also await the outcome of several legal proceedings.

➤ Applying a peer-level P/E-to-growth ratio of 1.2X, assuming three-year EPS growth of 22%, to our 2008 EPS estimate, we derive a 12-month target price of $75.

Qualitative Risk Assessment

LOW	MEDIUM	HIGH

Our risk assessment reflects our view of rising drug demand, and the company's improving financial performance and healthy operating cash flow. However, we believe that intense competition and increased government regulation of pharmacy benefit managers (PBMs), which we view as likely, could result in changes in industry conditions.

Quantitative Evaluations

S&P Quality Ranking   B+

D	C	B-	B	B+	A-	A	A+

Relative Strength Rank   STRONG
96
LOWEST = 1   HIGHEST = 99

Revenue/Earnings Data

Revenue (Million $)

	1Q	2Q	3Q	4Q	Year
2007	4,540	4,600	4,519	--	--
2006	4,380	4,421	4,330	4,529	17,660
2005	3,839	3,944	3,848	4,635	16,266
2004	3,628	3,780	3,768	3,940	15,115
2003	3,224	3,334	3,249	3,488	13,295
2002	2,540	3,178	3,177	3,366	12,261

Earnings Per Share ($)

	1Q	2Q	3Q	4Q	Year
2007	0.49	0.57	0.56	E0.64	E2.32
2006	0.35	0.38	0.42	0.54	1.67
2005	0.29	0.34	0.34	0.38	1.34
2004	0.22	0.21	0.20	0.27	0.90
2003	0.19	0.19	0.20	0.22	0.80
2002	0.14	0.15	0.17	0.18	0.64

Fiscal year ended Dec. 31. Next earnings report expected: Early February. EPS Estimates based on S&P Operating Earnings; historical GAAP earnings are as reported.

Dividend Data (Dates: mm/dd Payment Date: mm/dd/yy)

Amount ($)	Date Decl.	Ex-Div. Date	Stk. of Record	Payment Date
2-for-1	05/23	06/25	06/08	06/22/07

Source: Company reports.

Please read the Required Disclosures and Analyst Certification on the last page of this report.

The *McGraw-Hill* Companies

Express Scripts Inc

Business Summary November 29, 2007

CORPORATE OVERVIEW. Express Scripts is one of the largest U.S. pharmacy benefits managers (PBMs). Its PBM services (80.0% of 2006 revenue, versus 88.4% in 2005) include retail network pharmacy management, mail pharmacy services, benefit design consultation, drug utilization review, formulary management, disease management, and compliance and therapy management for thousands of client groups that include health insurers, third-party administrators, employers, union-sponsored benefit plans and government health programs.

The SAAS segment (20.0%, versus 11.6%) comprises specialty operations of CuraScript, and its SDS and PMG service lines. The segment's services include delivery of injectable and infusible drugs to patient homes, physician offices, clinics and infusion centers, third party logistics services, and biopharma services including reimbursement and customized logistics solutions. The segment also includes distribution of specialty pharmaceuticals requiring special handling or packaging; distribution of pharmaceuticals to low-income patients through manufacturer-sponsored branded and company-sponsored generic patient assistance programs; and distribution of sample units to

physicians and verification of practitioner licensure.

Revenues are generated primarily from the delivery of prescription drugs through 57,000 contracted retail pharmacies, four home delivery fulfillment pharmacies, and 38 specialty drug pharmacies, as of December 31, 2006. Revenues from the delivery of prescription drugs to members represented 98.3% of revenues in 2006, versus 98.2% in 2005. Revenues from services, such as the administration of some clients' retail pharmacy networks, and certain services provided by SAAS comprised the remainder.

The five largest clients accounted for 17.8% of revenues in 2006, compared to 23.6% in 2005. In 2006, the company processed 390 million network pharmacy claims, 41 million mail pharmacy claims and almost 6 million SAAS claims, compared to 437 million, 40 million and 5 million, respectively, in 2005.

Company Financials Fiscal Year Ended Dec. 31

Per Share Data ($)	2006	2005	2004	2003	2002	2001	2000	1999	1998	1997
Tangible Book Value	NM	NM	NM	NM	NM	NM	NM	NM	NM	0.77
Cash Flow	2.03	1.62	1.12	0.97	0.90	0.64	0.23	0.78	0.26	0.17
Earnings	1.67	1.34	0.90	0.79	0.64	0.39	-0.03	0.53	0.16	0.13
S&P Core Earnings	1.67	1.30	0.87	0.75	0.60	0.36	NA	NA	NA	NA
Dividends	Nil	Nil	Nil	Nil	Nil	Nil	Nil	Nil	Nil	Nil
Payout Ratio	Nil	Nil	Nil	Nil	Nil	Nil	Nil	Nil	Nil	Nil
Prices:High	47.50	45.40	20.30	18.86	16.48	15.36	13.38	13.19	8.63	4.05
Prices:Low	29.40	18.27	14.58	11.58	9.66	8.71	3.56	5.55	3.38	1.95
P/E Ratio:High	28	34	23	24	26	39	NM	25	54	32
P/E Ratio:Low	18	14	16	15	15	22	NM	10	21	15

Income Statement Analysis (Million $)										
Revenue	17,660	16,266	15,115	13,295	12,261	9,329	6,787	4,288	2,825	1,231
Operating Income	925	727	563	503	454	317	279	241	116	59.3
Depreciation	101	84.0	70.0	54.0	82.0	80.1	78.6	74.0	27.0	10.5
Interest Expense	95.7	37.0	41.7	41.4	42.2	34.2	47.9	60.0	20.2	0.23
Pretax Income	740	615	451	405	330	208	-4.47	265	76.2	54.7
Effective Tax Rate	35.9%	35.0%	38.3%	38.2%	38.2%	39.9%	NM	40.7%	44.0%	38.9%
Net Income	474	400	278	251	204	125	-8.02	157	42.7	33.4
S&P Core Earnings	474	389	270	239	192	115	NA	NA	NA	NA

Balance Sheet & Other Financial Data (Million $)										
Cash	131	478	166	396	191	178	53.2	283	123	64.2
Current Assets	1,772	2,257	1,443	1,560	1,394	1,213	998	1,066	657	364
Total Assets	5,108	5,493	3,600	3,409	3,207	2,500	2,277	2,487	1,095	403
Current Liabilities	2,429	2,394	1,813	1,626	1,544	1,246	1,116	1,100	539	198
Long Term Debt	1,270	1,401	412	455	563	346	396	636	306	Nil
Common Equity	1,125	1,465	1,196	1,194	1,003	832	705	699	250	204
Total Capital	2,395	2,866	1,608	1,649	1,565	1,178	1,102	1,335	556	204
Capital Expenditures	66.8	60.0	51.5	53.1	61.3	57.3	80.2	37.0	23.9	13.0
Cash Flow	575	484	348	305	286	205	70.6	231	69.7	43.9
Current Ratio	0.7	0.9	0.8	1.0	0.9	1.0	0.9	1.0	1.2	1.8
% Long Term Debt of Capitalization	53.0	48.9	25.6	27.6	35.9	29.4	36.0	47.6	55.1	Nil
% Net Income of Revenue	2.7	2.5	1.8	1.9	1.7	1.3	NM	3.7	1.5	2.7
% Return on Assets	8.9	8.8	7.9	7.6	7.1	5.2	NM	8.8	5.7	9.5
% Return on Equity	36.6	30.1	23.3	22.8	22.2	16.3	NM	33.2	18.8	18.2

Data as orig reptd.; bef. results of disc opers/spec. items. Per share data adj. for stk. divs.; EPS diluted. E-Estimated. NA-Not Available. NM-Not Meaningful. NR-Not Ranked. UR-Under Review.

Office: 13900 Riverport Drive, Maryland Heights, MO 63043-4804.
Telephone: 314-770-1666.
Email: investor.relations@express-scripts.com
Website: http://www.express-scripts.com

Chrmn, Pres & CEO: G. Paz
COO: D.A. Lowenberg
SVP & CFO: E. Stiften
SVP, Secy & General Counsel: T.M. Boudreau

VP, Chief Acctg Officer & Cntlr: K. Elliott
Investor Contact: D. Myers (314-702-7173)
Board Members: G. G. Benanav, F. J. Borelli, M. C. Breen, N. J. LaHowchic, T. P. Mac Mahon, W. A. Myers, J. O. Parker, Jr., G. Paz, S. Skinner, S. Sternberg, B. A. Toan, H. L. Waltman

Founded: 1986
Domicile: Delaware
Employees: 11,300

Exxon Mobil Corp

STANDARD &POOR'S

S&P Recommendation HOLD ★★★★★

Price	12-Mo. Target Price	Investment Style
$85.68 (as of Nov 26, 2007)	$98.00	Large-Cap Blend

GICS Sector Energy
Sub-Industry Integrated Oil & Gas

Summary XOM, formed through the merger of Exxon and Mobil in late 1999, is the world's largest publicly owned integrated oil company.

Key Stock Statistics (Source S&P, Vickers, company reports)

52-Wk Range	$95.27– 69.02	S&P Oper. EPS 2007**E**	6.95	Market Capitalization(B)	$468.123	Beta	0.72
Trailing 12-Month EPS	$6.91	S&P Oper. EPS 2008**E**	7.95	Yield (%)	1.63	S&P 3-Yr. Proj. EPS CAGR(%)	4.90
Trailing 12-Month P/E	12.4	P/E on S&P Oper. EPS 2007**E**	12.3	Dividend Rate/Share	$1.40	S&P Credit Rating	AAA
$10K Invested 5 Yrs Ago	$28,723	Common Shares Outstg. (M)	5,463.6	Institutional Ownership (%)	53		

Price Performance

30-Week Mov. Avg. ··· 10-Week Mov. Avg. - - **GAAP Earnings vs. Previous Year** Volume Above Avg. STARS
12-Mo. Target Price — Relative Strength — ▲ Up ▼ Down ▶ No Change Below Avg.

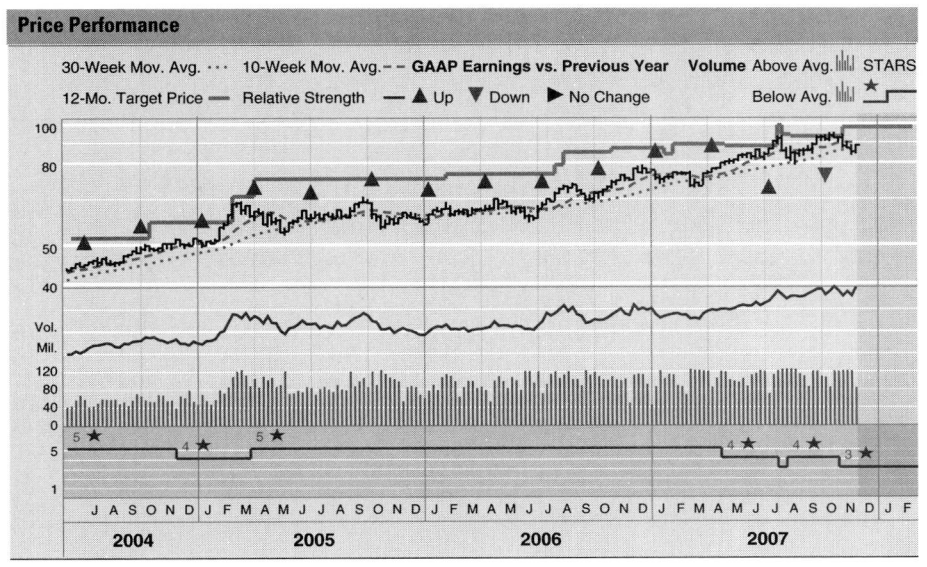

Options: ASE, CBOE, P, Ph

Analysis prepared by **Tina J. Vital** on November 26, 2007, when the stock traded at **$ 87.06**.

Highlights

➤ Third quarter oil and gas production declined 2.1%, below our expectations, reflecting the impact of high oil prices on entitlements in Africa, and the absence of Venezuelan crude. We expect full-year 2007 volumes to decline more than 2%, before rising about 1% in 2008. On September 6, XOM filed a request for arbitration with the International Center for Settlement of Investment Disputes following the expropriation of assets in Venezuela in June. XOM book exposure to Venezuela is about $750 million, related to its Cerro Negro project.

➤ Refining margins weakened in the 2007 second half, but were partially offset by strong crude oil price realizations. We expect 2008 U.S. refining margins to narrow more than 30% from 2007 levels on continued strong crude oil price realizations, but to remain relatively high compared to historical norms.

➤ We expect after-tax operating earnings to decline about 1.5% in 2007, before rising more than 13% in 2008 and remaining near that level in 2009.

Investment Rationale/Risk

➤ We believe XOM will benefit from "big-pocket" upstream growth opportunities in deepwater, liquefied natural gas (LNG), and ventures with state-owned oil companies. We expect its upstream to benefit from strong crude oil prices, and its complex refineries from significant cost discounts due to its ability to refine lower quality crude feedstocks. We estimate XOM's three-year (2004-06) finding and development costs at $7.00 per boe, below peers; its upstream production growth prospects as in line; and its three-year reserve replacement rate of 130% as above average.

➤ Risks to our recommendation and target price include changes in economic, industry and operating conditions, such as difficulty replacing reserves and geopolitical risk.

➤ A blend of our discounted cash flow model ($102 per share, assuming a WACC of 9.6% and terminal growth of 3%) and relative valuations leads to our 12-month target price of $98 per share, at an expected enterprise value of 7.7X our 2008 EBITDA estimate. This represents a premium to peers, warranted by our view of XOM's high and stable earnings quality.

Qualitative Risk Assessment

LOW	MEDIUM	HIGH

Our risk assessment reflects our view of the company's diversified and strong business profile in volatile, cyclical and capital-intensive segments of the energy industry. We view ExxonMobil's earnings stability and corporate governance practices as above average.

Quantitative Evaluations

S&P Quality Ranking   A

D	C	B-	B	B+	A-	A	A+

Relative Strength Rank   MODERATE

66

LOWEST = 1   HIGHEST = 99

Revenue/Earnings Data

Revenue (Million $)

	1Q	2Q	3Q	4Q	Year
2007	87,223	98,350	102,337	--	--
2006	86,317	96,024	96,268	86,858	377,635
2005	82,051	88,568	100,717	99,662	370,680
2004	67,602	70,693	76,375	83,357	298,035
2003	63,780	57,165	59,841	65,952	246,738
2002	43,531	50,909	54,182	56,211	204,506

Earnings Per Share ($)

2007	1.62	1.83	1.70	E1.80	E6.95
2006	1.37	1.72	1.77	1.76	6.62
2005	1.22	1.20	1.58	1.71	5.71
2004	0.83	0.88	0.88	1.30	3.89
2003	0.97	0.62	0.55	1.01	3.15
2002	0.30	0.38	0.39	0.54	1.61

Fiscal year ended Dec. 31. Next earnings report expected: Early February. EPS Estimates based on S&P Operating Earnings; historical GAAP earnings are as reported.

Dividend Data (Dates: mm/dd Payment Date: mm/dd/yy)

Amount ($)	Date Decl.	Ex-Div. Date	Stk. of Record	Payment Date
0.320	01/31	02/07	02/09	03/09/07
0.350	04/25	05/10	05/14	06/11/07
0.350	07/25	08/09	08/13	09/10/07
0.350	10/31	11/07	11/09	12/10/07

Dividends have been paid since 1882. Source: Company reports.

Exxon Mobil Corp

STANDARD &POOR'S

Business Summary November 26, 2007

CORPORATE OVERVIEW. In late 1999, the FTC allowed Exxon and Mobil to re-unite, creating Exxon Mobil Corp. (XOM). ExxonMobil's businesses include oil and natural gas exploration and production (9% of 2006 sales; 67% of 2006 segment earnings); refining and marketing (82%; 22%); chemicals (9%; 11%); and other operations, such as electric power generation, coal and minerals.

Excluding year-end price/cost effects, proved oil and gas (including tar sands and nonconsolidated) reserves rose 1.3% to 22.7 billion barrel oil equivalent (boe; 52% liquids, including 718 million barrels of oil sands), as of year-end 2006. Liquids production advanced 6.3%, to 2.681 million b/d in 2006, and natural gas production available for sale rose 0.9%, to 9.334 billion cubic feet per day (Bcf)/d in 2006. Using data from John S. Herold, we estimate XOM's three-year (2004-2006) reserve replacement at 130%, above the peer average; its three-year finding and development cost at $7.00 per boe, below the peer average; its proved acquisition costs at $0.56 per boe, below the peer average; and its reserve replacement costs at $6.07 per boe, below the peer average.

As of year-end 2006, the company had an ownership interest in 40 refineries in 20 countries, with 7.1 million b/d of atmospheric distillation capacity (U.S. 29%, Europe 29%, Asia Pacific 15%, Japan 12%, Canada 7%, and Latin America/other 8%). In April 2007, ExxonMobil sold its Ingolstadt refinery in Germany (rated capacity of 110,000 b/d) to Petroplus Holdings AG for about $627.5 million (including inventory).

MANAGEMENT. We believe XOM is one of the best managed companies in the energy sector. In January 2006, Lee R. Raymond retired and Rex W. Tillerson became chairman and CEO. We expect Mr. Tillerson to benefit from plans made by Mr. Raymond over the past 12 years, and we see Mr. Tillerson's diplomatic skills as playing an important role in enhancing those plans.

Company Financials Fiscal Year Ended Dec. 31

Per Share Data ($)	2006	2005	2004	2003	2002	2001	2000	1999	1998	1997
Tangible Book Value	19.87	18.13	15.90	13.69	11.13	10.74	10.21	9.13	8.83	8.69
Cash Flow	8.89	7.34	5.38	4.50	2.84	3.32	3.43	2.30	2.38	2.81
Earnings	6.62	5.71	3.89	3.15	1.61	2.18	2.27	1.13	1.31	1.69
S&P Core Earnings	6.75	5.72	4.01	3.03	1.52	2.03	NA	NA	NA	NA
Dividends	1.28	1.14	1.06	0.98	0.92	0.91	0.88	0.84	0.82	0.81
Payout Ratio	19%	20%	27%	31%	57%	42%	39%	74%	63%	48%
Prices:High	79.00	65.96	52.05	41.13	44.58	45.84	47.72	43.63	38.66	33.63
Prices:Low	56.42	49.25	39.91	31.58	29.75	35.01	34.94	32.16	28.31	24.13
P/E Ratio:High	12	12	13	13	28	21	21	39	30	20
P/E Ratio:Low	9	9	10	10	18	16	15	29	22	14

Income Statement Analysis (Million $)										
Revenue	377,635	370,680	298,035	246,738	204,506	213,488	232,748	185,527	117,772	137,242
Operating Income	150,107	59,255	45,639	32,230	23,280	29,602	33,309	17,921	12,326	16,993
Depreciation, Depletion and Amortization	11,416	10,253	9,767	9,047	8,310	7,944	8,130	8,304	5,340	5,474
Interest Expense	654	496	638	207	398	293	589	695	100	415
Pretax Income	68,453	60,231	42,017	32,660	17,719	24,688	27,493	11,295	9,241	13,204
Effective Tax Rate	40.8%	38.7%	37.9%	33.7%	36.7%	36.5%	40.3%	28.7%	28.3%	32.9%
Net Income	39,500	36,130	25,330	20,960	11,011	15,105	15,990	7,910	6,440	8,460
S&P Core Earnings	40,263	36,164	26,089	20,214	10,418	14,042	NA	NA	NA	NA

Balance Sheet & Other Financial Data (Million $)										
Cash	32,848	28,671	18,531	10,626	7,229	6,547	7,081	1,761	1,461	4,062
Current Assets	75,777	73,342	60,377	45,960	38,291	35,681	40,399	31,141	17,593	21,192
Total Assets	219,015	208,335	195,256	174,278	152,644	143,174	149,000	144,521	92,630	96,064
Current Liabilities	48,817	46,307	42,981	38,386	33,175	30,114	38,191	38,733	19,412	19,654
Long Term Debt	6,645	6,220	5,013	4,756	6,655	7,099	7,280	8,402	4,530	7,050
Common Equity	113,844	111,186	101,756	89,915	74,597	73,161	70,757	63,466	43,645	43,470
Total Capital	141,340	138,284	131,813	118,171	100,504	99,444	97,709	91,807	63,229	66,533
Capital Expenditures	15,462	13,839	11,986	12,859	11,437	9,989	8,446	10,849	8,359	7,393
Cash Flow	50,916	46,383	35,097	30,007	19,321	23,049	24,120	16,178	11,770	13,915
Current Ratio	1.6	1.6	1.4	1.2	1.2	1.2	1.1	0.8	0.9	1.1
% Long Term Debt of Capitalization	4.7	4.4	3.8	4.0	6.6	7.1	7.5	9.2	7.2	10.6
% Return on Assets	18.5	17.9	13.7	12.8	7.4	10.3	10.9	5.6	6.8	8.8
% Return on Equity	35.1	33.9	26.4	25.5	14.9	21.0	23.8	12.6	14.8	19.5

Data as orig reptd.; bef. results of disc opers/spec. items. Per share data adj. for stk. divs.; EPS diluted. E-Estimated. NA-Not Available. NM-Not Meaningful. NR-Not Ranked. UR-Under Review.

Office: 5959 Las Colinas Blvd, Irving, TX 75039-2298.
Telephone: 972-444-1000.
Website: http://www.exxonmobil.com
Chrmn, Pres & CEO: R.W. Tillerson

SVP & Treas: D.D. Humphreys
Investor Contact: P.T. Mulva (800-252-1800)
VP & Secy: P.T. Mulva
VP & General Counsel: C.W. Matthews

Board Members: M. J. Boskin, W. W. George, J. R. Houghton, W. R. Howell, R. C. King, P. E. Lippincott, H. A. McKinnell, Jr., M. C. Nelson, S. J. Palmisano, S. S. Reinemund, W. V. Shipley, J. S. Simon, R. W. Tillerson

Founded: 1870
Domicile: New Jersey
Employees: 82,100

The McGraw-Hill Companies

Family Dollar Stores Inc.

STANDARD &POOR'S

S&P Recommendation	HOLD ★★★☆☆	Price $22.82 (as of Nov 23, 2007)	12-Mo. Target Price $30.00	Investment Style Large-Cap Blend

GICS Sector Consumer Discretionary
Sub-Industry General Merchandise Stores

Summary This company operates a chain of more than 6,400 retail discount stores in 44 states across the U.S.

Key Stock Statistics (Source S&P, Vickers, company reports)

52-Wk Range	$35.42– 21.03	S&P Oper. EPS 2008**E**	1.85	Market Capitalization(B)	$3.206	Beta	0.99
Trailing 12-Month EPS	$1.62	S&P Oper. EPS 2009**E**	2.10	Yield (%)	2.02	S&P 3-Yr. Proj. EPS CAGR(%)	13.00
Trailing 12-Month P/E	14.1	P/E on S&P Oper. EPS 2008**E**	12.3	Dividend Rate/Share	$0.46	S&P Credit Rating	NA
$10K Invested 5 Yrs Ago	$8,143	Common Shares Outstg. (M)	140.5	Institutional Ownership (%)	NM		

Price Performance

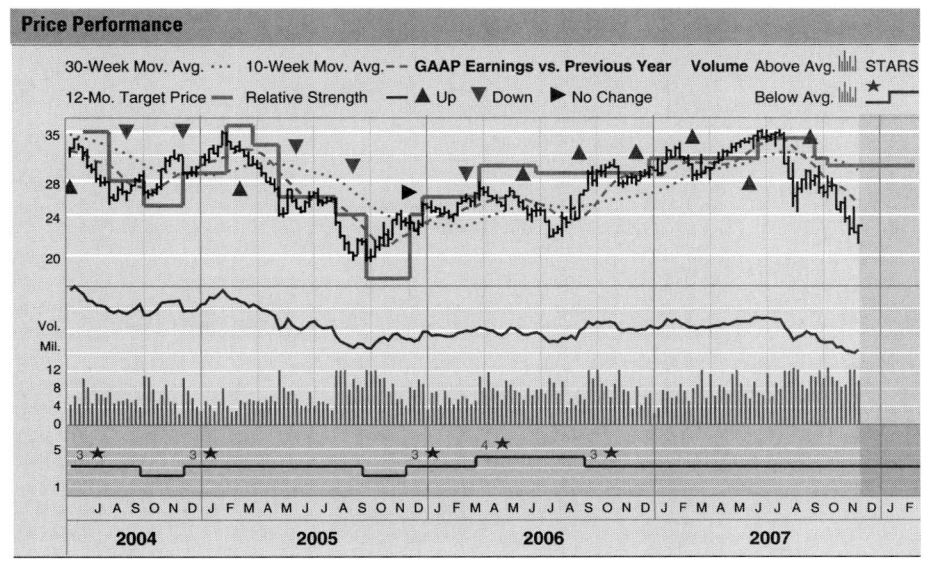

Options: ASE, CBOE, P, Ph

Analysis prepared by **Jason N. Asaeda** on October 11, 2007, when the stock traded at **$ 28.02**.

Highlights

➤ In FY 08 (Aug.), we look for sales to advance about 3.5%, to $7.1 billion. FDO plans to limit its expansion to 300 new stores in an effort to open stores more cost efficiently and on schedule. The company also intends to increase the selling space for food in approximately 2,800 stores, to install coolers in about 575 stores, and to improve its treasure-hunt assortments. Balancing these sales drivers against a challenging macro-economic environment, we look for same-store sales to rise 1% to 2%.

➤ As of FY 07, sales of prepaid cellular service cards are being recorded on a net basis--i.e., only the markup on the sales is posted as revenue. FDO estimates that this change in accounting has been modestly accretive to its operating margin. In FY 08, we anticipate operating margin expansion on higher initial markups, mainly supported by the company's treasure-hunt and global sourcing initiatives, lower shrinkage, and the cycling of FY 07 stock option review costs, partly offset by expenses related to implementation of strategic initiatives.

➤ FDO recently completed its share repurchase authorization. Assuming no additional buyback activity, we see FY 08 operating EPS of $1.85.

Investment Rationale/Risk

➤ FDO believes its low and low-middle income customers are consolidating shopping trips in response to pressures such as volatile energy costs. As a result, we foresee weak store traffic limiting same-store sales upside in the months ahead. Still, we look for an expanded food assortment and the promise of more compelling treasure-hunt merchandise supporting an increase in average customer transaction amount, another same-store sales driver. We are also encouraged by FDO's report of ongoing productivity gains at its Urban Initiative stores. We think these positive factors, coupled with tight inventory and expense controls, will drive an improvement in company fundamentals in FY 08. However, we do not see a near-term catalyst for the shares.

➤ Risks to our recommendation and target price include sales shortfalls due to a slowdown in consumer discretionary spending, delays in new store openings/product receipts, and increased competition.

➤ We derive our 12-month target price of $30 by applying a peer-median forward P/E multiple of 16X to our calendar 2008 operating EPS estimate of $1.88.

Qualitative Risk Assessment

LOW	MEDIUM	HIGH

Our risk assessment reflects our view of FDO's earnings erosion in recent years, partly a result of difficult economic conditions for core lower-income customers. This is offset by what we consider promising new merchandising and productivity initiatives that should, in our opinion, boost sales and profit margins going forward.

Quantitative Evaluations

S&P Quality Ranking   **A+**

D	C	B-	B	B+	A-	A	A+

Relative Strength Rank   **WEAK**

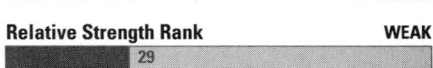

29

LOWEST = 1   HIGHEST = 99

Revenue/Earnings Data

Revenue (Million $)

	1Q	2Q	3Q	4Q	Year
2007	1,600	1,947	1,655	1,632	6,834
2006	1,511	1,736	1,570	1,578	6,395
2005	1,380	1,587	1,428	1,430	5,825
2004	1,245	1,403	1,310	1,324	5,282
2003	1,109	1,256	1,177	1,208	4,750
2002	977.1	1,105	1,022	1,058	4,163

Earnings Per Share ($)

2007	0.36	0.60	0.40	0.26	1.62
2006	0.32	0.35	0.37	0.21	1.26
2005	0.32	0.48	0.32	0.18	1.30
2004	0.37	0.47	0.43	0.26	1.53
2003	0.33	0.42	0.40	0.28	1.43
2002	0.29	0.37	0.35	0.24	1.25

Fiscal year ended Aug. 31. Next earnings report expected: Mid December. EPS Estimates based on S&P Operating Earnings; historical GAAP earnings are as reported.

Dividend Data (Dates: mm/dd Payment Date: mm/dd/yy)

Amount ($)	Date Decl.	Ex-Div. Date	Stk. of Record	Payment Date
0.115	01/19	03/12	03/14	04/13/07
0.115	03/28	06/13	06/15	07/13/07
0.115	08/29	09/12	09/14	10/15/07
0.115	11/05	12/12	12/14	01/15/08

Dividends have been paid since 1976. Source: Company reports.

The McGraw-Hill Companies

Family Dollar Stores Inc.

Business Summary October 11, 2007

CORPORATE OVERVIEW. FDO operates a chain of over 6,400 retail discount stores in 44 states. The company describes its typical customer as a woman in her mid-40s who is the head of her household and has an annual income of under $30,000. Family Dollar stores carry an assortment of hardlines and soft-lines priced from under $1 to $10 and are operated on a self-service basis, with limited advertising support and promotional activity. The once cash-only stores now accept PIN-based debit card payments in most locations. Food stamp acceptance is also being piloted. In our view, broader tender options offer the company an opportunity to improve its share of customer wallet as shopping is more convenient and available cash does not limit basket size.

PRIMARY BUSINESS DYNAMICS. FDO's primary growth drivers are same-store sales (sales results for stores open more than 13 months) and new store openings. In our opinion, the company is driving higher average customer transaction amounts through expanded offerings of frequently purchased hardline consumables such as food, household chemicals and paper products, as well as the addition of opportunistically purchased treasure-hunt items, which added interest to the merchandise mix over the past two years. However, FDO believes macro-economic concerns are prompting its customers to consolidate shopping trips in recent years. As a result, annual same-store sales growth weakened from an average 2.6% from FY 04 (Aug.)

through FY 06, to 0.9% in FY 07.

FDO continues to be one of the fastest growing retail chains in the U.S. The company's stores are located in rural, small town, suburban, and, increasingly, urban markets. A relatively small store size enables FDO to open new stores in locations that provide neighborhood convenience to its customers in each of these markets. Existing stores are either freestanding or located in shopping centers. From FY 00 through FY 05, the company increased its store count from 3,689 to 5,898 -- a compound annual growth rate (CAGR) of nearly 10%. FDO opened 350 new stores in FY 06, below its FY 04 and FY 05 run rate of 500 stores. The company slowed its pace of expansion in an effort to improve the timing of store openings over the course of the year. In prior years, about 30% of new store openings have occurred during the fourth quarter. This has added substantially to the cost of new store openings and made it challenging for FDO to staff and merchandise these stores, in our view. Only 300 new stores were opened in FY 07.

Company Financials Fiscal Year Ended Aug. 31

Per Share Data ($)	2007	2006	2005	2004	2003	2002	2001	2000	1999	1998
Tangible Book Value	8.19	8.04	8.64	8.13	7.61	6.66	5.57	4.66	4.00	3.36
Cash Flow	2.59	2.13	1.99	2.10	1.94	1.69	1.49	1.31	1.06	0.80
Earnings	1.62	1.26	1.30	1.53	1.43	1.25	1.10	1.00	0.81	0.60
S&P Core Earnings	1.71	1.44	1.21	1.45	1.39	1.22	1.08	NA	NA	NA
Dividends	0.44	0.40	0.36	0.32	0.28	0.25	0.23	0.22	0.20	0.17
Payout Ratio	27%	31%	28%	21%	20%	20%	21%	21%	24%	28%
Prices:High	35.42	30.91	35.25	39.66	44.13	37.25	31.35	24.50	26.75	22.44
Prices:Low	21.03	21.57	19.40	25.09	25.46	23.75	18.38	14.25	14.00	11.50
P/E Ratio:High	22	24	27	26	31	30	29	25	33	37
P/E Ratio:Low	13	17	15	16	18	19	17	14	17	19

Income Statement Analysis (Million $)										
Revenue	6,834	6,395	5,825	5,282	4,750	4,163	3,665	3,133	2,751	2,362
Operating Income	532	452	458	512	478	419	366	325	266	201
Depreciation	144	135	115	97.9	88.3	77.0	67.7	54.5	43.8	34.8
Interest Expense	17.0	13.1	Nil	Nil	Nil	Nil	Nil	Nil	Nil	0.01
Pretax Income	382	311	343	414	390	342	298	271	223	166
Effective Tax Rate	36.4%	37.3%	36.5%	36.6%	36.5%	36.5%	36.5%	36.5%	37.1%	37.8%
Net Income	243	195	218	263	247	217	190	172	140	103
S&P Core Earnings	257	223	202	250	241	213	186	NA	NA	NA

Balance Sheet & Other Financial Data (Million $)										
Cash	87.0	79.7	105	150	207	220	21.8	43.6	95.3	134
Current Assets	1,537	1,419	1,355	1,225	1,156	1,056	807	751	720	647
Total Assets	2,624	2,523	2,410	2,167	1,986	1,755	1,400	1,244	1,095	942
Current Liabilities	1,130	986	895	714	595	531	390	412	379	343
Long Term Debt	250	250	Nil	Nil	Nil	Nil	Nil	Nil	Nil	Nil
Common Equity	1,175	1,208	2,187	1,360	1,533	1,245	959	798	691	578
Total Capital	1,494	1,537	2,274	1,454	1,612	1,314	1,009	832	717	599
Capital Expenditures	132	192	229	218	220	187	163	172	125	96.4
Cash Flow	387	330	332	361	336	294	257	227	184	138
Current Ratio	1.4	1.4	1.5	1.7	1.9	2.0	2.1	1.8	1.9	1.9
% Long Term Debt of Capitalization	16.7	16.2	Nil	Nil	Nil	Nil	Nil	Nil	Nil	Nil
% Net Income of Revenue	3.5	3.1	3.7	5.0	5.2	5.2	5.2	5.5	5.1	4.4
% Return on Assets	9.4	7.9	9.4	12.7	13.2	13.8	14.3	14.7	13.7	12.0
% Return on Equity	20.3	8.9	10.6	19.7	17.8	18.9	21.6	23.1	22.1	19.2

Data as orig reptd.; bef. results of disc opers/spec. items. Per share data adj. for stk. divs.; EPS diluted. E-Estimated. NA-Not Available. NM-Not Meaningful. NR-Not Ranked. UR-Under Review.

Office: 10401 Monroe Rd, Matthews, NC 28105-5349.
Telephone: 704-847-6961.
Website: http://www.familydollar.com
Chrmn & CEO: H.R. Levine

Pres & COO: R.J. Kelly
Investor Contact: K.T. Smith (704-847-6961)
SVP & CFO: K.T. Smith
SVP, Secy & General Counsel: J.G. Kelley

Board Members: M. R. Bernstein, S. A. Decker, E. C. Dolby, G. A. Eisenberg, H. R. Levine, G. R. Mahoney, Jr., J. G. Martin, D. C. Pond

Founded: 1959
Domicile: Delaware
Employees: 44,000

Federal Home Loan Mortgage Corp.

STANDARD &POOR'S

S&P Recommendation	**SELL** ★★☆☆☆	Price $29.51 (as of Nov 29, 2007)	12-Mo. Target Price $25.00	Investment Style Large-Cap Blend

GICS Sector Financials
Sub-Industry Thrifts & Mortgage Finance

Summary Federal Home Loan Mortgage (Freddie Mac), a U.S. government-sponsored enterprise (GSE), buys mortgages from lenders to increase the supply of funds for housing.

Key Stock Statistics (Source S&P, Vickers, company reports)

52-Wk Range	$69.85– 22.90	S&P Oper. EPS 2007E	-4.99	Market Capitalization(B)	$19.522	Beta	0.85
Trailing 12-Month EPS	$-0.42	S&P Oper. EPS 2008E	-5.39	Yield (%)	3.39	S&P 3-Yr. Proj. EPS CAGR(%)	NM
Trailing 12-Month P/E	NM	P/E on S&P Oper. EPS 2007E	NM	Dividend Rate/Share	$1.00	S&P Credit Rating	AA-
$10K Invested 5 Yrs Ago	$5,020	Common Shares Outstg. (M)	661.6	Institutional Ownership (%)	96		

Price Performance

30-Week Mov. Avg. ···· 10-Week Mov. Avg. ─ ─ **GAAP Earnings vs. Previous Year**   Volume Above Avg. ⅢⅢ STARS
12-Mo. Target Price ── Relative Strength ── ▲ Up ▼ Down ► No Change   Below Avg. ⅢⅢ ★─

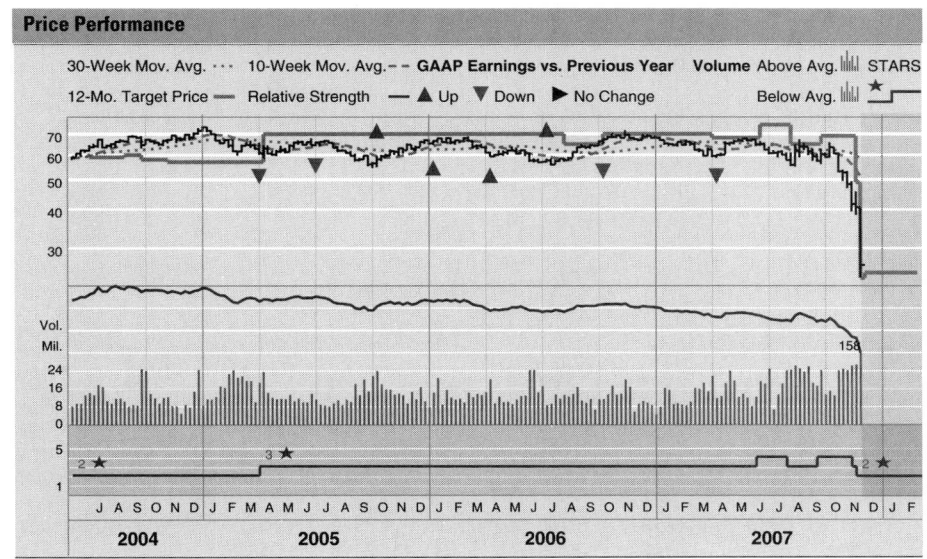

Options: ASE, CBOE, P, Ph

Analysis prepared by **Stuart Plesser** on November 29, 2007, when the stock traded at **$ 29.96**.

Qualitative Risk Assessment

LOW	MEDIUM	**HIGH**

Our risk assessment takes into account FRE's special position as a government-sponsored enterprise (GSE), offset by our view of a continued decline in home prices, and capital requirement issues.

Quantitative Evaluations

S&P Quality Ranking A-

D	C	B-	B	B+	**A-**	A	A+

Relative Strength Rank WEAK

4

LOWEST = 1   HIGHEST = 99

Revenue/Earnings Data

Revenue (Million $)

	1Q	2Q	3Q	4Q	Year
2007	10,235	--	--	--	--
2006	--	--	--	--	44,002
2005	--	--	--	--	36,653
2004	--	--	--	--	32,564
2003	--	--	--	--	36,839
2002	9,799	9,268	9,650	10,704	46,258

Earnings Per Share ($)

2007	-0.46	E1.48	E-3.29	E-2.71	E-4.99
2006	2.80	1.93	-1.17	--	2.84
2005	0.33	0.41	1.19	0.90	2.83
2004	1.82	3.91	-2.26	0.47	3.94
2003	--	--	--	--	6.68
2002	2.07	1.50	1.90	2.38	14.18

Fiscal year ended Dec. 31. Next earnings report expected: NA. EPS Estimates based on S&P Operating Earnings; historical GAAP earnings are as reported.

Highlights

► Ongoing losses due to higher credit costs will likely limit FRE's ability to grow its credit guarantee book of business. Based on our forecasts for lower interest expense and a modest rise in FRE's retained portfolio, we believe net interest income will increase in 2008. Despite recent price declines for mortgage-backed securities, a combination of FRE's voluntary limit on its retained portfolio and a dearth of capital due to the Office of Federal Housing Enterprise Oversight's (OFHEO) more stringent capital requirements will likely limit growth.

► We estimate higher management and guarantee income in 2008 due to continued growth in outstanding Participation Certificates (PCs) and structured securities and higher fees. Notwithstanding FRE's small exposure to interest only and option adjustable rate mortgages (ARMs) and low loan-to-value ratios, we foresee a significant increase in credit losses due to a difficult housing market. Loan-to-value ratios over 90% in its single-family portfolio now total 14%. With FRE's cost-control measures, we see non-interest expenses rising moderately in 2008.

► Assuming a 4.0% reduction in the share count, we see losses of $4.99 in 2007 and $5.39 in 2008.

Investment Rationale/Risk

► We believe credit issues are likely to continue to hurt FRE's results. FRE took provisions of $1.2 billion in the third quarter, up almost ten-fold from a year ago. Given our belief that default rates will increase in 2008, we look for provisions to remain at elevated levels. We also look for continued writedowns of mortgage-backed securities, as we do not foresee the secondary market improving anytime soon. Due to capital requirements, FRE recently halved its dividend and issued roughly $6 billion in preferred stock. Even with this additional capital, we think FRE will likely be circumspect and not be able to take advantage of attractive mortgage spreads.

► Risks to our recommendation and target price include an easing of government regulation, improvement in the pricing of mortgage-backed securities, and lower-than-projected credit losses.

► Our 12-month target price of $25 implies a price-to-book value multiple of roughly 0.91X applied to FRE's current book value of $27.42 (excluding preferred stock), a discount to its price-to-book multiple over the past three years.

Dividend Data (Dates: mm/dd Payment Date: mm/dd/yy)

Amount ($)	Date Decl.	Ex-Div. Date	Stk. of Record	Payment Date
0.500	03/05	03/08	03/12	03/30/07
0.500	06/08	06/14	06/18	06/29/07
0.500	09/07	09/13	09/17	09/28/07
0.250	11/27	12/13	12/17	12/31/07

Dividends have been paid since 1989. Source: Company reports.

Please read the Required Disclosures and Analyst Certification on the last page of this report.

The McGraw·Hill Companies

Federal Home Loan Mortgage Corp.

STANDARD
&POOR'S

Business Summary November 29, 2007

CORPORATE OVERVIEW. The Federal Home Loan Mortgage Corp., better known as Freddie Mac, is one of two public government-sponsored enterprises (the other is rival Fannie Mae) formed to promote home ownership by increasing the availability of mortgage financing. The company was originally part of the Federal Home Loan Bank Board, which was dismantled under the S&L bailout law of 1989.

PRIMARY BUSINESS DYNAMICS. The company generates income primarily from two business activities: portfolio investment activities and credit guarantee activities. With regard to investment activities, FRE purchases mortgage loans and mortgage-related securities and holds them in its retained portfolio. This business is quite profitable for Freddie Mac, because its cost of funds is, in a sense, subsidized by its quasi-agency status. While FRE functions in a manner similar to a savings and loan that originates home mortgage loans to hold for its own account, the major difference is that FRE uses capital market borrowings to finance its mortgage purchases, whereas thrifts use retail savings. Also, Freddie Mac purchases mortgages from various lenders, while thrifts actually issue mortgages to homebuyers. The retained portfolio business generates the majority of the company's profits.

The company also derives income from guaranteeing the payment of principal and interest on mortgage-related securities in exchange for a fee, which is referred to as a guarantee fee. The types of mortgage fee guarantees include: mortgage Participation Certificates (PCs), in which customers sell FRE mortgages in exchange for PCs; single-class and multi-class Structured Securities, which represent beneficial interests in pools of PCs; and securities related to tax-exempt multifamily housing revenue bonds.

The company's mortgage-backed securities (MBS) operation is best illustrated by an example. Typically, a bank or thrift decides that it prefers to hold MBSs, as opposed to originated loans. The institution then turns over the loan, or more often a pool of loans, to Freddie Mac, which gives the lender MBSs in return. The transaction helps both parties, in our opinion. Freddie Mac receives a fee of about one-fifth of 1% to guarantee the principal and interest on the MBSs. Meanwhile, the lender has a nearly risk-free instrument on which it receives principal and interest payments. Freddie Mac makes money in this business because its loss rate is very low: people will default on all sorts of bills, but the basic need for shelter provides a powerful incentive to keep mortgages more or less current.

Company Financials Fiscal Year Ended Dec. 31

Per Share Data ($)	2006	2005	2004	2003	2002	2001	2000	1999	1998	1997
Tangible Book Value	33.57	32.59	38.79	39.01	45.58	15.51	16.80	11.99	11.55	8.74
Earnings	2.84	2.83	3.94	6.68	14.18	5.96	3.39	2.95	2.31	1.88
S&P Core Earnings	2.83	3.16	3.95	6.70	14.22	5.91	NA	NA	NA	NA
Dividends	1.91	1.52	1.20	1.04	0.88	0.80	0.68	0.60	0.48	0.40
Payout Ratio	67%	54%	32%	16%	6%	13%	20%	20%	21%	21%
Prices:High	71.92	73.91	74.20	64.78	69.50	71.25	70.13	65.25	66.38	44.56
Prices:Low	55.64	54.50	56.45	46.48	52.60	58.75	36.88	45.38	38.69	26.69
P/E Ratio:High	25	26	19	10	5	12	21	22	29	24
P/E Ratio:Low	20	19	14	7	4	10	11	15	17	14

Income Statement Analysis (Million $)										
Interest on:Mortgages	38,825	33,721	32,467	33,302	34,239	30,180	23,989	19,714	14,269	11,030
Interest on:Investment	4,262	2,606	3,136	3,796	4,147	4,180	4,361	3,039	2,369	1,971
Interest Expense	37,270	29,899	26,566	28,150	26,564	28,808	25,512	20,213	14,711	11,119
Guaranty Fees	NA	NA	NA	NA	NA	1,639	1,489	1,405	1,307	1,298
Loan Loss Provision	215	251	143	10.0	128	45.0	40.0	60.0	190	310
Administration Expenses	2,774	2,666	2,242	2,064	1,553	1,020	883	655	578	495
Pretax Income	2,161	2,652	3,856	7,175	14,987	6,300	3,534	3,161	2,356	2,215
Effective Tax Rate	NM	13.8%	20.5%	30.7%	31.4%	30.6%	28.2%	29.8%	27.8%	25.7%
Net Income	2,211	2,189	2,937	4,816	10,090	4,373	2,539	2,218	1,700	1,395
S&P Core Earnings	1,926	2,194	2,737	4,605	9,881	4,121	NA	NA	NA	NA

Balance Sheet & Other Financial Data (Million $)										
Mortgages	700,543	709,503	664,582	660,531	589,722	494,585	385,117	322,569	255,348	164,250
Investment	56,945	57,324	62,027	83,936	124,245	75,894	40,718	31,747	44,753	13,402
Cash & Equivalent	11,359	10,468	35,253	23,142	10,792	1,508	366	5,144	2,565	438
Total Assets	813,081	806,222	795,284	803,449	752,249	617,340	459,297	386,684	321,421	194,597
Short Term Debt	294,861	288,532	282,303	295,262	244,429	250,338	183,576	175,525	193,871	85,128
Long Term Debt	459,077	460,260	449,394	444,351	421,267	311,608	243,178	185,056	Nil	83,446
Equity	22,192	22,582	26,807	26,878	24,381	10,777	11,642	8,330	8,028	5,934
% Return on Assets	0.3	0.3	0.4	0.6	1.4	0.8	0.6	0.6	0.7	0.8
% Return on Equity	8.7	8.0	10.2	17.2	49.3	37.1	23.6	25.2	22.6	20.6
Equity/Assets Ratio	36.2	32.4	29.8	29.0	34.9	2.1	2.4	2.3	2.7	3.1
Price Times Book Value:High	2.1	2.3	1.9	1.7	1.5	4.6	4.2	5.4	5.7	5.1
Price Times Book Value:Low	1.7	1.7	1.5	1.2	1.2	3.8	2.2	3.8	3.3	4.1

Data as orig reptd.; bef. results of disc opers/spec. items. Per share data adj. for stk. divs.; EPS diluted. E-Estimated. NA-Not Available. NM-Not Meaningful. NR-Not Ranked. UR-Under Review.

Office: 8200 Jones Branch Drive, McLean, VA 22102.
Telephone: 703-903-2000.
Website: http://www.freddiemac.com
Chrmn & CEO: R.F. Syron

Investor Contact: A.S. Piszel (703-903-2000)
EVP & CFO: A.S. Piszel
EVP & General Counsel: R. Bostrom

Board Members: B. T. Alexander, G. T. Boisi, M. Engler, R. Glauber, R. K. Goeltz, T. S. Johnson, W. M. Lewis, Jr., S. F. O'Malley, N. Retsinas, S. A. Ross, R. F. Syron

Auditor: PricewaterhouseCoopers
Founded: 1970
Domicile: United States
Employees: 5,400

Federal National Mortgage Association

STANDARD &POOR'S

S&P Recommendation **HOLD** ★★★★★	Price $32.20 (as of Nov 23, 2007)	12-Mo. Target Price $42.00	Investment Style Large-Cap Blend

GICS Sector Financials
Sub-Industry Thrifts & Mortgage Finance

Summary This government-sponsored enterprise (GSE) buys mortgage assets from other lenders and holds them in its portfolio or securitizes them for sale to investors.

Key Stock Statistics (Source S&P, Vickers, company reports)

52-Wk Range	$70.57– 26.38	S&P Oper. EPS 2007**E**	0.02	Market Capitalization(B)	$31.497	Beta	0.83
Trailing 12-Month EPS	$1.65	S&P Oper. EPS 2008**E**	-0.53	Yield (%)	6.21	S&P 3-Yr. Proj. EPS CAGR(%)	**NM**
Trailing 12-Month P/E	19.5	P/E on S&P Oper. EPS 2007**E**	**NM**	Dividend Rate/Share	$2.00	S&P Credit Rating	**AA-**
$10K Invested 5 Yrs Ago	$5,637	Common Shares Outstg. (M)	978.2	Institutional Ownership (%)	96		

Price Performance

30-Week Mov. Avg. · · · 10-Week Mov. Avg. - - **GAAP Earnings vs. Previous Year** Volume Above Avg. STARS
12-Mo. Target Price — Relative Strength — ▲ Up ▼ Down ► No Change Below Avg. ★

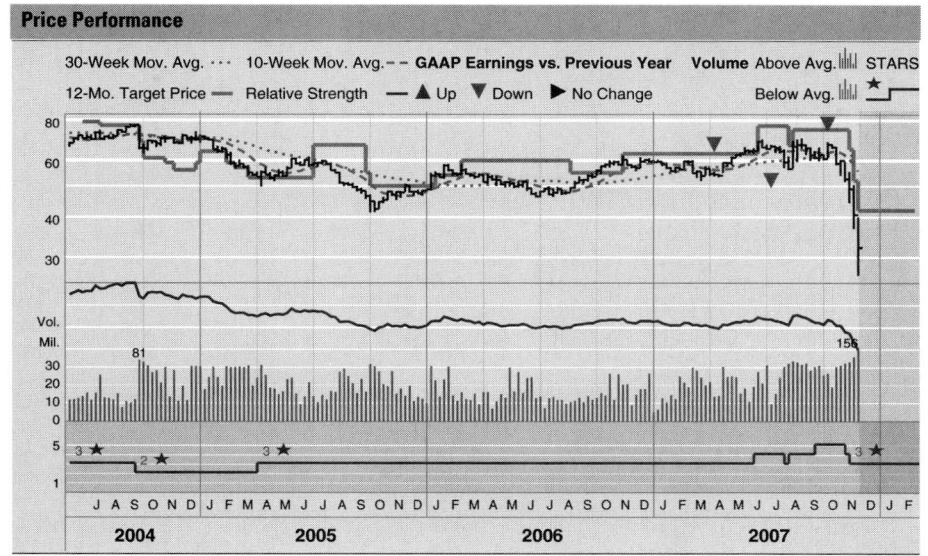

Options: ASE, CBOE, P, Ph

Analysis prepared by **Stuart Plesser** on November 20, 2007, when the stock traded at **$ 31.41**.

Qualitative Risk Assessment

LOW	**MEDIUM**	HIGH

Our risk assessment takes into account our projection of nationwide home price declines which will likely pressure FNM's credit guaranty business. FNM also has exposure to subprime loans in its held for investment portfolio. These issues are offset by FNM's attractive position as a government-sponsored enterprise.

Quantitative Evaluations

S&P Quality Ranking NR

D	C	B-	B	B+	A-	A	A+

Relative Strength Rank WEAK

3

LOWEST = 1   HIGHEST = 99

Revenue/Earnings Data

Revenue (Million $)

	1Q	2Q	3Q	4Q	Year
2007	--	--	--	--	--
2006	11,769	12,792	9,444	11,347	45,352
2005	--	--	--	--	43,702
2004	--	--	--	--	51,826
2003	--	--	--	--	52,685
2002	--	--	--	--	53,529

Earnings Per Share ($)

2007	0.85	1.86	-1.56	E-1.13	E0.02
2006	1.94	1.96	-0.79	0.49	3.64
2005	--	--	--	--	5.96
2004	-0.12	4.40	-0.92	1.59	4.94
2003	--	--	--	--	7.85
2002	--	--	--	--	3.81

Fiscal year ended Dec. 31. Next earnings report expected: NA. EPS Estimates based on S&P Operating Earnings; historical GAAP earnings are as reported.

Highlights

➤ Based on our expectations for a low single-digit increase in FNM's retained portfolio, and reduced interest expense, reflecting a more favorable interest-rate environment, we believe net interest income will increase in the fourth quarter and into 2008. Despite recent price declines for mortgage-backed securities, a regulatory cap on FNM's retained portfolio allowing the company to hold no more than $727 billion supports our projection for a low single-digit increase in assets.

➤ We estimate higher guarantee income in 2008 due to continued growth in outstanding Participation Certificates (PCs) and structured securities and higher fees. Notwithstanding FNM's small exposure to interest only and option adjustable rate mortgages (ARMs), and low loan-to-value ratios, we foresee a significant increase in provisions due to a tough housing environment. Given that FNM's earnings restatement is now complete, we see non-interest expenses declining in 2008, resulting in a modest improvement in operating margins.

➤ We forecast an operating loss of $0.02 per share for 2007, versus a profit of $3.64 in 2006. For 2008, we look for a loss of $0.53.

Investment Rationale/Risk

➤ Given credit market concerns over exotic mortgages, we see the likely return to fixed-rate mortgage products benefiting FNM's credit guaranty business. Although the company has roughly $11 a share in excess capital, we don't believe it will be returned to shareholders anytime soon in order to preserve capital and weather deteriorating credit markets. In view of the mortgage crisis, we believe regulators may allow FNM to expand its retained portfolio and possibly increase its lending cap ($417,000). We remain concerned, however, regarding deteriorating credit quality and the need for higher provisions, as well as possible writedowns in the roughly $56 billion of subprime loans that FNM holds in its retained portfolio.

➤ Risks to our recommendation and target price include more stringent regulation, and a worsening of credit conditions beyond our expectations.

➤ Our 12-month target price of $42 implies a price of about 1.3X book value per share of $31.75 (excluding preferred shares) as of September 30, 2007, a discount to FNM's one-year average, reflecting housing concerns.

Dividend Data (Dates: mm/dd Payment Date: mm/dd/yy)

Amount ($)	Date Decl.	Ex-Div. Date	Stk. of Record	Payment Date
0.400	04/20	04/26	04/30	05/25/07
.1 Spl.	05/04	05/16	05/18	05/25/07
0.500	07/17	07/27	07/31	08/27/07
0.500	10/16	10/29	10/31	11/26/07

Dividends have been paid since 1956. Source: Company reports.

Federal National Mortgage Association

**STANDARD
&POOR'S**

Business Summary November 20, 2007

CORPORATE OVERVIEW. The Federal National Mortgage Association (known as Fannie Mae) is a government-sponsored enterprise, chartered by Congress to increase the availability of mortgage credit for home buyers. Its mission is essentially to increase the rate of home ownership, making American society more stable. The company's predecessor was formed during the Great Depression, in an effort to make home ownership possible at a time when it was nearly impossible for people in certain parts of the U.S. to obtain a mortgage. FNM basically operates in two business segments.

PRIMARY BUSINESS DYNAMICS. In its retained mortgage portfolio business, which accounts for most of its profits, the company buys mortgages from lenders such as thrifts, banks and mortgage bankers, and holds them on account. It funds mortgage purchases with debt of various maturities, earning a spread on the difference between the yield on the mortgages and the cost of the debt. FNM purchased $197 billion of mortgages in 2006, and the gross ending balance of its mortgage portfolio totaled $724.4 billion, versus $727.5 billion the previous year.

In securitization operations, which account for much of FNM's remaining profits, the company swaps mortgage-backed securities (MBSs) for mortgages with various lending institutions, and in the process, earns a fee of about 0.20%. The main reason that lenders swap loans for MBSs is that the lending institution has a virtually risk-free liquid instrument that it can either sell or hold and collect interest. FNM functions as a mortgage insurer in that it accepts the risk of default on the mortgage in exchange for a fee or a premium. In 2006, its total single family MBS outstanding (including MBS held in portfolio) totaled roughly $2.0 trillion, compared to $1.9 trillion the previous year.

Company Financials Fiscal Year Ended Dec. 31

Per Share Data ($)	2006	2005	2004	2003	2002	2001	2000	1999	1998	1997
Tangible Book Value	33.33	31.10	30.43	29.02	29.55	15.86	18.58	16.03	13.95	12.34
Earnings	3.64	5.96	4.94	7.85	3.81	5.89	4.26	3.73	3.26	2.84
S&P Core Earnings	3.65	5.94	5.19	7.66	4.45	5.65	NA	NA	NA	NA
Dividends	1.18	1.04	2.08	1.68	1.32	1.20	1.12	1.08	0.96	0.84
Payout Ratio	32%	17%	42%	21%	35%	20%	26%	29%	29%	30%
Prices:High	62.37	71.70	80.82	75.95	84.10	87.94	89.38	75.88	76.19	57.31
Prices:Low	46.17	41.34	62.95	58.40	58.85	72.08	47.88	58.56	49.56	36.13
P/E Ratio:High	17	12	16	10	22	15	21	20	23	20
P/E Ratio:Low	13	7	13	7	15	12	11	16	15	13

Income Statement Analysis (Million $)										
Interest on:Mortgages	20,804	20,688	21,390	21,370	19,870	46,478	39,403	32,672	25,676	22,716
Interest on:Investment	22,823	24,156	26,428	27,694	31,054	2,692	3,378	2,823	4,319	3,662
Interest Expense	36,875	33,339	29,737	29,587	32,498	41,080	37,107	30,601	25,885	22,429
Guaranty Fees	3,735	3,779	3,604	3,281	2,516	1,482	1,351	1,282	1,229	1,274
Loan Loss Provision	589	441	362	365	284	Nil	Nil	-120	50.0	100
Administration Expenses	4,254	2,794	2,626	1,454	1,156	1,017	905	800	708	636
Pretax Income	4,223	7,569	5,991	10,286	4,754	8,291	5,982	5,440	4,645	4,337
Effective Tax Rate	3.93%	16.9%	17.1%	23.7%	17.7%	26.8%	26.2%	27.9%	25.9%	29.3%
Net Income	4,097	6,294	4,975	7,852	3,914	6,067	4,416	3,921	3,444	3,068
S&P Core Earnings	3,552	5,800	5,056	7,518	4,440	5,688	NA	NA	NA	NA

Balance Sheet & Other Financial Data (Million $)										
Mortgages	383,555	367,543	401,372	385,465	304,178	705,167	607,399	522,780	415,223	313,316
Investment	390,112	406,074	567,382	567,070	535,085	74,554	54,968	39,751	58,213	64,596
Cash & Equivalent	3,239	2,820	2,655	7,631	NA	1,518	617	2,099	743	2,205
Total Assets	843,936	834,168	1,020,934	1,022,275	904,739	799,791	675,072	575,167	485,014	391,673
Short Term Debt	166,510	173,891	320,280	343,662	293,538	343,492	280,322	226,582	205,413	175,400
Long Term Debt	601,236	590,824	632,831	617,618	547,755	419,975	362,360	321,037	254,878	194,374
Equity	32,398	30,194	29,794	28,160	29,221	15,815	18,560	16,329	14,303	12,793
% Return on Assets	4.9	0.7	0.5	0.8	0.5	0.8	0.7	0.7	0.8	0.8
% Return on Equity	13.1	19.4	16.6	27.4	15.6	34.5	24.6	25.1	25.4	24.4
Equity/Assets Ratio	37.3	30.9	35.3	3.0	2.9	2.3	3.6	2.9	3.1	3.6
Price Times Book Value:High	1.9	2.3	2.7	2.6	2.8	5.5	4.8	4.7	5.5	4.6
Price Times Book Value:Low	1.4	1.3	1.9	2.0	2.0	4.5	2.6	3.7	3.6	2.9

Data as orig reptd.; bef. results of disc opers/spec. items. Per share data adj. for stk. divs.; EPS diluted. 2003 and 2002 data have been restated from the 2004 10K to correct misstatements. E-Estimated. NA-Not Available. NM-Not Meaningful. NR-Not Ranked. UR-Under Review.

Office: 3900 Wisconsin Avenue NW, Washington, DC 20016-2892.
Telephone: 202-752-7000.
Email: investor_relations1@fanniemae.com
Website: http://www.fanniemae.com

Chrmn: S.B. Ashley
Pres & CEO: D.H. Mudd
COO & EVP: M.J. Williams
EVP & CFO: S.M. Swand

EVP, Secy & General Counsel: B.A. Wilkinson
Board Members: S. B. Ashley, D. R. Beresford, L. J. Freeh, B. Gaines, K. Horn, B. Macaskill, D. H. Mudd, J. K. Pickett, L. Rahl, G. C. Smith, H. P. Swygert, J. K. Wulff

Founded: 1938
Domicile: United States
Employees: 6,600

STANDARD &POOR'S

Federated Investors Inc.

S&P Recommendation	BUY ★★★★☆	Price	12-Mo. Target Price	Investment Style
		$37.91 (as of Nov 23, 2007)	$46.00	Large-Cap Growth

GICS Sector Financials
Sub-Industry Asset Management & Custody Banks

Summary This leading U.S. investment management company has a strong market share in money market products.

Key Stock Statistics (Source S&P, Vickers, company reports)

52-Wk Range	$43.35– 30.31	S&P Oper. EPS 2007E	2.20	Market Capitalization(B)	$3.904	Beta	0.96
Trailing 12-Month EPS	$2.11	S&P Oper. EPS 2008E	2.61	Yield (%)	2.22	S&P 3-Yr. Proj. EPS CAGR(%)	8.00
Trailing 12-Month P/E	18.0	P/E on S&P Oper. EPS 2007E	17.2	Dividend Rate/Share	$0.84	S&P Credit Rating	NA
$10K Invested 5 Yrs Ago	$15,292	Common Shares Outstg. (M)	103.0	Institutional Ownership (%)	64		

Price Performance

- 30-Week Mov. Avg.
- 10-Week Mov. Avg.
- GAAP Earnings vs. Previous Year
- Volume Above Avg.
- STARS
- 12-Mo. Target Price
- Relative Strength
- ▲ Up ▼ Down ▶ No Change
- Below Avg.

Options: ASE

Analysis prepared by **Matthew Albrecht** on November 06, 2007, when the stock traded at **$ 39.93**.

Highlights

- ➤ We believe Federated Investors should benefit from recent volatility in the markets, as the company's flagship money market and ultra-short term bond products may be relatively more attractive to investors. We also believe the company's recent focus on growing separate accounts and equity assets, which made up 17% of assets under management (AUM) at the end of 2006, but 40% of revenues, will be a profitable move. AUM increased 24% over the prior 12 months at the end of September, led by money market assets, and we look for more than 20% growth for 2007, before slower double-digit growth in 2008, with revenues advancing at a slightly slower rate due to a lower management fee capture rate.

- ➤ We look for a relatively flat pretax margin in each of 2007 and 2008. We anticipate modest growth in compensation and advertising expenses, offset by cost controls elsewhere, including general and administrative costs.

- ➤ We forecast EPS of $2.20 in 2007 and $2.61 in 2008, aided by modest share repurchases.

Investment Rationale/Risk

- ➤ We view a slightly discounted valuation on the shares relative to peers as appropriate, given the firm's focus on lower-margined money market funds. We view favorably the company's direct sales force and strong relationships with wholesalers and intermediaries in our valuation. We also applaud the recent moves to increase FII's exposure to equities, which should help margins. We view favorably the company's common share repurchase program, which we estimate could exceed 4 million shares per year.

- ➤ Risks to our recommendation and target price include potentially increased competition, lower short-term interest rates, and weaker equity fund performance. From a corporate governance perspective, we would like to see a greater percentage of independent directors on the board.

- ➤ These shares have recovered from late-summer concerns about the quality of money market investments, and have outperformed the market year to date. They recently traded at about 18.1X our 2007 EPS estimate. Our 12-month target price of $46 is equal to 17.6X our 2008 EPS estimate, a discount to peers.

Qualitative Risk Assessment

LOW	MEDIUM	HIGH

Our risk assessment reflects the company's relatively narrow product offering and significant competition from larger, more diversified fund management companies.

Quantitative Evaluations

S&P Quality Ranking A

D	C	B-	B	B+	A-	A	A+

Relative Strength Rank MODERATE

62

LOWEST = 1   HIGHEST = 99

Revenue/Earnings Data

Revenue (Million $)

	1Q	2Q	3Q	4Q	Year
2007	264.4	276.5	286.0	--	--
2006	238.8	236.4	243.9	259.7	978.9
2005	205.4	220.7	241.4	241.8	909.2
2004	220.7	213.1	205.2	208.1	847.0
2003	194.1	202.5	210.0	216.8	823.3
2002	181.6	182.4	173.2	173.8	711.1

Earnings Per Share ($)

2007	0.50	0.54	0.57	E0.59	E2.20
2006	0.43	0.44	0.43	0.51	1.80
2005	0.07	0.35	0.61	0.48	1.51
2004	0.46	0.44	0.43	0.29	1.62
2003	0.43	0.44	0.46	0.38	1.71
2002	0.44	0.45	0.43	0.42	1.74

Fiscal year ended Dec. 31. Next earnings report expected: Late January. EPS Estimates based on S&P Operating Earnings; historical GAAP earnings are as reported.

Dividend Data (Dates: mm/dd Payment Date: mm/dd/yy)

Amount ($)	Date Decl.	Ex-Div. Date	Stk. of Record	Payment Date
0.180	01/29	02/06	02/08	02/15/07
0.210	04/26	05/04	05/08	05/15/07
0.210	07/26	08/06	08/08	08/15/07
0.210	10/25	11/06	11/08	11/15/07

Dividends have been paid since 1998. Source: Company reports.

Federated Investors Inc.

STANDARD &POOR'S

Business Summary November 06, 2007

CORPORATE OVERVIEW. A leading provider of investment management products and related financial services, Federated Investors (FII) has been in the mutual fund business for more than 40 years. The company is one of the largest mutual fund managers in the United States, based on assets under management. Assets under management at the end of 2006 totaled $237 billion, up from $213 billion at the end of 2005.

Federated manages assets across a wide range of asset categories, including increasing participation in fast growing areas such as equity and international investments. It is among the industry leaders in money market funds, based on assets under management, and offers one of the industry's most comprehensive product lines. Assets under management by class at the end of 2006 included money market (73% of total), equity (17%), and fixed income (10%). By product type, mutual funds represented about 85% of total assets under man-

agement, with the balance held in separately managed accounts.

CORPORATE STRATEGY. Over the past several years, Federated has added several investment professionals and strengthened its equity and fixed-income product portfolio, in our opinion. The company has more than 170 investment professionals, which includes portfolio managers, analysts and traders. The company ended 2006 with 148 mutual funds and various separately managed accounts. FII has managed institutional separate accounts since 1973, and is focused on growing its managed account business for high-net-worth individuals with investable equity assets of $100,000 or more.

Company Financials Fiscal Year Ended Dec. 31

Per Share Data ($)	2006	2005	2004	2003	2002	2001	2000	1999	1998	1997
Tangible Book Value	0.39	1.59	1.36	2.05	1.46	0.79	0.86	0.62	0.28	NM
Cash Flow	2.07	1.75	1.79	1.95	1.90	1.65	1.40	1.10	0.88	0.70
Earnings	1.80	1.51	1.62	1.71	1.74	1.44	1.27	0.96	0.71	0.61
S&P Core Earnings	1.80	1.67	1.70	1.67	1.69	1.46	NA	NA	NA	NA
Dividends	0.69	0.58	0.41	0.30	0.22	0.22	0.14	0.11	0.05	0.07
Payout Ratio	38%	38%	26%	17%	12%	15%	11%	11%	7%	Nil
Prices:High	40.17	38.11	33.79	31.90	36.18	32.80	31.69	14.12	13.46	NA
Prices:Low	29.56	26.99	26.72	23.85	23.43	23.31	12.46	10.04	7.33	NA
P/E Ratio:High	22	25	21	19	21	23	25	15	19	NA
P/E Ratio:Low	16	18	16	14	13	16	10	10	10	NA

Income Statement Analysis (Million $)	2006	2005	2004	2003	2002	2001	2000	1999	1998	1997
Income Interest	2.51	8.73	3.39	2.15	2.40	9.74	19.0	13.9	8.88	3.03
Income Other	7.02	0.05	-0.11	0.00	2.27	706	662	587	513	401
Total Income	979	909	847	823	711	716	681	601	522	401
General Expenses	694	634	530	531	399	388	394	364	340	294
Interest Expense	8.19	17.9	21.0	4.71	4.79	29.7	34.2	31.8	27.6	20.1
Depreciation	24.1	24.0	19.0	20.6	19.2	26.0	15.8	18.1	22.9	22.4
Net Income	191	163	179	191	204	173	155	124	92.4	51.0
S&P Core Earnings	191	181	188	187	199	175	NA	NA	NA	NA

Balance Sheet & Other Financial Data (Million $)	2006	2005	2004	2003	2002	2001	2000	1999	1998	1997
Cash	119	246	258	234	151	73.5	150	171	186	NA
Receivables	23.3	45.8	33.8	38.3	31.2	32.6	36.9	35.2	31.0	NA
Cost of Investments	16.2	38.4	2.10	1.53	1.00	4.60	85.3	66.4	13.4	NA
Total Assets	810	897	955	879	530	432	705	673	580	NA
Loss Reserve	Nil	Nil	Nil	Nil	Nil	0.32	0.09	0.18	1.27	NA
Short Term Debt	Nil	Nil	Nil	Nil	Nil	Nil	14.3	14.3	0.24	0.28
Capitalization:Debt	113	160	285	328	59.2	55.0	394	394	372	284
Capitalization:Equity	529	540	458	396	341	237	148	119	88.7	-41.1
Capitalization:Total	671	723	767	744	416	299	583	551	491	244
Price Times Book Value:High	103	24.0	24.8	15.6	24.8	41.5	36.7	22.0	49.0	NA
Price Times Book Value:Low	76.0	17.0	19.6	11.6	16.0	29.5	14.5	16.0	27.0	NA
Cash Flow	215	187	198	212	223	199	171	142	115	73.4
% Expense/Operating Revenue	71.7	71.7	65.1	65.1	56.7	58.4	62.9	65.9	70.4	78.3
% Earnings & Depreciation/Assets	25.2	20.2	19.5	25.3	46.4	35.0	24.8	22.7	NA	NA

Data as orig reptd.; bef. results of disc opers/spec. items. Per share data adj. for stk. divs.; EPS diluted. E-Estimated. NA-Not Available. NM-Not Meaningful. NR-Not Ranked. UR-Under Review.

Office: 1001 Liberty Avenue, Pittsburgh, PA 15222-3779.
Telephone: 412-288-1900.
Email: investors@federatedinv.com
Website: http://www.FederatedInvestors.com

Chrmn: J.F. Donahue
Pres & CEO: J.C. Donahue
Vice Chrmn, EVP, Secy & Chief Lgl Officer: J.W. McGonigle
VP, CFO & Treas: T.R. Donahue

VP & CCO: B.P. Bouda
Investor Contact: R. Hanley (412-288-1920)
Board Members: J. C. Donahue, J. F. Donahue, M. J. Farrell, D. M. Kelly, J. W. McGonigle, J. L. Murdy, E. G. O'Connor

Founded: 1955
Domicile: Pennsylvania
Employees: 1,243

FedEx Corp.

S&P Recommendation	STRONG BUY ★★★★★	Price	12-Mo. Target Price	Investment Style
		$93.60 (as of Nov 23, 2007)	$140.00	Large-Cap Growth

GICS Sector Industrials
Sub-Industry Air Freight & Logistics

Summary This company provides guaranteed domestic and international air express, residential and business ground package delivery, heavy freight and logistics services.

Key Stock Statistics (Source S&P, Vickers, company reports)

52-Wk Range	$121.42– 91.56	S&P Oper. EPS 2008**E**	6.65	Market Capitalization(B)	$28.947	Beta	0.65
Trailing 12-Month EPS	$6.53	S&P Oper. EPS 2009**E**	7.65	Yield (%)	0.43	S&P 3-Yr. Proj. EPS CAGR(%)	11.00
Trailing 12-Month P/E	14.3	P/E on S&P Oper. EPS 2008**E**	14.1	Dividend Rate/Share	$0.40	S&P Credit Rating	BBB
$10K Invested 5 Yrs Ago	$18,049	Common Shares Outstg. (M)	309.3	Institutional Ownership (%)	73		

Price Performance

Options: ASE, CBOE, P, PH

Analysis prepared by **Jim Corridore** on October 09, 2007, when the stock traded at **$ 106.80**.

Highlights

➤ We see FY 08 (May) revenues rising about 7%, following 9% growth in FY 07. We view the economic outlook as supportive of growth in shipping demand, albeit at a slower pace than in FY 07. We expect about 8% volume growth at Ground, with revenues increasing about 5%, which should be aided by market share gains and price hikes. We look for 1% volume growth and 5% revenue growth at Express. We estimate that international revenues will continue to rise in the double digits, driven by export activity out of China.

➤ We think operating margins are likely to widen modestly, aided by lower salaries and benefits, purchased transportation, maintenance and depreciation as a percentage of revenues. We think efforts to focus on a better mix of products will help margins. The company is attempting to push lower margin shipments into ground and freight channels, which could also aid margins.

➤ We forecast FY 08 operating EPS of $7.00, which would represent 8% growth over FY 07 reported EPS of $6.48.

Investment Rationale/Risk

➤ We think FDX is likely to improve operating margins, which should help drive strong net income and free cash flow growth. We also believe the U.S. and global economies are likely to see accelerating growth as we enter 2008, which we think justifies a higher valuation for this cyclical stock. FDX was recently trading at a P/E below the S&P 500, while we expect that the company is likely to increase EPS faster than the overall market. In our opinion, FDX will achieve its goals of improving operating margins, cash flow, and return on invested capital.

➤ Risks to our recommendation and target price include a possible price war or a major economic slowdown. In addition, we are concerned about some of FDX's corporate governance practices, such as the presence of affiliated outsiders on the board of directors and the audit committee.

➤ Our 12-month target price of $140 is based on a P/E of 20X applied to our FY 08 EPS estimate, near the low end of the company's five-year historical P/E range of 16.3X-36.6X EPS, and below United Parcel Service (UPS: buy, $76).

Qualitative Risk Assessment

LOW	MEDIUM	HIGH

Our risk assessment reflects our view of the company's strong and stable balance sheet, healthy cash flow generation, and strong earnings growth potential amid the inherent cyclicality of its business segment. This is only partly offset by the potential that FDX could suffer from a material economic slowdown.

Quantitative Evaluations

S&P Quality Ranking B+

D	C	B-	B	B+	A-	A	A+

Relative Strength Rank MODERATE

34

LOWEST = 1 — HIGHEST = 99

Revenue/Earnings Data

Revenue (Million $)

	1Q	2Q	3Q	4Q	Year
2008	9,199	--	--	--	--
2007	8,545	8,926	8,592	9,151	35,214
2006	7,707	8,090	8,003	8,494	32,294
2005	6,975	7,334	7,339	7,715	29,363
2004	5,687	5,920	6,062	7,041	24,710
2003	5,445	5,667	5,545	5,830	22,487

Earnings Per Share ($)

2008	1.58	E1.55	E1.42	E2.10	E6.65
2007	1.53	1.64	1.35	1.96	6.48
2006	1.10	1.53	1.38	1.82	5.83
2005	1.08	1.15	1.03	1.46	4.72
2004	0.42	0.30	0.68	1.36	2.76
2003	0.52	0.81	0.49	0.92	2.74

Fiscal year ended May 31. Next earnings report expected: Mid December. EPS Estimates based on S&P Operating Earnings; historical GAAP earnings are as reported.

Dividend Data (Dates: mm/dd Payment Date: mm/dd/yy)

Amount ($)	Date Decl.	Ex-Div. Date	Stk. of Record	Payment Date
0.090	02/16	03/08	03/12	04/02/07
0.100	05/25	06/07	06/11	07/02/07
0.100	08/17	09/06	09/10	10/01/07
0.100	11/16	12/10	12/12	01/02/08

Dividends have been paid since 2002. Source: Company reports.

FedEx Corp.

STANDARD &POOR'S

Business Summary October 09, 2007

CORPORATE OVERVIEW. FedEx Corp. provides global time-definite air express services for packages, documents and freight in more than 220 countries, and ground-based delivery of small packages in North America. In addition, the company offers expedited critical shipment delivery, customs brokerage solutions, less-than-truckload (LTL) freight transportation, and customized logistics. In February 2004, FDX paid $2.4 billion in cash for Kinko's, which operates about 1,200 copy centers that also provide business services. Kinko's has annual revenues of about $2 billion. Kinko's joined three other FedEx companies: Express, Ground, and Freight.

CORPORATE STRATEGY. The company intends to leverage and extend the FedEx brand and to provide customers with seamless access to its entire

portfolio of integrated transportation services. Sales and marketing activities are coordinated among operating companies. Advanced information technology makes it convenient for customers to use the full range of FedEx services and provides a single point of contact for customers to access shipment tracking, customer service and invoicing information. The company intends to continue to operate independent express, ground and freight networks, but has increased its emphasis on having the individual business units work together to compete more effectively.

Company Financials Fiscal Year Ended May 31

Per Share Data ($)	2007	2006	2005	2004	2003	2002	2001	2000	1999	1998
Tangible Book Value	29.73	28.39	22.36	17.45	21.03	18.38	16.20	14.33	14.50	12.26
Cash Flow	12.20	10.83	9.48	7.28	7.20	6.89	6.35	6.23	5.55	4.91
Earnings	6.48	5.83	4.72	2.76	2.74	2.39	1.99	2.32	2.10	1.68
S&P Core Earnings	6.32	5.60	4.48	2.61	1.38	0.95	0.44	NA	NA	NA
Dividends	0.32	0.33	0.29	0.22	0.20	Nil	Nil	Nil	Nil	Nil
Payout Ratio	5%	6%	6%	8%	7%	Nil	Nil	Nil	Nil	Nil
Calendar Year	2006	2005	2004	2003	2002	2001	2000	1999	1998	1997
Prices:High	120.01	105.82	100.92	78.05	61.35	53.48	49.85	61.88	46.56	42.25
Prices:Low	96.50	76.81	64.84	47.70	42.75	33.15	30.56	34.88	21.81	21.00
P/E Ratio:High	19	18	21	28	22	22	25	27	22	25
P/E Ratio:Low	15	13	14	17	16	14	15	15	10	12

Income Statement Analysis (Million $)

	2007	2006	2005	2004	2003	2002	2001	2000	1999	1998
Revenue	35,214	32,294	29,363	24,710	22,487	20,607	19,629	18,257	16,773	15,873
Operating Income	5,018	4,564	3,933	3,250	2,822	2,804	2,347	2,376	2,198	2,047
Depreciation	1,742	1,550	1,462	1,375	1,351	1,364	1,276	1,155	1,035	964
Interest Expense	136	142	160	136	118	139	144	106	98.0	124
Pretax Income	3,215	2,899	2,313	1,319	1,338	1,160	928	1,138	1,061	899
Effective Tax Rate	37.3%	37.7%	37.4%	36.5%	38.0%	37.5%	37.0%	39.5%	40.5%	44.6%
Net Income	2,016	1,806	1,449	838	830	725	584	688	631	498
S&P Core Earnings	1,966	1,733	1,376	790	415	286	130	NA	NA	NA

Balance Sheet & Other Financial Data (Million $)

	2007	2006	2005	2004	2003	2002	2001	2000	1999	1998
Cash	1,569	1,937	1,039	1,046	538	331	121	68.0	325	230
Current Assets	6,629	6,464	5,269	4,970	3,941	3,665	3,449	3,285	3,141	2,880
Total Assets	24,000	22,690	20,404	19,134	15,385	13,812	13,340	11,527	10,648	9,686
Current Liabilities	5,428	5,473	4,734	4,732	3,335	2,942	3,250	2,891	2,785	2,804
Long Term Debt	2,662	1,592	2,427	2,837	1,709	1,800	1,900	1,776	1,360	1,385
Common Equity	12,656	11,511	9,588	8,036	7,288	6,545	5,900	4,785	4,664	3,961
Total Capital	16,215	14,470	13,221	12,054	9,879	8,944	8,256	6,906	6,317	5,620
Capital Expenditures	2,882	2,518	2,236	1,271	1,511	1,615	1,893	1,627	1,550	1,880
Cash Flow	3,758	3,356	2,911	2,213	2,181	2,089	1,860	1,843	1,665	1,462
Current Ratio	1.2	1.2	1.1	1.1	1.2	1.2	1.1	1.1	1.1	1.0
% Long Term Debt of Capitalization	16.4	11.0	18.3	23.5	17.2	20.1	23.0	25.7	21.5	24.6
% Net Income of Revenue	5.7	5.6	4.9	3.4	3.7	3.5	3.0	3.8	3.8	3.1
% Return on Assets	8.6	8.4	7.3	4.9	5.7	5.3	4.7	6.2	6.2	5.8
% Return on Equity	16.7	17.1	16.4	10.9	11.8	11.7	10.9	14.6	14.6	14.4

Data as orig reptd.; bef. results of disc opers/spec. items. Per share data adj. for stk. divs.; EPS diluted. E-Estimated. NA-Not Available. NM-Not Meaningful. NR-Not Ranked. UR-Under Review.

Office: 942 South Shady Grove Road, Memphis, TN 38120-4117.
Telephone: 901-818-7500.
Website: http://www.fedex.com
Chrmn, Pres & CEO: F.W. Smith

Investor Contact: A.B. Graf, Jr. (901-818-7388)
EVP & CFO: A.B. Graf, Jr.
EVP, Secy & General Counsel: C.P. Richards
EVP & CIO: R.B. Carter

Board Members: J. L. Barksdale, A. A. Busch, IV, J. A. Edwardson, J. L. Estrin, J. K. Glass, P. Greer, J. R. Hyde, III, S. A. Jackson, S. R. Loranger, C. T. Manatt, F. W. Smith, J. I. Smith, P. S. Walsh, P. S. Willmott

Founded: 1971
Domicile: Delaware
Employees: 143,000

The *McGraw-Hill* Companies

Fidelity National Information Services Inc

STANDARD &POOR'S

S&P Recommendation	**BUY** ★★★★☆	Price $42.89 (as of Nov 23, 2007)	12-Mo. Target Price $61.00	Investment Style Large-Cap Growth

GICS Sector Information Technology
Sub-Industry Data Processing & Outsourced Services

Summary This Florida-based company is a leading provider of core processing and mortgage-related processing services and products to financial institutions and lenders.

Key Stock Statistics (Source S&P, Vickers, company reports)

52-Wk Range	$57.80–39.33	S&P Oper. EPS 2007E	2.44	Market Capitalization(B)	$8.319	Beta	NA
Trailing 12-Month EPS	$2.69	S&P Oper. EPS 2008E	2.90	Yield (%)	0.47	S&P 3-Yr. Proj. EPS CAGR(%)	13.00
Trailing 12-Month P/E	15.9	P/E on S&P Oper. EPS 2007E	17.6	Dividend Rate/Share	$0.20	S&P Credit Rating	NA
$10K Invested 5 Yrs Ago	NA	Common Shares Outstg. (M)	194.0	Institutional Ownership (%)	77		

Price Performance

30-Week Mov. Avg. · · · 10-Week Mov. Avg. - - GAAP Earnings vs. Previous Year   Volume Above Avg. STARS
12-Mo. Target Price — Relative Strength — ▲ Up ▼ Down ► No Change   Below Avg.

Options: ASE, CBOE, P, Ph

Analysis prepared by **Zaineb Bokhari** on October 30, 2007, when the stock traded at **$ 45.66.**

Highlights

➤ We expect revenues to increase by 14% in 2007, to about $4.8 billion, as FIS continues to sell additional services to its existing customers and broadens its penetration of the mid-sized bank and lender markets. Our outlook includes contribution from the recent acquisition of eFunds (September 2007). We see the completion of the Bradesco card conversions supporting our outlook for revenue growth of 13% in 2008.

➤ We look for 2007 EBITDA margins to widen, helped by revenue growth and cost synergies from ongoing merger integration. We think the company's Brazilian item processing operation will aid margin expansion in late 2007. We look for modestly wider segment EBITDA margins in 2008, as FIS converts its Bradesco card portfolio and targets synergies from its eFunds acquisition.

➤ Our 2007 EPS estimate is $2.44, up from $2.10 in 2006, and we forecast $2.90 for 2008. Our estimates exclude projected merger and acquisition integration costs, one-time charges and purchase price amortization in both years.

Investment Rationale/Risk

➤ FIS shares have pulled back recently, we believe, due to investors' concerns about the subprime mortgage market. We are encouraged by ongoing cost-cutting efforts and believe that existing long-term and multi-year contracts will allow the company to generate recurring revenues. We have a favorable view of the growth FIS is delivering in its Lender Processing segment, despite softness in the domestic mortgage industry, on strong demand for default management and other information services. FIS has set a plan to spin off its lender unit by mid-2008, possibly removing some volatility from the shares.

➤ Risks to our recommendation and target price include a significant contraction in the U.S. housing market and mortgage origination volumes from recent levels. We also note that ongoing consolidation among financial services customers could lead to business disruption.

➤ We derive our 12-month target price of $61 by applying a 21.0X P/E to our 2008 EPS estimate of $2.90, below the 21.9X average P/E multiple for data processing and outsourced services peers, reflecting FIS's exposure to the mortgage industry.

Qualitative Risk Assessment

LOW	**MEDIUM**	HIGH

Our risk assessment reflects uncertainty surrounding the U.S. housing market, which could affect the company's lender processing segment. While the company faces ongoing acquisition integration risks, we think these concerns have faded somewhat after several quarters of what we consider consistent and improving financial performance.

Quantitative Evaluations

S&P Quality Ranking   NR

D	C	B-	B	B+	A-	A	A+

Relative Strength Rank   MODERATE

49

LOWEST = 1   HIGHEST = 99

Revenue/Earnings Data

Revenue (Million $)

	1Q	2Q	3Q	4Q	Year
2007	1,124	1,176	1,168	--	--
2006	900.9	1,022	1,081	1,129	4,133
2005	262.5	276.0	282.8	295.9	1,117
2004	--	--	--	--	1,040
2003	--	--	--	--	--
2002	--	--	--	--	--

Earnings Per Share ($)

2007	0.30	0.75	1.02	E0.68	E2.44
2006	0.23	0.34	0.41	0.39	1.37
2005	0.34	0.40	0.36	0.57	1.66
2004	--	--	--	--	0.92
2003	--	--	--	--	--
2002	--	--	--	--	--

Fiscal year ended Dec. 31. Next earnings report expected: Early February. EPS Estimates based on S&P Operating Earnings; historical GAAP earnings are as reported.

Dividend Data (Dates: mm/dd Payment Date: mm/dd/yy)

Amount ($)	Date Decl.	Ex-Div. Date	Stk. of Record	Payment Date
0.050	02/06	03/12	03/14	03/28/07
0.050	04/24	06/12	06/14	06/28/07
0.050	07/24	09/11	09/13	09/27/07
0.050	10/23	12/11	12/13	12/27/07

Dividends have been paid since 2006. Source: Company reports.

Fidelity National Information Services Inc

STANDARD &POOR'S

Business Summary October 30, 2007

CORPORATE OVERVIEW. Fidelity National Information Services, Inc. (FIS) was formed via the combination, on February 1, 2006, of the information processing subsidiary of Fidelity National Financial (FNF), a leading provider of title and specialty insurance, and Certegy, a provider of card and check processing services. As a result of the combination, the company is a leading provider of technology solutions, processing services, and information-based services to the financial industry. The company's primary services include core processing services, check services, card issuer and transaction processing services, risk management services, mortgage loan processing, mortgage-related information products, and outsourcing services.

FIS operates in two main business segments: Transaction Processing Services (TPS) and Lender Processing Services (LPS).

The Transaction Processing Services segment is comprised of Certegy's Card and Check Services businesses and the pre-merger financial institution processing businesses of FIS. The segment accounted for 60% of pro forma revenue in 2006 and is further segmented into integrated financial solutions

(independent community banks, credit unions, and savings banks), enterprise solutions (large North America-based financial institutions, commercial lenders, etc.), international, and other. At December 31, 2006, FIS had processing and technology relationships with 35 of the top 50 global banks, including nine of the top 10. Through its Lender Processing Services segment (40%), FIS offers a broad range of mortgage-related products and services to support origination, data gathering, risk management, servicing, default management among others. According to the company's 10-K filing for 2006, over 50% of all U.S. residential mortgages (by dollar volume) were processed using its loan servicing platform.

The company serves customers in more than 60 countries. No customer accounted for more than 10% of total revenue or total segment revenue in 2006.

Company Financials Fiscal Year Ended Dec. 31

Per Share Data ($)	2006	2005	2004	2003	2002	2001	2000	1999	1998	1997
Tangible Book Value	NM	3.53	0.55	NA	NA	NA	NA	NA	NA	NA
Cash Flow	3.66	2.48	2.40	NA	NA	NA	NA	NA	NA	NA
Earnings	1.37	1.66	0.92	NA	NA	NA	NA	NA	NA	NA
S&P Core Earnings	1.37	0.98	0.94	1.00	NA	NA	NA	NA	NA	NA
Dividends	0.20	Nil	Nil	NA	NA	NA	NA	NA	NA	NA
Payout Ratio	15%	Nil	Nil	NA	NA	NA	NA	NA	NA	NA
Prices:High	42.62	NA	NA	NA	NA	NA	NA	NA	NA	NA
Prices:Low	33.50	NA	NA	NA	NA	NA	NA	NA	NA	NA
P/E Ratio:High	31	NA	NA	NA	NA	NA	NA	NA	NA	NA
P/E Ratio:Low	24	NA	NA	NA	NA	NA	NA	NA	NA	NA

Income Statement Analysis (Million $)	2006	2005	2004	2003	2002	2001	2000	1999	1998	1997
Revenue	4,133	1,117	1,040	NA	NA	NA	NA	NA	NA	NA
Operating Income	1,025	248	227	NA	NA	NA	NA	NA	NA	NA
Depreciation	434	51.9	47.4	NA	NA	NA	NA	NA	NA	NA
Interest Expense	193	12.8	12.9	NA	NA	NA	NA	NA	NA	NA
Pretax Income	409	174	168	NA	NA	NA	NA	NA	NA	NA
Effective Tax Rate	36.7%	39.5%	37.0%	NA	NA	NA	NA	NA	NA	NA
Net Income	259	106	106	NA	NA	NA	NA	NA	NA	NA
S&P Core Earnings	259	196	189	200	NA	NA	NA	NA	NA	NA

Balance Sheet & Other Financial Data (Million $)	2006	2005	2004	2003	2002	2001	2000	1999	1998	1997
Cash	212	138	86.7	NA	NA	NA	NA	NA	NA	NA
Current Assets	1,301	445	409	NA	NA	NA	NA	NA	NA	NA
Total Assets	7,631	972	922	NA	NA	NA	NA	NA	NA	NA
Current Liabilities	881	234	290	NA	NA	NA	NA	NA	NA	NA
Long Term Debt	2,948	228	274	NA	NA	NA	NA	NA	NA	NA
Common Equity	3,548	459	300	NA	NA	NA	NA	NA	NA	NA
Total Capital	6,892	716	614	NA	NA	NA	NA	NA	NA	NA
Capital Expenditures	122	63.6	40.9	NA	NA	NA	NA	NA	NA	NA
Cash Flow	693	157	153	NA	NA	NA	NA	NA	NA	NA
Current Ratio	1.5	1.9	1.4	NA	NA	NA	NA	NA	NA	NA
% Long Term Debt of Capitalization	42.8	31.8	44.6	NA	NA	NA	NA	NA	NA	NA
% Net Income of Revenue	6.3	9.4	10.2	NA	NA	NA	NA	NA	NA	NA
% Return on Assets	4.4	11.1	12.4	NA	NA	NA	NA	NA	NA	NA
% Return on Equity	12.2	27.5	37.7	NA	NA	NA	NA	NA	NA	NA

Data as orig reptd.; bef. results of disc opers/spec. items. Per share data adj. for stk. divs.; EPS diluted. E-Estimated. NA-Not Available. NM-Not Meaningful. NR-Not Ranked. UR-Under Review.

Office: 601 Riverside Ave, Jacksonville, FL 32204-2901.
Telephone: 904-854-8100.
Website: http://www.fidelityinfoservices.com
Chrmn: W.P. Foley, II

Pres & CEO: L.A. Kennedy
EVP & CFO: J.S. Carbiener

Board Members: R. M. Clements, W. P. Foley, II, T. M. Hagerty, M. Haines, K. W. Hughes, D. K. Hunt, J. K. Hunt, L. A. Kennedy, D. D. Lane, R. N. Massey, C. H. Thompson

Founded: 2001
Domicile: Georgia
Employees: 24,871

Fifth Third Bancorp

STANDARD &POOR'S

S&P Recommendation	HOLD ★★★☆☆	Price $28.04 (as of Nov 23, 2007)	12-Mo. Target Price $39.00	Investment Style Large-Cap Blend

GICS Sector Financials
Sub-Industry Regional Banks

Summary This regional bank holding company operates banking centers in Ohio, Kentucky, Indiana, Michigan, Illinois, Florida, West Virginia, Pennsylvania, Missouri, and Tennessee.

Key Stock Statistics (Source S&P, Vickers, company reports)

52-Wk Range	$43.32–26.50	S&P Oper. EPS 2007**E**	2.70	Market Capitalization(B)	$14.936	Beta	0.47
Trailing 12-Month EPS	$2.06	S&P Oper. EPS 2008**E**	2.85	Yield (%)	5.99	S&P 3-Yr. Proj. EPS CAGR(%)	9.00
Trailing 12-Month P/E	13.6	P/E on S&P Oper. EPS 2007**E**	10.4	Dividend Rate/Share	$1.68	S&P Credit Rating	A+
$10K Invested 5 Yrs Ago	$5,763	Common Shares Outstg. (M)	532.7	Institutional Ownership (%)	76		

Price Performance

- 30-Week Mov. Avg. ···· 10-Week Mov. Avg.- - **GAAP Earnings vs. Previous Year** Volume Above Avg. ⅢⅠ STARS
- 12-Mo. Target Price — Relative Strength — ▲ Up ▼ Down ▶ No Change Below Avg. ⅢⅠ ★

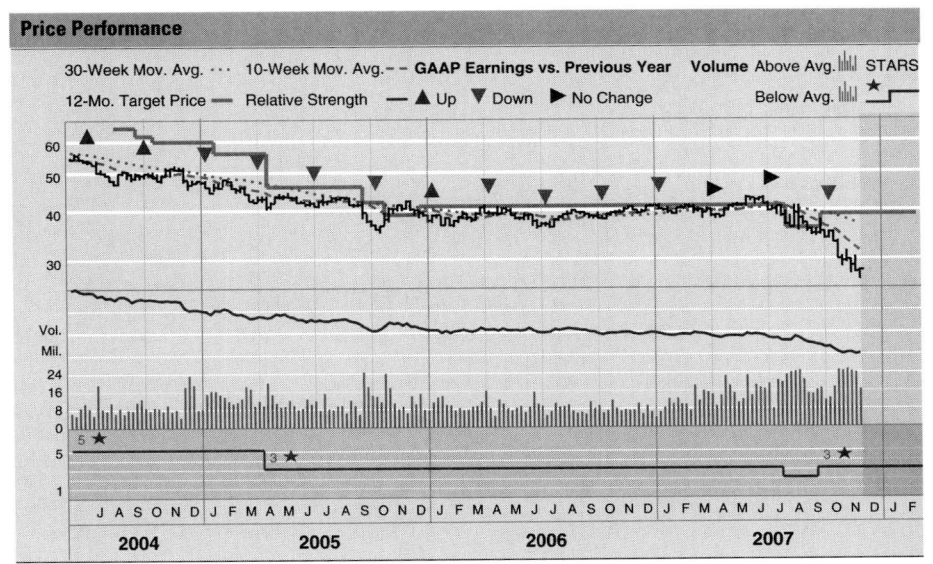

Options: ASE, CBOE, P, Ph

Analysis prepared by **Frank Braden, CFA** on November 08, 2007, when the stock traded at **$ 27.78**.

Highlights

➤ Reflecting a balance sheet restructuring and a more attractive yield curve, we expect an improvement in the net interest margin to 3.36% in 2007 and 3.42% in 2008, from 3.06% in 2006.

➤ We expect further deterioration in FITB's commercial mortgage and construction portfolio, particularly in the markets of Michigan, South Florida, and Northeast Ohio. We also see continued pressure on consumer real estate and auto loans, and we anticipate continued pressure on FITB's mortgage banking revenue as it shutters certain mortgage products and channels. We forecast expense growth to continue at a mid-single digit pace, driven by continuing de novo growth. We project that recent merchant contracts and increased demand by consumers for electronic payments will help support revenue growth in FITB's electronic payment processing segment.

➤ We project 2007 operating EPS of $2.70, assuming an effective tax rate of 29% and a 2% decrease in the share count. Our operating EPS estimate for 2008 is $2.88.

Investment Rationale/Risk

➤ We believe that FITB is experiencing a slowdown in both core deposit growth and loan growth, which is particularly experiencing a decline in real estate construction loans. We view positively management's focus on improving processes and raising customer satisfaction and loyalty, but we believe that will not be enough to counteract macroeconomic factors. We look for FITB to rely on cost cutting, share repurchases and electronic payment processing revenue to support EPS growth.

➤ Risks to our recommendation and target price include deterioration in economic conditions in the Midwest, a further decline in the housing market, and a decrease in consumer confidence that could affect consumer spending levels.

➤ We believe FITB is operating in a difficult environment, and we anticipate further deterioration in its real estate related portfolios. Our 12-month target price of $39 is equal to about 13.5X our 2008 EPS estimate, below FITB's historical average, reflecting continued mortgage pressures.

Qualitative Risk Assessment

LOW	MEDIUM	HIGH

Our risk assessment reflects what we see as solid business fundamentals and a strong customer base. We view FITB as well diversified and able to withstand a major regional or U.S. economic downturn.

Quantitative Evaluations

S&P Quality Ranking A

D	C	B-	B	B+	A-	A	A+

Relative Strength Rank WEAK

27

LOWEST = 1   HIGHEST = 99

Revenue/Earnings Data

Revenue (Million $)

	1Q	2Q	3Q	4Q	Year
2007	2,108	2,202	2,251	--	--
2006	2,015	2,132	2,196	1,765	8,108
2005	1,752	1,850	1,905	1,988	7,495
2004	1,617	1,749	1,654	1,560	6,579
2003	1,588	1,641	1,666	1,587	6,474
2002	1,514	1,554	1,644	1,611	6,324

Earnings Per Share ($)

2007	0.65	0.69	0.61	E0.66	E2.70
2006	0.65	0.69	0.68	0.12	2.12
2005	0.72	0.75	0.71	0.60	2.77
2004	0.75	0.79	0.83	0.31	2.68
2003	0.72	0.75	0.78	0.73	2.97
2002	0.66	0.68	0.70	0.72	2.76

Fiscal year ended Dec. 31. Next earnings report expected: Mid January. EPS Estimates based on S&P Operating Earnings; historical GAAP earnings are as reported.

Dividend Data (Dates: mm/dd Payment Date: mm/dd/yy)

Amount ($)	Date Decl.	Ex-Div. Date	Stk. of Record	Payment Date
0.400	12/19	12/27	12/29	01/18/07
0.420	03/20	03/28	03/30	04/19/07
0.420	06/19	06/27	06/29	07/19/07
0.420	09/18	09/26	09/28	10/19/07

Dividends have been paid since 1952. Source: Company reports.

The McGraw-Hill Companies

Fifth Third Bancorp

Business Summary November 08, 2007

CORPORATE OVERVIEW. FITB is divided into five segments: commercial banking, branch banking, consumer lending, investment advisors, and processing solutions. Commercial banking provides a comprehensive range of financial services and products to large and middle-market businesses, governments and professional customers. In addition to traditional lending and depository offerings, commercial banking products and services include cash management, foreign exchange and international trade finance, derivatives and capital markets services, asset-based lending, real estate finance, public finance, commercial leasing, and syndicated finance.

Branch banking provides deposit and loan and lease products to individuals and small businesses through over 1,100 banking centers. Branch banking offers depository and loan products, such as checking and savings accounts, home equity lines of credit, credit cards, and loans for automobiles and other personal financing needs, plus products designed to meet the specific needs of small businesses, including cash management services.

Consumer lending includes mortgage and home equity lending activities and other indirect lending activities. Mortgage and home equity lending activities include the origination, retention and servicing of mortgage and home equity

loans or lines of credit, sales and securitizations of those loans or pools of loans or lines of credit and all associated hedging activities. Other indirect lending activities include loans to consumers through dealers and federal and private student education loans.

Investment advisors provides a full range of investment alternatives for individuals, companies and not-for-profit organizations. Primary services include trust, asset management, retirement plans and custody. Fifth Third Securities, Inc., an indirect wholly-owned subsidiary, offers full service retail brokerage services to individual clients and broker dealer services to the institutional marketplace. Fifth Third Asset Management, Inc., an indirect wholly-owned subsidiary, provides asset management services and also advises a proprietary family of mutual funds, Fifth Third Funds. Fifth Third Processing Solutions provides electronic funds transfer, debit, credit and merchant transaction processing, operates the Jeanie ATM network, and provides other data processing services to affiliated and unaffiliated customers.

Company Financials Fiscal Year Ended Dec. 31

Per Share Data ($)	2006	2005	2004	2003	2002	2001	2000	1999	1998	1997
Tangible Book Value	13.78	12.72	13.33	13.46	13.12	13.09	10.50	8.79	7.04	8.47
Earnings	2.12	2.77	2.68	2.97	2.76	1.86	1.83	1.43	1.17	1.13
S&P Core Earnings	2.14	2.78	2.69	2.84	2.56	1.63	NA	NA	NA	NA
Dividends	1.58	1.46	1.31	1.13	0.98	0.83	0.70	0.56	0.44	0.38
Payout Ratio	75%	53%	49%	38%	36%	45%	38%	39%	37%	33%
Prices:High	41.57	48.12	60.00	62.15	69.70	64.77	60.88	50.29	49.42	37.11
Prices:Low	35.86	35.04	45.32	47.05	55.26	45.69	29.33	38.58	31.67	18.00
P/E Ratio:High	20	17	22	21	25	35	33	35	42	33
P/E Ratio:Low	17	13	17	16	20	25	16	27	27	16

Income Statement Analysis (Million $)										
Net Interest Income	2,873	2,965	3,012	2,905	2,700	2,433	1,470	1,405	1,003	745
Tax Equivalent Adjustment	26.0	31.0	36.0	39.0	39.5	45.5	93.0	73.0	49.2	43.0
Non Interest Income	1,657	2,461	2,502	2,399	2,047	1,626	1,013	876	626	439
Loan Loss Provision	343	330	268	399	247	236	89.0	134	109	80.3
% Expense/Operating Revenue	67.1%	53.6%	53.5%	46.0%	51.9%	57.7%	45.1%	47.7%	47.9%	42.7%
Pretax Income	1,627	2,208	2,237	2,547	2,432	1,653	1,275	1,026	726	604
Effective Tax Rate	27.2%	29.8%	31.8%	31.6%	31.2%	33.3%	32.3%	34.9%	34.4%	33.6%
Net Income	1,184	1,549	1,525	1,722	1,635	1,101	863	668	476	401
% Net Interest Margin	3.06	3.23	3.48	3.62	3.96	3.82	3.77	3.99	3.94	4.11
S&P Core Earnings	1,191	1,555	1,529	1,650	1,513	965	NA	NA	NA	NA

Balance Sheet & Other Financial Data (Million $)										
Money Market Assets	187	117	77.0	55.0	312	225	198	355	119	29.4
Investment Securities	12,218	22,471	25,474	29,402	25,828	20,748	15,827	12,817	8,539	6,469
Commercial Loans	36,114	33,214	30,601	28,242	22,614	10,839	12,382	11,141	9,093	5,684
Other Loans	39,485	38,024	29,207	25,493	23,314	30,709	13,570	14,746	9,375	7,555
Total Assets	100,669	105,225	94,456	91,143	80,894	71,026	45,857	41,589	28,922	21,375
Demand Deposits	38,584	39,020	37,288	31,899	11,139	10,595	5,604	8,011	6,355	2,426
Time Deposits	30,796	13,656	20,938	25,196	41,069	35,259	25,344	18,072	12,425	12,488
Long Term Debt	12,558	15,227	13,983	9,063	8,179	7,030	4,034	1,977	2,288	458
Common Equity	10,013	9,437	8,915	8,516	8,466	7,630	4,891	4,306	3,179	2,277
% Return on Assets	1.2	1.6	1.6	2.0	2.2	1.6	2.0	1.7	1.9	1.9
% Return on Equity	12.2	16.9	17.3	20.3	20.3	15.4	19.2	16.6	17.5	18.1
% Loan Loss Reserve	1.0	1.0	1.2	1.4	1.4	1.4	1.4	4.9	1.5	1.5
% Loans/Deposits	108.8	105.6	103.7	94.9	94.4	95.4	85.6	100.4	94.7	90.1
% Equity to Assets	9.4	9.2	9.5	9.9	10.6	10.2	10.3	10.3	10.8	10.5

Data as orig reptd.; bef. results of disc opers/spec. items. Per share data adj. for stk. divs.; EPS diluted. E-Estimated. NA-Not Available. NM-Not Meaningful. NR-Not Ranked. UR-Under Review.

Office: 38 Fountain Square Plaza, Cincinnati, OH 45263.
Telephone: 513-534-5300.
Website: http://www.53.com
Chrmn: G.A. Schaefer, Jr.

Pres & CEO: K.T. Kabat
COO & EVP: G.D. Carmichael
Sr EVP: R.A. Sullivan
EVP & CFO: C.G. Marshall

Investor Contact: J. Richardson (513-534-0983)
Board Members: D. F. Allen, J. F. Barrett, J. P. Hackett, G. R. Heminger, J. R. Herschede, A. M. Hill, K. T. Kabat, R. L. Koch, II, M. D. Livingston, H. G. Meijer, J. E. Rogers, G. A. Schaefer, Jr., J. J. Schiff, Jr., D. S. Taft, T. W. Traylor

Founded: 1862
Domicile: Ohio
Employees: 21,362

FirstEnergy Corp.

STANDARD &POOR'S

S&P Recommendation **HOLD** ★★★☆☆	Price $67.87 (as of Nov 23, 2007)	12-Mo. Target Price $76.00	Investment Style Large-Cap Blend

GICS Sector Utilities
Sub-Industry Electric Utilities

Summary This electric utility holding company serves about 4.5 million customers in portions of Ohio, Pennsylvania and New Jersey.

Key Stock Statistics (Source S&P, Vickers, company reports)

52-Wk Range	$72.90– 57.77	S&P Oper. EPS 2007**E**	4.25	Market Capitalization(B)	$20.689
Trailing 12-Month EPS	$4.19	S&P Oper. EPS 2008**E**	4.30	Yield (%)	2.95
Trailing 12-Month P/E	16.2	P/E on S&P Oper. EPS 2007**E**	16.0	Dividend Rate/Share	$2.00
$10K Invested 5 Yrs Ago	$25,068	Common Shares Outstg. (M)	304.8	Institutional Ownership (%)	77

Beta	0.26
S&P 3-Yr. Proj. EPS CAGR(%)	6.00
S&P Credit Rating	BBB

Price Performance

30-Week Mov. Avg. · · · 10-Week Mov. Avg. – – **GAAP Earnings vs. Previous Year** Volume Above Avg. |ıl|l| **STARS**
12-Mo. Target Price — Relative Strength — ▲ Up ▼ Down ► No Change Below Avg. |ıl|l| ★

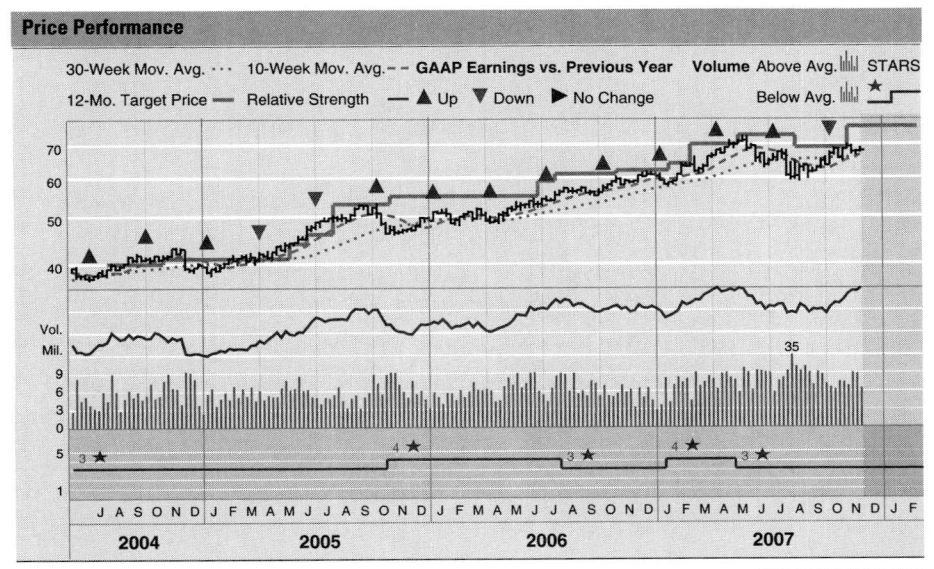

Options: ASE, CBOE, P, Ph

Analysis prepared by **Justin McCann** on November 08, 2007, when the stock traded at **$ 67.63**.

Highlights

➤ We expect 2007 operating EPS to increase about 11% from 2006's operating EPS of $3.82, driven by rate increases and fewer shares outstanding. We believe the 25 million shares the company has repurchased since August 2006 will add approximately $0.18 to 2007 EPS. Operating EPS of $3.35 in the first nine months of 2007 was aided by higher electric generation and distribution sales, lower fuel costs, and 5.5% fewer shares outstanding.

➤ For 2008, we expect only a slight increase in operating EPS. While we project growth in delivery sales, higher generation margins, and lower costs related to generation outages, we believe this will be largely offset by higher amortization, fuel and purchased power costs, as well as costs related to infrastructure investments.

➤ Under the coal supply agreement between FE's generation subsidiary and CONSOL Energy (CNX), which was reached in June 2006, CNX would supply a total of more than 128 million tons of high-BTU coal for the 20-year period 2009 through 2028. The agreement replaced an existing agreement that ran through 2020, and should result in the shipment of an additional two million tons per year.

Investment Rationale/Risk

➤ Although the stock is up approximately 12% year to date, we still expect the shares to realize an above-peers total return from the current level over the next 12 months. On March 2, 2007, FirstEnergy repurchased 14.4 million shares, about 4.5% of those outstanding. Earlier, on August 10, 2006, FE completed the repurchase of 10.6 million shares, about 3.2% of those then outstanding. We do not anticipate additional share buyback plans at this time.

➤ Risks to our recommendation and target price include the possibility of higher than anticipated or inadequately hedged replacement power costs, as well as a reduction in the average P/E of FE's electric utility peers.

➤ FE increased its dividend 11% with the March 2007 payment. This reflects the company's new dividend policy, which has targeted future annual increases of 4% to 5% and a dividend payout ratio of 50% to 60%. The targeted growth rate is above both the expected dividend growth rate of the industry and FE's own expected longer-term EPS growth rate of 3% to 4%. Our 12-month target price of $76 represents a modest premium-to-peers P/E of 17.7X our EPS estimate for 2008.

Qualitative Risk Assessment

LOW	MEDIUM	HIGH

Our risk assessment reflects the strong and steady cash flow we expect from the company's regulated electric utility subsidiaries; its low-cost baseload power generation in Ohio and Pennsylvania; its low-risk transmission distribution operations in New Jersey and Pennsylvania; and its rate certainty in Ohio. This is partially offset by the company's below average nuclear operations and our view of its high level of debt and environmental spending.

Quantitative Evaluations

S&P Quality Ranking B+

D	C	B-	B	**B+**	A-	A	A+

Relative Strength Rank STRONG

86

LOWEST = 1 HIGHEST = 99

Revenue/Earnings Data

Revenue (Million $)

	1Q	2Q	3Q	4Q	Year
2007	2,973	3,109	3,600	--	--
2006	2,705	2,751	3,365	2,680	11,501
2005	2,813	2,900	3,588	2,892	11,989
2004	3,183	3,150	3,536	2,950	12,453
2003	3,221	2,853	3,434	2,799	12,307
2002	2,762	2,899	3,451	3,040	12,152

Earnings Per Share ($)

2007	0.92	1.10	1.34	E0.96	E4.25
2006	0.67	0.93	1.40	0.84	3.82
2005	0.42	0.54	1.01	0.67	2.65
2004	0.53	0.62	0.91	0.61	2.66
2003	0.39	0.03	0.51	0.44	1.39
2002	0.29	0.79	1.05	0.20	2.33

Fiscal year ended Dec. 31. Next earnings report expected: NA. EPS Estimates based on S&P Operating Earnings; historical GAAP earnings are as reported.

Dividend Data (Dates: mm/dd Payment Date: mm/dd/yy)

Amount ($)	Date Decl.	Ex-Div. Date	Stk. of Record	Payment Date
0.500	12/19	02/05	02/07	03/01/07
0.500	03/22	05/03	05/07	06/01/07
0.500	07/17	08/03	08/07	09/01/07
0.500	09/18	11/05	11/07	12/01/07

Dividends have been paid since 1930. Source: Company reports.

FirstEnergy Corp.

STANDARD &POOR'S

Business Summary November 08, 2007

CORPORATE OVERVIEW. FirstEnergy (FE) is a diversified energy company involved in the generation, transmission and distribution of electricity as well as energy management and related services. The company operates primarily through two core business segments: Regulated Services, which is comprised of seven electric utility operating companies and provides transmission and distribution services, and Power Supply Management Services, which owns and operates the generation assets and wholesale purchase of electricity, energy management and other energy-related services.(PSM). Electric sales accounted for 92.8% of revenues in 2006.

CORPORATE STRATEGY. FE intends to be a leading regional supplier of energy services in the northeast quadrant of the U.S. On the generation front, the

company is working to optimize its generation portfolio and to effectively manage its commodity supplies and risks. FE is committed to reinvesting in the operations of its utilities for a continuous improvement in their customer service quality and reliability. To this end, FE is upgrading its transmission and distribution system, implementing new technologies and incorporating industry best practices. The company has made safety and environmental compliance one of its top priorities, both within the nuclear fleet and across the organization.

Company Financials Fiscal Year Ended Dec. 31

Per Share Data ($)	2006	2005	2004	2003	2002	2001	2000	1999	1998	1997
Tangible Book Value	9.83	9.63	7.70	6.55	4.11	6.04	11.42	10.47	9.62	8.91
Earnings	3.82	2.65	2.66	1.39	2.33	2.84	2.69	2.50	1.95	1.94
S&P Core Earnings	3.71	2.56	2.77	1.61	1.69	2.36	NA	NA	NA	NA
Dividends	NA	1.67	1.50	1.50	1.50	1.13	1.50	1.50	1.50	1.50
Payout Ratio	NA	63%	56%	108%	64%	40%	56%	60%	77%	77%
Prices:High	NA	53.36	43.41	38.90	39.12	36.98	32.13	33.19	34.06	29.00
Prices:Low	NA	37.70	35.24	25.82	24.85	25.10	18.00	22.13	27.06	19.25
P/E Ratio:High	NA	20	16	28	17	13	12	13	17	15
P/E Ratio:Low	NA	14	13	19	11	9	7	9	14	10
Income Statement Analysis (Million $)										
Revenue	11,501	11,989	12,453	12,307	12,152	7,999	7,029	6,320	5,861	2,821
Depreciation	1,457	1,870	1,756	1,282	1,106	890	934	938	741	475
Maintenance	NA	NA	NA	NA	NA	NA	NA	NA	NA	NA
Fixed Charges Coverage	3.78	3.39	3.25	1.88	2.25	2.85	2.71	2.62	2.21	2.64
Construction Credits	NA	NA	NA	NA	24.5	35.5	27.1	13.4	7.64	3.50
Effective Tax Rate	38.7%	46.3%	43.4%	49.0%	44.5%	42.0%	38.6%	41.0%	42.2%	40.5%
Net Income	1,258	873	874	422	686	655	599	568	441	306
S&P Core Earnings	1,211	841	911	492	496	546	NA	NA	NA	NA
Balance Sheet & Other Financial Data (Million $)										
Gross Property	24,722	23,790	22,892	22,374	21,231	20,589	12,839	15,013	15,255	17,516
Capital Expenditures	1,315	1,208	846	856	998	852	588	625	653	204
Net Property	14,667	13,998	13,478	13,269	12,680	12,428	7,575	9,093	9,243	11,880
Capitalization:Long Term Debt	8,535	8,339	10,348	9,789	11,636	12,508	6,552	6,906	7,307	6,970
Capitalization:% Long Term Debt	48.6	47.1	53.7	53.1	62.0	62.8	58.5	60.2	62.2	57.5
Capitalization:Preferred	NA	184	335	352	Nil	Nil	Nil	Nil	Nil	995
Capitalization:% Preferred	NA	1.04	1.74	1.91	Nil	Nil	Nil	Nil	Nil	8.20
Capitalization:Common	9,035	9,188	8,589	8,289	7,120	7,399	4,653	4,564	4,449	4,160
Capitalization:% Common	51.4	51.9	44.6	45.0	38.0	37.2	41.5	39.8	37.8	34.3
Total Capital	20,310	20,437	21,597	20,608	21,360	22,852	13,540	13,970	14,325	14,754
% Operating Ratio	84.3	89.0	87.3	90.4	86.6	50.8	37.8	82.0	82.2	81.2
% Earned on Net Property	18.2	15.0	16.5	11.2	17.4	16.8	18.1	16.7	NA	6.0
% Return on Revenue	10.9	7.3	7.0	3.4	5.6	8.2	8.5	9.0	7.5	10.8
% Return on Invested Capital	9.6	7.3	7.4	6.5	7.4	21.8	32.0	7.8	NA	5.5
% Return on Common Equity	13.8	9.8	10.4	5.5	9.5	10.9	13.0	12.6	NA	9.2

Data as orig reptd.; bef. results of disc opers/spec. items. Per share data adj. for stk. divs.; EPS diluted. E-Estimated. NA-Not Available. NM-Not Meaningful. NR-Not Ranked. UR-Under Review.

Office: 76 South Main Street, Akron, OH 44308-1890.
Telephone: 800-736-3402.
Website: http://www.firstenergycorp.com
Chrmn: G.M. Smart

Pres & CEO: A.J. Alexander
COO & EVP: R.R. Grigg
SVP & CFO: R.H. Marsh
SVP & General Counsel: L.L. Vespoli

Investor Contact: R.E. Seeholzer
Board Members: P. T. Addison, A. J. Alexander, M. J. Anderson, C. A. Cartwright, W. T. Cottle, R. B. Heisler Jr., R. W. Maier, E. J. Novak, Jr., R. N. Pokelwaldt, P. J. Powers, C. A. Rein, R. C. Savage, G. M. Smart, W. M. Taylor, J. T. Williams, Sr., P. K. Woolf

Founded: 1996
Domicile: Ohio
Employees: 13,739

First Horizon National Corp

STANDARD &POOR'S

S&P Recommendation SELL ★ ★ ☆ ☆ ☆	**Price** $21.09 (as of Nov 29, 2007)	**12-Mo. Target Price** $18.00	**Investment Style** Large-Cap Blend

GICS Sector Financials
Sub-Industry Regional Banks

Summary FHN (formerly First Tennessee National) owns First Tennessee Bank and First Horizon Home Loan Corporation.

Key Stock Statistics (Source S&P, Vickers, company reports)

52-Wk Range	$45.44– 19.31	S&P Oper. EPS 2007**E**	0.85	Market Capitalization(B)	$2.666	Beta	0.56
Trailing 12-Month EPS	$1.20	S&P Oper. EPS 2008**E**	1.58	Yield (%)	8.53	S&P 3-Yr. Proj. EPS CAGR(%)	NM
Trailing 12-Month P/E	17.6	P/E on S&P Oper. EPS 2007**E**	24.8	Dividend Rate/Share	$1.80	S&P Credit Rating	A-
$10K Invested 5 Yrs Ago	$6,751	Common Shares Outstg. (M)	126.4	Institutional Ownership (%)	59		

Price Performance

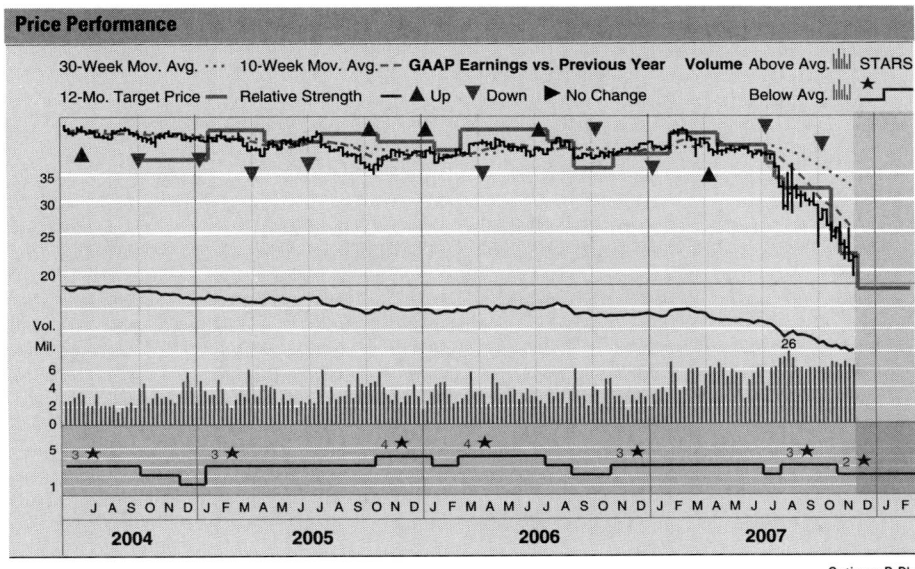

30-Week Mov. Avg. · · · 10-Week Mov. Avg. - - **GAAP Earnings vs. Previous Year** Volume Above Avg. STARS
12-Mo. Target Price — Relative Strength — ▲ Up ▼ Down ▶ No Change Below Avg. ★

Options: P, Ph

Qualitative Risk Assessment

LOW	MEDIUM	HIGH

Our risk assessment takes into account FHN's long-term trend of stability and moderate growth in earnings and its long-term trend of increasing dividends. While the company operates in a highly competitive and fragmented industry, that usually tends to produce relatively stable financial results, its exposure to a weak residential real estate market adds an element of risk.

Quantitative Evaluations

S&P Quality Ranking A+

D	C	B-	B	B+	A-	A	A+

Relative Strength Rank WEAK

16

LOWEST = 1   HIGHEST = 99

Revenue/Earnings Data

Revenue (Million $)

	1Q	2Q	3Q	4Q	Year
2007	866.4	875.2	786.2	--	--
2006	731.0	913.6	930.4	921.0	3,496
2005	728.3	781.8	867.0	862.9	3,240
2004	624.1	630.1	627.8	647.9	2,530
2003	685.6	698.3	669.7	639.8	2,693
2002	582.9	585.3	652.5	759.4	2,580

Earnings Per Share ($)

2007	0.55	0.17	-0.11	E0.24	E0.85
2006	0.03	0.82	0.53	0.60	3.61
2005	0.85	0.80	0.90	0.87	3.42
2004	0.92	0.92	0.89	0.81	3.54
2003	0.91	0.90	0.91	0.90	3.62
2002	0.67	0.69	0.73	0.80	2.89

Fiscal year ended Dec. 31. Next earnings report expected: Mid January. EPS Estimates based on S&P Operating Earnings; historical GAAP earnings are as reported.

Highlights

➤ The 12-month target price for FHN has recently been changed to $18.00 from $22.00. The Highlights section of this Stock Report will be updated accordingly.

Investment Rationale/Risk

➤ The Investment Rationale/Risk section of this Stock Report will be updated shortly. For the latest News story on FHN from MarketScope, see below.

➤ 11/29/07 01:38 pm EST... S&P MAINTAINS SELL OPINION ON SHARES OF FIRST HORIZON (FHN 21.15**): Based on a continued decline in home prices, we look for FHN's loan loss provisions to remain at elevated levels through '08. We note that its loan portfolio is roughly 45% residential loans, with a sizeable portion of home equity and construction loans. Non-performing loans jumped roughly 50% in Q3 from Q2, and we expect this figure will continue to rise in the coming quarters. Our '07 and '08 EPS estimates remain $0.85 and $1.58, respectively, but we are reducing our 12-month target price by $4 to $18, which at 11.4X our '08 EPS estimate, is a slight discount to peers. /S. Plesser

Dividend Data (Dates: mm/dd Payment Date: mm/dd/yy)

Amount ($)	Date Decl.	Ex-Div. Date	Stk. of Record	Payment Date
0.450	01/16	03/14	03/16	04/01/07
0.450	04/23	06/13	06/15	07/01/07
0.450	07/18	09/12	09/14	10/01/07
0.450	10/16	12/12	12/14	01/08/08

Dividends have been paid since 1895. Source: Company reports.

First Horizon National Corp

STANDARD
&POOR'S

Business Summary October 31, 2007

CORPORATE OVERVIEW. First Horizon National (formerly First Tennessee National) is a Memphis, TN-based regional bank holding company with $37.9 billion in assets at December 31, 2006. Through its three major brands--First Horizon Home Loan, First Tennessee National and FTN Financial--the bank provides retail commercial banking services, mortgage banking, and capital markets operations. During 2006, 54% of revenues came from fee income versus 58.7% in 2005. This contrasts with the average regional bank, which derives about 32% of its revenues from fee income sources.

Retail/commercial banking contributed 61% of revenues in 2006 (versus 58% in 2005), mortgage banking 22% (28%), and capital markets 17% (14%).

Income from capital markets operations was the largest contributor to fee income. As of December 2006, First Horizon Home Loan had 413 offices in 44 states, and ranked among the 25 U.S. leaders in mortgage loan originations and top 20 mortgage loan servicing, as reported by Inside Mortgage Finance.

CORPORATE STRATEGY. Unlike many of its competitors, the company has generally not grown through an aggressive acquisition strategy, but has fo-cused on expanding its nationally ranked specialty lines of business. FHN's strategy is to continue to expand and gain market share in its current markets, establish a large number of customers in those markets through its mortgage operations, and then cross-sell them other financial products.

RECENT DEVELOPMENTS. In January 2005, FTN Financial, FHN's capital markets division, acquired the fixed income business of Spear, Leeds & Kellogg, a division of Goldman Sachs, Inc. Following the acquisition, FTN Financial had about 1,000 employees in 15 states, with over 5,000 customers. In March 2006, FHN sold its merchant processing business--First Horizon Merchant Services--to NOVA Information Systems, a subsidiary of U.S. Bancorp. Partial proceeds from the sale were used to fund a 4 million common share accelerated repurchase program, which was estimated to cost $158 million, excluding transaction costs.

Company Financials Fiscal Year Ended Dec. 31

Per Share Data ($)	2006	2005	2004	2003	2002	2001	2000	1999	1998	1997
Tangible Book Value	17.00	15.19	14.73	13.43	11.92	10.27	9.81	8.53	2.34	3.38
Earnings	3.61	3.42	3.54	3.62	2.89	2.51	1.77	1.91	1.72	1.50
S&P Core Earnings	2.04	3.26	3.41	3.32	2.59	1.88	NA	NA	NA	NA
Dividends	1.80	1.74	1.63	1.30	1.05	0.91	0.88	0.76	0.66	0.62
Payout Ratio	50%	51%	46%	36%	36%	36%	50%	40%	38%	41%
Prices:High	43.07	44.80	48.65	48.50	41.00	37.49	29.31	45.38	38.38	34.81
Prices:Low	37.10	34.78	40.79	35.58	29.76	27.13	15.94	27.38	23.38	18.38
P/E Ratio:High	12	13	14	13	14	15	17	24	22	23
P/E Ratio:Low	10	10	12	10	10	11	9	14	14	12

Income Statement Analysis (Million $)

	2006	2005	2004	2003	2002	2001	2000	1999	1998	1997
Net Interest Income	997	984	856	806	753	686	598	590	541	483
Tax Equivalent Adjustment	NA	1.17	1.10	1.26	1.50	2.10	2.60	3.00	NA	NA
Non Interest Income	1,233	1,400	1,342	1,638	1,550	1,321	1,068	1,121	982	669
Loan Loss Provision	83.1	67.7	48.3	86.7	92.2	93.5	67.4	57.9	51.4	51.1
% Expense/Operating Revenue	78.2%	70.1%	68.4%	67.1%	71.3%	67.7%	75.5%	74.4%	73.7%	68.1%
Pretax Income	338	645	667	719	558	494	337	379	353	315
Effective Tax Rate	25.8%	31.6%	31.9%	34.2%	32.5%	33.2%	31.0%	34.8%	36.0%	37.3%
Net Income	251	441	454	473	376	330	233	248	226	197
% Net Interest Margin	2.93	3.08	3.62	3.78	4.33	4.27	3.73	3.80	3.80	4.23
S&P Core Earnings	261	423	438	434	337	248	NA	NA	NA	NA

Balance Sheet & Other Financial Data (Million $)

	2006	2005	2004	2003	2002	2001	2000	1999	1998	1997
Money Market Assets	1,221	3,629	1,676	1,182	1,157	877	380	430	484	482
Investment Securities	3,890	2,912	2,681	2,470	2,700	2,526	2,839	3,101	2,426	2,186
Commercial Loans	8,338	9,899	7,730	6,904	5,723	5,598	5,327	4,431	4,117	3,769
Other Loans	13,767	10,702	8,698	7,087	5,622	4,685	4,912	4,933	4,440	4,416
Total Assets	37,918	36,579	29,772	24,507	23,823	20,617	18,555	18,373	18,734	14,388
Demand Deposits	5,448	10,027	4,995	4,540	5,149	4,010	2,847	2,798	3,058	2,536
Time Deposits	14,766	13,411	14,788	11,140	10,564	9,596	9,342	8,560	8,665	7,136
Long Term Debt	6,132	3,733	2,617	1,117	1,074	3,066	3,119	459	514	169
Common Equity	2,462	2,312	2,041	1,850	1,691	1,478	1,384	1,241	1,100	954
% Return on Assets	0.7	1.3	1.7	2.0	1.7	1.7	1.3	1.3	1.4	1.4
% Return on Equity	10.4	20.3	23.1	26.7	23.8	23.0	17.7	21.1	23.0	20.7
% Loan Loss Reserve	0.9	0.8	0.7	0.9	0.9	1.1	1.2	1.2	1.6	1.5
% Loans/Deposits	123.6	106.8	109.2	108.2	102.7	100.6	98.2	100.5	78.3	85.9
% Equity to Assets	6.5	6.6	7.2	7.3	7.1	7.3	7.1	6.3	6.2	7.0

Data as orig reptd.; bef. results of disc opers/spec. items. Per share data adj. for stk. divs.; EPS diluted. E-Estimated. NA-Not Available. NM-Not Meaningful. NR-Not Ranked. UR-Under Review.

Office: 165 Madison Avenue, Memphis, TN 38103.
Telephone: 901-523-4444.
Website: http://www.firsttennessee.com
Chrmn: M.D. Rose

Pres & CEO: G.L. Baker
EVP & CFO: M.L. Mosby, III
EVP, Chief Acctg Officer & Cntlr: J.F. Keen
EVP & General Counsel: H.A. Johnson, III

Investor Contact: M. Yates (901-523-4068)
Board Members: G. L. Baker, R. C. Blattberg, S. F. Cooper, J. K. Glass, J. A. Haslam, III, R. B. Martin, V. R. Palmer, C. V. Reed, M. D. Rose, M. F. Sammons, W. B. Sansom, L. Yancy, III

Founded: 1968
Domicile: Tennessee
Employees: 12,131

The McGraw-Hill Companies

Fiserv Inc

STANDARD &POOR'S

S&P Recommendation **SELL** ★ ★ ☆ ☆ ☆	Price $51.26 (as of Nov 23, 2007)	12-Mo. Target Price $53.00	Investment Style Large-Cap Growth

GICS Sector Information Technology
Sub-Industry Data Processing & Outsourced Services

Summary This company provides account processing and integrated information management systems for financial institutions. In August 2007, FISV announced the proposed acquisition of CheckFree Corp. for about $4.4 billion.

Key Stock Statistics (Source S&P, Vickers, company reports)

52-Wk Range	$59.85–44.16	S&P Oper. EPS 2007E	2.75	Market Capitalization(B)	$8.554	Beta		1.00
Trailing 12-Month EPS	$2.76	S&P Oper. EPS 2008E	3.20	Yield (%)	Nil	S&P 3-Yr. Proj. EPS CAGR(%)		14.00
Trailing 12-Month P/E	18.6	P/E on S&P Oper. EPS 2007E	18.6	Dividend Rate/Share	Nil	S&P Credit Rating		BBB
$10K Invested 5 Yrs Ago	$14,772	Common Shares Outstg. (M)	166.9	Institutional Ownership (%)	78			

Price Performance

30-Week Mov. Avg. · · · 10-Week Mov. Avg. - - **GAAP Earnings vs. Previous Year** Volume Above Avg. ılıl STARS
12-Mo. Target Price — Relative Strength — ▲ Up ▼ Down ▶ No Change Below Avg. ılıl ★

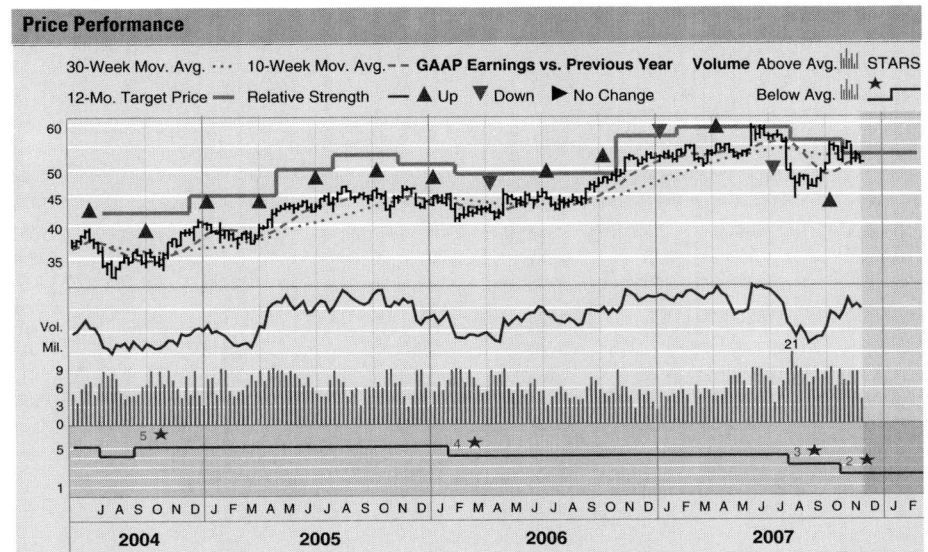

Options: ASE, CBOE, Ph

Analysis prepared by **Scott H. Kessler** on October 26, 2007, when the stock traded at **$ 54.01.**

Highlights

➤ We project that revenues will increase about 12% in 2007, with particular strength in core offerings from the financial segment (which accounted for 64% of revenues and 84% of operating income in the 2007 third quarter). We see comparable stand-alone growth in 2008.

➤ Historically, FISV has used its free cash flow to make acquisitions intended to broaden its offerings and customer base. Acquired companies and businesses once accounted for about 50% of FISV's annual revenue growth. However, in recent years the company de-emphasized acquisitions and focused more on efforts related to cross-selling software and services.

➤ In August 2007, FISV announced the planned acquisition of CheckFree Corp. (CKFR: hold, $47) for $4.4 billion. We believe this proposed combination would enable FISV to gain material market share, and we foresee consummation by December 2007, subject to necessary approvals. In January 2007, FISV announced a 10 million share repurchase program that we expect to contribute to EPS gains.

Investment Rationale/Risk

➤ We believe FISV will continue to benefit from demand for new financial institution products and services. Although we think the proposed purchase of CKFR has strategic merit, we see notable related risks related to the substantial value of the deal, FISV's need to raise a large amount of associated debt, and challenges related to integration and rationalization.

➤ Risks to our recommendation and target price include stronger demand than we expect for financial services technology offerings, substantial acceleration in internal growth, and a faster and more successful acquisition and integration of CKFR than we foresee.

➤ Our relative P/E and P/E to growth (PEG) analyses of FISV's peers in the S&P 500 Data Processing & Outsourced Services sub-industry yield a value of $46. Our DCF model (including assumptions of a discount rate of 11.6%, average growth of 13% over the next five years, and a terminal growth rate of 3%) leads to an intrinsic value calculation of $56. Based on a weighting of these methodologies, our 12-month target price is $53.

Qualitative Risk Assessment

LOW	**MEDIUM**	HIGH

Our risk assessment reflects our view of FISV's notable size, market position and flexible balance sheet, offset by what we consider its relatively modest internal growth rate and active acquisition strategy.

Quantitative Evaluations

S&P Quality Ranking B+

D	C	B-	B	**B+**	A-	A	A+

Relative Strength Rank MODERATE

69

LOWEST = 1 HIGHEST = 99

Revenue/Earnings Data

Revenue (Million $)

	1Q	2Q	3Q	4Q	Year
2007	1,219	1,180	1,174	--	--
2006	1,097	1,093	1,157	1,198	4,544
2005	973.1	996.4	1,012	1,078	4,059
2004	937.5	946.0	958.1	966.4	3,730
2003	707.5	738.6	796.1	837.3	3,034
2002	631.9	632.4	635.7	668.9	2,569

Earnings Per Share ($)

2007	0.66	0.62	0.72	E0.74	E2.75
2006	0.64	0.63	0.63	0.61	2.49
2005	0.71	0.59	0.58	0.80	2.68
2004	0.49	0.49	0.53	0.50	2.00
2003	0.38	0.40	0.41	0.42	1.61
2002	0.33	0.34	0.34	0.35	1.37

Fiscal year ended Dec. 31. Next earnings report expected: Early February. EPS Estimates based on S&P Operating Earnings; historical GAAP earnings are as reported.

Dividend Data

No cash dividends have been paid.

Fiserv Inc

STANDARD &POOR'S

Business Summary October 26, 2007

CORPORATE OVERVIEW. At the end of 2006, Fiserv made some adjustments to its operating segments. Most notably, it created a new insurance services unit, which includes the old health plan management services segment, and insurance operations that were previously classified in the financial institutions segment.

The newly constituted financial segment (accounting for 63% of 2006 revenues and 65% of 2005 revenues) provides solutions to thousands of financial institutions, including banks, credit unions, leasing companies, mortgage lenders, and savings institutions. "Core" products integrate account services and management information functions, and include systems to process accounts, general ledgers, central information files, and report generation. Complementary offerings allow financial institutions to provide additional services to their clients, such as home banking and ATM access; asset-liability modeling and cash management are also offered.

The insurance segment (34%, 31%) provides solutions for the administration of

health plans to customers nationwide, including claim adjudication and payment, customer service, reporting, and other related offerings. These offerings are provided to employers that self-fund their health plans, and to insurance companies and HMOs. Additional services include utilization and case management, health and prevention programs, prescription benefit management and pharmacy mail-order services, data management, and claim repricing. The unit also provides solutions to insurance-company clients.

IDC projects that U.S. IT outsourcing spending by banking and insurance firms will rise from $6.3 billion in 2004, to $7.8 billion in 2009. IDC also estimates that U.S. health care companies will increase their spending on IT outsourcing from $1.3 billion in 2004, to $1.7 billion in 2009.

Company Financials Fiscal Year Ended Dec. 31

Per Share Data ($)	2006	2005	2004	2003	2002	2001	2000	1999	1998	1997
Tangible Book Value	NM	NM	0.96	NM	2.60	2.60	2.18	1.57	1.57	1.50
Cash Flow	3.62	3.62	2.94	2.48	2.09	1.86	1.33	1.18	1.00	0.64
Earnings	2.49	2.68	2.00	1.61	1.37	1.09	0.93	0.73	0.60	0.50
S&P Core Earnings	2.50	2.28	1.91	1.47	1.26	1.00	NA	NA	NA	NA
Dividends	Nil	Nil	Nil	Nil	Nil	Nil	Nil	Nil	Nil	Nil
Payout Ratio	Nil	Nil	Nil	Nil	Nil	Nil	Nil	Nil	Nil	Nil
Prices:High	53.60	46.89	41.01	40.77	47.24	44.61	42.75	27.17	23.83	15.26
Prices:Low	40.29	36.33	32.20	27.23	22.50	29.08	16.21	16.08	13.33	9.63
P/E Ratio:High	21	17	21	25	34	41	46	37	40	30
P/E Ratio:Low	16	14	16	17	16	27	17	22	22	19

Income Statement Analysis (Million $)										
Revenue	4,544	4,059	3,730	3,034	2,569	1,890	1,654	1,408	1,234	974
Operating Income	943	925	845	704	734	501	429	347	282	229
Depreciation	199	179	185	172	141	148	70.1	86.3	76.5	63.2
Interest Expense	41.0	27.8	24.9	22.9	17.8	12.1	22.1	19.4	16.0	11.9
Pretax Income	710	818	641	516	436	347	300	234	194	154
Effective Tax Rate	37.6%	37.5%	38.4%	39.0%	39.0%	40.0%	41.0%	41.0%	41.0%	41.0%
Net Income	443	511	395	315	266	208	177	138	114	90.8
S&P Core Earnings	443	435	377	288	246	191	NA	NA	NA	NA

Balance Sheet & Other Financial Data (Million $)										
Cash	185	184	516	203	227	136	98.9	80.6	71.6	89.4
Current Assets	NA	NA	NA	NA	NA	NA	NA	NA	NA	NA
Total Assets	6,208	6,040	8,383	7,214	6,439	5,322	5,586	5,308	3,958	3,636
Current Liabilities	NA	NA	NA	NA	NA	NA	NA	NA	NA	NA
Long Term Debt	747	595	505	699	483	343	335	326	390	252
Common Equity	2,426	2,466	2,564	2,200	1,828	1,605	1,252	1,091	886	769
Total Capital	3,173	3,227	3,204	2,990	2,357	1,948	1,622	1,477	1,276	1,021
Capital Expenditures	187	165	161	143	142	68.0	73.0	69.7	77.5	39.8
Cash Flow	642	691	580	487	407	356	247	224	191	154
Current Ratio	NA	NA	NA	NA	NA	NA	NA	NA	NA	NA
% Long Term Debt of Capitalization	23.6	18.4	15.8	23.4	20.5	17.6	20.7	22.1	30.6	24.7
% Net Income of Revenue	9.8	12.6	10.6	10.4	10.4	11.0	10.7	9.8	9.3	9.3
% Return on Assets	7.2	7.1	5.1	4.6	4.5	3.8	3.2	3.0	3.0	3.3
% Return on Equity	18.1	20.3	16.6	15.6	15.5	14.6	15.1	13.9	13.8	14.2

Data as orig reptd.; bef. results of disc opers/spec. items. Per share data adj. for stk. divs.; EPS diluted. E-Estimated. NA-Not Available. NM-Not Meaningful. NR-Not Ranked. UR-Under Review.

Office: 255 Fiserv Drive, Brookfield, WI 53045.
Telephone: 262-879-5000.
Email: general_info@fiserv.com
Website: http://www.fiserv.com

Chrmn: D.F. Dillon
Pres & CEO: J.W. Yabuki
COO & Sr EVP: N.J. Balthasar
EVP & CFO: T. Hirsch

EVP, Chief Admin Officer, Secy & General Counsel: C.W. Sprague
Board Members: D. F. Dillon, K. R. Jensen, D. P. Kearney, G. J. Levy, G. M. Renwick, K. M. Robak, L. W. Seidman, T. C. Wertheimer, J. W. Yabuki

Founded: 1984
Domicile: Wisconsin
Employees: 23,000

Fluor Corp.

STANDARD &POOR'S

S&P Recommendation **BUY** ★★★★☆	Price $135.12 (as of Nov 23, 2007)	12-Mo. Target Price $175.00	Investment Style Large-Cap Blend

GICS Sector Industrials
Sub-Industry Construction & Engineering

Summary FLR is one of the world's largest engineering, procurement and construction companies.

Key Stock Statistics (Source S&P, Vickers, company reports)

52-Wk Range	$172.15– 75.22	S&P Oper. EPS 2007**E**	4.15	Market Capitalization(B)	$11.948	Beta	0.91
Trailing 12-Month EPS	$3.91	S&P Oper. EPS 2008**E**	5.25	Yield (%)	0.59	S&P 3-Yr. Proj. EPS CAGR(%)	NA
Trailing 12-Month P/E	34.6	P/E on S&P Oper. EPS 2007**E**	32.6	Dividend Rate/Share	$0.80	S&P Credit Rating	A
$10K Invested 5 Yrs Ago	$56,647	Common Shares Outstg. (M)	88.4	Institutional Ownership (%)	97		

Price Performance

30-Week Mov. Avg. · · · 10-Week Mov. Avg. - - **GAAP Earnings vs. Previous Year** Volume Above Avg. STARS
12-Mo. Target Price — Relative Strength — ▲ Up ▼ Down ► No Change Below Avg. ★

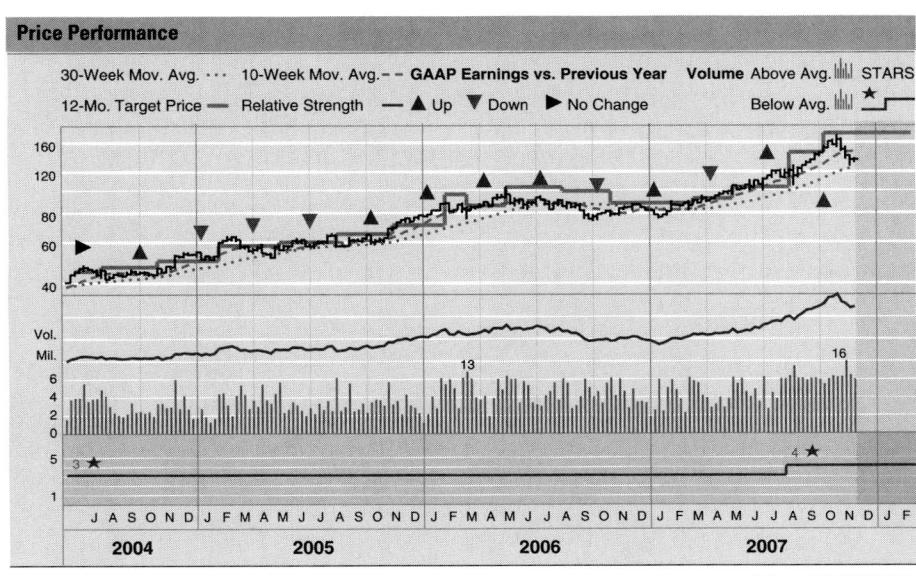

Options: ASE, CBOE, P, Ph

Analysis prepared by **Stewart Scharf** on November 14, 2007, when the stock traded at **$ 137.20**.

Highlights

➤ We project at least 15% revenue growth for 2007, rising to more than 20% in 2008, driven by strong global demand for oil and gas projects, and further growth in power and global services. We believe new awards will offset a decline in FEMA hurricane relief and other government work, and see favorable prospects for mining and transportation projects.

➤ In our view, quarterly operating margins may be uneven due to a mix shift during 2008, as several large oil and gas projects transition to the construction phase, with lower margins. However, we see higher-margin new awards for industrial, power and global services projects, and expect FLT to focus on growth in absolute operating profit and return on assets (ROA), rather than margins. In addition, with only one U.S. embassy project remaining to be completed (Haiti), we do not expect further cost overruns ($183 million in 2006).

➤ We project a higher effective tax rate of about 37.5% in 2007, and EPS of $4.15, advancing 27%, to $5.25, in 2008.

Investment Rationale/Risk

➤ We have a buy recommendation on the stock, based on our valuation models and favorable growth prospects for all segments except government. We think quarterly bookings could fluctuate due to the timing of new awards.

➤ Risks to our recommendation and target price include project delays, labor shortages, credit market issues, sharply lower oil prices and timing issues for new awards. We also are concerned about corporate governance practices, as three or more related-party transactions involved directors or officers other than the CEO.

➤ We attribute the stock's 10% premium forward multiple to our projected P/E for FLR's closest Construction & Engineering peers mainly to new awards for oil and gas projects, and target a value of $165. However, our discounted cash flow (DCF) model suggests the stock is well below its intrinsic value of $185, assuming a 3.5% terminal growth rate and an 8.3% weighted average cost of capital. We use a weighted blend of our DCF and relative P/E metrics to arrive at our 12-month target price of $175.

Qualitative Risk Assessment

LOW	MEDIUM	HIGH

Our risk assessment reflects the cyclical nature of the company's markets, and geopolitical issues, as more projects are in unstable regions of the world. In addition, we see a tight engineering labor market and lumpiness in new bookings. This is offset by our view of FLR's strong balance sheet, as debt levels are well controlled, and new bookings.

Quantitative Evaluations

S&P Quality Ranking B+

D	C	B-	B	B+	A-	A	A+

Relative Strength Rank MODERATE

56

LOWEST = 1   HIGHEST = 99

Revenue/Earnings Data

Revenue (Million $)

	1Q	2Q	3Q	4Q	Year
2007	3,642	4,222	4,155	--	--
2006	3,625	3,456	3,364	3,633	14,079
2005	2,860	2,920	3,419	3,963	13,161
2004	2,063	2,214	2,363	2,740	9,380
2003	2,077	2,243	2,121	2,365	8,806
2002	2,507	2,536	2,451	2,465	9,959

Earnings Per Share ($)

2007	0.94	1.05	1.02	E1.15	E4.15
2006	1.00	0.74	0.31	0.90	2.95
2005	0.56	-0.19	1.51	0.74	2.62
2004	0.57	0.54	0.57	0.57	2.25
2003	0.51	0.54	0.55	0.63	2.23
2002	0.45	0.54	0.58	0.56	2.13

Fiscal year ended Dec. 31. Next earnings report expected: Early March. EPS Estimates based on S&P Operating Earnings; historical GAAP earnings are as reported.

Dividend Data (Dates: mm/dd Payment Date: mm/dd/yy)

Amount ($)	Date Decl.	Ex-Div. Date	Stk. of Record	Payment Date
0.200	05/23	09/04	09/06	10/02/07
0.200	11/02	12/04	12/06	01/03/08

Dividends have been paid since 1974. Source: Company reports.

Fluor Corp.

Business Summary November 14, 2007

CORPORATE OVERVIEW. Fluor Corp. is one of the world's largest engineering, procurement, construction and maintenance companies. It has five principal operating segments. As of September 30, 2007, FLR's percentage of fixed price work in backlog decreased to 24%, from 27% at the end of the second quarter, and about 31% a year earlier, while 59% of work was outside the U.S., including 44% in Europe, Africa and the Middle East.

The Oil and Gas segment provides design and engineering, procurement and construction (EPC) services to oil, gas, refining, chemical, polymer and petrochemical customers. A new front-end oil & gas award typically takes six to 12 months to transition to a full EPC award. Industrial and Infrastructure provides EPC services to businesses, including industrial, commercial, telecommunications, mining and technology. Global Services provides operations and maintenance support, equipment and outsourcing, and asset management solutions through TRS Staffing Solutions. Government Services provides support services to the federal government and other government parties.

Contributions to revenues and operating profits in 2006 were as follows: Oil and Gas, 38% of revenues and 55% of operating profits ($306 million); Industrial and Infrastructure, 23% and 14% ($76 million); Power, 3.8% and 0.8% ($4.3 million); Global Services, 15% and 27% ($152 million); and Government Services, 20% and 3.2% ($18 million).

Total backlog of nearly $22 billion at year-end 2006, up 47% from a year earlier, was divided by segment as follows: Oil and Gas $12.0 billion, up 98%; Industrial and Infrastructure $5.4 billion, up 40%; Power $1.3 billion, up 15%; Global Services $2.3 billion, down 5.1%; and Government Services $840 million, down 41%. Backlog by geographic region at the end of 2006 was: U.S. 41%; the Americas 12%; Europe, Africa and the Middle East 42%; and Asia Pacific (including Australia) 5%. As of late 2007, backlog included a long cycle of large projects for refinery, coal plants and infrastructure. Larger projects tend to take three to five years to complete, versus the previous projects, which had an 18-to-36 month cycle.

FLR received new awards of $6.0 billion in the third quarter of 2007, including a major award for a new refinery in the Middle East, bringing backlog up to $27.9 billion, a 41% rise from a year earlier. New awards by segment in the third quarter of 2007 were: Oil and Gas, 72% of total awards; Industrial and Infrastructure, 6%; Government, 12%; Global Services, 9%; and Power, 1%.

Company Financials Fiscal Year Ended Dec. 31

Per Share Data ($)	2006	2005	2004	2003	2002	2001	2000	1999	1998	1997
Tangible Book Value	18.77	17.84	14.89	12.51	10.76	9.57	19.96	19.27	18.35	18.84
Cash Flow	4.37	3.82	3.36	3.22	3.11	2.52	5.39	5.56	6.63	4.64
Earnings	2.95	2.62	2.25	2.23	2.13	1.61	1.31	1.37	2.97	1.73
S&P Core Earnings	2.99	2.61	2.07	2.33	1.79	1.13	NA	NA	NA	NA
Dividends	0.20	0.64	0.64	0.64	0.64	0.64	1.00	0.80	0.80	0.76
Payout Ratio	7%	24%	28%	29%	30%	40%	76%	58%	27%	44%
Prices:High	103.85	79.10	55.19	40.82	44.95	63.20	48.50	46.50	52.50	75.88
Prices:Low	73.51	50.11	36.10	26.65	20.06	31.20	23.94	26.19	34.13	33.50
P/E Ratio:High	35	30	25	18	21	39	37	34	18	44
P/E Ratio:Low	25	19	16	12	9	19	18	19	11	19

Income Statement Analysis (Million $)

	2006	2005	2004	2003	2002	2001	2000	1999	1998	1997
Revenue	14,079	13,161	9,380	8,806	9,959	8,972	9,970	12,417	13,505	14,299
Operating Income	504	396	370	344	332	258	451	654	676	511
Depreciation	126	104	91.9	79.7	78.0	71.9	312	318	289	248
Interest Expense	23.0	16.3	15.4	10.1	8.93	25.0	26.3	50.9	45.0	31.0
Pretax Income	382	300	281	268	261	185	142	186	362	255
Effective Tax Rate	31.0%	24.1%	33.6%	33.0%	34.8%	31.1%	29.8%	44.0%	35.1%	42.7%
Net Income	263	227	187	180	170	128	99.8	104	235	146
S&P Core Earnings	267	226	171	188	143	90.2	NA	NA	NA	NA

Balance Sheet & Other Financial Data (Million $)

	2006	2005	2004	2003	2002	2001	2000	1999	1998	1997
Cash	976	789	605	497	753	573	69.4	210	341	309
Current Assets	3,324	3,108	2,723	2,214	1,941	1,851	1,448	1,910	2,277	2,226
Total Assets	4,875	4,574	3,970	3,449	3,142	3,091	3,653	4,886	5,019	4,698
Current Liabilities	2,406	2,339	1,764	1,829	1,756	1,811	1,620	2,204	2,496	1,991
Long Term Debt	187	92.0	348	44.7	17.6	17.6	17.6	318	300	301
Common Equity	1,730	1,631	1,336	1,082	884	789	1,609	1,581	1,526	1,741
Total Capital	1,918	1,723	1,683	1,126	901	807	1,627	2,061	1,932	2,108
Capital Expenditures	274	213	104	79.2	63.0	148	284	504	601	466
Cash Flow	390	331	279	259	248	200	412	422	524	394
Current Ratio	1.4	1.3	1.5	1.2	1.1	1.0	0.9	0.9	0.9	1.1
% Long Term Debt of Capitalization	9.8	5.3	20.7	4.0	2.0	2.2	1.1	15.4	15.5	14.3
% Net Income of Revenue	1.9	1.7	2.0	2.0	1.7	1.4	1.0	0.8	1.7	1.0
% Return on Assets	5.6	5.3	5.0	5.4	5.4	4.4	2.3	2.1	4.8	3.4
% Return on Equity	15.7	15.3	15.4	18.3	20.3	18.0	6.3	6.7	14.4	8.6

Data as orig reptd.; bef. results of disc opers/spec. items. Per share data adj. for stk. divs.; EPS diluted. E-Estimated. NA-Not Available. NM-Not Meaningful. NR-Not Ranked. UR-Under Review.

Office: 6700 Las Colinas Blvd, Irving, TX 75039-2902.
Telephone: 469-398-7000.
Email: investor@fluor.com
Website: http://www.fluor.com

Chrmn & CEO: A.L. Boeckmann
SVP & CFO: D.M. Steuert
VP & Cntlr: V.L. Prechtl
Secy & Chief Lgl Officer: L.N. Fisher

Investor Contact: K. Lockwood (949-349-3815)
Board Members: A. L. Boeckmann, P. J. Fluor, J. T. Hackett, K. Kresa, V. S. Martinez, D. R. O'Hare, J. W. Prueher, R. Renwick, P. S. Watson, S. H. Woolsey

Founded: 1924
Domicile: Delaware
Employees: 37,560

Ford Motor Co

STANDARD &POOR'S

S&P Recommendation	HOLD ★★★☆☆	Price	12-Mo. Target Price	Investment Style
		$7.19 (as of Nov 23, 2007)	$9.00	Large-Cap Value

GICS Sector Consumer Discretionary
Sub-Industry Automobile Manufacturers

Summary Ford, the world's second largest producer of cars and trucks, also has automotive financing and insurance operations.

Key Stock Statistics (Source S&P, Vickers, company reports)

52-Wk Range	$9.70–6.85	S&P Oper. EPS 2007E	-0.29	Market Capitalization(B)	$14.587	Beta	2.11
Trailing 12-Month EPS	$-3.12	S&P Oper. EPS 2008E	-0.52	Yield (%)	Nil	S&P 3-Yr. Proj. EPS CAGR(%)	NM
Trailing 12-Month P/E	NM	P/E on S&P Oper. EPS 2007E	NM	Dividend Rate/Share	Nil	S&P Credit Rating	B
$10K Invested 5 Yrs Ago	$8,083	Common Shares Outstg. (M)	2,099.6	Institutional Ownership (%)	93		

Price Performance

30-Week Mov. Avg. ···   10-Week Mov. Avg. - -   **GAAP Earnings vs. Previous Year**   Volume Above Avg. ⋯ STARS
12-Mo. Target Price —   Relative Strength   — ▲ Up ▼ Down ▶ No Change   Below Avg. ⋯ ★

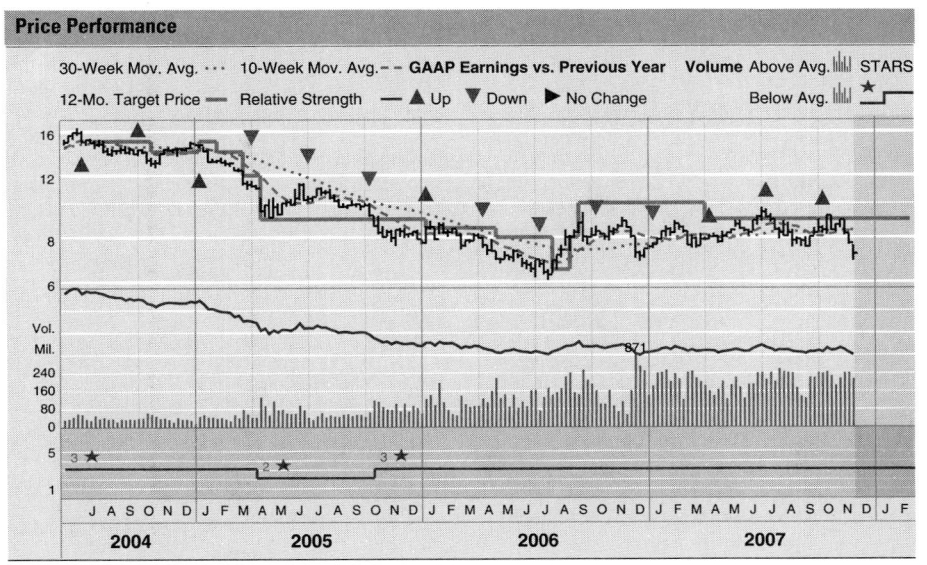

Options: ASE, CBOE, P, Ph

Analysis prepared by **Efraim Levy, CFA** on November 16, 2007, when the stock traded at **$ 7.74**.

Highlights

➤ In 2007, we see F's total revenues rising 7%, with growth slowing to about 3% in 2008. We believe F faces challenges from intense competition, lower market share, excess capacity and relatively high gasoline prices. The financial services segment has been an important contributor to recent sales and earnings, in our opinion, but we expect its income to fall in 2007 before rebounding in 2008.

➤ We see the ratification of F's contract with the United Auto Workers as a critical event that will enhance the profitability and competitiveness of the company. The agreement includes unprecedented union givebacks in terms of benefits and work rules, personalized to F's needs. In addition, the establishment of a healthcare trust to be managed by the union should free the company from onerous and uncertain obligations. Still, what is really needed, in our view, is increased demand for Ford's products on styling, quality and value improvements.

➤ We expect per share losses of $0.29 in 2007 and $0.52 in 2008.

Investment Rationale/Risk

➤ We think the new president and CEO, who is an automotive industry outsider with experience in turning around an international manufacturer, has enhanced Ford's improvement efforts. However, we are less confident in his or Ford's ability to consistently bring to market successful vehicles -- one of the company's most important challenges, in our view. In 2008, we expect the company to lose market share again. While we believe that Ford needs to stabilize volumes, we would hold the shares as we believe that net income will benefit from restructuring activities.

➤ Risks to our opinion and target price include increased competitive challenges, a decline in expected demand and production, and weaker than projected financial services income. We are also concerned about Ford's corporate governance that gives Ford family members greater voting rights than other shareholders.

➤ As we see losses in 2007 and 2008, P/E multiple valuation is not meaningful. The stock traded recently at a price to sales (P/S) multiple in line with GM. Based on peer comparative P/S multiples, our 12-month target price is $9, equal to 0.11X projected 2008 sales per share.

Qualitative Risk Assessment

LOW	MEDIUM	HIGH

Our risk assessment reflects the highly cyclical nature of Ford's markets as well as our view of the current and long-term challenges that it faces, with intensifying competition and high fixed and legacy costs.

Quantitative Evaluations

S&P Quality Ranking C

D	C	B-	B	B+	A-	A	A+

Relative Strength Rank WEAK

26

LOWEST = 1   HIGHEST = 99

Revenue/Earnings Data

Revenue (Million $)

	1Q	2Q	3Q	4Q	Year
2007	43,019	44,200	41,100	--	--
2006	41,055	41,965	37,110	40,318	160,123
2005	45,136	44,548	40,856	46,549	177,089
2004	44,691	42,802	38,996	44,930	171,652
2003	40,815	40,582	36,791	46,008	164,196
2002	39,541	42,127	39,338	41,580	163,420

Earnings Per Share ($)

	1Q	2Q	3Q	4Q	Year
2007	-0.15	0.30	-0.19	E-0.30	E-0.29
2006	-0.64	-0.14	-2.79	-2.98	-6.72
2005	0.58	0.47	-0.16	0.21	1.14
2004	0.95	0.57	0.25	0.03	1.80
2003	0.45	0.22	0.13	-0.35	0.50
2002	-0.05	0.31	-0.14	0.01	0.15

Fiscal year ended Dec. 31. Next earnings report expected: NA. EPS Estimates based on S&P Operating Earnings; historical GAAP earnings are as reported.

Dividend Data

No cash dividends have been paid since 2006.

Please read the Required Disclosures and Analyst Certification on the last page of this report.

Ford Motor Co

**STANDARD
&POOR'S**

Business Summary November 16, 2007

CORPORATE OVERVIEW. Ford is the world's second largest motor vehicle manufacturer. It produces cars and trucks, and many of the vehicles' plastic, glass and electronic components, and replacement parts. It also owns a 33% stake in Mazda Motor Corp. Financial services include Ford Motor Credit (automotive financing and insurance) and American Road Insurance Co.

Despite historically high new light vehicle industry volume, Ford's margins have been pressured by an increase in competition -- primarily from Asian companies -- and a shift away from the more profitable large SUV segment to smaller, less profitable crossover utility vehicles (CUVs), in our opinion. We think this is likely to hurt Ford's market share, at least until the company can introduce more of its own CUVs.

In recent years, the company's business and product portfolio has changed several times as Ford sought to optimize its financial health and performance. In December 2005, Ford sold its Hertz Corp. unit for about $15 billion, including around $5.6 billion in cash proceeds. We believe the sale diluted EPS in 2006, as Hertz had contributed $0.16 per share to EPS in 2004 and $0.19 in the first nine months of 2005, according to company estimates. In 1999, the company acquired the car operations of AB Volvo for $6.45 billion. In 2000, Ford acquired Land Rover from BMW Group for $1.9 billion. In July, the company said that it is in talks for the possible sale of Jaguar and Land Rover and that it is reviewing its strategy in regard to Volvo.

CORPORATE STRATEGY. Challenged by a shrinking U.S. market share, the company has announced restructuring plans in recent years in an attempt to lower its costs. However, even as Ford works to reduce its costs, the company now faces expenses stemming from assistance F is giving its former in-house parts manufacturing unit, Visteon Corp. In October 2005, Ford acquired 23 money-losing plants and facilities from Visteon. It also provided financial assistance to Visteon. In exchange, it received warrants to purchase Visteon common shares.

In March 2005, the company agreed to relieve Visteon of a portion (about $25 million per month) of its obligation to reimburse Ford for the costs of Ford's employees assigned to Visteon; to reduce by about one-fourth the number of days within which Ford will make payment to Visteon for materials and components it purchases from Visteon; and to acquire up to about $150 million of new machinery and equipment for use by Visteon necessary for its production of components for Ford. In exchange, Visteon agreed to continue to supply Ford with certain components without cost surcharges.

In January 2007, the company reported nearly $10 billion in restructuring related charges, after taxes. The costs included expenses related to the buyout of approximately 38,000 hourly U.S. as well additional employees outside the U.S and fixed asset impairment charges in North America and at Jaguar and Land Rover.

Company Financials Fiscal Year Ended Dec. 31

Per Share Data ($)	2006	2005	2004	2003	2002	2001	2000	1999	1998	1997
Tangible Book Value	NM	3.68	4.60	2.30	NM	NM	6.10	16.60	16.80	21.01
Cash Flow	-6.71	7.62	9.12	8.31	8.45	5.78	13.46	13.36	24.70	11.86
Earnings	-6.72	1.14	1.80	0.50	0.15	-3.02	3.59	5.86	17.76	5.62
S&P Core Earnings	-5.58	0.64	1.80	1.03	-1.16	-4.56	NA	NA	NA	NA
Dividends	0.35	0.40	0.40	0.40	0.40	1.05	2.30	1.88	2.18	1.65
Payout Ratio	NM	35%	22%	80%	NM	NM	64%	32%	12%	29%
Prices:High	9.48	14.75	17.34	17.33	18.23	31.42	57.25	67.88	65.94	50.25
Prices:Low	1.06	7.57	12.61	6.58	6.90	14.70	21.69	46.25	37.50	30.00
P/E Ratio:High	NM	13	10	35	NM	NM	16	12	4	9
P/E Ratio:Low	NM	7	7	13	NM	NM	6	8	2	5

Income Statement Analysis (Million $)										
Revenue	160,123	177,089	171,652	164,196	163,420	162,412	170,064	162,558	144,416	153,731
Operating Income	8,286	21,052	24,945	24,770	25,034	22,941	34,530	29,311	27,400	31,017
Depreciation	16,453	14,042	13,052	14,297	15,177	15,922	14,849	9,254	8,589	7,645
Interest Expense	8,783	7,643	7,071	7,690	8,824	10,848	10,902	9,076	8,865	10,500
Pretax Income	-15,051	1,996	4,853	1,370	953	-7,584	8,234	11,026	25,396	10,939
Effective Tax Rate	NM	NM	19.3%	9.85%	31.7%	NM	32.9%	33.3%	12.5%	34.2%
Net Income	-12,615	2,228	3,634	921	284	-5,453	5,410	7,237	22,071	6,920
S&P Core Earnings	-10,472	1,146	3,637	1,905	-2,202	-8,266	NA	NA	NA	NA

Balance Sheet & Other Financial Data (Million $)										
Cash	50,366	39,082	33,018	33,642	30,521	15,028	16,490	23,585	23,805	20,835
Total Assets	278,554	269,476	292,654	304,594	289,357	276,543	284,421	276,229	237,545	279,097
Long Term Debt	144,373	94,428	106,540	119,751	125,806	121,430	99,560	78,734	64,898	80,245
Total Debt	172,049	154,332	172,973	179,804	167,892	168,009	166,229	152,738	132,835	168,925
Common Equity	-3,465	12,957	16,045	11,651	5,590	7,786	18,610	27,537	23,409	30,734
Capital Expenditures	6,848	7,517	6,745	7,749	7,278	7,008	8,348	8,535	8,617	8,717
Cash Flow	-12,615	16,270	16,686	15,218	15,446	10,454	20,244	16,476	30,553	14,511
% Return on Assets	NM	0.8	1.2	0.3	0.1	NM	2.0	2.8	8.5	2.6
% Return on Equity	NM	15.4	26.2	10.7	4.0	NM	23.3	28.4	81.1	23.9
% Long Term Debt of Capitalization	83.7	82.9	82.2	87.5	87.8	87.2	78.3	68.6	73.5	68.5

Data as orig reptd.; bef. results of disc opers/spec. items. Per share data adj. for stk. divs.; EPS diluted. E-Estimated. NA-Not Available. NM-Not Meaningful. NR-Not Ranked. UR-Under Review.

Office: 1 American Rd, Dearborn, MI 48126-2798.
Telephone: 313-322-3000.
Website: http://www.ford.com
Exec Chrmn: W.C. Ford, Jr.

Pres & CEO: A. Mulally
Investor Contact: D.R. Leclair (800-555-5259)
EVP & CFO: D.R. Leclair
SVP & General Counsel: D. Leitch

Board Members: J. R. Bond, S. G. Butler, K. A. Casiano, E. B. Ford, II, W. C. Ford, Jr., I. O. Hockaday, Jr., R. A. Manoogian, E. R. Marram, A. Mulally, H. A. Neal, J. Ollila, G. L. Shaheen, J. L. Thorton

Founded: 1903
Domicile: Delaware
Employees: 283,000

Forest Laboratories Inc.

STANDARD &POOR'S

S&P Recommendation BUY ★★★★☆

Price	12-Mo. Target Price	Investment Style
$36.77 (as of Nov 23, 2007)	$50.00	Large-Cap Growth

GICS Sector Health Care
Sub-Industry Pharmaceuticals

Summary This company develops and makes branded and generic ethical drug products, sold primarily in the U.S., Puerto Rico, and Western and Eastern Europe.

Key Stock Statistics (Source S&P, Vickers, company reports)

52-Wk Range	$57.97–34.89	S&P Oper. EPS 2008E	3.15	Market Capitalization(B)	$11.625	Beta	1.19
Trailing 12-Month EPS	$1.59	S&P Oper. EPS 2009E	3.40	Yield (%)	Nil	S&P 3-Yr. Proj. EPS CAGR(%)	16.00
Trailing 12-Month P/E	23.1	P/E on S&P Oper. EPS 2008E	11.7	Dividend Rate/Share	Nil	S&P Credit Rating	NA
$10K Invested 5 Yrs Ago	$7,026	Common Shares Outstg. (M)	316.2	Institutional Ownership (%)	95		

Price Performance

30-Week Mov. Avg. · · · · 10-Week Mov. Avg. – – GAAP Earnings vs. Previous Year   Volume Above Avg. STARS
12-Mo. Target Price — Relative Strength — ▲ Up ▼ Down ▶ No Change   Below Avg.

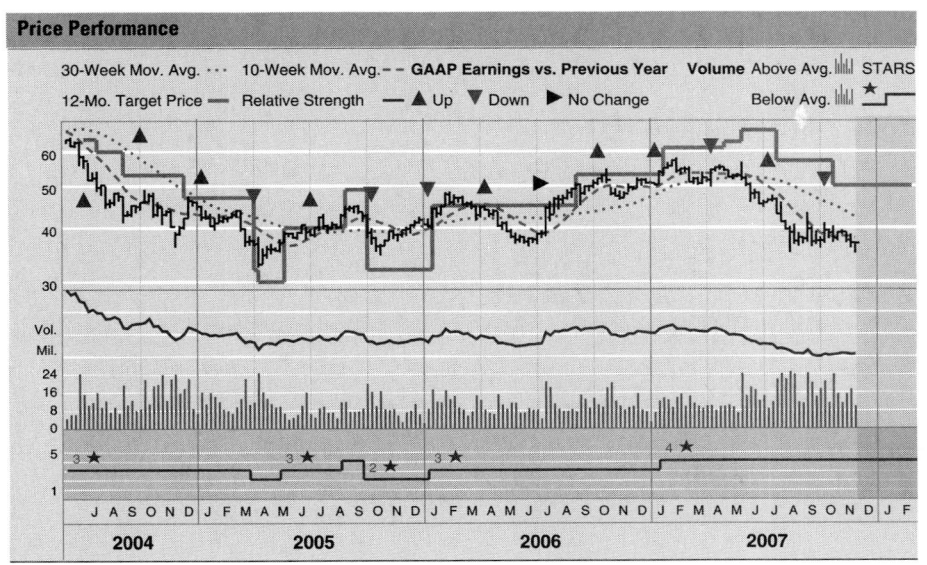

Options: ASE, CBOE, P, Ph

Analysis prepared by **Herman B. Saftlas** on October 17, 2007, when the stock traded at **$ 38.57**.

Highlights

➤ We expect revenues in FY 08 (Mar.) to rise 8%. Despite heightened competitive pressures, we project a 7% increase in Lexapro antidepressant sales, reflecting our view of that drug's efficacy and side effect advantages, an expanded salesforce, and higher prices. We look for sales of Namenda Alzheimer's drug to increase over 15%, lifted by projected greater acceptance of the drug by the medical community. A modest contribution is possible from nebivolol heart drug, assuming FDA clearance.

➤ We forecast a gross margin slightly above 77%, up from FY 07's 76.6%. SG&A spending will likely increase in line with sales, but R&D spending (excluding acquired in-process R&D charges) should increase sharply, reflecting stepped up investments on an expanding pipeline. We see other income augmented by increased alliance income from Benicar and Azor, heart drugs sold through a joint venture with Daiichi Sankyo.

➤ Our FY 08 operating EPS forecast is $3.15, after product licensing and milestone payments, up from FY 07's $2.89. We see further EPS progress, to $3.40 in FY 09.

Investment Rationale/Risk

➤ This leading specialty drugmaker faces a challenging future, with patent protection on its two principal products--Lexapro antidepressant and Namenda Alzheimer's treatment (combined sales accounting for 80% of FY 07 revenues)--expiring in 2012. However, we believe FRX's present strong lineup of promising pipeline products, combined with other in-licensing opportunities, will be able to replace the anticipated expiration losses. Key R&D products include milnacipran, a compound for fibromyalgia; nebivolol, a drug for hypertension and congestive heart failure; and RGH-188, an atypical antipsychotic.

➤ Risks to our recommendation and target price include greater than expected competition in principal markets, as well as possible setbacks in the R&D pipeline.

➤ Our 12-month target price of $50 applies a peer-level P/E of about 16X our FY 08 EPS estimate. This valuation is also supported by our DCF model, which assumes decelerated cash flow growth over the next 10 years, a weighted average cost of capital of 8%, and terminal growth of 1%, and leads to an estimated intrinsic value of $50.

Qualitative Risk Assessment

LOW	MEDIUM	HIGH

Our risk assessment reflects that we view positively the company's recent legal victory against generic challengers to its important Lexapro patent. We also think its R&D pipeline shows promise. However, Forest's relatively small size among big pharma competitors and our view of its somewhat limited product line represent negative risk factors.

Quantitative Evaluations

S&P Quality Ranking   B+

D	C	B-	B	B+	A-	A	A+

Relative Strength Rank   MODERATE

55

LOWEST = 1   HIGHEST = 99

Revenue/Earnings Data

Revenue (Million $)

	1Q	2Q	3Q	4Q	Year
2008	928.3	919.0	--	--	--
2007	816.3	847.0	893.0	885.4	3,442
2006	711.8	736.5	757.8	756.3	2,962
2005	--	--	--	640.6	3,114
2004	605.8	619.2	700.5	725.1	2,650
2003	467.2	531.6	586.8	621.1	2,207

Earnings Per Share ($)

2008	0.83	0.71	E0.75	E0.76	E3.15
2007	0.62	0.75	0.78	-0.75	1.41
2006	0.62	0.59	0.57	0.28	2.08
2005	0.60	0.79	0.70	0.15	2.25
2004	0.48	0.49	0.60	0.38	1.95
2003	0.34	0.39	0.47	0.48	1.66

Fiscal year ended Mar. 31. Next earnings report expected: Mid January. EPS Estimates based on S&P Operating Earnings; historical GAAP earnings are as reported.

Dividend Data

No cash dividends have been paid.

Forest Laboratories Inc.

STANDARD &POOR'S

Business Summary October 17, 2007

CORPORATE OVERVIEW. Forest Laboratories is a leading producer of niche-oriented branded and generic prescription pharmaceuticals. Most of Forest's products were developed in collaboration with licensing partners. FRX's most important products are antidepressants, which accounted for about 62% of net sales in FY 07 (Mar.).

Lexapro antidepressant is the company's single most important product. A single enanitomer version of Celexa (an older, off-patent FRX antidepressant), Lexapro is an advanced selective serotonin reuptake inhibitor (SSRI) indicated for the treatment of both depression and generalized anxiety disorder. Lexapro had sales of $2.1 billion in FY 07, up from $1.9 billion in FY 06. FRX licensed both Celexa and Lexapro from H. Lundbeck A/S, a Danish pharmaceutical company. As of March 2007, Lexapro had a 13.4% share of the relatively crowded U.S. prescription antidepressant drug market, based on data from IMS Health.

FRX's second most important product is Namenda (licensed from Merz Pharmaceuticals of Germany), a treatment for moderate to severe Alzheimer's disease. Sales of Namenda were $660 million in FY 07, up from $508 million in FY 06. As of March 2007, Namenda had about 33% of the Alzheimer's prescription drug market, according to IMS Health.

The company's third largest drug is Benicar, a antihypertensive co-promoted with Sankyo. FRX booked revenues of $175 million from Benicar in FY 07. Other products include Tiazac, an antihypertensive; Aerobid, an asthma drug; Campral for alcohol addiction; Combunox for the short-term management of severe pain; Aero-chamber, a device used to improve the delivery of aerosol products; and Cervidil, used to aid in cervical dilation.

COMPETITIVE LANDSCAPE. The U.S. antidepressant drug market totaled about $13.6 billion in 2006, based on data from IMS Health. We expect this market to shrink in terms of dollar sales over the coming years, reflecting the impact of inexpensive generic versions of many patent-expired branded antidepressants. Pfizer's popular Zoloft antidepressant lost patent protection in 2006, and Wyeth's patent on Effexor antidepressant expires in 2008. Generics now largely comprise previously branded Prozac and Paxil antidepressant markets.

Company Financials Fiscal Year Ended Mar. 31

Per Share Data ($)	2007	2006	2005	2004	2003	2002	2001	2000	1999	1998
Tangible Book Value	8.93	7.69	8.21	8.03	5.66	3.75	2.60	1.79	1.60	1.25
Cash Flow	1.55	2.20	2.32	2.01	1.80	1.06	0.71	0.44	0.29	0.17
Earnings	1.41	2.08	2.25	1.95	1.66	0.91	0.59	0.32	0.23	0.11
S&P Core Earnings	1.41	1.97	2.15	1.85	1.58	0.74	0.47	NA	NA	NA
Dividends	Nil	Nil	Nil	Nil	Nil	Nil	Nil	Nil	Nil	Nil
Payout Ratio	Nil	Nil	Nil	Nil	Nil	Nil	Nil	Nil	Nil	Nil
Calendar Year	2006	2005	2004	2003	2002	2001	2000	1999	1998	1997
Prices:High	54.70	45.21	78.81	63.23	54.99	41.60	35.33	15.44	13.31	6.16
Prices:Low	36.18	32.46	36.10	41.85	32.12	23.25	14.34	10.31	6.08	3.95
P/E Ratio:High	39	22	35	32	33	46	60	48	59	56
P/E Ratio:Low	26	16	16	21	19	26	24	32	27	36

Income Statement Analysis (Million $)										
Revenue	3,442	2,962	3,114	2,650	2,207	1,567	1,181	882	546	427
Operating Income	754	701	1,164	929	833	490	318	181	54.3	27.2
Depreciation	45.4	40.7	25.4	22.2	51.6	54.6	43.3	40.6	21.3	20.1
Interest Expense	Nil	Nil	Nil	Nil	Nil	Nil	Nil	Nil	Nil	Nil
Pretax Income	709	870	1,185	937	821	470	299	157	111	54.8
Effective Tax Rate	35.9%	18.5%	29.2%	21.5%	24.2%	28.1%	28.0%	28.4%	30.4%	33.0%
Net Income	454	709	839	736	622	338	215	113	77.2	36.7
S&P Core Earnings	454	673	800	697	589	272	170	NA	NA	NA

Balance Sheet & Other Financial Data (Million $)										
Cash	1,353	1,323	1,619	2,131	1,556	893	506	355	279	150
Current Assets	2,423	2,207	2,708	2,916	2,255	1,195	884	645	502	372
Total Assets	3,653	3,120	3,705	3,863	2,918	1,952	1,447	1,098	875	744
Current Liabilities	628	421	564	605	564	325	224	211	130	130
Long Term Debt	Nil	Nil	Nil	Nil	Nil	Nil	Nil	Nil	Nil	Nil
Common Equity	3,025	2,698	3,132	3,256	2,352	1,625	1,222	885	744	614
Total Capital	3,026	2,699	3,141	3,258	2,354	1,627	1,223	887	745	614
Capital Expenditures	30.0	55.0	89.0	102	79.6	36.4	30.9	35.3	17.2	6.89
Cash Flow	500	749	864	758	674	393	258	153	98.4	56.8
Current Ratio	3.9	5.2	4.8	4.8	4.0	3.7	4.0	3.1	3.9	2.9
% Long Term Debt of Capitalization	Nil	Nil	Nil	Nil	Nil	Nil	Nil	Nil	Nil	Nil
% Net Income of Revenue	13.5	24.3	26.9	27.8	28.2	21.6	18.2	12.8	14.1	8.6
% Return on Assets	13.4	20.8	22.2	21.7	25.5	19.9	16.7	11.4	9.5	5.1
% Return on Equity	15.9	24.3	26.3	26.2	31.3	23.7	20.4	13.8	11.4	5.9

Data as orig reptd.; bef. results of disc opers/spec. items. Per share data adj. for stk. divs.; EPS diluted. E-Estimated. NA-Not Available. NM-Not Meaningful. NR-Not Ranked. UR-Under Review.

Office: 909 3rd Ave, New York, NY 10022-4748.
Telephone: 212-421-7850.
Email: investor.relations@frx.com
Website: http://www.frx.com

Chrmn & CEO: H. Solomon
Pres & COO: L.S. Olanoff

Board Members: N. Basgoz, W. J. Candee, III, G. S. Cohan, D. L. Goldwasser, K. E. Goodman, L. S. Olanoff, L. B. Salans, H. Solomon

Founded: 1956
Domicile: Delaware
Employees: 5,126

Fortune Brands Inc.

S&P Recommendation HOLD ★★★☆☆	**Price** $77.76 (as of Nov 23, 2007)	**12-Mo. Target Price** $87.00	**Investment Style** Large-Cap Blend

GICS Sector Consumer Discretionary
Sub-Industry Housewares & Specialties

Summary This diversified holding company has interests in consumer businesses that include home improvement, spirits and wine, and golf-related products.

Key Stock Statistics (Source S&P, Vickers, company reports)

52-Wk Range	$90.80–76.58	S&P Oper. EPS 2007**E**	5.12	Market Capitalization(B)	$11.878	Beta	0.86
Trailing 12-Month EPS	$5.25	S&P Oper. EPS 2008**E**	5.62	Yield (%)	2.16	S&P 3-Yr. Proj. EPS CAGR(%)	9.00
Trailing 12-Month P/E	14.8	P/E on S&P Oper. EPS 2007**E**	15.2	Dividend Rate/Share	$1.68	S&P Credit Rating	BBB
$10K Invested 5 Yrs Ago	NA	Common Shares Outstg. (M)	152.8	Institutional Ownership (%)	73		

Price Performance

30-Week Mov. Avg. · · · 10-Week Mov. Avg. - - **GAAP Earnings vs. Previous Year** Volume Above Avg. STARS
12-Mo. Target Price — Relative Strength — ▲ Up ▼ Down ▶ No Change Below Avg.

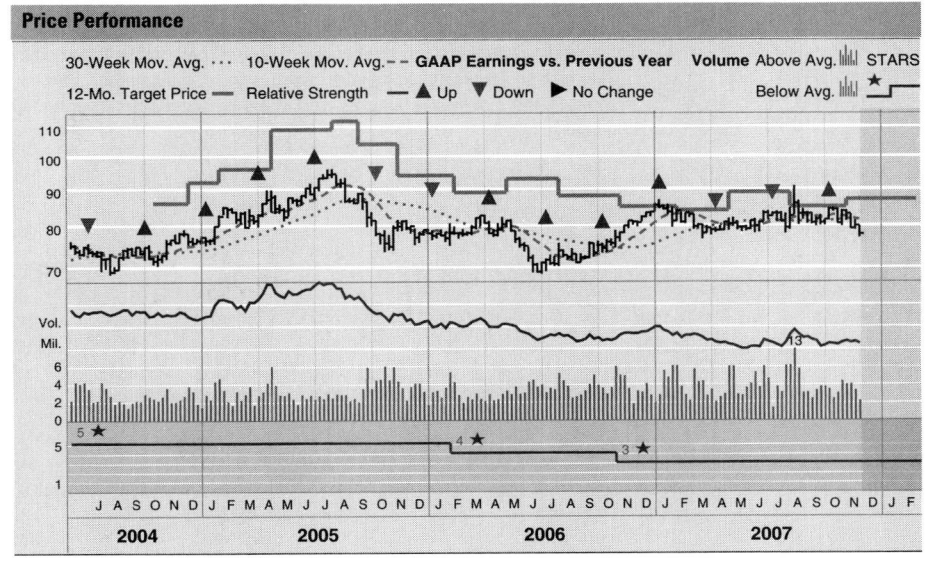

Options: ASE, CBOE, P, Ph

Analysis prepared by **Loran Braverman, CFA** on October 29, 2007, when the stock traded at **$ 83.07**.

Highlights

➤ For 2007, we project 1.2% total company sales growth. We think the Spirits & Wine segment will grow 1.5%, however this includes a 9% decline in the first quarter primarily due to distributors' inventory pipeline filling in 2006. We expect flat sales in the more cyclical Home & Hardware segment and 5.4% growth for the Golf business. For 2008, our projections are 3.6% overall growth, 4.6% for Spirits & Wine, 3.2% for Home & Hardware and 2.7% for Golf.

➤ We think the operating margin, before restructuring charges, will decrease to 16.9% in 2007 from 17.5%, due primarily to our projection of a 190 basis point drop in the operating margin in the Home & Hardware segment. We estimate an 80 basis point improvement in the Spirits & Wine segment margin and a slightly lower margin for the Golf segment. For 2008, we forecast an increase in the operating margin of 70 basis points, due to a 100 basis point improvment in the Home & Hardware segment and smaller gains in the other two businesses. Our effective tax rate assumption is about 32% in both years.

➤ We project that operating EPS will decrease 3.9% in 2007, to $5.12, from $5.33 in 2006, but then grow to $5.62 in 2008.

Investment Rationale/Risk

➤ Our hold opinion reflects our view that the stock price fairly reflects FO's growth prospects. We believe that, with its portfolio of diverse businesses, FO can continue to deliver earnings growth, on average, at least on par with the broader market. For 2007, although we think that consumers will continue to repair and remodel existing homes, we look for flat sales at best, and lower margins and earnings for the Home & Hardware segment.

➤ Risks to our recommendation and target price include a slowdown in the economy, a sharp increase in interest rates, and low consumer acceptance of new products.

➤ Our 12-month target price of $87 is based on a blend of our historical and peer analyses. Our historical analysis uses the 10-year historical median forward P/E on our 2008 estimate, implying a value of $88. Our sum-of-the-parts peer analysis, weighted by our relative segmental 2008 projected operating income percentages, uses a P/E of about 15X our 2008 EPS estimate, implying a value of $86.

Qualitative Risk Assessment

LOW	MEDIUM	HIGH

Our risk assessment reflects our view that FO has a long track record of consistent sales and earnings growth. While the company has exposure to the homebuilding market, more of its products are geared for remodeling. Its spirits and wine and golf businesses are generally stable, in our opinion.

Quantitative Evaluations

S&P Quality Ranking   B

D	C	B-	B	B+	A-	A	A+

Relative Strength Rank   MODERATE

55

LOWEST = 1   HIGHEST = 99

Revenue/Earnings Data

Revenue (Million $)

	1Q	2Q	3Q	4Q	Year
2007	1,949	2,355	2,198	--	--
2006	2,017	2,257	2,219	2,277	8,769
2005	1,518	1,783	1,802	1,959	7,061
2004	1,708	1,890	1,812	1,912	7,321
2003	1,392	1,582	1,584	1,657	6,215
2002	1,271	1,513	1,463	1,432	5,678

Earnings Per Share ($)

2007	0.77	1.48	1.33	E1.42	E5.12
2006	1.15	1.63	0.98	1.65	5.42
2005	0.95	1.22	0.52	1.17	3.87
2004	0.92	1.11	1.52	1.68	5.23
2003	0.66	1.18	0.98	1.04	3.86
2002	0.55	1.27	0.73	0.86	3.41

Fiscal year ended Dec. 31. Next earnings report expected: Late January. EPS Estimates based on S&P Operating Earnings; historical GAAP earnings are as reported.

Dividend Data (Dates: mm/dd Payment Date: mm/dd/yy)

Amount ($)	Date Decl.	Ex-Div. Date	Stk. of Record	Payment Date
0.390	01/25	02/05	02/07	03/01/07
0.390	04/24	05/07	05/09	06/01/07
0.420	07/31	08/13	08/15	09/04/07
0.420	09/25	11/05	11/07	12/03/07

Dividends have been paid since 1905. Source: Company reports.

Please read the Required Disclosures and Analyst Certification on the last page of this report.

The **McGraw-Hill** Companies

Fortune Brands Inc.

Business Summary October 29, 2007

CORPORATE OVERVIEW. Fortune Brands is a holding company with sub-sidiaries that produce home and hardware products, spirits and wine, and golf products.

Major units of FO's Home and Hardware products segment include Master-Brand Cabinets, Moen, Master Lock, Waterloo and Therma-Tru. In 2006, hard-ware and home improvement products accounted for 54% of total sales and 44% of operating company contributions (before corporate expenses).

Golf products (15%, 11%) operations are conducted through Acushnet, a lead-ing producer of golf balls (Titleist, Pinnacle), golf shoes (FootJoy), golf clubs (Cobra, Titleist), and golf gloves. Other products include bags, carts, dress and athletic shoes, socks and accessories.

Spirits and wine (31%, 45%) are sold through the Beam Global Spirits & Wine subsidiary. Leading brands include Jim Beam Bourbon whiskey, DeKuyper cordials, Gilbey's gin, Kamchatka vodka, and Geyser Peak wine. Principal markets are the U.S., the U.K., and Australia. About 25% of the division's sales come from international markets. In July 2005, the company acquired various spirits and wine brands from Pernod Ricard, which in turn were acquired by

Pernod from Allied Domecq PLC. This transaction more than doubled the sales of FO's Spirits and Wine segment. Some of the key brands that were acquired are Sauza tequila, Courvoisier cognac, Canadian Club whiskey, and Maker's Mark bourbon brand, which remains subject to regulatory clearance in the U.S.

In 2006, net sales by geographic region, based on country of destination, were the United States, with 79% of net sales, Canada 5%, the United Kingdom 3%, Australia 3%, Spain 2% and all other 8%.

CORPORATE STRATEGY. FO seeks to grow its sales and earnings through continued brand investment and to gain market share by developing and ex-panding customer relationships. Its first priority is internal growth, followed by expansion through acquisitions and joint ventures. Also, the company contin-uously looks to improve productivity, as well as the cost and asset structures, of its businesses.

Company Financials Fiscal Year Ended Dec. 31

Per Share Data ($)	2006	2005	2004	2003	2002	2001	2000	1999	1998	1997
Tangible Book Value	NM	NM	NM	NM	NM	2.06	0.89	0.83	1.91	1.93
Cash Flow	7.37	5.35	6.70	5.14	4.57	3.89	0.63	-3.96	3.09	1.64
Earnings	5.42	3.87	5.23	3.86	3.41	2.49	-0.88	-5.35	1.67	0.23
S&P Core Earnings	5.47	3.73	4.58	3.79	3.14	2.38	NA	NA	NA	NA
Dividends	1.50	1.38	1.26	1.14	1.02	0.97	0.93	0.89	0.85	1.41
Payout Ratio	28%	36%	24%	30%	30%	39%	NM	NM	51%	NM
Prices:High	85.96	96.18	80.50	71.80	57.86	40.54	33.25	45.88	42.25	56.00
Prices:Low	68.45	73.50	66.10	40.60	36.85	28.38	19.19	29.38	25.25	30.25
P/E Ratio:High	16	25	15	19	17	16	NM	NM	25	NM
P/E Ratio:Low	13	19	13	11	11	11	NM	NM	15	NM
Income Statement Analysis (Million $)										
Revenue	8,769	7,061	7,321	6,215	5,678	5,679	5,845	5,525	5,241	4,845
Operating Income	1,777	1,715	1,374	1,142	1,011	870	938	853	871	723
Depreciation	298	224	221	193	179	219	237	231	251	243
Interest Expense	332	159	87.9	73.8	74.1	96.8	134	107	103	117
Pretax Income	1,209	926	1,086	884	756	492	38.9	-721	512	140
Effective Tax Rate	25.7%	35.0%	26.1%	32.7%	28.3%	19.2%	NM	NM	42.6%	70.0%
Net Income	830	582	784	579	526	386	-138	-891	294	42.0
S&P Core Earnings	837	559	684	567	484	367	NA	NA	NA	NA
Balance Sheet & Other Financial Data (Million $)										
Cash	183	93.6	165	105	15.4	48.7	20.9	72.0	40.0	54.0
Current Assets	3,930	3,193	2,642	2,282	1,903	1,970	2,265	2,313	2,265	2,096
Total Assets	14,668	13,202	7,884	7,445	5,822	5,301	5,764	6,417	7,360	6,943
Current Liabilities	2,515	2,818	2,036	2,134	1,515	1,258	2,040	2,003	1,845	1,769
Long Term Debt	5,035	4,890	1,240	1,243	200	950	1,152	1,205	982	739
Common Equity	4,722	3,639	3,203	2,712	2,305	2,094	2,127	2,728	4,087	4,006
Total Capital	11,458	9,788	5,207	4,664	2,983	3,444	3,343	3,991	5,080	4,795
Capital Expenditures	266	222	242	194	194	207	227	241	252	197
Cash Flow	1,128	805	1,005	772	704	605	99.0	-661	544	284
Current Ratio	1.6	1.1	1.3	1.1	1.3	1.6	1.1	1.2	1.2	1.2
% Long Term Debt of Capitalization	43.9	50.0	23.8	26.6	6.7	27.6	34.5	30.2	19.3	15.4
% Net Income of Revenue	9.5	8.2	10.7	9.3	9.3	6.8	NM	NM	5.6	0.9
% Return on Assets	6.0	5.5	10.2	8.7	9.5	7.0	NM	NM	4.1	0.5
% Return on Equity	19.9	17.2	26.5	23.1	23.9	18.3	NM	NM	7.2	1.1

Data as orig reptd.; bef. results of disc opers/spec. items. Per share data adj. for stk. divs.; EPS diluted. E-Estimated. NA-Not Available. NM-Not Meaningful. NR-Not Ranked. UR-Under Review.

Office: 520 Lake Cook Rd, Deerfield, IL 60015-5611.
Telephone: 847-484-4400.
Email: investorrelations@fortunebrands.com
Website: http://www.fortunebrands.com

Chrmn & CEO: N.H. Wesley
Pres & COO: B.A. Carbonari
SVP & CFO: C.P. Omtvedt
SVP & Treas: M. Hausberg

SVP, Secy & General Counsel: M.A. Roche
Board Members: P. O. Ewers, R. A. Goldstein, P. E. Leroy, A. D. Mackay, E. A. Renna, A. M. Tatlock, D. M. Thomas, N. H. Wesley, P. M. Wilson

Founded: 1904
Domicile: Delaware
Employees: 36,251

FPL Group Inc.

STANDARD &POOR'S

S&P Recommendation HOLD ★★★☆☆	**Price** $68.49 (as of Nov 23, 2007)	**12-Mo. Target Price** $69.00	**Investment Style** Large-Cap Blend

GICS Sector Utilities
Sub-Industry Electric Utilities

Summary The holding company for Florida Power & Light and FPL Energy, FPL Group has agreed to the termination of its planned merger with Constellation Energy.

Key Stock Statistics (Source S&P, Vickers, company reports)

52-Wk Range	$70.12– 52.07	S&P Oper. EPS 2007**E**	3.45	Market Capitalization(B)	$27.864	Beta	0.47
Trailing 12-Month EPS	$3.39	S&P Oper. EPS 2008**E**	3.90	Yield (%)	2.39	S&P 3-Yr. Proj. EPS CAGR(%)	10.00
Trailing 12-Month P/E	20.2	P/E on S&P Oper. EPS 2007**E**	19.9	Dividend Rate/Share	$1.64	S&P Credit Rating	A
$10K Invested 5 Yrs Ago	$27,270	Common Shares Outstg. (M)	406.8	Institutional Ownership (%)	65		

Price Performance

30-Week Mov. Avg. · · · 10-Week Mov. Avg. – – **GAAP Earnings vs. Previous Year** Volume Above Avg. STARS
12-Mo. Target Price — Relative Strength — ▲ Up ▼ Down ► No Change Below Avg.

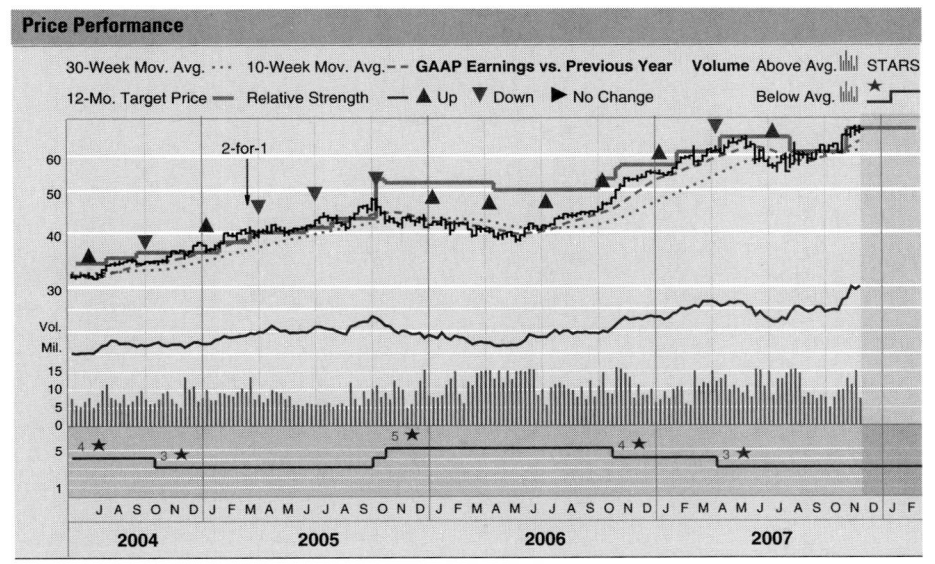

Options: ASE, CBOE, P, Ph

Analysis prepared by **Justin McCann** on November 15, 2007, when the stock traded at **$ 67.17**.

Qualitative Risk Assessment

LOW	MEDIUM	HIGH

Our risk assessment reflects our view of FPL's strong and steady cash flows from its Florida Power & Light utility, which enjoys well above average customer growth, and a generally supportive regulatory environment. We believe this largely offsets the fast growing but higher-risk cash flows from its independent power subsidiary.

Quantitative Evaluations

S&P Quality Ranking A-

D	C	B-	B	B+	A-	A	A+

Relative Strength Rank STRONG
92
LOWEST = 1   HIGHEST = 99

Revenue/Earnings Data

Revenue (Million $)

	1Q	2Q	3Q	4Q	Year
2007	3,075	3,929	--	--	--
2006	3,584	3,809	4,694	3,623	15,710
2005	2,437	2,741	3,504	3,164	11,846
2004	2,331	2,619	2,983	2,589	10,522
2003	2,082	2,339	2,775	2,435	9,630
2002	1,843	2,248	2,353	2,029	8,311

Earnings Per Share ($)

	1Q	2Q	3Q	4Q	Year
2007	0.38	1.01	E1.24	E0.66	E3.45
2006	0.64	0.60	1.32	0.67	3.23
2005	0.36	0.52	0.87	0.53	2.29
2004	0.39	0.72	0.88	0.47	2.46
2003	0.50	0.67	0.94	0.41	2.51
2002	0.49	0.73	0.43	0.37	2.00

Fiscal year ended Dec. 31. Next earnings report expected: NA. EPS Estimates based on S&P Operating Earnings; historical GAAP earnings are as reported.

Dividend Data (Dates: mm/dd Payment Date: mm/dd/yy)

Amount ($)	Date Decl.	Ex-Div. Date	Stk. of Record	Payment Date
0.410	02/16	02/28	03/02	03/15/07
0.410	05/25	06/06	06/08	06/15/07
0.410	08/03	08/29	08/31	09/17/07
0.410	10/19	11/28	11/30	12/17/07

Dividends have been paid since 1944. Source: Company reports.

Highlights

➤ We expect operating EPS in 2007 to rise about 13% from 2006 operating EPS of $3.04. Operating EPS in the first nine months of 2007 increased to $2.79, from $2.40 in 2006, driven by strong earnings growth at FPL Energy. FPL Energy benefited from new power generating facilities and growth in its wholesale market in the second quarter, despite weak wind source availability, and from very strong power marketing results in the third quarter, particularly in New England and Texas.

➤ For 2008, we see operating EPS of about $2.18 from Florida Power & Light; around $1.92 from FPL Energy; and a loss per share of about $0.20 from corporate and other operations. We expect earnings from the utility to continue to benefit from annual customer growth of more than 2% and a still strong Florida economy.

➤ We believe EPS growth in 2008 and 2009 will reflect sharp increases in earnings from FPL Energy, driven by the expansion of its wind power operations and from renewed higher-margin power contracts. It expects to add at least 2,000 megawatts (MW) of new wind projects by the end of 2008, and an additional 1,500 to 2,000 MW per year from 2009 through 2012.

Investment Rationale/Risk

➤ Following the recent rise in the shares, FPL is up around 23% year to date (after an approximate 31% gain in 2006), and we expect a roughly mid-single-digit total return over the next 12 months. While we believe the stock was aided in 2006 by the strong advance of around 19% for the electric utility sector, we also think it benefited from the termination of the planned merger with Constellation Energy. In our opinion, this enabled investors to focus more clearly on FPL's strong growth prospects on a stand-alone basis. After expected EPS growth of around 13% in both 2007 and 2008, we project growth of about 9% in 2009.

➤ Risks to our recommendation and target price include lower than expected results from the unregulated FPL Energy business, and a reduction in the average P/E of the group as a whole.

➤ Given the recent rise in the shares, the dividend yield declined to around 2.4%. However, we expect to see average annual dividend growth of about 8% over the next few years. Our 12-month target price of $69 reflects a modest premium to peers P/E of about 17.7X our EPS estimate for 2008, justified, in our view, by above-average earnings growth.

Please read the Required Disclosures and Analyst Certification on the last page of this report.

The McGraw-Hill Companies

FPL Group Inc.

STANDARD &POOR'S

Business Summary November 15, 2007

CORPORATE OVERVIEW. FPL Group, one of the largest providers of electricity-related services in the U.S., is the holding company for Florida Power & Light Co. (FP&L), a regulated and vertically integrated utility, and FPL Energy, a wholesale generator of electricity with operations in 24 states.

MARKET PROFILE. Florida Power & Light provides electricity to about 4.4 million customers in an area covering nearly all of Florida's eastern seaboard, as well as the southern part of the state. As is true of most states in the Southeast, Florida has shown little interest in restructuring its electric utility industry. Although there have been efforts to introduce a competitive wholesale generation market within the state, there has not been any legislation that would allow it to take place, and we do not expect to see any within the next several years.

Electric revenues by customer class in 2006 were: residential 54%; commercial 39%; industrial 3%; and other 4%. Given its unusually low level of exposure to industrial customers, we consider the company to be much less vulnerable to economic downturns. This, along with an above average customer growth rate (2.0% in 2006), and a recent regulatory ruling that has provided

rate certainty through 2009 and set up a storm cost recovery mechanism, helps to establish, we think, a more favorable foundation for the utility's long-term annual EPS growth, which we project at 3% to 4%.

IMPACT OF MAJOR DEVELOPMENTS. On October 25, 2006, the company and Baltimore-based Constellation Energy Group (CEG) announced the termination of the merger agreement that had been announced on December 19, 2005. Since CEG is not only the holding company for Baltimore Gas & Electric Company, but the nation's largest wholesale power seller and its greatest competitive supplier of electricity to large commercial and industrial customers, the merger would have made the combined entity one of the biggest electric companies in the U.S. Although we were disappointed that the merger was terminated, we believe the regulatory and judicial uncertainties surrounding the approval process in Maryland justified the decision.

Company Financials Fiscal Year Ended Dec. 31

Per Share Data ($)	2006	2005	2004	2003	2002	2001	2000	1999	1998	1997
Tangible Book Value	24.52	21.52	20.24	18.93	17.46	17.09	15.89	15.00	14.16	13.31
Earnings	3.23	2.29	2.46	2.51	2.01	2.31	2.07	2.04	1.93	1.79
S&P Core Earnings	3.00	2.06	2.17	2.21	1.52	1.83	NA	NA	NA	NA
Dividends	1.50	1.42	1.30	1.20	1.16	1.12	1.08	1.04	1.00	0.96
Payout Ratio	46%	62%	53%	48%	58%	48%	52%	51%	52%	54%
Prices:High	55.57	48.11	38.05	34.04	32.66	35.81	36.50	30.97	36.28	30.00
Prices:Low	37.81	35.90	30.10	26.78	22.50	25.61	18.19	20.56	28.03	21.31
P/E Ratio:High	17	21	15	14	16	16	18	15	19	17
P/E Ratio:Low	12	16	12	11	11	11	9	10	15	12

Income Statement Analysis (Million $)										
Revenue	15,710	11,846	10,522	9,630	8,311	8,475	7,082	6,438	6,661	6,369
Depreciation	1,185	1,285	1,198	1,105	952	983	1,032	1,040	1,284	1,061
Maintenance	NA	NA	NA	NA	NA	NA	NA	NA	NA	NA
Fixed Charges Coverage	3.30	2.87	3.26	3.95	4.52	4.51	4.55	4.96	NA	3.97
Construction Credits	21.0	28.0	37.0	NA	NA	NA	Nil	Nil	Nil	Nil
Effective Tax Rate	23.7%	23.5%	23.1%	29.2%	26.0%	32.7%	32.3%	31.7%	29.6%	33.0%
Net Income	1,281	885	887	893	695	781	704	697	664	618
S&P Core Earnings	1,187	797	782	786	527	616	NA	NA	NA	NA

Balance Sheet & Other Financial Data (Million $)										
Gross Property	36,152	33,351	31,720	30,272	26,505	23,388	21,022	19,554	17,952	17,820
Capital Expenditures	1,763	1,616	1,394	1,383	1,277	1,544	1,299	861	617	551
Net Property	24,499	22,463	21,226	20,297	14,304	11,662	9,934	9,264	8,555	9,354
Capitalization:Long Term Debt	9,591	8,039	8,027	8,728	6,016	5,084	4,202	3,704	2,347	2,949
Capitalization:% Long Term Debt	49.1	48.6	51.6	55.6	47.4	45.8	42.9	40.8	30.5	36.8
Capitalization:Preferred	Nil	Nil	Nil	Nil	Nil	Nil	Nil	Nil	226	226
Capitalization:% Preferred	Nil	Nil	Nil	Nil	Nil	Nil	Nil	Nil	2.90	2.80
Capitalization:Common	9,930	8,499	7,537	6,967	6,688	6,015	5,593	5,370	5,126	4,845
Capitalization:% Common	50.9	51.4	48.4	44.4	52.6	54.2	57.1	59.2	66.6	60.4
Total Capital	22,953	19,615	15,645	17,850	14,444	12,629	11,442	10,337	9,159	9,493
% Operating Ratio	87.1	88.6	87.8	87.9	85.7	87.6	86.3	88.0	85.4	85.5
% Earned on Net Property	8.9	6.7	7.1	8.1	9.5	10.3	12.9	18.2	14.0	13.1
% Return on Revenue	8.2	7.5	8.4	9.3	8.4	9.2	9.9	10.8	10.0	9.7
% Return on Invested Capital	10.9	8.6	9.2	8.1	9.0	9.6	9.7	11.4	10.7	9.4
% Return on Common Equity	13.9	11.0	12.0	13.4	10.7	13.5	12.8	13.3	13.3	13.1

Data as orig reptd.; bef. results of disc opers/spec. items. Per share data adj. for stk. divs.; EPS diluted. E-Estimated. NA-Not Available. NM-Not Meaningful. NR-Not Ranked. UR-Under Review.

Office: 700 Universe Boulevard, Juno Beach, FL 33408-0420.
Telephone: 561-694-4000.
Website: http://www.fplgroup.com
Chrmn & CEO: L. Hay, III

Pres & COO: J. Robo
VP & CFO: M.P. Dewhurst
VP & General Counsel: E.F. Tancer
Chief Acctg Officer: K.M. Davis

Investor Contact: P. Cutler (800-222-4511)
Board Members: S. S. Barrat, R. M. Beall, II, J. H. Brown, J. L. Camaren, J. B. Ferguson, L. Hay, III, T. Jennings, O. D. Kingsley, Jr., R. E. Schupp, M. Thaman, H. E. Tookes, II, P. R. Tregurtha

Founded: 1984
Domicile: Florida
Employees: 13,160

Franklin Resources Inc.

S&P Recommendation BUY ★★★★☆

Price $119.06 (as of Nov 23, 2007)	**12-Mo. Target Price** $155.00	**Investment Style** Large-Cap Growth

GICS Sector Financials
Sub-Industry Asset Management & Custody Banks

Summary This company is one of the world's largest asset managers, serving retail, institutional and high net worth clients.

Key Stock Statistics (Source S&P, Vickers, company reports)

52-Wk Range	$145.59– 103.43	S&P Oper. EPS 2008E	8.07	Market Capitalization(B)	$29.282	Beta	1.09
Trailing 12-Month EPS	$7.03	S&P Oper. EPS 2009E	NA	Yield (%)	0.50	S&P 3-Yr. Proj. EPS CAGR(%)	11.00
Trailing 12-Month P/E	16.9	P/E on S&P Oper. EPS 2008E	14.8	Dividend Rate/Share	$0.60	S&P Credit Rating	A+
$10K Invested 5 Yrs Ago	$33,956	Common Shares Outstg. (M)	245.9	Institutional Ownership (%)	50		

Price Performance

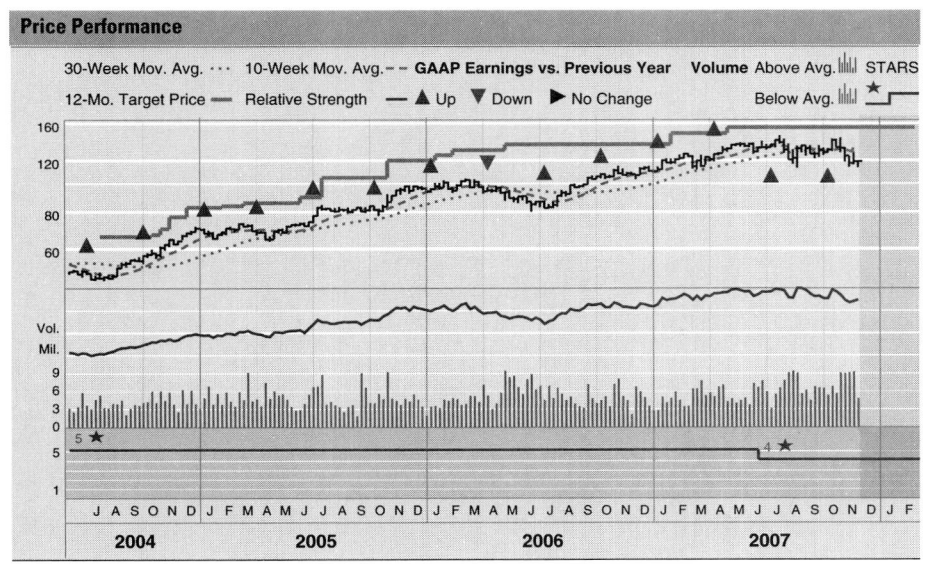

30-Week Mov. Avg. ··· 10-Week Mov. Avg. - - **GAAP Earnings vs. Previous Year** Volume Above Avg. STARS
12-Mo. Target Price — Relative Strength — ▲ Up ▼ Down ► No Change Below Avg. ★

Options: ASE, CBOE, P, Ph

Analysis prepared by **Matthew Albrecht** on November 08, 2007, when the stock traded at **$ 116.49.**

Highlights

▶ Franklin Resources continues to benefit from its exposure to international markets, a trend we expect will continue into 2008, considering the outsized growth of foreign economies. Net inflows have continued at a strong pace in recent quarters, and we believe investors are responding to strong fund performance in both equity and fixed income products. Its global expansion has also increased its visibility to investors outside the U.S. We expect the breadth and performance of its funds, particularly those under the Templeton brand, to help assets under management grow about 13% in FY 08 (Sep.), following 26% growth in FY 07.

▶ Compensation continued to decline in FY 07, to about 17.5% of operating revenues, and we look for it to flatten out in FY 08, as head count growth keeps the cost in line with revenue growth. We anticipate a 50 basis point contraction in the pretax margin for the year, however, as higher advertising costs combine with international expansion efforts to offset a slight improvement in the underwriting and distribution margin.

▶ We see earnings of $8.07 in FY 08.

Investment Rationale/Risk

▶ We have a buy recommendation on the shares, as we see BEN gaining market share due to better-than-average fund performance and international expansion. We believe the shares deserve to trade at a higher multiple, based on our view of BEN's consistent net client inflows, strong relative investment performance, and international exposure. We view favorably the company's strong operating free cash flow, but we would prefer that the company raise its dividend or repurchase additional shares, given increasing cash balances.

▶ Risks to our recommendation and target price include potential depreciation in global equity, bond and currency markets that can materially affect assets under management and net investor flows. In addition, we think the shift by investors toward discount brokerage firms could hurt net inflows, given that BEN's funds typically have front-end sales charges.

▶ The shares recently traded at about 14.5X our FY 08 EPS estimate, a discount to the peer group average. Our 12-month target price of $155 is equal to 19.2X our FY 08 EPS estimate, in line with the multiples of comparable peers.

Qualitative Risk Assessment

LOW	MEDIUM	HIGH

Our risk assessment reflects our view of the company's strong relative investment performance, consistent net client inflows, and low ratio of debt to total capitalization.

Quantitative Evaluations

S&P Quality Ranking A-

D	C	B-	B	B+	A-	A	A+

Relative Strength Rank MODERATE

47

LOWEST = 1   HIGHEST = 99

Revenue/Earnings Data

Revenue (Million $)

	1Q	2Q	3Q	4Q	Year
2007	1,428	1,509	1,640	1,629	6,206
2006	1,181	1,255	1,317	1,297	5,051
2005	986.0	1,051	1,110	1,163	4,310
2004	809.7	879.0	867.8	881.7	3,438
2003	605.5	613.1	683.9	722.0	2,624
2002	618.2	626.0	666.1	608.3	2,519

Earnings Per Share ($)

2007	1.67	1.73	1.91	1.76	7.03
2006	1.21	0.74	1.41	1.49	4.86
2005	0.92	0.85	1.00	1.28	4.06
2004	0.67	0.68	0.69	0.74	2.78
2003	0.43	0.43	0.52	0.61	1.97
2002	0.45	0.46	0.48	0.26	1.65

Fiscal year ended Sep. 30. Next earnings report expected: Late January. EPS Estimates based on S&P Operating Earnings; historical GAAP earnings are as reported.

Dividend Data (Dates: mm/dd Payment Date: mm/dd/yy)

Amount ($)	Date Decl.	Ex-Div. Date	Stk. of Record	Payment Date
0.150	12/13	12/26	12/28	01/12/07
0.150	03/13	03/28	03/30	04/13/07
0.150	06/19	06/27	06/29	07/13/07
0.150	09/19	10/02	10/04	10/12/07

Dividends have been paid since 1981. Source: Company reports.

Franklin Resources Inc.

**STANDARD
&POOR'S**

Business Summary November 08, 2007

CORPORATE OVERVIEW. Franklin Resources is one of the largest U.S. money managers, with $645.9 billion in assets under management at the end of FY 07 (Sep.), up from $511.3 billion at the end of FY 06. At the end of FY 07, equity-based investments accounted for 60% of assets under management, fixed income investments 21%, hybrid funds 18%, and money funds 1%. Global equity and fixed income accounted for 51% of assets under management. We think that a potential decline in the dollar relative to other major currencies would aid BEN, due to the high percentage of assets invested globally. At the end of FY 07, about 40% of assets under management were held by investors domiciled outside the U.S.

The company's sponsored investment products are distributed under five distinct names: Franklin, Templeton, Mutual Series, Bisset and Fiduciary. We are impressed with BEN's broad range of investment products, but we think the company lacks a compelling roster of growth equity products. BEN has targeted key market segments, including retail (57% of assets at the end of FY 07) and institutional and international (43%).

CORPORATE STRATEGY. Despite its acquisitive history, we think BEN's man-

agement favors organic growth. We believe that the interests of BEN's management are closely aligned with those of shareholders given that directors, director nominees and executive officers as a group owned about 34% of the common shares outstanding as of November 30, 2006. We expect BEN to be selective in any acquisition pursuits.

Through several acquisitions, BEN has shifted its asset mix from predominantly fixed-income securities toward equity-based investments. In April 2001, BEN acquired Fiduciary Trust Co. International, an investment management company catering to high net worth and institutional clients, for about $776 million. In 1996, BEN acquired certain assets and liabilities of Heine Securities Corp., which managed the value-oriented Mutual Series funds. The Templeton funds were acquired in 1992, with the purchase of Templeton, Galbraith & Hansberger.

Company Financials Fiscal Year Ended Sep. 30

Per Share Data ($)	2007	2006	2005	2004	2003	2002	2001	2000	1999	1998
Tangible Book Value	NA	18.57	14.39	12.23	9.31	8.69	7.23	7.37	5.79	4.08
Cash Flow	NA	5.86	5.02	3.51	2.67	2.35	2.79	3.13	2.48	2.74
Earnings	7.03	4.86	4.06	2.78	1.97	1.65	1.91	2.28	1.69	1.98
S&P Core Earnings	NA	4.78	3.97	2.47	1.70	1.56	1.61	NA	NA	NA
Dividends	0.57	0.36	0.40	0.33	0.29	0.28	0.26	0.24	0.22	0.20
Payout Ratio	8%	7%	10%	12%	15%	17%	14%	11%	13%	10%
Prices:High	145.59	114.98	98.86	71.45	52.25	44.48	48.30	45.63	45.00	57.88
Prices:Low	111.31	80.16	63.56	46.85	29.99	27.90	30.85	24.63	27.00	25.75
P/E Ratio:High	21	24	24	26	27	27	25	20	27	29
P/E Ratio:Low	16	16	16	17	15	17	16	11	16	13

Income Statement Analysis (Million $)										
Income Interest	NA	NA	NA	NA	NA	NA	NA	NA	NA	NA
Income Other	NA	NA	NA	NA	NA	NA	NA	NA	NA	NA
Total Income	NA	5,051	4,310	3,438	2,624	2,519	2,355	2,340	2,262	2,577
General Expenses	NA	NA	3,004	NA	NA	NA	NA	NA	NA	NA
Interest Expense	NA	29.2	34.0	30.7	19.9	12.3	10.6	14.0	21.0	22.5
Depreciation	NA	NA	17.5	NA	NA	NA	NA	200	200	191
Net Income	NA	1,268	1,058	702	503	433	485	562	427	500
S&P Core Earnings	NA	1,245	1,033	622	432	410	407	NA	NA	NA

Balance Sheet & Other Financial Data (Million $)										
Cash	NA	3,613	3,152	2,917	1,054	981	569	746	819	537
Receivables	NA	711	549	444	441	393	603	693	552	318
Cost of Investments	NA	NA	1,566	NA	NA	NA	NA	NA	NA	NA
Total Assets	NA	9,500	8,894	8,228	6,971	6,423	6,266	4,042	3,667	3,480
Loss Reserve	NA	NA	Nil	NA	NA	NA	NA	NA	NA	NA
Short Term Debt	NA	NA	169	NA	0.29	7.80	NA	NA	NA	NA
Capitalization:Debt	NA	628	1,208	1,196	1,109	595	566	294	294	612
Capitalization:Equity	NA	6,685	5,684	5,107	4,310	4,267	3,978	2,965	2,657	2,281
Capitalization:Total	NA	7,620	7,204	6,615	5,622	5,037	4,544	3,260	2,951	2,775
Price Times Book Value:High	NA	NA	6.9	NA	5.5	5.1	NA	NA	NA	NA
Price Times Book Value:Low	NA	NA	4.4	NA	3.2	3.2	NA	NA	NA	NA
Cash Flow	NA	NA	1,075	NA	NA	NA	NA	762	627	691
% Expense/Operating Revenue	NA	NA	70.1	NA	NA	NA	NA	NA	NA	NA
% Earnings & Depreciation/Assets	NA	NA	12.6	NA	NA	NA	NA	NA	NA	NA

Data as orig reptd.; bef. results of disc opers/spec. items. Per share data adj. for stk. divs.; EPS diluted. E-Estimated. NA-Not Available. NM-Not Meaningful. NR-Not Ranked. UR-Under Review.

Office: One Franklin Parkway, San Mateo, CA 94403.
Telephone: 650-312-2000.
Website: http://www.franklintempleton.com
Chrmn: C.B. Johnson

Pres & CEO: G.E. Johnson
Vice Chrmn: H.E. Burns
Vice Chrmn: R.H. Johnson, Jr.
Vice Chrmn: A.M. Tatlock

Board Members: S. H. Armacost, C. Crocker, J. R. Hardiman, R. Joffe, C. B. Johnson, R. H. Johnson, Jr., T. Kean, C. Ratnathicam, P. M. Sacerdote, L. Stein, A. M. Tatlock, L. E. Woodworth

Founded: 1947
Domicile: Delaware
Employees: 7,982

The McGraw-Hill Companies

Freeport-McMoran Copper & Gold Inc.

STANDARD &POOR'S

S&P Recommendation HOLD ★★★☆☆

Price	12-Mo. Target Price
$96.65 (as of Nov 29, 2007)	$100.00

GICS Sector Materials
Sub-Industry Diversified Metals & Mining

Summary Following its acquisition of Phelps Dodge on March 19, 2007, FCX is the world's second largest copper producer.

Key Stock Statistics (Source S&P, Vickers, company reports)

52-Wk Range	$120.20– 48.85	S&P Oper. EPS 2007**E**	9.68	Market Capitalization(B)	$36.894	Beta	1.35
Trailing 12-Month EPS	$8.57	S&P Oper. EPS 2008**E**	8.00	Yield (%)	1.29	S&P 3-Yr. Proj. EPS CAGR(%)	-6.30
Trailing 12-Month P/E	11.3	P/E on S&P Oper. EPS 2007**E**	10.0	Dividend Rate/Share	$1.25	S&P Credit Rating	BB+
$10K Invested 5 Yrs Ago	$76,363	Common Shares Outstg. (M)	381.7	Institutional Ownership (%)	96		

Price Performance

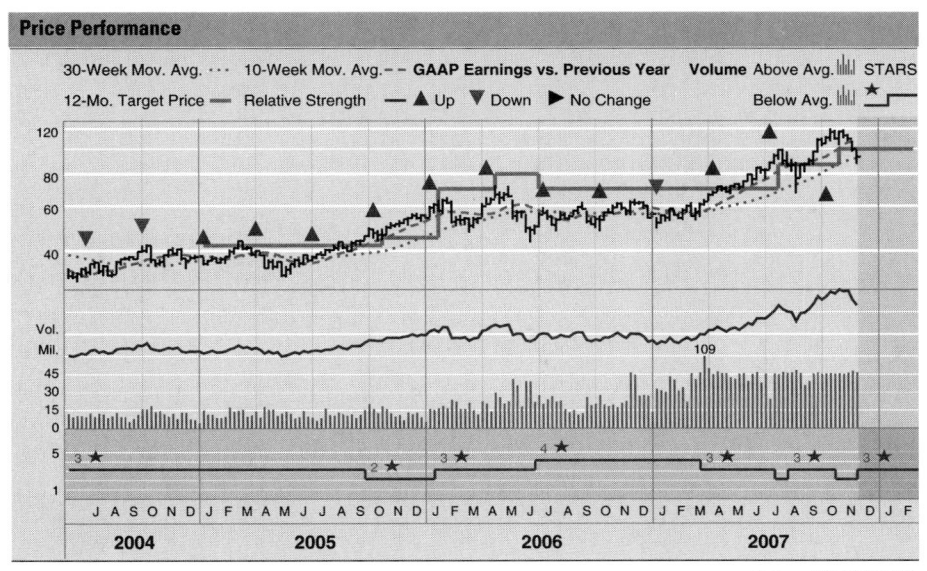

30-Week Mov. Avg. ··· 10-Week Mov. Avg. - - **GAAP Earnings vs. Previous Year** Volume Above Avg. STARS
12-Mo. Target Price — Relative Strength —▲ Up ▼ Down ► No Change Below Avg.

Options: ASE, CBOE, P, Ph

Analysis prepared by **Leo J. Larkin** on November 29, 2007, when the stock traded at **$ 94.35**.

Highlights

➤ Following an estimated gain of 210% in 2007, we look for sales to increase 25% in 2008 as the inclusion of Phelps Dodge (PD) for a full year offsets a lower average copper price. Our copper outlook is based on several assumptions. First, we believe that global demand in 2008 will trail 2007's rate of gain for two reasons. We think that Chinese consumption growth in 2008 will be substantially less than 2007's estimated increase of some 37%, and, given the S&P forecast for a 25.7% decline in housing starts in 2008 and less robust nonresidential construction spending, we believe that U.S. consumption will decline again in 2008. Second, we believe that strike-related supply disruptions will not be as long or as severe as those in 2007. Third, we believe that investment fund demand will cool.

➤ We look for operating EPS, penalized by a lower average copper price and a decline in byproduct credits stemming from lower gold production, to decrease in 2008 to $8.00, from 2007's estimated operating EPS of $9.68.

➤ We expect long-term EPS to increase on a secular rise in copper demand and consolidation of the base metals mining industry.

Investment Rationale/Risk

➤ Longer term, we think increased demand for durable goods in China and India, along with less rapid increases in the supply of copper, will support generally higher prices, sales and profits. Near term, we believe that the PD merger will be mildly dilutive, due to PD's cost of production being higher than that of FCX. But down the road, the merger should be positive given that it should achieve geographic diversification for FCX. In our opinion, the concentration of FCX's mining assets in Indonesia prior to the merger was a drag on its valuation. But with the shares recently selling with just modest upside to our 12-month target price, we would hold, but not add to positions.

➤ Risks to our opinion and target price include a decline in the price of copper in 2008 in excess of what we forecast.

➤ Our 12-month target price of $100 assumes that FCX will sell at 12.5X our 2008 EPS estimate, which is about in line with other base metal companies. Our target P/E is at the low end of FCX's historical range of the past 10 years.

Qualitative Risk Assessment

LOW	MEDIUM	HIGH

Our risk assessment for FCX reflects the exposure of its EPS to the cyclical demand for copper and gold along with a high debt level necessitated by the merger with Phelps Dodge. Offsetting this is FCX's sizable free cash flow generation and its large share of the global copper market.

Quantitative Evaluations

S&P Quality Ranking B

D	C	B-	B	B+	A-	A	A+

Relative Strength Rank MODERATE

49

LOWEST = 1   HIGHEST = 99

Revenue/Earnings Data

Revenue (Million $)

	1Q	2Q	3Q	4Q	Year
2007	2,303	5,807	5,066	--	--
2006	1,086	1,426	1,636	1,642	5,791
2005	803.1	902.9	983.3	1,490	4,179
2004	360.2	486.3	600.6	924.8	2,372
2003	524.6	609.5	632.0	446.1	2,212
2002	392.7	408.0	538.7	571.0	1,910

Earnings Per Share ($)

2007	2.02	2.62	1.85	E2.52	E9.68
2006	1.23	1.74	1.67	1.99	6.63
2005	0.70	0.91	0.86	2.19	4.67
2004	-0.10	-0.30	0.10	1.08	0.85
2003	0.28	0.37	0.41	Nil	1.07
2002	-0.01	0.04	0.39	0.41	0.89

Fiscal year ended Dec. 31. Next earnings report expected: Mid January. EPS Estimates based on S&P Operating Earnings; historical GAAP earnings are as reported.

Dividend Data (Dates: mm/dd Payment Date: mm/dd/yy)

Amount ($)	Date Decl.	Ex-Div. Date	Stk. of Record	Payment Date
0.313	12/28	01/11	01/16	02/01/07
0.313	03/29	04/12	04/16	05/01/07
0.313	06/28	07/12	07/16	08/01/07
0.313	09/27	10/11	10/15	11/01/07

Dividends have been paid since 2003. Source: Company reports.

Freeport-McMoRan Copper & Gold Inc.

STANDARD &POOR'S

Business Summary November 29, 2007

CORPORATE OVERVIEW. Freeport-McMoRan Copper & Gold is the world's second largest copper producer and is a major producer of gold and molybdenum. FCX has twelve producing mines located in Indonesia, North America, and South America along with exploration projects in Africa.

Following its takeover of Phelps Dodge in March 2007, FCX has proven and probable copper reserves of some 75 billion pounds, 41 million oz. of gold, 128 million oz. of silver and 1.9 billion pounds of molybdenum, net of minority interests. For 2006, the companies had combined revenues of $17.7 billion, combined net income of $4.4 billion and combined copper production of 1.7 million

metric tons. At the end of 2006, FCX's proven and probable reserves consisted of 38.7 billion lbs. of copper, 41.1 million oz. of gold and 128 million oz. of silver.

On a pro forma basis in 2006, copper comprised 78% of sales, molybdenum 12% and gold 10%. Pro forma sales by geographic region in 2006 were 38% Indonesia, 35% North America, 22% Chile, and 5% Peru.

Company Financials Fiscal Year Ended Dec. 31

Per Share Data ($)	2006	2005	2004	2003	2002	2001	2000	1999	1998	1997
Tangible Book Value	6.83	3.98	0.36	4.23	NM	NM	NM	NM	NM	NM
Cash Flow	7.33	5.38	1.96	2.52	2.67	2.49	2.09	2.39	2.25	2.32
Earnings	6.63	4.67	0.85	1.07	0.89	0.53	0.26	0.61	0.67	1.06
S&P Core Earnings	6.56	4.63	0.48	1.03	0.84	0.49	NA	NA	NA	NA
Dividends	1.25	1.25	0.85	0.27	Nil	Nil	Nil	Nil	0.20	0.90
Payout Ratio	19%	27%	100%	25%	Nil	Nil	Nil	Nil	30%	85%
Prices:High	72.20	56.35	44.90	46.74	20.83	17.15	21.44	21.38	21.44	34.88
Prices:Low	43.10	31.52	27.76	16.01	9.95	8.31	6.75	9.13	9.81	14.94
P/E Ratio:High	11	12	53	44	23	32	82	35	32	33
P/E Ratio:Low	7	7	33	15	11	16	26	15	15	14

Income Statement Analysis (Million $)										
Revenue	5,791	4,179	2,372	2,212	1,910	1,839	1,869	1,887	1,757	2,001
Operating Income	3,096	2,429	823	1,054	901	827	778	876	852	878
Depreciation	228	252	206	231	260	284	284	293	277	214
Interest Expense	75.6	132	148	197	171	174	205	194	225	175
Pretax Income	2,826	2,037	574	584	450	359	273	381	361	517
Effective Tax Rate	42.5%	44.9%	57.6%	57.9%	54.6%	56.6%	58.4%	51.4%	47.2%	44.8%
Net Income	1,457	995	202	197	168	113	77.0	136	154	245
S&P Core Earnings	1,381	919	77.7	167	123	70.8	NA	NA	NA	NA

Balance Sheet & Other Financial Data (Million $)										
Cash	907	764	551	464	7.84	7.59	7.97	6.70	5.90	9.00
Current Assets	2,151	2,022	1,460	1,100	638	548	569	564	46.0	463
Total Assets	5,390	5,550	5,087	4,718	4,192	4,212	3,951	4,083	4,193	4,152
Current Liabilities	972	1,369	698	632	538	628	634	515	518	476
Long Term Debt	661	1,003	1,874	2,076	1,961	2,133	1,988	2,033	2,329	2,308
Common Equity	1,345	743	63.6	776	-83.2	-246	-312	-153	-247	-71.1
Total Capital	4,119	3,971	4,189	3,925	3,514	3,464	3,204	3,453	3,599	3,551
Capital Expenditures	251	143	141	139	188	167	292	161	292	595
Cash Flow	1,624	1,186	363	401	391	360	323	394	395	459
Current Ratio	2.2	1.5	2.1	1.7	1.2	0.9	0.9	1.1	1.1	1.0
% Long Term Debt of Capitalization	16.0	25.2	44.7	52.9	55.8	61.6	62.0	58.9	64.7	65.0
% Net Income of Revenue	25.2	23.8	8.5	8.9	8.8	6.1	4.1	7.2	8.8	12.2
% Return on Assets	26.6	18.7	4.1	4.4	4.0	2.8	1.9	3.3	3.7	6.1
% Return on Equity	133.7	231.7	37.3	49.0	NM	NM	NA	NM	NM	NM

Data as orig reptd.; bef. results of disc opers/spec. items. Per share data adj. for stk. divs.; EPS diluted. E-Estimated. NA-Not Available. NM-Not Meaningful. NR-Not Ranked. UR-Under Review.

Office: 1615 Poydras Street, New Orleans, LA 70112-1254.
Telephone: 504-582-4000.
Email: ir@fmi.com
Website: http://www.fcx.com

Chrmn: J.R. Moffett
Pres & CEO: R.C. Adkerson
Vice Chrmn: B.M. Rankin, Jr.
COO & SVP: M.J. Johnson

Investor Contact: K.L. Quirk (504-582-4195)
Board Members: R. C. Adkerson, R. J. Allison, Jr., R. A. Day, G. J. Ford, H. D. Graham, Jr., J. B. Johnston, C. C. Krulak, B. L. Lackey, J. C. Madonna, D. E. McCoy, G. K. McDonald, J. R. Moffett, B. M. Rankin, Jr., J. S. Roy, S. H. Siegele, J. T. Wharton

Founded: 1987
Domicile: Delaware
Employees: 9,661

Gannett Co Inc.

STANDARD &POOR'S

| S&P Recommendation **BUY** ★★★★☆ | Price $37.72 (as of Nov 23, 2007) | 12-Mo. Target Price $56.00 | Investment Style Large-Cap Blend |

GICS Sector Consumer Discretionary
Sub-Industry Publishing

Summary Gannett publishes 90 daily U.S. newspapers, nearly 1,000 non-daily publications in the U.S., and close to 300 U.K. titles, and operates 23 TV stations in the U.S.

Key Stock Statistics (Source S&P, Vickers, company reports)

52-Wk Range	$63.50– 36.58	S&P Oper. EPS 2007**E**	4.52	Market Capitalization(B)	$8.785	Beta	0.49
Trailing 12-Month EPS	$4.96	S&P Oper. EPS 2008**E**	4.67	Yield (%)	4.24	S&P 3-Yr. Proj. EPS CAGR(%)	-1.70
Trailing 12-Month P/E	7.6	P/E on S&P Oper. EPS 2007**E**	8.3	Dividend Rate/Share	$1.60	S&P Credit Rating	A-
$10K Invested 5 Yrs Ago	$5,622	Common Shares Outstg. (M)	232.9	Institutional Ownership (%)	91		

Price Performance

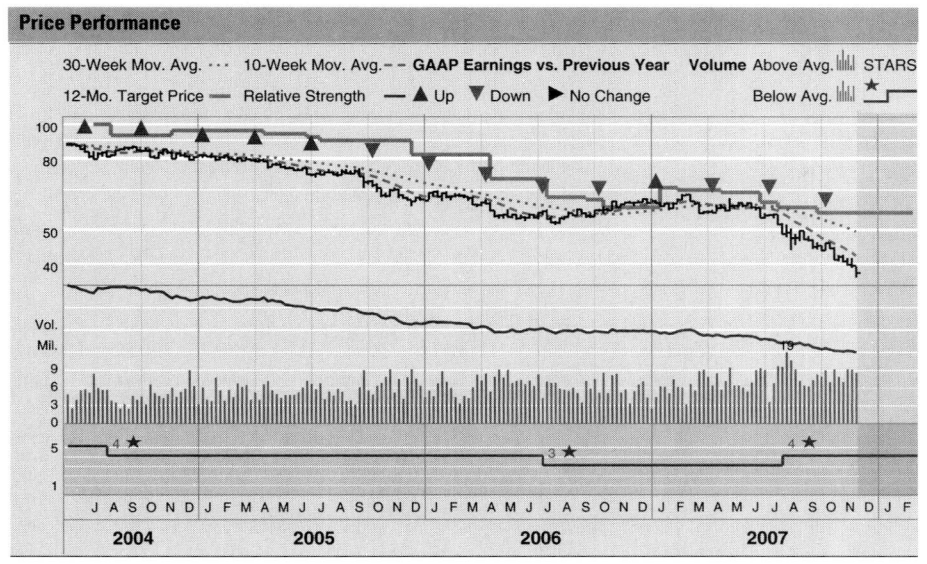

Legend:
30-Week Mov. Avg. ··· 10-Week Mov. Avg. – – **GAAP Earnings vs. Previous Year** Volume Above Avg. STARS
12-Mo. Target Price — Relative Strength — ▲ Up ▼ Down ► No Change Below Avg. ★

Options: ASE, CBOE, P, Ph

Analysis prepared by **James Peters, CFA** on October 18, 2007, when the stock traded at **$ 42.72**.

Highlights

➤ For 2007, we see an overall revenue decline of about 4.9%, hurt by one fewer reporting week than in 2006. For 2008, we foresee print publishing revenues remaining soft due to our view of a weak U.S. real estate environment persisting until the middle of the year, and as we expect classified advertising overall to continue migrating online. However, with a growing online presence, easier year-over-year comparisons, and a further projected improvement in the U.K., we think declines will moderate from 2007 levels. We look for strong broadcast revenue growth in 2008, mostly due to an anticipated boost from Olympic and election year advertising. Overall, we expect revenue growth of 2.1%.

➤ We forecast an operating margin of 23.7% in 2008, down slightly from our projection for 24.0% in 2007. We expect operating leverage from improvements in GCI's UK operations and from an increase in broadcast advertising to be offset by declines in profitable print classified advertising.

➤ We estimate 2008 EPS of $4.67, up from our forecast of $4.52 for 2007. Our 2008 S&P Core EPS estimate of $4.65 reflects $0.02 of projected pension adjustments.

Investment Rationale/Risk

➤ Although we remain concerned by what we see as a secular decline in newspaper advertising, we are encouraged by signs of classified advertising improvement at the company's U.K. operations, as we think this is a precursor for progress at GCI's U.S. publications once cyclical factors affecting domestic advertisers abate. We also continue to believe GCI will ultimately be successful in transitioning to a more Internet-based media company. With a cash flow yield of about 11%, we believe GCI shares are attractive at current levels.

➤ Risks to our recommendation and target price include greater than anticipated weakness in Detroit, declines in audience ratings at network-affiliated TV stations, and a weakening of the British pound versus the U.S. dollar.

➤ Our 12-month target price of $56 is derived by applying a peer average enterprise value/ EBITDA ratio of 8.1X to our 2008 EBITDA estimate of $2.1 billion. Our target price is supported by a $55 valuation we derive by applying GCI's two-year historical average P/E of about 11.8X to our 2008 EPS estimate.

Qualitative Risk Assessment

| LOW | MEDIUM | HIGH |

Our risk assessment reflects a highly competitive advertising environment, offset by our view of the company's consistently strong free cash flow and profitability, and its relatively low weighted average cost of capital.

Quantitative Evaluations

S&P Quality Ranking A

| D | C | B- | B | B+ | A- | A | A+ |

Relative Strength Rank WEAK

25

LOWEST = 1   HIGHEST = 99

Revenue/Earnings Data

Revenue (Million $)

	1Q	2Q	3Q	4Q	Year
2007	1,871	1,928	1,756	--	--
2006	1,883	2,028	1,915	2,208	8,033
2005	1,768	1,911	1,865	2,055	7,599
2004	1,730	1,873	1,816	1,962	7,381
2003	1,552	1,705	1,631	1,822	6,711
2002	1,513	1,613	1,570	1,726	6,422

Earnings Per Share ($)

	1Q	2Q	3Q	4Q	Year
2007	0.90	1.24	1.01	E1.37	E4.52
2006	0.99	1.31	1.11	1.51	4.90
2005	1.03	1.34	1.13	1.44	4.92
2004	1.00	1.30	1.18	1.47	4.92
2003	0.93	1.20	1.03	1.31	4.46
2002	0.91	1.13	0.99	1.29	4.31

Fiscal year ended Dec. 31. Next earnings report expected: Early February. EPS Estimates based on S&P Operating Earnings; historical GAAP earnings are as reported.

Dividend Data (Dates: mm/dd Payment Date: mm/dd/yy)

Amount ($)	Date Decl.	Ex-Div. Date	Stk. of Record	Payment Date
0.310	02/28	03/07	03/09	04/02/07
0.310	04/24	06/06	06/08	07/02/07
0.400	07/24	09/12	09/14	10/01/07
0.400	10/23	12/12	12/14	01/02/08

Dividends have been paid since 1929. Source: Company reports.

Please read the Required Disclosures and Analyst Certification on the last page of this report.

The McGraw-Hill Companies

Gannett Co Inc.

Business Summary October 18, 2007

CORPORATE OVERVIEW. Gannett is the largest newspaper publisher in the U.S. The company publishes newspapers, operates broadcasting stations, runs Web sites in connection with its newspaper and broadcast operations, and is engaged in marketing, commercial printing, a newswire service, data services, and news programming.

The newspaper publishing segment (89% of 2006 revenues) consists of the operations of 107 total daily newspapers, nearly 1,000 non-daily publications in the U.S. and Guam, and approximately 300 titles in the U.K. The segment includes the publication of USA TODAY, the nation's largest selling daily newspaper. The company's strategy for non-daily publications is to target these products at communities of interest, defined by geography, demographics or lifestyle. In the U.K., the company is the second largest regional publisher via its wholly owned subsidiary, Newsquest plc. The segment also includes PointRoll, an Internet ad services business, Planet Discover, a provider of local, integrated online search and advertising technology, commercial printing, newswire, marketing and data services operations.

Newspaper publishing revenues are derived principally from the sale of advertising (75% of 2006 revenues), including Internet advertising, and circulation revenues (18%). Within the advertising category, revenues were derived from local (43%), national (16%) and classified (41%) advertising. The remain-

ing segment revenues (7%) came from commercial printing operations, earnings from a 40.6% stake in the Texas-New Mexico Newspaper Partnership, a 50% owned Tucson joint operating agency, and a 19.49% equity interest in California Newspapers Partnership. Newsquest operations generated approximately 17% and 11% of segment advertising and circulation revenues, respectively.

The broadcast segment (11% of 2006 revenues) consists of 23 network-affiliated TV stations, including 12 NBC, six CBS, three ABC affiliates and two MyNetworkTV affiliates, and Captivate Network, a national news and entertainment network that delivers programming and full-motion video advertising through video screens located in office tower elevators across North America. The principal sources of GCI's television revenues are: local advertising focusing on the immediate geographic area of the stations; national advertising, compensation paid by the networks for carrying commercial network programs; advertising on the stations' Web sites; and payments by advertisers to television stations for other services, such as the production of advertising material. Captivate derives its revenue principally from national advertising.

Company Financials Fiscal Year Ended Dec. 31

Per Share Data ($)	2006	2005	2004	2003	2002	2001	2000	1999	1998	1997
Tangible Book Value	NM	NM	NM	NM	NM	NM	NM	NM	0.66	NM
Cash Flow	6.07	6.24	6.14	5.30	5.13	4.78	4.99	3.87	4.59	3.55
Earnings	4.90	4.92	4.92	4.46	4.31	3.12	3.63	3.26	3.50	2.50
S&P Core Earnings	4.86	4.43	4.45	4.23	3.70	2.39	NA	NA	NA	NA
Dividends	1.20	1.12	1.04	0.98	0.94	0.90	0.86	0.81	0.78	0.74
Payout Ratio	24%	23%	21%	22%	22%	29%	24%	25%	22%	30%
Prices:High	64.97	82.41	91.38	89.63	79.90	71.14	81.56	83.63	75.13	61.81
Prices:Low	51.65	58.37	78.84	66.70	62.76	53.00	48.38	60.63	47.63	35.69
P/E Ratio:High	13	17	19	20	19	23	22	26	21	25
P/E Ratio:Low	11	12	16	15	15	17	13	19	14	14

Income Statement Analysis (Million $)

	2006	2005	2004	2003	2002	2001	2000	1999	1998	1997
Revenue	8,033	7,599	7,381	6,711	6,422	6,344	6,222	5,260	5,121	4,729
Operating Income	2,275	2,322	2,392	2,213	2,149	2,034	2,190	1,843	1,754	1,617
Depreciation	277	274	244	232	215	444	376	169	310	301
Interest Expense	288	211	141	139	146	222	219	94.6	79.4	98.2
Pretax Income	1,719	1,818	1,995	1,840	1,765	1,371	1,609	1,527	1,669	1,209
Effective Tax Rate	32.5%	33.4%	34.0%	34.2%	34.3%	39.4%	39.6%	39.8%	40.1%	41.1%
Net Income	1,161	1,211	1,317	1,211	1,160	831	972	919	1,000	713
S&P Core Earnings	1,151	1,092	1,191	1,150	998	638	NA	NA	NA	NA

Balance Sheet & Other Financial Data (Million $)

	2006	2005	2004	2003	2002	2001	2000	1999	1998	1997
Cash	94.3	163	136	67.2	90.4	141	193	46.2	66.2	52.8
Current Assets	1,532	1,462	1,371	1,223	1,133	1,178	1,302	1,075	906	885
Total Assets	16,224	15,743	15,399	14,706	13,733	13,096	12,980	9,006	6,979	6,890
Current Liabilities	1,117	1,096	1,005	962	959	1,128	1,174	884	728	768
Long Term Debt	5,210	5,438	4,608	3,835	4,547	5,080	5,748	2,463	1,307	1,741
Common Equity	8,382	7,571	8,164	8,423	6,912	5,736	5,103	4,630	3,980	3,480
Total Capital	14,319	13,897	13,685	13,094	12,138	11,319	11,126	7,572	5,709	5,623
Capital Expenditures	201	263	280	281	275	325	351	258	244	221
Cash Flow	1,438	1,486	1,561	1,443	1,375	1,275	1,348	1,089	1,310	1,014
Current Ratio	1.4	1.3	1.4	1.3	1.2	1.0	1.1	1.2	1.2	1.2
% Long Term Debt of Capitalization	36.4	39.1	33.7	29.3	37.5	44.9	51.7	32.5	22.8	30.9
% Net Income of Revenue	14.4	15.9	17.8	18.0	18.1	13.1	15.6	17.5	19.5	15.1
% Return on Assets	7.3	7.8	8.8	8.5	8.6	6.4	8.8	11.5	14.4	10.8
% Return on Equity	14.6	15.4	15.9	15.8	18.3	15.3	20.0	21.4	26.8	22.2

Data as orig reptd.; bef. results of disc opers/spec. items. Per share data adj. for stk. divs.; EPS diluted. E-Estimated. NA-Not Available. NM-Not Meaningful. NR-Not Ranked. UR-Under Review.

Office: 7950 Jones Branch Dr, McLean, VA 22107-0910.
Telephone: 703-854-6000.
Email: gcishare@gannett.com
Website: http://www.gannett.com

Chrmn, Pres & CEO: C.A. Dubow
EVP & CFO: G.C. Martore
SVP & General Counsel: K. Wimmer
VP & Cntlr: G.R. Gavagan

Investor Contact: J. Heinz (703-854-6917)
Board Members: L. D. Boccardi, C. A. Dubow, C. B. Fruit, A. H. Harper, J. J. Louis, M. Magner, D. M. McFarland, D. Shalala, K. H. Williams

Founded: 1906
Domicile: Delaware
Employees: 49,675

Gap Inc. (The)

STANDARD &POOR'S

S&P Recommendation HOLD ★★★☆☆	**Price** $20.10 (as of Nov 28, 2007)	**12-Mo. Target Price** $20.00	**Investment Style** Large-Cap Blend

GICS Sector Consumer Discretionary
Sub-Industry Apparel Retail

Summary This specialty apparel retailer operates Gap, Banana Republic and Old Navy stores, offering casual clothing to moderate, upscale and value-oriented market segments.

Key Stock Statistics (Source S&P, Vickers, company reports)

52-Wk Range	$21.04–15.20	S&P Oper. EPS 2008E	1.01	Market Capitalization(B)	$16.044	Beta	1.49
Trailing 12-Month EPS	$0.97	S&P Oper. EPS 2009E	1.10	Yield (%)	1.59	S&P 3-Yr. Proj. EPS CAGR(%)	8.00
Trailing 12-Month P/E	20.7	P/E on S&P Oper. EPS 2008E	19.9	Dividend Rate/Share	$0.32	S&P Credit Rating	BB+
$10K Invested 5 Yrs Ago	$13,433	Common Shares Outstg. (M)	798.2	Institutional Ownership (%)	62		

Price Performance

30-Week Mov. Avg. · · · · 10-Week Mov. Avg. – – **GAAP Earnings vs. Previous Year** **Volume** Above Avg. ▁▌▋ **STARS**
12-Mo. Target Price — Relative Strength — ▲ Up ▼ Down ▶ No Change Below Avg. ▁▌▋ ★

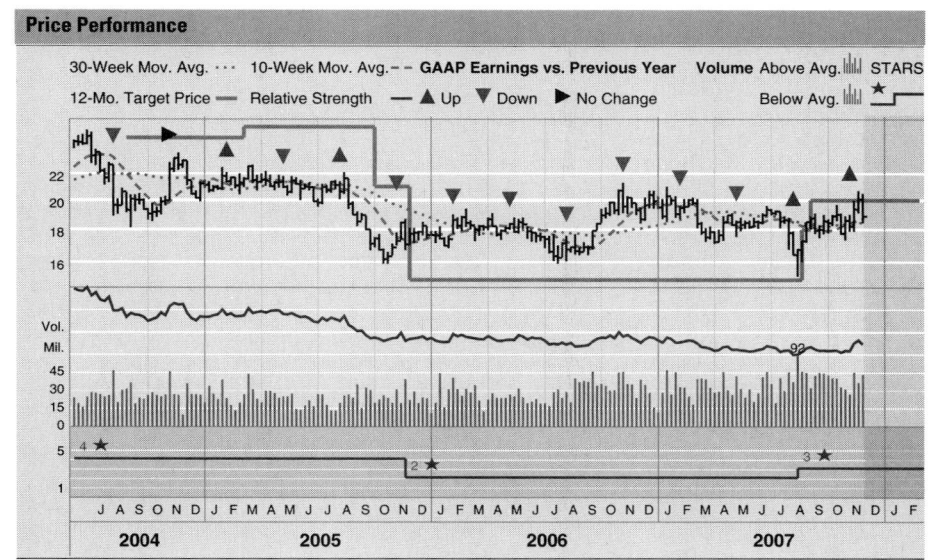

Options: ASE, CBOE, P, Ph

Analysis prepared by **Marie Driscoll, CFA** on November 28, 2007, when the stock traded at **$ 19.38**.

Highlights

➤ We believe that mature and overdistributed brands stymied GPS's FY 06 and FY 07 (Jan.) operating and financial results as sales were flat, at $16 billion in both years, and same-store sales were negative (down 5% and 7%, respectively), following a flat FY 05. Average store productivity declined 4%, to $395 per square foot, in FY 07.

➤ For FY 08, we project a 1% sales gain, to $16.2 billion; year to date through October, same-store sales fell 5%, on a 5% decline at Gap NA and a 7% drop at Old Navy; Banana Republic comp sales increased 1%. We see sales growth moderately accelerating to a 2%-3% annual pace in FY 09, with positive comps offsetting modest store fleet rationalization at Gap NA.

➤ We project a 20 basis point drop in the operating margin, to 7.2% of sales, in FY 08, reflecting an increase in occupancy costs. We expect an improvement in gross and operating margins as FY 09 progresses in tandem with the increased impact of new leadership at Gap on merchandise design and inventory flow. We see FY 09 operating margins expanding 50 basis points to 7.7%.

Investment Rationale/Risk

➤ Despite a 5% decline in same-store sales comparisons in the third quarter, we believe the worst is behind GPS and that we will begin to see data pointing to a turn in its operations. The merchandise is trend right at Old Navy, in our view, and we believe that marketing will drive store traffic this holiday. We are disappointed by traffic trends across all brands, but encouraged by improved merchandise margins and inventory management. We expect further Gap store closures in tandem with improved brand positioning.

➤ Risks to our recommendation and target price include adverse same-store sales trends and a slow learning curve for GPS's new CEO, in addition to typical risks associated with specialty retailers such as employment, consumer income and spending trends, an increase in promotional activity in the mall, and continued access to sourcing.

➤ Our 12-month target price of $20 assumes that GPS will trade in line with its historical five-year average forward multiple of 18.5X our FY 09 EPS estimate.

Qualitative Risk Assessment

LOW	MEDIUM	HIGH

Our risk assessment reflects our view of GPS's strong cash flow and balance sheet, offset by weakness in its two largest brands and increased competition.

Quantitative Evaluations

S&P Quality Ranking A-

D	C	B-	B	B+	A-	A	A+

Relative Strength Rank STRONG

92

LOWEST = 1 HIGHEST = 99

Revenue/Earnings Data

Revenue (Million $)

	1Q	2Q	3Q	4Q	Year
2008	3,558	3,685	3,854	--	--
2007	3,441	3,716	3,856	4,930	15,943
2006	3,626	3,716	3,860	4,821	16,023
2005	3,668	3,721	3,980	4,898	16,267
2004	3,353	3,685	3,929	4,886	15,854
2003	2,891	3,268	3,645	4,651	14,455

Earnings Per Share ($)

2008	0.22	0.19	0.30	E0.25	E1.01
2007	0.28	0.15	0.23	0.27	0.93
2006	0.31	0.30	0.24	0.39	1.24
2005	0.33	0.21	0.28	0.40	1.21
2004	0.22	0.22	0.28	0.37	1.09
2003	0.04	0.06	0.15	0.27	0.54

Fiscal year ended Jan. 31. Next earnings report expected: Early March. EPS Estimates based on S&P Operating Earnings; historical GAAP earnings are as reported.

Dividend Data (Dates: mm/dd Payment Date: mm/dd/yy)

Amount ($)	Date Decl.	Ex-Div. Date	Stk. of Record	Payment Date
0.080	03/27	04/05	04/10	05/01/07
0.080	06/06	07/06	07/10	07/31/07
0.080	10/02	10/12	10/16	10/30/07
0.080	11/27	01/07	01/09	01/30/08

Dividends have been paid since 1976. Source: Company reports.

Gap Inc. (The)

STANDARD
&POOR'S

Business Summary November 28, 2007

CORPORATE OVERVIEW. Gap is a specialty retailer that operates stores selling casual apparel, accessories, and personal care products for men, women and children. As of February 3, 2007, it operated 3,131 stores: 1,293 Gap North America; 521 Banana Republic North America; 1,012 Old Navy North America; 286 international locations, and 19 Forth & Towne stores (scheduled for closure in the second quarter), with 38.9 million sq. ft. of total retail space. In FY 07 (Jan.), North America accounted for an estimated 92% of sales.

MARKET PROFILE. GPS participates in the men's, women's and children's apparel market, which generated approximately $190 billion at U.S. retail in 2006, according to NPD Fashionworld consumer estimated data. The apparel market is fragmented, with national brands marketed by 20 companies accounting for about 30% of total apparel sales, and the remaining 70% comprised of smaller and/or private label "store" brands. The market is mature, in our view, with demand largely mirroring population growth, and fashion trends accounting for a modicum of incremental volume. Deflationary pricing pressure is a function of channel competition and production steadily moving offshore to

low-cost producers in India, Asia and China. S&P forecasts 2007 and 2008 apparel sales increasing in the low single digits, generally in line with GDP growth.

COMPETITIVE LANDSCAPE. By channel, specialty stores account for the largest share of apparel sales, at 31% in 2006, according to NPD. Mass merchants (e.g., Wal-Mart and Target) came in second, at 20%, up 100 basis points, and department stores came in third, at 16%, down from 19% in 2003. National chains (e.g., Sears and J C Penney) captured 15% of 2006 apparel sales, and off-price retailers (e.g., TJX and Ross Stores) were at 8%. The remaining 10% was divided among factory outlets and direct and e-mail pure plays. GPS is the largest U.S. specialty retailer, with an estimated 24% of the channel's volume.

Company Financials Fiscal Year Ended Jan. 31

Per Share Data ($)	2007	2006	2005	2004	2003	2002	2001	2000	1999	1998
Tangible Book Value	9.58	6.33	5.73	5.33	4.12	3.48	3.43	2.63	1.83	1.79
Cash Flow	1.57	1.93	1.79	1.71	1.43	0.93	1.67	1.75	1.25	0.87
Earnings	0.93	1.24	1.21	1.09	0.54	-0.01	1.00	1.26	0.91	0.58
S&P Core Earnings	0.93	1.15	1.13	1.03	0.50	-0.10	0.86	NA	NA	NA
Dividends	0.20	0.09	0.09	0.09	0.09	0.09	0.09	0.09	0.09	0.09
Payout Ratio	22%	7%	7%	8%	17%	NM	9%	7%	9%	15%
Calendar Year	2006	2005	2004	2003	2002	2001	2000	1999	1998	1997
Prices:High	21.39	22.70	25.72	23.47	17.14	34.98	53.75	52.69	40.92	17.15
Prices:Low	15.91	15.90	18.12	12.01	8.35	11.12	18.50	30.81	15.31	8.26
P/E Ratio:High	23	18	21	22	32	NM	54	42	45	30
P/E Ratio:Low	17	13	15	11	15	NM	18	24	17	14

Income Statement Analysis (Million $)

	2007	2006	2005	2004	2003	2002	2001	2000	1999	1998
Revenue	15,943	16,023	16,267	15,854	14,455	13,848	13,674	11,635	9,054	6,508
Operating Income	1,701	2,370	2,705	2,543	1,794	1,148	2,035	2,253	1,659	1,121
Depreciation	530	625	620	664	781	810	590	436	326	270
Interest Expense	49.0	45.0	167	234	249	109	74.9	31.8	13.6	Nil
Pretax Income	1,264	1,793	1,872	1,683	801	242	1,382	1,785	1,319	854
Effective Tax Rate	38.5%	37.9%	38.6%	38.8%	40.4%	NM	36.5%	36.9%	37.5%	37.5%
Net Income	778	1,113	1,150	1,030	477	-7.76	877	1,127	825	534
S&P Core Earnings	776	1,033	1,073	978	439	-89.1	760	NA	NA	NA

Balance Sheet & Other Financial Data (Million $)

	2007	2006	2005	2004	2003	2002	2001	2000	1999	1998
Cash	2,644	2,987	7,139	2,261	3,389	1,036	409	450	565	913
Current Assets	5,029	5,239	6,304	6,689	5,740	3,045	2,648	2,198	1,872	1,831
Total Assets	8,544	8,821	10,048	10,343	9,902	7,591	7,013	5,189	3,964	3,338
Current Liabilities	2,272	1,942	2,242	2,492	2,727	2,056	2,799	1,753	1,553	992
Long Term Debt	188	513	1,886	2,487	2,896	1,961	780	785	496	496
Common Equity	5,174	5,425	4,936	4,783	3,658	3,010	2,928	2,233	1,574	1,584
Total Capital	5,362	5,938	6,822	7,270	6,554	4,971	3,708	3,018	2,070	2,080
Capital Expenditures	572	600	442	272	303	940	1,859	1,239	798	466
Cash Flow	1,308	1,738	1,770	1,694	1,258	803	1,468	1,563	1,151	804
Current Ratio	2.2	2.7	2.8	2.7	2.1	1.5	0.9	1.3	1.2	1.8
% Long Term Debt of Capitalization	3.5	8.6	27.6	34.2	44.2	39.5	21.0	26.0	24.0	23.8
% Net Income of Revenue	4.9	6.9	7.1	6.5	3.3	NM	6.4	9.7	9.1	8.2
% Return on Assets	9.0	11.8	11.1	10.2	5.4	NM	14.4	24.6	22.6	17.9
% Return on Equity	14.7	21.5	24.0	24.4	14.3	NM	34.0	59.2	52.2	33.0

Data as orig reptd.; bef. results of disc opers/spec. items. Per share data adj. for stk. divs.; EPS diluted. E-Estimated. NA-Not Available. NM-Not Meaningful. NR-Not Ranked. UR-Under Review.

Office: 2 Folsom St, San Francisco, CA 94105-1205.
Telephone: 650-952-4400 .
Email: investor_relations@gap.com
Website: http://www.gapinc.com

Chrmn, Pres & CEO: R.J. Fisher
EVP & CFO: B.H. Pollitt
EVP, Secy, General Counsel & CCO: L. Shanahan
Investor Contact: E. Price (415-427-2360)

Board Members: H. Behar, A. D. Bellamy, D. De Sole, D.
G. Fisher, D. F. Fisher, R. J. Fisher, P. L. Hughes, B.
Martin, J. P. Montoya, J. M. Schneider, M. A. Shattuck,
III, K. C. Youngblood
Founded: 1969
Domicile: Delaware
Employees: 154,000

General Dynamics Corp

STANDARD &POOR'S

S&P Recommendation	BUY ★★★★☆	Price	12-Mo. Target Price	Investment Style
		$88.50 (as of Nov 23, 2007)	$98.00	Large-Cap Growth

GICS Sector Industrials
Sub-Industry Aerospace & Defense

Summary General Dynamics is the world's sixth largest military contractor and also one of the world's biggest makers of corporate jets.

Key Stock Statistics (Source S&P, Vickers, company reports)

52-Wk Range	$93.57– 70.61	S&P Oper. EPS 2007**E**	5.07	Market Capitalization(B)	$35.898	Beta	1.18
Trailing 12-Month EPS	$4.65	S&P Oper. EPS 2008**E**	5.65	Yield (%)	1.31	S&P 3-Yr. Proj. EPS CAGR(%)	13.00
Trailing 12-Month P/E	19.0	P/E on S&P Oper. EPS 2007**E**	17.5	Dividend Rate/Share	$1.16	S&P Credit Rating	A
$10K Invested 5 Yrs Ago	$23,024	Common Shares Outstg. (M)	405.6	Institutional Ownership (%)	81		

Price Performance

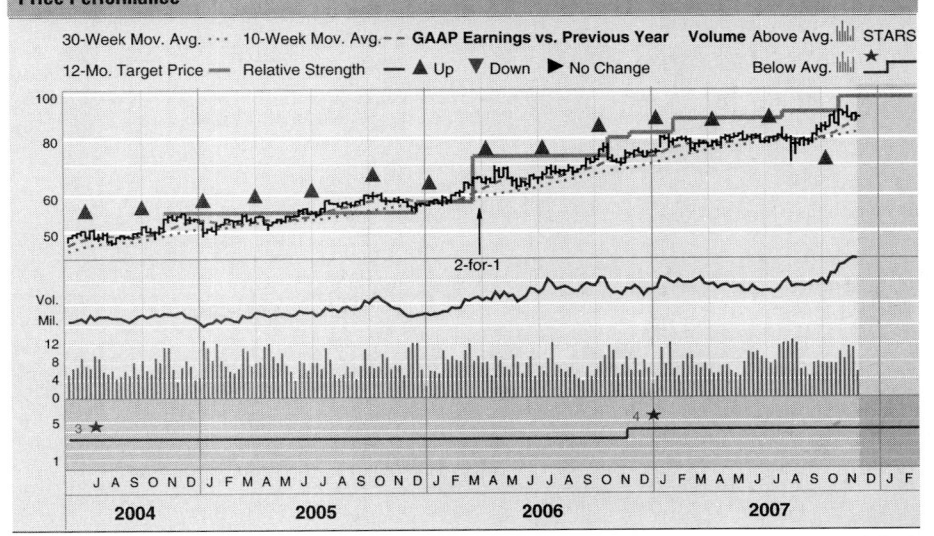

30-Week Mov. Avg. · · · 10-Week Mov. Avg. - - **GAAP Earnings vs. Previous Year** Volume Above Avg. STARS
12-Mo. Target Price — Relative Strength — ▲ Up ▼ Down ► No Change Below Avg.

2-for-1

Options: ASE, CBOE, Ph

Analysis prepared by **Richard Tortoriello** on October 29, 2007, when the stock traded at **$ 90.94**.

Highlights

➤ We look for sales to increase about 13% in 2007 and 11% in 2008. We expect the strongest growth in Combat Systems and Aerospace, with moderate growth in Information Systems & Technology and Marine Systems. We see increased spending by the Army and strong growth in the business jet market as multi-year drivers for revenue growth at GD. The September 30, 2007, funded backlog of $36.9 billion is 1.4X our 2007 revenue projection.

➤ We estimate a 2007 operating margin of 11.4%, up from 10.9% in 2006, and we see the possibility of further margin improvement in 2008, especially with additional improvement in Marine Systems (projected operating margin of 8.4% in 2007). We expect a 21% increase in EPS for 2007, to $5.07, and we forecast a further 11% increase, to $5.65, in 2008.

➤ GD has generated free cash flow (FCF; cash flow from operations less capital expenditures) per share in excess of EPS in each of the past four years. We expect FCF per share of just below EPS in 2007. We look for cash to be used for share repurchases, acquisitions, and dividend increases.

Investment Rationale/Risk

➤ Loner term, we see GD continuing to increase sales and EPS via acquisitions, growth in business jet sales, and strength in land vehicles and munitions needed for current operations in Iraq and the replacement of lost and damaged equipment afterward. We see strong supplemental spending by Congress for the ongoing wars funding increased defense spending at GD. We see a significant amount of this funding being used for land vehicles for the Army. Also, we expect continued strength in the IS&T segment, and we see increased potential for the Marine segment.

➤ Risks to our recommendation and target price include the potential for delays and/or cuts in military budgets and the failure to perform well on existing contracts or to win new contracts.

➤ At 16X our 2008 EPS estimate, GD recently traded in line with the average for "Big Five" defense contractor peers (15.9X). Given our view of strong EPS growth and cash flow generation, we believe that GD should trade above peers and above its 10-year historical average forward P/E ratio of 15.2X. Our 12-month target price of $98 represents a P/E of 17.3X our 2008 EPS estimate.

Qualitative Risk Assessment

LOW	MEDIUM	HIGH

Our risk assessment for GD is based on the company's long-term record of consistent earnings and dividend growth, as reflected in its S&P Quality Ranking of A+. In addition, we note the company's conservative capitalization, with a debt-to-total capital ratio of 18% as of September 2007.

Quantitative Evaluations

S&P Quality Ranking A+

D	C	B-	B	B+	A-	A	A+

Relative Strength Rank **STRONG**

87

LOWEST = 1   HIGHEST = 99

Revenue/Earnings Data

Revenue (Million $)

	1Q	2Q	3Q	4Q	Year
2007	6,300	6,591	6,834	--	--
2006	5,546	5,934	6,069	6,514	24,063
2005	4,819	5,214	5,380	5,831	21,244
2004	4,661	4,666	4,661	5,190	19,178
2003	3,421	3,935	4,427	4,834	16,617
2002	3,102	3,506	3,284	3,937	13,829

Earnings Per Share ($)

	1Q	2Q	3Q	4Q	Year
2007	1.07	1.27	1.34	E1.38	E5.07
2006	0.95	1.03	1.08	1.13	4.20
2005	0.85	0.85	0.92	1.00	3.63
2004	0.66	0.73	0.79	0.82	2.99
2003	0.56	0.61	0.64	0.70	2.50
2002	0.57	0.67	0.69	0.67	2.59

Fiscal year ended Dec. 31. Next earnings report expected: Late January. EPS Estimates based on S&P Operating Earnings; historical GAAP earnings are as reported.

Dividend Data (Dates: mm/dd Payment Date: mm/dd/yy)

Amount ($)	Date Decl.	Ex-Div. Date	Stk. of Record	Payment Date
0.230	12/06	01/17	01/19	02/09/07
0.290	03/07	04/11	04/13	05/11/07
0.290	06/06	07/03	07/06	08/10/07
0.290	08/01	10/03	10/05	11/09/07

Dividends have been paid since 1979. Source: Company reports.

Please read the Required Disclosures and Analyst Certification on the last page of this report.

The McGraw-Hill Companies

General Dynamics Corp

STANDARD
&POOR'S

Business Summary October 29, 2007

CORPORATE OVERVIEW. General Dynamics is a leading defense contractor and corporate jet maker that conducts business through four segments.

Information Systems & Technology (IS&T) (38% of sales and 37% of operating profits in 2006) primarily makes sophisticated electronics for land-, sea- and air-based weapons systems. Customers also include federal civilian agencies and commercial customers. Since it was created in 1997, the group has grown into a business that provides systems integration expertise; hardware and software products; and engineering, management, and support services. The group has over 5,000 active contracts. We believe the $60 billion U.S. government IT market is fragmented; IS&T's main competitors are the IT divisions of Northrop Grumman, Lockheed Martin and Boeing.

Marine Systems (20% and 14%) is the Pentagon's second largest military shipbuilder (Northrop Grumman is the largest). Major current programs include the Virginia-class submarine, Trident ballistic missile submarine conversions, the DDG 51 and DDG 1000 destroyers, the Littoral Combat Ship, and the T-AKE dry cargo/ammunition cargo ship. The U.S. military shipbuilding industry, which operates as a duopoly, suffered from low margins in 2003-2005, due to overcapacity, but margins improved significantly in 2006, and we project a further improvement in 2007.

Combat Systems (25% and 25%) makes, repairs and supports wheeled and tracked armored vehicles and munitions. GD is also the only U.S. tank maker. Reflecting the U.S. Army's desire to transform itself into a highly agile fighting force, demand is expected to slow for tanks, but to accelerate for its various wheeled combat vehicles. Major current programs include the M1 Abrams tank, the Stryker combat vehicle, and the Expeditionary Fighting Vehicle. CS's main competitor is BAE Systems' Land & Armaments division.

Aerospace (17% and 24%) makes the well known Gulfstream business jet. Based on revenues, Gulfstream is the world's third-largest corporate jet maker, behind Canada-based Bombardier and Textron's Cessna division. France's Dassault and Hawker Beechcraft Corp. (formerly Raytheon's aircraft-making unit) are also significant competitors. According to statistics from Bombardier, the total business aircraft market was $13.2 billion in 2005, with the top five manufacturers, given above, accounting for 91% of sales. Gulfstream sells business jets primarily to the high end of the market.

Company Financials Fiscal Year Ended Dec. 31

Per Share Data ($)	2006	2005	2004	2003	2002	2001	2000	1999	1998	1997
Tangible Book Value	0.25	1.40	NM	NM	2.81	1.92	3.22	1.64	2.74	2.83
Cash Flow	5.16	4.48	3.57	3.20	3.14	2.99	2.80	2.66	1.93	0.80
Earnings	4.20	3.63	2.99	2.50	2.59	2.33	2.24	2.18	1.43	1.25
S&P Core Earnings	4.08	3.34	2.81	2.34	1.62	1.57	NA	NA	NA	NA
Dividends	0.66	0.78	0.70	0.63	0.59	0.55	0.51	0.47	0.43	0.41
Payout Ratio	16%	22%	23%	25%	23%	24%	23%	22%	30%	33%
Prices:High	77.98	61.14	54.99	45.40	55.59	48.00	39.50	37.72	31.00	22.88
Prices:Low	56.68	48.80	42.48	25.00	36.63	30.25	18.13	23.09	20.13	15.78
P/E Ratio:High	19	17	18	18	21	21	18	17	22	18
P/E Ratio:Low	13	13	14	10	14	13	8	11	14	13

Income Statement Analysis (Million $)

	2006	2005	2004	2003	2002	2001	2000	1999	1998	1997
Revenue	24,063	21,244	19,178	16,617	13,829	12,163	10,356	8,959	4,970	4,062
Operating Income	3,009	2,539	2,173	1,744	1,795	1,756	1,555	1,396	668	549
Depreciation	384	342	232	277	213	271	226	193	126	91.0
Interest Expense	101	154	157	98.0	45.0	56.0	60.0	34.0	12.0	12.0
Pretax Income	2,527	2,100	1,785	1,372	1,584	1,424	1,262	1,126	549	479
Effective Tax Rate	32.3%	30.1%	32.6%	27.3%	33.6%	33.8%	28.6%	21.8%	33.7%	34.0%
Net Income	1,710	1,468	1,203	997	1,051	943	901	880	364	316
S&P Core Earnings	1,663	1,354	1,130	931	658	636	NA	NA	NA	NA

Balance Sheet & Other Financial Data (Million $)

	2006	2005	2004	2003	2002	2001	2000	1999	1998	1997
Cash	1,604	2,331	976	860	328	442	177	270	220	336
Current Assets	9,880	9,173	7,287	6,394	5,098	4,893	3,551	3,491	1,873	1,689
Total Assets	22,376	19,591	17,544	16,183	11,731	11,069	7,987	7,774	4,572	4,091
Current Liabilities	7,824	6,907	5,374	5,616	4,582	4,579	2,901	3,453	1,461	1,291
Long Term Debt	2,774	2,781	3,291	3,296	718	724	162	169	249	257
Common Equity	9,827	8,145	7,189	5,921	5,199	4,528	3,820	3,171	2,219	1,915
Total Capital	12,601	10,926	10,480	9,217	5,917	5,252	3,982	3,340	2,468	2,172
Capital Expenditures	334	279	266	224	264	356	288	197	158	83.0
Cash Flow	2,094	1,810	1,435	1,274	1,264	1,214	1,127	1,073	490	407
Current Ratio	1.3	1.3	1.4	1.1	1.1	1.1	1.2	1.0	1.3	1.3
% Long Term Debt of Capitalization	22.0	25.5	31.4	35.8	12.1	13.8	4.1	5.1	10.1	11.8
% Net Income of Revenue	7.1	6.9	6.3	6.0	7.6	7.8	8.7	9.8	7.3	7.8
% Return on Assets	8.1	7.9	7.1	7.1	9.2	9.9	11.4	12.6	8.4	8.6
% Return on Equity	19.0	19.1	18.4	17.9	21.6	22.6	25.8	31.5	17.6	17.4

Data as orig reptd.; bef. results of disc opers/spec. items. Per share data adj. for stk. divs.; EPS diluted. E-Estimated. NA-Not Available. NM-Not Meaningful. NR-Not Ranked. UR-Under Review.

Office: 2941 Fairview Park Dr Ste 100, Falls Church, VA 22042-4513.
Telephone: 703-876-3000.
Website: http://www.generaldynamics.com
Chrmn & CEO: N.D. Chabraja

SVP & CFO: L.H. Redd
SVP, Secy & General Counsel: D.A. Savner
Investor Contact: R. Lewis (703-876-3195)
VP & Cntlr: J.M. Schwartz

Board Members: N. D. Chabraja, J. S. Crown, W. P. Fricks, C. H. Goodman, J. L. Johnson, G. A. Joulwan, P. G. Kaminski, J. M. Keane, D. J. Lucas, L. L. Lyles, C. E. Mundy, Jr., R. Walmsley

Founded: 1899
Domicile: Delaware
Employees: 82,600

The McGraw-Hill Companies

General Electric Co

STANDARD &POOR'S

S&P Recommendation BUY ★★★★☆

Price	**12-Mo. Target Price**	**Investment Style**
$37.45 (as of Nov 27, 2007)	$45.00	Large-Cap Blend

GICS Sector Industrials
Sub-Industry Industrial Conglomerates

Summary This industrial conglomerate sells products ranging from jet engines and gas turbines to consumer appliances, railroad locomotives, and medical equipment. It also owns NBC Universal, and is one of the world's largest providers of consumer and commercial financing.

Key Stock Statistics (Source S&P, Vickers, company reports)

52-Wk Range	$42.15–33.90	S&P Oper. EPS 2007E	2.19	Market Capitalization(B)	$383.719	Beta	0.75
Trailing 12-Month EPS	$2.14	S&P Oper. EPS 2008E	2.49	Yield (%)	2.99	S&P 3-Yr. Proj. EPS CAGR(%)	12.00
Trailing 12-Month P/E	17.5	P/E on S&P Oper. EPS 2007E	17.1	Dividend Rate/Share	$1.12	S&P Credit Rating	AAA
$10K Invested 5 Yrs Ago	$16,325	Common Shares Outstg. (M)	10,246.2	Institutional Ownership (%)	60		

Price Performance

- 30-Week Mov. Avg. · · · 10-Week Mov. Avg. - - **GAAP Earnings vs. Previous Year** Volume Above Avg. STARS
- 12-Mo. Target Price — Relative Strength — ▲ Up ▼ Down ► No Change Below Avg.

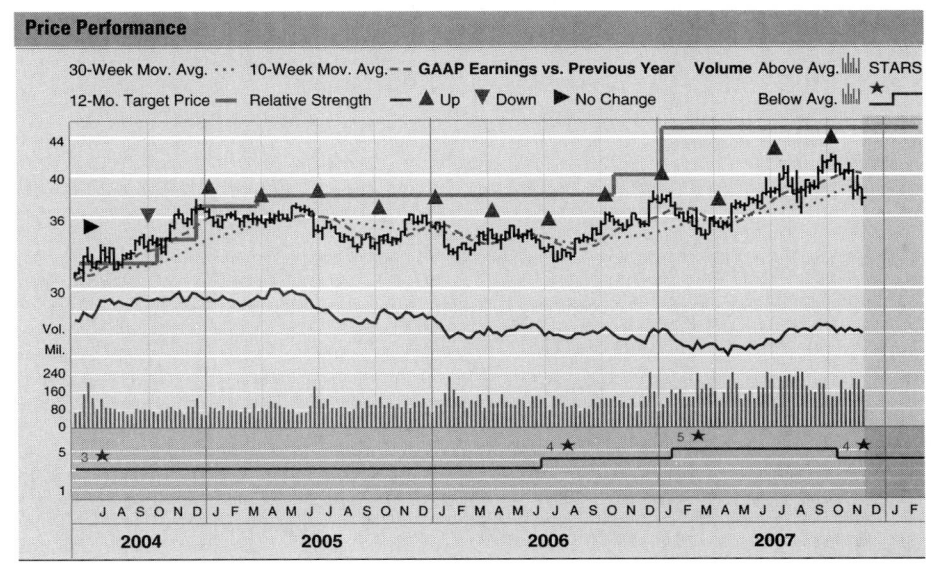

Analysis prepared by **Richard Tortoriello** on October 17, 2007, when the stock traded at **$ 40.93.**

Options: ASE, CBOE, P, Ph

Highlights

➤ We estimate about 7% revenue growth in 2007 and 8.2% in 2008, above S&P's estimate of U.S. real GDP growth of 2.0% in both 2007 and 2008. Global Insight, an economic forecasting firm, projects 1.9% real GDP growth for the 12 Euro-zone countries in 2007 and 2.5% in 2008 (24% of GE's sales are from Europe) and 3.3% in 2007 and 3.5% in 2008 in the Asia-Pacific region (11%). We see 2008 growth at GE driven by the infrastructure, health care, and commercial/consumer finance segments.

➤ We project that operating margins will widen to near 16% in 2007 and 16.4% in 2008, from 15.5% in 2006, as productivity increases and restructuring efforts aid profitability. We project EPS of $2.19 in 2007, with growth to $2.49 in 2008.

➤ We note that GE generated internal revenue growth (excluding recent acquisitions) of 8% in 2005 and 9% in 2006, more than double the rates of real U.S. GDP over those periods. We believe GE can continue to grow faster than U.S. GDP going forward, given its current portfolio of businesses, and we project average three-year earnings growth of 12%.

Investment Rationale/Risk

➤ Given what we see as an environment of increased investment risk, we view GE's S&P Quality Ranking of A+ as providing a measure of safety for shareholders. We also favor the repositioning of GE's portfolio of businesses that has taken place over the past few years, including recently announced acquisitions. We see reasons--including a strong aerospace market, increasing demand for energy infrastructure, high global liquidity and increased wealth--why we think GE's businesses should continue to show strong growth going forward.

➤ Risks to our recommendation and target price include slower than expected global economic growth, as well as manufacturing and regulatory problems, and the potential for further losses in GE's subprime lending unit.

➤ Our 12-month target price of $45 is based on a P/E multiple of 18X our 2008 EPS estimate. This compares to a 10-year average forward P/E for GE of 18X, with lows near 10X and highs (during 2000) near 40X. We believe GE deserves at least an average multiple due to our projection of strong earnings growth.

Qualitative Risk Assessment

LOW	MEDIUM	HIGH

Our risk assessment reflects our view of GE's long-term record of steady growth in earnings, cash flow and dividends, which we attribute to good management of a diversified portfolio of growing and profitable businesses, as well as GE's relatively low stock price volatility.

Quantitative Evaluations

S&P Quality Ranking A+

D	C	B-	B	B+	A-	A	A+

Relative Strength Rank MODERATE

54

LOWEST = 1   HIGHEST = 99

Revenue/Earnings Data

Revenue (Million $)

	1Q	2Q	3Q	4Q	Year
2007	40,195	42,316	42,534	--	--
2006	--	--	--	44,621	163,391
2005	--	--	--	40,705	149,702
2004	33,350	37,035	38,272	43,706	152,363
2003	30,456	33,373	33,394	36,964	134,187
2002	30,521	33,214	32,585	35,378	131,698

Earnings Per Share ($)

2007	0.44	0.52	0.50	E0.69	E2.19
2006	0.40	0.48	0.48	0.64	1.99
2005	0.33	0.41	0.43	0.55	1.72
2004	0.32	0.38	0.38	0.51	1.59
2003	0.32	0.38	0.40	0.45	1.55
2002	0.35	0.44	0.41	0.31	1.51

Fiscal year ended Dec. 31. Next earnings report expected: Mid January. EPS Estimates based on S&P Operating Earnings; historical GAAP earnings are as reported.

Dividend Data (Dates: mm/dd Payment Date: mm/dd/yy)

Amount ($)	Date Decl.	Ex-Div. Date	Stk. of Record	Payment Date
0.280	12/12	12/21	12/26	01/25/07
0.280	02/09	02/22	02/26	04/25/07
0.280	06/08	06/21	06/25	07/25/07
0.280	09/07	09/20	09/24	10/25/07

Dividends have been paid since 1899. Source: Company reports.

Please read the Required Disclosures and Analyst Certification on the last page of this report.

General Electric Co

STANDARD &POOR'S

Business Summary October 17, 2007

CORPORATE OVERVIEW. This multi-industry, media and financing giant does business through six segments: Infrastructure, Industrial, Healthcare, NBC Universal, Commercial Finance, and GE Money (formerly Consumer Finance).

The Infrastructure segment (30% of 2006 revenues, 34% of operating profits) produces, sells, finances and services equipment for the air transportation and energy generation industries (products include jet engines and maintenance services, gas turbines for power generation, windmills, and nuclear reactors). It also produces, sells and services equipment for the rail transportation (locomotives); oil & gas production, transportation, and refining; and water treatment industries. The Aviation and Energy sub-segments, excluding financial services, together made up 69% of 2006 segment revenues and 65% of operating profits.

The Industrial segment (21%, 10%) produces and sells products, including consumer appliances, industrial equipment and plastics, and related services. GE makes, sells and services major home appliances, under the Monogram, GE Profile, GE, and Hotpoint brands; it also produces a variety of electrical equipment and motors. Plastics are used for a number of applications, including automobile and appliance parts. In addition, it finances business equipment for a wide variety of customer applications. Consumer and industrial

products accounted for 51% of 2006 segment revenues and 34% of operating profits.

The Healthcare segment (10%, 12%) manufactures, sells and services a wide range of medical equipment, including equipment for magnetic resonance (MR), computed tomography (CT), positron emission tomography (PET) imaging, x-ray, patient monitoring, diagnostic cardiology, nuclear imaging, ultrasound, bone densitometry, anesthesiology and oxygen therapy, neonatal and critical care, and therapy.

NBC Universal (10%, 11%) is principally engaged in: the broadcast of network television services to affiliated television stations within the U.S.; the production of live and recorded TV programs; the production and distribution of motion pictures; the operation of TV broadcasting stations; the ownership of several cable/satellite networks around the world; the operation of theme parks; and investment and programming activities in multimedia and the Internet.

Company Financials Fiscal Year Ended Dec. 31

Per Share Data ($)	2006	2005	2004	2003	2002	2001	2000	1999	1998	1997
Tangible Book Value	2.52	2.64	2.55	2.40	1.76	2.34	2.32	1.68	1.55	1.56
Cash Flow	2.90	2.53	2.39	2.24	2.11	2.11	2.04	1.74	1.52	1.25
Earnings	1.99	1.72	1.59	1.55	1.51	1.41	1.27	1.07	0.93	0.82
S&P Core Earnings	1.90	1.66	1.54	1.41	1.10	0.98	NA	NA	NA	NA
Dividends	1.03	0.91	0.82	0.77	0.73	0.66	0.57	0.49	0.42	0.36
Payout Ratio	52%	53%	52%	50%	48%	47%	45%	46%	45%	44%
Prices:High	38.49	37.34	37.75	32.42	41.84	53.55	60.50	53.17	34.65	25.52
Prices:Low	32.06	32.67	28.88	21.30	21.40	28.50	41.65	31.35	23.00	15.98
P/E Ratio:High	19	22	24	21	28	38	48	50	37	31
P/E Ratio:Low	16	19	18	14	14	20	33	29	25	19

Income Statement Analysis (Million $)										
Revenue	163,391	149,702	152,363	134,187	131,698	125,913	129,853	111,630	100,469	90,840
Operating Income	53,972	46,840	40,262	36,792	35,431	38,200	38,329	32,646	29,355	23,885
Depreciation	9,158	8,538	8,385	6,956	5,998	7,089	7,736	6,691	5,860	4,082
Interest Expense	19,286	15,187	11,907	10,432	10,216	11,062	11,720	10,013	9,753	8,384
Pretax Income	25,528	23,115	21,034	20,194	19,217	20,049	18,873	15,577	13,742	11,419
Effective Tax Rate	15.5%	16.7%	16.7%	21.4%	19.6%	27.8%	30.3%	31.1%	30.4%	26.1%
Net Income	20,666	18,275	16,593	15,589	15,133	14,128	12,735	10,717	9,296	8,203
S&P Core Earnings	19,701	17,548	16,138	14,195	11,038	9,889	NA	NA	NA	NA

Balance Sheet & Other Financial Data (Million $)										
Cash	14,275	9,011	150,864	133,388	125,772	110,099	99,534	90,312	83,034	76,482
Current Assets	NA	NA	NA	NA	NA	NA	NA	NA	NA	NA
Total Assets	697,239	673,342	750,330	647,483	575,244	495,023	437,006	405,200	355,935	304,012
Current Liabilities	NA	NA	NA	NA	NA	NA	NA	NA	NA	NA
Long Term Debt	260,804	212,281	213,161	170,004	140,632	79,806	82,132	71,427	59,663	46,603
Common Equity	112,314	109,354	110,284	79,180	63,706	54,824	50,492	42,557	38,880	34,438
Total Capital	394,867	346,019	354,242	267,611	222,328	148,975	146,250	128,436	112,158	93,374
Capital Expenditures	16,650	14,441	13,118	9,767	13,351	15,520	13,967	15,502	8,982	8,388
Cash Flow	29,824	26,813	24,978	22,545	21,131	21,217	20,471	17,408	15,156	12,285
Current Ratio	NA	NA	NA	NA	NA	NA	NA	NA	NA	NA
% Long Term Debt of Capitalization	66.0	61.3	60.2	63.5	63.3	53.6	56.2	55.6	53.2	50.0
% Net Income of Revenue	12.8	12.2	10.8	11.6	11.5	11.2	9.8	9.6	9.3	9.0
% Return on Assets	3.0	2.6	2.4	2.5	2.8	3.0	3.0	2.8	2.8	2.8
% Return on Equity	18.6	16.6	17.5	21.8	25.5	26.8	27.4	26.3	25.4	25.0

Data as orig reptd.; bef. results of disc opers/spec. items. Per share data adj. for stk. divs.; EPS diluted. E-Estimated. NA-Not Available. NM-Not Meaningful. NR-Not Ranked. UR-Under Review.

Office: 3135 Easton Tpke, Fairfield, CT 06828-0001.
Telephone: 203-373-2211.
Website: http://www.ge.com
Chrmn & CEO: J.R. Immelt

Vice Chrmn: R.C. Wright
Vice Chrmn: L.G. Trotter
Vice Chrmn: D.L. Calhoun
Vice Chrmn: J. Rice

Investor Contact: D. Janki
Board Members: J. I. Cash, Jr., W. M. Castell, A. M. Fudge, C. X. Gonzalez, S. Hockfield, J. R. Immelt, A. Jung, A. G. Lafley, R. W. Lane, R. S. Larsen, R. B. Lazarus, S. Nunn, R. S. Penske, R. J. Swieringa, D. A. Warner, III, R. C. Wright

Founded: 1892
Domicile: New York
Employees: 319,000

The McGraw-Hill Companies

General Growth Properties Inc

S&P Recommendation	BUY ★★★★☆	Price $46.59 (as of Nov 23, 2007)	12-Mo. Target Price $62.00	Investment Style Large-Cap Blend

GICS Sector Financials
Sub-Industry Retail REITS

Summary This real estate investment trust owns, develops and operates regional shopping centers throughout the U.S.

Key Stock Statistics (Source S&P, Vickers, company reports)

52-Wk Range	$67.43– 42.40	S&P FFO/Sh. 2007E	3.27	Market Capitalization(B)	$11.413	Beta	0.58
Trailing 12-Month FFO/Share	NA	S&P FFO/Sh. 2008E	3.57	Yield (%)	4.29	S&P 3-Yr. FFO/Sh. Proj. CAGR(%)	10.00
Trailing 12-Month P/FFO	NA	P/FFO on S&P FFO/Sh. 2007E	14.2	Dividend Rate/Share	$2.00	S&P Credit Rating	BBB-
$10K Invested 5 Yrs Ago	$34,647	Common Shares Outstg. (M)	245.0	Institutional Ownership (%)	87		

Price Performance

30-Week Mov. Avg. · · · 10-Week Mov. Avg. - - **GAAP Earnings vs. Previous Year**   Volume Above Avg. |III STARS
12-Mo. Target Price — Relative Strength — ▲ Up ▼ Down ▶ No Change   Below Avg. |III ★

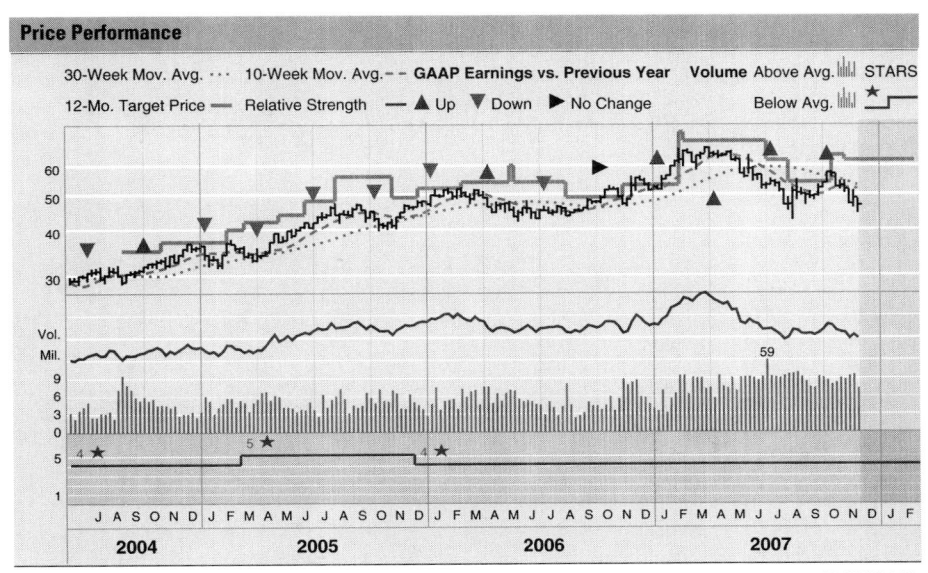

Options: ASE, CBOE, P, Ph

Analysis prepared by **Robert McMillan** on November 07, 2007, when the stock traded at **$ 49.81**.

Highlights

➤ We expect the trust to continue to benefit from its strategy of operating large and strategically located regional malls and shopping centers in major metropolitan markets.

➤ We see total revenues, after rising nearly 6% in 2006, rising just fractionally in 2007 owing to a steep drop in land sales, followed by nearly 11% growth in 2008 on gains in rental income. We believe real GDP expansion and moderate retail sales bode well for results in GGP's retail portfolio. We anticipate strong demand for space, enabling GGP to achieve moderate rent increases when expired leases are renewed. Retail center shop occupancy remained healthy, in our view, at 93.2% at the end of the third quarter of 2007, up from 92.4% a year earlier. We believe that the volatility of land sales and master planned community businesses could increase earnings volatility.

➤ We estimate operating EPS of $1.45 in 2007 and $0.74 in 2008, and we project funds from operations (FFO) of $3.27 for 2007 and $3.57 for 2008.

Investment Rationale/Risk

➤ We believe shareholders will benefit from what we view as GGP's position as a major owner and manager of shopping centers, an established array of relationships with retailers that are still expanding, and acumen in acquiring and developing shopping centers.

➤ Risks to our recommendation and target price include slower than expected growth in retailer revenues, a slowdown in retailer expansion, a large increase in shopping center supply, and increases in interest rates.

➤ The stock recently traded at about 15.8X GGP's trailing 12-month FFO. The shares and the multiple, after dropping sharply between May and August, have risen sharply recently. Our 12-month target price of $62 is equal to about 17.5X our four-quarter forward FFO estimate of $3.52. We think GGP will continue to deliver strong growth in operating results, driven by relatively robust rent growth and occupancy levels, and we think its valuation multiple will expand as concerns about the effect of the housing slowdown on retailer-dependent GGP's business continue to ease.

Qualitative Risk Assessment

LOW	MEDIUM	HIGH

Our risk assessment reflects GGP's position as a major owner and manager of geographically dispersed shopping centers with a mix of major retail tenants that generally have long-term leases for their space. We think that this diversification and what we see as a healthy balance sheet, with no overly burdensome near-term debt repayments, will generate relatively stable growth.

Quantitative Evaluations

S&P Quality Ranking   **B**

D	C	B-	B	B+	A-	A	A+

Relative Strength Rank   **MODERATE**

35

LOWEST = 1   HIGHEST = 99

Revenue/FFO Data

Revenue (Million $)

	1Q	2Q	3Q	4Q	Year
2007	728.8	740.1	864.3	--	--
2006	828.6	709.8	746.0	971.8	3,256
2005	709.5	766.9	756.7	862.2	3,073
2004	361.6	376.3	397.5	671.1	1,803
2003	273.9	284.7	327.4	384.8	1,271
2002	204.1	210.6	258.4	307.4	980.5

FFO Per Share ($)

2007	1.66	0.71	0.83	E1.07	E3.27
2006	0.77	0.62	0.65	1.02	3.07
2005	0.72	0.71	0.72	0.91	3.06
2004	0.60	0.61	0.66	0.90	2.77
2003	0.49	0.50	0.57	0.75	2.31
2002	0.37	0.39	0.47	0.65	1.86

Fiscal year ended Dec. 31. Next earnings report expected: Mid February. FFO Estimates based on S&P Funds From Operations Est..

Dividend Data (Dates: mm/dd Payment Date: mm/dd/yy)

Amount ($)	Date Decl.	Ex-Div. Date	Stk. of Record	Payment Date
0.450	01/05	01/12	01/17	01/31/07
0.450	04/05	04/12	04/16	04/30/07
0.450	07/05	07/13	07/17	07/31/07
0.500	10/04	10/15	10/17	10/31/07

Dividends have been paid since 1993. Source: Company reports.

General Growth Properties Inc

STANDARD &POOR'S

Business Summary November 07, 2007

General Growth Properties is a REIT that owns, develops, acquires and leases U.S. regional mall and community shopping centers. The trust makes all key strategic decisions for the properties in its portfolio. However, in connection with unconsolidated and joint venture properties, strategic decisions are made jointly with the respective stockholders or joint venture partners. GGP is also the asset manager of the properties in its portfolio, executing the strategic decisions and overseeing the day-to-day activities performed.

For GGP, as well as other retail related REITs, we believe that location and the financial health and growth of its retail tenants are among the most important factors affecting the success of its portfolio. Further, the companies in this industry enjoy relatively high barriers to entry, since developing new shopping centers requires large amounts of capital as well as time-consuming regulatory approval, which have been difficult to obtain in the recent past amid concerns about traffic and pollution. We expect GGP to continue to derive numerous growth opportunities from being large and from having a well-located and varied array of shopping center formats and relationships with a broad array of retailers.

At the end of 2006, the trust's portfolio was comprised primarily of over 200 regional shopping malls in 44 states. Most of the shopping centers in the trust's portfolio are strategically located in major and middle markets where we believe they have relatively strong competitive positions. The company also owns non-controlling interests in various international joint ventures in Brazil, Turkey and Costa Rica. We believe that the portfolio's geographic diversification will mitigate the effects of regional economic conditions and local factors.

In conjunction with the acquisition of the Rouse Company in 2004, GGP acquired several master-planned communities. GGP develops and sells land in these communities to builders and other developers for residential, commercial and other uses. It may also develop some of this land for its own purposes. These master-planned communities are located in and around Columbia, MD, Summerlin, NV, and Houston, TX.

Company Financials Fiscal Year Ended Dec. 31

Per Share Data ($)	2006	2005	2004	2003	2002	2001	2000	1999	1998	1997
Tangible Book Value	5.34	6.32	9.13	7.69	6.39	6.37	5.98	5.98	5.01	4.66
Earnings	0.24	0.27	1.15	1.20	0.99	0.54	0.73	0.65	0.53	0.92
S&P Core Earnings	0.24	0.27	1.15	1.20	0.99	0.54	NA	NA	NA	NA
Dividends	1.27	1.49	1.26	1.02	0.89	0.75	0.68	0.65	0.62	0.60
Payout Ratio	NM	NM	110%	85%	90%	139%	94%	99%	117%	65%
Prices:High	56.14	48.27	36.90	28.03	17.43	13.50	12.17	12.88	13.08	12.79
Prices:Low	41.92	31.38	24.31	15.90	12.67	10.93	8.79	8.33	10.83	10.08
P/E Ratio:High	NM	NM	32	23	18	25	17	20	25	14
P/E Ratio:Low	NM	NM	21	13	13	20	12	13	20	11

Income Statement Analysis (Million $)										
Rental Income	1,829	1,740	Nil	782	584	Nil	469	415	4.16	281
Mortgage Income	Nil	Nil	Nil	Nil	Nil	Nil	Nil	Nil	Nil	Nil
Total Income	3,256	3,073	1,803	1,271	980	804	699	612	427	291
General Expenses	1,159	1,136	567	397	308	389	226	206	118	88.9
Interest Expense	1,117	1,031	472	279	219	214	218	186	126	78.8
Provision for Losses	Nil	Nil	Nil	Nil	Nil	Nil	Nil	Nil	Nil	Nil
Depreciation	690	673	366	231	180	153	127	113	75.2	48.5
Net Income	60.1	63.9	254	259	211	110	138	115	71.2	90.7
S&P Core Earnings	60.1	63.9	254	246	186	84.9	NA	NA	NA	NA

Balance Sheet & Other Financial Data (Million $)										
Cash	23,491	23,399	39.6	10.7	6,980	5,394	5,045	25.6	3,866	2,011
Total Assets	25,241	25,307	25,719	9,583	7,281	5,647	5,284	4,955	4,027	2,098
Real Estate Investment	26,161	25,402	21,670	10,305	7,725	5,703	5,439	5,024	4,063	2,157
Loss Reserve	Nil	Nil	Nil	Nil	Nil	Nil	Nil	Nil	Nil	Nil
Net Investment	23,394	23,297	20,217	9,204	6,926	5,079	4,951	4,647	3,761	1,924
Short Term Debt	Nil	Nil	Nil	Nil	Nil	Nil	408	329	777	20.0
Capitalization:Debt	20,522	18,513	20,311	6,649	4,592	3,398	2,836	2,790	1,872	1,276
Capitalization:Equity	1,664	1,933	2,143	1,674	1,197	1,183	938	6,093	586	499
Capitalization:Total	24,019	22,369	24,823	9,228	6,972	5,474	4,642	3,094	3,872	2,515
% Earnings & Depreciation/Assets	2.9	2.8	3.5	5.8	6.0	4.8	5.2	4.8	4.1	7.2
Price Times Book Value:High	10.5	7.6	4.0	3.6	2.7	2.1	2.0	2.2	2.6	2.7
Price Times Book Value:Low	7.9	5.0	2.7	2.1	2.0	1.7	1.5	1.4	2.2	1.0

Data as orig reptd.; bef. results of disc opers/spec. items. Per share data adj. for stk. divs.; EPS diluted. E-Estimated. NA-Not Available. NM-Not Meaningful. NR-Not Ranked. UR-Under Review.

Office: 110 N. Wacker Dr, Chicago, IL 60606-1526.
Telephone: 312-960-5000.
Website: http://www.generalgrowth.com
Chrmn: M. Bucksbaum

Pres & COO: R.A. Michaels
CEO: J. Bucksbaum
EVP & CFO: B. Freibaum
Investor Contact: T. Goebel (312-960-5199)

Trustees: J. Bucksbaum, M. Bucksbaum, A. Cohen, A. Downs, B. Freibaum, A. Metz, R. Michaels, T. Nolan, J. T. Riordan, B. Stewart

Founded: 1986
Domicile: Delaware
Employees: 4,700

General Mills Inc.

STANDARD &POOR'S

S&P Recommendation	HOLD ★★★☆☆	Price $57.10 (as of Nov 23, 2007)	12-Mo. Target Price $63.00	Investment Style Large-Cap Blend

GICS Sector Consumer Staples
Sub-Industry Packaged Foods & Meats

Summary This company is a major producer of packaged consumer food products, including Big G cereals and Betty Crocker desserts/baking mixes.

Key Stock Statistics (Source S&P, Vickers, company reports)

52-Wk Range	$61.52– 54.17	S&P Oper. EPS 2008**E**	3.41	Market Capitalization(B)	$18.463	Beta	0.24
Trailing 12-Month EPS	$3.25	S&P Oper. EPS 2009**E**	NA	Yield (%)	2.73	S&P 3-Yr. Proj. EPS CAGR(%)	9.00
Trailing 12-Month P/E	17.6	P/E on S&P Oper. EPS 2008**E**	16.7	Dividend Rate/Share	$1.56	S&P Credit Rating	BBB+
$10K Invested 5 Yrs Ago	$14,126	Common Shares Outstg. (M)	323.3	Institutional Ownership (%)	80		

Price Performance

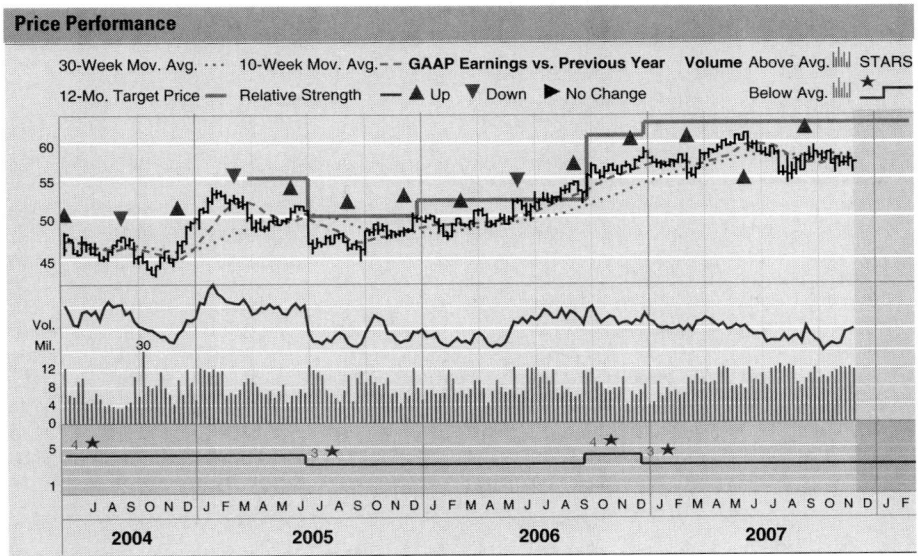

30-Week Mov. Avg. · · · 10-Week Mov. Avg. – – **GAAP Earnings vs. Previous Year** Volume Above Avg. ▍▍▍ STARS
12-Mo. Target Price — Relative Strength — ▲ Up ▼ Down ▶ No Change Below Avg. ▍▍▍ ★

Options: ASE, CBOE, P, Ph

Analysis prepared by **Tom Graves, CFA** on November 20, 2007, when the stock traded at **$ 55.87**.

Highlights

➤ In FY 08 (May), we look for net sales to advance moderately from FY 07's $12.4 billion, with unit volume growth and higher pricing. We expect operating margins to see some benefit from a combination of productivity gains and volume-based efficiencies and improved price realization.

➤ In FY 08, we expect that there will be more margin pressure from raw material and energy costs than there was in FY 07, but for this to be at least partly offset by price increases and a more favorable product mix. We expect higher spending on consumer marketing, and project that interest expense will rise.

➤ Including about $0.07 a share ($35 million pre-tax) of restructuring costs, we estimate FY 08 net income of $1.202 billion ($3.41, on about 2.1% fewer shares), up 7% from the $1.144 billion ($3.18) reported for FY 07. In FY 07, the adoption of a new accounting standard for stock-based compensation reduced earnings by about $0.12 per diluted share. We expect that this new accounting standard will stay in effect during FY 08. Also, in the first quarter of FY 08, GIS repurchased 20.9 million shares of common stock for $1.22 billion.

Investment Rationale/Risk

➤ Although we expect some near-term pressure from commodity costs, we believe the company has opportunities to bolster or expand longer-term profit margins through a focus on such areas as manufacturing and spending efficiency, global sourcing and sales mix. Also, we look for GIS to generate future free cash flow, with at least a portion being used for dividends and stock repurchases. A 5.7% quarterly dividend increase to $0.37 was paid in February 2007. In FY 07, GIS repurchased 24 million shares at an average price of $54.41 a share.

➤ Risks to our recommendation and target price include competitive pressures in General Mills' businesses, a lack of consumer acceptance of new product introductions, the potential for commodity cost inflation, and an inability to achieve sales and earnings growth forecasts.

➤ Our 12-month target price of $63 is 19X our calendar 2007 EPS estimate of $3.30, which includes some restructuring charges. This P/E is about 8% below the average P/E that we expect from a peer group of packaged food stocks, some of whose EPS estimates exclude various special item charges. GIS shares recently had an indicated dividend yield of about 2.8%.

Qualitative Risk Assessment

LOW	MEDIUM	HIGH

Our risk assessment reflects the relatively stable nature of the company's end markets, strong cash flows, and an S&P Quality Ranking of A- that reflects GIS's historical stability of earnings and dividends.

Quantitative Evaluations

S&P Quality Ranking A-

D	C	B-	B	B+	A-	A	A+

Relative Strength Rank STRONG

76

LOWEST = 1 HIGHEST = 99

Revenue/Earnings Data

Revenue (Million $)

	1Q	2Q	3Q	4Q	Year
2008	3,072	--	--	--	--
2007	2,860	3,467	3,054	3,061	12,442
2006	2,662	3,273	2,860	2,845	11,640
2005	2,585	3,168	2,772	2,719	11,244
2004	2,518	3,060	2,703	2,789	11,070
2003	2,362	2,953	2,645	2,546	10,506

Earnings Per Share ($)

2008	0.81	E1.12	E0.77	E0.71	E3.41
2007	0.74	1.08	0.74	0.62	3.18
2006	0.64	0.97	0.68	0.61	2.90
2005	0.45	0.92	0.58	1.14	3.08
2004	0.59	0.81	0.63	0.72	2.75
2003	0.47	0.73	0.63	0.59	2.43

Fiscal year ended May 31. Next earnings report expected: Late December. EPS Estimates based on S&P Operating Earnings; historical GAAP earnings are as reported.

Dividend Data (Dates: mm/dd Payment Date: mm/dd/yy)

Amount ($)	Date Decl.	Ex-Div. Date	Stk. of Record	Payment Date
0.370	12/11	01/08	01/10	02/01/07
0.370	03/12	04/05	04/10	05/01/07
0.390	06/25	07/06	07/10	08/01/07
0.390	09/24	10/05	10/10	11/01/07

Dividends have been paid since 1898. Source: Company reports.

General Mills Inc.

**STANDARD
&POOR'S**

Business Summary November 20, 2007

CORPORATE OVERVIEW. General Mills (GIS) is the second largest U.S. producer of ready-to-eat breakfast cereals, and a leading producer of other well known packaged consumer foods. The U.S. Retail segment, which we believe accounted for more than two-thirds of net sales in FY 06 (May), consists of cereals, meals, refrigerated and frozen dough products, baking products, snacks, yogurt and organic foods. The Bakeries and Foodservice segment consists of products marketed to retail and wholesale bakeries and offered to commercial and noncommercial foodservice sectors throughout the U.S. and Canada, such as restaurants and businesses and school cafeterias. The International segment is made up of retail business outside the U.S. and foodservice business outside of the U.S. and Canada.

Major cereal brands, most of which bear the Big G label, include Cheerios, Wheaties, Lucky Charms, Total and Chex cereals. Other consumer packaged food products include baking mixes (Betty Crocker, Bisquick); meals (Betty

Crocker dry packaged dinner mixes), Progresso soups, Green Giant canned and frozen vegetables; snacks (Pop Secret microwave popcorn, Bugles snacks, grain and fruit snack products); Pillsbury refrigerated and frozen dough products, frozen breakfast products and frozen pizza and snack products; and organic foods and other products, including Yoplait and Colombo yogurt. The company also engages in grain merchandising, produces its own ingredient flour requirements, and sells flour to bakeries. Products are also made and sold in Canada and Europe, Japan, Korea and Latin America.

During FY 06, Wal-Mart Stores, Inc. accounted for about 18% of GIS's consolidated net sales.

Company Financials Fiscal Year Ended May 31

Per Share Data ($)	2007	2006	2005	2004	2003	2002	2001	2000	1999	1998
Tangible Book Value	NM	NM	NM	NM	NM	NM	NM	NM	NM	NM
Cash Flow	4.59	3.99	4.11	3.79	3.39	2.21	3.04	2.68	4.63	1.90
Earnings	3.18	2.90	3.08	2.75	2.43	1.35	2.28	2.00	1.70	1.30
S&P Core Earnings	3.03	2.72	2.17	2.43	1.74	0.55	1.79	NA	NA	NA
Dividends	1.34	1.34	1.24	1.10	1.10	1.10	1.10	1.10	1.08	1.06
Payout Ratio	42%	46%	40%	40%	45%	81%	48%	55%	64%	82%
Calendar Year	2006	2005	2004	2003	2002	2001	2000	1999	1998	1997
Prices:High	59.23	53.89	49.96	49.66	51.73	52.86	45.31	43.94	39.84	39.13
Prices:Low	47.05	44.67	43.01	41.43	37.38	37.26	29.38	32.50	29.59	28.88
P/E Ratio:High	19	19	16	18	21	39	20	22	23	30
P/E Ratio:Low	15	15	14	15	15	28	13	16	17	22

Income Statement Analysis (Million $)										
Revenue	12,442	11,640	11,244	11,070	10,506	7,949	7,078	6,700	6,246	6,033
Operating Income	2,515	2,420	2,435	2,442	2,290	1,569	1,392	1,308	1,212	1,145
Depreciation	418	424	443	399	365	296	223	209	194	195
Interest Expense	427	427	488	537	589	445	223	168	134	130
Pretax Income	1,704	1,631	1,904	1,583	1,377	700	1,015	950	838	664
Effective Tax Rate	32.9%	33.2%	34.9%	33.4%	33.4%	34.1%	34.5%	35.3%	36.3%	36.4%
Net Income	1,144	1,090	1,240	1,055	917	461	665	614	535	422
S&P Core Earnings	1,089	1,024	863	931	652	189	512	NA	NA	NA

Balance Sheet & Other Financial Data (Million $)										
Cash	417	647	573	751	703	975	64.1	25.6	3.90	6.00
Current Assets	3,054	3,176	3,055	3,215	3,179	3,437	1,408	1,190	1,103	1,035
Total Assets	18,184	18,207	18,066	18,448	18,227	16,540	5,091	4,574	4,141	3,861
Current Liabilities	5,845	6,138	4,184	2,757	3,444	5,747	2,209	2,529	1,700	1,444
Long Term Debt	3,218	2,415	4,255	7,410	7,516	5,591	2,221	1,760	1,702	1,640
Common Equity	5,319	5,772	5,676	5,248	4,175	3,576	52.2	-289	164	190
Total Capital	11,109	11,145	12,915	14,730	13,652	9,727	2,696	1,859	2,156	2,244
Capital Expenditures	460	360	414	628	711	506	308	268	281	184
Cash Flow	1,562	1,514	1,683	1,454	1,282	757	888	823	729	617
Current Ratio	0.5	0.5	0.7	1.2	0.9	0.6	0.6	0.5	0.6	0.7
% Long Term Debt of Capitalization	28.9	21.7	32.9	50.3	55.1	57.5	82.4	94.7	79.0	73.1
% Net Income of Revenue	9.2	9.4	11.0	9.5	8.7	5.8	9.4	9.2	8.6	7.0
% Return on Assets	6.3	6.0	6.8	5.8	5.3	4.3	13.8	14.1	13.4	10.9
% Return on Equity	20.6	18.7	22.7	22.4	23.7	25.4	NM	NM	301.6	123.2

Data as orig reptd.; bef. results of disc opers/spec. items. Per share data adj. for stk. divs.; EPS diluted. E-Estimated. NA-Not Available. NM-Not Meaningful. NR-Not Ranked. UR-Under Review.

Office: 1 General Mills Blvd, Minneapolis, MN 55426-1348.
Telephone: 763-764-7600.
Website: http://www.generalmills.com
Chrmn & CEO: S.W. Sanger

Pres & COO: K.J. Powell
Vice Chrmn & CFO: J.A. Lawrence
SVP, Secy, General Counsel & CCO: S.S. Marshall
Investor Contact: K. Wenker (800-245-5703)

Board Members: P. Danos, W. T. Esrey, R. V. Gilmartin, J. R. Hope, H. G. Miller, H. Ochoa-Brillembourg, S. Odland, K. J. Powell, M. D. Rose, R. L. Ryan, S. W. Sanger, A. M. Spence, D. A. Terrell

Founded: 1928
Domicile: Delaware
Employees: 28,500

The McGraw·Hill Companies

General Motors Corp.

STANDARD &POOR'S

S&P Recommendation **SELL** ★ ★ ☆ ☆ ☆	Price $27.16 (as of Nov 23, 2007)	12-Mo. Target Price $32.00	Investment Style Large-Cap Value

GICS Sector Consumer Discretionary
Sub-Industry Automobile Manufacturers

Summary GM, the world's largest producer of cars and trucks, also has significant finance, aerospace, defense and electronics operations.

Key Stock Statistics (Source S&P, Vickers, company reports)

52-Wk Range	$43.20– 24.50	S&P Oper. EPS 2007 E	-0.27	Market Capitalization(B)	$15.369	Beta	1.42
Trailing 12-Month EPS	$-65.50	S&P Oper. EPS 2008 E	3.96	Yield (%)	3.68	S&P 3-Yr. Proj. EPS CAGR(%)	-5.00
Trailing 12-Month P/E	NM	P/E on S&P Oper. EPS 2007 E	NM	Dividend Rate/Share	$1.00	S&P Credit Rating	B
$10K Invested 5 Yrs Ago	$9,089	Common Shares Outstg. (M)	565.9	Institutional Ownership (%)	97		

Price Performance

30-Week Mov. Avg. · · · 10-Week Mov. Avg. - - GAAP Earnings vs. Previous Year   Volume Above Avg. ▌▌▌ STARS
12-Mo. Target Price — Relative Strength   — ▲ Up ▼ Down ► No Change   Below Avg. ▌▌▌ ★ ⌐

Options: ASE, CBOE, P, Ph

Analysis prepared by **Efraim Levy, CFA** on November 15, 2007, when the stock traded at **$ 30.16**.

Highlights

➤ We expect revenues to rise in the low single digits in 2008, led by non-U.S. sales, following a 13% projected decline in 2007. We forecast that U.S. car and light truck sales volume will dip 3.4%, to 16.0 million units in 2007, and stabilize at that level in 2008.

➤ We look for automotive profits, before special items, to improve in 2008, due to the more favorable recently ratified labor contract, offset by a less favorable product cycle in North America. However, we do not expect to see savings from the establishment of a healthcare trust before 2010. In addition, we see challenges to sustained profitability in North American automotive operations.

➤ Results from finance operations are no longer consolidated in GM's financial statements due to the sale of a 51% interest in General Motors Acceptance Corp. (GMAC). However, our 2007 loss per share estimate of $0.27, before unusual items, reflects GM's share of wider than expected losses at GMAC's mortgage unit. Our projected earnings improvement in 2008, to $3.96, includes savings from union concessions to GM, improved GMAC results, and expected strength in Asia and emerging markets.

Investment Rationale/Risk

➤ Even without the recent sale of the Allison Transmission business, we think GM has sufficient near-term liquidity for its operating needs. Our 2007 net loss forecast excludes a net non-cash charge of $38.6 billion due to a valuation allowance against deferred tax assets related to operations in the U.S., Canada and Germany.

➤ Risks to our recommendation and target price include stronger than expected demand for the company's vehicles, faster and higher cost and restructuring savings, and sharp decreases in gas prices. GMAC, GM's 49%-owned financial services division, could post stronger than projected net income, and savings and efficiencies from UAW negotiations may be more than we expect.

➤ Based on our 2008 EPS estimate, the stock recently traded in the lower portion of its recent historical P/E range, and below Daimler (DAI: hold, $99) and Japanese competitors. We project a loss for Ford (F: hold, $8). Based on historical and peer multiples, we apply a P/E of about 8X to our 2008 EPS forecast to arrive at our 12-month target price of $32.

Qualitative Risk Assessment

LOW	MEDIUM	**HIGH**

Our risk assessment reflects the highly cyclical nature of GM's markets as well as our view of the current and long-term challenges it faces, its highly leveraged balance sheet, intensifying competition, high fixed and legacy costs, and the risk of a strike at a bankrupt major parts supplier.

Quantitative Evaluations

S&P Quality Ranking B-

D	C	**B-**	B	B+	A-	A	A+

Relative Strength Rank WEAK

▌ 14

LOWEST = 1   HIGHEST = 99

Revenue/Earnings Data

Revenue (Million $)

	1Q	2Q	3Q	4Q	Year
2007	43,909	46,812	43,834	--	--
2006	52,376	54,464	49,300	51,209	207,349
2005	45,773	48,469	47,182	51,180	192,604
2004	47,862	49,293	44,934	51,428	193,517
2003	47,146	45,944	43,351	49,084	185,524
2002	46,264	48,265	43,578	48,656	186,763

Earnings Per Share ($)

2007	0.11	1.37	-75.12	E-0.12	E-0.27
2006	1.06	-5.98	-0.26	1.68	-3.50
2005	-2.22	-1.75	-2.94	-11.59	-18.50
2004	2.12	2.42	0.56	-0.17	4.95
2003	2.74	1.57	0.80	Nil	5.03
2002	0.57	2.43	-1.42	1.71	3.35

Fiscal year ended Dec. 31. Next earnings report expected: Mid March. EPS Estimates based on S&P Operating Earnings; historical GAAP earnings are as reported.

Dividend Data (Dates: mm/dd Payment Date: mm/dd/yy)

Amount ($)	Date Decl.	Ex-Div. Date	Stk. of Record	Payment Date
0.250	02/06	02/14	02/16	03/10/07
0.250	05/01	05/09	05/11	06/09/07
0.250	08/07	08/15	08/17	09/10/07
0.250	11/06	11/14	11/16	12/10/07

Dividends have been paid since 1915. Source: Company reports.

Please read the Required Disclosures and Analyst Certification on the last page of this report.

The McGraw-Hill Companies

General Motors Corp.

STANDARD &POOR'S

Business Summary November 15, 2007

CORPORATE OVERVIEW. Due to an adjustment in accounting methods, GM restated filed financial statements and financial information from 2002 through the third quarter of 2006 and delayed filing its full-year 2006 results. While we prefer to not see restatements of past filings, there was no material impact on cash flows, in our view, during the affected periods. However, we are concerned about GM's admission of a lack of effective internal accounting controls. GM is the world's largest manufacturer of cars and trucks. The majority of its business is derived from the automotive industry, but it also has financing and insurance and financial services operations through 49%-owned GMAC, and it produces products and provides services in other industries. Competition has been increasing for this once dominant market leader. With Toyota Motor (TM: hold, $111), already the world's most profitable automaker, in our opinion, steadily and rapidly expanding its global vehicle sales and production, we believe the Japanese company is likely to overtake GM as the undisputed world volume leader in vehicle production in 2007.

IMPACT OF MAJOR DEVELOPMENTS. GM's agreement with UAW should improve the company profits and competitiveness with foreign rivals. However, we do not expect GM to see the benefits from the establishment of a healthcare trust prior to 2010. The trust will managed by the UAW, but initially funded by GM. Also, what is really needed, in our view, is sustained improved demand for its products due to styling, quality and value improvements.

In November 2006, GM sold 51% of GMAC to an investor group. GM believes this will enhance GMAC's credit rating and thereby reduce the unit's borrowing costs, in addition to the funds it raises for the automaker. The downside of the transaction, in our view, is the partial loss of GMAC income contributions.

In October 2005, Delphi Corp. (formerly Delphi Automotive Systems) filed for Chapter 11 bankruptcy protection. Delphi is GM's largest parts supplier. Workers at GM's largest parts supplier have threatened to strike if a wage and benefits agreement cannot be worked out with Delphi. A work stoppage at General Motors in mid-1998 cost GM about $2 billion in lost profits; a strike against Delphi that could halt GM production could be even more costly for the struggling automaker, in our view. However, we think a strike is unlikely.

In November 2006, Kirk Kerkorian's Tracinda Corp. sold its entire 56 million GM share stake. This followed GM's rebuff of a Kerkorian-championed alliance with Renault S.A./Nissan Motors (NSANY: hold, $21) and the subsequent resignation of his representative, Jerome York, from GM's board of directors.

Company Financials Fiscal Year Ended Dec. 31

Per Share Data ($)	2006	2005	2004	2003	2002	2001	2000	1999	1998	1997
Tangible Book Value	NM	18.12	40.35	36.49	NM	1.93	13.60	16.03	6.25	5.80
Cash Flow	15.85	9.38	29.91	29.60	26.03	24.12	30.04	27.20	22.39	31.93
Earnings	-3.50	-18.50	4.95	5.03	3.35	1.77	6.68	8.53	4.18	8.62
S&P Core Earnings	3.48	-11.92	7.11	7.91	-1.49	-5.77	NA	NA	NA	NA
Dividends	1.00	2.00	2.00	2.00	2.00	2.00	2.00	2.00	2.00	2.00
Payout Ratio	NM	NM	40%	40%	60%	113%	30%	23%	48%	23%
Prices:High	36.56	40.80	55.55	54.39	68.17	67.80	94.63	94.88	76.69	72.44
Prices:Low	18.47	18.33	36.90	29.75	30.80	39.17	48.44	59.75	47.06	52.25
P/E Ratio:High	NM	NM	11	11	20	38	14	11	18	8
P/E Ratio:Low	NM	NM	7	6	9	22	7	7	11	6

Income Statement Analysis (Million $)										
Revenue	207,349	192,604	193,517	185,524	186,763	177,260	184,632	176,558	161,315	178,174
Operating Income	20,227	14,606	27,324	26,423	22,733	23,016	30,127	29,115	23,706	30,443
Depreciation	10,950	15,769	14,152	13,978	12,938	12,908	13,411	12,318	12,201	16,616
Interest Expense	16,945	15,768	11,980	9,464	7,715	8,590	9,552	7,750	6,893	6,113
Pretax Income	-4,763	-16,336	1,894	3,593	2,080	1,518	7,164	8,722	4,428	7,714
Effective Tax Rate	NM	NM	NM	20.3%	25.6%	50.6%	33.4%	35.7%	33.0%	13.9%
Net Income	-1,978	-10,458	2,805	2,862	1,736	601	4,452	5,576	2,956	6,698
S&P Core Earnings	1,972	-6,741	4,040	4,510	-838	-3,209	NA	NA	NA	NA

Balance Sheet & Other Financial Data (Million $)										
Cash	24,261	50,452	57,730	54,769	38,274	30,014	21,040	21,250	20,024	22,984
Total Assets	186,192	476,078	479,603	448,507	370,782	323,969	303,100	274,730	257,389	228,888
Long Term Debt	33,067	202,177	207,174	191,133	134,272	104,638	65,843	62,963	52,794	42,194
Total Debt	33,067	285,750	300,279	271,756	201,940	166,314	144,655	131,906	114,372	93,249
Common Equity	-5,441	14,597	27,726	25,268	6,814	19,707	30,175	20,644	14,983	17,505
Capital Expenditures	7,933	8,179	7,753	7,330	7,443	8,631	9,722	7,384	9,618	10,320
Cash Flow	8,972	5,311	16,957	16,840	14,627	13,410	17,753	17,814	15,094	23,216
% Return on Assets	NM	NM	0.6	0.7	0.5	0.2	1.5	2.1	1.2	3.0
% Return on Equity	NM	NM	10.6	17.8	12.7	2.0	17.1	30.8	17.8	32.4
% Long Term Debt of Capitalization	114.8	91.0	85.5	85.2	89.0	79.4	63.8	69.3	71.0	66.6

Data as orig reptd.; bef. results of disc opers/spec. items. Per share data adj. for stk. divs.; EPS diluted. E-Estimated. NA-Not Available. NM-Not Meaningful. NR-Not Ranked. UR-Under Review.

Office: 300 Renaissance Center, Detroit, MI 48265-3000.
Telephone: 313-556-5000.
Website: http://www.gm.com
Chrmn & CEO: G.R. Wagoner, Jr.

Vice Chrmn: R.A. Lutz
Vice Chrmn & CFO: F.A. Henderson
Chief Acctg Officer & Cntlr: N.S. Cyprus
Treas: W.G. Borst

Board Members: P. Barnevik, E. Bowles, J. H. Bryan, A. Codina, E. B. Davis, G. M. Fisher, K. Katen, K. Kresa, E. J. Kullman, P. A. Laskawy, K. V. Marinello, E. Pfeiffer, G. R. Wagoner, Jr.
Founded: 1908
Domicile: Delaware
Employees: 280,000

The McGraw-Hill Companies

Genuine Parts Co

STANDARD &POOR'S

S&P Recommendation HOLD ★★★☆☆	**Price** $47.72 (as of Nov 23, 2007)	**12-Mo. Target Price** $53.00	**Investment Style** Large-Cap Blend

GICS Sector Consumer Discretionary
Sub-Industry Distributors

Summary This company is a leading wholesale distributor of automotive replacement parts, industrial parts and supplies, and office products.

Key Stock Statistics (Source S&P, Vickers, company reports)

52-Wk Range	$51.68– 46.00	S&P Oper. EPS 2007**E**	2.99	Market Capitalization(B)	$8.109	Beta	0.56
Trailing 12-Month EPS	$2.93	S&P Oper. EPS 2008**E**	3.30	Yield (%)	3.06	S&P 3-Yr. Proj. EPS CAGR(%)	10.00
Trailing 12-Month P/E	16.3	P/E on S&P Oper. EPS 2007**E**	16.0	Dividend Rate/Share	$1.46	S&P Credit Rating	NA
$10K Invested 5 Yrs Ago	$17,781	Common Shares Outstg. (M)	169.9	Institutional Ownership (%)	75		

Price Performance

30-Week Mov. Avg. · · · 10-Week Mov. Avg. - - GAAP Earnings vs. Previous Year Volume Above Avg. STARS
12-Mo. Target Price — Relative Strength — ▲ Up ▼ Down ► No Change Below Avg.

Options: ASE, P, Ph

Analysis prepared by **Efraim Levy, CFA** on October 22, 2007, when the stock traded at **$ 48.06**.

Highlights

► We expect revenues to rise 7% in 2008 following forecasted 4% growth in 2007. We see sales gains in all four segments. We think pricing will remain competitive, and we foresee gross margins rising modestly as GPC divests some low-margin businesses and cuts costs. The gross margin improvement should be partially offset, as we see other lower margin businesses growing faster than higher margin segments.

► We expect longer-term prospects for GPC's auto parts segment to be enhanced by the rising number and increasing complexity of vehicles. The average vehicle in the U.S. is currently more than eight years old. We believe GPC will benefit from an expanding market share, as long-term industry consolidation continues to drive out smaller participants. We also foresee GPC as likely to use its distribution strength to leverage sales of acquired parts companies.

► What we view as GPC's solid balance sheet, low debt, and strong cash flow are resources that could be used to accelerate earnings growth in the longer term. We see GPC using cash flow to repurchase shares, invest in growing the business, make modest-sized acquisitions, and increase its dividend.

Investment Rationale/Risk

► Based on our 2008 EPS estimate, the stock's recent P/E of about 15X is above the average for peers and appropriate, in our view, given the company's greater earnings stability. Earnings quality appears high to us, and we look for only minor adjustments to reported EPS using Standard & Poor's Core Earnings methodology. An above-average dividend yield adds to GPC's total return potential.

► Risks to our recommendation and target price include weaker than expected demand for the company's products, and a less than anticipated improvement in operating margins.

► Our 12-month target price of $53 is based on a blend of our relative and DCF metrics. On a relative basis, we assume a P/E of about 17.9X applied to our 2008 EPS estimate of $3.30, reflecting historical P/E comparisons and leading to a value of about $59. Our DCF model, which assumes a weighted average cost of capital of 9.8%, a compound annual growth rate of 7.6% over the next 15 years, and a terminal growth rate of 3%, calculates an intrinsic value near $47.

Qualitative Risk Assessment

LOW	MEDIUM	HIGH

Our risk assessment reflects GPC's long-term record of rising sales and earnings and what we view as strong corporate leadership and a healthy balance sheet.

Quantitative Evaluations

S&P Quality Ranking A

D	C	B-	B	B+	A-	A	A+

Relative Strength Rank MODERATE

67

LOWEST = 1   HIGHEST = 99

Revenue/Earnings Data

Revenue (Million $)

	1Q	2Q	3Q	4Q	Year
2007	2,649	2,770	2,798	--	--
2006	2,554	2,662	2,700	2,543	10,458
2005	2,342	2,476	2,556	2,410	9,783
2004	2,197	2,298	2,349	2,253	9,097
2003	2,022	2,153	2,189	2,085	8,449
2002	1,978	2,131	2,157	1,994	8,259

Earnings Per Share ($)

2007	0.71	0.76	0.76	E0.77	E2.99
2006	0.66	0.70	0.71	0.70	2.76
2005	0.61	0.63	0.63	0.63	2.50
2004	0.57	0.58	0.56	0.55	2.25
2003	0.51	0.52	0.51	0.50	2.03
2002	0.50	0.55	0.54	0.52	2.10

Fiscal year ended Dec. 31. Next earnings report expected: Mid February. EPS Estimates based on S&P Operating Earnings; historical GAAP earnings are as reported.

Dividend Data (Dates: mm/dd Payment Date: mm/dd/yy)

Amount ($)	Date Decl.	Ex-Div. Date	Stk. of Record	Payment Date
0.365	02/19	03/07	03/09	04/02/07
0.365	04/23	06/06	06/08	07/02/07
0.365	08/20	09/05	09/07	10/01/07
0.365	11/19	12/05	12/07	01/02/08

Dividends have been paid since 1948. Source: Company reports.

The McGraw-Hill Companies

Genuine Parts Co

Business Summary October 22, 2007

CORPORATE OVERVIEW. Genuine Parts is the leading independent U.S. distributor of automotive replacement parts. It operates 58 NAPA warehouse distribution centers in the U.S., about 1,100 company-owned jobbing stores, five Rayloc auto parts rebuilding plants, four Balkamp distribution centers, and four Johnson Industries facilities. The company has been expanding via a combination of internal growth and acquisitions.

The automotive parts segment (49% of 2006 revenues, 47% of profits) serves about 5,800 NAPA Auto Parts stores, including about 1,100 company-owned stores, selling to garages, service stations, car and truck dealers, fleet operators, leasing companies, bus and truck lines, etc.

The industrial parts segment (30%, 30%) distributes around three million industrial replacement parts and related supply items, including bearings, power transmission equipment replacement parts, including hydraulic and pneu-

matic products, material handling components, agricultural and irrigation equipment, and related items from locations in the U.S. and Canada.

Through S. P. Richards Co., the office products group (17%, 20%) distributes more than 40,000 office product items, including information processing supplies and office furniture, machines and supplies to office suppliers, from facilities in the U.S. and Canada.

The EIS electrical/electronics materials group (4%, 3%) was formed via the 1998 acquisition of EIS, Inc., for $200 million. EIS is a wholesale distributor of material and supplies to the electrical and electronic industries.

Company Financials Fiscal Year Ended Dec. 31

Per Share Data ($)	2006	2005	2004	2003	2002	2001	2000	1999	1998	1997
Tangible Book Value	4.82	15.21	14.21	12.95	11.88	10.97	10.50	9.80	9.52	10.39
Cash Flow	3.18	2.87	2.61	2.42	2.50	2.21	2.72	2.61	2.36	2.23
Earnings	2.76	2.50	2.25	2.03	2.10	1.71	2.20	2.11	1.98	1.90
S&P Core Earnings	2.76	2.40	2.22	1.95	1.80	1.53	NA	NA	NA	NA
Dividends	1.35	1.25	1.20	1.18	1.16	1.14	1.10	1.03	0.99	0.96
Payout Ratio	49%	50%	53%	58%	55%	67%	50%	49%	50%	51%
Prices:High	48.34	46.64	44.32	33.75	38.80	37.94	26.69	35.75	38.25	35.88
Prices:Low	40.00	40.75	32.03	27.20	27.10	23.91	18.25	22.25	28.25	28.67
P/E Ratio:High	18	19	20	17	18	22	12	17	19	19
P/E Ratio:Low	14	16	14	13	13	14	8	11	14	15

Income Statement Analysis (Million $)	2006	2005	2004	2003	2002	2001	2000	1999	1998	1997
Revenue	10,458	9,783	9,097	8,449	8,259	8,221	8,370	7,982	6,614	6,005
Operating Income	870	804	698	641	676	656	739	718	658	624
Depreciation	73.4	65.5	62.2	69.0	70.2	85.8	92.3	90.0	69.3	58.9
Interest Expense	31.6	29.6	Nil	Nil	Nil	Nil	Nil	Nil	Nil	Nil
Pretax Income	771	709	636	572	606	496	647	628	589	566
Effective Tax Rate	38.3%	38.3%	37.8%	38.1%	39.3%	40.1%	40.4%	39.9%	39.6%	39.5%
Net Income	475	437	396	354	368	297	385	378	356	342
S&P Core Earnings	475	420	388	339	316	265	NA	NA	NA	NA

Balance Sheet & Other Financial Data (Million $)	2006	2005	2004	2003	2002	2001	2000	1999	1998	1997
Cash	136	189	135	15.4	20.0	85.8	27.7	45.7	85.0	72.8
Current Assets	3,835	3,807	3,633	3,418	3,336	3,146	3,019	2,895	2,683	2,094
Total Assets	4,497	4,772	4,455	4,116	4,020	4,207	4,142	3,930	3,600	2,754
Current Liabilities	1,199	1,249	1,133	1,017	1,070	919	988	916	818	557
Long Term Debt	500	500	500	625	675	836	771	702	589	210
Common Equity	2,550	2,694	2,544	2,312	2,130	2,345	2,261	2,178	2,053	1,859
Total Capital	3,111	3,408	3,212	3,100	2,950	3,287	3,154	3,014	2,782	2,198
Capital Expenditures	126	85.7	72.1	73.9	64.8	41.9	71.1	88.3	88.2	90.4
Cash Flow	549	503	458	423	438	383	478	468	425	401
Current Ratio	3.2	3.0	3.2	3.4	3.1	3.4	3.1	3.2	3.3	3.8
% Long Term Debt of Capitalization	16.1	14.7	15.6	20.2	22.9	25.4	24.4	23.3	21.1	9.5
% Net Income of Revenue	4.5	4.5	4.3	4.2	4.4	3.6	4.6	4.7	5.4	5.7
% Return on Assets	10.3	9.5	9.2	8.6	8.9	7.1	9.5	10.0	11.2	13.0
% Return on Equity	18.1	16.7	16.3	15.9	16.4	12.9	17.4	17.9	18.2	19.1

Data as orig reptd.; bef. results of disc opers/spec. items. Per share data adj. for stk. divs.; EPS diluted. E-Estimated. NA-Not Available. NM-Not Meaningful. NR-Not Ranked. UR-Under Review.

Office: 2999 Circle 75 Pkwy , Atlanta, GA 30339.
Telephone: 770-953-1700.
Website: http://www.genpt.com
Chrmn, Pres & CEO: T.C. Gallagher

Investor Contact: J.W. Nix (770-953-1700)
Vice Chrmn, EVP & CFO: J.W. Nix
SVP & Secy: C.B. Yancey

Board Members: M. B. Bullock, R. W. Courts, II, J. Douville, T. C. Gallagher, G. C. Guynn, J. D. Johns, M. M. Johns, J. H. Lanier, W. B. Needham, J. W. Nix, L. L. Prince, G. W. Rollins, L. G. Steiner

Founded: 1928
Domicile: Georgia
Employees: 32,000

Genworth Financial Inc

STANDARD &POOR'S

S&P Recommendation HOLD ★ ★ ★ ☆ ☆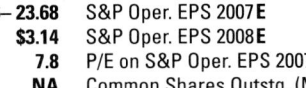

Price	12-Mo. Target Price	Investment Style
$24.60 (as of Nov 23, 2007)	**$30.00**	Large-Cap Blend

GICS Sector Financials
Sub-Industry Multi-line Insurance

Summary This insurance holding company serves lifestyle protection, retirement income, investment and mortgage insurance needs around the world.

Key Stock Statistics (Source S&P, Vickers, company reports)

52-Wk Range	**$37.16– 23.68**	S&P Oper. EPS 2007**E**	3.05	Market Capitalization(B)	**$10.890**	Beta 0.96
Trailing 12-Month EPS	**$3.14**	S&P Oper. EPS 2008**E**	3.30	Yield (%)	**1.63**	S&P 3-Yr. Proj. EPS CAGR(%) 13.00
Trailing 12-Month P/E	**7.8**	P/E on S&P Oper. EPS 2007**E**	8.1	Dividend Rate/Share	**$0.40**	S&P Credit Rating A
$10K Invested 5 Yrs Ago	**NA**	Common Shares Outstg. (M)	442.7	Institutional Ownership (%)	**99**	

Price Performance

30-Week Mov. Avg. · · · 10-Week Mov. Avg. - - **GAAP Earnings vs. Previous Year** Volume Above Avg. STARS
12-Mo. Target Price — Relative Strength — ▲ Up ▼ Down ► No Change Below Avg. ★

Options: ASE, P, Ph

Analysis prepared by **Tanjila Shafi** on November 12, 2007, when the stock traded at **$ 25.39**.

Highlights

➤ We believe that revenues will experience high single growth in 2008, driven by strength in GNW's retirement and protection and international businesses. We expect operating earnings in the retirement and protection business will benefit from strong growth in universal life sales, which should offset a challenging environment for term life and long-term care products. We also look for GNW to benefit from growth in its fee-based businesses.

➤ We expect operating earnings for the international business to benefit from the strong growth we foresee in the international mortgage unit, based on GNW's aggressive expansion into Europe, and growth in the payment protection business. However, we are concerned that disruptions in the housing environment will impede earnings growth at its U.S. mortgage insurance business. We see GNW reaching its management goal's of a 12% ROE by year-end 2008.

➤ We estimate a 4.8% increase in operating EPS in 2008, to $3.05 from $2.91 in 2006. Our operating EPS projection for 2008 is $3.30.

Investment Rationale/Risk

➤ Although we believe that the business units of GNW are fundamentally sound, we have a hold recommendation on the shares due to a weak housing market and our concerns regarding the overall mortgage credit environment, which may have a negative impact on its mortgage-related, and, specifically, subprime exposure. The company has subprime exposure in both its mortgage insurance business and its investments. Also, we expect that market concerns regarding the credit environment will result in share price volatility. However, we believe that the company will be able to weather housing and credit market problems, given what we see as its conservative business practices and the quality of its investment portfolio.

➤ Risks to our recommendation and target price include a low interest rate environment; increased investment portfolio risks; high concentrations of product line sales associated with certain third parties; and a prolonged slowdown in the housing market.

➤ Our 12-month target price is $30, 9.1X our 2008 operating EPS estimate, and below its historical multiples.

Qualitative Risk Assessment

LOW	MEDIUM	HIGH

Our risk assessment reflects what we see as GNW's strong balance sheet and large amount of excess capital. Also, we think the company will benefit from improved financial flexibility now that GE has fully divested its shares of GNW.

Quantitative Evaluations

S&P Quality Ranking NR

D	C	B-	B	B+	A-	A	A+

Relative Strength Rank WEAK

27

LOWEST = 1   HIGHEST = 99

Revenue/Earnings Data

Revenue (Million $)

	1Q	2Q	3Q	4Q	Year
2007	2,710	2,765	2,875	--	--
2006	2,625	2,754	2,804	2,846	11,029
2005	2,611	2,610	2,628	2,655	10,504
2004	3,024	2,921	2,470	2,642	11,057
2003	--	--	--	--	9,775
2002	--	--	--	--	--

Earnings Per Share ($)

2007	0.69	0.70	0.76	E0.69	E3.05
2006	0.69	0.68	0.65	0.81	2.83
2005	0.65	0.60	0.64	0.64	2.52
2004	0.53	0.55	0.55	0.70	2.34
2003	--	--	--	--	1.82
2002	--	--	--	--	--

Fiscal year ended Dec. 31. Next earnings report expected: Early February. EPS Estimates based on S&P Operating Earnings; historical GAAP earnings are as reported.

Dividend Data (Dates: mm/dd Payment Date: mm/dd/yy)

Amount ($)	Date Decl.	Ex-Div. Date	Stk. of Record	Payment Date
0.090	12/08	01/10	01/12	01/29/07
0.090	03/20	04/10	04/12	04/27/07
0.090	05/15	07/10	07/12	07/27/07
0.100	09/21	10/10	10/12	10/29/07

Dividends have been paid since 2004. Source: Company reports.

Genworth Financial Inc

STANDARD &POOR'S

Business Summary November 12, 2007

CORPORATE OVERVIEW. Genworth Financial, Inc., carved out from General Electric (GE) in May 2004, is a U.S. insurance company with an expanding international presence. As of February 2007, GNW had operations in 25 countries, and believed it was one of the largest providers of private mortgage insurance outside the U.S. based on new insurance written. According to reports by VARDS, LIMRA International, and Inside Mortgage Finance magazine, in 2005, GNW was the largest U.S. provider of variable income annuities and the second-largest provider of fixed immediate annuities, based on total premiums and deposits, and the fifth-largest provider of mortgage insurance, based on new insurance written.

The company conducts its business through three major segments. The first segment is retirement and protection (72% of 2006 total revenues, 70% of 2005 total revenues). This segment is comprised of managed money (1.9%, 1.3%); retirement income (21%, 24%); spread-based institutional (5.6%, 4.5%); life insurance (18%, 17%); and long-term care (26%, 24%). The second segment is international (21%, 21%). This segment consists of the company's mortgage

insurance business in Canada, Australia, and Europe, in addition to proposals for other target countries for mortgage insurance. The segment also includes payment protection insurance, which helps consumers meet their payment obligations in the event of illness, involuntary unemployment, disability or death. The third segment is U.S. mortgage insurance (6.3%, 6.2%). The mortgage insurance business facilitates home ownership by enabling borrowers to buy homes with low down-payment mortgages. These products also help financial institutions manage their capital efficiently by reducing the capital required for low down-payment mortgages. The company also has a corporate and other segment, which includes unallocated corporate income and expenses, results of a small, non-core business, and most interest and other financing expenses.

Company Financials Fiscal Year Ended Dec. 31

Per Share Data ($)	2006	2005	2004	2003	2002	2001	2000	1999	1998	1997
Tangible Book Value	24.20	24.51	21.69	20.18	NA	NA	NA	NA	NA	NA
Operating Earnings	NA	NA	NA	NA	NA	NA	NA	NA	NA	NA
Earnings	2.83	2.52	2.34	1.82	NA	NA	NA	NA	NA	NA
S&P Core Earnings	2.92	2.52	2.29	1.96	NA	NA	NA	NA	NA	NA
Dividends	0.32	0.27	0.07	NA	NA	NA	NA	NA	NA	NA
Relative Payout	11%	11%	3%	NA	NA	NA	NA	NA	NA	NA
Prices:High	36.47	35.25	27.84	NA	NA	NA	NA	NA	NA	NA
Prices:Low	31.00	25.72	18.75	NA	NA	NA	NA	NA	NA	NA
P/E Ratio:High	13	14	12	NA	NA	NA	NA	NA	NA	NA
P/E Ratio:Low	11	10	8	NA	NA	NA	NA	NA	NA	NA

Income Statement Analysis (Million $)										
Life Insurance in Force	NA	NA	NA	NA	NA	NA	NA	NA	NA	NA
Premium Income:Life A & H	NA	NA	NA	6,252	NA	NA	NA	NA	NA	NA
Premium Income:Casualty/Property.	NA	NA	NA	Nil	NA	NA	NA	NA	NA	NA
Net Investment Income	3,837	3,536	3,648	2,928	NA	NA	NA	NA	NA	NA
Total Revenue	11,029	10,504	11,057	9,775	NA	NA	NA	NA	NA	NA
Pretax Income	1,918	1,798	1,638	1,263	NA	NA	NA	NA	NA	NA
Net Operating Income	NA	NA	NA	NA	NA	NA	NA	NA	NA	NA
Net Income	1,324	1,221	1,145	892	NA	NA	NA	NA	NA	NA
S&P Core Earnings	1,369	1,221	1,126	956	NA	NA	NA	NA	NA	NA

Balance Sheet & Other Financial Data (Million $)										
Cash & Equivalent	3,222	2,608	2,125	1,630	NA	NA	NA	NA	NA	NA
Premiums Due	NA	NA	NA	NA	NA	NA	NA	NA	NA	NA
Investment Assets:Bonds	55,448	53,791	52,424	50,081	NA	NA	NA	NA	NA	NA
Investment Assets:Stocks	NA	367	374	387	NA	NA	NA	NA	NA	NA
Investment Assets:Loans	9,985	8,908	7,275	6,794	NA	NA	NA	NA	NA	NA
Investment Assets:Total	73,519	66,573	65,747	61,749	NA	NA	NA	NA	NA	NA
Deferred Policy Costs	NA	5,586	5,020	4,421	NA	NA	NA	NA	NA	NA
Total Assets	110,871	105,292	103,878	100,216	NA	NA	NA	NA	NA	NA
Debt	3,921	3,336	3,042	3,016	NA	NA	NA	NA	NA	NA
Common Equity	13,330	13,310	12,866	12,258	NA	NA	NA	NA	NA	NA
Combined Loss-Expense Ratio	NA	NA	NA	NA	NA	NA	NA	NA	NA	NA
% Return on Revenue	12.0	11.6	10.4	9.1	NA	NA	NA	NA	NA	NA
% Return on Equity	2.2	9.3	8.0	NA	NA	NA	NA	NA	NA	NA
% Investment Yield	NA	NA	NA	NA	NA	NA	NA	NA	NA	NA

Data as orig reptd.; bef. results of disc opers/spec. items. Per share data adj. for stk. divs.; EPS diluted. E-Estimated. NA-Not Available. NM-Not Meaningful. NR-Not Ranked. UR-Under Review.

Office: 6620 West Broad Street, Richmond, VA 23230.
Telephone: 804-281-6000.
Email: investorinfo@genworth.com
Website: http://www.genworth.com

Chrmn, Pres & CEO: M.D. Fraizer
SVP & CFO: P.B. Kelleher
SVP, Secy & General Counsel: L.E. Roday
Investor Contact: C. English (804-662-2614)

Board Members: F. J. Borelli, M. D. Fraizer, N. J. Karch, J. R. Kerrey, S. T. Naqvi, J. A. Parke, J. S. Riepe, B. A. Toan, T. B. Wheeler

Founded: 2003
Domicile: Delaware
Employees: 7,200

Genzyme Corp

STANDARD &POOR'S

S&P Recommendation BUY ★★★★☆	Price $72.17 (as of Nov 23, 2007)	12-Mo. Target Price $85.00	Investment Style Large-Cap Growth

GICS Sector Health Care
Sub-Industry Biotechnology

Summary This biopharmaceutical concern makes and markets human therapeutic and diagnostic products. Its largest selling product is Cerezyme, a drug to treat Gaucher disease.

Key Stock Statistics (Source S&P, Vickers, company reports)

52-Wk Range	$76.90–58.71	S&P Oper. EPS 2007**E**	2.84	Market Capitalization(B)	$19.031	Beta	1.58
Trailing 12-Month EPS	$0.46	S&P Oper. EPS 2008**E**	3.38	Yield (%)	Nil	S&P 3-Yr. Proj. EPS CAGR(%)	20.00
Trailing 12-Month P/E	NM	P/E on S&P Oper. EPS 2007**E**	25.4	Dividend Rate/Share	Nil	S&P Credit Rating	BBB
$10K Invested 5 Yrs Ago	$23,913	Common Shares Outstg. (M)	263.7	Institutional Ownership (%)	89		

Price Performance

30-Week Mov. Avg. · · · 10-Week Mov. Avg. – **GAAP Earnings vs. Previous Year** Volume Above Avg. ▌▌▌ STARS
12-Mo. Target Price — Relative Strength — ▲ Up ▼ Down ▶ No Change Below Avg. ▌▌▌ ★

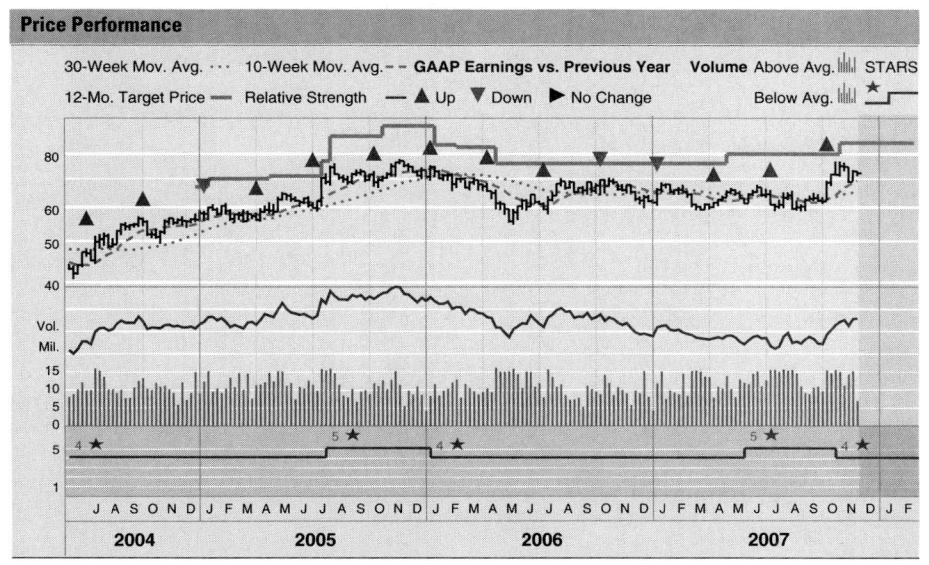

Options: ASE, CBOE, P, Ph

Analysis prepared by **Steven Silver** on October 25, 2007, when the stock traded at **$ 76.22**.

Highlights

➤ Genzyme delivered 19% higher third quarter sales, as most key products experienced double-digit year-over-year growth, led by Renagel, Cerezyme and Fabrazyme, up 14%, 13% and 12%, respectively. Myozyme sales of $53 million again showed solid growth, 15% above the preceding quarter. With clinical progress of Renvela, Synvisc-One and GENZ-112638, we see GENZ developing next-generation versions of key drugs to support future sales. We see 2007 revenues up about 18%, to $3.75 billion, and a further 15% rise in 2008, to $4.3 billion.

➤ In the third quarter, GENZ continued to maintain operating leverage, as revenues grew 19% while operating expenses rose only 14%. We see this trend continuing, as we see a robust late-stage pipeline enhancing margins by expanding sales within an established global infrastructure. Further, we see strong operational cash flows ($280 million in the third quarter) funding a $1.5 billion share repurchase program and further strategic acquisitions.

➤ Our 2007 and 2008 EPS estimates are $2.84 and $3.38. We expect GENZ to execute on its 20% goal for annual EPS growth through 2011.

Investment Rationale/Risk

➤ We consider Genzyme among the most diversified biotechs, with solid core product growth, a promising late-stage pipeline, and a strong financial position ($1.4 billion in cash at September 30, 2007). We believe GENZ is well positioned to expand and diversify its product portfolio, and we project long-term EPS growth of 20%. We see Mozobil as a key driver, in both oncology and transplant segments after positive Phase III data, and we see FDA approval for single-injection Synvisc-One in 2008. We view favorably recent developments including FDA approval of Renvela and label expansion for Campath, and the closing of the Bioenvision acquisition to gain worldwide rights to Clolar.

➤ Risks to our recommendation and target price include clinical or regulatory setbacks to the new product portfolio, and any slowdown in sales growth for key marketed products.

➤ Our 12-month target price of $85 applies a PEG multiple of 1.25X to our 20% long-term growth rate and our 2008 EPS estimate of $3.38. We think this valuation is warranted, given our view of diverse revenue streams and solid cash flow generation.

Qualitative Risk Assessment

LOW	MEDIUM	HIGH

Our risk assessment reflects our belief that Genzyme's portfolio of therapeutic products -- as well as its diagnostic business -- is diverse. With regard to the firm's individual drugs of importance, we think Renagel/Renvela faces the most immediate competition, and we see an increasingly competitive landscape for the foreseeable future, which may offset the benefits of product diversity.

Quantitative Evaluations

S&P Quality Ranking B-

D	C	B-	B	B+	A-	A	A+

Relative Strength Rank STRONG

89

LOWEST = 1   HIGHEST = 99

Revenue/Earnings Data

Revenue (Million $)

	1Q	2Q	3Q	4Q	Year
2007	883.2	933.4	960.2	--	--
2006	730.8	793.4	808.6	854.2	3,187
2005	630.0	668.1	708.1	728.7	2,735
2004	491.3	549.6	569.2	591.1	2,201
2003	381.9	418.9	437.0	476.1	1,714
2002	242.2	267.2	272.8	298.1	1,080

Earnings Per Share ($)

2007	0.57	0.51	0.58	E0.68	E2.84
2006	0.37	0.49	0.06	-1.02	-0.06
2005	0.36	0.46	0.43	0.39	1.65
2004	0.29	0.33	0.41	-0.68	0.37
2003	0.28	0.32	-0.43	0.25	0.42
2002	0.14	0.23	0.25	0.20	0.81

Fiscal year ended Dec. 31. Next earnings report expected: Mid February. EPS Estimates based on S&P Operating Earnings; historical GAAP earnings are as reported.

Dividend Data

No cash dividends have been paid.

The McGraw-Hill Companies

Genzyme Corp

STANDARD
&POOR'S

Business Summary October 25, 2007

CORPORATE OVERVIEW. Genzyme develops, manufactures and markets therapeutic and diagnostic products. GENZ's leading product is Cerezyme, an enzyme replacement therapy (ERT) for Gaucher disease, a debilitating genetic disorder causing fatigue, anemia and bone erosion. In 2006, Cerezyme sales totaled $1.0 billion (up from $933 million in 2005), accounting for 35% of total sales, down from 42%. In May 2007, GENZ announced positive initial Phase II data on GENZ-112638, an oral therapy for Gaucher disease for which Genzyme plans to meet with the FDA to discuss an expedited development program.

Renagel, which reduces elevated serum phosphorus levels in kidney dialysis patients, generated $515 million in 2006 sales (from $418 million). In April 2007, GENZ announced positive data for Renvela, a buffered form of Renagel and the FDA approved Renvela in October 2007. GENZ expects to launch Renvela in early 2008. Also in October 2007, an FDA renal committee recommended approval for Renagel/Renvela in earlier pre-dialysis stages of kidney disease.

Fabrazyme is approved in both Europe and the U.S. for the treatment of Fabry

disease, a rare genetic disorder. Fabrazyme sales were $359 million in 2006. Aldurazyme, an ERT for MPS-I, was approved by the FDA in April 2003. Aldurazyme is partnered with BioMarin through a 50%-owned joint venture. GENZ has developed Myozyme, for treating Pompe disease, a rare and often fatal disorder with an estimated worldwide patent population of less than 10,000. Myozyme was launched in the U.S. and Europe in mid-2006 and ended 2006 with more than 550 patients in 35 countries. Synvisc is an injectable biomaterial to treat knee osteoarthritis by improving joint lubrication. Synvisc sales were $233 million in 2006, compared with $219 million in the previous year. A follow-on version, Synvisc-One, showed positive Phase III results and is under FDA review while candidate Hylastan failed its Phase III trial in July 2007.

Company Financials Fiscal Year Ended Dec. 31

Per Share Data ($)	2006	2005	2004	2003	2002	2001	2000	1999	1998	1997
Tangible Book Value	10.91	7.99	8.11	6.31	NM	6.10	4.05	5.54	5.56	4.75
Cash Flow	2.00	2.67	1.24	0.41	1.16	0.75	0.91	1.27	1.02	0.77
Earnings	-0.06	1.65	0.37	0.42	0.81	0.19	0.68	1.00	0.74	0.49
S&P Core Earnings	0.32	1.23	-0.03	-0.26	0.59	0.02	NA	NA	NA	NA
Dividends	Nil	Nil	Nil	Nil	Nil	Nil	Nil	Nil	0.01	Nil
Payout Ratio	Nil	Nil	Nil	Nil	Nil	Nil	Nil	Nil	1%	Nil
Prices:High	75.34	77.82	59.14	52.45	58.55	64.00	51.88	31.56	25.00	16.50
Prices:Low	54.64	55.15	40.67	28.45	15.64	34.34	19.84	15.38	11.75	10.38
P/E Ratio:High	NM	47	NM	NM	72	NM	77	32	34	34
P/E Ratio:Low	NM	33	NM	NM	19	NM	29	15	16	21

Income Statement Analysis (Million $)										
Revenue	3,187	2,735	2,201	1,714	1,080	982	752	635	673	597
Operating Income	913	915	717	463	318	380	-185	280	185	140
Depreciation	541	285	205	160	96.0	118	41.2	50.2	45.8	43.7
Interest Expense	15.5	19.6	38.2	26.6	17.8	23.2	14.2	19.9	17.1	8.11
Pretax Income	-63.1	641	222	2.82	207	56.5	-179	226	164	90.6
Effective Tax Rate	NM	29.2%	63.7%	NM	27.3%	93.1%	51.9%	37.3%	38.2%	37.1%
Net Income	-16.8	441	86.5	-67.6	151	3.88	85.9	142	101	57.0
S&P Core Earnings	90.4	326	-6.61	-61.0	125	5.25	NA	NA	NA	NA

Balance Sheet & Other Financial Data (Million $)										
Cash	492	292	481	293	373	167	136	94.5	100	66.3
Current Assets	1,990	1,665	1,634	1,323	1,100	721	605	605	610	406
Total Assets	7,191	6,879	6,069	5,005	3,556	3,225	2,499	1,400	1,646	1,203
Current Liabilities	651	550	624	392	275	243	167	117	197	97.5
Long Term Debt	810	816	811	1,415	600	600	454	273	275	118
Common Equity	5,661	5,150	4,380	2,936	2,586	2,280	1,750	1,008	1,167	981
Total Capital	6,481	6,301	5,417	4,558	3,268	2,961	2,329	1,280	1,442	1,099
Capital Expenditures	334	19.2	187	260	220	171	72.6	52.9	55.3	28.5
Cash Flow	524	726	292	92.9	247	122	127	192	147	101
Current Ratio	3.1	3.0	2.6	3.4	4.0	3.0	3.6	5.2	3.1	4.2
% Long Term Debt of Capitalization	12.5	12.9	15.0	30.1	18.4	20.3	31.1	21.3	19.1	10.7
% Net Income of Revenue	NM	16.1	3.9	NM	14.0	0.4	11.4	22.4	15.0	9.5
% Return on Assets	NM	6.8	1.6	NM	4.4	0.2	4.0	10.1	7.1	4.7
% Return on Equity	NM	9.3	2.4	NM	6.2	0.1	5.5	14.6	9.4	6.1

Data as orig reptd.; bef. results of disc opers/spec. items. Per share data adj. for stk. divs.; EPS diluted. E-Estimated. NA-Not Available. NM-Not Meaningful. NR-Not Ranked. UR-Under Review.

Office: 500 Kendall St, Cambridge, MA 02142-1108.
Telephone: 617-252-7570.
Email: information@genzyme.com
Website: http://www.genzyme.com

Chrmn, Pres & CEO: H.A. Termeer
EVP, CFO & Chief Acctg Officer: M.S. Wyzga
EVP & Secy: P. Wirth
SVP & CSO: A.E. Smith

Investor Contact: K. Galfetti (617-768-6563)
Board Members: D. A. Berthiaume, H. E. Blair, G. K. Boudreaux, R. J. Carpenter, C. L. Cooney, V. J. Dzau, C. Mack, III, R. F. Syron, H. A. Termeer

Founded: 1991
Domicile: Massachusetts
Employees: 9,000

The McGraw-Hill Companies

STANDARD &POOR'S

Gilead Sciences Inc

S&P Recommendation **BUY** ★★★★☆	Price $43.32 (as of Nov 23, 2007)	12-Mo. Target Price $49.00	Investment Style Large-Cap Growth

GICS Sector Health Care
Sub-Industry Biotechnology

Summary This biopharmaceutical company is engaged in the discovery, development and commercialization of treatments to fight viral, bacterial and fungal infections.

Key Stock Statistics (Source S&P, Vickers, company reports)

52-Wk Range	$47.65– 30.96	S&P Oper. EPS 2007**E**	1.70	Market Capitalization(B)	$40.130	Beta	0.92
Trailing 12-Month EPS	$-0.52	S&P Oper. EPS 2008**E**	1.95	Yield (%)	Nil	S&P 3-Yr. Proj. EPS CAGR(%)	20.00
Trailing 12-Month P/E	NM	P/E on S&P Oper. EPS 2007**E**	25.5	Dividend Rate/Share	Nil	S&P Credit Rating	NA
$10K Invested 5 Yrs Ago	$43,902	Common Shares Outstg. (M)	926.4	Institutional Ownership (%)	92		

Price Performance

- 30-Week Mov. Avg. · · · 10-Week Mov. Avg. - - - **GAAP Earnings vs. Previous Year** Volume Above Avg. STARS
- 12-Mo. Target Price — Relative Strength — ▲ Up ▼ Down ► No Change Below Avg. ★

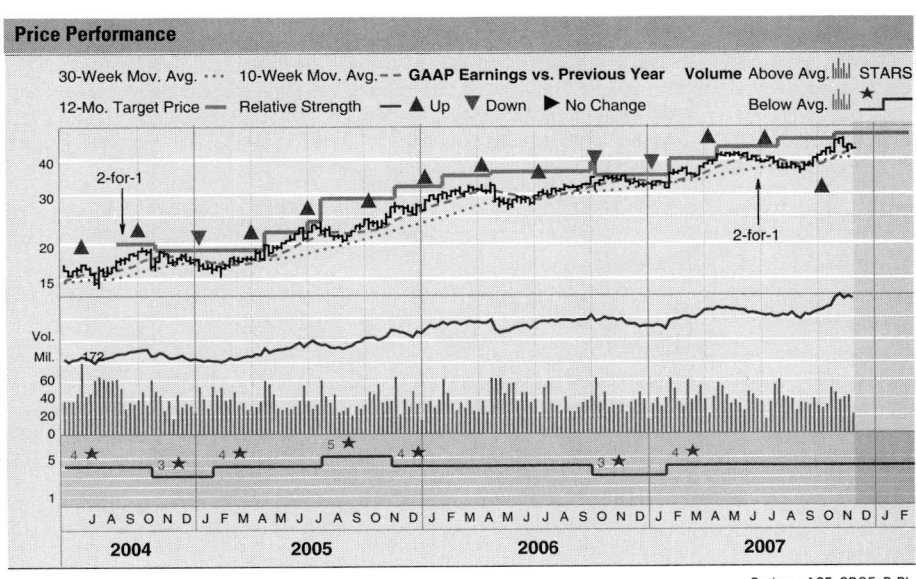

Options: ASE, CBOE, P, Ph

Analysis prepared by **Steven Silver** on October 22, 2007, when the stock traded at **$ 42.69**.

Highlights

➤ GILD's third quarter operating results exceeded our expectations. Truvada sales in Europe rose by 83% while U.S. Atripla sales more than tripled over 2006's third quarter. We expect EU Atripla approval near year end, and expect migration from Truvada to Atripla as the product rolls out across 2008 and beyond. GILD guided to the high end of 2007 product sales estimate of $3.6-$3.7 billion, and we see sales of $3.71 billion. We expect a further 27% increase in 2008 product sales, to $4.7 billion.

➤ We continue to view GILD's expense management favorably, despite year-over-year marketing and R&D expenses 31% and 50% higher in the third quarter, respectively, We see a strong late-stage pipeline in Aztreonam lysine and Darusentan, and earlier-stage candidates in HIV and growing Hepatitis-C market. Current operations drove operational cash flows of $251 million in the third quarter and $1.25 billion in the nine month period, and we see this positioning GILD for product growth, pipeline investment and share repurchases.

➤ Based on our view of continued strength in the HIV franchise, our 2007 EPS estimate is $1.70. Our 2008 EPS estimate is $1.95.

Investment Rationale/Risk

➤ We continue to view GILD's fundamentals among the strongest in the biotech industry. While HIV sales still account for over 80% of product sales, we see diversification from Letairis and Aztreonam lysine beginning to ease reliance on HIV sales in 2008. Initial Letairis sales of $6 million after June FDA approval disappointed us, but we see efforts to streamline safety monitoring improving GILD's ability to meet patient demand. GILD expects to file with the FDA for inhaled aztreonam lysine in cystic fibrosis by the end of 2007. We expect EPS growth of 15% in 2008 due to lower Tamiflu royalties and higher investment in future growth, but we maintain our view of 18%-20% long-term EPS growth and strong operational cash flows.

➤ Risks to our recommendation and target price include any slowdown in GILD's HIV product sales, failure of pipeline candidates to gain FDA approval, and increased competition in the heart failure market.

➤ Our 12-month target price of $49 is based on our P/E analysis, we apply a multiple of 25X our 2008 EPS estimate, in line with large-cap peers, reflecting our view of solid long-term prospects.

Qualitative Risk Assessment

LOW	MEDIUM	**HIGH**

Our risk assessment reflects Gilead's dependence on the growth of its anti-HIV drug portfolio. Also, the company operates in a highly competitive market, and a failure to successfully commercialize its pipeline candidates could diminish growth expectations in the future.

Quantitative Evaluations

S&P Quality Ranking   B-

D	C	**B-**	B	B+	A-	A	A+

Relative Strength Rank   STRONG

85

LOWEST = 1   HIGHEST = 99

Revenue/Earnings Data

Revenue (Million $)

	1Q	2Q	3Q	4Q	Year
2007	1,028	1,048	1,059	--	--
2006	692.9	685.3	748.7	899.2	3,026
2005	430.4	495.3	493.5	609.3	2,028
2004	309.1	319.7	326.2	369.6	1,325
2003	165.1	238.9	200.4	263.5	867.9
2002	78.42	109.4	134.0	145.0	466.8

Earnings Per Share ($)

2007	0.43	0.42	0.42	E0.43	E1.70
2006	0.28	0.28	-0.06	-1.81	-1.30
2005	0.17	0.21	0.19	0.29	0.86
2004	0.13	0.12	0.13	0.12	0.50
2003	-0.55	0.12	0.08	0.21	-0.09
2002	Nil	0.03	0.03	0.04	0.09

Fiscal year ended Dec. 31. Next earnings report expected: Early February. EPS Estimates based on S&P Operating Earnings; historical GAAP earnings are as reported.

Dividend Data (Dates: mm/dd Payment Date: mm/dd/yy)

Amount ($)	Date Decl.	Ex-Div. Date	Stk. of Record	Payment Date
2-for-1 Stk.	05/08	06/25	05/24	06/22/07

Source: Company reports.

Please read the Required Disclosures and Analyst Certification on the last page of this report.

Gilead Sciences Inc

Business Summary October 22, 2007

CORPORATE OVERVIEW. GILD focuses on the research, development and marketing of anti-infective medications, with a primary focus on treatments for HIV.

GILD's 2006 sales leader was Truvada, with sales of $1.19 billion, more than double 2005's $568 million. Truvada, approved in 2004, is a once-daily combination tablet formulated with previous-generation drugs Viread and Emtriva. Emtriva was the lead product of Triangle Pharmaceuticals, acquired in 2003. Viread was approved in 2001 to treat HIV patients who had become resistant to other reverse transcriptase inhibitors, as well as naive patients in a front-line treatment setting. Viread sales were $689 million in 2006, compared to $779 million in 2005.

In late 2004, GILD and Bristol-Myers Squibb (BMY) formed a joint venture to develop a combination tablet with Truvada and BMY's Sustiva. The formulation, marketed as Atripla, was approved and launched in July 2006. GILD books Atripla sales and then pays BMY its 37% share for the Sustiva portion of the drug, which GILD accounts for in cost of goods on its income statement. Atripla generated 2006 sales of $206 million. Atripla received a positive opinion from Europe's Committee for Medicinal Products in October 2007 and GILD expects EU approval by the end of 2007.

In September 2002, Hepsera was approved for treatment of Hepatitis B. In March 2003, it was approved in the European Union (EU). GILD recorded $231 million in Hepsera sales in 2006, up from $187 million in 2005. The company out-licensed rights to Hepsera for Asia and Latin America to GlaxoSmithKline (GSK) in exchange for milestones and royalties.

AmBisome is a liposomal formulation of amphotericin B, an antifungal agent that attacks a broad variety of life-threatening fungal infections. AmBisome is co-marketed in the U.S. with Fujisawa Healthcare, and is also approved by the FDA to treat cryptococcal meningitis in AIDS patients. Sales were $223 million in 2005, roughly flat with sales of $221 million in 2005.

Tamiflu, an orally administered treatment for influenza A and B, was developed with Roche and was approved by the FDA for adults in October 1999 and for children aged 1-12 in December 2005. Roche markets the drug, paying a 21-22% royalty to GILD. In April 2007, Roche said it would be decreasing near-term Tamiflu production because capacity has surpassed demand.

Company Financials Fiscal Year Ended Dec. 31

Per Share Data ($)	2006	2005	2004	2003	2002	2001	2000	1999	1998	1997
Tangible Book Value	1.97	3.30	2.09	1.17	0.72	0.58	0.47	0.42	0.47	0.58
Cash Flow	-1.24	0.90	0.51	-0.06	0.10	0.08	-0.04	-0.08	-0.11	0.07
Earnings	-1.30	0.86	0.50	-0.09	0.09	0.06	-0.06	-0.10	-0.12	-0.06
S&P Core Earnings	-1.29	0.78	0.39	-0.17	0.01	-0.14	NA	NA	NA	NA
Dividends	Nil	Nil	Nil	Nil	Nil	Nil	Nil	Nil	Nil	Nil
Payout Ratio	Nil	Nil	Nil	Nil	Nil	Nil	Nil	Nil	Nil	Nil
Prices:High	35.00	28.26	19.55	17.65	10.00	9.21	7.38	5.97	2.77	2.95
Prices:Low	26.24	15.20	12.88	7.81	6.52	3.11	2.70	2.20	1.13	1.32
P/E Ratio:High	NM	33	39	NM	NM	NM	NM	NM	NM	NM
P/E Ratio:Low	NM	18	26	NM	NM	NM	NM	NM	NM	NM

Income Statement Analysis (Million $)										
Revenue	3,026	2,028	1,325	868	467	234	196	169	32.6	40.0
Operating Income	1,683	1,148	656	361	95.4	-106	-40.3	-39.2	-71.6	-42.8
Depreciation	47.3	36.8	24.4	20.9	14.4	14.7	12.0	12.6	2.76	2.98
Interest Expense	20.4	0.44	7.35	21.9	13.9	14.0	Nil	6.52	0.19	0.49
Pretax Income	-644	1,158	656	-168	73.4	55.3	-41.9	-65.6	-56.1	28.0
Effective Tax Rate	NM	30.0%	31.5%	NM	1.77%	7.48%	NM	NM	NM	NM
Net Income	-1,190	814	449	-72.0	72.1	51.2	-43.1	-66.5	-56.1	28.0
S&P Core Earnings	-1,188	737	354	-133	8.55	-108	NA	NA	NA	NA

Balance Sheet & Other Financial Data (Million $)										
Cash	937	2,324	1,254	707	942	583	513	294	32.5	32.0
Current Assets	2,429	3,092	1,850	1,266	1,184	708	594	372	288	340
Total Assets	4,086	3,765	2,156	1,555	1,288	795	678	437	303	352
Current Liabilities	764	455	253	186	105	80.1	58.2	47.9	31.8	33.4
Long Term Debt	1,300	241	0.23	345	595	250	252	84.8	0.56	1.33
Common Equity	1,816	3,028	1,871	1,003	571	452	351	297	271	317
Total Capital	3,169	3,277	1,871	1,348	1,166	703	603	382	271	318
Capital Expenditures	105	2,226	51.4	38.6	17.6	26.3	15.6	12.5	2.50	3.86
Cash Flow	-1,143	851	474	-51.1	86.5	65.9	-31.1	-53.9	-53.3	31.0
Current Ratio	3.2	6.8	7.3	6.8	11.3	8.8	10.2	7.8	9.1	10.2
% Long Term Debt of Capitalization	41.0	7.3	NM	25.6	51.0	35.6	41.8	22.2	0.2	0.0
% Net Income of Revenue	NM	40.1	33.9	NM	15.4	21.9	NM	NM	NM	69.9
% Return on Assets	NM	27.5	24.2	NM	6.9	6.9	NM	NM	NM	8.4
% Return on Equity	NM	33.2	31.3	NM	14.1	12.7	NM	NM	NM	9.2

Data as orig reptd.; bef. results of disc opers/spec. items. Per share data adj. for stk. divs.; EPS diluted. E-Estimated. NA-Not Available. NM-Not Meaningful. NR-Not Ranked. UR-Under Review.

Office: 333 Lakeside Drive, Foster City, CA 94404.
Telephone: 650-574-3000.
Email: investor_relations@gilead.com
Website: http://www.gilead.com

Chrmn: J.M. Denny
Pres & CEO: J.C. Martin
COO, EVP & CFO: J.F. Milligan
SVP & General Counsel: G.H. Alton

Investor Contact: S. Hubbard ((650) 522-5715)
Board Members: P. Berg, J. F. Cogan, E. F. Davignon, J. M. Denny, C. A. Hills, J. W. Madigan, J. C. Martin, G. E. Moore, N. G. Moore, G. E. Wilson
Founded: 1987
Domicile: Delaware
Employees: 2,515

Goldman Sachs Group Inc. (The)

STANDARD &POOR'S

S&P Recommendation BUY ★★★★☆	**Price** $216.48 (as of Nov 23, 2007)	**12-Mo. Target Price** $250.00	**Investment Style** Large-Cap Growth

GICS Sector Financials
Sub-Industry Investment Banking & Brokerage

Summary Goldman Sachs is one of the world's leading investment banking and securities companies.

Key Stock Statistics (Source S&P, Vickers, company reports)

52-Wk Range	**$250.70– 157.38**	S&P Oper. EPS 2007**E**	23.14	Market Capitalization(B)	$86.089	Beta	1.50
Trailing 12-Month EPS	**$24.32**	S&P Oper. EPS 2008**E**	20.49	Yield (%)	0.65	S&P 3-Yr. Proj. EPS CAGR(%)	12.00
Trailing 12-Month P/E	**8.9**	P/E on S&P Oper. EPS 2007**E**	9.4	Dividend Rate/Share	$1.40	S&P Credit Rating	AA-
$10K Invested 5 Yrs Ago	**$28,590**	Common Shares Outstg. (M)	397.7	Institutional Ownership (%)	69		

Price Performance

30-Week Mov. Avg. ··· 10-Week Mov. Avg. -- **GAAP Earnings vs. Previous Year** Volume Above Avg. ▯▯▯ STARS
12-Mo. Target Price — Relative Strength — ▲ Up ▼ Down ▶ No Change   Below Avg. ▯▯▯ ★

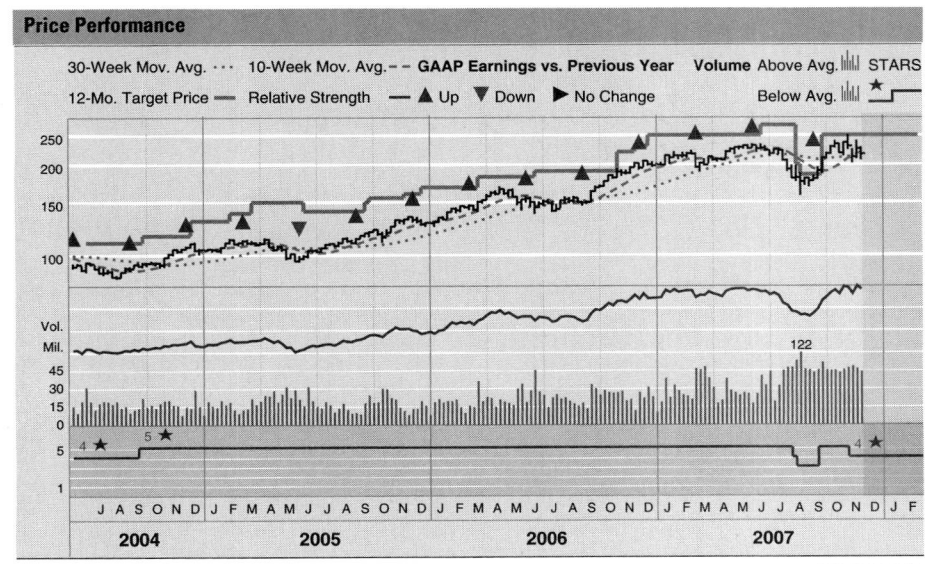

Options: ASE, CBOE, P, Ph

Analysis prepared by **Matthew Albrecht** on November 12, 2007, when the stock traded at **$ 211.33**.

Highlights

➤ We view Goldman Sachs as the best-in-breed of the investment banks and expect it to continue to benefit from capital market activities. We believe the company may be faced with additional markdowns of leveraged loan commitments and other securities, primarily related to sub-prime mortgages, in addition to those taken in its third quarter, because the market has not yet stabilized. We expect continued weakness in incentive fees from alternative investments due to relatively poor performance, but GS's asset management business continues to add client assets, and other operations should post year-over-year gains. All told, we look for net revenues to advance more than 20% in FY 07 (Nov.), before experiencing a decline in FY 08.

➤ We continue to expect compensation to approximate 47% of net revenues in each of FY 07 and FY 08, following a dip in the expense line in FY 06. We believe noncompensation expense growth will outpace net revenue growth due to international expansion, resulting in a slight compression in the pretax margin in each fiscal year.

➤ We expect GS to post EPS of $23.14 in FY 07 and $20.49 in FY 08.

Investment Rationale/Risk

➤ We believe the company's original partnership structure has contributed to an ownership viewpoint within the company, resulting in a competitive advantage for GS. We think the shares should trade at a premium valuation to peers, based on our view of the company's global reach, significant operating leverage, client relationships, and peer-best return on equity. Prudent growth in headcount and compensation should benefit GS's valuation, in our view. We also have a favorable view of the company's aggressive stock buyback program.

➤ Risks to our recommendation and target price include stock and bond market depreciation, sharply higher interest rates, widening credit spreads, and greater regulatory scrutiny. GS's global business model also adds risk due to its exposure to geopolitical issues.

➤ The shares recently traded at about 10.6X our FY 08 EPS estimate and 2.6X current book value, discounts to its historical multiples and that of the S&P 500. Our 12-month target price of $250 is based on a price-to-book multiple of about 2.5X applied to our 12-month book value projection, a premium multiple to peers.

Qualitative Risk Assessment

LOW	MEDIUM	HIGH

Our risk assessment reflects our view of the company's global footprint and strong client relationships.

Quantitative Evaluations

S&P Quality Ranking   NR

D	C	B-	B	B+	A-	A	A+

Relative Strength Rank   **STRONG**

76

LOWEST = 1   HIGHEST = 99

Revenue/Earnings Data

Revenue (Million $)

	1Q	2Q	3Q	4Q	Year
2007	22,280	20,351	23,803	--	--
2006	17,246	18,002	15,979	18,126	69,353
2005	9,964	8,949	12,333	12,145	43,391
2004	7,905	7,676	6,803	7,455	29,839
2003	6,094	5,985	5,715	5,829	23,623
2002	5,700	6,234	5,872	5,048	22,854

Earnings Per Share ($)

2007	6.67	4.93	6.13	E5.41	E23.14
2006	5.08	4.78	3.26	6.59	19.69
2005	2.94	1.71	3.25	3.35	11.21
2004	2.50	2.31	1.74	2.36	8.92
2003	1.29	1.36	1.32	1.89	5.87
2002	0.98	1.06	1.00	0.98	4.03

Fiscal year ended Nov. 30. Next earnings report expected: Mid December. EPS Estimates based on S&P Operating Earnings; historical GAAP earnings are as reported.

Dividend Data (Dates: mm/dd Payment Date: mm/dd/yy)

Amount ($)	Date Decl.	Ex-Div. Date	Stk. of Record	Payment Date
0.350	12/13	01/19	01/23	02/22/07
0.350	03/13	04/20	04/24	05/24/07
0.350	06/14	07/27	07/31	08/30/07
0.350	09/20	10/25	10/29	11/26/07

Dividends have been paid since 1999. Source: Company reports.

Goldman Sachs Group Inc. (The)

STANDARD &POOR'S

Business Summary November 12, 2007

CORPORATE OVERVIEW. Goldman Sachs (GS) is a global investment banking, securities and investment management firm that provides a wide range of services to corporations, financial institutions, governments and high-net-worth individuals. GS operates through three core businesses: Trading and Principal Investments, Investment Banking, and Asset Management and Securities Services.

The Trading and Principal Investments business (68% of FY 06-Nov. net revenues) facilitates customer transactions with a diverse group of corporations, financial institutions, governments and individuals, and takes proprietary positions through market making in, and trading of, fixed income and equity products, currencies, commodities and derivatives. The activities of the Trading and Principal Investments business can be grouped under three segments: Fixed Income, Currency and Commodities (FICC); Equities; and Principal Investments. The FICC business makes markets in and trades interest rate and credit products, mortgage-backed securities, loans and other asset-backed securities, currencies and commodities. The Equities business makes markets

in, trades, and acts as a specialist for equities and equity-related products. It generates commissions from executing and clearing client transactions on major stock, options, and futures exchanges worldwide through its Equities customer franchise and clearing activities.

The Principal Investments business primarily represents net revenues from corporate and real estate merchant banking investments. These net revenues are from three primary sources--returns on corporate and real estate investments, its investment in the convertible preferred stock of Sumitomo Mitsui Financial Group, Inc. (SMFG), and overrides. Overrides represent net revenues from the increased share of the income and gains derived from GS's merchant banking funds when the return on a fund's investments exceeds certain threshold returns.

Company Financials Fiscal Year Ended Nov. 30

Per Share Data ($)	2006	2005	2004	2003	2002	2001	2000	1999	1998	1997
Tangible Book Value	119.66	52.15	52.14	45.73	40.18	38.30	34.15	22.65	NA	NA
Cash Flow	20.78	12.22	9.90	6.97	5.20	5.39	6.94	6.27	NA	NA
Earnings	19.69	11.21	8.92	5.87	4.03	4.26	6.00	5.27	2.62	NA
S&P Core Earnings	19.72	11.12	8.63	5.26	3.30	3.60	NA	NA	NA	NA
Dividends	1.30	1.00	1.00	0.74	0.48	0.48	0.48	0.24	NA	NA
Payout Ratio	7%	9%	11%	13%	12%	11%	8%	4%	NA	NA
Prices:High	206.70	134.99	110.88	100.78	97.25	120.00	133.63	94.81	NA	NA
Prices:Low	124.23	94.75	83.29	61.02	58.57	63.27	65.50	53.00	NA	NA
P/E Ratio:High	10	12	12	17	24	28	22	17	NA	NA
P/E Ratio:Low	6	8	9	10	15	15	11	10	NA	NA

Income Statement Analysis (Million $)

	2006	2005	2004	2003	2002	2001	2000	1999	1998	1997
Commissions	10,140	6,689	5,941	4,317	3,273	3,020	2,307	Nil	NA	NA
Interest Income	35,186	21,250	11,914	10,751	11,269	16,620	17,396	12,722	NA	NA
Total Revenue	69,353	43,391	29,839	23,623	22,854	31,138	33,000	25,363	22,478	NA
Interest Expense	31,688	18,153	8,888	7,600	8,868	15,327	16,410	12,018	13,986	NA
Pretax Income	14,560	8,273	6,676	4,445	3,253	3,696	5,020	1,992	2,129	NA
Effective Tax Rate	34.5%	32.0%	31.8%	32.4%	35.0%	37.5%	38.9%	NM	41.0%	NA
Net Income	9,537	5,626	4,553	3,005	2,114	2,310	3,067	2,708	1,256	NA
S&P Core Earnings	9,416	5,560	4,406	2,693	1,737	1,949	NA	NA	NA	NA

Balance Sheet & Other Financial Data (Million $)

	2006	2005	2004	2003	2002	2001	2000	1999	1998	1997
Total Assets	838,201	706,804	531,379	403,799	355,574	312,218	289,760	250,491	231,796	NA
Cash Items	87,283	61,666	52,544	36,802	25,211	29,043	21,002	12,190	2,702	NA
Receivables	312,355	75,381	52,545	36,377	28,938	33,463	159,019	150,154	NA	NA
Securities Owned	416,687	238,043	183,880	160,719	129,775	108,885	95,260	81,809	NA	NA
Securities Borrowed	22,208	23,331	19,394	17,528	12,238	81,579	40,211	49,352	NA	NA
Due Brokers & Customers	223,874	188,318	161,221	109,028	95,590	97,297	82,148	59,534	NA	NA
Other Liabilities	31,866	13,830	10,360	8,144	6,002	7,129	11,116	110,508	NA	NA
Capitalization:Debt	122,842	100,007	80,696	57,482	38,711	31,016	31,395	20,952	20,776	NA
Capitalization:Equity	32,686	26,252	25,079	21,632	19,003	18,231	16,530	10,145	7,627	NA
Capitalization:Total	189,521	128,009	105,775	79,114	57,714	49,247	47,925	31,097	28,403	NA
% Return on Revenue	13.8	13.0	15.3	12.7	9.3	7.4	9.3	10.7	5.6	NA
% Return on Assets	1.2	0.9	1.0	0.8	0.6	0.8	1.1	1.2	NA	NA
% Return on Equity	31.9	21.9	19.5	14.8	11.4	13.3	23.0	30.4	NA	NA

Data as orig reptd.; bef. results of disc opers/spec. items. Per share data adj. for stk. divs.; EPS diluted. E-Estimated. NA-Not Available. NM-Not Meaningful. NR-Not Ranked. UR-Under Review.

Office: 85 Broad Street, New York, NY 10004.
Telephone: 212-902-1000.
Email: gs-investor-relations@gs.com
Website: http://www.gs.com

Chrmn & CEO: L.C. Blankfein
Pres & COO: G. Cohn
Vice Chrmn: J.S. Weinberg
EVP & CFO: D.A. Viniar

EVP & Chief Admin Officer: E.C. Forst
Investor Contact: J. Andrews (212-357-2674)
Auditor: PricewaterhouseCoopers
Board Members: L. C. Blankfein, J. H. Bryan, G. D. Cohn, C. Dahlback, S. Friedman, W. W. George, R. K. Gupta, J. A. Johnson, L. D. Juliber, E. M. Liddy, R. J. Simmons, J. Winkelried

Founded: 1869
Domicile: Delaware
Employees: 26,467

The **McGraw·Hill** Companies

Goodrich Corp

STANDARD
&POOR'S

S&P Recommendation STRONG BUY ★ ★ ★ ★ ★

Price	12-Mo. Target Price	Investment Style
$69.96 (as of Nov 23, 2007)	$80.00	Large-Cap Value

GICS Sector Industrials
Sub-Industry Aerospace & Defense

Summary This company is one of the world's largest providers of equipment, parts and services to the large commercial, regional, business, and military jet markets.

Key Stock Statistics (Source S&P, Vickers, company reports)

52-Wk Range	$73.43– 43.82	S&P Oper. EPS 2007**E**	3.67	Market Capitalization(B)	$8.762	Beta	0.88
Trailing 12-Month EPS	$3.52	S&P Oper. EPS 2008**E**	4.20	Yield (%)	1.29	S&P 3-Yr. Proj. EPS CAGR(%)	15.00
Trailing 12-Month P/E	19.9	P/E on S&P Oper. EPS 2007**E**	19.1	Dividend Rate/Share	$0.90	S&P Credit Rating	BBB
$10K Invested 5 Yrs Ago	$45,051	Common Shares Outstg. (M)	125.2	Institutional Ownership (%)	89		

Price Performance

30-Week Mov. Avg. ··· 10-Week Mov. Avg. — **GAAP Earnings vs. Previous Year** Volume Above Avg.|||| STARS
12-Mo. Target Price — Relative Strength — ▲ Up ▼ Down ► No Change Below Avg.|||| ★

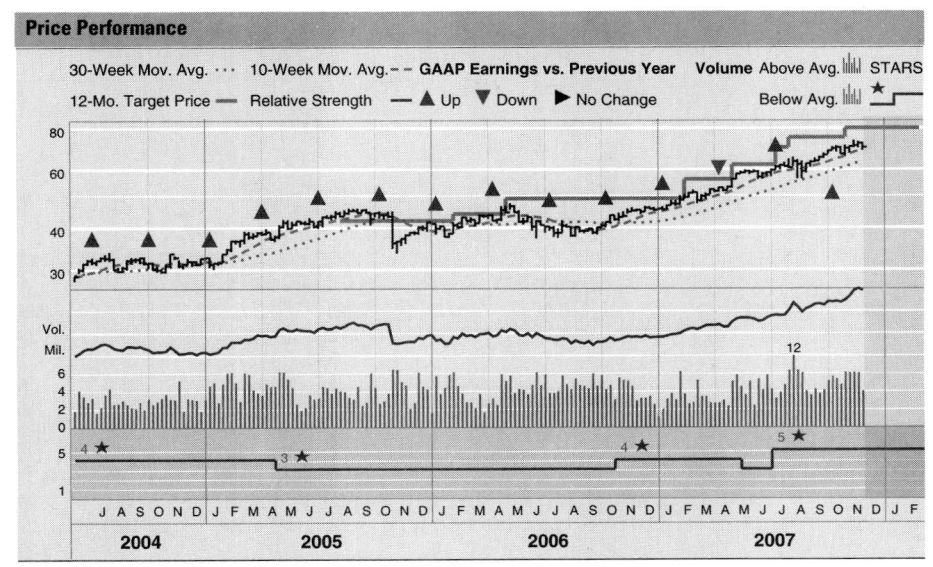

Options: ASE, CBOE, P, Ph

Analysis prepared by **Richard Tortoriello** on October 29, 2007, when the stock traded at **$ 69.97**.

Qualitative Risk Assessment

LOW	MEDIUM	HIGH

Our risk assessment reflects GR's history of cyclical earnings growth and its long record of dividend payments, offset by a lack of growth in dividends, as reflected in an S&P Quality Ranking of B (below average). We also take into account GR's recent long-term debt to capital ratio of 43%, which is above average for peers in the aerospace & defense subindustry.

Quantitative Evaluations

S&P Quality Ranking B

D	C	B-	B	B+	A-	A	A+

Relative Strength Rank STRONG

87

LOWEST = 1   HIGHEST = 99

Revenue/Earnings Data

Revenue (Million $)

	1Q	2Q	3Q	4Q	Year
2007	1,589	1,622	1,602	--	--
2006	1,424	1,483	1,436	1,535	5,878
2005	1,276	1,353	1,371	1,398	5,397
2004	1,162	1,134	1,167	1,262	4,725
2003	1,094	1,095	1,064	1,130	4,383
2002	921.2	925.5	882.1	1,181	3,910

Earnings Per Share ($)

2007	0.78	0.98	1.10	E0.81	E3.67
2006	1.59	0.64	0.80	0.78	3.80
2005	0.46	0.51	0.49	0.51	1.97
2004	0.26	0.32	0.41	0.30	1.30
2003	-0.28	0.12	0.29	0.19	0.33
2002	0.47	0.56	0.45	0.11	1.57

Fiscal year ended Dec. 31. Next earnings report expected: Early February. EPS Estimates based on S&P Operating Earnings; historical GAAP earnings are as reported.

Highlights

➤ We expect 2007 revenues to rise 12.2%, to $6.6 billion, driven by growth in all three business segments. We see a number of industry trends currently favoring GR's business lines, including a strong commercial jet demand cycle, increased global fleet sizes and utilization rates, aging aircraft in the U.S. (leading to rising demand for aftermarket parts), and strong demand for business aircraft. We project further revenue growth of 9% in 2008.

➤ We believe operating margins will improve to 15.5% in 2007, from 13.3% in 2006, based on GR's focus on volume growth, strong margin improvement in the Actuation & Landing Systems segment, and other cost-cutting initiatives across business segments. We see a further slight operating margin improvement in 2008. We think GR is on its way to achieving its 2009 operating margin goal of 15% early, and GR says it sees further room for improvement.

➤ We estimate 2007 EPS of $3.67, up from operating EPS of $2.63 in 2006 (excluding $1.17 of special tax gains), with growth to $4.20 in 2008. We expect free cash flow (cash generated from operations less capital expenditures) of about $2.50 in 2007.

Investment Rationale/Risk

➤ We believe that strong commercial aviation and business jet deliveries in 2007 and 2008, as well as strong demand for aftermarket parts and services, due to high global demand for air travel, will drive results. Goodrich sees total aftermarket sales rising 17% in 2007 and projects growth of 8% to 10% in 2008, as comparisons become more difficult. GR is using cash flow to expand its maintenance, repair, and overhaul facilities; move manufacturing to low-cost areas; and implement efficiency plans, all of which we view as good uses of cash in the current high-growth environment.

➤ Risks to our recommendation and target price include the potential for a global economic slowdown, rising raw material prices, and the possibility of slowing defense industry orders.

➤ Our 12-month target price of $80 is based on a P/E of 19X applied to our 2008 EPS estimate. This compares to a five-year historical average forward P/E of 15X for GR, with a high of 22X. We believe that GR deserves a P/E toward the upper end of this range, based on our view of the strength of the aerospace industry. Our target P/E of 19X is moderately above our three-year projected EPS growth rate for GR of 15%.

Dividend Data (Dates: mm/dd Payment Date: mm/dd/yy)

Amount ($)	Date Decl.	Ex-Div. Date	Stk. of Record	Payment Date
0.200	02/20	03/01	03/05	04/02/07
0.200	04/24	05/31	06/04	07/02/07
0.200	07/24	08/30	09/04	10/01/07
0.225	10/23	11/29	12/03	01/02/08

Dividends have been paid since 1939. Source: Company reports.

Goodrich Corp

Business Summary October 29, 2007

CORPORATE OVERVIEW. This $6 billion in revenues global aircraft components maker and services provider is also a leading supplier of systems and products to the global defense and space markets. Goodrich conducts business through three segments, shown below.

Nacelles and Interior Systems (32% of revenues and 52% of operating profits) consists of aerostructures and engineered polymer products; aircraft interior products, lighting systems, and cargo systems; and customer services. The aerostructures business includes nacelles (engine housings), thrust reversers, pylons, and maintenance, repair and overhaul services. Aircraft interior products include evacuation slides and life rafts, complete aircrew escape systems, and seating systems. Lighting systems includes interior lighting, external lighting, and night vision systems. The cargo systems business unit produces fully integrated main deck and lower lobe cargo systems for wide body aircraft. The customer service business unit sells aftermarket parts. N&IS's largest customers include Airbus, Boeing, Rolls-Royce and global airlines. Primary competitors in this market include United Technologies, BAE Systems and Honeywell.

Actuation and Landing Systems (40% and 18%) consists of landing gear, aircraft wheels and brakes, actuation systems, aviation technical services, and engine components, including turbine fuel technologies, turbomachinery products, and power transmission products. Several business units within the segment are linked by their ability to contribute to the integration, design, manufacture, and service of entire aircraft undercarriage systems, including landing gear, wheels and brakes, and certain brake controls. A&LS and Messier-Dowty (a division of France-based SNECMA) each control about 50% of the global landing gear market. The unit is also a major global provider of aircraft maintenance, repair and overhaul (MRO) services. A&LS's MRO customers mostly comprise the world's major airlines and aircraft leasing companies. Primary aircraft maintenance competitors include TIMCO Aviation Services, SIA Engineering Co., Singapore Technologies and Lufthansa Technik.

Company Financials Fiscal Year Ended Dec. 31

Per Share Data ($)	2006	2005	2004	2003	2002	2001	2000	1999	1998	1997
Tangible Book Value	1.31	NM	NM	NM	NM	4.66	3.48	1.41	9.63	11.35
Cash Flow	5.78	3.79	3.18	2.18	3.31	3.28	4.39	3.62	5.25	3.38
Earnings	3.80	1.97	1.30	0.33	1.57	1.65	2.68	1.53	3.04	1.53
S&P Core Earnings	3.94	2.10	1.57	0.42	0.42	0.41	NA	NA	NA	NA
Dividends	1.00	0.80	0.80	0.80	0.88	1.10	1.10	1.10	1.10	1.10
Payout Ratio	26%	41%	62%	242%	56%	67%	41%	72%	36%	72%
Prices:High	47.45	45.82	33.90	30.30	34.45	44.50	43.13	45.69	56.00	48.25
Prices:Low	37.15	30.11	26.60	12.20	14.17	15.91	21.56	21.00	26.50	35.13
P/E Ratio:High	12	23	26	92	22	27	16	30	18	32
P/E Ratio:Low	10	15	20	37	9	10	8	14	9	23

Income Statement Analysis (Million $)										
Revenue	5,878	5,397	4,725	4,383	3,910	4,185	4,364	5,538	3,951	3,373
Operating Income	886	759	636	515	586	666	830	973	653	501
Depreciation	240	226	223	219	184	174	193	231	165	139
Interest Expense	126	131	143	163	117	118	129	138	79.0	73.0
Pretax Income	462	375	199	61.3	259	271	443	316	374	207
Effective Tax Rate	NM	31.8%	21.7%	37.2%	36.0%	34.8%	35.4%	46.3%	39.1%	45.4%
Net Income	481	244	156	38.5	166	177	286	170	228	113
S&P Core Earnings	499	260	189	48.6	44.9	44.7	NA	NA	NA	NA

Balance Sheet & Other Financial Data (Million $)										
Cash	201	251	298	378	150	85.8	77.5	66.4	31.7	47.0
Current Assets	3,008	2,425	2,357	2,087	2,008	1,921	3,080	2,101	1,615	1,401
Total Assets	6,901	6,454	6,218	5,890	5,990	4,638	5,718	5,456	4,193	3,494
Current Liabilities	1,633	1,615	1,565	1,401	1,554	1,159	2,147	1,511	991	935
Long Term Debt	1,722	1,742	1,899	2,137	2,254	1,432	1,590	1,788	995	564
Common Equity	1,977	1,473	1,343	1,194	933	1,361	1,227	1,293	1,600	1,423
Total Capital	3,756	3,215	3,276	3,330	3,187	2,808	2,819	3,208	2,718	2,110
Capital Expenditures	257	216	152	125	107	191	148	246	209	160
Cash Flow	721	470	379	258	349	351	479	400	394	252
Current Ratio	1.8	1.5	1.5	1.5	1.3	1.7	1.4	1.4	1.6	1.5
% Long Term Debt of Capitalization	45.8	54.2	58.0	64.2	70.7	51.0	56.4	55.7	36.6	26.7
% Net Income of Revenue	8.2	4.5	3.3	0.9	4.2	4.2	6.6	3.1	5.8	3.4
% Return on Assets	7.2	3.8	2.6	0.6	3.0	3.6	5.3	3.2	5.9	3.7
% Return on Equity	27.9	17.3	12.3	3.6	14.5	13.7	22.7	13.4	15.1	9.2

Data as orig reptd.; bef. results of disc opers/spec. items. Per share data adj. for stk. divs.; EPS diluted. E-Estimated. NA-Not Available. NM-Not Meaningful. NR-Not Ranked. UR-Under Review.

Office: Four Coliseum Centre, Charlotte, NC 28217-4578.
Telephone: 704-423-7000.
Website: http://www.goodrich.com
Chrmn, Pres & CEO: M.O. Larsen

EVP & General Counsel: T.G. Linnert
SVP & CFO: S.E. Kuechle
VP & Cntlr: S. Cottrill
Investor Contact: P. Gifford (704-423-5517)

Board Members: D. C. Creel, G. A. Davidson, Jr., H. E. DeLoach, Jr., J. W. Griffith, W. R. Holland, J. P. Jumper, M. O. Larsen, L. W. Newton, D. E. Olesen, A. M. Rankin, Jr., J. R. Wilson, A. T. Young

Founded: 1912
Domicile: New York
Employees: 23,400

Goodyear Tire & Rubber Co

S&P Recommendation	HOLD ★★★☆☆	Price $26.58 (as of Nov 23, 2007)	12-Mo. Target Price $31.00	Investment Style Large-Cap Blend

GICS Sector Consumer Discretionary
Sub-Industry Tires & Rubber

Summary GT is the largest U.S. manufacturer of tires, and one of the biggest worldwide. Operations also include rubber and plastic products and chemicals.

Key Stock Statistics (Source S&P, Vickers, company reports)

52-Wk Range	**$36.90–16.60**	S&P Oper. EPS 2007**E**	**1.30**	Market Capitalization(B)	**$5.608**	Beta	**1.85**
Trailing 12-Month EPS	**$0.42**	S&P Oper. EPS 2008**E**	**2.74**	Yield (%)	**Nil**	S&P 3-Yr. Proj. EPS CAGR(%)	**NM**
Trailing 12-Month P/E	**63.3**	P/E on S&P Oper. EPS 2007**E**	**20.4**	Dividend Rate/Share	**Nil**	S&P Credit Rating	**BB-**
$10K Invested 5 Yrs Ago	**$33,142**	Common Shares Outstg. (M)	**211.0**	Institutional Ownership (%)	**99**		

Price Performance

30-Week Mov. Avg. · · · 10-Week Mov. Avg. - - GAAP Earnings vs. Previous Year Volume Above Avg. STARS
12-Mo. Target Price — Relative Strength ▲ Up ▼ Down ► No Change Below Avg.

Options: ASE, CBOE, P, Ph

Analysis prepared by **Efraim Levy, CFA** on November 16, 2007, when the stock traded at **$ 27.14**.

Highlights

➤ We expect 2008 sales to rise 7%, led by a better product mix and price increases. For 2007, we see 2% to 3% lower sales as revenues are restricted by lower heavy vehicle production. Profitability should benefit from a new union contract and a change in GT's pension plan. Although we see margins aided by increased selling prices and expense reduction due to restructuring activities, we think high raw material prices and rising pension expense will be partly offsetting. We expect interest expense increases to be limited by debt repurchases following an equity offering of 26 million shares. The equity improves GT's balance sheet, but will be dilutive to EPS.

➤ We see reductions in higher-cost plant capacity and a shift to Asian-based production providing savings. We expect all operating segments to be profitable in 2007 and 2008.

➤ We expect that the restructuring in its credit facilities will give GT more time and flexibility to make operating improvements in the key North American market.

Investment Rationale/Risk

➤ The August 2007 sale of the engineered products segment will provide cash to repay some debt, fund employee benefits, and invest in the tire business, in our view. GT has been extending its debt maturities, and we see a $350 million convertible debt offering helping liquidity, as does $833 million of net proceeds from a May equity issuance (including underwriter over-allotments). While we have increased confidence in GT's near-term liquidity, we regard liquidity challenges from debt and employee retirement obligations as matters of concern for the longer term.

➤ Risks to our recommendation and target price include an increase in GT's need for cash; weaker than anticipated demand for tires; lower than expected cost savings; and higher than projected raw material prices.

➤ We expect positive cash flow in 2008, even after cash contributions to fund GT's pension plan. However, applying a P/E of about 11.3X, in the middle to upper portion of the historical range, to our 2008 EPS estimate of $2.74 (which includes expected cost savings from a new union contract and changes in pension plans), we derive our 12-month target price of $31.

Qualitative Risk Assessment

LOW	MEDIUM	**HIGH**

Our risk assessment reflects the highly cyclical nature of the company's markets as well as the current and long-term challenges that GT faces due to our view of its highly leveraged balance sheet, intensifying competition, high fixed costs, and legacy costs.

Quantitative Evaluations

S&P Quality Ranking   **C**

D	**C**	B-	B	B+	A-	A	A+

Relative Strength Rank   **MODERATE**

44

LOWEST = 1   HIGHEST = 99

Revenue/Earnings Data

Revenue (Million $)

	1Q	2Q	3Q	4Q	Year
2007	4,499	4,921	5,064	--	--
2006	4,856	5,142	5,284	4,976	20,258
2005	4,767	4,992	5,030	4,934	19,723
2004	4,302	4,519	4,714	4,835	18,370
2003	3,546	3,753	3,906	3,914	15,119
2002	3,311	3,479	3,530	3,530	13,850

Earnings Per Share ($)

2007	-0.61	0.14	0.67	E0.48	E1.30
2006	0.37	0.01	-0.27	-2.02	-1.86
2005	0.35	0.34	0.70	-0.23	1.21
2004	-0.44	0.17	0.20	0.62	0.63
2003	-1.12	-0.30	-0.67	-2.49	-4.58
2002	-0.39	0.18	0.20	-6.30	-6.62

Fiscal year ended Dec. 31. Next earnings report expected: Mid February. EPS Estimates based on S&P Operating Earnings; historical GAAP earnings are as reported.

Dividend Data

Dividends were last paid in 2002.

Goodyear Tire & Rubber Co

STANDARD &POOR'S

Business Summary November 16, 2007

CORPORATE OVERVIEW. Goodyear Tire & Rubber is the largest U.S. manufacturer of tires, and one of the largest worldwide. Operations also include rubber and plastic products and chemicals. Despite efforts to rationalize operations, divest non-core operations, and explore international growth opportunities, the company posted annual losses during 2001 through 2003. However, Goodyear made operational progress and returned to profitability in 2004. Goodyear posted further income gains in 2005, but results in 2006 were dragged down by a fourth quarter strike against the company. We project an improvement for 2007 and 2008. GT holds the leading market share in North America, Latin America, China, and India.

In 2006, 93% of segment sales came from tire products. Engineered products, which the company has agreed to sell, accounted for the balance of revenues and contributed $74 million of segment operating income.

CORPORATE STRATEGY. The company sometimes uses joint ventures to facilitate the growth of its business. In 1999, GT and Sumitomo Rubber Industries (SRI) completed a global alliance that again made GT the world's leading tire manufacturer. GT created a European joint venture with SRI. GT and SRI

owned 75% and 25%, respectively, of both the North American and European joint ventures. In Japan, the ownership ratio is reversed.

GT and Pacific Dunlop Ltd. participate in equally owned joint ventures in South Pacific Tyres, an Australian partnership, and South Pacific Tyres N.Z. Ltd., a New Zealand company.

At December 31, 2004, the company said that it did not maintain effective control over the preparation and review of account reconciliations of certain general ledger accounts. This control deficiency resulted in misstatements that were part of the restatement of the company's consolidated financial statements for 2003, 2002 and 2001, for each of the quarters of 2003 and for the first, second and third quarters of 2004. In February 2006, GT said that the matters concerning weakness in internal controls had been fixed as of December 31, 2005.

Company Financials Fiscal Year Ended Dec. 31

Per Share Data ($)	2006	2005	2004	2003	2002	2001	2000	1999	1998	1997
Tangible Book Value	NM	NM	NM	NM	NM	14.06	18.49	19.87	24.01	21.68
Cash Flow	1.95	4.16	3.87	-0.62	-3.01	2.71	4.22	5.18	7.63	6.51
Earnings	-1.86	1.21	0.63	-4.58	-6.62	-1.27	0.26	1.52	4.53	3.53
S&P Core Earnings	-0.88	2.61	0.84	-3.32	-8.16	-3.09	NA	NA	NA	NA
Dividends	Nil	Nil	Nil	Nil	0.48	1.02	1.20	1.20	1.20	1.14
Payout Ratio	Nil	Nil	Nil	Nil	NM	NM	NM	79%	26%	32%
Prices:High	21.35	18.59	15.01	8.19	28.85	32.10	31.63	66.75	76.75	71.25
Prices:Low	9.75	11.24	7.06	3.35	6.50	17.37	15.60	25.50	45.88	49.25
P/E Ratio:High	NM	15	24	NM	NM	NM	NM	44	17	20
P/E Ratio:Low	NM	9	11	NM	NM	NM	NM	17	10	14

Income Statement Analysis (Million $)	2006	2005	2004	2003	2002	2001	2000	1999	1998	1997
Revenue	20,258	19,723	18,370	15,119	13,850	14,147	14,417	12,881	12,626	13,155
Operating Income	1,256	1,706	1,457	-549	915	916	1,173	1,094	1,560	1,689
Depreciation	675	630	629	693	603	637	630	582	488	469
Interest Expense	451	411	369	296	241	292	283	179	147	119
Pretax Income	-113	584	381	-655	37.9	-273	92.3	337	1,035	845
Effective Tax Rate	NM	42.8%	54.6%	NM	NM	NM	20.0%	16.5%	27.6%	28.5%
Net Income	-330	239	115	-802	-1,106	-204	40.3	241	717	559
S&P Core Earnings	-157	522	142	-584	-1,362	-495	NA	NA	NA	NA

Balance Sheet & Other Financial Data (Million $)	2006	2005	2004	2003	2002	2001	2000	1999	1998	1997
Cash	3,899	2,178	1,968	1,565	947	959	253	241	239	259
Current Assets	10,179	8,680	8,632	6,988	5,227	5,255	5,467	5,261	4,529	4,164
Total Assets	17,029	15,627	16,533	15,006	13,147	13,513	13,568	13,103	10,589	9,917
Current Liabilities	4,666	4,811	5,113	3,686	4,071	3,327	4,226	3,960	3,277	3,251
Long Term Debt	6,563	4,742	449	4,826	2,989	3,204	2,350	2,348	1,187	845
Common Equity	-758	73.0	72.8	-13.1	651	2,864	3,503	3,617	3,746	3,395
Total Capital	7,015	5,910	1,774	5,639	4,380	6,855	6,698	6,856	5,192	4,240
Capital Expenditures	671	634	519	375	458	435	614	805	838	699
Cash Flow	345	869	744	-109	-503	433	671	823	1,205	1,028
Current Ratio	2.2	1.8	1.7	1.9	1.3	1.6	1.3	1.3	1.4	1.3
% Long Term Debt of Capitalization	93.6	80.2	25.3	85.6	68.2	46.7	35.1	34.2	22.9	19.9
% Net Income of Revenue	NM	1.2	0.6	NM	NM	NM	0.3	1.9	5.7	4.2
% Return on Assets	NM	1.5	0.7	NM	NM	NM	0.3	2.0	7.0	5.7
% Return on Equity	NM	325.2	565.5	NM	NM	NM	1.1	6.5	20.1	16.7

Data as orig reptd.; bef. results of disc opers/spec. items. Per share data adj. for stk. divs.; EPS diluted. E-Estimated. NA-Not Available. NM-Not Meaningful. NR-Not Ranked. UR-Under Review.

Office: 1144 East Market Street, Akron, OH, USA 44316-0002.
Telephone: 330-796-2121.
Email: goodyear.investor.relations@goodyear.com
Website: http://www.goodyear.com

Chrmn, Pres & CEO: R.J. Keegan
EVP & CFO: R.J. Kramer
SVP, Secy & General Counsel: C.T. Harvie
VP & Treas: D. Audia

VP & Cntlr: T.A. Connell
Investor Contact: G. Dooley (330-796-6704)
Board Members: J. C. Boland, J. G. Breen, W. J. Hudson, Jr., R. J. Keegan, S. A. Minter, D. M. Morrison, R. O'Neal, S. D. Peterson, G. C. Sullivan, T. H. Weidemeyer, M. R. Wessel

Founded: 1898
Domicile: Ohio
Employees: 77,000

The McGraw-Hill Companies

Google Inc

STANDARD
&POOR'S

S&P Recommendation	HOLD ★★★☆☆	Price $676.70 (as of Nov 23, 2007)	12-Mo. Target Price $670.00	Investment Style Large-Cap Growth

GICS Sector Information Technology
Sub-Industry Internet Software & Services

Summary GOOG, which completed its initial public offering in August 2004, is the world's largest Internet company. It specializes in online search and advertising.

Key Stock Statistics (Source S&P, Vickers, company reports)

52-Wk Range	$747.24–437.00	S&P Oper. EPS 2007**E**	13.05	Market Capitalization(B)	$211.699	Beta	1.05
Trailing 12-Month EPS	$12.80	S&P Oper. EPS 2008**E**	16.62	Yield (%)	Nil	S&P 3-Yr. Proj. EPS CAGR(%)	32.00
Trailing 12-Month P/E	52.9	P/E on S&P Oper. EPS 2007**E**	51.9	Dividend Rate/Share	Nil	S&P Credit Rating	NA
$10K Invested 5 Yrs Ago	NA	Common Shares Outstg. (M)	312.8	Institutional Ownership (%)	62		

Price Performance

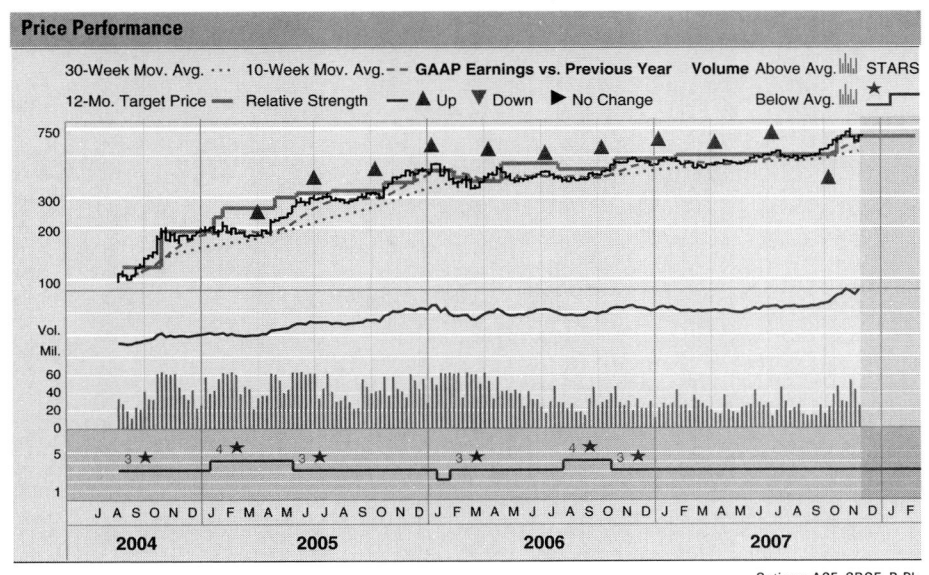

30-Week Mov. Avg. · · · 10-Week Mov. Avg. - - **GAAP Earnings vs. Previous Year** Volume Above Avg. STARS
12-Mo. Target Price — Relative Strength — ▲ Up ▼ Down ► No Change Below Avg.

Options: ASE, CBOE, P, Ph

Analysis prepared by **Scott H. Kessler** on October 23, 2007, when the stock traded at **$ 667.14**.

Highlights

➤ We expect gross revenues to increase 57% in 2007 and 39% in 2008, with revenues benefiting from higher spending on Internet advertising, the appeal of keyword search advertising, market share gains in some segments, new offerings, and international expansion. Revenue increases should continue to be paced, in our view, by revenues derived from GOOG's Web sites. We anticipate that GOOG will employ some of the proceeds from stock sales, including its IPO (completed in August 2004) for investments in, and acquisitions of, businesses and companies.

➤ We project that annual gross margins will narrow slightly through 2009, owing to a less favorable revenue mix that is becoming increasingly tied to large content partners. We expect operating margins to trend lower, reflecting continuing aggressive investments for business expansion.

➤ Our EPS estimates include notable expenses related to stock-based compensation. We foresee only moderate growth in diluted outstanding shares through 2009.

Investment Rationale/Risk

➤ We believe competitive pressures and broader concerns about GOOG's power could detract from revenue growth. However, we are constructive on GOOG's efforts to broaden its offering in Internet video and display advertising, but believe it is paying excessive prices to do so. In November 2006, GOOG acquired YouTube for $1.8 billion in stock, and in April 2007, the company announced the proposed purchase of DoubleClick for $3.1 billion (we foresee deal consummation possibly by year-end, pending approvals).

➤ Risks to our opinion and target price include possible market share losses, new product/service introductions or partnerships that do not succeed as some expect, and challenges related to more legal and regulatory issues.

➤ Our relative P/E analysis leads to a value of around $575. Comparable PEG considerations result in a price assessment of about $840. Our DCF model (assumptions include a WACC of 11.2%, five-year average annual growth of 41%, and a perpetuity growth rate of 3%) yields an intrinsic value of roughly $520. Using a blend of these methodologies, our 12-month target price is $670.

Qualitative Risk Assessment

LOW	MEDIUM	HIGH

Our risk assessment reflects what we see as the Internet segment's emerging nature and relatively low barriers to entry, significant and mounting competition, substantial and increasing investment and related new offerings, our view of somewhat lacking corporate governance practices, and notable share-price volatility.

Quantitative Evaluations

S&P Quality Ranking NR

D	C	B-	B	B+	A-	A	A+

Relative Strength Rank STRONG

95

LOWEST = 1   HIGHEST = 99

Revenue/Earnings Data

Revenue (Million $)

	1Q	2Q	3Q	4Q	Year
2007	3,664	3,872	4,231	--	--
2006	2,254	2,456	2,690	3,206	10,605
2005	1,257	1,385	1,578	1,919	6,139
2004	651.6	700.2	805.9	1,032	3,189
2003	248.6	311.2	393.9	512.2	1,466
2002	42.29	78.53	130.8	187.9	439.5

Earnings Per Share ($)

2007	3.18	2.93	3.38	E3.55	E13.05
2006	1.95	2.33	2.36	3.29	9.94
2005	1.29	1.19	1.32	1.22	5.02
2004	0.24	0.30	0.19	0.71	1.46
2003	--	--	--	--	0.51
2002	--	--	--	--	0.45

Fiscal year ended Dec. 31. Next earnings report expected: Early February. EPS Estimates based on S&P Operating Earnings; historical GAAP earnings are as reported.

Dividend Data

No cash dividends have been paid.

Google Inc

STANDARD &POOR'S

Business Summary October 23, 2007

CORPORATE OVERVIEW. Google is a global technology company whose stated mission is to organize the world's information and make it universally accessible and useful. GOOG has amassed and maintains what we believe is the Internet's largest index of information (consisting of billions of items, including Web pages, images and videos), and makes most of it freely accessible and usable to anyone with online access. GOOG's Web sites are a leading Internet destination, and its brand is one of the most recognized in the world. International sources contributed 48% of revenues in the 2007 third quarter, versus 44% in the prior-year period.

GOOG's advertising program, called AdWords, enables advertisers to present online ads when users are searching for related information. Advertisers employ GOOG's tools to create text-based ads, bid on keywords that trigger display of their ads, and set daily spending budgets. Ads are ranked for presentation based on the maximum cost per click set by the advertiser, click-through

rates, and other factors used to determine ad relevance. This process is designed to favor the most relevant ads. GOOG's AdSense technology enables Google Network Web sites to provide targeted ads from AdWords advertisers.

Advertising accounted for 99% of revenues in the third quarters of both 2007 and 2006. Google Web sites accounted for 64% of 2007 third quarter revenues and 60% of the prior year period's revenues. Google Network Web sites contributed 35% of 2007 third-quarter revenues and 39% in the 2006 quarter. S&P projects that U.S.-based spending on keyword search advertising will increase to $8.9 billion in 2008 from $6.8 billion in 2006.

Company Financials Fiscal Year Ended Dec. 31

Per Share Data ($)	2006	2005	2004	2003	2002	2001	2000	1999	1998	1997
Tangible Book Value	49.02	31.20	10.25	7.66	NA	NA	NA	NA	NA	NA
Cash Flow	11.79	5.90	1.93	0.75	NA	NA	NA	NA	NA	NA
Earnings	9.94	5.02	1.46	0.51	0.45	0.04	-0.22	-0.14	NA	NA
S&P Core Earnings	9.92	4.68	1.85	0.40	0.44	NA	NA	NA	NA	NA
Dividends	Nil	Nil	Nil	NA	NA	NA	NA	NA	NA	NA
Payout Ratio	Nil	Nil	Nil	NA	NA	NA	NA	NA	NA	NA
Prices:High	513.00	446.21	201.60	NA	NA	NA	NA	NA	NA	NA
Prices:Low	331.55	172.57	85.00	NA	NA	NA	NA	NA	NA	NA
P/E Ratio:High	52	89	NM	NA	NA	NA	NA	NA	NA	NA
P/E Ratio:Low	33	34	NM	NA	NA	NA	NA	NA	NA	NA

Income Statement Analysis (Million $)	2006	2005	2004	2003	2002	2001	2000	1999	1998	1997
Revenue	10,605	6,139	3,189	1,466	440	86.4	19.1	0.22	NA	NA
Operating Income	3,550	2,274	970	393	204	21.0	NA	NA	NA	NA
Depreciation	572	257	129	50.2	18.0	10.0	NA	NA	NA	NA
Interest Expense	0.26	0.78	0.86	1.93	2.57	1.76	NA	NA	NA	NA
Pretax Income	4,011	2,142	650	347	185	10.1	-14.7	-6.08	NA	NA
Effective Tax Rate	23.3%	31.6%	38.6%	69.5%	46.1%	30.6%	Nil	Nil	NA	NA
Net Income	3,077	1,465	399	106	99.7	6.99	-14.7	-6.08	NA	NA
S&P Core Earnings	3,071	1,366	503	103	97.4	NA	NA	NA	NA	NA

Balance Sheet & Other Financial Data (Million $)	2006	2005	2004	2003	2002	2001	2000	1999	1998	1997
Cash	11,244	8,034	2,132	1,712	146	33.6	19.1	20.0	NA	NA
Current Assets	13,040	9,001	2,693	NA	232	NA	NA	NA	NA	NA
Total Assets	18,473	10,272	3,313	2,492	286	84.5	46.9	25.8	NA	NA
Current Liabilities	1,305	745	340	NA	89.5	NA	NA	NA	NA	NA
Long Term Debt	Nil	Nil	Nil	NA	6.50	NA	NA	NA	NA	NA
Common Equity	17,040	9,419	2,929	2,181	130	NA	NA	NA	NA	NA
Total Capital	17,080	9,454	2,929	NA	178	50.2	27.2	20.0	NA	NA
Capital Expenditures	1,903	838	319	177	37.2	13.1	NA	NA	NA	NA
Cash Flow	3,649	1,722	528	156	118	17.0	NA	NA	NA	NA
Current Ratio	10.0	12.1	7.9	NA	2.6	NA	NA	NA	NA	NA
% Long Term Debt of Capitalization	Nil	Nil	Nil	NA	3.7	NA	NA	NA	NA	NA
% Net Income of Revenue	29.0	23.9	12.5	7.2	22.7	8.1	NM	NM	NA	NA
% Return on Assets	21.4	21.6	19.1	NA	NA	NA	NA	NA	NA	NA
% Return on Equity	23.3	23.7	23.0	NA	NA	NA	NA	NA	NA	NA

Data as orig reptd.; bef. results of disc opers/spec. items. Per share data adj. for stk. divs.; EPS diluted. E-Estimated. NA-Not Available. NM-Not Meaningful. NR-Not Ranked. UR-Under Review.

Office: 1600 Amphitheatre Parkway, Mountain View, CA 94043.
Telephone: 650-253-0000.
Email: info@google.com
Website: http://www.google.com

Exec Chrmn & CEO: E. Schmidt
Pres: S. Brin
Pres: L. Page
Investor Contact: G. Reyes (650-253-0000)

SVP & CFO: G. Reyes
Board Members: S. Brin, L. J. Doerr, J. L. Hennessy, A. D. Levinson, A. Mather, M. Moritz, P. S. Otellini, L. Page, E. Schmidt, K. R. Shriram, S. M. Tilghman

Employees: 10,674

The McGraw-Hill Companies

Grainger (W W) Inc.

STANDARD &POOR'S

S&P Recommendation BUY ★★★★☆

Price	12-Mo. Target Price	Investment Style
$86.84 (as of Nov 23, 2007)	$114.00	Large-Cap Blend

GICS Sector Industrials
Sub-Industry Trading Companies & Distributors

Summary Grainger is the largest global distributor of industrial and commercial supplies, such as hand tools, electric motors, light bulbs, and janitorial items.

Key Stock Statistics (Source S&P, Vickers, company reports)

52-Wk Range	$98.60–68.77	S&P Oper. EPS 2007E	4.98	Market Capitalization(B)	$6.882	Beta	1.05
Trailing 12-Month EPS	$4.80	S&P Oper. EPS 2008E	5.75	Yield (%)	1.61	S&P 3-Yr. Proj. EPS CAGR(%)	14.00
Trailing 12-Month P/E	18.1	P/E on S&P Oper. EPS 2007E	17.4	Dividend Rate/Share	$1.40	S&P Credit Rating	AA+
$10K Invested 5 Yrs Ago	$17,832	Common Shares Outstg. (M)	79.2	Institutional Ownership (%)	81		

Price Performance

30-Week Mov. Avg. · · ·   10-Week Mov. Avg. - -   GAAP Earnings vs. Previous Year   Volume Above Avg.▐▐▐ STARS
12-Mo. Target Price —   Relative Strength —   ▲ Up ▼ Down ▶ No Change   Below Avg.▐▐▐ ★

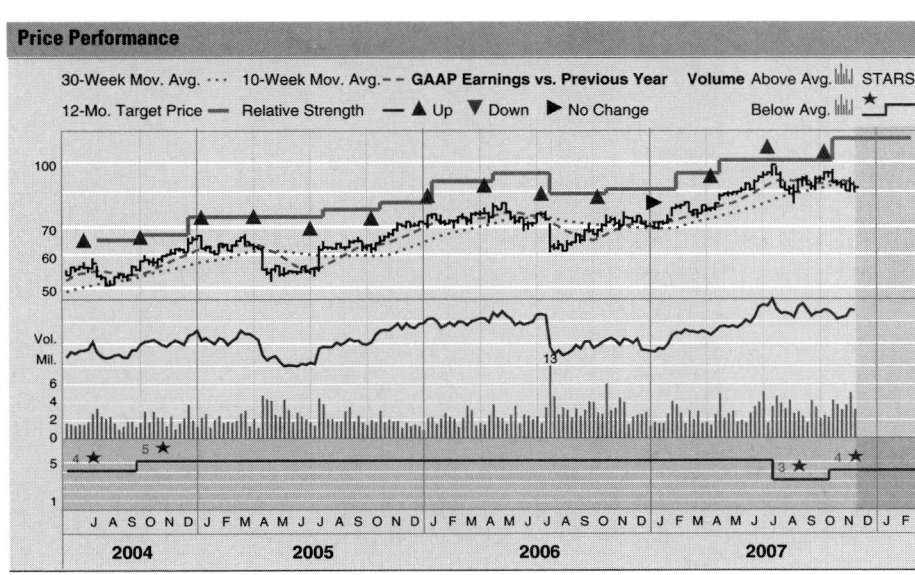

Options: CBOE, P, Ph

Analysis prepared by **Stewart Scharf** on October 17, 2007, when the stock traded at **$ 92.40**.

Highlights

► We expect sales to continue to advance in the high single digits through 2008, due to market and product line expansions in the U.S. branch-based business, driven by sales to governmental, light manufacturing and commercial customers, and growth in Mexico. We see slower growth in the retail and heavy manufacturing markets, especially on the West Coast and Mid-Atlantic regions. Sales in Canada should benefit from strength in oil and mining.

► We see wider gross margins in 2008 (40% projected for 2007), reflecting inflation recoveries and a more favorable product mix, as GWW continues to dissolve low-margin integrated supply and auto contracts. We believe EBITDA margins will expand further from our 12.4% forecast for 2007, based on supply chain cost savings, and nearly $30 million in savings from other technology programs and information technology staff cuts.

► We see a higher effective tax rate of 38.5% in 2007, and operating EPS of $4.98 (before a $0.04 severance charge), on nearly 6% fewer shares, advancing 15%, to $5.75, for 2008.

Investment Rationale/Risk

► Our buy recommendation is based on favorable market trends in the commercial and government markets, and our valuation metrics. We expect strategic initiatives to enhance the branch-based distribution network. We see strong free cash flow, targeted for internal investments and additional share buybacks, while ROIC continues to expand.

► Risks to our recommendation and target price include a significant downturn in industrial production; a greater than expected negative impact from entering new markets, especially China; and an inability to maintain GWW's large customer base.

► Our 12-month target price of $114 is based on a blend of our relative and DCF analyses. Based on historical P/E's and price-to-EBITDA ratios, and forward P/E-to-EPS growth, we believe the stock deserves a P/E of 19X our 2008 EPS estimate--modestly above GWW's five-year historical average--and we value the stock at $109. Our DCF-based model, assuming a 3.5% terminal growth rate and an 8.3% weighted average cost of capital, indicates intrinsic value of $119.

Qualitative Risk Assessment

LOW	MEDIUM	HIGH

Our risk assessment reflects uncertain economic conditions, pricing pressures, facilities disruptions or shutdowns, and corporate governance practices in which the positions of chairman and CEO are held by the same person. This is offset by an S&P Quality Ranking of A-, which indicates above average dividend and earnings growth.

Quantitative Evaluations

S&P Quality Ranking   A-

D	C	B-	B	B+	A-	A	A+

Relative Strength Rank   MODERATE

67

LOWEST = 1   HIGHEST = 99

Revenue/Earnings Data

Revenue (Million $)

	1Q	2Q	3Q	4Q	Year
2007	1,547	1,601	1,659	--	--
2006	1,419	1,483	1,520	1,462	5,884
2005	1,335	1,373	1,428	1,391	5,527
2004	1,228	1,256	1,301	1,265	5,050
2003	1,139	1,173	1,201	1,154	4,667
2002	1,125	1,195	1,203	1,120	4,644

Earnings Per Share ($)

2007	1.17	1.21	1.29	E1.31	E4.98
2006	0.93	1.02	1.16	1.13	4.24
2005	0.79	0.89	0.97	1.13	3.78
2004	0.69	0.72	0.74	0.98	3.13
2003	0.57	0.60	0.62	0.67	2.46
2002	0.61	0.57	0.64	0.67	2.50

Fiscal year ended Dec. 31. Next earnings report expected: Late January. EPS Estimates based on S&P Operating Earnings; historical GAAP earnings are as reported.

Dividend Data (Dates: mm/dd Payment Date: mm/dd/yy)

Amount ($)	Date Decl.	Ex-Div. Date	Stk. of Record	Payment Date
0.290	01/31	02/08	02/12	03/01/07
0.350	04/25	05/10	05/14	06/01/07
0.350	07/25	08/09	08/13	09/01/07
0.350	10/31	11/07	11/12	12/01/07

Dividends have been paid since 1965. Source: Company reports.

Grainger (W W) Inc.

STANDARD &POOR'S

Business Summary October 17, 2007

CORPORATE OVERVIEW. W.W. Grainger distributes facilities maintenance and other industrial and commercial supplies, including pumps, tools, motors, and electrical and safety products. It has more than 600 branches, 18 distribution centers and multiple Web sites. Starting in 2006, the company began reporting its Canadian branch-based business as a separate segment: Acklands-Grainger. The branch-based business segment mainly consists of 411 U.S. brick and mortar branch stores (two in Puerto Rico) and 22 Will Call Express branches, as well as 12 stores in Mexico, and one branch and five Will Call Express locations in China. These branches sell company-made--as well as third-party--industrial supplies, via in-store catalogs and Internet services. GWW estimates China's market for facilities maintenance supplies at $38 billion, and projects that it will exceed $70 billion by 2014.

During the first nine months of 2007, the branch-based unit accounted for nearly 84% of sales and had a pretax return on invested capital (ROIC) of 37.3%. The Acklands unit (154 branches) accounted for 10% of sales and had a ROIC of 12%. Lab Safety, a direct marketer of safety and other industrial products, was responsible for 7% of sales with a ROIC of 31.2%. Approximately 25% of GWW's sales consist of private label items. In 2006, 20% of sales

were derived from heavy manufacturing, 19% commercial, 18% government, 14% contractor, 10% light manufacturing, 8% retailer, 8% reseller, and 3% other.

The company's 2007 catalog features more than 139,000 products, a 20% increase from 2006. GWW expects to add 25,000 products in 2007. Product line expansion is forecast to contribute about 3% to sales growth for 2007.

In the first nine months of 2007, GWW bought back 7.1 million shares (5.3 million in August) for $647 million. Approximately 700,000 shares remain under this accelerated buyback plan, which GWW expects to complete by April 2008. In October 2007, GWW raised its EPS guidance for the second time in three months, to $4.85 to $4.95 (including a $0.04 projected fourth quarter charge related to about 125 information technology staff eliminations), from a range of $4.75 to $4.90.

Company Financials Fiscal Year Ended Dec. 31

Per Share Data ($)	2006	2005	2004	2003	2002	2001	2000	1999	1998	1997
Tangible Book Value	23.40	23.47	20.89	18.43	16.92	15.51	14.67	14.00	11.74	11.13
Cash Flow	5.35	4.85	4.06	3.28	3.30	2.73	3.01	2.85	3.20	3.05
Earnings	4.24	3.78	3.13	2.46	2.50	1.84	2.05	1.92	2.44	2.27
S&P Core Earnings	4.26	3.65	2.96	2.36	2.29	1.87	NA	NA	NA	NA
Dividends	1.11	0.92	0.79	0.74	0.72	0.70	0.67	0.63	0.58	0.53
Payout Ratio	26%	24%	25%	30%	29%	38%	33%	33%	24%	23%
Prices:High	79.95	72.45	66.99	53.30	59.40	48.99	56.88	58.13	54.72	49.88
Prices:Low	60.60	51.65	45.00	41.40	39.20	29.51	24.31	36.88	36.44	35.25
P/E Ratio:High	19	19	21	22	24	27	28	30	22	22
P/E Ratio:Low	14	14	14	17	16	16	12	19	15	16

Income Statement Analysis (Million $)

	2006	2005	2004	2003	2002	2001	2000	1999	1998	1997
Revenue	5,884	5,527	5,050	4,667	4,644	4,754	4,977	4,534	4,341	4,137
Operating Income	679	617	525	463	467	461	426	406	482	473
Depreciation	101	98.1	85.6	76.1	75.9	83.7	90.6	88.4	74.2	79.7
Interest Expense	1.93	1.86	4.39	6.02	6.16	10.7	24.4	15.6	6.65	5.46
Pretax Income	603	533	445	381	398	297	332	304	401	390
Effective Tax Rate	36.4%	35.0%	35.5%	40.4%	40.8%	41.3%	41.8%	40.5%	40.5%	40.5%
Net Income	383	346	287	227	235	175	193	181	239	232
S&P Core Earnings	385	336	272	217	213	177	NA	NA	NA	NA

Balance Sheet & Other Financial Data (Million $)

	2006	2005	2004	2003	2002	2001	2000	1999	1998	1997
Cash	361	545	429	403	209	169	63.4	62.7	43.1	46.9
Current Assets	1,862	1,998	1,755	1,633	1,485	1,393	1,483	1,471	1,206	1,183
Total Assets	3,046	3,108	2,810	2,625	2,437	2,331	2,460	2,565	2,104	1,998
Current Liabilities	706	727	662	707	586	554	747	871	664	534
Long Term Debt	4.90	4.90	Nil	4.90	120	118	125	125	123	131
Common Equity	2,178	2,289	2,068	1,845	1,668	1,603	1,537	1,481	1,279	1,295
Total Capital	2,189	2,301	2,072	1,850	1,787	1,723	1,663	1,654	1,402	1,429
Capital Expenditures	128	112	128	74.1	134	100	65.5	114	130	108
Cash Flow	484	444	372	303	311	258	284	269	313	311
Current Ratio	2.6	2.7	2.6	2.3	2.5	2.5	2.0	1.7	1.8	2.2
% Long Term Debt of Capitalization	0.2	0.2	Nil	0.3	6.7	6.9	7.5	7.6	8.8	9.2
% Net Income of Revenue	6.5	6.3	5.7	4.9	5.1	3.7	3.9	4.0	5.5	5.6
% Return on Assets	12.5	11.7	10.6	9.0	9.9	7.3	7.7	7.7	11.6	11.3
% Return on Equity	17.2	15.9	14.7	12.9	14.4	11.1	12.8	13.1	18.5	16.8

Data as orig reptd.; bef. results of disc opers/spec. items. Per share data adj. for stk. divs.; EPS diluted. E-Estimated. NA-Not Available. NM-Not Meaningful. NR-Not Ranked. UR-Under Review.

Office: 100 Grainger Pkwy, Lake Forest, IL 60045.
Telephone: 847-535-1000.
Website: http://www.grainger.com
Chrmn & CEO: R.L. Keyser

Pres & COO: J.T. Ryan
SVP & CFO: P.O. Loux
SVP & General Counsel: J.L. Howard
VP & Cntlr: R.L. Jadin

Investor Contact: W.D. Chapman (847-535-0881)
Board Members: B. P. Anderson, W. H. Gantz, V. A. Hailey, W. K. Hall, R. L. Keyser, S. L. Levenick, J. W. McCarter, Jr., N. S. Novich, M. J. Roberts, G. L. Rogers, J. T. Ryan, J. D. Slavik, H. B. Smith

Founded: 1927
Domicile: Illinois
Employees: 17,074

Halliburton Co

STANDARD &POOR'S

S&P Recommendation BUY ★★★★☆	**Price** $36.81 (as of Nov 23, 2007)	**12-Mo. Target Price** $45.00	**Investment Style** Large-Cap Growth

GICS Sector Energy
Sub-Industry Oil & Gas Equipment & Services

Summary This leading oilfield services company provides products and services to the global energy industry.

Key Stock Statistics (Source S&P, Vickers, company reports)

52-Wk Range	$41.95–27.65	S&P Oper. EPS 2007**E**	2.55	Market Capitalization(B)	$32.761	Beta	1.63
Trailing 12-Month EPS	$3.56	S&P Oper. EPS 2008**E**	3.21	Yield (%)	0.98	S&P 3-Yr. Proj. EPS CAGR(%)	20.00
Trailing 12-Month P/E	10.3	P/E on S&P Oper. EPS 2007**E**	14.4	Dividend Rate/Share	$0.36	S&P Credit Rating	A
$10K Invested 5 Yrs Ago	$41,912	Common Shares Outstg. (M)	890.0	Institutional Ownership (%)	84		

Price Performance

- 30-Week Mov. Avg. ···· 10-Week Mov. Avg. - - GAAP Earnings vs. Previous Year   Volume Above Avg. STARS
- 12-Mo. Target Price — Relative Strength — ▲ Up ▼ Down ► No Change   Below Avg.

2-for-1

214

J A S O N D J F M A M J J A S O N D J F M A M J J A S O N D J F M A M J J A S O N D J F
2004 **2005** **2006** **2007**

Options: ASE, CBOE, P, Ph

Analysis prepared by **Stewart Glickman, CFA** on November 16, 2007, when the stock traded at **$ 36.90**.

Highlights

➤ In the third quarter of 2007, HAL saw a narrowing of its North American operating margins by a mere 10 basis points, significantly better than its major oilfield services rivals. HAL said in October that it believed that it garnered market share in pressure pumping, which may have helped to generate this result. Internationally, HAL saw solid growth in the third quarter, and we anticipate continued strong growth in 2008, especially in the Middle East, Europe and Africa, with more modest growth in Asia.

➤ We view HAL's decision to open its headquarters in Dubai as a signal of the growing importance of the Middle East to its growth prospects. We think the acquisition of PSL Energy Services meshes with that strategic vision. We see the PSL transaction greatly boosting HAL's production enhancement headcount and equipment capacity in the Eastern Hemisphere.

➤ For 2007, we expect a decline of 34% in revenues, reflecting the separation of KBR (masking an expected 16% gain in oilfield services revenues), and EPS of $2.55. For 2008, we see oilfield services revenues up 16%, and EPS of $3.21.

Investment Rationale/Risk

➤ While the split-off of KBR shares eliminated a major overhang on the stock, we think the newly transformed HAL should still merit a valuation discount to peers (albeit smaller than before) due to its relatively lower Eastern Hemisphere exposure. We believe HAL is taking steps to enhance its leverage to overseas markets -- the recent PSL Energy acquisition being an example -- and we expect that over time it will gain market share and enhance its geographic footprint in frontier regions.

➤ Risks to our recommendation and target price include reduced oil and gas drilling activity, especially in North America; lower than expected oil and natural gas prices; and political risk.

➤ Our discounted cash flow (DCF) model, assuming a weighted average cost of capital of about 9% and terminal growth of 3%, shows intrinsic value of $44 per share. Despite the KBR spinoff, with higher exposure to North American oilfield activity, we think a valuation discount is merited. Using multiples of 9X estimated 2008 EBITDA and 11.5X projected 2008 cash flow (a modest discount to peers) and blending with our DCF model, our 12-month target price is $45.

Qualitative Risk Assessment

LOW	MEDIUM	**HIGH**

Our risk assessment reflects HAL's exposure to volatile crude oil and natural gas prices, leverage to the North American oilfield services market, and political risk associated with operating in frontier regions such as West Africa and the Middle East. A partial offset is HAL's strong number two position in oilfield services.

Quantitative Evaluations

S&P Quality Ranking   B

D	C	B-	**B**	B+	A-	A	A+

Relative Strength Rank   **MODERATE**

63

LOWEST = 1   HIGHEST = 99

Revenue/Earnings Data

Revenue (Million $)

	1Q	2Q	3Q	4Q	Year
2007	3,422	3,735	3,928	--	--
2006	5,184	5,545	5,831	6,016	22,576
2005	4,938	5,163	5,095	5,798	20,994
2004	5,519	4,956	4,790	5,201	20,466
2003	3,060	3,599	4,148	5,464	16,271
2002	3,007	3,235	2,982	3,348	12,572

Earnings Per Share ($)

2007	0.52	0.63	0.79	E0.72	E2.55
2006	0.45	0.48	0.58	0.65	2.16
2005	0.36	0.38	0.48	1.04	2.27
2004	0.09	-0.07	0.21	0.20	0.44
2003	0.07	0.05	0.11	0.17	0.39
2002	0.06	-0.42	0.11	-0.15	-0.40

Fiscal year ended Dec. 31. Next earnings report expected: Late January. EPS Estimates based on S&P Operating Earnings; historical GAAP earnings are as reported.

Dividend Data (Dates: mm/dd Payment Date: mm/dd/yy)

Amount ($)	Date Decl.	Ex-Div. Date	Stk. of Record	Payment Date
0.075	02/15	02/27	03/01	03/22/07
0.090	05/16	05/30	06/01	06/21/07
0.090	07/11	08/29	09/03	09/25/07
0.090	10/15	11/29	12/03	12/20/07

Dividends have been paid since 1947. Source: Company reports.

Halliburton Co

Business Summary November 16, 2007

CORPORATE OVERVIEW. HAL is a leading global provider of oilfield services to the energy industry, and until April 2007, provided engineering and construction expertise to energy, industrial and governmental customers. In 2006, HAL was comprised of two main business units: the Energy Services Group (ESG: 57% of 2006 revenues and 93% of segment operating income), and the KBR unit (KBR: 43%, 7%). ESG is further categorized by four operating segments: Production Optimization (24%, 42%), Fluid Systems (16%, 22%), Drilling & Formation Evaluation (14%, 23%), and Digital & Consulting Solutions (3%, 7%). KBR is further divided into two operating segments: the Energy & Chemicals segment (E&C: 11%, 1%) and the Government & Infrastructure segment (G&I: 32%, 6%). The former segment includes both upstream and downstream oil and gas projects, including liquefied natural gas (LNG) and gas-to-liquid (GTL) projects, while the latter segment includes reconstruction work in Iraq; Iraq generated 19% of total revenues in 2006, down from 24% in 2005.

UPCOMING CATALYSTS. In April 2007, HAL effected the complete separation of KBR via a split-off of its 135.6 million share stake in KBR (81% of KBR's outstanding shares) in exchange for HAL shares. Under the transaction, HAL exchanged its stake in KBR for about 85.3 million shares of HAL (about 8% of HAL shares outstanding), which were retired as treasury stock in early April. Following the separation, HAL was transformed into a pure-play oilfield services company. We believe that this separation advances HAL's shareholder value, given KBR's relatively lower operating margins and the corresponding valuation discount to HAL that had resulted, in our view, from KBR's presence. Operating margins at ESG reached 26% in 2006, significantly higher than the 1.6% for the E&C segment or 2.8% in the G&I segment. Also in April, HAL announced that it will recognize a gain of approximately $1.0 billion in the second quarter of 2007 due to the KBR split-off.

CORPORATE STRATEGY. HAL has transformed itself into a pure play oilfield services company, with a strong base in North America, but with a goal, in our view, of expanding its presence in the Eastern Hemisphere. Subsequent to the split-off, with HAL's financial obligations to KBR for the Barracuda-Caratinga project and the Foreign Corrupt Practices Act investigations limited by terms of the Master Separation Agreement with KBR, we view HAL's exposure to such issues as reduced. While we expect HAL to defend its strong market position in North America, we believe that future capital expenditures will increasingly flow to the Eastern Hemisphere, which we see as growing faster in the long term.

Company Financials Fiscal Year Ended Dec. 31

Per Share Data ($)	2006	2005	2004	2003	2002	2001	2000	1999	1998	1997
Tangible Book Value	6.61	5.46	3.55	2.14	3.25	4.65	3.90	3.98	3.74	4.32
Cash Flow	2.66	2.76	1.01	0.98	0.18	1.26	0.77	1.53	0.65	1.47
Earnings	2.16	2.27	0.44	0.39	-0.40	0.64	0.21	0.34	-0.02	0.88
S&P Core Earnings	2.12	2.11	0.37	0.34	-0.52	0.33	NA	NA	NA	NA
Dividends	0.30	0.25	0.25	0.25	0.25	0.25	0.25	0.25	0.25	0.25
Payout Ratio	14%	11%	57%	64%	NM	39%	119%	75%	NM	29%
Prices:High	41.99	34.89	20.85	13.60	10.83	24.63	27.59	25.88	28.63	31.63
Prices:Low	26.33	18.59	12.90	8.60	4.30	5.47	16.13	14.06	12.50	14.84
P/E Ratio:High	19	15	48	35	NM	38	NM	77	NM	36
P/E Ratio:Low	12	8	30	22	NM	9	NM	42	NM	17

Income Statement Analysis (Million $)

	2006	2005	2004	2003	2002	2001	2000	1999	1998	1997
Revenue	22,576	20,994	20,466	16,271	12,572	13,046	11,856	14,765	17,159	8,819
Operating Income	3,875	2,972	1,291	1,191	363	1,615	789	1,069	1,769	1,117
Depreciation, Depletion and Amortization	527	504	509	518	505	531	503	599	587	310
Interest Expense	175	207	229	139	113	147	146	144	137	43.0
Pretax Income	3,449	2,492	651	612	-228	954	335	1,012	278	766
Effective Tax Rate	33.2%	3.17%	37.0%	38.2%	NM	40.3%	38.5%	21.1%	NM	39.2%
Net Income	2,272	2,357	385	339	-346	551	188	755	-15.0	454
S&P Core Earnings	2,220	2,181	320	299	-445	287	NA	NA	NA	NA

Balance Sheet & Other Financial Data (Million $)

	2006	2005	2004	2003	2002	2001	2000	1999	1998	1997
Cash	4,379	2,391	2,808	1,815	1,107	290	231	466	203	221
Current Assets	11,183	9,327	9,962	7,919	5,560	5,573	5,568	6,022	6,083	2,972
Total Assets	16,820	15,010	15,796	15,463	12,844	10,966	10,103	10,728	11,112	5,603
Current Liabilities	4,727	4,437	7,064	6,542	3,272	2,908	3,826	3,693	4,004	1,773
Long Term Debt	2,786	2,813	3,593	3,415	1,181	1,403	1,049	1,056	1,370	539
Common Equity	7,376	6,372	3,932	2,547	3,558	4,752	5,618	4,287	4,061	2,585
Total Capital	10,609	9,330	7,633	6,062	4,810	6,196	6,705	5,496	5,601	3,144
Capital Expenditures	891	651	575	515	764	797	578	593	914	577
Cash Flow	2,799	2,861	894	857	159	1,082	691	1,354	572	764
Current Ratio	2.4	2.1	1.4	1.2	1.7	1.9	1.5	1.6	1.5	1.7
% Long Term Debt of Capitalization	26.3	30.2	47.1	56.3	24.6	22.6	15.6	19.2	24.5	17.1
% Return on Assets	14.3	15.3	2.5	2.4	NM	5.2	1.9	6.9	NM	9.0
% Return on Equity	33.1	45.7	14.4	11.1	NM	12.7	3.7	18.1	NM	19.1

Data as orig reptd.; bef. results of disc opers/spec. items. Per share data adj. for stk. divs.; EPS diluted. E-Estimated. NA-Not Available. NM-Not Meaningful. NR-Not Ranked. UR-Under Review.

Office: 1401 McKinney St Ste 2400, Houston, TX 77010-4040.
Telephone: 713-759-2600.
Email: investors@halliburton.com
Website: http://www.halliburton.com

Chrmn, Pres & CEO: D.J. Lesar
COO & EVP: A.R. Lane
EVP & CFO: C.C. Gaut
EVP & General Counsel: A.O. Cornelison, Jr.

SVP & Chief Acctg Officer: M.A. McCollum
Investor Contact: E. Angelle (713-759-2688)
Board Members: K. M. Bader, A. M. Bennett, J. R. Boyd, M. Carroll, R. L. Crandall, K. T. Derr, S. M. Gillis, W. R. Howell, D. J. Lesar, J. L. Martin, J. A. Precourt, D. L. Reed

Founded: 1919
Domicile: Delaware
Employees: 104,000

Harley-Davidson Inc.

STANDARD &POOR'S

S&P Recommendation SELL ★ ★ ☆ ☆ ☆	**Price** $46.53 (as of Nov 23, 2007)	**12-Mo. Target Price** $45.00	**Investment Style** Large-Cap Growth

GICS Sector Consumer Discretionary
Sub-Industry Motorcycle Manufacturers

Summary This leading maker of heavyweight motorcycles also produces a line of motorcycle parts and accessories.

Key Stock Statistics (Source S&P, Vickers, company reports)

52-Wk Range	$75.05– 44.37	S&P Oper. EPS 2007**E**	3.74	Market Capitalization(B)	$11.688	Beta	0.97
Trailing 12-Month EPS	$3.92	S&P Oper. EPS 2008**E**	3.93	Yield (%)	2.58	S&P 3-Yr. Proj. EPS CAGR(%)	9.00
Trailing 12-Month P/E	11.9	P/E on S&P Oper. EPS 2007**E**	12.4	Dividend Rate/Share	$1.20	S&P Credit Rating	A+
$10K Invested 5 Yrs Ago	$9,709	Common Shares Outstg. (M)	251.2	Institutional Ownership (%)	76		

Price Performance

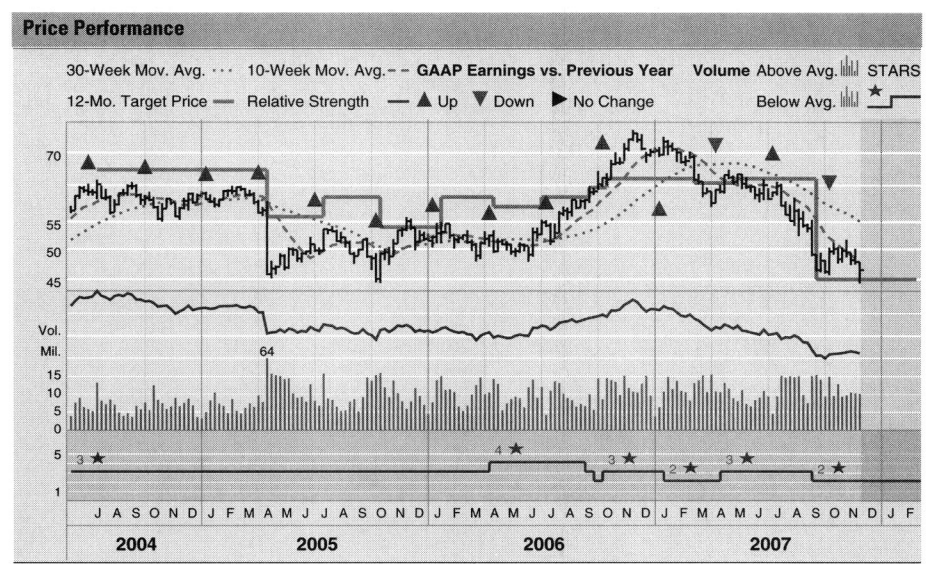

30-Week Mov. Avg. · · · 10-Week Mov. Avg. – – **GAAP Earnings vs. Previous Year** Volume Above Avg. |||| STARS
12-Mo. Target Price — Relative Strength — ▲ Up ▼ Down ► No Change Below Avg. |||| ★

Options: ASE, CBOE, P, Ph

Analysis prepared by **Erik Kolb** on October 25, 2007, when the stock traded at **$ 49.35**.

Highlights

➤ In October 2007, HOG said that it expected fourth quarter 2007 wholesale shipments of Harley-Davidson brand motorcycles to total between 87,600 and 82,600 units, which would compare with 92,848 units shipped in the fourth quarter of 2006.

➤ We look for revenues in 2007 to decrease 1.1% from the $5.8 billion reported for 2006, as consumers likely reduce their discretionary spending because of high interest rates and gasoline prices, and the downturn in the U.S. housing market continues. We see market conditions remaining challenging in 2008, and we are expecting a modest 2.0% revenue increase. We estimate EPS of $3.74 in 2007, on 3.6% fewer diluted shares, and EPS of $3.93 in 2008, on a fractional decline in shares.

➤ As of September 30, 2007, HOG had cash equivalents and marketable securities totaling about $457 million, down from $1.046 billion at year-end 2005. In 2006, the company repurchased 19.3 million shares of its common stock at a cost of $1.06 billion. In October 2006, directors authorized a new share repurchase program for up to 20 million additional shares.

Investment Rationale/Risk

➤ Although we continue to view positively HOG's strong brand and market leadership, we expect motorcycle sales, especially in the U.S., to be weak through 2008. Although the company made some headway clearing inventory in July, we expect building inventories to remain an ongoing concern.

➤ Risks to our recommendation and target price include the possibility that consumers increase their discretionary spending and demand for HOG bikes is stronger than expected.

➤ Our 12-month target price of $45 is based on our discounted cash flow model, which assumes a blended WACC of 9.9% and an annual perpetuity cash flow growth rate of 1.8%, and our relative analysis, which applies a P/E slightly below its peers given HOG's high U.S. exposure. HOG increased its quarterly dividend payment by 43% over the past nine months, continuing a series of payout hikes in recent years.

Qualitative Risk Assessment

LOW	MEDIUM	HIGH

Our risk assessment reflects our view that this company's market leadership position and strong brand should help offset the prospect that an aging U.S. population will limit future domestic demand for motorcycles. Also, we expect the company to generate free cash flow, with some of it likely to be used for dividend increases and to repurchase stock.

Quantitative Evaluations

S&P Quality Ranking   **A+**

D	C	B-	B	B+	A-	A	A+

Relative Strength Rank   **MODERATE**
                 44
LOWEST = 1   HIGHEST = 99

Revenue/Earnings Data

Revenue (Million $)

	1Q	2Q	3Q	4Q	Year
2007	1,179	1,620	1,541	--	--
2006	1,285	1,377	1,636	1,503	5,801
2005	1,235	1,333	1,431	1,342	5,342
2004	1,166	1,328	1,301	1,221	5,015
2003	1,114	1,219	1,134	1,158	4,624
2002	927.9	1,001	1,136	1,027	4,091

Earnings Per Share ($)

2007	0.74	1.14	1.07	E0.79	E3.74
2006	0.86	0.91	1.20	0.97	3.93
2005	0.77	0.84	0.96	0.84	3.41
2004	0.68	0.83	0.77	0.71	3.00
2003	0.61	0.66	0.62	0.60	2.50
2002	0.39	0.47	0.54	0.49	1.90

Fiscal year ended Dec. 31. Next earnings report expected: Mid January. EPS Estimates based on S&P Operating Earnings; historical GAAP earnings are as reported.

Dividend Data (Dates: mm/dd Payment Date: mm/dd/yy)

Amount ($)	Date Decl.	Ex-Div. Date	Stk. of Record	Payment Date
0.210	12/12	12/20	12/22	12/28/06
0.210	02/14	03/01	03/05	03/20/07
0.250	04/28	06/07	06/11	06/19/07
0.300	09/13	09/27	10/01	10/11/07

Dividends have been paid since 1993. Source: Company reports.

Harley-Davidson Inc.

STANDARD &POOR'S

Business Summary October 25, 2007

CORPORATE OVERVIEW. Harley-Davidson is a leading supplier of heavy-weight motorcycles (engine displacement exceeding about 651 cubic centimeters). The company also sells motorcycle parts, accessories, clothing and collectibles, and has a sizable financial services business.

HOG manufactures five families of Harley-Davidson brand motorcycles: Sportster, Dyna, Softail, Touring and VRSC. As of early 2007, the engines in these product lines ranged in size from 883 cc to 1800 cc. The company's 2007 model year line-up includes 35 models of Harley-Davidson heavyweight motorcycles, with domestic manufacturer's suggested retail prices ranging from $6,595 to $20,195. Also, as of early 2007, HOG was offering some limited-edition custom motorcycles having suggested retail prices ranging from $24,995 to $33,495.

In 2006, HOG shipped 349,196 Harley-Davidson brand motorcycles, up from 329,017 in 2005. Also, HOG shipped 12,460 Buell motorcycles in 2006, up from 11,166 in 2005.

In July 2007, the company said that its 2008 line of motorcycles would include nine new models, and that certain models available with a limited-edition 105th Anniversary styling package.

CORPORATE STRATEGY. We expect the company to focus on both current owners of HOG motorcycles and on potential new customers. We believe that many purchasers of a new Harley-Davidson motorcycle previously owned a HOG bike.

We expect HOG's marketing focus to include international markets, where we project that HOG's opportunities for growth are stronger than they are in the U.S. In 2006, HOG's international sales totaled about $1.18 billion, up from $1.04 million in 2005.

In addition to selling motorcycle-related products, we see HOG making a sizable profit related to financial services that it provides to independent dealers and to retail customers of those dealers. During 2006, Harley-Davidson Financial Services financed 48% of the new Harley-Davidson motorcycles retailed by independent dealers in the United States, as compared to 45% in 2005.

Company Financials Fiscal Year Ended Dec. 31

Per Share Data ($)	2006	2005	2004	2003	2002	2001	2000	1999	1998	1997
Tangible Book Value	10.46	11.05	10.73	9.63	7.21	5.64	4.47	3.65	3.20	2.59
Cash Flow	4.87	4.25	3.72	3.18	2.48	1.93	1.56	1.23	0.97	0.79
Earnings	3.93	3.41	3.00	2.50	1.90	1.43	1.13	0.87	0.69	0.57
S&P Core Earnings	3.95	3.44	2.98	2.51	1.85	1.34	NA	NA	NA	NA
Dividends	0.81	0.63	0.41	0.20	0.14	0.12	0.10	0.09	0.08	0.07
Payout Ratio	21%	18%	13%	8%	7%	8%	9%	10%	11%	12%
Prices:High	75.87	62.49	63.75	52.51	57.25	55.99	50.63	32.03	23.75	15.63
Prices:Low	47.86	44.40	45.20	35.01	42.60	32.00	29.53	21.38	12.47	8.34
P/E Ratio:High	19	18	21	21	30	39	45	37	34	28
P/E Ratio:Low	12	13	15	14	22	22	26	25	18	15

Income Statement Analysis (Million $)										
Revenue	5,801	5,342	5,015	4,624	4,091	3,363	2,906	2,453	2,064	1,763
Operating Income	1,431	1,676	1,576	1,346	1,059	816	648	530	421	340
Depreciation	214	206	214	197	176	153	133	114	87.4	70.2
Interest Expense	Nil	Nil	Nil	Nil	Nil	Nil	Nil	Nil	Nil	Nil
Pretax Income	1,624	1,488	1,379	1,166	886	673	549	421	336	276
Effective Tax Rate	35.8%	35.5%	35.5%	34.7%	34.5%	35.0%	36.6%	36.5%	36.5%	37.0%
Net Income	1,043	960	890	761	580	438	348	267	214	174
S&P Core Earnings	1,048	969	881	763	564	411	NA	NA	NA	NA

Balance Sheet & Other Financial Data (Million $)										
Cash	897	1,046	1,612	1,323	796	635	420	183	165	147
Total Assets	5,532	5,255	5,483	4,923	3,861	3,118	2,436	2,112	1,920	1,599
Long Term Debt	87.0	1,000	800	670	380	380	355	280	280	280
Total Debt	87.0	1,205	1,295	794	763	597	445	461	427	371
Common Equity	2,757	3,084	3,218	2,958	2,233	1,756	1,406	1,161	1,080	827
Capital Expenditures	220	198	214	227	324	204	204	166	183	186
Cash Flow	1,257	1,165	1,104	958	756	591	481	381	301	244
% Return on Assets	19.3	17.9	17.1	17.3	16.6	15.8	15.3	13.3	12.2	11.9
% Return on Equity	35.7	30.5	28.8	29.3	29.1	27.7	27.1	24.4	23.0	23.4
% Long Term Debt of Capitalization	3.1	23.6	19.7	17.8	14.4	17.6	20.2	19.4	21.4	25.3

Data as orig reptd.; bef. results of disc opers/spec. items. Per share data adj. for stk. divs.; EPS diluted. E-Estimated. NA-Not Available. NM-Not Meaningful. NR-Not Ranked. UR-Under Review.

Office: 3700 W Juneau Ave, Milwaukee, WI 53208.
Telephone: 414-342-4680.
Email: investor_relations@harley-davidson.com
Website: http://www.harley-davidson.com

Chrmn: J.L. Bleustein
Pres & CEO: J.L. Ziemer
Investor Contact: T.E. Bergmann (414-342-4680)
VP & CFO: T.E. Bergmann

VP, Chief Acctg Officer & Treas: J.M. Brostowitz
Board Members: B. K. Allen, R. I. Beattie, J. L. Bleustein, G. H. Conrades, J. C. Green, D. A. James, S. L. Levinson, G. L. Miles, Jr., J. A. Norling, J. L. Ziemer

Founded: 1903
Domicile: Wisconsin
Employees: 9,704

The McGraw-Hill Companies

Harman International Industries Inc.

STANDARD &POOR'S

S&P Recommendation **BUY** ★★★★☆	Price $73.61 (as of Nov 23, 2007)	12-Mo. Target Price $109.00	Investment Style Large-Cap Growth

GICS Sector Consumer Discretionary
Sub-Industry Consumer Electronics

Summary This company manufactures and markets high-fidelity audio products and electronic systems targeted at OEM, consumer and professional markets.

Key Stock Statistics (Source S&P, Vickers, company reports)

52-Wk Range	$125.13– 71.33	S&P Oper. EPS 2008**E**	4.35	Market Capitalization(B)	$4.802	Beta	1.60
Trailing 12-Month EPS	$4.42	S&P Oper. EPS 2009**E**	5.79	Yield (%)	0.07	S&P 3-Yr. Proj. EPS CAGR(%)	20.00
Trailing 12-Month P/E	16.7	P/E on S&P Oper. EPS 2008**E**	16.9	Dividend Rate/Share	$0.05	S&P Credit Rating	BB-
$10K Invested 5 Yrs Ago	$24,418	Common Shares Outstg. (M)	65.2	Institutional Ownership (%)	88		

Price Performance

30-Week Mov. Avg. · · · 10-Week Mov. Avg. - - **GAAP Earnings vs. Previous Year** Volume Above Avg. |ılıl STARS
12-Mo. Target Price — Relative Strength — ▲ Up ▼ Down ▶ No Change Below Avg. ılıl

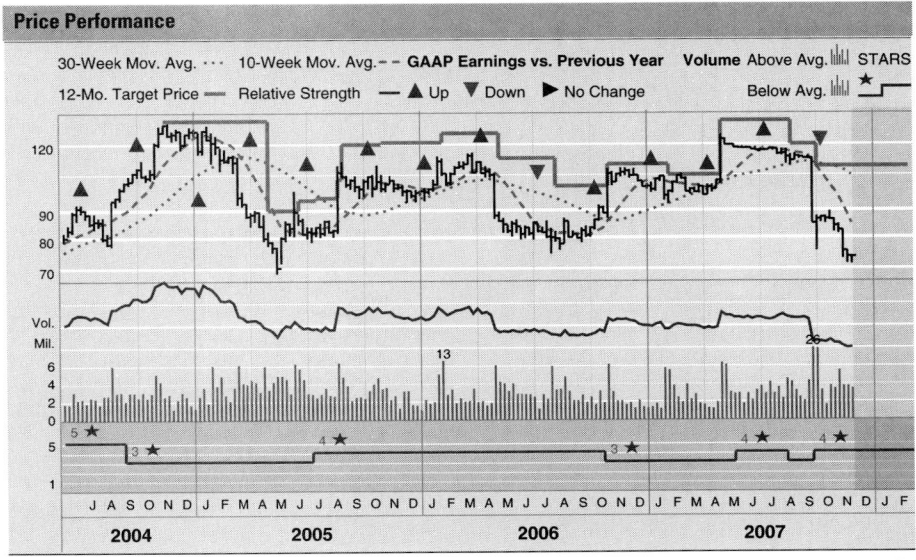

	2004	2005	2006	2007

Options: ASE, CBOE, P, Ph

Analysis prepared by **James Peters, CFA** on November 14, 2007, when the stock traded at **$ 73.61**.

Highlights

➤ For FY 08 (Jun.), we see overall revenue growth of about 15%, led by gains in the automotive segment. Given the long lead times required to fulfill infotainment awards programs, we believe there is high visibility into HAR's automotive segment, which represents about 70% of annual revenues. We note that HAR's original equipment manufacturing (OEM) pipeline for the automotive segment is booked through 2008 and is nearly full for 2009.

➤ We believe research and development expenses will rise in the first half of FY 08 as HAR prepares for recently awarded contracts as well as future growth opportunities by developing its infotainment and driver assistance capabilities. Overall, we see an operating margin contraction to 9.7% from 11.2% in FY 08, although we expect margin improvement as FY 08 progresses and into FY 09 as R&D expenses moderate and higher production volume improves capacity utilization.

➤ Excluding one-time expenses associated with the recently withdrawn takeover offer, we see operating EPS rising to $4.35, from $4.14 in FY 07, on fewer shares. Reported EPS in FY 07 included a net gain from one-time items of $0.58.

Investment Rationale/Risk

➤ Following a steep drop in the company's stock price at the end of September after KKR and GS Capital Partners backed out of a deal to acquire HAR for $120 per share, the company announced a deal termination fee in the form of a $400 million convertible note loan to HAR at an interest rate of 1.25%. On October 31, the company said it completed a program to repurchase shares with the loan proceeds, which we expect to add about $0.16 to FY 08 EPS. While costs will be higher than we originally anticipated this year, we are confident that the company's long-term business prospects remain solid. Our buy recommendation reflects our belief that the risk/reward quotient is positive at the current stock valuation.

➤ Risks to our recommendation and target price include higher-than-anticipated research and development costs, and a loss of customers.

➤ We derive our 12-month target price of $109 by applying an 11X multiple to our FY 09 EBITDA estimate of $660 million. The multiple is at the low end of HAR's historical range of 10X - 14X, reflecting the heightened near-term uncertainty we see in HAR's expense requirements.

Qualitative Risk Assessment

LOW	MEDIUM	HIGH

Our risk assessment reflects our view of HAR's strong balance sheet and what we consider high visibility into its revenue pipeline, offset by its large customer concentration in the automotive segment and sensitivity to the cyclical automobile industry.

Quantitative Evaluations

S&P Quality Ranking A-

D	C	B-	B	B+	A-	A	A+

Relative Strength Rank WEAK

18

LOWEST = 1   HIGHEST = 99

Revenue/Earnings Data

Revenue (Million $)

	1Q	2Q	3Q	4Q	Year
2008	947.0	--	--	--	--
2007	825.5	931.7	882.8	911.1	3,551
2006	754.7	832.7	801.5	859.1	3,248
2005	691.7	788.6	742.6	808.0	3,031
2004	597.3	691.6	690.4	732.0	2,711
2003	490.8	560.0	554.5	623.3	2,229

Earnings Per Share ($)

2008	0.55	E1.18	E1.22	E1.43	E4.35
2007	0.85	1.22	1.07	1.58	4.72
2006	0.79	1.07	0.94	0.95	3.75
2005	0.48	0.92	0.90	1.01	3.31
2004	0.29	0.60	0.63	0.76	2.27
2003	0.15	0.41	0.45	0.55	1.55

Fiscal year ended Jun. 30. Next earnings report expected: Late January. EPS Estimates based on S&P Operating Earnings; historical GAAP earnings are as reported.

Dividend Data (Dates: mm/dd Payment Date: mm/dd/yy)

Amount ($)	Date Decl.	Ex-Div. Date	Stk. of Record	Payment Date
0.013	01/29	02/05	02/07	02/21/07
0.013	05/01	05/07	05/09	05/23/07
0.013	07/30	08/06	08/08	08/22/07
0.013	10/30	11/06	11/08	11/21/07

Dividends have been paid since 1994. Source: Company reports.

Harman International Industries Inc.

STANDARD
&POOR'S

Business Summary November 14, 2007

CORPORATE OVERVIEW. HAR has three operating segments: Automotive (70% of FY 07 (Jun.) sales), Professional (16%), and Consumer (14%). Within Automotive, HAR designs, manufactures and markets audio, electronic and infotainment systems to be installed as original equipment by automotive manufacturers. Infotainment systems are a combination of information and entertainment components that may include or control GPS navigation, traffic information, voice-activated telephone and climate control, rear seat entertainment, wireless Internet access, hard disk recording, MP3 playback, and high-end branded audio systems. Brand names include JBL, Infinity, Mark Levinson, Harmon/Kardon, Logic 7, Lexicon and Becker. Customers include DaimlerChrysler, Mercedes Benz, the BMW Group, Toyota/Lexus, Audi/VW, Porsche, Land Rover, Hyundai and PSA Peugeot Citroen. HAR also produces an infotainment system for Harley-Davidson motorcycles, and produces personal navigation devices that are primarily sold in Europe.

In the Consumer segment, HAR makes audio, video and electronic systems for home, mobile and multimedia applications. Mobile products include an array of aftermarket systems to deliver audio entertainment and navigation in vehi-

cles. Products for multimedia applications are primarily focused on enhancing sound for Apple's iPods and iPhones, computers, headphones and MP3 players. Brands include JBL, Infinity, Harman/Kardon, Lexicon, Mark Levinson and Revel. The Professional segment produces loudspeakers and electronics used by audio professionals in concert halls, stadiums, and other buildings for recording, broadcast, cinema and music reproduction applications. In October 2007, the company noted that it had a professional services contract to install sound systems at venues in China for the 2008 Olympics. Brands include JBL Professional, Soundcraft, AKG, Lexicon, BSS and Studer.

DaimlerChrysler accounted for 25% of the company's net sales in FY 07, primarily from the Mercedes-Benz division. Thus, we believe HAR has a significant level of customer concentration risk, although we see no near-term threat to the business.

Company Financials Fiscal Year Ended Jun. 30

Per Share Data ($)	2007	2006	2005	2004	2003	2002	2001	2000	1999	1998
Tangible Book Value	16.71	12.82	10.74	9.43	6.66	5.04	4.33	4.69	4.61	4.70
Cash Flow	6.64	5.66	4.99	3.80	2.85	2.00	1.48	1.95	1.09	1.54
Earnings	4.72	3.75	3.31	2.27	1.55	0.85	0.48	1.03	0.16	0.72
S&P Core Earnings	4.75	3.75	3.28	2.27	1.51	0.76	0.41	NA	NA	NA
Dividends	0.05	0.05	0.05	0.05	0.05	0.05	0.05	0.04	0.05	0.05
Payout Ratio	1%	1%	2%	2%	3%	6%	10%	4%	31%	7%
Prices:High	125.13	115.85	130.45	131.74	75.35	32.65	23.31	25.18	14.03	11.70
Prices:Low	71.33	74.65	68.54	66.12	26.15	19.09	11.64	13.75	8.56	7.88
P/E Ratio:High	27	31	39	58	49	38	49	24	86	16
P/E Ratio:Low	15	20	21	29	17	22	24	13	53	11

Income Statement Analysis (Million $)										
Revenue	3,551	3,248	3,031	2,711	2,229	1,826	1,717	1,678	1,500	1,513
Operating Income	514	527	470	360	255	181	138	186	143	163
Depreciation	127	130	119	106	88.5	78.1	67.2	64.6	66.8	62.5
Interest Expense	1.50	13.0	10.5	17.2	22.6	22.4	25.0	18.5	23.6	24.9
Pretax Income	382	376	335	228	142	80.2	45.1	103	14.4	75.7
Effective Tax Rate	18.4%	32.4%	30.6%	30.6%	26.0%	28.2%	28.2%	29.1%	18.7%	28.9%
Net Income	314	255	233	158	105	57.5	32.4	72.8	11.7	53.8
S&P Core Earnings	316	256	231	158	102	51.5	27.3	NA	NA	NA

Balance Sheet & Other Financial Data (Million $)										
Cash	106	292	291	378	148	116	2.75	4.36	2.96	16.2
Current Assets	1,233	1,249	1,183	1,204	968	877	709	671	647	695
Total Assets	2,509	2,355	2,187	1,989	1,704	1,480	1,162	1,138	1,066	1,131
Current Liabilities	816	869	729	662	487	433	350	361	287	327
Long Term Debt	57.7	179	331	388	498	470	Nil	255	280	260
Common Equity	1,510	1,228	1,061	875	656	527	423	486	468	512
Total Capital	1,568	1,410	1,392	1,263	1,154	999	424	742	749	772
Capital Expenditures	175	131	176	135	116	114	88.1	80.4	67.8	57.5
Cash Flow	441	385	352	264	194	136	99.6	137	78.5	116
Current Ratio	1.5	1.4	1.6	1.8	2.0	2.0	2.0	1.9	2.3	2.1
% Long Term Debt of Capitalization	3.7	12.7	23.8	30.7	43.2	47.1	Nil	34.3	37.4	33.6
% Net Income of Revenue	8.8	7.9	7.7	5.8	4.7	3.1	1.9	4.3	0.8	3.6
% Return on Assets	12.9	11.2	11.2	8.6	6.6	4.4	2.8	6.6	1.1	5.0
% Return on Equity	22.8	22.3	24.1	20.6	17.8	12.1	7.1	15.3	2.4	11.0

Data as orig reptd.; bef. results of disc opers/spec. items. Per share data adj. for stk. divs.; EPS diluted. E-Estimated. NA-Not Available. NM-Not Meaningful. NR-Not Ranked. UR-Under Review.

Office: 1101 Pennsylvania Avenue, N.W., Washington, DC 20004.
Telephone: 202-393-1101.
Website: http://www.harman.com
Exec Chrmn: S. Harman

Pres, Vice Chrmn & CEO: D. Paliwal
EVP & CFO: K.L. Brown
EVP & CTO: E. Geiger
Investor Contact: S.B. Robinson (202-393-1101)

Board Members: S. Harman, S. M. Hufstedler, A. McLaughlin Korologos, E. H. Meyer, D. Paliwal

Founded: 1980
Domicile: Delaware
Employees: 11,688

The McGraw-Hill Companies

Harrah's Entertainment Inc

STANDARD &POOR'S

S&P Recommendation	HOLD ★★★☆☆	Price	12-Mo. Target Price	Investment Style
		$86.90 (as of Nov 26, 2007)	$90.00	Large-Cap Blend

GICS Sector Consumer Discretionary
Sub-Industry Casinos & Gaming

Summary This geographically diverse company, based in Las Vegas, operates and/or has ownership interests in more than 30 gaming properties.

Key Stock Statistics (Source S&P, Vickers, company reports)

52-Wk Range	$88.75– 75.70	S&P Oper. EPS 2007E	3.50	Market Capitalization(B)	$16.271	Beta	1.23
Trailing 12-Month EPS	$3.75	S&P Oper. EPS 2008E	4.05	Yield (%)	1.84	S&P 3-Yr. Proj. EPS CAGR(%)	13.00
Trailing 12-Month P/E	23.2	P/E on S&P Oper. EPS 2007E	24.8	Dividend Rate/Share	$1.60	S&P Credit Rating	BB
$10K Invested 5 Yrs Ago	$24,384	Common Shares Outstg. (M)	187.2	Institutional Ownership (%)	80		

Price Performance

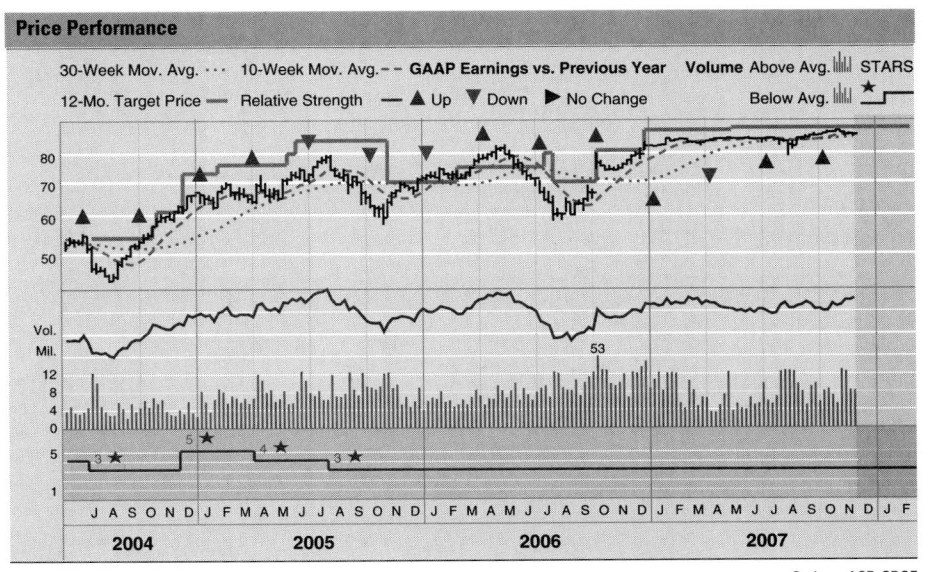

30-Week Mov. Avg. ···   10-Week Mov. Avg. - -   **GAAP Earnings vs. Previous Year**   Volume Above Avg. STARS
12-Mo. Target Price —   Relative Strength —   ▲ Up   ▼ Down   ► No Change   Below Avg.   ★

Options: ASE, CBOE

Analysis prepared by **Esther Y. Kwon, CFA** on November 26, 2007, when the stock traded at **$ 87.45**.

Highlights

➤ In June 2005, HET acquired gaming company Caesars Entertainment through a stock and cash transaction. This increased HET's presence in various markets, including Las Vegas and Atlantic City. In December 2006, HET acquired casino company London Clubs International plc.

➤ On December 19, 2006, HET entered into a definitive agreement to be acquired by affiliates of private equity firms Texas Pacific Group and Apollo Management, L.P., for $90 a share, subject to necessary approvals. Shareholders approved the deal in April.

➤ Before some special items, we look for 2007 operating EPS of $3.50, compared to $3.34 in 2006. Both years include costs related to master planning for prospective development in Las Vegas and Atlantic City. Among the special items excluded from 2006's $3.34 are $104.2 million of costs (net, pretax) related to writedowns, reserves and recoveries, and project opening costs. Also excluded are $37.0 million of merger and integration costs. We see 2008 EPS of $4.05.

Investment Rationale/Risk

➤ The stock recently traded below the $90 per share acquisition price, and we believe this partly reflects the relatively lengthy regulatory review process and the amount of time that investors would have to wait before the proposed acquisition is completed. Since October, the gaming commissions of New Jersey, Mississippi, Indiana and Illinois have approved the proposed transaction. HET said that it intends to pay its regular $0.40 per share quarterly dividend until the planned transaction closes.

➤ Risks to our recommendation and target price include a failure to consummate the planned deal or a similarly favorable one.

➤ Our 12-month target price of $90 reflects the proposed acquisition of HET. If the planned deal is not completed by about March 1, 2008, we think the acquisition price may be adjusted higher. The acquisition price is 26X our 2007 EPS estimate, which is modestly below the average P/E recently received by a small group of peer companies that we view as having primarily U.S. operations.

Qualitative Risk Assessment

LOW	MEDIUM	HIGH

Our risk assessment reflects our view that economic or regulatory changes in local or regional markets that can have an adverse impact on operating results are likely to be diluted by HET's geographic diversification. The development of new or expanded facilities by others is likely to increase competitive conditions in some gaming markets. However, we expect HET to generate a large amount of cash flow from operating activities, portions of which are likely to be used to help finance expansion projects.

Quantitative Evaluations

S&P Quality Ranking   **B**

D	C	B-	B	B+	A-	A	A+

Relative Strength Rank   **STRONG**

80

LOWEST = 1   HIGHEST = 99

Revenue/Earnings Data

Revenue (Million $)

	1Q	2Q	3Q	4Q	Year
2007	2,656	2,702	2,840	--	--
2006	2,357	2,374	2,513	2,431	9,674
2005	1,257	1,458	2,301	2,095	7,111
2004	1,012	1,037	1,310	1,189	4,548
2003	1,059	1,080	1,139	1,044	4,323
2002	974.7	1,021	1,124	1,016	4,136

Earnings Per Share ($)

2007	0.88	1.03	1.16	E0.80	E3.50
2006	0.95	0.69	0.96	0.21	2.79
2005	0.81	0.66	0.85	-0.39	1.75
2004	0.67	0.74	0.99	0.53	2.92
2003	0.73	0.70	0.89	0.32	2.64
2002	0.75	0.75	0.89	0.48	2.86

Fiscal year ended Dec. 31. Next earnings report expected: Late February. EPS Estimates based on S&P Operating Earnings; historical GAAP earnings are as reported.

Dividend Data (Dates: mm/dd Payment Date: mm/dd/yy)

Amount ($)	Date Decl.	Ex-Div. Date	Stk. of Record	Payment Date
0.400	01/31	02/08	02/12	02/21/07
0.400	04/27	05/07	05/09	05/23/07
0.400	07/24	08/06	08/08	08/22/07
0.400	10/29	11/06	11/08	11/21/07

Dividends have been paid since 2003. Source: Company reports.

Harrah's Entertainment Inc

STANDARD &POOR'S

Business Summary November 26, 2007

CORPORATE OVERVIEW. Harrah's Entertainment is the most geographically diversified casino company in North America. The company has ownership interests in and/or manages more than 30 gaming properties.

CORPORATE STRATEGY. This company has grown partly through acquisitions, the largest of which was the June 2005 acquisition of Caesars Entertainment. Earlier acquisitions included Horseshoe Gaming Holding Corp. (2004), Harveys Casino Resorts (2001), Players International (2000), Rio Hotel and Casino Inc. (1999), and Showboat Inc. (1998). In December 2006, HET acquired casino company London Clubs International plc. Also, outside the U.S., we have seen the company looking to participate in gaming development through joint ventures in various places. However, a joint venture proposal for a Singapore casino project was unsuccessful. In addition, we have seen the company looking to expand a number of existing U.S. properties. The company's future strategy could be affected if HET is acquired.

MARKET PROFILE. We estimate U.S. casino winnings in 2006 at $51 billion, which excludes gaming activity at racetracks. In the two largest U.S. gaming markets -- Las Vegas and Atlantic City -- HET operates a total of about 12 casino/hotels, including six that were part of the Caesars acquisition. In De-

cember 2005, HET acquired the Imperial Palace on the Las Vegas Strip, and we look for at least a portion of the 18.5-acre site to be used for future redevelopment. Also, in February 2007, HET acquired the Barbary Coast casino/hotel property in Las Vegas. In January 2007, a Harrah's slot machine casino opened at a racetrack property in Chester, PA. The "racino" there is 50% owned by HET.

PRIMARY BUSINESS DYNAMICS. HET operates casinos on boats or barges in Illinois, Indiana, Iowa, Louisiana, Mississippi and Missouri. However, three of HET's water-based gaming projects, plus a land-based casino in New Orleans, were closed following hurricane-related damage in the second half of 2005. The New Orleans casino and a Lake Charles, LA, hotel reopened in February 2006, and a Biloxi, MS, gaming project reopened in August 2006. HET has sold or has agreed to sell assets related to two of the closed gaming projects.

Company Financials Fiscal Year Ended Dec. 31

Per Share Data ($)	2006	2005	2004	2003	2002	2001	2000	1999	1998	1997
Tangible Book Value	1.81	2.78	NM	4.41	2.50	2.26	5.04	6.43	2.41	6.79
Cash Flow	6.59	5.32	6.12	5.75	5.55	4.68	2.30	3.40	2.77	2.27
Earnings	2.79	1.75	2.92	2.64	2.86	1.81	-0.09	1.71	1.19	1.06
S&P Core Earnings	3.01	1.53	2.66	2.51	2.66	1.62	NA	NA	NA	NA
Dividends	1.53	1.39	1.26	0.60	Nil	Nil	Nil	Nil	Nil	Nil
Payout Ratio	55%	79%	43%	23%	Nil	Nil	Nil	Nil	Nil	Nil
Prices:High	84.25	79.69	67.25	49.94	51.35	38.29	30.06	30.75	26.38	23.06
Prices:Low	58.22	57.29	43.94	30.30	34.95	22.00	17.00	14.19	11.06	15.50
P/E Ratio:High	30	46	23	19	18	21	NM	18	22	22
P/E Ratio:Low	21	33	15	11	12	12	NM	8	9	15

Income Statement Analysis (Million $)	2006	2005	2004	2003	2002	2001	2000	1999	1998	1997
Revenue	9,674	7,111	4,548	4,323	4,136	3,709	3,471	3,024	2,004	1,619
Operating Income	2,385	1,816	1,165	1,081	1,100	939	1,088	755	484	385
Depreciation	711	534	362	343	306	333	282	218	159	122
Interest Expense	670	481	272	234	240	256	227	193	117	79.1
Pretax Income	838	505	529	476	536	348	17.8	79.4	203	184
Effective Tax Rate	35.3%	45.1%	36.1%	36.2%	36.8%	36.4%	NM	NM	36.7%	37.4%
Net Income	527	265	330	292	325	209	-11.3	220	122	108
S&P Core Earnings	564	236	301	277	303	187	NA	NA	NA	NA

Balance Sheet & Other Financial Data (Million $)	2006	2005	2004	2003	2002	2001	2000	1999	1998	1997
Cash	800	724	489	410	416	361	299	234	159	116
Current Assets	1,631	1,629	787	685	686	618	583	487	279	212
Total Assets	22,285	20,518	8,586	6,579	6,350	6,129	5,166	4,767	3,286	2,006
Current Liabilities	2,241	1,598	754	583	626	569	778	372	233	211
Long Term Debt	11,639	11,039	5,151	3,672	3,763	3,719	2,836	2,540	1,999	924
Common Equity	6,071	5,665	2,035	1,738	1,471	1,374	12,853	1,486	851	736
Total Capital	19,659	18,583	7,632	5,791	5,538	5,386	15,794	4,274	2,941	1,696
Capital Expenditures	2,511	1,160	654	405	369	530	421	340	140	230
Cash Flow	1,238	799	691	635	631	542	270	438	281	230
Current Ratio	0.7	1.0	1.0	1.2	1.1	1.1	0.7	1.3	1.2	1.0
% Long Term Debt of Capitalization	59.2	59.4	67.5	63.4	68.0	69.1	17.9	59.4	68.0	54.5
% Net Income of Revenue	5.4	3.7	7.2	6.8	7.8	5.6	NM	7.3	6.1	6.6
% Return on Assets	2.5	1.8	4.3	4.5	5.2	3.7	NM	5.5	4.6	5.4
% Return on Equity	9.0	6.9	17.5	18.2	22.8	15.8	NM	18.8	15.3	14.8

Data as orig reptd.; bef. results of disc opers/spec. items. Per share data adj. for stk. divs.; EPS diluted. E-Estimated. NA-Not Available. NM-Not Meaningful. NR-Not Ranked. UR-Under Review.

Office: 1 Caesars Palace Dr, Las Vegas, NV 89109-8969.
Telephone: 702-407-6000.
Email: investors@harrahs.com
Website: http://www.harrahs.com

Chrmn, Pres & CEO: G.W. Loveman
Vice Chrmn: C.L. Atwood
SVP, CFO & Treas: J.S. Halkyard
SVP & General Counsel: S.H. Brammell

SVP & CIO: T.S. Stanley
Board Members: B. Alexander, C. L. Atwood, F. Biondi, S. F. Bollenbach, R. Horn, G. W. Loveman, R. B. Martin, G. Michael, R. G. Miller, B. A. Sells, C. J. Williams

Founded: 1989
Domicile: Delaware
Employees: 85,000

The McGraw-Hill Companies

STANDARD &POOR'S

Hartford Financial Services Group Inc. (The)

S&P Recommendation	STRONG BUY ★★★★★	Price $90.78 (as of Nov 23, 2007)	12-Mo. Target Price $115.00	Investment Style Large-Cap Blend

GICS Sector Financials
Sub-Industry Multi-line Insurance

Summary Based in Hartford, CT, HIG is one of the largest U.S. multi-line insurance holding companies, and a leading writer of individual variable annuities in the U.S. and Japan.

Key Stock Statistics (Source S&P, Vickers, company reports)

52-Wk Range	$106.23–83.00	S&P Oper. EPS 2007**E**	10.60	Market Capitalization(B)	$28.491	Beta	1.51
Trailing 12-Month EPS	$9.79	S&P Oper. EPS 2008**E**	10.45	Yield (%)	2.34	S&P 3-Yr. Proj. EPS CAGR(%)	NA
Trailing 12-Month P/E	9.3	P/E on S&P Oper. EPS 2007**E**	8.6	Dividend Rate/Share	$2.12	S&P Credit Rating	A
$10K Invested 5 Yrs Ago	$20,818	Common Shares Outstg. (M)	313.8	Institutional Ownership (%)	90		

Price Performance

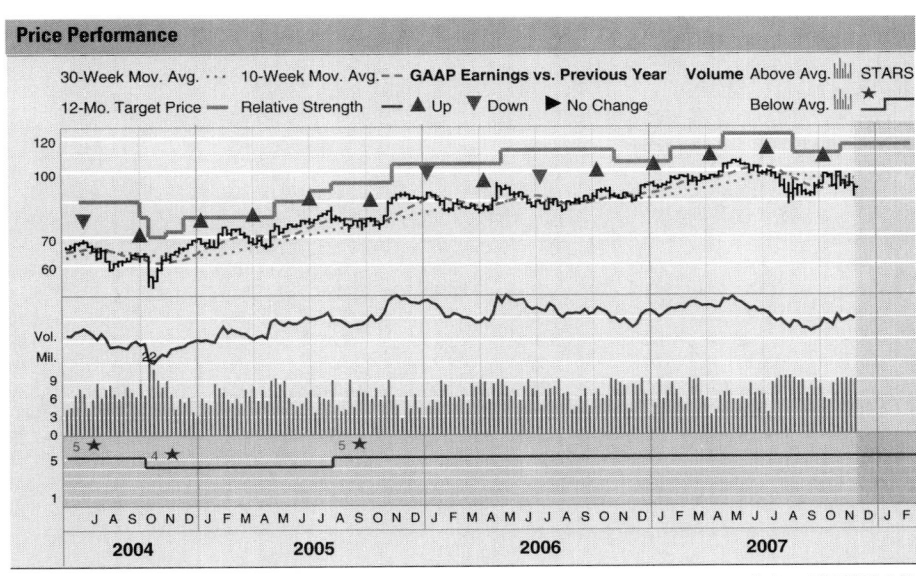

30-Week Mov. Avg. · · · · 10-Week Mov. Avg. - - **GAAP Earnings vs. Previous Year** Volume Above Avg. STARS
12-Mo. Target Price — Relative Strength — ▲ Up ▼ Down ▶ No Change Below Avg.

Options: ASE, CBOE, P, Ph

Analysis prepared by **Cathy A. Seifert** on November 16, 2007, when the stock traded at **$93.15**.

Qualitative Risk Assessment

LOW	MEDIUM	HIGH

Our risk assessment reflects our view of HIG's position as a leader in both the property-casualty and life insurance/retirement savings areas, combined with what we consider the company's diversified revenue and earnings streams and sound capital position. This is offset by its exposure to catastrophe losses and credit writedowns.

Quantitative Evaluations

S&P Quality Ranking — B+

D	C	B-	B	B+	A-	A	A+

Relative Strength Rank — MODERATE

66

LOWEST = 1   HIGHEST = 99

Revenue/Earnings Data

Revenue (Million $)

	1Q	2Q	3Q	4Q	Year
2007	6,759	7,573	5,823	--	--
2006	6,543	4,971	7,407	7,579	26,500
2005	6,002	6,064	7,307	7,710	27,083
2004	5,732	5,444	5,416	6,101	22,693
2003	4,331	4,682	4,947	4,773	18,733
2002	3,900	3,885	3,961	4,161	15,907

Earnings Per Share ($)

	1Q	2Q	3Q	4Q	Year
2007	2.71	1.96	2.68	E2.47	E10.60
2006	2.34	1.52	2.39	2.42	8.69
2005	2.21	1.98	1.76	1.51	7.44
2004	2.01	1.46	1.66	2.08	7.20
2003	-5.33	1.88	1.20	1.59	-0.33
2002	1.17	0.74	1.06	1.01	3.97

Fiscal year ended Dec. 31. Next earnings report expected: Late January. EPS Estimates based on S&P Operating Earnings; historical GAAP earnings are as reported.

Highlights

➤ We estimate property-casualty earned premiums will be flat to down slightly in 2008, versus a decline of 1% to 2% seen in 2007. This forecast assumes business insurance premiums decline by 2% to 3% in 2008; personal lines premiums rise by 3% to 5%; and specialty commercial premiums decline by 6%. We expect underwriting results to remain profitable in 2008, but an erosion in claim trends could cause underwriting margins to contract . Underwriting results year to date through September 30 were profitable in 2007, and the combined loss/expense ratio equaled 90.7%, versus 89.5% in the year-ago period.

➤ We expect life insurance operating revenues to advance 9% to 12% in 2008, reflecting double-digit premium and fee income growth, partly offset by a lower rate of net investment income growth . Margins will likely benefit from a more contained rise in benefit, claim and certain operating expenses.

➤ We estimate operating EPS of $10.60 in 2007 and $10.45 in 2008, versus the $9.07 operating EPS reported for 2006. Our estimate assumes a "normal" level of catastrophe losses and no large increases in loss reserves.

Investment Rationale/Risk

➤ Our strong buy opinion reflects our view that HIG is a well managed franchise with a number of positive catalysts, including an improved underwriting environment for some lines of property-casualty insurance, and continued favorable demand for savings and retirement products. We view positively the growth in HIG's fee-based businesses (including its mutual fund operations) and its presence in Japan. We see the shares as undervalued versus peers and in light of our view of HIG's favorable growth prospects.

➤ Risks to our recommendation and target price include a deterioration in claim trends, a continuation of heightened premium price competition, a continued downturn in the equity markets, a significant erosion in the credit quality of HIG's investment portfolio, and emergence or escalation of regulatory issues.

➤ Our 12-month target price of $115 assumes the shares will trade at approximately 11X our 2008 operating EPS estimate and about 1.8X our 2008 tangible book value per share estimate, both close to the average for most of the company's peers in our coverage universe.

Dividend Data (Dates: mm/dd Payment Date: mm/dd/yy)

Amount ($)	Date Decl.	Ex-Div. Date	Stk. of Record	Payment Date
0.500	02/22	02/27	03/01	04/02/07
0.500	05/17	05/30	06/01	07/02/07
0.500	07/19	08/30	09/04	10/01/07
0.530	10/18	11/29	12/03	01/02/08

Dividends have been paid since 1996. Source: Company reports.

Please read the Required Disclosures and Analyst Certification on the last page of this report.

The McGraw-Hill Companies

Hartford Financial Services Group Inc. (The)

STANDARD &POOR'S

Business Summary November 16, 2007

CORPORATE OVERVIEW. As a multi-line insurer, HIG underwrites life as well as property-casualty insurance. Segment revenues totaled $26.5 billion in 2006, of which life accounted for 53% and property-casualty for the remaining 47%.

HIG's property-casualty operation provides a wide range of commercial, personal, specialty and reinsurance coverages. It constitutes one of the largest U.S. property-casualty insurance organizations, and is the endorsed provider of automobile and homeowners coverages to members of AARP. Earned premiums of $10.4 billion in 2006 were derived from business insurance 49%, personal lines 36%, and specialty commercial 15%.

HIG's life insurance operations are conducted by Hartford Life, Inc. The Retail Investment Products Group (which accounted for 39% of the life divisions' more than $1.6 billion of segment operating profits in 2006) provides an array of investment and savings products to individual investors, including annuities, mutual funds, 401(k) plans and 529 college savings plans. Group Benefits

(19% of segment profits in 2006) offers short- and long-term disability insurance, group life and accident insurance, and other specialty products to employers, associations and affinity groups. The Individual Life segment (11%) offers an array of life insurance, including variable universal life, universal life, whole life and term life insurance. The Institutional Financial Solutions Group (6%) provides customized wealth creation and financial protection solutions for institutions, corporations and high net worth individuals. The Retirement Plans Group (7% of 2006 segment operating profits) provides retirement plans for corporate clients and non-profit organizations. The International unit (15%) offers fixed and variable annuities in Japan, Brazil and the U.K. Other operations accounted for the remaining 3% of segment operating profits in 2006.

Company Financials Fiscal Year Ended Dec. 31

Per Share Data ($)	2006	2005	2004	2003	2002	2001	2000	1999	1998	1997
Tangible Book Value	53.12	45.05	42.58	34.80	35.31	29.87	32.88	25.07	28.17	25.79
Operating Earnings	NA	NA	NA	-0.93	4.96	3.00	4.29	3.68	3.45	4.70
Earnings	8.69	7.44	7.20	-0.33	3.97	2.27	4.36	3.79	4.30	5.58
S&P Core Earnings	8.98	7.62	6.52	-1.15	4.27	2.22	NA	NA	NA	NA
Dividends	1.70	1.17	1.13	1.09	1.05	1.01	0.97	0.90	0.85	0.80
Relative Payout	20%	16%	16%	NM	26%	44%	22%	24%	20%	14%
Prices:High	94.03	89.49	69.57	59.27	70.24	71.15	80.00	66.44	60.00	47.25
Prices:Low	79.24	65.35	52.73	31.64	37.25	45.50	29.38	36.50	37.63	32.44
P/E Ratio:High	11	12	10	NM	18	31	18	18	14	8
P/E Ratio:Low	9	9	7	NM	9	20	7	10	9	6

Income Statement Analysis (Million $)	2006	2005	2004	2003	2002	2001	2000	1999	1998	1997
Life Insurance in Force	164,227	764,293	139,889	704,369	629,028	534,489	585,582	527,285	528,608	407,860
Premium Income:Life A & H	15,023	14,359	13,566	11,891	4,884	4,903	4,565	4,069	4,371	3,323
Premium Income:Casualty/Property.	NA	NA	NA	8,805	8,114	7,266	6,975	6,488	7,245	7,000
Net Investment Income	6,515	8,231	5,162	3,233	2,953	2,850	2,674	2,627	3,102	2,655
Total Revenue	26,500	27,083	22,693	18,733	15,907	15,147	14,703	13,528	15,022	13,305
Pretax Income	3,602	2,985	2,523	-550	1,068	354	1,418	1,235	1,475	1,703
Net Operating Income	NA	NA	NA	-253	1,250	724	962	837	816	1,117
Net Income	2,745	2,274	2,138	-91.0	1,000	549	974	862	1,015	1,332
S&P Core Earnings	2,839	2,335	1,936	-315	1,078	538	NA	NA	NA	NA

Balance Sheet & Other Financial Data (Million $)	2006	2005	2004	2003	2002	2001	2000	1999	1998	1997
Cash & Equivalent	1,424	1,273	1,148	462	377	353	227	182	123	140
Premiums Due	5,571	6,360	6,178	9,043	7,706	2,432	6,874	2,071	1,833	1,873
Investment Assets:Bonds	80,755	76,440	75,100	61,263	48,889	40,046	34,492	32,875	35,331	35,053
Investment Assets:Stocks	31,132	25,495	14,466	565	917	1,349	1,056	1,286	1,066	1,922
Investment Assets:Loans	5,369	3,747	2,662	2,512	2,934	3,317	3,610	4,222	6,687	3,759
Investment Assets:Total	119,173	106,935	94,408	65,847	54,530	46,689	40,669	39,141	43,696	37,363
Deferred Policy Costs	10,268	9,702	8,509	7,599	6,689	6,420	5,305	5,038	4,579	4,181
Total Assets	326,710	285,557	259,735	225,853	182,043	181,238	171,532	167,051	150,632	131,743
Debt	3,762	4,048	4,308	4,613	4,064	3,377	3,105	2,798	2,798	1,773
Common Equity	18,876	15,325	14,238	11,639	10,734	9,013	7,464	5,466	6,423	6,085
Combined Loss-Expense Ratio	89.3	93.2	95.3	98.0	99.2	112.4	102.4	103.3	102.9	102.3
% Return on Revenue	10.4	8.4	9.4	NM	6.3	3.6	6.6	6.4	6.8	10.0
% Return on Equity	16.1	15.4	16.5	NM	10.1	6.7	15.1	14.5	16.2	25.1
% Investment Yield	5.8	8.2	6.4	5.4	5.8	6.5	6.7	6.3	7.7	6.7

Data as orig reptd.; bef. results of disc opers/spec. items. Per share data adj. for stk. divs.; EPS diluted. E-Estimated. NA-Not Available. NM-Not Meaningful. NR-Not Ranked. UR-Under Review.

Office: Hartford Plaza, Hartford, CT 06115.
Telephone: 860-547-5000.
Website: http://www.thehartford.com
Chrmn, Pres & CEO: R. Ayer

EVP & CFO: D.M. Johnson
EVP & General Counsel: N.S. Wolin
Investor Contact: K. Johnson
SVP & Cntlr: B.A. Bombara

Board Members: R. Ayer, T. Fetter, E. J. Kelly, III, P. G. Kirk, Jr., T. M. Marra, G. J. McGovern, M. G. Morris, R. W. Selander, C. B. Strauss, H. P. Swygert, D. K. Zwiener, R. de Oliveira

Founded: 1810
Domicile: Delaware
Employees: 31,000

The **McGraw·Hill** Companies

Hasbro Inc.

STANDARD &POOR'S

S&P Recommendation **HOLD** ★★★☆☆	Price $27.01 (as of Nov 23, 2007)	12-Mo. Target Price $32.00

GICS Sector Consumer Discretionary
Sub-Industry Leisure Products

Summary This large toy company has brands that include Monopoly, Playskool and Tonka, as well as various items related to categories such as Star Wars and Pokemon.

Key Stock Statistics (Source S&P, Vickers, company reports)

52-Wk Range	$33.49– 25.25	S&P Oper. EPS 2007**E**	2.04	Market Capitalization(B)	$4.321	Beta	1.77
Trailing 12-Month EPS	$1.77	S&P Oper. EPS 2008**E**	1.89	Yield (%)	2.37	S&P 3-Yr. Proj. EPS CAGR(%)	12.00
Trailing 12-Month P/E	15.3	P/E on S&P Oper. EPS 2007**E**	13.2	Dividend Rate/Share	$0.64	S&P Credit Rating	BBB
$10K Invested 5 Yrs Ago	$22,631	Common Shares Outstg. (M)	160.0	Institutional Ownership (%)	95		

Price Performance

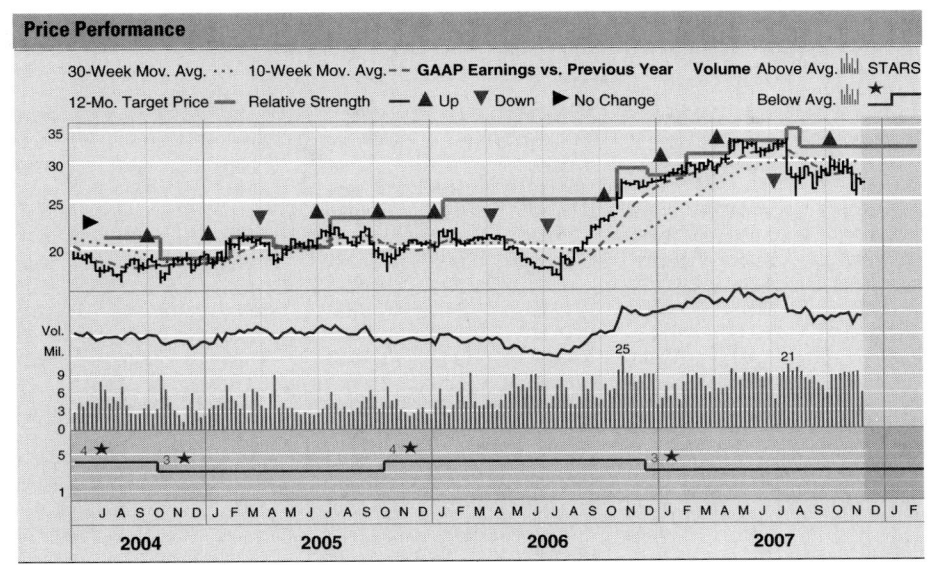

30-Week Mov. Avg. ··· 10-Week Mov. Avg. - - **GAAP Earnings vs. Previous Year** Volume Above Avg. STARS
12-Mo. Target Price — Relative Strength — ▲ Up ▼ Down ► No Change   Below Avg. ★

Options: CBOE, P, Ph

Analysis prepared by **Erik Kolb** on November 02, 2007, when the stock traded at **$ 28.50.**

Highlights

➤ We see revenues increasing about 18% in 2007, to $3.73 billion. We expect Star Wars revenue, which contributed almost $500 million, or 16%, to revenues in 2005, to continue to decline in 2007, although franchise revenues should remain significant. We think the alliance with Marvel Entertainment will help offset this projected decline, and we are anticipating that toy and gaming rights revenues for franchises such as Spider-Man, X-Men and Transformers will support growth in 2007 and beyond. Also, we expect the Littlest Pet Shop and Playskool toy brands to continue gaining ground. Visibility into 2008 is less clear, however, and we see increased competition in the already tight boys segment leading to about a 2.7% revenue decline.

➤ We expect 2007 gross margins to expand about 160 basis points, to 13.5%, on lower advertising and SD&A expense ratios. Also, we see a sales shift to higher margin licensed products in 2007. Lower revenues should compress margins to 12.3% in 2008, in our view.

➤ We estimate operating EPS of $2.04 and $1.89 for 2007 and 2008, respectively.

Investment Rationale/Risk

➤ We have a hold recommendation on HAS, which recently traded at about 15X our 2008 EPS estimate. We think HAS is well positioned to grow its market share in the toy category, particularly as it increases the use of technology in its offerings to make toys more interactive. We are looking for a ramp-up in 2007, partly tied to the Marvel licensing agreement, but for a modest decline in 2008. In addition, we believe HAS has strong cash flow and an improved balance sheet, which should enable the company to enhance shareholder value through its ongoing share repurchase program.

➤ Risks to our recommendation and target price include more store closings and tight inventory management at toy retailers, weak consumer spending and/or negative consumer sentiment, a lack of market demand for HAS products, and increased competition in the consumer electronic toy category from larger consumer electronics manufacturers.

➤ Our 12-month target price of $32 applies a P/E of about 17X to our 2008 EPS estimate, a premium to the S&P 500 and toy industry peers.

Qualitative Risk Assessment

LOW	**MEDIUM**	HIGH

Our risk assessment takes into account our view of HAS's strong market share position and healthy balance sheet, offset by intense industry rivalry and the concentrated buying power of U.S. toy retailers.

Quantitative Evaluations

S&P Quality Ranking   **B**

D	C	B-	**B**	B+	A-	A	A+

Relative Strength Rank   **MODERATE**

55

LOWEST = 1   HIGHEST = 99

Revenue/Earnings Data

Revenue (Million $)

	1Q	2Q	3Q	4Q	Year
2007	625.3	691.4	1,223	--	--
2006	468.2	527.8	1,039	1,116	3,151
2005	454.9	572.4	988.1	1,072	3,088
2004	474.3	516.4	947.3	1,060	2,998
2003	461.8	581.5	581.5	1,124	3,139
2002	452.3	546.0	820.5	997.4	2,816

Earnings Per Share ($)

2007	0.19	0.03	0.95	E0.83	E2.04
2006	-0.03	0.07	0.58	0.62	1.29
2005	-0.02	0.13	0.47	0.48	1.09
2004	0.03	0.06	0.43	0.44	0.96
2003	0.01	0.06	0.06	0.43	0.98
2002	-0.10	-0.15	0.32	0.36	0.43

Fiscal year ended Dec. 31. Next earnings report expected: Early February. EPS Estimates based on S&P Operating Earnings; historical GAAP earnings are as reported.

Dividend Data (Dates: mm/dd Payment Date: mm/dd/yy)

Amount ($)	Date Decl.	Ex-Div. Date	Stk. of Record	Payment Date
0.120	12/14	01/30	02/01	02/15/07
0.160	02/09	04/27	05/01	05/15/07
0.160	05/24	07/30	08/01	08/15/07
0.160	10/04	10/30	11/01	11/15/07

Dividends have been paid since 1981. Source: Company reports.

Please read the Required Disclosures and Analyst Certification on the last page of this report.

The McGraw-Hill Companies

Hasbro Inc.

STANDARD &POOR'S

Business Summary November 02, 2007

CORPORATE OVERVIEW. Hasbro is a worldwide leader in children's and family leisure time and entertainment products and services, including the design, manufacture and marketing of games and toys ranging from traditional to high-tech. Some of the company's widely recognized core brands, both internationally and in the U.S., are Playskool, Tonka, Super Soaker, Milton Bradley, Parker Brothers, Tiger And Wizards of the Coast. Offerings in the games segment include traditional board games, hand-held electronic, trading card, plug and play and DVD games, as well as electronic learning aids and puzzles. Toy offerings include boys' action figures, vehicles and playsets, girls' toys, electronic toys, plush products, preschool toys and infant products, children's consumer electronics, electronic interactive products and toy related specialty products.

Part of HAS's growth strategy includes licensing, which has been successful in the past for HAS. In 2005, revenues generated from the sale of Star Wars products produced under its license with Lucas Licensing and Lucasfilm represented approximately 16% of total company revenues. In January 2006, HAS completed a licensing agreement with Marvel Entertainment, Inc. to produce action figures and other toys and games based on their library of intellectual property, including Spiderman and the Fantastic 4. Products related to this license began shipping late in 2006, with the bulk of the licensed products expected in 2007 and thereafter.

Company Financials Fiscal Year Ended Dec. 31

Per Share Data ($)	2006	2005	2004	2003	2002	2001	2000	1999	1998	1997
Tangible Book Value	3.34	3.61	3.01	1.32	0.08	NM	NM	0.64	2.05	4.36
Cash Flow	2.35	2.20	1.75	2.37	0.95	1.66	0.69	2.31	1.48	1.20
Earnings	1.29	1.09	0.96	0.98	0.43	0.35	-0.82	0.93	1.01	0.68
S&P Core Earnings	1.29	1.02	0.90	0.93	0.44	0.19	NA	NA	NA	NA
Dividends	0.45	0.33	0.21	0.12	0.12	0.12	0.24	0.23	0.21	0.23
Payout Ratio	35%	30%	22%	12%	28%	34%	NM	25%	21%	33%
Prices:High	27.69	22.35	23.33	22.63	17.30	18.44	18.94	37.00	27.29	24.33
Prices:Low	17.00	17.75	16.90	11.23	9.87	10.31	8.38	16.88	18.67	15.25
P/E Ratio:High	21	21	24	23	40	53	NM	40	27	36
P/E Ratio:Low	13	16	18	11	23	29	NM	18	18	22

Income Statement Analysis (Million $)	2006	2005	2004	2003	2002	2001	2000	1999	1998	1997
Revenue	3,151	3,088	2,998	3,139	2,816	2,856	3,787	4,232	3,304	3,189
Operating Income	523	491	439	509	309	435	268	669	442	473
Depreciation	147	180	146	240	89.3	226	264	277	97.0	113
Interest Expense	27.5	30.5	31.7	52.5	77.5	104	114	69.3	36.1	27.5
Pretax Income	341	311	260	244	104	96.2	-226	274	303	205
Effective Tax Rate	32.6%	31.8%	24.6%	28.3%	27.9%	36.8%	NM	31.0%	32.0%	34.0%
Net Income	230	212	196	175	75.1	60.8	-145	189	206	135
S&P Core Earnings	230	199	184	166	79.1	33.8	NA	NA	NA	NA

Balance Sheet & Other Financial Data (Million $)	2006	2005	2004	2003	2002	2001	2000	1999	1998	1997
Cash	715	942	725	521	495	233	127	280	178	362
Current Assets	1,718	1,830	1,718	1,509	1,432	1,369	1,580	2,132	1,790	1,574
Total Assets	3,097	3,301	3,241	3,163	3,143	3,369	3,828	4,463	3,794	2,900
Current Liabilities	906	911	1,149	930	967	759	1,240	2,071	1,366	1,004
Long Term Debt	495	496	303	687	857	1,166	1,168	421	407	Nil
Common Equity	1,538	1,723	1,640	1,405	1,191	1,353	1,327	1,879	1,945	1,838
Total Capital	2,033	2,219	1,942	2,092	2,049	2,519	2,495	2,300	2,352	1,838
Capital Expenditures	82.1	70.6	79.2	63.1	58.7	50.0	125	107	142	99.3
Cash Flow	377	392	342	415	164	287	120	466	303	248
Current Ratio	1.9	2.0	1.5	1.6	1.5	1.8	1.3	1.0	1.3	1.6
% Long Term Debt of Capitalization	24.3	22.3	15.6	32.8	41.8	46.3	46.8	18.3	17.3	Nil
% Net Income of Revenue	7.3	6.9	6.5	5.6	2.7	2.1	NM	4.5	6.2	4.2
% Return on Assets	7.2	6.5	6.1	5.6	2.3	1.7	NM	4.6	6.2	4.8
% Return on Equity	14.1	12.6	12.9	13.5	5.9	4.5	NM	9.9	10.9	7.7

Data as orig reptd.; bef. results of disc opers/spec. items. Per share data adj. for stk. divs.; EPS diluted. E-Estimated. NA-Not Available. NM-Not Meaningful. NR-Not Ranked. UR-Under Review.

Office: 1027 Newport Ave, Pawtucket, RI, USA 02862.
Telephone: 401-431-8697.
Website: http://www.hasbro.com
Chrmn: A.G. Hassenfeld

Pres & CEO: A.J. Verrecchia
COO: B. Goldner
EVP & CFO: D.D. Hargreaves
SVP & Treas: M.R. Trueb

Board Members: B. L. Anderson, A. R. Batkin, F. J. Biondi, Jr., J. M. Connors, Jr., M. W. Garrett, E. G. Gee, J. M. Greenberg, A. G. Hassenfeld, C. B. Malone, E. M. Philip, P. Stern, A. J. Verrecchia

Founded: 1926
Domicile: Rhode Island
Employees: 5,800

Heinz (H J) Co

STANDARD &POOR'S

S&P Recommendation HOLD ★★★☆☆

Price	12-Mo. Target Price	Investment Style
$47.54 (as of Nov 29, 2007)	$50.00	Large-Cap Blend

GICS Sector Consumer Staples
Sub-Industry Packaged Foods & Meats

Summary This company produces a wide variety of food products worldwide, with a major presence in the U.S. in condiments, frozen potatoes, and convenience meals.

Key Stock Statistics (Source S&P, Vickers, company reports)

52-Wk Range	$48.73–41.82	S&P Oper. EPS 2008E	2.62	Market Capitalization(B)	$15.172	Beta		0.55
Trailing 12-Month EPS	$2.55	S&P Oper. EPS 2009E	2.85	Yield (%)	3.20	S&P 3-Yr. Proj. EPS CAGR(%)		8.00
Trailing 12-Month P/E	18.6	P/E on S&P Oper. EPS 2008E	18.1	Dividend Rate/Share	$1.52	S&P Credit Rating		BBB
$10K Invested 5 Yrs Ago	$18,859	Common Shares Outstg. (M)	319.1	Institutional Ownership (%)	72			

Price Performance

30-Week Mov. Avg. ··· 10-Week Mov. Avg. - - GAAP Earnings vs. Previous Year   Volume Above Avg. STARS
12-Mo. Target Price — Relative Strength — ▲ Up ▼ Down ▶ No Change   Below Avg.

Options: ASE, CBOE, P

Qualitative Risk Assessment

LOW	MEDIUM	HIGH

Our risk assessment for H. J. Heinz reflects the relatively stable nature of the company's end markets, our view of its strong cash flow, and corporate governance practices that we believe are favorable relative to peers.

Quantitative Evaluations

S&P Quality Ranking B+

D	C	B-	B	B+	A-	A	A+

Relative Strength Rank STRONG
86
LOWEST = 1   HIGHEST = 99

Highlights

➤ The 12-month target price for HNZ has recently been changed to $50.00 from $47.00. The Highlights section of this Stock Report will be updated accordingly.

Investment Rationale/Risk

➤ The Investment Rationale/Risk section of this Stock Report will be updated shortly. For the latest News story on HNZ from MarketScope, see below.

➤ 11/29/07 12:18 pm EST... S&P MAINTAINS HOLD OPINION ON SHARES OF H.J. HEINZ (HNZ 47.5***): Oct-Q EPS of $0.71 vs. $0.59 tops our estimate by $0.04, with impressive 8.1% underlying sales growth. Consumer marketing spend was up 23%, and margins faced pressure from higher commodity costs, but even so, operating profit rose 10%. We are raising our FY 08 (Apr.) EPS estimate to $2.62 from $2.60, and our FY 09's to $2.85 from $2.83. We are also increasing our 12-month target price to $50, from $47, putting our P/E target closer to what we expect from packaged food stock peers. The stock has an indicated dividend yield of about 3.2%. / TGraves-CFA

Revenue/Earnings Data

Revenue (Million $)

	1Q	2Q	3Q	4Q	Year
2008	2,248	2,523	--	--	--
2007	2,060	2,232	2,295	2,414	9,002
2006	2,110	2,339	2,187	2,400	8,643
2005	2,003	2,200	2,261	2,448	8,912
2004	1,896	2,090	2,097	2,331	8,415
2003	1,839	2,099	2,105	2,193	8,237

Earnings Per Share ($)

2008	0.63	0.71	E0.61	E0.67	E2.62
2007	0.58	0.59	0.66	0.55	2.38
2006	0.45	0.50	0.40	Nil	1.29
2005	0.55	0.56	0.50	0.58	2.08
2004	0.60	0.54	0.57	0.56	2.20
2003	0.50	0.60	0.37	0.29	1.57

Fiscal year ended Apr. 30. Next earnings report expected: NA. EPS Estimates based on S&P Operating Earnings; historical GAAP earnings are as reported.

Dividend Data (Dates: mm/dd Payment Date: mm/dd/yy)

Amount ($)	Date Decl.	Ex-Div. Date	Stk. of Record	Payment Date
0.350	03/14	03/21	03/24	04/10/07
0.380	05/31	06/21	06/25	07/10/07
0.380	08/15	09/19	09/21	10/10/07
0.380	11/14	12/19	12/21	01/10/08

Dividends have been paid since 1911. Source: Company reports.

The McGraw-Hill Companies

Heinz (H J) Co

**STANDARD
&POOR'S**

Business Summary November 19, 2007

CORPORATE OVERVIEW. Although largely known for its familiar ketchup, H.J. Heinz boasts many other branded food products, ranging from Ore-Ida frozen potatoes to Weight Watchers frozen dinners. Sales are broadly based geographically, with contributions by major region in FY 07 (Apr.) as follows: North America (47.7% of sales), Europe (34.2%), Asia/Pacific (13.4%), and other (4.7%). The North American sales included consumer products (30.4%) and foodservice (17.3%).

The company's revenues are generated via the manufacture and sale of products in the following categories: ketchup and sauces (40.9% of FY 07 sales), sold under names such as Heinz and Classico; meals and snacks (44.7%), which include items such as Boston Market HomeStyle Meals, Ore-Ida potatoes, and Smart Ones; infant foods (10%); and other products (4.9%).

CORPORATE STRATEGY. In June 2006, HNZ said that during the next two years, it planned to achieve $355 million in cost savings and $145 million in a

reduction in trade spending. HNZ said that it was committed to reinvesting a portion of the savings in growing a portfolio of leading brands. Also, HNZ said that it intended to return nearly $2 billion to shareholders over the next two years as a result of dividend payments and $1 billion of stock repurchases.

Heinz has focused on exiting non-strategic business operations. In the fourth quarter of FY 06, the company completed the sale of its European seafood business and its Tegel poultry business in New Zealand. Overall, portfolio realignment has resulted in the divesture of approximately 20 non-core product lines and businesses and has generated proceeds of about $1 billion. The company believed that by improving the focus of its product portfolio, it is better positioned to build consistent and sustainable growth.

Company Financials Fiscal Year Ended Apr. 30

Per Share Data ($)	2007	2006	2005	2004	2003	2002	2001	2000	1999	1998
Tangible Book Value	NM	NM	NM	NM	NM	NM	NM	NM	NM	NM
Cash Flow	3.88	2.07	2.82	2.86	2.17	3.22	2.26	3.32	2.11	2.99
Earnings	2.38	1.29	2.08	2.20	1.57	2.36	1.41	2.47	1.29	2.15
S&P Core Earnings	2.36	1.72	2.29	2.11	1.43	1.99	1.31	NA	NA	NA
Dividends	1.20	1.14	1.10	1.08	1.61	1.55	1.45	1.40	1.34	1.24
Payout Ratio	50%	88%	53%	49%	88%	65%	102%	56%	104%	57%
Calendar Year	2006	2005	2004	2003	2002	2001	2000	1999	1998	1997
Prices:High	46.75	39.13	40.61	36.82	43.48	47.94	48.00	58.81	61.75	56.69
Prices:Low	33.42	33.64	34.53	28.90	29.60	36.90	30.81	39.50	48.50	35.25
P/E Ratio:High	20	30	20	17	24	20	34	24	48	26
P/E Ratio:Low	14	26	17	13	16	16	22	16	38	16

Income Statement Analysis (Million $)										
Revenue	9,002	8,643	8,912	8,415	8,237	9,431	9,430	9,408	9,300	9,209
Operating Income	1,946	1,377	1,607	1,613	1,389	1,892	1,282	1,575	1,412	1,834
Depreciation	500	264	252	234	215	302	299	306	302	314
Interest Expense	333	316	232	212	224	294	333	270	259	259
Pretax Income	1,124	693	1,059	1,169	869	1,279	673	1,464	835	1,255
Effective Tax Rate	29.6%	36.2%	30.5%	33.3%	36.1%	34.8%	26.5%	39.2%	43.2%	36.1%
Net Income	792	443	736	779	555	834	495	891	474	802
S&P Core Earnings	784	587	809	747	500	702	458	NA	NA	NA

Balance Sheet & Other Financial Data (Million $)										
Cash	653	445	1,084	1,180	802	207	139	138	116	96.0
Current Assets	3,019	2,704	3,646	3,611	3,284	3,374	3,117	3,170	2,887	2,687
Total Assets	10,033	9,738	10,578	9,877	9,225	10,278	9,035	8,851	8,054	8,023
Current Liabilities	2,505	2,018	2,587	2,469	1,926	2,509	3,655	2,126	2,786	2,164
Long Term Debt	4,414	4,357	4,122	4,538	4,776	4,643	3,015	3,936	2,472	2,769
Common Equity	2,280	2,049	2,614	8,841	2,876	1,719	1,374	1,596	1,804	2,216
Total Capital	7,256	7,045	7,359	13,797	8,252	7,197	4,642	5,804	4,587	5,276
Capital Expenditures	245	231	241	232	154	213	411	452	317	374
Cash Flow	1,291	707	988	1,013	770	1,136	794	1,197	776	1,116
Current Ratio	1.2	1.3	1.4	1.5	1.7	1.3	0.9	1.5	1.0	1.2
% Long Term Debt of Capitalization	60.8	61.8	56.0	32.9	57.9	64.5	64.9	67.8	53.9	52.5
% Net Income of Revenue	8.8	5.1	8.3	9.3	6.7	8.8	5.2	9.5	5.1	8.7
% Return on Assets	8.0	4.4	7.2	8.2	5.7	8.6	5.5	10.5	5.9	9.7
% Return on Equity	34.0	19.0	26.3	8.9	17.9	53.9	33.3	52.4	23.6	34.5

Data as orig reptd.; bef. results of disc opers/spec. items. Per share data adj. for stk. divs.; EPS diluted. E-Estimated. NA-Not Available. NM-Not Meaningful. NR-Not Ranked. UR-Under Review.

Office: 600 Grant Street, Pittsburgh, PA 15219-2702.
Telephone: 412-456-5700.
Website: http://www.heinz.com
Chrmn, Pres & CEO: W.R. Johnson

EVP & CFO: A. Winkleblack
EVP & General Counsel: T. Bobby
SVP & Cntlr: E.J. McMenamin
Investor Contact: M.R. Nollen

Board Members: C. E. Bunch, L. S. Coleman, Jr., J. G. Drosdick, E. E. Holiday, W. R. Johnson, C. Kendle, D. R. O'Hare, N. Peltz, D. H. Reilley, L. C. Swann, T. J. Usher, M. F. Weinstein

Founded: 1869
Domicile: Pennsylvania
Employees: 33,000

Hercules Inc

STANDARD
&POOR'S

S&P Recommendation	HOLD ★★★☆☆	Price	12-Mo. Target Price	Investment Style
		$17.99 (as of Nov 27, 2007)	$22.00	Large-Cap Blend

GICS Sector Materials
Sub-Industry Diversified Chemicals

Summary This company manufactures and markets specialty chemicals globally used to make a variety of products for home, office, and industrial markets.

Key Stock Statistics (Source S&P, Vickers, company reports)

52-Wk Range	$22.48–17.49	S&P Oper. EPS 2007**E**	1.52	Market Capitalization(B)	$2.087	Beta	0.81
Trailing 12-Month EPS	$3.47	S&P Oper. EPS 2008**E**	1.60	Yield (%)	1.11	S&P 3-Yr. Proj. EPS CAGR(%)	10.00
Trailing 12-Month P/E	5.2	P/E on S&P Oper. EPS 2007**E**	11.8	Dividend Rate/Share	$0.20	S&P Credit Rating	BB
$10K Invested 5 Yrs Ago	$20,308	Common Shares Outstg. (M)	116.0	Institutional Ownership (%)	96		

Price Performance

Options: ASE, CBOE, P

Analysis prepared by **Richard O'Reilly, CFA** on November 27, 2007, when the stock traded at **$17.99**.

Highlights

➤ We expect sales in 2008 to rise at a mid-single digit rate, benefiting from stronger global demand. Reported sales will likely increase in 2007 despite the full-year absence of FiberVisions, which has been reported on an equity basis since March 2006, as we believe that sales for HPC's remaining businesses will be up about 8%. We think that price increases will offset increases in raw material costs.

➤ We see operating profits improving modestly as HPC continues to achieve productivity gains. HPC has implemented restructuring actions designed to generate annual overhead cost savings of $20 million by 2008. We think that raw material and freight costs could rise in 2008 at a faster pace than in 2007. It is our belief that a planned change in the pension investment policy will reduce annual expense by about $25 million beginning in 2008.

➤ We forecast that interest expense in 2008 will be lower than in 2007 as a result of debt repayment, and we believe that HPC will now focus on additional share repurchases. We see a tax rate of 26% in 2007, including 29% in the final quarter. Reported EPS for the first quarter of 2007 includes a $0.41 one-time tax benefit.

Investment Rationale/Risk

➤ We expect positive operating EPS comparisons to continue through 2008, driven by mid-single digit sales growth and lower interest expense. We anticipate that price boosts being implemented will begin to fully offset increases in raw material and freight costs. In 2007, the company resumed payment of a quarterly dividend and began a stock repurchase program.

➤ Risks to our recommendation and target price include the company's high net debt-to-capital ratio (64% as of September 2007), greater-than-expected increases in raw material costs, and a possible increase in asbestos-related legal exposure.

➤ We expect HPC to have free cash flow of about $200 million in 2008, including tax refunds, with funds used largely to buy back stock. We look for capital expenditures to increase, but we believe that asbestos-related spending will continue to be reimbursed. Assuming a multiple of 8.5X our 2008 EBITDA projection of $400 million, modestly below recent industry transactions, our 12-month target price is $22.

Qualitative Risk Assessment

LOW	MEDIUM	HIGH

Our risk assessment reflects the broad and stable nature of the company's end markets, with low exposure to petrochemicals, offset by our view of its high debt ratio and potentially large environmental claims.

Quantitative Evaluations

S&P Quality Ranking   B-

D	C	B-	B	B+	A-	A	A+

Relative Strength Rank   MODERATE

43

LOWEST = 1   HIGHEST = 99

Revenue/Earnings Data

Revenue (Million $)

	1Q	2Q	3Q	4Q	Year
2007	502.3	549.0	544.2	--	--
2006	527.3	501.0	513.1	493.9	2,035
2005	505.1	538.6	522.9	502.2	2,069
2004	475.0	510.0	501.0	511.0	1,997
2003	447.0	478.0	463.0	458.0	1,846
2002	402.0	437.0	443.0	423.0	1,705

Earnings Per Share ($)

2007	0.64	0.30	0.36	E0.35	E1.52
2006	0.13	-0.46	0.31	1.71	1.71
2005	0.04	0.08	0.22	-0.71	-0.25
2004	0.24	0.04	-0.47	0.44	0.25
2003	0.13	0.30	0.16	0.10	0.69
2002	-0.03	-0.19	-0.32	0.09	-0.45

Fiscal year ended Dec. 31. Next earnings report expected: Early February. EPS Estimates based on S&P Operating Earnings; historical GAAP earnings are as reported.

Dividend Data (Dates: mm/dd Payment Date: mm/dd/yy)

Amount ($)	Date Decl.	Ex-Div. Date	Stk. of Record	Payment Date
0.050	07/23	09/26	09/28	10/19/07
0.050	11/15	12/26	12/28	01/18/08

Dividends have been paid since 2007. Source: Company reports.

Please read the Required Disclosures and Analyst Certification on the last page of this report.

The McGraw-Hill Companies

Hercules Inc

STANDARD & POOR'S

Business Summary November 27, 2007

CORPORATE OVERVIEW. Hercules makes specialty chemicals that are used in a broad range of consumer and industrial markets. Key markets for the company's products include pulp and paper (45% of annual sales), industrial (25%), paints and adhesives (10%), construction materials (10%), and food, pharmaceutical and personal care (10%). International operations contributed 56% of sales in 2006, including 34% from Europe.

The paper technologies and ventures group (53% of sales and 30% of operating profits in 2006) consists of paper chemicals (42% -- sizing agents, coatings additives, emulsions, defoamers, deposit, corrosion and foam control, deinking, felt conditioning, fiber recovery). Ventures (11%) consists of water management chemicals (for utility systems, cooling water and water clarification), pulp and biorefining chemicals, synthetic lubricants, adhesives, and a water treatment chemicals-tolling business. Hercules is the largest global supplier in a fragmented $4.0 billion annual market for paper and pulp chemicals.

The Aqualon group (44%, 70%) is the global leader in water-soluble polymers and coatings derived from cellulose pulps and guar, and used in paints, adhesives, paper, construction materials, personal care products, drugs, food and beverages, inks, and oil well drilling and recovery. Coatings and construction markets account for almost 50% of annual sales. The group also includes the former Pinova resins unit, a maker of wood and gum rosin resins, and the world's only maker of pale wood rosin derivatives, for flavors and fragrances, adhesives and disinfectants for use in consumer and industrial products such as masking, packaging, and duct tapes, food and beverages, construction materials, and plastics. The global market size for the products in which Aqualon competes is about $2.5 billion. About 60% of Aqualon sales are outside the U.S.

In late March 2006, HPC sold for $109 million its 51% interest in FiberVisions (3%, Nil), one of the world's largest producers of polypropylene staple fiber used in disposable hygiene products and wipes, as well as olefin textile fibers and yarn. An option for the buyer to purchase an additional 14% interest for $7.4 million expired in early 2007. HPC reported a related pretax charge of $41.6 million in the 2005 fourth quarter. HPC's remaining 49% interest in FiberVisions is now reported using the equity earnings method. HPC's share of FiberVisions' net loss for the nine months ended December 2006 was $3.4 million.

Company Financials Fiscal Year Ended Dec. 31

Per Share Data ($)	2006	2005	2004	2003	2002	2001	2000	1999	1998	1997
Tangible Book Value	NM	NM	NM	NM	NM	NM	NM	NM	NM	7.18
Cash Flow	2.57	0.62	1.17	1.61	0.47	1.43	3.22	2.94	1.20	3.88
Earnings	1.71	-0.25	0.25	0.69	-0.45	-0.54	0.91	1.62	0.10	3.18
S&P Core Earnings	2.55	0.27	0.27	0.70	-0.58	-1.96	NA	NA	NA	NA
Dividends	Nil	Nil	Nil	Nil	Nil	Nil	0.62	1.08	1.08	1.00
Payout Ratio	Nil	Nil	Nil	Nil	Nil	Nil	68%	67%	NM	31%
Prices:High	19.87	15.55	15.25	12.50	13.70	20.00	28.00	40.69	51.38	54.50
Prices:Low	10.98	10.00	9.93	7.40	8.45	6.50	11.38	22.38	24.63	37.75
P/E Ratio:High	12	NM	61	18	NM	NM	31	25	NM	17
P/E Ratio:Low	6	NM	40	11	NM	NM	12	14	NM	12

Income Statement Analysis (Million $)										
Revenue	2,035	2,069	1,997	1,846	1,705	2,620	3,152	3,248	2,145	1,866
Operating Income	344	289	328	355	-323	482	598	624	506	466
Depreciation	95.3	106	101	100	100	212	246	144	108	73.0
Interest Expense	71.2	89.4	109	131	154	254	260	236	103	39.0
Pretax Income	Nil	-45.8	29.0	95.0	-53.0	14.0	164	243	77.0	593
Effective Tax Rate	NM	NM	6.90%	22.1%	NM	NM	40.2%	30.9%	88.3%	45.4%
Net Income	191	-38.6	27.0	74.0	-49.0	-58.0	98.0	168	9.00	324
S&P Core Earnings	285	28.3	28.9	76.1	-62.8	-212	NA	NA	NA	NA

Balance Sheet & Other Financial Data (Million $)										
Cash	172	77.3	127	125	334	76.0	54.0	63.0	68.0	17.0
Current Assets	984	843	772	820	907	842	1,022	1,338	1,240	689
Total Assets	2,809	2,569	2,710	2,766	2,693	5,049	5,309	5,896	5,833	2,411
Current Liabilities	630	512	477	457	616	917	922	1,559	1,317	799
Long Term Debt	960	1,092	1,210	1,326	1,362	2,583	2,964	2,769	3,296	799
Common Equity	243	-24.7	97.0	66.0	-123	4,402	4,600	4,733	559	690
Total Capital	1,285	1,143	1,384	1,470	1,319	7,319	7,751	7,789	4,080	1,649
Capital Expenditures	93.6	67.5	77.0	48.0	43.0	63.0	187	196	157	119
Cash Flow	286	67.3	128	174	51.0	154	344	312	117	397
Current Ratio	1.6	1.6	1.6	1.8	1.5	0.9	1.1	0.9	0.9	0.9
% Long Term Debt of Capitalization	74.7	95.5	87.4	90.2	103.3	35.3	38.2	35.6	80.8	48.5
% Net Income of Revenue	9.4	NM	1.4	4.0	NM	NM	3.1	5.2	0.4	17.4
% Return on Assets	7.1	NM	1.0	2.7	NM	NM	1.7	2.9	0.2	13.5
% Return on Equity	174.9	NM	50.0	NA	NM	NM	2.1	3.7	1.4	41.1

Data as orig reptd.; bef. results of disc opers/spec. items. Per share data adj. for stk. divs.; EPS diluted. E-Estimated. NA-Not Available. NM-Not Meaningful. NR-Not Ranked. UR-Under Review.

Office: 1313 N Market St Ofc, Wilmington, DE 19894-0001.
Telephone: 302-594-5000 .
Website: http://www.herc.com
Chrmn: J.K. Wulff

Pres & CEO: C.A. Rogerson
VP & CFO: A.A. Spizzo
VP & Treas: S.C. Shears
VP & Cntlr: F.G. Aanonsen

Investor Contact: S.L. Fornoff (302-594-7151)
Board Members: A. Cheng Catalano, T. P. Gerrity, J. C. Hunter, III, B. M. Joyce, R. D. Kennedy, J. M. Lipton, C. A. Rogerson, J. K. Wulff, J. B. Wyatt

Founded: 1912
Domicile: Delaware
Employees: 4,430

The McGraw-Hill Companies

Hershey Co (The)

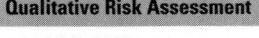

STANDARD &POOR'S

S&P Recommendation	HOLD ★★★☆☆	Price	12-Mo. Target Price	Investment Style
		$38.89 (as of Nov 23, 2007)	$43.00	Large-Cap Growth

GICS Sector Consumer Staples
Sub-Industry Packaged Foods & Meats

Summary Hershey is a major producer of chocolate or confectionery products.

Key Stock Statistics (Source S&P, Vickers, company reports)

52-Wk Range	$56.75– 38.30	S&P Oper. EPS 2007E	2.10	Market Capitalization(B)	$6.524
Trailing 12-Month EPS	$1.34	S&P Oper. EPS 2008E	2.20	Yield (%)	3.06
Trailing 12-Month P/E	29.0	P/E on S&P Oper. EPS 2007E	18.5	Dividend Rate/Share	$1.19
$10K Invested 5 Yrs Ago	$13,166	Common Shares Outstg. (M)	228.5	Institutional Ownership (%)	61

Beta	0.08
S&P 3-Yr. Proj. EPS CAGR(%)	3.00
S&P Credit Rating	A

Price Performance

30-Week Mov. Avg. · · · · 10-Week Mov. Avg. – – GAAP Earnings vs. Previous Year   Volume Above Avg. ▮▮▮ STARS
12-Mo. Target Price — Relative Strength — ▲ Up ▼ Down ► No Change   Below Avg. ▮▮▮ ★

2-for-1

Options: ASE, CBOE, P, Ph

Analysis prepared by **Tom Graves, CFA** on November 20, 2007, when the stock traded at **$ 38.88**.

Highlights

► We see HSY undergoing considerable change, and we believe there is increased pressure on management to deliver improved results and/or shareholder value. In November 2007, HSY said that six independent directors had resigned at the request of controlling shareholder The Hershey Trust. Also, in October, in a separate announcement, HSY's president and CEO said that he intended to retire.

► In 2008, we expect that efforts to bolster sales will include a growing presence in the premium chocolate category, and investment support of core brands, international expansion, and HSY's retail sales force. We expect that over the next couple of years, HSY will increasingly be looking to fund investments with savings from a supply chain transformation program.

► We look for HSY's sales to grow at least modestly in 2008, from the $4.95 billion projected for 2007. At least in the near term, we look for gross margins to be pressured by ingredient costs, especially dairy-related purchases. We estimate that EPS, before special items, will total $2.20 in 2008, up from the $2.10 projected for 2007. This excludes about $1.05 of business realignment charges expected in 2007.

Investment Rationale/Risk

► We see HSY's plan for an improved supply chain bolstering longer-term profit growth prospects. We expect a portion of anticipated manufacturing savings to be spent on areas such as brand support, new products and overseas expansion. In terms of corporate governance, the company has a dual class capital structure with unequal voting rights, which we view unfavorably.

► Risks to our recommendation and target price include the possibility that sales will be weaker than we anticipate and that profit margins will be less favorable.

► We think the recent replacement of eight directors increases the likelihood of the company being more aggressive in making moves to reduce costs and/or boost its stock price. This includes the possibility of HSY being more receptive or flexible regarding a merger or restructuring. Our 12-month target price of $43 is based on a P/E of 19.5X estimated 2008 EPS, which is relatively close to what we expect, on average, from a group of packaged food stock peers. Also, the stock recently had an indicated dividend yield of about 3.0%.

Qualitative Risk Assessment

LOW	MEDIUM	HIGH

Our risk assessment reflects what we see to be the relatively stable nature of Hershey's primary end markets, the strength of its U.S. business, and our view of the company's balance sheet and cash flow strength.

Quantitative Evaluations

S&P Quality Ranking B+

D	C	B-	B	B+	A-	A	A+

Relative Strength Rank MODERATE

31

LOWEST = 1   HIGHEST = 99

Revenue/Earnings Data

Revenue (Million $)

	1Q	2Q	3Q	4Q	Year
2007	1,153	1,052	1,399	--	--
2006	1,140	1,052	1,416	1,337	4,944
2005	1,126	988.5	1,368	1,353	4,836
2004	1,013	893.7	1,255	1,268	4,429
2003	953.2	849.1	1,191	1,179	4,173
2002	988.5	823.5	1,152	1,156	4,120

Earnings Per Share ($)

	1Q	2Q	3Q	4Q	Year
2007	0.40	0.01	0.27	E0.56	E2.10
2006	0.50	0.41	0.78	0.65	2.34
2005	0.47	0.39	0.48	0.70	1.99
2004	0.41	0.56	0.66	0.68	2.30
2003	0.37	0.27	0.58	0.55	1.76
2002	0.32	0.23	0.45	0.48	1.46

Fiscal year ended Dec. 31. Next earnings report expected: Late January. EPS Estimates based on S&P Operating Earnings; historical GAAP earnings are as reported.

Dividend Data (Dates: mm/dd Payment Date: mm/dd/yy)

Amount ($)	Date Decl.	Ex-Div. Date	Stk. of Record	Payment Date
0.270	02/16	02/21	02/23	03/15/07
0.270	04/16	05/23	05/25	06/15/07
0.298	08/07	08/22	08/24	09/14/07
0.298	10/02	11/19	11/21	12/14/07

Dividends have been paid since 1930. Source: Company reports.

Please read the Required Disclosures and Analyst Certification on the last page of this report.

The McGraw-Hill Companies

Hershey Co (The)

STANDARD &POOR'S

Business Summary November 20, 2007

CORPORATE OVERVIEW. This company produces and distributes a variety of chocolate, confectionery and grocery products. The companies brands include Hershey's, Kisses, and Reese's.

CORPORATE STRATEGY. In 2007, we expect the company's focus to include accelerating the growth of some core brands (e.g. Kisses, Hershey's and Reese's), and seeking growth from areas such as dark and premium chocolate, and portion control products (e.g., 60- or 100-calorie items).

In 2006, HSY derived about 10.9% of its net sales from customers located outside the U.S. Longer term, we expect international expansion to focus on emerging markets in Asia, particularly India and China, Mexico and selected markets in South America. In May 2007, HSY and Indian company Godrej Beverages and Foods, Ltd., entered into an agreement to manufacture and distribute confectionery products, snacks and beverages in India. Under the agreement, HSY invested $58.7 million during the second quarter of 2007, and owned a 51% controlling interest in a venture related to the agreement. Also in May 2007, HSY and Korean company Lotte Confectionery Co., LTD., entered into a manufacturing agreement related to the production of Hershey products and certain Lotte products for the market in China. HSY invested $18.3 million in the second quarter of 2007, and owned a 44% interest in a venture

related to the agreement.

In February 2007, HSY announced a supply chain transformation program that is expected to be completed by December 2009. HSY estimated that this program will incur pre-tax charges and non-recurring project implementation costs (including asset write-offs) of $525 million to $575 million over the three-year period. The program is projected to result in increased capital expenditures from 2007-2009. Under the program, HSY is expected to significantly increase manufacturing capacity utilization by reducing its number of production lines; outsource the production of low value-added items; and construct a production facility in Mexico.

As a result of the program, HSY estimated that the gross margin will improve significantly, with ongoing annual savings of about $170 million to $190 million generated by 2010. HSY says that it will invest a portion of these savings in strategic growth initiatives.

Company Financials Fiscal Year Ended Dec. 31

Per Share Data ($)	2006	2005	2004	2003	2002	2001	2000	1999	1998	1997
Tangible Book Value	0.18	1.63	2.03	3.29	3.55	2.65	2.57	2.34	1.79	1.05
Cash Flow	3.17	2.96	3.17	2.44	2.17	1.44	1.84	2.21	1.71	1.62
Earnings	2.34	1.99	2.30	1.76	1.46	0.75	1.21	1.63	1.17	1.12
S&P Core Earnings	2.26	1.94	2.23	1.73	1.37	0.94	NA	NA	NA	NA
Dividends	1.03	0.93	0.84	0.72	0.63	0.58	0.54	0.50	0.46	0.42
Payout Ratio	44%	47%	36%	41%	43%	78%	45%	31%	39%	38%
Prices:High	57.65	67.37	56.75	39.33	39.75	35.08	33.22	32.44	38.19	31.94
Prices:Low	48.20	52.49	37.28	30.35	28.23	27.56	18.88	22.88	29.84	21.06
P/E Ratio:High	25	34	25	22	27	47	27	20	33	29
P/E Ratio:Low	21	26	16	17	19	37	16	14	26	19

Income Statement Analysis (Million $)	2006	2005	2004	2003	2002	2001	2000	1999	1998	1997
Revenue	4,944	4,836	4,429	4,173	4,120	4,557	4,221	3,971	4,436	4,302
Operating Income	2,928	1,175	1,092	992	904	812	799	722	801	783
Depreciation	200	218	190	181	178	190	176	163	158	153
Interest Expense	116	89.5	66.5	63.5	60.7	71.5	81.0	77.3	88.6	79.1
Pretax Income	877	773	836	733	638	344	547	728	557	554
Effective Tax Rate	36.2%	36.2%	29.3%	36.6%	36.7%	39.7%	38.8%	36.8%	38.8%	39.3%
Net Income	559	493	591	465	404	207	335	460	341	336
S&P Core Earnings	540	482	573	455	377	258	NA	NA	NA	NA

Balance Sheet & Other Financial Data (Million $)	2006	2005	2004	2003	2002	2001	2000	1999	1998	1997
Cash	97.1	67.2	54.8	115	298	134	32.0	118	39.0	54.2
Current Assets	1,418	1,409	1,182	1,132	1,264	1,168	1,295	1,280	1,134	1,035
Total Assets	4,158	4,295	3,798	3,583	3,481	3,247	3,448	3,347	3,404	3,291
Current Liabilities	1,454	1,518	1,285	586	547	606	767	713	815	796
Long Term Debt	1,248	943	691	968	852	877	878	878	879	1,029
Common Equity	683	1,021	1,089	1,280	1,372	1,147	1,175	1,099	1,042	853
Total Capital	2,218	2,364	2,109	2,626	2,572	2,280	2,353	2,303	2,243	2,149
Capital Expenditures	183	181	182	219	133	160	138	115	161	173
Cash Flow	759	711	781	646	581	398	511	624	499	489
Current Ratio	1.0	0.9	0.9	1.9	2.3	1.9	1.7	1.8	1.4	1.3
% Long Term Debt of Capitalization	56.3	39.9	32.7	36.9	33.1	38.5	37.3	38.1	39.2	47.9
% Net Income of Revenue	11.3	10.2	13.3	11.1	9.8	4.5	7.9	11.6	7.7	7.8
% Return on Assets	13.3	12.2	16.0	13.2	12.0	6.2	9.8	13.6	10.2	10.4
% Return on Equity	65.8	45.7	46.4	35.1	32.0	17.8	29.4	43.0	36.0	33.4

Data as orig reptd.; bef. results of disc opers/spec. items. Per share data adj. for stk. divs.; EPS diluted. E-Estimated. NA-Not Available. NM-Not Meaningful. NR-Not Ranked. UR-Under Review.

Office: 100 Crystal A Dr, Hershey, PA 17033-0810.
Telephone: 717-534-4000.
Website: http://www.hersheys.com
Chrmn, Pres & CEO: R.H. Lenny

COO, EVP & CFO: D.J. West
SVP, Secy & General Counsel: B.H. Snyder
VP & Chief Acctg Officer: D.W. Tacka
Investor Contact: J.A. Edris (800-539-0261)

Board Members: J. A. Boscia, R. H. Campbell, R. F. Cavanaugh, G. P. Coughlan, H. Edelman, B. G. Hill, A. F. Kelly, Jr., R. H. Lenny, M. J. McDonald, M. J. Toulantis

Founded: 1893
Domicile: Delaware
Employees: 15,000

Hess Corp

STANDARD &POOR'S

S&P Recommendation HOLD ★★★☆☆	**Price** $70.26 (as of Nov 23, 2007)	**12-Mo. Target Price** $76.00	**Investment Style** Large-Cap Blend

GICS Sector Energy
Sub-Industry Integrated Oil & Gas

Summary This integrated oil and natural gas company has exploration and production activities worldwide, but markets refined petroleum products on the U.S. East Coast.

Key Stock Statistics (Source S&P, Vickers, company reports)

52-Wk Range	$74.95–45.96	S&P Oper. EPS 2007**E**	5.73	Market Capitalization(B)	$22.444	Beta	0.14
Trailing 12-Month EPS	$5.27	S&P Oper. EPS 2008**E**	5.80	Yield (%)	0.57	S&P 3-Yr. Proj. EPS CAGR(%)	1.94
Trailing 12-Month P/E	13.3	P/E on S&P Oper. EPS 2007**E**	12.3	Dividend Rate/Share	$0.40	S&P Credit Rating	BBB-
$10K Invested 5 Yrs Ago	$38,191	Common Shares Outstg. (M)	319.4	Institutional Ownership (%)	81		

Price Performance

30-Week Mov. Avg. · · · 10-Week Mov. Avg. - - **GAAP Earnings vs. Previous Year**   **Volume** Above Avg. STARS
12-Mo. Target Price — Relative Strength — ▲ Up ▼ Down ► No Change   Below Avg. ★

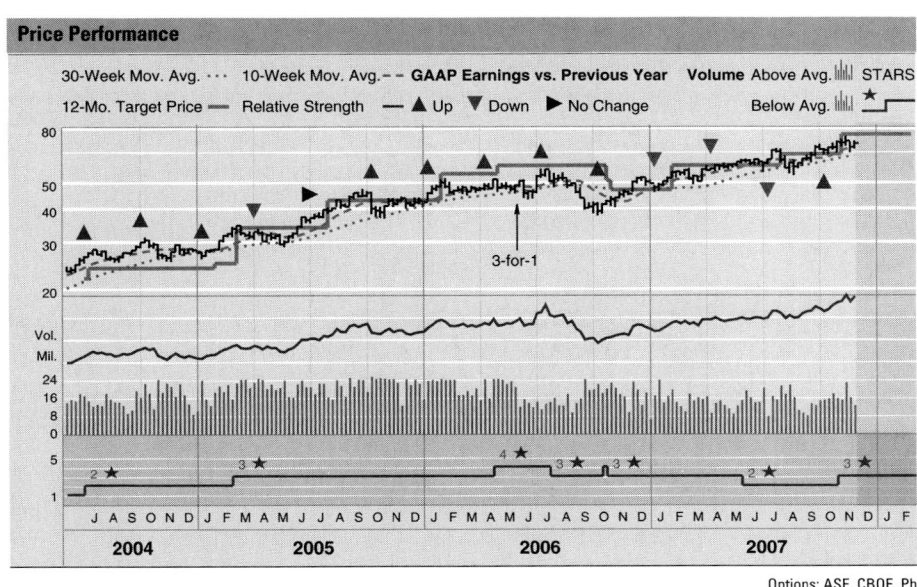

3-for-1

J A S O N D	J F M A M J J A S O N D	J F M A M J J A S O N D	J F M A M J J A S O N D	J F
2004	**2005**	**2006**	**2007**

Options: ASE, CBOE, Ph

Analysis prepared by **Tina J. Vital** on November 01, 2007, when the stock traded at **$ 70.02.**

Highlights

➤ Third quarter oil and gas production rose 1.4%, to 357,000 boe/d, but was slightly below our expectations. We expect production growth in 2007 and 2008 of over 5% and 6%. HES expects fourth quarter production will reach 390,000 boe/d, reflecting the resumption of natural gas production in the Cromarty Field in the U.K. North Sea and from the Malaysia-Thailand JDA, start-up of the Snohvit Field in Norway and from Genghis Khan in the U.S. Gulf of Mexico, and the ramp-up of crude production at the Okume Complex in Equatorial Guinea.

➤ Refining and marketing margins weakened in the 2007 second half, and we project 2008 refining margins will narrow over 30% from 2007 levels, as refined product prices have failed to keep pace with a sharp increase in crude oil prices.

➤ We expect after-tax operating earnings will decline over 8% in 2007, before rising slightly in 2008, reflecting weakened refining margins, partially offset by strong oil price realizations and improved volumes.

Investment Rationale/Risk

➤ We believe that HES's past reserve replacement rate is low compared to peers, and that its finding, development and reserve replacement costs are high. However, we think increased upstream spending by HES has improved its exploration success. In 2006, the company spent $3.7 billion on exploration and production, including $359 million for Libya's Waha concessions and $413 million in Egypt's West Med block, and plans to spend $3.9 billion in 2007, including $371 million for the Genghis Khan deepwater Gulf of Mexico development. In January 2007, HES estimated its three year (2004-2006) reserve replacement rate at a strong 162% at a finding & development cost of $12.50 per barrel.

➤ Risks to our recommendation and target price include changes in economic, industrial and operating conditions, including HES's ability to replace its oil and gas reserves.

➤ A blend of our discounted cash flow (assuming a WACC of 6.6%, and terminal growth of 3%) and our relative valuations leads us to our 12-month target of $76, representing an enterprise value of 5X our 2008 EBITDA estimate, a discount to peers.

Qualitative Risk Assessment

LOW	**MEDIUM**	HIGH

Our risk assessment reflects HES's diversified business profile in volatile, cyclical and capital intensive segments of the energy industry. However, we see increased risk from its investments in politically challenged locales, and a relatively high cost structure in exploration and production.

Quantitative Evaluations

S&P Quality Ranking   **B**

D	C	B-	**B**	B+	A-	A	A+

Relative Strength Rank   **STRONG**

90

LOWEST = 1   HIGHEST = 99

Revenue/Earnings Data

Revenue (Million $)

	1Q	2Q	3Q	4Q	Year
2007	7,319	7,274	7,451	--	--
2006	7,159	6,718	7,035	7,155	28,067
2005	4,956	4,963	5,769	7,059	22,747
2004	4,488	3,803	3,830	4,612	16,733
2003	4,254	3,199	3,230	3,628	14,480
2002	3,021	2,796	2,818	3,297	12,093

Earnings Per Share ($)

2007	1.17	1.75	1.23	E1.48	E5.73
2006	2.21	1.79	0.94	1.13	6.07
2005	0.71	0.92	0.87	1.44	3.98
2004	0.92	0.92	0.58	0.74	3.17
2003	0.81	0.24	0.55	0.24	1.72
2002	0.53	0.55	-0.51	-1.40	-0.83

Fiscal year ended Dec. 31. Next earnings report expected: Late January. EPS Estimates based on S&P Operating Earnings; historical GAAP earnings are as reported.

Dividend Data (Dates: mm/dd Payment Date: mm/dd/yy)

Amount ($)	Date Decl.	Ex-Div. Date	Stk. of Record	Payment Date
0.100	12/06	12/13	12/15	01/02/07
0.100	03/07	03/14	03/16	03/30/07
0.100	06/06	06/13	06/15	06/29/07
0.100	09/05	09/12	09/14	09/28/07

Dividends have been paid since 1922. Source: Company reports.

The McGraw·Hill Companies

Hess Corp

STANDARD &POOR'S

Business Summary November 01, 2007

Hess Corp. (HES; formerly Amerada Hess Corp.) has two operating segments: exploration and production (23 % of 2006 revenues; 82% of net income), and marketing and refining (77%; 18%). Business is conducted in the U.S., Europe, Africa, Asia and other countries. As of May 2007, the Hess family and related interests owned about 14% of the common shares.

We estimate HES's three-year (2003-2005, latest available) organic reserve replacement (including equity investees) at a subpar 68%. Crude oil and natural gas liquids production increased to 257,000 barrels per day (b/d) in 2006, from 244,000 b/d in 2005. Natural gas production rose to 612,000 thousand cubic feet (Mcf) per day in 2006, from 544,000 Mcf per day in 2005. HES estimates that its 2007 hydrocarbon production will average about 375,000 boe/d. Aver-

age selling prices in 2006 (including the effects of hedging) was $54.81 per barrel for liquids and $5.50 per Mcf for natural gas. Hedge losses totaled $285 million in 2006, and HES had $379 million of deferred hedging losses, after income taxes, included in accumulated other comprehensive income. As of December 31, 2006, the company's outstanding hedge positions included 24,000 b/d of crude oil for each year during 2007-2012. Three year (2004-2006) average production (lifting) costs were $8.02 per boe.

Company Financials Fiscal Year Ended Dec. 31

Per Share Data ($)	2006	2005	2004	2003	2002	2001	2000	1999	1998	1997
Tangible Book Value	21.77	16.61	14.34	13.62	12.17	14.70	14.59	11.17	9.99	11.72
Cash Flow	9.80	7.11	6.18	5.61	4.17	7.04	6.43	4.02	0.73	2.47
Earnings	6.07	3.98	3.17	1.72	-0.83	3.42	3.79	1.62	-1.71	0.03
S&P Core Earnings	5.38	3.78	3.06	1.75	-1.28	3.25	NA	NA	NA	NA
Dividends	0.40	0.40	0.40	0.40	0.40	0.40	0.20	0.20	0.20	0.20
Payout Ratio	7%	10%	13%	23%	NM	12%	5%	12%	NM	NM
Prices:High	56.45	47.50	31.30	19.07	28.23	30.13	25.42	22.10	20.35	21.50
Prices:Low	37.62	25.94	17.75	13.71	16.47	17.92	15.94	14.58	15.33	15.79
P/E Ratio:High	9	12	10	11	NM	9	7	14	NM	NM
P/E Ratio:Low	6	7	6	8	NM	5	4	9	NM	NM

Income Statement Analysis (Million $)										
Revenue	28,067	22,747	16,733	14,480	12,093	13,413	11,993	7,039	6,590	8,234
Operating Income	4,812	2,967	2,769	2,127	2,382	2,399	2,264	1,214	475	910
Depreciation, Depletion and Amortization	1,224	1,025	970	1,053	1,320	967	714	648	657	673
Interest Expense	201	224	241	293	269	194	162	158	153	136
Pretax Income	4,040	2,226	1,558	781	-51.0	1,438	1,672	702	-514	127
Effective Tax Rate	52.6%	44.2%	37.7%	40.2%	NM	36.4%	38.8%	37.6%	NM	93.7%
Net Income	1,916	1,242	970	467	-218	914	1,023	438	-459	8.00
S&P Core Earnings	1,657	1,131	888	468	-339	870	NA	NA	NA	NA

Balance Sheet & Other Financial Data (Million $)										
Cash	383	315	877	518	197	37.0	312	41.0	74.0	91.0
Current Assets	5,848	5,290	4,335	3,186	2,756	3,946	4,115	1,828	1,887	2,204
Total Assets	22,404	19,115	16,312	13,983	13,262	15,369	10,274	7,728	7,883	7,935
Current Liabilities	6,739	6,447	4,697	2,669	2,553	3,718	3,538	1,579	1,797	1,740
Long Term Debt	3,745	3,759	3,785	3,868	4,976	5,283	1,985	2,287	2,476	2,003
Common Equity	8,111	6,272	5,583	5,326	8,498	4,907	3,883	3,038	2,643	3,216
Total Capital	13,955	11,446	10,566	10,352	14,518	11,301	6,378	5,767	5,603	5,781
Capital Expenditures	3,844	2,341	1,521	1,358	1,404	2,501	938	797	1,439	1,346
Cash Flow	3,096	2,219	1,892	1,515	1,102	1,881	1,737	1,086	198	681
Current Ratio	0.9	0.8	0.9	1.2	1.1	1.1	1.2	1.2	1.1	1.3
% Long Term Debt of Capitalization	26.8	32.8	35.8	37.4	34.3	46.7	31.1	39.7	44.2	34.6
% Return on Assets	9.2	7.0	6.4	3.4	NM	7.1	11.4	5.6	NM	0.1
% Return on Equity	26.0	20.1	16.9	9.7	NM	20.8	29.6	15.4	NM	0.2

Data as orig reptd.; bef. results of disc opers/spec. items. Per share data adj. for stk. divs.; EPS diluted. E-Estimated. NA-Not Available. NM-Not Meaningful. NR-Not Ranked. UR-Under Review.

Office: 1185 Avenue Of The Americas, New York, NY 10036.
Telephone: 212-997-8500.
Email: investorrelations@hess.com
Website: http://www.hess.com

Chrmn & CEO: J.B. Hess
EVP & General Counsel: J.B. Collins, II
SVP & CFO: J.P. Reilly
VP & Treas: R.J. Vogel

Investor Contact: J.R. Wilson (212-536-8940)
Board Members: N. F. Brady, J. B. Collins, II, J. B. Hess, E. E. Holiday, T. H. Kean, R. Lavizzo-Mourey, C. G. Matthews, J. J. O'Connor, F. A. Olson, F. B. Walker, R. N. Wilson, E. H. von Metzsch

Founded: 1920
Domicile: Delaware
Employees: 13,700

Hewlett-Packard Co

STANDARD & POOR'S

S&P Recommendation **BUY** ★★★★☆	Price $49.17 (as of Nov 23, 2007)	12-Mo. Target Price $61.00	Investment Style Large-Cap Blend

GICS Sector Information Technology
Sub-Industry Computer Hardware

Summary This leading maker of computer products, including printers, servers, and PCs, has a large service and support network.

Key Stock Statistics (Source S&P, Vickers, company reports)

52-Wk Range	$53.48– 38.15	S&P Oper. EPS 2008E	3.40	Market Capitalization(B)	$126.763	Beta	2.04
Trailing 12-Month EPS	$2.68	S&P Oper. EPS 2009E	3.85	Yield (%)	0.65	S&P 3-Yr. Proj. EPS CAGR(%)	14.00
Trailing 12-Month P/E	18.4	P/E on S&P Oper. EPS 2008E	14.5	Dividend Rate/Share	$0.32	S&P Credit Rating	A
$10K Invested 5 Yrs Ago	$27,358	Common Shares Outstg. (M)	2,578.1	Institutional Ownership (%)	78		

Price Performance

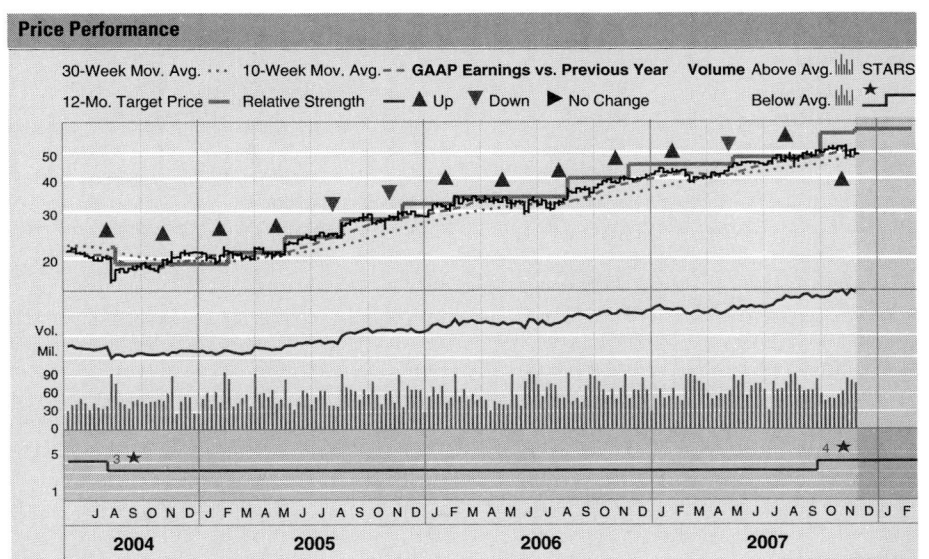

30-Week Mov. Avg. ··· 10-Week Mov. Avg. -- **GAAP Earnings vs. Previous Year**   Volume Above Avg. ||| STARS
12-Mo. Target Price — Relative Strength — ▲ Up ▼ Down ► No Change   Below Avg. ||| ★

Options: ASE, CBOE, P, Ph

Analysis prepared by **Thomas W. Smith, CFA** on November 21, 2007, when the stock traded at **$ 49.16**.

Highlights

► We project revenue growth of about 7% in FY 08 (Oct.) and 6% in FY 09, compared to a 14% increase in FY 07, which included unusually favorable foreign currency effects. We expect notebook PC sales and overall technology spending to receive a lift from the recent launch of Microsoft Corp.'s (MSFT: strong buy, $34) new operating system. In addition, we anticipate improved results from HPQ's software segment as it integrates acquisitions.

► We expect gross margins to widen a little, to 25.2% in FY 08, from about 24.4% in FY 07, on higher volumes and manufacturing efficiencies. We foresee steady R&D and SG&A expense levels ahead as a percentage of revenues, and we think that operating margins will widen toward 10% in FY 09, from FY 07's 9.2%. We believe results will be hindered by higher taxes, and aided by additional share buybacks.

► Based on these assumptions, we estimate FY 08 operating EPS of $3.40, and we project operating EPS of $3.85 for FY 09. EPS values exclude special charges that we estimate at $0.20 in each year.

Investment Rationale/Risk

► We believe that demand for PCs will grow at a strong pace over the next 12 months, with moderate growth for printers and most other segments. We expect HPQ's broad product and customer base to aid its efforts to add market share. We believe HPQ, under CEO Mark Hurd, has made substantial progress in its cost reduction efforts, and think expenses should remain under control.

► Risks to our recommendation and target price include what we view as HPQ's need to augment its capabilities in software and services in order to offer a more attractive long-term competitive position. In addition, we are concerned about any potential negative impact associated with an ongoing formal SEC investigation related to HPQ's boardroom activities and procedures.

► Our 12-month target price is based primarily on our P/E analysis. We apply a target P/E of 18X, in the bottom half of a four-year historical range for HPQ and near the average for S&P 500 Information Technology Sector companies, to our FY 08 operating EPS estimate of $3.40, to arrive at our 12-month target price of $61.

Qualitative Risk Assessment

LOW	**MEDIUM**	HIGH

Our risk assessment reflects the intensely price competitive environment in the computer hardware industry, balanced by our view of the company's successful efforts in reducing its cost structure.

Quantitative Evaluations

S&P Quality Ranking B+

D	C	B-	B	**B+**	A-	A	A+

Relative Strength Rank MODERATE

70

LOWEST = 1   HIGHEST = 99

Revenue/Earnings Data

Revenue (Million $)

	1Q	2Q	3Q	4Q	Year
2007	25,082	25,534	25,377	28,293	104,286
2006	22,659	22,554	21,890	24,555	91,658
2005	21,454	21,570	20,759	22,913	86,696
2004	19,514	20,113	18,889	21,389	79,905
2003	17,877	17,983	17,348	19,853	73,061
2002	11,383	10,621	16,536	18,048	56,588

Earnings Per Share ($)

2007	0.55	0.65	0.66	0.81	2.68
2006	0.42	0.66	0.48	0.60	2.18
2005	0.32	0.33	0.03	0.14	0.82
2004	0.30	0.29	0.19	0.37	1.15
2003	0.24	0.22	0.10	0.28	0.83
2002	0.25	0.12	-0.67	0.13	-0.37

Fiscal year ended Oct. 31. Next earnings report expected: Late February. EPS Estimates based on S&P Operating Earnings; historical GAAP earnings are as reported.

Dividend Data (Dates: mm/dd Payment Date: mm/dd/yy)

Amount ($)	Date Decl.	Ex-Div. Date	Stk. of Record	Payment Date
0.080	01/19	03/12	03/14	04/04/07
0.080	05/18	06/11	06/13	07/05/07
0.080	07/20	09/10	09/12	10/03/07
0.080	11/19	12/10	12/12	01/02/08

Dividends have been paid since 1965. Source: Company reports.

Please read the Required Disclosures and Analyst Certification on the last page of this report.

The McGraw-Hill Companies

Hewlett-Packard Co

Business Summary November 21, 2007

CORPORATE OVERVIEW. Hewlett-Packard provides computers and related products, technologies, solutions and services to all segments of the computer industry worldwide. The ongoing elimination of 15,200 positions through retirement programs and work force restructurings has enabled the company to develop a global delivery structure that has improved margins by taking advantage of low-cost technical expertise. In February 2005, chairman and CEO Carly Fiorina stepped down after the company's board was unable to agree on how to execute HPQ's strategy. Effective April 1, 2005, former NCR Corp. CEO Mark Hurd was named CEO and president. In addition, Mr. Hurd took over the chairman's role in late September 2006.

In July 2006, HPQ agreed to acquire Mercury Interactive Corp., a provider of software and services, for $4.5 billion. We believe the deal will strengthen and improve the profitability of HPQ's business mix, but we think the price paid is a bit steep, particularly given the ongoing formal SEC investigation of Mercury.

In November 2006, the company revealed that the SEC had begun a formal in-

vestigation of HPQ relating to procedures it used in trying to uncover the source of its boardroom leaks. In addition, the Federal Communications Commission has requested information relating to this matter. While these revelations do not affect HPQ's fundamental business, in our opinion, we are concerned about potential administrative costs and internal distractions associated with these probes.

PRIMARY BUSINESS DYNAMICS. Large corporations and small offices/home offices are the primary drivers of spending on information technology products and services. Industrywide trends, exchange rates, and distribution channels influence HPQ's financial performance. Most players sell broad product lines and have a global sourcing and distribution system.

Company Financials Fiscal Year Ended Oct. 31

Per Share Data ($)	2007	2006	2005	2004	2003	2002	2001	2000	1999	1998
Tangible Book Value	NA	6.57	6.04	6.06	6.08	5.35	7.20	7.30	9.10	8.33
Cash Flow	NA	3.00	1.63	1.93	1.65	0.48	1.01	2.37	2.10	2.25
Earnings	2.68	2.18	0.82	1.15	0.83	-0.37	0.32	1.73	1.49	1.39
S&P Core Earnings	NA	2.10	0.74	0.94	0.65	-0.65	0.16	NA	NA	NA
Dividends	0.32	0.32	0.32	0.32	0.32	0.32	0.32	0.32	0.32	0.30
Payout Ratio	12%	15%	39%	28%	39%	NM	100%	18%	22%	22%
Prices:High	53.48	41.70	30.25	26.28	23.90	24.12	37.95	77.75	59.22	41.19
Prices:Low	38.15	28.37	18.89	16.08	14.18	10.75	12.50	29.13	31.69	23.53
P/E Ratio:High	20	19	37	23	29	NM	NM	45	40	30
P/E Ratio:Low	14	13	23	14	17	NM	NM	17	21	17

Income Statement Analysis (Million $)										
Revenue	NA	91,658	86,696	79,905	73,061	56,588	45,226	48,782	42,370	47,061
Operating Income	NA	9,372	7,520	7,017	6,713	4,570	3,192	5,257	5,004	5,710
Depreciation	NA	2,353	2,344	2,395	2,527	2,119	1,369	1,368	1,316	1,869
Interest Expense	NA	249	334	247	277	212	234	233	202	235
Pretax Income	NA	7,191	3,543	4,196	2,888	-1,052	702	4,625	4,194	4,091
Effective Tax Rate	NA	13.8%	32.3%	16.7%	12.1%	NM	11.1%	23.0%	26.0%	28.0%
Net Income	NA	6,198	2,398	3,497	2,539	-923	624	3,561	3,104	2,945
S&P Core Earnings	NA	5,992	2,150	2,886	1,983	-1,635	285	NA	NA	NA

Balance Sheet & Other Financial Data (Million $)										
Cash	NA	16,400	13,911	12,663	14,188	11,192	4,197	3,415	5,411	4,046
Current Assets	NA	48,264	43,334	42,901	40,996	36,075	21,305	23,244	21,642	21,584
Total Assets	NA	81,981	77,317	76,138	74,708	70,710	32,584	34,009	35,297	33,673
Current Liabilities	NA	35,850	31,460	28,588	26,630	24,310	13,964	15,197	14,321	13,473
Long Term Debt	NA	2,490	3,392	4,623	6,494	6,035	3,729	3,402	1,764	2,063
Common Equity	NA	38,144	37,176	37,564	37,746	36,262	13,953	14,209	18,295	16,919
Total Capital	NA	40,634	40,568	42,187	44,240	42,297	17,682	17,611	20,059	18,982
Capital Expenditures	NA	2,536	1,995	2,126	1,995	1,710	1,527	1,737	1,134	1,997
Cash Flow	NA	8,551	4,742	5,892	5,066	1,196	1,993	4,929	4,420	4,814
Current Ratio	NA	1.3	1.4	1.5	1.5	1.5	1.5	1.5	1.5	1.6
% Long Term Debt of Capitalization	NA	6.1	8.4	11.0	14.7	14.3	21.1	19.3	8.8	10.9
% Net Income of Revenue	NA	6.8	2.8	4.4	3.5	NM	1.4	7.3	7.3	6.3
% Return on Assets	NA	7.8	3.1	4.6	3.5	NM	1.9	10.3	9.3	9.0
% Return on Equity	NA	16.5	6.4	9.3	6.9	NM	4.4	21.9	17.6	17.8

Data as orig reptd.; bef. results of disc opers/spec. items. Per share data adj. for stk. divs.; EPS diluted. E-Estimated. NA-Not Available. NM-Not Meaningful. NR-Not Ranked. UR-Under Review.

Office: 3000 Hanover Street, Palo Alto, CA 94304-1112.
Telephone: 650-857-1501.
Website: http://www.hp.com
Chrmn, Pres & CEO: M.V. Hurd

EVP & CFO: C.A. Lesjak
EVP & Chief Admin Officer: J.E. Flaxman
EVP & CTO: S.V. Robison
EVP & CIO: R.D. Mott

Investor Contact: B. Humphries (650-857-3342)
Board Members: L. T. Babbio, Jr., S. M. Baldauf, R. A. Hackborn, J. H. Hammergren, M. V. Hurd, R. Ryan, L. S. Salhany, G. K. Thompson

Founded: 1939
Domicile: Delaware
Employees: 156,000

Home Depot Inc. (The)

STANDARD &POOR'S

S&P Recommendation BUY ★★★★☆

Price	12-Mo. Target Price	Investment Style
$28.95 (as of Nov 23, 2007)	$38.00	Large-Cap Blend

GICS Sector Consumer Discretionary
Sub-Industry Home Improvement Retail

Summary HD operates a chain of about 2,100 retail warehouse-type stores, selling a wide variety of home improvement products for the do-it-yourself and home remodeling markets.

Key Stock Statistics (Source S&P, Vickers, company reports)

52-Wk Range	$42.01– 27.77	S&P Oper. EPS 2008E	2.31	Market Capitalization(B)	$48.767	Beta	1.15
Trailing 12-Month EPS	$2.41	S&P Oper. EPS 2009E	2.48	Yield (%)	3.11	S&P 3-Yr. Proj. EPS CAGR(%)	11.00
Trailing 12-Month P/E	12.0	P/E on S&P Oper. EPS 2008E	12.5	Dividend Rate/Share	$0.90	S&P Credit Rating	BBB+
$10K Invested 5 Yrs Ago	$12,290	Common Shares Outstg. (M)	1,684.5	Institutional Ownership (%)	76		

Price Performance

30-Week Mov. Avg. · · · 10-Week Mov. Avg. – – GAAP Earnings vs. Previous Year   Volume Above Avg. STARS
12-Mo. Target Price — Relative Strength   — ▲ Up ▼ Down ▶ No Change   Below Avg. ★

Options: ASE, CBOE, P, Ph

Analysis prepared by **Michael Souers** on November 13, 2007, when the stock traded at **$ 29.12**.

Highlights

▶ We expect retail sales to decline about 1% in FY 09 (Jan.), following our projection of a 1%-2% decrease in FY 08, excluding sales from HD Supply -- which is being treated as a discontinued operation. We see revenues being driven by about 90 new retail store additions, including international store openings and a same-store sales decline of about 3%, as we project continued deterioration in the housing market.

▶ We foresee FY 09 operating margins narrowing about 30 basis points, as expenses deleverage due to a projected decline in comp-store sales. Furthermore, reinvestment in stores to improve customer service should accelerate the margin decline. However, we believe this reinvestment will lead to longer-term margin improvement through customer retention and increased sales.

▶ After a diluted share count that is about 10% lower, reflecting our projection that HD will issue tranches of debt in the second half of 2008 in order to complete its recapitalization effort, we project FY 09 EPS of $2.48, a 7% increase from the $2.31 we project the company will earn in FY 08, excluding HD Supply.

Investment Rationale/Risk

▶ At about 11.7X our FY 09 EPS estimate, HD recently traded in line with key peer Lowe's (LOW: buy, $25) and at a modest discount to the S&P 500. We expect the housing market to bottom in late 2008, and believe HD will reap the rewards from an accelerated focus on customer service once the market recovers. Favorable demographic trends such as the aging of houses, historically high home ownership rates and relatively low interest rates should lead to continued home remodeling efforts longer term. Although we are concerned the bleak housing market outlook will limit share price upside over the near term, we favor what we see as HD's strong balance sheet, financial flexibility, and abundant free cash flow generation, and view the shares as attractive.

▶ Risks to our recommendation and target price include a sharp slowdown in the economy; a large rise in interest rates; and unfavorable currency movements.

▶ Our 12-month target price of $38 is equal to about 15.3X our FY 09 EPS estimate, and is derived from our DCF model, which assumes a weighted average cost of capital of 9.3% and a terminal growth rate of 3.0%.

Qualitative Risk Assessment

LOW	MEDIUM	HIGH

Our risk assessment for Home Depot reflects the cyclical nature of the home improvement retail industry, which is reliant on economic growth, more than offset by our view of ample opportunities for growth in the professional market domestically and the retail business overseas, and an S&P Quality Ranking of A+.

Quantitative Evaluations

S&P Quality Ranking   A+

D	C	B-	B	B+	A-	A	A+

Relative Strength Rank   MODERATE

34

LOWEST = 1   HIGHEST = 99

Revenue/Earnings Data

Revenue (Million $)

	1Q	2Q	3Q	4Q	Year
2008	21,585	22,184	18,961	--	--
2007	21,461	26,026	23,085	20,265	90,837
2006	18,973	22,305	20,744	19,489	81,511
2005	17,550	19,960	18,772	16,812	73,094
2004	15,104	17,989	16,598	15,125	64,816
2003	14,282	16,277	14,475	13,213	58,247

Earnings Per Share ($)

2008	0.53	0.77	0.59	E0.46	E2.31
2007	0.70	0.90	0.73	0.46	2.79
2006	0.57	0.82	0.72	0.60	2.72
2005	0.49	0.70	0.60	0.47	2.26
2004	0.39	0.56	0.50	0.42	1.88
2003	0.36	0.50	0.40	0.30	1.56

Fiscal year ended Jan. 31. Next earnings report expected: Mid February. EPS Estimates based on S&P Operating Earnings; historical GAAP earnings are as reported.

Dividend Data (Dates: mm/dd Payment Date: mm/dd/yy)

Amount ($)	Date Decl.	Ex-Div. Date	Stk. of Record	Payment Date
0.225	02/22	03/06	03/08	03/22/07
0.225	05/23	06/05	06/07	06/21/07
0.225	08/16	08/28	08/30	09/13/07
0.225	11/15	11/27	11/29	12/13/07

Dividends have been paid since 1987. Source: Company reports.

Please read the Required Disclosures and Analyst Certification on the last page of this report.

The McGraw-Hill Companies

Home Depot Inc. (The)

STANDARD &POOR'S

Business Summary November 13, 2007

CORPORATE OVERVIEW. Home Depot is the world's largest home improvement retailer, with revenues in excess of $90 billion. The company mainly operates retail warehouse-type stores that sell a wide assortment of building materials, home improvement and lawn and garden products. At January 28, 2007, HD operated 2,147 total stores, including 2,100 Home Depot Stores (155 in Canada, 61 in Mexico and 12 in China), 34 EXPO Design Centers, 11 Home Depot Landscape stores and two Home Depot Floor stores.

Home Depot stores average approximately 105,000 sq. ft., plus 23,000 sq. ft. of garden center and storage space. It stocks 35,000 to 45,000 items, including brand name and proprietary items. Home Depot stores serve three primary customer groups: Do-It-Yourself (DIY) customers, typically homeowners who complete their own projects and installations; Do-It-For-Me (DIFM) customers, usually homeowners who purchase materials and hire third parties to complete the project and/or installation; and Professional Customers, consisting of professional remodelers, general contractors, repairpeople and tradespeople. By product group, plumbing, electrical and kitchen (31% of FY 07 revenues) represented HD's largest source of revenue, followed by hardware and seasonal (27%), building materials, lumber and millwork (24%) and paint,

flooring and wall covering (19%).

CORPORATE STRATEGY. We believe HD is in a period of transition after years of expanding rapidly as a big-box retailer. We expect Home Depot to confront a rapidly saturating domestic market by accelerating its expansion efforts abroad. Domestically, HD is increasing its focus on service and customer retention as a means to gain market share.

At the end of 2006, Home Depot acquired The Home Way, a Chinese home improvement retailer, including 12 stores in six cities. We anticipate that HD will focus on learning from the Chinese market in FY 08 before embarking on an aggressive expansion of stores over several years starting in FY 09.

HD is currently evaluating strategic alternatives for HD Supply, including the possible sale or spin-off of the unit. This decision was reached due to the company's commitment to re-focus on its retail stores.

Company Financials Fiscal Year Ended Jan. 31

Per Share Data ($)	2007	2006	2005	2004	2003	2002	2001	2000	1999	1998
Tangible Book Value	11.81	11.12	9.54	9.56	8.39	7.53	6.32	5.22	3.83	3.17
Cash Flow	3.65	3.45	2.85	2.35	1.95	1.62	1.35	1.19	0.86	0.63
Earnings	2.79	2.72	2.26	1.88	1.56	1.29	1.10	1.00	0.71	0.52
S&P Core Earnings	2.79	2.68	2.19	1.78	1.46	1.18	1.01	NA	NA	NA
Dividends	0.68	0.40	0.33	0.26	0.21	0.17	0.16	0.11	0.08	0.06
Payout Ratio	24%	15%	15%	14%	13%	13%	15%	11%	11%	12%
Calendar Year	2006	2005	2004	2003	2002	2001	2000	1999	1998	1997
Prices:High	43.95	43.98	44.30	37.89	52.60	53.73	70.00	69.75	41.33	20.17
Prices:Low	32.85	34.56	32.34	20.10	23.01	30.30	34.69	34.58	18.44	10.61
P/E Ratio:High	16	16	20	20	41	43	64	70	58	39
P/E Ratio:Low	12	13	14	11	18	24	32	35	26	21

Income Statement Analysis (Million $)										
Revenue	90,837	81,511	73,094	64,816	58,247	53,553	45,738	38,434	30,219	24,156
Operating Income	11,435	10,942	9,245	7,922	6,733	5,696	4,792	4,258	3,034	2,299
Depreciation	1,762	1,579	1,319	1,076	903	764	601	463	373	283
Interest Expense	427	143	70.0	62.0	37.0	28.0	21.0	28.0	37.0	42.0
Pretax Income	9,308	9,282	7,912	6,843	5,872	4,957	4,217	3,804	2,654	1,914
Effective Tax Rate	38.1%	37.1%	36.8%	37.1%	37.6%	38.6%	38.8%	39.0%	39.2%	38.6%
Net Income	5,761	5,838	5,001	4,304	3,664	3,044	2,581	2,320	1,614	1,160
S&P Core Earnings	5,761	5,751	4,843	4,067	3,414	2,780	2,364	NA	NA	NA

Balance Sheet & Other Financial Data (Million $)										
Cash	614	793	506	2,826	2,188	2,477	167	168	62.0	172
Current Assets	18,000	15,346	14,190	13,328	11,917	10,361	7,777	6,390	4,933	4,460
Total Assets	52,263	44,482	38,907	34,437	30,011	26,394	21,385	17,081	13,465	11,229
Current Liabilities	12,931	12,901	10,529	9,554	8,035	6,501	4,385	3,656	2,857	2,456
Long Term Debt	11,643	2,672	2,148	856	1,321	1,250	1,545	750	1,566	1,303
Common Equity	25,030	26,909	24,158	22,407	19,802	18,082	15,004	12,341	8,740	7,098
Total Capital	38,089	30,604	27,615	24,230	21,485	19,521	16,755	13,188	10,400	8,595
Capital Expenditures	3,542	3,881	3,948	3,508	2,749	3,393	3,558	2,581	2,059	1,525
Cash Flow	7,523	7,417	6,320	5,380	4,567	3,808	3,182	2,783	1,987	1,443
Current Ratio	1.4	1.2	1.3	1.4	1.5	1.6	1.8	1.7	1.7	1.8
% Long Term Debt of Capitalization	31.8	8.7	7.8	3.5	6.1	6.4	9.2	5.7	15.1	15.2
% Net Income of Revenue	6.3	7.2	6.8	6.6	6.3	5.7	5.6	6.0	5.3	4.8
% Return on Assets	11.9	14.0	13.6	13.4	13.0	12.7	13.4	15.2	13.1	11.3
% Return on Equity	22.2	22.9	21.5	20.4	19.3	18.4	18.9	22.0	20.4	17.8

Data as orig reptd.; bef. results of disc opers/spec. items. Per share data adj. for stk. divs.; EPS diluted. E-Estimated. NA-Not Available. NM-Not Meaningful. NR-Not Ranked. UR-Under Review.

Office: 2455 Paces Ferry Rd, N.W., Atlanta, GA 30339-1834.
Telephone: 770-433-8211.
Website: http://www.homedepot.com
Chrmn & CEO: F.S. Blake

COO & EVP: J. DeAngelo
EVP & CFO: C.B. Tome
EVP & CIO: R.P. DeRodes
Investor Contact: D. Dayhoff (770-384-2666)

Board Members: D. H. Batchelder, F. Blake, G. D. Brenneman, J. L. Clendenin, C. X. Gonzalez, M. A. Hart, III, B. G. Hill, L. P. Jackson, Jr., H. Johnson-Leipold, L. R. Johnston, K. G. Langone, A. Mozilo, T. J. Ridge
Founded: 1978
Domicile: Delaware
Employees: 364,400

The McGraw-Hill Companies

Honeywell International Inc.

STANDARD & POOR'S

S&P Recommendation **BUY** ★★★★☆	Price $54.67 (as of Nov 23, 2007)	12-Mo. Target Price $66.00	Investment Style Large-Cap Value

GICS Sector Industrials
Sub-Industry Aerospace & Defense

Summary The world's largest maker of cockpit controls, small jet engines and climate control equipment, HON also makes industrial materials and automotive products.

Key Stock Statistics (Source S&P, Vickers, company reports)

52-Wk Range	$62.29–41.49	S&P Oper. EPS 2007**E**	3.15	Market Capitalization(B)	$40.826	Beta	1.48
Trailing 12-Month EPS	$2.96	S&P Oper. EPS 2008**E**	3.56	Yield (%)	1.83	S&P 3-Yr. Proj. EPS CAGR(%)	14.00
Trailing 12-Month P/E	18.5	P/E on S&P Oper. EPS 2007**E**	17.4	Dividend Rate/Share	$1.00	S&P Credit Rating	A
$10K Invested 5 Yrs Ago	$25,306	Common Shares Outstg. (M)	746.8	Institutional Ownership (%)	81		

Price Performance

- 30-Week Mov. Avg. ···
- 10-Week Mov. Avg. --
- **GAAP Earnings vs. Previous Year**
- Volume Above Avg. ▮▮▮ STARS
- 12-Mo. Target Price —
- Relative Strength —
- ▲ Up ▼ Down ▶ No Change
- Below Avg. ▮▮▮

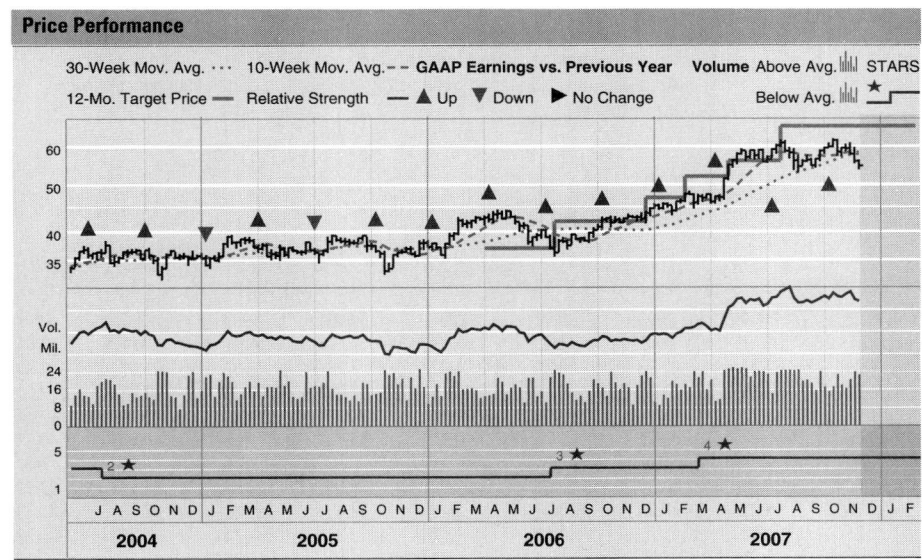

Options: ASE, CBOE, P, Ph

Analysis prepared by **Richard Tortoriello** on October 24, 2007, when the stock traded at **$ 57.99**.

Highlights

➤ We project revenue growth of 9.2% in 2007 and 8.2% in 2008, with growth driven primarily by the aerospace and automation & control systems segments (together about 70% of sales). We see the aerospace segment benefiting from high build rates for OEMs, including Boeing, Airbus, and business jet manufacturers, which are currently experiencing strong order rates and large backlogs of aircraft. We see ACS growth driven primarily by the need for industrial infrastructure globally, as emerging economies in China, India, and the Middle East expand.

➤ We expect margins to expand across the business segments in 2007, on volume growth and pricing and productivity gains, with a projected segment operating margin of 13.5%, up from 13.0% in 2006, and 12.2% in 2005. For 2008, we forecast further margin improvement, to 13.8%.

➤ We estimate a 25% rise in EPS, to $3.15 in 2007, from $2.51 in 2006, and we look for an 13% rise, to $3.56 in 2008. We expect free cash flow (cash flow from operating activities less capital expenditures) per share of about $3.75 in 2007 or about 120% of EPS.

Investment Rationale/Risk

➤ HON's return on invested capital (ROIC) rose from nearly 0% in 2001 and 2002 to 11.7% in 2005 and 15.4% in 2006. So far in 2007, ROIC has been about 16%. Given our expectation that growth in the global economy will benefit HON's ACS segment and that the aerospace segment, where business and commercial jet demand remains high, will continue to improve, we believe HON can continue to increase revenues and improve profitability. In addition, we see shareholders benefiting from HON's substantial cash generation in terms of share repurchases, dividend increases, and profitable reinvestment of capital in growing businesses.

➤ Risks to our recommendation and target price include a downturn in the global economy or in any of HON's core markets, the potential for competitive pressures in its core markets, as well as the possibility of manufacturing or other operational difficulties.

➤ Our 12-month target price of $66 is based on our discounted cash flow (DCF) analysis. Our DCF model assumes a cost of capital of 10.2%, compound annual growth in free cash flow for the first five years of 7.3%, growth of 4.5% for the next 15 years, and 4% growth in perpetuity.

Qualitative Risk Assessment

LOW	MEDIUM	HIGH

Our risk assessment reflects what we believe is above average exposure to market movements, sensitivity to economic cycles, currency fluctuations, and raw material costs. This is offset by what we view as HON's strong balance sheet and its ability to generate significant amounts of cash.

Quantitative Evaluations

S&P Quality Ranking   **B**

D	C	B-	B	B+	A-	A	A+

Relative Strength Rank   **MODERATE**

49

LOWEST = 1   HIGHEST = 99

Revenue/Earnings Data

Revenue (Million $)

	1Q	2Q	3Q	4Q	Year
2007	8,041	8,538	8,735	--	--
2006	7,241	7,898	7,952	8,276	31,367
2005	6,453	7,026	6,899	7,275	27,653
2004	6,178	6,388	6,395	6,640	25,601
2003	5,399	5,749	5,768	6,187	23,103
2002	5,199	5,651	5,569	5,855	22,274

Earnings Per Share ($)

	1Q	2Q	3Q	4Q	Year
2007	0.66	0.78	0.81	E0.89	E3.15
2006	0.51	0.63	0.66	0.72	2.51
2005	0.42	0.33	0.51	0.61	1.86
2004	0.34	0.42	0.43	0.30	1.49
2003	0.32	0.37	0.40	0.47	1.56
2002	0.46	0.56	0.50	-1.78	-0.27

Fiscal year ended Dec. 31. Next earnings report expected: Late January. EPS Estimates based on S&P Operating Earnings; historical GAAP earnings are as reported.

Dividend Data (Dates: mm/dd Payment Date: mm/dd/yy)

Amount ($)	Date Decl.	Ex-Div. Date	Stk. of Record	Payment Date
0.250	02/15	02/23	02/27	03/09/07
0.250	04/23	05/16	05/18	06/08/07
0.250	07/27	08/16	08/20	09/10/07
0.250	10/26	11/16	11/20	12/10/07

Dividends have been paid since 1887. Source: Company reports.

Honeywell International Inc.

Business Summary October 24, 2007

CORPORATE OVERVIEW. Honeywell International Inc., an aerospace and industrial conglomerate with $31 billion in revenues, conducts business through four operating segments.

The Aerospace segment (36% of 2006 revenues and 44% of operating profits, and 17% operating profit margins) primarily makes cockpit controls, power generation equipment, and wheels and brakes for commercial and military aircraft. It is also a leading maker of jet engines for regional and business jet manufacturers.

Demand for HON's aircraft equipment is driven primarily by growth in the global 100+ seat jetliner fleet.

The Aerospace segment is also a major player in the $39 billion global aircraft maintenance, repair and overhaul (MRO) industry. Research firm Aerostrategy projects 3.6% compound annual growth in the MRO market from 2005 to 2015. With airline fleet sizes growing globally, we believe that prospects for this market are favorable.

HON's Automation and Control Solutions segment (35%; 29%; 11%) is best

known as a global producer of home and office climate controls equipment. It also makes home automation systems, energy-efficient lighting controls, and security and fire alarms. Sweden's Securitas AB estimates that the $120 billion global security market is expanding by 6% to 8% per year, with the U.S. and Europe accounting for 75% of the market. It notes that the market is very fragmented.

The Specialty Materials segment (15%; 13%; 12%) makes specialty chemicals and fibers. HON sells its industrial materials primarily to the food, pharmaceutical, and electronic packaging industries.

The Transportation Systems segment (14%; 14%; 13%) consists of a portfolio of brand name car care products, such as FRAM filters, Prestone antifreeze, Autolite spark plugs, and Simoniz car waxes. The unit is also a large truck brake maker.

Company Financials Fiscal Year Ended Dec. 31

Per Share Data ($)	2006	2005	2004	2003	2002	2001	2000	1999	1998	1997
Tangible Book Value	0.09	1.95	4.70	4.46	2.52	3.45	4.71	4.95	4.12	3.47
Cash Flow	3.59	2.74	2.24	2.25	0.53	1.02	3.28	2.99	3.38	3.07
Earnings	2.51	1.86	1.49	1.56	-0.27	-0.12	2.05	1.90	2.32	2.02
S&P Core Earnings	2.62	1.83	1.42	1.57	0.15	-0.26	NA	NA	NA	NA
Dividends	0.91	1.03	0.75	0.75	0.75	0.75	0.75	0.68	0.60	0.52
Payout Ratio	36%	55%	50%	48%	NM	NM	37%	36%	26%	26%
Prices:High	45.77	39.50	38.46	33.50	40.95	53.90	60.50	68.63	47.56	47.13
Prices:Low	35.24	32.68	31.23	20.20	18.77	22.15	32.13	37.81	32.63	31.63
P/E Ratio:High	18	21	26	21	NM	NM	30	36	21	23
P/E Ratio:Low	14	18	21	13	NM	NM	16	20	14	16

Income Statement Analysis (Million $)										
Revenue	31,367	27,653	25,601	23,103	22,274	23,652	25,023	23,735	15,128	14,472
Operating Income	3,855	3,178	2,350	2,513	2,573	1,085	3,794	2,905	2,571	2,019
Depreciation	794	697	650	595	671	926	995	881	609	609
Interest Expense	374	356	331	335	344	405	481	265	162	175
Pretax Income	2,798	2,323	1,680	1,647	-945	-422	2,398	2,248	1,980	1,761
Effective Tax Rate	25.7%	31.9%	23.8%	18.0%	NM	NM	30.8%	31.5%	30.9%	31.0%
Net Income	2,078	1,581	1,281	1,344	-220	NA	1,659	1,541	1,331	1,170
S&P Core Earnings	2,168	1,554	1,225	1,363	119	-207	NA	NA	NA	NA

Balance Sheet & Other Financial Data (Million $)										
Cash	1,224	1,234	3,586	2,950	2,021	1,393	1,196	1,991	712	611
Current Assets	12,304	11,962	12,820	11,523	10,195	9,894	10,661	10,422	5,593	5,573
Total Assets	30,941	32,294	31,062	29,344	27,559	24,226	25,175	23,527	15,560	13,707
Current Liabilities	10,135	10,430	8,739	6,783	6,574	6,220	7,214	8,272	5,185	4,436
Long Term Debt	3,909	3,082	4,069	4,961	4,719	4,731	3,941	2,457	1,476	1,215
Common Equity	9,720	11,254	11,252	7,243	8,925	9,170	9,707	8,599	5,297	4,205
Total Capital	13,981	14,839	15,718	12,520	14,063	14,776	14,821	11,920	7,568	6,114
Capital Expenditures	733	684	629	655	671	876	853	986	684	717
Cash Flow	2,872	2,278	1,931	1,939	451	827	2,654	2,422	1,940	1,779
Current Ratio	1.2	1.1	1.5	1.7	1.6	1.6	1.5	1.3	1.1	1.3
% Long Term Debt of Capitalization	28.0	20.8	25.9	39.6	33.6	32.0	26.6	20.6	19.5	19.3
% Net Income of Revenue	6.6	5.7	5.0	5.8	NM	NM	6.6	6.5	8.8	8.1
% Return on Assets	6.5	5.0	4.2	4.7	NM	NM	6.8	6.7	9.1	8.8
% Return on Equity	20.3	14.0	11.7	21.1	NM	NM	18.1	18.5	28.0	27.9

Data as orig reptd.; bef. results of disc opers/spec. items. Per share data adj. for stk. divs.; EPS diluted. E-Estimated. NA-Not Available. NM-Not Meaningful. NR-Not Ranked. UR-Under Review.

Office: 101 Columbia Rd, Morristown, NJ 07960-4640.
Telephone: 973-455-2000.
Website: http://www.honeywell.com
Chrmn & CEO: D.M. Cote

SVP & CFO: D.J. Anderson
SVP & General Counsel: P.M. Kreindler
Investor Contact: N. Noviello (973-455-2222)
VP & Cntlr: T.A. Szlosek

Board Members: G. M. Bethune, D. M. Cote, D. S. Davis, L. F. Deily, C. Hollick, J. J. Howard, R. E. Palmer, J. C. Pardo, B. T. Sheares, E. K. Shinseki, J. R. Stafford, M. W. Wright

Founded: 1920
Domicile: Delaware
Employees: 118,000

Hospira Inc

STANDARD &POOR'S

S&P Recommendation BUY ★★★★☆	**Price** $42.38 (as of Nov 23, 2007)	**12-Mo. Target Price** $48.00	**Investment Style** Large-Cap Growth

GICS Sector Health Care
Sub-Industry Health Care Equipment

Summary Spun off from Abbott Laboratories in May 2004, this company provides a variety of hospital products, including injectable generic drugs, pumps and syringes.

Key Stock Statistics (Source S&P, Vickers, company reports)

52-Wk Range	$43.00– 32.14	S&P Oper. EPS 2007E	2.15	Market Capitalization(B)	$6.658	Beta	0.25
Trailing 12-Month EPS	$0.68	S&P Oper. EPS 2008E	2.50	Yield (%)	NA	S&P 3-Yr. Proj. EPS CAGR(%)	14.00
Trailing 12-Month P/E	62.3	P/E on S&P Oper. EPS 2007E	19.7	Dividend Rate/Share	NA	S&P Credit Rating	BBB
$10K Invested 5 Yrs Ago	NA	Common Shares Outstg. (M)	157.1	Institutional Ownership (%)	72		

Price Performance

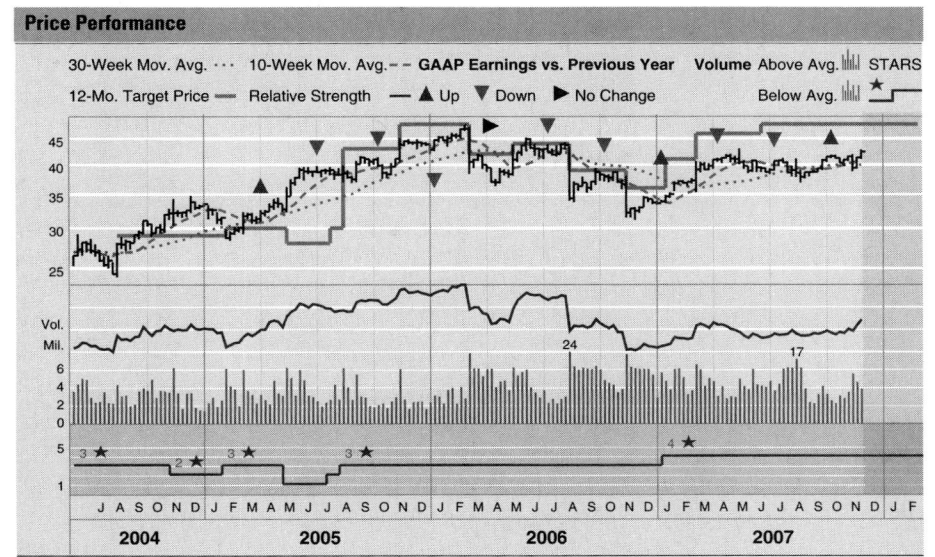

30-Week Mov. Avg. ··· 10-Week Mov. Avg. - - **GAAP Earnings vs. Previous Year** Volume Above Avg. STARS
12-Mo. Target Price — Relative Strength — ▲ Up ▼ Down ► No Change Below Avg. ★

Options: ASE, CBOE, P, Ph

Analysis prepared by **Jeffrey Englander, CFA** on November 19, 2007, when the stock traded at **$ 41.60**.

Highlights

➤ We expect revenues to rise about 26% in 2007, reflecting the acquisition of Mayne Pharma, followed by an increase of approximately 7.7% in 2008. We see growth driven by an improved pipeline and increased international penetration from the Mayne acquisition, partially offset by more gradual growth in medication management systems and the gradual replacement of lost business in the contract manufacturing area.

➤ We look for gross margins to widen in 2007 and increase further in 2008 as HSP realizes an anticipated $50 million in cost synergies from the Mayne acquisition as well as benefits of HSP's lean manufacturing programs. In addition, we look for HSP to transition to higher margin products, particularly in its medication management systems business. We see SG&A and R&D expenses declining as a percentage of revenues, as decreases in SG&A expenses are shifted toward R&D to enhance HSP's new product pipeline.

➤ After taxes at an effective rate of 27% in 2007 and 2008 (vs. 26% in 2006), we forecast operating EPS of $2.15 in 2007 and $2.50 in 2008.

Investment Rationale/Risk

➤ We think HSP is favorably positioned for growth, with sales contributions from the Mayne acquisition, a strong pipeline of new products (including 43 specialty injectable pharmaceuticals), and growth in oncologic products and generic injectables. We anticipate HSP (and it's partner Stada), will bring it's first biogeneric to market in the fist half of 2008 and expect the launch of a second biogeneric by 2010. In addition, we believe HSP is on track to reach its integration savings goals for the Mayne acquisition, and will be able to offset the impact of the $50 million of business lost in the contract manufacturing segment.

➤ Risks to our recommendation and target price include a failure to gain approval for injectable drugs, lack of approval or slower than anticipated approval for biogenerics, lower than anticipated drug pricing, and a decrease in demand for medication delivery products.

➤ Our 12-month target price of $48 assumes that HSP trades at 19X our 2008 EPS estimate of $2.50, below the historical P/E ratio afforded peers, given HSP's brief history as a public company and uneven performance.

Qualitative Risk Assessment

LOW	MEDIUM	HIGH

Our risk assessment reflects HSP's broad product portfolio, which reduces its dependence on any one product category. We see stable demand for hospital products due to our belief that demand for hospital services will remain strong. However, we see minimal growth in this industry.

Quantitative Evaluations

S&P Quality Ranking NR

D	C	B-	B	B+	A-	A	A+

Relative Strength Rank STRONG

89

LOWEST = 1   HIGHEST = 99

Revenue/Earnings Data

Revenue (Million $)

	1Q	2Q	3Q	4Q	Year
2007	782.8	869.4	838.0	--	--
2006	664.3	629.9	646.6	706.5	2,689
2005	662.1	618.5	656.6	646.2	2,627
2004	609.0	667.4	656.1	700.3	2,645
2003	--	--	--	--	2,545
2002	--	--	--	--	--

Earnings Per Share ($)

2007	-0.19	0.20	0.37	E0.58	E2.15
2006	0.49	0.34	0.35	0.30	1.48
2005	0.49	0.44	0.37	0.16	1.46
2004	0.43	0.80	0.39	0.31	1.92
2003	--	--	--	--	1.65
2002	--	--	--	--	--

Fiscal year ended Dec. 31. Next earnings report expected: Early March. EPS Estimates based on S&P Operating Earnings; historical GAAP earnings are as reported.

Dividend Data

No cash dividends have been paid.

Hospira Inc

STANDARD &POOR'S

Business Summary November 19, 2007

CORPORATE OVERVIEW. Hospira (HSP) was created on May 3, 2004, as a spin-off from Abbott Laboratories. Abbott shareholders received one share of Hospira for every 10 shares of Abbott. HSP provides medication delivery systems and specialty pharmaceuticals to hospitals, clinics and physicians. The legal separation to become a stand-alone company was completed in the second quarter of 2006.

Hospira has an international presence, with operations in close to 70 countries. International sales accounted for 17% of total revenues in 2006, unchanged from 2005. The company operates 14 manufacturing facilities domestically and internationally.

Operating segments include specialty injectable pharmaceuticals (2006 sales of $807 million, 30% of sales), medication delivery systems ($855 million, 32%), and injectable pharmaceutical contract manufacturing services ($183 million, 7%). Sales to Abbott Laboratories totaled $161 million in 2006, down from $169

million in 2005. Sales in the other category and to international third parties constitute the remainder of total sales. Major competitors include Baxter International, Becton Dickinson, Edwards Lifesciences, Fresenius AG, Patheon, and Sicor.

The specialty injectable pharmaceuticals division provides over 130 generic injectable drugs available in a wide array of dosages and formulations. Therapeutic areas of focus include cardiovascular, anesthesia, anti-infectives, analgesics, and other. Some other products include Carpuject prefilled syringes; patient-controlled analgesia syringes for use with its LifeCare PCA drug delivery pumps; and the ADD-Vantage System, which aids in the preparation of drug solutions from prepackaged powders or concentration.

Company Financials Fiscal Year Ended Dec. 31

Per Share Data ($)	2006	2005	2004	2003	2002	2001	2000	1999	1998	1997
Tangible Book Value	8.03	7.57	5.74	NM	NA	NA	NA	NA	NA	NA
Cash Flow	2.45	2.42	2.84	NA	NA	NA	NA	NA	NA	NA
Earnings	1.48	1.46	1.92	1.65	NA	NA	NA	NA	NA	NA
S&P Core Earnings	1.45	1.35	1.31	1.46	NA	NA	NA	NA	NA	NA
Dividends	Nil	Nil	Nil	NA	NA	NA	NA	NA	NA	NA
Payout Ratio	Nil	Nil	Nil	NA	NA	NA	NA	NA	NA	NA
Prices:High	47.99	45.10	34.86	NA	NA	NA	NA	NA	NA	NA
Prices:Low	31.15	28.35	24.02	NA	NA	NA	NA	NA	NA	NA
P/E Ratio:High	32	31	18	NA	NA	NA	NA	NA	NA	NA
P/E Ratio:Low	21	19	13	NA	NA	NA	NA	NA	NA	NA

Income Statement Analysis (Million $)	2006	2005	2004	2003	2002	2001	2000	1999	1998	1997
Revenue	2,689	2,627	2,645	2,624	NA	NA	NA	NA	NA	NA
Operating Income	506	493	509	506	NA	NA	NA	NA	NA	NA
Depreciation	157	156	146	146	NA	NA	NA	NA	NA	NA
Interest Expense	31.0	28.3	18.8	Nil	NA	NA	NA	NA	NA	NA
Pretax Income	324	322	412	359	NA	NA	NA	NA	NA	NA
Effective Tax Rate	26.9%	26.8%	26.7%	27.5%	NA	NA	NA	NA	NA	NA
Net Income	237	236	302	260	NA	NA	NA	NA	NA	NA
S&P Core Earnings	233	217	206	231	187	NA	NA	NA	NA	NA

Balance Sheet & Other Financial Data (Million $)	2006	2005	2004	2003	2002	2001	2000	1999	1998	1997
Cash	322	521	200	Nil	NA	NA	NA	NA	NA	NA
Current Assets	1,523	1,561	1,198	1,075	NA	NA	NA	NA	NA	NA
Total Assets	2,848	2,789	2,343	2,250	NA	NA	NA	NA	NA	NA
Current Liabilities	606	596	536	360	NA	NA	NA	NA	NA	NA
Long Term Debt	702	695	699	Nil	NA	NA	NA	NA	NA	NA
Common Equity	1,361	1,328	984	1,453	NA	NA	NA	NA	NA	NA
Total Capital	2,066	2,027	1,687	1,453	NA	NA	NA	NA	NA	NA
Capital Expenditures	235	256	229	197	NA	NA	NA	NA	NA	NA
Cash Flow	393	392	447	406	NA	NA	NA	NA	NA	NA
Current Ratio	2.5	2.6	2.2	3.0	NA	NA	NA	NA	NA	NA
% Long Term Debt of Capitalization	34.0	34.3	41.4	Nil	NA	NA	NA	NA	NA	NA
% Net Income of Revenue	8.8	9.0	11.4	9.9	NA	NA	NA	NA	NA	NA
% Return on Assets	8.4	9.2	13.1	11.8	NA	NA	NA	NA	NA	NA
% Return on Equity	17.6	20.4	24.7	18.7	NA	NA	NA	NA	NA	NA

Data as orig reptd.; bef. results of disc opers/spec. items. Per share data adj. for stk. divs.; EPS diluted. E-Estimated. NA-Not Available. NM-Not Meaningful. NR-Not Ranked. UR-Under Review.

Office: 275 North Field Drive, Lake Forest, IL 60045.
Telephone: 847-937-6100.
Chrmn: D.A. Jones
CEO: C.B. Begley

COO: T.C. Kearney
SVP & CFO: T.E. Werner
SVP, Secy & General Counsel: B.J. Smith
Investor Contact: L. McHugh (224-212-2363)

Board Members: I. W. Bailey, II, C. B. Begley, C. R. Curran, R. W. Hale, D. A. Jones, R. A. Matricaria, J. J. Sokolov, J. C. Staley, M. F. Wheeler

Founded: 2003
Domicile: Delaware
Employees: 13,000

Host Hotels & Resorts Inc

STANDARD &POOR'S

S&P Recommendation HOLD ★★★☆☆	**Price** $18.31 (as of Nov 23, 2007)	**12-Mo. Target Price** $20.00	**Investment Style** Large-Cap Value

GICS Sector Financials
Sub-Industry Specialized REITS

Summary This real estate investment trust owns a portfolio of luxury and upper-upscale full service hotels.

Key Stock Statistics (Source S&P, Vickers, company reports)

52-Wk Range	$28.98–17.55	S&P Oper. EPS 2007**E**	0.93	Market Capitalization(B)	$9.565	Beta		0.87
Trailing 12-Month EPS	$1.15	S&P Oper. EPS 2008**E**	1.16	Yield (%)	4.37	S&P 3-Yr. Proj. EPS CAGR(%)		15.00
Trailing 12-Month P/E	15.9	P/E on S&P Oper. EPS 2007**E**	19.7	Dividend Rate/Share	$0.80	S&P Credit Rating		BB
$10K Invested 5 Yrs Ago	$21,562	Common Shares Outstg. (M)	522.4	Institutional Ownership (%)	NM			

Price Performance

30-Week Mov. Avg. ··· 10-Week Mov. Avg. ─ ─ **GAAP Earnings vs. Previous Year** Volume Above Avg. ⅢⅢ STARS
12-Mo. Target Price ── Relative Strength ─ ▲ Up ▼ Down ▶ No Change Below Avg. ⅢⅢ ★

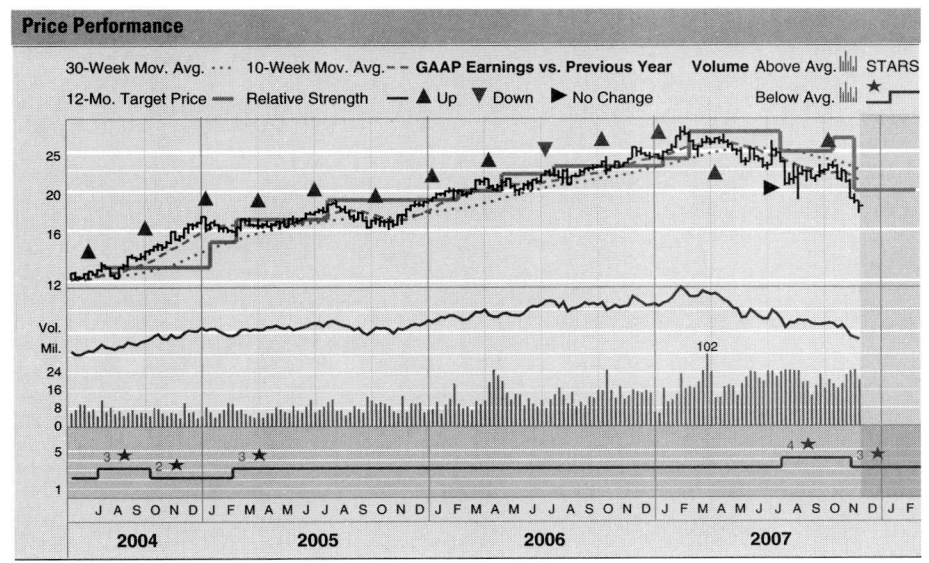

Options: ASE, CBOE, P, Ph

Analysis prepared by **Jason Willey** on November 12, 2007, when the stock traded at **$ 18.78**.

Highlights

➤ We believe HST has benefited from a healthy economy and strong corporate spending, driving growth in business and leisure travel. This positive demand environment has been accompanied by limited new hotel supply in areas where HST's portfolio is concentrated. However, we expect a higher level of new supply in 2008, and we are growing more pessimistic about the level of demand growth, particularly in the leisure and group segments.

➤ In the third quarter, comparable RevPAR expanded 7.2%, driven primarily by an improvement in the average daily rate. Demand remained strong across HST's urban properties, with slower growth in the resort/conference segment. Strong transient demand more than offset slower group business and results benefited from lower insurance and utility costs, a trend we see continuing in 2008. We are monitoring trends in group bookings and cancellations for signs of weakness in this key segment.

➤ Our forecast of 9.7% revenue growth, combined with some margin expansion, supports our 2007 continuing EPS and FFO per share estimates of $0.93 and $1.88, respectively. In 2008, we see continuing EPS of $1.16 and FFO of $2.21.

Investment Rationale/Risk

➤ We expect overall industry growth rates to moderate in 2008, and we believe HST will see a further decline in the rate of growth of its key fundamentals. We see rate increases, driven by transient demand, continuing to drive RevPAR in 2008, as we expect occupancy to decline slightly year over year and we anticipate a weaker leisure market. We believe HST owns one of the best-positioned luxury and upper-upscale portfolios in the industry, and we view positively its exposure to corporate travel and European properties.

➤ Risks to our recommendation and target price include sharp economic weakness; terrorist attacks directed toward the travel industry; slowing business or leisure travel demand; and the failure of third-party hotel management companies to perform up to expectations.

➤ Our 12-month target price of $20 is based on a multiple of 9X our 2008 FFO per share estimate, which is in line with the lodging REIT group. While HST has historically traded at a premium to peers, we believe a number of its competitors have closed the gap in terms of property location and quality.

Qualitative Risk Assessment

LOW	MEDIUM	HIGH

Our risk assessment reflects the highly cyclical nature of the lodging industry and the volatility that this may create in earnings and dividends. Offsetting this is what we consider HST's large and well-diversified portfolio.

Quantitative Evaluations

S&P Quality Ranking B-

D	C	B-	B	B+	A-	A	A+

Relative Strength Rank WEAK
24
LOWEST = 1   HIGHEST = 99

Revenue/Earnings Data

Revenue (Million $)

	1Q	2Q	3Q	4Q	Year
2007	1,037	1,391	1,206	--	--
2006	840.0	1,195	1,119	1,734	4,888
2005	802.0	976.0	831.0	1,272	3,881
2004	777.0	898.0	784.0	1,181	3,640
2003	779.0	840.0	737.0	1,092	3,448
2002	790.0	920.0	789.0	1,181	3,680

Earnings Per Share ($)

2007	0.08	0.17	0.17	E0.41	E0.93
2006	0.03	0.17	0.05	0.31	0.60
2005	-0.05	0.21	-0.03	0.17	0.30
2004	-0.14	-0.05	-0.17	0.05	-0.31
2003	-0.16	-0.09	-0.26	-0.36	-0.92
2002	-0.08	0.06	-0.18	-0.04	-0.24

Fiscal year ended Dec. 31. Next earnings report expected: Late February. EPS Estimates based on S&P Operating Earnings; historical GAAP earnings are as reported.

Dividend Data (Dates: mm/dd Payment Date: mm/dd/yy)

Amount ($)	Date Decl.	Ex-Div. Date	Stk. of Record	Payment Date
.05 Spl.	12/12	12/27	12/31	01/16/07
0.200	03/15	03/28	03/31	04/16/07
0.200	06/15	06/27	06/30	07/16/07
0.200	09/17	09/26	09/30	10/15/07

Dividends have been paid since 2004. Source: Company reports.

Host Hotels & Resorts Inc

STANDARD &POOR'S

Business Summary November 12, 2007

CORPORATE OVERVIEW. Host Hotels & Resorts operates as a self-managed and self-administered real estate investment trust (REIT). At September 30, 2007, HST owned a portfolio consisting of 121 luxury and upper-upscale hotels containing approximately 64,000 rooms. HST's hotels operate under a number of well-known brands, including Marriott, Ritz-Carlton, Hyatt, Swissotel, Four Seasons, Hilton, Fairmont and Westin. Seventy-five of the company's properties were operated under the Marriott brand name. HST also holds a minority interest in a joint venture that owns 10 hotels in Europe with approximately 3,000 rooms. HST is geographically diversified, with hotels in most of the major metropolitan areas. The company's locations primarily include central business districts of major cities, airport areas, and resort/conference destinations.

HST's hotel revenue has traditionally experienced moderate seasonality, with a greater percentage of revenue falling in the second and fourth quarters. In addition, the fourth quarter reflects 16 or 17 weeks of results, versus 12 weeks in each of the first three fiscal quarters.

MARKET PROFILE. We believe the lodging industry is in the midst of a strong recovery following a downturn after September 11, 2001. In the early part of 2004, the industry began to see positive trends in the three key metrics for lodging companies: occupancy, average daily rate (ADR), and revenue per available room (RevPAR). Along with strong demand for both business and leisure travel, lodging companies have benefited from a limited new supply of rooms. A number of factors have kept the supply pipeline slow, including, in our view, the depressed demand environment in 2002 and 2003, increasing construction costs, difficulty obtaining construction financing, and the demand for alternative real estate such as condo conversions.

According to industry data provider Smith Travel Research, the U.S. lodging industry experienced 7.5% RevPAR growth in 2006, compared to growth of 8.4% in 2005, 7.8% in 2004, and 0.4% in 2003. Driving the recent growth has been, in our view, additional room demand, a significant improvement in the ADR, and minimal new supply. The ADR in the U.S. reached $97.31 in 2006, and occupancy increased to 63.4%, the highest level since 2000. In 2006, the industry sold 1.1% more room nights than in 2005, while available rooms rose 0.6%, well below the 2.1% annual average since 1989.

Company Financials Fiscal Year Ended Dec. 31

Per Share Data ($)	2006	2005	2004	2003	2002	2001	2000	1999	1998	1997
Tangible Book Value	9.83	NM	5.64	5.57	4.87	4.77	5.50	5.82	5.81	5.89
Earnings	0.60	0.30	-0.31	-0.92	-0.24	0.09	0.64	0.87	0.84	0.23
S&P Core Earnings	0.57	0.27	-0.31	-0.95	-0.25	0.09	NA	NA	NA	NA
Dividends	0.71	0.41	0.10	Nil	Nil	0.78	0.86	0.63	Nil	Nil
Payout Ratio	118%	137%	NM	Nil	Nil	NM	106%	72%	Nil	Nil
Prices:High	25.79	19.24	17.40	12.33	12.25	13.95	12.93	14.81	22.13	23.75
Prices:Low	18.77	15.46	11.16	6.07	7.50	6.22	8.00	7.38	9.88	15.25
P/E Ratio:High	43	64	NM	NM	NM	NM	20	17	26	103
P/E Ratio:Low	31	52	NM	NM	NM	NM	13	8	12	66

Income Statement Analysis (Million $)										
Rental Income	Nil	Nil	Nil	110	101	126	1,390	1,295	NA	NA
Mortgage Income	Nil	Nil	Nil	Nil	Nil	Nil	Nil	Nil	NA	NA
Total Income	4,888	3,881	3,640	3,448	3,680	3,754	1,473	1,295	3,456	1,147
General Expenses	3,665	2,936	2,812	2,765	2,823	2,821	337	318	2,659	NA
Interest Expense	450	443	483	523	498	492	465	467	335	NA
Provision for Losses	Nil	Nil	Nil	Nil	Nil	Nil	Nil	Nil	Nil	NA
Depreciation	459	368	354	367	372	378	331	289	243	240
Net Income	309	138	-64.0	-225	-29.0	53.0	159	196	194	47.0
S&P Core Earnings	276	98.0	-106	-267	-65.0	20.0	NA	NA	NA	NA

Balance Sheet & Other Financial Data (Million $)										
Cash	524	225	416	838	627	608	566	326	469	865
Total Assets	11,808	8,245	8,421	8,592	8,316	8,338	8,396	8,202	8,268	6,526
Real Estate Investment	13,897	10,382	9,924	9,511	9,193	8,828	8,599	8,329	8,171	NA
Loss Reserve	Nil	Nil	Nil	Nil	Nil	Nil	Nil	Nil	Nil	NA
Net Investment	10,584	7,434	7,274	7,085	7,031	6,999	7,110	49.0	72.0	NA
Short Term Debt	Nil	Nil	Nil	Nil	Nil	148	54.0	180	405	NA
Capitalization:Debt	5,610	5,370	5,523	3,976	5,638	5,929	5,743	5,386	5,276	NA
Capitalization:Equity	5,125	2,176	2,058	1,797	1,271	1,270	1,225	1,309	1,311	NA
Capitalization:Total	11,045	7,932	8,126	6,112	7,471	7,748	7,649	7,448	7,199	5,491
% Earnings & Depreciation/Assets	7.6	6.0	3.4	1.7	4.1	5.2	5.9	5.9	6.1	NA
Price Times Book Value:High	2.6	NM	3.1	2.2	2.5	2.9	2.4	2.5	3.8	NA
Price Times Book Value:Low	1.9	NM	2.0	1.1	1.5	1.3	1.5	1.3	1.7	NA

Data as orig reptd.; bef. results of disc opers/spec. items. Per share data adj. for stk. divs.; EPS diluted. E-Estimated. NA-Not Available. NM-Not Meaningful. NR-Not Ranked. UR-Under Review.

Office: 6903 Rockledge Drive, Bethesda, MD 20817.
Telephone: 240-744-5121.
Website: http://www.hostmarriott.com
Chrmn: R.E. Marriott

Pres & CEO: W.E. Walter
EVP, Secy & General Counsel: E.A. Abdoo
SVP & Chief Acctg Officer: L. Harvey
Investor Contact: G.J. Larson (240-744-5800)

Founded: 1927
Domicile: Maryland
Employees: 229

Block (H&R) Inc.

STANDARD &POOR'S

S&P Recommendation HOLD ★★★☆☆	Price $18.96 (as of Nov 27, 2007)	12-Mo. Target Price $22.00	Investment Style Large-Cap Blend

GICS Sector Consumer Discretionary
Sub-Industry Specialized Consumer Services

Summary This diversified company provides a wide range of financial products and services, including income tax preparation, banking, brokerage and investment planning services.

Key Stock Statistics (Source S&P, Vickers, company reports)

52-Wk Range	$24.95–17.96	S&P Oper. EPS 2008**E**	1.42	Market Capitalization(B)	$6.155	Beta	0.37
Trailing 12-Month EPS	$-1.85	S&P Oper. EPS 2009**E**	1.50	Yield (%)	3.01	S&P 3-Yr. Proj. EPS CAGR(%)	-11.00
Trailing 12-Month P/E	NM	P/E on S&P Oper. EPS 2008**E**	13.4	Dividend Rate/Share	$0.57	S&P Credit Rating	BBB-
$10K Invested 5 Yrs Ago	$10,987	Common Shares Outstg. (M)	324.6	Institutional Ownership (%)	100		

Price Performance

30-Week Mov. Avg. · · · 10-Week Mov. Avg. - - **GAAP Earnings vs. Previous Year** Volume Above Avg. ⦙⦙⦙⦙ STARS

12-Mo. Target Price — Relative Strength — ▲ Up ▼ Down ▶ No Change   Below Avg. ⦙⦙⦙ ★

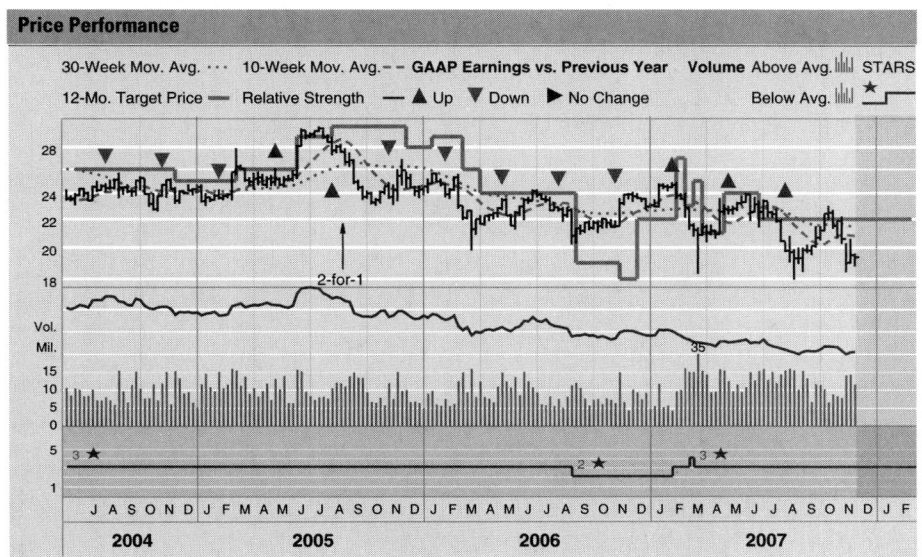

Options: ASE, CBOE, P, Ph

Analysis prepared by **Esther Y. Kwon, CFA** on September 17, 2007, when the stock traded at **$ 20.83**.

Qualitative Risk Assessment

LOW	MEDIUM	HIGH

Despite HRB's leading position in its market, our risk assessment reflects its heightened emphasis on cross-selling financial products to its tax service clients and, until recently, on its subprime variable rate mortgage and refinancing businesses. We are also concerned about internal accounting control issues, which in 2006 caused HRB to restate almost three years of results, and recent lawsuits targeting the company.

Quantitative Evaluations

S&P Quality Ranking A-

D	C	B-	B	B+	A-	A	A+

Relative Strength Rank MODERATE

43

LOWEST = 1   HIGHEST = 99

Highlights

➤ In April, HRB announced a definitive agreement to sell its Option One Mortgage unit for cash to a company associated with Cerebrus Capital. With the subsequent deterioration in the mortgage market, HRB announced in August that it was in discussions with Cerebrus to modify the agreement. Excluding Option One, we look for an 11% increase in total revenues in FY 08 (Apr.) after a 12% increase in FY 07. We see a 6.5% advance in the Tax Services unit.

➤ We look for FY 08 pretax margins to increase over 400 basis points, on about a 50-75 basis point improvement in Tax Services on changes in the refund anticipation loan program. We look for strong margin improvement in the Consumer Financial Services unit, driven by expansion of the bank and further progress at Financial Advisors and, to a lesser extent, improvement in the Investment Services unit.

➤ For FY 08, we estimate operating EPS of $1.42, compared to $1.15 in FY 07, on a slightly higher tax rate and without any share repurchases due to HRB's failure to maintain minimal capital levels in compliance with the Office of Thrift Supervision regulations.

Investment Rationale/Risk

➤ We believe HRB has an opportunity to gain market share due to an ongoing government investigation at key competitor Jackson Hewitt (JTX: hold, $28). In our opinion, the planned deal to sell Option One should remove some uncertainty, and we think proceeds will likely be used for share repurchases some time after the end of FY 08. However, we are unable to estimate the financial impact of this divestiture until the sale because of the conditions of the agreement.

➤ Risks to our opinion and target price include increased competition. Continued softening in the mortgage market could also lower the selling price for Option One. In February 2006, HRB announced that it was restating results for FY 04, FY 05 and FY 06 to date, principally due to errors in determining its effective state income tax rate.

➤ Our 12-month target price of $22 is based on a slight discount to HRB's historical forward P/E valuation.

Revenue/Earnings Data

Revenue (Million $)

	1Q	2Q	3Q	4Q	Year
2008	381.2	--	--	--	--
2007	342.8	396.1	931.2	2,351	4,021
2006	615.0	605.0	1,157	2,496	4,873
2005	482.7	539.3	1,032	2,357	4,420
2004	494.8	579.9	977.2	2,192	4,206
2003	431.4	471.4	958.4	1,919	3,780

Earnings Per Share ($)

	1Q	2Q	3Q	4Q	Year
2008	-0.34	E-0.41	E0.13	E2.04	E1.42
2007	-0.36	-0.38	0.07	1.81	1.15
2006	-0.08	-0.25	0.04	1.77	1.47
2005	-0.13	-0.16	0.28	1.83	1.88
2004	0.03	0.03	0.29	1.62	1.95
2003	-0.03	-0.11	0.37	1.36	1.58

Fiscal year ended Apr. 30. Next earnings report expected: Early December. EPS Estimates based on S&P Operating Earnings; historical GAAP earnings are as reported.

Dividend Data (Dates: mm/dd Payment Date: mm/dd/yy)

Amount ($)	Date Decl.	Ex-Div. Date	Stk. of Record	Payment Date
0.135	12/04	12/08	12/12	01/02/07
0.135	02/22	03/08	03/12	04/02/07
0.135	05/17	06/07	06/11	07/02/07
0.143	06/06	09/06	09/10	10/01/07

Dividends have been paid since 1962. Source: Company reports.

Please read the Required Disclosures and Analyst Certification on the last page of this report.

The **McGraw-Hill** Companies

Block (H&R) Inc.

Business Summary September 17, 2007

CORPORATE OVERVIEW. HRB provides various financial products and services, which the company believes are complementary. In FY 07 (Apr.), Tax Services accounted for 67% of revenues and 111% of profits, Business Services 23% and 9%, and Consumer Financial Services 10% and 10%; the corporate division was (23)% of profits. The Tax Services division served about 22.9 million clients in FY 07 vs. 21.9 million in FY 06, including 15.9 million retail clients (up 1.3%) and more than 4.4 million digital clients (up 19%). Tax Services also offers refund anticipation loans (RALs), which accounted for about 5% of total revenue and almost 20% of total pretax profits in FY 07. There were 12,784 company-owned and franchised U.S. H&R Block offices at April 30, 2007. In addition, HRB offers tax preparation services at hundreds of H&R Block Premium offices for more complex returns. International operations are located primarily in Australia, Canada, and the U.K., with combined company owned and franchise offices numbering 1,430 at April 30, 2007. Tax Services also offers online tax preparation, tax preparation software, and guarantee programs.

HRB also provides brokerage services, investment planning, accounting, tax and consulting services, and tax, estate planning, and financial planning services.

MARKET PROFILE. HRB's largest segment, Tax Services, has competition from other tax service chains, professional CPA/accounting firms, "mom and pop" local tax service providers and do-it-yourselfers (DIYers). In addition, HRB and some other online tax service product providers participate in the Free Filing Alliance, which offers free online federal return preparation with no income limitations. We believe HRB competes successfully by offering many services at what customers believe is an acceptable price-to-value relationship. These services include: the convenience of the largest retail tax office network in the U.S.; a "Peace of Mind" Guarantee" (POM) whereby HRB commits to representing its clients if audited by the IRS and to assuming the cost of additional taxes resulting from errors attributable to an HRB tax professional; "Refund Anticipation Loans" and "Refund Anticipation Checks" and a service whereby DIYers using HRB's online service can have an HRB tax professional check their returns and receive the POM guarantee. By offering increased value, HRB has been able to raise rates 5%-7% annually since 2002.

Company Financials Fiscal Year Ended Apr. 30

Per Share Data ($)	2007	2006	2005	2004	2003	2002	2001	2000	1999	1998
Tangible Book Value	0.74	1.90	1.64	1.41	1.69	0.73	0.67	0.32	1.68	2.46
Cash Flow	1.62	2.05	2.43	2.42	2.02	1.57	2.61	1.01	0.77	0.53
Earnings	1.15	1.47	1.88	1.95	1.58	1.16	0.76	0.64	0.59	0.41
S&P Core Earnings	1.15	1.53	1.76	1.85	1.44	1.07	0.73	NA	NA	NA
Dividends	0.49	0.54	0.39	0.39	0.35	0.29	0.27	0.26	0.21	0.20
Payout Ratio	42%	37%	21%	20%	22%	25%	35%	40%	36%	49%
Calendar Year	2006	2005	2004	2003	2002	2001	2000	1999	1998	1997
Prices:High	25.75	30.00	30.50	27.89	26.75	23.19	12.38	14.88	12.27	11.44
Prices:Low	19.80	22.99	22.08	17.64	14.50	9.16	6.73	9.50	8.83	7.00
P/E Ratio:High	22	20	16	14	17	20	16	23	21	28
P/E Ratio:Low	17	16	12	9	9	8	9	15	15	17

Income Statement Analysis (Million $)										
Revenue	4,021	4,873	4,420	4,206	3,780	3,318	3,002	2,452	1,645	1,307
Operating Income	810	128	215	1,411	240	987	913	704	499	364
Depreciation	150	192	184	172	162	155	206	147	74.6	55.8
Interest Expense	46.9	49.1	62.4	84.6	92.6	116	243	154	69.3	52.3
Pretax Income	636	827	1,018	1,164	987	717	473	412	384	281
Effective Tax Rate	41.1%	40.7%	37.5%	39.5%	41.2%	39.4%	41.5%	38.9%	38.0%	38.0%
Net Income	374	490	636	704	580	434	277	252	238	174
S&P Core Earnings	374	509	593	665	527	400	268	NA	NA	NA

Balance Sheet & Other Financial Data (Million $)										
Cash	1,254	1,088	1,617	1,617	1,337	617	326	442	250	901
Current Assets	3,454	2,824	3,071	2,961	2,747	2,245	2,271	3,864	1,087	2,143
Total Assets	7,499	5,989	5,539	5,380	4,604	4,231	4,122	5,699	1,910	2,904
Current Liabilities	5,176	2,893	2,209	2,472	1,897	1,880	1,988	3,520	554	1,277
Long Term Debt	520	418	923	546	822	868	871	872	250	250
Common Equity	1,414	2,148	1,976	1,897	1,664	1,369	1,174	1,219	1,062	1,342
Total Capital	1,934	2,565	2,899	2,443	2,486	2,238	2,045	2,091	1,312	1,591
Capital Expenditures	161	251	209	128	151	112	90.0	113	78.8	44.3
Cash Flow	525	682	820	876	742	590	482	399	312	230
Current Ratio	0.7	1.0	1.4	1.2	1.4	1.2	1.1	1.1	2.0	1.7
% Long Term Debt of Capitalization	26.9	16.3	31.8	22.3	33.1	38.8	42.6	41.7	19.0	15.7
% Net Income of Revenue	9.3	12.4	14.3	16.7	21.4	13.1	9.2	10.3	14.5	13.3
% Return on Assets	5.6	8.5	11.8	13.9	13.1	10.4	5.6	6.6	9.9	7.2
% Return on Equity	21.0	23.9	33.5	39.6	38.2	34.2	23.1	22.1	19.8	14.9

Data as orig reptd.; bef. results of disc opers/spec. items. Per share data adj. for stk. divs.; EPS diluted. E-Estimated. NA-Not Available. NM-Not Meaningful. NR-Not Ranked. UR-Under Review.

Office: 1 H&R Block Way, Kansas City, MO 64105.
Telephone: 816-854-3000.
Email: investorrelations@hrblock.com
Website: http://www.hrblock.com
Chrmn, Pres & CEO: M.A. Ernst
EVP & CFO: W. Trubeck
EVP & General Counsel: C.F. Graebner
SVP & Cntlr: J. Nachbor
Investor Contact: S. Dudley (816-854-4505)
Board Members: T. M. Bloch, J. D. Choate, D. R. Ecton, M. A. Ernst, H. F. Frigon, R. W. Hale, L. Lauer, D. B. Lewis, T. D. Seip, L. W. Smith, R. Wilkins, Jr
Founded: 1946
Domicile: Missouri
Employees: 136,600

Hudson City Bancorp Inc

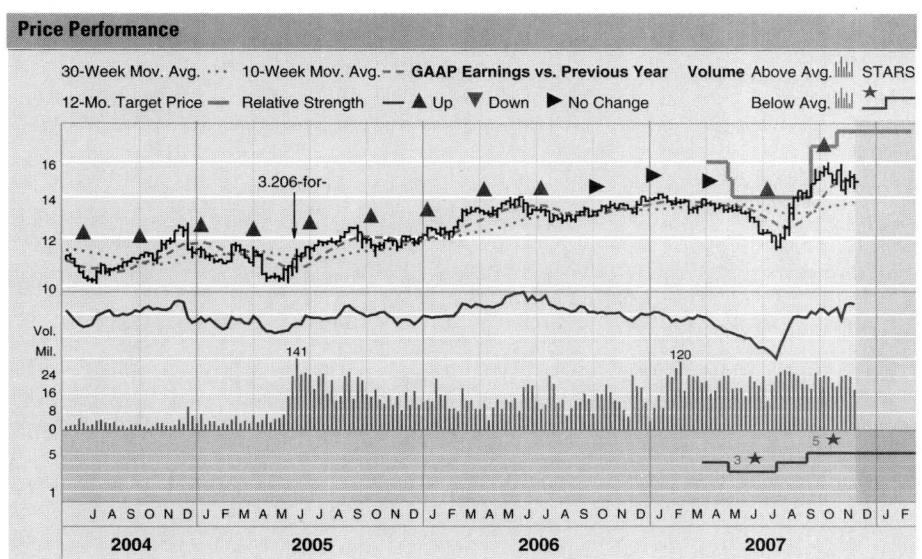

STANDARD &POOR'S

S&P Recommendation	**STRONG BUY** ★ ★ ★ ★ ★	Price $14.85 (as of Nov 23, 2007)	12-Mo. Target Price $18.00	Investment Style Large-Cap Blend

GICS Sector Financials
Sub-Industry Thrifts & Mortgage Finance

Summary Hudson City Bancorp, through Hudson City Savings Bank, operates over 100 branches in the New York metropolitan area. It caters to high median household income counties and focuses on jumbo mortgage loan funding, largely through time deposits.

Key Stock Statistics (Source S&P, Vickers, company reports)

52-Wk Range	$16.08– 11.45	S&P Oper. EPS 2007**E**	0.60	Market Capitalization(B)	$7.898	Beta	0.94
Trailing 12-Month EPS	$0.55	S&P Oper. EPS 2008**E**	0.90	Yield (%)	2.29	S&P 3-Yr. Proj. EPS CAGR(%)	14.00
Trailing 12-Month P/E	27.0	P/E on S&P Oper. EPS 2007**E**	24.8	Dividend Rate/Share	$0.34	S&P Credit Rating	NA
$10K Invested 5 Yrs Ago	$28,017	Common Shares Outstg. (M)	531.8	Institutional Ownership (%)	65		

Price Performance

30-Week Mov. Avg. ···· 10-Week Mov. Avg. – – GAAP Earnings vs. Previous Year   Volume Above Avg. STARS
12-Mo. Target Price — Relative Strength — ▲ Up ▼ Down ► No Change   Below Avg. ★

Options: ASE, CBOE, Ph

Analysis prepared by **Stuart Plesser** on November 05, 2007, when the stock traded at **$ 14.64**.

Highlights

➤ We anticipate that loan growth and higher fee income will result in revenues increasing 32% in 2008 versus a projected 7.0% in 2007. Our 2008 estimate includes a net interest margin of 1.75% (up from projected 1.67% in 2007), average earning asset growth of 26% and non-interest income growth of roughly 1%. We look for HCBK to take advantage of attractive spreads and add to its securities portfolio.

➤ HCBK has a strong record of expense control, in our view. We look for HCBK's efficiency ratio to total roughly 20% in 2008, at the low end of the industry, due largely to a higher revenue base. Given the company's concentration on fixed rate mortgages for higher median income families, we see relatively modest net charge-offs in 2008. Nonperforming assets to total assets is running toward the low end of the industry at 0.15%, reflecting HCBK's higher loan standards. As a result, we expect HCBK to add only modestly to provisions this year and next.

➤ Assuming an effective tax rate of 37.0%, and share buybacks of 6.0%, we see 2007 operating EPS of $0.60, up from 2006's $0.53. Our 2008 EPS estimate is $0.90.

Investment Rationale/Risk

➤ We believe HCBK will benefit from recent problems in the mortgage market. HCBK holds most of the loans it originates and thus should not be adversely affected by the secondary market, which we believe has priced some loans irrationally of late. We think that spreads on the loans HCBK originates will widen, which should result in a higher net interest margin. Also, with what we see as its strong capital base, HCBK should significantly add to its earning assets in the quarters ahead. Given HCBK's lending practices, we think chargeoffs will be minimal in 2007 and 2008. Finally, we think that additional stock buybacks will lend support to the shares.

➤ Risks to our opinion and target price include a further inversion in the slope of the yield curve or operational performance that does not meet our expectations.

➤ Our 12-month target price of $18 is based on tangible book value. Our target price indicates a multiple of 1.9X our 2007 tangible book value estimate of $9.40 a share, slightly above peers, justified, we think, by our view of HCBK's strong credit quality and capital base.

Qualitative Risk Assessment

LOW	MEDIUM	HIGH

Our risk assessment reflects our view of the solid credit quality of HCBK's loan portfolio and its history of profitability. While the company operates in a highly competitive and fragmented industry, companies in the industry tend to produce relatively stable financial results.

Quantitative Evaluations

S&P Quality Ranking NR

D	C	B-	B	B+	A-	A	A+

Relative Strength Rank STRONG

81

LOWEST = 1   HIGHEST = 99

Revenue/Earnings Data

Revenue (Million $)

	1Q	2Q	3Q	4Q	Year
2007	481.2	513.3	550.3	--	--
2006	361.0	385.6	423.7	449.0	1,621
2005	257.5	280.5	315.2	333.8	1,187
2004	216.7	224.7	239.2	251.1	931.6
2003	204.0	202.6	196.1	204.3	807.0
2002	189.8	197.2	210.7	203.0	792.2

Earnings Per Share ($)

2007	0.13	0.14	0.15	E0.17	E0.60
2006	0.13	0.13	0.13	0.13	0.53
2005	0.11	0.11	0.13	0.13	0.48
2004	0.09	0.10	0.11	0.11	0.40
2003	0.09	0.09	0.08	0.09	0.35
2002	0.07	0.07	0.08	0.08	0.32

Fiscal year ended Dec. 31. Next earnings report expected: Late January. EPS Estimates based on S&P Operating Earnings; historical GAAP earnings are as reported.

Dividend Data (Dates: mm/dd Payment Date: mm/dd/yy)

Amount ($)	Date Decl.	Ex-Div. Date	Stk. of Record	Payment Date
0.080	01/24	01/31	02/02	03/01/07
0.080	04/24	04/30	05/02	06/01/07
0.085	07/25	08/08	08/10	09/05/07
0.085	10/24	11/08	11/13	12/01/07

Dividends have been paid since 1999. Source: Company reports.

Please read the Required Disclosures and Analyst Certification on the last page of this report.

The McGraw·Hill Companies

Hudson City Bancorp Inc

STANDARD
&POOR'S

Business Summary November 05, 2007

CORPORATE OVERVIEW. Hudson City Bancorp, Inc. (HCBK), a community- and consumer-oriented retail savings bank holding company, offers traditional deposit products, residential real estate mortgage loans and consumer loans. In addition, HCBK purchases mortgages, mortgage-backed securities, securities issued by the U.S. government and government-sponsored agencies and other investments permitted by applicable laws and regulations. HCBK is the holding company of its only subsidiary, Hudson City Savings Bank (Hudson City). The company's revenues are derived principally from interest on mortgage loans & mortgage-backed securities and interest & dividends on investment securities. The bank's primary sources of funds are customer deposits, borrowings, scheduled amortization and prepayments of mortgage loans and mortgage-backed securities, maturities and calls of investment securities and funds provided by operations.

PRIMARY BUSINESS DYNAMICS. As of December 31, 2006, HCBK had total loans of $19.08 billion. Hudson's loan portfolio primarily consists of one-to-four family residential first mortgage loans. HCBK's first mortgage loans totaled $18.6 billion as of December 31, 2006, thereby contributing to 97.5% of the total loan portfolio. Of the first mortgage loans outstanding at that date, fixed-rate mortgage loans represented 82.7%, while adjustable-rate mortgage loans ac-

counted for the remaining 17.3%. HCBK's loan portfolio also includes consumer and other loans, which primarily consist of fixed-rate second mortgage loans and home equity credit lines. The company does not originate commercial real estate loans, loans secured by multi-family residences, construction loans or commercial/industrial business loans though it has the legal authority to make such loans.

CORPORATE STRATEGY. HCBK seeks to continue its growth by focusing on the origination and purchase of mortgage loans, while purchasing mortgage-backed securities and investment securities as a supplement. It intends to fund its growth with customer deposits and borrowed funds. The company aims to increase customer deposits by continuing to offer desirable products at competitive rates and by opening new branch offices. It plans to open approximately ten branch locations in 2007 in selected market areas. HCBK continues to focus on high median household income counties, which complements its jumbo mortgage loan and consumer deposit business model.

Company Financials Fiscal Year Ended Dec. 31

Per Share Data ($)	2006	2005	2004	2003	2002	2001	2000	1999	1998	1997
Tangible Book Value	8.54	8.83	2.35	2.18	2.14	2.03	2.04	NA	NA	NA
Earnings	0.53	0.48	0.40	0.35	0.32	0.21	0.16	NA	NA	NA
S&P Core Earnings	0.53	0.47	0.39	0.34	0.31	0.20	NA	NA	NA	NA
Dividends	0.30	0.27	0.22	0.16	0.11	0.07	0.03	NA	NA	NA
Payout Ratio	57%	56%	54%	47%	34%	35%	21%	NA	NA	NA
Prices:High	14.09	12.61	12.79	12.00	6.71	4.14	3.16	NA	NA	NA
Prices:Low	11.90	10.09	9.79	5.79	4.04	2.72	1.97	NA	NA	NA
P/E Ratio:High	27	26	32	35	21	20	19	NA	NA	NA
P/E Ratio:Low	22	21	24	17	13	13	12	NA	NA	NA

Income Statement Analysis (Million $)										
Net Interest Income	613	562	485	401	388	287	254	NA	NA	NA
Loan Loss Provision	Nil	0.07	0.79	0.90	1.50	1.88	2.13	NA	NA	NA
Non Interest Income	6.29	5.27	16.6	5.34	5.95	4.69	4.54	NA	NA	NA
Non Interest Expenses	159	128	118	103	93.5	81.8	79.0	NA	NA	NA
Pretax Income	461	442	382	327	301	208	177	NA	NA	NA
Effective Tax Rate	37.3%	37.6%	37.4%	36.6%	36.3%	35.3%	35.3%	NA	NA	NA
Net Income	289	276	239	207	192	135	115	NA	NA	NA
% Net Interest Margin	1.96	2.35	3.66	2.65	3.10	2.87	2.90	NA	NA	NA
S&P Core Earnings	287	272	235	204	186	128	NA	NA	NA	NA

Balance Sheet & Other Financial Data (Million $)										
Total Assets	35,507	28,075	20,146	17,033	14,145	11,427	9,380	NA	NA	NA
Loans	19,069	15,037	11,328	8,766	6,932	5,932	4,841	NA	NA	NA
Deposits	13,416	11,383	11,477	10,454	9,139	7,913	6,604	NA	NA	NA
Capitalization:Debt	16,966	11,350	7,150	5,150	3,600	2,150	650	NA	NA	NA
Capitalization:Equity	4,930	5,201	1,403	1,329	1,316	1,289	1,465	NA	NA	NA
Capitalization:Total	21,896	16,551	8,553	6,479	4,916	3,439	2,115	NA	NA	NA
% Return on Assets	0.9	1.1	1.3	1.3	1.5	1.3	1.3	NA	NA	NA
% Return on Equity	5.7	8.4	17.5	15.7	14.7	9.8	7.8	NA	NA	NA
% Loan Loss Reserve	0.2	0.2	0.2	0.2	0.4	0.4	NA	NA	NA	NA
% Risk Based Capital	31.0	41.3	17.5	7.5	26.8	32.0	43.0	NA	NA	NA
Price Times Book Value:High	1.6	1.4	5.4	5.5	3.1	2.0	1.5	NA	NA	NA
Price Times Book Value:Low	1.4	1.1	4.2	2.7	1.9	1.3	0.9	NA	NA	NA

Data as orig reptd.; bef. results of disc opers/spec. items. Per share data adj. for stk. divs.; EPS diluted. E-Estimated. NA-Not Available. NM-Not Meaningful. NR-Not Ranked. UR-Under Review.

Office: 80 W Century Rd, Paramus, NJ, USA 07652-1405.
Telephone: 201-967-1900.
Website: http://www.hcbk.com
Chrmn, Pres & CEO: R.E. Hermance, Jr.

COO & Sr EVP: D.J. Salamone
EVP & Treas: J.M. Tassillo
SVP & Secy: V.A. Olszewski
Investor Contact: S. Munhall (201-967-8290)

Board Members: M. W. Azzara, W. G. Bardell, S. A. Belair, V. H. Bruni, W. J. Cosgrove, R. E. Hermance, Jr., D. O. Quest, D. J. Salamone, J. G. Sponholz

Founded: 1868
Domicile: Delaware
Employees: 1,319

The McGraw-Hill Companies

Humana Inc.

STANDARD &POOR'S

S&P Recommendation BUY ★★★★☆	**Price** $71.19 (as of Nov 23, 2007)	**12-Mo. Target Price** $88.00	**Investment Style** Large-Cap Growth

GICS Sector Health Care
Sub-Industry Managed Health Care

Summary This company provides a broad range of managed health care services to more than 11 million individuals.

Key Stock Statistics (Source S&P, Vickers, company reports)

52-Wk Range	$81.50– 51.00	S&P Oper. EPS 2007E	4.55	Market Capitalization(B)	$12.062	Beta	0.43
Trailing 12-Month EPS	$4.40	S&P Oper. EPS 2008E	5.50	Yield (%)	Nil	S&P 3-Yr. Proj. EPS CAGR(%)	23.00
Trailing 12-Month P/E	16.2	P/E on S&P Oper. EPS 2007E	15.6	Dividend Rate/Share	Nil	S&P Credit Rating	BBB
$10K Invested 5 Yrs Ago	$66,347	Common Shares Outstg. (M)	169.4	Institutional Ownership (%)	94		

Price Performance

30-Week Mov. Avg. ···· 10-Week Mov. Avg. - - ● GAAP Earnings vs. Previous Year Volume Above Avg. ▥ STARS
12-Mo. Target Price — Relative Strength — ▲ Up ▼ Down ► No Change Below Avg. ▥ ★

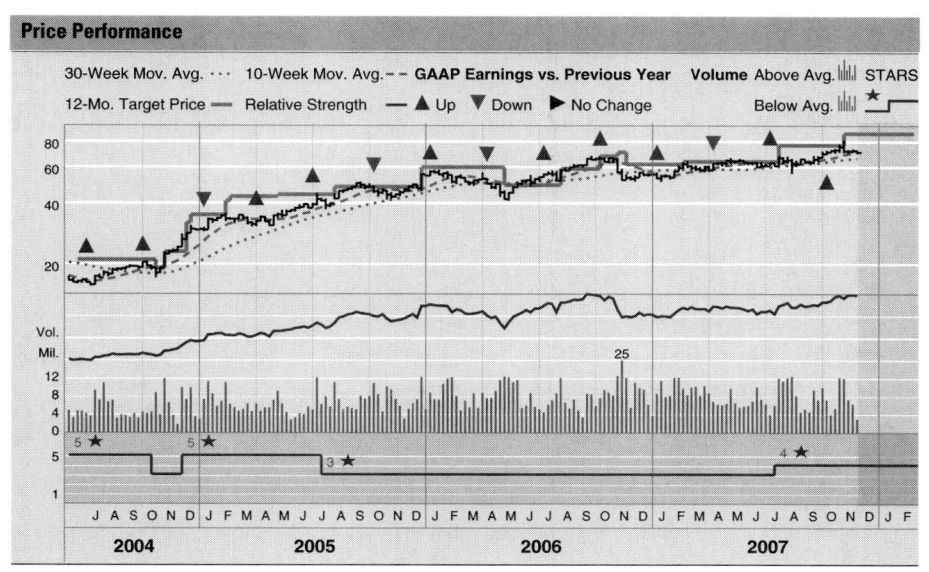

Options: ASE, CBOE, Ph

Analysis prepared by **Phillip M. Seligman** on November 05, 2007, when the stock traded at **$ 71.39.**

Highlights

➤ We look for premium and fee revenues to advance by 13% in 2008, to about $28.0 billion, from $24.8 billion that we project for 2007. Drivers we see include up to 225,000 additional Medicare Advantage (MA) and 65,000 additional commercial members, but 300,000 fewer Medicare stand-alone PDP members and no change in Medicaid and TRICARE enrollment. We also see growth benefiting from the recent acquisition of CompBenefits, a dental and vision benefits provider. In addition, HUM raised prices of its Medicare PDP plans. On the commercial side, we see premium yields (rates minus buydowns) in line with expected 4.5% to 5.0% medical cost trends, similar to 2007 levels.

➤ We believe the consolidated medical cost ratio (MCR) will be flat to slightly down from 2007 levels, with the negative impact from HUM's Medicare plan design changes offset by a lower commercial MCR. We see a modest decline in the SG&A cost ratio, as benefits from IT improvements and revenue leverage are muted by higher selling costs and a slightly less favorable revenue mix.

➤ We see EPS of $4.55 in 2007 and $5.50 in 2008, versus 2006 operating EPS of $2.79.

Investment Rationale/Risk

➤ We continue to see a multi-year growth opportunity for HUM's MA business, partly due to the underpenetration of the expanding Medicare population. Still, we view its strong reliance on MA for growth as carrying heightened risks, as we believe government reimbursement for MA could decline to the same level as traditional Medicare fee-for-service payouts. We do not see the potential rate cuts before 2009 and, should they occur, expect HUM to attempt to adapt. One way would be to transition MA private-fee-for-service members to MA PPO products. Meanwhile, we are encouraged by HUM's plans to leverage the nationwide provider network of its MA business to help expand its commercial business geographically. In addition, we view its acquisition of CompBenefits as a diversification move.

➤ Risks to our recommendation and target price include intensified competition, higher than expected medical costs, and MA rate cuts.

➤ Our 12-month target price of $88 assumes a P/E of 16X, at the midpoint of the historical 15X to 17X managed care range, applied to our 2008 EPS estimate.

Qualitative Risk Assessment

LOW	MEDIUM	HIGH

Our risk assessment reflects HUM's product, market and geographic diversity and its competitive strength in the Medicare market. However, despite HUM being a pioneer in consumer-directed health plans, we believe that intense competition will continue to limit commercial enrollment growth.

Quantitative Evaluations

S&P Quality Ranking   **B**

D	C	B-	B	B+	A-	A	A+

Relative Strength Rank   **STRONG**

83

LOWEST = 1   HIGHEST = 99

Revenue/Earnings Data

Revenue (Million $)

	1Q	2Q	3Q	4Q	Year
2007	6,205	6,427	6,320	--	--
2006	4,704	5,407	5,650	5,655	21,417
2005	3,887	3,546	3,821	3,663	14,418
2004	3,287	3,431	3,176	3,210	13,104
2003	2,932	3,030	3,112	3,153	12,226
2002	2,733	2,832	2,842	2,855	11,261

Earnings Per Share ($)

2007	0.42	1.28	1.78	E1.35	E4.55
2006	0.50	0.53	0.95	0.92	2.90
2005	0.54	0.51	0.30	0.39	1.87
2004	0.41	0.50	0.52	0.29	1.72
2003	0.19	0.43	0.38	0.41	1.41
2002	0.28	0.27	0.31	Nil	0.85

Fiscal year ended Dec. 31. Next earnings report expected: Early February. EPS Estimates based on S&P Operating Earnings; historical GAAP earnings are as reported.

Dividend Data

No cash dividends have been paid since 1993.

Humana Inc.

STANDARD &POOR'S

Business Summary November 05, 2007

CORPORATE OVERVIEW. Humana is one of the largest managed care organizations, with medical membership of 11,320,800 (7,861,100 excluding Medicare Prescription Drug Program (PDP) enrollment) as of September 30, 2007, versus 11,272,100 (7,735,500) at December 31, 2006.

The Commercial segment consists of members enrolled in products marketed to employer groups and individuals, including fully insured medical (1,765,200 versus 1,754,200), administrative services only (ASO; 1,533,900 versus 1,529,600), and specialty (1,930,100 versus 1,902,800). Health maintenance organizations (HMOs; 9.6% of total premium and fee revenues in 2006) require members to use only doctors in their networks and generally reimburse providers on a capitated basis. Preferred provider organizations (PPOs; 17.4%) allow members the option to go to doctors outside of the network, with the members paying a portion of the provider's fees. ASO products (1.4%), which include HMOs, PPOs and consumer-directed health plans, are offered to employers that self-insure their employee health plans. Specialty products (2.0%) include dental, group and individual life, and short-term disability.

The Government segment consists of Medicare Advantage (MA; HMO: 451,700 versus 457,900; PPO: 71,100 versus 71,700; private-fee-for-service, or PFFS: 615,200 versus 473,000); Medicare PDP (Standard: 2,148,900 versus 2,097,200, Enhanced: 1,085,100 versus 1,025,400, Complete: 225,700 versus 414,000); Medicaid (insured: 383,800 versus 390,700; ASO: 182,800 versus 178,400), and the Dept. of Defense health program, TRICARE (fully insured: 1,720,400 versus 1,716,400; ASO: 1,137,000 versus 1,163,600).

In 2006, MA revenues were $8.5 billion (40.3%). Florida contracts covered approximately 324,600 members and accounted for premium revenues of $3.5 billion (41.2% of MA premium revenues, or 16.6% of the total). As of January 1, 2007, MA plans included 12 local HMOs, 12 local PPOs, a regional PPO in 23 states, and private fee-for-service (PFFS) programs in 50 states, and HUM offered the Medicare Prescription Drug Program in 50 states.

The Medicaid unit (2.5%) has contracts in Puerto Rico and Florida.

HUM's current TRICARE South Region contract (fully insured: 12.1%; administrative services fees: 0.2%) covers beneficiaries in 10 states.

Company Financials Fiscal Year Ended Dec. 31

Per Share Data ($)	2006	2005	2004	2003	2002	2001	2000	1999	1998	1997
Tangible Book Value	10.46	7.41	7.52	6.54	5.09	4.33	3.43	2.75	2.98	1.68
Cash Flow	3.79	2.68	2.45	2.20	1.57	1.67	1.42	-1.53	1.53	1.69
Earnings	2.90	1.87	1.72	1.41	0.85	0.70	0.54	-2.28	0.77	1.05
S&P Core Earnings	2.64	1.99	1.55	1.23	0.87	0.63	NA	NA	NA	NA
Dividends	Nil	Nil	Nil	Nil	Nil	Nil	Nil	Nil	Nil	Nil
Payout Ratio	Nil	Nil	Nil	Nil	Nil	Nil	Nil	Nil	Nil	Nil
Prices:High	68.24	55.70	31.02	23.39	17.45	15.63	15.81	20.75	32.13	25.31
Prices:Low	41.08	28.92	15.20	8.68	9.78	8.38	4.75	5.88	12.25	17.38
P/E Ratio:High	24	30	18	17	21	22	29	NM	42	24
P/E Ratio:Low	14	15	9	6	12	12	9	NM	16	17

Income Statement Analysis (Million $)	2006	2005	2004	2003	2002	2001	2000	1999	1998	1997
Revenue	21,417	14,418	13,104	12,226	11,261	10,195	10,395	9,959	9,597	7,880
Operating Income	974	590	415	489	384	114	171	59.0	228	242
Depreciation	149	129	118	127	121	162	147	124	128	108
Interest Expense	63.1	39.3	23.2	17.4	17.0	25.0	29.0	33.0	47.0	20.0
Pretax Income	762	422	416	345	210	183	114	-404	203	270
Effective Tax Rate	36.0%	26.9%	32.7%	33.6%	32.0%	36.1%	21.1%	NM	36.5%	35.9%
Net Income	487	308	280	229	143	117	90.0	-382	129	173
S&P Core Earnings	443	330	252	200	145	104	NA	NA	NA	NA

Balance Sheet & Other Financial Data (Million $)	2006	2005	2004	2003	2002	2001	2000	1999	1998	1997
Cash	1,740	732	580	931	721	651	2,067	2,485	2,812	627
Current Assets	7,333	4,206	3,596	3,321	2,795	2,623	2,499	3,064	3,119	2,750
Total Assets	10,127	6,870	5,658	5,293	4,600	4,404	4,167	4,900	5,496	5,418
Current Liabilities	5,192	3,220	2,327	2,265	2,390	2,307	2,665	3,164	2,643	2,263
Long Term Debt	1,269	514	637	643	340	315	Nil	324	1,011	1,486
Common Equity	3,054	2,474	2,090	1,836	1,606	1,508	1,374	1,268	1,688	1,501
Total Capital	4,323	2,988	2,727	2,479	1,946	1,823	1,374	1,592	2,699	2,987
Capital Expenditures	193	166	114	101	112	115	135	89.0	104	73.0
Cash Flow	636	437	398	356	264	279	237	-258	257	281
Current Ratio	1.4	1.3	1.5	1.5	1.2	1.1	0.9	1.0	1.2	1.2
% Long Term Debt of Capitalization	29.4	17.2	23.3	25.9	17.5	17.3	Nil	20.4	37.5	49.7
% Net Income of Revenue	2.3	2.1	102.6	1.9	1.3	1.2	0.9	NM	1.3	2.2
% Return on Assets	5.7	4.9	5.1	4.5	3.2	2.7	2.0	NM	2.4	4.0
% Return on Equity	17.5	13.5	14.3	13.3	9.2	8.2	6.8	NM	8.1	12.4

Data as orig reptd.; bef. results of disc opers/spec. items. Per share data adj. for stk. divs.; EPS diluted. E-Estimated. NA-Not Available. NM-Not Meaningful. NR-Not Ranked. UR-Under Review.

Office: 500 W Main St Ste, Louisville, KY 40202-4268.
Telephone: 502-580-1000.
Website: http://www.humana.com
Chrmn: D.A. Jones, Jr.

Pres & CEO: M.B. McCallister
COO: J.E. Murray
SVP, CFO & Treas: J.H. Bloem
SVP & General Counsel: A.P. Hipwell

Investor Contact: R.C. Nethery (502-580-3644)
Board Members: F. A. D'Amelio, W. R. Dunbar, K. J. Hilzinger, D. A. Jones, Jr., M. B. McCallister, J. J. O'Brien, W. A. Reynolds, J. O. Robbins

Founded: 1964
Domicile: Delaware
Employees: 22,300

The McGraw-Hill Companies

Huntington Bancshares Inc

STANDARD &POOR'S

S&P Recommendation SELL ★★★★★

Price $14.56 (as of Nov 23, 2007)

12-Mo. Target Price $12.00

Investment Style Large-Cap Blend

GICS Sector Financials
Sub-Industry Regional Banks

Summary This $33 billion regional bank holding company has a network of branches throughout the Midwest.

Key Stock Statistics (Source S&P, Vickers, company reports)

52-Wk Range	$24.97– 13.50	S&P Oper. EPS 2007E	0.89	Market Capitalization(B)	$5.328	Beta	0.57
Trailing 12-Month EPS	$1.48	S&P Oper. EPS 2008E	1.73	Yield (%)	7.28	S&P 3-Yr. Proj. EPS CAGR(%)	8.00
Trailing 12-Month P/E	9.8	P/E on S&P Oper. EPS 2007E	16.4	Dividend Rate/Share	$1.06	S&P Credit Rating	BBB+
$10K Invested 5 Yrs Ago	$8,920	Common Shares Outstg. (M)	365.9	Institutional Ownership (%)	44		

Price Performance

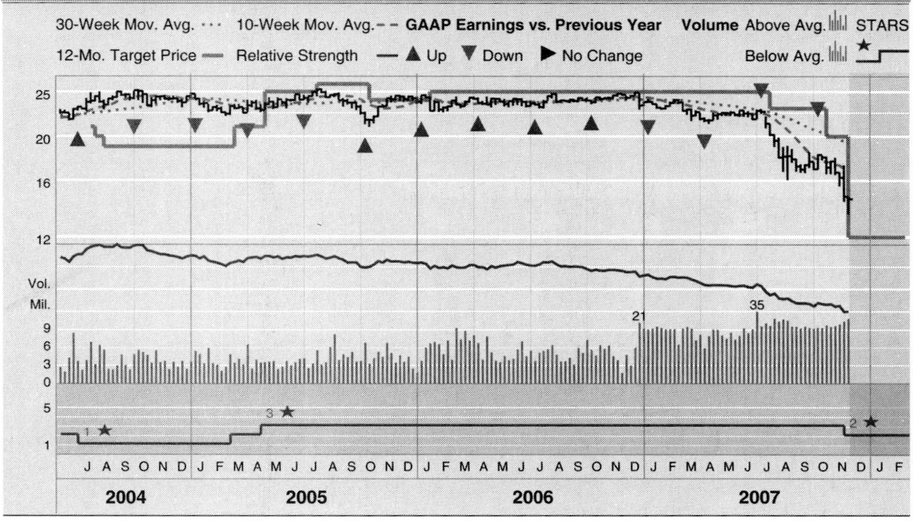

30-Week Mov. Avg. ··· 10-Week Mov. Avg. - - GAAP Earnings vs. Previous Year Volume Above Avg. STARS
12-Mo. Target Price — Relative Strength — ▲ Up ▼ Down ▶ No Change Below Avg.
25
20
16
12
Vol. Mil.
9
6
3
0
21
35
5
1
1 ★
3 ★
2 ★
J A S O N D J F M A M J J A S O N D J F M A M J J A S O N D J F M A M J J A S O N D J F
2004 2005 2006 2007

Options: CBOE, Ph

Analysis prepared by **Frank Braden, CFA** on November 19, 2007, when the stock traded at **$ 14.28**.

Highlights

- HBAN's $1.5 billion loan exposure to Franklin Credit Management (FCMC) diminishes the company's near-term earnings visibility and calls into question its due diligence practices surrounding its acquisition of Sky Financial, in our view. Based on our expectations for moderate growth in average earning assets and stable to slightly improving margins, we forecast that HBAN's net interest income will increase in the low- to mid-single digits in 2008, excluding the impact of the Sky Financial acquisition.
- We expect HBAN to see continued pressure in its residential mortgage and home equity portfolio in 2008 as the markets in Ohio and Michigan continue to suffer from a downturn in home sales activities. For 2008, we see solid growth in trust services, reflecting more assets under management, and moderately higher brokerage and insurance income and other service fees. We forecast mid-single digit loan growth, driven by middle market commercial and small business loans.
- We see operating EPS of $0.89 in 2007, excluding Sky Financial merger-related expenses. Our operating EPS estimate for 2008 is $1.73.

Investment Rationale/Risk

- We view HBAN's lack of geographic diversification as adding to its risks based on its large exposure to the Midwestern markets. The merger with Sky Financial, completed in July, further builds its presence in Ohio, Indiana and Pennsylvania. Although commercial loan growth has remained strong, we believe this loan growth further exposes HBAN to the challenging real estate market. We are also concerned about potential asset quality issues, given our view of HBAN's somewhat lackluster markets in the Midwest, as well as the company's relatively high proportion of borrowings as a funding source.
- Risks to our recommendation and target price include an improving interest rate environment, higher than expected revenue synergies from the Sky Financial acquisition, and rising employment in the Midwest.
- Our 12-month target price of $12 represents a P/E of about 7.0X our 2008 EPS estimate, a hefty discount to HBAN's historical average, given lower near-term earnings viability and large Midwestern exposure.

Qualitative Risk Assessment

LOW	MEDIUM	HIGH

Our risk assessment reflects what we see as solid business fundamentals and a strong customer base. We view HBAN as able to withstand a major economic downturn.

Quantitative Evaluations

S&P Quality Ranking B+

D	C	B-	B	B+	A-	A	A+

Relative Strength Rank WEAK

21

LOWEST = 1 HIGHEST = 99

Revenue/Earnings Data

Revenue (Million $)

	1Q	2Q	3Q	4Q	Year
2007	680.2	698.7	1,056	--	--
2006	624.3	684.9	636.9	685.5	2,632
2005	544.2	558.5	581.6	589.8	2,274
2004	553.6	542.3	527.9	542.2	2,166
2003	599.6	604.7	606.1	564.6	2,375
2002	695.0	491.8	522.7	506.9	2,216

Earnings Per Share ($)

	1Q	2Q	3Q	4Q	Year
2007	0.40	0.34	0.38	E-0.38	E0.89
2006	0.45	0.46	0.65	0.37	1.92
2005	0.41	0.45	0.47	0.44	1.77
2004	0.45	0.47	0.40	0.39	1.71
2003	0.39	0.42	0.45	0.40	1.67
2002	0.39	0.33	0.41	0.36	1.49

Fiscal year ended Dec. 31. Next earnings report expected: Mid January. EPS Estimates based on S&P Operating Earnings; historical GAAP earnings are as reported.

Dividend Data (Dates: mm/dd Payment Date: mm/dd/yy)

Amount ($)	Date Decl.	Ex-Div. Date	Stk. of Record	Payment Date
0.265	01/18	03/13	03/15	04/02/07
0.265	04/18	06/13	06/15	07/02/07
0.265	07/17	09/12	09/14	10/01/07
0.265	10/16	12/12	12/14	01/02/08

Dividends have been paid since 1912. Source: Company reports.

Please read the Required Disclosures and Analyst Certification on the last page of this report.

Redistribution or reproduction is prohibited without written permission. Copyright ©2007 The McGraw-Hill Companies, Inc.

The McGraw-Hill Companies

Huntington Bancshares Inc

Business Summary November 19, 2007

CORPORATE OVERVIEW. Huntington Bancshares Inc. (HBAN) is a multi-state diversified financial holding company focused on the Midwest region of the United States. It provides full-service commercial and consumer banking services, mortgage banking services, automobile financing, equipment leasing, investment management, trust services, and brokerage services. The company also offers insurance services.

The regional banking line of business provides traditional banking products and services to consumer, small business, and commercial customers located in its eight operating regions within the five states of Ohio, Michigan, West Virginia, Indiana, and Kentucky. It provides these services through a banking network of 371 branches, over 980 ATMs, along with Internet and telephone banking channels. It also provides certain services outside of these five states, including mortgage banking and equipment leasing. Each region is further divided into retail and commercial banking units.

In July 2007, HBAN acquired Sky Financial Group for $3.6 billion, in a 90%

stock, 10% cash deal. We expect the deal to add $0.01 to 2007 results. While we believe the merger will allow the combined company to cut costs through consolidation and to increase customer convenience, we question HBAN's strategy of expanding its concentration in the highly competitive Midwestern markets.

On March 1, 2006, Unizan Financial Corp. (UNIZ) was merged into HBAN. UNIZ shareholders were entitled to receive 1.1424 shares of HBAN common stock for each share of UNIZ held. The deal added 42 offices, 48 automated teller machines (ATMs), $2.5 billion in total assets, $1.7 billion in loans, and $1.8 billion in deposits. Furthermore, the combination added leading positions in Muskingum and Stark counties in Ohio, increased market share in the Dayton and Columbus areas, and created a new Eastern Ohio region.

Company Financials Fiscal Year Ended Dec. 31

Per Share Data ($)	2006	2005	2004	2003	2002	2001	2000	1999	1998	1997
Tangible Book Value	10.12	11.41	10.02	8.99	8.95	6.77	9.43	8.66	8.43	7.93
Earnings	1.92	1.77	1.71	1.67	1.49	0.71	1.32	1.65	1.17	1.14
S&P Core Earnings	1.95	1.73	1.66	1.56	0.67	0.60	NA	NA	NA	NA
Dividends	1.00	0.85	0.75	0.67	0.64	0.72	0.74	0.68	0.62	0.57
Payout Ratio	52%	48%	44%	40%	43%	101%	56%	41%	53%	50%
Prices:High	24.97	25.41	25.38	22.55	21.77	19.28	21.82	30.89	28.55	29.21
Prices:Low	22.56	20.97	20.89	17.78	16.00	12.63	12.52	19.49	18.18	17.08
P/E Ratio:High	13	14	15	14	15	27	17	19	25	26
P/E Ratio:Low	12	12	12	11	11	18	9	12	16	15

Income Statement Analysis (Million $)

	2006	2005	2004	2003	2002	2001	2000	1999	1998	1997
Net Interest Income	1,019	962	911	849	984	996	942	1,042	1,021	1,027
Tax Equivalent Adjustment	16.0	13.4	NA	9.68	5.21	6.35	8.31	9.42	10.3	11.9
Non Interest Income	634	640	803	1,064	680	509	494	561	408	335
Loan Loss Provision	65.2	81.3	55.1	164	227	309	90.5	88.4	105	108
% Expense/Operating Revenue	60.0%	60.5%	65.5%	64.3%	50.6%	67.4%	61.7%	56.6%	63.9%	59.0%
Pretax Income	514	544	553	524	589	173	460	615	440	459
Effective Tax Rate	10.3%	24.2%	27.8%	26.4%	38.4%	NM	28.6%	31.3%	31.4%	36.3%
Net Income	461	412	399	386	363	179	328	422	302	293
% Net Interest Margin	3.29	3.33	3.33	3.49	4.19	4.02	3.73	4.11	4.28	4.44
S&P Core Earnings	467	405	388	360	165	152	NA	NA	NA	NA

Balance Sheet & Other Financial Data (Million $)

	2006	2005	2004	2003	2002	2001	2000	1999	1998	1997
Money Market Assets	551	105	960	138	86.6	118	143	28.9	243	556
Investment Securities	4,363	4,527	4,239	4,929	3,411	2,862	4,107	4,889	4,806	5,743
Commercial Loans	12,354	10,845	10,303	9,486	9,336	10,415	8,887	8,452	6,027	5,271
Other Loans	13,799	13,627	13,257	11,590	11,619	11,187	11,723	12,216	13,428	12,468
Total Assets	35,329	32,765	32,565	30,484	27,579	28,500	28,599	29,037	28,296	26,731
Demand Deposits	15,145	3,390	3,392	2,987	3,074	3,741	3,505	7,594	7,771	2,550
Time Deposits	9,903	19,020	17,376	15,500	14,425	16,446	16,272	11,613	11,951	3,768
Long Term Debt	4,513	4,597	6,227	6,808	3,304	3,039	3,338	4,269	3,247	2,886
Common Equity	3,014	2,594	2,538	2,275	2,304	2,416	2,366	2,182	2,149	2,025
% Return on Assets	1.4	1.3	1.3	1.3	1.3	0.6	1.1	1.5	1.1	1.2
% Return on Equity	16.6	16.0	16.6	17.3	15.4	7.5	14.4	19.5	14.5	16.5
% Loan Loss Reserve	1.0	-0.7	1.1	1.6	1.7	1.8	1.4	-1.4	1.5	1.5
% Loans/Deposits	105.5	171.3	114.5	115.2	122.8	110.1	105.0	NA	98.6	98.6
% Equity to Assets	8.2	7.8	7.6	7.7	8.4	8.4	7.9	7.6	7.6	7.4

Data as orig reptd.; bef. results of disc opers/spec. items. Per share data adj. for stk. divs.; EPS diluted. E-Estimated. NA-Not Available. NM-Not Meaningful. NR-Not Ranked. UR-Under Review.

Office: Huntington Center, Columbus, OH 43287.
Telephone: 614-480-8300.
Website: http://www.huntington.com
Chrmn, Pres & CEO: T.E. Hoaglin

Vice Chrmn: R. Baldwin
Investor Contact: M.J. McMennamin (614-480-5676)
Sr EVP: D. Benhase
Sr EVP: N. Stanhutz

Board Members: R. Biggs, D. M. Casto, III, M. J. Endres, J. B. Gerlach, Jr., T. E. Hoaglin, K. A. Holbrook, D. P. Lauer, W. J. Lhota, G. E. Little, D. L. Porteous, K. H. Ransier

Founded: 1966
Domicile: Maryland
Employees: 8,081

IAC/InterActiveCorp

S&P Recommendation	BUY ★★★★☆	Price $27.35 (as of Nov 23, 2007)	12-Mo. Target Price $40.00	Investment Style Large-Cap Blend

GICS Sector Consumer Discretionary
Sub-Industry Internet Retail

Summary This company operates several interactive commerce and content businesses. In November 2007, it announced the proposed spin-offs of four of its businesses as publicly traded companies.

Key Stock Statistics (Source S&P, Vickers, company reports)

52-Wk Range	$40.99– 25.08	S&P Oper. EPS 2007E	1.50	Market Capitalization(B)	$7.163	Beta	2.57
Trailing 12-Month EPS	$0.82	S&P Oper. EPS 2008E	1.80	Yield (%)	Nil	S&P 3-Yr. Proj. EPS CAGR(%)	11.00
Trailing 12-Month P/E	33.4	P/E on S&P Oper. EPS 2007E	18.2	Dividend Rate/Share	Nil	S&P Credit Rating	BB
$10K Invested 5 Yrs Ago	$56,852	Common Shares Outstg. (M)	293.9	Institutional Ownership (%)	79		

Price Performance

Options: ASE, CBOE, P, Ph

Analysis prepared by **Scott H. Kessler** on November 14, 2007, when the stock traded at **$ 29.41**.

Highlights

➤ We project revenues will rise 5% in 2007 and 8% in 2008, reflecting challenges at Home Shopping Network (HSN) and LendingTree. We believe HSN's performance has been improving, and are positive on the prospects for Ask.com and some of the other Internet properties, especially following the November 2007 announcement of a new five-year sponsored listings deal with Google (GOOG: hold, $661), valued at no less than $3.5 billion.

➤ In November 2007, IACI announced the proposed spin-off of four of its businesses as separate publicly traded companies -- HSN, LendingTree, Ticketmaster and Interval. IACI expects the IPOs to be completed by the fall of 2008, pending approvals. We believe this breakup plan will create value for IACI, which will retain the more Internet-oriented businesses including Ask.com and Match.com.

➤ In October 2006, IACI announced a buyback of up to 60 million shares, but we expect such efforts to be curtailed until the spin-offs are consummated. We expect IACI to employ some of the proceeds to resume repurchase activity.

Investment Rationale/Risk

➤ We have concerns about competition, but expect many of IACI's businesses to retain market leadership. We think Ask.com has benefited from the June 2007 launch of a new search engine, and should be aided by the new GOOG contract. We also think IACI's plan to spin-off many of its businesses will enable it to better monetize those assets, and execute regarding its remaining operations.

➤ Risks to our recommendation and target price include the potential lack of demand for ownership of any of the proposed spin-off companies, and corporate governance practices regarding IACI's ownership structure and board of directors that we believe are somewhat lacking.

➤ IACI's recent P/E was well below those of Internet sub-industry peers, but its P/E to growth ratio was higher, and related analyses lead to a value of $37. Our DCF model (including a WACC of 10.4%, average annual free cash flow growth of 8% from 2007 to 2011, and a terminal growth rate of 3%) yields an intrinsic value of $43. Given these considerations, our 12-month target price is $40.

Qualitative Risk Assessment

LOW	MEDIUM	HIGH

Our risk assessment reflects the changing nature and significant competition that the company faces in many of its segments, offset by what we consider market leading brands and business in a number of its categories, and what we view as a strong balance sheet being employed to repurchase stock.

Quantitative Evaluations

S&P Quality Ranking   B-

D	C	B-	B	B+	A-	A	A+

Relative Strength Rank   MODERATE

48

LOWEST = 1   HIGHEST = 99

Revenue/Earnings Data

Revenue (Million $)

	1Q	2Q	3Q	4Q	Year
2007	1,595	1,512	1,516	--	--
2006	1,449	1,510	1,494	1,824	6,278
2005	1,136	1,375	1,450	1,792	5,754
2004	1,471	1,501	1,505	1,716	6,193
2003	1,387	1,527	1,610	1,805	6,328
2002	972.0	1,118	1,193	1,339	4,621

Earnings Per Share ($)

	1Q	2Q	3Q	4Q	Year
2007	0.22	0.16	0.25	E0.54	E1.50
2006	0.14	0.18	0.22	0.01	0.55
2005	0.07	1.17	0.10	0.37	1.68
2004	0.10	0.24	0.24	-0.12	0.46
2003	-0.44	0.18	0.04	0.38	0.34
2002	0.02	-0.56	-0.16	0.60	-0.04

Fiscal year ended Dec. 31. Next earnings report expected: Early February. EPS Estimates based on S&P Operating Earnings; historical GAAP earnings are as reported.

Dividend Data

No cash dividends have been paid.

IAC/InterActiveCorp

Business Summary November 14, 2007

CORPORATE OVERVIEW. The former USA Networks underwent a major transformation in May 2002, when it contributed its Entertainment Group to a new joint venture, Vivendi Universal Entertainment. The company was then renamed USA Interactive. In June 2003, it changed its name again, to InterActiveCorp, to reflect its focus on interactive commerce. In July 2004, it was renamed IAC/InterActiveCorp. In August 2005, the company spun off its travel business as a publicly traded company called Expedia, Inc. (EXPE: $29, hold). As a result, IACI does not own an interest in EXPE.

IACI operates leading businesses in sectors being transformed by the Internet, and its stated mission is to harness the power of interactivity to make people's daily lives easier and more productive. Primary operations include Ask.com, Citysearch, Entertainment Publications (publisher of the Entertainment Book), Home Shopping Network (HSN), Interval (a timeshare exchange company), LendingTree, Match.com, and Ticketmaster. In 2006, IACI took a $214 million impairment charge related to Entertainment Publications.

CORPORATE STRATEGY. IACI was largely built through a series of acquisitions. From 2003 to 2005 alone, IACI acquired Ask Jeeves, Entertainment Publications, Expedia, Hotels.com, Ticketmaster and TripAdvisor in transactions worth billions of dollars (in some of these cases, IACI already owned partial stakes in the companies). However, in August 2005, IACI spun off its travel businesses, including many of which it had recently acquired. In July 2005, it sold interests in Vivendi Universal Entertainment for some $3.4 billion in consideration (including cash, stock, and television advertising time from NBC Universal). We believe these divestitures marked a change in the company's strategy away from acquisitions and more toward financial clarity and internal development. We think these changes will contribute to more consistent execution and multiple expansion. In 2005, the company introduced Gifts.com (which provides users with ideas for gifts) and relaunched RealEstate.com (which offers resources related to buying/selling a house). In 2006, IACI introduced a new Ask.com (formerly Ask Jeeves), AskCity (a local search offering), and Ask X (a next-generation version of Ask.com). In 2007, IACI launched Ask3D, a new version of its flagship search engine. The company has employed its NBC advertising time to promote Ask.com. In 2007, the company has focused more on original content than it has in the past.

In November 2007, IACI announced that it would spin-off HSN, Interval, LendingTree and Ticketmaster and Interval as four publicly traded companies. We expect their initial public offerings to be completed by the fall of 2008, barring possible M&A activity that we think is possible. Although we believe this plan was surprising and may be complicated and confusing, we expect it to help IACI actualize value.

Company Financials Fiscal Year Ended Dec. 31

Per Share Data ($)	2006	2005	2004	2003	2002	2001	2000	1999	1998	1997
Tangible Book Value	1.11	0.99	2.18	1.76	2.30	NM	NM	NM	NM	NM
Cash Flow	1.72	3.18	0.95	1.24	1.44	2.37	3.36	1.97	1.09	0.98
Earnings	0.55	1.68	0.46	0.34	-0.04	-0.66	-0.30	0.08	0.43	0.12
S&P Core Earnings	0.93	0.75	0.74	0.10	-0.64	-1.38	NA	NA	NA	NA
Dividends	Nil	Nil	Nil	Nil	Nil	Nil	Nil	Nil	Nil	Nil
Payout Ratio	Nil	Nil	Nil	Nil	Nil	Nil	Nil	Nil	Nil	Nil
Prices:High	38.66	55.74	69.86	85.76	67.06	56.88	58.13	56.88	37.63	25.88
Prices:Low	23.54	23.49	38.32	41.46	30.62	32.90	32.38	31.13	13.81	10.00
P/E Ratio:High	70	33	NM	NM	NM	NM	NM	NM	87	NM
P/E Ratio:Low	43	14	NM	NM	NM	NM	NM	NM	32	NM

Income Statement Analysis (Million $)										
Revenue	6,278	5,754	6,193	6,328	4,621	5,285	4,601	3,236	2,634	1,262
Operating Income	782	888	929	827	614	807	750	573	464	192
Depreciation	339	544	180	286	323	573	694	360	246	97.0
Interest Expense	60.3	77.7	87.4	92.9	44.8	78.6	75.2	79.7	121	31.6
Pretax Income	299	987	379	262	47.0	-383	71.4	161	284	56.5
Effective Tax Rate	41.8%	39.6%	47.3%	26.9%	11.8%	NM	NM	NM	45.0%	72.7%
Net Income	175	598	186	127	7.38	-125	-88.6	-21.6	76.9	13.1
S&P Core Earnings	298	260	271	35.1	-132	-255	NA	NA	NA	NA

Balance Sheet & Other Financial Data (Million $)										
Cash	2,326	2,475	3,567	3,319	3,968	1,159	373	424	445	116
Current Assets	3,812	3,994	4,885	4,215	4,622	2,976	1,776	1,338	1,268	421
Total Assets	13,194	13,918	22,399	21,587	15,663	11,703	10,474	9,213	8,327	2,671
Current Liabilities	2,253	2,233	2,646	1,878	1,541	1,595	1,173	1,042	863	360
Long Term Debt	857	959	797	1,120	1,211	545	848	515	776	448
Common Equity	8,769	9,231	14,605	14,415	7,931	3,946	3,440	2,710	2,571	1,447
Total Capital	10,781	11,461	18,173	18,212	12,602	9,771	9,203	7,842	6,981	2,267
Capital Expenditures	251	241	224	187	166	144	177	139	87.0	NA
Cash Flow	514	1,134	352	400	319	448	605	332	323	110
Current Ratio	1.7	1.8	1.8	2.2	3.0	1.9	1.5	1.3	1.5	1.2
% Long Term Debt of Capitalization	8.0	8.4	4.4	6.2	9.6	5.6	9.2	7.1	11.1	19.8
% Net Income of Revenue	2.8	10.4	3.0	2.0	0.2	NM	NM	NM	2.9	1.0
% Return on Assets	1.3	3.3	0.8	0.7	0.1	NM	NM	NM	1.4	0.5
% Return on Equity	1.9	5.0	1.2	1.0	0.1	NM	NM	NM	3.8	1.0

Data as orig reptd.; bef. results of disc opers/spec. items. Per share data adj. for stk. divs.; EPS diluted. E-Estimated. NA-Not Available. NM-Not Meaningful. NR-Not Ranked. UR-Under Review.

Office: 152 West 57th St., New York, NY 10019.
Telephone: 212-314-7300.
Website: http://www.iac.com
Chrmn & CEO: B. Diller

Vice Chrmn: V.A. Kaufman
EVP & CFO: T.J. McInerney
SVP, Chief Acctg Officer & Cntlr: M.H. Schwerdtman

Board Members: W. H. Berkman, E. Bronfman, Jr., B. Diller, V. A. Kaufman, D. R. Keough, B. Lourd, J. C. Malone, A. C. Martinez, S. Rattner, H. N. Schwarzkopf, A. G. Spoon, D. Von Furstenberg

Founded: 1986
Domicile: Delaware
Employees: 20,000

Illinois Tool Works Inc.

STANDARD &POOR'S

S&P Recommendation **HOLD** ★★★☆☆	Price $54.62 (as of Nov 23, 2007)	12-Mo. Target Price $64.00	Investment Style Large-Cap Growth

GICS Sector Industrials
Sub-Industry Industrial Machinery

Summary This diversified manufacturer operates a portfolio of about 750 industrial and consumer businesses located throughout the world.

Key Stock Statistics (Source S&P, Vickers, company reports)

52-Wk Range	$60.00–45.60	S&P Oper. EPS 2007**E**	3.37	Market Capitalization(B)	$29.711	Beta	0.90
Trailing 12-Month EPS	$3.27	S&P Oper. EPS 2008**E**	3.83	Yield (%)	2.05	S&P 3-Yr. Proj. EPS CAGR(%)	13.00
Trailing 12-Month P/E	16.7	P/E on S&P Oper. EPS 2007**E**	16.2	Dividend Rate/Share	$1.12	S&P Credit Rating	AA
$10K Invested 5 Yrs Ago	$17,780	Common Shares Outstg. (M)	544.0	Institutional Ownership (%)	85		

Price Performance

30-Week Mov. Avg. · · · 10-Week Mov. Avg. - - GAAP Earnings vs. Previous Year Volume Above Avg. STARS
12-Mo. Target Price — Relative Strength — ▲ Up ▼ Down ▶ No Change Below Avg.

2-for-1

Options: ASE, CBOE, Ph

Analysis prepared by **Christopher Lippincott** on October 18, 2007, when the stock traded at **$ 57.66**.

Highlights

➤ We see revenues increasing 13% and 7% in 2007 and 2008, respectively, driven by contributions from acquisitions, combined with strength in ITW's international end markets, especially its commercial construction, automotive and industrial markets in Europe and Asia, as well as foreign currency translation. We foresee these drivers outweighing what we view as deteriorating end-market conditions in the North American auto and residential housing sectors. We expect ITW's U.S. housing sales to modestly benefit from renovation products, while we see ITW's domestic auto revenues hampered by soft demand and high inventories.

➤ We expect operating margins to expand in 2008, due to projected benefits from ongoing cost-cutting measures, combined with operating leverage from a forecast improvement in volumes. In addition, we see EPS benefiting from a lower anticipated share count in 2007 and 2008, as we believe the company will likely continue its share repurchase program.

➤ On a steady interest expense and tax rate, we forecast EPS of $3.37 and $3.83 in 2007 and 2008, respectively.

Investment Rationale/Risk

➤ While we expect contributions from acquisitions, share repurchases, and favorable international conditions in many of ITW's end markets to continue over the next 12 months, we believe that our outlook is largely reflected in the price of the stock.

➤ Risks to our recommendation and target price include an unexpected downturn in industrial activity and/or capital spending; execution risk associated with acquisitions; continued escalation of raw material costs; and a greater than anticipated slowing of the residential housing and/or automotive markets.

➤ Our 12-month target price of $64 represents a combination of two valuation metrics. Our discounted cash flow model, which assumes 3% growth in perpetuity, and a 10% weighted average cost of capital, indicates intrinsic value of about $65. In terms of relative valuation, applying a target P/E multiple of about 16.4X, in line with peers, to our 2008 EPS estimate of $3.83, suggests a value of about $63 a share.

Qualitative Risk Assessment

LOW	MEDIUM	HIGH

Our risk assessment reflects an S&P Quality Ranking of A+ for ITW, a balance sheet we see as strong with a relatively low amount of debt, and free cash flow that has averaged about 97% of net income over the past 10 years.

Quantitative Evaluations

S&P Quality Ranking A+

D	C	B-	B	B+	A-	A	**A+**

Relative Strength Rank MODERATE

63

LOWEST = 1 HIGHEST = 99

Revenue/Earnings Data

Revenue (Million $)

	1Q	2Q	3Q	4Q	Year
2007	3,759	4,160	4,094	--	--
2006	3,297	3,579	3,538	3,641	14,055
2005	3,074	3,296	3,258	3,294	12,922
2004	2,710	3,002	2,967	3,052	11,731
2003	2,314	2,564	2,532	2,626	10,036
2002	2,205	2,435	2,401	2,427	9,468

Earnings Per Share ($)

2007	0.71	0.90	0.89	E0.87	E3.37
2006	0.65	0.81	0.78	0.77	3.01
2005	0.53	0.65	0.72	0.71	2.60
2004	0.47	0.58	0.55	0.61	2.20
2003	0.33	0.46	0.44	0.47	1.69
2002	0.32	0.43	0.40	0.37	1.51

Fiscal year ended Dec. 31. Next earnings report expected: Late January. EPS Estimates based on S&P Operating Earnings; historical GAAP earnings are as reported.

Dividend Data (Dates: mm/dd Payment Date: mm/dd/yy)

Amount ($)	Date Decl.	Ex-Div. Date	Stk. of Record	Payment Date
0.210	02/09	03/28	03/31	04/16/07
0.210	05/04	06/27	06/30	07/16/07
0.280	08/03	09/26	09/30	10/15/07
0.280	10/25	12/27	12/31	01/14/08

Dividends have been paid since 1933. Source: Company reports.

The **McGraw-Hill** Companies

Illinois Tool Works Inc.

STANDARD &POOR'S

Business Summary October 18, 2007

CORPORATE OVERVIEW. ITW operates about 750 small industrial businesses in a highly decentralized structure that places responsibility on managers at the lowest level possible, in order to focus each business unit on the needs of its particular customers. Each business unit manager is responsible, and is held strictly accountable, for the results of his or her individual business.

ITW is diversified not only by customer and industry, but also by geographic region, with about 40% of revenues derived overseas.

The Specialty Systems segment (52% of revenues in 2006, and 53% of operating income; 17% operating profit margin) produces longer lead time systems and related consumables for consumer and industrial packaging; marking, labeling and identification systems; welding equipment and metal consumables, industrial spray coating equipment and systems; and quality assurance equipment and systems. Important markets are food retail and service, general industrial, food and beverage, construction, and industrial capital goods. International sales and profits accounted for 39% and 32% of 2006 Specialty Sys-

tems revenues and earnings, respectively.

The Engineered Products segment (48%, 47%, 16% operating profit margin in 2006) produces short lead time plastic and metal components, fasteners and assemblies, industrial fluids and adhesives, fastening tools, and welding products. The largest markets served are construction, automotive, general industrial, consumer durables and electronics. International sales and profits accounted for 41% and 38% of 2006 Engineered Products revenues and earnings, respectively.

In late 2001, ITW classified its Consumer Products (CP) division as discontinued. The segment was made up of companies that make small electric appliances, physical fitness equipment, and ceramic tile.

Company Financials Fiscal Year Ended Dec. 31

Per Share Data ($)	2006	2005	2004	2003	2002	2001	2000	1999	1998	1997
Tangible Book Value	6.94	6.89	7.59	8.22	6.90	5.42	4.82	4.64	4.30	4.07
Cash Flow	3.79	3.26	2.78	2.18	2.01	1.94	2.25	1.94	1.75	1.54
Earnings	3.01	2.60	2.20	1.69	1.51	1.31	1.58	1.38	1.34	1.17
S&P Core Earnings	3.03	2.60	2.13	1.63	1.38	1.13	NA	NA	NA	NA
Dividends	0.92	0.61	0.52	0.47	0.45	0.42	0.38	0.34	0.26	0.23
Payout Ratio	30%	23%	24%	28%	30%	32%	24%	25%	19%	20%
Prices:High	53.54	47.32	48.35	42.35	38.90	36.00	34.50	41.00	36.59	30.06
Prices:Low	41.54	39.25	36.46	27.28	27.52	24.58	24.75	29.06	22.59	18.69
P/E Ratio:High	18	18	22	25	26	27	22	30	27	26
P/E Ratio:Low	14	15	17	16	18	19	16	21	17	16

Income Statement Analysis (Million $)										
Revenue	14,055	12,922	11,731	10,036	9,468	9,293	9,984	9,333	5,648	5,220
Operating Income	2,865	2,558	2,410	1,940	1,812	1,692	1,977	1,830	1,291	1,113
Depreciation	444	383	353	307	306	386	413	343	212	185
Interest Expense	85.6	87.0	69.2	70.7	68.5	68.1	72.4	67.5	14.2	19.4
Pretax Income	2,445	2,182	1,999	1,576	1,434	1,231	1,478	1,353	1,060	924
Effective Tax Rate	29.8%	31.5%	33.0%	34.0%	35.0%	34.8%	35.2%	37.8%	36.5%	36.5%
Net Income	1,718	1,495	1,340	1,040	932	802	958	841	673	587
S&P Core Earnings	1,729	1,493	1,299	1,009	851	691	NA	NA	NA	NA

Balance Sheet & Other Financial Data (Million $)										
Cash	590	370	667	1,684	1,058	282	151	233	93.5	186
Current Assets	5,206	4,112	4,322	4,783	3,879	3,163	3,329	3,273	1,834	1,859
Total Assets	13,880	11,446	11,352	11,193	10,623	9,822	9,603	9,060	6,118	5,395
Current Liabilities	2,637	2,001	1,851	1,489	1,567	1,518	1,818	2,045	1,222	1,158
Long Term Debt	956	958	921	920	1,460	1,267	1,549	1,361	947	854
Common Equity	9,018	7,547	7,628	7,874	6,649	6,041	5,401	4,815	3,338	2,806
Total Capital	9,973	8,505	8,549	8,795	8,109	7,308	6,950	6,176	4,285	3,660
Capital Expenditures	301	293	283	258	271	257	314	336	208	179
Cash Flow	2,162	1,878	1,693	1,347	1,238	1,189	1,371	1,184	885	772
Current Ratio	2.0	2.1	2.3	3.2	2.5	2.1	1.8	1.6	1.5	1.6
% Long Term Debt of Capitalization	9.6	11.3	10.8	10.5	18.0	17.3	22.3	22.0	22.1	23.3
% Net Income of Revenue	12.2	11.6	11.4	10.4	9.8	8.6	9.6	9.0	11.9	11.3
% Return on Assets	13.6	13.1	11.9	9.5	9.1	8.3	10.3	9.7	11.7	11.5
% Return on Equity	20.7	19.7	17.3	14.3	14.7	14.0	18.8	18.6	21.9	22.6

Data as orig reptd.; bef. results of disc opers/spec. items. Per share data adj. for stk. divs.; EPS diluted. E-Estimated. NA-Not Available. NM-Not Meaningful. NR-Not Ranked. UR-Under Review.

Office: 3600 W. Lake Avenue, Glenview, IL 60026-5811.
Telephone: 847-724-7500.
Website: http://www.itwinc.com
Chrmn & CEO: D.B. Speer

SVP, Secy & General Counsel: J.H. Wooten, Jr.
Investor Contact: J. Brooklier (847-657-4104)

Board Members: W. F. Aldinger, M. J. Birck, M. D. Brailsford, S. Crown, D. H. Davis, Jr., R. C. McCormack, R. S. Morrison, J. A. Skinner, H. B. Smith, D. B. Speer

Founded: 1912
Domicile: Delaware
Employees: 55,000

The **McGraw·Hill** Companies

IMS Health Inc

STANDARD &POOR'S

S&P Recommendation	HOLD ★★★☆☆	Price $24.30 (as of Nov 23, 2007)	12-Mo. Target Price $26.00	Investment Style Large-Cap Growth

GICS Sector Health Care
Sub-Industry Health Care Technology

Summary IMS provides information solutions to the health care sector.

Key Stock Statistics (Source S&P, Vickers, company reports)

52-Wk Range	$33.12– 21.20	S&P Oper. EPS 2007**E**	1.50	Market Capitalization(B)	$4.738	Beta	0.81
Trailing 12-Month EPS	$1.41	S&P Oper. EPS 2008**E**	1.60	Yield (%)	0.49	S&P 3-Yr. Proj. EPS CAGR(%)	9.00
Trailing 12-Month P/E	17.2	P/E on S&P Oper. EPS 2007**E**	16.2	Dividend Rate/Share	$0.12	S&P Credit Rating	NA
$10K Invested 5 Yrs Ago	$14,757	Common Shares Outstg. (M)	195.0	Institutional Ownership (%)	92		

Price Performance

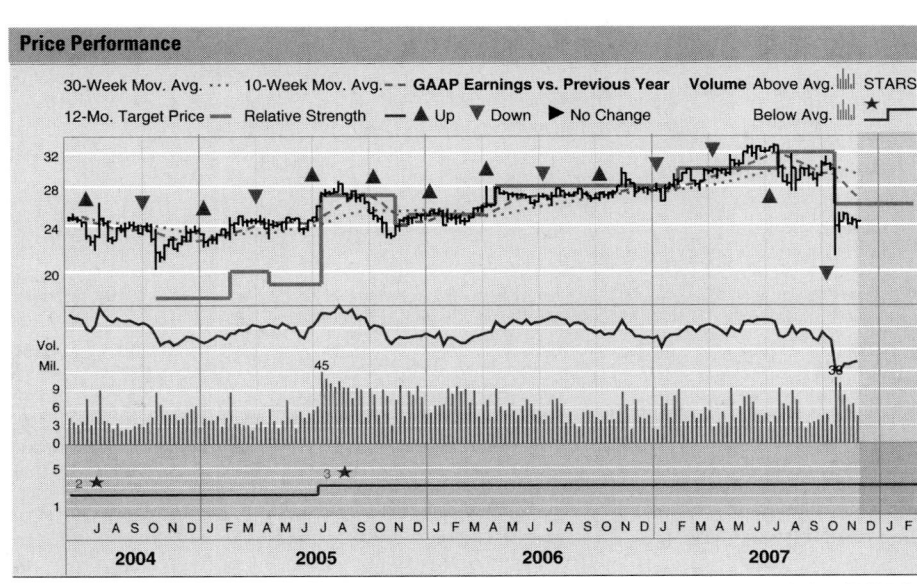

30-Week Mov. Avg. · · · 10-Week Mov. Avg. - - **GAAP Earnings vs. Previous Year** Volume Above Avg. ||||| STARS
12-Mo. Target Price — Relative Strength — ▲ Up ▼ Down ► No Change   Below Avg. ||||| ★

Options: CBOE, P, Ph

Analysis prepared by **Michael W. Jaffe** on November 08, 2007, when the stock traded at **$ 23.94.**

Highlights

➤ We expect revenues to increase 6% in 2008, based on our outlook for a modest pickup in demand, plus RX's expansion efforts. We see the strongest growth in the U.S. and emerging markets, and we think RX's consulting offerings will be the most favorable business area. At the same time, we believe the level of RX's growth will be limited by moderating demand in Europe, where we see the company's business being held back by healthcare reforms and caution among RX's clients.

➤ We see relatively flat operating margins in 2008. We think profits will be limited somewhat by the moderating growth we forecast for RX's products and services, particularly in Europe. We foresee that expectation offset by the solid demand we see for RX in a number of geographies, and ongoing cost cutting initiatives.

➤ We think RX's business will be restricted by the likelihood that the global pharmaceutical market will grow at a below historical pace. In early November 2007, IMS Health released its global pharmaceutical forecast, in which it sees a 5% to 6% rise in global pharmaceutical sales in 2008, versus an expected 6% to 7% gain in 2007, and higher totals in prior years.

Investment Rationale/Risk

➤ We believe IMS Health has been facing challenging business trends in its client base, as sales growth has slowed at many pharmaceutical companies in recent years. However, we have a favorable view of RX's ongoing efforts to design new products that should better enable its clients to prosper during more demanding times. Based on these factors and valuation considerations, we believe the shares are near an appropriate valuation.

➤ Risks to our recommendation and target price include weaker than anticipated conditions in the health care and pharmaceutical markets served by RX, and a resultant weakening in demand for information and decision support services in these areas.

➤ The shares recently traded at about 15X our 2008 EPS forecast, a small premium to the S&P 500, but at the low end of RX's historical range. Based on our belief that RX will face challenging industry conditions for some time, but still manage to record modest EPS growth, we think the stock is near a fair valuation. Our 12-month target price is $26, or 16X our 2008 forecast.

Qualitative Risk Assessment

LOW	MEDIUM	HIGH

Our risk assessment reflects our view of RX's usually solid levels of free cash flow, offset by the company's relatively high level of debt leverage. Also, its income statements typically have numerous one-time items, which raises questions about earnings quality.

Quantitative Evaluations

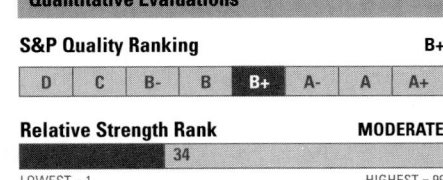

S&P Quality Ranking B+

D	C	B-	B	B+	A-	A	A+

Relative Strength Rank MODERATE

34

LOWEST = 1   HIGHEST = 99

Revenue/Earnings Data

Revenue (Million $)

	1Q	2Q	3Q	4Q	Year
2007	510.4	537.5	538.8	--	--
2006	446.2	486.2	482.7	543.5	1,959
2005	411.0	433.3	432.8	477.7	1,755
2004	361.6	379.6	384.2	443.7	1,569
2003	313.9	337.8	346.0	384.1	1,382
2002	331.6	353.1	361.8	381.9	1,428

Earnings Per Share ($)

2007	0.43	0.36	0.29	E0.40	E1.50
2006	0.56	0.30	0.34	0.32	1.53
2005	0.13	0.41	0.30	0.38	1.22
2004	0.34	0.27	0.28	0.32	1.20
2003	-0.20	0.23	0.29	0.28	0.56
2002	0.20	0.21	0.29	0.22	0.93

Fiscal year ended Dec. 31. Next earnings report expected: Early February. EPS Estimates based on S&P Operating Earnings; historical GAAP earnings are as reported.

Dividend Data (Dates: mm/dd Payment Date: mm/dd/yy)

Amount ($)	Date Decl.	Ex-Div. Date	Stk. of Record	Payment Date
0.030	02/13	02/27	03/01	03/29/07
0.030	04/17	04/27	05/01	06/08/07
0.030	07/17	07/30	08/01	09/07/07
0.030	10/15	10/26	10/30	12/07/07

Dividends have been paid since 1997. Source: Company reports.

Please read the Required Disclosures and Analyst Certification on the last page of this report.

The McGraw-Hill Companies

IMS Health Inc

STANDARD &POOR'S

Business Summary November 08, 2007

IMS Health is a global provider of market intelligence to the pharmaceutical and health care industries, with operations covering more than 100 countries (63% of revenues in 2006 from foreign operations). In November 2005, the company's planned agreement to be acquired by VNU N.V., a global information and media company, was mutually terminated. The cash and stock deal, valued at $7.0 billion at the time it was announced, was called off because of opposition from a group of major VNU shareholders.

IMS provides critical business intelligence, including information, analytics and consulting services, to the pharmaceutical and health care industries worldwide. This includes offerings in the areas of sales force effectiveness (47% of revenues in 2006), portfolio optimization (28%), and launch, brand management and other (24%). During the first quarter of 2005, RX started to incorporate revenues from its consulting and services operations into its business lines.

The company's sales force effectiveness services are used principally by pharmaceutical manufacturers to measure, forecast and optimize the effectiveness and efficiency of sales representatives, and to focus on sales and marketing efforts. They include sales territory and prescription tracking reports.

RX's portfolio optimization services provide customers with the intelligence and tools to identify and optimize pharmaceutical product portfolios, including currently marketed products and the new product pipeline. Integrating prescriptions, sales, disease/treatment and industry intelligence, RX's portfolio optimization services provide a comprehensive picture of the worldwide market. The company's offerings include syndicated pharmaceutical, medical, hospital and prescription audits.

In the area of launch, brand management and other services, RX's offerings combine information and analytical tools to address client needs relevant to each stage in the life of a pharmaceutical product. The areas covered include brand planning, pricing and market access, promotion management, and performance management.

Company Financials Fiscal Year Ended Dec. 31

Per Share Data ($)	2006	2005	2004	2003	2002	2001	2000	1999	1998	1997
Tangible Book Value	NM	NM	NM	NM	0.13	0.24	NM	0.51	1.45	2.21
Cash Flow	1.88	1.67	1.65	0.87	1.14	0.69	0.69	1.10	0.82	1.28
Earnings	1.53	1.22	1.20	0.56	0.93	0.46	0.39	0.78	0.53	1.40
S&P Core Earnings	1.36	1.09	0.95	0.47	0.82	0.52	NA	NA	NA	NA
Dividends	0.12	0.08	0.08	0.08	0.08	0.08	0.08	0.08	0.06	0.06
Payout Ratio	8%	7%	7%	14%	9%	17%	21%	10%	11%	4%
Prices:High	30.13	28.60	26.80	25.07	22.59	30.50	28.69	39.19	38.46	22.75
Prices:Low	23.94	22.01	20.16	13.68	12.90	17.30	14.25	21.50	21.34	14.00
P/E Ratio:High	20	23	22	45	24	66	74	50	73	16
P/E Ratio:Low	16	18	17	24	14	38	37	28	40	10

Income Statement Analysis (Million $)	2006	2005	2004	2003	2002	2001	2000	1999	1998	1997
Revenue	1,959	1,755	1,569	1,382	1,428	1,333	1,424	1,398	1,187	1,418
Operating Income	524	543	517	437	510	494	459	439	310	453
Depreciation	73.8	105	93.5	75.1	61.8	69.2	92.0	100	96.4	117
Interest Expense	40.4	22.7	19.5	15.4	14.4	18.1	17.6	7.59	1.17	2.29
Pretax Income	449	454	415	305	397	177	257	152	271	430
Effective Tax Rate	29.7%	37.5%	31.2%	54.4%	32.9%	21.7%	54.7%	NM	34.1%	27.4%
Net Income	316	284	285	139	266	138	116	250	178	312
S&P Core Earnings	282	252	226	116	236	155	NA	NA	NA	NA

Balance Sheet & Other Financial Data (Million $)	2006	2005	2004	2003	2002	2001	2000	1999	1998	1997
Cash	157	363	460	385	415	268	119	116	206	318
Current Assets	693	821	937	779	827	657	569	607	634	694
Total Assets	1,907	1,973	1,891	1,644	1,619	1,368	1,243	451	1,732	1,580
Current Liabilities	543	549	554	837	679	635	827	723	550	441
Long Term Debt	975	611	627	152	325	150	Nil	Nil	Nil	Nil
Common Equity	33.9	415	256	190	222	218	147	494	825	802
Total Capital	1,110	1,126	984	443	727	513	282	519	972	915
Capital Expenditures	27.5	52.0	22.5	23.7	44.4	34.3	33.4	33.0	30.9	72.0
Cash Flow	389	389	379	214	328	208	208	351	275	430
Current Ratio	1.3	1.5	1.7	0.9	1.2	1.0	0.7	0.8	1.2	1.6
% Long Term Debt of Capitalization	87.9	54.3	63.7	34.3	44.7	29.2	Nil	Nil	Nil	Nil
% Net Income of Revenue	16.1	16.2	18.2	10.1	18.6	10.4	8.2	7.9	15.0	22.0
% Return on Assets	16.3	14.7	16.1	8.5	17.8	10.3	8.7	5.8	11.0	18.1
% Return on Equity	140.6	84.7	128.2	67.6	120.8	86.0	34.7	8.0	21.9	37.3

Data as orig reptd.; bef. results of disc opers/spec. items. Per share data adj. for stk. divs.; EPS diluted. E-Estimated. NA-Not Available. NM-Not Meaningful. NR-Not Ranked. UR-Under Review.

Office: 901 Main Ave, Norwalk, CT 06851-1168.
Telephone: 203-845-5200.
Website: http://www.imshealth.com
Chrmn, Pres & CEO: D.R. Carlucci

COO & EVP: G.V. Pajot
SVP & CFO: L.G. Katz
SVP, Secy & General Counsel: R.H. Steinfeld
VP & Treas: J.J. Ford

Investor Contact: D. Peck (203-319-4766)
Board Members: D. R. Carlucci, C. L. Clemente, J. D. Edwards, K. E. Giusti, J. P. Imlay, Jr., R. J. Kamerschen, H. E. Lockhart, M. B. Puckett, W. C. Van Faasen, B. W. Wise

Founded: 1998
Domicile: Delaware
Employees: 7,600

Ingersoll-Rand Co Ltd

STANDARD &POOR'S

S&P Recommendation HOLD ★★★☆☆	**Price** $48.70 (as of Nov 23, 2007)	**12-Mo. Target Price** $52.00	**Investment Style** Large-Cap Blend

GICS Sector Industrials
Sub-Industry Industrial Machinery

Summary IR manufactures a wide range of industrial and commercial products, including refrigeration and construction equipment, compact vehicles and security products.

Key Stock Statistics (Source S&P, Vickers, company reports)

52-Wk Range	$56.66– 37.52	S&P Oper. EPS 2007E	2.67	Market Capitalization(B)	$13.960	Beta	1.60
Trailing 12-Month EPS	$5.54	S&P Oper. EPS 2008E	3.33	Yield (%)	1.48	S&P 3-Yr. Proj. EPS CAGR(%)	8.00
Trailing 12-Month P/E	8.8	P/E on S&P Oper. EPS 2007E	18.2	Dividend Rate/Share	$0.72	S&P Credit Rating	NA
$10K Invested 5 Yrs Ago	$23,884	Common Shares Outstg. (M)	286.7	Institutional Ownership (%)	79		

Price Performance

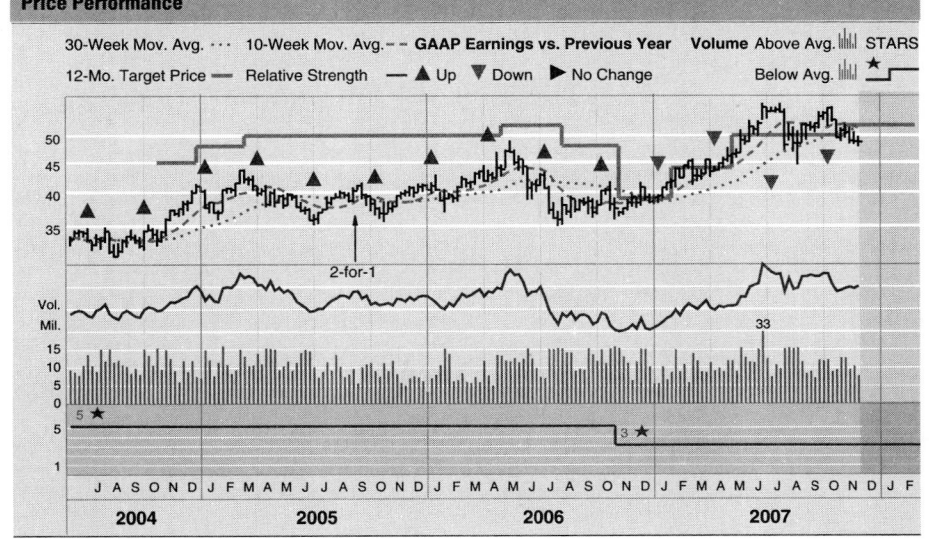

Analysis prepared by **Christopher Lippincott** on October 30, 2007, when the stock traded at **$ 50.05**.

Options: ASE, CBOE, Ph

Highlights

➤ We expect revenues to increase approximately 9% in 2007 and 5% in 2008, led by growth in the Industrial Solutions and Security segments. We see solid demand for security systems from strong commercial construction markets in the U.S. and Europe, and industrial market growth in all geographies. We expect particular strength from international markets in all areas, which may help partly offset a decline in the U.S. refrigerated trailer business.

➤ We see EBIT margins expanding to 12% in 2007 and 13% in 2008, from just under 12% in 2006. We think benefits from better capacity utilization, higher productivity and cost controls will be largely offset by raw material cost inflation. We expect most of the cost inflation from non-ferrous materials. We believe IR will try to minimize the impact of raw material cost increases through pricing, higher productivity, and relationships with its sourcing partners.

➤ Due to our forecast of share repurchases worth $2.4 billion in 2007 and $1.4 billion in 2008, we project EPS from continuing operations of $2.67 in 2007 and $3.33 in 2008. These estimates do not include benefits from discontinued operations.

Investment Rationale/Risk

➤ We believe IR's broad short-term organic growth prospects remain healthy primarily due to overseas strength, although some of its U.S. business units -- such as refrigerated trailers -- may display slower growth. We think that material cost inflation will have a modest impact on 2007 earnings growth potential, although good operating leverage should help profitability expand. In our view, the sale of the Road Development and Bobcat businesses will reduce IR's capital intensity and cyclicality. However, we believe much of the appreciation potential stemming from these positive developments is now fully reflected in the price of the stock.

➤ Risks to our recommendation and target price include sharply weaker than expected global economic growth, softer industrial, energy and electronics markets, and potential value-diminishing acquisitions.

➤ Our 12-month target price of $52 is based on our discounted cash flow model, which assumes a 3% growth rate in perpetuity and an 11.8% discount rate.

Our risk assessment reflects the cyclical nature of several of IR's major end markets, and its active acquisition strategy, offset by an expanding recurring revenue base and an S&P Quality Ranking of A, which indicates above-average stability in earnings and dividend growth.

Quantitative Evaluations

S&P Quality Ranking A

D	C	B-	B	B+	A-	A	A+

Relative Strength Rank MODERATE

56

LOWEST = 1   HIGHEST = 99

Revenue/Earnings Data

Revenue (Million $)

	1Q	2Q	3Q	4Q	Year
2007	2,668	2,225	2,239	--	--
2006	2,711	3,042	2,766	2,891	11,409
2005	2,459	2,760	2,615	2,713	10,547
2004	2,292	2,714	2,368	2,459	9,394
2003	2,182	2,509	2,520	2,666	9,876
2002	2,017	2,666	2,223	2,245	8,951

Earnings Per Share ($)

2007	0.70	0.68	0.68	E0.79	E2.67
2006	0.79	0.97	0.79	0.74	3.31
2005	0.67	0.86	0.75	0.81	3.09
2004	0.47	0.72	0.59	0.64	2.37
2003	0.28	0.45	0.44	0.56	1.72
2002	0.13	0.32	0.26	0.37	1.08

Fiscal year ended Dec. 31. Next earnings report expected: Late January. EPS Estimates based on S&P Operating Earnings; historical GAAP earnings are as reported.

Dividend Data (Dates: mm/dd Payment Date: mm/dd/yy)

Amount ($)	Date Decl.	Ex-Div. Date	Stk. of Record	Payment Date
0.180	10/02	11/09	11/13	12/01/06
0.180	02/09	02/14	02/16	03/01/07
0.180	04/05	11/08	11/13	12/03/07

Dividends have been paid since 1910. Source: Company reports.

Please read the Required Disclosures and Analyst Certification on the last page of this report.

The McGraw·Hill Companies

Ingersoll-Rand Co Ltd

Business Summary October 30, 2007

CORPORATE OVERVIEW. Ingersoll-Rand is a global provider of climate control equipment, compact vehicles, construction equipment, industrial solutions, and security and safety products. The Climate Control segment (39% of 2006 revenue; 36% of operating profits; 11% margin) makes transport temperature control units, HVAC systems, refrigerated display merchandisers, beverage coolers, and walk-in storage coolers and freezers. Its brand names include Hussmann and Thermo-King. Thermo-King is the world's largest maker of commercial refrigeration equipment used in truck trailers, seagoing containers, and railcars. Hussmann is one of the world's largest makers of refrigerated supermarket displays. The Compact Vehicle segment (41%; 43%; 13%) manufactures skid-steer loaders, all-wheel steer loaders, compact truck loaders, compact excavators, attachments and golf and utility vehicles. Brands include Bobcat and Club Car. On July 30, IR announced plans to sell this seg-

ment to Doosan Infracore for $4.9 billion, subject to necessary approvals. The Industrial Solutions segment (33%; 33%; 12%) provides solutions to enhance customer industrial efficiency in the areas of air solutions, productivity solutions and energy systems, and makes air compressors, fluid products, energy generation systems and industrial tools. The Security segment (28%; 41%; 18%) makes doors and locks for the commercial and do-it-yourself markets, electronic security products, and security and scheduling software. The segment makes products that include Schlage locks, door control hardware, and steel and power-operated doors.

Company Financials Fiscal Year Ended Dec. 31

Per Share Data ($)	2006	2005	2004	2003	2002	2001	2000	1999	1998	1997
Tangible Book Value	0.21	1.60	2.54	NM	NM	NM	NM	NM	NM	NM
Cash Flow	4.10	3.66	2.81	2.28	1.68	1.83	2.60	2.46	2.39	1.80
Earnings	3.31	3.09	2.37	1.72	1.08	0.74	1.68	1.65	1.54	1.16
Dividends	0.68	0.57	0.44	0.36	0.34	0.34	0.34	0.32	0.30	0.29
Payout Ratio	21%	18%	19%	21%	31%	46%	20%	19%	19%	25%
Prices:High	49.00	43.96	41.45	34.10	27.20	25.14	28.88	36.91	27.00	23.13
Prices:Low	34.95	35.13	29.52	17.26	14.85	15.20	14.75	22.31	17.00	13.92
P/E Ratio:High	15	14	18	20	25	34	17	22	18	20
P/E Ratio:Low	11	11	12	10	14	21	9	14	11	12

Income Statement Analysis (Million $)

	2006	2005	2004	2003	2002	2001	2000	1999	1998	1997
Revenue	11,409	10,547	9,394	9,876	8,951	9,682	8,798	7,667	8,292	7,103
Operating Income	1,632	1,558	1,295	1,061	891	979	1,488	1,372	1,327	973
Depreciation	191	196	174	194	206	363	297	272	283	212
Interest Expense	132	144	153	177	230	253	254	203	226	140
Pretax Income	1,315	1,270	984	703	402	263	869	874	843	614
Effective Tax Rate	17.6%	16.1%	14.1%	13.4%	5.05%	NM	32.6%	34.3%	33.2%	38.0%
Net Income	1,068	1,053	830	594	367	246	546	545	509	381

Balance Sheet & Other Financial Data (Million $)

	2006	2005	2004	2003	2002	2001	2000	1999	1998	1997
Cash	363	1,037	1,704	460	342	121	200	223	77.6	112
Current Assets	4,096	4,248	4,610	3,539	4,112	3,188	3,323	2,868	2,428	2,545
Total Assets	12,146	11,756	11,415	10,665	10,810	11,064	10,529	8,400	8,310	8,416
Current Liabilities	3,614	3,200	2,877	3,053	3,798	2,851	3,967	1,739	1,849	2,328
Long Term Debt	905	1,184	1,268	1,519	2,092	2,901	1,943	2,516	2,569	2,528
Common Equity	5,405	5,762	5,734	4,493	3,478	3,917	3,495	3,083	2,708	2,341
Total Capital	6,310	6,946	7,001	6,133	5,685	7,098	5,548	5,695	5,410	4,997
Capital Expenditures	212	112	109	108	123	201	187	191	14.5	186
Cash Flow	1,259	1,249	1,004	788	573	609	843	817	792	593
Current Ratio	1.1	1.3	1.6	1.2	1.1	1.1	0.8	1.6	1.3	1.1
% Long Term Debt of Capitalization	14.3	17.0	18.1	24.8	36.8	40.9	35.0	44.2	47.5	50.5
% Net Income of Revenue	9.4	10.0	8.8	6.0	4.1	2.5	6.2	7.1	6.1	5.4
% Return on Assets	8.9	9.1	7.5	5.5	3.3	2.2	5.8	6.7	6.1	5.4
% Return on Equity	19.1	18.3	16.2	14.9	9.9	6.7	16.6	18.7	20.2	17.2

Data as orig reptd.; bef. results of disc opers/spec. items. Per share data adj. for stk. divs.; EPS diluted. E-Estimated. NA-Not Available. NM-Not Meaningful. NR-Not Ranked. UR-Under Review.

Office: Clarendon House 2 Church Street, Hamilton, Bermuda HM 11.
Telephone: 441-295-2838.
Email: seekinfo@irco.com
Website: http://www.ingersollrand.com

Chrmn, Pres & CEO: H.L. Henkel
SVP & CFO: T.R. McLevish
SVP & General Counsel: P. Nachtigal
VP & Cntlr: R.W. Randall

Investor Contact: J. Fimbianti (201-573-3113)
Board Members: A. C. Berzin, P. C. Godsoe, H. L. Henkel, C. J. Horner, H. W. Lichtenberger, T. E. Martin, P. Nachtigal, O. R. Smith, R. J. Swift, T. L. White

Founded: 5
Domicile: Bermuda
Employee 3,000

Integrys Energy Group Inc

STANDARD &POOR'S

S&P Recommendation BUY ★★★★☆

Price	12-Mo. Target Price	Investment Style
$51.19 (as of Nov 23, 2007)	$56.00	Large-Cap Blend

GICS Sector Utilities
Sub-Industry Multi-Utilities

Summary This utility holding company serves about 481,000 regulated electric and 684,000 regulated gas customers. The company also operates an unregulated energy supply and services business.

Key Stock Statistics (Source S&P, Vickers, company reports)

52-Wk Range	$60.63– 48.10	S&P Oper. EPS 2007 **E**	2.60	Market Capitalization(B)	$3.890	Beta	0.39
Trailing 12-Month EPS	$2.84	S&P Oper. EPS 2008 **E**	3.90	Yield (%)	5.16	S&P 3-Yr. Proj. EPS CAGR(%)	7.00
Trailing 12-Month P/E	18.0	P/E on S&P Oper. EPS 2007 **E**	19.7	Dividend Rate/Share	$2.64	S&P Credit Rating	A-
$10K Invested 5 Yrs Ago	$16,546	Common Shares Outstg. (M)	76.0	Institutional Ownership (%)	57		

Price Performance

30-Week Mov. Avg. ··· 10-Week Mov. Avg. - - GAAP Earnings vs. Previous Year   Volume Above Avg. STARS
12-Mo. Target Price — Relative Strength — ▲ Up ▼ Down ► No Change   Below Avg.

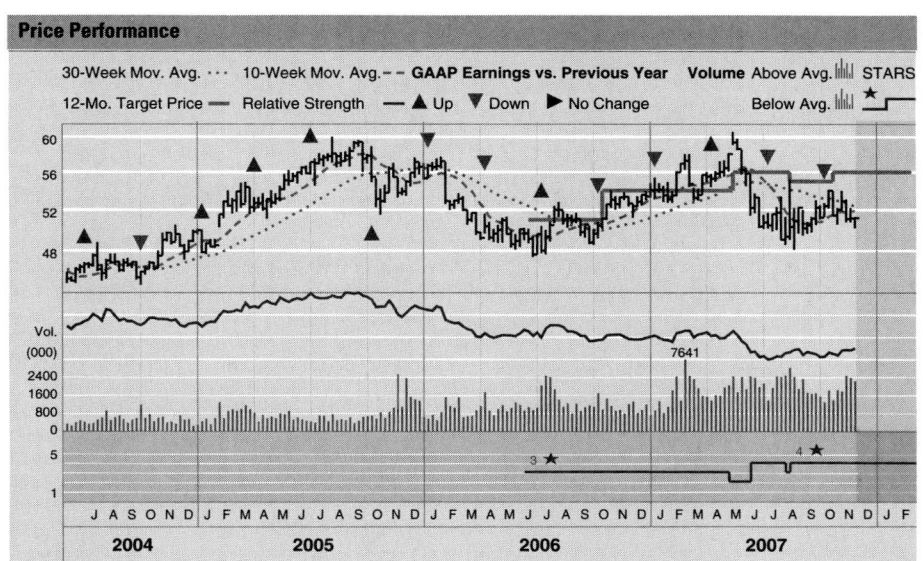

Options: P, Ph

Analysis prepared by **Christopher B. Muir** on October 19, 2007, when the stock traded at **$ 52.15**.

Highlights

➤ We expect revenues to increase 38% in 2007 and 15% in 2008, reflecting the inclusion of a full year of operations from the 2006 Minnesota gas distribution operations acquisition and the February 2007 Peoples Energy purchase. We see utility revenues rising 101% in 2007 and 24% in 2008. We see unregulated revenues advancing 17% in 2007 and 10% in 2008, as a result of our expectations for greater plant availability and higher power prices during peak periods.

➤ Our operating profit margin forecasts for 2008 and 2007 are 5.7% and 4.0% versus 2006's 3.6%, driven mostly by inclusion of higher margins from the recently acquired Peoples Energy Corp's (PGL). Our 2008 and 2007 pretax profit margin estimates are 4.4% and 2.7% versus 2.7% in 2006. In 2008, the company will receive the benefit of a full first quarter earnings compared to 2007, which missed nearly two months of one of the PGL's most profitable quarters.

➤ Assuming an effective tax rate, excluding tax credits from synfuel, of 36.9%, our 2007 operating EPS projection is $2.65, a 22% decrease from 2006's $3.40. We see EPS of $3.96 in 2008, an increase of 49%.

Investment Rationale/Risk

➤ In February 2007, WPS Resources acquired PGL and changed its name to Integrys Energy Group. We expect TEG to spend about $200 million in one-time costs related to the acquisition and integration of PGL in an effort to achieve annual cost savings and revenue enhancements of around $80 million. We think this merger, as well as the 2006 acquisition of Aquila's natural gas distribution properties, represents a good economic and strategic fit. TEG's shares recently traded at about 13.5X our 2008 EPS estimate, or a 7% discount to its multi-utility peers.

➤ Risks to our recommendation and target price include lower-than-expected merger cost savings, unfavorable regulatory decisions, and higher interest rates.

➤ Our 12-month target price of $56 is about 14.3X our 2008 EPS estimate, or a 5% premium to our average peer forecast. Despite our relatively slow EPS growth expectations, we view the above average recent 5.0% dividend yield as attractive. The company increased its quarterly dividend to $0.66 following the close of the PGL merger.

Qualitative Risk Assessment

LOW	MEDIUM	HIGH

Our risk assessment reflects what we see as a balanced portfolio of operations, which includes lower risk gas and electric utility businesses as well as higher risk unregulated wholesale and retail energy marketing services.

Quantitative Evaluations

S&P Quality Ranking A-

D	C	B-	B	B+	A-	A	A+

Relative Strength Rank STRONG
72
LOWEST = 1   HIGHEST = 99

Revenue/Earnings Data

Revenue (Million $)

	1Q	2Q	3Q	4Q	Year
2007	2,747	2,362	2,123	--	--
2006	2,038	1,479	1,561	1,865	6,891
2005	1,462	1,328	1,757	2,391	6,826
2004	1,373	1,046	1,073	1,399	4,891
2003	1,283	981.8	1,012	1,121	4,321
2002	671.3	579.4	609.6	814.6	2,675

Earnings Per Share ($)

	1Q	2Q	3Q	4Q	Year
2007	2.01	-0.53	0.14	E1.20	E2.60
2006	1.48	0.96	0.65	0.49	3.50
2005	1.62	0.62	1.25	0.53	4.11
2004	1.22	0.26	0.99	1.60	4.07
2003	0.92	0.08	1.04	0.91	3.24
2002	0.89	0.68	0.95	0.91	3.42

Fiscal year ended Dec. 31. Next earnings report expected: Late January. EPS Estimates based on S&P Operating Earnings; historical GAAP earnings are as reported.

Dividend Data (Dates: mm/dd Payment Date: mm/dd/yy)

Amount ($)	Date Decl.	Ex-Div. Date	Stk. of Record	Payment Date
0.524	--	02/22	02/28	03/12/07
0.660	04/12	05/29	05/31	06/20/07
0.660	07/16	08/29	08/31	09/20/07
0.660	10/24	11/28	11/30	12/20/07

Dividends have been paid since 1940. Source: Company reports.

Integrys Energy Group Inc

STANDARD &POOR'S

Business Summary October 19, 2007

CORPORATE OVERVIEW. Integrys Energy Group (TEG) is a holding company with regulated and unregulated business units. As of December 31, 2006, the company's subsidiaries included four regulated utilities:

Wisconsin Public Service Corporation (WPSC), an electric and natural gas utility; Michigan Gas Utilities Corporation (MGUC), a gas utility; Minnesota Energy Resources Corporation, (MERC), a gas utility; and Upper Peninsula Power Company (UPPCO), an electric utility. Integrys Energy Services, Inc. (ESI) is an unregulated subsidiary that operates electric generation facilities and energy marketing operations and provides energy generation and management services. In 2006, ESI was the largest contributor to TEG's revenues, at 75%. WPSC contributed 21%, while MGUC, MERC and UPPCO contributed 2% each.

IMPACT OF MAJOR DEVELOPMENTS. On July 10, 2006, TEG announced a merger agreement with Chicago-based Peoples Energy Corporation (PGL), which distributes natural gas to approximately 970,000 customers in Chicago and northeastern Illinois. The companies completed the merger on February 21, 2007. Under the agreement, PGL shareholders received 0.825 of a share of TEG common stock for each PGL share. Following the completion of the merger, former PGL shareholders became owners of about 42% of the company.

We believe the combined entity will be able realize cost savings through the elimination of overlapping functions. The combination adds nearly 970,000 natural gas customers to the 360,000 from the recently completed acquisitions from Aquila, and increases TEG's total natural gas customer base to more than 1,630,000, more than four times the level at the end of 2005.

On July 3, 2006, TEG completed the acquisition (announced in September 2005) of Aquila's natural gas distribution operations in Minnesota for $333 million in cash. Earlier, on April 3, 2006, it completed the acquisition of Aquila's Michigan operations for nearly $270 million plus an adjustment for working capital. The Minnesota and Michigan operations provide gas services to 200,000 and 161,000 customers, respectively. We believe the acquisitions have greatly expanded TEG's utility operations in a growing region and are helping to realize the company's strategy to become a strong regional energy company.

Company Financials Fiscal Year Ended Dec. 31

Per Share Data ($)	2006	2005	2004	2003	2002	2001	2000	1999	1998	1997
Tangible Book Value	28.36	31.69	29.12	27.25	24.48	22.91	20.42	19.97	19.45	19.96
Earnings	3.50	4.11	4.07	3.24	3.42	2.74	2.53	2.24	1.76	2.25
S&P Core Earnings	3.58	2.86	3.82	3.12	1.48	0.99	NA	NA	NA	NA
Dividends	2.28	2.24	2.20	2.16	2.12	2.08	2.04	2.00	1.96	1.92
Payout Ratio	62%	55%	54%	67%	62%	76%	81%	89%	111%	85%
Prices:High	57.75	60.00	50.53	46.80	42.68	36.80	39.00	35.75	37.50	34.25
Prices:Low	47.39	47.67	43.50	36.80	30.47	31.00	22.63	24.44	29.94	23.38
P/E Ratio:High	16	15	12	14	12	13	15	16	21	15
P/E Ratio:Low	13	12	11	11	9	11	9	11	17	10

Income Statement Analysis (Million $)										
Revenue	6,891	6,826	4,891	4,321	2,675	2,676	1,952	516	1,064	878
Depreciation	106	142	107	138	98.0	86.6	99.8	83.7	86.3	77.5
Maintenance	NA	NA	NA	NA	NA	NA	73.0	60.6	52.8	41.7
Fixed Charges Coverage	NA	3.80	4.31	3.55	3.97	2.32	2.14	3.03	3.56	3.77
Construction Credits	NA	NA	NA	NA	NA	NA	4.46	3.62	0.35	0.23
Effective Tax Rate	23.3%	20.7%	16.1%	22.0%	18.5%	5.83%	8.23%	3.3%	33.8%	35.6%
Net Income	152	148	153	114	109	77.6	67.0	59.6	46.6	53.7
S&P Core Earnings	152	111	144	103	47.1	28.2	NA	NA	NA	NA

Balance Sheet & Other Financial Data (Million $)										
Gross Property	NA	3,099	3,308	3,065	3,186	2,979	2,716	2,444	2,045	1,784
Capital Expenditures	NA	414	290	176	229	249	191	273	111	2.03
Net Property	NA	2,044	2,003	1,829	1,610	1,464	1,351	1,319	839	752
Capitalization:Long Term Debt	NA	918	866	923	926	829	761	686	394	304
Capitalization:% Long Term Debt	NA	41.3	42.0	47.9	53.7	53.7	58.4	56.1	40.9	36.4
Capitalization:Preferred	NA	Nil	Nil	Nil	Nil	Nil	Nil	Nil	51.2	51.2
Capitalization:% Preferred	NA	Nil	Nil	Nil	Nil	Nil	Nil	Nil	5.30	6.10
Capitalization:Common	NA	1,304	1,114	1,003	798	716	543	536	517	478
Capitalization:% Common	NA	58.7	58.0	52.1	46.3	46.3	41.6	43.9	53.8	57.3
Total Capital	2,970	2,317	2,062	2,024	1,816	1,635	1,428	1,359	1,061	986
% Operating Ratio	NA	98.2	96.7	97.8	95.3	96.2	94.5	95.4	92.8	91.9
% Earned on Net Property	NA	9.2	9.9	7.4	9.8	7.6	8.6	9.2	12.6	13.0
% Return on Revenue	NA	2.2	3.1	2.6	4.1	2.9	3.4	11.5	4.4	6.1
% Return on Invested Capital	NA	25.0	18.6	9.3	10.1	9.1	9.1	8.2	10.3	11.3
% Return on Common Equity	NA	13.3	14.5	12.8	14.5	12.3	12.4	11.3	9.4	11.4

Data as orig reptd.; bef. results of disc opers/spec. items. Per share data adj. for stk. divs.; EPS diluted. E-Estimated. NA-Not Available. NM-Not Meaningful. NR-Not Ranked. UR-Under Review.

Office: 130 E Randolph St, Chicago, IL 60601-6207.
Telephone: 800-699-1269.
Email: investor@integrysgroup.com
Website: http://www.integrysgroup.com

Chrmn: J.R. Boris
Pres & CEO: L.L. Weyers
SVP & CFO: J.P. O'Leary
Investor Contact: S.P. Eschbach (312-228-5408)

Secy: P. Kauffman
Board Members: K. E. Bailey, R. A. Bemis, J. R. Boris, W. J. Brodsky, A. J. Budney, Jr., P. S. Cafferty, E. Carnahan, D. S. Ferguson, R. C. Gallagher, K. M. Hasselblad-Pascale, J. W. Higgins, J. L. Kemerling, M. E. Lavin, J. C. Meng, W. F. Protz, Jr., L. L. Weyers

Founded: 18
Domicile: Wisconsin
Employees: 00

The McGraw-Hill Companies

STANDARD &POOR'S

Intel Corp

S&P Recommendation	**BUY** ★★★★☆	Price	12-Mo. Target Price	Investment Style
		$25.07 (as of Nov 23, 2007)	$30.00	Large-Cap Growth

GICS Sector Information Technology
Sub-Industry Semiconductors

Summary This company is the world's largest manufacturer of microprocessors, the central processing units of PCs, and also produces other semiconductor products.

Key Stock Statistics (Source S&P, Vickers, company reports)

52-Wk Range	$27.71– 18.75	S&P Oper. EPS 2007**E**	1.24	Market Capitalization(B)	$144.930	Beta	2.07
Trailing 12-Month EPS	$1.07	S&P Oper. EPS 2008**E**	1.48	Yield (%)	2.03	S&P 3-Yr. Proj. EPS CAGR(%)	18.00
Trailing 12-Month P/E	23.4	P/E on S&P Oper. EPS 2007**E**	20.2	Dividend Rate/Share	$0.51	S&P Credit Rating	A+
$10K Invested 5 Yrs Ago	$13,318	Common Shares Outstg. (M)	5,781.0	Institutional Ownership (%)	65		

Price Performance

30-Week Mov. Avg. · · · 10-Week Mov. Avg. - - **GAAP Earnings vs. Previous Year** Volume Above Avg. STARS
12-Mo. Target Price — Relative Strength — ▲ Up ▼ Down ► No Change Below Avg.

Options: ASE, CBOE, P, Ph

Analysis prepared by **Clyde Montevirgen** on October 19, 2007, when the stock traded at **$ 26.97**.

Qualitative Risk Assessment

LOW	**MEDIUM**	HIGH

Our view is that Intel's results reflect the sales cycles of the semiconductor industry and demand trends for personal computers. In addition, its above-average beta reflects high share price volatility. This is offset, in our opinion, by its large size, long corporate history, and its low debt levels compared to peers.

Quantitative Evaluations

S&P Quality Ranking B+

D	C	B-	B	**B+**	A-	A	A+

Relative Strength Rank MODERATE

68

LOWEST = 1   HIGHEST = 99

Revenue/Earnings Data

Revenue (Million $)

	1Q	2Q	3Q	4Q	Year
2007	8,852	868.0	10,090	--	--
2006	8,940	8,009	8,739	9,694	35,382
2005	9,434	9,231	9,960	10,201	38,826
2004	8,091	8,049	8,471	9,598	34,209
2003	6,751	6,816	7,833	8,741	30,141
2002	6,781	6,319	6,504	7,160	26,764

Earnings Per Share ($)

2007	0.28	0.22	0.31	E0.42	E1.24
2006	0.23	0.15	0.22	0.26	0.86
2005	0.35	0.33	0.32	0.40	1.40
2004	0.26	0.27	0.30	0.33	1.16
2003	0.14	0.14	0.25	0.33	0.85
2002	0.14	0.07	0.10	0.16	0.46

Fiscal year ended Dec. 31. Next earnings report expected: Mid January. EPS Estimates based on S&P Operating Earnings; historical GAAP earnings are as reported.

Highlights

➤ Following a 9% revenue decrease in 2006, we think sales will rebound about 6% in 2007 and rise 12% in 2008. We see healthy unit sales for chips over the next couple of years, supported by positive effects from accelerating traction for Microsoft's Vista operating system and the growing popularity of laptop computers. Although we see pricing pressure, we think enterprise spending on higher-end computers, release of new chips, and market share gains will balance some of the negative impact of eroding ASPs.

➤ Gross margins narrowed to 51% in 2006, owing to plant expansion costs, new product ramp-up expenses, lower ASPs, and lower plant utilization. Although we are projecting similar gross margins for 2007, we see potential catalysts that could eventually expand gross margins to the mid-50s in 2008, including a reduction in capital spending, improving plant utilization, and a potential easing in the price wars. We also see rising sales and cost containment efforts supporting higher operating margins going forward.

➤ We estimate operating EPS of $1.24 for 2007 and $1.48 for 2008.

Investment Rationale/Risk

➤ Through process manufacturing and chip technology advances, we think Intel is effectively positioning itself to increase its leadership as we head towards an industry cyclical peak. Although pricing pressure should limit results, we believe INTC has a number of options to preserve and expand profitability by the end of 2007. We also think Intel's competitive position will benefit from what we see as Advanced Micro Devices' growing financial concerns, inferior product portfolio and limited production capabilities. Anticipating wider margins, we believe INTC shares are undervalued relative to peers, historical averages and the broader market.

➤ Risks to our recommendation and target price include possible downward swings in demand for PCs, accelerated ASP erosion, and less traction for its latest chips.

➤ Applying a P/E of 21X to our 2008 EPS estimate indicates a value of about $30. Using a price-to-sales multiple of about 4X our forward 12-month sales per share estimate, we also derive a value of $29. Both target multiples are near peer averages. Blending these metrics, we arrive at our 12-month target price of $30.

Dividend Data (Dates: mm/dd Payment Date: mm/dd/yy)

Amount ($)	Date Decl.	Ex-Div. Date	Stk. of Record	Payment Date
0.113	01/18	02/05	02/07	03/01/07
0.113	03/22	05/03	05/07	06/01/07
0.113	07/12	08/03	08/07	09/01/07
0.113	09/12	11/05	11/07	12/01/07

Dividends have been paid since 1992. Source: Company reports.

Please read the Required Disclosures and Analyst Certification on the last page of this report.

The McGraw-Hill Companies

Intel Corp

STANDARD &POOR'S

Business Summary October 19, 2007

CORPORATE OVERVIEW. Intel is the world's largest semiconductor chip maker based on revenue and unit shipments, and is well known for its dominant market share in microprocessors for personal computers (PCs). In the first quarter of 2005, the company reorganized its operating segments to reflect a more customer-focused strategy.

The Digital Enterprise Group, or DEG (56% of 2006 total sales), designs and delivers computing and communications platforms for business and service providers. Revenues from microprocessors within DEG represented 41% of total sales in 2006. DEG serves the desktop computing market, including consumer and enterprise desktops, as well as the networking and storage markets.

The Mobility Group (35%) makes microprocessors and related chipsets and motherboards primarily for the notebook computing market. Intel's Centrino mobile platform, consisting of a processor, chipset, and wireless network connection, represented most of the revenue for the Mobility Group in 2006.

The Flash Memory Group (6%) makes NOR and NAND flash memory products for a variety of digital devices including: cellular phones, set-top boxes, networking equipment, DVD players, modems, digital audio devices, among others.

Intel also has three other operating segmen[ts] the Digital Home Group, Digital Health Group, and Channel Platform Group, [wh]ich have made limited contributions to total revenues.

CORPORATE STRATEGY. Intel's stated missi[on] is to be the preeminent supplier of silicon chips and platform solutions to [the] worldwide digital economy. Owning 75% of total microprocessors shippe[d] in late 2006, the company is a clear share leader in the worldwide micropr[oce]ssor market. Although INTC has a sizable lead over competitors, runner-[up] Advanced Micro Devices (AMD), with about 25% of market share, has [eff]ectively increased its presence over the past couple of years. In 2005, [wh]en Intel was focusing on creating faster microprocessors, AMD went a dif[fer]ent direction and focused on creating chips that were not only fast but als[o] power efficient, a quality that became increasingly attractive to enterprise[s] with large energy bills because of computing activities, and to laptop custom[er]s who faced short battery lives, among others.

Company Financials Fiscal Year Ended Dec. 31

Per Share Data ($)	2006	2005	2004	2003	2002	2001	2000	1999	1998	1997
Tangible Book Value	5.70	5.46	5.57	5.26	4.74	4.59	4.67	4.14	3.53	2.96
Cash Flow	1.65	2.15	1.91	1.62	1.25	1.13	2.20	1.57	0.63	1.27
Earnings	0.86	1.40	1.16	0.85	0.46	0.19	1.51	1.05	0.87	0.97
S&P Core Earnings	0.77	1.22	0.99	0.83	0.35	0.11	NA	NA	NA	NA
Dividends	0.40	0.32	0.16	0.08	0.08	0.08	0.07	0.07	0.03	0.03
Payout Ratio	47%	23%	14%	9%	17%	42%	4%	7%	4%	3%
Prices:High	26.63	28.84	34.60	34.51	36.78	38.59	75.81	44.75	31.55	25.50
Prices:Low	16.75	21.94	19.64	14.88	12.95	18.96	29.81	25.06	16.41	15.72
P/E Ratio:High	31	21	30	41	80	NM	50	42	37	26
P/E Ratio:Low	19	16	17	18	28	NM	20	24	19	16

Income Statement Analysis (Million $)

	2006	2005	2004	2003	2002	2001	2000	1999	1998	1997
Revenue	35,382	38,826	34,209	30,141	26,764	26,539	33,726	29,389	26,273	25,070
Operating Income	10,861	16,685	15,019	13,225	9,746	8,923	15,339	13,756	11,351	12,079
Depreciation	4,654	4,595	4,889	5,070	5,344	6,469	4,835	3,597	2,807	2,192
Interest Expense	1,202	19.0	50.0	62.0	84.0	56.0	35.0	36.0	34.0	27.0
Pretax Income	7,068	12,610	10,417	7,442	4,204	2,183	15,141	11,228	9,137	10,659
Effective Tax Rate	28.6%	31.3%	27.8%	24.2%	25.9%	40.9%	30.4%	34.9%	33.6%	34.8%
Net Income	5,044	8,664	7,516	5,641	3,117	1,291	10,535	7,314	6,068	6,945
S&P Core Earnings	4,518	7,555	6,374	5,467	2,332	740	NA	NA	NA	NA

Balance Sheet & Other Financial Data (Million $)

	2006	2005	2004	2003	2002	2001	2000	1999	1998	1997
Cash	6,598	7,324	8,407	7,971	7,404	7,970	2,976	3,695	2,038	4,102
Current Assets	18,280	21,194	24,058	22,882	18,925	17,633	21,150	17,819	13,475	15,867
Total Assets	48,368	48,314	48,143	47,143	44,224	44,395	47,945	43,849	31,471	28,880
Current Liabilities	8,514	9,234	8,006	6,879	6,595	6,570	8,650	7,099	5,804	6,020
Long Term Debt	1,848	2,106	703	936	929	1,050	707	955	702	448
Common Equity	36,752	36,182	38,579	37,846	35,468	35,830	37,322	32,535	23,377	19,295
Total Capital	38,865	38,991	40,137	40,264	37,629	37,825	39,295	36,750	25,667	22,860
Capital Expenditures	5,779	5,818	3,843	3,656	4,703	7,309	6,674	3,403	3,557	4,501
Cash Flow	9,698	13,259	12,405	10,711	8,461	7,760	15,370	10,911	8,875	9,137
Current Ratio	2.1	2.3	3.0	3.3	2.9	2.7	2.4	2.5	2.3	2.6
% Long Term Debt of Capitalization	4.8	5.4	1.8	2.3	2.5	2.8	1.8	2.6	2.7	1.9
% Net Income of Revenue	14.3	22.3	22.0	18.7	11.6	4.9	31.2	24.9	23.1	27.7
% Return on Assets	10.4	18.0	15.8	12.3	7.0	2.8	23.0	19.4	20.1	26.4
% Return on Equity	13.8	23.2	19.7	15.4	8.7	3.5	30.1	26.0	27.0	36.1

Data as orig reptd.; bef. results of disc opers/spec. items. Per share data adj. for stk. divs.; EPS diluted. E-Estimated. NA-Not Available. NM-Not Meaningful. NR-Not Ranked. UR- [un]der Review.

Office: 2200 Mission College Boulevard, Santa Clara, CA 95054-1549.
Telephone: 408-765-8080.
Website: http://www.intc.com
Chrmn: C.R. Barrett

Pres & CEO: P.S. Otellini
EVP & CFO: A.D. Bryant
SVP & General Counsel: D.B. Sewell
Investor Contact: N. Knupffer (408-653-5324)

Board Members: C. R. Barrett, C. Barshefsky, S. L. Decker, D. J. Guzy, R. E. Hundt, P. S. Otellini, J. D. Plummer, D. S. Pottruck, J. E. Shaw, J. L. Thornton, D. B. Yoffie

Founded: [19]68
Domicile: [D]elaware
Employe[es]: [?]94,100

IntercontinentalExchange Inc

STANDARD &POOR'S

S&P Recommendation	HOLD ★★★☆☆	Price $168.00 (as of Nov 23, 2007)	12-Mo. Target Price $175.00	Investment Style Large-Cap Growth

GICS Sector Financials
Sub-Industry Specialized Finance

Summary ICE is a fully electronic marketplace that offers exchange-based and over-the-counter trading of a variety of energy and soft commodity products.

Key Stock Statistics (Source S&P, Vickers, company reports)

52-Wk Range	$184.53– 93.40	S&P Oper. EPS 2007**E**	3.47	Market Capitalization(B)	$11.640	Beta	NA
Trailing 12-Month EPS	$3.40	S&P Oper. EPS 2008**E**	5.01	Yield (%)	Nil	S&P 3-Yr. Proj. EPS CAGR(%)	35.00
Trailing 12-Month P/E	49.4	P/E on S&P Oper. EPS 2007**E**	48.4	Dividend Rate/Share	Nil	S&P Credit Rating	NA
$10K Invested 5 Yrs Ago	NA	Common Shares Outstg. (M)	69.3	Institutional Ownership (%)	88		

Price Performance

- 30-Week Mov. Avg. · · ·
- 10-Week Mov. Avg. - -
- **GAAP Earnings vs. Previous Year**
- Volume Above Avg. ▮▮▮ STARS
- 12-Mo. Target Price —
- Relative Strength —
- ▲ Up ▼ Down ► No Change
- Below Avg. ▮▮▮

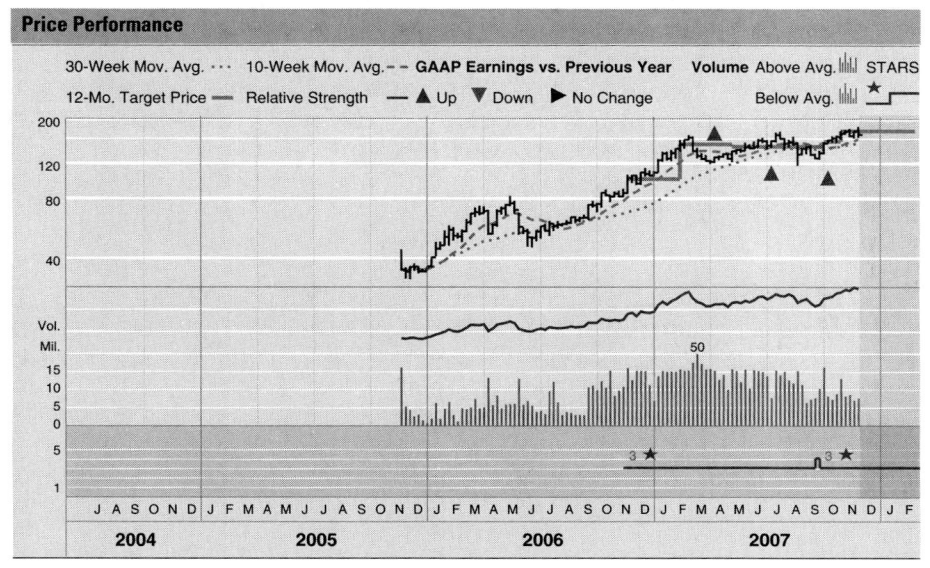

Options: ASE, CBOE, P, Ph

Analysis prepared by **Jason Willey** on October 25, 2007, when the stock traded at **$ 168.66**.

Highlights

► By embracing electronic trading and being an innovator with its centrally cleared over-the-counter (OTC) offerings, ICE has established itself as a leading marketplace for trading energy products. With its exchange and OTC product offerings, fully electronic platform, and leading position in energy and soft commodity products, we believe ICE's marketplaces are attractive to a growing pool of traders looking at alternative investments.

► Trading in ICE's futures and OTC products has increased substantially over the year, aided, in our view, by volatility in the energy markets, increased interest in alternative investments, and an expansion of its offerings. We expect revenue to grow 83% in 2007 and 33% in 2008. We see margins and earnings benefiting from ICE's decision to bring all of its clearing in-house by the third quarter of 2008, and continued progress on its integration of NYBOT.

► We are forecasting EPS of $3.47 in 2007 and $5.01 in 2008. Driving our earnings projections are growing average daily volumes in both the futures and OTC energy businesses, contribution from soft commodities, and the transition to in-house clearing.

Investment Rationale/Risk

► ICE has established itself as the leading marketplace for key Brent crude oil futures contracts, OTC Henry Hub natural gas contracts, and a number of soft commodities. We believe trading volumes will benefit from increased volatility in the global energy and commodity markets. We see ICE's acquisition of NYBOT, renamed ICE Futures U.S., providing key internal clearing capabilities and diversifying ICE's product offering by adding non-energy commodities. We believe ICE remains well positioned to grow as a standalone entity or provide strong technology capabilities and product diversification for a potential partner, as we expect further consolidation among exchanges.

► Risks to our recommendation and target price include slower trading volumes, enhanced regulatory scrutiny of OTC markets, increasing competition, and migration to in-house clearing.

► Our 12-month target price of $175 is based on a P/E of 35X our 2008 EPS estimate, which is a small premium to the current peer average. We believe this premium is justified by ICE's strong operating margins and leading market share across a number of futures products.

Qualitative Risk Assessment

LOW	MEDIUM	HIGH

Our risk assessment reflects the potential volatility in results due to changes in energy product trading volumes, recent acquisition activity in the sector, and a changing regulatory environment.

Quantitative Evaluations

S&P Quality Ranking NR

D	C	B-	B	B+	A-	A	A+

Relative Strength Rank STRONG

89

LOWEST = 1   HIGHEST = 99

Revenue/Earnings Data

Revenue (Million $)

	1Q	2Q	3Q	4Q	Year
2007	126.6	136.7	151.7	--	--
2006	73.59	73.59	94.66	95.26	313.8
2005	--	--	--	--	155.9
2004	--	--	--	--	108.4
2003	--	--	--	--	93.70
2002	--	--	--	--	125.0

Earnings Per Share ($)

2007	0.80	0.75	0.93	E0.98	E3.47
2006	0.33	0.52	0.73	0.81	2.40
2005	--	--	--	--	0.39
2004	--	--	--	--	0.41
2003	--	--	--	--	0.37
2002	--	--	--	--	0.37

Fiscal year ended Dec. 31. Next earnings report expected: Early February. EPS Estimates based on S&P Operating Earnings; historical GAAP earnings are as reported.

Dividend Data

No cash dividends have been paid.

IntercontinentalExchange Inc

STANDARD &POOR'S

Business Summary October 25, 2007

CORPORATE OVERVIEW. IntercontinentalExchange, Inc. operates a fully electronic marketplace offering exchange-based and over-the-counter (OTC) trading of a variety of energy products, and is the leading global exchange for soft commodities. The company's primary products include futures contracts for Brent crude oil and West Texas Intermediary crude oil, OTC trading of Henry Hub natural gas contracts, and various soft commodity futures. ICE provides trading for financial settlement and contracts for physical delivery of the underlying commodity.

ICE was formed in May 2000, to provide a platform for OTC energy trading. In June 2001, the company acquired the International Petroleum Exchange (IPE), which was mainly a floor-based futures exchange. In early 2002, the company introduced the industry's first cleared OTC contract through its partnership with LCH.Clearnet. In April 2005, ICE closed the IPE trading floor and moved to an entirely electronic marketplace. In January 2007, ICE acquired the New York Board of Trade (NYBOT) for approximately $1.1 billion. NYBOT, which has been renamed ICE Futures U.S., is a leading soft commodity exchange for products such as sugar, coffee, cocoa, orange juice, pulp, and cotton, as well as several financial products.

In 2006, ICE derived approximately 87% of its revenue from commission fees associated with trading its products on its [ex]change and OTC platforms. ICE generates a majority of its trading commiss[io]ns from a relatively small amount of crude, gas oil, and North American pow[er] futures and OTC contracts. The majority of the company's non-trading reve[nu]e is generated by the resale of market data information.

We view ICE's move to offer cleared OTC c[on]tracts as one of the key growth drivers for the OTC business. Transaction fe[e]s for cleared OTC contracts grew from $6.0 million in 2003 to $121 millio[n i]n 2006, and now represent almost 72% of OTC revenue, up from 14% in 2[00]3. By offering cleared contracts for the traditionally bilaterally settled OTC m[ar]ket, we believe ICE has helped to simplify and reduce the credit risk for OT[C t]ransactions, facilitating greater trading activity. Through its current OTC cle[ar]ing arrangement with LCH.Clearnet, ICE does not receive any of th[e] clearing fees associated with the centrally cleared products on its OTC pl[atf]orm. ICE does receive its standard commissions on these transactions.

Company Financials Fiscal Year Ended Dec. 31

Per Share Data ($)	2006	2005	2004	2003	2002	2001	2000	1999	1998	1997
Tangible Book Value	6.42	2.82	2.56	NA	NA	NA	NA	NA	NA	NA
Cash Flow	2.63	1.04	0.73	0.72	0.89	NA	NA	NA	NA	NA
Earnings	2.40	0.39	0.41	0.37	0.37	NA	NA	NA	NA	NA
S&P Core Earnings	2.39	0.82	0.32	0.18	NA	NA	NA	NA	NA	NA
Dividends	Nil	Nil	NA	NA	NA	NA	NA	NA	NA	NA
Payout Ratio	Nil	Nil	NA	NA	NA	NA	NA	NA	NA	NA
Prices:High	113.85	44.21	NA	NA	NA	NA	NA	NA	NA	NA
Prices:Low	36.00	26.00	NA	NA	NA	NA	NA	NA	NA	NA
P/E Ratio:High	47	NM	NA	NA	NA	NA	NA	NA	NA	NA
P/E Ratio:Low	15	NM	NA	NA	NA	NA	NA	NA	NA	NA

Income Statement Analysis (Million $)	2006	2005	2004	2003	2002	2001	2000	1999	1998	1997
Revenue	314	156	108	93.7	125	NA	NA	NA	NA	NA
Operating Income	218	91.1	49.4	38.3	65.3	NA	NA	NA	NA	NA
Depreciation	13.7	15.1	17.0	19.3	14.4	NA	NA	NA	NA	NA
Interest Expense	0.23	0.61	0.14	0.08	0.40	NA	NA	NA	NA	NA
Pretax Income	213	60.0	33.7	19.9	25.4	NA	NA	NA	NA	NA
Effective Tax Rate	32.6%	32.6%	34.7%	32.7%	33.8%	NA	NA	NA	NA	NA
Net Income	143	40.4	21.9	13.4	34.7	NA	NA	NA	NA	NA
S&P Core Earnings	143	43.8	17.0	9.81	NA	NA	NA	NA	NA	NA

Balance Sheet & Other Financial Data (Million $)	2006	2005	2004	2003	2002	2001	2000	1999	1998	1997
Cash	204	32.6	89.2	NA	NA	NA	NA	NA	NA	NA
Current Assets	341	164	NA	NA	NA	NA	NA	NA	NA	NA
Total Assets	493	266	NA	NA	NA	NA	NA	NA	NA	NA
Current Liabilities	37.9	26.4	NA	NA	NA	NA	NA	NA	NA	NA
Long Term Debt	Nil	Nil	Nil	NA	NA	NA	NA	NA	NA	NA
Common Equity	454	233	221	NA	NA	NA	NA	NA	NA	NA
Total Capital	454	238	221	NA	NA	NA	NA	NA	NA	NA
Capital Expenditures	12.4	8.61	NA	NA	NA	NA	NA	NA	NA	NA
Cash Flow	157	55.5	38.9	39.3	49.1	NA	NA	NA	NA	NA
Current Ratio	9.0	6.2	NA	NA	NA	NA	NA	NA	NA	NA
% Long Term Debt of Capitalization	Nil	Nil	Nil	NA	NA	NA	NA	NA	NA	NA
% Net Income of Revenue	45.5	25.9	20.3	14.3	27.8	NA	NA	NA	NA	NA
% Return on Assets	37.7	NM	NA	NA	NA	NA	NA	NA	NA	NA
% Return on Equity	41.6	NM	NA	NA	NA	NA	NA	NA	NA	NA

Data as orig reptd.; bef. results of disc opers/spec. items. Per share data adj. for stk. divs.; EPS diluted. E-Estimated. NA-Not Available. NM-Not Meaningful. NR-Not Ranked. UR-[Un]der Review.

Office: 2100 RiverEdge Parkway, Atlanta, GA 30328.
Telephone: 770-857-4700.
Email: ir@theice.com
Website: http://www.theice.com

Chrmn & CEO: J.C. Sprecher
Pres & COO: C.A. Vice
Vice Chrmn: R.V. Spencer
SVP & CFO: S.A. Hill

SVP & CTO: E.D. Marcial
Board Members: C. R. Crisp, J. Forneri, R. Reid, F. V. Salerno, R. L. Sandor, J. C. Sprecher

Founded: [0]0
Domicile: [De]laware
Employee[s]: [8]26

The *McGraw-Hi[ll]* Companies

STANDARD &POOR'S

International Business Machines Corp

| S&P Recommendation | STRONG BUY ★★★★★ | Price $104.05 (as of Nov 23, 2007) | 12-Mo. Target Price $138.00 | Investment Style Large-Cap Growth |

GICS Sector Information Technology
Sub-Industry Computer Hardware

Summary IBM, the world's largest technology company, offers a diversified line of computer hardware equipment, application and system software, and related services.

Key Stock Statistics (Source S&P, Vickers, company reports)

52-Wk Range	$121.46– 88.77	S&P Oper. EPS 2007E	7.02	Market Capitalization(B)	$143.376
Trailing 12-Month EPS	$6.72	S&P Oper. EPS 2008E	8.10	Yield (%)	1.54
Trailing 12-Month P/E	15.5	P/E on S&P Oper. EPS 2007E	14.8	Dividend Rate/Share	$1.60
$10K Invested 5 Yrs Ago	$12,981	Common Shares Outstg. (M)	1,378.0	Institutional Ownership (%)	66

Beta	1.20
S&P 3-Yr. Proj. EPS CAGR(%)	15.00
S&P Credit Rating	A+

Price Performance

30-Week Mov. Avg. ···· 10-Week Mov. Avg. -- **GAAP Earnings vs. Previous Year** Volume Above Avg. Below Avg. STARS
12-Mo. Target Price — Relative Strength — ▲ Up ▼ Down ► No Change

Options: ASE, CBOE, P, Ph

Analysis prepared by **Thomas W. Smith, CFA** on October 17, 2007, when the stock traded at **$ 115.09**.

Highlights

➤ We project revenues to rise 7.4% in 2007, then grow at 4.9% in 2008 amid a slower U.S. economy that we foresee, and then resume growth above 7% in 2009. The performance of the services units began to pick up in the second quarter, a trend we expect to continue into 2008, as IBM has been able to increase sales to existing clients and has a $116 billion backlog. We expect growth in IBM's Software division to be robust, reflecting recent acquisitions and the strength of some of the company's key middleware platforms (including WebSphere and Tivoli). We look for a mixed performance in Systems & Technology as new hardware products come on stream.

➤ We look for the gross margin for 2008 and 2009 to widen modestly, on ongoing cost reduction efforts, including increasing use of overseas labor, and an improved sales mix. We think pretax margins will improve slightly as a percentage of sales. Tax rates may benefit from more international business.

➤ We estimate 2008 EPS of $8.10 and 2009 EPS at $9.20. Our S&P Core EPS estimates are $0.20 lower each year, reflecting estimated pension costs.

Investment Rationale/Risk

➤ IBM's results should benefit, in our view, from a widening of margins reflecting cost cutting and improved profitability of its portfolio lines. We project modest, but relatively consistent, near-term revenue growth. Share buybacks have been pronounced so far in 2007, and we anticipate additional support of EPS from buybacks in 2008.

➤ Risks to our recommendation and target price include execution risks with regard to the global services operations, which might further elongate the sales cycle. Managing a transition to new hardware products, and pricing pressures are also risks. Regarding corporate governance practices, we are somewhat concerned that the roles of chairman and CEO are combined.

➤ Our 12-month target price of $138 reflects a target P/E of 17X, which is toward the low end of a recent 5-year historical range for IBM, applied to our $8.10 EPS estimate for 2008. Our target P/E is below a recent P/E level near 20X for Information Technology companies in the S&P 500 Index, which adds to our view of attractive valuation for IBM shares despite modest revenue growth.

Qualitative Risk Assessment

| LOW | MEDIUM | HIGH |

Our risk assessment reflects what we view as IBM's competitively positioned solutions offerings, offset by what we see as an intensely competitive pricing environment.

Quantitative Evaluations

S&P Quality Ranking   A

| D | C | B- | B | B+ | A- | A | A+ |

Relative Strength Rank   MODERATE

47

LOWEST = 1   HIGHEST = 99

Revenue/Earnings Data

Revenue (Million $)

	1Q	2Q	3Q	4Q	Year
2007	22,029	23,772	24,119	--	--
2006	20,659	21,890	22,617	26,257	91,424
2005	22,908	22,270	21,529	24,427	91,134
2004	22,175	23,098	23,349	27,671	96,293
2003	20,065	21,631	21,522	25,913	89,131
2002	18,030	19,651	19,821	23,684	81,186

Earnings Per Share ($)

	1Q	2Q	3Q	4Q	Year
2007	1.21	1.55	1.68	E2.62	E7.02
2006	1.08	1.30	1.45	2.30	6.06
2005	0.85	1.14	0.94	2.01	4.91
2004	0.93	1.16	1.06	1.81	4.94
2003	0.79	0.98	1.02	1.56	4.34
2002	0.73	0.25	0.99	1.11	3.07

Fiscal year ended Dec. 31. Next earnings report expected: Mid January. EPS Estimates based on S&P Operating Earnings; historical GAAP earnings are as reported.

Dividend Data (Dates: mm/dd Payment Date: mm/dd/yy)

Amount ($)	Date Decl.	Ex-Div. Date	Stk. of Record	Payment Date
0.300	01/30	02/07	02/09	03/10/07
0.400	04/24	05/08	05/10	06/09/07
0.400	07/31	08/08	08/10	09/10/07
0.400	10/30	11/07	11/09	12/10/07

Dividends have been paid since 1916. Source: Company reports.

The McGraw·Hill Companies

International Business Machines Corp

Business Summary October 17, 2007

CORPORATE OVERVIEW. In an information technology (IT) market estimated at $1 trillion, International Business Machines, with about $90 billion in annual sales, is a major contributor to each major category that comprises the total IT market: hardware, software, and services. The company is a leading server vendor, among the largest software vendors (behind Microsoft Corp. and Oracle Corp.), and has the largest global services organization.

CORPORATE STRATEGY. IBM has evolved from being a computer hardware vendor to a systems, services and software company. While computer hardware (included in the Systems & Technology Group) accounted for about 25% of sales in 2006, IBM has emphasized -- through acquisitions and investments -- services and software. These areas have gained momentum as IBM leverages these assets to offer total solutions to customers. IBM's focus on these higher value added segments such as services and software resulted in these areas representing some 73% of revenues and 67% of pretax profits during 2006.

The Systems group, once thought of principa[ll]y as mainframes (zSeries) and minicomputers (AS/400), has made a transit[ion] to more open systems. IBM, a leader in UNIX systems (pSeries), also offer[s] [e]ntry level servers. While IBM introduced the PC, it sold this business to L[en]ovo Group Ltd. in May 2005, for $1.75 billion.

However, hardware remains a critical part [of] [I]BM's portfolio of businesses, and the company has tried to be innovative [thr]ough its microelectronics division and early adoption of Linux to differentiate its products in a commoditizing market. The Hardware division, in the Systems & Technology Group, includes IBM's Shark storage offering and its semiconductor unit (custom logic and communications, and with exposure to gaming consoles). The focus to improve the profitability of this business led to IBM's sale of its PC business.

Company Financials Fiscal Year Ended Dec. 31

Per Share Data ($)	2006	2005	2004	2003	2002	2001	2000	1999	1998	1997
Tangible Book Value	8.93	13.97	11.86	12.36	10.84	12.96	11.08	10.65	9.84	9.62
Cash Flow	9.39	8.10	7.82	7.01	5.61	7.08	6.95	7.40	5.64	4.99
Earnings	6.06	4.91	4.94	4.34	3.07	4.35	4.44	4.12	3.28	3.01
S&P Core Earnings	5.88	3.93	4.06	3.00	0.08	1.33	NA	NA	NA	NA
Dividends	1.10	0.78	0.70	0.63	0.59	0.55	0.51	0.47	0.44	0.39
Payout Ratio	18%	16%	14%	15%	19%	13%	11%	11%	13%	13%
Prices:High	97.88	99.10	100.43	94.54	126.39	124.70	134.94	139.19	94.97	56.75
Prices:Low	72.73	71.85	90.82	73.17	54.01	83.75	80.06	80.88	47.81	31.78
P/E Ratio:High	16	20	20	22	41	29	30	34	29	19
P/E Ratio:Low	12	15	18	17	18	19	18	20	15	11

Income Statement Analysis (Million $)

	2006	2005	2004	2003	2002	2001	2000	1999	1998	1997
Revenue	91,424	91,134	96,293	89,131	81,186	85,866	88,396	87,548	81,667	78,508
Operating Income	16,912	14,564	15,890	14,790	11,175	14,115	16,147	18,086	13,639	13,116
Depreciation	4,983	5,188	4,915	4,701	4,379	4,820	4,513	6,159	4,475	4,018
Interest Expense	278	220	139	145	145	238	717	727	713	760
Pretax Income	13,317	12,226	12,028	10,874	7,524	10,953	11,534	11,757	9,040	9,027
Effective Tax Rate	29.3%	34.6%	29.8%	30.0%	29.1%	29.5%	29.8%	34.4%	30.0%	32.5%
Net Income	9,416	7,994	8,448	7,613	5,334	7,723	8,093	7,712	6,328	6,093
S&P Core Earnings	9,116	6,395	6,923	5,270	111	2,302	NA	NA	NA	NA

Balance Sheet & Other Financial Data (Million $)

	2006	2005	2004	2003	2002	2001	2000	1999	1998	1997
Cash	10,656	13,686	10,570	7,647	5,975	6,393	3,722	5,831	5,768	7,553
Current Assets	44,660	45,661	46,970	44,998	41,652	42,461	43,880	43,155	42,360	40,418
Total Assets	103,234	105,748	109,183	104,457	96,484	88,313	88,349	87,495	86,100	81,499
Current Liabilities	40,091	35,152	39,798	37,900	34,550	35,119	36,406	39,578	36,827	33,507
Long Term Debt	13,780	15,425	14,828	16,986	19,986	15,963	18,371	14,124	15,508	13,696
Common Equity	28,506	33,098	29,747	27,864	22,782	23,614	20,624	20,264	19,186	19,564
Total Capital	42,286	48,523	44,575	44,850	42,768	39,577	38,995	36,236	36,455	34,999
Capital Expenditures	4,362	3,842	4,368	4,393	4,753	5,660	5,616	5,959	6,520	6,793
Cash Flow	14,399	13,182	13,363	12,314	9,713	12,533	12,586	13,851	10,783	10,091
Current Ratio	1.1	1.3	1.2	1.2	1.2	1.2	1.2	1.1	1.2	1.2
% Long Term Debt of Capitalization	32.6	31.7	33.3	37.9	46.7	40.3	47.1	39.2	42.5	39.1
% Net Income of Revenue	10.3	8.8	8.8	8.5	6.6	9.0	9.2	8.8	7.7	7.8
% Return on Assets	9.0	7.4	7.9	7.6	5.7	8.7	9.2	8.9	7.6	7.5
% Return on Equity	30.6	24.7	29.3	30.1	23.1	35.1	39.7	39.0	32.7	29.8

Data as orig reptd.; bef. results of disc opers/spec. items. Per share data adj. for stk. divs.; EPS diluted. E-Estimated. NA-Not Available. NM-Not Meaningful. NR-Not Ranked. UR-Under Review.

Office: New Orchard Road, Armonk, NY 10504.
Telephone: 914-499-1900.
Website: http://www.ibm.com
Chrmn, Pres & CEO: S.J. Palmisano

SVP & CFO: M. Loughridge
VP & Treas: J.J. Greene, Jr.
VP & Secy: D.E. O'Donnell
VP & Cntlr: T.S. Shaughnessy

Board Members: C. Black, K. I. Chenault, J. Dormann, M. L. Eskew, S. A. Jackson, M. Makihara, L. A. Noto, J. W. Owens, S. J. Palmisano, J. E. Spero, S. Taurel, C. M. Vest, L. H. Zambrano

Founded: 1910
Domicile: New York
Employees: 355,766

International Flavors & Fragrances Inc.

STANDARD &POOR'S

S&P Recommendation HOLD ★★★☆☆	Price $48.28 (as of Nov 23, 2007)	12-Mo. Target Price $52.00	Investment Style Large-Cap Growth

GICS Sector Materials
Sub-Industry Specialty Chemicals

Summary This leading producer of flavors and fragrances used in a wide variety of consumer goods derives over two-thirds of its sales and earnings from operations outside the U.S.

Key Stock Statistics (Source S&P, Vickers, company reports)

52-Wk Range	$54.75– 45.71	S&P Oper. EPS 2007**E**	2.65	Market Capitalization(B)	$3.927	Beta	0.51
Trailing 12-Month EPS	$2.76	S&P Oper. EPS 2008**E**	2.85	Yield (%)	1.91	S&P 3-Yr. Proj. EPS CAGR(%)	10.00
Trailing 12-Month P/E	17.5	P/E on S&P Oper. EPS 2007**E**	18.2	Dividend Rate/Share	$0.92	S&P Credit Rating	BBB
$10K Invested 5 Yrs Ago	$15,797	Common Shares Outstg. (M)	81.3	Institutional Ownership (%)	95		

Price Performance

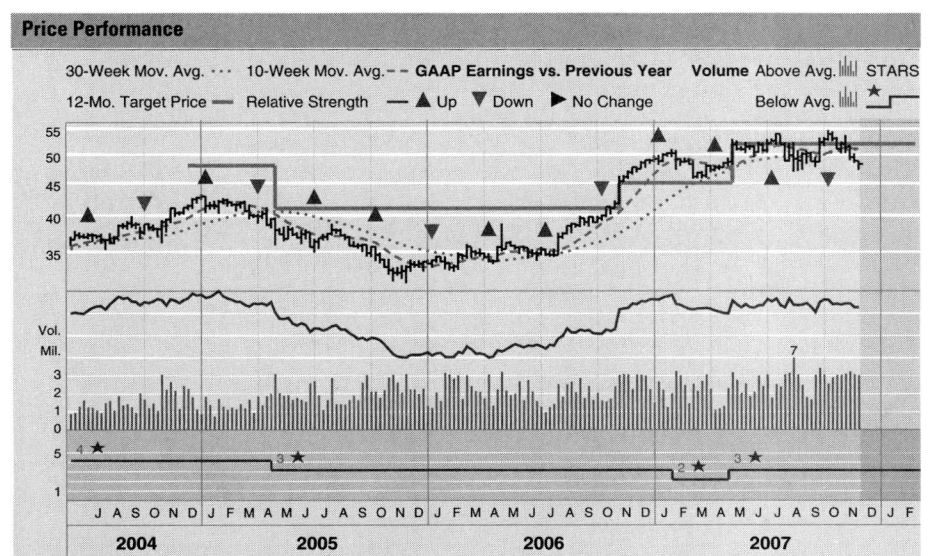

30-Week Mov. Avg. ··· 10-Week Mov. Avg. - - GAAP Earnings vs. Previous Year Volume Above Avg. STARS
12-Mo. Target Price — Relative Strength — ▲ Up ▼ Down ► No Change Below Avg.

Options: CBOE

Analysis prepared by **Richard O'Reilly, CFA** on November 16, 2007, when the stock traded at **$48.97**.

Highlights

➤ We expect sales in 2008 to grow almost 10%, including favorable exchange rates, on gains in both fragrances and flavors and aided by new customer products and higher selling prices. We believe that IFF has gained share with major customers in both segments. Sales growth of 9% in the first nine months of 2007 was helped by favorable currency rates.

➤ We forecast a gross margin for 2008 of 42.5%, despite possible higher costs for raw materials and freight. Third quarter 2007 pretax profits included a $6 million pension curtailment loss, and income for 2006 included about $0.14 a share from the sale of real estate. We see 2008 interest expense of about $65 million, as a result of increased debt incurred in an accelerated stock buyback plan.

➤ We project that the effective tax rate for 2008 will be about 27%, up from the 25.5% rate expected for 2007, which includes a one-time benefit in the second quarter. EPS comparisons should be helped by fewer average shares outstanding as a result of the company's stock repurchase program.

Investment Rationale/Risk

➤ IFF has reported better than expected results thus far in 2007. We see the company continuing to achieve sales growth, driven by an improved win rate of new business. In addition, it has announced an expanded stock repurchase program.

➤ Risks to our recommendation and target price include increased economic and political uncertainties in global markets, greater currency fluctuations, an inability to maintain close relationships with customers, lack of customers' success in new product launches, and increases in raw material costs.

➤ The shares recently yielded 1.9% and traded at a P/E of 18.5X our 2007 EPS estimate, modestly higher than the corresponding multiples accorded to the shares of other major specialty chemical concerns, based on our estimates. We think the stock will be an average performer, reflecting what we see as a favorable EPS outlook for 2008. Assuming a similar P/E multiple, our 12-month target price is $52.

Qualitative Risk Assessment

LOW	MEDIUM	HIGH

Our risk assessment reflects our view of the stable nature of the company's businesses and end markets, and its leadership positions, offset by a somewhat concentrated customer base.

Quantitative Evaluations

S&P Quality Ranking B+

D	C	B-	B	B+	A-	A	A+

Relative Strength Rank MODERATE

54

LOWEST = 1   HIGHEST = 99

Revenue/Earnings Data

Revenue (Million $)

	1Q	2Q	3Q	4Q	Year
2007	566.1	573.7	583.3	--	--
2006	511.4	530.5	539.1	514.3	2,095
2005	523.1	515.6	493.1	461.7	1,993
2004	535.0	524.2	506.2	468.2	2,034
2003	466.2	482.6	480.9	471.8	1,902
2002	445.8	476.3	462.8	424.3	1,809

Earnings Per Share ($)

2007	0.69	0.87	0.67	E0.52	E2.65
2006	0.58	0.67	0.70	0.53	2.48
2005	0.55	0.60	0.72	0.16	2.04
2004	0.59	0.59	0.44	0.43	2.05
2003	0.34	0.54	0.54	0.40	1.83
2002	0.44	0.47	0.52	0.41	1.84

Fiscal year ended Dec. 31. Next earnings report expected: Late January. EPS Estimates based on S&P Operating Earnings; historical GAAP earnings are as reported.

Dividend Data (Dates: mm/dd Payment Date: mm/dd/yy)

Amount ($)	Date Decl.	Ex-Div. Date	Stk. of Record	Payment Date
0.210	10/11	12/19	12/21	01/08/07
0.210	03/07	03/20	03/22	04/05/07
0.210	05/08	06/19	06/21	07/05/07
0.230	07/25	09/18	09/20	10/04/07

Dividends have been paid since 1956. Source: Company reports.

Please read the Required Disclosures and Analyst Certification on the last page of this report.

International Flavors & Fragrances Inc.

Business Summary November 16, 2007

CORPORATE OVERVIEW. International Flavors & Fragrances, founded in 1909, is a leading global maker of products used by other manufacturers to enhance the aromas and tastes of consumer products. The November 2000 purchase of Bush Boake Allen Inc. (BOA) for $970 million boosted annual sales to nearly $2 billion. With this purchase, IFF became the world's leading flavors company.

IFF receives about 70% of sales from outside the U.S. In 2006, North America contributed 31% of sales and 15% of operating profits; Europe 37% and 57%; India 3% and 3%; Latin America 13% and 9%; and Asia-Pacific 16% and 16%.

Fragrance products accounted for 57% of sales in 2006. Fragrances are used in the manufacture of soaps, detergents, cosmetic creams, lotions and powders, lipsticks, after shave lotions, deodorants, hair preparations, air fresheners, perfumes and colognes and other consumer products. Most major U.S. companies in these industries are IFF customers. Cosmetics (including perfumes and toiletries) and household products (soaps and detergents) are the two largest customer groups.

Flavor products account for IFF's remaining sales. Flavors are sold principally

to the food, beverage and other industries for use in consumer products such as soft drinks, candies, cake mixes, desserts, prepared foods, dietary foods, dairy products, drink powders, pharmaceuticals, oral care products, alcoholic beverages and tobacco. Two of the largest customers for flavor products are major U.S. producers of prepared foods and beverages.

By category, 43% of sales in 2006 were from flavor compounds, 25% functional fragrances, 20% fine fragrances and toiletries, and 12% ingredients.

The company uses both synthetic and natural ingredients in its compounds. IFF manufactures most of the synthetic ingredients, of which a substantial portion (45% in 2006) is sold to others. It has had a consistent commitment to R&D spending, and anticipates that R&D expense will approximate 9% of annual sales over the next several years. R&D is conducted in 32 laboratories in 23 countries.

Company Financials Fiscal Year Ended Dec. 31

Per Share Data ($)	2006	2005	2004	2003	2002	2001	2000	1999	1998	1997
Tangible Book Value	1.78	1.54	1.28	NM	NM	NM	NM	8.19	8.91	9.17
Cash Flow	3.46	3.07	3.01	2.77	2.72	2.47	1.90	2.06	2.35	2.45
Earnings	2.48	2.04	2.05	1.83	1.84	1.20	1.22	1.53	1.90	1.99
S&P Core Earnings	2.35	2.04	1.82	1.70	1.37	0.70	NA	NA	NA	NA
Dividends	0.77	0.73	0.69	0.63	0.60	0.60	1.52	1.52	1.48	1.45
Payout Ratio	31%	36%	33%	34%	33%	50%	125%	99%	78%	73%
Prices:High	49.88	42.90	43.20	36.61	37.45	31.69	37.94	48.50	51.88	53.44
Prices:Low	32.53	31.19	32.77	29.18	26.05	19.75	14.69	33.63	32.06	39.88
P/E Ratio:High	20	21	21	20	20	26	31	32	27	27
P/E Ratio:Low	13	15	16	16	14	16	12	22	17	20

Income Statement Analysis (Million $)										
Revenue	2,095	1,993	2,034	1,902	1,809	1,844	1,463	1,439	1,407	1,427
Operating Income	421	382	433	415	396	409	322	338	356	382
Depreciation	89.7	91.9	91.0	86.7	84.5	123	69.3	56.4	49.0	50.3
Interest Expense	25.5	24.0	24.0	28.5	37.0	70.4	25.1	5.15	2.04	2.42
Pretax Income	313	246	281	252	266	188	184	243	311	340
Effective Tax Rate	27.7%	21.6%	30.2%	31.5%	34.0%	38.2%	33.2%	33.5%	34.5%	35.9%
Net Income	227	193	196	173	176	116	123	162	204	218
S&P Core Earnings	214	193	174	161	131	68.5	NA	NA	NA	NA

Balance Sheet & Other Financial Data (Million $)										
Cash	115	273	32.6	12.1	14.9	48.5	129	62.1	116	217
Current Assets	1,080	1,191	961	903	867	896	1,019	835	848	935
Total Assets	2,479	2,638	2,363	2,307	2,233	2,268	2,489	1,401	1,388	1,422
Current Liabilities	447	1,203	400	526	359	560	1,179	370	273	265
Long Term Debt	791	131	669	690	1,007	939	417	3.83	4.34	5.11
Common Equity	873	915	910	743	575	524	631	858	945	1,000
Total Capital	1,665	1,047	1,579	1,433	1,582	1,508	1,152	895	1,084	1,029
Capital Expenditures	58.3	93.4	70.6	6.40	81.8	52.0	60.7	102	89.7	58.2
Cash Flow	316	285	287	259	260	239	192	218	253	269
Current Ratio	2.4	1.0	2.4	1.7	2.4	1.6	0.9	2.3	3.1	3.5
% Long Term Debt of Capitalization	47.5	12.5	42.4	48.2	63.7	62.3	36.2	0.4	0.4	0.5
% Net Income of Revenue	10.8	9.7	9.6	9.1	9.7	6.3	8.4	11.3	14.5	15.3
% Return on Assets	8.9	7.7	8.4	7.6	7.8	4.9	6.3	11.6	14.5	14.9
% Return on Equity	26.0	21.1	23.7	26.2	32.0	20.1	16.5	18.0	20.9	21.0

Data as orig reptd.; bef. results of disc opers/spec. items. Per share data adj. for stk. divs.; EPS diluted. E-Estimated. NA-Not Available. NM-Not Meaningful. NR-Not Ranked. UR-Under Review.

Office: 521 W 57th St, New York, NY 10019-2960.	**Chrmn & CEO:** R.M. Amen	**Investor Contact:** J. Fingeroth (212-521-4800)	**Founded:** 1909
Telephone: 212-765-5500.	**COO:** J.H. Dunsdon	**Board Members:** R. Amen, G. Blobel, J. M. Cook, P. A.	**Domicile:** New York
Email: investor.relations@iff.com	**SVP & CFO:** D.J. Wetmore	Georgescu, M. Hayes Adame, A. A. Herzan, H. W.	**Employees:** 5,087
Website: http://www.iff.com	**SVP, Secy & General Counsel:** D.M. Meany	Howell, Jr., A. C. Martinez, B. M. Tansky	

International Game Technology

STANDARD &POOR'S

S&P Recommendation	HOLD ★★★☆☆	Price $41.74 (as of Nov 23, 2007)	12-Mo. Target Price $43.00	Investment Style Large-Cap Growth

GICS Sector Consumer Discretionary
Sub-Industry Casinos & Gaming

Summary This company is a leading maker of gaming machines and proprietary software systems for gaming machine networks.

Key Stock Statistics (Source S&P, Vickers, company reports)

52-Wk Range	$48.79–33.57	S&P Oper. EPS 2008**E**	1.76	Market Capitalization(B)	$14.008	Beta	1.13
Trailing 12-Month EPS	$1.51	S&P Oper. EPS 2009**E**	2.02	Yield (%)	1.34	S&P 3-Yr. Proj. EPS CAGR(%)	14.00
Trailing 12-Month P/E	27.6	P/E on S&P Oper. EPS 2008**E**	23.7	Dividend Rate/Share	$0.56	S&P Credit Rating	BBB
$10K Invested 5 Yrs Ago	$22,422	Common Shares Outstg. (M)	335.6	Institutional Ownership (%)	75		

Price Performance

30-Week Mov. Avg. · · · 10-Week Mov. Avg. – – **GAAP Earnings vs. Previous Year** Volume Above Avg. STARS
12-Mo. Target Price — Relative Strength — ▲ Up ▼ Down ▶ No Change Below Avg. ★

Options: ASE, CBOE

Analysis prepared by **Esther Y. Kwon, CFA** on November 14, 2007, when the stock traded at **$ 42.27.**

Qualitative Risk Assessment

LOW	**MEDIUM**	HIGH

Our risk assessment reflects that the company has an industry-leading position as a supplier of gaming machines. We expect the company to generate free cash flow, with at least some of it used for stock repurchases. This is offset as we project that IGT will continue to spend a sizable amount of money on research and development. We see the company's growth prospects being partly dependent on regulatory factors and technology changes, including the legalization of gaming markets.

Quantitative Evaluations

S&P Quality Ranking   B+

D	C	B-	B	**B+**	A-	A	A+

Relative Strength Rank   **STRONG**

78

LOWEST = 1   HIGHEST = 99

Highlights

➤ In the third quarter of FY 07 (Sep.), IGT invested $104.8 million in China LotSynergy Holdings in an effort to enter the Chinese lottery market. We look for FY 08 revenues to rise about 5% from the $2.6 billion reported for FY 07, on sales of gaming machines for markets in PA, NY, FL, OK and CA, leases in Mexico, and a replacement cycle in Japan. While we see a shift toward sales or licensing of server-based games boosting revenue from replacement machines and games, we look for this shift to be a more meaningful growth driver in FY 09.

➤ We estimate FY 08 net income of $550 million ($1.76 a share), versus the $508 million ($1.51) reported for FY 07. Our FY 08 forecast is based on 7% fewer diluted shares, following a 5% decline in FY 07, reflecting expected stock repurchases. In FY 09, we look for EPS of $2.02.

➤ In April 2007, directors approved the repurchase of an additional 50 million shares. As of September 30, 2007, IGT had a remaining stock repurchase authorization totaling 33.2 million shares. The company repurchased 28.2 million shares in FY 07, for $1.1 billion.

Investment Rationale/Risk

➤ We see favorable prospects for sales of replacement gaming machines and sales of new gaming facilities. Overall, during the next few years, we see a shift toward sales or licensing of server-based games boosting revenue. Also, we expect further growth in IGT's installed base of recurring revenue machines. However, in our view, the company's market leadership and longer-term growth prospects are fully reflected in the stock's premium P/E to the S&P 500.

➤ Risks to our recommendation and target price include the possibility that IGT's sales and profits will be weaker than expected, and that prospects for growth from new or expanded gaming markets will become less favorable than we anticipate.

➤ Our 12-month target price of $43 reflects our view that there will be a narrowing of the stock's P/E premium to the S&P 500. Based on our calendar 2008 EPS estimate, the stock recently traded at a significant P/E premium. We expect support for the stock to be limited by its P/E and by questions about the speed and scope at which demand for new gaming machines or systems will develop.

Revenue/Earnings Data

Revenue (Million $)

	1Q	2Q	3Q	4Q	Year
2007	642.3	609.7	706.5	662.9	2,621
2006	616.2	644.4	612.4	638.7	2,512
2005	641.2	551.0	579.6	607.6	2,379
2004	608.1	636.1	618.9	621.7	2,485
2003	489.6	529.1	561.9	547.5	2,128
2002	301.5	500.9	522.4	522.8	1,848

Earnings Per Share ($)

2007	0.35	0.38	0.41	0.38	1.51
2006	0.34	0.35	0.33	0.33	1.34
2005	0.33	0.26	0.32	0.30	1.20
2004	0.33	0.32	0.38	0.15	1.18
2003	0.25	0.27	0.30	0.29	1.07
2002	0.18	0.20	0.23	0.20	0.80

Fiscal year ended Sep. 30. Next earnings report expected: Mid January. EPS Estimates based on S&P Operating Earnings; historical GAAP earnings are as reported.

Dividend Data (Dates: mm/dd Payment Date: mm/dd/yy)

Amount ($)	Date Decl.	Ex-Div. Date	Stk. of Record	Payment Date
0.130	12/05	12/15	12/19	01/02/07
0.130	03/05	03/15	03/19	04/02/07
0.130	06/25	07/05	07/09	07/23/07
0.140	09/25	10/04	10/09	10/23/07

Dividends have been paid since 2003. Source: Company reports.

Please read the Required Disclosures and Analyst Certification on the last page of this report.

The McGraw·Hill Companies

International Game Technology

Business Summary November 14, 2007

CORPORATE OVERVIEW. International Game Technology (IGT) is a leading maker of gaming machines. In addition to selling machines, IGT's business includes the placement of machines from which it receives recurring revenues.

In FY 06 (Sep.), 50% of IGT revenues came from product sales, and the remainder from gaming operations, including progressive systems.

Product sales in FY 06 included the sale of 112,000 machines, down from 141,900 in FY 05. FY 06 sales included 51,100 machines for the North American market, versus 50,500 in FY 05. Shipments to international markets totaled 60,900 machines in FY 06, down from 91,400 in FY 05. International sales may include some lower-priced machines with relatively low-value prizes. In addition to machines for casinos, IGT has made video gaming terminals (VGTs) for government-sponsored programs, including lotteries.

IGT's gaming operations segment includes the placement of games in both casinos and government-sponsored gaming markets, under a variety of recurring revenue pricing arrangements, including wide-area progressive systems, standalone participation and flat fee, equipment leasing and rental, as well as hybrid pricing or premium products that include a product sale and a recurring fee.

CORPORATE STRATEGY. In FY 06, IGT's research and development spending totaled $188.5 million (about 7.5% of revenues), up from $138.4 million (5.8%) in FY 05. We expect that the company's ability to develop successful machines and games, with features that appeal to gamblers and casinos, will be a significant factor in the amount of product sales it has.

PRIMARY BUSINESS DYNAMICS. In our view, new market opportunities for IGT include the expected debut of slot machines at various locations in Pennsylvania, and the forecast introduction of gaming machines at racetracks in Florida and New York. Also, in FY 07, we look for IGT to have increased sales of replacement machines for the Japanese market.

Overall, during the next few years, we expect a shift toward sales or licensing of server-based games to become more evident, creating opportunities for increased IGT revenues from sales or licensing of replacement machines or games for use in such locations as U.S. casinos.

Company Financials Fiscal Year Ended Sep. 30

Per Share Data ($)	2007	2006	2005	2004	2003	2002	2001	2000	1999	1998
Tangible Book Value	NA	2.06	1.56	1.98	1.42	0.55	0.40	NM	0.26	0.94
Cash Flow	NA	1.99	1.78	1.56	1.45	1.23	0.91	0.67	0.29	0.42
Earnings	1.51	1.34	1.20	1.18	1.07	0.80	0.70	0.50	0.16	0.33
S&P Core Earnings	NA	1.33	1.15	1.11	1.02	0.79	0.67	NA	NA	NA
Dividends	0.52	0.50	0.48	0.30	0.18	Nil	Nil	Nil	0.03	0.03
Payout Ratio	34%	37%	40%	25%	16%	Nil	Nil	Nil	18%	9%
Prices:High	48.79	46.76	34.63	47.12	37.00	20.03	17.99	12.34	6.03	7.17
Prices:Low	33.57	30.12	24.20	28.22	18.05	11.94	8.93	4.36	3.53	4.03
P/E Ratio:High	32	35	29	40	35	25	26	25	37	22
P/E Ratio:Low	22	22	20	24	17	15	13	9	22	12

Income Statement Analysis (Million $)										
Revenue	NA	2,512	2,379	2,485	2,128	1,848	1,199	1,004	930	824
Operating Income	NA	960	886	964	800	646	315	343	267	260
Depreciation	NA	235	222	150	134	146	63.3	54.4	52.3	41.5
Interest Expense	NA	50.8	58.1	90.5	117	117	102	102	72.8	41.0
Pretax Income	NA	747	681	653	599	110	339	245	101	235
Effective Tax Rate	NA	36.6%	35.9%	34.2%	37.3%	NM	37.0%	36.0%	35.6%	35.0%
Net Income	NA	474	437	430	375	277	214	157	65.3	152
S&P Core Earnings	NA	470	415	405	357	273	204	NA	NA	NA

Balance Sheet & Other Financial Data (Million $)										
Cash	NA	295	289	765	1,316	424	364	245	426	175
Current Assets	NA	1,376	1,437	1,510	2,078	1,195	968	814	975	671
Total Assets	NA	3,903	3,864	3,873	4,185	3,316	1,923	1,624	1,765	1,544
Current Liabilities	NA	1,247	1,218	560	945	511	371	259	213	201
Long Term Debt	NA	200	200	792	1,146	971	985	992	990	323
Common Equity	NA	2,042	1,906	1,977	1,687	1,433	296	96.6	242	541
Total Capital	NA	2,242	2,106	2,768	2,833	2,413	1,281	1,088	1,233	865
Capital Expenditures	NA	311	239	211	30.8	33.8	34.7	18.5	17.8	16.8
Cash Flow	NA	709	659	580	509	423	277	211	118	194
Current Ratio	NA	1.1	1.2	2.7	2.2	2.3	2.6	3.1	4.6	3.3
% Long Term Debt of Capitalization	NA	8.9	9.5	28.6	40.4	40.3	76.9	91.1	80.3	37.3
% Net Income of Revenue	NA	18.9	18.3	17.3	17.6	15.0	17.8	15.6	7.0	18.5
% Return on Assets	NA	12.2	11.3	10.7	10.0	10.6	12.1	9.3	3.9	11.1
% Return on Equity	NA	24.0	22.5	23.5	24.1	32.0	109.0	92.6	16.7	28.7

Data as orig reptd.; bef. results of disc opers/spec. items. Per share data adj. for stk. divs.; EPS diluted. E-Estimated. NA-Not Available. NM-Not Meaningful. NR-Not Ranked. UR-Under Review.

Office: 9295 Prototype Drive, Reno, NV 89521.
Telephone: 775-448-7777.
Website: http://www.igt.com
Chrmn, Pres & CEO: T.J. Matthews

COO: S.W. Morro
EVP, Secy & General Counsel: D.D. Johnson
Investor Contact: P. Cavanaugh (866-296-4232)
CFO, Chief Acctg Officer & Treas: D.R. Siciliano

Board Members: N. Barsky, R. A. Bittman, R. R. Burt, P. S. Hart, L. S. Heisz, R. A. Mathewson, T. J. Matthews, R. Miller, F. B. Rentschler
Founded: 1980
Domicile: Nevada
Employees: 5,200

International Paper Co

STANDARD &POOR'S

S&P Recommendation **BUY** ★★★★☆	Price $32.89 (as of Nov 23, 2007)	12-Mo. Target Price $43.00	Investment Style Large-Cap Value

GICS Sector Materials
Sub-Industry Paper Products

Summary This company is a leading worldwide producer and distributor of printing papers and packaging products.

Key Stock Statistics (Source S&P, Vickers, company reports)

52-Wk Range	$41.57–31.05	S&P Oper. EPS 2007**E**	2.15	Market Capitalization(B)	$14.633	Beta	1.15
Trailing 12-Month EPS	$6.02	S&P Oper. EPS 2008**E**	2.75	Yield (%)	3.04	S&P 3-Yr. Proj. EPS CAGR(%)	7.00
Trailing 12-Month P/E	5.5	P/E on S&P Oper. EPS 2007**E**	15.3	Dividend Rate/Share	$1.00	S&P Credit Rating	BBB
$10K Invested 5 Yrs Ago	$10,217	Common Shares Outstg. (M)	444.9	Institutional Ownership (%)	91		

Price Performance

30-Week Mov. Avg. · · · · 10-Week Mov. Avg. – – **GAAP Earnings vs. Previous Year** Volume Above Avg. STARS
12-Mo. Target Price — Relative Strength — ▲ Up ▼ Down ► No Change Below Avg. ★

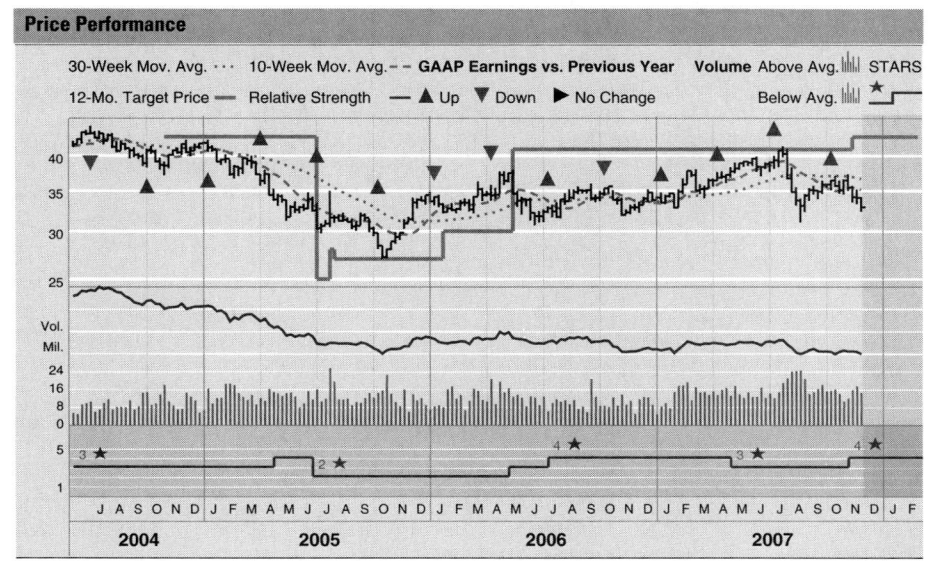

Options: ASE, CBOE, P, Ph

Analysis prepared by **Stuart J. Benway, CFA** on November 13, 2007, when the stock traded at **$ 34.05**.

Highlights

➤ IP has undergone a major restructuring that has shifted its product mix over the past 12 to 18 months. From its continuing operations, we expect sales in 2008 to rise about 3%-5% after an estimated 1%-2% increase in 2007. This projected improvement should come from higher prices for uncoated free sheet and container-board and from expanded volume in the distribution business. We also look for an increasing contribution from overseas businesses.

➤ We expect operating margins from continuing operations to expand moderately in 2008, following the steady progress seen in recent quarters. This projected widening should come from a continuing cost-reduction program that targeted $400 million of savings in 2007. We think that price increases will also help margins, but higher raw materials costs will likely be a partial offset. We believe that debt reduction will lead to lower interest expense.

➤ We see operating EPS of $2.15 for 2007 and $2.75 for 2008, following EPS of $1.33 in 2006. Comparisons should be helped modestly be a lower share count.

Investment Rationale/Risk

➤ We believe that IP's restructuring moves have allowed it to strengthen its balance sheet, make investments in faster growing regions, and re-purchase shares. The company has investments and joint ventures in Brazil, China, and Russia that will begin to contribute meaningfully to earnings growth in 2008, in our opinion. Moreover, based on our outlook for a favorable supply and demand situation in IP's major markets, we think that the paper and packaging environment will remain stable in 2008.

➤ Risks to our recommendation and target price include sharply reduced economic strength, worse than projected demand and pricing trends for uncoated paper and packaging, and the failure of new ventures to achieve targeted returns.

➤ Our DCF model, which assumes an 8.8% weighted average cost of capital, strong free cash flow generation in 2007 and 2008, and a 3.0% terminal growth rate, calculates intrinsic value of $42. Applying a peer forward P/E of 16.2 to our 2008 EPS estimate, we derive a value of $45. Our 12-month target price of $43 is a blend of these two measures.

Qualitative Risk Assessment

LOW	MEDIUM	HIGH

IP operates in a cyclical and capital intensive industry and is affected by changes in industrial production, interest rates, and economic growth. However, this is offset as it is one of the largest companies in the sector, and has greater economies of scale than many of its competitors.

Quantitative Evaluations

S&P Quality Ranking   **B**

D	C	B-	**B**	B+	A-	A	A+

Relative Strength Rank   **MODERATE**

46

LOWEST = 1   HIGHEST = 99

Revenue/Earnings Data

Revenue (Million $)

	1Q	2Q	3Q	4Q	Year
2007	5,217	5,291	5,541	--	--
2006	5,668	6,270	5,867	5,324	21,995
2005	6,011	5,916	6,036	6,134	24,097
2004	6,138	6,229	6,578	6,603	25,548
2003	6,075	6,264	6,373	6,500	25,179
2002	6,038	6,305	6,343	6,290	24,976

Earnings Per Share ($)

2007	1.02	0.46	0.52	E0.61	E2.15
2006	0.14	0.24	0.23	4.53	2.65
2005	0.22	0.19	1.48	-0.17	1.74
2004	0.10	0.13	0.42	0.32	0.98
2003	0.11	0.19	0.25	0.11	0.66
2002	0.13	0.45	0.30	-0.27	0.61

Fiscal year ended Dec. 31. Next earnings report expected: Early February. EPS Estimates based on S&P Operating Earnings; historical GAAP earnings are as reported.

Dividend Data (Dates: mm/dd Payment Date: mm/dd/yy)

Amount ($)	Date Decl.	Ex-Div. Date	Stk. of Record	Payment Date
0.250	02/13	02/14	02/16	03/15/07
0.250	05/07	05/16	05/18	06/15/07
0.250	07/10	08/13	08/15	09/17/07
0.250	10/09	11/14	11/16	12/14/07

Dividends have been paid since 1946. Source: Company reports.

Please read the Required Disclosures and Analyst Certification on the last page of this report.

The McGraw-Hill Companies

International Paper Co

STANDARD &POOR'S

Business Summary November 13, 2007

CORPORATE OVERVIEW. International Paper is the world's largest paper and forest products company. According to Pulp & Paper magazine, its market share is about 25% in uncoated free sheet (UFS), used in copiers and for envelopes and forms, giving it the number-two position in that major category. It is the third-largest linerboard producer, used to make corrugated boxes, with nearly 13% of the market. It also manufactures bleached paperboard used to package cosmetics, food, beverages, and pharmaceuticals, and is the second-largest boxboard producer in the U.S., with a share of 11%.

MARKET PROFILE. IP operates in a highly cyclical and capital-intensive industry. Demand for the company's products are dependent on a number of factors, including industrial non-durable goods production, consumer spending, commercial printing and advertising activity, and white collar employment levels. Historical prices for paper and wood products have been volatile, and, de-

spite its size, IP has had only a limited direct influence over the timing and extent of price changes for its products. Pricing is significantly affected by the relationship between supply and demand, and supply is mainly influenced by fluctuations in available manufacturing capacity. Technology seems to be having an impact on paper demand, especially in UFS, IP's largest category, where shipments have been down recently despite growth in the economy. We doubt the trend is likely to improve, as industry forecaster Resource Information Systems Inc. (RISI) projects that demand for UFS will grow at less than a 0.5% compound annual growth rate (CAGR) through 2009.

Company Financials Fiscal Year Ended Dec. 31

Per Share Data ($)	2006	2005	2004	2003	2002	2001	2000	1999	1998	1997
Tangible Book Value	11.10	6.75	6.69	6.01	4.31	7.78	11.89	18.65	20.45	20.36
Cash Flow	4.99	4.38	4.19	4.07	3.90	1.51	4.28	4.16	4.65	3.68
Earnings	2.65	1.74	0.98	0.66	0.61	-2.37	0.82	0.48	0.77	-0.50
S&P Core Earnings	1.13	1.67	0.84	0.51	0.92	-2.25	NA	NA	NA	NA
Dividends	1.00	1.00	1.00	1.00	1.00	1.00	1.00	1.00	1.00	1.00
Payout Ratio	38%	57%	102%	152%	164%	NM	122%	NM	130%	NM
Prices:High	37.98	42.59	45.01	43.32	46.20	43.31	60.00	59.50	55.25	61.00
Prices:Low	30.69	26.97	37.12	33.09	31.35	30.70	26.31	39.50	35.50	38.63
P/E Ratio:High	14	24	46	66	76	NM	73	NM	72	NM
P/E Ratio:Low	12	15	38	50	51	NM	32	NM	46	NM

Income Statement Analysis (Million $)										
Revenue	21,995	24,097	25,548	25,179	24,976	26,363	28,180	24,573	19,541	20,096
Operating Income	2,609	3,228	3,251	3,293	3,576	3,305	5,432	3,061	2,202	2,404
Depreciation	1,158	1,376	1,565	1,644	1,587	1,870	1,916	1,520	1,186	1,258
Interest Expense	651	593	743	766	783	929	791	541	496	490
Pretax Income	3,188	586	746	346	371	-1,265	497	448	392	16.0
Effective Tax Rate	59.3%	NM	27.6%	NM	NM	NM	23.5%	19.2%	20.4%	237.5%
Net Income	1,282	859	478	315	295	-1,142	142	199	236	-151
S&P Core Earnings	539	819	402	242	444	-1,091	NA	NA	NA	NA

Balance Sheet & Other Financial Data (Million $)										
Cash	1,624	1,641	2,596	2,363	1,074	1,224	1,198	453	477	398
Current Assets	8,637	7,409	9,319	9,337	7,738	8,312	10,455	7,241	6,010	5,945
Total Assets	24,034	28,771	34,217	35,525	33,792	37,158	42,109	30,268	26,356	26,754
Current Liabilities	4,641	4,844	4,872	6,803	4,579	5,374	7,413	4,382	3,636	4,880
Long Term Debt	6,531	11,023	14,132	13,450	13,042	14,262	14,453	9,325	8,212	7,154
Common Equity	10,839	8,351	8,254	8,237	7,374	10,291	12,034	10,304	8,902	8,710
Total Capital	19,816	20,311	25,631	25,085	25,435	29,804	32,541	24,554	21,582	20,188
Capital Expenditures	1,009	1,155	1,262	1,166	1,009	1,049	1,352	1,139	1,049	1,111
Cash Flow	2,440	2,235	2,043	1,959	1,882	728	2,058	1,719	1,422	1,107
Current Ratio	1.9	1.5	1.9	1.4	1.7	1.5	1.4	1.7	1.7	1.2
% Long Term Debt of Capitalization	33.0	54.3	55.1	53.6	51.3	47.9	44.4	38.0	38.1	35.4
% Net Income of Revenue	5.8	3.6	1.9	1.3	1.2	NM	0.5	0.8	1.2	NM
% Return on Assets	4.9	2.7	1.4	0.9	0.8	NM	0.4	0.6	0.9	NM
% Return on Equity	13.4	10.3	5.8	4.0	3.3	NM	1.3	1.9	2.7	NM

Data as orig reptd.; bef. results of disc opers/spec. items. Per share data adj. for stk. divs.; EPS diluted. E-Estimated. NA-Not Available. NM-Not Meaningful. NR-Not Ranked. UR-Under Review.

Office: 6400 Poplar Ave, Memphis, TN 38197-0198.
Telephone: 901-419-7000.
Email: comm@ipaper.com
Website: http://www.internationalpaper.com

Chrmn & CEO: J.V. Faraci
Pres: R.M. Amen
EVP & CFO: M.M. Parrs
SVP, Secy & General Counsel: M.A. Smith

SVP & CIO: J.N. Balboni
Investor Contact: B.N. McDonald (901-419-4957)
Board Members: D. J. Bronczek, M. F. Brooks, L. L. Elsenhans, J. V. Faraci, S. G. Gibara, D. F. McHenry, J. L. Townsend, III, J. F. Turner, W. G. Walter, A. Weisser

Founded: 1898
Domicile: New York
Employees: 60,600

The McGraw-Hill Companies

Interpublic Group of Companies Inc. (The)

STANDARD &POOR'S

S&P Recommendation HOLD ★★★☆☆	**Price** $9.02 (as of Nov 23, 2007)	**12-Mo. Target Price** $12.00	**Investment Style** Large-Cap Blend

GICS Sector Consumer Discretionary
Sub-Industry Advertising

Summary Interpublic is one of the world's largest organizations of advertising agencies and marketing communications companies.

Key Stock Statistics (Source S&P, Vickers, company reports)

52-Wk Range	$13.94– 8.69	S&P Oper. EPS 2007**E**	0.16	Market Capitalization(B)	$4.253	Beta	1.38
Trailing 12-Month EPS	$0.06	S&P Oper. EPS 2008**E**	0.45	Yield (%)	Nil	S&P 3-Yr. Proj. EPS CAGR(%)	NM
Trailing 12-Month P/E	NM	P/E on S&P Oper. EPS 2007**E**	56.4	Dividend Rate/Share	Nil	S&P Credit Rating	B
$10K Invested 5 Yrs Ago	$6,261	Common Shares Outstg. (M)	471.5	Institutional Ownership (%)	NM		

Price Performance

30-Week Mov. Avg. · · · ·   10-Week Mov. Avg. – –   **GAAP Earnings vs. Previous Year**   Volume Above Avg. ılıl   STARS
12-Mo. Target Price —   Relative Strength —   ▲ Up   ▼ Down   ► No Change   Below Avg. ılıl   ★

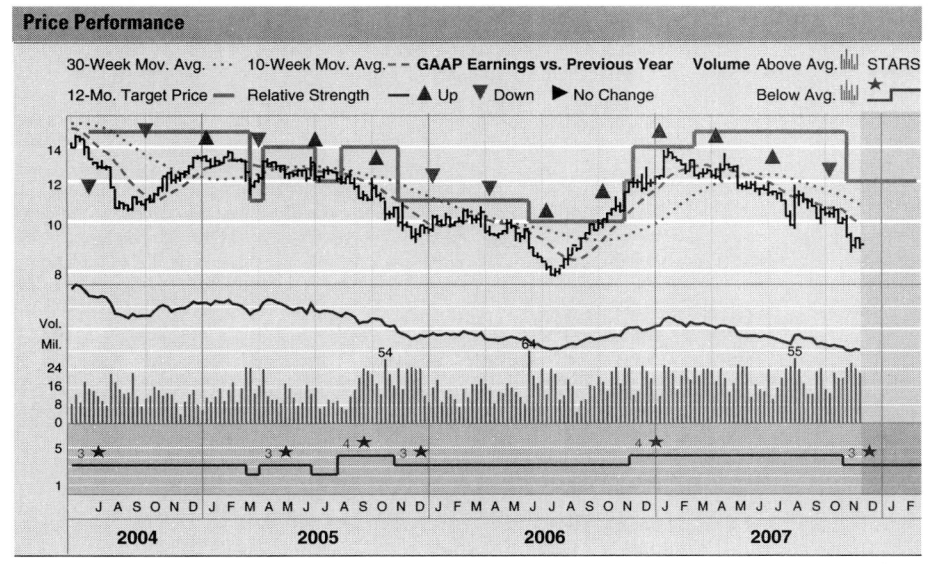

Options: ASE, CBOE, Ph

Analysis prepared by **James Peters, CFA** on November 05, 2007, when the stock traded at **$ 9.22**.

Highlights

➤ We see revenues rising about 6.0% in 2008, following an advance of about 5.7% we forecast for 2007. While we don't expect progress to be linear, we think organic revenue growth momentum that began in 2007 will continue in 2008. With nearly half of its revenues from overseas, we also expect IPG to continue benefiting from a weak U.S. dollar. We believe the company will be slightly more acquisitive in 2008 following several years of net divestitures that restrained overall revenue growth.

➤ We anticipate IPG's operating margin rising to 8.6%, up from our projection for 5.1% in 2007. We see higher revenues leading to fixed cost leverage, and believe less restructuring requirements will lead to lower severance expense. We believe IPG will finally be Sarbanes-Oxley compliant in early 2008, and as a result, we see professional fees falling to about 2.0% of sales from our 2.7% projection for 2007.

➤ We forecast EPS rising to $0.45, up from $0.16 we see for 2007, on more shares. We calculate EPS using a normalized effective tax rate of 37%, and include recurring severance expense.

Investment Rationale/Risk

➤ We believe investments in infrastructure helped IPG turn the corner competitively in 2007 after several years of organic growth that significantly trailed peers. Although IPG lost some clients at the end of the second quarter, the company remains net new business positive for 2007, in part due to winning incremental business from existing clients. We think revenue growth momentum will continue in 2008, aided by additional investments we expect IPG to make in order to acquire highly sought after digital advertising expertise. However, we also believe that the company's profitability level, while improving, will remain below peer levels for the next few years.

➤ Risks to our recommendation and target price include significant business losses, adverse accounting-related developments, and a delay in becoming Sarbanes-Oxley compliant.

➤ Our 12-month target price of $12 is derived by applying a discount to peer average enterprise value / EBITDA multiple of 8.5X to our 2008 EBITDA estimate of $880 million. We believe a discount is warranted to reflect IPG's lower than peer level profitability.

Qualitative Risk Assessment

LOW	MEDIUM	HIGH

Our risk assessment reflects our view of a highly competitive advertising industry, and economic cyclicality associated with advertising spending.

Quantitative Evaluations

S&P Quality Ranking   **C**

D	C	B-	B	B+	A-	A	A+

Relative Strength Rank   **MODERATE**

34

LOWEST = 1   HIGHEST = 99

Revenue/Earnings Data

Revenue (Million $)

	1Q	2Q	3Q	4Q	Year
2007	1,359	1,653	1,560	--	--
2006	1,327	1,533	1,454	1,877	6,191
2005	1,328	1,611	1,440	1,896	6,274
2004	1,389	1,513	1,519	1,966	6,387
2003	1,316	1,499	1,419	1,629	5,863
2002	1,420	1,613	1,502	1,669	6,204

Earnings Per Share ($)

2007	-0.29	0.24	-0.06	E0.22	E0.16
2006	-0.43	0.09	-0.03	0.11	-0.20
2005	-0.36	0.01	-0.25	-0.10	-0.70
2004	-0.21	-0.23	-1.22	0.22	-1.36
2003	-0.03	-0.06	-1.08	-0.26	-1.43
2002	0.16	0.29	-0.24	0.05	0.26

Fiscal year ended Dec. 31. Next earnings report expected: Late February. EPS Estimates based on S&P Operating Earnings; historical GAAP earnings are as reported.

Dividend Data

No cash dividends have been paid since 2002.

Interpublic Group of Companies Inc. (The)

STANDARD &POOR'S

Business Summary November 05, 2007

CORPORATE OVERVIEW. The Interpublic Group of Companies, along with its subsidiaries, is one of the world's largest advertising and marketing services companies, made up of communication agencies around the world that deliver custom marketing solutions to clients. These agencies cover the spectrum of marketing disciplines and specialties, from traditional services such as consumer advertising and direct marketing, to emerging services such as mobile and search engine marketing.

The company generates revenue from planning, creating and placing advertising in various media and from planning and executing other communications or marketing programs. IPG also receives commissions from clients for planning and supervising work done by outside contractors in the physical preparation of finished print advertisements and the production of TV and radio commercials and other forms of advertising. In addition, IPG derives revenue in a number of other ways, including the planning and placement in media of advertising produced by unrelated advertising agencies, the creation and publication of brochures, billboards, point of sale materials and direct marketing pieces for clients, the planning and carrying out of specialized marketing research, public relations campaigns, and creating and managing special events at which client products are featured.

IPG has two reportable segments: the Integrated Agency Network (IAN), comprised of Draftfcb, Lowe, McCann, media agencies and other standalone agencies, and the Constituent Management Group (CMG), which is made up of the bulk of IPG's specialist marketing service offerings. Draftfcb was formed from the merger of two IPG companies in 2006, and is focused on consumer advertising and behavioral, data-driven direct marketing. Lowe is a creative advertising agency operating in the world's largest advertising markets. McCann is a marketing communications company that consists of McCann Erickson Advertising, MRM Worldwide for relationship marketing and digital expertise, Momentum Worldwide for experiential marketing, and McCann Healthcare for health care communications, as well as various other brands. Interpublic also has two leading media specialists, Initiative (which was aligned with Draftfcb in 2006) and Universal McCann (aligned with McCann Erickson). The company maintains separate brands in competing disciplines in order to serve a broad range of clients.

Company Financials Fiscal Year Ended Dec. 31

Per Share Data ($)	2006	2005	2004	2003	2002	2001	2000	1999	1998	1997
Tangible Book Value	NM	NM	NM	NM	NM	NM	NM	NM	NM	0.32
Cash Flow	0.21	-0.30	-0.91	-0.90	0.83	-0.36	1.99	1.77	1.67	1.21
Earnings	-0.20	-0.70	-1.36	-1.43	0.26	-1.37	1.15	1.11	1.11	0.95
S&P Core Earnings	-0.18	-0.62	-0.82	-0.84	0.36	-0.60	NA	NA	NA	NA
Dividends	Nil	Nil	Nil	Nil	0.38	0.38	0.37	0.33	0.29	0.25
Payout Ratio	Nil	Nil	Nil	Nil	146%	NM	32%	30%	26%	26%
Prices:High	12.83	13.80	17.31	16.50	34.98	47.44	57.69	58.38	40.31	26.50
Prices:Low	7.79	9.08	10.47	7.20	9.85	18.25	32.69	34.41	22.56	15.67
P/E Ratio:High	NM	NM	NM	NM	NM	NM	50	53	36	28
P/E Ratio:Low	NM	NM	NM	NM	NM	NM	28	31	20	16

Income Statement Analysis (Million $)										
Revenue	6,191	6,274	6,387	5,863	6,204	6,727	5,626	4,427	3,844	2,997
Operating Income	341	156	589	719	762	1,113	1,096	791	656	437
Depreciation	174	169	185	204	218	372	263	190	159	75.0
Interest Expense	219	182	172	173	146	165	109	66.4	58.7	49.4
Pretax Income	2.00	-173	-261	-330	271	-519	672	592	570	448
Effective Tax Rate	NM	NM	NM	NM	51.8%	NM	40.7%	39.9%	40.7%	41.3%
Net Income	-36.7	-272	-545	-553	99.5	-505	359	322	310	239
S&P Core Earnings	-75.8	-265	-363	-325	136	-217	NA	NA	NA	NA

Balance Sheet & Other Financial Data (Million $)										
Cash	1,957	2,192	1,970	2,006	933	935	748	1,018	841	715
Current Assets	7,209	7,497	7,637	7,350	6,322	6,467	6,026	5,768	4,777	4,026
Total Assets	11,864	11,945	12,272	12,235	11,794	11,515	10,238	8,727	6,943	5,703
Current Liabilities	6,663	6,857	7,563	6,625	7,090	6,434	6,106	5,637	4,658	3,752
Long Term Debt	2,249	2,183	Nil	2,192	1,818	2,481	1,505	867	507	453
Common Equity	1,416	1,047	1,345	2,721	2,100	2,384	2,046	2,407	1,265	1,355
Total Capital	4,236	4,178	1,773	5,356	3,988	4,953	3,637	3,394	1,828	1,592
Capital Expenditures	128	141	194	160	183	268	202	150	137	96.9
Cash Flow	89.3	-129	-380	-349	317	-133	622	512	469	314
Current Ratio	1.1	1.1	1.0	1.1	0.9	1.0	1.0	1.0	1.0	1.1
% Long Term Debt of Capitalization	53.1	52.3	Nil	40.9	45.6	50.1	41.4	25.5	27.7	28.4
% Net Income of Revenue	NM	NM	NM	NM	1.6	NM	6.4	7.3	8.1	8.0
% Return on Assets	NM	NM	NM	NM	0.9	NM	3.7	4.1	4.9	4.6
% Return on Equity	NM	NM	NM	NM	5.1	NM	18.8	14.7	23.7	19.6

Data as orig reptd.; bef. results of disc opers/spec. items. Per share data adj. for stk. divs.; EPS diluted. E-Estimated. NA-Not Available. NM-Not Meaningful. NR-Not Ranked. UR-Under Review.

Office: 1114 Avenue Of The Americas, New York, NY 10020-1300.
Telephone: 212-704-1200.
Website: http://www.interpublic.com
Chrmn & CEO: M.I. Roth

EVP & CFO: F. Mergenthaler
SVP, Chief Acctg Officer & Cntlr: C. Carroll
SVP, Secy & General Counsel: N.J. Camera
Investor Contact: J. Leshne (212-704-1439)

Board Members: F. J. Borelli, R. K. Brack, J. M. Considine, R. A. Goldstein, H. J. Greeniaus, W. T. Kerr, M. I. Roth, J. P. Samper, D. M. Thomas

Founded: 1902
Domicile: Delaware
Employees: 42,000

The McGraw-Hill Companies

Intuit Inc

STANDARD &POOR'S

S&P Recommendation	HOLD ★★★☆☆	Price $29.17 (as of Nov 23, 2007)	12-Mo. Target Price $32.00	Investment Style Large-Cap Growth

GICS Sector Information Technology
Sub-Industry Application Software

Summary This company develops and markets small business accounting and management, tax preparation and personal finance software.

Key Stock Statistics (Source S&P, Vickers, company reports)

52-Wk Range	$33.10–26.14	S&P Oper. EPS 2008**E**	1.35	Market Capitalization(B)	$9.886	Beta	1.29
Trailing 12-Month EPS	$1.35	S&P Oper. EPS 2009**E**	1.53	Yield (%)	Nil	S&P 3-Yr. Proj. EPS CAGR(%)	15.00
Trailing 12-Month P/E	21.6	P/E on S&P Oper. EPS 2008**E**	21.6	Dividend Rate/Share	Nil	S&P Credit Rating	NA
$10K Invested 5 Yrs Ago	$11,008	Common Shares Outstg. (M)	338.9	Institutional Ownership (%)	85		

Price Performance

30-Week Mov. Avg. · · · 10-Week Mov. Avg. - - **GAAP Earnings vs. Previous Year** Volume Above Avg. STARS
12-Mo. Target Price — Relative Strength — ▲ Up ▼ Down ► No Change Below Avg.

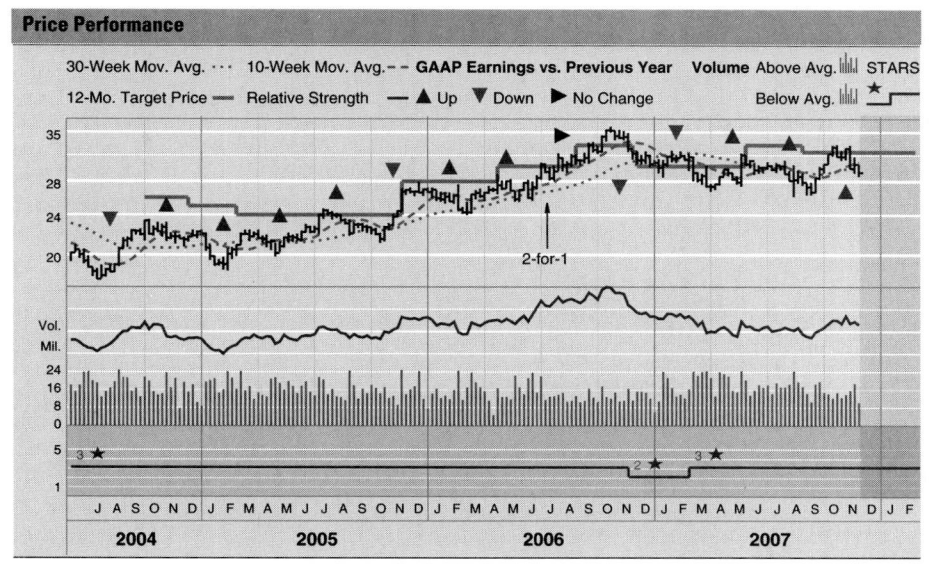

Options: ASE, CBOE, P, Ph

Analysis prepared by **Zaineb Bokhari** on November 20, 2007, when the stock traded at **$ 29.74**.

Highlights

➤ We estimate total revenue will rise 14% in FY 08 (Jul.). We forecast that the consumer tax business will grow 12%, reflecting modest increases in the number of units sold and a stable to modestly higher average selling price. We expect QuickBooks revenue to rise 10%, the midpoint of company guidance, based on our view of a maturing market, and to some extent, competition from Microsoft. We estimate that Digital Insight will add about $302 million in revenue for FY 08. We project revenue growth of about 10% for FY 09.

➤ We expect gross margins to narrow modestly in both FY 08 and FY 09, due to a higher proportion of revenue contribution from services. We also see non-GAAP operating margins narrowing slightly in both years, reflecting Digital Insight's lower operating margin and higher marketing expenses, partially offset by continued growth from INTU's core tax franchise.

➤ Our operating EPS estimate for FY 08 is $1.35, compared to FY 07 operating EPS of $1.23. We expect EPS to be aided by share repurchases under a recent $800 million share repurchase plan. We forecast EPS of $1.53 in FY 09.

Investment Rationale/Risk

➤ Our hold recommendation reflects our expectation that acquisitions will continue to contribute to revenues as INTU's underlying growth rate levels off and competitive pressures mount. We expect FY 08's revenue growth to moderate from FY 07's 17% rise. We believe the increase will be derived from contributions from recent acquisitions, offset by the sale or discontinuation of certain non-core businesses. We think there may be potential integration issues related to the acquisition of Digital Insight. However, we believe the stock is fairly valued at current levels.

➤ Risks to our recommendation and target price include the possibility of increased competition in the consumer tax market and small business accounting segments, and integration problems related to the acquisition of Digital Insight.

➤ Our 12-month target price of $32 is based on a blend of our discounted cash flow (DCF) and P/E analyses. Our DCF model assumes an 11.6% weighted average cost of capital and 3% terminal growth, yielding an intrinsic value of $32. For our P/E analysis, we derive a value of $32 based on an industry P/E to growth ratio of about 1.6X, or 24X our FY 08 EPS estimate.

Qualitative Risk Assessment

LOW	MEDIUM	HIGH

Our risk assessment reflects our view of the company's strong market position within the consumer tax and small business accounting software segments, and its liquid balance sheet. Our optimism is tempered by what we see as challenges that the company faces as it tries to grow beyond its core market segments.

Quantitative Evaluations

S&P Quality Ranking B

D	C	B-	B	B+	A-	A	A+

Relative Strength Rank MODERATE

59

LOWEST = 1 HIGHEST = 99

Revenue/Earnings Data

Revenue (Million $)

	1Q	2Q	3Q	4Q	Year
2008	444.9	--	--	--	--
2007	350.5	750.6	1,139	432.7	2,673
2006	304.1	742.7	952.6	342.9	2,342
2005	266.0	662.6	849.5	301.8	2,038
2004	242.5	636.3	713.0	275.9	1,868
2003	223.3	558.1	634.7	245.1	1,651

Earnings Per Share ($)

	1Q	2Q	3Q	4Q	Year
2008	-0.14	E0.29	E1.29	E-0.07	E1.35
2007	-0.17	0.40	1.04	-0.04	1.25
2006	-0.17	0.43	0.84	-0.06	1.05
2005	-0.11	0.39	0.81	-0.06	1.00
2004	-0.14	0.37	0.67	-0.11	0.79
2003	-0.13	0.29	0.53	-0.06	0.82

Fiscal year ended Jul. 31. Next earnings report expected: Late February. EPS Estimates based on S&P Operating Earnings; historical GAAP earnings are as reported.

Dividend Data

No cash dividends have been paid.

The McGraw-Hill Companies

Intuit Inc

Business Summary November 20, 2007

CORPORATE OVERVIEW. Intuit is a leading provider of accounting, financial management, personal finance and tax software for consumers and small businesses. The company's flagship products include QuickBooks, TurboTax, Lacerte, and Quicken, among others. In FY 06, the company had five business segments including: QuickBooks, Payroll and Payments, Consumer tax, Professional tax and Other Businesses.

QuickBooks products and services (which accounted for 23% of total net revenues in FY 06 (Jul.), down from 25% in FY 05) provide bookkeeping capabilities and business management tools. As part of the company's "Right for Me" strategy, INTU offers QuickBooks Simple Start for very small, less complex businesses; QuickBooks Pro, for slightly larger businesses that have additional payroll needs, QuickBooks Pro for Mac; QuickBooks Premier, to support businesses that need advanced accounting capabilities and business planning tools; and QuickBooks Enterprise Solutions, designed for mid-sized companies. INTU also offers an online version of Quickbooks and Premier and Enterprise versions that cater to specific industries, such as Accountant, Manufacturing and Wholesale, Retail, Non-Profit, Contractor, and Professional Services.

Payroll and Payments (20% and 18%) consist of miscellaneous business management solutions. Outsourced payroll services include QuickBooks Payroll in different varieties and QuickBooks Online Payroll, for use with QuickBooks Online Edition. Direct deposit and electronic tax payment and filing services are available with some of these offerings for additional fees. This segment also includes Innovative Merchant Solutions (IMS), which offers credit card, debit card, electronic benefits, check guarantee and gift card processing, Web-based transaction processing services for online merchants as well as customer service, charge-back retrieval and support, and fraud and loss prevention screening.

The Consumer Tax segment (30% and 28%) is centered on TurboTax. TurboTax software enables individuals and small businesses to prepare and file income tax returns using computers. TurboTax for the Web allows individuals to prepare tax returns online. Versions of TurboTax Premier software are designed to address the special income tax needs of different types of users, including investors, those planning for retirement, and rental property owners. Electronic tax filing services are also provided.

Company Financials Fiscal Year Ended Jul. 31

Per Share Data ($)	2007	2006	2005	2004	2003	2002	2001	2000	1999	1998
Tangible Book Value	0.66	3.41	3.61	2.75	3.44	4.02	4.15	4.00	2.75	2.01
Cash Flow	1.51	1.34	1.31	1.03	0.81	0.30	-0.09	1.23	1.36	0.14
Earnings	1.25	1.05	1.00	0.79	0.82	0.16	-0.24	0.73	0.99	-0.04
S&P Core Earnings	1.19	1.04	0.86	0.61	0.41	NA	-0.32	NA	NA	NA
Dividends	Nil	Nil	Nil	Nil	Nil	Nil	Nil	Nil	Nil	Nil
Payout Ratio	Nil	Nil	Nil	Nil	Nil	Nil	Nil	Nil	Nil	Nil
Prices:High	33.10	35.98	27.97	26.63	26.95	27.52	23.69	45.00	32.00	12.23
Prices:Low	26.14	23.99	18.62	17.92	16.65	17.26	11.31	12.88	11.25	5.65
P/E Ratio:High	26	34	28	34	33	NM	NM	62	32	NM
P/E Ratio:Low	21	23	19	23	20	NM	NM	18	11	NM

Income Statement Analysis (Million $)	2007	2006	2005	2004	2003	2002	2001	2000	1999	1998
Revenue	2,673	2,342	2,038	1,868	1,651	1,358	1,261	1,094	848	593
Operating Income	773	677	659	561	461	343	265	200	254	70.5
Depreciation	135	104	118	97.0	76.5	59.9	59.9	213	141	53.2
Interest Expense	27.1	Nil	Nil	Nil	Nil	Nil	Nil	Nil	Nil	Nil
Pretax Income	696	610	556	453	393	84.9	-96.5	513	617	-19.8
Effective Tax Rate	36.1%	38.0%	32.6%	30.0%	33.0%	17.9%	NM	40.4%	39.0%	NM
Net Income	443	377	375	317	263	69.8	-97.1	306	377	-12.2
S&P Core Earnings	422	372	323	245	172	-0.77	-129	NA	NA	NA

Balance Sheet & Other Financial Data (Million $)	2007	2006	2005	2004	2003	2002	2001	2000	1999	1998
Cash	255	180	83.8	27.2	1,207	452	535	643	950	138
Current Assets	1,952	1,817	1,614	1,517	1,669	1,995	2,148	2,129	1,586	980
Total Assets	4,252	2,770	2,716	2,696	2,790	2,963	2,962	2,879	2,328	1,499
Current Liabilities	1,160	1,016	1,003	857	796	733	788	807	781	375
Long Term Debt	998	15.4	17.5	5.77	29.3	14.6	12.4	0.54	36.3	35.6
Common Equity	2,035	1,738	1,695	1,822	1,965	2,216	2,170	4,143	1,511	1,088
Total Capital	3,034	1,754	1,713	1,828	1,994	2,230	2,182	4,143	1,547	1,124
Capital Expenditures	105	44.6	38.2	52.3	50.4	42.6	77.1	94.9	80.0	69.3
Cash Flow	538	482	493	414	340	130	-37.2	519	518	41.1
Current Ratio	1.7	1.8	1.6	1.8	2.1	2.7	2.7	2.6	2.0	2.6
% Long Term Debt of Capitalization	32.9	0.9	1.0	0.3	1.5	0.7	0.6	0.0	2.3	NA
% Net Income of Revenue	16.6	16.1	18.4	17.0	15.9	5.1	NM	27.9	44.4	NM
% Return on Assets	24.1	13.8	13.8	11.6	9.2	2.4	NM	11.4	19.7	NM
% Return on Equity	23.5	22.0	21.3	16.7	12.6	3.2	NM	8.4	29.0	NM

Data as orig reptd.; bef. results of disc opers/spec. items. Per share data adj. for stk. divs.; EPS diluted. E-Estimated. NA-Not Available. NM-Not Meaningful. NR-Not Ranked. UR-Under Review.

Office: 2700 Coast Ave, Mountain View, CA 94043-1140.
Telephone: 650-944-6000.
Email: investor_relations@intuit.com
Website: http://www.intuit.com

Chrmn: W.V. Campbell
Pres & CEO: S.M. Bennett
Investor Contact: K. Patel (650-944-3560)
SVP & CFO: K. Patel

SVP & CTO: P. Halvorsen
Board Members: S. M. Bennett, C. W. Brody, W. V. Campbell, S. D. Cook, L. J. Doerr, D. Greene, M. R. Hallman, E. Kangas, D. Powell, S. D. Sclavos

Founded: 1984
Domicile: Delaware
Employees: 8,200

ITT Corp

STANDARD &POOR'S

S&P Recommendation BUY ★★★★☆	**Price** $61.17 (as of Nov 23, 2007)	**12-Mo. Target Price** $73.00	**Investment Style** Large-Cap Growth

GICS Sector Industrials
Sub-Industry Industrial Machinery

Summary This company is a diversified industrial manufacturer of advanced technology products.

Key Stock Statistics (Source S&P, Vickers, company reports)

52-Wk Range	$73.44–52.50	S&P Oper. EPS 2007 **E**	3.65	Market Capitalization(B)	$11.077	Beta	1.05
Trailing 12-Month EPS	$3.92	S&P Oper. EPS 2008 **E**	4.10	Yield (%)	0.92	S&P 3-Yr. Proj. EPS CAGR(%)	14.00
Trailing 12-Month P/E	15.6	P/E on S&P Oper. EPS 2007 **E**	16.8	Dividend Rate/Share	$0.56	S&P Credit Rating	BBB+
$10K Invested 5 Yrs Ago	$19,884	Common Shares Outstg. (M)	181.1	Institutional Ownership (%)	79		

Price Performance

30-Week Mov. Avg. ···   10-Week Mov. Avg. - -   **GAAP Earnings vs. Previous Year**   Volume Above Avg. ▐▌▐ STARS
12-Mo. Target Price —   Relative Strength —   ▲ Up   ▼ Down   ► No Change   Below Avg. ▐▌▐ ★

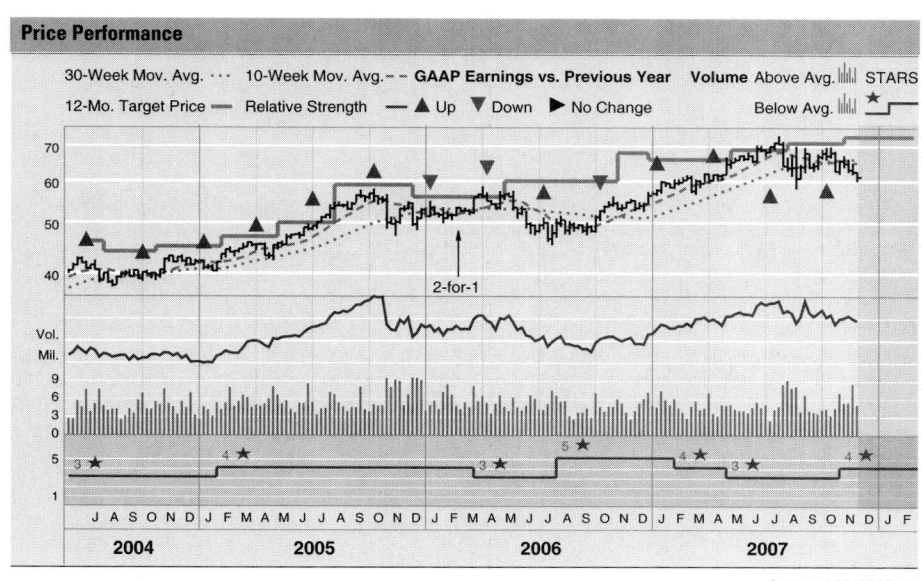

Options: ASE, CBOE, Ph

Analysis prepared by **Efraim Levy, CFA** on November 15, 2007, when the stock traded at **$ 63.84**.

Highlights

➤ Despite the sale of certain operations, we project 9% revenue expansion in 2007. In July, the company sold its switches business. Our forecasts exclude the switches and other divested businesses, but do not assume other divestitures. Rising order flow in most of the company's businesses supports our view that strong end-market demand will help sales increase 10% in 2008.

➤ Aided by higher sales, an improved cost structure, and the absence of certain one-time expenses, operating margins before R&D costs should widen in 2007 and 2008. We expect interest and R&D expenses to rise in both years. We also estimate an unadjusted 27.4% (about 32% adjusted) effective tax rate in 2007, rising to a 32.5% rate in 2008, as the proportion of profits taxed at the relatively higher U.S. statutory tax rate rises.

➤ For the longer term, we expect company revenues to post 8% to 10% average annual growth, reflecting new products, expanded markets, and likely acquisitions. In November, ITT said it expects 8% to 10% revenue growth in the defense segment through its short-term planning horizon.

Investment Rationale/Risk

➤ We believe strong cash flow will support a modest cash dividend, debt reduction, share buybacks and strategic acquisitions. We think the cash dividend payment will be increased on an annual basis. We expect the current $1 billion share buyback authorization to be accretive to 2007 EPS. With long-term debt at less than 15% of capitalization, below that of most peers, the balance sheet appears healthy to us.

➤ Risks to our recommendation and target price include reduced demand at ITT's operating segments, and competitive price pressures.

➤ Our use of a P/E of 17X applied to our 2008 EPS estimate reflects peer and historical P/E comparisons, and leads to a value of about $70. Our discounted cash flow model, which assumes a weighted average cost of capital of 10.7%, compound annual growth of about 6% over the next 15 years, and a terminal growth rate of 4%, generates intrinsic value of about $77. Based on a blend of these metrics, our 12-month target price is $73.

Qualitative Risk Assessment

LOW	MEDIUM	HIGH

Our risk assessment reflects our view of ITT's favorable growth prospects in most of the markets it serves and what we see as strong management and a healthy balance sheet. This is offset by our outlook for U.S. defense spending growth, which we think may slow in coming years.

Quantitative Evaluations

S&P Quality Ranking   B

D	C	B-	B	B+	A-	A	A+

Relative Strength Rank   MODERATE

50

LOWEST = 1   HIGHEST = 99

Revenue/Earnings Data

Revenue (Million $)

	1Q	2Q	3Q	4Q	Year
2007	2,070	2,223	2,181	--	--
2006	1,792	1,964	2,001	2,051	7,808
2005	1,776	1,874	1,828	1,950	7,427
2004	1,511	1,647	1,663	1,943	6,764
2003	1,296	1,438	1,375	1,517	5,627
2002	1,186	1,320	1,235	1,244	4,985

Earnings Per Share ($)

2007	0.74	1.08	0.92	E0.91	E3.65
2006	0.55	0.72	0.75	0.65	2.67
2005	0.65	0.70	0.79	-0.48	1.67
2004	0.47	0.60	0.58	0.66	2.32
2003	0.46	0.49	0.55	0.58	2.08
2002	0.39	0.50	0.50	0.51	2.03

Fiscal year ended Dec. 31. Next earnings report expected: Early February. EPS Estimates based on S&P Operating Earnings; historical GAAP earnings are as reported.

Dividend Data (Dates: mm/dd Payment Date: mm/dd/yy)

Amount ($)	Date Decl.	Ex-Div. Date	Stk. of Record	Payment Date
0.140	02/02	03/07	03/09	04/01/07
0.140	05/08	05/16	05/18	07/01/07
0.140	08/03	08/22	08/24	10/01/07
0.140	10/09	11/14	11/16	01/01/08

Dividends have been paid since 1996. Source: Company reports.

Please read the Required Disclosures and Analyst Certification on the last page of this report.

The McGraw-Hill Companies

ITT Corp

Business Summary November 15, 2007

CORPORATE OVERVIEW. ITT Corp. (name changed from ITT Industries in July 2006) is primarily a producer of defense electronics and fluid technology products.

Fluid technology products (39% of 2006 sales) include pumps, valves, heat exchangers, mixers and fluid measuring instruments and controls for residential, agricultural, commercial, municipal and industrial applications. The fluid technology segment became the world's largest pump manufacturer (formerly third largest) following its 1997 acquisition of Goulds Pumps, Inc.

Defense electronics and services (47%) are sold to the military and to government agencies. Products include traffic control systems, jamming devices that guard military planes against radar guided missiles, digital combat radios, night vision devices, radar, satellite instruments and other. About 83% of segment sales in 2006 were to the U.S. government.

Motion and flow control (14%) products include switches and valves for in-

dustrial and aerospace applications, products for the marine and leisure markets, and fluid handling materials such as tubing systems and connectors for various automotive and industrial markets for the transportation industry.

CORPORATE STRATEGY. The company's strategy is to expand revenues through a combination of internal growth and acquisitions. We expect the company to continue its tradition of successful acquisition integrations.

At the same time, ITT plans to divest operations that do not fit its strategic goals or provide adequate returns. One current example is the 2007 divestiture of the switches components operations, which accounted for about half of the electronics segment's 2006 revenues.

Company Financials Fiscal Year Ended Dec. 31

Per Share Data ($)	2006	2005	2004	2003	2002	2001	2000	1999	1998	1997
Tangible Book Value	1.72	1.38	NM	0.78	NM	NM	NM	NM	2.27	NM
Cash Flow	3.58	2.71	3.37	3.08	2.94	2.37	2.59	2.25	0.43	2.03
Earnings	2.67	1.67	2.32	2.08	2.03	1.20	1.47	1.27	-0.43	0.47
S&P Core Earnings	2.74	2.28	2.13	1.94	0.69	-0.18	NA	NA	NA	NA
Dividends	0.55	0.36	0.34	0.32	0.30	0.30	0.30	0.30	0.30	0.30
Payout Ratio	21%	22%	15%	15%	15%	25%	20%	24%	NM	64%
Prices:High	58.73	58.05	43.36	37.70	35.43	26.00	19.81	20.75	20.44	16.84
Prices:Low	45.34	40.24	35.52	25.06	22.90	17.78	11.19	15.25	14.06	11.06
P/E Ratio:High	22	35	19	18	17	22	13	16	NM	36
P/E Ratio:Low	17	24	15	12	11	15	8	12	NM	24

Income Statement Analysis (Million $)	2006	2005	2004	2003	2002	2001	2000	1999	1998	1997
Revenue	7,808	7,427	6,764	5,627	4,985	4,676	4,829	4,632	4,493	8,777
Operating Income	1,024	985	871	559	706	707	695	592	525	904
Depreciation	172	197	199	188	171	213	202	181	196	378
Interest Expense	86.2	75.0	50.4	Nil	68.8	85.5	93.1	84.8	126	133
Pretax Income	727	448	610	531	509	333	420	370	-160	187
Effective Tax Rate	31.3%	29.8%	28.3%	26.3%	25.3%	35.0%	37.0%	37.0%	NM	39.0%
Net Income	500	314	438	391	380	217	265	233	-98.0	114
S&P Core Earnings	512	429	400	364	129	-31.7	NA	NA	NA	NA

Balance Sheet & Other Financial Data (Million $)	2006	2005	2004	2003	2002	2001	2000	1999	1998	1997
Cash	937	451	263	414	202	121	88.7	182	880	192
Current Assets	3,348	2,772	2,329	2,106	1,701	1,459	1,506	1,628	2,382	2,377
Total Assets	7,430	7,063	7,277	5,938	5,390	4,508	4,611	4,530	5,049	6,221
Current Liabilities	2,759	2,560	2,446	1,687	1,730	1,897	2,233	2,110	2,151	3,545
Long Term Debt	500	516	543	461	492	456	408	479	516	532
Common Equity	3,362	2,723	2,343	1,848	1,137	1,376	1,211	1,099	1,299	822
Total Capital	3,863	3,240	2,886	2,309	1,630	1,832	1,620	1,578	1,815	1,386
Capital Expenditures	177	179	165	154	153	174	181	228	213	460
Cash Flow	671	511	636	579	551	430	466	414	98.0	492
Current Ratio	1.2	1.1	1.0	1.2	1.0	0.8	0.7	0.8	1.1	0.7
% Long Term Debt of Capitalization	13.0	15.9	18.8	20.0	30.2	24.9	25.2	30.3	28.4	38.4
% Net Income of Revenue	6.4	4.2	6.5	6.9	7.6	4.6	5.5	5.0	NM	1.3
% Return on Assets	6.9	4.4	6.6	6.9	7.7	4.8	5.8	4.9	NM	1.9
% Return on Equity	16.1	12.4	20.9	26.2	30.2	16.8	22.9	19.4	NM	14.1

Data as orig reptd.; bef. results of disc opers/spec. items. Per share data adj. for stk. divs.; EPS diluted. E-Estimated. NA-Not Available. NM-Not Meaningful. NR-Not Ranked. UR-Under Review.

Office: 4 West Red Oak Lane, White Plains, NY 10604-3617.
Telephone: 914-641-2000.
Website: http://www.itt.com
Chrmn, Pres & CEO: S.R. Loranger

SVP & CTO: B.L. Reichelderfer
SVP & Treas: D.E. Foley
SVP & General Counsel: V.A. Maffeo
VP & Cntlr: R.J. Pagano, Jr.

Investor Contact: P.J. Milligan
Board Members: C. J. Crawford, C. A. Gold, R. F. Hake, J. J. Hamre, R. W. LeBoeuf, S. R. Loranger, F. T. MacInnis, L. S. Sanford, M. I. Tambakeras

Founded: 1920
Domicile: Indiana
Employees: 37,500

Jabil Circuit Inc

STANDARD &POOR'S

S&P Recommendation **HOLD** ★★★☆☆	Price $17.35 (as of Nov 23, 2007)	12-Mo. Target Price $25.00	Investment Style Large-Cap Growth

GICS Sector Information Technology
Sub-Industry Electronic Manufacturing Services

Summary This company manufactures circuit board assemblies for international OEMs in the PC, peripheral, communications, and automotive markets.

Key Stock Statistics (Source S&P, Vickers, company reports)

52-Wk Range	$29.48– 16.62	S&P Oper. EPS 2008**E**	1.33	Market Capitalization(B)	$3.610	Beta	1.92
Trailing 12-Month EPS	$0.35	S&P Oper. EPS 2009**E**	1.70	Yield (%)	1.61	S&P 3-Yr. Proj. EPS CAGR(%)	15.00
Trailing 12-Month P/E	49.6	P/E on S&P Oper. EPS 2008**E**	13.0	Dividend Rate/Share	$0.28	S&P Credit Rating	BBB-
$10K Invested 5 Yrs Ago	$8,056	Common Shares Outstg. (M)	208.1	Institutional Ownership (%)	88		

Price Performance

30-Week Mov. Avg. · · · 10-Week Mov. Avg. - - **GAAP Earnings vs. Previous Year**   **Volume** Above Avg. STARS
12-Mo. Target Price — Relative Strength — ▲ Up ▼ Down ► No Change   Below Avg. ★

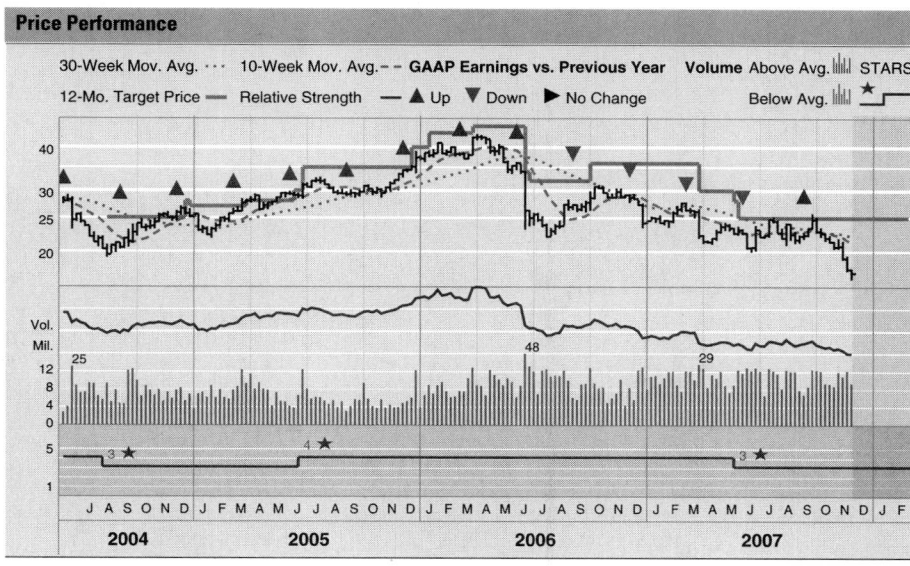

Options: ASE, CBOE, P, Ph

Analysis prepared by **Thomas W. Smith, CFA** on October 12, 2007, when the stock traded at **$ 21.77.**

Highlights

➤ We forecast a 12% revenue increase for FY 08 (Aug.), followed by a rise of 12% for FY 09. We project that recent pressure on consumer segment revenues will extend into FY 08, due to a realignment in operations. We see operational efficiencies and a continued push into low cost geographies offsetting a slowing economy and moderate enterprise spending. JBL benefits from being an industry leader providing end-to-end solutions to a well diversified customer base.

➤ We see gross margins improving to about 7.5% for FY 08, following a dip to 6.6% in FY 07, as higher volumes combine with fewer costs associated with the buildout of its electromechanical business and benefit from restructuring activities at existing facilities. We see restructuring actions continuing in FY 08, along with pressure on operating margins.

➤ We anticipate an effective tax rate of 18%, as we see JBL benefiting from favorable tax jurisdictions in offshore locations. We project FY 08 operating EPS of $1.33, excluding certain one-time charges and including stock-based compensation, and we estimate EPS of $1.70 for FY 09.

Investment Rationale/Risk

➤ We believe the longer-term outlook for the electronic manufacturing services industry remains favorable; however, near term, we think that market segments affected by U.S. consumer and enterprise spending are experiencing a slowdown. In spite of JBL's push to diversify its business mix, the consumer segment accounts for almost 30% of revenues, which creates an overall drag on revenues and margins.

➤ Risks to our recommendation and target price include potential market share losses, delays in the implementation of new contracts and facilities, possible financial restatements resulting from an investigation into the company's stock option granting practices, and acquisition integration risk.

➤ Our 12-month target price of $25 is based mainly on our P/E analysis. Applying a target P/E multiple of 19X, which is below the P/E for Information Technology Sector companies in the S&P 500 Index and above the P/E for electronic manufacturing services (EMS) peers, to our FY 08 operating EPS estimate, we arrive at our 12-month target price of $25.

Qualitative Risk Assessment

LOW	MEDIUM	HIGH

Our risk assessment reflects our view of the historically volatile nature of the electronic manufacturing services industry as well as what we see as the company's relatively high exposure to fluctuations in commodity prices.

Quantitative Evaluations

S&P Quality Ranking B

D	C	B-	**B**	B+	A-	A	A+

Relative Strength Rank WEAK

17

LOWEST = 1   HIGHEST = 99

Revenue/Earnings Data

Revenue (Million $)

	1Q	2Q	3Q	4Q	Year
2007	3,224	2,935	3,002	3,130	12,291
2006	2,404	2,315	2,592	2,954	10,265
2005	1,833	1,716	1,938	2,037	7,524
2004	1,509	1,492	1,626	1,626	6,253
2003	1,068	1,146	1,219	1,296	4,729
2002	884.6	822.1	850.6	988.2	3,545

Earnings Per Share ($)

2007	0.20	0.07	0.03	0.06	0.35
2006	0.37	0.32	0.30	-0.22	0.77
2005	0.27	0.22	0.29	0.34	1.12
2004	0.20	0.19	0.19	0.22	0.81
2003	0.04	0.05	0.02	0.10	0.21
2002	0.04	0.02	0.10	0.01	0.17

Fiscal year ended Aug. 31. Next earnings report expected: NA. EPS Estimates based on S&P Operating Earnings; historical GAAP earnings are as reported.

Dividend Data (Dates: mm/dd Payment Date: mm/dd/yy)

Amount ($)	Date Decl.	Ex-Div. Date	Stk. of Record	Payment Date
0.070	01/22	02/13	02/15	03/01/07
0.070	04/30	05/11	05/15	06/01/07
0.070	08/02	08/13	08/15	09/04/07
0.070	11/01	11/13	11/15	12/03/07

Dividends have been paid since 2006. Source: Company reports.

Jabil Circuit Inc

STANDARD &POOR'S

Business Summary October 12, 2007

CORPORATE OVERVIEW. This provider of electronic manufacturing services (EMS) works with customers in a variety of industries at facilities around the world. Between 2000 and 2005, sales doubled to more than $7.5 billion, with the vast majority of the growth generated internally.

In FY 06 (Aug.), Nokia Corp. and Royal Philips Electronics were the only customers accounting for greater than 10% of sales, with Nokia Corp. at 21% and Royal Philips at 12%. In 2005, 40 customers accounted for 90% of JBL's revenues, with Nokia at 13%, Royal Philips at 14%, and Hewlett-Packard at 10%. We think the 2006 acquisition of Taiwan Greenpoint enhanced JBL's position with most of its existing customers, and brought higher operating margins to JBL's core business.

MARKET PROFILE. We believe the EMS industry remains well positioned to capture new business from original equipment manufacturers (OEMs). This is due to our view that the cost advantages associated with the outsourcing model are beginning to be understood by potential participants. We think the benefits of this strategy are ample, with companies being able to reduce costs and reallocate resources toward their core competencies (e.g., marketing and research and development). We see the industry growing at a low double digit annual rate over the next several years and achieving nearly $180 billion in revenue by 2009.

We see a number of key trends emerging in the EMS landscape. For instance, OEMs have begun to limit the number of EMS providers with which they conduct business. We think this move results from the customer's desire to streamline its operations. While in the past, they may have utilized five or six vendors, many now seek to limit that total to just one or two. We believe this development bodes well for larger EMS companies such as JBL, as their broad range of service offerings and worldwide presence enable them to fulfill an entire slate of customer requests.

Company Financials Fiscal Year Ended Aug. 31

Per Share Data ($)	2007	2006	2005	2004	2003	2002	2001	2000	1999	1998
Tangible Book Value	5.97	8.26	8.22	7.29	6.06	6.63	6.43	6.68	3.32	1.67
Cash Flow	1.51	1.71	2.18	1.89	1.32	1.11	1.35	1.31	0.90	0.60
Earnings	0.35	0.77	1.12	0.81	0.21	0.17	0.59	0.78	0.56	0.37
S&P Core Earnings	0.35	0.77	0.64	0.59	0.04	NA	0.46	NA	NA	NA
Dividends	0.28	0.14	Nil	Nil	Nil	Nil	Nil	Nil	Nil	Nil
Payout Ratio	80%	18%	Nil	Nil	Nil	Nil	Nil	Nil	Nil	Nil
Prices:High	27.86	43.70	39.00	32.40	31.66	26.79	40.99	68.00	38.97	18.72
Prices:Low	16.62	22.01	21.80	19.18	21.20	11.13	14.00	18.63	14.25	5.75
P/E Ratio:High	80	57	35	40	NM	NM	69	87	70	51
P/E Ratio:Low	47	29	19	24	NM	65	24	24	25	16

Income Statement Analysis (Million $)	2007	2006	2005	2004	2003	2002	2001	2000	1999	1998
Revenue	12,291	10,265	7,524	6,253	4,729	3,545	4,331	3,558	2,000	1,277
Operating Income	494	522	507	439	369	296	353	317	197	142
Depreciation	240	199	220	222	224	188	155	99.3	56.0	35.7
Interest Expense	86.1	23.5	24.8	19.4	17.0	13.1	5.86	7.61	1.69	3.12
Pretax Income	94.5	225	276	198	37.0	44.8	166	213	140	82.0
Effective Tax Rate	22.6%	26.9%	16.1%	15.5%	NM	22.4%	28.7%	31.5%	34.4%	30.6%
Net Income	73.2	165	232	167	43.0	34.7	119	146	91.5	56.9
S&P Core Earnings	73.9	165	134	122	8.12	-0.11	93.4	NA	NA	NA

Balance Sheet & Other Financial Data (Million $)	2007	2006	2005	2004	2003	2002	2001	2000	1999	1998
Cash	664	774	796	621	700	641	431	338	114	23.1
Current Assets	3,666	3,679	2,686	2,183	2,094	1,588	1,447	1,387	588	290
Total Assets	6,295	5,412	4,077	3,329	3,245	2,548	2,358	2,018	921	527
Current Liabilities	2,991	2,701	1,568	1,159	1,263	593	505	692	331	187
Long Term Debt	760	330	327	305	297	355	362	25.0	33.3	81.7
Common Equity	2,443	2,294	2,135	1,819	1,588	1,507	1,414	1,270	546	248
Total Capital	3,226	2,632	2,462	2,125	1,905	1,903	1,813	1,323	588	338
Capital Expenditures	302	280	257	218	117	85.5	309	333	150	99.8
Cash Flow	313	363	452	389	267	223	274	245	147	92.6
Current Ratio	1.2	1.4	1.7	1.9	1.7	2.7	2.9	2.0	1.8	1.6
% Long Term Debt of Capitalization	23.6	12.5	13.3	14.4	15.6	18.6	20.0	1.9	5.7	24.2
% Net Income of Revenue	0.6	1.6	3.1	2.7	0.9	1.0	2.7	4.1	4.6	4.5
% Return on Assets	1.3	3.5	6.3	5.1	1.5	1.4	5.4	9.5	12.7	12.2
% Return on Equity	3.1	7.4	11.7	9.8	2.8	2.4	8.8	15.8	23.0	26.5

Data as orig reptd.; bef. results of disc opers/spec. items. Per share data adj. for stk. divs.; EPS diluted. E-Estimated. NA-Not Available. NM-Not Meaningful. NR-Not Ranked. UR-Under Review.

Office: 10560 Dr. Martin Luther King Jr. Street North, St. Petersburg, FL 33716.
Telephone: 727-577-9749.
Email: investor_relations@jabil.com
Website: http://www.jabil.com

Chrmn: W.D. Morean
Pres & CEO: T.L. Main
Vice Chrmn: T.A. Sansone
COO: M. Mondello

Investor Contact: B. Walters (727-803-3349)
Board Members: L. S. Grafstein, M. S. Lavitt, T. L. Main, W. D. Morean, L. J. Murphy, F. A. Newman, S. A. Raymund, T. A. Sansone, K. A. Walters

Founded: 1969
Domicile: Delaware
Employees: 61,000

Jacobs Engineering Group Inc.

STANDARD
&POOR'S

S&P Recommendation	STRONG BUY ★★★★★	Price $77.61 (as of Nov 23, 2007)	12-Mo. Target Price $106.00	Investment Style Large-Cap Growth

GICS Sector Industrials
Sub-Industry Construction & Engineering

Summary This company provides engineering, construction and maintenance services to private industry and federal government agencies on a worldwide basis.

Key Stock Statistics (Source S&P, Vickers, company reports)

52-Wk Range	$89.64– 38.25	S&P Oper. EPS 2008**E**	3.05	Market Capitalization(B)	$9.306	Beta	0.61
Trailing 12-Month EPS	$2.35	S&P Oper. EPS 2009**E**	3.65	Yield (%)	Nil	S&P 3-Yr. Proj. EPS CAGR(%)	22.00
Trailing 12-Month P/E	33.0	P/E on S&P Oper. EPS 2008**E**	25.4	Dividend Rate/Share	Nil	S&P Credit Rating	NA
$10K Invested 5 Yrs Ago	$48,071	Common Shares Outstg. (M)	119.9	Institutional Ownership (%)	84		

Price Performance

30-Week Mov. Avg. ··· 10-Week Mov. Avg. - - **GAAP Earnings vs. Previous Year** **Volume** Above Avg. ▐▐▌ **STARS**
12-Mo. Target Price — Relative Strength — ▲ Up ▼ Down ▶ No Change Below Avg. ▐▐▌ ★ ▗▗

Options: ASE, CBOE, Ph

Analysis prepared by **Stewart Scharf** on November 08, 2007, when the stock traded at **$ 87.01**.

Highlights

➤ We expect total revenues to rise close to 20% in FY 08 (Sep.), mainly reflecting strong demand for upstream oil & gas and downstream petroleum refining projects, chemical projects in the Middle East and Europe, environmental nuclear cleanup work in the U.K. and U.S. defense work, and public transportation infrastructure projects.

➤ In our view, gross margins will continue to widen during FY 08, albeit at a slower rate, from 14.3% in FY 07, as the mix gradually shifts toward the lower-margin construction phase from professional services. We expect operating margins to improve on increased global engineering work at low-cost centers mainly in India, higher wage rates and synergies from acquisitions; we expect SG&A expenses (largely salaries) to stabilize at less than 10.5% of revenues as the field services mix increases.

➤ We project an unchanged effective tax rate of about 36% in FY 08, and EPS of $3.05 for FY 08, advancing 20%, to $3.65 in FY 09. JEC continues to target average annual growth of at least 15%.

Investment Rationale/Risk

➤ We maintain our strong buy recommendation, based on our view that favorable core market trends will lead to increased capital spending for projects worldwide, as well as our valuation metrics.

➤ Risks to our recommendation and target price include a downturn in some core markets; project delays or cancellations due in part to customer liquidity issues; an inability to offset a shortage of skilled labor via outsourcing overseas; and a lack of acquisition opportunities.

➤ Our discounted cash flow (DCF) model suggests that the stock is more than 20% below our intrinsic value estimate of $113, assuming a perpetual growth rate of 4% and a weighted average cost of capital of about 8%. Based on our view of favorable prospects in almost all of its markets, JEC's low-risk relationship-based business model, and above historical average projected earnings growth, we think the stock deserves a premium P/E to peers of 32X our FY 08 EPS estimate, targeting a value of $98. Blending these metrics, we arrive at our 12-month target price of $106.

Qualitative Risk Assessment

LOW	MEDIUM	HIGH

Our risk assessment reflects the cyclical nature of the company's various markets, its growth by acquisition strategy, changes in global political conditions, timing issues related to new awards, and fluctuations in interest rates and foreign currencies. These factors are offset by what we see as JEC's strong cash position and virtually no debt.

Quantitative Evaluations

S&P Quality Ranking B+

D	C	B-	B	B+	A-	A	A+

Relative Strength Rank STRONG

77

LOWEST = 1 HIGHEST = 99

Revenue/Earnings Data

Revenue (Million $)

	1Q	2Q	3Q	4Q	Year
2007	2,019	2,092	2,084	2,280	8,474
2006	1,683	1,832	1,926	1,979	7,421
2005	1,283	1,383	1,449	1,519	5,635
2004	1,135	1,124	1,120	1,216	4,594
2003	1,135	1,203	1,131	1,063	4,616
2002	1,028	1,147	1,169	1,212	4,556

Earnings Per Share ($)

2007	0.51	0.55	0.61	0.68	2.35
2006	0.36	0.37	0.42	0.49	1.64
2005	0.28	0.31	0.34	0.36	1.29
2004	0.29	0.31	0.26	0.26	1.13
2003	0.29	0.28	0.29	0.29	1.14
2002	0.24	0.25	0.25	0.26	0.99

Fiscal year ended Sep. 30. Next earnings report expected: Late January. EPS Estimates based on S&P Operating Earnings; historical GAAP earnings are as reported.

Dividend Data (Dates: mm/dd Payment Date: mm/dd/yy)

Amount ($)	Date Decl.	Ex-Div. Date	Stk. of Record	Payment Date
2-for-1 Stk.	01/26	03/16	02/15	03/15/07

Source: Company reports.

Please read the Required Disclosures and Analyst Certification on the last page of this report.

Jacobs Engineering Group Inc.

STANDARD &POOR'S

Business Summary November 08, 2007

CORPORATE OVERVIEW. Jacobs Engineering focuses on providing a broad range of technical, professional and construction services to a large number of industrial, commercial and governmental clients worldwide. The company offers project services; consulting services; operations and maintenance services; and construction services via offices primarily in North America, Europe, Asia and Australia.

In FY 07 (Sep.), revenues by sector were: chemicals, 15%; buildings, 5%; national government (environmental, defense and NASA), 18%; pharmaBio (pharmaceutical and biotech), 9%; oil & gas (upstream), 11%; refining (downstream), 30%; infrastructure, 8%; and pulp and paper, high tech, food, consumer products, 4%. Technical professional services accounted for 52% of revenues, with the balance derived from field services. At September 30, 2007, total backlog was $13.6 billion, up 39% from $9.8 billion a year earlier, reflecting new awards for federal and petroleum projects. JEC expects solid and steady backlog growth to continue during FY 08 (Sep.), although quarterly backlog could be uneven. We think this is normal for E&C companies, and, in our view, projections should be based on full fiscal year comparisons. The company expects about 65% of its backlog to be realized as revenues within the next fiscal year. In FY 07, about 40% of revenues were generated from operations outside of the U.S., up from 35% in FY 06.

Project services include the engineering and design of process plants and high-technology facilities. Construction services offers traditional field services to private and public sector clients. Process, scientific and systems consulting includes market analyses to determine the feasibility of a project. Operations and maintenance services include all tasks required to keep a process plant in day-to-day operation.

In FY 06 (latest available), revenues derived from agencies of the U.S. government accounted for 16.4% of the total, down from over 21% in FY 05. JEC sees total federal contracts (40%) gradually rising to 50% of its business. In FY 06, Valero Energy Corp. accounted for in excess of 10% of JEC's total revenues.

In FY 06, stock option expense was $0.08 a share (adjusted for a 2-for-1 split in March 2007). FY 06 EPS of $1.64 included a $0.03 tax benefit. At the end of FY 06, the company's pension plans were underfunded by $184 million, down from $229 million a year earlier.

Company Financials Fiscal Year Ended Sep. 30

Per Share Data ($)	2007	2006	2005	2004	2003	2002	2001	2000	1999	1998
Tangible Book Value	NA	7.36	5.10	4.04	4.00	2.73	2.55	2.15	1.95	2.87
Cash Flow	NA	2.04	1.70	1.44	1.45	1.31	1.16	0.86	0.92	0.74
Earnings	2.35	1.64	1.29	1.13	1.14	0.99	0.81	0.48	0.62	0.52
S&P Core Earnings	NA	1.68	1.16	1.02	0.91	0.75	0.53	NA	NA	NA
Dividends	Nil	Nil	Nil	Nil	Nil	Nil	Nil	Nil	Nil	Nil
Payout Ratio	Nil	Nil	Nil	Nil	Nil	Nil	Nil	Nil	Nil	Nil
Prices:High	89.64	46.64	34.71	24.11	24.97	21.45	18.92	12.30	10.69	10.19
Prices:Low	38.25	33.90	22.33	18.43	17.48	13.05	10.56	6.55	7.31	6.19
P/E Ratio:High	38	29	27	21	22	22	24	25	17	20
P/E Ratio:Low	16	21	17	16	15	13	13	14	12	12

Income Statement Analysis (Million $)										
Revenue	NA	7,421	5,635	4,594	4,616	4,556	3,957	3,419	2,875	2,101
Operating Income	NA	350	288	232	232	207	183	165	140	110
Depreciation	NA	48.3	46.4	34.2	35.4	35.1	38.9	40.1	31.6	23.2
Interest Expense	NA	7.50	6.47	3.57	3.25	7.50	11.7	11.4	8.77	2.36
Pretax Income	NA	305	236	198	197	169	138	81.3	105	88.8
Effective Tax Rate	NA	35.5%	36.0%	35.0%	35.0%	35.0%	36.5%	37.3%	37.4%	38.7%
Net Income	NA	197	151	129	128	110	87.8	51.0	65.4	54.4
S&P Core Earnings	NA	202	136	118	102	82.3	57.5	NA	NA	NA

Balance Sheet & Other Financial Data (Million $)										
Cash	NA	434	240	100	126	48.5	49.3	65.8	53.5	101
Current Assets	NA	1,818	1,337	1,084	970	975	946	851	730	566
Total Assets	NA	2,854	2,354	2,071	1,671	1,674	1,557	1,384	1,220	807
Current Liabilities	NA	1,041	785	686	611	740	701	684	585	368
Long Term Debt	NA	77.7	89.6	78.8	17.8	85.7	164	147	135	26.2
Common Equity	NA	1,423	1,141	1,005	842	690	592	496	449	371
Total Capital	NA	1,508	1,237	1,089	865	781	761	648	590	404
Capital Expenditures	NA	54.0	43.9	37.1	25.8	37.2	28.8	44.4	39.0	46.3
Cash Flow	NA	245	197	163	163	145	127	91.1	97.0	77.6
Current Ratio	NA	1.7	1.7	1.6	1.6	1.3	1.4	1.2	1.2	1.5
% Long Term Debt of Capitalization	NA	5.2	7.2	7.2	2.1	11.0	21.6	22.7	22.9	6.5
% Net Income of Revenue	NA	2.7	2.7	2.8	2.8	2.4	2.2	1.5	2.3	2.6
% Return on Assets	NA	7.5	6.8	6.9	7.7	6.8	6.0	3.9	6.5	7.0
% Return on Equity	NA	15.2	14.1	14.0	16.7	17.1	16.1	10.8	16.0	15.6

Data as orig reptd.; bef. results of disc opers/spec. items. Per share data adj. for stk. divs.; EPS diluted. E-Estimated. NA-Not Available. NM-Not Meaningful. NR-Not Ranked. UR-Under Review.

Office: 1111 South Arroyo Parkway, Pasadena, CA, USA 91105.
Telephone: 626-578-3500.
Website: http://www.jacobs.com
Chrmn: N.G. Watson

Pres & CEO: C.L. Martin
Investor Contact: J.W. Prosser, Jr. (626-578-6803)
EVP & Treas: J.W. Prosser, Jr.
SVP, Secy & General Counsel: W.C. Markley, III

Board Members: J. R. Bronson, R. C. Davidson, Jr., E. V. Fritzky, R. B. Gwyn, L. K. Jacobs, J. P. Jumper, D. R. Laurance, L. F. Levinson, C. Martin, B. F. Montoya, T. M. Niles, T., N. G. Watson
Founded: 1957
Domicile: Delaware
Employees: 43,800

The McGraw-Hill Companies

Janus Capital Group Inc.

STANDARD &POOR'S

S&P Recommendation HOLD ★★★☆☆	**Price** $30.39 (as of Nov 23, 2007)	**12-Mo. Target Price** $36.00	**Investment Style** Large-Cap Blend

GICS Sector Financials
Sub-Industry Asset Management & Custody Banks

Summary Janus is a U.S.-based investment management company that focuses on growth equity and quantitative strategies.

Key Stock Statistics (Source S&P, Vickers, company reports)

52-Wk Range	$37.08–19.35	S&P Oper. EPS 2007E	1.09	Market Capitalization(B)	$5.330	Beta	1.93
Trailing 12-Month EPS	$0.71	S&P Oper. EPS 2008E	1.65	Yield (%)	0.13	S&P 3-Yr. Proj. EPS CAGR(%)	18.00
Trailing 12-Month P/E	42.8	P/E on S&P Oper. EPS 2007E	27.9	Dividend Rate/Share	$0.04	S&P Credit Rating	BBB+
$10K Invested 5 Yrs Ago	$20,308	Common Shares Outstg. (M)	175.4	Institutional Ownership (%)	NM		

Price Performance

30-Week Mov. Avg. · · · 10-Week Mov. Avg. - - **GAAP Earnings vs. Previous Year** **Volume** Above Avg. |l|l| **STARS**
12-Mo. Target Price — Relative Strength — ▲ Up ▼ Down ► No Change Below Avg. |l|l| ★

Options: CBOE, P, Ph

Analysis prepared by **Matthew Albrecht** on November 06, 2007, when the stock traded at **$ 36.26**.

Highlights

➤ We think Janus has improved its fund performance in recent years, and investors have taken notice. The company posted positive fund flows to its long-term funds for the second consecutive quarter in the third quarter of 2007, helped by investors' recent preference for growth funds. We think growth at INTECH, although in generally lower-margined quantitative funds, should continue to support growth. We anticipate assets under management will increase more than 30% in 2007, followed by 20% growth in 2008. We look for revenues to advance at a slower pace, however, as the its fee capture rate declines.

➤ We anticipate a slight reduction in compensation as a percentage of net revenues in 2007, before an increase in 2008. We look for the removal of costs associated with the for-sale printing and fulfillment operation to be the major driver of a pretax margin expansion in 2007 and 2008, despite stable expenditures for marketing and general and administrative needs.

➤ We forecast EPS of $1.09 in 2007 and $1.65 in 2008, as significant share repurchases support earnings over both years.

Investment Rationale/Risk

➤ As of September 30, 2007, 89% and 73% of the company's primary retail fund family were in the top half of their categories on a one-year and three-year performance basis, respectively, which we believe should help attract additional capital in the quarters to come. Client redemptions in legacy products have only recently been stemmed, however. We view Janus's corporate governance negatively; we would like to see a higher proportion of independent directors. Although the stock trades at a premium multiple to peers, a recent investor shift to growth products and the company's strong fund performance of late suggests to us that it deserves its lofty multiple.

➤ Risks to our recommendation and target price include potential equity and bond market depreciation, and increasing competition.

➤ The shares recently traded at 32.8X our 2007 EPS estimate, a wide premium to the peer group average. Our 12-month target price of $36 is equal to 21.8X our 2008 EPS estimate, which is more closely aligned with peers.

Qualitative Risk Assessment

LOW	MEDIUM	**HIGH**

Our risk assessment reflects the company's lack of product diversification, previous regulatory issues, and turnover of investment personnel.

Quantitative Evaluations

S&P Quality Ranking NR

D	C	B-	B	B+	A-	A	A+

Relative Strength Rank MODERATE

56

LOWEST = 1   HIGHEST = 99

Revenue/Earnings Data

Revenue (Million $)

	1Q	2Q	3Q	4Q	Year
2007	271.4	294.9	284.6	--	--
2006	256.1	254.6	250.1	265.9	1,027
2005	239.0	229.3	237.5	247.3	953.1
2004	274.4	258.8	237.8	239.8	1,011
2003	231.2	245.5	256.6	261.4	994.7
2002	328.3	310.4	257.8	248.3	1,145

Earnings Per Share ($)

	1Q	2Q	3Q	4Q	Year
2007	0.19	0.27	0.29	E0.34	E1.09
2006	0.17	0.15	0.15	0.19	0.66
2005	0.09	0.12	0.15	0.05	0.40
2004	-0.10	0.54	0.20	0.08	0.73
2003	0.17	0.22	0.24	3.51	4.17
2002	0.42	0.30	-0.60	0.20	0.38

Fiscal year ended Dec. 31. Next earnings report expected: Late January. EPS Estimates based on S&P Operating Earnings; historical GAAP earnings are as reported.

Dividend Data (Dates: mm/dd Payment Date: mm/dd/yy)

Amount ($)	Date Decl.	Ex-Div. Date	Stk. of Record	Payment Date
0.040	05/01	05/16	05/18	05/31/07

Dividends have been paid since 2000. Source: Company reports.

Please read the Required Disclosures and Analyst Certification on the last page of this report.

The McGraw·Hill Companies

Janus Capital Group Inc.

STANDARD &POOR'S

Business Summary November 06, 2007

CORPORATE OVERVIEW. Janus Capital Group, a single-branded global asset management company, was created through the January 1, 2003 merger of Janus Capital Corp. into its parent company, Stilwell Financial Inc., which had been spun off from Kansas City Southern Industries in July 2000 via a stock offering. The company had total assets under management of nearly $168 billion at the end of 2006, down from $193 billion at the end of 2001. The company distributes its products through one global distribution network directly to investors, and through advisers and financial intermediaries.

Wholly owned Janus Capital Management focuses on growth equities, and uses both fundamental and quantitative investment research. It also offers core, international, specialty fixed-income, and money market products. Its largest funds include Janus Fund (JANSX), Janus Worldwide (JAWWX) and Janus Twenty (JAVLX).

The company owns 82.5% of Enhanced Investment Technologies, LLC (INTECH), which focuses on mathematically driven equity investing strategies. INTECH's assets under management totaled about $62 billion at the end of 2006, up from $7.3 billion at the end of 2002. INTECH, which manages assets for large institutions and endowments, seeks to achieve long-term returns

that outperform a passive index, while controlling risks and trading costs.

JNS owns about 30% of Perkins, Wolf, McDonnell and Co., which focuses on value investing and sub-advises a number of Janus's small- and mid-cap value products. Bay Isle employs a bottom-up analysis, with a focus on what it believes to be quality companies that trade at discounts to their fair market value. Vontobel Asset Management is a sub-adviser for several Janus mutual funds and products, focusing on value equities.

In December 2003, JNS exchanged 32.3 million DST Systems shares for all shares of a DST unit, referred to as JCG Partners, which owns a commercial printing business worth about $115 million, and has $999 million in cash. In December 2003, JNS said it would no longer use the equity method to account for its remaining investment. In 2004, JNS sold its remaining 7.4 million shares of DST stock.

Company Financials Fiscal Year Ended Dec. 31

Per Share Data ($)	2006	2005	2004	2003	2002	2001	2000	1999	1998	1997
Tangible Book Value	NM	0.88	1.43	1.00	NM	NM	3.50	NA	NA	NA
Cash Flow	0.93	0.64	0.99	4.46	0.70	1.93	3.30	1.51	NA	NA
Earnings	0.66	0.40	0.73	4.17	0.38	1.31	2.90	1.31	NA	NA
S&P Core Earnings	0.57	0.42	0.32	1.60	0.42	1.18	NA	NA	NA	NA
Dividends	0.04	0.04	0.04	0.04	0.05	0.04	0.01	NA	NA	NA
Payout Ratio	6%	10%	5%	1%	13%	3%	NM	NA	NA	NA
Prices:High	24.20	20.59	17.90	19.00	29.24	46.63	54.50	NA	NA	NA
Prices:Low	15.50	12.75	12.60	9.46	8.97	18.20	30.75	NA	NA	NA
P/E Ratio:High	37	51	25	5	77	36	19	NA	NA	NA
P/E Ratio:Low	23	32	17	2	24	14	11	NA	NA	NA

Income Statement Analysis (Million $)										
Revenue	1,027	953	1,011	995	1,145	1,556	2,248	1,212	671	485
Operating Income	267	224	264	396	441	872	1,118	554	297	212
Depreciation	47.1	50.1	60.4	67.6	72.3	131	81.2	35.4	16.8	13.1
Interest Expense	32.3	28.6	38.4	60.5	57.8	34.8	7.70	5.90	6.50	10.4
Pretax Income	237	176	272	895	320	620	1,202	587	289	230
Effective Tax Rate	34.5%	38.6%	33.9%	NM	72.6%	35.1%	35.5%	36.8%	35.8%	37.8%
Net Income	134	87.8	170	956	84.7	302	664	313	152	118
S&P Core Earnings	117	92.5	74.1	367	92.4	276	NA	NA	NA	NA

Balance Sheet & Other Financial Data (Million $)										
Cash	560	553	527	1,223	161	237	364	324	139	NA
Current Assets	925	1,004	1,065	1,466	346	478	641	525	259	NA
Total Assets	3,538	3,629	3,768	4,332	3,322	3,392	1,581	1,232	823	NA
Current Liabilities	186	268	155	301	185	881	196	163	71.1	NA
Long Term Debt	537	262	378	769	856	400	Nil	Nil	16.6	NA
Common Equity	2,306	2,581	2,735	2,661	1,508	1,363	1,058	815	540	NA
Total Capital	3,261	3,283	3,553	3,997	3,097	2,466	1,342	1,024	710	NA
Capital Expenditures	17.0	23.6	26.5	23.9	16.3	34.3	107	50.5	35.0	NA
Cash Flow	181	138	230	1,023	157	433	745	348	169	NA
Current Ratio	5.0	3.7	6.9	4.9	1.9	0.5	3.3	3.2	3.6	NA
% Long Term Debt of Capitalization	16.5	8.0	10.6	19.2	27.6	16.2	Nil	Nil	2.3	NA
% Net Income of Revenue	13.0	9.2	16.8	96.1	7.4	19.4	29.5	25.8	22.7	NA
% Return on Assets	3.7	2.4	4.2	25.0	2.5	12.2	47.2	30.5	NA	NA
% Return on Equity	5.5	3.3	6.3	45.9	5.9	25.0	70.9	46.2	NA	NA

Data as orig reptd.; bef. results of disc opers/spec. items. Per share data adj. for stk. divs.; EPS diluted. E-Estimated. NA-Not Available. NM-Not Meaningful. NR-Not Ranked. UR-Under Review.

Office: 151 Detroit St, Denver, CO 80206-4928.
Telephone: 303-333-3863.
Website: http://www.janus.com
Chrmn: S.L. Scheid

CEO: G.D. Black
EVP & CFO: D.R. Martin
SVP & Cntlr: G.A. Frost

Board Members: P. F. Balser, G. D. Black, G. A. Cox, J. R. Fredericks, D. R. Gatzek, R. T. Parry, J. Patton, L. H. Rowland, S. L. Scheid, R. Skidelsky

Founded: 1998
Domicile: Delaware
Employees: 1,518

The McGraw-Hill Companies

STANDARD &POOR'S

JDS Uniphase Corp

S&P Recommendation	HOLD ★★★☆☆	Price	12-Mo. Target Price	Investment Style
		$12.95 (as of Nov 23, 2007)	$15.00	Large-Cap Blend

GICS Sector Information Technology
Sub-Industry Communications Equipment

Summary This company manufactures fiber optic products and communications test and measurement solutions.

Key Stock Statistics (Source S&P, Vickers, company reports)

52-Wk Range	$19.15– 12.41	S&P Oper. EPS 2008**E**	0.36	Market Capitalization(B)	$2.741	Beta	2.60
Trailing 12-Month EPS	$-0.07	S&P Oper. EPS 2009**E**	0.70	Yield (%)	Nil	S&P 3-Yr. Proj. EPS CAGR(%)	22.00
Trailing 12-Month P/E	NM	P/E on S&P Oper. EPS 2008**E**	36.0	Dividend Rate/Share	Nil	S&P Credit Rating	NA
$10K Invested 5 Yrs Ago	$5,213	Common Shares Outstg. (M)	211.7	Institutional Ownership (%)	78		

Price Performance

30-Week Mov. Avg. ···· 10-Week Mov. Avg. – – **GAAP Earnings vs. Previous Year** Volume Above Avg. STARS
12-Mo. Target Price — Relative Strength — ▲ Up ▼ Down ► No Change Below Avg. ★

Options: ASE, CBOE, P, Ph

Analysis prepared by **Ari Bensinger** on November 01, 2007, when the stock traded at **$ 14.66**.

Highlights

➤ Following a 16% sales increase in FY 07 (Jun.), we see sales advancing 8% in FY 08. Demand for optical communication products, particularly tunable laser and ROADMs, should benefit from accelerated buildouts of broadband networks. Recent sales growth has been hampered by weak optical component sales, as customers work through excess inventory. JDSU continues to expand its test and measurement business toward IP network services.

➤ The company is in the midst of a major restructuring program. As a result of a favorable product mix and continued cost cutting, we believe FY 08 gross margins will widen to the 40% level, up from the 37% registered in FY 07, albeit lower than the industry average of the mid-40% area. We expect operating expenses as a percentage of sales to decline moderately from the level of FY 07.

➤ After minimal taxes due to loss carryovers and higher interest income, we forecast FY 08 operating EPS of $0.36, versus the $0.18 of FY 07. Our FY 08 estimate includes projected stock option expense of $0.16.

Investment Rationale/Risk

➤ We see JDSU benefiting from increased demand for optical systems and test measurement systems as service operators expand their network bandwidth capabilities and begin to offer triple play services. However, we expect sales growth to fluctuate quarter to quarter, reflecting the uneven timing of carrier network rollouts. We see significant operating leverage in the company's business model, and believe earnings can ramp materially over the next two years.

➤ Risks to our recommendation and target price include a decline in capital spending by telecom operators, market share losses, and slower than expected margin improvement.

➤ Our 12-month target price of $15 is largely based on a forward P/E of 21X applied to our FY 09 EPS estimate of $0.70, which we view as a more normalized earnings level for the company given the restructuring initiatives under way. Our target price also reflects 2.2X our FY 08 sales per share estimate, below the industry average. We think this discount is warranted by our view of JDSU's inconsistencies in its operations.

Qualitative Risk Assessment

LOW	MEDIUM	HIGH

Our risk assessment reflects the highly competitive nature of the industry, the company's dependence on telecom carrier spending, which tends to be uneven due to the uncertain timing of network projects and upgrades, and a high degree of stock price volatility.

Quantitative Evaluations

S&P Quality Ranking C

D	C	B-	B	B+	A-	A	A+

Relative Strength Rank MODERATE

34

LOWEST = 1 HIGHEST = 99

Revenue/Earnings Data

Revenue (Million $)

	1Q	2Q	3Q	4Q	Year
2008	356.7	--	--	--	--
2007	318.1	366.3	361.7	350.7	1,397
2006	258.3	312.9	314.9	318.2	1,204
2005	194.5	180.5	166.3	170.9	712.2
2004	147.4	152.6	161.4	174.5	635.9
2003	193.0	156.6	165.7	160.6	675.9

Earnings Per Share ($)

	1Q	2Q	3Q	4Q	Year
2008	-0.03	E0.07	E0.09	E0.14	E0.36
2007	-0.08	0.10	-0.07	-0.08	-0.12
2006	-0.32	-0.24	0.02	-0.24	-0.72
2005	-0.16	-0.24	-0.24	-0.80	-1.44
2004	-0.16	-0.32	-0.08	-0.16	-0.64
2003	-2.96	-1.20	-0.80	-0.32	-5.28

Fiscal year ended Jun. 30. Next earnings report expected: Early February. EPS Estimates based on S&P Operating Earnings; historical GAAP earnings are as reported.

Dividend Data

No cash dividends have been paid.

The **McGraw-Hill** Companies

JDS Uniphase Corp

**STANDARD
&POOR'S**

Business Summary November 01, 2007

CORPORATE OVERVIEW. JDS Uniphase supplies optical components, as well as communications test and measurement solutions for the communications market. The company also leverages its optical science capabilities on non-communications applications, offering products for display, security, medical environmental instrumentation, decorative, aerospace and defense applications.

The company operates in three principal segments: optical communications, (37% of FY 07 (Jun.)revenue); communications test and measurement (44%); and advanced optical technologies (12%). In addition, the commercial lasers business unit accounted for approximately 7% of net revenue in FY 07.

PRIMARY BUSINESS DYNAMICS. JDSU supplies the basic building blocks for fiber optic networks, which enable the rapid transmission of large amounts of data over long distances via light waves. The optical communications product group provides fiber optic components, modules and subsystems. Products include tunable transmitters, receivers, amplifiers, multiplexers and demultiplexers, reconfigurable optical add/drop multiplexers (ROADMs), switches, optical performance monitors, couplers, splitters and circulators. In addition, the company provides optical communications solutions required to build and maintain Agile Optical Networks (AONs). AONs are designed to be dynamically and remotely reconfigurable, so that they can quickly and easily meet changes in network traffic patterns and demand. We believe that a growing

demand for network capacity and bandwidth will result in increased demand on the metro and long-haul infrastructures into which these services feed.

The communications test and measurement segment provides instruments, software, systems and services that help communications equipment manufacturers and service providers accelerate the deployment of broadband networks and services from the core of the network to the home, including deployment over fiber to the curb, node or premise and digital networks.

The advanced optical technologies segment provides document authentication, brand protection and product differentiation solutions for a range of commercial and consumer applications. It also offers thin film coated optics for applications, including computer monitors and flat panel displays, projection systems, photocopiers, facsimile machines, scanners, as well as optically variable micro flakes for security applications and decorative surface treatments. JDSU's technology protects approximately 100 currencies worldwide and has been widely adopted by leading pharmaceutical and biotechnology companies on prescription drug packaging.

Company Financials Fiscal Year Ended Jun. 30

Per Share Data ($)	2007	2006	2005	2004	2003	2002	2001	2000	1999	1998
Tangible Book Value	2.80	2.72	5.76	7.12	7.92	11.44	22.24	20.88	2.16	4.56
Cash Flow	0.48	-0.46	-1.11	-0.32	-4.82	-42.21	-370.58	0.52	-3.52	-2.04
Earnings	-0.12	-0.72	-1.44	-0.64	-5.28	-52.00	-411.20	-10.08	-4.30	-2.34
S&P Core Earnings	-0.21	-0.88	-2.24	-2.56	-7.84	-32.88	-175.60	NA	NA	NA
Dividends	Nil	Nil	Nil	Nil	Nil	Nil	Nil	Nil	Nil	Nil
Payout Ratio	Nil	Nil	Nil	Nil	Nil	Nil	Nil	Nil	Nil	Nil
Prices:High	17.99	34.40	26.08	47.08	37.68	82.72	519.50	1227	710.00	71.50
Prices:Low	12.41	13.93	10.56	22.72	19.84	12.64	40.96	296.00	59.25	31.25
P/E Ratio:High	NM	NM	NM	NM	NM	NM	NM	NM	NM	NM
P/E Ratio:Low	NM	NM	NM	NM	NM	NM	NM	NM	NM	NM

Income Statement Analysis (Million $)										
Revenue	1,397	1,204	712	636	676	1,098	3,233	1,430	283	176
Operating Income	36.8	-107	-83.9	-58.5	-306	-374	-62.5	446	94.6	36.7
Depreciation	128	57.4	61.3	55.9	79.2	1,645	5,542	951	30.7	10.1
Interest Expense	7.10	27.7	Nil	Nil	Nil	Nil	Nil	0.50	0.02	0.07
Pretax Income	-24.3	-152	-255	-128	-920	-8,501	-56,494	-830	-151	-69.8
Effective Tax Rate	NM	NM	NM	NM	NM	NM	NM	NM	NM	NM
Net Income	-26.3	-151	-261	-113	-934	-8,738	-56,122	-905	-171	-81.1
S&P Core Earnings	-45.7	-181	-394	-446	-1,399	-5,534	-23,966	NA	NA	NA

Balance Sheet & Other Financial Data (Million $)										
Cash	363	365	511	328	242	412	763	319	75.4	39.8
Current Assets	1,661	1,805	1,588	1,866	1,515	1,857	3,036	1,973	928	165
Total Assets	3,025	3,065	2,080	2,422	2,138	3,005	12,245	26,389	8,192	269
Current Liabilities	348	422	240	350	423	483	848	647	298	45.8
Long Term Debt	808	900	467	465	Nil	5.50	12.8	41.0	Nil	Nil
Common Equity	1,736	1,584	1,335	1,571	1,671	2,471	10,706	24,779	3,619	218
Total Capital	2,544	2,484	1,802	2,063	1,699	2,519	11,392	25,722	3,937	218
Capital Expenditures	75.7	67.2	35.8	66.4	47.2	133	732	280	46.6	24.0
Cash Flow	102	-93.8	-200	-56.7	-855	-7,093	-50,580	46.0	-140	-71.0
Current Ratio	4.8	4.3	6.6	5.3	3.6	3.8	3.6	3.0	3.1	3.6
% Long Term Debt of Capitalization	31.8	36.2	25.9	22.5	Nil	0.2	0.1	0.2	Nil	Nil
% Net Income of Revenue	NM	NM	NM	NM	NM	NM	NM	NM	NM	NM
% Return on Assets	NM	NM	NM	NM	NM	NM	NM	NM	NM	NM
% Return on Equity	NM	NM	NM	NM	NM	NM	NM	NM	NM	NM

Data as orig reptd.; bef. results of disc opers/spec. items. Per share data adj. for stk. divs.; EPS diluted. E-Estimated. NA-Not Available. NM-Not Meaningful. NR-Not Ranked. UR-Under Review.

Office: 430 N McCarthy Blvd, Milpitas, CA 95035-5116.
Telephone: 408-546-5000.
Email: investor.relations@jdsu.com
Website: http://www.jdsu.com

Chrmn: M.A. Kaplan
CEO: K.J. Kennedy
SVP & General Counsel: C.S. Dewees
Investor Contact: D. Vellequette (408-546-4445)

CTO: S. Lumish
Board Members: R. E. Belluzzo, H. L. Covert, B. D. Day, K. A. DeNuccio, P. A. Guglielmi, M. Jabbar, M. A. Kaplan, K. J. Kennedy, R. T. Liebhaber, C. S. Skrzypczak

Founded: 1979
Domicile: Delaware
Employees: 7,000

Johnson Controls Inc.

STANDARD &POOR'S

S&P Recommendation **HOLD** ★★★☆☆	Price $36.61 (as of Nov 23, 2007)	12-Mo. Target Price $45.00	Investment Style Large-Cap Blend

GICS Sector Consumer Discretionary
Sub-Industry Auto Parts & Equipment

Summary This company supplies building controls and energy management systems, automotive seating, and batteries.

Key Stock Statistics (Source S&P, Vickers, company reports)

52-Wk Range	$44.46– 26.82	S&P Oper. EPS 2008**E**	2.53	Market Capitalization(B)	$21.746	Beta	0.78
Trailing 12-Month EPS	$2.09	S&P Oper. EPS 2009**E**	NA	Yield (%)	1.42	S&P 3-Yr. Proj. EPS CAGR(%)	16.00
Trailing 12-Month P/E	17.5	P/E on S&P Oper. EPS 2008**E**	14.5	Dividend Rate/Share	$0.52	S&P Credit Rating	A-
$10K Invested 5 Yrs Ago	$28,733	Common Shares Outstg. (M)	594.0	Institutional Ownership (%)	76		

Price Performance

30-Week Mov. Avg. ··· 10-Week Mov. Avg. − − **GAAP Earnings vs. Previous Year**   Volume Above Avg. |||| **STARS**
12-Mo. Target Price — Relative Strength — ▲ Up ▼ Down ► No Change   Below Avg. |||| ★

3-for-1

J A S O N D J F M A M J J A S O N D J F M A M J J A S O N D J F M A M J J A S O N D J F
2004   **2005**   **2006**   **2007**

Options: ASE, CBOE, Ph

Analysis prepared by **Efraim Levy, CFA** on November 02, 2007, when the stock traded at **$ 42.60**.

Highlights

➤ We expect FY 08 (Sep.) sales to advance about 10%, reflecting an expansion of the facilities management business, expected new automotive business, higher global automobile production, and acquisitions. We see facilities management benefiting from new customers as outsourcing trends continue and the backlog of orders for installed systems continues to grow. Automotive revenues will likely benefit from new contracts and expanding business with Asian and European vehicle makers.

➤ We see operating margins widening, as JCI should benefit from the higher revenues we anticipate, plus restructuring activities, especially in Europe. We project a partial offset in higher health care expenses and pricing pressures from customers, and higher raw material costs.

➤ Our FY 08 EPS estimate is $2.53, up from $2.09 in FY 07, which excludes non-recurring tax benefits. We view the company's balance sheet as strong, and with about $1.5 billion in projected FY 08 free cash flow, we think a sizable acquisition in calendar 2008 is likely.

Investment Rationale/Risk

➤ We expect growth to exceed that of peers, and with greater earnings stability. We project that diversification in geography, products and customers will help JCI withstand weakness at the domestic auto manufacturers. The stock recently exceeded the P/E multiple of the S&P 500 based on our calendar 2007 estimates. We view the balance sheet as strong, with long-term debt generally at 20% to 36% of capitalization over the past decade.

➤ Risks to our recommendation and target price include lower than expected demand, especially for automotive parts, higher raw material costs, failure to achieve expected acquisition synergies, and pricing pressure from customers.

➤ Applying a P/E multiple of 17.8X to our FY 08 EPS estimate of $2.53, in line with peers and historical averages, leads us to a value of about $45, which is our 12-month target price. Our DCF model, which assumes a weighted average cost of capital of 9.6%, a compound annual growth rate of 10.4% over the next 15 years, and a terminal growth rate of 4%, leads to an intrinsic value of about $45 as well.

Qualitative Risk Assessment

LOW	**MEDIUM**	HIGH

Our risk assessment reflects favorable growth prospects in the building controls markets that JCI serves and what we view as a strong management team and a healthy balance sheet, offset by the challenges faced by the automotive operations.

Quantitative Evaluations

S&P Quality Ranking   **A+**

D	C	B-	B	B+	A-	A	**A+**

Relative Strength Rank   **MODERATE**

42

LOWEST = 1   HIGHEST = 99

Revenue/Earnings Data

Revenue (Million $)

	1Q	2Q	3Q	4Q	Year
2007	8,210	8,492	8,911	9,011	34,624
2006	7,528	8,167	8,390	8,150	32,235
2005	6,618	6,899	7,062	6,900	27,479
2004	6,384	6,620	6,792	6,757	26,553
2003	5,183	5,503	5,960	6,000	22,646
2002	4,818	4,811	5,257	5,218	20,103

Earnings Per Share ($)

2007	0.28	0.44	0.66	0.77	2.09
2006	0.29	0.28	0.57	0.62	1.75
2005	0.28	0.09	0.44	0.50	1.30
2004	0.29	0.27	0.38	0.47	1.41
2003	0.25	0.23	0.33	0.39	1.20
2002	0.21	0.20	0.31	0.34	1.06

Fiscal year ended Sep. 30. Next earnings report expected: Mid January. EPS Estimates based on S&P Operating Earnings; historical GAAP earnings are as reported.

Dividend Data (Dates: mm/dd Payment Date: mm/dd/yy)

Amount ($)	Date Decl.	Ex-Div. Date	Stk. of Record	Payment Date
0.330	05/22	06/13	06/15	06/29/07
0.110	07/25	10/03	09/14	10/02/07
3-for-1	07/25	10/03	09/14	10/02/07
0.130	11/14	12/12	12/14	01/03/08

Dividends have been paid since 1887. Source: Company reports.

Please read the Required Disclosures and Analyst Certification on the last page of this report.

The **McGraw·Hill** Companies

Johnson Controls Inc.

Business Summary November 02, 2007

CORPORATE OVERVIEW. Johnson Controls, founded in 1885, is a leading manufacturer of automotive interior systems, automotive batteries and automated building control systems. It also provides facility management services for commercial buildings. In FY 07 (Sep.), the automotive segment accounted for 63% of sales and 55% of income, with the balance coming from controls and facility management.

The automotive interior segment manufactures complete seats and seating components for North American and European car and light-truck manufacturers. The segment has grown rapidly in recent years, gaining contracts to produce seats formerly manufactured in-house by automakers, and expanding in Europe. Seating accounted for nearly 51% of sales in FY 07.

The power solutions unit, the largest automotive battery operation in North America, makes lead-acid batteries primarily for the automotive replacement market and for OEMs. Batteries accounted for about 12% of FY 07 sales and the unit is expanding operations in Europe.

The building efficiency (formerly called controls) segment manufactures, in-

stalls and services controls and control systems, principally for nonresidential buildings, which are used for temperature and energy management, and fire safety and security maintenance. The segment also includes custom engineering, installation and servicing of process control systems and a growing facilities management business. Building efficiency sales accounted for 37% of FY 07 revenues. At September 30, 2007, JCI had an unearned backlog of building systems and services contracts totaling $4.2 billion.

Government building trends promoting facility management outsourcing and energy efficiency programs are creating, in our view, additional opportunities.

GM, DaimlerChrysler and Ford accounted respectively for 11%, 11% and 10% of FY 06 sales. We expect the share of revenues from the largest three customers to shrink as the company expands its sales outside the U.S. and with non-domestic customers expanding in the U.S.

Company Financials Fiscal Year Ended Sep. 30

Per Share Data ($)	2007	2006	2005	2004	2003	2002	2001	2000	1999	1998
Tangible Book Value	NA	1.10	3.52	1.93	1.27	0.74	1.17	0.61	0.08	NM
Cash Flow	NA	2.95	2.41	2.48	2.17	1.97	1.77	1.79	1.55	1.29
Earnings	2.09	1.75	1.30	1.41	1.20	1.06	0.85	0.85	0.75	0.61
S&P Core Earnings	NA	1.74	1.31	1.42	1.16	0.89	0.70	NA	NA	NA
Dividends	0.33	0.37	0.33	0.30	0.24	0.22	0.21	0.19	0.17	0.15
Payout Ratio	16%	21%	26%	21%	20%	21%	24%	22%	22%	25%
Prices:High	44.46	30.00	25.07	21.33	19.37	15.53	13.78	10.85	12.78	10.31
Prices:Low	28.09	22.12	17.52	16.52	11.96	11.52	8.66	7.64	8.17	6.75
P/E Ratio:High	21	17	19	15	16	15	16	13	17	17
P/E Ratio:Low	13	13	13	12	10	11	10	9	11	11

Income Statement Analysis (Million $)										
Revenue	NA	32,235	27,479	26,553	22,646	20,103	18,427	17,155	16,139	12,587
Operating Income	NA	2,184	1,913	1,918	1,720	1,639	1,477	1,427	1,300	1,048
Depreciation	NA	705	636	617	558	517	516	462	446	384
Interest Expense	NA	248	121	111	114	122	129	128	153	134
Pretax Income	NA	1,138	1,003	1,212	1,058	1,006	867	856	770	617
Effective Tax Rate	NA	5.54%	20.4%	26.0%	31.0%	34.6%	38.7%	39.6%	40.5%	41.5%
Net Income	NA	1,033	757	818	683	600	478	472	420	338
S&P Core Earnings	NA	1,025	764	818	650	497	385	NA	NA	NA

Balance Sheet & Other Financial Data (Million $)										
Cash	NA	293	171	170	136	262	375	276	276	134
Current Assets	NA	9,264	7,139	6,377	5,620	4,946	4,544	4,277	3,849	3,404
Total Assets	NA	21,921	16,144	15,091	13,127	11,165	9,912	9,428	8,614	7,942
Current Liabilities	NA	8,146	6,841	6,602	5,584	4,806	4,580	4,510	4,267	4,288
Long Term Debt	NA	4,166	1,578	1,631	1,777	1,827	1,395	1,315	1,283	998
Common Equity	NA	7,355	6,058	5,206	4,164	3,396	2,862	2,447	2,135	1,801
Total Capital	NA	11,650	7,831	7,106	6,260	5,515	4,588	3,891	3,553	2,939
Capital Expenditures	NA	711	664	862	664	496	622	547	514	468
Cash Flow	NA	1,738	1,394	1,434	1,234	1,110	985	924	856	712
Current Ratio	NA	1.1	1.0	1.0	1.0	1.0	1.0	0.9	0.9	0.8
% Long Term Debt of Capitalization	NA	35.8	20.1	22.9	28.4	33.1	30.4	33.8	36.1	34.0
% Net Income of Revenue	NA	3.2	2.8	3.1	3.0	3.0	2.6	2.8	2.6	2.7
% Return on Assets	NA	5.4	4.9	5.8	5.6	5.7	4.9	5.2	5.1	4.8
% Return on Equity	NA	15.4	13.4	17.4	17.9	18.9	17.7	20.2	20.8	19.6

Data as orig reptd.; bef. results of disc opers/spec. items. Per share data adj. for stk. divs.; EPS diluted. E-Estimated. NA-Not Available. NM-Not Meaningful. NR-Not Ranked. UR-Under Review.

Office: 5757 N. Green Bay Avenue, Milwaukee, WI 53201.
Telephone: 414-524-1200.
Website: http://www.johnsoncontrols.com
Chrmn & CEO: J.M. Barth

Pres & COO: K.E. Wandell
Vice Chrmn & EVP: S.A. Roell
EVP & CFO: R.B. McDonald
VP & Treas: F.A. Voltolina

Investor Contact: D.M. Zutz (414-524-1200)
Board Members: D. W. Archer, R. L. Barnett, J. M. Barth, N. A. Black, P. A. Brunner, E. R. Clariond, R. A. Cornog, W. D. Davis, J. A. Joerres, W. H. Lacy, S. J. Morcott, S. A. Roell, R. F. Teerlink

Founded: 1900
Domicile: Wisconsin
Employees: 136,000

Johnson & Johnson

STANDARD &POOR'S

S&P Recommendation **BUY** ★★★★☆	Price $66.88 (as of Nov 23, 2007)	12-Mo. Target Price $74.00	Investment Style Large-Cap Growth

GICS Sector Health Care
Sub-Industry Pharmaceuticals

Summary This company is a leader in the pharmaceutical, medical device and consumer products industries. Its stock has one of the largest market caps in the S&P 500.

Key Stock Statistics (Source S&P, Vickers, company reports)

52-Wk Range	$68.22– 59.72	S&P Oper. EPS 2007E	4.14	Market Capitalization(B)	$191.394	Beta	0.33
Trailing 12-Month EPS	$3.55	S&P Oper. EPS 2008E	4.35	Yield (%)	2.48	S&P 3-Yr. Proj. EPS CAGR(%)	9.00
Trailing 12-Month P/E	18.8	P/E on S&P Oper. EPS 2007E	16.2	Dividend Rate/Share	$1.66	S&P Credit Rating	AAA
$10K Invested 5 Yrs Ago	$12,689	Common Shares Outstg. (M)	2,861.8	Institutional Ownership (%)	65		

Price Performance

30-Week Mov. Avg. · · · 10-Week Mov. Avg. – – GAAP Earnings vs. Previous Year   Volume Above Avg. STARS
12-Mo. Target Price — Relative Strength — ▲ Up ▼ Down ► No Change   Below Avg.

Options: ASE, CBOE, P, Ph

Analysis prepared by **Robert M. Gold** on October 16, 2007, when the stock traded at **$ 64.96**.

Highlights

➤ We see 2007 revenues of $60.5 billion, including approximately $4.0 billion in sales from the consumer products business acquired from Pfizer, and we think 2008 revenues can expand by approximately 5%, including $4.3 billion in sales from the Pfizer assets. We expect that foreign currency fluctuations will benefit reported sales by about 3% in 2007.

➤ We expect that gross margins in 2007 and 2008 will be pressured by lower pricing in some medical device and pharmaceutical product categories and a rising proportion of consumer product sales. However, we think synergies from recent acquisitions along with reduced staffing levels and lower other operating expenses will help drive earnings growth at a higher pace than revenues through 2008. We think JNJ will reinvest a substantial portion of the $1.3 billion to $1.6 billion of pretax savings tied to restructuring actions into R&D and share buybacks.

➤ We see 2007 operating EPS of $4.14, as expected dilution from the Pfizer and Conor deals is largely offset by higher investment and other income, a reduced share count, and a lower effective tax rate. Our 2008 EPS estimate is $4.35.

Investment Rationale/Risk

➤ JNJ's deal with Pfizer added brands such as Listerine, Nicorette, Visine and Neosporin. We believe revenue and cost synergies will drive cash EPS accretion by 2008, and we think the deal will boost revenue and cash flow visibility amid challenging medical device and pharmaceutical conditions. The Conor deal improves JNJ's competitive standing in interventional cardiology, in our opinion. Elsewhere, we view the reinvestment of some of JNJ's restructuring savings as necessary to help build its drug pipeline.

➤ Risks to our recommendation and target price include a faster than expected loss of drug sales to generic competition, an inability to sustain growth in the device area, a failure to commercialize compounds in the R&D pipeline, and an expanded SEC and DOJ investigation of the overseas medical device unit.

➤ Our 12-month target price of $74 is about 17X our 2008 EPS estimate, and represents a P/E to growth ratio of 1.5X, in line with pharmaceutical and consumer product peers and modestly below medical device peers. Our DCF analysis calculates intrinsic value of $75, assuming a 7.7% WACC and terminal growth of 3%.

Qualitative Risk Assessment

LOW	MEDIUM	HIGH

Our risk assessment reflects our belief that JNJ has products that are largely immune from economic cycles, its modest reliance on any single product category or customer for sustained growth, and competitive advantages owing to its large financial resources, business scale and global sales capabilities.

Quantitative Evaluations

S&P Quality Ranking   A+

D	C	B-	B	B+	A-	A	A+

Relative Strength Rank   STRONG
87
LOWEST = 1   HIGHEST = 99

Revenue/Earnings Data

Revenue (Million $)

	1Q	2Q	3Q	4Q	Year
2007	15,037	15,131	14,970	--	--
2006	12,992	13,363	13,287	13,682	53,324
2005	12,832	12,762	12,310	12,610	50,514
2004	11,559	11,484	11,553	12,752	47,348
2003	9,821	10,332	10,455	11,254	41,862
2002	8,743	9,073	9,079	9,403	36,298

Earnings Per Share ($)

2007	0.88	1.05	0.88	E0.87	E4.14
2006	1.10	0.95	0.94	0.74	3.73
2005	0.97	0.89	0.87	0.73	3.46
2004	0.83	0.82	0.78	0.41	2.84
2003	0.69	0.40	0.69	0.62	2.40
2002	0.59	0.54	0.57	0.46	2.16

Fiscal year ended Dec. 31. Next earnings report expected: Late January. EPS Estimates based on S&P Operating Earnings; historical GAAP earnings are as reported.

Dividend Data (Dates: mm/dd Payment Date: mm/dd/yy)

Amount ($)	Date Decl.	Ex-Div. Date	Stk. of Record	Payment Date
0.375	01/02	02/23	02/27	03/13/07
0.415	04/26	05/24	05/29	06/12/07
0.415	07/16	08/24	08/28	09/11/07
0.415	10/18	11/23	11/27	12/11/07

Dividends have been paid since 1944. Source: Company reports.

Please read the Required Disclosures and Analyst Certification on the last page of this report.

The McGraw-Hill Companies

Johnson & Johnson

STANDARD &POOR'S

Business Summary October 16, 2007

CORPORATE OVERVIEW. Johnson & Johnson ranks as one of the largest and most diversified health care firms, with products spanning across the pharmaceutical and medical device industries. The company is also a major participant in the global consumer products business, and, in December 2006, purchased the consumer products unit of Pfizer for $16.6 billion. In February 2007, JNJ consummated its acquisition of Conor Medsystems, Inc. for $1.4 billion in cash.

The pharmaceutical segment (44% of 2006 sales) focuses on the antifungal, anti-infective, cardiovascular, contraceptive, dermatology, gastrointestinal, hematology, immunology, neurology, oncology, pain management, central nervous system and urology fields. In 2006, eight products each generated at least $1 billion of sales: Risperdal/Risperdal Consta ($4.2 billion, up 18% from 2005, ex-currency), Procrit/Eprex ($3.2 billion, down 4%), Remicade ($3.0 billion, up 19%), Topamax ($2.0 billion, up 21%), Floxin/Levaquin ($1.5 billion, up

3%), Duragesic ($1.3 billion, down 18%), Aciphex/Pariet ($1.2 billion, up 6%), and hormonal contraceptives ($1.0 billion, down 11%). JNJ estimates that inroads made by generic drug launches negatively affected its 2006 pharmaceutical segment sales by about 3%.

The medical devices and diagnostics segment (38%) sells a wide range of products, including Ethicon's wound care, surgical sports medicine and women's health care products; Cordis's circulatory disease management products; Lifescan's blood glucose monitoring products; Ortho-Clinical Diagnostic's professional diagnostic products; Depuy's orthopaedic joint reconstruction and spinal products; and Vistakon's disposable contact lenses.

Company Financials Fiscal Year Ended Dec. 31

Per Share Data ($)	2006	2005	2004	2003	2002	2001	2000	1999	1998	1997
Tangible Book Value	3.67	8.64	6.72	5.17	4.53	4.97	4.15	3.11	2.38	3.38
Cash Flow	4.57	4.20	3.58	3.01	2.67	2.35	2.23	1.98	1.57	1.59
Earnings	3.73	3.46	2.84	2.40	2.16	1.84	1.70	1.47	1.12	1.21
S&P Core Earnings	3.65	3.38	2.77	2.26	1.99	1.66	NA	NA	NA	NA
Dividends	1.46	1.28	1.10	0.93	0.80	0.70	0.62	0.55	0.49	0.43
Payout Ratio	39%	37%	39%	39%	37%	38%	36%	37%	43%	35%
Prices:High	69.41	69.99	64.25	59.08	65.89	60.97	52.97	53.44	44.88	33.66
Prices:Low	56.65	59.76	49.25	48.05	41.40	40.25	33.06	38.50	31.69	24.31
P/E Ratio:High	19	20	23	25	31	33	31	36	40	28
P/E Ratio:Low	15	17	17	20	19	22	19	26	28	20

Income Statement Analysis (Million $)										
Revenue	53,324	50,514	47,348	41,862	36,298	33,004	29,139	27,471	23,657	22,629
Operating Income	15,886	15,464	14,987	12,740	11,340	9,490	7,992	7,370	6,291	5,689
Depreciation	2,177	2,093	2,124	1,869	1,662	1,605	1,515	1,444	1,246	1,067
Interest Expense	63.0	54.0	187	207	160	153	146	197	110	120
Pretax Income	14,587	13,656	12,838	10,308	9,291	7,898	6,622	5,753	4,269	4,576
Effective Tax Rate	24.2%	23.8%	33.7%	30.2%	29.0%	28.2%	27.5%	27.6%	28.3%	27.8%
Net Income	11,053	10,411	8,509	7,197	6,597	5,668	4,800	4,167	3,059	3,303
S&P Core Earnings	10,814	10,161	8,263	6,785	6,052	5,090	NA	NA	NA	NA

Balance Sheet & Other Financial Data (Million $)										
Cash	4,084	16,138	12,884	9,523	7,596	8,941	6,013	4,320	2,994	3,284
Current Assets	22,975	31,394	27,320	22,995	19,266	18,473	15,450	13,200	11,132	10,563
Total Assets	70,556	58,025	53,317	48,263	40,556	38,488	31,321	29,163	26,211	21,453
Current Liabilities	19,161	12,635	13,927	13,448	11,449	8,044	7,140	7,454	8,162	5,283
Long Term Debt	2,014	2,017	2,565	2,955	2,022	2,217	2,037	2,450	1,269	1,126
Common Equity	61,266	37,871	31,813	26,869	22,697	24,233	18,808	16,213	13,590	12,359
Total Capital	64,599	40,099	34,781	30,604	25,362	26,943	21,100	18,950	15,437	13,660
Capital Expenditures	2,666	2,632	2,175	2,262	2,099	1,731	1,646	1,728	1,460	1,391
Cash Flow	13,230	12,504	10,633	9,066	8,259	7,273	6,315	5,611	4,305	4,370
Current Ratio	1.2	2.5	2.0	1.7	1.7	2.3	2.2	1.8	1.4	2.0
% Long Term Debt of Capitalization	3.1	5.0	7.4	9.7	8.0	8.2	9.7	12.9	8.2	8.2
% Net Income of Revenue	20.7	20.6	18.0	17.2	18.2	17.2	16.5	15.2	12.9	14.6
% Return on Assets	17.1	18.7	16.8	16.2	16.7	15.6	15.9	14.8	12.8	15.9
% Return on Equity	19.8	29.9	29.0	29.0	28.1	25.4	27.4	27.5	23.6	28.5

Data as orig reptd.; bef. results of disc opers/spec. items. Per share data adj. for stk. divs.; EPS diluted. E-Estimated. NA-Not Available. NM-Not Meaningful. NR-Not Ranked. UR-Under Review.

Office: One Johnson & Johnson Plaza, New Brunswick, NJ 08933.
Telephone: 732-524-0400.
Website: http://www.jnj.com
Chrmn & CEO: W.C. Weldon

Vice Chrmn: C.A. Poon
Vice Chrmn: R.J. Darretta
VP & CFO: D.J. Caruso
VP, General Counsel & CCO: R.C. Deyo

Investor Contact: L. Mehrotra (732-524-6491)
Board Members: M. Coleman, J. G. Cullen, R. J. Darretta, M. M. Johns, A. D. Jordan, A. G. Langbo, S. L. Lindquist, L. F. Mullin, C. A. Poon, C. Prince, S. S. Reinemund, D. Satcher, W. C. Weldon

Founded: 1887
Domicile: New Jersey
Employees: 122,200

The McGraw-Hill Companies

Jones Apparel Group Inc.

STANDARD &POOR'S

S&P Recommendation `HOLD` ★★★☆☆

Price	12-Mo. Target Price	Investment Style
$19.29 (as of Nov 23, 2007)	$25.00	Large-Cap Blend

GICS Sector Consumer Discretionary
Sub-Industry Apparel, Accessories & Luxury Goods

Summary JNY is a leading designer, marketer and wholesaler of women's apparel, footwear and accessories, with brands that include Jones New York, Nine West and Evan-Picone.

Key Stock Statistics (Source S&P, Vickers, company reports)

52-Wk Range	$35.54–16.73	S&P Oper. EPS 2007E	1.22	Market Capitalization(B)	$1.802	Beta	1.31
Trailing 12-Month EPS	$1.37	S&P Oper. EPS 2008E	1.35	Yield (%)	2.90	S&P 3-Yr. Proj. EPS CAGR(%)	NM
Trailing 12-Month P/E	14.1	P/E on S&P Oper. EPS 2007E	15.8	Dividend Rate/Share	$0.56	S&P Credit Rating	BB+
$10K Invested 5 Yrs Ago	$5,618	Common Shares Outstg. (M)	93.4	Institutional Ownership (%)	NM		

Price Performance

30-Week Mov. Avg. · · · 10-Week Mov. Avg. - - **GAAP Earnings vs. Previous Year** Volume Above Avg. STARS
12-Mo. Target Price — Relative Strength — ▲ Up ▼ Down ► No Change Below Avg. ★

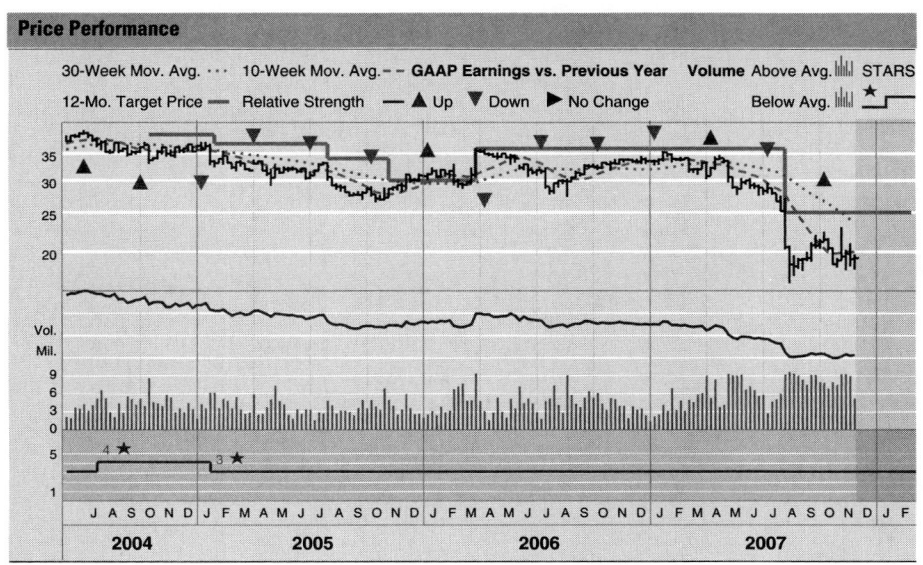

Options: ASE, P, Ph

Analysis prepared by **Marie Driscoll, CFA** on November 19, 2007, when the stock traded at **$18.66**.

Highlights

➤ 2007 is turning out to be another tough year for JNY, and we expect 2008 to be transitional as well, as the company right-sizes its wholesale apparel business and restores its specialty retail segment to profitability. JNY will focus on a handful of core brands-Jones New York, Anne Klein, Nine West, Gloria Vanderbilt and l.e.i.-as growth opportunities, and will exit most of its moderate sportswear business (about $1 billion) by 2007 year end. The company completed the sale of Barneys on September 6, 2007.

➤ We see sales from continuing operations of $3.9 billion in 2007 and $4 billion in 2008. The 2007 operating margin is expected to contract, reflecting an operating loss in the retail segment and a high level of markdown dollars for JNY's wholesale segment. We expect the company will begin to recoup margin contraction as 2008 progresses.

➤ We see share buybacks in 2007 and 2008, partly funded by a portion of the proceeds from the Barneys sale, benefiting per-share results, which we estimate at $1.22 and $1.35, respectively, versus an adjusted $2.19 in 2006.

Investment Rationale/Risk

➤ We regard many of JNY's 20-some apparel and footwear brands as mature and regard the decision to exit them as difficult but correct. As the company rationalizes its portfolio of branded apparel, we believe it will be able to focus better on a few recently acquired businesses that could provide significant growth opportunity along with potential cost synergies. We expect JNY to make further inroads into better apparel with multiple lines acquired with Kasper, and Anne Klein. We view Anne Klein as especially promising with new design talent and favorable retail response to recent fashion products. Maxwell Shoe provides increased market penetration and line extension potential, in our view.

➤ Risks to our opinion and target price include changes in consumer spending, fashion and inventory risk, and management's ability to integrate recent acquisitions.

➤ Our 12-month target price of $25 is derived by applying the peer apparel and footwear group forward 2008 multiple of about 18X to our 2008 EPS estimate.

Qualitative Risk Assessment

LOW	MEDIUM	HIGH

Our risk assessment is based on exposure to department store channel contraction offset by a diversified brand portfolio spanning multiple channels.

Quantitative Evaluations

S&P Quality Ranking B

D	C	B-	B	B+	A-	A	A+

Relative Strength Rank MODERATE

50

LOWEST = 1 HIGHEST = 99

Revenue/Earnings Data

Revenue (Million $)

	1Q	2Q	3Q	4Q	Year
2007	1,248	903.9	1,028	--	--
2006	1,215	1,074	1,241	1,213	4,743
2005	1,349	1,176	1,328	1,221	5,074
2004	1,218	1,053	1,296	1,083	4,650
2003	1,234	980.4	1,181	980.2	4,375
2002	1,127	972.1	1,278	964.5	4,341

Earnings Per Share ($)

2007	0.44	-0.48	1.37	E0.09	E1.22
2006	0.21	0.32	0.56	-2.51	-1.32
2005	0.71	0.46	0.65	0.48	2.30
2004	0.73	0.61	0.77	0.28	2.39
2003	0.90	0.54	0.71	0.33	2.48
2002	0.63	0.49	0.95	0.39	2.46

Fiscal year ended Dec. 31. Next earnings report expected: Mid February. EPS Estimates based on S&P Operating Earnings; historical GAAP earnings are as reported.

Dividend Data (Dates: mm/dd Payment Date: mm/dd/yy)

Amount ($)	Date Decl.	Ex-Div. Date	Stk. of Record	Payment Date
0.140	02/14	02/28	03/02	03/16/07
0.140	05/03	05/16	05/18	06/01/07
0.140	08/01	08/15	08/17	08/31/07
0.140	10/31	11/14	11/16	11/30/07

Dividends have been paid since 2003. Source: Company reports.

Jones Apparel Group Inc.

STANDARD &POOR'S

Business Summary November 19, 2007

CORPORATE OVERVIEW. Jones Apparel Group, Inc. (JNY) is a multi-branded apparel and accessories company operating on both the wholesale and retail level.

MARKET PROFILE. JNY participates in the women's apparel market, which represented 54% of domestic apparel retail purchases, or $102 billion, in 2006, according to NPD Fashionworld consumer estimated data. The apparel market is fragmented, with national brands marketed by 20 companies accounting for about 30% of total apparel sales, and the remaining 70% comprised of smaller and/or private label "store" brands. The market is mature, in our view, with demand largely mirroring population growth and fashion trends accounting for a modicum of incremental volume. Deflationary pricing pressure is a function, we think, of channel competition and production steadily moving offshore to low-cost producers in India, Asia and China. S&P forecasts 2007 apparel sales increasing in the low single digits, generally in line with GDP growth. This compares with a 5% year-to-year advance in 2006 and 4% gains in both 2004 and 2005.

COMPETITIVE LANDSCAPE. By channel, specialty stores account for the

largest share of apparel sales, at 31% in 2006, up from 30% in 2005 according to NPD. Mass merchants (Wal-Mart and Target) came in second at 20%, up 100 basis points and department stores, JNY's primary channel, came in third at 16%, losing 100 basis points of market share. National chains (Sears and JC Penney) captured 15% of 2006 apparel sales and off-price retailers (TJX and Ross Stores) 8%. The remaining 10% is divided among factory outlets and direct and email pure plays. JNY holds meaningful market shares in department stores and national chains, where it competes with Liz Claiborne, Polo Ralph Lauren and VF Corp., as well as private label offerings, which garner about a third of total apparel purchases and are an important differentiator for retailers. JNY also sells directly to consumers through 1,018 specialty retail and outlet stores in the U.S. and Canada. The company formerly participated in the luxury retail market via Barneys New York flagship store, three regional stores and eight Barneys New York CO-OP stores.

Company Financials Fiscal Year Ended Dec. 31

Per Share Data ($)	2006	2005	2004	2003	2002	2001	2000	1999	1998	1997
Tangible Book Value	1.30	NM	NM	0.98	0.66	0.03	0.16	NM	2.33	3.98
Cash Flow	-0.37	3.16	3.24	3.04	3.03	1.96	3.37	2.05	1.68	1.26
Earnings	-1.32	2.30	2.39	2.48	2.46	1.82	2.48	1.60	1.47	1.13
S&P Core Earnings	2.92	2.32	2.34	2.40	2.35	1.63	NA	NA	NA	NA
Dividends	0.50	0.44	0.36	0.16	Nil	Nil	Nil	Nil	Nil	Nil
Payout Ratio	NM	19%	15%	6%	Nil	Nil	Nil	Nil	Nil	Nil
Prices:High	36.10	37.48	40.00	37.44	41.68	47.43	35.00	35.88	37.75	28.72
Prices:Low	27.30	26.47	33.00	25.61	26.18	23.75	20.13	21.50	15.88	16.06
P/E Ratio:High	NM	16	17	15	17	26	14	22	26	25
P/E Ratio:Low	NM	12	14	10	11	13	8	13	11	14

Income Statement Analysis (Million $)	2006	2005	2004	2003	2002	2001	2000	1999	1998	1997
Revenue	4,743	5,074	4,650	4,375	4,341	4,073	4,143	3,151	1,685	1,387
Operating Income	475	600	636	664	679	506	714	431	283	211
Depreciation	105	103	108	84.3	88.8	25.7	109	53.1	21.2	14.6
Interest Expense	58.2	76.2	51.2	58.8	62.7	84.6	104	66.9	11.8	3.58
Pretax Income	-200	425	483	529	534	400	503	315	252	195
Effective Tax Rate	NM	35.5%	37.5%	37.5%	37.7%	40.9%	40.0%	40.1%	38.5%	37.5%
Net Income	-146	274	302	331	332	236	302	188	155	122
S&P Core Earnings	322	275	295	318	318	210	NA	NA	NA	NA

Balance Sheet & Other Financial Data (Million $)	2006	2005	2004	2003	2002	2001	2000	1999	1998	1997
Cash	71.5	34.9	45.0	350	283	76.5	60.5	47.0	129	51.3
Current Assets	1,279	1,284	1,296	1,456	1,318	1,141	1,182	1,131	632	441
Total Assets	3,787	4,578	4,551	4,188	3,853	3,374	2,979	2,792	1,189	581
Current Liabilities	615	836	684	629	427	378	887	661	174	110
Long Term Debt	Nil	790	1,017	835	978	977	576	834	415	27.3
Common Equity	2,212	2,666	2,654	2,538	2,304	1,905	1,477	1,241	594	436
Total Capital	2,254	3,632	3,806	3,503	3,380	2,963	2,053	2,075	1,009	463
Capital Expenditures	171	87.5	56.6	53.3	52.6	56.4	46.8	29.7	48.5	32.1
Cash Flow	-40.8	377	410	415	421	262	411	242	176	136
Current Ratio	2.1	1.5	1.9	2.3	3.1	3.0	1.3	1.7	3.6	4.0
% Long Term Debt of Capitalization	Nil	21.7	26.7	23.8	28.9	33.0	28.1	40.2	41.1	5.9
% Net Income of Revenue	NM	5.4	6.5	7.6	7.7	5.8	7.3	6.0	9.2	8.8
% Return on Assets	NM	6.0	6.9	8.2	9.2	7.4	10.5	9.5	17.5	22.8
% Return on Equity	NM	10.3	11.6	13.7	15.8	14.0	22.2	20.5	30.1	30.0

Data as orig reptd.; bef. results of disc opers/spec. items. Per share data adj. for stk. divs.; EPS diluted. E-Estimated. NA-Not Available. NM-Not Meaningful. NR-Not Ranked. UR-Under Review.

Office: 1411 Broadway, New York, NY 10018-3496.
Telephone: 212-642-3860.
Website: http://www.jny.com
Chrmn: S. Kimmel

Pres & CEO: P. Boneparth
COO & CFO: W.R. Card
EVP, Secy & General Counsel: I.M. Dansky
EVP & Cntlr: P.M. Farrell

Board Members: P. Boneparth, G. C. Crotty, H. Gittis, M. H. Kamens, J. R. Kerrey, S. Kimmel, A. I. Questrom, A. N. Reese, L. W. Robinson, A. F. Scarpa, F. D. van Paasschen

Founded: 1975
Domicile: Pennsylvania
Employees: 16,485

The McGraw-Hill Companies

JPMorgan Chase & Co.

STANDARD
&POOR'S

S&P Recommendation **BUY** ★★★★☆	Price $41.95 (as of Nov 23, 2007)	12-Mo. Target Price $58.00	Investment Style Large-Cap Value

GICS Sector Financials
Sub-Industry Other Diversified Financial Services

Summary JPMorgan Chase is a leading global financial services firm with assets of $1.3 trillion and operations in more than 50 countries.

Key Stock Statistics (Source S&P, Vickers, company reports)

52-Wk Range	$53.25– 40.15	S&P Oper. EPS 2007E	4.62	Market Capitalization(B)	$142.569	Beta	1.41
Trailing 12-Month EPS	$4.78	S&P Oper. EPS 2008E	4.90	Yield (%)	3.62	S&P 3-Yr. Proj. EPS CAGR(%)	10.00
Trailing 12-Month P/E	8.8	P/E on S&P Oper. EPS 2007E	9.1	Dividend Rate/Share	$1.52	S&P Credit Rating	AA-
$10K Invested 5 Yrs Ago	$20,116	Common Shares Outstg. (M)	3,398.5	Institutional Ownership (%)	69		

Price Performance

30-Week Mov. Avg. ··· 10-Week Mov. Avg. -- **GAAP Earnings vs. Previous Year** Volume Above Avg. STARS
12-Mo. Target Price — Relative Strength — ▲ Up ▼ Down ► No Change Below Avg. ★

Options: ASE, CBOE, P, Ph

Analysis prepared by **Frank Braden, CFA** on November 01, 2007, when the stock traded at **$ 47.00**.

Highlights

➤ We expect that strong growth in asset management fees and treasury and securities services revenue will more than offset pressure on JPM's investment banking business and weakness in credit quality. We look for JPM's asset management business to benefit from higher assets under management and larger performance fees, partially offset by increased compensation expense. We believe growth in commercial banking and treasury and security services will remain strong in 2008. While we view JPM's strategy of continued de novo branch building favorably, we believe it will take several years to make a material impact.

➤ In our view, resilient credit quality trends at the retail bank, as well as in commercial lending, along with healthy capital markets activity in a stable economy, will position the company to show solid earnings growth in 2008. However, we think deteriorating results in the mortgage banking, auto financing, and leveraged loan businesses will act as a near-term drag on earnings.

➤ We estimate operating EPS of $4.62 in 2007 and $4.90 in 2008.

Investment Rationale/Risk

➤ We believe JPM has solid growth prospects and diverse geographic product lines. We think its large customer base and what we see as its strong fundamentals will allow it the flexibility to move toward higher growth products and markets as well as absorb potential challenges that may be ahead. We further expect near-term results to be buoyed by recent expense management initiatives. However, we view market conditions as highly competitive, and we see the interest rate environment as challenging.

➤ Risks to our recommendation and target price include legal and regulatory risk; a failure to realize projected cost savings; continued turmoil in the credit markets; a severe economic downturn in combination with higher short-term interest rates that could result in a prolonged inverted yield curve; and any serious event that could adversely affect equity markets.

➤ Our 12-month target price of $58 is equal to 11.8X our 2008 operating EPS estimate, in line with JPM's historical average.

Qualitative Risk Assessment

LOW	MEDIUM	HIGH

Our risk assessment of JPMorgan Chase reflects our view of the company's strong fundamentals, solid credit quality, and a large customer base, and a relatively healthy economy. We also believe JPM's diversity in its geographic presence and product offerings provides significant protection from a local or regional downturn.

Quantitative Evaluations

S&P Quality Ranking B

D	C	B-	B	B+	A-	A	A+

Relative Strength Rank MODERATE

45

LOWEST = 1 HIGHEST = 99

Revenue/Earnings Data

Revenue (Million $)

	1Q	2Q	3Q	4Q	Year
2007	29,486	30,082	16,112	--	--
2006	23,477	24,175	24,957	26,693	99,302
2005	19,054	18,691	21,048	21,109	79,902
2004	11,625	11,227	16,546	17,483	56,931
2003	11,454	11,842	10,396	10,671	44,363
2002	10,957	11,190	7,301	--	43,372

Earnings Per Share ($)

2007	1.34	1.20	0.97	E1.09	E4.62
2006	0.86	0.98	0.90	1.26	3.82
2005	0.63	0.28	0.71	0.76	2.38
2004	0.92	-0.27	0.39	0.46	1.55
2003	0.69	0.89	0.78	0.89	3.24
2002	0.48	0.50	0.01	-0.20	0.80

Fiscal year ended Dec. 31. Next earnings report expected: Mid January. EPS Estimates based on S&P Operating Earnings; historical GAAP earnings are as reported.

Dividend Data (Dates: mm/dd Payment Date: mm/dd/yy)

Amount ($)	Date Decl.	Ex-Div. Date	Stk. of Record	Payment Date
0.340	12/12	01/03	01/05	01/31/07
0.340	03/20	04/03	04/05	04/30/07
0.380	04/18	07/03	07/06	07/31/07
0.380	09/18	10/03	10/05	10/31/07

Dividends have been paid since 1827. Source: Company reports.

Please read the Required Disclosures and Analyst Certification on the last page of this report.

The McGraw-Hill Companies

JPMorgan Chase & Co.

STANDARD &POOR'S

Business Summary November 01, 2007

CORPORATE OVERVIEW. JPMorgan's operations are divided into six major business lines: Investment Banking, Retail Financial Services (RFS), Card Services (CS), Commercial Banking (CB), Treasury & Securities Services (TSS), and Asset Management (AM).

JPM is one of the world's leading investment banks, with clients consisting of corporations, financial institutions, governments, and institutional investors worldwide. Its products and services include advising on corporate strategy and structure, equity and debt capital raising, sophisticated risk management, research, and market making in cash securities and derivative instruments.

RFS includes Home Finance, Consumer & Small Business Banking, Auto & Education Finance and Insurance. At year-end 2006, RFS had over 3,000 bank

branches, 8,500 ATMs and 270 mortgage offices. In 2006 JPM added 438 net new branches, including 339 acquired from The Bank of New York.

CS had over 154 million cards in circulation and $153 billion in managed loans as of December 31, 2006. Card Services offers a wide variety of products to satisfy the needs of its card members, including cards issued on behalf of many well-known partners, such as major airlines, hotels, universities, retailers, and other financial institutions. As of year-end 2006, CS was the second-largest MasterCard/Visa credit card issuer in the United States.

Company Financials Fiscal Year Ended Dec. 31

Per Share Data ($)	2006	2005	2004	2003	2002	2001	2000	1999	1998	1997
Tangible Book Value	16.11	15.88	14.77	14.77	15.82	12.54	12.95	18.59	17.93	15.84
Earnings	3.82	2.38	1.55	3.24	0.80	0.81	2.86	4.18	2.83	2.68
S&P Core Earnings	3.88	2.76	2.25	3.12	0.65	0.34	NA	NA	NA	NA
Dividends	1.36	1.36	1.36	1.36	1.36	1.34	1.23	1.06	0.93	0.81
Payout Ratio	34%	57%	88%	42%	170%	165%	43%	25%	33%	30%
Prices:High	49.00	40.56	43.84	38.26	39.68	57.33	67.17	60.75	51.71	42.19
Prices:Low	37.88	32.92	34.62	20.13	15.26	29.04	32.38	43.87	23.71	28.21
P/E Ratio:High	12	17	28	12	50	71	23	15	18	16
P/E Ratio:Low	9	14	22	6	19	36	11	10	8	11

Income Statement Analysis (Million $)										
Net Interest Income	21,242	19,831	16,761	12,337	11,526	10,802	9,512	8,744	8,566	8,158
Tax Equivalent Adjustment	NA	269	NA	NA	NA	NA	NA	NA	NA	NA
Non Interest Income	17,959	34,702	26,336	19,473	16,525	17,382	23,193	13,372	9,692	8,313
Loan Loss Provision	3,270	3,483	NA	NA	4,331	3,185	1,377	1,621	1,343	804
% Expense/Operating Revenue	97.7%	66.5%	85.6%	73.0%	81.2%	82.7%	69.8%	55.3%	63.5%	61.1%
Pretax Income	19,886	12,215	6,194	10,028	2,519	2,566	8,733	8,375	5,930	5,910
Effective Tax Rate	31.4%	30.6%	27.9%	33.0%	34.0%	33.0%	34.4%	35.0%	36.2%	37.6%
Net Income	13,649	8,483	4,466	6,719	1,663	1,719	5,727	5,446	3,782	3,708
% Net Interest Margin	2.16	2.19	NA	NA	2.09	1.99	1.87	2.98	2.89	2.86
S&P Core Earnings	13,852	9,802	6,456	6,439	1,290	698	NA	NA	NA	NA

Balance Sheet & Other Financial Data (Million $)										
Money Market Assets	506,262	432,358	390,168	329,739	314,110	265,875	293,429	115,168	83,391	106,207
Investment Securities	172,022	128,578	149,675	109,328	126,834	105,537	117,494	61,513	64,490	52,738
Commercial Loans	249,996	150,111	135,067	83,097	91,548	104,864	119,460	88,120	88,056	88,906
Other Loans	233,131	269,037	267,047	136,421	124,816	112,580	96,590	88,039	83,756	79,548
Total Assets	1,351,520	1,198,942	1,157,248	770,912	758,800	693,575	715,348	406,105	365,875	365,521
Demand Deposits	140,443	143,075	136,188	79,465	82,029	76,974	62,713	55,529	51,623	49,808
Time Deposits	498,345	411,916	385,268	247,027	222,724	216,676	216,652	186,216	160,814	143,880
Long Term Debt	117,358	119,886	105,718	54,782	45,190	44,172	47,788	20,690	18,375	15,127
Common Equity	115,790	107,072	105,314	45,145	41,297	40,090	40,818	22,689	22,810	20,002
% Return on Assets	1.1	0.7	0.5	0.9	0.2	0.2	0.8	1.4	1.0	1.1
% Return on Equity	12.2	8.0	5.9	15.4	4.0	4.1	15.2	23.6	17.2	18.4
% Loan Loss Reserve	1.5	1.7	1.8	2.1	2.5	2.1	1.7	2.0	2.1	2.2
% Loans/Deposits	75.6	75.5	77.1	67.2	71.0	74.0	77.3	72.9	84.0	87.0
% Equity to Assets	8.7	9.0	7.8	5.7	5.6	5.7	5.4	5.9	5.9	5.5

Data as orig reptd.; bef. results of disc opers/spec. items. Per share data adj. for stk. divs.; EPS diluted. E-Estimated. NA-Not Available. NM-Not Meaningful. NR-Not Ranked. UR-Under Review.

Office: 270 Park Ave, New York, NY 10017-2070.
Telephone: 212-270-6000.
Website: http://www.jpmorganchase.com
Chrmn & CEO: J. Dimon

EVP & CFO: M.J. Cavanagh
EVP & General Counsel: S.M. Cutler
EVP & Cntlr: J.L. Sclafani
Chief Admin Officer: F. Bisignano

Investor Contact: J. Bates (212-270-7318)
Board Members: J. H. Biggs, C. C. Bowles, S. B. Burke, J. S. Crown, J. Dimon, E. V. Futter, W. H. Gray, III, L. P. Jackson, Jr., J. W. Kessler, R. I. Lipp, R. A. Manoogian, D. C. Novak, L. R. Raymond, W. C. Weldon

Founded: 1823
Domicile: Delaware
Employees: 174,360

The McGraw-Hill Companies

Juniper Networks Inc

STANDARD &POOR'S

S&P Recommendation SELL ★ ★ ☆ ☆ ☆	Price $29.49 (as of Nov 23, 2007)	12-Mo. Target Price $28.00	Investment Style Large-Cap Blend

GICS Sector Information Technology
Sub-Industry Communications Equipment

Summary This company provides Internet Protocol networking products and services, with a specific emphasis on telecom routing solutions.

Key Stock Statistics (Source S&P, Vickers, company reports)

52-Wk Range	$37.95–17.21	S&P Oper. EPS 2007**E**	0.74	Market Capitalization(B)	$15.161	Beta	2.70
Trailing 12-Month EPS	$0.54	S&P Oper. EPS 2008**E**	1.02	Yield (%)	Nil	S&P 3-Yr. Proj. EPS CAGR(%)	15.00
Trailing 12-Month P/E	54.6	P/E on S&P Oper. EPS 2007**E**	39.9	Dividend Rate/Share	Nil	S&P Credit Rating	BB
$10K Invested 5 Yrs Ago	$33,780	Common Shares Outstg. (M)	514.1	Institutional Ownership (%)	NM		

Price Performance

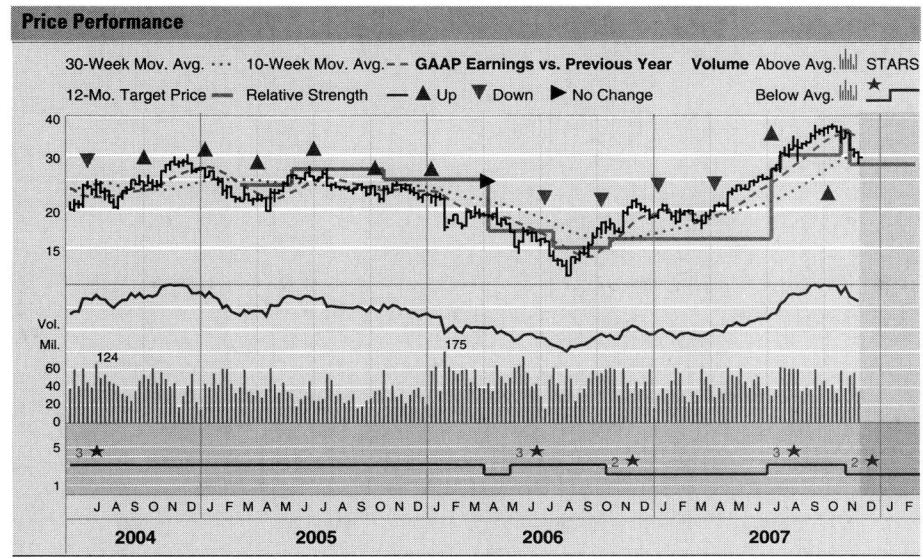

- 30-Week Mov. Avg. ···· 10-Week Mov. Avg. ─ ─ **GAAP Earnings vs. Previous Year**   Volume Above Avg. STARS
- 12-Mo. Target Price ─ Relative Strength ─ ▲ Up ▼ Down ▶ No Change   Below Avg.

Options: ASE, CBOE, P, Ph

Analysis prepared by **Ari Bensinger** on November 09, 2007, when the stock traded at **$ 31.98**.

Highlights

➤ Following an estimated 22% sales increase in 2007, we forecast sales advancing 16% in 2008, mainly reflecting accelerating demand for network infrastructure products from the service provider market. We believe JNPR needs to expand its distribution base and product application features to better compete in the enterprise market. We are optimistic about recent portfolio enhancements and new product introductions, specifically, the launch of a new ethernet switch and core router.

➤ We expect 2008 gross margins to remain flat with our 2007 estimate, at the 67% level, as the higher sales volume offsets an increasing mix of lower-margin enterprise sales and industry pricing pressure. We look for 2008 operating expenses as a percentage of sales to decrease moderately.

➤ After a decline in interest income on what we see as a lower cash balance, reflecting stock repurchases, we look for EPS of $1.02 in 2008, up from the $0.74 that we forecast for 2007. Estimates for both years include projected stock option expense of $0.12.

Investment Rationale/Risk

➤ We think recent product upgrades in core routing, as well as new opportunities in the carrier ethernet space, bode well for future growth opportunities. However, we see the enterprise business at risk from a more disciplined information technology spending environment. With JNPR's need for increased investments in the enterprise market, we see minimal operating leverage in the company's business model.

➤ Risks to our recommendation and target price include an increase in carrier spending, material market share gains in the routing market, and stronger than expected sales traction into the enterprise sector.

➤ Our 12-month target price of $28 is largely based on a P/E of 27X our 2008 EPS estimate of $1.02, above the industry average. This is warranted, in our view, by JNPR's strong position in IP transport, which is expanding at a rapid rate due to the proliferation of digital video. Using our three-year earnings growth estimate of 16%, our target price represents a P/E to growth ratio of 1.7X, in line with peers.

Qualitative Risk Assessment

LOW	MEDIUM	HIGH

Our risk assessment reflects the highly competitive nature of the industry and execution risks related to the company's planned expansion into the enterprise market.

Quantitative Evaluations

S&P Quality Ranking   NR

D	C	B-	B	B+	A-	A	A+

Relative Strength Rank   WEAK

29

LOWEST = 1   HIGHEST = 99

Revenue/Earnings Data

Revenue (Million $)

	1Q	2Q	3Q	4Q	Year
2007	626.9	664.9	735.1	--	--
2006	566.7	567.5	573.6	595.8	2,304
2005	449.1	493.0	546.4	575.5	2,064
2004	224.1	306.9	375.0	430.1	1,336
2003	157.2	165.1	172.1	207.0	701.4
2002	122.2	117.0	152.0	155.3	546.6

Earnings Per Share ($)

2007	0.11	0.15	0.15	E0.23	E0.74
2006	0.13	-2.13	0.10	0.12	-1.76
2005	0.13	0.15	0.14	0.17	0.59
2004	0.08	-0.02	0.08	0.11	0.25
2003	0.01	0.03	0.02	0.04	0.10
2002	-0.14	0.02	-0.24	0.02	-0.34

Fiscal year ended Dec. 31. Next earnings report expected: NA. EPS Estimates based on S&P Operating Earnings; historical GAAP earnings are as reported.

Dividend Data

No cash dividends have been paid.

The McGraw-Hill Companies

Juniper Networks Inc

STANDARD &POOR'S

Business Summary November 09, 2007

CORPORATE OVERVIEW. Juniper Networks, founded in 1996, makes secure Internet Protocol (IP) networking solutions that are designed to address the needs at the core and at the edge of the network, and for wireless access. The company's core product is IP backbone routers for service providers. The acquisition of NetScreen in 2004 added a broad family of network security solutions aimed at enterprises, service providers, and government entities.

JNPR has strategic distribution relationships with Ericsson A.B., Lucent Technologies and Siemens A.G, allowing for the resale of its products on a worldwide, non-exclusive basis, providing for discounts based upon the volume of products sold and specifying other general terms of sale. Operations are organized into three operating segments: infrastructure, service layer technologies (SLT), and service.

PRIMARY BUSINESS DYNAMICS. The infrastructure segment (66% of total sales in 2006) primarily offers scalable router products that are used to control and direct network traffic from the core, through the edge, aggregation and the customer premise equipment level. The company has experienced an increased demand for infrastructure products due to the adoption and expan-

sion of IP networks as a result of peer to peer interaction, increased broadband usage, video, and IP television.

Infrastructure products include the M-series and T-series routers, geared to service providers, offering carrier class reliability and scalability. The M-series, which can be deployed at the edge of operator networks, in small and medium core networks, includes the M320, M160, M40e, M20, M10i and M7i platforms. The MX-Series is a new product family developed as a platform to address the Carrier Ethernet market. The T-series, T640 and T320, and TX Matrix are primarily designed for core IP infrastructures. Other product platforms include E-series and J-series (wireless routers, developed through JNPR's joint venture with Ericsson). All routers run on JNPR's JUNOS Internet software, and are differentiated from their competition in that they also feature the company's high-performance, ASIC-based packet forwarding technology.

Company Financials Fiscal Year Ended Dec. 31

Per Share Data ($)

	2006	2005	2004	2003	2002	2001	2000	1999	1998	1997
Tangible Book Value	4.08	3.04	2.89	1.48	1.18	2.36	1.87	1.47	0.80	2.41
Cash Flow	-1.46	0.82	0.52	0.27	-0.16	0.42	0.53	-0.01	-1.35	-0.51
Earnings	-1.76	0.59	0.25	0.10	-0.34	-0.04	0.43	-0.05	-0.14	-0.20
S&P Core Earnings	-0.27	0.26	0.12	-0.06	-0.51	-0.38	NA	NA	NA	NA
Dividends	Nil	Nil	Nil	Nil	Nil	Nil	Nil	Nil	NA	NA
Payout Ratio	Nil	Nil	Nil	Nil	Nil	Nil	Nil	Nil	NA	NA
Prices:High	22.63	27.65	31.25	19.38	23.01	145.00	244.50	64.06	NA	NA
Prices:Low	12.09	19.65	18.75	6.88	4.15	8.90	48.83	5.67	NA	NA
P/E Ratio:High	NM	47	NM	NM	NM	NM	NM	NM	NA	NA
P/E Ratio:Low	NM	33	NM	NM	NM	NM	NM	NM	NA	NA

Income Statement Analysis (Million $)

	2006	2005	2004	2003	2002	2001	2000	1999	1998	1997
Revenue	2,304	2,064	1,336	701	547	887	674	103	3.81	Nil
Operating Income	496	595	376	141	42.2	205	249	-9.31	-30.1	-10.9
Depreciation	173	139	145	70.0	63.0	148	34.8	5.31	2.17	0.71
Interest Expense	3.59	3.93	5.38	39.1	55.6	61.4	52.7	Nil	Nil	0.33
Pretax Income	-897	502	219	59.0	-115	16.5	230	-6.61	-31.0	-10.4
Effective Tax Rate	NM	29.5%	38.0%	33.6%	NM	NM	35.8%	NM	NM	NM
Net Income	-1,001	354	136	39.2	-120	-13.4	148	-9.03	-31.0	-10.4
S&P Core Earnings	-156	156	65.9	-25.6	-180	-122	NA	NA	NA	NA

Balance Sheet & Other Financial Data (Million $)

	2006	2005	2004	2003	2002	2001	2000	1999	1998	1997
Cash	1,596	918	713	396	194	607	563	158	20.1	46.2
Current Assets	2,522	1,818	1,414	691	681	1,126	1,349	378	28.8	46.8
Total Assets	7,368	8,027	7,000	2,411	2,615	2,390	2,103	513	36.7	50.2
Current Liabilities	763	627	503	291	242	242	216	55.7	14.4	2.08
Long Term Debt	400	400	Nil	558	942	1,150	1,120	Nil	5.20	2.08
Common Equity	6,115	6,900	5,993	1,562	1,431	997	730	458	17.1	46.0
Total Capital	6,515	7,300	5,993	2,120	2,373	2,147	1,850	458	22.3	48.1
Capital Expenditures	102	98.2	63.2	19.4	36.1	241	35.0	10.0	6.53	3.11
Cash Flow	-828	493	281	109	-56.6	134	183	-3.73	-28.8	-9.65
Current Ratio	3.3	2.9	2.8	2.4	2.8	4.6	6.2	6.8	2.0	22.5
% Long Term Debt of Capitalization	6.1	5.5	Nil	26.3	39.7	53.6	60.5	Nil	23.4	4.3
% Net Income of Revenue	NM	17.2	10.2	5.6	NM	NM	22.0	NM	NM	NM
% Return on Assets	NM	4.7	2.9	1.6	NM	NM	11.3	NM	NM	NM
% Return on Equity	NM	5.5	3.6	2.6	NM	NM	24.9	NM	NM	NM

Data as orig reptd.; bef. results of disc opers/spec. items. Per share data adj. for stk. divs.; EPS diluted. E-Estimated. NA-Not Available. NM-Not Meaningful. NR-Not Ranked. UR-Under Review.

Office: 1194 North Mathilda Avenue, Sunnyvale, CA 94089.
Telephone: 408-745-2000.
Email: investor-relations@juniper.net
Website: http://www.juniper.net

Chrmn & CEO: S. Kriens
Vice Chrmn & CTO: P. Sindhu
COO: S. Elop
EVP & CFO: R.R. Dykes

Board Members: R. M. Calderoni, K. Goldman, W. R. Hearst, III, S. Kriens, M. Lawrie, K. Levy, S. Sclavos, P. Sindhu, W. R. Stensrud

Founded: 1996
Domicile: Delaware
Employees: 4,833

The McGraw-Hill Companies

KB Home

STANDARD &POOR'S

S&P Recommendation	HOLD ★★★☆☆	Price $21.69 (as of Nov 23, 2007)	12-Mo. Target Price $27.00	Investment Style Large-Cap Blend

GICS Sector Consumer Discretionary
Sub-Industry Homebuilding

Summary This large, diversified homebuilder has operations in most of the largest markets in the U.S.

Key Stock Statistics (Source S&P, Vickers, company reports)

52-Wk Range	$56.08– 20.74	S&P Oper. EPS 2007**E**	-9.90	Market Capitalization(B)	$1.942	Beta	1.71
Trailing 12-Month EPS	$-2.57	S&P Oper. EPS 2008**E**	0.45	Yield (%)	4.61	S&P 3-Yr. Proj. EPS CAGR(%)	2.00
Trailing 12-Month P/E	NM	P/E on S&P Oper. EPS 2007**E**	NM	Dividend Rate/Share	$1.00	S&P Credit Rating	BB+
$10K Invested 5 Yrs Ago	$10,812	Common Shares Outstg. (M)	89.5	Institutional Ownership (%)	98		

Price Performance

- 30-Week Mov. Avg. ···· 10-Week Mov. Avg. - - **GAAP Earnings vs. Previous Year** Volume Above Avg. STARS
- 12-Mo. Target Price — Relative Strength — ▲ Up ▼ Down ► No Change Below Avg.

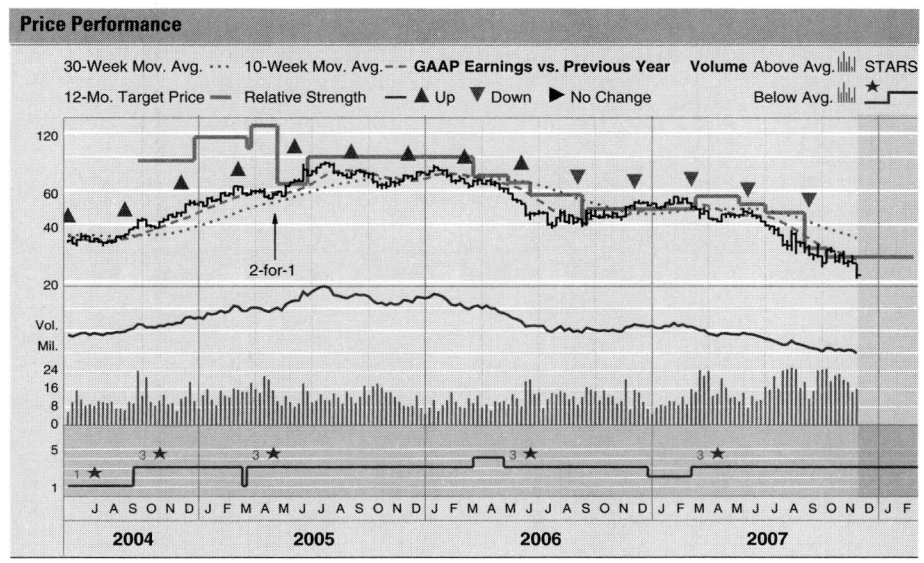

2-for-1

Options: ASE, CBOE, P, Ph

Analysis prepared by **Kenneth M. Leon, CPA** on October 01, 2007, when the stock traded at **$ 25.97**.

Qualitative Risk Assessment

LOW	MEDIUM	HIGH

Our risk assessment reflects our opinion that market conditions have worsened, and the visibility of a housing turnaround is not likely until sometime in 2008. KBH has taken large write-offs to adjust inventory, land and goodwill to its view of market value. Partly offsetting these risks is KBH's cash and borrowing capacity to run the business.

Quantitative Evaluations

S&P Quality Ranking A

D	C	B-	B	B+	A-	A	A+

Relative Strength Rank WEAK

13

LOWEST = 1   HIGHEST = 99

Revenue/Earnings Data

Revenue (Million $)

	1Q	2Q	3Q	4Q	Year
2007	1,767	1,413	1,544	--	--
2006	2,192	2,592	2,674	3,546	11,004
2005	1,636	2,130	2,525	3,150	9,442
2004	1,353	1,570	1,748	2,381	7,053
2003	1,095	1,440	1,442	1,873	5,851
2002	915.7	1,140	1,293	1,683	5,031

Earnings Per Share ($)

2007	0.34	-2.26	-6.19	E-1.79	E-9.90
2006	2.01	2.45	1.90	-0.64	5.82
2005	1.41	2.06	2.55	3.51	9.53
2004	0.88	1.20	1.42	2.21	5.70
2003	0.63	0.97	1.17	1.66	4.40
2002	0.48	0.71	0.94	1.46	3.58

Fiscal year ended Nov. 30. Next earnings report expected: Mid February. EPS Estimates based on S&P Operating Earnings; historical GAAP earnings are as reported.

Highlights

➤ We forecast that KB Home revenues will decrease 40% for FY 07 (Nov.), and decline 3% for FY 08, as the housing industry downturn plays out. We believe that KBH, like many homebuilders, is enduring weak orders and declining sales despite offering aggressive pricing. The company is responding to the depressed new housing market by booking near $800 million in asset write downs for home inventory, land acquisitions and goodwill.

➤ Gross proceeds of $800 million from the sale of its French operations that closed in July 2007 has enabled KBH to reduce its total debt outstanding to $2.2 billion, or to 45% of total capitalization, in line with peers. With $646 million in cash and no borrowings under a $1.5 billion revolving credit facility, we believe the company can survive the housing downturn and be well positioned for a recovery.

➤ We estimate a loss per share of $9.90 for FY 07 and EPS of $0.45 for FY 08. We note the possibility that KBH might be prompted to take additional write-downs, but we believe the worst was posted in the FY 07 third quarter.

Investment Rationale/Risk

➤ Earnings visibility has faded for homebuilders, including KBH, as the industry has experienced two years of a downturn, but we believe the rate of decline may ease for contract cancellations and order backlog in upcoming quarters. A strong balance sheet will enable KBH to withstand the housing downturn and be well positioned to gain market share when housing recovers, in our opinion.

➤ Risks to our recommendation and target price include higher mortgage rates, lower employment gains, and worse home affordability than we project. With KBH focused on entry-level and move-up products, its middle income base of buyers is relatively sensitive to these economic factors.

➤ Overall, we view risk and reward as roughly in balance for KBH shares. We apply a target price to book multiple of 1X--which is toward the low end of a historical range for KBH but still a premium to peers, warranted, we believe, as one of the largest homebuilders--to our 12-month forward book value estimate of $27 to derive our 12-month target price.

Dividend Data (Dates: mm/dd Payment Date: mm/dd/yy)

Amount ($)	Date Decl.	Ex-Div. Date	Stk. of Record	Payment Date
0.250	12/07	02/06	02/08	02/22/07
0.250	04/05	05/08	05/10	05/24/07
0.250	07/12	08/07	08/09	08/23/07
0.250	10/04	11/05	11/07	11/21/07

Dividends have been paid since 1986. Source: Company reports.

The McGraw·Hill Companies

KB Home

STANDARD &POOR'S

Business Summary October 01, 2007

CORPORATE OVERVIEW. From its base in California, KB Home has become one of the five largest single-family homebuilders in the country. In doing so, it has helped establish what has become the industry model for rapid growth: using the acquisition of smaller builders as platforms for growth into new markets. Since 1993, KBH has expanded into Nevada, Arizona, Colorado, New Mexico, Texas, Florida, Georgia, North Carolina, South Carolina, Illinois and Indiana.

KBH entered Georgia and North Carolina in March 2003, through the acquisition of Colony Homes; re-entered Illinois through the September 2003 takeover of Zale Homes in Chicago; South Carolina through the January 2004 purchase of Palmetto Traditional Homes; and Indiana through the June 2004 purchase of Dura Builders.

In FY 06 (Nov.), the company delivered a total of 39,013 homes, up from 37,140 for FY 05. The company reports in five geographic segments. In FY 06, the West Coast accounted for 18% of unit deliveries (18% in FY 05), the Southwest 18% (20%), Central 25% (27%), the Southeast 21% (19%), and France 18%

(16%).

Reflecting housing market conditions that show significant slowing, the number of lots under option was reduced to 56,316 at year-end FY (06) from 102,346. Similarly bracing for a slower market ahead, the company reduced its total lots owned or under option to 130,548 as of year-end FY 06, from 190,575 at year-end FY 05.

At the end of the FY 07 third quarter, KBH's backlog totaled 11,880 units, representing $3.07 billion. These levels are down 31% and 38%, respectively from the prior year's period. In our opinion, cancellation rates of 50% year over year for the quarter ending August 31, 2007 reflects the credit crunch which negatively affected mortgage availability and homebuyer demand.

Company Financials Fiscal Year Ended Nov. 30

Per Share Data ($)	2006	2005	2004	2003	2002	2001	2000	1999	1998	1997
Tangible Book Value	30.09	27.50	19.34	14.63	11.25	8.95	6.63	5.35	5.37	4.51
Cash Flow	6.11	9.76	5.96	4.65	3.77	3.32	3.14	1.95	1.38	0.87
Earnings	5.82	9.53	5.70	4.40	3.58	2.75	2.62	1.54	1.16	0.73
S&P Core Earnings	5.61	9.28	11.32	8.69	7.00	5.32	NA	NA	NA	NA
Dividends	1.00	0.56	0.15	0.15	0.15	0.15	0.15	0.15	0.15	0.15
Payout Ratio	17%	6%	3%	3%	4%	5%	6%	10%	13%	21%
Prices:High	81.99	85.45	53.76	37.48	27.20	20.72	19.16	15.13	17.50	11.56
Prices:Low	37.89	49.25	30.14	21.28	18.57	12.34	8.41	8.38	8.56	6.38
P/E Ratio:High	14	9	9	9	8	8	7	10	15	16
P/E Ratio:Low	7	5	5	5	5	4	3	5	7	9

Income Statement Analysis (Million $)										
Revenue	11,004	9,442	7,053	5,851	5,031	4,574	3,931	3,836	2,449	1,876
Operating Income	790	1,387	796	584	539	448	373	333	203	141
Depreciation	24.2	20.5	21.8	21.5	17.2	43.9	41.3	40.0	18.1	11.9
Interest Expense	18.8	24.0	22.7	30.2	44.2	59.5	50.9	45.0	38.4	42.5
Pretax Income	766	1,374	787	580	486	352	329	257	154	91.5
Effective Tax Rate	28.1%	33.0%	30.1%	31.5%	31.9%	31.3%	26.6%	30.7%	33.4%	35.9%
Net Income	482	842	481	371	314	214	210	147	95.3	58.2
S&P Core Earnings	465	808	467	357	302	207	NA	NA	NA	NA

Balance Sheet & Other Financial Data (Million $)										
Cash	655	145	234	138	330	281	33.1	28.0	63.4	68.2
Current Assets	NA	NA	NA	NA	NA	NA	NA	NA	NA	NA
Total Assets	9,014	7,747	5,836	4,236	4,026	3,693	2,829	2,664	1,860	1,419
Current Liabilities	NA	NA	NA	NA	NA	NA	NA	NA	NA	NA
Long Term Debt	3,027	2,433	2,048	1,393	1,181	1,111	1,208	1,308	800	698
Common Equity	2,923	2,852	2,056	1,593	1,274	1,092	655	676	475	383
Total Capital	6,139	5,429	4,231	3,075	2,530	2,267	1,919	1,994	1,472	1,083
Capital Expenditures	22.1	24.0	23.2	13.1	31.1	12.2	18.5	19.0	Nil	Nil
Cash Flow	503	863	503	392	332	258	251	187	113	70.1
Current Ratio	NA	NA	NA	NA	NA	NA	NA	NA	NA	NA
% Long Term Debt of Capitalization	49.3	44.8	48.4	45.3	46.7	49.0	62.9	65.6	54.3	64.5
% Net Income of Revenue	4.4	8.9	6.8	6.3	6.2	4.7	5.3	3.8	3.9	3.1
% Return on Assets	5.8	12.4	9.5	9.0	8.1	6.6	7.6	6.5	5.8	4.4
% Return on Equity	16.9	34.3	26.4	25.9	26.6	24.5	31.6	25.6	22.2	16.1

Data as orig reptd.; bef. results of disc opers/spec. items. Per share data adj. for stk. divs.; EPS diluted. E-Estimated. NA-Not Available. NM-Not Meaningful. NR-Not Ranked. UR-Under Review.

Office: 10990 Wilshire Blvd , Los Angeles, CA 90024.
Telephone: 310-231-4000.
Website: http://www.kbhome.com
Chrmn: S.F. Bollenbach

Pres & CEO: J.T. Mezger
EVP & CFO: D. Cecere
SVP & Chief Acctg Officer: W.R. Hollinger
Investor Contact: K. Masuda (310-893-7434)

Board Members: S. F. Bollenbach, R. Burkle, T. W. Finchem, R. R. Irani, K. M. Jastrow, II, J. A. Johnson, J. T. Lanni, M. Lora, M. G. McCaffery, J. T. Mezger, L. Moonves, L. G. Nogales

Founded: 1957
Domicile: Delaware
Employees: 5,100

The McGraw-Hill Companies

Kellogg Co

STANDARD &POOR'S

S&P Recommendation   HOLD ★★★☆☆

Price $52.96 (as of Nov 23, 2007)	**12-Mo. Target Price** $58.00	**Investment Style** Large-Cap Growth

GICS Sector Consumer Staples
Sub-Industry Packaged Foods & Meats

Summary Kellogg is a leading producer of ready-to-eat cereal, and also sells convenience foods such as cookies, crackers, cereal bars, fruit snacks, and frozen waffles.

Key Stock Statistics (Source S&P, Vickers, company reports)

52-Wk Range	$56.89– 48.68	S&P Oper. EPS 2007**E**	2.75	Market Capitalization(B)	$20.972
Trailing 12-Month EPS	$2.76	S&P Oper. EPS 2008**E**	2.95	Yield (%)	2.34
Trailing 12-Month P/E	19.2	P/E on S&P Oper. EPS 2007**E**	19.3	Dividend Rate/Share	$1.24
$10K Invested 5 Yrs Ago	$17,236	Common Shares Outstg. (M)	396.0	Institutional Ownership (%)	80

Beta	0.28
S&P 3-Yr. Proj. EPS CAGR(%)	9.00
S&P Credit Rating	BBB+

Price Performance

30-Week Mov. Avg. · · · · 10-Week Mov. Avg. ‑ ‑ **GAAP Earnings vs. Previous Year** Volume Above Avg. ▮▮▮ STARS
12-Mo. Target Price — Relative Strength — ▲ Up ▼ Down ▶ No Change   Below Avg. ▮▮▮ ★┌─

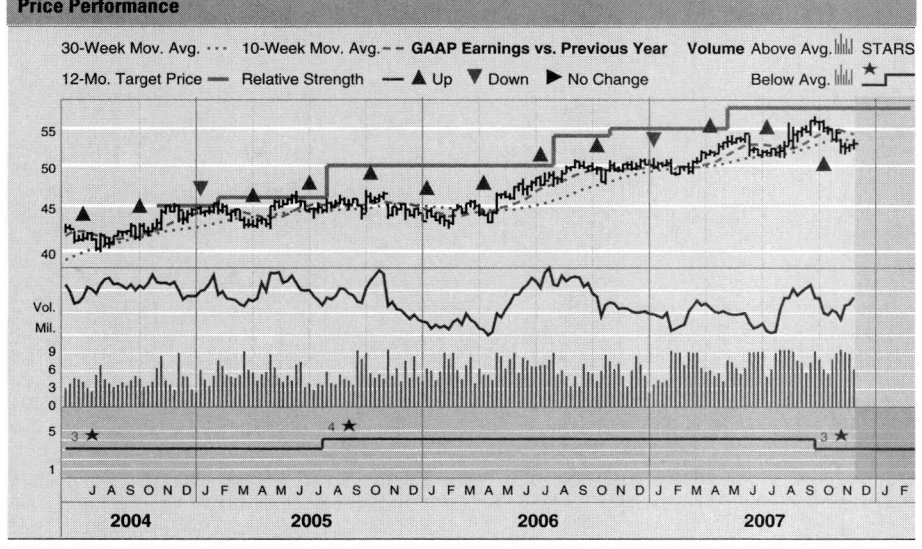

Options: CBOE, Ph

Analysis prepared by **Tom Graves, CFA** on September 28, 2007, when the stock traded at **$ 56.00**.

Highlights

► For 2008, we look for sales to increase moderately from the $11.75 billion projected for 2007. We expect that 2007 sales will include a favorable impact from currency exchange rates. In both years, we anticipate that profit margins will be pressured by commodity costs. However, at least in 2007, we look for less pressure from employee benefit costs. Also, we expect that Kellogg will receive benefits from cost-reduction projects, but that it will also incur expenses related to such initiatives. In 2007, we project that such per share expenses will total about $0.17, of which about $0.08 was incurred in 2007's second quarter. In full-year 2006, the company had about $0.14 of such costs.

► We estimate net income in 2008 of $1.17 billion ($2.97 a share), up from the $1.10 billion ($2.75) projected for 2007.

► For 2007, the company's board of directors has authorized a stock repurchase program of up to $650 million. As of June 30, 2007, the company had spent $264 million of this authorization to purchase about five million shares.

Investment Rationale/Risk

► Looking ahead, we expect profit growth to be bolstered by product innovation and expansion of Kellogg's snack product business. In 2007's first half, we were encouraged by overall revenue growth of 8.7%, which included a 2.2% benefit from currency fluctuation. The company's operating margin was flat, and net income was helped by an unusually low first quarter effective tax rate.

► Risks to our recommendation and target price include competitive pressures in K's businesses, consumer acceptance of new product introductions, commodity cost inflation, and the company's ability to achieve sales and earnings growth forecasts.

► In our view, projected strong company cash flow in 2007 (after capital expenditures) of close to $1 billion should help to give the stock appeal. Our 12-month target price of $58 reflects our view that the stock should receive a P/E valuation (on estimated 2007 EPS) that is similar to the average of what we expect from a peer group of packaged foods stocks. The stock recently had an indicated dividend yield of 2.2%.

Qualitative Risk Assessment

LOW	MEDIUM	HIGH

Our risk assessment for Kellogg Company reflects the relatively stable nature of the company's end markets, what we consider its strong balance sheet and cash flow, and corporate governance practices that we view as favorable versus peers.

Quantitative Evaluations

S&P Quality Ranking A-

D	C	B-	B	B+	A-	A	A+

Relative Strength Rank STRONG

73

LOWEST = 1   HIGHEST = 99

Revenue/Earnings Data

Revenue (Million $)

	1Q	2Q	3Q	4Q	Year
2007	2,963	3,015	3,004	--	--
2006	2,727	2,774	2,822	2,584	10,907
2005	2,572	2,587	2,623	2,394	10,177
2004	2,391	2,387	2,445	2,391	9,614
2003	2,148	2,247	2,282	2,135	8,812
2002	2,062	2,125	2,137	1,981	8,304

Earnings Per Share ($)

2007	0.80	0.75	0.76	E0.48	E2.75
2006	0.68	0.67	0.70	0.45	2.51
2005	0.61	0.62	0.66	0.47	2.36
2004	0.53	0.57	0.59	0.45	2.14
2003	0.40	0.50	0.56	0.46	1.92
2002	0.37	0.42	0.49	0.47	1.75

Fiscal year ended Dec. 31. Next earnings report expected: Late January. EPS Estimates based on S&P Operating Earnings; historical GAAP earnings are as reported.

Dividend Data (Dates: mm/dd Payment Date: mm/dd/yy)

Amount ($)	Date Decl.	Ex-Div. Date	Stk. of Record	Payment Date
0.291	04/27	05/30	06/01	06/15/07
0.291	04/27	05/30	06/01	06/15/07
0.310	04/27	08/29	08/31	09/14/07
0.310	10/26	11/29	12/03	12/14/07

Dividends have been paid since 1923. Source: Company reports.

Kellogg Co

Business Summary September 28, 2007

CORPORATE OVERVIEW. Kellogg Co., incorporated in 1922, is a leading producer of ready-to-eat cereal. Also, the company has expanded its operations to include convenience food products such as Pop-Tarts toaster pastries, Eggo frozen waffles, Nutri-Grain cereal bars, and Rice Krispies Treats squares.

With the 2001 acquisition of the Keebler Foods Co., the company also markets cookies, crackers and other convenience food products under brand names such as Keebler, Cheez-It, Murray and Famous Amos, and manufactures private label cookies, crackers and other products.

Sales contributions by geographic region in 2006 were: North America 67%, Europe 20%, Latin America 8%, and Asia Pacific 5%. Also, in 2006, cereal sold through North American retail channels represented 24% of total net sales, while international cereal sales represented 28%. Other sales categories in-

cluded North American retail snacks (30%), North American frozen and specialty channels (13%), and international convenience foods (5%).

In 2006, Kellogg's top five customers, collectively, accounted for about 33% of its net sales, and about 42% of U.S. net sales. Kellogg's largest customer, Wal-Mart Stores, Inc., and its affiliates, accounted for about 18% of net sales during 2006.

Kellogg's expenditures for research and development were about $190.6 million in 2006, and $181.0 million in 2005.

Company Financials Fiscal Year Ended Dec. 31

Per Share Data ($)	2006	2005	2004	2003	2002	2001	2000	1999	1998	1997
Tangible Book Value	NM	NM	NM	NM	NM	NM	1.21	1.28	1.26	2.42
Cash Flow	3.39	3.30	3.15	2.83	2.60	2.26	2.16	1.54	1.91	2.07
Earnings	2.51	2.36	2.14	1.92	1.75	1.18	1.45	0.83	1.23	1.32
S&P Core Earnings	2.62	2.29	2.10	1.86	1.24	0.77	NA	NA	NA	NA
Dividends	1.14	1.06	1.01	1.01	1.01	1.01	1.00	0.96	0.92	0.87
Payout Ratio	45%	45%	47%	53%	58%	86%	69%	116%	75%	66%
Prices:High	50.95	46.99	45.32	38.57	37.00	34.00	32.00	42.25	50.19	50.50
Prices:Low	42.41	42.35	37.00	27.85	29.02	24.25	20.75	30.00	28.50	32.00
P/E Ratio:High	20	20	21	20	21	29	22	51	41	38
P/E Ratio:Low	17	18	17	15	17	21	14	36	23	24

Income Statement Analysis (Million $)										
Revenue	10,907	10,177	9,614	8,812	8,304	8,853	6,955	6,984	6,762	6,830
Operating Income	2,119	2,142	2,091	1,917	1,857	1,640	1,367	1,361	1,243	1,480
Depreciation	353	392	410	373	348	439	291	288	278	287
Interest Expense	307	300	309	371	391	352	138	119	119	108
Pretax Income	1,471	1,425	1,366	1,170	1,144	804	868	537	783	905
Effective Tax Rate	31.7%	31.2%	34.8%	32.7%	37.0%	40.1%	32.3%	37.0%	35.8%	37.7%
Net Income	1,004	980	891	787	721	482	588	338	503	564
S&P Core Earnings	1,047	953	875	763	510	312	NA	NA	NA	NA

Balance Sheet & Other Financial Data (Million $)										
Cash	411	219	417	141	101	2,318	204	151	136	173
Current Assets	2,427	2,197	2,122	1,797	1,763	1,902	1,607	1,569	1,497	1,467
Total Assets	10,714	10,575	10,790	10,231	10,219	10,369	4,896	4,809	5,052	4,877
Current Liabilities	4,020	3,163	2,846	2,766	3,015	2,208	2,493	1,588	1,719	1,657
Long Term Debt	3,053	3,703	3,893	4,265	4,519	5,619	709	1,613	1,614	1,416
Common Equity	2,069	2,284	2,257	1,443	895	871	898	813	890	998
Total Capital	5,122	5,986	6,150	5,709	5,415	6,491	1,607	2,426	2,504	2,414
Capital Expenditures	453	374	279	247	254	277	231	266	344	312
Cash Flow	1,357	1,372	1,301	1,160	1,069	921	878	626	781	851
Current Ratio	0.6	0.7	0.7	0.6	0.6	0.9	0.6	1.0	0.9	0.9
% Long Term Debt of Capitalization	59.6	61.9	63.3	74.7	83.5	86.6	44.1	66.5	64.5	58.7
% Net Income of Revenue	9.2	9.6	9.3	8.9	8.7	5.4	8.5	4.8	7.4	8.3
% Return on Assets	9.4	9.3	8.5	7.7	7.0	6.3	12.1	6.9	10.1	11.4
% Return on Equity	46.1	43.2	48.1	67.3	81.6	54.5	68.7	39.7	53.3	49.5

Data as orig reptd.; bef. results of disc opers/spec. items. Per share data adj. for stk. divs.; EPS diluted. E-Estimated. NA-Not Available. NM-Not Meaningful. NR-Not Ranked. UR-Under Review.

Office: One Kellogg Sq, Battle Creek, MI, USA 49016-3599.
Telephone: 269-961-2000.
Website: http://www.kelloggcompany.com
Chrmn: J.M. Jenness

Pres & CEO: A.D. Mackay
Pres & EVP: J.W. Montie
EVP & CFO: J.A. Bryant
SVP, Secy & General Counsel: G.H. Pilnick

Board Members: B. S. Carson, Sr., J. T. Dillon, C. X. Gonzalez, G. Gund, J. M. Jenness, D. A. Johnson, L. D. Jorndt, A. D. Mackay, A. McLaughlin Korologos, W. D. Perez, W. C. Richardson, S. Speirn, R. A. Steele, J. L. Zabriskie

Founded: 1906
Domicile: Delaware
Employees: 25,856

KeyCorp

STANDARD
&POOR'S

S&P Recommendation **BUY** ★★★★☆	Price $23.47 (as of Nov 26, 2007)	12-Mo. Target Price $37.00	Investment Style Large-Cap Value

GICS Sector Financials
Sub-Industry Regional Banks

Summary This multiregional bank holding company, headquartered in Cleveland, operates over 950 branch offices in Ohio, New York, Washington State, Oregon, Maine, Indiana, and eight other states.

Key Stock Statistics (Source S&P, Vickers, company reports)

52-Wk Range	$39.90– 23.42	S&P Oper. EPS 2007**E**	2.80	Market Capitalization(B)	$9.138	Beta	0.77
Trailing 12-Month EPS	$2.61	S&P Oper. EPS 2008**E**	2.90	Yield (%)	6.22	S&P 3-Yr. Proj. EPS CAGR(%)	5.40
Trailing 12-Month P/E	9.0	P/E on S&P Oper. EPS 2007**E**	8.4	Dividend Rate/Share	$1.46	S&P Credit Rating	A-
$10K Invested 5 Yrs Ago	$11,925	Common Shares Outstg. (M)	389.4	Institutional Ownership (%)	59		

Price Performance

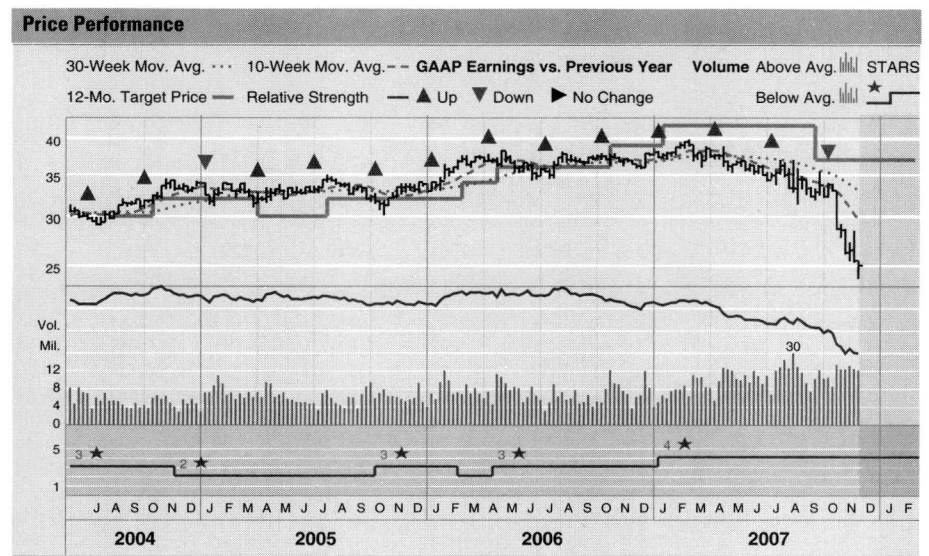

30-Week Mov. Avg. ···   10-Week Mov. Avg.- -   **GAAP Earnings vs. Previous Year**   Volume Above Avg. STARS
12-Mo. Target Price — Relative Strength — ▲ Up ▼ Down ► No Change   Below Avg. ★

Options: ASE, P, Ph

Analysis prepared by **Erik Oja** on November 26, 2007, when the stock traded at **$ 23.47**.

Highlights

➤ We forecast total loan portfolio growth of 6.1% in 2007, slowing to 4.8% in 2008, a growth rate that reflects KEY's Ohio and New York footprint. Recurring fee income has increased strongly in 2007 to date, while total fee income has been boosted by the sale of MasterCard shares, the sale of the McDonald Investments branch network, and principal investing gains. Our estimates for recurring fee income are a decline of 5.5% in 2007 and 6.0% growth in 2008. We expect 8.0% total fee income growth for all of 2007, followed by a decline of 1.4% in 2008.

➤ Credit quality declined in the third quarter, as 0.72% of loans were classified as non-performing, due to non-performing credits associated with housing developments. Accordingly, we expect loan loss provisions to rise to $236 million in 2007 and $290 million in 2008, from $147 million in 2006.

➤ We forecast share repurchases of 5.0 million in each of the next three quarters under the current share repurchase authorization of 16.0 million shares. We estimate 2007 EPS of $2.80, a 3.8% decrease from $2.91 earned in 2006. Our 2008 EPS estimate is $2.90, up 3.6%.

Investment Rationale/Risk

➤ Our buy recommendation reflects our view of KEY's better than peers credit quality, favorable non-interest expense controls, recurring fee income growth, an allowance for loan losses that is 1.9X the level of non-performing loans, an active share repurchase program, and a recent 5.8% dividend yield. We think KEY has kept loan growth relatively low in an attempt to stem the erosion of credit quality, a trend that may lead to less interest income currently, but lower loan loss provisions later, a trade-off that we favor as credit headwinds are increasing industry-wide.

➤ Risks to our recommendation and target price include a continuing flat or inverted yield curve further increasing the cost of deposits, and an economic slowdown further adversely affecting loan growth and credit quality.

➤ Our 12-month target price of $37 is derived by applying a slight premium-to-peers 12.8X multiple to our 2008 EPS estimate.

Qualitative Risk Assessment

LOW	MEDIUM	HIGH

Our risk assessment reflects our view of the company's large-cap valuation, the strong credit quality of its loan portfolio, and its history of profitability. While the company operates in a highly competitive and fragmented industry, the industry tends to produce relatively stable financial results.

Quantitative Evaluations

S&P Quality Ranking B+

D	C	B-	B	B+	A-	A	A+

Relative Strength Rank WEAK

15

LOWEST = 1   HIGHEST = 99

Revenue/Earnings Data

Revenue (Million $)

	1Q	2Q	3Q	4Q	Year
2007	2,022	2,044	1,872	--	--
2006	1,732	1,872	1,932	1,971	7,507
2005	1,565	1,602	1,705	1,823	6,695
2004	1,370	1,358	1,388	1,448	5,564
2003	1,418	1,456	1,434	1,422	5,730
2002	1,535	1,550	1,527	1,523	6,135

Earnings Per Share ($)

2007	0.89	0.85	0.57	E0.73	E2.80
2006	0.66	0.75	0.74	0.76	2.91
2005	0.64	0.70	0.67	0.72	2.73
2004	0.59	0.58	0.61	0.51	2.30
2003	0.51	0.53	0.53	0.55	2.12
2002	0.56	0.57	0.57	0.57	2.27

Fiscal year ended Dec. 31. Next earnings report expected: Mid January. EPS Estimates based on S&P Operating Earnings; historical GAAP earnings are as reported.

Dividend Data (Dates: mm/dd Payment Date: mm/dd/yy)

Amount ($)	Date Decl.	Ex-Div. Date	Stk. of Record	Payment Date
0.365	01/18	02/23	02/27	03/15/07
0.365	05/10	05/24	05/29	06/15/07
0.365	07/20	08/24	08/28	09/14/07
0.365	11/15	11/23	11/27	12/14/07

Dividends have been paid since 1963. Source: Company reports.

Please read the Required Disclosures and Analyst Certification on the last page of this report.

The McGraw-Hill Companies

KeyCorp

STANDARD &POOR'S

Business Summary November 26, 2007

CORPORATE OVERVIEW. KEY owns KeyBank, located in Ohio, New York, Washington, Oregon, Maine, Colorado, Indiana, Utah, Idaho, Vermont, Alaska and Kentucky. The company has two business groups: Community Banking, and National Banking.

The Community Banking segment generates about 52% of total revenues, and houses Regional Banking and Commercial Banking.

National Banking generates about 48% of total revenues, and houses Real Estate Capital, Equipment Finance, Institutional and Capital Markets, Consumer Finance, Indirect Lending, Commercial Floor Plan Lending, and National Home Equity.

MARKET PROFILE. As of June 30, 2007 (latest available FDIC data), KEY had 958 branches and $57.3 billion in deposits, with about 60% of its deposits and 45% of its branches concentrated in Ohio and New York, according to Highline Data. In Ohio, KEY had 227 branches, $18.1 billion in deposits, and a deposit market share of about 8.1%, which ranks third. In New York, KEY had 198 branches, $13.0 billion in deposits, and a deposit market share of about 1.7%, which ranks twelfth. In Washington State, KEY had 152 branches, $8.0 billion in deposits, and a deposit market share of about 6.4%, which ranks fourth. In Oregon, KEY had 64 branches, $3.2 billion in deposits, and a deposit market share of about 5.4%, which ranks sixth. In Maine, KEY had 63 branches, $2.6 billion in deposits, and a deposit market share of about 10.9%, which ranks second. In Indiana, KEY had 64 branches, $2.6 billion in deposits, and a deposit market share of about 2.5%, which ranks sixth. In Colorado, KEY had 48 branches, $2.3 billion in deposits, and a deposit market share of about 2.5%, which ranks seventh. In addition, KEY had a number three ranking in Idaho, and a number five market ranking in Vermont and in Alaska. Finally, KEY had offices in Utah, Michigan and Florida, with a small presence in Kentucky.

Company Financials Fiscal Year Ended Dec. 31

Per Share Data ($)	2006	2005	2004	2003	2002	2001	2000	1999	1998	1997
Tangible Book Value	15.99	15.05	13.91	13.87	13.34	11.85	12.39	11.13	10.28	9.14
Earnings	2.91	2.73	2.30	2.12	2.27	0.37	2.30	2.45	2.23	2.07
S&P Core Earnings	2.93	2.72	2.41	2.12	2.10	0.43	NA	NA	NA	NA
Dividends	1.38	1.30	1.24	1.22	1.20	1.18	1.12	1.04	0.94	0.84
Payout Ratio	47%	48%	54%	58%	53%	NM	49%	42%	42%	41%
Prices:High	38.63	35.00	34.50	29.41	29.40	29.25	28.50	38.13	44.88	36.59
Prices:Low	32.90	30.10	28.23	22.31	20.98	20.49	15.56	21.00	23.38	23.94
P/E Ratio:High	13	13	15	14	13	79	12	16	20	18
P/E Ratio:Low	11	11	12	11	9	55	7	9	10	12

Income Statement Analysis (Million $)										
Net Interest Income	2,815	2,790	2,637	2,725	2,749	2,825	2,730	2,787	2,749	2,794
Tax Equivalent Adjustment	103	121	94.0	71.0	120	45.0	28.0	32.0	34.0	44.0
Non Interest Income	2,126	2,077	1,742	1,749	1,763	1,690	2,222	2,265	1,566	1,305
Loan Loss Provision	150	143	185	501	553	1,350	490	348	297	320
% Expense/Operating Revenue	62.4%	64.5%	62.8%	60.3%	57.3%	64.5%	58.6%	60.0%	58.6%	59.4%
Pretax Income	1,643	1,588	1,388	1,242	1,312	259	1,517	1,684	1,479	1,345
Effective Tax Rate	27.4%	28.9%	31.3%	27.3%	25.6%	39.4%	33.9%	34.3%	32.7%	31.7%
Net Income	1,193	1,129	954	903	976	157	1,002	1,107	996	919
% Net Interest Margin	3.67	3.69	3.64	3.80	3.97	3.81	3.69	3.93	4.18	4.62
S&P Core Earnings	1,198	1,125	1,006	898	896	179	NA	NA	NA	NA

Balance Sheet & Other Financial Data (Million $)										
Money Market Assets	Nil	Nil	NA	NA	NA	NA	NA	NA	NA	NA
Investment Securities	13,409	12,974	13,023	12,944	13,592	10,676	12,626	9,511	6,254	8,938
Commercial Loans	48,306	39,291	43,276	36,189	36,612	38,063	39,610	36,672	22,685	18,013
Other Loans	17,520	20,078	25,188	26,522	25,845	25,246	27,295	27,550	39,327	35,367
Total Assets	92,337	93,126	90,739	84,487	85,202	80,938	87,270	83,395	80,020	73,699
Demand Deposits	15,237	13,335	11,581	11,175	10,630	23,128	9,076	8,607	9,540	9,368
Time Deposits	43,879	45,430	46,261	39,683	38,716	21,667	39,573	34,626	33,043	35,705
Long Term Debt	14,533	13,939	14,846	15,294	16,865	15,842	15,404	17,124	13,964	7,446
Common Equity	7,703	7,598	7,117	6,969	6,835	6,155	6,623	6,389	6,167	5,223
% Return on Assets	1.3	1.2	1.1	1.1	1.2	0.2	1.2	1.4	1.3	1.3
% Return on Equity	15.6	15.3	13.5	13.1	15.0	2.5	15.4	17.6	17.5	18.1
% Loan Loss Reserve	1.4	1.4	1.7	2.2	2.3	2.7	1.5	1.4	1.5	1.7
% Loans/Deposits	117.5	118.9	118.4	123.3	126.6	138.0	137.5	148.5	145.6	118.4
% Equity to Assets	8.3	8.0	8.0	8.1	7.8	7.6	7.6	7.7	7.4	7.2

Data as orig reptd.; bef. results of disc opers/spec. items. Per share data adj. for stk. divs.; EPS diluted. E-Estimated. NA-Not Available. NM-Not Meaningful. NR-Not Ranked. UR-Under Review.

Office: 127 Public Square, Cleveland, OH 44114-1306.
Telephone: 216-689-6300.
Website: http://www.key.com
Chrmn, Pres & CEO: H.L. Meyer, III

Vice Chrmn: T.W. Bunn
Vice Chrmn: B. Mooney
Vice Chrmn & Chief Admin Officer: T.C. Stevens
Sr EVP & CFO: J.B. Weeden

Board Members: R. Alvarez, W. G. Bares, E. P. Campbell, C. A. Cartwright, A. M. Cutler, H. J. Dallas, C. R. Hogan, L. E. Martin, E. R. Menasce, H. L. Meyer, III, B. R. Sanford, T. C. Stevens, P. G. Ten Eyck, II

Founded: 1849
Domicile: Ohio
Employees: 20,006

The McGraw-Hill Companies

Kimberly-Clark Corp

**STANDARD
&POOR'S**

| **S&P Recommendation** BUY ★★★★☆ | Price $68.25 (as of Nov 23, 2007) | 12-Mo. Target Price $79.00 | Investment Style Large-Cap Blend |

GICS Sector Consumer Staples
Sub-Industry Household Products

Summary This leading consumer products company's global tissue, personal care and healthcare brands include Huggies, Pull-Ups, Kotex, Depend, Kleenex, Scott and Kimberly-Clark.

Key Stock Statistics (Source S&P, Vickers, company reports)

52-Wk Range	$72.79– 63.79	S&P Oper. EPS 2007**E**	4.25	Market Capitalization(B)	$29.048	Beta	0.48
Trailing 12-Month EPS	$4.07	S&P Oper. EPS 2008**E**	4.68	Yield (%)	3.11	S&P 3-Yr. Proj. EPS CAGR(%)	8.00
Trailing 12-Month P/E	16.8	P/E on S&P Oper. EPS 2007**E**	16.1	Dividend Rate/Share	$2.12	S&P Credit Rating	A+
$10K Invested 5 Yrs Ago	NA	Common Shares Outstg. (M)	425.6	Institutional Ownership (%)	84		

Price Performance

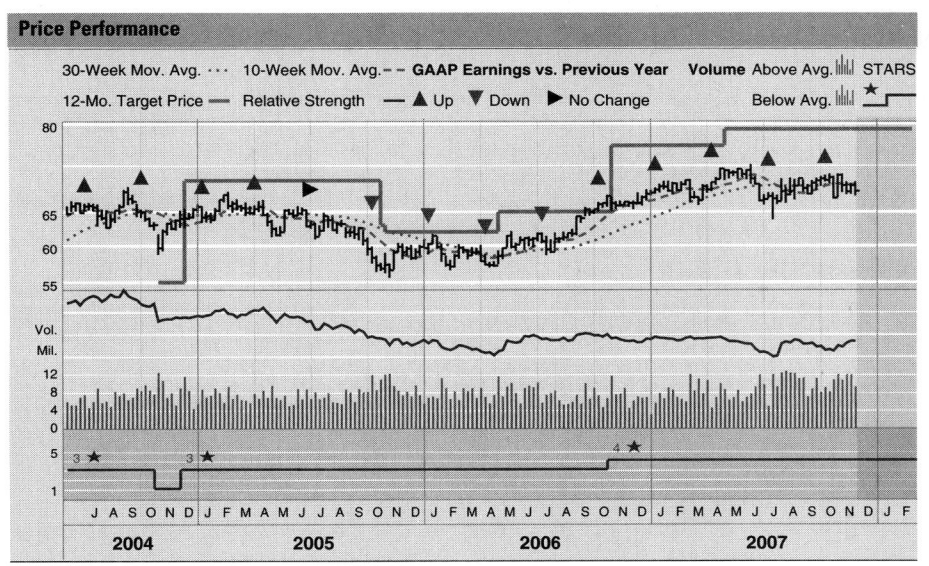

30-Week Mov. Avg. · · · 10-Week Mov. Avg. - - **GAAP Earnings vs. Previous Year** Volume Above Avg. STARS
12-Mo. Target Price — Relative Strength — ▲ Up ▼ Down ▶ No Change Below Avg.

Options: ASE, CBOE, P

Analysis prepared by **Loran Braverman, CFA** on October 22, 2007, when the stock traded at **$ 70.19**.

Qualitative Risk Assessment

| LOW | MEDIUM | HIGH |

Our risk assessment reflects that demand for household and personal care products is generally static, and that demand is usually not affected by changes in the economy or geopolitical factors.

Quantitative Evaluations

S&P Quality Ranking A

| D | C | B- | B | B+ | A- | **A** | A+ |

Relative Strength Rank STRONG

72

LOWEST = 1 HIGHEST = 99

Revenue/Earnings Data

Revenue (Million $)

	1Q	2Q	3Q	4Q	Year
2007	4,385	4,502	4,621	--	--
2006	4,068	4,161	4,210	4,307	16,747
2005	3,906	3,987	4,001	4,009	15,903
2004	3,712	3,687	3,783	3,901	15,083
2003	3,460	3,545	3,642	3,702	14,348
2002	3,331	3,409	3,487	3,340	13,566

Earnings Per Share ($)

2007	0.98	1.00	1.04	E1.11	E4.25
2006	0.60	0.82	0.79	1.05	3.25
2005	0.93	0.88	0.68	0.82	3.31
2004	0.88	0.88	0.87	0.92	3.55
2003	0.78	0.82	0.83	0.91	3.33
2002	0.86	0.81	0.85	0.72	3.24

Fiscal year ended Dec. 31. Next earnings report expected: Late January. EPS Estimates based on S&P Operating Earnings; historical GAAP earnings are as reported.

Highlights

➤ In 2007, we expect overall sales growth of 8%, including 3% from currency translation, with personal care division revenues up 10%, driven by new products and growth in developing markets. We also see consumer tissue segment sales up 7.5%, helped by growth in developing markets and price increases. For 2008, our forecast for overall growth is 5%, assuming no impact from currency and more difficult comparisons. Our sales growth outlook for the two largest divisions - personal care and consumer tissue - are 6.5% and 3%, respectively.

➤ We expect the operating margin to be flat in 2007, with commodity cost pressures from pulp and energy and planned strategic investments in advertising and promotions offsetting benefits from of a strategic cost reduction program, begun in late 2005, and price increases. For 2008, we see similar trends but with enough moderation in commodity cost pressures to allow for a 40 basis point improvement in the operating margin.

➤ We project that operating EPS will increase 9.7%, to $4.25, in 2007 and a further 10% in 2008, to $4.68.

Investment Rationale/Risk

➤ Although we continue to see intense competition in developed countries and in consumer tissue and personal care categories, we believe the company's efforts to expand in non-traditional (for KMB) categories and its focus on certain developing markets will support sales growth. In addition, we think KMB's earnings have started to benefit in 2007 from the strategic cost reduction program begun in late 2005.

➤ Risks to our recommendation and target price include increased promotional activity in the consumer paper category, higher commodity and energy costs, a lack of product innovation, and decreased consumer acceptance of KMB's products.

➤ Our 12-month target price of $79 is based on a blend of our historical and relative analyses. Our historical analysis suggests a value of $81, using a P/E that is slightly below the median of the last 10 years applied to our 2008 EPS forecast of $4.68. Our peer analysis applies a discount to the group average, implying a target price of $76.

Dividend Data (Dates: mm/dd Payment Date: mm/dd/yy)

Amount ($)	Date Decl.	Ex-Div. Date	Stk. of Record	Payment Date
0.530	02/21	03/07	03/09	04/03/07
0.530	04/26	06/06	06/08	07/03/07
0.530	08/01	09/05	09/07	10/02/07
0.530	11/14	12/05	12/07	01/03/08

Dividends have been paid since 1935. Source: Company reports.

Please read the Required Disclosures and Analyst Certification on the last page of this report.

The McGraw-Hill Companies

Kimberly-Clark Corp

STANDARD
&POOR'S

Business Summary October 22, 2007

CORPORATE OVERVIEW. Kimberly-Clark, best known for brand names such as Kleenex, Scott, Huggies and Kotex, sells consumer and other products in more than 150 countries. After operating as a broadly diversified enterprise, KMB made a major transition since the early 1990s, transforming itself into a global consumer products company. The company further developed its healthcare business through the acquisitions of Technol Medical Products, Ballard Medical Products, and Safeskin Corp. Reflecting more than 30 strategic acquisitions and 20 strategic divestitures since 1992, KMB has become a leading global manufacturer of tissue, personal care and healthcare products, manufactured in 37 countries. In 2004, KMB distributed to its shareholders all of the outstanding shares of Neenah Paper, Inc., which was formed in 2004 to facilitate the spin-off of KMB's U.S. fine paper and technical paper businesses and its Canadian pulp mills.

KMB classifies its business into four reportable global segments: Personal Care; Consumer Tissue; K-C Professional & Other; and Health Care. In 2006, Personal Care contributed 40% of sales and 47% of segment operating profits; Consumer Tissue 36% and 28%; K-C Professional & Other 16% and 16%; and Health Care 8% and 9%.

In 2006, sales in the U.S. and Canada contributed about 57% to sales, Europe 18%, and Asia, Latin America and other 25%. Wal-Mart Stores, Inc. is KMB's single largest customer, accounting for about 13% of net sales in each of 2004, 2005 and 2006.

CORPORATE STRATEGY. In mid-2003, KMB introduced a new strategic plan called the Global Business Plan (GBP), which involves prioritizing growth opportunities and applying greater financial discipline to KMB's global operations. The annual goals established by the GBP are: top-line growth of 3%-5%; EPS growth in the mid- to high-single digits; an operating margin improvement of 40 to 50 basis points; capital spending of 5%-6% of net sales; an ROIC improvement of 40 to 50 basis points; and dividend increases in the high single digits to the low double digits. On average, in the 2004 through 2006 period, we believe KMB met or exceeded all these goals but an operating margin improvement, which was adversely affected by unusually high inflationary cost pressures. Also, under the GBP, capital allocation focused on more targeted expansion activity and an increased emphasis on innovation and cost reduction. In the 2004 through 2006 period (2001 through 2003 period), capital was allocated as follows 29% (45%) for expansion, 29% (21%) for innovation, 24% (13%) for cost savings and 18% (21%) for other.

Company Financials Fiscal Year Ended Dec. 31

Per Share Data ($)	2006	2005	2004	2003	2002	2001	2000	1999	1998	1997
Tangible Book Value	7.10	6.22	8.13	8.21	6.65	7.10	7.04	7.12	6.12	6.35
Cash Flow	5.34	5.08	5.32	4.80	4.60	1.39	4.55	4.17	3.11	2.46
Earnings	3.25	3.31	3.55	3.33	3.24	3.02	3.34	3.09	2.13	1.58
S&P Core Earnings	3.27	3.32	3.56	3.35	2.74	2.49	NA	NA	NA	NA
Dividends	1.96	1.80	1.60	1.36	1.20	1.12	1.08	1.03	0.99	0.96
Payout Ratio	60%	54%	45%	41%	37%	37%	32%	33%	46%	61%
Prices:High	68.58	68.29	69.00	59.30	66.79	72.19	73.25	69.56	59.44	56.88
Prices:Low	56.59	55.60	56.19	42.92	45.30	52.06	42.00	44.81	35.88	43.25
P/E Ratio:High	21	21	19	18	21	24	22	23	28	36
P/E Ratio:Low	17	17	16	13	14	17	13	15	17	27

Income Statement Analysis (Million $)										
Revenue	16,747	15,903	15,083	14,348	13,566	14,524	13,982	13,007	12,298	12,547
Operating Income	3,034	3,155	3,358	3,158	3,170	3,162	3,203	2,815	2,320	2,276
Depreciation	933	844	800	746	707	740	673	586	542	491
Interest Expense	220	190	163	168	182	192	222	213	199	165
Pretax Income	2,064	2,106	2,328	2,153	2,411	2,319	2,622	2,441	1,763	1,345
Effective Tax Rate	22.7%	20.8%	20.8%	23.9%	27.7%	27.8%	28.9%	29.9%	31.9%	32.2%
Net Income	1,500	1,581	1,770	1,694	1,686	1,610	1,801	1,668	1,177	884
S&P Core Earnings	1,511	1,581	1,777	1,708	1,424	1,329	NA	NA	NA	NA

Balance Sheet & Other Financial Data (Million $)										
Cash	361	364	594	291	495	405	207	323	144	91.0
Current Assets	5,270	4,783	4,962	4,438	4,274	3,922	3,790	3,562	3,367	3,489
Total Assets	17,067	16,303	17,018	16,780	15,586	15,008	14,480	12,816	11,510	11,266
Current Liabilities	5,016	4,643	4,537	3,919	4,038	4,168	4,574	3,846	3,791	3,706
Long Term Debt	3,069	3,352	3,021	3,301	3,398	2,962	Nil	1,927	2,068	1,804
Common Equity	6,097	5,558	6,630	6,766	5,650	5,647	5,767	5,093	3,887	4,125
Total Capital	9,981	9,878	10,859	10,366	10,158	9,923	7,036	8,101	6,819	6,673
Capital Expenditures	972	710	535	878	871	1,100	1,170	786	670	944
Cash Flow	2,432	2,425	2,571	2,440	2,393	740	2,474	2,254	1,719	1,375
Current Ratio	1.1	1.0	1.1	1.1	1.1	0.9	0.8	0.9	0.9	0.9
% Long Term Debt of Capitalization	30.8	33.9	27.8	31.8	33.4	29.9	Nil	23.8	30.3	27.0
% Net Income of Revenue	9.0	9.9	11.7	11.8	12.4	11.1	12.9	12.8	9.6	7.0
% Return on Assets	9.0	9.5	10.5	10.5	11.0	10.9	13.2	13.6	10.3	7.6
% Return on Equity	25.7	25.9	26.4	27.3	29.8	28.2	33.2	37.1	29.4	20.5

Data as orig reptd.; bef. results of disc opers/spec. items. Per share data adj. for stk. divs.; EPS diluted. E-Estimated. NA-Not Available. NM-Not Meaningful. NR-Not Ranked. UR-Under Review.

Office: P.O. Box 619100, Dallas, TX 75261-9100.
Telephone: 972-281-1200.
Website: http://www.kimberly-clark.com
Chrmn, Pres & CEO: T.J. Falk

SVP & CFO: M.A. Buthman
SVP & CCO: R.D. McCray
VP & CIO: R. Baez
Investor Contact: M.D. Masseth (972-281-1478)

Board Members: J. R. Alm, D. R. Beresford, J. F. Bergstrom, A. E. Bru, R. W. Decherd, T. J. Falk, M. C. Jemison, J. M. Jenness, L. J. Rice, M. J. Shapiro, G. C. Sullivan

Founded: 1872
Domicile: Delaware
Employees: 55,000

The McGraw-Hill Companies

Kimco Realty Corp

STANDARD &POOR'S

S&P Recommendation **HOLD** ★★★☆☆	Price $37.82 (as of Nov 23, 2007)	12-Mo. Target Price $46.00	Investment Style Large-Cap Blend

GICS Sector Financials
Sub-Industry Retail REITS

Summary This REIT is one of the largest U.S. owners and operators of neighborhood and community shopping centers.

Key Stock Statistics (Source S&P, Vickers, company reports)

52-Wk Range	**$53.60–33.74**	S&P FFO/Sh. 2007**E**	2.59	Market Capitalization(B)	**$9.538**	Beta	0.52
Trailing 12-Month FFO/Share	**NA**	S&P FFO/Sh. 2008**E**	2.73	Yield (%)	**4.23**	S&P 3-Yr. FFO/Sh. Proj. CAGR(%)	6.00
Trailing 12-Month P/FFO	**NA**	P/FFO on S&P FFO/Sh. 2007**E**	14.6	Dividend Rate/Share	**$1.60**	S&P Credit Rating	A-
$10K Invested 5 Yrs Ago	**$29,894**	Common Shares Outstg. (M)	252.2	Institutional Ownership (%)	**78**		

Price Performance

30-Week Mov. Avg. ···· 10-Week Mov. Avg. – – **GAAP Earnings vs. Previous Year** Volume Above Avg. STARS
12-Mo. Target Price — Relative Strength — ▲ Up ▼ Down ► No Change Below Avg. ★

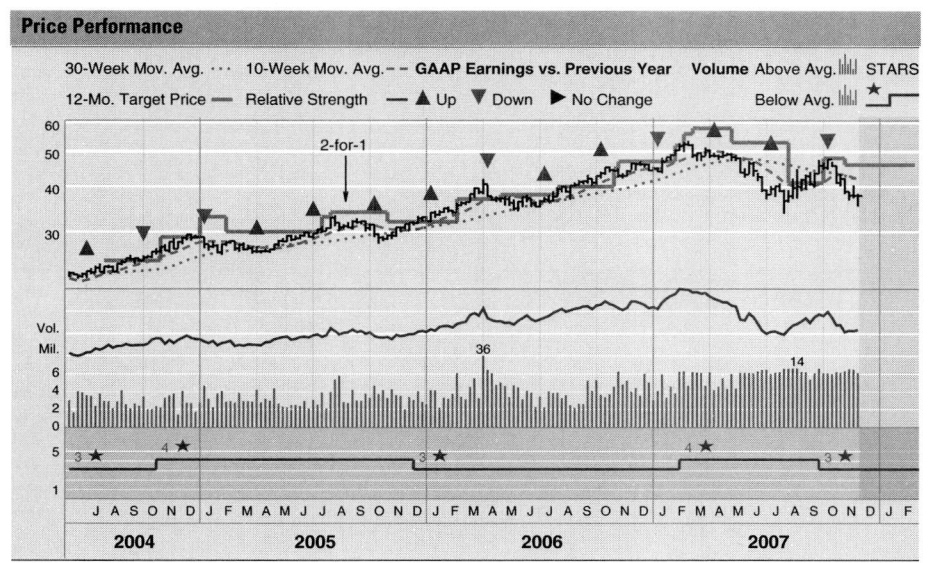

Options: ASE, CBOE, P, Ph

Analysis prepared by **Robert McMillan** on October 29, 2007, when the stock traded at **$41.15**.

Highlights

➤ We expect the trust to continue to benefit from what we view as a successful strategy of operating neighborhood and community shopping centers in North America and expanding into high growth international markets via joint ventures.

➤ We look for total revenues, after rising about 18% in 2006, to advance more than 14% in 2007 and about 13% in 2008, on higher rents at established properties, contributions from the acquisition of Pan Pacific Properties and other properties, and ongoing development activity. Occupancy at KIM's total portfolio rose to 96.2% at the end of the September quarter, from 95.3% a year earlier. We believe that a slowly expanding U.S. economy and continuing retailer expansion bode well for the trust's results. We anticipate strong demand for space, enabling KIM to continue to achieve healthy rent increases on new and renewal leases. Rents on new leases rose 17.1%, during the quarter.

➤ We estimate EPS from continuing operations of $1.22 and $1.51 for 2007 and 2008, respectively, and we project FFO per share of $2.59 for 2007 and $2.73 for 2008. We expect fourth quarter FFO of $0.53 per share.

Investment Rationale/Risk

➤ As one of the largest owners and operators of neighborhood and community shopping centers in the U.S. with a broad array of established relationships, we believe that KIM will generate above average rent growth, and that it deserves to trade at a premium to peers. We also view KIM's success in establishing portfolios in Canada and Mexico as a positive.

➤ Risks to our recommendation and target price include slower than expected growth in retailer expansion and rental rates, higher than normal retailer bankruptcies, and sharper than projected increases in interest rates.

➤ The shares recently traded at about 15.8X trailing 12-month FFO. The multiple for the shares as well as the sector, after dropping sharply between May and August, have rebounded sharply, driven, in our opinion, by the prospects of lower interest rates. Our 12-month target price of $46 is equal to about 18X our forward 12-month FFO estimate of $2.56. Given our projections of continued growth, we think that valuation multiples and the shares will advance as concerns about the housing market on KIM's retailer-dependent business and interest rates ease.

Qualitative Risk Assessment

LOW	MEDIUM	HIGH

Our risk assessment reflects our view of KIM's strong fundamentals, healthy credit quality, a diversified customer base, and rising GDP. We also believe KIM's diversity in its geographic presence helps provide significant protection from a local or regional downturn.

Quantitative Evaluations

S&P Quality Ranking A+

D	C	B-	B	B+	A-	A	A+

Relative Strength Rank MODERATE

40

LOWEST = 1 HIGHEST = 99

Revenue/FFO Data

Revenue (Million $)

	1Q	2Q	3Q	4Q	Year
2007	158.3	170.8	210.3	--	--
2006	138.1	147.9	150.7	157.3	653.0
2005	129.3	126.7	129.6	137.0	580.6
2004	139.9	129.7	122.7	124.7	517.0
2003	119.7	115.0	118.5	126.6	479.7
2002	112.3	112.5	110.2	115.9	450.8

FFO Per Share ($)

2007	0.78	0.71	0.57	E0.53	E2.59
2006	0.53	0.54	0.56	0.58	2.21
2005	0.53	0.54	0.56	0.55	2.00
2004	0.47	0.48	0.50	0.45	1.78
2003	0.39	0.40	0.41	0.43	1.62
2002	0.38	0.37	0.38	0.34	1.52

Fiscal year ended Dec. 31. Next earnings report expected: Mid February. FFO Estimates based on S&P Funds From Operations Est..

Dividend Data (Dates: mm/dd Payment Date: mm/dd/yy)

Amount ($)	Date Decl.	Ex-Div. Date	Stk. of Record	Payment Date
0.360	12/15	12/28	01/02	01/16/07
0.360	03/15	04/02	04/04	04/16/07
0.360	06/15	07/02	07/05	07/16/07
0.400	07/24	10/01	10/03	10/15/07

Dividends have been paid since 1992. Source: Company reports.

Please read the Required Disclosures and Analyst Certification on the last page of this report.

The McGraw-Hill Companies

Kimco Realty Corp

Business Summary October 29, 2007

Kimco Realty specializes in the acquisition, development and management of well located shopping centers with strong growth potential. At the end of 2006, KIM's real estate portfolio was comprised of interests in approximately 138 million square feet of gross leasable area (GLA) (not including interests in over 263 properties, ventures, land parcels and developments aggregating about 35.5 million square feet of GLA) in 1,061 operating properties primarily consisting of neighborhood and community shopping centers, 20 retail store leases and six parcels of undeveloped land located in 45 states, Canada, Mexico and Puerto Rico. Kim's portfolio also includes equity interests in other shopping center properties.

The trust's investment objective has been to increase cash flow, current income, and, consequently, the value of its existing portfolio of properties, and to seek continued growth through the strategic re-tenanting, renovation and expansion of its existing centers, and through the selective acquisition of established income-producing real estate properties and properties requiring significant re-tenanting and redevelopment. These properties are mainly located in neighborhood and community shopping centers in geographic regions in which KIM presently operates.

For KIM as well as other retail oriented REITs, we believe that location and the financial health and growth of its retail tenants are among the most important factors affecting the success of its portfolio. KIM's neighborhood and community shopping center properties are designed to attract local area customers and typically are anchored by a discount department store, a supermarket or a drugstore tenant offering day-to-day necessities rather than high-priced luxury items. The trust seeks to reduce operating and leasing risks through diversification achieved by the geographic distribution of its properties and a large tenant base. At December 31, 2006, the single largest neighborhood and community shopping center accounted for 1.2% of annualized base rental revenues and 0.8% of total shopping center GLA. At December 31, 2006, the five largest tenants were The Home Depot, TJX Companies, Sears Holdings, Kohl's, and Wal-Mart.

Company Financials Fiscal Year Ended Dec. 31

Per Share Data ($)	2006	2005	2004	2003	2002	2001	2000	1999	1998	1997
Tangible Book Value	13.24	9.70	9.17	8.87	8.04	7.95	7.26	6.98	6.94	4.28
Earnings	1.36	1.40	1.19	1.04	1.10	1.08	0.96	0.82	0.67	0.59
S&P Core Earnings	1.36	1.40	1.18	1.03	1.08	1.07	NA	NA	NA	NA
Dividends	1.38	1.27	1.16	1.10	1.05	0.98	0.91	0.79	0.66	0.59
Payout Ratio	101%	91%	97%	105%	96%	91%	95%	96%	98%	99%
Prices:High	47.13	33.35	29.64	22.93	16.94	17.03	14.92	13.58	13.88	12.06
Prices:Low	32.02	25.90	19.77	15.13	12.98	13.58	10.92	10.29	11.15	10.08
P/E Ratio:High	35	24	25	22	15	16	16	17	21	20
P/E Ratio:Low	24	18	17	14	12	13	11	13	17	17

Income Statement Analysis (Million $)										
Rental Income	594	523	517	480	451	469	459	434	339	199
Mortgage Income	Nil	Nil	Nil	Nil	Nil	Nil	Nil	Nil	Nil	Nil
Total Income	653	581	517	480	451	469	466	434	339	199
General Expenses	8.28	128	111	104	9.15	89.7	138	136	110	65.1
Interest Expense	173	128	108	103	86.9	89.4	92.1	83.6	64.9	31.7
Provision for Losses	Nil	Nil	Nil	Nil	Nil	Nil	Nil	Nil	Nil	Nil
Depreciation	141	106	102	86.2	76.7	74.2	71.1	67.4	51.3	30.1
Net Income	343	334	282	247	249	237	205	177	127	85.8
S&P Core Earnings	333	322	268	222	227	209	NA	NA	NA	NA

Balance Sheet & Other Financial Data (Million $)										
Cash	1,616	1,018	757	581	36.0	93.8	19.1	28.1	43.9	31.0
Total Assets	7,869	5,535	4,747	4,604	3,757	3,385	3,171	3,007	3,051	1,344
Real Estate Investment	6,002	4,560	4,877	4,137	3,399	3,201	3,112	2,951	3,024	1,213
Loss Reserve	Nil	Nil	Nil	Nil	Nil	Nil	Nil	Nil	Nil	Nil
Net Investment	5,195	3,820	4,242	3,569	2,882	2,748	2,720	2,627	2,768	1,197
Short Term Debt	Nil	Nil	Nil	570	147	123	4.60	229	129	7.90
Capitalization:Debt	3,378	2,397	1,860	1,585	1,430	1,205	1,321	1,021	1,169	524
Capitalization:Equity	3,366	2,387	2,236	2,135	1,906	1,889	1,703	1,604	1,584	742
Capitalization:Total	7,170	4,907	4,203	3,820	3,431	3,103	3,039	2,640	2,759	1,272
% Earnings & Depreciation/Assets	7.2	8.5	8.2	8.0	9.1	9.5	8.9	8.1	8.1	9.8
Price Times Book Value:High	3.6	3.4	3.2	2.6	2.1	2.1	2.1	2.0	2.0	2.8
Price Times Book Value:Low	2.4	2.7	2.2	1.7	1.6	1.7	1.5	1.5	1.6	2.4

Data as orig reptd.; bef. results of disc opers/spec. items. Per share data adj. for stk. divs.; EPS diluted. E-Estimated. NA-Not Available. NM-Not Meaningful. NR-Not Ranked. UR-Under Review.

Office: 3333 New Hyde Park Road, New Hyde Park, NY 11042-0020.
Telephone: 800-285-4626.
Email: ir@kimcorealty.com
Website: http://www.kimcorealty.com

Chrmn & CEO: M. Cooper
Pres, Vice Chrmn & COO: M.J. Flynn
Vice Chrmn: D.B. Henry
EVP & CFO: M.V. Pappagallo

VP & Treas: G.G. Cohen
Investor Contact: B. Pooley (516-869-2530)
Board Members: M. Cooper, R. G. Dooley, M. J. Flynn, J. Grills, D. B. Henry, F. P. Hughes, M. S. Kimmel, F. Lourenso, R. Saltzman

Founded: 1966
Domicile: Maryland
Employees: 618

King Pharmaceuticals Inc.

STANDARD &POOR'S

S&P Recommendation **HOLD** ★★★☆☆	Price $10.29 (as of Nov 23, 2007)	12-Mo. Target Price $15.00	Investment Style Large-Cap Blend

GICS Sector Health Care
Sub-Industry Pharmaceuticals

Summary This company makes and markets a line of prescription pharmaceuticals. Altace, a treatment for hypertension and congestive heart failure, is its most important product.

Key Stock Statistics (Source S&P, Vickers, company reports)

52-Wk Range	$22.25– 9.83	S&P Oper. EPS 2007**E**	1.75	Market Capitalization(B)	$2.512	Beta	0.77
Trailing 12-Month EPS	$0.72	S&P Oper. EPS 2008**E**	1.15	Yield (%)	Nil	S&P 3-Yr. Proj. EPS CAGR(%)	-20.00
Trailing 12-Month P/E	14.3	P/E on S&P Oper. EPS 2007**E**	5.9	Dividend Rate/Share	Nil	S&P Credit Rating	BB
$10K Invested 5 Yrs Ago	$5,568	Common Shares Outstg. (M)	244.2	Institutional Ownership (%)	NM		

Price Performance

30-Week Mov. Avg. ···· 10-Week Mov. Avg. -- GAAP Earnings vs. Previous Year   Volume Above Avg. STARS
12-Mo. Target Price — Relative Strength — ▲ Up ▼ Down ▶ No Change   Below Avg.

Options: ASE, CBOE, P, Ph

Analysis prepared by **Herman B. Saftlas** on November 19, 2007, when the stock traded at **$ 9.93**.

Qualitative Risk Assessment

LOW	MEDIUM	**HIGH**

Our risk assessment reflects King Pharmaceuticals' reliance on in-licensing drugs from other companies and on aggressive marketing for its sales growth. KG recently lost a key patent case on its principal Altace drug, and is awaiting a patent decision on Skelaxin, its second most important product. In view of these developments, we think KG's prospects are heavily dependent on the success of its R&D program and future in-licensing opportunities.

Quantitative Evaluations

S&P Quality Ranking   **B-**

D	C	**B-**	B	B+	A-	A	A+

Relative Strength Rank   **WEAK**

24

LOWEST = 1   HIGHEST = 99

Highlights

➤ Largely reflecting anticipated generic erosion in the principal Altace line, we expect revenues to drop about 25% in 2008 from the $2.1 billion indicated for 2007. In view of a recent court ruling that invalidated KG's Altace patent, we expect generic players to enter the Altace capsule market over the near term. However, some offset could come from the launch of KG's new Altace tablet formulation. We think Skelaxin may also be hit by generic erosion in 2008. With respect to other lines, we see sales growth for Thrombin-JMI critical care products, Avinza pain drug and Meridian Medical injection devices.

➤ We expect 2008 gross margins to contract to 73%, from an indicated 78% in 2007, on reduced volume and a less profitable sales mix. Although R&D spending will probably remain near the 2007 level, we think significant cost streamlining measures should result in sharp reductions in SG&A costs and other expenses.

➤ We project operating EPS of $1.15 for 2008, down from the $1.75 we expect in 2007. Our estimate for 2007 excludes asset impairment charges of about $0.22.

Investment Rationale/Risk

➤ Cobalt Pharmaceuticals recently notified King of its intent to launch a generic Altace not manufactured by KG, following an appellate court ruling that KG's Altace patent was invalid. Although KG may be able to salvage some of its Altace franchise with a new tablet formulation, we expect generics to severely cut into King's Altace sales in 2008. King is also in the midst of a major patent battle for Skelaxin, with a decision likely soon. On the plus side, we think KG still has several growing products, a decent pipeline, $1.1 billion of cash and investments, and what we believe to be significant opportunities for cost restructuring.

➤ Risks to our recommendation and target price include greater than expected competitive pressures in key lines, and uncertainties related to Remoxy and other pipeline drugs.

➤ Our 12-month target price of $15 applies a discount-to-peers P/E of about 13X to our 2008 EPS estimate. Our DCF model, which assumes decelerating cash flow growth over the next 10 years, a WACC of 8.5%, and terminal growth of 1%, also indicates intrinsic value of about $15.

Revenue/Earnings Data

Revenue (Million $)

	1Q	2Q	3Q	4Q	Year
2007	516.0	542.7	544.9	--	--
2006	484.2	499.7	491.7	512.9	1,989
2005	368.6	462.9	518.0	423.3	1,773
2004	291.5	275.1	394.7	342.6	1,304
2003	343.8	370.7	424.2	382.6	1,521
2002	258.1	282.5	315.7	272.0	1,128

Earnings Per Share ($)

2007	0.48	0.26	-0.17	E0.36	E1.75
2006	0.21	0.46	0.37	0.15	1.19
2005	0.28	0.08	0.50	-0.39	0.48
2004	-0.01	-0.27	-0.01	0.06	-0.21
2003	-0.03	-0.15	0.44	0.17	0.44
2002	0.29	0.24	0.35	-0.13	0.74

Fiscal year ended Dec. 31. Next earnings report expected: Late February. EPS Estimates based on S&P Operating Earnings; historical GAAP earnings are as reported.

Dividend Data

No cash dividends have been paid.

The McGraw-Hill Companies

King Pharmaceuticals Inc.

**STANDARD
&POOR'S**

Business Summary November 19, 2007

CORPORATE OVERVIEW. King Pharmaceuticals is a vertically integrated branded pharmaceutical company. A key part of its business strategy consists of the acquisition of branded prescription drugs being divested by large global pharmaceutical companies. To date, King has successfully acquired and commercialized more than 35 branded products, and has introduced several product line extensions.

Sales of branded pharmaceuticals accounted for 87% of total net revenues in 2006, Meridian Medical Technologies (a maker of autoinjectors acquired in January 2003) 8%, royalties from licensed drugs 4%, and contract manufacturing and other 1%.

The company's most important drug is Altace, a heart drug acquired together with two other products from Hoechst Marion Rousell in 1998, for $363 million. An angiotensin converting enzyme (ACE) inhibitor indicated for the treatment of hypertension and congestive heart failure, Altace had 2006 sales of $653 million, up from $554 million in 2005. Other cardiovascular drugs include Corzide and Corgard beta blocker treatments for high blood pressure. Altace sales in recent years have benefited from results of the Heart Outcomes Prevention Evaluation trial, which determined that Altace significantly reduces the rates of stroke, heart attack, and death in high-risk cardiovascular patients.

King's neuroscience products include Skelaxin, Avinza and Sonata. Skelaxin (sales of $415 million in 2006) is a muscle relaxant indicated for the relief of discomforts associated with acute, painful musculoskeletal conditions. Avinza, acquired from Ligand Pharmaceuticals in February 2007, is a once daily, extended release formulation of morphine for severe pain. Sonata ($86 million) is a nonbenzodiazepine treatment for insomnia. Levoxyl ($112 million) and Cytomel ($42 million) are treatments of thyroid disorders.

King's primary hospital/acute care product is Thrombin-JMI ($247 million), a drug used to control minor bleeding during surgery. Other products include Bicillin ($43 million), an anti-infective; Synercid, an injectable antibiotic; and Intal, an oral multi-dose inhaler of a non-steroidal anti-inflammatory agent to treat asthma. The Meridian Medical Technologies division markets autoinjectors, which are pre-filled, pen-like devices that allows patients or caregivers to automatically inject precise drug dosages.

Company Financials Fiscal Year Ended Dec. 31

Per Share Data ($)	2006	2005	2004	2003	2002	2001	2000	1999	1998	1997
Tangible Book Value	5.41	3.66	7.67	0.68	2.90	3.47	0.85	NM	NM	NM
Cash Flow	1.79	1.09	0.46	0.95	0.98	1.20	0.66	1.12	0.86	0.20
Earnings	1.19	0.48	-0.21	0.44	0.74	0.99	0.47	0.47	0.28	0.09
S&P Core Earnings	1.31	0.47	-0.06	0.41	0.71	0.94	NA	NA	NA	NA
Dividends	Nil	Nil	Nil	Nil	Nil	Nil	Nil	Nil	Nil	NA
Payout Ratio	Nil	Nil	Nil	Nil	Nil	Nil	Nil	Nil	Nil	NA
Prices:High	20.00	17.99	20.62	18.13	42.13	46.05	41.63	34.00	9.58	NA
Prices:Low	15.15	7.50	10.01	9.46	15.00	24.79	14.81	6.46	3.54	NA
P/E Ratio:High	17	37	NM	41	57	47	88	72	34	NA
P/E Ratio:Low	13	16	NM	22	20	25	31	14	13	NA

Income Statement Analysis (Million $)										
Revenue	1,989	1,773	1,304	1,521	1,128	872	620	348	163	123
Operating Income	700	551	272	403	426	429	326	155	64.7	35.4
Depreciation	148	147	162	125	59.3	48.0	41.9	26.9	9.30	9.80
Interest Expense	9.86	11.9	12.6	13.4	12.4	12.7	37.0	55.4	14.9	12.4
Pretax Income	424	178	-58.0	177	268	371	192	73.0	40.7	13.1
Effective Tax Rate	32.0%	34.5%	NM	40.2%	31.8%	37.2%	45.4%	37.5%	37.8%	38.1%
Net Income	289	117	-50.6	106	183	233	105	45.7	25.3	8.10
S&P Core Earnings	318	115	-13.1	98.4	175	222	NA	NA	NA	NA

Balance Sheet & Other Financial Data (Million $)										
Cash	114	48.5	359	146	815	924	76.4	8.50	1.16	12.5
Current Assets	1,673	1,248	1,127	946	1,262	1,238	317	131	75.6	NA
Total Assets	3,330	2,965	2,924	3,178	2,751	2,507	1,282	806	668	280
Current Liabilities	618	971	689	669	370	151	105	89.8	44.5	NA
Long Term Debt	400	Nil	345	345	345	346	99.0	553	514	150
Common Equity	2,289	1,973	1,849	2,042	1,931	1,908	988	148	101	83.3
Total Capital	2,689	1,973	2,194	2,387	2,310	2,292	1,104	716	623	NA
Capital Expenditures	45.8	53.3	55.1	51.2	73.6	40.2	25.1	8.80	81.1	NA
Cash Flow	436	264	111	230	242	281	147	22.6	34.6	17.9
Current Ratio	2.7	1.3	1.6	1.4	3.4	8.2	3.0	1.5	1.7	NA
% Long Term Debt of Capitalization	14.9	Nil	15.7	14.5	14.9	15.1	9.0	77.2	82.5	NA
% Net Income of Revenue	14.5	6.6	NM	7.0	16.2	26.7	16.9	13.1	15.5	6.6
% Return on Assets	9.2	4.0	NM	3.6	6.9	12.3	8.5	6.2	6.5	NA
% Return on Equity	13.5	6.1	NM	5.3	9.5	16.1	14.1	36.7	38.9	NA

Data as orig reptd.; bef. results of disc opers/spec. items. Per share data adj. for stk. divs.; EPS diluted. E-Estimated. NA-Not Available. NM-Not Meaningful. NR-Not Ranked. UR-Under Review.

Office: 501 Fifth Street, Bristol, TN 37620-2304.
Telephone: 423-989-8000.
Email: investorrelations@kingpharm.com
Website: http://www.kingpharm.com

Chrmn, Pres & CEO: B.A. Markison
Investor Contact: J.E. Green (423-989-8125)
CFO: J. Squicciarino
General Counsel: J.W. Elrod

Board Members: E. W. Deavenport, Jr., E. M. Greetham, P. A. Incarnati, G. D. Jordan, B. A. Markison, R. C. Moyer, D. G. Rooker, T. G. Wood

Founded: 1993
Domicile: Tennessee
Employees: 2,806

The McGraw·Hill Companies

KLA Tencor Corp

STANDARD & POOR'S

S&P Recommendation HOLD ★★★☆☆	**Price** $48.06 (as of Nov 23, 2007)	**12-Mo. Target Price** $55.00	**Investment Style** Large-Cap Growth

GICS Sector Information Technology
Sub-Industry Semiconductor Equipment

Summary This company is the world's leading manufacturer of yield monitoring and process control systems for the semiconductor industry.

Key Stock Statistics (Source S&P, Vickers, company reports)

52-Wk Range	$62.67– 46.59	S&P Oper. EPS 2008**E**	3.04	Market Capitalization(B)	$8.754
Trailing 12-Month EPS	$2.40	S&P Oper. EPS 2009**E**	3.40	Yield (%)	1.25
Trailing 12-Month P/E	20.0	P/E on S&P Oper. EPS 2008**E**	15.8	Dividend Rate/Share	$0.60
$10K Invested 5 Yrs Ago	$11,537	Common Shares Outstg. (M)	182.1	Institutional Ownership (%)	NM

Beta	2.31
S&P 3-Yr. Proj. EPS CAGR(%)	15.00
S&P Credit Rating	NA

Price Performance

30-Week Mov. Avg. ···· 10-Week Mov. Avg. — - **GAAP Earnings vs. Previous Year** Volume Above Avg. STARS
12-Mo. Target Price — Relative Strength — ▲ Up ▼ Down ► No Change Below Avg.

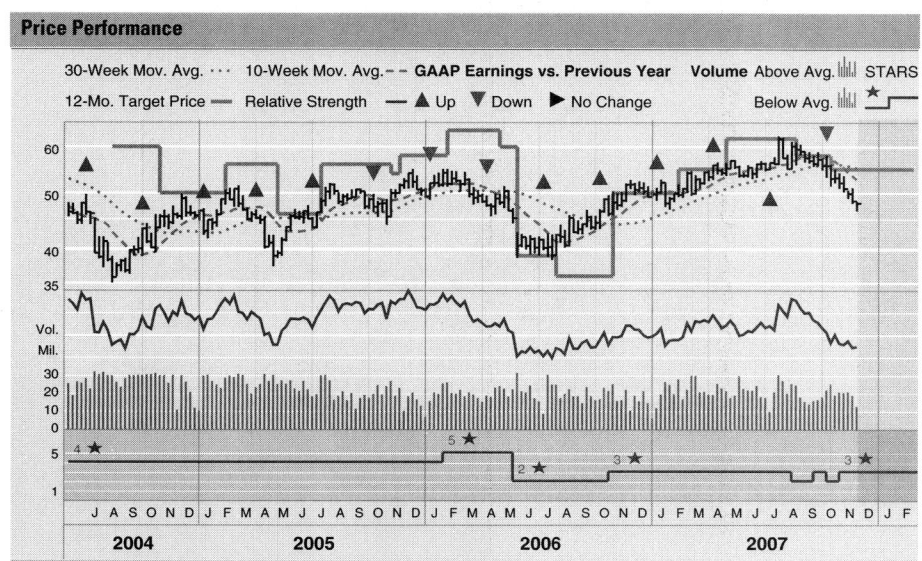

Options: ASE, CBOE, P, Ph

Analysis prepared by **Angelo Zino** on October 29, 2007, when the stock traded at **$ 51.97**.

Highlights

➤ Following revenue growth of 32% in FY 07 (Jun.), we see revenues falling slightly in FY 08. Although we expect the yield monitoring and process control systems products to do better than other types of front-end semiconductor equipment, we are concerned about the company's exposure to memory markets. We believe the transition to the 45-nanometer node from the 65-nanometer node will cause yield and defectivity challenges, which we anticipate will stimulate KLA-Tencor's customers to increase spending for better process control systems over the next several quarters.

➤ We see gross margins stable in the mid- to high 50s through FY 08, based on our view that KLAC's yield management and process control systems are only moderately susceptible to pricing pressure due to the critical value they add to semiconductor customers.

➤ We expect the effective tax rate to be 25%-28% in FY 08 and FY 09. We forecast EPS of $3.04 for FY 08, versus $2.61 reported for FY 07. For FY 09, we project EPS of $3.40.

Investment Rationale/Risk

➤ We view KLAC's competitive position in both inspection and metrology as strong, and we see longer-term growth in yield management and process control. Although we expect KLAC to benefit from challenges relating to new materials being used in the chip manufacturing process, we are concerned about near-term equipment spending, and think that the company's order declines may extend throughout the next few quarters. The shares are trading at a slight premium to peers, but we believe this is warranted at current levels given KLAC's market share and solid business model.

➤ Risks to our recommendation and target price include an industry downturn, competition pressuring KLAC's market share position, and a weakening of the global economy.

➤ We apply a risk-adjusted target P/E of approximately 18X to our FY 08 EPS estimate of $3.04, above the peer average, to derive our 12-month target price of $55. Given KLAC's market position and solid business model, we believe the shares should trade at a slight premium to peers.

Qualitative Risk Assessment

LOW	MEDIUM	**HIGH**

Our risk assessment reflects the company's exposure to the cyclicality of the semiconductor equipment industry and the amount of change in relevant technologies, only partially offset by limited pricing pressure and our view of KLAC's strong market position, size and financial condition.

Quantitative Evaluations

S&P Quality Ranking B

D	C	B-	**B**	B+	A-	A	A+

Relative Strength Rank MODERATE
35
LOWEST = 1   HIGHEST = 99

Revenue/Earnings Data

Revenue (Million $)

	1Q	2Q	3Q	4Q	Year
2008	693.0	--	--	--	--
2007	629.4	649.3	716.2	736.4	2,731
2006	484.3	487.7	519.7	579.0	2,071
2005	518.8	532.9	541.6	491.9	2,085
2004	318.0	338.5	389.8	450.4	1,497
2003	375.5	334.9	304.3	308.3	1,323

Earnings Per Share ($)

2008	0.46	E0.71	E0.79	E0.83	E3.04
2007	0.67	0.44	0.76	0.75	2.61
2006	0.37	0.38	0.47	0.65	1.86
2005	0.58	0.61	0.61	0.52	2.32
2004	0.18	0.22	0.33	0.48	1.21
2003	0.26	0.15	0.14	0.15	0.70

Fiscal year ended Jun. 30. Next earnings report expected: Early February. EPS Estimates based on S&P Operating Earnings; historical GAAP earnings are as reported.

Dividend Data (Dates: mm/dd Payment Date: mm/dd/yy)

Amount ($)	Date Decl.	Ex-Div. Date	Stk. of Record	Payment Date
0.120	02/02	02/13	02/15	03/01/07
0.120	05/04	05/11	05/15	06/01/07
0.150	08/09	08/16	08/20	09/01/07
0.150	11/08	11/15	11/19	12/03/07

Dividends have been paid since 2005. Source: Company reports.

KLA Tencor Corp

STANDARD
&POOR'S

Business Summary October 29, 2007

CORPORATE OVERVIEW. KLAC is the world's leading manufacturer of yield management and process monitoring systems for the semiconductor industry. While overall semiconductor equipment sales fell 60% from calendar 2000 to 2002, the company's sales declined only 19%, indicating, in our view, less exposure to the semiconductor cycle than peers. We believe this is a function of the pivotal role its products have in reducing manufacturing costs.

Maximizing yields, or the number of good die (chips) per wafer, is a key goal in manufacturing integrated circuits (ICs). Higher yields increase revenues obtained for each semiconductor wafer processed. As IC line widths decrease, yields become more sensitive to microscopic sized defects. KLAC's systems are used to improve yields by identifying defects, analyzing them to determine process problems and patterns, and facilitate corrective actions. These systems monitor subsequent results to ensure that problems have been contained. With in-line systems, corrections can be made while the wafer is still in the production line, rather than waiting for end-of-process testing and feedback.

KLAC offers a broad range of inspection and yield management. The company's wafer inspection systems include unpatterned and patterned wafer inspection tools used to find, count and characterize particles and pattern defects on wafers both in engineering applications and in-line at various stages during the semiconductor manufacturing process. Reticle inspection systems look for defects on the quartz plates used in copying circuit designs onto an IC during the photolithography process. Film measurement products measure a variety of optical and electrical properties of thin films. Finally, scanning electron beam microscopes (SEMs) can measure the critical dimensions (CDs) of tiny semiconductor features. For chip manufacturing below 90nm, e-beam inspection is becoming increasingly important, not only during the research and development phase, where the highest levels of sensitivity are needed to highlight and eradicate potential design problems, but also in production, where dedicated high-speed e-beam inspection systems.

Company Financials Fiscal Year Ended Jun. 30

Per Share Data ($)	2007	2006	2005	2004	2003	2002	2001	2000	1999	1998
Tangible Book Value	16.00	17.56	15.49	13.34	11.56	10.70	9.38	9.11	6.95	6.85
Cash Flow	3.15	2.20	2.67	1.62	1.07	1.45	2.22	1.65	0.48	0.98
Earnings	2.61	1.86	2.32	1.21	0.70	1.10	1.93	1.32	0.22	0.76
S&P Core Earnings	2.64	1.89	1.88	0.77	0.12	0.49	1.45	NA	NA	NA
Dividends	0.48	0.48	0.12	Nil	Nil	Nil	Nil	Nil	Nil	Nil
Payout Ratio	18%	26%	5%	Nil	Nil	Nil	Nil	Nil	Nil	Nil
Prices:High	62.67	55.03	55.00	62.82	61.25	70.58	61.00	97.75	56.56	24.00
Prices:Low	46.59	38.38	37.39	35.02	31.20	25.16	28.61	25.50	21.19	10.38
P/E Ratio:High	24	30	24	52	88	64	32	74	NM	32
P/E Ratio:Low	18	21	16	29	45	23	15	19	99	14

Income Statement Analysis (Million $)										
Revenue	2,731	2,071	2,085	1,497	1,323	1,637	2,104	1,499	843	1,166
Operating Income	699	379	653	380	201	314	512	370	80.6	226
Depreciation	109	69.4	70.9	82.9	71.4	69.6	55.6	63.3	48.2	38.9
Interest Expense	Nil	Nil	Nil	Nil	0.39	Nil	Nil	Nil	Nil	Nil
Pretax Income	680	378	627	325	181	287	513	353	50.3	206
Effective Tax Rate	22.1%	NM	25.0%	24.9%	24.0%	24.8%	27.2%	28.1%	22.1%	35.0%
Net Income	528	380	467	244	137	216	373	254	39.2	134
S&P Core Earnings	535	386	377	156	22.4	96.5	281	NA	NA	NA

Balance Sheet & Other Financial Data (Million $)										
Cash	1,711	2,326	2,195	1,876	1,488	1,334	697	844	696	216
Current Assets	3,253	3,543	3,203	2,192	1,806	1,619	1,897	1,552	942	956
Total Assets	4,623	4,576	3,986	3,539	2,867	2,718	2,745	2,204	1,585	1,548
Current Liabilities	1,073	1,002	932	912	651	687	984	495	352	351
Long Term Debt	Nil	Nil	Nil	Nil	Nil	Nil	Nil	Nil	Nil	Nil
Common Equity	3,550	3,568	3,045	2,628	2,216	2,030	1,760	1,709	1,233	1,198
Total Capital	3,550	3,573	3,055	2,628	2,216	2,030	1,760	1,709	1,233	1,198
Capital Expenditures	83.8	73.8	59.7	55.5	134	68.7	162	78.7	56.8	64.4
Cash Flow	637	450	538	327	209	286	429	317	87.4	173
Current Ratio	3.0	3.5	3.4	2.4	2.8	2.4	1.9	3.1	2.7	2.7
% Long Term Debt of Capitalization	Nil	Nil	Nil	Nil	Nil	Nil	Nil	Nil	Nil	Nil
% Net Income of Revenue	19.3	18.4	22.4	16.3	10.4	13.2	17.7	16.9	4.7	11.5
% Return on Assets	11.5	8.8	12.4	7.6	4.9	7.9	15.1	13.4	2.5	9.3
% Return on Equity	14.8	11.4	16.5	10.1	6.5	11.4	21.5	17.3	3.2	12.1

Data as orig reptd.; bef. results of disc opers/spec. items. Per share data adj. for stk. divs.; EPS diluted. E-Estimated. NA-Not Available. NM-Not Meaningful. NR-Not Ranked. UR-Under Review.

Office: 160 Rio Robles, San Jose, CA 95134.
Telephone: 408-875-3000.
Website: http://www.tencor.com
Chrmn: E.W. Barnholt

Pres & COO: J.H. Kispert
CEO: R.P. Wallace
Investor Contact: J. Hall (408-875-3600)
SVP & CFO: J. Hall

Board Members: E. W. Barnholt, H. R. Bingham, R. T. Bond, R. M. Calderoni, J. T. Dickson, S. P. Kaufman, K. J. Kennedy, L. Urbanek, R. P. Wallace, D. C. Wang

Founded: 1975
Domicile: Delaware
Employees: 6,000

Kohl's Corp

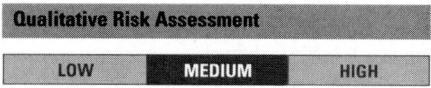

STANDARD &POOR'S

S&P Recommendation **BUY** ★★★★☆	Price $48.72 (as of Nov 23, 2007)	12-Mo. Target Price $60.00	Investment Style Large-Cap Growth

GICS Sector Consumer Discretionary
Sub-Industry Department Stores

Summary This company operates about 914 specialty department stores in 47 states, featuring moderately priced apparel, shoes, accessories, and products for the home.

Key Stock Statistics (Source S&P, Vickers, company reports)

52-Wk Range	$79.55– 46.99	S&P Oper. EPS 2008**E**	3.58	Market Capitalization(B)	$15.483	Beta	0.75
Trailing 12-Month EPS	$3.55	S&P Oper. EPS 2009**E**	4.45	Yield (%)	Nil	S&P 3-Yr. Proj. EPS CAGR(%)	16.00
Trailing 12-Month P/E	13.7	P/E on S&P Oper. EPS 2008**E**	13.6	Dividend Rate/Share	Nil	S&P Credit Rating	BBB+
$10K Invested 5 Yrs Ago	$7,444	Common Shares Outstg. (M)	317.8	Institutional Ownership (%)	89		

Price Performance

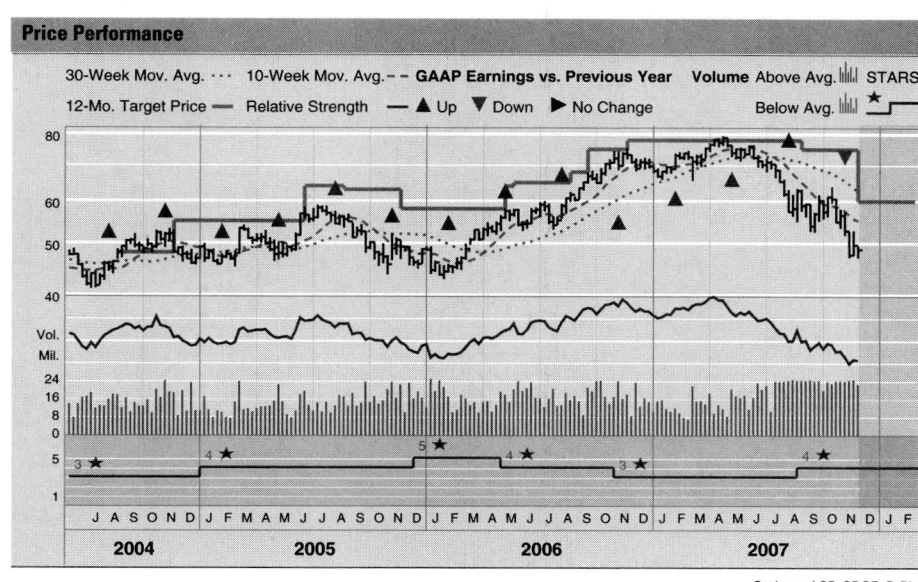

30-Week Mov. Avg. ··· 10-Week Mov. Avg. - - GAAP Earnings vs. Previous Year Volume Above Avg. STARS
12-Mo. Target Price — Relative Strength — ▲ Up ▼ Down ▶ No Change Below Avg. ★

Options: ASE, CBOE, P, Ph

Analysis prepared by **Jason N. Asaeda** on November 19, 2007, when the stock traded at **$ 47.57**.

Highlights

➤ From a projected $16.6 billion in FY 08 (Jan.), we look for sales to reach $18.4 billion in FY 09, driven mainly by new store growth. KSS plans to open about 90 new stores in FY 09. While consumer spending is slowing, we see the company's continuing effort to inject newness into its assortments, and in the process, broaden its customer base, supporting 2% to 3% same-store sales growth in FY 09. We expect same-store sales to decline 1.6% in FY 08.

➤ We believe that KSS's efforts to flow receipts more frequently in season and to allocate apparel inventory according to size profiles for individual stores will improve merchandise margins through lower levels of clearance. The implementation of markdown optimization software across all stores should improve the sell-through and profitability of clearance merchandise over the course of the year. However, we anticipate limited sales leverage on operating expenses, due to a projected increase in marketing spending in support of Kohl's media branding and the launch of new brands.

➤ Factoring in likely share buybacks, we see operating EPS of $3.58 in FY 08 rising to $4.45 in FY 09.

Investment Rationale/Risk

➤ Our buy recommendation is based on valuation. Despite a difficult retail environment, we believe KSS's focus on more exclusive, higher quality brands and products, lifestyle merchandising, and efforts to better tailor assortments to reflect regional market preferences will support improving sales and profit margin trends over the next 12 months. We expect all lines of business to perform well, including the home segment, which has been a challenging category for the company's competitors. We also think that KSS has the potential to gain market share from competitor Macy's, Inc. (M: hold, $28), as we believe Macy's has been repositioning its business toward a more upscale demographic, leaving a gap in the mid-market.

➤ Risks to our recommendation and target price include sales shortfalls due to unforeseen shifts in fashion trends and consumer discretionary spending patterns, as well as competitive pressures.

➤ We derive our 12-month target price of $60 by applying a forward P/E multiple of 13.5X, the low end of KSS's historical range, to our FY 09 EPS estimate.

Qualitative Risk Assessment

LOW	MEDIUM	HIGH

Our risk assessment reflects our view of KSS's improving sales and profit margins, increasing market share in the moderate department store sector, and healthy balance sheet and cash flow, offset by uncertainty over consumer discretionary spending in light of interest rates and debt levels.

Quantitative Evaluations

S&P Quality Ranking B+

D	C	B-	B	B+	A-	A	A+

Relative Strength Rank WEAK

27

LOWEST = 1   HIGHEST = 99

Revenue/Earnings Data

Revenue (Million $)

	1Q	2Q	3Q	4Q	Year
2008	3,572	3,589	3,825	--	--
2007	3,185	3,291	3,637	5,431	15,544
2006	2,743	2,888	3,119	4,652	13,402
2005	2,380	2,498	2,744	4,079	11,701
2004	2,118	2,208	2,394	3,562	10,282
2003	1,871	1,922	2,143	3,184	9,120

Earnings Per Share ($)

	1Q	2Q	3Q	4Q	Year
2008	0.64	0.83	0.61	E1.50	E3.58
2007	0.48	0.69	0.68	1.48	3.31
2006	0.36	0.54	0.45	1.08	2.43
2005	0.32	0.45	0.41	0.94	2.12
2004	0.32	0.33	0.35	0.72	1.72
2003	0.31	0.36	0.39	0.81	1.87

Fiscal year ended Jan. 31. Next earnings report expected: Early March. EPS Estimates based on S&P Operating Earnings; historical GAAP earnings are as reported.

Dividend Data

No cash dividends have been paid.

Please read the Required Disclosures and Analyst Certification on the last page of this report.

The McGraw-Hill Companies

Kohl's Corp

Business Summary November 19, 2007

CORPORATE OVERVIEW. KSS, with its "Expect Great Things" line, has positioned itself as a preferred shopping destination for busy women. Its traditional customers are married women aged 25 to 54. The company's stores feature easy-to-shop layouts and emphasize moderately priced exclusive and national brand family apparel and shoes, accessories, cosmetics, home furnishings, and housewares. KSS uses a "nine-box grid" merchandising strategy. Product assortments fall into three categories, "good," "better," and "best," differentiated by price and quality, and also reflect three distinct customer styles: the "classic" customer who wants a coordinated look without bending the rules; the "updated" customer who likes classic styles with a twist; and the more fashion-forward "contemporary" customer.

PRIMARY BUSINESS DYNAMICS. KSS is one of the fastest growing retail

chains in the U.S. From FY 01 through FY 06, the company increased its selling square footage at a compound annual growth rate (CAGR) of 19% as it expanded its store count from 320 to 732. From FY 07 through FY 11, KSS expects to open about 500 new stores. Based on this aggressive five-year growth plan, the company's store count should top 1,200 by the end of FY 11. As we see this level of expansion unlikely to be matched by other department stores, we think KSS is in a position to potentially capture market share. In FY 07, the company opened 85 new stores, including entries into the Portland, OR, Seattle, WA, and Tampa, FL markets, ending the year with 817 stores.

Company Financials Fiscal Year Ended Jan. 31

Per Share Data ($)	2007	2006	2005	2004	2003	2002	2001	2000	1999	1998
Tangible Book Value	18.32	16.62	13.78	11.60	9.85	7.78	6.21	4.70	3.55	2.88
Cash Flow	4.47	3.42	2.95	2.43	2.41	1.93	1.48	1.05	0.81	0.64
Earnings	3.31	2.43	2.12	1.72	1.87	1.35	1.10	0.78	0.59	0.46
S&P Core Earnings	3.31	2.43	2.04	1.62	1.78	1.38	1.04	NA	NA	NA
Dividends	Nil	Nil	Nil	Nil	Nil	Nil	Nil	Nil	Nil	Nil
Payout Ratio	Nil	Nil	Nil	Nil	Nil	Nil	Nil	Nil	Nil	Nil
Calendar Year	2006	2005	2004	2003	2002	2001	2000	1999	1998	1997
Prices:High	75.54	58.90	54.10	65.44	78.83	72.24	66.50	40.63	30.75	18.84
Prices:Low	42.78	43.63	39.59	42.40	44.00	41.95	33.50	28.63	16.20	9.06
P/E Ratio:High	23	24	26	38	42	54	60	52	52	42
P/E Ratio:Low	13	18	19	25	24	31	30	37	27	20

Income Statement Analysis (Million $)

	2007	2006	2005	2004	2003	2002	2001	2000	1999	1998
Revenue	15,544	13,402	11,701	10,282	9,120	7,489	6,152	4,557	3,682	3,060
Operating Income	2,202	1,755	1,525	1,260	1,282	1,002	779	537	408	316
Depreciation	388	339	288	237	191	152	128	83.3	70.0	57.4
Interest Expense	74.4	72.1	64.1	75.2	59.4	57.4	Nil	29.5	22.9	24.6
Pretax Income	1,774	1,346	1,174	950	1,034	800	605	421	317	235
Effective Tax Rate	37.5%	37.4%	37.8%	37.8%	37.8%	38.0%	38.5%	38.7%	39.3%	39.9%
Net Income	1,109	842	730	591	643	496	372	258	192	141
S&P Core Earnings	1,109	842	703	557	608	471	349	NA	NA	NA

Balance Sheet & Other Financial Data (Million $)

	2007	2006	2005	2004	2003	2002	2001	2000	1999	1998
Cash	620	127	117	113	90.1	107	124	12.6	29.6	44.2
Current Assets	3,401	4,266	3,643	3,025	3,284	2,464	1,922	1,367	939	811
Total Assets	9,041	9,153	7,979	6,698	6,316	4,930	3,855	2,915	1,936	1,620
Current Liabilities	1,919	1,746	1,456	1,122	1,508	880	723	634	380	286
Long Term Debt	1,040	1,046	1,103	1,076	1,059	1,095	803	495	311	310
Common Equity	5,603	5,957	4,967	4,191	3,512	2,791	2,203	1,686	1,163	955
Total Capital	6,887	7,221	6,367	5,504	4,743	4,001	3,090	2,247	1,527	1,310
Capital Expenditures	1,142	799	890	832	716	662	481	625	249	203
Cash Flow	1,496	1,181	1,019	828	835	648	500	341	262	199
Current Ratio	1.8	2.4	2.5	2.7	2.2	2.8	2.7	2.2	2.5	2.8
% Long Term Debt of Capitalization	15.7	14.5	17.3	19.5	22.3	27.4	26.0	22.0	20.4	23.6
% Net Income of Revenue	7.1	6.3	6.2	5.7	7.1	6.6	6.0	5.7	5.2	4.6
% Return on Assets	12.2	9.8	10.0	9.1	11.4	11.3	10.9	10.6	10.8	10.3
% Return on Equity	19.2	15.3	16.0	15.3	20.4	19.9	19.1	18.1	18.2	19.2

Data as orig reptd.; bef. results of disc opers/spec. items. Per share data adj. for stk. divs.; EPS diluted. E-Estimated. NA-Not Available. NM-Not Meaningful. NR-Not Ranked. UR-Under Review.

Office: N56W17000 Ridgewood Dr, Menomonee Falls, WI 53051-5660.
Telephone: 262-703-7000.
Website: http://www.kohls.com
Chrmn & CEO: R.L. Montgomery

Pres: K. Mansell
Sr EVP: T.A. Kingsbury
Investor Contact: W.S. McDonald (262-703-1893)
EVP & CFO: W.S. McDonald

Board Members: J. H. Baker, S. A. Burd, W. Embry, J. D. Ericson, J. F. Herma, W. S. Kellogg, K. Mansell, A. Meier, R. L. Montgomery, F. V. Sica, P. M. Sommerhauser, S. E. Watson, R. E. White

Founded: 1986
Domicile: Wisconsin
Employees: 114,000

Kraft Foods Inc.

STANDARD &POOR'S

S&P Recommendation	HOLD ★★★☆☆	Price	12-Mo. Target Price	Investment Style
		$33.44 (as of Nov 23, 2007)	$34.00	Large-Cap Blend

GICS Sector Consumer Staples
Sub-Industry Packaged Foods & Meats

Summary Kraft Foods is the largest U.S. branded food and beverage company, and the second largest in the world.

Key Stock Statistics (Source S&P, Vickers, company reports)

52-Wk Range	$37.20–29.95	S&P Oper. EPS 2007**E**	1.82	Market Capitalization(B)	$52.725	Beta	0.76
Trailing 12-Month EPS	$1.63	S&P Oper. EPS 2008**E**	1.94	Yield (%)	3.23	S&P 3-Yr. Proj. EPS CAGR(%)	3.00
Trailing 12-Month P/E	20.5	P/E on S&P Oper. EPS 2007**E**	18.4	Dividend Rate/Share	$1.08	S&P Credit Rating	A-
$10K Invested 5 Yrs Ago	$10,264	Common Shares Outstg. (M)	1,576.7	Institutional Ownership (%)	69		

Price Performance

30-Week Mov. Avg. ··· 10-Week Mov. Avg. - - **GAAP Earnings vs. Previous Year** Volume Above Avg. ▏▎▍ STARS
12-Mo. Target Price — Relative Strength — ▲ Up ▼ Down ▶ No Change Below Avg. ▏▎▍ ★

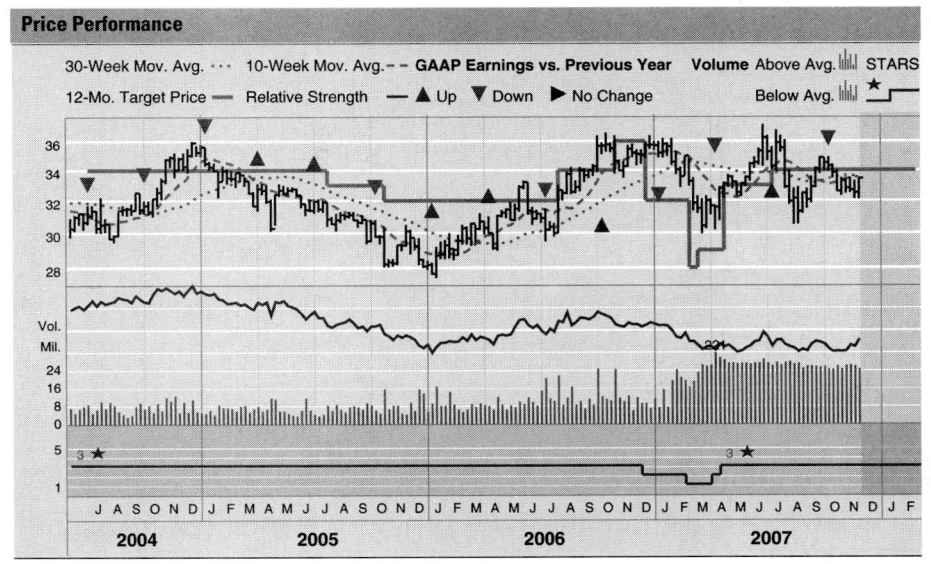

Options: ASE, CBOE, P, Ph

Analysis prepared by **Joseph Agnese** on November 20, 2007, when the stock traded at **$ 32.30**.

Highlights

➤ KFT is in the midst of a multi-year restructuring program that we expect will better position the company for growth. We see KFT's strategy including an emphasis on broadening some brands, leveraging scale, and focusing on quality.

➤ In 2008, for the company as currently constituted, we estimate revenue growth of about 5% from the $37 billion projected for 2007. However, this excludes KFT's planned acquisition of the Danone biscuit business, and KFT's planned divestiture of its Post cereal business. Subject to necessary approvals, the Danone transaction, for about $7.8 billion, is expected to close by the end of 2007, while the Post divestiture is expected to be completed in mid-2008. In the Post transaction, Kraft shareholders are expected to receive stock in food company Ralcorp Holdings, Inc. (RAH: hold, $60).

➤ Excluding special items, for Kraft as currently constituted, we estimate 2008 EPS at $1.94, up from the $1.82 that we project for 2007. In 2007, special items are expected to include $0.20 of restructuring costs, a $0.03 impairment charge, and $0.03 of one-time interest income.

Investment Rationale/Risk

➤ KFT shares have an above-average dividend yield, and we think the company has the potential for improved long-term EPS growth as it completes its restructuring plan. However, we have concerns about challenging competitive conditions we see in some product categories, plus some rising commodity costs, along with the operational and execution risk associated with the company's strategic growth plan and restructuring. Altria Group's majority ownership of KFT was spun off to Altria shareholders in March 2007.

➤ Risks to our recommendation and target price include higher than anticipated commodity costs, possible disappointing consumer acceptance of new product introductions, and the extent to which the company meets sales and earnings expectations.

➤ Our 12-month target price of $34 reflects our view that the stock should trade at about 17.5X our estimate of 2008 EPS, which is moderately below the average P/E that we expect from a peer group of food company stocks. Also, KFT recently had an indicated dividend yield of about 3.3%.

Qualitative Risk Assessment

LOW	MEDIUM	HIGH

Our risk assessment reflects the execution risk KFT faces not only from its internal restructuring but also from its spin-off from parent company Altria Group (MO). This is offset by the relatively stable nature of the company's end markets, our view of its strong balance sheet and cash flow, and its leading global market share positions.

Quantitative Evaluations

S&P Quality Ranking NR

D	C	B-	B	B+	A-	A	A+

Relative Strength Rank STRONG

81

LOWEST = 1   HIGHEST = 99

Revenue/Earnings Data

Revenue (Million $)

	1Q	2Q	3Q	4Q	Year
2007	8,586	9,205	9,054	--	--
2006	8,123	8,619	8,243	9,371	34,356
2005	8,059	8,334	8,057	9,663	34,113
2004	7,575	8,091	7,718	8,784	32,168
2003	7,359	7,841	7,480	8,330	31,010
2002	7,147	7,513	7,216	7,847	29,723

Earnings Per Share ($)

2007	0.43	0.44	0.38	E0.50	E1.82
2006	0.61	0.41	0.45	0.38	1.85
2005	0.41	0.45	0.40	0.46	1.72
2004	0.32	0.40	0.45	0.40	1.55
2003	0.49	0.55	0.47	0.50	2.01
2002	0.40	0.52	0.50	0.54	1.96

Fiscal year ended Dec. 31. Next earnings report expected: Late January. EPS Estimates based on S&P Operating Earnings; historical GAAP earnings are as reported.

Dividend Data (Dates: mm/dd Payment Date: mm/dd/yy)

Amount ($)	Date Decl.	Ex-Div. Date	Stk. of Record	Payment Date
0.250	12/08	12/22	12/27	01/05/07
0.250	03/05	03/13	03/15	04/04/07
0.250	06/15	06/26	06/28	07/06/07
0.270	08/28	09/06	09/10	10/05/07

Dividends have been paid since 2001. Source: Company reports.

Kraft Foods Inc.

STANDARD
&POOR'S

Business Summary November 20, 2007

CORPORATE OVERVIEW. Kraft Foods is one of the world's largest branded food and beverage companies. In 2006, U.S. operations accounted for $20.9 billion, or approximately 61%, of total company net revenues. European operations accounted for $7.8 billion (23%), and other operations provided $5.6 billion (16%).

Business segments include North America Beverages (9.0% of 2006 net revenues), North America Cheese & Foodservice (17.7%), North America Convenient Meals (14.2%), North America Grocery (7.9%), North America Snacks & Cereals (18.5%), European Union (19.4%), and Developing Markets, Oceania & North Asia (13.3%). Wal-Mart Stores, Inc. accounted for about 15% of KFT's net revenues in 2006.

Kraft has seven brands with annual revenue of at least approximately $1 billion each: Kraft, a leading brand of cheese, as well as salad and spoonable dressings, packaged dinners and barbecue sauce; Nabisco, the umbrella brand for a leading cookies and crackers business; Oscar Mayer, a leading U.S. processed meats brand; Philadelphia, a leading cream cheese brand;

Post, a major brand of ready-to-eat cereals in the U.S.; Jacobs; and Milka.

In 2006, the company completed the acquisition of the Spanish and Portuguese operations of United Biscuits for $1.07 billion. This acquisition included the rights to all Nabisco trademarks in Europe, the Middle East and Africa. Earlier, in December 2000, KFT acquired Nabisco Holdings Corp. for total consideration of $19.2 billion, comprised of $15.2 billion in cash and the assumption of approximately $4 billion of debt. In addition to expanding its global presence, the acquisition strengthened the company's position in the growing snacks segment.

Divestitures by KFT have included its hot cereal assets and trademarks, which were sold in the first quarter of 2007; and its pet snacks brand and assets, which were sold in the third quarter of 2006.

Company Financials Fiscal Year Ended Dec. 31

Per Share Data ($)	2006	2005	2004	2003	2002	2001	2000	1999	1998	1997
Tangible Book Value	NM	NM	NM	NM	NM	NM	NM	NA	NA	NA
Cash Flow	2.39	2.27	2.07	2.48	2.37	2.19	2.02	NA	NA	NA
Earnings	1.85	1.72	1.55	2.01	1.96	1.17	1.03	NA	NA	NA
S&P Core Earnings	1.80	1.74	1.53	1.93	1.65	0.81	NA	NA	NA	NA
Dividends	0.96	0.87	0.77	0.66	0.56	0.26	NA	NA	NA	NA
Payout Ratio	52%	51%	50%	33%	29%	22%	NA	NA	NA	NA
Prices:High	36.67	35.65	36.06	39.40	43.95	35.57	NA	NA	NA	NA
Prices:Low	27.44	27.88	29.45	26.35	32.50	29.50	NA	NA	NA	NA
P/E Ratio:High	20	21	23	20	22	30	NA	NA	NA	NA
P/E Ratio:Low	15	16	19	13	17	25	NA	NA	NA	NA
Income Statement Analysis (Million $)										
Revenue	34,356	34,113	32,168	31,010	29,723	33,875	34,679	NA	NA	NA
Operating Income	6,065	6,002	6,108	6,786	6,892	6,526	6,284	NA	NA	NA
Depreciation	898	879	879	813	716	1,642	1,722	NA	NA	NA
Interest Expense	510	636	666	678	854	1,437	NA	NA	NA	NA
Pretax Income	4,016	4,116	3,946	5,346	5,267	3,447	3,214	NA	NA	NA
Effective Tax Rate	23.7%	29.4%	32.3%	34.9%	35.5%	45.4%	44.4%	NA	NA	NA
Net Income	3,060	2,904	2,669	3,476	3,394	1,882	1,787	NA	NA	NA
S&P Core Earnings	2,963	2,930	2,632	3,337	2,861	1,308	NA	NA	NA	NA
Balance Sheet & Other Financial Data (Million $)										
Cash	239	316	282	514	215	162	NA	NA	NA	NA
Current Assets	8,254	8,153	9,722	8,124	7,456	7,006	NA	NA	NA	NA
Total Assets	55,574	57,628	59,928	59,285	57,100	55,798	NA	NA	NA	NA
Current Liabilities	10,473	8,724	9,078	7,861	7,169	8,875	NA	NA	NA	NA
Long Term Debt	7,081	8,475	9,723	11,591	10,416	13,134	15,677	NA	NA	NA
Common Equity	28,555	29,593	29,911	28,530	25,832	23,478	22,755	NA	NA	NA
Total Capital	39,566	44,135	45,484	45,977	41,676	41,643	38,432	NA	NA	NA
Capital Expenditures	1,169	1,171	1,006	1,085	1,184	1,101	1,151	NA	NA	NA
Cash Flow	3,958	3,783	3,548	4,289	4,110	3,524	3,509	NA	NA	NA
Current Ratio	0.8	0.9	1.1	1.0	1.0	0.8	NA	NA	NA	NA
% Long Term Debt of Capitalization	17.9	19.2	21.4	25.2	25.0	31.5	40.8	NA	NA	NA
% Net Income of Revenue	8.9	8.5	8.3	11.2	11.4	5.6	5.2	NA	NA	NA
% Return on Assets	5.4	4.9	4.5	6.0	6.0	3.5	NA	NA	NA	NA
% Return on Equity	10.5	9.8	9.1	12.8	13.8	10.0	NA	NA	NA	NA

Data as orig reptd.; bef. results of disc opers/spec. items. Per share data adj. for stk. divs.; EPS diluted. E-Estimated. NA-Not Available. NM-Not Meaningful. NR-Not Ranked. UR-Under Review.

Office: Three Lakes Drive, Northfield, IL 60093.
Telephone: 847-646-2000.
Website: http://www.kraft.com
Chrmn & CEO: I.B. Rosenfeld

EVP & CFO: J.P. Dollive
EVP, Secy & General Counsel: M.S. Firestone
EVP & CIO: A. Korby
Investor Contact: C. Jakubik (847-646-5494)

Board Members: A. Banga, J. Bennink, L. C. Camilleri, M. D. Ketchum, R. A. Lerner, J. C. Pope, I. B. Rosenfeld, M. L. Schapiro, D. C. Wright

Founded: 2000
Domicile: Virginia
Employees: 90,000

The McGraw·Hill Companies

Kroger Co. (The)

STANDARD
&POOR'S

S&P Recommendation BUY ★★★★☆

Price	**12-Mo. Target Price**	**Investment Style**
$28.00 (as of Nov 23, 2007)	$33.00	Large-Cap Blend

GICS Sector Consumer Staples
Sub-Industry Food Retail

Summary This supermarket operator, with about 2,500 stores in 31 states, also operates convenience stores, jewelry stores, supermarket fuel centers, and food processing plants.

Key Stock Statistics (Source S&P, Vickers, company reports)

52-Wk Range	$31.94– 21.12	S&P Oper. EPS 2008E	1.68	Market Capitalization(B)	$19.073	Beta	1.16
Trailing 12-Month EPS	$1.68	S&P Oper. EPS 2009E	1.90	Yield (%)	1.07	S&P 3-Yr. Proj. EPS CAGR(%)	11.00
Trailing 12-Month P/E	16.7	P/E on S&P Oper. EPS 2008E	16.7	Dividend Rate/Share	$0.30	S&P Credit Rating	BBB-
$10K Invested 5 Yrs Ago	$17,906	Common Shares Outstg. (M)	681.2	Institutional Ownership (%)	86		

Price Performance

30-Week Mov. Avg. · · · 10-Week Mov. Avg. - - **GAAP Earnings vs. Previous Year** **Volume** Above Avg. STARS
12-Mo. Target Price — Relative Strength — ▲ Up ▼ Down ► No Change Below Avg. ★

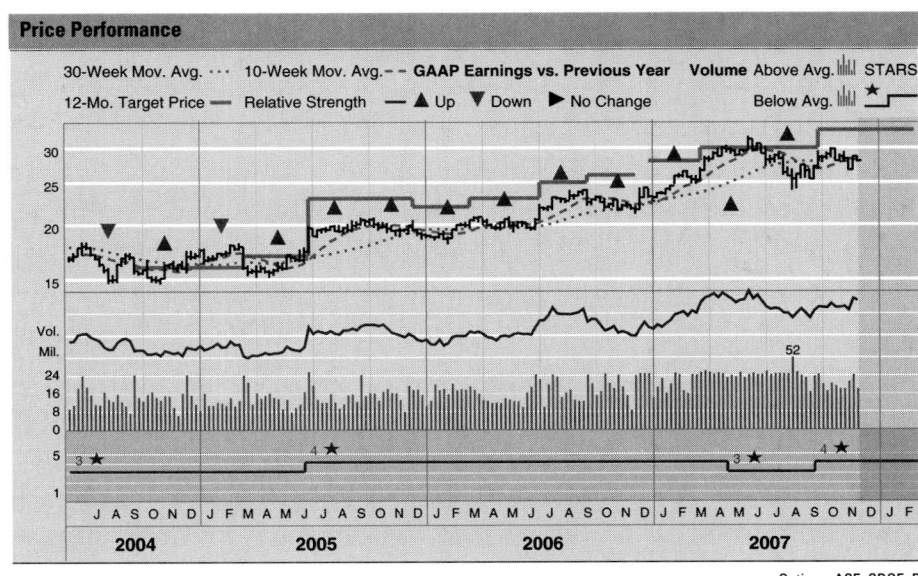

Options: ASE, CBOE, P

Analysis prepared by **Joseph Agnese** on September 19, 2007, when the stock traded at **$ 28.87**.

Highlights

➤ We expect sales growth of about 8% in FY 08 (Jan.), reflecting 2% square footage growth and mid-single digit comparable-store sales gains. Total sales should benefit from increased gasoline sales and from food cost inflation in the low single digits.

➤ We believe margins will be flat, reflecting the company's pursuit of a price reduction strategy, increased promotional spending and higher sales of lower margin gasoline. However, we see margin pressure partially offset by cost-saving opportunities that we forecast in areas such as administration, labor, shrinkage, warehousing and transportation. We think the company's sales growth strategy will focus on both service and merchandise improvements in addition to price reductions. In our opinion, these strategies will help the company compete against lower-priced mass merchants.

➤ After benefits from lower interest and rent expense and share repurchases, we expect FY 08 operating EPS to increase 11%, to $1.68, from $1.52 in FY 07.

Investment Rationale/Risk

➤ We have a buy recommendation on the shares, as we believe the company's outlook continues to improve. We think results will benefit from the company's strategy of boosting sales through targeted marketing, price reductions, and improved service levels which, in our view, should limit downside risk despite intense competition in the food/retail industry.

➤ Risks to our recommendation and target price include potential weakness in the economy that would cause consumers to become more price conscious, and increased price competition.

➤ Our discounted cash flow analysis, which assumes a weighted average cost of capital of 8.5% and a terminal growth rate of 3%, calculates intrinsic value of $34. Based on our expectations of improving trends, we think the shares should trade at about 17X our FY 09 EPS estimate of $1.90, a 10% premium to our estimated 12-month P/E multiple for the S&P 500, leading to a projected value of $32. Blending our two valuation metrics, we arrive at our 12-month target price of $33.

Qualitative Risk Assessment

LOW	MEDIUM	HIGH

Our risk assessment reflects our view of the company's diversification through multiple format offerings, strong market share positions, and potential opportunities from industry consolidation.

Quantitative Evaluations

S&P Quality Ranking B

D	C	B-	B	B+	A-	A	A+

Relative Strength Rank STRONG

78

LOWEST = 1 HIGHEST = 99

Revenue/Earnings Data

Revenue (Million $)

	1Q	2Q	3Q	4Q	Year
2008	20,726	16,139	--	--	--
2007	19,415	15,138	14,999	16,859	66,111
2006	17,948	13,865	14,021	14,720	60,553
2005	16,905	12,980	12,854	13,695	56,434
2004	16,266	12,351	12,141	13,034	53,791
2003	15,667	11,927	11,696	12,470	51,760

Earnings Per Share ($)

2008	0.47	0.38	E0.33	E0.50	E1.68
2007	0.42	0.29	0.30	0.54	1.54
2006	0.40	0.27	0.25	0.39	1.31
2005	0.35	0.19	0.19	-0.89	-0.14
2004	0.46	0.25	0.15	-0.45	0.42
2003	0.40	0.34	0.33	0.50	1.56

Fiscal year ended Jan. 31. Next earnings report expected: Early December. EPS Estimates based on S&P Operating Earnings; historical GAAP earnings are as reported.

Dividend Data (Dates: mm/dd Payment Date: mm/dd/yy)

Amount ($)	Date Decl.	Ex-Div. Date	Stk. of Record	Payment Date
0.065	01/19	02/13	02/15	03/01/07
0.075	03/15	05/11	05/15	06/01/07
0.075	06/29	08/13	08/15	09/01/07
0.075	09/20	11/13	11/15	12/01/07

Dividends have been paid since 2006. Source: Company reports.

Please read the Required Disclosures and Analyst Certification on the last page of this report.

Kroger Co. (The)

Business Summary September 19, 2007

Kroger is one of the largest U.S. supermarket chains, with 2,468 supermarkets as of February 2007. The company's principal operating format is combination food and drug stores (combo stores). In addition to combo stores, KR also operates multi-department stores, price-impact warehouses, convenience stores, fuel centers, jewelry stores, and food processing plants. Total food store square footage exceeded 42 million as of February 2007.

Retail food stores are operated under three formats: combo stores, multi-department stores, and price-impact warehouse stores. Combo stores are considered neighborhood stores, and include many specialty departments, such as whole health sections, pharmacies, general merchandise, pet centers, and perishables, such as fresh seafood and organic produce. Combo banners include Kroger, Ralphs, King Soopers, City Market, Dillons, Smith's, Fry's, QFC, Hilander, Owen's, Jay C, Cala Foods, Bell Markets, Pay Less and Gerbes.

Multi-department stores offer one-stop shopping, are significantly larger in size than combo stores, and sell a wider selection of general merchandise items, including apparel, home fashion and furnishings, electronics, automotive, toys, and fine jewelry. Multi-department formats include Fred Meyer, Fry's Marketplace, Smith's Marketplace and Kroger Marketplace. Many combination and multi-department stores include a fuel center.

Price-impact warehouse stores offer everyday low prices, plus promotions for a wide selection of grocery and health and beauty care items. Price-impact warehouse stores include Food 4 Less and Foods Co.

Company Financials Fiscal Year Ended Jan. 31

Per Share Data ($)	2007	2006	2005	2004	2003	2002	2001	2000	1999	1998
Tangible Book Value	5.61	3.04	1.85	1.18	0.36	NM	NM	NM	NM	NM
Cash Flow	3.30	3.04	1.57	2.02	2.93	2.44	2.11	1.86	1.66	1.57
Earnings	1.54	1.31	-0.14	0.42	1.56	1.26	1.04	0.74	0.85	0.85
S&P Core Earnings	1.59	1.27	0.99	0.98	1.40	1.12	0.96	NA	NA	NA
Dividends	Nil	Nil	Nil	Nil	Nil	Nil	Nil	Nil	Nil	Nil
Payout Ratio	Nil	Nil	Nil	Nil	Nil	Nil	Nil	Nil	Nil	Nil
Calendar Year	2006	2005	2004	2003	2002	2001	2000	1999	1998	1997
Prices:High	24.48	20.88	19.67	19.70	23.81	27.66	27.94	34.91	18.66	11.88
Prices:Low	18.05	15.15	14.65	12.05	11.00	19.60	14.06	14.88	11.34	8.38
P/E Ratio:High	16	16	NM	47	15	22	27	47	22	18
P/E Ratio:Low	12	12	NM	29	7	16	14	20	13	12

Income Statement Analysis (Million $)

	2007	2006	2005	2004	2003	2002	2001	2000	1999	1998
Revenue	66,111	60,553	56,434	53,791	51,760	50,098	49,000	45,352	28,203	26,567
Operating Income	3,508	3,300	3,003	3,147	3,676	3,567	3,397	3,125	1,410	1,377
Depreciation	1,272	1,265	1,256	1,209	1,087	973	907	961	430	380
Interest Expense	488	510	557	604	600	648	675	652	267	285
Pretax Income	1,748	1,525	290	770	1,973	1,711	1,508	1,129	713	712
Effective Tax Rate	36.2%	37.2%	NM	59.1%	37.5%	39.0%	41.6%	43.5%	36.9%	37.6%
Net Income	1,115	958	-100	315	1,233	1,043	880	638	450	444
S&P Core Earnings	1,155	928	720	745	1,105	914	816	NA	NA	NA

Balance Sheet & Other Financial Data (Million $)

	2007	2006	2005	2004	2003	2002	2001	2000	1999	1998
Cash	803	210	144	159	171	161	161	281	122	65.0
Current Assets	6,755	6,466	6,406	5,619	5,566	5,512	5,416	5,531	2,673	2,641
Total Assets	21,215	20,482	20,491	20,184	20,102	19,087	18,190	17,966	6,700	6,301
Current Liabilities	7,581	6,715	6,316	5,586	5,608	5,485	5,591	5,728	3,192	2,944
Long Term Debt	6,154	6,678	7,900	8,116	8,222	8,412	8,210	8,045	3,229	3,493
Common Equity	4,923	4,390	3,540	4,011	3,850	3,502	3,089	2,683	-388	-784
Total Capital	11,799	11,911	12,379	13,117	12,072	11,914	11,299	10,728	3,042	2,874
Capital Expenditures	1,683	1,306	1,634	2,000	1,891	2,139	1,623	1,701	923	612
Cash Flow	2,387	2,223	1,156	1,524	2,320	2,016	1,787	1,599	880	824
Current Ratio	0.9	1.0	1.0	1.0	1.0	1.0	1.0	1.0	0.8	0.9
% Long Term Debt of Capitalization	55.6	56.1	63.8	61.9	68.1	70.6	72.7	75.0	106.1	121.5
% Net Income of Revenue	1.7	1.6	NM	0.6	2.4	2.1	1.8	1.4	1.6	1.7
% Return on Assets	5.4	4.7	NM	1.6	6.3	5.6	4.9	3.7	6.9	7.3
% Return on Equity	24.0	23.9	NM	8.0	33.5	31.6	30.5	27.7	NM	NM

Data as orig reptd.; bef. results of disc opers/spec. items. Per share data adj. for stk. divs.; EPS diluted. E-Estimated. NA-Not Available. NM-Not Meaningful. NR-Not Ranked. UR-Under Review.

Office: 1014 Vine St, Cincinnati, OH 45202.
Telephone: 513-762-4000.
Email: investors@kroger.com
Website: http://www.kroger.com

Chrmn & CEO: D.B. Dillon
Pres & COO: D.W. McGeorge
Vice Chrmn: W.R. McMullen
EVP, Secy & General Counsel: P.W. Heldman

SVP & CFO: J.M. Schlotman
Investor Contact: C. Fike (513-762-4969)
Board Members: R. V. Anderson, R. D. Beyer, J. L. Clendenin, D. B. Dillon, J. T. LaMacchia, D. B. Lewis, D. W. McGeorge, W. R. McMullen, J. Montoya, C. R. Moore, K. D. Ortega, S. M. Phillips, S. R. Rogel, J. A. Runde, R. L. Sargent, B. S. Shackouls

Founded: 1883
Domicile: Ohio
Employees: 310,000

Laboratory Corporation of America Holdings

STANDARD &POOR'S

S&P Recommendation	**STRONG BUY** ★ ★ ★ ★ ★	Price $69.59 (as of Nov 23, 2007)	12-Mo. Target Price $90.00	Investment Style Large-Cap Growth

GICS Sector Health Care
Sub-Industry Health Care Services

Summary This clinical laboratory organization offers a broad range of clinical tests through a national network of laboratories.

Key Stock Statistics (Source S&P, Vickers, company reports)

52-Wk Range	$82.32– 65.13	S&P Oper. EPS 2007**E**	4.15	Market Capitalization(B)	$8.163	Beta	-0.07
Trailing 12-Month EPS	$3.76	S&P Oper. EPS 2008**E**	4.66	Yield (%)	Nil	S&P 3-Yr. Proj. EPS CAGR(%)	14.00
Trailing 12-Month P/E	18.5	P/E on S&P Oper. EPS 2007**E**	16.8	Dividend Rate/Share	Nil	S&P Credit Rating	BBB
$10K Invested 5 Yrs Ago	$30,126	Common Shares Outstg. (M)	117.3	Institutional Ownership (%)	100		

Price Performance

30-Week Mov. Avg. · · · 10-Week Mov. Avg. - - **GAAP Earnings vs. Previous Year** Volume Above Avg. STARS
12-Mo. Target Price — Relative Strength — ▲ Up ▼ Down ▶ No Change Below Avg. ★

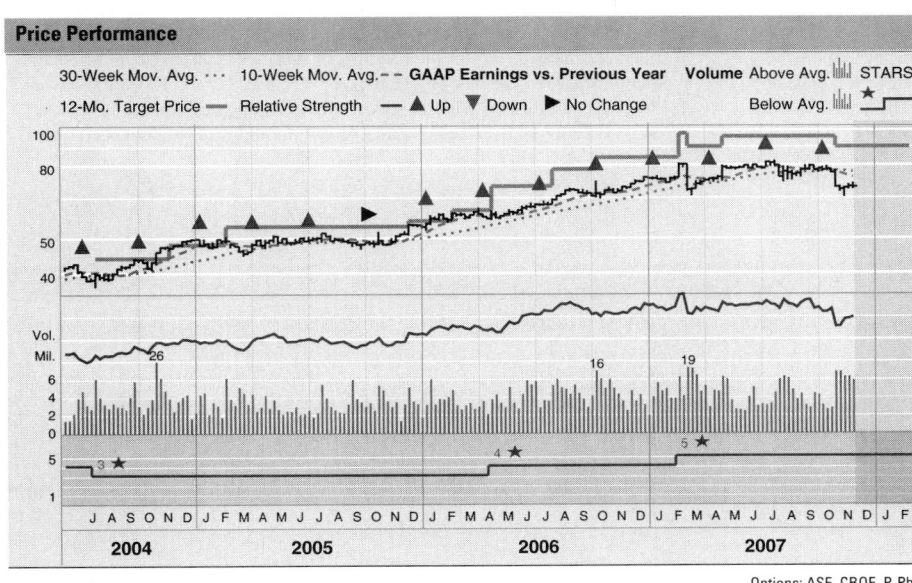

Options: ASE, CBOE, P, Ph

Analysis prepared by **Jeffrey Loo, CFA** on October 30, 2007, when the stock traded at **$ 67.62**.

Highlights

➤ We expect sales to increase 13% in 2007, to $4.07 billion, on low single digit organic growth and the 10-year exclusive national contract with United Healthcare (UNH) effective January 1, 2007, partially offset by the loss of the Aetna contract, effective July 1, 2007. For 2008, we see sales growth of 7%, to $4.36 billion. We think LH's agreement to reimburse UNH up to $200 million for transitional costs over three years (2007-2009) will limit margin expansion, but we think LH's rapid network buildout to minimize potential leakage will reduce transition costs. Despite our expectations of higher costs from expanding its network, we see a 40 basis point (bps) gain in the EBITDA margin in 2007, and a further 50 bps gain in 2008, primarily on leverage.

➤ In the first nine months of 2007, LH repurchased 7.3 million shares, with $329 million remaining under its repurchase program. In 2006, LH repurchased 6.7 million shares, and in the fourth quarter of 2006, it exchanged its liquid yield notes, which reduced its share count by 7.5 million shares.

➤ We forecast EPS of $4.15 for 2007 and $4.66 for 2008.

Investment Rationale/Risk

➤ We expect LH to expand faster than the industry's estimated low to mid-single digit growth rate, and we believe the UNH-related physician transition to LH is progressing well. But we think the rapid transition of UNH patients that LH benefited from in the first half 2007 is moderating. We also see better pricing stability and visibility, as we think most managed care contracts have been signed. We note that LH has submitted a proposal in response to Humana's RFP, but we do not expect further exclusive deals. We expect continued improvement in revenue per requisition, as we see more higher price esoteric testing. We think LH will continue to be acquisitive to supplement organic growth.

➤ Risks to our recommendation and target price include greater than expected pricing pressure and an inability to efficiently establish its lab network to absorb the UNH business.

➤ Our 12-month target price of $90 is based on our DCF analysis (assuming a WACC of 9.3% and a terminal growth rate of 3%) and a P/E to growth (PEG) ratio of 1.4X applied to our 2008 EPS estimate, in line with peers.

Qualitative Risk Assessment

LOW	MEDIUM	HIGH

Our risk assessment reflects LH's leadership position in a large, mature industry, its broad geographic service area with clients in all 50 states, and our view of its diverse and balanced payer mix.

Quantitative Evaluations

S&P Quality Ranking B

D	C	B-	**B**	B+	A-	A	A+

Relative Strength Rank MODERATE

52

LOWEST = 1 HIGHEST = 99

Revenue/Earnings Data

Revenue (Million $)

	1Q	2Q	3Q	4Q	Year
2007	998.7	1,043	1,021	--	--
2006	878.6	903.7	909.9	898.6	3,591
2005	799.1	853.3	852.9	822.3	3,328
2004	752.5	784.3	781.5	766.5	3,085
2003	712.2	743.7	752.0	731.5	2,939
2002	590.0	612.4	655.2	650.1	2,508

Earnings Per Share ($)

2007	0.98	1.09	0.92	E1.01	E4.15
2006	0.76	0.87	0.81	0.81	3.24
2005	0.67	0.74	0.66	0.64	2.71
2004	0.58	0.66	0.66	0.58	2.45
2003	0.51	0.60	0.58	0.54	2.22
2002	0.47	0.55	0.39	0.36	1.77

Fiscal year ended Dec. 31. Next earnings report expected: Mid February. EPS Estimates based on S&P Operating Earnings; historical GAAP earnings are as reported.

Dividend Data

No cash dividends have been paid.

Laboratory Corporation of America Holdings

STANDARD
&POOR'S

Business Summary October 30, 2007

CORPORATE OVERVIEW. Laboratory Corporation of America Holdings is the second largest independent U.S. clinical laboratory. Clinical laboratory tests are used by medical professionals in routine testing, patient diagnosis, and in the monitoring and treatment of disease. As of December 2006, LH had 36 primary testing facilities and more than 1,300 service sites consisting of branches, patient service centers, and STAT laboratories that have the ability to perform certain routine tests quickly and report results to the physician immediately. The company's laboratory services involve the testing of both bodily fluids and human tissues. LH offers more than 4,400 different tests, consisting of routine tests and specialty and niche testing (esoteric). The most frequently administered routine tests include blood chemistry analyses, urinalysis, blood cell counts, pap tests, HIV tests, microbiology cultures and procedures, and alcohol and other substance abuse tests. The company's esoteric tests include testing for infectious diseases, allergies, diagnostic genetics, identity, and oncology. An average of 370,000 specimens were being processed daily as of December 2006, with routine testing results generally available within 24 hours.

The company provides testing services to a broad range of health care providers, including independent physicians, hospitals, HMOs and other managed care groups, and governmental and other institutions. During 2005, no client accounted for over 4% of net sales. Most testing services are billed to a party other than the physician or other authorized person who ordered the test. Payers other than the direct patient include insurance companies, managed care organizations, Medicare and Medicaid. Client-billed accounted for 27% of revenue in 2006 (28% in 2005), and generated an average of $29.30 ($29.11 in 2005) in revenue per requisition; patients-billed 9% (9% in 2005) and $148.91 ($135.12 in 2005); managed care clients 43% (40% in 2005) and $37.01 ($34.98 in 2005); and Medicare, Medicaid and Insurance 21% (23% in 2005) and $40.11 ($38.49 in 2005). In May 2005, the company acquired Esoterix, Inc., a provider of specialty reference testing. In February 2005, LH bought US Labs, located in Irvine, CA. In March 2004, LH purchased laboratory operations in Poughkeepsie, NY, and Atlanta, GA, from MDS Diagnostic Services. In July 2007, LH acquired DSI Labs, expanding its operations in southwest Florida.

Company Financials Fiscal Year Ended Dec. 31

Per Share Data ($)	2006	2005	2004	2003	2002	2001	2000	1999	1998	1997
Tangible Book Value	NM	NM	1.04	0.27	2.67	0.83	0.09	NM	NM	NM
Cash Flow	4.80	4.24	3.33	3.18	2.47	2.03	1.74	0.19	2.17	-0.89
Earnings	3.24	2.71	2.45	2.22	1.77	1.29	0.81	0.29	0.50	-2.65
S&P Core Earnings	3.21	2.53	2.25	2.04	1.56	1.15	NA	NA	NA	NA
Dividends	Nil	Nil	Nil	Nil	Nil	Nil	Nil	Nil	Nil	Nil
Payout Ratio	Nil	Nil	Nil	Nil	Nil	Nil	Nil	Nil	Nil	Nil
Prices:High	74.30	55.00	50.03	37.72	52.38	45.68	45.75	9.69	6.88	10.00
Prices:Low	52.58	44.63	36.70	22.21	18.51	24.88	7.81	3.13	2.81	3.28
P/E Ratio:High	23	20	20	17	30	35	57	33	14	NM
P/E Ratio:Low	16	16	15	10	10	19	10	11	6	NM

Income Statement Analysis (Million $)										
Revenue	3,591	3,328	3,085	2,939	2,508	2,200	1,919	1,699	1,613	1,519
Operating Income	853	785	736	671	554	472	340	234	212	17.5
Depreciation	155	150	139	136	102	104	89.6	84.5	84.2	86.8
Interest Expense	47.8	34.4	36.1	40.9	19.2	27.0	38.5	41.6	48.7	71.7
Pretax Income	721	641	615	540	432	332	208	106	81.5	-161
Effective Tax Rate	40.1%	39.7%	41.0%	40.6%	41.1%	45.0%	46.0%	38.0%	15.6%	NM
Net Income	432	386	363	321	255	183	112	65.4	68.8	-107
S&P Core Earnings	428	368	339	295	226	162	NA	NA	NA	NA

Balance Sheet & Other Financial Data (Million $)										
Cash	51.5	45.4	187	123	56.4	149	48.8	40.3	22.7	23.3
Current Assets	887	702	740	658	597	624	512	500	519	528
Total Assets	4,001	3,876	3,601	3,415	2,612	1,930	1,667	1,590	1,641	1,659
Current Liabilities	931	888	301	758	229	201	312	246	251	197
Long Term Debt	603	604	892	361	522	509	354	483	576	650
Common Equity	1,977	1,886	1,999	1,896	1,612	1,085	877	176	154	129
Total Capital	2,989	2,899	3,213	2,530	2,133	1,594	1,231	1,217	1,257	779
Capital Expenditures	116	93.6	95.0	83.6	74.3	88.1	55.5	69.4	58.7	34.5
Cash Flow	587	536	502	457	356	287	167	99.5	109	-44.0
Current Ratio	1.0	0.8	2.5	0.9	2.6	3.1	1.6	2.0	2.1	2.7
% Long Term Debt of Capitalization	20.2	20.9	27.8	14.3	24.4	31.9	28.7	39.7	45.8	83.4
% Net Income of Revenue	12.0	11.6	11.8	10.9	10.2	8.3	5.8	3.9	4.3	NM
% Return on Assets	11.0	10.3	10.3	10.7	11.2	10.2	6.9	4.0	4.2	NM
% Return on Equity	22.3	19.9	18.6	18.3	18.9	18.6	14.8	9.1	17.2	NM

Data as orig reptd.; bef. results of disc opers/spec. items. Per share data adj. for stk. divs.; EPS diluted. E-Estimated. NA-Not Available. NM-Not Meaningful. NR-Not Ranked. UR-Under Review.

Office: 358 South Main Street, Burlington, NC 27215.
Telephone: 336-229-1127.
Website: http://www.labcorp.com
Chrmn: T.P. Mac Mahon

CEO: D.P. King
EVP, CFO & Treas: W.B. Hayes
EVP & CSO: M.P. Lai-Goldman
EVP & Secy: B.T. Smith

Investor Contact: S. Fleming (336-436-4879)
Board Members: K. B. Anderson, J. Belingard, W. E. Lane, T. P. Mac Mahon, R. E. Mittelstaedt, Jr., A. H. Rubenstein, B. T. Smith, A. G. Wallace, M. K. Weikel

Founded: 1971
Domicile: Delaware
Employees: 25,000

The *McGraw-Hill* Companies

Estee Lauder Companies Inc. (The)

STANDARD &POOR'S

S&P Recommendation	BUY ★★★★☆	Price $41.95 (as of Nov 23, 2007)	12-Mo. Target Price $51.00	Investment Style Large-Cap Growth

GICS Sector Consumer Staples
Sub-Industry Personal Products

Summary This company is one of the world's leading manufacturers and marketers of skin care, makeup, and fragrance products.

Key Stock Statistics (Source S&P, Vickers, company reports)

52-Wk Range	$52.31–38.41	S&P Oper. EPS 2008E	2.34	Market Capitalization(B)	$4.718	Beta	0.43
Trailing 12-Month EPS	$2.09	S&P Oper. EPS 2009E	NA	Yield (%)	1.31	S&P 3-Yr. Proj. EPS CAGR(%)	11.00
Trailing 12-Month P/E	20.1	P/E on S&P Oper. EPS 2008E	17.9	Dividend Rate/Share	$0.55	S&P Credit Rating	A
$10K Invested 5 Yrs Ago	$16,240	Common Shares Outstg. (M)	194.3	Institutional Ownership (%)	86		

Price Performance

30-Week Mov. Avg. · · ·   10-Week Mov. Avg. – – **GAAP Earnings vs. Previous Year**   Volume Above Avg. STARS
12-Mo. Target Price — Relative Strength — ▲ Up ▼ Down ▶ No Change   Below Avg. ★

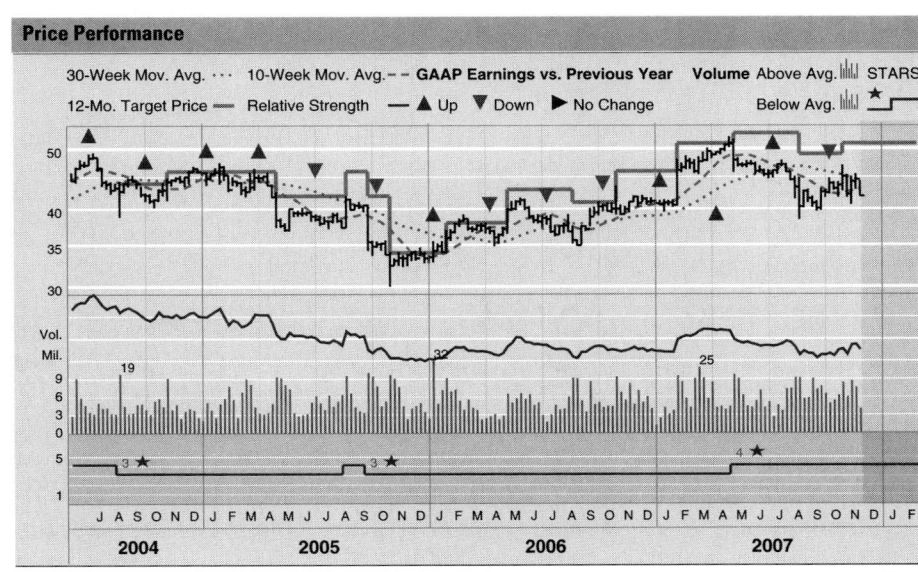

Options: ASE, CBOE, Ph

Analysis prepared by **Loran Braverman, CFA** on October 25, 2007, when the stock traded at **$44.72**.

Qualitative Risk Assessment

LOW	MEDIUM	HIGH

Our risk assessment reflects our view of EL's market share advantage, leading brands, scale leverage, and a strong balance sheet. However, the company is exposed to short-term events such as changes in the retail industry, geopolitical events, and consumer spending.

Quantitative Evaluations

S&P Quality Ranking   A-

D	C	B-	B	B+	A-	A	A+

Relative Strength Rank   MODERATE

64

LOWEST = 1   HIGHEST = 99

Revenue/Earnings Data

Revenue (Million $)

	1Q	2Q	3Q	4Q	Year
2008	1,710	--	--	--	--
2007	1,594	1,991	1,691	1,762	7,038
2006	1,497	1,784	1,578	1,605	6,464
2005	1,504	1,750	1,538	1,544	6,336
2004	1,352	1,619	1,422	1,403	5,790
2003	1,243	1,413	1,239	1,223	5,118

Earnings Per Share ($)

2008	0.20	E1.11	E0.49	E0.53	E2.34
2007	0.27	0.99	0.45	0.45	2.16
2006	0.28	0.70	0.28	0.23	1.49
2005	0.41	0.60	0.46	0.30	1.78
2004	0.34	0.54	0.43	0.31	1.62
2003	0.28	0.44	0.33	0.20	1.26

Fiscal year ended Jun. 30. Next earnings report expected: Late January. EPS Estimates based on S&P Operating Earnings; historical GAAP earnings are as reported.

Dividend Data (Dates: mm/dd Payment Date: mm/dd/yy)

Amount ($)	Date Decl.	Ex-Div. Date	Stk. of Record	Payment Date
0.500	10/25	12/06	12/08	12/27/06
0.550	11/09	12/05	12/07	12/27/07

Dividends have been paid since 1996. Source: Company reports.

Highlights

➤ We estimate sales will rise 8% in FY 08 (Jun.). We think there will continue to be a negative impact from U.S. department store closures and store conversions, but we expect these factors to be offset by strength in other channels in the Americas region and in other geographic regions. While we forecast 4% revenue growth from the Americas segment, we look for 12% and 13%, respectively, from Europe, the Middle East & Africa, and Asia/Pacific.

➤ We look for EL's operating margin to be about flat in FY 08 versus FY 07. Following better than expected December 2007 quarter results, EL announced its intention to accelerate and increase its investments in its business, particularly in foreign markets. We are projecting 40 basis points of margin pressure from higher interest expense and a 36% tax rate.

➤ Our EPS estimate for FY 08 is $2.34, up 8% from FY 07's $2.16. In March 2007, EL repurchased about 16 million shares at a cost of $750 million. Our FY 08 EPS estimate assumes an 85% increase in interest expense and a 5% drop in average shares outstanding.

Investment Rationale/Risk

➤ Our buy recommendation reflects our view of favorable growth prospects and an attractive valuation. We believe EL will eventually work out the challenging environment tied to department stores. We also expect that the expenses the company is incurring for its strategic initiatives program will drive future sales growth.

➤ Risks to our recommendation and target price include a sharp decline in the economy that could hurt EL's retail business. We are concerned about EL's corporate governance practices given the majority voting power of insiders.

➤ Our 12-month target price of $51 is based on a blend of our historical and relative analyses. Our historical analysis suggests a value of $55 based on a multiple of 23X, slightly below the 10-year median, applied to our calendar 2008 EPS estimate of $2.43. Our peer analysis uses a P/E of about 19X, a premium to the peer average, to value the stock at $47.

Estee Lauder Companies Inc. (The)

STANDARD &POOR'S

Business Summary October 25, 2007

CORPORATE OVERVIEW. The Estee Lauder Companies was founded in 1946 by Estee and Joseph Lauder. EL has grown into one of the world's largest manufacturers and marketers of skin care, makeup and fragrance products, sold in more than 135 countries and territories worldwide. EL has historically been a dominant player in the high end fragrance and cosmetic categories, with brand names such as Estee Lauder, Clinique, Aramis, Prescriptives, Origins, M.A.C, Bobbi Brown, La Mer, Aveda, Stila, Jo Malone, and Bumble and Bumble. EL is also the global licensee for fragrances and cosmetics sold under the Tommy Hilfiger, Donna Karan and Michael Kors brands. Each brand is distinctly positioned within the cosmetics market, according to the company.

The Americas comprise EL's most important operating region, accounting for 51% of sales and 45% of profits in FY 07 (Jun.). Other regions include Europe, the Middle East and Africa (35% of sales and 43% of profits), and Asia-Pacific (14% and 12%).

The skin care division (37% of FY 07 net sales) addresses various skin care needs of women and men. Products include moisturizers, creams, lotions, cleansers, sun screens and self-tanning products. The makeup division (39%) manufactures, markets and sells a full array of makeup products, including lipsticks, mascaras, foundations, eyeshadows, nail polishes and powders. The

fragrance division (18%) offers a variety of fragrance products, including eau de parfum sprays and colognes, as well as lotions, powders, creams and soaps that are based on a particular fragrance. The products of the hair care division (5%) are offered mainly in salons and in freestanding retail stores and include styling products, shampoos, conditioners and finishing sprays. Other is less than 1%.

As is customary in the cosmetics industry, EL accepts returns of its products from retailers under certain conditions. In recognition of this practice and in according with generally accepted accounting principals, EL reports sales on a net basis, which is computed by deducting the amount of actual returns received and an amount established for anticipated returns from gross sales. As a percentage of gross sales, returns were 4.2% in FY 07, 5.0% in FY 06 and 4.6% in FY 05.

In FY 07, Macy's, Inc. accounted for 12% of EL's accounts receivable and 14% of consolidated net sales.

Company Financials Fiscal Year Ended Jun. 30

Per Share Data ($)	2007	2006	2005	2004	2003	2002	2001	2000	1999	1998
Tangible Book Value	2.23	4.29	6.79	4.35	2.92	3.20	2.64	1.77	1.33	0.57
Cash Flow	3.16	2.41	2.64	2.45	2.01	1.46	1.82	1.73	1.45	1.22
Earnings	2.16	1.49	1.78	1.62	1.26	0.78	1.17	1.20	1.03	0.89
S&P Core Earnings	2.18	1.52	1.69	1.51	1.17	0.70	1.01	NA	NA	NA
Dividends	0.50	0.40	0.40	0.30	0.20	0.20	0.20	0.15	0.18	0.17
Payout Ratio	23%	27%	22%	19%	16%	26%	17%	12%	17%	19%
Prices:High	52.31	43.60	47.50	49.34	40.20	38.80	44.35	55.88	56.50	43.25
Prices:Low	38.41	32.79	29.98	37.55	25.73	25.20	29.25	33.75	37.25	23.34
P/E Ratio:High	24	29	27	30	32	50	38	47	55	49
P/E Ratio:Low	18	22	17	23	20	32	25	28	36	26

Income Statement Analysis (Million $)

	2007	2006	2005	2004	2003	2002	2001	2000	1999	1998
Revenue	7,038	6,464	6,336	5,790	5,118	4,744	4,608	4,367	3,962	3,618
Operating Income	958	910	917	836	712	614	706	645	556	489
Depreciation	207	198	197	192	175	162	156	129	99.6	79.8
Interest Expense	38.9	23.8	13.9	27.1	8.10	9.80	12.3	17.1	16.7	6.30
Pretax Income	711	596	707	617	474	332	483	499	440	403
Effective Tax Rate	35.9%	43.6%	41.2%	37.7%	33.9%	34.5%	36.0%	37.0%	38.0%	40.0%
Net Income	449	325	406	375	320	213	307	314	273	237
S&P Core Earnings	453	332	390	351	274	171	245	NA	NA	NA

Balance Sheet & Other Financial Data (Million $)

	2007	2006	2005	2004	2003	2002	2001	2000	1999	1998
Cash	254	369	553	612	364	547	347	320	348	278
Current Assets	2,239	2,177	2,303	2,199	1,845	1,928	1,739	1,619	1,570	1,455
Total Assets	4,126	3,784	3,886	3,708	3,350	3,417	3,219	3,043	2,747	2,513
Current Liabilities	1,501	1,438	1,498	1,322	1,054	960	857	902	862	837
Long Term Debt	1,028	432	451	462	284	404	411	418	423	425
Common Equity	1,199	1,622	1,693	1,733	1,424	1,462	1,352	1,160	924	696
Total Capital	2,248	2,079	2,160	2,211	2,080	2,226	2,123	1,939	1,707	1,481
Capital Expenditures	312	261	230	207	163	203	192	181	118	121
Cash Flow	656	523	603	567	471	351	440	420	349	293
Current Ratio	1.5	1.5	1.5	1.7	1.8	2.0	2.0	1.8	1.8	1.7
% Long Term Debt of Capitalization	45.7	20.8	20.9	20.9	13.6	18.1	19.4	21.6	24.8	28.6
% Net Income of Revenue	6.4	5.0	6.4	6.5	6.2	4.5	6.7	7.2	6.9	6.5
% Return on Assets	11.3	8.5	10.7	10.6	9.5	6.4	9.8	10.8	10.4	10.7
% Return on Equity	31.8	19.6	23.7	23.8	20.5	13.4	22.6	27.9	30.8	34.3

Data as orig reptd.; bef. results of disc opers/spec. items. Per share data adj. for stk. divs.; EPS diluted. E-Estimated. NA-Not Available. NM-Not Meaningful. NR-Not Ranked. UR-Under Review.

Office: 767 5th Avenue, New York, NY 10153-0023.
Telephone: 212-572-4200.
Email: irdept@estee.com
Website: http://www.elcompanies.com

Chrmn: L.A. Lauder
Pres & CEO: W.P. Lauder
COO: D. Brestle
EVP & CFO: R.W. Kunes

EVP, Secy & General Counsel: S.E. Moss
Investor Contact: D. D'Andrea (212-572-4384)
Board Members: C. Barshefsky, R. M. Bravo, L. Forester de Rothschild, P. Fribourg, M. Hobson, I. O. Hockaday, Jr., A. Lauder, L. A. Lauder, R. S. Lauder, W. P. Lauder, R. D. Parsons, B. S. Sternlicht

Founded: 1946
Domicile: Delaware
Employees: 28,500

The McGraw·Hill Companies

Leggett & Platt Inc

STANDARD &POOR'S

S&P Recommendation	HOLD ★★★☆☆	Price $20.25 (as of Nov 23, 2007)	12-Mo. Target Price $21.00	Investment Style Large-Cap Blend

GICS Sector Consumer Discretionary
Sub-Industry Home Furnishings

Summary This company makes a broad line of bedding and furniture components and other home, office and commercial furnishings, as well as diversified products for non-furnishings markets.

Key Stock Statistics (Source S&P, Vickers, company reports)

52-Wk Range	$24.73– 17.96	S&P Oper. EPS 2007**E**	1.35	Market Capitalization(B)	$3.538	Beta	1.20
Trailing 12-Month EPS	$1.49	S&P Oper. EPS 2008**E**	1.45	Yield (%)	4.94	S&P 3-Yr. Proj. EPS CAGR(%)	11.00
Trailing 12-Month P/E	13.6	P/E on S&P Oper. EPS 2007**E**	15.0	Dividend Rate/Share	$1.00	S&P Credit Rating	A
$10K Invested 5 Yrs Ago	$10,130	Common Shares Outstg. (M)	174.7	Institutional Ownership (%)	81		

Price Performance

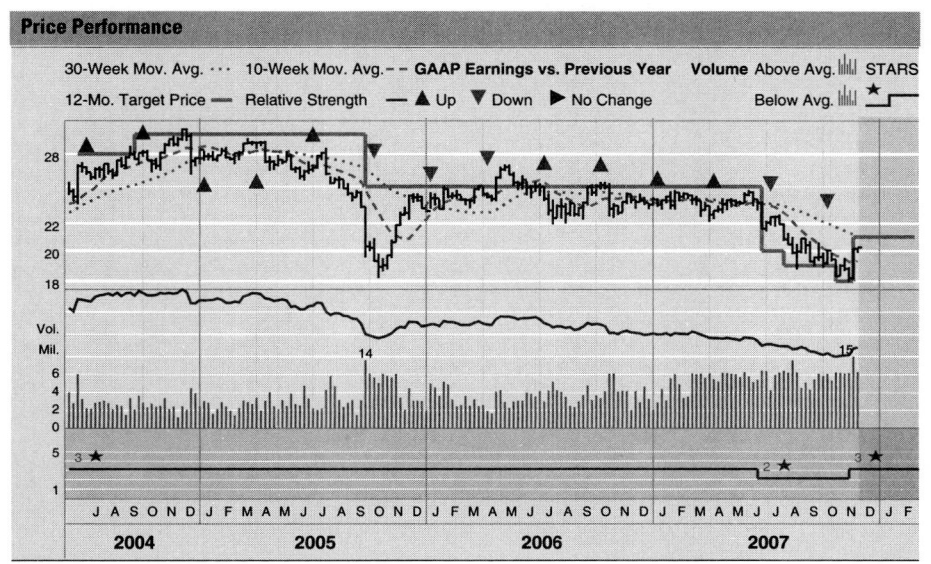

30-Week Mov. Avg. ··· 10-Week Mov. Avg. - - **GAAP Earnings vs. Previous Year** Volume Above Avg. STARS
12-Mo. Target Price — Relative Strength - ▲ Up ▼ Down ► No Change Below Avg.

Options: Ph

Analysis prepared by **Kenneth M. Leon, CPA** on November 15, 2007, when the stock traded at **$ 20.01**.

Highlights

➤ Excluding the planned divestment of the Aluminum Products segment and other plant closings, we project that revenue will decrease 5% in 2007 and increase about 2% in 2008, largely reflecting a slowdown in housing and home furnishing markets. Sales in the third quarter were down 3%, year to year, as a 5% dip in same-location sales was partly offset by a 2% boost from acquisitions.

➤ Facing weak volumes, high and rising raw material costs, and poor capacity utilization, LEG announced in November 2007 that it was seeking opportunities to consolidate, close or divest production or warehouse facilities. The timing of the divestitures or other productivity measures is uncertain.

➤ LEG believes the proposed elimination of businesses will cut approximately $1.2 billion from total sales, or 23% of our $5.3 billion sales estimate for 2008. We will update our financial forecast when the company reports Aluminum Products as a discontinued operation and provides restated financials for 2006 and 2007. Our current EPS estimates are $1.35 for 2007 and $1.45 for 2008.

Investment Rationale/Risk

➤ We believe LEG is still challenged by a slump in U.S. housing markets and rising prices for steel and other materials. Narrowing its focus to fewer businesses with the planned restructuring should enable the company to improve operating efficiencies, in our opinion. One caveat to LEG's bold new strategy is that the same management team that underperformed in past years will implement these new strategic actions.

➤ Risks to our recommendation and target price include any further weakness in economic and market conditions, and rising costs of raw materials, fuel and energy. We also see execution risk of the planned restructuring.

➤ Taking into account an above-average dividend yield (recently about 5% following a 39% dividend increase) and a forward P/E of 14.5X our 2008 EPS estimate of $1.45, our 12-month target price is $21. This is a discount to LEG's five-year historical average -- warranted, in our view, by a lack of visibility to improved sales growth.

Qualitative Risk Assessment

LOW	MEDIUM	HIGH

Our risk assessment takes into account our view of LEG's long history of profitability and strong free cash flow, offset by the cyclical industry in which the company operates. We believe LEG has execution risk on its planned corporate restructuring to drive improved returns on investment.

Quantitative Evaluations

S&P Quality Ranking   **B+**

D	C	B-	B	B+	A-	A	A+

Relative Strength Rank   **STRONG**

88

LOWEST = 1   HIGHEST = 99

Revenue/Earnings Data

Revenue (Million $)

	1Q	2Q	3Q	4Q	Year
2007	1,294	1,316	1,325	--	--
2006	1,378	1,403	1,415	1,311	5,505
2005	1,301	1,310	1,349	1,340	5,299
2004	1,187	1,278	1,338	1,282	5,086
2003	1,038	1,053	1,157	1,141	4,388
2002	1,023	1,115	1,121	1,013	4,272

Earnings Per Share ($)

2007	0.34	0.33	0.37	E0.24	E1.35
2006	0.33	0.45	0.45	0.38	1.61
2005	0.37	0.41	0.28	0.24	1.30
2004	0.32	0.39	0.41	0.33	1.45
2003	0.25	0.24	0.26	0.30	1.05
2002	0.28	0.35	0.29	0.25	1.17

Fiscal year ended Dec. 31. Next earnings report expected: Late January. EPS Estimates based on S&P Operating Earnings; historical GAAP earnings are as reported.

Dividend Data (Dates: mm/dd Payment Date: mm/dd/yy)

Amount ($)	Date Decl.	Ex-Div. Date	Stk. of Record	Payment Date
0.170	02/22	03/13	03/15	04/13/07
0.180	05/09	06/13	06/15	07/13/07
0.180	08/09	09/12	09/14	10/15/07
0.250	11/13	12/12	12/14	01/15/08

Dividends have been paid since 1939. Source: Company reports.

Please read the Required Disclosures and Analyst Certification on the last page of this report.

The McGraw-Hill Companies

Leggett & Platt Inc

Business Summary November 15, 2007

Leggett & Platt, founded in 1883, is a diversified manufacturer that conceives, designs and produces a wide range of engineered components and products that can be found in most homes, offices, retail stores and automobiles.

LEG's business is organized into five business segments. Residential Furnishings, which accounted for 47% of 2006 sales (46% in 2005), consists of the Bedding, Home Furniture & Consumer Products, and Fabric, Foam & Fiber Groups. The Commercial Fixturing and Components segment, 17% of 2006 sales (20%), consists of Fixture & Display and Office Furniture Components. Industrial Materials, 13% of 2006 sales (15%), consists of the Wire and Tubing Groups, while Specialized Products, 13% (10%), consists of the Automotive, Machinery, and Commercial Vehicles Groups, and Aluminum Products, 10% (9%), makes up the balance. The new strategy calls for divesting Aluminum Products and downsizing Commercial Fixturing.

In the past 20 years, about two-thirds of the company's sales growth has come from acquisitions. Over the past 10 years, the average acquisition target had revenues of $15 million to $20 million, which the company believes serves to minimize the risk of any single acquisition. The company plans to spend about $250 million to $300 million on acquisitions and share repurchases combined.

In 2006, LEG acquired five businesses representing $75 million in annualized sales, all within the Residential Furnishings segment. The largest acquisition was of a maker of rubber carpet underlay, a product type that accounts for 6% of LEG's overall revenue. In addition, the company divested five businesses in 2006 with annualized sales of about $45 million.

In 2005, LEG acquired 12 businesses representing approximately $320 million in annualized sales. The acquired businesses boosted annual sales by about $170 million for Residential Furnishings, and $150 million for Specialized Products.

In 2006, about 21% of sales were derived from foreign operations, similar to levels in recent years. Much of these international operations are in Canada, Europe and Mexico. However, the company has gone from having just three production facilities in China in 2003, to having 12 at the end of 2006.

Company Financials Fiscal Year Ended Dec. 31

Per Share Data ($)	2006	2005	2004	2003	2002	2001	2000	1999	1998	1997
Tangible Book Value	5.72	5.55	6.38	5.62	5.36	4.81	4.61	4.50	4.59	7.77
Cash Flow	2.67	2.18	2.35	1.89	1.99	1.92	2.18	2.19	1.87	3.25
Earnings	1.61	1.30	1.45	1.05	1.17	0.94	1.32	1.45	1.24	1.08
S&P Core Earnings	1.58	1.27	1.38	1.02	1.11	0.85	NA	NA	NA	NA
Dividends	0.84	0.63	0.58	0.54	0.50	0.48	0.42	0.35	0.31	0.27
Payout Ratio	52%	48%	40%	51%	43%	51%	32%	24%	25%	25%
Prices:High	27.04	29.61	30.68	23.69	27.40	24.45	22.56	28.31	28.75	23.88
Prices:Low	21.93	18.19	21.19	17.16	18.60	16.85	14.19	18.63	16.88	15.75
P/E Ratio:High	17	23	21	23	23	26	17	20	23	22
P/E Ratio:Low	14	14	15	16	16	18	11	13	14	15

Income Statement Analysis (Million $)	2006	2005	2004	2003	2002	2001	2000	1999	1998	1997
Revenue	5,505	5,299	5,086	4,388	4,272	4,114	4,276	3,779	3,370	2,909
Operating Income	666	605	622	520	582	558	660	650	555	467
Depreciation	175	171	177	167	165	197	173	149	128	106
Interest Expense	56.2	46.7	45.9	46.9	42.1	58.8	66.3	43.0	38.5	31.8
Pretax Income	435	356	423	315	364	297	419	463	396	333
Effective Tax Rate	30.9%	29.4%	32.5%	34.7%	35.9%	36.9%	36.9%	37.2%	37.3%	37.5%
Net Income	300	251	285	206	233	188	264	291	248	208
S&P Core Earnings	293	245	272	202	221	169	NA	NA	NA	NA

Balance Sheet & Other Financial Data (Million $)	2006	2005	2004	2003	2002	2001	2000	1999	1998	1997
Cash	132	64.9	491	444	225	187	37.3	20.6	83.5	7.70
Current Assets	1,894	1,763	2,065	1,819	1,488	1,422	1,405	1,256	1,137	945
Total Assets	4,265	4,053	4,197	3,890	3,501	3,413	3,373	2,978	2,535	2,106
Current Liabilities	691	738	960	626	598	457	477	432	401	373
Long Term Debt	1,060	922	779	1,012	809	978	988	787	574	466
Common Equity	2,351	2,249	2,313	2,114	1,977	1,867	1,794	1,646	1,437	1,174
Total Capital	3,478	3,230	3,178	3,221	2,865	2,909	2,854	2,502	2,086	1,693
Capital Expenditures	166	164	157	137	124	128	170	159	148	119
Cash Flow	476	422	463	373	398	384	437	440	376	314
Current Ratio	2.7	2.4	2.2	2.9	2.5	3.1	2.9	2.9	2.8	2.5
% Long Term Debt of Capitalization	30.5	28.5	24.5	31.4	28.2	33.6	34.6	31.5	27.5	27.5
% Net Income of Revenue	5.5	4.7	5.6	4.7	5.5	4.6	6.2	7.7	7.4	7.2
% Return on Assets	7.2	6.1	7.1	5.6	6.7	5.5	8.3	10.5	10.7	10.9
% Return on Equity	13.1	11.0	12.9	10.1	12.1	10.3	15.4	18.8	19.0	19.7

Data as orig reptd.; bef. results of disc opers/spec. items. Per share data adj. for stk. divs.; EPS diluted. E-Estimated. NA-Not Available. NM-Not Meaningful. NR-Not Ranked. UR-Under Review.

Office: No. 1 Leggett Road, Carthage, MO 64836-9649.
Telephone: 417-358-8131.
Email: invest@leggett.com
Website: http://www.leggett.com

Chrmn: F.E. Wright
Pres & CEO: D.S. Haffner
COO & EVP: K.G. Glassman
SVP & CFO: M.C. Flanigan

SVP, Secy & General Counsel: E.C. Jett
Investor Contact: S.R. McCoy (417-358-8131)
Board Members: R. F. Bentele, R. W. Clark, H. M. Cornell, Jr., R. T. Enloe, III, R. T. Fisher, K. G. Glassman, D. S. Haffner, J. W. McClanathan, J. C. Odom, M. E. Purnell, Jr., P. A. Wood, F. E. Wright

Founded: 1883
Domicile: Missouri
Employees: 32,828

Legg Mason Inc

STANDARD &POOR'S

S&P Recommendation BUY ★★★★☆

Price	**12-Mo. Target Price**	**Investment Style**
$70.04 (as of Nov 23, 2007)	$95.00	Large-Cap Growth

GICS Sector Financials
Sub-Industry Asset Management & Custody Banks

Summary This diversified investment manager serves individual and institutional investors through offices around the United States.

Key Stock Statistics (Source S&P, Vickers, company reports)

52-Wk Range	$110.17– 68.35	S&P Oper. EPS 2008**E**	5.25	Market Capitalization(B)	$9.299	Beta	1.56
Trailing 12-Month EPS	$4.95	S&P Oper. EPS 2009**E**	5.82	Yield (%)	1.37	S&P 3-Yr. Proj. EPS CAGR(%)	12.00
Trailing 12-Month P/E	14.2	P/E on S&P Oper. EPS 2008**E**	13.3	Dividend Rate/Share	$0.96	S&P Credit Rating	BBB+
$10K Invested 5 Yrs Ago	$20,757	Common Shares Outstg. (M)	132.8	Institutional Ownership (%)	83		

Price Performance

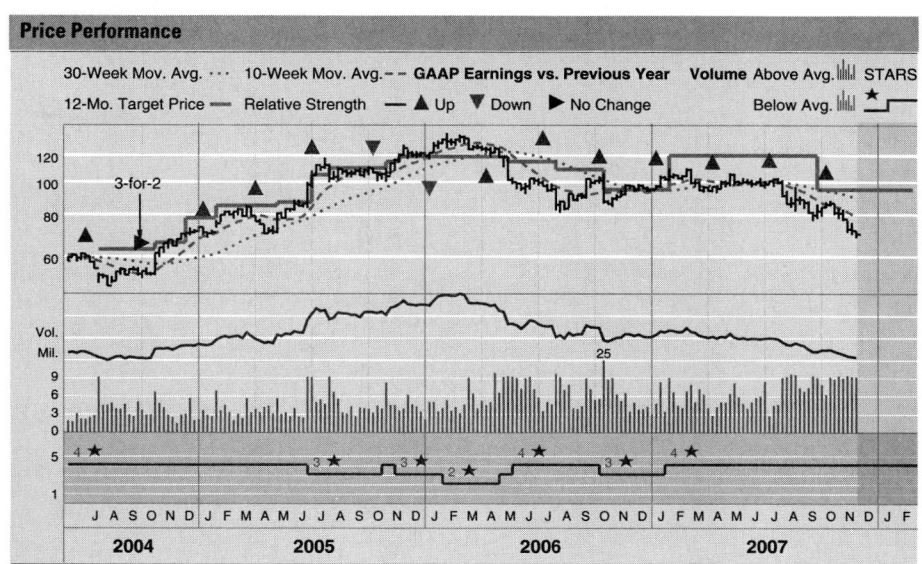

- 30-Week Mov. Avg. ··· 10-Week Mov. Avg. - - **GAAP Earnings vs. Previous Year** Volume Above Avg. STARS
- 12-Mo. Target Price — Relative Strength — ▲ Up ▼ Down ► No Change Below Avg.

Options: ASE, CBOE, P, Ph

Analysis prepared by **Matthew Albrecht** on October 31, 2007, when the stock traded at **$ 82.46**.

Highlights

➤ Despite recent volatility and lackluster client flows, we expect assets under management to grow about 10% in FY 08 (Mar.) before advancing more than 12% in FY 09. We look for the company to focus on expanding its distribution network, particularly for retail investors, and improving lagging fund performance, both of which should help attract client assets. LM recently received the necessary approvals to distribute its funds more extensively in a few Asian locales, and has also agreed to distribution plans with a number of large domestic adviser networks. All told, we expect a relatively stable realization rate and performance fee income to result in operating revenue growth of about 12% in FY 08 before 11% growth in FY 09.

➤ The net distribution expense ratio has decreased modestly in FY 08 to about 42%, and we anticipate a similar ratio in FY 09. We look for compensation to increase about 70 basis points on a percentage of net revenues basis in FY 08, before a slight decrease in FY 09. We look for pretax margins to expand modestly in each of the next two fiscal years.

➤ We forecast operating EPS of $5.25 in FY 08 and $5.82 in FY 09.

Investment Rationale/Risk

➤ We believe that Legg Mason is nearing the end of its integration of Citigroup's asset management division, and expected cost synergies are being realized. It has also overcome fund redemptions triggered by the deal, and assets under management are increasing. Equity fund performance has lagged peers, but improving fund performance and positive industry trends result in our buy recommendation.

➤ Risks to our recommendation and target price include potential market depreciation, a deterioration in relative investment performance, and various regulatory issues. We believe that unsuccessful integrations and a lower than expected rate of retaining clients from recent acquisitions also are risks. We view the retention of Bill Miller, a key portfolio manager, and his relatively concentrated investment strategy, as another risk.

➤ The shares recently traded at 15.7X our FY 08 EPS estimate, a discount to peers. Our 12-month target price of $95 is derived by applying a P/E multiple of 18.1X to our FY 08 EPS estimate, a discount to peer multiples due to recent fund underperformance and continued equity fund outflows.

Qualitative Risk Assessment

LOW	MEDIUM	HIGH

Our risk assessment reflects our view of the company's strong market share and impressive relative investment performance, offset by industry cyclicality and integration challenges we foresee from recent acquisitions.

Quantitative Evaluations

S&P Quality Ranking A

D	C	B-	B	B+	A-	A	A+

Relative Strength Rank WEAK

25

LOWEST = 1   HIGHEST = 99

Revenue/Earnings Data

Revenue (Million $)

	1Q	2Q	3Q	4Q	Year
2008	1,206	1,172	--	--	--
2007	1,038	1,031	1,133	1,142	4,344
2006	437.7	466.4	689.0	1,052	2,645
2005	554.9	585.5	658.3	690.8	2,490
2004	440.2	585.5	521.2	576.5	2,004
2003	417.4	395.5	401.0	401.5	1,615

Earnings Per Share ($)

2008	1.32	1.23	E1.36	E1.34	E5.25
2007	1.08	1.00	1.21	1.19	4.48
2006	0.93	0.75	0.77	1.04	3.30
2005	0.76	0.81	0.98	0.98	3.53
2004	0.55	0.81	0.71	0.81	2.64
2003	0.47	0.44	0.47	0.47	1.85

Fiscal year ended Mar. 31. Next earnings report expected: Late January. EPS Estimates based on S&P Operating Earnings; historical GAAP earnings are as reported.

Dividend Data (Dates: mm/dd Payment Date: mm/dd/yy)

Amount ($)	Date Decl.	Ex-Div. Date	Stk. of Record	Payment Date
0.210	01/23	03/06	03/08	04/09/07
0.240	04/24	06/08	06/12	07/09/07
0.240	07/19	09/25	09/27	10/15/07
0.240	10/16	12/03	12/05	12/31/07

Dividends have been paid since 1983. Source: Company reports.

Legg Mason Inc

STANDARD &POOR'S

Business Summary October 31, 2007

CORPORATE OVERVIEW. Legg Mason is a holding company which, through subsidiaries, is principally engaged in providing asset management and other related financial services to individuals, institutions, corporations, governments, and government agencies. We are pleased with the company's recent efforts to focus on its asset management business, which we think makes LM a much larger, broader, and more focused asset management company. At the end of FY 07 (Mar.), total assets under management were about $969 billion, up from nearly $868 billion a year earlier. Headquartered in Baltimore, MD, LM's offices are mainly in the U.S., as well as in the U.K., Canada and Singapore. At the end of March 2007, fixed income assets represented 49% of total assets under management, equity assets 35%, and liquidity assets 16%. We are pleased with the company's success in diversifying its product offerings, but would like to see more sector and industry specific mutual funds.

We think LM has a diverse collection of asset management subsidiaries, which include Western Asset, Legg Mason Capital Management, Brandywine, and Permal. LM's Asset Management business provides asset management services to institutional and individual clients and investment advisory services to company-sponsored investment funds. Investment products include proprietary mutual funds ranging from money market and fixed income funds to equity funds managed in a wide variety of investing styles, non-U.S. funds, and a number of unregistered, alternative investment products. LM's mutual funds group sponsors domestic and international equity, fixed income and money market mutual funds, closed-end funds, and other proprietary funds. Legg Mason Value Trust (LMVTX), managed by Bill Miller, had been the only equity mutual fund to have surpassed the S&P 500 Index for 15 straight years, with the streak ending in 2006. We do not doubt his investment strategy, however, and we still believe the fund will outperform the market frequently.

Company Financials Fiscal Year Ended Mar. 31

Per Share Data ($)	2007	2006	2005	2004	2003	2002	2001	2000	1999	1998
Tangible Book Value	NM	NM	11.66	6.50	3.32	1.52	8.25	7.07	5.89	5.31
Cash Flow	5.95	3.90	3.83	2.62	1.85	1.49	1.53	1.56	1.03	0.87
Earnings	4.48	3.30	3.53	2.64	1.85	1.49	1.53	1.55	1.03	0.88
S&P Core Earnings	4.48	3.25	3.41	2.57	1.63	1.35	1.44	NA	NA	NA
Dividends	0.69	0.40	0.37	0.29	0.29	0.23	0.20	0.18	0.15	0.11
Payout Ratio	15%	12%	11%	11%	15%	16%	13%	12%	15%	12%
Calendar Year	2006	2005	2004	2003	2002	2001	2000	1999	1998	1997
Prices:High	140.00	129.00	73.70	56.77	38.10	37.99	40.17	28.58	21.52	18.77
Prices:Low	81.01	68.10	48.95	29.47	24.74	22.83	20.46	17.62	11.54	9.44
P/E Ratio:High	31	39	21	22	21	25	26	18	24	21
P/E Ratio:Low	18	21	14	11	13	15	13	11	13	11

Income Statement Analysis (Million $)										
Commissions	Nil	Nil	358	344	317	331	359	363	279	241
Interest Income	58.9	48.0	119	84.3	109	168	282	223	160	127
Total Revenue	4,344	2,645	2,490	2,004	1,615	1,579	1,536	1,371	1,046	648
Interest Expense	71.5	52.6	80.8	63.2	87.1	127	175	134	94.9	73.7
Pretax Income	1,044	703	659	472	308	253	266	239	149	128
Effective Tax Rate	38.1%	39.2%	38.0%	38.5%	38.1%	39.6%	41.2%	40.4%	40.0%	40.7%
Net Income	646	434	408	291	191	153	156	143	89.3	76.1
S&P Core Earnings	646	421	394	283	168	138	146	NA	NA	NA

Balance Sheet & Other Financial Data (Million $)										
Total Assets	9,604	9,302	8,219	7,263	6,067	5,940	4,688	4,785	3,474	2,832
Cash Items	1,184	1,023	3,554	3,744	3,274	2,970	2,498	1,628	1,582	1,128
Receivables	852	850	1,564	1,458	1,155	1,230	1,333	1,652	921	713
Securities Owned	273	142	1,298	870	419	458	374	774	144	81.5
Securities Borrowed	Nil	Nil	588	488	220	280	253	688	309	448
Due Brokers & Customers	Nil	Nil	3,419	3,657	75.0	35.0	2,955	15.2	2,181	1,568
Other Liabilities	1,079	1,633	1,108	764	462	410	328	334	541	85.4
Capitalization:Debt	1,108	1,166	811	794	787	877	219	339	99.7	114
Capitalization:Equity	6,678	5,850	2,293	1,560	1,248	1,075	917	752	554	500
Capitalization:Total	8,229	7,016	3,104	2,354	2,035	1,952	1,136	1,091	654	600
% Return on Revenue	14.9	16.4	19.2	17.5	14.7	12.3	13.3	14.1	12.9	11.8
% Return on Assets	6.8	5.0	5.3	4.4	3.2	2.9	3.3	3.5	2.8	3.2
% Return on Equity	10.2	10.7	21.2	20.7	16.4	15.4	18.7	21.8	16.9	16.6

Data as orig reptd.; bef. results of disc opers/spec. items. Per share data adj. for stk. divs.; EPS diluted. E-Estimated. NA-Not Available. NM-Not Meaningful. NR-Not Ranked. UR-Under Review.

Office: 100 Light Street, Baltimore, MD 21202-1099.
Telephone: 410-539-0000.
Website: http://www.leggmason.com
Chrmn, Pres & CEO: R.A. Mason

Sr EVP: M.R. Fetting
Sr EVP: P.L. Bain
SVP, CFO & Treas: C.J. Daley, Jr.
Secy: R.F. Price

Board Members: H. L. Adams, R. E. Angelica, D. R. Beresford, C. Bildt, J. E. Koerner, III, C. G. Krongard, R. A. Mason, E. I. O'Brien, W. A. Reed, M. M. Richardson, R. W. Schipke, K. L. Schmoke, N. J. St. George, J. E. Ukrop

Founded: 1899
Domicile: Maryland
Employees: 4,030

The McGraw-Hill Companies

Lehman Brothers Holdings Inc.

STANDARD &POOR'S

S&P Recommendation SELL ★★☆☆☆	**Price** $60.86 (as of Nov 23, 2007)	**12-Mo. Target Price** $55.00	**Investment Style** Large-Cap Blend

GICS Sector Financials
Sub-Industry Investment Banking & Brokerage

Summary This major global investment bank serves institutional, corporate and government clients and high-net-worth individuals.

Key Stock Statistics (Source S&P, Vickers, company reports)

52-Wk Range	$86.18– 49.06	S&P Oper. EPS 2007**E**	7.36	Market Capitalization(B)	$32.258	Beta		1.58
Trailing 12-Month EPS	$7.43	S&P Oper. EPS 2008**E**	6.68	Yield (%)	0.99	S&P 3-Yr. Proj. EPS CAGR(%)		10.00
Trailing 12-Month P/E	8.2	P/E on S&P Oper. EPS 2007**E**	8.3	Dividend Rate/Share	$0.60	S&P Credit Rating		A+
$10K Invested 5 Yrs Ago	$20,339	Common Shares Outstg. (M)	530.0	Institutional Ownership (%)	68			

Price Performance

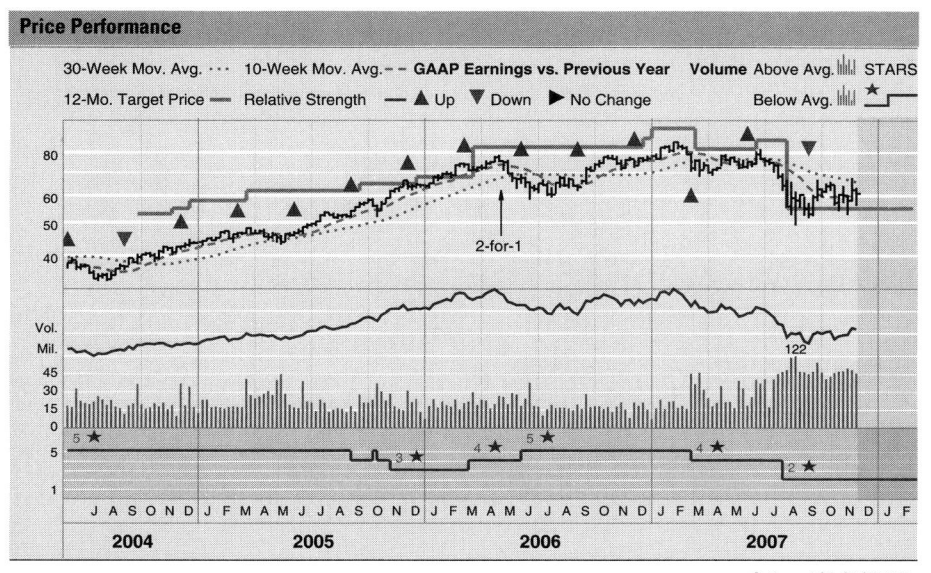

- 30-Week Mov. Avg. ··· 10-Week Mov. Avg. - - **GAAP Earnings vs. Previous Year** Volume Above Avg. STARS
- 12-Mo. Target Price — Relative Strength — ▲ Up ▼ Down ► No Change Below Avg.

2-for-1

Options: ASE, CBOE, P, Ph

Analysis prepared by **Matthew Albrecht** on September 26, 2007, when the stock traded at **$ 60.02**.

Highlights

➤ LEH's fixed income business has been hurt by exposure to mortgage markets through reduced volume in trading and originations. Although we think balance sheet write-downs in the third quarter may position the company more favorably going forward, we continue to expect reduced volume in its fixed income business late in FY 07 (Nov.) and into FY 08. Equity capital markets volume has been strong, but we anticipate somewhat reduced volatility in the fourth quarter and FY 08, particularly related to cash trading and derivatives, resulting in lower volume. And while investment banking fee income has held up well, we look for somewhat reduced advisory activity volume to result in lower fee income in coming quarters as recent record backlogs are realized.

➤ We expect compensation to be in line with LEH's historical range in FY 07 and FY 08, typically 49% to 50% of net revenues. We see a slight reduction in the FY 07 pretax margin on asset write-downs and global expansion, followed in FY 08 by a widening margin, despite additional costs related to global growth.

➤ We look for EPS of $7.36 in FY 07 and $6.68 in FY 08, supported by additional share repurchases.

Investment Rationale/Risk

➤ We think LEH's strong global competitive position, successful diversification efforts and significant scale are offset at the moment by hurdles in the capital markets. Executive compensation and stock option grants are generous, in our opinion, but we view favorably significant insider ownership (about 30%) and strong growth in the asset management business. However, we believe obstacles outnumber catalysts at this point, resulting in our sell recommendation.

➤ Risks to our recommendation and target price include lower credit spreads, stock and bond market appreciation, and growing trading revenues. The potential for government action that would benefit capital markets could also be detrimental to our sell recommendation.

➤ LEH shares were recently trading at 8.2X our FY 07 EPS estimate and 1.6X our FY 07 book value projection, a discount to peers. Our 12-month target price is $55, which is about 1.5X estimated 12-month book value, a discount to LEH's historical book value multiple and that of its peers, due primarily to its outsized exposure to fixed income capital markets relative to peers and that market's current struggles.

Qualitative Risk Assessment

LOW	MEDIUM	HIGH

Our risk assessment reflects our view of the company's long history of earnings growth, strong global competitive position, and successful diversification efforts, partially offset by industry cyclicality.

Quantitative Evaluations

S&P Quality Ranking   **A**

D	C	B-	B	B+	A-	**A**	A+

Relative Strength Rank   **STRONG**

76

LOWEST = 1   HIGHEST = 99

Revenue/Earnings Data

Revenue (Million $)

	1Q	2Q	3Q	4Q	Year
2007	13,795	15,579	14,739	--	--
2006	10,307	11,515	11,727	13,160	46,709
2005	7,391	7,335	8,639	9,055	32,420
2004	5,125	5,228	5,051	5,846	21,250
2003	4,100	4,470	4,463	4,254	17,287
2002	4,226	4,347	4,075	4,133	16,781

Earnings Per Share ($)

	1Q	2Q	3Q	4Q	Year
2007	1.96	2.21	1.54	E1.65	E7.36
2006	1.75	1.69	1.57	1.72	6.73
2005	1.46	1.13	1.47	1.38	5.44
2004	1.11	1.01	0.86	0.98	3.95
2003	0.58	0.84	0.91	0.86	3.18
2002	0.50	0.54	0.35	0.35	1.74

Fiscal year ended Nov. 30. Next earnings report expected: Mid December. EPS Estimates based on S&P Operating Earnings; historical GAAP earnings are as reported.

Dividend Data (Dates: mm/dd Payment Date: mm/dd/yy)

Amount ($)	Date Decl.	Ex-Div. Date	Stk. of Record	Payment Date
0.150	02/01	02/08	02/12	02/21/07
0.150	04/26	05/11	05/15	05/23/07
0.150	07/31	08/13	08/15	08/24/07
0.150	10/30	11/13	11/15	11/23/07

Dividends have been paid since 1994. Source: Company reports.

Please read the Required Disclosures and Analyst Certification on the last page of this report.

The McGraw·Hill Companies

Lehman Brothers Holdings Inc.

STANDARD
&POOR'S

Business Summary September 26, 2007

CORPORATE OVERVIEW. Lehman Brothers is a global investment bank, serving the needs of corporations, governments and municipalities, institutional clients and high-net-worth individuals. It provides a full suite of services, including equity and fixed income sales, trading and research, investment banking services and investment management and advisory services. Its world headquarters is in New York, and it has regional headquarters in London and Tokyo. Its principal business is divided into three segments: Capital Markets, Investment Banking, and Investment Management.

The Capital Markets segment (68% of net revenues in FY 06) represents institutional client-flow activities, including prime brokerage, research, mortgage origination and securitization, secondary-trading and financing activities in fixed income and equity products. These products include a wide range of cash, derivative, secured financing and structured instruments and investments. The segment also includes proprietary trading activities and principal investments, including investments in real estate, private equity and other long-term investments.

The Investment Banking segment (18%) provides advice to corporate, institu-

tional and government clients throughout the world on mergers, acquisitions, and other financial matters, and underwrites public and private debt and equity offerings to raise capital for clients.

The Investment Management segment (14%) provides strategic investment advice and services to institutional and high-net-worth clients around the globe. The asset management business offers proprietary asset management products across traditional and alternative asset classes through a variety of asset distribution channels to individuals and institutions. It includes the Neuberger Berman and Lehman Brothers Asset Management brands, as well as the Private Equity business. The private investment management business provides traditional brokerage services and comprehensive investment, wealth advisory, trust and capital markets execution services to both high-net-worth individuals and small and medium-size institutional clients.

Company Financials Fiscal Year Ended Nov. 30

Per Share Data ($)	2006	2005	2004	2003	2002	2001	2000	1999	1998	1997
Tangible Book Value	32.25	22.92	18.78	16.05	17.38	15.95	14.60	12.81	9.55	8.26
Cash Flow	6.74	5.43	4.19	3.09	1.96	2.45	3.54	2.01	1.48	1.36
Earnings	6.73	5.44	3.95	3.18	1.74	2.19	3.19	2.04	1.30	1.18
S&P Core Earnings	6.76	5.35	3.73	2.91	1.07	1.94	NA	NA	NA	NA
Dividends	0.48	0.40	0.32	0.24	0.18	0.14	0.11	0.09	0.08	0.06
Payout Ratio	7%	7%	8%	8%	10%	6%	3%	4%	6%	5%
Prices:High	78.89	66.58	44.86	38.85	34.95	43.10	40.06	21.39	21.25	14.13
Prices:Low	58.37	42.71	33.63	25.08	21.24	21.75	15.16	10.95	5.66	7.13
P/E Ratio:High	12	12	11	12	20	20	13	10	16	12
P/E Ratio:Low	9	8	9	8	12	10	5	5	4	6

Income Statement Analysis (Million $)

	2006	2005	2004	2003	2002	2001	2000	1999	1998	1997
Commissions	2,050	1,728	1,537	1,210	1,286	1,091	944	651	513	423
Interest Income	30,284	19,043	11,032	9,942	11,728	16,470	19,440	14,251	16,542	13,635
Total Revenue	46,709	32,420	21,250	17,287	16,781	22,392	26,447	18,989	19,894	16,883
Interest Expense	29,126	17,790	9,698	8,712	10,682	15,712	18,796	13,691	15,781	13,010
Pretax Income	5,905	4,829	3,494	2,464	1,343	1,692	2,523	1,589	1,052	937
Effective Tax Rate	32.9%	32.5%	32.2%	31.0%	27.4%	25.8%	29.6%	28.8%	30.0%	30.9%
Net Income	3,960	3,260	2,369	1,699	975	1,255	1,775	1,132	736	647
S&P Core Earnings	3,909	3,124	2,149	1,488	558	1,027	NA	NA	NA	NA

Balance Sheet & Other Financial Data (Million $)

	2006	2005	2004	2003	2002	2001	2000	1999	1998	1997
Total Assets	503,545	410,063	357,168	312,061	260,336	247,816	224,720	192,244	153,890	151,705
Cash Items	12,078	10,644	9,525	11,022	6,502	5,850	7,594	7,175	4,238	2,834
Receivables	129,538	21,643	18,763	15,310	13,964	17,057	10,382	12,360	11,965	12,838
Securities Owned	226,596	182,413	149,217	137,040	119,278	119,362	105,207	89,059	77,000	76,862
Securities Borrowed	17,883	13,154	115,188	89,870	8,137	12,541	7,242	127,693	96,533	93,284
Due Brokers & Customers	43,912	49,080	39,529	30,733	11,844	16,636	13,559	16,723	13,690	21,703
Other Liabilities	14,697	10,962	10,611	9,266	6,633	9,895	8,735	10,144	10,913	11,934
Capitalization:Debt	81,178	62,309	56,486	44,839	39,388	38,301	36,093	31,401	27,341	20,261
Capitalization:Equity	18,096	15,699	13,575	12,129	8,242	16,218	14,862	5,595	4,505	4,015
Capitalization:Total	101,777	79,103	71,406	58,013	48,330	55,219	51,655	37,684	32,754	24,276
% Return on Revenue	8.9	10.6	12.0	10.6	25.9	26.0	29.3	27.7	3.7	4.3
% Return on Assets	0.9	0.8	0.7	0.6	0.4	0.5	0.9	0.7	0.5	0.5
% Return on Equity	23.0	21.8	17.9	16.2	11.3	7.5	12.6	20.5	15.2	15.5

Data as orig reptd.; bef. results of disc opers/spec. items. Per share data adj. for stk. divs.; EPS diluted. E-Estimated. NA-Not Available. NM-Not Meaningful. NR-Not Ranked. UR-Under Review.

Office: 745 7th Ave, New York, NY 10019.
Telephone: 212-526-7000.
Email: inquiry@lehman.com
Website: http://www.lehman.com

Chrmn & CEO: R.S. Fuld, Jr.
Pres & COO: J.M. Gregory
EVP, CFO & Cntlr: C.M. O'Meara
EVP & Chief Lgl Officer: T.A. Russo

Chief Admin Officer: S.J. Freidheim
Investor Contact: S.K. Butler (212-526-3267)
Board Members: M. L. Ainslie, J. F. Akers, R. S. Berlind, T. H. Cruikshank, M. J. Evans, R. S. Fuld, Jr., C. Gent, R. A. Hernandez, H. Kaufman, J. D. Macomber

Founded: 1983
Domicile: Delaware
Employees: 25,936

The McGraw·Hill Companies

Lennar Corp

STANDARD &POOR'S

S&P Recommendation **HOLD** ★★★☆☆	Price $14.77 (as of Nov 29, 2007)	12-Mo. Target Price $16.00	Investment Style Large-Cap Blend

GICS Sector Consumer Discretionary
Sub-Industry Homebuilding

Summary Lennar, one of the largest, most geographically diversified U.S. home builders, concentrates on moderately priced homes.

Key Stock Statistics (Source S&P, Vickers, company reports)

52-Wk Range	$56.54– 14.00	S&P Oper. EPS 2007**E**	-7.40	Market Capitalization(B)	$1.904	Beta	1.32
Trailing 12-Month EPS	$-5.56	S&P Oper. EPS 2008**E**	-2.75	Yield (%)	4.33	S&P 3-Yr. Proj. EPS CAGR(%)	5.00
Trailing 12-Month P/E	NM	P/E on S&P Oper. EPS 2007**E**	NM	Dividend Rate/Share	$0.64	S&P Credit Rating	BB+
$10K Invested 5 Yrs Ago	$8,228	Common Shares Outstg. (M)	160.2	Institutional Ownership (%)	NM		

Price Performance

- 30-Week Mov. Avg. ···
- 10-Week Mov. Avg. - -
- **GAAP Earnings vs. Previous Year**
- Volume Above Avg. STARS
- 12-Mo. Target Price —
- Relative Strength —
- ▲ Up ▼ Down ► No Change
- Below Avg.

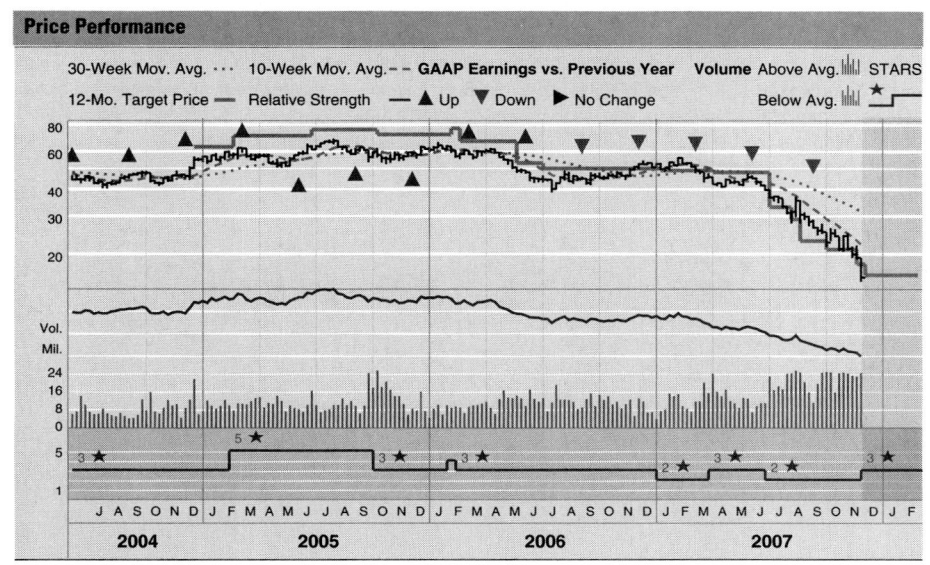

Options: ASE, CBOE, P, Ph

Analysis prepared by **Kenneth M. Leon, CPA** on November 29, 2007, when the stock traded at **$14.61**.

Qualitative Risk Assessment

LOW	MEDIUM	**HIGH**

Our risk assessment reflects that, at about 33% debt to capital, LEN is among the least leveraged homebuilders in our coverage universe. However, the company's off balance sheet operations, including a 50%-owned development joint venture and a relatively significant proportion of land controlled through option contracts, suggest to us relatively limited financial transparency.

Quantitative Evaluations

S&P Quality Ranking   A-

D	C	B-	B	B+	**A-**	A	A+

Relative Strength Rank   WEAK

5

LOWEST = 1   HIGHEST = 99

Revenue/Earnings Data

Revenue (Million $)

	1Q	2Q	3Q	4Q	Year
2007	2,792	2,876	2,342	--	--
2006	3,241	4,578	4,182	4,266	16,267
2005	2,406	2,933	3,498	5,030	13,867
2004	1,863	2,343	2,748	3,551	10,505
2003	1,600	2,103	2,268	2,936	8,908
2002	1,248	1,572	1,861	2,640	7,320

Earnings Per Share ($)

2007	0.43	-1.55	-3.25	E-1.91	E-7.40
2006	1.58	2.00	1.30	-1.24	3.69
2005	1.17	1.55	2.06	3.54	8.17
2004	0.84	1.22	1.36	2.29	5.70
2003	0.68	1.02	1.22	1.69	4.65
2002	0.52	0.76	1.01	1.58	3.86

Fiscal year ended Nov. 30. Next earnings report expected: Mid January. EPS Estimates based on S&P Operating Earnings; historical GAAP earnings are as reported.

Highlights

➤ We project that revenues will decrease 35% in FY 07 (Nov.) and be fractionally lower in FY 08, reflecting a deepening of the housing downturn. Home deliveries and average selling prices continued to decline in the third quarter of FY 07. Management described "weak and perhaps deteriorating market conditions" on September 25. The order cancellation rate was 32% for the third quarter, well above historical norms.

➤ We think high costs associated with attracting and retaining buyers will hurt gross margins, which we project in the low to mid-teens for FY 07 and FY 08, well below a cycle-top level of 26% in FY 05. Write-offs for land options and land have been significant since the fourth quarter of FY 06. The removal of land recently purchased at cycle-high values should aid the cost structure in future quarters.

➤ We estimate a loss per share of $7.40 for FY 07, including substantial inventory writedowns, and a loss of $2.75 for FY 08. We believe that additional homesite and lot inventory writedowns are possible over the next 6 months, creating low earnings visibility.

Investment Rationale/Risk

➤ Considering investments over $1 billion in joint venture homebuilding activities, we see the broader issue of transparency as a concern along with weakening of most of LEN's communities. Overall, in the context of a housing downturn that we project will last into 2008, we believe the share price reflects most of the negative drivers on LEN's fundamentals, and we see the company surviving.

➤ Risks to our recommendation and target price include higher levels for 30-year mortgage interest rates and the possibility that LEN's large land positions might increase further writedowns if industry conditions deteriorate more than we expect.

➤ With $847 million in asset impairments for the August quarter and assuming another $800 million in the November quarter from a total of $7.8 billion in goodwill, speculative homes owned, construction in progress, land under development and investment in joint ventures, our net tangible book value estimate is $26.80. Applying a 0.6X price-to-book value, near large homebuilders, our 12-month target price is $16.

Dividend Data (Dates: mm/dd Payment Date: mm/dd/yy)

Amount ($)	Date Decl.	Ex-Div. Date	Stk. of Record	Payment Date
0.160	01/10	02/01	02/05	02/15/07
0.160	03/28	05/02	05/04	05/14/07
0.160	06/28	08/01	08/03	08/15/07
0.160	09/27	11/01	11/05	11/15/07

Dividends have been paid since 1978. Source: Company reports.

Lennar Corp

STANDARD &POOR'S

Business Summary November 29, 2007

CORPORATE OVERVIEW. Lennar Corp., the second largest homebuilder in the U.S. (based on FY 06 U.S. home closings), constructs homes for first-time, move-up, and active adult buyers, and also provides various financial services. It takes part in all phases of planning and building, and subcontracts nearly all development and construction work.

The financial services division provides mortgage financing, title insurance, closing services and insurance agency services for LEN homebuyers and others, and sells the loans it originates in the secondary mortgage market.

CORPORATE STRATEGY. Lennar greatly expanded its operations through the May 2000 purchase of U.S. Home Corp. (UH), and has maintained an active acquisition program since, in our opinion. The company entered the North Carolina and South Carolina markets, and extended its positions in Colorado and Arizona, through the acquisition of various operations of Fortress Group in two separate transactions in late 2001 and mid-2002. It expanded its California business by acquiring Pacific Century Homes and Cambridge Homes (combined annual deliveries of about 2,000 homes) in 2002. LEN entered the Chicago market through the late 2002 purchase of Concord Homes and the fall

2002 takeover of Summit Homes. LEN acquired Seppala Homes and Coleman Homes in 2003, expanding its operations in South Carolina and California.

In early 2004, a venture owned 50% by the company and 50% by LNR Property, LEN's former commercial real estate unit (which agreed in August 2004 to be acquired by Riley Property Holdings LLC), purchased Newhall Land and Farming Co., for about $1 billion. Newhall develops master-planned communities in and around Los Angeles.

In 2005, the company entered the metropolitan New York City and Boston markets by acquiring rights to develop a portfolio of properties in New Jersey facing mid-town Manhattan and waterfront properties near Boston. It also entered the Reno, NV market through the acquisition of Barker Coleman. In addition, LEN expanded its presence in Jacksonville through the acquisition of Admiral Homes that same year.

Company Financials Fiscal Year Ended Nov. 30

Per Share Data ($)	2006	2005	2004	2003	2002	2001	2000	1999	1998	1997
Tangible Book Value	34.42	32.09	24.05	20.68	15.71	12.14	8.92	7.08	6.16	4.13
Cash Flow	4.03	8.60	5.98	5.11	4.32	3.45	2.23	1.69	1.44	0.79
Earnings	3.69	8.17	5.70	4.65	3.86	3.01	1.82	1.37	1.25	0.67
S&P Core Earnings	3.62	8.10	5.63	4.61	3.83	2.90	NA	NA	NA	NA
Dividends	0.64	0.57	0.39	0.14	0.03	0.03	0.03	0.03	0.03	0.04
Payout Ratio	17%	7%	7%	3%	1%	1%	1%	2%	2%	7%
Prices:High	66.44	68.86	57.20	50.90	31.99	24.94	19.69	13.94	18.09	22.34
Prices:Low	38.66	50.30	40.30	24.10	21.60	15.52	7.63	6.53	7.44	7.50
P/E Ratio:High	18	8	10	11	8	8	11	10	15	33
P/E Ratio:Low	10	6	7	5	6	5	4	5	6	11

Income Statement Analysis (Million $)										
Revenue	16,267	13,867	10,505	8,908	7,320	6,029	4,707	3,119	2,417	1,303
Operating Income	941	2,124	1,426	1,158	1,094	868	533	382	NA	149
Depreciation	56.5	79.6	55.6	54.5	72.4	68.7	58.5	47.7	24.4	9.00
Interest Expense	Nil	Nil	Nil	141	146	120	98.6	48.9	47.6	25.0
Pretax Income	956	2,205	1,519	1,207	876	679	376	285	240	85.7
Effective Tax Rate	36.5%	37.0%	37.8%	37.8%	37.8%	38.5%	39.0%	39.5%	40.0%	41.0%
Net Income	594	1,344	946	751	545	418	229	173	144	50.6
S&P Core Earnings	582	1,331	934	744	541	404	NA	NA	NA	NA

Balance Sheet & Other Financial Data (Million $)										
Cash	778	910	1,322	1,201	731	824	288	83.3	34.7	52.9
Current Assets	NA	NA	NA	NA	NA	NA	NA	NA	NA	NA
Total Assets	12,408	12,541	9,165	6,775	5,756	4,714	3,778	2,058	1,918	1,343
Current Liabilities	NA	NA	NA	NA	NA	NA	NA	NA	NA	NA
Long Term Debt	2,614	2,565	2,918	1,552	1,521	1,488	1,240	524	799	614
Common Equity	5,702	5,251	4,053	3,264	2,229	1,659	1,229	881	716	439
Total Capital	8,283	7,895	6,971	4,816	3,751	3,147	2,468	1,405	1,515	1,053
Capital Expenditures	26.8	21.7	NA	29.6	4.09	13.1	16.0	15.3	13.2	70.8
Cash Flow	650	1,424	1,001	806	618	487	288	220	168	59.6
Current Ratio	NA	NA	NA	NA	NA	NA	NA	NA	NA	NA
% Long Term Debt of Capitalization	31.2	32.5	41.9	32.2	40.6	47.3	50.2	37.3	52.7	41.7
% Net Income of Revenue	3.7	9.7	9.0	8.4	7.4	6.9	4.9	5.5	6.0	3.9
% Return on Assets	4.8	12.4	11.9	12.0	10.4	9.8	7.9	8.7	8.8	3.3
% Return on Equity	10.8	28.9	25.8	27.4	28.0	28.9	21.7	21.6	25.0	8.9

Data as orig reptd.; bef. results of disc opers/spec. items. Per share data adj. for stk. divs.; EPS diluted. E-Estimated. NA-Not Available. NM-Not Meaningful. NR-Not Ranked. UR-Under Review.

Office: 700 NW 107th Ave, Miami, FL 33172.
Telephone: 305-559-4000.
Website: http://www.lennar.com
Pres & CEO: S.A. Miller

COO & VP: J.M. Jaffe
VP & CFO: B.E. Gross
Investor Contact: M.H. Ames (800-741-4663)
VP & Cntlr: D.J. Bessette

Board Members: I. Bolotin, S. L. Gerard, R. K. Landon, S. Lapidus, S. A. Miller, D. E. Shalala, J. Sonnenfeld, R. J. Strudler

Founded: 1954
Domicile: Delaware
Employees: 12,605

The McGraw-Hill Companies

Leucadia National Corp

S&P Recommendation HOLD ★★★☆☆

Price $44.57 (as of Nov 23, 2007)	**12-Mo. Target Price** $48.00	**Investment Style** Large-Cap Growth

GICS Sector Financials
Sub-Industry Multi-Sector Holdings

Summary This diversified holding company has subsidiaries engaged in manufacturing, real estate, medical product development, gaming entertainment, mining, and energy.

Key Stock Statistics (Source S&P, Vickers, company reports)

52-Wk Range	$52.67–26.52	S&P Oper. EPS 2007E	0.26	Market Capitalization(B)	$9.655	Beta	1.09
Trailing 12-Month EPS	$0.48	S&P Oper. EPS 2008E	0.35	Yield (%)	0.56	S&P 3-Yr. Proj. EPS CAGR(%)	5.00
Trailing 12-Month P/E	92.9	P/E on S&P Oper. EPS 2007E	NM	Dividend Rate/Share	$0.25	S&P Credit Rating	BB+
$10K Invested 5 Yrs Ago	$35,722	Common Shares Outstg. (M)	216.6	Institutional Ownership (%)	66		

Price Performance

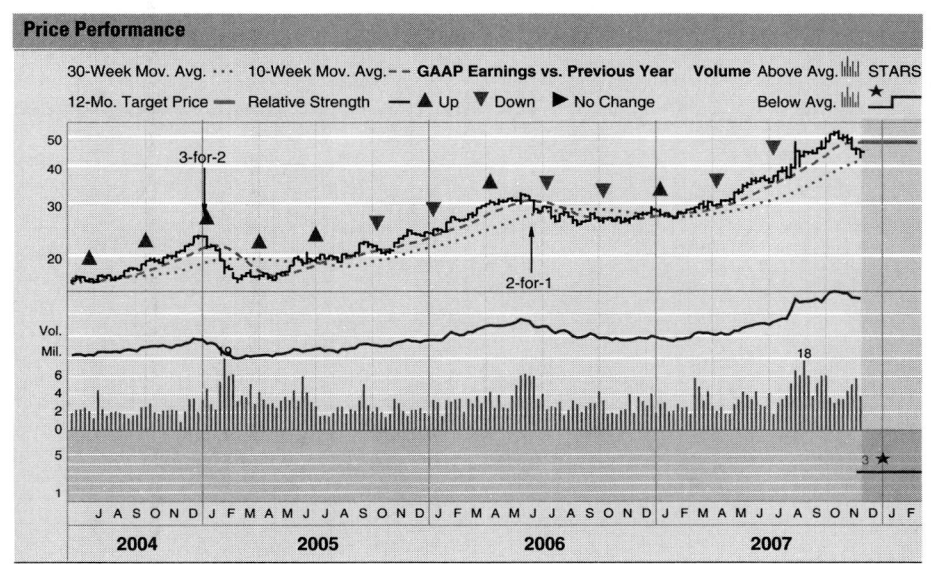

30-Week Mov. Avg. ··· 10-Week Mov. Avg. — GAAP Earnings vs. Previous Year Volume Above Avg. STARS
12-Mo. Target Price — Relative Strength ▲ Up ▼ Down ► No Change Below Avg.

Options: ASE, CBOE, Ph

Analysis prepared by **Stuart J. Benway, CFA** on November 21, 2007, when the stock traded at **$42.72**.

Highlights

➤ We see revenues from continuing operations increasing 8%-10% in 2008, fueled largely by a full year of revenues from the gaming business, which began operating in mid-2007. The plastics and timber remanufacturing units should generate only modest sales growth due to what we expect will be a sluggish housing market. Moreover, any acquisitions or divestitures could have a significant impact on revenue growth.

➤ We expect the gaming operations to turn profitable in 2008 after being rebuilt following damage from Hurricane Katrina. The medical business is likely to continue to generate losses unless and until its blood substitute product receives FDA approval. The timber and plastics businesses are likely to produce relatively stable profits in 2008.

➤ Our operating EPS forecast for 2008 is $0.35, up from the $0.26 we estimate for 2007, but still well below the $0.58 reported for 2006. We expect LUK to have a very uneven earnings pattern due to frequent changes in the number and types of businesses it operates.

Investment Rationale/Risk

➤ Leucadia has a strong record of stock market performance in recent years, due, we think, to its strategy of finding assets and companies that are out of favor or troubled and are therefore selling at a discount to their inherent value. While we believe the medical products and gaming businesses have significant growth potential, we see the shares as fully valued.

➤ Risks to our recommendation and target price include reliance on the two top executives for most of the company's investment decisions, the potential failure of a large investment to meet expected returns, and the need to develop commercially viable biopharmaceuticals.

➤ The company has exhibited strong growth in book value in recent years, with book value per share rising at a compound annual rate of 20% from 2001 through 2006. Over this time, its ratio of price/book value per share has ranged from 1.3X to 2.2X. Our 12-month target price of $48 is calculated using a 2X multiple, a modest premium to peers, of our 2008 book value per share estimate of $24.

Qualitative Risk Assessment

LOW	MEDIUM	HIGH

Our risk assessment reflects the broad diversity of the company's investments and what we view as a strong management team, offset by its exposure to certain development stage businesses.

Quantitative Evaluations

S&P Quality Ranking B-

D	C	B-	B	B+	A-	A	A+

Relative Strength Rank MODERATE

60

LOWEST = 1   HIGHEST = 99

Revenue/Earnings Data

Revenue (Million $)

	1Q	2Q	3Q	4Q	Year
2007	197.2	334.0	--	--	--
2006	291.6	224.4	170.2	176.4	862.7
2005	121.3	258.7	343.3	317.9	1,041
2004	509.7	569.6	633.6	549.2	2,262
2003	56.90	67.30	76.09	356.1	556.4
2002	57.57	70.32	52.37	61.55	241.8

Earnings Per Share ($)

	1Q	2Q	3Q	4Q	Year
2007	0.04	0.12	E0.02	E0.08	E0.26
2006	0.37	0.17	0.02	0.03	0.60
2005	-0.03	5.23	0.22	-0.10	5.35
2004	-0.06	0.17	0.34	0.24	0.70
2003	-0.08	0.06	0.30	0.16	0.46
2002	0.07	0.12	-0.01	0.73	0.91

Fiscal year ended Dec. 31. Next earnings report expected: NA. EPS Estimates based on S&P Operating Earnings; historical GAAP earnings are as reported.

Dividend Data (Dates: mm/dd Payment Date: mm/dd/yy)

Amount ($)	Date Decl.	Ex-Div. Date	Stk. of Record	Payment Date
0.250	12/07	12/14	12/18	12/29/06

Dividends have been paid since 1999. Source: Company reports.

Leucadia National Corp

**STANDARD
&POOR'S**

Business Summary November 21, 2007

CORPORATE OVERVIEW. Leucadia National is a diversified holding company that is involved in a wide variety of businesses, including timber and plastics manufacturing, telecommunications, real estate activities, medical product development, and winery operations. The company also owns equity interests in operating businesses and investment partnerships including gaming entertainment, land-based contract oil and gas drilling, real estate activities, and development of a copper mine in Spain. In addition, Leucadia has significant investments in several partnerships that invest in domestic and international debt and equity securities. Revenues by business segment in 2006 were as follows: Idaho Timber 40% (35% in 2005); Conwed Plastics 12% (14%); domestic real estate 10% (4%) other operations 5% (9%); and corporate 33% (38%).

CORPORATE STRATEGY. Leucadia's approach to its investments is to focus on return on investment and cash flow to build long-term shareholder value. Management continuously evaluates the retention and disposition of its existing operations, and investigates possible acquisition targets. In selecting potential acquisitions, LUK seeks assets and companies that are troubled or out of favor, and that are selling below apparent value as a result. We expect the composition of Leucadia's assets to change continuously as certain businesses are divested and others are acquired.

Company Financials Fiscal Year Ended Dec. 31

Per Share Data ($)	2006	2005	2004	2003	2002	2001	2000	1999	1998	1997
Tangible Book Value	17.72	16.87	17.32	10.04	8.78	7.05	7.26	6.58	9.97	9.72
Cash Flow	0.75	NA	NA	NA	NA	NA	NA	NA	NA	NA
Earnings	0.60	5.36	0.70	0.46	0.91	0.39	0.69	1.09	0.24	-0.12
S&P Core Earnings	NA	4.69	0.05	0.42	1.05	0.27	NA	NA	NA	NA
Dividends	0.25	0.13	0.13	0.08	0.08	0.08	0.08	4.53	Nil	0.08
Payout Ratio	42%	2%	18%	18%	9%	21%	12%	NM	Nil	NM
Prices:High	32.62	24.64	23.50	15.40	13.42	11.90	12.50	11.13	13.71	12.21
Prices:Low	23.26	16.20	15.02	10.86	9.21	8.77	6.88	6.71	8.75	8.58
P/E Ratio:High	54	5	34	34	15	31	18	10	56	NM
P/E Ratio:Low	39	3	21	24	10	22	10	6	36	NM

Income Statement Analysis (Million $)										
Revenue	863	1,041	2,262	556	242	375	715	710	507	700
Operating Income	222	NA	NA	NA	NA	NA	NA	NA	NA	NA
Depreciation	43.6	NA	NA	NA	NA	NA	NA	NA	NA	NA
Interest Expense	79.4	68.4	96.8	43.6	33.5	55.2	57.7	50.7	45.1	46.0
Pretax Income	172	93.0	132	42.9	13.2	53.7	193	243	29.4	-24.9
Effective Tax Rate	24.4%	NM	NM	NM	NM	NM	37.6%	18.3%	NM	NM
Net Income	130	1,224	152	84.4	153	64.8	115	193	46.2	-22.6
S&P Core Earnings	-9.43	1,071	5.47	77.7	177	45.7	NA	NA	NA	NA

Balance Sheet & Other Financial Data (Million $)										
Cash	3,430	3,063	2,781	2,033	1,044	1,183	1,613	1,467	2,230	2,563
Current Assets	1,366	NA	NA	NA	NA	NA	NA	NA	NA	NA
Total Assets	5,304	5,261	4,800	4,397	2,542	2,577	3,144	3,070	3,959	2,477
Current Liabilities	327	NA	NA	NA	NA	NA	NA	NA	NA	NA
Long Term Debt	975	NA	NA	NA	NA	NA	NA	NA	NA	NA
Common Equity	3,893	NA	NA	NA	NA	NA	NA	1,122	1,853	1,864
Total Capital	4,887	4,665	3,760	3,307	1,893	1,666	1,631	1,720	2,685	2,377
Capital Expenditures	111	NA	NA	NA	NA	NA	NA	NA	NA	NA
Cash Flow	173	NA	NA	NA	NA	NA	NA	NA	NA	NA
Current Ratio	4.2	NA	NA	NA	NA	NA	NA	NA	NA	NA
% Long Term Debt of Capitalization	19.9	NA	NA	NA	NA	NA	NA	NA	NA	NA
% Net Income of Revenue	15.7	NA	NA	NA	NA	NA	NA	NA	NA	NA
% Return on Assets	2.5	NA	NA	NA	NA	NA	NA	NA	NA	NA
% Return on Equity	3.4	NA	NA	NA	NA	NA	NA	NA	NA	NA

Data as orig reptd.; bef. results of disc opers/spec. items. Per share data adj. for stk. divs.; EPS diluted. E-Estimated. NA-Not Available. NM-Not Meaningful. NR-Not Ranked. UR-Under Review.

Office: 315 Park Ave S Fl, New York, NY 10010.
Telephone: 212-460-1900.
Chrmn: I.M. Cumming
Pres: J.S. Steinberg

EVP & Treas: T.E. Mara
VP & CFO: J.A. Orlando
Investor Contact: L.E. Ulbrandt (212-460-1900)

Board Members: I. M. Cumming, P. M. Dougan, L. D. Glaubinger, A. J. Hirschfield, J. E. Jordan, J. C. Keil, J. C. Nichols, III, J. S. Steinberg

Founded: 1854
Domicile: New York
Employees: 1,323

The McGraw-Hill Companies

Lexmark International Inc.

STANDARD
&POOR'S

S&P Recommendation SELL ★ ★ ☆ ☆ ☆	**Price** $36.37 (as of Nov 23, 2007)	**12-Mo. Target Price** $35.00	**Investment Style** Large-Cap Growth

GICS Sector Information Technology
Sub-Industry Computer Storage & Peripherals

Summary Lexmark develops, manufactures and supplies laser and inkjet printers and associated consumable supplies for the office and home markets.

Key Stock Statistics (Source S&P, Vickers, company reports)

52-Wk Range	$74.68– 35.08	S&P Oper. EPS 2007**E**	2.50	Market Capitalization(B)	$3.437	Beta	1.64
Trailing 12-Month EPS	$3.00	S&P Oper. EPS 2008**E**	2.20	Yield (%)	Nil	S&P 3-Yr. Proj. EPS CAGR(%)	-1.00
Trailing 12-Month P/E	12.1	P/E on S&P Oper. EPS 2007**E**	14.5	Dividend Rate/Share	Nil	S&P Credit Rating	NA
$10K Invested 5 Yrs Ago	$5,496	Common Shares Outstg. (M)	94.5	Institutional Ownership (%)	NM		

Price Performance

30-Week Mov. Avg. · · · 10-Week Mov. Avg. - - **GAAP Earnings vs. Previous Year** Volume Above Avg. STARS
12-Mo. Target Price — Relative Strength — ▲ Up ▼ Down ► No Change   Below Avg.

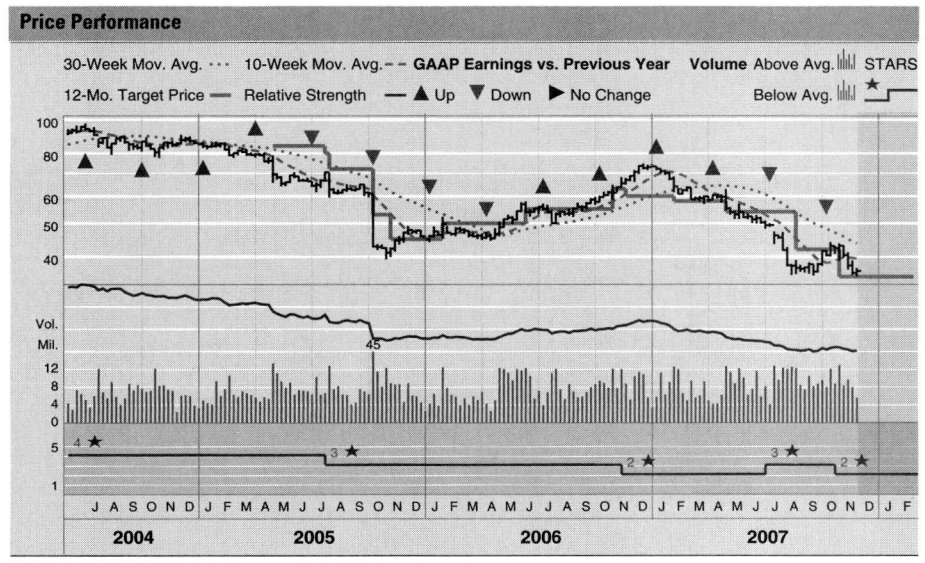

Options: ASE, CBOE, P, Ph

Analysis prepared by **Thomas W. Smith, CFA** on October 24, 2007, when the stock traded at **$ 40.60**.

Highlights

➤ We project that revenues will decrease about 2.5% for 2007, and rise 1% for 2008, continuing a recent trend of flattish top-line performance. We believe results will benefit from new product introductions, continued growth with laser units and supplies, and further penetration of its enterprise customer base. However, the inkjet printer business has been slowing and we expect the pricing environment to intensify, given updated offerings by competitors.

➤ We look for operating margins to narrow for 2007 and 2008, despite a restructuring plan announced October 23, 2007, that aims to shift about 1,650 jobs to plants in lower-cost countries. We think results are likely to be negatively affected by LXK's business mix, as the company increases its focus on the small- and midsize business market. In addition, we believe that share repurchases are not likely in 2008 as LXK's earnings remain under pressure.

➤ We estimate 2007 EPS of $2.50, reflecting both restructuring charges and a tax benefit in the third quarter. We project 2008 EPS of $2.20.

Investment Rationale/Risk

➤ Although we think that LXK has been innovative in its product line in the past, owns some important intellectual property, and should be able to expand its branded products and laser printer businesses, we believe that market conditions supporting low end systems will continue to pressure the company's growth over the next year. In our opinion, LXK faces considerable challenges from Hewlett-Packard (HPQ: buy, $52). Although we view LXK as a potential takeover candidate, we believe that it has some contractual agreements that may prevent such a deal from occurring.

➤ Risks to our recommendation and target price include the possibility that competition from HPQ will not be as great as we anticipate, that savings from restructuring exceed our estimates, and that penetration of high growth segments is faster than we project.

➤ Our 12-month target price of $35 reflects our P/E analysis. We apply a target P/E of 16X--which is toward the low end of a five-year historical range for LXK, to reflect a slow revenue environment that we foresee--to our 2008 EPS estimate.

Qualitative Risk Assessment

LOW	MEDIUM	HIGH

Our risk assessment reflects what we see as a difficult competitive pricing environment in the printer market, offset by our view of LXK's strides in improving its product portfolio and cost position.

Quantitative Evaluations

S&P Quality Ranking   B+

D	C	B-	B	B+	A-	A	A+

Relative Strength Rank   MODERATE

36

LOWEST = 1   HIGHEST = 99

Revenue/Earnings Data

Revenue (Million $)

	1Q	2Q	3Q	4Q	Year
2007	1,261	1,208	1,195	--	--
2006	1,275	1,229	1,235	1,369	5,108
2005	1,358	1,283	1,216	1,365	5,222
2004	1,256	1,248	1,266	1,544	5,314
2003	1,108	1,120	1,157	1,370	4,755
2002	1,050	1,058	1,041	1,207	4,356

Earnings Per Share ($)

2007	0.95	0.67	0.48	E0.41	E2.50
2006	0.78	0.74	0.85	0.91	3.27
2005	0.96	0.64	0.59	0.71	2.91
2004	0.91	1.02	1.17	1.18	4.28
2003	0.73	0.77	0.79	1.05	3.34
2002	0.53	0.67	0.70	0.90	2.79

Fiscal year ended Dec. 31. Next earnings report expected: Late January. EPS Estimates based on S&P Operating Earnings; historical GAAP earnings are as reported.

Dividend Data

No cash dividends have been paid.

Lexmark International Inc.

STANDARD &POOR'S

Business Summary October 24, 2007

CORPORATE OVERVIEW. Lexmark shook up the printer industry with the introduction of the first desktop color printer priced under $100 with its November 1997 launch of the $99 color inkjet printer, aimed at building brand awareness and an installed base. We think LXK's competitive advantage in the past was its low cost structure and its ability to price aggressively. However, in recent quarters, it has been on the defensive, in our view, as peers have undercut its prices and LXK's product mix was not focused on some of the more compelling printer areas. Going forward, LXK management believes that its commitment to R&D should bear fruit and help revive unit growth and subsequently high margin supplies sales, but we view this as a multi-year process.

In addition to its core printer business, the company makes supplies for IBM branded printers, after-market supplies for OEM products, and typewriters and typewriter supplies sold under the IBM trademark. Lexmark also has an agreement with Dell under which Dell rebrands Lexmark printers, although this is not an exclusive agreement. (Dell accounted for 15% of LXK revenues in 2006.)

MARKET PROFILE. The total revenue market opportunity for laser and inkjet hardware units is expected to rise at a compound annual growth rate (CAGR) of 4% from 2004 to 2009, to 135 million units, according to market research firm IDC, with growth in the laser market projected to be 6%. However, the revenue change over that period for laser and inkjets is forecast at -0.5%. The key is that printer vendors are cutting prices on printers to expand their installed base and subsequently capitalize on the growth in margin-rich supplies sales. A CAGR of 7% in revenue for supplies over the 2004 to 2009 time frame is expected, according to market research firm IDC.

Company Financials Fiscal Year Ended Dec. 31

Per Share Data ($)	2006	2005	2004	2003	2002	2001	2000	1999	1998	1997
Tangible Book Value	10.67	12.77	NM	17.46	NM	8.25	6.11	6.24	5.22	4.07
Cash Flow	5.21	4.21	5.29	4.48	3.84	2.98	2.80	2.89	2.23	1.60
Earnings	3.27	2.91	4.28	3.34	2.79	2.05	2.13	2.32	1.70	1.09
S&P Core Earnings	3.28	2.52	3.94	3.04	2.27	1.57	NA	NA	NA	NA
Dividends	Nil	Nil	Nil	Nil	Nil	Nil	Nil	Nil	Nil	Nil
Payout Ratio	Nil	Nil	Nil	Nil	Nil	Nil	Nil	Nil	Nil	Nil
Prices:High	74.68	86.62	97.50	79.65	69.50	70.75	135.88	104.00	51.00	19.00
Prices:Low	44.09	39.33	76.00	56.57	41.94	40.81	28.75	42.09	17.50	9.56
P/E Ratio:High	23	30	23	24	25	35	64	45	30	18
P/E Ratio:Low	13	14	18	17	15	20	13	18	10	9

Income Statement Analysis (Million $)	2006	2005	2004	2003	2002	2001	2000	1999	1998	1997
Revenue	5,108	5,222	5,314	4,755	4,356	4,143	3,807	3,452	3,021	2,494
Operating Income	715	692	867	743	643	525	548	557	458	352
Depreciation	201	159	135	149	138	126	91.2	80.1	75.6	77.5
Interest Expense	12.1	11.2	12.3	12.5	9.00	14.8	12.8	10.7	11.0	10.8
Pretax Income	459	554	746	594	496	318	396	459	365	255
Effective Tax Rate	26.3%	35.7%	23.8%	26.0%	26.0%	13.9%	28.0%	30.6%	33.5%	36.0%
Net Income	338	356	569	439	367	274	285	319	243	163
S&P Core Earnings	340	308	524	399	298	210	NA	NA	NA	NA

Balance Sheet & Other Financial Data (Million $)	2006	2005	2004	2003	2002	2001	2000	1999	1998	1997
Cash	551	889	1,567	1,196	498	90.7	68.5	93.9	149	43.0
Current Assets	1,830	2,170	3,001	2,444	1,799	1,493	1,244	1,089	1,020	776
Total Assets	2,849	3,330	4,124	3,450	2,808	2,450	2,073	1,703	1,483	1,208
Current Liabilities	1,324	1,234	1,468	1,183	1,099	931	979	736	606	548
Long Term Debt	150	150	150	149	149	149	149	149	149	57.0
Common Equity	1,035	1,429	2,083	1,643	1,082	1,076	777	659	578	501
Total Capital	1,185	1,578	2,232	1,792	1,231	1,225	926	808	727	558
Capital Expenditures	200	201	198	93.8	112	214	297	220	102	69.5
Cash Flow	539	515	704	588	505	399	377	399	319	241
Current Ratio	1.4	1.8	2.0	2.1	1.6	1.6	1.3	1.5	1.7	1.4
% Long Term Debt of Capitalization	12.6	9.5	6.7	8.3	12.1	12.2	16.1	18.4	20.5	10.2
% Net Income of Revenue	6.6	6.8	10.7	9.2	8.4	6.6	7.5	9.2	8.0	6.5
% Return on Assets	11.0	9.6	15.0	14.0	13.9	12.1	15.1	20.0	18.1	13.4
% Return on Equity	27.5	20.3	30.5	32.2	34.0	29.5	39.7	51.5	45.1	31.3

Data as orig reptd.; bef. results of disc opers/spec. items. Per share data adj. for stk. divs.; EPS diluted. E-Estimated. NA-Not Available. NM-Not Meaningful. NR-Not Ranked. UR-Under Review.

Office: 740 West New Circle Rd, Lexington, KY 40550.
Telephone: 859-232-2000.
Website: http://www.lexmark.com
Chrmn & CEO: P.J. Curlander

EVP & CFO: J.W. Gamble, Jr.
VP, Secy & General Counsel: V.J. Cole
VP & Cntlr: G.D. Stromquist

Board Members: B. C. Ames, T. Beck, P. J. Curlander, W. R. Fields, R. E. Gomory, S. R. Hardis, J. F. Hardymon, R. Holland, Jr., M. L. Mann, M. J. Maples, J. Montupet, K. P. Seifert, M. D. Walker

Founded: 1990
Domicile: Delaware
Employees: 14,900

Eli Lilly and Co

S&P Recommendation HOLD ★★★☆☆	**Price** $50.79 (as of Nov 23, 2007)	**12-Mo. Target Price** $59.00	**Investment Style** Large-Cap Blend

GICS Sector Health Care
Sub-Industry Pharmaceuticals

Summary Eli Lilly & Co. is a leading producer of prescription drugs, offering a wide range of treatments for neurological disorders, diabetes, cancer, and other conditions. Animal health products are also sold.

Key Stock Statistics (Source S&P, Vickers, company reports)

52-Wk Range	$61.00–49.09	S&P Oper. EPS 2007**E**	3.54	Market Capitalization(B)	$57.610	Beta	1.14
Trailing 12-Month EPS	$2.05	S&P Oper. EPS 2008**E**	3.85	Yield (%)	3.35	S&P 3-Yr. Proj. EPS CAGR(%)	9.00
Trailing 12-Month P/E	24.8	P/E on S&P Oper. EPS 2007**E**	14.3	Dividend Rate/Share	$1.70	S&P Credit Rating	AA
$10K Invested 5 Yrs Ago	$8,807	Common Shares Outstg. (M)	1,134.3	Institutional Ownership (%)	76		

Price Performance

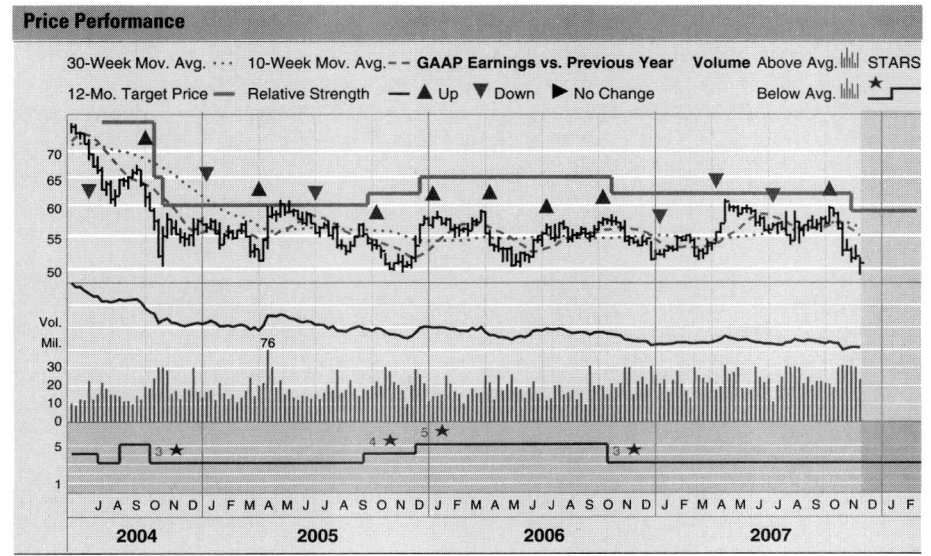

30-Week Mov. Avg. · · ·   10-Week Mov. Avg. – –   **GAAP Earnings vs. Previous Year**   Volume Above Avg. �𝄚 STARS
12-Mo. Target Price —   Relative Strength —   ▲ Up ▼ Down ► No Change   Below Avg. ⠿ ★

Options: ASE, CBOE, P, Ph

Analysis prepared by **Herman B. Saftlas** on November 06, 2007, when the stock traded at **$ 52.16**.

Highlights

➤ We expect revenues to rise 8% in 2008, following a projected 16% gain in 2007 (which reflects the full year inclusion of ICOS and a boost from foreign currency exchange). Sales of Cymbalta antidepressant should advance about 30% in 2008, boosted by expanded direct to consumer advertising, new indications and expansion in foreign markets. We also see growth in smaller drugs such as Forteo antiosteoporosis and Byetta diabetes treatment. We look for these gains to more than offset likely flat sales of Zyprexa antipsychotic and Humulin/Humulog insulin.

➤ Helped by manufacturing efficiencies, we expect a modest expansion in the gross margin. We see SG&A expenses and R&D spending increasing at rates comparable to our projected sales growth. We forecast that other net income will decline, but that the tax rate will probably be unchanged at about 22%.

➤ We project operating EPS of $3.85 for 2008, up from an estimated $3.54 for 2007, excluding merger, plant closing and other special charges in each year.

Investment Rationale/Risk

➤ Lilly has outperformed many of its peers in sales and EPS growth in recent quarters, and 2007 EPS guidance was recently raised for a third time this year. We attribute the strength to robust growth in newer products such as Cymbalta antidepressant, and a streamlined cost structure. However, we still think the shares are likely to be range-bound over the near term, pending further developments related to prasugrel anti-clotting drug, which recently had mixed Phase III results. Clinical data showed that while the drug was effective in reducing heart attacks and strokes, it was also linked with increased bleeding risks.

➤ Risks to our recommendation and target price include possible greater than expected competitive pressures, as well as the failure to develop and commercialize new drugs.

➤ Our 12-month target price of $59 applies a peer level P/E of 16.6X to our 2008 EPS estimate. Our DCF model, which assumes decelerating cash flow growth over the next 10 years, a WACC of 7.0%, and perpetuity growth of 1%, also indicates intrinsic value of about $59.

Qualitative Risk Assessment

LOW	MEDIUM	HIGH

Our risk assessment reflects that LLY, along with other major drug companies, is subject to generic challenges to branded patents, and drug development and regulatory risks. This is offset by our view of LLY's diverse drug portfolio, limited patent expiration exposure, and robust pipeline.

Quantitative Evaluations

S&P Quality Ranking   B+

D	C	B-	B	B+	A-	A	A+

Relative Strength Rank   MODERATE
44
LOWEST = 1   HIGHEST = 99

Revenue/Earnings Data

Revenue (Million $)

	1Q	2Q	3Q	4Q	Year
2007	4,226	4,631	4,587	--	--
2006	3,715	3,867	3,864	4,245	15,691
2005	3,497	3,668	3,601	3,879	14,645
2004	3,377	3,556	3,280	3,644	13,858
2003	2,889	3,088	3,139	3,466	12,583
2002	2,561	2,775	2,786	2,956	11,078

Earnings Per Share ($)

2007	0.47	0.61	0.85	E0.89	E3.54
2006	0.77	0.76	0.80	0.12	2.45
2005	0.68	-0.23	0.73	0.66	1.83
2004	0.37	0.60	0.69	Nil	1.66
2003	0.38	0.64	0.66	0.69	2.37
2002	0.58	0.61	0.63	0.68	2.50

Fiscal year ended Dec. 31. Next earnings report expected: Late January. EPS Estimates based on S&P Operating Earnings; historical GAAP earnings are as reported.

Dividend Data (Dates: mm/dd Payment Date: mm/dd/yy)

Amount ($)	Date Decl.	Ex-Div. Date	Stk. of Record	Payment Date
0.425	12/18	02/13	02/15	03/09/07
0.425	04/16	05/11	05/15	06/08/07
0.425	06/21	08/13	08/15	09/10/07
0.425	10/15	11/13	11/15	12/10/07

Dividends have been paid since 1885. Source: Company reports.

Eli Lilly and Co

STANDARD
&POOR'S

Business Summary November 06, 2007

CORPORATE OVERVIEW. Eli Lilly and Co. is a leading maker of prescription drugs, offering a wide range of treatments for neurological disorders, diabetes, cancer and other conditions. Animal health products are also sold. Foreign operations accounted for 45% of sales in 2006. In January 2007, the company acquired ICOS Corp. for $2.3 billion in cash. The acquisition gave LLY full ownership of Cialis, a treatment for erectile dysfunction, which had previously been marketed through a 50/50 venture with ICOS. Total Cialis sales were $971 million in 2006 (partially booked by LLY).

LLY's largest selling drug is Zyprexa, a treatment for schizophrenia and bipolar disorder that offers clinical advantages over older antipsychotic drugs. Sales of Zyprexa totaled $4.4 billion in 2006, up from $4.2 billion in 2005. Zyprexa accounted for about 13.3% of total U.S. antipsychotic prescriptions in December 2006, based on data from IMS Health, a pharmaceutical market intelligence firm. LLY also offers Symbyax, a combination of Zyprexa and Prozac, to treat bipolar depression. In August 2004, the company launched Cymbalta, a potent antidepressant. Cymbalta works on two body chemicals involved in depression--serotonin and norepinephrine--while most conventional antidepressants affect only serotonin. Sales of Cymbalta were $1.3 billion in 2006, up from $680 million in 2005.

Diabetes care products (sales of $2.9 billion in 2006) include Humulin, a human insulin produced through recombinant DNA technology; Humalog, a rapid-acting injectable human insulin analog; Iletin, an animal-source insulin; and Actos, an oral agent for Type 2 diabetes that is manufactured by Takeda Chemical Industries of Japan and co-marketed by Lilly and Takeda. In May 2005, the FDA approved Byetta (generically known as exenatide) for Type 2 diabetes. Lilly shares in the profits from Byetta with Amylin Pharmaceuticals, co-developer of the drug.

Other important drugs are Gemzar, a treatment for lung cancer and pancreatic cancer (sales of $1.4 billion); Evista, a drug used to prevent and treat osteoporosis in postmenopausal women ($1.0 billion); Strattera, a treatment for attention deficit hyperactivity disorder ($579 million); Forteo for severe osteoporosis ($594 million); Humatrope, a recombinant human growth hormone ($416 million); and a line of anti-infectives such as Ceclor/cefaclor, Vancocin HCI, and Keflex. Animal health products ($875 million) include cattle feed additives, antibiotics and related items.

Company Financials Fiscal Year Ended Dec. 31

Per Share Data ($)	2006	2005	2004	2003	2002	2001	2000	1999	1998	1997
Tangible Book Value	9.70	9.55	9.51	8.69	7.37	6.32	5.37	4.49	2.66	2.83
Cash Flow	3.06	2.41	2.21	2.87	2.85	2.91	3.18	2.70	2.31	0.11
Earnings	2.45	1.83	1.66	2.37	2.50	2.58	2.79	2.30	1.87	-0.35
S&P Core Earnings	2.90	1.85	1.42	2.09	1.96	2.17	NA	NA	NA	NA
Dividends	1.60	1.52	1.42	1.34	1.24	1.12	1.04	0.92	0.80	0.74
Payout Ratio	65%	83%	86%	57%	50%	43%	37%	40%	43%	NM
Prices:High	59.24	60.98	76.95	73.89	81.09	95.00	109.00	97.75	91.31	70.44
Prices:Low	50.19	49.47	50.34	52.77	43.75	70.01	54.00	60.56	57.69	35.56
P/E Ratio:High	24	33	46	31	32	37	39	42	49	NM
P/E Ratio:Low	20	27	30	22	17	27	19	26	31	NM

Income Statement Analysis (Million $)										
Revenue	15,691	14,645	13,858	12,583	11,078	11,543	10,862	10,003	9,237	8,518
Operating Income	4,927	4,375	4,256	4,050	3,821	4,185	3,996	3,803	3,315	2,968
Depreciation	802	726	598	548	493	455	436	440	490	510
Interest Expense	Nil	105	274	61.0	79.7	147	182	242	181	234
Pretax Income	3,418	2,718	2,942	3,262	3,458	3,552	3,859	3,245	2,665	510
Effective Tax Rate	22.1%	26.3%	38.5%	21.5%	21.7%	20.9%	20.8%	21.5%	21.4%	175.5%
Net Income	2,663	2,002	1,810	2,561	2,708	2,809	3,058	2,547	2,096	-385
S&P Core Earnings	3,153	2,016	1,558	2,261	2,128	2,359	NA	NA	NA	NA

Balance Sheet & Other Financial Data (Million $)										
Cash	3,109	3,007	5,365	2,756	1,946	2,702	4,115	3,700	1,496	1,948
Current Assets	9,694	10,796	12,836	8,759	7,804	6,939	7,943	7,056	5,407	5,321
Total Assets	21,955	24,581	24,867	21,678	19,042	16,434	14,691	12,825	12,596	12,577
Current Liabilities	5,086	5,716	7,594	5,551	5,064	5,203	4,961	3,935	4,607	4,192
Long Term Debt	3,494	5,764	4,492	4,688	4,358	3,132	2,634	2,812	2,186	2,326
Common Equity	11,081	11,000	10,920	9,765	8,274	7,104	8,682	5,013	4,430	4,645
Total Capital	14,638	17,459	16,032	14,453	12,632	10,236	11,407	7,962	6,864	7,187
Capital Expenditures	1,078	1,298	1,898	1,707	1,131	884	678	528	420	366
Cash Flow	3,465	2,728	2,408	3,109	3,201	3,264	3,494	2,986	2,586	125
Current Ratio	1.9	1.9	1.7	1.6	1.5	1.3	1.6	1.8	1.2	1.3
% Long Term Debt of Capitalization	23.9	33.0	28.0	32.4	34.5	30.6	23.1	35.3	31.8	32.4
% Net Income of Revenue	17.0	13.7	13.1	20.4	24.4	24.3	28.2	25.5	22.7	NM
% Return on Assets	11.4	8.1	7.8	12.6	15.3	18.1	22.2	20.0	16.7	NM
% Return on Equity	24.2	18.1	17.5	28.4	35.2	42.7	44.7	53.9	46.2	NM

Data as orig reptd.; bef. results of disc opers/spec. items. Per share data adj. for stk. divs.; EPS diluted. E-Estimated. NA-Not Available. NM-Not Meaningful. NR-Not Ranked. UR-Under Review.

Office: Lilly Corporate Center, Indianapolis, IN 46285.
Telephone: 317-276-2000.
Website: http://www.lilly.com
Chrmn & CEO: S. Taurel

Pres & COO: J.C. Lechleiter
SVP & CFO: D. Rice
SVP & General Counsel: R.A. Armitage
Investor Contact: P. Johnson (317-276-2000)

Board Members: S. Bischoff, J. M. Cook, M. S. Feldstein, G. M. Fisher, J. E. Fyrwald, A. G. Gilman, K. N. Horn, J. C. Lechleiter, E. R. Marram, F. G. Prendergast, K. P. Seifert, S. Taurel

Founded: 1876
Domicile: Indiana
Employees: 41,500

Limited Brands Inc.

STANDARD &POOR'S

S&P Recommendation	HOLD ★★★★★	Price $19.32 (as of Nov 29, 2007)	12-Mo. Target Price $24.00	Investment Style Large-Cap Blend

GICS Sector Consumer Discretionary
Sub-Industry Apparel Retail

Summary This specialty retailer of women's apparel, lingerie and personal care and beauty products operates about 3,000 specialty stores.

Key Stock Statistics (Source S&P, Vickers, company reports)

52-Wk Range	$31.96– 16.50	S&P Oper. EPS 2008**E**	1.35	Market Capitalization(B)	$7.000	Beta	1.33
Trailing 12-Month EPS	$1.94	S&P Oper. EPS 2009**E**	1.60	Yield (%)	3.11	S&P 3-Yr. Proj. EPS CAGR(%)	12.00
Trailing 12-Month P/E	10.0	P/E on S&P Oper. EPS 2008**E**	14.3	Dividend Rate/Share	$0.60	S&P Credit Rating	BBB-
$10K Invested 5 Yrs Ago	$13,283	Common Shares Outstg. (M)	362.3	Institutional Ownership (%)	89		

Price Performance

30-Week Mov. Avg. ··· 10-Week Mov. Avg. - - **GAAP Earnings vs. Previous Year**   Volume Above Avg. ▮▮▮ STARS
12-Mo. Target Price — Relative Strength — ▲ Up ▼ Down ► No Change   Below Avg. ▮▮▮ ★

Options: ASE, CBOE, P, Ph

Analysis prepared by **Marie Driscoll, CFA** on November 29, 2007, when the stock traded at **$ 19.21**.

Highlights

➤ We see FY 08 (Jan.) and FY 09 as a period of restructuring and investing in infrastructure as LTD prepares to grow businesses globally with its leading intimates and personal care retail brands, Victoria's Secret (VS) and Bath and Body Works (BBW). We see VS providing growth opportunities via line extensions, sub-brands, and additional fragrance and beauty launches in the intermediate term.

➤ We expect 1% sales declines in FY 08 and FY 09, reflecting modestly positive same store sales comparisons and increases in selling space at VS (9%), BBW (4%) and La Senza (8%), offset by the loss of approximately $529 million apparel retail sales due to the disposition of LTD's apparel brands in the second quarter of FY 08. Consolidated same-store sales for the first nine months of FY 08 increased 1%.

➤ We look for about 200 basis point operating margin contraction, to 8.8% of sales, in FY 08, with modest improvement in FY 09, as heightened competition and a difficult retail environment make price increases difficult and may necessitate additional marketing and sales support. We estimate a 5% decline in share count, benefiting per share results.

Investment Rationale/Risk

➤ We see no near-term catalyst for share outperformance, with the shares recently trading at 11X our FY 09 EPS estimate. We expect LTD's strategy to focus on increasing sales via new concepts and the recent La Senza acquisition in FY 08, then on margin expansion in FY 09. La Senza launched LTD into the international intimate apparel market and should provide a platform for further international expansion, which we believe will be important given the relative maturity of LTD's many domestic retail concepts. The dividend recently provided a yield of about 3.4%.

➤ Risks to our recommendation and target price include fashion and inventory risk, weakening trends in consumer spending, integration risk relative to La Senza, and weak same-store sales trends. With an estimated 65%+ of LTD's profits earned in the fiscal fourth quarter, earnings risk is heightened.

➤ We derive our 12-month target price of $24 by applying a peer 15X forward multiple to our FY 09 EPS estimate of $1.60.

Qualitative Risk Assessment

LOW	MEDIUM	HIGH

Our risk assessment reflects LTD's strong cash flow, offset by execution risk in the company's attempt to turn around its apparel businesses.

Quantitative Evaluations

S&P Quality Ranking B+

D	C	B-	B	B+	A-	A	A+

Relative Strength Rank MODERATE

33

LOWEST = 1   HIGHEST = 99

Revenue/Earnings Data

Revenue (Million $)

	1Q	2Q	3Q	4Q	Year
2008	2,311	2,624	1,923	--	--
2007	2,077	2,454	2,115	4,025	10,671
2006	1,975	2,291	1,892	3,542	9,699
2005	1,975	2,211	1,891	3,328	9,408
2004	1,842	2,014	1,847	3,231	8,934
2003	2,027	2,113	1,983	2,966	8,445

Earnings Per Share ($)

	1Q	2Q	3Q	4Q	Year
2008	0.13	0.67	-0.03	E1.00	E1.35
2007	0.25	0.28	0.06	1.08	1.68
2006	0.16	0.20	Nil	1.28	1.62
2005	0.06	0.31	0.16	0.87	1.47
2004	0.19	0.19	0.25	0.74	1.36
2003	0.10	0.16	0.03	0.66	0.95

Fiscal year ended Jan. 31. Next earnings report expected: Early March. EPS Estimates based on S&P Operating Earnings; historical GAAP earnings are as reported.

Dividend Data (Dates: mm/dd Payment Date: mm/dd/yy)

Amount ($)	Date Decl.	Ex-Div. Date	Stk. of Record	Payment Date
0.150	02/02	02/27	03/01	03/16/07
0.150	05/22	05/29	05/31	06/15/07
0.150	08/10	08/28	08/30	09/14/07
0.150	11/12	11/27	11/29	12/14/07

Dividends have been paid since 1970. Source: Company reports.

Limited Brands Inc.

STANDARD &POOR'S

Business Summary November 29, 2007

CORPORATE OVERVIEW. Limited Brands (formerly The Limited) is a specialty retailer that conducts its business in three primary segments: Victoria's Secret, a women's intimate apparel, personal care products and accessories retail brand; Bath & Body Works, a personal care and home fragrance products retail brand; and the Apparel segment, which operates Express and Limited Stores. At February 3, 2007, the store base consisted of 195 Express Women, 69 Express Men, 394 Express Dual Gender, 260 Limited Stores, 1,003 Victoria's Secret, and 1,537 Bath & Body Works locations. LTD also operates two Henri Bendel stores, nine C.O. Bigelows, an upscale apothecary, six Divas and 323 La Senza stores. The company adopted its current name in May 2002.

The Apparel businesses accounted for 21% of total sales in FY 07 (Jan.), Victoria's Secret 48%, and Bath & Body Works 24%. The remaining 7% was Mast Industries external sales to third parties as well as Avenues and Henri Bendel's sales. LTD has signed a definitive agreement to sell 67% of Express for $425 million (after tax), expected to close in July. In addition, it is exploring strategic options for Limited Stores.

Victoria's Secret is the leading specialty retailer of women's intimate apparel and beauty products, with FY 07 sales of $5,139 million, which includes $1,415 million at Victoria's Secret Direct, a catalog and e-commerce retailer of women's intimate and other apparel and beauty products. Bath & Body Works is a specialty retailer of personal care and home fragrance products. FY 07 sales were $2,555 million, including White Barn Candle Company. Express, launched in 1980, seeks to offer cutting edge style for casual, professional and urban customers, both men and women. Express had sales of $1,749 million in FY 07. Limited stores focus on sophisticated sportswear for modern American women, with FY 07 sales of $493 million.

Company Financials Fiscal Year Ended Jan. 31

Per Share Data ($)	2007	2006	2005	2004	2003	2002	2001	2000	1999	1998
Tangible Book Value	2.34	1.69	1.31	6.78	5.93	6.40	5.43	5.00	4.92	3.75
Cash Flow	2.46	2.45	2.17	1.90	1.48	1.83	1.58	1.61	4.76	0.97
Earnings	1.68	1.62	1.47	1.36	0.95	0.94	0.96	1.00	4.16	0.40
S&P Core Earnings	1.68	1.57	1.27	1.03	0.94	0.80	0.91	NA	NA	NA
Dividends	0.60	0.48	0.40	0.40	0.30	0.30	0.30	0.30	0.26	0.24
Payout Ratio	36%	30%	27%	29%	32%	32%	31%	30%	6%	61%
Calendar Year	2006	2005	2004	2003	2002	2001	2000	1999	1998	1997
Prices:High	32.60	25.50	27.89	18.46	22.34	21.29	27.88	25.31	18.25	12.88
Prices:Low	21.62	18.81	17.35	10.88	12.53	9.00	14.44	13.75	10.25	8.25
P/E Ratio:High	19	16	19	14	24	23	29	25	4	33
P/E Ratio:Low	13	12	12	8	13	10	15	14	2	21

Income Statement Analysis (Million $)

	2007	2006	2005	2004	2003	2002	2001	2000	1999	1998
Revenue	10,671	9,699	9,408	8,934	8,445	9,363	10,105	9,766	9,347	9,189
Operating Income	1,492	1,285	1,360	1,246	1,148	1,025	1,148	1,169	984	1,006
Depreciation	316	299	333	28.3	276	277	272	272	286	313
Interest Expense	102	94.0	58.0	62.0	30.0	34.0	58.0	78.0	69.0	69.0
Pretax Income	1,097	960	1,116	1,166	843	968	828	905	2,428	457
Effective Tax Rate	38.5%	30.3%	36.8%	38.5%	40.5%	39.8%	40.0%	41.0%	12.8%	40.0%
Net Income	675	669	705	717	496	519	428	461	2,054	217
S&P Core Earnings	675	638	609	540	492	352	406	NA	NA	NA

Balance Sheet & Other Financial Data (Million $)

	2007	2006	2005	2004	2003	2002	2001	2000	1999	1998
Cash	500	1,208	1,161	3,129	2,262	1,375	563	817	1,222	1,098
Current Assets	2,771	2,784	2,684	4,433	3,606	2,682	2,068	2,285	2,318	2,031
Total Assets	7,093	6,346	6,089	7,873	7,246	4,719	4,088	4,126	4,550	4,301
Current Liabilities	1,709	1,575	1,451	1,392	1,259	1,319	1,000	1,236	1,248	1,093
Long Term Debt	1,665	1,669	1,646	648	547	250	400	400	550	650
Common Equity	2,955	2,471	2,335	5,266	4,860	2,744	2,317	2,147	2,233	2,044
Total Capital	4,864	4,319	4,191	6,048	5,532	3,171	2,860	2,666	2,894	2,797
Capital Expenditures	548	480	431	293	306	337	446	375	347	405
Cash Flow	991	968	1,038	1,000	772	796	700	733	2,340	530
Current Ratio	1.6	1.8	1.8	3.2	2.9	2.0	2.1	1.8	1.9	1.9
% Long Term Debt of Capitalization	35.5	38.6	39.3	10.7	9.9	7.9	14.0	15.0	19.0	23.2
% Net Income of Revenue	6.3	6.9	7.5	8.0	5.9	5.5	4.2	4.7	22.0	2.4
% Return on Assets	10.1	10.8	10.1	9.5	8.0	11.8	10.4	10.7	46.4	5.2
% Return on Equity	24.9	27.9	18.6	14.2	13.0	20.5	19.2	21.4	96.0	10.9

Data as orig reptd.; bef. results of disc opers/spec. items. Per share data adj. for stk. divs.; EPS diluted. E-Estimated. NA-Not Available. NM-Not Meaningful. NR-Not Ranked. UR-Under Review.

Office: Three Limited Parkway, Columbus, OH 43216.
Telephone: 614-415-7000.
Website: http://www.limited.com
Chrmn & CEO: L.H. Wexner

Vice Chrmn & COO: L.A. Schlesinger
EVP & Chief Admin Officer: M.R. Redgrave
CFO: S. Burgdoerfer

Board Members: E. M. Freedman, E. G. Gee, D. S. Hersch, J. L. Heskett, D. A. James, D. T. Kollat, W. R. Loomis, Jr., J. H. Miro, L. A. Schlesinger, J. B. Swartz, A. R. Tessler, A. S. Wexner, L. H. Wexner, R. Zimmerman

Founded: 1967
Domicile: Delaware
Employees: 125,500

Lincoln National Corp

STANDARD &POOR'S

S&P Recommendation **BUY** ★★★★☆	Price $59.76 (as of Nov 23, 2007)	12-Mo. Target Price $73.00	Investment Style Large-Cap Value

GICS Sector Financials
Sub-Industry Life & Health Insurance

Summary This company offers annuities, life insurance, mutual funds, asset management and related advisory services to affluent individuals.

Key Stock Statistics (Source S&P, Vickers, company reports)

52-Wk Range	$74.72– 54.40	S&P Oper. EPS 2007E	5.49	Market Capitalization(B)	$16.176	Beta	1.50
Trailing 12-Month EPS	$5.37	S&P Oper. EPS 2008E	6.17	Yield (%)	2.78	S&P 3-Yr. Proj. EPS CAGR(%)	10.00
Trailing 12-Month P/E	11.1	P/E on S&P Oper. EPS 2007E	10.9	Dividend Rate/Share	$1.66	S&P Credit Rating	A+
$10K Invested 5 Yrs Ago	$20,246	Common Shares Outstg. (M)	270.7	Institutional Ownership (%)	69		

Price Performance

30-Week Mov. Avg. ···   10-Week Mov. Avg. --   **GAAP Earnings vs. Previous Year**   Volume Above Avg. ░ STARS
12-Mo. Target Price —   Relative Strength   — ▲ Up ▼ Down ▶ No Change   Below Avg. ░   ★

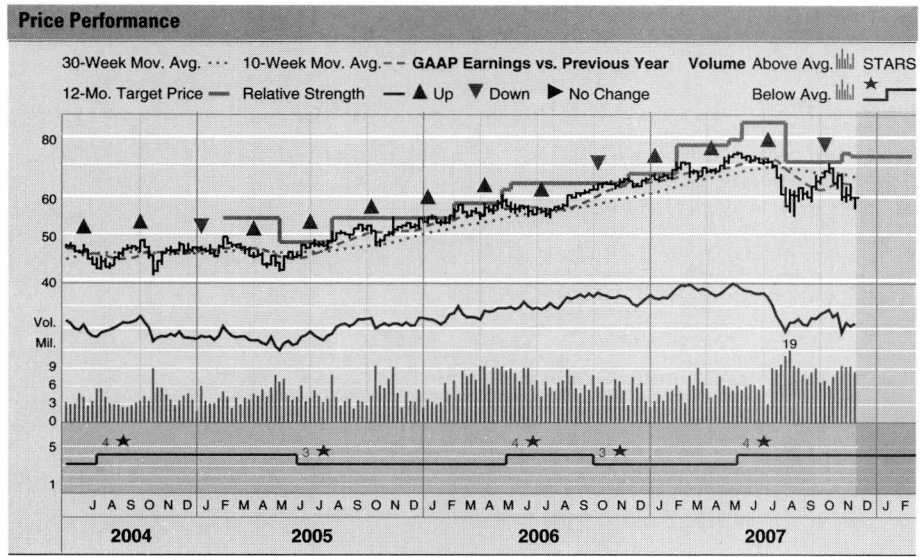

Options: ASE, CBOE, P, Ph

Analysis prepared by **Tanjila Shafi** on November 14, 2007, when the stock traded at **$ 62.80**.

Highlights

➤ We expect strong growth in premiums and operating earnings in 2008, driven by LNC's merger with Jefferson-Pilot, its continued distribution expansion, and its focus on high growth areas. We see operating earnings of the company's life insurance operations increasing at low double-digit rates in 2008. We believe that life sales will benefit from distribution expansion, particularly from the MGA channel, and a streamlined underwriting process. Given its improved distribution efforts and new product initiatives, we expect operating earnings of individual annuities operations to experience double-digit growth in 2008.

➤ We anticipate that operating earnings of the investment management segment will see low to mid single-digit growth, but personnel attrition in its institutional fixed income sub-segment may impact its net inflows in 2008. We are also concerned that its defined contribution business may face earnings pressure due to changes in its business mix.

➤ We forecast 2007 operating EPS of $5.49, up from 2006 operating EPS of $5.14. Our estimate for 2008 is $6.17.

Investment Rationale/Risk

➤ We believe that LNC will be able to increase its market share in the variable annuity business, given its strong distribution capabilities and innovative products. In addition, we anticipate that the company will benefit from strong prepayment income and solid institutional investment inflows. We see results benefiting from operational efficiencies following the merger with Jefferson-Pilot and continued stock repurchases. We further view the acquisition of Jefferson-Pilot as adding financial flexibility and distribution capabilities.

➤ Risks to our recommendation and target price include dynamic hedging for guaranteed minimum benefits; pressures on product spreads; difficulties in obtaining reinsurance for some products; currency risk; higher than expected losses in its investment portfolio; and potentially unfavorable tax law changes lessening product competitiveness.

➤ Our 12-month target price is $73, or 11.8X our 2008 EPS estimate, in line with historical multiples.

Qualitative Risk Assessment

LOW	**MEDIUM**	HIGH

Our risk assessment reflects our view of the company's solid balance sheet with low debt-to-total capitalization and a stable dividend policy, tempered by risks associated with the acquisition of Jefferson-Pilot and earnings volatility related to interest rate and equity market movements.

Quantitative Evaluations

S&P Quality Ranking   B+

D	C	B-	B	**B+**	A-	A	A+

Relative Strength Rank   MODERATE

52

LOWEST = 1   HIGHEST = 99

Revenue/Earnings Data

Revenue (Million $)

	1Q	2Q	3Q	4Q	Year
2007	2,670	2,740	2,681	--	--
2006	1,417	2,496	2,487	2,658	9,063
2005	1,313	1,373	1,413	1,388	5,488
2004	1,259	1,359	1,406	1,347	5,371
2003	1,099	1,213	1,269	1,327	5,284
2002	1,126	1,145	1,141	1,189	4,635

Earnings Per Share ($)

	1Q	2Q	3Q	4Q	Year
2007	1.42	1.37	1.21	E1.43	E5.49
2006	1.24	1.23	1.29	1.36	5.13
2005	1.01	1.13	1.30	1.28	4.72
2004	0.86	1.04	1.12	1.07	4.09
2003	0.23	0.80	0.74	1.08	2.85
2002	0.49	0.31	-0.68	0.35	0.49

Fiscal year ended Dec. 31. Next earnings report expected: Early February. EPS Estimates based on S&P Operating Earnings; historical GAAP earnings are as reported.

Dividend Data (Dates: mm/dd Payment Date: mm/dd/yy)

Amount ($)	Date Decl.	Ex-Div. Date	Stk. of Record	Payment Date
0.395	02/23	04/04	04/09	05/01/07
0.395	05/10	07/06	07/10	08/01/07
0.395	08/03	10/05	10/10	11/01/07
0.415	11/06	01/08	01/10	02/01/08

Dividends have been paid since 1920. Source: Company reports.

Lincoln National Corp

Business Summary November 14, 2007

CORPORATE OVERVIEW. Lincoln National is a holding company with subsidiaries that operate multiple insurance and investment management businesses. Primary operating subsidiaries include The Lincoln National Life Insurance Company, First Penn-Pacific Life Insurance Company, Lincoln Life & Annuity Company of New York, Delaware Management Holdings, Inc., Lincoln National (UK) plc, Lincoln Financial Advisors (LFA), a retailing distribution unit, and Lincoln Financial Distributors (LFD), a wholesaling distribution unit.

Following the acquisition of Jefferson-Pilot in April 2006, LNC's segments were restructured and currently operations are divided into six business segments: Individual Markets (60% of 2006 operating revenue), Employer Markets (26%), Investment Management (5.6%), Lincoln U.K. (3.2%), Lincoln Financial Media (2.7%), and Other Operations (1.7%).

The Individual Markets segment encompasses the Individual Annuities and Individual Life Insurance business lines. According to Variable Annuity Research and Data Services (VARDS), LNC ranked sixth in assets and fifth in individual variable annuity sales for 2005 in the U.S. The life insurance business targets the affluent market, and underwrites and sells universal life, variable universal life, interest-sensitive whole life, corporate-owned life insurance

(COLI), term-life insurance, and linked products such as universal life linked with long-term care benefits. The employer markets segment encompasses the retirement products, executive benefits, and benefit partners businesses.

The Investment Management segment offers retail and institutional mutual funds, separate and managed accounts, 529 college savings plans, and retirement plans and services, including 401(k) plans and administration services. Lincoln U.K. is licensed to do business throughout the U.K., and focuses primarily on retaining its existing customers and managing expenses for a closed block of business in the U.K., including accepting new deposits from, and offering new products to, existing policyholders. Offerings consist principally of unit-linked life and pension products, similar to U.S. variable life and annuity products. The Other Operations segment includes the financial data for the operations of Lincoln Financial Advisors (LFA) and Lincoln Financial Distributors (LFD), LNC's retail and wholesale distributors, operations that are not directly related to the business segments.

Company Financials Fiscal Year Ended Dec. 31

Per Share Data ($)	2006	2005	2004	2003	2002	2001	2000	1999	1998	1997
Tangible Book Value	27.92	22.47	22.25	18.74	15.62	14.10	11.06	5.59	10.17	19.34
Operating Earnings	NA	NA	NA	NA	2.56	3.56	3.27	2.32	2.61	-0.25
Earnings	5.13	4.72	4.09	2.85	0.49	3.13	3.19	2.30	2.51	0.11
S&P Core Earnings	5.05	4.71	3.78	4.36	1.16	3.10	NA	NA	NA	NA
Dividends	1.52	1.46	1.40	1.34	1.28	1.22	1.16	1.10	1.30	0.98
Payout Ratio	30%	31%	34%	47%	NM	39%	36%	48%	52%	NM
Prices:High	66.72	54.41	50.38	41.32	53.65	52.75	56.38	57.50	49.44	39.06
Prices:Low	52.00	41.59	39.98	24.73	25.11	38.00	22.63	36.00	33.50	24.50
P/E Ratio:High	13	12	12	14	NM	17	18	25	20	NM
P/E Ratio:Low	10	9	10	9	NM	12	7	16	13	NM

Income Statement Analysis (Million $)										
Life Insurance in Force	697,900	338,500	NA	307,800	874	651,900	637,100	516,600	400,800	249,800
Premium Income:Life	NA	NA	NA	1,694	1,730	2,907	3,064	2,721	2,260	1,588
Premium Income:A & H	NA	NA	NA	3.98	20.3	341	410	698	635	573
Net Investment Income	3,981	2,702	2,704	2,639	2,608	2,680	2,747	2,808	2,681	2,251
Total Revenue	9,063	5,488	5,371	5,284	4,635	6,381	6,852	6,798	6,087	4,898
Pretax Income	1,811	1,075	1,036	1,048	1.62	764	836	570	697	34.0
Net Operating Income	NA	NA	NA	NA	474	689	639	457	NA	257
Net Income	1,316	831	732	767	91.6	606	621	460	510	21.0
S&P Core Earnings	1,298	831	675	782	215	600	NA	NA	NA	NA

Balance Sheet & Other Financial Data (Million $)										
Cash & Equivalent	2,487	2,838	2,187	2,234	2,227	3,659	2,474	2,429	2,433	3,795
Premiums Due	356	343	233	352	213	400	297	260	775	621
Investment Assets:Bonds	55,853	33,443	34,701	32,769	32,767	28,346	27,450	27,689	30,233	24,066
Investment Assets:Stocks	701	3,391	3,399	3,319	337	471	550	604	543	660
Investment Assets:Loans	10,144	5,525	5,728	6,119	6,151	6,475	6,624	6,628	6,233	4,051
Investment Assets:Total	71,488	43,168	44,507	42,778	40,000	36,113	35,369	35,578	37,929	25,212
Deferred Policy Costs	8,420	4,092	3,445	3,192	2,971	2,885	3,071	2,800	1,964	1,624
Total Assets	178,494	124,788	116,219	106,745	93,133	98,001	99,844	103,096	99,836	77,175
Debt	4,116	1,333	1,083	1,459	1,512	1,336	1,457	1,457	712	808
Common Equity	71,017	6,384	6,175	5,811	5,296	5,263	4,953	4,264	5,388	4,983
% Return on Revenue	14.5	15.1	13.6	14.5	2.0	9.5	9.1	6.8	28.6	0.7
% Return on Assets	0.1	0.1	0.1	0.1	0.1	0.6	0.6	0.5	0.5	0.0
% Return on Equity	2.3	13.2	12.2	13.8	1.7	11.9	13.5	0.4	9.8	0.4
% Investment Yield	6.8	6.1	6.8	7.1	6.9	7.5	7.7	7.6	7.9	7.5

Data as orig reptd.; bef. results of disc opers/spec. items. Per share data adj. for stk. divs.; EPS diluted. E-Estimated. NA-Not Available. NM-Not Meaningful. NR-Not Ranked. UR-Under Review.

Office: 1500 Market Street, Philadelphia, PA 19102-2112.
Telephone: 215-448-1400.
Email: investorrelations@lnc.com
Website: http://www.lfg.com

Chrmn & CEO: J.A. Boscia
Pres & COO: D.R. Glass
SVP & CFO: F.J. Crawford
SVP & General Counsel: D.L. Schoff

SVP & CIO: C.C. Comelio
Board Members: W. J. Avery, J. P. Barrett, J. A. Boscia, W. H. Cunningham, D. R. Glass, G. W. Henderson, III, E. G. Johnson, M. L. Lachman, M. F. Mee, W. P. Payne, P. S. Pittard, J. S. Ruckelshaus, D. A. Stonecipher, I. Tidwell, G. F. Tilton

Founded: 1905
Domicile: Indiana
Employees: 10,744

Linear Technology Corp

STANDARD
&POOR'S

S&P Recommendation	HOLD ★★★☆☆	Price $30.47 (as of Nov 23, 2007)	12-Mo. Target Price $38.00	Investment Style Large-Cap Growth

GICS Sector Information Technology
Sub-Industry Semiconductors

Summary This company manufactures high-performance linear integrated circuits.

Key Stock Statistics (Source S&P, Vickers, company reports)

52-Wk Range	$38.84– 29.72	S&P Oper. EPS 2008**E**	1.72	Market Capitalization(B)	$6.764
Trailing 12-Month EPS	$1.42	S&P Oper. EPS 2009**E**	NA	Yield (%)	2.36
Trailing 12-Month P/E	21.5	P/E on S&P Oper. EPS 2008**E**	17.7	Dividend Rate/Share	$0.72
$10K Invested 5 Yrs Ago	$9,704	Common Shares Outstg. (M)	222.0	Institutional Ownership (%)	NM

Beta	1.66
S&P 3-Yr. Proj. EPS CAGR(%)	10.00
S&P Credit Rating	NA

Price Performance

30-Week Mov. Avg. ··· 10-Week Mov. Avg.- - **GAAP Earnings vs. Previous Year** **Volume** Above Avg. STARS
12-Mo. Target Price — Relative Strength — ▲ Up ▼ Down ► No Change   Below Avg. ★

Options: ASE, CBOE, P, Ph

Analysis prepared by **Clyde Montevirgen** on October 19, 2007, when the stock traded at **$ 33.39**.

Highlights

➤ After an inventory glut that led to quarters of sales decreases, we foresee healthy demand in most of LLTC's end markets providing above industry sales growth ahead. Although we are somewhat concerned that distributor's lean inventory strategies may lead to order volatility, we see solid yet seasonally lower industrial orders ahead. We also look for stronger communications orders and accelerating consumer order growth lifting revenues. We are modeling sales growth of 12% in FY 2008 (Jun.), compared to a sales decline of 1% in FY 2007.

➤ We anticipate gross margin in the upper-70% range over the next couple of years. We view favorably LLTC's focus on high-end analog, as pricing should remain relatively stable, helping to preserve margins. We think Linear is focused on protecting margins, and is fairly particular in choosing projects. Although we see R&D head count and related compensation costs increasing, we forecast that SG&A will grow at a slower pace than sales, providing healthy operating leverage and supporting overall profitability.

➤ We expect EPS of $1.72 in FY 2008, compared to $1.39 in FY 2007.

Investment Rationale/Risk

➤ We think Linear can capitalize on its entrenched customer base and will experience more notable top-line growth following the recent industrywide downswing. We believe that the company can gain market share and expand revenues in several end markets, but given our view of LLTC's well managed operations, evidenced by successful restructuring efforts, we see limited margin expansion. Also, we anticipate increasing pricing pressure as it further engages the consumer markets. As such, we believe the shares are appropriately valued at current price levels.

➤ Risks to our recommendation and target price include the possibility of a sharp downturn in semiconductor demand. We are concerned about LLTC's corporate governance regarding its reliance on stock-based compensation.

➤ Our 12-month target price of $38 is based on a blend of our DCF and P/E analyses. Our DCF model, which assumes a terminal growth rate of 4% and a WACC of 10%, produces a value of $39. We also apply a P/E of 22X, slightly higher than the peer average, to our FY 2008 EPS estimate to derive a value of $38.

Qualitative Risk Assessment

LOW	MEDIUM	HIGH

Our risk assessment reflects that Linear is subject to the sales cycles of the semiconductor industry. This is offset by stabilizing factors such as a high level of proprietary circuit design content, a varied customer base, diverse end markets, our view of an absence of long-term debt, and wider margins than most competitors.

Quantitative Evaluations

S&P Quality Ranking   A

D	C	B-	B	B+	A-	A	A+

Relative Strength Rank   MODERATE

37

LOWEST = 1   HIGHEST = 99

Revenue/Earnings Data

Revenue (Million $)

	1Q	2Q	3Q	4Q	Year
2008	281.5	--	--	--	--
2007	292.1	267.9	255.0	268.1	1,083
2006	256.0	265.2	278.9	292.9	1,093
2005	253.0	250.1	290.7	255.8	1,050
2004	174.1	186.0	209.1	238.1	807.3
2003	142.0	145.0	153.8	165.8	606.6

Earnings Per Share ($)

	1Q	2Q	3Q	4Q	Year
2008	0.40	E0.41	E0.45	E0.48	E1.72
2007	0.37	0.34	0.32	0.36	1.39
2006	0.31	0.33	0.35	0.37	1.37
2005	0.33	0.33	0.39	0.34	1.38
2004	0.22	0.23	0.27	0.31	1.02
2003	0.17	0.18	0.19	0.21	0.74

Fiscal year ended Jun. 30. Next earnings report expected: Mid January. EPS Estimates based on S&P Operating Earnings; historical GAAP earnings are as reported.

Dividend Data (Dates: mm/dd Payment Date: mm/dd/yy)

Amount ($)	Date Decl.	Ex-Div. Date	Stk. of Record	Payment Date
0.180	01/16	01/24	01/26	02/14/07
0.180	04/17	04/25	04/27	05/16/07
0.180	07/26	08/08	08/10	08/22/07
0.180	10/16	11/14	11/16	11/28/07

Dividends have been paid since 1992. Source: Company reports.

Linear Technology Corp

STANDARD
&POOR'S

Business Summary October 19, 2007

CORPORATE OVERVIEW. Linear Technology Corp. (LLTC) designs, makes and markets a broad line of high-performance standard linear integrated circuits (ICs) that address a wide range of real-world signal processing applications. Its principal product lines include operational and high-speed amplifiers, voltage regulators, voltage references, data converters, interface circuits, and other linear circuits, including buffers, battery monitors, comparators, drivers and filters. LLTC's products are used in a wide variety of applications, including wireless and wireline telecommunications, networking, satellite systems, notebook and desk-top PCs, computer peripherals, video/multimedia, industrial instrumentation, medical devices, and high-end consumer products such as digital cameras and MP3 players. The company has consistently expanded its customer base throughout its history. LLTC initially served primarily an indus-

trial customer base, with a high percentage of revenues from the military market. Since the late 1980s, new products led to growth in the PC and hand-held device markets, and communication and networking markets contributed to growth significantly in recent years. The company now sells its products to more than 15,000 original equipment manufacturers directly or through a sales distributor channel. Its largest customer in FY 06 (Jun.) was the distributor Arrow Electronics, which accounted for 14% of total revenue. No other single company comprised over 10% of sales.

Company Financials Fiscal Year Ended Jun. 30

Per Share Data ($)	2007	2006	2005	2004	2003	2002	2001	2000	1999	1998
Tangible Book Value	NM	6.94	6.55	5.87	5.80	5.63	5.59	4.20	2.95	2.46
Cash Flow	1.56	1.53	1.53	1.17	0.88	0.74	1.39	0.95	0.68	0.63
Earnings	1.39	1.37	1.38	1.02	0.74	0.60	1.29	0.88	0.61	0.57
S&P Core Earnings	1.39	1.37	0.99	0.79	0.50	0.40	1.10	NA	NA	NA
Dividends	0.66	0.50	0.36	0.28	0.21	0.17	0.13	0.08	0.08	0.06
Payout Ratio	47%	36%	26%	27%	28%	28%	10%	9%	12%	11%
Prices:High	38.84	39.35	41.67	45.09	44.80	47.50	65.13	74.75	41.59	22.63
Prices:Low	29.72	27.80	32.83	34.01	24.76	18.92	29.45	35.06	20.88	9.78
P/E Ratio:High	28	29	30	44	61	79	50	85	68	40
P/E Ratio:Low	21	20	24	33	33	32	23	40	34	17

Income Statement Analysis (Million $)

	2007	2006	2005	2004	2003	2002	2001	2000	1999	1998
Revenue	1,083	1,093	1,050	807	607	512	973	706	507	485
Operating Income	575	613	638	485	340	271	582	399	280	268
Depreciation	50.7	49.3	48.8	48.7	45.9	46.3	35.8	25.0	22.0	20.1
Interest Expense	12.1	Nil	Nil	Nil	Nil	Nil	Nil	Nil	Nil	Nil
Pretax Income	570	617	620	462	333	278	611	417	286	271
Effective Tax Rate	27.8%	30.5%	30.0%	29.0%	29.0%	29.0%	30.0%	31.0%	32.0%	33.3%
Net Income	412	429	434	328	237	198	427	288	194	181
S&P Core Earnings	412	429	311	253	161	132	366	NA	NA	NA

Balance Sheet & Other Financial Data (Million $)

	2007	2006	2005	2004	2003	2002	2001	2000	1999	1998
Cash	156	541	323	204	136	212	321	230	787	638
Current Assets	861	2,077	2,007	1,832	1,776	1,728	1,728	1,310	905	768
Total Assets	1,219	2,391	2,286	2,088	2,057	1,988	2,017	1,507	1,047	893
Current Liabilities	180	237	208	203	162	169	202	169	125	123
Long Term Debt	1,700	Nil	Nil	Nil	Nil	Nil	Nil	Nil	Nil	Nil
Common Equity	-708	2,104	2,007	1,811	1,815	1,781	1,782	1,322	907	756
Total Capital	1,005	2,104	2,007	1,811	1,815	1,819	1,815	1,339	922	770
Capital Expenditures	62.0	69.4	62.1	20.7	6.61	17.9	128	80.3	39.1	24.4
Cash Flow	462	478	483	377	282	244	463	313	216	201
Current Ratio	4.8	8.8	9.7	9.0	11.0	10.2	8.5	7.8	7.2	6.2
% Long Term Debt of Capitalization	169.2	Nil	Nil	Nil	Nil	Nil	Nil	Nil	Nil	Nil
% Net Income of Revenue	38.0	39.2	41.3	40.7	39.0	38.6	43.9	40.8	38.3	37.3
% Return on Assets	22.8	18.3	19.8	15.8	11.7	9.9	24.3	22.5	20.0	23.0
% Return on Equity	59.0	20.9	22.7	18.1	13.2	11.1	27.5	25.8	23.3	26.4

Data as orig reptd.; bef. results of disc opers/spec. items. Per share data adj. for stk. divs.; EPS diluted. E-Estimated. NA-Not Available. NM-Not Meaningful. NR-Not Ranked. UR-Under Review.

Office: 1630 McCarthy Boulevard, Milpitas, CA 95035-7487.
Telephone: 408-432-1900.
Website: http://www.linear.com
Exec Chrmn: R.H. Swanson, Jr.

CEO: L. Maier
COO & VP: A. McCann
Investor Contact: P. Coghlan (408-432-1900)
VP & CFO: P. Coghlan

Board Members: D. S. Lee, L. Maier, R. M. Moley, R. H. Swanson, Jr., T. S. Volpe

Founded: 1981
Domicile: Delaware
Employees: 3,837

Liz Claiborne Inc.

STANDARD &POOR'S

S&P Recommendation BUY ★★★★☆	**Price** $24.99 (as of Nov 23, 2007)	**12-Mo. Target Price** $38.00	**Investment Style** Large-Cap Blend

GICS Sector Consumer Discretionary
Sub-Industry Apparel, Accessories & Luxury Goods

Summary This company designs and markets women's and men's apparel made by independent suppliers and sold through department and specialty stores worldwide.

Key Stock Statistics (Source S&P, Vickers, company reports)

52-Wk Range	$46.84– 23.84	S&P Oper. EPS 2007**E**	1.70	Market Capitalization(B)	$2.556	Beta	0.80
Trailing 12-Month EPS	$1.33	S&P Oper. EPS 2008**E**	2.15	Yield (%)	0.90	S&P 3-Yr. Proj. EPS CAGR(%)	NM
Trailing 12-Month P/E	18.8	P/E on S&P Oper. EPS 2007**E**	14.7	Dividend Rate/Share	$0.23	S&P Credit Rating	BBB
$10K Invested 5 Yrs Ago	$8,047	Common Shares Outstg. (M)	102.3	Institutional Ownership (%)	NM		

Price Performance

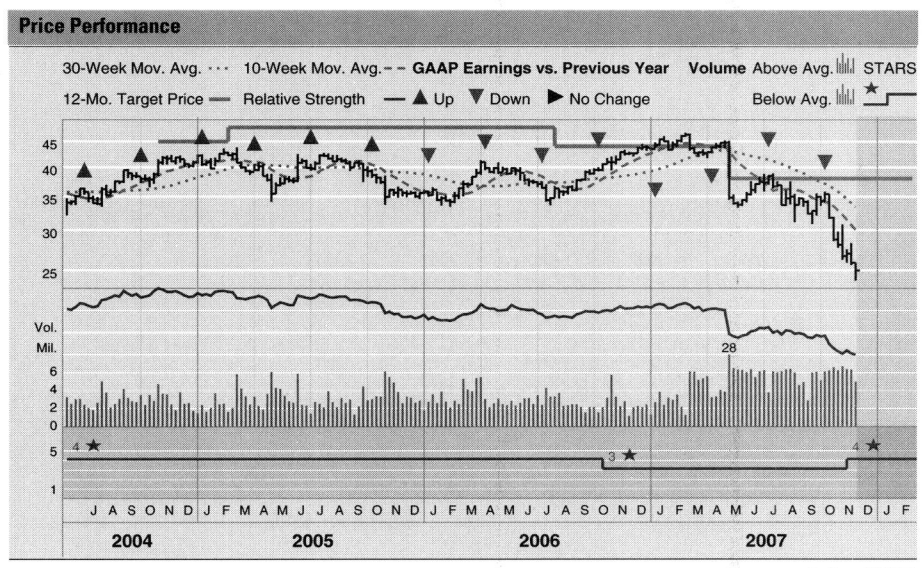

30-Week Mov. Avg. · · · 10-Week Mov. Avg. – – **GAAP Earnings vs. Previous Year** Volume Above Avg. STARS
12-Mo. Target Price — Relative Strength — ▲ Up ▼ Down ► No Change Below Avg. ★

Options: CBOE, P

Analysis prepared by **Marie Driscoll, CFA** on November 13, 2007, when the stock traded at **$ 27.80.**

Highlights

➤ CEO McComb put his stamp on LIZ by dividing the organization into Direct Brands and Partnered Brands this June. In the former reside LIZ's future: Juicy Couture, Lucky Brand, Kate Spade and Mexx in multi-channel distribution emphasizing specialty retail. Partnered Brands has about 16 brands (representing an estimated $800 million of unprofitable sales) under strategic review, with the remaining $2 billion (Liz Claiborne, DKNY Jeans, Monet, and cosmetics) operated to stabilize and reduce costs, and improve margins under the mantra of 'faster fashion.'

➤ We see 2007 and 2008 as transitional years, with Direct Brands achieving mid-teens sales gains, offset by double-digit sales declines in Partnered Brands. We see sales declining at a low single-digit pace in 2007 and 2008, excluding acquisitions and divestitures.

➤ We estimate a 7% operating margin in 2007 (vs. 8.7% in 2006), with modest improvement in 2008 reflecting $150 million of cost savings from a 7%-9% staff reduction, consolidation of the Partnered Brands structure, and rationalization of the supply chain.

Investment Rationale/Risk

➤ Despite the challenging retail environment of weak mall traffic and soft consumer spending trends, we see opportunity for LIZ's portfolio of Direct Brands in 2008-2010 and are encouraged by progress thus far on cost reductions ($130 million via staff reductions, two distribution centers closed, real estate rationalization and restructuring) and the strategic brand review process (sold four brands with nine brands in second round of management reviews). We concur with the radical decision to prune the portfolio and concentrate on the most meaningful growth opportunities.

➤ Risks to our recommendation and target price include execution risk in LIZ's strategic plan of accelerating specialty retail growth and de-emphasizing Partnered Brands, changes in consumer sentiment and spending trends, continued access to sourcing, as well as fashion and inventory risk.

➤ Our 12-month target price of $38 represents 17.7X our 2008 EPS estimate of $2.15, at the high end of LIZ's five-year average forward P/E multiple range of 9X-21X. We see the growing Direct Brands business providing for multiple expansion over the longer term.

Qualitative Risk Assessment

LOW	MEDIUM	HIGH

Our risk assessment reflects our view of LIZ's exposure to department store consolidation, offset by its broad diversification and strong cash flows.

Quantitative Evaluations

S&P Quality Ranking A

D	C	B-	B	B+	A-	A	A+

Relative Strength Rank WEAK

18

LOWEST = 1   HIGHEST = 99

Revenue/Earnings Data

Revenue (Million $)

	1Q	2Q	3Q	4Q	Year
2007	1,153	1,131	1,263	--	--
2006	1,171	1,125	1,370	1,329	4,994
2005	1,212	1,099	1,337	1,200	4,848
2004	1,103	1,026	1,307	1,198	4,633
2003	1,076	959.4	1,174	1,032	4,241
2002	892.9	789.5	1,041	993.9	3,718

Earnings Per Share ($)

2007	0.16	0.13	0.33	E0.60	E1.70
2006	0.45	0.38	0.93	0.71	2.46
2005	0.65	0.50	1.06	0.74	2.94
2004	0.62	0.46	1.03	0.75	2.85
2003	0.59	0.41	0.89	0.66	2.55
2002	0.48	0.36	0.78	0.54	2.16

Fiscal year ended Dec. 31. Next earnings report expected: Late February. EPS Estimates based on S&P Operating Earnings; historical GAAP earnings are as reported.

Dividend Data (Dates: mm/dd Payment Date: mm/dd/yy)

Amount ($)	Date Decl.	Ex-Div. Date	Stk. of Record	Payment Date
0.056	01/31	02/21	02/23	03/15/07
0.056	05/18	05/30	06/01	06/15/07
0.056	06/19	08/22	08/24	09/17/07
0.056	10/04	11/19	11/21	12/17/07

Dividends have been paid since 1984. Source: Company reports.

Liz Claiborne Inc.

STANDARD &POOR'S

Business Summary November 13, 2007

CORPORATE OVERVIEW. Liz Claiborne is one of the largest U.S. apparel suppliers, with a portfolio of more than 40 apparel and accessory brands.

MARKET PROFILE. The women's apparel market represented 54% of 2006 domestic apparel retail purchases, or $102 billion, according to NPD Fashionworld consumer estimated data. The apparel market is fragmented, with national brands marketed by 20 companies accounting for about 30% of total apparel sales, and the remaining 70% comprised of smaller and/or private label "store" brands. The market is mature, with demand largely mirroring population growth and fashion trends accounting for a modicum of incremental volume. Deflationary pricing pressure is a function of channel competition and production steadily moving offshore to low-cost producers in India, Asia and China. S&P forecasts 2007 apparel sales increasing in the low single digits, generally in line with GDP growth, versus a 5% year-to-year advance in 2006 and a 4% gain in both 2004 and 2005.

COMPETITIVE LANDSCAPE. By channel, specialty stores account for the

largest share of apparel sales, at 31% in 2006, up from 30% in 2005, according to NPD. Mass merchants (Wal-Mart and Target) came in second at 20%, up 100 basis points, and department stores came in third at 16%, losing 100 basis points of market share. National chains (Sears and JC Penney) captured 15% of 2006 apparel sales and off-price retailers (TJX and Ross Stores) 8%. The remaining 10% is divided among factory outlets and direct and email pure plays. LIZ holds meaningful market shares in department stores and national chains, where it competes with Jones Apparel Group, Polo Ralph Lauren and VF Corp., as well as private label offerings, which garner about a third of total apparel purchases and are an important differentiator for retailers. LIZ also sells directly to consumers through 399 specialty retail stores and 336 outlet stores throughout the world as well as 625 international concession stores.

Company Financials Fiscal Year Ended Dec. 31

Per Share Data ($)	2006	2005	2004	2003	2002	2001	2000	1999	1998	1997
Tangible Book Value	6.86	7.74	7.13	6.73	5.43	5.71	5.45	5.95	7.67	6.97
Cash Flow	3.82	4.12	3.95	3.51	3.06	2.79	2.43	2.11	1.71	1.64
Earnings	2.46	2.94	2.85	2.55	2.16	1.83	1.72	1.56	1.29	1.32
S&P Core Earnings	2.44	2.88	2.60	2.39	2.00	1.68	NA	NA	NA	NA
Dividends	0.23	0.23	0.23	0.23	0.23	0.23	0.23	0.23	0.23	0.23
Payout Ratio	9%	8%	8%	9%	10%	12%	13%	14%	18%	17%
Prices:High	44.50	43.82	42.47	38.90	33.25	27.48	24.16	20.34	27.44	28.97
Prices:Low	33.40	33.70	32.09	26.23	23.55	18.00	15.47	15.44	12.50	19.06
P/E Ratio:High	18	15	15	15	15	15	14	13	21	22
P/E Ratio:Low	14	11	11	10	11	10	9	10	10	14

Income Statement Analysis (Million $)	2006	2005	2004	2003	2002	2001	2000	1999	1998	1997
Revenue	4,994	4,848	4,633	4,241	3,718	3,449	3,104	2,807	2,535	2,413
Operating Income	576	652	628	575	493	780	402	368	340	323
Depreciation	140	128	116	105	96.4	101	77.0	67.8	55.8	46.0
Interest Expense	Nil	31.8	32.2	30.5	25.1	28.1	21.9	1.61	Nil	Nil
Pretax Income	407	491	480	438	362	300	288	302	267	293
Effective Tax Rate	37.4%	35.4%	34.7%	36.2%	36.2%	36.0%	36.0%	36.2%	36.5%	37.0%
Net Income	255	317	314	280	231	192	185	192	169	185
S&P Core Earnings	252	309	284	259	213	176	NA	NA	NA	NA

Balance Sheet & Other Financial Data (Million $)	2006	2005	2004	2003	2002	2001	2000	1999	1998	1997
Cash	195	343	393	344	276	161	54.4	37.9	230	138
Current Assets	1,470	1,457	1,509	1,348	1,203	1,106	911	859	1,075	1,057
Total Assets	3,496	3,152	3,030	2,607	2,296	1,951	1,512	1,412	1,393	1,305
Current Liabilities	674	608	638	527	591	447	358	352	363	328
Long Term Debt	570	418	485	440	378	387	269	116	Nil	Nil
Common Equity	2,130	2,003	1,812	1,600	1,286	1,056	834	902	981	922
Total Capital	2,758	2,478	2,359	2,094	1,705	1,480	1,139	1,044	999	932
Capital Expenditures	169	140	134	96.7	80.0	82.2	66.7	75.1	88.5	34.0
Cash Flow	395	445	429	385	328	294	262	260	225	231
Current Ratio	2.2	2.4	2.4	2.6	2.0	2.5	2.5	2.4	3.0	3.2
% Long Term Debt of Capitalization	20.7	16.9	20.6	21.0	22.2	26.1	23.6	11.1	Nil	Nil
% Net Income of Revenue	5.1	6.5	6.8	6.6	6.2	5.6	5.9	6.9	6.7	7.7
% Return on Assets	7.7	10.3	11.1	11.5	10.9	11.1	12.6	13.7	12.6	13.7
% Return on Equity	12.3	16.5	18.4	19.3	19.7	20.3	21.3	20.4	17.8	19.0

Data as orig reptd.; bef. results of disc opers/spec. items. Per share data adj. for stk. divs.; EPS diluted. E-Estimated. NA-Not Available. NM-Not Meaningful. NR-Not Ranked. UR-Under Review.

Office: 1441 Broadway, New York, NY 10018.
Telephone: 212-354-4900.
Email: investor_relations@liz.com
Website: http://www.lizclaiborne.com

Chrmn: K. Koplovitz
Pres: T.F. Sullivan
CEO: W.L. McComb
COO & CFO: M. Scarpa

SVP & CIO: J.J. Sullivan
Board Members: B. W. Aronson, D. A. Carp, R. J. Fernandez, M. Haben, N. J. Karch, K. P. Kopelman, K. Koplovitz, A. C. Martinez, W. L. McComb, O. R. Sockwell, P. E. Tierney, Jr.

Founded: 1976
Domicile: Delaware
Employees: 17,000

The **McGraw-Hill** Companies

Lockheed Martin Corp

**STANDARD
&POOR'S**

S&P Recommendation **BUY** ★★★★☆	Price $111.01 (as of Nov 23, 2007)	12-Mo. Target Price $120.00	Investment Style Large-Cap Growth

GICS Sector Industrials
Sub-Industry Aerospace & Defense

Summary This company is the world's largest military weapons manufacturer and is also a significant supplier to NASA and other government agencies.

Key Stock Statistics (Source S&P, Vickers, company reports)

52-Wk Range	$113.74–87.64	S&P Oper. EPS 2007E	6.85	Market Capitalization(B)	$45.886	Beta	-0.06
Trailing 12-Month EPS	$6.89	S&P Oper. EPS 2008E	7.20	Yield (%)	1.51	S&P 3-Yr. Proj. EPS CAGR(%)	11.00
Trailing 12-Month P/E	16.1	P/E on S&P Oper. EPS 2007E	16.2	Dividend Rate/Share	$1.68	S&P Credit Rating	A-
$10K Invested 5 Yrs Ago	$23,081	Common Shares Outstg. (M)	413.4	Institutional Ownership (%)	90		

Price Performance

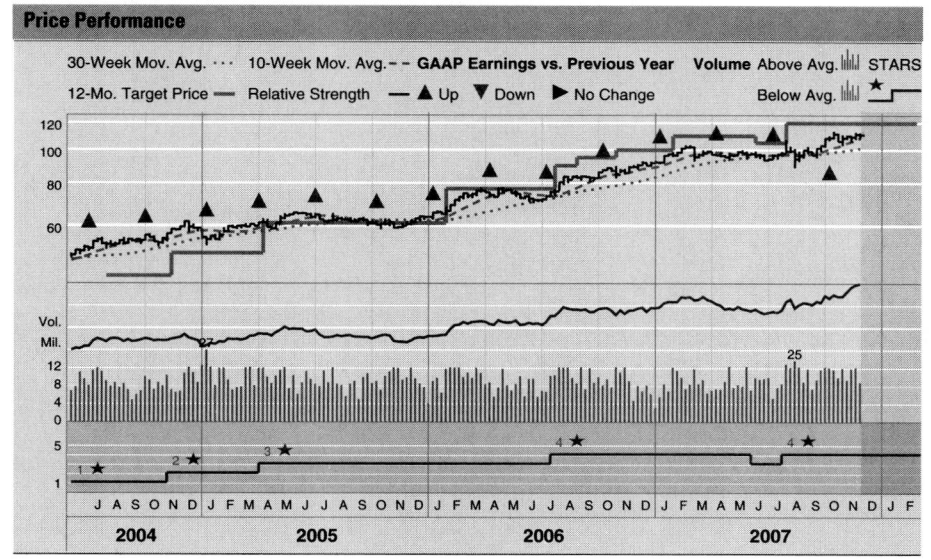

30-Week Mov. Avg. · · · 10-Week Mov. Avg. - - GAAP Earnings vs. Previous Year Volume Above Avg. STARS
12-Mo. Target Price — Relative Strength — ▲ Up ▼ Down ► No Change Below Avg. ★

Options: ASE, CBOE, P, Ph

Analysis prepared by **Richard Tortoriello** on October 26, 2007, when the stock traded at **$ 108.61**.

Highlights

➤ We project a 5.4% sales increase in 2007 slowing to a 2% rise in 2008, as we see growth in LMT's Information Systems & Global Services and Electronic Systems segments being offset by declines in Aeronautics and Space Systems. The anticipated decline in Space Systems revenues is due to the formation of the United Launch Alliance, a joint venture with Boeing, which was initiated at the end of 2006. We expect Aeronautics to be weak in the short term but to show strong growth in future years, with LMT expecting strong revenues from the F-22, F-35, and C-130J programs beginning in 2009.

➤ We expect operating margins to widen to 10.9% in 2007, from 10.0% in 2006 and 8% in 2005, with improvement in each of LMT's four operating segments. Margin improvement has been a big part of LMT's growth story in recent years, in our view, allowing for significantly better profitability and free cash flow. We expect margin improvement to continue in 2008.

➤ We project EPS growth of 18% in 2007, to $6.85, and 5.1% in 2008, to $7.20. We expect free cash flow per share of near $8.00 in 2007. We note that our 2008 estimate includes $0.21 of net gains taken in the first quarter of 2007.

Investment Rationale/Risk

➤ We see significant long-term opportunities for Lockheed in Aeronautics, given both the average age of the U.S. Air Force fleet of about 25 years and the need for next-generation fighter planes. We believe the F-35 Lightning II and the F-22 Raptor hold strong long-term promise for LMT. We also have a positive view of LMT's efforts to pursue more non-defense opportunities with the government, and see recent overall contract wins as a sign that LMT continues to execute well across its businesses.

➤ Risks to our recommendation and target price include the potential for decreases in defense spending, as recommended by the president or as enacted by Congress; time or cost overruns on major projects; and the failure to secure significant new contracted business.

➤ Our 12-month target price of $120 is based on a P/E of 16.7X our 2008 EPS estimate. This is below a 10-year average historical forward P/E of 17.7X for LMT, with highs near 29X and lows of 9X. Given our projection of a slowing in earnings growth in 2007 and 2008 for LMT, we believe a slightly lower than historical average multiple for LMT is warranted.

Qualitative Risk Assessment

LOW	MEDIUM	HIGH

Our risk assessment reflects the company's leading position in military markets and what we view as a healthy balance sheet, with long-term debt representing about 35% of LMT's total capitalization as of March 2007. However, our risk evaluation also factors in the cyclical nature of Lockheed's business, especially its dependence on government defense programs.

Quantitative Evaluations

S&P Quality Ranking B

D	C	B-	B	B+	A-	A	A+

Relative Strength Rank STRONG
89
LOWEST = 1   HIGHEST = 99

Revenue/Earnings Data

Revenue (Million $)

	1Q	2Q	3Q	4Q	Year
2007	9,275	10,651	11,095	--	--
2006	9,214	9,961	9,605	10,840	39,620
2005	8,488	9,295	9,201	10,229	37,213
2004	8,347	8,776	8,438	9,965	35,526
2003	7,059	7,709	8,078	8,978	31,824
2002	5,966	6,290	6,542	7,780	26,578

Earnings Per Share ($)

2007	1.60	1.82	1.80	E1.63	E6.85
2006	1.34	1.34	1.46	1.68	5.80
2005	0.83	1.02	0.96	1.29	4.10
2004	0.65	0.66	0.69	0.83	2.83
2003	0.55	0.54	0.48	0.77	2.34
2002	0.50	0.78	0.66	-0.76	1.18

Fiscal year ended Dec. 31. Next earnings report expected: Late January. EPS Estimates based on S&P Operating Earnings; historical GAAP earnings are as reported.

Dividend Data (Dates: mm/dd Payment Date: mm/dd/yy)

Amount ($)	Date Decl.	Ex-Div. Date	Stk. of Record	Payment Date
0.350	01/25	02/27	03/01	03/30/07
0.350	04/26	05/30	06/01	06/22/07
0.350	06/28	08/30	09/04	09/28/07
0.420	09/27	11/29	12/03	12/28/07

Dividends have been paid since 1995. Source: Company reports.

Please read the Required Disclosures and Analyst Certification on the last page of this report.

The **McGraw·Hill** Companies

Lockheed Martin Corp

STANDARD &POOR'S

Business Summary October 26, 2007

CORPORATE OVERVIEW. Lockheed Martin is the world's largest military weapons maker. During 2006, the company derived 84% of its net sales from the U.S. government, including both Department of Defense and non-Department of Defense agencies. Sales to foreign governments were 13% of net sales, with 3% of net sales to commercial and other customers. Lockheed Martin conducts business through four operating segments:

The Aeronautics segment (31% of revenues and 30% of operating profits in 2006) primarily makes fighter jets and military transport planes. Major development and production programs include the F-35 Lightning II, the F-22 Raptor, the F-16 Fighting Falcon, and the CJ-130 Super Hercules transport.

Electronic Systems (26% and 32%) primarily makes land-, sea- and air-based missiles and missile defense systems. Other offerings include various electronic surveillance and reconnaissance systems. Major current programs include the Terminal High-Altitude Area Defense System (THAAD), the Patriot Advanced Capability (PAC-3) missile, the VH-71 Presidential Helicopter, the AEGIS weapon system, and the Arrowhead fire control system for the Apache helicopter. The segment has over 1,000 programs.

Space Systems (20% and 18%) mostly makes satellites, strategic and defensive missile systems and space transportation systems. Satellites include both government and commercial products. Space transportation systems include NASA's next-generation space flight systems, including the Orion crew exploration vehicle and the Ares I launch system, and the Ares V launch system for the Space Shuttle. LMT is the prime contractor for the Space-Based Infrared System (SBIRS) missile detection program and the Advanced Extremely High Frequency (AEHF) communications system. LMT is the sole supplier of strategic fleet ballistic missiles to the U.S. Navy.

Information Systems & Global Services (23% and 20%) is engaged in a wide variety of information technology, IT services, and other technology services to federal agencies and other customers. Major product lines include: IT integration and management; enterprise solutions; application development and maintenance; business processing management; consulting on strategic programs for the Department of Defense and other civil government agencies; mission operations and engineering for the military, homeland security, and NASA; mission readiness, peacekeeping, and nation-building programs; and support of nuclear weapons stewardship and naval reactor programs.

Company Financials Fiscal Year Ended Dec. 31

Per Share Data ($)	2006	2005	2004	2003	2002	2001	2000	1999	1998	1997
Tangible Book Value	NM	NM	NM	NM	NM	NM	NM	NM	NM	NM
Cash Flow	7.55	5.68	4.39	3.69	2.40	2.08	1.36	3.30	5.27	5.37
Earnings	5.80	4.10	2.83	2.34	1.18	0.18	-1.05	1.92	2.63	3.05
S&P Core Earnings	5.70	4.11	3.23	2.20	-0.78	-2.29	NA	NA	NA	NA
Dividends	1.25	1.05	0.91	0.58	0.44	0.44	0.44	0.88	0.82	0.80
Payout Ratio	22%	26%	32%	25%	37%	NM	NM	46%	31%	26%
Prices:High	93.24	65.46	61.77	58.95	71.52	52.98	37.58	46.00	58.94	56.72
Prices:Low	62.52	52.54	43.10	40.64	45.85	31.00	16.50	16.38	41.00	39.13
P/E Ratio:High	16	16	22	25	61	NM	NM	24	22	19
P/E Ratio:Low	11	13	15	17	39	NM	NM	9	16	13

Income Statement Analysis (Million $)

	2006	2005	2004	2003	2002	2001	2000	1999	1998	1997
Revenue	39,620	37,213	35,526	31,824	26,578	23,990	25,329	25,530	26,266	28,069
Operating Income	4,198	3,242	2,624	2,585	2,507	2,366	2,582	2,634	3,357	3,349
Depreciation	764	705	656	609	558	823	968	969	1,005	1,052
Interest Expense	361	370	425	487	581	700	919	809	861	842
Pretax Income	3,592	2,616	1,664	1,532	577	188	286	1,200	1,661	1,937
Effective Tax Rate	29.6%	30.2%	23.9%	31.3%	7.63%	58.0%	NM	38.6%	39.7%	32.9%
Net Income	2,529	1,825	1,266	1,053	533	79.0	-424	737	1,001	1,300
S&P Core Earnings	2,486	1,830	1,448	994	-353	-989	NA	NA	NA	NA

Balance Sheet & Other Financial Data (Million $)

	2006	2005	2004	2003	2002	2001	2000	1999	1998	1997
Cash	1,912	2,244	1,060	1,010	2,738	912	1,505	455	285	Nil
Current Assets	10,164	10,529	8,953	9,401	10,626	10,778	11,259	10,696	10,611	10,105
Total Assets	28,231	27,744	25,554	26,175	25,758	27,654	30,349	30,012	28,744	28,361
Current Liabilities	9,553	9,428	8,566	8,893	9,821	9,689	10,175	8,812	10,267	9,189
Long Term Debt	4,405	4,784	5,104	6,072	6,217	7,422	9,065	11,427	8,957	10,528
Common Equity	6,884	7,867	7,021	6,756	5,865	6,443	7,160	6,361	6,137	5,176
Total Capital	11,289	12,651	12,125	12,828	12,082	14,857	16,961	17,788	15,094	15,704
Capital Expenditures	893	865	769	687	662	619	500	669	697	750
Cash Flow	3,293	2,530	1,922	1,662	1,091	902	544	1,266	2,006	2,299
Current Ratio	1.1	1.1	1.0	1.1	1.1	1.1	1.1	1.2	1.0	1.1
% Long Term Debt of Capitalization	39.0	37.8	42.1	47.3	51.5	50.0	53.4	64.2	59.3	67.0
% Net Income of Revenue	6.4	4.9	3.6	3.3	2.0	0.3	NM	2.9	3.8	4.6
% Return on Assets	9.0	6.8	4.9	4.0	2.0	0.3	NM	2.5	3.5	4.5
% Return on Equity	34.3	24.5	18.4	16.7	8.7	1.2	NM	11.8	17.7	22.6

Data as orig reptd.; bef. results of disc opers/spec. items. Per share data adj. for stk. divs.; EPS diluted. E-Estimated. NA-Not Available. NM-Not Meaningful. NR-Not Ranked. UR-Under Review.

Office: 6801 Rockledge Drive, Bethesda, MD 20817.
Telephone: 301-897-6000.
Website: http://www.lockheedmartin.com
Chrmn, Pres & CEO: R.J. Stevens

EVP & CFO: C.E. Kubasik
SVP & General Counsel: J.B. Comey
VP & Cntlr: M.T. Stanislav

Board Members: E. C. Aldridge, Jr., N. D. Archibald, M. C. Bennett, J. O. Ellis, Jr., G. S. King, J. M. Loy, D. H. McCorkindale, E. F. Murphy, J. W. Ralston, F. Savage, J. M. Schneider, A. Stevens, R. J. Stevens, J. R. Ukropina, D. C. Yearley

Founded: 1909
Domicile: Maryland
Employees: 140,000

The McGraw-Hill Companies

Loews Corp

STANDARD &POOR'S

S&P Recommendation BUY ★★★★☆	**Price** $45.31 (as of Nov 23, 2007)	**12-Mo. Target Price** $57.00	**Investment Style** Large-Cap Value

GICS Sector Financials
Sub-Industry Multi-line Insurance

Summary This conglomerate includes holdings in property/casualty insurance, tobacco, offshore drilling, hotels, and natural gas pipelines.

Key Stock Statistics (Source S&P, Vickers, company reports)

52-Wk Range	$53.46– 39.55	S&P Oper. EPS 2007**E**	4.12	Market Capitalization(B)	$24.270	Beta	0.72
Trailing 12-Month EPS	$4.03	S&P Oper. EPS 2008**E**	5.10	Yield (%)	0.55	S&P 3-Yr. Proj. EPS CAGR(%)	12.00
Trailing 12-Month P/E	11.2	P/E on S&P Oper. EPS 2007**E**	11.0	Dividend Rate/Share	$0.25	S&P Credit Rating	A
$10K Invested 5 Yrs Ago	$35,470	Common Shares Outstg. (M)	535.6	Institutional Ownership (%)	64		

Price Performance

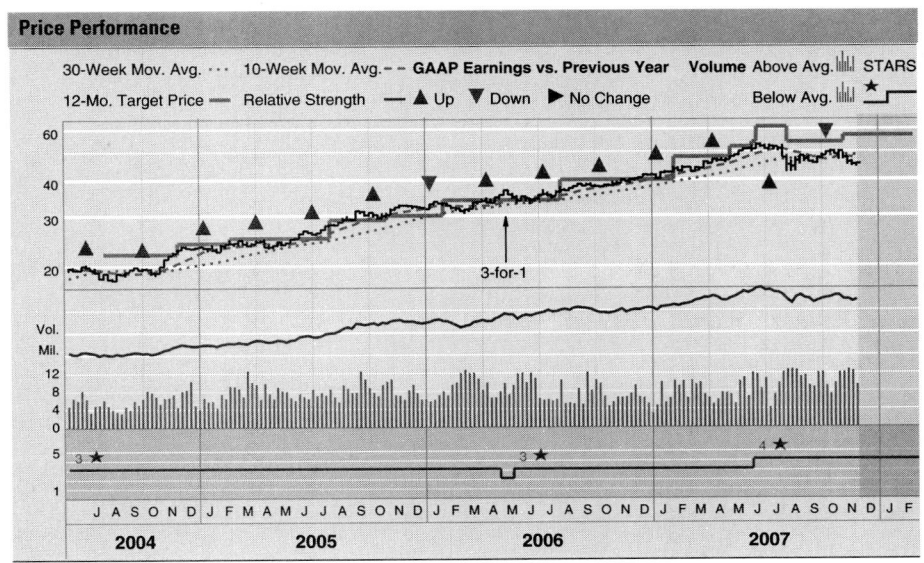

30-Week Mov. Avg. · · · 10-Week Mov. Avg. - - **GAAP Earnings vs. Previous Year** Volume Above Avg. STARS
12-Mo. Target Price — Relative Strength — ▲ Up ▼ Down ▶ No Change Below Avg.

3-for-1

2004 2005 2006 2007

Options: ASE, CBOE, P, Ph

Analysis prepared by **Tanjila Shafi** on November 15, 2007, when the stock traded at **$ 45.34**.

Highlights

➤ We expect Diamond Offshore (DO) to benefit from rising demand in deepwater floaters and midwater floaters and its ability to roll over rigs from expiring contracts at higher dayrates. We forecast solid operating earnings growth for Boardwalk Pipeline Partners (BWP), primarily based on our estimate of expanding natural gas storage capacity and improved operating efficiencies. We see operating earnings for the hotels segment benefiting from a stronger travel and leisure market, leading to higher revenue per available room (RevPAR).

➤ Despite a softening environment, we expect single-digit growth in operating earnings for the CNA Financial subsidiary in 2008, based on the company's underwriting discipline, diversified portfolio, and strong market franchise. We also anticipate the company's combined ratio to improve due to continuing expense control efforts. We see 2008 revenues at Lorillard benefiting from expected moderate growth in discount volumes and higher average pricing for premium brands.

➤ Our operating EPS forecast for 2007 is $4.12, and we see $5.10 for 2008.

Investment Rationale/Risk

➤ We believe that the demand for rigs will prove to be a boon for Diamond Offshore. In addition, we believe CNA Financial's cross-selling efforts and cost-cutting measures will increase its premium growth and operating earnings. We are encouraged by the company's capital management initiatives such as the recent share repurchases, and we expect buybacks to continue throughout the year. Furthermore, we believe the company is well positioned to make opportunistic investments, with $3.2 billion in cash and investments.

➤ Risks to our recommendation and target price include legal and regulatory risks associated with tobacco sales; extended periods of price promotions in the cigarette market; decreases in the global smoking population; higher than projected catastrophic losses; higher than expected losses in its investment portfolio; and asbestos and environmental losses for CNA.

➤ Our 12-month target price of $57 is based on our sum-of-the-parts valuation.

Qualitative Risk Assessment

LOW	MEDIUM	HIGH

Our risk assessment reflects the company's exposure to regulation risks, litigation risk, and catastrophic events. This is offset by the company's diversified group of holdings and its substantial free cash flow.

Quantitative Evaluations

S&P Quality Ranking   B

D	C	B-	B	B+	A-	A	A+

Relative Strength Rank   MODERATE

56

LOWEST = 1   HIGHEST = 99

Revenue/Earnings Data

Revenue (Million $)

	1Q	2Q	3Q	4Q	Year
2007	4,660	4,637	4,653	--	--
2006	4,245	4,277	4,507	4,882	17,911
2005	3,741	4,031	4,138	4,108	16,018
2004	3,491	3,915	3,785	4,051	15,242
2003	3,949	4,250	3,940	4,336	16,461
2002	4,792	4,652	4,079	3,972	17,495

Earnings Per Share ($)

	1Q	2Q	3Q	4Q	Year
2007	1.20	0.97	0.77	E1.19	E4.12
2006	0.86	0.85	0.93	1.15	3.80
2005	0.53	0.68	0.42	0.07	1.69
2004	0.02	0.66	0.40	0.80	1.88
2003	0.29	0.34	-2.53	0.60	-1.30
2002	0.46	0.28	0.35	0.40	1.50

Fiscal year ended Dec. 31. Next earnings report expected: Mid February. EPS Estimates based on S&P Operating Earnings; historical GAAP earnings are as reported.

Dividend Data (Dates: mm/dd Payment Date: mm/dd/yy)

Amount ($)	Date Decl.	Ex-Div. Date	Stk. of Record	Payment Date
0.063	02/13	02/27	03/01	03/12/07
0.063	05/08	05/30	06/01	06/11/07
0.063	08/14	08/30	09/04	09/13/07
0.063	11/13	11/29	12/03	12/14/07

Dividends have been paid since 1967. Source: Company reports.

Please read the Required Disclosures and Analyst Certification on the last page of this report.

The **McGraw-Hill** Companies

Loews Corp

STANDARD &POOR'S

Business Summary November 15, 2007

CORPORATE OVERVIEW. Loews Corp. is a holding company with interests in property/casualty insurance (CNA Financial Corp., 89% stake), cigarettes (Lorillard Inc.), hotels (Loews Hotels Holding Corp.), offshore oil and gas drilling (Diamond Offshore Drilling, Inc., 51% stake), interstate natural gas pipelines (Boardwalk Pipeline Partners, LP, 75% stake), and watches and clocks (Bulova Corp.).

Loews Corp. maintains a two class common stock structure. Carolina Group stock (NYSE: CG) is a tracking stock intended to reflect the economic performance of a defined group of assets and liabilities referred to as the Carolina Group, which includes Loews' equity interest in Lorillard Inc., $1.2 billion of notional intergroup debt owed by Carolina Group to the Loews Group, and any and all liabilities, costs and expenses arising out of or related to tobacco-related businesses. The Loews Group consists of all of the company's assets and liabilities other than the economic interest in the Carolina Group represented by the Carolina Group tracking stock and includes as an asset the notional intergroup debt of the Carolina Group. The Carolina Group and Loews Group are not separate legal entities, and holders of LTR's common stock and Carolina Group stock are both shareholders of Loews Corp. and are subject to the risks

related to an equity investment in Loews Corp. At December 31, 2006, CG tracking stock represented a 62.34% economic interest in the Carolina Group.

CNA Financial Corp. (NYSE: CNA; 58% of consolidated total revenue in 2006) is an insurance holding company with subsidiaries that primarily consist of property and casualty insurance companies. Lorillard, Inc. (22%) is a leading U.S. producer of tobacco products, with principal products marketed under the brand names Newport, Kent, True, Maverick, and Old Gold. The Loews Hotels division (2.1%) owns and/or operates 18 hotels in the U.S. and Canada. Diamond Offshore (NYSE: DO; 12%) operates 44 offshore drilling rigs that are chartered on a contract basis for fixed terms by energy exploration companies. Boardwalk Pipeline (NYSE: BWP; 3.5%) owns and operates two interstate natural gas pipeline systems, Gulf South Pipeline and Texas Gas Transmission. Bulova (1.2%) distributes and sells watches and clocks. Other activities accounted for about 1.2% of consolidated total revenue in 2006.

Company Financials Fiscal Year Ended Dec. 31

Per Share Data ($)	2006	2005	2004	2003	2002	2001	2000	1999	1998	1997
Tangible Book Value	NM	NM	21.35	NM	19.88	16.23	18.28	15.24	14.24	12.92
Operating Earnings	NA	NA	NA	NA	1.71	-2.27	1.90	1.01	0.66	1.38
Earnings	3.80	1.69	1.88	-1.30	1.50	-0.92	3.15	0.80	0.68	1.15
S&P Core Earnings	3.65	1.49	2.17	-2.00	2.63	-2.47	NA	NA	NA	NA
Dividends	0.18	0.20	0.20	0.20	0.20	0.19	0.17	0.17	0.17	0.17
Relative Payout	5%	12%	11%	NM	13%	NM	5%	21%	25%	14%
Prices:High	42.18	32.90	23.67	16.49	20.77	24.17	34.98	17.42	18.04	19.27
Prices:Low	30.42	22.35	16.36	12.75	12.50	13.68	12.75	9.75	13.00	14.25
P/E Ratio:High	11	19	13	NM	14	NM	11	22	27	17
P/E Ratio:Low	8	13	9	NM	8	NM	4	12	19	12

Income Statement Analysis (Million $)										
Life Insurance in Force	15,652	20,548	56,645	388,968	437,751	497,732	534,781	469,990	394,394	311,598
Premium Income:Life A & H	641	704	901	2,275	3,382	4,351	4,549	4,502	4,391	3,431
Premium Income:Casualty/Property.	6,962	6,865	7,304	6,935	6,828	5,010	6,923	8,775	8,979	NA
Net Investment Income	2,915	2,099	1,869	1,732	1,867	2,145	2,388	2,175	2,558	2,442
Total Revenue	3,866	3,640	15,242	16,461	17,495	19,417	21,338	21,465	21,208	20,139
Pretax Income	1,237	1,016	1,822	-751	1,647	-813	3,206	945	1,078	1,593
Net Operating Income	NA	NA	NA	NA	1,099	-1,328	1,134	658	452	954
Net Income	760	623	1,231	-468	983	-536	1,877	521	465	794
S&P Core Earnings	2,024	831	1,205	-1,112	1,594	-1,447	NA	NA	NA	NA

Balance Sheet & Other Financial Data (Million $)										
Cash & Equivalent	132	151	220	181	185	181	195	184	287	498
Premiums Due	12,423	15,314	18,807	20,468	16,601	19,453	15,302	13,529	13,071	NA
Investment Assets:Bonds	37,570	33,381	33,502	28,781	27,434	31,191	27,244	27,924	31,409	30,723
Investment Assets:Stocks	1,309	1,107	664	888	1,121	1,646	2,683	4,024	2,381	1,163
Investment Assets:Loans	Nil	Nil	Nil	Nil	NA	NA	NA	NA	NA	NA
Investment Assets:Total	52,020	43,547	44,299	42,515	40,137	41,159	40,396	40,633	42,705	41,618
Deferred Policy Costs	1,190	1,197	1,268	2,533	2,551	2,424	2,418	2,436	2,422	2,142
Total Assets	75,325	69,548	73,750	77,881	70,520	75,251	70,877	69,464	70,906	69,577
Debt	1,230	1,627	5,980	2,032	5,652	5,920	6,040	5,706	5,967	5,906
Common Equity	0.16	-201	45,428	-729	11,235	9,649	11,191	9,978	10,200	9,664
Combined Loss-Expense Ratio	109.1	120.3	105.9	146.6	110.3	158.6	113.6	120.9	114.2	108.2
% Return on Revenue	19.7	17.1	8.1	14.2	5.6	NM	8.8	2.4	2.2	4.5
% Return on Equity	14.2	2.6	2.8	NM	8.1	NM	4.9	5.2	4.7	8.6
% Investment Yield	6.1	2.6	4.3	4.2	4.6	5.2	5.9	5.2	6.1	5.9

Data as orig reptd.; bef. results of disc opers/spec. items. Per share data adj. for stk. divs.; EPS diluted. E-Estimated. NA-Not Available. NM-Not Meaningful. NR-Not Ranked. UR-Under Review.

Office: 667 Madison Ave , New York, NY 10021-8087.
Telephone: 212-521-2000.
Website: http://www.loews.com
Co-Chrmn: A.H. Tisch

Co-Chrmn: J.M. Tisch
Pres & CEO: J.S. Tisch
SVP & CFO: P.W. Keegan
SVP, Secy & General Counsel: G.W. Garson

Investor Contact: D. Daugherty (212-521-2788)
Board Members: A. E. Berman, J. L. Bower, C. M. Diker, P. J. Fribourg, W. L. Harris, P. A. Laskawy, G. R. Scott, A. H. Tisch, J. S. Tisch, J. M. Tisch

Founded: 1954
Domicile: Delaware
Employees: 21,600

Lowe's Companies Inc.

STANDARD &POOR'S

S&P Recommendation BUY ★★★★☆	**Price** $23.47 (as of Nov 28, 2007)	**12-Mo. Target Price** $32.00	**Investment Style** Large-Cap Growth

GICS Sector Consumer Discretionary
Sub-Industry Home Improvement Retail

Summary This company retails building materials and supplies, lumber, hardware and appliances through about 1,400 stores in 49 states.

Key Stock Statistics (Source S&P, Vickers, company reports)

52-Wk Range	$35.74– 21.76	S&P Oper. EPS 2008**E**	1.87	Market Capitalization(B)	$34.703	Beta	1.07
Trailing 12-Month EPS	$1.98	S&P Oper. EPS 2009**E**	1.94	Yield (%)	1.36	S&P 3-Yr. Proj. EPS CAGR(%)	12.00
Trailing 12-Month P/E	11.9	P/E on S&P Oper. EPS 2008**E**	12.6	Dividend Rate/Share	$0.32	S&P Credit Rating	A+
$10K Invested 5 Yrs Ago	$11,707	Common Shares Outstg. (M)	1,478.6	Institutional Ownership (%)	82		

Price Performance

30-Week Mov. Avg. · · · 10-Week Mov. Avg. - - **GAAP Earnings vs. Previous Year**   Volume Above Avg. STARS
12-Mo. Target Price — Relative Strength — ▲ Up ▼ Down ► No Change   Below Avg.

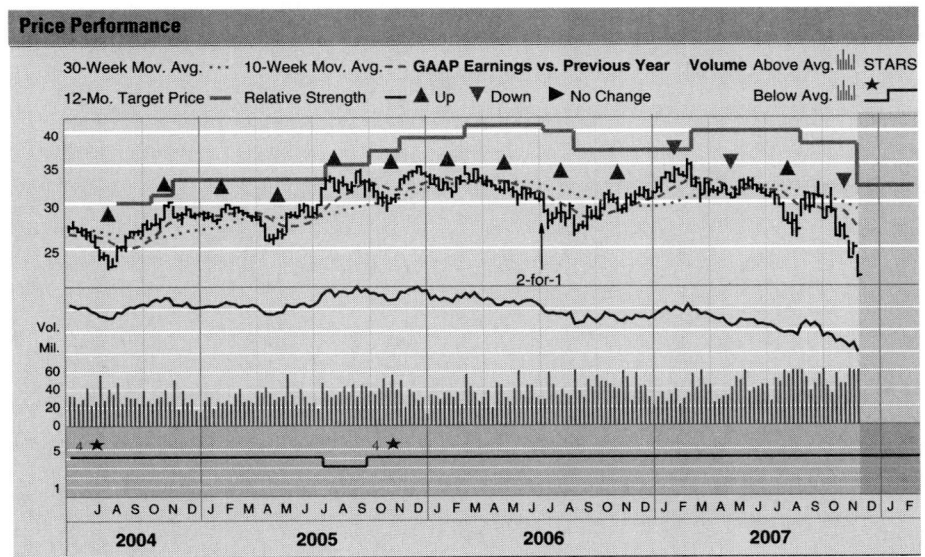

Options: ASE, CBOE, P, Ph

Analysis prepared by **Michael Souers** on November 28, 2007, when the stock traded at **$ 22.09**.

Highlights

➤ We forecast sales growth of between 6% and 7% in FY 09 (Jan.), following a projected 4% advance in FY 08. We expect this growth to be driven by an estimated 140 net store openings, reflecting an approximate 9% increase in total square footage. We look for same-store sales to decrease in the low single digits, as declines in foot traffic should more than offset expected gains in the average ticket. We expect the housing market to remain under pressure throughout 2008 and see a related slowdown in consumer spending.

➤ We project FY 09 operating margins to decline modestly, as higher occupancy costs, increasing payroll expenses and a deleveraging of expenses due to declining same-store sales results are only partially offset by lower sourcing costs and an improved product mix.

➤ We project slightly higher interest expense, taxes at an effective rate of 38.0%, and about 3% fewer shares outstanding, reflecting LOW's active share repurchase plan. Our FY 09 EPS estimate of $1.94 is a 4% increase from the $1.87 we expect LOW to earn in FY 08.

Investment Rationale/Risk

➤ We think the aging of homes, home ownership rates near historical highs, and the increased net worth of baby boomers are powerful long-term demographic drivers that should help mitigate the continued slowdown in housing turnover we see for 2007 and 2008. In addition, despite concerns about interest rates and overall consumer spending, we believe consumers will continue to allocate a fair portion of their discretionary income to home improvement projects, as they view their homes as investments.

➤ Risks to our recommendation and target price include a sharp slowdown in the economy; a large rise in long-term interest rates; and the failure to execute LOW's metro market expansion strategy.

➤ At about 11X our FY 09 EPS estimate, LOW's shares recently traded in line with key peer Home Depot (HD: buy, $27), but at a significant discount to the S&P 500. Our 12-month target price of $32 is derived from our discounted cash flow (DCF) analysis, which assumes a weighted average cost of capital of 9.3% and a terminal growth rate of 3.0%.

Qualitative Risk Assessment

LOW	**MEDIUM**	HIGH

Our risk assessment reflects the cyclical nature of the home improvement retail industry, which is reliant on economic growth, offset by our view of ample opportunities for retail growth both domestically and abroad, and an S&P Quality Ranking of A+, reflecting LOW's consistent historical earnings and dividend growth.

Quantitative Evaluations

S&P Quality Ranking A+

D	C	B-	B	B+	A-	A	**A+**

Relative Strength Rank WEAK

26

LOWEST = 1   HIGHEST = 99

Revenue/Earnings Data

Revenue (Million $)

	1Q	2Q	3Q	4Q	Year
2008	12,172	14,167	11,565	--	--
2007	11,921	13,389	11,211	10,406	46,927
2006	9,913	11,929	10,592	10,808	43,243
2005	8,681	10,169	9,064	8,550	36,464
2004	7,118	8,666	7,802	7,252	30,838
2003	6,471	7,488	6,415	6,118	26,491

Earnings Per Share ($)

2008	0.48	0.67	0.43	E0.28	E1.87
2007	0.53	0.60	0.46	0.40	1.99
2006	0.37	0.52	0.41	0.44	1.73
2005	0.28	0.44	0.32	0.32	1.36
2004	0.26	0.38	0.28	0.25	1.16
2003	0.22	0.29	0.22	0.20	0.93

Fiscal year ended Jan. 31. Next earnings report expected: Late February. EPS Estimates based on S&P Operating Earnings; historical GAAP earnings are as reported.

Dividend Data (Dates: mm/dd Payment Date: mm/dd/yy)

Amount ($)	Date Decl.	Ex-Div. Date	Stk. of Record	Payment Date
0.050	03/27	04/18	04/20	05/04/07
0.080	05/25	07/18	07/20	08/03/07
0.080	08/20	10/17	10/19	11/02/07
0.080	11/19	01/16	01/18	02/01/08

Dividends have been paid since 1961. Source: Company reports.

Lowe's Companies Inc.

STANDARD &POOR'S

Business Summary November 28, 2007

CORPORATE OVERVIEW. Lowe's Companies is the world's second largest home improvement retailer. It focuses on retail do-it-yourself (DIY) customers, do-it-for-me (DIFM) customers who utilize LOW's installation services, and commercial business customers. Lowe's offers a complete line of products and services for home decorating, maintenance, repair, remodeling, and the maintenance of commercial buildings.

As of February 2, 2007, LOW operated 1,385 stores in 49 states, representing 157 million sq. ft. of selling space. The company has two prototype stores—a 117,000-square-foot store for larger markets and a 94,000-square-foot store used primarily to serve smaller markets. Both prototypes include a lawn and garden center, averaging an additional 31,000 square feet for larger stores and 26,000 square feet for smaller stores. Of the total stores operating at February 2, 2007, approximately 86% were owned, including stores on leased land, while the remaining 14% were leased from unaffiliated third parties. Typical LOW stores stock more than 40,000 items, with hundreds of thousands of

items available through the company's special order system.

CORPORATE STRATEGY. LOW is focusing much of its future expansion on metropolitan markets with populations of 500,000 or more. Lowe's expects that approximately 80% of its FY 08 expansion plans will be comprised of the 117,000 square-foot stores in larger markets, and approximately 20% of its growth will be comprised of 94,000 square-foot stores in smaller markets.

Lowe's also intends to enter the home improvement market in Canada, and currently has plans to open between five and six stores in the greater Toronto area in the second half of 2007. Additionally, LOW plans on expanding into Mexico, with three to five stores expected to open in Monterrey in 2009.

Company Financials Fiscal Year Ended Jan. 31

Per Share Data ($)	2007	2006	2005	2004	2003	2002	2001	2000	1999	1998
Tangible Book Value	10.31	9.15	7.45	6.55	5.31	4.30	3.59	3.07	2.22	1.85
Cash Flow	2.73	2.44	1.92	1.68	1.32	0.98	0.79	0.66	0.53	0.43
Earnings	1.99	1.73	1.36	1.16	0.93	0.65	0.52	0.44	0.34	0.26
S&P Core Earnings	1.99	1.73	1.33	1.13	0.87	0.61	0.50	NA	NA	NA
Dividends	0.11	0.08	0.06	0.06	0.04	0.04	0.04	0.03	0.03	0.03
Payout Ratio	6%	4%	4%	5%	5%	0%	7%	7%	9%	11%
Calendar Year	2006	2005	2004	2003	2002	2001	2000	1999	1998	1997
Prices:High	34.83	34.85	30.27	30.21	25.00	24.44	16.81	16.61	13.05	6.14
Prices:Low	26.15	25.36	22.95	16.69	16.25	10.94	8.56	10.75	5.40	3.95
P/E Ratio:High	17	20	22	26	27	38	32	38	38	24
P/E Ratio:Low	13	15	17	14	18	17	16	25	16	15

Income Statement Analysis (Million $)										
Revenue	46,927	43,243	36,464	30,838	26,491	22,111	18,779	15,906	12,245	10,137
Operating Income	6,314	5,715	4,878	3,959	3,186	2,332	1,811	1,511	1,105	865
Depreciation	1,162	1,051	920	781	645	534	409	337	272	241
Interest Expense	238	158	176	180	203	199	146	123	95.0	73.3
Pretax Income	4,998	4,506	3,536	2,998	2,359	1,624	1,283	1,065	758	559
Effective Tax Rate	37.9%	38.5%	38.5%	37.9%	37.6%	37.0%	36.9%	36.8%	36.4%	36.0%
Net Income	3,105	2,771	2,176	1,862	1,471	1,023	810	673	482	357
S&P Core Earnings	3,105	2,763	2,134	1,801	1,386	968	773	NA	NA	NA

Balance Sheet & Other Financial Data (Million $)										
Cash	796	423	813	1,624	1,126	799	456	491	223	195
Current Assets	8,314	7,831	6,974	6,687	5,568	4,920	4,175	3,710	2,586	2,110
Total Assets	27,767	24,682	21,209	19,042	16,109	13,736	11,376	9,012	6,345	5,219
Current Liabilities	6,539	5,832	5,719	4,368	3,578	3,017	2,929	2,386	1,765	1,449
Long Term Debt	4,325	3,499	3,060	3,678	3,736	3,734	2,698	1,727	1,283	1,046
Common Equity	15,725	14,339	11,535	10,309	8,302	6,675	5,494	4,695	3,136	2,601
Total Capital	20,785	18,573	15,331	14,644	12,516	10,713	8,443	6,622	4,579	3,771
Capital Expenditures	3,916	3,379	2,927	2,444	2,362	2,199	2,332	1,472	928	773
Cash Flow	4,267	3,822	3,096	2,643	2,116	1,557	1,219	1,010	754	598
Current Ratio	1.3	1.3	1.2	1.5	1.6	1.6	1.4	1.6	1.5	1.5
% Long Term Debt of Capitalization	21.6	18.8	20.0	25.1	29.8	34.9	32.0	26.1	28.0	27.7
% Net Income of Revenue	6.6	6.4	6.0	6.0	5.6	4.6	4.3	4.2	3.9	3.5
% Return on Assets	11.9	12.1	10.9	10.6	9.9	8.2	7.9	8.4	8.3	7.4
% Return on Equity	20.7	21.4	20.0	20.0	19.6	16.8	15.9	16.2	16.8	14.8

Data as orig reptd.; bef. results of disc opers/spec. items. Per share data adj. for stk. divs.; EPS diluted. E-Estimated. NA-Not Available. NM-Not Meaningful. NR-Not Ranked. UR-Under Review.

Office: 1000 Lowes Blvd, Mooresville, NC 28117-8520.
Telephone: 704-758-1000.
Website: http://www.lowes.com
Chrmn & CEO: R.A. Niblock

Pres & COO: L.D. Stone
EVP & CFO: R.F. Hull, Jr.
SVP & Chief Acctg Officer: M.V. Hollifield
SVP, Secy & General Counsel: G. Keener, Jr.

Board Members: D. W. Bernauer, L. L. Berry, P. C. Browning, D. E. Hudson, R. A. Ingram, R. L. Johnson, M. O. Larsen, R. K. Lochridge, R. A. Niblock, S. F. Page, O. T. Sloan, Jr.
Founded: 1952
Domicile: North Carolina
Employees: 210,000

The McGraw-Hill Companies

L-3 Communications Holdings Inc

S&P Recommendation **BUY** ★★★★☆	Price $109.33 (as of Nov 23, 2007)	12-Mo. Target Price $118.00	Investment Style Large-Cap Blend

GICS Sector Industrials
Sub-Industry Aerospace & Defense

Summary This company is a provider of intelligence, surveillance, and reconnaissance systems; secure communications systems; aircraft modernization, training and government services; among other defense, intelligence, and security products.

Key Stock Statistics (Source S&P, Vickers, company reports)

52-Wk Range	$114.17– 78.00	S&P Oper. EPS 2007**E**	5.90	Market Capitalization(B)	$13.780	Beta		0.82
Trailing 12-Month EPS	$5.72	S&P Oper. EPS 2008**E**	6.50	Yield (%)	0.91	S&P 3-Yr. Proj. EPS CAGR(%)		11.00
Trailing 12-Month P/E	19.1	P/E on S&P Oper. EPS 2007**E**	18.5	Dividend Rate/Share	$1.00	S&P Credit Rating		BBB-
$10K Invested 5 Yrs Ago	$25,435	Common Shares Outstg. (M)	126.0	Institutional Ownership (%)	87			

Price Performance

30-Week Mov. Avg. ··· 10-Week Mov. Avg.— **GAAP Earnings vs. Previous Year** Volume Above Avg. |||| STARS
12-Mo. Target Price — Relative Strength — ▲ Up ▼ Down ► No Change Below Avg. |||| ★

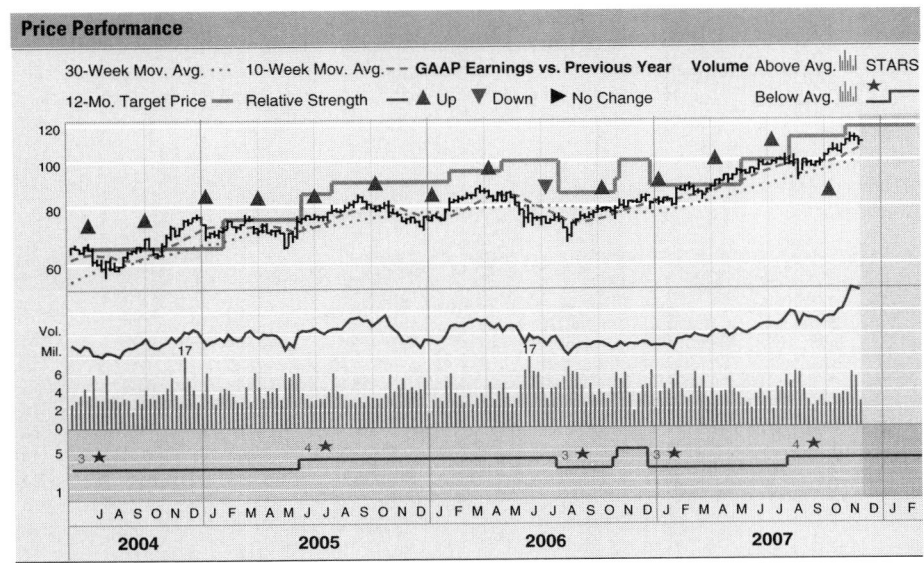

Options: ASE, CBOE, P

Analysis prepared by **Richard Tortoriello** on October 29, 2007, when the stock traded at **$ 108.53.**

Highlights

➤ We anticipate organic revenue growth, which excludes the effects of recent acquisitions, of about 9% in 2007 and 8% in 2008, versus organic growth of 9% that was recorded in 2006 (a total sales gain of 32% after the inclusion of acquisitions). For 2008, we expect strong growth in Government Services and Specialized Products, and moderate growth in C3ISR and Aircraft Modernization & Maintenance. We see Government Services growth driven by military training and support demand in Iraq and Afghanistan. In addition, we see growth in Specialized Products driven by demand for a variety of business lines, from undersea warfare products to simulation devices.

➤ For 2007, we expect a slight increase in operating margins, to 10.4% from 10.3% in 2006, on improved contract performance and cost efficiencies. We project a further modest increase, to 10.5%, in 2008.

➤ We project EPS of $5.90 in 2007 and $6.50 in 2008. We expect the company to generate free cash flow (cash from operations less capital expenditures) of over $8 per share in 2007.

Investment Rationale/Risk

➤ Following the June 2006 death of L-3's founder, we see new management focusing on more selective acquisitions, improving profit margins, creating more products that span business lines, and maximizing cash flow. We also see an increased focus on moderate share repurchases and dividend increases. We see L-3's mix of defense electronics and communications and government services as well matched with current military priorities, and expect investors to benefit from what we see as strong organic sales growth, strong cash flow generation, and an attractive valuation.

➤ Risks to our recommendation and target price include the potential for delays and/or cuts in military budgets and the failure to perform well on existing contracts or to win new contracts.

➤ Our 12-month target price of $118 is based on a P/E of 18X our 2008 EPS estimate, in line with LLL's 10-year historical average forward P/E. This compares to a recent P/E of around 16X for the "Big Five" defense contractors. We see earnings benefiting from increased outsourcing by the U.S. government, and believe LLL deserves a valuation near its historical average.

Qualitative Risk Assessment

LOW	**MEDIUM**	HIGH

Our risk assessment reflects our view of LLL's strong historical record of earnings growth, offset by the company's current low dividend payout ratio and relatively high financial leverage, and risks inherent in its dependence on government spending.

Quantitative Evaluations

S&P Quality Ranking   A-

D	C	B-	B	B+	**A-**	A	A+

Relative Strength Rank   **STRONG**

88

LOWEST = 1   HIGHEST = 99

Revenue/Earnings Data

Revenue (Million $)

	1Q	2Q	3Q	4Q	Year
2007	3,300	3,408	3,448	--	--
2006	2,904	3,083	3,105	3,385	12,477
2005	1,963	2,076	2,506	2,900	9,445
2004	1,522	1,680	1,784	1,911	6,897
2003	1,089	1,227	1,265	1,481	5,062
2002	696.8	955.2	1,054	1,306	4,011

Earnings Per Share ($)

2007	1.29	1.49	1.56	E1.56	E5.90
2006	1.13	0.40	1.31	1.37	4.22
2005	0.86	0.99	1.11	1.24	4.20
2004	0.67	0.81	0.93	1.01	3.33
2003	0.50	0.53	0.74	0.94	2.71
2002	0.36	0.49	0.62	0.79	2.29

Fiscal year ended Dec. 31. Next earnings report expected: Late January. EPS Estimates based on S&P Operating Earnings; historical GAAP earnings are as reported.

Dividend Data (Dates: mm/dd Payment Date: mm/dd/yy)

Amount ($)	Date Decl.	Ex-Div. Date	Stk. of Record	Payment Date
0.250	02/06	02/16	02/21	03/15/07
0.250	04/24	05/14	05/16	06/15/07
0.250	07/10	08/14	08/16	09/17/07
0.250	10/09	11/14	11/16	12/17/07

Dividends have been paid since 2004. Source: Company reports.

L-3 Communications Holdings Inc

STANDARD &POOR'S

Business Summary October 29, 2007

CORPORATE OVERVIEW. L-3 Communications (LLL), an acquisitive $13 billion in revenues maker of military and homeland security electronics, conducts business through four operating segments.

The Command, Control, Communications, Intelligence, Surveillance, and Reconnaissance (C3ISR) business segment (22% of sales and 22% of operating income in 2006), specializes in signals intelligence (SIGINT) and communications intelligence (COMINT) products. These products provide troops the ability to collect and analyze unknown electronic signals from command centers, communications nodes and air defense systems for real-time situation awareness and response. Major product groups are intelligence, surveillance and reconnaissance (ISR) systems, networked communications, C3ISR support services, and secure communications products.

The Government Services segment (25% of sales and 22% of operating profits) provides a wide range of support services to the Department of Defense (DoD), U.S. Government intelligence agencies, and allied foreign governments. Major product groups include military and law enforcement training and leadership development; communications systems and software engineering services; acquisition management and staff augmentation for the U.S.

Army; battlefield and weapon simulation; system support and concept operations; information technology (IT) modernization and operations; information management and IT systems support, and software design, development, and systems integration; systems acquisition and advisory support and comprehensive operational support services; and linguistic, interpretation, translation and analyst services.

The Aircraft Modernization & Maintenance segment (19% of sales and 19% of operating profits) provides modernization, upgrades and sustainment, maintenance and logistics support services for various government aircraft and other platforms. Services are sold primarily to the U.S. DoD, the Canadian Department of National Defense, and other allied foreign governments. Major products and services include aircraft modernization, including life extension maintenance upgrades and support; and base operations support and aircraft services, including logistics support, maintenance and refurbishment, quick response teams, and contractor operated and managed base supply.

Company Financials Fiscal Year Ended Dec. 31

Per Share Data ($)	2006	2005	2004	2003	2002	2001	2000	1999	1998	1997
Tangible Book Value	NM	NM	NM	NM	NM	NM	NM	NM	NM	NM
Cash Flow	5.30	5.46	4.27	3.52	2.96	2.37	2.25	16.75	1.41	NA
Earnings	4.22	4.20	3.33	2.71	2.29	1.48	1.18	0.88	0.63	0.22
S&P Core Earnings	4.93	4.07	3.22	2.66	1.87	1.08	NA	NA	NA	NA
Dividends	0.75	0.50	0.40	Nil	Nil	Nil	Nil	Nil	Nil	NA
Payout Ratio	18%	12%	12%	Nil	Nil	Nil	Nil	Nil	Nil	NA
Prices:High	88.50	84.84	77.26	51.83	66.78	49.04	39.66	27.13	24.75	NA
Prices:Low	66.50	64.66	49.31	34.22	40.60	30.35	17.84	17.13	11.00	NA
P/E Ratio:High	21	20	23	19	29	33	33	31	39	NA
P/E Ratio:Low	16	15	15	13	18	21	15	20	17	NA

Income Statement Analysis (Million $)										
Revenue	12,477	9,445	6,897	5,062	4,011	2,347	1,910	1,405	1,037	894
Operating Income	1,376	1,150	868	676	530	362	297	204	141	58.4
Depreciation	136	153	119	95.4	75.9	87.0	74.3	53.7	40.4	NA
Interest Expense	296	204	145	133	122	86.4	93.0	60.6	49.6	42.4
Pretax Income	835	798	606	437	336	191	134	95.4	53.5	15.9
Effective Tax Rate	35.7%	35.1%	35.5%	35.7%	35.0%	37.1%	38.3%	38.5%	39.1%	30.0%
Net Income	526	509	382	278	212	115	82.7	58.7	32.6	11.2
S&P Core Earnings	615	493	370	274	171	82.0	NA	NA	NA	NA

Balance Sheet & Other Financial Data (Million $)										
Cash	348	394	653	135	135	361	32.7	42.8	26.1	50.0
Current Assets	3,930	3,644	2,808	1,938	1,639	1,239	830	568	405	NA
Total Assets	13,287	11,909	7,781	6,493	5,242	3,335	2,464	1,634	1,285	NA
Current Liabilities	2,376	1,854	1,176	924	697	524	469	318	248	NA
Long Term Debt	4,535	4,634	2,190	2,457	1,848	1,315	1,095	605	605	413
Common Equity	5,306	4,491	3,800	2,574	2,202	1,214	693	583	300	235
Total Capital	10,069	9,325	6,067	5,108	4,123	2,599	1,788	1,188	905	649
Capital Expenditures	156	120	80.5	82.9	62.1	48.1	33.6	23.5	23.4	NA
Cash Flow	662	661	501	373	288	202	157	112	72.9	NA
Current Ratio	1.7	2.0	2.4	2.1	2.4	2.4	1.8	1.8	1.6	NA
% Long Term Debt of Capitalization	45.0	49.7	36.1	48.1	44.8	50.6	61.3	50.9	66.9	63.7
% Net Income of Revenue	4.2	5.4	5.5	5.5	5.3	4.9	4.3	4.2	3.1	NA
% Return on Assets	4.2	5.2	5.3	4.7	5.0	4.0	4.0	4.0	3.3	NA
% Return on Equity	10.7	12.3	12.0	11.6	12.4	12.1	13.0	13.3	15.0	NA

Data as orig reptd.; bef. results of disc opers/spec. items. Per share data adj. for stk. divs.; EPS diluted. E-Estimated. NA-Not Available. NM-Not Meaningful. NR-Not Ranked. UR-Under Review.

Office: 600 3rd Ave, New York, NY 10016.
Telephone: 212-697-1111.
Website: http://www.L3com.com
Chrmn: R.B. Millard

Pres & CEO: M.T. Strianese
SVP, Secy & General Counsel: K.E. Karellis
VP & CFO: R.G. D'Ambrosio
VP & Treas: S.M. Souza

Investor Contact: C. Mohrmann (212-850-5600)
Board Members: C. R. Canizares, P. A. Cohen, T. A. Corcoran, R. B. Millard, J. M. Shalikashvili, A. L. Simon, M. T. Strianese, A. H. Washkowitz, J. P. White

Founded: 1997
Domicile: Delaware
Employees: 63,700

The McGraw-Hill Companies

LSI Corp

STANDARD &POOR'S

S&P Recommendation	HOLD ★★★☆☆	Price $5.78 (as of Nov 23, 2007)	12-Mo. Target Price $7.50	Investment Style Large-Cap Blend

GICS Sector Information Technology
Sub-Industry Semiconductors

Summary This leading supplier of complex, high-performance semiconductors and storage systems, recently acquired Agere Systems.

Key Stock Statistics (Source S&P, Vickers, company reports)

52-Wk Range	$10.89– 5.56	S&P Oper. EPS 2007**E**	0.22	Market Capitalization(B)	$4.139	Beta	2.85
Trailing 12-Month EPS	$-0.63	S&P Oper. EPS 2008**E**	0.50	Yield (%)	Nil	S&P 3-Yr. Proj. EPS CAGR(%)	15.00
Trailing 12-Month P/E	NM	P/E on S&P Oper. EPS 2007**E**	26.3	Dividend Rate/Share	Nil	S&P Credit Rating	BB
$10K Invested 5 Yrs Ago	$7,556	Common Shares Outstg. (M)	716.1	Institutional Ownership (%)	89		

Price Performance

30-Week Mov. Avg. ··· 10-Week Mov. Avg. - - GAAP Earnings vs. Previous Year Volume Above Avg. ⅰⅼⅼⅼ STARS
12-Mo. Target Price — Relative Strength — ▲ Up ▼ Down ▶ No Change Below Avg. ⅰⅼⅼⅼ ★

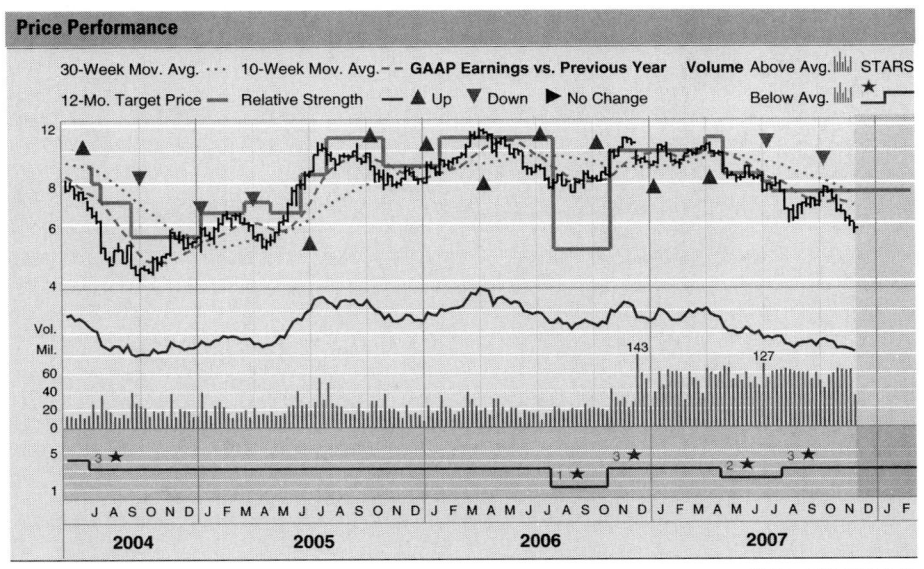

Options: ASE, CBOE, P, Ph

Analysis prepared by **Jawahar Hingorani** on October 31, 2007, when the stock traded at **$ 6.56**.

Highlights

➤ We project revenues of $2.9 billion in 2007, about 20% below LSI-Agere pro forma combined revenues of $3.6 billion in 2006, and see revenues of $3.1 billion in 2008. The sale of the consumer business, the mobility business and the Thai assembly operations, and the acquisition of Tarari, Inc., are steps in the right direction, in our opinion. However, we still think challenges persist in filling the resulting gap in revenues. We view the sequential increase in revenues in the networking and storage segments as positive.

➤ We do not expect synergies related to the acquisition of Agere to provide LSI with manufacturing and operating efficiencies until 2008. The combined company is among the top 20 global semiconductor makers by revenue, implying some scale advantages, in our estimation. We expect the acquisition to be dilutive to EPS in 2007 despite some cost savings, and accretive in 2008.

➤ We estimate operating EPS of $0.22 for 2007. This estimate does not include one-time acquisition-related charges. Our 2008 EPS estimate is $0.50.

Investment Rationale/Risk

➤ Our hold recommendation is based on our view of somewhat improving revenue opportunities in storage for LSI. We still see integration issues from the acquisition of Agere Systems, given uncertainties about the size and timing of potential cost savings. We believe the Store-Age acquisition adds expertise in SAN storage management, a growth area in storage, to LSI's product portfolio. We are concerned about top-line growth following the sale of the consumer business and lack of recognition of IP revenues.

➤ Risks to our recommendation and target price include slower-than-expected resolution of strategic options for the consumer business, weaker demand for semiconductors, slower realization of synergy cost savings from the Agere acquisition, and higher stock option expense.

➤ We arrive at our 12-month target price of $7.50 by applying a price-to-sales multiple of 1.7X, near the middle of LSI's four-year historical range for P/S multiples, to our 2007 sales per share estimate.

Qualitative Risk Assessment

LOW	MEDIUM	HIGH

LSI is subject to the sales cycles of the semiconductor industry and of consumer electronics and data storage end markets. The company faces competition from makers of programmable logic devices as well as from many custom logic chip makers. We view the balance sheet as weaker than the peer group average.

Quantitative Evaluations

S&P Quality Ranking   C

D	C	B-	B	B+	A-	A	A+

Relative Strength Rank   WEAK

22

LOWEST = 1   HIGHEST = 99

Revenue/Earnings Data

Revenue (Million $)

	1Q	2Q	3Q	4Q	Year
2007	465.4	669.9	727.4	--	--
2006	475.9	489.6	493.0	523.7	1,982
2005	450.0	481.3	481.7	506.2	1,919
2004	452.4	447.9	380.2	419.7	1,700
2003	372.8	407.2	450.2	462.9	1,693
2002	412.5	437.8	487.0	479.7	1,817

Earnings Per Share ($)

2007	0.07	-0.50	-0.20	E0.15	E0.22
2006	0.03	0.13	0.11	0.14	0.42
2005	0.01	0.06	-0.19	0.09	-0.01
2004	0.02	0.02	-0.73	-0.51	-1.21
2003	-0.33	-0.43	-0.08	0.02	-0.82
2002	-0.47	-0.17	-0.07	-0.08	-0.79

Fiscal year ended Dec. 31. Next earnings report expected: Late January. EPS Estimates based on S&P Operating Earnings; historical GAAP earnings are as reported.

Dividend Data

No cash dividends have been paid.

LSI Corp

STANDARD
&POOR'S

Business Summary October 31, 2007

CORPORATE OVERVIEW. LSI Corp. (formerly LSI Logic) is best known as a leading supplier of application-specific and standard integrated circuits, although since 1998 it has diversified into storage components. In March 2006, the company announced plans to focus on growth opportunities in storage and consumer markets. Through 2005, principal markets served include storage components, storage systems, consumers, and communications. Sales in 2005 by market segment were as follows: storage systems 35%, storage components 33%, consumer 18%, and communications 14%.

In 2006, the company operated in two main reporting segments: semiconductors, which accounted for 62% of revenues compared to 65% in 2005; and storage systems, which represented 38% (35%) in the same time period. Semiconductors posted operating income of $96.2 million in 2006, versus a loss from operations in 2005, 2004, 2003, and 2002. Storage systems had income of $62 million in 2006, and has maintained profitability.

MARKET PROFILE. Customers are generally electronic original equipment

manufacturers (OEMs). LSI focuses on larger companies that make products in high volume.

The company emphasizes complex system-on-a-chip products that employ its CoreWare design methodology. Using sophisticated electronic design automation tools, customers add product features to pre-wired cores of industry-standard architecture protocols and algorithms that are electronically stitched together on a single chip. CoreWare methodology is based on application-specific integrated circuit (ASIC) technology: these semiconductors are designed to satisfy particular customer requirements. LSI is a large player in the global ASIC market, competing with companies such as IBM, Philips Electronics, Texas Instruments, and Broadcom.

Company Financials Fiscal Year Ended Dec. 31

Per Share Data ($)	2006	2005	2004	2003	2002	2001	2000	1999	1998	1997
Tangible Book Value	2.24	1.66	1.38	2.39	2.80	3.15	5.96	5.21	4.17	5.59
Cash Flow	0.62	0.36	-0.75	-0.12	0.15	-1.32	1.81	1.62	0.41	1.14
Earnings	0.42	-0.01	-1.21	-0.82	-0.79	-2.84	0.70	0.52	-0.47	0.56
S&P Core Earnings	0.35	-0.20	-1.51	-1.33	-1.36	-3.47	NA	NA	NA	NA
Dividends	Nil	Nil	Nil	Nil	Nil	Nil	Nil	Nil	Nil	Nil
Payout Ratio	Nil	Nil	Nil	Nil	Nil	Nil	Nil	Nil	Nil	Nil
Prices:High	11.81	10.75	11.50	12.90	18.60	26.10	90.38	35.69	14.69	23.44
Prices:Low	7.41	4.92	4.01	3.78	3.97	9.70	16.30	8.06	5.25	9.31
P/E Ratio:High	28	NM	NM	NM	NM	NM	NM	69	NM	42
P/E Ratio:Low	18	NM	NM	NM	NM	NM	NM	16	NM	17

Income Statement Analysis (Million $)										
Revenue	1,982	1,919	1,700	1,693	1,817	1,785	2,738	2,089	1,491	1,290
Operating Income	236	283	172	171	155	-157	815	568	198	362
Depreciation	82.3	146	177	263	349	533	404	367	248	166
Interest Expense	24.3	25.3	25.3	30.7	52.0	44.6	41.6	40.0	8.48	1.50
Pretax Income	185	20.9	-439	-284	-291	-1,030	380	224	-124	224
Effective Tax Rate	8.46%	NM	NM	NM	NM	NM	37.6%	29.0%	NM	28.0%
Net Income	170	-5.62	-464	-309	-292	-992	237	159	-132	161
S&P Core Earnings	140	-80.0	-582	-505	-507	-1,214	NA	NA	NA	NA

Balance Sheet & Other Financial Data (Million $)										
Cash	328	265	219	270	449	757	236	251	200	105
Current Assets	1,636	1,620	1,365	1,390	1,626	1,769	2,072	1,288	820	870
Total Assets	2,852	2,796	2,874	3,448	4,143	4,626	4,197	3,207	2,800	2,127
Current Liabilities	527	743	396	391	398	510	627	475	593	438
Long Term Debt	350	350	782	866	1,241	1,336	846	672	556	67.3
Common Equity	1,896	1,628	1,618	2,042	2,300	2,480	2,498	1,856	1,510	1,566
Total Capital	2,246	1,978	2,400	2,916	3,665	3,995	3,481	2,610	2,207	1,689
Capital Expenditures	58.7	48.1	52.8	78.2	39.0	224	277	205	329	513
Cash Flow	252	141	-287	-45.8	57.0	-459	641	526	116	327
Current Ratio	3.1	2.2	3.4	3.6	4.1	3.5	3.3	2.7	1.4	2.0
% Long Term Debt of Capitalization	15.6	17.7	32.6	29.7	33.8	33.4	24.3	25.7	25.2	4.0
% Net Income of Revenue	8.6	NM	NM	NM	NM	NM	8.6	7.6	NM	12.5
% Return on Assets	6.0	NM	NM	NM	NM	NM	6.4	5.3	NM	7.9
% Return on Equity	9.6	NM	NM	NM	NM	NM	10.9	9.4	NM	11.2

Data as orig reptd.; bef. results of disc opers/spec. items. Per share data adj. for stk. divs.; EPS diluted. E-Estimated. NA-Not Available. NM-Not Meaningful. NR-Not Ranked. UR-Under Review.

Office: 1621 Barber Lane, Milpitas, CA 95035.
Telephone: 408-433-8000.
Email: investorrelations@lsil.com
Website: http://www.lsi.com

Chrmn: G. Reyes
Pres & CEO: A.Y. Talwalkar
EVP & CFO: B. Look
EVP & CTO: C. Simson

VP, Secy & General Counsel: A.S. Hughes
Board Members: T. Y. Chen, C. A. Haggerty, R. S. Hill, J. H. Keyes, M. J. Mancuso, J. H. Miner, A. Netravali, M. J. O'Rourke, G. Reyes, A. Y. Talwalkar

Founded: 1980
Domicile: Delaware
Employees: 4,010

Macy's Inc

STANDARD &POOR'S

S&P Recommendation	HOLD ★★★☆☆	Price	12-Mo. Target Price	Investment Style
		$30.03 (as of Nov 23, 2007)	$35.00	Large-Cap Blend

GICS Sector Consumer Discretionary
Sub-Industry Department Stores

Summary M operates over 800 department stores under the Macy's and Bloomingdale's names.

Key Stock Statistics (Source S&P, Vickers, company reports)

52-Wk Range	$46.70–27.18	S&P Oper. EPS 2008**E**	2.30	Market Capitalization(B)	$13.019	Beta	1.18
Trailing 12-Month EPS	$1.65	S&P Oper. EPS 2009**E**	2.60	Yield (%)	1.73	S&P 3-Yr. Proj. EPS CAGR(%)	9.00
Trailing 12-Month P/E	18.2	P/E on S&P Oper. EPS 2008**E**	13.1	Dividend Rate/Share	$0.52	S&P Credit Rating	BBB
$10K Invested 5 Yrs Ago	$18,706	Common Shares Outstg. (M)	433.5	Institutional Ownership (%)	91		

Price Performance

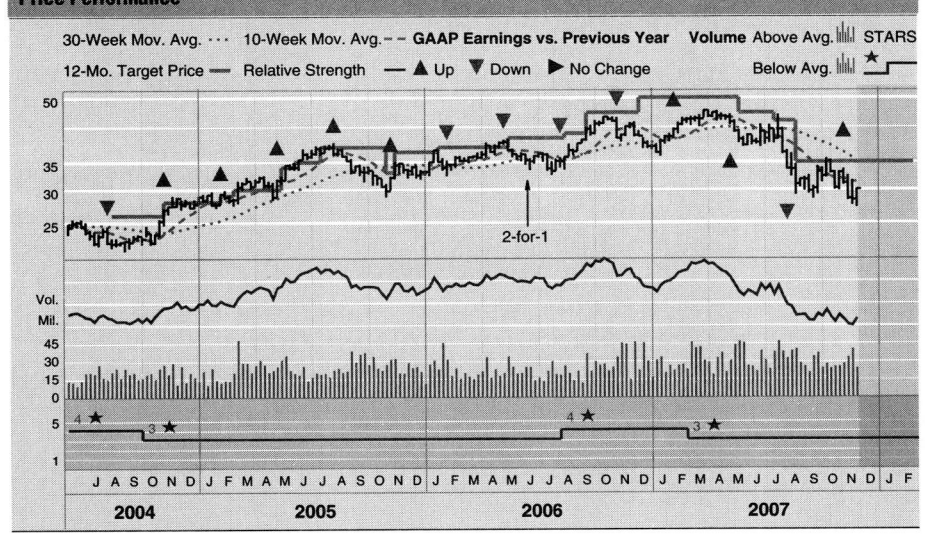

30-Week Mov. Avg. · · · 10-Week Mov. Avg. − − GAAP Earnings vs. Previous Year Volume Above Avg. STARS
12-Mo. Target Price — Relative Strength — ▲ Up ▼ Down ▶ No Change Below Avg.

2-for-1

Options: ASE, CBOE, P, Ph

Analysis prepared by **Jason N. Asaeda** on November 20, 2007, when the stock traded at **$ 28.03**.

Highlights

➤ From a projected $26.5 billion in FY 08 (Jan.), we expect net sales to rise 2.0% in FY 09, to $27.1 billion, supported by a 1% to 2% increase in same-store sales. Over the next 12 months, we look for improving performance of the core Macy's business and continued strength in results for the higher-end Bloomingdale's business.

➤ At "new Macy's" stores (the former May chains), which entered the same-store sales base in February 2007, we believe a lack of customer and employee buy-in into new national brand and private label assortments and lower promotional levels contributed to weak sales in FY 07. In response, M is attempting to increase customer conversion at new Macy's stores through better training of sales associates and the redirection of more of its marketing dollars from private sales to public couponing.

➤ While we see ongoing markdown exposure at Macy's, after factoring in our expectation of sales growth in private brands, a projected $450 million in annual cost savings from the Macy's-May merger, and likely share buybacks, we see operating EPS of $2.60 in FY 09, a 13% increase from our $2.30 estimate in FY 08.

Investment Rationale/Risk

➤ M reports that the performance gap between legacy and new Macy's doors is narrowing, which we view positively, as it implies to us an initial payoff of the company's efforts to drive store traffic with increased couponing. With over a year's worth of operating experience in new Macy's markets, we think M is becoming more effective in its assortment planning and store allocation. However, as we perceive Macy's as being positioned toward a more upscale demographic than the former May stores, we think M could lose market share to competitors J.C. Penney Company Inc. (JCP: buy, $42) and Kohl's Corp. (KSS: buy, $48) in the mid-market.

➤ Risks to our recommendation and target price include sales shortfalls due to fashion merchandising mistakes and cutbacks in consumer spending. Our corporate governance concerns include the non-disclosure of specific hurdle rates for performance-based equity awards and of stock ownership for executives.

➤ Our 12-month target price of $35 applies a premium to peers forward P/E of 13.5X--which we believe is justified by our view of M's turnaround potential--to our FY 09 EPS estimate.

Qualitative Risk Assessment

LOW	MEDIUM	HIGH

Our risk assessment reflects our view of M's strong brand and geographical presence in a consolidating industry, offset by potential merger-related integration challenges and uncertainty over consumer discretionary spending in light of interest rates and debt levels.

Quantitative Evaluations

S&P Quality Ranking   **B**

D	C	B-	B	B+	A-	A	A+

Relative Strength Rank   **MODERATE**

52

LOWEST = 1   HIGHEST = 99

Revenue/Earnings Data

Revenue (Million $)

	1Q	2Q	3Q	4Q	Year
2008	5,921	5,892	5,906	--	--
2007	5,930	5,995	5,886	9,159	26,970
2006	3,641	3,623	5,785	9,571	22,390
2005	3,517	3,548	3,491	5,074	15,630
2004	3,291	3,434	3,486	5,053	15,264
2003	3,453	3,486	3,479	5,017	15,435

Earnings Per Share ($)

	1Q	2Q	3Q	4Q	Year
2008	0.11	0.16	0.08	E1.75	E2.30
2007	-0.13	0.51	0.03	1.45	1.80
2006	0.36	0.84	0.89	1.23	3.16
2005	0.26	0.22	0.21	1.28	1.93
2004	0.12	0.32	0.18	1.25	1.86
2003	0.22	0.33	0.19	0.89	1.61

Fiscal year ended Jan. 31. Next earnings report expected: Late February. EPS Estimates based on S&P Operating Earnings; historical GAAP earnings are as reported.

Dividend Data (Dates: mm/dd Payment Date: mm/dd/yy)

Amount ($)	Date Decl.	Ex-Div. Date	Stk. of Record	Payment Date
0.128	10/26	12/13	12/15	01/02/07
0.128	02/27	03/13	03/15	04/02/07
0.130	08/24	09/12	09/14	10/01/07
0.130	10/26	12/12	12/14	01/02/08

Dividends have been paid since 2003. Source: Company reports.

Please read the Required Disclosures and Analyst Certification on the last page of this report.

The McGraw-Hill Companies

Macy's Inc

STANDARD
&POOR'S

Business Summary November 20, 2007

CORPORATE OVERVIEW. In February 2005, M and The May Department Stores Co. announced merger plans. At that time, May was in need of new leadership to revive its business, and M was in the midst of a successful turnaround and on the lookout for acquisitions that would expand its presence in underserved markets. Both companies viewed the merger as a win-win proposition, as M would roll out its profit-driving merchandising, pricing, and service initiatives to May's stores, and May would extend M's presence into 15 new states.

As a result of the $17 billion May merger, which closed in August 2005, M is now the fourth largest U.S. mass merchandiser in annual revenues, with over 800 department stores in 45 states under the Macy's and Bloomingdale's names.

CORPORATE STRATEGY. Since 2005, M has focused on three key priorities to better position its business for long-term growth: growing "better" and "affordable luxury" assortments, with an emphasis on private label merchandise; im-

proving customer perceptions of fair value in less discounted prices; and enriching the overall shopping experience. With its merger with May, the company also expanded its core Macy's brand nationwide.

Going forward, M sees an opportunity to accelerate the sales performance in about 400 former May locations that were rebranded Macy's on September 9, 2006. As part of its efforts to increase public awareness of Macy's, which contributes about 90% of the company's revenues, M changed its corporate name to Macy's, Inc. from Federated Department Stores, Inc. on June 1, 2007. On that date, the company's shares also began trading under the ticker symbol "M" (replacing "FD") on the New York Stock Exchange.

Company Financials Fiscal Year Ended Jan. 31

Per Share Data ($)	2007	2006	2005	2004	2003	2002	2001	2000	1999	1998
Tangible Book Value	5.56	5.34	16.55	NM	13.47	12.16	12.47	11.26	12.15	10.87
Cash Flow	4.11	4.29	4.09	3.92	3.31	2.94	1.32	3.49	2.91	2.61
Earnings	1.80	3.16	1.93	1.86	1.61	1.30	-0.45	1.81	1.53	1.29
S&P Core Earnings	1.62	2.21	1.83	1.69	1.24	0.91	0.25	NA	NA	NA
Dividends	0.45	0.26	0.19	Nil	Nil	Nil	Nil	Nil	Nil	Nil
Payout Ratio	25%	8%	10%	Nil	Nil	Nil	Nil	Nil	Nil	Nil
Calendar Year	2006	2005	2004	2003	2002	2001	2000	1999	1998	1997
Prices:High	45.01	39.03	29.08	25.30	22.13	24.95	26.94	28.53	28.09	24.44
Prices:Low	32.38	27.10	21.40	11.76	11.80	13.03	10.50	18.22	16.41	15.00
P/E Ratio:High	25	12	15	14	14	19	NM	16	18	19
P/E Ratio:Low	18	9	11	6	7	10	NM	10	11	12

Income Statement Analysis (Million $)

	2007	2006	2005	2004	2003	2002	2001	2000	1999	1998
Revenue	26,970	22,390	15,630	15,264	15,435	15,651	18,407	17,716	15,833	15,668
Operating Income	2,910	3,087	2,143	2,047	2,019	1,923	2,239	2,443	2,085	1,951
Depreciation	1,265	974	743	706	676	657	727	742	630	610
Interest Expense	520	422	299	266	311	331	444	368	304	418
Pretax Income	1,446	2,044	1,116	1,084	1,048	780	113	1,346	1,163	958
Effective Tax Rate	31.7%	32.8%	38.3%	36.1%	39.1%	33.6%	NM	40.9%	41.1%	40.0%
Net Income	988	1,373	689	693	638	518	-184	795	685	575
S&P Core Earnings	888	967	655	628	490	364	102	NA	NA	NA

Balance Sheet & Other Financial Data (Million $)

	2007	2006	2005	2004	2003	2002	2001	2000	1999	1998
Cash	1,211	248	868	925	716	636	322	218	307	142
Current Assets	7,422	10,145	7,510	7,452	7,154	7,280	8,700	8,522	5,972	6,194
Total Assets	29,550	33,168	14,885	14,550	14,441	15,044	17,012	17,692	13,464	13,738
Current Liabilities	6,359	7,590	4,301	3,883	3,601	3,714	4,869	4,552	3,068	3,060
Long Term Debt	7,847	8,860	2,637	3,151	3,408	3,859	4,374	4,589	3,057	3,919
Common Equity	12,254	13,519	6,167	5,940	5,762	5,564	5,822	6,552	5,709	5,256
Total Capital	21,829	24,083	10,003	10,089	10,168	10,768	11,589	12,585	9,826	10,114
Capital Expenditures	1,317	568	467	508	568	615	742	770	695	696
Cash Flow	2,253	2,347	1,432	1,399	1,314	1,175	543	1,537	1,315	1,185
Current Ratio	1.2	1.3	1.7	1.9	2.0	2.0	1.8	1.9	1.9	2.0
% Long Term Debt of Capitalization	39.0	36.8	26.4	31.2	33.5	35.8	37.7	36.5	31.1	38.7
% Net Income of Revenue	3.7	6.1	4.4	4.5	4.1	3.3	NM	4.5	4.3	3.7
% Return on Assets	3.2	5.7	4.7	4.8	4.2	3.4	NM	5.1	5.0	4.1
% Return on Equity	7.7	13.9	11.4	11.8	11.3	9.1	NM	13.0	12.5	11.6

Data as orig reptd.; bef. results of disc opers/spec. items. Per share data adj. for stk. divs.; EPS diluted. E-Estimated. NA-Not Available. NM-Not Meaningful. NR-Not Ranked. UR-Under Review.

Office: 7 W Seventh St, Cincinnati, OH 45202.
Telephone: 513-579-7000.
Website: http://www.fds.com
Chrmn, Pres & CEO: T.J. Lundgren

Vice Chrmn: T.G. Cody
Vice Chrmn: T.L. Cole
Vice Chrmn: J.E. Grove
Vice Chrmn: S.D. Kronick

Investor Contact: K.M. Hoguet (212-494-1602)
Board Members: M. Feldberg, S. Levinson, T. J. Lundgren, J. Neubauer, J. A. Pichler, J. M. Roche, W. P. Stiritz, C. E. Weatherup, M. C. Whittington, K. M. von der Heyden

Founded: 1858
Domicile: Delaware
Employees: 188,000

The McGraw-Hill Companies

Manitowoc Company Inc. (The)

STANDARD & POOR'S

S&P Recommendation STRONG BUY ★★★★★	**Price** $39.40 (as of Nov 23, 2007)	**12-Mo. Target Price** $64.00	**Investment Style** Large-Cap Growth

GICS Sector Industrials
Sub-Industry Construction & Farm Machinery & Heavy Trucks

Summary This Wisconsin company is a leading provider of cranes, commercial refrigeration equipment, and shipbuilding, ship repair and ship conversion services.

Key Stock Statistics (Source S&P, Vickers, company reports)

52-Wk Range	$49.40– 25.67	S&P Oper. EPS 2007E	2.50	Market Capitalization(B)	$4.914	Beta	1.12
Trailing 12-Month EPS	$2.23	S&P Oper. EPS 2008E	3.20	Yield (%)	0.20	S&P 3-Yr. Proj. EPS CAGR(%)	26.00
Trailing 12-Month P/E	17.7	P/E on S&P Oper. EPS 2007E	15.8	Dividend Rate/Share	$0.08	S&P Credit Rating	BB
$10K Invested 5 Yrs Ago	$64,007	Common Shares Outstg. (M)	124.7	Institutional Ownership (%)	77		

Price Performance

30-Week Mov. Avg. ··· 10-Week Mov. Avg.- - **GAAP Earnings vs. Previous Year** Volume Above Avg.|||| STARS
12-Mo. Target Price — Relative Strength — ▲ Up ▼ Down ► No Change Below Avg. ||||

Options: ASE, CBOE, P, Ph

Analysis prepared by **Michael W. Jaffe** on November 05, 2007, when the stock traded at **$ 44.27.**

Highlights

➤ We see revenues rising 18% in 2008. We look for the gains to come almost entirely from MTW's principal crane division, which we believe will benefit from healthy demand in foreign markets, expected ongoing strength in U.S. commercial construction activity, increased global distribution efforts, and new product introductions.

➤ We expect operating margins to expand in 2008, on the very solid demand that we see for MTW's cranes, combined with the likely incremental benefits of previously implemented cost reductions. We also see MTW benefiting from its current effort to increase production capacity, largely through equipment and tool additions, which should enable it to reduce its level of outsourcing (which carries lower margins than in-house production).

➤ We see sales growth in 2008 and subsequent years being driven in part by increased demand in emerging markets, which have been taking on a growing number of infrastructure and industrial projects. Demand for crane products in emerging markets is expected to outpace current industry production capacity for the next several years.

Investment Rationale/Risk

➤ We have a positive outlook for the company's operating prospects over the next few years, particularly as the use of MTW's crane products continues to increase in emerging markets. As such, we believe that the upcycle in MTW's principal business is only in its middle stages. Based on our resultant belief that MTW will record what we view as solid earnings growth for an extended period, our valuation model shows the company's shares to be greatly undervalued.

➤ Risks to our recommendation and target price include weakness in the global economy, and a resultant downturn in commercial construction markets.

➤ Manitowoc recently traded at about 14X our EPS estimate for 2008, which was in the low end of the company's range of multiples over the past decade. However, because we think that the current upturn still has a long way to run, we believe that a multiple in the middle part of MTW's range is more appropriate. We thus apply a P/E multiple of 20X to our 2008 EPS forecast, to arrive at our 12-month target price of $64.

Qualitative Risk Assessment

LOW	MEDIUM	HIGH

Our risk assessment for Manitowoc reflects the highly cyclical nature of the crane market, offset by our positive outlook for improving nonresidential construction activity over the next several years.

Quantitative Evaluations

S&P Quality Ranking   **B**

D	C	B-	B	B+	A-	A	A+

Relative Strength Rank   **MODERATE**

43

LOWEST = 1   HIGHEST = 99

Revenue/Earnings Data

Revenue (Million $)

	1Q	2Q	3Q	4Q	Year
2007	862.1	1,019	1,006	--	--
2006	633.0	746.2	779.0	775.2	2,933
2005	510.3	589.6	564.9	589.3	2,254
2004	411.8	526.2	491.2	534.9	1,964
2003	365.9	419.3	412.1	395.9	1,593
2002	283.0	328.3	394.9	400.4	1,407

Earnings Per Share ($)

2007	0.51	0.77	0.59	E0.64	E2.50
2006	0.24	0.34	0.40	0.35	1.33
2005	0.05	0.20	0.17	0.07	0.48
2004	0.06	0.14	0.12	0.05	0.37
2003	0.01	0.06	0.08	0.03	0.18
2002	0.06	0.20	0.14	Nil	0.39

Fiscal year ended Dec. 31. Next earnings report expected: Late January. EPS Estimates based on S&P Operating Earnings; historical GAAP earnings are as reported.

Dividend Data (Dates: mm/dd Payment Date: mm/dd/yy)

Amount ($)	Date Decl.	Ex-Div. Date	Stk. of Record	Payment Date
0.035	04/30	05/30	06/01	06/11/07
0.040	07/26	08/29	08/31	09/10/07
2-for-1	07/26	09/11	08/31	09/10/07
0.020	10/23	11/28	11/30	12/10/07

Dividends have been paid since 1945. Source: Company reports.

Manitowoc Company Inc. (The)

STANDARD &POOR'S

Business Summary November 05, 2007

CORPORATE OVERVIEW. The Manitowoc Co. is a diversified manufacturer of cranes, foodservice equipment and marine vessels. The company derived 48% of its sales in foreign markets in both 2005 and 2006, with Europe accounting for the majority (28% of total sales in 2006 and 30% in 2005).

The crane division (76% and 81% of 2006 sales and operating profits, respectively; 12.6% operating margin) designs and manufactures a diversified line of lattice-boom crawler cranes with lifting capacities of up to 1,433 U.S. tons, which are used to lift material and equipment in a wide variety of applications and end markets; tower cranes, which offer the ability to lift and distribute material at the point of use more quickly and accurately than other types of lifting machinery; mobile telescopic cranes, which are used to lift and move material at job sites; and boom trucks, of which telescopic boom trucks are used mostly for lifting material at a job site, and articulated boom trucks are used mostly to load and unload truck beds. MTW's crane segment also has a parts and services operation, through which it offers replacement parts, product services, and crane building and remanufacturing services. The division serves applications such as energy, petrochemical and industrial projects; infrastructure development; commercial and high-rise residential construction; and mining and dredging.

The foodservice segment (14% and 16%; 13.5%) is a leading broad-line producer of "cold-side" commercial foodservice products. The segment designs, makes, and sells commercial ice-cube machines and storage bins; refrigerators and freezers; refrigerated undercounters and food preparation tables; ice/beverage dispensers; cast aluminum cold plates; compressor racks; and modular refrigeration systems. The foodservice segment has sold products primarily in the U.S., but has been increasing its global focus in recent years. The division sells to lodging, restaurant, health care, convenience, and soft-drink bottling markets.

The marine division (10% and 3%; 4.0%) provides new construction services for commercial, government and military vessels, including inloading research vessels, ice breakers, ferries, patrol boats, self-unloading bulk carriers, double-hull tank barges, articulated tug/barges, and dredges. It also provides inspection, maintenance, conversion, and repair of freshwater and saltwater vessels.

Company Financials Fiscal Year Ended Dec. 31

Per Share Data ($)	2006	2005	2004	2003	2002	2001	2000	1999	1998	1997
Tangible Book Value	1.23	NM	NM	NM	NM	NM	NM	NM	NM	NM
Cash Flow	1.92	1.00	0.78	0.63	0.71	0.85	0.81	0.80	0.63	0.46
Earnings	1.33	0.48	0.36	0.17	0.39	0.50	0.60	0.64	0.49	0.35
S&P Core Earnings	1.33	0.51	0.32	0.14	0.34	0.48	NA	NA	NA	NA
Dividends	0.07	0.07	0.07	0.07	0.07	0.08	0.08	0.08	0.08	0.08
Payout Ratio	5%	15%	19%	41%	18%	15%	12%	12%	15%	22%
Prices:High	31.33	13.50	9.96	7.95	11.10	8.21	8.72	10.94	7.83	6.78
Prices:Low	12.41	8.58	6.90	4.18	5.53	5.58	4.41	6.05	4.08	3.71
P/E Ratio:High	24	28	27	46	28	17	15	17	16	19
P/E Ratio:Low	9	18	19	24	14	11	7	9	8	11

Income Statement Analysis (Million $)

	2006	2005	2004	2003	2002	2001	2000	1999	1998	1997
Revenue	2,933	2,254	1,964	1,593	1,407	1,117	873	805	695	546
Operating Income	375	200	162	132	159	152	131	136	107	76.7
Depreciation	72.3	63.5	54.0	48.4	35.1	33.4	18.1	16.7	14.6	11.7
Interest Expense	46.3	53.8	56.9	56.9	52.0	37.5	14.5	10.8	9.74	6.23
Pretax Income	245	73.9	49.1	22.6	62.8	79.7	96.1	106	81.4	57.8
Effective Tax Rate	32.0%	20.0%	19.0%	18.0%	36.0%	38.7%	37.3%	37.0%	36.9%	37.0%
Net Income	167	59.1	39.8	18.5	40.2	48.9	60.3	66.8	51.4	36.4
S&P Core Earnings	167	62.2	34.7	14.6	34.6	46.9	NA	NA	NA	NA

Balance Sheet & Other Financial Data (Million $)

	2006	2005	2004	2003	2002	2001	2000	1999	1998	1997
Cash	176	232	179	47.2	30.4	25.7	16.0	12.0	12.4	11.9
Current Assets	1,143	953	846	646	647	331	224	191	191	146
Total Assets	2,220	1,962	1,928	1,603	1,577	1,081	643	530	481	396
Current Liabilities	935	690	653	545	460	296	239	189	198	171
Long Term Debt	264	474	512	567	624	23.1	20.3	79.2	79.8	66.4
Common Equity	774	543	519	298	295	264	234	232	173	129
Total Capital	1,039	1,017	1,031	866	919	287	254	311	252	195
Capital Expenditures	67.6	54.9	44.4	32.0	33.0	29.3	13.4	13.7	11.7	12.0
Cash Flow	239	123	93.8	66.9	75.3	82.2	78.3	83.5	66.0	48.1
Current Ratio	1.2	1.4	1.3	1.2	1.4	1.1	0.9	1.0	1.0	0.9
% Long Term Debt of Capitalization	25.4	46.6	49.7	65.5	67.9	8.0	8.0	25.4	31.6	34.1
% Net Income of Revenue	5.7	2.6	2.0	1.2	2.9	4.4	6.9	8.3	7.4	6.7
% Return on Assets	8.0	3.0	2.2	1.2	3.0	5.7	10.3	13.2	11.7	10.2
% Return on Equity	25.3	11.1	9.1	6.2	14.4	19.6	25.9	33.0	34.1	31.8

Data as orig reptd.; bef. results of disc opers/spec. items. Per share data adj. for stk. divs.; EPS diluted. E-Estimated. NA-Not Available. NM-Not Meaningful. NR-Not Ranked. UR-Under Review.

Office: 2400 South 44th Street, Manitowoc, WI 54220-5846.
Telephone: 920-652-2222.
Website: http://www.manitowoc.com
Chrmn: T.D. Growcock

Pres & CEO: G.E. Tellock
SVP & CFO: C.J. Laurino
SVP, Secy & General Counsel: M.D. Jones
VP & Cntlr: D.J. Nolden

Investor Contact: S.C. Khail (920-684-4410)
Board Members: D. H. Anderson, V. W. Colbert, D. W. Duval, T. D. Growcock, K. W. Krueger, K. D. Nosbusch, J. L. Packard, R. C. Stift, G. E. Tellock, R. S. Throop

Founded: 1853
Domicile: Wisconsin
Employees: 9,500

The McGraw-Hill Companies

Marathon Oil Corp

STANDARD &POOR'S

S&P Recommendation **BUY** ★★★★☆	Price $56.37 (as of Nov 23, 2007)	12-Mo. Target Price $70.00	Investment Style Large-Cap Blend

GICS Sector Energy
Sub-Industry Integrated Oil & Gas

Summary MRO (formerly USX-Marathon Group, a part of USX Corp.) engages in worldwide oil and gas exploration and production, and domestic refining, marketing and transportation.

Key Stock Statistics (Source S&P, Vickers, company reports)

52-Wk Range	$67.04– 41.50	S&P Oper. EPS 2007**E**	5.89	Market Capitalization(B)	$40.034	Beta	0.62
Trailing 12-Month EPS	$6.31	S&P Oper. EPS 2008**E**	4.81	Yield (%)	1.70	S&P 3-Yr. Proj. EPS CAGR(%)	-8.70
Trailing 12-Month P/E	8.9	P/E on S&P Oper. EPS 2007**E**	9.6	Dividend Rate/Share	$0.96	S&P Credit Rating	BBB+
$10K Invested 5 Yrs Ago	$63,791	Common Shares Outstg. (M)	710.2	Institutional Ownership (%)	80		

Price Performance

30-Week Mov. Avg. ··· 10-Week Mov. Avg. - - **GAAP Earnings vs. Previous Year**   Volume Above Avg. STARS
12-Mo. Target Price — Relative Strength — ▲ Up ▼ Down ► No Change   Below Avg.

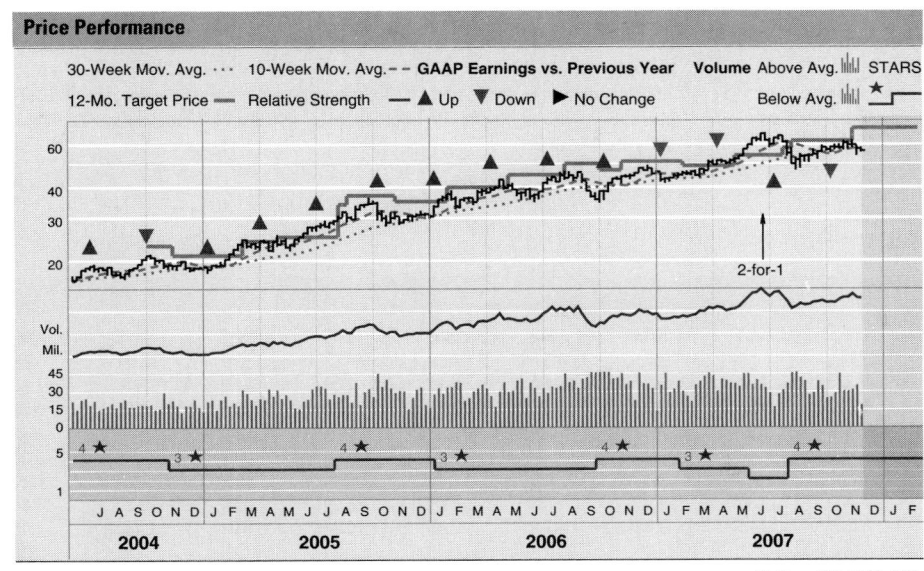

Options: ASE, CBOE, P, Ph

Analysis prepared by **Tina J. Vital** on November 16, 2007, when the stock traded at **$ 55.88**.

Highlights

➤ Third quarter oil and gas production rose 2.5%, in line with our expectations. However, we expect full-year output to decline about 1%. Over the period 2007-10, we expect about 6% growth per year, on international start-ups, at the low end of MRO's guidance of 6%-9%.

➤ On October 18, MRO acquired Western Oil Sands Inc. for about US$6.9 billion. We like the deal, as it will enable MRO to realize a greater portion of the oil sands resource value through its integrated strategy to link oil sands production with heavy oil upgrade projects at its refineries. Subsequently, on October 31, MRO's directors approved a $1.9 billion upgrade project at its Detroit refinery to increase its heavy oil processing capacity. In November, MRO said it expects minimal impact on its plans and operations from Alberta's royalty hikes in western Canada.

➤ Refining margins weakened in the 2007 second half, and we project that 2008 refining margins will narrow more than 30% from 2007 levels, as refined product prices have failed to keep pace with a sharp increase in crude oil prices. As a result, we see after-tax operating earnings down more than 15% in 2007 and 18% in 2008.

Investment Rationale/Risk

➤ We view MRO's business profile as solid, reflecting its large and geographically diverse exploration and production (54% liquids, 28% North America) and strong refining operations, with refineries advantageously situated within a high quality refining and marketing network that ranks near the top of most operating metrics. MRO has increased its exploration and production exposure toward more higher-growth but politically challenging regions (e.g., West Africa and Libya), and has placed greater emphasis on larger, longer lead time projects (e.g., deepwater Gulf of Mexico and western Canada).

➤ Risks to our recommendation and target price include changes in economic, industry and operating conditions, such as rising costs and difficulty replacing reserves.

➤ A blend of our discounted cash flow ($78; assuming a WACC of 7.6%, and terminal growth of 3%) and relative valuations leads to our 12-month target of $70. This represents an expected enterprise value of 7.2X our 2008 EBIT-DA estimate, a premium to peers.

Qualitative Risk Assessment

LOW	MEDIUM	HIGH

Our risk assessment reflects our view of the company's diversified and solid business profile in volatile and cyclical segments of the energy industry. We consider MRO's earnings stability to be good, and its corporate governance practices sound.

Quantitative Evaluations

S&P Quality Ranking B+

D	C	B-	B	B+	A-	A	A+

Relative Strength Rank MODERATE

69

LOWEST = 1   HIGHEST = 99

Revenue/Earnings Data

Revenue (Million $)

	1Q	2Q	3Q	4Q	Year
2007	13,002	16,887	76,964	--	--
2006	16,638	18,290	16,634	13,807	64,896
2005	12,932	16,019	17,248	17,314	63,673
2004	10,652	12,514	12,249	14,183	49,598
2003	10,033	9,643	10,253	11,034	40,963
2002	6,419	8,078	8,437	8,530	31,464

Earnings Per Share ($)

2007	1.04	2.24	1.49	E1.13	E5.89
2006	1.07	2.04	2.26	1.53	6.87
2005	0.47	0.96	1.04	1.74	4.25
2004	0.42	0.51	0.32	0.62	1.86
2003	0.49	0.40	0.45	0.32	1.63
2002	0.11	0.27	0.12	0.31	0.86

Fiscal year ended Dec. 31. Next earnings report expected: Early February. EPS Estimates based on S&P Operating Earnings; historical GAAP earnings are as reported.

Dividend Data (Dates: mm/dd Payment Date: mm/dd/yy)

Amount ($)	Date Decl.	Ex-Div. Date	Stk. of Record	Payment Date
0.480	04/25	05/14	05/16	06/11/07
2-for-1	04/25	06/19	05/23	06/18/07
0.240	07/25	08/14	08/16	09/10/07
0.240	10/31	11/19	11/21	12/10/07

Dividends have been paid since 1991. Source: Company reports.

Marathon Oil Corp

STANDARD
&POOR'S

Business Summary November 16, 2007

CORPORATE OVERVIEW. In January 2002, the integrated oil and gas company Marathon Oil (MRO; formerly USX-Marathon Group, a part of USX Corp.) began trading as a stand-alone company after USX-Marathon shareholders voted to separate USX's steel and energy businesses via a tax-free spinoff. On June 30, 2005, MRO acquired Ashland Inc.'s 38% interest in its Marathon Ashland Petroleum LLC (MAP) refining joint venture, ASH's maleic anhydride business, and 60 Valvoline Instant Oil Change retail outlets (located in Michigan and Ohio), for about $3.73 billion. As a result, the refining venture is now wholly owned by MRO. (MAP changed its name to Marathon Petroleum Co. LLC (MPC) on September 1, 2005.)

MARKET PROFILE. MRO is the fourth largest U.S.-based integrated oil company and the nation's fifth largest refiner. MRO is engaged in oil and gas exploration and production (E&P; 14% of 2006 revenues, 42% of segment income); refining, marketing and transportation (RM&T; 86%, 58%); and integrated gas operations (less than 1%, less than 1%).

At year-end 2006, net proved oil and gas reserves totaled 1.262 billion barrels (68% developed, 54% liquids), down 2.5% from a year earlier, reflecting disposals of 45 million barrels despite MRO's re-entry into Libya, extensions, dis-

coveries, and other additions. MRO's production operations are focused in the U.S., Europe, West Africa, Libya and Russia. In 2006, worldwide oil and gas production sales rose 9%, to 377,000 barrels per day (b/d; 62% liquids).

In 1998, the company and ASH combined their RM&T operations into the MAP joint venture, owned 62% by MRO. As of year-end 2006, MAP owned and operated seven refineries (245,000 b/d Garyville, LA; 222,000 b/d Catlettsburg, KY; 192,000 b/d Robinson, IL; 100,000 b/d Detroit, MI; 73,000 b/d Canton, OH; 72,000 b/d Texas City, TX; and 70,000 b/d St. Paul Park, MN), with throughput capacity of 974,000 b/d of crude oil. Its pipelines and terminals supplied petroleum products to 4,200 Marathon branded retail outlets, as of year-end 2006. Retail sales of gasoline and convenience store merchandise are also made through a wholly owned MAP subsidiary, Speedway SuperAmerica LLC., which had 1,636 retail outlets at the end of 2006 (primarily under the Speedway and SuperAmerica brand names). In addition, MRO owns a 50% interest in Pilot Travel Centers LLC.

Company Financials Fiscal Year Ended Dec. 31

Per Share Data ($)	2006	2005	2004	2003	2002	2001	2000	1999	1998	1997
Tangible Book Value	18.72	13.90	11.17	9.20	7.57	7.99	7.77	7.70	7.00	6.26
Cash Flow	9.30	6.14	3.57	3.53	2.80	4.12	2.69	2.59	2.14	1.95
Earnings	6.87	4.25	1.86	1.63	0.86	2.13	0.70	1.05	0.52	0.79
S&P Core Earnings	6.85	4.20	1.91	1.63	0.69	2.21	NA	NA	NA	NA
Dividends	0.77	0.61	0.52	0.48	0.46	0.46	0.44	0.42	0.42	0.38
Payout Ratio	11%	14%	28%	29%	53%	75%	63%	40%	80%	48%
Prices:High	49.37	36.34	21.30	16.81	15.15	16.87	15.19	16.94	20.25	19.44
Prices:Low	31.01	17.76	15.15	9.93	9.41	12.48	10.34	9.81	12.50	11.88
P/E Ratio:High	7	9	11	10	18	28	22	16	39	25
P/E Ratio:Low	5	4	8	6	11	20	15	9	24	15

Income Statement Analysis (Million $)										
Revenue	64,896	63,673	49,598	40,963	31,464	33,019	34,487	24,212	21,726	15,668
Operating Income	9,932	6,660	8,379	2,988	2,253	4,215	3,521	1,997	1,530	1,510
Depreciation, Depletion and Amortization	1,518	1,358	1,217	1,175	1,201	1,236	1,245	950	941	664
Interest Expense	108	145	161	238	288	196	260	290	311	285
Pretax Income	8,969	5,157	2,509	1,898	1,098	2,781	1,412	1,425	701	672
Effective Tax Rate	44.8%	33.5%	29.0%	30.8%	35.4%	27.3%	34.1%	22.7%	20.3%	32.1%
Net Income	4,957	3,051	1,257	1,012	536	1,318	432	654	310	456
S&P Core Earnings	4,949	3,013	1,290	1,014	428	1,367	NA	NA	NA	NA

Balance Sheet & Other Financial Data (Million $)										
Cash	2,585	2,617	3,369	1,396	488	657	340	111	137	36.0
Current Assets	10,096	9,383	8,867	6,040	4,479	4,411	4,985	4,102	2,976	2,018
Total Assets	30,831	28,498	23,423	19,482	17,812	16,129	15,232	15,705	14,544	10,565
Current Liabilities	8,061	8,154	5,253	4,207	3,659	3,468	4,012	3,149	2,610	2,262
Long Term Debt	3,061	3,698	4,057	4,085	4,410	3,432	4,196	3,504	3,640	2,476
Common Equity	14,607	11,705	8,111	6,075	5,082	4,940	4,845	4,800	4,312	3,618
Total Capital	20,083	17,868	16,411	12,171	12,908	11,632	12,235	11,552	10,992	7,596
Capital Expenditures	3,433	2,890	2,237	1,892	1,574	1,639	1,669	1,378	1,270	1,038
Cash Flow	6,475	4,409	2,474	2,187	1,737	2,546	1,677	1,604	1,251	1,120
Current Ratio	1.3	1.2	1.7	1.4	1.2	1.3	1.2	1.3	1.1	0.9
% Long Term Debt of Capitalization	15.2	20.7	24.7	33.6	34.2	29.5	34.3	30.3	33.1	32.6
% Return on Assets	16.7	11.8	5.9	5.4	3.2	7.9	2.8	4.3	2.5	4.4
% Return on Equity	37.7	30.8	17.7	18.1	10.7	22.4	9.0	14.4	7.8	13.1

Data as orig reptd.; bef. results of disc opers/spec. items. Per share data adj. for stk. divs.; EPS diluted. E-Estimated. NA-Not Available. NM-Not Meaningful. NR-Not Ranked. UR-Under Review.

Office: 5555 San Felipe Rd, Houston, TX 77056-2723.
Telephone: 713-629-6600.
Website: http://www.marathon.com
Chrmn: T.J. Usher

Pres & CEO: C.P. Cazalot, Jr.
SVP & CFO: J. Clark
VP & Treas: P.C. Reinbolt
VP, Secy & General Counsel: W.F. Schwind, Jr.

Investor Contact: K.L. Matheny (713-296-4114)
Board Members: C. F. Bolden, Jr., C. P. Cazalot, Jr., D. A. Daberko, W. L. Davis, S. Jackson, P. Lader, C. R. Lee, D. H. Reilley, S. E. Schofield, J. W. Snow, T. J. Usher, D. C. Yearley

Founded: 1901
Domicile: Delaware
Employees: 28,195

The McGraw·Hill Companies

Marriott International Inc.

STANDARD &POOR'S

S&P Recommendation HOLD ★★★☆☆	**Price** $35.11 (as of Nov 23, 2007)	**12-Mo. Target Price** $49.00	**Investment Style** Large-Cap Growth

GICS Sector Consumer Discretionary
Sub-Industry Hotels, Resorts & Cruise Lines

Summary MAR's lodging brands include nearly 2,950 properties, most of which are managed by the company or are operated by others through franchise relationships.

Key Stock Statistics (Source S&P, Vickers, company reports)

52-Wk Range	$52.00–33.05	S&P Oper. EPS 2007**E**	1.75	Market Capitalization(B)	$12.912	Beta	1.02
Trailing 12-Month EPS	$1.81	S&P Oper. EPS 2008**E**	2.05	Yield (%)	0.85	S&P 3-Yr. Proj. EPS CAGR(%)	8.00
Trailing 12-Month P/E	19.4	P/E on S&P Oper. EPS 2007**E**	20.1	Dividend Rate/Share	$0.30	S&P Credit Rating	BBB
$10K Invested 5 Yrs Ago	$20,962	Common Shares Outstg. (M)	367.8	Institutional Ownership (%)	53		

Price Performance

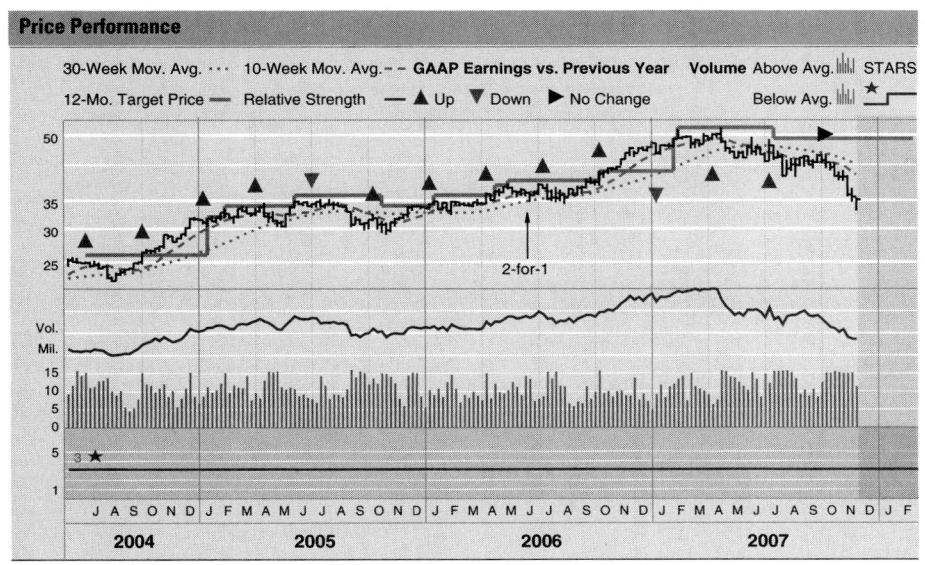

- 30-Week Mov. Avg. ····
- 10-Week Mov. Avg. ‑ ‑
- **GAAP Earnings vs. Previous Year**
- Volume Above Avg. ▐▐▐ STARS
- 12-Mo. Target Price —
- Relative Strength —
- ▲ Up ▼ Down ► No Change
- Below Avg. ▐▐▐ ★

2-for-1

2004   2005   2006   2007

Options: ASE, CBOE, P, Ph

Analysis prepared by **Mark S. Basham** on October 16, 2007, when the stock traded at **$ 40.72**.

Highlights

> In 2007, we look for hotel management income to rise about 15%, including 27% higher incentive management fees related to hotel profits. We expect growth drivers from MAR's lodging business to include 6%-7% higher comparable revenue per available room (RevPAR). We look for timeshare-related profits to increase by 2%. After sharply higher interest expense and lower other non-operating gains, partially reflecting $54 million in charges associated with a tax settlement with the IRS, we expect pretax income to be flat with 2006.

> We estimate 2007 EPS of $1.75, vs. $1.66 in 2006. Our 2007 estimate includes $0.13 in charges from an IRS settlement related to deductions claimed regarding the company's ESOP. Results exclude EPS of $0.12 and $0.01, respectively, from the company's synfuels business. Per share figures also reflect a 7% reduction in shares outstanding on ongoing share buybacks.

> In 2008, we see hotel related income up 9% on new property openings and about 5% higher RevPAR. We estimate EPS will increase 17% to $2.05 on fewer shares outstanding and the absence of the tax settlement charge.

Investment Rationale/Risk

> Our hold opinion on the stock reflects our view that the shares will get support from prospects for an improvement in lodging industry fundamentals, particularly in international markets. Also, we expect the company to repurchase additional stock in the year ahead.

> Risks to our recommendation and target price include the possibility that terrorism fears will heighten, leading to lower than anticipated demand for hotel rooms. New property development has increased dramatically recently, suggesting there is a growing risk that supply gains could outstrip demand growth.

> Our 12-month target price of $49 is based on a P/E of about 24X our 2008 EPS estimate, which reflects our view that the stock should receive a valuation modestly above the average P/E that we expect from a small group of peers. In our view, expectations of further RevPAR gains, particularly on MAR's foreign hotel portfolio, will help MAR shares retain most of their P/E premium. We are not attaching any value to MAR's synthetic fuel investments, as we expect that tax credits will not be available for synfuel produced by this investment after 2007.

Qualitative Risk Assessment

LOW	MEDIUM	HIGH

In our view, the company is subject to cyclical economic and industry changes. However, we believe that MAR's finances are relatively strong, and we expect that internal cash flow will be sufficient to finance future growth.

Quantitative Evaluations

S&P Quality Ranking A-

D	C	B-	B	B+	A-	A	A+

Relative Strength Rank WEAK

27

LOWEST = 1   HIGHEST = 99

Revenue/Earnings Data

Revenue (Million $)

	1Q	2Q	3Q	4Q	Year
2007	2,904	3,210	3,040	--	--
2006	2,705	2,891	2,703	3,861	12,160
2005	2,534	2,661	2,714	3,641	11,550
2004	2,252	2,402	2,304	3,141	10,099
2003	2,023	2,016	2,109	2,866	9,014
2002	1,808	2,034	1,924	2,675	8,441

Earnings Per Share ($)

	1Q	2Q	3Q	4Q	Year
2007	0.44	0.51	0.33	E0.62	E1.75
2006	0.39	0.43	0.33	0.52	1.66
2005	0.31	0.29	0.33	0.54	1.45
2004	0.24	0.34	0.28	0.40	1.24
2003	0.18	0.26	0.19	0.35	0.97
2002	0.16	0.25	0.23	0.24	0.87

Fiscal year ended Dec. 31. Next earnings report expected: Early February. EPS Estimates based on S&P Operating Earnings; historical GAAP earnings are as reported.

Dividend Data (Dates: mm/dd Payment Date: mm/dd/yy)

Amount ($)	Date Decl.	Ex-Div. Date	Stk. of Record	Payment Date
0.063	02/01	03/28	03/30	04/27/07
0.075	04/27	06/19	06/21	07/20/07
0.075	08/02	09/04	09/06	10/23/07
0.075	11/08	12/04	12/06	01/09/08

Dividends have been paid since 1998. Source: Company reports.

Please read the Required Disclosures and Analyst Certification on the last page of this report.

The McGraw-Hill Companies

Marriott International Inc.

STANDARD
&POOR'S

Business Summary October 16, 2007

CORPORATE OVERVIEW. As of September 7, 2007, Marriott International's lodging and timeshare businesses included 2,942 properties, with 527,307 rooms or suites. This compares with 2,832 properties with 518,832 rooms or suites as of year-end 2006, including 2,425 U.S. properties with 411,028 rooms or suites.

At year-end 2006, MAR had 1,035 properties (267,342 rooms or suites) that MAR operated under long-term management or lease agreements, and had 13 owned properties (3,156). With its management agreements, the company typically earns a base fee, and may receive an incentive management fee that is based on hotel profits. MAR also had 1,784 franchised properties, with 243,334 rooms, that were operated by other parties. With franchise properties, the company generally receives an initial application fee and continuing royalty fees.

By brand (including franchises), as of year-end 2006, MAR's business included 519 Marriott Hotels & Resorts, Marriott Conference Centers or JW Marriott Hotels & Resorts properties; 60 Ritz-Carlton hotels; 136 Renaissance hotels; 733 Courtyard hotels; 518 Fairfield Inn properties; 153 SpringHill Suites properties, 511 Residence Inn hotels; 123 TownPlace Suites properties; two Bulgari

Hotel & Resorts property, 57 timeshare properties; and some corporate housing rental units. In 2006, MAR's North American full-service lodging segment, which included Marriott full-service and Renaissance businesses, accounted for 43% of total revenues.

The company's international presence, as of year-end 2006, included 186 properties (38,242 rooms or suites) in Europe or the United Kingdom, 79 properties (28,172) in Asia, 34 (10,089) in the Middle East or Africa, 52 (11,397) in Canada, 13 (3,247) in Mexico, eight (2,354) in Australia, and 35 properties elsewhere.

CORPORATE STRATEGY. We look for MAR to emphasize managing and franchising, rather than owning, hotels. However, we expect that MAR will make loans and equity investments aimed at facilitating the growth and success of its lodging system. When MAR sells equity interests in hotels, it may hold management contracts for such properties.

Company Financials Fiscal Year Ended Dec. 31

Per Share Data ($)	2006	2005	2004	2003	2002	2001	2000	1999	1998	1997
Tangible Book Value	2.88	4.52	5.85	5.17	4.57	3.56	2.81	2.13	1.68	NA
Cash Flow	2.32	1.84	1.68	1.30	1.23	0.89	1.33	1.04	0.97	0.83
Earnings	1.66	1.45	1.24	0.97	0.87	0.46	0.95	0.76	0.73	0.60
S&P Core Earnings	1.57	1.25	1.00	0.68	0.77	0.35	NA	NA	NA	NA
Dividends	0.24	0.20	0.17	0.15	0.14	0.13	0.12	0.11	0.07	NA
Payout Ratio	14%	14%	13%	15%	16%	28%	12%	13%	10%	NA
Prices:High	48.31	35.39	32.00	23.60	23.23	25.25	21.75	22.25	18.97	NA
Prices:Low	32.31	29.01	20.32	14.28	13.13	13.65	13.06	14.50	9.69	NA
P/E Ratio:High	29	24	26	24	27	55	23	28	26	NA
P/E Ratio:Low	19	20	16	15	15	30	14	18	13	NA
Income Statement Analysis (Million $)										
Revenue	12,160	11,550	10,099	9,014	8,441	10,152	10,017	8,739	7,968	9,046
Operating Income	1,199	739	643	537	634	779	997	828	766	647
Depreciation	188	184	166	160	187	222	195	162	140	126
Interest Expense	124	106	99.0	110	86.0	109	100	61.0	30.0	22.0
Pretax Income	997	717	654	488	471	370	757	637	632	531
Effective Tax Rate	28.7%	13.1%	15.3%	NM	6.79%	36.2%	36.7%	37.2%	382.0%	39.0%
Net Income	717	668	594	476	439	236	479	400	390	324
S&P Core Earnings	680	579	484	330	381	180	NA	NA	NA	NA
Balance Sheet & Other Financial Data (Million $)										
Cash	193	203	770	229	198	817	334	489	390	289
Current Assets	3,314	2,010	1,946	1,235	1,744	2,130	1,415	1,600	1,333	1,367
Total Assets	8,588	8,530	8,668	8,177	8,296	9,107	8,237	7,324	6,233	5,557
Current Liabilities	2,522	1,992	2,356	1,770	2,207	1,802	1,917	1,743	1,412	1,639
Long Term Debt	1,818	1,681	836	1,391	1,553	2,815	2,016	1,676	1,267	422
Common Equity	2,618	3,252	4,081	3,838	3,573	3,478	3,267	2,908	2,570	2,586
Total Capital	4,436	4,944	4,929	5,398	5,232	6,293	5,283	4,584	3,837	3,008
Capital Expenditures	529	780	181	210	292	560	1,095	929	937	520
Cash Flow	905	852	760	636	626	458	674	562	530	450
Current Ratio	1.3	1.0	0.8	0.7	0.8	1.2	0.7	0.9	0.9	0.8
% Long Term Debt of Capitalization	41.0	34.0	16.9	25.7	29.7	44.7	38.2	36.6	33.0	14.0
% Net Income of Revenue	5.9	5.8	5.9	5.3	5.2	2.3	4.8	4.6	4.9	3.6
% Return on Assets	8.4	7.8	7.1	5.8	5.0	2.7	6.2	5.9	6.8	6.6
% Return on Equity	24.4	18.2	15.0	12.8	12.5	7.0	15.5	14.6	15.1	16.1

Data as orig reptd.; bef. results of disc opers/spec. items. Per share data adj. for stk. divs.; EPS diluted. E-Estimated. NA-Not Available. NM-Not Meaningful. NR-Not Ranked. UR-Under Review.

Office: 10400 Fernwood Road, Bethesda, MD 20817.
Telephone: 301-380-3000.
Website: http://www.marriott.com
Chrmn & CEO: J.W. Marriott, Jr.

Pres & COO: W.J. Shaw
EVP & CFO: A.M. Sorenson
EVP & General Counsel: E.A. Ryan
Secy: T.L. Turner

Investor Contact: T. Marder (301-380-2553)
Board Members: R. S. Braddock, F. Dukes McKenzie, L. W. Kellner, D. L. Lee, J. W. Marriott, III, J. W. Marriott, Jr., F. D. McKenzie, G. Munoz, H. J. Pearce, S. S. Reinemund, W. J. Shaw, L. M. Small

Founded: 1971
Domicile: Delaware
Employees: 150,600

The McGraw-Hill Companies

Marshall & Ilsley Corp

STANDARD &POOR'S

S&P Recommendation	SELL ★ ★ ☆ ☆ ☆	Price $30.30 (as of Nov 27, 2007)	12-Mo. Target Price $29.00	Investment Style Large-Cap Blend

GICS Sector Financials
Sub-Industry Regional Banks

Summary This bank holding company operates mainly in Wisconsin, and also in Arizona, Nevada, Minnesota, Missouri, Florida, Kansas and Oklahoma.

Key Stock Statistics (Source S&P, Vickers, company reports)

52-Wk Range	$51.48– 28.76	S&P Oper. EPS 2007**E**	3.33	Market Capitalization(B)	$7.797	Beta	0.84
Trailing 12-Month EPS	$3.28	S&P Oper. EPS 2008**E**	2.93	Yield (%)	Nil	S&P 3-Yr. Proj. EPS CAGR(%)	2.70
Trailing 12-Month P/E	9.2	P/E on S&P Oper. EPS 2007**E**	9.1	Dividend Rate/Share	Nil	S&P Credit Rating	A
$10K Invested 5 Yrs Ago	$15,076	Common Shares Outstg. (M)	257.3	Institutional Ownership (%)	55		

Price Performance

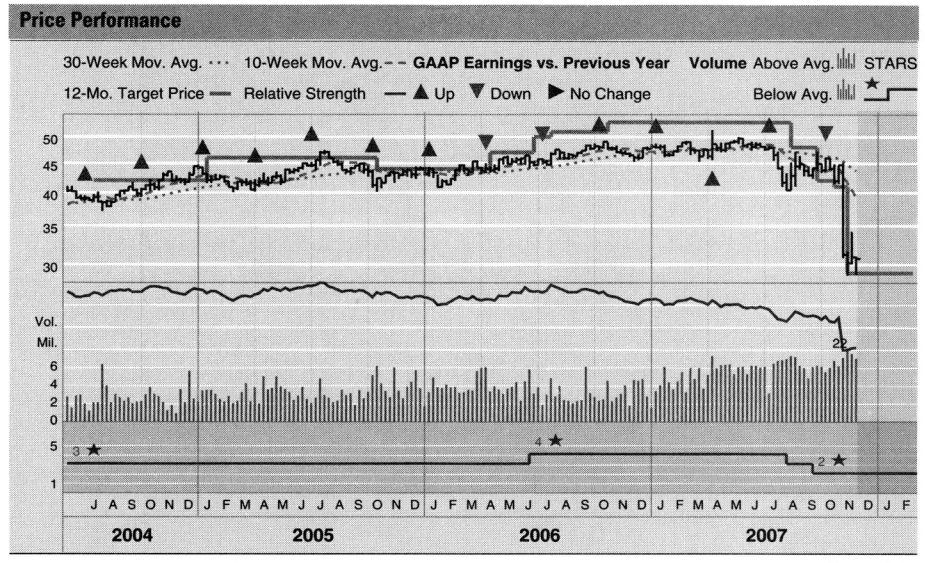

30-Week Mov. Avg. ···· 10-Week Mov. Avg. - - **GAAP Earnings vs. Previous Year** Volume Above Avg. STARS
12-Mo. Target Price ── Relative Strength ── ▲ Up ▼ Down ► No Change Below Avg. ★

Options: P, Ph

Qualitative Risk Assessment

LOW	MEDIUM	HIGH

Our risk assessment reflects our view of the company's large-cap valuation, the credit quality of its loan portfolio, and its history of profitability. While the company operates in a highly competitive and fragmented industry, the industry tends to produce relatively stable financial results.

Quantitative Evaluations

S&P Quality Ranking   **A**

D	C	B-	B	B+	A-	A	A+

Relative Strength Rank   **WEAK**

14

LOWEST = 1   HIGHEST = 99

Revenue/Earnings Data

Revenue (Million $)

	1Q	2Q	3Q	4Q	Year
2007	1,386	1,438	--	--	--
2006	1,139	1,290	1,381	1,317	5,128
2005	895.1	975.8	1,014	--	3,963
2004	702.5	728.0	792.2	--	3,112
2003	548.7	682.2	696.3	818.5	2,746
2002	639.4	654.3	665.3	--	2,650

Earnings Per Share ($)

	1Q	2Q	3Q	4Q	Year
2007	0.83	0.83	0.85	E0.86	E3.33
2006	0.72	0.74	0.92	0.79	3.17
2005	0.73	0.81	0.78	0.78	3.10
2004	0.65	0.67	0.69	0.76	2.77
2003	0.56	0.59	0.61	0.62	2.38
2002	0.53	0.54	0.54	0.55	2.16

Fiscal year ended Dec. 31. Next earnings report expected: Mid January. EPS Estimates based on S&P Operating Earnings; historical GAAP earnings are as reported.

Highlights

➤ The 12-month target price for MI has recently been changed to $29.00 from $41.00. The Highlights section of this Stock Report will be updated accordingly.

Investment Rationale/Risk

➤ The Investment Rationale/Risk section of this Stock Report will be updated shortly. For the latest News story on MI from MarketScope, see below.

➤ 11/19/07 09:35 am EST... S&P MAINTAINS SELL OPINION ON SHARES OF MARSHALL & ILSLEY (MI 30.4**): MI announces that it has lending exposure of $282 million with Franklin Credit Management (FCMC 0.52, NR), a troubled mortgage originator. At September 30, MI had nearly $45 billion in total loans outstanding, with a reserve for non-performing loans of $453 million, and therefore the exposure to FCMC is about 0.6% of MI's loans. MI says that all loans to FCMC are current, and estimates that the exposure to that company will not be material. We are keeping our '08 EPS estimate of $2.93, and our 12-month target price of $29, a discount-to-peers 10.0X our '08 EPS estimate. /E. Oja

Dividend Data (Dates: mm/dd Payment Date: mm/dd/yy)

Amount ($)	Date Decl.	Ex-Div. Date	Stk. of Record	Payment Date
0.270	02/15	02/27	03/01	03/09/07
0.310	04/24	05/23	05/25	06/08/07
0.310	08/16	08/29	08/31	09/14/07

Dividends have been paid since 1938. Source: Company reports.

Marshall & Ilsley Corp

STANDARD &POOR'S

Business Summary September 19, 2007

CORPORATE OVERVIEW. MI owns banking subsidiaries with operations in Wisconsin and the metropolitan areas of Phoenix and Tucson, AZ, Minneapolis/St. Paul, MN, St. Louis, MO, Las Vegas, NV, and Naples and Bonita Springs, FL. MI also owns nonbanking subsidiaries that are related or incidental to banking. The company has two reportable business segments: Banking (54% of total external revenues) and Data Services (37%). The company also has other business operations (8%) that include trust services, residential mortgage banking, capital markets, brokerage and insurance, commercial leasing, commercial mortgage banking, and community development investments.

The Metavante subsidiary is the Data Services segment of MI. Metavante delivers banking and payment technologies to financial services firms and businesses and organizes its business into two groups, Financial Solutions (FS) and Payment Solutions (PS). Metavante products and services drive account processing for deposit, loan and trust systems, image-based and conventional check processing, electronic funds transfer, consumer health care payments, and electronic presentment and payment.

PRIMARY BUSINESS DYNAMICS. On April 3, 2007, MI announced that it would separate MI and Metavante Corporation into two separate publicly held companies by the end of 2007.

Under an investment agreement with Warburg Pincus, a global private equity investor, Warburg Pincus has agreed to invest $625 million to acquire an equity stake of 25% in Metavante Corp. MI shareholders will own the remaining 75%. This plan will be implemented through the spinoff of MI and is intended to be tax-free to MI and its shareholders. In connection with the plan, approximately $1.75 billion of new Metavante debt will be arranged.

Upon completion of the transaction, shareholders will receive one share of the new Marshall & Ilsley Corp. stock for each one share of MI held and one share of Metavante Corp. stock for every three shares of MI stock held.

Company Financials Fiscal Year Ended Dec. 31

Per Share Data ($)	2006	2005	2004	2003	2002	2001	2000	1999	1998	1997
Tangible Book Value	11.51	9.02	7.76	9.96	8.61	9.00	9.06	8.12	8.67	7.43
Earnings	3.17	3.10	2.77	2.38	2.16	1.54	1.45	1.57	1.31	1.21
S&P Core Earnings	3.17	2.99	2.66	2.28	2.07	1.49	NA	NA	NA	NA
Dividends	1.05	0.93	0.81	0.70	0.55	0.57	0.52	0.47	0.43	0.39
Payout Ratio	33%	30%	29%	29%	25%	37%	36%	30%	33%	32%
Prices:High	49.10	47.40	44.70	38.46	32.12	32.12	31.13	36.38	31.13	31.13
Prices:Low	40.83	40.05	35.67	24.60	23.11	23.54	19.13	27.19	19.69	16.19
P/E Ratio:High	15	15	16	16	15	21	22	23	24	26
P/E Ratio:Low	13	13	13	10	11	15	13	17	15	13

Income Statement Analysis (Million $)										
Net Interest Income	1,490	1,233	1,132	1,057	1,006	843	673	705	676	564
Tax Equivalent Adjustment	NA	33.3	NA	NA	32.2	31.2	31.0	28.7	26.2	22.8
Non Interest Income	1,906	1,704	1,411	1,194	1,089	1,020	978	850	726	596
Loan Loss Provision	50.6	44.8	38.0	63.0	74.4	54.1	30.4	25.4	27.1	17.3
% Expense/Operating Revenue	63.6%	62.2%	62.7%	64.5%	61.9%	68.1%	65.4%	64.2%	67.1%	66.9%
Pretax Income	1,196	1,090	945	758	719	501	470	528	465	370
Effective Tax Rate	32.4%	33.3%	33.6%	28.3%	33.2%	32.6%	32.5%	32.9%	35.2%	33.8%
Net Income	808	727	627	544	480	338	317	355	301	245
% Net Interest Margin	3.27	3.31	3.52	3.65	3.96	3.67	2.81	3.58	3.69	4.00
S&P Core Earnings	808	705	605	519	453	319	NA	NA	NA	NA

Balance Sheet & Other Financial Data (Million $)										
Money Market Assets	293	330	191	163	250	947	163	175	146	81.0
Investment Securities	7,473	6,320	6,085	5,607	5,209	4,464	5,848	5,575	5,192	4,969
Commercial Loans	23,717	19,023	16,646	14,254	6,586	10,815	9,649	4,754	4,078	3,865
Other Loans	17,917	14,866	12,810	10,896	17,011	8,480	7,938	11,580	9,918	8,776
Total Assets	56,230	46,213	40,437	34,373	32,875	27,254	26,078	24,370	21,566	19,477
Demand Deposits	6,112	5,525	15,005	4,715	4,462	3,559	3,130	2,831	2,929	2,723
Time Deposits	27,972	22,149	11,450	17,555	15,932	12,934	16,119	13,604	12,991	11,633
Long Term Debt	8,026	6,669	5,027	2,735	2,284	1,560	921	665	794	791
Common Equity	6,151	4,769	3,970	3,329	3,037	2,536	3,200	2,117	2,282	1,919
% Return on Assets	1.6	1.7	1.7	1.6	1.6	1.3	1.3	1.5	1.5	1.4
% Return on Equity	14.7	16.6	17.1	17.1	17.4	13.8	10.6	13.8	14.0	15.1
% Loan Loss Reserve	1.0	1.1	1.2	1.4	1.4	1.4	1.3	1.4	1.6	1.6
% Loans/Deposits	123.0	123.5	111.6	113.1	117.2	117.0	91.4	99.4	88.0	87.4
% Equity to Assets	10.7	9.9	9.8	9.5	9.2	9.0	11.9	11.0	10.2	9.3

Data as orig reptd.; bef. results of disc opers/spec. items. Per share data adj. for stk. divs.; EPS diluted. E-Estimated. NA-Not Available. NM-Not Meaningful. NR-Not Ranked. UR-Under Review.

Office: 770 N Water St, Milwaukee, WI 53202.
Telephone: 414-765-7801.
Website: http://www.micorp.com
Chrmn: D.J. Kuester

Pres & CEO: M.F. Furlong
SVP & CFO: G.A. Smith
SVP & Treas: M.C. Smith
SVP & Cntlr: P.R. Justiliano

Investor Contact: D.L. Urban
Board Members: M. M. Aslin, A. N. Baur, J. F. Chait, J. W. Daniels, Jr., M. F. Furlong, B. E. Jacobs, T. D. Kellner, D. J. Kuester, D. J. Lubar, K. C. Lyall, J. A. Mellowes, E. L. Meyer, R. J. O'Toole, S. W. Orr, Jr., P. M. Platten III, J. S. Shiely, D. S. Waller, G. E. Wardeberg, J. B. Wigdale

Founded: 1959
Domicile: Wisconsin
Employees: 14,699

Marsh & McLennan Companies Inc.

STANDARD &POOR'S

S&P Recommendation HOLD ★★★☆☆	**Price** $24.92 (as of Nov 23, 2007)	**12-Mo. Target Price** $25.00	**Investment Style** Large-Cap Blend

GICS Sector Financials
Sub-Industry Insurance Brokers

Summary This global professional services concern provides risk and insurance services, investment management, and consulting services through its operating companies.

Key Stock Statistics (Source S&P, Vickers, company reports)

52-Wk Range	$33.90– 23.12	S&P Oper. EPS 2007**E**	1.16	Market Capitalization(B)	$13.507	Beta	1.11
Trailing 12-Month EPS	$4.71	S&P Oper. EPS 2008**E**	1.60	Yield (%)	3.05	S&P 3-Yr. Proj. EPS CAGR(%)	17.00
Trailing 12-Month P/E	5.3	P/E on S&P Oper. EPS 2007**E**	21.5	Dividend Rate/Share	$0.76	S&P Credit Rating	BBB
$10K Invested 5 Yrs Ago	$5,983	Common Shares Outstg. (M)	542.0	Institutional Ownership (%)	86		

Price Performance

30-Week Mov. Avg. · · · 10-Week Mov. Avg. – – **GAAP Earnings vs. Previous Year** **Volume** Above Avg. ▍▋▍ **STARS**
12-Mo. Target Price — Relative Strength – ▲ Up ▼ Down ▶ No Change Below Avg. ▍▋▍ ★

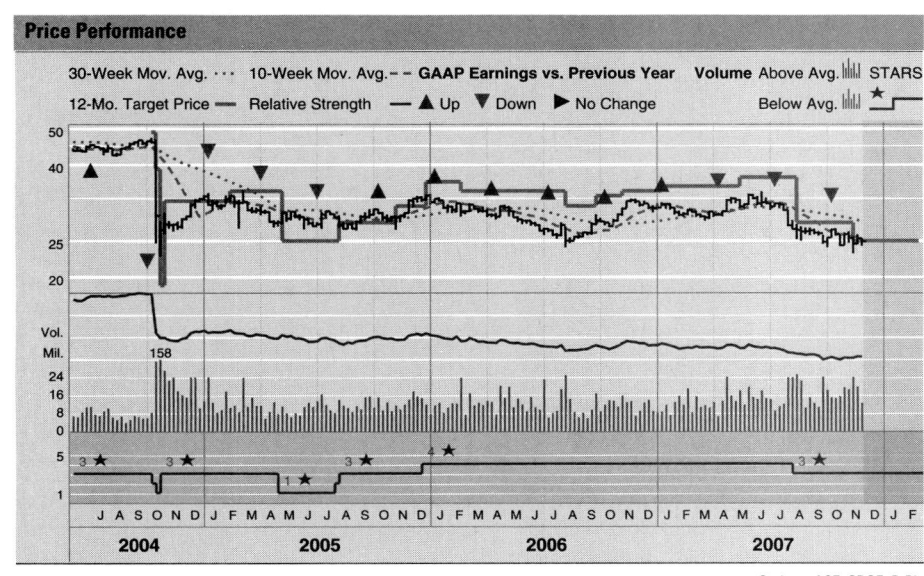

Options: ASE, CBOE, P, Ph

Analysis prepared by **Tanjila Shafi** on November 15, 2007, when the stock traded at **$ 25.38.**

Highlights

➤ We anticipate that total revenues in 2008 will grow in the single-digits, driven by the company's international and consumer businesses. We see risk and insurance services segment revenue increasing modestly in 2008, reflecting solid growth in EMEA and Asia-Pacific. However, we are concerned that retention rates may continue to decline in the U.S. and U.K., hindering revenue growth in the segment. We estimate a mid-single digit increase for total consulting revenues, based on the addition of new clients and an expansion of offerings in new geographic locations. Revenues in the risk consulting and technology segment should rise in the mid-single digits.

➤ We expect margin improvement for the company in 2008. We believe expenses will be lowered given the various cost-cutting initiatives set by the company, which we see resulting in $125 million of savings next year.

➤ We forecast 2007 EPS from continuing operations at $1.16, compared to 2006 EPS from continuing operations of $1.45. Our 2008 EPS from continuing operations estimate is $1.60.

Investment Rationale/Risk

➤ We believe that 2008 will be a transitional year for the MMC as it has implemented a five-step plan to improve its businesses, especially its brokerage operations. The company is seeking to 1) solidify its leadership team; 2) simplify its business practices allowing brokers to have more face time with clients; 3) focus on set of operational and IT initiatives; 4) implement a major cost-cutting plan, which should result in $125 million in savings for 2008; and 5) restructure its compensation initiatives. While we believe the plan will expand revenues and cut expenses, we still have concerns regarding the declining customer retention rates in the company's U.S. brokerage business.

➤ Risks to our recommendation and target price include lower-than-expected revenue on rate increases and/or deteriorating client retention; less-than-projected cost savings from restructurings and layoffs; lower-than-anticipated cost savings and growth at Kroll; and unfavorable legal and regulatory developments related to contingent commissions.

➤ Our 12-month target price is $25, about 15.6X estimated 2008 EPS from continuing operations, and in line with MMC's historical multiples.

Qualitative Risk Assessment

LOW	**MEDIUM**	HIGH

Our risk assessment reflects the company's leading market share position, diversified businesses, and global scale, offset by regulatory scrutiny and business model changes as a result of contingent commissions.

Quantitative Evaluations

S&P Quality Ranking A-

D	C	B-	B	B+	**A-**	A	A+

Relative Strength Rank MODERATE

59

LOWEST = 1 HIGHEST = 99

Revenue/Earnings Data

Revenue (Million $)

	1Q	2Q	3Q	4Q	Year
2007	2,812	2,819	2,794	--	--
2006	3,016	2,970	2,872	3,063	11,921
2005	3,070	2,977	2,779	2,826	11,652
2004	3,196	3,028	2,950	2,985	12,159
2003	2,852	2,865	2,837	3,034	11,588
2002	2,635	2,612	2,553	2,640	10,440

Earnings Per Share ($)

2007	0.41	0.25	0.15	E0.35	E1.16
2006	0.43	0.31	0.32	0.39	1.45
2005	0.24	0.30	0.11	0.03	0.67
2004	0.83	0.73	0.04	-1.29	0.33
2003	0.81	0.66	0.65	0.69	2.81
2002	0.74	0.60	0.55	0.57	2.45

Fiscal year ended Dec. 31. Next earnings report expected: Mid February. EPS Estimates based on S&P Operating Earnings; historical GAAP earnings are as reported.

Dividend Data (Dates: mm/dd Payment Date: mm/dd/yy)

Amount ($)	Date Decl.	Ex-Div. Date	Stk. of Record	Payment Date
0.190	01/17	01/22	01/24	02/15/07
0.190	03/14	04/03	04/06	05/15/07
0.190	05/17	07/03	07/06	08/15/07
0.190	09/19	10/11	10/15	11/15/07

Dividends have been paid since 1923. Source: Company reports.

Marsh & McLennan Companies Inc.

**STANDARD
&POOR'S**

Business Summary November 15, 2007

CORPORATE OVERVIEW. Marsh & McLennan is one of the world's largest in-surance brokers. The insurance brokerage industry has suffered in recent years from probes into bid rigging and contingent commissions. We believe recent settlements and corporate restructurings have improved the outlook at MMC, but ongoing legal and regulatory proceedings and uncertainty regard-ing implementing a new business model present weak near-term earnings vis-ibility, in our view.

MMC operates in four main segments: risk and insurance services, risk con-sulting and technology, investment management, and consulting. Risk and in-surance services (45% of operating segment revenues and 46% of operating segment operating income in 2006; 48% and 36% in 2005) includes insurance services, reinsurance services and risk capital holdings, risk management and consulting, insurance broking, and insurance program management. Reinsurance broking and catastrophe and financial modeling services are done under the Guy Carpenter name. Risk consulting and technology (8.1% and 10% in 2006; 7.4% and 14% in 2005) are performed under the Kroll name. Consulting and human resource outsourcing (35% and 32% in 2006; 32% and 53% in 2005) is done under the Mercer name.

Investment management (12% and 21% in 2006; 13% and 31% in 2005) is pri-marily carried out by Putnam Investments. At December 31, 2006, assets un-der management (AUM) amounted to $192 billion, a further decline from $196 billion at December 31, 2005, $217 billion at December 31, 2004, $240 billion at year-end 2003, and $251 billion at year-end 2002.

LEGAL/REGULATORY ISSUES. In April 2004, Putnam entered into the final set-tlements of charges by the SEC and the Massachusetts Secretary of the Com-monwealth related to alleged short-term trading of Putnam mutual funds by employees in their personal accounts. Under the settlements, Putnam agreed, without admitting or denying the charges, to pay $110 million in penalties and restitution, and to implement a number of remedial actions. In March 2005, an independent consultant concluded that Putnam should pay fund shareholders $108.5 million, of which $83.5 million was in addition to previous settlement amounts.

Company Financials Fiscal Year Ended Dec. 31

Per Share Data ($)	2006	2005	2004	2003	2002	2001	2000	1999	1998	1997
Tangible Book Value	NM	NM	NM	NM	NM	NM	9.47	NM	NM	1.53
Cash Flow	2.34	1.58	1.18	3.52	3.10	2.61	2.94	2.07	1.98	1.19
Earnings	1.45	0.67	0.33	2.81	2.45	1.70	2.05	1.31	1.49	0.80
S&P Core Earnings	1.30	0.38	1.11	2.29	1.60	0.91	NA	NA	NA	NA
Dividends	0.68	0.68	0.99	1.18	1.09	1.03	0.95	0.85	0.73	0.55
Payout Ratio	47%	101%	NM	42%	44%	61%	46%	65%	49%	69%
Prices:High	32.73	34.25	49.69	54.97	57.30	59.03	67.84	48.38	32.16	26.67
Prices:Low	24.00	26.67	22.75	38.27	34.61	39.50	35.25	28.56	21.69	17.10
P/E Ratio:High	23	51	NM	19	23	35	33	37	22	33
P/E Ratio:Low	17	40	NM	14	14	23	17	22	15	21

Income Statement Analysis (Million $)										
Revenue	11,921	11,652	12,159	11,588	10,440	9,943	10,157	9,157	7,190	6,009
Operating Income	1,946	1,386	2,073	2,887	2,633	2,283	2,179	1,859	1,671	944
Depreciation	488	490	456	391	359	520	488	400	251	199
Interest Expense	303	332	219	185	160	196	247	233	140	106
Pretax Income	1,219	571	450	2,335	2,133	1,590	1,955	1,247	1,305	662
Effective Tax Rate	31.8%	33.6%	57.6%	33.0%	35.0%	37.7%	38.5%	41.8%	39.0%	39.7%
Net Income	818	369	176	1,540	1,365	974	1,181	726	796	399
S&P Core Earnings	732	211	590	1,254	890	525	NA	NA	NA	NA

Balance Sheet & Other Financial Data (Million $)										
Cash	2,089	2,020	1,396	665	546	537	240	428	610	424
Current Assets	5,834	5,262	4,887	3,901	3,664	3,792	3,639	3,283	3,245	2,569
Total Assets	18,137	17,892	18,337	15,053	13,855	13,293	13,769	13,021	11,871	7,914
Current Liabilities	5,549	4,351	4,735	4,089	3,863	3,938	4,119	4,318	5,002	2,379
Long Term Debt	3,860	5,044	4,691	2,910	2,891	2,334	2,347	2,357	1,590	1,240
Common Equity	5,819	5,360	5,056	5,451	5,018	5,173	5,228	4,170	3,659	3,199
Total Capital	9,679	10,404	9,747	8,361	7,909	7,507	7,575	6,527	5,249	4,439
Capital Expenditures	307	345	376	436	423	433	472	358	297	202
Cash Flow	1,306	859	632	1,931	1,724	1,494	1,669	1,126	1,047	598
Current Ratio	1.1	1.2	1.0	1.0	0.9	1.0	0.9	0.8	0.6	1.1
% Long Term Debt of Capitalization	39.9	48.5	48.1	34.8	36.6	31.1	31.0	36.1	30.3	27.9
% Net Income of Revenue	6.9	3.2	1.4	13.3	13.1	9.8	11.6	7.9	11.1	6.6
% Return on Assets	4.5	2.0	1.1	10.7	10.1	7.2	8.8	5.8	8.0	6.4
% Return on Equity	14.6	7.1	3.4	29.4	26.8	18.7	25.1	18.5	23.2	15.7

Data as orig reptd.; bef. results of disc opers/spec. items. Per share data adj. for stk. divs.; EPS diluted. E-Estimated. NA-Not Available. NM-Not Meaningful. NR-Not Ranked. UR-Under Review.

Office: 1166 Avenue Of The Americas , New York, NY 10036-2774.
Telephone: 212-345-5000.
Email: shareowner-svcs@email.bankofny.com
Website: http://www.mmc.com

Chrmn: S.R. Hardis
Pres & CEO: M.G. Cherkasky
Vice Chrmn: D.A. Nadler
Vice Chrmn: M. Cabiallavetta

EVP & General Counsel: P.J. Beshar
Investor Contact: M.B. Bartley (212-345-5000)
Board Members: L. M. Baker, Jr., Z. W. Carter, M. G. Cherkasky, O. Fanjul, S. R. Hardis, G. S. King, M. D. Oken, D. A. Olsen, M. O. Schapiro, A. Simmons, L. of Monkton

Founded: 1923
Domicile: Delaware
Employees: 55,200

The McGraw-Hill Companies

Masco Corp

STANDARD &POOR'S

S&P Recommendation BUY ★★★★☆

Price	12-Mo. Target Price	Investment Style
$21.65 (as of Nov 23, 2007)	$31.00	Large-Cap Blend

GICS Sector Industrials
Sub-Industry Building Products

Summary This company is one of the world's leading makers of faucets, cabinets, coatings and other consumer brand-name home improvement and building products.

Key Stock Statistics (Source S&P, Vickers, company reports)

52-Wk Range	$34.72–20.89	S&P Oper. EPS 2007E	1.80	Market Capitalization(B)	$7.949	Beta	1.04
Trailing 12-Month EPS	$0.97	S&P Oper. EPS 2008E	1.95	Yield (%)	4.25	S&P 3-Yr. Proj. EPS CAGR(%)	-1.00
Trailing 12-Month P/E	22.3	P/E on S&P Oper. EPS 2007E	12.0	Dividend Rate/Share	$0.92	S&P Credit Rating	BBB+
$10K Invested 5 Yrs Ago	$12,962	Common Shares Outstg. (M)	367.1	Institutional Ownership (%)	100		

Price Performance

30-Week Mov. Avg. ··· 10-Week Mov. Avg. - - **GAAP Earnings vs. Previous Year** Volume Above Avg. STARS
12-Mo. Target Price — Relative Strength — ▲ Up ▼ Down ► No Change Below Avg. ★

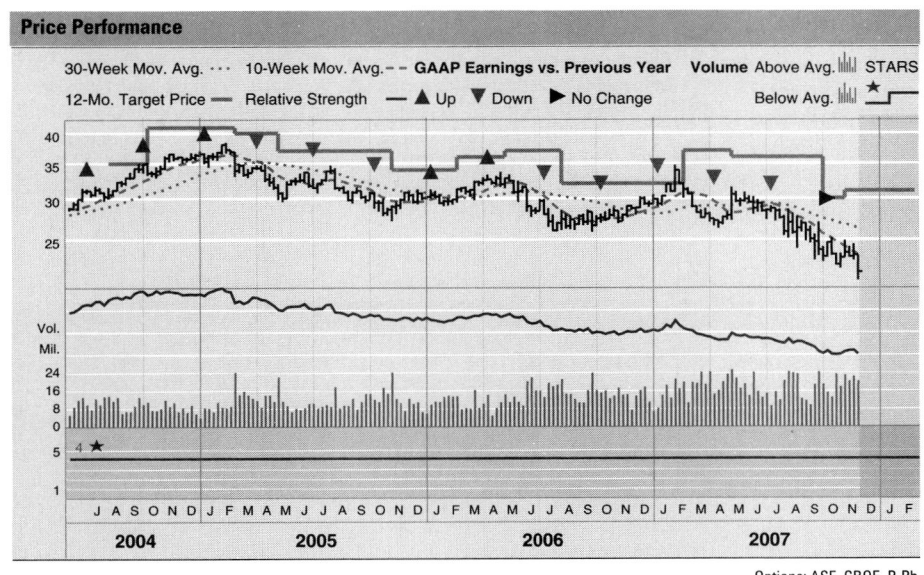

Options: ASE, CBOE, P, Ph

Analysis prepared by **Michael W. Jaffe** on November 14, 2007, when the stock traded at **$ 23.54**.

Highlights

➤ We forecast a flat level of sales in 2008. We expect demand to continue to be limited by a still very slow U.S. housing market. We see a lesser level of refinancings and home equity loans restricting big-ticket consumer spending for some time longer. On the other hand, we think sales will be aided by selling price increases, and, to a lesser extent, market share gains. We look for higher sales in Europe, on our forecast of ongoing economic growth in that region. In addition, we see European sales being aided by ongoing favorable currency exchange rates.

➤ We project slightly wider margins in 2008, on the price hikes that we foresee and expected benefits from cost-cutting initiatives put in place over the past year, particularly headcount reductions amounting to 17% of MAS's North American workforce.

➤ Our $1.80 EPS forecast for 2007 excludes $0.13 a share of one-time charges, including $0.10 recorded in the first nine months. We see 2008 EPS of $1.95.

Investment Rationale/Risk

➤ We think very soft U.S. housing markets will continue to limit MAS's sales through the end of 2008. Yet, we see its long-term outlook aided by its strong brand names and growing home center presence. Additionally, we have a favorable view of its business model. Based on these factors and valuation considerations, we believe MAS shares are undervalued.

➤ Risks to our recommendation and target price include a longer-than-expected housing market downturn; a larger-than-estimated impact from commodities prices; an inability to put through price hikes to offset these higher costs; and an unsuccessful executive transition.

➤ Recently trading at about 12X our 2008 EPS forecast, MAS was at a 14% discount to the S&P 500 and in the lower part of its range for the past decade. Masco's business has cyclical qualities, but we think it has very strong positions in many of the markets it serves, and that its aggressive cost cuts of the past year will bring its earnings to a trough in coming periods. As a result, we think the stock should trade at a small premium to the market. Using a multiple of 16X our 2008 EPS estimate, we arrive at our 12-month target price of $31.

Qualitative Risk Assessment

LOW	MEDIUM	HIGH

Our risk assessment for Masco reflects the company's relatively consistent generation of strong levels of free cash flow, and what we view as a very good business model. These factors have, in our view, been major contributors to Masco's 49 consecutive years of cash dividend increases. However, we think Masco's risk profile has been raised by an executive transition, with its chairman and CEO giving up his CEO role in July 2007, and its president planning to retire in early 2008.

Quantitative Evaluations

S&P Quality Ranking B+

D	C	B-	B	B+	A-	A	A+

Relative Strength Rank MODERATE

34

LOWEST = 1   HIGHEST = 99

Revenue/Earnings Data

Revenue (Million $)

	1Q	2Q	3Q	4Q	Year
2007	2,881	3,148	3,059	--	--
2006	3,167	3,370	3,295	2,946	12,778
2005	2,914	3,286	3,296	3,146	12,642
2004	2,806	3,061	3,173	3,034	12,074
2003	2,498	2,788	2,918	2,862	10,936
2002	2,100	2,314	2,518	2,487	9,419

Earnings Per Share ($)

2007	0.37	0.50	0.57	E0.26	E1.80
2006	0.50	0.53	0.57	-0.48	1.15
2005	0.47	0.62	0.60	0.34	2.03
2004	0.52	0.65	0.64	0.23	2.04
2003	0.32	0.46	0.53	0.19	1.51
2002	0.31	0.43	0.24	0.37	1.33

Fiscal year ended Dec. 31. Next earnings report expected: Mid February. EPS Estimates based on S&P Operating Earnings; historical GAAP earnings are as reported.

Dividend Data (Dates: mm/dd Payment Date: mm/dd/yy)

Amount ($)	Date Decl.	Ex-Div. Date	Stk. of Record	Payment Date
0.220	12/06	01/03	01/05	02/05/07
0.230	03/23	04/03	04/06	05/07/07
0.230	06/22	07/03	07/06	08/06/07
0.230	09/14	10/03	10/05	11/05/07

Dividends have been paid since 1944. Source: Company reports.

Masco Corp

STANDARD &POOR'S

Business Summary November 14, 2007

Masco is one of the largest U.S. makers of brand name consumer products for home improvement and new construction markets; it derives most of its revenues from the sale of faucets, kitchen and bath cabinets, plumbing supplies and architectural coatings. Operations are focused on North America (82% of 2006 sales) and Europe (most of the rest). Home Depot contributed 20% of 2006 sales.

The plumbing products division (26% of 2006 sales) is a major global faucet maker. Masco revolutionized faucets in 1954 with the Delta line, and also offers the Peerless, Brizo and Newport Brass brands, among others. In addition, the division offers other bath products, including plumbing fittings and valves, bathtubs and shower enclosures, and spa items; brand names include Alsons, Aqua Glass, and HotSpring. It makes cabinets and related products (26%), including cabinetry for kitchen, bath, storage, home office and home entertainment applications, featuring the Kraftmaid, Merillat, and Mill's Pride brands. According to the company, it is the largest U.S. maker of kitchen and bath cabinetry.

Masco sells decorative architectural items (14%), including paints and stains, and decorative bath and shower accessories. Trade names include Behr in paints and stains and Franklin Brass in bath and shower. It also supplies and installs insulation products and other building products such as fireplaces, cabinetry, gutters, shelving and windows (25%), and sells other specialty products (11%), such as windows and patio doors, electric staple guns, and radiators.

We believe that an aggressive acquisition program enabled Masco to build large positions in the markets it serves. Since 2003, however, the company adopted a business plan that shifted it away from a focus on takeovers. It now plans to concentrate on internal growth, with an increased emphasis on cash flow and return on invested capital.

In July 2007, Richard Manoogian, Masco's chairman and CEO, gave up his CEO duties and moved into a new post as executive chairman. Based on Mr. Manoogian's recommendation, Timothy Wadhams, Masco's senior vice president and CFO since 2001, was appointed to the CEO role. In addition, Alan Barry, Masco's president, informed the board in April 2007 of his desire to step down from his post in early 2008, when he reaches normal retirement age.

Company Financials Fiscal Year Ended Dec. 31

Per Share Data ($)	2006	2005	2004	2003	2002	2001	2000	1999	1998	1997
Tangible Book Value	0.54	0.88	1.54	1.36	1.31	1.30	2.78	3.14	4.99	4.53
Cash Flow	1.76	2.66	2.56	2.00	1.85	1.02	1.84	1.68	1.78	1.48
Earnings	1.15	2.03	2.04	1.51	1.33	0.42	1.31	1.28	1.39	1.17
S&P Core Earnings	2.15	2.17	2.25	1.67	1.52	1.12	NA	NA	NA	NA
Dividends	0.86	0.78	0.66	0.58	0.55	0.52	0.49	0.45	0.43	0.40
Payout Ratio	75%	38%	32%	38%	41%	125%	37%	35%	31%	34%
Prices:High	33.70	38.43	37.02	28.44	29.43	26.94	27.00	33.69	33.00	26.91
Prices:Low	25.85	27.15	25.88	16.59	17.25	17.76	14.50	22.50	20.75	16.88
P/E Ratio:High	29	19	18	19	22	64	21	26	24	23
P/E Ratio:Low	22	13	13	11	13	42	11	18	15	14

Income Statement Analysis (Million $)										
Revenue	12,778	12,642	12,074	10,936	9,419	8,358	7,243	6,307	4,345	3,760
Operating Income	1,700	1,881	1,944	1,738	1,683	1,309	1,295	1,093	817	703
Depreciation	244	241	237	244	220	269	238	182	136	116
Interest Expense	240	247	217	262	237	239	191	120	85.3	79.9
Pretax Income	900	1,412	1,518	1,216	1,031	301	893	904	755	631
Effective Tax Rate	45.8%	36.7%	37.5%	38.1%	33.8%	34.0%	33.8%	37.0%	37.0%	39.4%
Net Income	461	872	930	740	682	199	592	570	476	382
S&P Core Earnings	859	936	1,027	816	779	528	NA	NA	NA	NA

Balance Sheet & Other Financial Data (Million $)										
Cash	1,958	1,964	1,256	795	1,067	312	169	231	542	441
Current Assets	5,115	5,123	4,402	3,804	3,950	2,627	2,308	2,110	1,863	1,627
Total Assets	12,325	12,559	12,541	12,149	12,050	9,183	7,744	6,635	5,167	4,334
Current Liabilities	3,389	2,894	2,147	2,099	1,932	1,237	1,078	846	847	620
Long Term Debt	3,533	3,915	4,187	3,848	4,316	3,628	3,018	2,431	1,391	1,322
Common Equity	4,471	4,848	5,596	5,456	5,294	4,120	3,426	3,137	2,729	2,229
Total Capital	8,004	9,665	9,783	9,304	9,610	7,747	6,444	5,788	4,321	3,714
Capital Expenditures	388	282	310	271	285	274	388	351	189	167
Cash Flow	705	1,113	1,167	984	902	468	830	751	612	498
Current Ratio	1.5	1.8	2.1	1.8	2.0	2.1	2.1	2.5	2.2	2.6
% Long Term Debt of Capitalization	44.1	40.5	42.8	41.4	44.9	46.8	46.8	42.0	32.2	35.6
% Net Income of Revenue	3.6	6.9	7.7	6.8	7.2	2.4	8.2	9.0	11.0	10.2
% Return on Assets	3.7	6.9	7.5	6.1	6.5	2.3	8.2	9.3	10.0	9.5
% Return on Equity	9.9	17.0	16.6	13.8	14.7	5.3	18.0	19.3	19.2	18.8

Data as orig reptd.; bef. results of disc opers/spec. items. Per share data adj. for stk. divs.; EPS diluted. E-Estimated. NA-Not Available. NM-Not Meaningful. NR-Not Ranked. UR-Under Review.

Office: 21001 Van Born Road, Taylor, MI 48180.
Telephone: 313-274-7400.
Website: http://www.masco.com
Exec Chrmn: R.A. Manoogian

Pres & COO: A.H. Barry
CEO: T. Wadhams
SVP & General Counsel: J.R. Leekley
VP, CFO & Treas: J.G. Sznewajs

Investor Contact: M.C. Duey (313-274-7400)
Board Members: D. W. Archer, T. G. Denomme, P. A. Dow, A. F. Earley, Jr., V. G. Istock, D. L. Johnston, J. M. Losh, R. A. Manoogian, L. A. Payne, M. Van Lokeren, T. Wadhams

Founded: 1929
Domicile: Delaware
Employees: 57,000

Mattel Inc.

STANDARD &POOR'S

S&P Recommendation	**STRONG BUY** ★★★★★	Price	12-Mo. Target Price	Investment Style
		$20.47 (as of Nov 23, 2007)	$29.00	Large-Cap Blend

GICS Sector Consumer Discretionary
Sub-Industry Leisure Products

Summary This large toy company's brands and products include Barbie dolls, Fisher-Price toys, and Hot Wheels.

Key Stock Statistics (Source S&P, Vickers, company reports)

52-Wk Range	$29.71– 19.52	S&P Oper. EPS 2007**E**	1.51	Market Capitalization(B)	$7.509	Beta		0.80
Trailing 12-Month EPS	$1.42	S&P Oper. EPS 2008**E**	1.72	Yield (%)	3.66	S&P 3-Yr. Proj. EPS CAGR(%)		6.00
Trailing 12-Month P/E	14.4	P/E on S&P Oper. EPS 2007**E**	13.6	Dividend Rate/Share	$0.75	S&P Credit Rating		BBB-
$10K Invested 5 Yrs Ago	$11,254	Common Shares Outstg. (M)	366.8	Institutional Ownership (%)	98			

Price Performance

- 30-Week Mov. Avg. · · · 10-Week Mov. Avg. – – **GAAP Earnings vs. Previous Year**   **Volume** Above Avg. STARS
- 12-Mo. Target Price — Relative Strength — ▲ Up ▼ Down ► No Change   Below Avg. ★

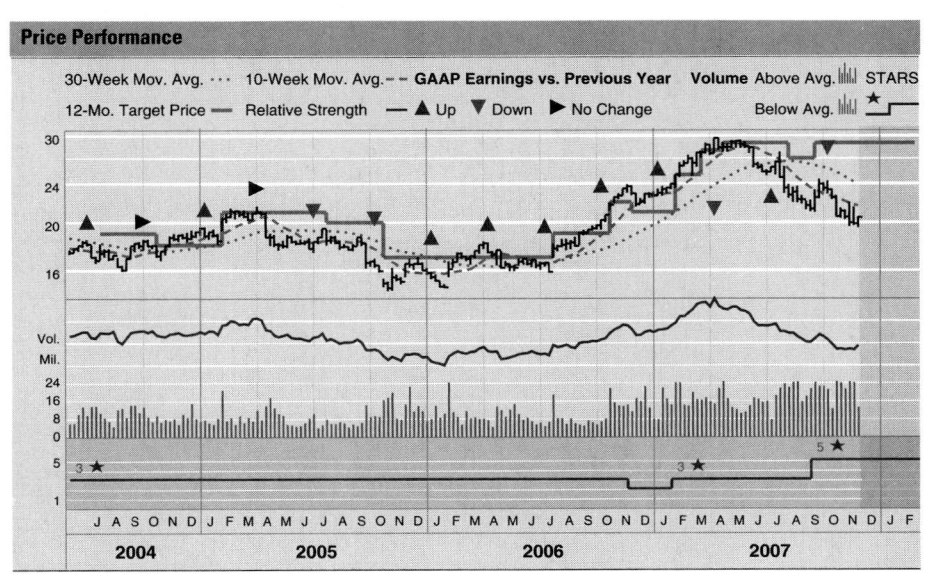

Options: CBOE, P, Ph

Analysis prepared by **Erik Kolb** on October 18, 2007, when the stock traded at **$ 21.51**.

Highlights

➤ We expect revenues to rise 5.8% in 2007 and 5.2% in 2008, compared to 2006 growth of 9.1%. While we see continued strength in Fisher-Price brands, we believe Fisher-Price has lower margins than some other MAT brands, resulting in a negative mix shift. We think the Hot Wheels property and girls' brands such as Polly Pocket should be strong contributors. Although we are encouraged by the increase in the U.S. Barbie business at the beginning of the year, we remain cautious regarding the segment. In addition to projected volume growth, we look for low single-digit price increases to help boost sales. Geographically, we expect international growth to significantly outpace domestic growth.

➤ We see profit margins expanding to 47.5% in 2007 and 48.0% in 2008, from 46.2% in 2006, on recent productivity initiatives related to reducing headcounts and administrative expenses. We also project that continued external cost pressures -- such as higher raw material and transportation costs, and a negative mix shift -- will be partly offset by price increases.

➤ We see 2007 EPS slipping to $1.51, from $1.53 in 2006. Our 2008 EPS estimate is $1.72.

Investment Rationale/Risk

➤ MAT recently recalled a substantial number of toys, some of which contained lead paint and were produced in China by third-party manufacturers. We believe the company will be able to restore consumer confidence in the safety of its products, and we expect only a minimal impact on holiday sales. Recognizing some recent share price improvement, we think current valuations represent a solid buying opportunity. Although MAT could face challenges in generating a sustained improvement to its top line, we have confidence in its strong portfolio of leading consumer brands and its strong cash flow, which has enabled it to raise the dividend and increase share buybacks.

➤ Risks to our recommendation and target price include an uncertain toy retailing environment and the possibility of continued toy store closings, an inability to reinvigorate the top line, continued cost pressures, and a material impact resulting from recent toy recalls.

➤ Our 12-month target price of $29 is based on a P/E of 17X applied to our 2008 EPS estimate. This represents a slight discount to historical multiples, reflecting the risk we see with the toy recalls and improving the top line.

Qualitative Risk Assessment

LOW	**MEDIUM**	HIGH

Our risk assessment reflects our favorable view of MAT's leading market share position and strong balance sheet, offset by our negative view of the intense industry rivalry and concentrated buying power of U.S. toy retailers.

Quantitative Evaluations

S&P Quality Ranking   **B**

D	C	B-	**B**	B+	A-	A	A+

Relative Strength Rank   **MODERATE**

49

LOWEST = 1   HIGHEST = 99

Revenue/Earnings Data

Revenue (Million $)

	1Q	2Q	3Q	4Q	Year
2007	940.3	1,020	1,839	--	--
2006	793.3	957.7	1,790	2,109	5,650
2005	783.1	886.8	1,666	1,843	5,179
2004	780.9	804.0	1,667	1,850	5,103
2003	745.3	769.0	1,705	1,741	4,960
2002	742.0	804.4	1,669	1,669	4,885

Earnings Per Share ($)

	1Q	2Q	3Q	4Q	Year
2007	0.03	0.11	0.61	E0.76	E1.51
2006	0.08	0.10	0.62	0.75	1.53
2005	0.02	-0.23	0.55	0.69	1.01
2004	0.02	0.06	0.61	0.68	1.35
2003	0.07	0.05	0.61	0.49	1.22
2002	-0.01	0.04	0.57	0.42	1.03

Fiscal year ended Dec. 31. Next earnings report expected: Late January. EPS Estimates based on S&P Operating Earnings; historical GAAP earnings are as reported.

Dividend Data (Dates: mm/dd Payment Date: mm/dd/yy)

Amount ($)	Date Decl.	Ex-Div. Date	Stk. of Record	Payment Date
0.650	11/17	11/29	12/01	12/15/06
0.750	11/16	11/28	11/30	12/14/07

Dividends have been paid since 1990. Source: Company reports.

Mattel Inc.

STANDARD
&POOR'S

Business Summary October 18, 2007

CORPORATE OVERVIEW. Mattel markets a wide variety of toy products on a worldwide basis. Brands are grouped in the following categories: Mattel Girls & Boys Brands, Fisher-Price Brands and American Girl Brands. Mattel brands include Barbie, Polly Pocket, Disney Classics, Hot Wheels, Matchbox and Tyco R/C vehicles and playsets, Nickelodeon, Harry Potter, Yu-Gi-Oh!, Batman, Justice League, and Megaman, among others. Fisher-Price brands includes Fisher-Price, Power Wheels, Sesame Street, Little People, Winnie the Pooh, Rescue Heroes, Barney, See 'N Say, Dora the Explorer, BabyGear, and View-Master. American Girl Brands are sold directly to consumers, and its children's publications are sold to certain retailers. Brand names include American Girl Today, the American Girls Collection, and Bitty Baby.

MAT operates in the U.S. and internationally. Revenues from the international segment provided 48% of consolidated gross sales in 2006. In the international segment, the geographic breakdown was as follows: Europe, 56% of 2006 sales; Latin America, 27%; Asia Pacific, 9%; and Other, 8%.

CORPORATE STRATEGY. We believe that two key elements of MAT's growth

strategy are to build its brands and cut costs. With declining sales in its core Barbie brand, MAT has been focused on reinvigorating this product line, while driving growth in other key brands. To further leverage its brands, MAT also pursues licensing arrangements and strategic partnerships, which we think helps to extend its portfolio of brands into areas outside of traditional toys.

Faced with a challenging sales environment and inflationary pricing, MAT is also focused on reducing costs as a means to deliver bottom-line growth. In keeping with this strategy, in October 2005, MAT announced the consolidation of its domestic Mattel Girls & Boys Brands and Fisher-Price Brands divisions into one division. We think this consolidation will help MAT to better leverage its scale. In connection with this consolidation, MAT also recently completed a workforce reduction, eliminating approximately 200 positions.

Company Financials Fiscal Year Ended Dec. 31

Per Share Data ($)	2006	2005	2004	2003	2002	2001	2000	1999	1998	1997
Tangible Book Value	4.13	3.51	3.97	3.49	2.92	1.46	0.59	1.36	1.64	4.06
Cash Flow	1.98	1.44	1.79	1.63	1.47	1.31	1.00	0.73	1.78	1.59
Earnings	1.53	1.01	1.35	1.22	1.03	0.71	0.40	-0.21	1.10	0.94
S&P Core Earnings	1.55	0.88	1.25	1.14	1.00	0.66	NA	NA	NA	NA
Dividends	0.65	0.50	0.45	0.40	0.05	0.05	0.27	0.34	0.30	0.27
Payout Ratio	42%	50%	33%	33%	5%	7%	67%	NM	27%	29%
Prices:High	23.98	21.64	19.79	23.20	22.36	19.92	15.13	30.31	46.56	42.25
Prices:Low	14.75	14.52	15.94	18.57	15.05	13.52	8.94	11.69	21.25	23.38
P/E Ratio:High	16	21	15	19	22	28	38	NM	42	45
P/E Ratio:Low	10	14	12	15	15	19	22	NM	19	25

Income Statement Analysis (Million $)

	2006	2005	2004	2003	2002	2001	2000	1999	1998	1997
Revenue	5,650	5,179	5,103	4,960	4,885	4,804	4,670	5,515	4,782	4,835
Operating Income	901	840	913	974	934	881	652	671	841	1,014
Depreciation	172	175	182	184	192	263	256	390	215	190
Interest Expense	79.9	76.5	77.8	80.6	114	155	153	152	111	90.1
Pretax Income	684	652	696	741	621	430	225	-111	465	425
Effective Tax Rate	13.3%	36.0%	17.7%	27.4%	26.8%	27.7%	24.5%	NM	28.6%	31.8%
Net Income	593	417	573	538	455	311	170	-82.4	332	290
S&P Core Earnings	600	359	531	502	439	288	NA	NA	NA	NA

Balance Sheet & Other Financial Data (Million $)

	2006	2005	2004	2003	2002	2001	2000	1999	1998	1997
Cash	1,206	998	1,157	1,153	1,267	617	232	275	212	695
Current Assets	2,850	2,413	2,637	2,395	2,389	2,093	1,751	2,420	2,058	2,462
Total Assets	4,956	4,372	4,756	4,511	4,460	4,541	4,313	5,127	4,262	3,804
Current Liabilities	1,583	1,463	1,727	1,468	1,649	1,597	1,502	1,818	1,317	1,173
Long Term Debt	636	525	400	589	640	1,021	1,242	1,184	984	664
Common Equity	2,433	2,102	2,386	2,216	1,979	1,738	1,403	1,963	1,819	1,726
Total Capital	3,069	2,627	2,786	2,805	2,619	2,759	2,645	3,147	2,804	2,486
Capital Expenditures	64.1	137	144	101	167	101	162	212	783	223
Cash Flow	765	592	755	721	647	573	427	304	539	469
Current Ratio	1.8	1.6	1.5	1.6	1.4	1.3	1.2	1.3	1.6	2.1
% Long Term Debt of Capitalization	20.7	20.0	14.4	21.0	24.4	37.0	47.0	37.6	35.1	26.7
% Net Income of Revenue	10.5	8.1	11.2	10.8	9.3	6.5	3.6	NM	6.9	6.0
% Return on Assets	12.7	9.1	12.4	12.0	10.1	7.0	3.8	NM	8.2	8.7
% Return on Equity	26.2	18.6	24.9	25.6	24.5	19.8	10.1	NM	17.8	17.1

Data as orig reptd.; bef. results of disc opers/spec. items. Per share data adj. for stk. divs.; EPS diluted. E-Estimated. NA-Not Available. NM-Not Meaningful. NR-Not Ranked. UR-Under Review.

Office: 333 Continental Boulevard, El Segundo, CA 90245-5012.
Telephone: 310-252-2000.
Website: http://www.mattel.com
Chrmn & CEO: R.A. Eckert

SVP & Treas: M.A. Salop
SVP, Secy & General Counsel: R. Normile
SVP & Cntlr: H.S. Topham
CFO: K.M. Farr

Board Members: E. P. Beard, K. Brittain White, M. J. Dolan, R. A. Eckert, F. D. Fergusson, T. M. Friedman, D. Ng, A. L. Rich, R. L. Sargent, D. A. Scarborough, C. A. Sinclair, G. C. Sullivan, J. L. Vogelstein

Founded: 1945
Domicile: Delaware
Employees: 32,000

MBIA Inc.

STANDARD &POOR'S

S&P Recommendation	HOLD ★★★☆☆	Price	12-Mo. Target Price	Investment Style
		$34.14 (as of Nov 23, 2007)	$40.00	Large-Cap Blend

GICS Sector Financials
Sub-Industry Property & Casualty Insurance

Summary This company is a leading provider of financial guarantee insurance and related services to public finance clients and financial institutions around the world.

Key Stock Statistics (Source S&P, Vickers, company reports)

52-Wk Range	$76.02– 29.50	S&P Oper. EPS 2007**E**	6.15	Market Capitalization(B)	$4.287	Beta	1.51
Trailing 12-Month EPS	$4.16	S&P Oper. EPS 2008**E**	6.65	Yield (%)	3.98	S&P 3-Yr. Proj. EPS CAGR(%)	7.00
Trailing 12-Month P/E	8.2	P/E on S&P Oper. EPS 2007**E**	5.6	Dividend Rate/Share	$1.36	S&P Credit Rating	AA
$10K Invested 5 Yrs Ago	$8,518	Common Shares Outstg. (M)	125.6	Institutional Ownership (%)	NM		

Price Performance

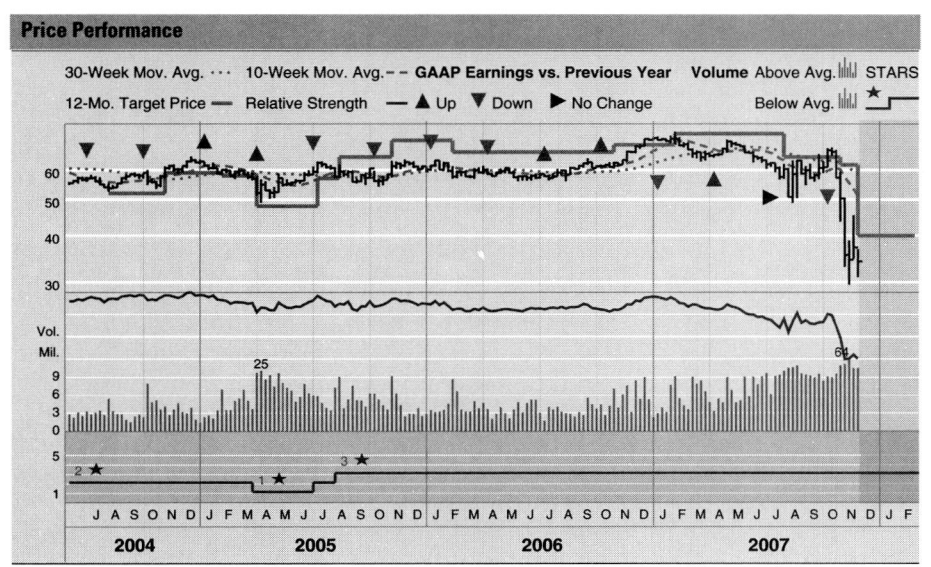

30-Week Mov. Avg. ··· 10-Week Mov. Avg.- - **GAAP Earnings vs. Previous Year** Volume Above Avg. STARS
12-Mo. Target Price — Relative Strength — ▲ Up ▼ Down ▶ No Change Below Avg.

Options: ASE, CBOE, P, Ph

Analysis prepared by **Cathy A. Seifert** on November 21, 2007, when the stock traded at **$ 34.34**.

Qualitative Risk Assessment

LOW	MEDIUM	HIGH

Our risk assessment reflects the company's involvement in municipal bond insurance and other financial guaranty products, exacerbated by issues related to certain regulatory investigations that were recently settled. We are also concerned that the company will face claims related to its portfolio of insured subprime mortgage-backed securities.

Quantitative Evaluations

S&P Quality Ranking   A

D	C	B-	B	B+	A-	A	A+

Relative Strength Rank   WEAK

6

LOWEST = 1   HIGHEST = 99

Revenue/Earnings Data

Revenue (Million $)

	1Q	2Q	3Q	4Q	Year
2007	369.6	779.1	428.3	--	--
2006	351.8	689.2	707.4	693.3	2,712
2005	326.0	339.3	605.2	600.0	2,301
2004	327.5	340.4	476.0	345.5	2,001
2003	280.9	310.7	313.0	325.8	1,770
2002	252.3	258.4	282.5	357.7	1,151

Earnings Per Share ($)

	1Q	2Q	3Q	4Q	Year
2007	1.46	1.61	-0.29	E1.58	E6.15
2006	1.45	1.61	1.58	1.30	5.95
2005	1.52	1.37	1.05	1.34	5.19
2004	1.42	1.47	1.29	1.36	5.61
2003	1.54	1.51	1.31	1.25	5.61
2002	1.08	0.97	1.11	0.84	3.98

Fiscal year ended Dec. 31. Next earnings report expected: Late January. EPS Estimates based on S&P Operating Earnings; historical GAAP earnings are as reported.

Highlights

➤ We estimate that earned premiums will advance 12% to 14% in 2008, versus a fractional drop in earned premiums expected in 2007 (reflecting a lower level of refunding premiums earned). Net written premiums advanced 17%, year to year, in the nine months ended September 30, 2007. Adjusted direct premiums (ADPs), which include both upfront premiums and the present value of estimated installment premiums for new business writings, more than doubled, year to year, in the first nine months of 2007. This growth reflected a 175% surge in global structured finance volume (both in the U.S. and abroad); and 38% higher global public finance activity.

➤ Margins in the investment management services unit are likely to come under continued pressure through 2007. We also anticipate that loss costs will rise amid an anticipated increase in claims related to mortgage-backed securities that the company insured.

➤ We forecast operating EPS of $6.15 in 2007 and $6.65 in 2008, versus operating EPS of $5.81 in 2006 and $5.23 in 2005. These estimates exclude the impact of mark-to-market adjustments on credit derivative portfolios.

Investment Rationale/Risk

➤ Our hold recommendation reflects what we view as a challenging near-term operating environment marked by headline risk associated with concerns that the company will incur claims related to the subprime mortgage market. The attendant widening of credit spreads, coupled with investors' reduced appetite for risk amid the problems in the mortgage market, could actually enhance demand for many of MBI's products. Our outlook is also tempered by MBI's restatement of results from 1998-2004 as part of a regulatory settlement. We cannot rule out the possibility of further regulatory probes.

➤ Risks to our opinion and target price include a greater than anticipated reduction in demand for credit enhancement products and an escalation in the scope of the regulatory investigations.

➤ Our 12-month target price of $40 assumes the shares will trade at 6.5X our 2007 operating EPS estimate and at 6.0X our 2008 operating EPS estimate. These valuation metrics are discounted to MBI's historical averages, but a premium to those of its closest peers.

Dividend Data (Dates: mm/dd Payment Date: mm/dd/yy)

Amount ($)	Date Decl.	Ex-Div. Date	Stk. of Record	Payment Date
0.310	12/07	12/20	12/22	01/16/07
0.340	02/27	03/21	03/23	04/16/07
0.340	06/07	06/20	06/22	07/16/07
0.340	09/06	09/19	09/21	10/15/07

Dividends have been paid since 1987. Source: Company reports.

MBIA Inc.

STANDARD &POOR'S

Business Summary November 21, 2007

MBIA Inc. (MBI), a dominant force in the municipal bond insurance market, has leveraged that strength and expanded into the structured finance market and into selected international markets. It is also engaged in asset management operations. At December 31, 2006, fixed income assets under management totaled $52.1 billion, versus $43.5 billion a year earlier.

MBI offers insurance for new issues of municipal bonds, and for bonds traded in the secondary market, including bonds held in unit investment trusts and mutual funds. The economic value of municipal bond insurance to the governmental unit or agency offering bonds is a saving in interest costs reflecting the difference in yield on an insured bond from that on the same bond if uninsured. The company's guarantee also increases market acceptance for complex financings, and for municipal bonds of issuers that are not well known.

At December 31, 2006, the net par value of the company's insured debt obligations was $617.6 billion, of which general obligation municipal bonds accounted for 27%, utility bonds 11%, special revenue bonds 7%, transportation bonds

5%, health care bonds 5%, other U.S. municipal bonds 8%, non-U.S. municipal obligations 5%, U.S. structured finance obligations (asset/mortgage backed) 20%, and international structured finance 12%. Of the $617.6 billion of net outstanding insured debt obligations at December 31, 2006, 18% had been issued outside the U.S., 11% had been issued by California, 6% by New York, 4% by Florida, and about 3% each by Texas, New Jersey and Illinois.

MBI in recent years has expanded its presence in the structured finance (or asset-backed) markets. Adjusted direct premiums (which include upfront and installment premiums) in the global public finance segment were down fractionally in 2006, to $578.9 million, from $580.4 million in 2005. Global structured finance adjusted direct premiums (including upfront and installment premiums) declined 13% in 2006, to $451.9 million, from $520.8 million in 2005.

Company Financials Fiscal Year Ended Dec. 31

Per Share Data ($)	2006	2005	2004	2003	2002	2001	2000	1999	1998	1997
Tangible Book Value	53.15	48.36	46.63	42.87	37.32	31.56	27.86	23.01	24.59	21.81
Operating Earnings	NA	NA	5.25	4.80	4.27	3.88	3.41	3.15	3.05	2.71
Earnings	5.95	5.19	5.61	5.61	3.98	3.91	3.55	2.13	2.88	2.81
S&P Core Earnings	5.88	5.75	5.33	5.25	3.91	3.81	NA	NA	NA	NA
Dividends	1.24	1.12	0.96	0.80	0.68	0.60	0.55	0.53	0.52	0.51
Payout Ratio	21%	22%	17%	14%	17%	15%	15%	25%	18%	18%
Prices:High	73.49	64.00	67.34	60.72	60.11	57.49	50.79	47.92	53.96	44.92
Prices:Low	56.00	49.07	52.55	34.14	34.93	36.00	24.21	30.08	30.71	30.29
P/E Ratio:High	12	12	12	11	15	15	14	23	19	16
P/E Ratio:Low	9	9	9	6	9	9	7	14	11	11

Income Statement Analysis (Million $)										
Premium Income	836	843	822	733	589	524	446	443	425	297
Net Investment Income	13.5	492	474	447	442	413	394	359	332	281
Other Revenue	1,863	1,458	704	590	120	197	217	605	156	75.1
Total Revenue	2,712	2,301	2,001	1,770	1,151	1,134	1,057	964	912	654
Pretax Income	1,133	1,016	1,130	1,149	793	791	715	388	565	480
Net Operating Income	NA	NA	NA	NA	NA	NA	NA	NA	NA	364
Net Income	813	712	813	814	587	583	529	321	433	374
S&P Core Earnings	804	789	773	761	577	568	NA	NA	NA	NA

Balance Sheet & Other Financial Data (Million $)										
Cash & Equivalent	796	629	678	452	298	297	246	229	148	23.2
Premiums Due	363	408	505	536	522	507	NA	NA	NA	13.4
Investment Assets:Bonds	27,756	23,747	19,680	17,391	16,195	14,087	11,737	10,274	9,562	4,867
Investment Assets:Stocks	Nil	Nil	Nil	Nil	Nil	Nil	Nil	Nil	Nil	Nil
Investment Assets:Loans	Nil	Nil	Nil	Nil	Nil	Nil	Nil	Nil	Nil	Nil
Investment Assets:Total	46,399	40,562	41,556	27,707	17,095	14,516	12,233	10,694	10,080	8,470
Deferred Policy Costs	450	427	360	320	302	278	274	252	230	154
Total Assets	39,763	34,561	33,027	30,268	18,852	16,200	13,894	12,264	11,797	9,811
Debt	13,619	10,033	8,877	8,870	1,033	805	795	689	689	474
Common Equity	7,204	6,592	6,579	6,259	5,493	4,783	4,223	3,513	3,792	3,048
Property & Casualty:Loss Ratio	9.7	10.0	10.0	9.2	9.4	9.3	6.2	12.3	8.0	6.3
Property & Casualty:Expense Ratio	26.6	24.9	22.0	12.8	16.8	13.4	22.1	23.6	16.8	26.2
Property & Casualty Combined Ratio	36.3	34.9	32.0	22.0	26.2	22.7	28.3	35.9	24.8	32.5
% Return on Revenue	30.0	31.0	40.6	46.0	51.0	51.4	50.0	33.2	47.5	57.2
% Return on Equity	11.8	10.8	12.7	13.8	11.4	13.0	13.7	8.8	12.7	13.5

Data as orig reptd.; bef. results of disc opers/spec. items. Per share data adj. for stk. divs.; EPS diluted. E-Estimated. NA-Not Available. NM-Not Meaningful. NR-Not Ranked. UR-Under Review.

Office: 113 King Street, Armonk, NY 10504-1610.
Telephone: 914-273-4545.
Website: http://www.mbia.com
Chrmn, Pres & CEO: G.C. Dunton

VP & CFO: C.E. Chaplin
VP & Chief Admin Officer: K.D. Silva
VP, Secy & General Counsel: R.D. Wertheim
CCO: D. McManus

Board Members: J. W. Brown, D. C. Clapp, G. C. Dunton, C. L. Gaudiani, D. P. Kearney, L. H. Meyer, D. M. Moffett, D. J. Perry, J. A. Rolls, R. H. Walker, J. W. Yabuki

Founded: 1973
Domicile: Connecticut
Employees: 492

The McGraw·Hill Companies

McCormick & Company Inc

STANDARD &POOR'S

S&P Recommendation	HOLD ★★★☆☆	**Price** $37.88 (as of Nov 23, 2007)	**12-Mo. Target Price** $41.00	**Investment Style** Large-Cap Growth

GICS Sector Consumer Staples
Sub-Industry Packaged Foods & Meats

Summary This company primarily produces spices, seasonings, and flavorings for the retail food, foodservice, and industrial markets. Trademarks include McCormick and Schilling.

Key Stock Statistics (Source S&P, Vickers, company reports)

52-Wk Range	$39.82– 33.89	S&P Oper. EPS 2007E	1.90	Market Capitalization(B)	$4.347	Beta	0.53
Trailing 12-Month EPS	$1.69	S&P Oper. EPS 2008E	2.08	Yield (%)	2.11	S&P 3-Yr. Proj. EPS CAGR(%)	10.00
Trailing 12-Month P/E	22.4	P/E on S&P Oper. EPS 2007E	19.9	Dividend Rate/Share	$0.80	S&P Credit Rating	A
$10K Invested 5 Yrs Ago	$17,675	Common Shares Outstg. (M)	127.7	Institutional Ownership (%)	79		

Price Performance

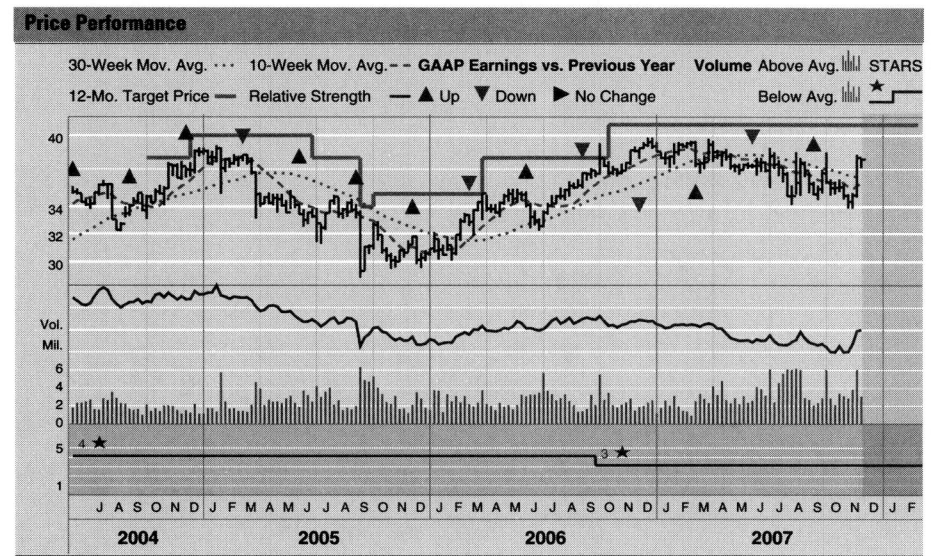

- 30-Week Mov. Avg. · · · 10-Week Mov. Avg. - - **GAAP Earnings vs. Previous Year** Volume Above Avg. STARS
- 12-Mo. Target Price — Relative Strength — ▲ Up ▼ Down ► No Change Below Avg. ★

Options: Ph

Analysis prepared by **Tom Graves, CFA** on July 23, 2007, when the stock traded at **$ 36.57.**

Qualitative Risk Assessment

LOW	MEDIUM	HIGH

Our risk assessment reflects the relatively stable nature of the company's end markets, our view of its strong balance sheet and cash flow, and an S&P Quality Ranking of A+ that reflects historical stability of earnings and dividends.

Quantitative Evaluations

S&P Quality Ranking **A+**

D	C	B-	B	B+	A-	A	A+

Relative Strength Rank **STRONG**

91

LOWEST = 1   HIGHEST = 99

Revenue/Earnings Data

Revenue (Million $)

	1Q	2Q	3Q	4Q	Year
2007	652.6	687.2	716.2	--	--
2006	609.7	639.9	663.1	803.7	2,716
2005	603.6	628.6	622.7	737.1	2,592
2004	572.4	596.2	613.5	744.1	2,526
2003	485.4	527.9	557.6	698.7	2,270
2002	518.9	552.6	545.0	703.4	2,320

Earnings Per Share ($)

2007	0.33	0.31	0.43	E0.73	E1.90
2006	0.11	0.46	0.32	0.62	1.50
2005	0.26	0.31	0.35	0.65	1.56
2004	0.27	0.30	0.33	0.62	1.52
2003	0.23	0.27	0.28	0.61	1.40
2002	0.24	0.24	0.25	0.54	1.26

Fiscal year ended Nov. 30. Next earnings report expected: Late January. EPS Estimates based on S&P Operating Earnings; historical GAAP earnings are as reported.

Highlights

- Before any additional acquisitions, we look for FY 07 (Nov.) net sales to increase about 6.6%, from the $2.7 billion reported for FY 06. We expect this to reflect a full-year's inclusion of the Simply Asia acquisition, which occurred in June 2006. We look for sales gains to be limited by the elimination of some lower-margin products.

- In FY 07, we expect profit margins (before restructuring costs) to be helped by cost reduction efforts and product mix. Excluding restructuring charges, we estimate EPS of $1.91, up from $1.72 in FY 06. In FY 07, we look for the company to have restructuring charges totaling about $0.18 a share, compared to a $0.22 net negative impact (including an asset sale gain) from restructuring activity in FY 06. For FY 08, we estimate EPS, before restructuring charges, of $2.10.

- In the first half of FY 07, MKC repurchased 1.52 million common shares for $57.5 million. As of May 31, 2007, $148 million remained under a $400 million share repurchase authorization that was approved by MKC's board of directors in June 2005.

Investment Rationale/Risk

- We believe long-term prospects for the company to generate free cash flow are favorable. In FY 07, we look for uses of cash to include about $45 million of payments related to restructuring activity, and around $85 million of net (after proceeds from the sale of fixed assets) capital expenditures. Other uses of cash could include stock repurchase and/or acquisition activity. With its restructuring program, MKC expects to reduce annual costs by $50 million (pretax) by the end of 2008.

- Risks to our recommendation and target price relate to competitive pressures in MKC's businesses, consumer acceptance of new product introductions, and commodity cost inflation. In terms of corporate governance, the company has a dual class capital structure with unequal voting rights, which we view unfavorably.

- Our 12-month target price of $41 is 21.4X our calendar year 2007 EPS estimate of $1.92, a moderate premium to what we expect, on average, from a small group of peers or competitors. The stock recently had an indicated dividend yield of about 2.2%.

Dividend Data (Dates: mm/dd Payment Date: mm/dd/yy)

Amount ($)	Date Decl.	Ex-Div. Date	Stk. of Record	Payment Date
0.200	11/28	12/27	12/29	01/19/07
0.200	03/28	04/04	04/09	04/20/07
0.200	06/26	07/03	07/06	07/20/07
0.200	09/26	10/03	10/05	10/19/07

Dividends have been paid since 1925. Source: Company reports.

The McGraw-Hill Companies

McCormick & Company Inc

Business Summary July 23, 2007

CORPORATE PROFILE. Founded by Willoughby M. McCormick in 1889, Mc-Cormick & Co. is the world's largest spice company, with operations in the manufacture, marketing and distribution of spices, seasonings, flavorings and other specialty food products. The company markets its products to retail food, foodservice, and industrial markets under the McCormick and Schilling names.

McCormick's consumer segment, which accounted for 57% of sales and 79% of operating profits (before restructuring costs) in FY 06 (Nov.), sells spices, herbs, extracts, seasoning blends, sauces, marinades and specialty foods to the consumer food market. The industrial segment (43%, 21%) sells seasoning blends, natural spices and herbs, wet flavors, coating systems and compound flavors to food manufacturers and the food service industry, both directly and through distributors. Many spices and herbs purchased by the company are imported into the U.S., although significant quantities of some materials, such as paprika, dehydrated vegetables, onion and garlic, and food ingredients other than spices and herbs, originate in the U.S.

MKC says that many of its products are prepared from confidential formulae developed by its research laboratories and product development teams. Ex-penditures for research and development were $43.6 million in FY 06, compared to $43.1 million in FY 05.

CORPORATE STRATEGY. We see MKC aiming to improve profitability with cost reduction efforts and a focus on higher-margin, higher value-added products.

A restructuring program was announced in 2005 and is expected to extend through 2008. Related to this plan, we look for MKC to have a total pretax negative impact (net) from restructuring charges and an asset sale gain of $110 million to $130 million. MKC's goal is to reduce annual costs by $50 million (pretax). We expect the restructuring plan to include the consolidation of global manufacturing, the rationalization of distribution facilities, efforts to improve its go-to-market strategy, the elimination of administrative redundancies, and the rationalization of joint venture partnerships. The company says that in FY 06, it realized $10 million ($7 million after tax) of savings, and estimates that another $30 million ($20 million after tax) will be realized in FY 07.

Company Financials Fiscal Year Ended Nov. 30

Per Share Data ($)	2006	2005	2004	2003	2002	2001	2000	1999	1998	1997
Tangible Book Value	NM	NM	0.45	0.28	0.62	NM	NM	1.70	1.57	1.59
Cash Flow	2.14	2.10	2.11	1.85	1.73	1.57	1.43	1.12	1.07	0.97
Earnings	1.50	1.56	1.52	1.40	1.26	1.05	0.99	0.72	0.71	0.65
S&P Core Earnings	1.40	1.51	1.43	1.28	1.12	0.90	NA	NA	NA	NA
Dividends	0.72	0.64	0.56	0.46	0.37	0.40	0.38	0.34	0.32	0.30
Payout Ratio	48%	41%	37%	33%	29%	38%	38%	48%	45%	47%
Prices:High	39.82	39.14	38.94	30.21	27.25	23.27	18.88	17.31	18.22	14.19
Prices:Low	30.09	28.95	28.60	21.71	20.70	17.00	11.88	13.31	13.53	11.31
P/E Ratio:High	27	25	26	22	22	22	19	24	26	22
P/E Ratio:Low	20	19	19	16	16	16	12	19	19	18

Income Statement Analysis (Million $)	2006	2005	2004	2003	2002	2001	2000	1999	1998	1997
Revenue	2,716	2,592	2,526	2,270	2,320	2,372	2,124	2,007	1,881	1,801
Operating Income	429	429	402	366	353	324	287	252	240	217
Depreciation	86.8	74.6	72.0	65.3	66.8	73.0	61.3	57.4	54.8	49.3
Interest Expense	53.7	48.2	41.0	38.6	43.6	52.9	39.7	32.4	36.9	36.3
Pretax Income	270	316	308	286	257	212	204	163	159	150
Effective Tax Rate	24.0%	30.6%	28.9%	29.1%	28.9%	29.7%	32.6%	36.8%	34.6%	35.1%
Net Income	202	215	215	199	180	147	138	103	104	97.4
S&P Core Earnings	189	208	202	182	158	126	NA	NA	NA	NA

Balance Sheet & Other Financial Data (Million $)	2006	2005	2004	2003	2002	2001	2000	1999	1998	1997
Cash	49.0	30.3	70.3	25.1	47.3	31.3	23.9	12.0	17.7	13.5
Current Assets	899	800	864	762	725	636	620	491	504	507
Total Assets	2,568	2,273	2,370	2,148	1,931	1,772	1,660	1,189	1,259	1,256
Current Liabilities	780	699	773	713	673	714	1,027	471	518	498
Long Term Debt	570	464	465	449	454	454	160	241	250	276
Common Equity	933	800	890	755	592	463	359	382	468	393
Total Capital	1,575	1,293	1,386	1,226	1,046	943	523	628	643	671
Capital Expenditures	84.8	73.8	69.8	91.6	111	112	53.6	49.3	54.8	43.9
Cash Flow	289	290	287	265	247	220	199	161	159	147
Current Ratio	1.2	1.1	1.1	1.1	1.1	0.9	0.6	1.0	1.0	1.0
% Long Term Debt of Capitalization	37.8	35.9	33.6	36.6	43.4	48.2	30.6	38.5	38.9	41.1
% Net Income of Revenue	7.4	8.3	8.5	8.8	7.8	6.2	6.5	5.1	5.5	5.4
% Return on Assets	8.4	9.3	9.5	9.8	9.7	8.5	9.7	8.4	8.3	7.5
% Return on Equity	23.3	25.4	26.1	29.6	34.1	35.7	37.1	26.8	24.1	23.1

Data as orig reptd.; bef. results of disc opers/spec. items. Per share data adj. for stk. divs.; EPS diluted. E-Estimated. NA-Not Available. NM-Not Meaningful. NR-Not Ranked. UR-Under Review.

Office: 18 Loveton Circle, Sparks, MD 21152-6000.
Telephone: 410-771-7301.
Website: http://www.mccormick.com
Chrmn, Pres & CEO: R.J. Lawless

Pres & COO: A.D. Wilson
EVP & CFO: F.A. Contino
SVP, Secy & General Counsel: R.W. Skelton
VP & Treas: P. Beard

Investor Contact: J. Brooks (410-771-7244)
Board Members: B. H. Beracha, J. P. Bilbrey, J. T. Brady, F. A. Contino, J. M. Fitzpatrick, F. A. Hrabowski, III, R. J. Lawless, M. D. Mangan, M. M. Preston, G. A. Roche, W. E. Stevens, K. D. Weatherholtz

Founded: 1889
Domicile: Maryland
Employees: 8,000

McDonald's Corp

STANDARD &POOR'S

S&P Recommendation **STRONG BUY** ★★★★★

Price	12-Mo. Target Price	Investment Style
$57.72 (as of Nov 23, 2007)	$68.00	Large-Cap Growth

GICS Sector Consumer Discretionary
Sub-Industry Restaurants

Summary MCD is the largest fast-food restaurant company in the world, with more than 30,000 restaurants in over 100 countries.

Key Stock Statistics (Source S&P, Vickers, company reports)

52-Wk Range	$59.92–40.79	S&P Oper. EPS 2007**E**	2.95	Market Capitalization(B)	$68.269	Beta	1.51
Trailing 12-Month EPS	$1.92	S&P Oper. EPS 2008**E**	3.30	Yield (%)	2.60	S&P 3-Yr. Proj. EPS CAGR(%)	16.00
Trailing 12-Month P/E	30.1	P/E on S&P Oper. EPS 2007**E**	19.6	Dividend Rate/Share	$1.50	S&P Credit Rating	A
$10K Invested 5 Yrs Ago	$34,325	Common Shares Outstg. (M)	1,182.8	Institutional Ownership (%)	77		

Price Performance

30-Week Mov. Avg. · · · 10-Week Mov. Avg. - - **GAAP Earnings vs. Previous Year** Volume Above Avg. STARS
12-Mo. Target Price — Relative Strength — ▲ Up ▼ Down ► No Change Below Avg.

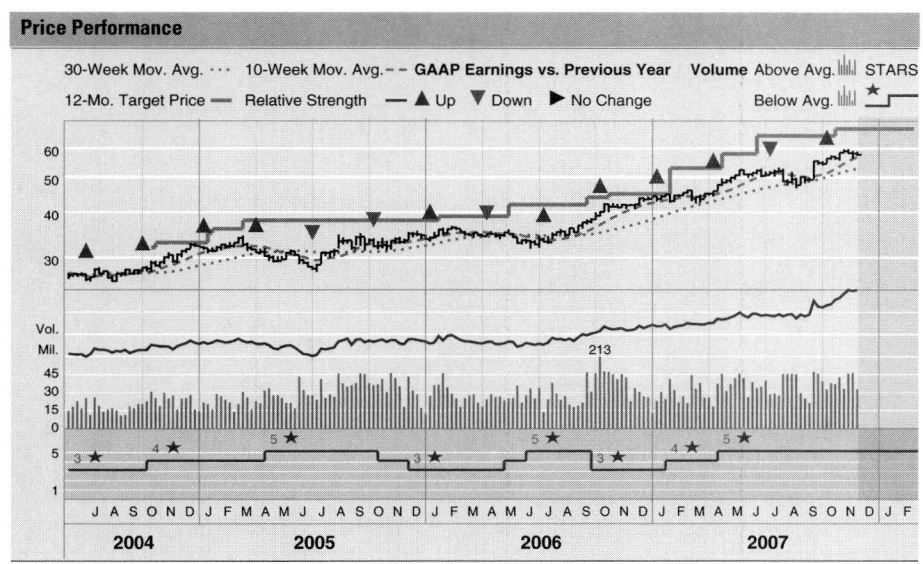

Options: ASE, CBOE, P, Ph

Analysis prepared by **Mark S. Basham** on October 29, 2007, when the stock traded at **$ 58.88**.

Highlights

➤ We see 2007 earnings benefiting from the sale of underperforming restaurants or of locations in higher-risk geographies to local licensees. Systemwide sales are likely to increase about 11%, including positive forex effects. Our 2007 EPS estimate of $2.95 excludes largely non-cash losses of $1.31 a share on the August sale of most Latin American operations to a developmental licensee.

➤ We expect the net number of systemwide restaurants to increase about 2% in 2008, reflecting the opening of up to 1,000 new restaurants, mostly in international markets, partly offset a smaller number of closures. We look for systemwide sales to increase 5.0%, 8.5% and 12.0% in the U.S., Europe and Asia Pacific/Middle East/Africa, respectively.

➤ We expect new salad offerings, snack wraps, breakfast items and coffees to drive an overall systemwide sales increase of 6% (exclusive of forex effects) in 2008. Aided by the elimination of expenses related to the Latin American locations sold in 2007, and by expected ongoing stock repurchases, we estimate 2008 EPS will increase 12%, to $3.30.

Investment Rationale/Risk

➤ We believe MCD's solid execution of its "Plan to Win" operating strategy has helped produce strong sales momentum over the past several years, and we expect healthy sales results to continue over the next few years. We think this has improved MCD's competitive position, and we expect it to step up expansion, particularly in Asia. In addition, from 2007 to 2009, MCD expects to expend $15 billion to $17 billion on dividends and stock repurchases.

➤ Risks to our recommendation and target price include the potential for higher food costs; a lack of customer acceptance of MCD's new menu offerings; and exchange rate risk, in light of MCD's substantial international business.

➤ Our 12-month target price of $68 is based on a forward P/E of approximately 21X applied to our 2008 EPS estimate of $3.30, a slight premium to the peer group average. Our target price is also supported by our discounted cash flow model, which assumes revenue growth of 6% to 7% over the 2008-2010 period and then gradually declining to a perpetuity growth rate of 2.0%, and a weighted average cost of equity of 9.6%.

Qualitative Risk Assessment

LOW	MEDIUM	HIGH

McDonald's competes in the global fast food industry, where it has a very strong brand name presence. However, results can vary widely due to fluctuations in food costs, competitive discounting, and exchange rate volatility.

Quantitative Evaluations

S&P Quality Ranking A

D	C	B-	B	B+	A-	**A**	A+

Relative Strength Rank **STRONG**

87

LOWEST = 1   HIGHEST = 99

Revenue/Earnings Data

Revenue (Million $)

	1Q	2Q	3Q	4Q	Year
2007	5,464	6,011	5,901	--	--
2006	4,914	5,367	5,671	5,634	21,586
2005	4,803	5,096	5,327	5,235	20,460
2004	4,400	4,729	4,926	5,010	19,065
2003	3,800	4,281	4,505	4,555	17,141
2002	3,597	3,862	4,047	3,899	15,406

Earnings Per Share ($)

2007	0.62	-0.60	0.83	E0.78	E2.95
2006	0.46	0.56	0.67	0.61	2.30
2005	0.56	0.42	0.58	0.48	2.04
2004	0.40	0.47	0.61	0.31	1.79
2003	0.29	0.37	0.43	0.10	1.18
2002	0.28	0.39	0.38	-0.27	0.77

Fiscal year ended Dec. 31. Next earnings report expected: Late January. EPS Estimates based on S&P Operating Earnings; historical GAAP earnings are as reported.

Dividend Data (Dates: mm/dd Payment Date: mm/dd/yy)

Amount ($)	Date Decl.	Ex-Div. Date	Stk. of Record	Payment Date
1.000	09/27	11/13	11/15	12/01/06
1.500	09/12	11/13	11/15	12/03/07

Dividends have been paid since 1976. Source: Company reports.

Please read the Required Disclosures and Analyst Certification on the last page of this report.

The **McGraw·Hill** Companies

McDonald's Corp

STANDARD
&POOR'S

Business Summary October 29, 2007

CORPORATE OVERVIEW. With one of the world's most widely known brand names, McDonald's operates and franchises more than 30,000 restaurants in over 100 countries. Systemwide sales totaled $57.5 billion in 2006, up from $53.6 billion in 2005.

In the U.S., the McDonald's chain dominates the $120 billion quick-service restaurant industry. With U.S. systemwide sales of more than $25 billion, its domestic business is approximately three times larger than its closest competitors, Burger King and Wendy's Old Fashioned Hamburgers. MCD's international segment has supplied much of its earnings growth over the past two decades, and, in 2006, contributed 46% of operating income (before corporate expenses and one-time charges). All restaurants are operated by MCD, franchisees, or affiliates under joint venture agreements.

In August, 2007, the company completed the sale of its existing businesses in Brazil, Argentina, Mexico, Puerto Rico, Venezuela and 13 other countries in Latin America and the Caribbean to a developmental licensee. The company recorded impairment charges totaling approximately $1.7 billion, substantially

all of which was noncash. The charges included approximately $892 million for the difference between the net book value of the Latam business and the approximately $680 million in cash proceeds, and $773 million in foreign currency translation losses previously included in comprehensive income.

CORPORATE STRATEGY. In 2003, the company introduced a new corporate strategy that focuses on product development and investment in existing properties, rather than on expansion and price discounting. MCD's stated operating priorities include fixing operating inadequacies in existing restaurants; taking a more integrated and focused approach to growth, with an emphasis on increasing sales, margins and returns in existing restaurants; and ensuring the correct operating structure and resources, aligned behind focusing priorities that create benefits for its customers and restaurants.

Company Financials Fiscal Year Ended Dec. 31

Per Share Data ($)	2006	2005	2004	2003	2002	2001	2000	1999	1998	1997
Tangible Book Value	11.01	10.45	9.74	8.18	6.88	6.30	5.86	6.20	6.26	5.86
Cash Flow	3.29	3.05	2.73	2.08	1.59	2.08	2.20	2.07	1.73	1.71
Earnings	2.30	2.04	1.79	1.18	0.77	1.25	1.46	1.39	1.10	1.15
S&P Core Earnings	2.28	2.00	1.66	0.96	0.51	1.01	NA	NA	NA	NA
Dividends	1.00	0.67	0.55	0.40	0.24	0.23	0.22	0.20	0.18	0.16
Payout Ratio	43%	33%	31%	34%	31%	18%	15%	14%	16%	14%
Prices:High	44.68	35.69	32.96	27.01	30.72	35.06	43.63	49.56	39.75	27.44
Prices:Low	31.73	27.36	24.54	12.12	15.17	24.75	26.38	35.94	22.31	21.06
P/E Ratio:High	19	17	18	23	40	28	30	36	36	24
P/E Ratio:Low	14	13	14	10	20	20	18	26	20	18

Income Statement Analysis (Million $)										
Revenue	21,586	20,460	19,065	17,141	15,406	14,870	14,243	13,259	12,421	11,409
Operating Income	5,829	5,243	4,742	3,980	3,164	3,983	4,144	4,171	3,903	3,488
Depreciation	1,250	1,250	1,201	1,148	1,051	1,086	1,011	956	881	794
Interest Expense	402	356	358	388	360	452	430	396	414	363
Pretax Income	4,166	3,702	3,202	2,346	1,662	2,330	2,882	2,884	2,307	2,408
Effective Tax Rate	31.0%	29.7%	28.9%	35.7%	40.3%	29.8%	31.4%	32.5%	32.8%	31.8%
Net Income	2,873	2,602	2,279	1,508	992	1,637	1,977	1,948	1,550	1,643
S&P Core Earnings	2,848	2,540	2,100	1,226	667	1,328	NA	NA	NA	NA

Balance Sheet & Other Financial Data (Million $)										
Cash	2,136	4,260	1,380	493	330	418	422	420	299	341
Current Assets	3,625	5,850	2,858	1,885	1,715	1,819	1,662	1,572	1,309	1,142
Total Assets	29,024	29,989	27,838	25,525	23,971	22,535	21,683	20,983	19,784	18,242
Current Liabilities	3,008	4,036	3,521	2,486	2,422	2,248	2,361	3,274	2,497	2,985
Long Term Debt	8,417	8,937	8,357	9,343	9,704	8,556	7,844	5,632	6,189	4,834
Common Equity	15,458	15,146	14,202	11,982	10,281	9,488	9,204	9,639	9,464	8,851
Total Capital	24,941	25,060	23,340	22,340	20,988	19,156	18,133	16,445	17,228	15,178
Capital Expenditures	1,742	1,607	1,419	1,307	2,004	1,906	1,945	1,868	1,879	2,111
Cash Flow	4,123	3,852	3,480	2,656	2,043	2,723	2,988	2,904	2,431	2,412
Current Ratio	1.2	1.4	0.8	0.8	0.7	0.8	0.7	0.5	0.5	0.4
% Long Term Debt of Capitalization	33.7	35.7	35.8	41.8	46.2	44.7	43.3	34.2	35.9	31.8
% Net Income of Revenue	13.3	12.7	12.0	8.8	6.4	11.0	13.9	14.7	12.5	14.4
% Return on Assets	9.7	9.0	8.5	6.1	4.3	7.4	9.3	9.6	8.2	9.2
% Return on Equity	18.8	17.7	17.4	13.5	10.0	17.5	21.0	20.4	16.9	18.8

Data as orig reptd.; bef. results of disc opers/spec. items. Per share data adj. for stk. divs.; EPS diluted. E-Estimated. NA-Not Available. NM-Not Meaningful. NR-Not Ranked. UR-Under Review.

Office: McDonald's Plaza, Oak Brook, IL 60523.
Telephone: 630-623-3000.
Website: http://www.mcdonalds.com
Chrmn: A.J. McKenna

Pres & COO: R. Alvarez
Vice Chrmn & CEO: J.A. Skinner
Sr EVP & CFO: M.H. Paull
EVP, Secy & General Counsel: G. Santona

Board Members: H. Adams, Jr., E. A. Brennan, R. A. Eckert, E. Hernandez, Jr., J. P. Jackson, R. H. Lenny, W. E. Massey, A. J. McKenna, C. D. McMillan, S. A. Penrose, J. W. Rogers, J. A. Skinner, R. W. Stone

Founded: 1948
Domicile: Delaware
Employees: 465,000

McGraw-Hill Companies Inc. (The)

STANDARD &POOR'S

S&P Recommendation	**NOT RANKED**	Price $46.18 (as of Nov 23, 2007)	Investment Style Large-Cap Growth

GICS Sector Consumer Discretionary
Sub-Industry Publishing

Summary This leading information services organization serves worldwide markets in education, business, industry, other professions and government.

Key Stock Statistics (Source S&P, Vickers, company reports)

52-Wk Range	$72.50– 44.96	S&P Oper. EPS 2007**E**	NA	Market Capitalization(B)	$15.193	Beta		0.71
Trailing 12-Month EPS	$3.06	S&P Oper. EPS 2008**E**	NA	Yield (%)	1.78	S&P 3-Yr. Proj. EPS CAGR(%)		
Trailing 12-Month P/E	15.1	P/E on S&P Oper. EPS 2007**E**	NA	Dividend Rate/Share	$0.82	S&P Credit Rating		NR
$10K Invested 5 Yrs Ago	$16,175	Common Shares Outstg. (M)	329.0	Institutional Ownership (%)	79			

Price Performance

30-Week Mov. Avg. · · · 10-Week Mov. Avg. - - **GAAP Earnings vs. Previous Year** Volume Above Avg. STARS
12-Mo. Target Price — Relative Strength — ▲ Up ▼ Down ► No Change Below Avg.

2-for-1

J A S O N D J F M A M J J A S O N D J F M A M J J A S O N D J F M A M J J A S O N D J F
2004   2005   2006   2007

Options: ASE, CBOE, P, Ph

Analysis prepared by **James Peters, CFA** on October 19, 2007, when the stock traded at **$50.21.**

Highlights

➤ MHP forecasts double-digit revenue growth for 2007. The company sees double-digit revenue growth in Financial Services on strength in ratings through the first three quarters of the year, although for the fourth quarter MHP expects a decline in Financial Services revenues due to weakness in the U.S. structured finance market. MHP sees various factors contributing to growth in Education, including a 14%-20% increase in the state new textbook adoption market, where the company recently said it had a 32% market share, and growing global growth prospects in the higher education and professional markets.

➤ MHP sees continued operating margin expansion in the Financial Services segment in 2007, from 43.8% in 2006. MHP expects operating margin expansion in the Education segment to about 20% by 2010, from 13% in 2006, including restructuring and stock option charges.

➤ In October, MHP reiterated that it expects double-digit EPS growth in 2007 from $2.50 in 2006. MHP's estimate excludes $0.06 of restructuring charges and a $0.04 charge for the elimination of the stock restoration program in 2006, and a $0.03 sale gain in 2007.

Investment Rationale/Risk

➤ Through mid-October 2007, MHP had repurchased 30 million of its shares for about $1.9 billion. For 2007, the company anticipates $310 million of pre-publication investments, up from $277 million in 2006, mainly for products MHP is developing to realize opportunities it sees in the elementary and high school market in 2007 through 2009. Property, plant and equipment purchases are expected to rise $123 million, to $250 million, and depreciation and amortization are expected to advance to $420 million, from $389 million.

➤ MHP noted in its 2006 10-K report filed with the SEC in February 2007 that among the risks facing its businesses are the level of educational funding both domestically and internationally, and the health of capital and equity markets, including future interest rate changes.

➤ EPS estimates for MHP from other analysts recently averaged about $3.01 for 2007 and $3.37 for 2008. Standard & Poor's is a division of MHP, and provides no EPS estimates, target price or recommendation for the company.

Qualitative Risk Assessment

A Qualitative Risk Assessment is not available for this company.

Quantitative Evaluations

S&P Quality Ranking   NR

D	C	B-	B	B+	A-	A	A+

Relative Strength Rank   MODERATE

38

LOWEST = 1   HIGHEST = 99

Revenue/Earnings Data

Revenue (Million $)

	1Q	2Q	3Q	4Q	Year
2007	1,296	1,718	2,188	--	--
2006	1,141	1,528	1,993	1,594	6,255
2005	1,029	1,456	1,977	1,541	6,004
2004	919.9	1,246	1,723	1,362	5,251
2003	830.8	1,172	1,603	1,222	4,828
2002	846.7	1,191	1,577	1,172	4,788

Earnings Per Share ($)

2007	0.40	0.79	1.34	--	--
2006	0.20	0.60	1.06	0.56	2.40
2005	0.21	0.51	1.00	0.50	2.21
2004	0.20	0.43	0.85	0.49	1.96
2003	0.11	0.37	0.76	0.56	1.79
2002	0.08	0.35	0.71	0.35	1.48

Fiscal year ended Dec. 31. Next earnings report expected: Late January. EPS Estimates based on S&P Operating Earnings; historical GAAP earnings are as reported.

Dividend Data (Dates: mm/dd Payment Date: mm/dd/yy)

Amount ($)	Date Decl.	Ex-Div. Date	Stk. of Record	Payment Date
0.205	01/31	02/22	02/26	03/12/07
0.205	04/25	05/24	05/29	06/12/07
0.205	07/25	08/24	08/28	09/12/07
0.205	10/24	11/26	11/28	12/12/07

Dividends have been paid since 1937. Source: Company reports.

Please read the Required Disclosures and Analyst Certification on the last page of this report.

The *McGraw-Hill* Companies

McGraw-Hill Companies Inc. (The)

STANDARD &POOR'S

Business Summary October 19, 2007

CORPORATE PROFILE. The McGraw-Hill Companies, Inc. is a leading provider of information products and services to business, professional and education markets worldwide. The company believes that through acquisitions, new product and service development and a strong commitment to customer service, many of its business units have grown to be leaders in their respective fields. Well known brands include BusinessWeek, Standard & Poor's, Platts, F.W. Dodge, and Sweet's. Operations are conducted through over 290 offices in 38 countries worldwide.

The Financial Services segment (44% of revenues and 76% of operating profit) operates under the Standard & Poor's brand and provides credit ratings, evaluation services and analyses globally on corporations, financial institutions, securitized and project financings, and local, state and sovereign governments. The company believes it is the world's leading provider of credit analysis and information, incorporating the largest global network of credit ratings professionals. In June 2005, MHP acquired majority ownership of Crisil Limited, a leading provider of credit ratings, financial news and risk and policy advisory services in India. In February 2007, the company announced the sale of its mutual fund data business to Morningstar, Inc. In April 2005, the company

acquired Vista Research Inc., a leading provider of primary research. In September 2004, the company acquired privately owned Capital IQ, a leading provider of high-impact information solutions to the global investment and financial services communities.

McGraw-Hill Education (40%, 21%) is comprised of two operating groups -- the School Education Group (SEG) and the Higher Education, Professional and International Group (HPI). SEG provides educational and professional materials in the U.S. to the pre-K to 12th grade market, and is a leading provider of assessment and reporting services. In July 2004, MHP acquired The Grow Network, a privately held company now part of SEG that provides assessment reporting and customized content for states and large school districts across the country.

Company Financials Fiscal Year Ended Dec. 31

Per Share Data ($)	2006	2005	2004	2003	2002	2001	2000	1999	1998	1997
Tangible Book Value	1.00	2.04	2.72	2.24	0.94	0.09	0.17	1.12	0.74	0.32
Cash Flow	2.85	3.21	2.98	2.84	1.71	2.04	2.13	1.85	1.61	1.46
Earnings	2.40	2.21	1.96	1.79	1.48	0.96	1.21	1.07	0.86	0.73
S&P Core Earnings	2.38	2.05	1.80	1.44	1.15	0.60	NA	NA	NA	NA
Dividends	0.73	0.66	0.60	0.54	0.51	0.49	0.47	0.43	0.39	0.36
Payout Ratio	30%	30%	31%	30%	34%	51%	39%	40%	46%	49%
Prices:High	69.25	53.97	46.06	35.00	34.85	35.44	33.84	31.56	25.83	18.84
Prices:Low	46.37	40.51	34.55	25.87	25.36	24.35	20.94	23.56	17.13	11.22
P/E Ratio:High	29	24	23	20	24	37	28	29	30	26
P/E Ratio:Low	19	18	18	14	17	25	17	22	20	15

Income Statement Analysis (Million $)										
Revenue	6,255	6,004	5,251	4,828	4,788	4,646	4,281	3,992	3,729	3,534
Operating Income	1,580	1,749	1,467	1,369	1,037	1,044	1,128	984	851	779
Depreciation	162	385	393	403	89.6	421	362	308	299	294
Interest Expense	13.6	5.20	5.79	7.10	22.5	55.1	52.8	42.0	48.0	52.5
Pretax Income	1,405	1,360	1,169	1,130	905	615	767	698	560	471
Effective Tax Rate	37.2%	37.9%	35.3%	39.1%	36.3%	38.7%	38.5%	39.0%	39.0%	38.3%
Net Income	882	844	756	688	577	377	472	426	342	291
S&P Core Earnings	874	786	694	552	446	233	NA	NA	NA	NA

Balance Sheet & Other Financial Data (Million $)										
Cash	353	749	681	696	58.2	53.5	3.17	6.49	10.5	4.77
Current Assets	2,258	2,591	2,448	2,256	1,674	1,813	1,802	1,554	1,429	1,464
Total Assets	6,043	6,396	5,863	5,394	5,032	5,161	4,931	4,089	3,788	3,724
Current Liabilities	2,468	2,225	1,969	1,994	1,775	1,876	1,781	1,525	1,291	1,206
Long Term Debt	0.31	0.34	0.51	0.39	459	834	818	355	452	607
Common Equity	7,785	3,113	4,952	2,557	2,202	1,884	1,761	1,691	1,565	1,435
Total Capital	7,936	3,432	5,185	2,758	2,861	2,908	2,742	2,182	2,147	2,153
Capital Expenditures	127	120	139	115	70.0	117	97.7	154	179	78.7
Cash Flow	1,044	1,230	1,149	1,091	666	798	834	734	641	584
Current Ratio	0.9	1.2	1.2	1.1	0.9	1.0	1.0	1.0	1.1	1.2
% Long Term Debt of Capitalization	0.0	0.0	0.0	0.0	16.0	28.7	29.8	16.3	21.1	28.2
% Net Income of Revenue	14.1	14.1	14.4	14.2	12.0	8.1	11.0	10.7	9.2	8.2
% Return on Assets	14.2	13.8	13.5	13.2	11.3	7.5	10.4	10.8	9.1	7.9
% Return on Equity	12.8	27.7	16.5	29.1	28.2	20.5	27.7	26.3	22.7	20.8

Data as orig reptd.; bef. results of disc opers/spec. items. Per share data adj. for stk. divs.; EPS diluted. E-Estimated. NA-Not Available. NM-Not Meaningful. NR-Not Ranked. UR-Under Review.

Office: 1221 Avenue Of The Americas, New York, NY 10020-1095.
Telephone: 212-512-2000.
Email: investor_relations@mcgraw-hill.com
Website: http://www.mcgraw-hill.com
Chrmn, Pres & CEO: H.W. McGraw, III
EVP & CFO: R.J. Bahash
EVP & General Counsel: K.M. Vittor
EVP & CIO: B.D. Marcus
Investor Contact: D.S. Rubin (212-512-4321)
Board Members: P. Aspe, W. F. Bischoff, W., D. N. Daft, L. K. Lorimer, R. P. McGraw, H. W. McGraw, III, H. W. McGraw, Jr., H. Ochoa-Brillembourg, J. H. Ross, E. B. Rust, Jr., K. L. Schmoke, S. Taurel
Founded: 1899
Domicile: New York
Employees: 20,214

The McGraw-Hill Companies

McKesson Corp

STANDARD &POOR'S

S&P Recommendation	STRONG BUY ★★★★★	Price $67.00 (as of Nov 23, 2007)	12-Mo. Target Price $74.00	Investment Style Large-Cap Blend

GICS Sector Health Care
Sub-Industry Health Care Distributors

Summary MCK (formerly McKesson HBOC) provides pharmaceutical supply management and information technologies to a broad range of health care customers.

Key Stock Statistics (Source S&P, Vickers, company reports)

52-Wk Range	$67.00– 47.59	S&P Oper. EPS 2008**E**	3.37	Market Capitalization(B)	$19.832
Trailing 12-Month EPS	$3.24	S&P Oper. EPS 2009**E**	3.85	Yield (%)	0.36
Trailing 12-Month P/E	20.7	P/E on S&P Oper. EPS 2008**E**	19.9	Dividend Rate/Share	$0.24
$10K Invested 5 Yrs Ago	$25,235	Common Shares Outstg. (M)	296.0	Institutional Ownership (%)	89

Beta	0.29
S&P 3-Yr. Proj. EPS CAGR(%)	15.00
S&P Credit Rating	BBB

Price Performance

30-Week Mov. Avg. · · · 10-Week Mov. Avg. – – **GAAP Earnings vs. Previous Year** Volume Above Avg. STARS
12-Mo. Target Price — Relative Strength — ▲ Up ▼ Down ► No Change Below Avg. ★

Options: ASE, CBOE, P, Ph

Analysis prepared by **Phillip M. Seligman** on November 06, 2007, when the stock traded at **$ 64.18**.

Highlights

➤ For FY 08 (Mar.), we now look for company-wide revenue growth to accelerate to 8.0%, from FY 07's 6.9%. Growth drivers we see include drug distribution account wins, rising generic drug sales, healthy medical-surgical (med-surg) sales, continued robust demand for McKesson Technology Solutions (MTS) services, and the October 2007 Oncology Therapeutics Network (OTN) and January 2007 Per-Se Technologies acquisitions, partly offset by the generic drugs' sharply lower prices than their brand equivalents.

➤ We expect the company-wide operating margin to widen gradually, as generic drug penetration and cost-control initiatives outweigh incremental internal investments and the absence of LIFO credits, which aided FY 07 margins. We also think that MTS, which has wider margins than McKesson Distribution Solutions (MDS), will continue to grow faster than MCK as a whole.

➤ We estimate FY 08 operating EPS of $3.37, versus FY 07's $2.85, and look for FY 09 EPS of $3.85. Our FY 08 estimate includes $21 million of revenue from a disease management contract, the costs of which were recognized previously. In addition, MCK sees $0.06 dilution from OTN.

Investment Rationale/Risk

➤ September quarter drug distribution revenue growth was stronger than we expected, indicating continuing momentum from the June quarter. Looking ahead, we expect MCK to continue to achieve above-average earnings growth by leveraging its leading positions in the drug distribution, alternate-site med-surg and health care IT arenas to penetrate its core markets via "one-stop shopping." We are encouraged by MCK's cash position, debt capacity and healthy cash flow, which provide financial flexibility. We view the capital deployment in internal investments, tuck-in acquisitions, dividends and share buybacks as reflecting good management execution and shareholder focus.

➤ Risks to our recommendation and target price include the loss of major accounts, unfavorable regulatory changes, and unfavorable changes in drugmaker-distributor agreements.

➤ Our 12-month target price of $74 is derived by applying an above-peer P/E of 20X to our calendar 2008 EPS estimate of $3.70. We believe MCK merits a premium multiple on the brighter long-term prospects we see for MTS, versus peers' non-distribution businesses.

Qualitative Risk Assessment

LOW	MEDIUM	HIGH

Our risk assessment reflects our view of MCK's improving profitability and the growing demand for its highly profitable IT products and services, offset by our belief that the company is more price competitive than peers and that future drugmaker-distributor contract negotiations might be less favorable for distributors.

Quantitative Evaluations

S&P Quality Ranking   B

D	C	B-	B	B+	A-	A	A+

Relative Strength Rank   STRONG

95

LOWEST = 1   HIGHEST = 99

Revenue/Earnings Data

Revenue (Million $)

	1Q	2Q	3Q	4Q	Year
2008	24,528	24,450	--	--	--
2007	23,315	22,386	23,111	24,165	92,977
2006	20,968	21,515	22,510	23,057	88,050
2005	19,187	19,934	20,782	20,612	80,515
2004	16,524	16,810	18,232	17,940	69,506
2003	13,623	13,690	14,921	14,886	57,121

Earnings Per Share ($)

2008	0.77	0.83	E0.84	E0.97	E3.37
2007	0.60	0.94	0.79	0.85	3.17
2006	0.55	0.49	0.61	0.70	2.34
2005	0.55	0.29	-2.26	0.85	-0.53
2004	0.53	0.53	0.41	0.73	2.19
2003	0.39	0.43	0.46	0.62	1.90

Fiscal year ended Mar. 31. Next earnings report expected: Late January. EPS Estimates based on S&P Operating Earnings; historical GAAP earnings are as reported.

Dividend Data (Dates: mm/dd Payment Date: mm/dd/yy)

Amount ($)	Date Decl.	Ex-Div. Date	Stk. of Record	Payment Date
0.060	01/24	02/27	03/01	04/02/07
0.060	05/23	06/06	06/08	07/02/07
0.060	07/25	08/29	09/03	10/01/07
0.060	10/26	11/29	12/03	01/02/08

Dividends have been paid since 1995. Source: Company reports.

The McGraw-Hill Companies

McKesson Corp

Business Summary November 06, 2007

CORPORATE OVERVIEW. McKesson Corp. is a leading distributor of medical products and supplies and health care information technology products and services. Beginning in FY 08 (Mar.), MCK started reporting its results in two segments:

McKesson Distribution Solutions (MDS; 97.5% of FY 07 revenue on a pro forma basis) includes what was previously reported as Pharmaceutical Solutions and Medical-Surgical Solutions, with the exception of its Payor business. The pharmaceutical distribution unit primarily distributes ethical and proprietary drugs and health and beauty care, and focuses on three customer segments: retail independent pharmacies, retail chains, and institutions, in all 50 states and Canada. The medical-surgical distribution unit provides medical-surgical supplies, equipment, logistics and related services to alternate-site health care providers, including physicians' offices, long-term care and home care. Through its investment in Parata Systems, MDS also markets automated pharmacy systems to hospitals and retail pharmacies.

McKesson Technology Solutions (MTS; 2.5%) consists primarily of the former

Provider Technologies segment and the aforementioned Payor business. MTS delivers enterprise-wide patient care, clinical, financial, supply chain, and strategic management software solutions, pharmacy automation for hospitals, as well as connectivity, outsourcing and other services, to healthcare organizations throughout North America, the United Kingdom and other European countries. Its customers include hospitals, physicians, homecare providers, retail pharmacies and payors.

CORPORATE STRATEGY. Distribution agreements between distributors and most drugmakers have transitioned toward a more fee-based approach, with the distributors appropriately and predictably compensated for distribution and related logistic and administrative services and data, in our opinion. MCK and its peers see over 80% of their drugmaker compensation as fixed and not dependent upon drug price inflation.

Company Financials Fiscal Year Ended Mar. 31

Per Share Data ($)	2007	2006	2005	2004	2003	2002	2001	2000	1999	1998
Tangible Book Value	9.10	13.36	12.47	12.66	10.57	9.81	8.55	8.40	5.89	7.11
Cash Flow	4.14	3.28	0.32	2.94	2.65	2.20	0.72	1.37	0.98	2.39
Earnings	3.17	2.34	-0.53	2.19	1.90	1.43	-0.15	0.66	0.31	1.59
S&P Core Earnings	3.16	2.07	1.93	1.29	1.24	0.87	-0.39	NA	NA	NA
Dividends	0.24	0.24	0.24	0.24	0.24	0.24	0.24	0.31	0.50	0.50
Payout Ratio	8%	10%	NM	11%	13%	17%	NM	46%	161%	31%
Calendar Year	2006	2005	2004	2003	2002	2001	2000	1999	1998	1997
Prices:High	55.10	52.89	35.90	37.14	42.09	41.50	37.00	89.75	96.25	56.88
Prices:Low	44.60	30.13	22.61	22.61	24.99	23.40	16.00	18.56	47.88	25.88
P/E Ratio:High	17	23	NM	17	22	29	NM	NM	NM	36
P/E Ratio:Low	14	13	NM	10	13	16	NM	NM	NM	16

Income Statement Analysis (Million $)										
Revenue	92,977	88,050	80,515	69,506	57,121	50,006	42,010	36,734	30,382	20,857
Operating Income	1,553	1,425	1,260	1,216	1,134	923	454	359	531	449
Depreciation	295	266	251	232	204	208	246	201	199	86.0
Interest Expense	99.0	94.0	118	120	121	119	118	120	124	103
Pretax Income	1,297	1,158	-240	911	855	601	9.60	307	202	254
Effective Tax Rate	25.4%	36.4%	NM	29.1%	34.3%	30.4%	NM	39.7%	57.9%	39.0%
Net Income	968	737	-157	646	562	419	-42.7	185	85.0	155
S&P Core Earnings	964	650	565	380	364	255	-113	NA	NA	NA

Balance Sheet & Other Financial Data (Million $)										
Cash	1,954	2,142	1,809	718	534	563	446	606	269	36.0
Current Assets	17,856	16,919	15,332	13,004	11,254	10,699	9,164	7,966	6,500	4,106
Total Assets	23,943	20,975	18,775	16,240	14,353	13,324	11,530	10,373	9,082	5,608
Current Liabilities	15,126	13,515	11,793	9,456	7,974	7,588	6,550	5,122	4,800	2,578
Long Term Debt	1,803	965	1,202	1,210	1,487	1,485	1,232	1,440	1,142	1,194
Common Equity	6,273	5,907	5,275	5,165	4,529	3,940	3,493	4,213	2,882	1,523
Total Capital	8,076	6,872	6,477	6,375	6,016	5,425	4,724	5,653	4,024	2,796
Capital Expenditures	126	167	140	115	116	132	159	145	251	130
Cash Flow	1,263	1,003	94.2	879	766	626	203	386	284	241
Current Ratio	1.2	1.3	1.3	1.4	1.4	1.4	1.4	1.6	1.4	1.6
% Long Term Debt of Capitalization	22.3	14.0	18.6	19.0	24.7	27.4	26.1	25.5	28.4	42.7
% Net Income of Revenue	1.0	0.8	NM	0.9	1.0	0.8	NM	0.5	0.3	0.7
% Return on Assets	4.3	3.7	NM	4.2	4.1	3.4	NM	1.9	1.2	2.9
% Return on Equity	15.9	13.2	NM	13.3	13.3	11.3	NM	4.8	3.9	10.7

Data as orig reptd.; bef. results of disc opers/spec. items. Per share data adj. for stk. divs.; EPS diluted. E-Estimated. NA-Not Available. NM-Not Meaningful. NR-Not Ranked. UR-Under Review.

Office: One Post St McKesson Plaza , San Francisco, CA 94104-5296.
Telephone: 415-983-8300.
Email: investors@mckesson.com
Website: http://www.mckesson.com

Chrmn, Pres & CEO: J.H. Hammergren
Investor Contact: J.C. Campbell (800-826-9360)
EVP & CFO: J.C. Campbell
EVP, Secy & General Counsel: L. Seeger

EVP & CIO: R.N. Spratt
Board Members: W. A. Budd, J. H. Hammergren, A. F. Irby, III, M. C. Jacobs, M. L. Knowles, D. M. Lawrence, R. W. Matshullat, J. V. Napier, J. E. Shaw

Founded: 1994
Domicile: Delaware
Employees: 31,800

MeadWestvaco Corp

STANDARD &POOR'S

S&P Recommendation HOLD ★★★☆☆	**Price** $30.83 (as of Nov 23, 2007)	**12-Mo. Target Price** $34.00	**Investment Style** Large-Cap Value

GICS Sector Materials
Sub-Industry Paper Products

Summary This company is primarily a major producer of paperboard packaging used in a variety of consumer markets.

Key Stock Statistics (Source S&P, Vickers, company reports)

52-Wk Range	$36.50– 28.39	S&P Oper. EPS 2007 E	1.10	Market Capitalization(B)	$5.655	Beta	1.22
Trailing 12-Month EPS	$1.55	S&P Oper. EPS 2008 E	1.50	Yield (%)	2.98	S&P 3-Yr. Proj. EPS CAGR(%)	21.00
Trailing 12-Month P/E	19.9	P/E on S&P Oper. EPS 2007 E	28.0	Dividend Rate/Share	$0.92	S&P Credit Rating	BBB
$10K Invested 5 Yrs Ago	$15,352	Common Shares Outstg. (M)	183.4	Institutional Ownership (%)	88		

Price Performance

- 30-Week Mov. Avg. ···
- 10-Week Mov. Avg. – –
- GAAP Earnings vs. Previous Year
- Volume Above Avg. ⅲ
- STARS
- 12-Mo. Target Price —
- Relative Strength —
- ▲ Up ▼ Down ► No Change
- Below Avg. ⅲ ★

Options: ASE, CBOE, P

Analysis prepared by **Stuart J. Benway, CFA** on November 07, 2007, when the stock traded at **$ 31.92**.

Highlights

➤ We expect sales from continuing operations to rise about 5% in 2007. In our view, this improvement will be largely due to the addition of a modest acquisition and higher average prices across most of MWV's businesses. We look for a moderate recovery in the beverage market, especially overseas. For 2008, we estimate 3%-5% growth in revenue, primarily due to expansion in consumer packaging.

➤ We anticipate higher margins in 2007 because of the positive impact of the higher prices that we see, improved manufacturing efficiencies from the shutdown of high-cost capacity, and the anticipated benefits of other cost-cutting initiatives. We see these factors being partly offset by higher costs for manufacturing inputs such as energy, chemicals, stainless steel, and wood fiber.

➤ Our operating EPS forecast for 2007 is $1.10, up 16% from operating EPS of $0.95 in 2006. For 2008, we estimate further growth to $1.50 a share. These estimates do not include land sales gains, which we expect to be significant in certain quarters.

Investment Rationale/Risk

➤ We believe that volume trends in the packaging sector will remain subdued in the near term due to reduced compact disc sales, an increased emphasis on packaging reduction, and higher Asian imports. However, we think that Mead-Westvaco is better positioned than many paper companies in our coverage universe, with its high market share in mostly non-commodity markets and its geographic diversification. We expect a recent acquisition to make a rising contribution to results.

➤ Risks to our recommendation and target price include a weaker-than-expected global economy, softer-than-projected demand and pricing trends for the company's packaging grades, higher energy and raw material costs, and poor execution of MWV's planned cost-cutting initiatives.

➤ The shares recently traded at about 22X our 2008 EPS forecast, which is a significant premium to its peer group. Our DCF model values the shares at $34, assuming a weighted average cost of capital of 8.9%, significant land sales, and growth in perpetuity of 3%; this is the basis for our 12-month target price of $34.

Qualitative Risk Assessment

LOW	MEDIUM	HIGH

MWV operates in a moderately cyclical and seasonal sector and is subject to swings in certain commodity prices. However, it has some pricing power due to its high market share, and we find its debt levels low relative to many of its peers.

Quantitative Evaluations

S&P Quality Ranking　　　　B-

D	C	B-	B	B+	A-	A	A+

Relative Strength Rank　　　MODERATE

68

LOWEST = 1　　　　　HIGHEST = 99

Revenue/Earnings Data

Revenue (Million $)

	1Q	2Q	3Q	4Q	Year
2007	1,552	1,706	1,796	--	--
2006	1,434	1,570	1,751	1,775	6,530
2005	1,373	1,587	1,583	1,627	6,170
2004	1,833	2,095	2,148	2,151	8,227
2003	1,694	1,915	1,999	1,945	7,553
2002	1,461	2,012	2,023	1,893	7,242

Earnings Per Share ($)

2007	-0.09	0.17	0.66	E0.43	E1.10
2006	0.02	-0.04	0.31	0.23	0.52
2005	0.08	-0.06	0.30	0.33	0.62
2004	-0.01	0.24	0.52	-2.45	-1.73
2003	-0.36	-0.04	0.14	0.25	-0.01
2002	-0.37	-0.04	0.09	0.21	-0.01

Fiscal year ended Dec. 31. Next earnings report expected: Late January. EPS Estimates based on S&P Operating Earnings; historical GAAP earnings are as reported.

Dividend Data (Dates: mm/dd Payment Date: mm/dd/yy)

Amount ($)	Date Decl.	Ex-Div. Date	Stk. of Record	Payment Date
0.230	10/24	11/01	11/03	12/01/06
0.230	01/23	11/07	11/11	12/03/07

Dividends have been paid since 1892. Source: Company reports.

MeadWestvaco Corp

**STANDARD
&POOR'S**

Business Summary November 07, 2007

CORPORATE OVERVIEW. Through a series of mergers and divestitures, Mead-Westvaco has molded itself into one of the largest producers of packaging products in the world, and it is also a major supplier of consumer and office products and specialty chemicals. The Packaging Resources segment (42% of 2006 revenues) produces bleached paperboard, coated paperboard, kraft paperboard, linerboard and saturating kraft, and packaging for consumer products including beverage and dairy, cosmetics, tobacco, pharmaceuticals, and health care products. Some of the company's major customers include Altria, Anheuser-Busch, Coca-Cola and Procter & Gamble. The Consumer Solutions segment (31%) sells a full range of consumer packaging products, including printed plastic packaging and injection-molded products used for packaging DVDs, CDs, cosmetics, and pharmaceuticals, and plastic dispensing and spraying systems for worldwide personal care, health care, fragrance, and lawn and garden markets. The Consumer and Office Products segment (16%) makes, markets and distributes school and office products, time management products, and envelopes. The Specialty Chemicals segment (7%) produces, markets and distributes specialty chemicals derived from sawdust and other by-products of the pulp and papermaking process. These chemicals include activated carbon, printing ink resins, emulsifiers used in asphalt paving, and dyestuffs. Corporate and other accounted for 4% of sales in 2006. The company also owns about 1.1 million acres of forest lands in the U.S.

MARKET PROFILE. MeadWestvaco is the largest producer of paperboard, also known as folding boxboard or cartonboard, in North America, with a share of about 17%, according to Pulp & Paper magazine. The market is somewhat fragmented, with more than 15 companies accounting for at least a 1% share, although the top three producers control 38% of the industry. Unlike containerboard, paperboard has a bendable quality for creasing, scoring and shaping, and usually packages single items meant for consumer purchase. It is used in a variety of consumer applications where print quality, strength and customer appeal are important. Folding carton demand is primarily driven by consumer spending and industrial production. We believe the company's market position, technical expertise and product line diversity give it a moderate level of control over pricing.

Company Financials Fiscal Year Ended Dec. 31

Per Share Data ($)	2006	2005	2004	2003	2002	2001	2000	1999	1998	1997
Tangible Book Value	14.74	14.58	18.44	19.89	20.44	17.34	23.17	21.65	22.39	22.35
Cash Flow	3.37	3.17	1.87	3.60	3.49	4.29	5.63	3.90	4.06	4.25
Earnings	0.52	0.62	-1.73	-0.01	-0.01	0.87	2.53	1.11	1.30	1.58
S&P Core Earnings	-0.11	0.27	-2.67	-0.81	-1.37	-1.01	NA	NA	NA	NA
Dividends	0.92	0.92	0.92	0.92	0.92	0.88	0.88	0.88	0.88	0.88
Payout Ratio	177%	148%	NM	NM	NM	101%	35%	79%	68%	55%
Prices:High	30.85	34.33	34.34	29.83	36.50	32.10	34.75	33.50	34.13	37.50
Prices:Low	24.76	25.06	25.16	21.37	15.57	22.68	24.06	20.81	21.00	25.00
P/E Ratio:High	59	55	NM	NM	NM	37	14	30	26	23
P/E Ratio:Low	48	40	NM	NM	NM	26	10	19	16	16

Income Statement Analysis (Million $)										
Revenue	6,530	6,170	8,227	7,553	7,242	3,935	3,663	2,802	2,886	2,982
Operating Income	743	818	1,042	855	859	677	869	601	577	580
Depreciation	517	491	726	724	674	347	314	280	281	269
Interest Expense	211	208	278	291	309	208	192	124	110	93.3
Pretax Income	98.0	135	-454	-29.0	-15.0	119	404	148	204	247
Effective Tax Rate	5.10%	11.9%	NM	NM	NM	25.6%	36.9%	24.9%	35.4%	34.0%
Net Income	93.0	119	-349	-2.00	-3.00	88.2	255	111	132	163
S&P Core Earnings	-22.1	50.6	-539	-164	-264	-104	NA	NA	NA	NA

Balance Sheet & Other Financial Data (Million $)										
Cash	156	297	270	225	372	81.2	255	109	105	175
Current Assets	2,015	2,030	2,562	2,426	2,431	1,016	1,064	738	739	805
Total Assets	9,285	8,908	11,681	12,487	12,921	6,787	6,570	4,897	5,009	4,899
Current Liabilities	1,465	1,042	1,751	1,501	1,620	701	567	425	467	406
Long Term Debt	2,372	2,417	3,427	3,969	4,233	2,660	2,687	1,502	1,526	1,513
Common Equity	3,533	3,483	4,317	4,768	4,831	2,341	2,333	2,171	2,246	2,279
Total Capital	7,082	7,052	9,249	10,415	10,821	6,009	5,927	4,472	4,541	4,494
Capital Expenditures	302	305	407	393	377	290	214	229	423	621
Cash Flow	610	610	377	722	671	436	569	392	413	432
Current Ratio	1.4	1.9	1.5	1.6	1.5	1.4	1.9	1.7	1.6	2.0
% Long Term Debt of Capitalization	33.5	34.3	37.1	38.1	39.1	44.3	45.3	33.6	33.6	33.7
% Net Income of Revenue	1.4	1.9	NM	NM	NM	2.2	7.0	4.0	4.6	5.5
% Return on Assets	1.0	1.2	NM	NM	NM	1.3	4.4	2.2	2.7	3.5
% Return on Equity	2.7	3.1	NM	NM	NM	3.8	11.3	5.0	5.8	7.3

Data as orig reptd.; bef. results of disc opers/spec. items. Per share data adj. for stk. divs.; EPS diluted. E-Estimated. NA-Not Available. NM-Not Meaningful. NR-Not Ranked. UR-Under Review.

Office: 11013 West Broad St, Glen Allen, VA 23060-5937.
Telephone: 804-327-5200.
Website: http://www.meadwestvaco.com
Chrmn & CEO: J.A. Luke, Jr.

Pres: J.A. Buzzard
SVP & CFO: E.M. Rajkowski
SVP, Secy & General Counsel: W.L. Willkie, II
Treas: R.E. Birkenholz

Investor Contact: J. Thompson
Board Members: M. E. Campbell, T. W. Cole, Jr., J. G. Kaiser, R. B. Kelson, J. M. Kilts, J. A. Krol, S. J. Kropf, D. S. Luke, J. A. Luke, Jr., R. C. McCormack, T. H. Powers, E. M. Straw, J. L. Warner

Founded: 1846
Domicile: Delaware
Employees: 24,000

Medco Health Solutions Inc.

STANDARD &POOR'S

S&P Recommendation	BUY ★★★★☆	Price $101.87 (as of Nov 29, 2007)	12-Mo. Target Price $112.00	Investment Style Large-Cap Blend

GICS Sector Health Care
Sub-Industry Health Care Services

Summary Medco, spun off from Merck & Co. in August 2003, is the largest U.S. pharmacy benefit manager (PBM) in terms of revenues and script count.

Key Stock Statistics (Source S&P, Vickers, company reports)

52-Wk Range	$102.74– 49.56	S&P Oper. EPS 2007**E**	3.60	Market Capitalization(B)	$27.584	Beta		0.28
Trailing 12-Month EPS	$3.26	S&P Oper. EPS 2008**E**	4.45	Yield (%)	Nil	S&P 3-Yr. Proj. EPS CAGR(%)		21.00
Trailing 12-Month P/E	31.3	P/E on S&P Oper. EPS 2007**E**	28.3	Dividend Rate/Share	Nil	S&P Credit Rating		BBB
$10K Invested 5 Yrs Ago	NA	Common Shares Outstg. (M)	270.8	Institutional Ownership (%)	81			

Price Performance

30-Week Mov. Avg. · · · 10-Week Mov. Avg. ▬ **GAAP Earnings vs. Previous Year** Volume Above Avg. ▮▮▮ STARS
12-Mo. Target Price ▬ Relative Strength ▬ ▲ Up ▼ Down ► No Change Below Avg. ▮▮▮ ★▬

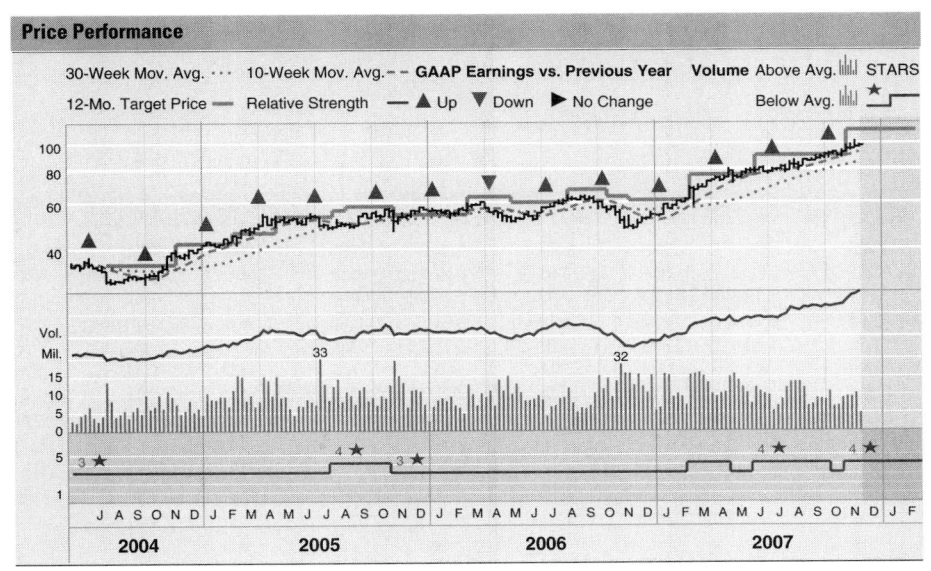

Options: ASE, CBOE, P, Ph

Analysis prepared by **Phillip M. Seligman** on November 05, 2007, when the stock traded at **$ 95.33**.

Highlights

➤ We expect revenues to increase about 11% in 2008, to $49.6 billion, from the $44.7 billion we estimate for 2007. Drivers we see include net new business of $3.9 billion for 2008 as of October 2007 and the recent acquisition of PolyMedica, a provider of direct-to-consumer diabetes testing supplies and drugs. We see revenue growth benefiting from the company's high account retention rate. However, we expect the growth to be tempered by the increasing penetration of generic drugs, which carry lower prices but wider margins than branded drugs.

➤ We believe EBITDA per adjusted prescription, the measure of a PBM's profitability, will expand modestly in 2008 as a whole. We see this due to the benefit from higher generic drug, specialty drug and mail order penetration rates being mostly offset by pricing pressure from 10 large contract renewals in 2007's first half, incremental SG&A spending for PolyMedica, and the new Federal Employee Program contract, which carries a below-average gross margin.

➤ We estimate 2007 operating EPS, before amortization charges, of $3.60, compared to 2006's $2.78, and look for $4.45 in 2008.

Investment Rationale/Risk

➤ We recently upgraded MHS shares to buy, from hold, partly on valuation. Fundamentals in the PBM space look healthy to us, and we are encouraged by MHS's high account retention rate and sizable new business netted. While we see tougher EPS comparisons in 2007's second half and 2008's first half on price concessions made in contract renewals, we expect the renewed accounts' margins to widen over time on generic drug and mail penetration. For 2008, we see fewer renewals and more new account opportunities, and note the recent wins of the $2.0 billion Federal Employee Program mail/specialty contract and the $1.6 billion State of New York contract. Meanwhile, we are encouraged by the PolyMedica acquisition, which provides MHS entry into the Medicare Part B drug market.

➤ Risks to our recommendation and target price include intensifying competition, more regulatory oversight, and the loss of MHS's largest client, UnitedHealth Group.

➤ Our 12-month target price of $112 is derived by applying a peer-level P/E-to-growth ratio of 1.2X, assuming three-year EPS growth of 21% and our 2008 operating EPS estimate of $4.45.

Qualitative Risk Assessment

LOW	MEDIUM	HIGH

Our risk assessment reflects rising drug demand and our view of MHS's improving financial performance and declining debt leverage. However, we believe that intense competition and increased government regulation of pharmacy benefit managers (PBMs), which we view as likely, could slow long-term progress in profits.

Quantitative Evaluations

S&P Quality Ranking   **NR**

D	C	B-	B	B+	A-	A	A+

Relative Strength Rank   **STRONG**

95

LOWEST = 1   HIGHEST = 99

Revenue/Earnings Data

Revenue (Million $)

	1Q	2Q	3Q	4Q	Year
2007	11,160	11,050	10,919	--	--
2006	10,564	10,589	10,461	10,930	42,544
2005	8,743	8,999	9,325	10,803	37,871
2004	8,906	8,836	8,697	8,913	35,352
2003	8,334	8,405	8,524	9,002	34,265
2002	--	--	--	--	32,959

Earnings Per Share ($)

2007	0.94	0.76	0.78	E0.87	E3.60
2006	0.15	0.56	0.62	0.77	2.09
2005	0.47	0.48	0.53	0.57	2.05
2004	0.38	0.46	0.43	0.48	1.75
2003	0.38	0.39	0.37	0.43	1.57
2002	--	--	--	--	1.18

Fiscal year ended Dec. 31. Next earnings report expected: Late February. EPS Estimates based on S&P Operating Earnings; historical GAAP earnings are as reported.

Dividend Data

No cash dividends have been paid.

Medco Health Solutions Inc.

STANDARD
&POOR'S

Business Summary November 05, 2007

CORPORATE OVERVIEW. Medco Health Solutions was spun off to Merck & Co. (MRK) shareholders in a tax-free transaction on August 19, 2003. The company is one of the largest U.S. pharmacy benefit managers (PBMs). It provides programs and services to clients and members of PBMs, and to physicians and pharmacies that they use.

In 2006, MHS processed about 553 million prescriptions, compared to 540 million in 2005. Revenues and net income are derived from: rebates and discounts on prescription drugs from pharmaceutical manufacturers; competitive discounts from retail pharmacies; the negotiation of favorable client pricing, including rebate sharing terms; the shift in dispensing volumes from retail to home delivery; and the provision of services in a cost-efficient manner.

We believe that MHS is facing some risks, including pending lawsuits by plaintiffs alleging that MHS breached fiduciary obligations under the Employee Retirement Income Security Act (ERISA).

Gross rebates recorded as received from MRK totaled $301.1 million through the separation date of August 19, 2003, $443.9 million in 2002, and $439.4 million in 2001. According to MHS, effective as of the end of March 2006, the agreement entered into with MRK in July 2002 was terminated. Under that agreement, MRK provided MHS with rebates based, in part, on whether MRK products were included in formularies that MHS offers clients, and on whether MRK products achieve specified market share targets under MHS's plans. If MHS had failed to achieve the targets, it may have had to pay damages. That agreement was replaced with one that is similar to other rebate agreements that MHS has with other major drugmakers.

Company Financials Fiscal Year Ended Dec. 31

Per Share Data ($)	2006	2005	2004	2003	2002	2001	2000	1999	1998	1997
Tangible Book Value	NM	NM	0.98	NM	NM	1.70	1.31	NA	NA	NA
Cash Flow	3.39	3.27	3.13	2.62	2.13	2.15	1.87	NA	NA	NA
Earnings	2.09	2.05	1.75	1.57	1.18	0.95	0.80	NA	NA	NA
S&P Core Earnings	2.41	1.86	1.48	1.03	1.07	0.71	NA	NA	NA	NA
Dividends	Nil	Nil	Nil	Nil	NA	NA	NA	NA	NA	NA
Payout Ratio	Nil	Nil	Nil	Nil	NA	NA	NA	NA	NA	NA
Prices:High	64.13	57.95	41.90	38.00	NA	NA	NA	NA	NA	NA
Prices:Low	47.08	40.55	29.40	20.20	NA	NA	NA	NA	NA	NA
P/E Ratio:High	31	28	24	24	NA	NA	NA	NA	NA	NA
P/E Ratio:Low	23	20	17	13	NA	NA	NA	NA	NA	NA

Income Statement Analysis (Million $)

	2006	2005	2004	2003	2002	2001	2000	1999	1998	1997
Revenue	42,544	37,871	35,352	34,265	32,959	29,071	22,266	NA	NA	NA
Operating Income	1,470	1,350	1,244	1,025	886	837	731	NA	NA	NA
Depreciation	392	358	378	283	257	323	289	NA	NA	NA
Interest Expense	65.9	73.9	Nil	Nil	73.5	Nil	Nil	NA	NA	NA
Pretax Income	1,012	953	806	729	547	518	448	NA	NA	NA
Effective Tax Rate	37.7%	36.8%	40.3%	41.6%	41.7%	50.5%	51.6%	NA	NA	NA
Net Income	630	602	482	426	319	257	217	NA	NA	NA
S&P Core Earnings	726	544	404	279	287	188	NA	NA	NA	NA

Balance Sheet & Other Financial Data (Million $)

	2006	2005	2004	2003	2002	2001	2000	1999	1998	1997
Cash	818	888	1,146	638	203	16.3	NA	NA	NA	NA
Current Assets	5,855	5,061	4,320	3,760	3,044	2,534	NA	NA	NA	NA
Total Assets	14,388	13,703	10,542	10,263	9,714	9,252	8,915	NA	NA	NA
Current Liabilities	4,827	3,761	2,645	2,605	2,370	1,809	NA	NA	NA	NA
Long Term Debt	866	944	1,093	1,346	1,385	Nil	Nil	NA	NA	NA
Common Equity	7,504	7,724	5,719	5,080	4,738	6,268	6,358	NA	NA	NA
Total Capital	9,531	9,882	6,812	7,604	7,305	7,423	7,502	NA	NA	NA
Capital Expenditures	151	132	98.1	125	NA	322	251	NA	NA	NA
Cash Flow	1,022	960	859	709	576	580	506	NA	NA	NA
Current Ratio	1.2	1.3	1.6	1.4	1.3	1.4	NA	NA	NA	NA
% Long Term Debt of Capitalization	9.1	9.6	16.0	17.7	19.0	Nil	Nil	NA	NA	NA
% Net Income of Revenue	1.5	1.6	1.4	1.2	1.0	0.9	1.0	NA	NA	NA
% Return on Assets	4.4	5.0	4.6	4.2	NA	2.8	NA	NA	NA	NA
% Return on Equity	8.3	9.0	8.9	7.3	NA	4.1	NA	NA	NA	NA

Data as orig reptd.; bef. results of disc opers/spec. items. Per share data adj. for stk. divs.; EPS diluted. E-Estimated. NA-Not Available. NM-Not Meaningful. NR-Not Ranked. UR-Under Review.

Office: 100 Parsons Pond Drive, Franklin Lakes, NJ 07417-2603.
Telephone: 201-269-3400.
Website: http://www.medco.com
Chrmn, Pres & CEO: D.B. Snow, Jr.

COO & EVP: K.O. Klepper
SVP & CFO: J.A. Reed
SVP, Secy & General Counsel: D.S. Machlowitz
Investor Contact: J. Pirro (201-269-6047)

Board Members: H. W. Barker, Jr., J. L. Cassis, M. Goldstein, L. S. Lewin, C. Lillis, E. H. Shortliffe, D. B. Snow, Jr., D. Stevens, B. L. Strom, B. J. Wilson

Founded: 1983
Domicile: Delaware
Employees: 15,700

The **McGraw-Hill** Companies

Medtronic Inc.

STANDARD &POOR'S

S&P Recommendation **HOLD** ★★★☆☆	Price $48.32 (as of Nov 23, 2007)	12-Mo. Target Price $50.00	Investment Style Large-Cap Growth

GICS Sector Health Care
Sub-Industry Health Care Equipment

Summary This global medical device manufacturer has leadership positions in the pacemaker, defibrillator, orthopedic, diabetes management and other medical markets.

Key Stock Statistics (Source S&P, Vickers, company reports)

52-Wk Range	$57.99– 44.87	S&P Oper. EPS 2008**E**	2.50	Market Capitalization(B)	$54.801	Beta	0.39
Trailing 12-Month EPS	$2.48	S&P Oper. EPS 2009**E**	2.95	Yield (%)	1.03	S&P 3-Yr. Proj. EPS CAGR(%)	13.00
Trailing 12-Month P/E	19.5	P/E on S&P Oper. EPS 2008**E**	19.3	Dividend Rate/Share	$0.50	S&P Credit Rating	AA-
$10K Invested 5 Yrs Ago	$10,278	Common Shares Outstg. (M)	1,134.1	Institutional Ownership (%)	78		

Price Performance

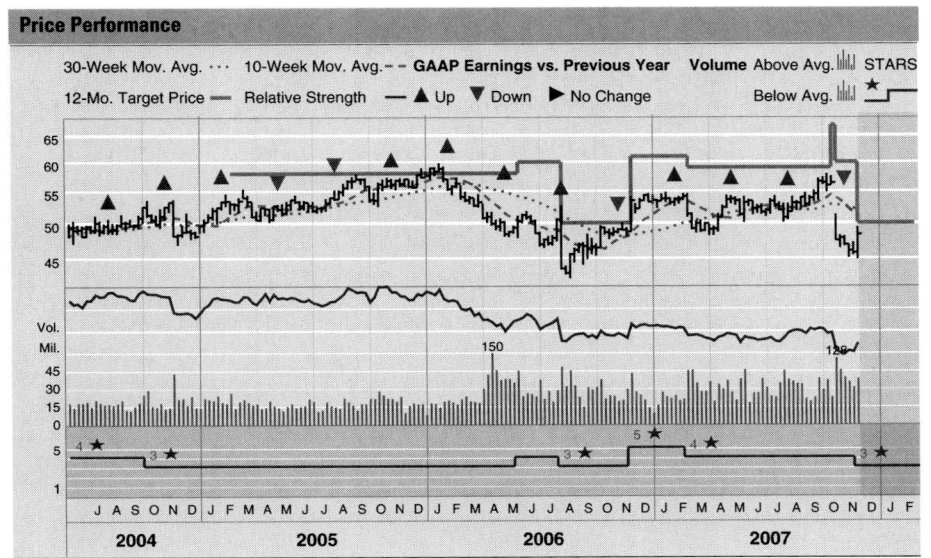

30-Week Mov. Avg. ··· 10-Week Mov. Avg. -- **GAAP Earnings vs. Previous Year** Volume Above Avg.|||| STARS
12-Mo. Target Price — Relative Strength — ▲ Up ▼ Down ► No Change Below Avg.|||| ★

Options: ASE, CBOE, P, Ph

Analysis prepared by **Robert M. Gold** on November 21, 2007, when the stock traded at **$ 48.42**.

Highlights

➤ We project FY 08 (Apr.) sales of $13.5 billion, reflecting a modest recovery in the domestic ICD market, substantial ICD growth overseas, and protracted strength in the diabetes, interventional cardiology and neurology categories. In our opinion, the company is likely to lose about 3% of ICD market share in 2008, and we project global share of about 45%, down from an estimated 49% in 2007. We think sales in the spinal/ear, nose and throat business unit will advance about 13%. Our revenue forecast includes about $310 million in sales from recently-acquired Kyphon Inc.

➤ We think FY 08 gross margins will continue to be hurt by sluggish sales performance in the U.S. ICD category, partially offset by manufacturing efficiencies. We expect R&D and SG&A costs to consume 10% and 32%, respectively, of sales. We see FY 08 free cash flow of $2.5 billion, and we think MDT may raise the dividend and/or pursue strategic acquisitions with the available cash.

➤ We see FY 08 operating EPS of $2.50, including $0.09 of dilution from the Kyphon deal and an approximate $0.12 impact from the recall of Fidelis ICD leads Our FY 09 estimate is $2.95.

Investment Rationale/Risk

➤ We believe the global ICD market will rise 3% in 2008, pressured by recent product recalls in the U.S. In our view, however, MDT has significant growth opportunities in the cardiac stent markets, driven by rising demand for its Endeavor drug coated product in Europe and an expected U.S. launch of Endeavor by late 2007 or early 2008. We look for contributions from the launch of new heart valve products, and we believe the diabetes franchise will continue to grow in excess of 20%.

➤ Risks to our recommendation and target price include a loss of share in key markets, unfavorable patent litigation, adverse reimbursement rate changes, and further weakness in the U.S. ICD market.

➤ Although we are cautious on the domestic ICD market and the impact of a recent ICD lead recall, we think the company's diversified product line, new product pipeline, and free cash flow generation warrants a forward P/E to growth (PEG) ratio only modestly below peers. Our 12-month target price is $50, or about 20X our FY 08 EPS estimate, resulting in a forward PEG ratio of 1.5X.

Qualitative Risk Assessment

LOW	MEDIUM	HIGH

Our risk assessment reflects MDT's exposure to intensely competitive areas of the medical equipment markets, which are typically characterized by relatively short product life cycles, pricing pressures, and the threat of new market entrants. However, we believe this is offset by MDT's many competitive advantages due to the scale of its operations and salesforce, product breadth and what we see as its financial strength.

Quantitative Evaluations

S&P Quality Ranking A

D	C	B-	B	B+	A-	A	A+

Relative Strength Rank MODERATE

60

LOWEST = 1   HIGHEST = 99

Revenue/Earnings Data

Revenue (Million $)

	1Q	2Q	3Q	4Q	Year
2008	3,127	3,124	--	--	--
2007	2,897	3,075	3,048	3,280	12,299
2006	2,690	2,765	2,770	3,077	11,292
2005	2,346	2,400	2,531	2,778	10,055
2004	2,064	2,164	2,194	2,665	9,087
2003	1,714	1,891	1,913	2,148	7,665

Earnings Per Share ($)

2008	0.59	0.58	E0.61	E0.72	E2.50
2007	0.51	0.59	0.61	0.70	2.41
2006	0.26	0.67	0.55	0.62	2.09
2005	0.43	0.44	0.45	0.16	1.48
2004	0.37	0.39	0.38	0.47	1.60
2003	0.31	0.25	0.35	0.40	1.30

Fiscal year ended Apr. 30. Next earnings report expected: Late February. EPS Estimates based on S&P Operating Earnings; historical GAAP earnings are as reported.

Dividend Data (Dates: mm/dd Payment Date: mm/dd/yy)

Amount ($)	Date Decl.	Ex-Div. Date	Stk. of Record	Payment Date
0.110	01/18	04/03	04/06	04/27/07
0.125	06/22	07/03	07/06	07/27/07
0.125	08/23	10/03	10/05	10/26/07
0.125	10/19	01/02	01/04	01/25/08

Dividends have been paid since 1977. Source: Company reports.

Medtronic Inc.

Business Summary November 21, 2007

Medtronic has leading positions in medical device categories, including cardiac rhythm management, ear, nose and throat, spinal, vascular, neurological, and cardiac surgery.

Cardiac rhythm management products (42% of FY 07 (Apr.) revenues) include implantable pacemakers to treat bradycardia (slow or irregular heartbeats). Bradycardia systems include pacemakers, leads and accessories. Some models are non-invasively programmed by a physician to adjust sensing, electrical pulse intensity, duration, rate and other factors, as well as pacers that can sense in both upper and lower heart chambers and produce appropriate impulses. In May 2005, FDA approval was received for EnRhythm, the company's newest dual-chamber pacemaker, and the first to offer an exclusive pacing mode, called Managed Ventricular Pacing, which enables the device to be programmed to minimize pacing pulses to the right ventricle.

Implantable cardioverter defibrillators (ICDs) treat abnormally fast heart beats (tachyarrhythmias) by monitoring the heart; when a rapid rhythm is detected, electrical impulses or shocks are delivered. Cardiac resynchronization thera-py (CRT) devices synchronize contractions of multiple heart chambers. The company's InSynch ICD offers CRT for heart failure, as well as advanced defibrillation capabilities for patients also at risk for potentially lethal tachyarrhythmias that may lead to cardiac arrest. The Insynch Marquis system combines the cardiac resynchronization of InSynch devices with defibrillation therapies of the Marquis ICD platform. During FY 05, MDT launched its highest energy CRT-D device, the InSynch Maximo, and the InSynch Sentry CRT-D, which incorporates automatic fluid status monitoring. It also added a ventricle-to-ventricle feature to both InSynch Maximo and InSynch Sentry that allows physicians to separately adjust the timing of electrical therapy delivered to the two ventricles to optimize the beating of the heart and enhance blood flow. MDT also sells external defibrillators.

Company Financials Fiscal Year Ended Apr. 30

Per Share Data ($)	2007	2006	2005	2004	2003	2002	2001	2000	1999	1998
Tangible Book Value	4.56	2.98	4.26	3.18	2.21	1.10	3.53	2.61	1.99	1.68
Cash Flow	2.91	2.54	1.86	1.96	1.64	1.07	1.10	1.10	0.58	0.63
Earnings	2.41	2.09	1.48	1.60	1.30	0.80	0.85	0.90	0.40	0.48
S&P Core Earnings	2.44	2.00	1.65	1.46	1.10	0.76	0.91	NA	NA	NA
Dividends	0.39	0.34	0.29	0.25	0.25	0.20	0.12	0.15	0.12	0.11
Payout Ratio	16%	16%	20%	16%	19%	25%	14%	16%	30%	23%
Calendar Year	2006	2005	2004	2003	2002	2001	2000	1999	1998	1997
Prices:High	59.87	58.91	53.70	52.92	50.69	60.81	62.00	44.63	38.38	26.38
Prices:Low	42.37	48.70	43.99	42.90	32.50	36.64	32.75	29.94	22.72	14.41
P/E Ratio:High	25	28	36	33	39	72	61	50	97	55
P/E Ratio:Low	18	23	30	27	25	43	32	33	58	30

Income Statement Analysis (Million $)										
Revenue	12,299	11,292	10,055	9,087	7,665	6,411	5,552	5,015	4,134	2,605
Operating Income	4,322	4,248	3,907	3,583	3,062	2,479	2,176	1,871	1,535	1,017
Depreciation	583	544	463	443	408	330	297	243	213	138
Interest Expense	228	Nil	55.1	56.5	7.20	Nil	74.0	13.0	28.8	8.16
Pretax Income	3,515	3,161	2,544	2,797	2,341	1,524	1,549	1,630	822	702
Effective Tax Rate	20.3%	19.4%	29.1%	29.9%	31.7%	35.4%	32.5%	32.6%	43.0%	34.8%
Net Income	2,802	2,547	1,804	1,959	1,600	984	1,046	1,099	468	457
S&P Core Earnings	2,841	2,450	2,006	1,790	1,347	936	1,121	NA	NA	NA

Balance Sheet & Other Financial Data (Million $)										
Cash	1,256	2,994	2,232	1,594	1,470	411	1,030	448	376	383
Current Assets	7,918	10,377	7,422	5,313	4,606	3,488	3,757	3,013	2,395	1,552
Total Assets	19,512	19,665	16,617	14,111	12,321	10,905	7,039	5,669	4,870	2,775
Current Liabilities	2,563	4,406	3,380	4,241	1,813	3,985	1,359	992	990	572
Long Term Debt	5,578	5,486	1,973	1.10	1,980	9.50	13.0	14.0	17.6	16.2
Common Equity	10,977	9,383	10,450	9,077	7,906	6,431	5,510	4,491	3,655	2,044
Total Capital	16,555	14,891	12,901	9,486	10,191	6,674	5,523	4,520	3,703	2,074
Capital Expenditures	573	407	452	425	380	386	440	342	226	148
Cash Flow	3,385	3,090	2,267	2,402	2,008	1,314	1,343	1,342	681	595
Current Ratio	3.1	2.4	2.2	1.3	2.5	0.9	2.8	3.0	2.4	2.7
% Long Term Debt of Capitalization	33.7	36.8	15.3	0.0	19.4	0.1	0.2	0.3	0.5	0.8
% Net Income of Revenue	22.8	22.6	17.9	21.6	20.9	15.3	18.8	21.9	11.3	17.6
% Return on Assets	14.3	14.0	11.7	14.8	13.8	11.0	16.5	20.6	11.0	17.6
% Return on Equity	27.5	25.7	18.5	23.1	22.3	16.5	20.9	26.6	14.8	24.1

Data as orig reptd.; bef. results of disc opers/spec. items. Per share data adj. for stk. divs.; EPS diluted. E-Estimated. NA-Not Available. NM-Not Meaningful. NR-Not Ranked. UR-Under Review.

Office: 710 Medtronic Parkway, Minneapolis, MN 55432-5604.
Telephone: 763-514-4000.
Website: http://www.medtronic.com
Chrmn & CEO: A.D. Collins, Jr.

Pres & COO: W.A. Hawkins III
Investor Contact: G.L. Ellis (763-505-2692)
SVP & CFO: G.L. Ellis
SVP, Secy & General Counsel: T.L. Carlson

Board Members: R. H. Anderson, M. R. Bonsignore, W. R. Brody, A. D. Collins, Jr., W. A. Hawkins, S. A. Jackson, J. T. Lenehan, D. M. O'Leary, R. C. Pozen, J. Rosso, J. W. Schuler, G. M. Sprenger

Founded: 1957
Domicile: Minnesota
Employees: 37,800

MEMC Electronic Materials Inc.

STANDARD &POOR'S

S&P Recommendation **STRONG BUY** ★★★★★	Price $67.53 (as of Nov 23, 2007)	12-Mo. Target Price $82.00	Investment Style Large-Cap Growth

GICS Sector Information Technology
Sub-Industry Semiconductor Equipment

Summary This company is a worldwide producer of silicon wafers used in semiconductors for microelectronic applications. It also provides silicon materials to the solar industry.

Key Stock Statistics (Source S&P, Vickers, company reports)

52-Wk Range	$78.50–37.30	S&P Oper. EPS 2007**E**	2.78	Market Capitalization(B)	$15.200	Beta	3.42
Trailing 12-Month EPS	$2.50	S&P Oper. EPS 2008**E**	3.86	Yield (%)	Nil	S&P 3-Yr. Proj. EPS CAGR(%)	25.00
Trailing 12-Month P/E	27.0	P/E on S&P Oper. EPS 2007**E**	24.3	Dividend Rate/Share	Nil	S&P Credit Rating	NA
$10K Invested 5 Yrs Ago	$78,982	Common Shares Outstg. (M)	225.1	Institutional Ownership (%)	92		

Price Performance

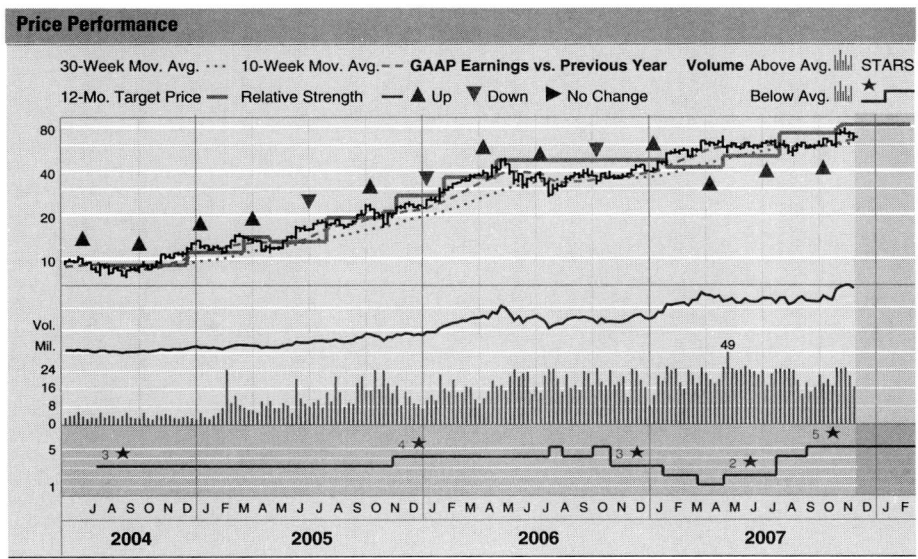

30-Week Mov. Avg. ··· 10-Week Mov. Avg. -- GAAP Earnings vs. Previous Year Volume Above Avg. STARS
12-Mo. Target Price — Relative Strength ▲ Up ▼ Down ▶ No Change Below Avg.

Options: ASE, CBOE, P, Ph

Analysis prepared by **Jim Yin** on October 29, 2007, when the stock traded at **$ 73.81**.

Highlights

➤ We estimate revenues will increase 25% in both 2007 and 2008, after 39% growth in 2006, driven by strength in demand for semiconductor chips and expansion in the solar panel market. WFR has signed separate agreements with Suntech, Gintech and Conergy to supply a total of $15.5 billion to $18 billion of solar wafers over a 10-year period. In addition to increased demand, we forecast better pricing due to a supply shortage.

➤ We expect the gross margin to expand to 52% and 56% in 2007 and 2008, respectively, from 45% in 2006. Even though we expect the industry to bring substantial capacity on line, we forecast that demand will exceed supply for the next few years. We expect non-GAAP operating margins to increase to 44% and 49% in 2007 and 2008, respectively, from 36% in 2006, reflecting stronger demand and operating leverage.

➤ Our EPS estimates are $2.78 for 2007 and $3.86 for 2008, compared to $1.61 in 2006. The projected increases are due to our expectations for higher revenues and expanding operating margins.

Investment Rationale/Risk

➤ Our strong buy recommendation is based on our positive outlook for the solar energy industry. We project the industry will grow at a 30% compound annual growth rate (CAGR) through 2010 with demand of polysilicon, the raw material for solar cell, outstripping supply. We expect WFR will benefit from rising prices of polysilicon, since the company signed long-term agreements to supply solar wafers to three solar manufacturing companies. We believe the shares are undervalued, trading at a discount to the S&P 500 on a P/E-to-growth ratio despite our view of higher growth opportunities.

➤ Risks to our recommendation and target price include an increase in industry capacity expansion earlier than expected, changes in governmental policy related to alternative energy technology, a slowdown in the global economy, and lower than expected growth in the solar or semiconductor industries.

➤ Our 12-month target price of $82 is based on a P/E-to-growth ratio of 0.85X, a discount to that of the S&P 500 to reflect WFR's higher risks, a long-term EPS growth rate of 25%, and our 2008 EPS estimate of $3.86.

Qualitative Risk Assessment

LOW	MEDIUM	HIGH

Our risk assessment reflects WFR's exposure to the historical cyclicality of the semiconductor equipment industry and intense competition, partly offset by what we view as WFR's strong market position and size.

Quantitative Evaluations

S&P Quality Ranking B-

D	C	B-	B	B+	A-	A	A+

Relative Strength Rank STRONG
88
LOWEST = 1   HIGHEST = 99

Revenue/Earnings Data

Revenue (Million $)

	1Q	2Q	3Q	4Q	Year
2007	440.4	472.7	472.8	--	--
2006	341.6	370.5	408.0	420.6	1,541
2005	250.9	272.3	280.7	303.4	1,107
2004	228.8	255.5	275.3	268.4	1,028
2003	188.4	191.8	195.9	205.0	781.1
2002	136.7	174.3	190.3	186.0	687.2

Earnings Per Share ($)

2007	0.58	0.70	0.65	E0.82	E2.78
2006	0.29	0.36	0.40	0.56	1.61
2005	0.25	0.18	0.45	0.22	1.10
2004	0.16	0.27	0.27	0.31	1.02
2003	0.09	0.13	0.16	0.15	0.53
2002	-0.26	0.07	-0.25	0.17	-0.17

Fiscal year ended Dec. 31. Next earnings report expected: Late January. EPS Estimates based on S&P Operating Earnings; historical GAAP earnings are as reported.

Dividend Data

No cash dividends have been paid.

Please read the Required Disclosures and Analyst Certification on the last page of this report.

The McGraw·Hill Companies

MEMC Electronic Materials Inc.

STANDARD &POOR'S

Business Summary October 29, 2007

CORPORATE OVERVIEW. MEMC Electronic Materials, Inc. (WFR) is a global leader in the manufacture of silicon wafers. The company designs, manufactures and provides wafers and intermediate products for use in the semiconductor, solar and related industries. WFR operates manufacturing facilities in every major semiconductor manufacturing region, including Europe, Japan, Malaysia, South Korea, Taiwan, and the U.S. Its customers include virtually all of the world's major semiconductor device manufacturers, such as the major memory, microprocessor, and applications specific integrated circuit (ASIC) manufacturers, as well as the world's largest foundries.

WFR's products include prime polish wafers, epitaxial wafers and test and monitor wafers. The company markets its products primarily through a global direct sales force, with about 66% of 2006 sales to customers outside the U.S., including 17% in Taiwan, 18% in Korea, and 14% in China. The company has a network of customer service and support centers globally.

COMPETITIVE LANDSCAPE. WFR competes in a highly competitive and commodity-like market for silicon wafers. Competition is global and intense involving competitors with substantial financial, technical, engineering and manufacturing resources. Among the six largest global wafer manufacturers, Shin-

Etsu Handotai, SUMCO and Siltronic are the biggest competitors. WFR has a granular polysilicon facility in Pasadena, TX, and a chunk polysilicon facility in Merano, Italy. WFR believes it has a competitive and cost advantage over peers, through its ability to manufacture the majority of its own polysilicon, the raw material used in the manufacture of silicon wafers.

MARKET PROFILE. Historically the silicon wafer industry correlated well with the demand for semiconductors. With a compound annual growth rate (CAGR) of 10% in units for the global semiconductor device industry from 1985 to 2005, the silicon wafer industry grew at a CAGR of 9% in volume over the same period. Growth in end demand for semiconductor chips, an industry shift to larger diameter wafers, and increasingly stringent technical specifications for wafers (a function of the drive for smaller geometries in the chip circuitry) are the current drivers of growth in the silicon wafer business, in our view. WFR provides wafers ranging from 100 millimeters (4 inch) to 300 millimeters (12 inch) in diameter.

Company Financials Fiscal Year Ended Dec. 31

Per Share Data ($)	2006	2005	2004	2003	2002	2001	2000	1999	1998	1997
Tangible Book Value	5.23	3.21	2.13	0.94	NM	NM	4.61	5.55	8.66	15.67
Cash Flow	1.91	1.35	1.22	0.68	0.09	-4.65	1.86	0.12	-3.95	2.91
Earnings	1.61	1.10	1.02	0.53	-0.17	-7.51	-0.62	-2.43	-7.80	-0.16
S&P Core Earnings	1.62	1.06	0.96	0.49	-0.33	-7.60	NA	NA	NA	NA
Dividends	Nil	Nil	Nil	Nil	Nil	Nil	Nil	Nil	Nil	Nil
Payout Ratio	Nil	Nil	Nil	Nil	Nil	Nil	Nil	Nil	Nil	Nil
Prices:High	48.90	24.68	13.28	14.51	11.50	11.90	24.25	21.62	19.00	38.94
Prices:Low	22.60	10.70	7.33	7.00	2.25	1.05	6.25	5.37	2.94	14.44
P/E Ratio:High	30	17	13	27	NM	NM	NM	NM	NM	NM
P/E Ratio:Low	14	7	7	13	NM	NM	NM	NM	NM	NM

Income Statement Analysis (Million $)										
Revenue	1,541	1,107	1,028	781	687	618	872	694	759	987
Operating Income	629	314	304	174	114	-9.69	161	0.11	-31.1	117
Depreciation	70.3	57.2	44.1	31.0	34.2	169	173	159	156	127
Interest Expense	2.43	7.26	13.5	12.9	73.4	78.4	78.8	66.1	45.8	14.7
Pretax Income	590	252	175	162	20.8	-259	-65.6	-222	-417	-7.08
Effective Tax Rate	36.4%	NA	NM	22.7%	NM	NM	NM	NM	NM	NM
Net Income	369	249	226	117	-5.07	-489	-43.4	-151	-316	-6.75
S&P Core Earnings	370	240	212	108	-41.9	-529	NA	NA	NA	NA

Balance Sheet & Other Financial Data (Million $)										
Cash	528	126	92.3	96.9	166	107	94.8	28.6	16.2	30.1
Current Assets	900	436	390	365	364	264	410	276	299	377
Total Assets	1,766	1,148	1,010	727	632	549	1,891	1,725	1,774	1,777
Current Liabilities	258	225	216	244	286	222	324	190	259	339
Long Term Debt	29.4	34.8	116	59.3	161	145	943	870	871	610
Common Equity	1,167	711	443	194	-24.7	-9.74	366	433	399	698
Total Capital	1,235	791	605	317	194	186	1,384	1,346	1,318	1,267
Capital Expenditures	148	163	150	85.2	22.0	7.00	57.8	49.3	195	372
Cash Flow	440	307	270	148	12.1	-324	130	7.60	-160	120
Current Ratio	3.5	1.9	1.8	1.5	1.3	1.2	1.3	1.5	1.2	1.1
% Long Term Debt of Capitalization	2.4	4.4	19.2	18.7	82.9	77.8	68.1	64.6	66.1	40.2
% Net Income of Revenue	24.0	22.5	22.0	14.9	NM	NM	NM	NM	NM	NM
% Return on Assets	25.3	22.9	26.0	17.2	NM	NM	NM	NM	NM	NM
% Return on Equity	39.3	43.2	71.1	138.1	NM	NM	NM	NM	NM	NM

Data as orig reptd.; bef. results of disc opers/spec. items. Per share data adj. for stk. divs.; EPS diluted. E-Estimated. NA-Not Available. NM-Not Meaningful. NR-Not Ranked. UR-Under Review.

Office: 501 Pearl Drive, St. Peters, MO 63376.
Telephone: 636-474-5000.
Email: invest@memc.com
Website: http://www.memc.com

Chrmn: J. Marren
Pres & CEO: N. Gareeb
SVP & CFO: K.H. Hannah
VP, Secy & General Counsel: B.D. Kohn

Investor Contact: B. Michalek (636-474-5443)
Board Members: P. Blackmore, R. J. Boehlke, N. Gareeb, J. Marren, C. D. Marsh, W. E. Stevens, M. Turner, J. B. Williams

Founded: 1984
Domicile: Delaware
Employees: 5,500

The McGraw-Hill Companies

Merck & Co Inc.

STANDARD &POOR'S

S&P Recommendation	STRONG BUY ★★★★★	Price $57.66 (as of Nov 23, 2007)	12-Mo. Target Price $66.00	Investment Style Large-Cap Blend

GICS Sector Health Care
Sub-Industry Pharmaceuticals

Summary Merck is one of the world's largest prescription pharmaceuticals concerns. The Medco pharmaceutical benefits management unit was spun off to shareholders in August 2003.

Key Stock Statistics (Source S&P, Vickers, company reports)

52-Wk Range	$58.89– 42.35	S&P Oper. EPS 2007**E**	3.13	Market Capitalization(B)	$125.068	Beta	0.98
Trailing 12-Month EPS	$2.46	S&P Oper. EPS 2008**E**	3.40	Yield (%)	2.64	S&P 3-Yr. Proj. EPS CAGR(%)	10.00
Trailing 12-Month P/E	23.4	P/E on S&P Oper. EPS 2007**E**	18.4	Dividend Rate/Share	$1.52	S&P Credit Rating	AA-
$10K Invested 5 Yrs Ago	$13,103	Common Shares Outstg. (M)	2,169.1	Institutional Ownership (%)	72		

Price Performance

30-Week Mov. Avg. ··· 10-Week Mov. Avg. -- GAAP Earnings vs. Previous Year Volume Above Avg. STARS
12-Mo. Target Price — Relative Strength — ▲ Up ▼ Down ► No Change Below Avg. ★

Options: ASE, CBOE, P, Ph

Analysis prepared by **Herman B. Saftlas** on November 13, 2007, when the stock traded at **$ 56.68**.

Highlights

➤ We expect revenues in 2008 to increase about 3%, with the projected advance reflecting robust showings by Singulair, a market-leading asthma/allergic rhinitis treatment, and the recently launched Januvia diabetes treatment. We see sales of vaccines climbing 40%, lifted by robust growth in Gardasil for cervical cancer, RotaTeq for rotavirus and Zostavax for shingles. Sales of Cozaar/Hyzaar cardiovascular should be relatively unchanged, but we expect volume in the older Fosamax, Proscar and Zocor lines to decline under generic pressure.

➤ By our analysis, gross margins in 2008 will likely narrow slightly from the 76.3% projected for 2007, due to a less profitable mix. However, results should benefit from controls over SG&A spending. We expect equity income from affiliates to increase, largely on higher income from Vytorin and Zetia cholesterol drugs, which are sold through a joint venture with Schering-Plough.

➤ We project 2008 operating EPS of $3.40, up from an estimated $3.13 for 2007 before restructuring charges and other nonrecurring items in each year.

Investment Rationale/Risk

➤ We commend top management for its handling of Vioxx litigation, new product development, and cost streamlining. On the new product front, we see much promise for Gardasil vaccine against cervical cancer, and Januvia for diabetes. Bolstered by restructuring savings, expected to reach $5 billion by 2010, we project improving growth in operating EPS over the coming years. In mid-November 2007, the company announced an agreement with claimant lawyers to pay $4.85 billion to settle the majority of Vioxx heart attack and stroke cases. While the deal must still be ratified by over 45,000 claimants, we think the settlement largely alleviates Vioxx related worries. We expect the plan to be implemented.

➤ Risks to our recommendation and target price include failure to implement the proposed Vioxx settlement, increased competitive pressures in principal markets, and possible R&D pipeline setbacks.

➤ Our 12-month target price of $66 applies a modest premium-to-peers P/E of 19.4X to our EPS estimate for 2008. Merck's $1.52 annual dividend recently provided a 2.7% yield.

Qualitative Risk Assessment

LOW	MEDIUM	HIGH

Our risk assessment for MRK reflects risks that the company shares with other major pharmaceutical producers such as challenges to branded patents, and new drug development and regulatory risks. In addition, MRK also faces litigations risk from its former Vioxx pain medicine. However, we believe the latter risk may be significantly mitigated, in view of a recently proposed $4.85 billion agreement to settle the majority of cases.

Quantitative Evaluations

S&P Quality Ranking A-

D	C	B-	B	B+	A-	A	A+

Relative Strength Rank STRONG

92

LOWEST = 1   HIGHEST = 99

Revenue/Earnings Data

Revenue (Million $)

	1Q	2Q	3Q	4Q	Year
2007	5,769	6,111	6,074	--	--
2006	5,410	5,772	5,410	6,044	22,636
2005	5,362	5,468	5,416	5,766	22,012
2004	5,631	6,022	5,538	5,748	22,939
2003	5,571	5,525	5,762	5,627	22,486
2002	12,169	12,810	12,893	13,918	51,790

Earnings Per Share ($)

2007	0.78	0.77	0.70	E0.73	E3.13
2006	0.69	0.69	0.43	0.22	2.03
2005	0.62	0.33	0.65	0.51	2.10
2004	1.06	1.26	1.28	0.50	2.61
2003	0.68	0.79	0.83	0.62	2.92
2002	0.71	0.77	0.83	0.83	3.14

Fiscal year ended Dec. 31. Next earnings report expected: Late January. EPS Estimates based on S&P Operating Earnings; historical GAAP earnings are as reported.

Dividend Data (Dates: mm/dd Payment Date: mm/dd/yy)

Amount ($)	Date Decl.	Ex-Div. Date	Stk. of Record	Payment Date
0.380	11/28	12/06	12/08	01/02/07
0.380	02/27	03/07	03/09	04/02/07
0.380	05/22	06/06	06/08	07/02/07
0.380	07/24	09/05	09/07	10/01/07

Dividends have been paid since 1935. Source: Company reports.

Merck & Co Inc.

STANDARD
&POOR'S

Business Summary November 13, 2007

CORPORATE OVERVIEW. Merck & Co. is a leading global drugmaker, producing a wide range of prescription drugs in many therapeutic classes in the U.S. and abroad. Foreign operations accounted for 39% of total pharmaceutical and vaccine sales in 2006.

MRK's largest-selling products include Singulair (sales of $3.5 billion in 2006), a treatment for asthma and seasonal allergic rhinitis; Cozaar/Hyzaar ($3.2 billion), treatments for high blood pressure and congestive heart failure; Fosamax ($3.1 billion), a drug for osteoporosis (a bone-thinning disease that affects postmenopausal women); and Zocor, a cholesterol-lowering agent ($2.8 billion). Zocor's U.S. patent expired in June 2006.

Other drugs include Vasotec/Vaseretic antihypertensives; Primaxin, an intravenous antibiotic; Proscar, a treatment for enlarged prostates; Cosopt/Trusopt, glaucoma treatments; and Januvia, a novel treatment for type 2 diabetes. Merck is also a leading maker of vaccines, which accounted for 8% of sales in 2006. New vaccines launched in 2006 include Gardasil for human papillomavirus (the main cause of cervical cancer), RotaTeq pediatric vaccine, and Zostavax for shingles.

Through a joint venture with Schering-Plough, Merck also markets Zetia--a new type of cholesterol therapy that works by blocking cholesterol absorption in the intestines--as well as Vytorin, a combination pill containing both Zocor and Zetia. Zetia had sales of $1.9 billion in 2006. Launched in July 2004, Vytorin had sales of $2.0 billion in 2006. Merck books only equity income from the Schering-Plough joint venture.

OTC medications such as Pepcid AC are offered through a venture with Johnson & Johnson. Merial, a leading animal health products company, is owned jointly by Merck and Rhone-Poulenc SA. Through a venture with Astra AB of Sweden, Merck books sales of Prilosec and other Astra drugs.

MARKET PROFILE. The dollar value of the global pharmaceutical market is estimated to reach over $665 billion in 2007, based on data from IMS Health. Although drug sales continue to grow faster than most segments of the world economy, we expect industry growth to decelerate over the balance of the decade, reflecting the loss of patent protection on many large selling drugs, tighter reimbursement from government and private health insurance payors, and relatively sluggish new product flow.

Company Financials Fiscal Year Ended Dec. 31

Per Share Data ($)	2006	2005	2004	2003	2002	2001	2000	1999	1998	1997
Tangible Book Value	7.00	7.48	7.03	6.13	4.88	3.77	3.23	2.43	1.91	2.45
Cash Flow	3.06	2.88	3.29	3.51	3.79	3.77	3.44	3.02	2.67	2.29
Earnings	2.03	2.10	2.61	2.92	3.14	3.14	2.90	2.45	2.15	1.87
S&P Core Earnings	2.28	2.09	2.56	2.71	2.81	2.87	NA	NA	NA	NA
Dividends	1.52	1.52	1.49	1.45	1.41	1.37	1.26	1.10	0.95	0.87
Payout Ratio	75%	72%	57%	50%	45%	44%	43%	45%	44%	47%
Prices:High	46.37	35.36	49.33	63.50	64.50	95.25	96.69	87.38	80.88	54.09
Prices:Low	31.81	25.50	25.60	40.57	38.50	56.80	52.00	60.94	50.69	39.00
P/E Ratio:High	23	17	19	22	21	30	33	36	38	29
P/E Ratio:Low	16	12	10	14	12	18	18	25	24	21

Income Statement Analysis (Million $)										
Revenue	22,636	22,012	22,939	22,486	51,790	47,716	40,363	32,714	26,898	23,637
Operating Income	5,955	7,567	8,074	9,912	11,361	11,192	10,686	9,056	7,655	6,701
Depreciation	2,268	1,708	1,451	1,314	1,488	1,464	1,277	1,145	1,279	1,034
Interest Expense	375	386	294	351	391	465	484	317	206	130
Pretax Income	6,342	7,486	8,129	9,220	10,428	10,693	10,133	8,842	8,295	6,594
Effective Tax Rate	28.2%	36.5%	26.6%	26.7%	29.3%	29.2%	29.6%	30.9%	34.8%	28.0%
Net Income	4,434	4,631	5,813	6,590	7,150	7,282	6,822	5,891	5,248	4,614
S&P Core Earnings	4,973	4,582	5,699	6,089	6,395	6,649	NA	NA	NA	NA

Balance Sheet & Other Financial Data (Million $)										
Cash	5,915	9,585	2,879	1,201	2,243	2,144	2,537	2,022	2,606	1,125
Current Assets	15,230	21,049	13,475	11,527	14,834	12,962	13,353	11,259	10,229	8,213
Total Assets	44,570	44,846	42,573	40,588	47,561	44,007	39,910	35,635	31,853	25,812
Current Liabilities	12,723	13,304	11,744	9,570	12,375	11,544	9,710	8,759	6,069	5,569
Long Term Debt	5,551	5,126	4,692	5,096	4,879	4,799	3,601	3,144	3,221	1,347
Common Equity	17,560	17,917	17,288	15,576	18,200	16,050	14,832	13,242	12,802	12,614
Total Capital	25,517	25,449	24,387	24,588	28,008	25,686	23,454	19,847	19,728	15,144
Capital Expenditures	980	1,403	1,726	1,916	2,370	2,725	2,728	2,561	1,973	1,449
Cash Flow	6,702	6,339	7,264	7,904	8,638	8,746	8,099	7,035	6,527	5,648
Current Ratio	1.2	1.6	1.1	1.2	1.2	1.1	1.4	1.3	1.7	1.5
% Long Term Debt of Capitalization	21.8	20.1	19.2	20.7	17.4	18.7	15.4	15.8	16.3	8.8
% Net Income of Revenue	19.6	21.0	25.3	29.3	13.8	15.3	16.9	18.0	19.5	19.5
% Return on Assets	9.9	10.6	14.0	15.0	15.6	17.3	18.1	17.4	18.2	18.4
% Return on Equity	25.0	26.3	35.4	39.0	41.7	47.2	48.6	20.1	41.3	37.5

Data as orig reptd.; bef. results of disc opers/spec. items. Per share data adj. for stk. divs.; EPS diluted. E-Estimated. NA-Not Available. NM-Not Meaningful. NR-Not Ranked. UR-Under Review.

Office: One Merck Drive, Whitehouse Station, NJ 08889-0100.
Telephone: 908-423-1000.
Website: http://www.merck.com
Chrmn, Pres & CEO: R.T. Clark

EVP & CFO: J.C. Lewent
EVP & General Counsel: K.C. Frazier
SVP & CIO: J.C. Scalet
VP & Treas: M.E. McDonough

Board Members: R. T. Clark, J. B. Cole, W. B. Harrison, Jr., W. N. Kelley, R. B. Lazarus, T. E. Shenk, A. M. Tatlock, S. O. Thier, W. P. Weeks, P. C. Wendell

Founded: 1891
Domicile: New Jersey
Employees: 60,000

The McGraw-Hill Companies

Meredith Corp

STANDARD & POOR'S

S&P Recommendation HOLD ★★★☆☆	**Price** $56.33 (as of Nov 23, 2007)	**12-Mo. Target Price** $64.00	**Investment Style** Large-Cap Growth

GICS Sector Consumer Discretionary
Sub-Industry Publishing

Summary This company derives the bulk of its earnings from publishing magazines (primarily Better Homes and Gardens and Ladies' Home Journal) and the ownership of 14 TV stations.

Key Stock Statistics (Source S&P, Vickers, company reports)

52-Wk Range	$63.41– 48.15	S&P Oper. EPS 2008**E**	3.56	Market Capitalization(B)	$2.151	Beta	0.89
Trailing 12-Month EPS	$3.37	S&P Oper. EPS 2009**E**	4.18	Yield (%)	1.31	S&P 3-Yr. Proj. EPS CAGR(%)	9.00
Trailing 12-Month P/E	16.7	P/E on S&P Oper. EPS 2008**E**	15.8	Dividend Rate/Share	$0.74	S&P Credit Rating	NA
$10K Invested 5 Yrs Ago	$13,071	Common Shares Outstg. (M)	47.4	Institutional Ownership (%)	90		

Price Performance

30-Week Mov. Avg. ··· 10-Week Mov. Avg. - - **GAAP Earnings vs. Previous Year** Volume Above Avg. | Below Avg. | STARS
12-Mo. Target Price — Relative Strength — ▲ Up ▼ Down ► No Change

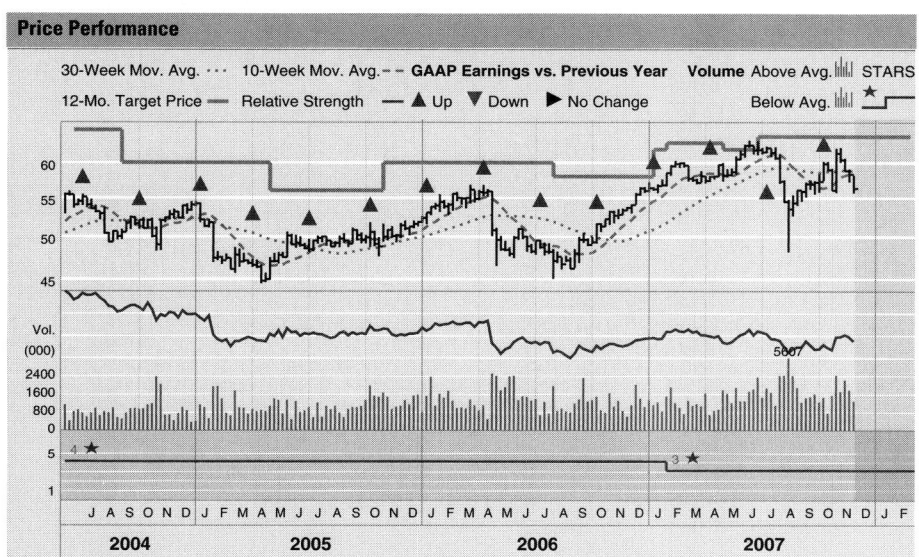

Options: ASE

Analysis prepared by **James Peters, CFA** on November 14, 2007, when the stock traded at **$ 58.61**.

Highlights

► For FY 08 (Jun.), we look for revenue growth of about 2.5%, including an advance in interactive media as the company incorporates recent acquisitions and deploys resources to this high-growth area. We see a 2.9% decline in broadcasting as the company mostly offsets difficult FY 07 political advertising comparisons by monetizing an increased level of news broadcasts. We forecast a 3.9% gain in publishing revenues, with an advertising revenue advance of about 5.3% outpacing a 1.7% circulation revenue decline.

► We see MDP's operating margin rising slightly to 18.4% from 18.0% in FY 07, with continued gains for integrating previous acquisitions and lower paper costs offsetting a rise in postal expense following a recent rate hike.

► We see MDP using free cash flow through FY 08 to pay down debt assumed in the 2005 Gruner & Jahr acquisition, and to pursue strategic acquisitions. After lower projected interest expense, we see FY 08 EPS growing about 8%, to $3.56, from $3.30 in FY 07.

Investment Rationale/Risk

► In October, MDP signed a multi-year brand licensing agreement with Wal-Mart, and announced that it will provide video on demand content to Comcast. We view these developments positively as we believe they demonstrate MDP's ability to leverage its strong brands and content into incremental and profitable revenue streams. We expect MDP to continue to supplement organic growth with special interest publication and interactive media acquisitions, and we are encouraged by MDP's plans to derive at least 10% of revenues from online sources by 2010, vs. 3.7% in FY 07.

► Risks to our recommendation and target price include a rapid rise in paper prices, an economic slowdown that hurts advertising demand, and a substantial decline in magazine circulation. We also are concerned about MDP's corporate governance, as we do not believe policies such as a dual class voting structure are in the best interests of common shareholders.

► Our 12-month target price of $64 is derived by applying a two-year sum-of-the-parts peer-average enterprise value/EBITDA ratio of 10.1X to our FY 08 EBITDA estimate of $356 million.

Qualitative Risk Assessment

LOW	MEDIUM	HIGH

Our risk assessment reflects a highly competitive environment for advertising among publishers and other media, offset by our view of the company's consistent record of earnings growth, its low weighted average cost of capital, and the stock's low beta.

Quantitative Evaluations

S&P Quality Ranking   A-

D	C	B-	B	B+	A-	A	A+

Relative Strength Rank   MODERATE

62

LOWEST = 1   HIGHEST = 99

Revenue/Earnings Data

Revenue (Million $)

	1Q	2Q	3Q	4Q	Year
2008	404.5	--	--	--	--
2007	386.4	399.4	401.8	428.5	1,616
2006	390.3	386.0	394.9	426.4	1,598
2005	288.9	294.6	305.5	332.4	1,221
2004	272.7	280.4	299.6	309.1	1,162
2003	250.1	251.7	278.2	300.2	1,080

Earnings Per Share ($)

2008	0.68	E0.72	E0.98	E1.19	E3.56
2007	0.62	0.73	1.08	1.01	3.44
2006	0.52	0.58	0.97	0.97	2.86
2005	0.46	0.52	0.69	0.83	2.50
2004	0.37	0.38	0.67	0.76	2.14
2003	0.32	0.38	0.50	0.58	1.78

Fiscal year ended Jun. 30. Next earnings report expected: Late January. EPS Estimates based on S&P Operating Earnings; historical GAAP earnings are as reported.

Dividend Data (Dates: mm/dd Payment Date: mm/dd/yy)

Amount ($)	Date Decl.	Ex-Div. Date	Stk. of Record	Payment Date
0.185	01/29	02/26	02/28	03/15/07
0.185	05/09	05/29	05/31	06/15/07
0.185	08/08	08/29	08/31	09/14/07
0.185	11/07	11/28	11/30	12/14/07

Dividends have been paid since 1930. Source: Company reports.

Meredith Corp

Business Summary November 14, 2007

CORPORATE OVERVIEW. Meredith Corp. is a diversified media and marketing company with operations in publishing (78% of FY 07 (Jun.) revenues) and broadcasting (22%). Advertising accounted for about 60% of total revenues, followed by magazine circulation (27%) and other (13%).

The publishing segment focuses on the home and family market. Meredith has more than 25 subscription-based magazines, including Better Homes and Gardens, Family Circle, Ladies' Home Journal and approximately 180 special interest publications. The segment also includes book publishing, integrated marketing, a large consumer database, 25 websites, brand licensing and other related activities. Books are published under the Better Homes and Gardens trademark and under licensed trademarks such as The Home Depot books. Meredith Integrated Marketing offers integrated promotional, database management, relationship and direct marketing capabilities for corporate customers. In April 2006, Meredith acquired O'Grady Meyers (OGM), an interactive marketing services agency that specializes in online customer relationship marketing. Overall FY 07 publishing segment revenues were derived from

advertising (50%), circulation (27%) and other (23%).

The broadcasting segment consists of 13 network-affiliated TV stations and one AM radio station. Broadcasting affiliations include CBS (six stations), FOX (three), MyNetwork TV (two), CW (one) and NBC (one). Local and national advertising contributed approximately 98% of segment revenues in FY 07, and the company states that 30% to 40% of a market's television ad revenues are generated by local news on major network-affiliated stations. The other 2% of revenues comes primarily from broadcast retransmission fees. Given current industry trends, we expect the company to negotiate substantially higher retransmission fees when most of its retransmission agreements expire in FY 09. The segment also includes 18 related websites.

Company Financials Fiscal Year Ended Jun. 30

Per Share Data ($)	2007	2006	2005	2004	2003	2002	2001	2000	1999	1998
Tangible Book Value	NM	NM	NM	NM	NM	NM	NM	NM	NM	NM
Cash Flow	4.94	3.76	3.19	2.82	2.40	3.64	2.39	3.01	3.20	2.64
Earnings	3.44	2.86	2.50	2.14	1.78	1.79	1.39	1.35	1.67	1.46
S&P Core Earnings	3.48	2.84	2.49	2.01	1.64	0.92	0.92	NA	NA	NA
Dividends	0.69	0.60	0.52	0.43	0.37	0.35	0.33	0.16	0.29	0.27
Payout Ratio	20%	20%	21%	20%	22%	20%	24%	12%	17%	18%
Prices:High	63.41	57.29	54.33	55.94	50.32	47.75	38.97	41.06	42.00	48.50
Prices:Low	48.15	45.04	44.51	48.24	47.09	33.42	26.50	22.38	30.63	26.69
P/E Ratio:High	18	20	22	26	28	27	28	30	25	33
P/E Ratio:Low	14	16	18	23	26	19	19	17	18	18

Income Statement Analysis (Million $)	2007	2006	2005	2004	2003	2002	2001	2000	1999	1998
Revenue	1,616	1,598	1,221	1,162	1,080	988	1,053	1,097	1,036	1,010
Operating Income	365	312	263	238	209	212	204	249	254	217
Depreciation	73.8	45.7	35.3	35.2	31.4	93.8	51.6	87.6	82.6	64.5
Interest Expense	27.2	30.2	Nil	22.7	27.8	33.2	32.9	34.9	22.0	14.7
Pretax Income	263	237	209	181	149	149	116	128	152	139
Effective Tax Rate	35.7%	39.0%	38.7%	38.7%	38.7%	38.7%	38.7%	44.3%	41.1%	42.6%
Net Income	169	145	128	111	91.1	91.4	71.3	71.0	89.7	79.9
S&P Core Earnings	171	144	127	104	83.5	46.8	47.6	NA	NA	NA

Balance Sheet & Other Financial Data (Million $)	2007	2006	2005	2004	2003	2002	2001	2000	1999	1998
Cash	39.2	30.7	29.8	58.7	22.3	28.2	36.3	22.9	11.0	4.95
Current Assets	453	432	304	314	268	272	291	289	256	247
Total Assets	2,090	2,041	1,491	1,466	1,437	1,460	1,438	1,440	1,423	1,067
Current Liabilities	487	464	439	371	297	307	371	359	344	347
Long Term Debt	375	515	125	225	375	385	400	455	485	175
Common Equity	833	698	652	589	501	508	448	423	413	378
Total Capital	1,375	1,338	871	912	948	985	907	926	932	372
Capital Expenditures	42.6	29.2	23.8	24.5	26.6	23.4	56.0	39.4	25.7	46.2
Cash Flow	243	190	163	146	123	185	123	159	172	144
Current Ratio	0.9	0.9	0.7	0.8	0.9	0.9	0.8	0.8	0.7	0.7
% Long Term Debt of Capitalization	27.3	38.5	14.4	24.7	39.6	39.1	44.1	49.1	52.0	47.0
% Net Income of Revenue	10.4	9.1	10.5	9.5	8.4	9.3	6.8	6.5	8.7	7.9
% Return on Assets	8.2	8.2	8.7	7.6	6.3	6.3	5.0	5.0	7.2	8.7
% Return on Equity	22.1	21.5	20.3	20.4	18.1	19.1	16.4	17.0	22.7	22.7

Data as orig reptd.; bef. results of disc opers/spec. items. Per share data adj. for stk. divs.; EPS diluted. E-Estimated. NA-Not Available. NM-Not Meaningful. NR-Not Ranked. UR-Under Review.

Office: 1716 Locust Street, Des Moines, IA 50309-3023.
Telephone: 515-284-3000.
Website: http://www.meredith.com
Chrmn: W.T. Kerr

Pres & CEO: S.M. Lacy
Investor Contact: S.V. Radia (515-284-3357)
VP & CFO: S.V. Radia
VP, Secy & General Counsel: J.S. Zieser

Board Members: H. M. Baum, M. S. Coleman, J. R. Craigie, A. H. Drewes, F. B. Henry, J. W. Johnson, W. T. Kerr, S. M. Lacy, R. E. Lee, D. J. Londoner, P. A. Marineau, M. Meredith Frazier, C. D. Peebler, Jr.

Founded: 1902
Domicile: Iowa
Employees: 3,166

Merrill Lynch & Co Inc

STANDARD &POOR'S

S&P Recommendation	SELL ★★☆☆☆	Price	12-Mo. Target Price	Investment Style
		$57.79 (as of Nov 28, 2007)	$48.00	Large-Cap Value

GICS Sector Financials
Sub-Industry Investment Banking & Brokerage

Summary Merrill Lynch is one of the world's largest and most diversified securities brokerage concerns.

Key Stock Statistics (Source S&P, Vickers, company reports)

52-Wk Range	$98.68– 50.50	S&P Oper. EPS 2007**E**	-0.17	Market Capitalization(B)	$49.658	Beta	1.83
Trailing 12-Month EPS	$4.43	S&P Oper. EPS 2008**E**	7.62	Yield (%)	2.42	S&P 3-Yr. Proj. EPS CAGR(%)	NA
Trailing 12-Month P/E	13.1	P/E on S&P Oper. EPS 2007**E**	NM	Dividend Rate/Share	$1.40	S&P Credit Rating	A+
$10K Invested 5 Yrs Ago	$13,285	Common Shares Outstg. (M)	859.3	Institutional Ownership (%)	74		

Price Performance

30-Week Mov. Avg. · · ·   10-Week Mov. Avg. - - - **GAAP Earnings vs. Previous Year**   Volume Above Avg. STARS

12-Mo. Target Price —   Relative Strength — ▲ Up ▼ Down ▶ No Change   Below Avg. ★

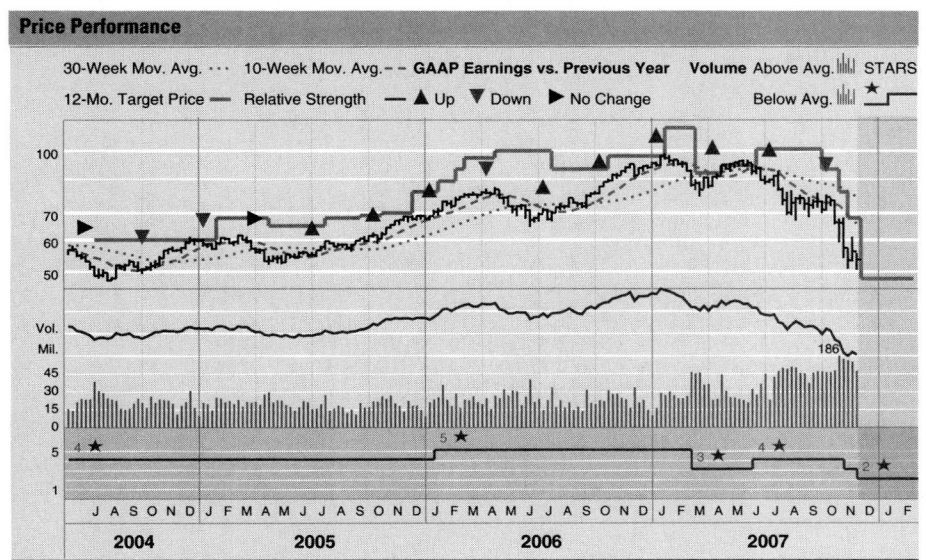

Options: ASE, CBOE, P, Ph

Qualitative Risk Assessment

LOW	MEDIUM	HIGH

Our risk assessment reflects our view of the company's broad business diversification, strong customer relationships, and significant proportion of asset management and portfolio fees, partially offset by industry cyclicality.

Quantitative Evaluations

S&P Quality Ranking   A

D	C	B-	B	B+	A-	A	A+

Relative Strength Rank   WEAK

27

LOWEST = 1   HIGHEST = 99

Revenue/Earnings Data

Revenue (Million $)

	1Q	2Q	3Q	4Q	Year
2007	21,475	23,806	577.0	--	--
2006	15,561	16,689	17,379	18,959	68,622
2005	10,562	11,326	12,395	13,500	47,783
2004	7,963	7,334	7,553	9,617	32,467
2003	6,923	7,292	6,857	6,673	27,745
2002	7,563	7,352	6,860	6,478	28,253

Earnings Per Share ($)

2007	2.26	2.24	-2.85	E-1.82	E-0.17
2006	0.44	1.63	3.17	2.41	7.59
2005	1.21	1.14	1.40	1.41	5.16
2004	1.21	1.05	0.93	1.19	4.38
2003	0.72	1.05	1.04	1.23	4.05
2002	0.67	0.66	0.73	0.56	2.63

Fiscal year ended Dec. 31. Next earnings report expected: Mid January. EPS Estimates based on S&P Operating Earnings; historical GAAP earnings are as reported.

Highlights

➤ The STARS recommendation for MER has recently been changed to 2 (sell) from 3 (hold) and the 12-month target price has recently been changed to $48.00 from $68.00. The Highlights section of this Stock Report will be updated accordingly.

Investment Rationale/Risk

➤ The Investment Rationale/Risk section of this Stock Report will be updated shortly. For the latest News story on MER from MarketScope, see below.

➤ 11/27/07 11:18 am EST... S&P DOWNGRADES SHARES OF MERRILL LYNCH TO SELL FROM HOLD (MER 52.91**): We believe further deterioration in the mortgage securities market has put further downward pressure on the value of ABS CDOs on the balance sheet at MER. Remaining net exposure to these products at the end of Q3 was more than $21 billion, and we expect additional write-downs in the range of 25%-30% of these assets in Q4. We are reducing our Q4 and '07 EPS estimates by $3.06 to losses of $1.82 and $0.17, respectively, and lower our '08 EPS estimate by $0.98 to $7.62. We are cutting our 12-month target price by $20 to $48, 1.3X projected book value, a discount to peers. /M.Albrecht

Dividend Data (Dates: mm/dd Payment Date: mm/dd/yy)

Amount ($)	Date Decl.	Ex-Div. Date	Stk. of Record	Payment Date
0.350	01/18	02/05	02/07	03/01/07
0.350	04/27	05/04	05/08	05/23/07
0.350	07/23	08/01	08/03	08/22/07
0.350	10/22	10/31	11/02	11/21/07

Dividends have been paid since 1961. Source: Company reports.

Please read the Required Disclosures and Analyst Certification on the last page of this report.

The McGraw-Hill Companies

Merrill Lynch & Co Inc

STANDARD &POOR'S

Business Summary November 12, 2007

CORPORATE OVERVIEW. Merrill Lynch is one of the world's largest financial management and advisory companies, consistently ranking among the largest debt and equity underwriters and mergers and acquisitions advisers on a global basis. MER has two operating segments: Global Markets and Investment Banking (GMI); and the Global Wealth Management group (GWM), including the Private Client Group (GPC) and its nearly 50% stake in BlackRock. In 2006, GMI accounted for 57% of total net revenues and GWM 43% (37% from GPC and 6% from the divested asset management business). GMI provides comprehensive investment banking and strategic advisory services, including debt and equity trading, underwriting and origination, and mergers and acquisitions. We remain concerned about rising competition from large commercial banks, which have been gaining market share in investment banking.

We think MER's Global Private Client Group is an undervalued franchise. We believe the company's Private Wealth and Wealth Management Advisors maintain strong relationships with MER's most affluent clients and high net worth individuals, respectively. MER's Financial Advisory Center serves more

than a million clients that have more basic financial needs. At the end of 2006, MER had about 15,880 private client advisers in around 700 offices, with nearly $1.6 trillion in total client assets in GPC. We think MER is focused on attracting higher net worth clients and emphasizing asset-priced accounts.

In early October 2006, MER combined its asset management business (MLIM) with BlackRock Inc. Although MER did not receive a majority stake or voting control, it did obtain approximately a 49% equity stake and a 45% voting stake in a premier asset management company, which we think should see improved growth opportunities. BlackRock is one of the world's largest investment managers, and it holds more than $1.1 trillion in assets under management as of December 31, 2006. MER reports its share of earnings from the investment, net of expenses and taxes, as revenues on its income statement.

Company Financials Fiscal Year Ended Dec. 31

Per Share Data ($)	2006	2005	2004	2003	2002	2001	2000	1999	1998	1997
Tangible Book Value	38.67	29.37	26.48	23.69	20.76	18.38	16.67	10.67	6.09	3.66
Cash Flow	7.59	5.16	5.77	4.05	2.63	0.57	4.11	3.09	1.50	3.00
Earnings	7.59	5.16	4.38	4.05	2.63	0.57	4.11	3.09	1.50	2.42
S&P Core Earnings	6.44	5.18	4.41	3.79	1.80	-0.51	NA	NA	NA	NA
Dividends	1.00	0.76	0.64	0.64	0.64	0.64	0.60	0.52	0.46	0.38
Payout Ratio	13%	15%	15%	16%	24%	112%	15%	17%	31%	16%
Prices:High	93.93	69.34	64.89	60.47	59.32	80.00	74.63	51.25	54.56	39.09
Prices:Low	64.58	52.00	47.35	30.75	28.21	33.50	36.31	31.00	17.88	19.63
P/E Ratio:High	12	13	15	15	23	NM	18	17	36	16
P/E Ratio:Low	9	10	11	8	11	NM	9	10	12	8

Income Statement Analysis (Million $)										
Commissions	5,952	5,371	4,877	4,396	4,657	5,266	6,977	6,334	5,779	4,667
Interest Income	40,588	26,571	14,973	11,678	13,178	20,143	21,196	15,097	19,314	17,087
Total Revenue	68,622	47,783	32,467	27,745	28,253	38,757	44,872	34,879	35,853	31,731
Interest Expense	35,932	21,774	10,444	7,782	9,836	17,072	18,280	13,205	18,306	16,109
Pretax Income	10,426	7,231	5,836	5,458	3,566	1,182	5,522	3,883	1,972	3,003
Effective Tax Rate	28.1%	29.2%	24.0%	26.9%	29.5%	51.5%	31.5%	32.6%	36.2%	36.5%
Net Income	7,499	5,116	4,436	3,988	2,513	573	3,784	2,618	1,259	1,906
S&P Core Earnings	6,191	5,066	4,418	3,689	1,694	-441	NA	NA	NA	NA

Balance Sheet & Other Financial Data (Million $)										
Total Assets	841,299	681,015	648,059	494,518	447,928	419,419	407,200	328,071	299,804	292,819
Cash Items	45,558	26,535	44,302	25,321	17,586	15,537	29,297	16,707	19,120	17,416
Receivables	459,388	134,238	124,988	105,182	100,462	86,039	103,482	77,336	135,422	114,315
Securities Owned	203,848	148,710	181,950	134,309	100,216	92,883	91,514	106,734	107,845	106,778
Securities Borrowed	266,116	217,487	177,032	107,219	93,018	87,186	103,883	99,741	81,417	122,725
Due Brokers & Customers	73,696	55,147	60,750	47,968	45,110	40,636	34,276	34,119	28,871	20,631
Other Liabilities	113,977	108,053	137,028	109,720	95,804	79,654	72,765	71,880	117,432	98,044
Capitalization:Debt	147,033	135,501	119,576	85,969	59,070	79,267	72,937	56,190	78,869	43,090
Capitalization:Equity	70,129	32,927	30,740	27,226	22,450	19,583	17,879	12,377	9,707	7,904
Capitalization:Total	220,307	171,101	150,946	113,620	81,945	99,275	91,241	68,992	85,576	52,055
% Return on Revenue	12.0	10.7	13.7	14.4	10.7	1.7	10.0	9.2	3.5	6.0
% Return on Assets	1.0	0.8	1.0	0.8	0.6	0.1	1.1	0.8	0.4	0.8
% Return on Equity	12.3	15.9	14.8	15.9	11.8	2.9	24.6	23.4	13.9	26.3

Data as orig reptd.; bef. results of disc opers/spec. items. Per share data adj. for stk. divs.; EPS diluted. E-Estimated. NA-Not Available. NM-Not Meaningful. NR-Not Ranked. UR-Under Review.

Office: 4 World Financial Ctr , New York, NY 10080-0002.
Telephone: 212-449-1000.
Website: http://www.ml.com
Chrmn: A. Cribiore

Vice Chrmn & General Counsel: R.T. Berkery
SVP & CFO: J. Edwards
VP & Chief Acctg Officer: L. Tosi
Secy: J. Witterschein

Investor Contact: J. Blum (866-607-1234)
Board Members: C. T. Christ, A. Codina, V. Colbert, A. Cribiore, J. D. Finnegan, J. M. Jonas, A. L. Peters, J. W. Prueher, A. N. Reese, C. O. Rossotti

Founded: 1820
Domicile: Delaware
Employees: 56,200

The *McGraw-Hill* Companies

STANDARD &POOR'S

Metlife Inc.

S&P Recommendation	**STRONG BUY** ★★★★★	Price $61.77 (as of Nov 23, 2007)	12-Mo. Target Price $82.00	Investment Style Large-Cap Blend

GICS Sector Financials
Sub-Industry Life & Health Insurance

Summary This company is a leading publicly traded diversified U.S. life insurance and financial services concern.

Key Stock Statistics (Source S&P, Vickers, company reports)

52-Wk Range	$71.23–57.21	S&P Oper. EPS 2007E	6.07	Market Capitalization(B)	$45.887	Beta	1.02
Trailing 12-Month EPS	$9.01	S&P Oper. EPS 2008E	6.20	Yield (%)	1.20	S&P 3-Yr. Proj. EPS CAGR(%)	10.00
Trailing 12-Month P/E	6.9	P/E on S&P Oper. EPS 2007E	10.2	Dividend Rate/Share	$0.74	S&P Credit Rating	A
$10K Invested 5 Yrs Ago	$24,176	Common Shares Outstg. (M)	742.9	Institutional Ownership (%)	59		

Price Performance

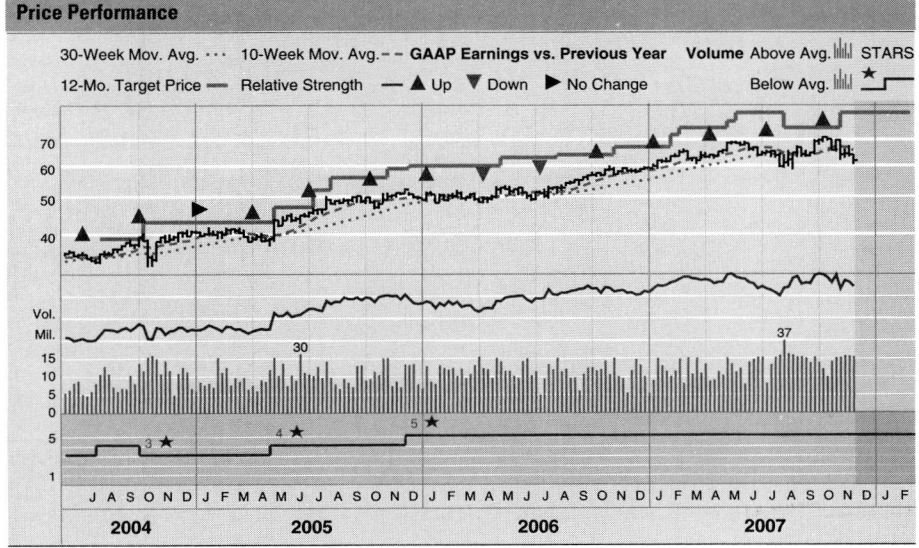

30-Week Mov. Avg. ··· 10-Week Mov. Avg. – – **GAAP Earnings vs. Previous Year** Volume Above Avg. STARS
12-Mo. Target Price — Relative Strength — ▲ Up ▼ Down ▶ No Change Below Avg.

Options: ASE, CBOE, P

Analysis prepared by **Tanjila Shafi** on November 06, 2007, when the stock traded at **$64.55.**

Highlights

➤ We expect operating earnings from institutional operations to experience double-digit growth in 2008, on improving results from the Travelers acquisition, growth in the non-medical health segment, better results in the retirement and savings segment, and improved mortality trends. We estimate single-digit growth in operating earnings from individual operations, driven by solid customer retention, increased productivity per agent, and a reorganized distribution network.

➤ We see double digit operating earnings growth in the company's international segment. We look for Korea, Mexico and Japan to contribute to operating earnings as MET focuses on increasing sales, expanding its marketing efforts, and upgrading its systems and services. We forecast that reinsurance operating earnings will see solid growth, based on higher international demand and favorable pricing conditions in the U.S.

➤ We forecast 2007 operating EPS of $6.07, which would represent more than 16% growth from 2006 operating EPS of $5.21. Our EPS estimate for 2008 is $6.20.

Investment Rationale/Risk

➤ We believe that the company is poised to benefit from its diverse business mix, strong organic growth, aggressive capital management initiatives, and improved operating efficiencies. We see the company benefiting from changing demographics. We anticipate that the company's retirement and savings segment will grow as an aging population seeks retirement-oriented financial products. In addition, we do not expect that the company's subprime exposure of $2.2 billion -- representing only 0.6% of total investments and mostly in higher-rated tranches -- to generate material losses that will negatively affect its investment portfolio.

➤ Risks to our recommendation and target price include credit and interest rate risk; exposure to asbestos-related liability claims; emerging market operations; investigations by attorneys general and insurance regulators into insurance broker relationships; and competition for large group insurance policies.

➤ Our 12-month target price of $82 is 13.2X our 2008 operating EPS forecast -- in line with historical multiples.

Qualitative Risk Assessment

LOW	MEDIUM	HIGH

Our risk assessment reflects our view of the company's consistent earnings growth, strong brand identity, diversified product offerings, and geographic footprint. MET has been able to keep its long-term debt to total capital ratio below 30%.

Quantitative Evaluations

S&P Quality Ranking NR

D	C	B-	B	B+	A-	A	A+

Relative Strength Rank MODERATE

47

LOWEST = 1   HIGHEST = 99

Revenue/Earnings Data

Revenue (Million $)

	1Q	2Q	3Q	4Q	Year
2007	12,912	13,219	13,055	--	--
2006	11,565	11,387	12,551	12,893	48,396
2005	10,257	10,961	12,012	11,546	44,776
2004	9,426	9,479	10,047	10,062	39,014
2003	8,364	8,862	8,816	9,747	35,790
2002	7,973	8,244	8,120	8,810	33,147

Earnings Per Share ($)

2007	1.29	1.48	1.52	E1.42	E6.07
2006	0.92	0.74	1.19	1.00	3.85
2005	1.08	1.36	0.96	0.77	4.16
2004	0.86	1.11	0.93	0.68	3.59
2003	0.38	0.78	0.74	0.68	2.57
2002	0.41	0.50	0.43	0.24	1.58

Fiscal year ended Dec. 31. Next earnings report expected: Mid February. EPS Estimates based on S&P Operating Earnings; historical GAAP earnings are as reported.

Dividend Data (Dates: mm/dd Payment Date: mm/dd/yy)

Amount ($)	Date Decl.	Ex-Div. Date	Stk. of Record	Payment Date
0.590	10/24	11/02	11/06	12/15/06
0.740	10/23	11/02	11/06	12/14/07

Dividends have been paid since 2000. Source: Company reports.

The McGraw-Hill Companies

Metlife Inc.

STANDARD &POOR'S

Business Summary November 06, 2007

CORPORATE OVERVIEW. MetLife (MET) is one of the largest insurance and financial services companies in the U.S. The company benefits from a strong brand, a solid financial position, and a large distribution network, in our view. According to the American Council of Life Insurers, MetLife was the largest life insurer in 2005, based on total assets. As of February 2006, MetLife had access to 71% of the world's life insurance markets, up from 36% in 2004. Formerly a mutual insurance company, MetLife demutualized and issued a publicly traded stock in April 2000.

MET is organized into five business segments: institutional, individual, auto and home, international, and reinsurance. The institutional segment accounted for 42% of consolidated revenues in 2006 (42% in 2005), the individual segment 30% (31%), the auto and home segment 6.2% (6.9%), the international segment 9.2% (8.1%), and the reinsurance segment 10% (10%). Corporate and

other activities, including MetLife Bank operations, accounted for 2.4% (1.9%) of consolidated revenues in 2006.

CORPORATE STRATEGY. On July 1, 2005, MET acquired Travelers Life & Annuity from Citigroup, Inc. and substantially all of Citigroup's international insurance businesses for $11.8 billion, including approximately $1 billion in MET shares and $10.8 billion in cash. The Travelers acquisition greatly enhances MET's size and scope in its core businesses, in our view. We also see the acquisition leading to strong top-line growth in MET's international operations.

Company Financials Fiscal Year Ended Dec. 31

Per Share Data ($)	2006	2005	2004	2003	2002	2001	2000	1999	1998	1997
Tangible Book Value	35.64	32.06	31.16	27.94	24.83	22.43	21.53	NA	NA	NA
Operating Earnings	NA	NA	NA	NA	NA	NA	NA	NA	NA	NA
Earnings	3.85	4.16	3.59	2.57	1.58	0.62	1.49	1.21	NA	NA
S&P Core Earnings	5.01	4.12	3.41	2.87	2.06	0.91	NA	NA	NA	NA
Dividends	0.59	0.52	0.46	0.23	0.21	0.20	0.20	NA	NA	NA
Payout Ratio	15%	13%	13%	9%	13%	32%	13%	NA	NA	NA
Prices:High	60.00	52.57	41.27	34.14	34.85	36.63	36.50	NA	NA	NA
Prices:Low	48.00	37.29	32.30	23.51	20.60	24.70	14.25	NA	NA	NA
P/E Ratio:High	16	13	11	13	22	59	24	NA	NA	NA
P/E Ratio:Low	12	9	9	9	13	40	10	NA	NA	NA

Income Statement Analysis (Million $)

	2006	2005	2004	2003	2002	2001	2000	1999	1998	1997
Life Insurance in Force	3,602,755	3,250,759	4,346,898	3,875,110	2,679,870	2,419,341	2,572,261	NA	NA	NA
Premium Income:Life	26,412	24,860	15,341	14,065	13,070	11,611	11,224	NA	NA	NA
Premium Income:A & H	NA	NA	4,016	3,537	3,052	2,744	2,377	NA	NA	NA
Net Investment Income	17,192	14,910	12,418	11,636	11,329	11,923	11,768	7,639	NA	NA
Total Revenue	49,746	44,869	39,014	36,147	33,147	31,928	31,947	19,244	NA	NA
Pretax Income	4,221	4,399	3,779	2,630	1,671	739	1,416	1,357	NA	NA
Net Operating Income	NA	NA	NA	NA	NA	NA	NA	NA	NA	NA
Net Income	3,105	3,139	2,708	1,943	1,155	473	953	918	NA	NA
S&P Core Earnings	3,867	3,123	2,574	2,144	1,512	697	NA	NA	NA	NA

Balance Sheet & Other Financial Data (Million $)

	2006	2005	2004	2003	2002	2001	2000	1999	1998	1997
Cash & Equivalent	10,454	7,054	6,389	5,919	4,411	9,535	5,484	4,097	NA	NA
Premiums Due	14,490	12,186	6,696	7,047	7,669	6,437	8,343	6,552	NA	NA
Investment Assets:Bonds	243,428	230,050	176,763	167,752	140,553	115,398	112,979	75,252	NA	NA
Investment Assets:Stocks	5,890	4,163	2,188	1,598	1,348	3,063	2,193	2,006	NA	NA
Investment Assets:Loans	52,467	47,170	41,305	34,998	33,666	31,893	30,109	16,805	NA	NA
Investment Assets:Total	324,689	301,709	234,985	218,099	188,335	162,222	156,527	105,187	NA	NA
Deferred Policy Costs	20,851	19,641	14,336	12,943	11,727	11,167	10,618	4,416	NA	NA
Total Assets	527,715	481,645	356,808	326,841	277,385	256,898	255,018	226,791	NA	NA
Debt	13,759	12,022	5,944	5,703	5,690	4,884	3,516	3,350	NA	NA
Common Equity	33,797	29,100	22,824	21,149	17,385	16,062	16,389	13,873	NA	NA
% Return on Revenue	6.2	7.0	6.9	5.4	3.5	1.5	3.0	4.8	NA	NA
% Return on Assets	0.6	0.7	0.8	0.6	0.4	0.2	0.4	NA	NA	NA
% Return on Equity	9.4	11.8	12.3	10.1	6.9	2.9	6.3	NA	NA	NA
% Investment Yield	5.5	5.6	6.8	5.7	6.5	7.5	8.0	NA	NA	NA

Data as orig reptd.; bef. results of disc opers/spec. items. Per share data adj. for stk. divs.; EPS diluted. E-Estimated. NA-Not Available. NM-Not Meaningful. NR-Not Ranked. UR-Under Review.

Office: 200 Park Ave, New York, NY 10166-0188.
Telephone: 212-578-2211.
Website: http://www.metlife.com
Chrmn, Pres & CEO: C.R. Henrikson

Sr EVP & Chief Admin Officer: C.A. Rein
Investor Contact: W.J. Wheeler (212-578-2211)
EVP & CFO: W.J. Wheeler
EVP & General Counsel: J.L. Lipscomb

Board Members: C. H. Barnette, B. A. Dole, Jr., C. W. Grise, C. R. Henrikson, J. R. Houghton, H. P. Kamen, H. L. Kaplan, J. M. Keane, J. M. Kilts, C. M. Leighton, S. M. Mathews, H. B. Price, D. Satcher, K. J. Sicchitano, W. C. Steere, Jr.

Founded: 1999
Domicile: Delaware
Employees: 47,000

MGIC Investment Corp

STANDARD &POOR'S

S&P Recommendation **HOLD** ★★★☆☆	Price $20.63 (as of Nov 23, 2007)	12-Mo. Target Price $23.00	Investment Style Large-Cap Blend

GICS Sector Financials
Sub-Industry Thrifts & Mortgage Finance

Summary Through its Mortgage Guaranty Insurance Corp. unit, this holding company is a leading U.S. provider of private mortgage insurance (PMI) coverage.

Key Stock Statistics (Source S&P, Vickers, company reports)

52-Wk Range	$70.10– 16.22	S&P Oper. EPS 2007**E**	-2.85	Market Capitalization(B)	$1.687	Beta	1.93
Trailing 12-Month EPS	$-1.02	S&P Oper. EPS 2008**E**	-1.03	Yield (%)	0.48	S&P 3-Yr. Proj. EPS CAGR(%)	NA
Trailing 12-Month P/E	NM	P/E on S&P Oper. EPS 2007**E**	NM	Dividend Rate/Share	$0.10	S&P Credit Rating	A-
$10K Invested 5 Yrs Ago	$4,681	Common Shares Outstg. (M)	81.8	Institutional Ownership (%)	NM		

Price Performance

30-Week Mov. Avg. · · · 10-Week Mov. Avg. - - **GAAP Earnings vs. Previous Year** Volume Above Avg. STARS
12-Mo. Target Price — Relative Strength — ▲ Up ▼ Down ► No Change Below Avg. ★

Options: ASE, CBOE, P

Analysis prepared by **Stuart Plesser** on October 30, 2007, when the stock traded at **$ 19.25**.

Highlights

➤ We see net premiums earned rising about 10% in 2008, despite a roughly 10% drop in new premiums written, mainly due to a decline in bulk business. We see persistency (insurance in force from one year prior) continuing to rise. We think that contributions from joint ventures will total roughly $60 million, versus a loss in 2007 as a result of the writedown of C-BASS, an acquirer of distressed loans. In the absence of any realized investment gains, we expect total revenues to be up slightly from 2007's level.

➤ We see net claims paid increasing almost 60% in 2008, reflecting deteriorating credit conditions and declining home prices, which should result in a higher severity of claims. We expect losses incurred to rise about 10%, with the assumption that claims paid will level off in the second half of 2008, reducing the need for a buildup in reserves. We expect a mid-single digit increase in expenses, stemming from greater staffing in MTG's international operations as well as higher operating costs, causing operating margins to narrow moderately.

➤ Assuming a 4% decline in diluted shares, we estimate a per share operating loss of $1.03 in 2008, versus a projected loss of $2.85 in 2007.

Investment Rationale/Risk

➤ We are concerned about MTG's exposure to the subprime market (roughly 13% of its risk in force). We expect housing prices to decline in 2008, which should result in an increase in the delinquency of the loans MTG insures and a higher severity of claims paid due to the high loan to value ratio of its book of business. On a positive note, MTG recently announced that it is terminating its planned agreement to merge with Radian (RDN: hold, $13), which, in our opinion, would have added considerable risk to MTG's insurance book. With the shares recently trading at less than 0.5X MTG's current book value of $49.30, we believe that most of our concerns regarding rising claims paid are already reflected in the stock price.

➤ Risks to our recommendation and target price include higher claims paid than expected due to a further than anticipated decline in U.S. home prices.

➤ Our 12-month target price of $23 is derived by using a price-to-book ratio of 0.47X--a significant discount to historical levels, reflecting a weak housing market--applied to MTG's current book value of $49.30.

Qualitative Risk Assessment

LOW	MEDIUM	HIGH

Our risk assessment reflects our view of MTG as a leading provider of private mortgage insurance, with sound risk and capital management practices and a leading market share, offset by declining home prices.

Quantitative Evaluations

S&P Quality Ranking A-

D	C	B-	B	B+	A-	A	A+

Relative Strength Rank WEAK

10

LOWEST = 1   HIGHEST = 99

Revenue/Earnings Data

Revenue (Million $)

	1Q	2Q	3Q	4Q	Year
2007	369.6	369.0	555.4	--	--
2006	369.0	363.5	369.4	367.2	1,469
2005	384.9	395.0	375.7	370.9	1,527
2004	415.4	403.2	391.0	403.1	1,613
2003	422.9	459.6	445.6	401.6	1,685
2002	375.6	383.8	390.8	415.6	1,566

Earnings Per Share ($)

2007	1.12	0.93	-4.61	E-0.37	E-2.85
2006	1.87	1.74	1.55	1.47	6.65
2005	1.90	1.87	1.55	1.44	6.78
2004	1.31	1.56	1.36	1.39	5.63
2003	1.42	1.46	1.06	1.05	4.99
2002	1.58	1.61	1.47	1.37	6.04

Fiscal year ended Dec. 31. Next earnings report expected: Mid January. EPS Estimates based on S&P Operating Earnings; historical GAAP earnings are as reported.

Dividend Data (Dates: mm/dd Payment Date: mm/dd/yy)

Amount ($)	Date Decl.	Ex-Div. Date	Stk. of Record	Payment Date
0.250	01/26	02/08	02/12	03/01/07
0.250	05/10	05/18	05/22	06/08/07
0.250	07/26	08/09	08/13	09/04/07
0.025	10/25	11/07	11/09	12/03/07

Dividends have been paid since 1991. Source: Company reports.

Please read the Required Disclosures and Analyst Certification on the last page of this report.

The McGraw-Hill Companies

MGIC Investment Corp

Business Summary October 30, 2007

COMPANY OVERVIEW. MTG is a leading provider of private mortgage insurance (PMI), which lets home buyers purchase homes with down payments of under 20% by reducing default risk borne by lenders. In addition, by improving the credit quality of the underlying loans, mortgage insurance facilitates the sale of mortgage loans in the secondary market.

PRIMARY BUSINESS DYNAMICS. There are two types of private mortgage insurance: primary and pool. Primary insurance provides default protection on individual loans and covers unpaid loan principal, interest, and certain expenses, with the insurer having the option to pay either the coverage percentage specified in the policy or 100% of the claim amount and acquire the title to the property. In general, a borrower may stop making mortgage insurance payments when the loan to value ratio (LTV) is scheduled to reach 80%. Primary insurance can be written on a flow basis, in which loans are insured in individual, loan-by-loan transactions, or on a bulk basis, in which a portfolio of loans is insured in a single bulk transaction. In 2006, new insurance written on

a flow basis totaled $39.2 billion versus $40.1 billion in 2005; new insurance written for bulk transactions totaled $19.0 billion ($21.4 billion). We expect flow business to pick up in 2007.

Pool insurance is mortgage insurance that is supplemental to other insurance or that reduces a lender's credit risk to less than 50% of the property value, and is generally used as an additional credit enhancement for certain secondary market mortgage transactions. It covers the loss on a defaulted mortgage loan that exceeds the claim payment under the primary coverage as well as the total loss on a defaulted mortgage that did not require primary coverage.

Company Financials Fiscal Year Ended Dec. 31

Per Share Data ($)	2006	2005	2004	2003	2002	2001	2000	1999	1998	1997
Tangible Book Value	51.88	47.30	43.05	38.58	33.87	28.47	23.07	16.79	15.05	13.07
Operating Earnings	NA	NA	NA	NA	NA	NA	NA	NA	3.29	2.73
Earnings	6.65	6.78	5.63	4.99	6.04	5.93	5.05	4.30	3.39	2.75
S&P Core Earnings	6.68	6.61	5.49	4.72	5.71	5.53	NA	NA	NA	NA
Dividends	1.00	0.52	0.23	0.11	0.10	0.10	0.10	0.10	0.10	0.10
Payout Ratio	15%	8%	4%	2%	2%	2%	2%	2%	3%	4%
Prices:High	72.73	70.99	78.95	58.77	74.40	77.31	71.50	62.75	74.50	66.94
Prices:Low	53.96	56.70	56.20	35.30	33.60	50.56	31.94	30.13	24.25	34.94
P/E Ratio:High	11	10	14	12	12	13	14	15	22	24
P/E Ratio:Low	8	8	10	7	6	9	6	7	7	13

Income Statement Analysis (Million $)										
Premium Income	1,187	1,239	1,329	1,366	1,182	1,042	890	793	763	709
Net Investment Income	241	229	215	203	208	204	179	153	143	124
Other Revenue	282	288	68.2	117	176	111	41.7	51.1	65.4	35.0
Total Revenue	1,469	1,527	1,613	1,685	1,566	1,358	1,110	997	972	869
Pretax Income	695	804	713	640	898	932	789	681	555	465
Net Operating Income	NA	NA	NA	NA	NA	NA	NA	NA	NA	NA
Net Income	565	627	553	494	629	639	542	470	385	324
S&P Core Earnings	567	611	539	468	595	597	NA	NA	NA	NA

Balance Sheet & Other Financial Data (Million $)										
Cash & Equivalent	358	71.0	70.1	83.2	69.5	85.4	57.0	49.0	46.1	40.4
Premiums Due	101	106	113	140	127	35.3	41.8	Nil	Nil	Nil
Investment Assets:Bonds	5,250	5,293	5,414	5,059	4,613	3,889	3,299	2,667	2,603	2,301
Investment Assets:Stocks	2.60	2.49	5.33	8.28	10.8	20.7	22.0	Nil	4.63	116
Investment Assets:Loans	Nil	Nil	Nil	Nil	Nil	Nil	Nil	Nil	Nil	Nil
Investment Assets:Total	5,908	5,968	5,997	5,513	5,069	4,231	3,472	2,790	2,780	2,417
Deferred Policy Costs	12.8	18.4	27.7	32.6	31.9	32.1	25.8	22.4	24.1	27.0
Total Assets	6,622	6,358	6,381	5,917	5,300	4,567	3,858	3,104	3,051	2,618
Debt	697	497	485	315	677	472	397	425	442	238
Common Equity	5,422	5,290	5,329	4,859	4,128	3,020	2,465	1,776	1,641	1,487
Property & Casualty:Loss Ratio	51.7	44.7	52.7	56.1	30.9	15.4	10.3	12.3	27.7	34.2
Property & Casualty:Expense Ratio	17.0	15.9	14.6	14.1	14.8	16.5	16.4	19.7	19.6	18.4
Property & Casualty Combined Ratio	68.7	60.6	67.3	70.2	45.7	31.9	26.7	32.0	47.3	52.6
% Return on Revenue	38.4	41.1	34.3	29.3	40.2	47.1	48.8	47.2	39.7	37.3
% Return on Equity	10.5	11.8	10.9	11.0	16.2	23.3	25.6	27.5	24.7	22.7

Data as orig reptd.; bef. results of disc opers/spec. items. Per share data adj. for stk. divs.; EPS diluted. E-Estimated. NA-Not Available. NM-Not Meaningful. NR-Not Ranked. UR-Under Review.

Office: 250 East Kilbourn Avenue, Milwaukee, WI 53202.
Telephone: 414-347-6480.
Website: http://www.mgic.com
Chrmn & CEO: C.S. Culver

Pres & COO: P. Sinks
EVP & CFO: J.M. Lauer
SVP & Treas: J.A. Karpowicz
SVP, Secy & General Counsel: J.H. Lane

Investor Contact: M.J. Zimmerman (414-347-6596)
Board Members: J. A. Abbott, K. E. Case, C. S. Culver, D. S. Engelman, T. M. Hagerty, K. M. Jastrow, II, D. P. Kearney, M. E. Lehman, W. A. McIntosh, L. M. Muma, D. T. Nicolaisen

Founded: 1984
Domicile: Wisconsin
Employees: 1,200

Microchip Technology Inc

STANDARD &POOR'S

S&P Recommendation	HOLD ★★★☆☆	Price $28.52 (as of Nov 23, 2007)	12-Mo. Target Price $32.00	Investment Style Large-Cap Growth

GICS Sector Information Technology
Sub-Industry Semiconductors

Summary This company supplies field programmable 8-bit microcontrollers and related analog and specialty memory products for high-volume embedded control applications.

Key Stock Statistics (Source S&P, Vickers, company reports)

52-Wk Range	$42.46–28.08	S&P Oper. EPS 2008**E**	1.38	Market Capitalization(B)	$6.201	Beta	1.62
Trailing 12-Month EPS	$1.54	S&P Oper. EPS 2009**E**	1.54	Yield (%)	4.35	S&P 3-Yr. Proj. EPS CAGR(%)	6.00
Trailing 12-Month P/E	18.5	P/E on S&P Oper. EPS 2008**E**	20.7	Dividend Rate/Share	$1.24	S&P Credit Rating	NA
$10K Invested 5 Yrs Ago	$10,923	Common Shares Outstg. (M)	217.4	Institutional Ownership (%)	93		

Price Performance

30-Week Mov. Avg. ··· 10-Week Mov. Avg. — — **GAAP Earnings vs. Previous Year** Volume Above Avg. STARS
12-Mo. Target Price — Relative Strength — ▲ Up ▼ Down ► No Change Below Avg. ★

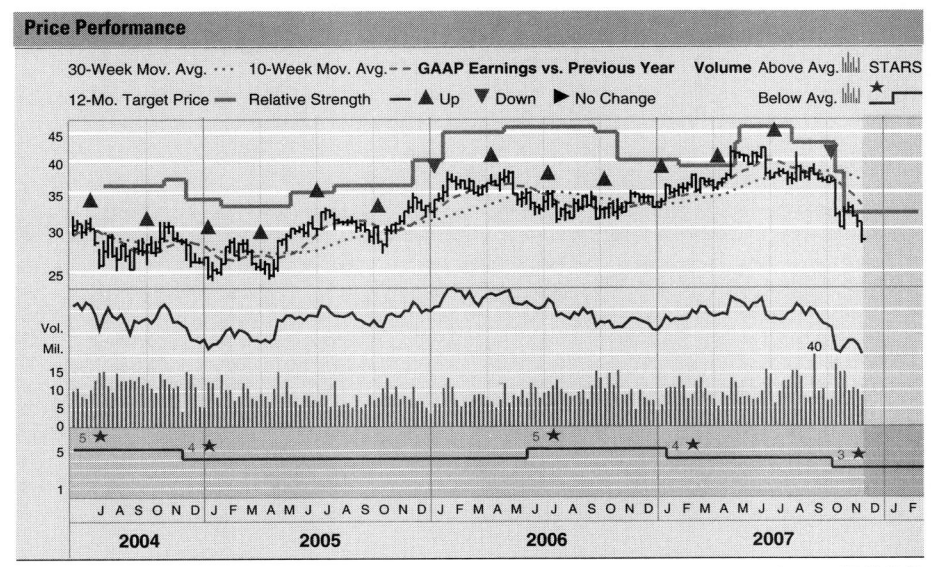

Options: ASE, CBOE, Ph

Analysis prepared by **Clyde Montevirgen** on October 25, 2007, when the stock traded at **$32.18**.

Highlights

➤ Following a sales increase of 12% in FY 07 (Mar.), we are looking for a modest decline in FY 08, as a slowdown in the U.S. housing market affects sales. MCHP has consistently taken market share in the 8-bit and 16-bit microprocessor segments and has unusually high exposure to a wide range of end-markets. Unfortunately, we think this may work against the company in the near term as a number of those markets are related to the U.S. housing industry, which we see continuing to show signs of weakness. However, we believe market share gains in microcontrollers and analog will help balance potential sales declines.

➤ We expect gross margins to widen to about 61% in FY 08, from 60% in FY 07. The company's long-term goal for gross margins is 62%, reflecting its expectations for a richer product mix, lower depreciation charges, and better efficiency at its newest wafer fabrication plant located in Gresham, OR. We are projecting operating margins to remain in the mid-30% area.

➤ We project FY 08 operating EPS of $1.38 and FY 09 EPS of $1.54.

Investment Rationale/Risk

➤ Although we think Microchip has a very profitable business model featuring unusually diverse end-markets and a low cost structure, we are concerned about revenue growth in the near term, given the company's exposure to the soft U.S. housing market. Throughout this period of softness, we think MCHP will likely manage operations more efficiently to preserve gross and operating margins. Longer term, we expect the company to continue to gain market share in its mainstay 8-bit microcontroller market and in the 16-bit microcontroller and analog markets. We also note that the company has one of the highest dividend yields in the semiconductor industry.

➤ Risks to our recommendation and target price include industry cyclicality, maintaining global operations, above-average share price volatility, numerous competitors, and the challenges of entering new markets for 16-bit microcontrollers.

➤ Applying a price/earnings multiple of 23X, above the peer average, to our FY 08 EPS estimate, we derive a value of approximately $32, which is our 12-month target price.

Qualitative Risk Assessment

LOW	MEDIUM	HIGH

Microchip operates in the cyclical semiconductor industry, and the shares have above-average volatility. Offsetting positive factors that we see include a very broad customer base, a breadth of end markets, a low cost structure, no debt, and one of the highest dividend yields among peers.

Quantitative Evaluations

S&P Quality Ranking   B+

D	C	B-	B	B+	A-	A	A+

Relative Strength Rank   WEAK

22

LOWEST = 1   HIGHEST = 99

Revenue/Earnings Data

Revenue (Million $)

	1Q	2Q	3Q	4Q	Year
2008	264.1	258.7	--	--	--
2007	262.6	267.9	251.0	258.2	1,040
2006	218.5	227.3	234.9	247.2	927.9
2005	212.8	220.7	205.4	208.1	846.9
2004	161.3	168.5	178.0	191.5	699.3
2003	157.5	166.8	167.5	159.7	651.5

Earnings Per Share ($)

	1Q	2Q	3Q	4Q	Year
2008	0.36	0.27	E0.34	E0.33	E1.38
2007	0.35	0.36	0.33	0.57	1.62
2006	0.29	0.31	0.19	0.35	1.13
2005	0.21	0.29	0.25	0.27	1.01
2004	0.06	0.17	0.19	0.23	0.65
2003	0.10	0.05	0.17	0.16	0.47

Fiscal year ended Mar. 31. Next earnings report expected: Early February. EPS Estimates based on S&P Operating Earnings; historical GAAP earnings are as reported.

Dividend Data (Dates: mm/dd Payment Date: mm/dd/yy)

Amount ($)	Date Decl.	Ex-Div. Date	Stk. of Record	Payment Date
0.265	01/31	02/12	02/14	02/28/07
0.280	04/26	05/08	05/10	05/24/07
0.295	07/26	08/07	08/09	08/23/07
0.310	10/23	11/02	11/06	11/20/07

Dividends have been paid since 2002. Source: Company reports.

Please read the Required Disclosures and Analyst Certification on the last page of this report.

The McGraw-Hill Companies

Microchip Technology Inc

STANDARD
&POOR'S

Business Summary October 25, 2007

CORPORATE OVERVIEW. Microchip Technology Inc. (MCHP) develops and manufactures specialized chips used in a wide variety of embedded control applications. MCHP is a leading microcontroller company, serving more than 56,000 end customers worldwide and having shipped over 5 billion PIC microcontrollers since 1990. MCHP also offers a broad range of high-performance linear, mixed-signal, power management, thermal management, battery management, and interface devices, and serial EEPROMs. Microcontrollers are low-cost components that form the brains of the vast majority of electronic devices, except for PCs. MCHP's signature products include a broad family of proprietary 8- and 16-bit field programmable microcontrollers under the PIC name, designed for applications requiring high performance, fast time-to-market, and user programmability. The company offers a comprehensive set of low cost and easy-to-learn application development tools that let system designers program a PIC microcontroller for specific applications. Over 500,000 development tools have been shipped.

By product line, microcontrollers provided 80.2% of sales in FY 07 (Mar.)

(79.3% in FY 06), memory products 11.8% (13.5%), and analog and interface products 8.0% (7.2%). Average selling prices are relatively stable for the microcontrollers and for analog products with significant proprietary content, which is about half the analog segment. Pricing for EEPROM products and the more commodity-type analog products tends to fluctuate.

The 10 largest customers represented about 10% of total revenue in FY 07. Foreign sales accounted for approximately 72% of FY 07 net sales, up from 71% in FY 06. By major region, FY 07 sales came from Asia (43.3%), Europe (29.1%), and the Americas (27.6%). About 18% of FY 07 sales were sourced from China, including Hong Kong, and Taiwan accounted for about 10% of sales. In FY 07, MCHP derived 65% of its net sales from sales through distributors.

Company Financials Fiscal Year Ended Mar. 31

Per Share Data ($)	2007	2006	2005	2004	2003	2002	2001	2000	1999	1998
Tangible Book Value	9.03	7.89	6.95	6.19	5.58	5.36	4.80	3.52	2.07	2.06
Cash Flow	2.14	1.64	1.58	1.32	1.00	0.98	1.20	0.93	0.64	0.62
Earnings	1.62	1.13	1.01	0.65	0.47	0.45	0.69	0.56	0.28	0.34
S&P Core Earnings	1.62	1.05	0.89	0.47	0.30	0.28	0.57	NA	NA	NA
Dividends	0.57	0.21	0.11	0.04	0.04	Nil	Nil	Nil	Nil	Nil
Payout Ratio	35%	18%	11%	6%	9%	Nil	Nil	Nil	Nil	Nil
Calendar Year	2006	2005	2004	2003	2002	2001	2000	1999	1998	1997
Prices:High	38.56	34.98	34.88	36.50	33.99	28.29	34.39	22.81	12.15	14.63
Prices:Low	30.63	24.06	25.12	17.85	15.02	14.00	12.92	7.54	5.04	6.93
P/E Ratio:High	24	31	35	56	72	62	50	41	44	43
P/E Ratio:Low	19	21	25	27	32	31	19	14	18	21

Income Statement Analysis (Million $)

	2007	2006	2005	2004	2003	2002	2001	2000	1999	1998
Revenue	1,040	928	847	699	651	571	716	496	406	397
Operating Income	464	567	400	314	286	232	304	204	164	145
Depreciation	116	111	120	142	111	109	104	68.5	65.2	53.8
Interest Expense	5.42	1.97	0.94	0.25	0.49	0.57	0.75	1.05	2.96	1.13
Pretax Income	401	359	277	178	128	127	196	140	68.6	88.2
Effective Tax Rate	11.0%	32.5%	22.9%	22.8%	22.3%	25.5%	27.2%	27.0%	27.0%	27.0%
Net Income	357	242	214	137	99.7	94.8	143	102	50.1	64.4
S&P Core Earnings	357	226	190	100	63.5	58.2	117	NA	NA	NA

Balance Sheet & Other Financial Data (Million $)

	2007	2006	2005	2004	2003	2002	2001	2000	1999	1998
Cash	167	565	68.7	105	53.9	281	130	188	30.8	32.2
Current Assets	1,085	1,119	1,075	884	609	549	372	365	203	195
Total Assets	2,270	2,351	1,818	1,622	1,428	1,276	1,161	812	505	525
Current Liabilities	256	609	307	270	215	168	195	169	110	139
Long Term Debt	Nil	Nil	Nil	Nil	Nil	Nil	Nil	Nil	25.0	8.77
Common Equity	2,004	1,726	1,486	1,321	1,179	1,076	943	624	359	367
Total Capital	2,013	1,741	1,510	1,351	1,212	1,107	966	643	396	384
Capital Expenditures	60.0	76.3	63.2	63.5	80.4	44.7	441	212	39.5	145
Cash Flow	473	353	334	279	211	204	247	171	115	118
Current Ratio	4.2	1.8	3.5	3.3	2.8	3.3	1.9	2.2	1.8	1.4
% Long Term Debt of Capitalization	Nil	Nil	Nil	Nil	Nil	Nil	Nil	Nil	6.3	2.2
% Net Income of Revenue	34.3	26.1	25.2	19.6	15.3	16.6	20.0	20.6	12.3	16.2
% Return on Assets	15.5	11.6	12.4	9.0	7.4	7.8	14.1	15.5	9.7	13.5
% Return on Equity	19.1	15.1	15.2	11.0	8.8	9.4	17.8	20.8	13.8	18.8

Data as orig reptd.; bef. results of disc opers/spec. items. Per share data adj. for stk. divs.; EPS diluted. E-Estimated. NA-Not Available. NM-Not Meaningful. NR-Not Ranked. UR-Under Review.

Office: 2355 West Chandler Boulevard, Chandler, AZ 85224-6199.
Telephone: 480-792-7200.
Email: ir@mail.microchip.com
Website: http://www.microchip.com

Chrmn, Pres & CEO: S. Sanghi
VP & CFO: G.W. Parnell
Investor Contact: D.L. Wussler (480-792-7373)

Board Members: M. W. Chapman, L. B. Day, A. J. Hugo-Martinez, W. F. Meyercord, S. Sanghi

Founded: 1989
Domicile: Delaware
Employees: 4,582

Micron Technology Inc.

STANDARD &POOR'S

S&P Recommendation HOLD ★★★☆☆	**Price** $8.37 (as of Nov 23, 2007)	**12-Mo. Target Price** $14.00	**Investment Style** Large-Cap Value

GICS Sector Information Technology
Sub-Industry Semiconductors

Summary MU is a manufacturer of semiconductor memory products, including DRAM and NAND flash memory, as well as image sensors.

Key Stock Statistics (Source S&P, Vickers, company reports)

52-Wk Range	$15.16– 7.90	S&P Oper. EPS 2008E	0.19	Market Capitalization(B)	$6.365	Beta	2.50
Trailing 12-Month EPS	$-0.42	S&P Oper. EPS 2009E	NA	Yield (%)	Nil	S&P 3-Yr. Proj. EPS CAGR(%)	9.00
Trailing 12-Month P/E	NM	P/E on S&P Oper. EPS 2008E	44.1	Dividend Rate/Share	Nil	S&P Credit Rating	BB-
$10K Invested 5 Yrs Ago	$5,225	Common Shares Outstg. (M)	760.4	Institutional Ownership (%)	89		

Price Performance

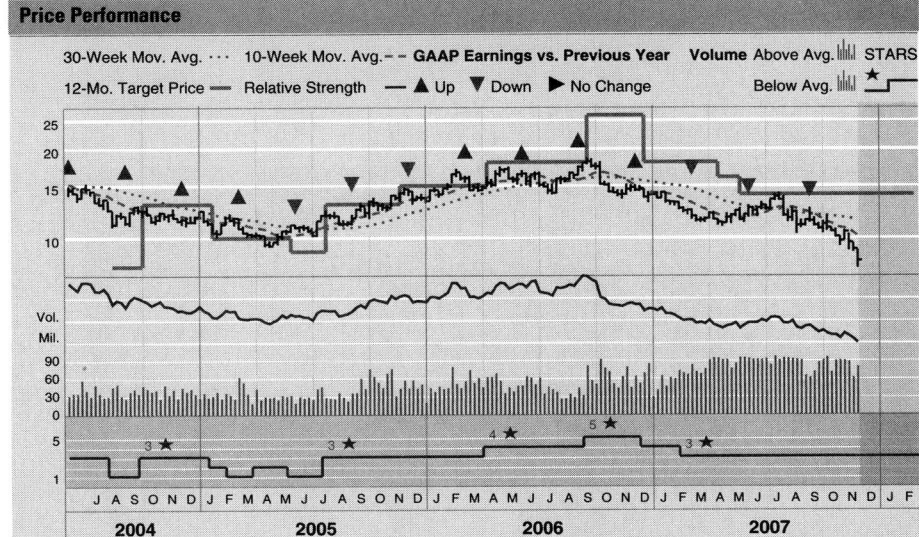

30-Week Mov. Avg. · · · 10-Week Mov. Avg. - – **GAAP Earnings vs. Previous Year** **Volume** Above Avg. STARS
12-Mo. Target Price — Relative Strength — ▲ Up ▼ Down ► No Change Below Avg.

Options: ASE, CBOE, P, Ph

Analysis prepared by **Clyde Montevirgen** on October 03, 2007, when the stock traded at **$ 10.72**.

Highlights

➤ After sales growth of about 8% in FY 07 (Aug.), we anticipate 21% in FY 08, reflecting anticipated healthy memory bit growth due to continuing strength in demand for PCs and electronic devices and more stable average selling prices (ASPs). We believe that Micron's continuing focus on NAND flash memories and CMOS image sensors will help diversify sales in the long term, but we see near-term results being affected by declining memory prices due to industry overcapacity.

➤ Gross margins for MU's main products are highly sensitive to industry factors such as inventory levels, demand for PCs and consumer electronics, and per-chip cost reduction, which affects movements in prices. Although we see brisk unit demand for DRAM and NAND flash memory chips, we see deteriorating ASPs pressuring margin expansion over the near-term. We project gross margins widening to the mid-20% in FY 08, following 19% in FY 07. Although we see lower unit costs and improving operational efficiency, we think industry-wide production capacity increases will pressure prices.

➤ We estimate EPS of $0.19 for FY 08.

Investment Rationale/Risk

➤ We believe MU will benefit from growing demand for DRAM chips due to strong PC sales growth, and from healthy unit growth of NAND flash memory due to robust demand for consumer electronic products. We also see more stable NAND pricing ahead as memory chipmakers have recently shifted production to DRAM. However, we think increasing capacity for memory and slower than expected traction for Microsoft Vista operating system by enterprise customers will lead to ASP deterioration for DRAM in the next quarter. We expect profits to be volatile and would not add to positions.

➤ Risks to our opinion and target price include sudden downturns in end-market demand for PCs, slower than expected sales of consumer electronic products, and sharp increases in DRAM production by competitors. Also, competition might be more intense than we anticipate for DRAM or NAND flash memory.

➤ Our 12-month target price of $14 mainly reflects our price-to-sales model, and is derived by applying a multiple of 1.6X, below the historical average, to our forward 12-month sales per share estimate.

Qualitative Risk Assessment

LOW	MEDIUM	HIGH

Micron is subject to semiconductor industry cyclicality and to sudden changes in pricing for commodity memory products. It is a relatively large semiconductor company and is the lone American survivor in the global DRAM industry, which has been consolidating in recent years.

Quantitative Evaluations

S&P Quality Ranking B-

D	C	B-	B	B+	A-	A	A+

Relative Strength Rank WEAK

16

LOWEST = 1   HIGHEST = 99

Revenue/Earnings Data

Revenue (Million $)

	1Q	2Q	3Q	4Q	Year
2007	1,530	1,427	1,294	1,437	5,688
2006	1,362	1,225	1,312	1,373	5,272
2005	1,260	1,308	1,054	1,258	4,880
2004	1,107	991.0	1,117	1,189	4,404
2003	685.1	785.0	732.7	888.5	3,091
2002	423.9	645.9	771.2	748.0	2,589

Earnings Per Share ($)

2007	0.15	-0.07	-0.29	-0.21	-0.42
2006	0.09	0.27	0.12	0.08	0.57
2005	0.23	0.17	-0.20	0.07	0.29
2004	Nil	-0.04	0.13	0.14	0.24
2003	-0.52	-1.02	-0.36	-0.20	-2.11
2002	-0.44	-0.05	-0.04	-0.97	-1.51

Fiscal year ended Aug. 31. Next earnings report expected: Late December. EPS Estimates based on S&P Operating Earnings; historical GAAP earnings are as reported.

Dividend Data

The most recent cash dividend was a payment of $0.05 a share in May 1996.

Micron Technology Inc.

STANDARD &POOR'S

Business Summary October 03, 2007

CORPORATE OVERVIEW. Micron Technology is a global manufacturer and marketer of dynamic random access memory (DRAM), NAND flash memory, and complementary metal-oxide semiconductor (CMOS) image sensors. The company's products are used in an increasingly broad range of electronic devices, including personal computers, workstations, network servers, mobile phones, digital still cameras, MP3 players and other consumer electronics products. About 70% of FY 06 total sales were to the computing market, and Hewlett-Packard accounted for 10% of FY 06 sales.

The company has been in the DRAM business since 1980, and is currently one of the world's largest DRAM suppliers. DRAM products are high-density, low-cost per bit, random access memory devices that provide high-speed data storage and retrieval. Micron offers DRAM products with a variety of performance, pricing, and other characteristics. The company's DRAM products may be classified as core DRAM or specialty memory.

Micron has two segments, memory, which includes both DRAM and NAND flash memory, and imaging. DRAM sales accounted for 76% of the total in FY 06 (Aug.), down from 87% in FY 05, reflecting an expansion into flash memory and CMOS image sensors over the last couple of years. NAND flash memory sales comprised 6% of sales in FY 06, reflecting growing market demand for memory devices that can retain memory when the power is turned off for use in handheld electronic devices such as digital still cameras. Many such consumer electronics products also use image sensors, and the company's CMOS image sensor products grew to 14% of FY 06 sales. The company is allocating more manufacturing capacity to NAND and image sensor products in FY 06 in response to the rising demand that it perceives.

Company Financials Fiscal Year Ended Aug. 31

Per Share Data ($)	2007	2006	2005	2004	2003	2002	2001	2000	1999	1998
Tangible Book Value	NA	9.64	9.07	8.73	7.68	9.93	11.59	11.34	7.00	6.31
Cash Flow	NA	2.33	2.07	2.13	-0.10	0.45	1.00	4.13	1.49	0.88
Earnings	-0.42	0.57	0.29	0.24	-2.11	-1.51	-0.88	2.56	-0.13	-0.55
S&P Core Earnings	-0.38	0.40	-0.12	-0.09	-2.60	-2.14	-1.06	NA	NA	NA
Dividends	Nil	Nil	Nil	Nil	Nil	Nil	Nil	Nil	Nil	Nil
Payout Ratio	Nil	Nil	Nil	Nil	Nil	Nil	Nil	Nil	Nil	Nil
Prices:High	14.31	18.65	14.82	18.25	15.66	39.50	49.61	97.50	42.50	27.81
Prices:Low	7.90	13.12	9.32	10.89	6.60	9.50	16.39	28.00	17.13	10.03
P/E Ratio:High	NM	33	51	76	NM	NM	NM	38	NM	NM
P/E Ratio:Low	NM	23	32	45	NM	NM	NM	11	NM	NM

Income Statement Analysis (Million $)

	2007	2006	2005	2004	2003	2002	2001	2000	1999	1998
Revenue	NA	5,272	4,880	4,404	3,091	2,589	3,936	7,336	3,764	3,012
Operating Income	NA	1,631	1,458	1,445	133	152	138	3,288	796	113
Depreciation	NA	1,281	1,265	1,218	1,210	1,177	1,114	994	843	607
Interest Expense	NA	25.0	46.9	36.0	36.5	17.1	16.7	104	130	49.4
Pretax Income	NA	433	199	232	-1,200	-998	-960	2,317	-91.5	-335
Effective Tax Rate	NA	4.16%	5.34%	32.2%	NM	NM	NM	34.4%	NM	NM
Net Income	NA	408	188	157	-1,273	-907	-521	1,504	-68.9	-234
S&P Core Earnings	-290	288	-75.8	-62.2	-1,578	-1,288	-626	NA	NA	NA

Balance Sheet & Other Financial Data (Million $)

	2007	2006	2005	2004	2003	2002	2001	2000	1999	1998
Cash	NA	1,431	525	486	570	398	469	702	295	559
Current Assets	NA	5,101	2,926	2,639	2,037	2,119	3,138	4,904	2,830	1,499
Total Assets	NA	12,221	8,006	7,760	7,158	7,555	8,363	9,632	6,965	4,688
Current Liabilities	NA	1,661	979	972	993	753	687	1,648	922	740
Long Term Debt	NA	405	1,020	1,028	997	361	445	934	1,528	757
Common Equity	NA	8,114	5,847	5,615	5,038	6,367	7,135	6,432	3,964	2,693
Total Capital	NA	10,115	6,902	6,685	6,035	6,727	7,599	7,899	5,969	3,887
Capital Expenditures	NA	1,365	1,065	1,081	822	760	1,489	1,188	804	707
Cash Flow	NA	1,689	1,453	1,375	-63.3	270	593	2,499	774	373
Current Ratio	NA	3.1	3.0	2.7	2.1	2.8	4.6	3.0	3.1	19.4
% Long Term Debt of Capitalization	NA	4.0	14.8	15.4	16.5	5.4	5.9	11.8	25.6	20.3
% Net Income of Revenue	NA	7.7	3.9	3.6	NM	NM	NM	20.5	NM	NM
% Return on Assets	NA	4.0	2.4	2.1	NM	NM	NM	18.1	NM	NM
% Return on Equity	NA	5.8	3.3	3.0	NM	NM	NM	28.9	NM	NM

Data as orig reptd.; bef. results of disc opers/spec. items. Per share data adj. for stk. divs.; EPS diluted. E-Estimated. NA-Not Available. NM-Not Meaningful. NR-Not Ranked. UR-Under Review.

Office: 8000 South Federal Way, Boise, ID 83716-7128.
Telephone: 208-368-4000.
Email: invrel@micron.com
Website: http://www.micron.com

Chrmn & CEO: S.R. Appleton
Pres & COO: D.M. Durcan
VP & CFO: W.G. Stover, Jr.
VP, Secy & General Counsel: R.W. Lewis

VP, Secy & General Counsel: R. Lewis
Investor Contact: K.A. Bedard (208-368-4400)
Board Members: T. Aoki, S. R. Appleton, J. W. Bagley, M. Johnson, L. N. Mondry, R. Switz

Founded: 1978
Domicile: Delaware
Employees: 23,500

The McGraw-Hill Companies

Microsoft Corp

STANDARD &POOR'S

S&P Recommendation	STRONG BUY ★★★★★	Price $33.06 (as of Nov 27, 2007)	12-Mo. Target Price $42.00	Investment Style Large-Cap Growth

GICS Sector Information Technology
Sub-Industry Systems Software

Summary Microsoft, the world's largest software company, develops PC software, including the Windows operating system and the Office application suite.

Key Stock Statistics (Source S&P, Vickers, company reports)

52-Wk Range	$37.50–26.60	S&P Oper. EPS 2008**E**	1.81	Market Capitalization(B)	$309.291
Trailing 12-Month EPS	$1.52	S&P Oper. EPS 2009**E**	2.04	Yield (%)	1.33
Trailing 12-Month P/E	21.8	P/E on S&P Oper. EPS 2008**E**	18.3	Dividend Rate/Share	$0.44
$10K Invested 5 Yrs Ago	$13,727	Common Shares Outstg. (M)	9,355.4	Institutional Ownership (%)	59

Beta	0.87
S&P 3-Yr. Proj. EPS CAGR(%)	13.00
S&P Credit Rating	NR

Price Performance

Options: ASE, CBOE, P, Ph

Analysis prepared by **Jim Yin** on October 29, 2007, when the stock traded at **$ 34.84**.

Highlights

➤ We see total revenues rising 16% in FY 08 (Jun.), driven by increasing market acceptance of Windows Vista. We expect client revenue to rise 14%. Our growth estimate is based on our forecast for 13%-15% growth in worldwide PC unit shipments and an increase in the OEM premium mix, offset by lower selling prices in emerging markets. We estimate Server and Tools revenue will rise 16%, Microsoft Business division 15%, and Entertainment and Devices Division (EDD) 20%, down from 31% in FY 07, due to slower sales of Xbox.

➤ We look for gross margins to increase to 81% in FY 08, from 79% in FY 07, reflecting margin improvement in its online business and EDD. We see operating margins widening to 39.2% from 36.2%, reflecting better monetization of its online advertising and search engine technology, better operating efficiency due to economies of scale, and one-time charges in FY 07 related to Xbox defects.

➤ We estimate EPS of $1.81 for FY 08, compared to $1.43 for FY 07, on 5% fewer shares due to the company's share repurchase program. MSFT had $21.6 billion in cash and short-term investments as of September 30, 2007.

Investment Rationale/Risk

➤ Our strong buy recommendation reflects our view of higher sales of PC units following the launch of Windows Vista, and valuation. We believe the adoption rate of Vista and Office 2007 will accelerate in the next 12 months when MSFT releases Windows Server 2008, enabling enterprises to upgrade Office, Vista, and back office applications simultaneously. We expect stronger growth of its online business following the FY 08 first quarter acquisition of aQuantive.

➤ Risks to our recommendation and target price include a lower than projected growth rate of PC sales, adverse outcomes from ongoing legal disputes, and the more rapid adoption of open-source software than we currently anticipate.

➤ Our 12-month target price of $42 is based on a blend of our discounted cash flow (DCF) and P/E analyses. Our DCF model assumes a 12% weighted average cost of capital and 3% terminal growth, yielding an intrinsic value of $41. Our P/E analysis derives a value of $42, based on an industry P/E to growth ratio of 1.8X, or 23.2X our FY 08 EPS estimate.

Qualitative Risk Assessment

LOW	MEDIUM	HIGH

Our risk assessment reflects MSFT's ongoing antitrust related issues, the risk that its applications and operating systems may lose market share to open source rivals, and potential difficulties releasing new products in a timely manner, mitigated by the company's present leading market positions and financial strength.

Quantitative Evaluations

S&P Quality Ranking   B+

D	C	B-	B	B+	A-	A	A+

Relative Strength Rank   STRONG

88

LOWEST = 1   HIGHEST = 99

Revenue/Earnings Data

Revenue (Million $)

	1Q	2Q	3Q	4Q	Year
2008	13,762	--	--	--	--
2007	10,811	12,542	14,398	13,371	51,122
2006	9,741	11,837	10,900	11,804	44,282
2005	9,189	10,818	9,620	10,161	39,788
2004	8,215	10,153	9,175	9,292	36,835
2003	7,746	8,541	7,835	8,065	32,187

Earnings Per Share ($)

2008	0.45	E0.46	E0.45	E0.46	E1.81
2007	0.35	0.26	0.50	0.31	1.42
2006	0.29	0.34	0.29	0.28	1.20
2005	0.23	0.32	0.23	0.34	1.12
2004	0.24	0.14	0.12	0.25	0.75
2003	0.25	0.23	0.26	0.18	0.92

Fiscal year ended Jun. 30. Next earnings report expected: Late January. EPS Estimates based on S&P Operating Earnings; historical GAAP earnings are as reported.

Dividend Data (Dates: mm/dd Payment Date: mm/dd/yy)

Amount ($)	Date Decl.	Ex-Div. Date	Stk. of Record	Payment Date
0.100	12/20	02/13	02/15	03/08/07
0.100	03/26	05/15	05/17	06/14/07
0.100	06/27	08/14	08/16	09/13/07
0.110	09/12	11/13	11/15	12/13/07

Dividends have been paid since 2003. Source: Company reports.

Please read the Required Disclosures and Analyst Certification on the last page of this report.

The McGraw-Hill Companies

Microsoft Corp

STANDARD &POOR'S

Business Summary October 29, 2007

CORPORATE OVERVIEW. Microsoft is the world's largest software maker, primarily as a result of its dominant position in operating systems, which run 90% of all PCs currently in use, and business productivity applications, where its Office productivity suite has over 400 million users. The combination of these two strongholds provides MSFT with a strong barrier to entry for competitors, in our opinion. With MSFT generating over $1 billion every month in free cash flow, it had $33.4 billion in cash and investments as of June 2007, despite having paid out more than $100 billion for dividends and share buybacks from FY 04 to FY 07 (Jun.).

MARKET PROFILE. According to IDC, global spending on packaged software totaled $211.3 billion in 2005, with MSFT's share totaling $35.0 billion or 17% of the total market. IDC expects the system infrastructure market, which comprises roughly half of MSFT's software revenues, to expand at a compound annual growth rate (CAGR) of 9.1% from 2005 through 2010. The applications market, which constitutes more than a third of revenues, is expected to increase 7.0%, and the application development and deployment market, more

than 10% of revenues, is forecast to rise 7.1%. We look for MSFT to expand at slightly faster rates for the most part, as the Windows platform continues to gain market share.

CORPORATE STRATEGY. Ray Ozzie, when he was MSFT's Chief Technical Officer (he replaced Bill Gates as Chief Software Architect in June 2006), described the core of the company's business strategy as centered on software as a service rather than as a transactional purchase. This strategy is a further refinement of the .NET strategy described by Gates in 2002, and essentially is driven by three key themes: the power of advertising-supported business models, the effectiveness of online discovery and trial-version downloads as a model for new software adoption, and the demand from users for integrated user experiences that "just work."

Company Financials Fiscal Year Ended Jun. 30

Per Share Data ($)	2007	2006	2005	2004	2003	2002	2001	2000	1999	1998
Tangible Book Value	2.71	3.55	4.14	6.55	5.34	2.05	4.39	3.92	2.69	1.59
Cash Flow	1.57	1.28	1.20	0.86	1.05	0.80	0.83	0.92	0.80	0.51
Earnings	1.42	1.20	1.12	0.75	0.92	0.71	0.66	0.85	0.71	0.42
S&P Core Earnings	1.38	1.27	1.20	0.83	0.75	0.65	0.58	NA	NA	NA
Dividends	0.40	0.35	3.40	0.16	0.08	Nil	Nil	Nil	Nil	Nil
Payout Ratio	28%	0%	NM	21%	9%	Nil	Nil	Nil	Nil	Nil
Prices:High	37.50	30.26	28.25	30.20	30.00	35.31	38.08	59.31	59.97	36.00
Prices:Low	26.60	21.46	23.82	24.86	22.55	20.71	21.44	20.13	34.00	15.55
P/E Ratio:High	26	25	25	40	33	50	58	70	84	86
P/E Ratio:Low	19	18	21	33	25	29	32	24	48	37

Income Statement Analysis (Million $)										
Revenue	51,122	44,282	39,788	36,835	32,187	28,365	25,296	22,956	19,747	14,484
Operating Income	19,964	17,375	15,416	10,220	14,656	12,994	13,256	11,685	10,938	7,734
Depreciation	1,440	903	855	1,186	1,439	1,084	1,536	748	1,010	1,024
Interest Expense	Nil	Nil	Nil	Nil	Nil	Nil	Nil	Nil	Nil	Nil
Pretax Income	20,101	18,262	16,628	12,196	14,726	11,513	11,525	14,275	11,891	7,117
Effective Tax Rate	30.0%	31.0%	26.3%	33.0%	32.1%	32.0%	33.0%	34.0%	34.5%	36.9%
Net Income	14,065	12,599	12,254	8,168	9,993	7,829	7,721	9,421	7,785	4,490
S&P Core Earnings	13,643	13,329	13,107	9,042	8,155	7,051	6,518	NA	NA	NA

Balance Sheet & Other Financial Data (Million $)										
Cash	6,111	6,714	4,851	15,982	6,438	3,016	3,922	4,846	17,236	13,927
Current Assets	40,168	49,010	48,737	70,566	58,973	48,576	39,637	30,308	20,233	15,889
Total Assets	63,171	69,597	70,815	92,389	79,571	67,646	59,257	52,150	37,156	22,357
Current Liabilities	23,754	22,442	16,877	14,969	13,974	12,744	11,132	9,755	8,718	5,730
Long Term Debt	Nil	Nil	Nil	Nil	Nil	Nil	Nil	Nil	Nil	Nil
Common Equity	31,097	40,104	48,115	74,825	61,020	52,180	47,289	41,368	27,458	15,647
Total Capital	31,097	40,104	48,115	74,825	62,751	52,578	48,125	42,753	28,438	16,627
Capital Expenditures	2,264	1,578	812	1,109	891	770	1,103	879	583	656
Cash Flow	15,505	13,502	13,109	9,354	11,432	8,913	9,257	10,156	8,767	5,486
Current Ratio	1.7	2.2	2.9	4.7	4.2	3.8	3.6	3.1	2.3	2.8
% Long Term Debt of Capitalization	Nil	Nil	Nil	Nil	Nil	Nil	Nil	Nil	Nil	Nil
% Net Income of Revenue	27.5	28.5	30.8	22.2	31.0	27.6	30.5	41.0	39.4	31.0
% Return on Assets	21.2	17.9	14.8	9.4	13.6	12.4	13.9	20.8	26.2	24.4
% Return on Equity	39.5	28.6	19.9	11.7	17.7	15.7	17.4	27.3	36.0	35.1

Data as orig reptd.; bef. results of disc opers/spec. items. Per share data adj. for stk. divs.; EPS diluted. E-Estimated. NA-Not Available. NM-Not Meaningful. NR-Not Ranked. UR-Under Review.

Office: 1 Microsoft Way, Redmond, WA 98052-8300.
Telephone: 425-882-8080.
Email: msft@microsoft.com
Website: http://www.microsoft.com

Chrmn: W.H. Gates
CEO: S.A. Ballmer
COO: K. Turner
SVP, Secy & General Counsel: B. Smith

CFO: C. Liddell
Investor Contact: F. Brod (800-285-7772)
Board Members: S. A. Ballmer, J. I. Cash, Jr., D. Dublon, W. H. Gates III, R. V. Gilmartin, r. Hastings, D. F. Marquardt, C. H. Noski, H. Panke, J. A. Shirley

Founded: 1975
Domicile: Washington
Employees: 79,000

Millipore Corp

STANDARD &POOR'S

S&P Recommendation **HOLD** ★★★☆☆	Price $80.06 (as of Nov 26, 2007)	12-Mo. Target Price $84.00	Investment Style Large-Cap Growth

GICS Sector Health Care
Sub-Industry Life Sciences Tools & Services

Summary This company provides technologies, tools and services for the discovery, development and production of new therapeutic drugs.

Key Stock Statistics (Source S&P, Vickers, company reports)

52-Wk Range	$83.20– 65.29	S&P Oper. EPS 2007**E**	3.40	Market Capitalization(B)	$4.319	Beta	0.89
Trailing 12-Month EPS	$2.00	S&P Oper. EPS 2008**E**	3.97	Yield (%)	Nil	S&P 3-Yr. Proj. EPS CAGR(%)	16.00
Trailing 12-Month P/E	40.0	P/E on S&P Oper. EPS 2007**E**	23.5	Dividend Rate/Share	Nil	S&P Credit Rating	BB+
$10K Invested 5 Yrs Ago	$22,022	Common Shares Outstg. (M)	54.0	Institutional Ownership (%)	NM		

Price Performance

Legend: 30-Week Mov. Avg. · · · 10-Week Mov. Avg. - - GAAP Earnings vs. Previous Year   Volume Above Avg. STARS
12-Mo. Target Price — Relative Strength — ▲ Up ▼ Down ▶ No Change   Below Avg.

Options: ASE, CBOE, P, Ph

Analysis prepared by **Jeffrey Loo, CFA** on November 26, 2007, when the stock traded at **$ 80.06**.

Highlights

➤ We see 2007 sales growth of 23%, to $1.54 billion, including a 10% contribution from Serologicals, acquired in July 2006. In 2008, we project an 8% rise in sales to $1.67 billion, reflecting solid 10% growth in Biosciences on strong demand from drug discovery, but we expect Bioprocess growth to moderate to 7% as we see continued sluggish demand from large biotech firms in North America, particularly in the 2008 first half. We foresee 2007 and 2008 operating margins improving 170 and 40 basis points, respectively, on product mix, including higher-margin Serologicals products, and on operating leverage, partially offset by greater R&D costs.

➤ The Serologicals integration is complete and we believe the combination will provide attractive product line expansion and geographic revenue synergies as the companies have minimal global sales overlap, particularly in Asia, where MIL has a strong presence. However, we have some concerns over sales force disruptions as MIL redeploys its sales force structure.

➤ Our 2007 and 2008 EPS estimates are $3.40 and $3.97 and take into account significantly higher interest expense from financing the Serologicals acquisition.

Investment Rationale/Risk

➤ We remain encouraged by MIL's product line expansion through internal and external growth efforts. We think these efforts will drive solid sales growth and we believe the product portfolio expansion better positions MIL for uncertainties in various units. But we continue to see sales force integration resulting in some disruption. We also believe some products acquired from Serologicals are not performing as well as originally expected. In addition, MIL's net debt obligation of about $1.26 billion as of September 30, 2007, primarily from financing the Serologicals deal, will likely hurt net margins by about 310 basis points. Nevertheless, we believe the longer-term benefits from an expanding life sciences product line and geographic sales penetration outweigh the potential negatives.

➤ Risks to our recommendation and target price include a deterioration in the pharmaceutical and biotech R&D spending environment.

➤ Our 12-month target price of $84 is based on an in line with peers P/E to growth (PEG) ratio of 1.3X, with a three-year EPS growth rate of 16%, applied to our 2008 EPS estimate.

Qualitative Risk Assessment

LOW	MEDIUM	HIGH

Our risk assessment reflects MIL's broad product line and geographic reach, offset by the highly competitive marketplace and its proactive acquisition strategy, which we believe increases its risk profile.

Quantitative Evaluations

S&P Quality Ranking   **B**

D	C	B-	B	B+	A-	A	A+

Relative Strength Rank   **STRONG**

90

LOWEST = 1   HIGHEST = 99

Revenue/Earnings Data

Revenue (Million $)

	1Q	2Q	3Q	4Q	Year
2007	372.0	383.2	371.2	--	--
2006	268.4	273.8	330.1	383.1	1,255
2005	250.2	245.0	293.6	256.3	991.0
2004	222.5	224.7	210.7	225.4	883.3
2003	187.5	196.4	200.1	215.8	799.6
2002	166.6	176.1	175.6	185.9	704.3

Earnings Per Share ($)

2007	0.49	0.52	0.66	E1.03	E3.40
2006	0.64	0.54	0.27	0.34	1.79
2005	0.64	0.47	0.44	0.02	1.55
2004	0.55	0.57	0.50	0.49	2.10
2003	0.44	0.46	0.50	0.66	2.06
2002	0.40	0.46	0.39	0.41	1.67

Fiscal year ended Dec. 31. Next earnings report expected: Early February. EPS Estimates based on S&P Operating Earnings; historical GAAP earnings are as reported.

Dividend Data

No cash dividends have been paid since January 2002.

The McGraw-Hill Companies

Millipore Corp

Business Summary November 26, 2007

COMPANY OVERVIEW. Millipore provides tools and services for the development and production of therapeutic drugs. MIL focuses on solutions for drug manufacturing and other production processes, and on research and development tools for the life science industry. MIL's offerings include consumable products, capital equipment, and services sold mainly to pharmaceutical, biotechnology and life science research companies. In 2006, consumables and services accounted for about 83% of sales, with the remaining 17% from hardware. The company sells more than 5,000 products, including process filtration and chromatography products, hardware components and systems used to manufacture and process biopharmaceuticals, process monitoring tools to test for contamination, laboratory sample preparation products, and laboratory water products used to create ultra pure water for laboratory analysis and clinical testing.

The company concentrates its in-house R&D on the development of new products and has augmented its product offerings and research capabilities through acquisitions and alliances, including the $1.5 billion acquisition of Serologicals in July 2006. MIL has said that its operations could be affected by an increasing number of biologic therapeutics being developed and approved over time, since its products are used in research laboratories, drug development programs, and drug manufacturing. According to the company, the drug industry is developing about 2,200 biologic compounds, including about 565 antibodies.

MIL sells its products through a global sales network. In the U.S., it mainly uses a direct sales force and Web site sales. Outside the U.S., MIL has subsidiaries and branches in more than 30 countries, and also employs independent distributors. Revenues by geographic region were as follows: the Americas 45% in 2006 (42% in 2005), Europe 39% (40%), and Asia Pacific (the majority derived from Japan) 16% (18%). Competitors include Amersham Biosciences, Apogent Technologies (now part of Thermo Fisher Scientific), Pall Corp., Qiagen, and United States Filter Corp.

Company Financials Fiscal Year Ended Dec. 31

Per Share Data ($)	2006	2005	2004	2003	2002	2001	2000	1999	1998	1997
Tangible Book Value	NM	12.74	12.24	8.72	5.16	7.60	5.25	2.36	1.37	1.64
Cash Flow	3.16	2.53	2.99	2.88	2.39	1.96	3.51	2.40	1.23	0.04
Earnings	1.79	1.55	2.10	2.06	1.67	1.32	2.53	1.42	0.22	-0.89
S&P Core Earnings	1.81	1.43	1.27	1.67	1.41	1.08	NA	NA	NA	NA
Dividends	Nil	Nil	Nil	Nil	Nil	0.44	0.44	0.44	0.42	0.49
Payout Ratio	Nil	Nil	Nil	Nil	Nil	33%	17%	31%	191%	NM
Prices:High	76.95	67.95	57.20	49.37	60.95	66.85	77.38	42.13	38.44	52.00
Prices:Low	59.58	42.01	42.13	29.90	27.25	42.65	36.25	23.44	17.25	33.50
P/E Ratio:High	43	44	27	24	36	51	31	30	NM	NM
P/E Ratio:Low	33	27	20	15	16	32	14	17	NM	NM

Income Statement Analysis (Million $)										
Revenue	1,255	991	883	800	704	657	954	771	699	759
Operating Income	219	195	182	166	160	150	216	149	89.2	41.8
Depreciation	74.4	50.7	44.5	40.5	35.0	30.7	46.1	44.3	44.4	40.7
Interest Expense	45.3	6.71	9.45	16.5	19.0	25.3	26.9	30.2	29.5	30.5
Pretax Income	120	138	130	112	104	78.4	154	82.4	8.54	-18.1
Effective Tax Rate	17.8%	41.7%	19.1%	10.1%	22.0%	19.0%	22.4%	21.9%	NA	NM
Net Income	97.0	80.2	106	101	80.8	63.5	119	64.3	9.86	-38.8
S&P Core Earnings	97.9	74.6	64.0	82.0	68.5	51.8	NA	NA	NA	NA

Balance Sheet & Other Financial Data (Million $)										
Cash	77.5	651	152	147	101	62.5	58.4	51.1	36.0	2.24
Current Assets	709	1,067	541	516	390	312	465	359	305	352
Total Assets	2,771	1,647	1,014	951	786	916	875	793	762	766
Current Liabilities	402	243	163	222	134	134	235	270	299	305
Long Term Debt	1,316	552	147	216	334	320	300	313	299	287
Common Equity	948	792	639	461	288	394	305	177	137	149
Total Capital	2,286	1,350	793	677	622	759	605	490	436	436
Capital Expenditures	110	86.4	63.7	71.9	79.3	72.3	52.2	31.3	59.8	41.1
Cash Flow	171	131	150	141	116	94.2	165	109	54.3	1.88
Current Ratio	1.8	4.4	3.3	2.3	2.9	2.3	2.0	1.3	1.0	1.2
% Long Term Debt of Capitalization	57.6	40.9	18.5	31.9	53.7	42.1	49.6	63.9	68.6	65.8
% Net Income of Revenue	7.7	8.1	12.0	12.6	11.5	9.7	12.5	8.3	1.4	NM
% Return on Assets	4.4	6.0	10.7	11.5	9.3	7.3	14.3	8.3	1.3	NM
% Return on Equity	11.1	11.2	19.1	26.9	23.7	18.2	49.4	41.4	6.9	NM

Data as orig reptd.; bef. results of disc opers/spec. items. Per share data adj. for stk. divs.; EPS diluted. E-Estimated. NA-Not Available. NM-Not Meaningful. NR-Not Ranked. UR-Under Review.

Office: 290 Concord Road, Billerica, MA 01821.
Telephone: 978-715-4321 .
Website: http://www.millipore.com
Chrmn, Pres & CEO: M.D. Madaus

Investor Contact: K.B. Allen (978-715-4321)
VP & CFO: K.B. Allen
VP, Secy & General Counsel: J. Rudin
Treas: G. Helliwell

Board Members: D. Bellus, R. C. Bishop, R. A. Classon, M. A. Hendricks, M. Hoffman, M. D. Madaus, J. F. Reno, E. M. Scolnick, K. E. Welke

Founded: 1954
Domicile: Massachusetts
Employees: 6,100

Molex Inc

STANDARD
&POOR'S

S&P Recommendation HOLD ★ ★ ★ ☆ ☆	**Price** $27.26 (as of Nov 23, 2007)	**12-Mo. Target Price** $30.00	**Investment Style** Large-Cap Growth

GICS Sector Information Technology
Sub-Industry Electronic Manufacturing Services

Summary This company makes electrical and electronic devices primarily for OEMs in the computer, telecommunications, home appliance and home entertainment industries.

Key Stock Statistics (Source S&P, Vickers, company reports)

52-Wk Range	$33.63–23.50	S&P Oper. EPS 2008E	1.40	Market Capitalization(B)	$2.711	Beta	1.56
Trailing 12-Month EPS	$1.18	S&P Oper. EPS 2009E	1.85	Yield (%)	1.65	S&P 3-Yr. Proj. EPS CAGR(%)	12.00
Trailing 12-Month P/E	23.1	P/E on S&P Oper. EPS 2008E	19.5	Dividend Rate/Share	$0.45	S&P Credit Rating	NA
$10K Invested 5 Yrs Ago	$10,019	Common Shares Outstg. (M)	184.1	Institutional Ownership (%)	58		

Price Performance

30-Week Mov. Avg. ··· 10-Week Mov. Avg. ― **GAAP Earnings vs. Previous Year** **Volume** Above Avg. STARS
12-Mo. Target Price ― Relative Strength ― ▲ Up ▼ Down ▶ No Change   Below Avg. ★

Options: CBOE, P, Ph

Analysis prepared by **Stewart Scharf** on October 22, 2007, when the stock traded at **$ 28.12**.

Highlights

➤ We project flat- to low-single digit organic revenue growth for FY 08 (Jun.), as growth in automotive, industrial, military, and medical electronics is offset by lower consumer, telecom and data sales. However, we expect these segments to rebound sequentially during the year, and we see demand for entry level phones with lower connector content picking up in developing global regions.

➤ We look for FY 08 gross margins to improve to near 32%, from 31% in FY 07, as new products, price hikes, gold hedges and increased bookings offset price erosion and higher raw material costs. We expect adjusted EBITDA margins to widen from 17.3% at June 30, based on restructuring cost savings of at least $20 million in FY 08; we project annualized savings of about $90 million when the plan is fully implemented by the end of FY 09.

➤ We estimate an effective tax rate of 30% in FY 08, and operating EPS of $1.40 (before a $0.15 restructuring charge); we forecast EPS of $1.85 for FY 09, before a charge of about $0.30.

Investment Rationale/Risk

➤ We base our hold recommendation on a recent sequential pickup in bookings for consumer, data and mobile products, potential cost benefits from a restructuring plan, and valuation metrics.

➤ Risks to our recommendation and target price include a further significant rise in copper, gold and plastics prices; a stronger dollar against the yen and the euro; and a sharp global economic downturn. Corporate governance practices are also a concern to us as MOLX has two classes of stock, and the board consists mostly of insiders. In addition, we caution that MOLX may restate financials related to misdated stock option grants.

➤ Based on our relative and historical valuation metrics, our 12-month target price is $30. We arrive at this calculation by applying a P/E of 21.5X to our FY 08 EPS estimate, blending the company's five-year average historical forward P/E of 26X with our projected P/E (as adjusted for the June fiscal year end) of near 16X for the S&P 500 and our sub-industry group's 15X multiple.

Qualitative Risk Assessment

LOW	MEDIUM	HIGH

Our risk assessment reflects the cyclicality in MOLX's global markets, price and product competition, volatile raw material costs, and weaker foreign currency exchange rates. However, we view the company's balance sheet as strong, as Molex is virtually debt free.

Quantitative Evaluations

S&P Quality Ranking B+

D	C	B-	B	B+	A-	A	A+

Relative Strength Rank STRONG

74

LOWEST = 1   HIGHEST = 99

Revenue/Earnings Data

Revenue (Million $)

	1Q	2Q	3Q	4Q	Year
2008	792.6	--	--	--	--
2007	829.6	837.5	807.0	791.9	3,266
2006	659.8	697.4	720.3	783.8	2,861
2005	640.2	651.8	612.8	643.8	2,549
2004	496.8	549.0	569.2	631.8	2,247
2003	469.3	454.6	443.2	476.1	1,843

Earnings Per Share ($)

2008	0.29	E0.33	E0.40	E0.37	E1.40
2007	0.41	0.36	0.35	0.18	1.30
2006	0.25	0.31	0.33	0.38	1.26
2005	0.29	0.27	0.24	0.03	0.81
2004	0.17	0.21	0.24	0.30	0.92
2003	0.15	0.15	0.13	0.01	0.44

Fiscal year ended Jun. 30. Next earnings report expected: Mid January. EPS Estimates based on S&P Operating Earnings; historical GAAP earnings are as reported.

Dividend Data (Dates: mm/dd Payment Date: mm/dd/yy)

Amount ($)	Date Decl.	Ex-Div. Date	Stk. of Record	Payment Date
0.075	04/26	12/27	12/29	01/25/07
0.075	03/16	03/28	03/30	04/25/07
0.075	04/26	06/27	06/29	07/25/07
0.113	08/01	09/26	09/30	10/25/07

Dividends have been paid since 1976. Source: Company reports.

Please read the Required Disclosures and Analyst Certification on the last page of this report.

The McGraw·Hill Companies

Molex Inc

STANDARD &POOR'S

Business Summary October 22, 2007

CORPORATE OVERVIEW. Molex is the world's second largest connector maker, operating 54 plants in 18 countries, and offering more than 100,000 products.

MOLX's products include electrical and electronic devices such as terminals, cable assemblies, interconnection systems, fiber-optic interconnection systems, and mechanical and electronic switches. In FY 07 (Jun.), these products were sold to the following industries: data products (21%), telecommunications (26%), consumer products (18%), automotive (18%), industrial (15%), and other (2%).

MOLX sells primarily to original equipment manufacturers (OEMs), subcontractors and suppliers. Customers include Arrow, Cisco, Dell, Ford, General Motors, Hewlett Packard, IBM, Matsushita, Motorola and Nokia.

Revenues outside the U.S. accounted for 73% of the FY 07 total, with 51% generated in Asia (16% in the Far East North and 35% in the Far East South), 20% in Europe and 7% in other regions.

At September 30, 2007, order backlog was $353 million, up 6.3% sequentially, but down 17% from a year earlier. New orders in the September period were $812 million, up 4.6% from the June quarter but down 6% from a year earlier. The book-to-bill ratio of 1.02 times was positive for the first time in four quar-

ters. The company expects nearly 30% of sales in FY 08 to come from new products.

In FY 07, MOLX repurchased 1,117,500 Class A common shares. In the first quarter of FY 08, MOLX repurchased 1.94 million Class A common shares and 500,000 common shares for $61 million. About $140 million remains under the $200 million program.

In FY 07, MOLX recorded a restructuring charge of $0.16 a share and a tax benefit of $0.04.

In August 2006, MOLX and a special committee found that the dates of some stock option grants to officers and other employees differed from the dates approved. The company ordered 14 executives to return a total of $685,000 to compensate for backdated stock options over a 12-year period. In October 2006, the U.S. Justice Department subpoenaed MOLX, seeking documents related to the company's review of stock options. The company noted that it may restate financial statements to reflect adjustments, and estimated non-cash charges of $18 million (after taxes), including $3.5 million in FY 03.

Company Financials Fiscal Year Ended Jun. 30

Per Share Data ($)	2007	2006	2005	2004	2003	2002	2001	2000	1999	1998
Tangible Book Value	10.64	11.60	10.78	10.05	9.10	8.64	8.25	7.83	6.94	6.47
Cash Flow	2.58	2.41	2.02	2.10	1.62	1.53	2.13	2.11	1.77	1.67
Earnings	1.30	1.26	0.81	0.92	0.44	0.39	1.03	1.12	0.91	0.92
S&P Core Earnings	1.30	1.27	0.76	0.85	0.39	0.39	1.01	NA	NA	NA
Dividends	0.30	0.23	0.15	0.10	0.10	0.10	0.10	0.07	0.04	0.05
Payout Ratio	23%	18%	19%	11%	23%	26%	10%	6%	4%	5%
Prices:High	32.34	40.10	30.00	36.10	35.12	39.61	48.00	63.75	45.60	31.20
Prices:Low	23.50	25.63	23.75	27.07	19.98	19.43	25.76	34.19	20.40	18.40
P/E Ratio:High	25	32	37	39	80	NM	47	57	50	34
P/E Ratio:Low	18	20	29	29	45	50	25	31	22	20

Income Statement Analysis (Million $)										
Revenue	3,266	2,861	2,549	2,247	1,843	1,712	2,366	2,217	1,712	1,623
Operating Income	596	552	481	450	-120	324	498	512	395	413
Depreciation	238	215	231	228	229	224	218	196	169	149
Interest Expense	Nil	Nil	Nil	Nil	Nil	Nil	Nil	Nil	Nil	Nil
Pretax Income	338	329	217	240	110	93.2	291	324	230	275
Effective Tax Rate	28.8%	28.0%	28.8%	26.5%	22.5%	17.9%	30.0%	31.1%	22.7%	33.7%
Net Income	241	237	154	176	84.9	76.5	204	222	178	182
S&P Core Earnings	241	238	143	164	76.1	76.7	200	NA	NA	NA

Balance Sheet & Other Financial Data (Million $)										
Cash	461	486	498	339	350	313	208	241	183	205
Current Assets	1,591	1,548	1,374	1,169	962	915	892	1,023	881	868
Total Assets	3,316	2,973	2,728	2,572	2,335	2,254	2,214	2,247	1,902	1,640
Current Liabilities	531	595	470	428	356	360	374	475	342	333
Long Term Debt	128	8.81	9.98	14.0	16.9	17.8	25.5	21.6	20.1	5.60
Common Equity	2,523	2,281	2,168	2,066	1,897	1,828	1,766	1,706	1,501	1,262
Total Capital	2,651	2,290	2,180	2,081	1,914	1,846	1,793	1,734	1,526	1,274
Capital Expenditures	297	277	231	190	171	172	376	337	229	227
Cash Flow	479	452	385	404	314	300	422	419	347	331
Current Ratio	3.0	2.6	2.9	2.7	2.7	2.5	2.4	2.2	2.6	2.6
% Long Term Debt of Capitalization	4.8	0.4	0.5	0.7	0.9	1.0	1.4	1.2	1.3	0.4
% Net Income of Revenue	7.4	8.3	6.1	7.8	4.6	4.5	8.6	10.0	10.4	11.2
% Return on Assets	7.7	8.3	5.8	7.2	3.7	3.4	9.1	10.7	10.1	11.1
% Return on Equity	10.0	10.7	7.3	8.9	4.6	4.3	11.7	13.9	12.9	14.6

Data as orig reptd.; bef. results of disc opers/spec. items. Per share data adj. for stk. divs.; EPS diluted. E-Estimated. NA-Not Available. NM-Not Meaningful. NR-Not Ranked. UR-Under Review.

Office: 2222 Wellington Court, Lisle, IL 60532.
Telephone: 630-969-4550.
Website: http://www.molex.com
Co-Chrmn: F.A. Krehbiel

Co-Chrmn: J.H. Krehbiel
Pres & COO: L. McCarthy
Vice Chrmn & CEO: M.P. Slark
Investor Contact: D.D. Johnson (630-969-4550)

Board Members: M. J. Birck, M. Collins, E. D. Jannotta, F. L. Krehbiel, F. A. Krehbiel, J. H. Krehbiel, Jr., K. Kusaka, D. L. Landsittel, J. W. Laymon, D. G. Lubin, R. J. Potter, M. P. Slark

Founded: 1938
Domicile: Delaware
Employees: 33,200

Molson Coors Brewing Co

STANDARD &POOR'S

S&P Recommendation	BUY ★★★★☆	Price $50.34 (as of Nov 26, 2007)	12-Mo. Target Price $65.00	Investment Style Large-Cap Blend

GICS Sector Consumer Staples
Sub-Industry Brewers

Summary TAP, the fifth largest brewer in the world, was formed in early 2005 via the combination of Adolph Coors Co. and Molson, Inc.

Key Stock Statistics (Source S&P, Vickers, company reports)

52-Wk Range	$57.70–34.72	S&P Oper. EPS 2007**E**	2.63	Market Capitalization(B)	$8.728	Beta	1.17
Trailing 12-Month EPS	$2.37	S&P Oper. EPS 2008**E**	3.03	Yield (%)	1.27	S&P 3-Yr. Proj. EPS CAGR(%)	10.00
Trailing 12-Month P/E	21.2	P/E on S&P Oper. EPS 2007**E**	19.1	Dividend Rate/Share	$0.64	S&P Credit Rating	BBB
$10K Invested 5 Yrs Ago	$16,790	Common Shares Outstg. (M)	179.4	Institutional Ownership (%)	71		

Price Performance

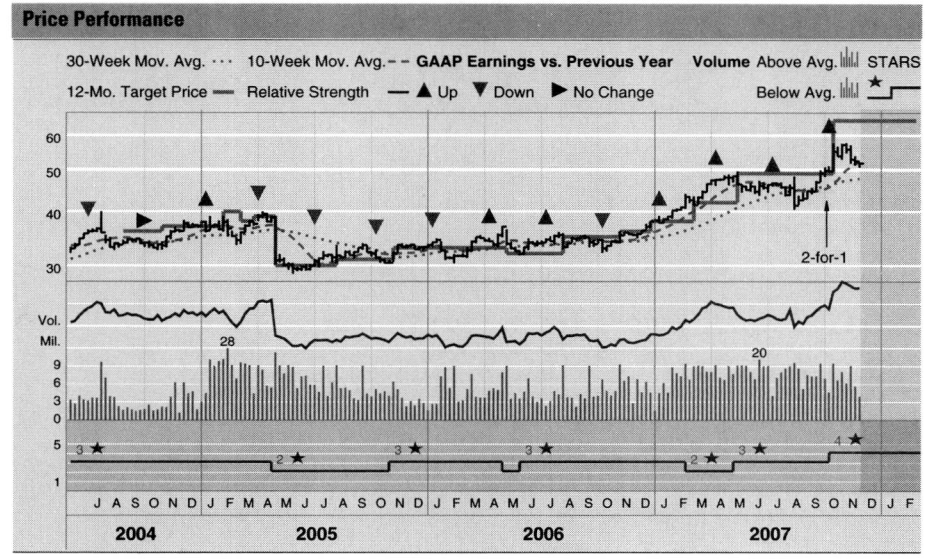

30-Week Mov. Avg. · · · 10-Week Mov. Avg. – – GAAP Earnings vs. Previous Year Volume Above Avg. STARS
12-Mo. Target Price — Relative Strength — ▲ Up ▼ Down ► No Change Below Avg. ★

Options: CBOE, P, Ph

Analysis prepared by **Esther Y. Kwon, CFA** on November 26, 2007, when the stock traded at **$ 51.79**.

Highlights

➤ TAP announced an agreement to combine its U.S. operations into a joint venture with SAB-Miller. By pooling the breweries, distribution resources, and brand marketing, the companies believe they can achieve $500 million of cost synergies annually. Pending customary approvals, the proposed deal will give TAP a 50% voting and 42% economic interest in the JV.

➤ Excluding the impact of the planned joint venture (JV), we see sales rising in the low single digits in 2008, mainly on volume increases. We expect continued growth for Coors Light in Canada, and double-digit growth for Blue Moon in the U.S.. However, we foresee continued pressures in the U.K. market hurting overall sales growth. We expect merger synergies, including efficiencies from supply chain improvements, increased productivity and volume growth, to offset cost pressures in packaging, grains, and energy.

➤ We expect interest expense to decline, and we project a lower effective tax rate. With an anticipated 2% rise in shares outstanding, we estimate 2007 operating EPS of $2.63, before special items, versus a split adjusted $2.13 in 2006. For 2008, we see EPS rising to $3.03.

Investment Rationale/Risk

➤ We expect continued market share gains in the U.S., on the strength of Coors Light, and Blue Moon. We think TAP's brands are capable of weathering the competition from imports and craft brews, and think volumes will remain strong even with price increases. We project income growth, aided by cost savings, ahead of peers' over the next few years.

➤ Risks to our opinion and target price include a weakening of Coors Light volumes in the U.S. and Canada. Commodity cost increases could pose additional risks. We see significant execution risk in the proposed joint venture.

➤ Our 12-month target price of $65 is supported by our discounted EV/EBITDA, DCF, and P/E analyses. Our DCF model derives an intrinsic value of $55, assuming a long-term revenue growth rate of 2.5% and a 9% weighted average cost of capital, and excluding the joint venture with SABMiller. Applying a forward P/E multiple of 20X, above peers, to our 2008 EPS estimate, we derive a value of $60. However, assuming the joint venture is approved, and TAP receives 42% of the economic benefit of $500 million cost savings, and applying a peer average 10.6X EBITDA, we see a value of $65.

Qualitative Risk Assessment

LOW	MEDIUM	HIGH

Our risk assessment reflects the stable revenue streams of the brewing industry, in which TAP is a major player. We have some corporate governance concerns with respect to TAP's multi-class stock structure and its more than 50% controlling family interest.

Quantitative Evaluations

S&P Quality Ranking A-

D	C	B-	B	B+	A-	A	A+

Relative Strength Rank STRONG

71

LOWEST = 1 HIGHEST = 99

Revenue/Earnings Data

Revenue (Million $)

	1Q	2Q	3Q	4Q	Year
2007	1,229	1,676	1,685	--	--
2006	1,154	1,583	1,577	1,531	5,845
2005	1,048	1,547	1,527	1,385	5,507
2004	923.5	1,151	1,104	1,127	4,306
2003	828.1	1,100	1,049	1,023	4,000
2002	745.8	1,048	1,002	981.1	3,776

Earnings Per Share ($)

2007	0.11	1.02	0.74	E0.60	E2.63
2006	-0.11	0.91	0.71	0.65	2.16
2005	-0.24	0.56	0.76	0.20	1.44
2004	0.07	0.95	0.84	0.73	2.60
2003	0.01	1.04	0.84	0.49	2.39
2002	0.38	0.92	0.64	0.28	2.21

Fiscal year ended Dec. 31. Next earnings report expected: Mid February. EPS Estimates based on S&P Operating Earnings; historical GAAP earnings are as reported.

Dividend Data (Dates: mm/dd Payment Date: mm/dd/yy)

Amount ($)	Date Decl.	Ex-Div. Date	Stk. of Record	Payment Date
0.320	05/18	05/29	05/31	06/15/07
0.320	08/02	08/29	08/31	09/14/07
2-for-1	--	10/04	09/19	10/03/07
0.160	11/16	11/28	11/30	12/14/07

Dividends have been paid since 1970. Source: Company reports.

Please read the Required Disclosures and Analyst Certification on the last page of this report.

The McGraw-Hill Companies

Molson Coors Brewing Co

STANDARD &POOR'S

Business Summary November 26, 2007

CORPORATE OVERVIEW. Molson Coors Brewing Company was formed in February 2005 by the combination of Adolph Coors Co. and Canadian brewer Molson, Inc. Total combined sales are estimated at about 61 million hectoliters, making it the fifth largest brewer in the world. The transaction resulted in each Molson Class B voting share being converted to shares with 0.126 voting rights and 0.234 non-voting rights of Molson Coors stock, and each Molson Class A converted to shares with a 0.360 non-voting share of Molson Coors.

Molson Inc. was the world's 14th largest brewer in 2004, pre-merger, with operations in Canada, Brazil and the United States. A global brewer with C$3.5 billion in gross annual sales, Molson traces its roots back to 1786, making it North America's oldest beer brand. Adolph Coors Co. was the third largest U.S. brewer, with a 10.3% share of the U.S. beer market in 2004, selling 32.7 million barrels of beer and other malt beverage products, up 3% from the level of 2003. The company was founded in 1873.

TAP's stable of well known U.S. brands includes Coors Light, Original Coors, and Coors Non-Alcoholic premium beers; above-premium brews such as George Killian's Irish Red and Blue Moon Belgian White Ale, and Aspen Edge; and lower-priced beers, including Extra Gold, Keystone Premium, Keystone

Light, and Keystone Ice. Coors produces Zima and Zima Citrus malt-based beverages. Brands sold primarily in Canada include Molson Canadian, Molson Dry, Molson Export, Creemore Springs, Rickard's Red Ale, Carling and Pilsner. Brands sold primarily in the U.K. include Carling, Coors Fine Light Beer, Worthington's Caffrey's, Reef, Screamers, and Stones. Approximately 56% of TAP's 2006 volume was sold in the United States segment, 19% in the Canada segment, and 25% in the Europe segment. In 2006, Coors Light accounted for approximately 45% of reported volume, Carling for 19%, and Keystone Light for approximately 8%.

CORPORATE STRATEGY. We look favorably on TAP's strategy to gain market share in each area by cross marketing its products. We are particularly pleased with the gains we see for Coors Light brand in Canada, where it now has a 10% market share, making it the largest selling light-beer, and second largest-selling beer brand overall in Canada.

Company Financials Fiscal Year Ended Dec. 31

Per Share Data ($)	2006	2005	2004	2003	2002	2001	2000	1999	1998	1997
Tangible Book Value	NM	NM	1.72	NM	NM	12.03	12.16	11.03	10.26	9.68
Cash Flow	4.68	3.89	6.13	5.71	5.36	3.28	3.19	2.88	2.45	2.62
Earnings	2.16	1.44	2.60	2.39	2.21	1.66	1.47	1.23	0.91	1.08
S&P Core Earnings	1.87	1.07	2.13	2.10	0.77	0.68	NA	NA	NA	NA
Dividends	0.64	0.64	0.41	0.41	0.41	0.40	0.36	0.32	0.30	0.28
Payout Ratio	31%	44%	16%	17%	19%	24%	25%	26%	33%	25%
Prices:High	38.50	40.00	40.06	32.41	35.08	40.59	41.16	32.91	28.38	20.63
Prices:Low	30.38	28.69	26.87	22.93	25.25	21.33	18.69	22.63	14.63	8.75
P/E Ratio:High	18	28	15	14	16	25	28	27	31	19
P/E Ratio:Low	15	20	10	10	11	13	13	18	16	8

Income Statement Analysis (Million $)										
Revenue	5,845	5,507	4,306	4,000	3,776	2,429	2,414	2,057	1,900	1,822
Operating Income	1,097	960	609	551	535	296	295	271	239	233
Depreciation	438	393	268	244	230	121	129	124	116	117
Interest Expense	143	131	72.4	81.2	70.9	2.01	6.41	4.36	9.80	13.6
Pretax Income	472	295	308	254	257	198	170	151	111	147
Effective Tax Rate	17.5%	17.0%	30.9%	31.2%	37.0%	37.9%	35.3%	38.7%	39.0%	44.0%
Net Income	374	230	197	175	162	123	110	92.3	67.8	82.3
S&P Core Earnings	324	172	161	154	56.1	50.7	NA	NA	NA	NA

Balance Sheet & Other Financial Data (Million $)										
Cash	182	39.4	123	19.4	59.2	310	120	164	256	169
Current Assets	1,458	1,468	1,268	1,079	1,054	607	498	613	549	517
Total Assets	11,603	11,799	4,658	4,486	4,297	1,740	1,629	1,546	1,461	1,412
Current Liabilities	1,800	2,237	1,177	1,134	1,148	518	379	393	384	359
Long Term Debt	2,130	2,137	894	1,160	1,383	20.0	105	105	105	145
Common Equity	5,817	5,325	1,601	1,267	982	951	932	842	775	737
Total Capital	8,601	8,151	2,682	2,623	2,522	1,033	1,127	1,025	946	958
Capital Expenditures	446	406	212	240	240	245	154	134	105	60.3
Cash Flow	812	623	465	418	392	244	239	216	184	199
Current Ratio	0.8	0.7	1.1	1.0	0.9	1.2	1.3	1.6	1.4	1.4
% Long Term Debt of Capitalization	24.8	26.2	33.3	44.2	54.9	1.9	9.3	10.2	11.1	15.1
% Net Income of Revenue	6.4	4.2	4.6	4.4	4.3	5.1	4.5	4.5	3.6	4.5
% Return on Assets	3.2	2.8	4.3	4.0	5.4	7.3	6.9	6.1	4.7	5.9
% Return on Equity	6.7	6.7	13.7	15.5	16.7	13.1	12.4	11.4	9.0	11.3

Data as orig reptd.; bef. results of disc opers/spec. items. Per share data adj. for stk. divs.; EPS diluted. E-Estimated. NA-Not Available. NM-Not Meaningful. NR-Not Ranked. UR-Under Review.

Office: 1225 17th St, Denver, CO 80202-5534.
Telephone: 303-279-6565.
Website: http://www.molsoncoors.com
Chrmn: E.H. Molson

Pres & CEO: W.L. Kiely III
Vice Chrmn: P.H. Coors
SVP, Secy & Chief Lgl Officer: S. Walker
VP & Chief Acctg Officer: M.L. Miller

Investor Contact: D. Dunnewald (303-279-6565)
Board Members: F. Bellini, R. G. Brewer, J. E. Cleghorn, P. H. Coors, M. E. Coors Osborn, C. M. Herington, F. W. Hobbs, W. L. Kiely III, G. S. Matthews, A. T. Molson, E. H. Molson, D. P. O'Brien, P. H. Patsley, H. S. Riley

Founded: 1873
Domicile: Delaware
Employees: 9,550

Monsanto Co

STANDARD
&POOR'S

S&P Recommendation HOLD ★★★☆☆

Price $90.41 (as of Nov 23, 2007)	**12-Mo. Target Price** $92.00	**Investment Style** Large-Cap Blend

GICS Sector Materials
Sub-Industry Fertilizers & Agricultural Chemicals

Summary This company is a global provider of agricultural products and integrated solutions for farmers.

Key Stock Statistics (Source S&P, Vickers, company reports)

52-Wk Range	$99.98– 46.75	S&P Oper. EPS 2008**E**	2.40	Market Capitalization(B)	$49.393	Beta	1.12
Trailing 12-Month EPS	$1.79	S&P Oper. EPS 2009**E**	2.71	Yield (%)	0.77	S&P 3-Yr. Proj. EPS CAGR(%)	24.00
Trailing 12-Month P/E	50.5	P/E on S&P Oper. EPS 2008**E**	37.7	Dividend Rate/Share	$0.70	S&P Credit Rating	A
$10K Invested 5 Yrs Ago	$122,759	Common Shares Outstg. (M)	546.3	Institutional Ownership (%)	86		

Price Performance

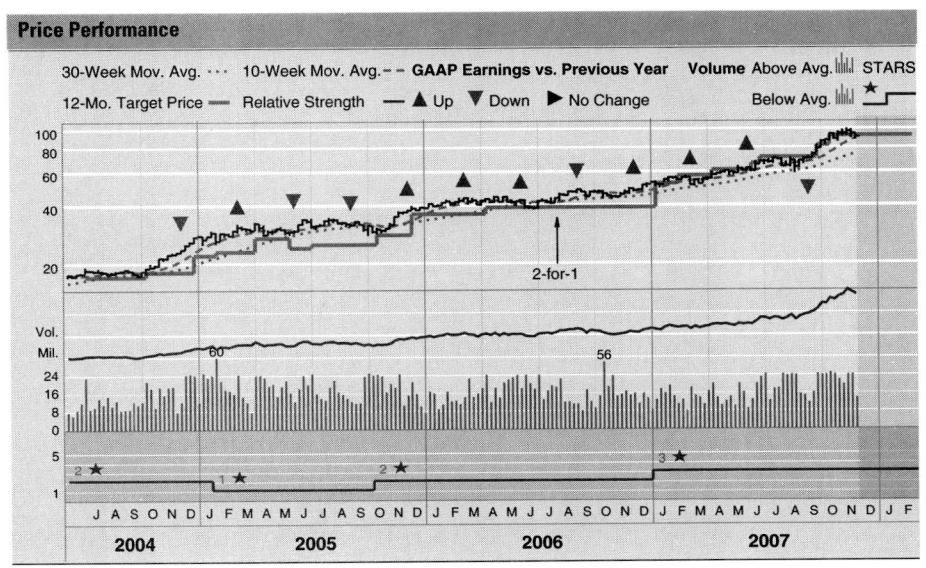

30-Week Mov. Avg. ··· 10-Week Mov. Avg.--- **GAAP Earnings vs. Previous Year** Volume Above Avg. STARS
12-Mo. Target Price — Relative Strength — ▲ Up ▼ Down ▶ No Change Below Avg.

2-for-1

2004 2005 2006 2007

Options: ASE, CBOE, P

Analysis prepared by **Kevin Kirkeby** on October 15, 2007, when the stock traded at **$ 91.62.**

Highlights

➤ Following a 16% proforma revenue increase in FY 07 (Aug.), we see revenue growth slowing to 10% in FY 08. We look for U.S. farmers to increase their usage of double and triple stacked seeds due to the yield advantage, but we believe overall corn acreage, already near record levels, is likely to be unchanged. Revenue resulting from the Delta & Pine Land Co. (DLP) acquisition completed in June 2007 is likely to be partly offset by the Stoneville and NexGen divestitures.

➤ We look for widening margins in FY 08 on growing sales of MON's higher value-added seeds and traits. However, we see margins in the chemical segments pressured by rising competition and production costs in FY 08. We believe these trends, combined with modestly lower selling and administrative expenses, will support a widening in the operating margin, after depreciation, to over 21%.

➤ We calculate that MON generated EPS in FY 07 of $1.94, after adjusting for the various acquisitions and divestitures. For FY 08, we project 24% growth in EPS, to $2.40. We see an effective tax rate of 30%.

Investment Rationale/Risk

➤ We think MON is likely to achieve above-average earnings growth over the coming decade due to the introduction of next-generation seeds, the development of its smaller product segments, such as cotton, vegetables and soy, as well as increases in crop penetration outside the United States. However, we believe this growth is already factored into the share price, as the stock is trading at a valuation premium to both the S&P 500 and peers.

➤ Risks to our recommendation and target price include unfavorable weather affecting planting and fertilizer usage, the possibility of lower than anticipated margin and market share growth, greater than expected legal and regulatory exposures, and exchange rate fluctuations.

➤ Our DCF model, which assumes a 9.3% weighted average cost of capital, annual free cash flow growth of 17% for 10 years, and 4% terminal growth, calculates intrinsic value of $95. Our relative valuation model targets a four-quarter forward enterprise value (EV)/EBITDA multiple of 19X, and produces a value of $90. Blending these two metrics results in our 12-month target price of $92.

Qualitative Risk Assessment

LOW	MEDIUM	HIGH

Our risk assessment for MON reflects its exposure to global agricultural markets and currencies, adverse weather, unfavorable legal and regulatory developments, and risks relating to the enforcement of intellectual property rights. This is offset by relatively low exposure to economic cycles and our view of consistent cash flow generation.

Quantitative Evaluations

S&P Quality Ranking NR

D	C	B-	B	B+	A-	A	A+

Relative Strength Rank STRONG
90
LOWEST = 1 HIGHEST = 99

Revenue/Earnings Data

Revenue (Million $)

	1Q	2Q	3Q	4Q	Year
2007	1,539	2,609	2,842	1,573	8,563
2006	1,405	2,200	2,348	1,391	7,344
2005	1,072	1,908	2,040	1,274	6,294
2004	1,028	1,492	1,679	1,258	5,457
2003	--	--	--	--	3,373
2002	1,221	1,553	679.0	1,220	4,673

Earnings Per Share ($)

	1Q	2Q	3Q	4Q	Year
2007	0.17	0.99	1.02	-0.52	1.66
2006	0.11	0.80	0.61	-0.25	1.27
2005	-0.24	0.68	0.08	-0.24	0.29
2004	-0.15	0.29	0.43	-0.07	0.51
2003	--	--	--	--	-0.02
2002	0.17	0.28	-0.32	0.12	0.25

Fiscal year ended Aug. 31. Next earnings report expected: Early January. EPS Estimates based on S&P Operating Earnings; historical GAAP earnings are as reported.

Dividend Data (Dates: mm/dd Payment Date: mm/dd/yy)

Amount ($)	Date Decl.	Ex-Div. Date	Stk. of Record	Payment Date
0.125	12/12	01/03	01/05	01/26/07
0.125	01/17	04/03	04/06	04/27/07
0.125	06/15	07/03	07/06	07/27/07
0.175	08/07	10/03	10/05	10/26/07

Dividends have been paid since 2001. Source: Company reports.

Monsanto Co

STANDARD &POOR'S

Business Summary October 15, 2007

CORPORATE OVERVIEW. MON produces leading seed brands and develops biotechnology traits that assist farmers in controlling insects and weeds, and provides other seed companies with genetic material and biotech traits. MON's Roundup herbicides are used for agricultural, industrial and residential weed control, and are sold in more than 80 countries.

MARKET PROFILE. MON operates in two segments: agricultural productivity, and seeds and genomics. Agricultural productivity (42% of sales and 30% of gross profits in FY 07 (Aug.) consists of MON's crop protection products (Roundup herbicide and other glyphosate products), its animal agriculture, and the Roundup lawn and garden products. In the year ended August 31, 2007, Roundup and other glyphosate-based herbicides accounted for 30% of total sales. Patent protection for the active ingredient in Roundup herbicides expired in the U.S. in 2000. Since then, MON has repositioned itself as one of the lowest cost producers in an effort to mitigate declining herbicide pricing and margins. MON's animal agriculture business focuses on improving animal productivity, producing the largest selling U.S. brand of recombinant bovine

growth hormone, which increases milk production in dairy cows. We believe this business is in its maturity phase, moving toward a decline.

Seeds and genomics (58% of sales and 70% of gross profits) consists of the global seeds and related traits businesses, and technology platforms based on plant genomics, which increases the speed and power of genetic research. MON's seeds and genomics segment focuses on corn, soybeans and other oilseeds, cotton, and wheat. Given the loss of patent protection for Roundup, we believe MON has focused on capturing value and profitability in its patent-protected seeds and traits business, and expanded its product line through its acquisition of Seminis in 2005. Given this trend, we think that the growth and margin outlook for MON's seeds and genomics segment is superior to that of its agricultural productivity segment.

Company Financials Fiscal Year Ended Aug. 31

Per Share Data ($)	2007	2006	2005	2004	2003	2002	2001	2000	1999	1998
Tangible Book Value	NA	6.95	5.99	7.71	7.26	7.24	7.84	7.24	NM	NA
Cash Flow	NA	2.25	1.21	1.37	0.56	1.12	1.61	1.40	1.59	NA
Earnings	1.66	1.27	0.29	0.51	-0.02	0.25	0.57	0.34	0.52	NA
S&P Core Earnings	1.72	1.36	0.67	0.68	0.61	0.01	0.52	NA	NA	NA
Dividends	0.48	0.39	0.33	0.27	0.25	0.24	0.23	Nil	NA	NA
Payout Ratio	29%	30%	113%	53%	NM	98%	40%	Nil	NA	NA
Prices:High	99.98	53.49	39.93	28.22	14.45	17.00	19.40	13.69	NA	NA
Prices:Low	49.10	37.91	25.00	14.04	6.78	6.60	13.44	9.88	NA	NA
P/E Ratio:High	60	42	NM	55	NM	69	34	40	NA	NA
P/E Ratio:Low	30	30	86	28	NM	27	24	29	NA	NA

Income Statement Analysis (Million $)

	2007	2006	2005	2004	2003	2002	2001	2000	1999	1998
Revenue	NA	7,344	6,294	5,457	3,373	4,673	5,462	5,493	5,248	NA
Operating Income	NA	1,694	1,503	1,254	768	882	1,335	1,216	1,179	NA
Depreciation	NA	519	488	452	302	460	554	546	547	NA
Interest Expense	NA	134	115	91.0	57.0	59.0	99.0	214	269	NA
Pretax Income	NA	1,055	261	402	-38.0	202	463	334	263	NA
Effective Tax Rate	NA	32.2%	39.8%	32.6%	NM	36.1%	35.9%	47.6%	43.0%	NA
Net Income	NA	698	157	271	-11.0	129	297	175	150	NA
S&P Core Earnings	951	745	363	362	317	5.45	277	NA	NA	NA

Balance Sheet & Other Financial Data (Million $)

	2007	2006	2005	2004	2003	2002	2001	2000	1999	1998
Cash	NA	1,460	525	1,037	511	428	307	131	26.0	NA
Current Assets	NA	5,461	4,644	4,931	4,962	4,424	4,797	4,973	4,027	NA
Total Assets	NA	11,728	10,579	9,164	9,461	8,890	11,429	11,726	11,101	NA
Current Liabilities	NA	2,279	2,159	1,894	1,944	1,810	2,377	2,757	1,704	NA
Long Term Debt	NA	1,639	1,458	1,075	1,258	851	893	962	4,278	NA
Common Equity	NA	6,680	5,613	5,258	5,156	5,180	7,483	7,341	4,645	NA
Total Capital	NA	8,319	7,071	6,333	6,414	6,031	8,376	8,303	8,923	NA
Capital Expenditures	NA	370	281	210	114	224	382	582	632	NA
Cash Flow	NA	1,217	645	723	291	589	851	721	697	NA
Current Ratio	NA	2.4	2.2	2.6	2.6	2.4	2.0	1.8	2.4	NA
% Long Term Debt of Capitalization	NA	19.7	20.6	17.0	19.6	14.1	10.7	11.6	47.9	NA
% Net Income of Revenue	NA	9.5	2.5	5.0	NM	2.8	5.4	3.2	2.9	NA
% Return on Assets	NA	6.3	1.6	2.9	NM	1.3	2.6	1.5	1.4	NA
% Return on Equity	NA	11.2	2.9	5.2	NM	2.0	4.0	2.9	3.4	NA

Data as orig reptd.; bef. results of disc opers/spec. items. Per share data adj. for stk. divs.; EPS diluted. E-Estimated. NA-Not Available. NM-Not Meaningful. NR-Not Ranked. UR-Under Review.

Office: 800 North Lindbergh Boulevard, St. Louis, MO 63167.
Telephone: 314-694-1000.
Email: info@monsanto.com
Website: http://www.monsanto.com

Chrmn, Pres & CEO: H. Grant
EVP & CFO: T.K. Crews
EVP & CTO: R.T. Fraley
SVP, Secy & General Counsel: D.F. Snively

VP & Treas: R.A. Paley
Investor Contact: S. Foster (314-694-8148)
Board Members: F. V. AtLee, III, J. Bachmann, H. Grant, A. H. Harper, G. S. King, S. R. Long, C. S. McMillan, W. U. Parfet, G. H. Poste, R. J. Stevens

Founded: 2000
Domicile: Delaware
Employees: 23,600

The McGraw·Hill Companies

Monster Worldwide Inc

S&P Recommendation	HOLD ★★★☆☆	Price $33.06 (as of Nov 23, 2007)	12-Mo. Target Price $43.00	Investment Style Large-Cap Blend

GICS Sector Industrials
Sub-Industry Human Resource & Employment Services

Summary Monster Worldwide operates a multinational online careers network. It also provides offerings to help consumers develop and direct their careers.

Key Stock Statistics (Source S&P, Vickers, company reports)

52-Wk Range	$54.79– 32.37	S&P Oper. EPS 2007 E	1.40	Market Capitalization(B)	$4.218	Beta	3.36
Trailing 12-Month EPS	$1.06	S&P Oper. EPS 2008 E	1.70	Yield (%)	Nil	S&P 3-Yr. Proj. EPS CAGR(%)	18.00
Trailing 12-Month P/E	31.2	P/E on S&P Oper. EPS 2007 E	23.6	Dividend Rate/Share	Nil	S&P Credit Rating	NA
$10K Invested 5 Yrs Ago	NA	Common Shares Outstg. (M)	132.4	Institutional Ownership (%)	95		

Price Performance

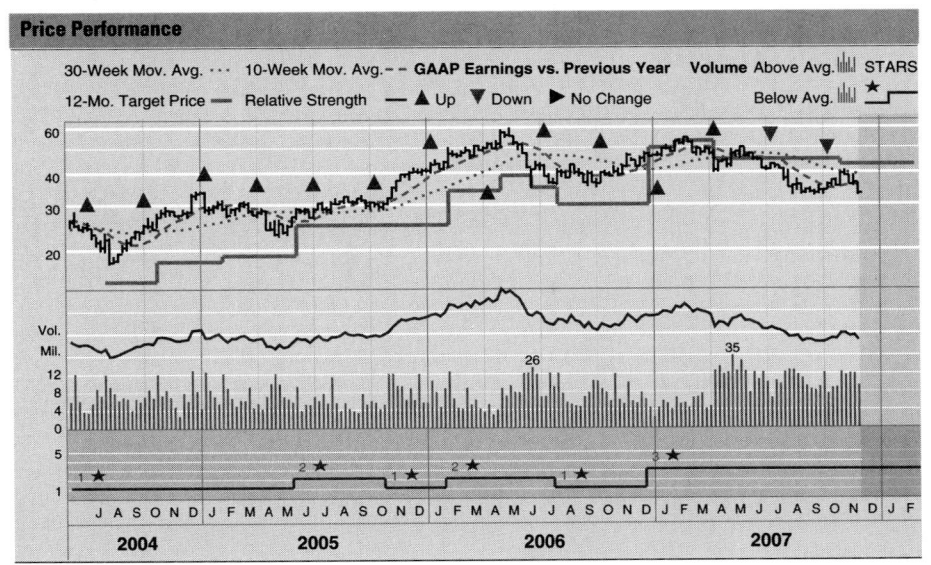

30-Week Mov. Avg. ···   10-Week Mov. Avg. - -   GAAP Earnings vs. Previous Year   Volume Above Avg. STARS
12-Mo. Target Price —   Relative Strength —   ▲ Up   ▼ Down   ▶ No Change   Below Avg.

Options: ASE, CBOE, P

Analysis prepared by **Michael W. Jaffe** on November 14, 2007, when the stock traded at **$ 38.37**.

Highlights

➤ We expect revenues to increase 17% in 2008. We see this projected improvement being driven mostly by ongoing strong growth in MNST's international business, and to a lesser extent, by more modest gains in its North American segment. We expect demand for MNST's services to be lifted by growth in global labor markets (despite some recent moderation in the U.S.), and we look for its foreign business to be aided by a strong marketing effort and ongoing geographic expansion.

➤ We see slightly wider net margins in 2008. We expect margins to benefit from the strong sales trends that we forecast in MNST's foreign business, as well as savings from its recently announced staff reduction program. We foresee these factors being partly offset by the negative impact of the only moderate growth that we forecast in MNST's North American Career operations.

➤ Our EPS forecast for 2007 excludes $0.06 of net charges recorded in the first nine months of the year, while our for 2008 estimate excludes further expected charges related to MNST's recently announced restructuring program.

Investment Rationale/Risk

➤ We think MNST's business is very cyclical, and that results in its North American business will stay unexceptional in coming periods. Yet, we also think favorable global trends will allow Monster to post ongoing solid profit gains for the next few years. MNST's recent discovery of substantial stock option backdating makes us question its corporate governance practices, but the executives involved are gone from the company. Based on these mixed factors and valuation, we would hold MNST shares.

➤ Risks to our recommendation and target price include weaker-than-projected global labor markets, a greater-than-expected impact from competitors, and a less successful expansion of MNST's business than we anticipate.

➤ The shares recently traded at 21.5X our 2008 EPS estimate, a large premium to MNST's peer group. We recognize several negative characteristics about Monster and its business, but think the stock's premium multiple is merited by a growth outlook in excess of most of its peers. Our 12-month target price is $43, or 25X our 2008 EPS estimate. Yet, given our high qualitative risk assessment, we do not think expected appreciation is enough to merit new positions.

Qualitative Risk Assessment

LOW	MEDIUM	HIGH

Our risk assessment reflects the cyclicality of the help wanted industry, as it strongly correlates with the economy. It also reflects that despite what we view as a solid earnings performance in 2006, MNST's return on invested capital in that year fell below its weighted average cost of capital. In addition, the company's foreign operations carry operating and exchange rate risks.

Quantitative Evaluations

S&P Quality Ranking   B-

D	C	B-	B	B+	A-	A	A+

Relative Strength Rank   MODERATE

34

LOWEST = 1   HIGHEST = 99

Revenue/Earnings Data

Revenue (Million $)

	1Q	2Q	3Q	4Q	Year
2007	329.0	331.2	337.1	--	--
2006	257.0	275.2	285.9	298.6	1,117
2005	232.1	239.0	249.3	266.6	986.9
2004	182.4	202.1	224.2	236.8	845.5
2003	168.5	166.7	173.7	170.8	679.6
2002	290.8	291.0	284.0	248.8	1,115

Earnings Per Share ($)

2007	0.30	0.21	0.25	E0.38	E1.40
2006	0.26	0.29	0.31	0.31	1.17
2005	0.19	0.21	0.25	0.28	0.92
2004	0.11	0.14	0.18	0.20	0.62
2003	-1.04	0.08	0.11	0.11	0.06
2002	0.06	-0.68	0.12	-0.46	-0.96

Fiscal year ended Dec. 31. Next earnings report expected: Early February. EPS Estimates based on S&P Operating Earnings; historical GAAP earnings are as reported.

Dividend Data

No cash dividends have been paid.

Monster Worldwide Inc

STANDARD & POOR'S

Business Summary November 14, 2007

CORPORATE OVERVIEW. Monster Worldwide is a leading online recruitment and career management services provider through its Monster.com Web site. MNST's clients range from Fortune 100 companies, to small and medium-sized enterprises and government agencies. During 2006, the company derived 59% of its revenues from its Monster Careers North America division, 27% from Monster Careers International, and 14% from its Advertising & Fees division. No client accounts for more than 5% of MNST's revenue base.

Among the most visited brands on the Internet, the Monster network is designed to connect companies with qualified job seekers, offering innovative technology and services that provide greater control over the recruiting process. At year-end 2006, the Monster.com global network was available in 36 countries.

Monster's job search, resume posting services and basic networking are free to the job seeker. It also offers premium career services to job seekers at a fee, including resume writing, resume priority listing, and premium network-

ing. MNST charges a fee to employers and human resources professionals who want to post jobs, search its resume database, and use its career site hosting and applicant tracking systems.

The company's Internet Advertising & Fees division provides consumers with content, services and offers, to help them manage the development and direction of their current and future careers. The majority of its services are free to users and are primarily available in North America at present, although MNST plans to expand its offerings across its global network. Revenues for the division are derived mostly from lead generation, display advertising, and products sold to consumers for a fee. To date, the Internet Advertising & Fees division's largest customer categories are employers, schools, financial services, and consumer products and services.

Company Financials Fiscal Year Ended Dec. 31

Per Share Data ($)	2006	2005	2004	2003	2002	2001	2000	1999	1998	1997
Tangible Book Value	3.65	1.47	0.27	0.18	2.02	2.61	5.16	0.18	NM	NM
Cash Flow	1.47	1.22	0.92	0.31	-0.46	1.28	1.11	0.35	0.43	0.48
Earnings	1.17	0.92	0.62	0.06	-0.96	0.61	0.53	-0.09	0.07	0.19
S&P Core Earnings	1.17	0.47	0.37	-0.08	-1.48	0.10	NA	NA	NA	NA
Dividends	Nil	Nil	Nil	Nil	Nil	Nil	Nil	Nil	Nil	Nil
Payout Ratio	Nil	Nil	Nil	Nil	Nil	Nil	Nil	Nil	Nil	Nil
Prices:High	59.99	42.03	34.25	29.65	48.13	68.73	94.69	80.50	21.31	14.38
Prices:Low	34.75	22.44	17.60	7.63	7.94	25.21	45.00	18.50	7.75	6.44
P/E Ratio:High	51	46	55	NM	NM	NM	NM	NM	NM	76
P/E Ratio:Low	30	24	28	NM	NM	NM	NM	NM	NM	34

Income Statement Analysis (Million $)

	2006	2005	2004	2003	2002	2001	2000	1999	1998	1997
Revenue	1,117	987	846	680	1,115	1,448	1,292	766	407	237
Operating Income	270	214	152	101	112	262	222	109	69.4	41.3
Depreciation	39.8	38.0	37.6	28.0	55.5	76.0	62.6	35.0	22.2	14.0
Interest Expense	Nil	Nil	Nil	Nil	4.90	10.6	9.49	17.0	13.7	11.0
Pretax Income	241	179	112	23.6	-130	125	114	-1.50	12.7	18.3
Effective Tax Rate	36.3%	35.8%	34.6%	69.0%	NM	46.1%	50.5%	NM	66.6%	46.7%
Net Income	154	115	73.1	7.32	-107	69.0	56.9	-7.40	4.25	9.62
S&P Core Earnings	154	59.2	44.0	-8.08	-165	11.4	NA	NA	NA	NA

Balance Sheet & Other Financial Data (Million $)

	2006	2005	2004	2003	2002	2001	2000	1999	1998	1997
Cash	58.7	320	198	142	192	341	572	57.0	28.9	5.94
Current Assets	1,124	773	704	567	809	1,006	1,248	557	343	288
Total Assets	1,970	1,679	1,544	1,122	1,631	2,206	1,992	945	608	495
Current Liabilities	826	697	731	640	799	930	853	565	360	282
Long Term Debt	0.42	15.7	34.0	2.09	3.93	9.13	28.0	71.0	118	116
Common Equity	1,110	920	756	468	813	1,229	1,058	281	123	96.9
Total Capital	1,143	981	789	470	817	1,238	1,086	352	241	213
Capital Expenditures	55.6	39.8	24.3	21.6	46.7	73.6	78.9	NA	21.7	18.3
Cash Flow	193	153	111	35.4	-51.0	145	119	27.6	26.4	23.5
Current Ratio	1.4	1.1	1.0	0.9	1.0	1.1	1.5	1.0	1.0	1.0
% Long Term Debt of Capitalization	0.0	1.6	4.3	0.4	0.5	0.7	2.6	NA	48.9	54.4
% Net Income of Revenue	13.8	11.7	8.6	1.1	NM	4.8	4.4	NM	1.0	4.1
% Return on Assets	8.4	7.1	5.5	0.5	NM	3.2	3.7	NM	0.8	2.3
% Return on Equity	15.0	13.7	11.9	1.1	NM	6.0	8.2	NM	3.9	14.8

Data as orig reptd.; bef. results of disc opers/spec. items. Per share data adj. for stk. divs.; EPS diluted. E-Estimated. NA-Not Available. NM-Not Meaningful. NR-Not Ranked. UR-Under Review.

Office: 622 Third Ave, New York, NY 10017-6707.
Telephone: 212-351-7000.
Email: corporate.communications@monsterworldwide.com
Website: http://www.monsterworldwide.com

Chrmn & CEO: S. Iannuzzi
Investor Contact: T.T. Yates
EVP & CFO: T.T. Yates
SVP & CIO: D. Dejanovic

Chief Acctg Officer & Cntlr: J. Trumbull
Board Members: R. J. Chrenc, G. R. Eisele, J. Gaulding, S. Iannuzzi, M. Kaufman, R. J. Kramer, P. R. Lochner, Jr., W. M. Pastore, D. A. Stein, J. Swann

Founded: 1967
Domicile: Delaware
Employees: 4,900

The McGraw-Hill Companies

STANDARD & POOR'S

Moody's Corp.

S&P Recommendation HOLD ★★★☆☆	Price	12-Mo. Target Price	Investment Style
	$37.24 (as of Nov 23, 2007)	$54.00	Large-Cap Growth

GICS Sector Financials
Sub-Industry Specialized Finance

Summary Moody's is a leading global credit rating, research, and risk analysis concern.

Key Stock Statistics (Source S&P, Vickers, company reports)

52-Wk Range	$76.09– 35.50	S&P Oper. EPS 2007**E**	2.42	Market Capitalization(B)	$9.939	Beta	1.02
Trailing 12-Month EPS	$3.05	S&P Oper. EPS 2008**E**	2.66	Yield (%)	0.86	S&P 3-Yr. Proj. EPS CAGR(%)	10.00
Trailing 12-Month P/E	12.2	P/E on S&P Oper. EPS 2007**E**	15.4	Dividend Rate/Share	$0.32	S&P Credit Rating	NA
$10K Invested 5 Yrs Ago	$17,523	Common Shares Outstg. (M)	266.9	Institutional Ownership (%)	95		

Price Performance

30-Week Mov. Avg. ··· 10-Week Mov. Avg. – – **GAAP Earnings vs. Previous Year** Volume Above Avg. STARS
12-Mo. Target Price — Relative Strength ▲ Up ▼ Down ▶ No Change Below Avg.

Options: ASE, CBOE, P, Ph

Analysis prepared by **James Peters, CFA** on October 29, 2007, when the stock traded at **$ 43.39**.

Highlights

➤ With a difficult U.S. credit environment and challenging year-over-year comparisons, we expect structured finance ratings revenues to substantially decline through the second quarter of 2008. We believe generally more favorable economic conditions outside the U.S. will result in continued overseas growth, and expect international results to be further buoyed by a weak U.S. dollar. Overall, we see revenues rising about 5.0% in 2008, following a 10% advance we project for 2007.

➤ We forecast an operating margin contraction to about 50.0%, down from our projection of 51.7% in 2007. MCO increased investments to support future growth in 2007 that we believe will eventually pay off. However, as these investments preceded a significantly tighter domestic credit environment, we expect the MCO's near term operating margin to fall.

➤ As part of the company's ongoing share buyback program, we expect MCO to continue to repurchase shares through 2008. On fewer shares, we see operating EPS rising to $2.66 in 2008, up from our forecast for $2.42 in 2007. EPS in 2007 excludes a one-time tax benefit of $0.19.

Investment Rationale/Risk

➤ We believe MCO is in a favorable position, with limited competition, high margins, and a risk-averse corporate environment that should lead to above average long-term growth. In addition, we expect growth to come from the need to rate new products and capital market development overseas. However, we expect slowing consumer spending and a tight U.S. credit market to reduce the near-term demand to rate securities.

➤ Risks to our recommendation and target price include significant decline in the volume of debt issued in domestic and global capital markets, regulatory changes that increase competition, and persistently high long-term interest rates.

➤ Our 12-month target price of $54 is derived from a blend of relative value and DCF analyses. Our DCF model yields an intrinsic value of $55, and includes assumptions of a 10.4% WACC and 4.0% terminal growth. We derive a $54 valuation by applying an 11.6X EV/EBITDA ratio to our 2008 EBITDA estimate of $1.2 billion. This is a discount to MCO's historical multiple that we believe is warranted by our outlook for operating margin contraction and slower revenue growth.

Qualitative Risk Assessment

LOW	**MEDIUM**	HIGH

Our risk assessment reflects Moody's significant market share in the high barrier to entry ratings industry, and what we consider the company's net positive balance sheet cash position, offset by ratings business sensitivity to higher interest rates, and the possibility of regulatory reform designed to increase competition.

Quantitative Evaluations

S&P Quality Ranking   B+

D	C	B-	B	**B+**	A-	A	A+

Relative Strength Rank   WEAK

17

LOWEST = 1   HIGHEST = 99

Revenue/Earnings Data

Revenue (Million $)

	1Q	2Q	3Q	4Q	Year
2007	583.0	646.1	525.0	--	--
2006	440.2	511.4	495.5	590.0	2,037
2005	390.5	446.8	421.1	473.2	1,732
2004	331.2	357.6	357.9	391.6	1,438
2003	278.2	312.7	305.0	350.7	1,247
2002	231.6	271.5	248.3	271.9	1,023

Earnings Per Share ($)

2007	0.62	0.95	0.51	E0.53	E2.42
2006	0.49	0.59	0.55	0.97	2.58
2005	0.39	0.47	0.48	0.50	1.84
2004	0.34	0.34	0.32	0.40	1.40
2003	0.31	0.33	0.28	0.28	1.20
2002	0.23	0.25	0.22	0.23	0.92

Fiscal year ended Dec. 31. Next earnings report expected: Early February. EPS Estimates based on S&P Operating Earnings; historical GAAP earnings are as reported.

Dividend Data (Dates: mm/dd Payment Date: mm/dd/yy)

Amount ($)	Date Decl.	Ex-Div. Date	Stk. of Record	Payment Date
0.080	12/13	02/15	02/20	03/10/07
0.080	04/24	05/16	05/20	06/10/07
0.080	08/01	08/16	08/20	09/10/07
0.080	10/24	11/16	11/20	12/10/07

Dividends have been paid since 1934. Source: Company reports.

Please read the Required Disclosures and Analyst Certification on the last page of this report.

The McGraw-Hill Companies

Moody's Corp.

STANDARD &POOR'S

Business Summary October 29, 2007

CORPORATE PROFILE. Moody's Investors Service and the Dun & Bradstreet (D&B) operating company were separated into stand-alone entities on September 30, 2000. Old D&B changed its name to Moody's Corp. (MCO), and new D&B assumed the name Dun & Bradstreet Corp. (DNB).

Moody's is a provider of credit ratings, research and analysis covering debt instruments and securities in the global capital markets, and a provider of quantitative credit assessment services, credit training services and credit process software to banks and other financial institutions. Moody's credit ratings and research help investors analyze the credit risks associated with fixed-income securities. Beyond credit rating services for issuers, Moody's provides research services, data, and analytic tools that are utilized by institutional investors and other credit and capital markets professionals.

Moody's provides ratings and credit research on governmental and commercial entities in approximately 100 countries, and its customers include a wide range of corporate and governmental issuers of securities as well as institu-

tional investors, depositors, creditors, investment banks, commercial banks, and other financial intermediaries. In 2006, no single customer accounted for 10% or more of total revenue.

Moody's operates in two reportable segments: Moody's Investors Service, and Moody's KMV. Moody's Investors Service consists of a research group (13% of 2006 revenues) and four ratings groups: structured finance (44%), corporate finance (19%), financial institutions and sovereign risk (13%), and public finance (4%). The research group primarily generates revenue from the sale of investor-oriented credit research, principally produced by the ratings groups. The ratings groups generate revenue mainly from the assignment of credit ratings on fixed-income instruments in the debt markets.

Company Financials Fiscal Year Ended Dec. 31

Per Share Data ($)	2006	2005	2004	2003	2002	2001	2000	1999	1998	1997
Tangible Book Value	NM	0.30	0.39	NM	NM	NM	NM	NM	NM	NM
Cash Flow	2.72	1.95	1.51	1.30	1.00	0.72	0.54	1.21	1.13	1.02
Earnings	2.58	1.84	1.40	1.20	0.92	0.66	0.49	0.78	0.72	0.64
S&P Core Earnings	2.26	1.83	1.35	1.12	0.85	0.64	NA	NA	NA	NA
Dividends	0.28	0.20	0.15	0.09	0.07	0.11	0.28	0.37	0.41	0.44
Payout Ratio	11%	11%	11%	8%	7%	17%	57%	47%	56%	69%
Prices:High	73.29	62.50	43.86	30.43	26.20	20.55	18.09	20.00	18.34	15.63
Prices:Low	49.76	39.55	29.85	19.75	17.90	12.78	11.31	11.69	10.88	11.56
P/E Ratio:High	28	34	31	25	29	31	37	26	25	36
P/E Ratio:Low	19	21	21	17	20	19	23	15	15	18

Income Statement Analysis (Million $)										
Revenue	2,037	1,732	1,438	1,247	1,023	797	602	1,972	1,935	1,811
Operating Income	1,138	975	820	696	563	416	305	621	591	536
Depreciation	39.5	35.2	34.1	32.6	25.0	17.0	16.6	141	142	132
Interest Expense	15.2	21.0	16.2	21.8	21.0	16.5	3.60	5.00	12.0	53.0
Pretax Income	1,261	935	771	656	517	382	284	457	400	332
Effective Tax Rate	40.2%	40.0%	44.9%	44.6%	44.1%	44.4%	44.2%	39.1%	38.5%	34.0%
Net Income	754	561	425	364	289	212	159	256	246	219
S&P Core Earnings	662	558	413	340	269	203	NA	NA	NA	NA

Balance Sheet & Other Financial Data (Million $)										
Cash	408	486	606	269	40.0	163	119	113	91.0	82.0
Current Assets	1,002	1,052	1,023	569	272	371	278	785	764	806
Total Assets	1,498	1,457	1,376	941	631	505	398	1,786	1,789	2,225
Current Liabilities	700	579	837	432	462	359	253	1,415	1,353	1,497
Long Term Debt	300	300	Nil	300	300	300	300	Nil	Nil	Nil
Common Equity	167	309	318	-32.1	-327	-304	-283	-417	-371	-490
Total Capital	467	609	318	268	-27.0	-4.10	17.5	-115	-70.0	-188
Capital Expenditures	31.1	31.3	21.3	17.9	18.0	14.8	12.3	44.1	55.0	51.0
Cash Flow	793	596	459	397	314	229	175	397	388	351
Current Ratio	1.4	1.8	1.2	1.3	0.6	1.0	1.1	0.6	0.6	0.5
% Long Term Debt of Capitalization	64.2	49.2	Nil	112.0	NM	NM	NM	Nil	Nil	Nil
% Net Income of Revenue	37.0	32.4	29.6	29.2	28.2	26.6	26.3	13.0	12.7	12.1
% Return on Assets	51.0	39.4	36.5	46.3	50.9	47.0	47.1	14.3	NA	10.2
% Return on Equity	316.2	178.9	297.9	NM	NM	NM	NM	NM	NM	NM

Data as orig reptd.; bef. results of disc opers/spec. items. Per share data adj. for stk. divs.; EPS diluted. E-Estimated. NA-Not Available. NM-Not Meaningful. NR-Not Ranked. UR-Under Review.

Office: 99 Church Street, New York, NY 10007-2703.
Telephone: 212-553-0300.
Website: http://www.moodys.com
Chrmn & CEO: R.W. McDaniel, Jr.

Investor Contact: L.S. Huber (212-553-0300)
EVP & CFO: L.S. Huber
SVP & General Counsel: J.J. Goggins
SVP & Cntlr: J. McCabe

Board Members: B. L. Anderson, R. R. Glauber, E. Kist, C. Mack, R. W. McDaniel, Jr., H. A. McKinnell, Jr., N. S. Newcomb, J. K. Wulff

Founded: 1998
Domicile: Delaware
Employees: 3,400

STANDARD &POOR'S

Morgan Stanley

S&P Recommendation **SELL** ★★☆☆☆	Price $53.50 (as of Nov 28, 2007)	12-Mo. Target Price $45.00	Investment Style Large-Cap Blend

GICS Sector Financials
Sub-Industry Investment Banking & Brokerage

Summary Morgan Stanley is among the largest financial services firms in the U.S., with operations in investment banking, securities, and investment and wealth management.

Key Stock Statistics (Source S&P, Vickers, company reports)

52-Wk Range	**$90.95– 47.56**	S&P Oper. EPS 2007**E**	**5.98**	Market Capitalization(B)	**$56.311**	Beta	**1.74**
Trailing 12-Month EPS	**$8.48**	S&P Oper. EPS 2008**E**	**7.45**	Yield (%)	**2.02**	S&P 3-Yr. Proj. EPS CAGR(%)	**10.00**
Trailing 12-Month P/E	**6.3**	P/E on S&P Oper. EPS 2007**E**	**8.9**	Dividend Rate/Share	**$1.08**	S&P Credit Rating	**A+**
$10K Invested 5 Yrs Ago	**NA**	Common Shares Outstg. (M)	**1,052.5**	Institutional Ownership (%)	**77**		

Price Performance

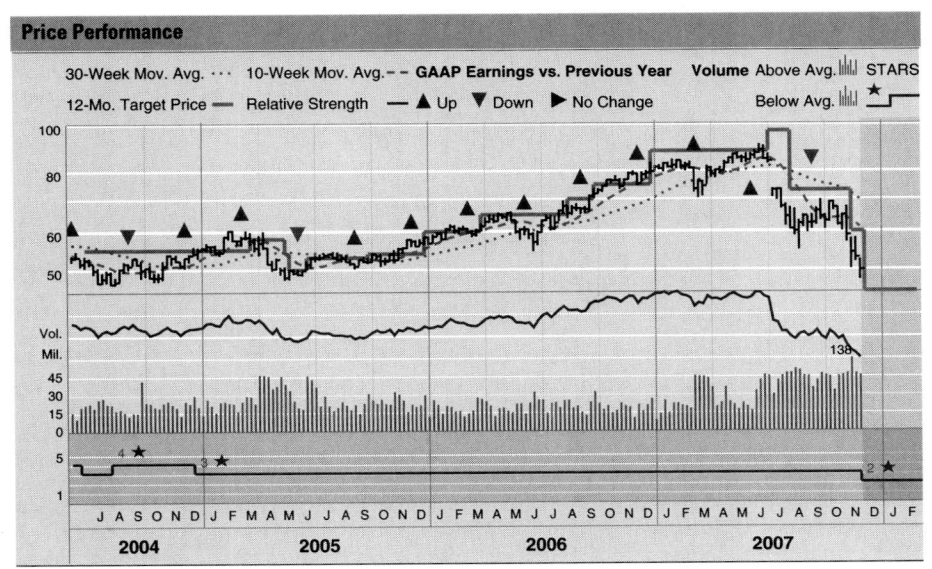

30-Week Mov. Avg. ··· 10-Week Mov. Avg. - - GAAP Earnings vs. Previous Year Volume Above Avg. STARS
12-Mo. Target Price — Relative Strength — ▲ Up ▼ Down ▶ No Change Below Avg. ★

Options: ASE, CBOE, P, Ph

Qualitative Risk Assessment

LOW	MEDIUM	HIGH

Our risk assessment reflects our favorable view of the company's diversification by product and by region, offset by our concerns about corporate governance and our view that certain segments lack competitive advantages.

Quantitative Evaluations

S&P Quality Ranking — A-

D	C	B-	B	B+	A-	A	A+

Relative Strength Rank — WEAK

27

LOWEST = 1   HIGHEST = 99

Revenue/Earnings Data

Revenue (Million $)

	1Q	2Q	3Q	4Q	Year
2007	24,678	27,734	21,230	--	--
2006	18,119	19,062	20,055	19,473	76,551
2005	11,641	11,845	13,157	15,525	52,081
2004	9,992	9,802	9,854	10,420	39,549
2003	8,502	8,418	8,929	9,092	34,933
2002	8,540	8,149	8,156	7,570	32,415

Earnings Per Share ($)

2007	2.40	2.45	1.38	E-0.25	E5.98
2006	1.50	1.85	1.75	2.08	7.09
2005	1.23	0.86	1.09	1.69	4.81
2004	1.11	1.10	0.78	1.09	4.08
2003	0.82	0.55	1.15	0.92	3.45
2002	0.76	0.72	0.55	0.67	2.69

Fiscal year ended Nov. 30. Next earnings report expected: Mid December. EPS Estimates based on S&P Operating Earnings; historical GAAP earnings are as reported.

Highlights

➤ The STARS recommendation for MS has recently been changed to 2 (sell) from 3 (hold) and the 12-month target price has recently been changed to $45.00 from $60.00. The Highlights section of this Stock Report will be updated accordingly.

Investment Rationale/Risk

➤ The Investment Rationale/Risk section of this Stock Report will be updated shortly. For the latest News story on MS from MarketScope, see below.

➤ 11/27/07 11:55 am EST... S&P DOWNGRADES OPINION ON SHARES OF MORGAN STANLEY TO SELL FROM HOLD (MS 50.21**): We believe additional write-downs to its mortgage-backed securities portfolio may be necessary beyond those forecast by MS at the end of Oct. We expect a further deterioration in the ABS collateralized debt obligation marketplace to put additional pressure on fair value measurements, and we now look for a write-down of about $4.2B, up from $3.7B figure at Oct. 31. We are widening our Nov-Q loss forecast by $0.19 to a loss of $0.25 and cutting FY 07 (Nov.) EPS est by $0.19 to $5.98. We are reducing our target price by $15 to $45, 1.5X projected book value, a discount to peers. /M.Albrecht

Dividend Data (Dates: mm/dd Payment Date: mm/dd/yy)

Amount ($)	Date Decl.	Ex-Div. Date	Stk. of Record	Payment Date
0.270	03/21	04/11	04/13	04/30/07
Stk.	06/01	07/02	06/18	06/30/07
0.270	06/21	07/11	07/13	07/31/07
0.270	09/19	10/10	10/12	10/31/07

Dividends have been paid since 1993. Source: Company reports.

The McGraw-Hill Companies

Morgan Stanley

STANDARD & POOR'S

Business Summary November 15, 2007

CORPORATE OVERVIEW. Morgan Stanley is a global financial services firm that provides a comprehensive suite of products to a diverse group of clients and customers, including corporations, governments, financial institutions and individuals. MS currently has three operating segments: Institutional Securities, Global Wealth Management Group and Asset Management.

The Institutional Securities segment includes capital raising; financial advisory services; corporate lending; sales, trading, financing and market-making activities for equity and fixed-income securities and related products such as foreign exchange and commodities; benchmark indices and risk management analytics; research; and investment activities. The investment banking business is included in this segment, and includes capital raising activities, financial advisory services and corporate lending. This business is one of the largest in the world, ranking second globally in 2006 in completed mergers and acquisitions and initial public offerings, and fifth in global debt issuance. This segment accounted for approximately 64% of net revenues and 74% of pretax profits in FY 06 (Nov.).

The Global Wealth Management Group provides brokerage and investment

advisory services; financial and wealth planning services; annuity and insurance products; credit and other lending products; banking and cash management services; retirement services; and trust and fiduciary services. It provides these services to clients through a network of more than 8,000 global representatives in over 500 locations, overseeing $686 billion in client assets at the end of FY 06. The segment accounted for about 16% of net revenues and 5% of pretax profits in FY 06.

The Asset Management segment provides global asset management products and services in equity, fixed income, alternative investments and private equity to institutional and retail clients through proprietary and third-party channels. It had $478 billion of assets under management or supervision at the end of FY 06, and its activities are principally conducted under the Morgan Stanley and Van Kampen brands. The segment accounted for 8% of net revenues and 7% of pretax profits in FY 06.

Company Financials Fiscal Year Ended Nov. 30

Per Share Data ($)	2006	2005	2004	2003	2002	2001	2000	1999	1998	1997
Tangible Book Value	34.89	25.23	23.93	21.52	19.43	17.36	16.91	14.79	11.88	10.99
Earnings	7.09	4.81	4.08	3.45	2.69	3.19	4.73	4.10	2.76	2.13
S&P Core Earnings	7.12	5.00	4.18	3.48	2.38	2.84	NA	NA	NA	NA
Dividends	1.08	1.08	1.00	0.92	0.92	0.92	0.80	0.48	0.40	0.28
Payout Ratio	15%	22%	25%	27%	34%	29%	17%	12%	14%	13%
Prices:High	83.40	60.51	62.83	58.78	60.02	90.49	110.00	71.44	48.75	29.75
Prices:Low	54.52	47.66	46.54	32.46	28.80	35.75	58.63	35.41	18.25	16.38
P/E Ratio:High	12	13	15	17	22	28	23	17	18	14
P/E Ratio:Low	8	10	11	9	11	11	12	9	7	8

Income Statement Analysis (Million $)										
Net Interest Income	3,279	3,750	3,731	2,935	3,896	3,348	3,058	2,365	2,922	2,777
Non Interest Income	45,558	23,906	20,959	19,189	16,549	19,600	24,179	20,110	14,656	13,549
Loan Loss Provision	756	878	925	1,267	1,336	1,052	810	529	1,173	1,493
Non Interest Expenses	23,614	20,857	18,333	16,636	15,725	17,264	18,746	14,281	15,530	12,052
% Expense/Operating Revenue	51.8%	84.2%	80.8%	79.9%	81.3%	84.6%	79.5%	75.7%	81.1%	78.7%
Pretax Income	10,772	7,050	6,312	5,334	4,633	5,684	8,526	7,728	5,385	4,274
Effective Tax Rate	30.4%	26.4%	28.6%	29.0%	35.5%	36.5%	36.0%	38.0%	37.0%	39.5%
Net Income	7,497	5,192	4,509	3,787	2,988	3,610	5,456	4,791	3,393	2,586
% Net Interest Margin	NA	NA	NA	5.40	5.50	5.57	6.08	8.47	9.00	8.45
S&P Core Earnings	7,511	5,401	4,624	3,830	2,658	3,203	NA	NA	NA	NA

Balance Sheet & Other Financial Data (Million $)										
Money Market Assets	174,866	174,330	123,041	78,205	76,910	54,618	50,992	70,366	90,101	6,890
Investment Securities	855,350	304,172	260,640	228,904	185,588	164,011	130,818	112,042	41,689	35,801
Earning Assets:Total Loans	24,173	23,754	21,169	20,384	24,322	20,955	21,870	20,229	22,388	24,499
Total Assets	1,120,645	898,523	775,410	602,843	529,499	482,628	426,794	366,967	317,590	302,287
Demand Deposits	14,872	2,629	1,117	1,264	1,441	1,741	1,589	1,458	1,355	1,210
Time Deposits	13,471	16,034	12,660	11,575	12,316	10,535	10,341	8,939	6,842	7,783
Long Term Debt	144,978	110,465	95,286	68,410	43,985	40,851	36,830	28,604	27,435	18,627
Common Equity	34,264	29,248	28,272	24,933	21,951	20,437	18,796	16,344	13,445	14,079
% Return on Assets	0.7	0.6	0.7	0.7	0.6	0.8	1.4	1.4	NA	1.5
% Return on Equity	23.5	18.9	16.9	16.2	14.1	18.2	30.3	30.3	25.2	26.2
% Loan Loss Reserve	3.3	3.5	4.5	4.9	3.8	4.0	3.6	3.7	NA	NA
% Loans/Deposits	85.2	127.3	153.7	158.8	176.8	170.7	183.3	229.2	272.8	294.2
% Loans/Assets	2.3	2.7	3.0	3.9	4.5	4.7	5.4	6.2	7.5	13.8
% Equity to Assets	3.1	3.3	3.9	4.1	4.2	4.3	4.5	4.4	4.3	5.6

Data as orig reptd.; bef. results of disc opers/spec. items. Per share data adj. for stk. divs.; EPS diluted. E-Estimated. NA-Not Available. NM-Not Meaningful. NR-Not Ranked. UR-Under Review.

Office: 1585 Broadway, New York, NY 10036.
Telephone: 212-761-4000.
Website: http://www.morganstanley.com
Chrmn & CEO: J.J. Mack

EVP & CFO: D.H. Sidwell
EVP, Chief Admin Officer & Secy: T.R. Nides
Chief Lgl Officer: G.G. Lynch
Investor Contact: W. Pike (212-761-0008)

Board Members: R. J. Bostock, E. B. Bowles, H. J. Davies, C. R. Kidder, J. J. Mack, D. T. Nicolaisen, C. H. Noski, H. S. Olayan, C. E. Phillips, Jr., O. G. Sexton, L. D. Tyson, K. Zumwinkel

Auditor: Deloitte & Touche
Founded: 1981
Domicile: Delaware
Employees: 55,310

The McGraw·Hill Companies

Motorola Inc.

STANDARD
&POOR'S

S&P Recommendation	HOLD ★★★☆☆	Price $15.71 (as of Nov 23, 2007)	12-Mo. Target Price $20.00	Investment Style Large-Cap Blend

GICS Sector Information Technology
Sub-Industry Communications Equipment

Summary This leading supplier of cellular telephone systems, semiconductors, two-way radios and paging equipment also offers information systems and other electronics products.

Key Stock Statistics (Source S&P, Vickers, company reports)

52-Wk Range	$22.55– 15.11	S&P Oper. EPS 2007**E**	0.21	Market Capitalization(B)	$36.362	Beta	1.12
Trailing 12-Month EPS	$0.19	S&P Oper. EPS 2008**E**	0.64	Yield (%)	1.27	S&P 3-Yr. Proj. EPS CAGR(%)	7.00
Trailing 12-Month P/E	82.7	P/E on S&P Oper. EPS 2007**E**	74.8	Dividend Rate/Share	$0.20	S&P Credit Rating	A-
$10K Invested 5 Yrs Ago	NA	Common Shares Outstg. (M)	2,314.6	Institutional Ownership (%)	78		

Price Performance

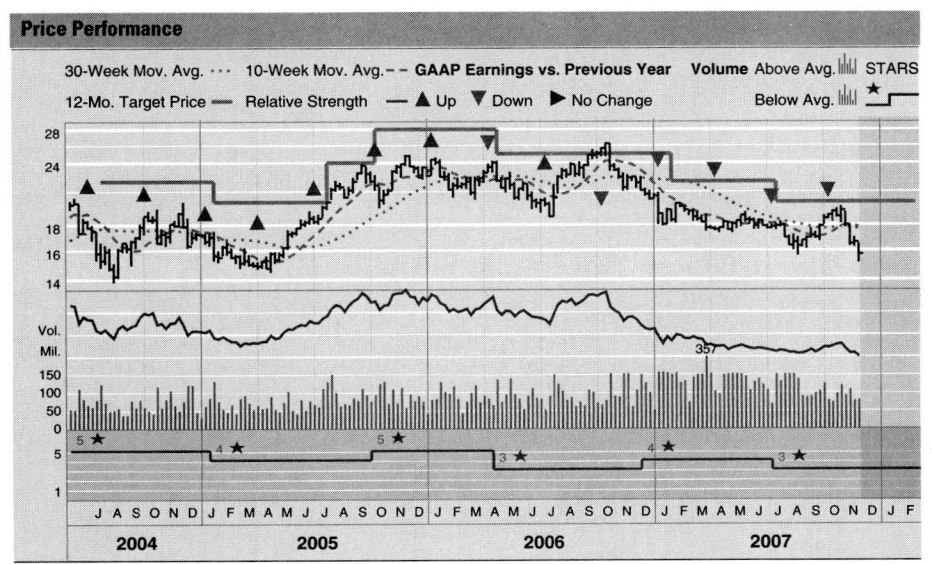

30-Week Mov. Avg. ···   10-Week Mov. Avg. – –   GAAP Earnings vs. Previous Year   Volume Above Avg. STARS
12-Mo. Target Price —   Relative Strength —   ▲ Up ▼ Down ▶ No Change   Below Avg.

Options: ASE, CBOE, P, Ph

Analysis prepared by **Todd Rosenbluth** on October 30, 2007, when the stock traded at **$ 18.95**.

Highlights

➤ Following a forecast sales decline of 17% in 2007, we expect sales to recover and rise 12% in 2008. We look for a modest recovery from MOT's mobile device unit after being challenged by an unfavorable product mix and pricing pressure in 2007; we see 9% handset growth and relatively stable average selling prices. We foresee 17% revenue growth in home and network mobility, and 9% for enterprise mobility, in 2008, following purchases that we think will have aided 2007 revenues.

➤ We expect a gross margin for 2008 of 28%, holding steady with our projected 2007 level but down compared to 30% in 2006. Despite a focus on profitable growth, we believe the gross margin will be hurt by a lower contribution from handset sales. We look for the operating margin to widen in 2008 on SG&A cost reductions, even as R&D costs rise.

➤ Our operating EPS estimates (excluding special items) are $0.21 for 2007 and $0.64 for 2008, including $0.08 for projected stock option expense in both years. With a strong cash balance, we think MOT will continue to repurchase its common shares.

Investment Rationale/Risk

➤ While third quarter results showed signs of improvement, particularly within its handset unit, we believe a turnaround is not yet complete. We expect that cost savings and growth in the home and network mobility segment will be the EPS driver in 2008. However, we contend that MOT will trade on the prospects of its handset business that has lost global market share, and, in our view, will lag the growth of peers. We expect the company to use part of its free cash flow to repurchase common shares.

➤ Risks to our recommendation and target price include execution risks of a turnaround in the handset unit, a failure to successfully introduce and ship new handset products, and a slowdown in telecom equipment capital spending.

➤ Based on our 12-month target price of $20, we value the shares at a below peers price to sales multiple of 1.1X, and we see support from a sizable current share repurchase plan. However, on our target P/E of more than 30X our 2008 EPS estimate, above peers whose revenues are increasing faster, we would not add to positions in MOT.

Qualitative Risk Assessment

LOW	MEDIUM	HIGH

Our risk assessment reflects the company's exposure to the economic health of the telecom and broadband industries and risks related to high volume manufacturing and distribution to service providers. This is offset by our view of MOT's product leadership and strong balance sheet.

Quantitative Evaluations

S&P Quality Ranking B+

D	C	B-	B	B+	A-	A	A+

Relative Strength Rank MODERATE

30

LOWEST = 1   HIGHEST = 99

Revenue/Earnings Data

Revenue (Million $)

	1Q	2Q	3Q	4Q	Year
2007	9,433	8,732	8,811	--	--
2006	9,608	10,876	10,603	11,792	42,879
2005	8,161	8,825	9,424	10,433	36,843
2004	7,441	7,541	7,499	8,842	31,323
2003	6,043	6,163	6,829	8,023	27,058
2002	6,021	6,741	6,371	7,546	26,679

Earnings Per Share ($)

2007	-0.09	0.02	0.02	E0.12	E0.21
2006	0.26	0.54	0.29	0.21	1.30
2005	0.28	0.38	0.69	0.47	1.82
2004	0.19	0.25	0.18	0.28	0.90
2003	0.07	0.05	0.05	0.20	0.38
2002	-0.20	-1.02	0.05	0.08	-1.09

Fiscal year ended Dec. 31. Next earnings report expected: Mid January. EPS Estimates based on S&P Operating Earnings; historical GAAP earnings are as reported.

Dividend Data (Dates: mm/dd Payment Date: mm/dd/yy)

Amount ($)	Date Decl.	Ex-Div. Date	Stk. of Record	Payment Date
0.050	02/12	03/13	03/15	04/13/07
0.050	05/08	06/13	06/15	07/13/07
0.050	07/25	09/12	09/14	10/15/07
0.050	11/13	12/12	12/14	01/14/08

Dividends have been paid since 1942. Source: Company reports.

Motorola Inc.

STANDARD
&POOR'S

Business Summary October 30, 2007

CORPORATE OVERVIEW. Motorola is a leader in wireless and networking solutions for cable, fixed-line, and wireless service providers. We believe all three markets are exposed to increased buyer's power due to the industry consolidation of service providers. The Mobile Devices segment (53% of sales in the nine months ended September 2007) primarily manufactures wireless handsets in all three major digital standards: GSM, TDMA and CDMA. We estimate that MOT's global handset market share declined to 13% in the third quarter of 2007, from 22% in 2006. MOT's Mobile Devices segment's operating margins remained weak in the third quarter of 2007, even as it worked through inventory. We expect a modest recovery in the fourth quarter and a greater one in 2008. We forecast that MOT will achieve a 14% share in 2008, with the shipment of 175 million handsets, up 9% from in 2007.

The remainder of revenues are broken into the Home and Networks Mobility (27%) and Enterprise Mobility (21%) segments. These businesses encompass products such as digital set-top box converters, cable modems and other home devices. We believe key customers may be boosting capital spending to compete against large telephone companies. Also, the wireless and wireline infrastructure businesses, large enterprises and governments are within these groups, where capital spending by major carriers improved sales

growth in 2007, in our opinion.

COMPETITIVE LANDSCAPE. Entry barriers are high in many of MOT's businesses due to economies of scale and strong customer relationships, but all markets are highly competitive, in our view. Service providers for broadband and mobility have high bargaining power over suppliers. Migration to next-generation products often leads to narrower margins in the early stages of the product cycle.

We believe MOT is well positioned for increased convergence of wireless and fixed line networks for broadband products. MOT is investing in emerging fourth generation wireless solutions. In August 2006, MOT announced plans to develop and deploy the first fourth generation (4G) nationwide broadband mobile network for Sprint Nextel (S: $17, hold), and despite management changes at S, we still expect MOT to be a key supplier.

Company Financials Fiscal Year Ended Dec. 31

Per Share Data ($)	2006	2005	2004	2003	2002	2001	2000	1999	1998	1997
Tangible Book Value	7.15	6.67	5.45	5.43	4.85	6.07	8.50	8.89	6.78	7.40
Cash Flow	1.53	2.06	1.15	1.09	-0.17	-0.63	1.70	1.60	0.69	1.91
Earnings	1.30	1.82	0.90	0.38	-1.09	-1.78	0.58	0.44	-0.54	0.65
S&P Core Earnings	1.24	1.18	0.78	0.08	-0.93	-2.23	NA	NA	NA	NA
Dividends	0.19	0.16	0.16	0.16	0.16	0.16	0.16	0.16	0.16	0.16
Payout Ratio	15%	9%	18%	42%	NM	NM	28%	37%	NM	25%
Prices:High	26.30	24.99	20.89	14.40	17.12	25.13	61.54	49.83	21.96	30.17
Prices:Low	18.66	14.48	13.83	7.59	7.30	10.50	15.81	20.85	12.79	18.00
P/E Ratio:High	20	14	23	38	NM	NM	NM	NM	NM	47
P/E Ratio:Low	14	8	15	20	NM	NM	NM	NM	NM	28

Income Statement Analysis (Million $)										
Revenue	42,879	36,843	31,323	27,058	26,679	30,004	37,580	30,931	29,398	29,794
Operating Income	4,675	4,851	3,887	2,694	2,059	-2,595	4,544	3,279	3,019	4,276
Depreciation	558	613	659	1,667	2,108	2,552	2,522	2,182	2,197	2,329
Interest Expense	335	325	199	295	668	645	494	305	301	216
Pretax Income	4,610	6,520	3,252	1,293	-3,446	-5,511	2,231	1,168	-1,374	1,816
Effective Tax Rate	29.3%	29.5%	32.6%	30.9%	NM	NM	40.9%	30.1%	NM	35.0%
Net Income	3,261	4,599	2,191	893	-2,485	-3,937	1,318	817	-962	1,180
S&P Core Earnings	3,132	2,964	1,899	164	-2,084	-4,893	NA	NA	NA	NA

Balance Sheet & Other Financial Data (Million $)										
Cash	15,416	14,641	10,556	7,877	6,507	6,082	3,301	3,345	1,453	1,445
Current Assets	30,975	27,869	21,082	17,907	17,134	17,149	19,885	16,503	13,531	13,236
Total Assets	38,593	35,649	30,889	32,098	31,152	33,398	42,343	37,327	28,728	27,278
Current Liabilities	15,425	12,488	10,573	9,433	9,810	9,698	16,257	12,416	11,440	9,055
Long Term Debt	2,704	3,806	4,578	7,161	7,674	8,857	4,778	3,573	2,633	2,144
Common Equity	17,142	16,673	13,331	12,689	11,239	13,691	18,612	16,344	12,222	13,272
Total Capital	19,846	20,479	17,909	19,850	18,913	22,548	24,894	23,398	16,043	17,038
Capital Expenditures	649	583	494	655	607	1,321	4,131	2,684	3,221	2,874
Cash Flow	3,819	5,212	2,850	2,560	-377	-1,385	3,840	2,999	1,235	3,509
Current Ratio	2.0	2.2	2.0	1.9	1.7	1.8	1.2	1.3	1.2	1.5
% Long Term Debt of Capitalization	13.6	18.6	25.6	36.1	40.6	39.3	19.2	15.3	16.4	12.6
% Net Income of Revenue	7.6	12.5	7.0	3.3	NM	NM	3.5	2.6	NM	4.0
% Return on Assets	8.8	13.8	7.0	2.8	NM	NM	3.2	2.5	NM	4.6
% Return on Equity	19.3	30.7	16.8	7.5	NM	NM	7.1	5.7	NM	9.4

Data as orig reptd.; bef. results of disc opers/spec. items. Per share data adj. for stk. divs.; EPS diluted. E-Estimated. NA-Not Available. NM-Not Meaningful. NR-Not Ranked. UR-Under Review.

Office: 1303 East Algonquin Road, Schaumburg, IL 60196.
Telephone: 800-262-8509.
Email: investors@motorola.com
Website: http://www.motorola.com

Chrmn & CEO: E.J. Zander
Pres & COO: G. Brown
EVP & CTO: P. Warrior
EVP, Secy & General Counsel: A.P. Lawson

Investor Contact: E. Gams (847-576-6873)
Board Members: D. W. Dorman, J. C. Lewent, T. J. Meredith, N. Negroponte, S. C. Scott, III, R. Sommer, J. R. Stengel, D. A. Warner, III, J. A. White, M. D. White, E. J. Zander

Founded: 1928
Domicile: Delaware
Employees: 66,000

The McGraw-Hill Companies

M&T Bank Corp

STANDARD
&POOR'S

S&P Recommendation	HOLD ★★★★★	Price	12-Mo. Target Price	Investment Style
		$89.97 (as of Nov 23, 2007)	$114.00	Large-Cap Blend

GICS Sector Financials
Sub-Industry Regional Banks

Summary This bank holding company for M&T Bank and M&T Bank, N.A. has offices in New York, Pennsylvania, Maryland, Virginia, West Virginia, New Jersey, Delaware, and DC.

Key Stock Statistics (Source S&P, Vickers, company reports)

52-Wk Range	$125.13–84.74	S&P Oper. EPS 2007E	7.34	Market Capitalization(B)	$9.640	Beta	0.36
Trailing 12-Month EPS	$7.22	S&P Oper. EPS 2008E	8.06	Yield (%)	3.11	S&P 3-Yr. Proj. EPS CAGR(%)	5.30
Trailing 12-Month P/E	12.5	P/E on S&P Oper. EPS 2007E	12.3	Dividend Rate/Share	$2.80	S&P Credit Rating	NA
$10K Invested 5 Yrs Ago	$12,148	Common Shares Outstg. (M)	107.1	Institutional Ownership (%)	71		

Price Performance

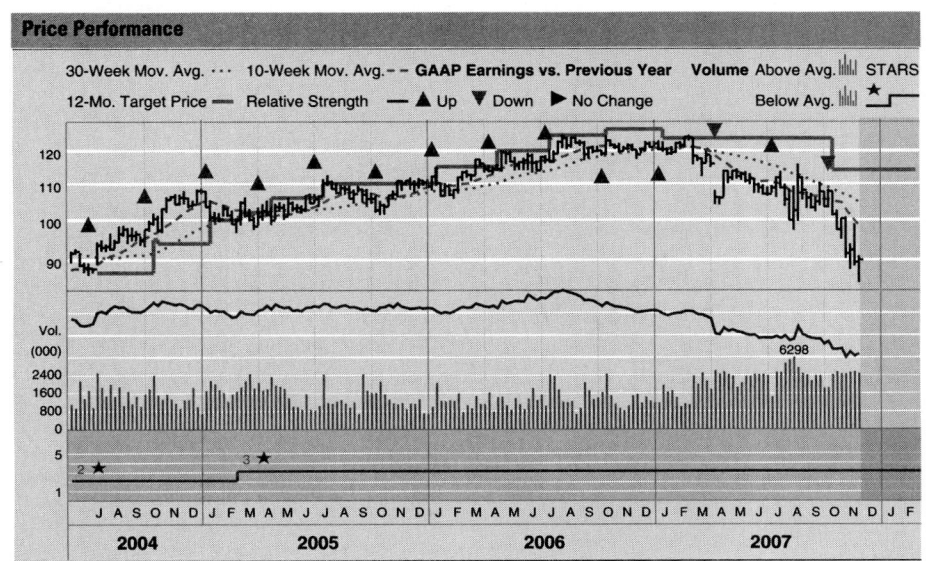

30-Week Mov. Avg. ··· 10-Week Mov. Avg.-- **GAAP Earnings vs. Previous Year** Volume Above Avg. STARS
12-Mo. Target Price — Relative Strength — ▲ Up ▼ Down ▶ No Change   Below Avg.

Options: P

Analysis prepared by **Erik Oja** on October 16, 2007, when the stock traded at **$ 97.94**.

Highlights

➤ Based on company guidance as well as our own forecasts, we estimate that loan growth will slow to 6.2% in 2007, and 5.1% in 2008, from 6.6% in 2006, reflecting business conditions in the Northeast, as well as MTB's cautionary stance on credit quality. We expect flat fee income growth in 2007, largely due to a slowdown in mortgage banking revenues, increasing to 6.5% in 2008, from deposit and other fees.

➤ We expect MTB's non-interest expense to total revenue (efficiency ratio) to remain low relative to other regional banks of similar size; our 2007 forecast is 54.2% and our 2008 projection is 53.5%, versus 2006's 54.2%. However, we project an increase in loan loss provisions in 2007 to $126 million, and $160 million in 2008, from $80 million in 2006, driven by a decrease in credit quality.

➤ MTB has 2.31 million shares remaining under a stock repurchase authorization, and we expect at least a 0.25 million net reduction in shares in each of the next four quarters. Including the repurchases, we expect EPS to fall 0.4% to $7.34 in 2007. In 2008, we expect EPS to increase 9.8%, to $8.06.

Investment Rationale/Risk

➤ Over the past four quarters, MTB's yield on earning assets has increased in lockstep with its rate on interest-bearing liabilities, causing MTB's net interest spread to stabilize at 3.06% as of September 30, 2007, equal to the level of a year earlier. We think this is largely due to a recent moderation in deposit costs at MTB, a trend which we believe may continue for several quarters. However, we are carefully watching credit trends and loan loss provisions at MTB. Non-performing loans are now 0.83% of total loans, up from 0.68% at June 30, and 0.52% at December 31, a rate of increase that leads to our hold recommendation.

➤ Risks to our recommendation and target price include a flat or inverted yield curve increasing the cost of deposits, and an economic slowdown affecting loan growth and credit quality.

➤ Our 12-month target price of $114 is based on a premium-to-peers 14.1X our 2008 EPS estimate of $8.06, which reflects our view of MTB's consistent record of credit quality monitoring and non-interest expense controls.

Qualitative Risk Assessment

LOW	MEDIUM	HIGH

Our risk assessment reflects the company's large-cap valuation, our view of the strong credit quality of its loan portfolio, and its history of profitability. While the company operates in a highly competitive and fragmented industry, the industry tends to produce relatively stable financial results.

Quantitative Evaluations

S&P Quality Ranking   A+

D	C	B-	B	B+	A-	A	A+

Relative Strength Rank   MODERATE

36

LOWEST = 1   HIGHEST = 99

Revenue/Earnings Data

Revenue (Million $)

	1Q	2Q	3Q	4Q	Year
2007	1,098	1,161	1,146	--	--
2006	1,030	1,076	1,127	1,127	4,360
2005	872.6	921.9	942.3	1,002	3,738
2004	774.3	792.9	828.0	846.5	3,242
2003	568.4	809.3	795.7	784.2	2,958
2002	585.4	582.6	589.6	596.4	2,354

Earnings Per Share ($)

2007	1.57	1.95	1.83	E2.01	E7.34
2006	1.77	1.87	1.85	1.88	7.37
2005	1.62	1.69	1.64	1.78	6.73
2004	1.30	1.53	1.56	1.62	6.00
2003	1.23	1.10	1.23	1.35	4.95
2002	1.25	1.26	1.23	1.33	5.07

Fiscal year ended Dec. 31. Next earnings report expected: Mid January. EPS Estimates based on S&P Operating Earnings; historical GAAP earnings are as reported.

Dividend Data (Dates: mm/dd Payment Date: mm/dd/yy)

Amount ($)	Date Decl.	Ex-Div. Date	Stk. of Record	Payment Date
0.600	02/20	02/26	02/28	03/30/07
0.600	04/18	05/30	06/01	06/29/07
0.700	07/18	08/30	09/04	09/28/07
0.700	11/20	12/13	12/17	12/31/07

Dividends have been paid since 1979. Source: Company reports.

M&T Bank Corp

STANDARD
&POOR'S

Business Summary October 16, 2007

CORPORATE OVERVIEW. M&T Bank Corporation is a New York-based bank holding company with $57 billion in assets as of December 31, 2006. Its primary subsidiaries are M&T Bank, a New York State chartered bank that focuses its lending on consumers and small and medium-sized businesses in the Mid-Atlantic region, and National Association (N.A.), a national banking association that offers selected deposit and loan products on a nationwide basis through direct mail and telephone marketing. MTB also operates other subsidiaries that provide insurance, securities, investments, leasing, mortgage, mortgage reinsurance, real estate and other financial products and services.

Following MTB's acquisition of Allfirst Financial Inc., a bank holding company in Baltimore, MD, from Allied Irish Banks, p.l.c. (AIB) on April 1, 2003, AIB gained a 22.5% stake in MTB. As of December 31, 2005, the foreign bank owned 23.8% of MTB's common stock. As long as AIB maintains a significant ownership in MTB, each bank will have representation on the other's board.

MARKET PROFILE. As of June 30, 2006, which is the latest available FDIC data,

MTB had 664 branches and $35.9 billion in deposits, with about 57% of its deposits and 41% of its branches concentrated in New York, according to Highline Data. In addition, 98.2% of MTB's deposits and 97.2% of branches were concentrated in the three adjoining states of New York, Pennsylvania, and Maryland. In New York, MTB had 269 branches, $20.4 billion in deposits, and a deposit market share of about 2.5%, ranking sixth. In Pennsylvania, MTB had 215 branches, $7.5 billion in deposits, and a deposit market share of about 2.8%, ranking seventh. In Maryland, MTB has 142 branches, $7.4 billion in deposits, and a deposit market share of about 7%, ranking fourth. Finally, MTB has a small presence in the District of Columbia, Virginia, West Virginia, and Delaware.

Company Financials Fiscal Year Ended Dec. 31

Per Share Data ($)	2006	2005	2004	2003	2002	2001	2000	1999	1998	1997
Tangible Book Value	30.05	25.56	24.52	21.43	20.23	17.84	16.10	14.88	13.72	15.59
Earnings	7.37	6.73	6.00	4.95	5.07	3.82	3.44	3.28	2.62	2.53
S&P Core Earnings	7.36	6.64	5.97	4.95	4.60	3.40	NA	NA	NA	NA
Dividends	2.25	1.75	1.60	1.20	1.05	1.00	0.62	0.45	0.38	0.32
Payout Ratio	31%	26%	27%	24%	21%	26%	18%	14%	15%	13%
Prices:High	124.98	112.50	108.75	98.98	90.05	82.11	68.42	58.25	58.20	46.80
Prices:Low	105.72	96.71	82.90	74.71	67.70	59.80	35.70	40.60	40.00	28.10
P/E Ratio:High	17	17	18	20	18	21	20	18	22	19
P/E Ratio:Low	14	14	14	15	13	16	10	12	15	11

Income Statement Analysis (Million $)										
Net Interest Income	1,818	1,794	1,735	1,599	1,248	1,158	854	759	664	557
Tax Equivalent Adjustment	NA	17.3	NA	16.3	14.0	17.5	10.5	7.71	7.19	5.84
Non Interest Income	1,043	978	940	831	513	476	325	282	269	161
Loan Loss Provision	80.0	88.0	95.0	131	122	104	NA	44.5	43.2	46.0
% Expense/Operating Revenue	54.2%	53.2%	56.7%	59.6%	51.9%	57.4%	61.6%	59.4%	60.2%	58.7%
Pretax Income	1,232	1,171	1,067	851	716	584	446	418	326	282
Effective Tax Rate	31.9%	33.2%	32.3%	32.5%	32.3%	35.2%	35.9%	36.5%	36.1%	37.5%
Net Income	839	782	723	574	485	378	286	266	208	176
% Net Interest Margin	3.70	3.77	3.88	4.09	4.36	4.23	4.02	4.02	3.97	4.38
S&P Core Earnings	838	772	718	574	440	336	NA	NA	NA	NA

Balance Sheet & Other Financial Data (Million $)										
Money Market Assets	143	211	199	250	380	84.4	57.8	1,286	403	111
Investment Securities	7,371	8,400	8,475	7,259	3,955	3,024	3,310	1,901	2,786	1,725
Commercial Loans	23,165	23,940	22,886	20,869	14,522	14,071	13,399	6,141	3,657	2,542
Other Loans	20,042	16,614	15,758	15,169	11,415	11,117	9,571	11,431	12,348	9,224
Total Assets	57,065	55,146	52,939	49,826	33,175	31,450	28,949	22,409	20,584	14,003
Demand Deposits	8,820	9,044	9,246	10,150	5,101	4,634	4,218	2,844	2,576	1,458
Time Deposits	25,660	28,056	26,183	20,756	16,564	16,946	16,014	12,530	12,161	9,705
Long Term Debt	6,891	5,586	6,349	5,535	4,497	3,462	3,415	1,744	1,568	428
Common Equity	6,281	5,876	5,730	5,717	3,182	2,939	38.0	44.5	1,602	1,018
% Return on Assets	1.5	1.4	1.4	1.4	1.5	1.3	1.1	1.2	1.2	1.3
% Return on Equity	13.8	13.5	12.6	12.9	15.8	13.4	12.7	15.6	15.9	18.3
% Loan Loss Reserve	1.5	1.6	1.6	1.7	1.7	1.7	1.6	-2.0	1.9	2.4
% Loans/Deposits	107.6	108.7	108.4	108.0	119.7	116.7	112.4	115.4	107.2	105.4
% Equity to Assets	10.8	10.7	11.1	10.8	9.5	9.3	8.8	7.9	7.6	7.1

Data as orig reptd.; bef. results of disc opers/spec. items. Per share data adj. for stk. divs.; EPS diluted. E-Estimated. NA-Not Available. NM-Not Meaningful. NR-Not Ranked. UR-Under Review.

Office: 1 M And T Plz , Buffalo, NY 14203-2399.
Telephone: 716-842-5445.
Email: ir@mandtbank.com
Website: http://www.mandtbank.com

Chrmn & CEO: R.G. Wilmers
Pres: M.J. Czarnecki
Vice Chrmn: M.P. Pinto
Vice Chrmn: J.G. Pereira

Vice Chrmn: R.E. Sadler, Jr.
Investor Contact: D. MacLeod (716-842-5462)
Board Members: B. D. Baird, R. J. Bennett, C. A. Bontempo, R. T. Brady, M. D. Buckley, T. J. Cunningham, III, M. J. Czarnecki, C. E. Doherty, R. E. Garman, D. C. Hathaway, D. R. Hawbaker, P. W. Hodgson, R. G. King, R. B. Newman, II, J. G. Pereira, M. P. Pinto, R. E. Sadler, Jr., E. J. Sheehy, S. G. Sheetz, H. L. Washington, R. G. Wilmers

Founded: 1969
Domicile: New York
Employees: 13,352

Murphy Oil Corp

S&P Recommendation **HOLD** ★★★☆☆	Price $72.94 (as of Nov 23, 2007)	12-Mo. Target Price $76.00	Investment Style Large-Cap Blend

GICS Sector Energy
Sub-Industry Integrated Oil & Gas

Summary This integrated oil company has exploration and production interests worldwide, and refining and marketing operations in the U.S.

Key Stock Statistics (Source S&P, Vickers, company reports)

52-Wk Range	$79.73– 45.45	S&P Oper. EPS 2007**E**	3.96	Market Capitalization(B)	$13.722	Beta	0.32
Trailing 12-Month EPS	$3.37	S&P Oper. EPS 2008**E**	6.06	Yield (%)	1.03	S&P 3-Yr. Proj. EPS CAGR(%)	14.25
Trailing 12-Month P/E	21.6	P/E on S&P Oper. EPS 2007**E**	18.4	Dividend Rate/Share	$0.75	S&P Credit Rating	BBB
$10K Invested 5 Yrs Ago	$38,026	Common Shares Outstg. (M)	188.1	Institutional Ownership (%)	81		

Price Performance

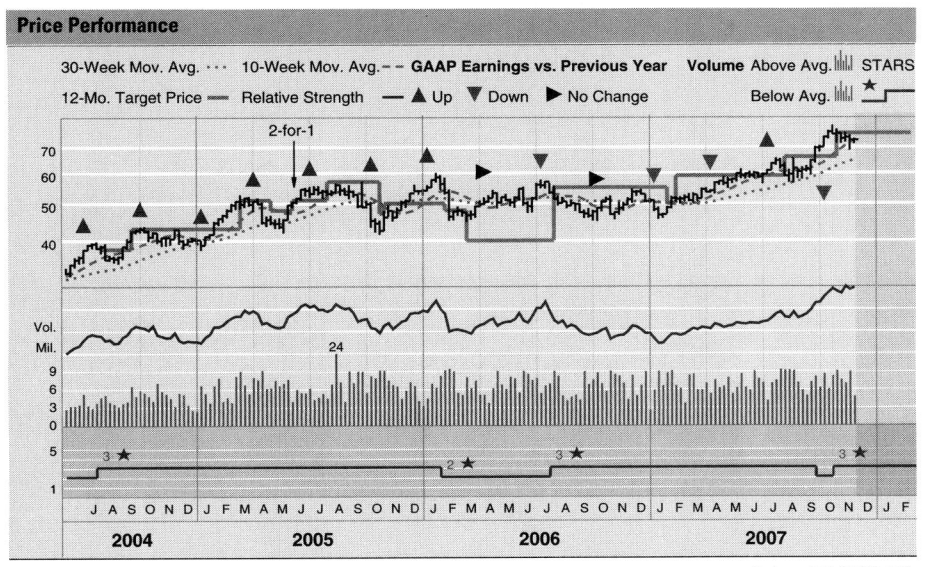

30-Week Mov. Avg. · · · 10-Week Mov. Avg. - - **GAAP Earnings vs. Previous Year** Volume Above Avg.▐▐ STARS
12-Mo. Target Price — Relative Strength — ▲ Up ▼ Down ► No Change Below Avg.▐▐ ★

Options: ASE, CBOE, P, Ph

Analysis prepared by **Tina J. Vital** on October 31, 2007, when the stock traded at **$ 73.46**.

Highlights

➤ Oil and gas production rose 5.8% in the third quarter, to 97,247 boe/d, above our expectations, reflecting the start-up of the Kikeh Field, offshore Sabah Malaysia. MUR expects fourth quarter production will top 118,000 boe/d. We see 2007 production levels about flat with 2006, but look for improved volumes in 2008. Looking ahead to 2008, we expect operating costs to trend below industry averages, reflecting new volumes from prolific fields in Malaysia and deepwater Gulf of Mexico.

➤ Refining margins have weakened in the 2007 second half, and we project 2008 refining margins will narrow over 30% from 2007 levels, as refined product prices have failed to keep pace with the sharp increase in crude oil prices.

➤ We expect after-tax operating earnings will climb 49% in 2007, and remain near those levels in 2008, as weakened refining margins are partially offset by strong crude oil price realizations and improved production levels.

Investment Rationale/Risk

➤ With MUR's reserves in the Gulf of Mexico, the North Sea, Canada, Malaysia and Ecuador, we believe a significant portion of its production as being derived from non-operating interests in large deepwater developments, particularly in the Gulf of Mexico, coastal Newfoundland and the North Sea. We estimate MUR's three-year (2004-06) finding and development costs at $23.12 per boe, above its peer average, and its three-year organic reserve replacement at a solid 113%, albeit below its peer average.

➤ Risks to our recommendation and target price include positive economic, industrial and operating conditions, stronger than anticipated production, higher oil and natural gas prices, and exploration success.

➤ A blend of our discounted cash flow (WACC of 7.3%, terminal growth of 3%) and relative valuations leads to our 12-month target price of $76. This represents an expected enterprise value of 6.3X our 2008 EBITDA estimate, a premium to peers.

Qualitative Risk Assessment

LOW	MEDIUM	**HIGH**

Our risk assessment reflects our view of MUR's moderate financial policies and integrated operations in a volatile, cyclical and capital intensive segment of the energy industry. We believe its low reserve-to-production ratio limits its operating flexibility, increasing dependence on long-term projects.

Quantitative Evaluations

S&P Quality Ranking   B+

D	C	B-	B	**B+**	A-	A	A+

Relative Strength Rank   **STRONG**

87

LOWEST = 1   HIGHEST = 99

Revenue/Earnings Data

Revenue (Million $)

	1Q	2Q	3Q	4Q	Year
2007	3,435	4,614	4,781	--	--
2006	2,991	3,799	4,153	3,364	14,307
2005	2,415	2,950	3,317	3,195	11,877
2004	1,628	2,096	2,291	2,301	8,360
2003	1,322	1,278	1,297	1,449	5,345
2002	748.4	1,035	1,044	1,139	3,967

Earnings Per Share ($)

2007	0.58	1.32	1.04	E0.92	E3.96
2006	0.60	1.13	1.18	0.46	3.37
2005	0.60	1.85	1.18	0.82	4.46
2004	0.43	0.90	0.62	0.71	2.66
2003	0.51	0.43	0.37	0.32	1.63
2002	0.02	0.07	0.20	0.25	0.53

Fiscal year ended Dec. 31. Next earnings report expected: Early February. EPS Estimates based on S&P Operating Earnings; historical GAAP earnings are as reported.

Dividend Data (Dates: mm/dd Payment Date: mm/dd/yy)

Amount ($)	Date Decl.	Ex-Div. Date	Stk. of Record	Payment Date
0.150	02/07	02/09	02/13	03/01/07
0.150	04/04	05/09	05/11	06/01/07
0.188	08/01	08/13	08/15	09/03/07
0.188	10/03	11/07	11/12	12/03/07

Dividends have been paid since 1961. Source: Company reports.

Please read the Required Disclosures and Analyst Certification on the last page of this report.

The McGraw-Hill Companies

Murphy Oil Corp

STANDARD &POOR'S

Business Summary October 31, 2007

CORPORATE OVERVIEW. As a U.S. integrated oil company, Murphy Oil explores for oil and gas worldwide, but operates in refining and marketing in the U.S.

During 2006, MUR's principal exploration and production activities were conducted in the U.S., Ecuador, Malaysia, Canada, and the U.K. North Sea. MUR owns a 5% undivided interest in Syncrude Canada Ltd. in northern Alberta, the world's largest producer of synthetic crude oil.

MUR owns and operates two U.S. refineries (a 125,000 b/d capacity facility at Meraux, LA, and a 35,000 b/d refinery at Superior, WI), and has a 30% stake in the 108,000 b/d U.K. Milford Haven, Wales refinery. On August 30, 2007, MUR agreed to purchase Total SA's 70% interest in the Milford Haven refinery for $250 million; closure is expected in the 2007 fourth quarter.

MUR markets refined products through a network of retail gasoline stations and branded and unbranded wholesale customers in 23 states, primarily located in the parking areas of Wal-Mart stores in 21 states and using the brand name Murphy USA. At December 31, 2006, the company marketed products through 987 Murphy USA stations and 169 branded wholesale SPUR stations.

MARKET PROFILE. With upstream operations worldwide, MUR has successfully found significant quantities of hydrocarbons in the deepwater Gulf of Mexico, and more recently in Malaysia (Kikeh field) and the Republic of the Congo. MUR booked proved oil reserves of 38.9 million bbl. in the Kikeh field at year-end 2005, with first production scheduled to begin in the second half of 2007.

In the past, MUR's strategy has emphasized organic production growth and reserve additions through high risk, but focused, exploration. However, given the increased cost of drilling and the difficulty of accessing new plays, MUR has begun to broaden its thinking to include acquisitions (both assets and companies), which would provide meaningful upside or entrance to a new targeted area or play.

Company Financials Fiscal Year Ended Dec. 31

Per Share Data ($)	2006	2005	2004	2003	2002	2001	2000	1999	1998	1997
Tangible Book Value	21.37	18.38	14.16	10.27	8.41	7.99	6.72	5.87	5.44	6.02
Cash Flow	5.40	6.57	4.38	3.39	2.16	3.07	2.87	1.80	1.05	1.90
Earnings	3.37	4.46	2.66	1.63	0.53	1.82	1.69	0.67	-0.08	0.74
S&P Core Earnings	3.32	3.85	2.40	1.40	0.39	1.30	NA	NA	NA	NA
Dividends	0.52	0.45	0.43	0.40	0.39	0.38	0.36	0.35	0.35	0.34
Payout Ratio	16%	10%	16%	25%	73%	21%	21%	53%	NM	46%
Prices:High	60.18	57.07	43.69	34.35	24.86	21.96	17.27	15.41	13.61	15.64
Prices:Low	44.72	37.80	28.45	19.27	15.95	13.81	12.05	8.22	8.63	10.75
P/E Ratio:High	18	13	16	21	47	12	10	23	NM	21
P/E Ratio:Low	13	8	11	12	30	8	7	12	NM	15

Income Statement Analysis (Million $)										
Revenue	14,307	11,877	8,360	5,345	3,967	4,479	4,639	2,037	1,694	2,132
Operating Income	1,514	1,854	1,110	781	492	768	723	400	288	444
Depreciation, Depletion and Amortization	384	397	321	328	300	229	213	204	203	209
Interest Expense	9.48	8.77	34.1	20.5	27.0	19.0	16.3	20.3	10.5	0.62
Pretax Income	1,028	1,372	805	419	152	506	465	179	-8.28	212
Effective Tax Rate	37.9%	38.9%	38.3%	28.1%	35.7%	34.6%	34.3%	32.9%	NM	37.4%
Net Income	638	838	496	301	97.5	331	306	120	-14.4	132
S&P Core Earnings	630	725	448	259	71.4	236	NA	NA	NA	NA

Balance Sheet & Other Financial Data (Million $)										
Cash	543	585	536	252	165	82.7	133	34.1	28.3	24.3
Current Assets	2,107	1,839	1,629	1,039	854	599	817	593	437	518
Total Assets	7,446	6,369	5,458	4,713	3,886	3,259	3,134	2,446	2,164	2,238
Current Liabilities	1,311	1,287	1,205	810	718	560	745	488	381	469
Long Term Debt	840	610	613	1,090	863	521	525	393	333	206
Common Equity	4,053	3,461	2,649	1,951	1,594	1,498	1,260	1,057	978	1,079
Total Capital	5,498	4,685	3,263	3,463	2,784	2,322	2,014	1,604	1,436	1,422
Capital Expenditures	1,192	1,246	938	938	834	814	512	387	389	468
Cash Flow	1,022	1,235	818	630	398	560	519	324	188	342
Current Ratio	1.6	1.4	1.4	1.3	1.2	1.1	1.1	1.2	1.1	1.1
% Long Term Debt of Capitalization	15.3	13.0	18.8	31.5	31.0	22.4	26.1	24.5	23.2	14.5
% Return on Assets	9.2	14.2	9.8	7.0	2.7	10.4	11.0	5.2	NM	5.9
% Return on Equity	17.0	27.4	21.6	17.0	6.3	24.0	26.4	11.8	NM	12.6

Data as orig reptd.; bef. results of disc opers/spec. items. Per share data adj. for stk. divs.; EPS diluted. E-Estimated. NA-Not Available. NM-Not Meaningful. NR-Not Ranked. UR-Under Review.

Office: 200 Peach Street, El Dorado, AR 71730-7000.
Telephone: 870-862-6411.
Email: murphyoil@murphyoilcorp.com
Website: http://www.murphyoilcorp.com

Chrmn: W.C. Nolan, Jr.
Pres & CEO: C.P. Deming
EVP & General Counsel: S.A. Cosse
SVP & CFO: K.G. Fitzgerald

Investor Contact: M. West (870-864-6315)
Board Members: F. W. Blue, G. S. Dembroski, C. P. Deming, R. A. Hermes, J. V. Kelley, R. M. Murphy, W. C. Nolan, Jr., I. B. Ramberg, N. E. Schmale, D. J. Smith, C. G. Theus

Founded: 1950
Domicile: Delaware
Employees: 7,296

Mylan Inc

S&P Recommendation HOLD ★ ★ ★ ☆ ☆

Price	12-Mo. Target Price	Investment Style
$13.61 (as of Nov 23, 2007)	$17.00	Large-Cap Growth

GICS Sector Health Care
Sub-Industry Pharmaceuticals

Summary This leading manufacturer of generic pharmaceuticals produces a broad range of generic drugs in varying strengths. In early October 2007, Mylan acquired the generic drug division of German drugmaker Merck KGaA for some $7.0 billion in cash.

Key Stock Statistics (Source S&P, Vickers, company reports)

52-Wk Range	$22.90– 12.93	S&P Oper. EPS 2008**E**	1.15	Market Capitalization(B)	$4.116	Beta	0.16
Trailing 12-Month EPS	$1.19	S&P Oper. EPS 2009**E**	0.70	Yield (%)	Nil	S&P 3-Yr. Proj. EPS CAGR(%)	7.00
Trailing 12-Month P/E	11.4	P/E on S&P Oper. EPS 2008**E**	11.8	Dividend Rate/Share	Nil	S&P Credit Rating	BB-
$10K Invested 5 Yrs Ago	$9,289	Common Shares Outstg. (M)	302.4	Institutional Ownership (%)	66		

Price Performance

30-Week Mov. Avg. ···· 10-Week Mov. Avg.-- **GAAP Earnings vs. Previous Year** Volume Above Avg.|||| STARS

12-Mo. Target Price — Relative Strength — ▲ Up ▼ Down ► No Change Below Avg. |||| ★

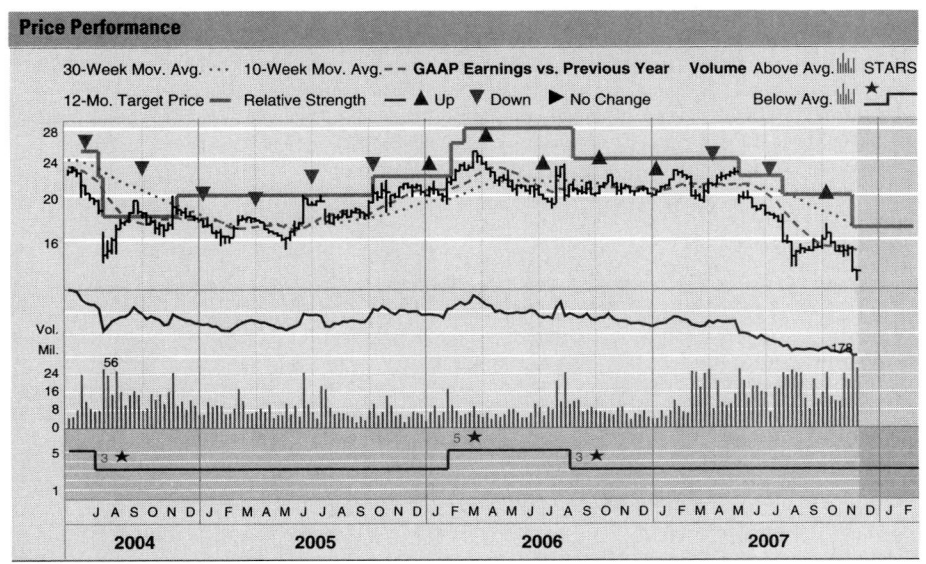

Options: ASE, CBOE, P, Ph

Analysis prepared by **Herman B. Saftlas** on November 16, 2007, when the stock traded at **$ 13.86**.

Highlights

➤ Mylan has changed its fiscal year end to December 31 from March 31. Boosted by the full year inclusion of the generic business of Merck KGaA (acquired in October 2007), we project total revenues of $4.6 billion for calendar 2008, up from a pro forma estimate of $2.6 billion for 2007. We also see higher sales from Matrix, an Indian producer of active pharmaceutical ingredients. However, sales of MYL's U.S. generics are expected to fall, reflecting projected declines in older products such as generic versions of Duragesic and Norvasc.

➤ We look for gross margins on generic sales to narrow in 2008, largely on expected reductions in sales of high-margin generics with extended exclusivities, as well as a higher proportion of lower-margin Matrix and Merck KGaA sales in the mix. We also project much higher SG&A expenses and interest charges, as well as reduced investment income.

➤ After dividend payments from a planned preferred offering, we project operating cash EPS of $0.70 in 2008, down from an indicated $1.15 in 2007, before acquisition-related charges and other specified items.

Investment Rationale/Risk

➤ In early October 2007, MYL purchased the generics unit of German drugmaker Merck KGaA for some $7.0 billion in cash. To help refinance bridge borrowings made to finance the acquisition, Mylan plans to generate $2.5 billion from offerings of 1.86 billion shares of a 6.50% convertible preferred stock, and 53.3 million MYL common shares. Factoring heavy financing costs and integration expenses, we do not expect this acquisition to become accretive to cash EPS until 2010. On the plus side, we think the acquisition has made Mylan a top tier global generic player, lessened its dependence on the U.S. market, and should provide important long-term operating synergies.

➤ Risks to our recommendation and target price include possible problems integrating the Merck KGaA business, as well as the need to obtain FDA approval for new generics and mount legal challenges to branded patents.

➤ Based on our analysis, MYL shares are valued in line with peers on an EV/EBITDA basis. Our 12 month target price of $17 is supported by our DCF model, which assumes a WACC of 8% and perpetuity growth of 1%.

Qualitative Risk Assessment

LOW	MEDIUM	HIGH

Our risk assessment reflects risks inherent in the generic pharmaceutical business, which include the ability to successfully develop generic products, obtain regulatory approvals, and legally challenge branded patents. However, we believe these risks are offset at Mylan, given its wide and diverse generic portfolio, and promising branded drug business. We also think the recent acquisition of Merck KGaA's generic business holds long-term promise.

Quantitative Evaluations

S&P Quality Ranking A-

D	C	B-	B	B+	A-	A	A+

Relative Strength Rank MODERATE

30

LOWEST = 1   HIGHEST = 99

Revenue/Earnings Data

Revenue (Million $)

	1Q	2Q	3Q	4Q	Year
2008	546.3	477.1	--	--	--
2007	356.1	366.7	401.8	487.3	1,612
2006	323.4	298.0	311.3	324.6	1,257
2005	339.0	307.0	291.0	316.4	1,253
2004	331.4	360.1	349.8	333.4	1,375
2003	275.5	319.5	320.5	353.7	1,269

Earnings Per Share ($)

2008	0.32	0.60	E-0.15	E0.16	E1.15
2007	0.35	0.36	0.63	-0.31	0.99
2006	0.16	0.16	0.22	0.27	0.79
2005	0.30	0.18	0.13	0.14	0.74
2004	0.31	0.33	0.31	0.27	1.21
2003	0.22	0.24	0.25	0.27	0.97

Fiscal year ended Mar. 31. Next earnings report expected: Early February. EPS Estimates based on S&P Operating Earnings; historical GAAP earnings are as reported.

Dividend Data (Dates: mm/dd Payment Date: mm/dd/yy)

Amount ($)	Date Decl.	Ex-Div. Date	Stk. of Record	Payment Date
0.060	12/19	12/27	12/29	01/16/07
0.060	03/15	03/28	03/30	04/16/07
0.060	06/18	06/27	06/29	07/16/07

Dividends have been paid since 1983. Source: Company reports.

Please read the Required Disclosures and Analyst Certification on the last page of this report.

Mylan Inc

STANDARD &POOR'S

Business Summary November 16, 2007

CORPORATE PROFILE. Mylan Laboratories is a leading manufacturer of generic pharmaceutical products in finished tablet, capsule and powder dosage forms. Generic drugs are the chemical equivalents of branded drugs, and are marketed after patents on the primary products expire. Generics are typically sold at prices significantly below those of comparable branded products.

MYL's U.S. generic division markets about 170 generic products, primarily solid oral dose drugs encompassing some 50 therapeutic categories. Some 15 generics are extended release drugs. UDL Laboratories is the largest U.S. repackager of pharmaceuticals in unit dose formats, which are used primarily in hospitals, nursing homes and similar settings. Mylan Technologies develops and markets products using transdermal drug delivery systems.

IMPACT OF MAJOR DEVELOPMENTS. With the early October 2007 acquisition of a generic drug business from German drugmaker Merck KGaA, Mylan now ranks as the third largest producer of generic pharmaceuticals in the world. The acquired business (now referred to as Merck Generics) markets over 400 products and had sales of $2.3 billion in 2006. The operation has a strong presence in key foreign generic markets, including France, the U.K., Japan, Canada and Australia. Under terms of the acquisition agreement, MYL has rights to purchase Merck KGaA's generic businesses in 17 additional countries in Latin America, Europe and Asia until October 2009.

As part of the Merck Generics acquisition, MYL also acquired Dey, a producer of branded specialty respiratory and allergy drugs. Key Dey products are EpiPen, an auto-injector treatment for allergic reactions; and DuoNeb, a nebulized treatment for COPD. On a pro forma basis (including Merck Generics), Mylan had sales of about $4.2 billion in the 12 months ended March 31, 2007. Mylan expects Merck Generics, which was acquired for some $7.0 billion in cash, to be dilutive to cash EPS in year one, to break even in year two, and to be significantly accretive thereafter.

In January 2007, MYL acquired about 72% of the voting shares of Indian drugmaker Matrix Laboratories for about $776 million in cash. Matrix is the second largest maker of active pharmaceutical ingredients (APIs) in the world. Matrix produces high quality APIs for Mylan's own generics, as well as for third parties. We think Matrix offers MYL significant long-term pluses in terms of geographic expansion and cost efficiencies.

Company Financials Fiscal Year Ended Mar. 31

Per Share Data ($)	2007	2006	2005	2004	2003	2002	2001	2000	1999	1998
Tangible Book Value	2.75	2.76	6.03	5.30	4.39	3.97	2.97	3.00	2.49	2.24
Cash Flow	1.27	0.99	0.91	1.37	1.11	1.07	0.28	0.65	0.50	0.44
Earnings	0.99	0.79	0.74	1.21	0.97	0.91	0.13	0.52	0.43	0.36
S&P Core Earnings	0.84	0.78	0.64	1.05	0.89	0.84	0.40	NA	NA	NA
Dividends	0.24	0.12	0.10	0.08	0.08	0.07	0.07	0.07	0.07	0.07
Payout Ratio	24%	15%	14%	7%	18%	8%	55%	14%	17%	20%
Calendar Year	2006	2005	2004	2003	2002	2001	2000	1999	1998	1997
Prices:High	25.00	21.69	26.35	28.75	16.56	16.94	14.33	14.22	15.97	11.25
Prices:Low	18.65	15.21	14.24	15.56	11.15	8.96	7.11	7.58	7.58	5.11
P/E Ratio:High	25	27	36	24	17	19	NM	27	37	31
P/E Ratio:Low	19	19	19	13	12	12	NM	14	18	14

Income Statement Analysis (Million $)										
Revenue	1,612	1,257	1,253	1,375	1,269	1,104	847	790	721	555
Operating Income	586	347	321	504	452	441	209	259	224	146
Depreciation	61.5	46.8	45.1	44.3	40.6	46.1	42.4	35.7	26.9	21.7
Interest Expense	52.3	31.3	Nil	Nil	Nil	Nil	Nil	Nil	Nil	Nil
Pretax Income	426	275	312	513	427	408	58.0	243	192	148
Effective Tax Rate	48.9%	32.8%	34.8%	34.7%	36.1%	36.3%	36.0%	36.5%	40.0%	32.1%
Net Income	217	185	204	335	272	260	37.1	154	115	101
S&P Core Earnings	185	184	175	286	247	241	113	NA	NA	NA

Balance Sheet & Other Financial Data (Million $)										
Cash	1,427	518	808	687	687	617	285	303	260	104
Current Assets	2,412	1,192	1,528	1,318	1,228	1,062	879	687	583	430
Total Assets	4,254	1,871	2,136	1,875	1,745	1,617	1,466	1,341	1,207	848
Current Liabilities	701	265	246	174	266	175	291	87.8	96.4	71.3
Long Term Debt	1,655	685	19.3	19.1	19.9	21.9	23.3	30.6	26.8	26.2
Common Equity	1,649	4,242	2,786	2,600	1,446	1,607	1,133	1,204	1,060	744
Total Capital	3,390	4,948	2,830	2,642	1,479	1,646	1,175	1,253	1,110	776
Capital Expenditures	162	104	90.7	118	32.6	20.6	24.7	28.8	16.7	28.9
Cash Flow	279	231	249	379	313	306	79.5	190	142	122
Current Ratio	3.4	4.5	6.2	7.6	4.6	6.1	3.0	7.8	6.0	6.0
% Long Term Debt of Capitalization	48.8	13.8	0.7	0.7	1.3	1.3	2.0	2.4	2.4	3.4
% Net Income of Revenue	13.5	14.7	16.2	24.3	21.5	23.6	4.4	19.5	16.0	18.1
% Return on Assets	7.1	9.2	10.1	18.5	16.2	16.9	2.6	12.1	11.2	12.4
% Return on Equity	17.8	5.3	7.6	14.1	19.1	17.7	3.2	13.6	12.8	14.4

Data as orig reptd.; bef. results of disc opers/spec. items. Per share data adj. for stk. divs.; EPS diluted. E-Estimated. NA-Not Available. NM-Not Meaningful. NR-Not Ranked. UR-Under Review.

Office: 1500 Corporate Dr, Canonsburg, PA 15317-8580.
Telephone: 724-514-1800.
Email: investor_relations@mylan.com
Website: http://www.mylan.com

Chrmn: M. Puskar
Vice Chrmn & CEO: R.J. Coury
VP & Cntlr: D.C. Rizzo, Jr.
CFO: E.J. Borkowski

Secy & Chief Lgl Officer: S.A. Williams
Investor Contact: K. King (724-514-1800)
Board Members: W. Cameron, R. J. Coury, N. Dimick, D. J. Leech, J. C. Maroon, R. L. Piatt, N. Prasad, M. Puskar, C. B. Todd, R. L. Vanderveen

Founded: 1970
Domicile: Pennsylvania
Employees: 6,400

The McGraw-Hill Companies

STANDARD &POOR'S

Nabors Industries Ltd

S&P Recommendation **BUY** ★★★★☆	Price $27.51 (as of Nov 23, 2007)	12-Mo. Target Price $33.00	Investment Style Large-Cap Growth

GICS Sector Energy
Sub-Industry Oil & Gas Drilling

Summary This Bermuda company, based in Barbados, is the world's largest oil and gas land drilling contractor.

Key Stock Statistics (Source S&P, Vickers, company reports)

52-Wk Range	$36.42– 26.82	S&P Oper. EPS 2007**E**	3.22	Market Capitalization(B)	$7.735
Trailing 12-Month EPS	$3.30	S&P Oper. EPS 2008**E**	4.23	Yield (%)	Nil
Trailing 12-Month P/E	8.3	P/E on S&P Oper. EPS 2007**E**	8.5	Dividend Rate/Share	Nil
$10K Invested 5 Yrs Ago	$15,283	Common Shares Outstg. (M)	281.2	Institutional Ownership (%)	86

Beta	0.85
S&P 3-Yr. Proj. EPS CAGR(%)	6.00
S&P Credit Rating	A-

Price Performance

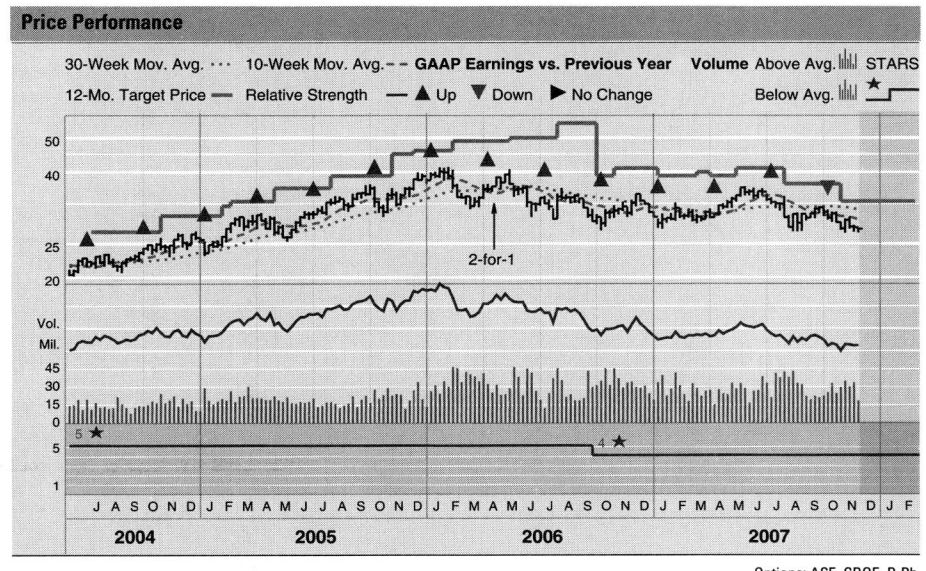

30-Week Mov. Avg. · · · 10-Week Mov. Avg. - - **GAAP Earnings vs. Previous Year** Volume Above Avg. STARS
12-Mo. Target Price — Relative Strength — ▲ Up ▼ Down ► No Change Below Avg.

2-for-1

Options: ASE, CBOE, P, Ph

Analysis prepared by **Michael Kay** on November 01, 2007, when the stock traded at **$ 28.17**.

Highlights

➤ Dayrates for U.S. land drilling rigs declined by $94 per day, to $20,431, in the third quarter, while cash margins fell by $767 per day, to $8,852, the third straight sequential decline after a string of unbroken gains since the 2003 fourth quarter. Although NBR has a high percentage of its domestic fleet secured to long-term contracts, and new rigs ready to begin similar term deals upon delivery, we expect a decline in Lower 48 operating income in 2007, as we believe spot-market exposed rigs will yield lower margins that offset volume growth. We see operating income increasing 36% in 2008 on an estimated 47% increase in U.S. land drilling and 36% in the International segment.

➤ Unlike U.S. markets, we believe that considerable pricing power still exists in NBR's international markets. We see operating income from international land drilling rivaling that of Lower 48 land drilling by 2008, and in so doing, raising NBR's crude oil-related exposure and reducing its exposure to natural gas. We look for significant gains from U.S. offshore and Alaska drilling operations.

➤ For 2007, we expect operating EPS of $3.22, rising to $4.23 in 2008.

Investment Rationale/Risk

➤ While U.S. onshore drilling appears to have slowed, we view NBR as somewhat protected through the use of long-term contracts, its emphasis on larger operators, and segment diversification (particularly its fast-growing international segment). In addition, we remain bullish on NBR's drilling prospects related to unconventional natural gas, given higher technology content needed for drilling such wells and NBR's ongoing newbuild program.

➤ Risks to our recommendation and target price include reduced oil and natural gas prices; lower land drilling dayrates; slower than expected deliveries of new rigs; and rising cost inflation.

➤ Our discounted cash flow (DCF) model shows intrinsic value of about $38 per share. NBR's forward multiples have compressed significantly over the past 12 months, which we attribute in part to concerns about natural gas storage levels and domestic weakness. We expect a recovery from current levels. Using multiples of 5X our 2008 EBITDA estimate and 6X our 2008 cash flow projection (a premium to current levels and peers), and our DCF model, we arrive at our 12-month target price of $33.

Qualitative Risk Assessment

LOW	MEDIUM	HIGH

Our risk assessment reflects NBR's sensitivity to volatile crude oil and natural gas prices (especially the latter), capital spending decisions made by oil and gas producing customers, and the rising number of newbuild land rigs on order. Partly offsetting these risks is NBR's diversified fleet, including overseas operations, and its leadership position in the industry.

Quantitative Evaluations

S&P Quality Ranking B

D	C	B-	**B**	B+	A-	A	A+

Relative Strength Rank MODERATE

50

LOWEST = 1   HIGHEST = 99

Revenue/Earnings Data

Revenue (Million $)

	1Q	2Q	3Q	4Q	Year
2007	1,261	1,157	1,226	--	--
2006	1,164	1,144	1,244	1,329	4,943
2005	783.7	786.1	893.3	1,016	3,551
2004	607.7	546.7	585.7	701.0	2,394
2003	455.7	433.4	476.0	524.6	1,880
2002	381.7	367.3	362.2	380.0	1,466

Earnings Per Share ($)

2007	0.92	0.79	0.68	E0.83	E3.22
2006	0.79	0.77	1.02	0.97	3.40
2005	0.40	0.41	0.56	0.65	2.00
2004	0.23	0.15	0.24	0.34	0.96
2003	0.16	0.10	0.17	0.21	0.63
2002	0.14	0.09	0.09	0.09	0.41

Fiscal year ended Dec. 31. Next earnings report expected: Early February. EPS Estimates based on S&P Operating Earnings; historical GAAP earnings are as reported.

Dividend Data

No cash dividends have been paid.

The McGraw-Hill Companies

Nabors Industries Ltd

**STANDARD
&POOR'S**

Business Summary November 01, 2007

CORPORATE OVERVIEW. The world's largest land drilling contractor, Nabors Industries Ltd. owns a fleet of about 615 land drilling rigs. Formed as a Bermuda-exempt company in December 2001, but operating continuously in the drilling sector since the early 1900s, Nabors conducts oil, gas and geothermal land drilling operations in the lower 48 U.S. states, Alaska and Canada, and internationally, mainly in South and Central America, the Middle East and Africa. NBR owns approximately 610 land workover and well servicing rigs in the U.S. Southwest and West, and approximately 190 well servicing and workover rigs in Canada. In addition, it markets 48 platform, 19 jackup and five barge rigs in the Gulf of Mexico and international markets; these rigs provide well servicing, workover and drilling services. NBR also has a 50% ownership interest in a joint venture in Saudi Arabia, which owns 18 rigs.

The contract drilling segment (90% of 2006 revenues, and 95% of segment operating income) provides drilling, workover, well servicing and related services in the U.S. (including the lower 48, Alaska and offshore), Canada, and internationally. During 2006, 59% of contract drilling revenues served customers in the Lower 48, either for land drilling or land well-servicing. Well servicing and workover services are provided for existing wells where some form of artificial lift is required to bring oil to the surface. To supplement its primary business, NBR offers ancillary wellsite services, such as oilfield management, engineering, transportation, construction, maintenance, and well logging. As of March 2007, NBR had a fleet of 29 marine transportation and support vessels, primarily in the Gulf of Mexico, Trinidad, and the Middle East, providing marine transportation of drilling materials, supplies and crews for offshore rig operations and support for other offshore facilities. The supply vessels are used as freight-carrying vessels for bringing drill pipe, tubing, casing, drilling mud, and other equipment to drilling rigs and production platforms.

Company Financials Fiscal Year Ended Dec. 31

Per Share Data ($)	2006	2005	2004	2003	2002	2001	2000	1999	1998	1997
Tangible Book Value	11.46	10.83	8.68	7.35	6.39	5.89	5.51	4.76	4.30	3.62
Cash Flow	4.77	3.04	1.84	1.36	1.06	1.59	0.94	0.53	0.93	0.80
Earnings	3.40	2.00	0.96	0.63	0.41	1.09	0.45	0.12	0.58	0.56
Dividends	Nil	Nil	Nil	Nil	Nil	Nil	Nil	Nil	Nil	Nil
Payout Ratio	Nil	Nil	Nil	Nil	Nil	Nil	Nil	Nil	Nil	Nil
Prices:High	41.35	39.94	27.13	22.93	24.99	31.56	30.24	15.63	15.78	23.41
Prices:Low	27.26	23.10	20.01	16.10	13.07	9.00	14.06	5.38	5.88	7.38
P/E Ratio:High	12	20	28	37	62	29	68	NM	27	42
P/E Ratio:Low	8	12	21	26	32	8	32	NM	10	13

Income Statement Analysis (Million $)										
Revenue	4,943	3,551	2,394	1,880	1,466	2,121	1,327	639	968	1,029
Operating Income	1,952	1,304	626	438	351	0.69	377	155	267	223
Depreciation, Depletion and Amortization	409	339	300	235	195	190	152	99.9	84.9	66.4
Interest Expense	46.6	44.8	48.5	70.7	67.1	60.7	35.4	30.4	15.5	16.5
Pretax Income	1,471	874	336	175	141	542	227	45.6	200	182
Effective Tax Rate	30.6%	25.8%	9.94%	NM	13.7%	35.9%	40.2%	39.3%	37.5%	37.1%
Net Income	1,021	649	302	192	121	348	135	27.7	125	115

Balance Sheet & Other Financial Data (Million $)										
Cash	701	565	1,253	1,532	1,331	919	551	112	47.3	3.92
Current Assets	2,505	2,617	1,581	1,516	1,370	1,031	1,018	461	266	306
Total Assets	9,142	7,230	5,863	5,603	5,064	4,152	3,137	2,398	1,450	1,234
Current Liabilities	854	1,352	1,199	598	751	330	279	265	244	235
Long Term Debt	4,004	1,252	1,202	1,986	1,615	1,568	855	483	217	230
Common Equity	3,537	3,758	2,929	2,490	2,158	1,858	1,806	1,470	867	728
Total Capital	8,125	5,727	4,517	4,849	4,175	3,711	2,759	2,046	1,157	986
Capital Expenditures	1,927	907	544	353	317	701	301	82.1	276	268
Cash Flow	1,430	987	603	427	317	538	288	128	210	181
Current Ratio	2.9	1.9	1.3	2.5	1.8	3.1	3.6	1.7	1.1	1.3
% Long Term Debt of Capitalization	49.3	21.9	26.6	41.0	38.7	42.2	31.0	23.6	18.8	23.3
% Return on Assets	12.5	9.9	5.3	3.6	2.6	9.5	4.9	1.4	9.3	10.9
% Return on Equity	28.0	19.4	11.2	8.3	6.0	19.0	8.3	2.4	15.7	19.4

Data as orig reptd.; bef. results of disc opers/spec. items. Per share data adj. for stk. divs.; EPS diluted. E-Estimated. NA-Not Available. NM-Not Meaningful. NR-Not Ranked. UR-Under Review.

Office: 8 Par-La_Ville Road, Hamilton, St. Michael , Barbados HM08.
Telephone: 441.292.1510.
Website: http://www.nabors.com
Chrmn & CEO: E.M. Isenberg

Pres & COO: A.G. Petrello
VP & CFO: B.P. Koch
Investor Contact: D.A. Smith (281-874-0035)

Board Members: E. M. Isenberg, A. M. Knaster, J. L. Payne, A. G. Petrello, H. Schmidt, M. M. Sheinfeld, M. J. Whitman

Founded: 1968
Domicile: Bermuda
Employees: 22,014

National City Corp

STANDARD &POOR'S

S&P Recommendation **SELL** ★★☆☆☆	Price $19.55 (as of Nov 23, 2007)	12-Mo. Target Price $21.00	Investment Style Large-Cap Blend

GICS Sector Financials
Sub-Industry Regional Banks

Summary The third largest Ohio bank holding company, NCC also has banking offices in Michigan, Kentucky, Indiana, Illinois, Missouri and Pennsylvania.

Key Stock Statistics (Source S&P, Vickers, company reports)

52-Wk Range	$38.94–18.00	S&P Oper. EPS 2007**E**	1.74	Market Capitalization(B)	$12.387	Beta	0.71
Trailing 12-Month EPS	$2.43	S&P Oper. EPS 2008**E**	2.05	Yield (%)	8.39	S&P 3-Yr. Proj. EPS CAGR(%)	8.00
Trailing 12-Month P/E	8.1	P/E on S&P Oper. EPS 2007**E**	11.2	Dividend Rate/Share	$1.64	S&P Credit Rating	A
$10K Invested 5 Yrs Ago	$8,615	Common Shares Outstg. (M)	633.6	Institutional Ownership (%)	53		

Price Performance

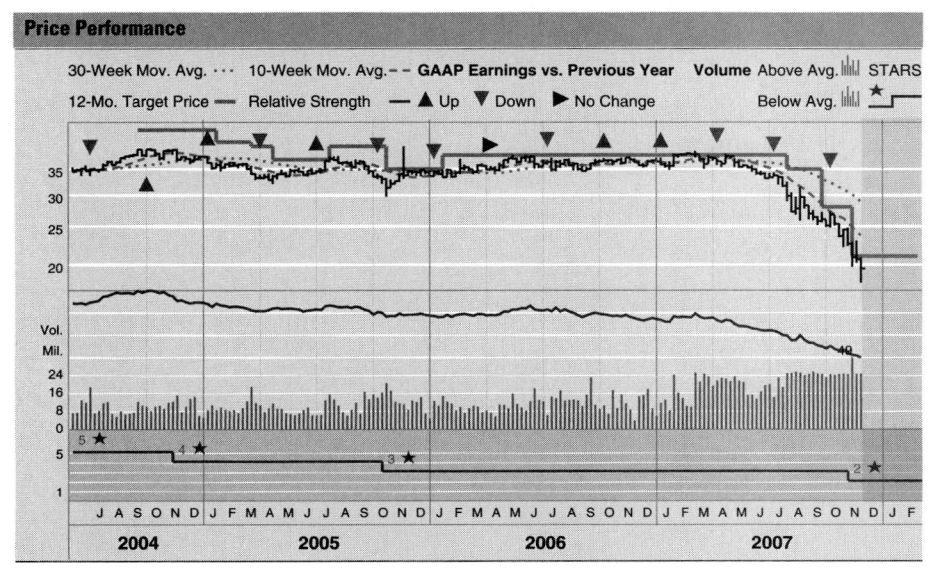

30-Week Mov. Avg. ··· 10-Week Mov. Avg. - - **GAAP Earnings vs. Previous Year** Volume Above Avg. STARS
12-Mo. Target Price — Relative Strength — ▲ Up ▼ Down ▶ No Change Below Avg.

Options: CBOE

Analysis prepared by **Frank Braden, CFA** on November 05, 2007, when the stock traded at **$ 22.55**.

Highlights

➤ We expect a modest 4% rise in total revenue in 2008, following an expected double-digit decline in 2007 from the First Franklin divestiture. We expect some of the revenue pressure in 2008 to come from the restructuring of NCC's mortgage business and the elimination of approximately 1,700 positions in the second half of 2007. We believe NCC's net interest margin will continue to be pressured in 2008, reflecting narrow loan spreads on commercial loans due to intense competition, partially offset by moves into more profitable areas and a more attractive interest rate environment.

➤ In September, NCC announced a mortgage banking restructuring that included suspension of broker-sourced originations of home equity loans, a reduction in non-agency eligible origination capacity and a reduction in staff. We believe that the restructuring of NCC's mortgage and home equity businesses was necessary to improve the business, but we expect difficulties to continue, given its midwestern mortgage exposure.

➤ We project EPS of $1.74 in 2007 and $2.05 in 2008.

Investment Rationale/Risk

➤ In our view, the stock's valuation and relative discount versus peers reflects challenging markets, due to increased competition, and a difficult interest rate and mortgage environment. We anticipate that consolidation in the Midwestern markets will help alleviate some of the competitive deposit pricing, but expect continued job losses in NCC's Midwestern footprint to put increasing pressure on the residential real estate market.

➤ Risks to our recommendation and target price include the possibility of a turn around in the Midwestern housing market; an improvement in economic conditions; an increase in credit quality; lower net hedging losses than we expect; and an improvement in corporate loan demand.

➤ Our 12-month target price of $21 reflects a P/E multiple of 10.2X our 2008 EPS estimate, a discount to its historical average, which we see as justified by our view of NCC's home equity and mortgage related issues.

Qualitative Risk Assessment

LOW	MEDIUM	HIGH

Our risk assessment reflects our view of NCC's solid fundamentals coupled with its strong customer base, and good diversification.

Quantitative Evaluations

S&P Quality Ranking A

D	C	B-	B	B+	A-	A	A+

Relative Strength Rank WEAK

15

LOWEST = 1　　　　　　　　　　　HIGHEST = 99

Revenue/Earnings Data

Revenue (Million $)

	1Q	2Q	3Q	4Q	Year
2007	2,831	3,012	2,977	--	--
2006	2,801	3,020	3,168	3,965	12,953
2005	2,554	2,839	2,773	2,883	11,036
2004	2,462	2,261	2,639	3,198	10,560
2003	2,622	2,534	2,037	2,400	9,594
2002	2,248	2,209	2,064	2,207	8,728

Earnings Per Share ($)

2007	0.50	0.60	-0.03	E0.46	E1.74
2006	0.74	0.77	0.86	1.36	3.72
2005	0.74	0.97	0.74	0.64	3.09
2004	1.16	0.83	0.86	1.46	4.31
2003	1.05	0.94	0.56	0.88	3.43
2002	0.73	0.63	0.61	0.62	2.59

Fiscal year ended Dec. 31. Next earnings report expected: Late January. EPS Estimates based on S&P Operating Earnings; historical GAAP earnings are as reported.

Dividend Data (Dates: mm/dd Payment Date: mm/dd/yy)

Amount ($)	Date Decl.	Ex-Div. Date	Stk. of Record	Payment Date
0.390	01/02	01/10	01/12	02/01/07
0.390	04/02	04/10	04/12	05/01/07
0.410	07/02	07/11	07/13	08/01/07
0.410	10/01	10/09	10/11	11/01/07

Dividends have been paid since 1936. Source: Company reports.

Please read the Required Disclosures and Analyst Certification on the last page of this report.

National City Corp

**STANDARD
&POOR'S**

Business Summary November 05, 2007

CORPORATE OVERVIEW. NCC operates five major lines of business: Retail Banking (RB), Commercial Banking - Regional, Commercial Banking - National, Mortgage Banking (NMB), and Asset Management. RB provides banking services to consumers and small businesses within NCC's seven-state footprint. In addition to deposit gathering and direct lending services provided through the retail bank branch network, call centers, and the Internet, RB's activities also include small business banking services, education finance, retail brokerage, and lending-related insurance services. Consumer lending products include home equity, government or privately guaranteed student loans, and credit cards and other unsecured personal and small business lines of credit.

Commercial banking provides credit-related and treasury management services, as well as capital markets and international services, to large- and medium-sized corporations. Major products and services include: lines of credit, term loans, leases, automobile floorplan lending, investment real estate

lending, asset-based lending, structured finance, syndicated lending, equity and mezzanine capital, treasury management, and international payment and clearing services.

The mortgage banking line primarily originates conventional residential mortgage and home equity loans both within NCC's banking footprint and nationally. NMB's activities also include servicing mortgage loans for third-party investors. Mortgage loans originated by NMB generally represent loans collateralized by one-to-four-family residential real estate and are made to borrowers in good credit standing. These loans are typically sold to primary mortgage market aggregators and jumbo loan investors.

Company Financials Fiscal Year Ended Dec. 31

Per Share Data ($)	2006	2005	2004	2003	2002	2001	2000	1999	1998	1997
Tangible Book Value	16.73	14.85	14.36	13.47	11.70	12.15	11.06	9.44	10.69	10.14
Earnings	3.72	3.09	4.31	3.43	2.59	2.27	2.13	2.22	1.61	1.83
S&P Core Earnings	2.67	2.99	3.44	3.30	2.31	1.95	NA	NA	NA	NA
Dividends	1.52	1.44	1.34	1.25	1.20	1.16	1.14	1.06	0.94	0.84
Payout Ratio	41%	47%	31%	36%	46%	51%	54%	48%	58%	46%
Prices:High	38.04	40.00	39.66	34.97	33.75	32.70	29.75	37.81	38.75	33.78
Prices:Low	33.26	29.75	32.14	26.53	24.60	23.69	16.00	22.13	28.47	21.25
P/E Ratio:High	10	13	9	10	13	14	14	17	24	18
P/E Ratio:Low	9	10	7	8	9	10	8	10	18	12

Income Statement Analysis (Million $)

	2006	2005	2004	2003	2002	2001	2000	1999	1998	1997
Net Interest Income	4,604	4,696	4,504	4,368	4,005	3,439	2,958	3,000	2,912	1,943
Tax Equivalent Adjustment	NA	31.3	NA	28.0	30.4	33.3	33.7	36.9	40.3	19.4
Non Interest Income	4,019	3,225	4,444	3,549	2,731	2,533	2,427	2,242	1,695	899
Loan Loss Provision	483	287	323	638	682	605	287	250	201	140
% Expense/Operating Revenue	54.7%	60.0%	51.0%	51.6%	55.4%	56.0%	59.1%	56.9%	73.3%	71.0%
Pretax Income	3,423	2,961	4,078	3,237	2,406	2,167	1,972	2,149	1,647	1,169
Effective Tax Rate	32.8%	33.0%	31.8%	34.6%	33.8%	35.9%	34.0%	34.6%	35.0%	31.0%
Net Income	2,300	1,985	2,780	2,117	1,594	1,388	1,302	1,405	1,071	807
% Net Interest Margin	3.75	3.74	4.09	4.11	4.34	4.71	3.85	3.99	4.11	4.25
S&P Core Earnings	1,607	1,924	2,225	2,038	1,429	1,201	NA	NA	NA	NA

Balance Sheet & Other Financial Data (Million $)

	2006	2005	2004	2003	2002	2001	2000	1999	1998	1997
Money Market Assets	1,551	301	303	162	136	171	81.0	556	930	600
Investment Securities	15,378	10,285	10,518	7,859	10,217	10,463	10,673	15,135	15,701	8,865
Commercial Loans	47,755	53,392	40,847	50,446	34,107	34,033	52,247	29,415	22,243	14,095
Other Loans	47,737	62,646	59,290	60,115	38,028	34,007	13,357	30,789	35,768	25,476
Total Assets	140,191	142,397	139,280	113,933	118,258	105,817	88,535	87,121	88,246	54,684
Demand Deposits	47,873	45,733	47,916	43,435	39,179	34,324	28,763	27,744	29,523	16,822
Time Deposits	39,361	38,253	38,039	20,495	25,940	28,806	26,494	22,322	28,724	20,039
Long Term Debt	18,656	19,370	28,444	23,666	22,730	17,316	18,145	15,038	9,009	4,810
Common Equity	14,581	12,613	12,804	9,329	8,308	7,381	6,740	5,698	6,977	4,281
% Return on Assets	1.6	1.4	2.2	1.8	1.4	1.4	1.5	1.6	1.5	1.5
% Return on Equity	16.9	15.6	25.1	24.2	20.3	19.7	20.9	22.2	18.7	18.5
% Loan Loss Reserve	1.0	10.3	1.2	1.2	1.1	1.2	1.3	1.5	1.7	1.8
% Loans/Deposits	124.2	126.3	116.5	148.0	141.7	130.0	125.3	114.9	106.3	103.5
% Equity to Assets	9.6	9.0	8.7	7.5	7.0	7.3	7.1	7.2	8.2	8.3

Data as orig reptd.; bef. results of disc opers/spec. items. Per share data adj. for stk. divs.; EPS diluted. E-Estimated. NA-Not Available. NM-Not Meaningful. NR-Not Ranked. UR-Under Review.

Office: 1900 E 9th St , Cleveland, OH, USA 44114-3484.
Telephone: 216-222-2000.
Email: investor.relation@nationalcity.com
Website: http://www.nationalcity.com

Chrmn & CEO: D.A. Daberko
Pres & Vice Chrmn: P.E. Raskind
Vice Chrmn & CFO: J.D. Kelly
EVP, Secy & General Counsel: D.L. Zoeller

SVP & Treas: T.A. Richlovsky
Investor Contact: J. Hammarlund (800-622-4204)
Board Members: J. E. Barfield, J. S. Broadhurst, C. M. Connor, D. A. Daberko, B. P. Healy, S. C. Lindner, M. B. McCallister, P. A. Ormond, R. A. Paul, P. E. Raskind, G. L. Shaheen, J. S. Thornton, M. Weiss

Founded: 1845
Domicile: Delaware
Employees: 31,270

The McGraw-Hill Companies

National Oilwell Varco Inc

S&P Recommendation **BUY** ★★★★☆	Price $68.06 (as of Nov 23, 2007)	12-Mo. Target Price $79.00	Investment Style Large-Cap Growth

GICS Sector Energy
Sub-Industry Oil & Gas Equipment & Services

Summary This company designs and manufactures drill rig equipment, provides downhole tools and services, and also provides supply chain integration services to the upstream oil and gas industry.

Key Stock Statistics (Source S&P, Vickers, company reports)

52-Wk Range	$82.00– 26.88	S&P Oper. EPS 2007**E**	3.77	Market Capitalization(B)	$24.244	Beta	0.58
Trailing 12-Month EPS	$3.39	S&P Oper. EPS 2008**E**	4.56	Yield (%)	Nil	S&P 3-Yr. Proj. EPS CAGR(%)	20.00
Trailing 12-Month P/E	20.1	P/E on S&P Oper. EPS 2007**E**	18.1	Dividend Rate/Share	Nil	S&P Credit Rating	NR
$10K Invested 5 Yrs Ago	$63,400	Common Shares Outstg. (M)	356.2	Institutional Ownership (%)	95		

Price Performance

30-Week Mov. Avg. ··· 10-Week Mov. Avg. - - **GAAP Earnings vs. Previous Year** Volume Above Avg. STARS
12-Mo. Target Price — Relative Strength ▲ Up ▼ Down ► No Change Below Avg. ★

Options: ASE, CBOE, P

Analysis prepared by **Stewart Glickman, CFA** on November 21, 2007, when the stock traded at **$ 67.93**.

Highlights

➤ New orders for capital equipment totaled $1.9 billion in the third quarter, up $100 million from the second quarter of 2007, and the total backlog at the end of September was a record $8.0 billion. A typical order for rig components for a newbuild jackup yields NOV approximately $50 million in revenue, while a similar order for a new floater could yield revenues of about $150 million. Although a large number of jackup newbuild announcements have occurred over the past 12 months (with the orderbook standing at about 154 new offshore rigs), we think there is the potential for further newbuilds, particularly on the floater side.

➤ Third-quarter 2007 operating margins widened in the Rig Technology segment, pacing an overall margin of about 21.1%, versus 20.8% in the second quarter of 2007. For full-year 2007, we see total revenue growth of approximately 41%, with a further 16% advance expected in 2008, and operating margins in the 22% area.

➤ We estimate split-adjusted operating EPS of $3.77 in 2007, with a rise of about 21% to $4.56 in 2008.

Investment Rationale/Risk

➤ We view NOV as an attractive way to play the growing need for new rig equipment for the oil and gas industry. While the current book of 154 rigs either on order or under construction (including 85 jackups, 44 semisubmersibles, and 25 drillships) implies about a 25% addition to the existing worldwide fleet, we believe that currently unsatisfied demand should absorb most new additions over the next several years, especially for deepwater-capable rigs.

➤ Risks to our opinion and target price include lower-than-expected prices for crude oil and natural gas; a slowdown in drilling activity; and delays in meeting capital equipment orders.

➤ Our discounted cash flow (DCF) model, assuming terminal growth of 3% and a WACC of 10.8%, yields an intrinsic value of about $76. We think NOV merits a premium-to-peers valuation given our view of its strong installed base of rig components. Based on an assumed 11X multiple of enterprise value to estimated 2008 EBITDA, 13.5X estimated 2008 cash flow (a slight premiums to peers), and our DCF model, our 12-month target price is $79.

Qualitative Risk Assessment

LOW	MEDIUM	HIGH

Our risk assessment reflects NOV's exposure to volatile crude oil and natural gas prices, and capital spending decisions made by its contract driller and exploration and production customers. Offsetting these risks is what we view as NOV's leading industry position as a manufacturer of rig capital equipment.

Quantitative Evaluations

S&P Quality Ranking B

D	C	B-	**B**	B+	A-	A	A+

Relative Strength Rank STRONG

75

LOWEST = 1 HIGHEST = 99

Revenue/Earnings Data

Revenue (Million $)

	1Q	2Q	3Q	4Q	Year
2007	2,166	2,385	2,580	--	--
2006	1,512	1,657	1,778	2,079	7,026
2005	814.9	1,216	1,237	1,377	4,645
2004	496.2	533.5	618.9	669.5	2,318
2003	500.6	475.4	498.6	530.4	2,005
2002	389.0	372.4	366.9	393.6	1,522

Earnings Per Share ($)

2007	0.78	0.90	1.02	E1.08	E3.77
2006	0.34	0.42	0.50	0.68	1.94
2005	0.17	0.18	0.25	0.29	0.91
2004	0.07	0.13	0.16	0.29	0.64
2003	0.12	0.12	0.14	0.09	0.45
2002	0.13	0.11	0.11	0.11	0.45

Fiscal year ended Dec. 31. Next earnings report expected: Early February. EPS Estimates based on S&P Operating Earnings; historical GAAP earnings are as reported.

Dividend Data (Dates: mm/dd Payment Date: mm/dd/yy)

Amount ($)	Date Decl.	Ex-Div. Date	Stk. of Record	Payment Date
2-for-1	08/22	10/01	09/07	09/28/07

Source: Company reports.

National Oilwell Varco Inc

Business Summary November 21, 2007

CORPORATE OVERVIEW. Formerly known as National-Oilwell, this company changed its name to National Oilwell Varco (NOV) on March 14, 2005, following the completion of the merger with Varco International. NOV, a worldwide designer, manufacturer and marketer of comprehensive systems and components used in oil and gas drilling and production, as well as a provider of downhole tools and services, also provides supply chain integration services to the upstream oil and gas industry. The company estimates that more than 90% of the mobile offshore rig fleet and the majority of the world's larger land rigs (2,000 horsepower and greater) manufactured in the past 20 years use drawworks, mud pumps and other drilling components manufactured by NOV.

The combined company generated 2006 revenues of about $7.0 billion, and operating income of $1.15 billion, for an operating margin of approximately 16.4%. The company's Rig Technology segment ($3.58 billion of revenue in

2006, and $621 million of 2006 segment operating income) designs, manufactures and sells drilling systems and components for both land and offshore drilling rigs, as well as complete land drilling and well servicing rigs. The major mechanical components include drawworks, mud pumps, power swivels, SCR houses, solids control equipment, traveling equipment and rotary tables. Many of these components are designed specifically for applications in offshore, extended reach and deep land drilling. This equipment is installed on new rigs and is often replaced during the upgrade and refurbishment of existing rigs. As of March 31, 2007, total backlog in this segment was about $6.4 billion.

Company Financials Fiscal Year Ended Dec. 31

Per Share Data ($)	2006	2005	2004	2003	2002	2001	2000	1999	1998	1997
Tangible Book Value	5.91	4.20	3.33	2.49	2.17	3.19	2.72	1.90	2.16	2.46
Cash Flow	2.39	1.27	0.89	0.68	0.60	0.87	0.30	0.21	0.83	0.64
Earnings	1.94	0.91	0.64	0.45	0.45	0.64	0.08	0.02	0.65	0.50
S&P Core Earnings	1.94	0.90	0.58	0.41	0.38	0.57	NA	NA	NA	NA
Dividends	Nil	Nil	Nil	Nil	Nil	Nil	Nil	Nil	Nil	Nil
Payout Ratio	Nil	Nil	Nil	Nil	Nil	Nil	Nil	Nil	Nil	Nil
Prices:High	38.80	34.17	18.69	12.43	14.41	20.62	19.84	9.25	20.22	22.22
Prices:Low	25.81	16.54	10.83	8.75	7.60	6.20	7.00	4.25	3.81	7.00
P/E Ratio:High	20	38	29	28	32	32	NM	NM	31	45
P/E Ratio:Low	13	18	17	19	17	10	NM	NM	6	14

Income Statement Analysis (Million $)	2006	2005	2004	2003	2002	2001	2000	1999	1998	1997
Revenue	7,026	4,645	2,318	2,005	1,522	1,747	1,150	745	1,172	1,006
Operating Income	1,280	623	213	198	159	228	97.6	45.1	157	113
Depreciation, Depletion and Amortization	161	115	44.0	39.2	25.0	38.9	35.0	23.2	19.2	14.7
Interest Expense	48.7	52.9	38.4	38.9	27.3	24.9	Nil	Nil	12.5	6.20
Pretax Income	1,049	430	132	117	112	168	27.0	4.52	109	82.5
Effective Tax Rate	33.9%	32.3%	14.6%	28.9%	35.0%	38.1%	51.4%	66.4%	36.9%	37.8%
Net Income	684	287	110	76.8	73.1	104	13.1	1.52	68.9	51.3
S&P Core Earnings	685	283	99.2	69.3	61.6	93.6	NA	NA	NA	NA

Balance Sheet & Other Financial Data (Million $)	2006	2005	2004	2003	2002	2001	2000	1999	1998	1997
Cash	957	209	143	74.2	118	43.2	42.5	12.4	11.4	19.8
Current Assets	4,966	2,998	1,537	1,246	1,115	909	743	478	558	464
Total Assets	9,019	6,679	2,599	2,243	1,969	1,472	1,279	782	818	568
Current Liabilities	2,665	1,187	800	452	346	277	263	176	211	211
Long Term Debt	835	836	350	594	595	300	222	196	206	61.6
Common Equity	5,024	4,194	1,296	1,090	933	868	767	395	387	278
Total Capital	6,283	5,428	1,767	1,753	1,592	1,188	1,006	597	597	342
Capital Expenditures	200	105	39.0	32.4	24.8	27.4	24.6	15.4	27.8	32.6
Cash Flow	845	402	154	116	98.1	143	48.2	24.8	88.1	66.0
Current Ratio	1.9	2.5	1.9	2.8	3.2	3.3	2.8	2.7	2.6	2.2
% Long Term Debt of Capitalization	13.3	15.4	19.8	33.9	37.3	25.3	22.1	32.8	34.5	18.0
% Return on Assets	8.7	6.2	4.6	3.6	4.2	7.6	1.2	0.2	9.9	12.3
% Return on Equity	14.8	10.5	9.2	7.6	8.1	12.7	1.9	0.4	20.7	26.5

Data as orig reptd.; bef. results of disc opers/spec. items. Per share data adj. for stk. divs.; EPS diluted. E-Estimated. NA-Not Available. NM-Not Meaningful. NR-Not Ranked. UR-Under Review.

Office: 10000 Richmond Avenue, Houston, TX 77042-4200.
Telephone: 713-346-7500.
Email: investor.relations@natoil.com
Website: http://www.natoil.com

Chrmn, Pres & CEO: M.A. Miller, Jr.
COO & EVP: J.C. Winkler
SVP & CFO: C.C. Williams
VP, Chief Acctg Officer & Cntlr: R. Blanchard

VP & General Counsel: D.W. Rettig
Board Members: G. L. Armstrong, R. E. Beauchamp, B. A. Guill, D. D. Harrison, R. L. Jarvis, E. L. Mattson, M. A. Miller, Jr., J. A. Smisek

Founded: 1987
Domicile: Delaware
Employees: 26,861

National Semiconductor Corp

STANDARD &POOR'S

S&P Recommendation	HOLD ★★★☆☆	Price	12-Mo. Target Price	Investment Style
		$22.36 (as of Nov 23, 2007)	$30.00	Large-Cap Growth

GICS Sector Information Technology
Sub-Industry Semiconductors

Summary This company is a leading manufacturer of a broad line of semiconductors, including analog, digital and mixed-signal integrated circuits.

Key Stock Statistics (Source S&P, Vickers, company reports)

52-Wk Range	$29.69– 21.65	S&P Oper. EPS 2008E	1.40	Market Capitalization(B)	$5.903	Beta	2.46
Trailing 12-Month EPS	$1.07	S&P Oper. EPS 2009E	1.79	Yield (%)	1.07	S&P 3-Yr. Proj. EPS CAGR(%)	3.00
Trailing 12-Month P/E	20.9	P/E on S&P Oper. EPS 2008E	16.0	Dividend Rate/Share	$0.24	S&P Credit Rating	BBB
$10K Invested 5 Yrs Ago	$24,115	Common Shares Outstg. (M)	264.0	Institutional Ownership (%)	97		

Price Performance

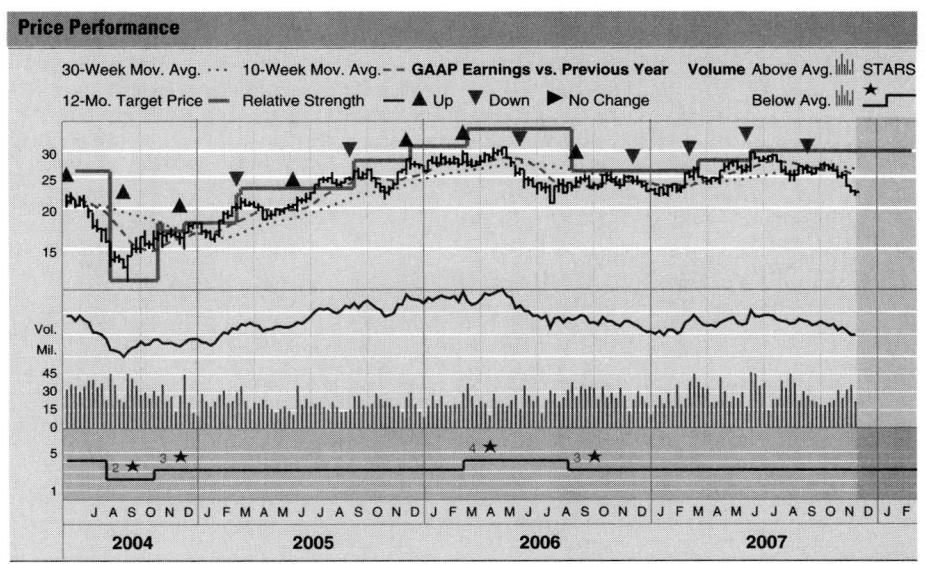

30-Week Mov. Avg. ··· 10-Week Mov. Avg. - - **GAAP Earnings vs. Previous Year**   Volume Above Avg. ⅠⅠⅠ STARS
12-Mo. Target Price — Relative Strength — ▲ Up ▼ Down ► No Change   Below Avg. ⅠⅠⅠ ★

Options: ASE, CBOE, P, Ph

Analysis prepared by **Clyde Montevirgen** on September 11, 2007, when the stock traded at **$ 25.96**.

Highlights

➤ Following a FY 07 (May) sales decline of about 11%, we project 5% growth in FY 08. NSM is winding down activity for certain older product lines, and we think the loss of revenues from these businesses dampened results in FY 07. However, we believe healthy sales growth in higher-margin analog businesses that the company is targeting for the long term should help balance the losses. A recent inventory glut also hurt sales, but we see a strengthening in wireless and portable electronics helping longer term results.

➤ After gross margin improvement to 61% in FY 07, we see further widening to 64% in FY 08, reflecting a continued focus on higher-margin analog products. However, we think the company will maintain its utilization rates at low levels in the near term, preventing it from exceeding its 65% gross margin target this fiscal year. Although we expect operating expenses to increase as a percentage of sales, increasing gross margins should support wider operating margins.

➤ We are forecasting operating EPS of $1.40 for FY 08 and $1.79 for FY 09.

Investment Rationale/Risk

➤ Although excess inventory appears to be burning off, we remain concerned about the rate of demand in the second half of the year due to end-market uncertainty and formidable competition. While we believe NSM is capable of gaining market share in the high-performance analog space, we believe that the company does not yet have the demand to drastically improve its utilization rates, which may limit sizable gross margin expansion. We also think that recent price appreciation provides a less compelling risk-reward payoff, given current valuations.

➤ Risks to our recommendation and target price include the possibility of a sudden deterioration in demand for electronic goods that contain NSM's chips and above-average share price volatility.

➤ Our 12-month target price of $30 is derived by applying a price-to-sales multiple of 3.8X, which is at the high end of historical averages and slightly above peer averages, to our forward 12-month sales per share estimate, implying a $30 value. We also apply a 21X P/E multiple, slightly above peers, to our FY 08 EPS estimate, implying a $29 value.

Qualitative Risk Assessment

LOW	MEDIUM	HIGH

NSM operates in the semiconductor industry, which historically has experienced industry cycles of about four years. Sudden slowdowns can result from downturns in demand for electronics or from chip inventory buildup and industry overcapacity. Share price volatility for the stock is well above average.

Quantitative Evaluations

S&P Quality Ranking   B-

D	C	B-	B	B+	A-	A	A+

Relative Strength Rank   MODERATE

30

LOWEST = 1   HIGHEST = 99

Revenue/Earnings Data

Revenue (Million $)

	1Q	2Q	3Q	4Q	Year
2008	471.5	--	--	--	--
2007	541.4	501.6	431.0	455.9	1,930
2006	493.8	544.0	547.7	572.6	2,158
2005	548.0	448.9	449.2	467.0	1,913
2004	424.8	473.5	513.6	571.2	1,983
2003	420.6	422.3	404.3	425.3	1,673

Earnings Per Share ($)

2008	0.30	E0.31	E0.38	E0.42	E1.40
2007	0.35	0.27	0.22	0.28	1.12
2006	0.24	0.32	0.37	0.34	1.26
2005	0.31	0.24	0.21	0.36	1.11
2004	0.08	0.17	0.24	0.24	0.74
2003	Nil	0.02	-0.10	-0.01	-0.09

Fiscal year ended May 31. Next earnings report expected: Early December. EPS Estimates based on S&P Operating Earnings; historical GAAP earnings are as reported.

Dividend Data (Dates: mm/dd Payment Date: mm/dd/yy)

Amount ($)	Date Decl.	Ex-Div. Date	Stk. of Record	Payment Date
0.040	03/12	03/15	03/19	04/09/07
0.040	06/11	06/14	06/18	07/09/07
0.040	09/07	09/13	09/17	10/09/07
0.060	09/28	12/13	12/17	01/07/08

Dividends have been paid since 2005. Source: Company reports.

National Semiconductor Corp

STANDARD &POOR'S

Business Summary September 11, 2007

CORPORATE OVERVIEW. National Semiconductor designs, develops, manufactures and markets a wide range of semiconductor products. Leading-edge products include power management circuits, display drivers, audio and operational amplifiers, communication interface products and data conversion solutions. The company targets a broad range of markets and applications such as wireless handsets, medical applications, displays, automotive applications, networks, test and measurement applications, industrial markets, and a broad range of portable applications. Most of its products are analog and mixed-signal integrated circuits, comprising 86% of FY 06 total revenue.

NSM classifies its product lines in two groups, Power Management and Analog Signal Path. The Power Management group makes products that converts and manages power consumption in electronic systems. The Analog Signal Path group makes analog technology that is used during the path that information or data enters the electronic products, is conditioned, converted and processed to the point it is sent out. This technology is used to connect and convert analog signals to digital information.

The company markets its products globally to original equipment manufacturers (OEMs) and original design manufacturers through a direct sales force. In FY 06, 49% of sales were made directly to OEMs and 51% came from distribu-

tors. Leading distributors include Avnet (which accounted for 12% of NSM's FY 06 sales) and Arrow (12%). International sales accounted for 80% of total sales in FY 06.

CORPORATE STRATEGY. National Semiconductor's CEO, Brian Halla, who joined the company in 1996, has led an effort to form a "new" NSM. The company's expertise has been primarily in analog intensive, digital and mixed-signal complex integrated circuits. In 1996, NSM spun off its logic, memory and discrete products (considered commodity-type components) as a separate company, Fairchild Semiconductor. The company now focuses on high-end analog chips.

Wafer fabrication is concentrated in two facilities in the U.S. and one in Scotland. Nearly all product assembly and final test operations are performed in several facilities in Asia. The Singapore assembly and test facility is scheduled for closure in 2007; most operations were transferred to the Malaysia and China plants during FY 06.

Company Financials Fiscal Year Ended May 31

Per Share Data ($)

	2007	2006	2005	2004	2003	2002	2001	2000	1999	1998
Tangible Book Value	5.43	5.57	5.65	4.21	4.18	4.46	4.70	4.63	2.67	5.62
Cash Flow	1.56	1.72	1.63	1.27	0.54	0.31	1.30	2.33	-1.81	0.59
Earnings	1.12	1.26	1.11	0.74	-0.09	-0.34	0.65	1.64	-3.02	-0.30
S&P Core Earnings	1.11	1.21	1.15	0.26	-0.59	-0.84	0.29	NA	NA	NA
Dividends	0.10	0.04	Nil	Nil	Nil	Nil	Nil	Nil	Nil	Nil
Payout Ratio	9%	3%	Nil	Nil	Nil	Nil	Nil	Nil	Nil	Nil
Calendar Year	2006	2005	2004	2003	2002	2001	2000	1999	1998	1997
Prices:High	30.93	28.75	24.35	22.63	18.65	17.55	42.97	25.94	14.13	21.44
Prices:Low	20.56	18.36	11.85	6.27	4.98	9.85	8.56	4.44	3.72	10.81
P/E Ratio:High	28	23	22	31	NM	NM	66	16	NM	NM
P/E Ratio:Low	18	15	11	8	NM	NM	13	3	NM	NM

Income Statement Analysis (Million $)

	2007	2006	2005	2004	2003	2002	2001	2000	1999	1998
Revenue	1,930	2,158	1,913	1,983	1,673	1,495	2,113	2,140	1,957	2,537
Operating Income	642	844	626	582	248	81.9	517	550	20.2	342
Depreciation	145	166	194	210	229	230	243	264	406	292
Interest Expense	Nil	Nil	Nil	Nil	Nil	3.90	5.00	17.9	Nil	26.3
Pretax Income	531	695	410	334	-23.3	-123	307	642	-1,085	-99.7
Effective Tax Rate	29.3%	35.4%	NM	14.7%	NM	NM	19.4%	2.32%	NM	NM
Net Income	375	449	415	285	-33.3	-122	246	628	-1,010	-98.6
S&P Core Earnings	372	433	430	102	-215	-298	108	NA	NA	NA

Balance Sheet & Other Financial Data (Million $)

	2007	2006	2005	2004	2003	2002	2001	2000	1999	1998
Cash	829	932	867	643	802	681	818	850	419	461
Current Assets	1,291	1,541	1,514	1,246	1,281	1,073	1,275	1,468	989	1,308
Total Assets	2,202	2,511	2,504	2,280	2,245	2,289	2,362	2,382	2,044	3,101
Current Liabilities	300	398	285	461	367	404	472	628	665	794
Long Term Debt	20.6	21.1	23.0	Nil	19.9	20.4	26.0	48.6	416	391
Common Equity	1,749	1,926	2,062	1,681	1,706	1,781	1,768	1,643	701	1,859
Total Capital	1,769	1,947	2,085	1,681	1,726	1,802	1,794	1,692	1,317	2,254
Capital Expenditures	107	163	96.6	215	171	138	228	170	303	622
Cash Flow	520	616	610	495	195	109	489	891	-604	194
Current Ratio	4.3	3.9	5.3	2.7	3.5	2.7	2.7	2.3	1.5	1.6
% Long Term Debt of Capitalization	1.2	1.1	1.1	Nil	1.2	1.1	1.4	2.9	31.6	17.3
% Net Income of Revenue	19.4	20.8	21.7	14.4	NM	NM	11.6	29.3	NM	NM
% Return on Assets	15.9	17.9	17.4	12.6	NM	NM	10.3	28.4	NM	NM
% Return on Equity	20.4	22.6	22.1	16.8	NM	NM	14.4	49.3	NM	NM

Data as orig reptd.; bef. results of disc opers/spec. items. Per share data adj. for stk. divs.; EPS diluted. E-Estimated. NA-Not Available. NM-Not Meaningful. NR-Not Ranked. UR-Under Review.

Office: 2900 Semiconductor Dr, Santa Clara, CA 95051-0695.
Telephone: 408-721-5000.
Email: invest.group@nsc.com
Website: http://www.national.com

Chrmn & CEO: B.L. Halla
Pres & COO: D. Macleod
SVP & CFO: L. Chew
SVP, Secy & General Counsel: J.M. Clark, III

SVP & CIO: U. Seif
Board Members: S. R. Appleton, G. P. Arnold, R. J. Danzig, J. T. Dickson, R. J. Frankenberg, B. L. Halla, E. F. Kvamme, M. A. Maidique, E. R. McCracken

Founded: 1959
Domicile: Delaware
Employees: 7,600

The McGraw-Hill Companies

Network Appliance Inc

STANDARD &POOR'S

S&P Recommendation HOLD ★★★☆☆	Price $24.81 (as of Nov 23, 2007)	12-Mo. Target Price $27.00	Investment Style Large-Cap Growth

GICS Sector Information Technology
Sub-Industry Computer Storage & Peripherals

Summary This company manufactures and supports high-performance network data storage devices that provide file service for data-intensive network environments.

Key Stock Statistics (Source S&P, Vickers, company reports)

52-Wk Range	$41.56– 22.51	S&P Oper. EPS 2008**E**	0.86	Market Capitalization(B)	$8.828
Trailing 12-Month EPS	$0.73	S&P Oper. EPS 2009**E**	1.07	Yield (%)	Nil
Trailing 12-Month P/E	34.0	P/E on S&P Oper. EPS 2008**E**	28.8	Dividend Rate/Share	Nil
$10K Invested 5 Yrs Ago	$17,289	Common Shares Outstg. (M)	355.8	Institutional Ownership (%)	81

Beta	2.69
S&P 3-Yr. Proj. EPS CAGR(%)	24.00
S&P Credit Rating	NA

Price Performance

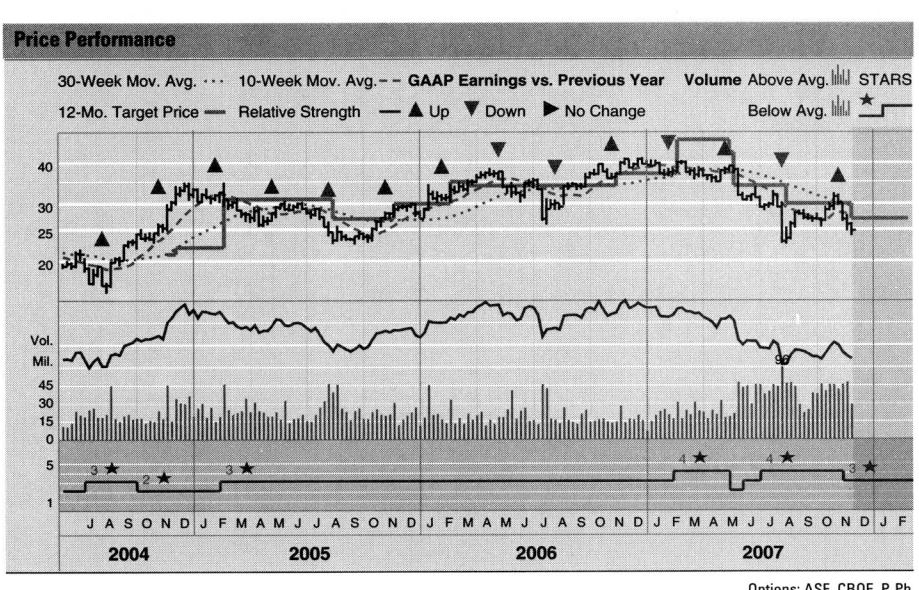

30-Week Mov. Avg. ··· 10-Week Mov. Avg. - - GAAP Earnings vs. Previous Year Volume Above Avg. STARS
12-Mo. Target Price — Relative Strength — ▲ Up ▼ Down ► No Change Below Avg.

Options: ASE, CBOE, P, Ph

Analysis prepared by **Jawahar Hingorani** on November 19, 2007, when the stock traded at **$ 25.92**.

Qualitative Risk Assessment

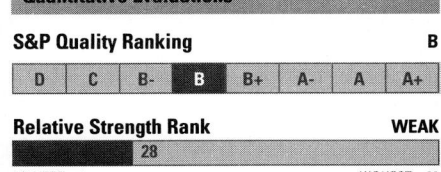

LOW	MEDIUM	HIGH

Our risk assessment takes into consideration the volatile nature of the data storage industry and the rapid pace of technological change. However, we believe these factors are offset by NTAP's strong market share position and earnings growth.

Quantitative Evaluations

S&P Quality Ranking   **B**

D	C	B-	B	B+	A-	A	A+

Relative Strength Rank   **WEAK**

28

LOWEST = 1   HIGHEST = 99

Revenue/Earnings Data

Revenue (Million $)

	1Q	2Q	3Q	4Q	Year
2008	689.2	792.2	--	--	--
2007	621.3	652.5	729.3	801.2	2,804
2006	448.4	483.1	537.0	598.0	2,066
2005	358.4	375.2	412.7	451.8	1,598
2004	260.5	275.6	297.3	337.0	1,170
2003	206.8	215.2	228.5	241.6	892.1

Earnings Per Share ($)

	1Q	2Q	3Q	4Q	Year
2008	0.09	0.23	E0.23	E0.33	E0.86
2007	0.14	0.22	0.17	0.23	0.77
2006	0.16	0.18	0.20	0.15	0.69
2005	0.13	0.15	0.16	0.16	0.59
2004	0.08	0.13	0.11	0.10	0.42
2003	0.05	0.05	0.06	0.07	0.22

Fiscal year ended Apr. 30. Next earnings report expected: Mid February. EPS Estimates based on S&P Operating Earnings; historical GAAP earnings are as reported.

Dividend Data

No cash dividends have been paid.

Highlights

➤ We expect revenues to advance about 17% in FY 08 (Apr.) and 18% in FY 09. We are somewhat concerned about a slowdown in certain market segments due to a weak US economy, offset by growth in global markets. We view NTAP's targeting of small and medium sized enterprises with new product introductions somewhat positively, but see increased competition in the space. We think NTAP's decision to pursue market share and revenue growth by lowering prices will result in lower margins.

➤ We see gross margins being down slightly in FY 08, largely related to business mix, pricing pressure and to an increasing focus on the small and mid-size business market. We expect NTAP to control hiring and operating expenses to bolster operating income. Following free cash flow of $190 million in the quarter ended October 31, 2007, we expect to see continuing free cash flow generation. We anticipate that additional share repurchases will take place during the remainder of calendar 2007.

➤ Our EPS estimate for FY 08 is $0.86, up 12% from FY 07's EPS of $0.77, followed by EPS of $1.07 in FY 09. Our estimates do not include acquisition and other one time costs and expenses.

Investment Rationale/Risk

➤ We lowered our opinion to hold, based on valuation, and based on lower EPS estimates. As we near the end of 2007, we see a slowing US economy, and weakness in market segments, like financial services, affecting near term revenue growth. In addition to slowing revenues, and together with pricing pressures, we do not foresee a return to year ago earnings growth levels of over 30%. We think focusing sales and product development on small and medium businesses makes sense, but believe the space is increasingly competitive.

➤ Risks to our recommendation and target price include decreased enterprise spending, reduced demand for network storage products, longer sales cycles, and losses in market share relative to competitors.

➤ Our 12-month target price of $27 is based on a combination of valuation metrics. The first, our discounted cash flow (DCF) analysis, leads to an intrinsic value of $27.50 and assumes a weighted average cost of capital of 11.7% and a terminal growth rate of 3%. The second is a relative P/E valuation in which we apply a ratio of 24.8X our forward twelve month EPS estimate, in line with peers, resulting in a value of $27.

Please read the Required Disclosures and Analyst Certification on the last page of this report.

The McGraw-Hill Companies

Network Appliance Inc

STANDARD &POOR'S

Business Summary November 19, 2007

CORPORATE OVERVIEW. Network Appliance supplies enterprise storage and data management software and hardware products and services. NTAP's solutions help global enterprises meet major information technology challenges such as managing the continued growth in the volume of data, scaling existing infrastructure, regulatory compliance and corporate security.

The NTAP family of modular, scalable, highly available, unified networked systems provides seamless access to a full range of enterprise data for users on a variety of platforms. These include Fibre Channel (FC), network-attached storage (NAS), storage area network (SAN), iSCSI environments, and Web data in central locations. NTAP refers to this as fabric-attached storage (FAS). Products include the 200, 900, 3000 and 6000 series.

NTAP's V-Series is a network-based solution that consolidates storage arrays from different suppliers, enabling unified SAN and file access to data stored in heterogeneous FC SAN storage arrays. The V-Series family supports products from Hewlett-Packard, Hitachi Data Systems and IBM.

CORPORATE STRATEGY. NearStore products focus on optimizing data protection and retention applications. This system offers an alternative to customers by providing faster data access than offline storage at a significantly lower cost than primary storage. Offerings in this category include the Virtual Tape Library (VTL), a disk-to-disk backup appliance that appears as a tape library to a back-up software application.

The NetCache suite of solutions is designed to manage, control and improve access to Web-based information. Working with a range of software partners, NetCache gives large enterprises the ability to manage Internet access and security, thereby enabling IT managers to control who in their user base is going where on the Internet, when, and what content is being accessed.

Company Financials Fiscal Year Ended Apr. 30

Per Share Data ($)	2007	2006	2005	2004	2003	2002	2001	2000	1999	1998
Tangible Book Value	3.56	3.62	3.67	2.91	2.75	2.39	2.21	1.54	1.02	0.64
Cash Flow	1.05	0.90	0.77	0.58	0.38	0.14	0.33	0.26	0.14	0.18
Earnings	0.77	0.69	0.59	0.42	0.22	0.01	0.21	0.21	0.12	0.07
S&P Core Earnings	0.73	0.45	0.39	0.16	-0.28	-0.77	-0.52	NA	NA	NA
Dividends	Nil	Nil	Nil	Nil	Nil	Nil	Nil	Nil	Nil	Nil
Payout Ratio	Nil	Nil	Nil	Nil	Nil	Nil	Nil	Nil	Nil	Nil
Calendar Year	2006	2005	2004	2003	2002	2001	2000	1999	1998	1997
Prices:High	41.56	34.98	34.99	26.69	27.95	74.98	152.75	45.94	12.00	4.50
Prices:Low	25.85	22.50	15.92	9.26	5.18	6.00	33.88	9.53	3.25	1.33
P/E Ratio:High	54	51	59	64	NM	NM	NM	NM	NM	62
P/E Ratio:Low	34	33	27	22	NM	NM	NM	NM	NM	18

Income Statement Analysis (Million $)										
Revenue	2,804	2,066	1,598	1,170	892	798	1,006	579	289	166
Operating Income	387	395	319	228	146	76.5	179	121	63.3	38.2
Depreciation	111	81.8	65.6	59.5	57.4	65.3	42.3	15.7	8.15	5.55
Interest Expense	11.6	1.28	Nil	Nil	Nil	Nil	Nil	Nil	0.78	0.21
Pretax Income	360	350	276	170	97.8	2.53	133	114	57.0	33.5
Effective Tax Rate	17.2%	23.9%	18.3%	10.8%	21.8%	NM	43.7%	35.5%	37.5%	37.5%
Net Income	298	266	226	152	76.5	3.03	74.9	73.8	35.6	21.0
S&P Core Earnings	282	175	148	59.5	-98.0	-256	-167	NA	NA	NA

Balance Sheet & Other Financial Data (Million $)										
Cash	489	461	194	241	284	211	272	279	221	37.3
Current Assets	2,241	2,033	1,576	1,089	853	679	636	533	315	98.9
Total Assets	3,658	3,261	2,373	1,877	1,319	1,109	1,036	592	346	116
Current Liabilities	1,188	917	520	344	265	216	219	113	50.5	29.3
Long Term Debt	Nil	138	4.47	4.86	3.10	3.73	0.15	0.05	0.09	0.16
Common Equity	1,989	1,923	1,661	1,416	987	858	804	479	296	86.3
Total Capital	1,989	2,061	1,665	1,421	990	862	805	479	296	86.4
Capital Expenditures	166	133	93.6	48.6	61.3	284	83.7	40.8	15.5	7.97
Cash Flow	409	348	291	212	134	47.4	117	89.5	43.8	26.5
Current Ratio	1.9	2.2	3.0	3.2	3.2	3.2	2.9	4.7	6.2	3.4
% Long Term Debt of Capitalization	Nil	6.7	0.3	0.3	0.3	0.4	0.0	0.0	0.0	Nil
% Net Income of Revenue	10.6	12.9	14.1	13.0	8.6	0.4	7.4	12.7	12.3	12.6
% Return on Assets	8.6	9.5	10.6	9.5	6.3	0.3	9.2	15.7	15.4	22.7
% Return on Equity	15.2	14.9	14.7	12.7	8.3	0.4	11.7	19.1	18.6	29.9

Data as orig reptd.; bef. results of disc opers/spec. items. Per share data adj. for stk. divs.; EPS diluted. E-Estimated. NA-Not Available. NM-Not Meaningful. NR-Not Ranked. UR-Under Review.

Office: 495 East Java Drive, Sunnyvale, CA 94089.
Telephone: 408-822-6000.
Email: investor_relations@netapp.com
Website: http://www.netapp.com

Chrmn: D.T. Valentine
Pres: T.F. Mendoza
CEO: D.J. Warmenhoven
EVP & CFO: S.J. Gomo

SVP & CTO: S. Kleinman
Investor Contact: K. McGaughey (408-822-3856)
Board Members: J. R. Allen, C. A. Bartz, A. L. Earhart, E. Kozel, M. Leslie, N. G. Moore, G. T. Shaheen, D. T. Valentine, R. T. Wall, D. J. Warmenhoven

Founded: 1992
Domicile: Delaware
Employees: 6,635

The McGraw-Hill Companies

Newell Rubbermaid Inc.

STANDARD &POOR'S

S&P Recommendation HOLD ★★★☆☆	**Price** $26.55 (as of Nov 26, 2007)	**12-Mo. Target Price** $32.00	**Investment Style** Large-Cap Value

GICS Sector Consumer Discretionary
Sub-Industry Housewares & Specialties

Summary This high-volume, brand-name consumer products concern has grown through acquisitions. Major product lines include housewares, home furnishings, office products and hardware.

Key Stock Statistics (Source S&P, Vickers, company reports)

52-Wk Range	$32.19–24.22	S&P Oper. EPS 2007**E**	1.79	Market Capitalization(B)	$7.336	Beta	0.92
Trailing 12-Month EPS	$1.67	S&P Oper. EPS 2008**E**	1.95	Yield (%)	3.16	S&P 3-Yr. Proj. EPS CAGR(%)	10.00
Trailing 12-Month P/E	15.9	P/E on S&P Oper. EPS 2007**E**	14.8	Dividend Rate/Share	$0.84	S&P Credit Rating	BBB+
$10K Invested 5 Yrs Ago	$10,931	Common Shares Outstg. (M)	276.3	Institutional Ownership (%)	88		

Price Performance

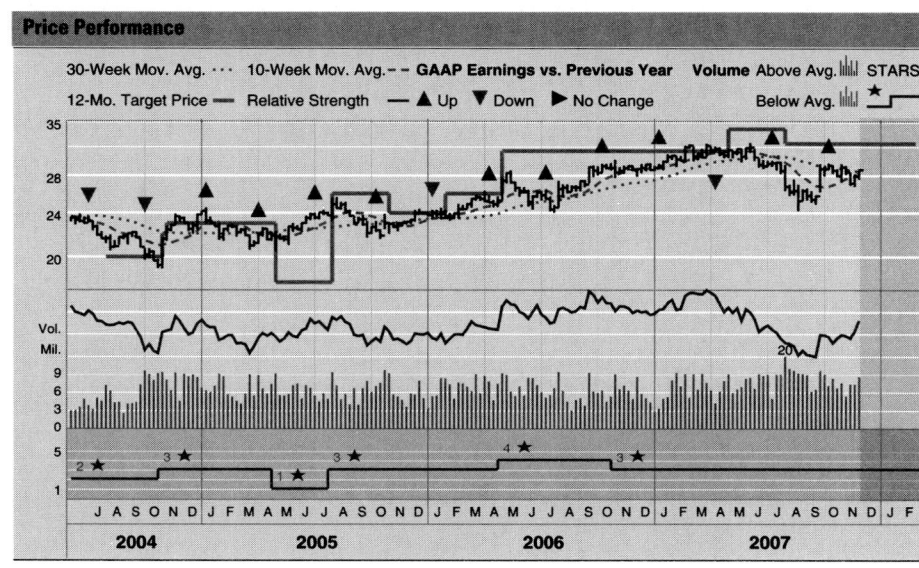

30-Week Mov. Avg. · · · 10-Week Mov. Avg. - - **GAAP Earnings vs. Previous Year** Volume Above Avg. STARS
12-Mo. Target Price — Relative Strength — ▲ Up ▼ Down ► No Change Below Avg. ★

Options: CBOE, P

Analysis prepared by **Loran Braverman, CFA** on October 26, 2007, when the stock traded at **$ 28.74**.

Highlights

➤ We see net sales increasing 3.8% in 2007, reflecting the elimination of non-strategic, low margin products, as well as acquisitions and our cautious outlook for discretionary spending. For 2008, we look for 4.3% growth, assuming a continuation of our concerns about consumer spending, but a modest recovery in housing-related expenditures in the second half.

➤ We expect the operating margin, excluding restructuring charges, to widen by 130 basis points in 2007, with higher pricing and productivity gains more than offsetting increases in brand building and other expenses. For 2008, we forecast another 60 basis point improvement in the operating margin, assuming that commodity cost pressures do not worsen. We look for an effective tax rate in both 2007 and 2008 of close to 30% versus 2006's effective tax rate of about 28.5%.

➤ We estimate that 2007 operating EPS will increase to $1.79, from $1.52 in 2006 (excluding charges and one-time tax benefits), on a 3% increase in average fully diluted shares outstanding. Our 2008 EPS estimate is $1.95.

Investment Rationale/Risk

➤ Our hold opinion reflects our view that, at the current price, the stock appropriately reflects what we view as improved long-term growth prospects. Under new leadership, we believe the company is poised for better innovation and efficiency. We think that NWL is shedding lower margin product lines and is investing in the more profitable categories. While the categories in which it competes are competitive, we believe NWL will be able to gain market share through better consumer research and greater product innovation.

➤ Risks to our recommendation and target price include poor consumer acceptance of new products, a low level of cost savings associated with the company's reorganization program, and a material increase in prices of key raw materials such as resin and steel.

➤ Our 12-month target price of $32 is a blend of our historical and relative analyses. Our historical model uses a P/E of about 18X our 2008 EPS estimate, close to the 10-year median, to arrive at a $36 valuation. Our relative analysis uses a multiple of about 14X, slightly above the peer average, implying a $27 value.

Qualitative Risk Assessment

LOW	MEDIUM	HIGH

Our risk assessment reflects that Housewares companies' products are generally affordable, low-priced goods that are modestly affected by swings in the economy. However, there is a greater level of import competition for commodity-type goods.

Quantitative Evaluations

S&P Quality Ranking B

D	C	B-	**B**	B+	A-	A	A+

Relative Strength Rank MODERATE

56

LOWEST = 1 HIGHEST = 99

Revenue/Earnings Data

Revenue (Million $)

	1Q	2Q	3Q	4Q	Year
2007	1,384	1,693	1,687	--	--
2006	1,343	1,634	1,586	1,638	6,201
2005	1,363	1,646	1,585	1,749	6,343
2004	1,541	1,736	1,672	1,809	6,748
2003	1,736	1,976	1,945	2,093	7,750
2002	1,597	1,895	1,948	2,014	7,454

Earnings Per Share ($)

2007	0.23	0.51	0.61	E0.45	E1.79
2006	0.47	0.49	0.41	0.33	1.71
2005	0.33	0.30	0.37	0.31	1.29
2004	0.12	0.21	-0.86	0.45	-0.07
2003	0.06	0.27	0.27	-0.77	-0.17
2002	0.19	0.33	0.29	0.36	1.16

Fiscal year ended Dec. 31. Next earnings report expected: Late January. EPS Estimates based on S&P Operating Earnings; historical GAAP earnings are as reported.

Dividend Data (Dates: mm/dd Payment Date: mm/dd/yy)

Amount ($)	Date Decl.	Ex-Div. Date	Stk. of Record	Payment Date
0.210	02/07	02/26	02/28	03/15/07
0.210	05/10	05/29	05/31	06/15/07
0.210	08/09	08/29	08/31	09/14/07
0.210	11/08	11/28	11/30	12/14/07

Dividends have been paid since 1946. Source: Company reports.

Please read the Required Disclosures and Analyst Certification on the last page of this report.

The McGraw-Hill Companies

Newell Rubbermaid Inc.

**STANDARD
&POOR'S**

Business Summary October 26, 2007

CORPORATE OVERVIEW. Newell Rubbermaid is a global manufacturer and marketer of name-brand consumer products and their commercial extensions, serving a wide array of retail channels including department stores, warehouse clubs, home centers, hardware stores, commercial distributors, office superstores, contract stationers, automotive stores and small superstores. Products are sold through four business segments: cleaning, organization & decor (32% of 2006 sales, 26% of segment operating profits), office products (33%, 36%), tools & hardware (20%, 23%), and home & family (15%, 15%). About 26% of 2006 sales and 21% of operating profits were made outside the U.S.

NWL's cleaning, organization & decor segment is made up of three businesses using the Rubbermaid name and the Levolor/Kirsch unit. These businesses design, manufacture or source, package and distribute semi-durable products primarily for use in the home and commercial settings. These products include indoor and outdoor organization, home storage, food storage, cleaning, refuse, material handling, drapery hardware, custom and stock horizontal and vertical blinds, as well as pleated, cellular and roller shades.

The office products segment is conducted by four geographic business units and primarily sells writing instruments, labeling solutions, and office organization products. Brands include Sharpie, Paper-Mate, Waterman, Parker, and DYMO.

The tools & hardware business sells hand tools, power tool accessories, propane torches, manual paint applicator products, cabinet hardware, and window hardware under brand names such as Irwin, Lenox, and BernzOmatic.

The home & family segment offers an extensive line of premium kitchenware (Calphalon brand), infant and juvenile products (Graco), and hair care accessories and grooming products (Goody).

During 2005, the company acquired DYMO, a maker of labeling products, and sold its Curver (home organization) business to Jar din International Holding BV. During 2006 and early 2007, NWL divested its European cookware, Little Tikes, and Home Decor Europe businesses.

Company Financials Fiscal Year Ended Dec. 31

Per Share Data ($)	2006	2005	2004	2003	2002	2001	2000	1999	1998	1997
Tangible Book Value	NM	NM	NM	NM	NM	0.44	0.97	2.38	1.57	2.20
Cash Flow	2.41	2.07	0.84	0.84	2.21	2.22	2.57	1.30	3.14	2.82
Earnings	1.71	1.29	-0.07	-0.17	1.16	0.99	1.57	0.34	2.38	1.82
S&P Core Earnings	1.73	1.22	0.56	0.39	0.86	0.71	NA	NA	NA	NA
Dividends	0.84	0.84	0.84	0.84	0.84	0.84	0.84	0.80	0.72	0.64
Payout Ratio	49%	65%	NM	NM	72%	85%	54%	235%	30%	35%
Prices:High	29.98	25.69	26.41	32.00	36.70	29.50	31.88	52.00	55.19	43.81
Prices:Low	23.25	20.50	19.05	20.27	26.11	20.50	18.25	25.25	35.69	30.13
P/E Ratio:High	18	20	NM	NM	32	30	20	NM	23	24
P/E Ratio:Low	14	16	NM	NM	23	21	12	NM	15	17

Income Statement Analysis (Million $)										
Revenue	6,201	6,343	6,748	7,750	7,454	6,909	6,935	6,413	3,720	3,234
Operating Income	916	843	870	992	1,033	966	1,173	862	736	702
Depreciation	193	214	249	278	281	329	293	272	148	162
Interest Expense	155	142	130	140	111	137	130	100	60.4	73.6
Pretax Income	515	418	86.3	20.1	495	443	685	231	685	482
Effective Tax Rate	8.58%	14.8%	NM	NM	31.7%	34.2%	38.5%	58.7%	42.1%	39.5%
Net Income	471	356	-19.1	-46.6	312	265	422	95.4	396	290
S&P Core Earnings	476	333	153	108	232	190	NA	NA	NA	NA

Balance Sheet & Other Financial Data (Million $)										
Cash	201	116	506	144	55.1	6.80	31.7	102	57.5	36.1
Current Assets	2,477	2,473	3,012	3,000	3,080	2,851	2,897	2,739	1,591	1,382
Total Assets	6,311	6,446	6,666	7,481	7,389	7,266	7,262	6,724	4,328	3,944
Current Liabilities	1,897	1,798	1,871	2,022	2,614	2,534	1,551	1,630	821	664
Long Term Debt	1,972	2,430	2,424	2,869	2,357	1,865	2,815	1,956	1,366	784
Common Equity	1,890	1,643	1,764	2,016	2,064	2,433	2,449	2,697	1,912	1,714
Total Capital	3,863	4,073	4,189	4,887	4,426	4,373	5,358	4,738	3,300	3,096
Capital Expenditures	138	92.2	122	300	252	250	317	200	148	98.4
Cash Flow	664	570	230	232	592	593	714	367	544	452
Current Ratio	1.3	1.4	1.6	1.5	1.2	1.1	1.9	1.7	1.9	2.1
% Long Term Debt of Capitalization	51.1	59.7	57.9	58.7	53.2	42.7	52.5	41.3	41.3	25.4
% Net Income of Revenue	7.6	5.6	NM	NM	4.2	3.8	6.1	1.5	10.6	9.0
% Return on Assets	7.4	5.4	NM	NM	4.3	3.6	6.0	1.5	9.5	8.4
% Return on Equity	26.6	20.9	NM	NM	13.9	10.8	16.4	3.4	21.7	18.1

Data as orig reptd.; bef. results of disc opers/spec. items. Per share data adj. for stk. divs.; EPS diluted. E-Estimated. NA-Not Available. NM-Not Meaningful. NR-Not Ranked. UR-Under Review.

Office: 10 B Glenlake Pkwy Ste 300, Atlanta, GA 30328-7266.
Telephone: 770-407-3800.
Email: investor.relations@newellco.com
Website: http://www.newellrubbermaid.com

Chrmn: W.D. Marohn
Pres & CEO: M.D. Ketchum
EVP & CFO: J.P. Robinson
VP, Chief Acctg Officer & Cntlr: R.T. Dillon

VP, Secy & General Counsel: D.L. Matschullat
Board Members: T. E. Clarke, S. S. Cowen, M. T. Cowhig, M. D. Ketchum, W. D. Marohn, E. C. Millett, C. A. Montgomery, A. P. Newell, S. J. Strobel, G. R. Sullivan, M. A. Todman, R. G. Viault

Founded: 1903
Domicile: Delaware
Employees: 23,500

The McGraw-Hill Companies

Newmont Mining Corp

STANDARD & POOR'S

S&P Recommendation HOLD ★★★☆☆	**Price** $52.09 (as of Nov 23, 2007)	**12-Mo. Target Price** $56.00	**Investment Style** Large-Cap Growth

GICS Sector Materials
Sub-Industry Gold

Summary Newmont is the world's second-largest gold producer.

Key Stock Statistics (Source S&P, Vickers, company reports)

52-Wk Range	$56.35–38.01	S&P Oper. EPS 2007E	1.14	Market Capitalization(B)	$22.155	Beta	-0.01
Trailing 12-Month EPS	$-3.04	S&P Oper. EPS 2008E	2.05	Yield (%)	0.77	S&P 3-Yr. Proj. EPS CAGR(%)	5.40
Trailing 12-Month P/E	NM	P/E on S&P Oper. EPS 2007E	45.7	Dividend Rate/Share	$0.40	S&P Credit Rating	BBB+
$10K Invested 5 Yrs Ago	$22,626	Common Shares Outstg. (M)	451.5	Institutional Ownership (%)	83		

Price Performance

30-Week Mov. Avg. · · · 10-Week Mov. Avg. - - **GAAP Earnings vs. Previous Year**   Volume Above Avg. ▌▌▌ STARS
12-Mo. Target Price — Relative Strength — ▲ Up ▼ Down ► No Change   Below Avg. ▌▌▌ ★

Options: ASE, CBOE, P, Ph

Analysis prepared by **Leo J. Larkin** on November 20, 2007, when the stock traded at **$50.00**.

Qualitative Risk Assessment

LOW	MEDIUM	HIGH

Our risk assessment is based on our belief that Newmont's current reserve growth profile is stagnant and could worsen if output from the Yanacocha mine declines more than currently expected. This is offset by our view of Newmont's strong balance sheet and future production from new mines.

Quantitative Evaluations

S&P Quality Ranking   B-

D	C	B-	B	B+	A-	A	A+

Relative Strength Rank   STRONG
95
LOWEST = 1   HIGHEST = 99

Revenue/Earnings Data

Revenue (Million $)

	1Q	2Q	3Q	4Q	Year
2007	1,256	1,302	1,646	--	--
2006	1,132	1,293	1,102	1,460	4,987
2005	945.0	998.0	1,158	1,305	4,406
2004	1,122	1,009	1,163	1,230	4,524
2003	748.5	747.2	897.0	821.4	3,214
2002	491.6	632.4	712.1	786.1	2,658

Earnings Per Share ($)

2007	0.15	-0.90	0.72	E0.38	E1.14
2006	0.46	0.34	0.59	0.47	1.86
2005	0.19	0.19	0.29	0.16	0.83
2004	0.30	0.08	0.29	0.43	1.10
2003	0.38	0.22	0.28	0.36	1.23
2002	-0.06	0.17	0.05	0.19	0.39

Fiscal year ended Dec. 31. Next earnings report expected: Late February. EPS Estimates based on S&P Operating Earnings; historical GAAP earnings are as reported.

Highlights

➤ Following an estimated sales increase of 20% in 2007, we look for a 12% rise in 2008, reflecting a higher average gold price. Our forecast assumes an average gold price of $730 an ounce for 2008, versus 2007's estimated average price of $670 an ounce. In our view, a higher average price of gold will offset a projected decline in the copper price in 2008 to $2.80 a pound from an estimated average price of $3.20 a pound in 2007. We look for NEM's production of gold and copper in 2008 to approximate 2007's levels. We believe global gold production will fall in 2008. By our analysis, lower global production along with a likely continued decline in short-term interest rates in the U.S. and continued downward pressure on the U.S. Dollar support another increase in the gold price in 2008.

➤ Benefiting from increased revenue per ounce and less rapidly rising raw material costs, we project an increase in EPS to $2.05 for 2008 from estimated operating EPS of $1.14 for 2007.

➤ Longer term, we see EPS aided by a projected rise in the price of gold, further consolidation of the industry, and profit contributions from copper operations.

Investment Rationale/Risk

➤ With all of NEM's output now exposed to spot gold, we think it is well positioned for a higher gold price. We believe that gold is in a bull market for several reasons: we expect the gap between consumption and production to widen as production worldwide likely declines; we think gold and gold shares will be viewed as attractive alternative investments, given our view that financial asset returns in the first decade of the 21st century will trail the high levels seen in the late 1990s; and we believe that currency instability will increase gold's role as a monetary reserve asset.

➤ Risks to our recommendation and target price include a drop in the price of gold and lower-than-expected output from Yanacocha.

➤ Given our view that its growth profile remains stagnant, we anticipate that NEM will not command a high P/E on its 2008 EPS. We believe NEM's weak growth prospects relative to peers will be a drag on its P/E. We expect NEM to trade at 27.3X our 2008 EPS estimate, leading to our 12-month target price of $56. Based on our projected P/E, NEM would sell at the low end of its historical range.

Dividend Data (Dates: mm/dd Payment Date: mm/dd/yy)

Amount ($)	Date Decl.	Ex-Div. Date	Stk. of Record	Payment Date
0.100	02/07	03/05	03/07	03/29/07
0.100	04/24	06/06	06/08	06/29/07
0.100	07/18	09/04	09/07	09/28/07
0.100	10/17	12/05	12/07	12/28/07

Dividends have been paid since 1934. Source: Company reports.

Please read the Required Disclosures and Analyst Certification on the last page of this report.

The McGraw-Hill Companies

Newmont Mining Corp

STANDARD &POOR'S

Business Summary November 20, 2007

CORPORATE OVERVIEW. Newmont Mining Corp. is the world's second-largest gold company. It has significant assets and operations in the in the United States, Australia, Peru, Indonesia, Ghana, Canada, Bolivia, New Zealand, and Mexico. The company has two large development projects in Ghana, West Africa. Newmont is also engaged in the production of copper, principally through its Batu Hijau operation in Indonesia. In 2007's second quarter, NEM incurred a charge to discontinue its Merchant Banking unit as part of its strategy to focus on core mining operations.

Proven and probable gold reserves totaled 93.9 million oz. at the end of 2006, using a gold price assumption of $500 an oz., versus 93.2 million oz. at the end of 2005, using a gold price assumption of $400 per oz.

At year-end 2006, 33.1 million oz. of NEM's gold reserves were located in Nevada, 15.1 million oz. in Peru, 20.3 million oz. in Ghana, 18.5 million oz. in Australia/New Zealand, 5.0 million oz. in Indonesia, and 1.9 million oz. in other operations located in Mexico and Bolivia.

Copper reserves totaled 8.0 billion lbs. at the end of 2006, using a copper price assumption of $1.25 a pound, versus 9.1 billion lbs. at the end of 2005, using a copper price assumption of $1.00 per lb.

About 29% of Newmont's equity gold sales in 2006 came from the United States, 31% from Peru, 16% from Australia/New Zealand, 19% from Indonesia, 2% from Ghana, and 3% from other. As of December 31, 2006, approximately 54% of the company's total long-lived assets were located in the U.S., 10% in Peru, 8% in Australia/New Zealand, 15% in Indonesia, 5% in Ghana and 8% in other.

CORPORATE STRATEGY. NEM's main strategy is to increase its portfolio of low-cost, long-life mines. In 2007's second quarter, NEM incurred a charge to eliminate its remaining gold hedges as it anticipates higher gold prices over the long term, and seeks to provide shareholders with maximum leverage to the price of gold. NEM plans to spend $1.8 billion in capital development from 2006 to 2010 to offset the decline in the production of mature operations. NEM estimates that its new mines will have project lives of over 16 years and add 2.6 million oz. of annual equity production at costs below the industry average.

Company Financials Fiscal Year Ended Dec. 31

Per Share Data ($)	2006	2005	2004	2003	2002	2001	2000	1999	1998	1997
Tangible Book Value	14.98	12.27	11.02	8.39	2.77	7.49	8.58	8.66	8.62	10.17
Cash Flow	3.27	2.27	2.66	2.60	1.75	1.38	1.61	1.58	-0.45	2.14
Earnings	1.86	0.83	1.10	1.23	0.39	-0.16	-0.06	0.15	-2.27	0.44
S&P Core Earnings	1.45	0.79	1.22	1.05	0.25	-0.26	NA	NA	NA	NA
Dividends	0.40	0.40	0.30	0.17	0.12	0.12	0.12	0.12	0.12	0.39
Payout Ratio	22%	48%	28%	14%	31%	NM	NM	80%	NM	89%
Prices:High	62.72	53.93	50.20	50.28	32.75	25.23	28.38	30.06	34.88	47.50
Prices:Low	39.84	34.90	34.70	24.08	18.52	14.00	12.75	16.38	13.25	26.56
P/E Ratio:High	34	65	46	41	84	NM	NM	NM	NM	NM
P/E Ratio:Low	21	42	32	20	47	NM	NM	NM	NM	NM

Income Statement Analysis (Million $)										
Revenue	4,987	4,406	4,524	3,214	2,658	1,656	1,555	1,399	1,454	1,573
Operating Income	2,059	1,621	1,878	1,219	852	435	502	493	500	582
Depreciation	636	644	697	564	506	300	293	240	289	266
Interest Expense	97.0	98.0	97.6	88.6	130	86.4	79.6	62.6	78.8	77.1
Pretax Income	1,627	1,068	1,102	890	268	-10.2	94.2	112	-471	132
Effective Tax Rate	26.1%	29.4%	25.0%	23.2%	7.43%	NM	12.1%	12.9%	NM	48.2%
Net Income	840	374	490	510	150	-23.3	-10.5	24.8	-360	68.4
S&P Core Earnings	657	356	540	435	96.7	-52.8	NA	NA	NA	NA

Balance Sheet & Other Financial Data (Million $)										
Cash	1,275	1,899	1,726	1,459	402	149	60.3	55.3	79.1	146
Current Assets	2,642	3,036	2,721	2,360	1,113	709	512	534	513	641
Total Assets	15,601	13,992	12,771	11,050	10,155	4,062	3,510	3,383	3,187	3,614
Current Liabilities	1,739	1,350	1,101	834	693	486	291	274	212	395
Long Term Debt	Nil	1,733	1,311	887	1,701	1,090	976	1,014	1,201	1,179
Common Equity	9,865	8,376	7,938	7,385	5,419	1,469	1,466	1,452	1,440	1,591
Total Capital	10,963	11,489	10,500	9,251	8,132	2,955	2,695	2,627	2,733	2,938
Capital Expenditures	1,551	1,226	718	501	300	402	378	221	216	415
Cash Flow	1,476	1,018	1,187	1,075	652	269	283	264	-71.4	334
Current Ratio	1.5	2.2	2.5	2.8	1.6	1.5	1.8	2.0	2.4	1.6
% Long Term Debt of Capitalization	Nil	15.1	12.5	9.6	20.9	40.3	36.2	38.6	43.9	40.1
% Net Income of Revenue	16.8	8.5	10.8	15.9	5.7	NM	NM	1.8	NM	4.3
% Return on Assets	5.7	2.8	4.2	4.8	2.1	NM	NM	0.7	NM	2.4
% Return on Equity	9.0	4.5	6.4	8.0	4.4	NM	NM	1.7	NM	5.2

Data as orig reptd.; bef. results of disc opers/spec. items. Per share data adj. for stk. divs.; EPS diluted. E-Estimated. NA-Not Available. NM-Not Meaningful. NR-Not Ranked. UR-Under Review.

Office: 1700 Lincoln Street, Denver, CO 80203-4500.
Telephone: 303-863-7414.
Website: http://www.newmont.com
Chrmn: W.W. Murdy

Pres & CEO: R.T. O'Brien
Vice Chrmn: P. Lassonde
SVP & CFO: R. Ball
VP & Treas: T.P. Mahoney

Investor Contact: R. Engel (303-837-6033)
Board Members: G. A. Barton, V. A. Calarco, N. Doyle, V. Hagen, M. S. Hamson, P. Lassonde, R. J. Miller, W. W. Murdy, R. A. Plumbridge, J. B. Prescott, D. C. Roth, S. Schulich, J. V. Taranik

Founded: 1916
Domicile: Delaware
Employees: 15,000

The McGraw-Hill Companies

New York Times Co (The)

STANDARD &POOR'S

S&P Recommendation **BUY** ★★★★☆	Price $17.26 (as of Nov 23, 2007)	12-Mo. Target Price $26.00	Investment Style Large-Cap Blend

GICS Sector Consumer Discretionary
Sub-Industry Publishing

Summary This diversified communications company publishes newspapers, operates radio and television stations, and has equity holdings in newsprint and paper mills.

Key Stock Statistics (Source S&P, Vickers, company reports)

52-Wk Range	$26.90– 16.75	S&P Oper. EPS 2007**E**	1.13	Market Capitalization(B)	$2.470	Beta	0.74
Trailing 12-Month EPS	$-3.40	S&P Oper. EPS 2008**E**	1.31	Yield (%)	5.33	S&P 3-Yr. Proj. EPS CAGR(%)	3.00
Trailing 12-Month P/E	NM	P/E on S&P Oper. EPS 2007**E**	15.3	Dividend Rate/Share	$0.92	S&P Credit Rating	BBB
$10K Invested 5 Yrs Ago	$3,948	Common Shares Outstg. (M)	143.9	Institutional Ownership (%)	NM		

Price Performance

30-Week Mov. Avg. · · · 10-Week Mov. Avg. – – **GAAP Earnings vs. Previous Year** Volume Above Avg. STARS
12-Mo. Target Price — Relative Strength — ▲ Up ▼ Down ► No Change Below Avg. ★

Options: ASE, CBOE, P, Ph

Analysis prepared by **James Peters, CFA** on October 25, 2007, when the stock traded at **$ 20.71**.

Highlights

➤ We anticipate revenues in 2008 of about the same level as 2007. We believe NYT will fare better than other pure play peers exposed to cyclical and secular challenges in the print publishing industry partly due to the company's above average revenues and revenue growth from fast growing Internet operations. We also expect revenue growth from higher circulation revenues following a price increase that took effect in the third quarter of 2007, from recently added print outsourcing contracts, and from incremental lease revenues associated with the company's new headquarters.

➤ We look for operating margins to expand to 11.0% in 2008, from our projection of 9.7% in 2007. Including an estimated 3% rate of expense inflation and excluding potential severance costs, we see overall expenses falling about $50 million in 2008 as the company implements various cost reduction initiatives.

➤ We forecast 2008 operating EPS of $1.31, up from our projection of $1.13 in 2007. Projected EPS in 2007 excludes a net benefit of $0.39, with one-time gains and earnings from discontinued operations offsetting severance expense.

Investment Rationale/Risk

➤ Following previously announced cost cutting actions we have observed taking hold in 2007, we are encouraged by NYT's announcement in July to reduce its annual cost structure by an additional $230 million, before inflation, by 2009. We think NYT distinguishes itself by deriving about 11% of overall revenues from its high growth Internet operations versus an estimated 6% for peers. We expect the company to utilize what we view as a conservative balance sheet, with a less than 2X debt/EBITDA ratio, to pursue online acquisitions. Our buy recommendation incorporates an above average dividend yield recently at 4.5%.

➤ Risks to our recommendation and target price include a decline in the health of the New York City and Boston economies, where NYT derives most of its newspaper advertising revenues.

➤ Our 12-month target price of $26 is derived from a blend of our relative valuation and DCF analyses. Our DCF model yields an intrinsic value of $29, and includes assumptions of a 7.2% WACC and 2.5% terminal growth. Applying a peer average 8X enterprise value/EBITDA multiple to our 2008 EBITDA estimate of $531 million, we derive a $23 valuation.

Qualitative Risk Assessment

LOW	MEDIUM	HIGH

Our risk assessment reflects our view of a highly competitive advertising environment for publishers and other media, offset by the company's better than peer opportunity, in our opinion, to leverage its brand, and NYT's low weighted average cost of capital.

Quantitative Evaluations

S&P Quality Ranking B+

D	C	B-	B	B+	A-	A	A+

Relative Strength Rank WEAK

25

LOWEST = 1   HIGHEST = 99

Revenue/Earnings Data

Revenue (Million $)

	1Q	2Q	3Q	4Q	Year
2007	786.0	788.9	754.4	--	--
2006	799.2	819.6	739.6	931.5	3,290
2005	805.6	845.1	791.1	931.0	3,373
2004	801.9	823.9	773.8	903.9	3,304
2003	783.7	801.9	759.3	882.3	3,227
2002	737.1	772.2	729.5	840.2	3,079

Earnings Per Share ($)

2007	0.14	0.15	0.10	E0.50	E1.13
2006	0.21	0.37	0.06	-4.59	-3.93
2005	0.76	0.42	0.16	0.49	1.82
2004	0.38	0.50	0.33	0.75	1.96
2003	0.45	0.47	0.33	0.73	1.98
2002	0.35	0.51	0.38	0.69	1.94

Fiscal year ended Dec. 31. Next earnings report expected: Late January. EPS Estimates based on S&P Operating Earnings; historical GAAP earnings are as reported.

Dividend Data (Dates: mm/dd Payment Date: mm/dd/yy)

Amount ($)	Date Decl.	Ex-Div. Date	Stk. of Record	Payment Date
0.175	02/22	02/27	03/01	03/13/07
0.230	03/22	05/30	06/01	06/13/07
0.230	06/21	08/30	09/04	09/12/07
0.230	11/15	11/29	12/03	12/12/07

Dividends have been paid since 1958. Source: Company reports.

Please read the Required Disclosures and Analyst Certification on the last page of this report.

The McGraw-Hill Companies

New York Times Co (The)

**STANDARD
&POOR'S**

Business Summary October 25, 2007

CORPORATE OVERVIEW. The New York Times Company is a media company that includes newspapers, Internet businesses, a radio station, investments in paper mills and other investments. In 2006, NYT classified its businesses into two segments, the News Media Group (about 98% of revenues) and About.com (2%).

The News Media Group primarily consists of The New York Times, the International Herald Tribune, The Boston Globe, the Worcester Telegram & Gazette, 14 daily newspapers in Alabama, California, Florida, Louisiana, North Carolina and South Carolina, and related print and digital businesses, such as NYT.com. The majority of the News Media Group's revenue comes from advertising sold in its newspapers and other publications and on its Web sites. In 2006, revenues were derived from national advertising (45%), classified (28%), retail and pre-print (24%), and other (3%). We note that as one of only three national newspapers (along with the USA Today and The Wall Street Journal), the New York Times garners a disproportionate amount of its advertising from national advertisers relative to most other newspapers. According to TNS Media Intelligence, the New York Times had a 49.6% market share of national advertising revenue among national newspapers in 2006.

About.com provides users with information and advice on thousands of top-

ics, and the site was one of the top 15 most visited Web sites in 2006. About.com generates revenues through display advertising relevant to adjacent content, cost-per-click advertising, and e-commerce. In September 2006, NYT acquired Calorie-Count.com, a site that offers weight loss tools and information. Calories-Count is part of the About.com segment.

The company also owns equity interests in a Canadian newsprint company and a supercalendered paper manufacturing partnership in Maine; New England Sports Ventures, LLC (NESV), which owns the Boston Red Sox, Fenway Park and adjacent real estate, approximately 80% of the New England Sports Network (the regional cable sports network that televises the Red Sox games) and 50% of Roush Fenway Racing, a leading NASCAR team; and Metro Boston LLC (Metro Boston), which publishes a free daily newspaper catering to young professionals and students in the Boston metropolitan area. In August 2006, the company acquired Baseline StudioSystems, an online database and research service for information on the film and television industries.

Company Financials Fiscal Year Ended Dec. 31

Per Share Data ($)	2006	2005	2004	2003	2002	2001	2000	1999	1998	1997
Tangible Book Value	0.25	NM	NM	NM	NM	NM	NM	0.83	1.12	1.77
Cash Flow	-2.76	2.81	2.94	2.95	2.93	2.48	3.65	2.83	2.46	2.21
Earnings	-3.93	1.82	1.96	1.98	1.94	1.26	2.32	1.73	1.49	1.33
S&P Core Earnings	1.13	1.41	1.62	1.77	1.35	0.72	NA	NA	NA	NA
Dividends	0.69	0.65	0.61	0.57	0.53	0.49	0.45	0.41	0.37	0.32
Payout Ratio	NM	36%	31%	29%	27%	39%	19%	24%	25%	24%
Prices:High	28.98	40.90	49.23	49.06	53.00	47.98	49.88	49.94	40.69	33.25
Prices:Low	21.54	26.09	38.47	43.29	38.60	35.48	32.63	26.50	20.50	18.19
P/E Ratio:High	NM	22	25	25	27	38	21	29	27	25
P/E Ratio:Low	NM	14	20	22	20	28	14	15	14	14

Income Statement Analysis (Million $)	2006	2005	2004	2003	2002	2001	2000	1999	1998	1997
Revenue	3,290	3,373	3,304	3,227	3,079	3,016	3,489	3,131	2,937	2,866
Operating Income	464	502	657	687	698	568	864	769	703	629
Depreciation	170	144	147	148	153	194	228	197	188	174
Interest Expense	50.7	49.2	44.2	44.8	48.7	51.4	64.1	52.5	46.9	45.0
Pretax Income	-552	446	477	500	491	340	673	538	506	437
Effective Tax Rate	NM	40.4%	38.5%	39.6%	39.0%	40.5%	40.9%	42.4%	43.3%	40.0%
Net Income	-568	266	293	303	300	202	398	310	287	262
S&P Core Earnings	164	205	242	268	208	116	NA	NA	NA	NA

Balance Sheet & Other Financial Data (Million $)	2006	2005	2004	2003	2002	2001	2000	1999	1998	1997
Cash	72.4	44.9	42.4	39.4	37.0	52.0	69.0	63.9	36.0	107
Current Assets	1,185	658	614	603	563	560	611	615	522	616
Total Assets	3,856	4,533	3,950	3,805	3,634	3,439	3,607	3,496	3,465	3,639
Current Liabilities	1,298	1,067	1,120	760	736	861	877	674	628	697
Long Term Debt	795	898	471	726	729	599	637	598	598	545
Common Equity	820	1,516	1,401	1,392	1,362	1,150	1,281	1,449	1,531	1,728
Total Capital	1,621	2,683	2,139	2,350	2,164	1,813	2,024	2,188	2,295	2,460
Capital Expenditures	332	221	154	121	161	90.4	85.3	73.4	82.6	153
Cash Flow	-398	409	439	450	453	396	626	508	475	436
Current Ratio	0.9	0.6	0.5	0.8	0.8	0.7	0.7	0.9	0.8	0.9
% Long Term Debt of Capitalization	49.1	33.5	22.0	30.9	33.7	33.0	31.5	27.3	26.1	22.2
% Net Income of Revenue	NM	7.9	8.9	9.4	9.7	6.7	11.4	9.9	9.8	9.2
% Return on Assets	NM	6.3	7.5	8.1	8.5	5.7	11.2	8.9	8.1	7.3
% Return on Equity	NM	18.2	21.0	22.7	23.9	16.6	29.1	20.8	17.6	15.6

Data as orig reptd.; bef. results of disc opers/spec. items. Per share data adj. for stk. divs.; EPS diluted. E-Estimated. NA-Not Available. NM-Not Meaningful. NR-Not Ranked. UR-Under Review.

Office: 229 W. 43rd St., New York, NY 10036.
Telephone: 212-556-1234.
Website: http://www.nytco.com
Chrmn: A. Sulzberger, Jr.

Pres & CEO: J. Robinson
Vice Chrmn: M. Golden
SVP & CFO: J.M. Follo
SVP & Chief Lgl Officer: S.B. Watson, IV

Investor Contact: C.J. Mathis (212-556-1981)
Board Members: B. C. Barnes, R. E. Cesan, L. G. Dolnick, M. Golden, W. E. Kennard, J. M. Kilts, D. E. Liddle, E. R. Marram, T. Middelhoff, J. Robinson, C. J. Sulzberger, A. Sulzberger, Jr., D. A. Toben

Founded: 1896
Domicile: New York
Employees: 11,585

News Corp

STANDARD &POOR'S

S&P Recommendation BUY ★★★★☆

Price	12-Mo. Target Price	Investment Style
$20.40 (as of Nov 23, 2007)	$25.00	Large-Cap Blend

GICS Sector Consumer Discretionary
Sub-Industry Movies & Entertainment

Summary With controlling interests in leading content and distribution assets across the globe, including Fox Entertainment, Sky Italia, BSkyB and STAR Asia, this leading media conglomerate recently agreed to acquire Dow Jones in a transaction valued at about $5.6 billion.

Key Stock Statistics (Source S&P, Vickers, company reports)

52-Wk Range	$25.40– 19.00	S&P Oper. EPS 2008**E**	1.19	Market Capitalization(B)	$43.694	Beta	1.40
Trailing 12-Month EPS	$1.09	S&P Oper. EPS 2009**E**	1.38	Yield (%)	0.59	S&P 3-Yr. Proj. EPS CAGR(%)	19.00
Trailing 12-Month P/E	18.7	P/E on S&P Oper. EPS 2008**E**	17.1	Dividend Rate/Share	$0.12	S&P Credit Rating	BBB+
$10K Invested 5 Yrs Ago	$18,069	Common Shares Outstg. (M)	3,128.4	Institutional Ownership (%)	71		

Price Performance

30-Week Mov. Avg. ··· 10-Week Mov. Avg. - - **GAAP Earnings vs. Previous Year** Volume Above Avg. ▯▮▯ STARS
12-Mo. Target Price — Relative Strength ▲ Up ▼ Down ▶ No Change Below Avg. ▯▯▯

Options: ASE, CBOE, P, Ph

Qualitative Risk Assessment

LOW	**MEDIUM**	HIGH

Our risk assessment reflects a portfolio of leading properties with balanced business and geographic diversification, and a strong balance sheet, offset by cyclical ad exposure, film volatility, currency risk, and some corporate governance issues.

Quantitative Evaluations

S&P Quality Ranking NR

D	C	B-	B	B+	A-	A	A+

Relative Strength Rank MODERATE

55

LOWEST = 1   HIGHEST = 99

Revenue/Earnings Data

Revenue (Million $)

	1Q	2Q	3Q	4Q	Year
2008	7,067	--	--	--	--
2007	5,914	7,844	7,530	7,367	28,655
2006	5,682	6,665	6,198	6,782	25,327
2005	5,191	6,562	6,043	6,108	23,859
2004	4,649	5,588	5,201	5,521	20,579
2003	3,813	4,681	4,388	4,592	20,157

Earnings Per Share ($)

	1Q	2Q	3Q	4Q	Year
2008	0.23	E0.29	E0.31	E0.34	E1.19
2007	0.28	0.27	0.29	0.30	1.14
2006	0.19	0.22	0.27	0.24	0.92
2005	0.16	0.56	0.14	0.23	0.73
2004	0.14	0.13	0.16	0.13	0.58
2003	0.06	0.09	0.11	0.13	0.46

Fiscal year ended Jun. 30. Next earnings report expected: NA. EPS Estimates based on S&P Operating Earnings; historical GAAP earnings are as reported.

Highlights

➤ The 12-month target price for NWS.A has recently been changed to $25.00 from $26.00. The Highlights section of this Stock Report will be updated accordingly.

Investment Rationale/Risk

➤ The Investment Rationale/Risk section of this Stock Report will be updated shortly. For the latest News story on NWS.A from MarketScope, see below.

➤ 11/08/07 08:20 am EST... UPDATE - S&P MAINTAINS BUY OPINION ON CLASS A SHRES OF NEWS CORPORATION (NWS.A 20.92****): CEO Murdoch addressed concerns about burgeoning social networking rivalry from Facebook on NWS.A's MySpace. With potential upside on new behavioral/hyper-targeted ads, and potentially complementary recent acquisitions, MySpace could drive FY 08 (Jun) revenues approaching $1B, likely a key turning point. Murdoch also alluded to plans for potentially radical WSJ makeover and international expansion, on likely '07 close of Dow Jones (Hold, $59.57) deal. With higher FY 08 TV-related start-up losses, we are trimming our target price by $1 to $25, on blend of DCF and sum-of-the-parts. /T. Amobi - CPA, CFA

Dividend Data (Dates: mm/dd Payment Date: mm/dd/yy)

Amount ($)	Date Decl.	Ex-Div. Date	Stk. of Record	Payment Date
0.060	03/07	03/12	03/14	04/18/07
0.060	08/08	09/10	09/12	10/17/07

Dividends have been paid since 1995. Source: Company reports.

Please read the Required Disclosures and Analyst Certification on the last page of this report.

The McGraw·Hill Companies

News Corp

Business Summary August 27, 2007

CORPORATE OVERVIEW. News Corp., once a small publisher of Australian newspapers, has grown into one of the world's premier media conglomerates. In December 2004, the company moved its domicile to the U.S., followed in March 2005 by a tender offer for the public's 18% minority stake in its Fox Entertainment Group, which we believe helped to simplify its corporate structure.

Key U.S. assets include Fox film studio and 20th Century Fox TV; Fox broadcast network and TV stations; Fox News, FX and regional sports networks (including FSN Ohio, FSN Florida and 40% of FSN Bay Area); HarperCollins (book publishers); the New York Post newspaper; and an inserts business. International assets include several newspaper businesses in the U.K. and Australia (including The Times, The Sun, News of the World and The Australian); the wholly owned DBS provider Sky Italia; a 37% controlling stake in U.K. DBS provider BSkyB; and several other associated entities in the U.S., Australia and Latin America. About 53% of FY 07 (Jun.) revenues were derived from the U.S. and Canada, 32% from Europe, and 15% from Australasia/other.

CORPORATE STRATEGY. We see an increased focus to capitalize on higher growth Internet distribution. In 2005, the company acquired MySpace.com, a leading social networking site, for about $650 million (now the core of its Fox Interactive Media unit), as well as IGN Entertainment for $650 million, and Scout Media for $65 million. MySpace is the nucleus of the Fox Interactive Media unit, which the company expects to generate over $800 million of FY 08 revenues (versus $550 million in FY 07), aided by a multi-year search deal with Google that provides for a minimum revenue guarantee of $900 million over the term. NWS's TV shows are also available from Apple's iTunes and mobile content destination Mobizzo.

Management adopts a generational approach to managing its cable channels that include fully distributed networks (e.g., Fox News and FX), those approaching full distribution (e.g., Speed and National Geographic), as well as newer start-ups (e.g., Fuel, Fox College Sports, Fox Reality Channel), including Fox Business Network, which is to debut on October 15, 2007.

Company Financials Fiscal Year Ended Jun. 30

Per Share Data ($)	2007	2006	2005	2004	2003	2002	2001	2000	1999	1998
Tangible Book Value	2.37	1.86	1.81	1.85	NM	0.68	3.34	0.76	1.67	NM
Cash Flow	1.38	1.62	1.40	0.79	0.65	-2.39	-0.01	0.48	0.58	0.29
Earnings	1.14	0.92	0.73	0.58	0.46	-2.75	0.32	0.39	0.50	0.52
Dividends	0.12	0.13	0.11	0.10	0.08	0.07	0.07	0.07	0.08	0.04
Payout Ratio	11%	14%	14%	17%	17%	NM	22%	18%	16%	8%
Prices:High	25.40	21.94	18.88	18.77	15.54	13.60	18.70	28.59	18.44	14.75
Prices:Low	19.00	15.17	13.94	14.57	9.33	7.54	9.80	13.44	11.47	9.06
P/E Ratio:High	22	24	26	32	34	NM	58	73	37	28
P/E Ratio:Low	17	16	19	25	20	NM	31	34	23	17

Income Statement Analysis (Million $)

	2007	2006	2005	2004	2003	2002	2001	2000	1999	1998
Revenue	28,655	25,327	23,859	29,428	29,913	29,014	25,578	22,443	21,774	21,206
Operating Income	5,331	4,643	4,329	5,146	4,372	4,291	3,799	2,913	NA	3,066
Depreciation	879	775	765	844	776	749	706	562	510	415
Interest Expense	843	791	736	958	1,094	1,384	1,358	1,248	NA	898
Pretax Income	5,306	4,405	3,561	3,855	3,000	-10,959	-562	1,587	1,913	2,142
Effective Tax Rate	34.2%	34.6%	34.3%	32.3%	25.8%	NM	NM	20.7%	15.0%	12.1%
Net Income	3,426	2,812	2,128	2,312	1,808	-11,962	-746	1,259	1,471	1,800

Balance Sheet & Other Financial Data (Million $)

	2007	2006	2005	2004	2003	2002	2001	2000	1999	1998
Cash	7,654	5,783	6,470	6,217	6,746	6,337	5,615	4,638	7,483	4,314
Current Assets	15,906	13,123	12,779	15,012	14,861	14,647	16,173	13,127	13,555	11,179
Total Assets	62,343	56,649	54,692	73,738	67,747	71,441	84,961	65,585	53,972	54,484
Current Liabilities	7,494	6,373	6,649	10,437	9,303	11,005	9,776	9,008	7,447	8,376
Long Term Debt	12,147	11,385	10,087	12,972	14,480	15,275	23,345	18,396	15,516	15,621
Common Equity	32,922	29,874	29,377	39,387	31,834	34,101	42,050	29,389	27,109	26,546
Total Capital	51,530	46,740	44,500	59,473	53,867	54,743	70,940	51,056	42,625	42,714
Capital Expenditures	1,308	976	901	517	551	505	1,113	671	702	848
Cash Flow	4,305	3,587	2,883	3,156	2,584	-11,213	-40.0	1,598	1,981	2,215
Current Ratio	2.1	2.1	1.9	1.4	1.6	1.3	1.7	1.5	1.8	1.3
% Long Term Debt of Capitalization	23.6	24.4	22.7	21.8	26.9	27.9	32.9	36.0	36.4	36.6
% Net Income of Revenue	12.0	11.1	8.9	7.9	6.0	NM	NM	5.6	6.8	8.5
% Return on Assets	5.8	5.1	4.1	3.3	2.6	NM	NM	2.1	2.7	3.8
% Return on Equity	10.9	9.5	8.4	6.5	5.5	NM	NM	4.0	4.4	7.7

Data as orig reptd.; bef. results of disc opers/spec. items. Per share data adj. for stk. divs.; EPS diluted. Income and balance sheet data in Australian $ prior to 2005. E-Estimated. NA-Not Available. NM-Not Meaningful. NR-Not Ranked. UR-Under Review.

Office: 1211 Avenue Of The Americas, New York, NY 10036-8701.
Telephone: 212-852-7000.
Website: http://www.newscorp.com
Chrmn & CEO: K.R. Murdoch

Pres & COO: P. Chernin
Sr EVP & CFO: D.F. DeVoe
Sr EVP & General Counsel: L.A. Jacobs
SVP & CCO: G. Gavenchak

Investor Contact: R. Nolte (212-852-7017)
Board Members: J. M. Aznar, P. Barnes, C. Carey, P. Cherin, K. E. Cowley, D. F. DeVoe, V. Dinh, R. I. Eddington, A. S. Knight, K. R. Murdoch, R. Paige, T. J. Perkins, A. M. Siskind, J. L. Thornton

Founded: 1922
Domicile: Delaware
Employees: 53,000

Nicor Inc.

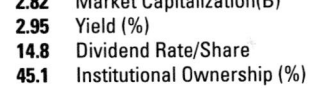
STANDARD &POOR'S

S&P Recommendation	**STRONG BUY** ★★★★★	Price $41.66 (as of Nov 23, 2007)	12-Mo. Target Price $50.00	Investment Style Large-Cap Blend

GICS Sector Utilities
Sub-Industry Gas Utilities

Summary This holding company's Nicor Gas subsidiary is one of the largest U.S. distributors of natural gas.

Key Stock Statistics (Source S&P, Vickers, company reports)

52-Wk Range	$53.66– 37.80	S&P Oper. EPS 2007E	2.82	Market Capitalization(B)	$1.879	Beta	0.61
Trailing 12-Month EPS	$3.06	S&P Oper. EPS 2008E	2.95	Yield (%)	4.46	S&P 3-Yr. Proj. EPS CAGR(%)	7.00
Trailing 12-Month P/E	13.6	P/E on S&P Oper. EPS 2007E	14.8	Dividend Rate/Share	$1.86	S&P Credit Rating	AA
$10K Invested 5 Yrs Ago	$16,790	Common Shares Outstg. (M)	45.1	Institutional Ownership (%)	78		

Price Performance

- 30-Week Mov. Avg. · · · 10-Week Mov. Avg. - - GAAP Earnings vs. Previous Year   Volume Above Avg. STARS
- 12-Mo. Target Price — Relative Strength — ▲ Up ▼ Down ▶ No Change   Below Avg.

2004 2005 2006 2007

Options: P

Analysis prepared by **Christopher B. Muir** on November 06, 2007, when the stock traded at **$ 40.26**.

Highlights

➤ We see a revenue increase of 6.3% in 2007, driven by our projection of higher revenues for all of the company's segments. We see the unregulated businesses as driving this growth, especially the Other Energy Ventures business. We think the regulated business will be helped by less mild weather. We expect revenue growth of 4.4% in 2008, aided by customer growth and unregulated business growth.

➤ We project an operating margin of 6.8% for 2007, down slightly from 7.1% in 2006, reflecting the higher cost of gas and Other Energy Ventures expenses, partly offset by lower per-revenue operations and maintenance costs and depreciation and amortization expense. We see an operating margin of 6.6% in 2008. We expect lower non-operating income, resulting in our projection of a decline in the pretax margins to 5.7% in 2008 and 5.5% in 2007 from 6.1% in 2006.

➤ Assuming an effective tax rate of 26.8% and a small increase in the number of shares outstanding, we estimate EPS of $2.82 in 2007, a 7.2% decline from 2006's $3.04. Our 2008 EPS estimate is $2.95, a rise of 4.6%.

Investment Rationale/Risk

➤ Our 2008 projected payout ratio of about 63% is higher than the peer average of around 53%, and we see no growth in dividends for 2008 and 2009. However, we expect dividend increases beyond 2009. We think the Chicago hub operations will see strong profit growth on greater demand for natural gas, and we expect continued volatility in the gas markets to benefit the wholesale and retail energy marketing and services business. In addition, the company's shipping business is poised to help drive GAS's earnings growth, in our view.

➤ Risks to our recommendation and target price include a possible unfavorable resolution of ongoing regulatory issues, and slower-than-projected growth in unregulated operations.

➤ The shares recently traded at about 14X our 2008 EPS estimate, a 15% discount to its natural gas utility peers. Our 12-month target price of $50 equals a P/E of around 17X our 2008 EPS estimate, a slight discount to our peer forecast. We think this valuation is warranted by the growth we see in GAS's unregulated businesses, partly offset by relatively slow growth at its utility. The shares recently yielded 4.6%.

Qualitative Risk Assessment

LOW	MEDIUM	HIGH

Our risk assessment reflects the low risk nature of the company's main subsidiary, a regulated natural gas distribution company, slightly offset by the higher risk nature of its much smaller competitive operations. The company benefits from being the lone delivery agent of natural gas to customers within its service territory.

Quantitative Evaluations

S&P Quality Ranking B

D	C	B-	**B**	B+	A-	A	A+

Relative Strength Rank STRONG

72

LOWEST = 1   HIGHEST = 99

Revenue/Earnings Data

Revenue (Million $)

	1Q	2Q	3Q	4Q	Year
2007	1,335	556.9	365.2	--	--
2006	1,319	451.3	351.1	838.2	2,960
2005	1,180	484.4	336.0	1,358	3,358
2004	1,116	429.5	299.9	894.6	2,740
2003	1,171	452.8	294.8	743.9	2,663
2002	588.0	352.2	252.4	704.7	1,897

Earnings Per Share ($)

2007	1.04	0.40	0.32	E1.17	E2.82
2006	0.99	0.19	0.39	1.29	2.87
2005	0.99	0.75	-0.06	1.40	3.07
2004	0.44	0.36	-0.26	1.08	1.70
2003	1.14	0.54	0.01	0.79	2.48
2002	0.82	0.50	0.67	0.89	2.88

Fiscal year ended Dec. 31. Next earnings report expected: NA. EPS Estimates based on S&P Operating Earnings; historical GAAP earnings are as reported.

Dividend Data (Dates: mm/dd Payment Date: mm/dd/yy)

Amount ($)	Date Decl.	Ex-Div. Date	Stk. of Record	Payment Date
0.465	11/16	12/27	12/29	02/01/07
0.465	03/22	03/28	03/30	05/01/07
0.465	04/26	06/27	06/29	08/01/07
0.465	07/26	09/26	09/28	11/01/07

Dividends have been paid since 1954. Source: Company reports.

Nicor Inc.

STANDARD &POOR'S

Business Summary November 06, 2007

CORPORATE OVERVIEW. Nicor Inc. is a holding company, whose principal subsidiaries are Northern Illinois Gas Company (doing business as Nicor Gas Company), one of the nation's largest distributors of natural gas, and Tropical Shipping, a transporter of containerized freight in the Bahamas and the Caribbean region. Nicor also owns several energy-related ventures, including Nicor Services and Nicor Solutions, which provide energy-related products and services to retail markets, and Nicor Enerchange, a wholesale natural gas marketing company.

PRIMARY BUSINESS DYNAMICS. Nicor seeks earnings growth through investment in unregulated operations, including its Tropical Shipping and Other Energy Ventures divisions. However, the company's main operating segment remains its regulated gas utility operations.

As of the end of 2006, Nicor Gas (61% of 2006 segment operating profits) served 2.2 million customers in a service area that covers most of northern Illinois, excluding Chicago. In 2006, gas deliveries declined to 438.7 billion cubic feet (Bcf) from 470.6 Bcf in 2005. The company has an extensive storage and transmission system that is directly connected to eight interstate

pipelines, and includes eight owned underground gas storage facilities, with about 150 Bcf of annual storage capacity. In addition, Nicor Gas has about 40 Bcf of purchased storage from an affiliated party under contracts that expire between 2009 and 2012.

Nicor Gas is also engaged in non-traditional natural gas storage and transportation activities through its Chicago Hub, which serves marketers, other distributors, and electric power facilities.

GAS's Tropical Shipping unit (23%) is one of the largest containerized cargo carriers in the Caribbean, with a fleet of 10 owned and eight chartered vessels, with total container capacity of about 5,800 20-foot equivalent units (TEU), serving 27 ports. Total volumes shipped in 2006 were 203,100 TEU, down from 214,200 TEU in 2005, but up from 198,000 TEU in 2004.

Company Financials Fiscal Year Ended Dec. 31

Per Share Data ($)	2006	2005	2004	2003	2002	2001	2000	1999	1998	1997
Tangible Book Value	19.43	18.36	16.99	17.15	16.55	16.39	15.56	16.76	15.97	15.43
Cash Flow	6.44	6.55	5.05	5.73	6.00	6.46	4.12	5.58	5.25	5.29
Earnings	2.87	3.07	1.70	2.48	2.88	3.17	1.00	2.62	2.42	2.61
S&P Core Earnings	2.83	2.47	1.97	2.45	2.30	1.99	NA	NA	NA	NA
Dividends	1.86	1.86	1.86	1.86	1.84	1.76	1.66	1.54	1.46	1.40
Payout Ratio	65%	61%	109%	75%	64%	56%	166%	59%	60%	54%
Prices:High	49.92	42.97	39.65	39.30	49.00	42.38	43.88	42.94	44.44	42.94
Prices:Low	38.72	35.50	32.04	23.70	18.09	34.00	29.38	31.19	37.13	30.00
P/E Ratio:High	17	14	23	16	17	13	44	16	18	16
P/E Ratio:Low	13	12	19	10	6	11	29	12	15	11

Income Statement Analysis (Million $)										
Revenue	2,960	3,358	2,740	2,663	1,897	2,544	2,298	1,615	1,465	1,993
Operating Income	366	202	138	189	227	244	507	352	345	361
Depreciation	160	155	149	144	138	149	144	140	137	131
Interest Expense	49.8	48.0	41.6	37.3	38.5	44.9	48.6	45.1	46.6	49.1
Pretax Income	174	171	105	169	186	217	61.1	190	178	197
Effective Tax Rate	26.3%	20.3%	28.7%	35.2%	31.0%	33.8%	23.6%	34.6%	34.4%	35.0%
Net Income	128	136	75.1	110	128	144	46.7	124	116	128
S&P Core Earnings	127	110	87.7	108	102	90.4	NA	NA	NA	NA

Balance Sheet & Other Financial Data (Million $)										
Cash	41.1	119	12.9	50.3	75.2	10.7	55.8	42.5	13.0	5.20
Current Assets	911	1,346	1,021	916	708	518	915	508	465	535
Total Assets	4,090	4,391	3,975	3,797	2,899	2,575	2,885	2,452	2,365	2,395
Current Liabilities	1,142	1,623	1,174	1,069	1,099	826	1,312	746	579	622
Long Term Debt	498	486	495	497	396	446	347	436	557	550
Common Equity	873	811	749	755	728	728	708	788	759	744
Total Capital	1,787	1,751	1,873	1,813	1,514	1,548	1,173	1,539	1,606	1,516
Capital Expenditures	592	202	190	181	193	186	158	154	136	113
Cash Flow	288	291	224	253	266	292	191	264	253	259
Current Ratio	0.8	0.8	0.9	0.9	0.6	0.6	0.7	0.7	0.8	0.9
% Long Term Debt of Capitalization	27.9	27.7	26.4	27.4	26.1	28.8	29.6	28.3	34.7	36.3
% Net Income of Revenue	4.3	4.5	2.7	4.1	6.7	5.6	2.0	7.7	7.9	6.4
% Return on Assets	3.0	11.4	7.8	3.3	4.7	5.3	1.8	5.1	4.9	5.3
% Return on Equity	15.2	17.4	9.9	14.8	12.3	20.0	6.2	16.0	15.4	17.3

Data as orig reptd.; bef. results of disc opers/spec. items. Per share data adj. for stk. divs.; EPS diluted. E-Estimated. NA-Not Available. NM-Not Meaningful. NR-Not Ranked. UR-Under Review.

Office: 1844 Ferry Road, Naperville, IL 60563-9600.
Telephone: 630-305-9500.
Website: http://www.nicorinc.com
Chrmn, Pres & CEO: R.M. Strobel

EVP & CFO: R.L. Hawley
VP, Secy & General Counsel: P.C. Gracey
VP & Cntlr: K. Pepping
Investor Contact: M. Knox (630-388-2529)

Board Members: R. M. Beavers, Jr., B. P. Bickner, J. H. Birdsall, III, N. R. Bobins, T. A. Donahoe, B. Gaines, R. A. Jean, D. J. Keller, R. E. Martin, G. R. Nelson, J. Rau, J. F. Riordan, R. M. Strobel

Founded: 1953
Domicile: Illinois
Employees: 3,900

NIKE Inc.

STANDARD &POOR'S

S&P Recommendation	**BUY** ★★★★☆	Price $63.75 (as of Nov 23, 2007)	12-Mo. Target Price $71.00	Investment Style Large-Cap Growth

GICS Sector Consumer Discretionary
Sub-Industry Footwear

Summary NIKE is the world's leading designer and marketer of high-quality athletic footwear, athletic apparel, and accessories.

Key Stock Statistics (Source S&P, Vickers, company reports)

52-Wk Range	$66.57– 47.40	S&P Oper. EPS 2008**E**	3.55	Market Capitalization(B)	$24.941	Beta	0.53
Trailing 12-Month EPS	$3.31	S&P Oper. EPS 2009**E**	3.82	Yield (%)	1.44	S&P 3-Yr. Proj. EPS CAGR(%)	15.00
Trailing 12-Month P/E	19.3	P/E on S&P Oper. EPS 2008**E**	18.0	Dividend Rate/Share	$0.92	S&P Credit Rating	A+
$10K Invested 5 Yrs Ago	$31,040	Common Shares Outstg. (M)	498.7	Institutional Ownership (%)	86		

Price Performance

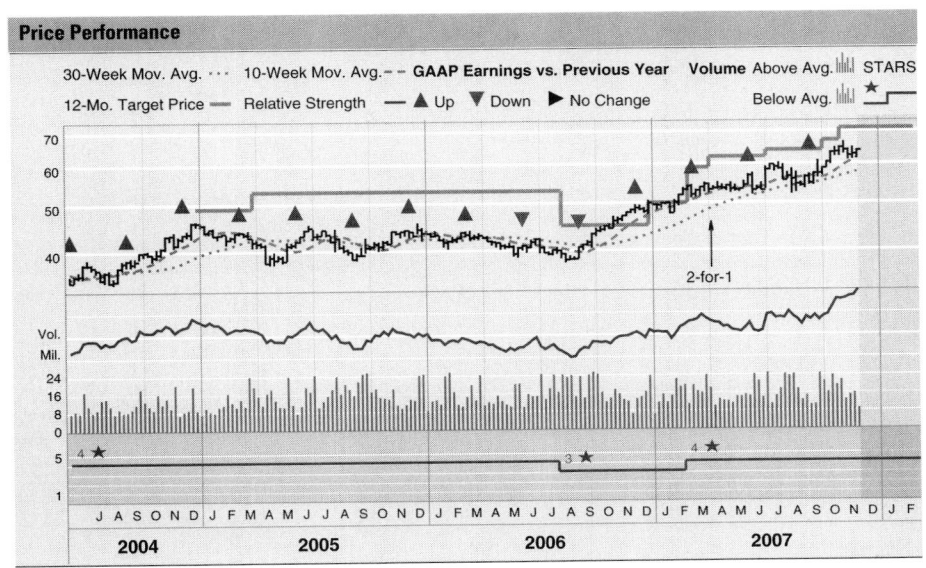

30-Week Mov. Avg. · · · 10-Week Mov. Avg. -- GAAP Earnings vs. Previous Year   Volume Above Avg. STARS
12-Mo. Target Price — Relative Strength ▲ Up ▼ Down ▶ No Change   Below Avg.

2-for-1

Options: ASE, CBOE, P, Ph

Analysis prepared by **Esther Y. Kwon, CFA** on October 24, 2007, when the stock traded at **$ 62.95**.

Highlights

➤ We project revenue growth of about 10% in FY 08 (May), to $18 billion, after 9% growth in FY 07. With over 60% of sales derived outside the U.S., we think NKE's broad geographic exposure positions it well for growth even with weakness in some of its markets, and we see the company continuing to benefit from foreign currency. We look for strong performance in its other brands, such as Converse, which grew 23% in FY 07.

➤ We forecast about flat operating margins of 13.0% in FY 08 as gross margin benefits from lean initiatives are offset by higher raw materials and labor costs. Although NKE anniversaries over $140 million in FY 08 in incremental stock option expense and increased demand creation spending for the World Cup, we project SG&A growth above revenue growth as it invests in store growth and in its brands.

➤ With almost $2 billion in cash on the balance sheet at fiscal year end and ample free cash flow of $1.6 billion generated in FY 07, we expect NKE to continue to increase its dividend and buy back shares. Incorporating share buy-backs and a lower effective tax rate than in FY 07, we estimate EPS of $3.55 and $3.82 in FY 08 and FY 09, respectively.

Investment Rationale/Risk

➤ NIKE increased its dividend 19% with the January 2007 quarterly payment, and in FY 07, repurchased $976 million of its shares. We see these factors supporting the stock price. Furthermore, NKE has launched key marketing and sales strategies to more closely align it with its key markets. We believe NKE's House of Hoops concept with Foot Locker will strengthen its position in basketball by allowing NKE to better control the merchandising of its brand.

➤ Risks to our recommendation and target price include an economic slowdown domestically and a greater than expected moderation in consumer spending. International risks include economic weakness, supply disruptions, and unfavorable currency fluctuations.

➤ Our 12-month target price of $71 is equal to 20X our FY 08 EPS estimate of $3.55, in the middle of the 14X-26X range in which the stock has traded over the past five years.

Qualitative Risk Assessment

LOW	**MEDIUM**	HIGH

Our risk assessment reflects what we see as NKE's strong financial and operating metrics, offset by an increasingly competitive global marketplace and prospects for slowing consumer spending in the U.S.

Quantitative Evaluations

S&P Quality Ranking   A+

D	C	B-	B	B+	A-	A	**A+**

Relative Strength Rank   **STRONG**

89

LOWEST = 1   HIGHEST = 99

Revenue/Earnings Data

Revenue (Million $)

	1Q	2Q	3Q	4Q	Year
2008	4,655	--	--	--	--
2007	4,194	3,822	3,927	4,383	16,326
2006	3,862	3,475	3,613	4,005	14,955
2005	3,562	3,148	3,308	3,721	13,740
2004	3,025	2,837	2,904	3,487	12,253
2003	2,796	2,515	2,401	2,985	10,697

Earnings Per Share ($)

	1Q	2Q	3Q	4Q	Year
2008	1.12	E0.67	E0.75	E0.99	E3.55
2007	0.74	0.64	0.68	0.86	2.93
2006	0.81	0.57	0.62	0.64	2.64
2005	0.61	0.49	0.51	0.65	2.24
2004	0.49	0.33	0.37	0.57	1.76
2003	0.41	0.29	0.24	0.46	1.39

Fiscal year ended May 31. Next earnings report expected: Late December. EPS Estimates based on S&P Operating Earnings; historical GAAP earnings are as reported.

Dividend Data (Dates: mm/dd Payment Date: mm/dd/yy)

Amount ($)	Date Decl.	Ex-Div. Date	Stk. of Record	Payment Date
2-for-1	--	04/03	03/12	04/02/07
0.185	05/14	06/07	06/11	07/02/07
0.185	08/13	09/06	09/10	10/01/07
0.230	11/16	12/06	12/10	01/02/08

Dividends have been paid since 1984. Source: Company reports.

NIKE Inc.

STANDARD &POOR'S

Business Summary October 24, 2007

CORPORATE OVERVIEW. Nike is the world's largest supplier of athletic footwear, with an estimated 30% of this $20 billion market (at wholesale). Sports apparel and equipment are also sold under the Nike banner, and the company's Other segment (13% of sales) houses its affiliated brands including Cole Haan, Converse and Hurley businesses.

MARKET PROFILE. Innovation, marketing and the sports cycle drive the global footwear and athletic apparel markets, in our view. Technologically superior performance products, we think, convey the idea of extraordinary ability to the wearer and are the root of the marketing campaigns aimed at lifestyle consumers (individuals attracted to a brand's attributes of an active lifestyle regardless of sports participation). The global market for athletic apparel is several times as large as the footwear market, and totals over a $100 billion according to industry sources. An estimated 30% of this market consists of active sports apparel (purchased with the intent to be used in an active sport), and the remainder is lifestyle or casual wear. We see apparel representing a significant opportunity for NKE via its brand extensions and market penetration. According to NPD Fashionworld consumer estimated data, U.S. athletic footwear sales increased 2.5% in 2006, following several years of low single digit gains, with skateboarding and soccer shoes enjoying the strongest momentum. Sales fell in the running, basketball, and tennis categories. Frequent technological innovation enables manufacturers to hold and increase prices while building brand equity. S&P projects mid-single digit gains for these markets in 2007.

COMPETITIVE LANDSCAPE. Both the athletic footwear and apparel markets are fragmented, providing opportunities for growing market share, in our view. Significant domestic footwear retail channels include athletic footwear specialty shops (20% market share), sporting goods stores (16%), and discounters or mass merchants (11%). Online athletic footwear retailers' sales grew 36% in 2006 and represented 2% of total sales.

Company Financials Fiscal Year Ended May 31

Per Share Data ($)	2007	2006	2005	2004	2003	2002	2001	2000	1999	1998
Tangible Book Value	12.93	11.23	9.77	8.14	7.22	6.39	5.77	5.05	5.14	4.91
Cash Flow	3.51	3.17	2.72	2.22	1.83	3.51	1.44	1.37	1.13	0.99
Earnings	2.93	2.64	2.24	1.76	1.39	1.23	1.08	1.04	0.79	0.68
S&P Core Earnings	2.89	2.56	2.14	1.68	1.31	1.16	1.03	NA	NA	NA
Dividends	0.56	0.45	0.45	0.34	0.26	0.24	0.24	0.24	0.24	0.22
Payout Ratio	19%	17%	20%	19%	19%	20%	22%	23%	31%	33%
Calendar Year	2006	2005	2004	2003	2002	2001	2000	1999	1998	1997
Prices:High	50.60	45.77	46.22	34.27	32.14	30.03	28.50	33.47	26.34	38.19
Prices:Low	37.76	37.55	32.91	21.19	19.27	17.75	12.91	19.38	15.50	18.88
P/E Ratio:High	17	17	21	20	26	24	26	32	34	57
P/E Ratio:Low	13	14	15	12	16	14	12	19	20	28

Income Statement Analysis (Million $)

	2007	2006	2005	2004	2003	2002	2001	2000	1999	1998
Revenue	16,326	14,955	13,740	12,253	10,697	9,893	9,489	8,995	8,777	9,553
Operating Income	2,402	23,912	2,151	1,802	1,485	1,291	1,212	1,150	1,054	1,049
Depreciation	270	282	257	252	239	224	197	188	198	185
Interest Expense	Nil	Nil	39.7	40.3	42.9	47.6	58.7	45.0	44.0	60.0
Pretax Income	2,200	2,142	1,860	1,450	1,123	2,035	921	919	745	653
Effective Tax Rate	32.2%	35.0%	34.9%	34.8%	34.1%	17.2%	36.0%	37.0%	39.5%	38.7%
Net Income	1,492	1,392	1,212	946	740	1,686	590	579	451	400
S&P Core Earnings	1,472	1,346	1,148	897	698	632	559	NA	NA	NA

Balance Sheet & Other Financial Data (Million $)

	2007	2006	2005	2004	2003	2002	2001	2000	1999	1998
Cash	1,857	954	1,388	828	634	576	304	254	198	109
Current Assets	8,077	7,359	6,351	5,512	4,680	4,158	3,625	3,596	3,265	3,533
Total Assets	10,688	9,870	8,794	7,892	6,714	6,443	5,820	5,857	5,248	5,397
Current Liabilities	2,584	2,623	1,999	2,009	2,015	1,836	1,787	2,140	1,447	1,704
Long Term Debt	Nil	Nil	687	682	552	626	436	470	386	379
Common Equity	7,025	6,285	5,644	4,782	3,991	3,839	3,495	3,136	3,335	3,262
Total Capital	7,026	6,286	6,332	5,464	4,543	4,465	3,931	3,607	3,721	3,641
Capital Expenditures	314	334	257	214	186	283	318	420	384	506
Cash Flow	1,761	1,674	1,469	1,198	979	1,909	787	767	645	585
Current Ratio	3.1	2.8	3.2	2.7	2.3	2.3	2.0	1.7	2.3	2.1
% Long Term Debt of Capitalization	Nil	Nil	10.9	12.5	12.1	14.0	11.1	13.0	10.4	10.4
% Net Income of Revenue	9.1	9.3	8.8	7.7	6.9	17.0	6.2	6.4	5.1	4.2
% Return on Assets	14.5	14.9	14.5	12.9	11.3	27.5	10.1	10.4	8.5	7.4
% Return on Equity	22.4	23.3	23.2	21.6	18.9	46.0	17.8	17.9	13.7	12.5

Data as orig reptd.; bef. results of disc opers/spec. items. Per share data adj. for stk. divs.; EPS diluted. E-Estimated. NA-Not Available. NM-Not Meaningful. NR-Not Ranked. UR-Under Review.

Office: 1 Bowerman Dr, Beaverton, OR 97005-0979.
Telephone: 503-641-6453.
Website: http://www.nikebiz.com
Chrmn: P.H. Knight

Pres & CEO: M.G. Parker
VP & CFO: D.W. Blair
VP, Chief Lgl Officer & General Counsel: J.C. Carter
Investor Contact: P.M. Catlett (800-640-8007)

Board Members: J. G. Connors, J. K. Conway, T. D. Cook, R. D. DeNunzio, A. B. Graf, Jr., D. G. Houser, J. P. Jackson, P. H. Knight, M. G. Parker, J. A. Rodgers, O. C. Smith, J. R. Thompson, Jr.
Founded: 1964
Domicile: Oregon
Employees: 30,200

The McGraw-Hill Companies

NiSource Inc.

STANDARD &POOR'S

S&P Recommendation HOLD ★★★☆☆

Price $18.31 (as of Nov 23, 2007)	**12-Mo. Target Price** $20.00	**Investment Style** Large-Cap Value

GICS Sector Utilities
Sub-Industry Multi-Utilities

Summary NI, the third largest U.S. gas distribution utility and the fourth largest gas pipeline company, also provides electric utility services.

Key Stock Statistics (Source S&P, Vickers, company reports)

52-Wk Range	$25.43– 17.49	S&P Oper. EPS 2007**E**	1.35	Market Capitalization(B)	$5.020	Beta	0.60
Trailing 12-Month EPS	$1.16	S&P Oper. EPS 2008**E**	1.35	Yield (%)	5.02	S&P 3-Yr. Proj. EPS CAGR(%)	2.00
Trailing 12-Month P/E	15.8	P/E on S&P Oper. EPS 2007**E**	13.6	Dividend Rate/Share	$0.92	S&P Credit Rating	NA
$10K Invested 5 Yrs Ago	$11,875	Common Shares Outstg. (M)	274.2	Institutional Ownership (%)	79		

Price Performance

30-Week Mov. Avg. · · · · 10-Week Mov. Avg. - - - **GAAP Earnings vs. Previous Year** Volume Above Avg. |||| STARS
12-Mo. Target Price — Relative Strength — ▲ Up ▼ Down ► No Change Below Avg. |||| ★

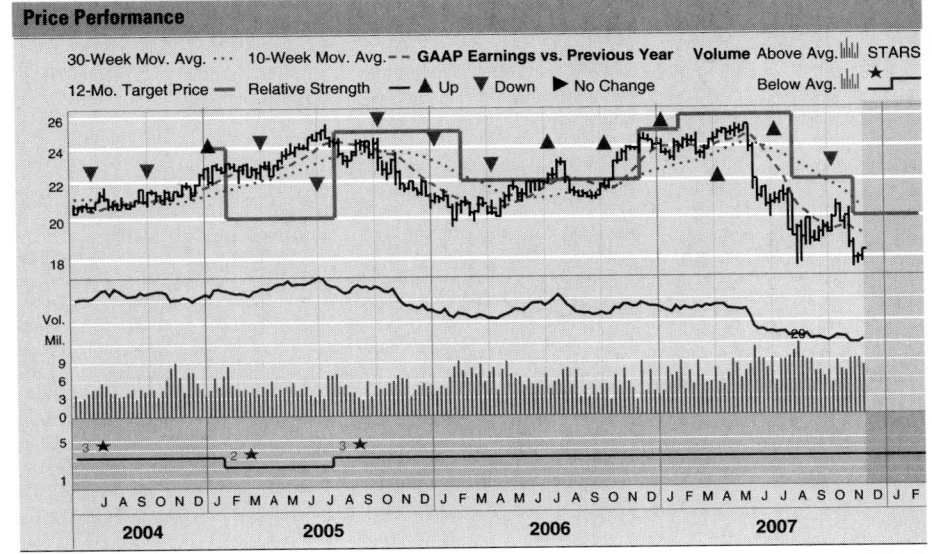

Options: ASE, CBOE, Ph

Analysis prepared by **Christopher B. Muir** on November 09, 2007, when the stock traded at **$ 18.02**.

Highlights

➤ We see total revenues growing by 4.7% in 2007 and 3.0% in 2008. For the regulated utilities, we expect growth to be helped by less mild weather in 2007 and customer growth in both periods. Gas transmission and storage revenues should benefit from higher short-term transportation and storage services, as well as increased subscriptions for demand services in both periods. We see non-regulated revenues rising due to higher gas marketing volumes, offset by lower prices in 2007, but helped by higher prices in 2008.

➤ We expect operating margins to remain relatively flat in both 2007 and 2008, versus 2006's 12.4%. We see per-revenue fuel and purchased power costs falling in 2007, partly offset by higher per-revenue operations and maintenance costs. We expect the opposite in 2008. We see pretax margins also remaining relatively flat, as we see higher interest expense in both periods.

➤ Assuming an effective tax rate of 36.8%, we forecast operating EPS of $1.35 in 2007, up 7.1% from 2006's $1.26. Our 2008 forecast is also $1.35.

Investment Rationale/Risk

➤ Although NI faces rising labor costs and declining usage per customer at the gas distribution segment, we expect expansion projects in transportation and storage to provide some growth. We forecast that investments in Millennium Pipeline and Hardy Storage will contribute a significant portion of EPS growth starting in 2007. We view NI's utility service territory as having relatively slow, but stable, customer growth. NI's non-utility operations may benefit from improved financial performance at the Whiting Clean Energy facility.

➤ Risks to our recommendation and target price include a decline in power margins, unusually mild winter and summer weather, a strong rise in natural gas prices, and sharply higher interest rates.

➤ The stock recently traded at about 11.9X our 2008 EPS estimate, a 19% discount to its multi-utility peers. Our 12-month target price of $20 is about 15X our 2008 EPS estimate, or about even with our peer target. We believe this is justified by what we see as the company's solid utility operations and the prospects for increased earnings from its unregulated business.

Qualitative Risk Assessment

LOW	MEDIUM	HIGH

Our risk assessment reflects the company's reliance on fairly stable regulated sources of earnings including gas distribution, gas transmission, and electric utility services.

Quantitative Evaluations

S&P Quality Ranking B

D	C	B-	**B**	B+	A-	A	A+

Relative Strength Rank MODERATE

55

LOWEST = 1   HIGHEST = 99

Revenue/Earnings Data

Revenue (Million $)

	1Q	2Q	3Q	4Q	Year
2007	2,894	1,577	1,241	--	--
2006	2,972	1,312	1,156	2,050	7,490
2005	2,683	1,356	1,165	2,695	7,899
2004	2,473	1,245	979.8	1,968	6,666
2003	2,525	1,141	898.3	1,683	6,247
2002	2,208	1,376	1,067	1,841	6,492

Earnings Per Share ($)

	1Q	2Q	3Q	4Q	Year
2007	0.76	0.11	0.03	E0.39	E1.35
2006	0.63	0.08	0.10	0.33	1.14
2005	0.77	0.03	-0.02	0.27	1.04
2004	0.82	0.13	0.08	0.58	1.62
2003	0.87	0.15	0.09	0.53	1.63
2002	1.17	0.11	0.12	0.59	2.00

Fiscal year ended Dec. 31. Next earnings report expected: Late January. EPS Estimates based on S&P Operating Earnings; historical GAAP earnings are as reported.

Dividend Data (Dates: mm/dd Payment Date: mm/dd/yy)

Amount ($)	Date Decl.	Ex-Div. Date	Stk. of Record	Payment Date
0.230	01/05	01/29	01/31	02/20/07
0.230	03/27	04/26	04/30	05/18/07
0.230	05/08	07/27	07/31	08/20/07
0.230	08/28	10/29	10/31	11/20/07

Dividends have been paid since 1987. Source: Company reports.

Business Summary November 09, 2007

CORPORATE OVERVIEW. NiSource is the third largest U.S. natural gas distributor (measured by customers served), the fourth largest owner of U.S. natural gas interstate pipelines (by route miles), and one of the largest owners of underground natural gas storage. It also provides electric utility services in northern Indiana. The company's operating divisions include Gas Distribution (33% of year end-2006 segment operating profits), Gas Transmission and Storage (39%), Electric Operations (35%), Other Operations (-5%) and Corporate (-2%).

Gas Distribution operations provide gas utility service to 3.4 million customers in nine states. The division owns and operates over 57,500 miles of pipeline, 28,479 acres of underground storage, and 90 storage wells. In 2006, total sales and transportation volumes were 827 MMDth, down from 864 MMDth in 2005.

Gas Transmission and Storage operates 15,532 miles of interstate natural gas pipelines and 870,000 acres of underground storage systems with a capacity of about 637 billion cubic feet (Bcf). In 2006, total throughput was 1,178 MMDth, up 0.5% from 2005. The division is working to develop the proposed Millennium Pipeline to access additional Canadian gas supply. The Millenni-

um project, a 186-mile section in New York state, is expected to be in service by November 2008 or earlier if feasible.

NI's Northern Indiana subsidiary, NIPSCO, generates and distributes electricity for 453,728 electric utility customers. The utility operates four coal-fired plants (2,574 MW), six gas-fired plants (323 MW), and two hydroelectric plants (10 MW). In 2006, the utility generated 81.1% of its electric requirements, and purchased 18.9%.

Other Operations include gas marketing, power and gas risk management and ventures focused on distributed power generation technologies, including a 525 MW gas fired cogeneration facility--the Whiting Clean Energy project. After being placed into service in 2002, Whiting was unable to deliver originally projected levels of steam. Whiting lost about $40.9 million after taxes in 2006 after losing about $21.5 million in 2005 and $32.8 million in 2004.

Company Financials Fiscal Year Ended Dec. 31

Per Share Data ($)	2006	2005	2004	2003	2002	2001	2000	1999	1998	1997
Tangible Book Value	3.29	2.79	2.14	0.70	NM	NM	NM	9.88	9.20	9.59
Cash Flow	3.16	3.04	3.54	3.53	4.70	4.07	3.84	NA	NA	NA
Earnings	1.14	1.04	1.62	1.63	2.00	1.01	1.08	1.27	1.59	1.53
S&P Core Earnings	1.13	1.20	1.62	1.67	1.43	0.32	NA	NA	NA	NA
Dividends	0.92	0.92	0.92	1.10	1.16	1.16	1.08	1.02	0.96	0.90
Payout Ratio	81%	88%	57%	67%	58%	115%	100%	80%	60%	59%
Prices:High	24.80	25.50	22.82	21.97	24.99	32.55	31.50	30.94	33.75	24.94
Prices:Low	19.51	20.44	19.65	16.39	14.51	18.25	12.75	16.38	24.66	19.00
P/E Ratio:High	22	25	14	13	12	32	29	24	21	16
P/E Ratio:Low	17	20	12	10	7	18	12	13	16	12

Income Statement Analysis (Million $)	2006	2005	2004	2003	2002	2001	2000	1999	1998	1997
Revenue	7,490	7,899	6,666	6,247	6,492	9,459	6,031	3,145	2,933	2,587
Operating Income	880	1,520	1,072	1,116	1,203	1,009	568	773	678	660
Depreciation	549	545	510	497	574	642	374	311	256	250
Interest Expense	7,304	425	408	469	533	605	325	184	129	121
Pretax Income	484	433	671	662	680	416	298	NA	NA	NA
Effective Tax Rate	35.3%	34.5%	35.9%	35.4%	34.4%	44.1%	43.7%	33.5%	34.2%	35.5%
Net Income	314	284	430	426	426	212	147	160	194	191
S&P Core Earnings	310	324	429	437	305	67.9	NA	NA	NA	NA

Balance Sheet & Other Financial Data (Million $)	2006	2005	2004	2003	2002	2001	2000	1999	1998	1997
Cash	33.1	69.4	30.1	27.3	56.2	128	193	NA	NA	NA
Current Assets	2,783	3,061	2,286	2,063	1,869	2,567	4,918	NA	NA	NA
Total Assets	18,157	17,959	16,988	16,624	16,897	17,374	19,697	NA	NA	NA
Current Liabilities	3,821	3,843	3,602	2,609	4,177	4,729	6,893	NA	NA	NA
Long Term Debt	5,146	5,271	4,917	6,075	5,448	6,214	6,148	NA	NA	NA
Common Equity	5,014	4,933	4,787	4,416	4,175	3,469	3,415	NA	NA	NA
Total Capital	11,775	11,866	11,448	10,490	11,581	11,515	11,483	4,903	3,725	2,370
Capital Expenditures	637	590	517	575	622	668	366	NA	NA	NA
Cash Flow	863	829	940	923	1,000	854	521	NA	NA	NA
Current Ratio	0.7	0.8	0.6	0.8	0.4	0.5	0.7	NA	NA	NA
% Long Term Debt of Capitalization	43.7	44.4	42.9	57.9	47.0	54.0	53.5	NA	NA	NA
% Net Income of Revenue	4.2	3.6	6.5	6.8	6.6	2.2	2.4	NA	NA	NA
% Return on Assets	1.7	1.6	2.6	2.5	2.5	1.1	1.1	NA	NA	NA
% Return on Equity	6.3	5.8	9.3	9.9	11.1	6.2	6.2	NA	NA	NA

Data as orig reptd.; bef. results of disc opers/spec. items. Per share data adj. for stk. divs.; EPS diluted. E-Estimated. NA-Not Available. NM-Not Meaningful. NR-Not Ranked. UR-Under Review.

Office: 801 East 86th Avenue, Merrillville, IN, USA 46410-6272.
Telephone: 877-647-5990.
Email: questions@nisource.com
Website: http://www.nisource.com

Chrmn: I.M. Rolland
Pres & CEO: R.C. Skaggs, Jr.
EVP & CFO: M.W. O'Donnell
Investor Contact: D.J. Vajda (877-647-5990)

VP & Treas: D.J. Vajda
Board Members: S. C. Beering, D. E. Foster, P. McCausland, S. R. McCracken, G. L. Neale, I. M. Rolland, R. C. Skaggs Jr., R. L. Thompson, R. J. Welsh, C. Y. Woo, R. A. Young

Founded: 1912
Domicile: Delaware
Employees: 7,439

Noble Corp

S&P Recommendation	**STRONG BUY** ★★★★★	Price $51.08 (as of Nov 23, 2007)	12-Mo. Target Price $66.00	Investment Style Large-Cap Growth

GICS Sector Energy
Sub-Industry Oil & Gas Drilling

Summary This company principally provides contract drilling services for the oil and gas industry worldwide.

Key Stock Statistics (Source S&P, Vickers, company reports)

52-Wk Range	$56.46–33.81	S&P Oper. EPS 2007**E**	4.62	Market Capitalization(B)	$13.692	Beta	0.84
Trailing 12-Month EPS	$3.92	S&P Oper. EPS 2008**E**	6.80	Yield (%)	0.31	S&P 3-Yr. Proj. EPS CAGR(%)	40.00
Trailing 12-Month P/E	13.0	P/E on S&P Oper. EPS 2007**E**	11.1	Dividend Rate/Share	$0.16	S&P Credit Rating	A-
$10K Invested 5 Yrs Ago	$30,418	Common Shares Outstg. (M)	268.0	Institutional Ownership (%)	86		

Price Performance

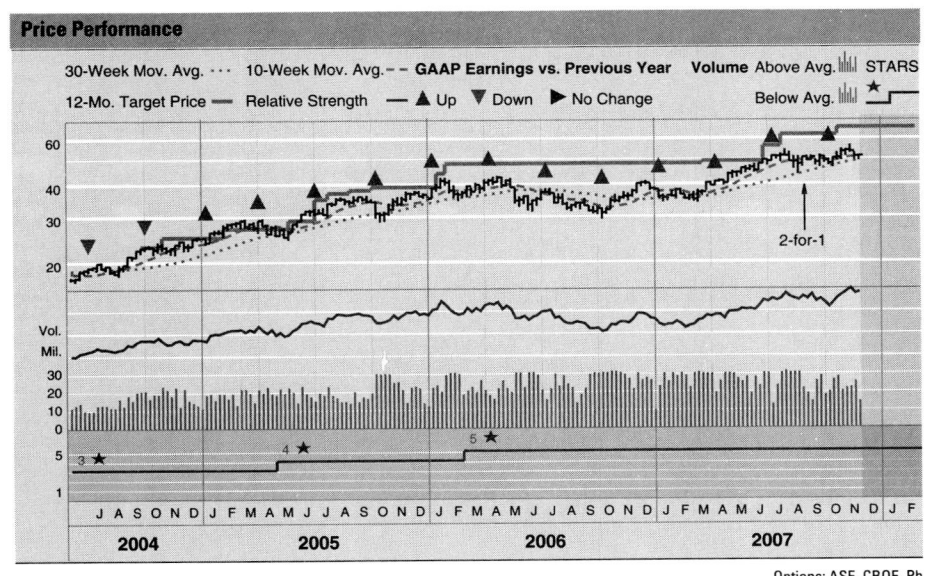

30-Week Mov. Avg. · · · 10-Week Mov. Avg. – – GAAP Earnings vs. Previous Year Volume Above Avg. STARS
12-Mo. Target Price — Relative Strength — ▲ Up ▼ Down ► No Change Below Avg.

Options: ASE, CBOE, Ph

Analysis prepared by **Stewart Glickman, CFA** on November 16, 2007, when the stock traded at **$ 50.69.**

Qualitative Risk Assessment

LOW	**MEDIUM**	HIGH

Our risk assessment reflects NE's exposure to volatile crude oil and natural gas prices, capital spending decisions made by its oil and gas producing customers, and political risk associated with operating in frontier regions. Offsetting these risks is the company's strong historical financial performance relative to peers.

Quantitative Evaluations

S&P Quality Ranking **B**

D	C	B-	**B**	B+	A-	A	A+

Relative Strength Rank **STRONG**

82

LOWEST = 1   HIGHEST = 99

Revenue/Earnings Data

Revenue (Million $)

	1Q	2Q	3Q	4Q	Year
2007	646.4	726.0	791.3	--	--
2006	461.9	517.5	562.0	558.8	2,100
2005	310.3	344.0	367.2	360.6	1,382
2004	245.4	253.0	265.6	302.2	1,066
2003	245.0	247.9	254.7	239.8	987.4
2002	235.5	247.4	234.7	251.1	986.4

Earnings Per Share ($)

2007	0.93	1.08	1.18	E1.43	E4.62
2006	0.52	0.65	0.76	0.74	2.66
2005	0.17	0.26	0.28	0.37	1.08
2004	0.11	0.13	0.12	0.20	0.55
2003	0.15	0.17	0.20	0.12	0.63
2002	0.20	0.22	0.19	0.20	0.79

Fiscal year ended Dec. 31. Next earnings report expected: Late January. EPS Estimates based on S&P Operating Earnings; historical GAAP earnings are as reported.

Highlights

➤ As of early November 2007, NE had nearly all of 2008 operating days for its floater rigs contracted, but only about 70% of its 2008 operating days for its jackup fleet. We view this as a positive, given our expectation for further improvements in leading edge dayrates in key regions such as Mexico, the Middle East, West Africa, and the North Sea. We project NE's jackup fleet to generate an average dayrate of about $118,000 in 2007, up about 30% over the fourth quarter of 2006, and to rise a further 29% in 2008, to $152,000 per day.

➤ In July, NE suspended its stock buyback program while an ongoing independent investigation continues into potentially illegal payments to customs agents in its Nigerian operations. We estimate that in the first half of 2007, NE repurchased about 1% of shares outstanding, largely in the first quarter.

➤ We see revenue growth of 46% in 2007, largely on projected contract drilling revenue gains, rising a further 35% in 2008. We estimate split-adjusted EPS of $4.62 in 2007, rising to $6.80 in 2008.

Investment Rationale/Risk

➤ With all of its active jackups located in international waters, we think NE is well insulated from recent weakness in U.S. Gulf of Mexico dayrates. We view Mexico in particular as a very promising market, given declines at Mexico's Cantarell field, and recent contract signings have been at attractive dayrates, including the semisubmersible Noble Max Smith for three years at $484,000 per day. Other strong markets, in our view, include the Middle East and West Africa. We expect NE to use cash from operations to fund capital spending plans, and would not be surprised if the company were to acquire newbuilds under construction by smaller players, especially deepwater assets.

➤ Risks to our recommendation and target price include reduced rig dayrates; higher than expected unscheduled shipyard repair days; and decreased oil and natural gas prices.

➤ We think the shares merit about peer valuations, given expected 2008 return on invested capital about in line with peers. Assuming multiples of 7.5X 2008 forecast EBITDA and 8.5X estimated 2008 cash flow (in line with peer averages), and blending with our net asset value model, our 12-month target price is $66.

Dividend Data (Dates: mm/dd Payment Date: mm/dd/yy)

Amount ($)	Date Decl.	Ex-Div. Date	Stk. of Record	Payment Date
0.040	02/02	02/12	02/14	03/01/07
0.040	04/25	05/03	05/07	06/01/07
2-for-1	07/27	08/29	08/07	08/28/07
0.040	10/25	11/05	11/07	12/03/07

Dividends have been paid since 2005. Source: Company reports.

Noble Corp

Business Summary November 16, 2007

CORPORATE OVERVIEW. In April 2002, Noble Drilling Corp. shareholders approved a corporate restructuring that effectively changed the company's place of incorporation from Delaware to the Cayman Islands. The restructuring was completed April 30, 2002, upon the merger of an indirect subsidiary of Noble Corp., a newly formed Cayman Islands company, with Noble Drilling. Noble Corp. (NE) became the parent holding company of Noble Drilling and the other companies in the Noble corporate group.

NE provides contract drilling services in offshore markets worldwide. The company has a fleet of 63 offshore drilling rigs. Company owned rigs include floating deepwater units, including 13 semisubmersibles and three dynamically positioned drillships, 44 independent leg, cantilever jackup rigs (including three under construction), and three submersibles. As of January 2007, approximately 85% of the fleet was deployed in international markets, mainly in the Middle East, Mexico, the North Sea, Brazil, West Africa, and India. Con-

tract drilling operations accounted for 92% of total revenues in 2006.

Within contract drilling operations, international activity accounted for 72% of revenues in 2006. PEMEX accounted for 12% of total revenues in 2006; no other customer comprised more than 10% of revenues.

In 2006, average utilization for NE's international fleet was flat at 97%, while U.S. utilization rose to 92%, from 91%. Dayrates for the international fleet rose to $83,417, from $60,922, while for the U.S. fleet, dayrates rose to $178,684, from $74,056.

Company Financials Fiscal Year Ended Dec. 31

Per Share Data ($)	2006	2005	2004	2003	2002	2001	2000	1999	1998	1997
Tangible Book Value	11.96	9.97	8.87	8.16	7.45	6.72	5.90	5.30	5.00	4.39
Cash Flow	3.66	1.97	1.32	1.18	1.25	1.43	1.02	0.69	0.89	1.28
Earnings	2.67	1.08	0.55	0.63	0.79	0.99	0.61	0.36	0.62	0.99
Dividends	0.08	0.05	Nil	Nil	Nil	Nil	Nil	Nil	Nil	Nil
Payout Ratio	3%	5%	Nil	Nil	Nil	Nil	Nil	Nil	Nil	Nil
Prices:High	43.08	37.81	25.27	19.20	22.98	27.00	26.75	16.44	17.34	19.09
Prices:Low	29.26	23.52	16.77	15.23	13.50	10.40	13.63	6.00	5.38	7.75
P/E Ratio:High	16	35	46	31	29	27	44	46	28	19
P/E Ratio:Low	11	22	31	24	17	11	22	17	9	8

Income Statement Analysis (Million $)										
Revenue	2,100	1,382	1,066	987	986	1,002	883	706	788	713
Operating Income	1,170	585	396	366	400	503	379	245	301	261
Depreciation, Depletion and Amortization	253	242	209	148	125	119	111	89.0	72.0	77.9
Interest Expense	16.2	19.8	34.4	40.3	42.6	47.8	54.6	33.2	5.20	12.9
Pretax Income	921	364	162	187	243	350	226	124	231	380
Effective Tax Rate	20.6%	18.5%	9.72%	11.0%	13.9%	24.6%	26.8%	24.3%	29.8%	30.5%
Net Income	732	297	146	166	210	264	166	95.3	162	264

Balance Sheet & Other Financial Data (Million $)										
Cash	61.7	166	58.8	139	274	288	177	137	217	66.4
Current Assets	570	522	425	422	466	494	379	291	438	265
Total Assets	4,586	4,346	3,308	3,190	3,066	2,751	2,596	2,432	2,179	1,506
Current Liabilities	426	259	214	244	281	208	205	233	350	153
Long Term Debt	684	1,129	503	542	590	550	650	731	461	138
Common Equity	3,229	2,732	2,384	2,178	1,989	1,778	1,577	1,398	1,310	1,149
Total Capital	4,126	4,097	3,086	2,927	2,779	2,526	2,372	2,197	1,828	1,351
Capital Expenditures	1,053	434	261	307	268	134	125	422	541	391
Cash Flow	985	538	355	315	335	382	276	184	234	342
Current Ratio	1.3	2.0	2.0	1.7	1.7	2.4	1.8	1.2	1.3	1.7
% Long Term Debt of Capitalization	16.6	27.6	16.3	18.5	21.2	21.8	27.4	33.3	25.2	10.2
% Return on Assets	16.4	7.8	4.5	5.3	7.2	9.9	6.6	4.1	8.8	18.4
% Return on Equity	24.6	11.6	6.4	8.0	11.1	15.7	11.1	7.0	13.2	25.5

Data as orig reptd.; bef. results of disc opers/spec. items. Per share data adj. for stk. divs.; EPS diluted. E-Estimated. NA-Not Available. NM-Not Meaningful. NR-Not Ranked. UR-Under Review.

Office: 13135 South Dairy Ashford, Sugar Land, TX, USA 77478.
Telephone: 281-276-6100.
Website: http://www.noblecorp.com
Chrmn, Pres & CEO: M.A. Jackson

COO & SVP: D.W. Williams
EVP & Secy: J.J. Robertson
SVP, CFO, Treas & Cntlr: T.L. Mitchell
SVP & General Counsel: R.D. Campbell

Investor Contact: L.M. Ahlstrom (281-276-6440)
Auditor: Pricewaterhousecoopers
Board Members: M. A. Cawley, L. J. Chazen, L. R. Corbett, J. C. Day, J. H. Edwards, M. A. Jackson, M. E. Leland, J. E. Little, M. P. Ricciardello, W. A. Sears

Founded: 1939
Domicile: Cayman Islands
Employees: 6,000

Noble Energy Inc

STANDARD &POOR'S

S&P Recommendation **BUY** ★★★★☆	Price $74.09 (as of Nov 23, 2007)	12-Mo. Target Price $86.00	Investment Style Large-Cap Growth

GICS Sector Energy
Sub-Industry Oil & Gas Exploration & Production

Summary This independent exploration and production company (formerly Noble Affiliates) is engaged in the exploration, production, and marketing of oil and natural gas worldwide.

Key Stock Statistics (Source S&P, Vickers, company reports)

52-Wk Range	$78.05– 46.04	S&P Oper. EPS 2007**E**	5.42	Market Capitalization(B)	$12.719	Beta	0.76
Trailing 12-Month EPS	$4.66	S&P Oper. EPS 2008**E**	6.16	Yield (%)	0.65	S&P 3-Yr. Proj. EPS CAGR(%)	5.00
Trailing 12-Month P/E	15.9	P/E on S&P Oper. EPS 2007**E**	13.7	Dividend Rate/Share	$0.48	S&P Credit Rating	BBB-
$10K Invested 5 Yrs Ago	$41,861	Common Shares Outstg. (M)	171.7	Institutional Ownership (%)	96		

Price Performance

30-Week Mov. Avg. · · · 10-Week Mov. Avg. - - GAAP Earnings vs. Previous Year   Volume Above Avg. STARS
12-Mo. Target Price — Relative Strength ▲ Up ▼ Down ▶ No Change   Below Avg.

Options: ASE, CBOE, P, Ph

Analysis prepared by **Michael Kay** on November 01, 2007, when the stock traded at **$ 76.81.**

Highlights

➤ Driven by developing Rocky Mountain assets, the start-up of Gulf of Mexico (GOM) projects, the start-up of Dumbarton in the North Sea, and increased sales in Israel, we see 2007 and 2008 production increases of 8% and 9%, respectively. We expect the completion of an LNG plant and improved volumes in Equatorial Guinea to boost West Africa operations and help offset production declines from the disposal of GOM assets. In 2008, NBL expects to drill three high impact exploration wells in Suriname, Norway and the Tamar prospect in offshore Israel.

➤ We see lease operating expense per unit declining 1% in 2007 and rising 2% in 2008, very impressive figures when considering a rising service cost environment. We see exploration expense up 7% in 2007 and flat in 2008, and DD&A up 10% and 3%, respectively. With moderating cost inflation, we see EBITDA increases of 23% in 2007 and 12% in 2008.

➤ NBL has increased drilling in the deepwater GOM and West Africa in light of recent exploration success and expects the majority of future spending to be allocated toward U.S. development projects, as it has what we see as a solid inventory of high impact prospects.

Investment Rationale/Risk

➤ In our view, acquisitions have extended NBL's reserve life and made its reserve replacement efforts less dependent on projects operated by other companies. As a result, we see an improvement in NBL's business profile due to increased U.S. onshore operations through organic growth and acquisitions, operational synergies, and a stronger balance sheet. We view NBL as a low-cost and geographically balanced producer with more financial flexibility than it previously had. We see catalysts for the stock in recent discoveries announced at Isabela (GOM) and Benita (Equatorial Guinea) and several development projects underway.

➤ Risks to our recommendation and target price include changes to economic, industrial or operating conditions, including difficulty in replacing reserves and heightened geopolitical risk.

➤ A blend of our discounted cash flow analysis (assuming a WACC of 9.3%, and terminal growth of 3%), which results in intrinsic value of $88, and our peer average relative valuations, including a target enterprise value to 2008 EBITDA of 6.5X and a target P/E of 13.5X our 2008 EPS estimate, leads to our 12-month target price of $86.

Qualitative Risk Assessment

LOW	MEDIUM	HIGH

Our risk assessment reflects our view of NBL's aggressive financial profile, and a satisfactory business profile limited by participation in the cyclical, competitive and capital intensive exploration and production sector, and by U.S. and international oil and gas operations that carry heightened political and operational risk.

Quantitative Evaluations

S&P Quality Ranking   B

D	C	B-	B	B+	A-	A	A+

Relative Strength Rank   STRONG
90
LOWEST = 1   HIGHEST = 99

Revenue/Earnings Data

Revenue (Million $)

	1Q	2Q	3Q	4Q	Year
2007	742.6	794.2	813.8	--	--
2006	712.0	772.6	741.3	714.2	2,940
2005	368.2	485.4	632.1	701.0	2,187
2004	317.6	335.2	320.2	378.2	1,351
2003	266.7	247.2	244.3	252.8	1,011
2002	317.7	330.3	339.7	456.1	1,444

Earnings Per Share ($)

	1Q	2Q	3Q	4Q	Year
2007	1.22	1.21	1.28	E1.45	E5.42
2006	1.26	-0.17	1.75	0.94	3.79
2005	0.92	0.91	0.99	1.18	4.12
2004	0.65	0.60	0.68	0.73	2.70
2003	0.28	0.23	0.28	Nil	0.78
2002	-0.13	0.15	-0.01	0.15	0.16

Fiscal year ended Dec. 31. Next earnings report expected: Late February. EPS Estimates based on S&P Operating Earnings; historical GAAP earnings are as reported.

Dividend Data (Dates: mm/dd Payment Date: mm/dd/yy)

Amount ($)	Date Decl.	Ex-Div. Date	Stk. of Record	Payment Date
0.075	01/23	02/01	02/05	02/20/07
0.120	04/23	05/03	05/07	05/21/07
0.120	07/24	08/02	08/06	08/20/07
0.120	10/23	11/01	11/05	11/19/07

Dividends have been paid since 1975. Source: Company reports.

Noble Energy Inc

STANDARD &POOR'S

Business Summary November 01, 2007

CORPORATE OVERVIEW. Noble Energy (NBL; formerly Noble Affiliates, Inc.) is a large international, independent exploration and production concern, engaged in exploration, production and marketing of oil and natural gas. The company has operations in the U.S. (offshore the Gulf of Mexico and California, the Gulf Coast region, the Mid-Continent region, and the Rocky Mountain region) and internationally (in Argentina, China, Ecuador, Equatorial Guinea, the Mediterranean Sea, and the North Sea).

In February 2007, NBL estimated its 2006 reserve replacement at 179%, which includes the effect of a negative revision of 10.8 million BOE due to low year-end North American natural gas prices. NBL organically replaced 139% of its North American production in 2006, and 74% of its international production. Reserve additions from all sources in North America were 104 million BOE; international reserve additions from all sources totaled 17.7 million BOE. Companywide at year-end 2006, reserves were 834.6 million BOE, and reserve additions from all sources were 122.1 million BOE, at a finding and development cost of $15.15 per BOE. NBL's 2006 production grew 28% relative to 2005, reflecting contributions from its Patina Oil and Gas acquisition. NBL has been reducing its investment in the Gulf of Mexico's conventional shallow shelf and shifting its domestic offshore exploration focus to deepwater Gulf of Mexico areas. NBL is now a larger, more diversified company with greater opportuni-

ties for both domestic and international growth, in our view, through high-impact exploration drilling as well as lower risk exploitation projects.

IMPACT OF MAJOR DEVELOPMENTS. On July 14, 2006, NBL closed on a $625 million sale of its Gulf of Mexico shelf assets to Coldren Resources LP. After-tax cash proceeds from the sale totaled $504 million, including proceeds received from parties that exercised preferential rights to purchase certain minor properties.

On May 16, 2005, NBL acquired Patina Oil and Gas Corp. As a result of the transaction, Patina shareholders received 0.6014 shares of NBL common stock, or $39.3398 in cash for their shares. NBL incurred about $1.7 billion of debt in the deal, of which $1.1 billion funded the cash contribution and $611 million repaid Patina's debt. We estimate that the Patina merger has extended NBL's reserve life and made its reserve replacement less dependent on international and Gulf of Mexico projects operated by other companies.

Company Financials Fiscal Year Ended Dec. 31

Per Share Data ($)	2006	2005	2004	2003	2002	2001	2000	1999	1998	1997
Tangible Book Value	19.35	12.68	12.37	9.38	8.80	8.86	7.58	5.99	5.64	7.10
Cash Flow	7.27	6.61	5.26	3.47	2.62	3.64	3.72	2.65	1.31	3.48
Earnings	3.79	4.12	2.70	0.78	0.16	1.17	1.69	0.43	-1.44	0.87
S&P Core Earnings	3.05	4.08	2.58	0.70	0.08	1.08	NA	NA	NA	NA
Dividends	0.28	0.15	0.10	0.09	0.08	0.08	0.08	0.08	0.08	0.08
Payout Ratio	7%	4%	4%	11%	52%	7%	5%	19%	NM	9%
Prices:High	54.64	48.75	32.30	23.00	20.38	25.55	24.19	17.50	23.09	25.00
Prices:Low	36.14	27.78	21.33	16.19	13.33	13.75	9.59	9.56	10.97	16.09
P/E Ratio:High	14	12	12	29	NM	22	14	41	NM	29
P/E Ratio:Low	9	7	8	21	NM	12	6	22	NM	19

Income Statement Analysis (Million $)										
Revenue	2,940	2,187	1,351	1,011	1,444	1,572	1,381	887	894	1,091
Operating Income	2,019	1,423	884	539	376	535	550	352	315	479
Depreciation, Depletion and Amortization	623	391	309	309	285	284	231	255	313	300
Interest Expense	117	87.5	48.2	47.0	47.7	26.0	31.6	43.0	43.8	46.8
Pretax Income	1,096	969	516	142	42.6	225	299	77.6	-247	158
Effective Tax Rate	38.1%	33.3%	39.2%	36.5%	58.6%	40.5%	36.0%	36.3%	NM	37.0%
Net Income	678	646	314	89.9	17.7	134	192	49.5	-164	99.3
S&P Core Earnings	548	640	305	81.0	8.88	123	NA	NA	NA	NA

Balance Sheet & Other Financial Data (Million $)										
Cash	153	110	180	62.4	15.4	73.2	23.2	2.93	19.1	55.1
Current Assets	1,069	1,176	734	478	310	352	271	148	188	259
Total Assets	9,589	8,878	3,443	2,843	2,730	2,480	1,879	1,450	1,686	1,875
Current Liabilities	1,184	1,240	665	655	472	381	325	184	139	217
Long Term Debt	1,801	2,031	880	776	977	837	525	445	745	645
Common Equity	4,114	3,231	1,460	1,074	1,009	1,010	850	2,134	642	813
Total Capital	7,673	5,262	2,524	2,013	2,188	2,024	1,492	2,662	1,494	1,602
Capital Expenditures	1,357	786	661	527	596	739	537	123	432	327
Cash Flow	1,301	1,036	623	399	303	418	422	304	149	400
Current Ratio	0.9	0.9	1.1	0.7	0.7	0.9	0.8	0.8	1.4	1.2
% Long Term Debt of Capitalization	23.5	38.6	34.9	38.6	44.6	41.4	35.2	16.7	49.9	40.3
% Return on Assets	7.3	10.5	10.0	3.2	0.7	6.1	11.6	3.2	NM	5.2
% Return on Equity	18.8	27.5	24.8	8.6	1.7	14.4	25.0	2.2	NM	13.0

Data as orig reptd.; bef. results of disc opers/spec. items. Per share data adj. for stk. divs.; EPS diluted. E-Estimated. NA-Not Available. NM-Not Meaningful. NR-Not Ranked. UR-Under Review.

Office: 100 Glenborough Drive, Houston, TX 77067.
Telephone: 281-872-3100.
Email: info@nobleenergyinc.com
Website: http://www.nobleenergyinc.com

Chrmn, Pres & CEO: C.D. Davidson
COO & EVP: D.L. Stover
SVP & CFO: C. Tong
VP, Secy & General Counsel: A.J. Johnson

Chief Acctg Officer: F.B. Bruning
Investor Contact: G. Panagos (281-872-3100)
Auditor: KPMG
Board Members: J. L. Berenson, M. A. Cawley, E. F. Cox, C. D. Davidson, T. J. Edelman, K. Hedrick, B. A. Smith, W. T. Van Kleef

Founded: 1969
Domicile: Delaware
Employees: 1,243

Nordstrom Inc.

STANDARD
&POOR'S

S&P Recommendation BUY ★★★★☆	Price $33.72 (as of Nov 29, 2007)	12-Mo. Target Price $45.00	Investment Style Large-Cap Growth

GICS Sector Consumer Discretionary
Sub-Industry Department Stores

Summary This Seattle-based specialty retailer of apparel and accessories, widely known for its emphasis on service, operates about 157 stores in 28 states.

Key Stock Statistics (Source S&P, Vickers, company reports)

52-Wk Range	**$59.70–30.46**	S&P Oper. EPS 2008**E**	2.80	Market Capitalization(B)	$8.235	Beta	1.48
Trailing 12-Month EPS	**$2.86**	S&P Oper. EPS 2009**E**	3.44	Yield (%)	1.60	S&P 3-Yr. Proj. EPS CAGR(%)	14.00
Trailing 12-Month P/E	**11.8**	P/E on S&P Oper. EPS 2008**E**	12.0	Dividend Rate/Share	$0.54	S&P Credit Rating	A-
$10K Invested 5 Yrs Ago	**$38,439**	Common Shares Outstg. (M)	244.2	Institutional Ownership (%)	70		

Price Performance

30-Week Mov. Avg. ··· 10-Week Mov. Avg. - - **GAAP Earnings vs. Previous Year**   Volume Above Avg. ⓘⓘⓘ STARS
12-Mo. Target Price — Relative Strength — ▲ Up ▼ Down ▶ No Change   Below Avg. ⓘⓘⓘ ★

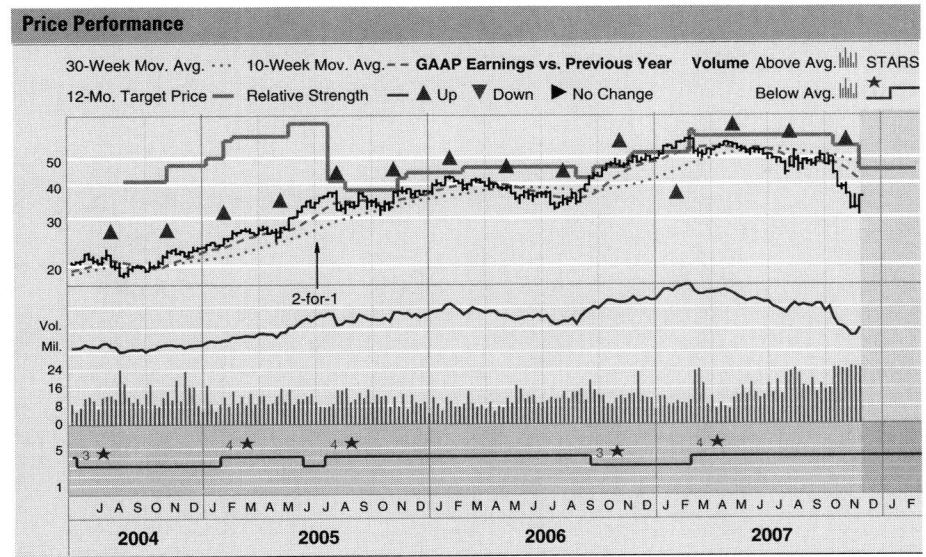

Options: ASE, CBOE, P, Ph

Analysis prepared by **Jason N. Asaeda** on November 29, 2007, when the stock traded at **$ 34.21**.

Highlights

➤ From a projected $8.9 billion in FY 08 (Jan.), we expect net sales to rise 7.7% in FY 09, to $9.6 billion, supported by a 4% increase in same-store sales and the opening of four new full-line stores and one relocated store. Based on our view that JWN has well-edited luxury-focused assortments and superior customer service, we see potential for the company to increase its share of wallet among wealthy baby boomers. We also look for a broader offering of designer apparel to attract a growing base of loyal younger customers.

➤ As a result of above-plan inventories at the start of the fall selling season, and unseasonably warm weather in September, which dampened apparel sales, JWN took additional markdowns during the FY 08 third quarter. However, we see full-year operating margins widening on increased full-price sales achieved in the spring and summer, as well as effective cost controls. In FY 09, we look for margins to expand further, supported by JWN's leveraging of technology to better plan and manage its merchandise assortments and inventory levels.

➤ After anticipated share buybacks, we see operating EPS of $2.80 in FY 08 and $3.44 in FY 09.

Investment Rationale/Risk

➤ JWN successfully worked through excess inventory during the recent third quarter, and we look for the company to post strong holiday sales results based on our view of on-trend fashions and expanded luxury and designer brand merchandise offerings. That said, we think investor concerns over an uncertain outlook for customer spending will pressure JWN shares over the near term. Looking ahead to FY 09, we expect the company's merchant team to continue to leverage systems investments to more accurately forecast sales trends and to better plan store-level inventory and expense. Enhanced online offerings and sales associates' use of the Personal Book tool should also drive incremental sales volume, we believe.

➤ Risks to our recommendation and target price include sales shortfalls due to unforeseen shifts in fashion trends, sharp cutbacks in consumer discretionary spending, and aggressive competition from peers such as Saks (SKS; hold, $20).

➤ Our 12-month target price of $45 applies a premium to peers forward P/E of 13X -- which we believe is warranted by our view of strong company fundamentals -- to our FY 09 EPS estimate.

Qualitative Risk Assessment

LOW	MEDIUM	HIGH

Our risk assessment reflects our view of JWN's improving sales and profit margins, increasing market share in the better department store sector, and healthy balance sheet and cash flow. This is offset by uncertainty over consumer discretionary spending in light of higher interest rates and debt levels.

Quantitative Evaluations

S&P Quality Ranking A-

D	C	B-	B	B+	A-	A	A+

Relative Strength Rank WEAK

18

LOWEST = 1   HIGHEST = 99

Revenue/Earnings Data

Revenue (Million $)

	1Q	2Q	3Q	4Q	Year
2008	1,954	2,390	1,970	--	--
2007	1,787	2,270	1,872	2,631	8,561
2006	1,654	2,106	1,666	2,296	7,723
2005	1,535	1,953	1,542	2,100	7,131
2004	1,344	1,795	1,421	1,933	6,492
2003	1,246	1,656	1,323	1,751	5,975

Earnings Per Share ($)

	1Q	2Q	3Q	4Q	Year
2008	0.60	0.71	0.68	E0.90	E2.80
2007	0.48	0.67	0.52	0.89	2.55
2006	0.38	0.53	0.39	0.69	1.98
2005	0.24	0.38	0.27	0.50	1.39
2004	0.10	0.24	0.17	0.37	0.88
2003	-0.04	0.14	0.07	0.22	0.38

Fiscal year ended Jan. 31. Next earnings report expected: Late February. EPS Estimates based on S&P Operating Earnings; historical GAAP earnings are as reported.

Dividend Data (Dates: mm/dd Payment Date: mm/dd/yy)

Amount ($)	Date Decl.	Ex-Div. Date	Stk. of Record	Payment Date
0.135	02/21	02/26	02/28	03/15/07
0.135	05/21	05/29	05/31	06/15/07
0.135	08/21	08/29	08/31	09/14/07
0.135	11/19	11/28	11/30	12/14/07

Dividends have been paid since 1971. Source: Company reports.

Nordstrom Inc.

STANDARD &POOR'S

Business Summary November 29, 2007

CORPORATE OVERVIEW. In our view, JWN is the clear leader in the U.S. better department store sector, reflecting its focus on high-quality, differentiated merchandise; personalized customer service; and a consistent upscale shopping experience across its entire Nordstrom store base. The company derives its revenues from retail, credit and direct sales channels, as well as Faconnable, a wholly owned wholesaler and retailer of apparel and accessories. In FY 07 (Jan.), merchandise category sales were: women's apparel 37.7%; accessories 19.3%; cosmetics 16.3%; men's apparel 13.9%; shoes 8.5%; and other 4.3%.

IMPACT OF MAJOR DEVELOPMENTS. JWN spends about $150 million annually on information technology (IT). In FY 03, the company invested in a perpetual inventory system that has enabled its merchant teams to more accurately forecast sales trends and to better track and plan store-level inventory and expenses, resulting in improved sales performance and profitability, in our opinion. In FY 05, JWN put into place a new point of sales system that in-

cludes Personal Book, a tool that allows salespeople to tailor service to the needs of each customer by organizing and tracking customer preferences, purchases, and contact information. The company has noted that Personal Book has driven incremental sales volume.

In July 2007, JWN agreed to sell Faconnable to M1 Group, a Lebanon-based, family-owned diversified business, for $210 million. As part of the agreement, JWN will continue to buy Faconnable merchandise at historical levels for at least the next three years and will continue to offer Faconnable in Nordstrom stores. The company anticipates realizing a gain of $0.08 to $0.10 per share on the sale, which is expected to close in the third quarter of FY 08, subject to closing conditions.

Company Financials Fiscal Year Ended Jan. 31

Per Share Data ($)	2007	2006	2005	2004	2003	2002	2001	2000	1999	1998
Tangible Book Value	7.90	7.26	6.10	5.40	4.55	4.38	4.06	4.49	4.63	4.84
Cash Flow	3.62	2.98	2.31	1.78	1.24	1.27	1.16	1.44	1.32	1.11
Earnings	2.55	1.98	1.39	0.88	0.38	0.46	0.39	0.73	0.71	0.60
S&P Core Earnings	2.55	1.93	2.62	1.67	0.62	0.80	0.83	NA	NA	NA
Dividends	0.32	0.24	0.21	0.21	0.19	0.18	0.16	0.18	0.15	0.13
Payout Ratio	13%	12%	15%	23%	50%	38%	41%	24%	21%	22%
Calendar Year	2006	2005	2004	2003	2002	2001	2000	1999	1998	1997
Prices:High	51.40	39.00	23.68	17.75	13.44	11.49	17.25	22.41	20.19	17.05
Prices:Low	31.77	22.71	16.55	7.50	7.80	6.90	7.06	10.84	10.71	8.47
P/E Ratio:High	20	20	17	20	35	25	44	31	29	28
P/E Ratio:Low	12	11	12	9	20	15	18	15	15	14

Income Statement Analysis (Million $)

	2007	2006	2005	2004	2003	2002	2001	2000	1999	1998
Revenue	8,794	7,723	7,131	6,492	5,975	5,634	5,529	5,124	5,028	4,852
Operating Income	1,427	1,010	817	585	424	363	335	467	458	393
Depreciation	285	276	265	251	234	218	203	194	180	160
Interest Expense	62.4	45.3	85.4	91.0	86.2	73.5	63.0	54.0	49.0	35.5
Pretax Income	1,106	885	647	398	196	204	167	332	338	307
Effective Tax Rate	38.7%	37.7%	39.2%	39.0%	47.1%	39.0%	38.9%	38.9%	38.8%	39.4%
Net Income	678	551	393	243	104	125	102	203	207	186
S&P Core Earnings	677	536	373	229	83.9	107	109	NA	NA	NA

Balance Sheet & Other Financial Data (Million $)

	2007	2006	2005	2004	2003	2002	2001	2000	1999	1998
Cash	403	463	361	476	208	331	25.0	27.0	241	24.8
Current Assets	2,742	2,874	2,572	2,455	2,073	2,055	1,813	1,565	1,680	1,595
Total Assets	4,822	4,921	4,605	4,466	4,096	4,049	3,608	3,062	3,115	2,865
Current Liabilities	1,433	1,623	1,341	1,050	870	948	951	867	769	943
Long Term Debt	624	628	929	1,605	1,342	1,351	1,100	747	805	320
Common Equity	2,169	2,093	1,789	1,634	1,372	1,314	1,229	1,185	1,317	1,475
Total Capital	2,792	2,720	2,718	3,239	2,714	2,666	2,329	1,932	2,122	1,775
Capital Expenditures	264	272	247	258	328	390	321	305	291	260
Cash Flow	963	828	658	494	338	342	305	397	387	346
Current Ratio	1.9	1.8	1.9	2.3	2.4	2.2	1.9	1.8	2.2	1.7
% Long Term Debt of Capitalization	22.3	23.1	34.2	49.5	49.4	50.7	47.2	38.7	37.9	17.8
% Net Income of Revenue	7.7	7.1	5.5	3.7	1.7	2.2	1.8	4.0	4.1	3.8
% Return on Assets	13.9	11.6	8.6	5.7	2.5	3.3	3.1	6.6	6.9	6.7
% Return on Equity	31.8	28.4	23.0	16.2	7.7	9.8	8.5	16.3	14.8	12.6

Data as orig reptd.; bef. results of disc opers/spec. items. Per share data adj. for stk. divs.; EPS diluted. E-Estimated. NA-Not Available. NM-Not Meaningful. NR-Not Ranked. UR-Under Review.

Office: 1617 Sixth Ave, Seattle, WA 98101-1707.
Telephone: 206-628-2111.
Email: invrelations@nordstrom.com
Website: http://www.nordstrom.com

Chrmn: B.A. Nordstrom
Pres: B.W. Nordstrom
EVP & CFO: M.G. Koppel
VP & Secy: D.L. Mackie

Chief Acctg Officer & Cntlr: P. Collins
Investor Contact: R. Jones (206-303-3007)
Board Members: P. Campbell, E. Hernandez, Jr., J. P. Jackson, R. G. Miller, B. W. Nordstrom, E. Nordstrom, P. Nordstrom, P. G. Satre, A. A. Winter

Founded: 1901
Domicile: Washington
Employees: 52,900

The McGraw-Hill Companies

Norfolk Southern Corp

STANDARD &POOR'S

S&P Recommendation **HOLD** ★★★☆☆	Price $49.55 (as of Nov 23, 2007)	12-Mo. Target Price $57.00	Investment Style Large-Cap Blend

GICS Sector Industrials
Sub-Industry Railroads

Summary This railroad operates 21,200 route miles serving 22 Eastern states, the District of Columbia, and Ontario, Canada.

Key Stock Statistics (Source S&P, Vickers, company reports)

52-Wk Range	$59.77– 45.38	S&P Oper. EPS 2007**E**	3.65	Market Capitalization(B)	$19.503	Beta	1.01
Trailing 12-Month EPS	$3.61	S&P Oper. EPS 2008**E**	4.17	Yield (%)	2.10	S&P 3-Yr. Proj. EPS CAGR(%)	10.00
Trailing 12-Month P/E	13.7	P/E on S&P Oper. EPS 2007**E**	13.6	Dividend Rate/Share	$1.04	S&P Credit Rating	BBB+
$10K Invested 5 Yrs Ago	$26,838	Common Shares Outstg. (M)	393.6	Institutional Ownership (%)	69		

Price Performance

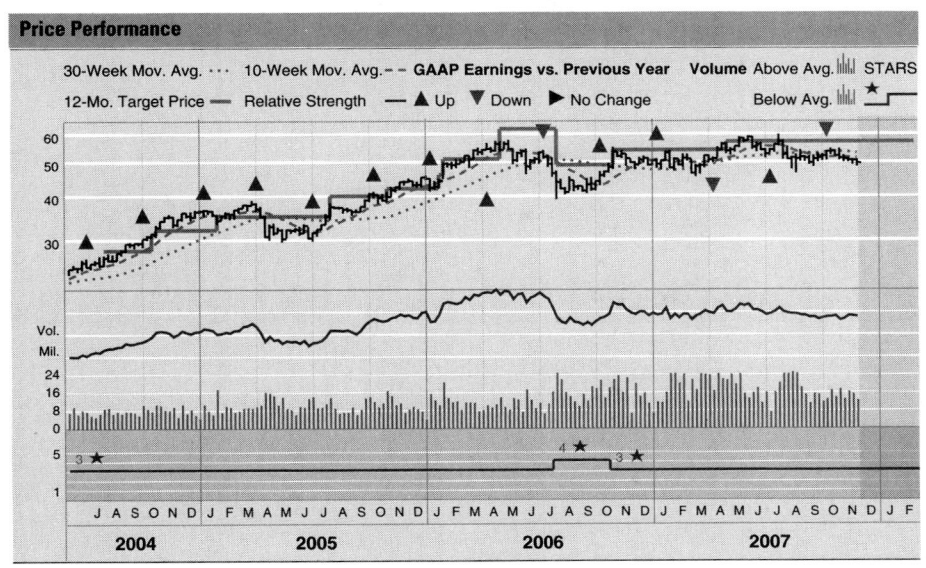

30-Week Mov. Avg. ··· 10-Week Mov. Avg. - - **GAAP Earnings vs. Previous Year** Volume Above Avg. STARS
12-Mo. Target Price — Relative Strength — ▲ Up ▼ Down ▶ No Change Below Avg.

2004 2005 2006 2007

Options: ASE, CBOE, P, Ph

Analysis prepared by **Kevin Kirkeby** on November 13, 2007, when the stock traded at **$ 49.70**.

Highlights

➤ We believe NSC can achieve revenue growth of 7% in 2008, through equal contributions from volume and yield. This is partly driven by our expectation that coal volumes will improve with the restart of several mines and growth in exports. While we think construction-related shipments will remain weak, we see automotive shipments starting to stabilize. Route changes by ocean carriers are likely to drive additional intermodal traffic through East Coast ports, but with a corresponding reduction in longer-haul transcontinental containers.

➤ We see 2008 operating margins widening modestly from the 27.3% we anticipate in 2007 due to cost control measures and improved utilization rates. Also, we expect little impact from fluctuations in fuel prices because over 90% of NSC's fuel needs are covered by surcharge mechanisms, and all its hedges have rolled off. Net interest expenses are likely to increase in 2008 as share repurchases reduce its cash position.

➤ We expect the effective tax rate to rise in 2008 on a reduction in synthetic fuel credits and recent state tax increases. Our 2008 EPS estimate incorporates a 1% reduction in share count.

Investment Rationale/Risk

➤ Medium-term trends in NSC's primary markets remain favorable and support rising traffic and prices, in our opinion. We see investments in its network improving capacity on heavily trafficked lines, and leading to higher railcar utilization and greater system fluidity. However, with valuations near historical averages and our forecast for a slower rate of pricing gains, we believe NSC is appropriately valued.

➤ Risks to our recommendation and target price include weaker than anticipated coal shipments, rising competition in its shorter routes where trucks are able to compete effectively, severe weather, a new round of production cuts by auto manufacturers, and declining railroad system fluidity.

➤ Blending a forward P/E of about 13.5X our next 12-month EPS estimate, above the five-year average but a modest discount to peers, with our DCF model, which assumes a 9% weighted average cost of capital, 10% average EPS growth over the next three years and a 3.5% terminal growth rate (yielding a value of $59), we arrive at our 12-month target price of $57.

Qualitative Risk Assessment

LOW	**MEDIUM**	HIGH

Our risk assessment reflects what we see as NSC's exposure to economic cycles, regulations, labor and fuel costs, significant capital expenditure requirements, and challenges in maintaining system fluidity, offset by our view of a diverse customer base, historically positive free cash flow, and moderate financial leverage.

Quantitative Evaluations

S&P Quality Ranking B+

D	C	B-	B	**B+**	A-	A	A+

Relative Strength Rank MODERATE

61

LOWEST = 1   HIGHEST = 99

Revenue/Earnings Data

Revenue (Million $)

	1Q	2Q	3Q	4Q	Year
2007	2,247	2,378	2,353	--	--
2006	2,303	2,392	2,393	2,319	9,407
2005	1,961	2,154	2,155	2,257	8,527
2004	1,693	1,813	1,857	1,949	7,312
2003	1,561	1,633	1,598	1,676	6,468
2002	1,498	1,593	1,598	1,581	6,270

Earnings Per Share ($)

2007	0.71	0.98	0.97	E0.99	E3.65
2006	0.72	0.89	1.02	0.95	3.57
2005	0.47	1.04	0.73	0.87	3.11
2004	0.40	0.54	0.72	0.65	2.31
2003	0.54	0.35	0.35	0.13	1.05
2002	0.22	0.31	0.32	0.33	1.18

Fiscal year ended Dec. 31. Next earnings report expected: Late January. EPS Estimates based on S&P Operating Earnings; historical GAAP earnings are as reported.

Dividend Data (Dates: mm/dd Payment Date: mm/dd/yy)

Amount ($)	Date Decl.	Ex-Div. Date	Stk. of Record	Payment Date
0.220	01/23	01/31	02/02	03/10/07
0.220	04/24	05/02	05/04	06/11/07
0.260	07/24	08/01	08/03	09/10/07
0.260	10/23	10/31	11/02	12/10/07

Dividends have been paid since 1901. Source: Company reports.

Please read the Required Disclosures and Analyst Certification on the last page of this report.

The McGraw-Hill Companies

Norfolk Southern Corp

STANDARD
&POOR'S

Business Summary November 13, 2007

CORPORATE OVERVIEW. Norfolk Southern provides rail transportation service in the eastern U.S., operating over 21,000 miles of road, with an extensive intermodal and coal service network and a significant general freight business, including an automotive business that is the largest in North America. NSC owns 58% of Conrail's shares, with CSX holding the remainder, and holds 50% voting rights. NSC and CSX operate separate portions of Conrail's rail routes and assets. NSC's non-rail activities includes real estate and natural resources.

MARKET PROFILE. We believe NSC's intermodal business, representing 21% of 2006 freight revenues, will be NSC's fastest growing segment longer term, driven by rising international trade and its cost savings over trucks for long-distance container movements. We think the superior system fluidity of its most extensive intermodal network on the East Coast, supported by ongoing investment in facilities, will provide NSC with a continuing edge in garnering east coast intermodal traffic. Coal, which we believe is NSC's most profitable segment, accounted for 25% of 2006 freight revenues. Most of this traffic originates from the Appalachian coal fields, and is primarily delivered to power utilities. General merchandise, sensitive to U.S. GDP trends, provided 54% of freight revenues in 2006. We believe chemicals and automotive, representing

11% and 10% of 2006 freight revenues, respectively, are significant general merchandise subsegments that are facing low long-term volume growth prospects. We consider NSC to have considerable exposure to the auto market since it serves 29 assembly plants, the majority of which belong to the domestic manufacturers Ford, Chrysler and General Motors.

COMPETITIVE LANDSCAPE. The U.S. rail industry has an oligopoly-like structure, with over 80% of revenues generated by the four largest railroads: NSC and CSX Corp. operating on the East Coast, and Union Pacific Corp. and Burlington Northern Santa Fe Corp. operating on the West Coast. Railroads simultaneously compete for customers while cooperating by sharing assets, interfacing systems, and completing customer movements. Key suppliers include locomotive and rail equipment manufacturers, fuel suppliers, and labor. NSC's employees, about 85% of whom are unionized, enjoy above national average compensation due to their significant bargaining power.

Company Financials Fiscal Year Ended Dec. 31

Per Share Data ($)	2006	2005	2004	2003	2002	2001	2000	1999	1998	1997
Tangible Book Value	24.19	22.66	19.98	17.83	16.71	15.78	15.17	15.53	15.61	14.44
Cash Flow	5.50	5.02	3.83	2.40	2.50	2.27	1.80	1.91	2.83	2.98
Earnings	3.57	3.11	2.31	1.05	1.18	0.94	0.45	0.63	1.65	1.84
S&P Core Earnings	3.43	2.97	2.13	0.95	0.70	0.41	NA	NA	NA	NA
Dividends	0.68	0.48	0.46	0.30	0.26	0.24	0.80	0.80	0.80	0.80
Payout Ratio	19%	15%	20%	29%	22%	26%	178%	127%	48%	43%
Prices:High	57.71	45.81	36.69	24.62	26.98	24.11	22.75	36.44	41.75	38.13
Prices:Low	39.10	29.60	20.38	17.35	17.20	13.41	11.94	19.63	27.44	28.21
P/E Ratio:High	16	15	16	23	23	26	51	58	25	21
P/E Ratio:Low	11	10	9	17	15	14	27	31	17	15

Income Statement Analysis (Million $)	2006	2005	2004	2003	2002	2001	2000	1999	1998	1997
Revenue	9,407	8,527	7,312	6,468	6,270	6,170	6,159	5,195	4,221	4,223
Operating Income	3,307	2,904	2,311	1,592	1,158	1,521	1,150	1,207	1,502	1,645
Depreciation	750	787	609	528	515	514	517	489	450	432
Interest Expense	493	500	506	497	518	553	551	561	516	385
Pretax Income	2,230	1,697	1,302	586	706	553	250	351	845	998
Effective Tax Rate	33.6%	24.5%	29.1%	29.9%	34.8%	34.5%	31.2%	31.9%	25.4%	30.0%
Net Income	1,481	1,281	923	411	460	362	172	239	630	699
S&P Core Earnings	1,417	1,224	849	365	270	155	NA	NA	NA	NA

Balance Sheet & Other Financial Data (Million $)	2006	2005	2004	2003	2002	2001	2000	1999	1998	1997
Cash	527	289	579	284	184	204	Nil	37.0	5.00	34.0
Current Assets	2,400	2,650	1,967	1,425	1,299	1,047	849	1,371	913	1,103
Total Assets	26,028	25,861	24,750	20,596	19,956	19,418	18,976	19,250	18,180	17,350
Current Liabilities	2,093	1,921	2,201	1,801	1,853	2,386	1,887	1,924	1,117	1,093
Long Term Debt	6,109	6,616	6,863	6,800	7,006	7,027	7,339	7,556	7,483	7,398
Common Equity	9,615	9,289	7,990	6,976	6,500	6,090	5,824	5,932	5,921	5,445
Total Capital	22,168	22,525	21,403	17,008	16,561	15,943	15,958	16,225	15,998	15,372
Capital Expenditures	1,178	1,025	1,041	720	689	746	731	912	956	875
Cash Flow	2,231	2,068	1,532	939	975	876	689	728	1,080	1,131
Current Ratio	1.1	1.4	0.9	0.8	0.7	0.4	0.4	0.7	0.8	1.0
% Long Term Debt of Capitalization	27.6	29.4	32.1	40.0	42.3	44.1	46.0	46.6	46.8	48.1
% Net Income of Revenue	15.7	15.0	12.6	6.4	7.3	5.9	2.8	4.6	14.9	16.6
% Return on Assets	5.7	5.1	4.1	2.0	2.3	1.9	0.9	1.3	3.5	4.9
% Return on Equity	15.7	14.8	12.3	6.1	7.3	6.1	2.9	4.0	11.1	13.4

Data as orig reptd.; bef. results of disc opers/spec. items. Per share data adj. for stk. divs.; EPS diluted. E-Estimated. NA-Not Available. NM-Not Meaningful. NR-Not Ranked. UR-Under Review.

Office: Three Commercial Pl, Norfolk, VA 23510-2191.
Telephone: 757-629-2680.
Website: http://www.nscorp.com
Chrmn, Pres & CEO: C.W. Moorman

Vice Chrmn & COO: S.C. Tobias
Vice Chrmn & CFO: H.C. Wolf
EVP & CIO: D.H. Butler
VP & Cntlr: M.R. Stewart

Investor Contact: L. Tyree (757-533-4810)
Board Members: G. L. Baliles, D. A. Carp, G. R. Carter, A. D. Correll, L. Hilliard, B. M. Joyce, S. F. Leer, C. W. Moorman, J. M. O'Brien, J. P. Reason

Founded: 1980
Domicile: Virginia
Employees: 30,541

The McGraw-Hill Companies

Northern Trust Corp

S&P Recommendation	BUY ★★★★☆	Price $76.94 (as of Nov 23, 2007)	12-Mo. Target Price $76.00	Investment Style Large-Cap Growth

GICS Sector Financials
Sub-Industry Asset Management & Custody Banks

Summary Northern Trust is a leading provider of fiduciary, asset management and private banking services.

Key Stock Statistics (Source S&P, Vickers, company reports)

52-Wk Range	$80.23– 56.00	S&P Oper. EPS 2007**E**	3.53	Market Capitalization(B)	$16.934	Beta	1.10
Trailing 12-Month EPS	$3.46	S&P Oper. EPS 2008**E**	3.93	Yield (%)	1.46	S&P 3-Yr. Proj. EPS CAGR(%)	12.00
Trailing 12-Month P/E	22.2	P/E on S&P Oper. EPS 2007**E**	21.8	Dividend Rate/Share	$1.12	S&P Credit Rating	AA-
$10K Invested 5 Yrs Ago	$21,096	Common Shares Outstg. (M)	220.1	Institutional Ownership (%)	73		

Price Performance

30-Week Mov. Avg. ··· 10-Week Mov. Avg. — **GAAP Earnings vs. Previous Year** Volume Above Avg. STARS
12-Mo. Target Price — Relative Strength — ▲ Up ▼ Down ► No Change Below Avg. ★

Options: ASE, CBOE, P, Ph

Analysis prepared by **Frank Braden, CFA** on October 19, 2007, when the stock traded at **$ 68.65**.

Highlights

➤ We continue to look for healthy investment asset growth, new business wins, and net interest income growth of 10% to 11% to support operating earnings growth in the quarters ahead. We expect new business wins to increase in light of disruptions at its competitors. We forecast a 13% increase in non-interest expense in 2008, as a result of higher performance-based compensation and increased staff levels. Although we view the increase in non-interest expense as a negative, we think it is a product of growth and believe the expenses will be relatively contained.

➤ Asset quality has remained solid, with nonperforming assets as a percent of total loans at 0.12% in the third quarter. New international business growth and foreign exchange trading income should support solid domestic growth, and we expect Northern Trust's private client business to make up an increasing portion of its business. We expect a slightly lower tax rate due to NTRS' growing international exposure.

➤ We estimate that operating EPS will advance to $3.53 in 2007 and $3.93 in 2008.

Investment Rationale/Risk

➤ Despite the recent run-up in non-interest expense, we view NTRS as a well-run custody bank with solid credit quality. We have a positive view of the company's product and geographic diversity, coupled with a healthy operating outlook. We believe the company's leading position in the affluent market, and its focus on ultra wealthy clients, should result in above peer average revenue and earnings growth in a stable or modestly rising equity market. We see pretax operating margins growing to 33.8% in 2008 from our expectation of 33.9% in 2007.

➤ Risks to our recommendation and target price include the failure to generate new business from existing and new clients, a significant decline in economic activity, higher growth in non-interest expenses, and integration, legal and regulatory risks.

➤ Over the past five years, on average, the shares have traded at 18.5X its 12-month forward EPS estimate. Our 12-month target price of $76 is equal to approximately 19.3X our 2008 EPS estimate, a slight premium to peers.

Qualitative Risk Assessment

LOW	MEDIUM	HIGH

Our risk assessment reflects what we see as solid business fundamentals and a strong customer base. We view NTRS as well diversified geographically and able to withstand a major economic downturn.

Quantitative Evaluations

S&P Quality Ranking   A-

D	C	B-	B	B+	A-	A	A+

Relative Strength Rank   STRONG

94

LOWEST = 1   HIGHEST = 99

Revenue/Earnings Data

Revenue (Million $)

	1Q	2Q	3Q	4Q	Year
2007	1,250	1,338	1,385	--	--
2006	1,030	1,134	1,117	1,192	4,473
2005	792.9	902.4	912.0	947.1	3,554
2004	680.9	695.9	686.7	765.6	2,829
2003	630.2	671.3	645.9	650.5	2,598
2002	714.2	719.3	678.6	663.0	2,775

Earnings Per Share ($)

2007	0.84	0.92	0.93	E0.90	E3.53
2006	0.74	0.76	0.74	0.77	3.00
2005	0.63	0.68	0.67	0.67	2.64
2004	0.57	0.59	0.52	0.59	2.26
2003	0.43	0.36	0.51	0.58	1.89
2002	0.56	0.56	0.43	0.43	1.97

Fiscal year ended Dec. 31. Next earnings report expected: Mid January. EPS Estimates based on S&P Operating Earnings; historical GAAP earnings are as reported.

Dividend Data (Dates: mm/dd Payment Date: mm/dd/yy)

Amount ($)	Date Decl.	Ex-Div. Date	Stk. of Record	Payment Date
0.250	02/20	03/07	03/09	04/02/07
0.250	04/17	06/06	06/08	07/02/07
0.250	07/17	09/06	09/10	10/01/07
0.280	10/16	12/06	12/10	01/02/08

Dividends have been paid since 1896. Source: Company reports.

Northern Trust Corp

STANDARD &POOR'S

Business Summary October 19, 2007

CORPORATE OVERVIEW. NTRS organizes its services globally around its two principal business units: Corporate and Institutional Services (C&IS) and Personal Financial Services (PFS). C&IS is a leading worldwide provider of asset administration, asset management and related services to corporate and public entity retirement funds, foundation and endowment clients, fund managers, insurance companies and government funds. C&IS also offers a full range of commercial banking services through the bank, placing special emphasis on developing and supporting institutional relationships in two target markets: large U.S. corporations and financial institutions (both U.S. and non-U.S.). Asset administration, asset management and related services encompass a full range of capabilities including: worldwide master trust, asset servicing, fund administration, settlement and reporting; cash management; and investment risk and performance analytical services.

In 2005, NTRS completed its acquisition of the Financial Services Group Limited (FSG) from Baring Asset Management Holdings Limited. The purchase of FSG brought to C&IS expanded capabilities in institutional fund administration,

custody, trust and related services as well as new capabilities in hedge fund and private equity administration, in our view.

PFS provides personal trust, custody and investment management services; individual retirement accounts; guardianship and estate administration; qualified retirement plans; banking (including private banking); personal lending; and residential real estate mortgage lending. PFS focuses on high net worth individuals, business owners, executives, retirees and established privately-held businesses in its target markets. PFS also includes the Wealth Management Group, which provides customized products and services to meet the complex financial needs of families and individuals in the U.S. and throughout the world, with assets typically exceeding $75 million.

Company Financials Fiscal Year Ended Dec. 31

Per Share Data ($)	2006	2005	2004	2003	2002	2001	2000	1999	1998	1997
Tangible Book Value	15.53	14.72	14.14	13.88	13.04	11.97	10.54	9.25	7.54	6.62
Earnings	3.00	2.64	2.26	1.89	1.97	2.11	2.08	1.74	1.52	1.33
S&P Core Earnings	3.04	2.51	2.19	1.63	1.64	1.82	NA	NA	NA	NA
Dividends	0.94	0.86	0.78	0.70	0.68	0.64	0.56	0.48	0.42	0.38
Payout Ratio	31%	33%	35%	37%	35%	30%	27%	28%	28%	28%
Prices:High	61.40	55.00	51.35	48.75	62.67	82.25	92.13	54.63	44.94	35.75
Prices:Low	49.12	41.60	38.40	27.64	30.41	41.40	46.75	40.16	27.88	17.00
P/E Ratio:High	20	21	23	26	32	39	44	31	30	27
P/E Ratio:Low	16	16	17	15	15	20	22	23	18	13

Income Statement Analysis (Million $)

	2006	2005	2004	2003	2002	2001	2000	1999	1998	1997
Net Interest Income	730	661	561	548	602	595	569	519	477	438
Tax Equivalent Adjustment	64.8	60.9	54.4	52.4	48.7	52.6	53.3	38.6	35.9	32.7
Non Interest Income	2,018	1,783	1,711	1,542	1,537	1,580	1,537	1,235	1,070	934
Loan Loss Provision	15.0	2.50	-15.0	2.50	37.5	66.5	24.0	12.5	9.00	9.00
% Expense/Operating Revenue	69.6%	69.2%	65.9%	68.1%	67.2%	61.8%	62.6%	62.8%	63.0%	65.0%
Pretax Income	1,024	888	754	631	669	732	730	616	543	472
Effective Tax Rate	35.0%	34.2%	33.1%	32.9%	33.2%	33.4%	33.6%	34.3%	34.8%	34.4%
Net Income	665	584	505	423	447	488	485	405	354	309
% Net Interest Margin	1.73	1.79	1.66	1.73	1.93	2.02	2.02	2.05	2.08	2.18
S&P Core Earnings	674	561	491	365	369	418	NA	NA	NA	NA

Balance Sheet & Other Financial Data (Million $)

	2006	2005	2004	2003	2002	2001	2000	1999	1998	1997
Money Market Assets	16,790	16,036	13,168	9,565	9,332	10,546	5,865	3,439	1,174	5,275
Investment Securities	12,365	11,109	9,042	9,471	6,594	6,331	7,270	6,244	5,848	4,198
Commercial Loans	6,515	5,064	4,498	4,702	5,137	5,767	5,708	5,485	4,615	4,082
Other Loans	16,094	14,905	13,445	13,111	12,927	12,213	12,437	9,890	9,032	8,506
Total Assets	60,712	53,414	45,277	41,450	39,478	39,665	36,022	28,708	27,870	25,315
Demand Deposits	9,315	7,427	6,377	5,767	6,602	7,110	5,375	4,945	3,928	3,961
Time Deposits	34,505	31,093	24,681	20,503	19,460	17,909	17,453	16,426	14,275	12,399
Long Term Debt	2,421	2,791	1,340	1,341	1,284	1,485	1,356	1,427	1,426	1,225
Common Equity	3,944	3,601	3,296	3,055	2,880	2,653	2,342	2,055	1,820	1,619
% Return on Assets	1.2	3.0	1.2	1.0	1.1	1.3	1.5	1.4	1.3	1.3
% Return on Equity	17.6	42.7	15.9	14.2	16.1	19.4	21.8	20.7	20.3	20.0
% Loan Loss Reserve	0.6	0.6	0.7	0.8	0.9	0.9	0.9	1.0	1.1	1.2
% Loans/Deposits	51.6	51.8	57.8	67.8	69.3	71.9	79.5	71.9	75.0	76.9
% Equity to Assets	6.6	7.0	7.3	7.3	7.0	6.6	6.8	6.8	6.5	6.5

Data as orig reptd.; bef. results of disc opers/spec. items. Per share data adj. for stk. divs.; EPS diluted. E-Estimated. NA-Not Available. NM-Not Meaningful. NR-Not Ranked. UR-Under Review.

Office: 50 S La Salle St , Chicago, IL 60603-1003.
Telephone: 312-630-6000.
Website: http://www.northerntrust.com
Chrmn & CEO: W.A. Osborn

Pres & COO: F.H. Waddell
Investor Contact: S.L. Fradkin (312-630-6000)
EVP & CFO: S.L. Fradkin
EVP & General Counsel: K.R. Welsh

Board Members: L. W. Bynoe, N. D. Chabraja, S. Crown, D. C. Jain, A. L. Kelly, R. C. McCormack, E. J. Mooney, W. A. Osborn, J. W. Rowe, H. B. Smith, W. D. Smithburg, E. J. Sosa, C. A. Tribbett III, F. H. Waddell

Founded: 1889
Domicile: Delaware
Employees: 9,726

Northrop Grumman Corp

STANDARD &POOR'S

S&P Recommendation	BUY ★★★★☆	Price $80.07 (as of Nov 23, 2007)	12-Mo. Target Price $89.00	Investment Style Large-Cap Blend

GICS Sector Industrials
Sub-Industry Aerospace & Defense

Summary This company is the world's third largest producer of military arms and equipment, and also has a government IT services business.

Key Stock Statistics (Source S&P, Vickers, company reports)

52-Wk Range	$85.21– 64.63	S&P Oper. EPS 2007**E**	5.11	Market Capitalization(B)	$27.093	Beta		0.41
Trailing 12-Month EPS	$5.09	S&P Oper. EPS 2008**E**	5.56	Yield (%)	1.85	S&P 3-Yr. Proj. EPS CAGR(%)		10.00
Trailing 12-Month P/E	15.7	P/E on S&P Oper. EPS 2007**E**	15.7	Dividend Rate/Share	$1.48	S&P Credit Rating		BBB+
$10K Invested 5 Yrs Ago	$18,119	Common Shares Outstg. (M)	338.4	Institutional Ownership (%)	92			

Price Performance

30-Week Mov. Avg. · · · 10-Week Mov. Avg. – – **GAAP Earnings vs. Previous Year** Volume Above Avg. ▯▯▯ STARS
12-Mo. Target Price — Relative Strength — ▲ Up ▼ Down ► No Change Below Avg. ▯▯▯ ★

Options: ASE, CBOE, P

Analysis prepared by **Richard Tortoriello** on October 29, 2007, when the stock traded at **$ 82.76**.

Highlights

➤ We project revenue growth of about 5% in 2007 and 6% in 2008, following flat revenues in 2006. We see growth primarily in Information & Services and Electronics, and a rebound in Ships, with NOC's Gulf Coast shipyards recovering from Hurricane Katrina damage. Over the longer term, we see Aerospace benefiting as aircraft such as the E-2D Hawkeye, the EA-18 Growler and the F-35 Joint Strike Fighter transition from development to production. We view NOC's order book as strong, with funded backlog equal to just under one year of sales as of September 2007.

➤ We project an operating margin of 9.6% in 2007, up from 9.3% in 2006. Operating margins have improved from 7.8% in 2005, and we see the potential for improved margins in 2008 and beyond, particularly in Ships and Aerospace.

➤ We estimate EPS of $5.11 in 2007, up from $4.44 in 2006, and $5.56 in 2008. We project free cash flow (cash flow from operating activities less capital expenditures) per share of about $5.30 in 2007.

Investment Rationale/Risk

➤ Our buy recommendation is based primarily on our view of a healthy outlook for U.S. defense spending, a strong order backlog, and the opportunities for margin expansion we see in the ships and aerospace segments and elsewhere in the company, as well as our view of an attractive valuation. We also have a positive view of NOC's cash deployment strategy, which consists of dividend increases, share repurchases, debt and pension funding, and select acquisitions.

➤ Risks to our recommendation and target price include the potential for delays and/or cuts in military budgets, and failure to perform well on existing contracts or to win new contracts.

➤ Our 12-month target price of $89 is based primarily on our discounted free cash flow valuation, which assumes 7.5% compound annual growth in free cash flow over the first 10 years, gradually declining to 3% in perpetuity. The weighted average cost of capital used is 8.5%. Based on our 2008 EPS estimate, NOC recently traded at a slight premium to its 10-year historical average two-year forward P/E ratio of 14X.

Qualitative Risk Assessment

LOW	MEDIUM	HIGH

Our risk assessment reflects our view of NOC's typically strong levels of cash flow and a solid balance sheet with a relatively low level of debt. This is offset by the highly cyclical nature of the company's business, particularly its dependence on government defense programs.

Quantitative Evaluations

S&P Quality Ranking   A-

D	C	B-	B	B+	A-	A	A+

Relative Strength Rank   STRONG

78

LOWEST = 1   HIGHEST = 99

Revenue/Earnings Data

Revenue (Million $)

	1Q	2Q	3Q	4Q	Year
2007	7,344	7,929	7,928	--	--
2006	7,093	7,601	7,433	8,021	30,148
2005	7,453	7,962	7,446	7,860	30,721
2004	7,105	7,374	7,408	7,846	29,853
2003	5,866	6,627	6,619	7,094	26,206
2002	3,931	4,231	4,214	4,830	17,206

Earnings Per Share ($)

2007	1.10	1.31	1.41	E1.29	E5.11
2006	1.03	1.26	0.87	1.29	4.44
2005	1.08	1.00	0.80	0.92	3.81
2004	0.63	0.79	0.80	0.81	2.99
2003	0.46	0.55	0.61	0.56	2.16
2002	0.64	0.77	0.58	0.87	2.86

Fiscal year ended Dec. 31. Next earnings report expected: Late January. EPS Estimates based on S&P Operating Earnings; historical GAAP earnings are as reported.

Dividend Data (Dates: mm/dd Payment Date: mm/dd/yy)

Amount ($)	Date Decl.	Ex-Div. Date	Stk. of Record	Payment Date
0.370	02/21	03/01	03/05	03/17/07
0.370	05/16	05/24	05/29	06/09/07
0.370	08/15	08/23	08/27	09/08/07
0.370	11/14	11/21	11/26	12/08/07

Dividends have been paid since 1951. Source: Company reports.

Northrop Grumman Corp

STANDARD
&POOR'S

Business Summary October 29, 2007

CORPORATE OVERVIEW. This $30 billion in revenues defense electronics and warship-making giant, which operated through seven reportable segments and four primary businesses in 2006, conducts most of its business with the U.S. government, principally the Department of Defense. NOC also transacts with foreign governments and makes commercial sales both domestically and overseas.

The Information & Services business consists of the Mission Systems (17% of 2006 revenue and 18% of operating profit), Information Technology (13% and 12%) and Technical Services (6% and 4%) segments. Mission Systems is a leading global integrator of complex, mission-enabling systems, in the areas of command, control and intelligence (C2I), missiles, and technical & management services. Information Technology provides IT services and solutions in four business areas: intelligence; defense; civilian agencies; and commercial, state & local. Technical Services provides infrastructure managment and maintenance, training and preparedness, and logistics and life-cycle management to a wide variety of government agencies and commercial and international customers.

The Aerospace business consists of the Integrated Systems (17% of revenue

and 19% of operating profit) and Space Technology (9% and 8%) segments. Integrated Systems designs, develops, produces and supports fully mission-ized integrated systems and subsystems in the areas of battlespace awareness, command and control systems, integrated combat systems, and airborne ground surveillance. Space Technology develops a broad range of systems at the leading edge of space, defense and electronics technology.

The Electronics business (21% of revenue and 25% of operating profit) develops, produces, integrates and supports high performance sensors, intelligence processing, and navigation systems operating in all environments from undersea to outer space and cyberspace. It also makes and supports power, power control and ship controls for commercial and naval ships. The segment is composed of five areas of business: Aerospace Systems; Defensive Systems; Government Systems; Naval & Marine Systems; and Navigation Systems.

Company Financials Fiscal Year Ended Dec. 31

Per Share Data ($)	2006	2005	2004	2003	2002	2001	2000	1999	1998	1997
Tangible Book Value	NM	NM	NM	NM	NM	NM	NM	NM	NM	NM
Cash Flow	6.34	5.94	5.01	4.05	5.29	6.31	7.08	6.23	4.25	6.16
Earnings	4.44	3.81	2.99	2.16	2.86	2.40	4.41	3.47	1.40	2.99
S&P Core Earnings	3.67	2.84	2.63	2.42	-0.95	-2.85	NA	NA	NA	NA
Dividends	1.16	1.01	0.89	0.80	0.80	0.80	0.80	0.80	0.80	0.80
Payout Ratio	26%	27%	30%	37%	28%	33%	18%	23%	57%	27%
Prices:High	71.37	60.26	58.15	50.55	67.50	55.28	46.94	37.97	69.50	63.94
Prices:Low	59.10	51.10	46.91	41.50	43.60	38.20	21.31	23.50	29.66	35.69
P/E Ratio:High	16	16	19	23	24	23	11	11	50	21
P/E Ratio:Low	13	13	16	19	15	16	5	7	21	12

Income Statement Analysis (Million $)										
Revenue	30,148	30,721	29,853	26,206	17,206	13,558	7,618	8,995	8,902	9,153
Operating Income	3,159	2,951	2,740	1,538	1,391	1,649	1,479	1,358	1,149	1,298
Depreciation	705	773	734	682	525	645	381	389	393	418
Interest Expense	347	388	431	497	422	373	175	224	233	257
Pretax Income	2,276	2,044	1,615	1,131	1,009	699	975	762	312	651
Effective Tax Rate	31.2%	32.3%	32.3%	28.6%	30.9%	38.9%	35.9%	36.6%	37.8%	37.5%
Net Income	1,567	1,383	1,093	808	697	427	625	483	194	407
S&P Core Earnings	1,288	1,026	961	892	-223	-487	NA	NA	NA	NA

Balance Sheet & Other Financial Data (Million $)										
Cash	1,015	1,605	1,230	342	1,412	464	319	142	44.0	63.0
Current Assets	6,719	7,549	6,907	5,745	15,835	4,589	2,526	2,793	3,033	2,936
Total Assets	32,009	34,214	33,361	33,009	42,266	20,886	9,622	9,285	9,536	9,677
Current Liabilities	6,753	7,974	6,223	6,361	11,373	5,132	2,688	2,464	2,367	2,715
Long Term Debt	3,992	3,881	5,116	5,410	9,398	5,033	1,605	2,000	2,562	2,500
Common Equity	16,615	16,825	16,970	15,785	14,322	7,391	3,919	3,257	2,850	2,623
Total Capital	20,957	21,651	22,942	22,067	24,209	13,443	5,800	5,321	5,412	5,198
Capital Expenditures	737	824	672	635	538	393	274	201	211	238
Cash Flow	2,272	2,156	1,827	1,490	1,222	1,072	1,006	872	587	825
Current Ratio	1.0	0.9	1.1	0.9	1.4	0.9	0.9	1.1	1.3	1.1
% Long Term Debt of Capitalization	19.0	17.9	22.3	24.5	38.8	37.4	27.7	37.6	47.3	48.1
% Net Income of Revenue	5.2	4.5	3.7	3.1	4.1	3.1	8.2	5.4	2.2	4.4
% Return on Assets	4.7	4.1	3.3	2.1	2.2	2.8	6.6	5.1	2.0	4.3
% Return on Equity	9.4	8.2	6.6	5.4	6.4	7.6	17.4	15.8	7.1	17.1

Data as orig reptd.; bef. results of disc opers/spec. items. Per share data adj. for stk. divs.; EPS diluted. E-Estimated. NA-Not Available. NM-Not Meaningful. NR-Not Ranked. UR-Under Review.

Office: 1840 Century Park E Ste, Los Angeles, CA 90067-2199.
Telephone: 310-553-6262.
Email: investor_relations@mail.northrgrum.com
Website: http://www.northropgrumman.com

Chrmn & CEO: R.D. Sugar
Pres & COO: W.G. Bush
VP & CFO: J.F. Palmer
VP, Chief Acctg Officer & Cntlr: K.N. Heintz

VP & Treas: J.L. Sanford
Investor Contact: G. Kent (310-553-6262)
Board Members: J. T. Chain, Jr., L. W. Coleman, V. Fazio, D. E. Felsinger, S. E. Frank, P. Frost, C. R. Larson, R. B. Myers, P. A. Odeen, A. L. Peters, K. W. Sharer, R. D. Sugar

Founded: 1939
Domicile: Delaware
Employees: 122,200

Novell Inc

STANDARD & POOR'S

S&P Recommendation HOLD ★★★☆☆

Price	**12-Mo. Target Price**	**Investment Style**
$6.70 (as of Nov 27, 2007)	$7.50	Large-Cap Blend

GICS Sector Information Technology
Sub-Industry Systems Software

Summary NOVL is a leading vendor of directory-enabled networking software, with its NetWare product line and Linux-based offerings.

Key Stock Statistics (Source S&P, Vickers, company reports)

52-Wk Range	$8.26–5.70	S&P Oper. EPS 2007E	0.04	Market Capitalization(B)	$2.344	Beta	2.26
Trailing 12-Month EPS	$-0.02	S&P Oper. EPS 2008E	0.11	Yield (%)	Nil	S&P 3-Yr. Proj. EPS CAGR(%)	NM
Trailing 12-Month P/E	NM	P/E on S&P Oper. EPS 2007E	NM	Dividend Rate/Share	Nil	S&P Credit Rating	NA
$10K Invested 5 Yrs Ago	$19,467	Common Shares Outstg. (M)	349.9	Institutional Ownership (%)	74		

Price Performance

- 30-Week Mov. Avg. ··· 10-Week Mov. Avg. – – GAAP Earnings vs. Previous Year Volume Above Avg. STARS
- 12-Mo. Target Price — Relative Strength — ▲ Up ▼ Down ▶ No Change Below Avg.

Options: ASE, CBOE, P, Ph

Analysis prepared by **Jim Yin** on November 27, 2007, when the stock traded at **$ 6.62**.

Highlights

➤ We project total revenue will increase 0.4% and 6.8% in FY 07 (Oct.) and FY 08, respectively. We see a 70% rise in open platform solutions revenue, which should be partially offset by declines in systems and resource management, workgroup, and business consulting. We believe NOVL will benefit from its partnership with Microsoft (MSFT: strong buy, $33). However, we expect the amount of invoicing will decline from the $73 million achieved in the first quarter of FY 07.

➤ We forecast gross margins in FY 07 to widen to 70% from 68% in FY 06 due to a favorable revenue mix. We expect total operating expenses to increase slightly as a result of a $23 million-$25 million temporary investment to transform its businesses and developing partnerships. We see the FY 07 non-GAAP operating margin narrowing to 2.1% from 3.9% in FY 06, but project it will widen to 6.7% in FY 08.

➤ We estimate operating EPS of $0.04 and $0.11 in FY 07 and FY 08, respectively. The expected increase in FY 08, reflects our view of higher revenues, a widening of the operating margin, and a lower effective tax rate.

Investment Rationale/Risk

➤ Our hold recommendation reflects our concern about NOVL's ability to transform itself into a solution provider in a mixed operating system environment from its NetWare business, which has been declining. We believe the company needs to continue developing solutions in areas such as system integration to counter increased competition from Red Hat (RHT: hold, $19) and Oracle (ORCL: strong buy, $20). However, we think the company has shown progress in recent quarters by stabilizing its NetWare product revenue. We also believe NOVL's net cash of $1.2 billion, about $3.44 per share, as of July 31, 2007, will lend some support to the share price.

➤ Risks to our opinion and target price include slower-than-expected growth in Linux products and lower-than-expected cost savings from cost-cutting initiatives.

➤ Our 12-month target price of $7.50 is based on an enterprise value/sales ratio of 1.6X, which is below the industry average of 2.7X. We believe this discount is appropriate due to our projection of NOVL's slower growth rate and lower profitability than its peers.

Qualitative Risk Assessment

LOW	MEDIUM	HIGH

Our risk assessment reflects the volatile market conditions in the Linux and open source software markets, the continuing decline in sales of NOVL's NetWare products, and our belief that NOVL is having difficulty gaining sufficient traction in Linux to offset the decrease in NetWare revenues.

Quantitative Evaluations

S&P Quality Ranking B-

D	C	B-	B	B+	A-	A	A+

Relative Strength Rank MODERATE

47

LOWEST = 1   HIGHEST = 99

Revenue/Earnings Data

Revenue (Million $)

	1Q	2Q	3Q	4Q	Year
2007	229.6	239.2	243.1	--	--
2006	274.4	278.3	241.4	244.9	967.3
2005	290.1	297.1	290.2	320.3	1,198
2004	267.1	293.6	304.6	300.7	1,166
2003	260.0	276.0	282.8	286.8	1,105
2002	277.9	273.9	282.3	300.3	1,134

Earnings Per Share ($)

2007	-0.06	Nil	-0.01	E0.01	E0.04
2006	Nil	0.01	0.03	0.06	0.02
2005	0.90	-0.04	Nil	-0.01	0.86
2004	0.03	-0.04	0.06	0.03	0.08
2003	-0.03	-0.08	-0.03	-0.29	-0.44
2002	0.03	-0.08	0.03	-0.25	-0.28

Fiscal year ended Oct. 31. Next earnings report expected: NA. EPS Estimates based on S&P Operating Earnings; historical GAAP earnings are as reported.

Dividend Data

No cash dividends have been paid.

Novell Inc

**STANDARD
&POOR'S**

Business Summary November 27, 2007

CORPORATE OVERVIEW. Novell, Inc. (NOVL) is a provider of security and identity management, resource management, desktop, workgroup, and data center solutions on several operating systems including Linux, NetWare, Windows, and Unix. Sales of NetWare, one of NOVL's key products, have been declining. According to IDC, the installed base of servers running NOVL's NetWare operating system peaked in 2001 at 1.35 million, and new shipments fell at a 17% compound annual growth rate (CAGR) from 1999 to 2005. IDC expects shipments to decline at a 9% CAGR through 2009, and sees spending on services declining at a 12% CAGR.

In the past few years, NOVL has embraced and promoted Linux and open source computing. The company is the second largest provider of Linux operating systems and subsystems, capturing 29% of the market by revenue in 2005 according to market research firm IDC, up from 21% in 2004. As a result of increased use of open source software in enterprise applications, NOVL has repositioned the company as a solution provider in a mixed operating system environment that includes open source and proprietary technologies, thus reducing reliance on its traditional product offerings, such as NetWare.

NOVL offers solutions in three categories: identity-driven solutions, offering

user authentication and provisioning and resource management capabilities; Linux and platform services solutions, which encompasses NOVL's two major operating systems, SUSE Linux and NetWare; and global services and support, including the Certified NOVL Engineer, Certified Linux Engineer, and Certified Linux Professional programs.

CORPORATE STRATEGY. NOVL relies on a series of alliances and partnerships to drive sales growth; its partners include IBM, HP, Dell, Intel, Oracle, SAP, AMD, CA, EMC and Adobe. NOVL believes it has created an ecosystem around it to combine its strengths with those of its partners; however, these partners are also counted among the strategic partners of many other software firms, and we doubt the partnerships provide a significant competitive advantage. In addition, NOVL's go-to market strategy embraces both a direct and indirect sales channel, with the indirect channel including independent distributors, value-added resellers, systems integrators, and hardware OEMs.

Company Financials Fiscal Year Ended Oct. 31

Per Share Data ($)	2006	2005	2004	2003	2002	2001	2000	1999	1998	1997
Tangible Book Value	1.86	2.42	1.39	1.89	2.31	2.98	3.80	4.57	4.42	4.46
Cash Flow	0.15	0.98	0.22	-0.27	-0.09	-0.53	0.39	0.75	0.50	0.04
Earnings	0.02	0.86	0.08	-0.44	-0.28	-0.79	0.15	0.55	0.29	-0.22
S&P Core Earnings	-0.02	-0.11	-0.07	-0.45	-0.47	-1.27	NA	NA	NA	NA
Dividends	Nil	Nil	Nil	Nil	Nil	Nil	Nil	Nil	Nil	Nil
Payout Ratio	Nil	Nil	Nil	Nil	Nil	Nil	Nil	Nil	Nil	Nil
Prices:High	9.83	9.27	14.24	10.77	5.64	9.13	44.56	41.19	19.00	13.00
Prices:Low	5.70	4.94	5.62	2.14	1.57	2.96	4.88	16.06	6.81	6.28
P/E Ratio:High	NM	11	NM	NM	NM	NM	NM	75	66	NM
P/E Ratio:Low	NM	6	NM	NM	NM	NM	33	29	23	NM

Income Statement Analysis (Million $)										
Revenue	967	1,198	1,166	1,105	1,134	1,040	1,162	1,273	1,084	1,007
Operating Income	27.8	99.3	140	52.3	103	46.1	98.2	293	175	-53.6
Depreciation	47.0	56.3	53.5	61.1	68.8	86.7	81.9	70.2	76.2	91.1
Interest Expense	8.02	9.63	Nil	Nil	Nil	Nil	Nil	Nil	Nil	Nil
Pretax Income	30.9	466	75.0	-55.0	-92.2	-277	70.7	244	142	-151
Effective Tax Rate	75.3%	19.2%	23.7%	NM	NM	NM	30.0%	21.8%	28.0%	NM
Net Income	7.63	377	57.2	-162	-103	-262	49.5	191	102	-78.3
S&P Core Earnings	-8.34	-52.6	-30.8	-167	-172	-384	NA	NA	NA	NA

Balance Sheet & Other Financial Data (Million $)										
Cash	676	811	434	752	636	705	698	895	1,007	1,033
Current Assets	1,761	2,009	1,535	1,031	920	1,027	1,007	1,336	1,436	1,470
Total Assets	2,450	2,762	2,292	1,568	1,665	1,904	1,712	1,942	1,924	1,911
Current Liabilities	686	753	693	626	592	611	455	440	415	322
Long Term Debt	600	600	600	Nil	Nil	Nil	Nil	Nil	Nil	Nil
Common Equity	1,105	1,386	963	934	1,066	1,271	1,245	1,492	1,493	1,565
Total Capital	1,718	2,004	1,599	941	1,074	1,293	1,257	1,503	1,509	1,589
Capital Expenditures	26.7	30.8	27.0	39.5	27.6	33.3	57.8	69.2	57.4	64.8
Cash Flow	54.6	433	84.6	-101	-34.3	-175	131	261	178	12.8
Current Ratio	2.6	2.7	2.2	1.6	1.6	1.7	2.2	3.0	3.5	4.6
% Long Term Debt of Capitalization	34.9	29.9	37.5	Nil	Nil	Nil	Nil	Nil	Nil	Nil
% Net Income of Revenue	0.8	31.5	4.9	NM	NM	NM	4.3	15.0	9.4	NM
% Return on Assets	0.3	14.9	3.0	NM	NM	NM	2.7	9.9	5.3	NM
% Return on Equity	0.6	32.1	3.3	NM	NM	NM	3.6	12.8	6.7	NM

Data as orig reptd.; bef. results of disc opers/spec. items. Per share data adj. for stk. divs.; EPS diluted. E-Estimated. NA-Not Available. NM-Not Meaningful. NR-Not Ranked. UR-Under Review.

Office: 404 Wyman St Ste 500, Waltham, MA 02451-1212.
Telephone: 781-464-8000.
Website: http://www.novell.com
Chrmn: T.G. Plaskett

Pres & CEO: R. Hovsepian
EVP & CTO: J. Jaffe
SVP, Secy & General Counsel: J.A. LaSala, Jr.
CFO: D.C. Russell

Investor Contact: E.M. Hennessy (781-464-8553)
Board Members: A. Aiello, F. Corrado, R. Crandall, R. W. Hovsepian, P. Jones, C. Malone, R. L. Nolan, T. G. Plaskett, J. W. Poduska, Sr., J. D. Robinson, III, K. B. White

Founded: 1983
Domicile: Delaware
Employees: 4,500

Novellus Systems Inc

STANDARD &POOR'S

S&P Recommendation **SELL** ★ ★ ★ ★ ★	Price $26.73 (as of Nov 23, 2007)	12-Mo. Target Price $25.00	Investment Style Large-Cap Growth

GICS Sector Information Technology
Sub-Industry Semiconductor Equipment

Summary This company manufactures, markets and services automated wafer fabrication systems for the deposition of thin films.

Key Stock Statistics (Source S&P, Vickers, company reports)

52-Wk Range	$35.00– 25.40	S&P Oper. EPS 2007**E**	1.64	Market Capitalization(B)	$3.378	Beta	2.77
Trailing 12-Month EPS	$1.62	S&P Oper. EPS 2008**E**	1.80	Yield (%)	Nil	S&P 3-Yr. Proj. EPS CAGR(%)	9.00
Trailing 12-Month P/E	16.5	P/E on S&P Oper. EPS 2007**E**	16.3	Dividend Rate/Share	Nil	S&P Credit Rating	NA
$10K Invested 5 Yrs Ago	$7,770	Common Shares Outstg. (M)	126.4	Institutional Ownership (%)	95		

Price Performance

30-Week Mov. Avg. · · · · 10-Week Mov. Avg. – – **GAAP Earnings vs. Previous Year**   **Volume** Above Avg. ||||| **STARS**
12-Mo. Target Price — Relative Strength — ▲ Up ▼ Down ▶ No Change   Below Avg. ||||| ★

Options: ASE, CBOE, P, Ph

Analysis prepared by **Clyde Montevirgen** on November 08, 2007, when the stock traded at **$ 26.25**.

Highlights

➤ We foresee flat industry sales in 2007 and 2008 as semiconductor companies digest capacity from the healthy capital investments of 2006 and early 2007. Although we see some positive growth indicators, such as rising utilization rates at foundries and more stable NAND flash memory prices, we believe that equipment sales will continue to be negatively affected by deteriorating DRAM prices and U.S. economic risks. We may also see customer orders pulled into late 2007 from 2008, but we think that capital expenditures will generally decrease next year, posing risk to our 2008 sales estimate.

➤ Following gross margins of around 50% in 2006, we see margins declining to the high-40% area in 2008. We anticipate slower sales, but we believe that NVLS has enough flexibility in its operations to adjust for order weakness. Although we see higher R&D expenses, we think that SG&A expenses will decrease with sales, helping to keep operating margins in the high teens over the next several quarters.

➤ We forecast EPS of $1.64 for 2007, rising to $1.80 in 2008.

Investment Rationale/Risk

➤ Although we view Novellus as a technology leader, we do not believe that the company's results will be immune to the demand weakness that the semiconductor equipment industry is currently experiencing. Due to uncertainty for DRAM pricing as inventory levels remain high, lower than expected capital expenditure projections by foundries for 2008, and economic risk, we forecast weakening order conditions over the next few quarters and believe that the industry upturn may occur later than originally expected. We view the shares as trading at a premium to peers on a relative basis, and think there is downside risk should earnings continue to weaken.

➤ Risks to our recommendation and target price include a shorter than expected semiconductor equipment downturn, a stronger than projected global economy, and an increase in interest in NVLS as a takeover target.

➤ We apply a target P/E multiple of approximately 14X, in line with peer average, to our 2008 EPS estimate to arrive at our 12-month target price of $25.

Qualitative Risk Assessment

LOW	MEDIUM	**HIGH**

Our risk assessment reflects the historical cyclicality of the semiconductor equipment industry, the lack of visibility in the medium term, the dynamic nature of semiconductor technology, and intense competition. We believe these risks are partially offset by our view of the company's strong market position, size, and financial condition.

Quantitative Evaluations

S&P Quality Ranking   B-

D	C	**B-**	B	B+	A-	A	A+

Relative Strength Rank   **MODERATE**

68

LOWEST = 1   HIGHEST = 99

Revenue/Earnings Data

Revenue (Million $)

	1Q	2Q	3Q	4Q	Year
2007	397.0	416.3	393.3	--	--
2006	365.9	410.1	444.0	438.5	1,659
2005	339.7	329.6	338.9	332.3	1,340
2004	262.9	338.2	415.9	340.3	1,357
2003	238.4	239.1	221.1	226.5	925.1
2002	169.7	222.2	230.5	217.6	840.0

Earnings Per Share ($)

2007	0.42	0.45	0.41	E0.35	E1.64
2006	0.18	0.42	0.57	0.34	1.49
2005	0.22	0.24	0.17	0.17	0.80
2004	0.11	0.25	0.45	0.27	1.06
2003	0.08	0.05	-0.23	0.07	-0.03
2002	0.03	0.08	0.03	0.02	0.15

Fiscal year ended Dec. 31. Next earnings report expected: Late January. EPS Estimates based on S&P Operating Earnings; historical GAAP earnings are as reported.

Dividend Data

No cash dividends have been paid.

Novellus Systems Inc

STANDARD &POOR'S

Business Summary November 08, 2007

CORPORATE OVERVIEW. Novellus is the second largest maker of deposition equipment used to deposit conductive and insulating layers on semiconductor wafers to form integrated circuits (ICs). The company entered the market for wafer surface preparation equipment in 2001. NVLS also entered the chemical mechanical planarization (CMP) equipment market in 2002. These two types of equipment are complementary to deposition equipment.

NVLS's product line of deposition equipment includes chemical vapor deposition (CVD), physical vapor deposition (PVD) and electroplating (ECD) equipment, all of which are used to form the layers of wiring and insulation, known as the interconnect, of ICs. High-density plasma CVD (HDP) and plasma-enhanced CVD (PECVD) systems employ a chemical plasma to deposit all of the insulating layers and some of the conductive layers on the surface of a wafer. PVD systems deposit conductive layers through a process known as sputtering. ECD systems deposit conductive layers of copper on wafers, through a process known as electrochemical deposition.

Although NVLS's original tool sets established it as a leader in CVD, the company has centered its product strategy around the emergence of the copper interconnect market. Copper has lower resistance and capacitance values

than aluminum, the conductive metal generally used in ICs, offering increased speed and decreased chip size. The company's SABRE tool offers a complete solution for the deposition of copper interconnects and holds the leading market share in copper.

Surface preparation products, including photoresist strip and clean, are becoming increasingly important with the industry's migration to copper interconnects. Surface preparation systems remove photoresist and other potential contaminants from a wafer before proceeding with the next deposition step. CMP systems polish the surface of a wafer after a deposition step to create a flat topography before moving on to subsequent manufacturing steps. Since copper is more difficult to polish and smooth than previous generation aluminum interconnects, and low-k dielectrics are much more porous than their predecessors, NVLS's product offerings in this category have become very important, in our view.

Company Financials Fiscal Year Ended Dec. 31

Per Share Data ($)	2006	2005	2004	2003	2002	2001	2000	1999	1998	1997
Tangible Book Value	12.54	11.29	11.06	12.42	12.69	13.04	11.49	6.47	3.63	2.98
Cash Flow	2.05	1.39	1.66	0.43	0.45	1.32	2.04	0.89	0.73	-0.78
Earnings	1.49	0.80	1.06	-0.03	0.15	0.97	1.75	0.64	0.50	-0.96
S&P Core Earnings	1.47	0.43	0.74	-0.42	-0.33	0.52	NA	NA	NA	NA
Dividends	Nil	Nil	Nil	Nil	Nil	Nil	Nil	Nil	Nil	Nil
Payout Ratio	Nil	Nil	Nil	Nil	Nil	Nil	Nil	Nil	Nil	Nil
Prices:High	35.00	30.77	44.52	45.50	54.48	58.70	70.25	42.79	19.77	22.13
Prices:Low	22.28	20.83	22.89	24.93	19.40	25.37	24.94	14.96	6.96	7.96
P/E Ratio:High	23	38	42	NM	NM	61	40	67	39	NM
P/E Ratio:Low	15	26	22	NM	NM	26	14	23	14	NM

Income Statement Analysis (Million $)										
Revenue	1,659	1,340	1,357	925	840	1,339	1,174	593	519	534
Operating Income	388	228	308	56.5	46.3	273	328	130	103	112
Depreciation	69.7	82.8	89.3	69.6	44.3	51.9	40.1	29.8	23.8	18.3
Interest Expense	4.29	3.51	2.13	0.91	1.02	1.15	2.34	1.70	4.87	2.74
Pretax Income	339	159	223	-15.3	22.9	209	342	114	80.0	-121
Effective Tax Rate	44.2%	30.6%	29.8%	NM	NM	31.0%	31.0%	33.0%	34.0%	NM
Net Income	189	110	157	-5.03	22.9	144	236	76.6	52.8	-95.7
S&P Core Earnings	186	59.8	108	-67.2	-50.7	81.6	NA	NA	NA	NA

Balance Sheet & Other Financial Data (Million $)										
Cash	58.5	649	106	497	616	551	571	182	81.2	59.3
Current Assets	1,505	1,364	1,369	1,572	1,634	2,517	1,827	733	399	351
Total Assets	2,362	2,290	2,402	2,339	2,494	3,010	2,015	910	552	493
Current Liabilities	361	344	324	221	382	1,138	505	140	111	127
Long Term Debt	128	125	161	Nil	Nil	Nil	Nil	Nil	65.0	65.0
Common Equity	1,835	1,779	1,862	2,072	2,056	1,872	1,511	770	375	301
Total Capital	1,963	1,904	2,023	2,072	2,075	1,872	1,511	770	440	366
Capital Expenditures	39.4	44.7	31.7	31.1	26.8	80.0	68.5	28.8	36.1	36.2
Cash Flow	259	193	246	64.5	67.2	196	276	106	76.7	-77.4
Current Ratio	4.2	4.0	4.2	7.1	4.3	2.2	3.6	5.2	3.6	2.8
% Long Term Debt of Capitalization	6.5	6.6	8.0	Nil	Nil	Nil	Nil	Nil	14.7	17.8
% Net Income of Revenue	11.4	8.2	11.5	NM	2.7	10.8	20.1	12.9	10.2	NM
% Return on Assets	8.1	4.7	6.6	NM	0.8	5.5	16.1	10.5	10.1	NM
% Return on Equity	10.5	6.0	8.0	NM	1.2	8.2	20.7	13.4	15.6	NM

Data as orig reptd.; bef. results of disc opers/spec. items. Per share data adj. for stk. divs.; EPS diluted. E-Estimated. NA-Not Available. NM-Not Meaningful. NR-Not Ranked. UR-Under Review.

Office: 4000 North First Street, San Jose, CA 95134-1568.
Telephone: 408-943-9700.
Email: info@novellus.com
Website: http://www.novellus.com

Chrmn & CEO: R.S. Hill
EVP & CFO: W.H. Kurtz
EVP & CTO: F. Chen
Investor Contact: R.S. Yim (408-943-9700)

VP & Treas: R.S. Yim
Board Members: N. R. Bonke, Y. A. El-Mansy, R. S. Hill, J. D. Litster, Y. Nishi, G. G. Possley, A. D. Rhoads, W. R. Spivey, D. A. Whitaker

Founded: 1984
Domicile: California
Employees: 3,725

The McGraw-Hill Companies

Nucor Corp

STANDARD &POOR'S

S&P Recommendation `HOLD` ★★★☆☆

Price	12-Mo. Target Price	Investment Style
$53.23 (as of Nov 23, 2007)	$66.00	Large-Cap Blend

GICS Sector Materials
Sub-Industry Steel

Summary Nucor Corp. is the largest minimill steelmaker in the U.S. and has one of the most diverse product lines of any steelmaker in the Americas.

Key Stock Statistics (Source S&P, Vickers, company reports)

52-Wk Range	$69.93–41.62	S&P Oper. EPS 2007**E**	4.84	Market Capitalization(B)	$16.060	Beta	2.25
Trailing 12-Month EPS	$5.02	S&P Oper. EPS 2008**E**	5.50	Yield (%)	0.83	S&P 3-Yr. Proj. EPS CAGR(%)	0.70
Trailing 12-Month P/E	10.6	P/E on S&P Oper. EPS 2007**E**	11.0	Dividend Rate/Share	$0.44	S&P Credit Rating	AA-
$10K Invested 5 Yrs Ago	$52,627	Common Shares Outstg. (M)	301.7	Institutional Ownership (%)	73		

Price Performance

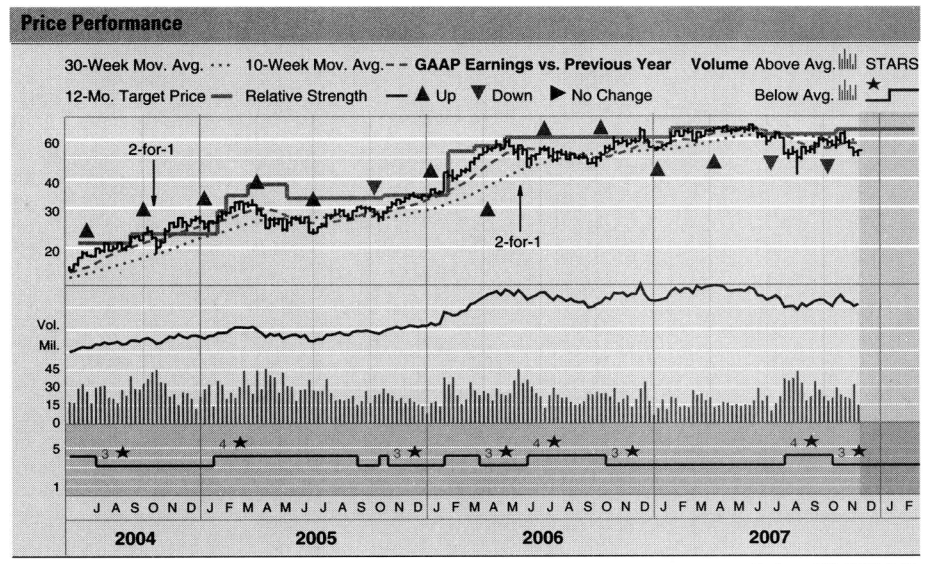

- 30-Week Mov. Avg. ···
- 10-Week Mov. Avg. --
- GAAP Earnings vs. Previous Year
- Volume Above Avg. |||| STARS
- 12-Mo. Target Price — Relative Strength — ▲ Up ▼ Down ► No Change
- Below Avg. |||| ★

Options: ASE, CBOE, P, Ph

Analysis prepared by **Leo J. Larkin** on October 22, 2007, when the stock traded at **$ 58.24.**

Highlights

➤ We look for a 10% sales increase in 2008, versus a projected rise of 7.5% in 2007. Part of the gain will reflect the inclusion of Harris Steel for a full year as well as other acquisitions. Also, we think that demand for beams and bars will remain strong in 2008 on continued gains in nonresidential construction. We also believe that sales will rise due to inventory rebuilding by distributors. We think that distributors will likely rebuild inventories in 2008 given that de-stocking has been ongoing since late 2006 and through nearly all of 2007. Finally, we anticipate that imports will be down again in 2008, helping boost sales as NUE and other domestic producers gain market share.

➤ Aided mostly by higher volume, we look for margin expansion and increased operating income in 2008. Following minimal interest expense and an unchanged tax rate, we project EPS of $5.50 in 2008, versus estimated EPS of $4.84 in 2007.

➤ Longer term, we see EPS being aided by industry consolidation, the introduction of new steel-making technology, a better product mix, acquisitions, and increased control of raw material costs.

Investment Rationale/Risk

➤ We view Nucor as a vehicle for capitalizing on the consolidation of the global steel industry. With the global steel industry becoming more consolidated via mergers, the increased concentration of production among fewer companies should result in greater pricing discipline. Also, we see free cash flow growth accelerating on a combination of rising net income and generally moderate capital spending for the next several years. We believe this will enable NUE to raise its dividend, make acquisitions and invest in new steelmaking technology. But, with the shares recently trading with just modest upside to our target price, our recommendation is hold.

➤ Risks to our opinion and target price include the possibility that distributor demand fails to recover in 2008 and that demand for construction related products declines.

➤ The P/E of 12X that we apply to our 2008 EPS estimate of $5.50 is toward the low end of the stock's historical range of the past 10 years, but at a slight premium to that of peers. On that basis, our 12-month target price is $66.

Qualitative Risk Assessment

LOW	MEDIUM	HIGH

Our risk assessment reflects that despite Nucor's exposure to cyclical markets such as non-residential construction, the company has a solid share of the markets in which it competes, has a very low ratio of total debt to assets, and generates what we view as substantial free cash flow.

Quantitative Evaluations

S&P Quality Ranking **B**

D	C	B-	B	B+	A-	A	A+

Relative Strength Rank **MODERATE**

49

LOWEST = 1   HIGHEST = 99

Revenue/Earnings Data

Revenue (Million $)

	1Q	2Q	3Q	4Q	Year
2007	3,769	4,168	4,259	--	--
2006	3,545	3,806	3,931	3,469	14,751
2005	3,323	3,145	3,026	3,207	12,701
2004	2,286	2,762	3,240	3,089	11,376
2003	1,480	1,520	1,604	1,661	6,266
2002	1,028	1,142	1,166	1,233	4,802

Earnings Per Share ($)

2007	1.26	1.14	1.29	E1.15	E4.84
2006	1.21	1.45	1.68	1.35	5.68
2005	1.10	1.02	0.93	1.09	4.13
2004	0.36	0.79	1.30	1.06	3.51
2003	0.06	0.03	0.05	0.07	0.20
2002	0.07	0.19	0.13	0.14	0.52

Fiscal year ended Dec. 31. Next earnings report expected: Late January. EPS Estimates based on S&P Operating Earnings; historical GAAP earnings are as reported.

Dividend Data (Dates: mm/dd Payment Date: mm/dd/yy)

Amount ($)	Date Decl.	Ex-Div. Date	Stk. of Record	Payment Date
.50 Ext.	06/05	06/27	06/29	08/10/07
0.110	06/05	06/27	06/29	08/10/07
.50 Ext.	09/06	09/26	09/28	11/09/07
0.110	09/06	09/26	09/28	11/09/07

Dividends have been paid since 1973. Source: Company reports.

The McGraw-Hill Companies

Nucor Corp

Business Summary October 22, 2007

CORPORATE OVERVIEW. Nucor is the largest U.S. minimill steelmaker. In 2006, production was 22.4 million tons and outside shipments were 20.6 million tons.

MARKET PROFILE. The primary factors affecting demand for steel products are economic growth in general and growth in demand for durable goods in particular. The two largest end markets for steel products in the U.S. are autos and construction. In 2006, these two markets accounted for 29.1% of shipments in the U.S. market. Other end markets include appliances, containers, machinery, and oil and gas. Distributors, also known as service centers, accounted for 21.8% of industry shipments in the U.S. market in 2006. Distributors are the largest single market for the steel industry in the U.S. Because distributors sell to a wide variety of OEMs, it is impossible to trace the final

destination of much of the industry's shipments. Consequently, demand for steel from the auto, construction and other industries may be higher than the shipment data would suggest. Construction accounts for some 60% of the demand for Nucor's products, oil and gas 15%, autos and appliances 15%, and other markets 10%. In terms of production, the size of the U.S. market was 105.1 million tons in 2006, and Nucor's market share was 21.3%. In the U.S. market, consumption increased at a compound annual growth rate (CAGR) of 1.4% from 1997 through 2006. Global steel production was 1.22 billion metric tons in 2006. Consumption grew at a CAGR of 5.2% from 1997 through 2006.

Company Financials Fiscal Year Ended Dec. 31

Per Share Data ($)	2006	2005	2004	2003	2002	2001	2000	1999	1998	1997
Tangible Book Value	15.56	13.80	10.84	7.45	7.43	7.07	6.87	6.49	5.93	5.33
Cash Flow	7.05	5.43	4.72	1.36	1.50	1.29	1.74	1.44	1.47	1.46
Earnings	5.68	4.13	3.51	0.20	0.52	0.36	0.95	0.70	0.75	0.84
S&P Core Earnings	5.68	4.09	3.49	0.15	0.46	0.33	NA	NA	NA	NA
Dividends	0.40	0.30	0.24	0.20	0.19	0.17	0.15	0.13	0.12	0.10
Payout Ratio	7%	7%	7%	100%	37%	47%	16%	18%	15%	12%
Prices:High	67.55	35.11	27.74	14.70	17.54	14.13	14.11	15.45	15.16	15.73
Prices:Low	33.63	22.78	13.04	8.76	9.00	8.36	7.38	10.41	8.81	11.19
P/E Ratio:High	12	9	8	73	34	39	15	22	20	19
P/E Ratio:Low	6	6	4	44	17	23	8	15	12	13

Income Statement Analysis (Million $)										
Revenue	14,751	12,701	11,377	6,266	4,802	4,139	4,586	4,009	4,151	4,184
Operating Income	3,240	2,497	2,216	468	601	469	737	631	665	678
Depreciation	364	375	383	364	307	289	259	257	253	218
Interest Expense	Nil	4.20	22.4	24.6	22.9	22.0	24.1	20.5	10.0	9.28
Pretax Income	2,913	2,127	1,812	90.8	310	174	478	379	415	460
Effective Tax Rate	32.1%	33.2%	33.6%	4.51%	22.0%	35.0%	35.0%	35.5%	36.5%	36.0%
Net Income	1,758	1,310	1,121	62.8	162	113	311	245	264	294
S&P Core Earnings	1,758	1,296	1,114	47.9	143	101	NA	NA	NA	NA

Balance Sheet & Other Financial Data (Million $)										
Cash	786	1,838	779	350	219	462	491	572	309	283
Current Assets	4,675	4,072	3,175	1,621	1,424	1,374	1,381	1,539	1,129	1,126
Total Assets	7,885	7,139	6,133	4,492	4,381	3,759	3,722	3,730	3,227	2,984
Current Liabilities	1,450	1,256	1,066	630	592	484	558	531	487	524
Long Term Debt	922	922	924	904	879	460	460	390	215	168
Common Equity	4,826	4,280	3,456	2,342	2,323	2,201	2,131	2,262	2,073	1,876
Total Capital	5,987	5,396	4,553	3,423	3,419	2,946	2,904	2,934	2,570	2,321
Capital Expenditures	338	331	286	215	244	261	415	375	503	307
Cash Flow	2,122	1,685	1,505	427	469	402	570	501	517	512
Current Ratio	3.2	3.2	3.0	2.6	2.4	2.8	2.5	2.9	2.3	2.1
% Long Term Debt of Capitalization	15.4	17.1	20.3	26.4	25.7	15.6	15.9	13.3	8.4	7.2
% Net Income of Revenue	11.9	10.3	9.9	1.0	3.4	2.7	6.8	6.1	6.4	7.0
% Return on Assets	23.4	19.7	21.1	1.4	4.0	3.0	8.3	7.0	8.5	10.5
% Return on Equity	38.6	33.9	38.7	2.7	5.1	5.2	14.2	11.3	13.4	16.9

Data as orig reptd.; bef. results of disc opers/spec. items. Per share data adj. for stk. divs.; EPS diluted. E-Estimated. NA-Not Available. NM-Not Meaningful. NR-Not Ranked. UR-Under Review.

Office: 1915 Rexford Rd, Charlotte, NC 28211-3441.
Telephone: 704-366-7000.
Email: info@nucor.com
Website: http://www.nucor.com

Chrmn, Pres & CEO: D.R. DiMicco
EVP, CFO & Treas: T.S. Lisenby
Cntlr: J. Frias

Board Members: P. C. Browning, C. C. Daley, Jr., D. R. DiMicco, H. B. Gantt, V. F. Haynes, J. D. Hlavacek, B. L. Kasriel, R. J. Milchovich

Founded: 1940
Domicile: Delaware
Employees: 11,900

STANDARD &POOR'S

NVIDIA Corp

S&P Recommendation	HOLD ★★★★★	Price	12-Mo. Target Price	Investment Style
		$30.22 (as of Nov 23, 2007)	$37.00	Large-Cap Growth

GICS Sector Information Technology
Sub-Industry Semiconductors

Summary This company develops and markets 3D graphics processors and related software for personal computers, workstations and digital entertainment platforms.

Key Stock Statistics (Source S&P, Vickers, company reports)

52-Wk Range	$39.67–18.69	S&P Oper. EPS 2008E	1.30	Market Capitalization(B)	$16.789	Beta	3.88
Trailing 12-Month EPS	$1.16	S&P Oper. EPS 2009E	1.47	Yield (%)	Nil	S&P 3-Yr. Proj. EPS CAGR(%)	18.00
Trailing 12-Month P/E	26.1	P/E on S&P Oper. EPS 2008E	23.2	Dividend Rate/Share	Nil	S&P Credit Rating	BB-
$10K Invested 5 Yrs Ago	$57,672	Common Shares Outstg. (M)	555.6	Institutional Ownership (%)	83		

Price Performance

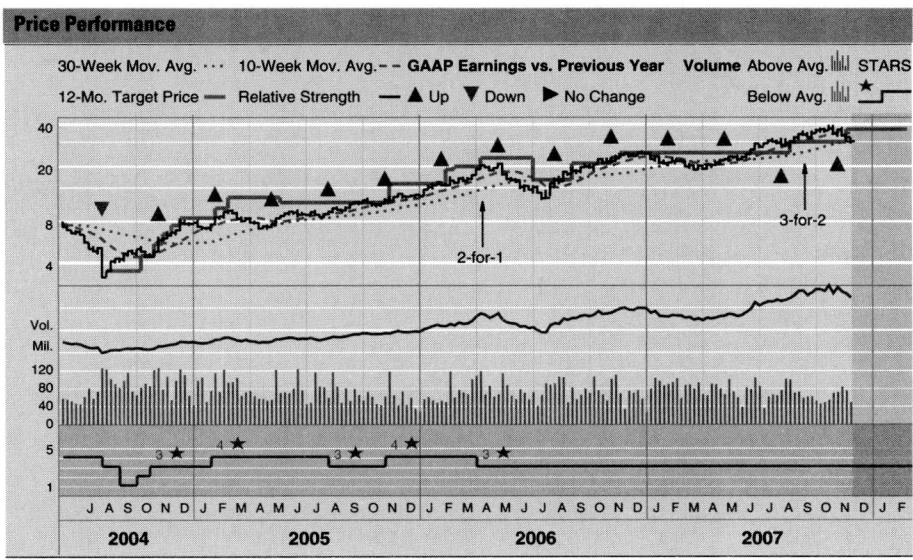

30-Week Mov. Avg. · · · 10-Week Mov. Avg. – – GAAP Earnings vs. Previous Year   Volume Above Avg. STARS
12-Mo. Target Price — Relative Strength — ▲ Up ▼ Down ▶ No Change   Below Avg.

Options: ASE, CBOE, P, Ph

Analysis prepared by **Clyde Montevirgen** on November 12, 2007, when the stock traded at **$ 33.36**.

Highlights

➤ We expect 33% and 15% sales growth for FY 08 and FY 09, respectively. Results have been stronger than expected due to accelerating growth for computers and graphics intensive applications, and although we see a strong demand environment ahead, the company will likely face increasing competition from AMD and Intel. Longer-term, we see sales supported by market share gains for notebook GPUs, growth for MCPs, royalties from PlayStation 3 sales, and traction for handheld device application processors.

➤ We believe gross margins will expand to around 46% in FY 08 and FY 09, as gross margins should be helped by a more favorable sales mix and reduced chip costs. However the sales mix may be more volatile, depending on higher-margin royalties from PlayStation 3 sales and lower-margin sales from its recently acquired Portal Player business. Although we see the acquisition adding operating costs, we are projecting operating margins in the high-teens range for over the next few quarters.

➤ We estimate FY 08 operating EPS of $1.30, and see $1.47 for FY 09.

Investment Rationale/Risk

➤ The company has been benefiting from strong computer growth, increasing graphics intensity in applications, and various miscues by competitors. We see NVDA gaining market share, as growth for graphics chips should continue to outpace that of the broader semiconductor industry, but we are somewhat concerned about potential pricing pressure as the company's competitors release competing graphics chips. We also think NVDA will likely face capacity constraints as foundries' utilization rates increase, potentially limiting sales growth ahead. Lastly, we think our longer-term growth view is largely reflected in current share prices.

➤ Risks to our opinion and target price include the possibility that relatively lower economic growth might slow PC sales more than we expect, and that Intel might develop its own graphics chips.

➤ Our 12-month target price of $37 is based mainly on our P/E analysis. We apply a target P/E ratio of about 25X to our FY 09 EPS estimate, above the peer average, given our view of strong growth and less variable results relative to peers.

Qualitative Risk Assessment

LOW	MEDIUM	HIGH

Our risk assessment reflects the cyclicality of the semiconductor industry and of demand trends for electronics goods that benefit from advanced visual displays, and revenue volatility resulting from wins and losses of deals with big accounts.

Quantitative Evaluations

S&P Quality Ranking   **B**

D	C	B-	B	B+	A-	A	A+

Relative Strength Rank   **MODERATE**

32

LOWEST = 1   HIGHEST = 99

Revenue/Earnings Data

Revenue (Million $)

	1Q	2Q	3Q	4Q	Year
2008	844.3	935.3	1,116	--	--
2007	681.8	687.5	820.6	878.9	3,069
2006	583.9	574.8	583.4	633.6	2,376
2005	471.9	456.1	515.6	566.5	2,010
2004	405.0	459.8	486.1	472.1	1,823
2003	582.9	427.3	430.3	469.0	1,909

Earnings Per Share ($)

2008	0.22	0.29	0.38	E0.41	E1.30
2007	0.15	0.15	0.18	0.27	0.77
2006	0.12	0.14	0.12	0.18	0.55
2005	0.04	0.01	0.05	0.09	0.19
2004	0.04	0.05	0.01	0.05	0.15
2003	0.16	0.01	-0.11	0.10	0.18

Fiscal year ended Jan. 31. Next earnings report expected: Early January. EPS Estimates based on S&P Operating Earnings; historical GAAP earnings are as reported.

Dividend Data (Dates: mm/dd Payment Date: mm/dd/yy)

Amount ($)	Date Decl.	Ex-Div. Date	Stk. of Record	Payment Date
3-for-2	08/08	09/11	08/20	09/10/07

Source: Company reports.

The **McGraw·Hill** Companies

NVIDIA Corp

Business Summary November 12, 2007

CORPORATE OVERVIEW. NVIDIA Corp. designs, develops and markets high-performance graphics processing units (GPUs), media and communications processors (MCPs), handheld GPUs, and related software for PCs and digital entertainment platforms, ranging from professional workstations to video game consoles to handheld electronic devices. It aims to be the leading supplier of performance GPUs, MCPs and handheld GPUs.

Interactive 3D graphics displays are an integral part of many computing applications for workstations, consumer and commercial desktop and laptop PCs, personal digital assistants, cellular phones, and gaming consoles. NVDA's products are designed into products offered by nearly all leading PC OEMs. Also, in March 2000, the company agreed to develop and supply graphics chips for Microsoft's Xbox video game console. The XGPU and MCP products form a two-processor chipset that powers the Xbox system's graphics, audio and networking capabilities. In August 2003, rival ATI Technologies won the contract for the GPU for the next-generation Xbox. The company presently supplies GPU products for Sony's PlayStation 3 video game console.

CORPORATE STRATEGY. Nvidia's goal is to become the leading supplier of performance GPUs, MCPs, and handheld GPUs and application processors. The elements behind the strategy include: building award winning and architecturally compatible graphics and media products for various platforms, targeting leading OEMs, ODMs, and system builders, sustaining technology and product leadership in graphics and media products, increasing market share, creating synergy by combining expertise in graphics and media, and using its intellectual property and resources to enter into license and development contracts.

Company Financials Fiscal Year Ended Jan. 31

Per Share Data ($)	2007	2006	2005	2004	2003	2002	2001	2000	1999	1998
Tangible Book Value	3.32	2.52	2.08	1.83	1.81	1.52	0.93	0.34	0.19	NM
Cash Flow	0.95	0.73	0.38	0.30	0.29	0.43	0.24	0.14	0.02	-0.02
Earnings	0.77	0.55	0.19	0.14	0.18	0.34	0.21	0.09	0.01	-0.02
S&P Core Earnings	0.79	0.42	0.03	-0.00	-0.22	0.10	0.12	NA	NA	NA
Dividends	Nil	Nil	Nil	Nil	Nil	Nil	Nil	Nil	Nil	NA
Payout Ratio	Nil	Nil	Nil	Nil	Nil	Nil	Nil	Nil	Nil	NA
Calendar Year	2006	2005	2004	2003	2002	2001	2000	1999	1998	1997
Prices:High	25.97	12.83	9.12	9.25	24.22	23.42	14.67	3.96	NA	NA
Prices:Low	11.45	6.82	3.10	3.11	2.40	4.71	2.92	1.00	NA	NA
P/E Ratio:High	34	23	48	65	NM	68	71	42	NA	NA
P/E Ratio:Low	15	12	16	22	NM	14	14	11	NA	NA

Income Statement Analysis (Million $)

	2007	2006	2005	2004	2003	2002	2001	2000	1999	1998
Revenue	3,069	2,376	2,010	1,823	1,909	1,369	735	375	158	29.1
Operating Income	593	452	216	172	202	299	146	63.4	8.52	-2.10
Depreciation	108	98.0	103	82.0	58.2	43.5	15.7	9.00	4.01	1.36
Interest Expense	0.02	0.07	0.16	12.0	Nil	16.2	4.85	Nil	Nil	Nil
Pretax Income	494	360	125	86.7	151	253	147	56.2	4.49	-3.60
Effective Tax Rate	9.37%	16.0%	20.0%	14.1%	39.7%	30.0%	31.9%	32.1%	7.96%	Nil
Net Income	448	301	100	74.4	90.8	177	100	38.1	4.13	-3.60
S&P Core Earnings	460	230	14.6	-1.44	-104	49.4	54.7	NA	NA	NA

Balance Sheet & Other Financial Data (Million $)

	2007	2006	2005	2004	2003	2002	2001	2000	1999	1998
Cash	1,118	950	670	604	1,028	791	674	61.6	50.3	6.60
Current Assets	2,032	1,549	1,305	1,053	1,352	1,234	930	173	101	19.3
Total Assets	2,675	1,915	1,629	1,399	1,617	1,503	1,017	203	113	25.0
Current Liabilities	639	439	421	334	379	433	110	76.2	47.1	3.20
Long Term Debt	Nil	Nil	Nil	0.86	305	306	300	1.46	2.00	1.90
Common Equity	2,007	1,458	1,178	1,051	933	764	406	125	64.2	6.90
Total Capital	2,007	1,466	1,199	1,061	1,238	1,070	706	126	66.2	8.80
Capital Expenditures	145	79.6	67.3	128	63.1	97.0	36.3	11.6	7.90	2.70
Cash Flow	556	401	203	156	149	220	114	50.0	8.14	-2.24
Current Ratio	3.2	3.5	3.1	3.2	3.6	2.8	8.4	2.3	2.1	6.0
% Long Term Debt of Capitalization	NA	Nil	Nil	0.1	24.6	28.6	42.4	1.2	3.0	21.5
% Net Income of Revenue	14.6	12.7	5.0	4.1	4.8	12.9	13.4	10.9	2.6	NM
% Return on Assets	19.4	17.1	6.6	4.9	5.8	14.0	16.1	25.9	5.8	NM
% Return on Equity	25.6	23.0	9.0	7.5	10.7	30.2	36.9	42.9	11.3	NM

Data as orig reptd.; bef. results of disc opers/spec. items. Per share data adj. for stk. divs.; EPS diluted. E-Estimated. NA-Not Available. NM-Not Meaningful. NR-Not Ranked. UR-Under Review.

Office: 2701 San Tomas Expressway, Santa Clara, CA 95050.
Telephone: 408-486-2000.
Email: ir@nvidia.com
Website: http://www.nvidia.com

Pres & CEO: J. Huang
SVP, Secy & General Counsel: D.M. Shannon
Investor Contact: M. Hara (408-486-2511)
VP & CIO: G.H. Stelling

CFO: M.D. Burkett
Board Members: S. Chu, T. Coxe, J. C. Gaither, J. Huang, H. C. Jones, W. J. Miller, M. L. Perry, A. B. Seawell

Founded: 1993
Domicile: Delaware
Employees: 4,083

NYSE Euronext

STANDARD &POOR'S

S&P Recommendation BUY ★★★★☆	**Price** $82.72 (as of Nov 23, 2007)	**12-Mo. Target Price** $105.00	**Investment Style** Large-Cap Growth

GICS Sector Financials
Sub-Industry Specialized Finance

Summary NYX is a holding company created by the merger of NYSE Group and Euronext. NYX operates six cash equities exchanges in five countries and six derivatives exchanges in six countries.

Key Stock Statistics (Source S&P, Vickers, company reports)

52-Wk Range	$109.50–64.26	S&P Oper. EPS 2007**E**	2.72	Market Capitalization(B)	$21.838	Beta	NA
Trailing 12-Month EPS	$2.41	S&P Oper. EPS 2008**E**	3.48	Yield (%)	1.21	S&P 3-Yr. Proj. EPS CAGR(%)	25.00
Trailing 12-Month P/E	34.3	P/E on S&P Oper. EPS 2007**E**	30.4	Dividend Rate/Share	$1.00	S&P Credit Rating	NA
$10K Invested 5 Yrs Ago	NA	Common Shares Outstg. (M)	264.0	Institutional Ownership (%)	52		

Price Performance

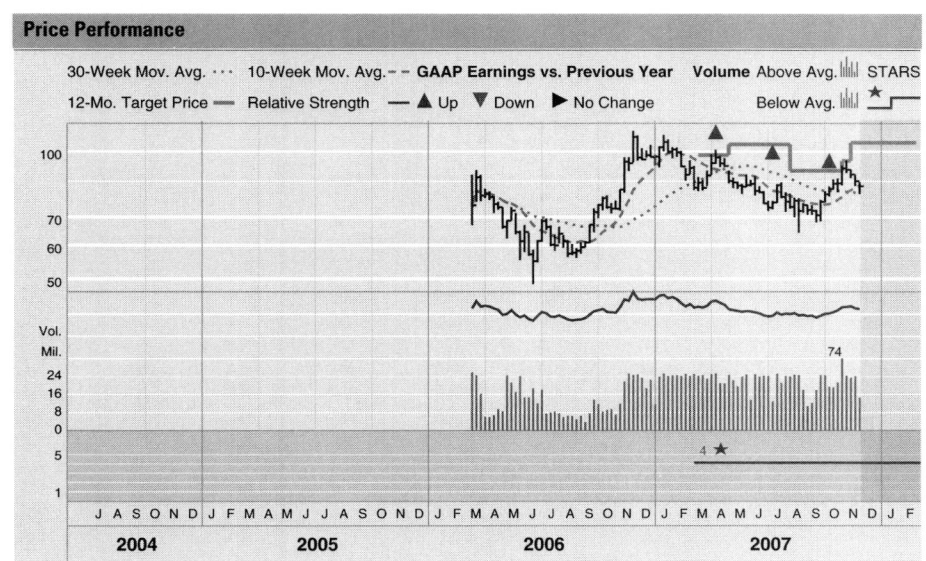

Analysis prepared by **Jason Willey** on November 02, 2007, when the stock traded at **$ 89.60**.

Highlights

➤ We view NYX and its New York Stock Exchange, NYSE Arca, and Euronext operations as the leading exchange group in the world. With the completion of its acquisition of Euronext in early April, we see NYX taking the lead in the rapidly consolidating global financial exchange landscape. While we view 2007 as a transitional year for NYX as it integrates Euronext, we still expect the company to deliver revenue and earnings expansion, and we see accelerated profit growth in 2008.

➤ In the third quarter, NYX saw record trading volumes across its U.S. and European equities and derivatives businesses, which all benefited from increased market volatility. We believe NYX's broad product and geographic exposure position it well for earnings growth, and we expect more significant expense synergies in 2008. We see a number of future growth drivers, including U.S. derivatives, bonds, and further geographic expansion.

➤ We forecast EPS of $2.72 in 2007, rising to $3.48 in 2008. Our estimates include results from Euronext, which we believe will be accretive to earnings in both years.

Investment Rationale/Risk

➤ We believe NYX is in the midst of a significant transformational phase, highlighted by its acquisition of European derivatives and equity exchange Euronext, and the implementation of Regulation National Market System in the U.S and MiFD in Europe. While we see risk from acquisition integration and regulatory changes, we believe NYX is taking the right steps to position itself for what we see as an increasingly global competitive environment. We see the Euronext acquisition broadening NYX's geographic footprint, providing strong multi-asset exposure, and delivering product diversification.

➤ Risks to our recommendation and target price include an uncertain regulatory environment, Euronext integration problems, migration to a hybrid trading model, and an industrywide slowdown in equity and option trading volumes.

➤ Our 12-month target price of $105 is based on a P/E multiple of 30X our 2008 EPS estimate, a small discount to the current peer average. We believe this discount is warranted by NYX's exposure to slower growing equity markets and the potential for the company to undertake a dilutive acquisition.

Qualitative Risk Assessment

LOW	MEDIUM	HIGH

Our risk assessment reflects the potential volatility in results due to changes in equity and equity options trading volumes, the impact of current and future regulatory changes, and the integration of a number of recent acquisitions.

Quantitative Evaluations

S&P Quality Ranking NR

D	C	B-	B	B+	A-	A	A+

Relative Strength Rank STRONG

77

LOWEST = 1   HIGHEST = 99

Revenue/Earnings Data

Revenue (Million $)

	1Q	2Q	3Q	4Q	Year
2007	702.0	1,078	1,198	--	--
2006	478.9	659.5	602.9	658.5	2,376
2005	--	--	--	--	1,667
2004	--	--	--	--	--
2003	--	--	--	--	--
2002	--	--	--	--	--

Earnings Per Share ($)

	1Q	2Q	3Q	4Q	Year
2007	0.43	0.62	0.97	E0.70	E2.72
2006	0.24	0.39	0.43	0.29	1.36
2005	--	--	--	--	0.58
2004	--	--	--	--	--
2003	--	--	--	--	--
2002	--	--	--	--	--

Fiscal year ended Dec. 31. Next earnings report expected: Early February. EPS Estimates based on S&P Operating Earnings; historical GAAP earnings are as reported.

Dividend Data (Dates: mm/dd Payment Date: mm/dd/yy)

Amount ($)	Date Decl.	Ex-Div. Date	Stk. of Record	Payment Date
0.250	06/06	06/26	06/28	07/13/07
0.250	09/10	09/12	09/14	09/28/07

Dividends have been paid since 2007. Source: Company reports.

Please read the Required Disclosures and Analyst Certification on the last page of this report.

The **McGraw-Hill** Companies

NYSE Euronext

STANDARD &POOR'S

Business Summary November 02, 2007

CORPORATE OVERVIEW. NYSE Euronext (NYX) is a holding company created by the combination of NYSE Group and Euronext on April 4, 2007. NYX operates the world's largest and most liquid exchange group and offers a diverse array of financial products and services. The company, which brings together six cash equities exchanges in five countries and six derivatives exchanges in six countries, offers listings, trading in cash equities, equity and interest rate derivatives, bonds and the distribution of market data. As of September 30, 2007, NYX combined listed companies represented over $30 trillion in total market capitalization and average daily trading value of approximately $139 billion.

NYX generates revenue primarily from transactions, company listing fees, market data, regulatory fees, and exchange licenses. The company also records activity assessment revenue, which is a pass through netted against section 31 fee expense. We have excluded this revenue line item when examining NYX's revenue from operations. Following the combination of the NYSE with Archipelago (now NYSE Arca), transaction fees have become the largest revenue driver for NYX (46% of total revenue for the three months ended December 31, 2006). Transaction revenue is generated from fees paid for trading

on NYX's exchanges, and benefits from higher trading volumes. Listing fees are NYX's second largest revenue contributor (19%) and include initial fees charged for companies listing on one of NYX's exchanges and an ongoing annual listing fee. We view transactional revenue as the key growth driver for NYX moving forward.

CORPORATE STRATEGY. We believe NYX is in the middle of a transformational phase as it fully integrates the NYSE Arca assets with the NYSE, transitions the NYSE from a floor-based trading system to a hybrid floor/electronic model, completes its merger with Euronext, and readies for significant regulatory and structural changes in U.S. and European equity and equity options trading. We expect the number and scope of ongoing projects and regulatory changes to likely make for uneven financial performance and difficult historical and peer comparisons in 2007.

Company Financials Fiscal Year Ended Dec. 31

Per Share Data ($)	2006	2005	2004	2003	2002	2001	2000	1999	1998	1997
Tangible Book Value	3.51	NA	NA	NA	NA	NA	NA	NA	NA	NA
Cash Flow	2.27	1.50	NA	NA	NA	NA	NA	NA	NA	NA
Earnings	1.36	0.58	NA	NA	NA	NA	NA	NA	NA	NA
S&P Core Earnings	1.28	0.35	0.31	NA	NA	NA	NA	NA	NA	NA
Dividends	Nil	NA	NA	NA	NA	NA	NA	NA	NA	NA
Payout Ratio	Nil	NA	NA	NA	NA	NA	NA	NA	NA	NA
Prices:High	112.00	NA	NA	NA	NA	NA	NA	NA	NA	NA
Prices:Low	48.62	NA	NA	NA	NA	NA	NA	NA	NA	NA
P/E Ratio:High	82	NA	NA	NA	NA	NA	NA	NA	NA	NA
P/E Ratio:Low	36	NA	NA	NA	NA	NA	NA	NA	NA	NA

Income Statement Analysis (Million $)										
Revenue	2,376	1,667	NA	NA	NA	NA	NA	NA	NA	NA
Operating Income	424	3.18	NA	NA	NA	NA	NA	NA	NA	NA
Depreciation	136	143	NA	NA	NA	NA	NA	NA	NA	NA
Interest Expense	Nil	Nil	NA	NA	NA	NA	NA	NA	NA	NA
Pretax Income	328	176	NA	NA	NA	NA	NA	NA	NA	NA
Effective Tax Rate	36.7%	47.6%	NA	NA	NA	NA	NA	NA	NA	NA
Net Income	205	90.0	NA	NA	NA	NA	NA	NA	NA	NA
S&P Core Earnings	193	54.1	42.3	NA	NA	NA	NA	NA	NA	NA

Balance Sheet & Other Financial Data (Million $)										
Cash	298	328	NA	NA	NA	NA	NA	NA	NA	NA
Current Assets	1,443	1,204	NA	NA	NA	NA	NA	NA	NA	NA
Total Assets	3,466	3,154	NA	NA	NA	NA	NA	NA	NA	NA
Current Liabilities	832	823	NA	NA	NA	NA	NA	NA	NA	NA
Long Term Debt	Nil	Nil	NA	NA	NA	NA	NA	NA	NA	NA
Common Equity	1,669	1,366	NA	NA	NA	NA	NA	NA	NA	NA
Total Capital	1,934	1,646	NA	NA	NA	NA	NA	NA	NA	NA
Capital Expenditures	97.8	NA	NA	NA	NA	NA	NA	NA	NA	NA
Cash Flow	341	233	NA	NA	NA	NA	NA	NA	NA	NA
Current Ratio	1.7	1.5	NA	NA	NA	NA	NA	NA	NA	NA
% Long Term Debt of Capitalization	Nil	Nil	NA	NA	NA	NA	NA	NA	NA	NA
% Net Income of Revenue	8.6	5.4	NA	NA	NA	NA	NA	NA	NA	NA
% Return on Assets	7.2	NA	NA	NA	NA	NA	NA	NA	NA	NA
% Return on Equity	16.6	NA	NA	NA	NA	NA	NA	NA	NA	NA

Data as orig reptd.; bef. results of disc opers/spec. items. Per share data adj. for stk. divs.; EPS diluted. E-Estimated. NA-Not Available. NM-Not Meaningful. NR-Not Ranked. UR-Under Review.

Office: 11 Wall Street, New York, NY 10005.
Telephone: 212-656-3000.
Website: http://www.nyse.com
Chrmn: J. Hessels

CEO: J.A. Thain
CFO: N. Chai
Investor Contact: R. Adamonis (212-656-2140)

Board Members: E. L. Brown, M. N. Carter, S. Cox, A. Dirckx, W. E. Ford, S. Hefes, J. Hessels, D. Hoenn, P. Houel, S. A. Jackson, J. S. McDonald, D. M. McFarland, J. J. McNulty, J. Peterbroeck, A. M. Rivlin, R. Salgado, R. B. Shapiro, J. A. Thain, J. Theodore, S. Williamson, R. van Tets, K. M. von der Heyden

Founded: 2006
Domicile: Delaware
Employees: 2,578

Occidental Petroleum Corp

STANDARD &POOR'S

S&P Recommendation **HOLD** ★★★☆☆	Price $72.10 (as of Nov 23, 2007)	12-Mo. Target Price $70.00	Investment Style Large-Cap Blend

GICS Sector Energy
Sub-Industry Integrated Oil & Gas

Summary This domestic integrated oil company has global operations in exploration & production and chemicals.

Key Stock Statistics (Source S&P, Vickers, company reports)

52-Wk Range	$74.33– 42.06	S&P Oper. EPS 2007**E**	5.51	Market Capitalization(B)	$59.897	Beta	0.46
Trailing 12-Month EPS	$5.77	S&P Oper. EPS 2008**E**	5.66	Yield (%)	1.39	S&P 3-Yr. Proj. EPS CAGR(%)	9.02
Trailing 12-Month P/E	12.5	P/E on S&P Oper. EPS 2007**E**	13.1	Dividend Rate/Share	$1.00	S&P Credit Rating	A-
$10K Invested 5 Yrs Ago	$56,894	Common Shares Outstg. (M)	830.7	Institutional Ownership (%)	81		

Price Performance

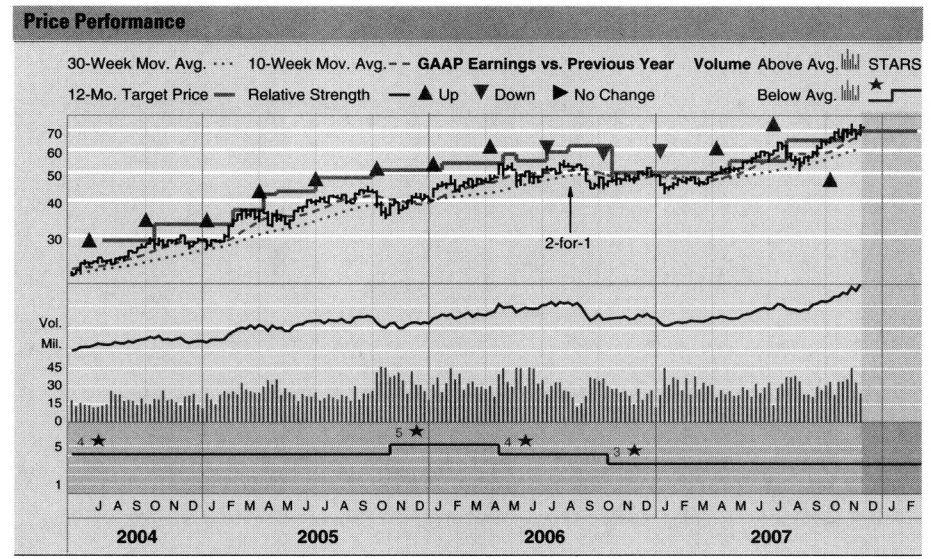

30-Week Mov. Avg. · · ·   10-Week Mov. Avg. – –   **GAAP Earnings vs. Previous Year**   **Volume** Above Avg. STARS
12-Mo. Target Price —   Relative Strength —   ▲ Up   ▼ Down   ▶ No Change   Below Avg.   ★

2-for-1

2004   2005   2006   2007

Options: ASE, CBOE, P, Ph

Analysis prepared by **Tina J. Vital** on November 06, 2007, when the stock traded at **$ 73.15.**

Highlights

➤ Third quarter oil and gas production rose 6.9%, to 570,000 boe/d, reflecting additions from the Dolphin Project in Qatar's North Field and other Middle East projects. However, third quarter levels were below our expectations due to the delayed closing of the acquisition of assets in Qatar from Anadarko, and the impact of product prices on OXY's production-sharing contracts.

➤ In October, OXY closed on the acquisition of blocks 12 and 13 in Qatar from Anadarko, which should add 5,000 boe/d to OXY's net production. Also, the company was recently awarded two offshore exploration areas in Bahrain, which are adjacent to major producing fields in Qatar. OXY said the two remaining trains of its Dolphin Project should come on line by year-end 2007, and reach full capacity in early 2008. Based on guidance from OXY, we expect fourth quarter production and year-end 2007 exit rates to approach 615,000 boe/d. As a result, we see a 3% decline in volume in 2007, before an advance of about 9% in 2008.

➤ We expect after-tax operating earnings to increase by almost 6% in 2007, and over 2% in 2008.

Investment Rationale/Risk

➤ We expect OXY's oil and gas production growth to be driven by new opportunities in the Middle East/North Africa region. In October, OXY said it expects to announce two new agreements in this region by 2007 year end. We estimate that OXY's three-year (2004-06) average finding and development costs were $12.26 per boe, in line with peers, with a strong, albeit below peers, three-year organic reserve replacement rate of 185%.

➤ Risks to our recommendation and target price include changes to economic, industrial and operating conditions, such as geopolitical risk and difficulty in organically replacing oil and gas reserves.

➤ A blend of our discounted cash flow (WACC of 7.7%, terminal growth of 3%) and relative valuations leads us to our 12-month target price of $70, which represents an expected enterprise value of 6.6X our 2008 EBITDA estimate, a premium to peers.

Qualitative Risk Assessment

LOW	MEDIUM	HIGH

Our risk assessment reflects our view of OXY's strong business profile and intermediate financial risk. The company has a large, geographically diverse reserve base, predictable production, and substantial liquidity, in our opinion. However, we believe its strengths are limited by participation in volatile, competitive and capital-intensive businesses, and a penchant for debt-financed acquisitions.

Quantitative Evaluations

S&P Quality Ranking   B+

D	C	B-	B	B+	A-	A	A+

Relative Strength Rank   STRONG
         95

LOWEST = 1   HIGHEST = 99

Revenue/Earnings Data

Revenue (Million $)

	1Q	2Q	3Q	4Q	Year
2007	4,108	4,411	4,841	--	--
2006	4,396	4,599	4,522	4,144	17,661
2005	3,303	3,518	4,057	4,330	15,208
2004	2,557	2,724	3,005	3,082	11,368
2003	2,371	2,266	2,319	2,370	9,326
2002	1,523	1,867	1,963	1,985	7,338

Earnings Per Share ($)

2007	1.43	1.68	1.57	E1.31	E5.51
2006	1.34	1.39	1.35	1.08	5.15
2005	1.04	1.89	2.12	1.40	6.45
2004	0.62	0.73	0.94	0.96	3.25
2003	0.52	0.49	0.57	0.49	2.06
2002	0.17	0.32	0.63	0.42	1.54

Fiscal year ended Dec. 31. Next earnings report expected: Early March. EPS Estimates based on S&P Operating Earnings; historical GAAP earnings are as reported.

Dividend Data (Dates: mm/dd Payment Date: mm/dd/yy)

Amount ($)	Date Decl.	Ex-Div. Date	Stk. of Record	Payment Date
0.220	02/15	03/07	03/09	04/15/07
0.220	05/03	06/06	06/08	07/15/07
0.250	07/19	09/06	09/10	10/15/07
0.250	10/11	12/06	12/10	01/15/08

Dividends have been paid since 1975. Source: Company reports.

Please read the Required Disclosures and Analyst Certification on the last page of this report.

The McGraw-Hill Companies

Occidental Petroleum Corp

**STANDARD
&POOR'S**

Business Summary November 06, 2007

CORPORATE OVERVIEW. Conducting business through subsidiaries, Occidental Petroleum Corp. (OXY) is a U.S. based integrated oil company with global operations in oil and gas exploration and production (72% of 2006 segment revenues; 89% of 2006 pretax operating profits) and chemicals (28%; 11%).

The oil and gas segment explores for, develops, produces, and markets crude oil and natural gas. OXY operates primarily in the U.S. as well as Qatar, Yemen, Colombia, Ecuador, and other international regions. OXY replaced 245% of worldwide oil and gas production from all sources in 2006. For the three-year period (2004-2006), OXY's consolidated proved reserve additions totaled 1.141 billion boe, and total production equaled 575 million BOE, for a three-year average organic reserve replacement rate of 185%. Using data from John S. Herold, we estimate OXY's finding and development costs at

$21.39 per boe in 2006, versus a three-year (2004-06) average of $12.26 per boe.

The OxyChem subsidiary manufactures basic chemicals (principally chlorine and caustic soda), vinyls, petrochemicals, and specialty products. OxyChem has enhanced its position in core markets by entering into alliances that offer cost savings. OXY manages this subsidiary to be self-funding during its down cycle, and a contributor of free cash to the parent company during the up cycle.

Company Financials Fiscal Year Ended Dec. 31

Per Share Data ($)	2006	2005	2004	2003	2002	2001	2000	1999	1998	1997
Tangible Book Value	22.84	18.69	13.30	10.25	8.35	7.53	6.45	4.79	4.49	4.23
Cash Flow	7.71	8.26	4.93	3.56	2.87	2.88	3.35	1.92	1.63	1.39
Earnings	5.15	6.45	3.25	2.06	1.54	1.59	2.13	0.79	0.44	0.20
S&P Core Earnings	4.97	5.78	3.26	2.03	1.28	1.70	NA	NA	NA	NA
Dividends	NA	0.65	0.41	0.52	0.50	0.50	0.50	0.50	0.50	0.50
Payout Ratio	NA	10%	13%	25%	33%	32%	23%	63%	114%	NM
Prices:High	NA	44.90	30.38	21.49	15.38	15.55	12.78	12.28	15.22	15.38
Prices:Low	NA	27.09	20.98	13.59	11.49	10.94	7.88	7.31	8.31	10.88
P/E Ratio:High	NA	7	9	10	10	10	6	16	35	79
P/E Ratio:Low	NA	4	6	7	7	7	4	9	19	56

Income Statement Analysis (Million $)										
Revenue	17,661	15,208	11,368	9,326	7,338	13,985	13,574	7,610	6,596	8,016
Operating Income	9,664	7,860	5,573	4,281	3,119	3,638	3,826	1,831	1,297	1,835
Depreciation, Depletion and Amortization	2,042	1,485	1,303	1,177	1,012	971	901	805	835	822
Interest Expense	291	293	260	332	295	392	518	498	559	434
Pretax Income	8,012	7,365	4,389	2,884	1,662	1,892	3,196	1,257	688	528
Effective Tax Rate	43.3%	27.4%	38.9%	42.5%	25.4%	29.8%	45.1%	50.2%	52.8%	58.9%
Net Income	4,435	5,272	2,606	1,595	1,163	1,186	1,569	568	325	217
S&P Core Earnings	4,280	4,729	2,607	1,568	963	1,273	NA	NA	NA	NA

Balance Sheet & Other Financial Data (Million $)										
Cash	1,339	2,189	1,449	683	146	199	97.0	214	96.0	113
Current Assets	6,006	6,574	4,431	2,474	1,873	1,483	2,067	1,688	2,795	1,916
Total Assets	32,355	26,108	21,391	18,168	16,548	17,850	19,414	14,125	15,252	15,282
Current Liabilities	4,724	4,280	3,423	2,526	2,235	1,890	2,740	1,967	2,931	1,870
Long Term Debt	2,619	2,873	3,345	3,993	4,452	4,528	5,658	4,854	5,367	4,925
Common Equity	19,184	15,032	10,550	7,929	6,318	5,634	4,774	3,523	3,120	2,304
Total Capital	24,470	19,207	15,470	13,235	12,085	13,489	13,977	9,372	9,555	10,239
Capital Expenditures	3,005	2,423	1,843	1,601	1,236	1,401	952	601	1,074	1,549
Cash Flow	6,477	6,757	3,909	2,772	2,175	2,157	2,470	1,366	1,143	951
Current Ratio	1.3	1.5	1.3	1.0	0.8	0.8	0.8	0.9	1.0	1.0
% Long Term Debt of Capitalization	10.7	15.0	21.6	30.2	36.8	33.6	40.5	51.8	56.2	48.1
% Return on Assets	15.2	22.2	13.2	9.2	6.8	6.4	9.4	3.9	2.1	1.3
% Return on Equity	25.9	41.2	28.2	22.4	19.5	22.8	37.8	16.9	12.6	6.2

Data as orig reptd.; bef. results of disc opers/spec. items. Per share data adj. for stk. divs.; EPS diluted. E-Estimated. NA-Not Available. NM-Not Meaningful. NR-Not Ranked. UR-Under Review.

Office: 10889 Wilshire Boulevard, Los Angeles, CA 90024-4201.
Telephone: 310-208-8800.
Email: investorrelations_newyork@oxy.com
Website: http://www.oxy.com

Chrmn, Pres & CEO: R.R. Irani
Sr EVP & CFO: S.I. Chazen
EVP, Secy & General Counsel: D.P. de Brier
VP & Treas: J.R. Havert

Investor Contact: C.G. Stavros (212-603-8184)
Board Members: S. Abraham, R. W. Burkle, J. S. Chalsty, E. P. Djerejian, R. C. Dreier, J. E. Feick, R. R. Irani, I. W. Maloney, R. Segovia, A. D. Syriani, R. Tomich, W. L. Weisman

Founded: 1920
Domicile: Delaware
Employees: 8,886

Officemax Inc

STANDARD &POOR'S

S&P Recommendation	HOLD ★★★☆☆	Price $23.97 (as of Nov 23, 2007)	12-Mo. Target Price $38.00	Investment Style Large-Cap Value

GICS Sector Consumer Discretionary
Sub-Industry Specialty Stores

Summary This retail and business-to-business office products distributor operates more than 900 superstores.

Key Stock Statistics (Source S&P, Vickers, company reports)

52-Wk Range	$55.40– 22.91	S&P Oper. EPS 2007**E**	2.30	Market Capitalization(B)	$1.806	Beta	1.06
Trailing 12-Month EPS	$2.51	S&P Oper. EPS 2008**E**	2.56	Yield (%)	2.50	S&P 3-Yr. Proj. EPS CAGR(%)	12.00
Trailing 12-Month P/E	9.6	P/E on S&P Oper. EPS 2007**E**	10.4	Dividend Rate/Share	$0.60	S&P Credit Rating	BB
$10K Invested 5 Yrs Ago	$10,049	Common Shares Outstg. (M)	75.3	Institutional Ownership (%)	100		

Price Performance

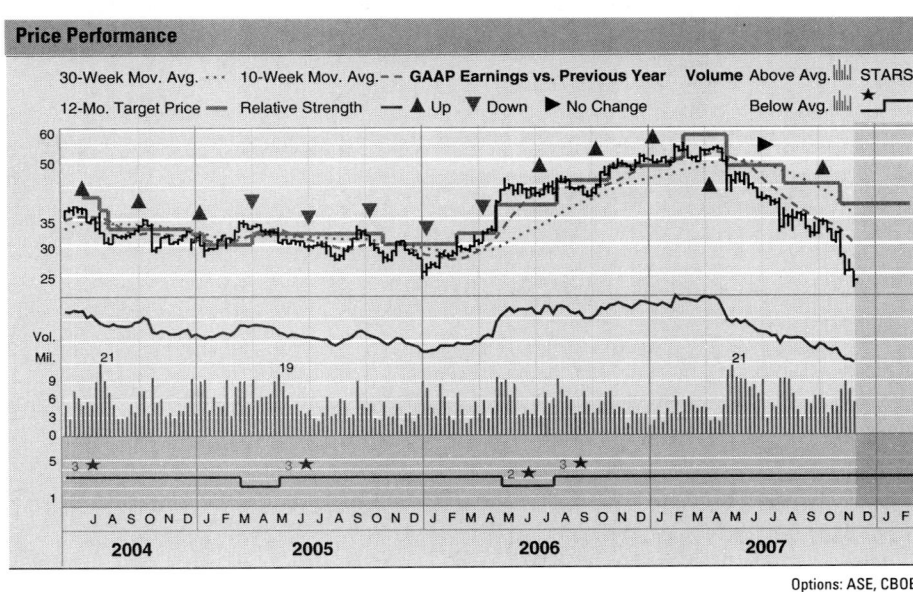

30-Week Mov. Avg. · · · 10-Week Mov. Avg. - - GAAP Earnings vs. Previous Year Volume Above Avg. STARS
12-Mo. Target Price — Relative Strength — ▲ Up ▼ Down ▶ No Change Below Avg.

Options: ASE, CBOE

Analysis prepared by **Michael Souers** on November 08, 2007, when the stock traded at **$ 25.95**.

Highlights

➤ We expect revenues to increase 3%-4% in 2008, following a projected 3% advance in 2007. We look for this growth to be driven by the opening of approximately 60 net new stores and low single-digit same-store sales growth. We expect sales growth in the contract segment to outpace that of retail due to macro factors negatively impacting consumers and small businesses.

➤ We see operating margins widening about 10 basis points, as recent initiatives to cut costs and improve operational efficiency should continue to bear fruit. We believe OMX's concerted efforts to increase private label brand sales and push to drive sales of higher-margin middle-market businesses should help boost profitability, but expect those efforts to be largely offset by increased occupancy costs.

➤ We project that flat interest expense and an effective tax rate of 38.0% will drive 2008 operating EPS to $2.56, an increase of 11% from the $2.30 we expect the company to earn in 2007, excluding extraordinary items.

Investment Rationale/Risk

➤ We think OMX's renewed focus on profitable growth, most notably on the contract side, will hasten its turnaround. However, we question whether OMX can compete effectively against larger peers Staples (SPLS: buy, $22) and Office Depot (ODP: hold, $18) over the longer term. In addition, since we think the office supply retailing industry is nearing saturation, we believe OMX will eventually have to re-focus on driving same-store sales growth in order to further improve margins -- as meager growth in sales does not bode well for future profitability, in our view.

➤ Risks to our recommendation and target price include a slowdown in consumer and business spending, sharply higher energy costs and increased paper costs, and a return to a more promotional environment in the office supply retailing industry.

➤ At about 10X our 2008 EPS estimate, the shares recently traded at a discount to both peers and the S&P 500. Our 12-month target price of $38 is based on our DCF model, which assumes a weighted average cost of capital of 10.0% and a terminal growth rate of 3%.

Qualitative Risk Assessment

LOW	MEDIUM	HIGH

Our risk assessment reflects the rather cyclical nature of the office supply retailing industry, which is highly dependent on continued consumer and business spending, and what we view as a slightly weaker competitive position compared to peers in terms of buyer power with vendors, offset by what we see as a rational pricing environment that should help boost margins.

Quantitative Evaluations

S&P Quality Ranking B

D	C	B-	B	B+	A-	A	A+

Relative Strength Rank WEAK

12

LOWEST = 1   HIGHEST = 99

Revenue/Earnings Data

Revenue (Million $)

	1Q	2Q	3Q	4Q	Year
2007	2,436	2,132	2,315	--	--
2006	2,424	2,041	2,244	2,257	8,966
2005	2,323	2,092	2,288	2,455	9,158
2004	3,530	3,401	3,651	2,688	13,270
2003	1,853	1,928	2,111	2,352	8,245
2002	1,788	1,888	1,935	1,801	7,412

Earnings Per Share ($)

2007	0.76	0.35	0.64	E0.55	E2.30
2006	-0.21	0.35	0.41	0.71	1.29
2005	-0.03	-0.23	-0.02	-0.33	-0.58
2004	0.67	0.58	0.69	0.51	2.44
2003	-0.38	-0.12	0.48	0.05	0.07
2002	-0.17	Nil	0.09	0.05	-0.03

Fiscal year ended Dec. 31. Next earnings report expected: Late February. EPS Estimates based on S&P Operating Earnings; historical GAAP earnings are as reported.

Dividend Data (Dates: mm/dd Payment Date: mm/dd/yy)

Amount ($)	Date Decl.	Ex-Div. Date	Stk. of Record	Payment Date
0.150	12/07	12/27	01/01	01/15/07
0.150	02/15	03/28	04/01	04/15/07
0.150	04/26	06/27	07/01	07/15/07
0.150	07/26	09/27	10/01	10/15/07

Dividends have been paid since 1935. Source: Company reports.

Officemax Inc

STANDARD &POOR'S

Business Summary November 08, 2007

CORPORATE OVERVIEW. OfficeMax (formerly Boise Cascade Corp.) is a leader in both business-to-business and retail office products distribution. It provides office supplies and paper, print and document services, technology products and solutions, and furniture to large, medium and small businesses, government offices, and consumers.

OfficeMax, Contract (53% of sales in 2006) distributes office supplies and paper, technology products and solutions, and office furniture. The segment sells directly to large corporate and government offices, as well as to small- and medium-sized offices in the U.S., Canada, Australia, New Zealand, and Mexico.

OfficeMax, Retail (47%) has operations in the U.S., Puerto Rico and the U.S. Virgin Islands. It also operates office products superstores in Mexico through

a 51% owned joint venture. As of January 27, 2007, OMX's retail segment operated 914 stores, three large distribution centers, and two small distribution centers in Mexico. Each superstore offers approximately 10,000 stock keeping units (SKUs) of name brand and OfficeMax private branded merchandise and a variety of business services targeted at serving the small business customer, including OfficeMax ImPress.

In October 2004, the company sold its paper, forest products, and timberland assets for about $3.7 billion to affiliates of Boise Cascade, LLC. Prior to the sale, the company reported business results using five reportable segments.

Company Financials Fiscal Year Ended Dec. 31

Per Share Data ($)	2006	2005	2004	2003	2002	2001	2000	1999	1998	1997
Tangible Book Value	6.86	4.41	13.20	9.55	14.72	18.07	21.81	18.10	14.93	17.47
Cash Flow	3.02	1.49	6.30	5.20	5.24	4.13	7.49	7.68	4.31	3.65
Earnings	1.29	-0.58	2.44	0.07	-0.03	-0.96	2.73	3.06	-0.85	-1.19
S&P Core Earnings	1.36	-0.31	2.45	0.39	-1.15	-1.84	NA	NA	NA	NA
Dividends	0.60	0.60	0.60	0.60	0.60	0.60	0.60	0.60	0.60	0.60
Payout Ratio	47%	NM	25%	NM	NM	NM	22%	20%	NM	NM
Prices:High	51.80	34.84	38.01	32.89	38.81	38.00	43.94	47.19	40.38	45.56
Prices:Low	24.72	24.20	28.58	20.72	19.61	26.99	21.75	28.75	22.25	27.75
P/E Ratio:High	40	NM	16	NM	NM	NM	16	15	NM	NM
P/E Ratio:Low	19	NM	12	NM	NM	NM	8	9	NM	NM

Income Statement Analysis (Million $)										
Revenue	8,966	9,158	13,270	8,245	7,412	7,422	7,807	6,953	6,162	5,494
Operating Income	294	155	656	483	459	515	656	704	495	365
Depreciation	128	151	355	308	307	296	298	289	283	256
Interest Expense	123	129	152	133	118	128	151	145	160	137
Pretax Income	172	-37.6	379	19.3	1.01	-47.6	298	356	-15.0	-28.0
Effective Tax Rate	40.0%	NM	37.5%	11.5%	NM	NM	39.0%	40.0%	NM	NM
Net Income	99.1	-41.2	234	17.1	11.3	-42.5	179	200	-25.7	-30.0
S&P Core Earnings	100	-24.4	223	22.6	-67.3	-106	NA	NA	NA	NA

Balance Sheet & Other Financial Data (Million $)										
Cash	282	72.2	1,243	125	65.2	56.7	62.8	66.9	74.4	64.0
Current Assets	2,097	1,942	3,259	2,501	1,296	1,245	1,577	1,531	1,368	1,354
Total Assets	6,216	6,272	7,543	7,376	4,947	4,934	5,267	5,138	4,967	4,970
Current Liabilities	1,529	1,588	1,857	1,977	1,054	1,266	1,014	1,125	1,130	894
Long Term Debt	1,854	1,877	2,055	2,191	1,611	1,144	1,823	1,717	1,734	1,903
Common Equity	1,931	1,681	2,549	2,157	1,258	1,458	1,654	1,523	1,187	1,251
Total Capital	3,870	3,640	4,689	4,598	3,176	3,203	3,973	3,774	3,535	3,852
Capital Expenditures	175	152	298	228	219	305	297	221	229	280
Cash Flow	223	106	577	312	305	238	460	472	241	190
Current Ratio	1.4	1.2	1.8	1.3	1.2	1.0	1.6	1.4	1.2	1.5
% Long Term Debt of Capitalization	47.9	51.6	43.8	47.7	50.7	35.7	45.9	45.5	49.1	49.4
% Net Income of Revenue	1.1	NM	1.8	0.2	0.2	NM	2.3	2.9	NM	NM
% Return on Assets	1.6	NM	3.1	0.3	0.2	NM	3.4	4.0	NM	NM
% Return on Equity	5.3	NM	9.5	0.2	0.8	NM	10.2	12.7	NM	NM

Data as orig reptd.; bef. results of disc opers/spec. items. Per share data adj. for stk. divs.; EPS diluted. E-Estimated. NA-Not Available. NM-Not Meaningful. NR-Not Ranked. UR-Under Review.

Office: 263 Shuman Blvd, Naperville, IL 60563-1255.
Telephone: 630-438-7800.
Website: http://www.officemax.com
Chrmn, Pres & CEO: S.K. Duncan

EVP & CFO: D. Civgin
EVP & General Counsel: M. Broad
EVP & CIO: R. Burdick
Investor Contact: J.S. Jennings (630-864-6800)

Board Members: D. J. Bern, W. F. Bryant, B. C. Cornell, J. M. DePinto, S. K. Duncan, R. Gangwal, G. G. Michael, D. M. Szymanski, F. R. de Luzuriaga

Founded: 1931
Domicile: Delaware
Employees: 36,000

The **McGraw·Hill** Companies

Office Depot Inc

STANDARD
&POOR'S

S&P Recommendation	HOLD ★★★☆☆	Price	12-Mo. Target Price	Investment Style
		$17.50 (as of Nov 23, 2007)	$22.00	Large-Cap Growth

GICS Sector Consumer Discretionary
Sub-Industry Specialty Stores

Summary Office Depot is a leading operator of office products superstores and mail order catalogs.

Key Stock Statistics (Source S&P, Vickers, company reports)

52-Wk Range	$41.06– 16.51	S&P Oper. EPS 2007**E**	1.72	Market Capitalization(B)	$4.773	Beta	1.91
Trailing 12-Month EPS	$1.85	S&P Oper. EPS 2008**E**	1.95	Yield (%)	Nil	S&P 3-Yr. Proj. EPS CAGR(%)	12.00
Trailing 12-Month P/E	9.5	P/E on S&P Oper. EPS 2007**E**	10.2	Dividend Rate/Share	Nil	S&P Credit Rating	BBB-
$10K Invested 5 Yrs Ago	$10,511	Common Shares Outstg. (M)	272.8	Institutional Ownership (%)	87		

Price Performance

30-Week Mov. Avg. · · · 10-Week Mov. Avg.- - GAAP Earnings vs. Previous Year Volume Above Avg. STARS
12-Mo. Target Price — Relative Strength — ▲ Up ▼ Down ▶ No Change Below Avg.

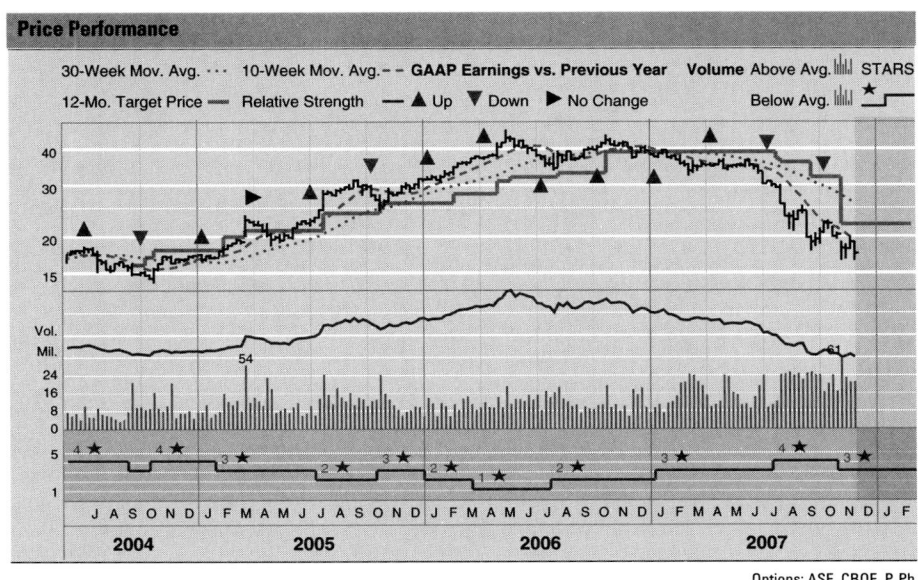

Options: ASE, CBOE, P, Ph

Analysis prepared by **Michael Souers** on November 06, 2007, when the stock traded at **$17.76**.

Highlights

➤ ODP announced that it is delaying the release of third quarter earnings due to a review of the timing and recognition of certain vendor program funds, and we anticipate restatements of past earnings as a result. We expect sales to rise 5%-6% in 2008, following our projections of a 4%-5% advance in 2007. We look for this growth to be achieved by expansion of ODP's retail and delivery operations in the Northeast, modest gains in the U.S. contract business, and continued international penetration. We see ODP opening 125 net new stores in 2008, and forecast a slight increase in same-store sales following a challenging 2007.

➤ We expect ODP's operating margins to widen modestly in 2008, led by aggressive cost-cutting efforts, inventory optimization, improved sourcing, and a continued push toward selling higher margin private label brands.

➤ We project an effective tax rate of 30% and approximately 3% fewer shares as a result of ODP's aggressive share repurchase plan. Our 2008 operating EPS estimate of $2.10 is a 12% increase from the $1.88 we project the company will earn in 2007, excluding extraordinary items.

Investment Rationale/Risk

➤ Following the announcement of potential accounting irregularities and restatements, we have downgraded the shares to hold, from buy. Due to the uncertainty created by this news, along with the macro challenges currently facing the retail side of ODP's business, we do not anticipate any near-term catalysts for the stock. In our view, ODP has realized significant operational improvement due to widespread cost-cutting efforts and a rational industry pricing environment, but we remain concerned that sales growth and expense leverage will be difficult to achieve over the longer-term due to our belief that the retail market for office supply stores may be approaching saturation levels.

➤ Risks to our recommendation and target price include a lower than expected increase in capital spending by businesses, an inability to post solid same-store sales gains in ODP's North America Retail division, and unfavorable currency fluctuations.

➤ Our 12-month target price of $22 is based on our DCF analysis, which assumes a weighted average cost of capital of 12.0% and a terminal growth rate of 4%.

Qualitative Risk Assessment

LOW	MEDIUM	HIGH

Our risk assessment for Office Depot reflects the cyclical nature of the office supply retailing industry, which is highly dependent on consumer and business spending, and a fairly large exposure to international markets, offset by what we view as a strong balance sheet.

Quantitative Evaluations

S&P Quality Ranking   B

D	C	B-	B	B+	A-	A	A+

Relative Strength Rank   WEAK

21

LOWEST = 1   HIGHEST = 99

Revenue/Earnings Data

Revenue (Million $)

	1Q	2Q	3Q	4Q	Year
2007	4,094	3,632	3,935	--	--
2006	3,816	3,495	3,857	3,843	15,011
2005	3,703	3,364	3,493	3,719	14,279
2004	3,605	3,162	3,328	3,469	13,565
2003	3,056	2,816	3,236	3,251	12,359
2002	3,022	2,622	2,871	2,842	11,357

Earnings Per Share ($)

2007	0.56	0.40	0.43	E0.41	E1.72
2006	0.43	0.41	0.47	0.48	1.79
2005	0.37	0.31	-0.15	0.34	0.87
2004	0.37	0.25	0.28	0.17	1.06
2003	0.33	0.19	0.29	0.15	0.96
2002	0.32	0.18	0.27	0.21	0.98

Fiscal year ended Dec. 31. Next earnings report expected: Mid February. EPS Estimates based on S&P Operating Earnings; historical GAAP earnings are as reported.

Dividend Data

No cash dividends have been paid.

Office Depot Inc

Business Summary November 06, 2007

CORPORATE OVERVIEW. Office Depot is a global supplier of office products and services. It generated net sales of $15.0 billion in 2006 to customers and businesses of all sizes through three business segments: the North America Retail division (45% of revenues), the North America Business Solutions division (31%), and the International group (24%). Sales by product group were as follows: supplies 61%; technology 26%; and furniture and other 13%.

At December 31, 2006, ODP's North America Retail division operated 1,158 office supply stores in 49 states, the District of Columbia and Canada. North America Retail sells a broad assortment of merchandise, including brand name and private brand office supplies, business machines and computers, computer software, office furniture, and other business-related products through its chain of office supply stores. Most stores also contain a copy and print center that offers printing, reproduction mailing, shipping, and other services.

ODP's International group served customers in 42 countries outside the U.S. and Canada through 125 company-owned stores and 153 additional stores operating under licensing and joint venture agreements as of December 31,

2006. It also participates in 70 franchised stores in South Korea. In 2007, ODP plans to open over 20 company-owned stores.

MARKET PROFILE. The U.S. office products industry totaled approximately $323 billion in sales in 2005, according to the School, Home and Office Products Association (SHOPA). The market is mature, and S&P forecasts an industry growth rate of 3% for the next five years. Growth in the higher-margin commercial segment (36% of the total industry) will likely continue to outpace that of the retail segment (64%) over the next several years due to a solid macro environment for capital spending. While behemoths Staples, Office Depot and OfficeMax are often regarded as the dominant players, the office products industry remains quite fragmented, with the aforementioned trio comprising an approximate 12.2% share of U.S. sales in 2005, including only about 9.5% of the retail channel.

Company Financials Fiscal Year Ended Dec. 31

Per Share Data ($)	2006	2005	2004	2003	2002	2001	2000	1999	1998	1997
Tangible Book Value	5.11	6.26	6.96	5.77	6.61	5.28	4.66	5.06	4.86	7.23
Cash Flow	2.76	1.72	1.92	1.75	1.59	1.27	0.86	1.08	0.93	1.49
Earnings	1.79	0.87	1.06	0.96	0.98	0.66	0.16	0.69	0.61	0.65
S&P Core Earnings	1.78	0.86	1.03	0.91	0.92	0.58	NA	NA	NA	NA
Dividends	Nil	Nil	Nil	Nil	Nil	Nil	Nil	Nil	Nil	Nil
Payout Ratio	Nil	Nil	Nil	Nil	Nil	Nil	Nil	Nil	Nil	Nil
Prices:High	46.52	31.76	19.50	18.50	21.96	18.70	14.88	26.00	24.83	16.00
Prices:Low	30.64	16.50	13.87	10.28	10.60	7.13	5.88	9.00	10.58	8.42
P/E Ratio:High	26	37	18	19	22	28	93	38	41	25
P/E Ratio:Low	17	19	13	11	11	11	37	13	17	13

Income Statement Analysis (Million $)										
Revenue	15,011	14,279	13,565	12,359	11,357	11,154	11,570	10,263	8,998	6,718
Operating Income	998	750	799	719	707	562	433	615	659	405
Depreciation	279	268	269	248	201	199	206	169	141	102
Interest Expense	40.8	32.4	61.1	54.8	46.2	44.3	33.9	26.1	22.4	21.6
Pretax Income	727	362	461	445	479	314	92.5	414	389	263
Effective Tax Rate	29.0%	24.3%	27.3%	32.1%	35.0%	36.0%	46.6%	37.8%	40.0%	39.4%
Net Income	516	274	336	302	311	201	49.3	258	233	160
S&P Core Earnings	513	270	327	286	292	178	NA	NA	NA	NA

Balance Sheet & Other Financial Data (Million $)										
Cash	174	703	794	791	877	563	151	219	705	200
Current Assets	3,455	3,530	3,916	3,577	3,210	2,806	2,699	2,631	2,780	2,021
Total Assets	6,570	6,099	6,767	6,145	4,766	4,332	4,196	4,276	4,113	2,981
Current Liabilities	2,970	2,469	2,618	2,277	1,992	2,102	1,908	1,944	1,531	1,138
Long Term Debt	571	569	584	829	412	318	598	321	471	447
Common Equity	2,610	2,739	3,223	2,794	2,297	1,848	1,601	1,908	2,029	1,329
Total Capital	3,197	3,308	3,957	3,868	2,774	2,230	2,200	2,229	2,500	1,777
Capital Expenditures	343	261	391	212	202	207	268	396	255	94.3
Cash Flow	795	542	605	550	512	400	255	426	374	262
Current Ratio	1.2	1.4	1.5	1.6	1.6	1.3	1.4	1.4	1.8	1.8
% Long Term Debt of Capitalization	17.9	17.2	14.8	21.4	14.9	14.2	27.2	14.4	18.8	25.2
% Net Income of Revenue	3.4	1.9	2.5	2.4	2.7	1.8	0.4	2.5	2.6	2.4
% Return on Assets	8.1	4.2	5.2	5.5	6.8	4.7	1.2	6.2	6.6	5.6
% Return on Equity	19.3	9.2	11.2	11.9	15.0	11.7	2.8	13.1	13.9	12.9

Data as orig reptd.; bef. results of disc opers/spec. items. Per share data adj. for stk. divs.; EPS diluted. E-Estimated. NA-Not Available. NM-Not Meaningful. NR-Not Ranked. UR-Under Review.

Office: 2200 Old Germantown Road, Delray Beach, FL 33445.
Telephone: 561-438-4800.
Email: investor.relations@officedepot.com
Website: http://www.officedepot.com

Chrmn & CEO: S. Odland
EVP & CFO: P.A. McKay
EVP, Secy & General Counsel: D.C. Fannin
SVP & Cntlr: J. Moline

Investor Contact: R. Tharpe (561-438-4540)
Board Members: L. A. Ault, III, N. R. Austrian, D. W. Bernauer, A. E. Bru, M. J. Evans, D. I. Fuente, B. J. Gaines, M. M. Hart, W. S. Hedrick, K. Mason, M. J. Myers, S. Odland

Founded: 1986
Domicile: Delaware
Employees: 52,000

Omnicom Group Inc.

STANDARD &POOR'S

S&P Recommendation BUY ★★★★☆	**Price** $46.80 (as of Nov 23, 2007)	**12-Mo. Target Price** $67.00	**Investment Style** Large-Cap Growth

GICS Sector Consumer Discretionary
Sub-Industry Advertising

Summary This company owns DDB Worldwide, BBDO Worldwide, and TBWA Worldwide advertising agency networks; it also owns more than 100 marketing and specialty services firms.

Key Stock Statistics (Source S&P, Vickers, company reports)

52-Wk Range	$55.45– 45.82	S&P Oper. EPS 2007**E**	2.97	Market Capitalization(B)	$15.364	Beta	1.28
Trailing 12-Month EPS	$2.81	S&P Oper. EPS 2008**E**	3.36	Yield (%)	1.28	S&P 3-Yr. Proj. EPS CAGR(%)	13.00
Trailing 12-Month P/E	16.7	P/E on S&P Oper. EPS 2007**E**	15.8	Dividend Rate/Share	$0.60	S&P Credit Rating	A-
$10K Invested 5 Yrs Ago	$14,848	Common Shares Outstg. (M)	328.3	Institutional Ownership (%)	86		

Price Performance

30-Week Mov. Avg. · · · 10-Week Mov. Avg. - - **GAAP Earnings vs. Previous Year** Volume Above Avg. STARS
12-Mo. Target Price — Relative Strength — ▲ Up ▼ Down ► No Change Below Avg. ★

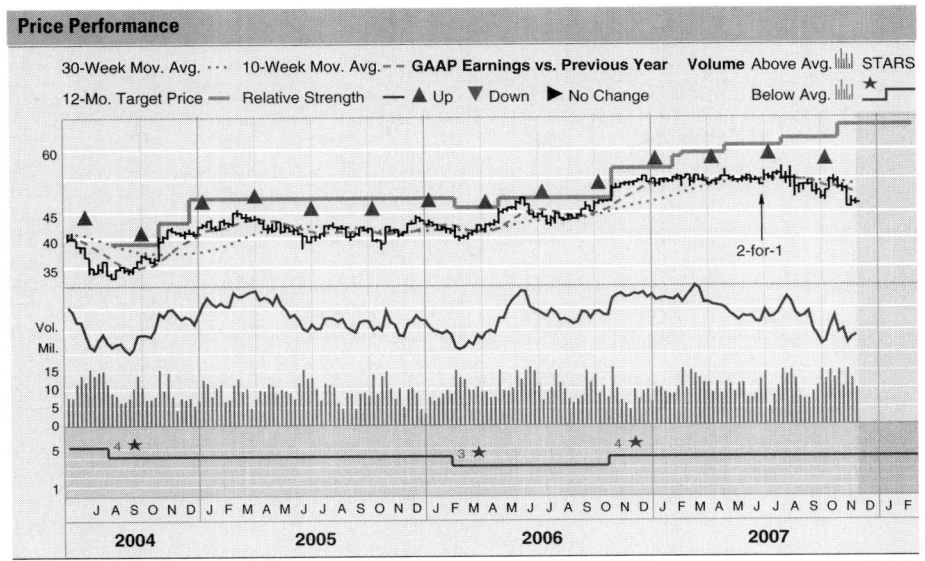

Options: ASE, CBOE, P, Ph

Analysis prepared by **James Peters, CFA** on October 29, 2007, when the stock traded at **$ 50.51**.

Highlights

➤ We forecast 2008 revenue growth of about 8%, following an 11.3% advance we see for 2007. We expect market share gains to boost domestic organic growth in 2008, although we anticipate a more moderate pace than our 7.7% projection for 2007 due to our expectations of a slowing U.S. economy. We see continued strong overseas gains in 2008, following a rise of 15.8% that we forecast for 2007, partly due to our outlook for a declining U.S. dollar. We also expect OMC to grow through acquisitions.

➤ We anticipate a modest operating margin advance, to about 13.2% in 2008, up from our forecast for 13.1% in 2007. While we expect OMC to realize operating leverage from higher revenues on its fixed costs, we also see the company continuing to invest heavily in its infrastructure in order to maintain above peer revenue growth and profitability.

➤ After lower projected interest expense, we see EPS rising to $3.36 in 2008, up from our $2.97 estimate for 2007. Following $1.3 billion of stock repurchases in 2006 and more than $800 million through the first three quarters of 2007, we see buybacks continuing in 2008.

Investment Rationale/Risk

➤ We see a slowing U.S. economy leading to a decelerating pace of domestic organic growth for OMC in 2008. However, we also believe a tighter credit environment in the U.S. is likely to reduce acquisition multiples and increase accretive acquisition opportunities. Thus, we see OMC utilizing what we view as a strong balance sheet to more aggressively pursue acquisition growth in 2008. We also believe OMC's geographic and product revenue stream will help shield it from potential domestic weakness and lead to continued market share gains.

➤ Risks to our recommendation and target price include a deterioration in global GDP, lost accounts, and possible stock dilution from convertible liquid yield options.

➤ Our 12-month target price of $67 is based on a blend of our DCF and relative value analyses. Our DCF model yields an intrinsic value of $68 and assumes a 7.6% WACC and 3.5% terminal growth. We derive a $67 value by applying an historical P/E of 20X to our 2008 EPS estimate, and note that OMC's P/E has been near 20X over the past 1, 2, 3, 4, and 5 year periods.

Qualitative Risk Assessment

LOW	MEDIUM	HIGH

Our risk assessment reflects a highly competitive advertising industry, offset by OMC's diversified geographic and product revenue sources coupled with its position as the world's largest advertising agency by revenue, and our view of its strong track record of EPS and free cash flow growth.

Quantitative Evaluations

S&P Quality Ranking A+

D	C	B-	B	B+	A-	A	A+

Relative Strength Rank MODERATE

51

LOWEST = 1　　　HIGHEST = 99

Revenue/Earnings Data

Revenue (Million $)

	1Q	2Q	3Q	4Q	Year
2007	2,841	3,126	3,101	--	--
2006	2,563	2,823	2,774	3,216	11,377
2005	2,403	2,616	2,523	2,939	10,481
2004	2,231	2,408	2,319	2,789	9,747
2003	1,937	2,150	2,029	2,506	8,621
2002	1,732	1,917	1,768	2,119	7,536

Earnings Per Share ($)

2007	0.55	0.84	0.62	E0.97	E2.97
2006	0.47	0.71	0.52	0.81	2.50
2005	0.41	0.62	0.45	0.71	2.18
2004	0.36	0.55	0.40	0.64	1.94
2003	0.35	0.51	0.36	0.58	1.80
2002	0.34	0.50	0.34	0.54	1.72

Fiscal year ended Dec. 31. Next earnings report expected: Mid February. EPS Estimates based on S&P Operating Earnings; historical GAAP earnings are as reported.

Dividend Data (Dates: mm/dd Payment Date: mm/dd/yy)

Amount ($)	Date Decl.	Ex-Div. Date	Stk. of Record	Payment Date
0.250	02/13	03/06	03/08	04/05/07
0.150	05/22	06/04	06/06	07/05/07
2-for-1	05/22	06/26	06/06	06/25/07
0.150	07/25	09/18	09/20	10/04/07

Dividends have been paid since 1986. Source: Company reports.

Please read the Required Disclosures and Analyst Certification on the last page of this report.

The **McGraw-Hill** Companies

Omnicom Group Inc.

STANDARD &POOR'S

Business Summary October 29, 2007

Omnicom Group, a global advertising and marketing services company, is one of the world's largest corporate communications companies. OMC is comprised of more than 1,500 subsidiary agencies, operating in over 100 countries. It operates as three independent global agency networks: the BBDO Worldwide Network, the DDB Worldwide Network, and the TBWA Worldwide Network. Each agency network has its own clients, and the networks compete with each other in the same markets.

OMC's companies provide an extensive range of services, which it groups into four disciplines: traditional media advertising (43% of 2006 revenues), customer relationship management (36%), public relations (10%), and specialty communications (11%) The services included in these categories are: advertising, brand consultancy, crisis communications, custom publishing, data-

base management, digital and interactive marketing, direct marketing, directory advertising, entertainment marketing, environmental design, experiential marketing, field marketing, financial/corporate business-to-business advertising, graphic arts, health care communications, instore design, investor relations, marketing research, media planning and buying, multi-cultural marketing, non-profit marketing, organizational communications, package design, product placement, promotional marketing, public affairs, public relations, real estate advertising and marketing, recruitment communications, reputation consulting, retail marketing, and sports and event marketing.

Company Financials Fiscal Year Ended Dec. 31

Per Share Data ($)	2006	2005	2004	2003	2002	2001	2000	1999	1998	1997
Tangible Book Value	NM	NM	NM	NM	NM	NM	NM	NM	NM	NM
Cash Flow	3.13	2.71	2.40	2.10	2.03	1.88	1.81	1.30	1.19	0.96
Earnings	2.50	2.18	1.94	1.80	1.72	1.35	1.37	1.01	0.84	0.69
S&P Core Earnings	2.50	2.18	1.92	1.69	1.56	1.24	NA	NA	NA	NA
Dividends	0.50	0.46	0.45	0.40	0.40	0.39	0.35	0.30	0.25	0.23
Payout Ratio	20%	21%	23%	22%	23%	29%	26%	30%	30%	33%
Prices:High	53.03	45.74	44.41	43.80	48.68	49.10	50.47	53.75	29.25	21.19
Prices:Low	39.38	37.88	33.22	23.25	18.25	29.55	34.06	27.97	18.50	11.13
P/E Ratio:High	21	21	23	24	28	36	37	53	35	31
P/E Ratio:Low	16	17	17	13	11	22	25	28	22	16

Income Statement Analysis (Million $)										
Revenue	11,377	10,481	9,747	8,621	7,536	6,889	6,154	5,131	4,092	3,125
Operating Income	1,674	1,515	1,388	1,289	1,224	1,179	1,065	821	693	506
Depreciation	190	175	172	124	120	211	187	97.1	133	103
Interest Expense	125	78.0	51.1	57.9	45.5	72.8	76.5	84.9	69.6	43.1
Pretax Income	1,422	1,308	1,196	1,137	1,087	908	923	689	545	411
Effective Tax Rate	32.8%	33.3%	33.1%	33.5%	34.5%	38.8%	40.0%	39.7%	39.6%	38.0%
Net Income	864	791	724	676	643	503	499	363	285	222
S&P Core Earnings	866	790	715	631	584	456	NA	NA	NA	NA

Balance Sheet & Other Financial Data (Million $)										
Cash	1,740	836	1,166	1,529	667	472	517	576	648	556
Current Assets	9,647	7,967	8,095	7,286	5,637	5,234	5,367	4,712	3,981	2,988
Total Assets	18,164	15,920	16,002	14,499	11,820	10,617	9,891	9,018	6,910	4,966
Current Liabilities	10,296	8,700	8,744	7,762	6,840	6,644	6,625	6,009	4,796	3,579
Long Term Debt	3,055	2,357	2,358	2,537	1,945	1,340	1,245	712	716	342
Common Equity	3,871	3,948	4,079	3,466	2,569	2,178	1,548	1,553	1,086	981
Total Capital	7,562	6,921	6,949	6,394	4,687	3,677	2,970	2,708	1,893	1,273
Capital Expenditures	178	163	160	141	117	149	150	130	89.7	76.1
Cash Flow	1,054	966	896	800	763	714	685	460	418	325
Current Ratio	0.9	0.9	0.9	0.9	0.8	0.8	0.8	0.8	0.8	0.8
% Long Term Debt of Capitalization	40.4	34.1	33.9	39.7	41.5	36.4	41.9	26.3	37.8	68.1
% Net Income of Revenue	7.6	7.5	7.4	7.8	8.5	7.3	8.1	7.1	7.0	7.1
% Return on Assets	5.1	5.0	4.7	5.1	5.7	4.9	5.3	4.5	4.8	4.9
% Return on Equity	22.1	19.7	18.8	22.4	27.1	27.0	32.2	27.9	27.6	23.3

Data as orig reptd.; bef. results of disc opers/spec. items. Per share data adj. for stk. divs.; EPS diluted. E-Estimated. NA-Not Available. NM-Not Meaningful. NR-Not Ranked. UR-Under Review.

Office: 437 Madison Ave , New York, NY 10022-7000.
Telephone: 212-415-3600.
Email: IR@OmnicomGroup.com
Website: http://www.omnicomgroup.com

Chrmn: B. Crawford
Pres & CEO: J.D. Wren
Vice Chrmn: M. Birkin
Vice Chrmn: P. Mead

Investor Contact: R.J. Weisenburger (212-415-3600)
Board Members: R. C. Clark, L. Coleman, Jr., E. M. Cook, B. Crawford, S. S. Denison, M. A. Henning, J. R. Murphy, J. R. Purcell, L. J. Rice, G. L. Roubos, J. D. Wren

Founded: 1944
Domicile: New York
Employees: 66,000

Oracle Corp

STANDARD &POOR'S

S&P Recommendation	STRONG BUY ★★★★★	Price	12-Mo. Target Price	Investment Style
		$19.89 (as of Nov 27, 2007)	$26.00	Large-Cap Growth

GICS Sector Information Technology
Sub-Industry Systems Software

Summary This company is a leading supplier of enterprise database management systems and business applications.

Key Stock Statistics (Source S&P, Vickers, company reports)

52-Wk Range	$23.00– 15.97	S&P Oper. EPS 2008**E**	1.21	Market Capitalization(B)	$101.863	Beta	1.82
Trailing 12-Month EPS	$0.84	S&P Oper. EPS 2009**E**	1.43	Yield (%)	Nil	S&P 3-Yr. Proj. EPS CAGR(%)	16.00
Trailing 12-Month P/E	23.7	P/E on S&P Oper. EPS 2008**E**	16.4	Dividend Rate/Share	Nil	S&P Credit Rating	A
$10K Invested 5 Yrs Ago	$17,539	Common Shares Outstg. (M)	5,121.3	Institutional Ownership (%)	57		

Price Performance

30-Week Mov. Avg. ··· 10-Week Mov. Avg. - - GAAP Earnings vs. Previous Year Volume Above Avg. STARS
12-Mo. Target Price — Relative Strength — ▲ Up ▼ Down ▶ No Change Below Avg.

Options: ASE, CBOE, P, Ph

Analysis prepared by **Zaineb Bokhari** on September 24, 2007, when the stock traded at **$21.95**.

Qualitative Risk Assessment

LOW	MEDIUM	HIGH

Our risk assessment reflects potential acquisition integration risks faced by the company following a series of large purchases over the past three years. This is offset by our view of ORCL's strong balance sheet, considerable free cash flow, and what we see as a deep management bench.

Quantitative Evaluations

S&P Quality Ranking B

D	C	B-	B	B+	A-	A	A+

Relative Strength Rank MODERATE

56

LOWEST = 1   HIGHEST = 99

Revenue/Earnings Data

Revenue (Million $)

	1Q	2Q	3Q	4Q	Year
2008	4,529	--	--	--	--
2007	3,591	4,163	4,414	5,828	17,996
2006	2,768	3,292	3,470	4,851	14,380
2005	2,215	2,756	2,950	3,878	11,799
2004	2,072	2,498	2,509	3,076	10,156
2003	2,028	2,309	2,307	2,832	9,475

Earnings Per Share ($)

	1Q	2Q	3Q	4Q	Year
2008	0.16	E0.26	E0.29	E0.44	E1.21
2007	0.13	0.18	0.20	0.31	0.81
2006	0.10	0.15	0.14	0.24	0.64
2005	0.10	0.16	0.10	0.20	0.55
2004	0.08	0.12	0.12	0.19	0.50
2003	0.06	0.10	0.11	0.16	0.43

Fiscal year ended May 31. Next earnings report expected: Mid December. EPS Estimates based on S&P Operating Earnings; historical GAAP earnings are as reported.

Dividend Data

No cash dividends have been paid.

Highlights

➤ Although we forecast healthy organic growth rates for the company, we expect recent acquisitions (Hyperion Solutions, April 2007, Agile Software, July 2007) to help drive the faster growth we project in ORCL's applications business in FY 08 (May) than in its core database operations. We look for middleware to remain an area of strong growth for the company. We see non-GAAP revenue growth of 19% in FY 08, to $21.7 billion; we forecast approximately 13% higher revenues in FY 09, as year-to-year comparisons become tougher.

➤ Despite our strong revenue growth outlook, we expect operating margins to widen by 1%, to 41.8%, in FY 08, as management continues to integrate and derive cost efficiencies from recent acquisitions. We expect operating margins to widen slightly in FY 09, as targeted cost synergies and scale benefits are achieved.

➤ With an effective tax rate of 28.9%, comparable to FY 07's, we expect pro forma operating EPS to rise 23% in FY 08, to $1.21. We expect an 18% rise in EPS in FY 09, to $1.43. We look for notable share repurchases to continue.

Investment Rationale/Risk

➤ We have a strong buy recommendation on the shares due to our view of ORCL's formidable market position, enviable operating margins, considerable free cash generation, and attractive valuation based on our discounted cash flow and relative analyses. While we continue to foresee potential acquisition integration risks, we believe the current discount to peers will continue to shrink.

➤ Risks to our recommendation and target price include acquisition integration risks, intense competition, and pricing pressure within the enterprise software market. We also note that while ORCL is diversified in its customer base, it has exposure to the financial services sector, which may be adversely affected by the downturn in the mortgage industry.

➤ Our 12-month target price of $26 is based on our valuation of discounted free cash flow, assuming a 10.6% weighted average cost of capital and 4% terminal growth. At this level, the shares would trade at about 18X our FY 09 estimate. On a forward 12-month basis, our target price assumes that ORCL will trade in line with the normalized average P/E for S&P 500 software peers of about 20.6X.

Oracle Corp

STANDARD &POOR'S

Business Summary September 24, 2007

CORPORATE OVERVIEW. Oracle Corp. is a leading provider of enterprise software. The company is organized into two main businesses: software and services. The company further segments its software business into new software licenses (32% of revenue in FY 07 (May) and 33% in FY 06) and software license updates, and product support (47% and 48% of revenue in FY 07 and FY 06, respectively). The company's services business is divided into consulting (16%, 14%), On Demand (3%, 3%), and education (2%, 2%). Oracle's software products fall into two broad categories: database and middleware and application software. Database and middleware products accounted for about 66% of software revenues in FY 07 (67% in FY 06).

CORPORATE STRATEGY. ORCL has acquired companies that it believes offer complementary products and services. In January 2005, ORCL purchased PeopleSoft Inc., a provider of enterprise application software products, for about $11.1 billion. In January 2006, ORCL bought Siebel Systems, a leading provider of customer relationship management software (CRM), for $5.85 billion in cash and stock. ORCL believes these acquisitions support its long-term

strategy, strengthen its competitive position in the enterprise applications market, and expand its customer base. In addition to these large deals, ORCL has acquired several smaller companies that provide software solutions targeted at specific industries in an effort to gain expertise in what it considers to be key verticals such as retail and financial services. In April 2005, ORCL purchased Retek, Inc., a provider of software and services to the retail industry, for approximately $700 million. In December 2005, ORCL acquired a 43% stake in i-Flex Solutions, an India-based provider of software solutions for the banking and insurance industries. The company has continued to add to this stake. In April 2007, ORCL acquired Hyperion Solutions Corp., a provider of business intelligence/corporate performance management software, for approximately $3.3 billion. In July 2007, ORCL acquired Agile Software, a provider of product lifecycle management software solutions for $495 million.

Company Financials Fiscal Year Ended May 31

Per Share Data ($)	2007	2006	2005	2004	2003	2002	2001	2000	1999	1998
Tangible Book Value	NM	0.13	0.09	1.55	1.21	1.13	1.12	1.15	1.29	0.51
Cash Flow	1.03	0.79	0.63	0.55	0.49	0.45	0.50	1.10	0.43	0.19
Earnings	0.81	0.64	0.55	0.50	0.43	0.39	0.44	1.05	0.22	0.14
S&P Core Earnings	0.80	0.62	0.52	0.46	0.37	0.34	0.36	NA	NA	NA
Dividends	Nil	Nil	Nil	Nil	Nil	Nil	Nil	Nil	Nil	Nil
Payout Ratio	Nil	Nil	Nil	Nil	Nil	Nil	Nil	Nil	Nil	Nil
Calendar Year	2006	2005	2004	2003	2002	2001	2000	1999	1998	1997
Prices:High	19.75	14.51	15.51	14.03	17.50	35.00	46.47	28.34	7.48	7.02
Prices:Low	12.06	11.25	9.78	10.64	7.25	10.16	21.50	5.25	2.96	3.49
P/E Ratio:High	24	23	28	28	41	90	NM	27	34	52
P/E Ratio:Low	15	18	18	21	17	26	NM	5	14	26

Income Statement Analysis (Million $)

	2007	2006	2005	2004	2003	2002	2001	2000	1999	1998
Revenue	17,996	14,380	11,799	10,156	9,475	9,673	10,860	10,130	8,827	7,144
Operating Income	726	5,764	4,802	4,098	3,767	3,934	4,124	3,472	2,248	1,740
Depreciation	1,127	806	425	234	327	363	347	391	375	329
Interest Expense	343	169	135	21.0	16.0	20.0	24.0	18.9	21.4	16.7
Pretax Income	5,986	4,810	4,051	3,945	3,425	3,408	3,971	10,123	1,982	1,328
Effective Tax Rate	28.6%	29.7%	28.8%	32.0%	32.6%	34.7%	35.5%	37.8%	34.9%	38.7%
Net Income	4,274	3,381	2,886	2,681	2,307	2,224	2,561	6,297	1,290	814
S&P Core Earnings	4,224	3,237	2,750	2,459	2,049	1,923	2,119	NA	NA	NA

Balance Sheet & Other Financial Data (Million $)

	2007	2006	2005	2004	2003	2002	2001	2000	1999	1998
Cash	7,020	7,605	4,802	4,138	4,737	3,095	4,449	7,429	1,786	1,274
Current Assets	12,883	11,974	8,479	11,336	9,227	8,728	8,963	10,883	5,447	4,323
Total Assets	34,572	29,029	20,687	12,763	11,064	10,800	11,030	13,077	7,260	5,819
Current Liabilities	9,387	6,930	8,063	4,272	4,158	3,960	3,917	5,862	3,046	2,484
Long Term Debt	6,235	5,735	159	163	175	298	301	301	304	304
Common Equity	16,919	15,012	10,837	7,995	6,320	6,117	6,278	6,461	3,695	2,958
Total Capital	24,275	21,311	12,006	8,217	6,681	6,619	6,906	7,028	4,135	3,278
Capital Expenditures	319	236	188	189	291	278	313	263	347	328
Cash Flow	5,401	4,187	3,311	2,915	2,634	2,587	2,908	6,611	1,290	1,142
Current Ratio	1.4	1.7	1.1	2.7	2.2	2.2	2.3	1.9	1.8	1.7
% Long Term Debt of Capitalization	25.7	26.9	1.3	2.0	2.6	4.5	4.4	4.3	7.3	9.3
% Net Income of Revenue	22.7	23.5	24.4	26.4	24.3	23.0	23.6	62.2	14.6	11.4
% Return on Assets	13.4	13.6	17.3	22.6	21.1	20.4	21.2	61.9	19.7	15.6
% Return on Equity	26.8	26.2	30.7	37.5	37.1	35.9	40.2	124.0	19.4	30.5

Data as orig reptd.; bef. results of disc opers/spec. items. Per share data adj. for stk. divs.; EPS diluted. E-Estimated. NA-Not Available. NM-Not Meaningful. NR-Not Ranked. UR-Under Review.

Office: 500 Oracle Parkway, Redwood Shores, CA 94065-1675.
Telephone: 650-506-7000.
Email: investor_us@oracle.com
Website: http://www.oracle.com

Chrmn: J.O. Henley
CEO: L.J. Ellison
SVP, Secy & General Counsel: D. Cooperman
VP, Chief Acctg Officer & Cntlr: W.C. West

CFO & Co-Pres: S. Catz
Investor Contact: K. Bessinger (650-506-4073)
Board Members: J. Berg, H. R. Bingham, M. J. Boskin, S. A. Catz, L. J. Ellison, H. Garcia-Molina, J. O. Henley, J. F. Kemp, D. L. Lucas, C. E. Phillips, Jr., N. O. Seligman

Founded: 1977
Domicile: Delaware
Employees: 74,674

PACCAR Inc

STANDARD &POOR'S

S&P Recommendation HOLD ★★★☆☆	**Price** $48.19 (as of Nov 23, 2007)	**12-Mo. Target Price** $63.00	**Investment Style** Large-Cap Blend

GICS Sector Industrials
Sub-Industry Construction & Farm Machinery & Heavy Trucks

Summary This heavy-duty truck manufacturer produces the well known Peterbilt and Kenworth brand heavy-duty highway trucks.

Key Stock Statistics (Source S&P, Vickers, company reports)

52-Wk Range	$65.75– 42.15	S&P Oper. EPS 2007**E**	3.40	Market Capitalization(B)	$17.970	Beta	1.37
Trailing 12-Month EPS	$3.60	S&P Oper. EPS 2008**E**	3.87	Yield (%)	1.49	S&P 3-Yr. Proj. EPS CAGR(%)	3.00
Trailing 12-Month P/E	13.4	P/E on S&P Oper. EPS 2007**E**	14.2	Dividend Rate/Share	$0.72	S&P Credit Rating	AA-
$10K Invested 5 Yrs Ago	$40,434	Common Shares Outstg. (M)	372.9	Institutional Ownership (%)	51		

Price Performance

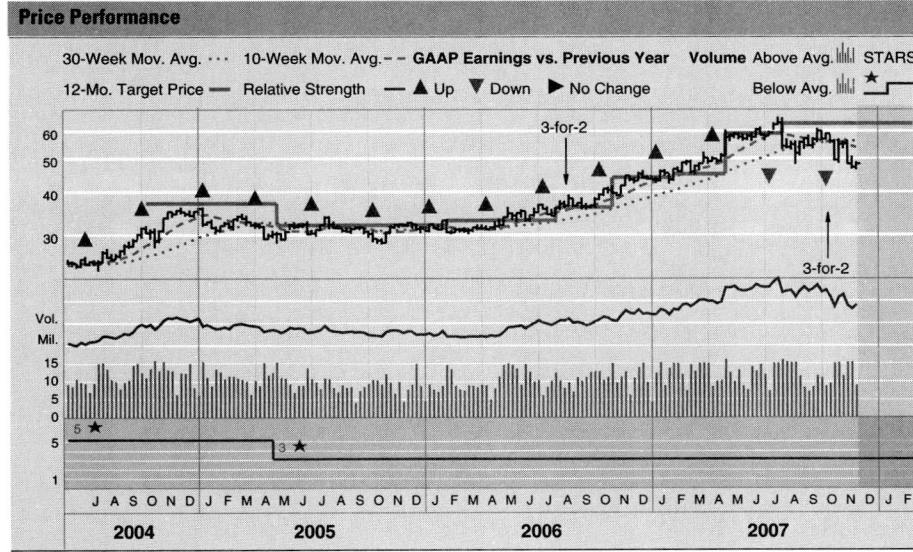

30-Week Mov. Avg. ··· 10-Week Mov. Avg.– – **GAAP Earnings vs. Previous Year** Volume Above Avg. STARS
12-Mo. Target Price — Relative Strength — ▲ Up ▼ Down ▶ No Change Below Avg.

Options: ASE, CBOE, P, Ph

Analysis prepared by **Pearl Wang** on November 19, 2007, when the stock traded at **$ 46.74.**

Highlights

➤ We see net sales declining about 11% in 2007, following a 17% increase in 2006 that was largely tied to pre-buying of heavy trucks in the U.S. ahead of changes in emissions regulations. However, we expect continued strength overseas to serve as a partial offset. In 2008, we anticipate a roughly 13% recovery in revenue as fleet owners begin replacing older vehicles and positioning their fleet ahead of an even more stringent set of emission standards scheduled to take effect in 2010.

➤ We anticipate a narrowing of operating margins in 2007 due to the significantly lower production volumes, widening slightly in 2008. Yet, we see ongoing cost-control efforts and lessening raw material cost pressures providing some support to margins in 2007. For the longer term, we think that margins (and earnings) will continue to exhibit large swings, due to the highly cyclical nature of the global truck industry.

➤ We regard the company's quality of earnings as high versus peers, with no difference between our Standard & Poor's Core EPS estimates and our operating EPS forecasts.

Investment Rationale/Risk

➤ We believe continued strength in international truck demand should help mitigate the industry downturn we project for the North American class 8 truck market in 2007. Moreover, we believe PCAR is well positioned to benefit from an eventual rebound in demand that we anticipate will begin to occur in 2008. We see businesses such as aftermarket parts and leasing in Europe providing additional areas for PCAR to augment growth.

➤ Risks to our recommendation and target price include a more severe than expected downturn in the North American and/or European truck markets; potential supply disruptions; and further increases in raw material costs.

➤ Our discounted cash flow model, which assumes a 9% compound annual growth rate in free cash flow over the next 10 years, 3.5% growth in perpetuity, and a 9% discount rate, indicates intrinsic value of about $64. In terms of relative valuation, applying a target P/E multiple of about 16.3X, in line with historical norms, to our 2008 EPS estimate of $3.87 suggests a value of $63. Blending these two valuation metrics results in our 12-month target price of $63.

Qualitative Risk Assessment

LOW	MEDIUM	HIGH

Our risk assessment for Paccar reflects the highly cyclical nature of the heavy-duty (class 8) truck market, offset by our view of a strong balance sheet with a relatively low amount of manufacturing debt and the company's above-average profitability. We estimate that over the past 10 years, the company has generated an average ROIC of 19% versus 11% for the S&P 1500 Industrials sector.

Quantitative Evaluations

S&P Quality Ranking B+

D	C	B-	B	B+	A-	A	A+

Relative Strength Rank MODERATE

33

LOWEST = 1 HIGHEST = 99

Revenue/Earnings Data

Revenue (Million $)

	1Q	2Q	3Q	4Q	Year
2007	3,985	3,429	3,449	--	--
2006	3,852	3,937	3,959	3,968	16,454
2005	3,422	3,555	3,541	3,426	14,057
2004	2,501	2,787	2,775	3,190	11,396
2003	1,803	1,895	1,940	2,083	8,195
2002	1,502	1,802	1,996	1,919	7,219

Earnings Per Share ($)

2007	0.97	0.79	0.81	E0.82	E3.40
2006	0.90	0.98	1.07	1.01	3.97
2005	0.69	0.62	0.79	0.81	2.91
2004	0.46	0.60	0.63	0.61	2.29
2003	0.28	0.31	0.33	0.40	1.33
2002	0.12	0.19	0.33	0.31	0.95

Fiscal year ended Dec. 31. Next earnings report expected: Late January. EPS Estimates based on S&P Operating Earnings; historical GAAP earnings are as reported.

Dividend Data (Dates: mm/dd Payment Date: mm/dd/yy)

Amount ($)	Date Decl.	Ex-Div. Date	Stk. of Record	Payment Date
0.250	04/24	05/16	05/18	06/05/07
0.250	07/10	08/15	08/17	09/05/07
3-for-2	09/11	10/10	09/25	10/09/07
0.180	09/11	11/15	11/19	12/05/07

Dividends have been paid since 1943. Source: Company reports.

Please read the Required Disclosures and Analyst Certification on the last page of this report.

The **McGraw-Hill** Companies

PACCAR Inc

Business Summary November 19, 2007

CORPORATE OVERVIEW. Originally incorporated in 1924 as the Pacific Car and Foundry Company, and tracing its roots back to the Seattle Car Manufacturing Company, PACCAR has grown into a multinational company with principal businesses that include the design, manufacture and distribution of high-quality light, medium and heavy-duty commercial trucks and related aftermarket parts. The company's heavy-duty (class 8) diesel trucks are marketed under the Peterbilt, Kenworth, DAF and Foden names. In addition, through its Peterbilt and Kenworth divisions, PCAR competes in the North American medium duty (class 6/7) markets and the European light/medium (6 to 15 metric ton) commercial vehicle market with DAF cab-over-engine trucks.

In 2006, the company's truck production and related aftermarket parts distribution businesses accounted for 94% of revenues and 88% of operating income. Segment profit margins in 2006, 2005, and 2004, were 11.9%, 11.5%, and 10.6%, respectively; in the previous cycle, during the boom years of 2000, 1999 and 1998, segment profit margins were 6.9%, 9.0% and 7.4%, respectively.

PCAR also manufactures industrial winches under the Braden, Carco and Gearmatic names. Sales of winches provided less than 1% of net sales in 2006, 2005 and 2004.

Like other big truck makers, the company aims to capitalize on a growing trend toward truck leasing and financing. The Finance Services segment accounted for 5.8% of 2006 revenues, but generated 12% of operating income; it posted 26%, 26%, and 30% operating margins in 2006, 2005, and 2004, respectively. In 2006, 2005, and 2004, provisions for loan losses were $34 million, $40 million, and $18 million, respectively.

Company Financials Fiscal Year Ended Dec. 31

Per Share Data ($)	2006	2005	2004	2003	2002	2001	2000	1999	1998	1997
Tangible Book Value	11.98	10.27	9.61	7.36	6.08	5.64	5.64	5.13	4.46	3.79
Cash Flow	5.12	3.87	3.09	2.00	1.50	0.91	1.54	1.85	1.37	1.16
Earnings	3.97	2.92	2.29	1.33	0.95	0.45	1.13	1.46	1.05	0.87
S&P Core Earnings	3.97	2.92	2.25	1.32	0.89	0.37	NA	NA	NA	NA
Dividends	0.64	0.39	0.33	0.46	0.29	0.24	0.24	0.47	0.41	0.41
Payout Ratio	16%	13%	15%	35%	30%	53%	21%	32%	40%	47%
Prices:High	46.17	36.17	36.19	25.95	15.70	13.68	10.72	12.44	13.19	11.75
Prices:Low	30.12	28.13	22.05	12.37	9.09	8.44	7.16	7.80	7.31	5.99
P/E Ratio:High	12	12	16	20	17	31	9	9	13	13
P/E Ratio:Low	8	10	10	9	10	19	6	5	7	7

Income Statement Analysis (Million $)

	2006	2005	2004	2003	2002	2001	2000	1999	1998	1997
Revenue	16,454	14,057	11,396	8,195	7,219	6,089	7,437	9,021	7,895	6,764
Operating Income	3,136	2,572	1,972	1,313	1,012	672	1,122	1,243	931	790
Depreciation	435	370	315	268	218	180	156	147	124	112
Interest Expense	573	445	331	3.50	249	275	294	223	192	170
Pretax Income	2,175	1,774	1,368	806	574	255	665	923	653	536
Effective Tax Rate	31.2%	36.1%	33.7%	34.6%	35.2%	32.0%	33.6%	36.8%	36.1%	35.5%
Net Income	1,496	1,133	907	527	372	174	442	584	417	346
S&P Core Earnings	1,496	1,134	889	523	349	145	NA	NA	NA	NA

Balance Sheet & Other Financial Data (Million $)

	2006	2005	2004	2003	2002	2001	2000	1999	1998	1997
Cash	2,628	2,290	2,220	1,724	1,308	1,062	910	1,059	837	676
Current Assets	4,200	3,508	3,332	2,599	2,102	1,834	1,861	2,119	2,070	1,756
Total Assets	16,107	13,715	12,228	9,940	8,703	7,914	8,271	7,933	6,795	5,600
Current Liabilities	2,738	2,182	2,151	1,482	1,258	1,134	1,268	1,534	1,519	1,214
Long Term Debt	498	936	2,314	1,557	1,552	1,547	1,655	1,475	1,311	1,334
Common Equity	4,456	3,901	3,762	3,246	2,601	2,253	2,249	2,111	1,764	1,498
Total Capital	4,954	4,837	6,077	4,803	4,152	3,800	3,904	3,585	3,075	2,987
Capital Expenditures	312	300	232	111	78.8	83.9	143	256	193	133
Cash Flow	1,931	1,503	1,222	794	590	354	598	730	541	458
Current Ratio	1.5	1.6	1.5	1.8	1.7	1.6	1.5	1.4	1.4	1.4
% Long Term Debt of Capitalization	10.1	19.3	38.1	32.4	37.4	40.7	42.4	41.1	42.6	44.7
% Net Income of Revenue	9.1	8.1	8.0	6.4	5.2	2.9	5.9	6.5	5.3	5.1
% Return on Assets	10.0	8.7	8.2	5.6	4.5	2.1	5.5	7.9	6.7	6.4
% Return on Equity	35.8	29.6	25.9	18.0	15.3	7.7	20.3	30.1	25.6	24.2

Data as orig reptd.; bef. results of disc opers/spec. items. Per share data adj. for stk. divs.; EPS diluted. E-Estimated. NA-Not Available. NM-Not Meaningful. NR-Not Ranked. UR-Under Review.

Office: 777 106th Avenue NE, Bellevue, WA 98004-5027.
Telephone: 425-468-7400.
Website: http://www.paccar.com
Chrmn & CEO: M.C. Pigott

Pres: T.E. Plimpton
Vice Chrmn: M.A. Tembreull
VP & General Counsel: D.C. Anderson
VP & Cntlr: M.T. Barkley

Investor Contact: R. Easton
Board Members: A. J. Carnwath, J. M. Fluke, Jr., D. K. Newbigging, S. F. Page, R. T. Parry, J. C. Pigott, M. C. Pigott, W. G. Reed, Jr., M. A. Tembreull, H. A. Wagner, C. R. Williamson

Founded: 1905
Domicile: Delaware
Employees: 21,000

Pactiv Corp

STANDARD &POOR'S

S&P Recommendation **HOLD** ★★★☆☆	Price $23.10 (as of Nov 23, 2007)	12-Mo. Target Price $32.00	Investment Style Large-Cap Growth

GICS Sector Materials
Sub-Industry Metal & Glass Containers

Summary Spun off by Tenneco in 1999, this company is a leading provider of advanced packaging solutions for consumer, institutional and industrial markets.

Key Stock Statistics (Source S&P, Vickers, company reports)

52-Wk Range	$36.91–22.79	S&P Oper. EPS 2007**E**	1.80	Market Capitalization(B)	$3.020	Beta	0.81
Trailing 12-Month EPS	$1.79	S&P Oper. EPS 2008**E**	2.05	Yield (%)	Nil	S&P 3-Yr. Proj. EPS CAGR(%)	12.00
Trailing 12-Month P/E	12.9	P/E on S&P Oper. EPS 2007**E**	12.8	Dividend Rate/Share	Nil	S&P Credit Rating	BBB
$10K Invested 5 Yrs Ago	$11,521	Common Shares Outstg. (M)	130.7	Institutional Ownership (%)	82		

Price Performance

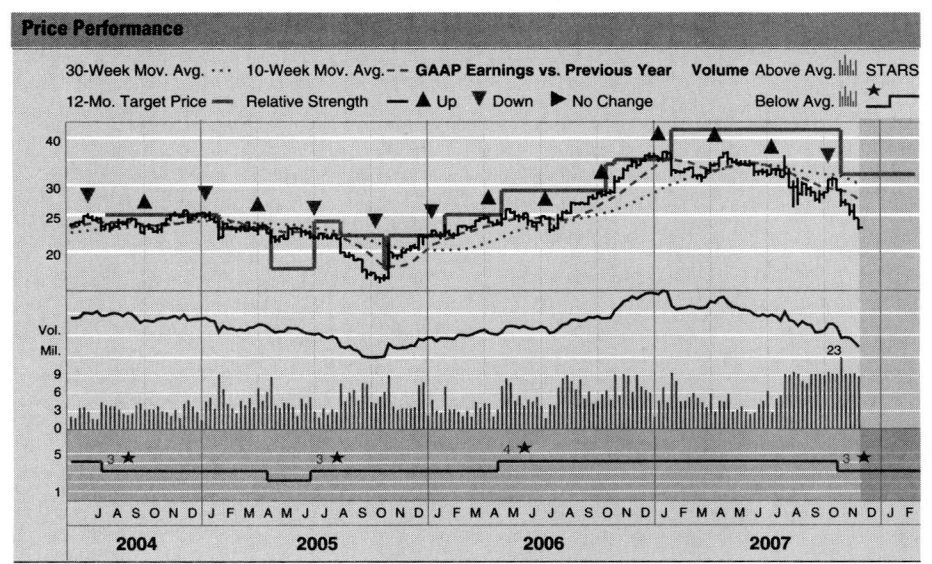

Options: ASE, CBOE, Ph

Analysis prepared by **Stewart Scharf** on October 24, 2007, when the stock traded at **$ 27.42**.

Highlights

➤ We expect organic sales growth of 3% (10% including Prairie Packaging) in 2007, with modest improvement in 2008, driven by pricing initiatives in the foodservice/food packaging unit. We also see a gradual sequential rebound in volume based on demand for Hefty's foam tableware, cups and food and waste bags, which should offset weak foam insulation sales due to a soft housing market.

➤ We look for gross margins (before D&A) to narrow in 2007 by more than 150 basis points from 30.5% in 2006, reflecting an unfavorable product mix, higher petrochemical and other raw material costs, and difficult comparisons. Pricing initiatives should offset these costs in 2008, and EBITDA margins should expand from our near projection of near 20% for 2007, on improved productivity and cost controls. We see pretax pension income adding $50 million to earnings ($0.23 a share, after tax).

➤ We estimate a tax rate of 36% in 2007, and operating EPS of $1.80 (including $0.02 to $0.04 of projected accretion from the Prairie acquisition), advancing to $2.05 in 2008.

Investment Rationale/Risk

➤ We base our hold recommendation on uncertain economic conditions and our valuation models. We still project strong cash flow generation targeted for debt paydowns.

➤ Risks to our recommendation and target price include a significant rise in resin prices and a soft global economy that may force some customers to shift to lower-priced private label products. Regarding corporate governance, we are somewhat concerned that the positions of chairman and CEO are held by the same person.

➤ We blend our DCF valuation with relative metrics to arrive at our 12-month target price of $32. Our DCF model, which assumes a 3% terminal growth rate and an 8.5% weighted average cost of capital (WACC), shows intrinsic value of $33. Based on relative metrics, we apply a peer-average P/E of 14.5X to our 2008 EPS estimate to arrive at a value of $30. We think this P/E, which is below PTV's five-year historical average and that of other packaging companies, is warranted by strong demand for new consumer products, brand loyalty, and well controlled operating expenses.

Qualitative Risk Assessment

LOW	**MEDIUM**	HIGH

Our risk assessment reflects increased foreign competition and demand for unbranded products, supplier and customer consolidation, and volatile energy costs. However, we believe the balance sheet is improving as the company generates cash to pay down debt.

Quantitative Evaluations

S&P Quality Ranking NR

D	C	B-	B	B+	A-	A	A+

Relative Strength Rank WEAK

19

LOWEST = 1   HIGHEST = 99

Revenue/Earnings Data

Revenue (Million $)

	1Q	2Q	3Q	4Q	Year
2007	677.0	828.0	872.0	--	--
2006	680.0	750.0	749.0	738.0	2,917
2005	613.0	707.0	695.0	741.0	2,756
2004	775.0	858.0	865.0	884.0	3,382
2003	717.0	810.0	793.0	818.0	3,138
2002	647.0	728.0	727.0	778.0	2,880

Earnings Per Share ($)

2007	0.43	0.52	0.45	E0.40	E1.80
2006	0.35	0.49	0.75	0.39	1.98
2005	0.14	0.24	0.28	0.30	0.96
2004	Nil	0.33	0.37	0.31	1.01
2003	0.27	0.37	0.16	0.41	1.21
2002	0.26	0.38	0.37	0.37	1.37

Fiscal year ended Dec. 31. Next earnings report expected: Late January. EPS Estimates based on S&P Operating Earnings; historical GAAP earnings are as reported.

Dividend Data

No cash dividends have been paid.

Pactiv Corp

Business Summary October 24, 2007

CORPORATE OVERVIEW. Pactiv Corp., a global supplier of specialty packaging and consumer products, derives more than 80% of its sales from markets in which it holds the No. 1 or No. 2 market-share position. It operates 39 manufacturing plants in North America, three in China and one in Germany. In October 2005, PTV sold most of its protective and flexible packaging divisions to a unit of AEA Investors LLC, an international private equity company. PTV retained its European molded fiber business and Asian operations. In 2006, Wal-Mart accounted for 16% of sales.

After discontinuing the protective and flexible packaging division during 2005, PTV operated two units: consumer products (Hefty) and foodservice/food packaging. Consumer products sales accounted for 37% of total sales in 2006 ($195 million of operating income, before restructuring charges), and foodservice/food packaging 63% ($244 million). In 2006, foreign sales accounted for about 10% of the total.

The company manufactures consumer products such as plastic storage bags and waste bags; foam and molded fiber disposable tableware; and disposable aluminum cookware. It sells many products under recognized brand names such as Hefty, Baggies, Hefty One-Zip, Zoo Pals, Kordite, The Gripper, and E-Z Foil. In early 2007, PTV rolled out Hefty One Zip travel bags for liquid carry-on

items at airports and OneZip big bags for storing or transporting large items. The company expects new product innovations to generate $100 million in annual retail sales over the next few years.

PTV makes food packaging products for the food processing industry, including molded fiber egg cartons, foam meat trays, aluminum containers, and modified atmosphere packaging. The company also offers tableware products such as plates, bowls, cups, and takeout-service containers.

We believe the company will maintain its leading brand name position in the specialty packaging industry and will continue to develop new products.

The company estimates that a 1% change in resin costs equates to a $0.03 effect on EPS on an annualized basis, assuming no pricing actions.

In 2006, EPS was $1.63, before a $0.14 foreign exchange gain and a $0.21 tax liability adjustment, on 6% more shares. The company's pension deficit was below $300 million at year-end 2006 as its return on assets (ROA) exceeded 9%.

Company Financials Fiscal Year Ended Dec. 31

Per Share Data ($)	2006	2005	2004	2003	2002	2001	2000	1999	1998	1997
Tangible Book Value	0.68	0.23	0.98	0.77	1.79	4.91	3.79	2.19	NA	NA
Cash Flow	3.02	1.94	2.10	2.24	2.35	2.14	1.84	0.43	1.43	NA
Earnings	1.98	0.96	1.01	1.21	1.37	1.03	0.70	-0.67	0.39	NA
S&P Core Earnings	1.71	0.56	0.64	1.00	-0.23	-0.57	NA	NA	NA	NA
Dividends	Nil	Nil	Nil	Nil	Nil	Nil	Nil	Nil	Nil	NA
Payout Ratio	Nil	Nil	Nil	Nil	Nil	Nil	Nil	Nil	Nil	NA
Prices:High	36.53	25.58	25.73	24.03	24.47	18.10	13.31	14.50	NA	NA
Prices:Low	21.50	16.50	19.80	17.55	15.35	11.26	7.50	9.31	NA	NA
P/E Ratio:High	18	27	25	20	18	18	19	NM	NA	NA
P/E Ratio:Low	11	17	20	15	11	11	11	NM	NA	NA

Income Statement Analysis (Million $)	2006	2005	2004	2003	2002	2001	2000	1999	1998	1997
Revenue	2,917	2,756	3,382	3,138	2,880	2,812	3,134	2,921	2,791	NA
Operating Income	568	452	954	630	617	574	570	498	466	NA
Depreciation	145	146	169	163	158	177	185	184	175	NA
Interest Expense	73.0	82.0	101	96.0	96.0	107	134	146	164	NA
Pretax Income	391	224	244	314	367	284	207	-159	124	NA
Effective Tax Rate	29.2%	36.2%	36.9%	37.6%	39.8%	41.5%	44.0%	NM	46.0%	NA
Net Income	277	143	155	195	220	165	113	-112	66.0	NA
S&P Core Earnings	239	82.3	96.9	160	-36.1	-91.1	NA	NA	NA	NA

Balance Sheet & Other Financial Data (Million $)	2006	2005	2004	2003	2002	2001	2000	1999	1998	1997
Cash	181	172	222	140	127	41.0	26.0	12.0	18.0	NA
Current Assets	838	820	1,079	982	904	740	900	866	1,031	NA
Total Assets	2,758	2,820	3,741	3,706	3,412	4,060	4,341	4,588	4,749	NA
Current Liabilities	549	456	984	474	501	459	512	920	1,703	NA
Long Term Debt	771	869	869	1,336	1,224	1,211	1,560	1,741	1,186	NA
Common Equity	853	820	1,083	1,061	897	1,689	1,539	1,350	1,286	NA
Total Capital	1,753	1,802	2,209	2,617	2,282	3,502	3,595	3,432	2,848	NA
Capital Expenditures	78.0	121	100	112	126	145	135	1,129	NA	NA
Cash Flow	422	289	324	358	378	342	298	72.0	241	NA
Current Ratio	1.5	1.8	1.1	2.1	1.8	1.6	1.8	0.9	0.6	NA
% Long Term Debt of Capitalization	44.0	48.2	39.3	51.1	53.6	34.6	43.4	50.7	41.6	NA
% Net Income of Revenue	9.5	5.2	4.6	6.2	7.6	5.9	3.6	NM	2.4	NA
% Return on Assets	9.9	4.4	4.2	5.5	5.9	4.0	2.5	NM	NA	NA
% Return on Equity	33.1	15.0	14.5	19.9	17.0	10.2	7.8	NM	NA	NA

Data as orig reptd.; bef. results of disc opers/spec. items. Per share data adj. for stk. divs.; EPS diluted. E-Estimated. NA-Not Available. NM-Not Meaningful. NR-Not Ranked. UR-Under Review.

Office: 1900 West Field Court, Lake Forest, IL 60045-4828.
Telephone: 847-482-2000.
Email: investorrelations@pactiv.com
Website: http://www.pactiv.com

Chrmn, Pres & CEO: R.L. Wambold
SVP & CFO: A.A. Campbell
VP, Secy & General Counsel: J.E. Doyle
Investor Contact: C. Hanneman (847-482-2429)

Board Members: L. D. Brady, K. D. Brooksher, R. J. Darnall, M. R. Henderson, N. T. Linebarger, R. B. Porter, R. L. Wambold, N. H. Wesley

Founded: 1965
Domicile: Delaware
Employees: 11,000

Pall Corp

STANDARD
&POOR'S

S&P Recommendation	HOLD ★★★☆☆	Price $37.49 (as of Nov 23, 2007)	12-Mo. Target Price $47.00

GICS Sector Industrials
Sub-Industry Industrial Machinery

Summary This company is a leading producer of filters for the health care, aerospace, microelectronics and other industries.

Key Stock Statistics (Source S&P, Vickers, company reports)

52-Wk Range	$49.00–30.58	S&P Oper. EPS 2007**E**	1.75	Market Capitalization(B)	$4.596	Beta	1.52
Trailing 12-Month EPS	$1.68	S&P Oper. EPS 2008**E**	1.95	Yield (%)	1.28	S&P 3-Yr. Proj. EPS CAGR(%)	15.00
Trailing 12-Month P/E	22.3	P/E on S&P Oper. EPS 2007**E**	21.4	Dividend Rate/Share	$0.48	S&P Credit Rating	BBB
$10K Invested 5 Yrs Ago	$21,495	Common Shares Outstg. (M)	122.6	Institutional Ownership (%)	86		

Price Performance

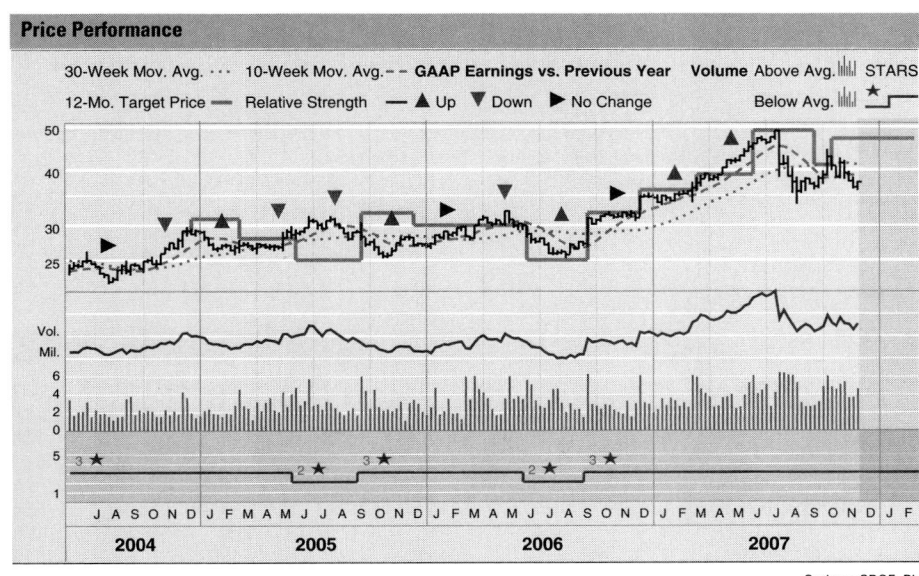

30-Week Mov. Avg. ··· 10-Week Mov. Avg. -- **GAAP Earnings vs. Previous Year** Volume Above Avg. STARS
12-Mo. Target Price — Relative Strength — ▲ Up ▼ Down ▶ No Change Below Avg.

Options: CBOE, Ph

Analysis prepared by **Stewart Scharf** on October 08, 2007, when the stock traded at **$ 42.96**.

Highlights

➤ We expect sales to advance about 6% in local currency in FY 08 (Jul.), and near 10% after foreign exchange, with general industrial driven by systems sales in the municipal water and industrial manufacturing markets. BioPharm sales should remain strong while aerospace returns to its mid-single digit historical growth rate. We see medical sales unchanged and expect microelectronics to remain soft before picking up later in FY 08.

➤ We foresee gross margins expanding by about 100 basis points in FY 08, from 47% in FY 07, based on better pricing in life sciences, as well as PLL's facilities rationalization program and better systems profits despite carrying lower margins. We expect operating margins (EBIT) to widen from 14.3% of sales in FY 07, on improved productivity and cost-cutting initiatives.

➤ As of early October 2007, PLL had not reported FY 07 EPS due to a pending auditors' review and restatements related to the understatement of taxes. We project FY 08 EPS of $1.95, advancing 18%, to $2.30 for FY 09.

Investment Rationale/Risk

➤ Our hold opinion is based on our valuation models and our view of favorable global market trends as PLL focuses on cost reductions during a transitional period that includes the pending restatement of financial statements due to the understatement of tax payments.

➤ Risks to our recommendation and target price include an extended cyclical downturn in semiconductors, negative foreign currency translations, and a significant rise in raw material costs. In addition, corporate governance practices are a concern to us as PLL believes it may have one or more material weaknesses in its internal controls over financial reporting, while at least one related party transaction appears to have involved the CEO.

➤ Our relative valuation targets a value of $45, using a P/E of 23X our FY 08 EPS estimate, near PLL's five-year historical forward average. Our intrinsic value estimate of $49 is based on our DCF model, which assumes a terminal growth rate of 3.5% and a cost of capital of 8.5%. Blending these metrics, our 12-month target price is $47.

Qualitative Risk Assessment

LOW	MEDIUM	HIGH

Our risk assessment reflects the historically cyclical semiconductor sector, exposure to foreign markets and currency swings, and certain concerns that we have related to corporate governance practices. This is offset by our view of PLL's reduced debt levels and strong cash generation.

Quantitative Evaluations

S&P Quality Ranking B+

D	C	B-	B	B+	A-	A	A+

Relative Strength Rank MODERATE

57

LOWEST = 1   HIGHEST = 99

Revenue/Earnings Data

Revenue (Million $)

	1Q	2Q	3Q	4Q	Year
2007	499.3	544.9	559.4	--	--
2006	431.2	478.4	510.0	597.3	2,017
2005	414.7	469.5	493.5	524.5	1,902
2004	374.3	428.1	463.9	504.5	1,771
2003	332.2	388.5	421.5	471.4	1,614
2002	274.1	285.4	302.4	428.9	1,291

Earnings Per Share ($)

2007	0.20	0.45	0.54	E0.50	E1.75
2006	0.20	0.26	0.20	0.50	1.16
2005	0.17	0.26	0.35	0.34	1.12
2004	0.19	0.20	0.37	0.44	1.20
2003	-0.19	0.25	0.33	0.44	0.83
2002	0.16	0.15	0.21	0.07	0.59

Fiscal year ended Jul. 31. Next earnings report expected: NA. EPS Estimates based on S&P Operating Earnings; historical GAAP earnings are as reported.

Dividend Data (Dates: mm/dd Payment Date: mm/dd/yy)

Amount ($)	Date Decl.	Ex-Div. Date	Stk. of Record	Payment Date
0.120	01/11	01/24	01/26	02/19/07
0.120	04/11	04/23	04/25	05/09/07
0.120	09/21	10/03	10/05	10/19/07
0.120	10/15	10/25	10/29	11/12/07

Dividends have been paid since 1974. Source: Company reports.

Pall Corp

Business Summary October 08, 2007

CORPORATE OVERVIEW. Pall Corp. is a global producer of filters for health care, aerospace and industrial markets. Pall divides these markets into the following subsegments: Medical and BioPharmaceuticals (Life Sciences), General Industrial, Aerospace & Transportation (formed in early FY 07 by integrating the sales and marketing teams of Aerospace and Commercial OEMs), and Microelectronics (the Industrial business). The company's Industrial group includes machinery and equipment, food and beverage, fuels and chemicals, power generation, and municipal water.

The Industrial segment (61% of segment revenues in FY 06; $166 million in profits) makes filters and separation products for three markets. Aerospace (16% of the segment; $32 million in profits) includes both commercial and military markets. General Industrial (63%; $72 million in profits) produces filters for the aluminum, paper, automobile, oil, gas, chemical, petrochemical and power industries. Microelectronics (21%; $63 million in profits) makes products for the semiconductor, data storage and photographic film industries. PLL noted that over $300 million in FY 06 sales were derived from water filtration, with municipalities accounting for 22%. Consumer electronics accounted for about 40% of division sales in FY 07, up from 25% in 2000.

The Life Sciences segment contributed 39% of total revenues ($142 million in operating profits) in FY 06 (Jul.). The BioPharmaceuticals division makes filter products used in the development of drugs, and food and beverage filters that help produce yeast- and bacteria-free water. The rapidly growing blood division offers hospitals and blood centers blood filters that reduce leukocyte (white cells) and other bloodborne viral contaminants, such as bacteria. Biopharmaceutical sales accounted for 44% of the segment's total sales in FY 06 ($88 million), while medical products (blood and cardiovascular filtration) accounted for 56% ($54 million). PLL estimates the market potential for medical filters at $4.3 billion.

In FY 06, sales were: Western Hemisphere, 40%; Europe 36%; and Asia 24%.

In June 2005, the company expanded its global strategic alliance with GE Infrastructure, Water & Process Technologies, a unit of General Electric (GE; NYSE).

The company incurred a charge of $0.14 a share in FY 06 related to its repatriation of $400 million in foreign earnings.

Company Financials Fiscal Year Ended Jul. 31

Per Share Data ($)	2006	2005	2004	2003	2002	2001	2000	1999	1998	1997
Tangible Book Value	7.21	6.73	6.21	5.16	NM	6.29	5.41	5.09	5.32	5.84
Cash Flow	1.92	1.85	1.90	1.51	1.19	1.53	1.68	1.01	1.33	1.03
Earnings	1.16	1.12	1.20	0.83	0.59	0.95	1.18	0.41	0.75	0.53
S&P Core Earnings	1.22	1.13	1.16	0.70	0.42	0.83	NA	NA	NA	NA
Dividends	0.53	0.38	0.27	0.36	0.52	0.68	0.50	0.64	0.61	0.54
Payout Ratio	46%	34%	23%	43%	88%	71%	42%	156%	81%	102%
Prices:High	35.57	31.52	29.80	27.00	24.48	26.25	25.00	26.19	26.63	26.13
Prices:Low	25.26	25.21	22.00	15.01	14.68	17.50	17.13	15.75	19.38	19.50
P/E Ratio:High	31	28	25	33	41	28	21	64	36	49
P/E Ratio:Low	22	23	18	18	25	18	15	38	26	37
Income Statement Analysis (Million $)										
Revenue	2,017	1,902	1,771	1,614	1,291	1,235	1,224	1,147	1,087	1,062
Operating Income	341	337	320	299	215	256	274	160	216	182
Depreciation	95.7	90.9	88.9	83.9	74.0	71.5	63.4	74.8	73.1	62.8
Interest Expense	23.0	26.0	20.5	24.4	14.3	16.6	14.1	18.4	7.87	2.84
Pretax Income	210	181	198	143	100.0	150	188	58.9	135	86.1
Effective Tax Rate	30.8%	22.2%	23.4%	27.9%	26.7%	21.5%	22.2%	12.6%	30.6%	21.8%
Net Income	145	141	152	103	73.2	118	147	51.5	93.6	67.3
S&P Core Earnings	153	142	148	87.4	52.1	102	NA	NA	NA	NA
Balance Sheet & Other Financial Data (Million $)										
Cash	318	165	199	127	105	54.9	81.0	86.7	12.1	18.0
Current Assets	1,377	1,160	1,070	938	916	779	753	744	602	607
Total Assets	2,553	2,265	2,140	2,017	2,027	1,549	1,507	1,488	1,347	1,266
Current Liabilities	531	457	419	421	438	314	438	558	394	301
Long Term Debt	640	510	489	490	620	359	224	117	112	62.1
Common Equity	1,179	1,140	1,054	935	820	770	761	731	766	825
Total Capital	1,826	1,660	1,559	1,439	1,478	1,149	1,006	869	899	915
Capital Expenditures	96.0	86.2	61.3	62.2	69.9	77.8	66.5	71.2	85.1	88.6
Cash Flow	241	232	241	187	147	190	210	126	167	130
Current Ratio	2.6	2.5	2.6	2.2	2.1	2.5	1.7	1.3	1.5	2.0
% Long Term Debt of Capitalization	35.0	30.7	31.3	34.0	41.9	31.2	22.3	13.4	12.4	6.8
% Net Income of Revenue	7.2	7.4	8.6	6.4	5.7	9.6	12.0	4.5	8.6	6.3
% Return on Assets	6.0	6.3	7.3	5.1	NA	7.7	9.8	3.6	7.2	5.5
% Return on Equity	12.5	12.8	15.2	11.8	NA	15.4	19.7	6.9	11.8	8.6

Data as orig reptd.; bef. results of disc opers/spec. items. Per share data adj. for stk. divs.; EPS diluted. E-Estimated. NA-Not Available. NM-Not Meaningful. NR-Not Ranked. UR-Under Review.

Office: 2200 Northern Boulevard, East Hills, NY 11548.
Telephone: 516-484-5400.
Email: invrel@pall.com
Website: http://www.pall.com

Chrmn, Pres & CEO: E. Krasnoff
COO: D. Stevens
SVP, Secy & General Counsel: M. Bartlett
CFO & Treas: L. McDermott

Investor Contact: P. Iannucci (866-898-7255)
Board Members: D. J. Carroll, Jr., C. W. Grise, J. H. Haskell, Jr., U. Haynes, Jr., E. Krasnoff, D. Longstreet, E. W. Martin, Jr., K. L. Plourde, H. Shelley, E. L. Snyder, E. Travaglianti, J. D. Watson

Founded: 1946
Domicile: New York
Employees: 10,828

Parker-Hannifin Corp

STANDARD &POOR'S

S&P Recommendation BUY ★★★★☆

Price	12-Mo. Target Price	Investment Style
$76.48 (as of Nov 23, 2007)	$84.00	Large-Cap Blend

GICS Sector Industrials
Sub-Industry Industrial Machinery

Summary This company is a global maker of industrial pumps, valves and hydraulics. Its products are used in everything from jet engines to trucks and autos and utility turbines.

Key Stock Statistics (Source S&P, Vickers, company reports)

52-Wk Range	$86.56– 50.41	S&P Oper. EPS 2008**E**	5.17	Market Capitalization(B)	$13.327	Beta	1.42
Trailing 12-Month EPS	$4.83	S&P Oper. EPS 2009**E**	5.65	Yield (%)	1.10	S&P 3-Yr. Proj. EPS CAGR(%)	9.00
Trailing 12-Month P/E	15.8	P/E on S&P Oper. EPS 2008**E**	14.8	Dividend Rate/Share	$0.84	S&P Credit Rating	A
$10K Invested 5 Yrs Ago	$26,327	Common Shares Outstg. (M)	174.3	Institutional Ownership (%)	84		

Price Performance

30-Week Mov. Avg. ···   10-Week Mov. Avg. --   **GAAP Earnings vs. Previous Year**   Volume Above Avg. STARS
12-Mo. Target Price —   Relative Strength —   ▲ Up   ▼ Down   ► No Change   Below Avg.

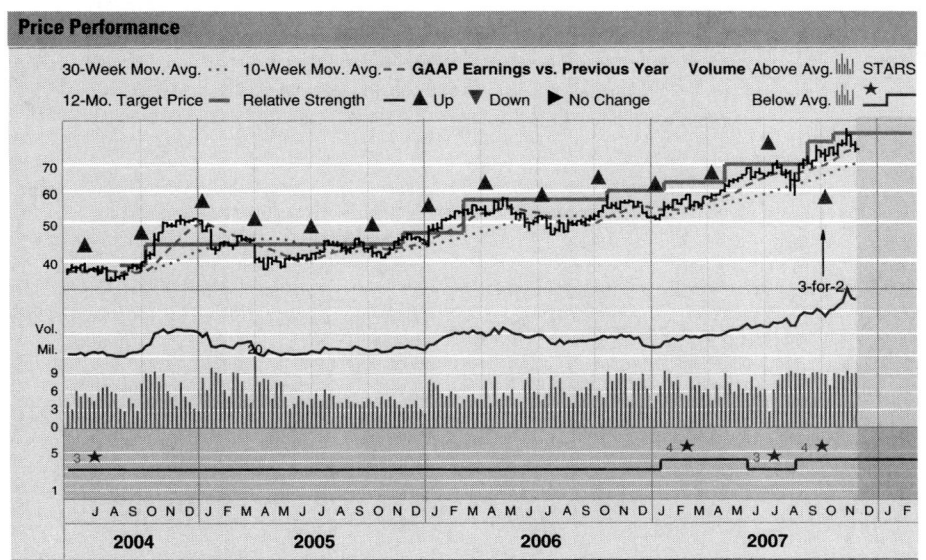

Options: ASE, CBOE, Ph

Analysis prepared by **Richard Tortoriello** on October 22, 2007, when the stock traded at **$ 75.70**.

Highlights

➤ We anticipate overall FY 08 (Jun.) revenue growth of 4%, with about half coming from acquisitions and favorable foreign exchange rates. We see growth driven primarily by the International Industrial and Aerospace segments, reflecting our view of solid international demand for industrial equipment and a very strong global aerospace cycle.

➤ Based on our projections of volume growth, a better product mix due to increased sales of higher-margin aircraft components, and improved operating efficiencies from ongoing cost containment programs, we expect segment profit margins to improve to 14.2% in FY 08 from 13.8% in FY 07.

➤ In August 2007, PH said it would undertake an accelerated repurchase of $500 million of common stock, or 4.6% of shares outstanding at the time of the announcement. We forecast an EPS increase of 11% in FY 08, to $5.17 (as adjusted), versus $4.67 reported in FY 07. For FY 09, we project a further 9.3% increase, to $5.65. We estimate FY 08 free cash flow (cash flow from operations less capital expenditures) per share of about 90% of EPS, and we expect continued share repurchases and dividend increases.

Investment Rationale/Risk

➤ Although we see weakness in the automotive, heavy truck, and residential housing markets affecting PH's orders, we continue to project very strong growth in its international industrial business segment. In addition, we view the aerospace cycle as strong, and with commercial airplane orders outpacing deliveries, and backlogs at aerospace OEMs expanding, we expect the solid cycle to continue for several years. We also note that PH's return on invested capital (after-tax operating earnings as a percent of debt plus equity) rose to 15% in FY 07, versus 12.9% in FY 06 and 13.9% in FY 05.

➤ Risks to our recommendation and target price include declines in global economic growth, a downturn in the aerospace market, and the potential for production and other problems at PH.

➤ Our 12-month target price of $84 is based on a P/E of about 15X our FY 09 EPS estimate. This is above PH's 10-year historical average forward P/E of 13.5X, but below historical highs of 21X. Given our belief that we are late in the industrial production economic cycle but still early in the aerospace cycle, we believe a near average historical P/E is appropriate for the shares.

Qualitative Risk Assessment

LOW	**MEDIUM**	HIGH

Our risk assessment reflects the highly cyclical nature of the company's industrial and aviation markets, volatile energy costs and a competitive environment. This is offset by our view of PH's favorable earnings and dividend track record.

Quantitative Evaluations

S&P Quality Ranking   A-

D	C	B-	B	B+	**A-**	A	A+

Relative Strength Rank   STRONG

81

LOWEST = 1   HIGHEST = 99

Revenue/Earnings Data

Revenue (Million $)

	1Q	2Q	3Q	4Q	Year
2008	2,787	--	--	--	--
2007	2,552	2,511	2,781	2,874	10,718
2006	2,114	2,158	2,498	2,617	9,386
2005	1,947	1,943	2,142	2,211	8,215
2004	1,587	1,621	1,906	1,993	7,107
2003	1,586	1,517	1,647	1,661	6,411

Earnings Per Share ($)

2008	1.33	E1.21	E1.28	E1.36	E5.17
2007	1.17	1.09	1.19	1.23	4.67
2006	0.79	0.71	0.97	1.03	3.52
2005	0.74	0.63	0.79	0.89	3.03
2004	0.32	0.31	0.60	0.70	1.94
2003	0.35	0.21	0.28	0.28	1.12

Fiscal year ended Jun. 30. Next earnings report expected: Mid January. EPS Estimates based on S&P Operating Earnings; historical GAAP earnings are as reported.

Dividend Data (Dates: mm/dd Payment Date: mm/dd/yy)

Amount ($)	Date Decl.	Ex-Div. Date	Stk. of Record	Payment Date
0.260	04/17	05/15	05/17	06/01/07
0.315	08/16	08/23	08/27	09/07/07
3-for-2	08/16	10/02	09/17	10/01/07
0.210	10/24	11/13	11/15	11/30/07

Dividends have been paid since 1949. Source: Company reports.

Please read the Required Disclosures and Analyst Certification on the last page of this report.

The *McGraw-Hill* Companies

Parker-Hannifin Corp

STANDARD &POOR'S

Business Summary October 22, 2007

CORPORATE OVERVIEW. With $10.7 billion in annual revenues in FY 07 (Jun.), Parker-Hannifin is one of the world's largest makers of components that control the flow of industrial fluids. It is also a major global maker of components that move and/or control the operation of a variety of machinery and equipment. In addition to motion control products, PH also produces fluid purification, fluid and fuel control, process instrumentation, air conditioning, refrigeration, electromagnetic shielding, and thermal management products and systems. PH's offerings include a wide range of valves, pumps, hydraulics, filters and related products. The company's components are used in everything from jet engines to medical devices, farm tractors and utility turbines.

Although U.S. markets still account for most of the company's revenues, PH is expanding its overseas presence; in FY 06, international sales accounted for 34% of total revenues.

PH's Industrial segment (73% of FY 06 revenues; 76% of earnings before interest and taxes (EBIT); and 14% EBIT margins) makes valves, pumps, filters, seals and hydraulic components for a broad range of industries, as well as pneumatic and electromechanical components and systems. The company's industrial components are sold to manufacturers (as part of original equipment) and to end users (as replacement parts). Replacement part sales are

generally more profitable than original equipment sales. PH's industrial components are designed for both standard and custom specifications. Custom-made components are typically more profitable than standard components.

Aerospace, PH's most profitable segment (16%; 17%; 15%) primarily makes hydraulic, pneumatic and fuel equipment used in civilian and military airframes and jet engines. It also makes aircraft wheels and brakes for small planes and military aircraft. PH sells aircraft components to aircraft manufacturers as new equipment, and to end-users (such as airlines) as replacement parts. As with industrial components, aircraft-related replacement parts sales are generally more profitable than are original equipment sales.

PH's Climate & Industrial Controls unit (11%; 7%; 9%) makes refrigeration and air conditioning systems and components and fluid control process systems used primarily in the mobile and stationary refrigeration and air conditioning industry.

Company Financials Fiscal Year Ended Jun. 30

Per Share Data ($)	2007	2006	2005	2004	2003	2002	2001	2000	1999	1998
Tangible Book Value	10.69	9.75	9.23	9.39	7.63	8.18	8.95	9.96	8.41	7.79
Cash Flow	6.45	5.07	4.50	3.34	2.57	2.37	3.53	3.44	3.12	3.01
Earnings	4.67	3.52	3.03	1.94	1.12	0.75	1.99	2.21	1.89	1.92
S&P Core Earnings	4.77	3.83	3.08	2.00	0.61	0.37	1.19	NA	NA	NA
Dividends	0.69	0.61	0.52	0.51	0.49	0.48	0.47	0.34	0.43	0.40
Payout Ratio	15%	17%	17%	26%	44%	64%	23%	15%	23%	21%
Prices:High	86.56	58.67	50.82	52.28	39.87	36.59	33.40	36.00	34.29	35.08
Prices:Low	50.41	43.44	37.87	34.49	23.88	23.01	20.27	20.67	19.67	17.71
P/E Ratio:High	19	17	17	27	36	49	17	16	18	18
P/E Ratio:Low	11	12	12	18	21	31	10	9	10	9

Income Statement Analysis (Million $)	2007	2006	2005	2004	2003	2002	2001	2000	1999	1998
Revenue	10,718	9,386	8,215	7,107	6,411	6,149	5,980	5,355	4,959	4,633
Operating Income	1,513	1,263	1,100	817	639	628	836	829	741	733
Depreciation	295	281	265	253	259	282	265	206	202	183
Interest Expense	83.4	75.8	67.0	73.4	81.6	82.0	90.4	59.2	63.7	52.8
Pretax Income	1,159	900	756	494	297	218	534	562	478	504
Effective Tax Rate	28.4%	NM	27.6%	30.0%	34.0%	40.3%	35.5%	34.5%	35.0%	35.9%
Net Income	830	638	548	346	196	130	344	368	311	323
S&P Core Earnings	846	694	557	357	107	65.0	204	NA	NA	NA

Balance Sheet & Other Financial Data (Million $)	2007	2006	2005	2004	2003	2002	2001	2000	1999	1998
Cash	173	172	336	184	246	46.0	23.7	68.5	33.3	30.5
Current Assets	3,386	3,139	2,786	2,537	2,397	2,236	2,196	2,153	1,775	1,780
Total Assets	8,441	8,173	6,899	6,257	5,986	5,733	5,338	4,646	3,706	3,525
Current Liabilities	1,925	1,681	1,336	1,260	1,424	1,360	1,413	1,186	755	989
Long Term Debt	1,087	1,059	938	954	966	1,089	857	702	725	513
Common Equity	4,712	4,241	3,340	2,982	2,521	2,584	2,529	2,309	1,854	1,683
Total Capital	5,913	5,419	4,314	4,015	3,508	3,750	3,518	3,089	2,610	2,226
Capital Expenditures	238	198	157	142	158	207	345	230	230	237
Cash Flow	1,125	919	813	599	455	412	609	575	513	506
Current Ratio	1.8	1.9	2.1	2.0	1.7	1.6	1.6	1.8	2.3	1.8
% Long Term Debt of Capitalization	18.4	19.6	21.8	23.8	27.5	29.0	24.4	22.7	27.8	23.0
% Net Income of Revenue	7.7	6.8	6.7	4.9	3.1	2.1	5.8	6.9	6.3	7.0
% Return on Assets	10.0	8.5	8.3	5.6	3.3	2.3	6.9	8.8	8.6	9.9
% Return on Equity	18.5	16.8	17.3	12.6	7.7	5.1	14.2	17.7	17.6	20.0

Data as orig reptd.; bef. results of disc opers/spec. items. Per share data adj. for stk. divs.; EPS diluted. E-Estimated. NA-Not Available. NM-Not Meaningful. NR-Not Ranked. UR-Under Review.

Office: 6035 Parkland Boulevard, Cleveland, OH 44124-4141.
Telephone: 216-896-3000.
Website: http://www.parker.com
Chrmn, Pres & CEO: D.E. Washkewicz

EVP & CFO: T.K. Pistell
VP & Treas: P. Huggins
VP, Secy & General Counsel: T.A. Piraino, Jr.
VP & Cntlr: D.A. Dennis

Investor Contact: C. Groudle (216-896-3000)
Board Members: L. S. Harty, W. E. Kassling, R. J. Kohlhepp, G. Mazzaupi, K. Mueller, C. Obourn, J. Scaminace, W. R. Schmitt, M. I. Tambakeras, D. E. Washkewicz

Founded: 1924
Domicile: Ohio
Employees: 57,338

STANDARD &POOR'S

Patterson Companies Inc

S&P Recommendation HOLD ★★★☆☆	Price	12-Mo. Target Price	Investment Style
	$32.53 (as of Nov 29, 2007)	$34.00	Large-Cap Growth

GICS Sector Health Care
Sub-Industry Health Care Distributors

Summary This company is one of the largest distributors of dental supplies in North America and also sells veterinary supplies and rehabilitative equipment.

Key Stock Statistics (Source S&P, Vickers, company reports)

52-Wk Range	$40.08– 28.32	S&P Oper. EPS 2008E	1.70	Market Capitalization(B)	$4.553	Beta	-0.22
Trailing 12-Month EPS	$1.60	S&P Oper. EPS 2009E	1.90	Yield (%)	Nil	S&P 3-Yr. Proj. EPS CAGR(%)	13.00
Trailing 12-Month P/E	20.3	P/E on S&P Oper. EPS 2008E	19.1	Dividend Rate/Share	Nil	S&P Credit Rating	NA
$10K Invested 5 Yrs Ago	$14,253	Common Shares Outstg. (M)	139.9	Institutional Ownership (%)	69		

Price Performance

30-Week Mov. Avg. · · · 10-Week Mov. Avg. - - **GAAP Earnings vs. Previous Year** Volume Above Avg. STARS
12-Mo. Target Price — Relative Strength — ▲ Up ▼ Down ▶ No Change Below Avg. ★

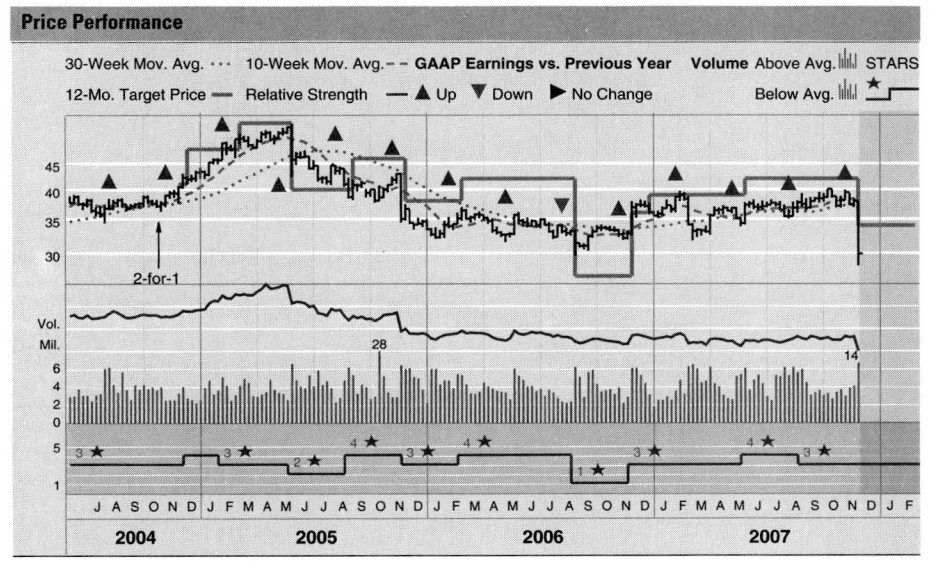

Options: CBOE, Ph

Analysis prepared by **Phillip M. Seligman** on November 29, 2007, when the stock traded at **$ 32.16**.

Highlights

➤ We project PDCO's sales will rise 7.6% in FY 08 (Apr.), above FY 07's 7% growth. We forecast dental equipment sales to remain soft until PDCO execute's better amid competition, and we see signs of a pick-up in consumers' discretionary spending. Moreover, while we see PDCO benefiting from upgrades to existing CEREC dental restorative systems and favorable FY 08 second-half sales comps for the product, given declines in CEREC sales in FY 07's second half, we think the pending launch of a rival system may hamper CEREC sales to prospective first-time buyers. However, we expect sales of consumable dental supplies to remain healthy.

➤ We forecast sales growth of the Medical segment will accelerate, aided by salesforce expansion. But we look for Veterinary segment sales, while still healthy in our view, to decelerate on the "law of large numbers." We now expect the FY 08 operating margin to expand by 30 basis points--to 12.3%--mainly as the addition of freight surcharges by the Medical segment and operating leverage outweigh the cost of internal investments.

➤ We look for EPS of $1.70 in FY 08 and $1.90 for FY 09.

Investment Rationale/Risk

➤ We see strong dental supply market fundamentals over the long term, driven by an aging population, increased cosmetic dentistry, and a dentist shortage (creating a need for equipment that increases their productivity). Meanwhile, we view PDCO's attribution of delayed capital spending by dentists due to certain economic conditions as one reason for the October quarter's 2% decline in its dental equipment sales. Still, rival Henry Schein's (HSIC: Hold; $58) 24.7% September-quarter dental equipment revenue growth suggests to us that PDCO's problem is company-specific. We are encouraged on the strength we see in its Veterinary and Medical segments and improving firmwide operating margins. But we see limited stock appreciation potential until we discern a turnaround in its dental equipment business.

➤ Risks to our recommendation and target price primarily include a worse than expected performance in PDCO's operating segments, leading to deteriorating profit margins and EPS growth.

➤ Our 12-month target price of $34 is based on a P/E of 19X our calendar 2008 EPS estimate of $1.80, below PDCO's 10-year average historical forward P/E of 22X.

Qualitative Risk Assessment

LOW	**MEDIUM**	HIGH

Our risk assessment is based on our view of PDCO's strong long-term record of earnings growth, offset by historically high valuation multiples relative to the overall stock market. Given high multiples, we view the stock as vulnerable to price declines in the event of an earnings disappointment. For example, this occurred when revenue and EPS posted for the quarter ending October 31, 2007 were below Street and our estimates.

Quantitative Evaluations

S&P Quality Ranking B+

D	C	B-	B	**B+**	A-	A	A+

Relative Strength Rank WEAK

26

LOWEST = 1   HIGHEST = 99

Revenue/Earnings Data

Revenue (Million $)

	1Q	2Q	3Q	4Q	Year
2008	701.4	742.0	--	--	--
2007	655.5	694.3	709.5	739.1	2,798
2006	595.9	641.7	682.4	695.2	2,615
2005	577.9	578.2	638.0	627.3	2,421
2004	433.3	477.5	521.2	537.4	1,969
2003	387.7	400.8	421.1	447.3	1,657

Earnings Per Share ($)

2008	0.35	0.39	E0.48	E0.52	E1.70
2007	0.30	0.35	0.43	0.44	1.51
2006	0.31	0.32	0.39	0.41	1.43
2005	0.29	0.31	0.36	0.36	1.32
2004	0.22	0.26	0.29	0.33	1.09
2003	0.19	0.20	0.22	0.25	0.85

Fiscal year ended Apr. 30. Next earnings report expected: Late February. EPS Estimates based on S&P Operating Earnings; historical GAAP earnings are as reported.

Dividend Data

No cash dividends have been paid.

Patterson Companies Inc

STANDARD
&POOR'S

Business Summary November 29, 2007

CORPORATE OVERVIEW. Patterson Companies (formerly Patterson Dental), one of two large distributors of dental products in North America, is a full-service supplier to dentists, dental laboratories, institutions, physicians, and other health care professionals. Through the July 2001 acquisition of J.A. Webster, PDCO became the second largest U.S. distributor of companion-pet veterinary supplies. Also, through the August 2003 acquisition of AbilityOne Products Corp. (now Patterson Medical), PDCO became the largest distributor of non-wheelchair assistive products for patient rehabilitation in the U.S. and the U.K.

PDCO's Patterson Dental subsidiary, 73.8% of FY 07 (Apr.) sales, versus 75.2% in FY 06, provides a broad range of consumables (X-ray film, restorative materials, and sterilization products), advanced technology dental equipment, practice management software, and office forms and stationery.

Consumables and printed products accounted for 55.9% of dental supply sales in FY 07, slightly above FY 06's 55.5%. The company offers its own private label line of anesthetics, instruments, preventative and restorative products, as well as brand name supplies, including X-ray film, protective clothing, toothbrushes, and other dental accessories. Printed products include insurance and billing forms, stationery, appointment books, and other stock office supply products.

PDCO offers a wide range of dental equipment, which accounted for 34.6% of dental supply sales in FY 07, down from 35.8% in FY 06. The product line includes X-ray machines, sterilizers, dental chairs, dental lights and diagnostic equipment. Two of PDCO's fastest growing product lines are the CEREC chairside ceramic dental-restorative system and digital radiography (X-ray) systems. However, sales of CEREC slowed in FY 07. Not only do we think that dentists were awaiting the launch of a rival's system, but, in addition, the manufacturer of CEREC had production glitches.

Other products, which accounted for 9.5% of dental supply sales in FY 07 and 8.7% in FY 06, include software services, equipment installation and repair, dental office design, and equipment financing.

Company Financials Fiscal Year Ended Apr. 30

Per Share Data ($)	2007	2006	2005	2004	2003	2002	2001	2000	1999	1998
Tangible Book Value	3.70	2.73	1.95	0.76	3.66	2.85	2.64	2.08	1.62	1.22
Cash Flow	1.70	1.60	1.52	1.27	0.94	0.80	0.65	0.55	0.43	0.36
Earnings	1.51	1.43	1.32	1.09	0.85	0.70	0.57	0.48	0.37	0.31
S&P Core Earnings	1.51	1.39	1.30	1.08	0.84	0.70	0.57	NA	NA	NA
Dividends	Nil	Nil	Nil	Nil	Nil	Nil	Nil	Nil	Nil	Nil
Payout Ratio	Nil	Nil	Nil	Nil	Nil	Nil	Nil	Nil	Nil	Nil
Calendar Year	2006	2005	2004	2003	2002	2001	2000	1999	1998	1997
Prices:High	38.28	53.85	44.20	35.75	27.56	21.03	17.25	12.53	11.59	7.63
Prices:Low	29.61	33.21	29.70	17.71	19.00	13.75	8.13	8.28	7.03	4.46
P/E Ratio:High	25	38	33	33	32	30	31	26	31	25
P/E Ratio:Low	20	23	22	16	22	20	14	17	19	14

Income Statement Analysis (Million $)

	2007	2006	2005	2004	2003	2002	2001	2000	1999	1998
Revenue	2,798	2,615	2,421	1,969	1,657	1,416	1,156	1,040	879	778
Operating Income	361	347	329	262	192	161	391	205	86.6	72.7
Depreciation	25.5	23.7	26.9	19.4	12.8	14.3	11.1	10.2	8.20	7.46
Interest Expense	14.2	13.4	15.1	9.60	0.07	0.11	0.12	0.13	0.52	0.67
Pretax Income	330	317	293	240	186	152	122	103	79.7	65.7
Effective Tax Rate	36.8%	37.4%	37.4%	37.6%	37.6%	37.4%	37.4%	37.4%	37.4%	38.0%
Net Income	208	198	184	150	116	95.3	76.5	64.5	49.9	40.8
S&P Core Earnings	208	194	180	147	115	95.3	76.5	NA	NA	NA

Balance Sheet & Other Financial Data (Million $)

	2007	2006	2005	2004	2003	2002	2001	2000	1999	1998
Cash	242	224	233	287	195	126	160	113	78.7	35.6
Current Assets	886	847	800	778	606	529	443	351	287	228
Total Assets	1,940	1,912	1,685	1,589	824	718	549	452	373	316
Current Liabilities	377	410	322	264	184	198	133	113	98.7	94.4
Long Term Debt	130	210	302	480	0.13	Nil	Nil	Nil	1.68	2.74
Common Equity	1,379	1,243	1,015	802	634	514	409	330	265	210
Total Capital	1,563	1,502	1,363	1,325	634	514	409	330	269	215
Capital Expenditures	19.5	49.2	31.5	19.6	11.4	11.1	10.0	15.4	7.09	5.96
Cash Flow	234	222	211	169	129	110	87.6	74.7	58.1	48.2
Current Ratio	2.3	2.1	2.5	2.9	3.3	2.7	3.3	3.1	2.9	2.4
% Long Term Debt of Capitalization	8.3	14.0	22.1	36.2	Nil	Nil	Nil	Nil	0.6	1.2
% Net Income of Revenue	7.4	7.6	7.6	7.6	7.0	6.7	6.6	6.2	5.7	5.2
% Return on Assets	10.8	11.0	11.2	12.4	15.1	15.0	15.3	15.6	14.5	14.5
% Return on Equity	15.9	17.6	20.2	20.8	20.3	20.7	20.7	21.6	21.0	21.9

Data as orig reptd.; bef. results of disc opers/spec. items. Per share data adj. for stk. divs.; EPS diluted. E-Estimated. NA-Not Available. NM-Not Meaningful. NR-Not Ranked. UR-Under Review.

Office: 1031 Mendota Heights Road, St. Paul, MN 55120-1419.
Telephone: 612-686-1600.
Email: investors@pattersondental.com
Website: http://www.pattersondental.com

Chrmn: P.L. Frechette
Pres & CEO: J.W. Wiltz
Investor Contact: R.S. Armstrong (651-686-1600)
EVP, CFO & Treas: R.S. Armstrong

Board Members: J. D. Buck, R. E. Ezerski, P. L. Frechette, A. B. Lacy, C. Reich, E. A. Rudnick, H. C. Slavkin, J. W. Wiltz

Founded: 1877
Domicile: Minnesota
Employees: 6,580

The McGraw-Hill Companies

Paychex Inc

STANDARD &POOR'S

| S&P Recommendation **BUY** ★★★★☆ | Price $38.19 (as of Nov 23, 2007) | 12-Mo. Target Price $48.00 | Investment Style Large-Cap Growth |

GICS Sector Information Technology
Sub-Industry Data Processing & Outsourced Services

Summary Paychex provides payroll accounting services to small and medium size concerns throughout the U.S.

Key Stock Statistics (Source S&P, Vickers, company reports)

52-Wk Range	$47.14–36.08	S&P Oper. EPS 2008E	1.59	Market Capitalization(B)	$14.310	Beta	0.81
Trailing 12-Month EPS	$1.40	S&P Oper. EPS 2009E	1.80	Yield (%)	3.14	S&P 3-Yr. Proj. EPS CAGR(%)	16.00
Trailing 12-Month P/E	27.3	P/E on S&P Oper. EPS 2008E	24.0	Dividend Rate/Share	$1.20	S&P Credit Rating	NA
$10K Invested 5 Yrs Ago	$14,324	Common Shares Outstg. (M)	374.7	Institutional Ownership (%)	72		

Price Performance

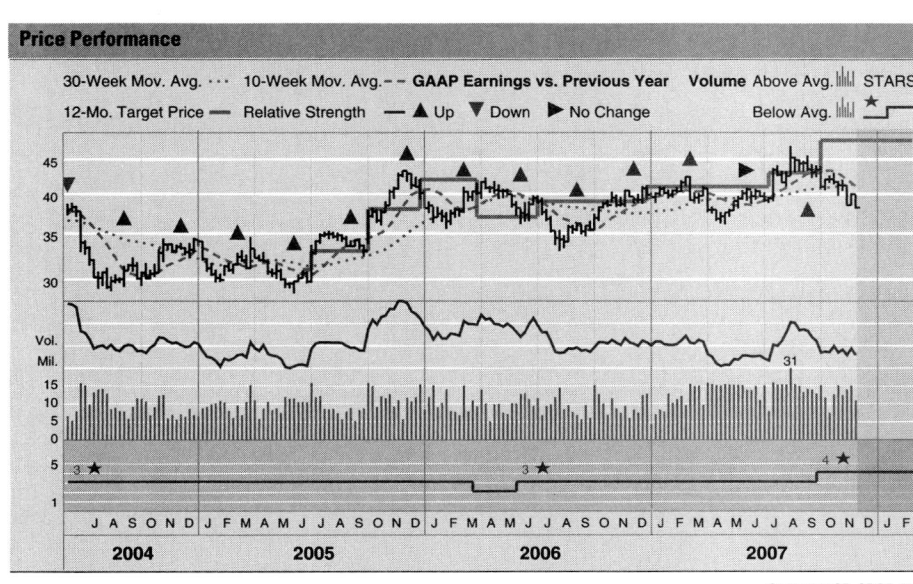

30-Week Mov. Avg. · · · 10-Week Mov. Avg. - - **GAAP Earnings vs. Previous Year** Volume Above Avg. STARS
12-Mo. Target Price — Relative Strength — ▲ Up ▼ Down ► No Change Below Avg. ★

Options: ASE, CBOE, Ph

Analysis prepared by **Dylan Cathers** on September 28, 2007, when the stock traded at **$ 41.00**.

Highlights

➤ We look for revenues to increase 11% in FY 08 (May) and in FY 09. We expect revenues in the Human Resources Services business to increase over 20%, and we look for payroll to increase around 9% in FY 08. Revenue in payroll should be aided by further penetration of add-on services such as Taxpay and direct deposit, higher check volume, and an increased client base. We expect income on funds held for clients to be flat this year, due to lower short-term interest rates.

➤ We look for an operating margin of 40% in FY 08, which would be modestly wider than FY 07. We believe expenses from rising personnel levels and the promotion of new products will be offset by solid cost controls, reduced attrition levels, and high customer retention rates.

➤ In July, PAYX announced a $1 billion share repurchase plan, and it intends to complete the purchases in calendar 2007. This, along with an increased dividend, will adversely affect corporate investment income this year, but the reduced share count should offset this decrease. We estimate EPS in FY 08 of $1.59, up from operating EPS of $1.41 in FY 07. For FY 09, we forecast EPS of $1.80.

Investment Rationale/Risk

➤ We recently upgraded our recommendation to buy from hold on valuation. We see the company's earnings benefiting from solid execution, higher retention rates, falling attrition, and strong profitability.

➤ Risks to our recommendation and target price stem from volatility in the small to medium sized business environment, and the impact of competition on pricing and margins. Automatic Data Processing (ADP: strong buy, $46) is the leader in the payroll processing space, and is promoting a payroll processing and tax filing software solution coupled with Microsoft's small business software. We see this product potentially affecting Paychex's growth in the small office market.

➤ Using our calendar 2008 EPS estimate of $1.68, we blend valuations using a peer-based P/E multiple of 28.6X, a P/E to growth (PEG) ratio of 2.05X, and an estimated three-year growth rate of 14%, to arrive at our 12-month target price of $48. This is a slight premium to its peers, which includes comparable data processing and outsourcing companies that offer solutions that compete with PAYX.

Qualitative Risk Assessment

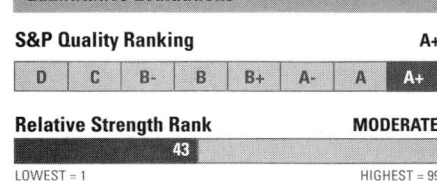

| LOW | MEDIUM | HIGH |

Our risk assessment reflects what we see as the company's strong balance sheet and regular cash inflows, offset by the highly competitive nature of the outsourcing industry as well as the threat of new entrants into the human resources segment.

Quantitative Evaluations

S&P Quality Ranking A+

| D | C | B- | B | B+ | A- | A | **A+** |

Relative Strength Rank MODERATE

43

LOWEST = 1 HIGHEST = 99

Revenue/Earnings Data

Revenue (Million $)

	1Q	2Q	3Q	4Q	Year
2008	507.1	--	--	--	--
2007	459.4	455.0	485.3	487.4	1,887
2006	403.7	399.8	430.6	440.5	1,675
2005	345.0	347.3	373.9	379.0	1,445
2004	309.3	312.1	342.6	330.4	1,294
2003	252.7	268.8	287.8	289.8	1,099

Earnings Per Share ($)

2008	0.40	E0.38	E0.40	E0.41	E1.59
2007	0.35	0.35	0.33	0.32	1.39
2006	0.30	0.30	0.30	0.32	1.22
2005	0.23	0.23	0.24	0.27	0.97
2004	0.21	0.21	0.21	0.16	0.80
2003	0.20	0.20	0.19	0.19	0.78

Fiscal year ended May 31. Next earnings report expected: Late December. EPS Estimates based on S&P Operating Earnings; historical GAAP earnings are as reported.

Dividend Data (Dates: mm/dd Payment Date: mm/dd/yy)

Amount ($)	Date Decl.	Ex-Div. Date	Stk. of Record	Payment Date
0.210	01/19	01/30	02/01	02/15/07
0.210	04/12	04/27	05/01	05/15/07
0.300	07/12	07/30	08/01	08/15/07
0.300	10/03	10/30	11/01	11/15/07

Dividends have been paid since 1988. Source: Company reports.

Please read the Required Disclosures and Analyst Certification on the last page of this report.

The McGraw-Hill Companies

Paychex Inc

STANDARD
&POOR'S

Business Summary September 28, 2007

CORPORATE OVERVIEW. Paychex is a leading provider of payroll processing, human resources and benefits services. The company was founded in 1971, and began by serving the payroll accounting services of businesses with fewer than 200 employees. It currently has more than 100 locations and serves over 561,000 clients throughout the U.S.

The company's payroll segment prepares payroll checks, earnings statements, internal accounting records, all federal, state and local payroll tax returns, and provides collection and remittance of payroll obligations. PAYX's tax filing and payment services provide automatic tax filing and payment, preparation and submission of tax returns, plus deposit of funds with tax authorities. Employee Payment Services provides a variety of ways for businesses to pay employees.

In our opinion, PAYX has shown an ability to expand its client base and increase the use of ancillary services, which we believe will lead to consistent growth for its mainstay payroll segment.

The Human Resources/Professional Employer Organization (HRS/PEO) segment provides employee benefits, management and human resources ser-

vices. The Paychex Administrative Services (PAS) product offers businesses a bundled package that includes payroll, employer compliance, and human resource and employee benefit administration. PAYX also offers 401(k) plan services.

MARKET PROFILE. The market for HR services totaled $88.7 billion worldwide in calendar 2006, according to market researcher IDC. Between 2006 and 2011, IDC expects this area to grow at a compound annual growth rate (CAGR) of 8.3%, with the market in the U.S. increasing at a CAGR of 9.4% from $44.9 billion in 2006. For the more narrow Processing services market, where we believe Automatic Data Processing is the market leader, IDC sees a CAGR of 6.8% in the U.S. between 2006 and 2011. In contrast, in the market for business process outsourcing (BPO) services, IDC expects a CAGR of 13.7% over the same time frame.

Company Financials Fiscal Year Ended May 31

Per Share Data ($)	2007	2006	2005	2004	2003	2002	2001	2000	1999	1998
Tangible Book Value	3.87	3.12	2.40	1.88	1.55	2.43	2.00	1.50	1.18	0.90
Cash Flow	1.54	1.39	1.13	1.02	0.89	0.80	0.75	0.57	0.43	0.33
Earnings	1.39	1.22	0.97	0.80	0.78	0.73	0.68	0.51	0.37	0.28
S&P Core Earnings	1.41	1.17	0.93	0.80	0.72	0.66	0.65	NA	NA	NA
Dividends	0.61	0.51	0.47	0.44	0.33	0.33	0.22	0.18	0.12	0.08
Payout Ratio	44%	42%	48%	55%	56%	45%	32%	35%	32%	29%
Calendar Year	2006	2005	2004	2003	2002	2001	2000	1999	1998	1997
Prices:High	42.37	43.37	39.12	40.54	42.15	51.00	61.25	29.92	24.47	15.33
Prices:Low	32.98	28.60	28.83	23.76	20.39	28.27	24.17	15.71	13.37	7.56
P/E Ratio:High	30	36	40	51	54	70	90	59	66	55
P/E Ratio:Low	24	23	30	30	26	39	36	31	36	27

Income Statement Analysis (Million $)

	2007	2006	2005	2004	2003	2002	2001	2000	1999	1998
Revenue	1,887	1,675	1,445	1,294	1,099	955	870	728	597	494
Operating Income	775	716	596	516	444	393	700	283	210	153
Depreciation	73.4	66.5	62.0	82.8	43.4	29.5	26.4	23.9	22.1	18.8
Interest Expense	Nil	Nil	Nil	Nil	Nil	Nil	Nil	Nil	Nil	Nil
Pretax Income	743	675	546	450	432	395	364	275	200	144
Effective Tax Rate	30.7%	31.1%	32.5%	32.6%	32.0%	30.5%	30.0%	31.0%	30.5%	29.1%
Net Income	515	465	369	303	293	275	255	190	139	102
S&P Core Earnings	537	445	353	304	272	252	243	NA	NA	NA

Balance Sheet & Other Financial Data (Million $)

	2007	2006	2005	2004	2003	2002	2001	2000	1999	1998
Cash	79.4	137	281	219	79.9	61.9	45.8	47.1	343	251
Current Assets	4,861	4,444	3,689	3,280	3,033	2,815	2,791	2,363	1,793	1,479
Total Assets	6,247	5,549	4,379	3,950	3,691	2,953	2,907	2,456	1,873	1,550
Current Liabilities	4,237	3,838	2,942	2,722	2,588	2,023	2,144	1,887	1,432	1,216
Long Term Debt	Nil	Nil	Nil	Nil	Nil	Nil	Nil	Nil	Nil	Nil
Common Equity	1,985	1,670	1,411	1,235	1,077	924	745	563	436	330
Total Capital	1,994	1,686	1,429	1,249	1,084	924	745	563	436	330
Capital Expenditures	79.0	81.1	70.7	50.6	60.2	54.4	45.3	32.9	22.1	28.2
Cash Flow	589	531	431	386	337	304	281	214	161	121
Current Ratio	1.1	1.2	1.3	1.2	1.2	1.4	1.3	1.3	1.3	1.2
% Long Term Debt of Capitalization	Nil	Nil	Nil	Nil	Nil	Nil	Nil	Nil	Nil	Nil
% Net Income of Revenue	27.3	27.8	25.5	23.4	26.7	28.7	29.3	26.1	23.3	20.7
% Return on Assets	8.7	9.1	8.9	7.9	8.8	9.4	9.5	8.8	8.1	7.4
% Return on Equity	28.2	30.2	27.9	26.2	29.3	32.6	38.7	38.0	36.3	35.2

Data as orig reptd.; bef. results of disc opers/spec. items. Per share data adj. for stk. divs.; EPS diluted. E-Estimated. NA-Not Available. NM-Not Meaningful. NR-Not Ranked. UR-Under Review.

Office: 911 Panorama Trail South, Rochester, NY 14625-2396.
Telephone: 585-385-6666.
Website: http://www.paychex.com
Chrmn: B.T. Golisano

Pres & CEO: J.J. Judge
SVP, CFO & Secy: J.M. Morphy
VP & Cntlr: M. Janik
Investor Contact: T.J. Allen (585-383-3406)

Board Members: D. J. Flaschen, B. T. Golisano, P. Horsley, G. M. Inman, P. A. Joseph, J. J. Judge, J. M. Tucci, J. M. Velli

Founded: 1979
Domicile: Delaware
Employees: 11,700

Peabody Energy Corp

STANDARD &POOR'S

| **S&P Recommendation** BUY ★★★★☆ | **Price** $52.61 (as of Nov 23, 2007) | **12-Mo. Target Price** $62.00 | **Investment Style** Large-Cap Blend |

GICS Sector Energy
Sub-Industry Coal & Consumable Fuels

Summary BTU is the world's largest private sector coal company, with 10.2 billion tons of coal reserves; its coal fuels about 10% of U.S. electricity generation and 3% of worldwide electricity generation.

Key Stock Statistics (Source S&P, Vickers, company reports)

52-Wk Range	$58.92– 36.20	S&P Oper. EPS 2007E	1.57	Market Capitalization(B)	$13.931	Beta	1.60
Trailing 12-Month EPS	$1.50	S&P Oper. EPS 2008E	1.99	Yield (%)	0.46	S&P 3-Yr. Proj. EPS CAGR(%)	26.00
Trailing 12-Month P/E	35.1	P/E on S&P Oper. EPS 2007E	33.5	Dividend Rate/Share	$0.24	S&P Credit Rating	BB
$10K Invested 5 Yrs Ago	NA	Common Shares Outstg. (M)	264.8	Institutional Ownership (%)	87		

Price Performance

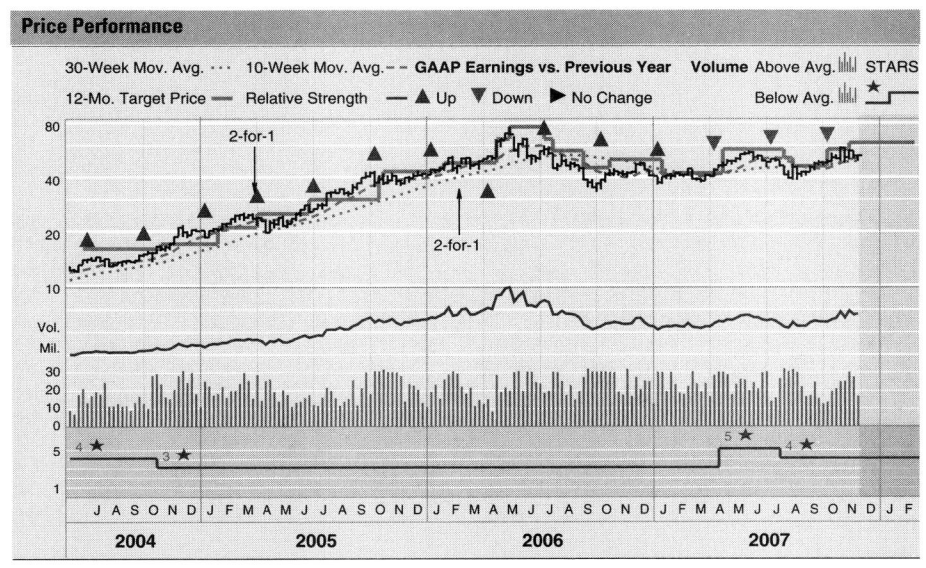

30-Week Mov. Avg. · · · 10-Week Mov. Avg. - - GAAP Earnings vs. Previous Year Volume Above Avg. STARS
12-Mo. Target Price — Relative Strength — ▲ Up ▼ Down ► No Change Below Avg. ★

Options: ASE, CBOE, P, Ph

Analysis prepared by **Christopher Lippincott** on November 16, 2007, when the stock traded at **$ 52.41**.

Highlights

➤ We expect revenues to increase 6% in 2007 and 13% in 2008, led by growth in produced tons sold of 3% in 2007 and 7% in 2008, driven by greater productivity and increased domestic and global demand. We believe BTU should realize higher pricing as supplies tighten due to shipment disruptions, production cutbacks and higher global demand, especially from the Pacific Rim. We are seeing premium prices for shipborne export coal and higher prices for domestic steam coal. We calculate that this should cause BTU's per-ton prices to increase 4% in 2007 and 5% in 2008.

➤ We look for the EBITDA margin to fall to 18% in 2007 as average cost per ton rises 13%. However, we forecast BTU's EBITDA margin to expand to nearly 21% in 2008 due to average cost per ton declining 1.5% and leverage from increasing volume and productivity. BTU is successfully reducing high-cost production, which we believe should help lower per-ton costs. We expect margins to expand, as we project a moderation in fuel and labor cost increases.

➤ We forecast that operating EPS will be $1.57 in 2007 and $1.99 in 2008.

Investment Rationale/Risk

➤ We believe BTU will benefit from improved pricing and demand in 2008, partly offset by shipment delays in Australia and resulting demurrage costs. We see accelerating global energy demand, especially from China and India, and rising costs for competing fuels driving demand. Conversely, the regulatory environment and rail and port congestion will limit supply, in our view. We anticipate this will increase both BTU's volume and realized pricing into 2008 and beyond. BTU's focus on its western and international assets should help solidify its profile in rapidly growing and increasingly profitable markets, thereby creating greater margin expansion opportunity, in our opinion.

➤ Risks to our recommendation and target price include lower-than-expected prices for steam and metallurgical grade coal, lower productivity and increased supply costs.

➤ Our 12-month target price of $62 is driven by our discounted cash flow model, which assumes a 4% perpetual growth rate and a 10.5% discount rate. This implies a P/E multiple of 31X our 2008 EPS estimate, a premium to peers due to BTU's scale and footprint.

Qualitative Risk Assessment

| LOW | MEDIUM | HIGH |

Our risk assessment reflects the industry's high cyclicality, extensive industry regulation, the potential for geological difficulties with mines, transportation problems, and volatility in the prices of competing fuels and a narrow customer focus. This is offset by the company's leading market position and geographically well-diversified coal holdings.

Quantitative Evaluations

S&P Quality Ranking NR

| D | C | B- | B | B+ | A- | A | A+ |

Relative Strength Rank STRONG

89

LOWEST = 1 HIGHEST = 99

Revenue/Earnings Data

Revenue (Million $)

	1Q	2Q	3Q	4Q	Year
2007	1,365	1,322	1,494	--	--
2006	1,312	1,316	1,265	1,363	5,256
2005	1,077	1,109	1,224	1,235	4,644
2004	788.6	920.1	923.1	1,024	3,632
2003	681.3	693.3	702.0	753.0	2,829
2002	675.8	656.9	714.6	669.8	2,717

Earnings Per Share ($)

2007	0.33	0.40	0.12	E0.73	E1.57
2006	0.48	0.57	0.53	0.65	2.23
2005	0.20	0.36	0.42	0.61	1.58
2004	0.10	0.16	0.17	0.27	0.70
2003	Nil	Nil	0.10	0.10	0.19
2002	0.11	0.11	0.14	0.14	0.49

Fiscal year ended Dec. 31. Next earnings report expected: Late January. EPS Estimates based on S&P Operating Earnings; historical GAAP earnings are as reported.

Dividend Data (Dates: mm/dd Payment Date: mm/dd/yy)

Amount ($)	Date Decl.	Ex-Div. Date	Stk. of Record	Payment Date
0.060	04/13	04/25	04/27	05/18/07
0.060	07/31	08/10	08/14	09/04/07
Stk.	10/12	11/01	10/22	10/31/07
0.060	10/18	11/05	11/01	11/23/07

Dividends have been paid since 2001. Source: Company reports.

Please read the Required Disclosures and Analyst Certification on the last page of this report.

The McGraw-Hill Companies

Peabody Energy Corp

STANDARD
&POOR'S

Business Summary November 16, 2007

CORPORATE OVERVIEW. Peabody Energy Corp. was founded in 1883 as Peabody, Daniels and Co., a retail coal supplier. BTU is currently the world's largest private sector coal company. In 2006, it produced over 225 million tons of coal, representing almost a 20% share of U.S. production, by our calculation. BTU sold 247.6 million tons of coal, almost double the its nearest U.S. competitor and 50% more than any global peer. It sold coal to more than 400 electricity generating and industrial plants in 20 countries, and fueled the generation of nearly 10% of all electricity in the U.S., and 2% of all electricity in the world. At December 31, 2006, BTU had 10.2 billion tons of proven and probable coal reserves. BTU owns majority interests in 40 coal operations located throughout all major U.S. coal producing regions and in Australia. It also owns a minority interest in one Venezuelan mine through a joint venture agreement. In 2006, 75% of the U.S. mining operation's coal sales were shipped from the U.S. West, and the remaining 25% from the East. Most production in the West is low sulfur coal from the Powder River Basin, which has seen the fastest growth of all U.S. coal regions, according to the Energy Information Administration (EIA). In the West, the company owns and operates mines in Arizona, Colorado, New Mexico and Wyoming. In the East, BTU owns and operates

mines in Illinois, Indiana, Kentucky and West Virginia.

In 2006, 87% of sales were to U.S. electricity generators, 4% to the U.S. industrial sector, and 9% to foreign customers. About 90% of 2006 coal sales were under long-term contracts with an average volume-weighted term of approximately five years, with terms ranging from one to 19 years. The company had a sales backlog of over 1 billion tons of coal. As of December 31, 2006, the company had 19 million to 29 million and 90 million to 102 million tons of total unpriced planned production for 2007 and 2008, respectively. In addition to its mining operations, BTU markets and trades coal and emission allowances. Total tons traded amounted to 79.1 million in 2006 (36.2 million tons in 2005). Other energy-related businesses include coalbed methane production, transportation services, and the development of coal-fueled generation plants.

Company Financials Fiscal Year Ended Dec. 31

Per Share Data ($)	2006	2005	2004	2003	2002	2001	2000	1999	1998	1997
Tangible Book Value	7.95	8.27	3.33	5.18	5.16	4.98	5.72	NA	NA	NA
Cash Flow	3.63	2.76	0.88	1.26	1.57	0.96	3.12	NA	NA	NA
Earnings	2.23	1.58	0.70	0.19	0.49	0.10	0.74	NA	NA	NA
S&P Core Earnings	2.00	1.43	0.63	0.11	0.27	-0.03	NA	NA	NA	NA
Dividends	0.24	0.17	0.13	0.11	0.10	0.05	0.05	NA	NA	NA
Payout Ratio	11%	11%	19%	59%	20%	53%	7%	NA	NA	NA
Prices:High	76.29	43.48	21.70	10.75	7.69	9.51	NA	NA	NA	NA
Prices:Low	32.94	18.37	9.10	6.13	4.38	5.55	NA	NA	NA	NA
P/E Ratio:High	34	28	31	57	16	NM	NA	NA	NA	NA
P/E Ratio:Low	15	12	13	32	9	NM	NA	NA	NA	NA

Income Statement Analysis (Million $)										
Revenue	5,256	4,644	3,632	2,829	2,717	2,027	2,670	NA	NA	NA
Operating Income	884	703	519	385	390	276	405	NA	NA	NA
Depreciation	377	316	270	234	232	175	241	NA	NA	NA
Interest Expense	143	103	96.8	98.5	102	89.0	198	NA	NA	NA
Pretax Income	531	426	153	-3.18	78.8	29.0	153	NA	NA	NA
Effective Tax Rate	NM	0.23%	NM	NM	NM	12.9%	27.9%	NA	NA	NA
Net Income	601	423	178	41.5	106	19.0	103	NA	NA	NA
S&P Core Earnings	541	382	160	23.9	58.5	-5.74	NA	NA	NA	NA

Balance Sheet & Other Financial Data (Million $)										
Cash	327	503	390	118	71.2	39.0	67.7	NA	NA	NA
Current Assets	1,274	1,325	1,055	683	550	527	630	NA	NA	NA
Total Assets	9,514	6,852	6,179	5,280	5,140	5,151	5,209	NA	NA	NA
Current Liabilities	1,368	1,023	774	632	632	684	777	NA	NA	NA
Long Term Debt	3,168	1,383	1,406	1,173	982	985	1,369	NA	NA	NA
Common Equity	2,339	2,178	1,725	1,132	1,081	1,040	631	NA	NA	NA
Total Capital	5,735	3,902	3,526	2,742	2,599	2,590	2,613	NA	NA	NA
Capital Expenditures	478	384	267	156	209	194	151	NA	NA	NA
Cash Flow	978	739	448	276	338	194	344	NA	NA	NA
Current Ratio	0.9	1.3	1.4	1.1	0.9	0.8	0.8	NA	NA	NA
% Long Term Debt of Capitalization	55.2	35.4	39.9	42.8	37.8	38.0	52.4	NA	NA	NA
% Net Income of Revenue	11.4	9.1	4.9	NM	3.9	0.1	3.8	NA	NA	NA
% Return on Assets	7.3	6.5	3.1	NM	2.1	0.3	1.9	NA	NA	NA
% Return on Equity	26.6	21.7	12.5	NM	10.0	2.3	18.0	NA	NA	NA

Data as orig reptd.; bef. results of disc opers/spec. items. Per share data adj. for stk. divs.; EPS diluted. E-Estimated. NA-Not Available. NM-Not Meaningful. NR-Not Ranked. UR-Under Review.

Office: 701 Market St, St. Louis, MO 63101-1826.
Telephone: 314-342-3400.
Email: publicrelations@peabodyenergy.com
Website: http://www.peabodyenergy.com

Chrmn: I.F. Engelhardt
Pres & CEO: G.H. Boyce
COO & EVP: E. Ford
EVP & CFO: R.A. Navarre

EVP & Chief Lgl Officer: A.C. Schoch
Board Members: G. H. Boyce, B. R. Brown, W. A. Coley, I. F. Engelhardt, H. Givens, Jr., W. E. James, R. B. Karn, III, H. E. Lentz, W. C. Rusnack, J. R. Schlesinger, B. M. Touhill, J. F. Turner, S. A. Van Trease, A. H. Washkowitz

Founded: 1883
Domicile: Delaware
Employees: 9,200

J. C. Penney Company Inc.

STANDARD &POOR'S

S&P Recommendation	BUY ★★★★☆	Price $44.53 (as of Nov 29, 2007)	12-Mo. Target Price $55.00	Investment Style Large-Cap Blend

GICS Sector Consumer Discretionary
Sub-Industry Department Stores

Summary JCP is the leading mall-based family department store operator in the U.S., with about 1,067 retail locations and catalog/Internet operations.

Key Stock Statistics (Source S&P, Vickers, company reports)

52-Wk Range	$87.18– 39.98	S&P Oper. EPS 2008**E** 4.55	Market Capitalization(B) $9.870	Beta	0.69
Trailing 12-Month EPS	$5.07	S&P Oper. EPS 2009**E** 5.20	Yield (%) 1.80	S&P 3-Yr. Proj. EPS CAGR(%)	12.00
Trailing 12-Month P/E	8.8	P/E on S&P Oper. EPS 2008**E** 9.8	Dividend Rate/Share $0.80	S&P Credit Rating	BBB-
$10K Invested 5 Yrs Ago	$19,364	Common Shares Outstg. (M) 221.6	Institutional Ownership (%) 96		

Price Performance

30-Week Mov. Avg. · · · 10-Week Mov. Avg. - - **GAAP Earnings vs. Previous Year** Volume Above Avg. STARS
12-Mo. Target Price — Relative Strength — ▲ Up ▼ Down ▶ No Change Below Avg.

2004 2005 2006 2007

Options: ASE, CBOE, P

Analysis prepared by **Jason N. Asaeda** on November 29, 2007, when the stock traded at **$ 44.53**.

Highlights

➤ From a projected $20 billion in FY 08 (Jan.), we expect net sales to reach $21 billion in FY 09, with $18 billion in retail sales and $3 billion in direct sales. At retail, we look for a low single-digit same-store sales gain, supported by JCP's efforts to raise newness in assortments through shorter merchandise cycle times and the launch of new exclusive brands, as well as a highly promotional calendar. We expect fine jewelry and women's apparel and accessories to be among the company's best-performing categories. We believe the home business for "big ticket" categories such as furniture will remain challenging, in line with industry trends.

➤ Despite additional markdowns being taken on heavier-weighted apparel this fall, reflecting unseasonably warm weather, we project full-year FY 08 operating margins to widen on increased sales penetration in higher-margin private brands, improved inventory planning and store allocation, expense controls, and efficiencies in JCP's growing direct business, partly offset by promotional events. We look for similar margin benefits in FY 09.

➤ Factoring in likely share buybacks, we see operating EPS of $4.55 in FY 08 and $5.20 in FY 09.

Investment Rationale/Risk

➤ In our view, the JCPenney brand is a leading shopping choice for middle-income families. Over the next 12 months, we see faster-turning assortments, a growing focus on more exclusive, higher-quality brands such as Ambrielle, Liz & Co. and American Living, and accelerated off-mall expansion strengthening JCP's competitive positioning. We also look for the company to leverage the Sephora store-within-store concept to become a shopping destination for younger, more-contemporary customers, which we see as critical to its long-term growth. In addition, we believe JCP has the potential to gain market share from competitor Macy's, Inc. (M: hold, $29), as we believe Macy's has been repositioning its business toward a more upscale demographic, leaving a gap in the mid-market.

➤ Risks to our recommendation and target price include a sharp decline in consumer spending due to economic uncertainties, and a loss of sales due to increased competition.

➤ Our 12-month target price of $55 applies a forward P/E multiple of 10.5X, the low end of JCP's three-year historical range, to our FY 09 operating EPS estimate.

Qualitative Risk Assessment

LOW	MEDIUM	HIGH

Our risk assessment reflects our view of JCP's improving sales and profit margins, increasing market share in the moderate department store sector, and what we see as a healthy balance sheet and cash flow, offset by uncertainty over consumer discretionary spending in light of higher interest rates and debt levels.

Quantitative Evaluations

S&P Quality Ranking B

D	C	B-	B	B+	A-	A	A+

Relative Strength Rank WEAK

14

LOWEST = 1   HIGHEST = 99

Revenue/Earnings Data

Revenue (Million $)

	1Q	2Q	3Q	4Q	Year
2008	4,350	4,391	4,729	--	--
2007	4,220	4,238	4,781	6,664	19,903
2006	4,192	3,981	4,479	6,203	18,781
2005	4,033	3,857	4,461	6,073	18,424
2004	7,493	7,313	7,985	6,098	17,786
2003	7,728	7,198	7,872	9,549	32,347

Earnings Per Share ($)

2008	1.04	0.78	1.17	E1.70	E4.55
2007	0.90	0.75	1.26	2.00	4.88
2006	0.63	0.46	0.94	1.92	3.83
2005	0.38	0.23	0.53	1.16	2.23
2004	0.05	-0.03	0.31	0.83	1.21
2003	0.29	-0.05	0.30	0.68	1.25

Fiscal year ended Jan. 31. Next earnings report expected: Late February. EPS Estimates based on S&P Operating Earnings; historical GAAP earnings are as reported.

Dividend Data (Dates: mm/dd Payment Date: mm/dd/yy)

Amount ($)	Date Decl.	Ex-Div. Date	Stk. of Record	Payment Date
0.180	12/13	01/08	01/10	02/05/07
0.200	03/29	04/05	04/10	05/01/07
0.200	05/18	07/06	07/10	08/01/07
0.200	09/21	10/05	10/10	11/01/07

Dividends have been paid since 1922. Source: Company reports.

Please read the Required Disclosures and Analyst Certification on the last page of this report.

The McGraw-Hill Companies

J. C. Penney Company Inc.

STANDARD
&POOR'S

Business Summary November 29, 2007

CORPORATE OVERVIEW. In our view, JCP is the leading mall-based family department store operator, with 1,067 JCPenney stores in 49 states and Puerto Rico, as of November 2007. The company is also adeptly addressing the needs of time-strapped shoppers with the shopping convenience afforded by its direct business, comprised of JCPenney catalogs and the jcpenney.com Web site, as well as its growing off-mall retail presence.

CORPORATE STRATEGY. From FY 01 (Jan.) to FY 06, JCP executed a turn-around plan to improve the profitability of its JCPenney stores. The company focused on delivering competitive, fashionable merchandise assortments; developing a compelling and appealing marketing program; improving store environments; reducing its expense structure; and attracting and retaining an experienced and professional work force. In support of these objectives, JCP moved from decentralized to centralized merchandising, marketing and operating functions, and invested in a new store distribution network and in new merchandise planning, allocation and replenishment systems.

With what we view as the success of its turnaround, JCP has mapped out a new FY 06-FY 10 plan for making JCPenney the preferred shopping choice for "Middle America", which it defines as customers aged 35 to 54 with annual household incomes of $35,000 to $85,000. Key strategies include offering styles that make an emotional connection with the customer; making it easier for the customer to shop seamlessly across store/catalog/Internet channels; creating and sustaining a customer-focused culture; and using the off-mall store format to expand the company's presence in high-potential markets. JCP plans to open 50 stores annually from FY 08 through FY 10, with the majority in off-mall locations. The company sees the potential for up to 400 new stores, relocations or expansions on a long-term basis.

Company Financials Fiscal Year Ended Jan. 31

Per Share Data ($)	2007	2006	2005	2004	2003	2002	2001	2000	1999	1998
Tangible Book Value	18.97	17.20	17.92	18.54	12.04	11.46	NM	14.28	15.04	15.50
Cash Flow	6.57	5.79	3.33	2.68	3.45	3.00	0.36	3.87	4.40	4.46
Earnings	4.88	3.83	2.23	1.21	1.25	0.32	-2.29	1.16	2.19	2.10
S&P Core Earnings	4.66	3.77	2.26	1.24	0.66	0.15	-2.47	NA	NA	NA
Dividends	0.50	0.50	0.50	0.50	0.50	0.50	0.50	2.19	2.18	2.14
Payout Ratio	10%	13%	22%	41%	40%	156%	NM	188%	100%	102%
Calendar Year	2006	2005	2004	2003	2002	2001	2000	1999	1998	1997
Prices:High	82.49	57.99	41.82	26.42	27.75	29.50	22.50	54.44	78.75	68.25
Prices:Low	54.18	40.26	25.29	15.57	14.07	10.50	8.63	17.69	42.63	44.88
P/E Ratio:High	17	15	19	22	22	92	NM	47	36	32
P/E Ratio:Low	11	11	11	13	11	33	NM	15	19	21

Income Statement Analysis (Million $)										
Revenue	19,903	18,781	18,424	17,786	32,347	32,004	31,846	32,510	30,678	30,546
Operating Income	2,277	1,949	1,680	1,184	1,681	1,473	873	1,681	2,253	1,687
Depreciation	389	372	368	394	667	717	695	710	637	584
Interest Expense	270	169	233	261	388	386	427	673	663	648
Pretax Income	1,792	1,444	1,020	546	584	203	-886	531	955	925
Effective Tax Rate	36.7%	32.3%	34.6%	33.3%	36.5%	43.8%	NM	36.7%	37.8%	38.8%
Net Income	1,134	977	667	345	371	114	-568	336	594	566
S&P Core Earnings	1,081	960	662	345	171	41.0	-650	NA	NA	NA

Balance Sheet & Other Financial Data (Million $)										
Cash	2,747	3,016	4,687	2,994	2,474	2,840	944	1,233	96.0	287
Current Assets	6,648	6,702	8,427	6,515	8,353	8,677	7,257	8,472	11,125	11,484
Total Assets	12,673	12,461	14,127	18,300	17,867	18,048	19,742	20,888	23,638	23,493
Current Liabilities	3,492	2,762	3,447	3,754	4,159	4,499	4,235	4,465	5,970	6,137
Long Term Debt	3,010	3,444	3,464	5,114	4,940	5,179	5,448	5,844	7,143	6,986
Common Equity	4,288	4,007	4,856	5,121	6,037	5,766	5,860	6,782	6,694	6,831
Total Capital	8,504	8,738	9,638	11,756	12,701	12,539	12,843	14,087	15,829	15,668
Capital Expenditures	772	535	412	373	658	631	648	631	744	824
Cash Flow	1,523	1,349	1,023	733	1,011	802	94.0	1,010	1,193	1,110
Current Ratio	1.9	2.4	2.4	1.7	2.0	1.9	1.7	1.9	1.9	1.9
% Long Term Debt of Capitalization	41.2	39.4	35.9	43.5	38.9	41.3	42.4	41.5	45.1	44.6
% Net Income of Revenue	5.7	5.2	3.6	2.0	1.1	0.4	NM	1.0	1.9	1.9
% Return on Assets	9.0	7.3	4.1	2.0	2.1	0.1	NM	1.5	2.5	2.5
% Return on Equity	27.3	22.0	13.1	6.1	5.8	1.9	NM	4.5	8.2	8.6

Data as orig reptd.; bef. results of disc opers/spec. items. Per share data adj. for stk. divs.; EPS diluted. E-Estimated. NA-Not Available. NM-Not Meaningful. NR-Not Ranked. UR-Under Review.

Office: 6501 Legacy Drive, Plano, TX 75024-3698.
Telephone: 972-431-1000.
Website: http://www.jcpenney.net
Chrmn & CEO: M.E. Ullman, III

Pres: K.C. Hicks
EVP & CFO: R.B. Cavanaugh
EVP, Secy & General Counsel: J.L. Bober
EVP & CIO: T.M. Nealon

Investor Contact: R. Johnson (972-431-8167)
Board Members: C. C. Barrett, A. Burns, M. Clark, T. J. Engibous, K. B. Foster, V. E. Jordan, Jr., B. Osborne, L. H. Roberts, A. M. Tallman, R. G. Turner, M. C. Ullman, III, M. West

Founded: 1902
Domicile: Delaware
Employees: 155,000

Pepco Holdings Inc.

STANDARD &POOR'S

S&P Recommendation **HOLD** ★★★☆☆	Price $27.15 (as of Nov 23, 2007)	12-Mo. Target Price $30.00	Investment Style Large-Cap Blend

GICS Sector Utilities
Sub-Industry Electric Utilities

Summary This electric utility holding company was formed through the 2002 merger of Potomac Electric Power Co. (Pepco) and Conectiv.

Key Stock Statistics (Source S&P, Vickers, company reports)

52-Wk Range	$30.71– 24.20	S&P Oper. EPS 2007**E**	1.62	Market Capitalization(B)	$5.254	Beta	0.54
Trailing 12-Month EPS	$1.62	S&P Oper. EPS 2008**E**	1.95	Yield (%)	3.83	S&P 3-Yr. Proj. EPS CAGR(%)	14.00
Trailing 12-Month P/E	16.8	P/E on S&P Oper. EPS 2007**E**	16.8	Dividend Rate/Share	$1.04	S&P Credit Rating	BBB
$10K Invested 5 Yrs Ago	$16,941	Common Shares Outstg. (M)	193.5	Institutional Ownership (%)	55		

Price Performance

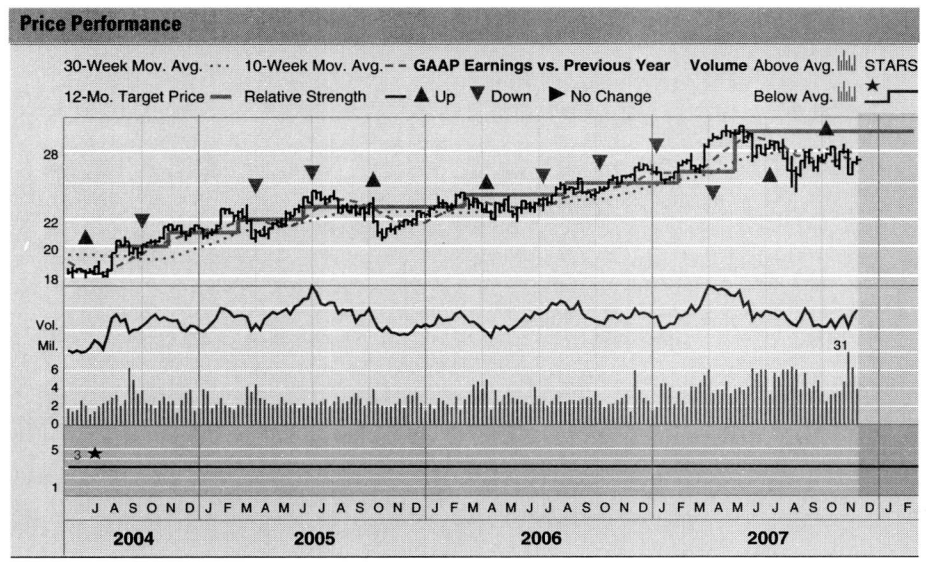

30-Week Mov. Avg. ··· 10-Week Mov. Avg. - - GAAP Earnings vs. Previous Year Volume Above Avg. STARS
12-Mo. Target Price — Relative Strength — ▲ Up ▼ Down ► No Change Below Avg. ★

Options: Ph

Analysis prepared by **Justin McCann** on November 14, 2007, when the stock traded at **$ 26.45**.

Highlights

- We expect EPS in 2007 to grow more than 20% from 2006 operating EPS of $1.33, reflecting a return to more normal weather and improved earnings at Conectiv Energy. We see Conectiv benefiting from higher power prices, improved margins on standard hedges, and higher generating output, most of which has already been contracted. Aided by more favorable weather, operating EPS in the first nine months of 2007 was $1.24, up $0.11 from the year-earlier period.

- For 2008, we expect operating EPS to increase approximately 20% from anticipated results in 2007. We see the growth being driven by rate increases at the utilities, and by higher-margin renewal contracts at Conectiv Energy.

- On August 8, 2007, a U.S. District Court dismissed an appeal by objecting creditors of the settlement agreement between Pepco and Mirant (MIR) that was affirmed by the District Court in December 2006. Under the agreement, MIR paid Pepco $414 million in exchange for the termination of certain power purchase contracts. This amount was dedicated to the payment of the liabilities of the contracts. MIR also paid Pepco $70 million for other claims.

Investment Rationale/Risk

- After an approximate 18% gain in the first five months of 2007 (which followed a 16% gain in 2006), the shares are down nearly 14% from their 2007 high, and up less than 2% year-to-date. We believe the decline reflected an investor shift away from the electric utility sector, just as the earlier strong performance had been aided, in our view, by a significant investor shift into the sector, as well as from an above-peers yield from the dividend.

- Risks to our recommendation and target price include the extent to which POM is unable to recover incremental purchased power costs; much weaker than expected earnings from the unregulated Conectiv Energy; and the potential for a significant shift in the average P/E of the group as a whole.

- With a recent slightly above-peer yield of about 3.9% from a dividend we consider secure, we would continue to hold the shares for total return potential. Looking forward, we expect the stock to trade at a discount-to-peers P/E of about 15.4X our EPS estimate for 2008 of $1.95. Our 12-month target price is $30.

Qualitative Risk Assessment

LOW	MEDIUM	HIGH

Our risk assessment reflects our view of the steady cash flows expected from the regulated electric transmission and distribution businesses, which account for approximately 70% of consolidated cash flows and reflect a healthy economy in the company's service territories. We believe this should largely offset the less predictable earnings and cash flow from the company's unregulated wholesale and retail power marketing businesses.

Quantitative Evaluations

S&P Quality Ranking B

D	C	B-	**B**	B+	A-	A	A+

Relative Strength Rank STRONG

76

LOWEST = 1   HIGHEST = 99

Revenue/Earnings Data

Revenue (Million $)

	1Q	2Q	3Q	4Q	Year
2007	2,179	2,084	2,770	--	--
2006	1,952	1,917	2,590	1,905	8,363
2005	1,805	1,712	2,489	2,063	8,066
2004	1,764	1,692	2,047	--	7,222
2003	1,929	1,698	2,131	1,514	7,271
2002	489.2	581.2	1,641	1,608	4,325

Earnings Per Share ($)

2007	0.27	0.30	0.87	E0.33	E1.62
2006	0.29	0.27	0.54	0.19	1.30
2005	0.24	0.34	0.90	0.43	1.91
2004	0.30	0.53	0.64	--	1.47
2003	-0.15	0.22	0.92	-0.36	0.63
2002	0.22	0.43	0.80	0.16	1.61

Fiscal year ended Dec. 31. Next earnings report expected: Early March. EPS Estimates based on S&P Operating Earnings; historical GAAP earnings are as reported.

Dividend Data (Dates: mm/dd Payment Date: mm/dd/yy)

Amount ($)	Date Decl.	Ex-Div. Date	Stk. of Record	Payment Date
0.260	10/26	12/06	12/10	12/29/06
0.260	01/25	03/08	03/12	03/30/07
0.260	04/26	06/07	06/11	06/29/07
0.260	07/26	12/06	12/10	12/31/07

Dividends have been paid since 1904. Source: Company reports.

Pepco Holdings Inc.

STANDARD
&POOR'S

Business Summary November 14, 2007

CORPORATE OVERVIEW. Pepco Holdings (POM) is an energy holding company involved in two principal business operations: power delivery and competitive energy. POM's power delivery business, which provides the transmission and distribution of electricity and the distribution of natural gas, contributed 56.7% of the company's consolidated operating revenues in 2006. Its operations are conducted through its three regulated utility subsidiaries: Potomac Electric Power Company (Pepco), Delmarva Power & Light Company (DPL), and Atlantic City Electric Company (ACE). POM'S competitive energy business provides non-regulated generation, marketing and supply of electricity and natural gas, and related energy management services through the subsidiaries of Conectiv Energy and Pepco Energy Services. In 2006, the competitive energy business contributed 43.3% of consolidated operating revenues.

CORPORATE STRATEGY. The company's business strategy is to stay focused on the low-risk, stable, power delivery business. Over the next five years, the company plans to invest $2.7 billion in the utility infrastructure. The utility business has targeted 4% annual average earnings growth by focusing on sales growth, operational excellence, and constructive regulatory outcomes. POM's financial strategy has been to reduce debt, which should result in a stronger balance sheet and enhanced returns for shareholders. The Conectiv Energy division plans to adopt a proactive hedging strategy for risk management and evaluate inorganic growth possibilities.

Company Financials Fiscal Year Ended Dec. 31

Per Share Data ($)	2006	2005	2004	2003	2002	2001	2000	1999	1998	1997
Tangible Book Value	11.48	11.34	10.28	9.12	9.20	17.01	16.77	16.05	15.84	15.72
Earnings	1.30	1.91	1.47	0.63	1.61	1.50	2.96	1.98	1.73	1.38
S&P Core Earnings	1.28	1.37	1.38	0.87	1.31	1.20	NA	NA	NA	NA
Dividends	1.04	1.00	1.00	1.00	0.92	1.17	1.66	1.66	1.66	1.66
Payout Ratio	80%	52%	68%	159%	57%	78%	56%	84%	96%	120%
Prices:High	26.99	24.46	21.71	20.56	23.83	24.90	27.88	31.75	27.81	26.81
Prices:Low	21.79	20.26	16.94	16.10	15.37	20.08	19.06	21.25	23.06	21.00
P/E Ratio:High	21	13	15	33	15	17	9	16	16	19
P/E Ratio:Low	17	11	12	26	10	13	6	11	13	15

Income Statement Analysis (Million $)

	2006	2005	2004	2003	2002	2001	2000	1999	1998	1997
Revenue	8,363	8,066	7,222	7,271	4,325	2,503	2,624	2,476	2,064	1,864
Depreciation	413	423	441	422	240	171	248	273	240	232
Maintenance	NA	NA	NA	NA	NA	NA	NA	NA	91.5	95.3
Fixed Charges Coverage	2.25	2.37	2.06	1.43	2.47	3.06	4.32	2.71	3.08	2.97
Construction Credits	NA	NA	NA	NA	NA	NA	NA	NA	5.50	14.5
Effective Tax Rate	39.4%	41.3%	40.1%	38.0%	37.1%	33.1%	49.2%	31.7%	36.0%	39.3%
Net Income	248	362	259	108	211	168	352	247	326	182
S&P Core Earnings	246	259	241	147	171	130	NA	NA	NA	NA

Balance Sheet & Other Financial Data (Million $)

	2006	2005	2004	2003	2002	2001	2000	1999	1998	1997
Gross Property	11,820	11,384	11,045	10,747	10,625	4,367	4,339	6,862	6,658	6,393
Capital Expenditures	475	467	517	564	504	245	226	200	212	232
Net Property	7,577	7,312	7,088	6,965	6,798	2,758	2,776	4,602	4,521	4,486
Capitalization:Long Term Debt	4,367	4,885	5,128	5,373	5,122	1,722	1,985	2,992	2,142	2,062
Capitalization:% Long Term Debt	54.7	57.7	60.4	63.7	62.2	45.9	50.4	59.8	51.4	49.2
Capitalization:Preferred	Nil	Nil	Nil	63.2	111	210	90.3	100	150	266
Capitalization:% Preferred	Nil	Nil	Nil	0.75	1.35	5.59	2.29	2.00	3.60	6.30
Capitalization:Common	3,612	3,584	3,366	3,003	2,996	1,823	1,863	1,910	1,877	1,863
Capitalization:% Common	45.3	42.3	39.6	35.6	36.4	48.5	47.3	38.2	45.0	44.5
Total Capital	10,134	10,455	10,532	8,439	9,833	4,282	4,384	6,105	5,272	5,277
% Operating Ratio	93.2	92.4	91.6	92.6	90.3	87.1	91.9	81.4	82.3	82.5
% Earned on Net Property	9.3	12.6	11.0	18.6	16.4	27.5	16.0	10.0	7.9	4.1
% Return on Revenue	3.0	4.5	3.6	1.5	4.9	6.7	13.4	10.0	10.9	9.8
% Return on Invested Capital	6.2	8.0	6.7	8.3	6.4	9.6	11.8	7.6	7.1	6.9
% Return on Common Equity	6.9	10.5	8.1	3.4	8.7	8.9	18.4	12.6	11.5	9.7

Data as orig reptd.; bef. results of disc opers/spec. items. Per share data adj. for stk. divs.; EPS diluted. E-Estimated. NA-Not Available. NM-Not Meaningful. NR-Not Ranked. UR-Under Review.

Office: 701 Ninth Street N.W., Washington, DC 20068.
Telephone: 202-872-2000.
Email: shareholder@pepco.com
Website: http://www.pepcoholdings.com

Chrmn, Pres, CEO & COO: D.R. Wraase
Vice Chrmn & General Counsel: W.T. Torgerson
SVP & CFO: J.M. Rigby
VP & Cntlr: R.K. Clark

Investor Contact: E.J. Bourscheid (202-872-2797)
Board Members: E. B. Cronin, Jr., J. B. Dunn, IV, T. C. Golden, F. O. Heintz, G. F. MacCormack, R. B. McGlynn, L. C. Nussdorf, P. F. O'Malley, F. K. Ross, P. A. Schneider, L. P. Silverman, W. T. Torgerson, D. R. Wraase

Founded: 1896
Domicile: Delaware
Employees: 5,156

PepsiCo Inc

STANDARD &POOR'S

S&P Recommendation HOLD ★★★☆☆	**Price** $75.51 (as of Nov 23, 2007)	**12-Mo. Target Price** $76.00	**Investment Style** Large-Cap Growth

GICS Sector Consumer Staples
Sub-Industry Soft Drinks

Summary This company is a major international producer of branded beverage and snack food products.

Key Stock Statistics (Source S&P, Vickers, company reports)

52-Wk Range	$76.29– 61.21	S&P Oper. EPS 2007**E**	3.36	Market Capitalization(B)	$121.549	Beta	0.58
Trailing 12-Month EPS	$3.72	S&P Oper. EPS 2008**E**	3.70	Yield (%)	1.99	S&P 3-Yr. Proj. EPS CAGR(%)	10.00
Trailing 12-Month P/E	20.3	P/E on S&P Oper. EPS 2007**E**	22.5	Dividend Rate/Share	$1.50	S&P Credit Rating	A+
$10K Invested 5 Yrs Ago	$19,597	Common Shares Outstg. (M)	1,609.7	Institutional Ownership (%)	68		

Price Performance

30-Week Mov. Avg. ··· 10-Week Mov. Avg. --- GAAP Earnings vs. Previous Year Volume Above Avg. STARS
12-Mo. Target Price — Relative Strength — ▲ Up ▼ Down ▶ No Change Below Avg. ★

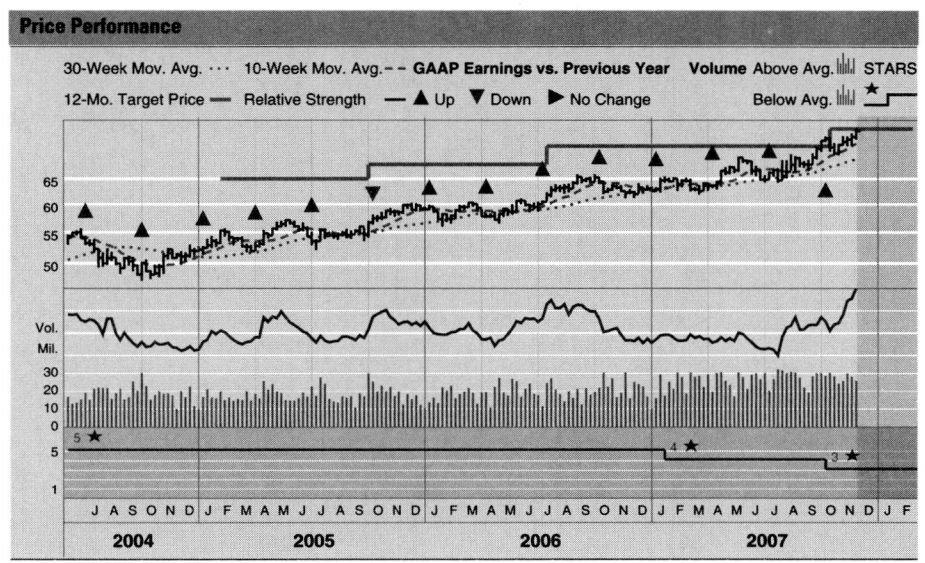

Options: ASE, CBOE, P, Ph

Analysis prepared by **Raymond Mathis** on October 12, 2007, when the stock traded at **$72.36**.

Highlights

▶ We expect net sales to rise nearly 10% in 2008, aided by new products, acquisitions, penetration of international markets, and a modest foreign currency benefit. We see segment operating income rising 9% to 10% on favorable pricing and product mix benefits, operating efficiencies, and productivity gains. Fuel, energy and PET resin costs will likely remain at elevated levels into 2008, and we see rising prices for other inputs such as corn, high fructose corn syrup and orange juice potentially pressuring margins.

▶ By segment, we see operating profits for Pepsi-Co Beverages North American (PBNA) rising 3% to 5% in 2008, and we expect profits at Frito-Lay North America (FLNA) to grow 6% to 7%. For the PepsiCo International (PI) segment, we believe profits will climb more than 15%, while we think the Quaker Foods (QFNA) business will see profits rise in the low single digits.

▶ With 1% to 2% fewer shares outstanding, we estimate 2007 operating EPS of $3.36, a 14% gain from operating EPS of $2.96 in 2006. We expect further growth to $3.70 in 2008. For the longer term, we expect annual EPS growth of 11% to 12%.

Investment Rationale/Risk

▶ Our recommendation reflects our view of strong pricing power and cash flow growth. In addition to the company's leading market positions, we view PEP's product innovation strategy as trend-setting for the industry. Its focus on health and wellness, not only at QFNA, but also at FLNA and PBNA, in addition to its continued penetration of international markets, should continue to drive the top line.

▶ Risks to our recommendation and target price include unfavorable weather conditions in the company's markets, increased competitive activity, and weak consumer acceptance of new product introductions. As PEP increases its exposure to foreign markets, political and currency risks also increase.

▶ Our DCF model, which assumes a cost of capital of 8.5% and a terminal growth rate of 4%, calculates intrinsic value of $76. Our relative valuation model, derived from an analysis of peer P/E and historical P/E multiples, indicates a value of $88 at a historical average high of 24X. At peer EV/EBITDA multiples, we see a value of $69. Blending our valuations, we arrive at our 12-month target price of $76.

Qualitative Risk Assessment

LOW	MEDIUM	HIGH

Our risk assessment reflects the relatively stable nature of the company's end markets, strong cash flow, leading global market positions, corporate governance practices that we view as favorable versus peers, and an S&P Quality Ranking of A+, reflecting historical growth and stability of earnings and dividends.

Quantitative Evaluations

S&P Quality Ranking A+

D	C	B-	B	B+	A-	A	A+

Relative Strength Rank STRONG

90

LOWEST = 1   HIGHEST = 99

Revenue/Earnings Data

Revenue (Million $)

	1Q	2Q	3Q	4Q	Year
2007	7,350	9,607	10,171	--	--
2006	7,205	8,599	8,950	10,383	35,137
2005	6,585	7,697	8,184	10,096	32,562
2004	6,131	7,070	7,257	8,803	29,261
2003	5,530	6,538	6,830	8,073	26,971
2002	5,101	6,178	6,376	7,457	25,112

Earnings Per Share ($)

2007	0.65	0.94	1.06	E0.81	E3.36
2006	0.60	0.80	0.88	1.06	3.34
2005	0.53	0.70	0.51	0.65	2.39
2004	0.46	0.61	0.79	0.55	2.41
2003	0.45	0.58	0.62	0.52	2.05
2002	0.36	0.49	0.54	0.46	1.85

Fiscal year ended Dec. 31. Next earnings report expected: Early February. EPS Estimates based on S&P Operating Earnings; historical GAAP earnings are as reported.

Dividend Data (Dates: mm/dd Payment Date: mm/dd/yy)

Amount ($)	Date Decl.	Ex-Div. Date	Stk. of Record	Payment Date
0.300	02/02	03/07	03/09	03/30/07
0.375	05/02	06/06	06/08	06/29/07
0.375	07/19	09/05	09/07	09/28/07
0.375	11/16	12/05	12/07	01/02/08

Dividends have been paid since 1952. Source: Company reports.

Please read the Required Disclosures and Analyst Certification on the last page of this report.

The McGraw-Hill Companies

PepsiCo Inc

STANDARD &POOR'S

Business Summary October 12, 2007

CORPORATE OVERVIEW. Originally incorporated in 1919, PepsiCo is a leader in the global snack and beverage industry. The company manufactures, markets and sells a variety of salty, convenient, sweet and grain-based snacks, carbonated and non-carbonated beverages, and foods. PepsiCo is organized into four business segments: Frito-Lay North America (FLNA), PepsiCo Beverages North America (PBNA), PepsiCo International (PI) and Quaker Foods North America (QFNA). The company's North American divisions operate in the U.S. and Canada. PepsiCo's international divisions operate in more than 200 countries, with its largest operations in Mexico and the United Kingdom.

FLNA (31% of 2006 net revenue, 41% of operating profits before corporate overhead) produces the best-selling line of snack foods in the U.S., including Fritos brand corn chips, Lay's and Ruffles potato chips, Doritos and Tostitos tortilla chips, Cheetos cheese-flavored snacks, Rold Gold pretzels, Sunchips multigrain snacks, Grandma's cookies, Quaker Fruit and Oatmeal bars, Quaker Chewy granola bars, Lay's Stax potato crisps, Cracker Jack candy-coated popcorn and Quaker Quakes corn and rice snacks. FLNA branded products are sold to independent distributors and retailers. Products are transported

from Frito-Lay's manufacturing plants to major distribution centers, principally by company-owned trucks.

PBNA (27%, 31%) manufactures or uses contract manufacturers, markets and sells beverage concentrates, fountain syrups and finished goods, under the brands Pepsi, Mountain Dew, Sierra Mist, Mug, SoBe, Gatorade, Slice, Tropicana Juice Drinks, Tropicana Pure Premium, Dole, Tropicana Season's Best, Tropicana Twister and Propel. PBNA also manufactures, markets and sells ready-to-drink tea and coffee products through joint ventures with Lipton and Starbucks. In addition, it markets the Aquafina water brand and licenses it to its bottlers. Pepsi-Cola bottlers are licensed by PepsiCo to manufacture, sell and distribute, within defined territories, beverages and syrups bearing the Pepsi-Cola beverage trademarks.

Company Financials Fiscal Year Ended Dec. 31

Per Share Data ($)	2006	2005	2004	2003	2002	2001	2000	1999	1998	1997
Tangible Book Value	1.93	2.17	1.96	3.82	2.37	1.90	1.91	1.48	NM	0.72
Cash Flow	4.30	3.25	2.45	2.75	2.47	2.07	2.13	2.06	2.12	1.65
Earnings	3.34	2.39	2.41	2.05	1.85	1.47	1.48	1.37	1.31	0.95
S&P Core Earnings	3.30	2.37	2.44	2.03	1.54	1.20	NA	NA	NA	NA
Dividends	1.16	1.01	0.85	0.63	0.60	0.58	0.56	0.53	0.51	0.49
Payout Ratio	35%	42%	35%	31%	32%	39%	38%	39%	39%	52%
Prices:High	65.99	60.34	55.71	48.88	53.50	50.46	49.94	42.56	44.81	41.31
Prices:Low	56.00	51.34	45.30	36.24	34.00	40.25	29.69	30.13	27.56	28.25
P/E Ratio:High	20	25	23	24	29	34	34	31	34	43
P/E Ratio:Low	17	21	19	18	18	27	20	22	21	30

Income Statement Analysis (Million $)										
Revenue	35,137	32,562	29,261	26,971	25,112	26,935	20,438	20,367	22,348	20,917
Operating Income	7,845	7,230	6,673	6,208	6,066	5,490	4,185	3,915	4,106	4,058
Depreciation	1,406	1,308	1,264	1,221	1,112	1,082	960	1,032	1,234	1,106
Interest Expense	239	256	167	163	178	219	221	363	395	478
Pretax Income	6,989	6,382	5,546	4,992	4,868	4,029	3,210	3,656	2,263	2,309
Effective Tax Rate	19.3%	36.1%	24.7%	28.5%	31.9%	33.9%	32.0%	43.9%	11.9%	35.4%
Net Income	5,642	4,078	4,174	3,568	3,313	2,662	2,183	2,050	1,993	1,491
S&P Core Earnings	5,565	4,028	4,191	3,543	2,749	2,164	NA	NA	NA	NA

Balance Sheet & Other Financial Data (Million $)										
Cash	1,651	1,716	1,280	820	1,638	683	864	964	311	2,883
Current Assets	9,130	10,454	8,639	6,930	6,413	5,853	4,604	4,173	4,362	6,251
Total Assets	29,930	31,727	27,987	25,327	23,474	21,695	18,339	17,551	22,660	20,101
Current Liabilities	6,860	9,406	6,752	6,415	6,052	4,998	3,935	3,788	7,914	4,257
Long Term Debt	2,550	2,313	2,397	1,702	2,187	2,651	2,346	2,812	4,028	4,946
Common Equity	15,327	14,210	13,572	11,896	9,250	8,648	7,249	6,881	6,401	6,939
Total Capital	18,446	17,998	17,226	14,837	13,196	12,821	10,956	10,902	12,432	13,582
Capital Expenditures	2,068	1,736	1,387	1,345	1,437	1,324	1,067	1,118	1,405	1,506
Cash Flow	7,047	5,384	4,109	4,786	4,421	3,744	3,143	3,082	3,227	2,597
Current Ratio	1.3	1.1	1.3	1.1	1.1	1.2	1.2	1.1	0.6	1.5
% Long Term Debt of Capitalization	13.8	12.9	13.9	11.5	16.6	20.7	21.4	25.8	32.4	36.4
% Net Income of Revenue	16.1	12.5	14.3	13.2	13.2	9.9	10.7	10.1	8.9	7.1
% Return on Assets	18.3	13.7	15.7	14.6	14.7	12.5	12.2	10.2	9.3	7.1
% Return on Equity	38.2	29.4	22.3	33.3	37.0	32.8	30.9	30.9	29.9	22.0

Data as orig reptd.; bef. results of disc opers/spec. items. Per share data adj. for stk. divs.; EPS diluted. E-Estimated. NA-Not Available. NM-Not Meaningful. NR-Not Ranked. UR-Under Review.

Office: 700 Anderson Hill Road, Purchase, NY 10577.
Telephone: 914-253-2000.
Website: http://www.pepsico.com
Chrmn, Pres & CEO: I.K. Nooyi

Vice Chrmn: M.D. White
SVP & Treas: L.L. Nowell, III
SVP, Secy & General Counsel: L.D. Thompson
SVP & Cntlr: P.A. Bridgman

Board Members: J. F. Akers, R. E. Allen, D. Dublon, V. J. Dzau, R. L. Hunt, A. Ibarguen, A. C. Martinez, I. K. Nooyi, S. S. Reinemund, S. P. Rockefeller, J. J. Schiro, F. A. Thomas, D. Vasella, M. D. White

Founded: 1916
Domicile: North Carolina
Employees: 168,000

The McGraw-Hill Companies

Pepsi Bottling Group Inc.

STANDARD &POOR'S

S&P Recommendation HOLD ★★★☆☆	**Price** $41.72 (as of Nov 23, 2007)	**12-Mo. Target Price** $41.00	**Investment Style** Large-Cap Blend

GICS Sector Consumer Staples
Sub-Industry Soft Drinks

Summary This company is the world's largest manufacturer, seller and distributor of carbonated and non-carbonated Pepsi-Cola beverages.

Key Stock Statistics (Source S&P, Vickers, company reports)

52-Wk Range	$43.38–30.13	S&P Oper. EPS 2007**E**	2.18	Market Capitalization(B)	$9.332	Beta	1.18
Trailing 12-Month EPS	$2.49	S&P Oper. EPS 2008**E**	2.25	Yield (%)	1.34	S&P 3-Yr. Proj. EPS CAGR(%)	9.00
Trailing 12-Month P/E	16.8	P/E on S&P Oper. EPS 2007**E**	19.1	Dividend Rate/Share	$0.56	S&P Credit Rating	A
$10K Invested 5 Yrs Ago	$16,374	Common Shares Outstg. (M)	223.7	Institutional Ownership (%)	62		

Price Performance

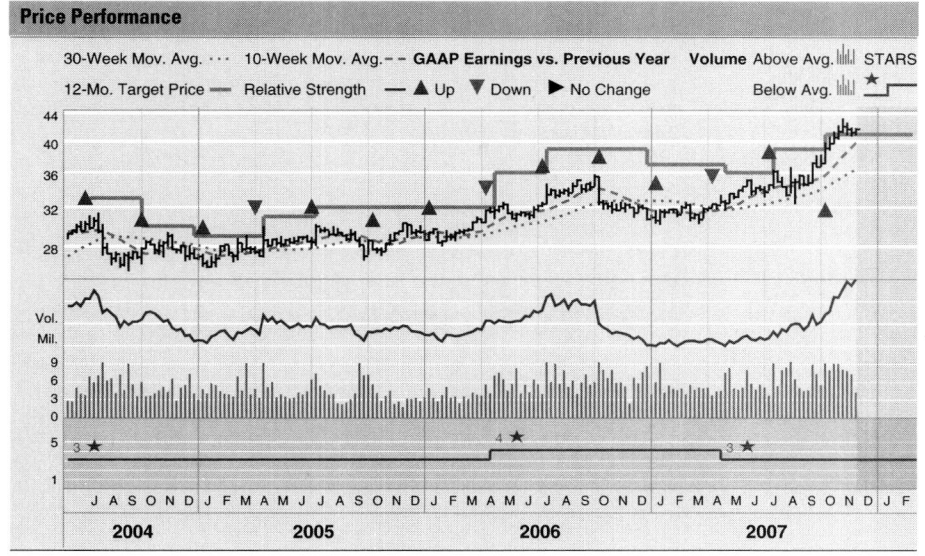

30-Week Mov. Avg. · · · 10-Week Mov. Avg. - - **GAAP Earnings vs. Previous Year** Volume Above Avg. STARS
12-Mo. Target Price — Relative Strength — ▲ Up ▼ Down ► No Change Below Avg. ★

Options: CBOE, P

Analysis prepared by **Raymond Mathis** on October 03, 2007, when the stock traded at **$ 37.97**.

Highlights

➤ We expect net revenues to rise 5% to 7%, primarily reflecting 1% to 2% comparable worldwide volume growth and a 4% to 5% increase in net revenues per case. Volume comparisons should benefit from strong bottled water growth and the addition of new beverage products, although we think carbonated soft drink (CSD) trends will remain sluggish. By geographic segment, we see volume flat in the U.S., but we project growth of 2% for Mexico and 5% for Europe. The anticipated introduction of Pepsi Max could provide a boost to CSD volumes.

➤ We expect margins to be aided by cost saving and efficiency initiatives. However, we think that higher raw material and packaging costs will likely lead to a 5% to 6% increase in cost of goods sold per case. With a growing percentage of sales coming from overseas, we see foreign currency contributing to margins as well.

➤ After expected higher interest expense and an effective tax rate of 34% to 35%, balanced against stock repurchases that we see reducing the number of shares outstanding by 1% to 2%, we forecast 2007 EPS of $2.18, rising to $2.25 in 2008. For the longer term, we project 8% to 10% annual EPS growth.

Investment Rationale/Risk

➤ Our hold recommendation reflects our expectation for strong brand momentum, cost structure improvements, and better EPS visibility in coming quarters, coupled with valuation. We expect to see modest market share gains behind new product introductions and line extensions, better revenue per case growth, and a continuing improvement in the Mexican business.

➤ Risks to our recommendation and target price include rising competitive pressures for PBG's business in Mexico, increasing commodity cost pressures, an inability to meet volume and revenue growth targets, and unfavorable weather conditions in the company's markets. In terms of corporate governance, the company has a dual class capital structure with unequal voting rights, which we view unfavorably. Former parent Pepsico (PEP) owns 100% of the class B shares.

➤ Our 12-month target price of $41 is derived from our analysis of comparable peer multiples and discounted free cash flows. Our DCF assumptions include a weighted average cost of capital of 9% and an expected terminal growth rate for cash flows of 3%.

Qualitative Risk Assessment

LOW	MEDIUM	HIGH

Our risk assessment reflects the relatively stable nature of the company's end markets, strong cash flows and market share positions, and its relationship with corporate partner PepsiCo.

Quantitative Evaluations

S&P Quality Ranking   NR

D	C	B-	B	B+	A-	A	A+

Relative Strength Rank   **STRONG**

91

LOWEST = 1   HIGHEST = 99

Revenue/Earnings Data

Revenue (Million $)

	1Q	2Q	3Q	4Q	Year
2007	2,466	3,360	3,729	--	--
2006	2,367	3,138	3,460	3,765	12,730
2005	2,147	2,862	3,214	3,662	11,885
2004	2,067	2,675	2,934	3,230	10,906
2003	1,874	2,532	2,810	3,049	10,265
2002	1,772	2,209	2,455	2,780	9,216

Earnings Per Share ($)

2007	0.12	0.70	1.12	E0.40	E2.18
2006	0.14	0.61	0.86	0.55	2.16
2005	0.15	0.59	0.82	0.30	1.86
2004	0.19	0.53	0.73	0.29	1.73
2003	0.14	0.47	0.67	0.26	1.52
2002	0.19	0.47	0.61	0.20	1.46

Fiscal year ended Dec. 31. Next earnings report expected: Late January. EPS Estimates based on S&P Operating Earnings; historical GAAP earnings are as reported.

Dividend Data (Dates: mm/dd Payment Date: mm/dd/yy)

Amount ($)	Date Decl.	Ex-Div. Date	Stk. of Record	Payment Date
0.110	02/21	03/07	03/09	03/30/07
0.140	03/22	06/06	06/08	06/29/07
0.140	07/25	09/05	09/07	09/28/07
0.140	10/12	12/05	12/07	01/02/08

Dividends have been paid since 1999. Source: Company reports.

The *McGraw-Hill* Companies

Pepsi Bottling Group Inc.

STANDARD &POOR'S

Business Summary October 03, 2007

CORPORATE OVERVIEW. The Pepsi Bottling Group is the world's largest manufacturer, seller and distributor of carbonated and non-carbonated Pepsi-Cola beverages. The company was separated from PepsiCo (PEP) via a March 1999 IPO. As of January 26, 2007, PepsiCo's ownership represented 44.4% of the voting power of all classes of PBG's voting stock. In addition, PEP owned a 6.7% interest in Bottling Group, LLC, PBG's main operating subsidiary.

The company has exclusive rights to manufacture, sell and distribute Pepsi-Cola beverages in all or a portion of 41 states, the District of Columbia, nine Canadian provinces, Spain, Greece, Turkey, Mexico and Russia. In 2006, approximately 78% of PBG's net revenues were generated in the U.S. and Canada, 12% were derived from Europe, and the remaining 10% came from Mexico.

The company's brands include some of the world's best recognized trademarks, and include Pepsi-Cola, Diet Pepsi, Mountain Dew, Lipton's Iced Tea, Slice, Sierra Mist, Tropicana juice drinks, Tropicana Twister, Mug Root Beer, SoBe, Dole, Aquafina, Starbucks Frappuccino and Miranda, which are bottled under licenses from PepsiCo or PepsiCo joint ventures. In some markets, PBG also has the rights to bottle and sell non-PEP beverages such as Dr. Pepper and 7UP.

The company has established an extensive production and distribution system

to deliver products directly to stores without using wholesalers or middlemen. In Europe, PBG uses a combination of direct store distribution and distribution through wholesalers, depending on local market conditions. At December 31, 2006, it operated 101 soft drink production facilities worldwide, as well as 546 distribution facilities. PBG also owns or leases and operates approximately 41,000 vehicles, and owns more than 2 million coolers and soft drink dispensing and vending machines.

While no customer accounted for 10% or more of PBG's net revenue in 2006, the company is highly reliant on PEP. Key to PBG's business, in our view, is its Master Bottling Agreement with PEP, under which the company has exclusive rights to manufacture, package, sell and distribute beverages bearing Pepsi trademarks. In addition to purchasing PEP concentrates to manufacture beverages, PBG relies on PEP as an agent for the procurement of other essential inputs from third parties, such as sweeteners, glass and plastic bottles, cans, and other packaging materials.

Company Financials Fiscal Year Ended Dec. 31

Per Share Data ($)	2006	2005	2004	2003	2002	2001	2000	1999	1998	1997
Tangible Book Value	NM	NM	NM	NM	NM	NM	NM	NM	NM	NA
Cash Flow	4.84	4.38	3.99	3.57	3.00	2.77	2.23	2.43	2.96	NA
Earnings	2.16	1.86	1.73	1.52	1.46	1.03	0.77	0.46	-0.39	NA
S&P Core Earnings	2.27	1.71	1.64	1.42	1.18	0.78	NA	NA	NA	NA
Dividends	0.52	0.29	0.16	0.04	0.04	0.04	0.04	0.02	NA	NA
Payout Ratio	24%	16%	9%	3%	3%	4%	5%	4%	NA	NA
Prices:High	35.83	30.35	31.40	27.62	34.80	25.00	21.25	12.63	NA	NA
Prices:Low	27.99	26.00	24.00	17.00	21.65	15.81	8.13	7.75	NA	NA
P/E Ratio:High	17	16	18	18	24	24	28	27	NA	NA
P/E Ratio:Low	13	14	14	11	15	15	11	17	NA	NA

Income Statement Analysis (Million $)										
Revenue	12,730	11,885	10,906	10,265	9,216	8,443	7,982	7,505	7,041	NA
Operating Income	1,666	1,653	1,568	1,524	1,349	1,190	1,025	901	749	NA
Depreciation	649	630	593	568	451	514	435	505	472	NA
Interest Expense	266	250	230	239	191	194	192	202	221	NA
Pretax Income	740	772	745	710	700	482	397	209	-192	NA
Effective Tax Rate	21.5%	32.0%	31.1%	33.5%	31.6%	28.2%	34.0%	33.5%	NM	NA
Net Income	522	466	457	422	428	305	229	118	-146	NA
S&P Core Earnings	549	431	435	394	347	229	NA	NA	NA	NA

Balance Sheet & Other Financial Data (Million $)										
Cash	629	502	305	1,235	222	277	318	190	36.0	NA
Current Assets	2,749	2,412	2,039	3,039	1,737	1,548	1,584	1,493	1,318	NA
Total Assets	11,927	11,524	10,793	11,544	10,027	7,857	7,736	7,619	7,322	NA
Current Liabilities	2,051	2,598	1,581	2,478	1,248	1,081	967	947	1,025	NA
Long Term Debt	4,754	3,939	4,489	4,493	4,523	3,285	3,271	3,268	3,361	NA
Common Equity	2,084	2,043	1,949	1,881	1,824	1,601	1,646	1,563	-238	NA
Total Capital	8,671	7,899	8,298	8,191	7,960	6,226	6,295	6,287	4,325	NA
Capital Expenditures	725	715	717	644	623	593	515	560	507	NA
Cash Flow	1,171	1,096	1,050	990	879	819	664	623	326	NA
Current Ratio	1.3	0.9	1.3	1.2	1.4	1.4	1.6	1.6	1.3	NA
% Long Term Debt of Capitalization	54.8	49.9	54.1	54.9	56.8	52.8	52.0	51.9	77.7	NA
% Net Income of Revenue	4.1	3.9	4.2	4.1	4.6	3.6	2.9	1.6	NM	NA
% Return on Assets	4.5	4.1	4.1	3.9	4.8	3.9	3.0	1.6	NM	NA
% Return on Equity	25.3	23.3	23.9	22.8	25.0	18.8	14.3	17.8	NM	NA

Data as orig reptd.; bef. results of disc opers/spec. items. Per share data adj. for stk. divs.; EPS diluted. E-Estimated. NA-Not Available. NM-Not Meaningful. NR-Not Ranked. UR-Under Review.

Office: 1 Pepsi Way, Somers, NY 10589-2204.
Telephone: 914-767-6000.
Email: shareholder.relations@pepsi.com
Website: http://www.pbg.com

Chrmn: B.H. Beracha
Pres & CEO: E.J. Foss
SVP & CFO: A.H. Drewes
SVP, Secy & General Counsel: S.M. Rapp

SVP & CIO: N.A. Bronzo
Investor Contact: M. Settino (914-767-7216)
Board Members: L. G. Alvarado, B. H. Beracha, E. J. Foss, I. D. Hall, H. F. Johnston, S. D. Kronick, B. J. McGarvie, M. D. Moore, J. D. Quelch, J. G. Teruel

Founded: 1999
Domicile: Delaware
Employees: 70,400

PerkinElmer Inc.

STANDARD &POOR'S

S&P Recommendation **BUY** ★★★★☆	Price $26.94 (as of Nov 23, 2007)	12-Mo. Target Price $35.00	Investment Style Large-Cap Value

GICS Sector Health Care
Sub-Industry Life Sciences Tools & Services

Summary This diversified technology company provides advanced scientific and technical products and services worldwide to the pharmaceutical and industrial industries.

Key Stock Statistics (Source S&P, Vickers, company reports)

52-Wk Range	$30.00–20.94	S&P Oper. EPS 2007E	1.29	Market Capitalization(B)	$3.268	Beta	1.72
Trailing 12-Month EPS	$0.99	S&P Oper. EPS 2008E	1.49	Yield (%)	1.04	S&P 3-Yr. Proj. EPS CAGR(%)	16.00
Trailing 12-Month P/E	27.2	P/E on S&P Oper. EPS 2007E	20.9	Dividend Rate/Share	$0.28	S&P Credit Rating	BBB
$10K Invested 5 Yrs Ago	$34,253	Common Shares Outstg. (M)	121.3	Institutional Ownership (%)	79		

Price Performance

- 30-Week Mov. Avg. ···
- 10-Week Mov. Avg. - -
- 12-Mo. Target Price —
- Relative Strength —
- GAAP Earnings vs. Previous Year
- ▲ Up ▼ Down ▶ No Change
- Volume Above Avg. ⫿⫿⫿
- Below Avg. ⫿⫿⫿
- STARS ★

Options: ASE, CBOE, Ph

Analysis prepared by **Jeffrey Loo, CFA** on November 05, 2007, when the stock traded at **$ 27.52**.

Highlights

➤ We see sales increasing 14% in 2007, to $1.76 billion, and 9.1% in 2008 to $1.92 billion, on contributions from acquisitions (exclusive of the proposed ViaCell deal, subject to necessary approvals) and organic growth within Life and Analytical Sciences, driven by new products. We think recent divestitures narrowed PKI's portfolio and should enable it to focus on higher-margin and faster-growing products. We see continued robust growth in genetic screening as developing countries increasingly adopt prenatal screening, and on strong medical imaging sales, partially offset by slow growth in bio-pharmaceuticals. We believe the planned ViaCell deal will expand PKI's neonatal and prenatal product lines. We look for high single-digit growth in optoelectronics on increased capacity in medical imaging.

➤ We see the 2007 and 2008 gross margin improving 50 and 110 basis points as a higher-margin product mix is partially offset by increased investments. We see operating margins rising 110 bps and 120 bps on operating leverage, partially offset by higher R&D costs.

➤ Excluding intangible amortization, we see 2007 and 2008 operating EPS at $1.29 and $1.49.

Investment Rationale/Risk

➤ We believe PKI is benefiting from its R&D investments, recent acquisitions and portfolio restructuring, which should result in improving sales and margins in the second half of 2007 and into 2008. We think PKI's acquisitions, product development efforts, and recent divestitures will allow the company to focus on the faster-growing, higher-margin health sciences end market, which should account for about 85% of sales. Separately, we believe PKI's management succession plan should lead to a smooth transition.

➤ Risks to our recommendation and target price include slower-than-anticipated growth in health sciences end markets, greater-than-expected integration challenges from recent acquisitions, and a slowdown in PKI's fastest-growing markets, including Asia.

➤ Our 12-month target price of $35 is based on a blend of our discounted cash flow analysis, using a weighted average cost of capital of 9.8% and a terminal growth rate of 3%, and our relative valuation analysis, using a P/E-to-growth ratio of 1.5X our 2008 EPS estimate, in line with peers, valuing the shares at $35.

Qualitative Risk Assessment

LOW	**MEDIUM**	HIGH

Our risk assessment reflects PKI's broad product mix and diverse global client base. However, the company has been actively restructuring its business units and product portfolio, which we believe could increase operating risks.

Quantitative Evaluations

S&P Quality Ranking   **B**

D	C	B-	**B**	B+	A-	A	A+

Relative Strength Rank   **MODERATE**

64

LOWEST = 1   HIGHEST = 99

Revenue/Earnings Data

Revenue (Million $)

	1Q	2Q	3Q	4Q	Year
2007	402.9	437.3	435.7	--	--
2006	355.5	377.0	386.9	427.0	1,546
2005	358.2	368.0	360.0	387.7	1,474
2004	392.6	412.6	403.4	478.6	1,687
2003	358.5	377.1	367.1	432.6	1,535
2002	346.3	383.1	366.0	409.6	1,505

Earnings Per Share ($)

	1Q	2Q	3Q	4Q	Year
2007	0.12	0.28	0.26	E0.45	E1.29
2006	0.17	0.21	0.23	0.33	0.94
2005	0.12	0.23	0.20	-0.05	0.51
2004	0.11	0.17	0.19	0.29	0.75
2003	0.03	0.08	0.11	0.21	0.43
2002	-0.23	0.03	0.08	0.01	-0.03

Fiscal year ended Dec. 31. Next earnings report expected: Late January. EPS Estimates based on S&P Operating Earnings; historical GAAP earnings are as reported.

Dividend Data (Dates: mm/dd Payment Date: mm/dd/yy)

Amount ($)	Date Decl.	Ex-Div. Date	Stk. of Record	Payment Date
0.070	01/25	04/18	04/20	05/11/07
0.070	05/16	07/18	07/20	08/10/07
0.070	07/25	10/17	10/19	11/09/07
0.070	10/24	01/16	01/18	02/08/08

Dividends have been paid since 1965. Source: Company reports.

Please read the Required Disclosures and Analyst Certification on the last page of this report.

The McGraw-Hill Companies

PerkinElmer Inc.

Business Summary November 05, 2007

CORPORATE OVERVIEW. PerkinElmer is a global technology company with operations in more than 125 countries. It develops, manufactures and provides scientific instruments, consumables and services to the pharmaceutical, biomedical, environmental testing and general industrial markets. Collectively, these markets are commonly referred to as the health sciences and industrial sciences markets. In 2005, PKI operated three business segments within its end markets: Life and Analytical Sciences, Optoelectronics, and Fluid Sciences. However, in 2005 and 2006, PKI divested its Fluid Sciences unit in an effort to focus on the health sciences market, which PKI believes has greater growth and profitability potential. The health sciences markets include all of the businesses in the Life and Analytical Sciences unit and the medical imaging, medical sensors and lighting business in the Optoelectronics unit. The industrial sciences markets include the remaining businesses in Optoelectronics.

Life and Analytical Sciences provides drug discovery, genetic screening, and environmental and chemical analysis tools, including instruments, reagents, consumables and services. Its instruments are used for scientific research and clinical applications. For drug discovery, PKI offers a wide range of in-

strumentation, software and consumables, including reagents, based on its core expertise in fluorescent, chemiluminescent and radioactive labeling, and the detection of nucleic acids and proteins. For genetic screening laboratories, it provides software, reagents and analysis tools to test for various inherited disorders. For chemical analysis, the company offers analytical tools employing technologies such as molecular and atomic spectroscopy, high-pressure liquid chromatography, gas chromatography and thermal analysis.

The Optoelectronics unit makes products that include digital imaging, sensor and specialty lighting components to customers in biomedical, consumer products and other specialty end markets. PKI supplies amorphous silicon digital X-ray detectors, a technology for medical imaging and radiation therapy. The company's specialty lighting technologies include xenon flashtubes, ceramic xenon light sources, and laser pump sources.

Company Financials Fiscal Year Ended Dec. 31

Per Share Data ($)	2006	2005	2004	2003	2002	2001	2000	1999	1998	1997
Tangible Book Value	0.45	1.91	NM	NM	NM	NM	NM	NM	0.92	2.75
Cash Flow	1.52	1.03	1.35	1.07	0.58	0.77	1.62	1.01	1.66	0.82
Earnings	0.94	0.51	0.75	0.43	-0.03	-0.01	1.32	0.31	1.11	0.34
S&P Core Earnings	0.91	0.40	0.63	0.25	-0.34	-0.68	NA	NA	NA	NA
Dividends	0.28	0.28	0.28	0.28	0.28	0.28	0.28	0.28	0.28	0.28
Payout Ratio	30%	55%	37%	65%	NM	NM	21%	92%	25%	84%
Prices:High	24.17	24.02	23.28	18.71	36.30	52.31	60.50	22.50	16.88	12.31
Prices:Low	16.31	17.92	15.05	7.22	4.28	21.28	19.00	12.75	9.44	9.00
P/E Ratio:High	26	47	31	44	NM	NM	46	74	15	37
P/E Ratio:Low	17	35	20	17	NM	NM	14	42	9	27

Income Statement Analysis (Million $)										
Revenue	1,546	1,474	1,687	1,535	1,505	1,330	1,695	1,363	1,408	1,461
Operating Income	221	229	253	211	131	196	263	177	144	132
Depreciation	69.2	67.0	76.2	80.2	76.6	80.5	79.1	66.1	50.4	44.6
Interest Expense	9.16	74.3	38.0	Nil	Nil	Nil	Nil	28.3	11.4	12.5
Pretax Income	151	66.7	137	80.9	-8.55	34.2	144	44.9	156	54.0
Effective Tax Rate	21.5%	0.19%	28.2%	32.0%	NM	NM	40.4%	36.8%	34.6%	43.3%
Net Income	118	66.5	98.3	55.0	-4.14	-0.62	86.1	28.4	102	30.6
S&P Core Earnings	114	53.8	81.3	31.2	-43.1	-71.3	NA	NA	NA	NA

Balance Sheet & Other Financial Data (Million $)										
Cash	199	502	208	202	317	138	126	127	95.6	57.9
Current Assets	745	999	748	766	991	997	893	815	565	488
Total Assets	2,510	2,693	2,576	2,608	2,836	2,919	2,260	1,715	1,185	832
Current Liabilities	477	495	446	452	698	708	718	852	524	286
Long Term Debt	152	243	365	544	614	598	583	115	130	114
Common Equity	1,578	1,651	1,460	1,349	1,252	1,364	728	551	400	328
Total Capital	1,730	1,894	1,825	1,893	1,866	1,962	1,312	666	530	443
Capital Expenditures	44.5	25.1	19.0	16.6	37.8	88.7	70.6	41.1	NA	48.7
Cash Flow	188	134	174	135	72.4	79.9	165	94.5	152	75.3
Current Ratio	1.6	2.0	1.7	1.7	1.4	1.4	1.2	1.0	1.1	1.7
% Long Term Debt of Capitalization	8.8	12.8	20.0	28.7	32.9	30.5	44.5	17.3	24.5	25.9
% Net Income of Revenue	7.7	4.5	5.8	3.6	NM	NM	5.1	2.1	7.2	2.1
% Return on Assets	4.5	2.5	3.8	2.0	NM	NM	4.3	2.0	10.1	3.7
% Return on Equity	7.3	4.3	7.0	4.2	NM	NM	13.5	6.0	28.0	8.8

Data as orig reptd.; bef. results of disc opers/spec. items. Per share data adj. for stk. divs.; EPS diluted. E-Estimated. NA-Not Available. NM-Not Meaningful. NR-Not Ranked. UR-Under Review.

Office: 940 Winter St, Wellesley, MA 02481-4008.
Telephone: 781-663-6900.
Website: http://www.perkinelmer.com
Chrmn, Pres & CEO: G.L. Summe

Vice Chrmn: R.F. Friel
SVP & CFO: J.D. Capello
SVP & Chief Admin Officer: R.F. Walsh
SVP, Secy & General Counsel: K.A. O'Hara

Board Members: R. F. Friel, N. A. Lopardo, A. P. Michas, J. C. Mullen, V. L. Sato, G. Schmergel, K. J. Sicchitano, G. L. Summe, G. R. Tod

Founded: 1947
Domicile: Massachusetts
Employees: 8,500

Pfizer Inc.

STANDARD &POOR'S

S&P Recommendation	HOLD ★★★☆☆	Price $22.98 (as of Nov 23, 2007)	12-Mo. Target Price $28.00	Investment Style Large-Cap Blend

GICS Sector Health Care
Sub-Industry Pharmaceuticals

Summary Pfizer is the world's largest pharmaceutical company, producing a wide range of drugs across a broad therapeutic spectrum. In December 2006, PFE sold its consumer products division to Johnson & Johnson for $16.6 billion in cash.

Key Stock Statistics (Source S&P, Vickers, company reports)

52-Wk Range	$27.88–22.29	S&P Oper. EPS 2007E	2.15	Market Capitalization(B)	$159.185	Beta	0.60
Trailing 12-Month EPS	$2.09	S&P Oper. EPS 2008E	2.33	Yield (%)	5.05	S&P 3-Yr. Proj. EPS CAGR(%)	7.00
Trailing 12-Month P/E	11.0	P/E on S&P Oper. EPS 2007E	10.7	Dividend Rate/Share	$1.16	S&P Credit Rating	AAA
$10K Invested 5 Yrs Ago	$8,263	Common Shares Outstg. (M)	6,927.1	Institutional Ownership (%)	68		

Price Performance

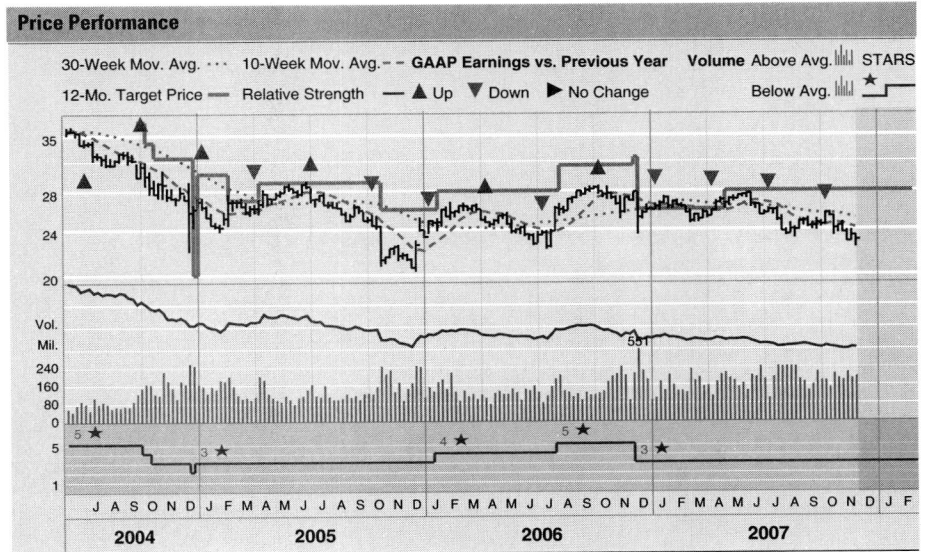

30-Week Mov. Avg. ··· 10-Week Mov. Avg. - - GAAP Earnings vs. Previous Year Volume Above Avg. STARS
12-Mo. Target Price — Relative Strength — ▲ Up ▼ Down ▶ No Change Below Avg.

Options: ASE, CBOE, P, Ph

Analysis prepared by **Herman B. Saftlas** on October 22, 2007, when the stock traded at **$24.05**.

Highlights

➤ We expect revenues in 2008 to decline modestly from the $47.8 billion that we estimate for 2007. We see the top line primarily affected by projected sharp declines in sales of Norvasc cardiovascular and Zyrtec allergy treatment, reflecting the effects of generic erosion in those lines. We also see further attrition in the Lipitor cholesterol lowering drug (estimated to account for about 25% of total revenues in 2007), reflecting increased competitive conditions in both domestic and foreign markets. On the plus side, we forecast growth for Celebrex and Geodon, as well as greater contributions from newer drugs such as Lyrica, Sutent and Chantix. Alliance revenues should also rise.

➤ We think gross margins will improve modestly in 2008, helped by cost efficiencies. SG&A and R&D spending should also decline under PFE's aggressive ongoing cost reduction program, which is expected to yield savings of up to $2.0 billion by the end of 2008.

➤ Helped by an estimated 5% reduction in average shares, we project operating EPS of $2.33 in 2008, up from an indicated $2.15 for 2007.

Investment Rationale/Risk

➤ We think PFE is struggling with huge expiration losses, including the loss of patent protection on Norvasc and Zyrtec. On the plus side, PFE has a cost restructuring program designed to yield up to $2 billion in savings by the end of 2008, as well as a large mid-stage pipeline. Helped by new drugs, cost savings and stock buybacks, PFE hopes to increase EPS from an estimated $2.10-$2.15 in 2007 to $2.31-$2.45 in 2008. We think this goal will be challenging, but attainable, as we believe sales will trend lower over the next few years. Lipitor loses patent protection in 2011, and PFE recently pulled Exubera inhaled insulin off the market due to disappointing sales.

➤ Risks to our recommendation and target price include competitive pressures in key drug lines, and possible pipeline setbacks.

➤ Our 12-month target price of $28 applies a below peer P/E of about 12X to our 2008 EPS estimate. Our target price is also close to our calculation of intrinsic value, derived from our DCF model, which assumes decelerating cash flow growth over 10 years and a WACC of 7.2%.

Qualitative Risk Assessment

LOW	MEDIUM	HIGH

Our risk assessment reflects PFE's lead position in the global pharmaceutical market, which we believe affords the company significant competitive advantages in terms of marketing and R&D. We also think PFE has unmatched financial flexibility in the pharmaceutical sector. However, we see these pluses offset by the effects of patent expirations and pipeline uncertainties.

Quantitative Evaluations

S&P Quality Ranking A-

D	C	B-	B	B+	A-	A	A+

Relative Strength Rank MODERATE

54

LOWEST = 1   HIGHEST = 99

Revenue/Earnings Data

Revenue (Million $)

	1Q	2Q	3Q	4Q	Year
2007	12,474	11,084	11,990	--	--
2006	11,747	11,741	12,280	12,603	48,371
2005	13,091	12,425	12,189	13,592	51,298
2004	12,487	12,274	12,831	14,924	52,516
2003	8,525	9,993	12,504	14,167	45,188
2002	7,747	7,296	7,996	9,333	32,373

Earnings Per Share ($)

2007	0.48	0.19	0.12	E0.47	E2.15
2006	0.55	0.31	0.44	0.21	1.52
2005	0.04	0.47	0.22	0.37	1.09
2004	0.30	0.38	0.43	0.39	1.49
2003	0.40	-0.49	0.29	0.08	0.22
2002	0.37	0.30	0.37	0.43	1.47

Fiscal year ended Dec. 31. Next earnings report expected: Late January. EPS Estimates based on S&P Operating Earnings; historical GAAP earnings are as reported.

Dividend Data (Dates: mm/dd Payment Date: mm/dd/yy)

Amount ($)	Date Decl.	Ex-Div. Date	Stk. of Record	Payment Date
0.290	12/18	02/07	02/09	03/06/07
0.290	04/26	05/09	05/11	06/05/07
0.290	06/28	08/08	08/10	09/05/07
0.290	10/25	11/07	11/09	12/04/07

Dividends have been paid since 1901. Source: Company reports.

Pfizer Inc.

STANDARD
&POOR'S

Business Summary October 22, 2007

CORPORATE OVERVIEW. Pfizer stands out above its peers in the $670 billion global pharmaceutical sector, in our opinion. Growth over the past 10 years was largely augmented by two major acquisitions--Warner-Lambert Co. in 2000 and Pharmacia Corp. in 2003--as well as by in-licensed products. In December 2006, PFE sold its consumer health care products business (sales of $3.9 billion in 2005) to Johnson & Johnson for $16.6 billion in cash.

MARKET PROFILE. Worldwide pharmaceutical industry revenue growth has slowed in recent years, reflecting the effects of tighter reimbursements from key managed care markets, the loss of patent protection on blockbuster drugs, and relatively sluggish new product flow stemming from reduced R&D productivity. IMS Health projects that the global drug market will grow 5%-6% in 2007, down from 6.8% in 2006. For the U.S. alone, IMS estimates market growth of 4%-5% in 2007, versus 8.3% in 2006, reflecting the loss of patent protection on several large selling drugs.

COMPETITIVE LANDSCAPE. We think Pfizer's size gives it important competitive advantages over peers, especially in terms of marketing prowess in managed care and Medicare markets. In our opinion, the company's size and fi-

nancial resources also empower it with a greater ability to make acquisitions and form strategic alliances with smaller pharmaceutical and biotechnology companies. Pfizer's drug portfolio is unmatched in terms of breadth and depth in the global drug market. Foreign sales accounted for 46% of total revenues in 2006.

Principal cardiovasculars include Lipitor, the world's largest selling cholesterol-lowering agent as well as the biggest drug in any therapeutic category in 2006 (sales of $12.9 billion in 2006), and antihypertensives such as Norvasc ($4.9 billion) and Cardura ($538 million). Infectious disease drugs consist of Zyvox ($782 million), a treatment for severe bacterial infections, and Zithromax, a now off-patent broad spectrum antibiotic ($638 million). Key central nervous system medicines include Zoloft, a now off patent antidepressant ($2.1 billion); Lyrica, a treatment for nerve pain and epileptic seizures ($1.2 billion); and Geodon, an antipsychotic ($758 million).

Company Financials Fiscal Year Ended Dec. 31

Per Share Data ($)	2006	2005	2004	2003	2002	2001	2000	1999	1998	1997
Tangible Book Value	3.65	1.91	1.48	0.85	3.04	2.64	2.26	2.11	2.06	2.03
Cash Flow	2.24	1.84	2.16	0.78	1.64	1.39	0.74	0.96	0.63	0.69
Earnings	1.52	1.09	1.49	0.22	1.47	1.22	0.59	0.82	0.49	0.57
S&P Core Earnings	1.53	1.02	1.45	0.29	1.35	1.09	NA	NA	NA	NA
Dividends	0.96	0.76	0.68	0.60	0.52	0.44	0.36	0.31	0.25	0.23
Payout Ratio	63%	70%	46%	273%	35%	36%	61%	37%	51%	40%
Prices:High	28.60	29.21	38.89	36.92	42.46	46.75	49.25	50.04	42.98	26.67
Prices:Low	22.16	20.27	21.99	27.90	25.13	34.00	30.00	31.54	23.69	13.44
P/E Ratio:High	19	27	26	NM	29	38	83	61	87	47
P/E Ratio:Low	15	19	15	NM	17	28	51	38	48	24

Income Statement Analysis (Million $)

	2006	2005	2004	2003	2002	2001	2000	1999	1998	1997
Revenue	48,371	51,298	52,516	45,188	32,373	32,259	29,574	16,204	13,544	12,504
Operating Income	19,575	20,501	22,117	17,061	13,436	12,147	9,758	5,091	4,092	3,848
Depreciation	5,293	5,576	5,093	4,078	1,036	1,068	968	542	489	502
Interest Expense	488	488	359	290	279	432	401	236	143	149
Pretax Income	13,028	11,534	14,007	3,263	11,796	10,329	5,781	4,448	2,594	3,088
Effective Tax Rate	15.3%	29.7%	19.0%	49.7%	22.1%	24.8%	35.4%	28.0%	24.7%	28.0%
Net Income	11,024	8,094	11,332	1,639	9,181	7,752	3,718	3,199	1,950	2,213
S&P Core Earnings	11,048	7,588	11,030	2,147	8,441	6,862	NA	NA	NA	NA

Balance Sheet & Other Financial Data (Million $)

	2006	2005	2004	2003	2002	2001	2000	1999	1998	1997
Cash	1,827	2,247	1,808	1,520	1,878	1,036	1,099	739	1,552	877
Current Assets	46,949	41,896	39,694	29,741	24,781	18,450	17,187	11,191	9,931	6,820
Total Assets	114,837	117,565	123,684	116,775	46,356	39,153	33,510	20,574	18,302	15,336
Current Liabilities	21,389	28,448	26,458	23,657	18,555	13,640	11,981	9,185	7,192	5,305
Long Term Debt	5,546	6,347	7,279	5,755	3,140	2,609	1,123	525	527	729
Common Equity	71,217	65,458	68,085	65,158	19,950	18,293	16,076	8,887	8,810	7,933
Total Capital	84,919	82,214	88,189	84,370	23,454	21,354	17,579	9,713	9,534	8,818
Capital Expenditures	2,050	2,106	2,601	2,641	1,758	2,203	2,191	1,561	1,198	943
Cash Flow	16,317	13,661	16,417	5,710	10,217	8,820	4,686	3,741	2,484	2,715
Current Ratio	2.2	1.5	1.5	1.3	1.3	1.4	1.4	1.2	1.4	1.3
% Long Term Debt of Capitalization	6.5	7.7	8.3	6.8	13.4	12.2	6.4	5.4	5.5	8.3
% Net Income of Revenue	22.8	15.8	21.6	3.6	28.4	24.0	12.6	19.7	14.4	17.7
% Return on Assets	9.5	6.7	9.4	2.0	21.5	21.3	11.5	16.5	11.6	14.8
% Return on Equity	16.1	12.1	17.0	3.8	48.0	45.1	24.8	36.2	23.3	29.7

Data as orig reptd.; bef. results of disc opers/spec. items. Per share data adj. for stk. divs.; EPS diluted. E-Estimated. NA-Not Available. NM-Not Meaningful. NR-Not Ranked. UR-Under Review.

Office: 235 East 42nd Street, New York, NY 10017-5703. **Telephone:** 212-573-2323. **Website:** http://www.pfizer.com **Chrmn & CEO:** J.B. Kindler	**Vice Chrmn:** D.L. Shedlarz **SVP & General Counsel:** A. Waxman **VP & Cntlr:** L.V. Cangialosi **Investor Contact:** A. Naj	**Board Members:** D. A. Ausiello, M. S. Brown, M. A. Burns, R. N. Burt, W. D. Cornwell, W. H. Gray III, C. J. Horner, W. R. Howell, S. O. Ikenberry, J. B. Kindler, G. A. Lorch, H. A. McKinnell, D. G. Mead, R. J. Simmons, W. C. Steere, Jr. **Founded:** 1849 **Domicile:** Delaware **Employees:** 98,000

PG&E Corp

STANDARD &POOR'S

S&P Recommendation **HOLD** ★★★☆☆	Price $46.01 (as of Nov 28, 2007)	12-Mo. Target Price $48.00	Investment Style Large-Cap Blend

GICS Sector Utilities
Sub-Industry Multi-Utilities

Summary This energy holding company is the parent of Pacific Gas and Electric Co., which emerged from a bankruptcy reorganization in April 2004.

Key Stock Statistics (Source S&P, Vickers, company reports)

52-Wk Range	$52.17– 42.58	S&P Oper. EPS 2007 **E**	2.77	Market Capitalization(B)	$16.258	Beta	0.84
Trailing 12-Month EPS	$2.65	S&P Oper. EPS 2008 **E**	3.00	Yield (%)	3.13	S&P 3-Yr. Proj. EPS CAGR(%)	6.00
Trailing 12-Month P/E	17.4	P/E on S&P Oper. EPS 2007 **E**	16.6	Dividend Rate/Share	$1.44	S&P Credit Rating	NR
$10K Invested 5 Yrs Ago	$36,480	Common Shares Outstg. (M)	353.4	Institutional Ownership (%)	65		

Price Performance

30-Week Mov. Avg. ··· 10-Week Mov. Avg. – – GAAP Earnings vs. Previous Year Volume Above Avg. STARS
12-Mo. Target Price — Relative Strength — ▲ Up ▼ Down ► No Change Below Avg. ★

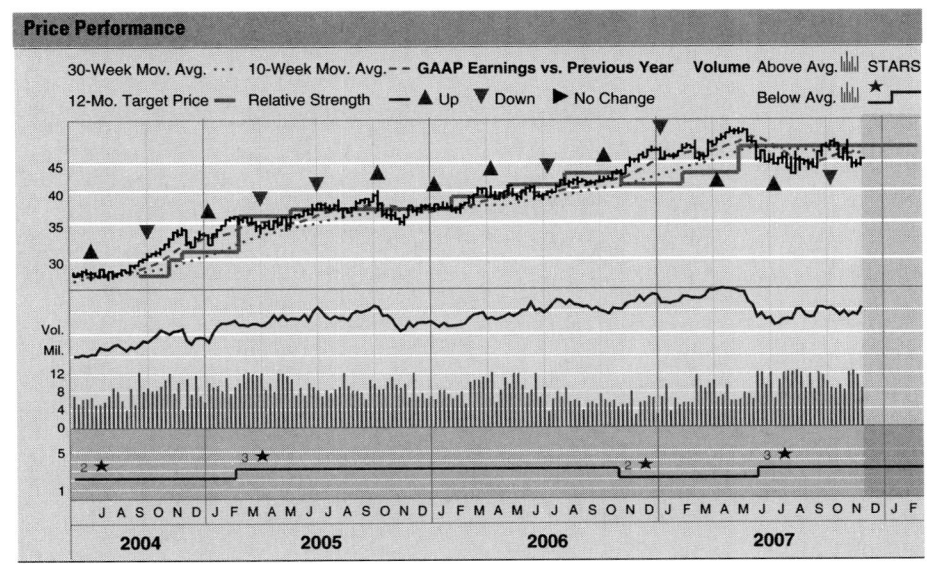

Options: ASE, CBOE, P

Analysis prepared by **Justin McCann** on November 28, 2007, when the stock traded at **$ 45.82**.

Highlights

➤ We expect operating EPS in 2007 to increase more than 7%, from 2006 operating EPS of $2.57, largely driven by rate increases retroactively authorized by the California Public Utility Commission (CPUC). In addition to higher rates, EPS in the first nine months of 2007 benefited from reduced natural gas costs and a lower tax rate.

➤ For 2008, we expect operating EPS to increase approximately 8% from anticipated results in 2007, primarily driven by higher electric revenues resulting from PCG's pre-approved rate base transmission and generation investments.

➤ On March 15, 2007, the CPUC approved a multi-party settlement resolving the 2007 General Rate Case for Pacific Gas & Electric (PG&E). The decision authorized a $222 million increase (to about $2.9 billion) for PG&E's electric distribution business, a $21 million increase (to around $1 billion) for its natural gas distribution segment, and a decrease of $30 million (to approximately $1 billion) for its electric generation operations. The net 4.5% increase, to about $4.9 billion, was made retroactively effective to January 1, 2007, and the new rates will remain in effect through the end of 2010.

Investment Rationale/Risk

➤ With the shares having declined nearly 4% year to date (following a 27% advance in 2006), we view them as appropriately valued, trading at a discount-to-peers P/E based on our 2007 EPS estimate. Although it has underperformed thus far in 2007, we expect the stock to perform more in line with its electric and gas utility peers over the next 12 months.

➤ Risks to our recommendation and target price include a much worse than expected earnings performance, and/or a major decline in the average P/E multiple of the group as a whole.

➤ The recent decline in the shares has reduced the P/E on our 2007 EPS estimate from a premium-to-peers' P/E of 18.6X in mid-May to a discount-to-peers P/E of about 16.5X. The decline also increased the recent yield from the dividend (from about 2.8% to around 3.2%), and slightly narrowed the spread with the recent peer yield (which has increased from approximately 3.3% to around 3.4%). We expect the shares to trade at a nearly 4% discount-to-peers P/E of around 16X our 2008 EPS estimate. Our 12-month target price is $48.

Qualitative Risk Assessment

LOW	MEDIUM	HIGH

Our risk assessment reflects our view of the company's: strong and steady cash flow from the regulated Pacific Gas & Electric subsidiary; a much improved balance sheet and credit profile; a healthy economy in its service territory; and a greatly improved regulatory environment.

Quantitative Evaluations

S&P Quality Ranking   B

D	C	B-	**B**	B+	A-	A	A+

Relative Strength Rank   STRONG

72

LOWEST = 1   HIGHEST = 99

Revenue/Earnings Data

Revenue (Million $)

	1Q	2Q	3Q	4Q	Year
2007	3,356	3,187	3,279	--	--
2006	3,148	3,017	3,168	3,206	12,539
2005	2,669	2,498	2,804	3,732	11,703
2004	2,722	2,749	2,623	2,986	11,080
2003	2,065	2,729	3,103	2,538	10,435
2002	2,935	2,938	3,654	2,968	12,495

Earnings Per Share ($)

	1Q	2Q	3Q	4Q	Year
2007	0.71	0.74	0.77	E0.55	E2.77
2006	0.60	0.65	1.09	0.43	2.76
2005	0.54	0.70	0.62	0.49	2.34
2004	7.15	0.88	0.53	0.44	8.97
2003	-0.21	0.81	1.24	0.09	1.96
2002	1.71	0.75	1.17	-3.72	-0.15

Fiscal year ended Dec. 31. Next earnings report expected: Late February. EPS Estimates based on S&P Operating Earnings; historical GAAP earnings are as reported.

Dividend Data (Dates: mm/dd Payment Date: mm/dd/yy)

Amount ($)	Date Decl.	Ex-Div. Date	Stk. of Record	Payment Date
0.330	12/20	12/27	12/29	01/15/07
0.360	03/16	03/28	03/30	04/15/07
0.360	06/20	06/28	07/02	07/15/07
0.360	09/19	09/27	10/01	10/15/07

Dividends have been paid since 2005. Source: Company reports.

Please read the Required Disclosures and Analyst Certification on the last page of this report.

The **McGraw-Hill** Companies

PG&E Corp

STANDARD
&POOR'S

Business Summary November 28, 2007

CORPORATE OVERVIEW. PG&E Corporation (PCG) is an energy-based holding company that conducts its business through Pacific Gas and Electric Company, a public utility operating in northern and central California. The utility's business consists of four main operational units: electricity and natural gas distribution, electricity generation, gas transmission, and electricity transmission. The utility is primarily regulated by the California Public Utilities Commission (CPUC) and the Federal Energy Regulatory Commission (FERC).

CORPORATE STRATEGY. In order to support anticipated customer growth and the improvement of its existing services, Pacific Gas & Electric plans to make major capital additions to its infrastructure. During 2007, it expects to connect about 75,000 new electric customers and around 62,000 new gas customers. The utility is also devoting substantial resources to the building and expansion of its transmission lines, which has become the fastest growing part of its business. It has proposed constructing additional gas and electric transmission arteries so as to create access to new supplies of renewable energy and new sources of natural gas. In addition to maintaining its ongoing investment in its existing hydroelectric and nuclear, the company is planning to build three new state-of-the-art power plants that are scheduled to come on line between 2009 and 2010, and to generate enough power for around 950,000 homes.

Company Financials Fiscal Year Ended Dec. 31

Per Share Data ($)	2006	2005	2004	2003	2002	2001	2000	1999	1998	1997
Tangible Book Value	20.89	19.67	20.60	10.11	8.92	11.87	8.74	19.13	21.06	21.28
Earnings	2.76	2.34	8.97	1.96	-0.15	2.99	-9.18	0.04	1.88	1.75
S&P Core Earnings	2.64	2.45	9.00	2.05	-1.08	1.59	NA	NA	NA	NA
Dividends	1.32	1.23	Nil	Nil	Nil	Nil	1.20	1.20	1.20	1.20
Payout Ratio	48%	53%	Nil	Nil	Nil	Nil	NM	NM	64%	69%
Prices:High	48.17	40.10	34.46	27.98	23.75	20.94	31.81	34.00	35.06	30.94
Prices:Low	36.25	31.83	25.90	11.69	8.00	6.50	17.00	20.25	29.06	20.88
P/E Ratio:High	17	17	4	14	NM	7	NM	NM	19	18
P/E Ratio:Low	13	14	3	6	NM	2	NM	NM	15	12

Income Statement Analysis (Million $)										
Revenue	12,539	11,703	11,080	10,435	12,495	22,959	26,232	20,820	19,942	15,400
Depreciation	1,709	1,735	1,497	1,222	1,309	1,068	3,659	1,780	1,609	1,889
Maintenance	NA	NA	NA	NA	NA	NA	NA	NA	NA	NA
Fixed Charges Coverage	3.09	3.48	2.75	2.23	2.94	2.48	3.01	2.99	2.65	2.90
Construction Credits	NA	NA	NA	NA	NA	NA	NA	Nil	Nil	Nil
Effective Tax Rate	35.9%	37.6%	39.2%	36.7%	NM	35.8%	NM	95.0%	44.2%	43.4%
Net Income	991	904	3,820	791	-57.0	1,090	-3,324	13.0	719	716
S&P Core Earnings	972	974	3,828	830	-404	580	NA	NA	NA	NA

Balance Sheet & Other Financial Data (Million $)										
Gross Property	34,214	32,030	30,509	29,222	31,179	33,012	28,469	28,067	29,844	20,472
Capital Expenditures	2,402	1,804	1,559	1,698	3,032	2,665	1,758	1,584	1,619	1,822
Net Property	21,785	19,955	18,989	18,107	16,928	19,167	16,591	16,776	17,633	20,472
Capitalization:Long Term Debt	8,885	9,794	8,311	9,924	11,590	9,527	5,516	9,484	10,523	7,659
Capitalization:% Long Term Debt	53.2	57.5	49.0	70.2	76.2	68.8	63.5	57.9	56.6	35.7
Capitalization:Preferred	Nil	Nil	Nil	Nil	Nil	Nil	Nil	Nil	Nil	539
Capitalization:% Preferred	Nil	Nil	Nil	Nil	Nil	Nil	Nil	Nil	Nil	2.71
Capitalization:Common	7,811	7,240	8,633	4,215	3,613	4,322	3,172	6,886	8,066	8,897
Capitalization:% Common	46.8	42.5	51.0	29.8	23.8	31.2	36.5	42.1	43.4	41.5
Total Capital	19,642	20,238	20,596	15,122	16,786	15,668	10,536	19,748	22,733	21,424
% Operating Ratio	87.6	87.8	102.2	80.4	67.2	90.3	84.1	90.9	92.8	92.3
% Earned on Net Property	10.1	10.1	38.4	14.6	31.2	15.0	34.7	5.1	5.0	8.8
% Return on Revenue	7.9	7.7	34.5	7.6	NM	4.7	NM	0.1	3.6	4.6
% Return on Invested Capital	8.7	7.3	15.6	13.9	22.8	16.7	29.1	9.7	6.4	9.0
% Return on Common Equity	13.2	11.4	59.5	20.2	NM	29.1	NM	0.2	8.5	8.3

Data as orig reptd.; bef. results of disc opers/spec. items. Per share data adj. for stk. divs.; EPS diluted. E-Estimated. NA-Not Available. NM-Not Meaningful. NR-Not Ranked. UR-Under Review.

Office: 1 Mkt Steuart Tower St Ste 2400, San Francisco, CA 94105-1415.
Telephone: 415-267-7000.
Email: invrel@pg-corp.com
Website: http://www.pgecorp.com

Chrmn, Pres & CEO: P.A. Darbee
SVP, CFO & Treas: C.P. Johns
SVP & General Counsel: H. Park
Investor Contact: G.B. Togneri (415-267-7080)

Board Members: D. R. Andrews, L. S. Biller, D. A. Coulter, C. L. Cox, P. A. Darbee, M. C. Herringer, R. A. Meserve, M. S. Metz, B. L. Rambo, B. L. Williams

Founded: 1995
Domicile: California
Employees: 20,400

The McGraw-Hill Companies

STANDARD &POOR'S

Pinnacle West Capital Corp

S&P Recommendation HOLD ★★★☆☆	**Price** $43.18 (as of Nov 23, 2007)	**12-Mo. Target Price** $42.00	**Investment Style** Large-Cap Value

GICS Sector Utilities
Sub-Industry Electric Utilities

Summary This utility holding company is the parent of Arizona Public Service (APS), Arizona's largest electric utility.

Key Stock Statistics (Source S&P, Vickers, company reports)

52-Wk Range	$51.67– 36.79	S&P Oper. EPS 2007**E**	2.90	Market Capitalization(B)	$4.331	Beta	0.63
Trailing 12-Month EPS	$3.19	S&P Oper. EPS 2008**E**	2.80	Yield (%)	4.86	S&P 3-Yr. Proj. EPS CAGR(%)	2.00
Trailing 12-Month P/E	13.5	P/E on S&P Oper. EPS 2007**E**	14.9	Dividend Rate/Share	$2.10	S&P Credit Rating	BBB-
$10K Invested 5 Yrs Ago	$17,712	Common Shares Outstg. (M)	100.3	Institutional Ownership (%)	89		

Price Performance

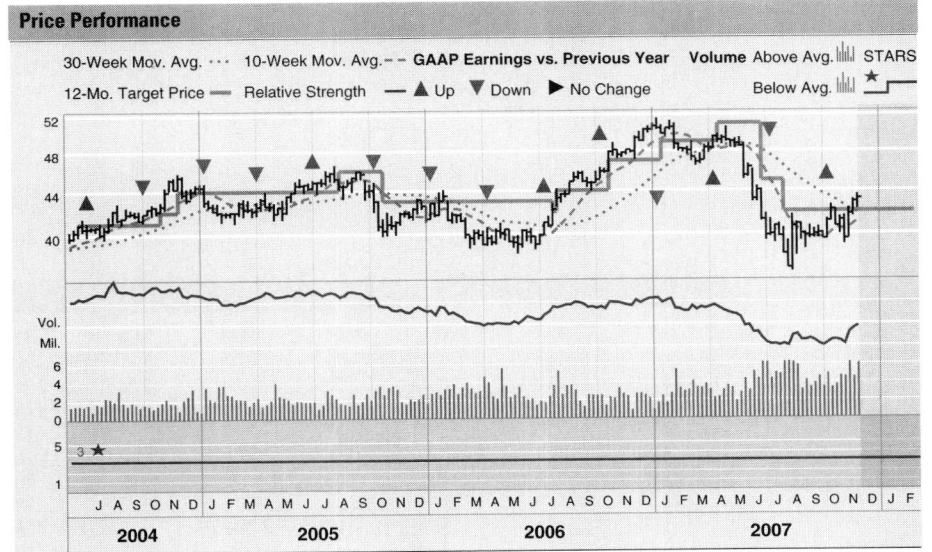

30-Week Mov. Avg. · · · 10-Week Mov. Avg. - - **GAAP Earnings vs. Previous Year** Volume Above Avg. STARS
12-Mo. Target Price — Relative Strength — ▲ Up ▼ Down ▶ No Change Below Avg. ★

Options: P

Analysis prepared by **Justin McCann** on October 31, 2007, when the stock traded at **$ 40.40.**

Qualitative Risk Assessment

LOW	MEDIUM	HIGH

Our risk assessment reflects the steady cash flow that we project from the electric utility operations of Arizona Public Service, which has one of the fastest growing service territories in the U.S. While the regulatory environment has often been difficult, we do not expect to see the general strength of the utility significantly impeded by regulatory rulings. This should help offset the less predictable earnings stream from the real estate business and the power marketing and trading operations.

Quantitative Evaluations

S&P Quality Ranking A-

D	C	B-	B	B+	A-	A	A+

Relative Strength Rank STRONG

89

LOWEST = 1   HIGHEST = 99

Highlights

▶ We expect operating EPS in 2007 to decline about 8% from the 2006 EPS from continuing operations of $3.17. We see higher earnings at the regulated Arizona Public Service utility (APS), aided by a very strong third quarter that benefited from the extremely hot weather. However, we believe this will be more than off-set by a very sharp decline at the SunCor real estate business and a continuing decline in earnings from the marketing and trading operations.

▶ For 2008, we see EPS growth being restricted by continuing weakness in the real estate seg-ment due to a significant slowdown in the re-gional market, which should partially offset the benefit from continuing strong customer growth at Arizona Public Service (APS).

▶ On June 19, 2007, the Arizona Corporation Com-mission approved a net retail rate rise of 6.8% for Arizona Public Service. The decision includ-ed a 15.1% increase ($322 million) in annual base rate revenues effective as of July 1, 2007. This was partially offset, however, by the con-current termination of the interim Power Supply Adjustor (PSA) that had represented an in-crease of 8.3%.

Investment Rationale/Risk

▶ Following a 22% gain in 2006, the stock is down approximately 20% year to date. The sharp drop reflects, in our view, the disappointment related to the APS rate case, the problems at the Palo Verde nuclear facility, and the weakness in the real estate business. Concurrent with the drop in the shares, however, has been a rise in the yield (recently at 5.1%). With the 15% federal tax rate on dividends extended through 2010, we expect the shares to be partially supported by the well-above-peers yield from the divi-dend.

▶ Risks to our recommendation and target price include worse than expected earnings from the real estate business, and a sharp decline in the average P/E multiple of the group as a whole.

▶ With the October declaration of a quarterly divi-dend of $0.525 a share, PNW discontinued its long-standing policy of increasing the annual dividend by $0.10 a year. We expect future de-cisions regarding the dividend to be dependent upon such factors as the company's free cash flow and payout ratio. Our 12-month target price is $42, reflecting a discount-to-peers P/E of approximately 15X our EPS estimate for 2008.

Revenue/Earnings Data

Revenue (Million $)

	1Q	2Q	3Q	4Q	Year
2007	695.1	863.4	1,206	--	--
2006	670.2	925.0	1,076	730.1	3,402
2005	585.4	755.3	955.6	691.7	2,988
2004	574.4	722.7	886.8	734.7	2,900
2003	552.6	683.3	847.7	734.2	2,818
2002	380.2	496.8	719.4	416.6	2,637

Earnings Per Share ($)

2007	0.16	0.78	1.99	E0.07	E2.90
2006	0.12	1.11	1.84	0.10	3.17
2005	0.32	0.88	0.86	0.24	2.31
2004	0.33	0.78	1.14	0.32	2.57
2003	0.22	0.60	1.20	0.50	2.52
2002	0.63	0.89	1.19	-0.17	2.53

Fiscal year ended Dec. 31. Next earnings report expected: Late January. EPS Estimates based on S&P Operating Earnings; historical GAAP earnings are as reported.

Dividend Data (Dates: mm/dd Payment Date: mm/dd/yy)

Amount ($)	Date Decl.	Ex-Div. Date	Stk. of Record	Payment Date
0.525	01/19	01/30	02/01	03/01/07
0.525	04/18	04/27	05/01	06/01/07
0.525	07/18	07/30	08/01	09/04/07
0.525	10/18	10/30	11/01	12/03/07

Dividends have been paid since 1993. Source: Company reports.

Please read the Required Disclosures and Analyst Certification on the last page of this report.

The McGraw·Hill Companies

Pinnacle West Capital Corp

STANDARD &POOR'S

Business Summary October 31, 2007

CORPORATE OVERVIEW. Pinnacle West Capital, formed in 1985, is the holding company for Arizona Public Service (APS), which, with about 1,052,000 customers, is Arizona's largest electric utility. PNW's other major subsidiaries are APS Energy Services, which provides competitive energy services, including wholesale marketing and trading, and SunCor, which is engaged in real estate development and investment activities. In 2006, the regulated electricity segment accounted for 77.4% of PNW's consolidated revenues (compared to 74.9% in 2005); the real estate segment, 11.8% (11.3%); the marketing and trading segment, 9.7% (11.8%); and other, 1.1% (2.0%).

MARKET PROFILE. APS provides vertically integrated retail and wholesale service to the entire state of Arizona, with the exception of Tucson and about 50% of the Phoenix area. In 2006, residential customers accounted for 48.2% of the utility's regulated electric sales (48.2% in 2005); business customers, 47.0% (46.5%); and wholesale and other, 4.7% (5.2%). APS has a 29.1% owned or leased interest in the Palo Verde Nuclear Generating Station's Units 1 and 3, and a 17.0% interest in Unit 2. It has a 100% interest in Units 1, 2 and 3; a 15% interest in Units 4 and 5 of the coal-fueled Four Corners Steam Generating Station; and a 14.0% interest in Units 1, 2 and 3 of the coal-fueled Navajo Steam Generating Station (NGS). Consolidated fuel sources for APS in 2006

were: purchased power, 35%; coal, 31.2%; gas, 17.3%; and nuclear, 16.5%. With APS dependent on purchased power for so much of its fuel sources, we believe that it has been hurt by the sharp rise in natural gas prices and by the time lags involved in being authorized to recover the difference between its actual fuel costs and the rates the company is allowed to charge its customers.

SunCor develops residential, commercial and industrial real estate projects in Arizona, Idaho, New Mexico and Utah. The company, which had total assets of $607 million at the end of 2006, intends to continue its focus on the development of master-planned communities, mixed-use residential, commercial, office and industrial projects. In 2006, SunCor's operating revenues increased to approximately $400 million, from $338 million in 2005, and its net income rose by $5 million, to $61 million. We believe the company will continue to be an important source of PNW's earnings and cash flow.

Company Financials Fiscal Year Ended Dec. 31

Per Share Data ($)	2006	2005	2004	2003	2002	2001	2000	1999	1998	1997
Tangible Book Value	34.48	34.58	30.99	29.81	28.23	29.46	28.09	26.00	25.50	23.90
Earnings	3.17	2.31	2.57	2.52	2.53	3.85	3.56	1.97	2.85	2.76
S&P Core Earnings	3.00	2.00	2.15	2.43	1.65	3.00	NA	NA	NA	NA
Dividends	2.03	1.93	1.83	1.73	1.63	1.53	1.43	1.33	1.23	1.13
Payout Ratio	64%	83%	71%	68%	64%	40%	40%	67%	43%	41%
Prices:High	51.00	46.68	45.84	40.48	46.68	50.70	52.69	43.38	49.25	42.75
Prices:Low	38.31	39.81	36.30	28.34	21.70	37.65	25.69	30.19	39.38	27.63
P/E Ratio:High	16	20	18	16	18	13	15	22	17	15
P/E Ratio:Low	12	17	14	11	9	10	7	15	14	10

Income Statement Analysis (Million $)										
Revenue	3,402	2,988	2,900	2,818	2,637	4,551	3,690	2,423	2,131	1,995
Depreciation	359	348	401	438	425	428	394	386	380	368
Maintenance	NA	NA	NA	NA	NA	NA	NA	NA	NA	NA
Fixed Charges Coverage	3.23	2.77	2.75	2.43	2.64	3.80	3.95	3.61	3.17	2.93
Construction Credits	14.3	11.2	4.89	14.2	NA	NA	NA	11.7	18.6	16.2
Effective Tax Rate	33.0%	36.2%	35.4%	31.4%	39.1%	39.5%	42.5%	38.4%	40.4%	38.9%
Net Income	317	223	235	231	215	327	302	270	243	236
S&P Core Earnings	300	193	197	223	140	255	NA	NA	NA	NA

Balance Sheet & Other Financial Data (Million $)										
Gross Property	11,679	11,200	18,280	10,470	16,316	9,285	8,383	7,805	7,876	7,730
Capital Expenditures	738	634	538	693	896	1,041	659	343	319	308
Net Property	7,882	7,577	14,914	7,310	12,842	5,907	5,133	4,779	5,062	5,043
Capitalization:Long Term Debt	3,233	2,608	2,585	2,898	2,882	2,673	1,955	2,206	2,144	2,244
Capitalization:% Long Term Debt	48.4	43.2	46.7	50.6	51.8	51.7	45.1	50.0	49.8	50.5
Capitalization:Preferred	Nil	Nil	Nil	Nil	Nil	Nil	Nil	Nil	Nil	171
Capitalization:% Preferred	Nil	Nil	Nil	Nil	Nil	Nil	Nil	Nil	Nil	3.80
Capitalization:Common	3,446	3,425	2,950	2,830	2,686	2,499	2,383	2,206	2,163	2,027
Capitalization:% Common	51.6	56.8	53.3	49.4	48.2	48.3	54.9	50.0	50.2	45.6
Total Capital	7,905	7,259	6,763	7,057	6,777	6,237	5,481	5,599	5,678	5,856
% Operating Ratio	85.6	82.4	85.8	86.6	81.7	89.9	87.7	83.1	75.7	74.0
% Earned on Net Property	8.0	6.8	3.4	6.8	4.2	24.6	13.6	12.2	11.2	11.0
% Return on Revenue	9.3	7.5	8.1	8.2	8.2	7.2	8.2	11.1	11.4	11.8
% Return on Invested Capital	7.2	8.0	6.9	6.2	7.7	7.9	8.2	7.5	13.9	7.0
% Return on Common Equity	9.2	7.0	8.1	8.4	8.3	13.4	13.2	12.3	11.6	11.8

Data as orig reptd.; bef. results of disc opers/spec. items. Per share data adj. for stk. divs.; EPS diluted. E-Estimated. NA-Not Available. NM-Not Meaningful. NR-Not Ranked. UR-Under Review.

Office: 400 N 5th St Frnt, Phoenix, AZ 85004-3902.
Telephone: 602-250-1000.
Website: http://www.pinnaclewest.com
Chrmn & CEO: W.J. Post

Pres & COO: J.E. Davis
EVP & CFO: D. Brandt
VP & Treas: B.M. Gomez
VP, Secy & General Counsel: N.C. Loftin

Investor Contact: R. Hickman (602-250-5668)
Board Members: E. N. Basha, Jr., J. E. Davis, M. L. Gallagher, P. Grant, R. A. Herberger, Jr., W. S. Jamieson, Jr., H. S. Lopez, K. L. Munro, B. J. Nordstrom, W. J. Post, W. L. Stewart

Founded: 1920
Domicile: Arizona
Employees: 7,400

The McGraw-Hill Companies

Pitney Bowes Inc.

STANDARD &POOR'S

S&P Recommendation HOLD ★★★☆☆

Price $37.73 (as of Nov 23, 2007)

12-Mo. Target Price $43.00

Investment Style Large-Cap Growth

GICS Sector Industrials
Sub-Industry Office Services & Supplies

Summary PBI, the world's largest maker of mailing systems, also provides production and document management equipment and facilities management services.

Key Stock Statistics (Source S&P, Vickers, company reports)

52-Wk Range	$49.70–36.40	S&P Oper. EPS 2007**E**	2.67	Market Capitalization(B)	$8.296	Beta	0.88
Trailing 12-Month EPS	$2.62	S&P Oper. EPS 2008**E**	2.90	Yield (%)	3.71	S&P 3-Yr. Proj. EPS CAGR(%)	9.00
Trailing 12-Month P/E	14.4	P/E on S&P Oper. EPS 2007**E**	14.1	Dividend Rate/Share	$1.40	S&P Credit Rating	A+
$10K Invested 5 Yrs Ago	$12,568	Common Shares Outstg. (M)	219.9	Institutional Ownership (%)	83		

Price Performance

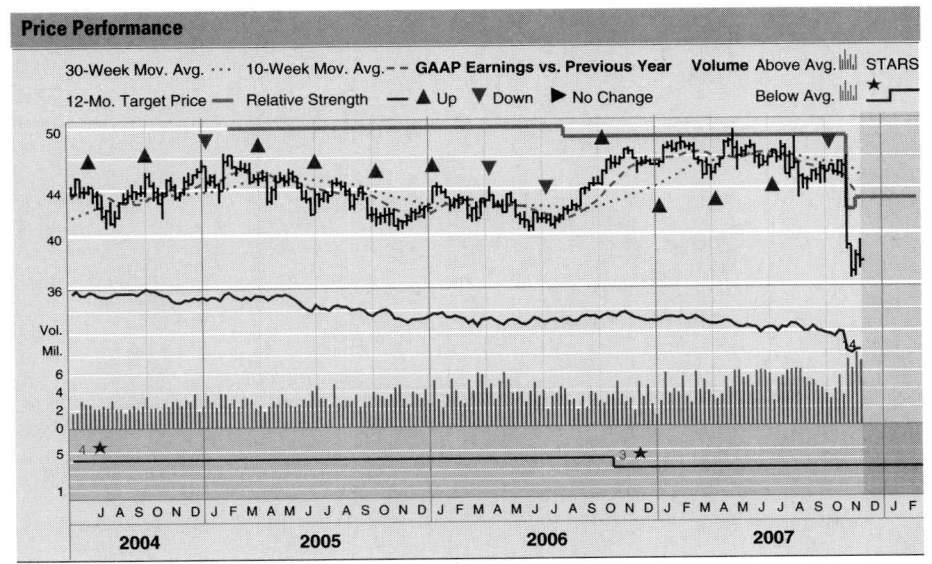

30-Week Mov. Avg. ··· 10-Week Mov. Avg. -- GAAP Earnings vs. Previous Year Volume Above Avg. STARS
12-Mo. Target Price — Relative Strength — ▲ Up ▼ Down ▶ No Change Below Avg.

Options: CBOE, P, Ph

Analysis prepared by **Thomas W. Smith, CFA** on November 19, 2007, when the stock traded at **$38.40**.

Highlights

➤ We look for revenue to rise about 6.6% in 2007 and 6.5% in 2008. We see results being aided by the recently completed acquisition of MapInfo, postal legislation reform, and further acquisition activity. However, third-quarter sales were up just 5%, year to year, below the longer-term trend we see. The company cited several areas of weakness, including a slow migration to digital meters, and delays in postal liberalization in Europe. On November 15, PBI announced 1,500 job cuts, or about 4% of global staff, as it makes product transitions and seeks lower costs.

➤ We see gross margins dipping toward 53% in 2007 and 2008, from almost 54% in 2006, as a less-favorable business mix outweighs the benefits of modest gains in volume. We believe PBI will maintain SG&A expenses near 31% of total revenue in both years. Results should continue to be favorably affected by share buybacks. A 6% increase in the quarterly cash dividend was announced November 15.

➤ We forecast 2007 EPS of $2.67, excluding restructuring and other special items. We expect EPS to improve to $2.90 in 2008 and $3.25 in 2009.

Investment Rationale/Risk

➤ PBI has a large recurring revenue stream and a leadership position within its market, in our view. We expect synergies from acquisitions, and from new product introductions focusing on digital technology, to aid future growth. However, sales weakness on several fronts appeared in the third quarter. On November 15, PBI announced a restructuring plan and an intention to explore strategic alternatives for its U.S. Management Services division, both of which could lead to greater efficiency in the longer term, in our view.

➤ Risks to our recommendation and target price include increased competition in the document management outsourcing market, which would have an impact on pricing within PBI's Management Services division, which contributes close to 20% of revenues. Postal regulatory changes in key countries are also a risk factor.

➤ Our 12-month target price of $43 is based mainly on our P/E analysis. We apply a target P/E of 15X, toward the low end of a five-year historical range for PBI to reflect near-term revenue weakness we foresee, to our 2008 EPS estimate of $2.90.

Qualitative Risk Assessment

LOW | **MEDIUM** | HIGH

Our risk assessment reflects our view of PBI's steady cash flow, recurring revenue streams, and history of a consistent dividend policy and share buyback programs. However, we think these factors are offset by a lackluster rate of revenue growth and integration risk associated with recent acquisitions.

Quantitative Evaluations

S&P Quality Ranking A-

D	C	B-	B	B+	**A-**	A	A+

Relative Strength Rank WEAK
29
LOWEST = 1   HIGHEST = 99

Revenue/Earnings Data

Revenue (Million $)

	1Q	2Q	3Q	4Q	Year
2007	1,414	1,543	1,508	--	--
2006	1,362	1,389	1,433	1,546	5,730
2005	1,318	1,360	1,356	1,458	5,492
2004	1,172	1,206	1,218	1,362	4,957
2003	1,091	1,134	1,137	1,215	4,577
2002	1,050	1,081	1,114	1,165	4,410

Earnings Per Share ($)

	1Q	2Q	3Q	4Q	Year
2007	0.66	0.69	0.59	E0.71	E2.67
2006	0.60	0.54	0.64	0.73	2.51
2005	0.64	0.60	0.62	0.41	2.27
2004	0.54	0.58	0.58	0.35	2.05
2003	0.48	0.50	0.50	0.61	2.10
2002	0.53	0.59	0.61	0.08	1.81

Fiscal year ended Dec. 31. Next earnings report expected: Early February. EPS Estimates based on S&P Operating Earnings; historical GAAP earnings are as reported.

Dividend Data (Dates: mm/dd Payment Date: mm/dd/yy)

Amount ($)	Date Decl.	Ex-Div. Date	Stk. of Record	Payment Date
0.330	04/09	05/16	05/18	06/12/07
0.330	07/09	08/15	08/17	09/12/07
0.330	11/12	11/20	11/23	12/12/07
0.350	11/15	02/13	02/18	03/12/08

Dividends have been paid since 1934. Source: Company reports.

Pitney Bowes Inc.

**STANDARD
&POOR'S**

Business Summary November 19, 2007

CORPORATE OVERVIEW. Pitney Bowes is a provider of global, integrated mail and document management offerings. The company operates in the following business groups: Global Mailstream Solutions and Global Business Services. A third division, Capital Services, was divested in July 2006.

The Global Mailstream Solutions segment, which accounted for 73% of 2006 revenue (73% in 2005), is comprised of three units. The first, Inside the U.S., includes U.S. revenue and related expenses from the sale, rental and financing of mail finishing, and mail creation and shipping equipment. The second, Document Messaging Technologies (DMT), includes U.S. revenue and related expenses from the sale, service and financing of high speed, production mail systems, sorting equipment, incoming mail systems, and electronic statement, billing and payment solutions. The third unit, Outside the U.S., encompasses the above mentioned products and services relative to overseas markets.

The Global Business Services segment (27%, 27%) is made up of three divisions: Management Services (PBMS), Mail Services and Marketing Services. The PBMS unit focuses on facilities management contracts for advanced

mailing, secure mail services, reprographic, document management and other high value services. The Mail Services group offers presort mail services and international outbound mail services. The Marketing Services business is comprised of direct mail and marketing campaign services.

IMPACT OF MAJOR DEVELOPMENTS. In April 2005, PBI entered into a definitive agreement with an affiliate of Cerberus Capital Management, L.P. for a sponsored spin-off of its Capital Services business. The transaction was completed in July 2006, with the unit becoming an independent company called EntreCap Financial Corp. PBI received a net amount of approximately $750 million as well as relinquished debt obligations of $470 million. PBI applied the proceeds toward a $1.1 billion tax settlement, about $900 million of which resulted from the Capital Services sale.

Company Financials Fiscal Year Ended Dec. 31

Per Share Data ($)	2006	2005	2004	2003	2002	2001	2000	1999	1998	1997
Tangible Book Value	NM	NM	NM	NM	0.10	1.05	4.34	5.28	5.26	5.96
Cash Flow	4.21	3.70	3.36	3.32	2.98	3.44	3.55	4.05	3.31	2.21
Earnings	2.51	2.27	2.05	2.10	1.81	2.08	2.18	2.42	2.03	1.80
S&P Core Earnings	2.50	2.09	1.94	1.87	1.34	0.81	NA	NA	NA	NA
Dividends	1.28	1.24	1.22	1.20	1.18	1.16	1.14	1.02	0.90	0.80
Payout Ratio	51%	55%	60%	57%	65%	56%	52%	42%	44%	44%
Prices:High	47.97	47.50	46.97	42.75	44.41	44.70	54.13	73.31	66.38	45.75
Prices:Low	40.18	40.34	38.88	29.45	28.55	32.00	24.00	40.88	42.22	26.81
P/E Ratio:High	19	21	23	20	25	21	25	30	33	25
P/E Ratio:Low	16	18	19	14	16	15	11	17	21	15

Income Statement Analysis (Million $)										
Revenue	5,730	5,492	4,957	4,577	4,410	4,122	3,881	4,433	4,221	4,100
Operating Income	1,487	1,435	1,352	1,291	1,276	1,046	1,316	1,526	1,375	1,303
Depreciation	363	332	307	289	264	317	321	412	361	300
Interest Expense	228	214	172	168	185	193	201	184	169	209
Pretax Income	914	867	699	721	619	766	803	985	864	803
Effective Tax Rate	36.6%	39.3%	31.3%	31.4%	29.3%	32.9%	29.9%	33.1%	34.3%	34.3%
Net Income	566	527	481	495	438	514	563	659	568	526
S&P Core Earnings	564	485	456	440	324	199	NA	NA	NA	NA

Balance Sheet & Other Financial Data (Million $)										
Cash	239	244	316	294	315	232	198	254	129	139
Current Assets	2,919	2,742	2,693	2,513	2,553	2,557	2,627	3,343	2,509	2,464
Total Assets	8,480	10,621	9,821	8,891	8,732	8,318	7,901	8,223	7,661	7,893
Current Liabilities	2,747	2,911	3,294	2,647	3,350	3,083	2,882	2,873	2,722	3,373
Long Term Debt	4,232	3,850	3,109	3,151	2,317	2,419	2,192	2,308	2,023	1,068
Common Equity	698	1,301	1,289	1,086	852	890	1,283	1,624	1,734	1,870
Total Capital	5,287	7,074	4,399	5,898	4,706	4,584	4,704	5,015	4,680	4,146
Capital Expenditures	328	292	317	286	225	256	269	305	298	244
Cash Flow	929	858	787	784	702	832	884	1,071	929	646
Current Ratio	1.1	0.9	0.8	0.9	0.8	0.8	0.9	1.2	0.9	0.7
% Long Term Debt of Capitalization	80.0	54.4	70.7	53.4	49.2	52.8	46.6	46.0	43.2	25.8
% Net Income of Revenue	9.9	11.2	9.7	10.8	9.9	12.5	14.5	14.9	13.5	12.8
% Return on Assets	5.9	5.1	5.1	5.6	5.1	6.3	7.0	8.3	7.3	6.6
% Return on Equity	54.9	40.7	40.5	51.1	50.3	47.3	38.7	40.3	31.5	25.6

Data as orig reptd.; bef. results of disc opers/spec. items. Per share data adj. for stk. divs.; EPS diluted. E-Estimated. NA-Not Available. NM-Not Meaningful. NR-Not Ranked. UR-Under Review.

Office: 1 Elmcroft Rd, Stamford, CT 06926-0700.
Telephone: 203-351-6858.
Email: investorrelations@pb.com
Website: http://www.pb.com

Exec Chrmn: M.J. Critelli
Pres & CEO: M.D. Martin
EVP & CFO: B.P. Nolop
SVP & CTO: J.E. Wall

SVP & General Counsel: M.C. Mayes
Investor Contact: C.F. McBride (203-351-6349)
Board Members: L. G. Alvarado, M. J. Critelli, A. S. Fuchs, E. Green, J. H. Keyes, M. D. Martin, J. S. McFarlane, E. R. Menasce, M. I. Roth, D. L. Shedlarz, D. B. Snow, Jr., R. E. Weissman

Founded: 1920
Domicile: Delaware
Employees: 34,454

The McGraw-Hill Companies

Plum Creek Timber Co Inc.

STANDARD
&POOR'S

S&P Recommendation `HOLD` ★★★☆☆

Price	$43.14 (as of Nov 23, 2007)
12-Mo. Target Price	$44.00
Investment Style	Large-Cap Blend

GICS Sector Financials
Sub-Industry Specialized REITS

Summary Plum Creek Timber Co., a real estate investment trust (REIT), is the largest private timberland owner in the United States, with about 8.2 million acres of timberlands in 18 states.

Key Stock Statistics (Source S&P, Vickers, company reports)

52-Wk Range	$46.16–36.37	S&P Oper. EPS 2007**E**	1.35	Market Capitalization(B)	$7.532	Beta	1.22
Trailing 12-Month EPS	$1.31	S&P Oper. EPS 2008**E**	1.60	Yield (%)	3.89	S&P 3-Yr. Proj. EPS CAGR(%)	6.00
Trailing 12-Month P/E	32.9	P/E on S&P Oper. EPS 2007**E**	32.0	Dividend Rate/Share	$1.68	S&P Credit Rating	NA
$10K Invested 5 Yrs Ago	$22,556	Common Shares Outstg. (M)	174.6	Institutional Ownership (%)	65		

Price Performance

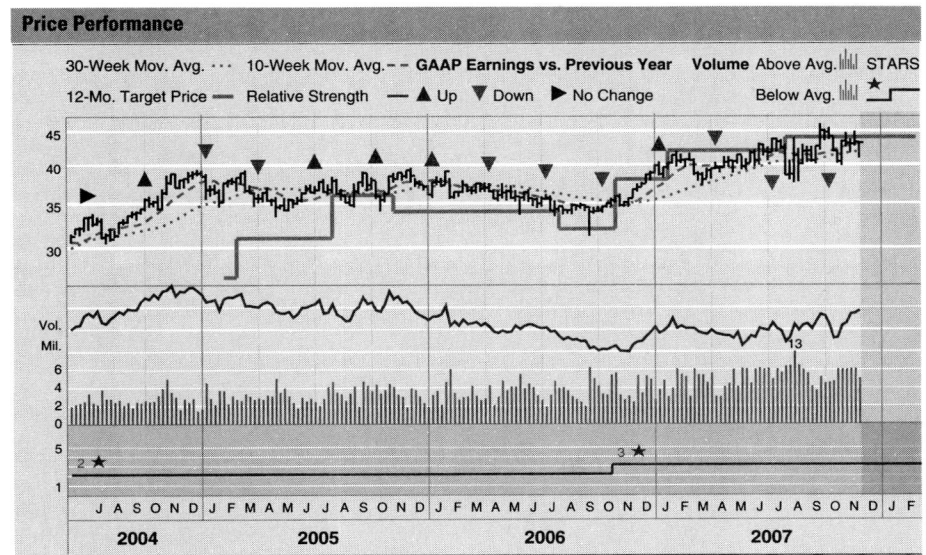

- 30-Week Mov. Avg. ⋯ 10-Week Mov. Avg. - - GAAP Earnings vs. Previous Year   Volume Above Avg. ▌▍▎ STARS
- 12-Mo. Target Price — Relative Strength — ▲ Up ▼ Down ▶ No Change   Below Avg. ▏▎▍ ★

Options: CBOE, P, Ph

Analysis prepared by **Stuart J. Benway, CFA** on October 23, 2007, when the stock traded at **$ 41.45**.

Highlights

➤ S&P projects that housing starts will decline more than 25% in 2007, to 1.34 million units, and a further 13% drop is forecast for 2008. We expect this to prevent any sustained increase in lumber and sawlog prices, which remain below historical levels. After an expected 2% decline in revenues in 2007, we look for about a 5% recovery in 2008, as harvest levels should rise slightly and we believe real estate revenues will be up nearly 10%.

➤ We think that average wood product prices in 2008 will be about in line with 2007, as demand from the housing market continues to be weak. In our view, this will allow for only modest margin recovery in the timberland operations. We see PCL capturing improved market prices for its higher and better use land sales, and for this business to expand gradually for many years.

➤ Our 2007 operating EPS estimate is $1.35, down 19% from $1.67 earned in 2006, and we note that the timing of real estate transactions could create some quarterly volatility. For 2008, we forecast operating EPS of $1.60.

Investment Rationale/Risk

➤ We believe PCL has significant value in its land holdings, and we expect real estate to become a rising source of earnings in coming years. PCL plans to develop 225,000 acres of land over the next 15 years, and we estimate that these properties can be sold at high margin levels. In our view, this will allow PCL to pay a rising dividend. In the near term, however, log prices are likely to be hurt by what we see as weak residential construction activity.

➤ Risks to our recommendation and target price include renewed declines in log demand and prices due to weakness in the U.S. housing market, and lower than projected profits on sales of higher and better use land.

➤ Our dividend discount model, which assumes a $1.72 dividend payout in 2008, a required rate of return of 9.2%, and constant dividend growth of 5.5%, indicates that the stock has an intrinsic value of $46. Applying a 10% premium to the peer P/E of 22.7X to our 2008 EPS estimate results in a value of $40. Our 12-month target price of $44 is a weighted blend of these two measures.

Qualitative Risk Assessment

LOW	MEDIUM	HIGH

Our risk assessment reflects that Plum Creek operates in a cyclical industry, with demand for its products tied to residential construction and paper manufacturing. It is subject to movements in interest rates, economic conditions and currency, and prices for its products have historically been volatile. However, it is a major landowner, and its debt levels are relatively low.

Quantitative Evaluations

S&P Quality Ranking   B+

D	C	B-	B	B+	A-	A	A+

Relative Strength Rank   STRONG

83

LOWEST = 1   HIGHEST = 99

Revenue/Earnings Data

Revenue (Million $)

	1Q	2Q	3Q	4Q	Year
2007	369.0	395.0	407.0	--	--
2006	414.0	380.0	454.0	379.0	1,627
2005	400.0	358.0	427.0	391.0	1,576
2004	497.0	341.0	363.0	327.0	1,528
2003	273.0	318.0	290.0	315.0	1,196
2002	275.0	271.0	310.0	281.0	1,137

Earnings Per Share ($)

2007	0.25	0.33	0.34	E0.42	E1.35
2006	0.50	0.34	0.51	0.39	1.74
2005	0.56	0.37	0.52	0.34	1.79
2004	0.84	0.31	0.42	0.28	1.84
2003	0.18	0.31	0.25	0.30	1.04
2002	0.30	0.29	0.38	0.29	1.26

Fiscal year ended Dec. 31. Next earnings report expected: Late January. EPS Estimates based on S&P Operating Earnings; historical GAAP earnings are as reported.

Dividend Data (Dates: mm/dd Payment Date: mm/dd/yy)

Amount ($)	Date Decl.	Ex-Div. Date	Stk. of Record	Payment Date
0.420	02/06	02/14	02/16	03/02/07
0.420	05/01	05/14	05/16	05/31/07
0.420	07/31	08/14	08/16	08/31/07
0.420	10/30	11/09	11/14	11/30/07

Dividends have been paid since 1989. Source: Company reports.

The **McGraw-Hill** Companies

Plum Creek Timber Co Inc.

Business Summary October 23, 2007

CORPORATE OVERVIEW. Plum Creek Timber Co., a real estate investment trust (REIT), is the largest private timberland owner in the United States, with about 8.2 million acres of timberlands in 18 states. In addition, the trust operates several wood products manufacturing facilities and is actively involved in land purchases and sales. The company conducts operations through four business segments: the timber operation accounted for 50% of 2006 revenues, manufacturing (30%), real estate (19%), and other (1%). The Northern Resources portion of the timber segment encompasses 3.9 million acres of timberlands, mostly in Maine, Michigan, Montana, and Wisconsin. The Southern Resources portion of the timber segment consists of 4.3 million acres of timberlands primarily in Arkansas, Florida, Georgia, Louisiana, and Mississippi.

MARKET PROFILE. The timber industry provides raw materials and manages resources for the paper and forest products industry. Harvested logs are sold to third party mills that produce lumber, plywood, oriented strand board, and pulp and paper products. There are five primary end markets for most of the timber harvested in the United States: new housing construction, home repair and remodeling, products for industrial uses, raw material for the manufacture of pulp and paper, and logs for export.

The demand for timber is directly related to the underlying demand for pulp and paper products, lumber, panels, and other wood products. The demand for pulp and paper is largely driven by population growth and per-capita income levels. The demand for lumber and manufactured wood products is primarily affected by the level of new residential construction activity and repair and remodeling activity, which, in turn, is affected by changes in general economic and demographic factors, including population growth and interest rates for home mortgages and construction loans. The market for wood fiber used in paper production and wood products manufacturing is very diverse, with many manufacturers of various sizes. We therefore believe that Plum Creek has only limited control over the prices that it can charge for timber and wood products.

Company Financials Fiscal Year Ended Dec. 31

Per Share Data ($)	2006	2005	2004	2003	2002	2001	2000	1999	1998	1997
Tangible Book Value	11.80	12.62	12.19	11.57	12.04	12.21	7.46	7.70	8.78	10.14
Cash Flow	2.45	1.92	2.46	1.63	1.82	3.00	2.47	3.10	3.12	3.93
Earnings	1.74	1.79	1.84	1.04	1.26	2.58	1.91	1.72	0.90	1.72
S&P Core Earnings	1.67	1.78	1.82	1.04	1.24	2.57	NA	NA	NA	NA
Dividends	1.60	1.52	1.42	1.40	1.49	2.85	2.28	2.28	2.26	2.16
Payout Ratio	92%	85%	77%	135%	118%	110%	119%	133%	NM	126%
Prices:High	40.00	39.63	39.45	30.75	31.98	30.00	29.81	32.13	34.88	36.00
Prices:Low	31.21	33.40	27.30	20.88	18.92	23.30	21.50	23.13	23.44	25.75
P/E Ratio:High	23	22	21	30	25	12	16	19	39	21
P/E Ratio:Low	18	19	15	20	15	9	11	13	26	15

Income Statement Analysis (Million $)										
Revenue	1,627	1,576	1,528	1,196	1,137	598	209	461	699	726
Operating Income	571	561	586	410	443	305	166	206	210	244
Depreciation	128	113	114	107	105	55.0	38.9	59.7	69.3	70.2
Interest Expense	133	109	111	117	103	54.0	46.8	63.5	60.6	60.4
Pretax Income	328	339	366	186	235	196	132	100	76.0	112
Effective Tax Rate	3.90%	2.30%	7.40%	NM	0.85%	NM	NM	NM	0.68%	0.07%
Net Income	315	331	339	192	233	338	132	113	75.4	112
S&P Core Earnings	301	329	336	193	229	336	NA	NA	NA	NA

Balance Sheet & Other Financial Data (Million $)										
Cash	301	395	376	260	246	193	181	115	114	135
Current Assets	513	574	499	405	378	306	195	133	210	232
Total Assets	4,661	4,812	4,378	4,387	4,289	4,122	1,250	1,251	1,438	1,301
Current Liabilities	281	375	184	168	155	149	180	74.2	80.9	74.0
Long Term Debt	1,617	1,524	1,853	2,031	1,839	1,667	560	643	943	745
Common Equity	2,089	2,325	2,240	2,119	2,222	2,247	507	533	405	470
Total Capital	3,731	3,888	4,138	4,187	4,105	3,952	1,066	1,176	1,348	1,215
Capital Expenditures	86.0	89.0	70.0	246	231	59.0	21.7	25.6	54.9	28.3
Cash Flow	443	444	453	299	338	393	171	173	145	182
Current Ratio	1.8	1.5	2.7	2.4	2.4	2.1	1.1	1.8	2.6	3.1
% Long Term Debt of Capitalization	43.3	39.1	44.8	48.5	44.8	42.2	52.5	54.7	69.9	61.3
% Net Income of Revenue	19.3	21.0	22.2	16.1	20.5	56.5	63.1	24.6	10.8	15.4
% Return on Assets	6.6	7.2	7.7	4.4	5.5	11.8	10.5	8.4	5.5	8.5
% Return on Equity	14.2	14.5	15.6	8.8	10.4	28.3	25.4	24.2	17.2	23.2

Data as orig reptd.; bef. results of disc opers/spec. items. Per share data adj. for stk. divs.; EPS diluted. E-Estimated. NA-Not Available. NM-Not Meaningful. NR-Not Ranked. UR-Under Review.

Office: 999 3rd Ave Ste 4300, Seattle, WA 98104-4096.
Telephone: 206-467-3600.
Email: info@plumcreek.com
Website: http://www.plumcreek.com

Chrmn: D.D. Leland
Pres & CEO: R.R. Holley
COO & EVP: T.M. Lindquist
SVP & CFO: D.W. Lambert

SVP, Secy & General Counsel: J.A. Kraft
Investor Contact: J. Hobbs (800-858-5347)
Board Members: I. B. Davidson, R. R. Holley, R. Josephs, J. G. McDonald, R. B. McLeod, J. H. Scully, S. C. Tobias, C. B. Webb, M. A. White

Founded: 1989
Domicile: Delaware
Employees: 2,000

PNC Financial Services Group Inc.

STANDARD &POOR'S

S&P Recommendation BUY ★★★★☆

Price $69.84 (as of Nov 23, 2007)	**12-Mo. Target Price** $80.00	**Investment Style** Large-Cap Value

GICS Sector Financials
Sub-Industry Regional Banks

Summary This bank holding company conducts regional banking, wholesale banking and asset management businesses, primarily in Pennsylvania, Maryland and New Jersey.

Key Stock Statistics (Source S&P, Vickers, company reports)

52-Wk Range	$76.41– 64.00	S&P Oper. EPS 2007**E**	5.39	Market Capitalization(B)	$24.414	Beta	0.51
Trailing 12-Month EPS	$5.12	S&P Oper. EPS 2008**E**	5.68	Yield (%)	3.61	S&P 3-Yr. Proj. EPS CAGR(%)	NM
Trailing 12-Month P/E	13.6	P/E on S&P Oper. EPS 2007**E**	13.0	Dividend Rate/Share	$2.52	S&P Credit Rating	A+
$10K Invested 5 Yrs Ago	$19,866	Common Shares Outstg. (M)	349.6	Institutional Ownership (%)	62		

Price Performance

- 30-Week Mov. Avg. ···· 10-Week Mov. Avg. - - **GAAP Earnings vs. Previous Year** Volume Above Avg. STARS
- 12-Mo. Target Price — Relative Strength — ▲ Up ▼ Down ► No Change Below Avg.

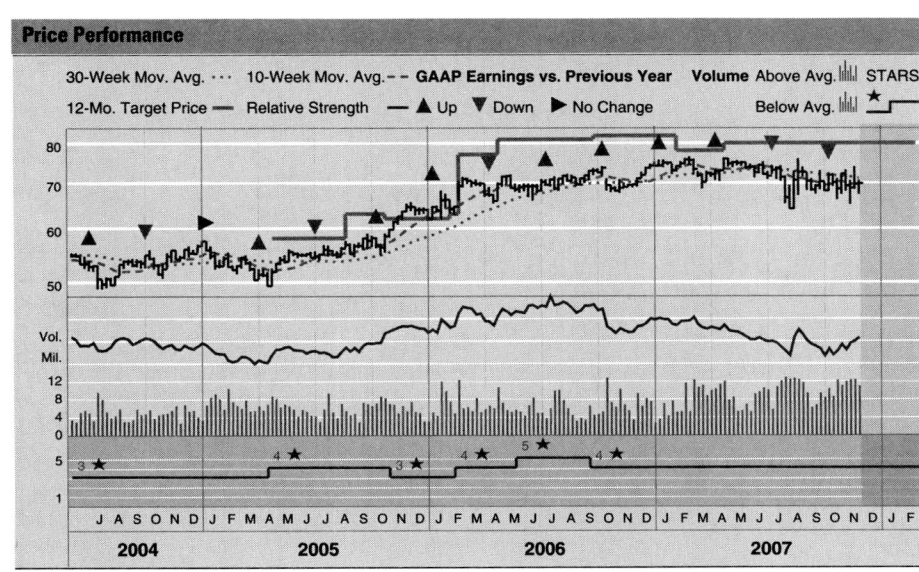

Options: ASE, CBOE, Ph

Analysis prepared by **Erik Oja** on November 19, 2007, when the stock traded at **$ 68.15.**

Highlights

➤ We expect earning asset growth of 5.5% in 2008, aided by a net interest margin of 3.14%, up from the 2.93% we expect for 2007 and the 2.92% recorded in 2006. We expect PNC to increase its loan portfolio at a mid-single digit rate in 2008, while resisting increases in deposit rates. In our estimation, this will lead to a gradual decrease in the deposit-to-loan ratio to 119% by the end of 2008, down from approximately 132% at the end of 2006, a manageable development, in our view.

➤ Our 2008 non-interest expense to total revenue forecast of 58.8% is lower than our 59.1% estimate for 2007, due to cost improvements generated by the One PNC initiative. Asset quality is high, in our view, with 0.22% of assets non-performing, which is well below industry averages. However, based on industywide credit trends, we look for higher loan loss provisions of about $193 million in 2007 and $262 million in 2008.

➤ We expect 2007 operating EPS of $5.39, a 6.5% increase from the $5.06 adjusted EPS in 2006, but a 38% decrease from $8.73 GAAP EPS, which included gains from the BlackRock transaction. Our 2008 EPS estimate is $5.68.

Investment Rationale/Risk

➤ We think the BlackRock deal will continue to create significant value for PNC, and we are similarly optimistic about the recently integrated Mercantile Bankshares, which we think gives PNC a solid base in Maryland. In our view, PNC has successfully avoided most of the sub-prime and collateralized debt obligation-based impairments to credit quality that have resulted in writedowns at many peers. In addition, PNC realized its goal of $400 million of total annual pretax earnings benefit by mid-2007 from the One PNC initiative, and expects to realize this amount annually, going forward.

➤ Risks to our recommendation and target price include a continuing flat or inverted yield curve, which could further increase the cost of deposits while keeping loan yields from increasing, plus an economic slowdown, which could adversely affect loan growth and credit quality.

➤ Our 12-month target price of $80 implies a P/E of 14.1X our 2008 EPS estimate, a premium to peers that takes into account PNC's relatively high proportion of fee income to total revenues and our view that asset quality at PNC is well above peers.

Qualitative Risk Assessment

LOW	MEDIUM	HIGH

Our risk assessment for PNC reflects our view of the company's large-cap valuation, strong loan portfolio credit quality, and history of profitability. While the industry in which PNC operates is highly competitive and fragmented, it tends to produce relatively stable financial results.

Quantitative Evaluations

S&P Quality Ranking   B+

D	C	B-	B	**B+**	A-	A	A+

Relative Strength Rank   **STRONG**

78

LOWEST = 1   HIGHEST = 99

Revenue/Earnings Data

Revenue (Million $)

	1Q	2Q	3Q	4Q	Year
2007	2,306	1,721	1,757	--	--
2006	2,251	2,356	4,146	2,186	10,939
2005	1,777	1,826	2,108	2,185	7,896
2004	1,577	1,395	1,523	1,413	6,315
2003	1,487	1,468	1,493	1,521	5,969
2002	1,648	1,674	1,540	1,507	6,369

Earnings Per Share ($)

	1Q	2Q	3Q	4Q	Year
2007	1.46	1.22	1.19	E1.52	E5.39
2006	1.19	1.28	5.01	1.27	8.73
2005	1.24	0.98	1.14	1.20	4.55
2004	1.15	1.07	0.91	1.08	4.21
2003	0.92	0.65	1.00	1.08	3.65
2002	1.11	1.12	1.00	0.97	4.20

Fiscal year ended Dec. 31. Next earnings report expected: Late January. EPS Estimates based on S&P Operating Earnings; historical GAAP earnings are as reported.

Dividend Data (Dates: mm/dd Payment Date: mm/dd/yy)

Amount ($)	Date Decl.	Ex-Div. Date	Stk. of Record	Payment Date
0.550	01/04	01/10	01/12	01/24/07
0.630	04/05	04/11	04/13	04/24/07
0.630	07/05	07/11	07/13	07/24/07
0.630	10/04	10/10	10/12	10/24/07

Dividends have been paid since 1865. Source: Company reports.

Please read the Required Disclosures and Analyst Certification on the last page of this report.

The McGraw-Hill Companies

PNC Financial Services Group Inc.

STANDARD
&POOR'S

Business Summary November 19, 2007

CORPORATE OVERVIEW. PNC is a bank holding company that operates businesses engaged in retail banking, corporate and institutional banking, asset management, and global fund processing services. The company has four primary reportable business segments: Retail Banking, Corporate and Institutional Banking, BlackRock, and PFPC.

The Retail Banking and Corporate and Institutional Banking segments generate about 53% of total revenues. Retail Banking (36%) provides deposit, lending, brokerage, trust, investment management and cash management services to consumers and small businesses. Corporate and Institutional Banking (17%) offers lending, treasury management and capital markets products and services to mid-sized corporations, government entities and selectively to large corporations. The BlackRock segment (14%) includes the operations of 37%-owned BlackRock, Inc. (BLK). BLK, with about $1.3 trillion in assets under management, provides diversified investment management services to institutional and individual investors worldwide through a variety of fixed income, cash management, equity and alternative investment products. PFPC (10%) provides mutual fund transfer agency and accounting and administration services.

MARKET PROFILE. As of June 30, 2007 (latest available FDIC branch-level data), PNC had 1,194 branches and $78.8 billion in deposits, including 231 branches and $13.4 billion in deposits acquired from Mercantile. According to Highline Data, 47.8% of deposits were concentrated in Pennsylvania, while 85.0% of deposits were in the three states of Pennsylvania, New Jersey and Maryland. In Pennsylvania, PNC had 409 branches, $37.7 billion in deposits, and a deposit market share of about 13.4%, ranking first, ahead of Wachovia (WB: buy, $39). In Maryland, PNC had 206 branches, including 187 from Mercantile, $11.0 billion in deposits, and a deposit market share of about 10.3%, ranking second, after Bank of America (BAC: strong buy, $44). In New Jersey, PNC had 329 branches, $18.3 billion in deposits, and a deposit market share of about 7.9%, ranking fourth. In the District of Columbia, PNC had 33 offices, deposits of $2.2 billion, and a deposit market share of 7.2%, ranking fourth. In addition, PNC had a total of 217 branches and $9.7 billion in deposits in Kentucky, Delaware, Virginia, Ohio, Indiana, and Florida.

Company Financials Fiscal Year Ended Dec. 31

Per Share Data ($)	2006	2005	2004	2003	2002	2001	2000	1999	1998	1997
Tangible Book Value	23.02	13.98	14.55	14.22	14.78	12.19	13.37	12.07	11.49	12.47
Earnings	8.73	4.55	4.21	3.65	4.20	1.26	4.09	4.15	3.60	3.28
S&P Core Earnings	8.63	4.43	4.00	3.53	3.83	0.92	NA	NA	NA	NA
Dividends	2.15	2.00	2.00	1.94	1.92	1.92	1.83	1.68	1.58	1.50
Payout Ratio	25%	44%	48%	53%	46%	152%	45%	40%	44%	46%
Prices:High	75.15	65.66	59.79	55.55	62.80	75.81	75.00	62.00	66.75	58.75
Prices:Low	61.78	49.35	48.90	41.63	32.70	51.14	36.00	43.00	38.75	36.50
P/E Ratio:High	9	14	14	15	15	60	18	15	19	18
P/E Ratio:Low	7	11	12	11	8	41	9	10	11	11

Income Statement Analysis (Million $)										
Net Interest Income	2,245	2,154	1,969	1,996	2,197	2,262	2,164	2,433	2,573	2,495
Tax Equivalent Adjustment	25.0	33.0	NA	NA	NA	NA	18.0	22.0	49.0	99.0
Non Interest Income	6,534	4,203	3,508	3,141	3,108	2,412	2,871	2,723	2,503	1,759
Loan Loss Provision	124	21.0	52.0	177	309	903	136	163	225	70.0
% Expense/Operating Revenue	50.5%	48.6%	68.2%	67.7%	60.8%	71.4%	60.8%	60.3%	63.6%	61.5%
Pretax Income	4,005	1,962	1,745	1,600	1,858	564	1,848	1,891	1,710	1,618
Effective Tax Rate	34.0%	30.8%	30.8%	33.7%	33.4%	33.2%	34.3%	33.2%	34.8%	35.0%
Net Income	2,595	1,325	1,197	1,029	1,200	377	1,214	1,264	1,115	1,052
% Net Interest Margin	2.92	3.00	3.22	3.64	3.99	3.84	3.64	3.68	3.85	3.94
S&P Core Earnings	2,565	1,294	1,134	993	1,093	270	NA	NA	NA	NA

Balance Sheet & Other Financial Data (Million $)										
Money Market Assets	1,763	350	1,635	50.0	3,658	1,335	1,151	1,148	1,014	1,526
Investment Securities	31,651	23,253	18,609	16,409	17,421	15,243	7,053	8,759	8,088	8,522
Commercial Loans	27,672	26,115	19,418	15,987	22,335	23,134	28,635	24,198	25,182	19,989
Other Loans	22,433	23,821	24,077	18,093	13,115	14,840	21,966	26,572	32,468	34,668
Total Assets	101,820	91,954	79,723	68,168	66,377	69,568	69,844	75,413	77,207	75,120
Demand Deposits	16,070	14,988	12,915	11,505	9,538	10,124	8,490	8,441	9,943	10,158
Time Deposits	50,231	45,287	40,354	33,736	35,444	37,180	39,174	38,227	37,553	37,491
Long Term Debt	10,266	6,797	8,684	7,667	9,112	8,922	7,266	9,395	10,994	11,523
Common Equity	10,788	8,563	7,548	6,735	6,943	5,822	6,649	5,939	6,036	5,377
% Return on Assets	2.7	1.5	1.6	1.5	1.8	0.5	1.7	1.7	1.5	1.4
% Return on Equity	26.8	16.5	16.8	15.0	18.7	5.9	19.0	20.8	19.2	18.4
% Loan Loss Reserve	1.1	1.2	1.3	1.8	1.8	1.5	1.3	1.2	1.3	1.8
% Loans/Deposits	79.1	123.7	84.8	78.4	82.4	89.1	109.6	119.7	121.4	111.8
% Equity to Assets	10.0	9.3	9.7	10.2	9.4	8.9	9.0	7.8	7.5	7.6

Data as orig reptd.; bef. results of disc opers/spec. items. Per share data adj. for stk. divs.; EPS diluted. E-Estimated. NA-Not Available. NM-Not Meaningful. NR-Not Ranked. UR-Under Review.

Office: 249 5th Ave, 1 PNC Plz, Pittsburgh, PA 15222-2707.
Telephone: 412-762-2000.
Email: corporate.communiations@pncbank.com
Website: http://www.pnc.com

Chrmn & CEO: J.E. Rohr
Pres: J. Guyaux
Vice Chrmn: W.S. Demchak
Vice Chrmn: W.C. Mutterperl

SVP & General Counsel: H.P. Pudlin
Investor Contact: W. Callihan (800-843-2206)
Board Members: R. O. Berndt, C. E. Bunch, P. W. Chellgren, R. N. Clay, G. A. Davidson, Jr., K. C. James, R. B. Kelson, B. C. Lindsay, A. A. Massaro, J. G. Pepper, J. E. Rohr, D. J. Shepard, L. K. Steffes, D. F. Strigl, S. G. Thieke, T. J. Usher, G. H. Walls, H. H. Wehmeier

Founded: 1922
Domicile: Pennsylvania
Employees: 23,783

Polo Ralph Lauren Corp

S&P Recommendation	HOLD ★★★☆☆	Price	12-Mo. Target Price	Investment Style
		$66.80 (as of Nov 23, 2007)	$80.00	Large-Cap Growth

GICS Sector Consumer Discretionary
Sub-Industry Apparel, Accessories & Luxury Goods

Summary This company designs, markets and distributes men's and women's clothing and other premium lifestyle products.

Key Stock Statistics (Source S&P, Vickers, company reports)

52-Wk Range	$102.58–63.43	S&P Oper. EPS 2008**E**	3.50	Market Capitalization(B)	$4.008	Beta	1.24
Trailing 12-Month EPS	$3.63	S&P Oper. EPS 2009**E**	4.10	Yield (%)	0.30	S&P 3-Yr. Proj. EPS CAGR(%)	15.00
Trailing 12-Month P/E	18.4	P/E on S&P Oper. EPS 2008**E**	19.1	Dividend Rate/Share	$0.20	S&P Credit Rating	NA
$10K Invested 5 Yrs Ago	$28,657	Common Shares Outstg. (M)	103.3	Institutional Ownership (%)	NM		

Price Performance

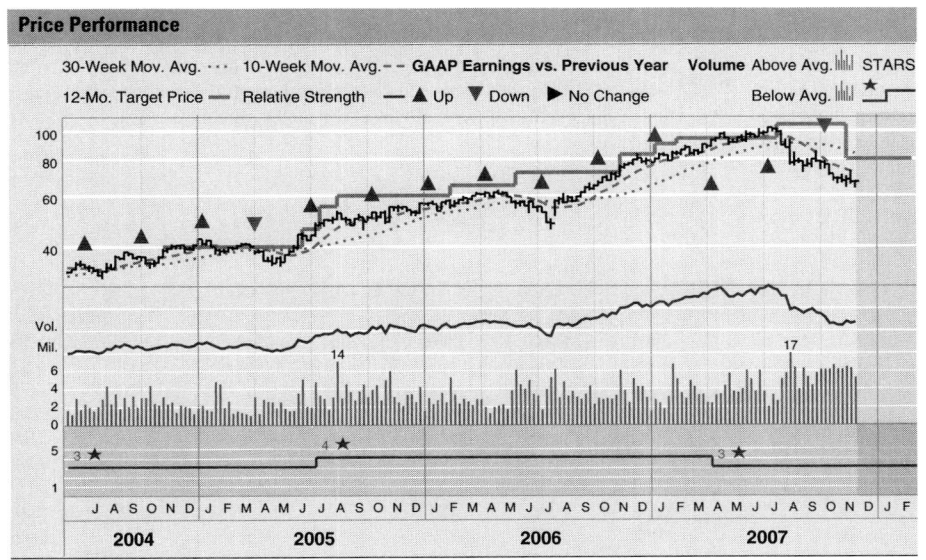

30-Week Mov. Avg. · · · 10-Week Mov. Avg. – – **GAAP Earnings vs. Previous Year** Volume Above Avg. STARS
12-Mo. Target Price — Relative Strength — ▲ Up ▼ Down ► No Change Below Avg.

Options: ASE, CBOE, Ph

Analysis prepared by **Marie Driscoll, CFA** on November 08, 2007, when the stock traded at **$66.68**.

Highlights

➤ Having successfully navigated a brand strategy in the past few years that included purchasing licenses, exiting tertiary doors, and decreasing exposure to the off-price channel, we see the direct-to-consumer channel, new product categories and the moderate channel providing incremental growth opportunities for RL. In addition to its exclusive arrangement with Kohl's and its Chap's brand, in 2008, RL's American Living (an exclusive lifestyle brand for JC Penney spanning multiple product categories) will launch.

➤ We see FY 08 (Mar.) sales growth of 9%, to $4.7 billion and earnings before interest and taxes (EBIT) margins declining about 210 basis points, reflecting a higher SG&A expense ratio as non-cash goodwill charges and investment in American Living have an impact on the operating margin.

➤ For FY 09 we see attenuated sales growth, to a 7% pace, with about 100 basis point EBIT margin expansion, assuming leveraging of fixed costs including goodwill. We anticipate improved merchandise and gross margins, reflecting supply chain and sourcing initiatives.

Investment Rationale/Risk

➤ RL intends to open about one store a month in the U.S. over the next few years, which should boost its retail business to about 50% of the total, and, we think, will allow for multiple expansion longer term. RL's women's apparel business currently represents less than 30% of total revenues, versus a 60% weighting for most dual-gender apparel brands, and, in our view, provides growth potential along with the significant opportunity we see in accessories for the Polo brands. We regard RL's brand positioning along with its specialty retail operations as strong positives as the department store retail channel consolidates.

➤ Risks to our recommendation and target price include the integration of recent licensee acquisitions. Regarding corporate governance, we are concerned that chairman, CEO and founder Ralph Lauren controls approximately 88% of the voting shares of the company.

➤ We think the recent share price decline reflects concerns about the negative wealth effect. Our 12-month target price of $80 is equal to about 20X our calendar 2008 EPS estimate of $3.95, about a 10% premium to its peer luxury brands.

Qualitative Risk Assessment

LOW	MEDIUM	HIGH

Our risk assessment reflects our view of RL's strong balance sheet with no long-term debt, offset by its exposure to the consolidating and contracting department store channel.

Quantitative Evaluations

S&P Quality Ranking NR

D	C	B-	B	B+	A-	A	A+

Relative Strength Rank MODERATE

38

LOWEST = 1   HIGHEST = 99

Revenue/Earnings Data

Revenue (Million $)

	1Q	2Q	3Q	4Q	Year
2008	1,070	1,299	--	--	--
2007	953.6	1,167	1,144	1,031	4,295
2006	751.9	964.8	995.5	971.6	3,746
2005	535.8	821.5	888.0	834.5	3,305
2004	477.7	707.8	645.4	818.8	2,650
2003	467.0	640.8	639.2	692.3	2,439

Earnings Per Share ($)

2008	0.82	1.09	E0.88	E0.70	E3.50
2007	0.74	1.28	1.03	0.68	3.73
2006	0.48	0.97	0.84	0.58	2.87
2005	0.13	0.78	0.72	0.22	1.83
2004	0.05	0.54	0.35	0.75	1.69
2003	0.07	0.52	0.43	0.74	1.76

Fiscal year ended Mar. 31. Next earnings report expected: Early February. EPS Estimates based on S&P Operating Earnings; historical GAAP earnings are as reported.

Dividend Data (Dates: mm/dd Payment Date: mm/dd/yy)

Amount ($)	Date Decl.	Ex-Div. Date	Stk. of Record	Payment Date
0.050	12/18	12/27	12/29	01/12/07
0.050	03/19	03/28	03/30	04/13/07
0.050	06/18	06/27	06/29	07/13/07
0.050	09/17	09/26	09/28	10/12/07

Dividends have been paid since 2003. Source: Company reports.

Please read the Required Disclosures and Analyst Certification on the last page of this report.

Polo Ralph Lauren Corp

STANDARD &POOR'S

Business Summary November 08, 2007

CORPORATE OVERVIEW. Since its modest beginnings in men's ties more than 30 years ago, Polo Ralph Lauren has grown into one of America's leading lifestyle brands encompassing multiple permutations targeted at specific demographics, usage occasions and price points. Licensor relationships extend the brand to fragrance, eyewear, leather goods, jewelry and an extensive home merchandise offering. In total, we believe the Polo Ralph Lauren brand generates about $8 billion at retail worldwide.

MARKET PROFILE. RL participates in the men's, women's and children's apparel market, which represented an estimated $190 billion at retail in 2006, according to NPD Fashionworld consumer estimated data. The apparel market is fragmented, with national brands marketed by 20 companies accounting for about 30% of total apparel sales, and the remaining 70% comprised of smaller and/or private label "store" brands. The market is mature, in our view, with demand largely mirroring population growth and fashion trends accounting for a modicum of incremental volume. Deflationary pricing pressure is a function, we think, of channel competition and production steadily moving offshore to low-cost producers in India, Asia and China. S&P forecasts 2007 apparel sales increasing in the low single digits, generally in line with GDP growth. This compares with a 5% year-to-year advance in 2006 following 4% incre-

ments in both 2004 and 2005.

COMPETITIVE LANDSCAPE. By channel, specialty stores account for the largest share of apparel sales, at 31% in 2006, according to NPD. Mass merchants (Wal-Mart and Target) came in second, at 20%, up 100 basis points, and department stores, RL's primary channel, came in third, at 16%, losing 100 basis points of market share, and down 400 basis points since 2003. National chains (Sears and JC Penney) captured 15% of 2006 apparel sales, and off-price retailers (TJX and Ross Stores) 8%. The remaining 11% is divided among factory outlets and direct and e-mail pure plays. RL holds leading market shares in department stores, where it competes with Jones Apparel Group, Liz Claiborne, and VF Corp., as well as private label offerings, which garner about a third of total apparel purchases and are an important differentiator for retailers. RL also sells directly to consumers through 292 specialty retail locations spanning the luxury, mid-market and factory channels.

Company Financials Fiscal Year Ended Mar. 31

Per Share Data ($)	2007	2006	2005	2004	2003	2002	2001	2000	1999	1998
Tangible Book Value	11.99	10.35	10.38	10.56	8.93	7.38	5.76	5.08	6.60	5.83
Cash Flow	5.07	4.06	2.83	2.52	2.55	2.60	1.41	2.16	1.37	1.75
Earnings	3.73	2.87	1.83	1.69	1.76	1.75	0.61	1.49	0.91	1.20
S&P Core Earnings	3.75	2.80	2.32	1.53	1.55	1.54	0.44	NA	NA	NA
Dividends	0.20	0.20	0.20	Nil	Nil	Nil	Nil	Nil	Nil	Nil
Payout Ratio	5%	7%	11%	Nil	Nil	Nil	Nil	Nil	Nil	Nil
Calendar Year	2006	2005	2004	2003	2002	2001	2000	1999	1998	1997
Prices:High	83.15	56.84	42.83	31.52	30.82	31.34	23.25	25.38	31.38	33.00
Prices:Low	45.65	34.19	27.28	19.30	16.49	17.80	12.75	16.06	15.88	21.75
P/E Ratio:High	22	20	23	19	18	18	38	17	34	27
P/E Ratio:Low	12	12	15	11	9	10	21	11	17	18

Income Statement Analysis (Million $)

	2007	2006	2005	2004	2003	2002	2001	2000	1999	1998
Revenue	4,295	3,746	3,305	2,650	2,439	2,364	2,226	1,956	1,713	1,471
Operating Income	802	663	406	377	382	393	319	330	247	227
Depreciation	145	127	104	83.2	78.6	83.9	78.6	66.3	46.4	27.4
Interest Expense	21.6	12.5	11.0	10.0	13.5	19.0	25.1	15.0	2.76	0.16
Pretax Income	659	516	298	266	274	276	98.0	249	153	200
Effective Tax Rate	36.8%	37.7%	36.0%	35.7%	36.5%	37.5%	39.5%	40.8%	40.7%	26.1%
Net Income	401	308	190	171	174	173	59.3	147	90.6	148
S&P Core Earnings	403	299	242	154	154	151	43.1	NA	NA	NA

Balance Sheet & Other Financial Data (Million $)

	2007	2006	2005	2004	2003	2002	2001	2000	1999	1998
Cash	564	286	350	343	344	239	102	165	88.7	58.8
Current Assets	1,686	1,379	1,414	1,271	1,166	1,008	902	853	679	556
Total Assets	3,758	2,089	2,727	2,270	2,039	1,749	1,626	1,621	1,105	825
Current Liabilities	640	844	622	501	500	392	440	406	348	202
Long Term Debt	399	Nil	291	277	248	285	297	343	44.2	Nil
Common Equity	2,335	2,050	1,676	1,422	1,209	998	809	772	659	584
Total Capital	2,734	2,070	1,967	1,699	1,457	1,284	1,106	1,115	703	584
Capital Expenditures	184	159	174	123	98.7	88.0	105	122	142	63.0
Cash Flow	546	435	294	254	253	256	138	214	137	175
Current Ratio	2.6	1.6	2.3	2.5	2.3	2.6	2.1	2.1	2.0	2.8
% Long Term Debt of Capitalization	14.6	Nil	14.8	16.3	17.1	22.2	26.8	30.7	6.3	Nil
% Net Income of Revenue	9.3	8.2	5.8	6.5	7.1	7.3	2.7	7.5	5.3	10.0
% Return on Assets	11.7	12.8	7.6	7.9	9.2	10.2	3.7	10.8	9.4	21.1
% Return on Equity	18.3	16.5	12.3	13.0	15.8	19.1	7.5	20.6	14.6	34.9

Data as orig reptd.; bef. results of disc opers/spec. items. Per share data adj. for stk. divs.; EPS diluted. E-Estimated. NA-Not Available. NM-Not Meaningful. NR-Not Ranked. UR-Under Review.

Office: 650 Madison Ave, New York, NY 10022-1062.
Telephone: 212-318-7000.
Website: http://www.polo.com
Chrmn & CEO: R. Lauren

Pres & COO: R.N. Farah
Investor Contact: T.C. Travis (212-318-7000)
SVP & CFO: T.C. Travis
SVP & General Counsel: J.D. Drucker

Board Members: J. R. Alchin, A. H. Aronson, F. A. Bennack, Jr., J. F. Brown, R. N. Farah, J. L. Fleishman, R. Lauren, J. A. McHale, S. P. Murphy, J. Nemerov, T. S. Semel, B. Wright

Founded: 1967
Domicile: Delaware
Employees: 14,000

The McGraw-Hill Companies

PPG Industries Inc.

STANDARD &POOR'S

S&P Recommendation HOLD ★★★☆☆	**Price** $66.50 (as of Nov 23, 2007)	**12-Mo. Target Price** $80.00	**Investment Style** Large-Cap Blend

GICS Sector Materials
Sub-Industry Diversified Chemicals

Summary PPG is a leading manufacturer of coatings and resins, flat and fiber glass, and industrial and specialty chemicals.

Key Stock Statistics (Source S&P, Vickers, company reports)

52-Wk Range	$82.42–63.02	S&P Oper. EPS 2007 **E** 4.85	Market Capitalization(B)	$10.889	Beta 0.88
Trailing 12-Month EPS	$4.76	S&P Oper. EPS 2008 **E** 5.60	Yield (%)	3.13	S&P 3-Yr. Proj. EPS CAGR(%) 8.00
Trailing 12-Month P/E	14.0	P/E on S&P Oper. EPS 2007 **E** 13.7	Dividend Rate/Share	$2.08	S&P Credit Rating A
$10K Invested 5 Yrs Ago	$16,505	Common Shares Outstg. (M) 163.7	Institutional Ownership (%)	69	

Price Performance

- 30-Week Mov. Avg. · · · 10-Week Mov. Avg. - - **GAAP Earnings vs. Previous Year** Volume Above Avg. STARS
- 12-Mo. Target Price — Relative Strength — ▲ Up ▼ Down ▶ No Change Below Avg.

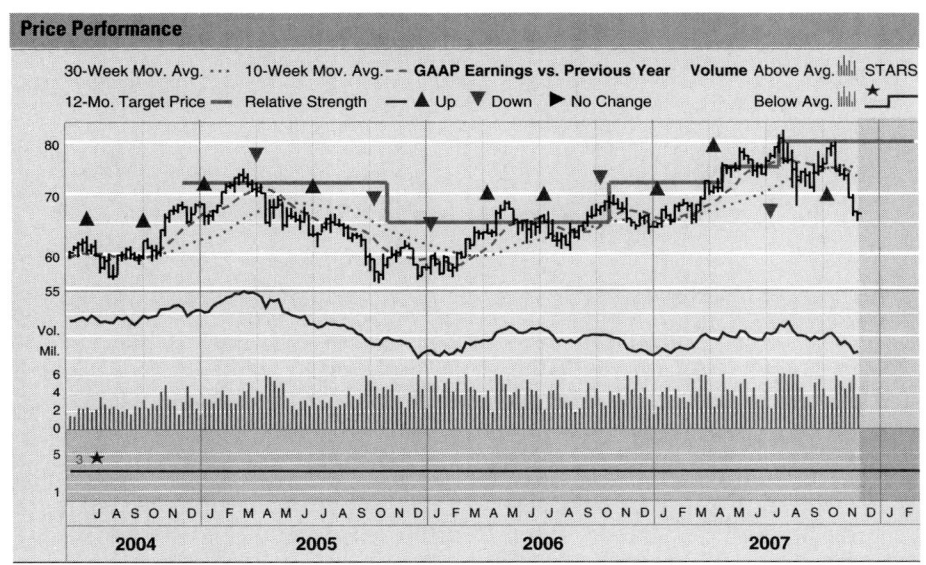

Options: ASE, CBOE, Ph

Analysis prepared by **Richard O'Reilly, CFA** on October 22, 2007, when the stock traded at **$ 74.15**.

Highlights

➤ PPG has agreed to buy SigmaKalon, a European-based coatings producer with annual sales of about $2.7 billion, for around $3.1 billion, and to sell its auto glass and fine chemicals businesses (total annual sales of about $1.2 billion; reported as discontinued operations in 2007) for a total of $565 million. Assuming these transactions are completed, we forecast sales of around $14 billion for 2008. We think coatings and glass will continue to be limited by downturns in U.S. auto and residential construction markets.

➤ We forecast that margins for the coatings units will continue to recover as additional price increases should help offset the large climb in raw material costs since mid-2004. Optical products should continue to post good sales growth. Chlor alkali profits fell sharply in the first half of 2007, partly due to lower prices, but we forecast a sequential improvement as prices recover.

➤ We see the effective tax rate before special items remaining at about 31%. We forecast that quarterly charges of a few cents related to PPG's asbestos settlement obligation will continue into 2008.

Investment Rationale/Risk

➤ We would hold the shares, based on valuation and an above average yield. The stock was recently trading at a P/E multiple, based on our 2007 EPS estimate, that was slightly below that of the S&P 500. If completed, the proposed purchase of SigmaKalon would greatly expand PPG's coatings business, while the sale of the auto glass businesses would greatly reduce its exposure to the domestic auto market. We believe that SigmaKalon would be accretive beginning in 2009.

➤ Risks to our recommendation and target price include slower than projected industrial activity, unplanned production outages and interruptions, exposure to domestic auto makers, and unexpected weakness in selling prices for commodity chemicals.

➤ Our 12-month target price of $80 assumes that the stock's P/E multiple of 14.5X, based on our 2008 operating EPS estimate of $5.60, will remain below that of the S&P 500 due to the unusually high profit contribution from cyclical commodity chemicals. Dividends have been increased for 36 consecutive years, and the recent yield was well above that of the S&P 500.

Qualitative Risk Assessment

LOW	MEDIUM	HIGH

Our risk assessment reflects the company's diversified business mix, large market shares in key products, and what we see as a strong balance sheet, offset by the cyclical nature of the commodity chemicals business and the auto and construction related end markets.

Quantitative Evaluations

S&P Quality Ranking B

D	C	B-	**B**	B+	A-	A	A+

Relative Strength Rank MODERATE

37

LOWEST = 1   HIGHEST = 99

Revenue/Earnings Data

Revenue (Million $)

	1Q	2Q	3Q	4Q	Year
2007	2,917	3,173	2,823	--	--
2006	2,638	2,824	2,802	2,773	11,037
2005	2,493	2,656	2,547	2,505	10,201
2004	2,264	2,429	2,409	2,411	9,513
2003	2,071	2,304	2,206	2,175	8,756
2002	1,875	2,134	2,068	1,990	8,067

Earnings Per Share ($)

2007	1.17	1.50	1.29	E1.10	E4.85
2006	1.11	1.68	0.54	0.94	4.27
2005	0.55	1.34	0.92	0.68	3.49
2004	0.69	1.08	1.12	1.06	3.95
2003	0.49	0.89	0.83	0.71	2.92
2002	0.25	-2.03	0.87	0.55	-0.36

Fiscal year ended Dec. 31. Next earnings report expected: Mid January. EPS Estimates based on S&P Operating Earnings; historical GAAP earnings are as reported.

Dividend Data (Dates: mm/dd Payment Date: mm/dd/yy)

Amount ($)	Date Decl.	Ex-Div. Date	Stk. of Record	Payment Date
0.500	01/18	02/14	02/16	03/12/07
0.500	04/19	05/08	05/10	06/12/07
0.520	07/19	08/08	08/10	09/12/07
0.520	10/18	11/07	11/12	12/12/07

Dividends have been paid since 1899. Source: Company reports.

Please read the Required Disclosures and Analyst Certification on the last page of this report.

*The **McGraw·Hill** Companies*

PPG Industries Inc.

Business Summary October 22, 2007

CORPORATE OVERVIEW. PPG Industries is a diversified producer of coatings, chemicals and glass products. International operations contributed 38% of sales and 29% of operating profits in 2006.

PPG Industries is one of the world's leading producers of protective and decorative coatings. Industrial coatings (29% of sales in 2006 and 23% of operating profits) is comprised of original automotive and industrial coatings (used in appliance, industrial equipment and packaging markets). Performance and applied coatings (28%, 34%) consists of automotive and industrial refinish coatings, aerospace coatings, and a major North American supplier of architectural coatings (Pittsburgh, Olympic, Porter and Lucite brands). The architectural finishes business operated 450 company-owned service centers at year-end 2006, which represented an increase of 72 over the prior year. The company is a global supplier of aircraft coatings, sealants, and transparencies to OEM, maintenance and aftermarket customers. PPG also produces metal pretreatments, adhesives and sealants for the automotive industry, and sealants for architectural insulating glass. The coatings industry is highly competitive and consists of a few large firms with a global presence and many smaller firms serving local or regional markets.

PPG's commodity chemicals business (14%, 19%) is the fourth largest U.S. producer of chlorine and caustic soda (used in a wide variety of industrial applications), vinyl chloride monomer (for use in polyvinyl chloride resins), calcium hypochlorite, and chlorinated solvents. These commodity chemicals are highly cyclical; PPG volumes fell 4% in 2006 following an 11% drop in 2005 due to a plant disruption caused by hurricanes. The company's electrochemical unit (ECU) average prices were at a record level in 2006.

Optical and specialty materials (9%, 14%) consists of optical resins (transitions photochromic lenses, sun lenses, and polarized film), silica compounds, and fine chemicals (to be sold, subject to normal approvals). With the introduction of new photochromic lenses, the optical products business grew at a compound annual growth rate of 18% for the fourth year through 2005. PPG plans to introduce the newest version of the product in early 2008.

Company Financials Fiscal Year Ended Dec. 31

Per Share Data ($)	2006	2005	2004	2003	2002	2001	2000	1999	1998	1997
Tangible Book Value	7.59	8.46	10.81	7.36	3.49	9.10	8.57	8.30	13.09	14.10
Cash Flow	6.61	5.66	6.19	5.23	1.99	4.93	6.20	12.99	6.69	6.04
Earnings	4.27	3.49	3.95	2.92	-0.36	2.29	3.57	3.23	4.48	3.94
S&P Core Earnings	4.78	4.57	4.42	3.48	1.76	1.17	NA	NA	NA	NA
Dividends	1.91	1.86	1.79	1.73	1.70	1.68	1.60	1.52	1.42	1.33
Payout Ratio	45%	53%	45%	59%	NM	73%	45%	47%	32%	34%
Prices:High	69.80	74.73	68.79	64.42	62.86	59.75	65.06	70.75	76.63	67.50
Prices:Low	56.53	55.64	54.81	42.61	41.39	38.99	36.00	47.94	49.13	48.63
P/E Ratio:High	16	21	17	22	NM	26	18	22	17	17
P/E Ratio:Low	13	16	14	15	NM	17	10	15	11	12

Income Statement Analysis (Million $)										
Revenue	11,037	10,201	9,513	8,756	8,067	8,169	8,629	7,757	7,510	7,379
Operating Income	1,703	1,648	1,496	1,367	1,309	1,371	1,649	1,528	1,659	1,689
Depreciation	380	372	388	394	398	447	447	419	383	373
Interest Expense	83.0	81.0	90.0	107	128	169	161	133	110	105
Pretax Income	1,060	947	1,063	843	-28.0	666	1,017	973	1,294	1,175
Effective Tax Rate	26.2%	29.8%	30.3%	34.8%	NM	37.1%	36.3%	38.7%	36.0%	37.0%
Net Income	711	596	683	500	-60.0	387	620	568	801	714
S&P Core Earnings	797	780	765	597	300	197	NA	NA	NA	NA

Balance Sheet & Other Financial Data (Million $)										
Cash	455	466	709	499	117	108	111	158	128	129
Current Assets	4,592	4,019	4,054	3,537	2,945	2,703	3,093	3,062	2,660	2,584
Total Assets	10,021	8,681	8,932	8,424	7,863	8,452	9,125	8,914	7,387	6,868
Current Liabilities	2,787	2,349	2,221	2,139	1,920	1,955	2,543	2,384	1,912	1,662
Long Term Debt	1,155	1,169	1,184	1,339	1,699	1,699	1,810	1,836	1,081	1,257
Common Equity	3,234	3,053	3,572	2,911	2,150	3,080	3,097	3,106	2,880	2,509
Total Capital	4,673	4,420	4,997	4,475	4,044	5,453	5,578	5,560	4,488	4,254
Capital Expenditures	372	288	244	217	238	291	561	490	487	466
Cash Flow	1,091	968	1,071	894	338	834	1,067	987	1,184	1,087
Current Ratio	1.6	1.7	1.8	1.7	1.5	1.4	1.2	1.3	1.4	1.6
% Long Term Debt of Capitalization	24.7	26.4	23.7	29.9	42.0	31.2	32.4	33.0	24.0	29.5
% Net Income of Revenue	6.4	5.8	7.2	5.7	NM	4.7	7.2	7.3	10.7	9.7
% Return on Assets	7.6	6.8	7.9	6.1	NM	4.4	6.9	7.0	11.2	10.7
% Return on Equity	22.6	18.0	21.1	19.8	NM	12.5	20.0	19.0	29.7	28.6

Data as orig reptd.; bef. results of disc opers/spec. items. Per share data adj. for stk. divs.; EPS diluted. E-Estimated. NA-Not Available. NM-Not Meaningful. NR-Not Ranked. UR-Under Review.

Office: 1 PPG Place, Pittsburgh, PA 15272.
Telephone: 412-434-3131.
Website: http://www.ppg.com
Chrmn & CEO: C.E. Bunch

Investor Contact: W.H. Hernandez (412-434-3131)
SVP & CFO: W.H. Hernandez
SVP & General Counsel: J.C. Diggs

Board Members: J. G. Berges, C. E. Bunch, E. B. Davis, Jr., H. Grant, V. F. Haynes, M. J. Hooper, R. Mehrabian, R. Ripp, T. J. Usher, D. R. Whitwam

Founded: 1883
Domicile: Pennsylvania
Employees: 32,200

PPL Corp

STANDARD &POOR'S

S&P Recommendation BUY ★★★★☆	**Price** $49.12 (as of Nov 23, 2007)	**12-Mo. Target Price** $57.00	**Investment Style** Large-Cap Blend

GICS Sector Utilities
Sub-Industry Electric Utilities

Summary This Pennsylvania-based holding company for PPL Utilities also has holdings in the U.K. and Latin America.

Key Stock Statistics (Source S&P, Vickers, company reports)

52-Wk Range	$52.79– 34.43	S&P Oper. EPS 2007**E**	2.55	Market Capitalization(B)	$18.818	Beta	0.14
Trailing 12-Month EPS	$2.71	S&P Oper. EPS 2008**E**	2.42	Yield (%)	2.48	S&P 3-Yr. Proj. EPS CAGR(%)	11.00
Trailing 12-Month P/E	18.1	P/E on S&P Oper. EPS 2007**E**	19.3	Dividend Rate/Share	$1.22	S&P Credit Rating	NA
$10K Invested 5 Yrs Ago	$33,846	Common Shares Outstg. (M)	383.1	Institutional Ownership (%)	61		

Price Performance

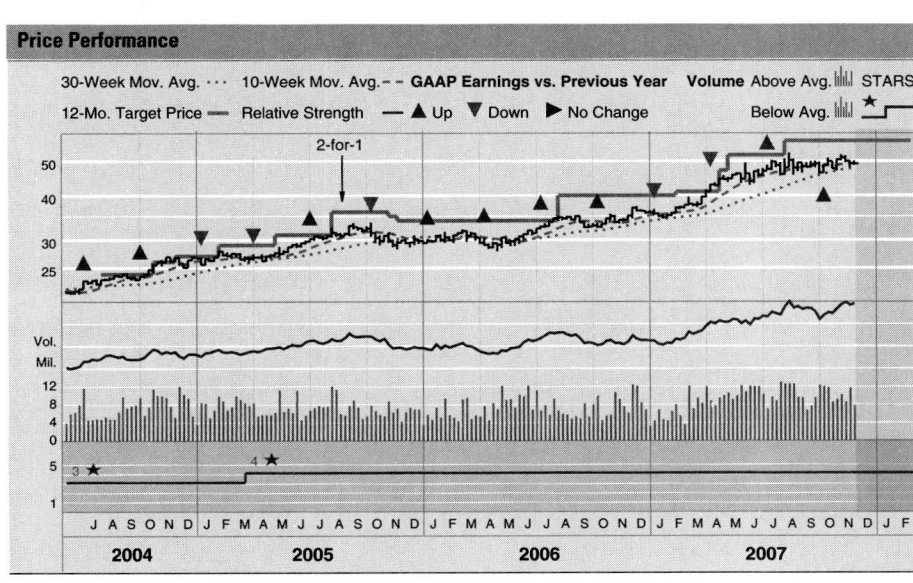

Options: P, Ph

Analysis prepared by **Justin McCann** on November 13, 2007, when the stock traded at **$ 48.08**.

Highlights

➤ We expect 2007 EPS to rise nearly 15% from 2006 operating EPS of $2.22, driven by the replacement of expiring wholesale energy contracts with higher-margin contracts, as well as higher earnings from the U.K., reflecting a favorable currency exchange rate and income tax benefits. We expect this to be partially offset by higher O&M and depreciation expenses at the Pennsylvania delivery business. Results in the first nine months of 2007 were aided by a one-time income tax benefit of $0.08 related to the international delivery business segment.

➤ We expect EPS in 2008 to decline about 5% from anticipated results in 2007, as higher wholesale margins are more than offset by the absence of prior-year tax benefits as well as earnings from the divested Latin American operations. We expect a modest increase in 2009 EPS, but then see a sharp increase in 2010 as expired energy contracts are replaced by much higher-margin contracts.

➤ We expect the proceeds from the now completed sale of the Latin American operations to be invested in either acquisitions or share buybacks, which could largely offset the loss of income from these businesses.

Investment Rationale/Risk

➤ After outperforming the S&P Index of Electric Utilities in each of the past three years, we expect the stock to continue to outperform over the next 12 months on a total return basis. We believe that after an expected EPS decline in 2008 from the 15% growth we see for 2007, the market will be looking beyond the modest EPS growth anticipated through 2009, to the substantial increase projected for 2010. The stock's dividend yield (recently 2.4%) remains below the peer average (3.7%), and the effective payout ratio (50% of our 2007 operating EPS estimate) is also below that of peers (60%).

➤ Risks to our recommendation and target price include potentially unfavorable regulatory rulings, significantly lower results from the unregulated operations, and a major shift in the average P/E multiple of the peer group as a whole.

➤ Our 12-month target price is $57. In light of PPL's strength in a strong wholesale power market and given our view of a sharp rise in EPS in 2010, we expect the shares to trade at nearly 24X our 2008 EPS estimate of $2.42, reflecting an approximate 35% premium to the average projected peer P/E multiple, based on our EPS estimates for 2008.

Qualitative Risk Assessment

LOW	**MEDIUM**	HIGH

Our risk assessment reflects the steady cash flow we expect from the regulated Pennsylvania and U.K. distribution segments, which operate within supportive regulatory environments. This is offset by the highly profitable but less predictable earnings and cash flow from the power supply segment, as well as the currency risks related to the U.K. and Latin American businesses.

Quantitative Evaluations

S&P Quality Ranking   **B+**

D	C	B-	B	**B+**	A-	A	A+

Relative Strength Rank   **STRONG**

79

LOWEST = 1   HIGHEST = 99

Revenue/Earnings Data

Revenue (Million $)

	1Q	2Q	3Q	4Q	Year
2007	1,638	1,613	1,763	--	--
2006	1,781	1,642	1,752	1,724	6,899
2005	1,602	1,476	1,643	1,498	6,219
2004	1,520	1,362	1,465	1,465	5,812
2003	1,487	1,338	1,456	1,296	5,587
2002	1,351	1,288	1,476	1,314	5,429

Earnings Per Share ($)

2007	0.58	0.63	0.72	E0.55	E2.55
2006	0.73	0.52	0.58	0.47	2.29
2005	0.44	0.47	0.51	0.50	1.92
2004	0.50	0.41	0.52	0.47	1.89
2003	0.53	0.34	0.49	0.72	2.08
2002	0.50	-0.09	0.40	0.36	1.17

Fiscal year ended Dec. 31. Next earnings report expected: Early February. EPS Estimates based on S&P Operating Earnings; historical GAAP earnings are as reported.

Dividend Data (Dates: mm/dd Payment Date: mm/dd/yy)

Amount ($)	Date Decl.	Ex-Div. Date	Stk. of Record	Payment Date
0.305	02/23	03/07	03/09	04/01/07
0.305	05/23	06/06	06/08	07/01/07
0.305	08/24	09/06	09/10	10/01/07
0.305	11/15	12/06	12/10	01/01/08

Dividends have been paid since 1946. Source: Company reports.

Please read the Required Disclosures and Analyst Certification on the last page of this report.

The McGraw-Hill Companies

PPL Corp

STANDARD
&POOR'S

Business Summary November 13, 2007

CORPORATE OVERVIEW. PPL Corporation (PPL) is an energy and utility holding company organized into three operating segments: the supply segment, the Pennsylvania delivery segment, and the international delivery segment. PPL's subsidiaries PPL Generation and PPL EnergyPlus comprise the supply segment. These units are involved in electricity generation and marketing of electricity and other power purchases to deregulated wholesale and retail markets. The Pennsylvania delivery segment operates through its subsidiaries PPL Electric and PPL Gas Utilities, which provide electric and gas utility services in the regulated Pennsylvania market. The international delivery segment is focused on electricity distribution in the U.K. and Latin America through its subsidiary PPL Global.

CORPORATE STRATEGY. The company's business strategy is to achieve stable growth in the regulated delivery business. It plans to earn long-term growth in delivery through efficient and low-cost operations while working to enhance strong customer and regulatory relations. In the unregulated supply business, PPL intends to reduce the volatility in both its cash flows and earnings and to ensure disciplined growth. The company's strategy for its electricity generation and marketing business is to build an effective risk management framework to handle energy price risk and counterparty risk. It will work to reduce risk by entering into supply contracts of varying duration, which should reflect fluctuations in demand.

MARKET PROFILE. PPL provides electricity delivery service to 1.4 million customers in a 10,000-square-mile territory covering 29 counties of eastern and central Pennsylvania. In 2006, about 42% of electricity revenues were from residential customers, 37% from commercial customers, 20% from industrial customers, and 1% from other customer classes. In 2005, PPL provided gas distribution services to 110,000 customers in Pennsylvania and parts of Maryland and Delaware. In addition, PPL Gas Utilities provides intra- and interstate storage services from its storage fields in Pennsylvania. PPL Generation owned or controlled 11,556 megawatts (mw) of generating capacity at the end of 2006, with 9,229 mw at its plants in Pennsylvania and 1,289 mw in Montana. In the U.K., PPL operates two distribution companies that serve 2.6 million customers.

Company Financials Fiscal Year Ended Dec. 31

Per Share Data ($)	2006	2005	2004	2003	2002	2001	2000	1999	1998	1997
Tangible Book Value	9.35	7.73	7.50	5.53	5.87	6.98	6.65	5.60	5.94	8.39
Earnings	2.29	1.92	1.89	2.08	1.17	0.58	1.68	1.57	1.15	0.90
S&P Core Earnings	2.33	1.87	1.74	1.95	0.79	0.90	NA	NA	NA	NA
Dividends	1.10	1.21	0.82	0.77	0.68	0.53	0.53	0.50	0.67	0.84
Payout Ratio	48%	63%	43%	37%	57%	92%	32%	32%	59%	93%
Prices:High	37.34	33.68	27.08	22.17	19.98	31.18	23.06	16.00	14.47	12.13
Prices:Low	27.83	25.52	19.92	15.83	13.00	15.50	9.19	10.19	10.44	9.50
P/E Ratio:High	16	18	14	11	17	54	14	10	13	13
P/E Ratio:Low	12	13	11	8	11	27	5	6	9	11

Income Statement Analysis (Million $)	2006	2005	2004	2003	2002	2001	2000	1999	1998	1997
Revenue	6,899	6,219	5,812	5,587	5,429	5,725	5,683	4,590	3,786	3,049
Depreciation	446	420	412	380	367	254	261	257	338	374
Maintenance	NA	NA	NA	NA	314	269	261	215	182	184
Fixed Charges Coverage	3.46	2.70	2.72	2.72	2.49	3.08	2.95	3.20	3.45	3.25
Construction Credits	NA	NA	NA	NA	NA	NA	NA	NA	Nil	NA
Effective Tax Rate	23.5%	14.0%	21.6%	18.5%	29.5%	54.4%	36.3%	26.1%	39.3%	42.7%
Net Income	885	737	700	748	425	221	513	478	379	296
S&P Core Earnings	897	716	645	674	240	262	NA	NA	NA	NA

Balance Sheet & Other Financial Data (Million $)	2006	2005	2004	2003	2002	2001	2000	1999	1998	1997
Gross Property	20,079	18,615	18,692	17,775	16,406	12,477	11,418	10,717	10,489	10,336
Capital Expenditures	1,394	811	703	771	648	565	460	318	304	310
Net Property	12,069	10,916	11,209	10,446	9,566	6,135	5,948	5,644	4,363	6,766
Capitalization:Long Term Debt	6,728	6,095	6,881	8,145	6,562	5,906	4,717	4,103	3,092	2,698
Capitalization:% Long Term Debt	56.8	58.0	61.6	71.1	74.0	75.3	69.1	71.8	60.3	47.0
Capitalization:Preferred	Nil	Nil	51.0	51.0	82.0	82.0	97.0	Nil	347	347
Capitalization:% Preferred	Nil	Nil	0.46	0.45	0.92	1.05	1.42	Nil	6.70	6.10
Capitalization:Common	5,122	4,418	4,239	3,259	2,224	1,857	2,012	1,613	1,790	2,809
Capitalization:% Common	43.2	42.0	37.9	28.5	25.1	23.7	29.5	28.2	34.9	49.0
Total Capital	14,241	12,766	13,653	13,710	11,274	9,332	6,880	7,328	5,317	8,075
% Operating Ratio	80.8	80.3	79.5	78.9	76.8	81.1	84.0	84.8	79.8	82.1
% Earned on Net Property	13.9	12.2	12.7	13.4	17.5	14.2	28.6	22.3	10.3	8.0
% Return on Revenue	12.8	11.9	12.0	13.4	7.8	3.9	9.0	10.4	10.0	9.7
% Return on Invested Capital	10.3	9.5	9.0	10.0	12.6	12.4	14.3	11.3	13.1	9.4
% Return on Common Equity	18.6	17.0	18.6	26.2	17.5	8.7	28.3	28.1	16.5	10.7

Data as orig reptd.; bef. results of disc opers/spec. items. Per share data adj. for stk. divs.; EPS diluted. E-Estimated. NA-Not Available. NM-Not Meaningful. NR-Not Ranked. UR-Under Review.

Office: 2 N 9th St, Allentown, PA, USA 18101-1170.
Telephone: 610-774-5151.
Email: invrel@pplweb.com
Website: http://www.pplweb.com

Chrmn, Pres & CEO: J.H. Miller
COO & EVP: W.H. Spence
EVP & CFO: P.A. Farr
SVP, Secy & General Counsel: R.J. Grey

VP & Treas: J.E. Abel
Investor Contact: T.J. Paukovits (610-774-4124)
Board Members: F. M. Bernthal, J. R. Biggar, J. W. Conway, E. A. Deaver, L. K. Goeser, S. Heydt, J. H. Miller, C. A. Rogerson, W. K. Smith, S. M. Stalnecker, K. H. Williamson

Founded: 1920
Domicile: Pennsylvania
Employees: 12,620

The McGraw-Hill Companies

Praxair Inc.

STANDARD &POOR'S

S&P Recommendation	SELL ★★☆☆☆	Price	12-Mo. Target Price	Investment Style
		$80.67 (as of Nov 23, 2007)	$80.00	Large-Cap Growth

GICS Sector Materials
Sub-Industry Industrial Gases

Summary This company is the largest producer of industrial gases in North and South America, and the second biggest worldwide. It also provides ceramic and metallic coatings.

Key Stock Statistics (Source S&P, Vickers, company reports)

52-Wk Range	$88.02–57.97	S&P Oper. EPS 2007E	3.60	Market Capitalization(B)	$25.485	Beta	0.73
Trailing 12-Month EPS	$3.46	S&P Oper. EPS 2008E	4.00	Yield (%)	1.49	S&P 3-Yr. Proj. EPS CAGR(%)	10.00
Trailing 12-Month P/E	23.3	P/E on S&P Oper. EPS 2007E	22.4	Dividend Rate/Share	$1.20	S&P Credit Rating	A
$10K Invested 5 Yrs Ago	$30,728	Common Shares Outstg. (M)	315.9	Institutional Ownership (%)	85		

Price Performance

30-Week Mov. Avg. ···   10-Week Mov. Avg. − −   **GAAP Earnings vs. Previous Year**   Volume Above Avg. STARS
12-Mo. Target Price —   Relative Strength —   ▲ Up ▼ Down ▶ No Change   Below Avg. ★

Options: ASE, CBOE, Ph

Analysis prepared by **Richard O'Reilly, CFA** on November 15, 2007, when the stock traded at **$ 81.83**.

Highlights

➤ We project that sales will rise about 10% in 2008, versus 12% seen for 2007, driven by the start-up of new projects, including about 40 major ones scheduled through 2009. We expect that North American gases volumes will continue to show low-single digit growth, reflecting moderate growth in industrial activity and the addition of new projects.

➤ We also see the European and South American regions posting good sales gains, while Asian growth should continue in the double digits, driven by new projects. We expect healthy increases in selling prices in most regions. We look for Surface Technologies' ongoing sales to expand close to 10% on stronger demand in coatings services for industrial equipment and OEM aircraft engines.

➤ We project that 2008 operating profit margins will remain at about 19%, assuming a neutral impact from the pass-through of natural gas costs to hydrogen customers. We look for the effective tax rate to remain at the 26% rate of 2007. A more aggressive stock buyback program initiated in mid-2007 should help to boost EPS comparisons.

Investment Rationale/Risk

➤ We have a sell opinion on the shares, based on what we view as its excessive valuation. The stock recently traded at about 23X our 2007 EPS estimate of $3.60, a sharp premium to the S&P 500. PX typically sold at a discount prior to 2004. We believe that the company's longer-term fundamentals remain sound, and that it is concentrating on several less capital-intensive, faster-growing global markets such as health care, as well as hydrogen for use by petroleum refiners.

➤ Risks to our recommendation and target price include an unexpected pickup in industrial activity, especially metals-related markets; lower than projected power and natural gas costs; and a more rapid ability to develop and successfully introduce new products and applications for industrial gases.

➤ The shares recently traded at a steep premium to the overall chemical industry and the S&P 500, based on our projections. Our 12-month target price of $80 assumes a narrowing of PX's P/E to about 20X, in line with its industrial gases peers, applied to our 2008 EPS forecast. The stock's S&P Quality Ranking is A.

Qualitative Risk Assessment

LOW	**MEDIUM**	HIGH

Our risk assessment reflects the relatively stable growth and cash flow nature of the industrial gases industry versus commodity chemicals, and PX's high S&P Quality Ranking of A. This is offset by its exposure to volatile energy costs.

Quantitative Evaluations

S&P Quality Ranking A

D	C	B-	B	B+	A-	**A**	A+

Relative Strength Rank STRONG

76

LOWEST = 1   HIGHEST = 99

Revenue/Earnings Data

Revenue (Million $)

	1Q	2Q	3Q	4Q	Year
2007	2,175	2,332	2,372	--	--
2006	2,026	2,076	2,099	2,123	8,324
2005	1,827	1,919	1,890	2,020	7,656
2004	1,531	1,603	1,674	1,786	6,594
2003	1,337	1,401	1,414	1,461	5,613
2002	1,232	1,307	1,292	1,297	5,128

Earnings Per Share ($)

	1Q	2Q	3Q	4Q	Year
2007	0.81	0.89	0.94	E0.96	E3.60
2006	0.68	0.75	0.75	0.82	3.00
2005	0.59	0.63	0.33	0.67	2.22
2004	0.49	0.53	0.53	0.55	2.10
2003	0.40	0.46	0.46	0.47	1.77
2002	0.39	0.46	0.40	0.43	1.66

Fiscal year ended Dec. 31. Next earnings report expected: Late January. EPS Estimates based on S&P Operating Earnings; historical GAAP earnings are as reported.

Dividend Data (Dates: mm/dd Payment Date: mm/dd/yy)

Amount ($)	Date Decl.	Ex-Div. Date	Stk. of Record	Payment Date
0.300	01/23	03/05	03/07	03/15/07
0.300	04/24	06/05	06/07	06/15/07
0.300	07/25	09/05	09/07	09/17/07
0.300	10/23	12/05	12/07	12/17/07

Dividends have been paid since 1992. Source: Company reports.

Praxair Inc.

STANDARD &POOR'S

Business Summary November 15, 2007

CORPORATE OVERVIEW. Since its 1992 spin-off from Union Carbide Corp., PX, the largest producer of industrial gases in North and South America, has expanded its operations to 40 countries. Foreign sales accounted for 55% of the total in 2006, with Brazil alone providing 13%.

PX conducts its industrial gases business through four operating segments: North America (56% of sales and 54% of profits in 2006); South America (16%, 17%); Europe (14%,18%); and Asia (8%, 7%). The capital intensive industrial gases business involves the production, distribution and sale of atmospheric gases (oxygen, nitrogen, argon and rare gases), carbon dioxide, hydrogen, helium, acetylene, and specialty and electronic gases. Atmospheric gases are produced through air separation processes, primarily cryogenic, while other gases are produced by various methods. PX also produces specialty products (sputtering targets, mechanical planarization slurries and polishing pads, and coatings) for use in semiconductor manufacturing. In addition, the business includes the construction and sale of equipment to produce industrial gases.

Industrial gases are supplied to customers through three basic methods: on-

site/pipeline (24% of total 2006 sales, sold under long-term contracts), merchant (30%, with three to five year contracts) and packaged (33%). At the end of 2006, the company had 260 major production facilities (air separation, hydrogen and carbon dioxide plants) in North America and five major pipeline complexes; 50 facilities and three pipeline complexes in Europe; more than 40 plants in South America, primarily in Brazil; and more than 25 plants in Asia, mainly in China, Korea and India. S.A. White Martins is the largest producer of industrial gases in South America.

The Surface Technologies business (6%, 4%) applies metallic and ceramic coatings and powders to parts and equipment provided by customers, including aircraft engine, printing, power generation and other industrial markets, and manufactures electric arc, plasma and oxygen fuel spray equipment. In July 2006, PX sold its aviation services business (annual sales of $80 million).

Company Financials Fiscal Year Ended Dec. 31

Per Share Data ($)	2006	2005	2004	2003	2002	2001	2000	1999	1998	1997
Tangible Book Value	8.91	7.05	6.08	6.00	4.03	7.59	3.97	3.70	3.36	2.89
Cash Flow	5.12	4.23	3.85	3.33	3.12	2.84	2.59	2.73	2.73	2.62
Earnings	3.00	2.22	2.10	1.77	1.66	1.32	1.13	1.37	1.30	1.27
S&P Core Earnings	2.99	2.16	2.02	1.67	1.38	1.04	NA	NA	NA	NA
Dividends	1.00	0.72	0.60	0.46	0.38	0.34	0.31	0.28	0.25	0.22
Payout Ratio	33%	32%	29%	26%	23%	26%	28%	21%	19%	17%
Prices:High	63.70	54.31	46.25	38.26	30.56	27.96	27.47	29.06	26.94	29.00
Prices:Low	50.36	41.06	34.52	25.02	22.28	18.25	15.16	16.00	15.34	19.63
P/E Ratio:High	21	24	22	22	18	21	24	21	21	23
P/E Ratio:Low	17	18	16	14	13	14	13	12	12	16

Income Statement Analysis (Million $)	2006	2005	2004	2003	2002	2001	2000	1999	1998	1997
Revenue	8,324	7,656	6,594	5,613	5,128	5,158	5,043	4,639	4,833	4,735
Operating Income	2,183	1,948	1,681	1,444	1,358	1,333	1,220	1,199	1,310	1,230
Depreciation	696	665	578	517	483	499	471	445	467	444
Interest Expense	155	163	155	151	206	224	224	204	260	216
Pretax Income	1,312	1,145	959	735	726	585	493	638	607	633
Effective Tax Rate	27.1%	32.8%	24.2%	23.7%	21.8%	23.1%	20.9%	23.8%	20.9%	23.9%
Net Income	988	732	697	585	548	432	363	441	425	416
S&P Core Earnings	983	711	671	552	454	343	NA	NA	NA	NA

Balance Sheet & Other Financial Data (Million $)	2006	2005	2004	2003	2002	2001	2000	1999	1998	1997
Cash	36.0	173	25.0	50.0	39.0	39.0	31.0	76.0	34.0	43.0
Current Assets	2,059	2,133	1,744	1,449	1,286	1,276	1,361	1,335	1,394	1,497
Total Assets	11,102	10,491	9,878	8,305	7,401	7,715	7,762	7,722	8,096	7,810
Current Liabilities	1,758	2,001	1,875	1,117	1,100	1,194	1,439	1,725	1,289	1,366
Long Term Debt	2,981	2,926	2,876	2,661	2,510	2,725	2,641	2,111	2,895	2,874
Common Equity	4,554	3,902	3,608	3,088	2,340	2,477	2,357	2,290	2,332	2,122
Total Capital	7,757	6,828	6,709	5,944	5,014	5,363	5,156	4,835	5,789	5,592
Capital Expenditures	1,100	877	668	983	498	595	704	653	781	902
Cash Flow	1,684	1,397	1,275	1,102	1,031	931	834	886	892	860
Current Ratio	1.2	1.1	0.9	1.3	1.2	1.1	0.9	0.8	1.1	1.1
% Long Term Debt of Capitalization	38.4	42.9	42.9	44.8	50.1	50.8	51.2	43.7	50.0	51.4
% Net Income of Revenue	11.9	9.6	10.6	10.4	10.7	8.4	7.2	9.5	8.8	8.8
% Return on Assets	9.2	7.2	7.7	7.4	7.3	5.6	4.7	5.6	5.3	5.4
% Return on Equity	23.4	19.5	20.8	21.6	22.8	17.9	15.6	19.1	19.1	20.6

Data as orig reptd.; bef. results of disc opers/spec. items. Per share data adj. for stk. divs.; EPS diluted. E-Estimated. NA-Not Available. NM-Not Meaningful. NR-Not Ranked. UR-Under Review.

Office: 39 Old Ridgebury Rd, Danbury, CT 06810-5113.
Telephone: 203-837-2000.
Website: http://www.praxair.com
Pres & CEO: S.F. Angel

EVP & CFO: J.S. Sawyer
VP & Treas: M.J. Allan
VP, Secy & General Counsel: D.H. Chaifetz
Investor Contact: E.T. Hirsch (203-837-2354)

Board Members: S. F. Angel, C. W. Gargalli, I. D. Hall, R. L. Kuehn, Jr., R. W. LeBoeuf, D. H. Reilley, W. T. Smith, H. M. Watson, Jr., R. L. Wood, J. P. de Oliveira Alves

Founded: 1988
Domicile: Delaware
Employees: 27,042

Precision Castparts Corp.

STANDARD &POOR'S

| **S&P Recommendation** HOLD ★★★☆☆ | **Price** $137.08 (as of Nov 23, 2007) | **12-Mo. Target Price** $152.00 | **Investment Style** Large-Cap Growth |

GICS Sector Industrials
Sub-Industry Aerospace & Defense

Summary This company is a provider of complex metal components used primarily in the manufacture of jet engines and industrial gas turbines, as well as in the oil & gas industry.

Key Stock Statistics (Source S&P, Vickers, company reports)

52-Wk Range	$160.73–72.32	S&P Oper. EPS 2008**E**	6.76	Market Capitalization(B)	$18.897	Beta	1.02
Trailing 12-Month EPS	$5.92	S&P Oper. EPS 2009**E**	7.83	Yield (%)	0.09	S&P 3-Yr. Proj. EPS CAGR(%)	18.00
Trailing 12-Month P/E	23.2	P/E on S&P Oper. EPS 2008**E**	20.3	Dividend Rate/Share	$0.12	S&P Credit Rating	BBB+
$10K Invested 5 Yrs Ago	$123,224	Common Shares Outstg. (M)	137.9	Institutional Ownership (%)	87		

Price Performance

30-Week Mov. Avg. ··· 10-Week Mov. Avg. -- **GAAP Earnings vs. Previous Year** Volume Above Avg. STARS
12-Mo. Target Price — Relative Strength — ▲ Up ▼ Down ▶ No Change Below Avg. ★

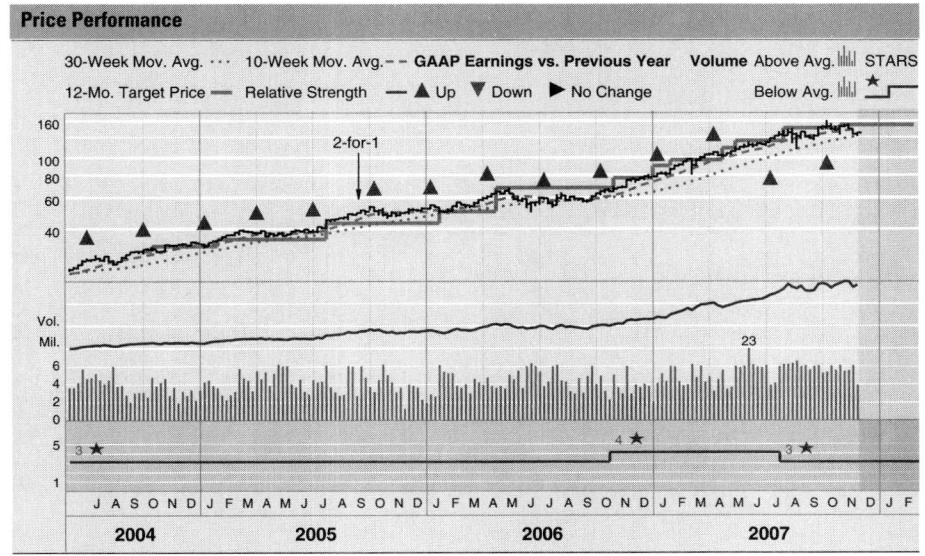

Options: ASE, CBOE, Ph

Analysis prepared by **Richard Tortoriello** on October 25, 2007, when the stock traded at **$ 150.04**.

Highlights

➤ Following a 51% revenue increase in FY 07 (Mar.), driven by the acquisition of Special Metals Corp. in May 2006, we look for sales to rise about 27% in FY 08, aided by acquisitions, and we project a further 14% increase in FY 09. Special Metals Corp., acquired for about $550 million, is the world's largest producer of high-performance nickel-based alloys, of which PCP is the leading user. We believe strong demand from aerospace OEMs and aftermarket parts makers will drive healthy sales growth at PCP for some time to come. In addition, we see strong global demand for gas turbines, another large market for PCP, aiding results.

➤ We foresee an operating margin of 21.5% in FY 08, up from 18.1% in FY 07, due to productivity and cost-savings programs, with particular margin improvement in the Special Metals business (now part of PCP's Forged Products segment). We are projecting an FY 09 operating margin of 21.3%.

➤ We project EPS growth of about 50% in FY 08, to $6.76, and see about 16% growth in FY 09, to $7.83. We expect free cash flow per share in FY 08 to be between 80% and 90% of reported EPS.

Investment Rationale/Risk

➤ We continue to have a favorable view of PCP's strong exposure to the jet engine and power generation markets, as well as expected continued cost savings that PCP should bring to the Special Metals acquisition. We see these factors resulting in EPS growth in the 15% to 25% range. Management has demonstrated a solid performance in turning top-line growth into bottom-line results, with operating margins rising from about 14% in FY 04 and FY 05 to 18% in FY 07.

➤ Risks to our recommendation and target price include a slowdown in either aerospace or gas turbine demand or an inability to successfully integrate acquisitions, as well as other operational difficulties, resulting in slower-than-anticipated sales and earnings growth.

➤ Given the company's performance, and our view of the current unusually strong aerospace cycle, we believe PCP deserves a multiple toward the high end of its 10-year historical range of between 6X and 25X (based on two-year forward P/E ratios). Our 12-month target price of $152 is based on a P/E of about 19X applied to our FY 09 EPS estimate.

Qualitative Risk Assessment

| LOW | **MEDIUM** | HIGH |

Precision Castparts operates in a cyclical and capital intensive industry and is subject to swings in commodity prices. However, due to PCP's large market share in most of its markets, we believe the company has significant pricing power over its products. We also consider its financial condition to be solid, with a relatively low level of debt.

Quantitative Evaluations

S&P Quality Ranking B

| D | C | B- | **B** | B+ | A- | A | A+ |

Relative Strength Rank MODERATE

66

LOWEST = 1   HIGHEST = 99

Revenue/Earnings Data

Revenue (Million $)

	1Q	2Q	3Q	4Q	Year
2008	1,660	1,727	--	--	--
2007	1,112	1,318	1,385	1,547	5,361
2006	854.6	874.9	864.4	952.6	3,546
2005	738.8	697.5	743.9	809.5	2,919
2004	475.7	476.3	517.6	705.1	2,175
2003	579.4	526.5	497.1	514.2	2,117

Earnings Per Share ($)

2008	1.61	1.67	E1.69	E1.79	E6.76
2007	0.83	1.03	1.15	1.44	4.45
2006	0.58	0.60	0.67	0.74	2.57
2005	0.40	0.43	0.47	0.52	1.80
2004	0.33	0.27	0.26	0.32	1.18
2003	0.40	0.40	0.36	0.36	1.51

Fiscal year ended Mar. 31. Next earnings report expected: Late January. EPS Estimates based on S&P Operating Earnings; historical GAAP earnings are as reported.

Dividend Data (Dates: mm/dd Payment Date: mm/dd/yy)

Amount ($)	Date Decl.	Ex-Div. Date	Stk. of Record	Payment Date
0.030	02/21	03/07	03/09	04/02/07
0.030	05/29	06/06	06/08	07/02/07
0.030	08/17	09/05	09/07	10/01/07
0.030	11/16	12/05	12/07	12/31/07

Dividends have been paid since 1978. Source: Company reports.

Precision Castparts Corp.

Business Summary October 25, 2007

COMPANY OVERVIEW. Precision Castparts, a manufacturer of jet engine and industrial gas turbine engine components, conducts business through four operating units. PCP's Investment Cast Products segment (34% and 37% of FY 07 (Mar.) revenues and operating earnings, respectively) makes cast components, primarily for aircraft jet engine and utility generator makers. PCP is the world's largest maker of jet engine structural castings (components made from molten metal poured into molds) used to strengthen sections of a jet engine. It is also the leading manufacturer of airfoils used in military and commercial jet engines. PCP's principal competitor is Alcoa's Howmet unit. PCP's Fastener Products segment (43% and 38%) primarily makes industrial fasteners for the aerospace, automotive, construction and power generation markets. The Forged Products segment (23% and 25%) produces forged components, which are used in jet engines, wings, fuselages and landing gear, and oil and gas pipe. Primary competitors include Ladish Co., Fortech, SA, Thyssen AG, Alcoa (AA: hold, $34), and Schultz Steel Co. in the aerospace market, and Mannesmann AG and Sumitomo Corp. in the power generation market.

MARKET PROFILE. Demand for PCP's aerospace components is primarily driven by growth of the global commercial aircraft fleet and the overall amount of aircraft usage in the industry. Aircraft fleet growth, in turn, is driven by airline industry profitability and passenger air traffic growth. Sales of industrial gas turbine engine components are tied to growth of global electricity consumption, while demand for replacement parts depends on the size and usage rate of the installed base. PCP relies heavily on aircraft components' business from GE, United Technologies' Pratt & Whitney jet engine unit, and Britain's Rolls-Royce plc. In FY 07, GE accounted for 11% of total revenues. Deliveries of large commercial aircraft from Boeing and Airbus rose 10% in 2005 and 25% in 2006, and we forecast a further increase of at least 8% to 10% in 2007 and 2008.

Company Financials Fiscal Year Ended Mar. 31

Per Share Data ($)	2007	2006	2005	2004	2003	2002	2001	2000	1999	1998
Tangible Book Value	5.37	3.56	1.51	0.62	0.74	NM	NM	NM	1.75	1.48
Cash Flow	5.27	3.30	2.53	1.73	2.28	1.37	2.23	1.62	1.61	1.33
Earnings	4.45	2.57	1.80	1.18	1.51	0.41	1.23	0.87	1.05	0.88
S&P Core Earnings	4.47	2.51	1.79	1.21	1.17	0.63	1.22	NA	NA	NA
Dividends	0.11	0.06	0.06	0.06	0.06	0.06	0.06	0.06	0.06	0.06
Payout Ratio	2%	2%	3%	5%	4%	15%	5%	7%	6%	7%
Calendar Year	2006	2005	2004	2003	2002	2001	2000	1999	1998	1997
Prices:High	80.90	53.91	34.19	22.97	19.00	24.75	22.78	11.81	16.06	16.92
Prices:Low	48.80	31.15	20.68	10.61	8.43	9.00	5.92	5.86	8.16	12.00
P/E Ratio:High	18	21	19	19	13	61	19	14	15	19
P/E Ratio:Low	11	12	11	9	6	22	5	7	8	14

Income Statement Analysis (Million $)

Revenue	5,361	3,546	2,919	2,175	2,117	2,557	2,326	1,674	1,472	1,317
Operating Income	1,086	656	517	380	390	448	401	267	246	208
Depreciation	113	99.2	97.0	88.2	82.5	101	102	74.2	54.1	43.5
Interest Expense	52.2	41.4	56.6	54.1	56.4	66.2	81.0	47.1	27.6	20.7
Pretax Income	918	513	360	212	242	135	209	139	151	135
Effective Tax Rate	33.2%	31.6%	33.7%	35.7%	34.5%	68.6%	40.1%	38.5%	31.5%	36.4%
Net Income	615	349	240	136	159	42.4	125	85.3	103	86.1
S&P Core Earnings	618	341	237	140	123	65.4	124	NA	NA	NA

Balance Sheet & Other Financial Data (Million $)

Cash	150	59.9	154	80.3	28.7	38.1	40.1	17.6	14.8	25.0
Current Assets	2,037	1,234	1,213	1,188	786	878	863	752	557	511
Total Assets	5,259	3,751	3,625	3,756	2,467	2,565	2,573	2,416	1,450	1,275
Current Liabilities	1,658	768	780	913	625	727	657	592	305	265
Long Term Debt	319	600	799	823	532	697	838	884	370	347
Common Equity	2,836	2,244	1,780	1,715	1,062	952	902	774	697	595
Total Capital	3,182	2,844	2,579	2,538	1,594	1,649	1,740	1,658	1,092	965
Capital Expenditures	222	99.2	61.7	65.5	70.5	125	90.2	49.3	74.8	82.9
Cash Flow	727	448	337	224	242	143	227	160	157	130
Current Ratio	1.2	1.6	1.6	1.3	1.3	1.2	1.3	1.3	1.8	1.9
% Long Term Debt of Capitalization	10.0	21.1	31.0	32.4	33.4	42.3	48.2	53.3	33.8	36.0
% Net Income of Revenue	11.5	9.8	8.2	6.2	7.5	1.7	5.4	5.1	7.0	6.5
% Return on Assets	13.6	9.5	6.5	4.4	6.3	1.7	5.0	4.4	7.6	7.3
% Return on Equity	24.7	17.0	13.7	9.8	15.8	4.6	14.9	11.6	16.0	15.7

Data as orig reptd.; bef. results of disc opers/spec. items. Per share data adj. for stk. divs.; EPS diluted. E-Estimated. NA-Not Available. NM-Not Meaningful. NR-Not Ranked. UR-Under Review.

Office: 4650 SW Macadam Avenue, Portland, OR 97239-4262.
Telephone: 503-417-4850.
Email: info@precastcorp.com
Website: http://www.precast.com
Chrmn & CEO: M. Donegan
Investor Contact: W.D. Larsson (503-417-4800)
SVP & CFO: W.D. Larsson
VP & Treas: G.A. Hawkes
VP & Secy: R.A. Cooke
Auditor: PricewaterhouseCoopers
Board Members: P. R. Bridenbaugh, M. Donegan, D. T. DuCray, D. R. Graber, D. Murphy, V. E. Oechsle, B. O. Pond, Jr., S. G. Rothmeier, U. Schmidt, J. F. Travis
Founded: 1949
Domicile: Oregon
Employees: 19,926

Principal Financial Group Inc.

STANDARD &POOR'S

S&P Recommendation HOLD ★★★☆☆	Price $66.24 (as of Nov 23, 2007)	12-Mo. Target Price $74.00	Investment Style Large-Cap Blend

GICS Sector Financials
Sub-Industry Life & Health Insurance

Summary PFG offers businesses, individuals and other clients various financial products and services, including insurance, retirement and investment services.

Key Stock Statistics (Source S&P, Vickers, company reports)

52-Wk Range	$68.43–51.52	S&P Oper. EPS 2007**E**	4.11	Market Capitalization(B)	$17.594	Beta	0.53
Trailing 12-Month EPS	$3.98	S&P Oper. EPS 2008**E**	4.50	Yield (%)	1.36	S&P 3-Yr. Proj. EPS CAGR(%)	13.00
Trailing 12-Month P/E	16.6	P/E on S&P Oper. EPS 2007**E**	16.1	Dividend Rate/Share	$0.90	S&P Credit Rating	NA
$10K Invested 5 Yrs Ago	$23,176	Common Shares Outstg. (M)	265.6	Institutional Ownership (%)	49		

Price Performance

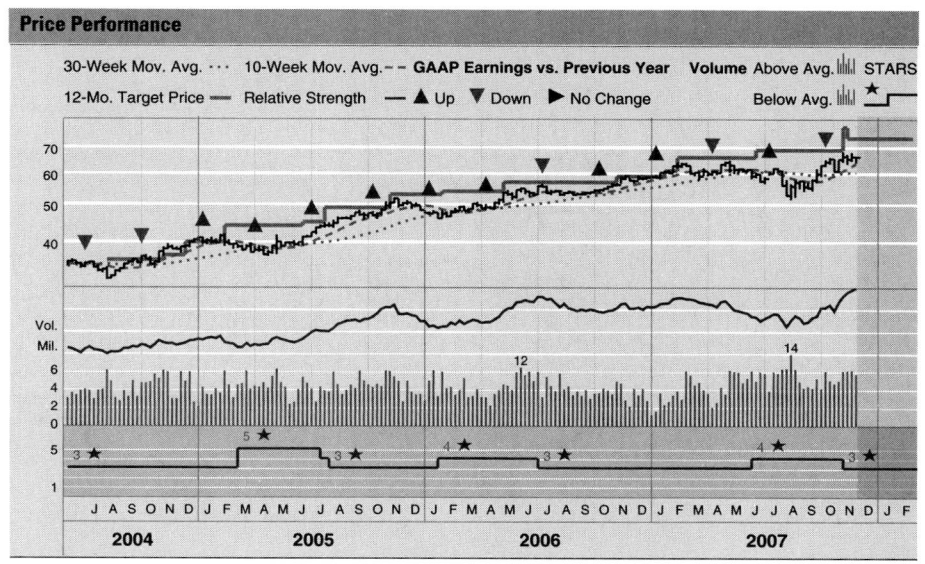

30-Week Mov. Avg. · · · 10-Week Mov. Avg. - - **GAAP Earnings vs. Previous Year** Volume Above Avg. STARS
12-Mo. Target Price — Relative Strength — ▲ Up ▼ Down ▶ No Change Below Avg. ★

Analysis prepared by **Tanjila Shafi** on November 15, 2007, when the stock traded at **$ 67.30.**

Highlights

➤ We expect operating earnings for the U.S. Asset Management and Accumulation (USAMA) segment to increase in the high single to low double digits in 2008, benefiting from higher fee income, stock market appreciation, and growth in assets under management. We believe that the Pension Protection Act of 2006 will help the company increase its market share in the small to medium-size employer market.

➤ We expect operating earnings for the International Asset Management and Accumulation (IAMA) segment to experience double-digit growth, based on strong growth in assets under management, and improving pension operations in Hong Kong and Brazil. We see the mutual fund joint venture with China Construction Bank as an area for growth. We expect operating earnings for the Life and Health segment to rise at a mid-single digit rate in 2008, as PFG continues to pursue new strategies to spur growth in the segment, including new products and refined product distribution.

➤ We forecast 2007 operating EPS of $4.11, which would represent more than 16% growth from 2006 operating EPS of $3.53. Our operating EPS estimate for 2008 is $4.50.

Investment Rationale/Risk

➤ We recently downgraded our recommendation to hold, from buy, based on valuation. PFG shares have risen more than 22% since their lows in August. We believe that the company will be able to grow organically by leveraging and expanding its distribution and sales network and by adding new funds and products. In addition, we anticipate that PFG will look to acquire new blocks of business, similar to its acquisition of WM Advisors, thereby increasing economies of scale. We do not believe that the company's $806 million of subprime exposure, representing 1.3% of invested assets, is a concern, given the level and quality of its holdings.

➤ Risks to our recommendation and target price include volatility in results due to large case sales for asset accumulation operations; sensitivity of operations to fluctuations in the equity markets and economic factors, particularly employment levels; credit risk; and purchase price and integration risks associated with potential acquisitions.

➤ Our 12-month target price is $74, 16.4X our 2008 operating EPS forecast, in line with historical multiples.

Qualitative Risk Assessment

LOW	MEDIUM	HIGH

Our risk assessment reflects our view of PFG's consistent earnings growth, diversified products, geographic scope, conservative debt to total capital ratio, and large excess capital. This is offset by several macroeconomic factors that affect the company, including decelerating job growth and the potential for rising interest rates.

Quantitative Evaluations

S&P Quality Ranking NR

D	C	B-	B	B+	A-	A	A+

Relative Strength Rank STRONG
90
LOWEST = 1   HIGHEST = 99

Revenue/Earnings Data

Revenue (Million $)

	1Q	2Q	3Q	4Q	Year
2007	2,661	2,832	2,850	--	--
2006	2,402	2,460	2,450	2,559	9,871
2005	2,144	2,200	2,218	2,445	9,008
2004	1,997	1,980	2,089	2,239	8,304
2003	2,297	2,412	2,266	2,479	9,404
2002	2,228	2,336	1,996	2,424	9,223

Earnings Per Share ($)

	1Q	2Q	3Q	4Q	Year
2007	0.95	1.12	0.87	E1.02	E4.11
2006	1.01	0.76	0.92	0.93	3.63
2005	0.68	0.77	0.74	0.83	3.02
2004	0.62	0.40	0.62	0.71	2.23
2003	0.47	0.62	0.68	0.60	2.23
2002	0.68	0.33	0.12	0.64	1.77

Fiscal year ended Dec. 31. Next earnings report expected: Early February. EPS Estimates based on S&P Operating Earnings; historical GAAP earnings are as reported.

Dividend Data (Dates: mm/dd Payment Date: mm/dd/yy)

Amount ($)	Date Decl.	Ex-Div. Date	Stk. of Record	Payment Date
0.800	11/07	11/20	11/22	12/15/06
0.900	10/29	11/14	11/16	12/07/07

Dividends have been paid since 2002. Source: Company reports.

Please read the Required Disclosures and Analyst Certification on the last page of this report.

The **McGraw-Hill** Companies

Principal Financial Group Inc.

STANDARD &POOR'S

Business Summary November 15, 2007

CORPORATE OVERVIEW. The Principal Financial Group is a leading provider of retirement savings, investment and insurance products and services, with approximately $257 billion in assets under management at December 31, 2006. The focus of the company is to provide retirement and employment products and services, specifically 401(k) plans, to small and medium-sized businesses.

PFG's businesses are organized into four operating segments. The U.S. Asset Management and Accumulation segment (USAMA), which accounted for 46% of operating revenue from continuing operations in 2006, provides retirement savings and related investment products and services, and asset management operations, with a concentration on small and medium-sized businesses with fewer than 1,000 employees. At year-end 2006, USAMA account values totaled $163.3 billion.

The International Asset Management and Accumulation segment (IAMA) con-

sists of Principal International and offers retirement products and services, annuities, mutual funds and life insurance through operations in Brazil, Chile, Mexico, China, Hong Kong and India. IAMA accounted for 6.2% of operating revenues from continuing operations in 2006.

The Life and Health Insurance segment, which accounted for 48% of operating revenues from continuing operations in 2006, offers individual and group life and disability insurance, as well as group health, dental and vision insurance. The Corporate and Other segment includes, among other things, inter-segment eliminations, income on capital not allocated to other segments, and the company's financing activities.

Company Financials Fiscal Year Ended Dec. 31

Per Share Data ($)	2006	2005	2004	2003	2002	2001	2000	1999	1998	1997
Tangible Book Value	22.24	24.14	23.67	22.12	19.32	10.59	14.89	NA	NA	NA
Operating Earnings	NA	NA	NA	NA	2.46	1.96	NA	NA	NA	NA
Earnings	3.63	3.02	2.23	2.23	1.77	1.02	1.74	NA	NA	NA
S&P Core Earnings	3.45	3.02	2.36	2.38	1.85	1.69	NA	NA	NA	NA
Dividends	0.80	0.65	0.55	0.45	0.25	Nil	NA	NA	NA	NA
Payout Ratio	22%	22%	25%	20%	14%	Nil	NA	NA	NA	NA
Prices:High	59.40	52.00	41.26	34.67	31.50	24.75	NA	NA	NA	NA
Prices:Low	45.91	36.80	32.00	25.21	22.00	18.50	NA	NA	NA	NA
P/E Ratio:High	16	17	19	16	18	24	NA	NA	NA	NA
P/E Ratio:Low	13	12	14	11	12	18	NA	NA	NA	NA

Income Statement Analysis (Million $)	2006	2005	2004	2003	2002	2001	2000	1999	1998	1997
Life Insurance in Force	218,947	197,690	180,344	136,530	137,794	62,309	60,389	NA	NA	NA
Premium Income:Life	4,305	3,975	3,710	1,500	1,824	2,089	1,792	NA	NA	NA
Premium Income:A & H	NA	NA	NA	2,135	2,058	2,033	2,205	NA	NA	NA
Net Investment Income	3,618	3,361	3,227	3,420	3,305	3,395	3,172	NA	NA	NA
Total Revenue	9,871	9,008	8,304	9,404	9,223	8,818	8,885	NA	NA	NA
Pretax Income	1,329	1,124	882	954	666	449	872	NA	NA	NA
Net Operating Income	NA	NA	NA	NA	864	711	NA	NA	NA	NA
Net Income	1,034	892	702	728	620	370	627	NA	NA	NA
S&P Core Earnings	951	871	742	778	647	608	NA	NA	NA	NA

Balance Sheet & Other Financial Data (Million $)	2006	2005	2004	2003	2002	2001	2000	1999	1998	1997
Cash & Equivalent	2,314	2,324	1,131	2,344	1,685	1,218	940	NA	NA	NA
Premiums Due	1,252	593	628	720	460	531	572	NA	NA	NA
Investment Assets:Bonds	44,727	42,117	40,916	37,553	34,287	30,030	29,328	NA	NA	NA
Investment Assets:Stocks	848	815	763	712	379	834	579	NA	NA	NA
Investment Assets:Loans	12,515	12,312	12,529	14,312	11,900	11,898	12,359	NA	NA	NA
Investment Assets:Total	60,367	57,583	57,012	55,578	48,996	44,773	44,403	NA	NA	NA
Deferred Policy Costs	2,419	2,174	1,838	1,572	1,414	1,373	1,338	NA	NA	NA
Total Assets	143,658	127,035	113,798	107,754	89,861	88,351	86,838	NA	NA	NA
Debt	1,554	899	844	2,767	1,333	1,378	1,391	NA	NA	NA
Common Equity	7,861	7,807	7,544	7,400	13,314	6,820	6,624	NA	NA	NA
% Return on Revenue	10.5	9.9	8.5	7.7	7.0	4.2	7.1	NA	NA	NA
% Return on Assets	0.8	0.7	0.6	0.7	0.7	0.4	NA	NA	NA	NA
% Return on Equity	12.8	11.4	9.4	10.4	4.6	5.7	NA	NA	NA	NA
% Investment Yield	6.1	5.9	5.8	6.5	7.0	7.8	NA	NA	NA	NA

Data as orig reptd.; bef. results of disc opers/spec. items. Per share data adj. for stk. divs.; EPS diluted. E-Estimated. NA-Not Available. NM-Not Meaningful. NR-Not Ranked. UR-Under Review.

Office: 711 High Street, Des Moines, IA 50392-9992.
Telephone: 515-247-5111.
Website: http://www.principal.com
Chrmn & CEO: J.B. Griswell

Pres & COO: L.D. Zimpleman
EVP & CFO: M.H. Gersie
EVP & General Counsel: K.E. Shaff
SVP & Cntlr: G. elming

Investor Contact: T. Graf (515-235-9500)
Board Members: B. J. Bernard, J. Carter-Miller, G. E. Costley, M. T. Dan, D. J. Drury, C. D. Gelatt, Jr., J. B. Griswell, S. L. Helton, W. T. Kerr, R. L. Keyser, A. K. Mathrani, E. E. Tallett, T. M. Vaughan, L. D. Zimpleman

Founded: 1998
Domicile: Delaware
Employees: 15,289

Procter & Gamble Co (The)

STANDARD &POOR'S

S&P Recommendation   STRONG BUY ★ ★ ★ ★ ★

Price	12-Mo. Target Price	Investment Style
$72.86 (as of Nov 23, 2007)	$81.00	Large-Cap Growth

GICS Sector Consumer Staples
Sub-Industry Household Products

Summary This leading consumer products company markets household and personal care products in more than 160 countries.

Key Stock Statistics (Source S&P, Vickers, company reports)

52-Wk Range	$73.85–60.42	S&P Oper. EPS 2008E	3.48	Market Capitalization(B)	$226.277	Beta	0.43
Trailing 12-Month EPS	$3.17	S&P Oper. EPS 2009E	NA	Yield (%)	1.92	S&P 3-Yr. Proj. EPS CAGR(%)	13.00
Trailing 12-Month P/E	23.0	P/E on S&P Oper. EPS 2008E	20.9	Dividend Rate/Share	$1.40	S&P Credit Rating	AA-
$10K Invested 5 Yrs Ago	$18,585	Common Shares Outstg. (M)	3,105.6	Institutional Ownership (%)	60		

Price Performance

30-Week Mov. Avg. · · ·   10-Week Mov. Avg. – –   GAAP Earnings vs. Previous Year   Volume Above Avg. ▐▌▌ STARS
12-Mo. Target Price —   Relative Strength —   ▲ Up ▼ Down ▶ No Change   Below Avg. ▐▌▌ ★

Options: ASE, CBOE, P, Ph

Analysis prepared by **Loran Braverman, CFA** on October 31, 2007, when the stock traded at **$ 69.43**.

Highlights

➤ For FY 08 (Jun.), we forecast growth of close to 7% for total company sales. We project the fastest growth from the Health Care, Fabric Care & Home Care, and Baby Care & Family Care segments, followed by the Beauty and Grooming segments, with the slowest growth expected for the Snacks, Coffee & Pet Care segment. In October 2007, PG announced price increases ranging from 3% to 12% for many of its products to start in the next few months, and we think the increases will stick.

➤ We look for the operating margin to widen, with the benefits from price increases, volume leveraging and cost saving programs more than offsetting increases in commodity costs and restructuring charges. Also, we believe the Gillette business negatively affected FY 07 EPS by close to $0.10 per share, and we look for a neutral effect this year and additive in FY 09 and beyond. Our tax rate assumption is 28.5%, versus 29.7% in FY 07.

➤ We project an increase in EPS to $3.48 in FY 08, from $3.04 in FY 07, on an estimated 3% lower share count. In August 2007, PG announced its plan to repurchase $8 billion to $10 billion of its shares each year for the next three years.

Investment Rationale/Risk

➤ Our strong buy opinion reflects our confidence that PG will deliver consistent sales and earnings growth near the high end of its peer group over the next several years, potential benefits of the Gillette acquisition, and growth prospects in new markets and categories. We think PG is well positioned to benefit from demand growth for household and personal care products in developing countries, given its broad product portfolio and sizable distribution network.

➤ Risks to our recommendation and target price include heightened competition, unfavorable currency translation, greater promotional spending, and low consumer acceptance of new products.

➤ Our 12-month target price of $81 is a blend of our relative and historical analyses. Based on the company's strong track record of earnings growth and leading market positions, we believe the stock should trade at a premium to peers. This, blended with a close to 10-year historical average forward P/E, leads us to apply a multiple of 22X our calendar 2008 EPS estimate of $3.69 to arrive at our target price.

Qualitative Risk Assessment

LOW	MEDIUM	HIGH

Our risk assessment reflects that demand for household and personal care products is generally stable and not affected by changes in the economy or geopolitical factors, except for select categories such as fragrances.

Quantitative Evaluations

S&P Quality Ranking   A+

D	C	B-	B	B+	A-	A	A+

Relative Strength Rank   STRONG

90

LOWEST = 1   HIGHEST = 99

Revenue/Earnings Data

Revenue (Million $)

	1Q	2Q	3Q	4Q	Year
2008	20,199	--	--	--	--
2007	18,785	19,725	18,694	19,272	76,476
2006	14,793	18,337	17,250	17,842	68,222
2005	13,744	14,452	14,287	14,258	56,741
2004	12,195	13,221	13,029	12,962	51,407
2003	10,796	11,005	10,656	10,920	43,377

Earnings Per Share ($)

2008	0.92	E0.95	E0.84	E0.79	E3.48
2007	0.79	0.84	0.74	0.67	3.04
2006	0.77	0.72	0.63	0.55	2.64
2005	0.73	0.74	0.63	0.56	2.66
2004	0.63	0.65	0.55	0.50	2.32
2003	0.52	0.53	0.46	0.34	1.85

Fiscal year ended Jun. 30. Next earnings report expected: Late January. EPS Estimates based on S&P Operating Earnings; historical GAAP earnings are as reported.

Dividend Data (Dates: mm/dd Payment Date: mm/dd/yy)

Amount ($)	Date Decl.	Ex-Div. Date	Stk. of Record	Payment Date
0.310	01/09	01/17	01/19	02/15/07
0.350	04/16	04/25	04/27	05/15/07
0.350	07/10	07/18	07/20	08/15/07
0.350	10/09	10/17	10/19	11/15/07

Dividends have been paid since 1891. Source: Company reports.

Procter & Gamble Co (The)

STANDARD &POOR'S

Business Summary October 31, 2007

CORPORATE OVERVIEW. Procter & Gamble's business is focused on providing branded products of what it considers superior quality and value to improve the lives of the world's consumers. By doing so successfully, the company believes this will result in leadership sales, profits, and value creation for employees, shareholders and the communities in which it operates. PG markets in more than 180 countries. In FY 07, North America accounted for 46% of total sales, Western Europe 23%, Northeast Asia 4%, and developing markets 27%.

PG's customers include mass merchandisers, grocery stores, membership club stores, drug stores and high-frequency stores. Sales to Wal-Mart Stores, Inc. and its affiliates represented approximately 15% of total FY 07 revenue. The top 10 customers accounted for about 30% of total unit volume.

In FY 07, PG business structure organization was three Global Business Units (GBUs) and seven reportable segments. The Beauty and Health Unit consisted of the Beauty segment (30% of FY 07 sales and 31% of net earnings) and the Health Care segment (12%, 13%); the Household Care Unit had the Fabric Care

and Home Care segment (24%, 25%), Baby Care and Family Care (16%, 13%) and Pet Health, Snacks and Coffee (6%, 4%); and the Gillette Unit had blades and razors (7%, 11%) and Duracell and Braun (5%, 3%). PG's new structure starting in FY 08 has three GBUs and six reportable segments: Beauty (Beauty and Grooming); Health and Well Being (Health Care and Snacks, Coffee & Pet Care); and Household Care (Fabric Care & Home Care and Baby Care & Family Care).

IMPACT OF MAJOR DEVELOPMENTS. On October 1, 2005, PG acquired The Gillette Company for approximately $54 billion. The Gillette Company is the world leader in the male and female grooming categories. Gillette also holds the number one position worldwide in alkaline batteries and toothbrushes. We expect the acquisition to add to shareholder value over time through cost synergies and sales growth opportunities.

Company Financials Fiscal Year Ended Jun. 30

Per Share Data ($)	2007	2006	2005	2004	2003	2002	2001	2000	1999	1998
Tangible Book Value	NM	NM	NM	NM	0.43	NM	0.78	0.68	1.31	1.28
Cash Flow	4.30	3.56	3.30	2.90	2.41	2.11	1.85	2.01	2.00	1.80
Earnings	3.04	2.64	2.66	2.32	1.85	1.54	1.04	1.24	1.30	1.28
S&P Core Earnings	2.96	2.60	2.45	2.17	1.58	1.28	0.81	NA	NA	NA
Dividends	1.28	1.15	1.03	0.93	0.82	0.76	0.70	0.64	0.57	0.51
Payout Ratio	42%	44%	39%	40%	44%	49%	68%	52%	44%	39%
Prices:High	73.85	64.73	59.70	57.40	49.97	47.38	40.86	59.19	57.81	47.41
Prices:Low	60.42	52.75	51.16	48.89	39.79	37.04	27.98	26.38	41.00	32.56
P/E Ratio:High	24	25	22	25	27	31	39	48	45	37
P/E Ratio:Low	20	20	19	21	22	24	27	21	32	25

Income Statement Analysis (Million $)	2007	2006	2005	2004	2003	2002	2001	2000	1999	1998
Revenue	76,476	68,222	56,741	51,407	43,377	40,238	39,244	39,951	38,125	37,154
Operating Income	18,580	15,876	12,811	11,560	9,556	8,371	7,007	8,145	8,401	7,653
Depreciation	3,130	2,627	1,884	1,733	1,703	1,693	2,271	2,191	2,148	1,598
Interest Expense	1,304	1,119	834	629	561	603	794	722	650	548
Pretax Income	14,710	12,413	10,439	9,350	7,530	6,383	4,616	5,536	5,838	5,708
Effective Tax Rate	29.7%	30.0%	30.5%	30.7%	31.1%	31.8%	36.7%	36.0%	35.5%	33.8%
Net Income	10,340	8,684	7,257	6,481	5,186	4,352	2,922	3,542	3,763	3,780
S&P Core Earnings	9,917	8,420	6,552	5,922	4,313	3,486	2,165	NA	NA	NA

Balance Sheet & Other Financial Data (Million $)	2007	2006	2005	2004	2003	2002	2001	2000	1999	1998
Cash	5,354	6,693	6,389	5,469	5,912	3,427	2,306	1,415	2,294	1,549
Current Assets	24,031	24,329	20,329	17,115	15,220	12,166	10,889	10,146	11,358	10,577
Total Assets	138,014	135,695	61,527	57,048	43,706	40,776	34,387	34,366	32,113	30,966
Current Liabilities	30,717	19,985	25,039	22,147	12,358	12,704	9,846	10,141	10,761	9,250
Long Term Debt	23,375	35,976	12,887	12,554	11,475	11,201	9,792	8,916	6,231	5,765
Common Equity	65,354	61,457	15,994	15,752	14,606	12,072	10,309	10,550	10,277	10,415
Total Capital	102,150	111,238	33,258	32,093	29,057	25,984	22,696	21,828	18,651	16,608
Capital Expenditures	2,945	2,667	2,181	2,024	1,482	1,679	2,486	3,018	2,828	2,559
Cash Flow	13,470	11,311	9,005	8,083	6,764	5,921	5,193	5,733	5,802	5,274
Current Ratio	0.8	1.2	0.8	0.8	1.2	1.0	1.1	1.0	1.1	1.1
% Long Term Debt of Capitalization	22.9	32.3	38.7	39.1	39.5	43.1	43.1	40.8	33.4	34.7
% Net Income of Revenue	13.5	12.7	12.8	12.6	12.0	10.8	7.4	8.9	9.9	10.2
% Return on Assets	7.6	8.8	12.2	12.9	12.3	11.6	8.5	10.7	11.9	12.9
% Return on Equity	16.3	22.1	45.7	41.8	37.9	37.8	28.0	34.0	35.3	35.7

Data as orig reptd.; bef. results of disc opers/spec. items. Per share data adj. for stk. divs.; EPS diluted. E-Estimated. NA-Not Available. NM-Not Meaningful. NR-Not Ranked. UR-Under Review.

Office: One Procter & Gamble Plaza, Cincinnati, OH 45202.
Telephone: 513-983-1100.
Website: http://www.pg.com
Chrmn, Pres & CEO: A.G. Lafley

Vice Chrmn & COO: R.A. McDonald
Vice Chrmn & CFO: C.C. Daley, Jr.
VP & Cntlr: V.L. Sheppard
CTO: C.G. Cloyd

Investor Contact: C. Peterson (800-742-6253)
Board Members: B. L. Byrnes, S. Cook, J. T. Gorman, R. Gupta, A. G. Lafley, C. R. Lee, L. M. Martin, W. J. McNerney, Jr., J. A. Rodgers, J. F. Smith, Jr., R. Snyderman, M. v. Whitman, E. Zedillo

Founded: 1837
Domicile: Ohio
Employees: 138,000

The **McGraw·Hill** Companies

Progressive Corp (The)

STANDARD &POOR'S

S&P Recommendation HOLD ★ ★ ★ ☆ ☆

Price	12-Mo. Target Price	Investment Style
$17.88 (as of Nov 23, 2007)	$21.00	Large-Cap Growth

GICS Sector Financials
Sub-Industry Property & Casualty Insurance

Summary This leading underwriter of nonstandard auto and other lines of coverage has expanded its product line and evolved into a full-service auto insurer.

Key Stock Statistics (Source S&P, Vickers, company reports)

52-Wk Range	$25.16– 17.28	S&P Oper. EPS 2007E	1.60	Market Capitalization(B)	$12.482	Beta	0.82
Trailing 12-Month EPS	$1.82	S&P Oper. EPS 2008E	1.55	Yield (%)	0.20	S&P 3-Yr. Proj. EPS CAGR(%)	NA
Trailing 12-Month P/E	9.8	P/E on S&P Oper. EPS 2007E	11.2	Dividend Rate/Share	$0.04	S&P Credit Rating	A+
$10K Invested 5 Yrs Ago	$13,954	Common Shares Outstg. (M)	698.1	Institutional Ownership (%)	71		

Price Performance

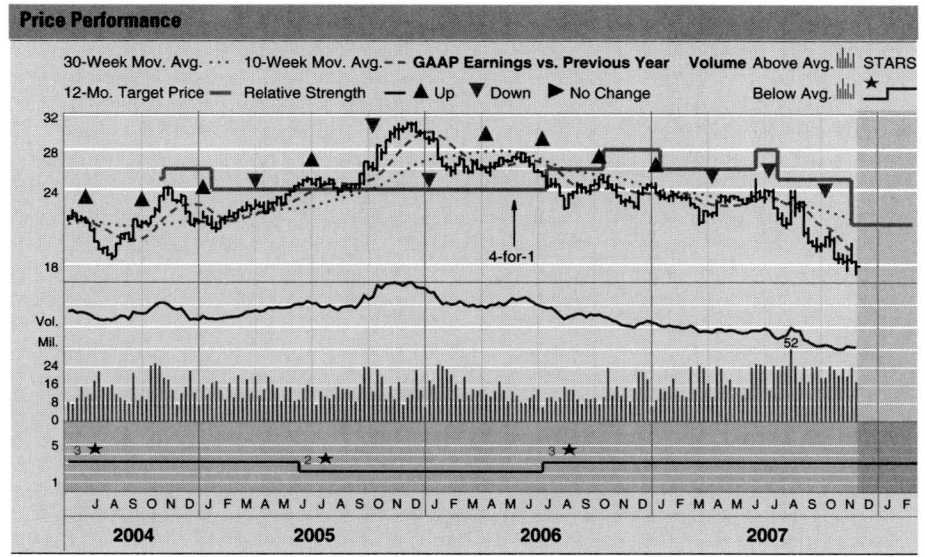

30-Week Mov. Avg. · · · 10-Week Mov. Avg. – – **GAAP Earnings vs. Previous Year** Volume Above Avg. STARS
12-Mo. Target Price — Relative Strength — ▲ Up ▼ Down ► No Change Below Avg. ★

Options: ASE, CBOE, P, Ph

Analysis prepared by **Cathy A. Seifert** on November 13, 2007, when the stock traded at **$ 19.35**.

Highlights

➤ We believe earned premiums in 2008 could decline modestly, amid heightened price competition that we expect will continue into at least mid-2008. We forecast earned premiums will also decline modestly in 2007. Earned premiums rose 3% in 2006 and nearly 5% in 2005, well below the 16% growth reported for 2004.

➤ Barring a surge in catastrophe losses, we expect underwriting results to remain profitable in 2008. However, we anticipate underwriting margins will remain under pressure amid an erosion in the until now extremely favorable claim trends, coupled with an increase in underwriting expenses. This is evidenced by the nine-month 2007 combined loss/expense ratio, which deteriorated to 91.9% in the 2007 interim, from 86.4% in the 2006 period.

➤ Our operating EPS estimates of $1.60 for 2007 and $1.55 for 2008 assume that an eroding premium base will be exacerbated by erosion in underwriting margins, amid an uptick in some competitive pressures and a slight deterioration in claim trends. An aggressive share buyback plan will mitigate the EPS impact of declining profitability, in our view.

Investment Rationale/Risk

➤ We view PGR's technology and marketing capabilities as superior to many of its peers. However, at current levels, the shares trade at premiums to most peers on both a forward price/earnings and a price/tangible book value basis. We do not believe such a large premium is warranted, particularly in light of the emerging evidence that indicates to us that the company's rates of growth are slowing. We also think that heightened competitive pressures will force PGR to incur higher policy acquisition costs. This will pressure margins, in our view.

➤ Risks to our recommendation and target price include a slowdown in premium growth. Increased competitive pressures in PGR's core personal auto line and a significant increase in claim costs could also pressure results. We also note that asset-backed securities (including mortgage-backed obligations) accounted for nearly 18% of the investment portfolio at September 30, 2007.

➤ Our 12-month target price of $21 assumes that the shares will continue to trade at a premium to their property-casualty insurance peers, albeit a smaller one, on a forward price/tangible book basis and a forward price/earnings basis.

Qualitative Risk Assessment

LOW	MEDIUM	HIGH

Our risk assessment reflects our view of PGR's position as a leading underwriter of personal lines coverage, combined with what we see as its superior financial strength. As primarily an auto insurer, PGR is less exposed to catastrophe losses than a number of its peers, in our view. Nonetheless, exposure to catastrophe losses always exists.

Quantitative Evaluations

S&P Quality Ranking B+

D	C	B-	B	B+	A-	A	A+

Relative Strength Rank MODERATE

42

LOWEST = 1 HIGHEST = 99

Revenue/Earnings Data

Revenue (Million $)

	1Q	2Q	3Q	4Q	Year
2007	3,687	3,671	3,710	--	--
2006	3,661	3,708	3,724	--	14,786
2005	3,492	3,590	3,623	3,599	14,303
2004	3,280	3,367	3,438	3,696	13,782
2003	2,720	2,921	3,081	3,170	11,892
2002	2,069	2,259	2,419	--	9,373

Earnings Per Share ($)

2007	0.49	0.39	0.42	E0.37	E1.60
2006	0.55	0.51	0.53	0.53	2.10
2005	0.51	0.49	0.39	0.36	1.75
2004	0.52	0.44	0.44	0.50	1.91
2003	0.33	0.32	0.36	0.41	1.42
2002	0.20	0.18	0.20	0.17	0.75

Fiscal year ended Dec. 31. Next earnings report expected: Mid January. EPS Estimates based on S&P Operating Earnings; historical GAAP earnings are as reported.

Dividend Data (Dates: mm/dd Payment Date: mm/dd/yy)

Amount ($)	Date Decl.	Ex-Div. Date	Stk. of Record	Payment Date
0.009	10/13	12/06	12/08	12/31/06
2.0 Ext.	06/14	08/29	08/31	09/14/07

Dividends have been paid since 1965. Source: Company reports.

Progressive Corp (The)

Business Summary November 13, 2007

CORPORATE OVERVIEW. Progressive has expanded from a specialty writer of nonstandard coverage into a full-service insurer. Net written premiums totaled $14.1 billion in 2006, of which personal lines accounted for 86% and commercial and other lines 14%.

PGR's core business (91% of 2006's $12.2 billion in personal lines net premiums written) consists of underwriting private passenger automobile insurance. Based on year-end 2005 industry net written premium data (latest available), the company was the third largest private U.S. passenger auto insurer, a position that PGR believes it retained in 2006. PGR's other lines of business include recreational vehicle, motorcycle and small commercial vehicle insurance, and, to a lesser degree, commercial indemnity insurance. PGR believes it is the market leader in providing coverage for watercraft vehicles and for motorcycles.

The company distributes its core personal lines products through the Drive

channel, which includes a network of more than 30,000, including independent agents, as well as brokers in New York and California, and strategic alliance business relationships with an array of financial institutions. During 2006, approximately 64% of total net written premiums were distributed through the Drive channel (66% in 2005). Distribution through direct channels, including a toll free telephone line and the Internet, accounted for 36% of net written premiums in 2006 (34% in 2005).

PGR conducts business in 49 states (all but Massachusetts) and in the District of Columbia. In 2006, Florida accounted for 13% of net premiums written, Texas 8%, California 8% New York 7%, and all other states the remaining 64%.

Company Financials Fiscal Year Ended Dec. 31

Per Share Data ($)	2006	2005	2004	2003	2002	2001	2000	1999	1998	1997
Tangible Book Value	9.15	7.74	6.43	5.85	4.32	3.69	3.25	3.14	2.94	2.46
Operating Earnings	NA	NA	NA	NA	0.81	0.54	0.06	0.30	0.50	0.37
Earnings	2.10	1.75	1.91	1.42	0.75	0.46	0.05	0.33	0.51	0.44
S&P Core Earnings	2.11	1.77	1.85	1.40	0.79	0.52	NA	NA	NA	NA
Dividends	0.06	0.03	0.04	0.03	0.02	0.02	0.02	0.02	0.02	0.02
Payout Ratio	3%	2%	2%	2%	3%	5%	44%	7%	4%	5%
Prices:High	30.09	31.23	24.32	21.17	15.12	12.65	9.25	14.52	14.33	10.07
Prices:Low	22.18	20.34	18.28	11.56	11.19	6.84	3.75	5.71	7.83	5.13
P/E Ratio:High	14	18	13	15	20	28	NM	44	28	23
P/E Ratio:Low	11	12	10	8	15	15	NM	17	15	12

Income Statement Analysis (Million $)										
Premium Income	14,118	13,764	13,170	11,341	8,884	7,162	6,348	5,684	4,948	4,190
Net Investment Income	648	537	484	465	455	414	385	341	295	275
Other Revenue	20.7	539	612	54.5	34.3	24.7	37.4	99.0	49.6	144
Total Revenue	14,786	14,303	13,782	11,892	9,373	7,488	6,771	6,124	5,292	4,608
Pretax Income	2,433	2,059	2,451	1,860	981	588	31.8	412	661	578
Net Operating Income	NA	NA	NA	NA	718	486	55.4	267	449	336
Net Income	1,648	1,394	1,649	1,255	667	411	46.1	295	457	400
S&P Core Earnings	1,654	1,415	1,591	1,234	702	469	NA	NA	NA	NA

Balance Sheet & Other Financial Data (Million $)										
Cash & Equivalent	140	139	124	110	94.8	86.4	73.1	68.2	71.7	23.3
Premiums Due	2,932	2,906	2,669	2,351	1,959	1,497	1,567	1,761	1,456	1,161
Investment Assets:Bonds	9,959	10,222	9,084	9,133	7,713	5,949	4,784	4,533	4,219	4,301
Investment Assets:Stocks	4,149	3,279	2,621	2,751	2,004	2,050	2,012	1,666	1,013	970
Investment Assets:Loans	Nil	Nil	Nil	Nil	Nil	Nil	Nil	Nil	Nil	Nil
Investment Assets:Total	14,689	14,275	13,082	12,532	10,284	8,226	6,983	6,428	5,674	5,270
Deferred Policy Costs	441	445	432	412	364	317	310	343	299	260
Total Assets	19,482	18,899	17,184	16,282	13,564	11,122	10,052	9,705	8,463	7,560
Debt	1,186	1,285	1,284	1,490	1,489	1,096	749	1,049	777	776
Common Equity	6,847	6,108	5,155	5,060	3,768	3,251	2,870	2,753	2,557	2,136
Property & Casualty:Loss Ratio	66.6	68.1	65.0	67.4	70.9	73.6	83.2	75.0	68.5	71.1
Property & Casualty:Expense Ratio	19.9	87.4	19.6	18.8	20.4	21.0	21.0	22.1	22.4	20.7
Property & Casualty Combined Ratio	86.5	19.3	84.6	86.2	91.3	94.7	104.2	97.1	90.9	91.8
% Return on Revenue	11.1	9.7	12.0	10.6	7.1	5.4	0.7	4.8	8.6	278.2
% Return on Equity	25.4	24.8	32.4	28.4	19.3	13.4	1.6	11.1	19.5	21.0

Data as orig reptd.; bef. results of disc opers/spec. items. Per share data adj. for stk. divs.; EPS diluted. E-Estimated. NA-Not Available. NM-Not Meaningful. NR-Not Ranked. UR-Under Review.

Office: 6300 Wilson Mills Road, Mayfield Village, OH 44143.
Telephone: 440-461-5000.
Website: http://www.progressive.com
Chrmn: P.B. Lewis

Pres & CEO: G.M. Renwick
Investor Contact: J.W. Basch (440-446-2851)
VP & Chief Acctg Officer: J.W. Basch
VP & Treas: T.A. King

Board Members: C. A. Davis, S. R. Hardis, B. P. Healy, J. D. Kelly, A. F. Kohnstamm, P. A. Laskawy, P. B. Lewis, N. S. Matthews, P. H. Nettles, G. M. Renwick, D. B. Shackelford, B. T. Sheares

Founded: 1965
Domicile: Ohio
Employees: 27,778

Progress Energy Inc.

S&P Recommendation	HOLD ★★★☆☆	Price	12-Mo. Target Price	Investment Style
		$48.57 (as of Nov 23, 2007)	$53.00	Large-Cap Blend

GICS Sector Utilities
Sub-Industry Electric Utilities

Summary This diversified energy company owns two electric utilities serving approximately 2.9 million customers in North Carolina, South Carolina and Florida.

Key Stock Statistics (Source S&P, Vickers, company reports)

52-Wk Range	$52.75– 43.12	S&P Oper. EPS 2007E	2.82	Market Capitalization(B)	$12.575	Beta	0.60
Trailing 12-Month EPS	$2.58	S&P Oper. EPS 2008E	3.05	Yield (%)	5.02	S&P 3-Yr. Proj. EPS CAGR(%)	5.00
Trailing 12-Month P/E	18.8	P/E on S&P Oper. EPS 2007E	17.2	Dividend Rate/Share	$2.44	S&P Credit Rating	BBB+
$10K Invested 5 Yrs Ago	$14,805	Common Shares Outstg. (M)	258.9	Institutional Ownership (%)	62		

Price Performance

30-Week Mov. Avg. · · ·   10-Week Mov. Avg. – –   **GAAP Earnings vs. Previous Year**   Volume Above Avg. STARS
12-Mo. Target Price —   Relative Strength — ▲ Up ▼ Down ► No Change   Below Avg. ★

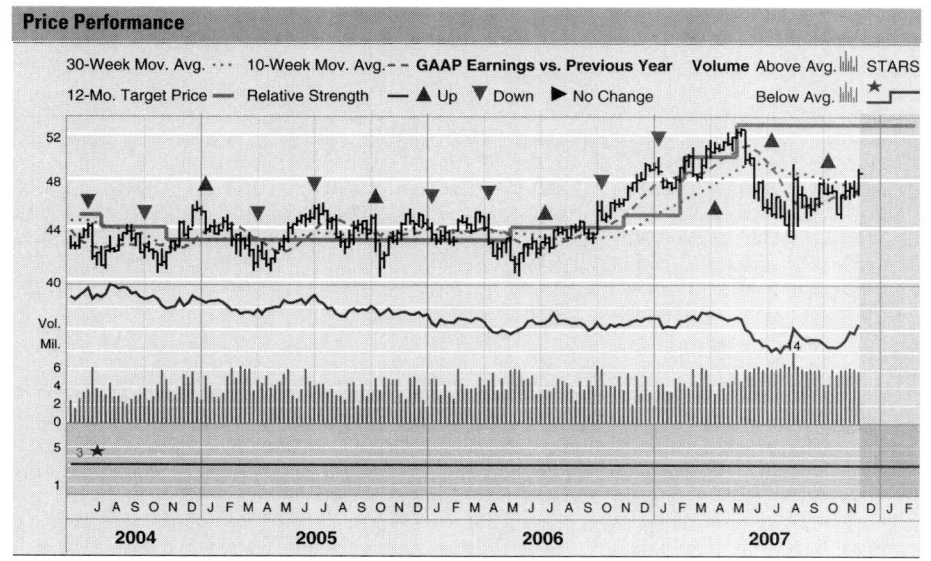

Options: ASE, CBOE, Ph

Analysis prepared by **Justin McCann** on November 19, 2007, when the stock traded at **$ 47.20.**

Highlights

➤ Excluding synfuel-related earnings, we expect 2007 EPS to increase about 8% from 2006 EPS from continuing operations of $2.60. We see ex-synfuel EPS in 2007 being aided by a return to normal weather, customer growth at the utilities, and a reduction in interest expense, reflecting the impact of the company's $1.3 billion redemption of debt in the fourth quarter of 2006. We believe synfuel-related tax credits could add $0.10 to $0.20 to reported EPS. However, PGN has entered into an oil hedge to provide protection for an equivalent of about 8 million tons of synfuel production in 2007.

➤ For 2008, we expect operating EPS to increase about 8% from anticipated results in 2007, primarily reflecting ongoing customer growth at the utilities and a further reduction in debt and interest expense. While synfuel-related tax credits will expire at the end of 2007, the company believes it will have produced approximately $800 million of deferred tax credits.

➤ We do not expect major equity issuances for the next several years. An agreement with regulators in Florida has provided rate certainty through 2009, and the utility may recover about 90% of its $252 million of storm-related costs.

Investment Rationale/Risk

➤ Although the shares are down approximately 4% year to date, we believe that given the well above peers yield from the dividend (recently at 5.2%), the stock should realize an above average total return over the next 12 months. While the transactions related to PGN's exit from its merchant energy segment resulted in a second quarter loss of $1.24 a share from its discontinued operations, the exit has now been completed. We believe the favorable IRS ruling on PGN's prior synfuel tax credits removed a major uncertainty from the shares, which should also benefit from the reduction of debt and related interest expense.

➤ Risks to our recommendation and target price include the possibility of unfavorable regulatory rulings as well as a sharp decline in the average P/E of the group as a whole.

➤ Our 12-month target price of $53 represents a peer-based P/E of about 17.4X our $3.05 EPS estimate for 2008, reflecting the recent recovery in electric utility stocks and the expansion of the average peer P/E. We believe the stock will be supported by its well above peers dividend yield.

Qualitative Risk Assessment

LOW	MEDIUM	HIGH

Our risk assessment reflects a balance between the strong and steady cash flow that we expect from the regulated utilities in both the Carolinas and Florida, which we believe have well above average customer growth and operate within a generally supportive regulatory environment, and the higher risk and much less predictable contribution that we anticipate from the synthetic fuel business.

Quantitative Evaluations

S&P Quality Ranking   B

D	C	B-	B	B+	A-	A	A+

Relative Strength Rank   STRONG

88

LOWEST = 1   HIGHEST = 99

Revenue/Earnings Data

Revenue (Million $)

	1Q	2Q	3Q	4Q	Year
2007	2,334	2,406	3,100	--	--
2006	2,433	2,499	2,913	2,273	9,570
2005	2,198	2,333	3,097	2,578	10,108
2004	2,234	2,430	2,775	2,358	9,772
2003	2,187	2,050	2,458	2,048	8,743
2002	1,787	1,959	2,277	1,922	7,945

Earnings Per Share ($)

2007	0.87	0.51	1.24	E0.54	E2.82
2006	0.19	0.06	0.97	0.51	2.05
2005	0.43	0.02	1.81	0.63	2.94
2004	0.45	0.63	1.24	0.78	3.10
2003	0.89	0.65	1.40	0.47	3.40
2002	0.58	0.56	0.72	0.66	2.53

Fiscal year ended Dec. 31. Next earnings report expected: Mid February. EPS Estimates based on S&P Operating Earnings; historical GAAP earnings are as reported.

Dividend Data (Dates: mm/dd Payment Date: mm/dd/yy)

Amount ($)	Date Decl.	Ex-Div. Date	Stk. of Record	Payment Date
0.610	05/09	10/05	10/10	11/01/07

Dividends have been paid since 1937. Source: Company reports.

Progress Energy Inc.

STANDARD &POOR'S

Business Summary November 19, 2007

CORPORATE OVERVIEW. Headquartered in Raleigh, NC, Progress Energy operates in retail utility markets in the southeastern U.S., and in competitive electricity, gas and other fuel markets in the eastern U.S. It is the holding company for the fully integrated regulated utilities Progress Energy Carolinas and Progress Energy Florida, which, together, serve approximately 3.1 million retail electric customers . It also has unregulated coal and synthetic fuel operations. In 2006, the regulated utility operations accounted for 91.1% of PGN's consolidated revenues, while the unregulated businesses accounted for 8.9%.

CORPORATE STRATEGY. As an integrated energy company, PGN has stated that its primary focus will be on the end-use and wholesale electricity markets in its service territory and region. It is intent on enhancing its operational excellence, strengthening its financial flexibility and growth, and preparing for future power generating capacity. Over the past few years, the company had reduced its business risk by exiting the majority of its non-regulated operations, and it completed the sale of the remaining businesses on June 13, 2007. PGN aims to achieve sustainable earnings growth from its regulated utilities and to continue its track record of having increased its dividend for 19 consecutive years. We believe the company has made great progress in reducing its debt and related interest expense through selected asset sales. It reduced its year-end 2005 debt by $1.7 billion by the end of 2006, and, received proceeds of $1.65 billion through asset sales in 2006.

Company Financials Fiscal Year Ended Dec. 31

Per Share Data ($)	2006	2005	2004	2003	2002	2001	2000	1999	1998	1997
Tangible Book Value	18.09	15.94	14.48	13.78	12.43	10.58	7.48	19.43	19.20	18.18
Earnings	2.05	2.94	3.10	3.40	2.53	2.64	3.03	2.55	2.75	2.66
S&P Core Earnings	1.95	2.94	2.93	3.44	2.04	2.59	NA	NA	NA	NA
Dividends	1.82	2.36	2.30	2.24	2.18	2.12	2.06	2.00	1.94	1.88
Payout Ratio	89%	80%	74%	66%	86%	80%	68%	78%	71%	71%
Prices:High	49.55	46.00	47.95	48.00	52.70	49.25	49.38	47.88	49.63	42.69
Prices:Low	40.27	40.19	40.09	37.45	32.84	38.78	28.25	29.25	39.19	32.75
P/E Ratio:High	24	16	15	14	21	19	16	19	18	16
P/E Ratio:Low	20	14	13	11	13	15	9	11	14	12
Income Statement Analysis (Million $)										
Revenue	9,570	10,108	9,772	8,743	7,945	8,461	4,119	3,358	3,130	3,024
Depreciation	1,032	1,074	1,068	1,040	820	1,090	740	496	487	482
Maintenance	NA	NA	NA	NA	NA	NA	NA	NA	NA	NA
Fixed Charges Coverage	2.28	1.93	2.21	2.16	1.64	1.75	2.60	4.23	4.50	4.25
Construction Credits	7.00	13.0	6.00	7.00	8.13	18.0	20.7	11.5	6.82	4.92
Effective Tax Rate	28.1%	NM	13.5%	NM	NM	NM	29.8%	40.3%	39.2%	37.6%
Net Income	514	727	753	811	552	542	478	382	399	388
S&P Core Earnings	487	726	712	819	445	532	NA	NA	NA	NA
Balance Sheet & Other Financial Data (Million $)										
Gross Property	25,796	26,401	25,602	25,172	23,021	22,541	21,028	12,233	10,797	10,475
Capital Expenditures	1,423	1,286	998	1,018	2,109	1,216	950	765	527	450
Net Property	15,732	16,799	16,819	17,056	12,541	12,445	11,677	7,257	6,300	6,294
Capitalization:Long Term Debt	8,928	10,539	9,650	10,027	9,840	9,577	5,983	3,029	2,614	2,416
Capitalization:% Long Term Debt	51.9	56.7	55.8	57.4	59.6	61.5	52.4	46.6	46.5	45.6
Capitalization:Preferred	NA	Nil	Nil	Nil	Nil	Nil	Nil	59.4	59.4	59.4
Capitalization:% Preferred	NA	Nil	Nil	Nil	Nil	Nil	Nil	0.91	1.06	1.10
Capitalization:Common	8,286	8,038	7,633	7,444	6,677	6,004	5,424	3,413	2,949	2,819
Capitalization:% Common	48.1	43.3	44.2	42.6	40.4	38.5	47.6	52.5	52.4	53.2
Total Capital	17,681	19,061	18,058	18,398	17,656	17,241	13,476	8,337	7,514	7,239
% Operating Ratio	87.5	87.2	86.7	66.8	85.4	83.5	87.1	82.4	79.3	80.6
% Earned on Net Property	8.5	7.7	8.8	8.2	8.3	10.3	7.6	12.1	10.2	8.9
% Return on Revenue	5.4	7.2	7.7	9.3	6.9	6.4	11.6	11.4	12.8	12.8
% Return on Invested Capital	6.8	7.3	7.6	8.2	7.2	9.2	7.1	7.3	7.8	7.7
% Return on Common Equity	6.3	9.3	10.0	11.5	8.7	9.4	10.8	11.9	13.7	13.9

Data as orig reptd.; bef. results of disc opers/spec. items. Per share data adj. for stk. divs.; EPS diluted. E-Estimated. NA-Not Available. NM-Not Meaningful. NR-Not Ranked. UR-Under Review.

Office: 410 S Wilmington St, Raleigh, NC 27601-1849.
Telephone: 919-546-6111.
Email: shareholder.relations@progress-energy.com
Website: http://www.progress-energy.com

Chrmn & CEO: R.B. McGehee
Pres & COO: W.D. Johnson
SVP, Secy & General Counsel: J.R. McArthur
VP & Treas: T.R. Sullivan

VP & General Counsel: F.A. Schiller
Investor Contact: B. Drennan (919-546-7474)
Board Members: E. B. Borden, J. E. Bostic, Jr., D. L. Burner, R. L. Daugherty, H. E. DeLoach Jr., W. D. Frederick, Jr., S. Jones, E. M. McKee, J. H. Mullin, III, C. A. Saladrigas, T. M. Stone, A. C. Tollison Jr., J. G. Wittner

Founded: 1926
Domicile: North Carolina
Employees: 11,000

ProLogis

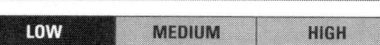
STANDARD &POOR'S

S&P Recommendation	**BUY** ★★★★☆	Price $65.07 (as of Nov 23, 2007)	12-Mo. Target Price $78.00

GICS Sector Financials
Sub-Industry Industrial REITS

Summary This REIT (formerly ProLogis Trust) is the largest publicly held, U.S.-based owner and operator of distribution facilities, with operations in North America, Europe and Asia.

Key Stock Statistics (Source S&P, Vickers, company reports)

52-Wk Range	$73.35– 51.64	S&P FFO/Sh. 2007E	4.48	Market Capitalization(B)	$16.721	Beta		0.70
Trailing 12-Month FFO/Share	NA	S&P FFO/Sh. 2008E	4.80	Yield (%)	2.83	S&P 3-Yr. FFO/Sh. Proj. CAGR(%)		7.00
Trailing 12-Month P/FFO	NA	P/FFO on S&P FFO/Sh. 2007E	14.5	Dividend Rate/Share	$1.84	S&P Credit Rating		BBB+
$10K Invested 5 Yrs Ago	$32,405	Common Shares Outstg. (M)	257.0	Institutional Ownership (%)	99			

Price Performance

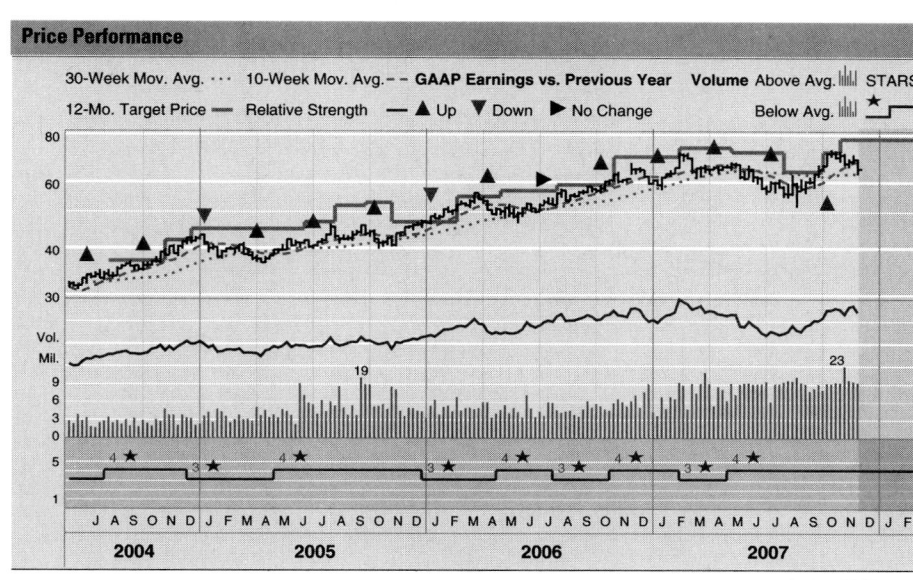

30-Week Mov. Avg. ··· 10-Week Mov. Avg. -- **GAAP Earnings vs. Previous Year** Volume Above Avg. STARS
12-Mo. Target Price — Relative Strength — ▲ Up ▼ Down ► No Change Below Avg.

Options: CBOE, P, Ph

Analysis prepared by **Robert McMillan** on October 25, 2007, when the stock traded at **$ 70.05**.

Highlights

➤ After rising 54% in 2006 on contributions from the acquisition of Catellus Development, we see rental income advancing 62% in 2007 and 8% in 2008 driven by a moderate increase in demand for industrial real estate, contributions from acquisitions and development activities, and income from the property funds business.

➤ We think expanding global trade levels will contribute to an increase in demand for PLD's properties. As of September 30, 2007, the trust's stabilized operating portfolio was 95.5% leased, up slightly from 95.2% in the prior quarter. We were encouraged that rents rose 9.6% in the quarter, with rent growth accelerating in many markets. We look for the company's acquisition and development program, particularly in Asia, to continue to benefit operations by enhancing PLD's economies of scale and geographic presence around the world. This should help insulate the company from the effects of a slowing US economy.

➤ We project EPS of $3.65 in 2007 and $4.22 in 2008, and funds from operations (FFO) per share of $4.48 and $4.80 in 2007 and 2008, respectively. We estimate fourth-quarter FFO of $0.66.

Investment Rationale/Risk

➤ We think PLD deserves to trade at a premium to peers due to its position as one of the largest owners of global distribution facilities, which are increasingly important, in our view, to global companies looking to increase efficiency by concentrating their business among fewer space providers. We view PLD's success in the property funds business, which allows it to expand its portfolio and collect management fees while using capital from institutional investors, as a positive factor in our valuation.

➤ Risks to our recommendation and target price include a sharp drop in demand and rental rates for industrial space, non-renewal of leases by customers, and a sharp increase in interest rates.

➤ The shares recently traded at about 14.6X PLD's trailing 12-month FFO per share. The valuation multiple had dropped sharply between May and August, and has risen considerably recently, driven in our opinion, by the prospects of lower interest rates. Our 12-month target price of $79 is equal to about 18.5X our forward 12-month FFO estimate of $4.24. We believe growth in PLD's business and overseas expansion will allow the multiple to expand.

Qualitative Risk Assessment

LOW	MEDIUM	HIGH

Our risk assessment reflects our view of PLD's position as one of the largest owners of industrial space in the world, its broad geographic and customer diversification, and what we view as its strong balance sheet.

Quantitative Evaluations

S&P Quality Ranking A-

D	C	B-	B	B+	A-	A	A+

Relative Strength Rank MODERATE

65

LOWEST = 1   HIGHEST = 99

Revenue/FFO Data

Revenue (Million $)

	1Q	2Q	3Q	4Q	Year
2007	958.4	989.4	3,462	--	--
2006	571.1	687.4	580.5	624.9	2,464
2005	431.9	469.6	532.0	434.6	1,868
2004	151.0	150.1	148.8	150.0	598.1
2003	159.9	169.4	116.8	213.1	734.1
2002	172.3	174.5	135.0	193.3	675.0

FFO Per Share ($)

	1Q	2Q	3Q	4Q	Year
2007	1.25	1.16	1.41	E0.66	E4.48
2006	0.90	0.90	0.79	1.11	3.69
2005	0.90	0.90	0.79	0.58	2.51
2004	0.63	0.67	0.74	0.56	2.11
2003	0.55	0.54	0.30	0.80	2.17
2002	0.59	0.59	0.40	0.58	2.39

Fiscal year ended Dec. 31. Next earnings report expected: Early February. FFO Estimates based on S&P Funds From Operations Est..

Dividend Data (Dates: mm/dd Payment Date: mm/dd/yy)

Amount ($)	Date Decl.	Ex-Div. Date	Stk. of Record	Payment Date
0.460	02/01	02/12	02/14	02/28/07
0.460	05/01	05/14	05/16	05/31/07
0.460	08/01	08/14	08/16	08/31/07
0.460	11/01	11/09	11/14	11/30/07

Dividends have been paid since 1994. Source: Company reports.

ProLogis

STANDARD &POOR'S

Business Summary October 25, 2007

ProLogis (formerly ProLogis Trust, and prior to that Security Capital Industrial Trust) is a real estate investment trust that owns and operates industrial distribution and temperature-controlled distribution facilities in North America, Europe and Japan. The trust's investment strategy focuses on generic industrial distribution facilities in markets that PLD thinks offer attractive long-term growth prospects, and in which it believes it can achieve a strong market position by acquiring and developing flexible facilities for warehousing and light manufacturing uses.

PLD's business is organized into three main operating segments: property operations, fund management, and corporate distribution facilities services and other (CDFS). The property operations segment (49% of 2006 operating income) is involved in long-term ownership, management and leasing of industrial distribution facilities, usually adaptable for both distribution and light manufacturing or assembly uses. The trust earns income from rents and reimbursement of property operating expenses from unaffiliated customers, and management fees from entities in which it has an ownership interest. At December 31, 2006, PLD's property operations segment consisted of 1,473 oper-

ating properties aggregating 204.7 million square feet in North America, Europe and Asia.

The fund management segment (23% of 2006 operating income) is involved in the long-term investment management of unconsolidated property funds, and the properties they own, with the objective of generating a high level of returns for PLD and its fund partners. It allows PLD, as the manager of the property funds, to maintain the market presence and customer relationships that are the key drivers of the ProLogis Operating System, and it enables the company to realize a portion of the development profits from its CDFS business activities by contributing its stabilized development properties to property funds. It also allows PLD to earn fees and incentives for providing services to the property funds and enables PLD to maintain a long-term ownership position in the properties.

Company Financials Fiscal Year Ended Dec. 31

Per Share Data ($)	2006	2005	2004	2003	2002	2001	2000	1999	1998	1997
Tangible Book Value	23.09	21.08	14.82	14.35	13.96	12.94	13.53	13.86	12.83	13.13
Earnings	2.71	1.39	1.09	1.16	1.20	0.52	0.96	0.81	0.51	0.04
S&P Core Earnings	2.71	1.39	1.06	1.14	1.17	0.49	NA	NA	NA	NA
Dividends	1.60	1.48	1.46	1.44	1.42	1.38	1.34	1.30	1.24	1.07
Payout Ratio	59%	106%	134%	124%	118%	NM	140%	160%	267%	245%
Prices:High	67.52	47.62	43.33	32.62	26.00	23.30	24.69	22.19	26.50	25.50
Prices:Low	46.29	36.50	27.62	23.63	20.96	19.35	17.56	16.75	19.75	18.88
P/E Ratio:High	25	34	40	28	22	45	26	27	52	NM
P/E Ratio:Low	17	26	25	20	17	37	18	20	39	NM

Income Statement Analysis (Million $)										
Rental Income	928	635	527	Nil	449	466	480	492	345	285
Mortgage Income	Nil	Nil	Nil	Nil	Nil	Nil	Nil	Nil	Nil	18.0
Total Income	2,464	1,868	598	734	675	574	644	567	368	302
General Expenses	1,403	1,210	224	210	91.0	83.0	78.0	76.7	58.1	51.7
Interest Expense	294	178	153	155	153	164	172	172	104	52.7
Provision for Losses	Nil	Nil	Nil	Nil	Nil	Nil	Nil	Nil	Nil	Nil
Depreciation	293	199	172	165	153	143	151	152	101	76.6
Net Income	718	318	234	251	249	128	214	182	111	39.7
S&P Core Earnings	692	292	199	208	210	86.8	NA	NA	NA	NA

Balance Sheet & Other Financial Data (Million $)										
Cash	1,775	1,241	1,145	1,009	111	28.0	57.9	69.3	63.1	25.0
Total Assets	15,904	13,114	7,098	6,369	5,924	5,604	5,946	5,848	4,331	3,034
Real Estate Investment	13,954	11,875	6,334	5,854	5,396	4,588	4,689	4,975	3,658	3,006
Loss Reserve	Nil	Nil	Nil	Nil	Nil	Nil	Nil	Nil	Nil	Nil
Net Investment	12,674	10,757	5,345	5,007	4,683	4,013	4,213	4,608	3,403	2,835
Short Term Debt	Nil	Nil	Nil	Nil	222	49.3	69.7	43.5	42.9	20.0
Capitalization:Debt	7,844	6,678	3,414	2,991	2,510	2,529	2,555	2,413	1,796	857
Capitalization:Equity	6,049	5,138	2,752	2,586	2,486	2,276	2,236	2,243	1,583	1,542
Capitalization:Total	14,295	12,225	6,583	6,089	5,439	5,251	5,574	5,428	4,104	2,379
% Earnings & Depreciation/Assets	4.7	5.1	6.0	6.8	7.0	4.7	6.2	6.6	5.7	4.2
Price Times Book Value:High	2.9	2.3	2.9	2.3	1.9	1.8	1.8	1.6	4.0	1.9
Price Times Book Value:Low	2.0	1.7	1.9	1.6	1.5	1.5	1.3	1.2	3.0	1.4

Data as orig reptd.; bef. results of disc opers/spec. items. Per share data adj. for stk. divs.; EPS diluted. E-Estimated. NA-Not Available. NM-Not Meaningful. NR-Not Ranked. UR-Under Review.

Office: 4545 Airport Way, Denver, CO 80239-5716.
Telephone: 303-567-5000.
Email: info@prologis.com
Website: http://www.prologis.com

Chrmn & CEO: J.H. Schwartz
Pres & COO: W.C. Rakowich
Investor Contact: M. Marsden (303-567-5622)
CFO: W.E. Sullivan

Secy & General Counsel: E.S. Nekritz
Trustees: K. D. Brooksher, S. L. Feinberg, G. L. Fotiades, C. N. Garvey, D. P. Jacobs, W. C. Rakowich, N. C. Rising, J. H. Schwartz, D. M. Steuert, J. A. Teixeira, W. D. Zollars, A. M. Zulberti

Founded: 1991
Domicile: Maryland
Employees: 1,300

Prudential Financial Inc

STANDARD &POOR'S

S&P Recommendation **BUY** ★★★★☆	Price **$93.87** (as of Nov 23, 2007)	12-Mo. Target Price **$115.00**	Investment Style Large-Cap Value

GICS Sector Financials
Sub-Industry Life & Health Insurance

Summary Through its subsidiaries, Prudential Financial provides a wide range of insurance, investment management and other financial products and services to customers in the U.S. and overseas.

Key Stock Statistics (Source S&P, Vickers, company reports)

52-Wk Range	$103.27– 79.13	S&P Oper. EPS 2007**E**	7.58	Market Capitalization(B)	$43.086	Beta	0.86
Trailing 12-Month EPS	$7.74	S&P Oper. EPS 2008**E**	8.20	Yield (%)	1.23	S&P 3-Yr. Proj. EPS CAGR(%)	14.00
Trailing 12-Month P/E	12.1	P/E on S&P Oper. EPS 2007**E**	12.4	Dividend Rate/Share	$1.15	S&P Credit Rating	A+
$10K Invested 5 Yrs Ago	$33,110	Common Shares Outstg. (M)	459.0	Institutional Ownership (%)	54		

Price Performance

30-Week Mov. Avg. ··· 10-Week Mov. Avg. - - **GAAP Earnings vs. Previous Year** Volume Above Avg. STARS
12-Mo. Target Price — Relative Strength — ▲ Up ▼ Down ► No Change Below Avg. ★

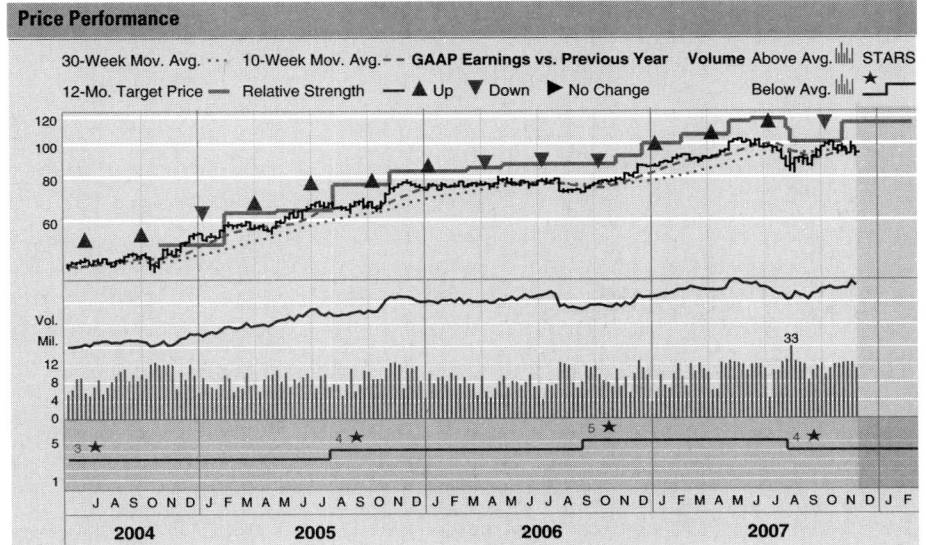

Options: ASE, CBOE, Ph

Analysis prepared by **Tanjila Shafi** on November 14, 2007, when the stock traded at **$ 99.42**.

Highlights

➤ We expect pretax adjusted operating income in the insurance division to experience high single to low double digit growth in 2008. We project that sales in this division will benefit from new annuity products and an expanded distribution network, aided by the acquisition of Allstate's variable annuity business. We forecast strong growth in pretax operating income for the investment division, helped by contributions from the Wachovia joint venture, and strong demand for retirement services products, driven by the Pension Protection Act.

➤ We estimate pretax adjusted operating income for the international insurance and investments division will see mid- to high-single digit growth in 2008, on improving retention rates, expanded distribution and strategic acquisitions, partially offset by higher expenses related to recruiting and client servicing. We expect strong growth to continue in Japan.

➤ We forecast 2007 operating EPS of $7.58, which would represent 23% growth from 2006 operating EPS of $6.15. Our EPS estimate for 2008 is $8.20.

Investment Rationale/Risk

➤ We believe that PRU's high-growth businesses and capital management initiatives will expand earnings and return on equity (ROE). We think the company has several sources of potential growth in 2008, including the June 2006 acquisition of Allstate Financial's variable annuity business; the Wachovia joint venture; and the passage of the Pension Protection Act. We do not expect that PRU's $8.3 billion of subprime exposure--representing 4.8% of invested assets--will create material losses that will negatively affect its investment portfolio.

➤ Risks to our recommendation and target price include currency risk; reserving risks for new guaranteed minimum benefits; integration risks from acquisitions; regulatory risks; credit risk; and litigation resulting from market timing issues at Prudential Securities.

➤ Our 12-month target price is $115, or 2.2X our 2008 book value forecast (excluding other comprehensive income), above PRU's historical multiples, which we believe is warranted given its strong earnings outlook and business mix.

Qualitative Risk Assessment

LOW	MEDIUM	HIGH

Our risk assessment reflects PRU's varied product offerings, geographic diversification, disciplined capital management, prominent market position, and high risk-based capital ratio.

Quantitative Evaluations

S&P Quality Ranking NR

D	C	B-	B	B+	A-	A	A+

Relative Strength Rank STRONG

71

LOWEST = 1 HIGHEST = 99

Revenue/Earnings Data

Revenue (Million $)

	1Q	2Q	3Q	4Q	Year
2007	8,821	8,425	6,658	--	--
2006	7,850	7,373	8,408	8,857	32,488
2005	7,721	8,318	7,787	7,882	31,708
2004	6,743	6,904	7,346	7,355	28,348
2003	6,785	7,304	6,693	7,125	27,907
2002	6,684	6,637	6,679	6,675	26,675

Earnings Per Share ($)

2007	2.10	1.86	1.74	E1.89	E7.58
2006	1.39	0.92	2.24	1.85	6.37
2005	1.47	1.56	2.61	0.78	6.46
2004	0.72	0.98	1.09	0.64	3.45
2003	0.42	0.21	0.48	0.95	2.06
2002	0.47	0.20	0.68	Nil	1.36

Fiscal year ended Dec. 31. Next earnings report expected: NA. EPS Estimates based on S&P Operating Earnings; historical GAAP earnings are as reported.

Dividend Data (Dates: mm/dd Payment Date: mm/dd/yy)

Amount ($)	Date Decl.	Ex-Div. Date	Stk. of Record	Payment Date
0.950	11/14	11/22	11/27	12/21/06
1.150	11/13	11/21	11/26	12/21/07

Dividends have been paid since 2002. Source: Company reports.

Prudential Financial Inc

STANDARD &POOR'S

Business Summary November 14, 2007

CORPORATE OVERVIEW. Prudential Financial is one of the largest U.S. financial services companies, with $616 billion in assets under management at year-end 2006, and it serves customers in roughly 30 other countries.

The financial services business operates through four segments: insurance (36% of 2006 operating revenues, 35% in 2005), investments (28%, 27%), international insurance and investments (33%, 35%), as well as a corporate and other segment (2.6%, 2.6%). The insurance segment consists of the individual life and annuities unit (49% of the division's 2005 operating revenues) and the group insurance unit (51%), which distributes group life, disability and related insurance products through employee and member benefit plans.

The asset management segment (29% of the division's 2006 operating revenues), the financial advisory segment (8.2%) and the retirement services segment (63%) comprise the investment division. International insurance and investments consists of insurance (93% of the division's 2006 operating revenues) and investments (7.1%).

The closed block businesses represent some insurance products no longer offered, including certain participating insurance and annuity policies. At De-

cember 31, 2005, PRU had reinsurance agreements covering about 90% of the closed block policies.

CORPORATE STRATEGY. We believe PRU is focused on two prime areas of growth: international businesses and domestic retirement and savings. To that end, Prudential has made strategic acquisitions to enhance these opportunities. In April 2004, the company acquired CIGNA's retirement business for $2.1 billion in cash.

At any time before July 1, 2008, PRU may, subject to limitations, require Wachovia to purchase its interest in Wachovia Securities. Prior to July 2008, the purchase price generally would equal $1 billion plus PRU's share of the joint venture's transition costs, adjusted for additional investments. On August 28, 2006, PRU announced a $600 million settlement with various regulatory agencies in connection with market timing activities at Prudential Securities.

Company Financials Fiscal Year Ended Dec. 31

Per Share Data ($)	2006	2005	2004	2003	2002	2001	2000	1999	1998	1997
Tangible Book Value	46.32	45.53	42.40	39.65	37.89	34.90	NA	NA	NA	NA
Operating Earnings	NA	NA	NA	NA	NA	NA	NA	NA	NA	NA
Earnings	6.37	6.46	3.45	2.06	1.36	0.07	0.82	NA	NA	NA
S&P Core Earnings	5.41	4.96	1.91	1.79	1.13	NA	NA	NA	NA	NA
Dividends	0.95	0.78	0.63	0.50	0.40	Nil	NA	NA	NA	NA
Payout Ratio	15%	12%	18%	24%	29%	Nil	NA	NA	NA	NA
Prices:High	87.18	78.62	55.62	42.21	36.00	33.74	NA	NA	NA	NA
Prices:Low	71.28	52.07	40.14	27.03	25.25	27.50	NA	NA	NA	NA
P/E Ratio:High	14	12	16	20	26	NM	NA	NA	NA	NA
P/E Ratio:Low	11	8	12	13	19	NM	NA	NA	NA	NA

Income Statement Analysis (Million $)										
Life Insurance in Force	NA	NA	NA	1,928,650	1,800,788	1,768,038	NA	NA	NA	NA
Premium Income:Life	13,908	13,685	12,580	10,972	10,897	10,078	NA	NA	NA	NA
Premium Income:A & H	NA	NA	NA	806	586	515	NA	NA	NA	NA
Net Investment Income	11,354	10,560	9,079	8,681	8,832	9,151	9,467	NA	NA	NA
Total Revenue	32,488	31,708	28,348	27,907	26,675	27,177	26,514	NA	NA	NA
Pretax Income	4,611	4,471	3,287	1,958	64.0	-227	525	NA	NA	NA
Net Operating Income	NA	NA	NA	NA	NA	NA	NA	NA	NA	NA
Net Income	3,363	3,602	2,332	1,308	256	-170	304	NA	NA	NA
S&P Core Earnings	2,675	2,580	1,022	981	650	-403	NA	NA	NA	NA

Balance Sheet & Other Financial Data (Million $)										
Cash & Equivalent	10,731	9,866	10,100	9,746	11,688	20,364	19,994	NA	NA	NA
Premiums Due	1,958	3,548	32,790	Nil	Nil	Nil	NA	NA	NA	NA
Investment Assets:Bonds	166,285	158,515	153,715	132,011	128,075	110,316	NA	NA	NA	NA
Investment Assets:Stocks	24,574	18,792	4,283	6,703	2,807	2,272	NA	NA	NA	NA
Investment Assets:Loans	8,887	32,811	32,761	27,621	22,094	28,299	NA	NA	NA	NA
Investment Assets:Total	245,349	221,401	216,624	181,041	183,094	165,834	169,251	NA	NA	NA
Deferred Policy Costs	10,863	9,438	8,847	7,826	7,031	6,868	6,751	NA	NA	NA
Total Assets	454,266	417,776	401,058	321,274	292,746	293,030	298,414	NA	NA	NA
Debt	11,423	8,270	7,627	5,610	4,757	5,304	14,812	NA	NA	NA
Common Equity	22,892	22,763	22,344	21,292	21,330	20,453	20,692	NA	NA	NA
% Return on Revenue	10.4	11.4	8.2	4.7	1.0	NM	1.1	NA	NA	NA
% Return on Assets	0.8	0.9	0.6	0.4	0.1	NM	NA	NA	NA	NA
% Return on Equity	14.7	16.0	10.7	6.1	1.2	NM	NA	NA	NA	NA
% Investment Yield	4.8	4.8	4.6	4.8	5.1	5.8	NA	NA	NA	NA

Data as orig reptd.; bef. results of disc opers/spec. items. Per share data adj. for stk. divs.; EPS diluted. E-Estimated. NA-Not Available. NM-Not Meaningful. NR-Not Ranked. UR-Under Review.

Office: 751 Broad St, Newark, NJ 07102.
Telephone: 973-802-6000.
Email: investor.relations@prudential.com
Website: http://www.investor.prudential.com

Chrmn, Pres & CEO: A.F. Ryan
Vice Chrmn: M.B. Grier
Vice Chrmn: V.L. Banta
Vice Chrmn: J.R. Strangfeld, Jr.

SVP & CFO: R.J. Carbone
Board Members: F. K. Becker, G. M. Bethune, G. Caperton, G. F. Casellas, J. G. Cullen, W. H. Gray, III, J. F. Hanson, C. J. Horner, K. J. Krapek, C. Poon, A. F. Ryan, J. A. Unruh

Founded: 1875
Domicile: New Jersey
Employees: 39,814

The McGraw-Hill Companies

STANDARD &POOR'S

Public Storage

S&P Recommendation	HOLD ★★★☆☆	Price	12-Mo. Target Price	Investment Style
		$76.25 (as of Nov 23, 2007)	$85.00	Large-Cap Blend

GICS Sector Financials
Sub-Industry Specialized REITS

Summary This real estate investment trust invests primarily in self-service storage facilities (mini-warehouses), but also in commercial and industrial properties.

Key Stock Statistics (Source S&P, Vickers, company reports)

52-Wk Range	$117.16– 68.09	S&P FFO/Sh. 2007E	4.71	Market Capitalization(B)	$13.002	Beta	0.47
Trailing 12-Month FFO/Share	NA	S&P FFO/Sh. 2008E	5.11	Yield (%)	2.62	S&P 3-Yr. FFO/Sh. Proj. CAGR(%)	9.00
Trailing 12-Month P/FFO	NA	P/FFO on S&P FFO/Sh. 2007E	16.2	Dividend Rate/Share	$2.00	S&P Credit Rating	A-
$10K Invested 5 Yrs Ago	$29,246	Common Shares Outstg. (M)	170.5	Institutional Ownership (%)	67		

Price Performance

30-Week Mov. Avg. ··· 10-Week Mov. Avg. - - GAAP Earnings vs. Previous Year Volume Above Avg. STARS
12-Mo. Target Price — Relative Strength — ▲ Up ▼ Down ► No Change Below Avg.

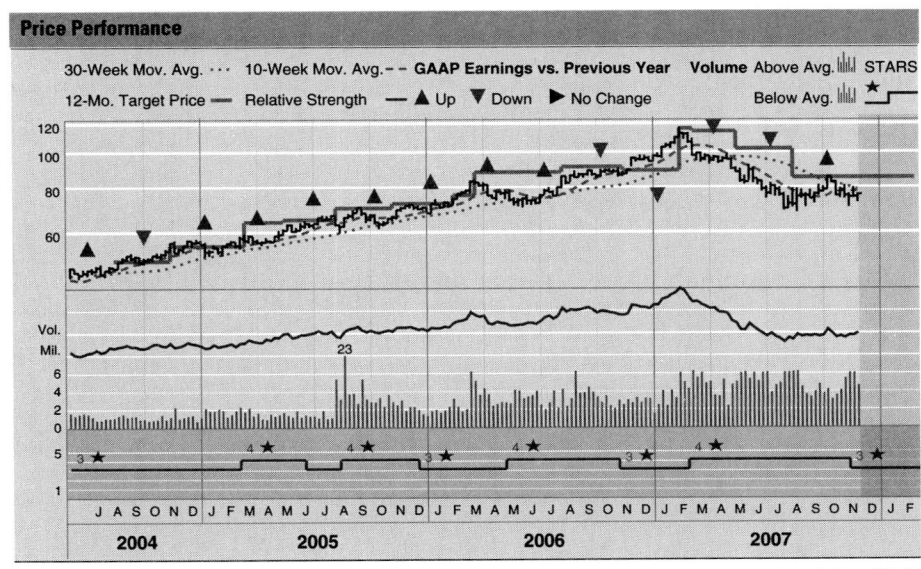

Options: ASE, Ph

Analysis prepared by **Robert McMillan** on November 12, 2007, when the stock traded at **$ 75.08**.

Highlights

➤ We expect PSA to benefit from moderately expanding economies in the U.S and Europe., which we see generating increased jobs and greater moving and re-location activity, which should translate into more demand for self-storage space.

➤ Following revenue growth of almost 29% in 2006, driven largely by, in our opinion, contributions from the August 2006 acquisition of Shurgard Storage Centers, we look for revenues to increase about 32% in 2007 on contributions from acquisitions as well as organic growth, followed by more normalized growth of 8% in 2008. Same-store domestic occupancy remained healthy, but declined slightly to 90.5% at the end of the third quarter of 2007, from 91.3% in the year-ago period, while revenue per available square foot rose 1.7%. European growth was more dynamic, with occupancy rising to 91.0% from 86.7% a year earlier, while revenue per available square foot rose 9.5%. We think continued turmoil in the U.S. housing market and management's promotional programs may crimp growth in the U.S. near term.

➤ We look for per share funds from operations (FFO) of $4.71 in 2007 and $5.11 in 2008.

Investment Rationale/Risk

➤ We believe that a moderately expanding economy will continue to generate moving activity. We see PSA benefiting from its ability to continue gaining share at the expense of smaller competitors by creating customer awareness in its markets and offering an array of customer services, such as container services, which many small competitors cannot provide.

➤ Risks to our recommendation and target price include slower than expected growth in rental rates and occupancy levels, a sharp drop in moving activity, and a rise in interest rates.

➤ The shares recently traded at about 16.8X trailing 12-month FFO. The shares and the valuation multiple have been volatile since May, reflecting changing views on the outlook for the economy and the housing market. Our 12-month target price of $85 is equal to about 17.2X our forward four quarter FFO estimate of $4.91. Although we expect a slight widening of the valuation multiple driven by continued operating improvements, we are concerned that earnings and the shares could be volatile, reflecting changing outlooks for the housing market and foreign currency gains.

Qualitative Risk Assessment

LOW	MEDIUM	HIGH

Our risk assessment reflects PSA's position as one of the largest providers of self storage space in a consolidating industry, as well as our view of its consistent growth and healthy balance sheet.

Quantitative Evaluations

S&P Quality Ranking B+

D	C	B-	B	B+	A-	A	A+

Relative Strength Rank STRONG

71

LOWEST = 1 HIGHEST = 99

Revenue/FFO Data

Revenue (Million $)

	1Q	2Q	3Q	4Q	Year
2007	434.4	449.2	469.0	--	--
2006	278.5	297.9	371.4	433.9	1,382
2005	243.8	254.3	264.9	273.6	1,061
2004	222.7	231.6	237.2	240.3	928.0
2003	206.9	217.1	228.0	223.1	875.1
2002	203.8	205.7	215.8	207.6	841.5

FFO Per Share ($)

2007	1.05	1.10	1.43	E1.14	E4.71
2006	0.94	0.99	0.77	0.89	3.57
2005	0.79	0.90	0.97	0.96	3.61
2004	0.58	0.77	0.76	0.82	2.93
2003	0.68	0.72	0.79	0.68	2.81
2002	0.73	0.70	0.65	0.60	2.74

Fiscal year ended Dec. 31. Next earnings report expected: Early March. FFO Estimates based on S&P Funds From Operations Est..

Dividend Data (Dates: mm/dd Payment Date: mm/dd/yy)

Amount ($)	Date Decl.	Ex-Div. Date	Stk. of Record	Payment Date
0.500	02/28	03/13	03/15	03/29/07
0.500	05/07	06/13	06/15	06/28/07
0.500	08/02	09/10	09/12	09/27/07
0.500	11/08	12/11	12/13	12/28/07

Dividends have been paid since 1981. Source: Company reports.

The **McGraw·Hill** Companies

Public Storage

STANDARD
&POOR'S

Business Summary November 12, 2007

Public Storage is an equity real estate investment trust that was organized as a corporation under the laws of California on July 10, 1980. It is a fully integrated, self-administered and self-managed REIT that acquires, develops, owns and operates storage facilities.

PSA is the largest U.S. owner and operator of storage space, with direct and indirect equity investments in 2,003 self-storage facilities located in 38 states within the U.S. operating under the "Public Storage" name. They contain approximately 125 million net rentable square feet of space, and 166 self-storage facilities are located in seven Western European countries, which operate under the "Shurgard Storage Centers" name, containing approximately 8.7 million net rentable square feet of space. The company also has direct and indirect equity interests in approximately 20 million net rentable square feet of commercial space located in 11 states in the U.S. operated under the "PS Business

Parks" and Public Storage, Inc. brands.

PSA's growth strategies consist of improving the operating performance of stabilized existing traditional self-storage properties; acquiring additional interests in entities that own properties operated by the trust; purchasing interests in properties that are owned or operated by others; developing properties in selected markets; improving the operating performance of the containerized storage operations; and participating in the growth of PS Business Parks, Inc.

Company Financials Fiscal Year Ended Dec. 31

Per Share Data ($)	2006	2005	2004	2003	2002	2001	2000	1999	1998	1997
Tangible Book Value	28.16	16.72	16.69	17.03	16.16	28.37	18.24	21.43	16.65	15.71
Earnings	0.32	1.92	1.39	1.27	1.28	1.51	1.41	1.52	1.30	0.91
S&P Core Earnings	0.32	1.91	1.38	1.25	1.26	1.48	NA	NA	NA	NA
Dividends	2.00	1.85	1.80	1.80	1.80	1.69	1.48	0.88	0.88	0.88
Payout Ratio	NM	97%	129%	142%	1%	112%	105%	58%	68%	97%
Prices:High	98.05	72.02	57.64	45.81	39.29	35.15	26.93	29.38	33.63	30.88
Prices:Low	67.72	51.50	39.50	28.25	27.98	24.13	20.87	20.81	22.63	25.88
P/E Ratio:High	NM	38	41	36	33	23	19	19	26	34
P/E Ratio:Low	NM	27	28	22	24	16	15	14	17	28

Income Statement Analysis (Million $)										
Rental Income	1,240	980	894	844	813	782	703	628	536	434
Mortgage Income	Nil	Nil	Nil	Nil	Nil	Nil	Nil	Nil	Nil	Nil
Total Income	1,382	1,061	928	875	841	835	757	677	582	471
General Expenses	585	400	349	336	311	297	273	229	223	182
Interest Expense	33.1	8.22	0.76	1.12	3.81	3.23	3.29	7.97	4.51	6.79
Provision for Losses	Nil	Nil	Nil	Nil	Nil	Nil	Nil	Nil	Nil	Nil
Depreciation	438	196	183	186	180	168	149	138	107	91.5
Net Income	312	450	367	335	319	324	297	288	227	179
S&P Core Earnings	44.7	247	179	157	156	183	NA	NA	NA	NA

Balance Sheet & Other Financial Data (Million $)										
Cash	857	329	708	205	103	49.3	89.5	55.1	51.2	41.5
Total Assets	11,198	5,552	5,205	4,968	4,844	4,626	4,514	4,214	3,404	3,312
Real Estate Investment	11,262	6,314	5,908	5,544	5,424	5,062	4,822	4,421	3,496	3,346
Loss Reserve	Nil	Nil	Nil	Nil	Nil	Nil	Nil	Nil	Nil	Nil
Net Investment	9,507	4,814	4,588	4,391	4,436	4,242	4,154	3,887	3,085	2,968
Short Term Debt	Nil	Nil	Nil	Nil	39.8	Nil	Nil	Nil	Nil	15.1
Capitalization:Debt	1,848	134	130	76.0	76.1	144	156	167	81.4	104
Capitalization:Equity	5,353	2,319	2,328	2,353	2,342	2,369	2,569	2,534	2,250	1,927
Capitalization:Total	8,785	5,205	4,989	4,722	4,675	4,508	4,413	4,043	3,340	3,225
% Earnings & Depreciation/Assets	8.9	12.0	10.8	10.6	10.5	7.1	10.2	11.2	7.6	9.2
Price Times Book Value:High	3.5	4.3	3.5	2.7	2.4	1.2	1.5	1.4	2.0	2.0
Price Times Book Value:Low	2.4	3.1	2.4	1.7	1.7	0.9	1.1	1.0	1.4	1.7

Data as orig reptd.; bef. results of disc opers/spec. items. Per share data adj. for stk. divs.; EPS diluted. E-Estimated. NA-Not Available. NM-Not Meaningful. NR-Not Ranked. UR-Under Review.

Office: 701 Western Ave, Glendale, CA 91201-2349.
Telephone: 818-244-8080.
Email: investor@publicstorage.com
Website: http://www.publicstorage.com

Chrmn: B.W. Hughes
Pres, Vice Chrmn & CEO: R.L. Havner, Jr.
Investor Contact: J. Reyes (818-244-8080)
SVP & CFO: J. Reyes

SVP & Chief Lgl Officer: J.S. Baumann
Trustees: D. V. Angeloff, W. C. Baker, J. T. Evans, U. P. Harkham, R. L. Havner, Jr., B. W. Hughes, B. W. Hughes, Jr., H. Lenkin, G. E. Pruitt, D. C. Staton

Founded: 1980
Domicile: California
Employees: 6,000

Public Service Enterprise Group Inc

STANDARD &POOR'S

S&P Recommendation **BUY** ★★★★☆	Price $92.20 (as of Nov 23, 2007)	12-Mo. Target Price $106.00	Investment Style Large-Cap Blend

GICS Sector Utilities
Sub-Industry Multi-Utilities

Summary PEG is the holding company for Public Service Electric and Gas (PSE&G), with a service area that encompasses 70% of New Jersey.

Key Stock Statistics (Source S&P, Vickers, company reports)

52-Wk Range	$98.61– 64.32	S&P Oper. EPS 2007**E**	5.35	Market Capitalization(B)	$23.445	Beta	0.05
Trailing 12-Month EPS	$4.18	S&P Oper. EPS 2008**E**	6.15	Yield (%)	2.54	S&P 3-Yr. Proj. EPS CAGR(%)	20.00
Trailing 12-Month P/E	22.1	P/E on S&P Oper. EPS 2007**E**	17.2	Dividend Rate/Share	$2.34	S&P Credit Rating	BBB
$10K Invested 5 Yrs Ago	$39,203	Common Shares Outstg. (M)	254.3	Institutional Ownership (%)	60		

Price Performance

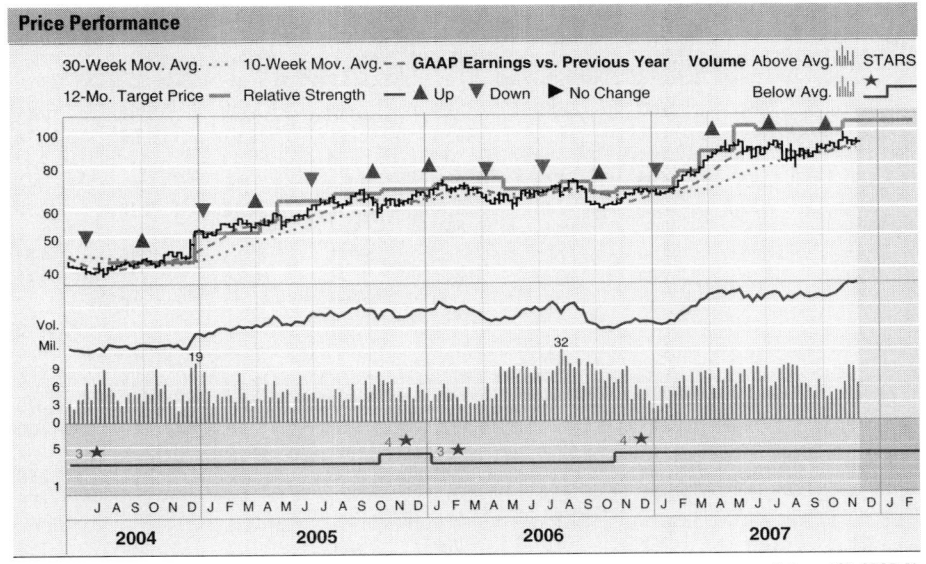

30-Week Mov. Avg. ··· 10-Week Mov. Avg. - - **GAAP Earnings vs. Previous Year** Volume Above Avg. ▐▐▌ STARS
12-Mo. Target Price — Relative Strength — ▲ Up ▼ Down ► No Change Below Avg. ▐▐▌ ★

Options: ASE, CBOE, Ph

Analysis prepared by **Justin McCann** on November 21, 2007, when the stock traded at **$ 92.15**.

Highlights

➤ We expect EPS in 2007 to grow approximately 44%, from 2006 EPS from continuing operations of $3.71. In addition to a return to normal weather (compared to the abnormally mild weather in the prior year), we see results benefiting from higher margins at the Power segment, and from the gas and electric rate increases that went into effect in the fourth quarter of 2006.

➤ For 2008, we expect operating EPS to increase around 15% from anticipated results in 2007, primarily driven by the renewal of expiring power contracts at higher commodity prices. We believe this trend will continue, and we expect PEG to realize double-digit earnings growth for the next few years.

➤ We believe the operating performance of PEG's previously troubled nuclear operations will continue to improve. This primarily reflects, in our opinion, the company's hiring of the senior personnel from the Exelon nuclear services team effective January 1, 2007, when PEG resumed direct management of its nuclear plants from the Exelon team. The company plans to spend approximately $50 million from 2007 though 2012 to explore an investment in new nuclear capacity.

Investment Rationale/Risk

➤ Although the shares are up around 40% year to date, we believe the stock is still attractive for above-average total return. The shares have fully recovered from the recent decline that had resulted, in our view, from speculation that private equity interest in certain utility assets had been deferred due to the recent credit tightening. We expect the stock to outperform PEG's peers over the next 12 months, aided by the strong EPS growth we see for the next few years and its competitive position in the Northeast power markets.

➤ Risks to our recommendation and target price include a failure to complete plants under construction on time, an inability to continue hedging over 75% of electric generating capacity, and narrower wholesale power margins.

➤ With the sharp year-to-date rise in the shares, the dividend yield declined from around 3.5% to 2.5% recently. While this is below the recent peer average of about 3.6%, we believe the stock will continue to benefit from a projected growth rate that is well above peers. Our 12-month target price of $106 reflects a premium-to-peers P/E of about 17X our EPS estimate for 2008.

Qualitative Risk Assessment

LOW	MEDIUM	HIGH

Our risk assessment reflects our view of the strong and steady cash flow from the regulated electric and gas utility operations of PSE&G, as well as the strong but less predictable earnings and cash flow from the non-regulated power generating operations. It also reflects what we see as a lowering of the company's risk profile through the divestiture of its non-core international investments.

Quantitative Evaluations

S&P Quality Ranking   **B+**

D	C	B-	B	**B+**	A-	A	A+

Relative Strength Rank   **STRONG**

86

LOWEST = 1   HIGHEST = 99

Revenue/Earnings Data

Revenue (Million $)

	1Q	2Q	3Q	4Q	Year
2007	3,614	2,810	3,475	--	--
2006	3,461	2,556	3,212	2,935	12,164
2005	3,310	2,442	3,376	3,472	12,430
2004	3,221	2,290	2,747	2,731	10,996
2003	3,364	2,419	2,805	--	11,116
2002	1,914	1,469	2,328	2,679	8,390

Earnings Per Share ($)

2007	1.32	1.15	1.97	E0.88	E5.35
2006	0.82	-0.01	1.49	0.69	2.98
2005	1.18	0.42	1.06	0.89	3.51
2004	1.14	0.50	1.03	0.38	3.03
2003	1.42	0.66	0.93	0.69	3.72
2002	0.87	-1.10	1.00	1.19	1.99

Fiscal year ended Dec. 31. Next earnings report expected: NA. EPS Estimates based on S&P Operating Earnings; historical GAAP earnings are as reported.

Dividend Data (Dates: mm/dd Payment Date: mm/dd/yy)

Amount ($)	Date Decl.	Ex-Div. Date	Stk. of Record	Payment Date
0.585	01/16	03/07	03/09	03/30/07
0.585	04/17	06/06	06/08	06/29/07
0.585	07/17	09/06	09/10	09/28/07
0.585	11/20	12/05	12/07	12/31/07

Dividends have been paid since 1907. Source: Company reports.

Please read the Required Disclosures and Analyst Certification on the last page of this report.

The **McGraw·Hill** Companies

Public Service Enterprise Group Inc

STANDARD &POOR'S

Business Summary November 21, 2007

CORPORATE OVERVIEW. Headquartered in Newark, NJ, Public Service Enterprise Group has three primary operating units: Public Service Electric and Gas Co. - PSE&G ($262 million of net income in 2006), Power ($515 million), and Energy Holdings ($227 million). The parent company and intersegment eliminations accounted for a loss of $66 million. PEG has sought to minimize its earnings and cash flow volatility by entering into long-term contracts for most of its competitive wholesale power generation, and by reducing its exposure to international operations over time.

IMPACT OF MAJOR DEVELOPMENTS. On September 14, 2006, the company and Exelon Corp.(EXC) announced the termination of the merger agreement

they had announced on December 20, 2004. While we view the termination of the merger as a negative for PEG shareholders (who would have received 1.225 shares of EXC for each PEG share), we believe the rate concessions and additional power plant divestitures required by the New Jersey regulators would have significantly diluted many of the expected benefits of the proposed transaction.

Company Financials Fiscal Year Ended Dec. 31

Per Share Data ($)	2006	2005	2004	2003	2002	2001	2000	1999	1998	1997
Tangible Book Value	24.45	21.57	21.41	20.84	14.78	16.93	19.21	18.50	21.86	21.72
Earnings	2.98	3.51	3.03	3.72	1.99	3.67	3.55	3.29	2.79	2.41
S&P Core Earnings	3.84	3.40	2.97	4.03	3.06	3.16	NA	NA	NA	NA
Dividends	2.28	2.24	2.20	2.16	2.16	2.16	2.16	2.16	2.16	2.16
Payout Ratio	77%	64%	73%	58%	109%	59%	61%	66%	77%	90%
Prices:High	72.61	68.47	52.64	44.50	47.25	51.55	50.00	42.63	42.75	31.81
Prices:Low	59.00	49.32	38.10	32.09	20.00	36.88	25.69	32.00	30.31	22.88
P/E Ratio:High	24	20	17	12	24	14	14	13	15	13
P/E Ratio:Low	20	14	13	9	10	10	7	10	11	9

Income Statement Analysis (Million $)

	2006	2005	2004	2003	2002	2001	2000	1999	1998	1997
Revenue	12,164	12,430	10,996	11,116	8,390	9,815	6,848	6,497	5,931	6,370
Depreciation	832	748	719	527	571	522	362	536	669	630
Maintenance	NA	NA	NA	NA	NA	NA	NA	NA	NA	281
Fixed Charges Coverage	2.73	2.55	2.21	2.43	2.38	2.46	2.88	3.20	2.87	2.69
Construction Credits	NA	NA	NA	NA	NA	NA	NA	NA	13.0	20.0
Effective Tax Rate	NM	38.7%	38.2%	35.3%	37.3%	NM	39.1%	43.8%	39.5%	37.0%
Net Income	752	858	721	852	416	763	764	723	644	560
S&P Core Earnings	967	834	708	925	638	656	NA	NA	NA	NA

Balance Sheet & Other Financial Data (Million $)

	2006	2005	2004	2003	2002	2001	2000	1999	1998	1997
Gross Property	18,851	18,896	19,121	17,406	16,562	14,886	11,968	11,156	18,386	17,982
Capital Expenditures	1,015	1,024	1,255	1,351	1,814	2,053	959	582	535	542
Net Property	13,002	13,336	13,750	12,422	11,449	10,064	7,702	7,078	11,026	11,217
Capitalization:Long Term Debt	10,450	11,359	13,005	13,025	12,391	11,061	6,505	5,783	4,813	4,925
Capitalization:% Long Term Debt	60.8	65.4	69.4	70.2	75.7	72.8	60.2	59.1	43.3	45.5
Capitalization:Preferred	Nil	Nil	Nil	Nil	Nil	Nil	Nil	Nil	1,208	683
Capitalization:% Preferred	Nil	Nil	Nil	Nil	Nil	Nil	Nil	Nil	10.9	6.30
Capitalization:Common	6,747	6,022	5,739	5,529	3,987	4,137	4,294	3,996	5,098	5,211
Capitalization:% Common	39.2	34.6	30.6	29.8	24.3	27.2	39.8	40.9	45.8	48.2
Total Capital	21,659	21,629	23,091	22,750	19,302	18,403	13,906	12,707	14,825	14,556
% Operating Ratio	78.7	88.6	87.5	86.5	78.8	76.9	79.6	80.4	80.0	82.5
% Earned on Net Property	15.1	15.9	14.9	17.3	14.3	21.3	18.9	20.4	10.7	9.9
% Return on Revenue	6.2	6.9	6.6	7.7	5.0	7.8	11.2	11.1	10.9	8.8
% Return on Invested Capital	9.3	7.6	6.9	8.1	9.3	9.6	10.8	9.5	8.1	10.1
% Return on Common Equity	11.8	14.6	12.8	18.1	10.2	18.8	18.4	15.9	12.5	10.7

Data as orig reptd.; bef. results of disc opers/spec. items. Per share data adj. for stk. divs.; EPS diluted. E-Estimated. NA-Not Available. NM-Not Meaningful. NR-Not Ranked. UR-Under Review.

Office: 80 Park Plaza, Newark, NJ 07102-4109.
Telephone: 973-430-7000.
Email: stkserv@pseg.com
Website: http://www.pseg.com

Chrmn, Pres & CEO: R. Izzo
EVP & CFO: T.M. O'Flynn
SVP & General Counsel: R.E. Selover
Investor Contact: K.A. Lally

VP & Cntlr: D.M. DiRisio
Board Members: C. Dorsa, E. H. Drew, A. R. Gamper, Jr., C. K. Harper, W. V. Hickey, R. Izzo, S. A. Jackson, T. A. Renyi, R. J. Swift

Founded: 1985
Domicile: New Jersey
Employees: 9,836

The McGraw·Hill Companies

STANDARD &POOR'S

Pulte Homes Inc.

S&P Recommendation **HOLD** ★★★☆☆	Price $9.63 (as of Nov 23, 2007)	12-Mo. Target Price $13.00	Investment Style Large-Cap Blend

GICS Sector Consumer Discretionary
Sub-Industry Homebuilding

Summary This builder of a wide range of single-family homes and condominiums throughout the country is the leading U.S. developer of active adult communities, and has a mortgage banking unit.

Key Stock Statistics (Source S&P, Vickers, company reports)

52-Wk Range	$35.56– 9.00	S&P Oper. EPS 2007**E**	-5.75	Market Capitalization(B)	$2.464	Beta	1.45
Trailing 12-Month EPS	$-5.51	S&P Oper. EPS 2008**E**	-1.10	Yield (%)	1.66	S&P 3-Yr. Proj. EPS CAGR(%)	-4.00
Trailing 12-Month P/E	NM	P/E on S&P Oper. EPS 2007**E**	NM	Dividend Rate/Share	$0.16	S&P Credit Rating	BB+
$10K Invested 5 Yrs Ago	$8,600	Common Shares Outstg. (M)	255.9	Institutional Ownership (%)	82		

Price Performance

30-Week Mov. Avg. ···· 10-Week Mov. Avg. - - GAAP Earnings vs. Previous Year   Volume Above Avg. ▮▮▮ STARS
12-Mo. Target Price — Relative Strength — ▲ Up ▼ Down ► No Change   Below Avg. ▮▮▮ ★ ┌┐

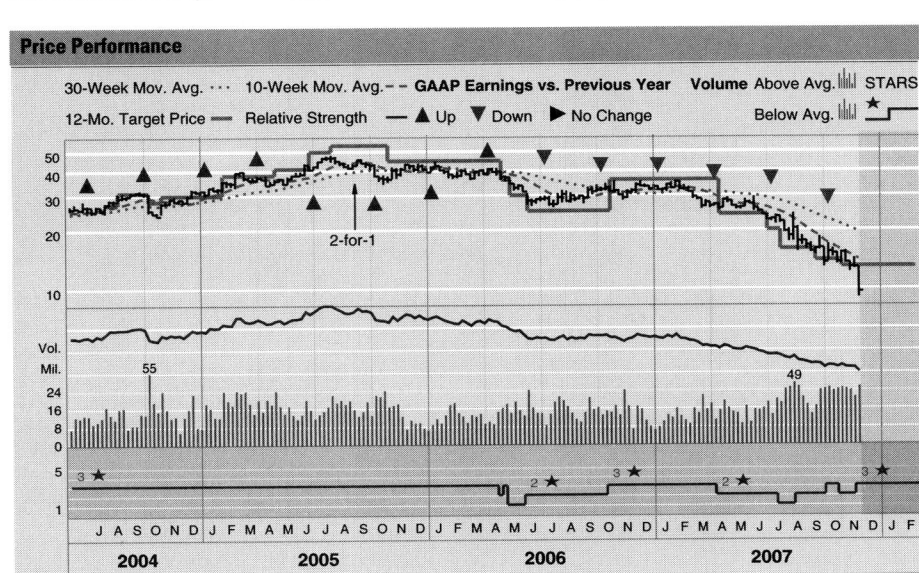

Options: ASE, CBOE, P, Ph

Analysis prepared by **Kenneth M. Leon, CPA** on November 21, 2007, when the stock traded at **$ 10.60**.

Highlights

➤ We forecast a 37% revenue decline in 2007 and a further 6% decrease in 2008, as a homebuilding industry slowdown plays out. Results for the third quarter show PHM's home closings down 28% from a year earlier, and a 4% drop in the average selling price per home, to $322,000. Also, net new orders decreased 37% in the third quarter, which we believe indicates a tough near-term outlook for sales.

➤ By our analysis, the gross margin should narrow in 2007 to the low single digit level, which is well below the 23% of the boom years of 2004 and 2005. We expect SG&A costs to rise as a percentage of sales, as we believe PHM is actively increasing sales incentives to close deals. We estimate that a 16% work force reduction announced May 30 will permit annual cost savings of around $200 million.

➤ We estimate a loss per share of $5.75 for 2007, including impairments and land-related charges of $3.33 a share in the third quarter, and we see a loss per share of $1.10 for 2008. We believe forward asset impairments will be lower than the $1.2 billion charges taken in the third quarter in 2007.

Investment Rationale/Risk

➤ We believe that the financial outlook for PHM and most of its homebuilding peers remains negative into 2008. On the plus side for PHM is its size, which carries many advantages, in our view, including access to capital and geographic diversity. In our opinion, asset impairment charges are likely for the next few quarters, but we expect them to be below the significant charge taken in the third quarter.

➤ Risks to our recommendation and target price include weakening in home demand, less availability of mortgage lending and future downward revaluations of PHM's land inventory. Asset impairment charges and contract cancellations may also be significantly higher in coming quarters.

➤ In our opinion, PHM's relatively large size in the industry should enable the company to weather the housing downturn. Our 12-month target price of $13 is derived by applying a target price-to-book multiple of just under 0.65X -- toward the low end of the historical range for PHM, but near other large homebuilder peers -- to our forward book value estimate of $20.

Qualitative Risk Assessment

LOW	MEDIUM	HIGH

Market conditions have worsened, especially in California and Florida, leading to a slower pace in completing communities. We believe PHM's cancellation rate of home closings will continue higher than its peers, especially with its intent to reduce sales incentives. The company is considering mothballing certain communities as well.

Quantitative Evaluations

S&P Quality Ranking   A+

D	C	B-	B	B+	A-	A	A+

Relative Strength Rank   WEAK

▮ 5

LOWEST = 1   HIGHEST = 99

Revenue/Earnings Data

Revenue (Million $)

	1Q	2Q	3Q	4Q	Year
2007	1,871	2,021	2,472	--	--
2006	2,963	3,359	3,564	4,389	14,274
2005	2,518	3,251	3,794	5,132	14,695
2004	2,032	2,515	2,960	4,205	11,711
2003	1,553	1,958	2,400	3,138	9,049
2002	1,379	1,686	1,860	2,548	7,472

Earnings Per Share ($)

2007	-0.34	-2.01	-3.12	E-0.28	E-5.75
2006	1.01	0.94	0.74	-0.03	2.67
2005	0.83	1.16	1.45	2.03	5.47
2004	0.51	0.73	1.00	1.60	3.84
2003	0.35	0.49	0.64	0.97	2.46
2002	0.28	0.36	0.46	0.70	1.80

Fiscal year ended Dec. 31. Next earnings report expected: Early February. EPS Estimates based on S&P Operating Earnings; historical GAAP earnings are as reported.

Dividend Data (Dates: mm/dd Payment Date: mm/dd/yy)

Amount ($)	Date Decl.	Ex-Div. Date	Stk. of Record	Payment Date
0.040	12/07	12/18	12/20	01/03/07
0.040	02/05	03/09	03/13	04/02/07
0.040	05/10	06/14	06/18	07/02/07
0.040	09/12	09/21	09/25	10/01/07

Dividends have been paid since 1977. Source: Company reports.

Pulte Homes Inc.

STANDARD &POOR'S

Business Summary November 21, 2007

CORPORATE OVERVIEW. Pulte Homes focuses on building single-family detached homes, which accounted for about 74% of unit volume in 2006, up slightly from 72% in 2005 but down from 86% in 2002. PHM's average price for U.S. homes sold in 2006 was $337,000, up from $315,000 in 2005 and considerably higher than the $242,000 figure for 2002, with about 70% of closings in 2006 ranging in price from $100,000 to $400,000. The company's operations are geographically diverse, with operations in 52 markets in 27 states at year-end 2006.

PHM targets buyers in nearly all home categories, but has recently concentrated its expansion efforts on affordable housing and on mature buyers (age 50 and over). In July 2001, it acquired Del Webb Corp., the leading U.S. builder of active adult communities, for a total of $1.9 billion in stock, cash, and the assumption of debt. Growth in this active adult segment and among first-time buyers, two groups that often prefer townhouses, condominiums or duplexes, helps to explain the decrease in single-family homes in PHM's product mix over the past five years.

CORPORATE STRATEGY. At December 31, 2006 and 2005, PHM controlled

about 232,223 and 362,615 lots, respectively, with the decrease reflecting an effort to bring land inventory in line with demand that was fading through 2006. Approximately 158,800 and 174,000 lots were owned, and around 63,700 and 133,400 lots were under option at December 31, 2006 and 2005, respectively. The total purchase price applicable to approved land under option approximated $3.9 billion at December 31, 2006. At that time, land option agreements -- which may be canceled at PHM's discretion, and are generally nonrefundable -- totaled $369.2 million.

To assist its home sales effort, PHM offers mortgage banking and title insurance services through Pulte Mortgage and other units mainly for the benefit of its domestic home buyers, but it also services the general public. In addition, it engages in the sale of loans and the related servicing rights. Mortgage underwriting, processing and closing functions are centralized in Denver, CO, and Charlotte, NC, using a mortgage operations center concept.

Company Financials Fiscal Year Ended Dec. 31

Per Share Data ($)	2006	2005	2004	2003	2002	2001	2000	1999	1998	1997
Tangible Book Value	23.82	21.49	15.95	12.13	9.41	7.64	7.51	6.32	5.34	4.78
Cash Flow	2.99	5.70	4.01	2.61	1.92	1.67	1.38	1.09	0.61	0.33
Earnings	2.67	5.47	3.84	2.46	1.80	1.50	1.30	1.02	0.58	0.29
S&P Core Earnings	2.59	5.46	3.82	2.45	1.76	1.43	NA	NA	NA	NA
Dividends	0.16	0.09	0.10	0.04	0.04	0.04	0.04	0.04	0.04	0.03
Payout Ratio	6%	2%	3%	2%	2%	3%	3%	4%	6%	11%
Prices:High	44.70	48.23	32.50	24.71	14.94	12.56	11.25	7.81	9.05	5.31
Prices:Low	26.02	30.01	20.00	11.36	9.05	6.53	3.81	4.19	4.98	3.41
P/E Ratio:High	17	9	8	10	8	8	9	8	16	19
P/E Ratio:Low	10	5	5	5	5	4	3	4	9	12

Income Statement Analysis (Million $)										
Revenue	14,274	14,695	11,711	9,049	7,472	5,382	4,159	3,730	2,867	2,524
Operating Income	2,678	244	1,587	997	746	601	429	350	222	135
Depreciation	83.7	62.0	46.3	40.2	29.8	32.9	14.2	13.5	5.04	7.81
Interest Expense	256	43.3	56.4	Nil	Nil	81.6	65.1	56.8	51.1	26.6
Pretax Income	1,083	2,277	1,601	996	729	492	355	286	166	81.0
Effective Tax Rate	36.3%	36.8%	37.6%	38.0%	39.0%	38.5%	38.5%	37.8%	39.0%	38.5%
Net Income	690	1,437	998	617	445	302	218	178	101	49.8
S&P Core Earnings	670	1,435	993	615	436	288	NA	NA	NA	NA

Balance Sheet & Other Financial Data (Million $)										
Cash	551	1,002	315	404	613	72.1	184	51.7	125	245
Current Assets	NA	NA	NA	NA	NA	NA	NA	NA	NA	NA
Total Assets	13,177	13,048	10,407	8,063	6,888	5,714	2,886	2,597	2,350	2,151
Current Liabilities	NA	NA	NA	NA	NA	NA	NA	NA	NA	NA
Long Term Debt	3,538	3,387	2,737	1,962	1,913	1,738	678	526	570	584
Common Equity	6,577	5,957	4,522	3,448	2,760	2,277	1,248	1,093	921	813
Total Capital	10,115	9,352	7,274	5,418	4,674	4,015	1,926	1,619	1,492	1,397
Capital Expenditures	98.6	88.9	75.2	39.1	NA	NA	NA	NA	NA	Nil
Cash Flow	773	1,499	1,044	657	474	335	233	192	106	57.6
Current Ratio	NA	NA	NA	NA	NA	NA	NA	NA	NA	NA
% Long Term Debt of Capitalization	35.0	36.2	37.6	36.2	40.9	43.3	35.2	32.5	38.2	41.8
% Net Income of Revenue	4.8	9.7	8.5	6.8	6.0	5.6	5.3	4.8	3.5	2.0
% Return on Assets	5.3	12.2	10.8	8.3	7.1	7.0	8.1	7.2	4.5	2.4
% Return on Equity	11.0	27.4	25.0	19.9	17.7	17.2	18.7	17.7	11.7	6.1

Data as orig reptd.; bef. results of disc opers/spec. items. Per share data adj. for stk. divs.; EPS diluted. E-Estimated. NA-Not Available. NM-Not Meaningful. NR-Not Ranked. UR-Under Review.

Office: 100 Bloomfield Hills Pkwy Ste 300, Bloomfield Hills, MI 48304-2950.
Telephone: 248-647-2750.
Website: http://www.pulte.com
Chrmn: W.J. Pulte

Pres & CEO: R.J. Dugas, Jr.
COO & EVP: S.C. Petruska
EVP & CFO: R.A. Cregg
VP & Treas: B.E. Robinson

Investor Contact: C. Boyd (248-647-2750)
Board Members: B. P. Anderson, D. K. Anderson, R. J. Dugas, Jr., D. Kelly-Ennis, D. N. McCammon, P. J. O'Leary, W. J. Pulte, B. W. Reznicek, A. E. Schwartz, F. J. Sehn, J. J. Shea, W. B. Smith

Founded: 1969
Domicile: Michigan
Employees: 12,400

The McGraw-Hill Companies

QLogic Corp

STANDARD &POOR'S

S&P Recommendation BUY ★★★★☆	**Price** $14.12 (as of Nov 23, 2007)	**12-Mo. Target Price** $17.00	**Investment Style** Large-Cap Growth

GICS Sector Information Technology
Sub-Industry Computer Storage & Peripherals

Summary This company designs and supplies semiconductor and board-level I/O (input/output) and enclosure management products.

Key Stock Statistics (Source S&P, Vickers, company reports)

52-Wk Range	$22.72–11.46	S&P Oper. EPS 2008E	0.71	Market Capitalization(B)	$1.933	Beta	2.65
Trailing 12-Month EPS	$0.62	S&P Oper. EPS 2009E	0.84	Yield (%)	Nil	S&P 3-Yr. Proj. EPS CAGR(%)	18.00
Trailing 12-Month P/E	22.8	P/E on S&P Oper. EPS 2008E	19.9	Dividend Rate/Share	Nil	S&P Credit Rating	NA
$10K Invested 5 Yrs Ago	$6,528	Common Shares Outstg. (M)	136.9	Institutional Ownership (%)	89		

Price Performance

30-Week Mov. Avg. · · · 10-Week Mov. Avg. - - **GAAP Earnings vs. Previous Year**   Volume Above Avg. ▦ STARS
12-Mo. Target Price — Relative Strength — ▲ Up ▼ Down ► No Change   Below Avg. ▥ ★

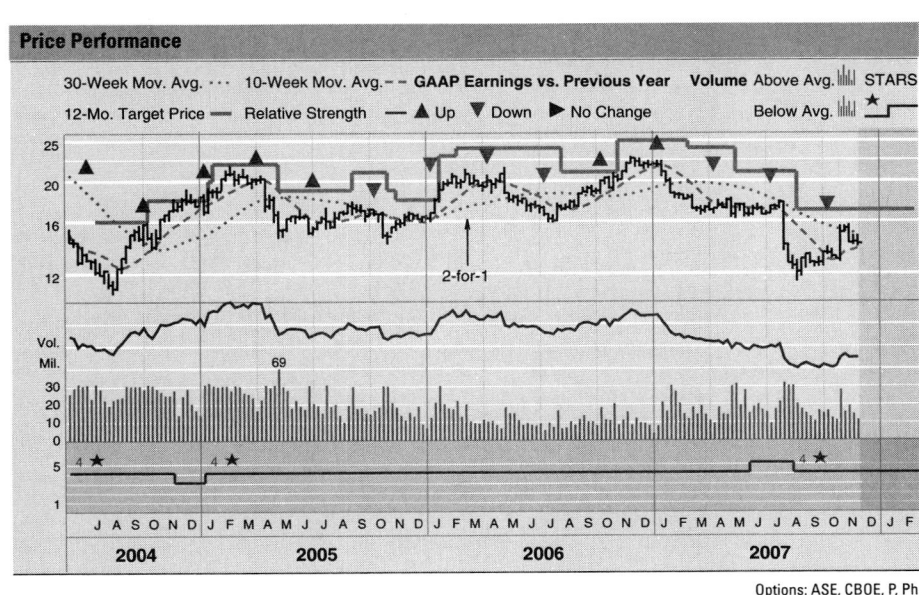

Options: ASE, CBOE, P, Ph

Analysis prepared by **Jawahar Hingorani** on November 12, 2007, when the stock traded at **$ 14.51**.

Highlights

➤ We expect a 1.2% revenue increase in FY 08 (Mar.), followed by a 15% rise in FY 09. We think QLGC continues to be a leader in the 4-Gbps space, but as the migration approaches maturity, we see its leadership position being challenged. We think new products like Infiniband will be a factor in 2008 and beyond. We believe the company has a strong balance sheet with over $3 per share in cash.

➤ We project that gross margins will remain around 67%, as higher volumes and manufacturing efficiencies are offset by a less favorable product mix. We believe declining blade server prices and a focus on the small and mid-size marketplace will drive revenue mix. We forecast that EPS will be aided by higher interest income and additional share repurchases, given that we anticipate continued positive free cash flow generation during FY 08.

➤ Our FY 08 operating EPS estimate is $0.71, a 7.6% increase from FY 07's operating EPS of $0.66. We estimate operating EPS of $0.84 in FY 09. EPS figures do not include acquisition and other one-time charges.

Investment Rationale/Risk

➤ We see challenges to QLGC's market leadership in the new upgrade cycle to 8Gb/s technology, and see Infiniband contributing to the revenue gap from the continued decline in Silicon products in 2008. We think share buybacks have somewhat benefited shareholders, but we would rather see investments in new strategic alternatives. We view QLGC's balance sheet as strong and as a positive, with over $3 per share in cash and no long-term debt.

➤ Risks to our recommendation and target price include a potential slowing of demand in storage networking and a greater than expected decline in average selling prices. Regarding corporate governance practices, we are concerned that the positions of chairman and CEO are held by the same individual.

➤ A blend of our P/E and discounted cash flow (DCF) based 12-month target price is $17. A P/E multiple of 24X our FY 08 EPS estimate of $0.71, a discount to the average P/E ratio for the S&P 500 Computer Storage & Peripherals sub-industry group, results in a price of $17. Our DCF analysis assumes a weighted average cost of capital of 11.5% and a terminal growth rate of 3%, also resulting in an intrinsic value of $17.

Qualitative Risk Assessment

LOW	MEDIUM	HIGH

Our risk assessment reflects the volatile nature of the data storage industry and the rapid pace of technological change. Offsetting these factors is our view of the company's significant market share and strong financial position.

Quantitative Evaluations

S&P Quality Ranking B+

D	C	B-	B	B+	A-	A	A+

Relative Strength Rank STRONG

77

LOWEST = 1   HIGHEST = 99

Revenue/Earnings Data

Revenue (Million $)

	1Q	2Q	3Q	4Q	Year
2008	139.8	140.3	--	--	--
2007	136.7	145.3	157.6	147.1	586.7
2006	158.8	119.0	129.2	130.5	494.1
2005	129.8	134.6	150.3	157.2	571.9
2004	126.2	132.3	137.1	128.3	523.9
2003	98.96	107.1	114.2	120.6	440.8

Earnings Per Share ($)

2008	0.12	0.16	E0.20	E0.23	E0.71
2007	0.13	0.19	0.22	0.12	0.66
2006	0.23	0.17	0.20	0.19	0.70
2005	0.17	0.19	0.23	0.25	0.84
2004	0.17	0.18	0.18	0.17	0.70
2003	0.12	0.12	0.15	0.16	0.55

Fiscal year ended Mar. 31. Next earnings report expected: Late January. EPS Estimates based on S&P Operating Earnings; historical GAAP earnings are as reported.

Dividend Data

No cash dividends have been paid.

QLogic Corp

Business Summary November 12, 2007

CORPORATE OVERVIEW. QLogic Corp. designs and develops storage networking infrastructure components sold to OEMs and distributors. QLGC produces host bus adapters (HBAs), fabric switches and management controller chips that provide the connectivity infrastructure for storage networks. The company serves customers with solutions based on various storage connectivity technologies, including Small Computer Systems Interface (SCSI), Internet SCSI (iSCSI), Fibre Channel and Infiniband.

International revenues accounted for 46% of net revenues in FY 07 (Mar.), up from 45% in FY 06. IBM, Hewlett-Packard and Sun Microsystems each accounted for over 10% of FY 07 sales. The 10 largest customers accounted for 80% of FY 07 revenues, up from 77% in FY 06. QLGC works closely with independent hardware and software vendors, as well as with developers and integrators who create, test and evaluate complementary storage networking products. Key alliance partners include Cisco Systems, Microsoft, and Symantec.

MARKET PROFILE. According to research firm IDC, growing server virtualization is driving an increase in storage area network (SAN) connectivity levels, more than offsetting moderating server growth rates through 2008. IDC pre-

dicts worldwide HBA port shipments will increase from 3.5 million to 5.2 million between 2007 and 2010, resulting in a compound annual growth rate (CAGR) of 23.2% for the 2005-2010 period. IDC expects single port and multi-port Fiber Channel (FC) HBA unit shipments to grow somewhat slower (a 2005-2010 CAGR of 18.1%), with 2010 shipments reaching 3.4 million. IDC estimated that worldwide external disk storage systems factory revenues in the third quarter of 2006 grew 9.9% from a year ago to $4.3 billion, marking 14 consecutive quarters of year-over-year growth. For the 2006 third quarter, the total disk storage systems market increased to $6.2 billion, up 7.9% from the prior year's quarter. For the first time, total disk storage systems capacity shipped was 783 petabytes, growing 50.2% from the year ago quarter. In 2005, IDC estimated shipped external SAN storage capacity at 660 petabytes (one petabyte is roughly equivalent to one billion books), an increase of 74% from 2004. Moreover, IDC projects that total capacity shipments will exceed 5,680 petabytes in 2009.

Company Financials Fiscal Year Ended Mar. 31

Per Share Data ($)	2007	2006	2005	2004	2003	2002	2001	2000	1999	1998
Tangible Book Value	4.61	5.10	5.19	4.61	4.00	3.33	2.84	1.64	1.06	1.71
Cash Flow	0.83	0.81	0.92	0.77	0.62	0.44	0.42	0.38	0.19	0.24
Earnings	0.66	0.70	0.84	0.70	0.55	0.37	0.36	0.35	0.17	0.10
S&P Core Earnings	0.70	0.49	0.67	0.52	0.35	0.22	0.16	NA	NA	NA
Dividends	Nil	Nil	Nil	Nil	Nil	Nil	Nil	Nil	Nil	Nil
Payout Ratio	Nil	Nil	Nil	Nil	Nil	Nil	Nil	Nil	Nil	Nil
Calendar Year	2006	2005	2004	2003	2002	2001	2000	1999	1998	1997
Prices:High	22.94	21.83	26.57	29.36	28.55	49.56	101.63	41.88	8.41	2.84
Prices:Low	15.86	14.10	10.72	16.07	9.83	8.60	19.84	5.81	1.50	1.16
P/E Ratio:High	35	31	32	42	52	NM	NM	NM	49	27
P/E Ratio:Low	24	20	13	23	18	NM	NM	NM	9	11

Income Statement Analysis (Million $)

	2007	2006	2005	2004	2003	2002	2001	2000	1999	1998
Revenue	587	494	572	524	441	344	358	203	117	81.4
Operating Income	169	196	240	214	157	99.5	132	78.8	36.7	20.9
Depreciation	27.6	17.9	15.6	14.8	14.7	13.0	10.8	4.80	3.37	2.43
Interest Expense	Nil	Nil	Nil	Nil	Nil	Nil	Nil	0.02	0.08	0.11
Pretax Income	155	200	242	216	159	106	117	81.7	38.9	21.8
Effective Tax Rate	31.9%	39.2%	35.0%	38.0%	35.0%	33.0%	41.2%	34.0%	34.0%	38.6%
Net Income	105	122	158	134	103	70.7	68.8	54.0	25.7	13.4
S&P Core Earnings	112	85.6	126	99.4	67.0	42.1	30.5	NA	NA	NA

Balance Sheet & Other Financial Data (Million $)

	2007	2006	2005	2004	2003	2002	2001	2000	1999	1998
Cash	544	125	166	157	138	76.1	128	64.1	43.2	64.1
Current Assets	697	819	940	854	748	587	490	177	131	108
Total Assets	971	938	1,026	929	817	670	571	267	173	136
Current Liabilities	94.5	78.4	68.8	60.8	66.7	51.0	47.8	24.2	20.2	17.6
Long Term Debt	Nil	Nil	Nil	Nil	Nil	Nil	Nil	Nil	Nil	0.14
Common Equity	875	859	956	868	751	619	524	243	153	118
Total Capital	877	859	958	868	751	619	524	243	153	118
Capital Expenditures	31.7	28.3	25.7	22.3	15.7	14.5	16.7	40.0	6.77	3.92
Cash Flow	133	140	173	149	118	83.7	79.6	58.8	29.1	15.8
Current Ratio	7.4	10.5	13.7	14.0	11.2	11.5	10.3	7.3	6.5	6.2
% Long Term Debt of Capitalization	Nil	Nil	Nil	Nil	Nil	Nil	Nil	Nil	Nil	0.1
% Net Income of Revenue	18.0	24.7	27.6	25.5	23.5	20.5	19.2	26.6	21.9	16.5
% Return on Assets	11.0	12.4	16.1	15.3	13.9	11.4	14.2	24.5	16.6	15.5
% Return on Equity	12.2	13.4	17.3	16.5	15.1	12.4	15.6	27.3	19.0	18.8

Data as orig reptd.; bef. results of disc opers/spec. items. Per share data adj. for stk. divs.; EPS diluted. E-Estimated. NA-Not Available. NM-Not Meaningful. NR-Not Ranked. UR-Under Review.

Office: 26650 Aliso Viejo Pkwy, Aliso Viejo, CA 92656-2674.
Telephone: 949-389-6000.
Website: http://www.qlogic.com
Chrmn & CEO: H.K. Desai

Investor Contact: A.J. Massetti (949-389-7533)
SVP & CFO: A.J. Massetti
VP, Secy & General Counsel: M.L. Hawkins

Auditor: KPMG
Board Members: J. S. Birnbaum, L. R. Carter, H. K. Desai, J. R. Fiebiger, B. S. Iyer, C. L. Miltner, G. D. Wells

Founded: 1992
Domicile: Delaware
Employees: 973

QUALCOMM Inc

STANDARD &POOR'S

S&P Recommendation	**HOLD** ★★★☆☆	Price $40.53 (as of Nov 23, 2007)	12-Mo. Target Price $40.00	Investment Style Large-Cap Growth

GICS Sector Information Technology
Sub-Industry Communications Equipment

Summary This company focuses on developing products and services based on its advanced wireless broadband technology.

Key Stock Statistics (Source S&P, Vickers, company reports)

52-Wk Range	$47.72–35.23	S&P Oper. EPS 2008**E**	1.70	Market Capitalization(B)	$66.327	Beta	1.73
Trailing 12-Month EPS	$1.95	S&P Oper. EPS 2009**E**	NA	Yield (%)	1.38	S&P 3-Yr. Proj. EPS CAGR(%)	10.00
Trailing 12-Month P/E	20.8	P/E on S&P Oper. EPS 2008**E**	23.8	Dividend Rate/Share	$0.56	S&P Credit Rating	NA
$10K Invested 5 Yrs Ago	$20,777	Common Shares Outstg. (M)	1,636.5	Institutional Ownership (%)	75		

Price Performance

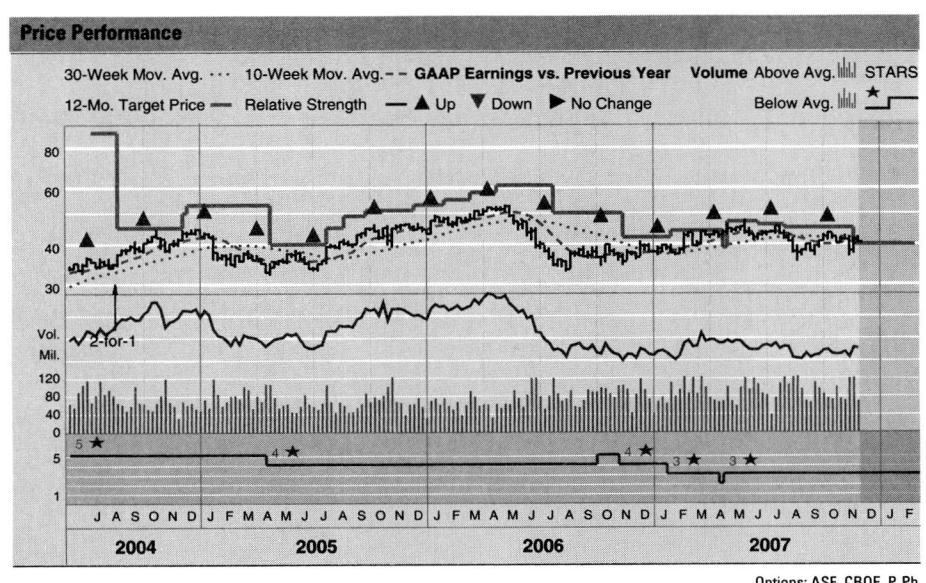

30-Week Mov. Avg. ··· 10-Week Mov. Avg. - - **GAAP Earnings vs. Previous Year** Volume Above Avg. STARS
12-Mo. Target Price — Relative Strength — ▲ Up ▼ Down ► No Change Below Avg.

Options: ASE, CBOE, P, Ph

Analysis prepared by **Todd Rosenbluth** on November 15, 2007, when the stock traded at **$ 40.68**.

Highlights

► A recent federal ruling banning certain chipsets from being imported into the U.S. may go into effect, creating uncertainty in the industry. We forecast 9% revenue growth in FY 08 (Sep.) revenues, following an 18% increase in FY 07, driven by chipset shipments in North America and Asia. We expect QCOM's licensing business to be weakened by the ending of its Nokia relationship in the fourth quarter of FY 07, which should limit overall revenue growth. We see emerging market growth pressuring selling prices.

► We believe QCOM will benefit as the CDMA handset market expands by an estimated 30% in FY 08, a similar pace to FY 07, as some top customers gain market share. However, the absence of industry leader Nokia should modestly pressure gross margins to 69% in FY 08, from 70% in FY 07.

► With an expected increase in R&D and costs to handle legal issues, we see net margins narrowing to 30% in FY 08, from 35% in FY 07. We estimate EPS of $1.70 for FY 08, with the inclusion of stock option expenses and strategic investment costs of $0.36 per share.

Investment Rationale/Risk

► We see continued revenue growth in FY 08, but the expected loss of Nokia as a customer and a possible U.S. ban on new QCOM-enabled handsets due to patent infringement creates operational risk and should limit earnings. We believe the fundamentals for QCOM's chipset business remain strong on sales of higher-priced 3G handsets in developed markets, and we see the license business, excluding Nokia, growing.

► Risks to our recommendation and target price include weaker demand in the replacement rate expected for more advanced CDMA handsets; lower selling prices for handsets in emerging markets; and prolonged legal risks related to QCOM's intellectual property rights.

► With its top customers reporting strong handset shipments during FY 07, we believe QCOM will realize increased CDMA chip orders and license fees from these companies. Applying a P/E of about 23.5X to our FY 08 EPS estimate--a premium to peers, reflecting QCOM's above-average margins--we arrive at our 12-month target price of $40.

Qualitative Risk Assessment

LOW	MEDIUM	HIGH

We believe QCOM's intellectual property rights and strong service provider relations give it a strong position in the industry. With our view of its healthy cash flow and no debt, we believe the company can support risks such as potentially weaker demand from customers and litigation risks related to its CDMA patents.

Quantitative Evaluations

S&P Quality Ranking B

D	C	B-	**B**	B+	A-	A	A+

Relative Strength Rank STRONG

74

LOWEST = 1 HIGHEST = 99

Revenue/Earnings Data

Revenue (Million $)

	1Q	2Q	3Q	4Q	Year
2007	2,019	2,221	2,325	2,306	8,871
2006	1,741	1,834	1,951	1,999	7,526
2005	1,390	1,365	1,358	1,560	5,673
2004	1,207	1,216	1,341	1,118	4,880
2003	1,097	1,043	921.6	908.8	3,971
2002	698.6	696.1	770.9	873.9	3,040

Earnings Per Share ($)

2007	0.38	0.43	0.47	0.67	1.95
2006	0.36	0.34	0.37	0.36	1.44
2005	0.30	0.31	0.33	0.32	1.26
2004	0.25	0.26	0.29	0.23	1.03
2003	0.15	0.07	0.12	0.18	0.51
2002	0.09	0.03	-0.01	0.12	0.22

Fiscal year ended Sep. 30. Next earnings report expected: Late January. EPS Estimates based on S&P Operating Earnings; historical GAAP earnings are as reported.

Dividend Data (Dates: mm/dd Payment Date: mm/dd/yy)

Amount ($)	Date Decl.	Ex-Div. Date	Stk. of Record	Payment Date
0.140	01/04	02/28	03/02	03/30/07
0.140	04/03	05/30	06/01	06/29/07
0.140	07/13	08/29	08/31	09/28/07
0.140	10/11	12/05	12/07	01/04/08

Dividends have been paid since 2003. Source: Company reports.

QUALCOMM Inc

Business Summary November 15, 2007

CORPORATE OVERVIEW. The company is organized by these operating segments: CDMA technology (QCT), technology licensing (QTL), wireless and Internet (QWI), and strategic initiatives (QSI). The QCT segment, which accounted for about 65% of total sales in FY 07 (Sep.), provides integrated circuits and system software solutions to top wireless handset and infrastructure manufacturers. QCOM uses a fabless business model, employing several independent semiconductor foundries to manufacture all of its semiconductor products. Approximately 68 million model station modem (MSM) integrated circuits were sold during the fourth quarter of FY 07, compared to approximately 56 million for the fourth quarter of FY 06.

The QTL business accounted for about 35% of total sales, with 84% operating margins. QCOM holds a number of patents related to CDMA, and derives royalties from licensing its technology. Royalties are paid when manufacturers earn revenue from the sale of CDMA-based equipment, including CDMA 2000 and WCDMA handsets made by Samsung, LG Electronics, Motorola, and others. QCOM expects 7% growth in CDMA 2000 handsets in 2008, but 56% growth in WCDMA handsets. Entry barriers are high, with QCOM's global franchise protected by legal patents.

QWI provides satellite based two-way data messaging and position reporting equipment to transportation companies. QWI includes the BREW product for software developers and interface device suppliers and OmniTRAC.

LEGAL/REGULATORY ISSUES. Qualcomm is involved in a number of legal issues involving patents on its chipsets and on competitor's chipsets. QCOM is involved in multiple disputes with Nokia, including litigation over Nokia's obligation to pay royalties for the use of certain of QCOM's patents. Without some license contract with QCOM, Nokia has opted to cancel its CDMA-related handset division. In the fourth quarter of FY 07, the loss of Nokia as a royalty customer negatively affected QCOM's EPS by $0.05. QCOM estimates that it will also result in a reduction in EPS of more than $0.25 in FY 08 as additional revenues would be lost. QCOM's complaint against Nokia in the International Trade Commission is expected to be completed in April 2008.

Company Financials Fiscal Year Ended Sep. 30

Per Share Data ($)	2007	2006	2005	2004	2003	2002	2001	2000	1999	1998
Tangible Book Value	8.82	7.37	6.43	5.69	4.54	2.77	2.82	3.14	2.22	0.83
Cash Flow	2.18	1.60	1.38	1.13	0.62	0.47	-0.14	0.57	0.28	0.21
Earnings	1.95	1.44	1.26	1.03	0.51	0.22	-0.36	0.43	0.16	0.09
S&P Core Earnings	1.86	1.40	1.03	0.83	0.74	0.34	-0.68	NA	NA	NA
Dividends	0.52	0.42	0.32	0.19	0.09	Nil	Nil	Nil	Nil	Nil
Payout Ratio	27%	29%	25%	18%	17%	Nil	Nil	Nil	Nil	Nil
Prices:High	NA	53.01	46.60	44.99	27.43	26.67	44.69	100.00	92.52	4.21
Prices:Low	NA	32.76	32.08	26.67	14.79	11.61	19.16	25.75	3.27	2.36
P/E Ratio:High	NA	37	37	44	54	NM	NM	NM	NM	46
P/E Ratio:Low	NA	23	25	26	29	NM	NM	NM	21	26

Income Statement Analysis (Million $)										
Revenue	8,871	7,526	5,673	4,880	3,971	3,040	2,680	3,197	3,937	3,348
Operating Income	3,266	2,962	2,586	2,266	1,684	1,068	877	1,105	564	385
Depreciation	383	272	200	163	180	394	320	244	158	142
Interest Expense	Nil	Nil	3.00	2.00	30.7	25.7	10.2	4.92	14.7	8.06
Pretax Income	3,626	3,156	2,809	2,313	1,285	461	-426	1,197	307	197
Effective Tax Rate	8.90%	21.7%	23.7%	25.4%	35.6%	22.0%	NM	44.0%	34.5%	20.4%
Net Income	3,303	2,470	2,143	1,725	827	360	-531	670	201	109
S&P Core Earnings	3,148	2,397	1,733	1,395	610	274	-512	NA	NA	NA

Balance Sheet & Other Financial Data (Million $)										
Cash	6,581	5,721	6,548	5,982	4,561	2,795	2,283	1,772	660	176
Current Assets	8,821	7,049	7,791	7,227	5,949	3,941	3,055	2,730	2,978	1,537
Total Assets	18,495	15,208	12,479	10,820	8,822	6,510	5,747	6,063	4,535	2,567
Current Liabilities	2,258	1,422	1,070	894	808	675	521	472	876	882
Long Term Debt	Nil	Nil	Nil	Nil	123	94.3	Nil	Nil	660	664
Common Equity	15,835	13,406	11,119	9,664	7,599	5,392	4,890	5,516	2,872	958
Total Capital	15,835	13,406	11,119	9,664	7,722	5,530	4,896	5,563	3,584	1,661
Capital Expenditures	818	685	576	332	231	142	114	163	180	322
Cash Flow	3,686	2,742	2,343	1,888	1,007	754	-211	914	359	250
Current Ratio	3.9	5.0	7.3	8.1	7.4	5.8	5.9	5.8	3.4	1.7
% Long Term Debt of Capitalization	Nil	Nil	Nil	Nil	1.6	1.7	Nil	Nil	18.4	39.9
% Net Income of Revenue	37.2	32.8	37.8	35.3	20.8	11.8	NM	21.0	5.1	3.2
% Return on Assets	19.6	17.8	18.4	17.6	10.8	5.9	NM	12.6	5.7	4.5
% Return on Equity	22.5	20.1	20.6	20.0	12.7	7.1	NM	16.0	10.5	11.0

Data as orig reptd.; bef. results of disc opers/spec. items. Per share data adj. for stk. divs.; EPS diluted. E-Estimated. NA-Not Available. NM-Not Meaningful. NR-Not Ranked. UR-Under Review.

Office: 5775 Morehouse Drive, San Diego, CA 92121-1714.
Telephone: 858-587-1121.
Email: ir@qualcomm.com
Website: http://www.qualcomm.com

Chrmn: I.M. Jacobs
Pres: S.R. Altman
CEO: P.E. Jacobs
COO & EVP: S.K. Jha

EVP & CFO: W.E. Keitel
Investor Contact: J. Gilbert (858-658-4813)
Board Members: B. T. Alexander, D. Cruickshank, R. V. Dittamore, I. M. Jacobs, P. E. Jacobs, R. E. Kahn, S. Lansing, D. A. Nelles, P. M. Sacerdote, B. Scowcroft, M. I. Stern

Founded: 1985
Domicile: Delaware
Employees: 12,800

Questar Corp

STANDARD &POOR'S

S&P Recommendation	HOLD ★★★☆☆	Price $54.86 (as of Nov 23, 2007)	12-Mo. Target Price $61.00	Investment Style Large-Cap Growth

GICS Sector Utilities
Sub-Industry Gas Utilities

Summary This integrated natural gas holding company is engaged in gas and oil exploration, energy marketing, gas gathering, transportation and storage, and retail gas distribution.

Key Stock Statistics (Source S&P, Vickers, company reports)

52-Wk Range	$58.75– 37.98	S&P Oper. EPS 2007E	2.77	Market Capitalization(B)	$9.471	Beta	0.34
Trailing 12-Month EPS	$2.84	S&P Oper. EPS 2008E	3.03	Yield (%)	0.89	S&P 3-Yr. Proj. EPS CAGR(%)	10.00
Trailing 12-Month P/E	19.3	P/E on S&P Oper. EPS 2007E	19.8	Dividend Rate/Share	$0.49	S&P Credit Rating	NR
$10K Invested 5 Yrs Ago	$45,985	Common Shares Outstg. (M)	172.6	Institutional Ownership (%)	77		

Price Performance

30-Week Mov. Avg. · · · 10-Week Mov. Avg. - - GAAP Earnings vs. Previous Year Volume Above Avg. STARS
12-Mo. Target Price — Relative Strength — ▲ Up ▼ Down ► No Change Below Avg.

Options: ASE, CBOE, Ph

Analysis prepared by **Christopher B. Muir** on November 06, 2007, when the stock traded at **$ 56.56**.

Highlights

► We forecast that revenues will fall about 5% in 2007 on lower oil and natural gas liquids prices, offset by continued growth at the exploration and production (E&P) and pipeline segments. We expect STR's E&P segment to benefit from higher volumes. Our pipeline growth estimate reflects our expectations for continued strong growth in contract transportation as well as higher natural gas liquids volumes. We see 2008 revenue growth of 7%, helped by higher realized gas and oil prices.

► We project a 2007 operating margin of 30.0%, versus 26.2% in 2006. We see STR benefiting from improved gross margins, partly offset by higher per-revenue non-fuel operating expenses. We see a 2008 operating margin of 31.1%, helped by improved per-revenue non-fuel expense ratios. We see 2008 and 2007 pretax profit margins rising to 29.4% and 28.7%, from 24.3%, as we expect interest expense to be mostly unchanged from 2006.

► Assuming an effective tax rate of 36.7% and small share increases, we project operating EPS of $2.77 in 2007, up 11% from 2006's $2.50. Our 2008 EPS forecast is $3.03, an additional increase of 9.4%.

Investment Rationale/Risk

► STR has posted steady production gains through an aggressive drilling program at its Rockies and Midcontinent assets. In 2006, production grew 13%, to 129.6 billion cubic feet equivalent (Bcfe), and we expect approximately 5% growth in 2007. Strong drilling activity by other companies in these regions should drive growth at STR's gas gathering and processing operations. Gas gathering volumes rose about 7% in 2006, while fee-based processing volumes increased 59%. We like STR's strong hedging program, which we believe will significantly reduce its 2007 and 2008 exposure to oil and gas price changes.

► Risks to our recommendation and target price include a prolonged drop in natural gas and oil prices, unusually mild winter weather, weaker than expected economic growth, and sharply higher interest rates.

► The stock recently traded at about 18.6X our 2008 EPS estimate, a 14% premium to its peers. Our 12-month target price of $61 is 20.1X our 2008 EPS estimate, or a 15% premium to our peer target. We think the premium is justified given our view of its EPS growth potential and lower risk operations.

Qualitative Risk Assessment

LOW	MEDIUM	HIGH

Our risk assessment is based on our view that the company's higher risk exploration and production and energy marketing operations are balanced by its lower-risk regulated gas transmission and distribution businesses.

Quantitative Evaluations

S&P Quality Ranking A

D	C	B-	B	B+	A-	A	A+

Relative Strength Rank STRONG

87

LOWEST = 1   HIGHEST = 99

Revenue/Earnings Data

Revenue (Million $)

	1Q	2Q	3Q	4Q	Year
2007	872.1	556.7	497.4	--	--
2006	911.4	596.2	555.1	772.9	2,836
2005	680.3	520.2	582.9	941.5	2,725
2004	563.6	369.5	360.2	608.1	1,901
2003	469.8	270.7	273.5	449.2	1,463
2002	402.5	224.6	190.7	382.9	1,201

Earnings Per Share ($)

2007	0.86	0.64	0.64	E0.63	E2.77
2006	0.79	0.52	0.54	0.70	2.54
2005	0.55	0.35	0.38	0.60	1.87
2004	0.45	0.25	0.22	0.43	1.34
2003	0.42	0.12	0.17	0.36	1.07
2002	0.31	0.18	0.14	0.41	1.04

Fiscal year ended Dec. 31. Next earnings report expected: Mid February. EPS Estimates based on S&P Operating Earnings; historical GAAP earnings are as reported.

Dividend Data (Dates: mm/dd Payment Date: mm/dd/yy)

Amount ($)	Date Decl.	Ex-Div. Date	Stk. of Record	Payment Date
0.245	05/14	05/23	05/25	06/11/07
2-for-1	05/14	06/19	06/04	06/18/07
0.123	08/07	08/15	08/17	09/10/07
0.123	10/23	11/14	11/16	12/10/07

Dividends have been paid since 1935. Source: Company reports.

Please read the Required Disclosures and Analyst Certification on the last page of this report.

The **McGraw-Hill** Companies

Questar Corp

STANDARD &POOR'S

Business Summary November 06, 2007

CORPORATE OVERVIEW. Questar Corp. (STR) is a natural gas energy entity operating three divisions: Questar Market Resources (QMR), Questar Gas Company (QGC), and Questar Pipeline Company (QPC). QMR, which is engaged in natural gas and oil exploration and production (E&P), energy marketing, gas gathering and processing services, contributed 80% of net income in 2006; QGC, which distributes natural gas as a public utility in Utah, southwestern Wyoming and a small portion of southeastern Idaho, contributed 8%; and QPC, an interstate pipeline company that provides natural gas transportation and underground storage services in Utah, Wyoming and Colorado, contributed 10%.

CORPORATE STRATEGY. STR's integrated model spans the entire natural gas value chain. The unregulated QMR businesses are the primary growth drivers for STR. The company believes these businesses -- which include E&P, gas gathering, and processing services -- have the potential to offer higher returns than the regulated utility and pipeline operations. STR expects the share of unconventional reservoirs to total natural gas production to increase to 50% in the next decade, from the current 10%. STR's properties in the Rockies

are expected to be a major contributor to this growth. The utility and pipeline operations are less sensitive to commodity prices and help fund dividend payouts.

MARKET PROFILE. QMR operates E&P properties, primarily natural gas, in the Rockies region of Wyoming, Utah and Colorado, and the Midcontinent region of Oklahoma, Texas and Louisiana. It has reported an estimated 1,631 Bcfe of proved reserves, with 81% of the proved reserves in the Rockies and the remainder in the Midcontinent region. As of 2006, QMR had developed 61% of the proved reserves, with most of the undeveloped reserves in the Pinedale Anticline property. Wexpro, a division of QMR, develops certain properties owned by QGC, and had proved reserves of 647 Bcfe as of year-end 2006. Wexpro charges the utility for costs plus a specified return, which averaged 19.9% (after tax) during 2006.

Company Financials Fiscal Year Ended Dec. 31

Per Share Data ($)	2006	2005	2004	2003	2002	2001	2000	1999	1998	1997
Tangible Book Value	12.43	8.60	8.03	7.06	6.41	6.07	6.01	5.69	5.31	5.08
Cash Flow	4.34	3.34	2.66	3.41	2.21	1.90	1.85	1.43	1.43	1.38
Earnings	2.54	1.87	1.34	1.07	1.04	0.97	0.97	0.60	0.47	0.63
S&P Core Earnings	2.49	1.88	1.37	1.08	0.77	0.82	NA	NA	NA	NA
Dividends	0.47	0.45	0.43	0.39	0.36	0.35	0.34	0.34	0.33	0.31
Payout Ratio	18%	24%	32%	37%	35%	36%	35%	56%	70%	49%
Prices:High	45.51	44.80	26.06	17.75	14.73	16.88	15.94	9.97	11.19	11.19
Prices:Low	33.69	23.37	16.91	13.02	9.01	9.29	6.78	7.38	7.91	8.56
P/E Ratio:High	18	24	20	17	14	17	16	17	24	18
P/E Ratio:Low	13	12	13	12	9	10	7	12	17	14

Income Statement Analysis (Million $)										
Revenue	2,836	2,725	1,901	1,463	1,201	1,439	1,266	924	906	933
Operating Income	1,156	841	646	557	524	482	453	180	133	170
Depreciation	316	256	226	394	194	152	142	138	159	124
Interest Expense	73.6	69.3	68.4	70.7	81.1	64.8	63.5	53.9	48.0	43.8
Pretax Income	700	514	359	282	262	246	242	147	106	150
Effective Tax Rate	36.5%	36.6%	36.1%	36.4%	34.8%	35.8%	35.3%	32.6%	27.4%	30.3%
Net Income	444	326	229	179	171	158	157	98.8	76.9	105
S&P Core Earnings	438	327	234	182	125	132	NA	NA	NA	NA

Balance Sheet & Other Financial Data (Million $)										
Cash	24.6	13.4	3.68	13.9	21.6	11.3	14.8	45.0	17.5	17.3
Current Assets	753	756	480	345	280	344	427	239	247	285
Total Assets	5,065	4,357	3,647	3,309	3,068	3,236	2,539	2,238	2,161	1,945
Current Liabilities	679	874	544	483	301	781	535	324	437	306
Long Term Debt	1,022	983	933	950	1,145	997	715	735	616	542
Common Equity	2,206	1,550	1,440	1,261	1,139	1,081	991	926	878	846
Total Capital	3,992	3,157	2,906	2,666	2,676	2,422	1,971	1,878	1,697	1,609
Capital Expenditures	910	716	442	335	358	871	314	268	461	200
Cash Flow	760	581	455	573	365	310	299	237	236	229
Current Ratio	1.1	0.9	0.9	0.7	0.9	0.4	0.8	0.7	0.6	0.9
% Long Term Debt of Capitalization	25.6	31.1	32.1	35.6	42.8	41.2	36.3	39.1	36.3	33.7
% Net Income of Revenue	15.7	12.0	12.1	12.2	14.2	11.0	12.4	10.7	8.5	11.2
% Return on Assets	9.4	8.1	6.6	5.6	5.4	5.5	6.6	4.5	3.7	5.6
% Return on Equity	23.7	21.8	17.0	14.9	15.4	15.6	16.4	11.0	8.9	12.9

Data as orig reptd.; bef. results of disc opers/spec. items. Per share data adj. for stk. divs.; EPS diluted. E-Estimated. NA-Not Available. NM-Not Meaningful. NR-Not Ranked. UR-Under Review.

Office: 180 East 100th Street, Salt Lake City, UT 84139-1500.
Telephone: 801-324-5000.
Website: http://www.questar.com
Chrmn, Pres & CEO: K.O. Rattie

SVP & CFO: S.E. Parks
VP & Secy: A. Jones
VP & General Counsel: T.C. Jepperson
Investor Contact: M. Craven (801-324-5077)

Board Members: P. S. Baker, Jr., T. Beck, R. D. Cash, L. R. Flury, J. A. Harmon, R. E. McKee, III, G. G. Michael, K. O. Rattie, M. W. Scoggins, H. H. Simmons, C. B. Stanley, B. A. Williamson
Founded: 1935
Domicile: Utah
Employees: 2,188

The McGraw-Hill Companies

Quest Diagnostics Inc

STANDARD & POOR'S

S&P Recommendation BUY ★★★★☆	**Price** $53.92 (as of Nov 23, 2007)	**12-Mo. Target Price** $66.00	**Investment Style** Large-Cap Growth

GICS Sector Health Care
Sub-Industry Health Care Services

Summary This company provides diagnostic testing, information and services to physicians, hospitals, managed care organizations, employers and government agencies.

Key Stock Statistics (Source S&P, Vickers, company reports)

52-Wk Range	**$58.63– 47.98**	S&P Oper. EPS 2007**E**	**2.88**	Market Capitalization(B)	**$10.406**
Trailing 12-Month EPS	**$2.53**	S&P Oper. EPS 2008**E**	**3.34**	Yield (%)	**0.74**
Trailing 12-Month P/E	**21.3**	P/E on S&P Oper. EPS 2007**E**	**18.7**	Dividend Rate/Share	**$0.40**
$10K Invested 5 Yrs Ago	**$19,738**	Common Shares Outstg. (M)	**193.0**	Institutional Ownership (%)	**74**

Beta	**0.03**
S&P 3-Yr. Proj. EPS CAGR(%)	**13.00**
S&P Credit Rating	**BBB+**

Price Performance

30-Week Mov. Avg. ··· 10-Week Mov. Avg. - - **GAAP Earnings vs. Previous Year** Volume Above Avg. STARS
12-Mo. Target Price — Relative Strength — ▲ Up ▼ Down ▶ No Change Below Avg.

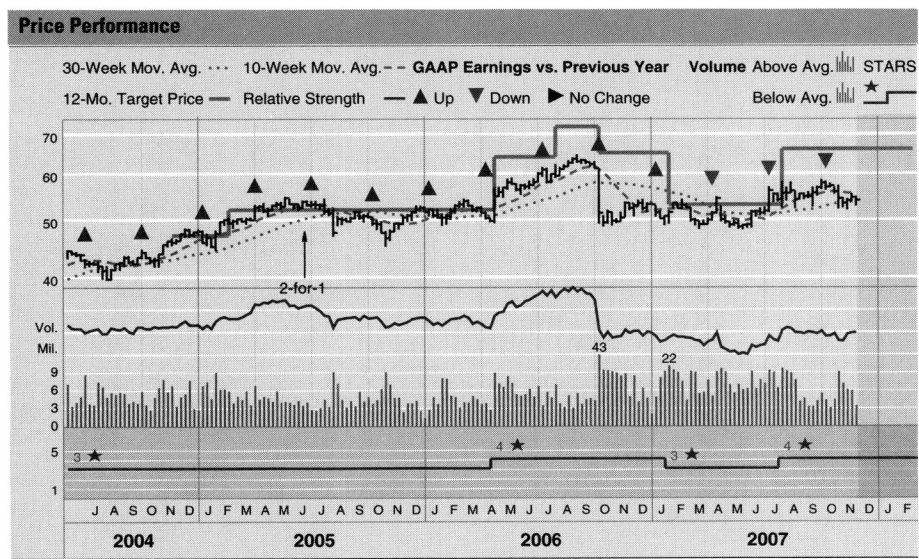

Options: ASE, CBOE, Ph

Analysis prepared by **Jeffrey Loo, CFA** on November 14, 2007, when the stock traded at **$ 54.80**.

Highlights

➤ We see 2007 sales increasing 6%, to $6.64 billion, and 2008 sales rising 10%, to $7.32 billion, on mid-single digit organic growth and contributions from the May acquisition of AmeriPath. We think AmeriPath and the five-year exclusive Aetna contract should more than offset the loss of the UnitedHealthcare (UNH) contract, which accounted for 7% of 2006 sales. But AmeriPath had lower margins, and we believe DGX priced the Aetna contract aggressively, limiting margin expansion. We see 2007 operating margins declining 90 basis points due to integrating the AmeriPath business, but expect a 60 basis point rebound in 2008, aided by aggressive cost cutting.

➤ DGX acquired AmeriPath for $2 billion in a deal financed with debt, significantly increasing interest costs. We do not expect DGX to pursue additional acquisitions over the next year due to its leverage, and as we believe it intends to pay down debt.

➤ Since May 2003, DGX repurchased 43.4 million shares, aiding EPS. However, with the large increase in debt, we see DGX limiting buybacks until some debt is paid down. Our 2007 and 2008 EPS forecasts are $2.88 and $3.34, respectively.

Investment Rationale/Risk

➤ We see better pricing stability, as we believe the majority of its managed care contracts have been signed, and we do not expect any additional exclusive national contracts, thereby alleviating, in our view, a major catalyst for pricing pressure. However, we note that managed care provider Humana recently requested lab proposals. We see some challenges for DGX, and we have a neutral view on the AmeriPath deal as we do not see material cost-saving synergies or margin expansion. We note that AmeriPath has bad debt expense of about 14%, but we see improvement in 2008. We view the five-year contract with Aetna as only slightly positive, as we believe DGX provided very favorable terms but the national exclusivity may limit losses from potential physician lab consolidation from the lost UNH contract.

➤ Risks to our recommendation and target price include the loss of more contracts and greater pricing pressure from third-party payers.

➤ Our 12-month target price of $66 is based a P/E to growth ratio of 1.5X, applied to our 2008 EPS estimate and assuming a three-year EPS growth rate of 13%, in line with peers.

Qualitative Risk Assessment

LOW	MEDIUM	HIGH

Our risk assessment reflects our view of DGX's leadership position in this large, mature industry; the company's broad geographic service area; its diverse and balanced payer mix; and the growing recognition of the importance and significance of diagnostic testing.

Quantitative Evaluations

S&P Quality Ranking **B**

D	C	B-	**B**	B+	A-	A	A+

Relative Strength Rank **MODERATE**

70

LOWEST = 1 HIGHEST = 99

Revenue/Earnings Data

Revenue (Million $)

	1Q	2Q	3Q	4Q	Year
2007	1,526	1,641	1,767	--	--
2006	1,553	1,583	1,583	1,549	6,269
2005	1,319	1,378	1,372	1,435	5,504
2004	1,256	1,298	1,290	1,283	5,127
2003	1,093	1,220	1,221	1,204	4,738
2002	946.8	1,069	1,059	1,034	4,108

Earnings Per Share ($)

2007	0.55	0.73	0.77	E0.79	E2.88
2006	0.77	0.78	0.82	0.77	3.14
2005	0.64	0.72	0.66	0.64	2.66
2004	0.54	0.59	0.62	0.60	2.35
2003	0.43	0.56	0.56	0.51	2.06
2002	0.34	0.44	0.44	0.41	1.62

Fiscal year ended Dec. 31. Next earnings report expected: Late January. EPS Estimates based on S&P Operating Earnings; historical GAAP earnings are as reported.

Dividend Data (Dates: mm/dd Payment Date: mm/dd/yy)

Amount ($)	Date Decl.	Ex-Div. Date	Stk. of Record	Payment Date
0.100	12/14	01/08	01/10	01/24/07
0.100	02/13	04/02	04/04	04/18/07
0.100	05/08	07/02	07/05	07/18/07
0.100	08/17	10/01	10/03	10/17/07

Dividends have been paid since 2004. Source: Company reports.

Please read the Required Disclosures and Analyst Certification on the last page of this report.

The McGraw-Hill Companies

Quest Diagnostics Inc

STANDARD
&POOR'S

Business Summary November 14, 2007

CORPORATE OVERVIEW. Quest Diagnostics is the largest independent U.S. clinical lab provider. The clinical laboratory market is estimated to be about a $40 billion market, with hospital-based labs accounting for about 60% of the market, independent commercial labs, such as DGX, accounting for 33%, and physician-office labs the rest. DGX offers a broad range of clinical laboratory testing services used by physicians in the detection, diagnosis, and treatment of diseases and other medical conditions. Tests range from routine (such as blood cholesterol tests) to highly complex esoteric (such as gene-based testing and molecular diagnostics testing). At the end of 2006, DGX had a network of 35 principal laboratories throughout the U.S., 150 smaller "rapid response" (STAT) laboratories, and over 2,100 patient service centers, along with facilities in Mexico, Puerto Rico, and England. DGX also operates two esoteric testing laboratories and has R&D facilities at its Nichols Institute unit.

The company processes more than 151 million requisitions (order forms completed by physicians indicating tests to be performed) annually. Routine testing generated 75% of net sales in 2006 (78% in 2005), esoteric testing 17% (17% in 2005), clinical trials and risk assessment services from recently acquired LabOne (acquired in November 2005) 8% (3%). Routine tests measure important health parameters such as the function of the kidney, heart, liver, thyroid and other organs. Esoteric tests are performed less frequently than routine tests, and/or require more sophisticated equipment and materials, professional hands-on attention, and more highly skilled personnel. As a result, they are generally priced substantially higher than routine tests.

Company Financials Fiscal Year Ended Dec. 31

Per Share Data ($)	2006	2005	2004	2003	2002	2001	2000	1999	1998	1997
Tangible Book Value	NM	NM	NM	NM	NM	NM	NM	NM	0.60	0.23
Cash Flow	4.24	3.51	3.12	2.79	2.31	1.70	1.27	0.64	0.79	0.45
Earnings	3.14	2.66	2.35	2.06	1.62	0.94	0.56	-0.01	0.22	-0.19
S&P Core Earnings	3.17	2.57	2.13	1.80	1.42	0.83	NA	NA	NA	NA
Dividends	0.39	0.26	0.30	Nil	Nil	Nil	Nil	Nil	Nil	Nil
Payout Ratio	12%	10%	13%	Nil	Nil	Nil	Nil	Nil	Nil	Nil
Prices:High	64.69	54.80	48.41	37.50	48.07	37.88	36.56	8.23	5.77	5.22
Prices:Low	48.59	44.32	35.94	23.68	24.55	18.30	7.28	4.44	3.63	3.56
P/E Ratio:High	21	21	21	18	30	40	66	NM	26	NM
P/E Ratio:Low	15	17	15	11	15	19	13	NM	16	NM

Income Statement Analysis (Million $)	2006	2005	2004	2003	2002	2001	2000	1999	1998	1997
Revenue	6,269	5,504	5,127	4,738	4,108	3,628	3,421	2,205	1,459	1,529
Operating Income	1,325	1,144	1,060	950	724	559	452	243	163	151
Depreciation	197	176	169	154	131	148	134	90.8	68.8	76.4
Interest Expense	96.5	61.4	57.9	59.8	53.7	70.5	120	69.8	44.0	46.0
Pretax Income	1,057	930	854	755	557	343	210	19.8	53.9	-19.1
Effective Tax Rate	38.6%	39.2%	39.3%	39.9%	39.5%	43.4%	45.7%	NM	50.1%	NM
Net Income	626	546	499	437	322	184	105	-1.27	26.9	-22.3
S&P Core Earnings	632	531	456	377	279	162	NA	NA	NA	NA

Balance Sheet & Other Financial Data (Million $)	2006	2005	2004	2003	2002	2001	2000	1999	1998	1997
Cash	150	92.1	73.3	155	96.8	122	171	27.3	203	162
Current Assets	1,191	1,069	931	996	824	877	981	873	578	572
Total Assets	5,661	5,306	4,204	4,301	3,324	2,931	2,865	2,878	1,360	1,401
Current Liabilities	1,151	1,101	1,044	724	636	659	955	701	309	295
Long Term Debt	1,239	1,255	724	1,029	797	820	761	1,171	413	482
Common Equity	3,019	2,763	2,289	2,397	1,769	1,336	1,031	862	567	541
Total Capital	4,258	4,018	3,013	3,426	2,565	2,156	1,793	2,046	2,034	1,024
Capital Expenditures	193	224	176	175	155	149	116	76.0	39.6	30.8
Cash Flow	823	722	668	591	454	332	239	89.6	95.7	54.1
Current Ratio	1.0	1.0	0.9	1.4	1.3	1.3	1.0	1.2	1.9	1.9
% Long Term Debt of Capitalization	29.1	31.2	24.0	30.0	31.0	38.0	42.4	57.6	42.1	47.1
% Net Income of Revenue	10.0	9.9	9.7	9.2	7.8	5.1	3.1	NM	1.8	NM
% Return on Assets	11.4	11.5	11.7	11.5	10.3	6.3	3.7	NM	1.9	NM
% Return on Equity	21.6	21.6	21.3	20.9	20.8	15.5	11.1	NM	4.9	NM

Data as orig reptd.; bef. results of disc opers/spec. items. Per share data adj. for stk. divs.; EPS diluted. E-Estimated. NA-Not Available. NM-Not Meaningful. NR-Not Ranked. UR-Under Review.

Office: 1290 Wall St W, Lyndhurst, NJ 07071-3683.
Telephone: 201-393-5000.
Email: investor@questdiagnostics.com
Website: http://www.questdiagnostics.com

Chrmn, Pres & CEO: S.N. Mohapatra
SVP & CFO: R.A. Hagemann
SVP & General Counsel: M.E. Prevoznik
VP, Chief Acctg Officer & Cntlr: T.F. Bongiomo

Investor Contact: L. Park (201-393-5030)
Board Members: J. C. Baldwin, J. K. Britell, W. F. Buehler, W. R. Grant, R. Haggerty, S. N. Mohapatra, G. M. Pfeiffer, D. C. Stanzione, G. R. Wilensky, J. B. Ziegler

Founded: 1967
Domicile: Delaware
Employees: 41,000

The McGraw-Hill Companies

Qwest Communications International Inc.

STANDARD &POOR'S

S&P Recommendation **HOLD** ★★★☆☆	Price $6.58 (as of Nov 23, 2007)	12-Mo. Target Price $7.00	Investment Style Large-Cap Blend

GICS Sector Telecommunication Services
Sub-Industry Integrated Telecommunication Services

Summary This company provides wireline and wireless services, primarily serving customers in 14 western and midwestern U.S. states.

Key Stock Statistics (Source S&P, Vickers, company reports)

52-Wk Range	$10.45– 6.23	S&P Oper. EPS 2007E	0.53	Market Capitalization(B)	$12.084	Beta	2.50
Trailing 12-Month EPS	$1.41	S&P Oper. EPS 2008E	0.55	Yield (%)	Nil	S&P 3-Yr. Proj. EPS CAGR(%)	6.00
Trailing 12-Month P/E	4.7	P/E on S&P Oper. EPS 2007E	12.4	Dividend Rate/Share	Nil	S&P Credit Rating	BB
$10K Invested 5 Yrs Ago	$14,242	Common Shares Outstg. (M)	1,836.4	Institutional Ownership (%)	97		

Price Performance

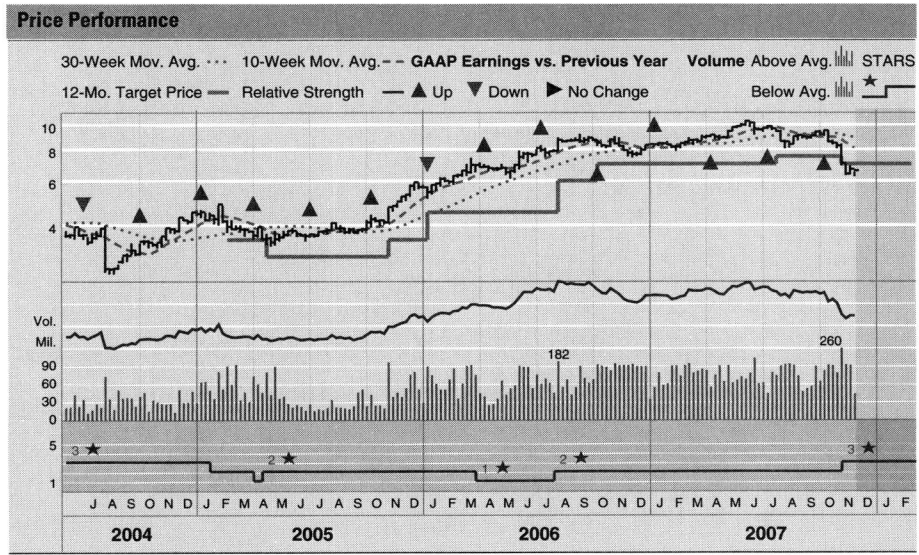

30-Week Mov. Avg. · · · 10-Week Mov. Avg. ─ ─ **GAAP Earnings vs. Previous Year**   **Volume** Above Avg. ⊪⊪ STARS
12-Mo. Target Price ─ Relative Strength ─ ▲ Up ▼ Down ▶ No Change   Below Avg. ⊪⊪ ✦

Options: ASE, CBOE, P, Ph

Analysis prepared by **Todd Rosenbluth** on November 06, 2007, when the stock traded at **$ 6.73**.

Highlights

➤ Following an expected 1% decline in revenues in 2007, we see fractional growth in 2008. We forecast pressure on voice services from access line losses, due to competition and slowing housing sales, and from wholesale weakness amid carrier customer consolidation. However, we expect data services growth from broadband additions, and we project gains in the enterprise segment from new contracts.

➤ We look for EBITDA margins to expand to 34% in 2008, from a projected 33% in 2007 and 31% in 2006. We believe 2007 margins are being helped as lower pension and facility costs are outweighing the effects of expanded lower margin services. We believe future savings will be more difficult, as we forecast a more aggressive broadband strategy in 2008. After lower depreciation charges in 2007, we see stability in 2008 on increased capital spending.

➤ We estimate operating EPS of $0.53 in 2007, and we see $0.55 in 2008, including our estimate of a $0.20 tax credit. The impact of modest share repurchases has been muted by a convertible bond.

Investment Rationale/Risk

➤ We were not surprised by Q's late October indication of higher capital spending in 2008 and the lack of a decision on a dividend or added share repurchases, although we believe the uncertainty has pressured the stock. Given that Q has a new CEO and sluggish revenue growth, we believe a strategic review will be completed by year end. With the stock down more than 16% since the release of third quarter results, we believe the valuation reflects our concerns. We also believe Q's share buyback program will provide some support.

➤ Risks to our recommendation and target price include a slowing of revenue growth, and lower demand for Q's bundled services, which would hurt margins.

➤ With the operational challenges we foresee, we believe Q warrants trading at a discount to peers using our enterprise value (EV)/EBITDA multiple analysis. We apply a 5.5X peer group EV multiple to our 2008 EBITDA estimate to arrive at our 12-month target price of $7. However, at our target price, Q would still trade in line with peers on a P/E basis.

Qualitative Risk Assessment

LOW	MEDIUM	**HIGH**

Our risk assessment reflects the highly competitive nature of the industry, our view of the above average debt load that Q carries, and the lack of a dividend to lend support to the share price.

Quantitative Evaluations

S&P Quality Ranking   C

D	**C**	B-	B	B+	A-	A	A+

Relative Strength Rank   WEAK

  18

LOWEST = 1   HIGHEST = 99

Revenue/Earnings Data

Revenue (Million $)

	1Q	2Q	3Q	4Q	Year
2007	3,446	3,463	3,434	--	--
2006	3,476	3,472	3,487	3,488	13,923
2005	3,449	3,470	3,504	3,480	13,903
2004	3,481	3,442	3,449	3,437	13,809
2003	3,624	3,596	3,570	3,498	14,288
2002	3,985	3,915	3,776	3,709	15,385

Earnings Per Share ($)

2007	0.12	0.13	1.08	E0.14	E0.53
2006	0.05	0.06	0.09	0.10	0.30
2005	0.03	-0.09	-0.08	-0.27	-0.41
2004	-0.17	-0.43	-0.31	-0.09	-1.00
2003	-0.07	-0.07	-0.39	-0.22	-0.76
2002	-0.59	-10.48	-0.07	0.62	-10.48

Fiscal year ended Dec. 31. Next earnings report expected: Early February. EPS Estimates based on S&P Operating Earnings; historical GAAP earnings are as reported.

Dividend Data

A dividend of $0.05 a share was paid in June 2001.

Qwest Communications International Inc.

Business Summary November 06, 2007

CORPORATE OVERVIEW. Following the June 2000 acquisition of Baby Bell U.S. WEST, Inc., Qwest Communications International (Q) provides telecommunications services in 14 midwestern and western states. Q had 13 million local access lines for consumers and businesses and 2.5 million DSL broadband customers as of September 2007, with approximately 80% of its access lines in its eight largest markets, including Denver, Portland, and Seattle. In March 2004, Q began offering wireless services under the Qwest name using Sprint's network but retaining control of all marketing, customer services, pricing and promotional offerings. In the quarter ended September 2007, 58% of Q's revenues were derived from a declining wireline voice services segment, a higher percentage than most peers, while 4% was derived from wireless service that is only used in Q's bundle. The remaining revenues are from data, Internet, and video services.

COMPETITIVE LANDSCAPE. We believe Q faces competitive challenges partly due to low barriers to entry and characteristics unique to the company. As of September 2007, Q's access line count was 7.2% lower than a year earlier, as wireless substitution was intense, and we believe fewer housing sales in core markets limited new customer additions. As a reseller of wireless services, we believe Q is at a competitive disadvantage to peers. In addition, we think Q will face added competition from cable providers such as Cox Communications and Comcast that offer broadband services and are rolling out telephony products. To offset possible customer migration to cable, Q is offering a triple-play package of voice, data and video services through a partnership with satellite provider Direct TV (634,000 customers). At the end of September 2007, 61% of its retail customers were receiving a bundle of two or more services from the company.

CORPORATE STRATEGY. During 2006 and the first half of 2007, Q focused on reducing its operating expenses, aiming to improve its below average EBITDA margin. Q's headcount was reduced by 5.5% during the 12 months ended September 2007 and the company lowered its wireline facility costs. In addition, Q expects a $150 million reduction in its cost of sales due to adjustments to its pension accounting. Unlike large telecom peers such as Verizon and AT&T that have invested in their own video offerings, to offset competitive pressure, Qwest has long pursued a wholesale strategy to offer bundled services. However, in late 2007, Q announced plans to invest $300 million in deploying fiber broadband services to 1.5 homes that we expect will result in modestly higher capital spending in 2008.

Company Financials Fiscal Year Ended Dec. 31

Per Share Data ($)	2006	2005	2004	2003	2002	2001	2000	1999	1998	1997
Tangible Book Value	NM	NM	NM	NM	NM	1.28	5.37	4.95	0.82	0.93
Cash Flow	1.51	1.26	0.74	1.07	-7.65	0.83	2.56	1.13	-1.15	0.09
Earnings	0.30	-0.41	-1.00	-0.76	-10.48	-2.38	-0.06	0.60	-1.51	0.04
S&P Core Earnings	0.25	-0.68	-0.81	-0.81	-7.38	-1.39	NA	NA	NA	NA
Dividends	Nil	Nil	Nil	Nil	Nil	0.05	Nil	Nil	Nil	Nil
Payout Ratio	Nil	Nil	Nil	Nil	Nil	Nil	NM	Nil	Nil	Nil	Nil
Prices:High	9.22	5.95	5.00	6.15	15.19	48.19	66.00	52.38	25.66	17.22
Prices:Low	5.10	3.30	2.56	3.01	1.07	11.08	32.13	25.03	11.00	5.50
P/E Ratio:High	31	NM	NM	NM	NM	NM	NM	87	NM	NM
P/E Ratio:Low	17	NM	NM	NM	NM	NM	NM	42	NM	NM

Income Statement Analysis (Million $)

	2006	2005	2004	2003	2002	2001	2000	1999	1998	1997
Revenue	13,923	13,903	13,809	14,288	15,385	19,695	16,610	3,928	2,243	697
Depreciation	2,381	3,065	3,123	3,167	3,847	5,335	3,342	404	202	20.3
Maintenance	NA	NA	NA	NA	NA	NA	NA	NA	NA	NA
Construction Credits	NA	NA	NA	NA	NA	NA	NA	NA	NA	NA
Effective Tax Rate	NM	NM	NM	NM	NM	NM	NM	21.4%	NM	38.4%
Net Income	593	-757	-1,794	-1,313	-17,625	-3,958	-81.0	459	-844	14.5
S&P Core Earnings	492	-1,154	-1,465	-1,382	-12,411	-2,327	NA	NA	NA	NA

Balance Sheet & Other Financial Data (Million $)

	2006	2005	2004	2003	2002	2001	2000	1999	1998	1997
Gross Property	46,374	45,954	45,428	45,094	44,580	55,099	48,318	4,469	2,811	657
Net Property	14,579	15,568	16,853	18,149	18,995	29,977	25,583	4,109	2,655	615
Capital Expenditures	1,632	1,613	1,731	2,088	2,764	8,543	6,597	1,900	1,413	346
Total Capital	11,761	11,751	14,078	14,744	16,924	59,046	58,493	9,370	6,545	1,012
Fixed Charges Coverage	1.4	0.6	NM	NM	0.2	1.3	2.5	4.9	1.0	2.2
Capitalization:Long Term Debt	13,206	14,968	16,690	15,639	19,754	20,197	15,421	2,368	2,307	630
Capitalization:Preferred	Nil	Nil	Nil	Nil	Nil	Nil	Nil	Nil	Nil	Nil
Capitalization:Common	-1,445	-3,217	-2,612	-1,016	-2,830	36,655	41,304	7,001	4,238	382
% Return on Revenue	4.3	NM	NM	NM	NM	NM	NM	11.7	NM	2.1
% Return on Invested Capital	15.0	8.1	NM	NM	12.4	NM	7.6	9.3	0.0	NA
% Return on Common Equity	NM	NM	NM	NM	NM	NM	NM	8.2	NM	NA
% Earned on Net Property	26.1	24.2	NM	17.5	16.9	26.4	32.9	22.4	18.0	NA
% Long Term Debt of Capitalization	112.3	127.4	118.6	106.9	116.7	34.2	27.2	25.3	35.2	62.3
Capital % Preferred	Nil	Nil	Nil	Nil	Nil	Nil	Nil	Nil	Nil	Nil
Capitalization:% Common	-12.3	-27.4	-18.6	-6.9	-16.7	62.0	72.8	74.7	64.8	37.7

Data as orig reptd.; bef. results of disc opers/spec. items. Per share data adj. for stk. divs.; EPS diluted. E-Estimated. NA-Not Available. NM-Not Meaningful. NR-Not Ranked. UR-Under Review.

Office: 1801 California St, Denver, CO 80202-5555.
Telephone: 303-992-1400.
Email: investor.relations@qwest.com
Website: http://www.qwest.com

Chrmn & CEO: R.C. Notebaert
EVP & CFO: J.W. Richardson
EVP, Secy & General Counsel: R.N. Baer
VP & CTO: P. Poll

VP & Cntlr: R.W. Johnston
Investor Contact: S. Comfort (800-567-7296)
Board Members: L. G. Alvarado, C. L. Biggs, K. D. Brooksher, P. S. Hellman, R. D. Hoover, P. J. Martin, C. Matthews, W. W. Murdy, R. C. Notebaert, F. Popoff, J. A. Unruh, A. Welters

Founded: 1983
Domicile: Delaware
Employees: 38,000

RadioShack Corp

STANDARD &POOR'S

S&P Recommendation	HOLD ★★★☆☆	Price	12-Mo. Target Price	Investment Style
		$18.55 (as of Nov 23, 2007)	$22.00	Large-Cap Blend

GICS Sector Consumer Discretionary
Sub-Industry Computer & Electronics Retail

Summary This consumer electronics retailer operates the RadioShack chain, which has about 7,000 outlets (including dealers/franchises).

Key Stock Statistics (Source S&P, Vickers, company reports)

52-Wk Range	$35.00– 16.42	S&P Oper. EPS 2007E	1.62	Market Capitalization(B)	$2.432	Beta	1.33
Trailing 12-Month EPS	$1.61	S&P Oper. EPS 2008E	1.65	Yield (%)	1.35	S&P 3-Yr. Proj. EPS CAGR(%)	9.00
Trailing 12-Month P/E	11.5	P/E on S&P Oper. EPS 2007E	11.5	Dividend Rate/Share	$0.25	S&P Credit Rating	BB
$10K Invested 5 Yrs Ago	$8,509	Common Shares Outstg. (M)	131.1	Institutional Ownership (%)	NM		

Price Performance

30-Week Mov. Avg. ··· 10-Week Mov. Avg. -- GAAP Earnings vs. Previous Year Volume Above Avg. STARS
12-Mo. Target Price — Relative Strength — ▲ Up ▼ Down ► No Change Below Avg.

Options: ASE, CBOE, P

Analysis prepared by **Michael Souers** on November 05, 2007, when the stock traded at **$ 19.30**.

Highlights

➤ We project that sales will decline 3% to 4% in 2008, following an 11% drop in 2007. We expect RSH to continue to focus on increasing profitability by closing underperforming stores. We also look for kiosk expansion and RSH's more recent focus on faster-moving categories--such as MP3 players and digital cameras--to partly offset lost sales from anticipated store closures and weakness in wireless within RSH's core retail operations. We expect comp-store sales to decline in the low single-digits.

➤ In spite of continued expected same-store-sales declines, we expect that RSH's cost-cutting initiatives will result in a slight widening of operating margins, following significant projected margin improvement in 2007. However, we think that RSH will struggle to achieve historical gross margins going forward due to the company's focus on faster-moving, but typically lower-margin, categories.

➤ After taxes that we forecast at 38.0% and a slight decline in net interest expense, we project operating EPS of $1.65 in 2008, a 2% increase from the $1.62 we expect the company to earn in 2007, excluding one-time items.

Investment Rationale/Risk

➤ We view the company as in the early stages of a potential turnaround plan, which is focused on increasing average unit volume, rationalizing its cost structure, and growing profitable square footage. While RSH's CEO has extensive retail experience with turnaround situations, we think the longer-term outlook for the company is uncertain, due to a highly competitive environment that includes behemoths Best Buy (BBY: strong buy, $47) and Circuit City (CC: buy, $7). Given the company's lackluster sales growth, we believe the risk/reward quotient for owning the shares is neutral, with the stock recently trading at about 12X our 2008 EPS estimate, in line with peers.

➤ Risks to our recommendation and target price include management's inability to rapidly execute its turnaround plan, and macroeconomic factors that could result in weaker than anticipated consumer spending levels.

➤ Our 12-month target price of $22, or about 13X our 2008 EPS estimate, is derived from our discounted cash flow analysis. Our DCF model assumes a weighted average cost of capital of 10.2% and a terminal growth rate of 3.0%.

Qualitative Risk Assessment

LOW	MEDIUM	HIGH

The company is the fifth largest player in a fragmented industry, with numerous suppliers and buyers, and a history of profitability. However, we view consumer electronics retailing as highly competitive, with numerous rivals and strong price competition.

Quantitative Evaluations

S&P Quality Ranking B+

D	C	B-	B	B+	A-	A	A+

Relative Strength Rank WEAK

28

LOWEST = 1 HIGHEST = 99

Revenue/Earnings Data

Revenue (Million $)

	1Q	2Q	3Q	4Q	Year
2007	992.3	934.8	960.3	--	--
2006	1,160	1,100	1,060	1,458	4,778
2005	1,123	1,092	1,195	1,672	5,082
2004	1,093	1,054	1,102	1,593	4,841
2003	1,070	1,025	1,064	1,490	4,649
2002	1,034	998.1	1,047	1,498	4,577

Earnings Per Share ($)

2007	0.31	0.34	0.34	E0.73	E1.62
2006	0.06	-0.02	-0.12	0.62	0.54
2005	0.34	0.33	0.75	0.40	1.81
2004	0.41	0.42	0.43	0.81	2.08
2003	0.33	0.34	0.34	0.77	1.77
2002	0.31	0.28	0.25	0.63	1.45

Fiscal year ended Dec. 31. Next earnings report expected: Late February. EPS Estimates based on S&P Operating Earnings; historical GAAP earnings are as reported.

Dividend Data (Dates: mm/dd Payment Date: mm/dd/yy)

Amount ($)	Date Decl.	Ex-Div. Date	Stk. of Record	Payment Date
0.250	11/06	11/29	12/01	12/20/06
0.250	11/12	11/27	11/29	12/19/07

Dividends have been paid since 1987. Source: Company reports.

RadioShack Corp

STANDARD &POOR'S

Business Summary November 05, 2007

CORPORATE OVERVIEW. As of December 31, 2006, this consumer electronics retailer had 4,467 company-operated stores located through the U.S., including Puerto Rico and the U.S. Virgin Islands. RSH also had a network of 1,587 dealer/franchise stores, including 36 located outside the U.S. At the end of 2006, RSH operated 772 non-RadioShack branded kiosks, which offer product lines such as wireless phones and associated accessories.

Each store carries an assortment of electronic parts, batteries and accessories; wireless and conventional phones; flat panel televisions; DVD players; direct-to-home (DTH) satellite systems; PCs; home entertainment, wireless and other computer accessories; wire, cable and connectivity products; digital cameras; and specialized products such as home air cleaners and unique toys. RSH also provides access to third-party services, such as cellular and PCS phone and DTH satellite activation, long-distance telephone service, prepaid wireless airtime, and extended service plans. We believe that RSH is focusing on revamping its product offerings in order to enhance its competitive position within the consumer electronics industry. For example, in the second half of 2005, RSH began dedicating floor space to Apple's iPod and accessories, a rapidly growing consumer electronics category.

MARKET PROFILE. The domestic consumer electronics industry generated $145 billion in sales in 2006, according to the Consumer Electronics Association (CEA), a 15.1% increase from the $125.9 billion generated in 2005. Total industry sales are forecast to grow 7% in 2007, to approximately $155 billion. For 2006, we estimate that RSH will have a market share of approximately 3%, trailing competitors such as Best Buy, Wal-Mart, Circuit City, and Dell. We expect pure-play electronics retailers to see increased competition from discounters and mass merchants as these companies have been ramping up their consumer electronics offerings to take advantage of what we view as a strong technology cycle. We believe that, historically, RSH has differentiated itself from big box competitors due to its heavy emphasis on high margin, smaller ticket items such as batteries and accessories. Along these lines, RSH's smaller store format does not afford the company the opportunity to capitalize on the strong demand for advanced televisions.

Company Financials Fiscal Year Ended Dec. 31

Per Share Data ($)	2006	2005	2004	2003	2002	2001	2000	1999	1998	1997
Tangible Book Value	4.81	4.36	5.83	4.73	4.24	4.04	4.46	3.70	3.84	4.69
Cash Flow	1.48	2.65	2.70	2.31	1.97	1.41	2.38	1.87	0.73	1.24
Earnings	0.54	1.81	2.08	1.77	1.45	0.85	1.84	1.43	0.27	0.82
S&P Core Earnings	0.67	1.69	1.94	1.49	1.18	1.06	NA	NA	NA	NA
Dividends	0.25	0.25	0.25	0.25	0.22	0.22	0.22	0.15	0.20	0.20
Payout Ratio	46%	14%	12%	14%	15%	25%	12%	10%	74%	25%
Prices:High	23.37	34.48	36.24	32.48	36.21	56.50	72.94	79.50	31.94	23.00
Prices:Low	13.73	20.55	26.04	18.74	16.99	20.10	35.06	20.59	15.19	10.16
P/E Ratio:High	43	19	17	18	25	66	40	56	NM	28
P/E Ratio:Low	25	11	13	11	12	24	19	14	NM	12

Income Statement Analysis (Million $)	2006	2005	2004	2003	2002	2001	2000	1999	1998	1997
Revenue	4,778	5,082	4,841	4,649	4,577	4,776	4,795	4,126	4,788	5,372
Operating Income	329	474	660	576	510	583	736	597	424	434
Depreciation	128	124	101	92.0	94.7	108	107	90.2	99.0	97.2
Interest Expense	44.3	44.5	29.6	35.7	43.4	50.8	53.9	37.2	45.4	46.1
Pretax Income	111	322	542	473	425	292	594	481	99.7	304
Effective Tax Rate	34.1%	16.0%	37.8%	36.9%	38.0%	42.8%	38.0%	38.0%	38.5%	38.5%
Net Income	73.4	270	337	299	263	167	368	298	61.3	187
S&P Core Earnings	92.0	251	315	252	211	200	NA	NA	NA	NA

Balance Sheet & Other Financial Data (Million $)	2006	2005	2004	2003	2002	2001	2000	1999	1998	1997
Cash	472	224	438	635	447	401	131	165	64.5	106
Current Assets	1,600	1,627	1,775	1,667	1,707	1,714	1,818	1,403	1,299	1,716
Total Assets	2,070	2,205	2,517	2,244	1,707	2,245	2,577	2,142	1,994	2,318
Current Liabilities	984	986	957	858	829	826	1,232	925	880	976
Long Term Debt	346	495	507	541	591	565	303	319	235	236
Common Equity	654	589	922	769	729	714	812	758	748	959
Total Capital	1,000	1,084	1,429	1,311	1,320	1,344	1,284	1,150	1,083	1,295
Capital Expenditures	91.0	171	229	190	107	139	120	102	132	118
Cash Flow	202	394	439	391	354	270	470	383	155	278
Current Ratio	1.6	1.6	1.9	1.9	2.1	2.1	1.5	1.5	1.5	1.8
% Long Term Debt of Capitalization	34.6	45.7	35.5	41.3	44.8	42.1	23.6	27.8	21.7	18.2
% Net Income of Revenue	1.5	5.3	7.0	6.4	5.8	3.5	7.7	7.2	1.3	3.5
% Return on Assets	3.4	11.4	14.2	13.4	13.3	6.9	15.6	14.4	2.8	7.6
% Return on Equity	11.8	35.7	39.9	39.9	35.9	21.2	46.2	38.8	6.5	17.0

Data as orig reptd.; bef. results of disc opers/spec. items. Per share data adj. for stk. divs.; EPS diluted. E-Estimated. NA-Not Available. NM-Not Meaningful. NR-Not Ranked. UR-Under Review.

Office: 300 Radioshack Cir, Fort Worth, TX 76102-1964.
Telephone: 817-415-3011.
Email: investor.relations@radioshack.com
Website: http://www.radioshack.com

Chrmn & CEO: J. Day
EVP & CFO: J. Gooch
SVP, Secy & General Counsel: D.S. Goldberg
SVP & Cntlr: D.P. Johnson

Board Members: F. J. Belatti, J. C. Day, R. S. Falcone, D. R. Feehan, R. J. Hernandez, H. E. Lockhart, J. L. Messman, W. G. Morton, Jr., T. G. Plaskett, E. D. Woodbury

Founded: 1899
Domicile: Delaware
Employees: 43,000

The McGraw-Hill Companies

Raytheon Co.

STANDARD &POOR'S

S&P Recommendation BUY ★★★★☆	Price $62.09 (as of Nov 23, 2007)	12-Mo. Target Price $73.00	Investment Style Large-Cap Value

GICS Sector Industrials
Sub-Industry Aerospace & Defense

Summary Raytheon, one of the world's largest U.S. military contractors, specializes in making high-tech missiles and electronics.

Key Stock Statistics (Source S&P, Vickers, company reports)

52-Wk Range	$65.94–50.03	S&P Oper. EPS 2007**E**	3.16	Market Capitalization(B)	$27.140	Beta	0.49
Trailing 12-Month EPS	$5.23	S&P Oper. EPS 2008**E**	3.60	Yield (%)	1.64	S&P 3-Yr. Proj. EPS CAGR(%)	11.00
Trailing 12-Month P/E	11.9	P/E on S&P Oper. EPS 2007**E**	19.6	Dividend Rate/Share	$1.02	S&P Credit Rating	BBB+
$10K Invested 5 Yrs Ago	$23,910	Common Shares Outstg. (M)	437.1	Institutional Ownership (%)	82		

Price Performance

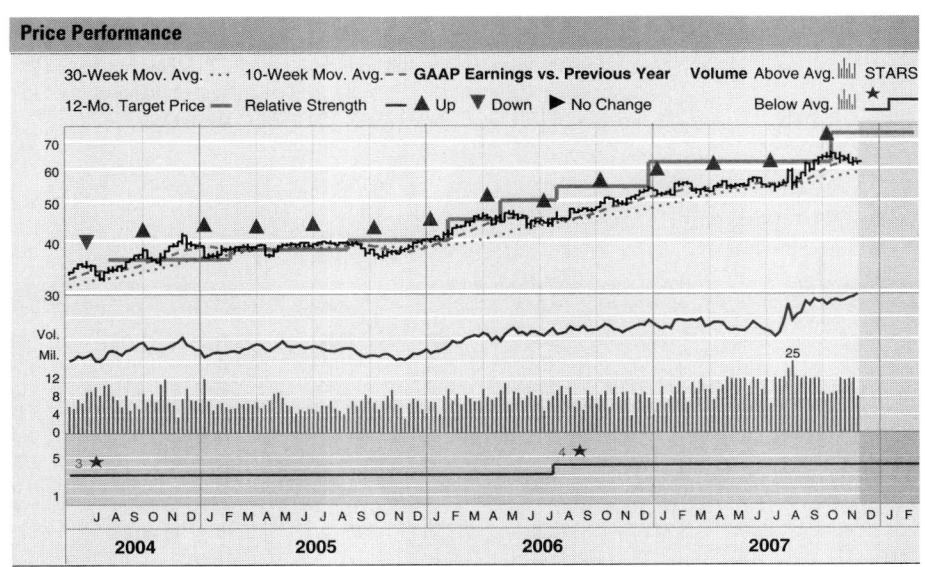

30-Week Mov. Avg. · · · · 10-Week Mov. Avg. - - - **GAAP Earnings vs. Previous Year** Volume Above Avg. STARS
12-Mo. Target Price — Relative Strength — ▲ Up ▼ Down ▶ No Change Below Avg. ★

Options: ASE, CBOE, P

Analysis prepared by **Richard Tortoriello** on October 30, 2007, when the stock traded at **$ 63.65**.

Highlights

➤ We estimate that increased demand for RTN's missiles and defense electronics (about 70% of revenues) will lead to a 7% revenue rise in 2007 and a 6% gain in 2008. With the planned sale of the Flight Options business, we see RTN fully focused on defense contracting. We continue to see good order growth at RTN, with a year-to-date book-to-bill ratio of 1.06-to-1 and a total backlog of 1.6X our 2007 sales estimate (funded backlog is 0.8X sales).

➤ We see operating profit margins expanding to 10.3% in 2007 and 10.5% in 2008, from 9.1% in 2006, on the strength of the increased sales volume and productivity improvements that we forecast (the 2006 figure is restated to exclude the RTN Aircraft business, which was sold in March 2007). We see a 28% rise in EPS in 2007, to $3.16, and a further 14% increase in 2008, to $3.60.

➤ We look for free cash flow (cash generated by operations less capital expenditures) of $1.1 billion, or $2.59 per share, in 2007, including $473 million in cash taxes on the RTN Aircraft sale and $400 million in voluntary pension contributions. For 2008, we project free cash flow of about $2.2 billion, or $4.85 per share.

Investment Rationale/Risk

➤ Despite recent changes in Congressional leadership, we think defense budgets will continue to increase at least moderately, given our view of significant current and potential future military threats. We also believe that RTN's leading positions in missiles and defense electronics situate it well to provide products for defense against these threats. We also see RTN as well positioned to capture foreign business, for missile defense and other defense products, with allies including Australia, the U.K., Japan, and other countries in the Middle East and Asia.

➤ Risks to our recommendation and target price include the potential for delays and/or cuts in military budgets and the failure to perform well on existing contracts or to win new contracts.

➤ Our 12-month target price of $73 is based on a P/E of about 20X our 2008 EPS estimate. This valuation is above RTN's 10-year average historical forward P/E ratio of 16X, reflecting our positive view of the defense market in general and RTN's product portfolio in particular.

Qualitative Risk Assessment

LOW	MEDIUM	HIGH

Our risk assessment reflects RTN's exposure to economic cycles and changes in defense spending, significant off balance sheet liabilities, and historically below average earnings stability, offset by its leading defense contractor status and large project backlog.

Quantitative Evaluations

S&P Quality Ranking B

D	C	B-	B	B+	A-	A	A+

Relative Strength Rank STRONG

80

LOWEST = 1 HIGHEST = 99

Revenue/Earnings Data

Revenue (Million $)

	1Q	2Q	3Q	4Q	Year
2007	4,928	5,419	5,355	--	--
2006	4,660	4,973	4,936	5,722	20,291
2005	4,944	5,409	5,331	6,210	21,894
2004	4,676	4,929	4,936	5,704	20,245
2003	4,201	4,429	4,378	5,101	18,109
2002	3,911	4,095	4,092	4,662	16,760

Earnings Per Share ($)

2007	0.69	0.79	0.69	E0.99	E3.16
2006	0.61	0.61	0.59	0.81	2.46
2005	0.43	0.51	0.51	0.63	2.08
2004	0.24	-0.22	0.41	0.54	0.99
2003	0.27	0.45	0.05	0.52	1.29
2002	0.37	0.54	0.56	0.38	1.85

Fiscal year ended Dec. 31. Next earnings report expected: Early February. EPS Estimates based on S&P Operating Earnings; historical GAAP earnings are as reported.

Dividend Data (Dates: mm/dd Payment Date: mm/dd/yy)

Amount ($)	Date Decl.	Ex-Div. Date	Stk. of Record	Payment Date
0.240	12/13	12/29	01/03	01/31/07
0.255	03/21	03/30	04/03	05/01/07
0.255	06/21	06/29	07/03	08/02/07
0.255	09/18	09/28	10/02	11/01/07

Dividends have been paid since 1964. Source: Company reports.

Raytheon Co.

Business Summary October 30, 2007

CORPORATE OVERVIEW. Raytheon, a leading missile and military electronics manufacturer, conducts business through six business segments.

Integrated Defense Systems (20% of sales and 27% of operating profits in 2007) is a leading provider of integrated joint battlespace (e.g., space, air, surface, and subsurface) and homeland security solutions. Customers include the U.S. Missile Defense Agency (MDA) and the U.S. Armed Forces, as well as key international customers. Business areas include future naval capability, focusing on the DDG-1000, the Navy's next-generation naval destroyer; integrated air defense, including the Patriot Air & Missile Defense System; missile defense, including Early Warning Radars and the X-band family of Radars; international operations; maritime mission systems; and joint battlespace integration.

Intelligence Information Systems (12% of sales and 9% of profits) provides systems, subsystems, and software engineering services for national and tactical intelligence systems, as well as for homeland security and information technology (IT) solutions. Areas of concentration include processing, analysis, and dissemination of signals and imagery, production of geospatial intelligence, command and control of airborne and space borne platforms, and inte-

grated ground systems for weather and environmental programs.

Missile Systems (11% of sales and 19% of profits) makes and supports a broad range of leading-edge solutions and products for the armed forces of the U.S. and other countries. Business areas include naval weapon systems, which provides defensive missiles and guided projectiles to the navies of over 30 countries; strike, with products focused on ground-based targets, including the Tomahawk cruise missile; air-to-air missiles; land combat, which includes the Javelin anti-tank missile; and other programs.

Network Centric Systems (17% of sales and 15% of profits) makes net-centric mission solutions for network sensors, command and control communications, air traffic management, and homeland security. Customers include all branches of the Department of Defense, the Department of Homeland Security, the Federal Aviation Administration, and other customers.

Company Financials Fiscal Year Ended Dec. 31

Per Share Data ($)	2006	2005	2004	2003	2002	2001	2000	1999	1998	1997
Tangible Book Value	NM	NM	NM	NM	NM	NM	NM	NM	NM	NM
Cash Flow	3.28	3.19	1.93	2.22	2.74	2.03	3.50	3.46	4.75	4.07
Earnings	2.46	2.08	0.99	1.29	1.85	0.01	1.46	1.34	2.53	2.18
S&P Core Earnings	3.10	2.61	1.96	1.11	-0.25	-2.68	NA	NA	NA	NA
Dividends	0.96	0.86	0.80	0.80	0.80	0.80	0.80	0.80	0.80	0.80
Payout Ratio	34%	41%	81%	62%	43%	NM	55%	60%	32%	37%
Prices:High	54.17	40.57	41.89	33.97	45.70	37.44	35.81	76.56	60.75	60.50
Prices:Low	39.43	35.96	29.28	24.31	26.30	23.95	17.50	22.19	40.69	41.75
P/E Ratio:High	19	21	42	26	25	NM	25	57	24	28
P/E Ratio:Low	14	19	30	19	14	NM	12	17	16	19

Income Statement Analysis (Million $)										
Revenue	20,291	21,894	20,245	18,109	16,760	16,867	16,895	19,841	19,530	13,673
Operating Income	2,213	2,131	1,822	1,709	2,118	1,488	2,319	2,251	2,797	2,036
Depreciation	373	444	434	393	364	729	694	724	761	457
Interest Expense	273	312	418	537	497	660	736	713	739	397
Pretax Income	1,688	1,440	579	762	1,074	117	877	828	1,467	790
Effective Tax Rate	34.4%	34.6%	24.2%	29.8%	29.7%	95.7%	43.2%	44.8%	41.1%	33.3%
Net Income	1,107	942	439	535	755	5.00	498	457	864	527
S&P Core Earnings	1,392	1,180	866	460	-105	-970	NA	NA	NA	NA

Balance Sheet & Other Financial Data (Million $)										
Cash	2,460	1,202	556	661	544	1,214	871	230	421	296
Current Assets	9,517	7,567	7,124	6,585	7,190	8,362	8,013	8,931	8,637	9,233
Total Assets	25,491	24,381	24,153	23,668	23,946	26,636	26,777	28,110	27,939	28,598
Current Liabilities	6,715	5,900	5,644	3,849	5,107	5,753	4,865	7,886	6,680	11,886
Long Term Debt	3,278	3,969	4,637	7,376	7,138	6,875	9,054	7,298	8,163	4,406
Common Equity	11,101	10,798	10,611	9,162	8,870	11,290	10,823	10,959	10,856	10,425
Total Capital	14,544	15,011	15,345	16,538	16,008	18,743	20,650	18,810	19,580	15,617
Capital Expenditures	295	75.0	363	428	458	486	431	532	509	459
Cash Flow	1,480	1,386	873	928	1,119	734	1,192	1,181	1,625	984
Current Ratio	1.4	1.3	1.3	1.7	1.4	1.5	1.6	1.1	1.3	0.8
% Long Term Debt of Capitalization	22.5	26.4	30.2	44.6	44.6	36.7	43.8	38.8	41.7	28.2
% Net Income of Revenue	5.5	4.3	2.2	3.0	4.5	0.0	2.9	2.3	4.4	3.9
% Return on Assets	4.4	3.9	1.8	2.2	3.0	0.0	1.8	1.6	3.1	2.7
% Return on Equity	10.2	8.8	4.4	5.9	7.5	0.0	4.6	4.2	8.1	7.0

Data as orig reptd.; bef. results of disc opers/spec. items. Per share data adj. for stk. divs.; EPS diluted. E-Estimated. NA-Not Available. NM-Not Meaningful. NR-Not Ranked. UR-Under Review.

Office: 870 Winter St, Waltham, MA 02451-1449.
Telephone: 781-522-3000.
Email: invest@raytheon.com
Website: http://www.raytheon.com

Chrmn & CEO: W.H. Swanson
SVP & CFO: D.C. Wajsgras
SVP & General Counsel: J.B. Stephens
VP & Chief Acctg Officer: M.J. Wood

VP & Treas: R.A. Goglia
Investor Contact: T. Rutledge (781-522-3000)
Board Members: B. M. Barrett, V. Clark, F. Colloredo-Mansfeld, J. M. Deutch, F. M. Poses, M. C. Ruettgers, R. L. Skates, W. R. Spivey, L. G. Stuntz, W. H. Swanson

Founded: 1928
Domicile: Delaware
Employees: 71,351

Regions Financial Corp

STANDARD
&POOR'S

S&P Recommendation	HOLD ★★★☆☆	Price	12-Mo. Target Price	Investment Style
		$24.22 (as of Nov 23, 2007)	$29.00	Large-Cap Value

GICS Sector Financials
Sub-Industry Regional Banks

Summary This major southeastern bank holding company, with 1,938 offices in 16 Sunbelt states, completed a merger with AmSouth Corp. in 2006.

Key Stock Statistics (Source S&P, Vickers, company reports)

52-Wk Range	$38.17– 22.84	S&P Oper. EPS 2007**E**	2.70	Market Capitalization(B)	$17.061	Beta	0.60
Trailing 12-Month EPS	$2.15	S&P Oper. EPS 2008**E**	2.81	Yield (%)	6.28	S&P 3-Yr. Proj. EPS CAGR(%)	4.90
Trailing 12-Month P/E	11.3	P/E on S&P Oper. EPS 2007**E**	9.0	Dividend Rate/Share	$1.52	S&P Credit Rating	A
$10K Invested 5 Yrs Ago	$10,536	Common Shares Outstg. (M)	704.4	Institutional Ownership (%)	40		

Price Performance

30-Week Mov. Avg. · · · 10-Week Mov. Avg. – – GAAP Earnings vs. Previous Year   Volume Above Avg. ▏▮▏ STARS
12-Mo. Target Price — Relative Strength — ▲ Up ▼ Down ▶ No Change   Below Avg. ▏▮▏ ★

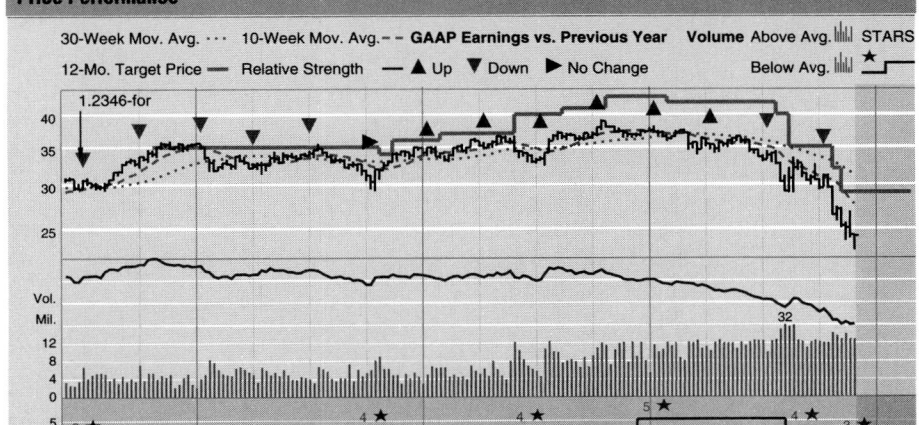

Options: C, Ph

Analysis prepared by **Stuart Plesser** on November 06, 2007, when the stock traded at **$ 24.82**.

Highlights

➤ Loan growth in the third quarter was 1.5% on an annualized basis, as an increase in real estate mortgage lending was partly offset by a dropoff in commercial lending. For 2008, we forecast low single digit loan growth, as RF strives to protect credit quality. Our net interest margin assumption for 2008 is 2.70% (versus a projected 3.80% in 2007), mostly due to higher funding costs and loan repricing. We expect non-interest income to rise 2%, to 40% of revenues, from a projected 39.2% of revenues in 2007.

➤ We believe that the 2006 merger with AmSouth will deliver the expected cost savings of $400 million annually beginning in 2008, offset somewhat by branch expansion. All told, we look for expenses to total 56% of revenue in 2008, versus a projected 57.1% in 2007. However, we expect credit quality to decline in 2008, in line with industry trends, which should result in loan loss provisions of $365 million, versus $280 million projected for 2007.

➤ Assuming a 1% decline in diluted shares, we estimate 2008 operating EPS of $2.81, up 4.1% from our estimate of $2.70 for 2007.

Investment Rationale/Risk

➤ In 2007, RF has deliberately reduced loan growth in an attempt to preserve credit quality, a trade-off we support. Furthermore, credit quality remains relatively high, with the ratio of net chargeoffs to loans at 0.27% at the end of the third quarter. However, we think credit quality will deteriorate in 2008, largely due to RF's exposure to the real estate market. With the shares trading at 9X our 2008 EPS estimate, a discount to peers and the historical average, we think the current stock price compensates for RF's real estate exposure.

➤ Risks to our recommendation and target price include shortfalls at the Morgan Keegan brokerage unit, worse credit deterioration than we expect, cost-cutting falling short of the company's forecasts, integration and customer retention difficulties stemming from the AmSouth merger, and operational performance that fails to meet our expectations.

➤ Our 12-month target price of $29 reflects a peer discount P/E multiple of 10.3X our 2008 EPS estimate of $2.81. The shares recently yielded about 6%.

Qualitative Risk Assessment

LOW	MEDIUM	HIGH

Our risk assessment reflects our view of the strong credit quality of the company's loan portfolio, and the bank's history of profitability.

Quantitative Evaluations

S&P Quality Ranking   A-

D	C	B-	B	B+	A-	A	A+

Relative Strength Rank   WEAK

25

LOWEST = 1   HIGHEST = 99

Revenue/Earnings Data

Revenue (Million $)

	1Q	2Q	3Q	4Q	Year
2007	2,797	2,724	2,742	--	--
2006	1,666	1,756	1,806	2,529	7,756
2005	1,423	1,565	1,564	1,572	6,124
2004	893.7	868.8	1,432	1,416	4,610
2003	917.6	940.1	888.6	871.7	3,618
2002	920.2	929.4	967.4	978.9	3,796

Earnings Per Share ($)

2007	0.65	0.63	0.56	E0.67	E2.70
2006	0.64	0.75	0.77	0.56	2.67
2005	0.51	0.53	0.55	0.55	2.15
2004	0.61	0.58	0.55	0.50	2.19
2003	0.58	0.59	0.59	0.59	2.35
2002	0.53	0.54	0.57	0.57	2.20

Fiscal year ended Dec. 31. Next earnings report expected: Mid January. EPS Estimates based on S&P Operating Earnings; historical GAAP earnings are as reported.

Dividend Data (Dates: mm/dd Payment Date: mm/dd/yy)

Amount ($)	Date Decl.	Ex-Div. Date	Stk. of Record	Payment Date
0.360	01/18	03/15	03/19	04/02/07
0.360	04/19	06/14	06/18	07/02/07
0.360	07/19	09/13	09/17	10/01/07
0.380	10/17	12/17	12/19	01/02/08

Dividends have been paid since 1968. Source: Company reports.

Regions Financial Corp

Business Summary November 06, 2007

CORPORATE OVERVIEW. Regions Financial is a bank holding company that operates primarily in the southeastern U.S., with operations consisting of banking, brokerage and investment services, mortgage banking, insurance brokerage, credit life insurance, commercial accounts receivable factoring and specialty financing. RF conducts its banking operations through Regions Bank, an Alabama chartered commercial bank that is a member of the Federal Reserve System, and Union Planters Bank, National Association (UPBNA), a national bank.

Banking operations also include Regions Mortgage (RMI) and EquiFirst Corp. (EFC), which are involved in mortgage banking. RMI's primary business is the origination and servicing of mortgage loans for long-term investors. EFC typically originates mortgage loans that are sold to third-party investors with servicing released. RMI and EFC generally provide services in the same states in which RF has banking operations.

Financial services operations include Morgan Keegan, a regional full-service brokerage and investment bank, which was acquired in 2001.

MARKET PROFILE. As of June 30, 2006, which is the latest available FDIC data, RF, together with AmSouth, on a pro forma basis, had 1,938 branches and $88.5 billion in deposits. These numbers reflect the divestiture of 52 branches in Alabama, Mississippi and Tennessee, which was imposed by regulatory agencies as a condition of the merger. About 60% of its deposits and 51% of branches were concentrated in the adjoining states of Tennessee, Alabama and Florida, by our calculations.

Company Financials Fiscal Year Ended Dec. 31

Per Share Data ($)	2006	2005	2004	2003	2002	2001	2000	1999	1998	1997
Tangible Book Value	11.74	11.55	11.58	16.25	15.29	10.58	11.00	9.75	9.72	9.56
Earnings	2.67	2.15	2.19	2.35	2.20	1.81	1.93	1.90	1.52	1.74
S&P Core Earnings	2.67	2.11	2.17	2.32	2.11	1.63	NA	NA	NA	NA
Dividends	2.11	1.36	0.93	1.00	0.94	0.91	0.87	0.79	0.72	0.62
Payout Ratio	79%	63%	43%	43%	43%	50%	45%	42%	47%	36%
Prices:High	39.15	35.54	35.97	30.70	31.10	26.72	22.68	33.72	36.96	36.45
Prices:Low	32.37	29.16	27.26	24.16	21.95	20.84	14.83	18.78	23.39	20.81
P/E Ratio:High	15	17	16	13	14	15	12	18	24	21
P/E Ratio:Low	12	14	12	10	10	11	8	10	15	12

Income Statement Analysis (Million $)										
Net Interest Income	3,353	2,821	2,113	1,475	1,498	1,425	1,389	1,426	1,325	829
Tax Equivalent Adjustment	NA	NA	NA	NA	NA	NA	NA	NA	NA	NA
Non Interest Income	2,054	1,832	1,591	1,373	1,207	950	641	537	468	258
Loan Loss Provision	143	165	129	122	128	165	127	114	60.5	41.8
% Expense/Operating Revenue	61.3%	65.5%	66.5%	64.6%	65.1%	64.2%	55.2%	54.2%	61.6%	55.2%
Pretax Income	1,959	1,422	1,176	912	869	718	742	785	635	445
Effective Tax Rate	30.9%	29.6%	29.9%	28.5%	28.7%	29.1%	28.9%	33.1%	33.6%	32.7%
Net Income	1,353	1,001	824	652	620	509	528	525	422	300
% Net Interest Margin	4.17	3.91	3.66	3.49	3.73	3.66	3.55	3.94	4.25	4.20
S&P Core Earnings	1,355	983	811	647	592	458	NA	NA	NA	NA

Balance Sheet & Other Financial Data (Million $)										
Money Market Assets	2,610	1,794	1,761	1,491	1,424	1,502	112	90.3	427	127
Investment Securities	18,562	11,979	12,617	9,088	8,995	7,847	8,994	10,913	7,969	4,451
Commercial Loans	24,145	14,728	15,180	9,914	10,842	9,912	9,070	8,230	7,144	3,856
Other Loans	70,360	43,677	42,556	22,501	20,144	21,225	22,402	19,992	17,286	12,572
Total Assets	143,369	84,786	84,106	48,598	47,939	45,383	43,688	42,714	36,832	23,034
Demand Deposits	20,709	13,699	11,424	5,718	5,148	5,085	4,513	4,420	4,577	2,368
Time Deposits	80,519	46,679	47,243	27,015	27,779	26,463	27,510	25,569	23,773	15,383
Long Term Debt	8,643	11,938	7,240	5,712	5,386	4,748	4,478	1,751	571	400
Common Equity	20,701	10,614	10,749	4,452	4,178	4,036	3,458	3,065	3,000	1,913
% Return on Assets	1.2	1.2	1.2	1.4	1.3	1.1	1.2	1.3	1.4	1.4
% Return on Equity	8.6	9.4	10.8	15.1	15.1	13.6	16.2	17.3	17.2	17.1
% Loan Loss Reserve	1.1	1.3	1.3	1.4	1.3	1.3	1.2	1.2	1.3	1.2
% Loans/Deposits	98.3	99.3	101.1	102.1	98.7	100.7	98.7	95.7	85.9	91.5
% Equity to Assets	13.7	12.6	11.5	8.9	8.8	8.4	7.5	7.6	8.2	8.4

Data as orig reptd.; bef. results of disc opers/spec. items. Per share data adj. for stk. divs.; EPS diluted. E-Estimated. NA-Not Available. NM-Not Meaningful. NR-Not Ranked. UR-Under Review.

Office: 1900 5th Ave N, Birmingham, AL 35203-2610.
Telephone: 205-944-1300.
Email: askus@regionsbank.com
Website: http://www.regions.com

Chrmn: J.W. Moore
Pres & CEO: C. Ritter
Vice Chrmn: A.B. Morgan, Jr.
Sr EVP: D.C. Gordon

Sr EVP: W. Mayer, III
Investor Contact: M.G. Underwood, Jr. (205-244-2823)
Board Members: S. W. Bartholomew, Jr., G. W. Bryan, D. J. Cooper, Sr., D. DeFosset, E. W. Deavenport, Jr., J. S. French, M. H. Greene, J. E. Harwood, R. D. Horsley, M. R. Ingram, P. S. Lewis, Jr., J. R. Malone, S. W. Matlock, C. D. McCray, J. W. Moore, A. B. Morgan, Jr., C. B. Nelsen, J. M. Perez, M. Portera, C. Ritter, J. R. Roberts, M. S. Starnes, W. W. Stewart, L. J. Styslinger, III, R. A. Trippeer, Jr., R. W. Waller, J. H. Watson, S. L. Wilson, H. W. Witt

Founded: 1970
Domicile: Delaware
Employees: 35,904

Reynolds American Inc

STANDARD &POOR'S

S&P Recommendation **BUY** ★★★★☆	Price $64.32 (as of Nov 26, 2007)	12-Mo. Target Price $71.00	Investment Style Large-Cap Value

GICS Sector Consumer Staples
Sub-Industry Tobacco

Summary RAI, the second largest U.S. cigarette manufacturer, was formed via the mid-2004 merger of R.J. Reynolds and Brown & Williamson.

Key Stock Statistics (Source S&P, Vickers, company reports)

52-Wk Range	$67.60–58.55	S&P Oper. EPS 2007**E**	4.55	Market Capitalization(B)	$18.974	Beta	0.18
Trailing 12-Month EPS	$4.04	S&P Oper. EPS 2008**E**	4.82	Yield (%)	5.29	S&P 3-Yr. Proj. EPS CAGR(%)	6.00
Trailing 12-Month P/E	15.9	P/E on S&P Oper. EPS 2007**E**	14.1	Dividend Rate/Share	$3.40	S&P Credit Rating	BB+
$10K Invested 5 Yrs Ago	$40,008	Common Shares Outstg. (M)	295.0	Institutional Ownership (%)	61		

Price Performance

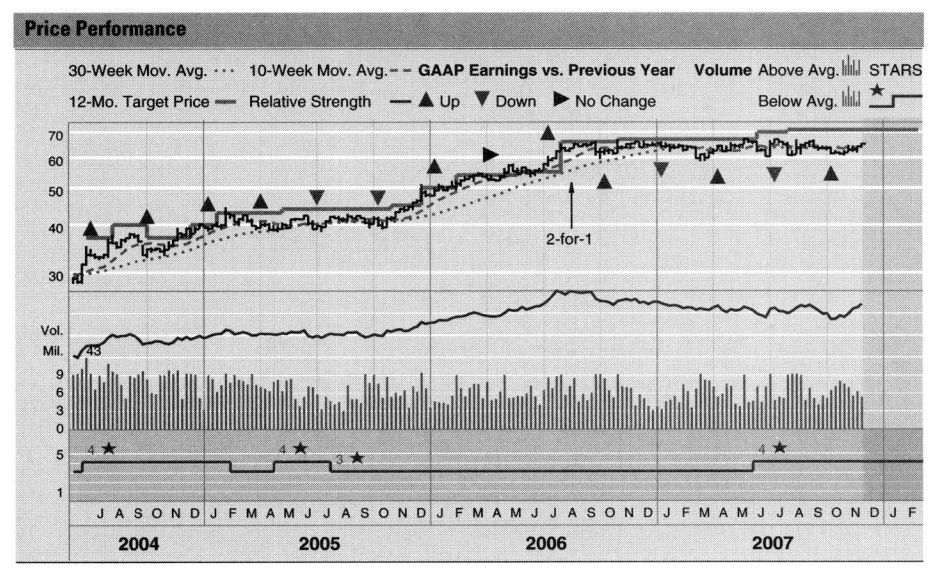

30-Week Mov. Avg. ··· 10-Week Mov. Avg. --- GAAP Earnings vs. Previous Year Volume Above Avg. STARS
12-Mo. Target Price — Relative Strength — ▲ Up ▼ Down ▶ No Change Below Avg.

2-for-1

J A S O N D J F M A M J J A S O N D J F M A M J J A S O N D J F M A M J J A S O N D J F
2004 2005 2006 2007

Options: ASE, CBOE, P, Ph

Analysis prepared by **Esther Y. Kwon, CFA** on November 26, 2007, when the stock traded at **$64.75**.

Highlights

➤ We expect revenues to rise about 6% in 2007, on a favorable product mix shift, price increases, new product introductions and acquisitions, partly offset by a shipment decline of 4% to 5%. We see a likely rise in volumes for growth brands Camel, Kool, Pall Mall and American Spirit, but anticipate declines for other brands, as marketing efforts are reduced. We see Conwood, which RAI acquired in mid-2006 for $3.5 billion, continuing to gain market share in a growing industry. For 2008, we project a 2% increase in revenue.

➤ While we anticipate that the bulk of the $75 million to $100 million of cost synergies from the merger between RJR and B&W will have been realized by 2007 year end, we see incremental improvement in operating profits as SG&A cost savings are likely to continue in 2008.

➤ We see higher interest expense in 2007 following the Conwood acquisition, and a higher effective tax rate of 38% due to the absence of a 2006 tax benefit. We see EPS rising to $4.55, reflecting further merger-related cost savings. We estimate that the Conwood acquisition will add $0.05 to quarterly EPS. In 2008, we expect EPS of $4.82.

Investment Rationale/Risk

➤ We are encouraged by RAI's new marketing strategy, as price increases have held, and we expect focus brands to continue to gain share. Although we believe overall domestic industry volumes will decline, we see a favorable mix shift and new product launches supporting RAI's bottom line. Further, we believe RAI will achieve its $600 million of anticipated synergies in two years, and see wider margins in the longer term. With the Price and Engle cases dismissed, we are more confident of an improving litigation environment for tobacco.

➤ Risks to our recommendation and target price include additional regulation and taxation of tobacco products, in addition to near-term pressure on trading multiples due to ongoing litigation.

➤ Assuming a perpetuity growth rate of 2% and a weighted average cost of capital of 8.25%, our discounted cash flow analysis calculates intrinsic value of $69 a share. Applying a forward P/E multiple of about 15X, slightly above RAI's historical average but in line with peers, to our 2008 EPS estimate, we arrive at a relative valuation of $72. Blending these values, we arrive at our 12-month target price of $71.

Qualitative Risk Assessment

LOW	**MEDIUM**	HIGH

The domestic tobacco industry typically produces stable revenue streams and strong cash flow. While the industry is involved in significant litigation, recent rulings have led to an improvement in the litigation environment. However, we think RAI's "poison pill" anti-takeover provision is not in its shareholders' best interests.

Quantitative Evaluations

S&P Quality Ranking NR

D	C	B-	B	B+	A-	A	A+

Relative Strength Rank STRONG

86

LOWEST = 1 HIGHEST = 99

Revenue/Earnings Data

Revenue (Million $)

	1Q	2Q	3Q	4Q	Year
2007	2,148	2,348	2,297	--	--
2006	1,960	2,291	2,190	2,069	8,510
2005	1,957	2,103	2,149	2,047	8,256
2004	1,218	1,352	1,866	2,001	6,437
2003	1,218	1,431	1,384	1,234	5,267
2002	1,515	1,705	1,585	1,406	6,211

Earnings Per Share ($)

	1Q	2Q	3Q	4Q	Year
2007	1.11	1.10	1.21	E1.09	E4.55
2006	0.95	1.24	1.05	0.61	3.85
2005	0.95	0.85	0.72	0.82	3.34
2004	0.72	0.88	1.14	0.22	2.81
2003	0.42	0.42	-20.66	-2.27	-22.04
2002	0.90	1.15	0.78	-0.58	2.32

Fiscal year ended Dec. 31. Next earnings report expected: Early February. EPS Estimates based on S&P Operating Earnings; historical GAAP earnings are as reported.

Dividend Data (Dates: mm/dd Payment Date: mm/dd/yy)

Amount ($)	Date Decl.	Ex-Div. Date	Stk. of Record	Payment Date
0.750	11/29	12/07	12/11	01/02/07
0.750	02/06	03/13	03/15	04/02/07
0.750	05/11	06/07	06/11	07/02/07
0.850	07/25	09/06	09/10	10/01/07

Dividends have been paid since 1999. Source: Company reports.

Please read the Required Disclosures and Analyst Certification on the last page of this report.

Reynolds American Inc

STANDARD
&POOR'S

Business Summary November 26, 2007

CORPORATE OVERVIEW. On July 30, 2004, R.J. Reynolds Tobacco Co. (RJRT) merged with Brown & Williamson (B&W), the U.S. operations of British American Tobacco (BTI), to form a new publicly traded company, Reynolds American, Inc. Combining RJRT and B&W, the second and third largest players, RAI is the second largest U.S. cigarette manufacturer, having a combined market share of approximately 30%.

RAI is the parent company of RJRT, Santa Fe Natural Tobacco, which RJRT acquired in 2002, and Lane Limited, which was purchased from BTI for $400 million as part of the merger. In 2003, prior to the merger, RJRT began a significant restructuring plan, targeting cost savings of $1 billion by the end of 2005 through a significant work force reduction, asset divestitures and associated exit activities. Full integration of RJRT and B&W was expected to be completed in 2006, however realization of cost savings continue into 2007. The business combination was expected to result in approximately $600 million in annualized savings, including headcount reductions and operations consolidation, when compared with a separate entity basis.

In May 2006, RAI completed the acquisition of Conwood, the second largest manufacturer of smokeless tobacco products in the U.S., for $3.5 billion. RAI plans to combine Conwood with its Lane Limited subsidiary into an Other Tobacco Products division in 2007. RAI's reportable segments are RJRT and Conwood.

The company's leading products are its Camel and Salem brand cigarettes. The company's other brands include Winston, Pall Mall, Kool, Doral, Vantage, More, Eclipse, American Spirit, and Now. Eclipse, a cigarette that primarily heats rather than burns tobacco in an effort to reduce second-hand smoke, is offered in selected retail chain outlets.

CORPORATE STRATEGY. RAI's management has stated that its strategy is to generate sustainable earnings growth and strong cash flow in order to maximize shareholder value. To that end, RAI implemented a new portfolio strategy, designed to improve profitability, which established three categories for the combined brands of RJRT and B&W. The investment brand category, which includes Camel and Kool, receive the majority of resources to promote market share growth. The selective support brands, which includes Winston, Salem, Doral and Pall Mall, receive limited support to optimize profitability; and the remaining brands are called non-support brands, which are managed to maximize profitability.

Company Financials Fiscal Year Ended Dec. 31

Per Share Data ($)	2006	2005	2004	2003	2002	2001	2000	1999	1998	1997
Tangible Book Value	NM	NM	NM	NM	NM	NM	NM	NM	NM	NA
Cash Flow	4.39	4.00	2.65	-20.81	3.34	4.72	4.10	3.11	NA	NA
Earnings	3.85	3.34	2.81	-22.04	2.32	2.24	1.73	0.90	-1.38	NA
S&P Core Earnings	3.95	3.96	3.59	2.13	1.73	1.52	NA	NA	NA	NA
Dividends	1.38	2.10	0.95	1.90	1.86	1.65	1.55	0.39	NA	NA
Payout Ratio	36%	63%	34%	NM	80%	74%	90%	43%	NA	NA
Prices:High	67.09	51.19	40.27	30.07	35.95	31.35	25.13	17.00	NA	NA
Prices:Low	47.48	38.24	26.69	13.76	17.42	22.09	7.88	8.00	NA	NA
P/E Ratio:High	17	15	14	NM	15	14	15	19	NA	NA
P/E Ratio:Low	12	11	9	NM	8	10	5	9	NA	NA

Income Statement Analysis (Million $)										
Revenue	8,510	8,256	6,437	5,267	6,211	8,585	8,167	7,567	5,716	NA
Operating Income	2,183	1,880	1,239	873	1,200	1,409	1,399	1,368	NA	NA
Depreciation	162	195	153	151	184	491	485	482	NA	NA
Interest Expense	270	113	85.0	111	147	150	168	268	176	NA
Pretax Income	1,809	1,416	829	-3,918	683	892	748	510	-340	NA
Effective Tax Rate	37.2%	30.4%	24.4%	NM	38.8%	50.2%	52.9%	61.8%	NM	NA
Net Income	1,136	985	627	-3,689	418	444	352	195	-299	NA
S&P Core Earnings	1,167	1,167	800	357	313	301	NA	NA	NA	NA

Balance Sheet & Other Financial Data (Million $)										
Cash	1,433	1,333	1,499	1,523	1,584	2,020	2,543	1,177	3,036	NA
Current Assets	4,935	5,065	4,624	3,331	3,992	3,856	3,871	2,468	4,138	NA
Total Assets	18,178	14,519	14,428	9,677	14,651	15,050	15,554	14,377	16,301	NA
Current Liabilities	4,092	4,149	4,055	2,865	3,427	2,792	2,776	3,068	3,885	NA
Long Term Debt	4,389	1,558	1,595	1,671	1,755	1,631	1,674	1,653	2,065	NA
Common Equity	7,043	6,553	6,176	3,057	6,716	8,026	8,436	7,064	7,555	NA
Total Capital	12,599	8,750	8,576	5,534	9,707	11,383	11,966	10,347	11,073	NA
Capital Expenditures	136	105	92.0	70.0	111	74.0	60.0	55.0	NA	NA
Cash Flow	1,298	1,180	780	-3,538	602	935	837	677	NA	NA
Current Ratio	1.2	1.2	1.1	1.2	1.2	1.4	1.4	0.8	1.1	NA
% Long Term Debt of Capitalization	34.8	17.8	18.6	30.2	18.1	14.3	14.0	16.0	18.6	NA
% Net Income of Revenue	13.3	11.9	9.7	NM	6.7	5.2	4.3	2.6	NM	NA
% Return on Assets	6.9	6.8	5.2	NM	2.8	2.9	2.4	1.2	NM	NA
% Return on Equity	16.7	15.5	13.6	NM	5.7	5.4	4.5	2.3	NM	NA

Data as orig reptd.; bef. results of disc opers/spec. items. Per share data adj. for stk. divs.; EPS diluted. E-Estimated. NA-Not Available. NM-Not Meaningful. NR-Not Ranked. UR-Under Review.

Office: 401 North Main Street, Winston-Salem, NC 27102-2866.
Telephone: 336-741-2000.
Email: talktorjrt@rjrt.com
Website: http://www.reynoldsamerican.com

Chrmn, Pres & CEO: S.M. Ivey
EVP & CFO: D.M. Neal
EVP & General Counsel: E.J. Lambeth
SVP & Chief Acctg Officer: M.S. Desmond

SVP & Treas: D.A. Fawley
Board Members: B. Atkins, J. T. Chain, Jr., M. D. Feinstein, S. M. Ivey, N. Mensah, A. Monteiro de Castro, H. G. Powell, J. P. Viviano, T. C. Wajnert, N. R. Withington

Auditor: KPMG, Greensboro
Founded: 1875
Domicile: Delaware
Employees: 7,800

Robert Half International Inc.

STANDARD &POOR'S

S&P Recommendation HOLD ★★★☆☆

Price	12-Mo. Target Price	Investment Style
$25.48 (as of Nov 23, 2007)	$32.00	Large-Cap Blend

GICS Sector Industrials
Sub-Industry Human Resource & Employment Services

Summary This company is the world's largest specialized provider of temporary and permanent personnel in the fields of accounting and finance.

Key Stock Statistics (Source S&P, Vickers, company reports)

52-Wk Range	$42.21– 24.83	S&P Oper. EPS 2007**E**	1.79	Market Capitalization(B)	$4.177	Beta	1.94
Trailing 12-Month EPS	$1.77	S&P Oper. EPS 2008**E**	2.00	Yield (%)	1.57	S&P 3-Yr. Proj. EPS CAGR(%)	17.00
Trailing 12-Month P/E	14.4	P/E on S&P Oper. EPS 2007**E**	14.2	Dividend Rate/Share	$0.40	S&P Credit Rating	NA
$10K Invested 5 Yrs Ago	$13,123	Common Shares Outstg. (M)	163.9	Institutional Ownership (%)	83		

Price Performance

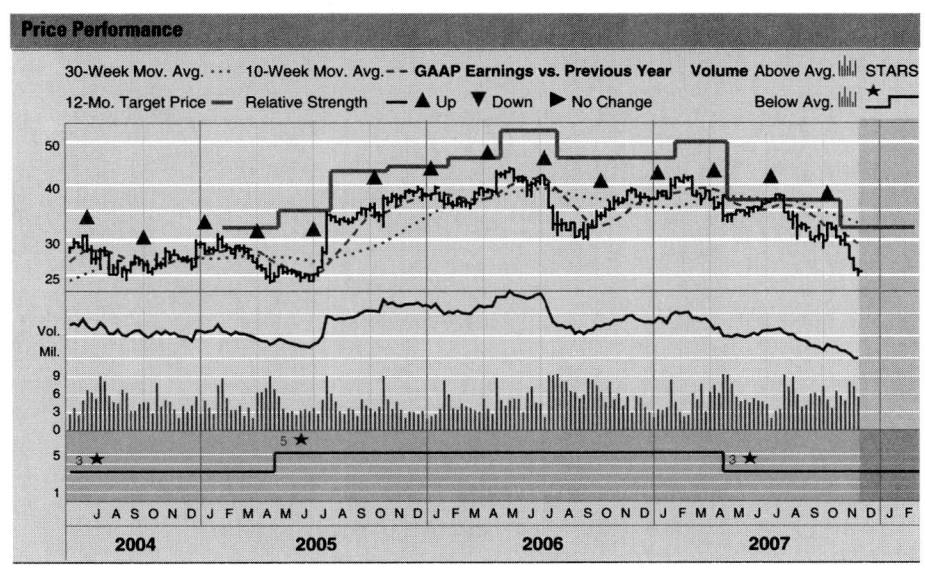

30-Week Mov. Avg. · · · 10-Week Mov. Avg. ‑ ‑ **GAAP Earnings vs. Previous Year** Volume Above Avg. STARS
12-Mo. Target Price — Relative Strength — ▲ Up ▼ Down ▶ No Change Below Avg.

Options: ASE, CBOE, Ph

Analysis prepared by **Michael W. Jaffe** on October 31, 2007, when the stock traded at **$29.99**.

Highlights

► We expect an 11% revenue rise in 2008, on our outlook for ongoing global economic gains. We also see demand being lifted by a focus on internal accounting controls and other corporate governance requirements, in light of various governance problems in the business world that were largely discovered several years ago. We expect flattish revenues at Protiviti, with reduced assignments related to the Sarbanes-Oxley Act likely to be offset by office additions.

► We expect flat operating margins in 2008. We see profits limited by the cost of investments in Protiviti's foreign operations, and the reduced utilization rates that we see at the unit. On the other hand, RHI will likely be assisted by the increased demand we anticipate for its human resource services and a larger proportion of permanent placements (which have better margins than temporary placements). Newly hired permanent hire recruiters have recently hampered margins, but we see their efficiency improving over the next year.

► In 2008, we expect low-teens revenue growth at RHI's temporary services businesses, and gains solidly higher than those at its permanent placement business.

Investment Rationale/Risk

► RHI's operating performance has been in an uptrend since early 2004, aided by, in our view, expanding labor markets and a greater need for internal accounting controls in U.S. companies. We see conditions remaining positive in RHI's staffing business through at least 2008, but we expect them to be partly offset by our outlook for soft results at Protiviti. Based on these factors and valuation considerations, we think the shares are near an appropriate valuation.

► Risks to our recommendation and target price include softer economic conditions and a worse than expected impact from Protiviti.

► The shares recently traded at 15X our 2008 EPS forecast, about in line with RHI's peers. We expect ongoing solid growth in RHI's staffing business over the next few years, especially since we believe current corporate trends will keep demand strong in its primary business areas. However, we see a likely sluggish performance at Protiviti limiting EPS gains. We think RHI should trade at about a peer multiple, and have a 12-month target price of $32, or 16X our 2008 EPS estimate.

Qualitative Risk Assessment

LOW	MEDIUM	HIGH

Our risk assessment reflects what we view as RHI's strong position in accounting and finance placements and a healthy balance sheet. This is offset by the highly cyclical nature of the company's business, which is largely dependent on the U.S. economy and the health of labor markets.

Quantitative Evaluations

S&P Quality Ranking   **B**

D	C	B-	B	B+	A-	A	A+

Relative Strength Rank   **WEAK**

22

LOWEST = 1   HIGHEST = 99

Revenue/Earnings Data

Revenue (Million $)

	1Q	2Q	3Q	4Q	Year
2007	1,097	1,149	1,179	--	--
2006	943.9	981.8	1,028	1,060	4,014
2005	770.0	816.7	867.0	884.8	3,338
2004	572.3	641.2	708.0	754.2	2,676
2003	473.2	483.0	501.1	517.7	1,975
2002	468.5	473.1	484.8	478.6	1,905

Earnings Per Share ($)

	1Q	2Q	3Q	4Q	Year
2007	0.42	0.44	0.46	E0.47	E1.79
2006	0.38	0.39	0.43	0.45	1.65
2005	0.29	0.33	0.37	0.37	1.36
2004	0.09	0.18	0.24	0.28	0.79
2003	-0.02	Nil	0.03	0.03	0.04
2002	0.05	0.02	-0.02	-0.04	0.01

Fiscal year ended Dec. 31. Next earnings report expected: Late January. EPS Estimates based on S&P Operating Earnings; historical GAAP earnings are as reported.

Dividend Data (Dates: mm/dd Payment Date: mm/dd/yy)

Amount ($)	Date Decl.	Ex-Div. Date	Stk. of Record	Payment Date
0.100	02/13	02/22	02/26	03/15/07
0.100	05/03	05/23	05/25	06/15/07
0.100	07/31	08/22	08/24	09/14/07
0.100	10/31	11/21	11/26	12/14/07

Dividends have been paid since 2004. Source: Company reports.

Please read the Required Disclosures and Analyst Certification on the last page of this report.

The **McGraw·Hill** Companies

Robert Half International Inc.

STANDARD &POOR'S

Business Summary October 31, 2007

Robert Half International is the world's largest specialized staffing service in the fields of accounting and finance. In May 2002, RHI expanded its offerings to include risk consulting and internal audit services through its Protiviti unit. In 2006, the company derived 78% of its revenue base from activities in temporary and consultant staffing, 8% from permanent placement staffing, and the remaining 14% from risk consulting and internal audit services. Foreign operations accounted for 21% of RHI's revenues in 2006. As of 2006 year end, the company's staffing businesses had more than 350 offices in 42 states, the District of Columbia and 17 foreign countries, while Protiviti had more than 55 offices in 22 states and 14 foreign countries.

RHI's Accountemps temporary services division offers customers an economical means of dealing with uneven or peak work loads for accounting, tax and finance personnel. The temporary workers are employees of Accountemps, and are paid by Accountemps only when working on customer assignments. The customer pays a fixed rate for hours worked. If the client converts the temporary hire to a permanent worker, it typically pays a one-time fee for the conversion.

RHI offers permanent placement services through Robert Half Finance & Accounting, which specializes in accounting, financial, tax and banking personnel. Fees for successful permanent placements are paid only by the employer and are usually a percentage of the new employee's annual salary.

Since the early 1990s, the company has expanded into additional specialty fields. OfficeTeam, formed in 1991, provides skilled temporary and full-time administrative and office personnel. In 1992, RHI acquired Robert Half Legal (formerly The Affiliates), which places temporary and regular employees in attorney, paralegal, legal administrative and other legal support positions. In 1994, Robert Half Technology (formerly RHI Consulting) was created to concentrate on the placement of contract and full-time information technology consultants. In 1997, the company established Robert Half Management Resources (formerly RHI Management Resources) to provide senior level project professionals specializing in the accounting and finance fields. The Creative Group, which started up in 1999, provides project staffing in the advertising, marketing and Web design fields. In 2006, Accountemps provided 37% of revenues, OfficeTeam 19%, other placement businesses 30%, and Protiviti 14%.

Company Financials Fiscal Year Ended Dec. 31

Per Share Data ($)	2006	2005	2004	2003	2002	2001	2000	1999	1998	1997
Tangible Book Value	5.15	4.72	4.30	3.65	3.41	3.69	3.13	2.28	1.89	1.33
Cash Flow	2.00	1.66	1.07	0.42	0.42	1.07	1.30	0.98	0.82	0.59
Earnings	1.65	1.36	0.79	0.04	0.01	0.67	1.00	0.77	0.70	0.50
S&P Core Earnings	1.65	1.29	0.71	-0.11	-0.17	0.51	NA	NA	NA	NA
Dividends	0.32	0.28	0.18	Nil	Nil	Nil	Nil	Nil	Nil	Nil
Payout Ratio	19%	21%	23%	Nil	Nil	Nil	Nil	Nil	Nil	Nil
Prices:High	43.94	39.86	30.98	25.18	30.90	30.90	38.63	24.19	30.13	21.53
Prices:Low	29.91	23.95	20.69	11.44	11.94	18.50	12.34	10.22	14.50	11.13
P/E Ratio:High	27	29	39	NM	NM	46	39	32	43	43
P/E Ratio:Low	18	18	26	NM	NM	28	12	13	21	22

Income Statement Analysis (Million $)										
Revenue	4,014	3,338	2,676	1,975	1,905	2,453	2,699	2,081	1,793	1,303
Operating Income	511	433	280	75.0	71.2	261	348	268	240	172
Depreciation	61.1	51.3	49.1	65.9	72.3	73.1	56.6	39.1	24.6	17.7
Interest Expense	Nil	Nil	Nil	Nil	Nil	Nil	Nil	Nil	Nil	Nil
Pretax Income	466	392	235	11.7	3.50	196	302	235	221	159
Effective Tax Rate	39.3%	39.3%	40.1%	45.5%	38.0%	38.3%	38.3%	39.7%	40.5%	41.0%
Net Income	283	238	141	6.39	2.17	121	186	141	132	93.7
S&P Core Earnings	283	224	125	-18.4	-30.2	91.1	NA	NA	NA	NA

Balance Sheet & Other Financial Data (Million $)										
Cash	447	458	437	377	317	347	239	151	166	131
Current Assets	1,112	1,017	916	699	643	686	672	491	430	334
Total Assets	1,459	1,319	1,199	980	936	994	971	777	704	561
Current Liabilities	403	337	280	189	184	177	237	176	153	122
Long Term Debt	3.83	2.70	2.27	2.34	2.40	2.48	2.54	2.60	3.40	4.53
Common Equity	1,043	971	912	789	745	806	719	576	522	419
Total Capital	1,047	974	914	791	747	808	721	601	551	439
Capital Expenditures	80.4	61.8	32.9	36.5	48.3	84.7	74.0	52.6	67.2	32.0
Cash Flow	344	289	190	72.3	74.5	194	243	181	156	111
Current Ratio	2.8	3.0	3.3	3.7	3.5	3.9	2.8	2.8	2.8	2.7
% Long Term Debt of Capitalization	0.4	0.3	0.2	0.3	0.3	0.3	0.4	0.4	0.6	1.1
% Net Income of Revenue	7.1	7.1	5.3	0.3	0.1	4.9	6.9	6.8	7.3	7.2
% Return on Assets	20.4	18.9	12.9	0.7	0.2	12.3	21.3	19.1	20.8	19.2
% Return on Equity	28.1	25.3	16.5	0.8	0.3	15.9	28.7	25.7	28.0	25.8

Data as orig reptd.; bef. results of disc opers/spec. items. Per share data adj. for stk. divs.; EPS diluted. E-Estimated. NA-Not Available. NM-Not Meaningful. NR-Not Ranked. UR-Under Review.

Office: 2884 Sand Hill Rd , Menlo Park, CA 94025-7072.
Telephone: 650-234-6000.
Website: http://www.rhi.com
Chrmn & CEO: H.M. Messmer, Jr.

Pres, Vice Chrmn & CFO: M.K. Waddell
EVP & Treas: M.C. Buckley

Board Members: A. S. Berwick, Jr., F. P. Furth, E. W. Gibbons, H. M. Messmer, Jr., T. J. Ryan, J. S. Schaub, M. K. Waddell

Founded: 1967
Domicile: Delaware
Employees: 255,400

The **McGraw·Hill** Companies

Rockwell Automation Inc.

STANDARD
&POOR'S

S&P Recommendation	**BUY** ★★★★☆	Price $64.97 (as of Nov 26, 2007)	12-Mo. Target Price $81.00	Investment Style Large-Cap Blend

GICS Sector Industrials
Sub-Industry Electrical Components & Equipment

Summary This former aerospace and defense contractor (formerly Rockwell International) now primarily manufactures automated industrial equipment and power generators.

Key Stock Statistics (Source S&P, Vickers, company reports)

52-Wk Range	$75.60–56.73	S&P Oper. EPS 2008**E**	4.37	Market Capitalization(B)	$9.695	Beta	1.24
Trailing 12-Month EPS	$9.23	S&P Oper. EPS 2009**E**	5.04	Yield (%)	1.79	S&P 3-Yr. Proj. EPS CAGR(%)	20.00
Trailing 12-Month P/E	7.0	P/E on S&P Oper. EPS 2008**E**	14.9	Dividend Rate/Share	$1.16	S&P Credit Rating	A
$10K Invested 5 Yrs Ago	$35,062	Common Shares Outstg. (M)	149.2	Institutional Ownership (%)	69		

Price Performance

30-Week Mov. Avg. ··· 10-Week Mov. Avg. -- **GAAP Earnings vs. Previous Year** Volume Above Avg. ▐▐▌ STARS
12-Mo. Target Price — Relative Strength — ▲ Up ▼ Down ► No Change Below Avg. ▐▐▌ ★

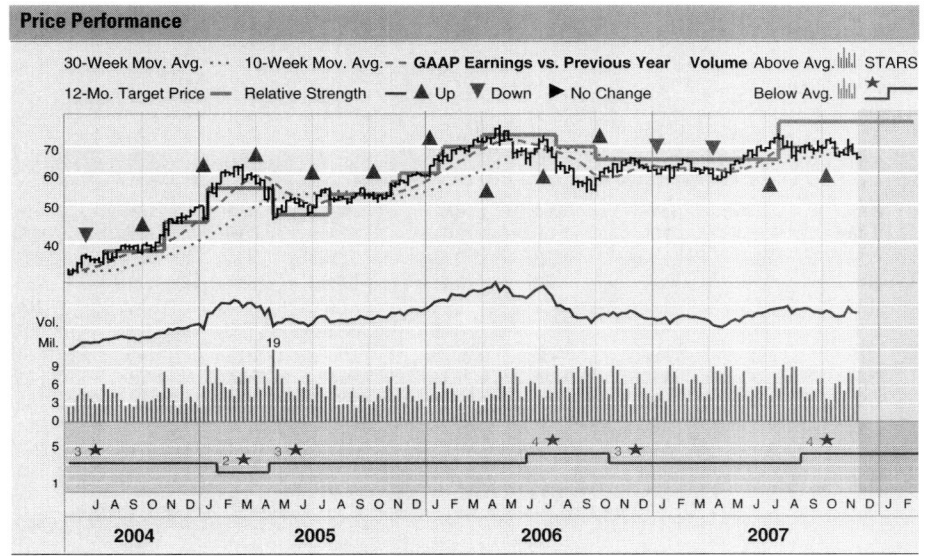

Options: ASE, CBOE, Ph

Analysis prepared by **Christopher Lippincott** on November 26, 2007, when the stock traded at **$65.58**.

Highlights

➤ We expect revenues to increase 11% in FY 08 (Sep.) and 9% in FY 09 on a continuing operations basis, driven primarily by strong order growth in the Control Products and Solutions segment, international demand and contributions from recent acquisitions. In our view, ROK will benefit from strength in Asia, the Middle East and Latin America, expanding market share, and internal growth initiatives. We believe this will help to partially offset moderating U.S. industrial growth and U.S. automotive weakness, and slightly lower growth rates in developed economies.

➤ In our opinion, EBIT margins will remain flat in FY 08 and expand slightly in FY 09. We see headwinds including modest dilution from recent acquisitions, globalization impacts and material cost inflation. In FY 09, however, we expect ROK to benefit from greater operating leverage as volumes increase, higher productivity, and an improved product mix as the company focuses on higher margin products in the Architecture and Software segment and as a result of its Power Systems divestiture.

➤ Assuming steady tax rates, we project operating EPS of $4.37 in FY 08 and $5.04 in FY 09.

Investment Rationale/Risk

➤ We believe ROK's divestiture of its Power Systems segment will enable it to improve its focus on sales growth, accelerate structural cost reduction, amplify its productivity, and generate greater free cash flow. We think international demand will continue to drive revenue growth, especially in Asia, Latin America, and Eastern Europe, where we anticipate manufacturers will continue to invest in automation projects to improve plant efficiency. We are positive on ROK's share repurchase program, and its strong balance sheet and attractive free cash flow and dividend yield.

➤ Risks to our recommendation and target price include weaker than expected global economic growth, rising raw material costs, and lower than forecast benefits from rationalization plans.

➤ Our 12-month price target of $81 represents a blend of two valuation metrics. Our DCF model, which assumes a 3% perpetual growth rate and a 10.9% discount rate, indicates an intrinsic value of $82. We also apply a target EV/EBITDA multiple of 12.4X--a premium to ROK's peers--to our calendar 2008 EBITDA estimate, implying a value of $80.

Qualitative Risk Assessment

LOW	**MEDIUM**	HIGH

Our risk assessment reflects the company's highly cyclical end market demand, offset by corporate governance practices that we view as favorable and an S&P Quality Ranking of B+, reflecting average stability in earnings and dividend growth.

Quantitative Evaluations

S&P Quality Ranking   B+

D	C	B-	B	**B+**	A-	A	A+

Relative Strength Rank   MODERATE

56

LOWEST = 1   HIGHEST = 99

Revenue/Earnings Data

Revenue (Million $)

	1Q	2Q	3Q	4Q	Year
2007	1,146	1,207	1,281	1,371	5,004
2006	1,301	1,378	1,428	1,454	5,561
2005	1,185	1,218	1,265	1,335	5,003
2004	990.3	1,080	1,135	1,206	4,411
2003	984.0	1,029	1,033	1,058	4,104
2002	939.0	958.0	995.0	1,017	3,909

Earnings Per Share ($)

2007	0.76	0.65	1.07	1.07	3.53
2006	0.80	0.83	0.83	1.04	3.49
2005	0.65	0.75	0.68	0.69	2.77
2004	0.30	0.39	0.66	0.51	1.85
2003	0.22	0.26	0.67	0.33	1.49
2002	0.16	0.31	0.47	0.26	1.20

Fiscal year ended Sep. 30. Next earnings report expected: Late January. EPS Estimates based on S&P Operating Earnings; historical GAAP earnings are as reported.

Dividend Data (Dates: mm/dd Payment Date: mm/dd/yy)

Amount ($)	Date Decl.	Ex-Div. Date	Stk. of Record	Payment Date
0.290	02/07	02/15	02/20	03/12/07
0.290	04/04	05/10	05/14	06/04/07
0.290	06/08	08/09	08/13	09/04/07
0.290	11/07	11/15	11/19	12/10/07

Dividends have been paid since 1948. Source: Company reports.

Rockwell Automation Inc.

STANDARD
&POOR'S

Business Summary November 26, 2007

CORPORATE OVERVIEW. In the early 1990s, Rockwell Automation (formerly Rockwell International) operated a broad range of manufacturing businesses. Following a series of divestitures that included the 2001 spin-off of Rockwell Collins and the 2006 divestiture of Power Systems, it now operates two business segments: Control Products and Solutions and Architecture and Software.

The Control Products and Solutions (CS) segment accounted for 55% of FY 07 (Sep.) total revenues and 40% of total operating profits, with 14% profit margins. CS supplies industrial control products and services focused on helping customers control, monitor and improve manufacturing processes. Products include industrial controls, variable frequency drives, smart motor controls, electronic overload controls, power control and motor control centers, drive systems, custom OEM panels, information systems and systems integration. Major markets served include consumer products, food and beverage, trans-

portation, metals, mining, pulp and paper, and oil and gas. Competitors include Emerson Electric, GE, and Schneider Electric.

The Architecture and Software segment (A&S) generated 60% of FY 07 sales and 60% of operating profits, with 26% operating margins. The division offers control platforms and software as well as bundled automation products for enterprise business systems, distribution and supply chains. Offerings include controllers, motor control sensors, programmable logic controllers (PLCs), input/output devices, sensors and software, networks, packaged software and safety components.

Company Financials Fiscal Year Ended Sep. 30

Per Share Data ($)	2007	2006	2005	2004	2003	2002	2001	2000	1999	1998
Tangible Book Value	NA	4.40	2.95	3.95	2.41	2.61	2.23	6.90	6.56	10.05
Cash Flow	NA	4.35	3.68	2.83	2.53	2.29	5.39	4.80	4.74	0.99
Earnings	3.53	3.49	2.77	1.85	1.49	1.20	0.68	3.35	3.01	-0.55
S&P Core Earnings	NA	3.48	2.68	1.88	1.16	0.75	-0.06	NA	NA	NA
Dividends	1.16	0.90	0.78	0.66	0.66	0.66	0.93	1.02	1.02	1.02
Payout Ratio	33%	26%	28%	36%	44%	55%	137%	30%	34%	NM
Prices:High	75.60	79.47	63.30	49.97	36.10	22.79	49.45	54.50	64.94	61.63
Prices:Low	56.73	53.49	45.40	28.45	18.75	14.71	11.78	27.69	39.94	32.13
P/E Ratio:High	21	23	23	27	24	19	73	16	22	NM
P/E Ratio:Low	16	15	16	15	13	12	17	8	13	NM

Income Statement Analysis (Million $)

	2007	2006	2005	2004	2003	2002	2001	2000	1999	1998
Revenue	NA	5,561	5,003	4,411	4,104	3,909	4,279	7,151	7,043	6,752
Operating Income	NA	1,073	944	691	543	488	1,079	1,223	1,203	1,001
Depreciation	NA	154	171	187	198	206	872	276	337	306
Interest Expense	NA	58.4	45.8	41.7	52.0	66.0	83.0	73.0	84.0	58.0
Pretax Income	NA	365	737	438	299	233	168	943	890	25.0
Effective Tax Rate	NA	NM	29.7%	19.2%	5.69%	3.00%	25.6%	32.6%	34.6%	536.0%
Net Income	NA	628	518	354	282	226	125	636	582	-109
S&P Core Earnings	NA	628	498	361	221	142	-12.0	NA	NA	NA

Balance Sheet & Other Financial Data (Million $)

	2007	2006	2005	2004	2003	2002	2001	2000	1999	1998
Cash	NA	415	464	474	226	289	121	190	356	103
Current Assets	NA	2,188	2,187	2,026	1,736	1,775	1,697	3,206	3,582	4,096
Total Assets	NA	4,735	4,525	4,201	3,986	4,024	4,074	6,390	6,704	7,170
Current Liabilities	NA	1,293	941	864	820	966	867	1,820	2,108	1,983
Long Term Debt	NA	748	748	758	764	767	922	924	911	908
Common Equity	NA	1,918	1,649	1,861	1,587	1,609	1,600	2,669	2,637	3,245
Total Capital	NA	2,822	2,397	2,708	2,388	2,534	2,693	3,593	3,548	4,153
Capital Expenditures	NA	150	124	98.0	109	104	157	315	377	408
Cash Flow	NA	782	690	541	480	432	997	912	919	197
Current Ratio	NA	1.7	2.3	2.3	2.1	1.8	2.0	1.8	1.7	2.1
% Long Term Debt of Capitalization	NA	26.5	31.2	28.0	32.0	30.3	34.2	25.7	25.7	21.9
% Net Income of Revenue	NA	11.3	10.4	8.0	6.9	5.8	2.9	8.9	8.3	NM
% Return on Assets	NA	13.6	11.9	8.7	7.1	5.6	2.7	9.8	8.4	NM
% Return on Equity	NA	35.2	29.5	20.5	17.6	14.1	5.9	24.4	19.8	NM

Data as orig reptd.; bef. results of disc opers/spec. items. Per share data adj. for stk. divs.; EPS diluted. E-Estimated. NA-Not Available. NM-Not Meaningful. NR-Not Ranked. UR-Under Review.

Office: 1201 S 2nd St, Milwaukee, WI 53204-2498.
Telephone: 414-382-2000.
Website: http://www.rockwellautomation.com
Chrmn, Pres & CEO: K.D. Nosbusch

SVP & CFO: T.D. Crandall
SVP, Secy & General Counsel: D.M. Hagerman
VP & Treas: S.W. Etzel
VP & Cntlr: D.M. Dorgan

Board Members: B. C. Alewine, D. H. Davis, Jr., B. C. Johnson, W. T. McCormick, Jr., K. D. Nosbusch, B. M. Rockwell, D. Speer, J. F. Toot, Jr., K. F. Yontz

Founded: 1928
Domicile: Delaware
Employees: 23,000

Rockwell Collins Inc.

STANDARD &POOR'S

S&P Recommendation **BUY** ★★★★☆	Price $71.90 (as of Nov 23, 2007)	12-Mo. Target Price $84.00	Investment Style Large-Cap Growth

GICS Sector Industrials
Sub-Industry Aerospace & Defense

Summary This company is one of the world's largest makers of military and commercial avionics and electronics, including cockpit controls, communications and navigation systems, and in-flight entertainment systems.

Key Stock Statistics (Source S&P, Vickers, company reports)

52-Wk Range	$76.00–59.15	S&P Oper. EPS 2008**E**	3.92	Market Capitalization(B)	$11.714	Beta	0.91
Trailing 12-Month EPS	$3.45	S&P Oper. EPS 2009**E**	4.45	Yield (%)	0.89	S&P 3-Yr. Proj. EPS CAGR(%)	14.00
Trailing 12-Month P/E	20.8	P/E on S&P Oper. EPS 2008**E**	18.3	Dividend Rate/Share	$0.64	S&P Credit Rating	NA
$10K Invested 5 Yrs Ago	$31,668	Common Shares Outstg. (M)	162.9	Institutional Ownership (%)	68		

Price Performance

30-Week Mov. Avg. ··· 10-Week Mov. Avg. -- **GAAP Earnings vs. Previous Year** Volume Above Avg. STARS
12-Mo. Target Price — Relative Strength — ▲ Up ▼ Down ► No Change Below Avg. ★

Options: ASE, Ph

Analysis prepared by **Richard Tortoriello** on November 01, 2007, when the stock traded at **$ 75.40**.

Highlights

➤ We project that sales will rise about 10% in FY 08 (Sep.), driven by 15% growth in commercial-aerospace related systems and 5% growth in government/military aircraft systems. Sales increased 14% in FY 07, with a 9% gain in government systems and a 20% expansion in commercial systems. We expect FY 08 commercial systems growth to be driven by strong commercial aerospace and business jet markets, and strong demand for aftermarket parts and services due to increased air travel. We also expect continued demand for military aircraft upgrade programs and defense communications.

➤ We project a 100 basis point (bp) increase in operating margins in FY 08, to 22%, on volume growth and continued improvement in efficiency. COL increased margins by 100 bps in FY 07, despite sharply higher R&D expenditures versus FY 06.

➤ We forecast EPS of $3.92 for FY 08, followed by a 14% increase, to $4.45, in FY 09. We project free cash flow (cash flow from operating activities less capital expenditures) will total about $3.00 per share in FY 08, up from $2.84 in FY 07.

Investment Rationale/Risk

➤ We continue to see COL benefiting from what we view as a very strong aerospace market and favorable execution by management. COL's return on invested capital was 33% in FY 06, and we estimate it was near 35% in FY 07. We look for solid demand from the commercial aerospace, business jet, and military markets, as well as what we view as the company's excellent operational management, to aid COL in continuing to achieve returns of triple its cost of capital, which we estimate at about 10%.

➤ Risks to our recommendation and target price include an unanticipated deterioration in COL's primary commercial and military avionics end markets, the loss of government contracts, competitive threats, and the possibility of operational missteps.

➤ Our 12-month target price of $84 is based on a P/E of about 19X our FY 09 EPS estimate. This compares to a five-year historical average forward P/E of about 17X for COL, with highs above 20X. We believe that COL deserves this premium due to what we view as its well-above-average recent record of growth in earnings.

Qualitative Risk Assessment

LOW	**MEDIUM**	HIGH

Our risk assessment reflects the company's exposure to the airline industry, dependence on U.S. military procurement and R&D budgets, and high fixed-cost structure, offset by what we view as a solid balance sheet, strong returns, and corporate governance practices that we consider favorable versus peers.

Quantitative Evaluations

S&P Quality Ranking NR

D	C	B-	B	B+	A-	A	A+

Relative Strength Rank STRONG

74

LOWEST = 1   HIGHEST = 99

Revenue/Earnings Data

Revenue (Million $)

	1Q	2Q	3Q	4Q	Year
2007	993.0	1,083	1,113	1,226	4,415
2006	881.0	957.0	964.0	1,061	3,863
2005	763.0	829.0	890.0	963.0	3,445
2004	628.0	719.0	744.0	839.0	2,930
2003	561.0	618.0	620.0	743.0	2,542
2002	563.0	608.0	623.0	698.0	2,492

Earnings Per Share ($)

2007	0.84	0.82	0.86	0.93	3.45
2006	0.59	0.65	0.70	0.79	2.73
2005	0.50	0.52	0.56	0.62	2.20
2004	0.38	0.39	0.42	0.48	1.67
2003	0.27	0.33	0.43	0.40	1.43
2002	0.26	0.31	0.33	0.38	1.28

Fiscal year ended Sep. 30. Next earnings report expected: Late January. EPS Estimates based on S&P Operating Earnings; historical GAAP earnings are as reported.

Dividend Data (Dates: mm/dd Payment Date: mm/dd/yy)

Amount ($)	Date Decl.	Ex-Div. Date	Stk. of Record	Payment Date
0.160	01/29	02/08	02/12	03/05/07
0.160	04/26	05/10	05/14	06/04/07
0.160	07/30	08/09	08/13	09/04/07
0.160	11/01	11/07	11/12	12/03/07

Dividends have been paid since 2001. Source: Company reports.

Please read the Required Disclosures and Analyst Certification on the last page of this report.

Rockwell Collins Inc.

Business Summary November 01, 2007

CORPORATE OVERVIEW. This global $4 billion revenue aircraft electronics (avionics) maker conducts its business through two segments: Commercial Systems (CS) and Government Systems (GS). CS (53% of revenues and 48% of operating earnings, and operating margins of 20% in FY 06 (Sep.)) primarily makes flight deck electronic systems and in-flight entertainment systems. CS also provides a range of repair and overhaul services. GS (47%; 52%; 20%) primarily makes communication radios and cockpit displays installed in military jets. GS also makes navigation equipment embedded in guided missiles.

Commercial Systems products include integrated avionics systems, which include liquid crystal flight displays, flight management, integrated flight control, automatic flight controls, engine indications, and crew alerts; cabin electronics, including passenger connectivity and entertainment, business support systems, networks, and environmental controls; communications products and systems; navigation products and systems; and situational awareness and surveillance products and systems, such as Heads-Up Guidance Systems, weather radar, and collision avoidance systems; flight deck systems; simulation and training systems; and maintenance, repair, parts, and support services. Customers include large commercial airplane, regional jet, and business jet makers; commercial airlines; regional airlines; fractional jet operators; and business jet operators.

Government Systems products include communications systems and products; military data link products; navigation systems and products, including radio navigation systems, global positioning systems (GPS), handheld navigation systems, and multi-mode receivers; subsystems for the flight deck that combine flight operations with navigation and guidance functions; cockpit display systems, including helmet-mounted and other displays for fighter/attack aircraft; simulation and training systems; and maintenance, repair, parts, and support services. Customers include the U.S. Department of Defense, other government agencies, civil agencies, defense contractors, and foreign ministries of defense. Products are used for airborne, ground, and shipboard applications.

In FY 06, U.S. Government sales accounted for 39% of total COL sales. Export sales and products made abroad accounted for 32% of total sales. About 89% of FY 06 sales were from fixed-price contracts, which allow benefits of cost savings but carry the burden of potential cost overruns.

Company Financials Fiscal Year Ended Sep. 30

Per Share Data ($)	2007	2006	2005	2004	2003	2002	2001	2000	1999	1998
Tangible Book Value	NA	3.30	2.13	3.29	2.21	2.93	4.48	NA	NA	NA
Cash Flow	NA	3.34	2.86	2.28	2.02	1.85	1.47	1.87	NA	NA
Earnings	3.45	2.73	2.20	1.67	1.43	1.28	0.72	1.35	NA	NA
S&P Core Earnings	NA	2.66	2.04	1.47	0.82	0.46	NA	NA	NA	NA
Dividends	0.64	0.56	0.48	0.39	0.36	0.36	Nil	NA	NA	NA
Payout Ratio	19%	21%	22%	23%	25%	28%	Nil	NA	NA	NA
Prices:High	76.00	64.31	49.80	40.94	30.10	28.00	27.12	NA	NA	NA
Prices:Low	61.25	43.49	37.22	29.16	17.20	18.50	11.80	NA	NA	NA
P/E Ratio:High	22	24	23	25	21	22	38	NA	NA	NA
P/E Ratio:Low	18	16	17	17	12	14	16	NA	NA	NA

Income Statement Analysis (Million $)										
Revenue	NA	3,863	3,445	2,930	2,542	2,492	2,820	2,510	NA	NA
Operating Income	NA	776	660	539	440	427	492	492	NA	NA
Depreciation	NA	106	119	109	105	105	131	99.0	NA	NA
Interest Expense	NA	13.0	11.0	8.00	3.00	6.00	3.00	20.0	NA	NA
Pretax Income	NA	689	547	430	368	341	224	381	NA	NA
Effective Tax Rate	NA	30.8%	27.6%	30.0%	29.9%	30.8%	37.9%	32.5%	NA	NA
Net Income	NA	477	396	301	258	236	139	257	NA	NA
S&P Core Earnings	NA	465	367	264	148	86.8	59.2	NA	NA	NA

Balance Sheet & Other Financial Data (Million $)										
Cash	NA	144	145	196	66.0	49.0	60.0	20.0	NA	NA
Current Assets	NA	1,927	1,775	1,663	1,427	1,438	1,639	1,531	NA	NA
Total Assets	NA	3,278	3,140	2,874	2,591	2,560	2,628	2,628	NA	NA
Current Liabilities	NA	1,324	1,177	964	901	1,043	1,135	1,073	NA	NA
Long Term Debt	NA	245	200	201	Nil	Nil	Nil	Nil	NA	NA
Common Equity	NA	1,206	939	1,133	833	987	1,110	1,086	NA	NA
Total Capital	NA	1,451	1,139	1,334	833	987	1,110	1,086	NA	NA
Capital Expenditures	NA	144	111	94.0	72.0	62.0	110	NA	NA	NA
Cash Flow	NA	583	515	410	363	341	270	356	NA	NA
Current Ratio	NA	1.5	1.5	1.7	1.6	1.4	1.4	1.4	NA	NA
% Long Term Debt of Capitalization	NA	16.9	17.6	15.1	Nil	Nil	Nil	Nil	NA	NA
% Net Income of Revenue	NA	12.3	11.5	10.3	10.1	9.5	4.9	10.2	NA	NA
% Return on Assets	NA	14.8	13.2	11.0	10.0	9.1	5.9	NA	NA	NA
% Return on Equity	NA	44.5	38.2	30.6	28.4	22.5	13.8	NA	NA	NA

Data as orig reptd.; bef. results of disc opers/spec. items. Per share data adj. for stk. divs.; EPS diluted. E-Estimated. NA-Not Available. NM-Not Meaningful. NR-Not Ranked. UR-Under Review.

Office: 400 Collins Rd NE, Cedar Rapids, IA 52498-0503.
Telephone: 319-295-1000.
Email: investorrelations@rockwellcollins.com
Website: http://www.rockwellcollins.com

Chrmn, Pres & CEO: C.M. Jones
COO & EVP: G.S. Churchill
COO & EVP: R.K. Ortberg
SVP & CFO: P.E. Allen

SVP, Secy & General Counsel: G.R. Chadick
Investor Contact: D. Crookshank (319-295-7575)
Board Members: D. R. Beall, A. J. Carbone, M. P. Carns, C. A. Davis, M. Donegan, R. E. Eberhart, C. M. Jones, A. J. Policano, C. L. Shavers, J. F. Toot, Jr.

Employees: 18,600

STANDARD &POOR'S

Rohm and Haas Co

S&P Recommendation HOLD ★★★★★

Price $53.22 (as of Nov 29, 2007)

12-Mo. Target Price $55.00

GICS Sector Materials
Sub-Industry Specialty Chemicals

Summary ROH, one of the world's largest producers of specialty chemicals and plastics, also supplies salt products.

Key Stock Statistics (Source S&P, Vickers, company reports)

52-Wk Range	$62.68– 47.05	S&P Oper. EPS 2007**E**	3.28	Market Capitalization(B)	$10.560	Beta	1.03
Trailing 12-Month EPS	$3.04	S&P Oper. EPS 2008**E**	3.80	Yield (%)	2.78	S&P 3-Yr. Proj. EPS CAGR(%)	10.00
Trailing 12-Month P/E	17.5	P/E on S&P Oper. EPS 2007**E**	16.2	Dividend Rate/Share	$1.48	S&P Credit Rating	BBB
$10K Invested 5 Yrs Ago	$16,398	Common Shares Outstg. (M)	198.4	Institutional Ownership (%)	90		

Price Performance

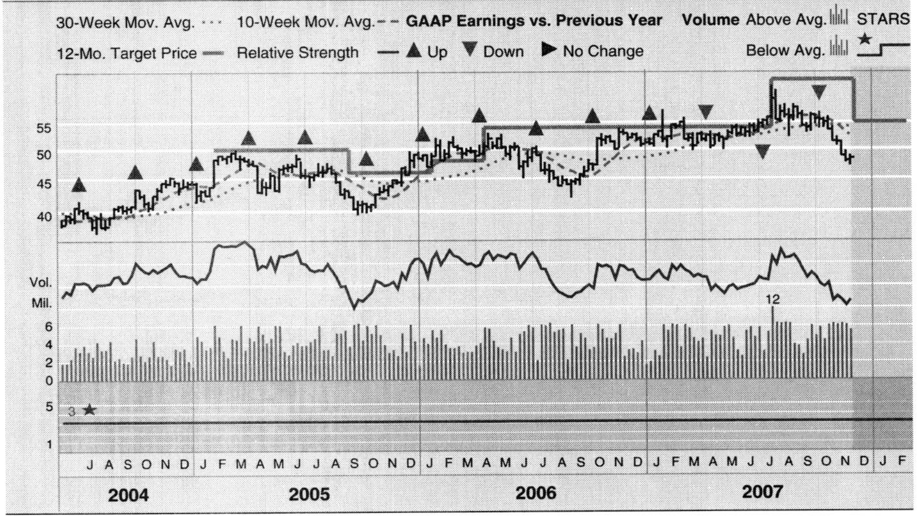
30-Week Mov. Avg. ··· 10-Week Mov. Avg.- - GAAP Earnings vs. Previous Year Volume Above Avg. STARS
12-Mo. Target Price — Relative Strength — ▲ Up ▼ Down ▶ No Change Below Avg.
55
50
45
40
Vol.
Mil.
12
6
4
2
0
5
3 ★
1
J A S O N D J F M A M J J A S O N D J F M A M J J A S O N D J F M A M J J A S O N D J F
2004
2005
2006
2007

Options: ASE, Ph

Analysis prepared by **Richard O'Reilly, CFA** on November 29, 2007, when the stock traded at **$ 53.22**.

Highlights

- We expect sales in 2008 to rise about 10% from the $8.8 billion we project for 2007, driven by gains in European and emerging markets, small acquisitions made in 2007, and price increases for chemical products, offsetting the continued impact of reduced U.S. construction related markets. We see electronic materials sales continuing to grow at a high single digit rate. While we expect modestly higher contract prices for ice-control salt in 2008, the salt business may have a difficult comparison following an expected 20% sales gain in 2007.
- We estimate gross margins will improve sequentially during the year, helped by a continued shift in the product mix and as price increases are achieved. Results in 2007 were hurt by about $0.17 from extended operating problems at ROH's largest monomer plant and by unexpected higher raw material costs. Selling and R&D expenses in total are projected to be 15% of sales.
- We believe that EPS comparisons will benefit from ROH's accelerated stock repurchases, outweighing higher interest expense as a result of increased debt.

Investment Rationale/Risk

- We have a hold opinion on the shares, based on total return potential. We view the company's fundamentals as favorable, although we expect volume growth to remain modest in 2008. We project that the company will largely recover through price increases a renewal surge in raw material and energy costs in late 2007. The company plans to have a less conservative debt ratio than usual as a result of its expanded stock repurchase program. It may also sell its salt business to finance potential acquisitions in chemicals.
- Risks to our recommendation and target price include unexpected cost increases and/or supply shortages for raw materials, unsuccessful new product introductions, unusually mild winter weather and soft demand for ice-control salt, and unscheduled plant outages and interruptions by the company and/or its suppliers.
- Our 12-month target price of $55 is based on a P/E of about 14.5X, below peers, applied to our 2008 EPS estimate. The dividend, increased in 2007 for the 30th consecutive year, provides an above-market yield, and we expect it to continue to rise over the long term.

Qualitative Risk Assessment

LOW | **MEDIUM** | HIGH

Our risk assessment reflects our view of the broad mix and cash flow generation ability of the company's business segments, offset by the cyclical nature of many of the product lines and exposure to volatile raw material and energy costs.

Quantitative Evaluations

S&P Quality Ranking A

D | C | B- | B | B+ | A- | **A** | A+

Relative Strength Rank STRONG

82

LOWEST = 1 HIGHEST = 99

Revenue/Earnings Data

Revenue (Million $)

	1Q	2Q	3Q	4Q	Year
2007	2,160	2,190	2,204	--	--
2006	2,058	2,081	2,065	2,026	8,230
2005	2,022	2,007	1,953	2,012	7,994
2004	1,832	1,801	1,803	1,864	7,300
2003	1,613	1,570	1,591	1,647	6,421
2002	1,381	1,457	1,454	1,435	5,727

Earnings Per Share ($)

2007	0.86	0.75	0.61	**E**0.78	**E**3.28
2006	0.93	0.87	0.86	0.76	3.41
2005	0.70	0.80	0.76	0.59	2.86
2004	0.51	0.52	0.61	0.56	2.21
2003	0.37	-0.02	0.45	0.49	1.30
2002	0.38	0.42	0.35	0.16	0.98

Fiscal year ended Dec. 31. Next earnings report expected: Late January. EPS Estimates based on S&P Operating Earnings; historical GAAP earnings are as reported.

Dividend Data (Dates: mm/dd Payment Date: mm/dd/yy)

Amount ($)	Date Decl.	Ex-Div. Date	Stk. of Record	Payment Date
0.370	05/07	05/16	05/18	06/01/07
0.370	05/07	05/16	05/18	06/01/07
0.370	07/16	08/08	08/10	09/04/07
0.370	09/28	10/31	11/02	12/01/07

Dividends have been paid since 1927. Source: Company reports.

Rohm and Haas Co

STANDARD &POOR'S

Business Summary November 29, 2007

CORPORATE OVERVIEW. Rohm & Haas is one of the world's largest specialty chemical companies, with annual sales of almost $9.0 billion. As a result of the 1999 purchase of Morton International Inc., the company is now a leading global maker of chemicals used in coatings, adhesives, sealants, plastics, and electronic materials. International operations accounted for 53% of sales in 2006.

As a result of a reorganization in January 2007, the company will report six new segments beginning in 2007 (electronic materials and salt segments remain unchanged). Paint and coatings materials (22% of sales and 28% of income in 2006) includes polymers and resins (including opaque polymers, emulsions, rheology modifiers, binders, thickeners, dispersants) for use in architectural and industrial paints and coatings. Packaging and building materials (19%, 15%) consists of the plastic additives business (7% of total sales - impact modifiers, processing aids, thermal stabilizers and lubricants); the former adhesives and sealants segment (8%) consisting of materials for use in pressure sensitive tapes and labels, laminated food packaging, graphic arts, and industrial products; and specialty polymers and coatings for use in leather, textile, graphic arts, paper, and packaging applications.

The primary materials segment (21%, 17%) consists of the former monomers business (20% of sales), which produces methyl methacrylate, acrylic acid

and specialty monomers, as well as polyacrylic acid dispersants. ROH uses these products in many of its acrylic technologies in other segments, and they are also sold externally (44% in 2006) for use in superabsorbent polymers and acrylic resins and sheet.

The performance materials segment (12%, 9%) largely consists of process chemicals and biocides (62% of segment sales - ion exchange and fluid process chemicals for water treatment and food and chemical processing; inorganic chemicals (sodium borohydride); and antimicrobials, water-soluble emulsions, dispersants, and scale inhibitors for cleaning and personal care products). The segment also includes powder coatings (29%) for automobile parts, building products, appliances, furniture and machinery; and other niche technologies such as the AgroFresh business. In October 2006, ROH sold its automotive liquids coatings business (excluding European operations) for $230 million (reported as discontinued operations in 2006; sales of $109 million in 2005). In June 2007, ROH sold its European automotive coatings business to the Mader Group.

Company Financials Fiscal Year Ended Dec. 31

Per Share Data ($)	2006	2005	2004	2003	2002	2001	2000	1999	1998	1997
Tangible Book Value	4.58	3.14	1.37	0.13	NM	NM	NM	NM	8.77	8.51
Cash Flow	5.52	5.00	4.36	3.44	3.04	2.24	4.39	5.87	4.04	3.67
Earnings	3.41	2.86	2.21	1.30	0.98	-0.31	1.61	1.27	2.52	2.13
S&P Core Earnings	3.45	2.81	1.98	0.90	0.23	-0.91	NA	NA	NA	NA
Dividends	1.28	1.12	0.97	0.86	0.82	0.80	0.78	0.74	0.69	0.63
Payout Ratio	38%	39%	44%	66%	84%	NM	48%	58%	27%	30%
Prices:High	53.99	50.00	45.41	43.05	42.60	38.70	49.44	49.25	38.88	33.75
Prices:Low	41.92	39.47	35.90	26.26	30.19	24.90	24.38	28.13	26.00	23.54
P/E Ratio:High	16	17	21	33	43	NM	31	39	15	16
P/E Ratio:Low	12	14	16	20	31	NM	15	22	10	11

Income Statement Analysis (Million $)	2006	2005	2004	2003	2002	2001	2000	1999	1998	1997
Revenue	8,230	7,994	7,300	6,421	5,727	5,666	6,879	5,339	3,720	3,999
Operating Income	1,565	1,522	1,291	1,264	1,066	973	1,395	1,220	898	896
Depreciation	465	481	481	478	457	562	613	902	276	279
Interest Expense	94.0	117	133	126	132	182	241	159	34.0	39.0
Pretax Income	1,042	872	692	415	320	-64.0	576	465	690	616
Effective Tax Rate	26.3%	25.7%	29.9%	30.6%	31.9%	NM	39.4%	46.2%	34.1%	32.6%
Net Income	755	638	496	288	218	-70.0	354	249	453	410
S&P Core Earnings	763	627	446	209	50.9	-202	NA	NA	NA	NA

Balance Sheet & Other Financial Data (Million $)	2006	2005	2004	2003	2002	2001	2000	1999	1998	1997
Cash	593	566	625	196	295	92.0	92.0	57.0	16.0	40.0
Current Assets	3,411	3,205	3,247	2,527	2,543	2,421	2,781	2,497	1,287	1,397
Total Assets	9,553	9,727	10,095	9,445	9,706	10,350	11,267	11,256	3,648	3,900
Current Liabilities	1,988	1,694	1,740	1,797	1,621	1,624	2,194	2,510	875	850
Long Term Debt	1,688	2,074	2,563	2,468	2,872	2,720	3,225	3,122	409	509
Common Equity	4,031	3,917	3,697	3,357	3,333	3,815	3,693	3,475	1,488	1,671
Total Capital	6,595	7,089	7,423	6,775	7,402	7,831	8,228	7,847	2,157	2,510
Capital Expenditures	404	333	5.00	339	407	401	391	323	229	254
Cash Flow	1,220	1,119	977	766	675	492	967	1,149	723	682
Current Ratio	1.7	1.9	1.9	1.4	1.6	1.5	1.3	1.0	1.5	1.6
% Long Term Debt of Capitalization	25.6	29.3	34.5	36.4	38.8	34.7	39.2	39.8	19.0	20.2
% Net Income of Revenue	9.2	8.0	6.8	4.5	3.8	NM	5.1	4.7	12.2	10.3
% Return on Assets	7.8	6.4	5.1	3.0	2.2	NM	3.1	3.3	12.0	10.5
% Return on Equity	19.0	16.8	14.1	8.9	5.9	NM	9.8	10.0	28.3	24.7

Data as orig reptd.; bef. results of disc opers/spec. items. Per share data adj. for stk. divs.; EPS diluted. E-Estimated. NA-Not Available. NM-Not Meaningful. NR-Not Ranked. UR-Under Review.

Office: 100 S Independence Mall W , Philadelphia, PA 19106.
Telephone: 215-592-3000.
Website: http://www.rohmhaas.com
Chrmn, Pres & CEO: R.L. Gupta

VP & CFO: J.M. Croisetiere
VP, Secy & General Counsel: R.A. Lonergan
Investor Contact: A.D. Sandifer

Board Members: W. J. Avery, R. L. Gupta, D. W. Haas, T. W. Haas, R. L. Keyser, R. J. Mills, J. P. Montoya, S. O. Moose, G. S. Omenn, G. L. Rogers, R. H. Schmitz, G. M. Whitesides, M. C. Whittington

Founded: 1909
Domicile: Delaware
Employees: 15,815

Rowan Companies Inc.

STANDARD &POOR'S

S&P Recommendation **HOLD** ★★★☆☆	Price $36.99 (as of Nov 23, 2007)	12-Mo. Target Price $43.00	Investment Style Large-Cap Value

GICS Sector Energy
Sub-Industry Oil & Gas Drilling

Summary This company performs contract oil and natural gas drilling, and builds heavy equipment and offshore drilling rigs.

Key Stock Statistics (Source S&P, Vickers, company reports)

52-Wk Range	$46.16– 29.48	S&P Oper. EPS 2007E	4.20	Market Capitalization(B)	$4.088	Beta	1.10
Trailing 12-Month EPS	$3.64	S&P Oper. EPS 2008E	4.64	Yield (%)	1.08	S&P 3-Yr. Proj. EPS CAGR(%)	30.00
Trailing 12-Month P/E	10.2	P/E on S&P Oper. EPS 2007E	8.8	Dividend Rate/Share	$0.40	S&P Credit Rating	NR
$10K Invested 5 Yrs Ago	$18,021	Common Shares Outstg. (M)	110.5	Institutional Ownership (%)	76		

Price Performance

30-Week Mov. Avg. ··· 10-Week Mov. Avg. - - **GAAP Earnings vs. Previous Year** Volume Above Avg. STARS
12-Mo. Target Price — Relative Strength — ▲ Up ▼ Down ▶ No Change Below Avg. ★

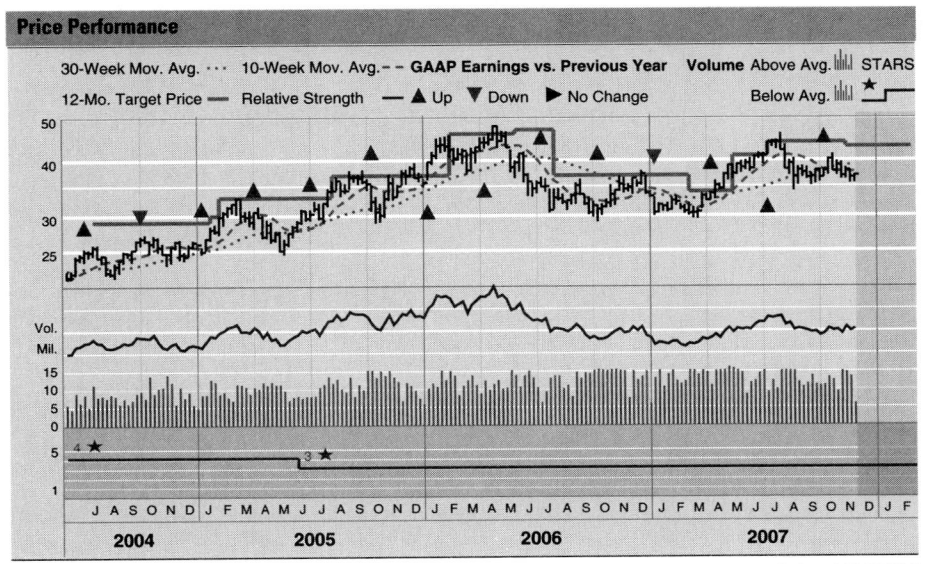

Options: ASE, CBOE, P

Analysis prepared by **Stewart Glickman, CFA** on November 20, 2007, when the stock traded at **$ 35.93**.

Highlights

➤ In November, RDC announced an aggressive expansion program, under which it will build six new high-specification jackup rigs (including two at its own shipyard in Vicksburg, MS), as well as plans to double the size of its fleet over the next 10 years. We view RDC as possessing a competitive advantage in newbuild activity versus peers, by virtue of its in-house shipyard and rig equipment manufacturing capabilities, and believe that the risks associated with a large fleet expansion are mitigated, to some extent, by these capabilities.

➤ After protracted weakness in jackup dayrates in the U.S. Gulf of Mexico (GOM), we think the GOM jackup market has largely stabilized due to the high number of rig mobilizations out of the region. We think RDC should have opportunities to mobilize more rigs out of the region, and believe that the company will take steps to do so, given the likelihood of superior dayrates and contract terms in overseas markets such as the Middle East.

➤ For 2007, we estimate total revenue growth of 35%, with a further 15% gain in 2008. We see operating EPS of $4.20 in 2007, rising to $4.64 in 2008.

Investment Rationale/Risk

➤ With recent stabilization in Gulf jackup dayrates, we think RDC's near-term prospects are improving. RDC has successfully diversified its fleet geographically, with 12 of 21 rigs working in non-U.S. waters (versus just 3 of 19 rigs two years ago), and with a fleet of largely premium assets, we also believe further rig mobilizations away from the Gulf are possible. While global newbuild jackup deliveries loom on the horizon, mainly in 2008-2010, we believe the potential for delays in deliveries, natural rig attrition, and rising demand for rigs should mitigate some of this concern.

➤ Risks to our recommendation and target price include lower dayrates and utilization; reduced drilling activity in the GOM; and shipyard delays.

➤ Our net asset valuation model, assuming terminal growth of 3% per year and a weighted average cost of capital of 11.1%, indicates that the shares have an intrinsic value of $39. Assuming relative multiples of 6X estimated 2008 EBITDA and 8X projected 2008 cash flow (a slight discount to peers, warranted by below-peer ROIC), and blending with our NAV model, our 12-month target price is $43.

Qualitative Risk Assessment

LOW	MEDIUM	HIGH

Our risk assessment reflects RDC's exposure to volatile crude oil and natural gas prices, capital spending decisions made by its oil and gas producing customers, and risks associated with operating in frontier regions. Offsetting these risks is the company's relatively higher specification jackup rig fleet than peers.

Quantitative Evaluations

S&P Quality Ranking B-

D	C	B-	B	B+	A-	A	A+

Relative Strength Rank MODERATE

68

LOWEST = 1 HIGHEST = 99

Revenue/Earnings Data

Revenue (Million $)

	1Q	2Q	3Q	4Q	Year
2007	465.3	507.0	502.2	--	--
2006	299.8	382.9	417.1	411.0	1,511
2005	222.4	244.6	284.4	317.4	1,069
2004	170.5	190.9	234.6	202.2	708.5
2003	131.4	158.1	193.9	195.8	679.1
2002	137.8	148.5	184.2	146.8	617.3

Earnings Per Share ($)

2007	0.77	1.14	1.16	E1.13	E4.20
2006	0.53	0.98	0.77	0.56	2.84
2005	0.28	0.39	0.67	0.63	1.97
2004	-0.11	-0.02	0.09	0.15	0.25
2003	-0.18	-0.07	0.12	0.05	-0.08
2002	0.92	-0.09	0.11	-0.03	0.90

Fiscal year ended Dec. 31. Next earnings report expected: Late February. EPS Estimates based on S&P Operating Earnings; historical GAAP earnings are as reported.

Dividend Data (Dates: mm/dd Payment Date: mm/dd/yy)

Amount ($)	Date Decl.	Ex-Div. Date	Stk. of Record	Payment Date
0.100	01/22	02/01	02/05	02/20/07
0.100	05/09	05/18	05/22	06/06/07
0.100	07/31	08/10	08/14	08/29/07
0.100	10/30	11/09	11/14	11/30/07

Dividends have been paid since 2005. Source: Company reports.

Rowan Companies Inc.

STANDARD &POOR'S

Business Summary November 20, 2007

CORPORATE OVERVIEW. Rowan Companies, a major provider of international and domestic contract drilling services, also operates a mini-steel mill, a manufacturing facility that produces heavy equipment, and a marine construction division. At June 20, 2007, RDC owned 17 cantilever jackups, four conventional jackups, three jackups under construction, and a fleet of 27 land rigs. Of the 21 active jackups in the fleet, nine were in the Gulf of Mexico (GOM), eight were in the Middle East, three were in the North Sea, and one was in Central America. Drilling operations generated 71% of total revenues and 92% of total segment operating income in 2006. The company's jackup rigs perform both exploratory and development drilling and, in certain areas, well workover operations. Its larger, deepwater jackups can drill to depths of 20,000 ft. to 30,000 ft. in maximum water depths of 250 ft. to 490 ft. Of the 17 active cantilever jackup rigs, three are harsh environment Gorilla Class rigs, four are enhanced Super Gorilla Class rigs, and three are Tarzan Class rigs. The Gorilla Class rigs (Gorillas II, III and IV) are heavier duty rigs intended to drill up to 30,000 ft. in water depths up to 328 ft. in extreme hostile environments (winds up to 100 miles per hour and seas up to 90 ft.). During 1998, RDC launched the first of three Super Gorilla Class rigs, Rowan Gorilla V, an enhanced Gorilla Class rig; it completed the Rowan Gorilla VI in 2000 and the Super Gorilla VII in 2001. The Super Gorilla VIII was completed in the 2003 third quarter. The Tarzan class

jackup rigs are designed specifically for deeper drilling (more than 25,000 ft.) in water depths less than 300 ft. in the GOM. The first such rig (the Scooter Yeargain) was delivered in April 2004; the second, the Bob Keller, was delivered in August 2005, and the third, the Hank Boswell, was delivered in September 2006.

RDC's worldwide rig utilization rate fell to 86% in 2006, from 96% in 2005; average dayrates increased about 81%, to $141,500. Land rig utilization was 97% in 2006 (versus 98% in 2005), with an average day rate of $22,600 ($18,400). The manufacturing division (29% of total revenues, 8% of segment operating income) operates a mini-steel mill that recycles scrap and produces steel plate; a manufacturing facility that produces heavy equipment such as front-end loaders; and a marine group that built the Gorilla V in late 1998, the Gorilla VI in June 2000, the Gorilla VII in December 2001, the Bob Palmer in August 2003, the Scooter Yeargain in April 2004, the Bob Keller in August 2005, and the Hank Boswell in September 2006.

Company Financials Fiscal Year Ended Dec. 31

Per Share Data ($)	2006	2005	2004	2003	2002	2001	2000	1999	1998	1997
Tangible Book Value	16.97	14.75	12.97	11.95	12.09	11.84	11.17	8.69	8.77	7.53
Cash Flow	3.64	2.71	1.14	0.84	1.72	1.52	1.36	0.54	2.00	2.28
Earnings	2.84	1.97	0.25	-0.08	0.90	0.80	0.74	-0.12	1.43	1.76
S&P Core Earnings	2.76	1.63	0.28	-0.05	-0.31	0.65	NA	NA	NA	NA
Dividends	0.30	Nil	Nil	Nil	Nil	Nil	Nil	Nil	Nil	Nil
Payout Ratio	11%	Nil	Nil	Nil	Nil	Nil	Nil	Nil	Nil	Nil
Prices:High	48.15	39.50	27.26	26.72	27.03	33.89	34.25	21.69	32.50	43.93
Prices:Low	29.03	24.53	20.44	17.70	16.04	11.10	19.06	8.50	9.00	16.75
P/E Ratio:High	17	20	NM	NM	30	42	46	NM	23	25
P/E Ratio:Low	10	12	NM	NM	18	14	26	NM	6	10
Income Statement Analysis (Million $)										
Revenue	1,511	1,069	709	679	617	731	646	461	706	695
Operating Income	555	355	152	89.0	65.1	193	170	45.1	232	230
Depreciation, Depletion and Amortization	90.0	81.3	95.7	86.9	78.1	68.5	58.9	54.7	49.7	47.1
Interest Expense	20.6	22.0	18.7	15.9	15.9	13.1	12.1	11.5	1.24	16.2
Pretax Income	493	345	42.8	-12.0	133	120	111	-14.5	194	173
Effective Tax Rate	35.8%	36.9%	38.4%	NM	35.0%	35.9%	36.7%	NM	35.7%	9.73%
Net Income	317	218	26.4	-7.77	86.3	77.0	70.2	-9.67	124	156
S&P Core Earnings	308	181	28.9	-4.74	-30.2	62.8	NA	NA	NA	NA
Balance Sheet & Other Financial Data (Million $)										
Cash	258	676	466	58.2	179	237	193	87.1	149	108
Current Assets	1,103	1,208	815	444	470	507	483	325	366	412
Total Assets	3,435	2,975	2,492	2,191	2,055	1,939	1,678	1,356	1,249	1,122
Current Liabilities	517	341	235	150	116	201	104	202	79.6	81.5
Long Term Debt	485	550	574	569	513	438	372	297	310	256
Common Equity	1,874	1,620	1,409	1,137	1,132	1,108	1,053	724	730	653
Total Capital	2,707	2,485	2,147	1,924	1,811	1,674	1,516	1,099	1,116	984
Capital Expenditures	479	200	137	250	243	305	216	205	248	181
Cash Flow	407	299	122	79.1	164	145	129	45.0	174	204
Current Ratio	2.1	3.5	3.5	3.0	4.1	2.5	4.6	1.6	4.6	5.1
% Long Term Debt of Capitalization	17.9	22.1	26.8	29.6	28.3	26.2	24.5	27.0	27.8	26.0
% Return on Assets	9.9	8.0	1.1	NM	4.3	4.3	4.6	NM	10.5	15.5
% Return on Equity	18.1	14.4	2.1	NM	7.7	7.1	7.9	NM	18.0	27.2

Data as orig reptd.; bef. results of disc opers/spec. items. Per share data adj. for stk. divs.; EPS diluted. E-Estimated. NA-Not Available. NM-Not Meaningful. NR-Not Ranked. UR-Under Review.

Office: 2800 Post Oak Blvd Ste 5450, Houston, TX 77056-6127.
Telephone: 713-621-7800.
Email: ir@rowancompanies.com
Website: http://www.rowancompanies.com

Chrmn, Pres & CEO: D.F. McNease
Vice Chrmn & Chief Admin Officer: R.G. Croyle
VP & CFO: W. Wells
Investor Contact: W.C. Provine (713-960-7575)

Secy: M. Trent
Board Members: R. G. Croyle, W. T. Fox III, G. Hearne, J. Huff, R. E. Kramek, F. R. Lausen, H. E. Lentz, D. F. McNease, L. Moynihan, C. R. Palmer, P. D. Peacock

Founded: 1923
Domicile: Delaware
Employees: 5,160

The McGraw-Hill Companies

Ryder System Inc

STANDARD &POOR'S

S&P Recommendation	BUY ★★★★☆	Price $40.24 (as of Nov 27, 2007)	12-Mo. Target Price $61.00	Investment Style Large-Cap Value

GICS Sector Industrials
Sub-Industry Trucking

Summary This company provides truck leasing and rental, logistics, and supply chain management solutions worldwide.

Key Stock Statistics (Source S&P, Vickers, company reports)

52-Wk Range	$57.70–38.95	S&P Oper. EPS 2007**E**	4.14	Market Capitalization(B)	$2.335	Beta	0.82
Trailing 12-Month EPS	$4.08	S&P Oper. EPS 2008**E**	4.73	Yield (%)	2.09	S&P 3-Yr. Proj. EPS CAGR(%)	11.00
Trailing 12-Month P/E	9.9	P/E on S&P Oper. EPS 2007**E**	9.7	Dividend Rate/Share	$0.84	S&P Credit Rating	BBB+
$10K Invested 5 Yrs Ago	$18,800	Common Shares Outstg. (M)	58.0	Institutional Ownership (%)	NM		

Price Performance

30-Week Mov. Avg. · · · 10-Week Mov. Avg. - - GAAP Earnings vs. Previous Year   Volume Above Avg. STARS
12-Mo. Target Price — Relative Strength   ▲ Up ▼ Down ► No Change   Below Avg.

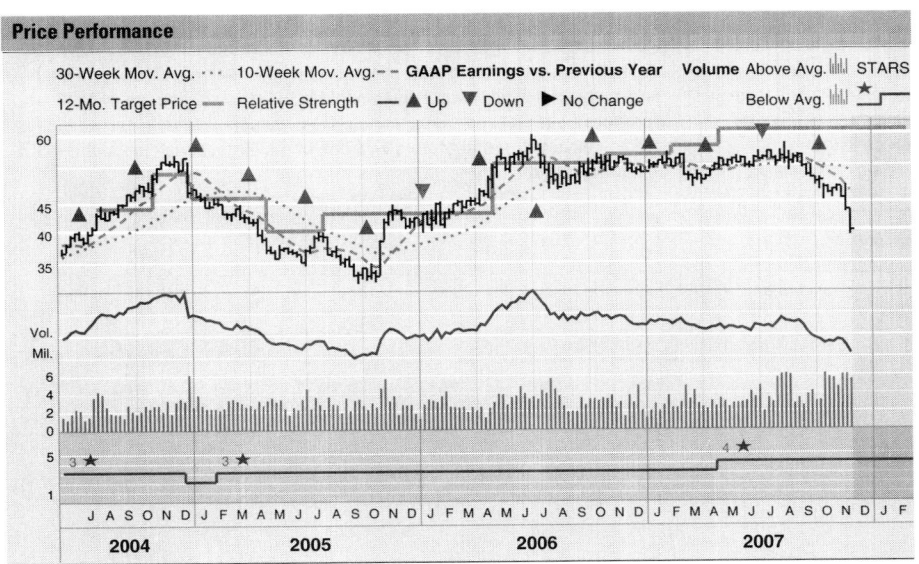

Options: ASE, CBOE, P

Analysis prepared by **Kevin Kirkeby** on November 27, 2007, when the stock traded at **$ 39.89**.

Highlights

➤ Following a 3.5% revenue increase we expect for 2007, we see a further gain of 6.6% in 2008. Within its largest segment, fleet management solutions, we see new client wins and expanded contracts with existing customers more than offsetting softness in commercial rentals. We also look for a higher growth rate in the smaller supply chain solutions segment. Fleet size, in our view, will expand modestly in 2008, but will remain closely tied to customer additions. In October 2007, R completed its acquisition of Pollock NationaLease, which adds approximately $43 million in annualized revenues.

➤ We anticipate a widening in margins during 2008, largely related to cost cutting measures and reductions in fleet size implemented late in 2007. Interest expense should increase due to a rise in average debt levels following the recent acquisition and as R expands its lease business.

➤ We forecast EPS of $4.73, representing a 14% increase over the $4.14, excluding special items, we expect for 2007. This incorporates a slightly higher tax rate, due to one-time favorable adjustments made in 2007, and a 2% reduction in average share count.

Investment Rationale/Risk

➤ Following a number of restructurings in the past decade, we believe R has passed the peak of its cost-cutting phase, and we expect the company to focus more on a strategy of profitable revenue growth. Its lease and supply chain segments have provided earnings support during the recent trucking sector slowdown. We believe the more economically sensitive segments, such as commercial rentals, will begin to improve in late 2008 and contribute to faster earnings growth.

➤ Risks to our recommendation and target price include weaker than expected economic growth; declining leasing demand and lease rates; increased competition from traditional truckload providers; higher interest rates, to which R is exposed in light of its financial leverage; and declining used vehicle prices.

➤ Our DCF model assumes a WACC of 7.2% and terminal growth of 3.5%, and calculates intrinsic value of $64. Our relative valuation model, relating historical peer group valuations to profitability and leverage, estimates a forward P/E of about 12.5X ($58). Blending these models, we arrive at our 12-month target price of $61.

Qualitative Risk Assessment

LOW	MEDIUM	HIGH

Our risk assessment reflects our view of the company's large amount of financial leverage, exposure to low-margin businesses, and heavy capital spending needs to maintain its fleet, offset by its strong market position in truck leasing and what we see as steady cash flow generated by multi-year lease contracts.

Quantitative Evaluations

S&P Quality Ranking   B+

D	C	B-	B	B+	A-	A	A+

Relative Strength Rank   WEAK

23

LOWEST = 1   HIGHEST = 99

Revenue/Earnings Data

Revenue (Million $)

	1Q	2Q	3Q	4Q	Year
2007	1,594	1,658	1,648	--	--
2006	1,496	1,596	1,621	1,594	6,307
2005	1,316	1,390	1,491	1,545	5,741
2004	1,212	1,269	1,306	1,363	5,150
2003	1,194	1,197	1,194	1,217	4,802
2002	1,150	1,209	1,212	1,205	4,776

Earnings Per Share ($)

2007	0.84	1.07	1.11	E1.10	E4.14
2006	0.77	1.13	1.06	1.08	4.04
2005	0.64	0.98	0.98	0.93	3.53
2004	0.53	0.97	0.83	0.96	3.28
2003	0.33	0.55	0.63	0.61	2.12
2002	0.27	0.47	0.54	0.52	1.80

Fiscal year ended Dec. 31. Next earnings report expected: Early February. EPS Estimates based on S&P Operating Earnings; historical GAAP earnings are as reported.

Dividend Data (Dates: mm/dd Payment Date: mm/dd/yy)

Amount ($)	Date Decl.	Ex-Div. Date	Stk. of Record	Payment Date
0.210	02/09	02/15	02/20	03/16/07
0.210	05/08	05/17	05/21	06/15/07
0.210	07/13	08/16	08/20	09/14/07
0.210	10/12	11/15	11/19	12/14/07

Dividends have been paid since 1976. Source: Company reports.

Ryder System Inc

STANDARD &POOR'S

Business Summary November 27, 2007

Ryder System has undertaken a series of corporate restructurings and asset divestitures in the past. During the 1990s, it sold assets accounting for over 50% of revenues. A reorganizational plan was implemented in January 2000 that was designed to make the company's earnings less cyclical and seasonal and its business less capital intensive, and to allow for better client service. Business operations are currently full-service leasing, short-term truck rental, truck maintenance services, logistics services, and dedicated contract carriage.

Fleet management solutions (FMS; 61% of revenues and 78% of pretax profits in 2006) provides full service truck leasing to more than 13,300 customers worldwide, ranging from large national enterprises to small companies, with a fleet of 154,100 trucks, tractors and trailers at June 30, 2007. Under a full service lease, the company provides customers with vehicles, maintenance, supplies and related equipment necessary for operation, while customers furnish and supervise their own drivers, and dispatch and exercise control over the vehicles. R leased approximately 114,400 vehicles under full service leases at June 30, 2007.

FMS also services customer vehicles under maintenance contracts, and provides short-term truck rental to commercial customers to supplement their fleets during peak periods. A range of vehicles, from heavy-duty tractors and trailers to light-duty trucks, is available for commercial short-term rental. Commercial rentals represented about 10% of Ryder's total revenue in 2006. Approximately 50% of Ryder's lease customers in 2006 were also customers of the rental unit. At June 30, 2007, the commercial rental fleet had about 36,200 units. This is down from about 43,200 at June 30, 2005, since the company has been more focused on the longer-term, contractual portions of its business.

Supply chain solutions (SCS; 30%, 13%) provides global integrated logistics support of entire customer supply chains, from inbound raw materials supply through finished goods distribution, management of carriers, and inventory deployment and overall supply chain design and management. Services include combinations of logistics systems and information technology design, the provision of vehicles and equipment (including maintenance and drivers), warehouse and transportation management, vehicle dispatch, and just-in-time delivery. General Motors was one of the largest customers of the SCS unit during 2006.

Company Financials Fiscal Year Ended Dec. 31

Per Share Data ($)	2006	2005	2004	2003	2002	2001	2000	1999	1998	1997
Tangible Book Value	25.48	21.81	20.65	18.09	14.97	17.51	17.43	16.87	11.51	11.17
Cash Flow	10.57	15.65	14.03	11.90	10.65	9.30	11.20	10.12	11.12	10.29
Earnings	4.04	3.53	3.28	2.12	1.80	0.31	1.49	1.06	2.16	2.05
S&P Core Earnings	3.72	3.09	2.80	2.26	0.84	-0.76	NA	NA	NA	NA
Dividends	0.72	0.64	0.60	0.60	0.60	0.60	0.60	0.60	0.60	0.60
Payout Ratio	18%	18%	18%	28%	33%	194%	40%	57%	28%	29%
Prices:High	59.93	47.82	55.55	34.65	31.09	23.19	25.13	28.75	40.56	37.13
Prices:Low	39.61	32.00	33.61	20.00	21.05	16.06	14.81	18.81	19.44	27.13
P/E Ratio:High	15	14	17	16	17	75	17	27	19	18
P/E Ratio:Low	10	9	10	9	12	52	10	18	9	13

Income Statement Analysis (Million $)										
Revenue	6,307	5,741	5,150	4,802	4,776	5,006	5,337	4,952	5,189	4,894
Operating Income	1,218	1,165	1,076	905	854	798	906	997	1,115	1,097
Depreciation	743	740	706	625	552	545	580	623	665	654
Interest Expense	141	120	100	96.2	91.7	119	154	184	199	189
Pretax Income	786	357	331	212	176	30.7	141	117	258	264
Effective Tax Rate	18.3%	36.3%	34.9%	36.2%	36.0%	39.2%	37.0%	37.9%	38.4%	39.4%
Net Income	642	228	216	136	113	18.7	89.0	72.9	159	160
S&P Core Earnings	229	200	184	145	53.1	-46.3	NA	NA	NA	NA

Balance Sheet & Other Financial Data (Million $)										
Cash	129	129	101	141	104	118	122	113	138	78.0
Current Assets	1,262	1,164	1,228	1,107	1,024	982	928	1,209	1,110	1,092
Total Assets	6,829	6,033	5,638	5,279	4,767	4,924	5,475	5,770	5,709	5,509
Current Liabilities	1,268	1,253	1,455	1,074	862	1,014	1,302	1,450	1,363	1,090
Long Term Debt	2,484	1,916	1,394	1,449	1,389	1,392	1,604	1,819	2,100	2,268
Common Equity	1,721	1,527	1,510	1,344	1,108	1,231	1,253	1,205	1,095	1,061
Total Capital	5,112	4,293	3,775	3,688	3,431	3,625	3,874	4,035	4,003	4,054
Capital Expenditures	1,695	1,399	1,092	725	600	657	1,289	1,734	1,369	1,042
Cash Flow	642	968	922	760	665	564	669	696	824	813
Current Ratio	1.0	0.9	0.8	1.0	1.2	1.0	0.7	0.8	0.8	1.0
% Long Term Debt of Capitalization	48.6	44.6	36.9	39.3	40.5	38.4	41.4	45.1	52.5	55.9
% Net Income of Revenue	10.2	4.0	4.2	2.8	2.4	0.4	1.7	1.5	3.1	3.3
% Return on Assets	10.0	3.9	3.9	2.7	2.3	0.4	1.6	1.3	2.8	2.9
% Return on Equity	39.5	15.0	15.1	11.1	9.6	1.5	7.2	1.1	14.7	14.8

Data as orig reptd.; bef. results of disc opers/spec. items. Per share data adj. for stk. divs.; EPS diluted. E-Estimated. NA-Not Available. NM-Not Meaningful. NR-Not Ranked. UR-Under Review.

Office: 11690 NW 105th St, Medley, FL 33178-1103.
Telephone: 305-593-3726.
Email: ryderforinvestor@ryder.com
Website: http://www.ryder.com

Chrmn & CEO: G.T. Swienton
EVP & CFO: M.T. Jamieson
EVP, Secy & General Counsel: R.D. Fatovic
SVP & Cntlr: A.A. Garcia

Investor Contact: B. Brunn (305-500-4053)
Board Members: J. M. Berra, D. I. Fuente, L. P. Hassey, L. M. Martin, D. Mudd, L. P. Nieto, Jr., E. A. Renna, A. J. Smith, E. F. Smith, G. Swienton, H. E. Tookes, II, C. A. Varney

Founded: 1955
Domicile: Florida
Employees: 28,600

SAFECO Corp

STANDARD &POOR'S

S&P Recommendation `HOLD` ★ ★ ★ ☆ ☆

Price	12-Mo. Target Price	Investment Style
$55.42 (as of Nov 23, 2007)	$64.00	Large-Cap Value

GICS Sector Financials
Sub-Industry Property & Casualty Insurance

Summary This Seattle-based property and casualty insurance company sells insurance to drivers, homeowners and owners of small- and medium-sized businesses.

Key Stock Statistics (Source S&P, Vickers, company reports)

52-Wk Range	$69.15– 53.18	S&P Oper. EPS 2007**E**	6.20	Market Capitalization(B)	$5.240	Beta	0.53
Trailing 12-Month EPS	$7.34	S&P Oper. EPS 2008**E**	6.10	Yield (%)	2.89	S&P 3-Yr. Proj. EPS CAGR(%)	NA
Trailing 12-Month P/E	7.6	P/E on S&P Oper. EPS 2007**E**	8.9	Dividend Rate/Share	$1.60	S&P Credit Rating	BBB+
$10K Invested 5 Yrs Ago	$16,731	Common Shares Outstg. (M)	94.6	Institutional Ownership (%)	80		

Price Performance

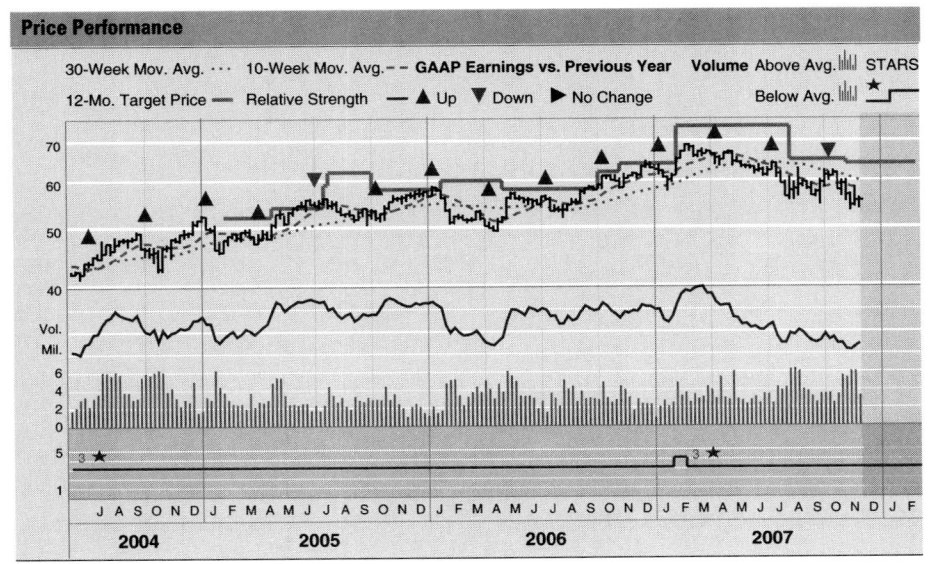

- 30-Week Mov. Avg. · · · 10-Week Mov. Avg. – – **GAAP Earnings vs. Previous Year**   Volume Above Avg.▮▮▮ STARS
- 12-Mo. Target Price — Relative Strength — ▲ Up ▼ Down ▶ No Change   Below Avg.▮▮▮ ★

Options: CBOE

Analysis prepared by **Cathy A. Seifert** on November 15, 2007, when the stock traded at **$ 56.07**.

Qualitative Risk Assessment

LOW	**MEDIUM**	HIGH

Our risk assessment reflects our view of SAF as an underwriter with acceptable risk and capital management practices. Offsetting this is our concern over SAF's exposure to catastrophe losses and the execution risk we see as SAF attempts a turnaround under a new management team and amid some heightened price competition and loss trend erosion in several core lines.

Quantitative Evaluations

S&P Quality Ranking   B+

D	C	B-	B	**B+**	A-	A	A+

Relative Strength Rank   **MODERATE**

`57`

LOWEST = 1   HIGHEST = 99

Highlights

➤ We expect earned premiums to decline by 1% to 3% in both 2007 and 2008 (versus a decrease of 3.4% in 2006.), amid ongoing price competition. Net written premiums fell 2.8% in 2006, and were unchanged in the first nine months of 2007.

➤ We believe margins in coming periods may contract amid growing competitive pressures. An erosion in non-catastrophe-related claim trends will also impair underwriting margins, in our view. Cost cuts should help offset this somewhat. Underwriting results in the first nine months of 2007 deteriorated, despite a continued low level of catastrophe losses, and the combined ratio increased (worsened) to 90.7% from 87.4%. Our outlook for 2008 assumes that catastrophes return to "normal" levels. Per share results will also be aided by share repurchases. SAF reacquired 20.7 million shares in 2006 for $1.17 billion, and 6.4 million shares for $373.1 million in the first nine months of 2007.

➤ We are forecasting operating EPS of $6.20 in 2007 and $6.10 in 2008, versus $6.67 of operating EPS in 2006. These estimates assume SAF will not incur any large, one-time reserve boosts.

Investment Rationale/Risk

➤ Our hold recommendation reflects our view that the positive catalysts of an aggressive cost-cutting and capital management plan are already reflected in the shares' current valuation. Moreover, our outlook is tempered by our view that the company's margins will likely contract slightly in coming periods amid an eroding premium base, higher marketing and underwriting costs, and an erosion in certain claim trends.

➤ Risks to our recommendation and target price include a deterioration in claim trends, a sharp increase in premium price competition; and a deterioration in the credit quality of SAF's investment portfolio, 11% of which was comprised of mortgage-backed securities at September 30, 2007.

➤ Our 12-month target price of $64 assumes the shares will trade at a forward P/E of 10.5X our 2008 operating EPS estimate. This multiple is in line with the average of most of the company's peers, and we believe reflects the impact of some positive steps that SAFECO's new management team has taken.

Revenue/Earnings Data

Revenue (Million $)

	1Q	2Q	3Q	4Q	Year
2007	1,507	1,540	1,638	--	--
2006	1,562	1,536	1,660	1,533	6,290
2005	1,581	1,591	1,586	1,594	6,351
2004	1,498	1,556	1,567	1,574	6,195
2003	1,763	1,872	1,781	1,943	7,358
2002	1,713	1,798	1,795	1,760	7,065

Earnings Per Share ($)

	1Q	2Q	3Q	4Q	Year
2007	1.71	1.75	1.93	E1.40	E6.20
2006	1.69	1.68	2.20	1.96	7.51
2005	1.65	1.46	0.80	1.53	5.43
2004	1.33	1.78	0.04	1.41	4.59
2003	0.65	0.81	-0.21	1.19	2.44
2002	0.50	0.82	0.59	0.42	2.33

Fiscal year ended Dec. 31. Next earnings report expected: Late January. EPS Estimates based on S&P Operating Earnings; historical GAAP earnings are as reported.

Dividend Data (Dates: mm/dd Payment Date: mm/dd/yy)

Amount ($)	Date Decl.	Ex-Div. Date	Stk. of Record	Payment Date
0.300	02/07	04/03	04/06	04/23/07
0.400	05/02	07/03	07/06	07/23/07
0.400	08/01	10/03	10/05	10/22/07
0.400	10/30	01/09	01/11	01/28/08

Dividends have been paid since 1933. Source: Company reports.

SAFECO Corp

STANDARD
&POOR'S

Business Summary November 15, 2007

Seattle-based insurer SAFECO has undergone a number of transitions in recent years, culminating in the sale of its non-core operations to better focus on the property-casualty insurance business. SAF was the 15th largest U.S. property-casualty (p-c) insurance company, based on 2006 net written premiums (latest available data). Earned premiums exceeded $5.6 billion in 2006, down 3.4% from earned premiums of over $5.8 billion in 2005. Through a network of independent agents and brokers and through the Internet, most major lines of personal and commercial p-c coverage are offered in nearly all states, although much of SAF's business is concentrated in the Pacific Northwest.

Safeco Personal Insurance (66% of 2006 earned premiums) primarily underwrites personal auto insurance and homeowners' coverage. The division also offers an array of umbrella, earthquake, dwelling fire, inland marine, recreational vehicle, motorcycle and boat insurance coverage for individuals. Underwriting results (as measured by the combined loss and expense ratio) in this line have been profitable in recent years. The combined ratio equaled 88.3% in 2006, versus 91.0% in 2005. (A combined ratio of under 100% indicates

an underwriting profit, while one in excess of 100% points to an underwriting loss).

Safeco Business Insurance (27% of 2006 earned premiums) offers a line of commercial insurance products designed for small to medium sized businesses. Principal products offered include commercial multi-peril, workers' compensation, property, general liability, and commercial auto. Underwriting results here were profitable in 2006, with a combined ratio of 84.7%, versus 85.6% in 2005. The Surety and Other segment (7% of earned premiums in 2006) provides surety bonds for construction, performance, and legal matters that include appeals, probate and bankruptcies; and includes businesses being run-off. The surety line's combined ratio was 66.9% in 2006, versus 78.9% in 2005.

Company Financials Fiscal Year Ended Dec. 31

Per Share Data ($)

	2006	2005	2004	2003	2002	2001	2000	1999	1998	1997
Tangible Book Value	37.29	33.37	30.87	34.92	30.69	27.70	26.48	22.80	31.01	29.28
Operating Earnings	NA	NA	NA	NA	NA	NA	0.19	1.32	2.07	3.02
Earnings	7.51	5.43	4.59	2.44	2.33	-8.18	0.90	1.90	2.51	3.31
S&P Core Earnings	6.39	5.02	3.60	2.80	1.77	-1.43	NA	NA	NA	NA
Dividends	1.10	0.94	0.78	0.74	0.74	0.93	1.48	1.44	1.34	1.22
Relative Payout	15%	17%	17%	30%	32%	NM	164%	76%	53%	37%
Prices:High	64.85	58.35	52.65	39.79	38.00	32.95	35.88	46.75	56.00	55.38
Prices:Low	49.09	45.18	37.95	32.50	24.99	21.50	18.00	21.81	38.25	36.50
P/E Ratio:High	9	11	11	16	16	NM	40	25	22	17
P/E Ratio:Low	7	8	8	13	11	NM	20	11	15	11

Income Statement Analysis (Million $)

	2006	2005	2004	2003	2002	2001	2000	1999	1998	1997
Life Insurance in Force	Nil	Nil	Nil	66,738	67,001	57,511	55,262	48,175	45,206	NA
Premium Income:Life A & H	5,642	5,805	Nil	868	778	637	503	361	353	290
Premium Income:Casualty/Property.	Nil	Nil	5,529	4,902	4,521	4,473	4,563	4,383	4,208	2,817
Net Investment Income	509	485	465	1,680	1,672	1,649	1,627	1,585	1,519	1,245
Total Revenue	6,290	6,351	6,195	7,358	7,065	6,863	7,118	31.0	6,547	4,709
Pretax Income	1,240	986	893	441	418	-1,458	114	287	418	573
Net Operating Income	NA	NA	NA	NA	27.8	-1,062	69.0	221	335	366
Net Income	880	691	620	339	301	-1,045	115	252	352	430
S&P Core Earnings	750	639	485	388	229	-184	NA	NA	NA	NA

Balance Sheet & Other Financial Data (Million $)

	2006	2005	2004	2003	2002	2001	2000	1999	1998	1997
Cash & Equivalent	414	688	382	550	3,482	593	529	440	398	728
Premiums Due	1,087	1,085	1,147	1,640	1,626	973	1,063	1,058	978	954
Investment Assets:Bonds	9,119	9,362	9,294	26,207	24,278	21,444	20,830	19,564	20,576	19,987
Investment Assets:Stocks	1,530	1,124	1,101	1,279	1,083	1,597	1,816	2,005	2,037	1,880
Investment Assets:Loans	Nil	Nil	Nil	936	926	924	823	861	630	584
Investment Assets:Total	10,663	1,124	11,506	28,807	26,771	24,875	23,811	22,931	24,160	22,451
Deferred Policy Costs	384	376	382	639	626	627	605	599	521	545
Total Assets	14,199	14,887	14,586	35,845	34,656	30,093	31,512	30,573	30,892	29,468
Debt	1,053	1,307	1,333	1,966	1,968	1,592	1,617	3,159	3,458	2,360
Common Equity	3,928	4,125	3,921	5,023	4,432	3,635	4,695	4,295	5,576	5,462
Combined Loss-Expense Ratio	82.0	78.3	77.3	100.1	105.3	118.7	111.4	108.4	102.6	98.7
% Return on Revenue	14.4	10.9	10.0	4.6	4.3	NM	1.6	3.8	5.4	9.1
% Return on Equity	21.9	17.2	13.9	7.2	7.5	NM	2.6	5.1	12.6	0.0
% Investment Yield	4.8	4.7	4.2	6.0	5.1	6.8	7.0	6.7	12.6	6.5

Data as orig reptd.; bef. results of disc opers/spec. items. Per share data adj. for stk. divs.; EPS diluted. E-Estimated. NA-Not Available. NM-Not Meaningful. NR-Not Ranked. UR-Under Review.

Office: Safeco Plaza, Seattle, WA 98185.
Telephone: 206-545-5000.
Website: http://www.safeco.com
Chrmn: J.W. Brown

Pres & CEO: P.R. Reynolds
EVP & CFO: R. Kari
EVP & General Counsel: A. Chong
VP & Cntlr: K.L. Hill

Investor Contact: N. Fuller (206-545-5537)
Board Members: J. W. Brown, R. S. Cline, P. Currie, M. S. Eitel, J. Green, III, J. Hamlin, G. T. Hutton, K. Killinger, G. Locke, W. G. Reed, Jr., P. R. Reynolds, C. Rinehart, J. M. Runstad

Founded: 1929
Domicile: Washington
Employees: 7,208

The McGraw-Hill Companies

Safeway Inc

STANDARD &POOR'S

S&P Recommendation	BUY ★★★★☆	Price	12-Mo. Target Price	Investment Style
		$33.69 (as of Nov 23, 2007)	$38.00	Large-Cap Blend

GICS Sector Consumer Staples
Sub-Industry Food Retail

Summary This major food retailer operates about 1,750 stores in the U.S. and Canada.

Key Stock Statistics (Source S&P, Vickers, company reports)

52-Wk Range	$38.31–29.92	S&P Oper. EPS 2007**E**	2.00	Market Capitalization(B)	$14.904	Beta	0.54
Trailing 12-Month EPS	$2.01	S&P Oper. EPS 2008**E**	2.25	Yield (%)	0.82	S&P 3-Yr. Proj. EPS CAGR(%)	13.00
Trailing 12-Month P/E	16.8	P/E on S&P Oper. EPS 2007**E**	16.8	Dividend Rate/Share	$0.28	S&P Credit Rating	BBB-
$10K Invested 5 Yrs Ago	$14,680	Common Shares Outstg. (M)	442.4	Institutional Ownership (%)	89		

Price Performance

30-Week Mov. Avg. ···· 10-Week Mov. Avg. – – **GAAP Earnings vs. Previous Year** Volume Above Avg. ▥▥ STARS
12-Mo. Target Price — Relative Strength — ▲ Up ▼ Down ▶ No Change Below Avg. ▥▥ ★

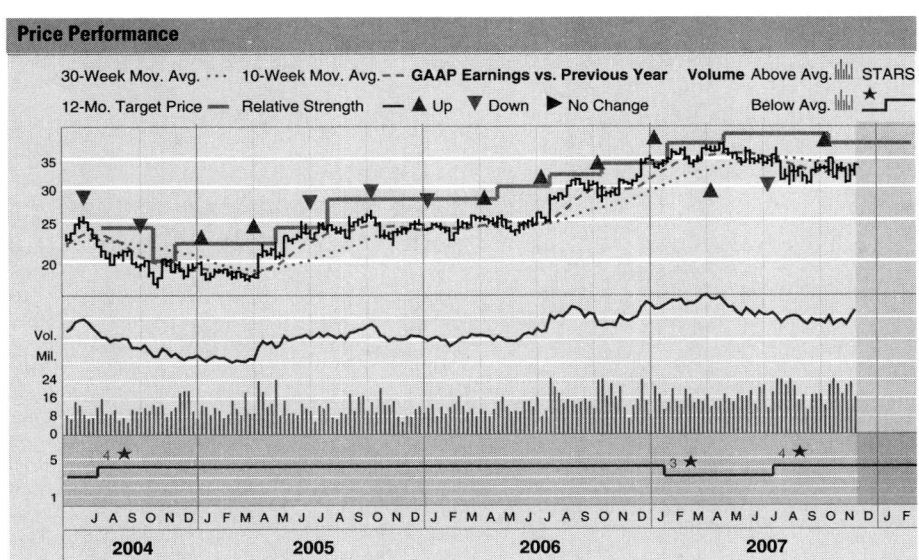

Options: ASE, CBOE, P

Analysis prepared by **Joseph Agnese** on October 22, 2007, when the stock traded at **$ 31.53**.

Highlights

➤ We expect sales to rise about 4.1% in 2008 to nearly $43.6 billion from our estimate of $41.9 billion in 2007 as benefits from the ongoing Lifestyle remodeling campaign are expected to help fuel identical-store sales growth of around 3.5%. We project that square footage will increase about 1% to 2%, reflecting the completion of a significant number of store remodelings and the opening of new stores.

➤ Gross margins should be about flat, reflecting reduced shrink and advertising expense, offset by a more aggressive pricing strategy and a shift in mix due to increased sales of lower margin fuel sales. We look for operating margins to widen as a significant restructuring of labor contracts, coupled with efficiency gains stemming from centralized marketing and procurement functions, should help the company leverage growth in sales while offsetting increased operating expenses associated with the expansion of new store formats.

➤ Interest expense will be lower, in our opinion, as a reduction in debt levels is partially offset by higher interest rates. We project 2008 operating EPS of $2.25, up 13% from our estimate of $2.00 in 2007.

Investment Rationale/Risk

➤ We expect earnings trends to improve, reflecting the company's aggressive rollout of its Lifestyle stores and better sales leverage due to the restructuring of labor contracts.

➤ Risks to our recommendation and target price include a more intense competitive environment than we anticipate, and a sharp slowdown in the economy. In addition, we have concerns with regard to corporate governance because the CEO and chairman of the board positions are not separate.

➤ Despite the stock recently trading at about 16X our 2007 EPS estimate, above its five-year historical average forward P/E multiple of 15X, we believe the shares are attractively valued. Due to favorable sales trends and increased contributions from its Blackhawk gift card business that we foresee, we project five-year annual EPS growth of at least 13%. Our 12-month target price of $38, equal to about 17X our 2008 EPS estimate of $2.25, is based on our assumption that the shares will trade above their historical forward 12-month P/E, as we expect favorable trends to continue.

Qualitative Risk Assessment

LOW	MEDIUM	HIGH

Our risk assessment reflects our view of an improved shopping experience associated with new Lifestyle store remodelings as well as potential opportunities to gain market share following the consolidation of a major rival. This is offset by a continued intense competitive environment as new entrants enter the company's markets.

Quantitative Evaluations

S&P Quality Ranking B

D	C	B-	B	B+	A-	A	A+

Relative Strength Rank STRONG

87

LOWEST = 1   HIGHEST = 99

Revenue/Earnings Data

Revenue (Million $)

	1Q	2Q	3Q	4Q	Year
2007	9,322	9,823	9,785	--	--
2006	8,895	9,367	9,420	12,504	40,185
2005	8,621	8,803	8,946	12,046	38,416
2004	7,639	8,361	8,297	11,390	35,823
2003	8,043	8,248	8,277	10,985	35,553
2002	7,367	7,514	7,508	10,011	32,399

Earnings Per Share ($)

2007	0.39	0.49	0.44	E0.68	E2.00
2006	0.32	0.55	0.39	0.69	1.94
2005	0.29	0.30	0.27	0.39	1.25
2004	0.10	0.35	0.35	0.45	1.25
2003	0.36	0.36	0.45	-1.57	-0.38
2002	0.66	0.62	0.60	-0.77	1.20

Fiscal year ended Dec. 31. Next earnings report expected: Late February. EPS Estimates based on S&P Operating Earnings; historical GAAP earnings are as reported.

Dividend Data (Dates: mm/dd Payment Date: mm/dd/yy)

Amount ($)	Date Decl.	Ex-Div. Date	Stk. of Record	Payment Date
0.058	12/08	12/27	12/29	01/19/07
0.058	03/09	03/28	03/30	04/20/07
0.069	05/16	06/27	06/29	07/19/07
0.069	08/29	09/25	09/27	10/18/07

Dividends have been paid since 2005. Source: Company reports.

Please read the Required Disclosures and Analyst Certification on the last page of this report.

The McGraw-Hill Companies

Safeway Inc

Business Summary October 22, 2007

CORPORATE OVERVIEW. Safeway is one of the largest U.S. food and drug re-tailers, operating about 1,750 stores principally in California, Oregon, Washington, Alaska, Colorado, Arizona, Texas, the Chicago metropolitan area, and the Mid-Atlantic region in the U.S., and in British Columbia, Alberta and Manitoba/Saskatchewan in Canada. To support its store network, SWY has a network of distribution, manufacturing and food processing facilities. The company seeks to provide value to customers by maintaining high store standards and a wide selection of high quality produce and meat at competitive prices. The company also provides third-party gift cards, prepaid cards and sports and entertainment cards to retailers for sales to customers in North America and the U.K. through its Blackhawk subsidiary.

MARKET PROFILE. The U.S. grocery industry was a $907 billion business in 2006, according to Progressive Grocer. Supermarkets generated $500 billion, or 55% of total grocery industry sales, followed by convenience stores ($291 billion, 32%) and warehouse clubs ($96 billion, 11%). When supermarkets are

broken down by format, conventional supermarkets have the largest market share, holding 69% of the supermarket category, with $345 billion in sales. However, supercenters are quickly gaining market share, and generated a 25% market share in 2006 ($124 billion in sales).

With $40.2 billion in sales in 2006, Safeway held an 8% market share within the supermarket category and 4.4% of total grocery sales. The average size of Safeway's stores (46,000 square feet) exceeded the industry average (33,400 square feet). Additionally, the company's sales per square foot ($496 per square foot) is higher than the supermarket average of $439 per square foot in 2006).

Company Financials Fiscal Year Ended Dec. 31

Per Share Data ($)	2006	2005	2004	2003	2002	2001	2000	1999	1998	1997
Tangible Book Value	7.44	5.60	4.24	2.79	1.77	1.67	1.35	NM	NM	0.68
Cash Flow	4.16	3.32	3.24	1.57	2.91	4.29	3.77	3.24	2.63	2.38
Earnings	1.94	1.25	1.25	-0.38	1.20	2.44	2.13	1.88	1.59	1.25
S&P Core Earnings	1.91	1.26	1.15	1.21	2.42	2.19	NA	NA	NA	NA
Dividends	0.22	0.15	Nil	Nil	Nil	Nil	Nil	Nil	Nil	Nil
Payout Ratio	11%	12%	Nil	Nil	Nil	Nil	Nil	Nil	Nil	Nil
Prices:High	35.61	26.46	25.64	25.83	46.90	61.38	62.69	62.44	61.38	31.72
Prices:Low	22.23	17.85	17.26	16.20	18.45	37.44	30.75	29.31	30.50	21.06
P/E Ratio:High	18	21	21	NM	39	25	29	33	39	25
P/E Ratio:Low	11	14	14	NM	15	15	14	16	19	17

Income Statement Analysis (Million $)										
Revenue	40,185	38,416	35,823	35,553	32,399	34,301	31,977	28,860	24,484	22,484
Operating Income	2,591	2,147	2,067	2,167	3,190	3,535	3,119	2,698	2,134	1,841
Depreciation	991	933	895	864	812	946	838	700	533	561
Interest Expense	396	403	411	442	369	447	457	362	244	247
Pretax Income	1,240	849	794	141	1,320	2,095	1,867	1,674	1,397	1,076
Effective Tax Rate	29.8%	33.9%	29.4%	NM	56.9%	40.1%	41.5%	42.0%	42.2%	42.3%
Net Income	871	561	560	-170	568	1,254	1,092	971	807	622
S&P Core Earnings	859	566	517	538	1,140	1,122	NA	NA	NA	NA

Balance Sheet & Other Financial Data (Million $)										
Cash	217	373	267	175	73.7	68.5	91.7	106	46.0	77.0
Current Assets	3,566	3,702	3,598	3,508	4,259	3,312	3,224	3,052	2,320	2,030
Total Assets	16,274	15,757	15,377	15,097	16,047	17,463	15,965	14,900	11,390	8,494
Current Liabilities	4,601	4,264	3,792	3,464	3,936	3,883	3,780	3,583	2,894	2,539
Long Term Debt	5,037	5,605	6,124	7,072	7,522	6,712	5,822	6,357	4,651	3,041
Common Equity	5,667	4,920	4,307	3,644	3,628	5,890	5,390	4,086	3,082	2,149
Total Capital	10,821	10,748	10,894	11,139	11,727	13,100	11,721	10,822	7,950	5,487
Capital Expenditures	1,674	1,384	1,213	936	1,371	1,793	1,573	1,334	1,075	758
Cash Flow	1,862	1,494	1,455	694	1,381	2,200	1,930	1,671	1,340	1,183
Current Ratio	0.8	0.9	0.9	1.0	1.1	0.9	0.9	0.9	0.8	0.8
% Long Term Debt of Capitalization	46.5	52.2	56.2	63.5	64.1	51.2	49.7	58.7	58.5	55.4
% Net Income of Revenue	2.2	1.5	1.6	NM	1.8	3.7	3.4	3.4	3.3	2.8
% Return on Assets	5.4	3.6	3.7	NM	3.4	7.5	7.1	7.4	8.1	8.9
% Return on Equity	16.4	12.2	14.1	NM	11.9	22.2	23.0	27.1	30.9	37.3

Data as orig reptd.; bef. results of disc opers/spec. items. Per share data adj. for stk. divs.; EPS diluted. E-Estimated. NA-Not Available. NM-Not Meaningful. NR-Not Ranked. UR-Under Review.

Office: 5918 Stoneridge Mall Road, Pleasanton, CA 94588-3229.
Telephone: 925-467-3000.
Website: http://www.safeway.com
Chrmn, Pres & CEO: S.A. Burd

EVP & CFO: R.L. Edwards
SVP & General Counsel: R.A. Gordon
Investor Contact: M.C. Plaisance (925-467-3790)

Board Members: S. A. Burd, J. E. Grove, M. Gyani, P. Hazen, R. I. MacDonnell, D. J. Mackenzie, R. A. Stirn, W. Y. Tauscher, R. G. Viault

Founded: 1915
Domicile: Delaware
Employees: 207,000

St. Jude Medical Inc.

S&P Recommendation **HOLD** ★★★☆☆	Price $38.95 (as of Nov 23, 2007)	12-Mo. Target Price $47.00	Investment Style Large-Cap Growth

GICS Sector Health Care
Sub-Industry Health Care Equipment

Summary St. Jude, the leading maker of mechanical heart valves, also produces pacemakers, defibrillators and other cardiac devices.

Key Stock Statistics (Source S&P, Vickers, company reports)

52-Wk Range	$48.10–34.90	S&P Oper. EPS 2007**E**	1.78	Market Capitalization(B)	$13.278	Beta	0.29
Trailing 12-Month EPS	$1.67	S&P Oper. EPS 2008**E**	2.05	Yield (%)	Nil	S&P 3-Yr. Proj. EPS CAGR(%)	15.00
Trailing 12-Month P/E	23.3	P/E on S&P Oper. EPS 2007**E**	21.9	Dividend Rate/Share	Nil	S&P Credit Rating	BBB+
$10K Invested 5 Yrs Ago	$24,170	Common Shares Outstg. (M)	340.9	Institutional Ownership (%)	85		

Price Performance

30-Week Mov. Avg. ···	10-Week Mov. Avg. - -	GAAP Earnings vs. Previous Year	Volume Above Avg. ⅲⅲ STARS
12-Mo. Target Price —	Relative Strength —	▲ Up ▼ Down ▶ No Change	Below Avg. ⅲⅲ ★

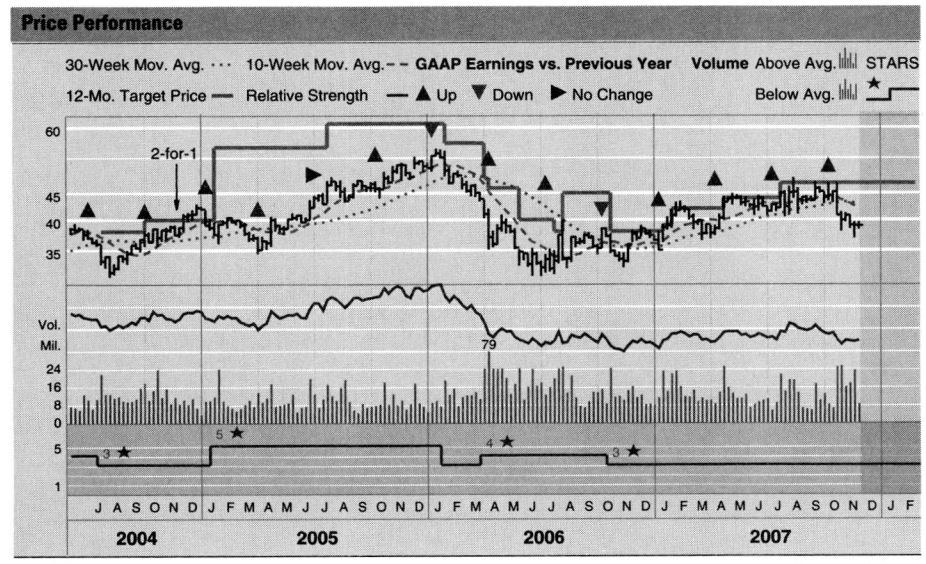

Options: ASE, CBOE

Analysis prepared by **Robert M. Gold** on October 30, 2007, when the stock traded at **$ 40.05**.

Highlights

➤ In our opinion, new product introductions and enhancements to existing products will allow STJ to capture additional share in the global ICD market during the fourth quarter of 2007 and into 2008, with some incremental share gains expected following the recall of some defibrillator leads by Medtronic (MDT: buy, $47). However, we are concerned about potential backlash in the market from cardiologists and patients. Our 2008 revenue forecast of about $4.2 billion, up from a projected $3.6 billion in 2007, assumes $1.4 billion of ICD sales (up about 9% from 2007) and $1.1 billion of pacemaker revenues (up 4%). We also see atrial fibrillation sales of $460 million, neuromodulation of $250 million, cardiac surgery of $340 million and cardiology and vascular access of $530 million.

➤ We expect the 2007 and 2008 gross margin to range from 73% to 74%, with SG&A expenses consuming 36% of sales and R&D outlays representing about 13% of sales. We expect that the effective tax rate will remain at 26.5% through 2008.

➤ We project 2007 operating EPS of $1.78, and believe that EPS in 2008 will reach $2.05.

Investment Rationale/Risk

➤ We are concerned about the sluggishness that we see throughout ICD markets and believe the Medtronic lead recall could potentially derail the early signs we have seen of a market recovery. However, we think the global ICD market can grow by about 7% in 2008, and we expect faster growth from St. Jude as it continues to gain market share. We believe revised Medicare reimbursement guidelines to hospitals for ICDs calling for an approximate 3% reimbursement reduction versus an earlier proposal for a cut of up to 23% is positive and could spur some incremental ICD implantations. Nevertheless, we think the market will be challenged to resume growth in excess of 10% in the foreseeable future.

➤ Risks to our recommendation and target price include the failure to successfully commercialize new products, adverse changes to Medicare and private pay reimbursement rates, and negative patent litigation outcomes.

➤ Our 12-month target price of $47 applies a peer-average P/E to growth (PEG) ratio of 1.5X to our 2008 EPS estimate. We project three-year EPS growth of 15%, which is approximately in line with peers in our coverage universe.

Qualitative Risk Assessment

LOW	MEDIUM	HIGH

The company operates in a highly competitive industry characterized by relatively short product life cycles and volatile market share fluctuations. However, there are significant barriers to entry in the company's core markets, as products must obtain FDA approval prior to launch and they require a large investment in both research and development, and sales.

Quantitative Evaluations

S&P Quality Ranking B

D	C	B-	B	B+	A-	A	A+

Relative Strength Rank MODERATE

47

LOWEST = 1   HIGHEST = 99

Revenue/Earnings Data

Revenue (Million $)

	1Q	2Q	3Q	4Q	Year
2007	887.0	947.3	926.8	--	--
2006	784.4	832.9	821.3	863.8	3,302
2005	663.9	723.7	737.8	789.9	2,915
2004	548.6	556.6	578.3	610.7	2,294
2003	441.4	495.1	477.5	518.6	1,933
2002	371.2	404.4	404.9	409.5	1,590

Earnings Per Share ($)

	1Q	2Q	3Q	4Q	Year
2007	0.41	0.39	0.46	E0.47	E1.78
2006	0.36	0.38	0.32	0.42	1.47
2005	0.32	0.27	0.44	0.01	1.04
2004	0.26	0.27	0.25	0.33	1.10
2003	0.22	0.22	0.23	0.26	0.92
2002	0.17	0.19	0.20	0.20	0.76

Fiscal year ended Dec. 31. Next earnings report expected: Late January. EPS Estimates based on S&P Operating Earnings; historical GAAP earnings are as reported.

Dividend Data

No cash dividends have been paid since 1994.

St. Jude Medical Inc.

STANDARD &POOR'S

Business Summary October 30, 2007

CORPORATE OVERVIEW. St. Jude Medical sells medical devices in the cardiac rhythm management (CRM), cardiac surgery, atrial fibrillation, and pain management categories. Although the company has a diversified product line, the principal driver of growth in recent years has been the CRM segment, where it sells pacemakers and defibrillators.

CRM products (62% of 2006 sales) include implantable cardioverter defibrillators (ICDs) that are used to treat hearts that beat too fast (tachycardia) by monitoring the heartbeat and delivering high energy electrical impulses to terminate ventricular tachycardia and ventricular fibrillation. ICD products include the Atlas, Photon, and Contour lines, as well as the Epic HF and Atlas+ HF ICDs with the ventricle-to-ventricle (V-to-V) timing feature.

Also within the CRM division, pacemakers and related systems are sold to treat patients with hearts that beat too slowly (bradycardia). Current pacemakers include the Victory and Victory XL models that provide the enhancements of earlier STJ models, plus new capabilities such as automatic P-wave and R-wave measurements with trends, lead monitoring and automatic polarity switch, follow-up electrograms, and Ventricular Intrinsic Preference (VIP) to reduce right ventricle pacing and a ventricular rate during an automatic mode switch histogram.

Other pacemakers offer features such as AF Suppression Pacing Algorithm and the beat-by-beat Autocapture pacing system that lets the pacemaker monitor each paced beat to verify heart stimulation, deliver a back-up pulse in the event of non-stimulation, continuously measure the threshold, and adjust energy output to match changing patient needs. The Identity pacemaker line expands the feature set to include a suite of arrhythmia diagnostics. Outside the U.S., STJ sells the Genesis System, a device-based ventricular resynchronization system designed to treat congestive heart failure and suppress atrial fibrillation.

The company also offers low voltage device-based ventricular resynchronization systems (bi-ventricular) designed to treat heart failure and suppress atrial fibrillation. In the U.S., the company's pacemakers are the only bi-ventricular pacing devices indicated for use in patients with chronic atrial fibrillation who have been treated with atrioventricular nodal ablation.

Company Financials Fiscal Year Ended Dec. 31

Per Share Data ($)	2006	2005	2004	2003	2002	2001	2000	1999	1998	1997
Tangible Book Value	2.23	1.84	4.27	3.02	3.27	2.28	1.50	1.02	1.44	1.75
Cash Flow	1.92	1.38	1.34	1.12	0.96	0.74	0.65	0.32	0.57	0.33
Earnings	1.47	1.04	1.10	0.92	0.76	0.48	0.38	0.07	0.38	0.15
S&P Core Earnings	1.47	0.90	1.03	0.82	0.63	0.38	NA	NA	NA	NA
Dividends	Nil	Nil	Nil	Nil	Nil	Nil	Nil	Nil	Nil	Nil
Payout Ratio	Nil	Nil	Nil	Nil	Nil	Nil	Nil	Nil	Nil	Nil
Prices:High	54.75	52.80	42.90	32.00	21.56	19.52	15.63	10.19	9.92	10.73
Prices:Low	31.20	34.48	29.90	19.38	15.26	11.11	5.91	5.73	4.80	6.75
P/E Ratio:High	37	51	39	35	29	41	41	NM	26	73
P/E Ratio:Low	21	33	27	21	20	23	16	NM	13	46

Income Statement Analysis (Million $)	2006	2005	2004	2003	2002	2001	2000	1999	1998	1997
Revenue	3,302	2,915	2,294	1,933	1,590	1,347	1,179	1,115	1,016	994
Operating Income	945	911	672	533	445	347	326	300	263	212
Depreciation	167	130	85.8	76.7	74.9	90.3	92.3	85.7	68.9	66.1
Interest Expense	33.9	Nil	Nil	Nil	Nil	Nil	Nil	Nil	23.7	14.4
Pretax Income	721	621	537	459	373	228	177	67.0	186	88.2
Effective Tax Rate	23.9%	36.7%	23.7%	26.0%	26.0%	24.3%	27.2%	63.8%	30.5%	38.0%
Net Income	548	393	410	339	276	173	129	24.2	129	54.7
S&P Core Earnings	548	341	377	302	231	136	NA	NA	NA	NA

Balance Sheet & Other Financial Data (Million $)	2006	2005	2004	2003	2002	2001	2000	1999	1998	1997
Cash	79.9	535	688	461	402	148	108	88.9	88.0	28.5
Current Assets	1,690	1,941	1,863	1,492	1,114	798	705	690	682	743
Total Assets	4,790	4,845	3,231	2,556	1,951	1,629	1,533	1,554	1,385	1,459
Current Liabilities	676	1,534	605	510	375	322	297	283	203	252
Long Term Debt	859	177	235	352	Nil	123	295	477	375	220
Common Equity	2,969	2,883	2,334	1,604	1,577	1,184	941	794	806	987
Total Capital	3,992	3,217	2,625	2,046	1,577	1,307	1,235	1,272	1,181	1,207
Capital Expenditures	268	159	89.5	49.6	62.2	63.1	39.7	69.4	74.2	94.0
Cash Flow	715	524	496	416	351	263	221	110	198	121
Current Ratio	2.5	1.3	3.1	2.9	3.0	2.5	2.4	2.4	3.4	3.0
% Long Term Debt of Capitalization	21.5	5.5	8.9	17.2	Nil	9.4	23.8	37.6	31.7	18.2
% Net Income of Revenue	16.6	13.5	17.9	17.6	17.4	12.8	11.0	2.2	12.7	5.5
% Return on Assets	11.4	9.7	14.2	15.1	15.4	10.9	8.4	1.6	9.1	4.0
% Return on Equity	18.7	15.1	20.8	21.3	20.0	16.2	14.9	3.0	14.4	6.0

Data as orig reptd.; bef. results of disc opers/spec. items. Per share data adj. for stk. divs.; EPS diluted. E-Estimated. NA-Not Available. NM-Not Meaningful. NR-Not Ranked. UR-Under Review.

Office: One Lillehei Plaza, St. Paul, MN 55117.
Telephone: 651-483-2000.
Website: http://www.sjm.com
Chrmn, Pres & CEO: D.J. Starks.

Investor Contact: J.C. Heinmiller (651-483-2000)
EVP, CFO & Treas: J.C. Heinmiller
VP, Secy & General Counsel: P.S. Krop
VP & Cntlr: D. Zurbay

Board Members: J. W. Brown, R. Devenuti, S. M. Essig, T. H. Garrett, III, M. A. Rocca, D. J. Starks, D. A. Thompson, S. Widensohler, W. Yarno

Founded: 1976
Domicile: Minnesota
Employees: 11,000

SanDisk Corp

STANDARD &POOR'S

S&P Recommendation **BUY** ★★★★☆	Price $36.11 (as of Nov 23, 2007)	12-Mo. Target Price $59.00	Investment Style Large-Cap Growth

GICS Sector Information Technology
Sub-Industry Computer Storage & Peripherals

Summary This company designs, makes and markets flash memory storage products used in a wide variety of electronic systems.

Key Stock Statistics (Source S&P, Vickers, company reports)

52-Wk Range	$59.75– 34.43	S&P Oper. EPS 2007**E**	2.00	Market Capitalization(B)	$8.241	Beta	3.03
Trailing 12-Month EPS	$0.29	S&P Oper. EPS 2008**E**	2.24	Yield (%)	Nil	S&P 3-Yr. Proj. EPS CAGR(%)	20.00
Trailing 12-Month P/E	NM	P/E on S&P Oper. EPS 2007**E**	18.1	Dividend Rate/Share	Nil	S&P Credit Rating	BB-
$10K Invested 5 Yrs Ago	$27,141	Common Shares Outstg. (M)	228.2	Institutional Ownership (%)	93		

Price Performance

30-Week Mov. Avg. · · · 10-Week Mov. Avg. - - GAAP Earnings vs. Previous Year Volume Above Avg. STARS
12-Mo. Target Price — Relative Strength — ▲ Up ▼ Down ► No Change Below Avg. ★

Options: ASE, CBOE, P, Ph

Analysis prepared by **Jawahar Hingorani** on October 23, 2007, when the stock traded at **$ 44.01**.

Highlights

➤ We project a 25% rise in 2007 revenues, followed by an advance of 20% in 2008. We see growth from increased demand for flash memory in a variety of consumer products, including cellular handsets, digital cameras and music players, being somewhat offset by capacity constraints and price erosion. In our view, a focus on international sales has resulted in market share gains in Europe, and strong sales growth in Asia, which is expected to continue in 2008. We think using non-captive capacity to fill demand in the short term could temporarily affect North American market share.

➤ We see gross margins increasing slightly as prices stabilize and cost reduction efforts continue, aided as well by a better product mix. Longer term, we expect margins to remain near 30%. Average selling prices per megabyte declined by 16% - 20% in the third quarter of 2007, and we think this trend will continue in the fourth quarter.

➤ We estimate 2007 operating EPS of $2.00, which does not include one-time expenses related to restructuring and integration costs. We see 2008 operating EPS of $2.24.

Investment Rationale/Risk

➤ Our buy opinion is based on valuation and on our view of SNDK's market leading position in an environment of growing demand and constrained supply. We think changes in technology, and the increased use of flash as a storage medium, will lead to long term growth for the industry. We believe SNDK is well positioned competitively, with its captive market share, branded products and retail presence, and technology leadership.

➤ Risks to our recommendation and target price include the potential for more aggressive price erosion than we foresee, a deceleration in the adoption rate of flash memory in the cellular phone market, and a decline in market share.

➤ Our 12-month target price of $59 is based on a combination of valuation metrics. The first is a relative P/E analysis that values SNDK at 26.3X our FY 08 EPS estimate, above the S&P 500 Computer Storage sub-industry group, which leads to a value of $59. The second, our discounted cash flow analysis, results in an intrinsic value of $58, assuming a weighted average cost of capital of 11.2% and a terminal growth rate of 3%.

Qualitative Risk Assessment

LOW	MEDIUM	**HIGH**

Our risk assessment takes into consideration the volatile nature of the flash memory space, an intensifying competitive environment, and what we deem to be significant price erosion within the industry.

Quantitative Evaluations

S&P Quality Ranking   B

D	C	B-	**B**	B+	A-	A	A+

Relative Strength Rank   WEAK

14

LOWEST = 1   HIGHEST = 99

Revenue/Earnings Data

Revenue (Million $)

	1Q	2Q	3Q	4Q	Year
2007	786.1	827.0	1,037	--	--
2006	623.3	719.2	751.4	1,164	3,258
2005	451.0	514.9	589.6	750.6	2,306
2004	386.9	433.3	408.0	548.9	1,777
2003	174.5	234.6	281.4	389.3	1,080
2002	92.62	127.7	141.1	179.8	541.3

Earnings Per Share ($)

2007	Nil	0.12	0.36	E0.45	E2.00
2006	0.17	0.47	0.51	-0.17	0.96
2005	0.39	0.37	0.55	0.68	2.00
2004	0.34	0.38	0.29	0.42	1.44
2003	0.17	0.26	0.09	0.47	1.02
2002	-0.03	0.07	0.08	0.13	0.26

Fiscal year ended Dec. 31. Next earnings report expected: Late January. EPS Estimates based on S&P Operating Earnings; historical GAAP earnings are as reported.

Dividend Data

No cash dividends have been paid.

SanDisk Corp

Business Summary October 23, 2007

CORPORATE OVERVIEW. SanDisk Corp. designs, makes and markets flash storage card products used in a wide variety of consumer electronics products such as digital cameras, mobile phones, Universal Serial Bus, or USB, drives, gaming devices and MP3 players. The company's strategy focuses on identifying and developing current and emerging mass consumer markets for flash storage products and -- through its vertical integration supply strategy -- selling all major card formats in high volumes.

CORPORATE STRATEGY. SNDK focuses primarily on five consumer electronics markets: imaging, mobile phones, USB flash drives, gaming devices, and digital audio players. In the imaging market, the company makes cards used in all major brands of digital cameras. For mobile phones, SNDK's cards are experiencing increasing demand as multimedia features such as video and Internet access become more prevalent. Finally, SNDK offers a number of digital audio players, which allow consumers to download, store and play music.

Products are available to end users at approximately 200,000 retail storefronts around the globe and as data storage cards bundled with host products by SNDK's OEM customers. In 2006, the retail market accounted for 68% of prod-

uct revenues, compared to 78% in 2005, while the OEM channel comprised 32% (22%). SNDK's top 10 customers and licensees in 2006 accounted for 52% of total revenues, up from 50% in 2005. Best Buy (BBY: strong buy, $48) was the only customer during 2005 that accounted for more than 10% of total revenues.

SNDK develops and owns leading edge technology and patents for flash memory and data storage cards. One key technology patented and successfully commercialized by the company is multi-level cell technology, or MLC, which allows a flash memory cell to be programmed to store two or more bits of data in about the same area of silicon that is typically required to store one bit of data. SNDK has an extensive patent portfolio that has been licensed by three of the four largest semiconductor companies based on revenues. Over the past three years, on a cumulative basis, the company's license and royalty revenues exceeded $500 million.

Company Financials Fiscal Year Ended Dec. 31

Per Share Data ($)	2006	2005	2004	2003	2002	2001	2000	1999	1998	1997
Tangible Book Value	15.31	13.41	10.78	9.32	4.54	4.93	6.40	4.38	1.95	1.85
Cash Flow	1.61	2.34	1.62	1.12	0.40	-2.04	2.17	0.26	0.17	0.23
Earnings	0.96	2.00	1.44	1.02	0.26	-2.19	2.06	0.22	0.11	0.20
S&P Core Earnings	0.94	1.76	1.29	0.89	0.18	-1.05	NA	NA	NA	NA
Dividends	Nil	Nil	Nil	Nil	Nil	Nil	Nil	Nil	Nil	Nil
Payout Ratio	Nil	Nil	Nil	Nil	Nil	Nil	Nil	Nil	Nil	Nil
Prices:High	79.80	65.49	36.35	43.15	14.60	24.34	84.81	25.16	6.56	10.00
Prices:Low	37.34	20.25	19.28	7.39	4.80	4.30	13.75	3.31	1.28	2.22
P/E Ratio:High	83	33	25	42	57	NM	41	NM	61	51
P/E Ratio:Low	39	10	13	7	19	NM	7	NM	12	11

Income Statement Analysis (Million $)										
Revenue	3,258	2,306	1,777	1,080	541	366	602	247	136	125
Operating Income	688	642	457	280	79.5	-124	141	37.2	18.6	23.7
Depreciation	136	65.8	38.9	23.0	21.3	20.5	15.9	7.15	5.84	3.99
Interest Expense	Nil	0.57	5.95	6.75	6.70	Nil	Nil	Nil	Nil	NA
Pretax Income	431	613	423	242	40.0	-442	492	39.6	18.5	23.3
Effective Tax Rate	53.4%	37.0%	37.0%	30.2%	9.35%	NM	39.3%	33.0%	36.0%	15.0%
Net Income	199	386	267	169	36.2	-298	299	26.6	11.8	19.8
S&P Core Earnings	195	339	239	149	25.7	-144	NA	NA	NA	NA

Balance Sheet & Other Financial Data (Million $)										
Cash	1,581	762	464	734	267	254	106	146	15.4	20.9
Current Assets	4,242	2,576	1,880	1,725	757	542	697	568	186	188
Total Assets	6,968	3,120	2,320	2,024	976	932	1,108	658	256	245
Current Liabilities	896	571	353	347	173	127	171	85.6	47.9	54.1
Long Term Debt	1,225	Nil	Nil	150	150	125	Nil	Nil	Nil	Nil
Common Equity	4,768	2,524	1,940	1,501	628	675	863	572	208	191
Total Capital	5,999	2,524	1,940	1,651	778	800	863	572	208	191
Capital Expenditures	176	134	126	52.5	16.6	26.2	26.6	21.4	7.49	9.60
Cash Flow	334	452	305	192	57.6	-277	315	33.7	17.7	23.8
Current Ratio	4.7	4.5	5.3	5.0	4.4	4.3	4.1	6.6	3.9	3.5
% Long Term Debt of Capitalization	20.4	Nil	Nil	9.1	19.3	15.6	Nil	Nil	Nil	Nil
% Net Income of Revenue	6.1	16.8	15.0	15.6	6.7	NM	49.6	10.7	8.7	15.8
% Return on Assets	3.9	14.2	12.2	11.3	3.8	NM	33.8	5.8	4.7	11.2
% Return on Equity	5.5	17.3	15.4	15.9	5.6	NM	41.6	6.8	5.9	14.2

Data as orig reptd.; bef. results of disc opers/spec. items. Per share data adj. for stk. divs.; EPS diluted. E-Estimated. NA-Not Available. NM-Not Meaningful. NR-Not Ranked. UR-Under Review.

Office: 601 McCarthy Blvd, Milpitas, CA 95035-7932.
Telephone: 408-801-1000.
Email: investor_relations@sandisk.com
Website: http://www.sandisk.com

Chrmn & CEO: E. Harari
Pres & COO: S. Mehrotra
Vice Chrmn: I. Federman
EVP, CFO & Chief Acctg Officer: J. Bruner

Investor Contact: L.B. Padon (408-542-0585)
Board Members: I. Federman, S. J. Gomo, E. Harari, C. P. Lego, M. Marks, J. D. Meindl

Founded: 1988
Domicile: Delaware
Employees: 2,586

Sara Lee Corp

STANDARD &POOR'S

S&P Recommendation	SELL ★★☆☆☆	Price $16.12 (as of Nov 23, 2007)	12-Mo. Target Price $15.00	Investment Style Large-Cap Blend

GICS Sector Consumer Staples
Sub-Industry Packaged Foods & Meats

Summary This diversified provider of branded food products (e.g., meats, fresh and frozen baked goods, and coffee) also sells household and body care products.

Key Stock Statistics (Source S&P, Vickers, company reports)

52-Wk Range	$18.15– 14.75	S&P Oper. EPS 2008**E**	0.88	Market Capitalization(B)	$11.679	Beta	0.98
Trailing 12-Month EPS	$0.52	S&P Oper. EPS 2009**E**	NA	Yield (%)	2.61	S&P 3-Yr. Proj. EPS CAGR(%)	0
Trailing 12-Month P/E	31.0	P/E on S&P Oper. EPS 2008**E**	18.3	Dividend Rate/Share	$0.42	S&P Credit Rating	BBB+
$10K Invested 5 Yrs Ago	NA	Common Shares Outstg. (M)	724.5	Institutional Ownership (%)	69		

Price Performance

30-Week Mov. Avg. ··· 10-Week Mov. Avg. –– GAAP Earnings vs. Previous Year Volume Above Avg. STARS
12-Mo. Target Price — Relative Strength — ▲ Up ▼ Down ▶ No Change Below Avg.

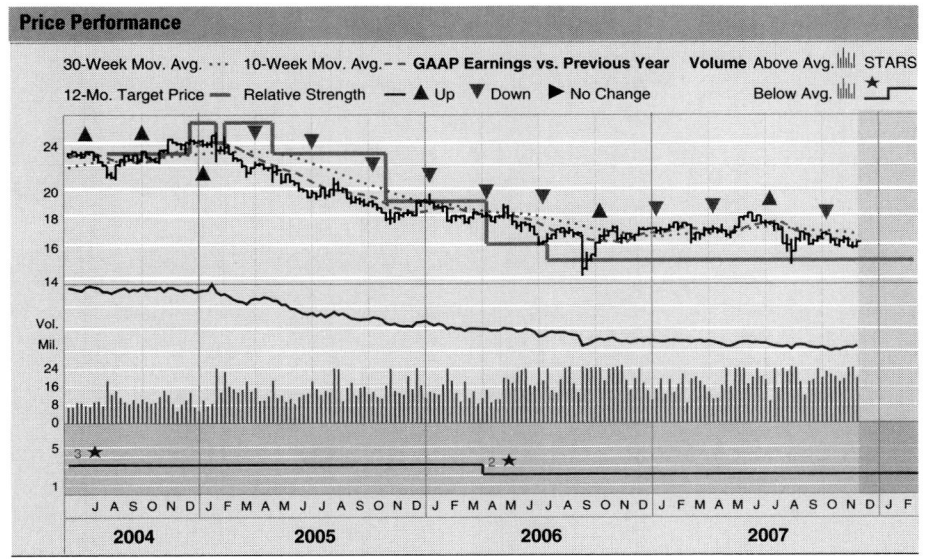

Options: ASE, CBOE, P

Analysis prepared by **Tom Graves, CFA** on November 20, 2007, when the stock traded at **$ 15.81**.

Highlights

➤ This company is implementing a multi-year transformation plan, which has resulted in special charges, and has included the divestiture of various businesses, including its Hanesbrands apparel, European meats, direct selling, European branded apparel, U.K. apparel, U.S. retail coffee, European snacks & nuts, and U.S. meat snacks businesses.

➤ In FY 08 (Jun.), we look for net sales from continuing operations to increase moderately from the $12.3 billion reported for FY 07, including a benefit from currency fluctuation. Also, we think the decline from the $15.9 billion of sales reported for FY 06 was primarily due to the September 2006 spinoff of the Hanesbrands business, which is now being treated as a discontinued operation. Before special items, we look for SLE's operating profit margin to improve in FY 08.

➤ Excluding special items, we forecast FY 08 EPS at $0.88, up from $0.72 for FY 07. Our estimate assumes a core effective tax rate of about 33%.

Investment Rationale/Risk

➤ In our view, this company has been significantly reshaped, and we see SLE making progress with its transformation plan. However, we believe that our expectations of additional progress are amply reflected in the stock price.

➤ Risks to our recommendation and target price include a significant improvement in the commodity cost environment, better than forecast sales trends for key businesses, and the realization of cost savings from restructuring actions at a faster than expected pace.

➤ The stock recently traded at about 22X our calendar 2007 EPS estimate of about $0.71 (before some special items). This was a roughly 15% premium to the valuation we saw being given to a group of food company peers. Our 12-month target price of $15 is based on our belief that the stock should trade at closer to the peer average P/E. Following the Hanesbrand spinoff, SLE reduced its dividend by about 49%. With the new dividend rate, the stock recently had an indicated dividend yield of about 2.7%.

Qualitative Risk Assessment

LOW	MEDIUM	HIGH

Our risk assessment for Sara Lee reflects the relatively stable nature of the company's end markets, strong cash flow, and corporate governance practices that we view as favorable relative to peers.

Quantitative Evaluations

S&P Quality Ranking   B+

D	C	B-	B	B+	A-	A	A+

Relative Strength Rank   STRONG

75

LOWEST = 1   HIGHEST = 99

Revenue/Earnings Data

Revenue (Million $)

	1Q	2Q	3Q	4Q	Year
2008	3,131	--	--	--	--
2007	2,891	3,182	3,006	3,199	12,278
2006	3,900	2,974	3,789	4,100	15,944
2005	4,861	5,199	4,785	4,754	19,254
2004	4,666	5,017	4,745	5,138	19,566
2003	4,534	4,776	4,350	4,631	18,291

Earnings Per Share ($)

	1Q	2Q	3Q	4Q	Year
2008	0.28	E0.22	E0.21	E0.31	E0.88
2007	0.34	-0.08	0.15	0.16	0.57
2006	0.25	-0.06	0.18	-0.15	0.53
2005	0.44	0.41	0.24	-0.14	0.92
2004	0.29	0.39	0.47	0.44	1.59
2003	0.38	0.42	0.33	0.37	1.50

Fiscal year ended Jun. 30. Next earnings report expected: Early February. EPS Estimates based on S&P Operating Earnings; historical GAAP earnings are as reported.

Dividend Data (Dates: mm/dd Payment Date: mm/dd/yy)

Amount ($)	Date Decl.	Ex-Div. Date	Stk. of Record	Payment Date
0.100	01/25	02/27	03/01	04/06/07
0.100	04/26	06/06	06/08	07/09/07
0.100	06/28	08/30	09/04	10/05/07
0.105	10/25	11/29	12/03	01/08/08

Dividends have been paid since 1946. Source: Company reports.

Sara Lee Corp

STANDARD
&POOR'S

Business Summary November 20, 2007

CORPORATE PROFILE. Sara Lee, best known for its baked goods, also has various other branded food and non-food businesses. In North America, this includes Jimmy Dean and Hillshire Farm meat products, while outside the U.S., it includes coffee and tea, and household and body care products. In North America, in addition to providing products to retailers, SLE provides coffee, meats and bakery products to foodservice operators.

At the beginning of FY 06, Sara Lee reorganized its businesses around distinct customers and geographic markets. The company's new structure was organized around the following business segments: North American Retail Meats (21% of FY 07 sales); North American Retail Bakery (16%); Foodservice (18%); International Beverage (21%); International Bakery (7%); and Household and Body Care (17%). SLE's Branded Apparel business, which had sales of $4.5 billion in FY 06, was spun off in September 2006.

CORPORATE STRATEGY. In February 2005, the company announced a comprehensive restructuring program, involving a reorganization of business units and plans to dispose of various businesses. The key components of this plan are to transform the company's portfolio, reorganize continuing operations,

improve operational efficiency, and consolidate the North American and European headquarters. We look for the transformation plan to be completed by 2010.

During FY 06 (Jun.), Sara Lee disposed of its direct selling, European branded apparel, U.K. apparel, U.S. retail coffee, European snacks & nuts, and U.S. meat snacks businesses. In August 2006, Sara Lee completed the sale of its European meats business. Also, in September 2006, the company completed the spinoff of its branded apparel Americas/Asia business. This business was spun off as an independent company named Hanesbrands Inc.

We expect SLE spending on information technology initiatives to include the implementation of a standardized information technology platform in North American operations and continued consolidation of information processing in both the U.S. and Europe.

Company Financials Fiscal Year Ended Jun. 30

Per Share Data ($)	2007	2006	2005	2004	2003	2002	2001	2000	1999	1998
Tangible Book Value	NM	NM	NM	NM	NM	NM	NM	NM	NM	NM
Cash Flow	1.33	1.46	1.87	2.53	2.44	1.94	2.80	1.92	1.83	0.08
Earnings	0.57	0.53	0.92	1.59	1.50	1.23	1.87	1.27	1.26	-0.57
S&P Core Earnings	0.50	0.44	0.86	1.67	1.30	1.00	0.92	NA	NA	NA
Dividends	0.50	0.79	0.78	0.60	0.62	0.60	0.57	0.54	0.49	0.45
Payout Ratio	88%	149%	85%	38%	41%	48%	30%	43%	39%	NM
Prices:High	18.15	19.64	25.00	24.49	23.13	23.84	24.75	25.31	28.75	31.81
Prices:Low	14.75	14.08	17.31	20.17	16.25	16.15	18.26	13.38	21.06	22.16
P/E Ratio:High	32	37	27	15	15	19	13	20	23	NM
P/E Ratio:Low	26	27	19	13	11	13	10	11	17	NM

Income Statement Analysis (Million $)										
Revenue	12,278	15,944	19,254	19,566	18,291	17,628	17,747	17,511	20,012	20,011
Operating Income	1,242	1,779	2,183	2,386	2,345	2,138	2,191	2,345	2,304	2,391
Depreciation	539	701	737	734	674	582	599	602	553	618
Interest Expense	265	308	290	271	276	304	270	252	237	224
Pretax Income	419	683	934	1,542	1,484	1,185	1,851	1,567	1,671	-443
Effective Tax Rate	NM	40.0%	21.7%	17.5%	17.7%	14.8%	13.4%	26.1%	28.7%	NM
Net Income	426	410	731	1,272	1,221	1,010	1,603	1,158	1,191	-523
S&P Core Earnings	385	339	684	1,336	1,047	806	768	NA	NA	NA

Balance Sheet & Other Financial Data (Million $)										
Cash	2,520	2,231	545	638	942	298	548	314	279	273
Current Assets	5,643	6,774	5,811	5,746	5,953	4,986	5,083	5,974	4,987	5,220
Total Assets	12,190	14,522	14,412	14,883	15,084	13,753	10,167	11,611	10,521	10,989
Current Liabilities	4,301	6,277	4,968	5,423	5,199	5,463	4,958	6,759	5,953	5,733
Long Term Debt	2,803	3,807	4,115	4,171	5,157	4,326	2,640	2,248	1,892	2,270
Common Equity	2,615	2,449	2,938	2,948	1,870	1,534	899	1,007	1,034	1,561
Total Capital	6,066	6,324	7,134	7,194	7,806	7,252	4,646	4,271	3,866	4,718
Capital Expenditures	529	625	538	530	746	669	532	647	535	474
Cash Flow	965	1,111	1,468	2,006	1,895	1,592	2,191	1,748	1,732	71.0
Current Ratio	1.3	1.1	1.2	1.1	1.1	0.9	1.0	0.9	0.8	0.9
% Long Term Debt of Capitalization	46.2	60.2	57.6	58.0	66.1	59.7	56.8	52.6	48.9	48.1
% Net Income of Revenue	3.5	2.6	3.8	6.5	6.7	5.7	9.0	6.6	6.0	NM
% Return on Assets	3.2	2.8	5.0	8.4	8.5	8.4	14.7	10.6	11.1	NM
% Return on Equity	16.8	15.2	24.7	52.8	71.7	83.0	167.1	112.3	90.9	NM

Data as orig reptd.; bef. results of disc opers/spec. items. Per share data adj. for stk. divs.; EPS diluted. E-Estimated. NA-Not Available. NM-Not Meaningful. NR-Not Ranked. UR-Under Review.

Office: 3500 Lacey Rd, Downers Grove, IL 60515-5422.
Telephone: 630-598-6000.
Website: http://www.saralee.com
Chrmn & CEO: B.C. Barnes

Investor Contact: L.M. de Kool (630-598-8100)
EVP & CFO: L.M. de Kool
EVP, Secy & General Counsel: R.A. Palmore
SVP, Chief Acctg Officer & Cntlr: R. Hoker

Board Members: B. C. Barnes, C. B. Begley, C. B. Carroll, V. Colbert, J. S. Crown, W. D. Davis, L. T. Koellner, I. Prosser, R. L. Ridgway, J. P. Ward, C. J. van Lede

Founded: 1941
Domicile: Maryland
Employees: 52,000

Schering-Plough

STANDARD &POOR'S

S&P Recommendation	**STRONG BUY** ★ ★ ★ ★ ★	Price $28.80 (as of Nov 26, 2007)	12-Mo. Target Price $37.00	Investment Style Large-Cap Blend

GICS Sector Health Care
Sub-Industry Pharmaceuticals

Summary This leading producer of prescription and OTC pharmaceuticals also has important interests in sun care, animal health, and foot care products.

Key Stock Statistics (Source S&P, Vickers, company reports)

52-Wk Range	$33.81– 21.21	S&P Oper. EPS 2007**E**	1.34	Market Capitalization(B)	$46.639	Beta	0.79
Trailing 12-Month EPS	$1.27	S&P Oper. EPS 2008**E**	1.60	Yield (%)	0.90	S&P 3-Yr. Proj. EPS CAGR(%)	25.00
Trailing 12-Month P/E	22.7	P/E on S&P Oper. EPS 2007**E**	21.5	Dividend Rate/Share	$0.26	S&P Credit Rating	A-
$10K Invested 5 Yrs Ago	$13,527	Common Shares Outstg. (M)	1,619.4	Institutional Ownership (%)	79		

Price Performance

30-Week Mov. Avg. · · · 10-Week Mov. Avg. - - **GAAP Earnings vs. Previous Year** Volume Above Avg. STARS
12-Mo. Target Price — Relative Strength — ▲ Up ▼ Down ► No Change Below Avg.

Options: ASE, CBOE, P, Ph

Analysis prepared by **Herman B. Saftlas** on October 26, 2007, when the stock traded at **$ 29.99**.

Highlights

➤ We project that revenues from present operations (excluding the planned acquisition of Organon BioSciences) will increase 5% in 2008. We see the advance led by an estimated 20% gain in Remicade, helped by new indications and expansion in foreign markets. We also forecast higher sales in the Nasonex, Asmanex and Temodar lines, and modest gains for animal health products and consumer healthcare products. However, we think sales of Rebetol and PEG-Intron may be lower.

➤ SGP's gross margins are well below those of peer drugmakers because most of its earnings are derived from equity income. Nonetheless, we see overall profitability benefiting from cost-cutting measures, as well as from increased equity income from SGP's joint venture with Merck. The latter reflects our projection of higher sales from the venture's Zetia and Vytorin cholesterol-lowering drugs. However, we believe that interest expense and the tax rate will be higher.

➤ We project operating EPS of $1.60 for 2008, up from the $1.34 that we estimate for 2007. Our estimates exclude nonrecurring items.

Investment Rationale/Risk

➤ Despite modestly disappointing third quarter operating EPS, we continue to see SGP delivering on its turnaround strategy over the coming quarters. Key growth drivers include Remicade, Nasonex, and Temodar, as well as the important Vytorin/Zetia joint venture with Merck. SGP plans to acquire Organon BioSciences from Akzo Nobel N.V. for some $15 billion in cash, subject to necessary approvals. Assuming cost synergies, SGP expects the proposed deal (forecast to close in late 2007) to add about $0.10 to EPS in 2008. We think the planned deal, valued at an attractive 2.9X sales, makes strategic sense since it should broaden SGP's sales base into new women's health and other areas. We believe SGP has takeover appeal at current levels.

➤ Risks to our recommendation and target price include slowing in sales of Vytorin and Zetia, worsening competitive pressures in other lines, and possible pipeline setbacks.

➤ Our 12-month target price of $37 is based on our DCF model, which assumes steady free cash flow growth over 10 years, a WACC of 7.3%, and terminal growth of 2%.

Qualitative Risk Assessment

LOW	MEDIUM	**HIGH**

Our risk assessment incorporates our view that SGP's turnaround phase will continue for several more years. We also think the company is dependent on a relatively small number of drugs to support future growth.

Quantitative Evaluations

S&P Quality Ranking   A-

D	C	B-	B	B+	**A-**	A	A+

Relative Strength Rank   MODERATE

58

LOWEST = 1   HIGHEST = 99

Revenue/Earnings Data

Revenue (Million $)

	1Q	2Q	3Q	4Q	Year
2007	2,975	3,178	2,812	--	--
2006	2,551	2,818	2,574	2,650	10,594
2005	2,369	2,532	2,284	2,324	9,508
2004	1,963	2,147	1,978	2,184	8,272
2003	2,082	2,338	1,998	1,948	8,334
2002	2,556	2,833	2,421	2,370	10,180

Earnings Per Share ($)

	1Q	2Q	3Q	4Q	Year
2007	0.36	0.34	0.45	E0.32	E1.34
2006	0.22	0.16	0.19	0.12	0.69
2005	0.07	-0.05	0.03	0.07	0.12
2004	-0.05	-0.04	0.01	-0.58	-0.67
2003	0.12	0.12	-0.18	-0.12	-0.06
2002	0.41	0.43	0.29	0.21	1.34

Fiscal year ended Dec. 31. Next earnings report expected: Late January. EPS Estimates based on S&P Operating Earnings; historical GAAP earnings are as reported.

Dividend Data (Dates: mm/dd Payment Date: mm/dd/yy)

Amount ($)	Date Decl.	Ex-Div. Date	Stk. of Record	Payment Date
0.055	12/15	01/31	02/02	02/27/07
0.065	02/27	05/02	05/04	05/29/07
0.065	06/26	08/01	08/03	08/28/07
0.065	09/19	10/31	11/02	11/27/07

Dividends have been paid since 1952. Source: Company reports.

Schering-Plough

Business Summary October 26, 2007

CORPORATE PROFILE. Schering-Plough is a leading maker of niche-oriented prescription pharmaceuticals. It also has interests in animal health products, over-the-counter (OTC) medications, and consumer products. In mid-April 2003, Fred Hassan (formerly chairman and CEO of Pharmacia Corp.) was elected chairman and CEO of SGP.

Prescription pharmaceuticals accounted for about 81% of total sales in 2006, consumer health care products for 11%, and animal health items for 8%. Sales outside of the U.S. represented 60% of total sales in 2006.

Through a joint venture with Merck & Co., Schering-Plough shares in the profits of two cholesterol-lowering drugs. These are Zetia, a novel lipid-lowering agent that works by blocking the absorption of cholesterol in the intestines, and Vytorin, a combination of Zetia with Merck's Zocor statin cholesterol agent that was introduced in July 2004. SGP booked equity income of $1.46 billion from this venture in 2006, up from $873 million in 2005. Sales of Zetia and Vytorin (not booked by SGP) totaled $3.9 billion in 2006. As of February 2007, combined sales of Zetia and Vytorin accounted for close to about 20% of total U.S. cholesterol drug sales, up from some 11% in July 2005, based on IMS data. The joint venture plans to launch a combination of Zetia with generic Lipi-

tor, after Pfizer's patent on Lipitor expires in 2010 or 2011.

SGP is a global leader in treatments for hepatitis C with its PEG-Intron (sales of $837 million in 2006), a once-weekly alpha interferon, combined with Rebetol antiviral agent ($311 million). In the anti-inflammatory area, SGP offers Remicade ($1.2 billion), a TNF-alpha treatment for rheumatoid arthritis and Crohn's disease. Other important products are Temodar ($703 million), a treatment for brain tumors; Integrilin ($329 million) for cardiovascular problems; Avelox, a treatment for bacterial infections; Intron A for cancer and viral infections; Subutex for opiate dependence; Caelyx for skin cancer; Cipro, an antibiotic; and Elocon, for inflammatory skin conditions.

A longtime leader in the U.S. respiratory/allergy market, SGP's most important prescription drugs in that area are Nasonex corticosteroid nasal spray ($944 million) and Clarinex/Aerius nonsedating antihistamine ($722 million). Other important allergy/respiratory drugs include Asmanex and Foradil.

Company Financials Fiscal Year Ended Dec. 31

Per Share Data ($)	2006	2005	2004	2003	2002	2001	2000	1999	1998	1997
Tangible Book Value	4.04	3.64	4.73	4.57	4.07	4.41	3.75	3.11	2.33	1.60
Cash Flow	1.08	0.45	-0.36	0.22	1.28	1.54	1.84	1.60	0.44	1.11
Earnings	0.69	0.12	-0.67	-0.06	1.34	1.32	1.64	1.42	1.18	0.98
S&P Core Earnings	0.72	0.19	-0.72	0.16	1.17	1.41	NA	NA	NA	NA
Dividends	0.22	0.22	0.22	0.57	0.67	0.62	0.55	0.49	0.43	0.55
Payout Ratio	32%	183%	NM	NM	50%	47%	33%	34%	36%	56%
Prices:High	24.07	22.53	21.37	23.75	36.25	57.25	60.00	60.81	57.75	32.00
Prices:Low	17.88	17.67	15.45	14.16	16.10	32.35	30.50	40.25	30.34	15.88
P/E Ratio:High	35	NM	NM	NM	27	43	37	43	49	33
P/E Ratio:Low	26	NM	NM	NM	12	25	19	28	26	16

Income Statement Analysis (Million $)										
Revenue	10,594	9,508	8,272	8,334	10,180	9,802	9,815	9,176	8,077	6,778
Operating Income	559	409	237	975	2,941	3,248	3,394	3,015	2,566	2,159
Depreciation	568	486	453	417	372	320	299	264	238	200
Interest Expense	Nil	Nil	Nil	81.0	Nil	Nil	44.0	29.0	19.0	40.0
Pretax Income	1,483	497	-168	-46.0	2,563	2,523	3,188	2,795	2,326	1,913
Effective Tax Rate	24.4%	45.9%	NM	NM	23.0%	23.0%	24.0%	24.5%	24.5%	24.5%
Net Income	1,121	269	-947	-92.0	1,974	1,943	2,423	2,110	1,756	1,444
S&P Core Earnings	1,077	279	-1,052	247	1,717	2,070	NA	NA	NA	NA

Balance Sheet & Other Financial Data (Million $)										
Cash	2,666	4,767	4,984	4,218	3,521	2,716	2,397	1,876	1,259	714
Current Assets	10,423	9,732	10,003	9,147	8,272	6,519	5,720	4,909	3,958	2,920
Total Assets	16,071	15,469	15,911	15,102	14,136	12,174	10,805	9,375	7,840	6,507
Current Liabilities	4,162	4,659	5,208	4,609	4,729	3,917	3,645	3,209	3,032	2,891
Long Term Debt	2,414	2,399	2,392	2,410	Nil	Nil	Nil	Nil	4.00	46.0
Common Equity	6,470	16,825	6,118	7,337	8,142	7,125	6,119	5,165	4,002	2,821
Total Capital	10,444	20,779	10,059	9,981	8,500	7,427	6,333	5,449	4,297	3,145
Capital Expenditures	458	478	489	701	770	759	763	543	389	405
Cash Flow	1,603	669	-528	325	2,346	2,263	2,722	2,374	1,994	1,644
Current Ratio	2.5	2.1	1.9	2.0	1.7	1.7	1.6	1.5	1.3	1.0
% Long Term Debt of Capitalization	23.1	11.5	23.8	24.1	Nil	Nil	Nil	Nil	0.1	1.4
% Net Income of Revenue	10.6	2.8	NM	NM	19.4	19.8	24.7	23.0	21.7	21.3
% Return on Assets	7.1	1.7	NM	NM	15.0	16.9	24.0	24.5	24.5	24.3
% Return on Equity	16.7	1.1	NM	NM	25.9	29.3	42.9	46.0	51.5	59.2

Data as orig reptd.; bef. results of disc opers/spec. items. Per share data adj. for stk. divs.; EPS diluted. E-Estimated. NA-Not Available. NM-Not Meaningful. NR-Not Ranked. UR-Under Review.

Office: 2000 Galloping Hill Road, Kenilworth, NJ 07033.
Telephone: 908-298-4000.
Website: http://www.schering-plough.com
Chrmn & CEO: F. Hassan

EVP & CFO: R.J. Bertolini
EVP & General Counsel: T.J. Sabatino, Jr.
Investor Contact: E.K. Moore (908-298-4000)
VP & Treas: E.K. Moore

Board Members: H. W. Becherer, T. J. Colligan, F. Hassan, C. R. Kidder, P. Leder, E. R. McGrath, C. E. Mundy, Jr., P. F. Russo, K. C. Turner, A. Weinbach, R. F. van Oordt

Founded: 1970
Domicile: New Jersey
Employees: 33,500

STANDARD &POOR'S

Schlumberger Ltd

S&P Recommendation BUY ★★★★☆	**Price** $94.11 (as of Nov 23, 2007)	**12-Mo. Target Price** $116.00	**Investment Style** Large-Cap Blend

GICS Sector Energy
Sub-Industry Oil & Gas Equipment & Services

Summary This leading oilfield services company provides equipment and technology to the oil and gas industry worldwide.

Key Stock Statistics (Source S&P, Vickers, company reports)

52-Wk Range	$114.84–55.68	S&P Oper. EPS 2007**E**	4.22	Market Capitalization(B)	$112.543	Beta	1.02
Trailing 12-Month EPS	$4.00	S&P Oper. EPS 2008**E**	5.09	Yield (%)	0.74	S&P 3-Yr. Proj. EPS CAGR(%)	25.00
Trailing 12-Month P/E	23.5	P/E on S&P Oper. EPS 2007**E**	22.3	Dividend Rate/Share	$0.70	S&P Credit Rating	A+
$10K Invested 5 Yrs Ago	$45,832	Common Shares Outstg. (M)	1,195.9	Institutional Ownership (%)	81		

Price Performance

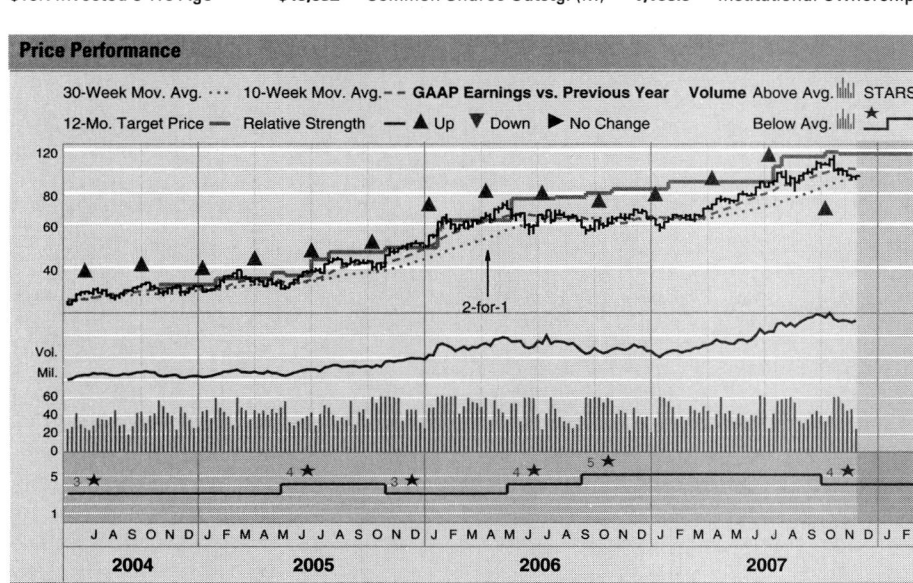

Options: ASE, CBOE, P, Ph

Analysis prepared by **Stewart Glickman, CFA** on October 19, 2007, when the stock traded at **$100.15**.

Highlights

▶ Third quarter operating results for SLB's WesternGeco seismic segment showed a 19% gain in revenues versus the second quarter, supporting our view that seismic demand would pick up in the second half of 2007 and into 2008. Oilfield services margins narrowed 110 basis points in the third quarter, to 29.3%, from the record 30.4% in the second quarter, but the decline was entirely due to a nearly 430 basis point drop in North America; in international markets, margins widened. For 2008, we expect oilfield services revenues to increase about 13%, with operating margins around 30%.

▶ We believe North American weakness reflects rising capacity by domestic oilfield services providers, and expect domestic margins to remain under pressure in the near term. However, we also believe that SLB is strategically geared toward growth in international markets, particularly in the Eastern Hemisphere, where we see margins continuing to widen as demand outstrips supply, particularly for services with high technology content.

▶ For 2007, we see EPS of $4.22, rising to $5.09 in 2008.

Investment Rationale/Risk

▶ We believe SLB is well positioned to benefit from growing demand for oilfield services technology, particularly in frontier regions such as the Middle East, Africa and Eastern Europe. Worldwide, we anticipate an increasing trend toward new oil and gas development opportunities that require higher levels of technology content, which we believe plays to the benefit of larger oilfield service providers.

▶ Risks to our recommendation and target price include a decline in oil and gas exploration and production activity; reduced demand for integrated systems in oilfield services; and political risk in emerging markets.

▶ Our DCF model, assuming free cash flow growth of about 15% per year for 10 years and 3% thereafter, discounted by a WACC of 10.2%, shows an intrinsic value of about $127 per share. On a relative basis, we think the shares merit a premium to peers on the strength of SLB's leadership position. Applying an enterprise value of 14X to our 2008 EBITDA estimate, a multiple of 16X projected 2008 cash flow (both premiums to peer averages), and blending with our DCF model, our 12-month target price is $116.

Qualitative Risk Assessment

LOW	MEDIUM	HIGH

Our risk assessment reflects the company's exposure to volatile crude oil and natural gas prices; its dependence on capital spending decisions by its oil and gas producing customers; and political risk associated with operating in frontier regions around the world. This is offset by the company's leading industry position.

Quantitative Evaluations

S&P Quality Ranking   B

D	C	B-	B	B+	A-	A	A+

Relative Strength Rank   MODERATE

62

LOWEST = 1   HIGHEST = 99

Revenue/Earnings Data

Revenue (Million $)

	1Q	2Q	3Q	4Q	Year
2007	5,464	5,639	5,926	--	--
2006	4,239	4,687	4,955	5,350	19,230
2005	3,159	3,429	3,698	4,023	14,309
2004	2,673	2,833	2,906	3,068	11,480
2003	3,263	3,485	3,474	3,671	14,059
2002	3,257	3,337	3,446	3,434	13,474

Earnings Per Share ($)

2007	0.96	1.02	1.09	E1.16	E4.22
2006	0.59	0.69	0.81	0.92	3.01
2005	0.44	0.39	0.45	0.54	1.81
2004	0.09	0.22	0.25	0.29	0.85
2003	0.13	0.12	-0.05	0.20	0.41
2002	0.15	0.17	0.15	-2.46	-2.09

Fiscal year ended Dec. 31. Next earnings report expected: Mid January. EPS Estimates based on S&P Operating Earnings; historical GAAP earnings are as reported.

Dividend Data (Dates: mm/dd Payment Date: mm/dd/yy)

Amount ($)	Date Decl.	Ex-Div. Date	Stk. of Record	Payment Date
0.175	01/18	02/16	02/21	04/06/07
0.175	04/19	06/04	06/06	07/06/07
0.175	07/19	08/31	09/05	10/05/07
0.175	10/18	12/03	12/05	01/04/08

Dividends have been paid since 1957. Source: Company reports.

Schlumberger Ltd

STANDARD &POOR'S

Business Summary October 19, 2007

CORPORATE OVERVIEW. As a global oilfield and information services company with major activity in the energy industry, Schlumberger operates in two primary business segments: Oilfield Services (87% of 2006 revenues; 84% of 2006 segment operating income), and WesternGeco (13%, 16%). Oilfield Services provides exploration and production services, solutions and technology to the petroleum industry. It is managed through four geographic areas (North America, South America, Europe/CIS/Africa, and the Middle East/Asia). The company is largely focused on international operations; North America generated only 32% of Oilfield Services' total revenues in 2006, and only 35% of the segment's pretax operating income. The Middle East/Asia region generated the highest operating margins in 2006, at 32.6%, with North America second, at 30.3%. Operations within oilfield services are organized into six technology segments: wireline services, providing information technology to evaluate the reservoir, plan and monitor wells, and evaluate and monitor production; drilling and measurements, including directional drilling, measurement while drilling and logging while drilling services; well services, constructing mostly oil and gas wells; well completions and productivity; data and consulting ser-

vices; and Schlumberger Information Solutions. Supporting these six technologies are 23 R&D centers.

In addition, SLB operates its WesternGeco seismic segment. WesternGeco provides worldwide comprehensive reservoir imaging, monitoring and development services, with seismic crews and data processing centers, as well as a large multiclient seismic library. Services include 3D and time-lapse (4D) seismic surveys, and multi-component surveys for delineating prospects and reservoir management. In January 2007, SLB announced that it would construct its eighth and ninth Q-marine seismic vessels for this segment, due in 2008 and 2009, respectively, and would deploy its sixth and seventh Q-land seismic crews in 2007.

Company Financials Fiscal Year Ended Dec. 31

Per Share Data ($)	2006	2005	2004	2003	2002	2001	2000	1999	1998	1997
Tangible Book Value	3.84	3.63	2.54	1.87	0.70	1.14	5.87	5.65	6.24	5.55
Cash Flow	4.24	2.89	1.89	1.74	-0.75	2.08	1.73	1.20	1.91	2.21
Earnings	3.01	1.81	0.85	0.41	-2.09	0.46	0.64	0.29	0.91	1.26
Dividends	0.50	0.42	0.38	0.38	0.38	0.38	0.38	0.38	0.38	0.56
Payout Ratio	17%	23%	44%	93%	NM	82%	59%	129%	41%	45%
Prices:High	74.75	51.49	34.95	28.12	31.22	41.41	44.44	35.34	43.22	47.22
Prices:Low	49.20	31.57	26.27	17.81	16.70	20.42	26.75	22.72	20.03	24.50
P/E Ratio:High	25	28	41	69	NM	91	70	NM	48	37
P/E Ratio:Low	16	17	31	44	NM	45	42	NM	22	19

Income Statement Analysis (Million $)										
Revenue	19,230	14,309	11,480	14,059	13,474	13,746	9,611	8,395	11,816	10,648
Operating Income	6,458	4,520	2,895	2,474	-456	3,165	2,084	1,327	2,428	2,622
Depreciation, Depletion and Amortization	1,561	1,351	1,308	1,571	1,545	1,896	1,271	1,021	1,137	973
Interest Expense	235	197	272	334	368	385	276	193	150	87.0
Pretax Income	4,948	2,972	1,327	568	-2,230	1,126	959	470	1,323	1,669
Effective Tax Rate	24.0%	22.9%	20.9%	36.9%	NM	51.1%	23.8%	29.9%	23.4%	22.3%
Net Income	3,710	2,199	1,014	473	-2,418	522	733	329	1,014	1,296

Balance Sheet & Other Financial Data (Million $)										
Cash	166	191	224	234	168	178	3,040	4,390	3,957	1,761
Current Assets	9,186	8,554	7,060	10,369	7,185	7,705	7,493	8,606	8,805	6,071
Total Assets	22,832	18,077	16,001	20,041	19,435	22,326	17,173	15,081	16,078	12,097
Current Liabilities	6,455	5,515	4,701	6,795	6,451	6,218	3,991	3,474	3,919	3,630
Long Term Debt	4,664	3,591	3,944	6,097	6,029	6,216	3,573	3,183	3,285	1,069
Common Equity	10,420	7,592	6,117	5,881	5,606	8,378	8,295	7,721	8,119	6,695
Total Capital	15,084	11,688	10,477	12,376	12,188	15,231	12,474	10,904	11,404	7,764
Capital Expenditures	2,457	1,593	1,216	1,025	1,366	2,053	1,323	792	1,887	1,496
Cash Flow	5,271	3,550	2,322	2,044	-872	2,418	2,003	1,350	2,151	2,269
Current Ratio	1.4	1.6	1.5	1.5	1.1	1.2	1.9	2.5	2.2	1.7
% Long Term Debt of Capitalization	30.9	30.7	37.6	49.3	49.5	40.8	28.6	29.2	28.8	13.8
% Return on Assets	18.1	12.9	5.6	2.4	NM	2.6	4.5	2.1	7.2	11.6
% Return on Equity	41.2	32.1	16.9	8.2	NM	6.3	9.1	4.2	13.7	21.0

Data as orig reptd.; bef. results of disc opers/spec. items. Per share data adj. for stk. divs.; EPS diluted. E-Estimated. NA-Not Available. NM-Not Meaningful. NR-Not Ranked. UR-Under Review.

Office: 5599 San Felipe St 17th Fl, Houston, TX 77056-2724.
Telephone: 713-513-2000.
Email: irsupport@slb.com
Website: http://www.slb.com

Chrmn & CEO: A. Gould
EVP & CFO: J. Perraud
VP & CTO: A. Belani
VP & Treas: S. Ayat

Investor Contact: J. Poupeau (713-375-3535)
Board Members: P. Camus, J. S. Gorelick, A. Gould, T. Isaac, N. Kudryavtsev, A. Lajous, M. E. Marks, D. Primat, L. .. Reif, T. Sandvold, N. Seydoux, L. G. Stuntz, R. Talwar

Founded: 1956
Domicile: Netherlands Antilles
Employees: 70,000

Schwab (Charles) Corp

STANDARD &POOR'S

S&P Recommendation	HOLD ★★★☆☆	Price $22.54 (as of Nov 26, 2007)	12-Mo. Target Price $24.00	Investment Style Large-Cap Blend

GICS Sector Financials
Sub-Industry Investment Banking & Brokerage

Summary This company's Charles Schwab & Co. subsidiary is among the largest brokerage companies in the U.S., primarily serving retail clients.

Key Stock Statistics (Source S&P, Vickers, company reports)

52-Wk Range	**$24.34– 17.41**	S&P Oper. EPS 2007**E**	0.97	Market Capitalization(B)	**$26.263**	Beta	2.28
Trailing 12-Month EPS	**$2.05**	S&P Oper. EPS 2008**E**	1.13	Yield (%)	**0.89**	S&P 3-Yr. Proj. EPS CAGR(%)	12.00
Trailing 12-Month P/E	**11.0**	P/E on S&P Oper. EPS 2007**E**	23.2	Dividend Rate/Share	**$0.20**	S&P Credit Rating	A-
$10K Invested 5 Yrs Ago	**$21,855**	Common Shares Outstg. (M)	1,165.2	Institutional Ownership (%)	71		

Price Performance

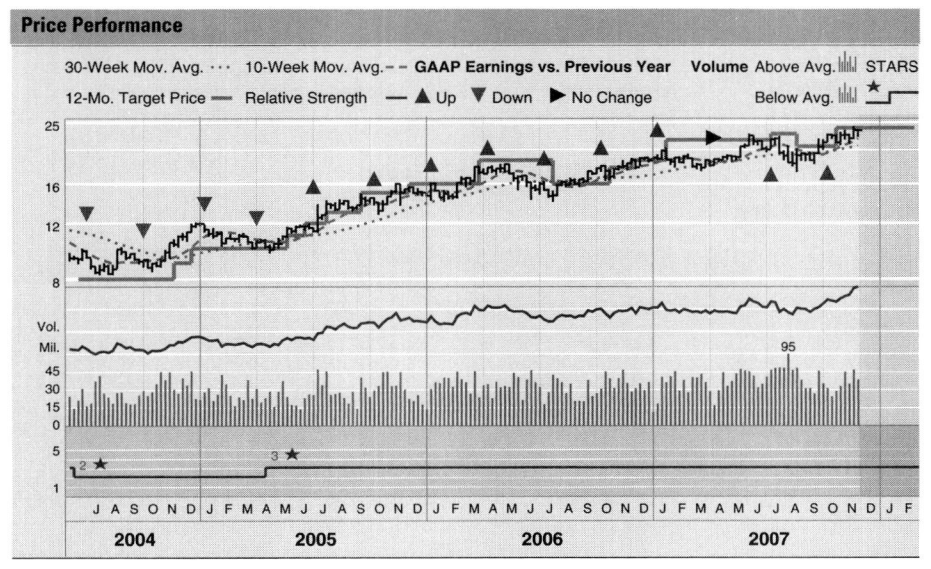

Options: ASE, CBOE, P, Ph

Analysis prepared by **Jason Willey** on October 15, 2007, when the stock traded at **$ 22.36**.

Highlights

➤ At the end of the third quarter, total client assets had increased 8.2% over the prior year, including acquired assets, helping asset management and administration fees rise. Deposit and loan growth have each advanced rapidly, and we expect this trend to continue into 2008 as the company expands the breadth of its relationships with clients and enhances its product line-up. Retirement plan participants have more than doubled in the past year, owing to acquisitions, and we look for these clients to provide meaningful long-term returns to the firm.

➤ We expect compensation costs as a percentage of revenue to decline significantly in 2007 and deliver an additional 60 basis point improvement in 2008. We look for advertising spending to continue to increase in 2008 as the company continues its "Talk To Chuck" campaign, but we see other expense savings more than offsetting this growth.

➤ We expect SCHW to earn $0.97 a share in 2007 and $1.13 in 2008, aided by trading volume growth, higher asset-based revenues, increased profitability in the banking segment, and additional cost reductions.

Investment Rationale/Risk

➤ We think the premium multiple afforded these shares compared to peers is appropriate in view of the company's brand recognition, affluent client base, and high proportion of recurring asset-based fees. We also see SCHW's success servicing the rapidly growing independent investment adviser channel as a positive, but we think that the banking segment, although growing, merits a lower valuation. We view the recent divestiture of its U.S. Trust wealth management subsidiary as a positive. While trading volumes have benefited from the recent market volatility, we believe prolonged market uncertainty may be a negative for retail activity.

➤ Risks to our recommendation and target price include reduced trading volumes, equity market declines, and a potentially more onerous regulatory environment. Our corporate governance concerns revolve primarily around the combined role of chairman and CEO.

➤ Our 12-month target price of $24 is 21X our 2008 EPS estimate, a premium to its discount brokerage peers, warranted, we think, by SCHW's leading market position and strong client asset base.

Qualitative Risk Assessment

LOW	MEDIUM	HIGH

Our risk assessment reflects our view of the company's strong competitive position, brand recognition and affluent client base, offset by industry cyclicality and our concerns about corporate governance.

Quantitative Evaluations

S&P Quality Ranking B+

D	C	B-	B	B+	A-	A	A+

Relative Strength Rank STRONG

87

LOWEST = 1   HIGHEST = 99

Revenue/Earnings Data

Revenue (Million $)

	1Q	2Q	3Q	4Q	Year
2007	1,153	1,205	1,291	--	--
2006	1,054	1,093	1,066	1,096	4,309
2005	1,059	1,087	1,138	1,180	4,464
2004	1,108	1,034	1,000	1,060	4,202
2003	900.0	1,018	1,051	1,118	4,087
2002	1,059	1,049	1,031	996.0	4,135

Earnings Per Share ($)

2007	0.19	0.23	0.27	E0.26	E0.97
2006	0.19	0.19	0.21	0.37	0.69
2005	0.11	0.14	0.16	0.14	0.56
2004	0.12	0.08	-0.03	0.04	0.30
2003	0.05	0.09	0.09	0.11	0.35
2002	0.07	0.07	Nil	-0.06	0.07

Fiscal year ended Dec. 31. Next earnings report expected: Mid January. EPS Estimates based on S&P Operating Earnings; historical GAAP earnings are as reported.

Dividend Data (Dates: mm/dd Payment Date: mm/dd/yy)

Amount ($)	Date Decl.	Ex-Div. Date	Stk. of Record	Payment Date
0.050	04/25	05/09	05/11	05/25/07
1.0 Spl.	07/02	07/20	07/24	08/24/07
0.050	07/02	07/20	07/24	08/24/07
0.050	10/18	11/07	11/09	11/23/07

Dividends have been paid since 1989. Source: Company reports.

Please read the Required Disclosures and Analyst Certification on the last page of this report.

The McGraw-Hill Companies

Schwab (Charles) Corp

STANDARD & POOR'S

Business Summary October 15, 2007

CORPORATE OVERVIEW. SCHW is a financial holding company that provides securities brokerage and related financial services through two segments, Schwab Investor Services and Schwab Institutional. Other subsidiaries include Charles Schwab Investment Management, the investment adviser for Schwab's proprietary mutual funds; and CyberTrader, Inc., an electronic trading technology and brokerage concern, acquired in 2000, which provides services to highly active, online traders.

Through the Schwab Investor Services segment (75% of 2006 net revenue), the company provides retail brokerage and banking services, as well as its retirement plan services division. Through various types of brokerage accounts, Schwab offers the purchase and sale of securities, including Nasdaq, exchange-listed and other equity securities, options, mutual funds, unit investment trusts, variable annuities and fixed income investments. At the end of 2006, the company, through subsidiaries, served 7.4 million active client accounts, and held client assets of $1.2 trillion.

Through its Schwab Institutional segment (22%), SCHW provides custodial, trade execution and support services to investment advisers, serves company

401(k) plan sponsors and third-party administrators, and supports company stock option plans. The company's Institutional segment had more than $502 billion in assets under management as of December 31, 2006. SCHW launched Schwab Advisor Network in May 2002, which refers affluent investors to local investment advisers.

The U.S. Trust Corp. business was sold for $3.3 billion to Bank of America at the beginning of the third quarter of 2007. In October 2004, Schwab sold its Capital Markets segment, which provided trade execution services in Nasdaq, exchange-listed and other securities primarily to broker-dealers, to UBS for $265 million. SCHW incurred a $49 million after-tax charge on the sale of its capital markets group (a strategic business, in our view). The sale of the Capital Markets segment included SoundView Technology Group, a research-oriented securities firm, which Schwab had acquired in January 2004, for about $340 million in cash.

Company Financials Fiscal Year Ended Dec. 31

Per Share Data ($)	2006	2005	2004	2003	2002	2001	2000	1999	1998	1997
Tangible Book Value	3.63	2.71	2.57	2.56	0.55	2.58	2.69	1.81	1.15	0.91
Cash Flow	0.81	0.72	0.47	0.35	0.30	0.30	0.70	0.59	0.39	0.32
Earnings	0.69	0.56	0.30	0.35	0.07	0.06	0.51	0.47	0.28	0.22
S&P Core Earnings	0.68	0.53	0.23	0.27	-0.02	-0.09	NA	NA	NA	NA
Dividends	0.14	0.09	0.07	0.05	0.04	0.04	0.04	0.04	0.04	0.03
Payout Ratio	14%	16%	25%	14%	63%	73%	8%	8%	13%	13%
Prices:High	19.49	16.14	13.92	14.20	19.00	33.00	44.75	51.67	22.83	9.83
Prices:Low	14.00	9.65	8.25	6.25	7.22	8.13	22.46	16.96	6.17	4.50
P/E Ratio:High	21	29	46	41	NM	NM	88	NM	81	45
P/E Ratio:Low	15	17	28	18	NM	NM	44	NM	22	20

Income Statement Analysis (Million $)

	2006	2005	2004	2003	2002	2001	2000	1999	1998	1997
Commissions	785	779	936	1,207	1,206	1,355	2,294	1,863	1,309	1,174
Interest Income	2,113	1,944	1,213	970	1,186	1,857	2,589	1,471	1,127	900
Total Revenue	4,988	5,151	4,479	4,328	4,480	5,281	7,139	4,713	3,388	2,845
Interest Expense	679	687	277	241	345	928	1,352	768	652	546
Pretax Income	1,476	1,185	645	710	168	135	1,231	971	577	447
Effective Tax Rate	39.6%	38.4%	35.8%	33.5%	42.3%	42.2%	41.7%	39.4%	39.6%	39.6%
Net Income	891	730	414	472	97.0	78.0	718	589	348	270
S&P Core Earnings	875	678	314	357	-31.5	-131	NA	NA	NA	NA

Balance Sheet & Other Financial Data (Million $)

	2006	2005	2004	2003	2002	2001	2000	1999	1998	1997
Total Assets	48,992	47,351	47,133	45,866	39,705	40,464	38,154	29,299	22,264	16,482
Cash Items	15,369	17,589	21,797	24,175	24,119	22,148	14,300	10,547	11,399	7,571
Receivables	11,577	11,600	10,323	9,137	7,067	10,066	16,680	17,543	9,980	8,019
Securities Owned	6,386	6,857	5,335	4,023	1,716	1,700	1,603	340	242	283
Securities Borrowed	Nil	Nil	Nil	Nil	Nil	Nil	Nil	Nil	Nil	Nil
Due Brokers & Customers	1,498	25,994	28,622	29,845	27,877	27,822	26,785	25,171	19,867	14,228
Other Liabilities	1,069	1,388	1,396	1,330	1,302	1,327	1,277	931	618	478
Capitalization:Debt	388	514	585	772	642	730	770	455	351	361
Capitalization:Equity	5,008	4,450	4,386	4,461	4,011	4,163	4,230	2,274	1,429	1,145
Capitalization:Total	5,396	4,964	4,971	5,233	4,653	4,893	5,000	2,729	1,780	1,506
% Return on Revenue	17.9	14.2	9.2	15.1	3.0	2.0	14.8	20.7	10.3	9.4
% Return on Assets	1.8	1.5	0.9	1.1	0.2	0.2	2.0	2.3	1.8	1.8
% Return on Equity	18.8	16.5	9.4	11.1	2.4	1.9	21.1	31.8	27.5	27.0

Data as orig reptd.; bef. results of disc opers/spec. items. Per share data adj. for stk. divs.; EPS diluted. Quarterly revs. excl. interest expense. E-Estimated. NA-Not Available. NM-Not Meaningful. NR-Not Ranked. UR-Under Review.

Office: 120 Kearny St , San Francisco, CA 94108-4899.
Telephone: 415-636-7000.
Email: investor.relations@schwab.com
Website: http://www.aboutschwab.com

Chrmn & CEO: C.R. Schwab
Pres & COO: W. Bettinger
EVP, Secy & General Counsel: C.E. Dwyer
EVP & CIO: G. Sasson

SVP & CFO: J.R. Martinetto
Investor Contact: R.G. Fowler (415-636-9869)
Board Members: W. F. Adlinger III, N. H. Bechtle, C. P. Butcher, D. G. Fisher, F. C. Herringer, M. Magner, S. T. McLin, C. R. Schwab, P. A. Sneed, R. O. Walther, R. N. Wilson, D. B. Yoffie

Founded: 1971
Domicile: Delaware
Employees: 12,400

The McGraw-Hill Companies

Scripps (E.W.) Co. (The)

S&P Recommendation	HOLD ★★★☆☆	Price	12-Mo. Target Price	Investment Style
		$44.46 (as of Nov 23, 2007)	$51.00	Large-Cap Growth

GICS Sector Consumer Discretionary
Sub-Industry Broadcasting & Cable TV

Summary This diversified media concern operates in the broadcasting, entertainment, publishing and interactive media industries.

Key Stock Statistics (Source S&P, Vickers, company reports)

52-Wk Range	$53.39– 37.89	S&P Oper. EPS 2007E	2.19	Market Capitalization(B)	$5.629	Beta	0.76
Trailing 12-Month EPS	$2.36	S&P Oper. EPS 2008E	2.45	Yield (%)	1.26	S&P 3-Yr. Proj. EPS CAGR(%)	6.00
Trailing 12-Month P/E	18.8	P/E on S&P Oper. EPS 2007E	20.3	Dividend Rate/Share	$0.56	S&P Credit Rating	A
$10K Invested 5 Yrs Ago	$11,857	Common Shares Outstg. (M)	163.2	Institutional Ownership (%)	73		

Price Performance

30-Week Mov. Avg. ···· 10-Week Mov. Avg. – – GAAP Earnings vs. Previous Year Volume Above Avg. ▮▮▮ STARS
12-Mo. Target Price — Relative Strength — ▲ Up ▼ Down ► No Change Below Avg. ▮▮▮ ★

Options: Ph

Analysis prepared by **James Peters, CFA** on October 30, 2007, when the stock traded at **$ 44.02**.

Highlights

➤ We see revenue growth of about 5.4% in 2008, following a 1.3% rise we project for 2007. We expect significant election year advertising gains to lead to strong growth for the broadcast television business. We anticipate high single digit percentage growth for Scripps Networks, driven by advertising rate gains for SSP's higher rated programming and improved penetration for the company's less distributed programming. Following significant marketing investments in 2007, we expect the company's interactive segment to post a modest revenue advance in 2008, and we forecast a slight decline in newspaper segment revenues.

➤ We forecast an operating margin of 26.7% in 2008, up from our projection of 24.8% for 2007. We see margin expansion being generated primarily from gains in profitable election year advertising and a reduced level of marketing investment spending to support uSwitch and Shopzilla.

➤ Including expected lower interest expense and higher minority interest, we see 2008 EPS of $2.45, up from our projection of $2.19 for 2007.

Investment Rationale/Risk

➤ On October 16, SSP announced plans to split the company into two: Scripps Networks Interactive and the E.W. Scripps Company. Contingent upon shareholder and board approval of the final plan as well as confirmation from the IRS that the transaction can be completed as a tax-free dividend, the planned split is expected to be completed in the second quarter of 2008. We view the separation plan positively, as we believe it unlocks value for SSP by allowing Scripps Networks Interactive to trade at a multiple associated with its higher growth potential unencumbered by the lower trading multiples associated with slower growth traditional media assets. We also are in favor of the company's plan to return about 50% of E.W. Scripps' free cash flow to shareholders in the form of dividends.

➤ Risks to our recommendation and target price include lower than expected advertising spending, and failure to consummate the planned company split.

➤ By applying a blended sum-of-the-parts peer average EBITDA multiple of 10X to our 2008 EBITDA estimate of $900 million, we derive our 12-month target price of $51.

Qualitative Risk Assessment

LOW	MEDIUM	HIGH

Our risk assessment reflects our view of a highly competitive environment for advertising among newspapers, television networks and other media, and the cyclical nature of advertising spending, offset by what we see as better growth prospects for the company than for its peers and the stock's low beta.

Quantitative Evaluations

S&P Quality Ranking A-

D	C	B-	B	B+	A-	A	A+

Relative Strength Rank STRONG

86

LOWEST = 1 HIGHEST = 99

Revenue/Earnings Data

Revenue (Million $)

	1Q	2Q	3Q	4Q	Year
2007	601.4	640.1	596.5	--	--
2006	589.7	641.9	583.5	683.0	2,498
2005	585.1	627.3	594.7	706.8	2,514
2004	513.7	547.3	499.8	606.7	2,168
2003	445.2	474.9	440.5	514.3	1,875
2002	359.8	399.9	371.5	478.1	1,536

Earnings Per Share ($)

2007	0.39	0.59	0.54	E0.69	E2.19
2006	0.49	0.64	0.48	0.80	2.41
2005	0.42	0.58	0.35	-0.01	1.35
2004	0.43	0.52	0.34	0.55	1.84
2003	0.33	0.40	0.32	0.62	1.66
2002	0.25	0.17	0.29	0.47	1.17

Fiscal year ended Dec. 31. Next earnings report expected: Late January. EPS Estimates based on S&P Operating Earnings; historical GAAP earnings are as reported.

Dividend Data (Dates: mm/dd Payment Date: mm/dd/yy)

Amount ($)	Date Decl.	Ex-Div. Date	Stk. of Record	Payment Date
0.120	02/09	02/21	02/23	03/09/07
0.140	05/10	05/23	05/25	06/08/07
0.140	07/31	08/29	08/31	09/10/07
0.140	11/07	11/28	11/30	12/10/07

Dividends have been paid since 1922. Source: Company reports.

Scripps (E.W.) Co. (The)

STANDARD &POOR'S

Business Summary October 30, 2007

CORPORATE OVERVIEW. The E.W. Scripps Co. is a diversified media company that has interests in national television networks (Scripps Networks), newspaper publishing (in 18 markets), broadcast television (10 stations), interactive media, including online comparison shopping (Shopzilla) and an online site for comparing and switching essential home services (uSwitch), and licensing and syndication. All of the media businesses provide content and advertising services on the Web. The Scripps Networks segment includes Home and Garden Television (HGTV), the Food Network (TFN), the Do It Yourself (DIY) Network, Fine Living, Great American Country (GAC), and a 12% interest in FOX Sports Net South, a regional television network. The Shop At Home television retailing network was reclassified as a discontinued operation in April 2006 and sold in June 2006 for $17 million.

In 2004, Scripps Networks surpassed newspapers as the largest reportable segment in both revenues and profits. In 2006, Scripps Networks accounted for 42% of revenues, while newspapers accounted for 29%, broadcast television 15%, interactive 11%, and licensing and other media 4%.

Advertising remains the most important source of revenue to SSP, accounting, we believe, for close to 67% of total revenues. In 2006, advertising provid-

ed about 80% of the revenues for both the Scripps Network and the newspaper segments and 97% of the revenues of the broadcast television segment. Shopzilla earns revenues primarily from lead referrals provided to participating online merchants. uSwitch provides consumers with a free utility comparison and switching service, and earns commissions from the utility suppliers for each switch or referral based on the terms of the contract. Approximately 95% of the licensing revenues are provided by Peanuts.

IMPACT OF MAJOR DEVELOPMENTS. Management has changed the profile of SSP significantly in the past 10 years, primarily through internal development and acquisitions. In 1996, Newspapers accounted for about half of total revenues and 57% of profits, with broadcast TV accounting for most of the rest. The licensing and other media segment was a similarly small contributor then as it is now. Scripps Network had $30 million in revenues then and reported a loss of $14 million.

Company Financials Fiscal Year Ended Dec. 31

Per Share Data ($)	2006	2005	2004	2003	2002	2001	2000	1999	1998	1997
Tangible Book Value	NM	NM	0.72	1.22	NM	0.23	0.44	NM	NM	NM
Cash Flow	3.11	1.90	2.28	2.05	1.56	1.48	1.72	1.34	1.45	1.44
Earnings	2.41	1.35	1.84	1.66	1.17	0.87	1.03	0.93	0.81	0.97
S&P Core Earnings	2.39	1.78	1.63	1.61	1.31	0.48	NA	NA	NA	NA
Dividends	0.47	0.43	0.39	0.30	0.30	0.30	0.28	0.28	0.27	0.26
Payout Ratio	20%	32%	21%	18%	26%	35%	27%	30%	33%	27%
Prices:High	51.09	52.91	54.65	47.58	43.75	35.85	31.63	26.50	29.25	24.47
Prices:Low	40.86	44.85	44.73	36.95	32.56	27.35	21.19	20.25	19.25	16.13
P/E Ratio:High	21	39	30	29	37	41	31	28	36	25
P/E Ratio:Low	17	33	24	22	28	32	21	22	24	17

Income Statement Analysis (Million $)

	2006	2005	2004	2003	2002	2001	2000	1999	1998	1997
Revenue	2,498	2,514	2,168	1,875	1,536	1,437	1,719	1,571	1,455	1,242
Operating Income	797	638	538	435	401	374	454	400	380	328
Depreciation	115	91.2	71.8	63.5	62.8	99.1	109	65.3	104	77.6
Interest Expense	56.0	38.8	30.9	31.6	28.3	39.2	51.9	45.2	47.1	18.5
Pretax Income	690	472	543	423	309	241	276	255	229	280
Effective Tax Rate	31.8%	40.5%	36.1%	32.6%	37.4%	41.3%	39.2%	40.7%	40.6%	41.9%
Net Income	397	223	304	271	188	138	163	147	131	158
S&P Core Earnings	394	293	269	263	211	76.8	NA	NA	NA	NA

Balance Sheet & Other Financial Data (Million $)

	2006	2005	2004	2003	2002	2001	2000	1999	1998	1997
Cash	30.5	19.2	12.3	18.2	15.5	17.4	14.1	10.5	14.4	14.3
Current Assets	875	797	643	562	500	451	524	477	407	379
Total Assets	4,344	4,033	3,425	3,009	2,870	2,644	2,573	2,520	2,345	2,281
Current Liabilities	399	348	375	331	426	906	533	577	532	430
Long Term Debt	766	826	533	509	650	110	502	502	502	60˝
Common Equity	2,580	2,287	2,096	1,823	1,515	1,352	1,278	1,164	1,065	1,049
Total Capital	3,803	3,562	2,629	2,524	2,308	1,609	1,910	1,810	1,682	1,739
Capital Expenditures	109	72.1	76.8	89.3	88.4	68.2	74.6	79.8	67.0	56.6
Cash Flow	512	314	376	334	251	237	273	212	235	235
Current Ratio	2.2	2.3	1.7	1.7	1.2	0.5	1.0	0.8	0.8	0.9
% Long Term Debt of Capitalization	20.2	23.2	20.3	20.2	28.2	6.8	26.3	27.7	29.8	34.6
% Net Income of Revenue	15.9	8.9	14.0	14.4	12.3	9.6	9.5	9.4	9.0	12.7
% Return on Assets	9.5	6.0	9.4	9.2	6.8	5.3	6.4	6.0	5.7	8.4
% Return on Equity	16.3	10.2	15.5	16.2	13.1	10.5	13.4	13.2	12.4	15.8

Data as orig reptd.; bef. results of disc opers/spec. items. Per share data adj. for stk. divs.; EPS diluted. E-Estimated. NA-Not Available. NM-Not Meaningful. NR-Not Ranked. UR-Under Review.

Office: 312 Walnut Street, Cincinnati, OH 45201.
Telephone: 513-977-3000.
Email: ir@scripps.com
Website: http://www.scripps.com

Chrmn: W.R. Burleigh
Pres & CEO: K.W. Lowe
COO & EVP: R.A. Boehne
EVP & CFO: J.G. NeCastro

SVP & General Counsel: A.B. Cruz, III
Investor Contact: T.E. Stautberg (513-977-3826)
Board Members: W. R. Burleigh, J. H. Burlingame, D. A. Galloway, K. W. Lowe, D. M. Moffett, J. Mohn, N. B. Paumgarten, J. Sagansky, N. E. Scagliotti, E. W. Scripps, P. K. Scripps, R. W. Tysoe, J. A. Wrigley

Founded: 1878
Domicile: Ohio
Employees: 9,000

The McGraw-Hill Companies

Sealed Air Corp

S&P Recommendation **BUY** ★★★★☆	Price $23.18 (as of Nov 23, 2007)	12-Mo. Target Price $29.00	Investment Style Large-Cap Growth

GICS Sector Materials
Sub-Industry Paper Packaging

Summary This company is a leading global manufacturer of a wide range of food and protective packaging materials and systems.

Key Stock Statistics (Source S&P, Vickers, company reports)

52-Wk Range	$33.87– 22.80	S&P Oper. EPS 2007E	1.65	Market Capitalization(B)	$3.744	Beta	2.20
Trailing 12-Month EPS	$1.90	S&P Oper. EPS 2008E	1.85	Yield (%)	1.73	S&P 3-Yr. Proj. EPS CAGR(%)	13.00
Trailing 12-Month P/E	12.2	P/E on S&P Oper. EPS 2007E	14.0	Dividend Rate/Share	$0.40	S&P Credit Rating	BBB
$10K Invested 5 Yrs Ago	$22,196	Common Shares Outstg. (M)	161.5	Institutional Ownership (%)	92		

Price Performance

30-Week Mov. Avg. ··· 10-Week Mov. Avg. - - **GAAP Earnings vs. Previous Year** Volume Above Avg. STARS
12-Mo. Target Price — Relative Strength — ▲ Up ▼ Down ► No Change Below Avg. ★

Options: CBOE, P, Ph

Analysis prepared by **Stewart Scharf** on October 30, 2007, when the stock traded at **$ 24.75**.

Highlights

➤ We project 3% to 5% organic sales growth in 2007 (before at least 3% favorable foreign currency effect), with a gradual rebound in 2008, driven by demand for new food products and solutions overseas, especially in Latin America and Asia/Pacific. We expect modest unit volume growth for protective packaging in North America.

➤ We believe gross margins will narrow to near 28% in 2007 from 28.7% in 2006, with sequential improvement during 2008, as pricing pass through and a better mix, and improved supply chain efficiencies offset high, albeit stabilizing, resin-based raw material costs. We expect EBITDA margins to expand in 2008 from about 15.5% projected for 2007, as SEE shifts production to more efficient locations overseas. We forecast that a global manufacturing strategy will lead to about $60 million in annual cost savings by 2009.

➤ We project an effective tax rate of 25.2% in 2007, and operating EPS of $1.65 (before a net gain of $0.23). We see growth of about 12%, to $1.85, in 2008.

Investment Rationale/Risk

➤ We have a buy recommendation based on our view of favorable growth prospects and a global manufacturing strategy, as well as our valuation models. We expect SEE to develop technologies and innovative new products.

➤ Risks to our recommendation and target price include a severe global economic downturn, a further significant increase in resin costs, a stronger U.S. dollar, and another mad cow disease scare. We have some concern regarding corporate governance issues, as at least one former CEO serves on the board.

➤ Using a P/E of 12.5X our 2008 EPS estimate--a discount to historical and peer levels--we arrive at a value of $23. The shares recently traded at a 24% discount to their intrinsic value of $32, based on our DCF model, which assumes a perpetual growth rate of 3.5% and a weighted average cost of capital of 8.3%. Our 12-month target price is $29, based on a weighted blend of these two metrics.

Qualitative Risk Assessment

LOW	MEDIUM	HIGH

Our risk assessment reflects asbestos litigation, volatile energy prices, and food-related health issues that could lead to restrictions on imports and exports, and some corporate governance concerns. This is offset by our view of the company's sound balance sheet and cash flow generation.

Quantitative Evaluations

S&P Quality Ranking NR

D	C	B-	B	B+	A-	A	A+

Relative Strength Rank MODERATE

36

LOWEST = 1 HIGHEST = 99

Revenue/Earnings Data

Revenue (Million $)

	1Q	2Q	3Q	4Q	Year
2007	1,095	1,145	1,161	--	--
2006	1,019	1,082	1,081	1,146	4,328
2005	969.8	1,020	1,020	1,076	4,085
2004	913.1	923.7	944.2	1,017	3,798
2003	822.9	865.6	908.7	934.8	3,532
2002	746.1	786.3	825.8	846.1	3,204

Earnings Per Share ($)

2007	0.67	0.40	0.39	E0.45	E1.65
2006	0.30	0.31	0.41	0.45	1.47
2005	0.29	0.33	0.34	0.39	1.35
2004	0.31	0.32	0.35	0.17	1.13
2003	0.26	0.28	0.21	0.25	1.00
2002	0.28	0.31	0.31	-3.07	-2.15

Fiscal year ended Dec. 31. Next earnings report expected: Late January. EPS Estimates based on S&P Operating Earnings; historical GAAP earnings are as reported.

Dividend Data (Dates: mm/dd Payment Date: mm/dd/yy)

Amount ($)	Date Decl.	Ex-Div. Date	Stk. of Record	Payment Date
2-for-1	02/16	03/19	03/02	03/16/07
0.100	04/12	05/30	06/01	06/15/07
0.100	08/09	09/05	09/07	09/21/07
0.100	11/16	12/05	12/07	12/21/07

Dividends have been paid since 2006. Source: Company reports.

Business Summary October 30, 2007

CORPORATE OVERVIEW. Sealed Air Corp., a leading protective and specialty packaging company, expects an increasing proportion of sales to come from outside the U.S. Foreign operations (excluding Canada, with about 3%) accounted for over 50% of sales in 2006, with Europe accounting for 29% of total sales, Latin America 8%, and Asia Pacific 12%. As of October 2007, more than 50% of sales came from outside the U.S.

As of the second quarter of 2007, the company realigned its segment reporting to reflect its growth strategies in core markets and new business opportunities, as it focuses on long-term global trends, including higher living standards in emerging markets, conservation and energy efficiency, convenience and longevity. The food packaging segment (40% of net sales in the first nine months of 2007) focuses on industrial products and new technologies that enable food processors to package and ship fresh and processed meats and cheeses through their supply chain. Food Solutions (20%) targets advancements in food packaging technologies that provide consumers with fresh meals from food service outlets or expanding retail cases at grocery stores. Protective Packaging (33%) includes core packaging technologies and solutions slated for traditional industrial applications while emphasizing consumer-oriented packaging solutions. Other sales accounted for 6.5%.

In 2006, the company operated in two business segments: protective packaging products (38% of net sales in 2006; 14.1% of segment operating profits) and food packaging products (62%; 11.5%). Food packaging products primarily consist of flexible materials and related systems marketed mainly under the Cryovac trademark for a broad range of perishable food applications. The segment also manufactures polystyrene foam trays that are used by supermarkets and food processors to protect and display fresh meat, poultry and produce. The U.S. Department of Agriculture (USDA) projects increases in U.S. protein consumption. Case-ready packaging sales exceeded $400 million in 2006. The protective packaging products segment includes surface protection and other cushioning products such as air cellular packaging materials, and plastic sheets containing encapsulated air bubbles that protect products from damage during shipment, under the Bubble Wrap and Air Cap brand names.

Company Financials Fiscal Year Ended Dec. 31

Per Share Data ($)	2006	2005	2004	2003	2002	2001	2000	1999	1998	1997
Tangible Book Value	NM	NM	NM	NM	NM	NM	NM	NM	NM	2.85
Cash Flow	2.30	2.64	1.99	1.95	-1.17	1.92	2.16	1.70	1.22	1.19
Earnings	1.47	1.35	1.13	1.00	-2.15	0.61	0.97	0.84	0.06	0.58
S&P Core Earnings	1.49	1.37	1.14	1.03	1.29	0.63	NA	NA	NA	NA
Dividends	0.30	Nil	Nil	Nil	Nil	Nil	Nil	Nil	Nil	NA
Payout Ratio	20%	Nil	Nil	Nil	Nil	Nil	Nil	Nil	Nil	NA
Prices:High	32.88	28.32	27.45	27.24	24.20	23.55	30.94	34.22	34.00	NA
Prices:Low	22.81	22.78	22.03	17.50	6.35	14.40	13.19	22.25	13.69	NA
P/E Ratio:High	22	21	24	27	NM	39	32	41	NM	NA
P/E Ratio:Low	16	17	20	17	NM	24	14	26	NM	NA

Income Statement Analysis (Million $)										
Revenue	4,328	4,085	3,798	3,532	3,204	3,067	3,068	2,840	2,507	1,480
Operating Income	707	687	716	693	1,766	641	687	648	524	155
Depreciation	168	175	180	154	166	221	220	147	178	93.0
Interest Expense	148	150	154	134	65.3	76.4	64.5	58.1	53.6	19.0
Pretax Income	400	377	323	377	-392	297	413	396	199	143
Effective Tax Rate	31.5%	32.1%	33.2%	36.2%	NM	47.3%	45.5%	46.6%	63.3%	38.5%
Net Income	274	256	216	240	-309	157	225	211	73.0	88.0
S&P Core Earnings	278	259	219	192	227	111	NA	NA	NA	NA

Balance Sheet & Other Financial Data (Million $)										
Cash	407	456	412	365	127	13.8	11.2	13.7	45.0	48.0
Current Assets	1,757	1,695	1,611	1,428	1,056	776	877	803	845	2,176
Total Assets	5,021	4,864	4,855	4,704	4,261	3,908	4,048	3,855	4,040	3,773
Current Liabilities	1,406	1,534	1,304	1,190	1,153	627	675	582	535	1,358
Long Term Debt	1,827	1,813	2,088	2,260	868	788	944	665	997	48.5
Common Equity	1,530	1,392	1,334	1,124	813	850	753	551	437	468
Total Capital	3,364	3,229	3,448	3,418	3,039	3,215	3,301	3,193	3,425	322
Capital Expenditures	168	96.9	103	124	91.6	146	114	75.1	82.4	24.3
Cash Flow	442	430	395	366	-197	322	381	287	179	181
Current Ratio	1.2	1.1	1.2	1.2	0.9	1.2	1.3	1.4	1.6	1.6
% Long Term Debt of Capitalization	54.3	56.1	60.5	66.1	28.6	24.5	28.6	20.8	29.1	15.1
% Net Income of Revenue	6.3	6.3	5.7	6.8	NM	5.1	7.3	7.4	2.9	5.9
% Return on Assets	5.5	5.3	4.5	5.4	NM	3.9	5.7	5.3	1.9	2.0
% Return on Equity	19.9	18.8	17.5	21.9	NM	12.7	24.7	28.3	0.2	16.0

Data as orig reptd.; bef. results of disc opers/spec. items. Per share data adj. for stk. divs.; EPS diluted. E-Estimated. NA-Not Available. NM-Not Meaningful. NR-Not Ranked. UR-Under Review.

Office: 200 Riverfront Blvd, Elmwood Park, NJ 07407-1033.
Telephone: 201-791-7600.
Website: http://www.sealedair.com
Pres & CEO: W.V. Hickey

SVP & CFO: D. Kelsey
VP, Secy & General Counsel: H.K. White
Treas: T.S. Christie
Investor Contact: E.D. Burrell (201-791-7600)

Board Members: H. Brown, M. Chu, L. R. Codey, T. D. Dunphy, C. F. Farrell, Jr., W. V. Hickey, J. B. Kosecoff, K. P. Manning, W. J. Marino
Founded: 1996
Domicile: Delaware
Employees: 17,400

Sears Holdings Corp

STANDARD
&POOR'S

S&P Recommendation	SELL ★ ★ ★ ★ ★	Price	12-Mo. Target Price	Investment Style
		$104.09 (as of Nov 29, 2007)	$90.00	Large-Cap Blend

GICS Sector Consumer Discretionary
Sub-Industry Department Stores

Summary Through its wholly owned Sears and Kmart subsidiaries, Sears Holdings is the third largest broadline retailer in the U.S.

Key Stock Statistics (Source S&P, Vickers, company reports)

52-Wk Range	$195.18–98.25	S&P Oper. EPS 2008**E**	6.75	Market Capitalization(B)	$14.868
Trailing 12-Month EPS	$7.94	S&P Oper. EPS 2009**E**	6.55	Yield (%)	Nil
Trailing 12-Month P/E	13.1	P/E on S&P Oper. EPS 2008**E**	15.4	Dividend Rate/Share	Nil
$10K Invested 5 Yrs Ago	NA	Common Shares Outstg. (M)	142.8	Institutional Ownership (%)	94

Beta	0.22
S&P 3-Yr. Proj. EPS CAGR(%)	-10.00
S&P Credit Rating	NA

Price Performance

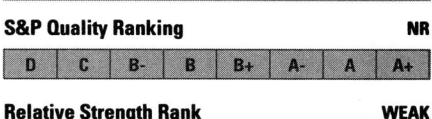

30-Week Mov. Avg. · · · 10-Week Mov. Avg. – – GAAP Earnings vs. Previous Year Volume Above Avg. STARS
12-Mo. Target Price — Relative Strength — ▲ Up ▼ Down ► No Change Below Avg. ★

Options: ASE, CBOE, P, Ph

Highlights

► The STARS recommendation for SHLD has recently been changed to 2 (sell) from 3 (hold) and the 12-month target price has recently been changed to $90.00 from $130.00. The Highlights section of this Stock Report will be updated accordingly.

Investment Rationale/Risk

► The Investment Rationale/Risk section of this Stock Report will be updated shortly. For the latest News story on SHLD from MarketScope, see below.

► 11/29/07 10:19 am EST... S&P DOWNGRADES SHARES OF SEARS HOLDINGS TO SELL FROM HOLD (SHLD 101.12**): Oct-Q operating EPS of $0.01 vs. $0.80 misses our $0.48 estimate on heavy seasonal merchandise markdowns and lack of expense leverage off of a 4.1% same-store sales decline. Given limited success of re-merchandising efforts at Sears and Kmart segments, increased competition, and a projected slowdown in consumer spending, we think SHLD's chances of executing a turnaround are slim. We are cutting our FY 08 (Jan.) operating EPS estimate by $1.00 to $6.75, FY 09's by $1.65 to $6.55, and lower our 12-month target price by $40 to $90 on a revised peer-P/E-based valuation. /J.Asaeda

Qualitative Risk Assessment

LOW	MEDIUM	HIGH

Our risk assessment reflects our view of SHLD's significant opportunity to leverage Kmart's and Sears's best practices and brands, as well as merger-related cost synergies, and to strengthen its competitive positioning. This is offset by what we consider the two units' long records of inconsistent sales and earnings.

Quantitative Evaluations

S&P Quality Ranking   NR

D	C	B-	B	B+	A-	A	A+

Relative Strength Rank   WEAK

13

LOWEST = 1   HIGHEST = 99

Revenue/Earnings Data

Revenue (Million $)

	1Q	2Q	3Q	4Q	Year
2008	11,702	12,239	11,548	--	--
2007	11,998	12,785	11,941	16,288	53,012
2006	7,626	13,192	12,202	16,086	49,124
2005	4,615	4,785	4,392	5,909	19,701
2004	--	5,652	5,092	6,328	17,072
2003	--	--	--	--	30,762

Earnings Per Share ($)

2008	1.40	1.17	0.01	E4.47	E6.75
2007	1.14	1.88	1.27	5.33	9.57
2006	0.65	0.98	0.35	4.03	6.17
2005	0.94	1.54	5.45	3.09	11.00
2004	--	-0.06	-0.26	2.78	2.52
2003	--	--	--	--	NA

Fiscal year ended Jan. 31. Next earnings report expected: Early March. EPS Estimates based on S&P Operating Earnings; historical GAAP earnings are as reported.

Dividend Data

No cash dividends have been paid.

Sears Holdings Corp

Business Summary November 27, 2007

CORPORATE OVERVIEW. Through the March 2005 merger of Kmart Holding Corp. and Sears, Roebuck and Co., which continue to operate under their separate brand names, Sears Holdings has emerged as the third largest broadline retailer in the U.S. based on FY 06 (Jan.) reported revenues. As of May 5, 2007, the company operated 2,410 Sears-branded full line and specialty stores in the U.S. and Canada (operated by Sears Canada), and 1,388 Kmart-branded discount stores and supercenters across the U.S. SHLD completed the integration of the Sears and Kmart supply chain, IT, finance, legal, human resources, marketing, and merchandising functions during FY 06, and the combination of store operations in February 2006.

CORPORATE STRATEGY. SHLD believes it has an opportunity to leverage Kmart's off-mall locations to expand the distribution of Sears products and services at a more rapid pace and at a lower cost than Sears would have been able to accomplish on its own. The company also sees the potential for

Kmart to improve its value proposition and competitive positioning through the addition of Sears-owned brands and services (cross-selling).

In FY 06, SHLD introduced select Sears private label branded products, including Kenmore appliances and Craftsman tools, into about 100 Kmart stores. The company further completed a national roll-out of Sears credit card acceptance to all Kmart locations, and tested certain Sears customer services at select Kmart locations. In FY 07, SHLD completed a national roll-out of Craftsman tools to Kmart locations, and expanded the number of Kmart stores carrying home appliances to 180. We look for SHLD to continue to roll out Sears brand products into Kmart locations in FY 08.

Company Financials Fiscal Year Ended Jan. 31

Per Share Data ($)	2007	2006	2005	2004	2003	2002	2001	2000	1999	1998
Tangible Book Value	49.25	41.80	50.21	24.36	NA	NA	NA	NA	NA	NA
Cash Flow	16.90	12.24	11.59	2.81	NA	NA	NA	NA	NA	NA
Earnings	9.57	6.17	11.00	2.52	NA	NA	NA	NA	NA	NA
S&P Core Earnings	9.24	4.53	4.51	-4.53	-6.80	-5.74	-0.55	NA	NA	NA
Dividends	Nil	Nil	Nil	Nil	Nil	NA	NA	NA	NA	NA
Payout Ratio	Nil	Nil	Nil	Nil	Nil	NA	NA	NA	NA	NA
Calendar Year	2006	2005	2004	2003	2002	2001	2000	1999	1998	1997
Prices:High	182.38	163.50	119.69	34.55	NA	NA	NA	NA	NA	NA
Prices:Low	114.90	84.51	22.41	12.00	NA	NA	NA	NA	NA	NA
P/E Ratio:High	19	26	11	14	NA	NA	NA	NA	NA	NA
P/E Ratio:Low	12	14	2	5	NA	NA	NA	NA	NA	NA

Income Statement Analysis (Million $)

	2007	2006	2005	2004	2003	2002	2001	2000	1999	1998
Revenue	53,012	49,124	19,701	17,072	30,762	NA	NA	NA	NA	NA
Operating Income	3,611	2,901	944	442	-1,303	NA	NA	NA	NA	NA
Depreciation	1,142	932	69.0	31.0	737	NA	NA	NA	NA	NA
Interest Expense	337	322	146	105	155	NA	NA	NA	NA	NA
Pretax Income	2,464	1,965	1,775	400	-3,286	NA	NA	NA	NA	NA
Effective Tax Rate	37.7%	36.4%	37.7%	38.0%	NM	NA	NA	NA	NA	NA
Net Income	1,490	948	1,106	248	-3,262	NA	NA	NA	NA	NA
S&P Core Earnings	1,439	696	448	-405	-3,439	-2,840	-260	NA	NA	NA

Balance Sheet & Other Financial Data (Million $)

	2007	2006	2005	2004	2003	2002	2001	2000	1999	1998
Cash	3,968	4,440	3,435	2,088	613	NA	NA	NA	NA	NA
Current Assets	15,406	15,207	7,541	5,811	6,102	NA	NA	NA	NA	NA
Total Assets	30,066	30,573	8,651	6,084	11,238	NA	NA	NA	NA	NA
Current Liabilities	10,052	10,350	2,086	1,776	2,120	NA	NA	NA	NA	NA
Long Term Debt	2,849	3,268	661	819	623	NA	NA	NA	NA	NA
Common Equity	12,714	11,611	4,469	2,192	-301	NA	NA	NA	NA	NA
Total Capital	15,563	14,879	5,130	3,011	322	NA	NA	NA	NA	NA
Capital Expenditures	513	546	230	108	252	NA	NA	NA	NA	NA
Cash Flow	2,632	1,880	1,175	279	-2,525	NA	NA	NA	NA	NA
Current Ratio	1.5	1.5	3.6	3.3	2.9	NA	NA	NA	NA	NA
% Long Term Debt of Capitalization	18.3	22.0	12.9	27.2	NM	NA	NA	NA	NA	NA
% Net Income of Revenue	2.8	1.9	5.6	1.5	NM	NA	NA	NA	NA	NA
% Return on Assets	4.9	4.8	15.0	3.9	NM	NA	NA	NA	NA	NA
% Return on Equity	12.3	11.8	33.1	12.7	NM	NA	NA	NA	NA	NA

Data as orig reptd.; bef. results of disc opers/spec. items. Per share data adj. for stk. divs.; EPS diluted. E-Estimated. NA-Not Available. NM-Not Meaningful. NR-Not Ranked. UR-Under Review.

Office: 3333 Beverly Rd, Hoffman Estates, IL 60179-0001.
Telephone: 847-286-2500.
Website: http://www.searsholdings.com
Chrmn: E.S. Lampert

Pres & CEO: A. Lewis
EVP, CFO & Chief Admin Officer: W.C. Crowley
EVP & CIO: K.A. Austin
SVP & Treas: A.R. Ravas

Board Members: W. C. Crowley, E. S. Lampert, A. Lewis, S. T. Mnuchin, R. C. Perry, A. N. Reese, E. Scott, T. J. Tisch

Founded: 1899
Domicile: Delaware
Employees: 352,000

Sempra Energy

STANDARD &POOR'S

S&P Recommendation	BUY ★★★★☆	Price	12-Mo. Target Price	Investment Style
		$60.58 (as of Nov 23, 2007)	$68.00	Large-Cap Blend

GICS Sector Utilities
Sub-Industry Multi-Utilities

Summary This gas and electric utility is also engaged in unregulated power, liquefied natural gas and international energy projects.

Key Stock Statistics (Source S&P, Vickers, company reports)

52-Wk Range	$66.38–50.95	S&P Oper. EPS 2007E	4.02	Market Capitalization(B)	$15.995	Beta	0.59
Trailing 12-Month EPS	$3.52	S&P Oper. EPS 2008E	3.92	Yield (%)	2.05	S&P 3-Yr. Proj. EPS CAGR(%)	0
Trailing 12-Month P/E	17.2	P/E on S&P Oper. EPS 2007E	15.1	Dividend Rate/Share	$1.24	S&P Credit Rating	BBB+
$10K Invested 5 Yrs Ago	$30,229	Common Shares Outstg. (M)	264.0	Institutional Ownership (%)	66		

Price Performance

30-Week Mov. Avg. · · · 10-Week Mov. Avg. - - GAAP Earnings vs. Previous Year Volume Above Avg. STARS
12-Mo. Target Price — Relative Strength — ▲ Up ▼ Down ▶ No Change Below Avg. ★

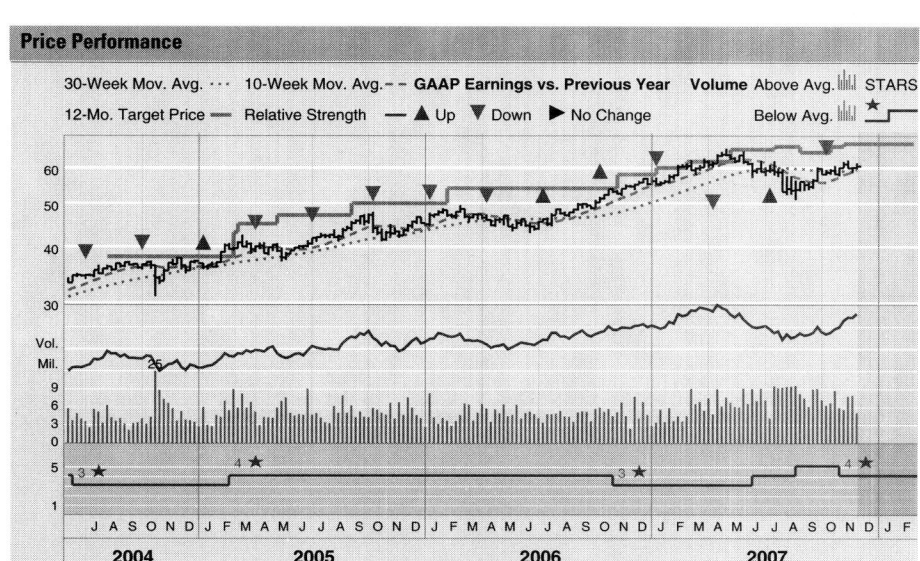

Options: CBOE

Analysis prepared by **Christopher B. Muir** on November 05, 2007, when the stock traded at **$61.02**.

Highlights

➤ We see revenues falling 4.4% in 2007, with customer growth more than offset by lower commodity prices. We forecast a 4.3% decrease in revenues in 2008 due to the expected placement of the commodities trading business into a joint venture with Royal Bank of Scotland (RBS) partly offset by higher commodity prices and customer growth.

➤ We expect that operating margins will decline to 12.2% in 2008 and 14.5% in 2007 from 15.1% in 2006, due to the placement of SRE's higher margin commodities business into a joint venture for 2008 and higher per-revenue cost of gas, depreciation and amortization and other operating expenses for 2007. We see pretax margins rising to 14.1% in 2008 and 14.2% in 2007, from 13.8% in 2006, as we expect substantially lower interest expense in both years.

➤ Assuming an effective tax rate of 33.6% and a slight increase in shares outstanding, we forecast operating EPS of $4.02 in 2007, down 4.5% from 2006's strong $4.21. Our 2008 forecast is $3.92, a 2.5% decrease related to the expected decline in SRE's commodity trading business earnings.

Investment Rationale/Risk

➤ We view the agreement that SRE has with RBS very favorably. The proposed deal to place its commodities business in a joint venture should substantially lower SRE's risk profile, free up about $1.0 billion in collateral payments, and still allow it to participate in the upside of the business. We also think the unique profit-sharing mechanism of the joint venture provides incentive for RBS to give its full support to the business. Separately, we expect two LNG projects under construction to add $0.30 to $0.35 per share to earnings starting in late 2009, with the first project ramping up in 2008.

➤ Risks to our recommendation and target price include a failure to complete LNG projects, declining wholesale power margins, potential losses from energy and metals trading, and a weaker economy.

➤ The stock recently traded at a P/E of 15.6X our 2008 EPS estimate, a 5% premium to multi-utility peers. Our 12-month target price of $68 is 17.4X our 2008 EPS estimate, a 27% premium to our peer P/E forecast. We think the premium is warranted by SRE's prospects for stronger-than-peers EPS growth beyond 2008, and an expected large share repurchase program.

Qualitative Risk Assessment

LOW	MEDIUM	HIGH

Our risk assessment reflects a balance between stable and steady earnings provided by SRE's regulated gas and electric utility operations and cyclical and volatile earnings from unregulated businesses, including power generation, energy marketing and trading, and international energy investments.

Quantitative Evaluations

S&P Quality Ranking B+

D	C	B-	B	B+	A-	A	A+

Relative Strength Rank STRONG

86

LOWEST = 1   HIGHEST = 99

Revenue/Earnings Data

Revenue (Million $)

	1Q	2Q	3Q	4Q	Year
2007	3,004	2,661	2,663	--	--
2006	3,336	2,486	2,694	3,245	11,761
2005	2,697	2,276	2,770	3,994	11,737
2004	2,360	1,996	2,165	2,889	9,410
2003	1,923	1,840	2,058	2,066	7,887
2002	1,460	1,488	1,384	1,688	6,020

Earnings Per Share ($)

2007	0.86	1.06	1.24	E1.03	E4.02
2006	0.90	0.71	2.07	0.49	4.17
2005	0.92	0.49	0.86	1.40	3.69
2004	0.96	0.55	0.98	1.43	3.93
2003	0.56	0.56	1.00	1.11	3.24
2002	0.71	0.70	0.73	0.65	2.79

Fiscal year ended Dec. 31. Next earnings report expected: Late February. EPS Estimates based on S&P Operating Earnings; historical GAAP earnings are as reported.

Dividend Data (Dates: mm/dd Payment Date: mm/dd/yy)

Amount ($)	Date Decl.	Ex-Div. Date	Stk. of Record	Payment Date
0.300	12/05	12/19	12/21	01/15/07
0.310	02/15	03/20	03/22	04/15/07
0.310	06/05	06/19	06/21	07/15/07
0.310	09/12	09/25	09/27	10/15/07

Dividends have been paid since 1998. Source: Company reports.

Please read the Required Disclosures and Analyst Certification on the last page of this report.

The McGraw-Hill Companies

Sempra Energy

Business Summary November 05, 2007

CORPORATE OVERVIEW. Sempra Energy (SRE) is a holding company with diverse interests in the energy domain. The company's business segments include California Utilities (CU), which contributed 59% of the revenues in 2006, and Sempra Global and parent division (SG), which contributed 41%. The CU segment includes regulated public utilities Southern California Gas Company (SCG) and San Diego Gas & Electric Company (SDGE), which provide electricity and natural gas services in the southern half of California. The unregulated business of SG includes Sempra Generation, which develops and operates power plants and energy infrastructure; Sempra Commodities, which provides marketing and risk management services for energy products and base metals; Sempra LNG, which constructs and operates LNG receipt terminals in North America; and Sempra Pipelines & Storage, which operates in Mexico and the US.

CORPORATE STRATEGY. Sempra seeks to increase earnings through a mix of moderate growth at its regulated utilities and faster growth in non-regulated businesses. In the utility segment, the company focuses on managing regulatory risk as well as operating and capital expenditures.

During 2003 to 2005, SRE focused on acquisitions as well as on new construc-

tion in generation, LNG, and pipelines and storage segments. However, starting in 2006, the company changed course related to generation, selling ownership interest in plants. The company remains focused on building new NGL projects.

On July 9, 2007, the company announced a deal with the Royal Bank of Scotland (RBS) that will place its commodity trading business in a joint venture. Upon closing, expected in December 2007, SRE will receive about $1 billion in cash that had been used as collateral. Earnings from the joint venture are to be divided into tranches so that each partner receives pretax 15% return on capital. SRE is to receive 70% of the first $500 million in pretax income above that threshold and then 30% of any pretax income above that level. We think this structure gives RBS a huge incentive to commit its substantial resources to growing the business. The company plans to increase its dividend and repurchase shares as a result of the deal.

Company Financials Fiscal Year Ended Dec. 31

Per Share Data ($)	2006	2005	2004	2003	2002	2001	2000	1999	1998	1997
Tangible Book Value	28.67	23.97	20.79	17.14	13.78	13.17	12.27	12.60	12.14	12.56
Cash Flow	6.70	6.25	6.59	6.12	5.68	5.35	NA	NA	NA	NA
Earnings	4.17	3.69	3.93	3.24	2.79	2.52	2.06	1.66	1.24	1.82
S&P Core Earnings	4.19	3.44	3.65	3.29	2.16	1.76	NA	NA	NA	NA
Dividends	1.20	1.16	1.00	1.00	1.00	1.00	1.00	1.56	1.56	1.27
Payout Ratio	29%	31%	25%	31%	36%	40%	49%	94%	126%	70%
Prices:High	57.35	47.86	37.93	30.90	26.25	28.61	24.88	26.00	29.31	NA
Prices:Low	42.90	35.53	29.51	22.25	15.50	17.31	16.19	17.13	23.75	NA
P/E Ratio:High	14	13	10	10	9	11	12	16	24	NA
P/E Ratio:Low	10	10	8	7	6	7	8	10	19	NA

Income Statement Analysis (Million $)	2006	2005	2004	2003	2002	2001	2000	1999	1998	1997
Revenue	11,761	11,737	9,410	7,887	6,020	8,029	7,143	5,360	5,481	5,069
Operating Income	1,785	1,111	1,272	939	987	993	NA	1,617	1,536	1,503
Depreciation	657	646	621	615	596	579	563	879	929	604
Interest Expense	361	321	332	327	323	352	301	229	207	107
Pretax Income	1,732	971	1,113	742	721	731	NA	NA	NA	NA
Effective Tax Rate	37.0%	4.33%	17.3%	6.33%	20.2%	29.1%	38.6%	31.2%	31.9%	41.1%
Net Income	1,091	929	920	695	575	518	429	394	294	432
S&P Core Earnings	1,096	866	855	708	445	362	NA	NA	NA	NA

Balance Sheet & Other Financial Data (Million $)	2006	2005	2004	2003	2002	2001	2000	1999	1998	1997
Cash	920	772	419	432	455	605	NA	NA	NA	NA
Current Assets	12,016	13,318	8,776	7,886	7,010	4,808	NA	NA	NA	NA
Total Assets	28,949	29,213	23,643	22,009	17,757	15,156	NA	NA	NA	NA
Current Liabilities	10,349	12,157	9,082	8,348	7,247	5,524	NA	NA	NA	NA
Long Term Debt	4,704	5,002	4,371	4,199	4,487	3,840	NA	NA	NA	NA
Common Equity	7,511	6,160	4,865	3,890	2,825	2,692	NA	NA	NA	NA
Total Capital	12,694	11,480	9,734	8,807	8,202	7,474	7,093	6,813	6,489	7,309
Capital Expenditures	1,907	1,404	1,083	1,049	1,214	1,068	NA	NA	NA	NA
Cash Flow	1,748	1,575	1,541	1,310	1,171	1,097	NA	NA	NA	NA
Current Ratio	1.2	1.1	1.0	0.9	1.0	0.9	NA	NA	NA	NA
% Long Term Debt of Capitalization	37.1	43.6	44.9	47.7	54.7	51.4	NA	NA	NA	NA
% Net Income of Revenue	9.3	7.9	9.8	8.8	9.6	6.5	NA	NA	NA	NA
% Return on Assets	3.7	3.5	4.0	3.3	3.5	3.4	NA	NA	NA	NA
% Return on Equity	16.0	16.9	21.0	20.7	20.8	20.0	NA	NA	NA	NA

Data as orig reptd.; bef. results of disc opers/spec. items. Per share data adj. for stk. divs.; EPS diluted. E-Estimated. NA-Not Available. NM-Not Meaningful. NR-Not Ranked. UR-Under Review.

Office: 101 Ash Street, San Diego, CA 92101-3017.
Telephone: 619-696-2000.
Email: investor@sempra.com
Website: http://www.sempra.com

Chrmn & CEO: D.E. Felsinger
Pres & COO: N.E. Schmale
EVP & CFO: M. Snell
EVP & General Counsel: M.J. Chaudhri

VP & Treas: C. McMonagle
Investor Contact: J. Martin (619-696-2901)
Board Members: J. G. Brocksmith, Jr., R. A. Collato, D. E. Felsinger, W. D. Godbold, Jr., W. D. Jones, R. G. Newman, W. G. Ouchi, W. C. Rusnack, W. P. Rutledge, N. E. Schmale

Founded: 1998
Domicile: California
Employees: 14,061

Sherwin-Williams Co (The)

STANDARD &POOR'S

S&P Recommendation HOLD ★★★☆☆	**Price** $60.62 (as of Nov 23, 2007)	**12-Mo. Target Price** $75.00	**Investment Style** Large-Cap Growth

GICS Sector Consumer Discretionary
Sub-Industry Home Improvement Retail

Summary This company, the largest U.S. producer of paints, is also a major seller of wallcoverings and related products.

Key Stock Statistics (Source S&P, Vickers, company reports)

52-Wk Range	$73.96– 58.53	S&P Oper. EPS 2007**E**	4.72	Market Capitalization(B)	$7.930	Beta		0.77
Trailing 12-Month EPS	$4.61	S&P Oper. EPS 2008**E**	5.20	Yield (%)	2.08	S&P 3-Yr. Proj. EPS CAGR(%)		9.00
Trailing 12-Month P/E	13.2	P/E on S&P Oper. EPS 2007**E**	12.8	Dividend Rate/Share	$1.26	S&P Credit Rating		A-
$10K Invested 5 Yrs Ago	$23,567	Common Shares Outstg. (M)	130.8	Institutional Ownership (%)	75			

Price Performance

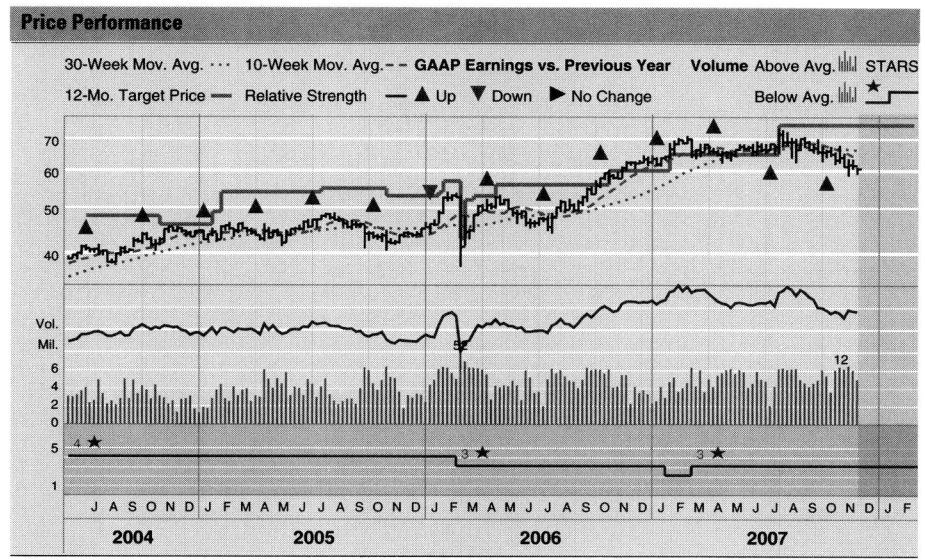

30-Week Mov. Avg. ··· 10-Week Mov. Avg.- - **GAAP Earnings vs. Previous Year** Volume Above Avg.||| STARS
12-Mo. Target Price— Relative Strength — ▲ Up ▼ Down ▶ No Change Below Avg.|||| ★

Options: CBOE

Analysis prepared by **Michael Souers** on October 31, 2007, when the stock traded at **$ 63.95.**

Highlights

➤ We expect sales growth of 5%-6% in 2008, following our projection of a 3% advance in 2007. We forecast continued softness in residential construction, which will likely negatively affect architectural sales, and we also foresee slowing demand in do-it-yourself (DIY) paint sales. Paint store segment sales gains will likely be driven by the addition of approximately 100 net new stores, but we expect flattish same-store sales results for this segment. In addition, we expect SHW to make several small acquisitions throughout the year.

➤ We see a slight widening in gross margins in 2008 due to improved pricing and product mix, partially offset by a projected increase in raw material costs. We also anticipate a slight increase in operating margins, as gross margin gains and cost-cutting initiatives are partially offset by a deleveraging of expenses due to our projection of flattish same-store sales.

➤ With a projected 32.0% tax rate and a diluted share count that is about 3% lower, reflecting SHW's buyback program, we estimate 2008 EPS of $5.20, a 10% increase from the $4.72 we expect the company to earn in 2007.

Investment Rationale/Risk

➤ We view the risk/reward quotient for owning SHW shares as neutral. While we continue to have a favorable view of the company's market niche, balance sheet and generation of free cash flow, we are concerned that a slowing housing market will limit sales and earnings growth potential over the next 12 months. In addition, we believe that much of the lead litigation risk is not being recognized in the current share price, and we see further risk as a distinct possibility.

➤ Risks to our recommendation and target price include a significant decrease in economic growth; sharply higher interest rates, which could cause further weakness to the slowing housing market; and any negative rulings on other lead pigment litigation cases outside of Rhode Island.

➤ At about 12X our 2008 EPS estimate, SHW shares recently traded in line with faster-growing peers but at a significant discount to the S&P 500. Our 12-month target price of $75 is based on our DCF analysis, assuming a weighted average cost of capital of 10.3% and a terminal growth rate of 3%.

Qualitative Risk Assessment

LOW	MEDIUM	HIGH

Our risk assessment for Sherwin-Williams reflects the cyclical nature of the company, which is reliant on new housing starts and remodeling, and lead pigment litigation risk, offset by an S&P Quality Ranking of A.

Quantitative Evaluations

S&P Quality Ranking A

D	C	B-	B	B+	A-	A	A+

Relative Strength Rank MODERATE

51

LOWEST = 1 HIGHEST = 99

Revenue/Earnings Data

Revenue (Million $)

	1Q	2Q	3Q	4Q	Year
2007	1,756	2,198	2,197	--	--
2006	1,769	2,130	2,117	1,795	7,810
2005	1,539	1,965	1,977	1,710	7,191
2004	1,320	1,618	1,677	1,499	6,114
2003	1,148	1,472	1,503	1,285	5,408
2002	1,149	1,453	1,426	1,156	5,185

Earnings Per Share ($)

2007	0.83	1.52	1.55	E0.83	E4.72
2006	0.82	1.33	1.30	0.73	4.19
2005	0.58	1.08	1.07	0.54	3.28
2004	0.35	0.87	0.92	0.57	2.72
2003	0.21	0.75	0.82	0.48	2.26
2002	0.23	0.70	0.74	0.38	2.04

Fiscal year ended Dec. 31. Next earnings report expected: Late January. EPS Estimates based on S&P Operating Earnings; historical GAAP earnings are as reported.

Dividend Data (Dates: mm/dd Payment Date: mm/dd/yy)

Amount ($)	Date Decl.	Ex-Div. Date	Stk. of Record	Payment Date
0.315	02/21	02/28	03/02	03/16/07
0.315	04/18	05/16	05/18	06/08/07
0.315	07/18	08/22	08/24	09/14/07
0.315	10/19	11/14	11/16	12/07/07

Dividends have been paid since 1979. Source: Company reports.

Please read the Required Disclosures and Analyst Certification on the last page of this report.

The McGraw-Hill Companies

Sherwin-Williams Co (The)

Business Summary October 31, 2007

CORPORATE PROFILE. Sherwin-Williams manufactures, distributes and sells paints, coatings and related products to professional, industrial, commercial and retail customers primarily in North and South America. The company is structured into five reportable segments: Paint Stores, Consumer, Automotive Finishes, International Coatings, and Administrative.

Paint Stores (62% of revenues in 2006) offer Sherwin-Williams branded architectural and industrial paints, stains and related products. Its diverse customer base includes architectural and industrial painting contractors, residential and commercial builders, property owners and managers, OEM product finishers and do-it-yourself (DIY) homeowners. In 2006, SHW opened 117 net new stores, bringing the North America Paint Stores store count to 3,046.

The Consumer segment (18%) makes architectural paints, stains, varnishes, industrial maintenance products, wood finishing products, paint applicators, corrosion inhibitors and paint related products. Brands include Dutch Boy, Krylon, Minwax, Thompson's Water Seal and Pratt & Lambert, as well as pri-

vate label brands.

Global Group (20%) sells paints, stains, coatings, varnishes, industrial products, wood finishing products, applicators, aerosols, high performance interior and exterior coatings for the automotive, aviation, fleet and heavy truck markets, OEM product finishes and related products. SHW sells these products through 469 company-operated architectural, automotive, industrial and chemical coatings branches and other operations in the United States, Canada, Mexico, Jamaica, Argentina, Brazil, Chile, Peru, Uruguay and China. It also distributes these products to 20 other countries through wholly owned subsidiaries, joint ventures and licensees of technology, trademarks and tradenames.

Company Financials Fiscal Year Ended Dec. 31

Per Share Data ($)	2006	2005	2004	2003	2002	2001	2000	1999	1998	1997
Tangible Book Value	2.67	3.83	3.12	2.95	4.05	3.69	3.18	2.32	1.76	0.86
Cash Flow	5.41	4.30	3.59	3.13	2.86	2.39	0.77	2.42	2.17	2.48
Earnings	4.19	3.28	2.72	2.26	2.04	1.68	0.10	1.80	1.57	1.50
S&P Core Earnings	4.10	3.24	2.60	2.15	1.81	1.62	NA	NA	NA	NA
Dividends	1.00	0.82	0.68	0.62	0.60	0.58	0.54	0.48	0.45	0.50
Payout Ratio	24%	25%	25%	27%	29%	35%	NM	27%	29%	33%
Prices:High	64.76	48.84	45.61	34.77	33.24	28.23	27.63	32.88	37.88	33.38
Prices:Low	37.40	40.47	32.95	24.42	21.75	19.73	17.13	18.75	19.44	24.13
P/E Ratio:High	15	15	17	15	16	17	NM	18	24	22
P/E Ratio:Low	9	12	12	11	11	12	NM	10	12	16

Income Statement Analysis (Million $)										
Revenue	7,810	7,191	6,114	5,408	5,185	5,067	5,212	5,004	4,934	4,881
Operating Income	1,024	898	758	690	670	599	676	680	629	613
Depreciation	146	144	126	117	116	109	109	105	97.8	90.2
Interest Expense	67.2	49.6	39.9	38.7	40.5	54.6	62.0	61.2	72.0	80.8
Pretax Income	834	656	580	523	497	424	143	490	440	427
Effective Tax Rate	31.0%	29.2%	32.0%	36.5%	37.5%	38.0%	88.8%	38.0%	38.0%	39.0%
Net Income	576	463	393	332	311	263	16.0	304	273	261
S&P Core Earnings	562	458	376	317	276	254	NA	NA	NA	NA

Balance Sheet & Other Financial Data (Million $)										
Cash	469	36.0	45.9	303	164	119	2.90	18.6	19.1	3.53
Current Assets	2,450	1,891	1,782	1,715	1,506	1,507	1,552	1,597	1,547	1,532
Total Assets	4,995	4,369	4,274	3,683	3,432	3,628	3,751	4,052	4,065	4,036
Current Liabilities	2,075	1,554	1,520	1,154	1,083	1,141	1,115	1,190	1,112	1,116
Long Term Debt	292	487	488	503	507	504	624	624	730	844
Common Equity	1,559	1,696	1,475	1,174	1,300	1,319	1,472	1,699	1,716	1,592
Total Capital	2,284	2,218	2,139	1,962	1,849	1,991	2,095	2,323	2,446	2,436
Capital Expenditures	210	143	107	117	127	82.6	133	134	146	164
Cash Flow	722	607	519	449	426	372	125	409	371	351
Current Ratio	1.2	1.2	1.2	1.5	1.4	1.3	1.4	1.3	1.4	1.4
% Long Term Debt of Capitalization	12.8	22.0	22.8	25.6	27.4	25.3	29.8	26.9	29.9	34.6
% Net Income of Revenue	7.4	6.4	6.4	6.1	6.0	5.2	0.3	6.1	5.5	5.3
% Return on Assets	12.3	10.7	9.9	9.3	8.8	7.1	0.4	7.5	6.7	7.4
% Return on Equity	35.4	29.2	29.7	26.8	23.7	18.9	1.0	17.8	16.5	17.4

Data as orig reptd.; bef. results of disc opers/spec. items. Per share data adj. for stk. divs.; EPS diluted. E-Estimated. NA-Not Available. NM-Not Meaningful. NR-Not Ranked. UR-Under Review.

Office: 101 Prospect Avenue N.W., Cleveland, OH 44115-1075.
Telephone: 216-566-2000.
Website: http://www.sherwin.com
Chrmn & CEO: C.M. Connor

Pres & COO: J.G. Morikis
SVP, CFO & Treas: S. Hennessy
Investor Contact: C.G. Ivy (216-566-2140)
VP, Secy & General Counsel: L.E. Stellato

Board Members: A. F. Anton, J. C. Boland, C. M. Connor, D. E. Evans, D. F. Hodnik, S. J. Kropf, R. W. Mahoney, G. E. McCullough, A. M. Mixon III, C. E. Moll, R. K. Smucker

Founded: 1866
Domicile: Ohio
Employees: 30,767

Sigma Aldrich Corporation

S&P Recommendation HOLD ★★★☆☆	Price $50.70 (as of Nov 23, 2007)	12-Mo. Target Price $52.00	Investment Style Large-Cap Growth

GICS Sector Materials
Sub-Industry Specialty Chemicals

Summary This company makes and sells a wide range of biochemicals, organic chemicals and chromatography products.

Key Stock Statistics (Source S&P, Vickers, company reports)

52-Wk Range	$53.01–37.40	S&P Oper. EPS 2007E	2.30	Market Capitalization(B)	$6.657	Beta	0.64
Trailing 12-Month EPS	$2.23	S&P Oper. EPS 2008E	2.50	Yield (%)	0.91	S&P 3-Yr. Proj. EPS CAGR(%)	10.00
Trailing 12-Month P/E	22.7	P/E on S&P Oper. EPS 2007E	22.0	Dividend Rate/Share	$0.46	S&P Credit Rating	NA
$10K Invested 5 Yrs Ago	$21,830	Common Shares Outstg. (M)	131.3	Institutional Ownership (%)	75		

Price Performance

30-Week Mov. Avg. · · · 10-Week Mov. Avg. - - GAAP Earnings vs. Previous Year Volume Above Avg. STARS
12-Mo. Target Price — Relative Strength — ▲ Up ▼ Down ▶ No Change Below Avg. ★

Options: ASE, CBOE

Analysis prepared by **Richard O'Reilly, CFA** on November 06, 2007, when the stock traded at **$ 52.34**.

Highlights

➤ We expect sales for 2008 to rise about 7%, before contributions from any additional acquisitions and currency exchange rates, versus the 13% growth expected for 2007. The February 2007 purchase of a supplier of semiconductor chemicals should add about 2% to sales growth in 2007, by our estimation. Currency exchange rates will also be a 4% positive factor for 2007, in our opinion. We believe volumes for the rest of 2007 will show continued mid-single digit growth after the improvements of the past two years, on new products and marketing initiatives. We project continued double digit gains in key international markets outside Europe.

➤ We see annual price increases remaining at about 2% for the research units, similar to 2006. We expect pretax margins in 2008 to be in line with the 21.5% expected for 2007, as process improvements offset additions to the sales and technical staffs.

➤ We foresee an effective tax rate of 30.0% for 2007, followed by a possibly higher rate in 2008, up from the 26.9% rate in 2006, which included one-time tax benefits. We think EPS comparisons will benefit from additional modest share repurchases.

Investment Rationale/Risk

➤ Since early 2005, the company has achieved its strongest organic revenue growth (7%-8%) in several years, boosted by new marketing initiatives and an expanded sales force; we expect this trend to continue in 2008. The company is reemphasizing an annual sales growth target of 10%, including a 3% contribution from acquisitions.

➤ Risks to our recommendation and target price include unexpected weakness in key markets such as pharmaceutical and academia, greater price competition, adverse currency exchange movements, an inability to successfully introduce new products, and failure to successfully integrate future acquisitions.

➤ The shares have advanced about 34% year to date in 2007, and recently traded at around 22X our 2007 EPS estimate of $2.30, below the life science peer average of 23X. Our 12-month target price of $52 assumes a P/E of around 21X our 2008 EPS estimate, a premium to the S&P 500 that we think is warranted in view of what we believe is an attractive earnings record.

Qualitative Risk Assessment

LOW	MEDIUM	HIGH

Our risk assessment reflects the stable nature of the company's laboratory chemicals business, its broad geographic sales mix, and our view of its strong balance sheet.

Quantitative Evaluations

S&P Quality Ranking A+

D	C	B-	B	B+	A-	A	A+

Relative Strength Rank STRONG

87

LOWEST = 1   HIGHEST = 99

Revenue/Earnings Data

Revenue (Million $)

	1Q	2Q	3Q	4Q	Year
2007	495.9	507.5	503.2	--	--
2006	443.1	448.5	441.4	464.5	1,798
2005	399.8	444.0	412.2	410.5	1,667
2004	368.1	348.6	340.6	351.9	1,409
2003	334.7	327.1	314.2	322.2	1,298
2002	301.6	304.3	304.8	296.3	1,207

Earnings Per Share ($)

2007	0.56	0.60	0.54	E0.60	E2.30
2006	0.49	0.52	0.51	0.53	2.05
2005	0.54	0.46	0.47	0.42	1.88
2004	0.45	0.43	0.41	0.40	1.67
2003	0.36	0.34	0.33	0.34	1.34
2002	0.27	-0.15	0.32	0.46	0.89

Fiscal year ended Dec. 31. Next earnings report expected: Mid February. EPS Estimates based on S&P Operating Earnings; historical GAAP earnings are as reported.

Dividend Data (Dates: mm/dd Payment Date: mm/dd/yy)

Amount ($)	Date Decl.	Ex-Div. Date	Stk. of Record	Payment Date
0.115	02/13	02/27	03/01	03/15/07
0.115	05/01	05/30	06/01	06/15/07
0.115	08/14	08/29	08/31	09/14/07
0.115	11/13	11/28	11/30	12/14/07

Dividends have been paid since 1970. Source: Company reports.

Sigma Aldrich Corporation

STANDARD &POOR'S

Business Summary November 06, 2007

CORPORATE OVERVIEW. Sigma-Aldrich, well known for its extensive catalog business, is one of the world's largest providers of research chemicals, reagents, chromatography products, and related products.

Foreign sales accounted for 60% of the total in 2006, with about 42% from Europe.

SIAL distributes more than 100,000 chemical products, under the Sigma, Aldrich, Fluka and Supelco brands names, for use primarily in research and development, diagnosis of disease, and as specialty chemicals for manufacturing. About 75% of sales are to customers in the life sciences, with the remaining 25% used in high technology applications. Customer sectors include pharmaceutical (40% of sales), academia and government (30%), chemical industry (20%), and hospitals and commercial laboratories (10%). The company itself produces about 46,000 products, accounting for 60% of 2006 net sales of chemical products. Remaining products are purchased from outside sources. The company also supplies 30,000 equipment products.

The Research Essentials unit (20% of sales in 2006) sells biological buffers, cell culture reagents, biochemicals, chemicals, solvents, and other reagents and kits. The Research Specialties unit (37%) sells organic chemicals, bio-

chemicals, analytical reagents, chromatography consumables, reference materials and high-purity products. The Research Biotech unit (15%) supplies immunochemical, molecular biology, cell signaling and neuroscience biochemicals and kits used in biotechnology, genomic, proteomic and other life science research applications. Sigma-Genosys (acquired in 1998) is a major maker of custom synthetic DNA products, synthetic peptides and genes to the life science product categories. SIAL believes it is the leading supplier of products used in cell signaling and neuroscience. The SAFC (Fine Chemicals) unit (28%) is a top 10 supplier of large-scale organic chemicals and biochemicals used in development and production by pharmaceutical, biotechnology, industrial and diagnostic companies. The February 2007 purchase of Epichem Group (with annual sales of $40 million) greatly expanded SAFC's high technology sales.

SIAL also offers about 80,000 esoteric chemicals (less than 1% of total sales) as a special service to customers that screen them for potential applications.

Company Financials Fiscal Year Ended Dec. 31

Per Share Data ($)	2006	2005	2004	2003	2002	2001	2000	1999	1998	1997
Tangible Book Value	7.00	5.71	7.67	6.42	5.45	3.38	3.67	5.79	5.48	5.28
Cash Flow	1.37	2.54	2.19	1.83	1.72	1.41	1.24	1.07	1.13	1.04
Earnings	2.05	1.88	1.67	1.34	0.89	0.94	0.83	0.74	0.82	0.81
S&P Core Earnings	2.05	1.81	1.58	1.28	1.05	0.88	NA	NA	NA	NA
Dividends	0.42	0.38	0.34	0.25	0.17	0.17	0.16	0.15	0.14	0.13
Payout Ratio	20%	20%	20%	19%	19%	18%	19%	20%	17%	16%
Prices:High	39.68	33.55	30.81	28.96	26.40	25.75	20.44	17.63	21.38	20.56
Prices:Low	31.27	27.67	26.61	20.47	19.08	18.13	10.09	12.25	12.88	13.44
P/E Ratio:High	19	18	18	22	30	28	25	24	26	25
P/E Ratio:Low	15	15	16	15	21	19	12	17	16	17

Income Statement Analysis (Million $)	2006	2005	2004	2003	2002	2001	2000	1999	1998	1997
Revenue	1,798	1,667	1,409	1,298	1,207	1,179	1,096	1,038	1,194	1,127
Operating Income	494	452	392	353	323	291	284	275	305	302
Depreciation	90.9	90.1	73.4	69.3	66.3	71.4	67.6	66.9	61.8	48.1
Interest Expense	24.0	18.1	7.20	10.1	13.8	18.2	10.2	Nil	0.92	0.73
Pretax Income	379	343	312	273	272	202	203	204	243	253
Effective Tax Rate	26.9%	24.8%	25.3%	30.2%	31.4%	30.2%	31.5%	27.1%	31.4%	34.3%
Net Income	277	258	233	190	187	141	139	149	166	166
S&P Core Earnings	276	249	221	180	155	133	NA	NA	NA	NA

Balance Sheet & Other Financial Data (Million $)	2006	2005	2004	2003	2002	2001	2000	1999	1998	1997
Cash	174	98.6	169	128	52.4	37.6	31.1	43.8	24.3	46.2
Current Assets	1,113	950	893	815	695	727	714	775	773	707
Total Assets	2,334	2,131	1,745	1,548	1,390	1,440	1,348	1,432	1,433	1,244
Current Liabilities	443	461	231	257	266	398	335	106	142	119
Long Term Debt	338	283	177	176	177	178	101	0.21	0.42	0.55
Common Equity	1,411	1,233	1,212	999	882	810	859	1,259	1,216	1,073
Total Capital	1,797	1,597	1,389	1,176	1,059	987	960	1,260	1,217	1,061
Capital Expenditures	74.5	92.2	70.3	57.7	60.7	110	69.2	91.8	130	109
Cash Flow	368	348	306	260	253	212	207	216	228	214
Current Ratio	2.5	2.1	3.9	3.2	2.6	1.8	2.1	7.3	5.4	5.9
% Long Term Debt of Capitalization	18.8	17.7	12.8	15.0	16.7	18.0	10.5	0.0	0.0	0.0
% Net Income of Revenue	15.4	15.5	16.5	14.7	15.5	11.9	12.7	14.3	13.9	14.7
% Return on Assets	12.4	13.3	14.1	12.7	13.2	10.1	10.0	10.4	12.4	14.2
% Return on Equity	20.9	21.1	21.1	20.2	22.1	16.9	13.1	12.0	14.5	16.4

Data as orig reptd.; bef. results of disc opers/spec. items. Per share data adj. for stk. divs.; EPS diluted. E-Estimated. NA-Not Available. NM-Not Meaningful. NR-Not Ranked. UR-Under Review.

Office: 3050 Spruce Street, St. Louis, MO 63103.
Telephone: 314-771-5765.
Website: http://www.sigma-aldrich.com
Chrmn: D.R. Harvey

Pres & CEO: J.P. Nagarkatti
VP, Secy & General Counsel: R.A. Keffer
CFO & Chief Admin Officer: M.R. Hogan
Investor Contact: K.A. Richter (314-286-8004)

Board Members: N. V. Fedoroff, D. R. Harvey, W. L. McCollum, J. P. Nagarkatti, A. M. Nash, W. C. O'Neil, Jr., S. M. Paul, J. P. Reinhard, T. R. Sear, D. D. Spatz, B. A. Toan

Founded: 1951
Domicile: Delaware
Employees: 7,299

STANDARD &POOR'S

Simon Property Group Inc.

S&P Recommendation	STRONG BUY ★★★★★	Price $90.75 (as of Nov 23, 2007)	12-Mo. Target Price $115.00	Investment Style Large-Cap Blend

GICS Sector Financials
Sub-Industry Retail REITS

Summary This real estate investment trust owns, develops and manages retail real estate, primarily regional malls, outlet centers and community/lifestyle centers, across the U.S.

Key Stock Statistics (Source S&P, Vickers, company reports)

52-Wk Range	$123.96– 82.60	S&P FFO/Sh. 2007E	5.85	Market Capitalization(B)	$20.272
Trailing 12-Month FFO/Share	NA	S&P FFO/Sh. 2008E	6.37	Yield (%)	3.70
Trailing 12-Month P/FFO	NA	P/FFO on S&P FFO/Sh. 2007E	15.5	Dividend Rate/Share	$3.36
$10K Invested 5 Yrs Ago	$33,171	Common Shares Outstg. (M)	233.4	Institutional Ownership (%)	97

Beta	0.76
S&P 3-Yr. FFO/Sh. Proj. CAGR(%)	9.00
S&P Credit Rating	A-

Price Performance

30-Week Mov. Avg. · · · 10-Week Mov. Avg. - - GAAP Earnings vs. Previous Year   Volume Above Avg. ▦ STARS
12-Mo. Target Price — Relative Strength — ▲ Up ▼ Down ► No Change   Below Avg. ▦ ★

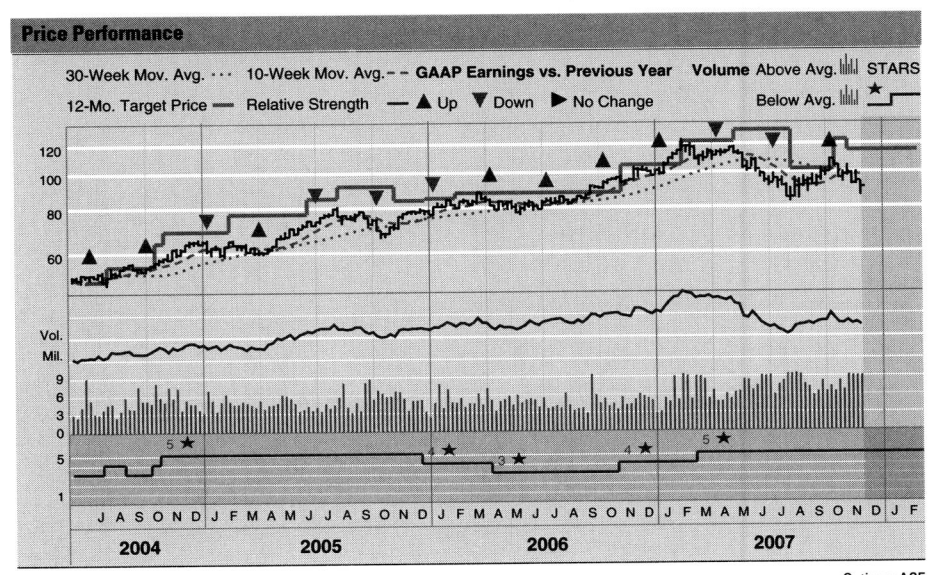

Options: ASE

Analysis prepared by **Robert McMillan** on October 30, 2007, when the stock traded at **$ 102.39.**

Highlights

➤ We expect the company to continue to benefit from what we view as a successful strategy of operating large and strategically located regional malls and shopping centers in major metropolitan markets.

➤ We look for total revenues, after increasing 5.2% in 2006, to rise about 9% in 2007 and 7% in 2008, reflecting expected higher rents and tenant reimbursements, and new domestic and international developments. In the third quarter of 2007, comparable sales per square foot increased 3.6%, year to year, in SPG's regional mall portfolio, and 8% in its premium outlet center portfolio, while total blended portfolio occupancy rose to 95.0% from 94.2%; average rent per square foot was 4.8% higher, year to year, for the regional malls, 5.8% for the Premium Outlet centers, and 3.9% for the community and lifestyle centers. We look for the ongoing development and redevelopment activity in the U.S. and overseas to further enhance growth.

➤ We see EPS of $1.65 in 2007 and $2.08 in 2008, with respective FFO per share of $5.85 and $6.37. We anticipate 2007 fourth quarter FFO of $1.71.

Investment Rationale/Risk

➤ We think SPG's position as one of the largest owners and managers of shopping centers in the U.S. and its established relationships with numerous retailers will allow it to continue to generate robust growth. We also view the geographic, customer and format diversity of SPG's portfolio and management's acquisitions and developments in both the U.S. and overseas as positive factors in our valuation.

➤ Risks to our recommendation and target price include slower than expected growth in retailer expansion, higher than normal retailer bankruptcies, and a rise in interest rates.

➤ The shares recently traded at about 17.9X SPG's trailing 12-month FFO. The shares and the valuation multiple, after dropping sharply between May and August, have risen sharply recently, due, in our opinion, to easing interest rate concerns. Our 12-month target price of $115 is equal to about 18.5X our forward 12-month FFO estimate of $6.24. We believe that the valuation multiple will expand based on improvements in the company's operating performance, and on the continued easing of concerns about the impact of the housing market on SPG's retailer-dependent business.

Qualitative Risk Assessment

LOW	MEDIUM	HIGH

Our risk assessment reflects SPG's position as one of the largest owners of shopping centers with a diverse tenant and geographic mix and a variety of shopping center formats. The majority of SPG's customers are under long-term leases, which helps lessen short-term volatility. The company also has a strong balance sheet, in our view.

Quantitative Evaluations

S&P Quality Ranking   B+

D	C	B-	B	B+	A-	A	A+

Relative Strength Rank   MODERATE

45

LOWEST = 1   HIGHEST = 99

Revenue/FFO Data

Revenue (Million $)

	1Q	2Q	3Q	4Q	Year
2007	852.1	855.9	907.2	--	--
2006	787.7	798.7	818.7	927.0	3,332
2005	756.9	756.3	786.8	889.8	3,167
2004	582.1	600.6	623.0	836.1	2,642
2003	547.8	566.3	566.6	659.9	2,314
2002	495.0	517.5	550.8	622.6	2,186

FFO Per Share ($)

	1Q	2Q	3Q	4Q	Year
2007	1.37	1.31	1.46	E1.71	E5.85
2006	1.26	1.26	1.30	1.57	5.39
2005	1.12	1.18	1.19	1.47	4.96
2004	0.96	1.01	1.04	1.36	4.39
2003	0.89	0.96	0.93	1.26	4.04
2002	0.77	0.81	0.93	1.17	3.79

Fiscal year ended Dec. 31. Next earnings report expected: Mid December. FFO Estimates based on S&P Funds From Operations Est..

Dividend Data (Dates: mm/dd Payment Date: mm/dd/yy)

Amount ($)	Date Decl.	Ex-Div. Date	Stk. of Record	Payment Date
0.840	02/02	02/12	02/14	02/28/07
0.840	04/27	05/15	05/17	05/31/07
0.840	07/30	08/15	08/17	08/31/07
0.840	10/29	11/14	11/16	11/30/07

Dividends have been paid since 1994. Source: Company reports.

Simon Property Group Inc.

STANDARD &POOR'S

Business Summary October 30, 2007

CORPORATE OVERVIEW. Simon Property Group is a real estate investment trust that owns, develops, manages, leases and acquires primarily regional malls and community shopping centers. It is one of the largest owners of shopping centers in the world. At December 31, 2006, SPG owned 286 income-producing properties in the U.S. SPG also had ownership interests in 59 shopping centers and Premium Outlet Centers in Europe, Japan, Canada and Mexico. The company's other properties include office space, hotel components as well as interests in land held for future development.

SPG's regional malls typically contain at least one traditional department store anchor or a combination of anchors and big box retailers with a wide variety of smaller stores located in enclosed malls connecting the anchors. Additional freestanding stores are usually located along the perimeter of the parking area. SPG's 171 regional malls range in size from approximately 400,000 to 2.0 million square feet of gross leasable area (GLA) and contain more than 18,300 occupied stores, including approximately 700 anchors, which are mostly national retailers. The regional mall totals include certain lifestyle centers when the center contains a traditional department store anchor.

SPG's Premium Outlet Centers contain a wide variety of retailers located in open-air manufacturers' outlet centers. The company's 36 Premium Outlet Centers range in size from approximately 200,000 to 600,000 square feet of GLA and are generally located near metropolitan areas .

SPG's 79 community and lifestyle shopping centers are generally unenclosed and smaller than its regional malls. The community and lifestyle centers usually range in size from approximately 100,000 to 600,000 square feet of GLA and are designed to serve a larger trade area, and typically contain at least two anchors and other tenants that are usually national retailers among the leaders in their markets. These tenants generally occupy a significant portion of the GLA of the center. The company also owns traditional community shopping centers that focus primarily on value-oriented and convenience goods and services. These centers are usually anchored by a supermarket, discount retailer, or drugstore and are designed to service a neighborhood area. Finally, the trust owns open-air centers adjacent to its regional malls designed to take advantage of the drawing power of the mall.

Company Financials Fiscal Year Ended Dec. 31

Per Share Data ($)	2006	2005	2004	2003	2002	2001	2000	1999	1998	1997
Tangible Book Value	13.98	14.64	16.21	14.66	13.87	13.00	14.29	15.36	15.70	11.11
Earnings	2.19	1.27	1.44	1.53	1.93	0.87	1.13	1.00	1.01	1.08
S&P Core Earnings	2.19	1.12	1.44	1.55	2.07	0.97	NA	NA	NA	NA
Dividends	3.04	2.80	2.60	2.40	2.18	2.08	2.02	2.02	2.02	2.01
Payout Ratio	139%	NM	181%	157%	113%	NM	179%	202%	200%	186%
Prices:High	104.08	80.97	65.87	48.59	36.95	30.97	27.13	30.94	34.88	34.38
Prices:Low	76.14	58.29	44.39	31.70	28.80	23.75	21.50	20.44	25.81	27.88
P/E Ratio:High	48	64	46	32	19	36	24	31	34	32
P/E Ratio:Low	35	46	31	21	15	27	19	20	26	26

Income Statement Analysis (Million $)										
Rental Income	3,063	2,920	2,411	1,423	1,386	1,320	1,284	1,207	900	680
Mortgage Income	Nil	Nil	Nil	Nil	Nil	Nil	Nil	Nil	Nil	Nil
Total Income	3,145	3,167	2,642	2,314	2,186	2,045	2,013	1,895	1,405	1,054
General Expenses	856	820	675	611	788	712	674	655	495	228
Interest Expense	822	799	662	615	603	622	667	580	420	288
Provision for Losses	9.50	8.10	17.7	Nil	8.97	8.41	9.64	8.50	6.60	Nil
Depreciation	856	850	623	498	423	453	420	382	268	201
Net Income	563	457	450	339	1,109	201	242	210	160	137
S&P Core Earnings	486	247	301	288	371	169	NA	NA	NA	NA

Balance Sheet & Other Financial Data (Million $)										
Cash	20,713	19,836	520	536	397	255	214	155	130	787
Total Assets	22,084	21,131	22,070	15,685	14,905	13,794	13,911	14,199	13,277	7,663
Real Estate Investment	24,390	23,307	23,175	14,972	14,250	13,187	13,038	12,794	11,850	6,867
Loss Reserve	Nil	Nil	Nil	Nil	20.5	24.7	20.1	14.6	14.5	Nil
Net Investment	19,784	19,499	20,012	12,415	12,027	11,311	11,558	11,697	11,127	6,406
Short Term Debt	Nil	Nil	Nil	1,481	940	665	1,164	1,162	1,030	390
Capitalization:Debt	13,711	14,106	13,044	8,786	8,606	8,176	7,904	9,109	7,973	5,078
Capitalization:Equity	3,095	3,227	3,580	2,971	2,653	2,327	2,515	3,246	3,409	2,465
Capitalization:Total	18,885	19,681	19,065	13,241	12,074	11,381	10,958	12,355	11,382	6,939
% Earnings & Depreciation/Assets	6.7	6.0	5.7	5.5	10.7	4.7	4.7	4.3	4.1	5.0
Price Times Book Value:High	7.4	5.5	4.1	3.3	2.7	2.4	1.9	2.0	2.2	3.1
Price Times Book Value:Low	5.4	4.0	2.7	2.2	2.1	1.8	1.5	1.3	1.6	2.5

Data as orig reptd.; bef. results of disc opers/spec. items. Per share data adj. for stk. divs.; EPS diluted. E-Estimated. NA-Not Available. NM-Not Meaningful. NR-Not Ranked. UR-Under Review.

Office: 225 W Washington St, Indianapolis, IN 46204-3438.
Telephone: 317-636-1600.
Website: http://www.simon.com
Co-Chrmn: M. Simon

Co-Chrmn: H. Simon
Pres & COO: R.S. Sokolov
CEO: D. Simon
EVP & CFO: S.E. Sterrett

Investor Contact: S.J. Doran (317-685-7330)
Trustees: B. Bayh, M. E. Bergstein, M. D. DeBartolo York, K. N. Horn, R. S. Leibowitz, F. W. Petri, D. Simon, H. Simon, M. Simon, J. A. Smith, Jr., R. S. Sokolov, L. Walker Bynoe, P. S. van den Berg

Founded: 1993
Domicile: Delaware
Employees: 4,500

SLM Corp

STANDARD &POOR'S

S&P Recommendation HOLD ★★★☆☆	**Price** $38.76 (as of Nov 23, 2007)	**12-Mo. Target Price** $45.00	**Investment Style** Large-Cap Growth

GICS Sector Financials
Sub-Industry Consumer Finance

Summary This company (formerly USA Education), the leading U.S. provider of post-secondary educational financial services, has agreed to be taken private at $60 per share.

Key Stock Statistics (Source S&P, Vickers, company reports)

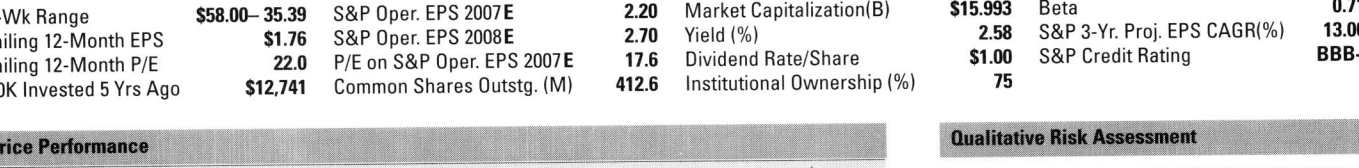

52-Wk Range	$58.00– 35.39	S&P Oper. EPS 2007**E**	2.20	Market Capitalization(B)	$15.993	Beta	0.71
Trailing 12-Month EPS	$1.76	S&P Oper. EPS 2008**E**	2.70	Yield (%)	2.58	S&P 3-Yr. Proj. EPS CAGR(%)	13.00
Trailing 12-Month P/E	22.0	P/E on S&P Oper. EPS 2007**E**	17.6	Dividend Rate/Share	$1.00	S&P Credit Rating	BBB+
$10K Invested 5 Yrs Ago	$12,741	Common Shares Outstg. (M)	412.6	Institutional Ownership (%)	75		

Price Performance

- 30-Week Mov. Avg. · · · 10-Week Mov. Avg. – – **GAAP Earnings vs. Previous Year** **Volume** Above Avg. STARS
- 12-Mo. Target Price — Relative Strength — ▲ Up ▼ Down ▶ No Change Below Avg.

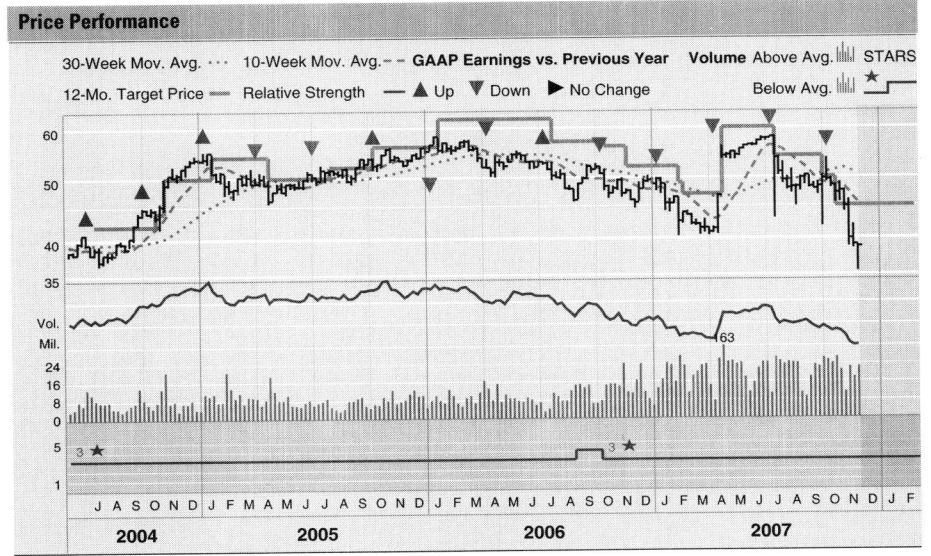

Options: ASE, CBOE, P

Analysis prepared by **Stuart Plesser** on October 16, 2007, when the stock traded at **$ 47.09**.

Highlights

➤ We believe that private student loans will continue to grow as a percentage of loans under management in 2008 and total roughly 16.0%, versus projected 15.5% of average assets under management at the end of 2007. Based on our expectations of a stabilization in student loan spreads and continued strength in loan origination volumes, we see SLM's core net interest income growing over 11% in 2007. We believe loan loss provisions will increase, largely due to growth of the private education loan portfolio as well as SLM's establishment of a risk-sharing allowance for losses on federal student loans, as default insurance coverage on such loans fell by 1%, to 99%, on loans originated after July 1, 2006.

➤ We project a 5% increase in other income in 2008, reflecting mostly organic growth from collections services. Due to the company's focus on controlling costs, we expect modest improvements in operating margins.

➤ Taking into account moderate share repurchase activity and assuming an effective 37% tax rate, we forecast operating EPS of $2.70 in 2008, 23% higher than projected for 2007.

Investment Rationale/Risk

➤ In April 2007, SLM agreed to be taken private, subject to necessary approvals, for $25 billion, or $60 per share. However, adverse legislation pertaining to cutbacks in subsidies for Federal Family Education Loan Program providers has resulted in the buyers' (JC Flowers and a consortium of investors) claim that they can back out of the deal. The buyers have since offered $50 a share for SLM with warrants valued at up to $10 a share based on performance metrics. In response, SLM filed a lawsuit seeking termination of the agreement and a $900 million termination fee. Given SLM's resolute stance regarding a renegotiation of the deal, we don't believe the buyout will be consummated and it is in question whether a breakup fee will be paid.

➤ Risks to our recommendation and target price include greater-than-expected deterioration of net income due to adverse government legislation, and higher funding costs than expected.

➤ Our 12-month target price of $45 is 16.7X our 2008 EPS estimate of $2.70, a discount to its historical average, due to adverse legislation.

Qualitative Risk Assessment

LOW	MEDIUM	HIGH

Our risk assessment for SLM reflects its leading position in education finance and its participation in the Federal Family Education Loan Program, offset by the possibility of adverse legislation.

Quantitative Evaluations

S&P Quality Ranking B+

D	C	B-	B	B+	A-	A	A+

Relative Strength Rank WEAK

22

LOWEST = 1   HIGHEST = 99

Revenue/Earnings Data

Revenue (Million $)

	1Q	2Q	3Q	4Q	Year
2007	2,466	2,495	2,119	--	--
2006	1,766	2,695	2,252	2,038	8,751
2005	1,285	1,506	1,715	2,012	6,518
2004	915.1	1,509	1,047	1,525	4,997
2003	1,109	1,047	1,013	955.9	4,160
2002	1,158	702.2	404.0	968.1	3,232

Earnings Per Share ($)

2007	0.26	1.03	-0.85	E0.63	E2.20
2006	0.34	1.52	0.60	0.02	2.63
2005	0.49	0.66	0.95	0.96	3.05
2004	0.64	1.36	0.80	1.40	4.04
2003	0.88	0.80	0.76	0.57	3.01
2002	0.88	0.26	-0.14	0.64	1.64

Fiscal year ended Dec. 31. Next earnings report expected: Mid January. EPS Estimates based on S&P Operating Earnings; historical GAAP earnings are as reported.

Dividend Data (Dates: mm/dd Payment Date: mm/dd/yy)

Amount ($)	Date Decl.	Ex-Div. Date	Stk. of Record	Payment Date
0.250	10/26	11/29	12/01	12/15/06
0.250	01/25	02/28	03/02	03/16/07

Dividends have been paid since 1983. Source: Company reports.

SLM Corp

STANDARD &POOR'S

Business Summary October 16, 2007

CORPORATE OVERVIEW. SLM Corp., formerly USA Education Inc., is the largest U.S. private source of funding, delivery and service support for higher education loans, primarily through its participation in the Federal Family Education Loan Program (FFELP). The company's main business is to originate, acquire and hold student loans with the net interest income and gains on the sales of student loans in securitization, the primary source of earnings. The company funds its operation through student loan asset-backed securities and unsecured debt securities. SLM was chartered by an Act of Congress in 1972, but in 1996 it was rechartered as a private sector corporation and completed its privatization process in December 2004.

The company is divided into two business segments: Lending and Debt Management Operations (DMO). According to the company, the SLM Lending segment manages the largest portfolio of FFELP and Private Education Loans in the student loan industry. As of December 31, 2006, the company served nearly ten million borrowers, and managed $142.1 billion in student loans, of which 84% were federally insured. In 2006, 76% of its student loan acquisitions were

through its Preferred Channel. Its DMO segment provides a wide range of accounts receivable and collections services.

PRIMARY BUSINESS DYNAMICS. There are two competing programs that divide student loans where the ultimate risk lies with the federal government: the FFELP and the Federal Direct Lending program (FDLP). FFELP loans are provided by private sector institutions, such as SLM, and are ultimately guaranteed by the U.S. Department of Education (ED). FDLP loans are funded by taxpayers and provided to borrowers directly by ED. Private Education Loans are originated by financial institutions where the lender assumes the credit risk of the borrower. SLM's position as an Exceptional Performer enables the company to receive a guarantee of 100% and 99% for student loans and accrued interest, originated before and after July 1, 2006, respectively.

Company Financials Fiscal Year Ended Dec. 31

Per Share Data ($)	2006	2005	2004	2003	2002	2001	2000	1999	1998	1997
Tangible Book Value	5.90	5.13	4.81	4.55	3.08	3.59	2.54	1.43	1.33	1.30
Earnings	2.63	3.05	4.04	3.01	1.64	0.76	0.92	1.02	0.98	0.93
S&P Core Earnings	2.62	2.98	3.95	2.75	1.40	0.53	NA	NA	NA	NA
Dividends	0.97	0.85	0.74	0.59	0.28	0.24	0.22	0.20	0.19	0.17
Payout Ratio	37%	28%	18%	20%	17%	32%	24%	20%	19%	19%
Prices:High	58.35	56.48	54.44	42.92	35.65	29.33	22.75	17.98	17.13	15.73
Prices:Low	44.65	45.56	36.43	33.73	25.67	18.63	9.27	13.17	9.17	8.48
P/E Ratio:High	22	19	13	14	22	39	25	18	17	17
P/E Ratio:Low	17	15	9	11	16	25	10	13	9	9

Income Statement Analysis (Million $)										
Interest on:Mortgages	6,074	4,233	2,500	2,197	2,124	2,625	2,977	2,569	2,293	2,711
Interest on:Investment	503	277	233	151	87.9	373	501	240	295	573
Interest Expense	5,123	3,059	1,434	1,022	1,203	2,124	2,837	2,115	1,925	2,526
Guaranty Fees	Nil	Nil	Nil	Nil	Nil	Nil	Nil	Nil	Nil	Nil
Loan Loss Provision	287	203	111	147	117	66.0	32.1	34.4	Nil	Nil
Administration Expenses	1,346	1,138	895	808	690	708	586	359	361	269
Pretax Income	1,995	2,117	2,557	2,183	1,223	617	712	752	750	765
Effective Tax Rate	41.8%	34.4%	25.1%	35.7%	35.3%	36.2%	33.1%	31.9%	31.7%	31.8%
Net Income	1,157	1,382	1,913	1,404	792	384	465	501	501	511
S&P Core Earnings	1,119	1,324	1,853	1,276	664	261	NA	NA	NA	NA

Balance Sheet & Other Financial Data (Million $)										
Mortgages	97,228	83,980	66,161	51,078	43,541	42,037	38,635	34,852	29,825	32,765
Investment	5,986	4,775	3,579	5,268	4,231	5,072	5,206	5,185	3,990	5,076
Cash & Equivalent	2,621	2,499	3,395	1,652	758	715	734	590	116	54.0
Total Assets	116,136	99,339	84,094	64,611	53,175	52,874	48,792	44,025	37,210	39,909
Short Term Debt	Nil	3,810	2,208	18,735	25,619	31,065	30,464	37,491	26,588	23,176
Long Term Debt	104,559	88,119	75,915	23,211	22,242	17,285	14,911	4,496	8,811	14,541
Equity	3,795	3,226	2,937	3,564	1,833	1,507	1,250	676	654	675
% Return on Assets	1.1	1.5	2.6	2.4	1.5	0.8	1.0	1.2	1.3	1.2
% Return on Equity	31.9	44.1	70.4	25.8	47.4	27.8	48.2	75.1	75.5	67.7
Equity/Assets Ratio	30.7	29.8	27.5	10.9	3.1	2.7	2.1	1.6	1.7	1.7
Price Times Book Value:High	9.9	11.0	11.3	9.4	11.6	8.2	8.9	12.6	12.9	12.1
Price Times Book Value:Low	7.6	8.9	7.6	7.4	8.3	5.2	3.6	9.2	6.9	6.5

Data as orig reptd.; bef. results of disc opers/spec. items. Per share data adj. for stk. divs.; EPS diluted. E-Estimated. NA-Not Available. NM-Not Meaningful. NR-Not Ranked. UR-Under Review.

Office: 12061 Bluemont Way, Reston, VA 20190-5684.
Telephone: 703-810-3000.
Website: http://www.salliemae.com
Chrmn: A.L. Lord

CEO: C.E. Andrews
EVP & CIO: R. Auter
Investor Contact: S. McGarry (703-810-7746)

Board Members: C. L. Daley, W. M. Diefenderfer, III, T. J. Fitzpatrick, D. S. Gilleland, E. A. Goode, R. F. Hunt, B. J. Lambert, III, A. L. Lord, B. A. Munitz, A. A. Porter, Jr., W. Schoellkopf, S. L. Shapiro, A. Torre Bates, B. L. Williams

Founded: 1972
Domicile: Delaware
Employees: 11,000

The McGraw-Hill Companies

Smith International Inc.

STANDARD &POOR'S

S&P Recommendation HOLD ★★★☆☆

Price $63.86 (as of Nov 23, 2007)	**12-Mo. Target Price** $66.00	**Investment Style** Large-Cap Growth

GICS Sector Energy
Sub-Industry Oil & Gas Equipment & Services

Summary This company is an international supplier of products and services primarily used in drilling of oil and gas.

Key Stock Statistics (Source S&P, Vickers, company reports)

52-Wk Range	$76.99– 36.13	S&P Oper. EPS 2007**E**	3.23	Market Capitalization(B)	$12.805
Trailing 12-Month EPS	$3.09	S&P Oper. EPS 2008**E**	3.99	Yield (%)	0.63
Trailing 12-Month P/E	20.7	P/E on S&P Oper. EPS 2007**E**	19.8	Dividend Rate/Share	$0.40
$10K Invested 5 Yrs Ago	$39,779	Common Shares Outstg. (M)	200.5	Institutional Ownership (%)	96

Beta	0.71
S&P 3-Yr. Proj. EPS CAGR(%)	20.00
S&P Credit Rating	BBB+

Price Performance

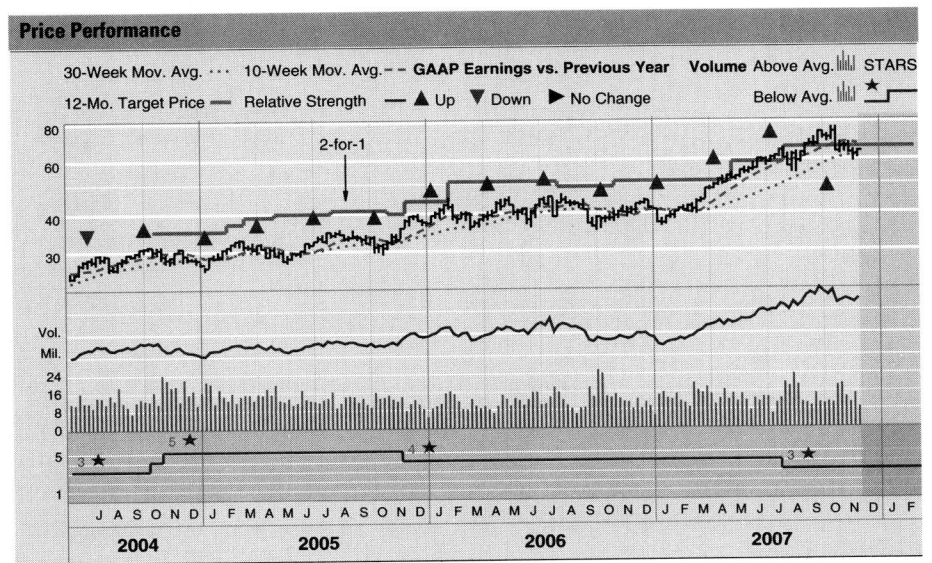

30-Week Mov. Avg. ··· 10-Week Mov. Avg. - - GAAP Earnings vs. Previous Year   Volume Above Avg. STARS
12-Mo. Target Price — Relative Strength — ▲ Up ▼ Down ► No Change   Below Avg.

Options: ASE, CBOE, P, Ph

Analysis prepared by **Stewart Glickman, CFA** on November 19, 2007, when the stock traded at **$ 61.57**.

Highlights

➤ We see higher drilling activity in deepwater fields in the near term and expect SII to benefit, given a strong position in drilling fluids and drill bit technology. Typically, deepwater drilling and completion projects demand more advanced equipment, reflecting the relatively harsh environments found in such projects. Given that much of the shallower reservoirs around the world are in mature production, we believe that significant growth opportunities lie mainly in deeper waters.

➤ We expect total revenues to increase about 20% in 2007 (with a 22% gain in oilfield services) and to grow a further 11% in 2008. We see a modest improvement in margins in oilfield services, rising 120 basis points to 20% in 2007, with a further 150 basis point gain in 2008. Margins in the distribution business are markedly lower than those in oilfield services, although third quarter margins rose to 4.4% (versus 4.0% in the second quarter), and we see a further recovery in this segment to about 4.7% in 2007 and 6.0% in 2008.

➤ For 2007, we estimate operating EPS of $3.23, rising to $3.99 in 2008.

Investment Rationale/Risk

➤ On a fundamental basis, we believe SII is well positioned to benefit from ongoing secular trends in oil and gas exploration and production towards deeper, more challenging plays. However, with the shares up 47% year to date, 5th best amongst our coverage universe of oilfield services companies, we would not add to positions.

➤ Risks to our recommendation and target price include political risk in frontier regions; reduced demand for drilling fluids and drill bits; and increased competition from larger companies in the drilling fluids business.

➤ Our DCF model, assuming free cash flow growth of 17% per year for 10 years, and a WACC of 10.5%, indicates intrinsic value of about $60. On a relative valuation basis, we think the shares should trade slightly below peers, as we project return on invested capital of 17% in 2008, below the peer average. Assuming a 9X multiple on projected 2008 EBITDA and a 12X multiple on estimated 2008 cash flow (both below peers), and blending with our DCF model, we derive our 12-month target price of $66.

Qualitative Risk Assessment

LOW	MEDIUM	HIGH

Our risk assessment reflects SII's exposure to volatile crude oil and natural gas prices, capital spending decisions made by its oil and gas producing customers, and political risk associated with operating in frontier regions. Offsetting these risks is SII's strong position in drill bits and drilling fluids.

Quantitative Evaluations

S&P Quality Ranking B+

D	C	B-	B	B+	A-	A	A+

Relative Strength Rank MODERATE
66
LOWEST = 1   HIGHEST = 99

Revenue/Earnings Data

Revenue (Million $)

	1Q	2Q	3Q	4Q	Year
2007	2,108	2,114	2,245	--	--
2006	1,682	1,738	1,914	1,999	7,334
2005	1,288	1,350	1,410	1,530	5,579
2004	1,018	1,064	1,119	1,218	4,419
2003	808.8	877.7	924.8	983.5	3,595
2002	827.4	801.0	777.2	764.4	3,170

Earnings Per Share ($)

2007	0.80	0.76	0.83	E0.85	E3.23
2006	0.53	0.59	0.66	0.71	2.49
2005	0.33	0.33	0.39	0.44	1.48
2004	0.22	0.14	0.26	0.29	0.89
2003	0.11	0.15	0.18	0.19	0.62
2002	0.15	0.14	0.10	0.09	0.47

Fiscal year ended Dec. 31. Next earnings report expected: Late January. EPS Estimates based on S&P Operating Earnings; historical GAAP earnings are as reported.

Dividend Data (Dates: mm/dd Payment Date: mm/dd/yy)

Amount ($)	Date Decl.	Ex-Div. Date	Stk. of Record	Payment Date
0.100	02/07	03/13	03/15	04/16/07
0.100	04/27	06/13	06/15	07/16/07
0.100	07/18	09/12	09/14	10/15/07
0.100	10/17	12/12	12/14	01/14/08

Dividends have been paid since 2005. Source: Company reports.

Please read the Required Disclosures and Analyst Certification on the last page of this report.

The McGraw·Hill Companies

Smith International Inc.

Business Summary November 19, 2007

CORPORATE OVERVIEW. Driven by exploration and production activities worldwide, Smith International manufactures and markets technologically advanced products and services to the oil and gas industry. Approximately 54% of total 2006 revenues were derived from equipment sold or services provided to customers outside the United States (versus 55% in 2005). In 2006, top non-U.S. regions included Europe/Africa (22%), Canada (12%), the Middle East (12%), and Latin America (8%). The Oilfield Products and Services segment (73% of 2006 revenues, and 91% of segment operating profits) consists of three businesses: M-I SWACO (49% of 2006 revenues); Smith Technologies (11%); and Smith Services (14%).

M-I SWACO provides drilling and completion fluid systems and services, solids control equipment and waste management services. Drilling fluid products and systems are used to cool and lubricate the bit during drilling, contain formation pressures, remove rock cuttings, and maintain the stability of the wellbore. Engineering services ensure that products are applied to optimize operations.

Smith Technologies is a worldwide leader in the design, manufacture and marketing of drilling bits primarily used in drilling oil and natural gas wells. In addition, Smith Technologies is the leading provider of downhole turbine products and services that enhance the operating performance of drillbits.

Smith Services manufactures and markets products used in the oil and gas industry for drilling, workover, well completion, and well re-entry. Drilling Optimization Solutions provides a broad range of downhole impact tools for drilling applications. Fishing and Remedial Solutions removes obstructions from the wellbore that may arise during drilling, completion or workover activities, and manufactures and markets hole openers and underreamers that create larger hole diameters in certain sections of the wellbore. Casing Exit and Multilateral Solutions manufactures proprietary casing exit tools. Completion Solutions specializes in providing fit-for-purpose liner hangers, liner cementing equipment, isolation packers, retrievable and permanent packers, packer products and multilateral completion equipment.

The Distribution segment (27% of total 2006 revenues, and 9% of total segment operating profits) consists of Wilson, a supply-chain management company that markets pipe, valves, fittings, and mill and safety products.

Company Financials Fiscal Year Ended Dec. 31

Per Share Data ($)	2006	2005	2004	2003	2002	2001	2000	1999	1998	1997
Tangible Book Value	4.89	3.40	3.06	2.72	2.23	1.90	1.83	1.89	1.79	1.64
Cash Flow	3.23	2.05	1.41	1.12	0.91	1.22	0.76	0.67	0.54	0.93
Earnings	2.49	1.48	0.89	0.62	0.47	0.76	0.36	0.29	0.18	0.64
S&P Core Earnings	2.49	1.41	0.94	0.57	0.42	0.72	NA	NA	NA	NA
Dividends	0.32	0.24	Nil	Nil	Nil	Nil	Nil	Nil	Nil	Nil
Payout Ratio	13%	16%	Nil	Nil	Nil	Nil	Nil	Nil	Nil	Nil
Prices:High	46.48	40.08	31.49	21.59	19.36	21.13	22.13	13.02	16.13	21.97
Prices:Low	34.87	25.80	20.03	14.75	11.60	8.08	11.25	5.89	4.31	9.63
P/E Ratio:High	19	27	35	35	42	28	61	45	92	34
P/E Ratio:Low	14	17	23	24	25	11	31	20	25	15

Income Statement Analysis (Million $)	2006	2005	2004	2003	2002	2001	2000	1999	1998	1997
Revenue	7,334	5,579	4,419	3,595	3,170	3,551	2,761	1,806	2,119	1,563
Operating Income	1,230	788	545	430	345	464	280	310	278	264
Depreciation, Depletion and Amortization	150	118	106	102	89.3	92.9	80.7	76.0	70.3	46.7
Interest Expense	63.0	44.4	38.8	41.0	40.9	45.4	36.8	40.8	46.0	26.9
Pretax Income	1,020	628	401	290	218	329	164	111	81.9	193
Effective Tax Rate	32.0%	32.3%	32.3%	32.2%	30.6%	32.3%	33.5%	43.2%	32.1%	26.3%
Net Income	502	302	182	125	93.2	152	72.8	56.7	34.1	102
S&P Core Earnings	503	290	192	115	84.6	145	NA	NA	NA	NA

Balance Sheet & Other Financial Data (Million $)	2006	2005	2004	2003	2002	2001	2000	1999	1998	1997
Cash	80.4	62.5	53.6	51.3	86.8	44.7	36.5	24.1	22.7	29.0
Current Assets	3,271	2,437	2,020	1,680	1,427	1,523	1,310	1,055	997	851
Total Assets	5,335	4,060	3,507	3,097	2,750	2,736	2,295	1,895	1,759	1,396
Current Liabilities	1,379	933	887	631	595	666	643	457	693	373
Long Term Debt	801	611	388	489	442	539	375	347	369	306
Common Equity	1,987	1,365	1,401	1,236	1,064	949	817	720	634	469
Total Capital	3,710	2,827	2,537	2,392	2,087	2,019	1,615	1,422	1,012	999
Capital Expenditures	308	178	111	98.9	97.1	128	94.6	57.2	119	82.8
Cash Flow	652	420	289	226	183	245	153	133	104	149
Current Ratio	2.4	2.6	2.3	2.7	2.4	2.3	2.0	2.3	1.4	2.3
% Long Term Debt of Capitalization	21.6	21.6	15.3	20.4	21.2	26.7	23.2	24.4	36.4	30.7
% Return on Assets	10.7	8.0	5.5	4.3	3.4	6.0	3.5	3.1	2.2	8.3
% Return on Equity	28.2	21.9	13.8	10.8	9.3	17.2	9.5	8.4	6.2	24.4

Data as orig reptd.; bef. results of disc opers/spec. items. Per share data adj. for stk. divs.; EPS diluted. E-Estimated. NA-Not Available. NM-Not Meaningful. NR-Not Ranked. UR-Under Review.

Office: 411 N Sam Houston Pkwy Ste 600, Houston, TX 77060-3545.
Telephone: 281-443-3370.
Website: http://www.smith.com
Chrmn, Pres, CEO & COO: D.L. Rock

Investor Contact: M.K. Dorman (281-443-3370)
SVP, CFO & Treas: M.K. Dorman
SVP, Secy & General Counsel: R.E. Chandler, Jr.
VP & Cntlr: J.S. Rinando, III

Board Members: G. C. Buck, L. K. Carroll, D. A. Fraser, J. R. Gibbs, R. Kelley, J. W. Neely, D. L. Rock, J. Yearwood

Founded: 1937
Domicile: Delaware
Employees: 17,377

Snap-On Inc

STANDARD &POOR'S

S&P Recommendation	BUY ★★★★☆	Price	12-Mo. Target Price	Investment Style
		$47.07 (as of Nov 23, 2007)	$60.00	Large-Cap Value

GICS Sector Consumer Discretionary
Sub-Industry Household Appliances

Summary This company is the largest manufacturer and distributor of hand tools, storage units and diagnostic equipment for professional mechanics.

Key Stock Statistics (Source S&P, Vickers, company reports)

52-Wk Range	$57.81– 45.03	S&P Oper. EPS 2007**E**	3.04	Market Capitalization(B)	$2.712	Beta	1.35
Trailing 12-Month EPS	$2.75	S&P Oper. EPS 2008**E**	3.50	Yield (%)	2.55	S&P 3-Yr. Proj. EPS CAGR(%)	15.00
Trailing 12-Month P/E	17.1	P/E on S&P Oper. EPS 2007**E**	15.5	Dividend Rate/Share	$1.20	S&P Credit Rating	A-
$10K Invested 5 Yrs Ago	$18,829	Common Shares Outstg. (M)	57.6	Institutional Ownership (%)	92		

Price Performance

30-Week Mov. Avg. · · · 10-Week Mov. Avg. — GAAP Earnings vs. Previous Year   Volume Above Avg. STARS
12-Mo. Target Price — Relative Strength — ▲ Up ▼ Down ▶ No Change   Below Avg.

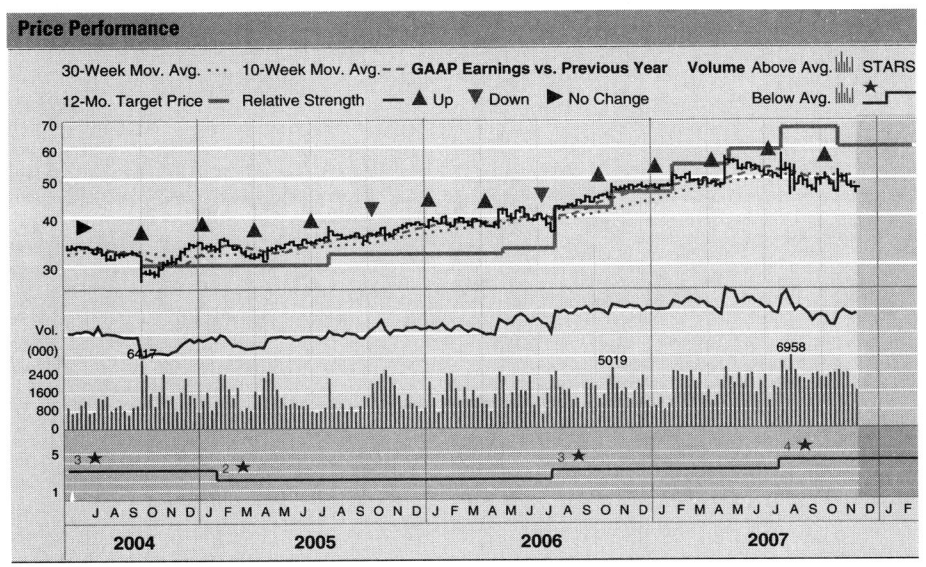

Options: ASE

Analysis prepared by **Kenneth M. Leon, CPA** on October 24, 2007, when the stock traded at **$ 50.50.**

Qualitative Risk Assessment

LOW	MEDIUM	HIGH

Our risk assessment is based on our view of SNA's strong brand equity and healthy balance sheet, offset by intense competition.

Quantitative Evaluations

S&P Quality Ranking   B+

D	C	B-	B	B+	A-	A	A+

Relative Strength Rank   MODERATE

62

LOWEST = 1   HIGHEST = 99

Revenue/Earnings Data

Revenue (Million $)

	1Q	2Q	3Q	4Q	Year
2007	709.7	711.9	680.7	--	--
2006	593.5	624.4	599.5	656.0	2,522
2005	612.8	608.6	567.2	573.6	2,362
2004	616.3	612.1	568.8	610.0	2,407
2003	543.1	565.2	525.6	599.3	2,233
2002	510.0	547.2	502.4	549.5	2,109

Earnings Per Share ($)

2007	0.66	0.90	0.70	E0.80	E3.04
2006	0.37	0.20	0.48	0.64	1.69
2005	0.31	0.46	0.36	0.47	1.59
2004	0.22	0.38	0.39	0.42	1.40
2003	0.37	0.38	0.30	0.30	1.35
2002	0.37	0.50	0.33	0.56	1.76

Fiscal year ended Dec. 31. Next earnings report expected: Early February. EPS Estimates based on S&P Operating Earnings; historical GAAP earnings are as reported.

Highlights

➤ We project sales growth of 13% to 14% in 2007 and high single digit growth in 2008, as moderate international industry growth is dampened by a housing slowdown in the U.S. The company continues to focus on improving its dealer business, which we think will ultimately benefit future sales. We foresee contributions to growth from all segments, with particular strength in Diagnostics and Information, which includes operations acquired from ProQuest Business Solutions in November 2006.

➤ We think SNA has done a good job of improving its cost structure, particularly while facing external cost pressures. In the Tools Group, we believe that investments to improve the franchise system in 2006 will aid the segment's margins.

➤ We believe that investment spending in SNA's other segments will be offset by expected productivity gains, resulting in better segment operating earnings. SNA's goal of at least 10% operating margins (versus 8% in 2006) was achieved in the second and third quarters in 2007. We forecast operating EPS of $3.04 for 2007 and $3.50 for 2008.

Investment Rationale/Risk

➤ We believe SNA is undergoing a transformation to become a leaner organization, with a high priority on bettering customer responsiveness and top-line growth. We expect these ongoing improvements to ultimately restore margins to prior levels. We think the November 2006 acquisition of ProQuest's business solutions unit will help the company expand revenues and profits.

➤ Risks to our recommendation and target price include weaker than expected results in SNA's major markets, failure to successfully introduce new products into the pipeline, an inability to achieve goals for revenue growth or productivity initiatives, and any negative effects from currency fluctuations.

➤ With the stock recently trading at 16X our 2007 EPS estimate, a more modest premium to peers than recently, we view the shares as attractively valued, despite some concern about modest growth for the industry. Our 12-month target price of $60 is based on our historical P/E model, which applies a target P/E of about 17X to our 2008 operating EPS estimate of $3.50.

Dividend Data (Dates: mm/dd Payment Date: mm/dd/yy)

Amount ($)	Date Decl.	Ex-Div. Date	Stk. of Record	Payment Date
0.270	02/15	02/22	02/26	03/12/07
0.270	04/30	05/17	05/21	06/11/07
0.270	08/02	08/16	08/20	09/10/07
0.300	11/01	11/15	11/19	12/10/07

Dividends have been paid since 1939. Source: Company reports.

Please read the Required Disclosures and Analyst Certification on the last page of this report.

The McGraw-Hill Companies

Snap-On Inc

Business Summary October 24, 2007

CORPORATE OVERVIEW. Snap-On Inc. is a major global manufacturer and marketer of high-quality tool, diagnostic, service and equipment solutions for professional tool and equipment users under various brands and trade names. Product lines include a broad range of hand and power tools, tool storage, saws and cutting tools, pruning tools, vehicle service diagnostics equipment, vehicle service equipment, including wheel service, safety testing and collision repair equipment, vehicle service information, business management systems, equipment repair services, and other tool and equipment solutions. SNA's customers include automotive technicians, vehicle service centers, manufacturers, industrial tool and equipment users, and those involved in commercial applications such as construction, electrical and agriculture. SNA services these customers through three primary channels of distribution: the mobile dealer van channel, including the company's technical representatives; company direct sales; and distributors.

SNA has four reportable business segments. The Snap-on Tools Group, formerly the Dealer Group (41% of 2006 sales, 43% of 2005 sales) consists of

SNA's business operations serving the worldwide franchised dealer van channel. The Commercial and Industrial Group (42%, 43%) provides tools, equipment products and equipment repair services to industrial and commercial customers worldwide through direct, distributor and other non-franchised distribution channels. The Diagnostics and Information Group (16%, 13%) provides diagnostic equipment, vehicle service information, business management systems and other solutions for customers in the vehicle service and repair marketplace. Financial Services (2%, 2%) is a relatively new business segment, which was originated in 2004. It consists of Snap-on Credit LLC, a consolidated 50%-owned joint venture between SNA and The CIT Group, and SNA's wholly owned finance subsidiaries in international markets where SNA has dealer operations. SNA groups its products and services into two categories: tools (58% of 2006 sales, 61% of 2005 sales) and equipment (42%, 39%).

Company Financials Fiscal Year Ended Dec. 31

Per Share Data ($)	2006	2005	2004	2003	2002	2001	2000	1999	1998	1997
Tangible Book Value	0.72	8.17	9.67	8.29	6.27	6.01	6.53	6.69	9.60	12.74
Cash Flow	2.57	2.48	2.45	2.38	2.65	1.54	3.23	3.10	0.68	3.06
Earnings	1.69	1.59	1.40	1.35	1.76	0.37	2.10	2.16	-0.08	2.44
S&P Core Earnings	2.07	1.56	1.35	1.31	0.92	0.09	NA	NA	NA	NA
Dividends	1.08	1.00	1.00	1.00	0.97	0.96	0.94	0.90	0.86	0.82
Payout Ratio	64%	63%	71%	74%	55%	NM	45%	42%	NM	34%
Prices:High	48.65	38.71	34.67	32.38	35.15	34.40	32.44	37.81	46.44	46.31
Prices:Low	36.38	30.57	27.15	22.60	20.71	21.15	20.88	26.44	25.50	34.25
P/E Ratio:High	29	24	25	24	20	93	15	18	NM	19
P/E Ratio:Low	22	19	19	17	12	57	10	12	NM	14

Income Statement Analysis (Million $)										
Revenue	2,522	2,362	2,407	2,233	2,109	2,096	2,176	1,946	1,773	1,672
Operating Income	217	220	203	167	217	168	270	228	102	232
Depreciation	51.9	52.2	61.0	60.3	51.7	68.0	66.2	55.4	45.0	38.4
Interest Expense	20.6	21.7	23.0	24.4	28.7	35.5	40.7	27.4	21.3	17.7
Pretax Income	146	148	120	117	161	47.6	193	198	10.8	239
Effective Tax Rate	31.4%	37.2%	32.1%	32.6%	36.0%	54.8%	36.1%	35.7%	NM	37.0%
Net Income	100	92.9	81.7	78.7	103	21.5	123	127	-4.78	150
S&P Core Earnings	123	91.6	78.3	76.6	53.9	5.49	NA	NA	NA	NA

Balance Sheet & Other Financial Data (Million $)										
Cash	63.4	170	150	96.1	18.4	6.70	6.10	17.6	15.0	25.7
Current Assets	1,113	1,073	1,193	1,132	1,051	1,139	1,186	1,206	1,080	1,022
Total Assets	2,655	2,008	2,290	2,139	1,994	1,974	2,050	2,150	1,675	1,641
Current Liabilities	682	506	674	567	552	549	538	453	458	353
Long Term Debt	506	202	203	303	304	446	473	247	247	151
Common Equity	1,076	962	1,111	1,011	830	868	844	825	762	892
Total Capital	1,671	1,239	1,390	1,348	1,168	1,339	1,342	1,099	1,018	1,055
Capital Expenditures	50.5	40.1	38.7	29.4	45.8	53.6	57.6	35.4	46.8	55.4
Cash Flow	152	145	143	139	155	89.5	189	183	40.2	189
Current Ratio	1.6	2.1	1.8	2.0	1.9	2.1	2.2	2.7	2.4	2.9
% Long Term Debt of Capitalization	30.3	16.3	14.6	22.5	26.0	33.3	35.3	22.4	24.2	14.3
% Net Income of Revenue	4.0	3.9	3.4	3.5	4.9	1.0	5.7	6.5	NM	9.0
% Return on Assets	4.3	4.3	3.7	3.8	5.2	1.1	5.9	6.7	NM	9.5
% Return on Equity	9.8	9.0	7.7	8.5	12.9	2.4	14.7	16.0	NM	17.5

Data as orig reptd.; bef. results of disc opers/spec. items. Per share data adj. for stk. divs.; EPS diluted. E-Estimated. NA-Not Available. NM-Not Meaningful. NR-Not Ranked. UR-Under Review.

Office: 2801 80th St, Kenosha, WI 53143-5656.
Telephone: 262-656-5200.
Website: http://www.snapon.com
Chrmn & CEO: J.D. Michaels

Pres & COO: N.T. Pinchuk
Investor Contact: M.M. Ellen (262-656-6462)
SVP & CFO: M.M. Ellen
VP, Secy & Chief Lgl Officer: S.F. Marrinan

Board Members: B. S. Chelberg, K. L. Daniel, R. J. Decyk, J. F. Fiedler, A. L. Kelly, W. D. Lehman, J. D. Michaels, L. Nyberg, N. T. Pinchuk, E. H. Rensi, R. F. Teerlink

Founded: 1920
Domicile: Delaware
Employees: 12,400

Southern Co (The)

STANDARD &POOR'S

S&P Recommendation	**BUY** ★★★★☆	Price $38.04 (as of Nov 23, 2007)	12-Mo. Target Price $39.00	Investment Style Large-Cap Value

GICS Sector Utilities
Sub-Industry Electric Utilities

Summary This Atlanta-based energy holding company is one of the largest producers of electricity in the U.S.

Key Stock Statistics (Source S&P, Vickers, company reports)

52-Wk Range	$38.90–33.16	S&P Oper. EPS 2007**E**	2.18	Market Capitalization(B)	$28.775
Trailing 12-Month EPS	$2.27	S&P Oper. EPS 2008**E**	2.31	Yield (%)	4.23
Trailing 12-Month P/E	16.8	P/E on S&P Oper. EPS 2007**E**	17.4	Dividend Rate/Share	$1.61
$10K Invested 5 Yrs Ago	$17,997	Common Shares Outstg. (M)	756.4	Institutional Ownership (%)	47

Beta	0.06
S&P 3-Yr. Proj. EPS CAGR(%)	4.00
S&P Credit Rating	A

Price Performance

30-Week Mov. Avg. ··· 10-Week Mov. Avg. – – GAAP Earnings vs. Previous Year   Volume Above Avg. STARS
12-Mo. Target Price — Relative Strength — ▲ Up ▼ Down ▶ No Change   Below Avg. ★

Options: ASE, CBOE, P, Ph

Analysis prepared by **Justin McCann** on October 26, 2007, when the stock traded at **$ 36.17**.

Highlights

➤ Excluding synthetic fuel related earnings, we expect 2007 EPS to increase nearly 4% from 2006 operating EPS of $2.10. We see Southern Power, which has been separated from the competitive generation business, earning about $115 million, with the remaining generation businesses earning around $155 million. We look for SO's synfuel-related tax credits to contribute about $0.07 to 2007 EPS, compared to $0.02 in 2006 and $0.12 in 2005.

➤ We project that EPS in 2008 will continue to benefit from a strong service territory economy and steady customer growth, partially offset by higher interest and operation and maintenance expenses. We see the utilities recording annual customer growth of about 1.7% and demand growth of around 2%, and we expect SO to post average annual EPS growth of 4% to 6% for the longer term.

➤ We forecast capital expenditures of about $13.2 billion in the 2007 through 2009 period, with the largest expenditures directed to the company's environmental construction program ($4.6 billion), the distribution operations ($2.3 billion), Southern Power ($1.6 billion), transmission ($1.5 billion), and fossil/hydro retrofits ($1 billion).

Investment Rationale/Risk

➤ With an above-peers yield from the dividend, we believe the stock is attractive for above-average total return. Although the shares have underperformed the S&P Index of Electric Utilities year to date (after having also underperformed in 2006), we believe SO's stock could outperform its peers over the next 12 months. We expect SO to trade at a premium to peers multiple, reflecting, in part, the relative predictability of its earnings and dividend stream (reflected in an S&P Quality Ranking of A-).

➤ Risks to our recommendation and target price include a possible economic downturn in the company's service territory, and a significant decline in the average P/E of the electric utility group as a whole.

➤ SO increased its dividend 3.9% with the June 2007 payment. This roughly equals the prior 4.0% increase, and with the payout ratio (at 73% of our 2007 EPS estimate) within SO's targeted range of 70% to 75%, we expect future dividends to rise at around 4% annually. We see the stock trading at an approximate peers' P/E of about 17X our 2008 EPS estimate. Our 12-month target price is $39.

Qualitative Risk Assessment

LOW	MEDIUM	HIGH

Our risk assessment reflects our view of: the company's strong and steady cash flow from the regulated electric utility operations, solid balance sheet, a healthy economy in most of its service territories, and a generally supportive regulatory environment.

Quantitative Evaluations

S&P Quality Ranking A-

D	C	B-	B	B+	A-	A	A+

Relative Strength Rank STRONG

90

LOWEST = 1   HIGHEST = 99

Revenue/Earnings Data

Revenue (Million $)

	1Q	2Q	3Q	4Q	Year
2007	3,409	3,772	4,832	--	--
2006	3,063	3,592	4,549	3,152	14,356
2005	2,864	3,144	4,378	3,287	13,554
2004	2,732	3,009	3,441	2,720	11,902
2003	2,553	2,859	3,319	2,564	11,251
2002	2,214	2,631	3,248	2,457	10,549

Earnings Per Share ($)

	1Q	2Q	3Q	4Q	Year
2007	0.45	0.57	1.00	E0.22	E2.18
2006	0.35	0.52	0.99	0.25	2.10
2005	0.43	0.52	0.97	0.21	2.14
2004	0.45	0.47	0.87	0.27	2.06
2003	0.41	0.59	0.84	0.17	2.02
2002	0.32	0.46	0.83	0.23	1.85

Fiscal year ended Dec. 31. Next earnings report expected: Late November. EPS Estimates based on S&P Operating Earnings; historical GAAP earnings are as reported.

Dividend Data (Dates: mm/dd Payment Date: mm/dd/yy)

Amount ($)	Date Decl.	Ex-Div. Date	Stk. of Record	Payment Date
0.388	01/12	02/01	02/05	03/06/07
0.403	04/16	05/03	05/07	06/06/07
0.403	07/16	08/02	08/06	09/06/07
0.403	10/15	11/01	11/05	12/06/07

Dividends have been paid since 1948. Source: Company reports.

Southern Co (The)

**STANDARD
&POOR'S**

Business Summary October 26, 2007

CORPORATE OVERVIEW. The Southern Company is one of the largest producers of electricity in the U.S. Based in Atlanta, GA, this utility holding company has approximately 41,785 megawatts of generating capacity and provides electricity to around 4.3 million customers in the Southeast through the following integrated utilities: Alabama Power, Georgia Power, Gulf Power (located in the northwestern portion of Florida), and Mississippi Power. Savannah Electric & Power was merged into Georgia Power on July 1, 2006.

MARKET PROFILE. Southern Power Company (SPC) was formed by SO in January 2001 to own, manage and finance wholesale generating assets in the Southeast. It serves both the utility units and the wholesale power market. Energy from SPC's assets, which included 6,733 megawatts of generating capacity at the end of 2006, was to be marketed to wholesale customers through the Southern Company Generation and Energy Marketing unit. SPC and the utility units enter into contracts for power purchases, sales and exchange

among themselves, as well as with other utilities in the Southeast. Southern Company Gas was formed by SO in June 2002 as a retail gas marketer in Georgia, and began operations in August 2002. In January 2006, SO sold nearly all the assets of Southern Company Gas to Gas South.

SO is also the parent company for Southern Telecom, which provides wholesale fiber optic solutions to telecommunication providers in the Southeast; Southern Communications Services (Southern LINC), which provides digital, wireless communications services to SO's four utility units, as well as to the general public within the Southeast; and Southern Nuclear, which provides services to SO's nuclear power plants.

Company Financials Fiscal Year Ended Dec. 31

Per Share Data ($)	2006	2005	2004	2003	2002	2001	2000	1999	1998	1997
Tangible Book Value	15.00	14.19	13.65	12.92	11.56	10.87	15.12	6.14	8.77	10.52
Earnings	2.10	2.14	2.06	2.02	1.85	1.61	1.52	1.86	1.40	1.42
S&P Core Earnings	2.06	2.04	1.93	1.85	1.35	1.12	NA	NA	NA	NA
Dividends	1.54	1.48	1.77	1.39	1.36	1.34	1.34	1.34	1.34	1.30
Payout Ratio	72%	69%	86%	69%	74%	83%	88%	72%	96%	92%
Prices:High	37.40	36.47	33.96	32.00	31.14	35.72	35.00	29.63	31.56	26.25
Prices:Low	30.48	31.14	27.44	27.00	23.22	20.89	20.38	22.06	23.94	19.88
P/E Ratio:High	18	17	16	16	17	22	23	16	23	18
P/E Ratio:Low	14	15	13	13	13	13	13	12	17	14

Income Statement Analysis (Million $)										
Revenue	70.3	13,554	11,902	11,251	10,549	10,155	10,066	11,585	11,403	12,611
Depreciation	1,200	1,176	955	1,027	1,047	1,173	1,171	1,307	1,539	1,246
Maintenance	1,096	1,116	1,027	937	961	909	852	945	887	763
Fixed Charges Coverage	3.73	3.90	4.11	4.21	3.80	3.25	2.87	2.71	2.63	2.68
Construction Credits	50.0	51.0	47.0	25.0	22.0	NA	NA	NA	NA	20.0
Effective Tax Rate	33.2%	27.2%	27.7%	29.3%	28.6%	33.3%	37.2%	33.2%	38.8%	42.7%
Net Income	1,574	1,591	1,532	1,474	1,318	1,119	994	1,276	977	972
S&P Core Earnings	1,551	1,532	1,436	1,351	964	776	NA	NA	NA	NA

Balance Sheet & Other Financial Data (Million $)										
Gross Property	50,167	47,580	45,585	43,722	41,764	38,104	35,972	38,620	37,363	34,044
Capital Expenditures	2,994	2,370	2,110	2,002	2,717	2,617	2,225	2,560	2,005	1,859
Net Property	33,585	31,853	30,634	29,418	26,315	23,084	21,622	24,544	24,124	22,110
Capitalization:Long Term Debt	13,247	13,442	13,010	10,587	8,956	10,941	10,457	14,443	13,020	10,274
Capitalization:% Long Term Debt	53.8	55.7	55.9	52.3	50.7	57.8	49.4	60.8	57.1	46.3
Capitalization:Preferred	Nil	Nil	Nil	Nil	Nil	Nil	Nil	Nil	Nil	2,237
Capitalization:% Preferred	Nil	Nil	Nil	Nil	Nil	Nil	Nil	Nil	Nil	10.0
Capitalization:Common	11,371	10,689	10,278	9,648	8,710	7,984	10,690	9,296	9,797	9,647
Capitalization:% Common	46.2	44.3	44.1	47.7	49.3	42.2	50.6	39.2	42.9	43.5
Total Capital	31,110	30,394	29,077	25,809	22,937	24,147	26,436	29,662	24,790	27,997
% Operating Ratio	83.0	82.5	81.2	79.7	80.5	81.9	82.0	81.7	82.6	84.6
% Earned on Net Property	9.9	9.5	9.4	10.0	10.1	10.7	11.4	8.5	7.3	8.6
% Return on Revenue	11.0	11.7	12.9	13.1	12.5	11.0	9.9	11.0	8.6	7.7
% Return on Invested Capital	8.0	8.0	7.9	8.9	8.5	7.4	7.3	9.6	13.8	10.4
% Return on Common Equity	14.3	15.2	15.4	16.1	15.8	12.0	10.0	13.4	10.0	10.3

Data as orig reptd.; bef. results of disc opers/spec. items. Per share data adj. for stk. divs.; EPS diluted. E-Estimated. NA-Not Available. NM-Not Meaningful. NR-Not Ranked. UR-Under Review.

Office: 30 Ivan Allen Jr Blvd NW, Atlanta, GA 30308-3003.
Telephone: 404-506-5000.
Email: investors@southerncompany.com
Website: http://www.southernco.com

Chrmn, Pres & CEO: D. Ratcliffe
EVP, CFO & Treas: T.A. Fanning
Investor Contact: G. Kundert (404-506-5135)

Board Members: J. P. Baranco, D. J. Bern, F. S. Blake, T. F. Chapman, B. Habermeyer, Jr., D. M. James, J. N. Purcell, D. M. Ratcliffe, W. G. Smith, Jr., G. J. St. Pe

Founded: 1945
Domicile: Delaware
Employees: 26,091

The McGraw-Hill Companies

Southwest Airlines Co.

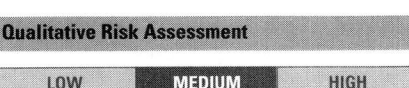
STANDARD &POOR'S

S&P Recommendation BUY ★★★★☆

Price
$13.73 (as of Nov 23, 2007)

12-Mo. Target Price
$22.00

GICS Sector Industrials
Sub-Industry Airlines

Summary LUV, the sixth largest U.S. airline, offers discounted fares, primarily for short-haul, point-to-point flights.

Key Stock Statistics (Source S&P, Vickers, company reports)

52-Wk Range	$16.96– 12.89	S&P Oper. EPS 2007**E**	0.69	Market Capitalization(B)	$10.078	Beta	0.84
Trailing 12-Month EPS	$0.77	S&P Oper. EPS 2008**E**	0.85	Yield (%)	0.13	S&P 3-Yr. Proj. EPS CAGR(%)	20.00
Trailing 12-Month P/E	17.8	P/E on S&P Oper. EPS 2007**E**	19.9	Dividend Rate/Share	$0.02	S&P Credit Rating	A-
$10K Invested 5 Yrs Ago	$8,836	Common Shares Outstg. (M)	734.0	Institutional Ownership (%)	83		

Price Performance

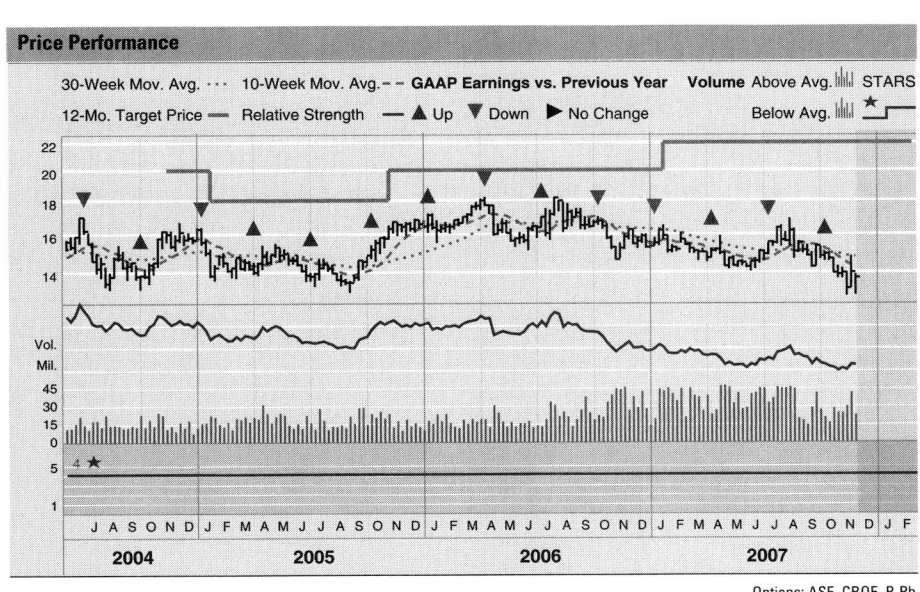

30-Week Mov. Avg. ···· 10-Week Mov. Avg.--- **GAAP Earnings vs. Previous Year** Volume Above Avg. STARS
12-Mo. Target Price — Relative Strength — ▲ Up ▼ Down ► No Change Below Avg. ★

Options: ASE, CBOE, P, Ph

Analysis prepared by **Jim Corridore** on November 08, 2007, when the stock traded at **$ 13.25.**

Highlights

➤ We look for 2008 revenues to rise about 10%, on top of estimated 8% growth in 2007. We expect 6% capacity growth in 2008, versus 8% capacity growth in 2007. We expect 2008 revenues to benefit from higher average fares as LUV rolls out its new business fares and starts selling assigned boarding slots. We also expect higher load factors as LUV slows its capacity growth in 2008.

➤ We see margins likely to benefit from increased revenue yields, efficiency gains and cost savings, modestly outweighing our estimate of about a 20% increase in fuel costs. LUV is about 70% hedged on estimated jet fuel consumption for 2008 at an average price of $51 a barrel, and 90% for 2007 at $51 a barrel, well below prevailing market rates. We think this is substantially better than any other U.S. airline, but compares unfavorably with 2006's average hedge price of about $38 a barrel for 85% of consumption.

➤ We estimate 2008 EPS of $0.85, up from our 2007 estimate of $0.69.

Investment Rationale/Risk

➤ We believe LUV is the financially strongest U.S. airline. LUV has posted 34 consecutive years and 66 consecutive quarters of profitable operations, and we see the quality of those earnings as high. In our view, LUV has ample cash, and its debt to total capitalization is significantly below peer levels. We think these measures warrant a premium valuation to peers and the S&P 500. We believe Southwest has the ability to participate in industry consolidation, should that occur, as it has the ability to fund potential asset purchases.

➤ Risks to our recommendation and target price include a possible price war with one or more competitors, and further increases in oil prices from recent record high levels. We are concerned about LUV's corporate governance relating to its use of affiliated outsiders on its board of directors' nominating and compensation committees.

➤ Our 12-month target price of $22 is equal to about 26X our 2008 EPS estimate, near the midpoint of LUV's five-year historical P/E range. We expect the shares to be volatile due to difficult industry conditions and fluctuating oil prices, but less so than peers.

Qualitative Risk Assessment

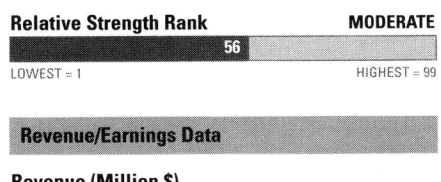

LOW	MEDIUM	HIGH

Even though Southwest participates in the highly volatile airline industry, our view of its conservative balance sheet, with low debt to total capitalization, its track record of 34 consecutive years of profitability, and the industry's leading fuel hedge position offset this risk.

Quantitative Evaluations

S&P Quality Ranking B+

D	C	B-	B	B+	A-	A	A+

Relative Strength Rank MODERATE

56

LOWEST = 1   HIGHEST = 99

Revenue/Earnings Data

Revenue (Million $)

	1Q	2Q	3Q	4Q	Year
2007	2,198	2,583	2,588	--	--
2006	2,019	2,449	2,342	2,276	9,086
2005	1,663	1,944	1,989	1,987	7,584
2004	1,484	1,716	1,674	1,633	6,530
2003	1,351	1,515	1,553	1,517	5,937
2002	1,257	1,473	1,391	1,401	5,522

Earnings Per Share ($)

2007	0.12	0.36	0.22	E0.10	E0.69
2006	0.07	0.40	0.06	0.07	0.61
2005	0.09	0.20	0.28	0.10	0.67
2004	0.03	0.14	0.15	0.07	0.38
2003	0.03	0.30	0.13	0.08	0.54
2002	0.03	0.13	0.09	0.05	0.30

Fiscal year ended Dec. 31. Next earnings report expected: Mid January. EPS Estimates based on S&P Operating Earnings; historical GAAP earnings are as reported.

Dividend Data (Dates: mm/dd Payment Date: mm/dd/yy)

Amount ($)	Date Decl.	Ex-Div. Date	Stk. of Record	Payment Date
0.005	01/18	02/27	03/01	03/22/07
0.005	05/16	06/05	06/07	06/28/07
0.005	07/19	08/28	08/30	09/20/07
0.005	11/15	12/04	12/06	01/03/08

Dividends have been paid since 1976. Source: Company reports.

Please read the Required Disclosures and Analyst Certification on the last page of this report.

The McGraw-Hill Companies

Southwest Airlines Co.

Business Summary November 08, 2007

CORPORATE OVERVIEW. Southwest Airlines was the sixth largest U.S. airline in 2006, based on revenue passenger miles. At December 31, 2006, it served 63 cities in 32 states. LUV specializes in low fare, point-to-point, short-haul, high-frequency service. Since 1993, it has concentrated its expansion program on markets in the East. Although 80% of its work force belongs to unions, the company believes that it has generally enjoyed harmonious labor relations. LUV began service to Philadelphia in May 2004, and started service to Pittsburgh in May 2005 and Ft. Meyers, FL in October 2005, Denver in January 2006, and Washington D.C. (Dulles) in October 2006.

MARKET PROFILE. The U.S. airline industry is a $164 billion market, according to 2006 data from the Air Transport Association. With 2006 revenues of $9.1

billion, LUV comprised around 5.5% of total industry revenues. Southwest also has an approximate 8.9% market share when measured by RPMs, as of February 2007. Southwest was profitable in 2006 for the 34rd consecutive year and was profitable throughout the industry downturn that took place after 9/11. Over the same period (2001-2005) S&P believes the 10 largest U.S. airlines lost about $58.6 billion. Over the same time period, LUV's net income totaled $2.1 billion.

Company Financials Fiscal Year Ended Dec. 31

Per Share Data ($)	2006	2005	2004	2003	2002	2001	2000	1999	1998	1997
Tangible Book Value	8.23	8.38	7.04	6.40	5.69	5.23	4.57	3.79	3.21	2.69
Cash Flow	1.23	1.25	0.91	1.00	0.74	1.03	1.14	0.90	0.83	0.67
Earnings	0.61	0.67	0.38	0.54	0.30	0.63	0.79	0.59	0.55	0.41
S&P Core Earnings	0.60	0.62	0.30	0.48	0.23	0.61	NA	NA	NA	NA
Dividends	0.02	0.02	0.02	0.02	0.02	0.01	0.01	0.01	0.01	0.01
Payout Ratio	3%	3%	5%	3%	6%	2%	1%	2%	2%	2%
Prices:High	18.20	16.95	17.06	19.69	22.00	23.32	23.32	15.72	10.56	7.78
Prices:Low	14.61	13.05	12.88	11.72	10.90	11.25	10.00	9.58	6.81	4.20
P/E Ratio:High	30	25	45	36	73	37	30	26	19	19
P/E Ratio:Low	24	19	34	22	36	18	13	16	12	10

Income Statement Analysis (Million $)										
Revenue	9,086	7,584	6,530	5,937	5,522	5,555	5,650	4,736	4,164	3,817
Operating Income	1,449	1,289	985	867	774	949	1,302	1,030	909	720
Depreciation	515	469	431	384	356	318	281	249	225	196
Interest Expense	77.0	83.0	49.0	58.0	89.3	49.3	42.3	22.9	30.7	43.7
Pretax Income	790	874	489	708	393	828	1,017	774	705	517
Effective Tax Rate	36.8%	37.3%	36.0%	37.6%	38.6%	38.2%	38.5%	38.7%	38.5%	38.5%
Net Income	499	548	313	442	241	511	625	474	433	318
S&P Core Earnings	489	504	236	385	188	486	NA	NA	NA	NA

Balance Sheet & Other Financial Data (Million $)										
Cash	1,390	2,280	1,305	1,865	1,815	2,280	523	419	379	623
Current Assets	2,601	3,620	2,172	2,313	2,232	2,520	832	631	574	806
Total Assets	13,460	14,218	11,337	9,878	8,954	8,997	6,670	5,652	4,716	4,246
Current Liabilities	2,887	3,848	2,142	172	1,434	2,239	1,298	960	851	869
Long Term Debt	1,567	1,394	1,700	1,332	1,553	1,327	761	872	623	628
Common Equity	6,449	6,675	5,524	5,052	4,422	4,014	3,451	2,836	2,398	2,009
Total Capital	10,120	9,965	8,834	7,804	7,202	6,399	5,065	4,400	3,570	3,076
Capital Expenditures	1,399	1,210	1,775	1,238	603	998	1,135	1,168	947	689
Cash Flow	1,014	1,017	744	826	597	829	906	723	659	513
Current Ratio	0.9	0.9	1.0	13.4	1.6	1.1	0.6	0.7	0.7	0.9
% Long Term Debt of Capitalization	15.5	14.0	19.2	17.1	21.6	20.7	15.0	19.8	17.5	20.4
% Net Income of Revenue	5.5	7.2	4.8	7.4	4.4	9.2	11.1	10.0	10.4	8.3
% Return on Assets	3.6	4.3	3.0	4.7	2.7	6.5	10.1	9.2	9.7	8.0
% Return on Equity	7.6	9.0	5.9	9.3	5.7	13.7	19.9	18.1	19.7	17.4

Data as orig reptd.; bef. results of disc opers/spec. items. Per share data adj. for stk. divs.; EPS diluted. E-Estimated. NA-Not Available. NM-Not Meaningful. NR-Not Ranked. UR-Under Review.

Office: P.O. Box 36611, Dallas, TX 75235-1611.
Telephone: 214-792-4000.
Website: http://www.southwest.com
Chrmn: H.D. Kelleher

Pres, COO & Secy: C.C. Barrett
Vice Chrmn & CEO: G.C. Kelly
Investor Contact: L. Wright (214-792-4415)
SVP & CFO: L. Wright

Board Members: C. C. Barrett, D. Biegler, L. Caldera, C. W. Crockett, W. H. Cunningham, T. C. Johnson, H. D. Kelleher, G. Kelly, N. Loeffler, J. T. Montford

Founded: 1967
Domicile: Texas
Employees: 32,664

Sovereign Bancorp Inc.

STANDARD &POOR'S

S&P Recommendation **HOLD** ★★★☆☆	Price $10.96 (as of Nov 23, 2007)	12-Mo. Target Price $16.00	Investment Style Large-Cap Blend

GICS Sector Financials
Sub-Industry Thrifts & Mortgage Finance

Summary This $90 billion bank holding company has branches in Pennsylvania, New Jersey, Connecticut, New Hampshire, Rhode Island, Massachusetts, New York, Maryland, and Delaware.

Key Stock Statistics (Source S&P, Vickers, company reports)

52-Wk Range	$26.70– 10.28	S&P Oper. EPS 2007**E**	1.10	Market Capitalization(B)	$5.251	Beta	0.92
Trailing 12-Month EPS	$0.19	S&P Oper. EPS 2008**E**	1.09	Yield (%)	2.92	S&P 3-Yr. Proj. EPS CAGR(%)	NA
Trailing 12-Month P/E	57.7	P/E on S&P Oper. EPS 2007**E**	10.0	Dividend Rate/Share	$0.32	S&P Credit Rating	BBB
$10K Invested 5 Yrs Ago	$8,584	Common Shares Outstg. (M)	479.2	Institutional Ownership (%)	49		

Price Performance

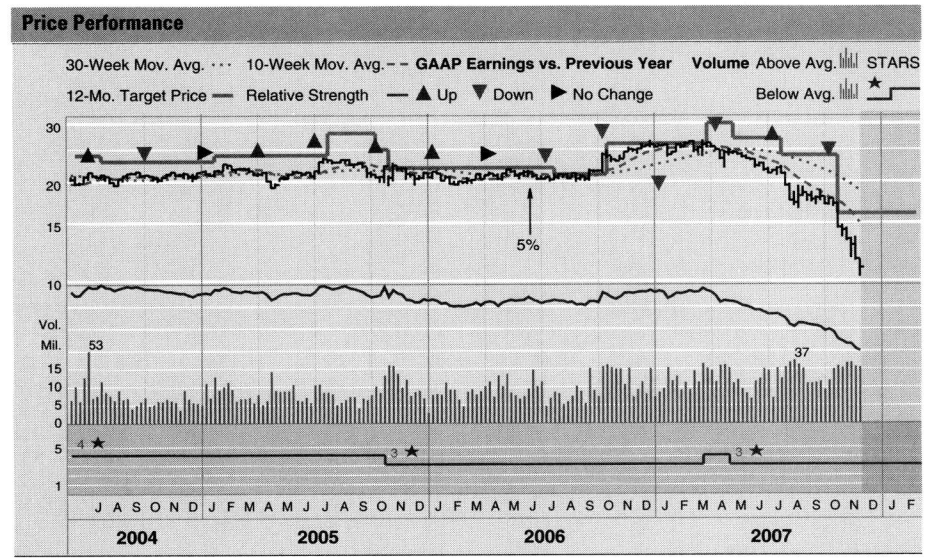

- 30-Week Mov. Avg. ···· 10-Week Mov. Avg. – – GAAP Earnings vs. Previous Year   Volume Above Avg. STARS
- 12-Mo. Target Price — Relative Strength — ▲ Up ▼ Down ▶ No Change   Below Avg. ★

Options: ASE, CBOE, P, Ph

Analysis prepared by **Stuart Plesser** on October 24, 2007, when the stock traded at **$14.09**.

Highlights

➤ We believe SOV's total revenue will likely rise modestly in 2008, helped by growth in net interest income, but offset by higher loss provisions and a reduction in output from the mortgage banking unit. Our 2008 estimates include a net interest margin of 2.80% (up from projected 2.7% in 2007 due to lower funding costs and repositioning of the balance sheet), earning asset growth of 3%, and a 3.0% increase in non-interest income.

➤ We look for SOV's expenses as a percentage of revenue to hold steady at 61.5% in 2008 from a projected 61.4% in 2007, assuming only modest revenue growth. Credit quality will likely deteriorate in 2008, and charge-offs should continue to rise necessitating a high level of provisions. Specifically, we expect loan loss provisions of about $380 million in 2008, up from a projected $340 million in 2007. Reserves seem a bit light, by our analysis, totaling roughly 240% of non-performing loans.

➤ Assuming a 16.0% effective tax rate for 2007, we estimate operating EPS of $1.10, versus $1.46 in 2006. Our 2008 EPS estimate is $1.09.

Investment Rationale/Risk

➤ Higher provisions due to deteriorating credit conditions will likely hamper SOV's earnings growth over the near term. We believe the company will need to continue to boost reserves in the quarters to come. Some of the added expenses should be offset by a higher net interest margin largely due to balance sheet repositioning. Also, expense initiatives implemented last year are gaining traction and should bolster the bottom line. We note that Banco Santander (STD: buy, $20) has an option to buy SOV at $40 a share starting in June 2008. However, we believe that STD's involvement in the buyout of another European bank could limit its appetite for SOV over the near term.

➤ Risks to our recommendation and target price include an inverted yield curve, and an operating performance that fails to meet our expectations. Regarding corporate governance, we are concerned about SOV's practice of staggering annual elections for directors.

➤ Our 12-month target price of $16 is derived by applying a multiple of 14.7X our 2008 EPS estimate, a premium to peers, due to the possibility of a buyout.

Qualitative Risk Assessment

LOW	MEDIUM	HIGH

Our risk assessment reflects SOV's mid-cap valuation and our view of the strong credit quality of the company's loan portfolio and its history of profitability. While the industry in which the company operates is highly competitive and fragmented, it tends to produce relatively stable financial results.

Quantitative Evaluations

S&P Quality Ranking B+

D	C	B-	B	B+	A-	A	A+

Relative Strength Rank WEAK

8

LOWEST = 1   HIGHEST = 99

Revenue/Earnings Data

Revenue (Million $)

	1Q	2Q	3Q	4Q	Year
2007	1,274	1,330	1,293	--	--
2006	973.9	829.0	1,442	1,367	4,612
2005	802.5	872.0	921.2	969.6	3,565
2004	627.6	639.7	714.1	726.0	2,706
2003	621.6	621.5	601.8	607.2	2,452
2002	602.4	622.1	634.5	633.1	2,492

Earnings Per Share ($)

	1Q	2Q	3Q	4Q	Year
2007	0.09	0.29	0.11	E0.28	E1.10
2006	0.36	-0.15	0.37	-0.28	0.30
2005	0.36	0.45	0.46	0.42	1.69
2004	0.31	0.40	0.23	0.36	1.30
2003	0.26	0.35	0.35	0.36	1.31
2002	0.24	0.30	0.31	0.31	1.17

Fiscal year ended Dec. 31. Next earnings report expected: Mid January. EPS Estimates based on S&P Operating Earnings; historical GAAP earnings are as reported.

Dividend Data (Dates: mm/dd Payment Date: mm/dd/yy)

Amount ($)	Date Decl.	Ex-Div. Date	Stk. of Record	Payment Date
0.080	01/23	01/31	02/02	02/15/07
0.080	04/17	04/27	05/01	05/15/07
0.080	07/17	07/30	08/01	08/15/07
0.080	10/18	10/30	11/01	11/15/07

Dividends have been paid since 1987. Source: Company reports.

Please read the Required Disclosures and Analyst Certification on the last page of this report.

The McGraw-Hill Companies

Sovereign Bancorp Inc.

Business Summary October 24, 2007

CORPORATE OVERVIEW. Sovereign Bancorp, once a small thrift, has grown into a large banking franchise, with nearly $90 billion in assets as of December 2006. The company has grown largely through acquisitions. From 1990 through December 2005, SOV acquired 27 financial institutions, branch networks and/or related businesses. From 1995, 17 of these acquisitions had assets totaling approximately $35 billion.

The company has nearly 800 community banking offices, and over 2,000 ATMs located principally in Pennsylvania, New Jersey, Connecticut, New Hampshire, Rhode Island, Massachusetts New York, and Maryland. SOV, which gathers substantially all of its deposits in these market areas, uses them, as well as other financing sources, to fund its loan and investment portfolios. SOV earns interest on its loan portfolio. In addition, the company generates non-interest income from a number of sources, including deposit and loan services, sales of residential loans and investment securities, capital markets products and bank-owned life insurance. SOV's principal non-interest expense includes employee compensation and benefits, occupancy and facility-related costs, technology and other administrative expenses.

PRIMARY BUSINESS DYNAMICS. SOV's financial results highly correlate with the economic environment, including interest rates, consumer and business confidence and spending, as well as competitive conditions. The company be-

lieves that its major strengths are: strong franchise value in terms of market share and demographics; a stable low-cost core deposit base; a diversified loan portfolio and products; a strong service culture; and the ability to cross-sell multiple product lines.

As of December 31, 2006, total loans of $62.5 billion were 28% residential real estate loans, 39.5% commercial loans, and 32.5% consumer loans (mostly home equity and auto loans). We look for residential loans to decline in 2007 as the company will likely deemphasize its multi-family loan business. As of December 31, 2006, deposits totaling $52.4 billion consisted of 13% demand accounts, 57% core accounts, and 31% CDs. The company is attempting to attract more low-cost deposits by launching new products and services such as remote image capture, remote check clearing, and health savings accounts. We think this will help widen net margins. The allowance for loan losses at December 31, 2006 was $471.0 million (equal to 2.1X total non-performing assets), up from $419.6 million (2.0X) a year earlier. Net charge-offs in 2006 totaled $139.4 million (0.25 of average loans), compared to $81.7 million (0.20) in 2005.

Company Financials Fiscal Year Ended Dec. 31

Per Share Data ($)	2006	2005	2004	2003	2002	2001	2000	1999	1998	1997
Tangible Book Value	5.75	7.60	7.11	6.30	5.02	3.24	2.04	5.74	4.51	4.78
Earnings	0.30	1.69	1.30	1.31	1.17	0.46	-0.17	0.96	0.81	0.60
S&P Core Earnings	0.30	1.68	1.28	1.31	1.15	0.38	NA	NA	NA	NA
Dividends	0.29	0.16	0.11	0.10	0.10	0.10	0.10	0.09	0.07	0.07
Payout Ratio	98%	10%	8%	7%	8%	21%	NM	9%	9%	11%
Prices:High	26.60	23.61	23.57	24.00	15.14	12.86	9.49	25.00	21.67	17.56
Prices:Low	19.47	19.10	18.39	12.00	10.67	6.82	5.95	6.67	8.33	8.52
P/E Ratio:High	89	14	18	18	13	28	NM	26	27	29
P/E Ratio:Low	65	11	14	9	9	15	NM	7	10	14

Income Statement Analysis (Million $)	2006	2005	2004	2003	2002	2001	2000	1999	1998	1997
Net Interest Income	1,822	1,588	1,405	1,206	1,160	1,054	855	615	494	341
Loan Loss Provision	484	90.0	127	162	147	97.1	56.5	30.0	28.0	37.2
Non Interest Income	598	635	468	456	381	411	230	130	106	38.5
Non Interest Expenses	1,547	2,319	2,100	968	979	1,175	1,013	446	360	212
Pretax Income	19.1	915	603	598	467	209	-106	269	211	130
Effective Tax Rate	NM	23.6%	21.2%	25.6%	26.7%	12.7%	NM	33.3%	35.4%	40.3%
Net Income	137	676	454	402	342	123	-41.0	179	136	77.6
% Net Interest Margin	2.75	3.09	3.24	3.42	3.61	3.57	3.19	2.86	2.56	2.68
S&P Core Earnings	127	669	450	401	336	101	NA	NA	NA	NA

Balance Sheet & Other Financial Data (Million $)	2006	2005	2004	2003	2002	2001	2000	1999	1998	1997
Total Assets	89,642	63,679	54,471	43,505	39,524	35,475	33,458	26,607	21,914	14,336
Loans	62,118	43,384	36,222	25,821	22,829	20,135	21,656	14,094	11,152	9,833
Deposits	52,385	37,978	32,556	27,344	26,785	23,298	24,499	11,720	12,323	7,890
Capitalization:Debt	9,181	9,330	9,642	12,124	6,240	6,869	5,367	316	4,108	858
Capitalization:Equity	8,449	5,811	4,988	3,260	2,764	2,202	1,949	1,821	1,204	682
Capitalization:Total	17,982	15,347	14,834	15,587	9,205	2,202	7,315	2,138	5,312	1,733
% Return on Assets	0.2	1.1	0.9	1.0	0.9	0.4	NM	19.2	82.7	12.6
% Return on Equity	1.9	12.5	11.0	13.3	13.8	5.9	NM	11.9	13.8	13.5
% Loan Loss Reserve	0.8	1.0	1.1	1.3	1.3	1.3	1.2	-0.9	1.2	0.9
% Risk Based Capital	10.1	10.7	11.6	12.1	7.6	10.7	10.3	14.9	10.3	12.2
Price Times Book Value:High	4.6	3.1	3.3	3.8	3.0	2.9	4.6	4.4	4.8	4.4
Price Times Book Value:Low	3.4	2.5	2.6	1.9	2.1	1.8	2.9	1.2	1.9	2.1

Data as orig reptd.; bef. results of disc opers/spec. items. Per share data adj. for stk. divs.; EPS diluted. E-Estimated. NA-Not Available. NM-Not Meaningful. NR-Not Ranked. UR-Under Review.

Office: 1500 Market St, Philadelphia, PA 19102-2100.
Telephone: 215-557-4630.
Email: investor@sovereignbank.com
Website: http://www.sovereignbank.com

Chrmn: P.M. Ehlerman
Pres & CEO: J.P. Campanelli
Vice Chrmn: J.J. Lynch
Vice Chrmn & Chief Admin Officer: L.M. Thompson, Jr.

CFO: M.R. McCollum
Investor Contact: S. Weikel (610-208-6112)
Board Members: J. P. Campanelli, P. M. Ehlerman, B. Hard, M. L. Heard, A. C. Hove, Jr., W. J. Moran, M. F. Ramirez, J. Rodriguez-Inciarte, D. K. Rothermel, A. Sanchez, J. S. Sidhu, C. C. Troilo, Sr., R. V. Whitworth

Founded: 1984
Domicile: Pennsylvania
Employees: 12,513

Spectra Energy Corp

**STANDARD
&POOR'S**

S&P Recommendation	HOLD ★★★☆☆	Price	12-Mo. Target Price	Investment Style
		$24.48 (as of Nov 23, 2007)	$29.00	Large-Cap Blend

GICS Sector Energy
Sub-Industry Oil & Gas Storage & Transportation

Summary This integrated natural gas holding company is engaged in gas gathering and processing and gas transportation and storage in the U.S. and Canada, and retail gas distribution to 1.3 million customers in Ontario, Canada.

Key Stock Statistics (Source S&P, Vickers, company reports)

52-Wk Range	$30.00– 21.24	S&P Oper. EPS 2007E	1.43	Market Capitalization(B)	$15.474	Beta		NA
Trailing 12-Month EPS	NA	S&P Oper. EPS 2008E	1.52	Yield (%)	3.59	S&P 3-Yr. Proj. EPS CAGR(%)		NM
Trailing 12-Month P/E	NM	P/E on S&P Oper. EPS 2007E	17.1	Dividend Rate/Share	$0.88	S&P Credit Rating		NA
$10K Invested 5 Yrs Ago	NA	Common Shares Outstg. (M)	632.1	Institutional Ownership (%)	68			

Price Performance

30-Week Mov. Avg. ···   10-Week Mov. Avg. - -   **GAAP Earnings vs. Previous Year**   Volume Above Avg. ▌▋▍▐ STARS
12-Mo. Target Price —   Relative Strength —   ▲ Up   ▼ Down   ► No Change   Below Avg. ▌▋▍▐ ★

Options: ASE, CBOE

Analysis prepared by **Stephen Ham, CFA** on November 15, 2007, when the stock traded at **$ 24.56**.

Highlights

➤ SE, which had its initial public offering in January 2007, reported third quarter continuing EPS of $0.37 with a 22% increase in continuing net income, above with our $0.25 estimate on 10% higher revenue. We expect revenues to be flat in 2007 with 6.4% growth in 2008. The company's largest segment, U.S. Transmission, is expected to have solid results in 2007 as throughput for the first nine months of 2007 was up 14%. We see the company's reorganization efforts of 2007 beginning to have an impact on its growth strategy in 2008.

➤ SE expects to spend about $ 3.0 billion on capital expenditures from 2007-2009 with $1.0 billion in 2007. Expansion projects include the $240 million pipeline connecting Excelerate's deepwater LNG port in Massachusetts Bay to the Algonquin pipeline (2007), the $210 million pipeline expansion between Ohio and New Jersey (2007, 2008), and the $320 million Maritimes & Northeast pipeline expansion connecting with an LNG port in New Brunswick, Canada (2008).

➤ We estimate 2007 operating EPS of $1.43, compared to our pro forma 2006 estimate of $1.44. We expect 2008 EPS to increase 6.3%, to $1.52.

Investment Rationale/Risk

➤ SE became an independent company on January 2, 2007, after Duke Energy's spinoff of its natural gas businesses. SE operates a large and diverse portfolio of natural gas transportation and storage assets in various parts of the U.S. and Canada. In July 2007, the company spun off some assets into Spectra Energy Partners L.P. and received $345 million. With over $3 billion in expansion projects planned for the next three years, including $1 billion to be spent in 2007, we believe SE is well positioned for continued cash flow and distribution growth. Our hold opinion is based on valuation.

➤ Risks to our opinion and target price include a slowdown in natural gas production growth, declines in long-term natural gas prices, higher interest rates than expected, and warmer than normal winter weather.

➤ Our 12-month target price of $29 is 19X our 12-month forward EPS estimate, a discount to peers. We believe the discount is warranted by our forecast for a slightly below-average EPS growth rate for the company and SE's current reorganization.

Qualitative Risk Assessment

LOW	MEDIUM	HIGH

Our risk assessment reflects the company's large market capitalization and the lower risk inherent in its regulated gas transmission and distribution businesses, offset by its investments in higher-risk gas gathering and processing businesses.

Quantitative Evaluations

S&P Quality Ranking   NR

D	C	B-	B	B+	A-	A	A+

Relative Strength Rank   MODERATE

69

LOWEST = 1   HIGHEST = 99

Revenue/Earnings Data

Revenue (Million $)

	1Q	2Q	3Q	4Q	Year
2007	1,401	985.0	959.0	--	--
2006	NA	NA	NA	--	4,532
2005	--	--	--	--	4,132
2004	--	--	--	--	--
2003	--	--	--	--	--
2002	--	--	--	--	--

Earnings Per Share ($)

2007	0.37	0.29	0.38	E0.37	E1.43
2006	NA	NA	NA	--	NA
2005	--	--	--	--	1.07
2004	--	--	--	--	--
2003	--	--	--	--	--
2002	--	--	--	--	--

Fiscal year ended Dec. 31. Next earnings report expected: NA. EPS Estimates based on S&P Operating Earnings; historical GAAP earnings are as reported.

Dividend Data (Dates: mm/dd Payment Date: mm/dd/yy)

Amount ($)	Date Decl.	Ex-Div. Date	Stk. of Record	Payment Date
0.220	01/08	02/14	02/16	03/15/07
0.220	04/04	05/09	05/11	06/18/07
0.220	07/02	08/15	08/17	09/17/07
0.220	10/31	11/14	11/16	12/17/07

Dividends have been paid since 2007. Source: Company reports.

Please read the Required Disclosures and Analyst Certification on the last page of this report.

The McGraw-Hill Companies

Spectra Energy Corp

STANDARD &POOR'S

Business Summary November 15, 2007

CORPORATE OVERVIEW. SE owns and operates a diversified portfolio of natural gas-related energy assets and is primarily a natural gas midstream company. The company operates in three areas of the natural gas industry: transmission and storage, distribution, and gathering and processing. SE also owns a natural gas distribution company, Union Gas, and participates in a 50%-owned joint venture, DCP Midstream.

MARKET PROFILE. The company manages its business in four segments: U.S. Transmission, Distribution, Western Canada Transmission and Processing, and Field Services.

The U.S. Transmission segment provides transportation and storage of natural gas for customers in the eastern and southeastern U.S. and the Maritime provinces of Canada. The segment has 12,915 miles of natural gas pipelines and 85 billion cubic feet (bcf) of storage capacity. The company's largest pipeline, Texas Eastern Transmission, is 9,040 miles, has a capacity of 6.2 billion cubic feet per day (bcf/d), and has 75.1 bcf of storage capacity. The pipeline connects Gulf Coast gas supply to demand centers in the Northeast, as well as to the East Tennessee Natural Gas and Algonquin Gas Transmission pipelines. The Algonquin pipeline can transport 1.9 bcf/d and connects to both the Texas Eastern and Maritimes and Northeast pipelines to provide gas

to areas between Boston, MA, and northern New Jersey. The East Tennessee pipeline brings gas from the Texas Eastern pipeline through eastern Tennessee as far as Roanoke, VA. The 50%-owned Gulfstream pipeline brings natural gas into the fast growing state of Florida. The Maritimes and Northeast pipeline provides Sable Island area Canadian natural gas down into the Boston area and helps to supply the Algonquin pipeline. The segment also operates other pipeline interconnection assets and storage assets.

The Distribution segment provides retail natural gas distribution in Ontario, Canada, as well as natural gas transportation and storage services to other utilities and energy market participants in Ontario, Quebec and the U.S. Union Gas is the company's regulated transmission and distribution subsidiary, serving 1.3 million customers in 400 communities throughout Ontario, Canada. Union Gas distributes its gas through 21,600 miles of distribution pipelines and owns 2,750 miles of transmission pipelines and 150 bcf of high deliverability storage.

Company Financials Fiscal Year Ended Dec. 31

Per Share Data ($)	2006	2005	2004	2003	2002	2001	2000	1999	1998	1997
Tangible Book Value	NM	NA	NA	NA	NA	NA	NA	NA	NA	NA
Cash Flow	NA	2.04	NA	NA	NA	NA	NA	NA	NA	NA
Earnings	NA	1.07	NA	NA	NA	NA	NA	NA	NA	NA
S&P Core Earnings	NA	NA	NA	NA	NA	NA	NA	NA	NA	NA
Dividends	Nil	Nil	NA	NA	NA	NA	NA	NA	NA	NA
Payout Ratio	Nil	Nil	NA	NA	NA	NA	NA	NA	NA	NA
Prices:High	29.00	NA	NA	NA	NA	NA	NA	NA	NA	NA
Prices:Low	27.50	NA	NA	NA	NA	NA	NA	NA	NA	NA
P/E Ratio:High	NA	NA	NA	NA	NA	NA	NA	NA	NA	NA
P/E Ratio:Low	NA	NA	NA	NA	NA	NA	NA	NA	NA	NA

Income Statement Analysis (Million $)										
Revenue	4,532	4,132	NA	NA	NA	NA	NA	NA	NA	NA
Operating Income	1,804	1,697	NA	NA	NA	NA	NA	NA	NA	NA
Depreciation	606	458	NA	NA	NA	NA	NA	NA	NA	NA
Interest Expense	605	607	NA	NA	NA	NA	NA	NA	NA	NA
Pretax Income	1,376	862	NA	NA	NA	NA	NA	NA	NA	NA
Effective Tax Rate	28.7%	41.7%	NA	NA	NA	NA	NA	NA	NA	NA
Net Income	936	502	NA	NA	NA	NA	NA	NA	NA	NA
S&P Core Earnings	926	NA	NA	NA	NA	NA	NA	NA	NA	NA

Balance Sheet & Other Financial Data (Million $)										
Cash	299	NA	NA	NA	NA	NA	NA	NA	NA	NA
Current Assets	1,625	18,601	NA	NA	NA	NA	NA	NA	NA	NA
Total Assets	20,345	21,442	NA	NA	NA	NA	NA	NA	NA	NA
Current Liabilities	2,358	2,052	NA	NA	NA	NA	NA	NA	NA	NA
Long Term Debt	7,726	7,957	NA	NA	NA	NA	NA	NA	NA	NA
Common Equity	5,639	5,225	NA	NA	NA	NA	NA	NA	NA	NA
Total Capital	16,910	16,100	NA	NA	NA	NA	NA	NA	NA	NA
Capital Expenditures	987	NA	NA	NA	NA	NA	NA	NA	NA	NA
Cash Flow	1,542	960	NA	NA	NA	NA	NA	NA	NA	NA
Current Ratio	0.7	NA	NA	NA	NA	NA	NA	NA	NA	NA
% Long Term Debt of Capitalization	45.7	NA	NA	NA	NA	NA	NA	NA	NA	NA
% Net Income of Revenue	20.7	NA	NA	NA	NA	NA	NA	NA	NA	NA
% Return on Assets	3.4	NA	NA	NA	NA	NA	NA	NA	NA	NA
% Return on Equity	10.9	NA	NA	NA	NA	NA	NA	NA	NA	NA

Data as orig reptd.; bef. results of disc opers/spec. items. Per share data adj. for stk. divs.; EPS diluted. E-Estimated. NA-Not Available. NM-Not Meaningful. NR-Not Ranked. UR-Under Review.

Office: 5400 Westheimer Court, Houston, TX 77056-5310.
Telephone: 713-627-5400 .
Website: http://www.spectraenergy.com
Chrmn: P.M. Anderson

Pres & CEO: F.J. Fowler
VP & Treas: K.A. Crane
VP & Cntlr: S.L. Harrington
CFO: G.L. Ebel

Investor Contact: J. Arensdorf (713-627-4600)
Board Members: A. A. Adams, R. Agnelli, P. M. Anderson, P. L. Carter, W. T. Esrey, F. J. Fowler, P. B. Hamilton, D. R. Hendrix, M. E. Phelps, M. B. Wyrsch

Founded: 2006
Domicile: Delaware
Employees: 4,950

Sprint Nextel Corp

STANDARD &POOR'S

| S&P Recommendation **HOLD** ★★★★☆ | Price $15.08 (as of Nov 23, 2007) | 12-Mo. Target Price $18.00 | Investment Style Large-Cap Value |

GICS Sector Telecommunication Services
Sub-Industry Wireless Telecommunication Services

Summary This leading provider of wireless and other telecommunications services was formed in August 2005 via the merger of Sprint Corp. and Nextel Communications, Inc.

Key Stock Statistics (Source S&P, Vickers, company reports)

52-Wk Range	$23.42– 14.67	S&P Oper. EPS 2007**E**	0.88	Market Capitalization(B)	$42.432	Beta	1.65
Trailing 12-Month EPS	$0.16	S&P Oper. EPS 2008**E**	0.93	Yield (%)	0.66	S&P 3-Yr. Proj. EPS CAGR(%)	4.00
Trailing 12-Month P/E	94.3	P/E on S&P Oper. EPS 2007**E**	17.1	Dividend Rate/Share	$0.10	S&P Credit Rating	BBB
$10K Invested 5 Yrs Ago	NA	Common Shares Outstg. (M)	2,891.0	Institutional Ownership (%)	91		

Price Performance

30-Week Mov. Avg. ···   10-Week Mov. Avg.- -   GAAP Earnings vs. Previous Year   Volume Above Avg. STARS
12-Mo. Target Price —   Relative Strength —   ▲ Up ▼ Down ► No Change   Below Avg.

Options: ASE, CBOE, P, Ph

Analysis prepared by **James Moorman** on November 05, 2007, when the stock traded at **$ 17.01**.

Highlights

► We project a decline in revenues of 1.0% in 2007 and then an increase of 1.2% in 2008, as S begins to reposition its wireless business (86% of projected revenues), which is expected to result in above average customer churn. We believe the company will continue to have difficulty balancing between expanding its postpaid customer base in 2008 and retaining customers as the company migrates its subscriber base. In addition, we believe the increased focus on growth in prepaid operations could weigh on ARPU. Within global markets, we see slight declines in revenues from competitive pressures.

► We estimate total EBITDA margins of 26.3% in 2007 and 26.8% in 2008, versus 29.4% in 2006, as we think S needs more time to realize cost savings from multiple acquisitions and the cost of slowly migrating its customer base to one network. We believe controlling marketing costs could improve margins, but we see challenges as S looks to regain wireless market share. We believe margins will be supported by cost reductions in the global markets segment.

► We estimate operating EPS of $0.88 in 2007 and $0.93 in 2008.

Investment Rationale/Risk

► In our opinion, the company is in a transition, trying to regain favor with customers as competitors take market share, and spending on new unproven technology. We expect S to offer handset subsidies to stimulate subscriber growth, which should limit wireless EBITDA growth even as cost reduction efforts are under way. We believe that continued uncertainty due to the change in management and the related potential change in corporate direction will prevent the shares from appreciating in the near term.

► Risks to our recommendation and target price include weaker execution in realizing merger cost savings, higher capital spending to deploy new services, a significant change in S's WiMAX strategy, and increased competition from nationwide peers that could lead to delayed growth in subscriber additions.

► Our 12-month target price of $18 assumes an enterprise value of 6.5X our 2008 EBITDA estimate, in line with larger-cap telecom peers, due to S's higher wireless exposure, but below smaller pure-play wireless carriers that we think have stronger growth prospects.

Qualitative Risk Assessment

| LOW | **MEDIUM** | HIGH |

As one of the weakest national wireless carriers, S's free cash flow could be pressured in the near term, in our view. We believe these risks are offset by a strong balance sheet and a reduction in its operating expenses.

Quantitative Evaluations

S&P Quality Ranking B

| D | C | B- | **B** | B+ | A- | A | A+ |

Relative Strength Rank WEAK

23

LOWEST = 1   HIGHEST = 99

Revenue/Earnings Data

Revenue (Million $)

	1Q	2Q	3Q	4Q	Year
2007	10,096	10,162	10,044	--	--
2006	11,548	10,014	10,496	10,444	41,028
2005	6,936	7,113	9,335	11,296	34,680
2004	6,707	6,869	6,922	6,930	27,428
2003	3,581	3,530	3,538	3,536	14,185
2002	4,029	3,965	3,805	3,659	15,182

Earnings Per Share ($)

2007	-0.07	0.01	0.02	E0.24	E0.88
2006	0.14	0.10	0.08	0.09	0.34
2005	0.32	0.40	0.23	0.07	0.87
2004	0.16	0.16	-1.32	0.29	-0.71
2003	0.31	0.10	-0.48	0.40	0.33
2002	0.32	0.12	0.54	0.28	1.18

Fiscal year ended Dec. 31. Next earnings report expected: Late February. EPS Estimates based on S&P Operating Earnings; historical GAAP earnings are as reported.

Dividend Data (Dates: mm/dd Payment Date: mm/dd/yy)

Amount ($)	Date Decl.	Ex-Div. Date	Stk. of Record	Payment Date
0.025	02/27	03/07	03/09	03/30/07
0.025	05/08	06/06	06/08	06/29/07
0.025	08/07	09/05	09/07	09/28/07
0.025	11/05	12/05	12/07	12/28/07

Dividends have been paid since 1939. Source: Company reports.

Sprint Nextel Corp

Business Summary November 05, 2007

CORPORATE OVERVIEW. On August 15, 2005, the shares of Sprint Nextel Corp. began trading under the symbol S. The company has a balanced mix of consumer, business and government wireless customers. S spun off to shareholders the local telephone business in May 2006. As of the 2007 third quarter, S provided service to just under 54 million wireless subscribers, with 77% of them direct post-paid customers, while 8% were prepaid (Boost Mobile), and 13% were wholesale customers (from Virgin Mobile, Qwest Communications and others). S also generates revenues from wireline voice and data communication services and services to the cable multiple systems operators that use S's network and back-office capabilities.

COMPETITIVE LANDSCAPE. In most major U.S. metropolitan markets, four national carriers offer competing wireless services to customers along with some regional carriers. Wireless carriers such as S have adjusted to potential substitutes by integrating the service features into the handsets. Until recently, S had a unique service with push-to-talk service through Nextel's iDEN network, but AT&T (formerly Cingular) has launched a competing nationwide service aimed at the consumer segment, in contrast to S's dominant position with small business and enterprise firms. In our opinion, S needs to better in-

tegrate Nextel and other affiliates into a unified brand and improve quality of service to its customers.

Wireless services are very price elastic. For the consumer market, service rate plans have taken on new features such as $9.99 for each family member added to the account. S realized 2.3% post-paid churn in the third quarter of 2007, above that of its larger peers, but generated $59 in average revenue per user (ARPU). Pre-paid customers had a 6.2% churn rate and generated $30 in ARPU. The company plans to expand its Boost Unlimited plan to an additional 10 states, which we believe will add to subscriber growth but could reduce ARPU. Expanding its post-paid customer base and retaining its high-end subscribers will be key priorities for S, in our opinion. In the first nine months of 2007, S had a net loss of roughly 541,000 post-paid customers, while peers added 3 million to 4 million.

Company Financials Fiscal Year Ended Dec. 31

Per Share Data ($)	2006	2005	2004	2003	2002	2001	2000	1999	1998	1997
Tangible Book Value	NM	0.88	3.85	14.40	11.45	11.41	13.95	10.42	10.45	10.52
Cash Flow	3.67	3.93	2.56	3.12	4.14	2.60	4.00	-4.35	7.19	3.07
Earnings	0.34	0.87	-0.71	0.33	1.18	-0.16	1.45	1.97	1.78	1.09
S&P Core Earnings	0.30	0.86	-0.72	1.20	1.26	-0.12	NA	NA	NA	NA
Dividends	0.13	0.30	0.50	0.50	0.50	0.50	0.50	0.50	0.50	0.50
Payout Ratio	37%	34%	NM	152%	42%	NM	34%	25%	28%	46%
Prices:High	26.89	27.20	25.80	16.76	20.47	29.31	67.81	75.94	42.66	30.31
Prices:Low	15.92	21.57	15.74	10.22	6.65	18.50	19.63	36.88	27.63	19.19
P/E Ratio:High	79	31	NM	51	17	NM	47	39	24	28
P/E Ratio:Low	47	25	NM	31	6	NM	14	19	16	18

Income Statement Analysis (Million $)										
Revenue	41,028	34,680	27,428	14,185	15,182	16,924	17,688	17,016	17,135	14,874
Operating Income	12,283	10,220	8,148	4,376	4,488	4,238	5,101	-5,059	3,075	4,178
Depreciation	9,592	6,269	4,720	2,519	2,645	2,449	2,267	2,129	2,705	1,726
Interest Expense	1,533	1,351	1,248	236	295	57.0	76.0	182	895	280
Pretax Income	1,817	2,906	-1,603	434	1,453	-129	2,170	-2,797	698	1,583
Effective Tax Rate	26.9%	38.0%	NM	32.3%	28.0%	NM	40.5%	37.9%	56.2%	39.8%
Net Income	1,329	1,801	-1,012	294	1,046	-146	1,292	-1,736	457	953
S&P Core Earnings	849	1,772	-1,036	1,096	1,132	-112	NA	NA	NA	NA

Balance Sheet & Other Financial Data (Million $)										
Cash	2,061	10,665	4,556	1,635	641	134	122	104	605	102
Current Assets	10,304	19,092	9,975	4,378	3,327	3,485	4,512	4,282	4,388	3,773
Total Assets	97,161	102,580	41,321	21,862	23,043	24,164	23,649	21,803	33,231	18,185
Current Liabilities	9,798	14,050	6,902	2,359	4,320	6,298	5,004	4,301	4,551	3,077
Long Term Debt	21,011	Nil	15,916	2,627	2,736	3,258	3,482	4,531	11,942	3,755
Common Equity	53,131	51,937	13,521	13,372	11,814	11,704	12,343	10,514	12,202	9,025
Total Capital	84,237	52,184	29,684	17,632	16,385	16,514	17,101	15,980	26,221	13,809
Capital Expenditures	7,556	5,057	3,980	1,674	2,181	5,295	4,105	3,534	42,311	2,863
Cash Flow	10,919	8,063	3,701	2,821	3,698	2,310	3,566	-3,858	3,156	2,678
Current Ratio	1.1	1.4	1.4	1.9	0.8	0.6	0.9	1.0	1.0	1.2
% Long Term Debt of Capitalization	24.9	Nil	53.6	14.9	16.7	19.7	20.4	28.4	45.5	27.1
% Net Income of Revenue	3.2	5.2	NM	2.1	6.9	NM	7.3	10.2	2.6	6.4
% Return on Assets	1.3	2.5	NM	1.3	4.4	NM	5.7	8.5	1.8	5.4
% Return on Equity	2.5	5.5	NM	2.3	8.8	NM	11.2	17.7	4.2	10.8

Data as orig reptd.; bef. results of disc opers/spec. items. Per share data adj. for stk. divs.; EPS diluted. E-Estimated. NA-Not Available. NM-Not Meaningful. NR-Not Ranked. UR-Under Review.

Office: 2001 Edmund Halley Dr, Reston, VA 20191-3436.
Telephone: 703-433-4000.
Email: investorrelation.sprintcom@mail.sprint.com
Website: http://www.sprint.com

Chrmn, Pres & CEO: G.D. Forsee
VP & Secy: C.A. Hill
CFO: P.N. Selah
CTO: B. West

General Counsel: L.J. Kennedy
Board Members: K. J. Bane, R. R. Bennett, G. M. Bethune, F. M. Drendel, G. D. Forsee, J. H. Hance, Jr., V. J. Hill, I. O. Hockaday, Jr., L. K. Lorimer, W. H. Swanson

Founded: 1925
Domicile: Kansas
Employees: 64,600

Stanley Works (The)

STANDARD &POOR'S

S&P Recommendation STRONG BUY ★★★★★	**Price** $49.84 (as of Nov 23, 2007)	**12-Mo. Target Price** $72.00	**Investment Style** Large-Cap Blend

GICS Sector Consumer Discretionary
Sub-Industry Household Appliances

Summary This company is a worldwide producer of tools, hardware and specialty hardware for home improvement, consumer, industrial and professional use.

Key Stock Statistics (Source S&P, Vickers, company reports)

52-Wk Range	$64.25– 48.61	S&P Oper. EPS 2007**E**	4.00	Market Capitalization(B)	$4.096	Beta	1.30
Trailing 12-Month EPS	$3.92	S&P Oper. EPS 2008**E**	4.70	Yield (%)	2.49	S&P 3-Yr. Proj. EPS CAGR(%)	15.00
Trailing 12-Month P/E	12.7	P/E on S&P Oper. EPS 2007**E**	12.5	Dividend Rate/Share	$1.24	S&P Credit Rating	A
$10K Invested 5 Yrs Ago	$16,163	Common Shares Outstg. (M)	82.2	Institutional Ownership (%)	81		

Price Performance

30-Week Mov. Avg. ··· 10-Week Mov. Avg. -- **GAAP Earnings vs. Previous Year** Volume Above Avg. STARS
12-Mo. Target Price — Relative Strength — ▲ Up ▼ Down ► No Change Below Avg. ★

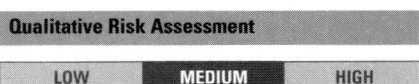

Options: P

Analysis prepared by **Kenneth M. Leon, CPA** on October 24, 2007, when the stock traded at **$ 57.67**.

Highlights

➤ We project that total sales will rise about 6% to 8% in 2008, after a 10% increase forecast in 2007 from volume growth, price increases, and acquisitions. Should the housing market rebound in 2008, we think the company would grow faster than our base line sales forecast of upper single digit growth.

➤ We expect the sales advance in Construction and Security Solutions to outpace total company growth, while Industrial Tools segment may lag, as we think the fastening area will remain a challenge in the near term. We believe that benefits achieved from recent acquisitions will outweigh restructuring charges. SWK closed on its acquisition of HSM Electronic Protection Services, a Chicago-based provider of security control systems, for about $545 million in January 2007.

➤ We look for operating margins to widen to 14.6% in 2007 and 14.8% in 2008, from 2006's 12.5%. After taxes we expect at an effective rate near 27%, higher than the 21% rate of 2006, we see operating EPS of $4.00 in 2007 rising to $4.70 in 2008.

Investment Rationale/Risk

➤ We are positive on SWK's ability to profitably grow its diversified businesses that are benefiting from strong economies outside the U.S. market and focused cost control efforts and synergies from acquisitions. Despite a weakening U.S. economy, we believe SWK is well positioned to take advantage of stable demand from the commercial construction market and a potential rebound in the U.S. housing market in 2008.

➤ Risks to our recommendation and target price include the possibility of an unexpected weakening in the company's major markets, lower-than-projected synergies from SWK's recent acquisitions, an inability to achieve the Security Solutions segment's target margin, and intense competition.

➤ Our 12-month target price of $72 applies a P/E of 15.3X to our 12-month forward operating EPS estimate of $4.70. This is approximately in line with SWK's peer group multiple and SWK's five-year historical average, a level we believe that is merited by a mix of growth opportunities and challenging macroeconomic factors we foresee.

Qualitative Risk Assessment

LOW	MEDIUM	HIGH

Our risk assessment takes into account our positive view of SWK's strong brand name and solid competitive position, offset by our negative view of industry cyclicality.

Quantitative Evaluations

S&P Quality Ranking B+

D	C	B-	B	B+	A-	A	A+

Relative Strength Rank MODERATE

35

LOWEST = 1   HIGHEST = 99

Revenue/Earnings Data

Revenue (Million $)

	1Q	2Q	3Q	4Q	Year
2007	1,062	1,123	1,131	--	--
2006	968.7	1,018	1,013	1,019	4,019
2005	796.3	814.7	834.9	839.4	3,285
2004	734.8	753.9	751.8	802.9	3,043
2003	632.2	652.6	665.6	727.7	2,678
2002	616.7	649.1	665.5	661.7	2,594

Earnings Per Share ($)

2007	0.80	1.01	1.09	E1.11	E4.00
2006	0.45	0.90	1.09	1.04	3.47
2005	0.78	0.77	0.89	0.75	3.18
2004	0.66	0.70	0.73	0.77	2.85
2003	0.22	0.11	0.46	0.38	1.14
2002	0.56	0.72	0.62	0.20	2.10

Fiscal year ended Dec. 31. Next earnings report expected: Late January. EPS Estimates based on S&P Operating Earnings; historical GAAP earnings are as reported.

Dividend Data (Dates: mm/dd Payment Date: mm/dd/yy)

Amount ($)	Date Decl.	Ex-Div. Date	Stk. of Record	Payment Date
0.300	02/21	03/05	03/07	03/27/07
0.300	04/25	06/04	06/06	06/26/07
0.310	07/20	09/05	09/07	09/25/07
0.310	10/19	12/05	12/07	12/18/07

Dividends have been paid since 1877. Source: Company reports.

Please read the Required Disclosures and Analyst Certification on the last page of this report.

The McGraw-Hill Companies

Stanley Works (The)

STANDARD & POOR'S

Business Summary October 24, 2007

The Stanley Works is a worldwide supplier of industrial tools and security solutions for professional, industrial and consumer use. The company offers a broad line of hand tools and has many well known brands. SWK's operations are classified into three business segments: Consumer Products (33% of 2006 sales), Industrial Tools (45%), and Security Solutions (22%).

In Consumer Products, SWK manufactures and markets hand tools, consumer mechanics tools and storage units, and hardware. Products are distributed directly to retailers (including home centers, mass merchants, hardware stores, and retail lumber yards) as well as third-party distributors, and include measuring instruments, hammers, knives and blades, screwdrivers, sockets and tool boxes. Among the company's brands are Stanley, FatMax, Powerlock, IntelliTools, ZAG, and National.

The Industrial Tools segment manufactures and markets professional mechanics tools and storage systems, pneumatic tools and fasteners, hydraulic tools and accessories, assembly tools and systems, and electronic measuring tools. Products are distributed primarily through third-party distributors.

Brands include Stanley, Proto, Facom, USAG, MAC, Jensen, Bostich, Virax, CST, David White and Rolatape.

The Security Solutions segment is a provider of access and security solutions primarily for retailers, educational and healthcare institutions, government, financial institutions, and commercial and industrial customers. Products include security integration systems, software, related installation and maintenance services, automatic doors, and locking mechanisms, and are sold on a direct sales basis. Brands include Stanley, Blick, Frisco Bay, PAC, ISR, WanderGuard, StanVision, Sargent and Greenleaf, and BEST.

About 60% of 2006 sales were made in the U.S., 9% in Other Americas, 11% in France, 15% in Other Europe, and 5% in Asia.

Company Financials Fiscal Year Ended Dec. 31

Per Share Data ($)	2006	2005	2004	2003	2002	2001	2000	1999	1998	1997
Tangible Book Value	NM	4.59	3.56	2.65	5.05	7.05	6.59	6.18	5.33	5.67
Cash Flow	4.92	4.40	4.07	2.16	2.90	2.76	3.17	2.62	2.41	0.34
Earnings	3.47	3.18	2.85	1.14	2.10	1.81	2.22	1.67	1.53	-0.47
S&P Core Earnings	3.57	3.16	2.49	1.12	1.43	1.30	NA	NA	NA	NA
Dividends	1.18	1.14	1.08	1.03	0.99	0.94	0.90	0.87	0.83	0.77
Payout Ratio	34%	36%	38%	90%	47%	52%	41%	52%	54%	NM
Prices:High	54.59	51.75	49.33	37.87	52.00	46.97	31.88	35.00	57.25	47.38
Prices:Low	41.60	41.51	36.42	20.84	27.31	28.06	18.44	22.00	23.50	28.00
P/E Ratio:High	16	16	17	33	25	26	14	21	37	NM
P/E Ratio:Low	12	13	13	18	13	16	8	13	15	NM

Income Statement Analysis (Million $)	2006	2005	2004	2003	2002	2001	2000	1999	1998	1997
Revenue	4,019	3,285	3,043	2,678	2,594	2,624	2,749	2,752	2,729	2,670
Operating Income	567	493	513	342	360	412	424	321	331	331
Depreciation	121	96.5	95.0	86.5	71.2	82.9	83.3	86.0	79.7	72.4
Interest Expense	69.3	40.4	38.6	34.2	28.5	18.9	34.6	33.0	31.0	24.7
Pretax Income	367	358	329	133	273	237	294	231	215	-18.6
Effective Tax Rate	20.8%	24.1%	27.0%	27.3%	32.1%	33.1%	33.8%	35.1%	36.0%	NM
Net Income	291	272	240	96.7	185	158	194	150	138	-41.9
S&P Core Earnings	299	270	209	94.7	127	113	NA	NA	NA	NA

Balance Sheet & Other Financial Data (Million $)	2006	2005	2004	2003	2002	2001	2000	1999	1998	1997
Cash	177	658	250	204	122	115	93.6	88.0	110	152
Current Assets	1,639	1,826	1,372	1,201	1,190	1,141	1,094	1,091	1,086	1,005
Total Assets	3,935	3,545	2,851	2,424	2,418	2,056	1,885	1,891	1,933	1,759
Current Liabilities	1,251	875	819	754	681	826	707	693	702	623
Long Term Debt	679	895	482	535	564	197	249	290	345	284
Common Equity	1,552	1,946	1,388	1,032	1,165	844	933	737	669	608
Total Capital	2,298	2,925	1,960	1,567	1,729	1,041	1,181	1,027	1,014	892
Capital Expenditures	59.6	53.3	47.6	31.4	37.2	55.7	59.8	78.0	56.9	73.3
Cash Flow	412	368	335	183	256	241	278	236	218	30.5
Current Ratio	1.3	2.1	1.7	1.6	1.7	1.4	1.5	1.6	1.5	1.6
% Long Term Debt of Capitalization	29.6	30.6	24.6	34.1	32.6	18.9	21.1	28.2	34.0	31.8
% Net Income of Revenue	7.2	8.3	7.9	3.6	7.1	6.0	7.1	5.5	5.0	NM
% Return on Assets	7.8	8.5	9.1	4.0	8.3	8.0	10.3	7.8	7.5	NM
% Return on Equity	19.4	14.4	19.8	8.8	16.9	20.0	20.8	20.8	21.6	NM

Data as orig reptd.; bef. results of disc opers/spec. items. Per share data adj. for stk. divs.; EPS diluted. E-Estimated. NA-Not Available. NM-Not Meaningful. NR-Not Ranked. UR-Under Review.

Office: 1000 Stanley Dr, New Britain, CT 06053.
Telephone: 860-225-5111.
Website: http://www.stanleyworks.com
Chrmn & CEO: J.F. Lundgren

EVP & CFO: J.M. Loree
VP, Secy & General Counsel: B.H. Beatt
Investor Contact: G. Gould (860-827-3833)
VP & Cntlr: D. Allan Jr.

Board Members: J. G. Breen, S. B. Brown, V. W. Colbert, E. A. Kampouris, E. S. Kraus, J. F. Lundgren, K. D. Wriston, L. A. Zimmerman

Founded: 1843
Domicile: Connecticut
Employees: 21,000

The McGraw-Hill Companies

Staples Inc

STANDARD &POOR'S

S&P Recommendation BUY ★★★★☆	**Price** $21.85 (as of Nov 27, 2007)	**12-Mo. Target Price** $29.00	**Investment Style** Large-Cap Growth

GICS Sector Consumer Discretionary
Sub-Industry Specialty Stores

Summary This leading operator of office products superstores has about 1,800 units in the U.S. and internationally.

Key Stock Statistics (Source S&P, Vickers, company reports)

52-Wk Range	$28.00– 19.69	S&P Oper. EPS 2008**E**	1.43	Market Capitalization(B)	$15.599	Beta	1.39
Trailing 12-Month EPS	$1.38	S&P Oper. EPS 2009**E**	1.64	Yield (%)	1.33	S&P 3-Yr. Proj. EPS CAGR(%)	13.00
Trailing 12-Month P/E	15.8	P/E on S&P Oper. EPS 2008**E**	15.3	Dividend Rate/Share	$0.29	S&P Credit Rating	BBB+
$10K Invested 5 Yrs Ago	$17,255	Common Shares Outstg. (M)	713.9	Institutional Ownership (%)	84		

Price Performance

30-Week Mov. Avg. · · · 10-Week Mov. Avg. - - GAAP Earnings vs. Previous Year Volume Above Avg. STARS
12-Mo. Target Price — Relative Strength — ▲ Up ▼ Down ▶ No Change Below Avg. ★

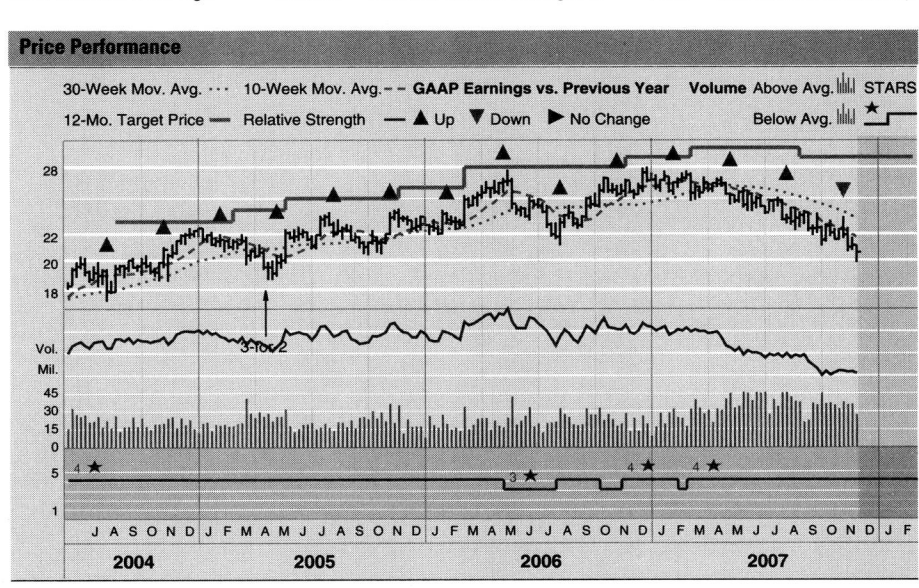

Options: ASE, CBOE, P, Ph

Analysis prepared by **Michael Souers** on November 27, 2007, when the stock traded at **$ 21.85**.

Highlights

➤ We estimate sales growth of between 9% and 10% in FY 09 (Jan.), following our projections of an 8%-9% advance in FY 08. Sales growth should be achieved by account growth in the delivery business, continued international penetration, and about 100 net new store additions in North America. We see North American Retail same-store sales gains of approximately 1%-2%, as customer traffic has weakened along with an overall slowdown in consumer spending.

➤ We expect a slight widening of gross margins on benefits from a growing private label business, supply chain initiatives, and lower sourcing costs, offset by higher occupancy costs. We also anticipate slightly higher operating margins as tighter expense controls are partially offset by a deleveraging of G&A expenses due to meager same-store-sales gains.

➤ We project modestly higher net interest income, an effective tax rate of 36%, and approximately 2% fewer shares outstanding. We estimate FY 09 operating EPS of $1.64, a 15% increase from the $1.43 we expect the company to earn in FY 08, excluding one-time items.

Investment Rationale/Risk

➤ We believe business spending trends and a solid job market bode well for SPLS. The North American Delivery division's recent performance has been stellar, in our opinion, and we anticipate continued strong results. In addition, we think strong results from new Chicago, Miami and Denver stores indicate further growth in untapped domestic metropolitan areas. Longer term, we believe China and South America will provide SPLS with additional growth avenues. At about 12X our FY 09 EPS estimate, the shares recently traded at a modest discount to the S&P 500. We think a premium valuation is merited due to what we see as SPLS's strong balance sheet and growth prospects.

➤ Risks to our recommendation and target price include a sharp slowdown in economic growth and slower than expected capital spending and hiring by businesses. International risks include economic instability and unfavorable currency movements.

➤ Our 12-month target price of $29, about 18X our FY 09 EPS estimate, is derived from our discounted cash flow model, which assumes a weighted average cost of capital of 10.1% and a terminal growth rate of 3.0%.

Qualitative Risk Assessment

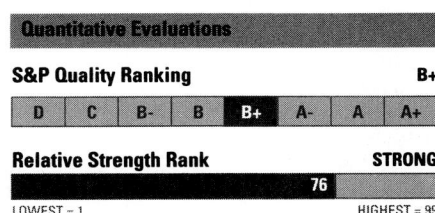

LOW	MEDIUM	HIGH

Our risk assessment reflects the rather cyclical nature of the company, which relies on consumer as well as business spending, and investments in emerging markets for future growth. This is offset by untapped growth areas in major domestic metro markets.

Quantitative Evaluations

S&P Quality Ranking B+

D	C	B-	B	B+	A-	A	A+

Relative Strength Rank STRONG

76

LOWEST = 1   HIGHEST = 99

Revenue/Earnings Data

Revenue (Million $)

	1Q	2Q	3Q	4Q	Year
2008	4,589	4,290	5,168	--	--
2007	4,238	3,881	4,757	5,286	18,161
2006	3,899	3,472	4,246	4,462	16,079
2005	3,452	3,089	3,830	4,077	14,448
2004	3,147	2,869	3,485	3,681	13,181
2003	2,745	2,426	3,090	3,335	11,596

Earnings Per Share ($)

2008	0.29	0.25	0.38	E0.48	E1.43
2007	0.25	0.22	0.39	0.46	E1.29
2006	0.20	0.20	0.32	0.39	1.12
2005	0.17	0.16	0.27	0.33	0.93
2004	0.03	0.12	0.22	0.28	0.66
2003	0.13	0.09	0.18	0.23	0.63

Fiscal year ended Jan. 31. Next earnings report expected: Early March. EPS Estimates based on S&P Operating Earnings; historical GAAP earnings are as reported.

Dividend Data (Dates: mm/dd Payment Date: mm/dd/yy)

Amount ($)	Date Decl.	Ex-Div. Date	Stk. of Record	Payment Date
0.290	03/01	03/28	03/30	04/19/07

Dividends have been paid since 2004. Source: Company reports.

Please read the Required Disclosures and Analyst Certification on the last page of this report.

The McGraw-Hill Companies

Staples Inc

STANDARD &POOR'S

Business Summary November 27, 2007

CORPORATE OVERVIEW. Staples is the world's leading office products company, with net sales of nearly $18.2 billion in FY 07 (Jan.). Staples operates under three segments: North American Retail (55% of total revenues in FY 07); North American Delivery (32%); and International Operations (13%). Sales by product line were: office supplies and services 39%; business machines and related products 31%; computers and related products 22%; and office furniture 8%.

At February 3, 2007, SPLS operated 1,884 superstores, mostly in North America (1,620 stores), but also in five European countries: the U.K. (137), Germany (57), the Netherlands (45), Portugal (22) and Belgium (3).

SPLS has approximately 8,000 stock keeping units (SKUs) stocked in each of its typical North American retail stores and approximately 15,000 SKUs stocked in its North American Delivery fulfillment centers. On Staples.com, the company's Internet site, approximately 50,000 SKUs are available to cus-tomers.

CORPORATE STRATEGY. Staples seeks to maintain its leadership position in the office products industry by differentiating itself from the competition, delivering industry-best execution and expanding its market share. In FY 08, it plans to add over 100 new stores in North America, filling in existing markets along with an expansion into untapped metro markets. Staples entered Chicago in March 2005, and initial results exceeded expectations, according to the company. We believe significant growth opportunities remain in other metropolitan markets where SPLS has yet to venture, and we expect the company to establish a strong Midwest presence over the next several years. SPLS also plans to open approximately 10 stores in Europe in FY 08.

Company Financials Fiscal Year Ended Jan. 31

Per Share Data ($)	2007	2006	2005	2004	2003	2002	2001	2000	1999	1998
Tangible Book Value	4.64	3.84	3.45	3.01	1.74	2.63	2.19	1.99	2.18	1.46
Cash Flow	1.78	1.56	1.33	1.03	1.01	0.73	0.42	0.67	0.69	0.35
Earnings	1.32	1.12	0.93	0.66	0.63	0.42	0.10	0.45	0.27	0.23
S&P Core Earnings	1.32	1.05	0.88	0.61	0.58	0.32	0.21	NA	NA	NA
Dividends	0.17	0.17	0.13	Nil	Nil	Nil	Nil	Nil	Nil	Nil
Payout Ratio	13%	15%	14%	Nil	Nil	Nil	Nil	Nil	Nil	Nil
Calendar Year	2006	2005	2004	2003	2002	2001	2000	1999	1998	1997
Prices:High	28.00	24.14	22.57	18.58	14.97	12.97	19.17	23.96	20.53	8.93
Prices:Low	21.08	18.64	15.79	10.49	7.79	7.35	6.83	10.96	7.06	5.07
P/E Ratio:High	21	22	24	28	24	31	NM	54	75	39
P/E Ratio:Low	16	17	17	16	12	17	NM	25	26	22

Income Statement Analysis (Million $)

Revenue	18,161	16,079	14,448	13,181	11,596	10,744	10,674	8,937	7,123	5,181
Operating Income	1,802	1,617	1,405	1,081	950	768	719	708	514	355
Depreciation	339	304	279	283	267	249	231	174	99.2	83.4
Interest Expense	47.8	56.8	39.9	20.2	20.6	27.2	45.2	17.1	17.4	23.1
Pretax Income	1,471	1,314	1,116	778	662	431	244	516	306	213
Effective Tax Rate	33.8%	36.5%	36.5%	37.0%	32.6%	38.5%	75.5%	39.0%	39.5%	38.5%
Net Income	974	834	708	490	446	265	59.7	315	185	131
S&P Core Earnings	974	784	667	450	413	221	147	NA	NA	NA

Balance Sheet & Other Financial Data (Million $)

Cash	1,018	978	997	457	596	395	264	110	358	355
Current Assets	4,431	4,145	3,782	3,479	2,717	2,403	2,356	2,192	2,064	1,666
Total Assets	8,397	7,677	7,071	6,503	5,721	4,093	3,989	3,814	3,179	2,455
Current Liabilities	2,788	2,480	2,197	2,123	2,175	1,596	1,711	1,455	1,265	941
Long Term Debt	569	528	558	567	732	350	441	501	205	509
Common Equity	5,022	4,425	4,115	3,663	2,659	2,054	1,764	1,829	1,657	967
Total Capital	5,600	4,963	4,696	4,230	3,441	2,411	2,205	2,330	1,862	1,476
Capital Expenditures	528	456	335	278	265	340	450	355	322	183
Cash Flow	1,313	1,138	987	773	713	514	291	489	285	214
Current Ratio	1.6	1.7	1.7	1.6	1.2	1.5	1.4	1.5	1.6	1.8
% Long Term Debt of Capitalization	10.2	10.6	11.9	13.4	21.3	14.5	20.0	21.5	11.0	34.5
% Net Income of Revenue	5.4	5.2	4.9	3.7	3.8	2.5	0.6	3.5	2.6	2.5
% Return on Assets	12.1	11.3	10.4	8.0	9.1	6.6	1.5	9.0	6.6	6.2
% Return on Equity	20.5	19.5	18.2	15.5	18.9	13.9	3.3	18.1	14.1	15.1

Data as orig reptd.; bef. results of disc opers/spec. items. Per share data adj. for stk. divs.; EPS diluted. E-Estimated. NA-Not Available. NM-Not Meaningful. NR-Not Ranked. UR-Under Review.

Office: Five Hundred Staples Dr, Framingham , MA 01702.
Telephone: 508-253-5000.
Email: investor@staples.com
Website: http://www.staples.com

Chrmn & CEO: R.L. Sargent
Pres & COO: M.A. Miles
Vice Chrmn & CFO: J.J. Mahoney
EVP, Secy & General Counsel: J.A. VanWoerkom

SVP & General Counsel: K. Campbell
Board Members: B. L. Anderson, A. M. Blank, M. E. Burton, G. L. Crittenden, R. T. Moriarty, R. C. Nakasone, R. L. Sargent, M. Trust, V. Vishwanath, P. F. Walsh

Founded: 1985
Domicile: Delaware
Employees: 73,646

The McGraw-Hill Companies

Starbucks Corp

S&P Recommendation	STRONG BUY ★★★★★	Price	12-Mo. Target Price	Investment Style
		$22.18 (as of Nov 26, 2007)	$34.00	Large-Cap Growth

GICS Sector Consumer Discretionary
Sub-Industry Restaurants

Summary This company purchases and roasts high-quality whole bean coffees, which it sells -- together with rich-brewed coffees -- primarily through its more than 15,000 retail stores.

Key Stock Statistics (Source S&P, Vickers, company reports)

52-Wk Range	$37.14– 21.77	S&P Oper. EPS 2008E	1.02	Market Capitalization(B)	$16.531	Beta		0.53
Trailing 12-Month EPS	$0.87	S&P Oper. EPS 2009E	1.25	Yield (%)	Nil	S&P 3-Yr. Proj. EPS CAGR(%)		19.00
Trailing 12-Month P/E	25.5	P/E on S&P Oper. EPS 2008E	21.7	Dividend Rate/Share	Nil	S&P Credit Rating		BBB+
$10K Invested 5 Yrs Ago	$21,155	Common Shares Outstg. (M)	745.3	Institutional Ownership (%)	60			

Price Performance

30-Week Mov. Avg. · · · 10-Week Mov. Avg. - - GAAP Earnings vs. Previous Year   Volume Above Avg. STARS
12-Mo. Target Price — Relative Strength — ▲ Up ▼ Down ► No Change   Below Avg.

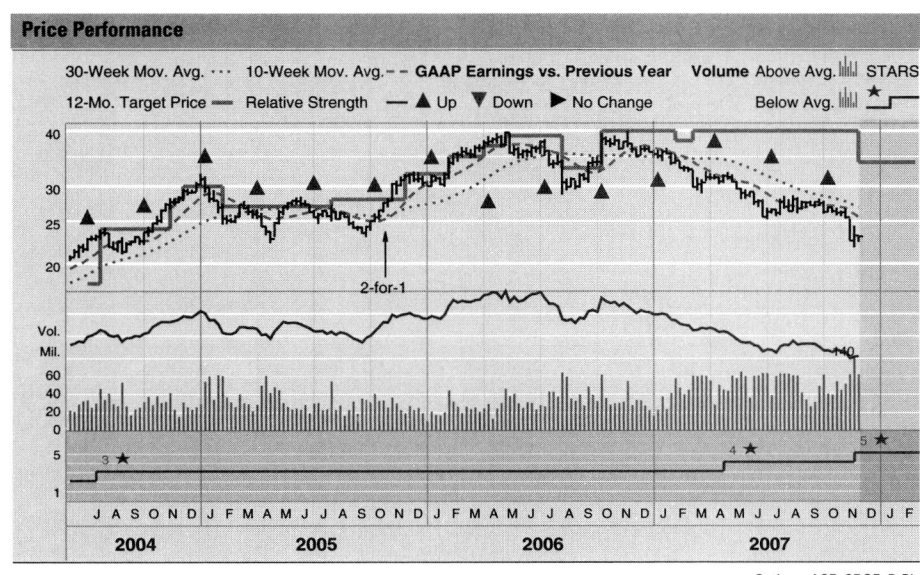

Options: ASE, CBOE, P, Ph

Analysis prepared by **Mark S. Basham** on November 26, 2007, when the stock traded at **$ 22.56**.

Highlights

➤ SBUX plans to add at least 2,400 retail units annually for the next several years as it expands operations worldwide, and has a long-term global target of 40,000 locations. Partially in response to slowing U.S. economic growth, in our view, SBUX recently reduced its targeted new store openings for FY 08 (Sep.) slightly, to 2,500, from 2,600, including shifts to more cafe openings in international markets as well as to more licensed stores as opposed to company owned locations.

➤ We expect retail revenues to be up in FY 08 by 17% in the U.S. and 21% internationally, due to expansion. Average unit sales are expected to be unchanged, reflecting prices increases and lower U.S. traffic. We see specialty revenues rising about 16%.

➤ Our FY 08 EPS estimate is $1.02, versus $0.87 in FY 07. We believe operating margins will narrow slightly, with higher store operating costs partly offset by a price increase taken in Fall 2007. From a Q1 high in dairy costs, the company expects some moderation through the rest of the fiscal year.

Investment Rationale/Risk

➤ At about 22X our calendar 2008 EPS estimate of $1.05, the shares recently traded at a premium to industry peers and the S&P 500, but at the low end of the company's historical valuation range. Given what we believe is much better visibility for earnings in FY 08, we recently upgraded the shares to strong buy, from buy. We consider SBUX's long-term growth prospects to be strong, with growth prospects in international markets particularly appealing.

➤ Risks to our recommendation and target price include the potentially negative impact of price increases on customer traffic, lack of customer acceptance of SBUX's food initiatives, and the possibility that aggressive expansion in the U.S. will increase cannibalization rates.

➤ Our 12-month target price of $34 is based on our discounted cash flow analysis, which assumes a weighted average cost of capital of 10.4%, and 2007 cash flow growth of 37% falling over 20 years to a perpetuity rate of 4%. Our target implies a P/E multiple of 32X applied to our calendar 2008 EPS estimate of $1.05.

Qualitative Risk Assessment

LOW	MEDIUM	HIGH

Our risk assessment reflects SBUX's relatively high P/E multiple compared to the 500, which we believe suggests that much of the company's value rests on its growth prospects. We also see a threat from gourmet coffee offerings by competitors. Partly offsetting these concerns, we think the company has significant financial strength, affording it the capacity to continue on its growth trajectory.

Quantitative Evaluations

S&P Quality Ranking B+

D	C	B-	B	B+	A-	A	A+

Relative Strength Rank WEAK

27

LOWEST = 1   HIGHEST = 99

Revenue/Earnings Data

Revenue (Million $)

	1Q	2Q	3Q	4Q	Year
2007	2,356	2,256	2,359	2,441	9,412
2006	1,934	1,886	1,964	2,003	7,787
2005	1,590	1,519	1,602	1,659	6,369
2004	1,281	1,241	1,319	1,453	5,294
2003	1,004	954.2	1,037	1,081	4,076
2002	805.3	783.2	835.2	865.2	3,289

Earnings Per Share ($)

2007	0.26	0.19	0.21	0.21	0.87
2006	0.22	0.16	0.18	0.17	0.73
2005	0.17	0.12	0.16	0.16	0.61
2004	0.14	0.10	0.12	0.13	0.48
2003	0.10	0.07	0.09	0.09	0.34
2002	0.09	0.04	0.07	0.08	0.27

Fiscal year ended Sep. 30. Next earnings report expected: Early February. EPS Estimates based on S&P Operating Earnings; historical GAAP earnings are as reported.

Dividend Data

No cash dividends have been paid.

Starbucks Corp

STANDARD
&POOR'S

Business Summary November 26, 2007

CORPORATE OVERVIEW. Starbucks Corp.'s rapid growth in retail outlets throughout the U.S. has made its name synonymous with specialty coffee. A caffeine-fueled expansion has brought the number of Starbucks retail stores to 15,011 at September 30, 2007, from 165 stores at the end of FY 92 (Sep.). Company revenues grew 21% in FY 07, to $9.4 billion, and posted a compound annual growth rate (CAGR) of about 23% over the past five years.

Company-operated retail stores accounted for 85% of FY 07 net sales (also 85% in FY 06). Stores are typically clustered in high-traffic, high-visibility locations in each market. They are located in office buildings, downtown and suburban retail centers, and kiosks placed in building lobbies, airport terminals and supermarkets. In FY 06 (latest available), the retail store sales mix by product type was 77% beverages, 15% food items, 3% whole bean coffees, and 5% coffee-related hardware items. The company is currently expanding its food menu at many of its U.S. retail locations.

At September 30, 2007, SBUX owned and operated 6,793 of its stores in the U.S., and 1,712 stores in international markets, including Canada, the U.K., Germany, Australia and China. SBUX seeks to expand its retail business by increasing its share in existing markets and opening stores in new markets in which it sees an opportunity to become the leading specialty coffee retailer. It opened a total of 1,342 company-owned stores in FY 07, and plans to open

1,200 in FY 08.

Revenue from retail licensees was approximately 7% of total revenues in FY 07 (7% in FY 06). As of September 30, 2007, there were 6,506 licensed retail stores worldwide. Licensees are expected to open 1,300 stores in FY 08.

The Global Consumer Products Group, which accounted for 4% of total revenues in FY 07 (4% in FY 06), aims to develop the Starbucks brand outside the company-owned retail store environment through a number of channels. Key initiatives include a licensing agreement with Kraft, Inc., which markets and distributes the company's whole bean and ground coffees to approximately 31,900 grocery and warehouse club accounts.

The company has approximately 16,200 foodservice accounts, through which it sells whole bean and ground coffee to various coffee distributors, hotels, airlines and restaurants. Foodservice revenues were 4.1% of total revenues in FY 07 (4.4% in FY 06).

Company Financials Fiscal Year Ended Sep. 30

Per Share Data ($)	2007	2006	2005	2004	2003	2002	2001	2000	1999	1998
Tangible Book Value	NA	2.68	2.56	3.00	2.52	2.20	1.78	1.50	1.29	1.11
Cash Flow	NA	1.25	1.06	0.85	0.66	0.55	0.45	0.48	0.28	0.20
Earnings	0.87	0.73	0.61	0.48	0.34	0.27	0.23	0.12	0.14	0.09
S&P Core Earnings	NA	0.73	0.53	0.42	0.29	0.23	0.18	NA	NA	NA
Dividends	Nil	Nil	Nil	Nil	Nil	Nil	Nil	Nil	Nil	Nil
Payout Ratio	Nil	Nil	Nil	Nil	Nil	Nil	Nil	Nil	Nil	Nil
Prices:High	36.61	40.01	32.46	32.13	16.72	12.85	12.83	12.70	10.25	7.49
Prices:Low	21.77	28.72	22.29	16.45	9.81	9.22	6.73	5.78	4.97	3.59
P/E Ratio:High	42	55	53	68	50	48	56	NM	76	80
P/E Ratio:Low	25	39	37	35	29	34	29	NM	37	38

Income Statement Analysis (Million $)										
Revenue	NA	7,787	6,369	5,294	4,076	3,289	2,649	2,169	1,680	1,309
Operating Income	NA	1,213	1,071	854	646	504	430	334	264	199
Depreciation	NA	413	367	305	259	221	177	142	108	80.9
Interest Expense	NA	Nil	Nil	Nil	Nil	Nil	Nil	Nil	1.36	1.38
Pretax Income	NA	906	796	624	436	341	289	161	164	116
Effective Tax Rate	NA	35.8%	37.9%	37.2%	38.5%	37.0%	37.3%	41.1%	38.0%	41.2%
Net Income	NA	581	494	392	268	215	181	94.6	102	68.4
S&P Core Earnings	NA	579	437	346	231	181	143	NA	NA	NA

Balance Sheet & Other Financial Data (Million $)										
Cash	NA	313	174	299	201	175	113	70.8	66.4	102
Current Assets	NA	1,530	1,209	1,368	924	848	594	460	387	337
Total Assets	NA	4,429	3,514	3,328	2,730	2,293	1,851	1,493	1,253	993
Current Liabilities	NA	1,936	1,227	783	609	537	445	313	252	179
Long Term Debt	NA	1.96	2.87	3.62	4.35	5.08	5.79	6.48	7.02	Nil
Common Equity	NA	2,229	2,091	2,487	2,082	1,727	1,376	1,148	961	794
Total Capital	NA	2,230	2,094	2,537	2,120	1,754	1,406	1,180	1,001	813
Capital Expenditures	NA	771	644	386	357	375	384	316	262	202
Cash Flow	NA	994	862	697	528	436	358	367	209	149
Current Ratio	NA	0.8	1.0	1.7	1.5	1.6	1.3	1.5	1.5	1.9
% Long Term Debt of Capitalization	NA	0.1	0.1	0.1	0.2	0.3	0.4	0.5	0.7	Nil
% Net Income of Revenue	NA	7.5	7.8	7.4	6.6	6.5	6.8	4.4	6.1	5.2
% Return on Assets	NA	14.6	14.3	12.9	10.9	10.4	10.8	6.9	9.1	7.4
% Return on Equity	NA	26.9	21.7	17.1	14.1	13.9	14.4	9.0	11.6	10.3

Data as orig reptd.; bef. results of disc opers/spec. items. Per share data adj. for stk. divs.; EPS diluted. E-Estimated. NA-Not Available. NM-Not Meaningful. NR-Not Ranked. UR-Under Review.

Office: 2401 Utah Avenue South, Seattle, WA 98134.
Telephone: 206-447-1575.
Email: investorrelations@starbucks.com
Website: http://www.starbucks.com

Chrmn: H. Schultz
Pres & CEO: O.C. Smith
EVP & CFO: P. Bocian
EVP, Secy & General Counsel: P.E. Boggs

CIO: B. Crynes
Auditor: Deloitte & Touche
Board Members: B. Bass, H. P. Behar, W. W. Bradley, J. Donald, M. Hobson, O. Lee, H. Schultz, J. G. Shennan, Jr., J. G. Teruel, M. E. Ullman, III, C. E. Weatherup

Founded: 1985
Domicile: Washington
Employees: 145,800

Starwood Hotels & Resorts Worldwide Inc.

STANDARD &POOR'S

S&P Recommendation **HOLD** ★★★☆☆	Price	12-Mo. Target Price	Investment Style
	$53.50 (as of Nov 23, 2007)	$65.00	Large-Cap Blend

GICS Sector Consumer Discretionary
Sub-Industry Hotels, Resorts & Cruise Lines

Summary Starwood is one of the world's largest lodging companies, with about 900 hotels in more than 100 countries, including the Sheraton, Westin, St. Regis, W, and Four Points by Sheraton brands.

Key Stock Statistics (Source S&P, Vickers, company reports)

52-Wk Range	$75.45– 50.26	S&P Oper. EPS 2007**E**	2.50	Market Capitalization(B)	$11.226	Beta	0.89
Trailing 12-Month EPS	$2.78	S&P Oper. EPS 2008**E**	2.55	Yield (%)	6.73	S&P 3-Yr. Proj. EPS CAGR(%)	11.00
Trailing 12-Month P/E	19.2	P/E on S&P Oper. EPS 2007**E**	21.4	Dividend Rate/Share	$3.60	S&P Credit Rating	BBB-
$10K Invested 5 Yrs Ago	$29,636	Common Shares Outstg. (M)	209.8	Institutional Ownership (%)	94		

Price Performance

30-Week Mov. Avg. ··· 10-Week Mov. Avg. - - GAAP Earnings vs. Previous Year Volume Above Avg. STARS
12-Mo. Target Price — Relative Strength — ▲ Up ▼ Down ▶ No Change Below Avg. ★

Options: CBOE, Ph

Analysis prepared by **Mark S. Basham** on November 02, 2007, when the stock traded at $ **55.00**.

Highlights

➤ Reflecting less emphasis on hotel ownership, we estimate revenue from owned and joint venture hotels will fall 11% in 2007, while management fees increase 20%. For 2008, we expect owned and J.V. revenues to be flat, while management fees rise 12%. Vacation ownership revenues are projected to decline 15% in 2008 after rising 6% in 2007, due to lower inventory of ownership interests, as well as uncertainty regarding the timing of sales of securitized receivables.

➤ We estimate 2007 EPS of $2.50, excluding charges of $0.14 primarily related to accelerated depreciation associated with hotel renovations, versus $2.73 in 2006, which excludes $2.28 of special items, but includes about $0.14 of tax benefits. In 2008, we expect operating profit from vacation ownership to fall 26%, but with hotel segment operating profit up 5.9%, we estimate EPS will rise to $2.55.

➤ During the first nine months of 2007, HOT bought back 19.2 million shares of its common stock for $1.22 billion. As of September 30, 2007, HOT was authorized to buy back up to an additional $156 million of its stock.

Investment Rationale/Risk

➤ We have lowered our recommendation to hold, from buy, reflecting issues with project delays and receivables securitizations in the vacation ownership segment, even as hotel operations, particularly international, show continued strength. In addition, credit market dislocations during August have caused the "M&A premium" that we saw in HOT shares to disappear, and we think it less likely that a strategic buyer will step in and possibly take advantage of the recent share weakness.

➤ Risks to our recommendation and target price include the possibility that terrorism fears could reduce demand for hotel rooms, as well as further economic fallout from the late summer financial crisis.

➤ Our 12-month target price of $65 is based on a multiple of 12.5X our 2008 EBITDA estimate, which is, in our estimation, about in line with peer valuations. Although lodging industry fundamentals remain strong globally, albeit with some moderation in the U.S. market, we think it unlikely that the shares will garner a buyout valuation premium until and unless credit market conditions improve substantially.

Qualitative Risk Assessment

LOW	MEDIUM	HIGH

In our view, Starwood's ongoing divestiture of non-strategic hotels has moved the company's business mix more toward management and franchising of hotels, with less emphasis on real estate ownership. We view the company's operations as being sensitive to macroeconomic conditions. However, over the long term, we expect the company to generate a sizable amount of cash flow, some of which we expect will be used for growth initiatives, payment of dividends, and possibly stock repurchases.

Quantitative Evaluations

S&P Quality Ranking NR

D	C	B-	B	B+	A-	A	A+

Relative Strength Rank MODERATE

47

LOWEST = 1 HIGHEST = 99

Revenue/Earnings Data

Revenue (Million $)

	1Q	2Q	3Q	4Q	Year
2007	1,431	1,572	1,540	--	--
2006	1,441	1,505	1,461	1,572	5,979
2005	1,406	1,559	1,496	1,516	5,977
2004	1,227	1,363	1,336	1,442	5,368
2003	1,073	1,220	1,140	1,197	4,630
2002	1,096	1,232	1,157	1,174	4,659

Earnings Per Share ($)

2007	0.56	0.67	0.61	E0.66	E2.50
2006	0.34	3.01	0.71	0.94	5.01
2005	0.36	0.65	0.18	0.72	1.88
2004	0.16	0.56	0.49	0.51	1.72
2003	-0.58	0.42	0.23	0.42	0.51
2002	0.16	0.37	0.26	0.42	1.20

Fiscal year ended Dec. 31. Next earnings report expected: Early February. EPS Estimates based on S&P Operating Earnings; historical GAAP earnings are as reported.

Dividend Data (Dates: mm/dd Payment Date: mm/dd/yy)

Amount ($)	Date Decl.	Ex-Div. Date	Stk. of Record	Payment Date
0.900	11/08	12/27	12/31	01/11/08

Dividends have been paid since 1995. Source: Company reports.

Please read the Required Disclosures and Analyst Certification on the last page of this report.

The McGraw·Hill Companies

Starwood Hotels & Resorts Worldwide Inc.

**STANDARD
&POOR'S**

Business Summary November 02, 2007

CORPORATE OVERVIEW. Starwood Hotels is one of the world's largest hotel companies, with owned, leased, managed or franchised hotels in approximately 100 countries. At September 30, 2007, the company's business included 896 hotels, with 274,085 rooms. Also, including an unconsolidated joint venture, HOT had 28 vacation ownership resorts in operation. Some of these resorts, plus some additional HOT-related resorts, were actively selling inventory.

HOT's business includes owned, managed and franchised properties. Its brands include St. Regis (luxury full-service hotels and resorts), The Luxury Collection (luxury full-service hotels and resorts), Westin (luxury and upscale full-service hotels and resorts), Sheraton (full-service hotels and resorts), W (boutique full-service urban hotels), and Four Points (moderately priced full-service hotels). At September 30, 2007, the company's hotel business included 403 Sheratons (140,018 rooms), 147 Westins (60,089 rooms), 70 properties (11,968 rooms) in the St. Regis or Luxury Collection groups, 128 Four Points (22,321 rooms), 20 hotels (6,014 rooms) in the W chain, 117 Le Meridien properties (31,262 rooms), and 11 other hotels (2,413 rooms).

The company's top five domestic markets by percentage of total owned revenues during 2006 were: New York (12.6%), Phoenix (5.1%), Boston (4.6%), San Francisco (4.3%), and Atlanta (4.0%). The top five international markets were Italy (7.9%), Canada (6.3%), Mexico (4.5%), the U.K. (3.0%), and Australia (3.0%).

Worldwide operating statistics for HOT's owned hotels operating in both 2005 and 2006 (74 properties with 25,000 rooms) were: average daily rate of $191.56 in 2006, up 8.2% from $177.04 in 2005, and occupancy of 71.2% vs. 69.9%, which resulted in revenue per available room (RevPAR) of $136.33, up 10% from $123.80.

Statistics on a same-store basis for the nine months ended September 30, 2007, for 72 owned hotels were: average daily rate of $211.16 (up 7.6% from the nine months ended September 30, 2006), and occupancy of 72.3% (vs. 71.6%), resulting in RevPAR rising 8.6%, from $140.43 to $152.57.

Company Financials Fiscal Year Ended Dec. 31

Per Share Data ($)	2006	2005	2004	2003	2002	2001	2000	1999	1998	1997
Tangible Book Value	3.31	13.59	10.73	4.55	3.57	2.35	2.50	2.16	1.43	NA
Cash Flow	6.37	3.69	3.72	2.58	2.28	3.29	4.30	-0.86	3.73	NA
Earnings	5.01	1.88	1.72	0.51	1.20	0.73	1.96	-3.41	0.67	NA
S&P Core Earnings	4.87	1.66	1.37	0.12	0.77	0.52	NA	NA	NA	NA
Dividends	0.84	0.84	0.84	0.84	0.84	0.80	0.69	0.60	2.04	NA
Payout Ratio	17%	45%	49%	165%	70%	110%	35%	NM	NM	NA
Prices:High	68.87	65.22	59.50	37.60	39.94	40.89	37.50	37.75	57.88	61.50
Prices:Low	49.68	51.50	34.81	21.68	19.00	17.10	19.75	19.50	18.75	33.50
P/E Ratio:High	14	35	35	74	33	56	19	NM	86	NA
P/E Ratio:Low	10	27	20	43	16	23	10	NM	28	NA

Income Statement Analysis (Million $)										
Revenue	5,979	5,977	5,368	4,630	4,659	3,967	4,345	3,862	4,710	NA
Operating Income	1,145	1,242	1,047	1,698	1,856	1,191	1,509	1,329	1,361	NA
Depreciation	306	407	431	429	222	526	481	476	556	NA
Interest Expense	244	258	257	287	338	369	439	516	639	NA
Pretax Income	682	642	412	-5.00	252	200	610	533	43.0	NA
Effective Tax Rate	NM	34.1%	10.4%	NM	1.59%	23.0%	33.0%	NM	NM	NA
Net Income	1,115	423	369	105	246	151	401	-638	141	NA
S&P Core Earnings	1,084	376	291	27.7	157	107	NA	NA	NA	NA

Balance Sheet & Other Financial Data (Million $)										
Cash	183	897	326	508	216	157	189	436	290	NA
Current Assets	1,810	2,283	1,683	1,245	950	897	1,048	1,176	1,077	NA
Total Assets	9,280	12,454	12,298	11,894	12,259	12,461	12,660	12,923	16,101	NA
Current Liabilities	2,461	2,879	2,128	1,644	2,199	1,587	1,805	2,303	2,074	NA
Long Term Debt	1,827	2,926	3,823	4,393	4,449	5,269	5,074	4,779	8,111	NA
Common Equity	3,008	5,211	4,788	4,326	6,357	3,756	3,851	3,690	4,202	NA
Total Capital	4,891	8,724	9,518	9,676	11,882	10,380	10,417	10,167	13,580	NA
Capital Expenditures	371	464	333	307	82.0	477	544	521	832	NA
Cash Flow	1,421	830	800	534	468	677	882	-162	697	NA
Current Ratio	0.7	0.8	0.8	0.8	0.4	0.6	0.6	0.5	0.5	NA
% Long Term Debt of Capitalization	37.4	33.5	40.2	45.4	37.4	50.8	48.7	47.0	59.7	NA
% Net Income of Revenue	18.6	7.1	6.9	NM	5.3	3.8	9.2	NM	3.0	NA
% Return on Assets	10.2	3.4	3.1	NM	2.0	1.2	3.1	NM	NA	NA
% Return on Equity	27.1	8.5	8.1	NM	3.9	4.0	10.6	NM	NA	NA

Data as orig reptd.; bef. results of disc opers/spec. items. Per share data adj. for stk. divs.; EPS diluted. E-Estimated. NA-Not Available. NM-Not Meaningful. NR-Not Ranked. UR-Under Review.

Office: 1111 Westchester Avenue, White Plains, NY 10604.
Telephone: 914-640-8100.
Website: http://www.starwoodhotels.com
Chrmn & CEO: B.W. Duncan

EVP & CFO: V.M. Prabhu
Chief Admin Officer, Secy & General Counsel: K.S. Siegal

Board Members: A. M. Aron, C. Barshefsky, J. Chapus, B. W. Duncan, L. Galbreath, E. Hippeau, S. R. Quazzo, T. O. Ryder, D. W. Yih, K. C. Youngblood

Founded: 1969
Domicile: Maryland
Employees: 145,000

The McGraw-Hill Companies

State Street Corp

STANDARD &POOR'S

S&P Recommendation	BUY ★★★★☆	Price	12-Mo. Target Price	Investment Style
		$77.76 (as of Nov 23, 2007)	$83.00	Large-Cap Growth

GICS Sector Financials
Sub-Industry Asset Management & Custody Banks

Summary This bank holding company, with about $11 trillion in assets under custody, is a leading servicer of financial assets worldwide.

Key Stock Statistics (Source S&P, Vickers, company reports)

52-Wk Range	$80.01– 59.13	S&P Oper. EPS 2007**E**	4.24	Market Capitalization(B)	$30.289	Beta	1.39
Trailing 12-Month EPS	$3.82	S&P Oper. EPS 2008**E**	4.65	Yield (%)	1.13	S&P 3-Yr. Proj. EPS CAGR(%)	12.00
Trailing 12-Month P/E	20.4	P/E on S&P Oper. EPS 2007**E**	18.3	Dividend Rate/Share	$0.88	S&P Credit Rating	AA-
$10K Invested 5 Yrs Ago	$18,182	Common Shares Outstg. (M)	389.5	Institutional Ownership (%)	85		

Price Performance

30-Week Mov. Avg. · · · 10-Week Mov. Avg. - - **GAAP Earnings vs. Previous Year**   Volume Above Avg. STARS
12-Mo. Target Price — Relative Strength — ▲ Up ▼ Down ► No Change   Below Avg.

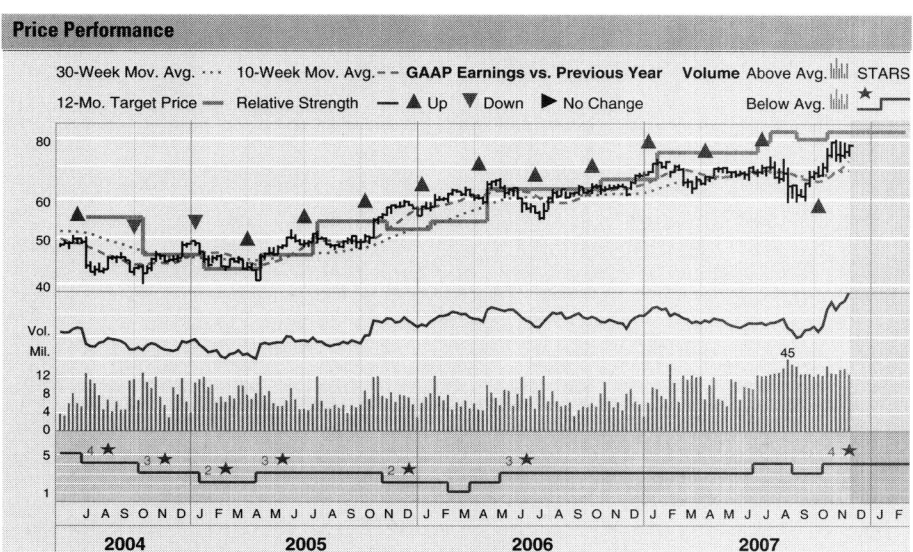

Options: Ph

Analysis prepared by **Frank Braden, CFA** on October 17, 2007, when the stock traded at **$ 74.68**.

Highlights

➤ We expect revenue growth of 28% in 2007 and 17% in 2008, driven by the Investors Financial acquisition and STT's success in gaining new assets both in the U.S. and internationally from existing and new clients. We believe that long-term macro trends affecting STT remain intact, including the outsourcing of custody services, growth in worldwide pension systems, the development of more complex investment vehicles, consolidation among financial processing providers, and increasing pressure on public retirement systems. We think STT has the potential to improve its new business growth in light of the July 2007 merger between Bank of New York and Mellon Financial (now Bank of New York Mellon (BK: hold, $44)).

➤ We remain confident in management's ability to better align operating expenses with its market-sensitive revenue model in a challenging interest rate environment. We expect the pretax operating margin to remain steady, at around 30%, in 2008.

➤ We project operating EPS of $4.25 in 2007 and $4.65 in 2008, on a relatively flat share count and assuming a healthy and stable global economy.

Investment Rationale/Risk

➤ We believe management is making the right moves by expanding its international presence, as well as increasing its services to hedge funds and private equity funds. While we do not think cost-cutting initiatives are hurting longer-term growth prospects, we continue to monitor spending levels needed to sustain growth. We expect the shares to remain under some near-term pressure, given STT's significant exposure to asset-backed commercial paper.

➤ Risks to our recommendation and target price include a significant slowdown in capital markets; a severe tightening of the asset-backed commercial paper markets; litigation arising from its enhanced index bond funds; and a slower than projected implementation of announced cost-cutting initiatives.

➤ Our 12-month target price is $83, or approximately 17.8X our 2008 EPS estimate, in line with peers and STT's historical average. We believe this multiple is appropriate based on our view of the company's operating outlook and the progress it has reported in reducing its expenses.

Qualitative Risk Assessment

LOW	MEDIUM	HIGH

Our risk assessment reflects our view of solid fundamentals coupled with a strong customer base and good diversification. We believe STT has a well established business and has maintained healthy earnings growth.

Quantitative Evaluations

S&P Quality Ranking   A

D	C	B-	B	B+	A-	A	A+

Relative Strength Rank   STRONG
93
LOWEST = 1   HIGHEST = 99

Revenue/Earnings Data

Revenue (Million $)

	1Q	2Q	3Q	4Q	Year
2007	1,696	2,740	3,165	--	--
2006	2,218	2,409	2,349	2,531	9,510
2005	1,699	1,837	1,925	2,035	7,496
2004	1,400	1,469	1,424	1,604	5,897
2003	1,213	1,290	1,287	1,673	5,463
2002	1,225	1,265	1,208	1,697	5,395

Earnings Per Share ($)

2007	0.93	1.07	0.91	E1.09	E4.24
2006	0.84	0.68	0.83	0.91	3.26
2005	0.67	0.66	0.75	0.74	2.82
2004	0.63	0.65	0.52	0.55	2.35
2003	0.29	-0.07	0.60	1.33	2.15
2002	0.54	0.54	0.56	1.46	3.10

Fiscal year ended Dec. 31. Next earnings report expected: Mid January. EPS Estimates based on S&P Operating Earnings; historical GAAP earnings are as reported.

Dividend Data (Dates: mm/dd Payment Date: mm/dd/yy)

Amount ($)	Date Decl.	Ex-Div. Date	Stk. of Record	Payment Date
0.210	12/21	12/28	01/02	01/16/07
0.210	03/15	03/29	04/02	04/16/07
0.220	06/21	06/27	06/29	07/16/07
0.220	09/19	09/27	10/01	10/15/07

Dividends have been paid since 1910. Source: Company reports.

State Street Corp

**STANDARD
&POOR'S**

Business Summary October 17, 2007

CORPORATE OVERVIEW. STT is a leading specialist in meeting the needs of institutional investors worldwide. Its customers include mutual funds and other collective investment funds, corporate and public pension funds, investment managers, and others. STT operates in the U.S., Australia, Austria, Belgium, Canada, the Cayman Islands, Chile, France, Germany, India, Ireland, Italy, Japan, Luxembourg, Mauritius, the Netherlands, New Zealand, China, Singapore, South Africa, South Korea, Switzerland, Taiwan, Thailand, the United Arab Emirates, and the United Kingdom.

STT reports two lines of business: Investment Servicing and Investment Management. Investment Servicing provides services for mutual funds and collective investment funds, corporate and public retirement plans, insurance companies, foundations, endowments, and other investment pools worldwide. Products include custody, product- and participant-level accounting, daily pricing and administration; master trust and master custody; record keeping;

foreign exchange, brokerage and other trading services; securities finance; deposit and short-term investment facilities; loans and lease financing; investment manager and hedge fund manager operations outsourcing; and performance, risk and compliance analytics to support institutional investors.

Investment Management offers a broad array of services for managing financial assets, including investment management and investment research services, primarily for institutional investors worldwide. These services include passive and active U.S. and non-U.S. equity and fixed income strategies, and other related services, such as securities finance.

Company Financials Fiscal Year Ended Dec. 31

Per Share Data ($)	2006	2005	2004	2003	2002	2001	2000	1999	1998	1997
Tangible Book Value	16.37	13.73	12.49	11.66	12.92	11.87	10.13	8.31	7.19	6.20
Earnings	3.26	2.82	2.35	2.15	3.10	1.90	1.82	1.89	1.33	1.16
S&P Core Earnings	3.30	2.80	2.30	1.41	2.01	1.83	NA	NA	NA	NA
Dividends	0.80	0.72	0.64	0.56	0.48	0.41	0.35	0.29	0.25	0.22
Payout Ratio	25%	26%	27%	26%	15%	21%	19%	15%	19%	19%
Prices:High	68.56	59.80	56.90	53.63	58.36	63.93	68.40	47.63	37.16	31.84
Prices:Low	54.39	40.62	39.91	30.37	32.11	36.25	31.22	27.75	23.94	15.66
P/E Ratio:High	21	21	24	25	19	34	38	25	28	27
P/E Ratio:Low	17	14	17	14	10	19	17	15	18	13

Income Statement Analysis (Million $)	2006	2005	2004	2003	2002	2001	2000	1999	1998	1997
Net Interest Income	1,110	907	859	810	979	1,025	894	781	745	641
Tax Equivalent Adjustment	NA	42.0	45.0	51.0	61.0	67.0	65.0	40.0	40.0	44.0
Non Interest Income	5,201	4,566	4,074	3,925	3,421	2,782	2,665	2,255	1,997	1,673
Loan Loss Provision	Nil	Nil	-18.0	Nil	4.00	10.0	9.00	80.0	17.0	16.0
% Expense/Operating Revenue	71.9%	73.8%	76.2%	76.5%	64.6%	75.3%	74.3%	76.9%	75.4%	73.5%
Pretax Income	1,771	1,432	1,192	1,112	1,555	930	906	968	657	564
Effective Tax Rate	38.1%	34.0%	33.1%	35.1%	34.7%	32.5%	34.3%	36.1%	33.6%	32.6%
Net Income	1,096	945	798	722	1,015	628	595	619	436	380
% Net Interest Margin	1.25	1.08	1.08	1.17	1.42	1.66	1.66	1.66	1.90	2.18
S&P Core Earnings	1,107	939	782	473	658	604	NA	NA	NA	NA

Balance Sheet & Other Financial Data (Million $)	2006	2005	2004	2003	2002	2001	2000	1999	1998	1997
Money Market Assets	6,021	12,039	26,829	31,694	46,342	37,991	44,083	35,616	26,399	16,450
Investment Securities	64,992	59,870	37,571	38,215	28,071	20,781	13,740	14,703	9,737	10,375
Commercial Loans	6,617	4,152	2,352	2,768	2,052	3,289	3,476	2,326	4,721	3,919
Other Loans	2,329	2,312	2,277	2,253	2,122	2,052	1,797	1,967	1,588	1,643
Total Assets	107,353	97,968	94,040	87,534	85,794	69,896	69,298	60,896	47,082	37,975
Demand Deposits	10,194	9,402	13,671	7,893	7,279	9,390	10,009	8,943	8,386	7,785
Time Deposits	55,452	50,244	41,458	39,623	38,189	29,169	27,928	25,202	19,153	17,093
Long Term Debt	2,616	2,659	2,458	2,222	1,270	1,217	1,219	921	922	774
Common Equity	7,252	6,367	6,159	5,747	4,787	3,845	3,262	2,652	2,311	1,995
% Return on Assets	1.1	1.0	0.9	0.8	1.3	0.9	0.9	1.1	1.0	1.1
% Return on Equity	16.1	15.1	13.4	13.7	23.5	17.7	20.1	24.9	20.3	20.2
% Loan Loss Reserve	0.2	0.3	0.4	1.2	1.5	1.1	1.1	1.1	1.3	1.5
% Loans/Deposits	13.6	10.9	8.4	10.6	9.2	13.9	13.9	12.6	22.9	22.4
% Equity to Assets	6.6	6.5	6.6	6.1	5.5	5.1	4.5	4.6	5.1	5.4

Data as orig reptd.; bef. results of disc opers/spec. items. Per share data adj. for stk. divs.; EPS diluted. E-Estimated. NA-Not Available. NM-Not Meaningful. NR-Not Ranked. UR-Under Review.

Office: One Lincoln St, Boston, MA 02111-2901.
Telephone: 617-786-3000.
Email: ir@statestreet.com
Website: http://www.statestreet.com

Chrmn & CEO: R.E. Logue
Vice Chrmn: J.L. Hooley
Vice Chrmn: W.W. Hunt
Vice Chrmn & CIO: J.C. Antonellis

EVP & CFO: E.J. Resch
Investor Contact: S.K. MacDonald (617-664-2888)
Board Members: T. E. Albright, K. F. Burnes, P. Coym, N. F. Darehshori, A. Fawcett, A. L. Goldstein, D. P. Gruber, L. A. Hill, C. R. LaMantia, R. E. Logue, M. Miskovic, R. P. Sergel, R. L. Skates, G. L. Summe, D. C. Walsh, R. E. Weissman

Founded: 1832
Domicile: Massachusetts
Employees: 21,700

The McGraw·Hill Companies

Stryker Corp

STANDARD &POOR'S

S&P Recommendation **HOLD** ★★★☆☆	Price $70.64 (as of Nov 23, 2007)	12-Mo. Target Price $77.00	Investment Style Large-Cap Growth

GICS Sector Health Care
Sub-Industry Health Care Equipment

Summary This company makes specialty surgical and medical products such as orthopedic implants, endoscopic items, and hospital beds. A division that operates outpatient physical therapy clinics was divested in June 2007.

Key Stock Statistics (Source S&P, Vickers, company reports)

52-Wk Range	$74.67– 51.20	S&P Oper. EPS 2007**E**	2.41	Market Capitalization(B)	$28.897	Beta	0.66
Trailing 12-Month EPS	$2.33	S&P Oper. EPS 2008**E**	2.87	Yield (%)	0.31	S&P 3-Yr. Proj. EPS CAGR(%)	18.00
Trailing 12-Month P/E	30.3	P/E on S&P Oper. EPS 2007**E**	29.3	Dividend Rate/Share	$0.22	S&P Credit Rating	A+
$10K Invested 5 Yrs Ago	$22,136	Common Shares Outstg. (M)	409.1	Institutional Ownership (%)	51		

Price Performance

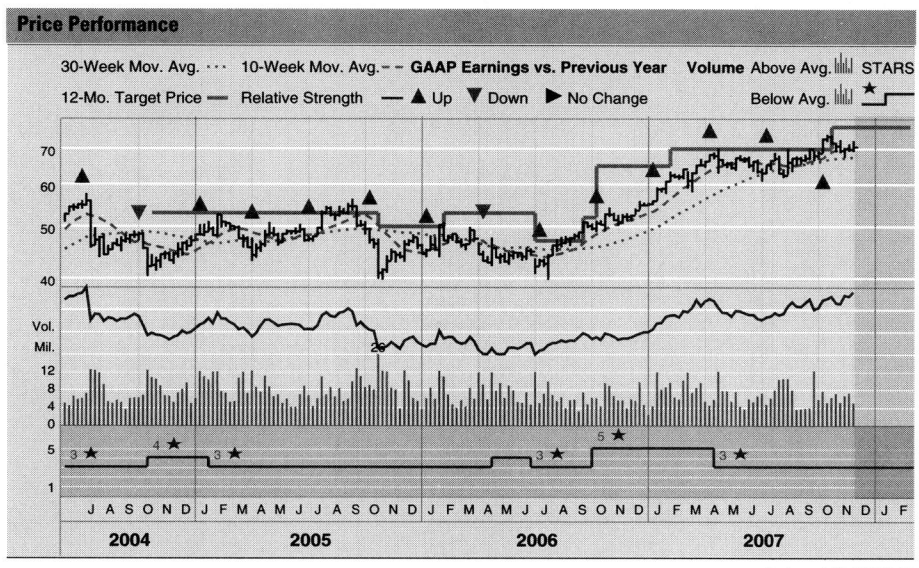

30-Week Mov. Avg. ··· 10-Week Mov. Avg. - - **GAAP Earnings vs. Previous Year** Volume Above Avg. STARS
12-Mo. Target Price — Relative Strength — ▲ Up ▼ Down ► No Change Below Avg. ★

Options: ASE, CBOE, Ph

Analysis prepared by **Robert M. Gold** on October 31, 2007, when the stock traded at **$ 71.00.**

Highlights

➤ We anticipate that 2008 sales will approximate $6.7 billion, up from an estimated $5.9 billion in 2007, driven by growth of approximately 12% in the orthopedic implant business and 13% to 14% growth in the medical/surgical (arthroscopy, endoscopy, surgical instrument, hospital beds and stretchers) division. We do not anticipate any contributions from the company's OP-1 bone growth compound prior to 2009, due to ongoing struggles in obtaining FDA approval. Based on recent trends and our expectation of new product launches, we think the company will experience modest unit price increases globally in 2008.

➤ We anticipate steady gross margin expansion through 2008, driven by manufacturing efficiencies and new product introductions. We expect that SG&A costs will absorb about 37% of sales over the coming three years, and we see R&D costs consuming between 5% and 6% of sales. We think the company will generate free cash flow of about $1.0 billion in 2008.

➤ After taxes estimated at 28.0%, our 2008 EPS estimate is $2.87, up from an estimated $2.41 in 2007 (before non-operating charges).

Investment Rationale/Risk

➤ We think Stryker will sustain high double digit earnings growth through 2009, driven by new product launches, rising gross margins and well managed operating costs. We believe the company can meaningfully expand its implant segment operating margins, in particular, and we expect that SYK will generate sales and EPS growth at the high end of the orthopedic device peer group. We anticipate that the company will utilize its free cash flow and cash on hand to make strategic acquisitions and repurchase common stock in coming years. We believe the orthopedics group offers consistent unit growth of 10% to 11%, and that global pricing will be a modest benefit through 2009.

➤ Risks to our recommendation and target price include unfavorable patent litigation outcomes, Medicare reimbursement rate reductions, and greater than expected price erosion in core markets.

➤ Our 12-month target price of $77 is based on a forward P/E-to-earnings growth ratio of about 1.5X, a modest premium to peers, applied to our 2008 EPS estimate and assuming three-year EPS growth of 18%.

Qualitative Risk Assessment

LOW	**MEDIUM**	HIGH

Stryker operates in very competitive areas of the global medical device industry, characterized by rapid technological innovation and relatively high levels of market share volatility. However, we believe that demand for the company's orthopedic products is largely immune from economic cycles, and that long-term unit demand drivers are more closely related to an aging global population.

Quantitative Evaluations

S&P Quality Ranking   A

D	C	B-	B	B+	A-	**A**	A+

Relative Strength Rank   **STRONG**

83

LOWEST = 1   HIGHEST = 99

Revenue/Earnings Data

Revenue (Million $)

	1Q	2Q	3Q	4Q	Year
2007	1,489	1,464	1,453	--	--
2006	1,321	1,328	1,294	1,463	5,406
2005	1,203	1,219	1,172	1,279	4,872
2004	1,035	1,043	1,029	1,156	4,262
2003	846.9	891.7	885.4	1,001	3,625
2002	702.9	733.9	745.6	829.2	3,012

Earnings Per Share ($)

2007	0.59	0.58	0.55	E0.67	E2.41
2006	0.36	0.52	0.46	0.55	1.89
2005	0.42	0.45	0.32	0.45	1.64
2004	0.33	0.37	0.04	0.40	1.14
2003	0.26	0.26	0.26	0.33	1.12
2002	0.20	0.21	0.18	0.26	0.85

Fiscal year ended Dec. 31. Next earnings report expected: Late January. EPS Estimates based on S&P Operating Earnings; historical GAAP earnings are as reported.

Dividend Data (Dates: mm/dd Payment Date: mm/dd/yy)

Amount ($)	Date Decl.	Ex-Div. Date	Stk. of Record	Payment Date
0.220	12/06	12/27	12/29	01/31/07

Dividends have been paid since 1992. Source: Company reports.

Stryker Corp

STANDARD &POOR'S

Business Summary October 31, 2007

Stryker Corp. traces its origins to a business founded in 1941 by Dr. Homer H. Stryker, a leading orthopedic surgeon and the inventor of several orthopedic products. The company has significant exposure to the artificial hip, prosthetic knee and trauma product areas. International sales accounted for 34% of the total in 2006 .

Orthopedic implants (57% of 2006 sales) consist of products such as hip, knee, shoulder and spinal implants, associated implant instrumentation, trauma-related products, and bone cement. Artificial joints are made of cobalt chromium, titanium alloys, ceramics, or ultra-high molecular weight polyethylene, and are implanted in patients whose natural joints have been damaged by arthritis, osteoporosis, other diseases, or injury. SYK also sells trauma-related products, used primarily in the fixation of fractures resulting from sudden injury, including internal fixation devices such as nails, plates and screws, and

external fixation devices such as pins, wires and connection bars. In addition, the division sells Simplex bone cement, a material used to secure cemented implants to bone, and the OP-1 Bone Growth Device. Composed of recombinant human osteogenic protein-1 and a bioresorbable collagen matrix, the product induces the formation of new bone when implanted into existing bone, and is approved to treat long bone fractures in patients in whom use of autograft treatments has failed or is not a feasible option. Stryker continues to develop OP-1 for spinal indications, including spinal stenosis, and is working with the FDA to obtain U.S. marketing clearance. In 2006, SYK began the initial launch of a hip resurfacing product in certain international markets.

Company Financials Fiscal Year Ended Dec. 31

Per Share Data ($)	2006	2005	2004	2003	2002	2001	2000	1999	1998	1997
Tangible Book Value	7.98	5.75	4.44	2.98	1.42	0.65	0.04	NM	NM	1.48
Cash Flow	2.69	2.34	1.78	1.71	1.30	1.09	0.97	0.46	0.20	0.40
Earnings	1.89	1.64	1.14	1.12	0.85	0.67	0.55	0.05	0.10	0.32
S&P Core Earnings	1.89	1.57	1.08	1.08	0.80	0.63	NA	NA	NA	NA
Dividends	0.22	0.11	0.09	0.07	0.06	0.05	0.03	0.03	0.03	0.03
Payout Ratio	12%	7%	8%	6%	7%	7%	5%	60%	27%	9%
Prices:High	55.92	56.32	57.66	42.68	33.74	31.60	28.88	18.31	13.94	11.33
Prices:Low	39.77	39.74	40.30	29.83	21.93	21.65	12.22	11.11	7.75	6.06
P/E Ratio:High	30	34	51	38	40	47	52	NM	NM	35
P/E Ratio:Low	21	24	35	27	26	32	22	NM	NM	19

Income Statement Analysis (Million $)	2006	2005	2004	2003	2002	2001	2000	1999	1998	1997
Revenue	5,406	4,872	4,262	3,625	3,012	2,602	2,289	2,104	1,103	980
Operating Income	1,459	1,305	1,092	901	751	645	600	329	226	217
Depreciation	332	290	251	230	186	172	169	163	37.6	33.3
Interest Expense	Nil	7.70	6.80	22.6	40.3	67.9	96.6	123	12.2	4.12
Pretax Income	1,104	1,003	717	652	507	406	335	29.8	60.0	196
Effective Tax Rate	29.5%	32.7%	35.0%	30.5%	31.8%	33.0%	34.0%	34.9%	34.0%	35.7%
Net Income	778	675	466	454	346	272	221	19.4	39.6	125
S&P Core Earnings	779	645	441	436	324	257	NA	NA	NA	NA

Balance Sheet & Other Financial Data (Million $)	2006	2005	2004	2003	2002	2001	2000	1999	1998	1997
Cash	1,415	1,057	349	65.9	37.8	50.1	54.0	80.0	142	351
Current Assets	3,534	2,870	2,143	1,398	1,151	993	997	1,110	1,312	757
Total Assets	5,874	4,944	4,084	3,159	2,816	2,424	2,431	2,581	2,886	985
Current Liabilities	1,352	1,249	1,114	850	708	533	617	670	699	303
Long Term Debt	Nil	184	0.70	18.8	491	721	876	1,181	1,488	4.45
Common Equity	4,191	3,252	2,752	2,155	1,498	1,056	855	672	643	657
Total Capital	4,191	3,436	2,753	2,174	1,989	1,777	1,731	1,853	2,148	653
Capital Expenditures	218	272	188	145	139	162	80.7	76.2	51.2	35.2
Cash Flow	1,110	965	717	683	532	444	390	182	77.2	159
Current Ratio	2.6	2.3	1.9	1.6	1.6	1.9	1.6	1.7	1.9	2.5
% Long Term Debt of Capitalization	Nil	5.4	0.0	0.9	24.7	40.6	50.6	63.8	69.3	0.7
% Net Income of Revenue	14.4	13.9	10.9	12.5	11.5	10.4	9.7	0.9	3.6	12.8
% Return on Assets	14.3	15.0	12.9	15.2	13.2	11.2	8.8	0.7	2.0	12.7
% Return on Equity	20.8	22.5	19.0	24.8	27.1	28.4	29.0	2.9	6.1	20.5

Data as orig reptd.; bef. results of disc opers/spec. items. Per share data adj. for stk. divs.; EPS diluted. E-Estimated. NA-Not Available. NM-Not Meaningful. NR-Not Ranked. UR-Under Review.

Office: 2825 Airview Blvd, Portage, MI 49002-1802.
Telephone: 269-385-2600.
Website: http://www.stryker.com
Chrmn: J.W. Brown

Pres & CEO: S.P. MacMillan
Investor Contact: D.H. Bergy (269-385-2600)
VP & CFO: D.H. Bergy
VP & General Counsel: C.E. Hall

Board Members: J. W. Brown, H. E. Cox, Jr., D. M. Engelman, L. L. Francesconi, J. H. Grossman, S. P. MacMillan, W. U. Parfet, R. E. Stryker

Founded: 1946
Domicile: Michigan
Employees: 18,806

The McGraw-Hill Companies

Sunoco Inc.

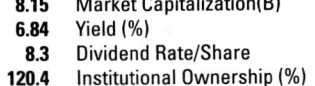

STANDARD &POOR'S

S&P Recommendation	BUY ★★★★☆	Price $67.73 (as of Nov 23, 2007)	12-Mo. Target Price $84.00	Investment Style Large-Cap Blend

GICS Sector Energy
Sub-Industry Oil & Gas Refining & Marketing

Summary The seventh largest refiner in the U.S., Sunoco has diversified operations in refining, marketing, chemicals, logistics and cokemaking.

Key Stock Statistics (Source S&P, Vickers, company reports)

52-Wk Range	$86.40– 56.68	S&P Oper. EPS 2007**E**	8.15	Market Capitalization(B)	$8.152	Beta	0.48
Trailing 12-Month EPS	$8.52	S&P Oper. EPS 2008**E**	6.84	Yield (%)	1.62	S&P 3-Yr. Proj. EPS CAGR(%)	-11.00
Trailing 12-Month P/E	8.0	P/E on S&P Oper. EPS 2007**E**	8.3	Dividend Rate/Share	$1.10	S&P Credit Rating	BBB
$10K Invested 5 Yrs Ago	$50,228	Common Shares Outstg. (M)	120.4	Institutional Ownership (%)	81		

Price Performance

- 30-Week Mov. Avg. · · · 10-Week Mov. Avg. ─ ─ **GAAP Earnings vs. Previous Year** Volume Above Avg. ▍▍▍ STARS
- 12-Mo. Target Price ── Relative Strength ─ ▲ Up ▼ Down ▶ No Change Below Avg. ▍▍▍ ★

2-for-1

J A S O N D J F M A M J J A S O N D J F M A M J J A S O N D J F M A M J J A S O N D J F

2004   2005   2006   2007

Options: CBOE, Ph

Analysis prepared by **Tina J. Vital** on November 19, 2007, when the stock traded at **$ 70.26.**

Highlights

➤ Third quarter refining throughputs rose 2.8%, above our expectations. Using guidance from SUN, we expect 2007 levels to decline over 2%, reflecting planned and unplanned maintenance activities, before rising slightly in 2008.

➤ SUN's refining margins narrowed in the third quarter, as refined product prices failed to keep pace with a sharp increase in crude oil prices. Industrywide, U.S. refining margins have weakened in the 2007 second half, and we project that 2008 refining margins will narrow more than 30% from 2007 levels, reflecting strong crude oil prices; however, we believe they will remain relatively high compared to historical norms, on continued strong demand and limited upgrading capacity.

➤ We project that 2007 after-tax operating earnings will remain about flat with 2006 levels, as weakened refining earnings are offset by market improvements in chemicals and logistics, before declining about 15% in 2008, reflecting narrowed refining margins.

Investment Rationale/Risk

➤ While we believe SUN's focus on light sweet crude oil feedstocks has limited its ability to lower costs and take advantage of the wider sour crude refining margins, it has permitted a relatively high volume of higher grade products. We think its strong East Coast and Midwest retail distribution provides long-term earnings stability, and its stake in Sunoco Logistics Partners L.P. provides a stable source of distributions. We see limited internal growth opportunities, and expect SUN to pursue acquisitions across all of its business lines.

➤ Risks to our recommendation and target price include changes in economic, industry and operating conditions that could lead to a narrowing of refining, chemical, coke or logistics margins, or overpaying for an acquisition.

➤ A blend of our discounted cash flow analysis (assuming a weighted average cost of capital of 7.2%, and a terminal growth rate of 3%) and relative valuation leads to our 12-month target of $84 per share. This result represents an expected enterprise value of 6.9X our 2008 EBITDA estimate, a premium to peers.

Revenue/Earnings Data

Revenue (Million $)

	1Q	2Q	3Q	4Q	Year
2007	9,305	10,764	11,497	--	--
2006	8,569	10,575	10,480	9,012	38,715
2005	7,209	7,990	9,295	9,270	33,764
2004	5,245	6,276	6,558	7,429	25,508
2003	4,570	4,189	4,594	4,576	17,929
2002	2,931	3,556	3,812	4,085	14,384

Earnings Per Share ($)

2007	1.44	4.20	1.81	E1.44	E8.15
2006	0.59	3.22	2.76	1.00	7.59
2005	0.84	1.75	2.39	2.12	7.08
2004	0.58	1.54	0.70	1.24	4.04
2003	0.56	0.52	0.70	0.24	2.02
2002	-0.70	0.06	-0.07	0.40	-0.31

Fiscal year ended Dec. 31. Next earnings report expected: Early February. EPS Estimates based on S&P Operating Earnings; historical GAAP earnings are as reported.

Dividend Data (Dates: mm/dd Payment Date: mm/dd/yy)

Amount ($)	Date Decl.	Ex-Div. Date	Stk. of Record	Payment Date
0.250	01/04	02/07	02/09	03/09/07
0.275	02/01	05/07	05/09	06/08/07
0.275	07/03	08/06	08/08	09/07/07
0.275	10/04	11/05	11/07	12/07/07

Dividends have been paid since 1904. Source: Company reports.

Sunoco Inc.

STANDARD &POOR'S

Business Summary November 19, 2007

CORPORATE OVERVIEW. Sunoco Inc. (SUN) has been active in the petroleum industry since 1886, and conducts its business through five operating segments: Refining and Supply (47% of 2006 revenues; 81% of 2006 after-tax segment income); Retail Marketing (35%; 7%); Chemicals (7%; 4%); Logistics (10%; 3%); and Coke (1%; 5%).

Refining and Supply manufactures petroleum products and commodity petrochemicals. As of December 31, 2006, SUN owned and operated five refineries with a crude unit capacity of about 900,000 barrels per day (b/d), located in the Northeast (655,000 b/d; in Marcus Hook, PA, Philadelphia, PA, and "Eagle Point" in Westville, NJ), and the MidContinent (245,000 b/d; Toledo, OH, and Tulsa, OK). Products manufactured fell 3.0%, to 946,700 b/d in 2006 (gasoline 46%, middle distillates 32%, residual fuels 8%, petrochemicals 4%, lubricants 1%, and other 9%).

SUN meets all of its crude oil requirements through purchases from third parties. Approximately 67% of SUN's 2006 crude oil supply came from West Africa (45% from Nigeria), 15% from the U.S., 9% from Canada, 3% from Central Asia, 1% from the North Sea, 4% from South and Central America, and 1% from lubes extracted gasoil/naphtha intermediate feedstock. In the 2004 second half, the company began processing limited amounts of lower value high acid sweet crude oils in some of its Northeast refineries; during 2006, about 63,000 b/d of high acid crude oil was processed.

SUN manufactures, distributes and markets commodity and intermediate petrochemicals, consisting of aromatic derivatives (cumene, phenol, acetone and bispenol-A) and polypropylene. At year end 2006, chemical plant capacity totaled 9.01 billion pounds. During 2006 chemicals production rose 1% to 7.216 billion pounds (31% polypropylene, 22% cumene, 21% phenol, 13% acetone, 9% propylene, 3% bisphenol-A, and 1% other phenol derivatives) .

Company Financials Fiscal Year Ended Dec. 31

Per Share Data ($)	2006	2005	2004	2003	2002	2001	2000	1999	1998	1997
Tangible Book Value	17.01	15.42	11.65	10.23	9.05	10.88	10.03	8.37	8.41	5.21
Cash Flow	11.15	10.20	9.50	4.35	1.85	4.38	4.05	2.05	2.72	2.46
Earnings	7.59	7.08	4.04	2.02	-0.31	2.43	2.35	0.54	1.48	1.35
S&P Core Earnings	7.63	7.56	4.19	2.13	-0.70	1.88	NA	NA	NA	NA
Dividends	0.95	0.75	0.58	0.51	0.50	0.50	0.50	0.50	0.50	0.50
Payout Ratio	13%	11%	14%	25%	NM	21%	21%	93%	34%	37%
Prices:High	97.25	85.29	42.26	26.30	21.13	21.37	17.28	19.72	22.16	23.19
Prices:Low	57.50	38.10	25.26	14.84	13.51	14.56	10.97	11.44	14.75	12.00
P/E Ratio:High	13	12	10	13	NM	9	7	37	15	17
P/E Ratio:Low	8	5	6	7	NM	6	5	21	10	9

Income Statement Analysis (Million $)										
Revenue	38,715	33,764	25,508	17,929	14,384	14,063	14,300	10,068	8,413	10,464
Operating Income	2,049	2,078	1,501	934	313	954	948	331	605	680
Depreciation, Depletion and Amortization	459	429	818	363	329	321	298	276	257	259
Interest Expense	89.0	69.0	97.0	111	108	103	78.0	82.0	71.0	71.0
Pretax Income	1,580	1,580	995	495	-73.0	587	596	150	389	385
Effective Tax Rate	38.0%	38.4%	39.2%	37.0%	NM	32.2%	31.0%	35.3%	28.0%	31.7%
Net Income	979	974	605	312	-47.0	398	411	97.0	280	263
S&P Core Earnings	984	1,040	626	330	-106	307	NA	NA	NA	NA

Balance Sheet & Other Financial Data (Million $)										
Cash	263	919	405	431	390	42.0	239	87.0	38.0	33.0
Current Assets	4,015	3,687	2,551	2,068	1,898	1,510	1,683	1,456	1,180	1,248
Total Assets	10,982	9,931	8,079	6,922	6,441	5,932	5,426	5,196	4,849	4,667
Current Liabilities	4,755	4,210	3,022	2,170	1,776	1,778	1,646	1,766	1,384	1,464
Long Term Debt	1,705	1,234	1,379	1,350	1,453	1,142	933	878	823	824
Common Equity	2,075	2,051	1,607	1,556	1,394	1,642	1,702	4,782	1,514	739
Total Capital	5,227	4,749	4,271	3,940	3,816	3,335	2,885	5,897	2,512	2,359
Capital Expenditures	1,019	970	832	425	385	331	465	374	457	380
Cash Flow	1,438	1,403	1,423	675	282	719	709	373	517	478
Current Ratio	0.8	0.9	0.8	1.0	1.1	0.8	1.0	0.8	0.9	0.9
% Long Term Debt of Capitalization	32.6	26.0	32.3	34.3	38.1	34.2	32.3	14.9	32.8	34.9
% Return on Assets	9.4	10.8	8.0	4.7	NM	7.0	7.7	1.9	5.9	5.4
% Return on Equity	47.5	53.3	38.3	21.2	NM	23.8	25.6	2.0	23.1	30.7

Data as orig reptd.; bef. results of disc opers/spec. items. Per share data adj. for stk. divs.; EPS diluted. E-Estimated. NA-Not Available. NM-Not Meaningful. NR-Not Ranked. UR-Under Review.

Office: 1735 Market St Ste LL, Philadelphia, PA 19103-7583.
Telephone: 215-977-3000.
Email: sunocoonline@sunocoinc.com
Website: http://www.sunocoinc.com

Chrmn, Pres & CEO: J.G. Drosdick
SVP & CFO: T.W. Hofmann
SVP & Chief Admin Officer: C.K. Valutas
SVP & General Counsel: M.S. Kuritzkes

Treas: P. Mulholland
Investor Contact: T. Harr (215-977-6764)
Board Members: R. J. Darnall, J. G. Drosdick, U. F. Fairbairn, T. P. Gerrity, R. Greco, J. P. Jones, III, J. G. Kaiser, R. A. Pew, G. J. Ratcliffe, J. G. Rowe, J. K. Wulff

Founded: 1886
Domicile: Pennsylvania
Employees: 14,000

STANDARD &POOR'S

Sun Microsystems Inc

S&P Recommendation **BUY** ★★★★☆	Price $19.16 (as of Nov 23, 2007)	12-Mo. Target Price $24.00	Investment Style Large-Cap Blend

GICS Sector Information Technology
Sub-Industry Computer Hardware

Summary This company makes high-performance servers, workstations and operating system software, and invented the Java programming language.

Key Stock Statistics (Source S&P, Vickers, company reports)

52-Wk Range	$27.12– 18.00	S&P Oper. EPS 2008**E**	0.56	Market Capitalization(B)	$15.876	Beta	2.59
Trailing 12-Month EPS	$0.72	S&P Oper. EPS 2009**E**	0.69	Yield (%)	Nil	S&P 3-Yr. Proj. EPS CAGR(%)	NM
Trailing 12-Month P/E	26.6	P/E on S&P Oper. EPS 2008**E**	34.2	Dividend Rate/Share	Nil	S&P Credit Rating	BB+
$10K Invested 5 Yrs Ago	$12,377	Common Shares Outstg. (M)	828.6	Institutional Ownership (%)	NA		

Price Performance

| 30-Week Mov. Avg. ··· 10-Week Mov. Avg. - - GAAP Earnings vs. Previous Year   Volume Above Avg. ⅲⅲ STARS |
| 12-Mo. Target Price — Relative Strength ▲ Up ▼ Down ▶ No Change   Below Avg. ⅲⅲ ★ |

Options: ASE, CBOE, P, Ph

Analysis prepared by **Jawahar Hingorani** on November 14, 2007, when the stock traded at **$ 20.62**.

Highlights

➤ We expect revenue to increase 5.5% in FY 08 (Jun.), followed by a gain of 8.6% in FY 09. We believe partnerships and new products will drive global revenue growth, offset by a slowing economy and potential weakness in enterprise IT spending in the U.S. going into 2008. We see the ongoing restructuring efforts aiding future profitability by lowering costs. In our view, the recently effected 1-for-4 reverse stock split, undertaken to encourage institutional ownership and reduce share price volatility, is neutral for shareholders.

➤ We look for strong pricing competition and the impact of Sun's increased low-end sales mix to be offset by higher volumes and manufacturing efficiencies. As a result, we anticipate that the gross margin level will remain around 44% in FY 08. We see SG&A expenses declining further as a percentage of revenue due to the company's ongoing restructuring efforts.

➤ Our split-adjusted EPS estimate for FY 08 is $0.56, before restructuring expense, to be followed by EPS of $0.69 in FY 09.

Investment Rationale/Risk

➤ We are encouraged by Sun's turnaround efforts, improving margin profile, and cash flow generation. In addition, we expect further work force reductions, beyond those taken in FY 07, to continue to realign its cost structure and improve overall profitability. We expect sales growth due to a focus on the low- and mid-range segment, which we think will keep Sun profitable. We believe the company's openness to partnering with current and former rivals will help it achieve its goals.

➤ Risks to our recommendation and target price include the possibility of an accelerated migration away from UNIX systems, elongating sales cycles, and server market share erosion.

➤ Our 12-month target price of $24 is based on a blend of our price-to-sales and discounted cash flow (DCF) analyses. We believe a ratio of 1.37X our calendar 2008 revenue per share estimate is appropriate, based on our review of the stock's one-year monthly historical average. This leads to a value of $24. Our DCF model, which assumes a weighted average cost of capital (WACC) of 11% and an expected terminal growth rate of 3%, also results in a value of $24.

Qualitative Risk Assessment

LOW	MEDIUM	**HIGH**

Our risk assessment reflects the losses the company has sustained over the past several years, our view of its reliance on high-end systems sales, and the difficult pricing pressures we see in the computer hardware industry.

Quantitative Evaluations

S&P Quality Ranking   C

D	**C**	B-	B	B+	A-	A	A+

Relative Strength Rank   WEAK

28

LOWEST = 1   HIGHEST = 99

Revenue/Earnings Data

Revenue (Million $)

	1Q	2Q	3Q	4Q	Year
2008	3,219	--	--	--	--
2007	3,189	3,566	3,283	3,835	13,873
2006	2,726	3,337	3,177	3,828	13,068
2005	2,628	2,841	2,627	2,974	11,070
2004	2,536	2,888	2,651	3,110	11,185
2003	2,747	2,915	2,790	2,982	11,434

Earnings Per Share ($)

	1Q	2Q	3Q	4Q	Year
2008	0.12	E0.16	E0.12	E0.18	E0.56
2007	-0.08	0.16	0.08	0.36	0.52
2006	-0.16	-0.28	-0.24	-0.36	-1.00
2005	-0.16	Nil	-0.04	0.04	-0.12
2004	-0.36	-0.16	-0.92	0.92	-0.48
2003	-0.16	-2.88	Nil	-1.28	-4.28

Fiscal year ended Jun. 30. Next earnings report expected: Late January. EPS Estimates based on S&P Operating Earnings; historical GAAP earnings are as reported.

Dividend Data (Dates: mm/dd Payment Date: mm/dd/yy)

Amount ($)	Date Decl.	Ex-Div. Date	Stk. of Record	Payment Date
1-for-4 REV.	--	11/12	--	11/12/07

Source: Company reports.

Please read the Required Disclosures and Analyst Certification on the last page of this report.

The McGraw-Hill Companies

Sun Microsystems Inc

STANDARD
&POOR'S

Business Summary November 14, 2007

CORPORATE OVERVIEW. Sun Microsystems (JAVA), founded in 1982, invented the workstation, but became known in the late 1990s for its higher-end systems, which experienced significant growth in demand during the build out of the Internet. The company serves a variety of markets, including financial services, government, manufacturing, retail and telecommunications, as it continues to focus on a single vision--that the network is the computer.

Sun is a primary supplier of networked computing products, including workstations, servers and storage products--which had primarily used the company's own Scaleable Processor Architecture (SPARC) microprocessors and its Solaris software--but this has been expanded to include other chips and operating system software. Computer systems accounted for 46% of net revenues in FY 07 (Jun.), storage 17%, support services 29%, and client solutions and educational services 8%. In FY 07, Avnet accounted for 11% of total revenue, due to its acquisition of Access Distribution from General Electric.

In January 2007, private equity firm Kohlberg Kravis Roberts & Co. (KKR) in-

vested $700 million in JAVA via convertible senior notes. We view this news positively, and we think it helps to validate JAVA's long-term growth strategy.

CORPORATE STRATEGY. We believe the company has undertaken a number of restructuring initiatives over the past several years in an effort to offset slowing demand trends, notably a nearly 40% decline in total revenues between 2001 and 2005. Sun's most recent plan, Restructuring Plan VII, initiated in August 2007, has a goal of reducing its employee base by an additional 600 employees. In the first fiscal quarter of 2008 ended September 30, 2007, total severance and benefit costs of $104 million were recognized, in addition to $4 million in expenses related to other restructuring related charges. Through the end of the FY 07, JAVA had reduced its work force by 2,150 and had recognized $192 million in expenses, largely related to the work force reduction.

Company Financials Fiscal Year Ended Jun. 30

Per Share Data ($)	2007	2006	2005	2004	2003	2002	2001	2000	1999	1998
Tangible Book Value	4.56	3.20	7.20	7.08	7.52	9.28	10.52	8.90	6.19	4.67
Cash Flow	1.45	-0.34	0.67	0.42	-3.15	0.47	2.59	3.11	2.04	1.53
Earnings	0.52	-1.00	-0.12	-0.48	-4.28	-0.72	1.16	2.20	1.28	0.96
S&P Core Earnings	0.48	-1.04	-1.00	-2.68	-3.24	-1.52	0.56	NA	NA	NA
Dividends	Nil	Nil	Nil	Nil	Nil	Nil	Nil	Nil	Nil	Nil
Payout Ratio	Nil	Nil	Nil	Nil	Nil	Nil	Nil	Nil	Nil	Nil
Prices:High	27.12	23.52	21.04	23.72	22.56	57.64	140.50	258.63	166.03	44.19
Prices:Low	18.00	14.96	13.68	13.16	12.08	9.36	30.08	100.50	43.56	18.81
P/E Ratio:High	52	NM	NM	NM	NM	NM	NM	NM	NM	46
P/E Ratio:Low	35	NM	NM	NM	NM	NM	26	46	34	19

Income Statement Analysis (Million $)

	2007	2006	2005	2004	2003	2002	2001	2000	1999	1998
Revenue	13,873	13,068	11,070	11,185	11,434	12,496	18,250	15,721	11,726	9,791
Operating Income	1,236	119	556	3.00	694	239	2,617	3,181	2,269	1,746
Depreciation	830	575	671	730	918	970	1,229	776	627	440
Interest Expense	Nil	55.0	49.0	37.0	43.0	58.0	100	84.0	0.68	1.57
Pretax Income	583	-675	-184	437	-2,653	-1,048	1,584	2,771	1,606	1,176
Effective Tax Rate	18.9%	NM	NM	NM	NM	NM	38.1%	33.1%	35.8%	35.1%
Net Income	473	-864	-107	-388	-3,429	-587	981	1,854	1,031	763
S&P Core Earnings	426	-904	-864	-2,166	-2,581	-1,253	471	NA	NA	NA

Balance Sheet & Other Financial Data (Million $)

	2007	2006	2005	2004	2003	2002	2001	2000	1999	1998
Cash	4,582	4,065	3,396	3,601	3,062	2,885	1,472	1,849	1,089	822
Current Assets	9,328	8,273	7,191	7,303	6,779	7,777	7,934	6,877	6,116	4,148
Total Assets	15,838	15,082	14,190	14,503	12,985	16,522	18,181	14,152	8,420	5,711
Current Liabilities	5,451	6,165	4,766	5,113	4,129	5,057	5,146	4,759	3,227	2,123
Long Term Debt	1,264	575	1,123	1,175	1,531	1,449	1,705	1,720	Nil	Nil
Common Equity	7,179	6,344	6,674	6,438	6,491	9,801	10,586	7,309	4,812	3,514
Total Capital	8,443	6,919	7,797	7,613	8,022	11,250	13,035	9,393	4,812	3,514
Capital Expenditures	488	315	257	249	373	559	1,292	982	739	830
Cash Flow	1,303	-289	564	342	-2,511	383	2,210	2,630	1,658	1,203
Current Ratio	1.7	1.3	1.5	1.4	1.6	1.5	1.5	1.4	1.9	2.0
% Long Term Debt of Capitalization	15.0	8.3	14.4	15.4	19.1	12.8	13.1	18.3	Nil	Nil
% Net Income of Revenue	3.4	NM	NM	NM	NM	NM	5.4	11.8	8.8	7.8
% Return on Assets	3.1	NM	NM	NM	NM	NM	6.1	16.4	14.6	14.7
% Return on Equity	7.0	NM	NM	NM	NM	NM	11.0	30.5	24.8	24.4

Data as orig reptd.; bef. results of disc opers/spec. items. Per share data adj. for stk. divs.; EPS diluted. E-Estimated. NA-Not Available. NM-Not Meaningful. NR-Not Ranked. UR-Under Review.

Office: 4150 Network Circle, Santa Clara, CA 95054.
Telephone: 650-960-1300.
Email: investor-relations@sun.com
Website: http://www.sun.com

Chrmn: S.G. McNealy
Pres & CEO: J.I. Schwartz
EVP & CFO: M. Lehman
EVP & CTO: G.M. Papadopoulos

EVP, Secy & General Counsel: M.A. Dillon
Board Members: J. L. Barksdale, S. Bennett, P.
Currie, R. Finocchio, Jr., M. E. Marks, S. G. McNealy, P.
E. Mitchell, M. K. Oshman, T. Ridder, J. I. Schwartz

Founded: 1982
Domicile: Delaware
Employees: 34,200

The McGraw-Hill Companies

SunTrust Banks Inc.

STANDARD &POOR'S

S&P Recommendation SELL ★ ★ ☆ ☆ ☆	Price $69.05 (as of Nov 29, 2007)	12-Mo. Target Price $68.00	Investment Style Large-Cap Blend

GICS Sector Financials
Sub-Industry Regional Banks

Summary This bank holding company has $176 billion in assets and $116 billion in deposits, and operates in eleven Southeastern states and DC.

Key Stock Statistics (Source S&P, Vickers, company reports)

52-Wk Range	$94.18– 64.34	S&P Oper. EPS 2007**E**	5.51	Market Capitalization(B)	$24.116	Beta	0.57
Trailing 12-Month EPS	$5.93	S&P Oper. EPS 2008**E**	6.06	Yield (%)	4.23	S&P 3-Yr. Proj. EPS CAGR(%)	1.30
Trailing 12-Month P/E	11.6	P/E on S&P Oper. EPS 2007**E**	12.5	Dividend Rate/Share	$2.92	S&P Credit Rating	AA-
$10K Invested 5 Yrs Ago	$13,096	Common Shares Outstg. (M)	349.3	Institutional Ownership (%)	57		

Price Performance

30-Week Mov. Avg. ···· 10-Week Mov. Avg. — **GAAP Earnings vs. Previous Year**   Volume Above Avg. ▌▌▌ STARS
12-Mo. Target Price — Relative Strength — ▲ Up ▼ Down ► No Change   Below Avg. ▌▌▌ ★

Options: CBOE, P, Ph

Analysis prepared by **Erik Oja** on November 29, 2007, when the stock traded at **$ 69.05**.

Highlights

➤ We believe STI's loan portfolio will grow 0.7% in 2007 and 5.1% in 2008, led by commercial lending, which is about 29% of the portfolio. We expect net interest income to rise 2.8% in 2007 and 7.7% in 2008, as we expect deposit rates to moderate. We project non-interest income will grow 8.0% in 2007, but only 1.3% in 2008. Together, this should result in revenue growth of 5.0% in 2007 and 4.9% in 2008.

➤ Our 2007 non-interest expense to total revenue (efficiency ratio) forecast is 58.7%, compared to 2006's 59.4% and 2005's 60.1%, including merger charges, or 58.8% excluding merger charges. STI has numerous non-interest expense reduction programs ongoing, and we think they will drive the efficiency ratio down to a level of below 57% starting in 2008. However, based on weakening credit trends, we expect loan loss provisions of about $479 million in 2007 and $842 million in 2008, up from about $263 million in 2006.

➤ Assuming some share repurchases under a 30 million share authorization approved August 2007, we project operating EPS of $5.51 in 2007, down 5.3% from $5.82 in 2006. Our 2008 EPS estimate is $6.06, up 10%.

Investment Rationale/Risk

➤ STI has made excellent progress, in our opinion, with non-interest expense reductions and in deposit and fee income growth, and can realize further gains should it choose to continue selling its holdings of Coca-Cola stock. However, we are concerned about STI's relatively low yields on loans and total assets, and by the decline in its credit quality in the last two quarters. Although STI estimates that Alt-A portfolio loans (which are 1.5% of STI's total loan portfolio) accounted for 60% of the non-performing residential mortgage loans, and that future exposure is manageable, we are concerned about credit quality in home equity lines of credit, and in smaller commercial loans. Credit quality further weakened in the third quarter, as non-performing loans increased to 0.83% of total loans, up from 0.64% at June 30 and 0.44% at December 31, 2007.

➤ Risks to our recommendation and target price include a takeover at a substantial premium, loan yields higher than our forecasts, and better than expected credit quality.

➤ Our 12-month target price is $68, based on a P/E of 11.2X our 2008 EPS estimate of $6.45, a multiple in line with STI's regional banking peers.

Qualitative Risk Assessment

LOW	MEDIUM	HIGH

Our risk assessment reflects the company's large-cap valuation, the strong credit quality of its loan portfolio, and its history of profitability. While the company operates in a highly competitive and fragmented industry, the industry tends to produce relatively stable financial results.

Quantitative Evaluations

S&P Quality Ranking   A+

D	C	B-	B	B+	A-	A	A+

Relative Strength Rank   MODERATE

46

LOWEST = 1   HIGHEST = 99

Revenue/Earnings Data

Revenue (Million $)

	1Q	2Q	3Q	4Q	Year
2007	3,407	3,698	3,334	--	--
2006	3,130	3,299	3,384	3,447	13,260
2005	2,470	2,614	2,829	2,973	10,886
2004	1,769	1,811	1,880	2,363	7,823
2003	1,766	1,771	1,752	1,783	7,072
2002	1,913	1,918	1,852	1,845	7,527

Earnings Per Share ($)

2007	1.44	1.89	1.18	E1.45	E5.51
2006	1.46	1.49	1.47	1.39	5.82
2005	1.36	1.28	1.40	1.43	5.47
2004	1.26	1.29	1.30	1.26	5.19
2003	1.17	1.17	1.18	1.21	4.73
2002	1.06	1.20	1.21	1.20	4.66

Fiscal year ended Dec. 31. Next earnings report expected: Mid January. EPS Estimates based on S&P Operating Earnings; historical GAAP earnings are as reported.

Dividend Data (Dates: mm/dd Payment Date: mm/dd/yy)

Amount ($)	Date Decl.	Ex-Div. Date	Stk. of Record	Payment Date
0.730	02/13	02/27	03/01	03/15/07
0.730	04/17	05/30	06/01	06/15/07
0.730	08/14	08/29	09/01	09/14/07
0.730	11/15	11/28	11/30	12/14/07

Dividends have been paid since 1985. Source: Company reports.

Please read the Required Disclosures and Analyst Certification on the last page of this report.

The McGraw-Hill Companies

SunTrust Banks Inc.

STANDARD
&POOR'S

Business Summary November 29, 2007

CORPORATE OVERVIEW. STI owns SunTrust Bank, an organization aligned by geographic region: the Carolinas Group (North and South Carolina), the Central Group (Georgia, Tennessee), the Florida Group, and the Mid-Atlantic Group (D.C., Maryland, Virginia and West Virginia). The company has five lines of business: Retail Banking, Commercial Banking, Corporate and Investment Banking, Mortgage Banking, and Wealth and Investment Management. With Corporate/Other, there are six reportable business segments.

The Retail and Commercial Banking segments generate about 55% of total segment net income. Retail Banking (35%) provides lending and deposit gathering as well as other banking-related products and services to consumers and small businesses with sales up to $10 million. Commercial Banking (20%) offers financial products and services, including commercial lending, treasury management, financial risk management, and corporate bankcard services, to enterprises with sales up to $250 million.

The Corporate and Investment Banking segment (10%) houses the company's corporate banking, investment banking, capital markets, commercial leasing, and merchant banking activities. This segment focuses on companies with sales in excess of $250 million, and concentrates on small-cap and mid-cap

growth companies, raising public and private equity, and providing merger and acquisition advisory services for investment banking.

The Mortgage Banking segment (12%) offers residential mortgage products nationally through its retail, broker and correspondent channels. The Wealth and Investment Management segment (13%) provides wealth management products and professional services to both individual and institutional clients. The remaining 10% of segment net income is allocated to corporate, other, treasury, and reconciling items.

The company has adopted an enterprise risk management model, which seeks to synthesize, assess, report and mitigate the full set of risks at the enterprise level and to provide management with an overall picture of the company's risk profile. The model incorporates an analysis of credit risk, organizational risk, market risk from trading activities, market risk from non-trading activities, and market liquidity risk.

Company Financials Fiscal Year Ended Dec. 31

Per Share Data ($)	2006	2005	2004	2003	2002	2001	2000	1999	1998	1997
Tangible Book Value	26.04	24.67	23.13	29.73	25.46	26.67	25.07	22.13	22.99	23.38
Earnings	5.82	5.47	5.19	4.73	4.66	4.70	4.30	3.50	3.04	3.13
S&P Core Earnings	5.64	5.39	5.17	4.80	4.38	4.50	NA	NA	NA	NA
Dividends	2.44	2.20	2.00	1.80	1.72	1.60	1.48	1.38	1.00	0.93
Payout Ratio	42%	40%	39%	38%	37%	34%	34%	39%	33%	30%
Prices:High	85.64	75.77	76.65	71.73	70.20	72.35	68.06	79.81	87.75	75.25
Prices:Low	69.68	65.32	61.27	51.44	51.48	57.29	41.63	60.44	54.00	44.13
P/E Ratio:High	15	14	15	15	15	15	16	23	26	24
P/E Ratio:Low	12	12	12	11	11	12	10	17	16	14

Income Statement Analysis (Million $)	2006	2005	2004	2003	2002	2001	2000	1999	1998	1997
Net Interest Income	4,660	4,579	3,685	3,320	3,244	3,253	3,108	3,145	2,929	1,894
Tax Equivalent Adjustment	87.9	75.5	NA	45.0	39.5	40.8	40.4	42.5	46.4	36.6
Non Interest Income	3,519	3,162	2,646	2,179	2,187	2,003	1,767	1,769	1,708	933
Loan Loss Provision	263	177	136	314	470	275	134	170	215	117
% Expense/Operating Revenue	59.0%	60.6%	67.3%	68.4%	61.5%	59.2%	58.0%	59.3%	62.8%	59.6%
Pretax Income	2,986	2,866	2,257	1,909	1,823	2,020	1,920	1,696	1,498	1,026
Effective Tax Rate	29.1%	30.7%	30.3%	30.2%	27.0%	32.2%	32.6%	33.7%	35.2%	35.0%
Net Income	2,117	1,987	1,573	1,332	1,332	1,369	1,294	1,124	971	667
% Net Interest Margin	3.00	3.16	3.15	3.08	3.41	NA	3.55	3.88	3.97	4.11
S&P Core Earnings	2,045	1,957	1,570	1,351	1,253	1,310	NA	NA	NA	NA

Balance Sheet & Other Financial Data (Million $)	2006	2005	2004	2003	2002	2001	2000	1999	1998	1997
Money Market Assets	3,849	4,457	3,796	3,243	2,820	3,025	2,223	1,869	2,027	1,180
Investment Securities	25,102	26,526	28,941	25,607	23,445	19,656	18,810	18,317	17,559	11,729
Commercial Loans	47,182	33,764	31,824	30,682	28,694	28,946	30,781	26,933	24,590	14,387
Other Loans	74,273	80,791	69,602	50,050	44,474	40,013	41,459	39,069	40,496	25,749
Total Assets	182,162	179,714	158,870	125,393	117,323	104,741	103,496	95,390	93,170	57,983
Demand Deposits	22,887	41,973	30,979	24,185	21,250	19,200	15,064	14,201	14,066	8,928
Time Deposits	101,134	80,081	72,382	57,004	58,456	48,337	54,469	45,900	44,968	29,270
Long Term Debt	18,993	20,779	22,127	15,314	11,880	12,661	8,945	6,017	5,808	3,172
Common Equity	17,314	16,887	15,987	9,731	16,030	15,064	14,536	13,691	8,179	5,199
% Return on Assets	1.2	1.2	1.1	1.1	1.2	1.3	1.3	1.2	1.3	1.2
% Return on Equity	12.3	12.1	12.2	14.4	8.6	9.3	9.2	8.0	14.5	13.2
% Loan Loss Reserve	0.8	0.5	1.0	1.1	1.1	1.2	1.2	1.3	1.5	1.9
% Loans/Deposits	107.4	171.3	104.5	106.3	101.5	108.5	106.4	112.4	110.3	137.1
% Equity to Assets	9.5	9.7	9.1	7.6	14.0	14.2	14.2	14.8	8.9	9.1

Data as orig reptd.; bef. results of disc opers/spec. items. Per share data adj. for stk. divs.; EPS diluted. E-Estimated. NA-Not Available. NM-Not Meaningful. NR-Not Ranked. UR-Under Review.

Office: 303 Peachtree St NE, Atlanta, GA 30308-3201.
Telephone: 404-588-7711.
Website: http://www.suntrust.com
Exec Chrmn: L.P. Humann

Pres & CEO: J.M. Wells III
Vice Chrmn: W.R. Reed, Jr.
EVP & CFO: M.A. Chancy
EVP & Chief Admin Officer: D.F. Dierker

Investor Contact: G. Ketron (404-827-6714)
Board Members: R. M. Beall II, J. H. Brown, A. D. Correll, J. C. Crowe, T. Farnsworth, Jr., P. C. Frist, B. Garrett, Jr., D. H. Hughes, L. P. Humann, E. N. Isdell, M. D. Ivester, J. H. Lanier, G. G. Minor III, L. L. Prince, F. S. Royal, J. M. Wells III, K. H. Williams, P. Wynn, Jr.

Founded: 1891
Domicile: Georgia
Employees: 33,599

SUPERVALU INC.

STANDARD &POOR'S

S&P Recommendation BUY ★★★★☆	**Price** $41.02 (as of Nov 23, 2007)	**12-Mo. Target Price** $44.00	**Investment Style** Large-Cap Blend

GICS Sector Consumer Staples
Sub-Industry Food Retail

Summary One of the largest U.S. food wholesalers, this company is also one of the biggest supermarket retailers in the U.S.

Key Stock Statistics (Source S&P, Vickers, company reports)

52-Wk Range	$49.78–33.75	S&P Oper. EPS 2008**E**	2.99	Market Capitalization(B)	$8.672	Beta	1.42
Trailing 12-Month EPS	$2.48	S&P Oper. EPS 2009**E**	3.20	Yield (%)	1.66	S&P 3-Yr. Proj. EPS CAGR(%)	12.00
Trailing 12-Month P/E	16.5	P/E on S&P Oper. EPS 2008**E**	13.7	Dividend Rate/Share	$0.68	S&P Credit Rating	BB-
$10K Invested 5 Yrs Ago	$27,132	Common Shares Outstg. (M)	211.4	Institutional Ownership (%)	88		

Price Performance

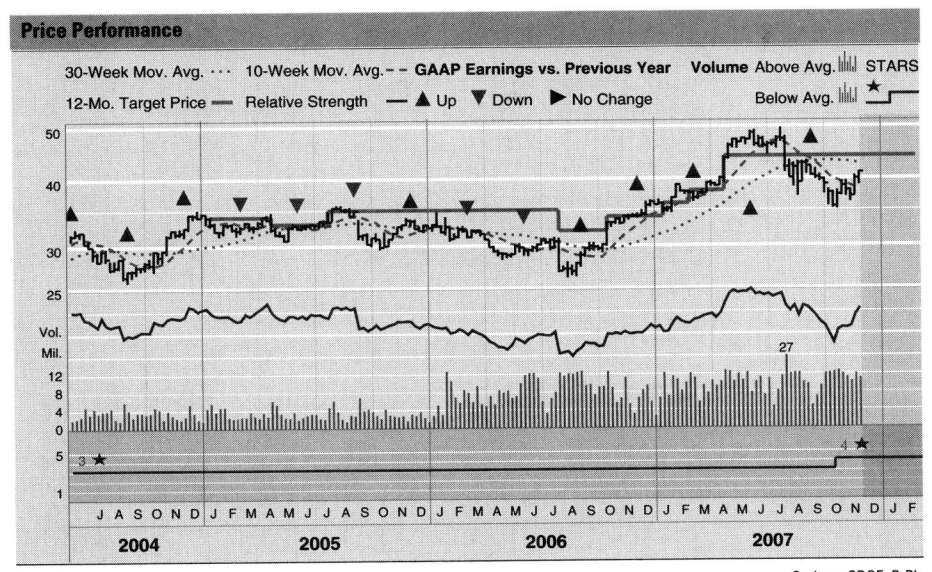

30-Week Mov. Avg. · · · 10-Week Mov. Avg. - - **GAAP Earnings vs. Previous Year** **Volume** Above Avg. STARS
12-Mo. Target Price — Relative Strength — ▲ Up ▼ Down ► No Change Below Avg. ★

Options: CBOE, P, Ph

Analysis prepared by **Joseph Agnese** on October 16, 2007, when the stock traded at **$ 37.44.**

Highlights

➤ We see FY 08 (Feb.) revenues increasing to about $44 billion, reflecting the integration of acquired Albertson's stores, identical store growth of about 1%, the opening of 20 to 22 standard stores, and 110 to 120 major remodels. We think food distribution sales will increase in the low single digits, as a result of new business wins, and should be offset by continued customer attrition.

➤ Margins should widen as we look for the company to benefit from initial synergies due to leveraging its larger scale through better purchasing, the removal of duplicate administrative expenses, the enhancement of Albertson's advanced information technology investments, and the rationalization of its current supply chain network. However, we expect interest expense to rise significantly as a result of the inclusion of debt from the Albertson's acquisition.

➤ Following an increase in shares outstanding, we look for FY 08 operating EPS of $2.99, up from $2.36 in FY 07 (excluding $0.20 and $0.32 of one-time transaction costs in the respective years due to acquisitions and divestitures).

Investment Rationale/Risk

➤ We believe SVU is well positioned, with strong regional market shares despite an intensely competitive environment. We see significant benefits from synergies over the next three years as well as from an increased focus on improving the in-store shopping experience at newly acquired stores.

➤ Risks to our recommendation and target price include difficulty integrating newly acquired stores, a sharp deterioration in the economic environment, and a slower than expected improvement in results due to increased competition.

➤ The shares traded recently at about 12.5X our FY 08 operating EPS estimate, below the three-year historical average of 13.5X. Due to our expectations for potential significant synergy savings from acquisitions, we believe the stock's valuation should exceed its historical average multiple, despite potential integration risks. Applying a P/E of about 14X to our forward 12-month EPS estimate of $3.11, we arrive at our 12-month target price of $44. The shares recently offered a dividend yield of 1.9%.

Qualitative Risk Assessment

LOW	MEDIUM	HIGH

Our risk assessment for SUPERVALU reflects the company's strong market share positions, and S&P's Quality Ranking of B+, partially offset by an intensely competitive environment and threats of new entrants into its markets.

Quantitative Evaluations

S&P Quality Ranking   B+

D	C	B-	B	B+	A-	A	A+

Relative Strength Rank   STRONG

90

LOWEST = 1   HIGHEST = 99

Revenue/Earnings Data

Revenue (Million $)

	1Q	2Q	3Q	4Q	Year
2008	13,292	10,159	--	--	--
2007	5,783	10,666	10,657	10,301	37,406
2006	5,972	4,556	4,695	4,640	19,864
2005	5,911	4,487	4,555	4,591	19,543
2004	5,836	4,591	4,739	5,044	20,210
2003	5,654	4,340	4,553	4,613	19,160

Earnings Per Share ($)

2008	0.69	0.69	E0.64	E0.85	E2.99
2007	0.57	0.61	0.54	0.57	2.32
2006	0.64	0.24	0.53	0.04	1.46
2005	1.04	0.55	0.46	0.65	2.71
2004	0.55	0.46	0.36	0.70	2.07
2003	0.57	0.44	0.43	0.48	1.91

Fiscal year ended Feb. 28. Next earnings report expected: Early January. EPS Estimates based on S&P Operating Earnings; historical GAAP earnings are as reported.

Dividend Data (Dates: mm/dd Payment Date: mm/dd/yy)

Amount ($)	Date Decl.	Ex-Div. Date	Stk. of Record	Payment Date
0.165	02/08	02/27	03/01	03/15/07
0.165	04/18	05/30	06/01	06/15/07
0.170	08/08	08/29	09/03	09/17/07
0.170	10/05	11/29	12/03	12/17/07

Dividends have been paid since 1936. Source: Company reports.

SUPERVALU INC.

STANDARD
&POOR'S

Business Summary October 16, 2007

CORPORATE OVERVIEW. SUPERVALU, organized in 1925 as the successor to two wholesale grocery concerns established in the 1870s, has grown into the largest U.S. food distributor to supermarkets, and the second largest conventional food retailer in the U.S. Retail operations are conducted through limited assortment stores, food stores, and combination food and drug stores. As of October 2007, the company operated about 2,500 multi-format retail food stores and was the primary grocery supplier to approximately 2,200 stores in addition to its own retail operations.

CORPORATE STRATEGY. The company aims to leverage its retail food and supply chain services by benefiting from economies of scale and its low-cost supply chain network. The company operated 877 combination stores, 403 food stores, and 325 limited assortment food stores through 71 million square feet of space as of October 2007. Combination food store banners (bigg's, for example) typically carry 50,000 items and average 60,000 square feet. Food store banners (Bristol Farms, Jewel, Hornbacher's, and Lucky) typically carry 40,000 items and average approximately 40,000 square feet. Other major banners that operate both combination food store and food stores include Albert-

son's, Sav-On, Jewel-Osco, Shaw's Supermarkets, Acme Markets, Cub Foods, Shoppers Food & Pharmacy, Farm Fresh, Shop n' Save, and Star Market banners.

Limited assortment food stores include Save-A-Lot stores and Sunflower Food Market stores. The company licenses 858 Save-A-Lot stores to independent operators. Save-A-Lot food stores are typically 15,000 square feet and stock 1,400 high volume food items as well as a limited number of general merchandise items. The majority of food products offered for sale are private label products. The company positions itself to offer low prices by carrying a limited selection of the most frequently purchased goods. The Sunflower Market banner is a fresh food focused banner also aimed at price conscious consumers. The majority of Save-A-Lot stores are found in small town/rural communities as opposed to urban and suburban locations.

Company Financials Fiscal Year Ended Feb. 28

Per Share Data ($)	2007	2006	2005	2004	2003	2002	2001	2000	1999	1998
Tangible Book Value	NM	7.37	6.52	4.84	3.24	2.54	1.43	1.40	6.10	5.81
Cash Flow	6.79	3.55	4.75	4.34	4.14	4.08	3.20	4.03	3.48	3.66
Earnings	2.32	1.46	2.71	2.07	1.91	1.53	0.62	1.87	1.57	1.82
S&P Core Earnings	2.45	1.90	2.21	2.03	1.61	1.24	0.39	NA	NA	NA
Dividends	0.64	0.60	0.58	0.57	0.56	0.55	0.54	0.54	0.52	0.52
Payout Ratio	28%	41%	21%	27%	29%	36%	87%	29%	33%	28%
Calendar Year	2006	2005	2004	2003	2002	2001	2000	1999	1998	1997
Prices:High	36.59	35.88	35.15	28.84	30.81	24.10	22.88	28.88	28.94	21.13
Prices:Low	26.14	29.55	25.70	12.60	14.75	12.60	11.75	16.81	20.19	14.06
P/E Ratio:High	16	25	13	14	16	16	37	15	18	12
P/E Ratio:Low	11	20	9	6	8	8	19	9	13	8

Income Statement Analysis (Million $)										
Revenue	37,406	19,864	19,543	20,210	19,160	20,909	23,194	20,339	17,421	17,201
Operating Income	2,058	750	936	919	870	904	860	800	652	636
Depreciation	879	311	303	302	297	341	344	277	234	230
Interest Expense	600	139	138	166	182	194	213	154	124	134
Pretax Income	747	329	601	455	408	344	154	448	316	385
Effective Tax Rate	39.5%	37.4%	35.8%	38.4%	37.0%	40.1%	46.8%	45.8%	39.6%	40.0%
Net Income	452	206	386	280	257	206	82.0	243	191	231
S&P Core Earnings	477	269	313	276	217	166	51.2	NA	NA	NA

Balance Sheet & Other Financial Data (Million $)										
Cash	285	686	464	292	29.2	12.0	11.0	11.0	8.00	6.00
Current Assets	4,460	2,168	2,127	2,037	1,647	1,604	2,092	2,178	1,583	1,612
Total Assets	21,702	6,038	6,278	6,153	5,896	5,825	6,407	6,495	4,266	4,093
Current Liabilities	4,705	1,507	1,632	1,872	1,525	1,701	2,341	2,510	1,522	1,457
Long Term Debt	9,192	1,406	1,579	1,634	2,020	1,875	2,008	1,954	1,246	1,261
Common Equity	5,306	2,619	2,511	2,210	2,009	1,918	1,793	1,821	1,300	1,196
Total Capital	15,006	4,079	4,240	3,986	4,146	3,873	3,831	3,778	2,606	2,499
Capital Expenditures	837	308	233	328	383	293	398	408	240	231
Cash Flow	1,331	517	689	582	554	547	426	520	425	461
Current Ratio	0.9	1.4	1.3	1.1	1.1	0.9	0.9	0.9	1.0	1.1
% Long Term Debt of Capitalization	61.3	34.5	37.2	41.0	48.7	48.4	52.4	51.7	47.8	50.5
% Net Income of Revenue	1.2	1.0	2.0	1.4	1.3	1.0	0.4	1.2	1.1	1.3
% Return on Assets	3.2	3.3	6.2	4.6	4.4	3.4	1.3	4.5	4.6	5.5
% Return on Equity	11.4	8.0	16.3	13.3	13.2	11.1	4.5	15.6	15.3	18.5

Data as orig reptd.; bef. results of disc opers/spec. items. Per share data adj. for stk. divs.; EPS diluted. E-Estimated. NA-Not Available. NM-Not Meaningful. NR-Not Ranked. UR-Under Review.

Office: 11840 Valley View Road, Eden Prairie, MN 55344.
Telephone: 952-828-4000.
Website: http://www.supervalu.com
Chrmn & CEO: J. Noddle

Pres & COO: M.L. Jackson
EVP & CFO: P.K. Knous
SVP & CIO: P. Singer
VP & Secy: B. Fealing

Investor Contact: Y. Scharton (952-828-4540)
Board Members: A. G. Ames, I. Cohen, R. E. Daly, L. A. Del Santo, S. E. Engel, P. L. Francis, E. C. Gage, G. L. Keith, Jr., C. M. Lillis, J. Noddle, M. Peterson, S. S. Rogers, W. Sales, K. P. Seifert

Founded: 1871
Domicile: Delaware
Employees: 191,400

The McGraw-Hill Companies

Symantec Corp

STANDARD &POOR'S

S&P Recommendation HOLD ★★★☆☆	**Price** $17.55 (as of Nov 23, 2007)	**12-Mo. Target Price** $21.00	**Investment Style** Large-Cap Blend

GICS Sector Information Technology
Sub-Industry Systems Software

Summary This company provides software solutions that enable customers to protect their network infrastructure from potential threats and to store their data.

Key Stock Statistics (Source S&P, Vickers, company reports)

52-Wk Range	$21.90– 16.20	S&P Oper. EPS 2008E	1.03	Market Capitalization(B)	$15.785	Beta	0.99
Trailing 12-Month EPS	$0.35	S&P Oper. EPS 2009E	1.16	Yield (%)	Nil	S&P 3-Yr. Proj. EPS CAGR(%)	10.00
Trailing 12-Month P/E	50.1	P/E on S&P Oper. EPS 2008E	17.0	Dividend Rate/Share	Nil	S&P Credit Rating	NR
$10K Invested 5 Yrs Ago	$15,418	Common Shares Outstg. (M)	899.4	Institutional Ownership (%)	96		

Price Performance

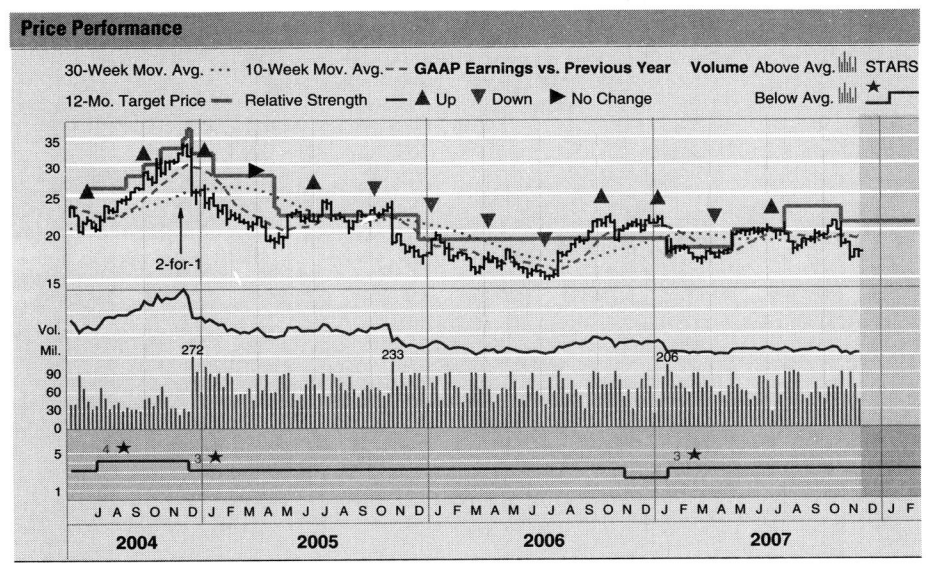

30-Week Mov. Avg. ···· 10-Week Mov. Avg. – – GAAP Earnings vs. Previous Year Volume Above Avg. STARS
12-Mo. Target Price — Relative Strength — ▲ Up ▼ Down ► No Change Below Avg. ★

Options: ASE, CBOE, P, Ph

Analysis prepared by **Jim Yin** on October 26, 2007, when the stock traded at **$ 18.20.**

Highlights

➤ We see total revenues increasing 10% in FY 08 (Mar.), with product revenue rising 12% and license revenue up 3.8%. We expect consumer revenue to increase 13%, with data center management and security and data management growing in the low single digits. We believe the company has partially addressed differences between its sales approach and that of Veritas. The Altiris acquisition should contribute incremental revenue growth. However, we believe growth will decelerate in FY 09 due to economic uncertainty.

➤ We look for non-GAAP gross margins in FY 08 to increase to 84%, from 83% last year, due to higher product revenue, which has higher gross margins. We see operating expenses as a percentage of revenues remaining steady at 67% even though the company has implemented cost-saving initiatives. We expect non-GAAP operating margins to narrow to 25%, from 26% in FY 07.

➤ Our estimate of FY 08 operating EPS is $1.03, compared to operating EPS of $0.90 in FY 07. The increase reflects higher revenues and fewer shares outstanding, partially offset by a lower operating margin.

Investment Rationale/Risk

➤ We believe SYMC has stabilized the business that was obtained from the acquisition of Veritas. The company has altered its sales approach to focus more on building long-term relationships with customers. We believe SYMC can generate cross-selling opportunities from the Altiris acquisition. However, we believe enterprise IT spending will weaken in 2008 due to a slowdown in the economy.

➤ Risks to our recommendation and target price include intense competition in the Internet security software industry, a potential slowdown in corporate information technology spending, and integration risk associated with acquisitions.

➤ Our 12-month target price of $21 is based on a blend of our discounted cash flow (DCF) and P/E analyses. Our DCF model assumes a 12% WACC and 3% terminal growth, yielding an intrinsic value of $21. For our P/E analysis, we derive a value of $20 based on an industry P/E-to-growth ratio of 1.8X, or 19.4X our FY 08 operating EPS estimate of $1.03.

Qualitative Risk Assessment

LOW	MEDIUM	**HIGH**

Our risk assessment for Symantec reflects the highly competitive market in which the company operates and integration risks from recent acquisitions.

Quantitative Evaluations

S&P Quality Ranking B

D	C	B-	**B**	B+	A-	A	A+

Relative Strength Rank **MODERATE**
46
LOWEST = 1 HIGHEST = 99

Revenue/Earnings Data

Revenue (Million $)

	1Q	2Q	3Q	4Q	Year
2008	1,400	--	1,419	--	--
2007	1,259	1,262	1,313	1,357	5,199
2006	699.9	1,056	1,149	1,239	4,143
2005	556.6	618.3	695.2	712.7	2,583
2004	391.1	428.7	493.9	556.4	1,870
2003	316.0	325.2	375.6	390.0	1,407

Earnings Per Share ($)

	1Q	2Q	3Q	4Q	Year
2008	0.10	E0.27	0.06	E0.27	E1.03
2007	0.09	0.12	0.12	0.07	0.41
2006	0.27	-0.21	0.08	0.11	0.15
2005	0.16	0.19	0.22	0.16	0.74
2004	0.09	0.12	0.16	0.16	0.54
2003	0.09	0.08	0.11	0.10	0.38

Fiscal year ended Mar. 31. Next earnings report expected: Late January. EPS Estimates based on S&P Operating Earnings; historical GAAP earnings are as reported.

Dividend Data

No cash dividends have been paid.

Please read the **Required Disclosures and Analyst Certification on the last page of this report.**

The McGraw-Hill Companies

Symantec Corp

STANDARD &POOR'S

Business Summary October 26, 2007

CORPORATE OVERVIEW. SYMC is a provider of software solutions that enable enterprises and consumers to protect their network infrastructure from potential threats and to archive and recover their data. Its products include virus protection, firewall, virtual private network, vulnerability management, intrusion detection, remote management technologies, and security services.

The company is organized into five operating segments:

Consumer Products -- focuses on Internet security. Key products include Norton Internet Security, which protects against viruses, worms and other security risks; Norton AntiVirus, which removes viruses, Trojan horses and worms; and Norton SystemWorks, which enables users to maintain and optimize their computers. The Consumer Products segment accounted for 34% and 30% of total revenue in FY 06 and FY 07, respectively.

Security and Data Management -- provides security throughout the network, including behind the gateway and at the client level including desktop PCs, laptops and handhelds. The company's enterprise security solutions address the following areas: Antivirus, Antispam, Compliance, and Managed Security

Services. The Security segment accounted for 41% and 39% of total revenue in FY 06 and FY 07, respectively.

Data Center Management -- provides software solutions designed to protect, back up, archive and restore data across the enterprise. It also helps customers manage heterogeneous storage and server environments. This segment accounted for 21% and 26% of total revenue in FY 06 and FY 07, respectively.

Services -- assists SYMC's customers in implementing, supporting and maintaining their security, storage and infrastructure software solutions. Services accounted for 4% and 5% of total revenue in FY 06 and FY 07, respectively.

The Other segment is comprised of products nearing the end of their life cycle. Revenues were insignificant during FY 06 and FY 07.

Company Financials Fiscal Year Ended Mar. 31

Per Share Data ($)	2007	2006	2005	2004	2003	2002	2001	2000	1999	1998
Tangible Book Value	NM	0.63	3.07	1.97	2.89	1.26	0.97	1.11	0.59	0.70
Cash Flow	1.24	0.48	0.86	0.62	0.45	0.37	0.18	0.43	0.16	0.23
Earnings	0.41	0.15	0.74	0.54	0.38	-0.05	0.12	0.34	0.11	0.18
S&P Core Earnings	0.40	-0.06	0.59	0.43	0.26	-0.19	0.03	NA	NA	NA
Dividends	Nil	Nil	Nil	Nil	Nil	Nil	Nil	Nil	Nil	Nil
Payout Ratio	Nil	Nil	Nil	Nil	Nil	Nil	Nil	Nil	Nil	Nil
Calendar Year	2006	2005	2004	2003	2002	2001	2000	1999	1998	1997
Prices:High	22.19	26.60	34.05	17.50	11.55	9.19	10.20	8.66	4.08	3.47
Prices:Low	14.78	16.32	17.27	9.09	6.80	3.90	3.42	1.56	1.09	1.50
P/E Ratio:High	54	NM	46	33	30	78	NM	25	38	20
P/E Ratio:Low	36	NM	23	17	18	33	NM	5	10	8

Income Statement Analysis (Million $)

	2007	2006	2005	2004	2003	2002	2001	2000	1999	1998
Revenue	5,199	4,143	2,583	1,870	1,407	1,071	854	746	593	578
Operating Income	1,402	942	926	611	417	269	240	191	90.0	126
Depreciation	811	340	96.3	78.8	59.6	238	105	42.9	30.2	25.2
Interest Expense	27.2	18.0	12.3	21.2	21.2	9.17	Nil	0.02	1.80	1.22
Pretax Income	632	363	858	542	364	45.5	141	257	83.2	112
Effective Tax Rate	36.0%	56.8%	37.5%	31.6%	31.7%	NM	54.6%	33.9%	39.6%	24.1%
Net Income	404	157	536	371	248	-28.2	63.9	170	50.2	85.1
S&P Core Earnings	393	-51.0	423	284	157	-106	14.8	NA	NA	NA

Balance Sheet & Other Financial Data (Million $)

	2007	2006	2005	2004	2003	2002	2001	2000	1999	1998
Cash	2,559	2,316	1,091	2,410	1,706	1,375	557	432	193	226
Current Assets	4,071	3,908	3,688	2,842	1,988	1,563	782	546	316	329
Total Assets	17,751	17,913	5,614	4,456	3,266	2,503	1,792	846	563	476
Current Liabilities	3,318	3,478	1,701	1,287	895	579	413	227	217	153
Long Term Debt	2,100	24.9	4.41	606	607	604	2.36	1.55	1.50	6.00
Common Equity	11,602	13,668	3,705	2,426	1,764	1,320	1,377	618	345	318
Total Capital	14,045	14,187	3,798	3,077	2,371	1,924	1,379	620	347	323
Capital Expenditures	420	267	91.5	111	192	141	61.2	28.5	25.1	26.3
Cash Flow	1,216	497	633	453	308	210	95.9	213	74.2	110
Current Ratio	1.2	1.1	2.2	2.2	2.2	31.3	1.9	2.4	1.5	2.1
% Long Term Debt of Capitalization	15.0	0.2	0.1	19.7	25.6	0.3	0.2	0.3	2.1	1.8
% Net Income of Revenue	7.8	3.8	20.8	19.8	17.7	NM	7.5	22.8	8.5	14.7
% Return on Assets	2.3	1.3	10.6	9.6	8.6	NM	4.8	24.1	9.7	20.8
% Return on Equity	3.2	1.8	17.5	17.7	16.1	NM	6.4	35.3	15.2	31.8

Data as orig reptd.; bef. results of disc opers/spec. items. Per share data adj. for stk. divs.; EPS diluted. E-Estimated. NA-Not Available. NM-Not Meaningful. NR-Not Ranked. UR-Under Review.

Office: 20330 Stevens Creek Boulevard, Cupertino, CA 95014-2132.
Telephone: 408-517-8000.
Email: investor-relations@symantec.com
Website: http://www.symantec.com

Chrmn & CEO: J.W. Thompson
EVP & CFO: J.A. Beer
SVP & Chief Acctg Officer: G.W. Harrington
Investor Contact: H. Corcos (408-517-8324)

Board Members: M. A. Brown, W. T. Coleman, III, F. E. Dangeard, D. L. Mahoney, R. S. Miller, G. Reyes, D. J. Roux, D. H. Schulman, J. W. Thompson, V. P. Unruh

Founded: 1983
Domicile: Delaware
Employees: 17,100

The McGraw-Hill Companies

Synovus Financial Corp.

STANDARD &POOR'S

S&P Recommendation HOLD ★★★☆☆	**Price** $23.79 (as of Nov 23, 2007)	**12-Mo. Target Price** $27.00	**Investment Style** Large-Cap Blend

GICS Sector Financials
Sub-Industry Regional Banks

Summary Synovus owns about 40 community banks in Georgia and four other southern states, and has an 81% interest in one of the world's largest bank payment processing companies.

Key Stock Statistics (Source S&P, Vickers, company reports)

52-Wk Range	$33.82– 22.40	S&P Oper. EPS 2007**E**	1.85	Market Capitalization(B)	$7.789	Beta	0.84
Trailing 12-Month EPS	$1.90	S&P Oper. EPS 2008**E**	1.80	Yield (%)	3.45	S&P 3-Yr. Proj. EPS CAGR(%)	4.20
Trailing 12-Month P/E	12.5	P/E on S&P Oper. EPS 2007**E**	12.9	Dividend Rate/Share	$0.82	S&P Credit Rating	A
$10K Invested 5 Yrs Ago	$13,210	Common Shares Outstg. (M)	327.4	Institutional Ownership (%)	56		

Price Performance

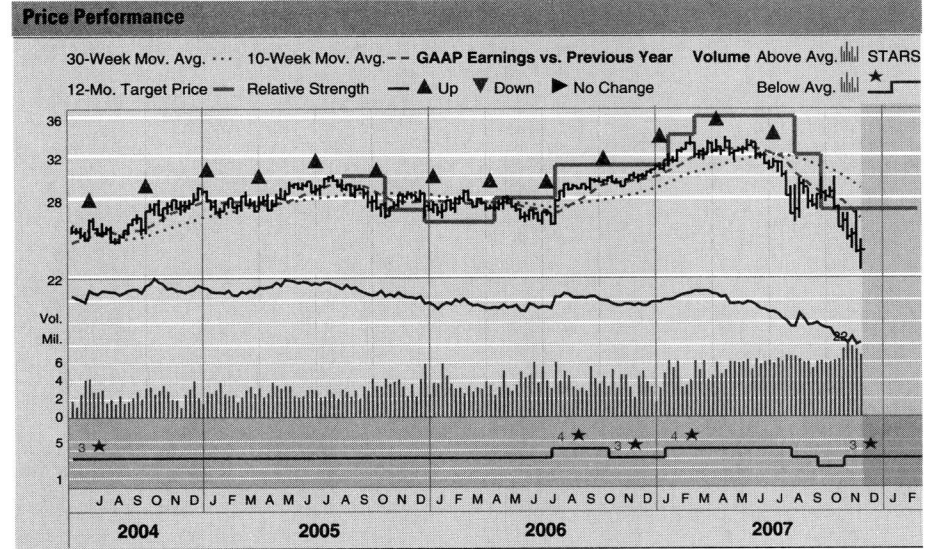

30-Week Mov. Avg. · · · 10-Week Mov. Avg. - - GAAP Earnings vs. Previous Year Volume Above Avg. STARS
12-Mo. Target Price — Relative Strength — ▲ Up ▼ Down ► No Change Below Avg. ★

Options: CBOE

Analysis prepared by **Stuart Plesser** on November 05, 2007, when the stock traded at **$ 24.58**.

Highlights

➤ We see total revenues rising 6.0% in 2008, driven by a 7.9% increase in fee income and a 5.4% increase in net interest income. Our 2008 estimates include a net interest margin of 3.95%, down from our estimate of 4.05% in 2007 and actual results of 4.30% in 2006, due to our concern that SNV's loan yields may reprice more rapidly downward than funding costs, should the Federal Reserve make further cuts in the Fed Funds target.

➤ Non-performing loans jumped to 0.87% of total loans at September 30, from 0.71% at June 30, and 0.39% at December 31. We forecast that loan loss provisions will increase to $160 million in 2007, and $180 million in 2008, from $75 million in 2006, due to increases in the level of non-performing loans resulting from a weak housing market.

➤ Assuming an effective tax rate of 37.5%, we estimate 2007 EPS of $1.85, down from the $1.90 earned in 2006. Our 2008 EPS estimate is $1.80, a modest decrease.

Investment Rationale/Risk

➤ SNV's loan portfolio has a significant concentration in Florida and Atlanta, GA, two areas that have seen residential and commercial over-construction, according to our research. The magnitude of the increase in non-performing loans concerns us, despite management's attempts to assure investors that the problems are focused in narrow geographic areas, and with a small number of clients. Our concerns regarding credit quality are offset somewhat by SNV's low valuation and the recent announcement that it will spin off to shareholders its 80.8% ownership of TSYS (TSS: hold, $28.85), pending necessary approvals. In conjunction with the spinoff, shareholders will receive a special dividend of $485 million. .

➤ Risks to our recommendation and target price include a deterioration in credit quality beyond expectations, and failure to win approval for the spinoff of TSYS.

➤ Our 12-month target price of $27 is equal to 14.5X our 2008 EPS estimate of $1.82. The multiple is modestly higher than industry peers, which we believe is justified by the likely benefits of the TSYS spinoff.

Qualitative Risk Assessment

LOW	MEDIUM	HIGH

Our risk assessment for SNV reflects our view of the company's large investment in its payment processing subsidiary, its large cap valuation, good credit quality of its loan portfolio, and history of profitability. While the company operates in a highly competitive and fragmented industry, the industry tends to produce relatively stable financial results, in our view.

Quantitative Evaluations

S&P Quality Ranking   A+

D	C	B-	B	B+	A-	A	A+

Relative Strength Rank   MODERATE

32

LOWEST = 1   HIGHEST = 99

Revenue/Earnings Data

Revenue (Million $)

	1Q	2Q	3Q	4Q	Year
2007	1,062	1,118	1,979	--	--
2006	932.9	1,015	1,062	1,146	4,150
2005	756.4	845.5	891.8	921.0	3,415
2004	646.8	648.6	684.0	700.7	2,680
2003	585.0	612.0	613.4	620.3	2,431
2002	547.4	558.1	580.7	603.7	2,290

Earnings Per Share ($)

	1Q	2Q	3Q	4Q	Year
2007	0.45	0.48	E0.45	E0.46	E1.85
2006	0.43	0.47	0.47	0.54	1.90
2005	0.37	0.41	0.43	0.44	1.64
2004	0.34	0.34	0.35	0.38	1.41
2003	0.30	0.32	0.33	0.34	1.28
2002	0.28	0.29	0.31	0.35	1.21

Fiscal year ended Dec. 31. Next earnings report expected: Mid January. EPS Estimates based on S&P Operating Earnings; historical GAAP earnings are as reported.

Dividend Data (Dates: mm/dd Payment Date: mm/dd/yy)

Amount ($)	Date Decl.	Ex-Div. Date	Stk. of Record	Payment Date
0.195	11/21	12/19	12/21	01/02/07
0.205	03/08	03/20	03/22	04/02/07
0.205	05/24	06/19	06/21	07/02/07
0.205	09/05	09/18	09/20	10/01/07

Dividends have been paid since 1930. Source: Company reports.

Synovus Financial Corp.

STANDARD &POOR'S

Business Summary November 05, 2007

CORPORATE OVERVIEW. Synovus is a bank holding company with 39 wholly owned bank subsidiaries in five southeastern states. The company has seven non-bank financial services subsidiaries that provide securities, trust, mortgage banking, insurance, financial planning, asset management and investment advisory services, and an 80% stake in a transaction processing company. The company's two segments are Financial Services and Transaction Processing Services. The company operates in Georgia, South Carolina, Florida, Alabama and Tennessee.

The Financial Services segment accounted for about 55% of 2006 revenues. Banking operations consist of lending and deposit gathering as well as other banking-related products and services, including investment, trust, insurance, and mortgage services. SNV's banking subsidiaries operate independently, with decentralized decision-making processes in place that allow each subsidiary to act independently.

The Transaction Processing Services segment (about 45% of revenues) owns 80.8% of the common stock of Total System Services (TSS), which provides electronic payment processing and associated services to financial and non-financial institutions in the U.S., Canada, Mexico, Honduras, Puerto Rico and Europe. Services provided include processing for consumer, debit, commer-

cial, stored value and retail cards, as well as for student loans. The company divides its services into three operating segments: domestic-based support services (75% of 2006 revenues), international-based support services (9% of 2006 revenues), and merchant processing services (16% of 2006 revenues).

In October 2007, SNV announced that it will spinoff its ownership of TSYS to shareholders pending the necessary approvals. SNV expects that it will distribute 0.49 share of TSYS for each share of SNV stock. Pursuant to the agreement, TSYS will pay a one-time dividend to SNV of $485 million.

SNV uses derivative instruments, including commitments to sell fixed-rate mortgage loans and interest rate swaps, to manage its exposure to various types of interest rate risks and to meet the financing and interest rate risk management needs of its customers. When using derivative instruments on behalf of its customers, SNV enters into offsetting transactions to minimize its risk.

Company Financials Fiscal Year Ended Dec. 31

Per Share Data ($)	2006	2005	2004	2003	2002	2001	2000	1999	1998	1997
Tangible Book Value	9.14	7.82	7.04	6.50	6.40	5.75	4.98	4.35	3.96	3.43
Earnings	1.90	1.64	1.41	1.28	1.21	1.05	0.92	0.80	0.70	0.62
S&P Core Earnings	1.90	1.60	1.33	1.23	1.17	0.97	NA	NA	NA	NA
Dividends	0.78	0.73	0.69	0.66	0.59	0.51	0.44	0.34	0.28	0.24
Payout Ratio	41%	45%	49%	52%	49%	49%	48%	43%	40%	39%
Prices:High	31.13	30.10	29.09	29.25	31.93	34.74	27.38	25.13	25.92	22.42
Prices:Low	25.74	26.30	22.50	17.24	16.48	22.75	14.00	17.25	17.25	13.11
P/E Ratio:High	16	18	21	23	26	33	30	31	37	36
P/E Ratio:Low	14	16	16	13	14	22	15	22	25	21
Income Statement Analysis (Million $)										
Net Interest Income	1,134	969	861	763	718	630	562	513	441	412
Tax Equivalent Adjustment	NA	6.44	6.96	7.39	7.27	7.25	6.00	5.30	4.54	4.42
Non Interest Income	2,136	1,918	1,521	1,592	1,009	936	833	739	561	489
Loan Loss Provision	75.1	82.5	75.3	71.8	65.3	51.7	44.3	34.0	26.7	32.3
% Expense/Operating Revenue	66.4%	67.2%	66.5%	50.7%	62.1%	64.0%	66.2%	68.4%	67.0%	66.7%
Pretax Income	1,022	861	718	638	588	510	428	363	302	268
Effective Tax Rate	34.9%	35.7%	35.1%	34.9%	33.8%	35.0%	34.8%	34.2%	34.6%	34.9%
Net Income	617	516	437	389	365	312	263	225	187	165
% Net Interest Margin	4.30	4.19	4.22	NA	4.65	4.65	4.70	5.07	5.22	5.26
S&P Core Earnings	617	502	413	375	351	286	NA	NA	NA	NA
Balance Sheet & Other Financial Data (Million $)										
Money Market Assets	136	99.2	140	177	97.8	27.6	380	94.0	54.1	93.3
Investment Securities	3,352	2,958	2,696	2,529	2,238	2,088	2,078	1,994	1,818	1,655
Commercial Loans	21,042	18,091	16,340	13,686	11,791	9,809	8,495	6,789	5,225	4,411
Other Loans	3,612	3,301	3,140	2,779	2,673	2,609	2,257	2,289	2,195	2,204
Total Assets	31,855	27,621	25,050	21,633	19,036	16,658	14,908	12,547	10,498	9,260
Demand Deposits	3,539	3,701	3,338	2,834	2,303	1,985	1,727	1,625	1,362	2,385
Time Deposits	20,756	17,084	15,240	13,108	11,625	10,162	9,435	7,815	7,180	5,323
Long Term Debt	1,350	1,252	1,880	1,576	1,336	1,053	841	319	127	126
Common Equity	3,709	2,949	2,641	2,245	2,041	1,695	1,417	1,227	1,071	904
% Return on Assets	2.1	2.0	3.3	1.9	2.0	2.0	1.9	1.9	1.9	1.8
% Return on Equity	18.5	18.5	17.9	18.1	19.6	20.0	19.9	19.3	19.0	19.6
% Loan Loss Reserve	-1.3	1.3	1.4	1.4	1.4	1.3	1.4	1.4	1.5	1.6
% Loans/Deposits	102.2	103.6	105.5	104.1	105.6	105.5	96.3	97.1	86.8	85.8
% Equity to Assets	11.2	10.6	18.3	10.5	10.5	9.9	9.6	10.0	10.0	9.4

Data as orig reptd.; bef. results of disc opers/spec. items. Per share data adj. for stk. divs.; EPS diluted. E-Estimated. NA-Not Available. NM-Not Meaningful. NR-Not Ranked. UR-Under Review.

Office: 1111 Bay Ave Ste 500, Columbus, GA 31901-5269.
Telephone: 706-649-5220.
Website: http://www.synovus.com
Chrmn & CEO: R.E. Anthony

Pres & COO: F.L. Green III
Vice Chrmn & CIO: E.R. James
Sr EVP, Secy & General Counsel: G.S. Griffith, III
EVP & CFO: T.J. Prescott

Investor Contact: P.A. Reynolds (706-649-5220)
Board Members: D. P. Amos, R. E. Anthony, J. H. Blanchard, R. Y. Bradley, F. W. Brumley, E. W. Camp, G. W. Garrard, Jr., T. M. Goodrich, F. Green, III, V. N. Hansford, A. W. Jones, III, M. H. Lampton, E. C. Ogie, H. L. Page, J. N. Purcell, M. T. Stith, W. B. Turner, Jr., J. D. Yancey

Founded: 1888
Domicile: Georgia
Employees: 13,178

The McGraw-Hill Companies

Sysco Corp

STANDARD &POOR'S

S&P Recommendation	HOLD ★★★☆☆	Price $31.87 (as of Nov 23, 2007)	12-Mo. Target Price $35.00	Investment Style Large-Cap Blend

GICS Sector Consumer Staples
Sub-Industry Food Distributors

Summary This company is the largest U.S. marketer and distributor of foodservice products.

Key Stock Statistics (Source S&P, Vickers, company reports)

52-Wk Range	$37.04–29.90	S&P Oper. EPS 2008**E**	1.79	Market Capitalization(B)	$19.382	Beta	0.91
Trailing 12-Month EPS	$1.66	S&P Oper. EPS 2009**E**	NA	Yield (%)	2.76	S&P 3-Yr. Proj. EPS CAGR(%)	13.00
Trailing 12-Month P/E	19.2	P/E on S&P Oper. EPS 2008**E**	17.8	Dividend Rate/Share	$0.88	S&P Credit Rating	AA-
$10K Invested 5 Yrs Ago	$11,334	Common Shares Outstg. (M)	608.2	Institutional Ownership (%)	77		

Price Performance

30-Week Mov. Avg. ··· 10-Week Mov. Avg. − − **GAAP Earnings vs. Previous Year** Volume Above Avg. STARS
12-Mo. Target Price — Relative Strength — ▲ Up ▼ Down ▶ No Change Below Avg.

Options: ASE, CBOE, P

Analysis prepared by **Tom Graves, CFA** on October 04, 2007, when the stock traded at **$ 34.74**.

Highlights

➤ In FY 08 (Jun), we look for sales to increase moderately from the $35.0 billion reported for FY 07. Also, in FY 07, the company's sales growth was reduced by about 0.7% due to an accounting change.

➤ Over time, we look for SYY's profitability to benefit from an increased amount of consolidated purchasing, the addition of regional distribution centers, improved management of freight costs, and better inventory management. We expect a second regional distribution center in Florida to open in FY 08, with some start-up costs. In addition, in March 2007, SYY purchased a site for the construction of a third regional distribution center in Indiana.

➤ Before special items, we estimate FY 08 net income of $1.1 billion ($1.78 a share), up from the $1.00 billion ($1.60) reported FY 07. In FY 08, we look for capital expenditures to be in the range of $625 million to $650 million, compared to $603.2 million in FY 07.

Investment Rationale/Risk

➤ We expect results of this leading U.S. food distributor to include both internal growth and additional acquisitions, with SYY increasing its market share.

➤ Risks to our recommendation and target price include a slowing of growth rates given SYY's significant size and reach, sharp increases in gas prices, and a potential slowdown in restaurant sales.

➤ We favor the company's lengthy history of an annual return on equity above 25%. Our 12-month target price for the stock of $35, about 21X our $1.68 calendar year 2007 EPS estimate, is similar to the average P/E that we expect for a peer group of food distributor stocks. In FY 07, SYY repurchased 16.231 million common shares at a cost of $550.9 million. An additional 3.157 million shares were repurchased at a cost of $101.7 million through August 15, 2007. It is authorized to repurchase 19.95 million shares. SYY shares recently had an indicated dividend yield of 2.2%.

Qualitative Risk Assessment

LOW	MEDIUM	HIGH

Our risk assessment reflects that SYY operates in a relatively stable industry, in which we believe it has the largest market share. It is a large cap company and its shares exhibit a relatively low beta, in our opinion.

Quantitative Evaluations

S&P Quality Ranking A+

D	C	B-	B	B+	A-	A	A+

Relative Strength Rank MODERATE

54

LOWEST = 1   HIGHEST = 99

Revenue/Earnings Data

Revenue (Million $)

	1Q	2Q	3Q	4Q	Year
2008	9,406	--	--	--	--
2007	8,672	8,569	8,573	9,228	35,042
2006	8,010	7,971	8,138	8,509	32,628
2005	7,532	7,331	7,437	7,981	30,282
2004	7,134	7,037	7,026	8,139	29,335
2003	6,424	6,349	6,395	6,972	26,140

Earnings Per Share ($)

	1Q	2Q	3Q	4Q	Year
2008	0.43	E0.42	E0.40	E0.54	E1.79
2007	0.37	0.39	0.35	0.49	1.60
2006	0.31	0.33	0.30	0.41	1.35
2005	0.35	0.36	0.34	0.44	1.47
2004	0.32	0.34	0.30	0.43	1.37
2003	0.28	0.28	0.26	0.37	1.18

Fiscal year ended Jun. 30. Next earnings report expected: Late January. EPS Estimates based on S&P Operating Earnings; historical GAAP earnings are as reported.

Dividend Data (Dates: mm/dd Payment Date: mm/dd/yy)

Amount ($)	Date Decl.	Ex-Div. Date	Stk. of Record	Payment Date
0.190	02/09	04/03	04/06	04/27/07
0.190	05/11	07/03	07/06	07/27/07
0.190	09/19	10/03	10/05	10/26/07
0.220	11/09	01/02	01/04	01/25/08

Dividends have been paid since 1970. Source: Company reports.

Sysco Corp

Business Summary October 04, 2007

CORPORATE OVERVIEW. Sysco is the largest distributor of foodservice products in the U.S. and Canada. As of June 2007, SYY operated 177 distribution facilities in the U.S. and Canada. The company provides products and services to about 391,000 customers, including restaurants (64% of FY 07 sales), hospitals and nursing homes (10%), schools and colleges (5%), hotels and motels (6%), and others (15%).

Sysco distributes food products, including frozen foods such as meats, fully prepared entrees, fruits, vegetables and desserts; canned and dry foods; fresh meats; imported specialties; and fresh produce. The company also distributes non-food products. These include paper products, tableware such as china and silverware, cookware, restaurant and kitchen equipment and supplies, and cleaning supplies. The company stresses prompt and accurate delivery of orders, and close contact with customers, and also provides customers with ancillary services, such as providing product usage reports, menu-planning advice, food safety training, and assistance in inventory control. No single customer accounted for more than 10% of sales in FY 07.

CORPORATE STRATEGY. SYY seeks to expand its business by gaining an increased share of products purchased by existing customers, the development of new customers, the use of foldouts (new facilities built in established markets), and an acquisition program. Over time, we look for SYY's profitability to benefit from an increased amount of consolidated purchasing, the addition of regional distribution centers, improved management of freight costs, and better inventory management.

SYY distributes nationally-branded merchandise, as well as products packaged under SYY private brands. We expect that Sysco-branded products typically carry wider profit margins than other branded products distributed by the company.

Company Financials Fiscal Year Ended Jun. 30

Per Share Data ($)	2007	2006	2005	2004	2003	2002	2001	2000	1999	1998
Tangible Book Value	2.99	2.67	2.35	2.11	1.68	1.85	2.07	1.90	1.71	1.57
Cash Flow	2.23	1.89	1.96	1.80	1.59	1.47	1.27	1.02	0.84	0.74
Earnings	1.60	1.35	1.47	1.37	1.18	1.01	0.88	0.68	0.54	0.48
S&P Core Earnings	1.59	1.38	1.39	1.31	1.08	0.92	0.82	NA	NA	NA
Dividends	0.72	0.64	0.56	0.48	0.40	0.32	0.23	0.22	0.19	0.16
Payout Ratio	45%	47%	38%	35%	34%	32%	26%	32%	35%	33%
Prices:High	36.74	37.04	38.04	41.27	37.57	32.58	30.12	30.44	20.56	14.34
Prices:Low	29.90	26.50	29.98	29.48	22.90	21.25	21.75	13.06	12.47	9.97
P/E Ratio:High	23	27	26	30	32	32	34	45	38	30
P/E Ratio:Low	19	20	20	22	19	21	25	19	23	21

Income Statement Analysis (Million $)										
Revenue	35,042	32,628	30,282	29,335	26,140	23,351	21,784	19,303	17,423	15,328
Operating Income	2,071	1,840	1,906	1,816	1,597	1,439	1,286	1,030	873	772
Depreciation	363	345	317	284	273	278	248	220	206	181
Interest Expense	105	109	75.0	69.9	72.2	62.9	71.0	71.0	73.0	58.0
Pretax Income	1,621	1,395	1,525	1,475	1,260	1,101	967	738	594	533
Effective Tax Rate	38.3%	39.3%	37.0%	38.5%	38.3%	38.3%	38.3%	38.5%	39.1%	39.0%
Net Income	1,001	846	961	907	778	680	597	454	362	325
S&P Core Earnings	995	866	890	868	710	618	559	NA	NA	NA

Balance Sheet & Other Financial Data (Million $)										
Cash	208	202	192	200	421	230	136	159	149	110
Current Assets	4,676	4,400	4,002	3,851	3,630	3,185	2,985	2,733	2,409	2,180
Total Assets	9,519	8,992	8,268	7,848	6,937	5,990	5,469	4,814	4,097	3,780
Current Liabilities	3,415	3,226	3,458	3,127	2,701	2,239	2,090	1,783	1,428	1,324
Long Term Debt	1,758	1,627	956	1,231	1,249	1,176	961	1,024	998	867
Common Equity	3,278	3,052	2,759	2,565	2,198	2,133	2,148	1,762	1,427	1,357
Total Capital	5,037	5,403	4,440	4,483	3,945	3,750	3,379	3,032	2,669	2,456
Capital Expenditures	603	515	390	530	436	416	341	266	287	259
Cash Flow	1,364	1,191	1,278	1,191	1,051	958	845	674	567	506
Current Ratio	1.4	1.4	1.2	1.2	1.3	1.4	1.4	1.5	1.7	1.6
% Long Term Debt of Capitalization	34.9	30.1	21.5	27.4	31.7	31.4	28.4	33.8	37.4	35.3
% Net Income of Revenue	2.9	2.6	3.2	3.1	3.0	2.9	2.7	2.4	2.1	2.1
% Return on Assets	10.8	9.8	11.9	12.3	12.0	12.0	11.6	10.2	9.2	9.0
% Return on Equity	31.6	29.1	36.1	38.1	35.9	32.1	30.5	28.5	26.0	23.6

Data as orig reptd.; bef. results of disc opers/spec. items. Per share data adj. for stk. divs.; EPS diluted. E-Estimated. NA-Not Available. NM-Not Meaningful. NR-Not Ranked. UR-Under Review.

Office: 1390 Enclave Parkway, Houston, TX, USA 77077-2099.
Telephone: 281-584-1390.
Website: http://www.sysco.com
Chrmn, Pres & CEO: R.J. Schneiders

EVP & CFO: W. Delaney, III
EVP & Chief Admin Officer: K.J. Carrig
SVP & Treas: D.D. Sanders
SVP & CIO: K.G. Drummond

Board Members: J. M. Cassaday, J. B. Craven, M. A. Fernandez, J. Golden, J. A. Hafner, R. G. Merrill, N. S. Newcomb, R. J. Schnieders, P. S. Sewell, R. G. Tilghman, J. M. Ward

Founded: 1969
Domicile: Delaware
Employees: 50,900

Target Corp

STANDARD & POOR'S

S&P Recommendation **HOLD** ★★★☆☆	Price $59.44 (as of Nov 29, 2007)	12-Mo. Target Price $60.00	Investment Style Large-Cap Growth

GICS Sector Consumer Discretionary
Sub-Industry General Merchandise Stores

Summary This company operates about 1,381 Target and 210 SuperTarget general merchandise stores across the U.S.

Key Stock Statistics (Source S&P, Vickers, company reports)

52-Wk Range	$70.75– 50.25	S&P Oper. EPS 2008**E**	3.41	Market Capitalization(B)	$50.322	Beta	1.35
Trailing 12-Month EPS	$3.40	S&P Oper. EPS 2009**E**	4.10	Yield (%)	0.94	S&P 3-Yr. Proj. EPS CAGR(%)	13.00
Trailing 12-Month P/E	17.5	P/E on S&P Oper. EPS 2008**E**	17.4	Dividend Rate/Share	$0.56	S&P Credit Rating	A+
$10K Invested 5 Yrs Ago	$18,027	Common Shares Outstg. (M)	846.6	Institutional Ownership (%)	89		

Price Performance

- 30-Week Mov. Avg. · · · 10-Week Mov. Avg. - - **GAAP Earnings vs. Previous Year** Volume Above Avg. STARS
- 12-Mo. Target Price — Relative Strength — ▲ Up ▼ Down ▶ No Change Below Avg. ★

Options: ASE, CBOE, Ph

Analysis prepared by **Jason N. Asaeda** on November 29, 2007, when the stock traded at **$ 59.44**.

Highlights

➤ From a projected $63.5 billion in FY 08 (Jan.), we look for revenues to reach $69.2 billion in FY 09. For retail operations, we see on an annual basis 3.0% to 4.0% same-store sales growth, which includes sales from Target.com, and the net addition of about 8% retail square footage. TGT planned to open 100 net new stores, including 30 to 35 SuperTarget locations in FY 08. We think improved in-stock levels, a continued focus on value and differentiation in merchandising, and an expanded assortment of food/consumables will drive shopping frequency ahead.

➤ Operating margins should widen modestly on higher merchandise markups, supported by direct imports and better inventory management, partly offset by sales growth in lower-margin food/consumables, markdown exposure on seasonal items, and higher marketing expenses. In FY 08, we also see margin pressure from increased investment in "Phoenix" rebuild stores--mature stores that were closed in January and completely rebuilt as new Target or SuperTarget stores that reopened this fall.

➤ Factoring in likely share buybacks, we see operating EPS of $3.41 in FY 08 and $4.10 in FY 09.

Investment Rationale/Risk

➤ Over the next 12 months, we anticipate both tighter spending by lower-income customers on macroeconomic concerns, and aggressive pricing by Wal-Mart Stores (WMT: hold, $47). That said, we look for marketing efforts that better convey TGT's "Expect More. Pay Less." brand message to sustain the company's positive same-store sales trend over the balance of FY 08 and into FY 09. We also think TGT will benefit from some trading down by consumers for consumables and positive customer response to ongoing refinements of its more discretionary-purchase categories such as apparel and electronics. In addition, we believe the company will do a good job in managing its flow of goods, which helps to keep inventories in line with sales trends, and in controlling expense growth.

➤ Risks to our recommendation and target price include sales shortfalls due to reduced consumer discretionary spending, and competition from Wal-Mart Stores.

➤ Our 12-month target price of $60 is based on our discounted cash flow model, which assumes a weighted average cost of capital of 8.5% and a terminal growth rate of 3.0%.

Qualitative Risk Assessment

LOW	MEDIUM	HIGH

Our risk assessment reflects our view of TGT's improving sales and profit margins, and healthy balance sheet and cash flow, offset by uncertainty over consumer discretionary spending in light of higher interest rates and debt levels.

Quantitative Evaluations

S&P Quality Ranking A+

D	C	B-	B	B+	A-	A	A+

Relative Strength Rank MODERATE

65

LOWEST = 1   HIGHEST = 99

Revenue/Earnings Data

Revenue (Million $)

	1Q	2Q	3Q	4Q	Year
2008	14,041	14,620	14,835	--	--
2007	12,863	13,347	13,570	19,710	59,490
2006	11,477	11,990	12,206	16,947	52,620
2005	11,587	10,556	10,909	15,194	46,839
2004	10,322	10,984	11,286	15,571	48,163
2003	9,594	10,068	10,194	14,061	43,917

Earnings Per Share ($)

2008	0.75	0.80	0.56	E1.30	E3.41
2007	0.63	0.70	0.59	1.29	3.21
2006	0.55	0.61	0.49	1.06	2.71
2005	0.48	0.40	0.37	0.90	2.07
2004	0.38	0.39	0.33	0.91	2.01
2003	0.38	0.38	0.30	0.75	1.81

Fiscal year ended Jan. 31. Next earnings report expected: Late February. EPS Estimates based on S&P Operating Earnings; historical GAAP earnings are as reported.

Dividend Data (Dates: mm/dd Payment Date: mm/dd/yy)

Amount ($)	Date Decl.	Ex-Div. Date	Stk. of Record	Payment Date
0.120	01/11	02/15	02/20	03/10/07
0.120	03/15	05/16	05/20	06/10/07
0.140	06/14	08/16	08/20	09/10/07
0.140	09/12	11/16	11/20	12/10/07

Dividends have been paid since 1965. Source: Company reports.

Please read the Required Disclosures and Analyst Certification on the last page of this report.

The McGraw-Hill Companies

Target Corp

Business Summary November 29, 2007

CORPORATE PROFILE. In FY 05 (Jan.), TGT shed its non-core legacy department store operations, retaining only its eponymous chain of upscale general merchandise stores that cater to middle- and upper-income consumers. As of November 3, 2007, the company operated 1,381 Target locations, and 210 SuperTarget stores. SuperTarget stores combine a full line of groceries with fashion apparel, electronics, home furnishings and other general merchandise found in Target stores. TGT's Web site serves as both a sales driver and a marketing vehicle. Target.com offers a more extensive selection of merchandise than the company's physical stores, including exclusive online products. To support sales and earnings growth, TGT offers credit to qualified customers. In FY 07, its credit card operations contributed $1.1 billion of revenues in finance charges.

CORPORATE STRATEGY. The monetizing of assets has provided TGT with

cash to invest in its core business and to fund capital repositioning--actions that improve shareholder value. TGT sold its entire Marshall Field's business unit, including about $600 million of credit card receivables, as well as its Mervyn's stores in Minnesota, to The May Department Stores Co. in July 2004 and August 2004, respectively, for a total of $3.24 billion in cash. Also in August 2004, TGT sold the balance of its Mervyn's stores to an investment consortium that includes Sun Capital Partners, Inc., Cerberus Capital Management, L.P., and Lubert-Adler/Klaff and Partners, L.P., and Mervyn's credit card receivables unit to GE Consumer Finance for a total of $1.65 billion in cash.

Company Financials Fiscal Year Ended Jan. 31

Per Share Data ($)	2007	2006	2005	2004	2003	2002	2001	2000	1999	1998
Tangible Book Value	18.17	16.25	14.63	12.14	10.38	8.68	7.27	6.43	5.71	4.78
Cash Flow	4.93	4.29	3.45	3.45	3.14	2.70	2.41	2.19	1.87	1.61
Earnings	3.21	2.71	2.07	2.01	1.81	1.51	1.38	1.27	1.02	0.85
S&P Core Earnings	3.21	2.68	2.06	1.95	1.70	1.42	1.37	NA	NA	NA
Dividends	0.36	0.30	0.26	0.26	0.24	0.21	0.20	0.20	0.18	0.17
Payout Ratio	11%	11%	13%	13%	13%	14%	14%	16%	18%	19%
Calendar Year	2006	2005	2004	2003	2002	2001	2000	1999	1998	1997
Prices:High	60.34	60.00	54.14	41.80	46.15	41.74	39.19	38.50	27.13	18.50
Prices:Low	44.70	45.55	36.63	25.60	24.90	26.00	21.63	25.03	15.72	8.97
P/E Ratio:High	19	22	26	21	25	28	28	30	27	22
P/E Ratio:Low	14	17	18	13	14	17	16	20	15	11

Income Statement Analysis (Million $)

	2007	2006	2005	2004	2003	2002	2001	2000	1999	1998
Revenue	59,490	52,620	46,839	48,163	43,917	39,888	36,903	33,702	30,951	27,757
Operating Income	6,565	5,732	4,860	4,839	4,476	3,759	3,418	3,183	2,734	2,435
Depreciation	1,496	1,409	1,259	1,320	1,212	1,079	940	854	780	693
Interest Expense	597	532	674	559	588	464	425	393	398	416
Pretax Income	4,497	3,860	3,031	2,960	2,676	2,216	2,053	1,936	1,556	1,326
Effective Tax Rate	38.0%	37.6%	37.8%	37.8%	38.2%	38.0%	38.4%	38.8%	38.2%	39.5%
Net Income	2,787	2,408	1,885	1,841	1,654	1,374	1,264	1,185	962	802
S&P Core Earnings	2,784	2,383	1,876	1,791	1,553	1,289	1,247	NA	NA	NA

Balance Sheet & Other Financial Data (Million $)

	2007	2006	2005	2004	2003	2002	2001	2000	1999	1998
Cash	813	1,648	2,245	716	758	499	356	220	255	211
Current Assets	14,706	14,405	13,922	12,928	11,935	9,648	7,304	6,483	6,005	5,561
Total Assets	37,349	34,995	32,293	31,392	28,603	24,154	19,490	17,143	15,666	14,191
Current Liabilities	11,117	9,588	8,220	8,314	7,523	7,054	6,301	5,850	5,057	4,556
Long Term Debt	8,675	9,119	9,034	10,217	10,186	8,088	5,634	4,521	4,452	4,425
Common Equity	15,633	14,205	13,029	11,065	9,443	7,860	6,519	5,862	5,043	4,180
Total Capital	24,885	24,175	23,036	21,282	21,080	15,948	12,153	10,383	10,585	9,635
Capital Expenditures	3,928	3,388	3,068	3,004	3,221	3,163	2,528	1,918	1,657	1,354
Cash Flow	4,283	3,817	3,144	3,161	2,866	2,453	2,204	2,039	1,742	1,495
Current Ratio	1.3	1.5	1.7	1.6	1.6	1.4	1.2	1.1	1.2	1.2
% Long Term Debt of Capitalization	34.9	37.7	39.2	48.0	48.3	50.7	46.4	43.5	42.1	45.9
% Net Income of Revenue	4.7	4.5	4.0	3.8	3.8	3.4	3.4	3.5	3.1	2.9
% Return on Assets	7.7	7.1	5.9	6.1	6.3	6.3	6.9	7.2	6.4	6.0
% Return on Equity	18.7	17.6	15.6	18.0	19.1	19.1	20.4	21.7	20.8	20.8

Data as orig reptd.; bef. results of disc opers/spec. items. Per share data adj. for stk. divs.; EPS diluted. E-Estimated. NA-Not Available. NM-Not Meaningful. NR-Not Ranked. UR-Under Review.

Office: 1000 Nicollet Mall, Minneapolis, MN 55403-2467.
Telephone: 612-304-6073.
Website: http://www.target.com
Chrmn & CEO: R.J. Ulrich

Pres: G.W. Steinhafel
Investor Contact: D.A. Scovanner
EVP & CFO: D.A. Scovanner
SVP, Secy & General Counsel: T.R. Baer

Board Members: R. Austin, C. Darden, J. A. Johnson, R. M. Kovacevich, M. E. Minnick, A. M. Mulcahy, S. W. Sanger, W. R. Staley, G. Steinhafel, G. W. Tamke, S. D. Trujillo, R. J. Ulrich

Founded: 1902
Domicile: Minnesota
Employees: 352,000

TECO Energy Inc.

STANDARD & POOR'S

S&P Recommendation **HOLD** ★★★☆☆	Price $17.12 (as of Nov 23, 2007)	12-Mo. Target Price $18.00	Investment Style Large-Cap Value

GICS Sector Utilities
Sub-Industry Multi-Utilities

Summary This company owns Tampa Electric Co., which serves the Tampa Bay region in west central Florida and has significant diversified operations related to its core business.

Key Stock Statistics (Source S&P, Vickers, company reports)

52-Wk Range	$18.58– 14.84	S&P Oper. EPS 2007**E**	1.04	Market Capitalization(B)	$3.604
Trailing 12-Month EPS	$1.37	S&P Oper. EPS 2008**E**	1.09	Yield (%)	4.56
Trailing 12-Month P/E	12.5	P/E on S&P Oper. EPS 2007**E**	16.5	Dividend Rate/Share	$0.78
$10K Invested 5 Yrs Ago	$15,192	Common Shares Outstg. (M)	210.5	Institutional Ownership (%)	58

Beta	0.65
S&P 3-Yr. Proj. EPS CAGR(%)	7.00
S&P Credit Rating	BBB-

Price Performance

30-Week Mov. Avg. · · · 10-Week Mov. Avg. - - **GAAP Earnings vs. Previous Year** Volume Above Avg. STARS
12-Mo. Target Price — Relative Strength — ▲ Up ▼ Down ► No Change Below Avg. ★

Options: Ph

Analysis prepared by **Justin McCann** on November 07, 2007, when the stock traded at **$ 17.02**.

Highlights

➤ Excluding tax credits related to synthetic fuel production (which are dependent on the price of oil and are set to expire at the end of 2007), we expect 2007 operating EPS to achieve only a low single-digit increase from 2006's EPS from continuing operations of $1.02. Due to oil price hedge instruments the company's TECO Coal subsidiary had entered into, TE expects net cash benefits of about $100 million from the production of synfuel in 2007, as well as net income of about $0.31 a share.

➤ On October 29, 2007, TE announced that it had agreed to sell its TECO Transport subsidiary for $405 million in cash. TECO intends to use a large portion of the estimated $375 million in after-tax proceeds for debt reduction.

➤ For 2008, we see EPS up 4.8% from forecast results in 2007. We believe Tampa Electric's customer base will continue to increase at around 2.5%, and that its sales will rise at about 3.0%. For Peoples Gas, we see 2.1% customer growth, and, assuming a return to normal winter weather, an approximate 10% increase in EPS. We expect the absence of earnings from TECO Transport to be partially offset by the reduction of debt and interest expense.

Investment Rationale/Risk

➤ We believe the shares are fairly valued relative to TE's electric and gas utility peers. After underperforming peers in 2006 and thus far in 2007, we expect TE's stock to perform closer to its peers over the next 12 months. While the stock had been restricted by the uncertainties related to the planned sale of its TECO Transport operations, we believe it will be partially supported by the expected completion of the agreed-to sale, as well as by the yield from the dividend (recently at 4.6%), which is well above that of TE's electric and gas utility peers.

➤ Risks to our recommendation and target price include significantly lower than expected synfuel-related tax credits, a sharp decrease in the average P/E of the Electric Utility group as a whole, and much worse than expected earnings from TE's non-regulated operations.

➤ TE's dividend represents nearly 75% of our estimate for 2007 operating EPS (excluding synfuel), well above the peer payout ratio average of 58%. Despite an above-peer yield from the dividend, we believe the shares will trade at a discount-to-peers P/E of about 16.5X our EPS estimate for 2008. Our 12-month target price is $18.

Qualitative Risk Assessment

LOW	**MEDIUM**	HIGH

Our risk assessment reflects the steady cash flow that we expect from the regulated electric and gas utilities, which operate within a generally supportive regulatory environment, offset by our view of the much less predictable earnings and cash flow from the unregulated coal and transport operations, particularly given the uncertainties concerning the tax credits related to the synthetic fuel operations.

Quantitative Evaluations

S&P Quality Ranking B

D	C	B-	**B**	B+	A-	A	A+

Relative Strength Rank STRONG

87

LOWEST = 1 HIGHEST = 99

Revenue/Earnings Data

Revenue (Million $)

	1Q	2Q	3Q	4Q	Year
2007	821.3	866.5	990.0	--	--
2006	836.4	862.6	922.9	826.2	3,448
2005	684.7	719.0	836.4	770.0	3,010
2004	642.3	713.0	742.3	660.2	2,669
2003	651.8	695.3	759.1	633.8	2,740
2002	606.6	677.7	731.0	660.5	2,676

Earnings Per Share ($)

2007	0.35	0.28	0.44	E0.18	E1.04
2006	0.26	0.29	0.38	0.23	1.17
2005	0.25	0.04	0.45	0.24	1.00
2004	0.15	-0.44	0.27	-2.05	-2.10
2003	-0.12	0.03	0.03	-0.02	-0.08
2002	0.50	0.56	0.72	0.20	1.95

Fiscal year ended Dec. 31. Next earnings report expected: Early February. EPS Estimates based on S&P Operating Earnings; historical GAAP earnings are as reported.

Dividend Data (Dates: mm/dd Payment Date: mm/dd/yy)

Amount ($)	Date Decl.	Ex-Div. Date	Stk. of Record	Payment Date
0.190	01/31	02/13	02/15	02/28/07
0.195	05/02	05/11	05/15	05/28/07
0.195	08/01	08/13	08/15	08/28/07
0.195	11/01	11/13	11/15	11/28/07

Dividends have been paid since 1900. Source: Company reports.

Please read the Required Disclosures and Analyst Certification on the last page of this report.

The **McGraw-Hill** Companies

TECO Energy Inc.

STANDARD &POOR'S

Business Summary November 07, 2007

CORPORATE OVERVIEW. TECO Energy (TE) is a holding company for a diverse set of energy companies including the regulated utility subsidiary Tampa Electric Company, which provides retail electric service in west central Florida. TE's other regulated utility is Peoples Gas System, which distributes natural gas in Florida's metropolitan areas. TE's unregulated businesses include TECO Coal, which has coal-mining operations and synthetic fuel facilities; TECO Transport, which provides shipping and storage services for coal and other dry-bulk commodities; and TECO Guatemala, which participates in independent power projects and electric distribution in Guatemala. In 2006, Tampa Electric accounted for 60.4% of TE's consolidated revenues; Peoples Gas System 16.8%; TECO Coal 16.7%; TECO Transport 5.9%; and TECO Guatemala 0.2%.

CORPORATE STRATEGY. With the divestiture of its non-core operations completed in January 2006, TE eliminated its exposure to the merchant power sec-

tor. This enabled it to strengthen its balance sheet and to meet its goal of repaying all the debt that is maturing in 2007, in our opinion. This was, in our view, a major step in reducing the company's business risk, improving its cash flows, and eventually restoring its investment grade credit rating. On October 29, 2007, the company announced that it had reached an agreement to sell its TECO Transport subsidiary to an investment group for approximately $405 million. TE expects the sale to be completed by the end of 2007 and, should it close successfully, it plans to use the after-tax proceeds (projected to be at around $375 million) to further reduce its debt, and realize a portion of the capital that would be needed for the expansion of its generating capacity and the upgrading of its infrastructure.

Company Financials Fiscal Year Ended Dec. 31

Per Share Data ($)	2006	2005	2004	2003	2002	2001	2000	1999	1998	1997
Tangible Book Value	7.97	7.36	6.13	8.55	13.75	12.94	11.93	11.19	11.42	11.04
Earnings	1.17	1.00	-2.10	-0.08	1.95	2.24	1.97	1.53	1.52	1.61
S&P Core Earnings	1.19	1.00	-1.58	0.24	1.75	2.04	NA	NA	NA	NA
Dividends	0.76	0.76	0.76	0.93	1.41	1.37	1.33	1.29	1.23	1.17
Payout Ratio	65%	76%	NM	NM	72%	61%	68%	84%	81%	72%
Prices:High	17.73	19.30	15.49	17.00	29.05	32.97	33.19	28.00	30.63	28.19
Prices:Low	14.40	14.87	11.30	9.47	10.02	24.75	17.25	18.38	24.75	22.75
P/E Ratio:High	15	19	NM	NM	15	15	17	18	20	18
P/E Ratio:Low	12	15	NM	NM	5	11	9	12	16	14

Income Statement Analysis (Million $)										
Revenue	3,448	3,010	2,669	2,740	2,676	2,649	2,295	1,983	1,958	1,862
Depreciation	282	282	282	326	303	298	268	232	228	225
Maintenance	183	168	141	152	162	151	140	125	129	114
Fixed Charges Coverage	1.42	1.25	1.26	2.30	2.43	2.51	2.59	3.30	3.95	3.88
Construction Credits	3.80	Nil	1.00	27.4	9.60	2.60	0.70	0.50	Nil	0.20
Effective Tax Rate	40.2%	45.1%	NM	NM	NM	NM	6.87%	30.2%	28.8%	30.9%
Net Income	246	211	-404	-14.7	298	304	251	201	200	211
S&P Core Earnings	248	212	-306	44.4	267	277	NA	NA	NA	NA

Balance Sheet & Other Financial Data (Million $)										
Gross Property	7,084	6,755	6,723	8,040	8,215	7,544	6,560	8,501	5,601	5,360
Capital Expenditures	456	295	273	591	1,065	966	688	426	296	213
Net Property	4,767	4,567	4,658	5,679	5,464	4,838	3,970	6,064	3,308	3,237
Capitalization:Long Term Debt	3,213	3,709	3,880	4,393	3,973	2,043	1,575	1,208	1,280	1,080
Capitalization:% Long Term Debt	65.0	70.0	75.1	73.0	43.2	50.9	51.1	46.0	45.9	42.8
Capitalization:Preferred	Nil	Nil	Nil	Nil	Nil	Nil	Nil	Nil	Nil	Nil
Capitalization:% Preferred	Nil	Nil	Nil	Nil	Nil	Nil	Nil	Nil	Nil	Nil
Capitalization:Common	1,729	1,592	1,284	1,622	5,223	1,972	1,507	1,418	1,508	1,445
Capitalization:% Common	35.0	30.0	24.9	27.0	56.8	49.1	48.9	54.0	54.1	57.2
Total Capital	4,957	5,318	5,691	6,537	9,719	4,545	3,564	3,284	3,334	3,048
% Operating Ratio	91.9	91.4	80.2	83.7	84.0	83.7	82.8	83.0	82.6	82.9
% Earned on Net Property	9.0	7.7	NA	0.3	7.6	9.6	10.9	7.3	12.1	13.3
% Return on Revenue	7.1	7.0	NA	NM	11.1	11.5	10.9	10.1	10.2	11.4
% Return on Invested Capital	8.5	9.3	14.2	9.6	6.4	11.9	12.4	9.7	11.3	10.9
% Return on Common Equity	14.8	14.7	NA	NM	6.5	17.5	17.2	13.7	13.6	15.6

Data as orig reptd.; bef. results of disc opers/spec. items. Per share data adj. for stk. divs.; EPS diluted. E-Estimated. NA-Not Available. NM-Not Meaningful. NR-Not Ranked. UR-Under Review.

Office: 702 N Franklin St , Tampa, FL 33602.
Telephone: 813-228-1111.
Website: http://www.tecoenergy.com
Chrmn & CEO: S. Hudson

Pres & COO: J.B. Ramil
EVP & CFO: G.L. Gillette
SVP & General Counsel: S.M. McDevitt
Investor Contact: M.M. Kane (813-228-1772)

Board Members: C. D. Ausley, S. L. Baldwin, J. L. Ferman, Jr., L. Guinot, Jr., S. Hudson, J. Lacher, L. A. Penn, T. L. Rankin, W. D. Rockford, W. P. Sovey, J. T. Touchton, P. L. Whiting

Founded: 1899
Domicile: Florida
Employees: 5,200

The McGraw-Hill Companies

STANDARD &POOR'S

Tellabs Inc

S&P Recommendation `HOLD` ★★★☆☆

Price
$7.03 (as of Nov 23, 2007)

12-Mo. Target Price
$10.00

GICS Sector Information Technology
Sub-Industry Communications Equipment

Summary This company manufactures voice and data equipment used in public and private communications networks worldwide.

Key Stock Statistics (Source S&P, Vickers, company reports)

52-Wk Range	$13.67– 6.72	S&P Oper. EPS 2007**E**	0.17	Market Capitalization(B)	$3.081	Beta	2.90
Trailing 12-Month EPS	$0.20	S&P Oper. EPS 2008**E**	0.35	Yield (%)	Nil	S&P 3-Yr. Proj. EPS CAGR(%)	4.00
Trailing 12-Month P/E	35.2	P/E on S&P Oper. EPS 2007**E**	41.4	Dividend Rate/Share	Nil	S&P Credit Rating	NA
$10K Invested 5 Yrs Ago	$7,717	Common Shares Outstg. (M)	438.3	Institutional Ownership (%)	76		

Price Performance

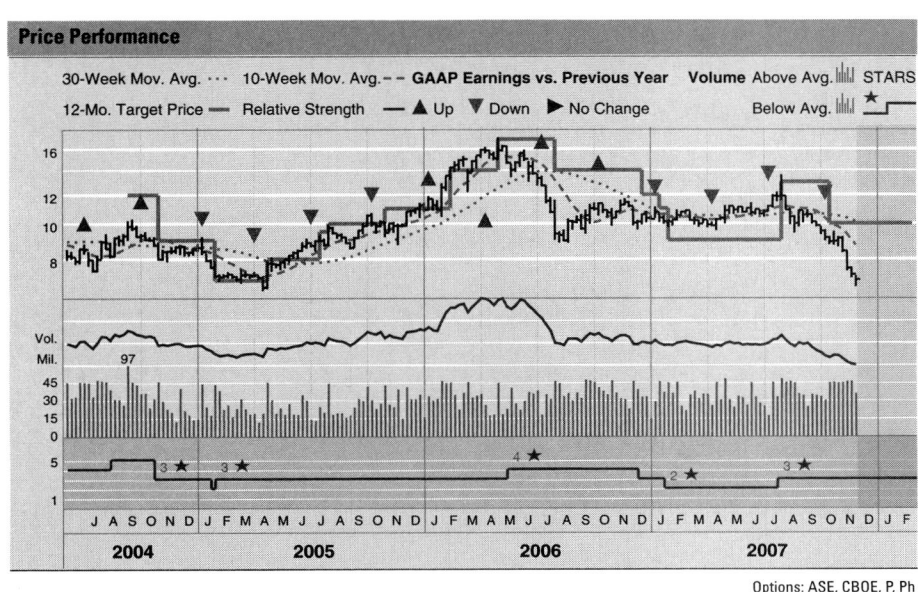

30-Week Mov. Avg. ··· 10-Week Mov. Avg. -- **GAAP Earnings vs. Previous Year** Volume Above Avg. STARS
12-Mo. Target Price — Relative Strength — ▲ Up ▼ Down ► No Change Below Avg.

Options: ASE, CBOE, P, Ph

Analysis prepared by **Ari Bensinger** on October 08, 2007, when the stock traded at **$ 8.82**.

Highlights

➤ Following an estimated 3% sales decline during 2007, we expect revenues to increase roughly 10% in 2008, reflecting a pick-up in wireless equipment sales following a carrier spending pause during 2007, partly reflecting integration issues due to the consolidation of top North American customers. We expect broadband data products to become a bigger part of the company's sales mix.

➤ We expect the 2008 gross margin to widen about 400 basis points, to 40%, up from the 36% that we forecast for 2007, albeit still below the industry average. Current profitability is being hurt by an increasing mix of lower-margin products and weaker revenues. We forecast 2008 operating margins under the 10% level, below peers, hurt by high research and development costs.

➤ After higher interest income and an effective tax rate of 30%, which helped 2005 and 2006 results, we project 2008 EPS of $0.35, up from the $0.17 that we estimate for 2007. Our earnings estimates for both years include annual projected stock option expense of $0.07.

Investment Rationale/Risk

➤ Current results are being hurt by poor sales visibility and a lower margin product mix. However, longer term, we view TLAB as well positioned to benefit from accelerating telecom spending on the access portion of the network, the company's core target market. We also view the company as an acquisition candidate, given its strong market position in the fiber-to-the-home and IP television markets.

➤ Risks to our recommendation and target price include a decreased pace of market penetration in the company's new broadband products; slower growth for its core transport products; and the loss of a major customer.

➤ Incorporating the company's nearly $3 a share in cash, our 12-month target price of $10 reflects a P/E of 27X our 2008 EPS estimate, after subtracting $0.09 of associated interest income. Our target price values TLAB at 2.2X our 2008 sales per share estimate, near its wireline equipment peers.

Qualitative Risk Assessment

LOW	MEDIUM	**HIGH**

Our risk assessment reflects the competitive pressure the company faces, and its dependence on a consolidating telecom industry.

Quantitative Evaluations

S&P Quality Ranking B-

D	C	**B-**	B	B+	A-	A	A+

Relative Strength Rank WEAK
`14`
LOWEST = 1 HIGHEST = 99

Revenue/Earnings Data

Revenue (Million $)

	1Q	2Q	3Q	4Q	Year
2007	451.9	469.0	457.9	--	--
2006	514.7	549.3	522.5	454.7	2,041
2005	435.6	462.5	463.9	521.4	1,883
2004	263.8	304.3	284.3	379.4	1,232
2003	222.5	234.1	244.5	279.3	980.4
2002	371.5	344.6	288.1	312.8	1,317

Earnings Per Share ($)

2007	0.06	0.07	0.01	E0.05	E0.17
2006	0.11	0.12	0.13	0.07	0.43
2005	Nil	0.09	0.09	0.20	0.39
2004	0.03	0.12	0.11	-0.32	-0.07
2003	-0.10	-0.27	-0.16	-0.06	-0.58
2002	0.01	-0.35	-0.22	-0.21	-0.76

Fiscal year ended Dec. 31. Next earnings report expected: Late January. EPS Estimates based on S&P Operating Earnings; historical GAAP earnings are as reported.

Dividend Data

No cash dividends have been paid.

The McGraw-Hill Companies

Tellabs Inc

STANDARD &POOR'S

Business Summary October 08, 2007

CORPORATE OVERVIEW. Tellabs designs, manufactures, markets and ser- vices optical networking, next-generation switching and broadband access solutions. The company's transport systems (41% of sales in 2006) are de- signed to help service providers lower their costs, generate more revenues, and efficiently manage bandwidth as end-user demand for communication services grows. TLAB's managed access solutions (17%) provide seamless in- tegration of circuit-switched voice and data, Internet Protocol (IP) data and voice over Internet Protocol (VoIP) services, and access capacity expansion through digital subscriber line (DSL) technology.

MARKET PROFILE. In our opinion, one of the most important fundamental changes in the telecom sector has been the rapid consolidation of service providers. The largest single group of customers for TLAB in 2006 was the In- cumbent Local Exchange Carriers (ILECs), which include AT&T, BellSouth (which was acquired by AT&T in late 2006), Verizon, and Qwest Communica- tions. We believe the balance of power resides with the service provider. In our view, due to their size, these large ILECs and their respective wireless segments have pricing power over suppliers, with a decision to slow down spending putting pressure on TLAB's revenue in the first quarter of 2007 and our outlook for the full year. We expect flat- to mid-single digit capital spend-

ing growth in 2007 to be largely focused on broadband and fiber-based initia- tives.

COMPETITIVE LANDSCAPE. Competition for new telecom customers as well as for new infrastructure deployments is particularly intense and increasingly focused on price, in our view. We believe customer concentration has raised customer buying power, with more demanding requirements from the largest service providers. Some of TLAB's peers, such as Alcatel, have made acquisi- tions to gain scale. It seems to us that capital spending decisions are more challenging and more competitive from service providers that use an open standard platform in which to choose network solutions from different equip- ment suppliers, leading to longer sales cycles. For example, after conducting a supplier search for a year, in July 2006, Verizon selected TLAB as a supplier of its reconfigurable optical add/drop multiplexer (ROADM) service, helping Verizon reshape its metro core optical network, although in early 2007, there were delays in offering the service.

Company Financials Fiscal Year Ended Dec. 31

Per Share Data ($)	2006	2005	2004	2003	2002	2001	2000	1999	1998	1997
Tangible Book Value	3.97	3.53	3.34	3.76	4.45	5.55	6.26	4.85	3.40	2.40
Cash Flow	0.66	0.66	0.12	-0.32	-0.41	-0.06	2.09	1.56	1.18	0.83
Earnings	0.43	0.39	-0.07	-0.58	-0.76	-0.44	1.82	1.36	1.03	0.71
S&P Core Earnings	0.44	0.38	-0.14	-0.71	-1.03	-0.68	NA	NA	NA	NA
Dividends	Nil	Nil	Nil	Nil	Nil	Nil	Nil	Nil	Nil	Nil
Payout Ratio	Nil	Nil	Nil	Nil	Nil	Nil	Nil	Nil	Nil	Nil
Prices:High	17.28	11.49	11.37	9.73	17.47	67.13	76.94	77.25	46.56	32.50
Prices:Low	8.84	6.56	7.40	5.07	4.00	8.98	37.63	32.38	15.69	16.00
P/E Ratio:High	40	29	NM	NM	NM	NM	42	57	45	46
P/E Ratio:Low	21	17	NM	NM	NM	NM	21	24	15	23

Income Statement Analysis (Million $)										
Revenue	2,041	1,883	1,232	980	1,317	2,200	3,387	2,319	1,660	1,204
Operating Income	358	330	152	-77.1	-12.7	70.9	1,117	832	593	410
Depreciation	104	126	82.3	110	143	158	116	84.6	56.1	46.9
Interest Expense	Nil	Nil	Nil	0.70	0.90	0.51	0.63	0.58	0.29	0.41
Pretax Income	285	213	-10.2	-245	-328	-245	1,109	816	590	400
Effective Tax Rate	31.8%	17.5%	NM	NM	NM	NM	31.5%	31.5%	32.5%	34.0%
Net Income	194	176	-29.8	-242	-313	-182	760	559	398	264
S&P Core Earnings	198	171	-58.9	-295	-427	-277	NA	NA	NA	NA

Balance Sheet & Other Financial Data (Million $)										
Cash	154	1,371	293	246	1,019	1,102	1,022	966	643	109
Current Assets	2,233	1,873	1,819	1,499	1,534	1,945	2,322	1,786	1,253	863
Total Assets	3,922	3,515	3,523	2,608	2,623	2,866	3,073	2,353	1,628	1,183
Current Liabilities	762	525	524	208	257	320	412	274	218	226
Long Term Debt	Nil	Nil	Nil	Nil	Nil	3.39	2.85	2.85	2.85	2.90
Common Equity	2,938	2,815	2,797	2,219	2,290	2,466	2,628	2,048	1,377	933
Total Capital	2,938	2,815	2,797	2,319	2,290	2,490	2,637	2,058	1,391	936
Capital Expenditures	67.2	61.8	41.4	9.50	34.1	208	208	98.9	75.9	84.7
Cash Flow	298	302	52.5	-131	-171	-24.5	876	644	454	311
Current Ratio	2.9	3.6	3.5	7.2	6.0	6.1	5.6	6.5	5.7	3.8
% Long Term Debt of Capitalization	Nil	Nil	Nil	Nil	Nil	0.1	0.1	0.1	0.2	0.0
% Net Income of Revenue	9.5	9.3	NM	NM	NM	NM	22.4	24.1	24.0	21.9
% Return on Assets	5.2	5.0	NM	NM	NM	NM	28.0	28.0	28.3	27.4
% Return on Equity	6.7	6.3	NM	NM	NM	NM	32.5	32.5	34.5	34.6

Data as orig reptd.; bef. results of disc opers/spec. items. Per share data adj. for stk. divs.; EPS diluted. E-Estimated. NA-Not Available. NM-Not Meaningful. NR-Not Ranked. UR-Under Review.

Office: 1415 W Diehl Rd, Naperville, IL 60563-2349.
Telephone: 630-798-8800.
Website: http://www.tellabs.com
Chrmn: M.J. Birck

Pres & CEO: K.A. Prabhu
EVP & CFO: T.J. Wiggins
EVP & CTO: T. Gruenwald
Chief Admin Officer, Secy & General Counsel: J. Sheehan

Investor Contact: T. Scottino (630-798-3602)
Board Members: L. Beck, M. J. Birck, B. Hedfors, F. Ianna, F. A. Krehbiel, M. E. Lavin, S. P. Marshall, K. A. Prabhu, W. F. Souders, J. H. Suwinski

Founded: 1974
Domicile: Delaware
Employees: 3,713

Temple-Inland Inc.

STANDARD &POOR'S

S&P Recommendation HOLD ★★★☆☆	**Price** $42.83 (as of Nov 23, 2007)	**12-Mo. Target Price** $60.00	**Investment Style** Large-Cap Value

GICS Sector Materials
Sub-Industry Paper Packaging

Summary This major producer of corrugated containers and containerboard also makes building products, provides financial services, and develops real estate.

Key Stock Statistics (Source S&P, Vickers, company reports)

52-Wk Range	$66.28– 38.74	S&P Oper. EPS 2007**E**	2.00	Market Capitalization(B)	$4.539	Beta	1.58
Trailing 12-Month EPS	$2.26	S&P Oper. EPS 2008**E**	2.50	Yield (%)	2.61	S&P 3-Yr. Proj. EPS CAGR(%)	2.00
Trailing 12-Month P/E	19.0	P/E on S&P Oper. EPS 2007**E**	21.4	Dividend Rate/Share	$1.12	S&P Credit Rating	BBB-
$10K Invested 5 Yrs Ago	$20,978	Common Shares Outstg. (M)	106.0	Institutional Ownership (%)	76		

Price Performance

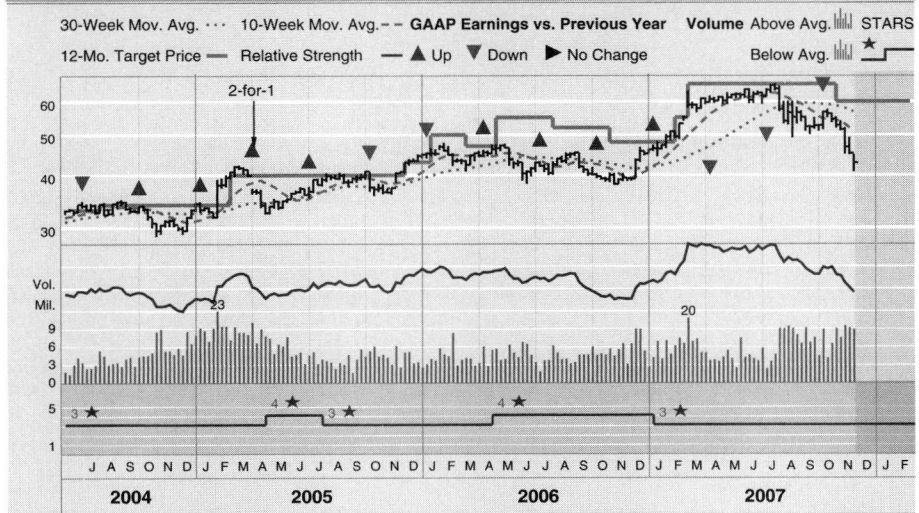

- 30-Week Mov. Avg. ··· 10-Week Mov. Avg. - - **GAAP Earnings vs. Previous Year** Volume Above Avg. STARS
- 12-Mo. Target Price — Relative Strength — ▲ Up ▼ Down ► No Change   Below Avg. ★

Options: ASE

Analysis prepared by **Stuart J. Benway, CFA** on October 30, 2007, when the stock traded at **$ 52.48**.

Highlights

➤ We see about a 5% decline in revenues in 2007 from ongoing operations. As for 2008, the company is expected to be split up into three separate entities. The real estate business will likely generate solid revenue growth with increased land sales. The financial services business is expected to suffer from the weak housing market. We see modest revenue growth from the containerboard business, and little improvement in the forest products sector.

➤ Following a nearly 400 basis point improvement in the operating margin in 2006, we see a contraction of about 350 basis points in 2007, to 9.9%. We forecast sharply lower profits in the forest products sector due to falling demand and prices. However, we believe that higher results in packaging will allow for reasonable levels of profitability.

➤ Our operating EPS estimate for 2007 is $2.00, following EPS of $3.33 in 2006, and our 2008 forecast is $2.60.

Investment Rationale/Risk

➤ On February 26, 2007, Temple-Inland announced a major transformational plan (subject to regulatory approval), which involves a separation of the company into three publicly traded entities and the sale of timberlands. The company would retain its corrugated packaging and building products manufacturing operations. We believe the planned deal would allow management to focus on its packaging and wood product businesses, but could lead to a more volatile earnings stream.

➤ Risks to our recommendation and target price include an unexpected downturn in packaging prices and demand, an escalation in input costs, a reduction in real estate values, and an inability of the company to complete its restructuring as currently planned.

➤ Our sum of the parts analysis--which assesses the financial services unit at 1.4X book value, assumes cash proceeds from timberland sales of about $1.8 billion, and values the real estate business at about $2.7 billion, including high values for residential properties--values the shares at $60, which is our 12-month target price.

Qualitative Risk Assessment

LOW	MEDIUM	HIGH

Our risk assessment reflects our view that Temple-Inland's manufacturing businesses are cyclical and capital intensive, while its financial services unit is subject to interest rate risk. Although we believe that both businesses are economically sensitive, this unusual mix of operations reduces Temple-Inland's overall business risk, in our opinion.

Quantitative Evaluations

S&P Quality Ranking   **B+**

D	C	B-	B	B+	A-	A	A+

Relative Strength Rank   **WEAK**

18

LOWEST = 1   HIGHEST = 99

Revenue/Earnings Data

Revenue (Million $)

	1Q	2Q	3Q	4Q	Year
2007	1,321	1,358	1,299	--	--
2006	1,384	1,433	1,409	1,332	5,558
2005	1,203	1,255	1,218	1,212	4,888
2004	1,148	1,218	1,194	1,190	4,750
2003	1,135	1,182	1,170	1,166	4,653
2002	1,020	1,190	1,157	1,151	4,518

Earnings Per Share ($)

2007	0.35	0.62	0.41	E0.51	E2.00
2006	0.67	1.71	0.87	0.98	4.23
2005	0.39	0.59	0.32	0.23	1.54
2004	0.12	0.49	0.36	0.47	1.44
2003	-0.16	1.43	-0.03	-0.35	0.89
2002	0.15	0.16	0.14	0.18	0.62

Fiscal year ended Dec. 31. Next earnings report expected: Early February. EPS Estimates based on S&P Operating Earnings; historical GAAP earnings are as reported.

Dividend Data (Dates: mm/dd Payment Date: mm/dd/yy)

Amount ($)	Date Decl.	Ex-Div. Date	Stk. of Record	Payment Date
0.280	02/02	02/27	03/01	03/15/07
0.280	05/04	05/30	06/01	06/15/07
0.280	08/03	08/29	08/31	09/14/07
0.280	11/02	11/28	11/30	12/14/07

Dividends have been paid since 1984. Source: Company reports.

The McGraw-Hill Companies

Temple-Inland Inc.

STANDARD &POOR'S

Business Summary October 30, 2007

CORPORATE OVERVIEW. With its operations in the areas of forest products and financial services, Temple-Inland has a diverse combination of business-es. Its corrugated packaging segment (54% of 2006 sales, 30% of operating in-come) makes containerboard and converts it into boxes. The forest products segment (22%, 37%) produces wood products, including lumber, particle-board, medium density fiberboard, gypsum wallboard and fiberboard. The fi-nancial services segment (21%, 26%) includes Guaranty Bank, which has $16 billion in assets and conducts business in Texas and California, where some of the fastest growing markets in the country are located. The newly formed real estate division (3%, 7%) develops the company's high value timberland in-to residential properties.

MARKET PROFILE. TIN's corrugated containers range from commodity brown boxes to intricate die-cut packages that can be printed with multi-color graphics. Sales of corrugated packaging follow changing population patterns and other demographic trends. Historically, there has been a correlation be-

tween the demand for corrugated packaging and orders for nondurable goods. With its 12% share of total industry shipments in 2006, we believe TIN is the fourth largest producer of corrugated packaging in the United States. However, because of the fragmented and commodity-oriented nature of the packaging industry, TIN has little control over the pricing or demand for its products. TIN's building products are used primarily in home construction, re-modeling and repair, and cabinet and furniture production. The forest prod-ucts business is heavily dependent on the level of residential housing expen-ditures, and, like the packaging sector, the forest products industry is fairly fragmented and commodity oriented, and pricing varies with the supply and demand balance.

Company Financials Fiscal Year Ended Dec. 31

Per Share Data ($)	2006	2005	2004	2003	2002	2001	2000	1999	1998	1997
Tangible Book Value	17.72	14.90	15.22	14.67	14.42	17.45	18.71	17.84	17.97	18.15
Cash Flow	6.50	3.71	3.71	3.40	3.13	3.34	4.12	3.71	3.06	2.84
Earnings	4.23	1.54	1.44	0.89	0.62	1.13	1.92	1.72	0.61	0.45
S&P Core Earnings	3.56	1.77	1.53	0.92	0.10	0.48	NA	NA	NA	NA
Dividends	1.00	0.90	0.72	0.85	0.64	0.64	0.64	0.64	0.64	0.64
Payout Ratio	24%	58%	50%	96%	103%	57%	33%	37%	106%	142%
Prices:High	47.92	45.28	35.01	31.43	30.00	31.08	33.84	38.75	33.63	34.72
Prices:Low	37.84	31.58	28.63	18.43	16.34	20.17	17.31	26.81	21.34	24.81
P/E Ratio:High	11	29	24	35	48	27	18	23	56	77
P/E Ratio:Low	9	21	20	21	26	18	9	16	35	55

Income Statement Analysis (Million $)										
Revenue	5,558	4,888	4,750	4,653	4,518	4,172	4,286	3,682	3,740	3,625
Operating Income	964	620	612	316	511	491	654	610	546	467
Depreciation	251	249	254	270	260	216	225	225	275	268
Interest Expense	128	109	125	135	133	98.0	104	95.0	106	110
Pretax Income	677	262	233	-97.0	107	177	320	306	124	95.0
Effective Tax Rate	30.7%	32.8%	30.5%	NM	39.3%	37.3%	39.1%	37.6%	46.0%	46.3%
Net Income	469	176	162	97.0	65.0	111	195	191	67.0	51.0
S&P Core Earnings	395	203	171	99.4	10.9	46.0	NA	NA	NA	NA

Balance Sheet & Other Financial Data (Million $)										
Cash	405	444	372	399	455	590	322	284	244	188
Current Assets	NA	NA	NA	NA	NA	NA	NA	NA	NA	NA
Total Assets	20,413	21,633	20,119	21,143	21,760	18,687	18,142	16,186	15,990	14,364
Current Liabilities	NA	NA	NA	NA	NA	NA	NA	NA	NA	NA
Long Term Debt	7,252	8,906	1,996	2,155	6,124	1,859	1,897	1,691	2,018	1,605
Common Equity	2,189	2,080	2,092	1,968	1,949	1,896	1,833	1,927	1,998	2,045
Total Capital	9,615	11,129	4,167	4,130	8,309	4,059	4,002	3,814	4,258	3,873
Capital Expenditures	233	265	264	159	125	210	257	204	214	251
Cash Flow	720	425	416	367	325	327	420	416	342	319
Current Ratio	NA	NA	NA	NA	NA	NA	NA	NA	NA	NA
% Long Term Debt of Capitalization	75.4	80.0	47.9	52.2	73.7	45.8	47.4	44.3	47.4	41.4
% Net Income of Revenue	8.4	3.6	3.4	NM	1.4	2.7	4.5	5.2	1.8	1.4
% Return on Assets	2.2	0.8	0.8	NM	0.3	0.6	1.1	1.2	0.4	0.4
% Return on Equity	20.2	8.4	8.0	NM	3.4	6.0	10.4	9.7	3.3	2.5

Data as orig reptd.; bef. results of disc opers/spec. items. Per share data adj. for stk. divs.; EPS diluted. E-Estimated. NA-Not Available. NM-Not Meaningful. NR-Not Ranked. UR-Under Review.

Office: 1300 MoPac Expressway South, Austin, TX 78746.
Telephone: 512-434-5800.
Email: investorrelations@templeinland.com
Website: http://www.temple-inland.com

Chrmn & CEO: K.M. Jastrow, II
VP & Chief Acctg Officer: L.R. Brill
VP & Secy: L.K. O' Neal
CFO: R.D. Levy

Chief Admin Officer & General Counsel: J.B. Johnston
Investor Contact: C.L. Nines (512-434-5587)
Board Members: A. M. Beschloss, D. M. Carlton, C. C. Carr, E. L. Draper, Jr., L. R. Faulkner, J. T. Hackett, J. M. Heller, K. M. Jastrow, II, J. A. Johnson, W. A. Reed, R. M. Smith, L. E. Temple, A. Temple, III

Founded: 1983
Domicile: Delaware
Employees: 15,500

Tenet Healthcare Corp

STANDARD &POOR'S

S&P Recommendation HOLD ★★★☆☆	Price $3.97 (as of Nov 23, 2007)	12-Mo. Target Price $5.00	Investment Style Large-Cap Value

GICS Sector Health Care
Sub-Industry Health Care Facilities

Summary This Dallas-based company is the second largest U.S. for-profit hospital manager.

Key Stock Statistics (Source S&P, Vickers, company reports)

52-Wk Range	$7.80–3.06	S&P Oper. EPS 2007E	-0.18	Market Capitalization(B)	$1.881	Beta	-0.15
Trailing 12-Month EPS	$-0.85	S&P Oper. EPS 2008E	0.02	Yield (%)	Nil	S&P 3-Yr. Proj. EPS CAGR(%)	NM
Trailing 12-Month P/E	NM	P/E on S&P Oper. EPS 2007E	NM	Dividend Rate/Share	Nil	S&P Credit Rating	B
$10K Invested 5 Yrs Ago	$2,421	Common Shares Outstg. (M)	473.9	Institutional Ownership (%)	NM		

Price Performance

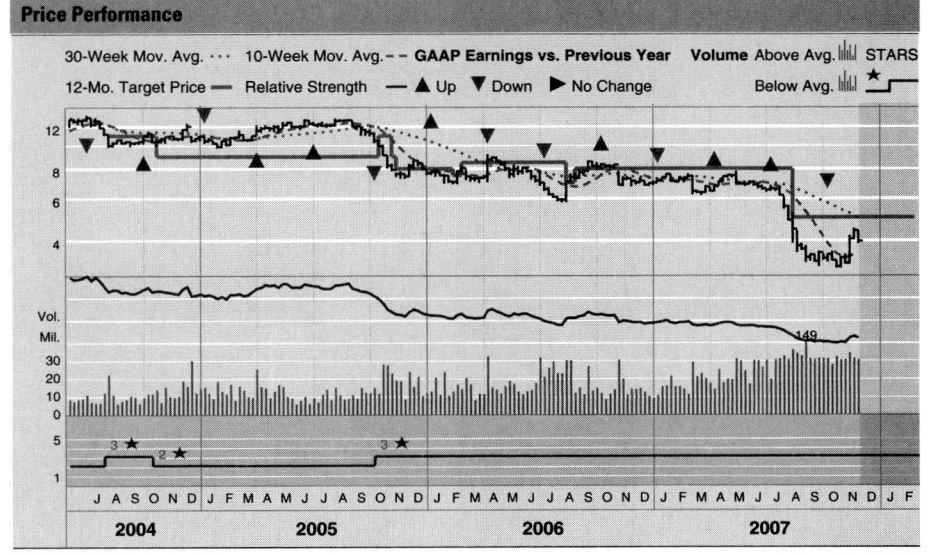

Options: ASE, CBOE, P

Analysis prepared by **Jeffrey Englander, CFA** on November 20, 2007, when the stock traded at **$ 4.01**.

Highlights

➤ We look for revenues to increase approximately 0.8% in 2007, vs. a 2.7% decrease in 2006, as the company continues to pursue its turnaround efforts amid a difficult market environment and continued challenges in its key California and Florida markets. We look for revenue growth to accelerate to 3.6% in 2008 as management's efforts to improve quality and physician recruitment and referrals improve admissions growth.

➤ We see EBITDA margins narrowing in 2007 as increases in payroll expenses, supplies and other operating costs as well as provisions for doubtful accounts negatively impact results. While we believe THC's Targeted Growth Initiative (TGI) may result in a greater focus on high-demand services and rationalization of underperforming facilities, it may be into 2008 before TGI produces meaningful results. Accordingly, we see EBITDA margins improving in 2008, reflecting a decrease in salaries and a leveling off of bad debt expense, both as a percent of revenues.

➤ We forecast an operating loss per share of $0.18 in 2007 and EPS of $0.02 in 2008, as THC's quality initiatives have greater impact.

Investment Rationale/Risk

➤ We continue to believe that 2007 will be a difficult year for THC as the company struggles with inconsistent volume growth, which we see as the key to any turnaround plans. In addition, while we believe that management is taking steps to improve quality as well as relationships with physicians and managed care payors, we anticipate that these initiatives will take time to have an impact, leaving THC to serve lower-margin Medicare and Medicaid patients.

➤ Risks to our opinion and target price include potential reimbursement cuts in Medicare and/or Medicaid, continued difficulty in managed care negotiations, and the potential for physicians to refer patients to competing facilities. In addition, the rising number of uninsured patients could negatively affect bad debt expense beyond our expectations.

➤ Our 12-month target price of $5 assumes an EV/EBITDA multiple of approximately 8X based on our 2008 EBITDA estimate, a discount to THC's historical levels, reflecting our view of its increased incidence of bad debts, low adjusted admissions growth and payor mix.

Qualitative Risk Assessment

LOW	MEDIUM	HIGH

Our risk assessment for THC reflects our view of stable demand for health care services and its generally favorable corporate governance practices. This is offset by the company's strong dependence on third-party reimbursements, including Medicare and Medicaid, which can be unpredictable, as well as its high level of debt.

Quantitative Evaluations

S&P Quality Ranking C

D	C	B-	B	B+	A-	A	A+

Relative Strength Rank STRONG

84

LOWEST = 1 HIGHEST = 99

Revenue/Earnings Data

Revenue (Million $)

	1Q	2Q	3Q	4Q	Year
2007	2,279	2,228	2,212	--	--
2006	2,414	2,195	2,117	2,179	8,701
2005	2,501	2,420	2,394	2,299	9,614
2004	2,574	2,505	2,428	2,412	9,919
2003	3,417	3,346	3,268	3,181	13,212
2002	--	--	--	--	8,743

Earnings Per Share ($)

	1Q	2Q	3Q	4Q	Year
2007	0.20	-0.06	-0.07	E-0.04	E-0.18
2006	-0.03	-0.95	-0.06	-0.83	-1.85
2005	0.04	Nil	-0.82	-0.54	-1.32
2004	-0.04	-0.45	-0.11	-3.43	-3.85
2003	0.03	-0.28	-0.50	-2.34	-3.01
2002	--	--	--	--	0.93

Fiscal year ended Dec. 31. Next earnings report expected: Late February. EPS Estimates based on S&P Operating Earnings; historical GAAP earnings are as reported.

Dividend Data

Dividends, initiated in 1973, were omitted beginning in 1993. A special dividend of $0.01 a share was paid in March 2000.

Please read the Required Disclosures and Analyst Certification on the last page of this report.

The McGraw-Hill Companies

Tenet Healthcare Corp

STANDARD &POOR'S

Business Summary November 20, 2007

CORPORATE OVERVIEW. Tenet Healthcare ranks as the second largest U.S. for-profit hospital manager. At December 31, 2006, it owned or operated 57 hospitals (excluding the 11 hospitals whose sale was announced in June 2006 and whose sale is expected to be completed in 2007), with 14,941 licensed beds. The largest concentrations of hospital beds were in California, Florida and Texas. THC also owns and operates a small number of rehabilitation hospitals, a specialty hospital, skilled nursing facilities, and medical office buildings located on or near the general hospital properties. In 2006, on a same-facility basis, admissions fell 2.5% and equivalent admissions declined 21.7%. In 2005, total admissions were down 2.9% and equivalent admissions decreased 2.2%.

In January 2003, THC was sued by the U.S. Justice Department for allegedly submitting false claims to Medicare. In October 2003, the Justice Department served THC with a subpoena related to its investigation of Medicare outlier payments. In September 2003, the U.S. Senate launched an investigation into the company's corporate governance practices with respect to federal health care programs. In October 2004, additional investigations were announced into THC's medical directorship arrangements and physician relocation agreements.

In January 2006, THC reached an agreement to settle federal securities class action lawsuits as well as shareholder derivative litigation for $215 million in cash; insurance proceeds covered $75 million of the this amount. The lawsuits were filed against the company beginning in 2002 and were consolidated in January 2003. In June 2006, THC and the U.S. Department of Justice reached an agreement to settle the ongoing investigation into Medicare outlier billing. The company agreed to pay $725 million over a period of four years, plus interest, and to waive its right to collect $175 million in Medicare payments for past services. In order to fund the settlement, at that time THC announced it would sell 11 hospitals, 10 of which whose sale has been completed. The settlement does not involve the Securities and Exchange Commission, which is investigating THC's financial disclosures surrounding the Medicare outlier payments. In our view, the Justice Department settlement removes some risk in the stock, but we expect its valuation to continue to be driven by the company's underlying operating fundamentals.

Company Financials Fiscal Year Ended Dec. 31

Per Share Data ($)	2006	2005	2004	2003	2002	2001	2000	1999	1998	1997
Tangible Book Value	NM	NM	1.63	4.85	4.40	4.40	3.45	1.57	1.01	0.31
Cash Flow	-1.12	-0.51	-3.02	-2.00	1.54	3.24	2.51	1.85	1.71	1.79
Earnings	-1.85	-1.32	-3.85	-3.01	0.93	2.04	1.39	0.72	0.53	0.81
S&P Core Earnings	-0.34	-1.14	-2.28	0.27	1.54	1.24	NA	NA	NA	NA
Dividends	Nil	Nil	Nil	Nil	Nil	Nil	Nil	0.01	Nil	Nil
Payout Ratio	Nil	Nil	Nil	Nil	Nil	Nil	Nil	1%	Nil	Nil
Prices:High	9.27	13.06	18.73	19.25	52.50	41.85	30.50	18.12	27.29	23.25
Prices:Low	5.77	7.27	9.15	11.32	13.70	24.67	11.29	10.25	15.83	14.25
P/E Ratio:High	NM	NM	NM	NM	56	21	22	25	52	29
P/E Ratio:Low	NM	NM	NM	NM	15	12	8	14	30	18

Income Statement Analysis (Million $)	2006	2005	2004	2003	2002	2001	2000	1999	1998	1997
Revenue	8,701	9,614	9,919	13,212	8,743	13,913	12,053	11,414	10,880	9,895
Operating Income	687	571	434	1,072	1,676	2,797	2,244	1,935	1,858	1,809
Depreciation	342	382	388	471	302	604	554	533	556	460
Interest Expense	409	405	333	296	147	327	456	479	485	464
Pretax Income	-1,129	-701	-1,616	-1,829	777	1,799	1,156	639	481	669
Effective Tax Rate	NM	NM	NM	NM	38.5%	40.9%	40.1%	43.5%	46.8%	40.2%
Net Income	-871	-621	-1,797	-1,404	459	1,025	678	340	249	378
S&P Core Earnings	-159	-561	-1,061	123	760	607	NA	NA	NA	NA

Balance Sheet & Other Financial Data (Million $)	2006	2005	2004	2003	2002	2001	2000	1999	1998	1997
Cash	784	1,373	654	619	210	38.0	62.0	135	29.0	155
Current Assets	3,025	3,508	3,992	4,248	3,792	3,394	3,226	3,594	3,962	2,890
Total Assets	8,539	9,812	10,078	12,298	13,780	13,814	12,995	13,161	13,771	12,833
Current Liabilities	1,925	2,292	2,130	2,394	2,381	2,584	2,166	1,912	2,022	1,767
Long Term Debt	4,760	4,784	4,395	4,039	3,872	3,919	4,202	5,668	6,391	5,829
Common Equity	995	1,760	2,460	4,361	5,723	5,619	5,079	4,066	3,870	3,558
Total Capital	5,862	6,756	7,166	8,404	10,121	10,227	9,835	10,225	10,701	9,810
Capital Expenditures	631	568	454	753	490	889	601	619	592	534
Cash Flow	-529	-239	-1,409	-933	761	1,629	1,232	873	805	838
Current Ratio	1.6	1.5	1.9	1.8	1.6	1.3	1.5	1.9	2.0	1.6
% Long Term Debt of Capitalization	81.2	70.8	61.3	48.1	38.3	38.3	42.7	55.4	59.7	59.4
% Net Income of Revenue	NM	NM	NM	NM	5.2	7.4	5.6	3.0	2.3	3.8
% Return on Assets	NM	NM	NM	NM	NM	7.6	5.2	2.5	1.9	3.1
% Return on Equity	NM	NM	NM	NM	NM	19.2	14.8	8.6	6.7	11.1

Data as orig reptd.; bef. results of disc opers/spec. items. Per share data adj. for stk. divs.; EPS diluted. E-Estimated. NA-Not Available. NM-Not Meaningful. NR-Not Ranked. UR-Under Review.

Office: 13737 Noel Rd, Dallas, TX 75240-2019.
Telephone: 469-893-2200.
Email: feedback@tenethealth.com
Website: http://www.tenethealth.com

Chrmn: E.A. Kangas
Pres & CEO: T. Fetter
Vice Chrmn: R.J. Jennings
COO: S.L. Newman

VP, Chief Acctg Officer & Cntlr: D.J. Cancelmi
Investor Contact: T. Rice (469-893-2522)
Board Members: J. E. Bush, T. Fetter, B. J. Gaines, K. M. Garrison, E. A. Kangas, J. R. Kerrey, F. D. Loop, R. R. Pettingill, J. A. Unruh, J. M. Williams

Founded: 1967
Domicile: Nevada
Employees: 68,952

The McGraw-Hill Companies

Teradata Corp

STANDARD &POOR'S

S&P Recommendation BUY ★★★★☆	**Price** $24.84 (as of Nov 23, 2007)	**12-Mo. Target Price** $28.00	**Investment Style** Large-Cap Blend

GICS Sector Information Technology
Sub-Industry Computer Hardware

Summary This Ohio-based company has global operations focused on data warehousing and enterprise analytics. Teradata was spun off from NCR Corporation in 2007.

Key Stock Statistics (Source S&P, Vickers, company reports)

52-Wk Range	$30.08–22.35	S&P Oper. EPS 2007**E** 1.17	Market Capitalization(B) $4.496	Beta	**NA**
Trailing 12-Month EPS	$1.01	S&P Oper. EPS 2008**E** 1.40	Yield (%) Nil	S&P 3-Yr. Proj. EPS CAGR(%)	13.00
Trailing 12-Month P/E	24.6	P/E on S&P Oper. EPS 2007**E** 21.2	Dividend Rate/Share Nil	S&P Credit Rating	**NA**
$10K Invested 5 Yrs Ago	**NA**	Common Shares Outstg. (M) 181.0	Institutional Ownership (%) 1		

Price Performance

30-Week Mov. Avg. ··· 10-Week Mov. Avg. - - **GAAP Earnings vs. Previous Year** Volume Above Avg. STARS
12-Mo. Target Price — Relative Strength — ▲ Up ▼ Down ► No Change Below Avg. ★

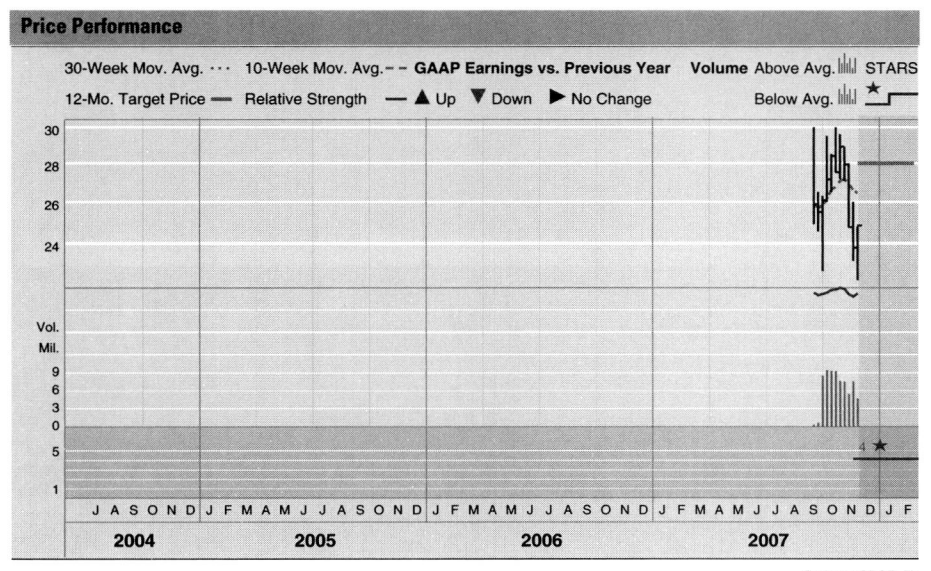

Options: CBOE, Ph

Analysis prepared by **Thomas W. Smith, CFA** on November 20, 2007, when the stock traded at **$ 23.93**.

Highlights

➤ We project revenue will rise 8% in both 2008 and 2009, compared to an almost 11% increase seen for 2007. The company operated as the Data Warehousing segment of NCR Corporation (NCR: hold, $24) through September 2007. A primary force driving sales is rising interest among enterprises in using their data to study and improve their patterns of operation.

➤ We anticipate margins will improve to about 54% for 2008 and 54.5% for 2009, from the 53% we forecast for 2007, as the company seeks efficiencies as a standalone operation. We similarly project progress in reducing SG&A to about 25.6% for 2009, from about 27% that we see for 2007. We expect R&D costs to be steady as a percentage of sales. A lack of long-term debt and the establishment of a $300 million credit facility indicates that presently negligible interest expense could rise.

➤ We estimate operating EPS of $1.17 for 2007, excluding certain separation-related expenses and one-time tax items. We forecast EPS of $1.40 for 2008 and $1.60 for 2009.

Investment Rationale/Risk

➤ We view Teradata as operating in a fairly steady, moderate growth information technology business. It serves a global, broad base of enterprise customers. We believe it has the potential to do well as a stand-alone company based on its one-stop shopping approach to offering business intelligence hardware, software and consulting. We think being one of a small number of pure-play investments in the industry, with no debt, will add to investor interest.

➤ Risks to our recommendation and target price include slowdowns in the general pace of spending on information technology for business, any failure to keep pace with rapidly evolving computer and analytical technology, competition on price and quality of products and services, and possible disruptions from the shift to being independent.

➤ Applying a peer-based target P/E multiple of 20X, which is also close to TDC's P/E based on our $1.17 EPS estimate for 2007, to our $1.40 EPS estimate for 2008, we arrive at our 12-month target price of $28.

Qualitative Risk Assessment

LOW	MEDIUM	HIGH

The newly independent Teradata participates in a large and growing global market we see for storing, retrieving, and analyzing data produced by businesses. However, competition is lively for technology and pricing. But we believe a stream of revenue from services, and a lack of debt, lends some stability.

Quantitative Evaluations

S&P Quality Ranking NR

D	C	B-	B	B+	A-	A	A+

Relative Strength Rank NA

Revenue/Earnings Data

Revenue (Million $)

	1Q	2Q	3Q	4Q	Year
2007	354.0	--	439.0	--	--
2006	323.0	396.0	375.0	466.0	1,560
2005	347.0	357.0	358.0	405.0	1,467
2004	--	--	--	--	1,349
2003	--	--	--	--	--
2002	--	--	--	--	--

Earnings Per Share ($)

2007	0.20	E0.31	0.16	E0.36	E1.17
2006	0.20	--	--	--	1.09
2005	--	--	--	--	1.14
2004	--	--	--	--	0.76
2003	--	--	--	--	--
2002	--	--	--	--	--

Fiscal year ended Dec. 31. Next earnings report expected: NA. EPS Estimates based on S&P Operating Earnings; historical GAAP earnings are as reported.

Dividend Data

No cash dividends have been paid.

Teradata Corp

STANDARD &POOR'S

Business Summary November 20, 2007

CORPORATE OVERVIEW: Teradata Corporation aims to help its enterprise customers make smarter and faster use of their stored data to improve decision-making. It views itself as a global leader in data warehousing and analytic technologies. The company offers hardware and software, as well as services including consulting, customer support and training. In the first nine months of 2007, almost 52% of revenues were derived from products (53% for full-year 2006), and 48% came from services (47%).

Headquartered in Dayton, Ohio, the company has offices throughout the Americas and operates in 60 countries worldwide. Teradata has more than 850 customers and over 1,900 project implementations. In the first nine months of 2007, revenue came 57% from the Americas, 25% from EMEA (Europe, Middle East, Africa), and 18% from APJ (Asia Pacific/Japan). Gross margins have typically been widest for the Americas region.

Data warehousing is the process of capturing, storing and analyzing data to gain insight, according to the company. This activity can be a significant source of intelligence for the enterprise and become a competitive advantage. Beyond mere storage of data, modern solutions allow for near real-time information access and analysis. Predictive analytics on customer or business activity may be run. Both long-term strategic and short-term tactical inquiries may be pursued.

In one example of active data warehousing, a business's call center could produce raw data on call attributes (e.g., number of calls, duration, agent, customer, dropped calls, results), which could be a starting point for mapping and analyzing overall interactions with customers, including Internet communications, which could then become the basis for a plan to improve customer satisfaction. The company serves many large clients in the communications industry, as well as in media and entertainment, financial services, government, health care, manufacturing, retail, and transportation.

Company Financials Fiscal Year Ended Dec. 31

Per Share Data ($)	2006	2005	2004	2003	2002	2001	2000	1999	1998	1997
Tangible Book Value	2.15	NA	NA	NA	NA	NA	NA	NA	NA	NA
Cash Flow	1.40	1.44	1.03	NA	NA	NA	NA	NA	NA	NA
Earnings	1.09	1.14	0.76	NA	NA	NA	NA	NA	NA	NA
S&P Core Earnings	1.09	1.10	NA	NA	NA	NA	NA	NA	NA	NA
Dividends	NA	NA	NA	NA	NA	NA	NA	NA	NA	NA
Payout Ratio	NA	NA	NA	NA	NA	NA	NA	NA	NA	NA
Prices:High	NA	NA	NA	NA	NA	NA	NA	NA	NA	NA
Prices:Low	NA	NA	NA	NA	NA	NA	NA	NA	NA	NA
P/E Ratio:High	NA	NA	NA	NA	NA	NA	NA	NA	NA	NA
P/E Ratio:Low	NA	NA	NA	NA	NA	NA	NA	NA	NA	NA

Income Statement Analysis (Million $)	2006	2005	2004	2003	2002	2001	2000	1999	1998	1997
Revenue	1,560	1,467	1,349	NA	NA	NA	NA	NA	NA	NA
Operating Income	367	339	247	NA	NA	NA	NA	NA	NA	NA
Depreciation	55.0	55.0	48.0	NA	NA	NA	NA	NA	NA	NA
Interest Expense	Nil	Nil	Nil	NA	NA	NA	NA	NA	NA	NA
Pretax Income	312	284	199	NA	NA	NA	NA	NA	NA	NA
Effective Tax Rate	36.5%	27.5%	30.7%	NA	NA	NA	NA	NA	NA	NA
Net Income	198	206	138	NA	NA	NA	NA	NA	NA	NA
S&P Core Earnings	198	200	NA	NA	NA	NA	NA	NA	NA	NA

Balance Sheet & Other Financial Data (Million $)	2006	2005	2004	2003	2002	2001	2000	1999	1998	1997
Cash	200	NA	NA	NA	NA	NA	NA	NA	NA	NA
Current Assets	645	NA	NA	NA	NA	NA	NA	NA	NA	NA
Total Assets	983	NA	NA	NA	NA	NA	NA	NA	NA	NA
Current Liabilities	428	NA	NA	NA	NA	NA	NA	NA	NA	NA
Long Term Debt	Nil	NA	NA	NA	NA	NA	NA	NA	NA	NA
Common Equity	477	NA	NA	NA	NA	NA	NA	NA	NA	NA
Total Capital	477	NA	NA	NA	NA	NA	NA	NA	NA	NA
Capital Expenditures	20.0	18.0	14.0	NA	NA	NA	NA	NA	NA	NA
Cash Flow	253	261	186	NA	NA	NA	NA	NA	NA	NA
Current Ratio	1.5	NA	NA	NA	NA	NA	NA	NA	NA	NA
% Long Term Debt of Capitalization	Nil	NA	10.2	NA	NA	NA	NA	NA	NA	NA
% Net Income of Revenue	12.7	14.0	NA	NA	NA	NA	NA	NA	NA	NA
% Return on Assets	NM	NM	NA	NA	NA	NA	NA	NA	NA	NA
% Return on Equity	NM	NM	NA	NA	NA	NA	NA	NA	NA	NA

Data as orig reptd.; bef. results of disc opers/spec. items. Per share data adj. for stk. divs.; EPS diluted. E-Estimated. NA-Not Available. NM-Not Meaningful. NR-Not Ranked. UR-Under Review.

Office: 1700 S. Patterson Blvd., Dayton, OH 45479.
Telephone: 937-445-5000.
Website: http://www.teradata.com
Chrmn: J.M. Ringler

Pres & CEO: M. Koehler
COO: B. Langos
EVP & CFO: S. Scheppmann
CTO: S. Brobst

Board Members: E. P. Boykin, M. Koehler, V. L. Lund, C. K. Prahalad, J. M. Ringler, W. S. Stavropoulos

Founded: 1979
Domicile: Delaware
Employees: 5,300

The McGraw·Hill Companies

Teradyne Inc.

STANDARD &POOR'S

S&P Recommendation BUY ★★★★☆	**Price** $10.77 (as of Nov 29, 2007)	**12-Mo. Target Price** $13.00	**Investment Style** Large-Cap Blend

GICS Sector Information Technology
Sub-Industry Semiconductor Equipment

Summary This maker of automatic test equipment (ATE), used primarily by the semiconductor and telecommunications industries, recently sold its connection systems business.

Key Stock Statistics (Source S&P, Vickers, company reports)

52-Wk Range	$18.53– 10.10	S&P Oper. EPS 2007**E**	0.48	Market Capitalization(B)	$2.043	Beta	3.19
Trailing 12-Month EPS	$0.39	S&P Oper. EPS 2008**E**	0.65	Yield (%)	Nil	S&P 3-Yr. Proj. EPS CAGR(%)	5.00
Trailing 12-Month P/E	27.6	P/E on S&P Oper. EPS 2007**E**	22.4	Dividend Rate/Share	Nil	S&P Credit Rating	NR
$10K Invested 5 Yrs Ago	$6,633	Common Shares Outstg. (M)	189.7	Institutional Ownership (%)	99		

Price Performance

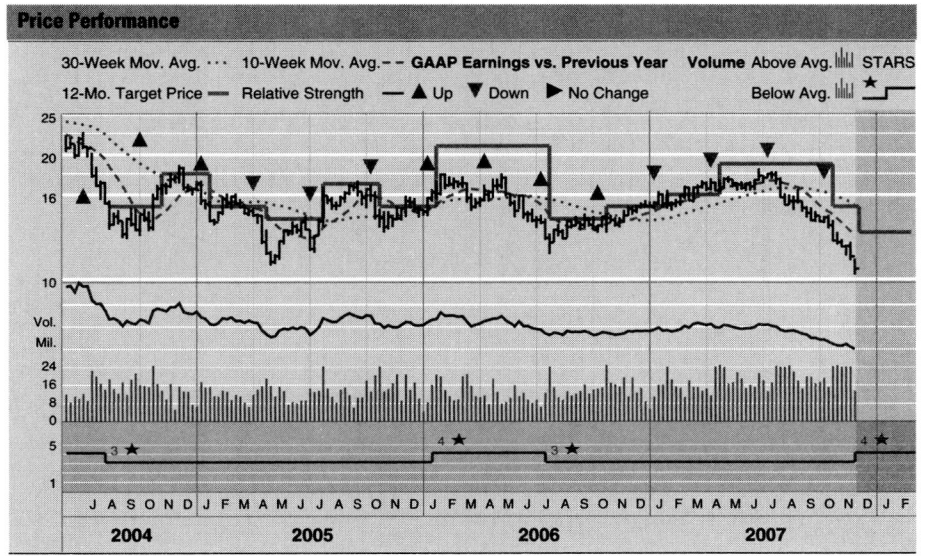

30-Week Mov. Avg. · · · 10-Week Mov. Avg. – – **GAAP Earnings vs. Previous Year** Volume Above Avg. STARS
12-Mo. Target Price — Relative Strength — ▲ Up ▼ Down ► No Change Below Avg. ★

Options: ASE, CBOE, P, Ph

Qualitative Risk Assessment

LOW	MEDIUM	**HIGH**

Our risk assessment reflects the historical cyclicality of the semiconductor equipment industry, the lack of visibility in the medium term, and intense competition, only partially offset by Teradyne's market position and current asset to liability ratio.

Quantitative Evaluations

S&P Quality Ranking   **B-**

D	C	**B-**	B	B+	A-	A	A+

Relative Strength Rank   **WEAK**

18

LOWEST = 1   HIGHEST = 99

Revenue/Earnings Data

Revenue (Million $)

	1Q	2Q	3Q	4Q	Year
2007	258.1	288.7	299.5	--	--
2006	362.9	391.6	359.1	263.2	1,377
2005	210.4	226.2	293.6	345.2	1,075
2004	430.6	526.5	457.8	377.0	1,792
2003	334.6	331.5	329.2	357.6	1,353
2002	248.0	309.9	330.7	333.6	1,222

Earnings Per Share ($)

	1Q	2Q	3Q	4Q	Year
2007	-0.04	0.14	0.19	E0.07	E0.48
2006	0.23	0.40	0.33	0.06	1.03
2005	-0.28	-0.26	-0.22	0.44	-0.31
2004	0.20	0.39	0.21	0.02	0.84
2003	-0.41	-0.28	-0.28	-0.06	-1.03
2002	-0.42	-0.28	-0.91	-2.31	-3.93

Fiscal year ended Dec. 31. Next earnings report expected: Late January. EPS Estimates based on S&P Operating Earnings; historical GAAP earnings are as reported.

Dividend Data

No cash dividends have been paid.

Highlights

➤ The STARS recommendation for TER has recently been changed to 4 (buy) from 3 (hold) and the 12-month target price has recently been changed to $13.00 from $15.00. The Highlights section of this Stock Report will be updated accordingly.

Investment Rationale/Risk

➤ The Investment Rationale/Risk section of this Stock Report will be updated shortly. For the latest News story on TER from MarketScope, see below.

➤ 11/29/07 12:11 pm EST... S&P UPGRADES OPINION ON SHARES OF TERADYNE TO BUY FROM HOLD, ON VALUATION (TER 10.9****): TER's shares have fallen more than 40% since peaking in June, and recently reached a four year low. Although we remain wary of near-term weakness in the semiconductor equipment sub-industry, we see a potential turnaround in the second half of 2008. Also, we expect TER shares to be aided by a $400 million stock buyback program, announced in November, that is roughly 22% of TER's existing market cap. We are cutting our '08 EPS estimate by $0.08 to $0.65 and lowering our 12-month target price to $13 from $15, applying a discount to our historical price/sales ratio. /A.Zino-CFA

Please read the Required Disclosures and Analyst Certification on the last page of this report.

The McGraw-Hill Companies

Teradyne Inc.

STANDARD &POOR'S

Business Summary October 22, 2007

CORPORATE OVERVIEW. Founded in 1960, Teradyne is a leading global supplier of automatic test equipment (ATE) for the electronics industry. As electronic systems have become more complex, the need for products to test the systems has grown dramatically. TER's product segments include systems to test semiconductors (76% of 2005 revenue, 81% in 2004), assemble test systems (14%, 11%), and other test systems (10%, 8%).

Semiconductor test systems products test system on a chip (SOC) semiconductor devices during the manufacturing process. These systems are used for wafer level and device packaging testing and span a broad range of end users and functionality. TER's systems help customers improve and control quality, reduce time to market, increase production yields, and improve product performance. TER's FLEX Test platform is designed for scalability and allows for simultaneous parallel testing, reducing costs. The versatility of the FLEX system to handle a wide range of devices makes it attractive to subcontracting test-houses. Other systems include the J750 system for higher volume

and the Catalyst system for higher performance SOC devices.

The Assembly test systems group of products test and inspect printed circuit boards (PCBs), which are thin plates or cards on which semiconductor chips and other electronic components are placed. In-circuit test systems assess electrical interconnections, verify inter-operation on PCBs, and are used both in prototype testing and high volume board manufacturing. Imaging inspection systems, such as the Xstation MX, use a 3-dimensional X-ray system for higher density double sided boards where half of all solder connections are invisible to optical inspection systems. Military/aerospace test systems are used by Department of Defense programs across U.S. military branches and allied military services worldwide.

Company Financials Fiscal Year Ended Dec. 31

Per Share Data ($)	2006	2005	2004	2003	2002	2001	2000	1999	1998	1997
Tangible Book Value	6.84	5.75	5.00	4.33	4.97	8.69	9.89	6.77	6.13	5.63
Cash Flow	1.35	0.16	1.47	-0.22	-3.06	-0.36	3.42	1.56	1.04	1.08
Earnings	1.03	-0.31	0.84	-1.03	-3.93	-1.15	2.86	1.07	0.60	0.74
S&P Core Earnings	0.92	-0.80	0.37	-1.44	-4.25	-1.65	NA	NA	NA	NA
Dividends	Nil	Nil	Nil	Nil	Nil	Nil	Nil	Nil	Nil	Nil
Payout Ratio	Nil	Nil	Nil	Nil	Nil	Nil	Nil	Nil	Nil	Nil
Prices:High	18.08	17.33	30.70	26.31	40.20	47.21	115.44	66.00	24.22	29.59
Prices:Low	11.50	10.80	12.53	8.75	7.10	18.43	23.00	20.63	7.50	11.81
P/E Ratio:High	18	NM	37	NM	NM	NM	40	62	41	40
P/E Ratio:Low	11	NM	15	NM	NM	NM	8	19	13	16

Income Statement Analysis (Million $)										
Revenue	1,377	1,075	1,792	1,353	1,222	1,441	3,044	1,791	1,489	1,266
Operating Income	236	27.1	318	47.3	-192	-1.54	813	345	210	234
Depreciation	73.5	91.2	124	152	160	139	102	86.4	76.3	59.2
Interest Expense	11.1	16.2	18.8	20.9	21.8	4.09	1.84	1.66	1.57	2.24
Pretax Income	230	-80.1	188	-186	-561	-326	740	274	146	193
Effective Tax Rate	12.0%	NM	12.1%	NM	NM	NM	30.0%	30.0%	30.0%	34.0%
Net Income	203	-60.5	165	-194	-718	-202	518	192	102	128
S&P Core Earnings	179	-161	73.3	-270	-777	-290	NA	NA	NA	NA

Balance Sheet & Other Financial Data (Million $)										
Cash	945	695	285	586	541	586	464	387	298	74.7
Current Assets	889	1,095	806	769	809	1,207	1,378	908	759	727
Total Assets	1,721	1,860	1,923	1,785	1,895	2,542	2,356	1,568	1,313	1,252
Current Liabilities	260	515	277	281	279	296	619	392	256	278
Long Term Debt	Nil	1.82	399	408	451	452	8.35	8.95	13.2	13.1
Common Equity	1,361	1,243	1,134	950	1,028	1,764	1,707	1,153	1,026	937
Total Capital	1,361	1,244	1,532	1,357	1,479	2,216	1,737	1,176	1,057	974
Capital Expenditures	110	113	165	30.8	46.4	198	235	120	119	106
Cash Flow	276	30.7	290	-41.5	-559	-63.5	620	278	178	187
Current Ratio	3.4	2.1	2.9	2.7	2.9	4.1	2.2	2.3	3.0	2.6
% Long Term Debt of Capitalization	Nil	0.1	26.0	30.0	30.5	20.4	0.5	0.8	1.2	1.4
% Net Income of Revenue	14.7	NM	9.2	NM	NM	NM	17.0	10.7	6.9	10.1
% Return on Assets	11.3	NM	8.9	NM	NM	NM	26.4	13.3	8.0	10.9
% Return on Equity	15.6	NM	15.9	NM	NM	NM	36.2	17.6	10.4	14.3

Data as orig reptd.; bef. results of disc opers/spec. items. Per share data adj. for stk. divs.; EPS diluted. E-Estimated. NA-Not Available. NM-Not Meaningful. NR-Not Ranked. UR-Under Review.

Office: 600 Riverpark Dr, North Reading, MA 01864-2634.
Telephone: 978-370-2700.
Email: investorrelations@teradyne.com
Website: http://www.teradyne.com

Chrmn: P. Wolpert
Pres & CEO: M.A. Bradley
VP, CFO & Treas: G.R. Beecher
VP, Secy & General Counsel: E. Casal

Investor Contact: J. Moore
Board Members: J. W. Bagley, M. A. Bradley, A. Carnesale, E. J. Gillis, V. M. O'Reilly, P. J. Tufano, R. A. Vallee, P. S. Wolpert

Founded: 1960
Domicile: Massachusetts
Employees: 3,800

The McGraw-Hill Companies

Terex Corp

STANDARD &POOR'S

S&P Recommendation	**STRONG BUY** ★★★★★	Price	12-Mo. Target Price	Investment Style
		$63.59 (as of Nov 29, 2007)	$78.00	Large-Cap Growth

GICS Sector Industrials
Sub-Industry Construction & Farm Machinery & Heavy Trucks

Summary Terex is a diversified global manufacturer of a broad range of heavy-duty off-road trucks, mobile cranes and aerial work platforms.

Key Stock Statistics (Source S&P, Vickers, company reports)

52-Wk Range	**$96.94– 54.65**	S&P Oper. EPS 2007**E**	5.58	Market Capitalization(B)	**$6.480**	Beta		1.13
Trailing 12-Month EPS	**$5.17**	S&P Oper. EPS 2008**E**	6.75	Yield (%)	**Nil**	S&P 3-Yr. Proj. EPS CAGR(%)		25.00
Trailing 12-Month P/E	**12.3**	P/E on S&P Oper. EPS 2007**E**	11.4	Dividend Rate/Share	**Nil**	S&P Credit Rating		BB
$10K Invested 5 Yrs Ago	**$100,400**	Common Shares Outstg. (M)	101.9	Institutional Ownership (%)	89			

Price Performance

30-Week Mov. Avg. · · · 10-Week Mov. Avg.- - **GAAP Earnings vs. Previous Year** Volume Above Avg. STARS
12-Mo. Target Price — Relative Strength — ▲ Up ▼ Down ► No Change Below Avg. ★

Options: ASE, Ph

Analysis prepared by **Christopher Lippincott** on November 29, 2007, when the stock traded at **$ 62.15.**

Highlights

➤ We project net sales growth of 16% for 2007, and see 12% growth in 2008, based on substantial exposure to later cycle businesses and overseas markets (nearly 62% of sales are international). We see strong global demand, particularly for cranes, due to large infrastructure projects in Asia, Europe and the Middle East, as well as aerial work platforms and construction equipment, driven by European projects as economic conditions remain favorable. Backlog as of September 30, 2007 was $4.1 billion, up 65% from a year ago, an indicator in our view of the strength of the global business environment. Backlog growth has been near these levels for the past five quarters.

➤ We expect gross margins in 2007 to expand to 21% and remain steady in 2008, as price increases and mix shifts should offset high, but stabilizing, raw material costs and supplier constraint impacts. We forecast further improvement in EBIT margins, reflecting pricing initiatives, along with improved manufacturing efficiencies and cost controls, which should be partly offset by marketing expenses.

➤ We estimate EPS of $5.58 in 2007, advancing 21% to $6.75 in 2008.

Investment Rationale/Risk

➤ We believe Terex will see double-digit order and sales growth over the next several years, driven by worldwide crane demand and particularly from large infrastructure projects in Asia, Europe, and the Middle East. We think greater demand for aerial work platforms in Europe and construction equipment in Europe, Asia, and the Middle East will also fuel sales growth. In our view, the global construction cycle is still in its early stages with solid growth, which should more than offset moderating North American demand.

➤ Risks to our recommendation and target price include a slowdown in global economic growth, lower demand for construction or mining machinery, and rising steel prices.

➤ Our 12-month target price of $78 is based on a blend of valuation methods. Our sum-of-the-parts model, which values each of TEX's five segments individually, indicates a value of $79. Our DCF model, which assumes a 3.5% perpetual growth rate and a 12.1% WACC, suggests a $78 value. In terms of relative valuation, applying a target EV/EBITDA multiple of 7.2X to our 2008 EBITDA estimate, a 6% discount to peers, indicates a value of $78.

Qualitative Risk Assessment

LOW	MEDIUM	**HIGH**

Our risk assessment reflects the highly cyclical nature of the company's businesses, TEX's small scale relative to several large competitors, and an S&P Quality Ranking of B-, which indicates low stability of earnings growth.

Quantitative Evaluations

S&P Quality Ranking   B-

D	C	**B-**	B	B+	A-	A	A+

Relative Strength Rank   WEAK

23

LOWEST = 1   HIGHEST = 99

Revenue/Earnings Data

Revenue (Million $)

	1Q	2Q	3Q	4Q	Year
2007	2,013	2,342	2,197	--	--
2006	1,694	2,021	1,904	2,030	7,648
2005	1,451	1,759	1,541	1,629	6,380
2004	1,059	1,333	1,252	1,376	5,020
2003	927.7	1,049	906.3	1,014	3,897
2002	582.0	690.2	674.1	851.1	2,797

Earnings Per Share ($)

2007	1.09	1.66	1.45	E1.38	E5.58
2006	0.75	1.10	1.02	0.97	3.85
2005	0.30	0.70	0.51	0.34	1.85
2004	0.19	0.62	0.44	1.94	3.17
2003	0.12	-0.55	0.15	Nil	-0.26
2002	0.08	0.06	0.13	-0.43	-0.21

Fiscal year ended Dec. 31. Next earnings report expected: Mid February. EPS Estimates based on S&P Operating Earnings; historical GAAP earnings are as reported.

Dividend Data

No cash dividends have been paid.

Please read the Required Disclosures and Analyst Certification on the last page of this report.

The **McGraw-Hill** Companies

Terex Corp

STANDARD &POOR'S

Business Summary November 29, 2007

CORPORATE OVERVIEW. Terex Corporation manufactures a broad range of equipment primarily for use in the construction, infrastructure and surface mining industries. Terex operates in five business segments: Terex Aerial Work Platforms; Terex Construction; Terex Cranes; Terex Materials Processing & Mining; and Terex Roadbuilding, Utility Products and Other. In terms of geography, 2006 net sales broke down as follows: United States 38%, United Kingdom 8%, Germany 7%, other European countries 25%, and Rest of World 21%.

The Aerial Work Platform segment (27% of 2006 net sales with 18% EBIT margins), formed following the September 2002 acquisition of Genie Holdings, Inc., manufactures work platform equipment and telehandlers. Products are used by customers in the construction and building maintenance industries to lift people and equipment to build and maintain large physical assets and structures.

Terex Construction (21%; 1%) manufactures heavy construction equipment, compact construction equipment, and crushing and screening equipment. The products are used primarily by construction, logging, mining, industrial and government customers in construction and infrastructure projects and for supplying coal, minerals, sand and gravel.

Terex Cranes (23%; 9%) supplies cranes for use in construction, repair and maintenance of infrastructure, building and manufacturing facilities. Products include mobile telescopic cranes, tower cranes, lattice boom crawler cranes, truck mounted cranes, telescopic container cranes, and related replacement parts and components.

Terex Materials Processing & Mining (21%; 12%) markets large hydraulic excavators and high capacity surface mining trucks, related components and replacement parts to construction, mining, quarrying and government customers for construction, excavation and supplying coal and minerals.

Terex Roadbuilding, Utility Products and Other segment (10%; 3%) manufactures fixed installation crushing and screening equipment, asphalt and concrete equipment, utility equipment, light construction equipment, construction trailers and heavy-duty vehicles. The products are intended primarily for government, utility and construction customers to build roads, maintain utility lines, trim trees, and for commercial and military applications.

Company Financials Fiscal Year Ended Dec. 31

Per Share Data ($)	2006	2005	2004	2003	2002	2001	2000	1999	1998	1997
Tangible Book Value	11.06	6.14	4.80	2.80	1.55	NM	NM	NM	NM	NM
Cash Flow	4.56	2.58	3.81	0.31	0.32	0.99	2.61	4.01	2.08	1.33
Earnings	3.85	1.85	3.17	-0.26	-0.21	0.29	1.86	3.38	1.63	0.81
S&P Core Earnings	3.96	1.93	3.02	0.23	-0.20	0.10	NA	NA	NA	NA
Dividends	Nil	Nil	Nil	Nil	Nil	Nil	Nil	Nil	Nil	Nil
Payout Ratio	Nil	Nil	Nil	Nil	Nil	Nil	Nil	Nil	Nil	Nil
Prices:High	66.52	31.22	24.12	14.83	13.75	12.25	14.44	17.75	15.75	12.75
Prices:Low	29.58	17.92	13.03	4.75	4.92	7.22	5.56	11.06	6.69	4.75
P/E Ratio:High	17	17	8	NM	NM	43	8	5	10	16
P/E Ratio:Low	8	10	4	NM	NM	25	3	3	4	6

Income Statement Analysis (Million $)	2006	2005	2004	2003	2002	2001	2000	1999	1998	1997
Revenue	7,648	6,380	5,020	3,897	2,797	1,813	2,087	1,857	1,233	842
Operating Income	782	454	280	180	114	145	240	211	140	85.4
Depreciation	73.0	75.6	65.6	55.2	45.0	40.3	41.5	32.2	20.5	16.9
Interest Expense	93.9	101	96.7	105	97.7	90.5	103	85.4	47.2	39.4
Pretax Income	615	290	147	-35.3	-25.8	24.6	160	98.4	74.5	31.0
Effective Tax Rate	35.5%	35.0%	NM	NM	NM	32.1%	34.9%	NM	2.28%	2.26%
Net Income	397	189	324	-25.5	-17.5	16.7	104	173	72.8	30.3
S&P Core Earnings	408	197	309	21.4	-17.5	5.76	NA	NA	NA	NA

Balance Sheet & Other Financial Data (Million $)	2006	2005	2004	2003	2002	2001	2000	1999	1998	1997
Cash	677	554	419	468	352	250	181	133	25.1	28.7
Current Assets	3,433	2,904	2,647	2,194	2,221	1,383	1,242	1,315	772	427
Total Assets	4,786	4,200	4,179	3,724	3,626	2,387	1,984	2,178	1,151	588
Current Liabilities	2,027	1,525	1,530	1,159	1,106	627	576	580	425	236
Long Term Debt	536	1,076	1,114	1,275	1,487	1,021	882	1,099	587	274
Common Equity	1,751	1,161	1,135	877	769	595	452	433	98.1	59.6
Total Capital	2,287	2,237	2,249	2,152	2,256	1,616	1,334	1,532	685	334
Capital Expenditures	78.9	48.6	35.5	27.1	29.2	13.5	24.2	21.4	13.1	9.90
Cash Flow	470	264	390	29.7	27.5	57.0	145	205	93.3	47.2
Current Ratio	1.7	1.9	1.7	1.9	2.0	2.2	2.2	2.3	1.8	1.8
% Long Term Debt of Capitalization	23.4	48.1	49.5	59.3	65.9	63.2	66.1	71.7	85.7	82.0
% Net Income of Revenue	5.2	3.0	6.5	NM	NM	0.9	4.9	9.3	5.9	3.6
% Return on Assets	8.8	4.5	8.4	NM	NM	0.8	5.0	10.4	8.4	5.7
% Return on Equity	27.2	16.4	35.8	NM	NM	3.2	23.5	65.1	92.3	NM

Data as orig reptd.; bef. results of disc opers/spec. items. Per share data adj. for stk. divs.; EPS diluted. E-Estimated. NA-Not Available. NM-Not Meaningful. NR-Not Ranked. UR-Under Review.

Office: 200 Nyala Farms Rd, Westport, CT 06880-6267.
Telephone: 203-222-7170.
Website: http://www.terex.com
Chrmn, Pres, CEO & COO: R.M. DeFeo

SVP & CFO: P.C. Widman
SVP, Secy & General Counsel: E.I. Cohen
VP, Chief Acctg Officer & Cntlr: J.D. Carter
Investor Contact: E. Gaal (203-222-5942)

Board Members: G. C. Andersen, P. H. Cholmondeley, R. M. DeFeo, D. DeFosset, W. H. Fike, D. P. Jacobs, D. A. Sachs, O. G. Shaffer, J. C. Watts, Jr., H. C. Wehmeier

Founded: 1925
Domicile: Delaware
Employees: 18,200

The McGraw-Hill Companies

Tesoro Corp

STANDARD &POOR'S

S&P Recommendation **SELL** ★★☆☆☆	Price $55.92 (as of Nov 23, 2007)	12-Mo. Target Price $54.00	Investment Style Large-Cap Blend

GICS Sector Energy
Sub-Industry Oil & Gas Refining & Marketing

Summary Tesoro is one of the largest independent refiners and marketers of petroleum products in the U.S., with operations focused on the West Coast.

Key Stock Statistics (Source S&P, Vickers, company reports)

52-Wk Range	$65.98– 31.47	S&P Oper. EPS 2007**E**	4.73	Market Capitalization(B)	$7.652	Beta	1.14
Trailing 12-Month EPS	$5.50	S&P Oper. EPS 2008**E**	4.27	Yield (%)	0.72	S&P 3-Yr. Proj. EPS CAGR(%)	-1.10
Trailing 12-Month P/E	10.2	P/E on S&P Oper. EPS 2007**E**	11.8	Dividend Rate/Share	$0.40	S&P Credit Rating	BB+
$10K Invested 5 Yrs Ago	$310,096	Common Shares Outstg. (M)	136.8	Institutional Ownership (%)	88		

Price Performance

Options: ASE, CBOE, Ph

Analysis prepared by **Tina J. Vital** on November 12, 2007, when the stock traded at **$ 55.74.**

Highlights

➤ Third quarter refining throughputs rose by 14%, above our expectations, despite unplanned downtime at the Anacortes and Golden Eagle refineries, reflecting contributions from the May acquisition of the 100,000 b/d Wilmington refinery in Los Angeles. We expect fourth quarter throughputs to be about flat with third quarter levels.

➤ In November, TSO said volumes and margins performed as expected following its May 2007 acquisition of 138 gasoline stations from USA Petroleum; however, these assets are now incurring expenses to improve their operating standards. TSO estimates these cost hikes will negatively affect operating earnings by $7 million to $9 million per quarter over the next three quarters.

➤ U.S. refining and marketing margins weakened in the 2007 second half, and we project that 2008 U.S. refining margins will narrow more than 30% from 2007 levels, but remain high relative to historical norms. We expect after-tax operating earnings to drop about 20% in 2007 and more than 9% in 2008.

Investment Rationale/Risk

➤ On October 29, TSO said its directors would review Kirk Kerkorian's Tracinda Corp.'s proposed unsolicited partial tender offer to purchase up to 21,875,000 shares of TSO common stock (or 16% of its common shares) for $64/share in cash. (Tracinda already owns a 4% stake in TSO's common stock.) With a significant portion of TSO's refining capacity of lower complexity, we expect it will achieve greater operational efficiencies from recent upgrades at several of its refineries. About 58% of its refining capacity is concentrated in three refineries (Martinez and Los Angeles, CA, and Anacortes, WA).

➤ Risks to our recommendation and target price include better than expected economic, industry and operating conditions that could lead to stronger than expected margins or production.

➤ A blend of our discounted cash flow ($52; assuming a WACC of 11.9% and terminal growth of 3%) and relative valuations leads to our 12-month target price of $54, or an expected enterprise value of 6.4X our 2008 EBITDA estimate, a premium to peers.

Qualitative Risk Assessment

LOW	MEDIUM	HIGH

Our risk assessment reflects our view of TSO's solid business profile in a competitive and volatile refining industry. We believe the company has strong asset quality and solid liquidity.

Quantitative Evaluations

S&P Quality Ranking   B

D	C	B-	**B**	B+	A-	A	A+

Relative Strength Rank   **STRONG**

88

LOWEST = 1   HIGHEST = 99

Revenue/Earnings Data

Revenue (Million $)

	1Q	2Q	3Q	4Q	Year
2007	3,876	5,604	5,902	--	--
2006	3,877	4,929	5,278	4,020	18,104
2005	3,171	4,033	5,017	4,360	16,581
2004	2,430	3,155	3,289	3,389	12,262
2003	2,286	2,116	2,330	2,113	8,846
2002	1,233	1,737	2,149	2,001	7,119

Earnings Per Share ($)

2007	0.84	3.17	0.34	E0.38	E4.73
2006	0.31	2.33	1.96	1.14	5.73
2005	0.20	1.31	1.60	0.49	3.60
2004	0.38	1.56	0.47	Nil	2.38
2003	0.16	-0.06	0.55	-0.06	0.58
2002	-0.58	-0.14	-0.12	-0.22	-0.97

Fiscal year ended Dec. 31. Next earnings report expected: Late January. EPS Estimates based on S&P Operating Earnings; historical GAAP earnings are as reported.

Dividend Data (Dates: mm/dd Payment Date: mm/dd/yy)

Amount ($)	Date Decl.	Ex-Div. Date	Stk. of Record	Payment Date
2-for-1	05/01	05/30	05/14	05/29/07
0.100	05/02	06/01	06/05	06/15/07
0.100	08/07	08/29	09/03	09/17/07
0.100	11/01	11/29	12/03	12/17/07

Dividends have been paid since 2005. Source: Company reports.

Please read the Required Disclosures and Analyst Certification on the last page of this report.

The McGraw·Hill Companies

Tesoro Corp

Business Summary November 12, 2007

CORPORATE OVERVIEW. Tesoro Corp. (TSO; formerly Tesoro Petroleum Corp.) is one of the largest independent refiners and marketers of petroleum products in the U.S. The company operates in two business segments: refining (94% of 2006 revenues; $1.476 billion of 2006 operating income) and retail (6%; loss of $21 million).

TSO refines crude oil and other feedstocks, and sells petroleum products in bulk and wholesale markets. As of December 31, 2006, the company owned and operated six U.S. refineries, located in California (Martinez, CA; 166,000 b/d), the Pacific Northwest (Anacortes, WA; 115,000 b/d; Kenai, AK; 72,000 b/d), the Mid-Pacific (Kapolei, HI; 94,000 b/d) and the Mid-Continent (Mandan, ND; 58,000 b/d; Salt Lake City, UT; 58,000 b/d). Refined product volumes were 549,000 b/d in 2006 (gasoline and gasoline blendstocks 45%, jet fuel 12%, diesel fuel 22%, and heavy oils, residual products, and other 21%), the same as in 2005.

The company purchases its crude oil and other feedstocks for its refineries from various domestic (about 53% of its 2006 crude oil, including 16% from

Alaska's North Slope) and foreign sources (around 47%, including 14% from Canada) through term agreements (approximately 43% of 2006 crude oil) with renewal provisions, and in the spot market. About 49% of its total refining throughput was heavy oil (API specific gravity of 32 or less) in 2006, down from 50% in 2005 and 2004 and 58% in 2003.

Through its network of retail stations, TSO sells gasoline and diesel fuel in the western and mid-continental U.S. As of December 31, 2006, TSO's retail segment included 460 branded retail stations (under the Tesoro and Mirastar brands, with the latter developed exclusively for use at Wal-Mart stores), comprising 194 company-operated retail gasoline stations and 266 jobber/dealer stations. About 434 million gallons of fuel were sold during 2006, down from 449 million gallons in 2005.

Company Financials Fiscal Year Ended Dec. 31

Per Share Data ($)	2006	2005	2004	2003	2002	2001	2000	1999	1998	1997
Tangible Book Value	17.09	12.12	8.31	5.70	5.00	6.75	7.17	8.57	8.65	6.33
Cash Flow	7.50	4.92	3.50	1.72	0.11	2.07	1.28	0.96	0.87	1.42
Earnings	5.73	3.60	2.38	0.58	-0.97	1.05	0.88	0.31	-0.36	0.57
S&P Core Earnings	5.73	3.65	2.42	0.78	-0.97	1.00	NA	NA	NA	NA
Dividends	0.20	0.10	Nil	Nil	Nil	Nil	Nil	Nil	Nil	Nil
Payout Ratio	3%	3%	Nil	Nil	Nil	Nil	Nil	Nil	Nil	Nil
Prices:High	38.40	35.91	17.33	7.56	7.65	8.25	6.50	9.41	10.69	9.09
Prices:Low	26.48	14.13	7.00	1.69	0.62	4.85	4.47	3.72	4.78	5.13
P/E Ratio:High	7	10	7	13	NM	8	7	30	NM	16
P/E Ratio:Low	5	4	3	3	NM	5	5	12	NM	9

Income Statement Analysis (Million $)										
Revenue	18,104	16,581	12,262	8,846	7,119	5,218	5,104	3,000	1,469	938
Operating Income	1,614	1,232	881	638	120	290	205	140	144	99.3
Depreciation, Depletion and Amortization	247	186	154	148	131	91.2	45.5	42.9	66.0	45.7
Interest Expense	77.0	211	167	212	166	52.8	32.7	37.6	33.0	6.70
Pretax Income	1,286	831	547	123	-181	147	124	51.2	-15.5	49.1
Effective Tax Rate	37.7%	39.0%	40.0%	38.2%	NM	40.1%	40.6%	37.1%	NM	37.5%
Net Income	801	507	328	76.1	-117	88.0	73.3	32.2	-15.0	30.7
S&P Core Earnings	800	514	333	101	-117	77.2	NA	NA	NA	NA

Balance Sheet & Other Financial Data (Million $)										
Cash	986	440	185	77.2	110	51.9	14.1	142	12.9	8.35
Current Assets	2,811	2,215	1,393	1,024	1,054	878	630	612	391	182
Total Assets	5,904	5,097	4,075	3,661	3,759	2,662	1,544	1,487	1,428	628
Current Liabilities	1,672	1,502	993	687	608	538	382	322	208	107
Long Term Debt	1,029	1,044	1,215	1,605	1,907	1,113	307	390	531	115
Common Equity	2,502	1,887	1,327	965	888	757	505	463	394	333
Total Capital	3,908	3,320	2,835	2,750	2,923	2,006	1,084	1,099	1,161	477
Capital Expenditures	436	258	179	101	204	210	94.0	84.7	185	147
Cash Flow	1,048	693	482	224	13.7	173	107	63.1	51.0	76.4
Current Ratio	1.7	1.5	1.4	1.5	1.7	1.6	1.6	1.9	1.9	1.7
% Long Term Debt of Capitalization	26.3	31.4	42.9	58.4	65.2	55.4	28.3	35.5	45.7	24.1
% Return on Assets	14.6	11.1	8.5	2.1	NM	4.2	4.8	2.2	NM	5.1
% Return on Equity	36.5	31.5	28.6	8.2	NM	13.0	12.7	4.7	NM	9.6

Data as orig reptd.; bef. results of disc opers/spec. items. Per share data adj. for stk. divs.; EPS diluted. E-Estimated. NA-Not Available. NM-Not Meaningful. NR-Not Ranked. UR-Under Review.

Office: 300 Concord Plaza Drive, San Antonio, TX 78216-6999 .
Telephone: 210-828-8484.
Email: investor_relations@tesoropetroleum.com
Website: http://www.tsocorp.com

Chrmn, Pres & CEO: B.A. Smith
COO & EVP: W.J. Finnerty
EVP & CFO: G.A. Wright
SVP, Secy & General Counsel: C.S. Parrish

VP & Treas: O.C. Schwethelm
Investor Contact: S. Phipps (800-837-6788)
Board Members: J. F. Bookout III, R. F. Chase, R. W. Goldman, S. H. Grapstein, W. J. Johnson, A. M. Myers, J. W. Nokes, D. H. Schmude, B. A. Smith, P. J. Ward, M. E. Wiley

Founded: 1939
Domicile: Delaware
Employees: 3,950

Texas Instruments Inc

STANDARD &POOR'S

S&P Recommendation HOLD ★★★☆☆

Price	12-Mo. Target Price	Investment Style
$30.91 (as of Nov 23, 2007)	$36.00	Large-Cap Growth

GICS Sector Information Technology
Sub-Industry Semiconductors

Summary One of the world's largest manufacturers of semiconductors, this company also produces handheld graphing calculator products.

Key Stock Statistics (Source S&P, Vickers, company reports)

52-Wk Range	$39.63–28.24	S&P Oper. EPS 2007**E**	1.79	Market Capitalization(B)	$44.173	Beta	2.34
Trailing 12-Month EPS	$1.78	S&P Oper. EPS 2008**E**	2.09	Yield (%)	1.29	S&P 3-Yr. Proj. EPS CAGR(%)	11.00
Trailing 12-Month P/E	17.4	P/E on S&P Oper. EPS 2007**E**	17.3	Dividend Rate/Share	$0.40	S&P Credit Rating	A
$10K Invested 5 Yrs Ago	$16,489	Common Shares Outstg. (M)	1,429.1	Institutional Ownership (%)	77		

Price Performance

30-Week Mov. Avg. · · · 10-Week Mov. Avg. - - **GAAP Earnings vs. Previous Year**   Volume Above Avg. STARS
12-Mo. Target Price — Relative Strength — ▲ Up ▼ Down ► No Change   Below Avg.

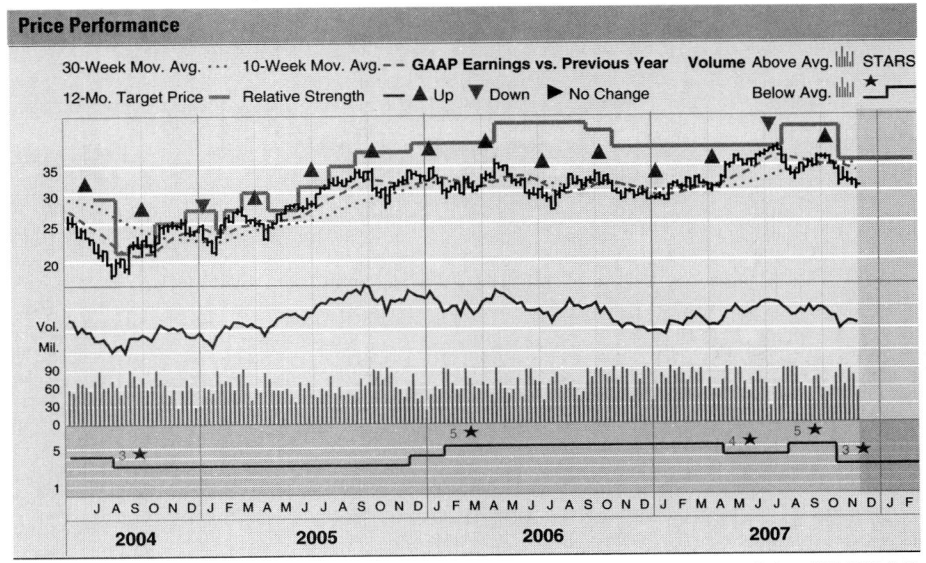

Options: ASE, CBOE, P, Ph

Analysis prepared by **Clyde Montevirgen** on October 24, 2007, when the stock traded at **$31.46**.

Highlights

➤ We see a 3% sales decline in 2007 and a 7% increase in 2008. We believe that TXN is gaining market share in the analog market, but believe that its digital signal processors (DSP) business will face challenges as wireless customers look to diversify their supply bases. Although growth of higher-end wireless handsets, which generally carry more chip content, is taking longer than expected, we believe TXN will have sales opportunities next year as we project accelerating growth. We also see one of TXN's large underperforming customers improving sales, also providing growth opportunities.

➤ We see gross margins of 53% and 54% in 2007 and 2008, respectively, as sales of higher-end analog products increase as a proportion of total revenue. We also expect increasing plant utilization and decreasing depreciation to contribute to improved results. Although operating expenses have increased as a percentage of sales, collaborations with suppliers on new technologies and other restructuring activities should lead to lower R&D expenses, aiding profitability.

➤ We estimate operating EPS of $1.79 for 2007, and $2.09 for 2008.

Investment Rationale/Risk

➤ As a market share leader in DSP and analog chips, TXN is well positioned to benefit from improving demand for higher-end phones and high-performance analog products over the next few quarters, in our opinion. While we see the company taking market share in a fragmented analog market, our optimism is tempered by our view of share losses in the wireless DSP market, where customers have recently diversified their supply bases. We think TXN has a profitable business model and see a healthy handset market ahead, but we are concerned about heightened competition.

➤ Risks to our recommendation and target price include possible sudden downturns in demand for semiconductors, competition in chip design and price, and the challenges of operating wafer plants.

➤ Applying a target P/E of about 18X, which is near the peer average, to our 2008 EPS estimate, we see a value of $37. We also apply a price-to-sales ratio of about 3.5X, below the historical range, to our 12-month forward sales per share estimate, deriving a value of $35. By combining both multiples, we arrive at our 12-month target price of $36.

Qualitative Risk Assessment

LOW	MEDIUM	HIGH

Our risk assessment reflects the cyclicality of the industry in which TXN operates and the volatility of its shares, offset by the large number of company operations, TXN's diverse line of semiconductor products with exposure to many end markets and customers, our view of its low debt levels, and its long corporate history.

Quantitative Evaluations

S&P Quality Ranking B+

D	C	B-	B	B+	A-	A	A+

Relative Strength Rank MODERATE
41
LOWEST = 1   HIGHEST = 99

Revenue/Earnings Data

Revenue (Million $)

	1Q	2Q	3Q	4Q	Year
2007	3,191	3,424	3,663	--	--
2006	3,334	3,697	3,761	3,463	14,255
2005	2,972	3,239	3,590	3,591	13,392
2004	2,936	3,241	3,250	3,153	12,580
2003	2,192	2,339	2,533	2,770	9,834
2002	1,827	2,162	2,248	2,146	8,383

Earnings Per Share ($)

2007	0.35	0.42	0.52	E0.50	E1.79
2006	0.33	0.47	0.45	0.45	1.69
2005	0.24	0.38	0.38	0.40	1.39
2004	0.21	0.25	0.32	0.28	1.05
2003	0.07	0.07	0.25	0.29	0.68
2002	-0.02	0.05	0.11	-0.34	-0.20

Fiscal year ended Dec. 31. Next earnings report expected: Late November. EPS Estimates based on S&P Operating Earnings; historical GAAP earnings are as reported.

Dividend Data (Dates: mm/dd Payment Date: mm/dd/yy)

Amount ($)	Date Decl.	Ex-Div. Date	Stk. of Record	Payment Date
0.040	01/18	01/29	01/31	02/12/07
0.080	04/18	04/26	04/30	05/21/07
0.080	07/19	07/27	07/31	08/20/07
0.100	09/21	10/29	10/31	11/19/07

Dividends have been paid since 1962. Source: Company reports.

Please read the Required Disclosures and Analyst Certification on the last page of this report.

The McGraw-Hill Companies

Texas Instruments Inc

STANDARD &POOR'S

Business Summary October 24, 2007

CORPORATE OVERVIEW. Texas Instruments is the world's third largest semi-conductor company, in terms of 2005 revenues. It has design, sales or manu-facturing operations in more than 25 countries. The company has increasingly concentrated on digital signal processors (DSPs), and on analog and mixed-signal integrated circuits. Semiconductors grew from less than 60% of rev-enues in 1996 to 87% in the boom year of 2000, and accounted for 96% in 2006 (96% in 2005). The Educational Technology segment represented 4% of 2006 sales (4%) and is a leading supplier of graphing calculators used in education, science and business.

On April 27, 2006, the company closed on its sale of the Sensors & Controls segment to Bain Capital for $3 billion in cash ($1.6 billion to $1.7 billion after tax). The company began treating the Sensors segment as discontinued oper-

ations as of the first quarter of 2006. Sensors & Controls had 2005 revenue of almost $1.2 billion and about 5,400 employees. The radio frequency identifica-tion (RFID) operations included within the Sensors segment were not part of the sale and were transferred to the Semiconductors segment.

End markets for TXN's chips in 2006 included communications, at 50% of Semiconductor sales, computing 25%, consumer electronics 10%, industrial 10%, and automotive 5%.

Company Financials Fiscal Year Ended Dec. 31

Per Share Data ($)	2006	2005	2004	2003	2002	2001	2000	1999	1998	1997
Tangible Book Value	7.08	6.99	7.13	6.35	5.73	6.42	6.71	5.39	4.19	3.80
Cash Flow	2.37	2.32	1.93	1.54	0.78	0.94	2.49	1.47	0.97	0.89
Earnings	1.69	1.39	1.05	0.68	-0.20	-0.12	1.73	0.84	0.26	0.19
S&P Core Earnings	1.68	1.26	0.86	0.40	-0.16	-0.34	NA	NA	NA	NA
Dividends	0.13	0.11	0.09	0.09	0.09	0.09	0.09	0.09	0.06	0.09
Payout Ratio	8%	8%	9%	13%	NM	NM	5%	10%	24%	45%
Prices:High	36.40	34.68	33.98	31.67	35.94	54.69	99.78	55.75	22.61	17.81
Prices:Low	26.77	20.70	18.06	13.90	13.10	20.10	35.00	21.50	10.06	7.77
P/E Ratio:High	22	25	32	47	NM	NM	58	66	89	94
P/E Ratio:Low	16	15	17	20	NM	NM	20	26	39	41

Income Statement Analysis (Million $)										
Revenue	14,255	13,392	12,580	9,834	8,383	8,201	11,875	9,468	8,460	9,750
Operating Income	4,419	4,222	3,756	2,493	1,977	1,246	3,715	2,751	1,568	1,724
Depreciation	1,052	1,431	1,549	1,528	1,689	1,828	1,376	1,055	1,169	1,109
Interest Expense	7.00	9.00	21.0	39.0	57.0	61.0	75.0	75.0	75.0	94.0
Pretax Income	3,625	2,988	2,421	1,250	-346	-426	4,578	2,019	617	713
Effective Tax Rate	27.2%	22.2%	23.1%	4.16%	NM	NM	32.6%	30.4%	34.0%	57.6%
Net Income	2,638	2,324	1,861	1,198	-344	-201	3,087	1,406	407	302
S&P Core Earnings	2,614	2,110	1,516	701	-275	-587	NA	NA	NA	NA

Balance Sheet & Other Financial Data (Million $)										
Cash	1,183	1,219	2,668	1,818	949	431	745	662	540	1,015
Current Assets	7,854	9,185	10,190	7,709	6,126	5,775	8,115	6,055	4,846	6,103
Total Assets	13,930	15,063	16,299	15,510	14,679	15,779	17,720	15,028	11,250	10,849
Current Liabilities	2,078	2,346	1,925	2,200	1,934	1,580	2,813	2,628	2,196	2,496
Long Term Debt	Nil	360	368	395	833	1,211	1,216	1,097	1,027	1,286
Common Equity	11,711	11,937	13,063	11,864	10,734	11,879	12,588	9,255	6,527	5,914
Total Capital	11,734	12,320	13,471	12,318	11,696	13,421	14,273	11,346	7,935	7,200
Capital Expenditures	1,272	1,330	1,298	800	802	1,790	2,762	1,373	1,031	1,238
Cash Flow	3,690	3,882	3,410	2,726	1,345	1,627	4,463	2,461	1,551	1,411
Current Ratio	3.8	3.9	5.3	3.5	3.2	3.7	2.9	2.3	2.2	2.4
% Long Term Debt of Capitalization	Nil	2.9	2.7	3.2	7.1	9.0	8.5	9.7	12.9	17.9
% Net Income of Revenue	18.5	17.4	14.8	12.2	NM	NM	26.0	14.9	4.8	3.1
% Return on Assets	18.2	14.8	11.7	7.9	NM	NM	18.6	10.6	3.7	3.0
% Return on Equity	22.2	18.6	14.9	10.6	NM	NM	27.9	17.6	6.5	6.0

Data as orig reptd.; bef. results of disc opers/spec. items. Per share data adj. for stk. divs.; EPS diluted. E-Estimated. NA-Not Available. NM-Not Meaningful. NR-Not Ranked. UR-Under Review.

Office: 12500 Ti Blvd, Dallas, TX 75243-0592.
Telephone: 972-995-3773.
Website: http://www.ti.com
Chrmn: T.J. Engibous

Pres & CEO: R.K. Templeton
SVP & CFO: K. March
SVP, Secy & General Counsel: J.F. Hubach
Investor Contact: T. West

Board Members: J. R. Adams, D. L. Boren, D. A. Carp, C. S. Cox, T. J. Engibous, D. R. Goode, P. H. Patsley, W. R. Sanders, R. J. Simmons, R. K. Templeton, C. Whitman
Founded: 1938
Domicile: Delaware
Employees: 30,986

Textron Inc.

STANDARD &POOR'S

S&P Recommendation BUY ★★★★☆

Price	12-Mo. Target Price	Investment Style
$66.98 (as of Nov 23, 2007)	$72.00	Large-Cap Value

GICS Sector Industrials
Sub-Industry Industrial Conglomerates

Summary This aerospace and industrial conglomerate makes Cessna business jets, Bell helicopters, and industrial equipment and components. It also operates a diversified commercial finance company.

Key Stock Statistics (Source S&P, Vickers, company reports)

52-Wk Range	$70.82– 43.60	S&P Oper. EPS 2007**E**	3.47	Market Capitalization(B)	$16.726	Beta	1.55
Trailing 12-Month EPS	$3.36	S&P Oper. EPS 2008**E**	4.00	Yield (%)	1.37	S&P 3-Yr. Proj. EPS CAGR(%)	16.00
Trailing 12-Month P/E	19.9	P/E on S&P Oper. EPS 2007**E**	19.3	Dividend Rate/Share	$0.92	S&P Credit Rating	A-
$10K Invested 5 Yrs Ago	$34,444	Common Shares Outstg. (M)	249.7	Institutional Ownership (%)	73		

Price Performance

30-Week Mov. Avg. ···   10-Week Mov. Avg. --   **GAAP Earnings vs. Previous Year**   Volume Above Avg. STARS
12-Mo. Target Price —   Relative Strength —   ▲ Up ▼ Down ► No Change   Below Avg. ★

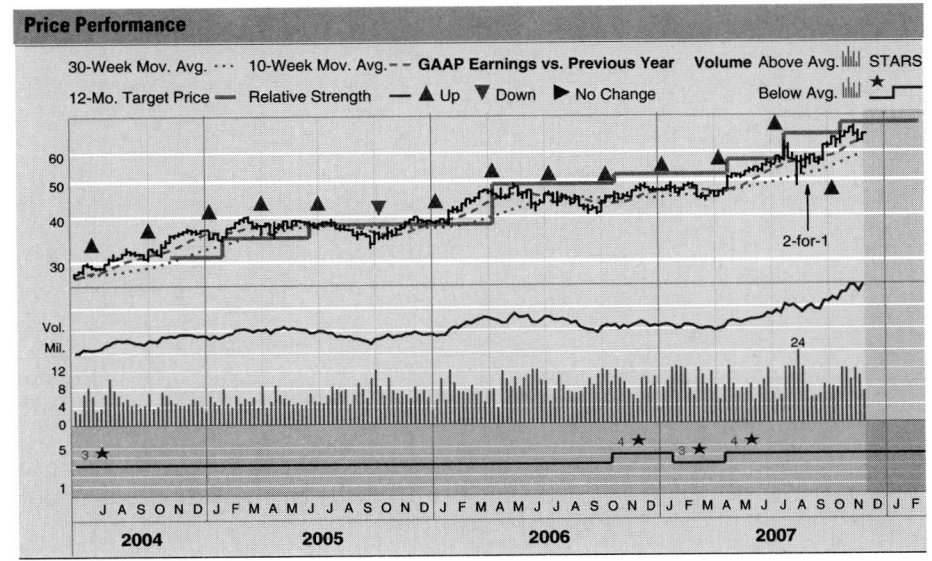

2-for-1

Options: ASE, CBOE, P, Ph

Analysis prepared by **Richard Tortoriello** on October 22, 2007, when the stock traded at **$ 65.51**.

Highlights

➤ We project sales growth of 13% in 2007 and 11% in 2008. Our growth forecasts reflect expected strong growth at Cessna (18% in 2007 and 17% in 2008) and moderately strong growth at Bell (12.5% and 8%) and Industrial (8% in both years). We continue to see aerospace growth driven by high business jet demand, strong demand for commercial helicopters, and good demand for military helicopters. In particular, we see the Bell segment aided by recent product introductions.

➤ We project operating margins of 12.2% in 2007 and 12.4% in 2008, up from 11.1% in 2006. We see margin improvements in all three segments, due to volume increases and efficiency programs. We estimate EPS of $3.47 in 2007, and we project growth of about 15%, to $4.00, in 2008. We project free cash flow of about $640 million, or about $2.50 per share, in 2007, up from $2.07 per share in 2006.

➤ We expect the current strong aerospace cycle to last for at least the next three to four years, and we project three-year average annual EPS growth of about 16% for TXT.

Investment Rationale/Risk

➤ Given our expectation of continued strong global economic growth, we expect continued strong demand in the business jet market, and we see TXT benefiting from our view of Cessna's well-respected brand name and strong product line. We also see good demand for both military and civilian helicopters going forward, and we believe Bell is making progress in overcoming military helicopter production problems. In January 2007, TXT replaced Bell's CEO. We also see signs of margin improvement in TXT's lagging industrial business.

➤ Risks to our recommendation and target price include an unexpected slowdown in the global economy, continued problems with TXT's military helicopter programs, and operational difficulties in any of TXT's business segments.

➤ Our 12-month target price of $72 is based on a P/E of 18X our 2008 EPS estimate. Our target P/E is 1.1X our three-year projected EPS growth rate for TXT (16%) compared to a recent 2008 P/E to growth ratio of 1.2X for the S&P 500. A recent 2008 P/E ratio for a group of 22 aerospace & defense peers was 16.8X.

Qualitative Risk Assessment

LOW	MEDIUM	HIGH

Our risk assessment reflects our view of TXT's cyclical earnings and the stock's above average volatility, offset by a stable or rising dividend over the past 10 years.

Quantitative Evaluations

S&P Quality Ranking   B+

D	C	B-	B	B+	A-	A	A+

Relative Strength Rank   **STRONG**

90

LOWEST = 1   HIGHEST = 99

Revenue/Earnings Data

Revenue (Million $)

	1Q	2Q	3Q	4Q	Year
2007	2,964	3,235	3,263	--	--
2006	2,632	2,820	2,837	3,201	11,490
2005	2,791	3,188	2,862	2,701	10,043
2004	2,354	2,547	2,569	2,833	10,242
2003	2,399	2,530	2,231	2,699	9,859
2002	2,418	2,824	2,554	2,862	10,658

Earnings Per Share ($)

2007	0.78	0.85	0.95	E0.90	E3.47
2006	0.60	0.67	0.68	0.77	2.72
2005	0.29	0.47	-0.63	0.63	1.89
2004	0.13	0.36	0.37	0.44	1.33
2003	0.25	0.31	0.17	0.30	1.03
2002	0.20	0.37	0.26	0.48	1.30

Fiscal year ended Dec. 31. Next earnings report expected: Late January. EPS Estimates based on S&P Operating Earnings; historical GAAP earnings are as reported.

Dividend Data (Dates: mm/dd Payment Date: mm/dd/yy)

Amount ($)	Date Decl.	Ex-Div. Date	Stk. of Record	Payment Date
0.388	04/25	06/13	06/15	07/01/07
2-for-1	07/19	08/27	08/03	08/24/07
0.230	07/19	09/12	09/14	10/01/07
0.230	10/24	12/12	12/14	01/01/08

Dividends have been paid since 1942. Source: Company reports.

Textron Inc.

STANDARD &POOR'S

Business Summary October 22, 2007

CORPORATE OVERVIEW. This $12 billion in revenue aerospace and industrial conglomerate conducts business through the following four operating segments.

The Bell segment (30% of 2006 sales and 19% of operating profits) is comprised of Bell Helicopter and Textron Systems. Bell Helicopter, the third largest helicopter maker behind United Technologies' Sikorsky Unit and EADS's Eurocopter unit AgustaWestland, makes helicopters and tiltrotor aircraft (the V-22 Osprey) for both military and commercial applications, and provides spare parts and service. Bell supplies advanced military helicopters and support (including spare parts, support equipment, technical data, trainers, etc.) to the U.S. government and to military customers outside the U.S. Bell is also a leading supplier of commercially certified helicopters to corporate, offshore petroleum exploration and development, utility, charter, police, fire, rescue and emergency medical helicopter operators. Bell Helicopter revenue accounted for 20% of total TXT revenues in 2006. The V-22 Osprey is a military tiltrotor aircraft built in conjunction with Boeing.

Textron Systems manufactures "smart" weapons, airborne and ground-based surveillance systems, aircraft landing systems, hovercraft, search and rescue vessels, armored vehicles and turrets, reciprocating piston aircraft engines, and aircraft and missile control actuators, valves, and components.

The Cessna segment (36% of sales and 51% of profits) primarily makes the Cessna brand aircraft (Citation business jets and Cessna single-piston airplanes). Based on revenues, Cessna is the world's third-largest corporate jet maker. Canada's Bombardier and General Dynamics' Gulfstream division are the world's first- and second-largest corporate aircraft makers, respectively. Forecast International projects the value of the business aviation market at $80 billion over the five years from 2007-2011 and sees Cessna garnering a 14.5% market share during this period.

Company Financials Fiscal Year Ended Dec. 31

Per Share Data ($)	2006	2005	2004	2003	2002	2001	2000	1999	1998	1997
Tangible Book Value	4.86	8.02	7.35	8.09	6.46	6.20	5.80	5.28	2.77	4.55
Cash Flow	3.95	3.15	2.69	2.32	2.61	2.38	2.64	3.45	2.43	2.92
Earnings	2.72	1.89	1.33	1.03	1.30	0.58	0.95	2.03	1.34	1.65
S&P Core Earnings	2.66	2.06	1.01	0.59	0.14	-0.70	NA	NA	NA	NA
Dividends	0.78	0.70	0.66	0.65	0.65	0.65	0.65	0.63	0.55	0.50
Payout Ratio	29%	37%	50%	63%	50%	NM	68%	9%	41%	30%
Prices:High	49.48	40.36	37.46	29.00	26.80	30.24	38.75	49.00	40.47	35.38
Prices:Low	37.76	32.60	25.30	13.00	16.10	15.65	20.34	32.94	26.03	22.50
P/E Ratio:High	18	21	28	28	21	52	41	24	30	22
P/E Ratio:Low	14	17	19	13	12	27	21	16	19	14

Income Statement Analysis (Million $)

	2006	2005	2004	2003	2002	2001	2000	1999	1998	1997
Revenue	11,490	10,043	10,242	9,859	10,658	12,321	13,090	11,579	9,683	10,544
Operating Income	1,703	1,450	1,260	1,171	1,285	1,461	2,074	1,702	1,439	2,109
Depreciation	290	303	353	356	368	514	494	440	361	435
Interest Expense	438	290	248	283	330	459	492	260	315	726
Pretax Income	437	739	528	388	464	393	585	1,004	737	922
Effective Tax Rate	NM	30.2%	29.4%	27.6%	21.6%	57.8%	52.6%	37.9%	39.9%	39.5%
Net Income	706	516	373	281	364	166	277	623	443	558
S&P Core Earnings	690	565	282	161	38.6	-202	NA	NA	NA	NA

Balance Sheet & Other Financial Data (Million $)

	2006	2005	2004	2003	2002	2001	2000	1999	1998	1997
Cash	780	796	732	843	307	260	289	209	53.0	87.0
Current Assets	4,287	4,975	4,168	3,592	3,887	4,017	3,914	3,735	4,355	NA
Total Assets	17,550	16,499	15,875	15,090	15,505	16,052	16,370	16,393	13,721	18,610
Current Liabilities	2,994	3,147	2,975	2,256	2,239	3,075	3,263	3,256	3,919	NA
Long Term Debt	6,150	7,079	6,141	6,144	7,038	5,962	6,648	6,142	4,192	10,496
Common Equity	2,639	3,266	3,642	3,680	3,395	3,923	3,982	4,365	2,984	3,215
Total Capital	8,799	10,816	10,246	10,224	10,842	10,253	10,957	10,826	7,511	14,207
Capital Expenditures	431	365	302	301	296	532	527	532	475	412
Cash Flow	996	819	726	637	732	680	771	1,062	803	992
Current Ratio	1.4	1.6	1.4	1.6	1.7	1.3	1.2	1.1	1.1	NA
% Long Term Debt of Capitalization	69.9	65.4	59.9	60.1	64.9	58.1	60.7	56.7	55.8	73.9
% Net Income of Revenue	6.1	5.1	3.6	2.9	3.4	1.3	2.1	5.4	4.6	5.3
% Return on Assets	4.1	3.2	2.4	1.8	2.3	1.0	1.7	4.1	2.7	3.0
% Return on Equity	23.9	14.9	10.2	7.9	9.9	4.2	6.6	16.9	14.3	17.4

Data as orig reptd.; bef. results of disc opers/spec. items. Per share data adj. for stk. divs.; EPS diluted. E-Estimated. NA-Not Available. NM-Not Meaningful. NR-Not Ranked. UR-Under Review.

Office: 40 Westminster Street, Providence, RI 02903-2525.
Telephone: 401-421-2800.
Website: http://www.textron.com
Chrmn, Pres & CEO: L.B. Campbell

EVP & CFO: T.R. French
EVP & General Counsel: T. O'Donnell
SVP & Cntlr: R.L. Yates
VP & Treas: M.F. Lovejoy

Investor Contact: D.R. Wilburne (401-457-2353)
Board Members: H. J. Arnelle, K. M. Bader, L. B. Campbell, L. B. Campbell, R. K. Clark, I. J. Evans, L. K. Fish, J. T. Ford, P. E. Gagne, D. M. Hancock, T. B. Wheeler, J. L. Ziemer, P. of Bayswater

Founded: 1928
Domicile: Delaware
Employees: 40,000

The *McGraw-Hill* Companies

Thermo Fisher Scientific Inc

S&P Recommendation **STRONG BUY** ★★★★★	Price $57.21 (as of Nov 23, 2007)	12-Mo. Target Price $78.00	Investment Style Large-Cap Growth

GICS Sector Health Care
Sub-Industry Life Sciences Tools & Services

Summary Thermo Fisher Scientific was formed through the November 2006 merger of Thermo Electron and Fisher Scientific. TMO is a leading manufacturer and developer of analytical and laboratory instruments and supplies for life science, drug discovery and industrial applications.

Key Stock Statistics (Source S&P, Vickers, company reports)

52-Wk Range	$62.02– 42.99	S&P Oper. EPS 2007**E**	2.58	Market Capitalization(B)	$24.139	Beta	1.28
Trailing 12-Month EPS	$1.13	S&P Oper. EPS 2008**E**	3.05	Yield (%)	Nil	S&P 3-Yr. Proj. EPS CAGR(%)	18.00
Trailing 12-Month P/E	50.6	P/E on S&P Oper. EPS 2007**E**	22.2	Dividend Rate/Share	Nil	S&P Credit Rating	BBB+
$10K Invested 5 Yrs Ago	$29,673	Common Shares Outstg. (M)	421.9	Institutional Ownership (%)	97		

Price Performance

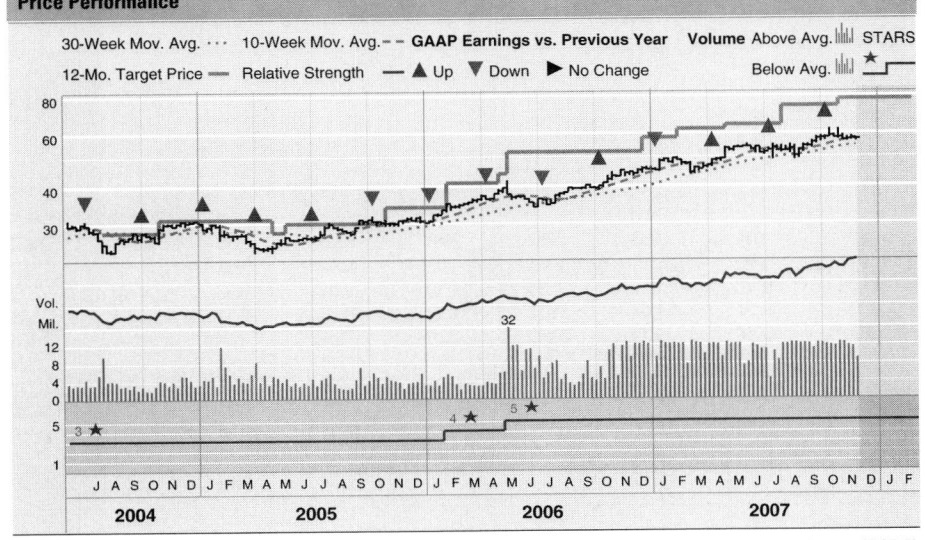

30-Week Mov. Avg. · · · 10-Week Mov. Avg. – – **GAAP Earnings vs. Previous Year** Volume Above Avg. STARS
12-Mo. Target Price — Relative Strength — ▲ Up ▼ Down ► No Change Below Avg. ★

Options: CBOE, Ph

Analysis prepared by **Jeffrey Loo, CFA** on November 08, 2007, when the stock traded at **$ 56.63**.

Highlights

➤ We see sales of $9.64 billion in 2007 growing 8% to $10.4 billion in 2008, driven by new products, broad geographic coverage and cross-selling opportunities. We expect Lab Products and Services (LPS), primarily from legacy Fisher business, to account for about 57% of 2008 sales, down about 100 basis points. We expect Analytical Technologies (AT) sales to grow at a much faster rate than LPS on robust life science and industrial demand. We view this growth rate positively as AT's operating margins are significantly higher than LPS.

➤ We believe TMO's estimates of $150 million in cost saving and $50 million in revenue synergies within three years of the Fisher merger will prove conservative, and we expect higher sales synergies in 2008 and 2009. We see 2007 operating margins of 16.7%, an improvement of 160 basis points from pro forma 2006 results, and see margins expanding 80 bps in 2008.

➤ We anticipate 2007 and 2008 operating EPS of $2.58 and $3.05, respectively, before accounting for the amortization of acquisition-related intangible assets.

Investment Rationale/Risk

➤ We think the integration of Fisher Scientific is progressing well, as nine month 2007 pro forma sales rose 9.2% while operating margins expanded 200 basis points. We see these trends continuing, with TMO's comprehensive life sciences product offering driving sales and operating leverage and purchasing power improving margins. We expect further margin expansion from better efficiency as the integration progresses. We think the companies can use their extensive global sales and distribution network to drive cost and revenue synergies, enabling a potential operating margin expansion of over 300 basis points within three years.

➤ Risks to our recommendation and target price include a slowdown in pharmaceutical R&D spending; an inability to achieve expected costs and revenue synergies; and the potential for a negative foreign currency impact.

➤ Our 12-month target price of $78 assumes a P/E-to-growth (PEG) ratio of 1.4X, based on our 2008 EPS estimate of $3.05, slightly below peers, as we take some integration risks into account.

Qualitative Risk Assessment

LOW	MEDIUM	HIGH

Our risk assessment reflects TMO's broad product lines and geographic coverage, spread across the life sciences, healthcare and industrial marketplaces, which we believe reduces risk. However, TMO has a proactive acquisition strategy that we believe raises its risk profile.

Quantitative Evaluations

S&P Quality Ranking B-

D	C	**B-**	B	B+	A-	A	A+

Relative Strength Rank STRONG

82

LOWEST = 1   HIGHEST = 99

Revenue/Earnings Data

Revenue (Million $)

	1Q	2Q	3Q	4Q	Year
2007	2,338	2,386	2,401	--	--
2006	684.3	713.5	725.0	1,669	3,792
2005	559.2	653.6	679.4	740.8	2,633
2004	525.0	525.3	542.3	613.3	2,206
2003	500.2	516.4	497.1	583.4	2,097
2002	491.3	509.1	517.2	568.8	2,086

Earnings Per Share ($)

2007	0.31	0.42	0.51	E0.69	E2.58
2006	0.26	0.30	0.30	0.08	0.82
2005	0.28	0.35	0.25	0.34	1.21
2004	0.24	0.30	0.26	0.52	1.31
2003	0.19	0.32	0.24	0.30	1.04
2002	0.34	0.23	0.23	0.25	1.12

Fiscal year ended Dec. 31. Next earnings report expected: Early February. EPS Estimates based on S&P Operating Earnings; historical GAAP earnings are as reported.

Dividend Data

No cash dividends have been paid.

The McGraw-Hill Companies

Thermo Fisher Scientific Inc

Business Summary November 08, 2007

CORPORATE OVERVIEW. In November 2006, Thermo Electron Corp. and Fisher Scientific completed a stock-for-stock merger. The combined company was renamed Thermo Fisher Scientific (TMO) and is a leading provider of life science and laboratory analytical instruments, equipment, reagents and consumables, software and services for research, analysis, discovery and diagnosis. We expect annual revenues in excess of $9 billion, with over 30,000 employees in 38 countries providing services and sales in over 150 countries. Major end markets served include drug discovery, proteomics research, biopharma services, molecular diagnostics, immunohistochemistry, cell screening, environmental regulatory compliance, and food safety. TMO believes these markets represent a combined $70 billion to $80 billion annual marketplace. We believe TMO is the largest company within its marketplace, with the broadest product offering and geographic coverage.

The legacy Thermo Electron business focuses primarily on the development and manufacture of analytical systems, instruments and components and provides solutions to monitor, collect and analyze data. These instruments are used primarily in life science, drug discovery, clinical, environmental and industrial laboratory applications. The legacy Fisher Scientific business focuses on providing a broad range of over 600,000 scientific research, healthcare and safety-related products and services. Customers included pharmaceutical and biotechnology companies, colleges and universities, medical research institutions, hospitals and reference labs, and research and development labs.

The company now reports through two business segments: Analytical Technologies and Laboratory Products and Services. Analytical Technologies should account for about 40% of sales and focuses on scientific instruments, bioscience reagents, lab informatics and automation, diagnostics, environmental monitoring instruments and industrial process instruments. Analytical Technologies is comprised primarily of the legacy Thermo Electron business. Laboratory Products and Services, comprised primarily of legacy Fisher Scientific business should account for about 60% of sales and focuses on lab equipment and consumables and biopharma outsourcing services.

Company Financials Fiscal Year Ended Dec. 31

Per Share Data ($)	2006	2005	2004	2003	2002	2001	2000	1999	1998	1997
Tangible Book Value	NM	2.32	6.19	5.00	3.79	1.33	6.34	5.03	1.51	1.60
Cash Flow	2.00	1.95	1.70	1.35	1.35	0.81	0.94	0.63	1.90	2.13
Earnings	0.82	1.21	1.31	1.04	1.12	0.27	0.36	-0.11	1.04	1.41
S&P Core Earnings	0.83	1.01	1.18	0.79	0.50	0.02	NA	NA	NA	NA
Dividends	Nil	Nil	Nil	Nil	Nil	Nil	Nil	Nil	Nil	Nil
Payout Ratio	Nil	Nil	Nil	Nil	Nil	Nil	Nil	Nil	Nil	Nil
Prices:High	46.34	31.87	31.40	25.40	24.60	30.62	31.24	20.25	44.25	44.50
Prices:Low	29.95	23.94	24.00	16.89	14.33	16.55	14.00	12.50	13.56	28.38
P/E Ratio:High	57	26	24	24	22	NM	87	NM	43	32
P/E Ratio:Low	37	20	18	16	13	NM	39	NM	13	20

Income Statement Analysis (Million $)										
Revenue	3,792	2,633	2,206	2,097	2,086	2,188	2,281	2,471	3,868	3,558
Operating Income	528	404	319	292	264	265	296	362	538	543
Depreciation	241	123	66.1	58.5	56.4	98.5	97.5	114	162	136
Interest Expense	51.9	26.7	11.0	18.7	Nil	71.8	Nil	Nil	104	93.1
Pretax Income	209	286	259	219	288	70.7	185	37.5	392	488
Effective Tax Rate	20.6%	30.6%	15.8%	21.0%	32.3%	38.1%	60.7%	NM	43.6%	35.8%
Net Income	166	198	218	173	195	49.6	62.0	-14.6	177	239
S&P Core Earnings	169	164	196	131	79.3	5.63	NA	NA	NA	NA

Balance Sheet & Other Financial Data (Million $)										
Cash	667	214	327	304	339	298	506	282	397	594
Current Assets	3,660	1,354	1,470	1,395	1,772	1,965	2,466	2,517	3,301	3,094
Total Assets	21,262	4,252	3,577	3,389	3,647	3,825	4,863	5,182	6,332	5,796
Current Liabilities	2,152	792	579	685	1,104	1,142	729	1,066	1,138	1,092
Long Term Debt	2,181	469	226	230	451	728	1,528	1,566	2,026	1,743
Common Equity	13,912	2,793	2,666	2,383	2,033	1,908	2,534	2,014	2,248	1,998
Total Capital	18,650	3,327	2,907	2,624	2,495	2,650	4,098	4,026	5,025	3,925
Capital Expenditures	76.8	43.5	50.0	46.1	51.2	84.8	74.0	87.2	148	112
Cash Flow	407	322	285	231	252	148	160	99.1	339	375
Current Ratio	1.7	1.7	2.5	2.0	1.6	1.7	3.4	2.4	2.9	2.8
% Long Term Debt of Capitalization	11.7	14.1	7.8	8.7	18.1	27.4	37.3	38.9	40.3	44.4
% Net Income of Revenue	4.4	7.5	9.9	8.2	9.4	2.3	2.7	NM	4.6	6.7
% Return on Assets	1.3	5.1	6.3	4.9	5.2	1.1	1.2	NM	2.9	4.1
% Return on Equity	2.0	7.3	8.7	7.8	9.9	2.2	2.7	NM	8.3	12.0

Data as orig reptd.; bef. results of disc opers/spec. items. Per share data adj. for stk. divs.; EPS diluted. E-Estimated. NA-Not Available. NM-Not Meaningful. NR-Not Ranked. UR-Under Review.

Office: 81 Wyman St PO Box 9046, Waltham, MA 02254-9046.
Telephone: 781-622-1000.
Website: http://www.fishersci.com
Chrmn: J.P. Manzi

Pres & CEO: M.E. Dekkers
VP & CFO: P.M. Wilver
VP, Secy & General Counsel: S.H. Hoogasian
Chief Acctg Officer & Cntlr: P.E. Hornstra

Investor Contact: K.J. Apicerno (781-622-1111)
Board Members: M. E. Dekkers, B. Koepfgen, P. J. Manning, J. P. Manzi, P. M. Meister, M. E. Porter, S. Sperling, E. S. Ullian

Founded: 1956
Domicile: Delaware
Employees: 30,500

3M Co

STANDARD &POOR'S

S&P Recommendation	HOLD ★★★☆☆	Price $82.75 (as of Nov 23, 2007)	12-Mo. Target Price $92.00	Investment Style Large-Cap Growth

GICS Sector Industrials
Sub-Industry Industrial Conglomerates

Summary This diversified global company has operations in electronics, health care, industrial, consumer and office, telecommunications, safety and security, and other markets.

Key Stock Statistics (Source S&P, Vickers, company reports)

52-Wk Range	$97.00– 72.90	S&P Oper. EPS 2007**E**	4.95	Market Capitalization(B)	$59.020	Beta	0.65
Trailing 12-Month EPS	$5.98	S&P Oper. EPS 2008**E**	5.26	Yield (%)	2.32	S&P 3-Yr. Proj. EPS CAGR(%)	7.00
Trailing 12-Month P/E	13.8	P/E on S&P Oper. EPS 2007**E**	16.7	Dividend Rate/Share	$1.92	S&P Credit Rating	AA
$10K Invested 5 Yrs Ago	$14,178	Common Shares Outstg. (M)	713.2	Institutional Ownership (%)	70		

Price Performance

30-Week Mov. Avg. · · · · 10-Week Mov. Avg. - - **GAAP Earnings vs. Previous Year** Volume Above Avg. STARS
12-Mo. Target Price — Relative Strength — ▲ Up ▼ Down ► No Change Below Avg. ★

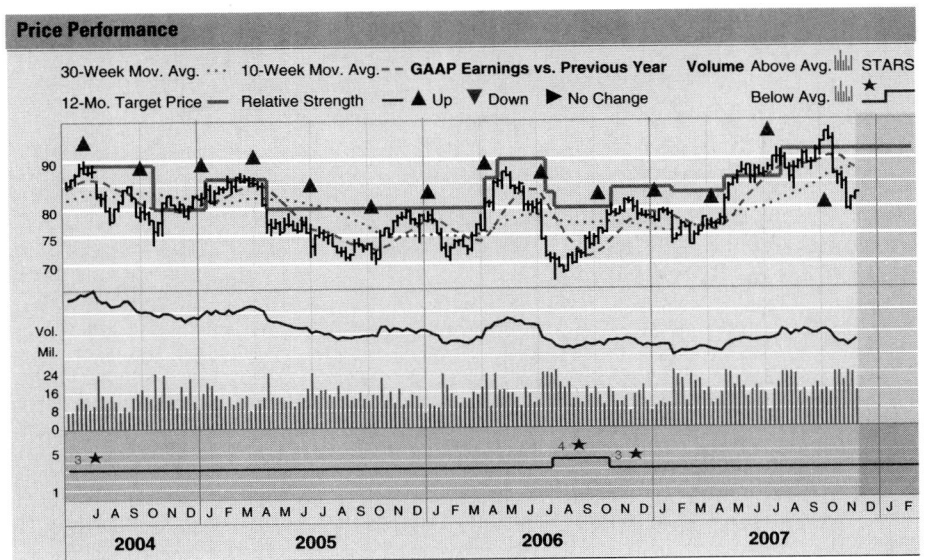

Options: ASE, CBOE, P, Ph

Analysis prepared by **Christopher Lippincott** on November 19, 2007, when the stock traded at **$ 81.99**.

Highlights

➤ We see revenues increasing about 6% in 2007 and 2008. We expect top line growth in 2007 and 2008 to benefit from further penetration of the Asia-Pacific and Latin America regions, the development of adjacent market opportunities, and an expanding pipeline of new products. We calculate organic growth of about 4% and expect contributions from acquisitions to total almost 2%.

➤ We foresee EBIT margins narrowing fractionally in 2007, as projected benefits from Six Sigma and higher volumes are more than offset by an expected decline in profitability in the Display and Graphics segment. However, we see 2008's EBIT margins expanding beyond 2006 levels. MMM's operating margin (before one-time items), which averaged about 19% from 1996 to 2005, was 22.4% in 2006. Over the next few years, we believe that continued efforts to streamline this diverse company will enable MMM to maintain above-average profitability.

➤ Assuming a steady 32.6% effective tax rate, we forecast MMM's operating EPS estimates for 2007 and 2008 will be $4.95 and $5.26, respectively.

Investment Rationale/Risk

➤ We expect favorable end market conditions to continue over the next 12 months, based on our outlook for ongoing global economic growth. We think 3M's global footprint positions the company well to participate in markets that are likely to grow faster than the U.S. over the next several years. However, we believe the shares are fully valued.

➤ Risks to our recommendation and target price include an unexpected downturn in the global economy; a greater than projected moderation of growth in the optical display business; execution risk associated with acquisitions and/or cost saving initiatives; and weaker than anticipated commercialization of the R&D pipeline.

➤ Our 12-month target price of $92 is based on a blend of valuations. Our DCF model, which assumes a 9% average annual free cash flow growth rate over the next 10 years, 3.5% growth in perpetuity, and a 9.3% discount rate, indicates intrinsic value of about $91. In terms of relative valuation, we apply an enterprise value multiple of 10.5X, in line with peers, to our 2008 EBITDA estimate, which suggests a value of $93.

Qualitative Risk Assessment

LOW	MEDIUM	HIGH

Our risk assessment reflects our view of the company's historical stability in earnings and dividends, its leading position in many of the end markets that it serves, a strong balance sheet with a relatively low amount of debt, and free cash flow that has averaged about 95% of net income over the past 10 years.

Quantitative Evaluations

S&P Quality Ranking A

D	C	B-	B	B+	A-	A	A+

Relative Strength Rank MODERATE

55

LOWEST = 1 HIGHEST = 99

Revenue/Earnings Data

Revenue (Million $)

	1Q	2Q	3Q	4Q	Year
2007	5,937	6,142	6,177	--	--
2006	5,595	5,688	5,858	5,782	22,923
2005	5,166	5,294	5,382	5,325	21,167
2004	4,939	5,012	4,969	5,091	20,011
2003	4,318	4,580	4,616	4,718	18,232
2002	3,890	4,161	4,143	4,138	16,332

Earnings Per Share ($)

2007	1.85	1.25	1.32	E1.13	E4.95
2006	1.17	1.15	1.18	1.57	5.06
2005	1.03	1.00	1.10	1.04	4.16
2004	0.90	0.97	0.97	0.91	3.75
2003	0.63	0.78	0.83	0.77	3.02
2002	0.57	0.59	0.69	0.65	2.49

Fiscal year ended Dec. 31. Next earnings report expected: Late January. EPS Estimates based on S&P Operating Earnings; historical GAAP earnings are as reported.

Dividend Data (Dates: mm/dd Payment Date: mm/dd/yy)

Amount ($)	Date Decl.	Ex-Div. Date	Stk. of Record	Payment Date
0.480	02/12	02/21	02/23	03/12/07
0.480	05/08	05/16	05/18	06/12/07
0.480	08/13	08/22	08/24	09/12/07
0.480	11/12	11/20	11/23	12/12/07

Dividends have been paid since 1916. Source: Company reports.

Please read the Required Disclosures and Analyst Certification on the last page of this report.

Business Summary November 19, 2007

CORPORATE OVERVIEW. During the first quarter of 2006, 3M combined its Industrial and Transportation segments. The new reportable business units are Industrial and Transportation; Health Care; Display and Graphics; Consumer and Office; Electro and Communications; and Safety, Security and Protection Services.

The Industrial and Transportation segment (29% of 2006 revenues and 20% operating margin) serves a broad range of markets, from appliances and electronics to paper and packaging, food and beverages, automotive, automotive aftermarket, aerospace and marine, and other transportation-related industries. Products include pressure-sensitive tapes, abrasives, adhesives, specialty materials, supply chain management software and solutions, insulation components, films, masking tapes, fasteners, adhesives and abrasives used in the repair and maintenance of automotive, marine, aircraft and other specialty vehicles.

The Health Care segment (17% and 29%) serves markets worldwide, including medical and surgical, pharmaceutical, dental, health information systems and personal care. Products provided include medical and surgical, infection pre-

vention, pharmaceuticals, drug delivery systems, dental products, health information systems, personal care and other products.

The Display and Graphics segment (16% and 29%) serves markets that include electronic display, touch screen, commercial graphics and traffic control materials. Optical products include Vikkuiti display enhancement films for electronic displays, lens systems for projection televisions, and 3M MicroTouch touch screens and touch monitors. Other products include 3M Scotchlite reflective sheeting for transportation safety and Scotchprint commercial graphics systems.

The Consumer and Office segment (14% and 18%) serves markets that include consumer, office, education, home improvement, building maintenance, food service and other markets. Offerings consist of office supplies, construction and home improvement products, protective materials, and visual systems.

Company Financials Fiscal Year Ended Dec. 31

Per Share Data ($)	2006	2005	2004	2003	2002	2001	2000	1999	1998	1997
Tangible Book Value	7.04	8.13	9.62	6.62	4.91	6.23	7.17	7.06	7.39	7.32
Cash Flow	6.48	5.43	5.01	4.23	3.70	3.15	3.60	3.28	2.55	3.57
Earnings	5.06	4.16	3.75	3.02	2.49	1.79	2.32	2.17	1.49	2.53
S&P Core Earnings	4.26	4.13	3.66	2.91	1.71	0.94	NA	NA	NA	NA
Dividends	1.84	1.68	1.44	1.32	1.24	1.20	1.16	1.12	1.10	1.06
Payout Ratio	36%	40%	38%	44%	50%	67%	50%	52%	74%	42%
Prices:High	88.35	87.45	90.29	85.40	65.78	63.50	61.47	51.69	48.94	52.75
Prices:Low	67.05	69.71	73.31	59.73	50.00	42.93	39.09	34.66	32.81	40.00
P/E Ratio:High	17	21	24	28	26	35	26	24	33	21
P/E Ratio:Low	13	17	20	20	20	24	17	16	22	16

Income Statement Analysis (Million $)										
Revenue	22,923	21,167	20,011	18,232	16,332	16,079	16,724	15,659	15,021	15,070
Operating Income	6,252	5,995	5,577	4,677	4,000	3,274	3,898	3,828	3,398	3,545
Depreciation	1,079	986	999	964	954	1,089	1,025	900	866	870
Interest Expense	122	82.0	69.0	84.0	80.0	124	111	109	139	94.0
Pretax Income	5,625	4,983	4,555	3,657	3,005	2,186	2,974	2,880	1,952	3,440
Effective Tax Rate	30.6%	34.0%	33.0%	32.9%	32.1%	32.1%	34.5%	35.8%	35.1%	36.1%
Net Income	3,851	3,234	2,990	2,403	1,974	1,430	1,857	1,763	1,213	2,121
S&P Core Earnings	3,242	3,227	2,918	2,319	1,356	750	NA	NA	NA	NA

Balance Sheet & Other Financial Data (Million $)										
Cash	1,918	1,072	2,757	1,836	618	616	302	387	448	477
Current Assets	8,946	7,115	8,720	7,720	6,059	6,296	6,379	6,066	6,318	6,168
Total Assets	21,294	20,513	20,708	17,600	15,329	14,606	14,522	13,896	14,153	13,238
Current Liabilities	7,323	5,238	6,071	5,082	4,457	4,509	4,754	3,819	4,386	3,983
Long Term Debt	1,047	1,309	727	1,735	2,140	1,520	971	1,480	1,614	1,015
Common Equity	10,097	10,100	10,378	7,885	5,993	6,086	6,531	6,289	5,936	5,926
Total Capital	11,433	11,409	11,105	9,620	8,133	7,606	7,502	7,769	7,550	6,941
Capital Expenditures	1,168	943	937	677	763	980	1,115	1,039	1,430	1,406
Cash Flow	4,930	4,220	3,989	3,367	2,928	2,519	2,882	2,663	2,079	2,991
Current Ratio	1.2	1.4	1.4	1.5	1.4	1.4	1.3	1.6	1.4	1.5
% Long Term Debt of Capitalization	9.4	11.5	6.5	18.0	26.3	20.0	12.9	19.1	21.3	14.6
% Net Income of Revenue	16.8	15.3	14.9	13.2	12.1	8.9	11.1	11.3	8.1	14.1
% Return on Assets	18.4	15.7	15.6	14.6	13.2	9.8	13.1	12.6	8.9	15.9
% Return on Equity	37.3	31.6	32.7	34.6	32.7	22.7	29.0	28.8	20.5	34.7

Data as orig reptd.; bef. results of disc opers/spec. items. Per share data adj. for stk. divs.; EPS diluted. E-Estimated. NA-Not Available. NM-Not Meaningful. NR-Not Ranked. UR-Under Review.

Office: 3M Center, St. Paul, MN 55144-1000.
Telephone: 651-733-1110.
Email: innovation@mmm.com
Website: http://www.3m.com

Chrmn, Pres & CEO: G.W. Buckley
EVP & CTO: F.J. Palensky
SVP & CFO: P.D. Campbell
SVP & General Counsel: R.F. Ziegler

Investor Contact: M. Colin (651-733-8206)
Board Members: L. G. Alvarado, G. W. Buckley, V. D. Coffman, M. L. Eskew, W. J. Farrell, E. M. Liddy, R. S. Morrison, A. L. Peters, R. L. Ridgway, K. W. Sharer

Founded: 1902
Domicile: Delaware
Employees: 75,333

Tiffany & Co.

STANDARD &POOR'S

S&P Recommendation	**STRONG BUY** ★ ★ ★ ★ ★	Price $47.99 (as of Nov 23, 2007)	12-Mo. Target Price $63.00	Investment Style Large-Cap Growth

GICS Sector Consumer Discretionary
Sub-Industry Specialty Stores

Summary Tiffany is a leading international retailer, designer, manufacturer and distributor of fine jewelry and gift items.

Key Stock Statistics (Source S&P, Vickers, company reports)

52-Wk Range	$57.34– 35.71	S&P Oper. EPS 2008**E**	2.25	Market Capitalization(B)	$6.561	Beta	1.64
Trailing 12-Month EPS	$1.83	S&P Oper. EPS 2009**E**	2.52	Yield (%)	1.25	S&P 3-Yr. Proj. EPS CAGR(%)	13.00
Trailing 12-Month P/E	26.2	P/E on S&P Oper. EPS 2008**E**	21.3	Dividend Rate/Share	$0.60	S&P Credit Rating	NR
$10K Invested 5 Yrs Ago	$18,015	Common Shares Outstg. (M)	136.7	Institutional Ownership (%)	90		

Price Performance

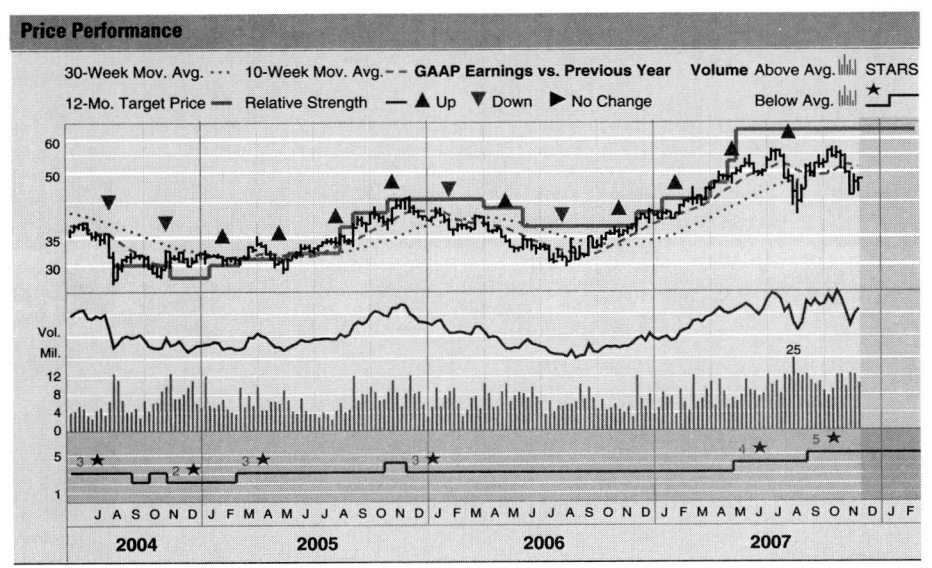

30-Week Mov. Avg. ···· 10-Week Mov. Avg. - - **GAAP Earnings vs. Previous Year** Volume Above Avg. STARS
12-Mo. Target Price — Relative Strength — ▲ Up ▼ Down ▶ No Change Below Avg. ★

2004 2005 2006 2007

Options: CBOE, P, Ph

Analysis prepared by **Esther Y. Kwon, CFA** on September 04, 2007, when the stock traded at **$ 52.28**.

Highlights

➤ We see about a 17% increase in TIF's FY 08 (Jan.) retail sales, to $2.7 billion, from $2.3 billion in FY 07. We project sales strength in the U.S. and across all international markets except Japan, where consumer spending continues to be soft. Combined with estimated direct marketing and other sales of $298 million, versus $311 million in FY 07, down on the sale of the Little Switzerland operation, we look for TIF's net sales to reach $2.98 billion in FY 08, up from $2.65 billion in FY 07.

➤ We expect operating margins to widen on efficiencies from the company's internal manufacturing and diamond sourcing capabilities and cost control, partly offset by an anticipated increase in wholesale diamond sales, a mix shift to higher-priced, lower-margin jewelry, and costs tied to accelerated new store openings. The company expects to open seven new stores in the United States and 11 stores and boutiques internationally in FY 08, equating to 11% unit growth and about 8% worldwide square footage growth.

➤ Factoring in anticipated share buybacks, we forecast FY 08 operating EPS of $2.25. We estimate FY 09 operating EPS of $2.52.

Investment Rationale/Risk

➤ We recently raised our recommendation to strong buy, from buy, based on valuation. In FY 08, we see TIF's solid U.S. and other international operations offering downside protection in a slowing U.S. economy. Same-store sales comparisons are notably easier in the U.S. as remodeling efforts, particularly in the flagship New York store, restricted traffic in the first half last year. While we remain concerned about the product mix shift toward higher-priced, lower-margin jewelry and high precious metal costs, we believe these factors will be offset by improved manufacturing efficiency from moving incremental production in-house.

➤ Risks to our recommendation and target price include sales weakness due to a severe downturn in consumer spending and/or increased competition from European luxury brands and independent high-end jewelers. Our corporate governance concerns include a lack of performance reviews of individual directors and the non-disclosure of specific hurdle rates for performance-based equity incentive awards.

➤ We derive our 12-month target price of $63 by applying a P/E of about 25X to our FY 09 EPS estimate, in line with the historical average.

Qualitative Risk Assessment

LOW	**MEDIUM**	HIGH

Our risk assessment reflects TIF's favorable market position as a premier global luxury brand, as well as its improving profit margin trends, offset by our view of the company's inconsistent sales and earnings record, and an uncertain outlook for U.S. consumer discretionary spending.

Quantitative Evaluations

S&P Quality Ranking A

D	C	B-	B	B+	A-	**A**	A+

Relative Strength Rank MODERATE

54

LOWEST = 1 HIGHEST = 99

Revenue/Earnings Data

Revenue (Million $)

	1Q	2Q	3Q	4Q	Year
2008	620.9	662.6	--	--	--
2007	539.2	574.9	547.8	986.4	2,648
2006	509.9	526.7	500.1	858.5	2,395
2005	457.0	476.6	461.2	810.1	2,205
2004	395.8	442.5	430.1	731.6	2,000
2003	347.1	374.4	366.0	619.0	1,707

Earnings Per Share ($)

2008	0.36	0.45	E0.23	E1.21	E2.25
2007	0.30	0.29	0.21	1.02	1.80
2006	0.27	0.35	0.16	0.97	1.75
2005	0.25	0.22	0.12	1.48	2.05
2004	0.24	0.28	0.19	0.74	1.45
2003	0.22	0.22	0.24	0.60	1.28

Fiscal year ended Jan. 31. Next earnings report expected: Late November. EPS Estimates based on S&P Operating Earnings; historical GAAP earnings are as reported.

Dividend Data (Dates: mm/dd Payment Date: mm/dd/yy)

Amount ($)	Date Decl.	Ex-Div. Date	Stk. of Record	Payment Date
0.100	02/15	03/16	03/20	04/10/07
0.120	05/17	06/18	06/20	07/10/07
0.150	08/16	09/18	09/20	10/10/07
0.150	11/15	12/18	12/20	01/10/08

Dividends have been paid since 1988. Source: Company reports.

Please read the Required Disclosures and Analyst Certification on the last page of this report.

Tiffany & Co.

STANDARD & POOR'S

Business Summary September 04, 2007

CORPORATE OVERVIEW. Charles Lewis Tiffany founded Tiffany & Co. in 1837. Jewelry is the company's primary sales driver, accounting for 83% of FY 07 (Jan.) net sales. The Tiffany & Co. brand also encompasses timepieces, sterling silver merchandise, china, crystal, stationery, fragrances, and personal accessories. TIF additionally sells other brands of timepieces and tableware in its U.S. stores.

Products are sold via four distribution channels: U.S. retail, comprised of company-owned stores and non-Internet, business-to-business sales (50% of FY 07 net sales); international retail (38%), including both retail and wholesale sales and a limited amount of business-to-business and Internet sales; U.S. direct marketing (less than 7%), consisting of Internet, direct mail catalog and business-to-business Internet sales; and other (5%), which reflects sales transacted under trademarks and trade names other than Tiffany & Co., as well as wholesale sales of diamonds that do not meet the company's quality standards.

CORPORATE STRATEGY. Diamonds are at the heart of TIF's merchandise offering, which also includes colored gemstones and silver and gold fashion

jewelry. In FY 07, the company produced 58% of its jewelry merchandise, based on cost, and purchased almost all non-jewelry merchandise from third-party vendors. To drive sales, TIF introduces new products annually. Last year, the company added architect Frank Gehry to its list of outside designers (which includes Jean Schlumberger, Elsa Peretti and Paloma Picasso) whose jewelry is licensed and sold exclusively under the Tiffany & Co. brand.

TIF believes that its multi-channel distribution represents a competitive advantage in a large and fragmented industry. In recent years, the company has expanded its direct marketing business, with a focus on e-commerce. TIF offers over 3,500 products through its U.S. consumer Web site, www.tiffany.com, which was launched in FY 00. The company extended e-commerce purchase capabilities to the U.K. in FY 02 and to both Japan and Canada in FY 06, and launched an informational Web site for China in FY 07.

Company Financials Fiscal Year Ended Jan. 31

Per Share Data ($)	2007	2006	2005	2004	2003	2002	2001	2000	1999	1998
Tangible Book Value	13.28	12.85	11.77	10.01	8.34	7.15	6.34	5.23	3.72	3.18
Cash Flow	2.64	2.50	2.79	2.06	1.80	1.58	1.56	1.25	0.83	0.66
Earnings	1.80	1.75	2.05	1.45	1.28	1.15	1.26	0.98	0.63	0.51
S&P Core Earnings	1.84	1.80	1.22	1.37	1.16	1.09	1.20	NA	NA	NA
Dividends	0.30	0.30	0.23	0.19	0.16	0.16	0.15	0.11	0.09	0.07
Payout Ratio	17%	17%	11%	13%	13%	14%	12%	11%	14%	13%
Calendar Year	2006	2005	2004	2003	2002	2001	2000	1999	1998	1997
Prices:High	41.29	43.80	45.22	49.45	41.00	38.25	45.38	45.00	13.00	12.16
Prices:Low	29.63	28.60	27.00	21.60	19.40	19.90	27.09	12.63	6.75	8.44
P/E Ratio:High	23	25	22	34	32	33	36	46	21	24
P/E Ratio:Low	16	16	13	15	15	17	22	13	11	17

Income Statement Analysis (Million $)										
Revenue	2,648	2,395	2,205	2,000	1,707	1,607	1,668	1,462	1,169	1,018
Operating Income	533	492	403	446	397	375	374	298	191	155
Depreciation	118	109	108	90.4	78.0	64.6	46.7	41.5	29.7	22.1
Interest Expense	26.1	23.1	22.0	14.9	15.1	19.8	16.2	15.0	9.33	8.04
Pretax Income	404	368	472	343	300	289	318	248	156	128
Effective Tax Rate	37.2%	30.8%	35.6%	37.1%	36.6%	40.0%	40.0%	41.3%	42.1%	43.0%
Net Income	254	255	304	216	190	174	191	146	90.1	72.8
S&P Core Earnings	260	261	181	204	173	164	181	NA	NA	NA

Balance Sheet & Other Financial Data (Million $)										
Cash	177	394	188	276	156	174	196	217	189	107
Current Assets	1,707	1,699	1,608	1,348	1,070	954	1,005	892	816	631
Total Assets	2,846	2,777	2,666	2,391	1,924	1,630	1,568	1,344	1,057	827
Current Liabilities	453	365	400	395	300	341	337	281	293	250
Long Term Debt	406	427	398	393	297	179	242	250	194	91.0
Common Equity	1,805	1,831	1,701	1,468	1,208	1,037	925	757	516	444
Total Capital	2,211	2,257	2,132	1,884	1,505	1,216	1,168	1,007	711	535
Capital Expenditures	182	157	142	273	220	171	108	171	62.8	51.0
Cash Flow	372	364	412	306	268	238	237	187	120	94.9
Current Ratio	3.8	4.7	4.0	3.4	3.6	2.8	3.0	3.2	2.8	2.5
% Long Term Debt of Capitalization	18.4	18.9	18.7	20.9	19.7	14.7	20.7	24.8	27.3	17.0
% Net Income of Revenue	9.6	10.6	13.8	10.8	11.1	10.8	11.4	10.0	7.7	7.2
% Return on Assets	9.0	9.4	12.0	10.0	10.7	10.9	13.1	12.1	9.6	9.3
% Return on Equity	14.0	14.4	19.2	16.1	16.9	17.7	22.7	22.9	18.8	17.7

Data as orig reptd.; bef. results of disc opers/spec. items. Per share data adj. for stk. divs.; EPS diluted. E-Estimated. NA-Not Available. NM-Not Meaningful. NR-Not Ranked. UR-Under Review.

Office: 727 Fifth Avenue, New York, NY 10022.
Telephone: 212-755-8000.
Website: http://www.tiffany.com
Chrmn & CEO: M.J. Kowalski

Pres: J.E. Quinn
EVP & CFO: J.N. Fernandez
SVP, Secy & General Counsel: P.B. Dorsey
Investor Contact: M.L. Aaron (212-230-5301)

Board Members: R. Bravo, W. R. Chaney, S. L. Hayes, III, A. F. Kohnstamm, M. J. Kowalski, C. K. Marquis, J. T. Presby, J. E. Quinn, W. A. Shutzer

Founded: 1837
Domicile: Delaware
Employees: 8,900

Time Warner Inc.

STANDARD &POOR'S

S&P Recommendation HOLD ★★★☆☆	**Price** $16.72 (as of Nov 23, 2007)	**12-Mo. Target Price** $22.00	**Investment Style** Large-Cap Blend

GICS Sector Consumer Discretionary
Sub-Industry Movies & Entertainment

Summary The world's largest media company, TWX has diversified interests in web properties, filmed entertainment content, cable systems, television networks and publishing.

Key Stock Statistics (Source S&P, Vickers, company reports)

52-Wk Range	$23.15– 16.47	S&P Oper. EPS 2007**E**	1.00	Market Capitalization(B)	$62.979
Trailing 12-Month EPS	$1.31	S&P Oper. EPS 2008**E**	1.14	Yield (%)	1.50
Trailing 12-Month P/E	12.8	P/E on S&P Oper. EPS 2007**E**	16.7	Dividend Rate/Share	$0.25
$10K Invested 5 Yrs Ago	$10,798	Common Shares Outstg. (M)	3,727.0	Institutional Ownership (%)	74

Beta	2.11
S&P 3-Yr. Proj. EPS CAGR(%)	13.00
S&P Credit Rating	BBB+

Price Performance

30-Week Mov. Avg. ··· 10-Week Mov. Avg. - - **GAAP Earnings vs. Previous Year** Volume Above Avg. STARS
12-Mo. Target Price — Relative Strength — ▲ Up ▼ Down ► No Change Below Avg. ★

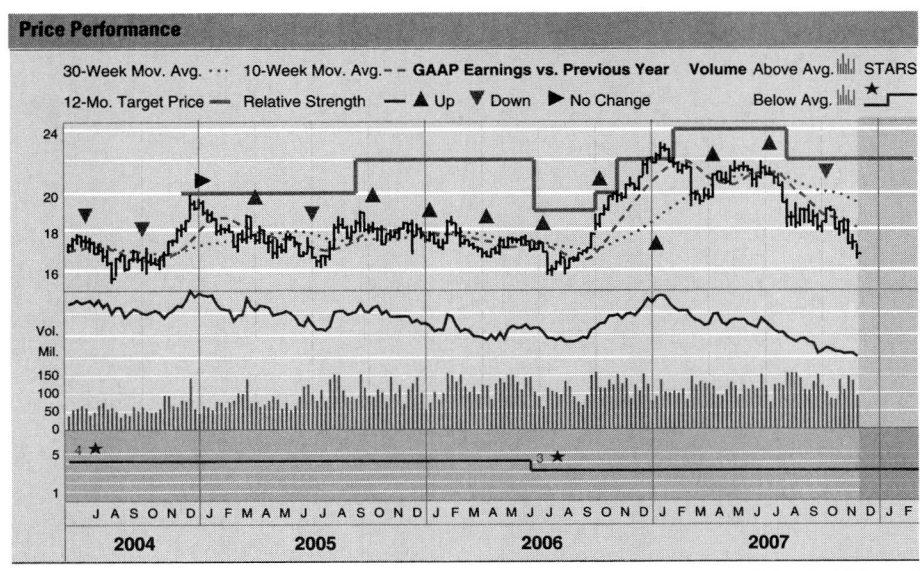

Options: ASE, CBOE, P, Ph

Analysis prepared by **Tuna N. Amobi, CFA, CPA** on November 19, 2007, when the stock traded at **$ 16.82**.

Highlights

➤ From a projected $46.6 billion in 2007 (including acquired cable systems), we see total revenues rising to $48.9 billion in 2008, aided by strong double-digit growth at the cable division, as well as ad and affiliate revenues at the networks, and a strong film/DVD slate for 2007 into the 2008 first half. We project sharp revenue declines at AOL, as further subscriptions erosion outweighs modest gains in online ads. We see easier comparisons for 2008 publishing revenues, on print ads and circulation.

➤ We expect a margin expansion in 2007 led by the film as well as networks businesses, with the AOL and publishing units also likely to drive some gains on recent cost reductions. We see 2008 margin upside from the acquired cable systems, but against otherwise relatively limited opportunities for margin expansion, we project total EBITDA to be essentially flat with 2007 at about $13.6 billion.

➤ With significantly higher cable depreciation & amortization (D&A), we forecast EPS of $1.00 in 2007 and $1.14 in 2008, assuming continued share buybacks under a current $5 billion program, which could be substantially completed by the end of 2008.

Investment Rationale/Risk

➤ In early November 2007, TWX reported what we saw as relatively healthy third-quarter gains for the film and networks businesses, against mixed results for its 84%-owned Time Warner Cable (TWC: hold, $25), and sub-par 13% ad revenue growth at AOL, where fourth-quarter growth could stay weak. However, we see a strong holiday DVD slate, and a relatively healthy cable ads market. Also, the shares increasingly could reflect expectations of a major strategic shift by CEO-elect Jeffrey Bewkes, who will replace Richard Parsons effective January 1, 2008. We believe TWX has ample financial flexibility for continued stock buybacks, select acquisitions and modest dividends.

➤ Risks to our recommendation and target price include continued uncertainties concerning AOL's turnaround strategy, increased competition for cable's triple-play offerings (from satellite TV and telcos), a soft advertising market, and volatility in film results.

➤ Our 12-month target price of $22 is based on a blend of our DCF model, which shows intrinsic value of $20 (with a 12% WACC, low double-digit growth in free cash flow, and 3% terminal growth), and a $24 sum-of-the-parts valuation.

Qualitative Risk Assessment

LOW	**MEDIUM**	HIGH

Our risk assessment reflects our view of the company's leading content and distribution businesses and ample financial flexibility, offset by increased competition, cyclical advertising exposure, a volatile stock price, and a continued audience fragmentation for traditional media platforms.

Quantitative Evaluations

S&P Quality Ranking   **B**

D	C	B-	**B**	B+	A-	A	A+

Relative Strength Rank   **MODERATE**

39

LOWEST = 1   HIGHEST = 99

Revenue/Earnings Data

Revenue (Million $)

	1Q	2Q	3Q	4Q	Year
2007	11,184	10,980	11,676	--	--
2006	10,327	10,519	10,912	12,466	44,224
2005	10,483	10,744	10,538	11,887	43,652
2004	10,178	10,858	9,936	11,109	42,081
2003	--	--	--	--	39,496
2002	--	--	--	--	36,955

Earnings Per Share ($)

	1Q	2Q	3Q	4Q	Year
2007	0.30	0.25	0.24	E0.29	E1.00
2006	0.26	0.20	0.33	0.43	1.21
2005	0.20	-0.07	0.19	0.29	0.62
2004	0.15	0.19	0.11	0.24	0.69
2003	0.09	0.23	0.12	0.24	0.68
2002	--	--	--	--	-9.43

Fiscal year ended Dec. 31. Next earnings report expected: Early February. EPS Estimates based on S&P Operating Earnings; historical GAAP earnings are as reported.

Dividend Data (Dates: mm/dd Payment Date: mm/dd/yy)

Amount ($)	Date Decl.	Ex-Div. Date	Stk. of Record	Payment Date
0.055	01/25	02/26	02/28	03/15/07
0.055	04/26	05/29	05/31	06/15/07
0.063	07/26	08/29	08/31	09/15/07
0.063	10/25	11/28	11/30	12/15/07

Dividends have been paid since 2005. Source: Company reports.

Time Warner Inc.

STANDARD & POOR'S

Business Summary November 19, 2007

CORPORATE OVERVIEW. In January 2001, online access and content company America Online (AOL) merged with cable systems and media concern Time Warner, forming AOL Time Warner (later changed to Time Warner in October 2003), in a $106 billion transaction. Revenues consist of subscriptions (54% of 2006 revenues), content (24%), advertising (19%), and other (3%).

AOL had 10.1 million subscribers in the U.S. at September 30, 2007. It owns the AOL, CompuServe and Netscape access brands, and the AOL.com, AIM and MapQuest portals and Web sites. Time Warner Cable serves about 13.5 million basic subscribers, also offering high-speed data, digital video (including SVOD/VOD, DVRs, HDTV), and digital (VoIP) phone. In July 2006, Time Warner Cable closed on the Adelphia/Comcast transactions to consolidate its position as the second-largest U.S. cable multiple system operator (MSO), with about 13.3 million subscribers.

Filmed Entertainment includes the Warner Bros. and New Line Cinema (independent) studios and home entertainment businesses, with key franchises such as Harry Potter, Lord of the Rings and Batman. The Networks segment includes cable networks CNN, HBO/Cinemax and Turner (TNT, TBS). In

September 2006, TWX's WB broadcast network merged with CBS's UPN to create the CW network. Publishing includes Time Inc., with over 130 magazine titles worldwide, including Time, People, Sports Illustrated and Fortune (77 titles in the U.K. and Australia).

CORPORATE STRATEGY. Under CEO Richard Parsons and President/COO Jeffrey Bewkes (who will become CEO on January 1, 2008), TWX aims to be a market leader in its various businesses. In August 2006, AOL unveiled a strategy to capitalize on the rapid growth in online advertising, enticing its broadband users with free access services such as software and e-mail. Management set key financial targets for AOL, including $1 billion in cost cuts by the end of 2007, EBITDA growth for 2007-2009, and revenue growth by 2009. In March 2006, Google invested $1 billion for a 5% stake in AOL, which has recently made a number of potentially complementary acquisitions.

Company Financials Fiscal Year Ended Dec. 31

Per Share Data ($)	2006	2005	2004	2003	2002	2001	2000	1999	1998	1997
Tangible Book Value	NM	NM	NM	NM	NM	NM	2.51	2.44	1.17	0.12
Cash Flow	2.86	2.06	2.13	2.00	NA	NA	0.62	0.61	0.42	0.11
Earnings	1.21	0.62	0.69	0.68	-9.43	-1.20	0.45	0.48	0.30	0.05
S&P Core Earnings	1.07	0.83	0.62	0.42	-3.44	-1.08	NA	NA	NA	NA
Dividends	0.21	0.10	Nil	Nil	Nil	Nil	Nil	Nil	Nil	Nil
Payout Ratio	17%	16%	Nil	Nil	Nil	Nil	Nil	Nil	Nil	Nil
Prices:High	22.25	19.64	19.90	18.32	32.92	58.51	83.38	83.38	95.81	40.00
Prices:Low	15.70	16.10	15.41	9.90	8.70	27.40	32.75	32.75	32.50	5.16
P/E Ratio:High	18	32	29	27	NM	NM	NM	NM	NM	NM
P/E Ratio:Low	13	26	22	15	NM	NM	NM	NM	NM	NM

Income Statement Analysis (Million $)

	2006	2005	2004	2003	2002	2001	2000	1999	1998	1997
Revenue	44,224	43,652	42,081	39,496	36,955	33,765	7,703	6,886	4,777	2,600
Operating Income	14,837	14,312	13,535	11,839	NA	NA	2,271	1,776	851	341
Depreciation	6,953	6,781	6,743	6,086	NA	NA	444	363	298	132
Interest Expense	1,971	1,622	1,754	1,926	1,900	1,576	55.0	40.0	20.0	13.0
Pretax Income	6,826	4,007	5,206	4,763	NA	NA	1,884	2,014	1,096	92.0
Effective Tax Rate	19.6%	27.2%	33.0%	29.0%	NM	NM	38.9%	38.8%	30.5%	NM
Net Income	5,114	2,921	3,239	3,164	-42,003	-5,313	1,152	1,232	762	92.0
S&P Core Earnings	4,551	3,929	2,938	1,999	-15,240	-4,771	NA	NA	NA	NA

Balance Sheet & Other Financial Data (Million $)

	2006	2005	2004	2003	2002	2001	2000	1999	1998	1997
Cash	1,549	4,220	6,139	3,040	1,730	771	2,610	2,490	887	631
Current Assets	10,851	13,463	14,639	12,268	11,155	10,274	4,671	4,428	1,979	930
Total Assets	131,669	122,745	123,149	121,748	115,508	209,429	10,827	10,673	5,348	2,214
Current Liabilities	12,780	12,608	14,673	NA	NA	NA	2,328	2,395	1,725	894
Long Term Debt	35,233	20,238	20,703	23,458	27,354	22,792	1,411	1,630	348	372
Common Equity	60,389	62,679	60,719	56,131	52,891	150,667	6,778	6,161	3,033	598
Total Capital	112,857	103,760	103,285	NA	NA	NA	8,189	7,791	3,381	970
Capital Expenditures	4,085	3,246	3,024	2,761	3,023	3,634	485	642	301	297
Cash Flow	12,067	9,702	9,982	9,250	NA	NA	1,596	1,595	1,060	224
Current Ratio	0.8	1.1	1.0	NA	NA	NA	2.0	1.8	1.1	1.0
% Long Term Debt of Capitalization	31.2	19.5	20.0	NA	NA	NA	17.2	20.9	10.3	38.4
% Net Income of Revenue	11.6	6.7	7.7	8.0	NM	NM	15.0	17.9	16.0	3.5
% Return on Assets	4.0	2.4	2.6	2.7	NM	NM	10.9	15.3	18.5	6.0
% Return on Equity	8.2	4.7	5.5	5.8	NM	NM	17.6	26.6	37.8	25.3

Data as orig reptd.; bef. results of disc opers/spec. items. Per share data adj. for stk. divs.; EPS diluted. E-Estimated. NA-Not Available. NM-Not Meaningful. NR-Not Ranked. UR-Under Review.

Office: 1 Time Warner Ctr, New York, NY 10019-6038.
Telephone: 212-484-8000.
Email: aoltwir@aoltw.com
Website: http://www.timewarner.com

Chrmn & CEO: R.D. Parsons
Pres & COO: J.L. Bewkes
EVP & CFO: W.H. Pace
EVP & General Counsel: P.T. Cappuccio

Board Members: J. L. Barksdale, J. L. Bewkes, S. F. Bollenbach, F. J. Caufield, R. C. Clark, M. Dopfner, J. P. Einhorn, R. Mark, M. A. Miles, K. J. Novack, R. D. Parsons, F. T. Vincent, Jr., D. C. Wright, E. J. Zander

Founded: 1985
Domicile: Delaware
Employees: 92,700

Titanium Metals Corp

S&P Recommendation HOLD ★★★☆☆

Price	12-Mo. Target Price	Investment Style
$26.33 (as of Nov 26, 2007)	$28.00	Large-Cap Blend

GICS Sector Materials
Sub-Industry Diversified Metals & Mining

Summary This company is a worldwide integrated producer of titanium metal products.

Key Stock Statistics (Source S&P, Vickers, company reports)

52-Wk Range	**$39.80–25.26**	S&P Oper. EPS 2007**E**	**1.48**	Market Capitalization(B)	**$4.270**	Beta	**-0.36**
Trailing 12-Month EPS	**$1.74**	S&P Oper. EPS 2008**E**	**1.66**	Yield (%)	**Nil**	S&P 3-Yr. Proj. EPS CAGR(%)	**NA**
Trailing 12-Month P/E	**15.1**	P/E on S&P Oper. EPS 2007**E**	**17.8**	Dividend Rate/Share	**Nil**	S&P Credit Rating	**NR**
$10K Invested 5 Yrs Ago	**$728,392**	Common Shares Outstg. (M)	**162.2**	Institutional Ownership (%)	**38**		

Price Performance

- 30-Week Mov. Avg. · · ·
- 10-Week Mov. Avg. ‑ ‑
- **GAAP Earnings vs. Previous Year**
- Volume Above Avg. ▮▮▮
- 12-Mo. Target Price ——
- Relative Strength ——
- ▲ Up
- ▼ Down
- ► No Change
- Below Avg. ▮▮▮
- STARS

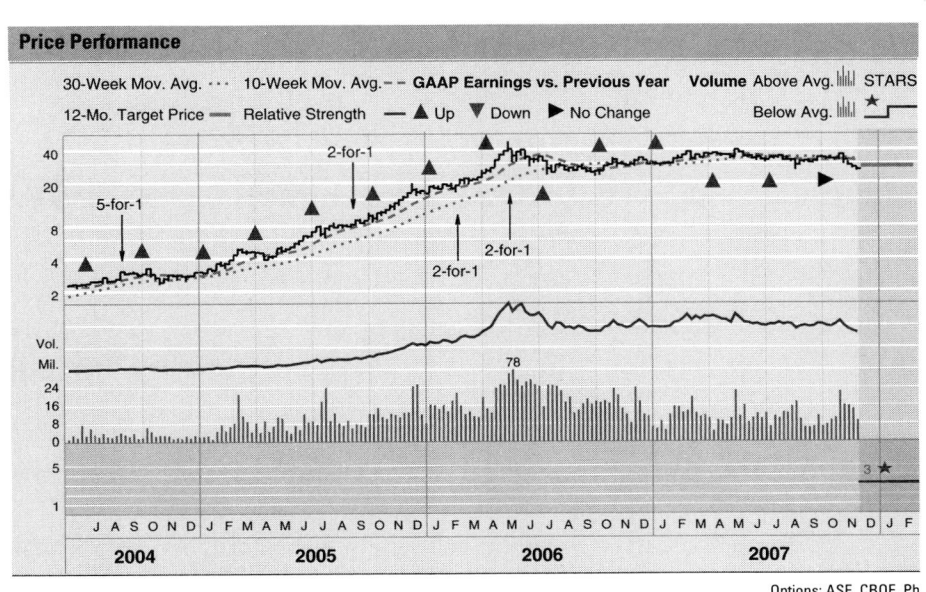

Options: ASE, CBOE, Ph

Analysis prepared by **Leo J. Larkin** on November 26, 2007, when the stock traded at **$26.90**.

Highlights

➤ Following an estimated sales gain of 14% in 2007, we look for a 9% rise in 2008 on increases in the average realized price of both melted and mill products. Due to delayed construction of Boeing Company's 787 airplane, volume of shipments will likely match or drop slightly from 2007's levels and cause the rate of gain in 2008's sales to trail 2007's projected increase. Our sales estimate assumes no other delays in airline construction and also looks for firm demand from defense and other non commercial aerospace markets. S&P forecasts GDP growth of 1.9% in 2008, versus estimated GDP growth of 2.1% in 2007.

➤ Aided by a more lucrative product mix stemming from greater sales of mill products along with less rapidly rising raw material costs, we project better margins and higher operating income. Following no interest expense and a flat tax rate, we estimate EPS of $1.66 in 2008, versus estimated operating EPS of $1.48 in 2007.

➤ Long-term, we look for higher EPS on a continued upturn in the commercial aerospace industry and increased use of titanium in other industrial sectors and in Asia.

Investment Rationale/Risk

➤ We view TIE as a vehicle for participation in a continued upturn in construction of new planes for commercial aerospace, growing acceptance of titanium in other industrial markets and rising Asian demand for titanium. In our view, demand for titanium in commercial aerospace will increase in 2008, 2009 and 2010. According to the Airline Monitor, an industry trade association, delivery of commercial aircraft will rise steadily through 2010. Higher deliveries along with rising demand from other industrial sectors should provide a firm base for EPS growth through 2010. Other positive factors include TIE's low debt levels and authorization of a stock repurchase program. But, with the shares trading with just modest upside to our target price, we would hold, but not add to positions.

➤ Risks to our recommendation and target price include the possibility of additional delays in construction of commercial aircraft.

➤ We project that TIE's P/E on our 2008 estimate will be 16.9X, which is just above the mid-point of its historical range and would be at a slight premium to its peers. On that basis, our 12 month target price is $28.

Qualitative Risk Assessment

LOW	MEDIUM	HIGH

Our risk assessment reflects the heavy reliance of this company's sales and earnings on demand from the aerospace industry and the volatility of its raw material costs. Partly offsetting this is its low debt levels and its large share of the markets it serves.

Quantitative Evaluations

S&P Quality Ranking   B-

D	C	B-	B	B+	A-	A	A+

Relative Strength Rank   WEAK

24

LOWEST = 1   HIGHEST = 99

Revenue/Earnings Data

Revenue (Million $)

	1Q	2Q	3Q	4Q	Year
2007	341.7	341.2	297.3	--	--
2006	286.9	300.9	271.8	323.5	1,183
2005	155.2	183.8	190.0	220.8	749.8
2004	120.5	124.1	120.3	137.0	501.8
2003	99.30	101.8	83.64	100.6	385.3
2002	104.4	94.30	82.79	85.00	366.5

Earnings Per Share ($)

2007	0.41	0.42	0.29	E0.36	E1.48
2006	0.32	0.31	0.29	0.61	1.53
2005	0.23	0.21	0.20	0.23	0.86
2004	-0.01	0.02	0.17	0.08	0.28
2003	-0.11	-0.05	-0.02	0.08	-0.11
2002	-0.29	-0.10	-0.07	-0.08	-0.53

Fiscal year ended Dec. 31. Next earnings report expected: Mid February. EPS Estimates based on S&P Operating Earnings; historical GAAP earnings are as reported.

Dividend Data

The company has not paid a dividend since 1999.

Titanium Metals Corp

STANDARD &POOR'S

Business Summary November 26, 2007

CORPORATE OVERVIEW: Titanium Metals Corp. is the one of the world's largest producers of titanium melted and mill products and the largest U.S. producer of titanium sponge (the raw material for titanium). The company estimates that it accounted for some 20% of global industry shipments of titanium mill products in 2006 and 7% of worldwide sponge production. Melted and mill products and sponge are sold principally to the commercial aerospace industry. Other sources of product demand include the military, industrial and emerging markets. As of September 30, 2007, 32.5% of TIE's common shares were held by Contran Corporation and its subsidiaries, and an additional 9.5% of TIE's shares were held by a trust sponsored by Contran.

Products include titanium sponge; melted products (ingot, electrodes and slab), mill products, including billet and bar, plate, strip and pipe and fabricated products such as spools, pipe fittings, manifolds and vessels. In 2006, mill products accounted for 69% of sales, melted products 19% and other prod-

ucts (titanium fabrications, titanium scrap and titanium tetrachloride), 12%.

Sales by market sector in 2006 were: aerospace, 57%; military, 15%; chemical products, oil and gas, consumer, sporting goods, automotive and power generation 17%; other 11%. In 2006, North American accounted for 59% of sales, Europe, 32% and other regions, 9%.

CORPORATE STRATEGY: The company's long-term strategy is to maximize the value of its core aerospace business while expanding its presence in non-aerospace markets. Additionally, the company seeks to develop new applications for its products.

Company Financials Fiscal Year Ended Dec. 31

Per Share Data ($)	2006	2005	2004	2003	2002	2001	2000	1999	1998	1997
Tangible Book Value	4.92	2.91	1.41	1.20	1.18	1.92	2.32	2.69	2.94	2.63
Cash Flow	1.68	0.96	0.47	0.19	-0.24	-0.01	0.03	0.08	0.53	0.75
Earnings	1.53	0.86	0.28	-0.11	-0.53	-0.33	-0.30	-0.25	0.37	0.62
S&P Core Earnings	1.29	0.82	0.29	-0.08	-0.37	-0.41	NA	NA	NA	NA
Dividends	Nil	Nil	Nil	Nil	Nil	Nil	Nil	0.03	0.03	Nil
Payout Ratio	Nil	Nil	Nil	Nil	Nil	Nil	Nil	13%	8%	Nil
Prices:High	47.63	19.86	3.33	1.51	1.35	3.60	2.23	3.31	8.25	9.59
Prices:Low	15.96	2.91	1.06	0.39	0.23	0.59	0.78	0.89	1.78	6.13
P/E Ratio:High	31	23	12	NM	NM	NM	NM	NM	23	15
P/E Ratio:Low	10	3	4	NM	NM	NM	NM	NM	5	10

Income Statement Analysis (Million $)										
Revenue	1,183	750	502	385	367	487	427	480	708	734
Operating Income	403	177	43.8	17.2	-9.02	28.2	1.81	19.6	138	162
Depreciation	34.1	31.5	32.8	36.6	37.1	40.1	41.9	42.7	32.5	28.4
Interest Expense	3.43	3.96	12.5	16.4	3.38	4.06	7.70	7.09	2.92	2.07
Pretax Income	418	185	39.0	-11.3	-54.5	4.47	-43.1	-33.7	85.8	135
Effective Tax Rate	30.7%	13.2%	NM	NM	NM	NM	NM	NM	34.0%	30.3%
Net Income	281	156	39.9	-12.9	-67.2	-41.8	-38.0	-31.4	45.8	83.0
S&P Core Earnings	229	136	37.9	-9.92	-46.4	-51.7	NA	NA	NA	NA

Balance Sheet & Other Financial Data (Million $)										
Cash	86.2	17.6	54.4	35.0	6.21	24.5	9.80	20.7	95.5	69.0
Current Assets	758	550	344	276	263	309	248	343	396	414
Total Assets	1,217	907	666	567	564	699	759	883	953	793
Current Liabilities	211	167	162	78.5	92.6	122	116	194	137	124
Long Term Debt	Nil	57.2	12.2	9.77	217	221	229	233	311	11.4
Common Equity	804	430	206	159	159	298	357	408	448	409
Total Capital	918	660	404	180	388	533	604	662	782	628
Capital Expenditures	101	61.1	23.6	12.5	7.77	16.1	11.2	24.8	115	66.3
Cash Flow	309	175	68.4	23.7	-30.1	-1.63	3.91	11.3	78.3	111
Current Ratio	3.6	3.3	2.1	3.5	2.8	2.5	2.1	1.8	2.9	3.3
% Long Term Debt of Capitalization	Nil	8.7	3.0	5.4	56.0	41.4	37.9	35.3	39.8	1.8
% Net Income of Revenue	23.8	20.8	8.0	NM	NM	NM	NM	NM	6.5	11.3
% Return on Assets	26.5	19.4	6.5	NM	NM	NM	NM	NM	5.2	11.1
% Return on Equity	44.5	43.4	19.5	NM	NM	NM	NM	NM	10.7	22.6

Data as orig reptd.; bef. results of disc opers/spec. items. Per share data adj. for stk. divs.; EPS diluted. E-Estimated. NA-Not Available. NM-Not Meaningful. NR-Not Ranked. UR-Under Review.

Office: 5430 Lbj Fwy Ste 1700, Dallas, TX 75240-2620.
Telephone: 972-233-1700.
Website: http://www.timet.com
Chrmn: H.C. Simmons

Pres & COO: C... Entrekin
Vice Chrmn & CEO: S.L. Watson
EVP & CFO: B.D. O'Brien
VP & Treas: J.A. St. Wrba

Board Members: K. R. Coogan, N. N. Green, G. R. Simmons, H. C. Simmons, T. P. Stafford, S. L. Watson, P. J. Zucconi

Founded: 1950
Domicile: Delaware
Employees: 2,380

The McGraw-Hill Companies

TJX Companies Inc. (The)

STANDARD &POOR'S

S&P Recommendation [BUY] ★★★★☆

Price	12-Mo. Target Price	Investment Style
$28.52 (as of Nov 23, 2007)	$35.00	Large-Cap Growth

GICS Sector Consumer Discretionary
Sub-Industry Apparel Retail

Summary TJX operates seven chains of off-price apparel and home fashion specialty stores in the U.S., Canada, Ireland and the U.K.

Key Stock Statistics (Source S&P, Vickers, company reports)

52-Wk Range	$32.46–25.74	S&P Oper. EPS 2008**E**	1.88	Market Capitalization(B)	$12.681	Beta	0.65
Trailing 12-Month EPS	$1.43	S&P Oper. EPS 2009**E**	2.28	Yield (%)	1.26	S&P 3-Yr. Proj. EPS CAGR(%)	15.00
Trailing 12-Month P/E	19.9	P/E on S&P Oper. EPS 2008**E**	15.2	Dividend Rate/Share	$0.36	S&P Credit Rating	A
$10K Invested 5 Yrs Ago	$15,213	Common Shares Outstg. (M)	444.6	Institutional Ownership (%)	100		

Price Performance

30-Week Mov. Avg. ··· 10-Week Mov. Avg. - - **GAAP Earnings vs. Previous Year** Volume Above Avg. ▮▮▮ STARS
12-Mo. Target Price — Relative Strength — ▲ Up ▼ Down ▶ No Change Below Avg. ▮▮▮

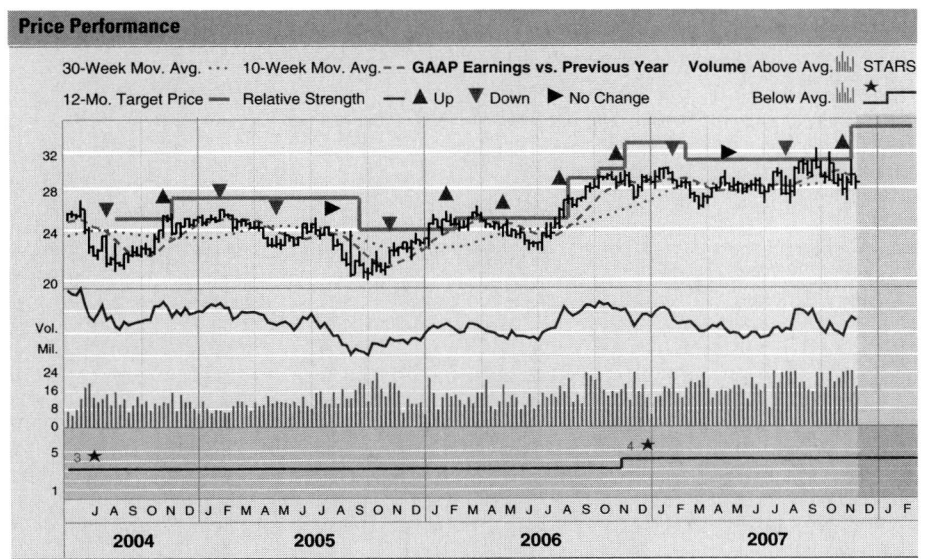

2004   2005   2006   2007

Options: ASE, CBOE

Analysis prepared by **Jason N. Asaeda** on November 14, 2007, when the stock traded at **$ 29.25**.

Highlights

➤ From a projected $18.7 billion in FY 08 (Jan.), we expect net sales to advance 6.4% in FY 09, to $19.9 billion, on expected contributions from new stores and a 3% to 4% consolidated same-store sales increase. In TJX's core Marmaxx division, we believe that a continued focus on off-price buys (purchases made opportunistically and closer to need during a season), as well as from moderate to better brands, will drive improved sales productivity. We also look for the company to leverage the talents of its HomeGoods merchant team to improve home merchandise assortments at Marmaxx.

➤ Based on what we see as improving merchandise margins, supported by an increase in off-price buys, which carry higher mark-ups than upfront buys (purchases made before or early in a season), and effective expense controls, we look for operating margins to widen.

➤ Excluding potential liabilities, costs and expenses arising from the company's computer system intrusion, which was announced on January 17, 2007, but factoring in likely share buybacks, we see operating EPS of $1.88 in FY 08 and $2.28 in FY 09.

Investment Rationale/Risk

➤ We see TJX's strong value proposition, opportunistic buying, and increased merchandising focus on affordable luxury sustaining the company's positive same-store sales trend this holiday selling season and through FY 09. We also see ample operating cash flow funding new store openings across brands, investments in infrastructure, and additional share buybacks. In addition, we look for the expansion of promising growth categories at A.J. Wright, T.K. Maxx and Winners, and "treasure hunt" assortments at HomeGoods and HomeSense, to support improving operations.

➤ Risks to our recommendation and target price include a sharp decline in consumer confidence, changes in spending habits and buying preferences, as well as merchandise availability. There is also the risk that the company could lose business from customers affected by the unauthorized computer system intrusion.

➤ Our 12-month target price of $35 applies the stock's historical average forward P/E of 15.5X to our FY 09 operating EPS estimate. Factoring in a recent 1.2% dividend yield, we believe the shares are attractive on a total return basis.

Qualitative Risk Assessment

LOW	MEDIUM	HIGH

Our risk assessment reflects our view of TJX's leadership position in off-price retail and promising new merchandising and productivity initiatives that could boost sales and profit margins. This is offset by what we see as an inconsistent earnings track record and an uncertain outlook for consumer discretionary spending.

Quantitative Evaluations

S&P Quality Ranking A+

D	C	B-	B	B+	A-	A	A+

Relative Strength Rank MODERATE

70

LOWEST = 1   HIGHEST = 99

Revenue/Earnings Data

Revenue (Million $)

	1Q	2Q	3Q	4Q	Year
2008	4,108	4,313	4,737	--	--
2007	3,871	3,964	4,473	5,097	17,405
2006	3,652	3,648	4,042	4,716	16,058
2005	3,353	3,414	3,817	4,329	14,913
2004	2,789	3,046	3,387	4,106	13,328
2003	2,666	2,765	3,045	3,505	11,981

Earnings Per Share ($)

2008	0.34	0.13	0.54	E0.59	E1.88
2007	0.34	0.29	0.48	0.51	1.63
2006	0.28	0.23	0.32	0.60	1.41
2005	0.32	0.23	0.40	0.35	1.30
2004	0.22	0.24	0.36	0.47	1.28
2003	0.27	0.24	0.28	0.29	1.08

Fiscal year ended Jan. 31. Next earnings report expected: Late February. EPS Estimates based on S&P Operating Earnings; historical GAAP earnings are as reported.

Dividend Data (Dates: mm/dd Payment Date: mm/dd/yy)

Amount ($)	Date Decl.	Ex-Div. Date	Stk. of Record	Payment Date
0.070	12/05	02/06	02/08	03/01/07
0.090	04/09	05/08	05/10	05/31/07
0.090	06/05	08/07	08/09	08/30/07
0.090	09/11	11/06	11/08	11/29/07

Dividends have been paid since 1980. Source: Company reports.

Please read the Required Disclosures and Analyst Certification on the last page of this report.

The McGraw-Hill Companies

TJX Companies Inc. (The)

STANDARD &POOR'S

Business Summary November 14, 2007

COMPANY PROFILE. With $17.4 billion in annual revenues, TJX is the largest U.S. off-price family apparel and home fashion retailer via its seven retail concepts. As of August 14, 2007, the company's core Marmaxx Group division operated 830 T.J. Maxx and 764 Marshalls stores. TJX also operated 128 A.J. Wright units, 34 Bob's Stores, and 273 HomeGoods stores in the U.S. The company's international operations were comprised of 212 T.K. Maxx stores in Europe, and 185 Winners and 70 HomeSense stores in Canada.

TJX believes it derives a competitive advantage by offering rapidly changing assortments of affordable, quality brand name and designer merchandise. Prices at T.J. Maxx and Marshalls are usually 20% to 60% below department and specialty store regular prices. With over 2,400 stores, the company has substantial buying power with more than 10,000 vendors worldwide. TJX purchases later in the buying cycle than department and specialty stores. Generally, purchases are for current selling seasons, with a limited quantity of packaway inventory intended for a future selling season. A combination of opportunistic buying, an expansive distribution infrastructure, and a low expense structure enable the company to offer everyday savings to its customers.

PRIMARY BUSINESS DYNAMICS. TJX's primary growth drivers are new store openings and same-store sales (sales results for stores open for all or a portion of two consecutive fiscal years). From FY 00 through FY 06, the company increased its consolidated store count from 1,493 to 2,381 at a compound annual growth rate (CAGR) of about 12%. TJX reported a 7.1% increase in FY 06, down from 7.8% in FY 05, and an 11% run rate from FY 00 through FY 04. Growth has slowed with the maturing of the core Marmaxx division. From FY 07 through FY 09, the company plans to further slow its new store growth to 4% to 5% annually as it implements changes at A.J. Wright and HomeGoods to improve store operations. Store expansion fell below plan in FY 07, with the consolidated store count rising only 3.6%, due to the closure of 34 underperforming A.J. Wright locations in January 2007.

Company Financials Fiscal Year Ended Jan. 31

Per Share Data ($)	2007	2006	2005	2004	2003	2002	2001	2000	1999	1998
Tangible Book Value	4.65	3.71	3.06	2.74	2.36	2.14	1.85	1.55	1.59	1.39
Cash Flow	2.35	2.23	1.86	1.75	1.46	1.34	1.23	1.08	0.85	0.60
Earnings	1.63	1.41	1.30	1.28	1.08	0.97	0.93	0.83	0.65	0.44
S&P Core Earnings	1.64	1.40	1.22	1.21	1.01	0.91	0.90	NA	NA	NA
Dividends	0.23	0.17	0.14	0.13	0.12	0.11	0.07	0.07	0.06	0.07
Payout Ratio	14%	12%	10%	10%	11%	11%	7%	8%	9%	15%
Calendar Year	2006	2005	2004	2003	2002	2001	2000	1999	1998	1997
Prices:High	29.84	25.96	26.82	23.70	22.45	20.30	15.75	18.50	15.00	9.64
Prices:Low	22.16	19.95	20.64	15.54	15.30	13.56	6.97	8.25	7.75	4.78
P/E Ratio:High	18	18	21	19	21	21	17	22	23	22
P/E Ratio:Low	14	14	16	12	14	14	7	10	12	11

Income Statement Analysis (Million $)

	2007	2006	2005	2004	2003	2002	2001	2000	1999	1998
Revenue	17,405	16,058	14,913	13,328	11,981	10,709	9,579	8,795	7,949	7,389
Operating Income	1,616	1,444	1,394	1,334	1,171	1,104	1,064	1,022	842	652
Depreciation	353	405	288	238	208	204	176	160	137	125
Interest Expense	39.2	39.0	33.5	27.3	25.4	25.6	34.7	20.4	1.69	4.50
Pretax Income	1,247	1,009	1,080	1,068	938	874	865	854	704	522
Effective Tax Rate	37.7%	31.6%	38.5%	38.4%	38.3%	38.2%	37.8%	38.3%	38.5%	41.3%
Net Income	777	690	664	658	578	540	538	527	433	307
S&P Core Earnings	778	687	615	619	546	506	519	NA	NA	NA

Balance Sheet & Other Financial Data (Million $)

	2007	2006	2005	2004	2003	2002	2001	2000	1999	1998
Cash	857	466	307	246	492	493	133	372	461	404
Current Assets	3,749	3,140	2,905	2,452	2,241	2,116	1,722	1,701	1,743	1,683
Total Assets	6,086	5,496	5,075	4,397	3,940	3,596	2,932	2,805	2,748	2,610
Current Liabilities	2,383	2,252	2,204	1,691	1,566	1,315	1,229	1,366	1,307	1,218
Long Term Debt	808	807	599	692	694	702	319	319	220	221
Common Equity	2,290	1,893	1,653	1,552	1,409	1,341	1,219	1,119	1,221	1,091
Total Capital	3,120	2,700	2,405	2,369	2,145	2,043	1,538	1,439	1,441	1,392
Capital Expenditures	378	496	429	409	397	449	257	239	208	192
Cash Flow	1,130	1,096	953	897	786	744	714	687	566	420
Current Ratio	1.6	1.4	1.3	1.5	1.4	1.6	1.4	1.2	1.3	1.4
% Long Term Debt of Capitalization	25.9	29.9	24.9	29.2	32.3	34.4	20.8	22.2	15.3	15.8
% Net Income of Revenue	4.5	4.3	4.5	4.9	4.8	5.0	5.6	6.0	5.4	4.1
% Return on Assets	13.4	13.1	14.0	15.8	15.3	16.6	18.8	19.0	16.2	11.9
% Return on Equity	37.1	37.9	41.4	44.5	42.1	42.2	46.0	45.0	37.2	28.5

Data as orig reptd.; bef. results of disc opers/spec. items. Per share data adj. for stk. divs.; EPS diluted. E-Estimated. NA-Not Available. NM-Not Meaningful. NR-Not Ranked. UR-Under Review.

Office: 770 Cochituate Road, Framingham, MA 01701-4666.
Telephone: 508-390-1000.
Website: http://www.tjx.com
Chrmn: B. Cammarata

Pres & CEO: C. Meyrowitz
Vice Chrmn: D. Cambell
Sr EVP: A. Barron
Sr EVP: J. Rossi

Investor Contact: S. Lang (508-390-2323)
Board Members: D. Brandon, B. Cammarata, G. Deegan, A. .. Lane, R. G. Lesser, C. Meyrowitz, J. F. O'Brien, R. F. Shapiro, W. B. Shire, F. H. Wiley

Founded: 1956
Domicile: Delaware
Employees: 125,000

The McGraw-Hill Companies

Torchmark Corp

S&P Recommendation	HOLD ★★★☆☆	Price	12-Mo. Target Price	Investment Style
		$60.60 (as of Nov 23, 2007)	$71.00	Large-Cap Blend

GICS Sector Financials
Sub-Industry Life & Health Insurance

Summary This financial services company derives most of its earnings from life and health insurance operations.

Key Stock Statistics (Source S&P, Vickers, company reports)

52-Wk Range	$70.54– 58.50	S&P Oper. EPS 2007E	5.43	Market Capitalization(B)	$5.799	Beta	0.68
Trailing 12-Month EPS	$5.52	S&P Oper. EPS 2008E	5.85	Yield (%)	0.86	S&P 3-Yr. Proj. EPS CAGR(%)	8.00
Trailing 12-Month P/E	11.0	P/E on S&P Oper. EPS 2007E	11.2	Dividend Rate/Share	$0.52	S&P Credit Rating	A
$10K Invested 5 Yrs Ago	$16,766	Common Shares Outstg. (M)	95.7	Institutional Ownership (%)	74		

Price Performance

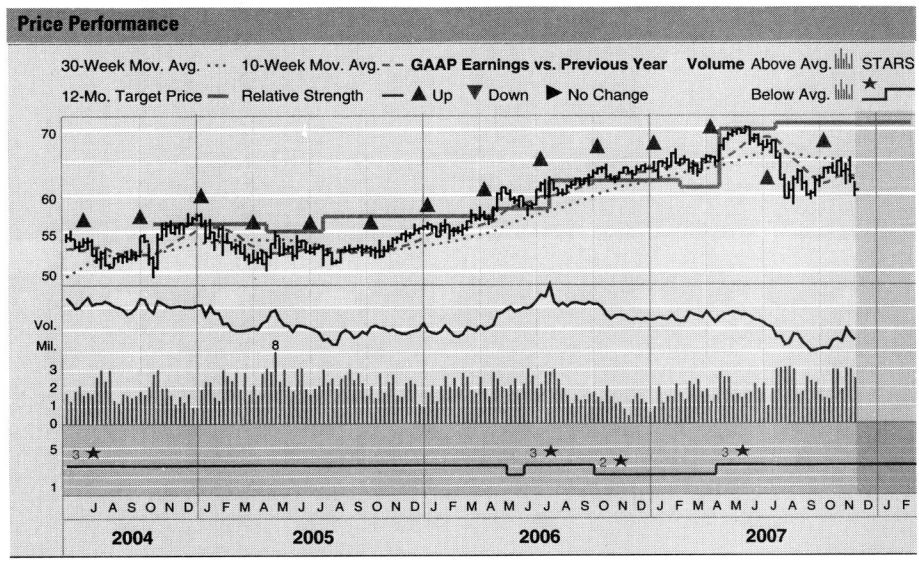

30-Week Mov. Avg. ··· 10-Week Mov. Avg. --- **GAAP Earnings vs. Previous Year** Volume Above Avg. STARS
12-Mo. Target Price — Relative Strength — ▲ Up ▼ Down ▶ No Change Below Avg.

Options: ASE

Analysis prepared by **Tanjila Shafi** on October 29, 2007, when the stock traded at **$ 64.38**.

Highlights

➤ We expect life underwriting margins to increase in the low single digits, based on solid premium growth in 2008. We expect new life sales to experience high single digit to low double digit growth in the second half of the year, based on improvements in the company's distribution channels. We also anticipate that the company's insert media circulation effort will boost new life sales in 2008. However, even though the number of agents is increasing in Liberty National, we are concerned that this unit is having difficulty retaining its experienced agents due to changes in the compensation structure.

➤ We expect premium growth in the company's health business to experience single digit growth in 2008, reflecting the prior year's recruitment efforts. We believe premiums in the Medicare Part D business will experience modest gains in 2008.

➤ We forecast 2007 operating EPS of $5.43, which represents an 8.8% gain from 2006 operating EPS of $4.99. Our EPS estimate for 2008 is $5.85.

Investment Rationale/Risk

➤ We view TMK's focus and commitment to recruiting and retaining agents favorably, as we believe that an increasing agent count acts as a positive indicator for future sales growth. We expect Medicare Part D enrollment to stabilize in 2008 and we anticipate that the company will be able to meet its underwriting margin target of 11% for its Medicare Part D business. We believe that the company will continue to maintain its 15%-plus ROE in 2008.

➤ Risks to our recommendation and target price include increased competition for some products; a decline in recruitment of agents; higher loss ratios for TMK's Medicare Part D business; and adverse mortality.

➤ Our 12-month target price of $71, based on 1.76X our 2008 projected book value (excluding SFAS 115), is in line with TMK's historical multiples.

Qualitative Risk Assessment

LOW	MEDIUM	HIGH

Our risk assessment for Torchmark reflects our view of its varied product lineup and diversified distribution network. TMK generates strong cash flow growth, in our opinion, and uses excess cash flow to repurchase shares and pay its dividend.

Quantitative Evaluations

S&P Quality Ranking   A

D	C	B-	B	B+	A-	A	A+

Relative Strength Rank   MODERATE

59

LOWEST = 1   HIGHEST = 99

Revenue/Earnings Data

Revenue (Million $)

	1Q	2Q	3Q	4Q	Year
2007	906.0	876.6	863.6	--	--
2006	857.0	869.1	837.9	857.1	3,421
2005	783.0	804.8	769.0	769.1	3,126
2004	772.5	764.0	774.2	760.8	3,072
2003	718.4	734.3	730.4	747.5	2,931
2002	689.7	633.5	715.8	699.0	2,738

Earnings Per Share ($)

2007	1.37	1.32	1.41	E1.39	E5.43
2006	1.16	1.26	1.28	1.43	5.13
2005	1.09	1.25	1.14	1.21	4.68
2004	1.05	1.04	1.12	1.05	4.25
2003	0.85	0.95	0.94	0.98	3.73
2002	0.80	0.52	0.98	0.89	3.18

Fiscal year ended Dec. 31. Next earnings report expected: Early February. EPS Estimates based on S&P Operating Earnings; historical GAAP earnings are as reported.

Dividend Data (Dates: mm/dd Payment Date: mm/dd/yy)

Amount ($)	Date Decl.	Ex-Div. Date	Stk. of Record	Payment Date
0.130	02/21	04/03	04/06	05/01/07
0.130	04/26	07/03	07/06	08/01/07
0.130	07/30	10/03	10/05	11/01/07
0.130	11/08	01/02	01/04	02/01/08

Dividends have been paid since 1933. Source: Company reports.

Torchmark Corp

Business Summary October 29, 2007

CORPORATE OVERVIEW. TMK's subsidiaries offer a full line of nonparticipating ordinary individual life products and health insurance, as well as fixed and variable annuities. Traditional whole life insurance constituted 58% of life insurance in force at the end of 2006, as measured by annualized premiums, with interest-sensitive whole life 7.7%, term life 31%, and other life products 3.1%. Medicare supplemental insurance accounted for 43% of supplemental health insurance in force at the end of 2006, as measured by annualized premiums, limited-benefit plans accounted for 39% of premiums in force, and Medicare Part D accounted for 18% of premiums in force. The number of individual health policies in force (excluding Medicare Part D) was 1.6 million at December 31, 2006, the same as the prior year-end. Medicare Part D enrollees were 189,000 at December 31, 2006. Annuity separate account assets totaled $1.498 billion at December 31, 2006, down 4.0% from the year-earlier level.

Life segment premium revenue accounted for 55% of total premium revenue in 2006 (59% in 2005), with the health segment at 37% (40%), Medicare Part D at 7.6% (0.0%) and the annuity segment at 0.8% (1.0%).

CORPORATE STRATEGY. A key corporate strategy for TMK is to improve its

distribution system. Distribution is through direct solicitation, independent agents, and exclusive agents. The Liberty National exclusive agency markets products to middle-income families in the Southeastern U.S. through full-time sales representatives. The American Income exclusive agency focuses on members of labor unions, credit unions, and other associations in the U.S., Canada, and New Zealand. The United Investors agency markets to middle-income Americans through independent agents. The military agency consists of a nationwide independent agency comprised of former commissioned and noncommissioned military officers who sell exclusively to military officers and their families. The United American independent agency focuses primarily on health insurance in the U.S. and Canada to individuals over the age of 50. The United American branch office agency also focuses on health insurance to over-age 50 individuals through exclusive producing agents.

Company Financials Fiscal Year Ended Dec. 31

Per Share Data ($)	2006	2005	2004	2003	2002	2001	2000	1999	1998	1997
Tangible Book Value	31.39	29.49	28.16	25.39	20.91	17.24	14.34	12.05	13.48	10.05
Operating Earnings	NA	NA	NA	3.87	3.51	3.12	2.85	2.45	2.29	NA
Earnings	5.13	4.68	4.25	3.73	3.18	3.11	2.82	1.93	1.81	2.56
S&P Core Earnings	5.07	4.29	4.03	3.68	3.39	2.73	NA	NA	NA	NA
Dividends	0.48	0.44	0.44	0.38	0.36	0.36	0.36	0.36	0.58	0.59
Payout Ratio	9%	9%	10%	10%	11%	12%	13%	19%	32%	23%
Prices:High	64.59	57.50	57.57	45.75	42.17	43.25	41.19	38.00	49.81	42.81
Prices:Low	53.91	50.05	44.61	33.00	30.02	32.56	18.75	24.56	31.81	25.00
P/E Ratio:High	13	12	14	12	13	14	15	20	28	17
P/E Ratio:Low	11	11	10	9	9	10	7	13	18	10

Income Statement Analysis (Million $)										
Life Insurance in Force	NA	137,668	133,064	126,737	118,660	113,055	108,319	101,846	96,339	91,870
Premium Income:Life	2,785	2,508	2,472	1,246	1,221	1,144	1,082	1,018	960	910
Premium Income:A & H	NA	NA	NA	1,034	1,019	1,011	911	825	760	739
Net Investment Income	629	603	577	557	519	492	472	447	460	434
Total Revenue	3,421	3,126	3,072	2,931	2,738	2,707	2,516	2,220	2,158	1,849
Pretax Income	774	732	721	655	580	597	553	393	410	516
Net Operating Income	NA	NA	NA	446	424	393	365	328	324	336
Net Income	519	495	476	430	383	391	362	259	256	338
S&P Core Earnings	512	455	452	424	408	343	NA	NA	NA	NA

Balance Sheet & Other Financial Data (Million $)										
Cash & Equivalent	185	178	164	155	140	129	154	127	104	126
Premiums Due	78.8	67.3	73.4	80.7	70.4	67.5	75.0	53.5	130	127
Investment Assets:Bonds	9,127	8,837	8,715	8,103	7,194	6,526	5,950	5,680	5,768	5,860
Investment Assets:Stocks	41.2	48.0	36.9	57.4	24.5	0.57	0.54	29.0	10.0	12.0
Investment Assets:Loans	329	317	338	704	401	393	374	245	358	301
Investment Assets:Total	9,703	9,649	9,405	8,795	7,784	7,154	6,471	6,399	6,413	6,538
Deferred Policy Costs	2,956	2,768	2,506	2,330	2,184	2,066	1,942	1,742	1,503	1,371
Total Assets	14,980	14,769	14,252	13,461	12,361	12,428	12,963	12,132	11,249	10,967
Debt	598	353	540	693	552	681	366	372	383	564
Common Equity	3,459	3,433	6,840	3,240	2,851	2,497	2,202	1,993	2,260	1,933
% Return on Revenue	15.2	15.8	15.5	14.7	14.0	14.4	14.4	11.7	11.9	18.3
% Return on Assets	3.5	3.4	3.4	3.3	3.1	3.1	2.9	2.2	2.3	3.3
% Return on Equity	15.1	14.5	7.1	14.1	14.3	16.6	17.2	12.2	12.2	19.0
% Investment Yield	6.5	6.3	6.4	6.7	7.0	7.2	7.5	6.8	7.1	7.0

Data as orig reptd.; bef. results of disc opers/spec. items. Per share data adj. for stk. divs.; EPS diluted. E-Estimated. NA-Not Available. NM-Not Meaningful. NR-Not Ranked. UR-Under Review.

Office: 3700 S Stonebridge Dr, McKinney, TX 75070-5934.
Telephone: 972-569-4000.
Website: http://www.torchmarkcorp.com
Chrmn & CEO: M.S. McAndrew

EVP & CFO: G.L. Coleman
EVP & Chief Admin Officer: V.D. Herbel
EVP & General Counsel: L.M. Hutchison
VP & Chief Acctg Officer: D.H. Almond

Investor Contact: J.L. Lane (972-569-3627)
Board Members: C. E. Adair, D. L. Boren, M. J. Buchan, R. W. Ingram, J. L. Lanier, Jr., M. S. McAndrew, L. W. Newton, S. R. Perry, L. C. Smith, P. J. Zucconi

Founded: 1900
Domicile: Delaware
Employees: 3,758

Trane Inc

STANDARD &POOR'S

S&P Recommendation HOLD ★★★☆☆	**Price** $37.12 (as of Nov 28, 2007)	**12-Mo. Target Price** $35.00	**Investment Style** Large-Cap Growth

GICS Sector Industrials
Sub-Industry Building Products

Summary During 2007, ASD separated into three businesses, with the company retaining its air-conditioning systems operations. It planned to change its name to Trane.

Key Stock Statistics (Source S&P, Vickers, company reports)

52-Wk Range	$63.74–32.09	S&P Oper. EPS 2007**E**	1.95	Market Capitalization(B)	$7.149	Beta	0.94
Trailing 12-Month EPS	$2.55	S&P Oper. EPS 2008**E**	2.60	Yield (%)	1.72	S&P 3-Yr. Proj. EPS CAGR(%)	NA
Trailing 12-Month P/E	14.6	P/E on S&P Oper. EPS 2007**E**	19.0	Dividend Rate/Share	$0.64	S&P Credit Rating	BBB-
$10K Invested 5 Yrs Ago	NA	Common Shares Outstg. (M)	192.6	Institutional Ownership (%)	NM		

Price Performance

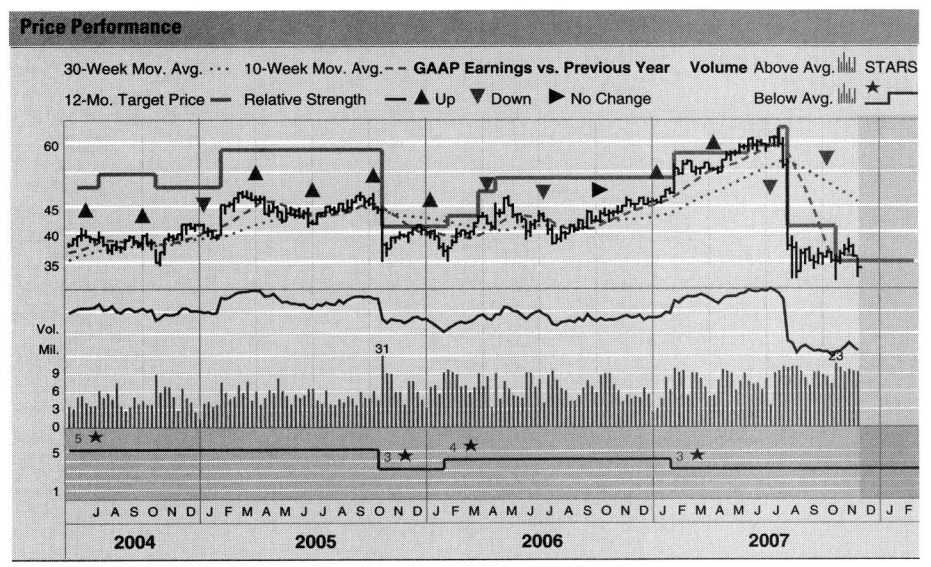

- 30-Week Mov. Avg. ··· 10-Week Mov. Avg. - - **GAAP Earnings vs. Previous Year** Volume Above Avg. ⅢⅢ STARS
- 12-Mo. Target Price — Relative Strength — ▲ Up ▼ Down ▶ No Change Below Avg. ⅢⅢ ★

Options: ASE, CBOE, P, Ph

Analysis prepared by **Michael W. Jaffe** on November 19, 2007, when the stock traded at **$34.36**.

Highlights

➤ ASD spun off its vehicle controls unit on July 31, 2007, and completed the sale of its bath and kitchen business on October 31. We expect sales from its ongoing air-conditioning operations to rise 7% in 2008. We see the forecasted gain driven mostly by continuing growth in commercial air conditioning sales, on our outlook for still strong U.S. commercial building markets. We see that likely commercial strength partly offset by ongoing softness that we expect in residential air conditioner sales, as home sales remain sluggish. We see slightly higher average sales prices in both commercial and residential.

➤ We expect slightly wider operating margins in 2008, on our outlook for higher commercial air conditioning sales. We see that factor outweighing the impact of the ongoing softness in demand for residential air conditioning that we forecast, and expected still-high materials costs.

➤ We see net margins widening considerably, as we expect accretion of about $0.35 a share from the sale of the bath and kitchen business, with proceeds to be used for the repurchase of shares and long-term debt.

Investment Rationale/Risk

➤ We think ASD will benefit from its just-completed plan to split into three separate businesses. The company retained its air-conditioning systems business, which we see being aided by what we expect to be ongoing gains in its primary commercial segment. We think ASD's sale of its struggling bath and kitchen business will be highly accretive. However, our valuation models show most of these positives to be already reflected in the shares.

➤ Risks to our recommendation and target price include a major slowdown in U.S. commercial construction markets and weaker than anticipated growth in global economies.

➤ The shares recently traded at a little over 13X our 2008 EPS forecast, a small discount to the S&P 500. We believe that valuation is about appropriate. We base that opinion on the highly cyclical nature of the company's business. However, our valuation also takes into account our positive view of ASD's commercial air-conditioning business, which now composes the large majority of the company's operations. Our 12-month target price is $35, or 13.5X our 2008 EPS forecast.

Qualitative Risk Assessment

LOW	MEDIUM	HIGH

Our risk assessment reflects that despite the cyclicality of ASD's businesses, we believe its risk is greatly reduced by what we view as a very strong business model, which has led to consistently strong levels of free cash flow over the past decade.

Quantitative Evaluations

S&P Quality Ranking B+

D	C	B-	B	B+	A-	A	A+

Relative Strength Rank MODERATE

70

LOWEST = 1   HIGHEST = 99

Revenue/Earnings Data

Revenue (Million $)

	1Q	2Q	3Q	4Q	Year
2007	2,166	2,620	1,982	--	--
2006	2,552	2,991	2,965	2,701	11,208
2005	2,340	2,755	2,624	2,545	10,264
2004	2,185	2,575	2,396	2,352	9,509
2003	1,951	2,265	2,234	2,118	8,568
2002	1,762	2,087	2,070	1,877	7,795

Earnings Per Share ($)

	1Q	2Q	3Q	4Q	Year
2007	0.49	0.90	0.63	E0.32	E1.95
2006	0.40	0.93	0.74	0.56	2.62
2005	0.57	0.95	0.74	0.30	2.56
2004	0.38	0.73	0.71	-0.41	1.42
2003	0.29	0.61	0.55	0.38	1.83
2002	0.26	0.57	0.52	0.34	1.68

Fiscal year ended Dec. 31. Next earnings report expected: Early February. EPS Estimates based on S&P Operating Earnings; historical GAAP earnings are as reported.

Dividend Data (Dates: mm/dd Payment Date: mm/dd/yy)

Amount ($)	Date Decl.	Ex-Div. Date	Stk. of Record	Payment Date
0.180	05/03	05/30	06/01	06/20/07
0.160	07/12	08/30	09/04	09/20/07
0.160	10/05	11/29	12/03	12/20/07
Stk.	07/12	--	07/19	07/31/07

Dividends have been paid since 2005. Source: Company reports.

Trane Inc

STANDARD
&POOR'S

Business Summary November 19, 2007

American Standard Companies undertook a separation of its portfolio of businesses in 2007. Under the plan, it retained its air-conditioning systems and services business, and planned to change the company's name to Trane, ASD's flagship air-conditioning brand, by year-end. In accordance with the plan, on July 31, ASD spun off its global vehicle control systems business as an independent publicly traded company called WABCO. Moreover, in October 2007, it sold its bath and kitchen business to Bain Capital Partners, LLC, a global private investment firm, for $1.745 billion in cash. It had also sold a small part of bath and kitchen to another entity in March 2007, for about $160 million. Under the separation plan, Fred Poses was to continue as chairman and CEO of the company through 2007, before stepping down as previously planned.

The company is a leading manufacturer of heating, ventilating and air-conditioning (HVAC) systems, with factories in the U.S. and in foreign markets. It also provides aftermarket services to the HVAC industry, including replacement parts and retrofit products, maintenance services for its and other man-

ufacturers' commercial products, and contracting services for the installation, upgrade and replacement of commercial HVAC systems featuring its products.

American Standard derived 27% of air-conditioning sales outside the U.S. in 2006. ASD makes unitary systems, which are factory-assembled central air-conditioning systems; and applied systems, which are custom-engineered for commercial use. Some 70% of segment sales came from commercial markets in 2006. About 59% of air-conditioning sales for the year came from replacement, renovation and repair markets, with the remainder from new construction. The company's air-conditioning business recorded sales of $6.8 billion in 2006. According to ASD, Trane products are present in over half of all commercial buildings in North America.

Company Financials Fiscal Year Ended Dec. 31

Per Share Data ($)	2006	2005	2004	2003	2002	2001	2000	1999	1998	1997
Tangible Book Value	NM	NM	NM	NM	NM	NM	NM	NM	NM	NM
Cash Flow	3.99	3.98	2.61	2.95	2.36	2.40	2.44	2.14	1.01	1.24
Earnings	2.62	2.56	1.42	1.83	1.68	1.35	1.45	1.21	0.15	0.52
S&P Core Earnings	2.62	2.60	2.37	1.82	1.44	1.07	NA	NA	NA	NA
Dividends	0.72	0.60	Nil	Nil	Nil	Nil	Nil	Nil	Nil	Nil
Payout Ratio	27%	23%	Nil	Nil	Nil	Nil	Nil	Nil	Nil	Nil
Prices:High	47.14	48.39	41.82	34.00	26.33	23.63	16.58	16.48	16.42	17.21
Prices:Low	35.01	35.01	33.10	21.28	19.40	15.58	11.44	10.38	7.21	11.54
P/E Ratio:High	18	19	29	19	16	18	11	14	NM	33
P/E Ratio:Low	13	14	23	12	12	12	8	9	NM	22

Income Statement Analysis (Million $)										
Revenue	11,208	10,264	9,509	8,568	7,795	7,465	7,598	7,190	6,654	6,008
Operating Income	1,108	1,112	1,060	924	842	886	916	839	748	711
Depreciation	282	268	262	247	150	232	213	202	190	164
Interest Expense	121	118	115	117	129	169	199	188	188	192
Pretax Income	746	726	363	549	556	476	509	452	167	247
Effective Tax Rate	27.5%	23.4%	13.6%	26.2%	33.3%	38.1%	38.1%	41.5%	79.0%	47.4%
Net Income	541	556	313	405	371	295	315	264	33.6	120
S&P Core Earnings	539	562	524	403	319	234	NA	NA	NA	NA

Balance Sheet & Other Financial Data (Million $)										
Cash	294	391	229	112	96.6	82.1	85.4	61.2	64.8	28.8
Current Assets	3,437	3,066	2,890	2,491	2,014	1,896	1,878	1,726	1,591	1,394
Total Assets	7,413	6,868	6,842	5,879	5,144	4,831	4,745	4,686	4,156	3,669
Current Liabilities	2,568	2,229	2,347	2,034	1,666	1,688	1,807	2,287	2,351	1,841
Long Term Debt	1,601	1,676	1,429	1,627	1,918	2,142	2,376	1,887	1,528	1,551
Common Equity	923	922	930	714	230	-90.1	-393	-497	-701	-610
Total Capital	2,662	2,730	2,454	2,559	2,257	2,137	2,028	1,445	875	941
Capital Expenditures	244	294	216	171	165	167	219	274	255	245
Cash Flow	823	824	575	652	521	527	529	466	224	284
Current Ratio	1.3	1.4	1.2	1.2	1.2	1.1	1.0	0.8	0.7	0.8
% Long Term Debt of Capitalization	60.1	61.4	58.2	63.6	85.0	100.2	117.1	130.5	174.6	165.0
% Net Income of Revenue	4.8	5.4	3.3	4.7	4.8	4.0	4.1	3.7	0.5	2.0
% Return on Assets	7.6	8.1	4.9	7.4	7.4	6.2	6.7	6.0	0.9	3.3
% Return on Equity	58.6	60.0	38.1	85.9	531.1	NM	NM	NM	NM	NM

Data as orig reptd.; bef. results of disc opers/spec. items. Per share data adj. for stk. divs.; EPS diluted. E-Estimated. NA-Not Available. NM-Not Meaningful. NR-Not Ranked. UR-Under Review.

Office: 1 Centennial Ave, Piscataway, NJ 08855-6820.
Telephone: 732-980-6000.
Website: http://www.americanstandard.com
Chrmn & CEO: F.M. Poses

SVP & CFO: G. D'Aloia
SVP, Secy & General Counsel: M.E. Gustafsson
VP & Treas: D.S. Kuhl
Investor Contact: E. Schlesinger (888-273-6397)

Board Members: S. E. Anderson, J. L. Cohon, P. J. Curlander, S. F. Goldstone, K. S. Hachigian, E. E. Hagenlocker, J. F. Hardymon, R. Marshall, D. F. Morrison, F. M. Poses

Founded: 1899
Domicile: Delaware
Employees: 29,000

Transocean Inc

STANDARD &POOR'S

S&P Recommendation	**BUY** ★★★★☆	Price	12-Mo. Target Price	Investment Style
		$135.92 (as of Nov 29, 2007)	$164.00	Large-Cap Blend

GICS Sector Energy
Sub-Industry Oil & Gas Drilling

Summary RIG is a leading provider of contract drilling services for the oil and gas industry, with the world's largest fleet of mobile offshore drilling units.

Key Stock Statistics (Source S&P, Vickers, company reports)

52-Wk Range	$187.98–103.59	S&P Oper. EPS 2007**E**	8.41	Market Capitalization(B)	$43.223	Beta	1.11
Trailing 12-Month EPS	$12.70	S&P Oper. EPS 2008**E**	14.26	Yield (%)	Nil	S&P 3-Yr. Proj. EPS CAGR(%)	60.00
Trailing 12-Month P/E	10.7	P/E on S&P Oper. EPS 2007**E**	16.2	Dividend Rate/Share	Nil	S&P Credit Rating	NA
$10K Invested 5 Yrs Ago	$52,053	Common Shares Outstg. (M)	318.0	Institutional Ownership (%)	89		

Price Performance

- 30-Week Mov. Avg. · · · 10-Week Mov. Avg. - - **GAAP Earnings vs. Previous Year** Volume Above Avg. STARS
- 12-Mo. Target Price — Relative Strength ▲ Up ▼ Down ► No Change Below Avg. ★

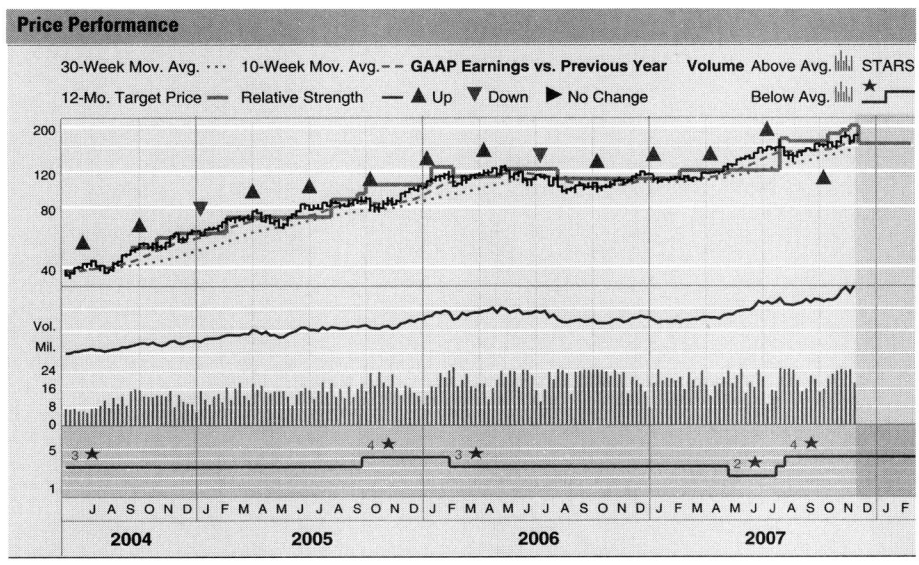

Options: ASE, CBOE, P, Ph

Qualitative Risk Assessment

LOW	MEDIUM	HIGH

Our risk assessment reflects RIG's exposure to volatile crude oil and natural gas prices, capital spending decisions by oil and gas producing customers, and risks associated with operating in frontier regions. Offsetting these risks is RIG's leadership position in deepwater drilling.

Quantitative Evaluations

S&P Quality Ranking   B-

D	C	B-	B	B+	A-	A	A+

Relative Strength Rank   WEAK

17	

LOWEST = 1   HIGHEST = 99

Revenue/Earnings Data

Revenue (Million $)

	1Q	2Q	3Q	4Q	Year
2007	1,328	1,434	1,538	--	--
2006	817.0	854.0	1,025	1,186	3,882
2005	630.5	727.4	762.6	771.2	2,892
2004	652.0	633.2	651.8	676.9	2,614
2003	616.0	603.9	622.9	591.5	2,434
2002	667.9	646.2	695.2	664.6	2,674

Earnings Per Share ($)

	1Q	2Q	3Q	4Q	Year
2007	2.63	2.63	4.63	E2.44	E8.41
2006	0.87	1.07	1.37	2.93	6.12
2005	0.40	1.29	0.71	0.64	3.04
2004	0.10	0.21	0.69	-0.33	0.67
2003	0.21	-0.20	0.04	0.03	0.09
2002	0.34	0.36	1.13	-12.45	-10.61

Fiscal year ended Dec. 31. Next earnings report expected: Mid February. EPS Estimates based on S&P Operating Earnings; historical GAAP earnings are as reported.

Highlights

➤ The 12-month target price for RIG has recently been changed to $164.00 from $202.00. The Highlights section of this Stock Report will be updated accordingly.

Investment Rationale/Risk

➤ The Investment Rationale/Risk section of this Stock Report will be updated shortly. For the latest News story on RIG from MarketScope, see below.

➤ 11/29/07 01:51 pm EST... S&P REITERATES BUY OPINION ON SHARES OF TRANSOCEAN, RAISES TARGET PRICE (RIG 135.35****): Leading offshore driller RIG has completed the merger with former rival GlobalSantaFe, previously the #2 player in this niche. In order to resolve U.K. antitrust concerns, the two parties agreed to divest two floater rigs currently working in the North Sea. Updating our models to reflect the net addition of GlobalSantaFe rigs, we are raising our '08 EPS estimate by $2.34 to $14.26. Based on an assumed 8X projected '08 EBITDA, 12X '08 P/E (above peers, merited in our view by strength in deepwater drilling), and our NAV model, we are raising our 12-mo target price by $23, to $164. /S. Glickman

Dividend Data (Dates: mm/dd Payment Date: mm/dd/yy)

Amount ($)	Date Decl.	Ex-Div. Date	Stk. of Record	Payment Date
0.6996-for-1 REV.	--	11/27	--	11/27/07

Source: Company reports.

Please read the Required Disclosures and Analyst Certification on the last page of this report.

The McGraw-Hill Companies

Transocean Inc

STANDARD &POOR'S

Business Summary November 12, 2007

CORPORATE OVERVIEW. Transocean (formerly Transocean Sedco Forex), the world's largest offshore drilling company, acquired R&B Falcon (FLC) on January 31, 2001, for about $9.6 billion. In May 2002, the company adopted its current name. Transocean Sedco Forex had been formed in December 1999, upon the merger of Transocean Offshore and Sedco Forex Holdings (the former offshore contract drilling unit of Schlumberger). RIG focuses mainly on deepwater drilling activity, where the deepwater sector is defined by the company as that which begins in water depths of 4,500 ft., and extending to practical maximum depth, which is currently at about 10,000 ft. of water. The mid-water market typically covers water depths of 400 ft. to 4,500 ft., while the shallow water market covers water depths of up to 400 ft.

COMPETITIVE LANDSCAPE. RIG's addressable market for offshore drilling rigs is global in nature, given that rigs can be mobilized from region to region.

Active offshore drilling regions around the globe include the U.S. Gulf of Mexico, the North Sea, West Africa, Southeast Asia, the Mediterranean, the Caspian Sea, and the Middle East. With 78 actively marketed mobile offshore drilling rigs as of March 2007, RIG is the leading player in this market. Of the 78 rigs, 53 are "floater" rigs--semisubmersibles and drillships--of which 28 are rated for deepwater drilling. The company has the vast majority of its drilling rigs located in seven regions: Northwest Europe (12 rigs), the U.S. Gulf of Mexico (10), Southeast Asia (11), India (12) West Africa (13), South America (7), and Egypt/the Middle East/the Mediterranean (6).

Company Financials Fiscal Year Ended Dec. 31

Per Share Data ($)	2006	2005	2004	2003	2002	2001	2000	1999	1998	1997
Tangible Book Value	22.71	25.41	22.86	22.23	22.04	19.93	20.13	26.60	18.52	13.28
Cash Flow	7.86	4.72	2.97	2.35	-8.37	4.07	2.48	1.29	6.52	3.41
Earnings	6.12	3.04	0.67	0.09	-10.61	1.23	0.71	0.76	4.87	1.97
Dividends	Nil	Nil	Nil	Nil	0.09	0.17	0.17	0.17	0.17	0.17
Payout Ratio	Nil	Nil	Nil	Nil	NM	14%	24%	23%	4%	9%
Prices:High	128.87	101.39	61.82	37.02	56.18	82.46	93.62	52.17	85.67	86.48
Prices:Low	92.22	56.88	33.02	26.30	25.87	32.95	41.81	28.05	32.88	37.34
P/E Ratio:High	21	33	92	NM	NM	67	NM	69	18	44
P/E Ratio:Low	15	19	49	NM	NM	27	NM	37	7	19

Income Statement Analysis (Million $)										
Revenue	3,882	2,892	2,614	2,434	2,674	2,820	1,230	648	1,090	892
Operating Income	1,637	1,096	821	759	1,114	1,159	375	181	577	320
Depreciation, Depletion and Amortization	401	406	525	508	500	625	259	132	117	103
Interest Expense	115	111	172	202	212	224	3.03	10.3	23.9	22.9
Pretax Income	1,607	802	240	21.6	-2,489	361	144	48.8	487	207
Effective Tax Rate	13.8%	10.8%	38.0%	13.9%	NM	23.8%	25.4%	NM	29.5%	31.5%
Net Income	1,385	716	152	18.4	-2,368	272	107	58.1	343	142

Balance Sheet & Other Financial Data (Million $)										
Cash	467	445	451	474	1,214	853	34.5	166	69.5	54.2
Current Assets	1,656	1,279	1,109	1,179	1,912	1,737	448	559	362	307
Total Assets	11,476	10,457	10,758	11,663	12,665	17,020	6,359	6,140	3,251	2,755
Current Liabilities	1,039	924	430	511	1,504	1,144	495	529	192	185
Long Term Debt	3,200	1,197	2,462	3,612	3,630	4,539	1,430	1,188	814	728
Common Equity	6,836	7,982	7,393	7,193	7,141	10,910	4,004	3,910	1,979	1,621
Total Capital	10,094	9,247	9,983	10,848	10,879	15,767	5,794	5,482	3,023	2,521
Capital Expenditures	876	182	127	496	141	506	575	537	573	406
Cash Flow	1,786	1,121	677	527	-1,868	897	367	190	460	245
Current Ratio	1.6	1.4	2.6	2.3	1.3	1.5	0.9	1.1	1.9	1.7
% Long Term Debt of Capitalization	31.7	12.9	24.7	33.3	33.4	28.7	24.7	21.7	26.9	28.9
% Return on Assets	12.6	6.7	1.4	0.2	NM	2.3	1.7	1.5	11.4	5.5
% Return on Equity	18.7	9.3	2.1	0.3	NM	3.6	2.7	2.6	19.1	8.7

Data as orig reptd.; bef. results of disc opers/spec. items. Per share data adj. for stk. divs.; EPS diluted. E-Estimated. NA-Not Available. NM-Not Meaningful. NR-Not Ranked. UR-Under Review.

Office: 4 Greenway Plaza, Houston, TX 77046.
Telephone: 713-232-7500.
Email: lmilner@mail.deepwater.com
Website: http://www.deepwater.com

Chrmn: J.M. Talbert
Pres: J.P. Cahuzac
CEO: R.L. Long
COO & EVP: S.L. Newman

SVP & CFO: G.L. Cauthen
Investor Contact: G.S. Panagos (713-232-7500)
Board Members: V. E. Grijalva, M. A. Hellerstein, J. J. Kelly, A. Lindenauer, R. Long, M. E. McMahon, M. B. McNamara, R. L. Monti, K. Siem, R. M. Sprague, I. C. Strachan, J. M. Talbert

Founded: 1953
Domicile: Cayman Islands
Employees: 12,500

Travelers Companies Inc (The)

STANDARD &POOR'S

S&P Recommendation **BUY** ★★★★☆	Price $51.61 (as of Nov 23, 2007)	12-Mo. Target Price $60.00	Investment Style Large-Cap Value

GICS Sector Financials
Sub-Industry Property & Casualty Insurance

Summary Formed via the 2004 merger of Travelers Property Casualty Corp. and Saint Paul Cos., TRV is a leading provider of commercial property-liability and homeowners and auto insurance.

Key Stock Statistics (Source S&P, Vickers, company reports)

52-Wk Range	$56.99– 47.26	S&P Oper. EPS 2007**E**	6.55	Market Capitalization(B)	$33.286	Beta	1.04
Trailing 12-Month EPS	$6.90	S&P Oper. EPS 2008**E**	6.15	Yield (%)	2.25	S&P 3-Yr. Proj. EPS CAGR(%)	NA
Trailing 12-Month P/E	7.5	P/E on S&P Oper. EPS 2007**E**	7.9	Dividend Rate/Share	$1.16	S&P Credit Rating	A-
$10K Invested 5 Yrs Ago	$33,301	Common Shares Outstg. (M)	645.0	Institutional Ownership (%)	87		

Price Performance

30-Week Mov. Avg. ···· 10-Week Mov. Avg. – – GAAP Earnings vs. Previous Year Volume Above Avg. STARS
12-Mo. Target Price — Relative Strength — ▲ Up ▼ Down ► No Change Below Avg. ★

Options: ASE, CBOE, Ph

Analysis prepared by **Cathy A. Seifert** on November 16, 2007, when the stock traded at **$ 52.72**.

Qualitative Risk Assessment

LOW	**MEDIUM**	HIGH

Our risk assessment reflects our view of TRV as a leading property-casualty underwriter with a diversified mix of business and sound capital management practices. Offsetting this is our view that TRV may have to add to loss reserves for certain "long tail" liability lines of coverage; and could see impairments to its fixed income investment portfolio..

Quantitative Evaluations

S&P Quality Ranking NR

D	C	B-	B	B+	A-	A	A+

Relative Strength Rank STRONG

75

LOWEST = 1 HIGHEST = 99

Revenue/Earnings Data

Revenue (Million $)

	1Q	2Q	3Q	4Q	Year
2007	6,427	6,612	6,526	--	--
2006	6,050	6,255	6,316	6,469	25,090
2005	6,105	6,037	6,042	6,181	24,365
2004	4,128	6,181	6,261	6,365	22,934
2003	3,603	3,749	3,746	4,042	15,139
2002	3,233	3,320	3,564	4,153	14,270

Earnings Per Share ($)

2007	1.56	1.86	1.81	E1.47	E6.55
2006	1.41	1.36	1.47	1.68	5.91
2005	1.25	1.33	0.11	0.26	2.95
2004	1.34	-0.42	0.50	0.44	1.53
2003	0.34	0.44	0.42	0.49	1.68
2002	0.43	0.33	0.33	-0.79	0.23

Fiscal year ended Dec. 31. Next earnings report expected: Early February. EPS Estimates based on S&P Operating Earnings; historical GAAP earnings are as reported.

Highlights

➤ We expect earned premium growth (from continuing operations) of 3% to 5% in 2008, versus growth of 4% to 5% forecasted for 2007. Earned premiums rose 7% in 2005. The rate of growth we expect for TRV is slightly ahead of what we forecast for the entire property-casualty industry. We attribute this to TRV's mix of business, partly offset by some heightened price competition.

➤ Total revenue growth in 2008 will likely be aided by an expected double-digit rise in net investment income. We think underwriting results in 2008 could deteriorate slightly from unusually favorable results posted in 2007. However, an expected uptick in catastrophe claims may be offset by continued favorable prior-year loss trends in certain casualty lines.

➤ We estimate operating EPS of $6.55 in 2007 and $6.15 in 2008. This compares with operating EPS of $5.90 for 2006; $2.90 in operating EPS from continuing operations was reported in 2005. Our operating EPS estimates assume a "normal" level of catastrophe losses and no significant reserve boosts.

Investment Rationale/Risk

➤ Our buy recommendation reflects our view that TRV's shares are undervalued on a price/ tangible book and price/earnings basis, versus most of its peers. We are encouraged by what we see as TRV's improved underwriting results, and by TRV's ability to withstand what we see as heightened competitive pressures. We believe a continuation of favorable loss trends in many of TRV's casualty lines will provide the shares with a catalyst, in our view.

➤ Risks to our recommendation and target price include a deterioration in asbestos and environmental claims and reserve development, an erosion in underwriting trends, a surge in catastrophe losses, and an erosion in the credit quality of TRV's investment portfolio.

➤ Our 12-month target price of $60 assumes a forward price/tangible book value multiple of approximately 1.7X our estimate of 2008 year-end tangible book value, which is closer to the peer group average. We believe this expansion is warranted in light of the improved underwriting trends that we see emerging.

Dividend Data (Dates: mm/dd Payment Date: mm/dd/yy)

Amount ($)	Date Decl.	Ex-Div. Date	Stk. of Record	Payment Date
0.260	02/07	03/07	03/09	03/30/07
0.290	05/02	06/06	06/08	06/29/07
0.290	08/01	09/06	09/10	09/28/07
0.290	11/06	12/06	12/10	12/31/07

Dividends have been paid since 2003. Source: Company reports.

Travelers Companies Inc (The)

STANDARD &POOR'S

CORPORATE OVERVIEW. TRV is a leading property-casualty underwriter. Net written premiums of $21.2 billion in 2006 were divided as follows: business insurance 52%; personal lines 32%; and financial, professional and international lines 16%.

The business insurance lines segment offers a broad array of coverages that are distributed through approximately 6,300 independent brokers and agencies throughout the United States. Business insurance net written premiums totaled $11.0 billion in 2006 and were divided as follows: commercial multi-peril 28%, workers' compensation 19%, commercial automobile 18%, commercial property 18%, and general liability and other 17%. This segment's underwriting results in 2006 improved amid a lower level of catastrophe losses and some favorable reserve development. As such, the combined loss and expense ratio improved to 90.9% in 2006, from 110.4% in 2005.

The financial, professional and international segment underwrites a number of specialized lines of business, including lines of coverage related to the surety bond business, the construction industry, and certain types of professional and managerial liability lines of coverage. This unit operates throughout the U.S. and in the United Kingdom, Canada and Ireland. Net written premiums totaled $3.4 billion in 2006 and were divided as follows: general liability 30%, fidelity and surety 33%, international 33%, and other 4%. During 2006, the bond and financial products business (including surety bonds) accounted for 66% of this unit's premium volume, while international and Lloyd's of London business for the remaining 34%. Underwriting results in this segment improved in 2006, as evidenced by the combined loss and expense ratio of 89.0% in 2006, compared with 92.5% in 2005.

The personal lines segment underwrites an array of coverage for personal risks (primarily personal automobile and homeowners' coverage) via a network of independent agencies. Net premiums written of $6.7 billion in 2006 were divided as follows: personal auto 55% and homeowners' and other 45%. At year-end 2006, automobile policies in force increased to about 2.6 million (from 2.3 million in 2005), while homeowners' and other policies in force rose to 4.6 million (from 4.2 million in 2005). Underwriting results in 2006 improved, as lower loss costs (primarily due to lower catastrophe losses) offset the impact of higher underwriting expenses. As a result, the combined ratio ended 2006 at 83.1%, versus 89.1% at the end of 2005.

Company Financials Fiscal Year Ended Dec. 31

Per Share Data ($)	2006	2005	2004	2003	2002	2001	2000	1999	1998	1997
Tangible Book Value	31.85	25.66	20.93	9.52	10.29	6.66	NA	NA	NA	NA
Operating Earnings	NA	NA	NA	NA	NA	NA	NA	NA	NA	NA
Earnings	5.91	2.95	1.53	1.68	0.23	1.06	NA	NA	NA	NA
S&P Core Earnings	5.87	2.87	1.50	3.71	0.14	2.42	NA	NA	NA	NA
Dividends	1.01	0.91	0.74	0.28	Nil	NA	NA	NA	NA	NA
Payout Ratio	17%	31%	48%	17%	Nil	NA	NA	NA	NA	NA
Prices:High	55.00	46.97	43.31	17.42	19.50	NA	NA	NA	NA	NA
Prices:Low	40.23	33.70	16.55	12.98	12.09	NA	NA	NA	NA	NA
P/E Ratio:High	9	16	28	10	85	NA	NA	NA	NA	NA
P/E Ratio:Low	7	11	11	8	53	NA	NA	NA	NA	NA

Income Statement Analysis (Million $)										
Premium Income	20,760	20,341	19,038	12,545	11,155	9,411	NA	NA	NA	NA
Net Investment Income	3,517	3,165	2,663	1,869	1,881	2,034	NA	NA	NA	NA
Other Revenue	813	859	20,271	725	1,234	786	NA	NA	NA	NA
Total Revenue	25,090	24,365	22,934	15,139	14,270	12,231	NA	NA	NA	NA
Pretax Income	5,725	2,671	1,128	2,229	-260	1,389	NA	NA	NA	NA
Net Operating Income	NA	NA	NA	NA	NA	NA	NA	NA	NA	NA
Net Income	4,208	2,061	955	1,696	216	1,062	NA	NA	NA	NA
S&P Core Earnings	4,171	2,001	937	1,615	41.1	803	NA	NA	NA	NA

Balance Sheet & Other Financial Data (Million $)										
Cash & Equivalent	1,286	1,098	933	714	432	NA	NA	NA	NA	NA
Premiums Due	6,181	6,124	6,201	4,090	3,861	NA	NA	NA	NA	NA
Investment Assets:Bonds	62,666	58,983	54,256	33,046	30,003	NA	NA	NA	NA	NA
Investment Assets:Stocks	476	579	791	733	852	NA	NA	NA	NA	NA
Investment Assets:Loans	Nil	145	191	211	258	32,843	NA	NA	NA	NA
Investment Assets:Total	72,268	68,287	64,710	38,652	38,425	NA	NA	NA	NA	NA
Deferred Policy Costs	1,615	1,527	1,559	925	873	NA	NA	NA	NA	NA
Total Assets	113,761	113,187	111,815	64,872	64,138	57,599	NA	NA	NA	NA
Debt	4,588	5,850	5,709	2,675	2,744	3,755	NA	NA	NA	NA
Common Equity	25,006	33,077	32,323	11,987	10,137	9,729	NA	NA	NA	NA
Property & Casualty:Loss Ratio	575.0	71.9	NA	NA	NA	80.7	NA	NA	NA	NA
Property & Casualty:Expense Ratio	30.6	29.4	NA	NA	NA	27.3	NA	NA	NA	NA
Property & Casualty Combined Ratio	88.1	101.3	107.7	96.9	117.4	108.0	NA	NA	NA	NA
% Return on Revenue	20.3	8.5	4.2	11.2	1.6	8.7	NA	NA	NA	NA
% Return on Equity	17.8	6.3	3.7	15.3	NA	NA	NA	NA	NA	NA

Data as orig reptd.; bef. results of disc opers/spec. items. Per share data adj. for stk. divs.; EPS diluted. E-Estimated. NA-Not Available. NM-Not Meaningful. NR-Not Ranked. UR-Under Review.

Office: 385 Washington Street, Saint Paul, MN 55102.
Telephone: 651-310-7911.
Website: http://www.stpaultravelers.com
Chrmn, Pres & CEO: J.S. Fishman

Vice Chrmn: C.J. Clarke
Vice Chrmn: W.H. Heyman
Vice Chrmn: I.R. Ettinger
Vice Chrmn & CFO: J.S. Benet

Investor Contact: M. Parr (860-277-0779)
Board Members: J. H. Dasburg, L. B. Disharoon, J. M. Dolan, K. M. Duberstein, J. S. Fishman, L. G. Graev, T. R. Hodgson, R. I. Lipp, B. J. McGarvie, G. D. Nelson, L. J. Thomsen

Auditor: KPMG, Minneapolis, MN
Founded: 1853
Domicile: Minnesota
Employees: 32,800

The McGraw·Hill Companies

Tribune Co

STANDARD &POOR'S

S&P Recommendation BUY ★★★★☆	**Price** $30.00 (as of Nov 28, 2007)	**12-Mo. Target Price** $34.00	**Investment Style** Large-Cap Blend

GICS Sector Consumer Discretionary
Sub-Industry Publishing

Summary This leading media company has interests in radio and television broadcasting, newspaper publishing, and the Internet. In April 2007, TRB announced plans to go private.

Key Stock Statistics (Source S&P, Vickers, company reports)

52-Wk Range	$33.30– 22.78	S&P Oper. EPS 2007**E**	1.68	Market Capitalization(B)	$3.553	Beta	0.75
Trailing 12-Month EPS	$1.80	S&P Oper. EPS 2008**E**	1.74	Yield (%)	2.40	S&P 3-Yr. Proj. EPS CAGR(%)	-2.00
Trailing 12-Month P/E	16.7	P/E on S&P Oper. EPS 2007**E**	17.9	Dividend Rate/Share	$0.72	S&P Credit Rating	BB-
$10K Invested 5 Yrs Ago	$6,662	Common Shares Outstg. (M)	118.4	Institutional Ownership (%)	68		

Price Performance

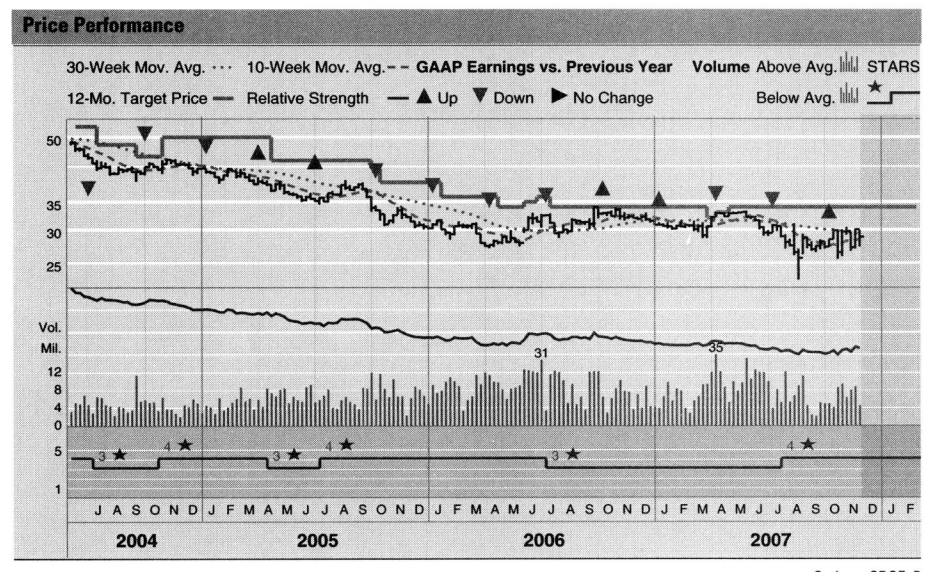

Options: CBOE, P

Analysis prepared by **James Peters, CFA** on October 25, 2007, when the stock traded at **$ 29.10**.

Highlights

➤ We see a modest revenue decline of about 1% in 2008, following a drop of about 6.7% we see for 2007. We expect improvement in the company's broadcast segment on the heels of new programming introductions in the fall of 2007, and from higher anticipated advertising rates that we believe will result from lower overall television advertising inventory once political advertising resumes ahead of 2008 elections. We expect cyclical and secular weakness to result in further print classified advertising, though to a lesser extent than the 19% drop we forecast for 2007.

➤ We expect TRB to continue reducing its cost structure and redeploying resources to areas of growth as it focuses on meeting debt covenants associated with its plan to go private. As a stand alone entity, we anticipate an operating margin expansion in 2008 to 19.3% from our forecast of 18.6% for 2007.

➤ Incorporating significantly fewer shares, higher interest expense and higher anticipated equity income, we forecast 2008 EPS of $1.74. Our forecast assumes TRB continues as a publicly traded entity, although we expect the company to go private at the end of 2007.

Investment Rationale/Risk

➤ TRB completed a tender offer for 52% of its outstanding shares in June as part of a proposal announced on April 2 to go private. In August, shareholders overwhelmingly approved the proposal. Pending necessary approvals, the company's employee stock ownership plan (ESOP) would merge with TRB and repurchase all remaining TRB shares at $34 per share by year end. The shares were recently trading about 15% below the announced deal price, reflecting concerns about TRB's ability to meet debt covenants given a sharply declining operating environment, in our opinion. However, on August 21, the company reiterated that financing is fully committed, and we continue to believe the deal will be consummated.

➤ Risks to our recommendation and target price include failure to gain the needed approvals or financing to allow TRB to consummate its plan to go private.

➤ Our 12-month target price of $34 represents our belief that TRB is likely to go private for $34 per share. Our valuation is supported by our DCF valuation of $32 that incorporates assumptions of a 6.6% WACC and 3.0% terminal growth.

Qualitative Risk Assessment

LOW	MEDIUM	**HIGH**

Our risk assessment reflects a highly competitive environment for advertising among broadcasters, publishers and other media, an uncertain regulatory outlook for cross-media ownership, and uncertainty we see regarding obtaining necessary approvals as well as financing for the proposed transaction to take Tribune private.

Quantitative Evaluations

S&P Quality Ranking   B

D	C	B-	**B**	B+	A-	A	A+

Relative Strength Rank   **STRONG**

89

LOWEST = 1   HIGHEST = 99

Revenue/Earnings Data

Revenue (Million $)

	1Q	2Q	3Q	4Q	Year
2007	1,215	1,313	1,277	--	--
2006	1,299	1,432	1,349	1,467	5,518
2005	1,316	1,462	1,403	1,415	5,596
2004	1,332	1,496	1,414	1,484	5,726
2003	1,290	1,450	1,386	1,470	5,595
2002	1,234	1,381	1,340	1,430	5,384

Earnings Per Share ($)

2007	0.05	0.17	0.69	--	E1.68
2006	0.33	0.53	0.65	0.96	2.39
2005	0.44	0.73	0.07	0.43	1.67
2004	0.35	0.29	0.37	0.72	1.72
2003	0.41	0.67	0.53	1.00	2.61
2002	0.18	0.33	0.71	0.57	1.80

Fiscal year ended Dec. 31. Next earnings report expected: Early February. EPS Estimates based on S&P Operating Earnings; historical GAAP earnings are as reported.

Dividend Data (Dates: mm/dd Payment Date: mm/dd/yy)

Amount ($)	Date Decl.	Ex-Div. Date	Stk. of Record	Payment Date
0.180	10/18	11/28	11/30	12/14/06
0.180	02/13	02/20	02/22	03/08/07

Dividends have been paid since 1902. Source: Company reports.

Please read the Required Disclosures and Analyst Certification on the last page of this report.

The **McGraw·Hill** Companies

Tribune Co

STANDARD &POOR'S

Business Summary October 25, 2007

CORPORATE OVERVIEW. Tribune Company is a media and entertainment company engaged through its subsidiaries in newspaper publishing, television and radio broadcasting and entertainment. The company's operations are divided into two segments: publishing (74% of 2006 revenues) and broadcasting and entertainment (26%).

About 80% of 2006 publishing segment revenues came from the sale of advertising in newspapers and interactive Web sites, 14% from the sale of newspapers, and about 6% from a variety of other activities. Tribune Publishing's primary daily newspapers include the Los Angeles Times, Chicago Tribune, Newsday (New York), South Florida Sun-Sentinel, the Orlando Sentinel, The Sun (Baltimore), The Morning Call (Pennsylvania), The Hartford Courant, The Advocate (Stamford), Greenwich Time, and Daily Press (VA). The publishing segment also manages the Web sites of the company's daily newspapers and television stations, as well as other branded sites targeting specific communities of interest.

The broadcasting and entertainment segment consists of 23 television stations, one radio station, the Chicago Cubs, and Tribune Entertainment, a company that develops and distributes first-run television programming for the

company's station group and national syndication. In 2006, 83% of segment revenues came from TV, with the remaining 17% from radio and entertainment. Fourteen of the company's stations are affiliated with The CW Network, six are affiliated with FOX, two with MyNetworkTV (MNTV), and one with ABC. The company sold three television stations in the second half of 2006, located in Atlanta, Albany and Boston, for an aggregate total of $311 million.

In 2006, the company repurchased 71 million of its shares outstanding for $2.3 billion, including 45 million shares repurchased as part of a tender offer initiated in May 2006, and 10 million shares bought from the McCormick Tribune Foundation and Cantigny Foundation in July 2006.

In September 2005, TRB announced an adverse U.S. tax court ruling on its 1998 tax-free reorganization; the company appealed the decision but also issued commercial paper to cover an estimated net cash liability of $840 million for this and a similar transaction.

Company Financials Fiscal Year Ended Dec. 31

Per Share Data ($)	2006	2005	2004	2003	2002	2001	2000	1999	1998	1997
Tangible Book Value	NM	NM	NM	NM	NM	NM	NM	NM	NM	NA
Cash Flow	3.70	2.51	2.52	3.26	2.43	1.82	2.27	6.44	2.21	2.02
Earnings	2.39	1.67	1.72	2.61	1.80	0.28	0.99	5.62	1.51	1.41
S&P Core Earnings	2.19	1.35	1.64	2.02	1.06	0.05	NA	NA	NA	NA
Dividends	0.72	0.72	0.48	0.44	0.44	0.44	0.40	0.36	0.34	0.32
Payout Ratio	30%	43%	28%	17%	24%	157%	40%	6%	23%	23%
Prices:High	34.28	42.17	53.00	51.77	49.49	45.90	55.19	60.88	37.53	31.34
Prices:Low	27.09	30.05	39.20	41.60	35.66	29.71	27.88	30.16	22.38	17.75
P/E Ratio:High	14	25	31	20	27	NM	56	11	25	22
P/E Ratio:Low	11	18	23	16	20	NM	28	5	15	13

Income Statement Analysis (Million $)										
Revenue	5,518	5,596	5,726	5,595	5,384	5,253	4,910	3,222	2,981	2,720
Operating Income	1,314	1,391	1,451	1,589	1,499	1,244	1,404	993	898	815
Depreciation	229	244	233	228	223	442	371	222	196	173
Interest Expense	274	155	153	198	213	255	241	113	88.5	86.5
Pretax Income	1,009	1,110	941	1,415	940	269	597	526	705	659
Effective Tax Rate	34.5%	51.8%	39.1%	37.0%	35.3%	58.7%	45.3%	NM	41.2%	40.3%
Net Income	661	535	573	891	609	111	310	1,483	414	394
S&P Core Earnings	597	424	536	669	337	17.1	NA	NA	NA	NA

Balance Sheet & Other Financial Data (Million $)										
Cash	175	151	124	248	106	65.8	116	631	12.4	66.6
Current Assets	1,377	1,493	1,452	1,605	1,525	1,364	1,491	2,085	945	848
Total Assets	13,401	14,546	14,168	14,280	14,078	14,505	14,676	8,798	5,936	4,778
Current Liabilities	2,547	1,447	1,370	1,264	1,154	1,533	1,449	861	828	706
Long Term Debt	3,576	2,959	2,318	2,350	3,227	3,685	4,007	2,694	1,616	1,521
Common Equity	4,320	6,619	6,730	6,941	5,806	5,294	5,513	3,189	2,063	1,522
Total Capital	9,870	12,037	11,433	11,635	11,448	11,479	12,039	7,415	4,675	3,710
Capital Expenditures	222	206	217	194	187	266	302	135	140	104
Cash Flow	884	770	798	1,095	807	553	681	1,687	591	547
Current Ratio	0.5	1.0	1.1	1.3	1.3	0.9	1.0	2.4	1.1	1.2
% Long Term Debt of Capitalization	36.2	24.6	20.3	20.2	28.2	32.1	33.3	36.3	34.6	41.0
% Net Income of Revenue	12.0	9.6	10.0	15.9	11.3	2.1	6.3	46.0	13.9	14.5
% Return on Assets	4.7	3.7	4.0	6.3	4.3	0.8	2.7	20.1	7.7	9.3
% Return on Equity	12.0	7.9	8.3	13.6	10.5	2.1	7.1	55.8	22.1	27.3

Data as orig reptd.; bef. results of disc opers/spec. items. Per share data adj. for stk. divs.; EPS diluted. E-Estimated. NA-Not Available. NM-Not Meaningful. NR-Not Ranked. UR-Under Review.

Office: 435 North Michigan Avenue, Chicago, IL 60611.
Telephone: 312-222-9100.
Website: http://www.tribune.com
Chrmn, Pres & CEO: D.J. FitzSimons

SVP, Secy & General Counsel: C.H. Kenney
Investor Contact: R. Musil (312-222-3787)
VP & Cntlr: R.M. Mallory

Board Members: D. J. FitzSimons, E. Hernandez, Jr., B. D. Holden, R. S. Morrison, W. A. Osborn, D. S. Taft, M. D. White, S. Zell
Founded: 1847
Domicile: Delaware
Employees: 21,000

The McGraw·Hill Companies

STANDARD &POOR'S

T. Rowe Price Group Inc

S&P Recommendation	**HOLD** ★★★☆☆	Price $59.05 (as of Nov 23, 2007)	12-Mo. Target Price $66.00	Investment Style Large-Cap Growth

GICS Sector Financials
Sub-Industry Asset Management & Custody Banks

Summary This company (formerly T. Rowe Price Associates) operates one of the largest no-load mutual fund complexes in the United States.

Key Stock Statistics (Source S&P, Vickers, company reports)

52-Wk Range	$65.28– 42.53	S&P Oper. EPS 2007E	2.34	Market Capitalization(B)	$15.658	Beta	1.60
Trailing 12-Month EPS	$2.25	S&P Oper. EPS 2008E	2.73	Yield (%)	1.15	S&P 3-Yr. Proj. EPS CAGR(%)	14.00
Trailing 12-Month P/E	26.2	P/E on S&P Oper. EPS 2007E	25.2	Dividend Rate/Share	$0.68	S&P Credit Rating	NA
$10K Invested 5 Yrs Ago	$41,793	Common Shares Outstg. (M)	265.2	Institutional Ownership (%)	67		

Price Performance

30-Week Mov. Avg. ··· 10-Week Mov. Avg. – – **GAAP Earnings vs. Previous Year** Volume Above Avg. |||| STARS
12-Mo. Target Price — Relative Strength — ▲ Up ▼ Down ▶ No Change Below Avg. |||| ★

2-for-1

Options: ASE, CBOE, P, Ph

Analysis prepared by **Matthew Albrecht** on October 30, 2007, when the stock traded at **$ 62.87**.

Highlights

➤ We believe that despite recent market volatility, T. Rowe Price will post growth in assets under management in 2007 of more than 20%, followed by somewhat slower growth in 2008. We think that investors will continue to migrate towards target-date retirement funds, particularly considering the increasing number of defined contribution sponsors opting for automatic enrollment. Global and international funds should also continue to see strong flows due to their recent outperformance of domestic equity funds. We also expect continued flows from customers domiciled outside the U.S., considering the disparity in savings rates and the low penetration of mutual funds. Furthermore, the asset mix is growing more favorable, which should allow fee capture rates to improve.

➤ We expect compensation expense to decrease slightly in this year and next, as the company realizes some leverage in its operating structure, despite modest headcount growth. We anticipate a flat pretax margin in 2007 and 2008, versus 2006, based on a slight uptick in non-compensation costs.

➤ We forecast earnings per share of $2.34 for 2007 and $2.73 for 2008.

Investment Rationale/Risk

➤ We believe that TROW's relative investment performance is strong and will continue to drive net client inflows into its mutual funds and separately managed accounts. We also view favorably the company's low debt levels, as well as its consistently growing dividend payout and recent increase in its share repurchase authorization. The stock has outperformed peers thus far in 2007, but we think that its strong fund performance and consistent flows are appropriately reflected in the current share price.

➤ Risks to our recommendation and target price include stock and bond market volatility. Regarding corporate governance, we view stock option grants as generous, especially given reductions at competitors, and we would like to see more independent directors on the board.

➤ The shares recently traded at 26.7X our 2007 EPS estimate. Our 12-month target price of $66 is equal to 24.2X our 2008 EPS estimate, which is in line with TROW's five year historical P/E multiple, and a premium multiple to peers based on its equity focus and strong fund performance.

Qualitative Risk Assessment

LOW	MEDIUM	HIGH

Our risk assessment reflects the company's strong market share and our view of its consistent net client inflows and impressive relative investment performance, taking into account industry cyclicality.

Quantitative Evaluations

S&P Quality Ranking A

D	C	B-	B	B+	A-	A	A+

Relative Strength Rank STRONG

85

LOWEST = 1 HIGHEST = 99

Revenue/Earnings Data

Revenue (Million $)

	1Q	2Q	3Q	4Q	Year
2007	509.6	551.1	572.2	--	--
2006	429.3	446.0	450.6	489.1	1,819
2005	358.0	364.5	389.6	403.8	1,516
2004	306.5	310.5	317.0	346.4	1,280
2003	219.5	238.3	259.1	364.5	996.5
2002	242.0	240.3	221.6	219.6	925.8

Earnings Per Share ($)

2007	0.51	0.58	0.63	E0.62	E2.34
2006	0.42	0.49	0.46	0.53	1.90
2005	0.35	0.38	0.43	0.43	1.58
2004	0.29	0.30	0.31	0.36	1.26
2003	0.16	0.21	0.26	0.26	0.89
2002	0.21	0.20	0.17	0.19	0.76

Fiscal year ended Dec. 31. Next earnings report expected: Late January. EPS Estimates based on S&P Operating Earnings; historical GAAP earnings are as reported.

Dividend Data (Dates: mm/dd Payment Date: mm/dd/yy)

Amount ($)	Date Decl.	Ex-Div. Date	Stk. of Record	Payment Date
0.170	09/07	09/19	09/21	10/05/07

Dividends have been paid since 1986. Source: Company reports.

Please read the Required Disclosures and Analyst Certification on the last page of this report.

The McGraw-Hill Companies

T. Rowe Price Group Inc

STANDARD
&POOR'S

Business Summary October 30, 2007

CORPORATE OVERVIEW. T. Rowe Price Group (TROW) is the successor to an investment counseling business formed by the late Thomas Rowe Price, Jr. in 1937. It is now the investment adviser to the T. Rowe Price family of no-load mutual funds, and is one of the largest publicly held U.S. mutual fund complexes. At the end of 2006, TROW had about $335 billion in assets under management, up from $270 billion at the end of 2005. At the end of 2006, 80% of assets under management were invested in equity securities, and 20% were invested in bond and money market securities.

T. Rowe Price offers mutual funds that employ a broad range of investment styles, including growth, value, sector-focused, tax-efficient, and quantitative index-oriented approaches. The company's investment approach is based upon a strong commitment to proprietary research, sophisticated risk-management processes, and a strict adherence to stated investment objectives. The company employs both fundamental and quantitative methods in performing security analyses, using internal equity and fixed income investment research capabilities. We believe T. Rowe Price's broad line of no-load mutual funds makes it easy for investors to reallocate assets among funds

(which is not the case at some smaller fund companies), contributing to increased client retention.

All of the company's funds are sold without a sales commission, known as no-load funds. TROW also manages private accounts for individuals and institutions. At the end of 2005, assets under management were sourced about 20%-30% from each of the following: individual U.S. investors, U.S. defined contribution retirement plans, third-party distributors, and institutional investors. Revenues primarily come from investment advisory fees for managing portfolios, which depend largely on the total value and composition of assets under management. At December 31, 2005, the five largest Price funds--Equity Income, Mid-Cap Growth, Growth Stock, Blue Chip Growth, and Small-Cap Stock---accounted for 24% of assets under management and nearly 30% of 2005 investment advisory revenues.

Company Financials Fiscal Year Ended Dec. 31

Per Share Data ($)	2006	2005	2004	2003	2002	2001	2000	1999	1998	1997
Tangible Book Value	6.63	5.21	3.98	2.66	1.91	1.68	1.21	3.18	2.53	2.05
Cash Flow	2.07	1.80	1.48	1.11	0.96	20.71	1.33	1.13	0.80	1.36
Earnings	1.90	1.58	1.26	0.89	0.76	0.76	1.04	0.93	0.67	0.56
S&P Core Earnings	1.90	1.43	1.16	0.78	0.67	0.65	NA	NA	NA	NA
Dividends	0.38	0.49	0.40	0.35	0.33	0.31	0.27	0.20	0.17	0.14
Payout Ratio	20%	31%	32%	40%	43%	40%	26%	22%	25%	25%
Prices:High	48.50	37.70	31.70	23.80	21.35	21.97	24.97	21.63	21.44	18.44
Prices:Low	34.87	27.10	21.92	19.19	10.63	11.72	15.03	12.94	10.44	9.13
P/E Ratio:High	26	24	25	27	28	29	24	23	32	33
P/E Ratio:Low	18	17	17	22	14	15	14	14	16	16

Income Statement Analysis (Million $)										
Income Interest	Nil	Nil	Nil	1.54	3.06	32.8	59.1	37.5	28.5	22.0
Income Other	Nil	Nil	Nil	995	923	995	1,153	999	858	733
Total Income	1,819	1,516	1,280	996	926	1,028	1,212	1,036	886	755
General Expenses	982	814	638	585	552	603	690	589	540	461
Interest Expense	4.30	4.03	3.30	3.29	4.96	12.7	9.72	Nil	Nil	Nil
Depreciation	47.0	42.0	40.0	45.3	50.6	80.5	53.7	32.6	32.6	29.0
Net Income	530	431	337	227	194	196	269	239	174	144
S&P Core Earnings	530	391	309	198	169	167	NA	NA	NA	NA

Balance Sheet & Other Financial Data (Million $)										
Cash	773	804	500	237	111	79.7	80.5	358	284	200
Receivables	224	175	158	121	96.8	104	131	122	101	86.8
Cost of Investments	762	378	329	273	216	154	250	279	220	193
Total Assets	2,765	2,311	1,929	1,547	1,370	1,313	1,469	998	797	646
Loss Reserve	Nil	Nil	Nil	Nil	Nil	Nil	Nil	Nil	Nil	Nil
Short Term Debt	Nil	Nil	Nil	Nil	Nil	Nil	Nil	Nil	Nil	NA
Capitalization:Debt	Nil	Nil	Nil	Nil	Nil	104	312	17.7	Nil	Nil
Capitalization:Equity	2,427	2,036	1,697	1,329	1,189	1,078	991	770	614	487
Capitalization:Total	2,427	2,036	1,697	1,329	1,189	1,181	1,304	848	667	537
Price Times Book Value:High	7.3	7.2	7.9	9.0	11.2	13.1	20.6	6.8	8.5	9.0
Price Times Book Value:Low	5.3	5.2	5.5	7.2	5.6	7.0	12.4	4.1	4.1	4.5
Cash Flow	577	473	377	273	245	276	323	272	207	173
% Expense/Operating Revenue	52.3	56.7	63.8	65.8	65.7	67.8	62.2	60.0	64.7	64.9
% Earnings & Depreciation/Assets	22.7	22.3	21.7	18.7	18.3	19.9	26.2	30.3	28.6	30.8

Data as orig reptd.; bef. results of disc opers/spec. items. Per share data adj. for stk. divs.; EPS diluted. E-Estimated. NA-Not Available. NM-Not Meaningful. NR-Not Ranked. UR-Under Review.

Office: 100 East Pratt Street, Baltimore, MD 21202.
Telephone: 410-345-2000.
Email: info@troweprice.com
Website: http://www.troweprice.com

Chrmn: B.C. Rogers
Pres & CEO: J.A. Kennedy
Vice Chrmn: E.C. Bernard
VP & CFO: K.V. Moreland

Investor Contact: J.P. Croteau (410-345-2000)
Board Members: E. C. Bernard, J. T. Brady, J. A. Broaddus, Jr., D. B. Hebb, Jr., J. A. Kennedy, C., B. C. Rogers, A. Sommer, D. S. Taylor, A. M. Whittemore

Founded: 1937
Domicile: Maryland
Employees: 4,605

Tyco Electronics Ltd

STANDARD &POOR'S

S&P Recommendation HOLD ★★★☆☆	**Price** $35.43 (as of Nov 23, 2007)	**12-Mo. Target Price** $37.00	**Investment Style** Large-Cap Blend

GICS Sector Information Technology
Sub-Industry Electronic Manufacturing Services

Summary This company designs, manufactures and markets engineered electronic components, network solutions, and wireless systems for the automotive, appliances, aerospace and defense, telecommunications, computers and consumer electronics industries.

Key Stock Statistics (Source S&P, Vickers, company reports)

52-Wk Range	$41.28–31.31	S&P Oper. EPS 2007E	2.08	Market Capitalization(B)	$17.560	Beta	NA
Trailing 12-Month EPS	NA	S&P Oper. EPS 2008E	2.44	Yield (%)	1.58	S&P 3-Yr. Proj. EPS CAGR(%)	15.00
Trailing 12-Month P/E	NM	P/E on S&P Oper. EPS 2007E	17.0	Dividend Rate/Share	$0.56	S&P Credit Rating	NA
$10K Invested 5 Yrs Ago	NA	Common Shares Outstg. (M)	495.6	Institutional Ownership (%)	53		

Price Performance

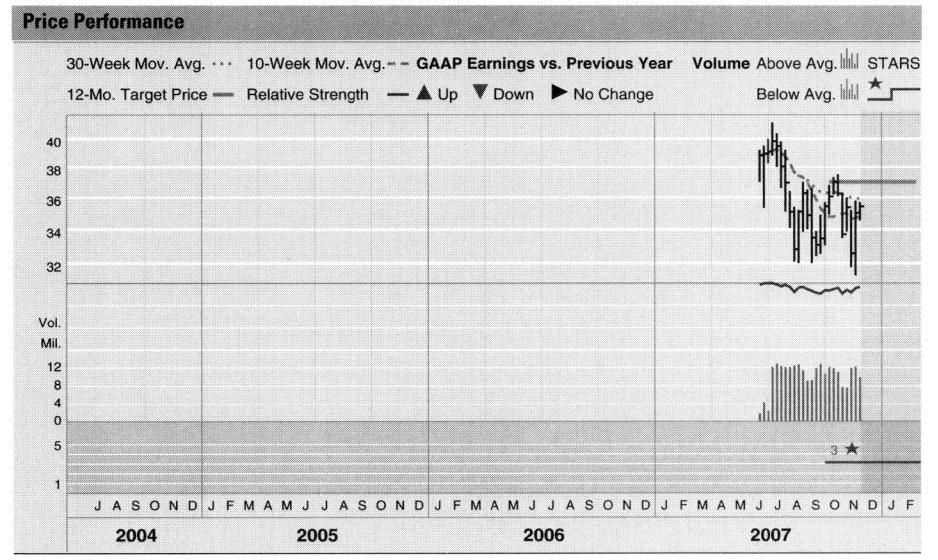

30-Week Mov. Avg. ··· 10-Week Mov. Avg. -- GAAP Earnings vs. Previous Year Volume Above Avg. STARS
12-Mo. Target Price — Relative Strength — ▲ Up ▼ Down ▶ No Change Below Avg. ★

Options: ASE, CBOE, P

Analysis prepared by **Jawahar Hingorani** on November 21, 2007, when the stock traded at **$ 35.20**.

Highlights

➤ Revenues rose 6.1% in the fourth quarter ended September 30, 2007, largely from growth in the undersea communications and wireless segments, offset by declines in the computer segment. We see FY 08 (Sep.) revenues increasing 7%, impacted by weakness in the U.S., and as TEL continues to divest non-strategic businesses, which account for nearly 15% of annual revenues. We think TEL's three-pronged strategy to improve margins by focusing on its portfolio of businesses, optimizing its manufacturing operations, and improving efficiencies is positive, and will bear fruit in the long run.

➤ We see gross profit margins slightly below 25% in FY 08, on lower North American production levels and the overall business mix. We expect operating profit margins to remain above 12% in FY 08, on improving operating efficiencies. We are pleased with free cash flow generation of $545 million and $324 million in the September and June quarters of 2007, respectively.

➤ We forecast FY 08 operating EPS of $2.44 not including one-time charges and costs, a 19% increase over FY 07.

Investment Rationale/Risk

➤ Our hold opinion is based on our view of slow growth in the TEL's main electronics component business, as growth in Asia and Europe is offset by a continuing decline in North America. We think near-term revenues will decline slightly, as the company reorganizes to address additional revenue sources and organic growth after divestitures, offset by double-digit growth in the undersea telecommunications business. We believe gains from moving to low-cost regions and exiting low-margin businesses will be offset by restructuring charges.

➤ Risks to our recommendation and target price include delays in divesting non-strategic businesses, challenges in the macroeconomic environment, and delays in placing its debt offering.

➤ Our 12-month target price of $37 is based on a blend of two valuation metrics. The first, a relative P/E measure, values TEL at 14.75X our FY 08 EPS estimate of $2.44, in line with peers, resulting in a price of $36. The second, our discounted cash flow analysis, uses a weighted average cost of capital of 10.7% and a terminal growth rate of 3%, leading to an intrinsic value of $38.

Qualitative Risk Assessment

LOW	MEDIUM	HIGH

Our risk assessment is based on our view of the company's reliance on cyclical businesses that are largely affected by the North American macroeconomic environment, offset by its efforts to reorganize its operations and target greater profitability. We see TEL's major electronic component business continuing to effect overall mix and profitability.

Quantitative Evaluations

S&P Quality Ranking NR

D	C	B-	B	B+	A-	A	A+

Relative Strength Rank STRONG
84
LOWEST = 1   HIGHEST = 99

Revenue/Earnings Data

Revenue (Million $)

	1Q	2Q	3Q	4Q	Year
2007	--	--	3,412	--	--
2006	--	--	--	--	12,812
2005	--	--	--	--	--
2004	--	--	--	--	--
2003	--	--	--	--	--
2002	--	--	--	--	--

Earnings Per Share ($)

	1Q	2Q	3Q	4Q	Year
2007	--	--	-1.88	E0.57	E2.08
2006	--	--	--	--	2.24
2005	--	--	--	--	--
2004	--	--	--	--	--
2003	--	--	--	--	--
2002	--	--	--	--	--

Fiscal year ended Sep. 30. Next earnings report expected: NA. EPS Estimates based on S&P Operating Earnings; historical GAAP earnings are as reported.

Dividend Data (Dates: mm/dd Payment Date: mm/dd/yy)

Amount ($)	Date Decl.	Ex-Div. Date	Stk. of Record	Payment Date
0.140	09/27	09/28	10/02	11/01/07

Dividends have been paid since 2007. Source: Company reports.

Please read the Required Disclosures and Analyst Certification on the last page of this report.

The McGraw-Hill Companies

Tyco Electronics Ltd

STANDARD &POOR'S

Business Summary November 21, 2007

CORPORATE OVERVIEW. TEL came into existence as a stand-alone entity following the January 13, 2006 decision by the company's former parent, Tyco International, to separate into three companies: Tyco Electronics, Tyco Healthcare, and Tyco International. Subsequently, Tyco Electronics separated from Tyco International on June 29, 2007, and began trading on the NYSE on July 2, 2007.

Tyco Electronics Ltd. designs, manufactures and markets engineered electronic components, network solutions, and wireless systems for customers in the automotive, appliances, aerospace and defense, telecommunications, computers and consumer electronics industries. TEL operates through four reporting segments: Electronic Components, Network Solutions, Wireless Systems, and Other.

Electronic Components supplies passive electronic components, including connectors and interconnect systems, relays, switches, circuit protection devices, touch screens, sensors, and wires and cable, primarily to the automotive, computer, consumer electronics, communication equipment, appliance, aerospace and defense, industrial machinery and instrumentation markets.

Network Solutions is a global supplier of infrastructure components for the telecommunications and energy markets. Its products include connectors, above- and below-ground enclosures, heat shrink tubing, cable accessories, surge arrestors, fiber optic cabling, copper cabling, and racks for copper and fiber networks.

Wireless Systems products include radio frequency and RFID components, radar sensors, microwave subsystems, and land mobile radio systems and networks sold primarily to the aerospace and defense, public safety, communication equipment and automotive markets.

Tyco Electronics also includes several other businesses, which manufacture, distribute, maintain and install power systems and undersea telecommunication systems. The Power Systems business is currently being treated as a discontinued operation.

Company Financials Fiscal Year Ended Sep. 30

Per Share Data ($)	2006	2005	2004	2003	2002	2001	2000	1999	1998	1997
Tangible Book Value	NM	NA	NA	NA	NA	NA	NA	NA	NA	NA
Cash Flow	3.29	NA	NA	NA	NA	NA	NA	NA	NA	NA
Earnings	2.24	NA	NA	NA	NA	NA	NA	NA	NA	NA
Dividends	NA	NA	NA	NA	NA	NA	NA	NA	NA	NA
Payout Ratio	NA	NA	NA	NA	NA	NA	NA	NA	NA	NA
Prices:High	NA	NA	NA	NA	NA	NA	NA	NA	NA	NA
Prices:Low	NA	NA	NA	NA	NA	NA	NA	NA	NA	NA
P/E Ratio:High	NA	NA	NA	NA	NA	NA	NA	NA	NA	NA
P/E Ratio:Low	NA	NA	NA	NA	NA	NA	NA	NA	NA	NA
Income Statement Analysis (Million $)										
Revenue	12,812	NA	NA	NA	NA	NA	NA	NA	NA	NA
Operating Income	2,269	NA	NA	NA	NA	NA	NA	NA	NA	NA
Depreciation	531	NA	NA	NA	NA	NA	NA	NA	NA	NA
Interest Expense	256	NA	NA	NA	NA	NA	NA	NA	NA	NA
Pretax Income	1,201	NA	NA	NA	NA	NA	NA	NA	NA	NA
Effective Tax Rate	2.66%	NA	NA	NA	NA	NA	NA	NA	NA	NA
Net Income	1,163	NA	NA	NA	NA	NA	NA	NA	NA	NA
Balance Sheet & Other Financial Data (Million $)										
Cash	470	NA	NA	NA	NA	NA	NA	NA	NA	NA
Current Assets	6,040	NA	NA	NA	NA	NA	NA	NA	NA	NA
Total Assets	19,091	NA	NA	NA	NA	NA	NA	NA	NA	NA
Current Liabilities	9,142	NA	NA	NA	NA	NA	NA	NA	NA	NA
Long Term Debt	3,371	NA	NA	NA	NA	NA	NA	NA	NA	NA
Common Equity	11,160	NA	NA	NA	NA	NA	NA	NA	NA	NA
Total Capital	14,927	NA	NA	NA	NA	NA	NA	NA	NA	NA
Capital Expenditures	560	NA	NA	NA	NA	NA	NA	NA	NA	NA
Cash Flow	1,694	NA	NA	NA	NA	NA	NA	NA	NA	NA
Current Ratio	1.0	NA	NA	NA	NA	NA	NA	NA	NA	NA
% Long Term Debt of Capitalization	22.6	NA	NA	NA	NA	NA	NA	NA	NA	NA
% Net Income of Revenue	9.1	NA	NA	NA	NA	NA	NA	NA	NA	NA
% Return on Assets	6.2	NA	NA	NA	NA	NA	NA	NA	NA	NA
% Return on Equity	11.1	NA	NA	NA	NA	NA	NA	NA	NA	NA

Data as orig reptd.; bef. results of disc opers/spec. items. Per share data adj. for stk. divs.; EPS diluted. E-Estimated. NA-Not Available. NM-Not Meaningful. NR-Not Ranked. UR-Under Review.

Office: 96 Pitts Bay Road, Pembroke, Bermuda HM 08.
Telephone: 441-294-0607.
Website: http://www.tycoelectronics.com
Chrmn: F.M. Poses

Pres: J.W. Gromer
CEO: T.J. Lynch
EVP & CFO: T.R. Curtin
EVP & General Counsel: R.A. Scott

Investor Contact: J. Roselli (610-893-9559)
Board Members: P. R. Brondeau, R. Charan, J. W. Gromer, R. M. Hernandez, T. J. Lynch, D. J. Phelan, F. M. Poses, L. S. Smith, P. A. Sneed, D. P. Steiner, S. S. Wijnberg

Founded: 2000
Domicile: Bermuda
Employees: 99,600

The McGraw-Hill Companies

Tyco International Ltd

STANDARD &POOR'S

S&P Recommendation HOLD ★★★☆☆	**Price** $39.83 (as of Nov 23, 2007)	**12-Mo. Target Price** $42.00	**Investment Style** Large-Cap Blend

GICS Sector Industrials
Sub-Industry Industrial Conglomerates

Summary Tyco split into three separate publicly traded companies in June 2007, with TYC maintaining its former Fire & Security and Engineered Products divisions.

Key Stock Statistics (Source S&P, Vickers, company reports)

52-Wk Range	$137.92– 37.46	S&P Oper. EPS 2008**E**	2.55	Market Capitalization(B)	$19.740	Beta	2.24
Trailing 12-Month EPS	$-3.52	S&P Oper. EPS 2009**E**	2.85	Yield (%)	1.51	S&P 3-Yr. Proj. EPS CAGR(%)	21.00
Trailing 12-Month P/E	NM	P/E on S&P Oper. EPS 2008**E**	15.6	Dividend Rate/Share	$0.60	S&P Credit Rating	BBB
$10K Invested 5 Yrs Ago	NA	Common Shares Outstg. (M)	495.6	Institutional Ownership (%)	89		

Price Performance

30-Week Mov. Avg. · · · 10-Week Mov. Avg. - - **GAAP Earnings vs. Previous Year** Volume Above Avg. �📊 STARS
12-Mo. Target Price — Relative Strength — ▲ Up ▼ Down ▶ No Change Below Avg. �📊 ★

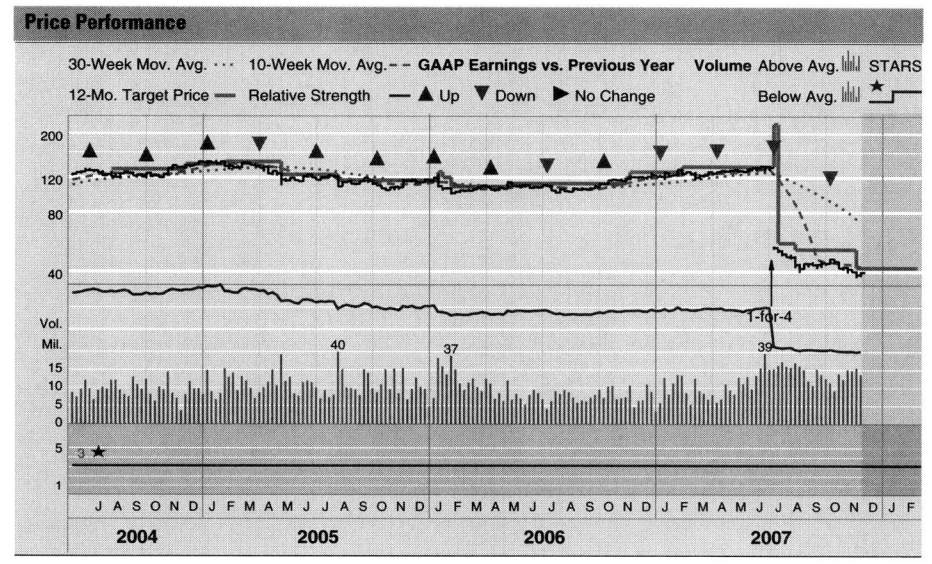

Options: ASE, CBOE, P, Ph

Analysis prepared by **Michael W. Jaffe** on November 16, 2007, when the stock traded at **$ 37.88**.

Highlights

➤ We see revenues from continuing operations increasing 7% in FY 08 (Sep.). We look for the largest percentage gains to come from the Flow Control and Fire Protection areas. We think Flow Control, which makes assorted valves and related equipment, will be assisted by favorable conditions in end markets such as oil and gas, commercial construction, and water and wastewater systems. We see Fire Protection being aided by a greater marketing effort, its large footprint, and its broad offering of products and services. We also see a modest gain at ADT Worldwide, as TYC has taken steps to reduce its attrition rate and to improve the quality of its accounts.

➤ We project wider net margins in FY 08, on the modest revenue gain that we forecast and the steps being taken to improve ADT's business model. We also see results being assisted by Tyco's actions to downsize its corporate office.

➤ Our FY 08 estimate of $2.55 a share compares with EPS from continuing operations of $1.93 in FY 07. The $7.02 a share of one-time charges in FY 07 were primarily a $5.83 a share charge for TYC's $3 billion class action settlement, and $0.85 a share of separation costs.

Investment Rationale/Risk

➤ We think TYC will record high levels of cash flow, especially if it can achieve success in its effort to improve the business model of its ADT security unit. However, we also believe Tyco has some ongoing work to improve what was, in our view, a highly inefficient operating model put together by its former executive team. We believe the shares are near a fair valuation.

➤ Risks to our recommendation and target price include a worse than expected global economy, and management's inability to improve TYC's business model through current initiatives.

➤ The stock recently traded at 15X our calendar 2008 EPS forecast of $2.60, a moderate premium to the S&P 500. We believe the reorganized Tyco merits that small premium, as we think the company's business has been on the right path since Edward Breen's July 2002 appointment as chairman and CEO, and that considerable concerns were resolved by its class action settlement agreement in May 2007. However, we also believe that there is a lack of near-term catalysts to drive the price of TYC's shares. Based on these factors, our 12-month target price is $42, or 16X our calendar 2008 forecast.

Qualitative Risk Assessment

LOW	**MEDIUM**	HIGH

Our risk assessment reflects what we see as strong cash flow characteristics and high levels of recurring revenues in a number of Tyco's businesses. However, the company has also been in the process of trying to repair what we view as an inefficient operating model, which was put together by an executive team that was replaced some five years ago.

Quantitative Evaluations

S&P Quality Ranking B

D	C	B-	**B**	B+	A-	A	A+

Relative Strength Rank WEAK
25
LOWEST = 1 HIGHEST = 99

Revenue/Earnings Data

Revenue (Million $)

	1Q	2Q	3Q	4Q	Year
2007	10,329	10,838	5,085	5,028	18,781
2006	9,603	10,093	10,504	10,760	40,960
2005	10,065	10,456	10,562	10,030	39,727
2004	9,665	9,821	10,225	10,442	40,153
2003	8,927	8,989	9,413	9,473	36,801
2002	8,579	8,611	9,104	9,350	35,644

Earnings Per Share ($)

2007	1.48	1.68	-6.13	0.42	-5.09
2006	1.56	2.08	1.72	2.52	7.88
2005	1.40	0.44	2.24	1.68	6.04
2004	1.36	1.36	1.72	1.08	5.64
2003	1.12	0.24	1.08	-0.44	2.08
2002	1.88	-4.12	-0.92	-3.00	-6.16

Fiscal year ended Sep. 30. Next earnings report expected: Early February. EPS Estimates based on S&P Operating Earnings; historical GAAP earnings are as reported.

Dividend Data (Dates: mm/dd Payment Date: mm/dd/yy)

Amount ($)	Date Decl.	Ex-Div. Date	Stk. of Record	Payment Date
1-for-4 REV.	--	07/02	--	07/02/07
0.150	09/13	09/27	10/01	11/01/07
0.150	09/14	09/27	10/01	11/01/07
Stk.	06/08	--	06/18	06/29/07

Dividends have been paid since 1975. Source: Company reports.

Please read the Required Disclosures and Analyst Certification on the last page of this report.

The McGraw-Hill Companies

Tyco International Ltd

STANDARD
&POOR'S

Business Summary November 16, 2007

CORPORATE OVERVIEW. At the close of trading on June 29, 2007, Tyco International divided its portfolio of businesses into three separate publicly traded companies. TYC maintained the units that had been part of its Fire & Security and Engineered Products & Services divisions, and spun off its Healthcare (now Covidien; COV) and Electronics (trading as Tyco Electronics; TEL) units. The businesses retained by Tyco recorded pro forma revenues of $18.6 billion in FY 06 (Sep.), with the former Fire & Security units accounting for 66% of that total, and the former Engineered Products & Services businesses accounting for 34%; Tyco now divides its businesses into five separate segments. These units derived 50% of their revenues outside the U.S. in FY 06 (latest available).

In the former Fire & Security businesses, Tyco is the world's leading provider of both electronic security services and fire protection contracting and services. Its security services, provided through its ADT Worldwide unit, include the monitoring of burglar alarms, fire alarms, medical alert systems, and other activities where around the clock monitoring and response are required. In fire protection contracting and services, Tyco fabricates, installs and services automatic fire sprinkler systems, fire alarm and detection systems and special hazard suppression systems, as well as respiratory systems and other life-saving devices. TYC's security businesses serve residential, commercial and government customers, and its fire protection units serve commercial and government customers.

The company's former Engineered Products & Services businesses manufacture and service industrial, commercial, water and wastewater valves and related devices; manufacture steel pipe and tubular goods, security fence products and electrical raceway products; provide a broad range of consulting, engineering and construction management and operating services for water, wastewater, environmental, transportation and infrastructure markets; and manufacture and distribute fire sprinkler devices, valves, pipe fittings and couplings used in commercial, residential and industrial fire protection systems.

IMPACT OF MAJOR DEVELOPMENTS. TYC's business separation was accomplished through the payment of tax-free stock dividends to its shareholders. Under the separation, each TYC shareholder received one share of the Covidien health care business and one share of Tyco Electronics for each four TYC shares held as of June 18. In addition, every four shares of the reorganized Tyco were converted into one TYC share in a reverse stock split.

Company Financials Fiscal Year Ended Sep. 30

Per Share Data ($)	2007	2006	2005	2004	2003	2002	2001	2000	1999	1998
Tangible Book Value	NA	10.92	5.56	NM	NM	NM	NM	1.68	0.40	NM
Cash Flow	NA	11.79	9.78	9.35	5.01	-2.09	14.88	14.39	5.62	5.94
Earnings	-5.09	7.88	6.04	5.64	2.08	-6.16	10.20	10.56	2.48	4.04
Dividends	1.90	1.20	1.60	0.20	0.20	0.20	0.20	0.20	0.20	0.20
Payout Ratio	NM	15%	26%	4%	10%	NM	2%	2%	8%	5%
Prices:High	137.92	127.44	146.32	145.68	108.72	235.24	252.84	236.75	215.50	156.36
Prices:Low	37.46	98.60	102.64	104.04	44.80	27.92	156.96	128.00	90.00	80.50
P/E Ratio:High	NM	16	24	26	52	NM	25	22	87	39
P/E Ratio:Low	NM	13	17	18	22	NM	15	12	36	20

Income Statement Analysis (Million $)

	2007	2006	2005	2004	2003	2002	2001	2000	1999	1998
Revenue	NA	40,960	39,727	40,153	36,801	35,644	34,037	28,932	22,497	12,311
Operating Income	NA	7,754	7,637	7,957	5,568	6,509	8,865	7,393	4,977	2,490
Depreciation	NA	2,065	2,100	2,176	1,472	2,033	2,141	1,644	1,322	566
Interest Expense	NA	713	815	963	1,148	1,077	776	845	547	236
Pretax Income	NA	4,884	4,192	4,159	1,803	-2,811	6,004	6,465	1,651	1,718
Effective Tax Rate	NA	16.4%	23.5%	27.4%	42.4%	NM	21.4%	29.8%	37.6%	31.5%
Net Income	NA	4,075	3,199	3,005	1,035	-3,070	4,671	4,520	1,031	1,177

Balance Sheet & Other Financial Data (Million $)

	2007	2006	2005	2004	2003	2002	2001	2000	1999	1998
Cash	NA	2,926	3,196	4,467	4,329	6,383	2,587	1,265	1,762	820
Current Assets	NA	18,785	18,537	18,545	17,240	19,765	NA	12,816	11,163	5,743
Total Assets	NA	63,722	62,621	63,667	63,545	66,414	111,287	40,404	32,362	16,527
Current Liabilities	NA	11,066	11,835	11,152	10,572	19,632	NA	11,679	9,179	5,048
Long Term Debt	NA	9,365	10,600	14,617	18,251	16,487	38,503	9,462	9,109	4,652
Common Equity	NA	35,419	32,450	30,292	26,369	24,791	31,737	17,033	12,333	6,137
Total Capital	NA	44,838	43,111	44,977	44,733	41,320	70,542	27,630	21,946	10,847
Capital Expenditures	NA	1,569	1,272	1,015	1,170	1,709	1,798	1,704	1,633	781
Cash Flow	NA	6,140	5,299	5,181	2,507	-1,037	6,812	6,165	2,353	1,743
Current Ratio	NA	1.7	1.6	1.7	1.6	1.0	NA	1.1	1.2	1.1
% Long Term Debt of Capitalization	NA	20.9	24.6	32.5	40.8	39.9	54.6	34.2	41.5	42.9
% Net Income of Revenue	NA	9.9	8.1	7.5	2.8	NM	13.7	15.6	4.6	9.6
% Return on Assets	NA	6.4	5.1	4.7	1.6	NM	6.2	12.4	3.7	8.7
% Return on Equity	NA	12.0	10.2	10.6	4.1	NM	19.2	30.7	9.3	24.6

Data as orig reptd.; bef. results of disc opers/spec. items. Per share data adj. for stk. divs.; EPS diluted. E-Estimated. NA-Not Available. NM-Not Meaningful. NR-Not Ranked. UR-Under Review.

Office: 90 Pitts Bay Road, Pembroke, Bermuda HM 08.
Telephone: 441-292-8674.
Email: info@tyco.com
Website: http://www.tyco.com

Chrmn & CEO: E. Breen
EVP & CFO: C.J. Coughlin
EVP & General Counsel: J.A. Reinsdorf
SVP & Chief Acctg Officer: C.A. Davidson

SVP & Treas: M. Hund-Mejean
Investor Contact: E.C. Arditte (609-720-4621)
Board Members: D. C. Blair, E. D. Breen, B. Duperreault, B. Gordon, R. L. Gupta, J. A. Krol, H. C. McCall, M. J. McDonald, B. R. O'Neill, S. S. Wijnberg, J. B. York

Founded: 1960
Domicile: Bermuda
Employees: 115,000

STANDARD &POOR'S

Tyson Foods Inc.

S&P Recommendation HOLD ★★★☆☆	**Price** $14.83 (as of Nov 23, 2007)	**12-Mo. Target Price** $15.00	**Investment Style** Large-Cap Blend

GICS Sector Consumer Staples
Sub-Industry Packaged Foods & Meats

Summary Tyson is the world's largest supplier of beef, chicken and pork products.

Key Stock Statistics (Source S&P, Vickers, company reports)

52-Wk Range	$24.32– 13.50	S&P Oper. EPS 2008**E**	0.50	Market Capitalization(B)	$4.236	Beta		0.65
Trailing 12-Month EPS	$0.75	S&P Oper. EPS 2009**E**	1.00	Yield (%)	1.08	S&P 3-Yr. Proj. EPS CAGR(%)		NM
Trailing 12-Month P/E	19.8	P/E on S&P Oper. EPS 2008**E**	29.7	Dividend Rate/Share	$0.16	S&P Credit Rating		BBB-
$10K Invested 5 Yrs Ago	$12,940	Common Shares Outstg. (M)	355.6	Institutional Ownership (%)	92			

Price Performance

30-Week Mov. Avg. · · · · 10-Week Mov. Avg. - - **GAAP Earnings vs. Previous Year** Volume Above Avg. |||| STARS
12-Mo. Target Price — Relative Strength — ▲ Up ▼ Down ▶ No Change Below Avg. |||| ★

Options: ASE, CBOE, P

Analysis prepared by **Joseph Agnese** on November 12, 2007, when the stock traded at **$ 13.85**.

Highlights

➤ We expect sales to rise to $28.0 billion in FY 08 (Sep.) from $26.9 billion in FY 07, reflecting strengthening international demand and increased average protein industry pricing. Although beef export markets are slow to reopen, we believe international pork demand will remain strong in FY 08.

➤ We expect chicken margins to narrow significantly, reflecting increased feed prices despite higher end product prices. We believe beef margins will also be pressured as higher costs for feed results in higher raw material costs for live cattle. However, we believe margins will improve in both the pork and prepared food segments. Pork results should benefit from strong international demand and lower live hog prices. Prepared foods should benefit from lower protein prices. We expect interest expense to decline, as TSN remains focused on paying down debt.

➤ We see FY 08 operating EPS of $0.50, down significantly from an operating EPS of $0.75 a share in FY 07.

Investment Rationale/Risk

➤ We believe the company is well positioned to benefit in the longer term from reduced commodity exposure due to a strategy focused on expansion in value-added prepared food products. As the largest protein supplier in the U.S., we believe the company is well positioned to sustain a difficult intermediate term environment due to rising grain costs.

➤ Risks to our recommendation and target price include significant uncertainty surrounding resumption of trade in international markets and corporate governance concerns that we have, which are related to board issues.

➤ Despite higher grain costs in the intermediate term, we believe increased pricing power will eventually drive a recovery in chicken and beef margins. Due to the recovery that we expect over the next 18 months, our P/E analysis assumes that the shares will trade at a multiple of 15X our FY 09 EPS estimate of $1.00, at the midpoint of the company's historical trading range of 8X-22X. This suggests a value of $15, which is our 12-month target price.

Qualitative Risk Assessment

LOW	MEDIUM	HIGH

Our risk assessment reflects the company's cyclical operations, which are significantly affected by exposure to commodity crop and meat markets, and international trade restrictions.

Quantitative Evaluations

S&P Quality Ranking B

D	C	B-	B	B+	A-	A	A+

Relative Strength Rank WEAK

24

LOWEST = 1 HIGHEST = 99

Revenue/Earnings Data

Revenue (Million $)

	1Q	2Q	3Q	4Q	Year
2007	6,558	6,501	6,958	6,883	26,900
2006	6,454	6,251	6,383	6,471	25,559
2005	6,452	6,359	6,708	6,495	26,014
2004	6,505	6,153	6,634	7,149	26,441
2003	5,802	5,845	6,330	6,572	24,549
2002	5,865	5,839	5,902	5,761	23,367

Earnings Per Share ($)

2007	0.16	0.20	0.31	0.09	0.75
2006	0.11	-0.37	-0.15	-0.15	-0.56
2005	0.14	0.21	0.36	0.28	0.99
2004	0.16	0.33	0.45	0.19	1.13
2003	0.11	0.20	0.23	0.42	0.96
2002	0.36	0.18	0.30	0.24	1.08

Fiscal year ended Sep. 30. Next earnings report expected: Late January. EPS Estimates based on S&P Operating Earnings; historical GAAP earnings are as reported.

Dividend Data (Dates: mm/dd Payment Date: mm/dd/yy)

Amount ($)	Date Decl.	Ex-Div. Date	Stk. of Record	Payment Date
0.040	02/08	05/30	06/01	06/15/07
0.040	05/07	08/29	09/01	09/15/07
0.040	08/03	11/28	12/01	12/15/07
0.040	11/15	02/27	03/01	03/15/08

Dividends have been paid since 1976. Source: Company reports.

Please read the Required Disclosures and Analyst Certification on the last page of this report.

The McGraw-Hill Companies

Tyson Foods Inc.

**STANDARD
&POOR'S**

Business Summary November 12, 2007

Tyson Foods is the world's largest supplier of beef, chicken and pork products. The company holds about 27% of the U.S. beef market, 23% of the chicken market, and 19% of the pork market. Its goal is to become the primary protein provider for its customers. The company exports to more than 80 countries including Canada, China, Europe, Japan, Mexico, Russia and South Korea. Operations are conducted through five segments: beef, chicken, pork, prepared foods, and other.

The beef segment (47% of FY 07 (Sep.) revenues) includes the slaughter of live cattle and fabrication into primal and sub-primal meat cuts and case-ready products. Operations reduce live cattle to dressed carcasses and allied products for sales to further processors. The company markets its products to food retailers, distributors, wholesalers, restaurants and hotel chains, and other food processors. Allied products are marketed to manufacturers of pharmaceuticals and animal feeds. The company's primary supply of live cat-

tle is purchased on a daily basis.

The chicken segment (30%) includes fresh, frozen and value-added chicken products sold through domestic foodservice, domestic retail markets for at-home consumption, wholesale club markets targeted to small food service operations, and individuals and distributors that deliver to restaurants, schools and international markets throughout the world. Also included in this segment are sales from allied products and TSN's chicken breeding stock subsidiary. The segment's primary raw material is live chickens that are raised by independent contractors. Profitability is partially dependent on corn and soybean meal, which represents about 40% of the cost of growing a chicken.

Company Financials Fiscal Year Ended Sep. 30

Per Share Data ($)		2007	2006	2005	2004	2003	2002	2001	2000	1999	1998
Tangible Book Value		NA	5.05	5.66	4.49	3.17	2.92	1.71	NM	5.09	4.05
Cash Flow		NA	1.31	2.39	2.50	2.26	2.39	1.91	-1.97	2.26	1.32
Earnings		0.75	-0.56	0.99	1.13	0.96	1.08	0.40	0.68	1.00	0.11
S&P Core Earnings		NA	-0.56	1.06	1.10	0.64	1.02	0.39	NA	NA	NA
Dividends		0.16	0.16	0.16	0.16	0.16	0.16	0.16	0.16	0.13	0.10
Payout Ratio		21%	NM	16%	14%	17%	15%	40%	24%	13%	91%
Prices:High		24.32	17.33	19.91	21.28	15.10	15.71	14.20	17.38	23.75	26.00
Prices:Low		13.50	12.57	12.50	12.97	7.25	9.27	8.10	8.50	14.88	16.31
P/E Ratio:High		32	NM	20	19	16	15	35	26	24	NM
P/E Ratio:Low		18	NM	13	11	8	9	20	13	15	NM

Income Statement Analysis (Million $)											
Revenue		NA	25,559	26,014	26,441	24,549	23,367	10,751	7,268	7,363	7,414
Operating Income		NA	510	1,266	1,415	837	1,407	650	643	854	622
Depreciation		NA	517	501	490	458	467	335	294	291	276
Interest Expense		NA	268	227	275	592	305	144	116	124	139
Pretax Income		NA	-293	528	635	523	593	165	234	371	71.0
Effective Tax Rate		NA	NM	33.1%	36.5%	35.6%	35.4%	35.2%	35.5%	34.9%	64.8%
Net Income		NA	-191	353	403	337	383	88.0	151	230	25.0
S&P Core Earnings		NA	-190	379	392	224	365	87.5	NA	NA	NA

Balance Sheet & Other Financial Data (Million $)											
Cash		NA	28.0	40.0	33.0	25.0	51.0	70.0	43.0	30.0	47.0
Current Assets		NA	4,187	3,485	3,532	3,371	3,144	3,290	1,576	1,727	1,765
Total Assets		NA	11,121	10,504	10,464	10,486	10,372	10,632	4,854	5,083	5,243
Current Liabilities		NA	2,846	2,157	2,293	2,475	2,093	2,416	886	987	831
Long Term Debt		NA	2,987	2,869	3,024	3,114	3,733	4,016	1,357	1,515	1,967
Common Equity		NA	4,900	4,615	4,912	3,954	3,662	3,354	2,175	2,128	1,971
Total Capital		NA	8,382	8,141	8,631	7,790	8,038	7,979	3,917	4,041	4,371
Capital Expenditures		NA	531	571	486	402	433	261	196	363	310
Cash Flow		NA	326	854	893	795	850	423	445	521	301
Current Ratio		NA	1.5	1.6	1.5	1.4	1.5	1.4	1.8	1.7	2.1
% Long Term Debt of Capitalization		NA	35.6	35.2	35.0	40.0	46.4	50.3	34.6	37.5	45.0
% Net Income of Revenue		NA	NM	1.4	1.5	1.4	1.6	0.8	2.1	3.1	0.3
% Return on Assets		NA	NM	3.4	3.8	3.2	3.6	1.1	3.0	4.5	0.5
% Return on Equity		NA	NM	7.9	8.5	8.8	10.9	3.2	7.0	11.2	1.4

Data as orig reptd.; bef. results of disc opers/spec. items. Per share data adj. for stk. divs.; EPS diluted. E-Estimated. NA-Not Available. NM-Not Meaningful. NR-Not Ranked. UR-Under Review.

Office: 2210 West Oaklawn Drive, Springdale, AR 72762-6999.
Telephone: 479-290-4000.
Email: tysonir@tyson.com
Website: http://www.tyson.com

Chrmn: J.H. Tyson
Pres & CEO: R.L. Bond
EVP & CFO: W.D. Miquelon
EVP & General Counsel: J.A. Gonzalez-Pita

SVP, Chief Acctg Officer & Cntlr: C.J. Hart
Investor Contact: R.A. Wisener (479-290-4235)
Board Members: R. L. Bond, S. Ford, L. V. Hackley, J. Kever, J. R. Smith, L. E. Tollett, B. A. Tyson, D. Tyson, J. H. Tyson, A. C. Zapanta

Founded: 1935
Domicile: Delaware
Employees: 107,000

The McGraw-Hill Companies

Union Pacific Corp

STANDARD &POOR'S

S&P Recommendation HOLD ★★★☆☆

Price $124.68 (as of Nov 23, 2007)	**12-Mo. Target Price** $130.00	**Investment Style** Large-Cap Blend

GICS Sector Industrials
Sub-Industry Railroads

Summary Union Pacific operates the largest U.S. railroad, with over 32,000 miles of rail serving the western two-thirds of the country.

Key Stock Statistics (Source S&P, Vickers, company reports)

52-Wk Range	$130.00–89.01	S&P Oper. EPS 2007E	7.00	Market Capitalization(B)	$32.744	Beta	0.90
Trailing 12-Month EPS	$6.84	S&P Oper. EPS 2008E	7.85	Yield (%)	1.41	S&P 3-Yr. Proj. EPS CAGR(%)	13.00
Trailing 12-Month P/E	18.2	P/E on S&P Oper. EPS 2007E	17.8	Dividend Rate/Share	$1.76	S&P Credit Rating	BBB
$10K Invested 5 Yrs Ago	$23,950	Common Shares Outstg. (M)	262.6	Institutional Ownership (%)	85		

Price Performance

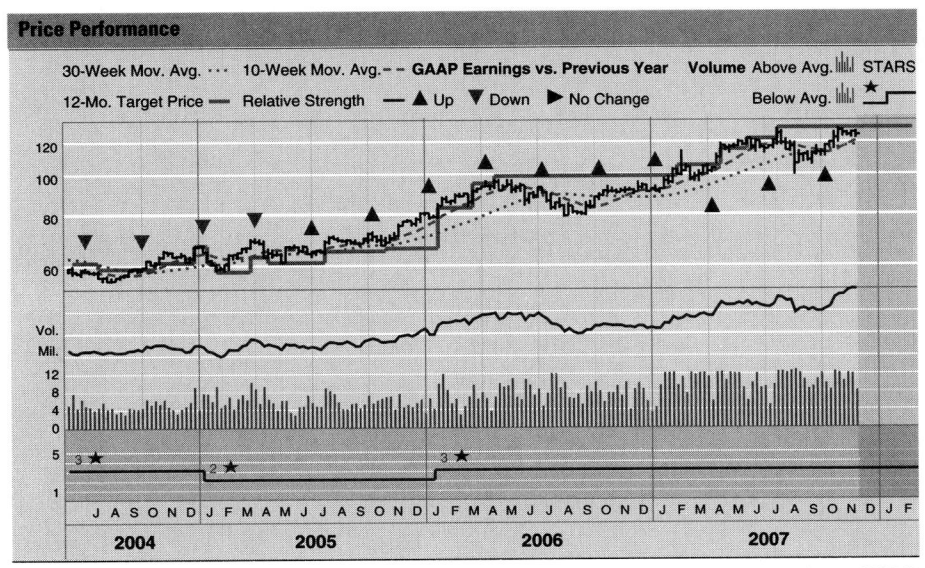

- 30-Week Mov. Avg. · · · 10-Week Mov. Avg. – – GAAP Earnings vs. Previous Year Volume Above Avg. STARS
- 12-Mo. Target Price — Relative Strength — ▲ Up ▼ Down ▶ No Change Below Avg.

2004   2005   2006   2007

Options: CBOE, Ph

Analysis prepared by **Kevin Kirkeby** on November 01, 2007, when the stock traded at **$ 128.04**.

Highlights

- Following a projected 4.7% revenue increase in 2007, we see revenue growth improving to 6.6% in 2008, mostly on a recovery in volumes, which we expect to be up 2%. We look for the yield to rise, although less than in 2007, as an expected increase in coal carloadings is likely to limit average revenue per car. We see coal shipments benefiting from investments made over the past year in its Powder River Basin infrastructure. However, UNP's intermodal and industrial shipments are likely to remain muted by the slowing economy.

- Improved asset utilization and a focus on higher-margin business are contributing to a widening of operating margins in 2007; however, fuel costs are a partial offset. For 2008, we see a further widening of margins, coming largely from additional productivity improvements. We believe opportunities for contract repricings are relatively limited in 2008, with about 7% of contracts up for renewal.

- We forecast 2007 operating EPS of $7.00, up about 20% from adjusted operating EPS of $5.82 in 2006. We estimate a 12% increase in 2008, to $7.85, including a 3% reduction in the average share count.

Investment Rationale/Risk

- For the period 2008-2012, we forecast compound annual growth in revenue of 7%. We think some of the revenue drivers are the expanding international trade with Asia and NAFTA, and a shifting of long-haul volumes from trucks to the railroads. However, as we forecast that pricing gains will slow, valuations near their 10-year average, and an increasing proportion of EPS growth coming from share buybacks, we view current valuations as fair.

- Risks to our recommendation and target price include sharply weaker than expected economic growth, shifts in shipping volumes away from UNP served ports, unusually severe weather, rapid fluctuations in fuel prices, and labor disruptions at key ports.

- Our relative valuation model suggests a forward enterprise value to EBITDA multiple of about 8.6X, which is the 10-year historical average, and a value of $136. Our discounted cash flow model, which assumes an 8.6% weighted average cost of capital and a 3.5% terminal growth rate, estimates an intrinsic value of $123. Blending these models, we arrive at our 12-month target price of $130.

Qualitative Risk Assessment

LOW	MEDIUM	HIGH

Our risk assessment reflects UNP's exposure to economic cycles, regulations, and labor and fuel costs, coupled with significant capital expenditure requirements, and challenges in maintaining system fluidity, offset by our view of the company's historically positive cash flow generation and moderate financial leverage.

Quantitative Evaluations

S&P Quality Ranking A-

D	C	B-	B	B+	A-	A	A+

Relative Strength Rank STRONG

88

LOWEST = 1   HIGHEST = 99

Revenue/Earnings Data

Revenue (Million $)

	1Q	2Q	3Q	4Q	Year
2007	3,849	4,046	4,191	--	--
2006	3,710	3,923	3,983	3,962	15,578
2005	3,152	3,344	3,461	3,621	13,578
2004	2,893	3,029	3,076	3,217	12,215
2003	2,736	2,894	2,956	2,965	11,551
2002	2,967	3,154	3,199	3,171	12,491

Earnings Per Share ($)

	1Q	2Q	3Q	4Q	Year
2007	1.41	1.65	2.00	E1.94	E7.00
2006	1.15	1.44	1.54	1.78	5.91
2005	0.48	0.88	1.38	1.10	3.85
2004	0.63	0.60	0.77	0.30	2.30
2003	0.60	1.10	1.21	1.28	4.07
2002	0.86	1.15	1.63	1.41	5.05

Fiscal year ended Dec. 31. Next earnings report expected: Late January. EPS Estimates based on S&P Operating Earnings; historical GAAP earnings are as reported.

Dividend Data (Dates: mm/dd Payment Date: mm/dd/yy)

Amount ($)	Date Decl.	Ex-Div. Date	Stk. of Record	Payment Date
0.350	01/30	02/26	02/28	04/02/07
0.350	05/03	05/25	05/30	07/02/07
0.350	07/31	08/28	08/30	10/01/07
0.440	11/15	11/27	11/29	01/02/08

Dividends have been paid since 1900. Source: Company reports.

Please read the Required Disclosures and Analyst Certification on the last page of this report.

The McGraw-Hill Companies

Union Pacific Corp

STANDARD &POOR'S

Business Summary November 01, 2007

CORPORATE OVERVIEW. We believe that Union Pacific, operating the largest U.S. railroad, will focus on improving service levels, system fluidity, and removing bottlenecks--challenges that we believe hampered its results in 2004 and 2005. UNP's system spans about 32,000 miles, linking pacific coast and gulf coast ports to midwestern and eastern gateways, and schedules are coordinated with other carriers.

MARKET PROFILE. We believe UNP's intermodal business, representing 18% of 2006 revenue, will be UNP's fastest growing segment longer term, driven by rising international trade and the outsourcing of manufacturing to Asia. However, weak service and timeliness levels in 2004 and 2005 restricted its ability to effectively compete with other railroad and trucking companies, in our view. Industrial products, sensitive to GDP trends, provided 20% of freight revenues in 2006, and included building products, metals and minerals. Energy, which we believe is UNP's most profitable segment, accounted for 19% of 2006 freight revenues. UNP is a major transporter of low-sulfur coal, with about 67% of its energy traffic consisting of coal originating in the Powder River Basin of Wyoming and Montana, primarily delivered to power utilities.

We believe chemicals, agricultural products, and automotive, representing 13%, 15%, and 9% of 2006 freight revenues, respectively, all face low long-term volume growth prospects.

COMPETITIVE LANDSCAPE. The U.S. rail industry has an oligopoly-like structure, with over 80% of revenues generated by the four largest railroads: UNP and Burlington Northern Santa Fe Corp. operating on the West Coast, and CSX Corp. and Norfolk Southern Corp. operating on the East Coast. Railroads simultaneously compete for customers while cooperating by sharing assets, interfacing systems, and completing customer movements. Key suppliers include locomotive and rail equipment manufacturers, fuel suppliers, and labor. UNP's employees, about 85% of whom are unionized, enjoy above national average compensation due to their significant bargaining power.

Company Financials Fiscal Year Ended Dec. 31

Per Share Data ($)	2006	2005	2004	2003	2002	2001	2000	1999	1998	1997
Tangible Book Value	56.68	51.15	48.49	47.85	41.99	38.30	35.07	32.29	29.93	30.79
Cash Flow	10.45	8.26	6.54	7.92	9.19	7.87	7.34	6.91	1.78	5.97
Earnings	5.91	3.85	2.30	4.07	5.05	3.77	3.34	3.12	-2.57	1.74
S&P Core Earnings	5.72	3.32	2.11	3.76	3.83	2.82	NA	NA	NA	NA
Dividends	1.20	1.20	1.20	0.99	0.83	0.80	0.80	0.80	1.03	1.72
Payout Ratio	20%	31%	52%	24%	16%	21%	24%	26%	NM	99%
Prices:High	97.49	81.26	69.56	69.50	65.15	60.70	52.81	67.88	63.75	72.98
Prices:Low	77.62	58.18	54.80	50.90	53.00	43.75	34.25	39.00	37.31	56.25
P/E Ratio:High	16	21	30	17	13	16	16	22	NM	42
P/E Ratio:Low	13	15	24	13	10	12	10	13	NM	32

Income Statement Analysis (Million $)

	2006	2005	2004	2003	2002	2001	2000	1999	1998	1997
Revenue	15,578	13,578	12,215	11,551	12,491	11,973	11,878	11,273	10,553	11,079
Operating Income	4,121	2,970	2,406	3,200	3,530	2,072	2,043	2,887	1,446	2,296
Depreciation	1,237	1,175	1,111	1,067	1,206	1,174	1,140	1,083	1,070	1,043
Interest Expense	477	504	527	574	633	701	723	733	714	605
Pretax Income	2,525	1,436	856	1,637	2,016	1,533	1,310	1,202	-696	676
Effective Tax Rate	36.4%	28.6%	29.4%	35.5%	33.5%	37.0%	35.7%	34.9%	NM	36.1%
Net Income	1,606	1,026	604	1,056	1,341	966	842	783	-633	432
S&P Core Earnings	1,553	886	551	972	1,003	708	NA	NA	NA	NA

Balance Sheet & Other Financial Data (Million $)

	2006	2005	2004	2003	2002	2001	2000	1999	1998	1997
Cash	827	773	977	527	369	113	105	175	176	90.0
Current Assets	2,411	2,325	2,290	2,089	2,152	1,542	1,285	1,314	1,502	1,415
Total Assets	36,515	35,620	34,589	33,460	32,764	31,551	30,499	29,888	29,374	28,764
Current Liabilities	3,539	3,384	2,516	2,456	2,701	2,692	2,962	2,885	2,932	3,247
Long Term Debt	6,000	6,760	7,981	7,822	8,928	9,386	9,644	9,926	10,011	8,285
Common Equity	15,312	13,707	12,655	12,354	10,651	9,575	8,662	8,001	7,393	8,225
Total Capital	31,008	29,949	29,816	29,345	28,057	26,843	25,449	24,642	23,712	22,762
Capital Expenditures	2,242	2,169	1,876	1,752	1,887	1,736	1,783	1,834	2,111	2,101
Cash Flow	2,843	2,201	1,715	2,123	2,547	2,140	1,982	1,866	437	1,475
Current Ratio	0.7	0.7	0.9	0.9	0.8	0.6	0.4	0.5	0.5	0.4
% Long Term Debt of Capitalization	19.3	22.6	26.8	26.7	31.8	35.0	37.9	40.3	42.2	36.3
% Net Income of Revenue	10.3	7.6	4.9	9.1	10.7	8.1	7.1	6.9	NM	3.9
% Return on Assets	4.5	2.9	1.8	3.2	4.2	3.1	2.8	2.6	NM	1.5
% Return on Equity	11.1	7.8	4.8	9.2	13.3	10.6	10.1	10.2	NM	5.3

Data as orig reptd.; bef. results of disc opers/spec. items. Per share data adj. for stk. divs.; EPS diluted. E-Estimated. NA-Not Available. NM-Not Meaningful. NR-Not Ranked. UR-Under Review.

Office: 1400 Douglas St, Omaha, NE 68179-0002.
Telephone: 402-544-5000.
Website: http://www.up.com
Chrmn, Pres & CEO: J.R. Young

EVP & CFO: R. Knight, Jr.
SVP & General Counsel: J.M. Hemmer
SVP & CIO: L. Tennison
Investor Contact: M.S. Jones (402-544-6111)

Board Members: A. Card, R. K. Davidson, E. B. Davis, Jr., T. J. Donohue, A. W. Dunham, J. R. Hope, C. C. Krulak, M. McConnell, T. McLarty, S. R. Rogel, J. R. Young

Founded: 1862
Domicile: Utah
Employees: 50,739

The McGraw-Hill Companies

Unisys Corp

STANDARD &POOR'S

S&P Recommendation HOLD ★★★☆☆	**Price** $5.14 (as of Nov 23, 2007)	**12-Mo. Target Price** $7.50	**Investment Style** Large-Cap Value

GICS Sector Information Technology
Sub-Industry IT Consulting & Other Services

Summary Unisys is a leading worldwide supplier of information services and technology solutions to more than 60,000 customers in 100 countries.

Key Stock Statistics (Source S&P, Vickers, company reports)

52-Wk Range	$9.70– 4.85	S&P Oper. EPS 2007**E**	-0.18	Market Capitalization(B)	$1.787	Beta	2.27
Trailing 12-Month EPS	$-0.21	S&P Oper. EPS 2008**E**	0.33	Yield (%)	Nil	S&P 3-Yr. Proj. EPS CAGR(%)	NM
Trailing 12-Month P/E	NM	P/E on S&P Oper. EPS 2007**E**	NM	Dividend Rate/Share	Nil	S&P Credit Rating	B+
$10K Invested 5 Yrs Ago	$4,729	Common Shares Outstg. (M)	347.8	Institutional Ownership (%)	87		

Price Performance

30-Week Mov. Avg. · · · 10-Week Mov. Avg. - - **GAAP Earnings vs. Previous Year** Volume Above Avg. STARS
12-Mo. Target Price — Relative Strength — ▲ Up ▼ Down ► No Change Below Avg. ★

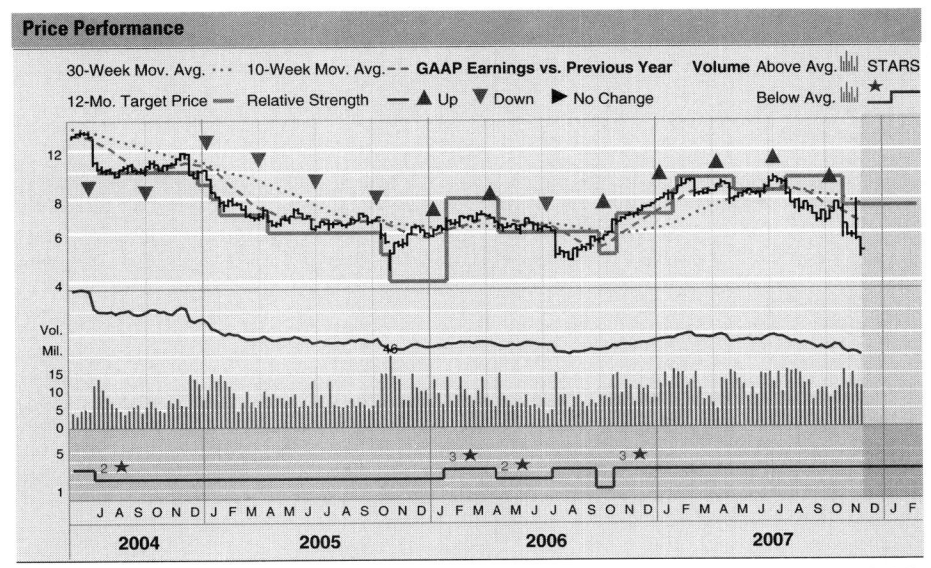

Options: ASE, CBOE, P, Ph

Analysis prepared by **Dylan Cathers** on October 25, 2007, when the stock traded at **$ 6.06**.

Highlights

➤ We expect revenues to be down 1% in 2007 and up 3.5% in 2008, following no growth in 2006. We think UIS's outsourcing segment of its services business is gaining momentum, but infrastructure and core maintenance are particularly weak. We expect continued softness in these areas, although we note orders have improved at a single digit pace through the first nine months of the year.

➤ We see a gross margin of 21.5% this year and we look for another roughly 200 basis point improvement in 2008, which would be far wider than the 14% in 2006 (using GAAP figures). UIS is still working to cut costs, primarily through the increased use of global sourcing, savings from the layoff of 5,600 employees, and improvements of problematic contracts. We think gains will be partially offset by additional severance and restructuring charges, as well as the use of temporary labor and weak revenues from higher-margined businesses.

➤ We project a loss of $0.18 per share in 2007 and a $0.33 profit in 2008, including pension and restructuring expenses.

Investment Rationale/Risk

➤ Our hold opinion is based on valuation. UIS has been pursuing efficiencies for many years, and while we see improvements such as increased contract wins and cost reductions, we think the next few quarters will continue to be challenging for the company. We expect UIS's large retirement expenses to persist, particularly overseas. We think demand in the tech segment will continue to be a drag on results, worsened by declining sales at high-margin businesses. UIS intends to expand its offshore presence to 6,000 workers by 2008.

➤ Risks to our recommendation and target price include more intense competition in outsourcing and IT services, a further weakening in demand for the company's server and software offerings, and a slower than expected reduction in costs from the ongoing restructuring program.

➤ Our 12-month target price of $7.50 is based on our discounted cash flow (DCF) analysis. Our DCF assumptions include a weighted average cost of capital of 11%, a terminal growth rate of 3%, and compound annual free cash growth of 15.5% over the next 15 years (from a low base).

Qualitative Risk Assessment

LOW	MEDIUM	HIGH

Our risk assessment for Unisys centers around the highly competitive nature of the IT consulting and services market, as well as the weak demand for the company's technology offerings.

Quantitative Evaluations

S&P Quality Ranking C

D	C	B-	B	B+	A-	A	A+

Relative Strength Rank WEAK

13

LOWEST = 1 HIGHEST = 99

Revenue/Earnings Data

Revenue (Million $)

	1Q	2Q	3Q	4Q	Year
2007	1,348	1,376	1,393	--	--
2006	1,388	1,407	1,410	1,552	5,757
2005	1,367	1,436	1,387	1,570	5,759
2004	1,463	1,388	1,446	1,524	5,821
2003	1,399	1,425	1,450	1,638	5,911
2002	1,363	1,360	1,332	1,553	5,607

Earnings Per Share ($)

2007	0.01	-0.19	-0.09	E0.08	E-0.18
2006	-0.08	-0.57	-0.23	0.06	-0.81
2005	-0.13	-0.08	-4.78	-0.09	-5.09
2004	0.09	0.06	0.07	-0.10	0.11
2003	0.12	0.16	0.17	0.33	0.78
2002	0.10	0.13	0.18	0.27	0.69

Fiscal year ended Dec. 31. Next earnings report expected: Late January. EPS Estimates based on S&P Operating Earnings; historical GAAP earnings are as reported.

Dividend Data

Common dividends, paid since 1895, were omitted in September 1990.

The McGraw-Hill Companies

Unisys Corp

**STANDARD
&POOR'S**

Business Summary October 25, 2007

CORPORATE OVERVIEW. Unisys is a technology services and solutions company, which operates through two business units: services and technology.

The services segment provides end-to-end services and solutions designed to help clients improve their competitiveness and efficiency in the global marketplace. UIS's portfolio of offerings includes systems integration and consulting; outsourcing, which includes the management of a customer's internal information systems and specific business processes such as payment processing, mortgage administration, and cargo management; infrastructure services involving the design, management and support of customer desktops, servers, mobile and wireless systems, and networks; and enterprise-wide security solutions to protect systems, networks, applications and data. Services revenue provide over 80% of total revenue.

The technology group develops servers and related products designed to operate in transaction intensive, mission critical environments. Major offerings

include enterprise class servers; operating system software and middleware to power high-end servers; and specialized technologies, including payment systems, chip testing, and peripheral support products. The company has entered into a series of agreements with NEC in an effort to cut costs by sharing server technology, research and development, manufacturing, and solutions delivery. Revenues from the technology group account for less than one-fifth of the company's total revenues.

The primary vertical markets served by the company worldwide include financial services, communications, transportation, commercial, and the public sector, including the U.S. federal government. Products and services are marketed primarily through a direct sales force.

Company Financials Fiscal Year Ended Dec. 31

Per Share Data ($)	2006	2005	2004	2003	2002	2001	2000	1999	1998	1997
Tangible Book Value	NM	NM	3.88	3.65	2.12	6.06	6.89	6.29	0.38	NM
Cash Flow	0.32	-3.99	1.27	1.81	1.16	0.79	1.63	2.51	2.04	1.39
Earnings	-0.81	-5.09	0.11	0.78	0.69	-0.16	0.77	1.63	1.06	-5.30
S&P Core Earnings	-1.03	-5.21	-0.02	0.39	-0.56	-1.46	NA	NA	NA	NA
Dividends	Nil	Nil	Nil	Nil	Nil	Nil	Nil	Nil	Nil	Nil
Payout Ratio	Nil	Nil	Nil	Nil	Nil	Nil	Nil	Nil	Nil	Nil
Prices:High	7.87	10.24	15.88	16.85	13.84	19.70	36.06	49.69	35.38	16.50
Prices:Low	4.72	4.38	9.50	8.25	5.92	7.70	9.13	20.94	13.31	5.75
P/E Ratio:High	NM	NM	NM	22	20	NM	47	30	33	NM
P/E Ratio:Low	NM	NM	NM	11	9	NM	12	13	13	NM

Income Statement Analysis (Million $)										
Revenue	5,757	5,759	5,821	5,911	5,607	6,018	6,885	7,545	7,208	6,636
Operating Income	61.7	212	359	770	578	298	698	1,226	1,076	1,722
Depreciation	389	374	394	343	155	302	271	265	266	1,218
Interest Expense	77.2	64.7	69.0	69.6	66.5	70.0	79.8	128	172	233
Pretax Income	-251	-171	-76.0	381	333	-46.5	379	770	604	-759
Effective Tax Rate	NM	NM	NM	32.0%	33.0%	NM	35.4%	32.1%	35.9%	NM
Net Income	-279	-1,732	38.6	259	223	-49.9	245	523	387	-854
S&P Core Earnings	-358	-1,772	-7.26	132	-183	-463	NA	NA	NA	NA

Balance Sheet & Other Financial Data (Million $)										
Cash	719	642	660	636	302	326	378	464	605	803
Current Assets	2,239	2,153	2,418	2,258	1,946	2,204	2,587	2,846	2,817	2,887
Total Assets	4,038	4,029	5,621	5,475	4,981	5,769	5,718	5,890	5,578	5,591
Current Liabilities	1,932	1,815	2,023	2,054	2,185	2,323	2,686	2,619	2,583	2,577
Long Term Debt	1,049	1,049	898	1,048	748	745	536	950	1,105	1,438
Common Equity	-64.2	-32.6	1,507	1,395	856	2,113	2,186	1,953	97.0	-214
Total Capital	985	1,016	2,405	2,444	1,604	2,858	2,722	2,904	2,622	2,644
Capital Expenditures	70.1	256	315	251	196	199	198	220	207	302
Cash Flow	110	-1,358	433	601	378	252	516	751	546	253
Current Ratio	1.2	1.2	1.2	1.1	0.9	0.9	1.0	1.1	1.1	1.1
% Long Term Debt of Capitalization	106.5	103.2	37.4	42.9	46.6	26.1	19.7	32.7	42.1	54.4
% Net Income of Revenue	NM	NM	NM	4.4	4.0	NM	3.6	6.9	5.4	NM
% Return on Assets	NM	NM	NM	4.9	4.1	NM	4.2	9.1	6.9	NM
% Return on Equity	NM	NM	NM	23.0	15.0	NM	11.8	47.6	NA	NM

Data as orig reptd.; bef. results of disc opers/spec. items. Per share data adj. for stk. divs.; EPS diluted. E-Estimated. NA-Not Available. NM-Not Meaningful. NR-Not Ranked. UR-Under Review.

Office: Unisys Way, Blue Bell, PA 19424.
Telephone: 215-986-4011.
Website: http://www.unisys.com
Chrmn: H.C. Duques

Pres & CEO: J.W. McGrath
SVP & CFO: J.B. Haugen
SVP, Secy & General Counsel: N.S. Sundheim
VP & Treas: S.A. Battersby

Investor Contact: J.F. McHale (215-986-4011)
Board Members: J. P. Bolduc, J. J. Duderstadt, H. C. Duques, M. J. Espe, D. K. Fletcher, E. A. Huston, C. M. Jones, L. F. Kenne, T. E. Martin, J. W. McGrath

Founded: 1886
Domicile: Delaware
Employees: 31,500

The **McGraw·Hill** Companies

STANDARD &POOR'S

UnitedHealth Group Inc

S&P Recommendation **BUY** ★★★★☆	Price **$54.07** (as of Nov 23, 2007)	12-Mo. Target Price **$62.00**	Investment Style Large-Cap Growth

GICS Sector Health Care
Sub-Industry Managed Health Care

Summary This leading health care services company provides health benefit services to more than 28.5 million individuals across the U.S.

Key Stock Statistics (Source S&P, Vickers, company reports)

52-Wk Range	$57.10–45.82	S&P Oper. EPS 2007**E**	3.50	Market Capitalization(B)	$71.913	Beta	0.25
Trailing 12-Month EPS	$3.34	S&P Oper. EPS 2008**E**	3.95	Yield (%)	0.06	S&P 3-Yr. Proj. EPS CAGR(%)	16.00
Trailing 12-Month P/E	16.2	P/E on S&P Oper. EPS 2007**E**	15.4	Dividend Rate/Share	$0.03	S&P Credit Rating	A-
$10K Invested 5 Yrs Ago	$25,616	Common Shares Outstg. (M)	1,330.0	Institutional Ownership (%)	85		

Price Performance

30-Week Mov. Avg. ··· 10-Week Mov. Avg. – – **GAAP Earnings vs. Previous Year** Volume Above Avg. ▌▌▌ STARS
12-Mo. Target Price — Relative Strength — ▲ Up ▼ Down ▶ No Change Below Avg. ▌▌▌ ★

Options: ASE, CBOE, P

Analysis prepared by **Phillip M. Seligman** on October 23, 2007, when the stock traded at **$ 48.43**.

Highlights

➤ We forecast that total revenue will rise 7.4% in 2008, to $81.2 billion, from the $75.6 billion we expect in 2007. Drivers we see include premium pricing above medical cost trends and strong Medicare Advantage (MA) and Medicaid enrollment growth. We look for commercial risk enrollment growth to be flat by year-end 2008, as UNH expects enrollment to decline in January due to pricing discipline and to strengthen modestly afterward. We estimate 1% to 2% higher commercial fee-based enrollment, which UNH also expects to decline in January and then grow throughout the year, more than offsetting attrition during the period.

➤ We see the consolidated medical loss ratio (MLR) remaining stable in 2008, with a slight uptick in cost trends from 2007's 7.5% that UNH sees due to changes in public policy and evidence-based care guidelines offset by higher premium pricing. We look for the SG&A cost ratio to decline modestly on revenue leverage.

➤ We estimate EPS of $3.50 in 2007, versus 2006's $2.98, and $3.95 in 2008, aided also by a $7 billion share buyback program. Our model excludes the planned acquisition of Sierra Health (SIE: $42), subject to necessary approvals.

Investment Rationale/Risk

➤ We are encouraged by UNH's attempts to resolve its execution issues. We believe execution shortcomings amid distractions from ongoing government probes of past stock option grants led to lower MA enrollment in 2007. In this regard, we think UNH's new products and service improvements will help lift commercial enrollment in 2008 following a dip at the start of the year, while its expanded agreement with AARP helps revitalize its MA business. We are also encouraged by its focus on profitability, as reflected by its pricing discipline even at the cost of enrollment growth. Finally, we view favorably UNH's diversification, which has enabled challenges faced by some businesses to be outweighed by strength exhibited by others, and its financial flexibility, aided by strong cash flow.

➤ Risks to our recommendation and target price include a sharp rise in medical costs, unfavorable regulatory changes, and unfavorable rulings in government stock-option probes.

➤ Our 12-month target price of $62 is derived by applying a forward P/E multiple of 15.7X, near the mid-point of the 15X to 17X historical managed care range, to our 2008 EPS estimate.

Qualitative Risk Assessment

LOW	MEDIUM	HIGH

Our risk assessment reflects UNH's leadership in the highly fragmented managed care market and its wide geographic, market and product diversity, which we believe permits stable operational performance even during periods of economic downturn. However, we see commercial enrollment growth slowing from an expanding base and as a result of intensifying competition.

Quantitative Evaluations

S&P Quality Ranking   **A+**

D	C	B-	B	B+	A-	A	A+

Relative Strength Rank   **STRONG**

93

LOWEST = 1   HIGHEST = 99

Revenue/Earnings Data

Revenue (Million $)

	1Q	2Q	3Q	4Q	Year
2007	19,047	18,926	18,679	--	--
2006	17,581	17,863	17,970	18,128	71,542
2005	10,887	11,111	11,322	12,045	45,365
2004	8,144	8,704	9,859	10,511	37,218
2003	6,975	7,087	7,238	7,523	28,823
2002	6,013	6,078	6,247	6,682	25,020

Earnings Per Share ($)

	1Q	2Q	3Q	4Q	Year
2007	0.66	0.87	0.95	E0.92	E3.50
2006	0.63	0.70	0.80	0.84	2.97
2005	0.58	0.61	0.64	0.65	2.48
2004	0.44	0.47	0.52	0.55	1.97
2003	0.33	0.36	0.39	0.42	1.48
2002	0.23	0.25	0.28	0.30	1.07

Fiscal year ended Dec. 31. Next earnings report expected: Early March. EPS Estimates based on S&P Operating Earnings; historical GAAP earnings are as reported.

Dividend Data (Dates: mm/dd Payment Date: mm/dd/yy)

Amount ($)	Date Decl.	Ex-Div. Date	Stk. of Record	Payment Date
0.030	01/31	03/29	04/02	04/16/07

Dividends have been paid since 1990. Source: Company reports.

The McGraw-Hill Companies

UnitedHealth Group Inc

STANDARD &POOR'S

Business Summary October 23, 2007

CORPORATE OVERVIEW. UnitedHealth Group, a U.S. leader in health care management, provides a broad range of health care products and services, including health maintenance organizations (HMOs), point of service (POS) plans, preferred provider organizations (PPOs), and managed fee for service programs.

The company reports results in four business segments, organized by product and/or market basis:

The Health Care Services segment (85% of 2006 revenues and 73% of operating earnings) consists of the following business units: UnitedHealthcare coordinates network-based health and well-being services on behalf of multistate mid-sized and local employers and for consumers. AmeriChoice facilitates and manages health care services for state Medicaid programs and their beneficiaries. Ovations delivers health and well-being services to Americans over the age of 50. At September 30, 2007, risk and fee-based Health care Services enrollment totaled 17,495,000, versus 17,610,000 at December 31, 2006, including risk-based commercial (9,625,000 versus 10,040,000), fee-based commercial (4,880,000 versus 4,735,000), Medicare Advantage (1,340,000 versus 1,410,000) and Medicaid (1,650,000 versus 1,425,000) members.

Uniprise (8% and 13%) provides network-based health services, consumer connectivity, and technology support services to large, self-insured accounts in return for administrative fees; it generally assumes no responsibility for health care costs. At September 30, 2007, segment enrollment was 11,070,000, versus 10,925,000.

Specialized Care Services (6% and 11%) offers a comprehensive array of specialized benefits, networks, services and resources.

Ingenix (1% and 3%) is a leader in the field of health care data, analysis and application, serving pharmaceutical companies, health insurers and other payers, physicians and other health care providers, large employers and governments. We view Ingenix as key to the other segments' competitive strengths.

Company Financials Fiscal Year Ended Dec. 31

Per Share Data ($)	2006	2005	2004	2003	2002	2001	2000	1999	1998	1997
Tangible Book Value	1.55	NM	0.04	1.24	0.79	0.88	0.61	0.75	1.03	1.47
Cash Flow	3.44	2.82	2.26	1.72	1.26	0.90	0.73	0.56	-0.01	0.38
Earnings	2.97	2.48	1.97	1.48	1.07	0.70	0.55	0.40	-0.14	0.28
S&P Core Earnings	2.94	2.36	1.86	1.37	0.99	0.62	NA	NA	NA	NA
Dividends	0.03	0.02	0.02	0.01	0.01	0.01	0.00	0.00	0.00	0.00
Payout Ratio	1%	1%	1%	1%	1%	1%	1%	1%	NM	1%
Prices:High	62.93	64.61	44.38	29.34	25.25	18.20	15.86	8.75	9.24	7.52
Prices:Low	41.44	42.63	27.73	19.60	16.96	12.63	5.80	4.92	3.70	5.30
P/E Ratio:High	21	26	23	20	24	26	29	22	NM	27
P/E Ratio:Low	14	17	14	13	16	18	11	12	NM	19

Income Statement Analysis (Million $)

	2006	2005	2004	2003	2002	2001	2000	1999	1998	1997
Revenue	71,542	45,365	37,218	28,823	25,020	23,454	21,122	19,343	17,106	11,563
Operating Income	6,783	5,826	4,475	3,234	2,441	1,831	1,215	957	619	657
Depreciation	670	453	374	299	255	265	247	233	185	146
Interest Expense	456	241	128	95.0	90.0	94.0	72.0	49.0	4.00	NM
Pretax Income	6,528	5,132	3,973	2,840	2,096	1,472	1,155	894	-46.0	742
Effective Tax Rate	36.3%	35.7%	34.9%	35.7%	35.5%	38.0%	36.3%	36.5%	NM	38.0%
Net Income	4,159	3,300	2,587	1,825	1,352	913	736	568	-166	460
S&P Core Earnings	4,108	3,137	2,443	1,689	1,260	812	NA	NA	NA	NA

Balance Sheet & Other Financial Data (Million $)

	2006	2005	2004	2003	2002	2001	2000	1999	1998	1997
Cash	10,940	5,421	3,991	2,262	1,130	1,540	1,419	1,605	1,644	750
Current Assets	16,044	10,640	8,241	6,120	5,174	4,946	4,405	4,568	4,280	2,193
Total Assets	48,320	41,374	27,879	17,634	14,164	12,486	11,053	10,273	9,701	7,623
Current Liabilities	18,497	16,644	11,329	8,768	8,379	7,491	6,570	5,892	5,342	2,570
Long Term Debt	5,973	3,850	3,350	1,750	950	900	650	400	249	19.0
Common Equity	20,810	17,733	10,717	5,128	4,428	3,891	3,688	3,863	4,038	4,534
Total Capital	26,783	21,583	14,067	6,878	5,378	4,791	4,338	4,263	4,287	4,553
Capital Expenditures	728	5,876	350	352	419	425	245	196	210	187
Cash Flow	4,829	3,753	2,961	2,124	1,607	1,178	983	801	-9.00	577
Current Ratio	0.9	0.6	0.7	0.7	0.6	0.7	0.7	0.8	0.8	0.9
% Long Term Debt of Capitalization	22.3	17.8	23.8	25.4	17.7	18.8	15.0	9.4	5.8	0.4
% Net Income of Revenue	5.9	7.3	7.0	6.3	5.4	3.9	3.5	2.9	NM	4.0
% Return on Assets	9.3	9.5	11.4	11.5	10.1	7.8	6.9	5.7	NM	6.3
% Return on Equity	21.5	23.2	32.7	38.2	32.5	24.1	19.5	14.4	NM	10.3

Data as orig reptd.; bef. results of disc opers/spec. items. Per share data adj. for stk. divs.; EPS diluted. E-Estimated. NA-Not Available. NM-Not Meaningful. NR-Not Ranked. UR-Under Review.

Office: 9900 Bren Rd E, Minnetonka, MN 55343.
Telephone: 952-936-1300.
Website: http://www.unitedhealthgroup.com
Chrmn: R.T. Burke

Pres & CEO: S.J. Hemsley
EVP & CFO: G.M. Mikan
EVP & Chief Lgl Officer: T.L. Strickland
General Counsel: F. Burke

Investor Contact: P.J. Erlandson (952-936-1300)
Board Members: W. C. Ballard, Jr., R. T. Burke, R. J. Darretta, S. Hemsley, J. A. Johnson, T. H. Kean, D. W. Leatherdale, M. O. Mundinger, R. L. Ryan, D. E. Shalala, G. R. Wilensky

Founded: 1974
Domicile: Minnesota
Employees: 58,000

United Parcel Service Inc.

STANDARD &POOR'S

| S&P Recommendation **BUY** ★★★★☆ | Price $70.92 (as of Nov 23, 2007) | 12-Mo. Target Price $89.00 | Investment Style Large-Cap Growth |

GICS Sector Industrials
Sub-Industry Air Freight & Logistics

Summary UPS is the world's largest express delivery company, and has established itself as a facilitator of e-commerce.

Key Stock Statistics (Source S&P, Vickers, company reports)

52-Wk Range	$79.50– 68.66	S&P Oper. EPS 2007E	4.17	Market Capitalization(B)	$48.366	Beta	0.91
Trailing 12-Month EPS	$3.88	S&P Oper. EPS 2008E	4.55	Yield (%)	2.37	S&P 3-Yr. Proj. EPS CAGR(%)	11.00
Trailing 12-Month P/E	18.3	P/E on S&P Oper. EPS 2007E	17.0	Dividend Rate/Share	$1.68	S&P Credit Rating	AAA
$10K Invested 5 Yrs Ago	$12,217	Common Shares Outstg. (M)	1,049.8	Institutional Ownership (%)	70		

Price Performance

30-Week Mov. Avg. ··· 10-Week Mov. Avg. - - GAAP Earnings vs. Previous Year Volume Above Avg. STARS
12-Mo. Target Price — Relative Strength — ▲ Up ▼ Down ► No Change Below Avg. ★

Options: ASE, CBOE, P, Ph

Analysis prepared by **Jim Corridore** on November 19, 2007, when the stock traded at **$ 71.75**.

Highlights

➤ We expect 2007 revenues to rise 5%. We look for international revenues to be up 10%, aided by strong export activity from China. We see 2% domestic revenue growth, with faster growth in deferred and ground, and slower growth at express. UPS announced a general rate increase of 4.9% for 2008, in line with 2007's increase and about in line with expectations. We think that UPS may have trouble getting customers to absorb this increase, given recent weakness in shipping volumes domestically. We foresee 7% growth in the supply chain and freight segment.

➤ We expect operating margins to widen. We anticipate improved productivity, partly offset by a weaker package mix due to a likely shift to deferred and ground delivery options, from next day air. UPS's implementation of its package flow technology is targeted to save the company $700 million annually. UPS is also implementing a restructuring program in its supply chain business, designed to save $100 million annually.

➤ We estimate 2008 EPS of $4.55, up 9.1% from out 2007 EPS estimate of $4.17. We see UPS growing EPS at a compound annual growth rate of about 11% over the next three years.

Investment Rationale/Risk

➤ We believe UPS will continue to increase domestic revenues faster than U.S. GDP growth. The company should also benefit from a strong global economy and export activity out of Asia. In our view, the company has a healthy balance sheet and generates a great deal of cash from operations, which it has used historically to increase its dividend and make acquisitions. An ongoing stock repurchase program has been successful in reducing the share count.

➤ Risks to our recommendation and target price include a more severe economic slowdown and a possible price war with competitors. Regarding corporate governance, we are concerned that Class A shareholders have 10 votes per share on many matters.

➤ Our 12-month target price of $89 values the stock at 19.6X our 2008 EPS estimate of $4.55, near the low end of the company's five-year historical P/E range of 17.0X-30.4X earnings, due to our concerns about a potential P/E contraction related to the late stage of the economic cycle. This is still a premium to the S&P 500, which we see as warranted by UPS's high return on assets and what we view as strong cash flow from operations.

Qualitative Risk Assessment

| LOW | MEDIUM | HIGH |

Our risk assessment reflects what we see as: UPS's geographically diversified and increasing revenue base, a strong balance sheet with ample cash, low debt relative to total capitalization, and a track record of earnings and cash flow growth.

Quantitative Evaluations

S&P Quality Ranking NR

| D | C | B- | B | B+ | A- | A | A+ |

Relative Strength Rank MODERATE

56

LOWEST = 1 HIGHEST = 99

Revenue/Earnings Data

Revenue (Million $)

	1Q	2Q	3Q	4Q	Year
2007	11,906	12,189	12,205	--	--
2006	11,521	11,736	11,662	12,628	47,547
2005	9,886	10,191	10,550	11,954	42,581
2004	8,919	8,871	8,952	9,840	36,582
2003	8,015	8,226	8,312	8,932	33,485
2002	7,579	7,682	7,754	8,257	31,272

Earnings Per Share ($)

2007	0.78	1.04	1.02	E1.13	E4.17
2006	0.89	0.97	0.96	1.04	3.86
2005	0.78	0.88	0.86	0.95	3.47
2004	0.67	0.72	0.78	0.76	2.93
2003	0.54	0.61	0.65	0.75	2.55
2002	0.50	0.54	0.51	1.32	2.87

Fiscal year ended Dec. 31. Next earnings report expected: Late January. EPS Estimates based on S&P Operating Earnings; historical GAAP earnings are as reported.

Dividend Data (Dates: mm/dd Payment Date: mm/dd/yy)

Amount ($)	Date Decl.	Ex-Div. Date	Stk. of Record	Payment Date
0.420	02/08	02/15	02/20	03/06/07
0.420	05/10	05/17	05/21	06/05/07
0.420	08/29	09/06	09/10	09/17/07
0.420	11/08	11/15	11/19	01/03/08

Dividends have been paid since 2000. Source: Company reports.

The McGraw·Hill Companies

United Parcel Service Inc.

STANDARD &POOR'S

Business Summary November 19, 2007

United Parcel Service is the world's largest express and package delivery company. It is also a leading commerce facilitator, offering various logistics and financial services. The company, which was privately held since its founding in 1907, had its IPO of Class B stock in November 1999.

The company seeks to position itself as the primary coordinator of the flow of goods, information and funds throughout the entire supply chain (the movement from the raw materials and parts stage through final consumption of the finished product).

Domestic package delivery services accounted for 64% of revenues in 2006. About 84% of the 13.8 million daily domestic shipments handled by the company in 2006 was moved by its ground delivery service, which is available to every address in the 48 contiguous states in the U.S. Domestic air delivery is provided throughout the U.S., including next-day air, which is guaranteed by 10:30 a.m. to more than 75% of the U.S. population, and by noon to an additional 15% of the population.

UPS entered the international arena in 1975. In 2006, it handled 1.8 million international shipments per day. Its international package delivery service (19% of total revenues in 2006) is growing faster than its domestic business. UPS delivers international shipments to more than 200 countries and territories worldwide and provides delivery within one to two business days to the world's major business centers. Services include export (packages that cross national borders), and domestic (packages that stay within a single country's boundaries). UPS has a portfolio of domestic services in 20 major countries. Transborder services within the European Union are expected to continue to be a growth engine for the company. Asia continues to be an area in which UPS is investing in infrastructure and technology.

Company Financials Fiscal Year Ended Dec. 31

Per Share Data ($)	2006	2005	2004	2003	2002	2001	2000	1999	1998	1997
Tangible Book Value	11.46	12.44	12.84	12.03	11.09	9.14	8.58	10.31	13.10	5.42
Cash Flow	5.46	4.94	4.33	3.91	4.20	3.41	3.50	1.77	5.15	1.77
Earnings	3.86	3.47	2.93	2.55	2.87	2.12	2.50	0.77	1.57	0.81
S&P Core Earnings	3.78	3.40	2.87	2.46	2.48	1.70	NA	NA	NA	NA
Dividends	1.52	1.32	1.12	0.92	0.76	0.76	0.81	Nil	NA	NA
Payout Ratio	39%	38%	38%	36%	26%	36%	32%	Nil	NA	NA
Prices:High	83.99	85.84	89.11	74.87	67.10	62.50	69.75	76.94	NA	NA
Prices:Low	65.50	66.10	67.51	53.00	54.25	46.15	49.50	50.00	NA	NA
P/E Ratio:High	22	25	30	29	23	29	28	NM	NA	NA
P/E Ratio:Low	17	19	23	21	19	22	20	NM	NA	NA

Income Statement Analysis (Million $)	2006	2005	2004	2003	2002	2001	2000	1999	1998	1997
Revenue	47,547	42,581	36,582	33,485	31,272	30,646	29,771	27,052	24,788	22,458
Operating Income	8,383	7,787	6,532	5,994	5,560	5,358	5,685	5,127	4,202	2,761
Depreciation	1,748	1,644	1,543	1,549	1,464	1,396	1,173	1,139	1,112	1,063
Interest Expense	211	172	149	121	173	184	205	228	227	187
Pretax Income	6,510	6,075	4,922	4,370	5,009	3,937	4,834	2,088	2,902	1,553
Effective Tax Rate	35.5%	36.3%	32.3%	33.7%	35.0%	38.4%	39.3%	57.7%	40.0%	41.5%
Net Income	4,202	3,870	3,333	2,898	3,254	2,425	2,934	883	1,741	909
S&P Core Earnings	4,109	3,784	3,261	2,790	2,820	1,948	NA	NA	NA	NA

Balance Sheet & Other Financial Data (Million $)	2006	2005	2004	2003	2002	2001	2000	1999	1998	1997
Cash	794	1,369	5,197	2,951	2,211	1,616	1,952	6,278	1,629	460
Current Assets	9,377	11,003	12,605	9,853	8,738	7,597	7,124	11,138	5,425	4,477
Total Assets	33,210	35,222	33,026	28,909	26,357	24,636	21,662	23,043	17,067	15,912
Current Liabilities	6,719	6,793	6,483	5,518	5,555	4,629	4,501	4,198	3,717	3,398
Long Term Debt	3,133	3,159	3,261	3,149	3,495	4,648	2,981	1,912	2,191	2,583
Common Equity	15,482	16,884	16,384	14,852	12,455	10,248	9,735	12,474	7,598	6,087
Total Capital	21,144	20,043	25,027	18,001	15,950	14,896	12,716	14,386	9,789	8,676
Capital Expenditures	3,085	2,187	2,127	1,947	1,658	2,372	2,147	1,476	1,645	1,984
Cash Flow	5,950	5,514	4,876	4,447	4,718	3,821	4,107	2,022	2,853	1,972
Current Ratio	1.4	1.6	1.9	1.8	1.6	1.6	1.6	2.7	1.5	1.3
% Long Term Debt of Capitalization	14.8	15.8	13.0	17.5	21.9	31.2	23.4	13.3	22.4	29.8
% Net Income of Revenue	8.8	9.1	9.1	8.7	10.4	7.9	9.9	3.3	7.0	4.0
% Return on Assets	12.3	11.3	10.6	10.5	12.8	10.5	13.1	4.4	10.6	5.9
% Return on Equity	26.0	23.3	21.3	21.2	28.7	24.3	26.4	8.8	25.4	21.0

Data as orig reptd.; bef. results of disc opers/spec. items. Per share data adj. for stk. divs.; EPS diluted. E-Estimated. NA-Not Available. NM-Not Meaningful. NR-Not Ranked. UR-Under Review.

Office: 55 Glenlake Parkway N.E., Atlanta, GA 30328.
Telephone: 404-828-6000.
Website: http://www.shareholder.com/ups
Chrmn & CEO: M. Eskew

Investor Contact: D.S. Davis (404-828-6000)
Vice Chrmn & CFO: D.S. Davis
COO: D. Abney
SVP, Secy & General Counsel: T.P. McClure

Board Members: M. J. Burns, S. Davis, S. E. Eizenstat, M. L. Eskew, J. P. Kelly, A. M. Livermore, V. A. Pelson, J. W. Thompson, C. B. Tome, B. Verwaayen

Founded: 1907
Domicile: Delaware
Employees: 428,000

U.S. Bancorp

STANDARD &POOR'S

S&P Recommendation	HOLD ★★★☆☆	Price	12-Mo. Target Price	Investment Style
		$31.21 (as of Nov 23, 2007)	$37.00	Large-Cap Blend

GICS Sector Financials
Sub-Industry Diversified Banks

Summary This bank holding company was formed through the February 2001 merger of Minneapolis-based U.S. Bancorp and Milwaukee-based Firstar Corp.

Key Stock Statistics (Source S&P, Vickers, company reports)

52-Wk Range	$36.85–29.09	S&P Oper. EPS 2007E	2.63	Market Capitalization(B)	$53.889	Beta	1.14
Trailing 12-Month EPS	$2.55	S&P Oper. EPS 2008E	2.87	Yield (%)	5.13	S&P 3-Yr. Proj. EPS CAGR(%)	9.00
Trailing 12-Month P/E	12.2	P/E on S&P Oper. EPS 2007E	11.9	Dividend Rate/Share	$1.60	S&P Credit Rating	AA
$10K Invested 5 Yrs Ago	NA	Common Shares Outstg. (M)	1,726.7	Institutional Ownership (%)	63		

Price Performance

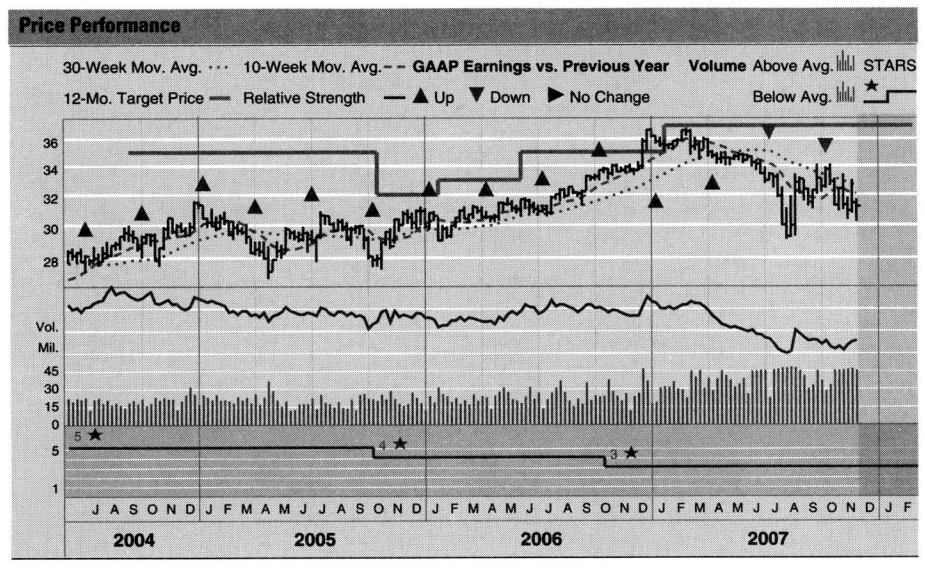

30-Week Mov. Avg. ··· 10-Week Mov. Avg. - - GAAP Earnings vs. Previous Year Volume Above Avg. STARS
12-Mo. Target Price — Relative Strength — ▲ Up ▼ Down ► No Change Below Avg.

Options: ASE, CBOE, Ph

Analysis prepared by **Frank Braden, CFA** on October 17, 2007, when the stock traded at **$32.18**.

Highlights

▶ USB remains one of the most profitable large cap banks in our coverage universe, in terms of returns on equity and assets, which highlights the company's focus on revenue growth and cost controls, and what we see as its attractive mix of high margin fee businesses. We look for revenues and earnings to increase steadily in 2008, in line with the higher middle market and corporate commercial loan growth that we expect, partially offset by a challenging real estate market.

▶ We forecast a slight increase in net interest margin in 2008 from our 2007 estimate of 3.46%, as an improvement in the yield curve environment is partially offset by competitive pricing and mix shift. We view USB as well-capitalized, with a Tier 1 capital ratio of 8.6%, and we think it is likely to remain an active acquirer of its common stock and should exceed its plan to return at least 80% of its earnings to shareholders.

▶ We expect operating EPS of $2.63 for 2007, and $2.87 in 2008.

Investment Rationale/Risk

▶ We believe that the company's diversified revenue model of economically sensitive businesses, combined with our projection of accelerating growth in commercial lending and USB's strong focus on expense management, will generate above industry average profitability. We expect credit quality to remain resilient, but we forecast higher commercial and commercial real estate net charge-offs in 2008, as USB focuses on loan quality over loan growth. We also project mortgage banking revenue to gradually increase from depressed levels.

▶ Risks to our recommendation and target price include a severe economic downturn, a further tightening of the credit markets, a marked decline in consumer spending, a significant deterioration in credit quality, legal and regulatory risks, and any serious event that could hurt U.S. equity markets.

▶ Our 12-month target price of $37 equates to approximately 12.9X our 2008 EPS estimate, in line with its historical average.

Qualitative Risk Assessment

LOW	MEDIUM	HIGH

Our risk assessment for U.S. Bancorp reflects our view of the company's solid fundamentals, along with good geographic and product diversification. We think USB would sustain a downturn in the U.S. economy better than many peers.

Quantitative Evaluations

S&P Quality Ranking A-

D	C	B-	B	B+	A-	A	A+

Relative Strength Rank MODERATE

66

LOWEST = 1   HIGHEST = 99

Revenue/Earnings Data

Revenue (Million $)

	1Q	2Q	3Q	4Q	Year
2007	4,883	5,091	5,178	--	--
2006	4,505	4,773	4,897	4,934	19,109
2005	3,817	4,106	4,294	4,379	16,596
2004	3,576	3,478	3,827	3,825	14,706
2003	3,697	3,801	3,489	3,584	14,571
2002	3,690	3,813	3,978	3,492	15,422

Earnings Per Share ($)

2007	0.65	0.65	0.62	E0.68	E2.63
2006	0.63	0.66	0.66	0.66	2.61
2005	0.57	0.60	0.62	0.62	2.42
2004	0.52	0.54	0.56	0.56	2.18
2003	0.46	0.48	0.49	0.50	1.92
2002	0.41	0.43	0.45	0.44	1.73

Fiscal year ended Dec. 31. Next earnings report expected: Mid January. EPS Estimates based on S&P Operating Earnings; historical GAAP earnings are as reported.

Dividend Data (Dates: mm/dd Payment Date: mm/dd/yy)

Amount ($)	Date Decl.	Ex-Div. Date	Stk. of Record	Payment Date
0.400	12/12	12/27	12/29	01/16/07
0.400	03/20	03/28	03/30	04/16/07
0.400	06/19	06/27	06/29	07/16/07
0.400	09/18	09/26	09/28	10/15/07

Dividends have been paid since 1863. Source: Company reports.

U.S. Bancorp

Business Summary October 17, 2007

CORPORATE OVERVIEW. USB consists of several major lines of business, which include wholesale banking, consumer banking, private client, trust and asset management, payment services, and treasury and corporate support. Wholesale banking offers lending, depository, treasury management and other financial services to middle market, large corporate and public sector clients. Consumer banking delivers products and services through banking offices, telephone servicing and sales, on-line services, direct mail and ATMs. It encompasses community banking, metropolitan banking, in-store banking, small business banking, including lending guaranteed by the Small Business Administration, small-ticket leasing, consumer lending, mortgage banking, consumer finance, workplace banking, student banking, 24-hour banking, and investment product and insurance sales.

Private client, trust and asset management provides trust, custody, private banking, financial advisory, investment management and mutual fund servicing through five businesses: private client group, corporate trust, FAF Advi-

sors, institutional trust and custody, and fund services. Payment services includes consumer and business credit cards, stored-value cards, debit cards, corporate and purchasing card services, consumer lines of credit, ATM processing and merchant processing.

CORPORATE STRATEGY. USB has several goals in order to achieve long-term success, including: 10% plus EPS growth, a 20% plus ROE, reducing credit and earnings volatility, providing high-quality customer service, investing in future growth, and targeting an 80% return on earnings to shareholders. In banking, USB is maintaining what we view as its low-cost, highly efficient model and plans to grow organically and through smaller, fill-in acquisitions in higher growth markets.

Company Financials Fiscal Year Ended Dec. 31

Per Share Data ($)	2006	2005	2004	2003	2002	2001	2000	1999	1998	1997
Tangible Book Value	5.34	5.62	5.87	5.77	4.93	4.64	7.11	4.66	5.38	NA
Earnings	2.61	2.42	2.18	1.92	1.73	0.88	1.32	0.87	0.65	0.78
S&P Core Earnings	2.59	2.41	2.16	1.89	1.59	0.66	NA	NA	NA	NA
Dividends	1.39	1.23	1.02	0.86	0.78	0.75	0.65	0.40	Nil	NA
Payout Ratio	53%	51%	47%	45%	45%	85%	49%	46%	Nil	NA
Prices:High	36.85	31.36	31.65	30.00	24.50	26.06	28.00	35.33	31.31	NA
Prices:Low	28.99	26.80	24.89	18.56	16.05	16.50	15.38	19.56	23.50	NA
P/E Ratio:High	14	13	15	16	14	30	21	41	48	NA
P/E Ratio:Low	11	11	11	10	9	19	12	22	36	NA

Income Statement Analysis (Million $)										
Net Interest Income	6,741	7,055	7,111	7,189	6,840	6,409	2,699	2,643	1,413	1,366
Tax Equivalent Adjustment	49.0	33.0	28.6	28.2	36.6	55.9	45.1	54.3	43.3	40.6
Non Interest Income	6,832	6,151	5,624	5,068	5,569	5,030	1,505	1,388	859	770
Loan Loss Provision	544	666	670	1,254	1,349	2,529	222	187	114	124
% Expense/Operating Revenue	45.4%	44.3%	45.3%	45.7%	83.7%	57.5%	55.0%	59.9%	65.7%	57.3%
Pretax Income	6,863	6,571	6,176	5,651	5,103	2,634	1,927	1,413	638	785
Effective Tax Rate	30.8%	31.7%	32.5%	34.4%	34.8%	35.2%	31.4%	38.0%	32.6%	34.0%
Net Income	4,751	4,489	4,167	3,710	3,326	1,707	1,284	875	430	519
% Net Interest Margin	3.65	3.97	4.25	4.49	4.61	4.45	4.73	4.83	4.46	NA
S&P Core Earnings	4,674	4,470	4,135	3,655	3,062	1,280	NA	NA	NA	NA

Balance Sheet & Other Financial Data (Million $)										
Money Market Assets	NA	Nil	Nil	Nil	1,332	1,607	200	897	2.75	150
Investment Securities	40,117	39,768	41,481	43,334	28,488	26,608	13,866	13,114	6,432	7,196
Commercial Loans	74,835	71,405	67,758	65,768	68,811	71,703	28,498	26,198	15,241	NA
Other Loans	68,762	66,401	58,557	52,467	47,440	42,702	25,208	24,428	10,627	NA
Total Assets	219,232	209,465	195,104	189,286	180,027	171,390	77,585	72,788	38,476	37,100
Demand Deposits	32,128	32,214	30,756	32,470	35,106	31,212	10,980	10,300	10,498	6,181
Time Deposits	92,754	92,495	89,985	86,582	80,428	74,007	45,298	41,586	18,353	21,658
Long Term Debt	37,602	37,069	22,807	33,816	31,582	28,542	3,877	5,038	1,709	1,371
Common Equity	20,197	20,086	19,539	19,242	18,101	16,461	6,528	6,309	3,530	3,185
% Return on Assets	2.2	2.2	2.2	2.0	1.9	1.0	1.7	1.2	1.2	NA
% Return on Equity	23.6	22.7	21.5	19.7	19.2	10.8	20.0	13.6	13.7	NA
% Loan Loss Reserve	-1.4	1.5	1.6	2.0	2.0	2.1	1.3	1.4	1.5	1.6
% Loans/Deposits	117.6	111.9	105.8	100.5	100.6	111.4	95.4	98.8	89.7	NA
% Equity to Assets	9.4	9.8	10.1	10.2	9.8	9.4	8.5	8.8	8.8	NA

Data as orig reptd.; bef. results of disc opers/spec. items. Per share data adj. for stk. divs.; EPS diluted. E-Estimated. NA-Not Available. NM-Not Meaningful. NR-Not Ranked. UR-Under Review.

Office: 800 Nicollet Mall, Minneapolis, MN 55402-7000.
Telephone: 651-466-3000.
Website: http://www.usbank.com
Chrmn: J.A. Grundhofer

Pres & CEO: R.K. Davis
Vice Chrmn: W.L. Chenevich
Vice Chrmn: J. Otting
Vice Chrmn: R.B. Payne, Jr.

Investor Contact: J.T. Murphy (612-303-0783)
Board Members: A. D. Collins, Jr., P. H. Coors, R. K. Davis, V. B. Gluckman, J. A. Grundhofer, J. W. Johnson, O. F. Kirtley, J. W. Levin, D. B. O'Maley, O. M. Owens, R. G. Reiten, C. D. Schnuck, W. R. Staley, P. T. Stokes

Founded: 1929
Domicile: Delaware
Employees: 50,423

STANDARD &POOR'S

United States Steel Corp

S&P Recommendation	BUY ★★★★☆	Price	12-Mo. Target Price	Investment Style
		$93.90 (as of Nov 23, 2007)	$120.00	Large-Cap Value

GICS Sector Materials
Sub-Industry Steel

Summary This company manufactures and sells a wide variety of steel sheet, plate, tubular and tin products, coke, and taconite pellets.

Key Stock Statistics (Source S&P, Vickers, company reports)

52-Wk Range	$127.26– 68.83	S&P Oper. EPS 2007E	9.54	Market Capitalization(B)	$11.100	Beta	3.65
Trailing 12-Month EPS	$9.61	S&P Oper. EPS 2008E	9.90	Yield (%)	0.85	S&P 3-Yr. Proj. EPS CAGR(%)	0.90
Trailing 12-Month P/E	9.8	P/E on S&P Oper. EPS 2007E	9.8	Dividend Rate/Share	$0.80	S&P Credit Rating	BB+
$10K Invested 5 Yrs Ago	$75,292	Common Shares Outstg. (M)	118.2	Institutional Ownership (%)	83		

Price Performance

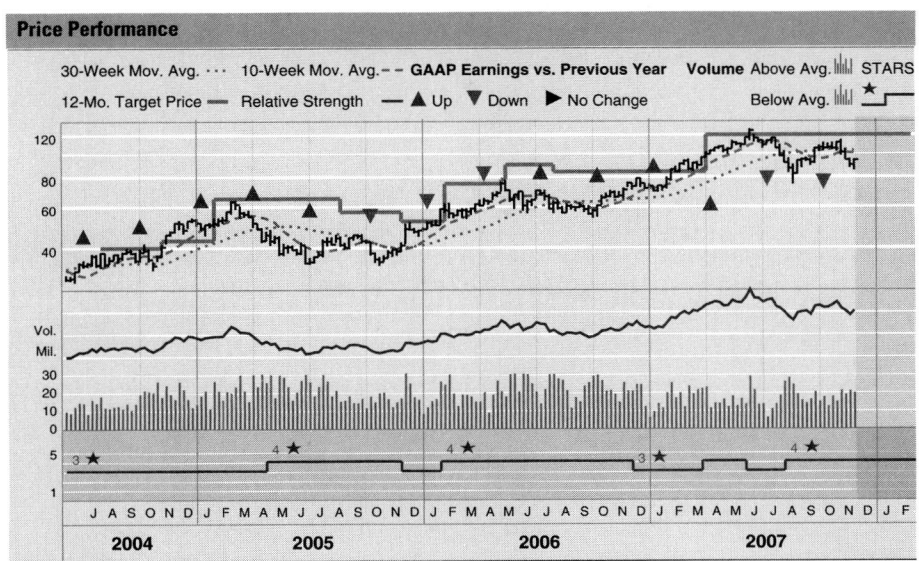

30-Week Mov. Avg. · · · 10-Week Mov. Avg. – – **GAAP Earnings vs. Previous Year** Volume Above Avg. ▐▌▌ STARS
12-Mo. Target Price — Relative Strength — ▲ Up ▼ Down ▶ No Change Below Avg. ▐▌▌ ★

Options: ASE, CBOE

Analysis prepared by **Leo J. Larkin** on November 07, 2007, when the stock traded at **$ 100.10**.

Highlights

➤ We project a 14% sales rise in 2008, mostly reflecting acquisitions. Other factors we see lifting sales include a projected recovery in demand from distributors, another decline in the level of imports and a small increase in auto production. In our view, distributor inventories reached unsustainably low levels in late 2007 and we think they will rebuild inventory beginning in 2008's first quarter. We anticipate that continued weakness in the U.S. dollar combined with higher shipping costs will lead to another decline in imports. Our broad economic assumption is for GDP growth of 2.1% in 2008, versus estimated GDP growth of 2.0% in 2007. Finally, we see another increase in sales in European operations on continued economic growth and less import competition.

➤ Penalized by acquisition costs, we look for margin contraction and estimate EPS of $9.90 in 2008, versus estimated operating EPS of $9.54 in 2007.

➤ We think EPS over the longer term will benefit from industry consolidation and a gradual decline in costs for employee pension and health care.

Investment Rationale/Risk

➤ We view X as a way to capitalize on the ongoing consolidation of the global steel industry. In our view, sharply higher costs for raw materials will prompt further merger activity as a means to obtain better terms from suppliers or produce raw materials internally. Also, we believe that consolidation will help the industry regain some pricing power. We also see X benefiting from a gradual decline in pension and health care costs and rising demand for oil country tubular goods used for oil and gas exploration. Recently selling at about 10.3X our 2008 EPS estimate, we think X is attractively valued.

➤ Risks to our recommendation and target price include the possibility that X fails to profitably integrate Lone Star and Stelco. Also, in 2003, X incurred litigation expenses totaling $25 million to settle an asbestos-related lawsuit. While the 2003 settlement may prove to be an aberration, we see it as a cause for caution.

➤ We look for X to trade at about 12.1X our 2008 EPS estimate, which is toward the low end of the historical range and about in line with our projected P/E level for peers. On that basis, our 12-month target price is $120.

Qualitative Risk Assessment

LOW	MEDIUM	**HIGH**

Our risk assessment reflects the company's exposure to highly cyclical industries such as autos and construction. While X has reduced debt and improved free cash flow in recent years, its unfunded health care liabilities totaled $2.2 billion at the end of 2006.

Quantitative Evaluations

S&P Quality Ranking B-

D	C	**B-**	B	B+	A-	A	A+

Relative Strength Rank MODERATE

51

LOWEST = 1   HIGHEST = 99

Revenue/Earnings Data

Revenue (Million $)

	1Q	2Q	3Q	4Q	Year
2007	3,756	4,228	4,354	--	--
2006	3,728	4,107	4,106	3,774	15,715
2005	3,787	3,582	3,200	3,470	14,039
2004	2,963	3,466	3,729	3,932	14,108
2003	1,907	2,362	2,508	2,681	9,458
2002	1,434	1,807	1,914	1,899	7,054

Earnings Per Share ($)

2007	2.30	2.54	2.27	E2.25	E9.54
2006	2.04	3.22	3.42	2.50	11.18
2005	3.51	1.91	0.71	0.85	7.00
2004	0.36	1.62	2.72	3.59	8.37
2003	-0.35	-0.01	-3.47	-0.26	-4.09
2002	-0.93	0.28	1.04	0.10	0.62

Fiscal year ended Dec. 31. Next earnings report expected: Late January. EPS Estimates based on S&P Operating Earnings; historical GAAP earnings are as reported.

Dividend Data (Dates: mm/dd Payment Date: mm/dd/yy)

Amount ($)	Date Decl.	Ex-Div. Date	Stk. of Record	Payment Date
0.200	07/25	05/14	05/16	06/09/07
0.200	07/31	08/13	08/15	09/10/07
0.200	10/30	11/09	11/14	12/10/07

Dividends have been paid since 1991. Source: Company reports.

The McGraw-Hill Companies

United States Steel Corp

Business Summary November 07, 2007

CORPORATE OVERVIEW. U.S. Steel is the second largest integrated steel company in the U.S. and has operations in Central Europe. In 2006, X produced 16.4 million tons in the U.S. and 7.1 million tons in Europe.

On October 31, 2007, X announced that it had completed the acquisition of Canada based steelmaker Stelco Inc. in an all cash transaction valued at $1.2 billion. Following the merger, X will have annual raw steel capacity of some 33 million tons,versus 26.8 at 2006's year end. On June 14, 2007, X announced that it had completed the acquisition of Lone Star Technologies in an all-cash transaction totaling $2.1 billion. Following the transaction, X will have annual North American tubular manufacturing capability of approximately 2.8 million tons. X's tubular shipments totaled 1.2 million tons in 2006.

MARKET PROFILE. The primary factor affecting demand for steel products is economic growth in general, and growth in demand for durable goods in particular. The two largest end markets for steel products in the U.S. are autos and construction, which together accounted for 29.1% of shipments in 2006. Other end markets include appliances, containers, machinery, and oil and

gas. Distributors, also known as service centers, accounted for 21.8% of industry shipments in the U.S. in 2006. Distributors are the largest single market for the steel industry in the U.S. Because distributors sell to a wide variety of OEMs, it is impossible to trace the final destination of much of the industry's shipments. Consequently, consumption of steel by the auto, construction and other industries may be higher than the shipment data would suggest. U.S. production was 105.1 million tons in 2006, and X's market share was 15.6%. X's largest end markets in 2006 were distributors (21% of revenues), appliances (8%), converters (23%), construction (13%), automotive (13%), containers (9%), oil and gas (5%), and other (8%). U.S. consumption increased at a compound annual growth rate (CAGR) of 1.4% from 1997 through 2006. Global steel consumption rose at a CAGR of 5.2% from 1997 through 2006.

Company Financials Fiscal Year Ended Dec. 31

Per Share Data ($)	2006	2005	2004	2003	2002	2001	2000	1999	1998	1997
Tangible Book Value	36.82	25.63	32.30	7.98	15.81	28.16	21.54	23.22	22.22	18.78
Cash Flow	14.69	11.54	11.17	-0.57	4.24	1.42	3.72	3.93	6.72	7.89
Earnings	11.18	7.00	8.37	-4.09	0.62	-2.45	-0.33	0.48	3.92	4.88
S&P Core Earnings	11.76	6.64	8.74	-1.06	-4.10	-8.47	NA	NA	NA	NA
Dividends	0.25	0.28	0.20	0.20	0.20	0.55	1.00	1.00	1.00	1.00
Payout Ratio	2%	4%	2%	NM	32%	NM	NM	NM	26%	20%
Prices:High	79.01	63.90	54.06	37.05	22.00	22.00	32.94	34.25	43.06	40.75
Prices:Low	48.05	33.59	25.22	9.61	10.66	13.00	12.69	21.75	20.44	25.38
P/E Ratio:High	7	9	6	NM	35	NM	NM	71	11	8
P/E Ratio:Low	4	5	3	NM	17	NM	NM	45	5	5

Income Statement Analysis (Million $)										
Revenue	15,715	14,039	14,108	9,458	7,054	6,375	6,090	5,380	6,189	6,814
Operating Income	2,143	1,740	1,964	316	478	-61.0	422	520	763	949
Depreciation	441	366	382	363	350	344	360	304	283	303
Interest Expense	Nil	107	138	148	136	153	115	75.0	53.0	98.0
Pretax Income	1,723	1,312	1,461	-860	13.0	-546	-1.00	76.0	537	686
Effective Tax Rate	18.8%	27.8%	24.0%	NM	NM	NM	NM	32.9%	32.2%	34.1%
Net Income	1,374	910	1,077	-406	61.0	-218	-21.0	51.0	364	452
S&P Core Earnings	1,438	847	1,104	-109	-398	-755	NA	NA	NA	NA

Balance Sheet & Other Financial Data (Million $)										
Cash	1,422	1,479	1,037	316	243	147	219	22.0	9.00	18.0
Current Assets	5,196	4,831	4,243	3,107	2,440	2,073	2,717	1,981	1,275	1,531
Total Assets	10,586	9,822	10,956	7,838	7,977	8,337	8,711	7,525	6,693	6,694
Current Liabilities	2,702	2,749	2,531	2,130	1,372	1,259	1,391	1,266	1,016	1,334
Long Term Debt	943	1,363	1,363	1,890	1,408	1,434	2,485	1,151	712	456
Common Equity	4,365	3,108	3,754	867	2,027	2,506	1,917	2,053	2,090	1,634
Total Capital	5,346	4,719	5,959	2,989	3,658	4,672	5,070	3,555	2,805	2,486
Capital Expenditures	612	741	579	316	258	287	244	287	310	261
Cash Flow	1,807	1,258	1,441	-59.0	411	126	331	346	638	742
Current Ratio	1.9	1.8	1.7	1.5	1.8	1.6	2.0	1.6	1.3	1.1
% Long Term Debt of Capitalization	17.6	28.9	22.9	63.2	38.5	30.7	49.0	32.4	25.4	18.3
% Net Income of Revenue	8.7	6.5	7.8	NM	0.9	NM	NM	0.9	5.9	6.6
% Return on Assets	13.5	8.7	11.5	NM	0.7	NM	NM	0.7	5.4	6.8
% Return on Equity	36.6	25.6	45.8	NM	2.7	NM	NM	2.0	18.4	31.7

Data as orig reptd.; bef. results of disc opers/spec. items. Per share data adj. for stk. divs.; EPS diluted. E-Estimated. NA-Not Available. NM-Not Meaningful. NR-Not Ranked. UR-Under Review.

Office: 600 Grant Street, Pittsburgh, PA 15219-2702.
Telephone: 412-433-1121.
Email: shareholderservices@uss.com
Website: http://www.ussteel.com

Chrmn, Pres & CEO: J.P. Surma, Jr.
COO & EVP: J.H. Goodish
EVP & CFO: G.R. Haggerty
SVP & General Counsel: J.D. Garraux

VP & Treas: L.T. Brockway
Investor Contact: N. Harper (412-433-1184)
Board Members: J. G. Cooper, R. J. Darnall, J. Drosdick, R. A. Gephardt, C. R. Lee, J. M. Lipton, F. Lucchino, S. E. Schofield, J. P. Surma, D. C. Yearley

Founded: 2001
Domicile: Delaware
Employees: 44,000

United Technologies Corp

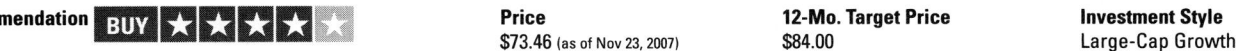

STANDARD
&POOR'S

S&P Recommendation	BUY ★★★★☆	Price	12-Mo. Target Price	Investment Style
		$73.46 (as of Nov 23, 2007)	$84.00	Large-Cap Growth

GICS Sector Industrials
Sub-Industry Aerospace & Defense

Summary This aerospace-industrial conglomerate's portfolio includes Pratt & Whitney jet engines, Sikorsky helicopters, Otis elevators and Carrier air conditioners, among other products.

Key Stock Statistics (Source S&P, Vickers, company reports)

52-Wk Range	$82.50–61.80	S&P Oper. EPS 2007**E**	4.24	Market Capitalization(B)	$72.616	Beta	0.87
Trailing 12-Month EPS	$4.06	S&P Oper. EPS 2008**E**	4.76	Yield (%)	1.74	S&P 3-Yr. Proj. EPS CAGR(%)	12.00
Trailing 12-Month P/E	18.1	P/E on S&P Oper. EPS 2007**E**	17.3	Dividend Rate/Share	$1.28	S&P Credit Rating	A
$10K Invested 5 Yrs Ago	$25,022	Common Shares Outstg. (M)	988.5	Institutional Ownership (%)	82		

Price Performance

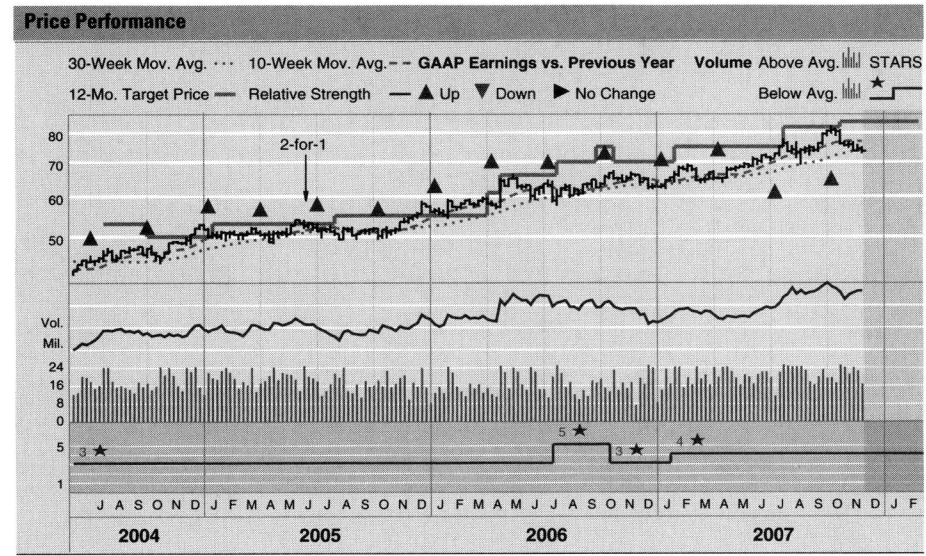

30-Week Mov. Avg. ··· 10-Week Mov. Avg. - - **GAAP Earnings vs. Previous Year** Volume Above Avg. ▮▮▮ STARS
12-Mo. Target Price — Relative Strength — ▲ Up ▼ Down ▶ No Change Below Avg. ▮▮▮

Options: ASE, CBOE, P, Ph

Analysis prepared by **Richard Tortoriello** on October 19, 2007, when the stock traded at **$ 76.32**.

Highlights

➤ After a projected 12% increase in 2007, we see sales growth slowing to about 7% in 2008, due to moderating growth across UTX's business segments, including Otis, Carrier, UTC Fire & Security and the aerospace businesses. We expect growth in the industrial businesses of about 6%, led by UTC Fire & Security. New orders at Otis increased 24% in the first nine months of 2007. We expect high single digit growth in the aerospace businesses, where we see continued strong demand for jet engines and gas turbines, OEM parts, and aftermarket parts and service.

➤ We project a 2007 operating profit margin of 13.1%, up from 12.7% in 2006 and 12.1% in 2005. For 2008, we project margin improvement to about 13.5%, on volume increases, restructuring, and productivity improvements. We project an EPS increase of 14%, to $4.24, in 2007, and we see 12% growth, to $4.76, in 2008.

➤ From a longer-term perspective, we believe UTX can sustain earnings growth of about 12% over the next three years, as we expect strong global trends in aerospace and infrastructure growth to continue.

Investment Rationale/Risk

➤ We believe a combination of strong management and favorable global trends, including global aerospace and commercial construction and infrastructure demand, will lead to above average growth for UTX going forward. We are encouraged by the continued improvement we saw in commercial HVAC and refrigeration markets at Carrier thus far in 2007. In addition, we think management's focus on production issues and bolstering profits at Sikorsky will continue to result in improved growth and profit margins in this segment.

➤ Risks to our recommendation and target price include an unanticipated slowdown in the growth of the global economy, competitive pressures in UTX's core businesses, and industry-specific slowdowns, such as further deterioration in the U.S. residential housing market.

➤ Our 12-month target price of $84 is based on a P/E of 17.6X our 2008 EPS estimate, slightly above UTX's 10-year historical average forward P/E ratio of 16X, with a high of 22X and a low of 11X. We believe UTX's earnings growth outlook and current economic conditions justify a slightly better than average P/E valuation.

Qualitative Risk Assessment

LOW	MEDIUM	HIGH

Our risk assessment is based on our view of UTX's history of steady growth in both earnings and dividends over the past 10 years, as reflected in an S&P Quality Ranking of A+. We also consider UTX's balance sheet strong, with 25% long-term debt to total capital and 5.3% cash to assets as of September 2007.

Quantitative Evaluations

S&P Quality Ranking A+

D	C	B-	B	B+	A-	A	A+

Relative Strength Rank MODERATE

64

LOWEST = 1   HIGHEST = 99

Revenue/Earnings Data

Revenue (Million $)

	1Q	2Q	3Q	4Q	Year
2007	12,278	13,904	13,863	--	--
2006	10,446	12,046	11,972	12,654	47,829
2005	9,309	10,974	10,832	11,172	42,725
2004	8,646	9,622	9,339	8,938	37,445
2003	6,702	7,790	7,954	8,588	31,034
2002	6,374	7,324	7,299	7,215	28,212

Earnings Per Share ($)

2007	0.82	1.16	1.21	E1.02	E4.24
2006	0.76	1.09	0.99	0.87	3.71
2005	0.64	0.95	0.81	0.71	3.12
2004	0.57	0.83	0.72	0.65	2.76
2003	0.50	0.63	0.64	0.58	2.35
2002	0.46	0.62	0.61	0.53	2.21

Fiscal year ended Dec. 31. Next earnings report expected: Late January. EPS Estimates based on S&P Operating Earnings; historical GAAP earnings are as reported.

Dividend Data (Dates: mm/dd Payment Date: mm/dd/yy)

Amount ($)	Date Decl.	Ex-Div. Date	Stk. of Record	Payment Date
0.265	02/05	02/14	02/16	03/10/07
0.265	04/11	05/16	05/18	06/10/07
0.320	06/13	08/15	08/17	09/10/07
0.320	10/10	11/14	11/16	12/10/07

Dividends have been paid since 1936. Source: Company reports.

Please read the Required Disclosures and Analyst Certification on the last page of this report.

The McGraw-Hill Companies

United Technologies Corp

STANDARD &POOR'S

Business Summary October 19, 2007

CORPORATE OVERVIEW. This $50 billion in annual sales multi-industry holding company conducts business through six business segments: Carrier, Otis, Pratt & Whitney, UTC Fire & Security, Hamilton Sundstrand, and Sikorsky.

Carrier (28% of sales and 20% of operating profits) is the world's largest maker of commercial and residential heating, ventilating and air-conditioning (HVAC) systems. It also offers refrigeration and food service equipment, and related controls for residential, commercial, industrial and transportation applications. In addition, carrier provides installation, retrofit, and parts and services for its products, as well as those of other HVAC and refrigeration makers. International sales, including U.S. export sales, accounted for 54% of segment sales in 2006.

Otis (22% of 2005 sales, 30% of operating profits) is the world's largest maker of elevators and escalators. Otis designs, manufactures, sells and installs a wide range of passenger and freight elevators for low-, medium-, and high-speed applications, as well as a broad line of escalators and moving walkways. International revenues were 80% of total segment revenues in 2006.

Pratt & Whitney (23% of sales and 29% of operating profits) is a major supplier of jet engines for commercial, general aviation, and military aircraft. P&W al-

so sells engines for auxiliary power units, industrial applications, and space propulsion systems. P&W's Global Service Partners provides maintenance, repair, and overhaul services, including the sale of spare parts for non-P&W engines, as well as fleet management services. Boeing and Airbus accounted for 6% and 12%, respectively, of segment sales in 2006, and the U.S. government accounted for 33%. Aircraft spare parts and overhaul service operations are an important source of high-margin, recurring revenues. International revenues were 53% of total segment revenues in 2006.

UTC Fire & Security (10% of sales and 5% of operating profits) is a global provider of security and fire safety products and services. This segment was created in the second quarter of 2005 following the acquisition of Kidde plc, a provider of fire safety products and services to commercial, industrial, aerospace and retail customers in 29 countries. International sales accounted for 84% of total segment sales in 2006.

Company Financials Fiscal Year Ended Dec. 31

Per Share Data ($)	2006	2005	2004	2003	2002	2001	2000	1999	1998	1997
Tangible Book Value	NM	0.91	1.84	2.32	1.46	1.66	0.95	0.80	2.92	3.37
Cash Flow	4.74	4.09	3.73	3.14	2.93	2.81	2.63	1.66	2.13	1.86
Earnings	3.71	3.12	2.76	2.35	2.21	1.92	1.78	0.83	1.26	1.05
S&P Core Earnings	3.64	3.05	2.59	2.16	1.32	1.14	NA	NA	NA	NA
Dividends	1.02	0.88	0.70	0.57	0.49	0.45	0.41	0.38	0.35	0.31
Payout Ratio	27%	28%	25%	24%	22%	23%	23%	46%	28%	29%
Prices:High	67.47	58.89	53.14	48.38	38.88	43.75	39.88	37.98	28.13	22.23
Prices:Low	54.20	48.43	40.34	26.76	24.42	20.05	23.25	25.81	16.75	16.28
P/E Ratio:High	18	19	19	21	18	23	22	46	22	21
P/E Ratio:Low	15	16	15	11	11	10	13	31	13	15

Income Statement Analysis (Million $)

	2006	2005	2004	2003	2002	2001	2000	1999	1998	1997
Revenue	47,829	42,725	37,445	31,034	28,212	27,897	26,583	23,844	25,687	24,495
Operating Income	7,131	6,166	5,448	4,644	4,384	4,138	3,999	2,361	2,993	2,598
Depreciation	1,033	984	978	799	727	905	859	844	854	848
Interest Expense	606	498	363	375	381	426	382	260	204	195
Pretax Income	5,492	4,684	4,107	3,470	3,276	2,807	2,758	1,257	1,963	1,764
Effective Tax Rate	27.2%	26.8%	26.4%	27.1%	27.1%	26.9%	30.9%	25.9%	31.7%	32.5%
Net Income	3,732	3,164	2,788	2,361	2,236	1,938	1,808	841	1,255	1,072
S&P Core Earnings	3,653	3,089	2,619	2,147	1,298	1,113	NA	NA	NA	NA

Balance Sheet & Other Financial Data (Million $)

	2006	2005	2004	2003	2002	2001	2000	1999	1998	1997
Cash	2,546	2,247	2,265	1,623	2,080	1,558	748	957	550	755
Current Assets	18,844	17,206	15,522	12,364	11,751	11,263	10,662	10,627	9,355	9,248
Total Assets	47,141	45,925	40,035	34,648	29,090	26,969	25,364	24,366	18,375	16,719
Current Liabilities	15,208	15,345	12,947	10,295	7,903	8,371	9,344	9,215	7,735	7,311
Long Term Debt	7,037	5,935	4,231	4,257	4,632	4,237	3,476	3,086	1,575	1,275
Common Equity	17,297	16,991	14,008	11,707	10,506	8,369	7,662	7,117	3,998	3,658
Total Capital	25,170	23,704	19,149	16,673	16,445	13,899	12,514	11,664	6,994	6,362
Capital Expenditures	954	929	795	530	586	793	937	762	866	843
Cash Flow	4,765	4,148	3,766	3,160	2,963	2,843	2,667	1,685	2,109	1,888
Current Ratio	1.2	1.1	1.2	1.2	1.5	1.3	1.1	1.2	1.2	1.3
% Long Term Debt of Capitalization	28.0	25.0	22.1	25.5	28.2	30.5	27.8	26.5	22.5	20.0
% Net Income of Revenue	7.8	7.4	7.4	7.6	7.9	6.9	6.8	3.5	4.9	4.4
% Return on Assets	8.0	7.3	7.4	7.4	8.0	7.4	7.3	4.0	7.2	6.4
% Return on Equity	21.8	20.2	21.7	23.9	23.0	24.2	24.5	14.6	32.8	27.7

Data as orig reptd.; bef. results of disc opers/spec. items. Per share data adj. for stk. divs.; EPS diluted. E-Estimated. NA-Not Available. NM-Not Meaningful. NR-Not Ranked. UR-Under Review.

Office: 1 Financial Plz , Hartford, CT 06103.
Telephone: 860-728-7000.
Email: invrelations@corphq.utc.com
Website: http://www.utc.com

Chrmn & CEO: G. David
Pres & COO: L.R. Chenevert
SVP & General Counsel: C.D. Gill
VP & Treas: T.I. Rogan

VP & Secy: D. Valentine
Investor Contact: P. Jackson (860-728-7912)
Board Members: L. R. Chenevert, G. David, J. V. Faraci, J. Garnier, J. S. Gorelick, C. R. Lee, R. D. McCormick, H. W. McGraw III, R. B. Myers, F. P. Popoff, H. P. Swygert, A. Villeneuve, H. A. Wagner, C. T. Whitman

Founded: 1934
Domicile: Delaware
Employees: 214,500

The McGraw-Hill Companies

Unum Group

STANDARD &POOR'S

S&P Recommendation `HOLD` ★★★☆☆

Price	12-Mo. Target Price	Investment Style
$23.43 (as of Nov 23, 2007)	$29.00	Large-Cap Value

GICS Sector Financials
Sub-Industry Life & Health Insurance

Summary This leading provider of individual and group disability coverage was formed through the June 1999 merger of Provident Cos. and UNUM Corp.

Key Stock Statistics (Source S&P, Vickers, company reports)

52-Wk Range	$28.20– 19.79	S&P Oper. EPS 2007**E**	2.14	Market Capitalization(B)	$8.453	Beta	1.21
Trailing 12-Month EPS	$2.29	S&P Oper. EPS 2008**E**	2.40	Yield (%)	1.28	S&P 3-Yr. Proj. EPS CAGR(%)	10.00
Trailing 12-Month P/E	10.2	P/E on S&P Oper. EPS 2007**E**	10.9	Dividend Rate/Share	$0.30	S&P Credit Rating	BB+
$10K Invested 5 Yrs Ago	$14,407	Common Shares Outstg. (M)	360.8	Institutional Ownership (%)	96		

Price Performance

- 30-Week Mov. Avg. ··· 10-Week Mov. Avg. - - GAAP Earnings vs. Previous Year   Volume Above Avg. STARS
- 12-Mo. Target Price — Relative Strength — ▲ Up ▼ Down ▶ No Change   Below Avg.

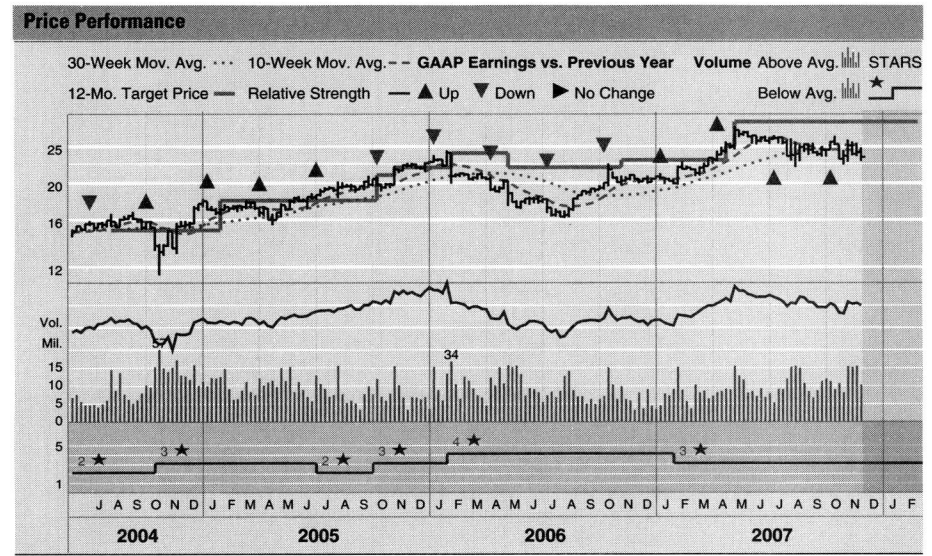

Options: ASE, CBOE, P

Analysis prepared by **Tanjila Shafi** on November 19, 2007, when the stock traded at **$ 24.24**.

Highlights

➤ We expect 2008 pretax operating earnings for the Unum U.S. segment to increase, as the group income protection sub-segment benefits from an improving benefit ratio. We believe that case sales will experience low double-digit growth based on new product initiatives such as Simply Unum. We see moderate pretax operating earnings growth for the Unum U.K. segment on a steady benefit ratio and a declining expense ratio.

➤ We look for operating earnings for the Colonial segment to rise modestly in 2008, based on its improved distribution efforts and diversified products. For the run-off closed block individual income protection segment, we estimate flat pretax operating earnings, reflecting lower net investment income and continued run-off.

➤ We project EPS from continuing operations in 2007 of $2.14. Our forecast for 2008 EPS from continuing operations is $2.40.

Investment Rationale/Risk

➤ We believe that UNM's recent securitization of its individual disability income closed block is favorable, as it releases $1.1 billion in capital that can be used for share buybacks. We expect that the group income protection sub-segment will achieve its stated goal of an 88% to 89% benefit ratio by late 2008 to early 2009, reflecting changes in sales mix, underwriting discipline, and operational improvements. Also, we anticipate that the company's goals of improving its risk-based capital (RBC) ratio to 315% to 325%, decreasing its debt to capital ratio, and increasing excess capital at the holding company level will help improve its return on equity (ROE).

➤ Risks to our recommendation and target price include worse than expected client retention and sales following income protection product price increases; unfavorable claims handling in the group income protection area; and higher than forecast costs for reassessed claims under recent market conduct exam settlements.

➤ Our 12-month target price is $29, 12.1X our 2008 operating EPS and in line with its historical multiples.

Qualitative Risk Assessment

LOW	MEDIUM	HIGH

Our risk assessment for UNM reflects regulatory scrutiny surrounding certain claims practices. Although the largest suits have been settled, UNM faces the possibility of additional suits and increased reserving for benefit costs in its claims reassessment.

Quantitative Evaluations

S&P Quality Ranking   B-

D	C	B-	B	B+	A-	A	A+

Relative Strength Rank   MODERATE

59

LOWEST = 1   HIGHEST = 99

Revenue/Earnings Data

Revenue (Million $)

	1Q	2Q	3Q	4Q	Year
2007	2,601	2,666	2,610	--	--
2006	2,600	2,622	2,617	2,696	10,535
2005	2,572	2,657	2,544	2,665	10,437
2004	2,624	2,509	2,655	2,677	10,465
2003	2,395	2,529	2,556	2,511	9,992
2002	2,331	2,402	2,450	2,431	9,613

Earnings Per Share ($)

	1Q	2Q	3Q	4Q	Year
2007	0.49	0.43	0.52	E0.53	E2.14
2006	0.23	0.37	-0.19	0.79	1.21
2005	0.49	0.55	0.17	0.43	1.64
2004	-1.93	0.25	0.55	0.45	-0.65
2003	-1.02	0.36	0.36	-0.71	-0.96
2002	0.30	0.40	0.45	0.39	1.68

Fiscal year ended Dec. 31. Next earnings report expected: Late January. EPS Estimates based on S&P Operating Earnings; historical GAAP earnings are as reported.

Dividend Data (Dates: mm/dd Payment Date: mm/dd/yy)

Amount ($)	Date Decl.	Ex-Div. Date	Stk. of Record	Payment Date
0.075	01/17	01/25	01/29	02/16/07
0.075	04/16	04/26	04/30	05/18/07
0.075	07/17	07/26	07/30	08/17/07
0.075	10/15	10/25	10/29	11/16/07

Dividends have been paid since 1925. Source: Company reports.

Unum Group

STANDARD &POOR'S

Business Summary November 19, 2007

CORPORATE OVERVIEW. UNM provides group and individual income protection insurance in North America and the U.K. through its subsidiaries. The company offers other products, including long-term care insurance, life insurance, group benefits, and related services.

The company has six operating segments: Unum US, Unum UK, Colonial, individual income protection - closed block, other, and corporate. Unum US accounted for 60% of operating revenue in 2006, Unum UK 9.7%, Colonial 8.9%, individual income protection - closed block 19%, other 1.4%, and corporate 0.6%. In 2006, premium income for Unum US declined 0.6%, Unum UK premium income rose 7.3%, and Colonial premium income increased 7.0%.

The Unum US segment includes group income protection insurance, group life and accidental death and dismemberment products, and supplemental and voluntary lines of business. The Unum UK segment includes group long-term income protection insurance, group life products, and individual income pro-

tection products issued by Unum Limited and sold primarily in the U.K. through field sales personnel and independent brokers and consultants. The Colonial segment includes a broad line of products sold mainly to employees at their workplaces, including income protection, life, and cancer and critical illness products. The other segment includes products that are no longer actively marketed, with the exception of the closed block business, including individual life and corporate-owned life insurance, reinsurance pools and management operations, group pension, health insurance, and individual annuities. The corporate segment includes investment income on unallocated corporate assets, interest expense, and certain unallocated corporate income and expense items.

Company Financials Fiscal Year Ended Dec. 31

Per Share Data ($)	2006	2005	2004	2003	2002	2001	2000	1999	1998	1997
Tangible Book Value	21.93	23.76	23.45	22.94	25.58	21.74	20.29	17.82	20.05	17.69
Operating Earnings	NA	NA	NA	NA	2.52	2.44	2.37	-1.00	2.14	1.77
Earnings	1.21	1.64	-0.65	-0.96	1.68	2.39	2.33	-0.77	1.82	1.84
S&P Core Earnings	1.29	1.81	-0.26	-0.54	2.35	2.30	NA	NA	NA	NA
Dividends	0.30	0.30	0.30	0.37	0.59	0.59	0.59	0.35	0.40	0.38
Payout Ratio	25%	18%	NM	NM	35%	25%	25%	NM	22%	21%
Prices:High	24.44	22.90	18.25	19.54	29.70	33.75	31.94	56.88	42.44	39.06
Prices:Low	16.15	15.50	11.41	5.91	16.30	22.25	11.94	26.00	26.13	23.19
P/E Ratio:High	20	14	NM	NM	18	14	14	NM	23	21
P/E Ratio:Low	13	9	NM	NM	10	9	5	NM	14	13

Income Statement Analysis (Million $)	2006	2005	2004	2003	2002	2001	2000	1999	1998	1997
Life Insurance in Force	NA	833,363	908,034	787,199	712,826	642,988	583,848	567,215	158,317	138,341
Premium Income:Life	NA	7,816	5,985	1,800	1,683	1,554	1,448	1,452	503	1,287
Premium Income:A & H	NA	1,787	1,855	5,816	5,770	5,524	5,608	5,391	1,845	NA
Net Investment Income	2,321	2,188	2,159	2,158	2,086	2,003	2,060	2,060	1,374	1,355
Total Revenue	10,535	10,437	10,465	9,992	9,613	9,395	9,432	9,330	3,938	3,553
Pretax Income	465	710	-260	-435	1,019	825	866	-166	403	380
Net Operating Income	NA	NA	NA	NA	614	593	NA	NA	368	NA
Net Income	404	514	-192	-265	817	582	564	-183	254	247
S&P Core Earnings	428	570	-77.1	-150	568	564	NA	NA	NA	NA

Balance Sheet & Other Financial Data (Million $)	2006	2005	2004	2003	2002	2001	2000	1999	1998	1997
Cash & Equivalent	768	688	719	663	734	2,515	1,958	836	366	401
Premiums Due	5,512	5,609	6,969	6,243	5,986	6,224	6,047	765	98.4	73.9
Investment Assets:Bonds	35,002	34,857	32,488	31,187	27,486	24,393	22,589	22,357	15,142	17,342
Investment Assets:Stocks	Nil	13.6	12.9	39.1	27.9	10.9	24.5	38.0	2.10	10.0
Investment Assets:Loans	944	3,941	3,572	3,353	3,344	3,510	3,679	3,595	2,107	1,984
Investment Assets:Total	40,163	39,357	36,588	35,028	31,152	28,324	26,604	26,549	17,333	19,434
Deferred Policy Costs	2,983	2,913	2,883	3,052	2,982	2,675	2,424	2,391	465	363
Total Assets	52,823	51,867	50,832	49,718	45,260	42,443	40,364	38,448	23,088	23,178
Debt	2,660	3,262	2,862	2,789	1,914	2,304	1,915	1,467	900	725
Common Equity	7,719	7,364	7,224	7,271	9,398	5,940	5,576	4,983	3,409	3,123
% Return on Revenue	3.9	4.9	NM	NM	8.5	6.2	6.0	NM	6.5	7.0
% Return on Assets	0.8	1.0	NM	NM	1.9	1.4	1.4	NM	1.1	1.3
% Return on Equity	5.4	7.0	NM	NM	9.1	10.1	10.7	NM	7.7	10.0
% Investment Yield	5.8	5.8	6.0	6.5	7.0	7.3	7.8	NM	7.9	7.6

Data as orig reptd.; bef. results of disc opers/spec. items. Per share data adj. for stk. divs.; EPS diluted. E-Estimated. NA-Not Available. NM-Not Meaningful. NR-Not Ranked. UR-Under Review.

Office: 1 Fountain Square, Chattanooga, TN 37402-1307.
Telephone: 423-294-1011.
Website: http://www.unum.com
Pres & CEO: T.R. Watjen

EVP & CFO: R.C. Greving
EVP & General Counsel: C.L. Glick

Board Members: E. M. Caulfield, J. S. Fossel, P. H. Godwin, R. E. Goldsberry, T. Kinser, G. C. Larson, A. S. MacMillan, Jr., H. O. Maclellan, Jr., E. J. Muhl, M. J. Passarella, W. J. Ryan, T. R. Watjen

Founded: 1887
Domicile: Delaware
Employees: 11,100

UST Inc.

STANDARD &POOR'S

S&P Recommendation **BUY** ★★★★☆

Price	12-Mo. Target Price	Investment Style
$54.68 (as of Nov 26, 2007)	$62.00	Large-Cap Blend

GICS Sector Consumer Staples
Sub-Industry Tobacco

Summary UST is a leading producer of moist smokeless tobacco products, marketed under leading brand names such as Copenhagen and Skoal. It also produces and imports wines.

Key Stock Statistics (Source S&P, Vickers, company reports)

52-Wk Range	$61.17– 47.40	S&P Oper. EPS 2007**E**	3.44	Market Capitalization(B)	$8.715	Beta	0.51
Trailing 12-Month EPS	$3.22	S&P Oper. EPS 2008**E**	3.60	Yield (%)	4.39	S&P 3-Yr. Proj. EPS CAGR(%)	7.00
Trailing 12-Month P/E	17.0	P/E on S&P Oper. EPS 2007**E**	15.9	Dividend Rate/Share	$2.40	S&P Credit Rating	A
$10K Invested 5 Yrs Ago	$21,621	Common Shares Outstg. (M)	159.4	Institutional Ownership (%)	NM		

Price Performance

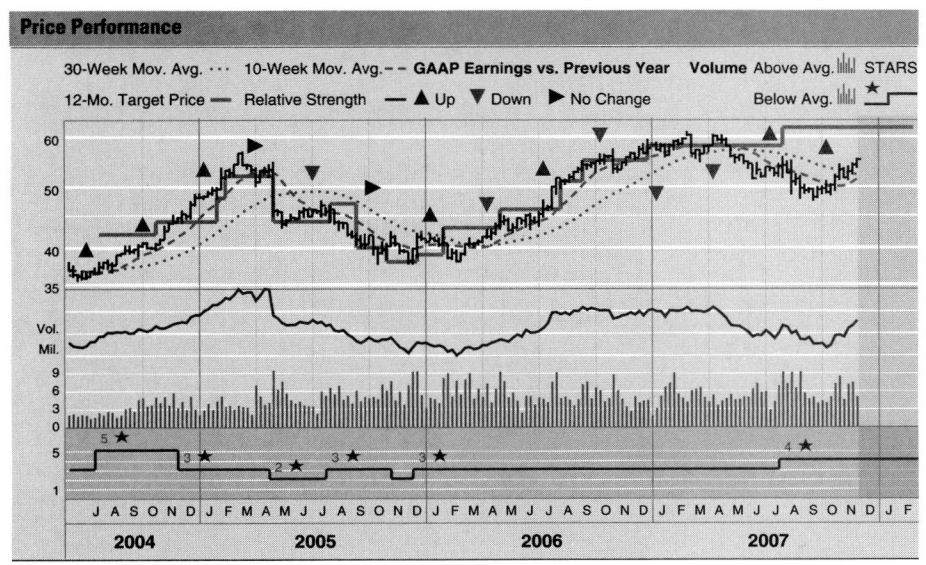

30-Week Mov. Avg. · · · 10-Week Mov. Avg. - - GAAP Earnings vs. Previous Year   Volume Above Avg. STARS
12-Mo. Target Price — Relative Strength — ▲ Up ▼ Down ▶ No Change   Below Avg. ★

Options: ASE, CBOE, P

Analysis prepared by **Esther Y. Kwon, CFA** on November 26, 2007, when the stock traded at **$ 54.73**.

Highlights

➤ With moist smokeless tobacco (MST) volume trends improving, and growth in the wine segment, we see net sales increases of about 5% in 2007 and 4% in 2008. With planned marketing increases, we foresee volume trends improving for higher margin premium MST brands, although we expect continued pricing pressure as UST focuses on shoring up market share. We look for price-value segment volume to continue to expand. We see new line extensions, pouches, and other product innovations contributing to sales growth longer term.

➤ We look for a stabilizing of tobacco gross margins, as increased promotional activity offsets possible volume growth in the price-value brand. However, we see momentum in wine volume building and pressuring overall corporate gross margins, offset slightly by cost savings from UST's Project Momentum initiative.

➤ Aided by lower interest expense due to reduced debt levels, and stock repurchases anticipated to be in the range of $200 million to $300 million, we estimate 2007 operating EPS of $3.44, up from 2006's $3.10. For 2008, we see sales momentum, cost savings initiatives, and share repurchases boosting EPS to $3.60.

Investment Rationale/Risk

➤ With increased marketing efforts on premium products, we look for a recovery in this category over the long term. Furthermore, we see UST's efforts to build the smokeless category supporting long-term industry growth. However, we remain concerned about competitive pressures in the form of discounting in the price-value category and new product introductions by peers.

➤ Risks to our recommendation and target price include the possibility of volume declines in the premium category, despite increased marketing efforts, and continued trading-down to price value brands, which would pressure margins further. Also, the Project Momentum restructuring plan might not achieve the expected cost benefits.

➤ Our 12-month target price of $62 is based on a weighted blend of two metrics. Our DCF model, which assumes a weighted average cost of capital of 8%, five-year annual sales growth of 3%, and a terminal growth rate of 2.5%, derives an intrinsic value of $60. By applying a forward peer P/E of 18X to our 2008 EPS estimate, we arrive at a value of $63. The stock recently yielded 4.4%.

Qualitative Risk Assessment

LOW	MEDIUM	**HIGH**

Our risk assessment reflects that the tobacco industry is typified by relatively stable revenue streams, while tobacco company stocks typically have below average betas. Although the smokeless tobacco industry is not subject to as much litigation as cigarette manufacturers, there is a risk, in our opinion, that future litigation could affect cash flow. Also, due to its large market share, UST has been subject to antitrust actions.

Quantitative Evaluations

S&P Quality Ranking   B+

D	C	B-	B	**B+**	A-	A	A+

Relative Strength Rank   **STRONG**
                                                     91
LOWEST = 1   HIGHEST = 99

Revenue/Earnings Data

Revenue (Million $)

	1Q	2Q	3Q	4Q	Year
2007	447.0	491.3	479.6	--	--
2006	433.6	472.9	458.7	485.7	1,851
2005	440.5	480.1	456.8	474.4	1,852
2004	433.3	464.7	462.0	478.3	1,838
2003	420.0	438.9	437.6	446.2	1,743
2002	375.2	432.3	451.3	424.0	1,683

Earnings Per Share ($)

2007	0.67	0.87	0.84	E0.92	E3.44
2006	0.71	0.83	0.71	0.85	3.10
2005	0.73	0.82	0.80	0.88	3.23
2004	0.73	0.92	0.80	0.77	3.23
2003	0.66	0.77	0.74	-0.27	1.90
2002	0.61	0.80	0.77	-3.82	-1.61

Fiscal year ended Dec. 31. Next earnings report expected: Late January. EPS Estimates based on S&P Operating Earnings; historical GAAP earnings are as reported.

Dividend Data (Dates: mm/dd Payment Date: mm/dd/yy)

Amount ($)	Date Decl.	Ex-Div. Date	Stk. of Record	Payment Date
0.600	02/22	03/13	03/15	03/30/07
0.600	05/01	06/13	06/15	06/29/07
0.600	08/02	09/12	09/14	09/28/07
0.600	11/01	12/12	12/14	12/28/07

Dividends have been paid since 1912. Source: Company reports.

UST Inc.

Business Summary November 26, 2007

CORPORATE OVERVIEW. UST is the holding company for United States Smokeless Tobacco Company, which was formed in 1911. The company's three segments include Smokeless Tobacco Products, Wine, and Other operations including international tobacco.

The company's moist smokeless tobacco products include Copenhagen and Skoal, the world's two best selling brands of moist smokeless tobacco. Moist brands also include Skoal Long Cut, Skoal Bandits, Copenhagen Long Cut, Rooster, and Husky. Dry tobacco products carry the names Bruton, CC, and Red Seal. The company's tobacco products (82.3% of 2006 revenues) are sold throughout the U.S., principally to chain stores and tobacco and grocery wholesalers.

In addition to its smokeless tobacco offerings, UST is also a significant importer and producer of wines, and has other operations. Wines (15.3% of 2006 revenues) consist of premium varietal and blended wines dominated by Washington State-produced Chateau Ste. Michelle and Columbia Crest, and Villa Mt. Eden, a premium-quality California wine. In the third quarter of 2006, the company acquired the Erath label, an Oregon wine.

Other businesses (2.4% of 2006 revenues) include UST's international opera-

tion, which markets moist smokeless tobacco, and formerly included the manufacture and marketing of premium cigars (Don Tomas, Astral, and Hellix). In March 2004, UST paid $200 million and transferred its cigar operations to Swedish Match North America, to dismiss a case brought by that company.

CORPORATE STRATEGY. UST's objective in the Smokeless Tobacco segment is to continue to grow the moist smokeless tobacco category by building awareness and social acceptability of smokeless tobacco products among adult smokers, and by being competitive in every moist smokeless tobacco category segment. The company believes its future growth and profitability is in attracting growing numbers of adult consumers, primarily smokers, as approximately every 1% of adult smokers who convert to moist smokeless tobacco represents a 10% increase in the segment's adult consumer base. In addition to advertising initiatives, in 2004 and 2005 UST began a direct mail program to over 1 million adult smokers and began an advertising campaign to promote the convenience of smokeless tobacco relative to cigarettes.

Company Financials Fiscal Year Ended Dec. 31

Per Share Data ($)	2006	2005	2004	2003	2002	2001	2000	1999	1998	1997
Tangible Book Value	0.40	0.46	0.06	NM	NM	3.47	1.66	1.20	2.57	2.37
Cash Flow	3.38	3.51	3.52	2.15	-1.31	3.23	2.94	2.89	2.61	2.53
Earnings	3.10	3.23	3.23	1.90	-1.61	2.97	2.70	2.68	2.44	2.37
S&P Core Earnings	3.14	3.20	3.24	1.93	3.13	2.84	NA	NA	NA	NA
Dividends	2.28	2.20	2.08	2.00	1.92	1.84	1.76	1.68	1.62	1.62
Payout Ratio	74%	68%	64%	105%	NM	62%	65%	63%	66%	68%
Prices:High	59.49	56.90	48.97	37.79	41.35	36.00	28.88	34.94	36.88	36.94
Prices:Low	37.96	37.59	34.00	26.73	25.30	23.38	13.88	24.06	24.56	25.50
P/E Ratio:High	19	18	15	20	NM	12	11	13	15	16
P/E Ratio:Low	12	12	11	14	NM	8	5	9	10	11

Income Statement Analysis (Million $)										
Revenue	1,851	1,852	1,838	1,743	1,683	1,670	1,548	1,512	1,423	1,402
Operating Income	905	936	960	958	912	876	792	813	764	742
Depreciation	45.8	46.4	47.6	41.6	49.7	43.2	39.6	37.0	31.7	30.5
Interest Expense	57.1	50.6	75.0	76.9	46.1	66.2	47.4	13.5	4.42	8.40
Pretax Income	793	828	838	515	-444	799	718	763	734	704
Effective Tax Rate	36.7%	35.4%	35.8%	38.1%	NM	38.5%	38.5%	38.5%	38.0%	37.6%
Net Income	502	534	538	319	-271	492	442	469	455	439
S&P Core Earnings	509	529	540	323	528	470	NA	NA	NA	NA

Balance Sheet & Other Financial Data (Million $)										
Cash	254	202	510	438	382	272	96.0	75.0	33.2	6.93
Current Assets	998	890	1,173	1,248	2,291	892	691	580	507	442
Total Assets	1,440	1,367	1,659	1,726	2,765	2,012	1,646	1,016	913	827
Current Liabilities	300	259	619	521	1,462	222	170	261	197	167
Long Term Debt	840	840	840	1,140	1,140	863	869	411	100	100
Common Equity	3,373	75.1	9.66	-115	-47.0	581	271	201	468	438
Total Capital	4,213	927	859	-47.0	1,093	1,627	1,326	612	568	538
Capital Expenditures	37.0	89.9	70.3	45.1	57.2	47.2	51.1	59.3	56.3	58.1
Cash Flow	548	581	586	360	-222	535	481	506	487	470
Current Ratio	3.3	3.4	1.9	2.4	1.6	4.0	4.1	2.2	2.6	2.7
% Long Term Debt of Capitalization	19.9	90.6	97.8	110.8	104.3	53.0	65.5	67.2	17.6	18.6
% Net Income of Revenue	27.1	28.9	29.3	18.3	NM	29.4	28.6	31.0	32.0	31.3
% Return on Assets	35.8	35.3	31.8	14.2	NM	26.9	33.2	48.7	52.3	53.7
% Return on Equity	15.8	12.6	NM	NM	NM	115.4	187.5	19.3	100.5	122.0

Data as orig reptd.; bef. results of disc opers/spec. items. Per share data adj. for stk. divs.; EPS diluted. E-Estimated. NA-Not Available. NM-Not Meaningful. NR-Not Ranked. UR-Under Review.

Office: 100 West Putnam Ave, Greenwich, CT 06830.
Telephone: 203-661-1100.
Website: http://www.ustinc.com
Chrmn: V.A. Gierer, Jr.

Pres & CEO: M.S. Kessler
SVP, Secy & General Counsel: R.A. Kohlberger
CFO & Chief Acctg Officer: J.D. Patracuolla
Investor Contact: M. Rozelle (203-622-3520)

Board Members: J. D. Barr, J. P. Clancey, P. Diaz Dennis, V. A. Gierer, Jr., J. E. Heid, M. S. Kessler, P. J. Mannelly, P. J. Neff, A. J. Parsons, R. J. Rossi

Founded: 1911
Domicile: Delaware
Employees: 5,008

Valero Energy Corp

STANDARD &POOR'S

S&P Recommendation HOLD ★★★☆☆	**Price** $65.96 (as of Nov 23, 2007)	**12-Mo. Target Price** $77.00	**Investment Style** Large-Cap Blend

GICS Sector Energy
Sub-Industry Oil & Gas Refining & Marketing

Summary Valero is the largest oil refiner in North America, one of the largest independent U.S. refined petroleum products retailers, and operates refineries that can process sour and acidic crude oils.

Key Stock Statistics (Source S&P, Vickers, company reports)

52-Wk Range	$78.68– 47.66	S&P Oper. EPS 2007**E**	7.88	Market Capitalization(B)	$36.530	Beta	-0.22
Trailing 12-Month EPS	$9.61	S&P Oper. EPS 2008**E**	7.26	Yield (%)	0.73	S&P 3-Yr. Proj. EPS CAGR(%)	-11.50
Trailing 12-Month P/E	6.9	P/E on S&P Oper. EPS 2007**E**	8.4	Dividend Rate/Share	$0.48	S&P Credit Rating	BBB
$10K Invested 5 Yrs Ago	$83,984	Common Shares Outstg. (M)	553.8	Institutional Ownership (%)	74		

Price Performance

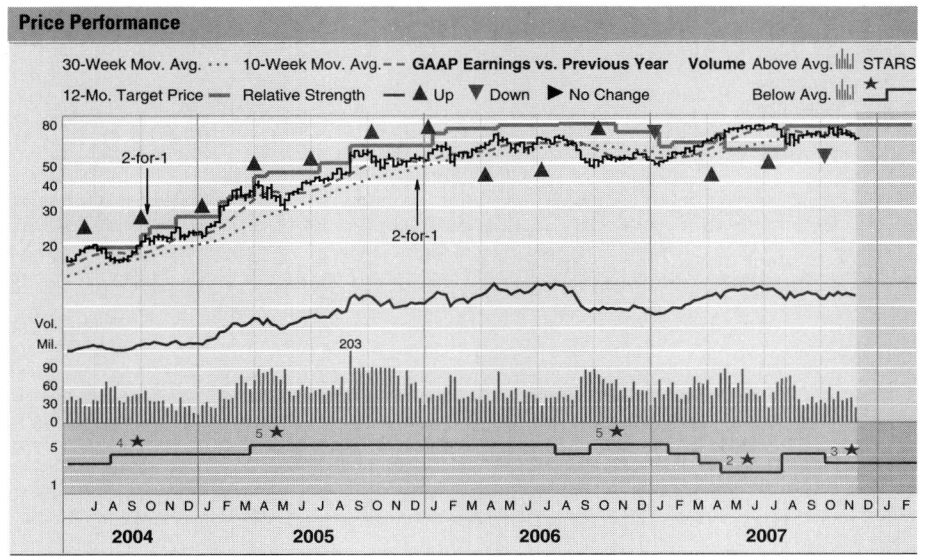

- 30-Week Mov. Avg. ··· 10-Week Mov. Avg. - - **GAAP Earnings vs. Previous Year** Volume Above Avg. ▥▥ STARS
- 12-Mo. Target Price — Relative Strength — ▲ Up ▼ Down ▶ No Change Below Avg. ▥▥ ★

Options: ASE, CBOE, P, Ph

Analysis prepared by **Tina J. Vital** on November 19, 2007, when the stock traded at **$ 65.98.**

Highlights

➤ Third-quarter refining throughputs declined 0.3%, and were below our expectations, reflecting weather and operational difficulties. During the fourth quarter, VLO plans to execute several major unit turnarounds, which will impact throughput rates at its West Coast refineries. Using guidance from VLO, we expect overall fourth-quarter refining throughputs to rise about 0.4% from third-quarter levels.

➤ VLO's refining margins weakened in the third quarter due to substantially higher feedstock costs resulting from increased premiums for light sweet crude oils and narrower discounts for sour crude oils. On the refined products side, product prices have not increased at the same pace as prices for crude oil. Going forward, we estimate that U.S. refining margins in 2008 will narrow more than 30% from 2007 levels, but remain relatively high compared to historical norms, reflecting strong demand and limited upgrading capacity.

➤ We expect after-tax operating earnings will decline 13% in 2007 and 11% in 2008.

Investment Rationale/Risk

➤ As VLO is the largest refiner in North America, we believe its size and ability to refine heavy sour crude feedstocks offer strategic and economic advantages. With the majority of refining costs focused on feedstocks, we think VLO's ability to refine lower-quality crudes (about 56% of its 2006 feedstocks were sour or acidic) is a competitive advantage. We estimate that VLO holds an above-average level of conversion capacity (near 1.6 million b/d), and the company's board recently approved a major $1.4 billion expansion at its St. Charles refinery.

➤ Risks to our recommendation and target price include changes in economic, industry and operating conditions that could lead to a narrowing of margins or a decrease in production.

➤ A blend of our discounted cash flow ($75; assuming a weighted average cost of capital of 7.4% and terminal growth of 3%) and relative valuations leads us to our 12-month target price of $77. This result represents an expected enterprise value of 6.7X our 2008 EBITDA estimate, slightly below peers.

Qualitative Risk Assessment

LOW	MEDIUM	HIGH

Our risk assessment reflects our view of VLO's strong business profile in the volatile and competitive oil refining industry. The company is the largest oil refiner in the U.S. and possesses above-average refining complexity, which allows it to process a large amount of lower-cost heavy and sour crudes.

Quantitative Evaluations

S&P Quality Ranking   B+

D	C	B-	B	**B+**	A-	A	A+

Relative Strength Rank   MODERATE

54

LOWEST = 1   HIGHEST = 99

Revenue/Earnings Data

Revenue (Million $)

	1Q	2Q	3Q	4Q	Year
2007	19,698	23,999	23,699	--	--
2006	20,941	26,781	24,319	19,792	91,833
2005	14,943	18,032	23,283	25,894	82,162
2004	11,082	13,808	14,339	15,390	54,619
2003	9,693	8,844	9,922	9,509	37,969
2002	5,122	6,522	7,192	8,110	26,976

Earnings Per Share ($)

2007	1.86	3.57	1.34	E0.94	E7.88
2006	1.32	2.98	2.55	1.80	8.64
2005	0.96	1.53	1.47	2.06	6.10
2004	0.46	1.14	0.79	0.88	3.27
2003	0.38	0.27	0.38	0.25	1.27
2002	-0.09	0.03	0.07	0.20	0.21

Fiscal year ended Dec. 31. Next earnings report expected: Early February. EPS Estimates based on S&P Operating Earnings; historical GAAP earnings are as reported.

Dividend Data (Dates: mm/dd Payment Date: mm/dd/yy)

Amount ($)	Date Decl.	Ex-Div. Date	Stk. of Record	Payment Date
0.120	01/18	02/12	02/14	03/14/07
0.120	04/26	05/14	05/16	06/13/07
0.120	07/12	08/06	08/08	09/06/07
0.120	10/25	11/05	11/07	12/12/07

Dividends have been paid since 1997. Source: Company reports.

Valero Energy Corp

STANDARD &POOR'S

Business Summary November 19, 2007

CORPORATE OVERVIEW. Incorporated in 1981 under the name Valero Refining and Marketing Co., the company changed its name to Valero Energy Co. (VLO) in 1997. In 2001, VLO merged with Ultramar Diamond Shamrock, and in September 2005 with Premcor Inc., creating the largest refiner in North America, based on atmospheric distillation capacity.

The company's business segments are refining (91% of 2006 revenues, 98% of operating income) and retail (9%, 2%). VLO serves customers in the U.S. (88% of 2006 revenues), Canada (8%), and other countries (4%); no single customer accounted for over 10% of consolidated operating revenues.

The refining segment includes refining operations, wholesale marketing, product supply and distribution, and transportation operations. As of year-end 2006, the company owned and operated 18 refineries in the U.S., Canada and Aruba, with a combined throughput capacity of 3.26 million barrels per day (b/d). The refining segment by region consisted of the Gulf Coast (nine refineries, 53% of 2006 throughput capacity), the Mid-Continent (four, 19%), the West Coast (two, 9%) and the Northeast (three, 19%). During 2006, sour crude oils

represented 47% of VLO's throughput volumes, acidic sweet crude oils 9%, sweet crude oil 29%, residual fuel oil 4%, other feedstocks 3%, and the remaining 8% was composed of blendstocks. About 65% of VLO's current crude oil feedstock requirements were purchased through term contracts, with the remainder generally purchased on the spot market. About 75% of these crude oil feedstocks are imported from foreign sources, and around 25% are domestic.

Average refinery yields for 2006 were composed of 48% gasoline and blendstocks, 32% distillates such as home heating oil, diesel fuel and jet fuel, 3% petrochemicals, and 17% other products (including vacuum gas oil, no. 6 fuel oil, petroleum coke, and asphalt).

Company Financials Fiscal Year Ended Dec. 31

Per Share Data ($)	2006	2005	2004	2003	2002	2001	2000	1999	1998	1997
Tangible Book Value	23.33	15.82	9.55	5.86	3.24	3.90	6.28	4.84	4.85	5.16
Cash Flow	10.47	7.57	3.24	2.31	1.23	2.75	1.86	0.47	0.14	0.78
Earnings	8.64	6.10	3.27	1.27	0.21	2.21	1.40	0.06	-0.21	0.51
S&P Core Earnings	8.32	6.02	3.25	1.25	0.14	2.14	NA	NA	NA	NA
Dividends	0.30	0.19	0.15	0.15	0.10	0.09	0.08	0.08	0.06	0.04
Payout Ratio	3%	3%	4%	11%	48%	4%	6%	128%	NM	8%
Prices:High	70.75	58.63	23.91	11.77	12.49	13.15	9.66	6.33	9.13	8.78
Prices:Low	46.84	21.01	11.43	8.05	5.79	7.88	4.63	4.17	4.41	6.73
P/E Ratio:High	8	10	7	9	60	6	7	NM	NM	17
P/E Ratio:Low	5	3	3	6	28	4	3	NM	NM	13

Income Statement Analysis (Million $)										
Revenue	91,833	82,162	54,619	37,969	26,976	14,988	14,671	7,961	5,539	5,756
Operating Income	9,165	6,334	2,979	1,733	920	1,139	723	162	198	276
Depreciation, Depletion and Amortization	1,155	875	NA	511	449	138	112	92.4	78.7	65.2
Interest Expense	210	266	260	278	256	102	83.0	55.4	32.5	42.5
Pretax Income	8,196	5,287	2,710	989	164	895	528	20.2	-83.1	176
Effective Tax Rate	33.3%	32.1%	33.4%	36.9%	35.5%	37.0%	35.8%	29.2%	NM	36.3%
Net Income	5,463	3,590	1,804	622	91.5	564	339	14.3	-47.3	112
S&P Core Earnings	5,258	3,534	1,785	604	60.0	547	NA	NA	NA	NA

Balance Sheet & Other Financial Data (Million $)										
Cash	1,590	436	864	369	409	346	14.6	60.1	11.2	9.94
Current Assets	10,760	8,276	5,264	3,817	3,536	4,113	1,285	829	640	789
Total Assets	37,753	32,728	19,392	15,664	14,465	14,337	4,308	2,979	2,726	2,493
Current Liabilities	8,822	7,305	4,534	3,064	3,007	4,730	1,039	719	498	597
Long Term Debt	4,657	5,156	3,901	4,245	4,867	2,805	1,042	785	822	430
Common Equity	18,605	14,982	7,590	5,535	4,308	4,203	1,527	1,085	1,085	1,159
Total Capital	27,309	20,206	13,710	11,585	10,592	8,884	3,149	2,146	2,117	1,846
Capital Expenditures	3,187	2,133	1,292	976	628	394	195	101	166	69.2
Cash Flow	6,616	4,452	1,791	1,128	541	701	451	107	31.4	172
Current Ratio	1.2	1.1	1.2	1.2	1.2	0.9	1.2	1.2	1.3	1.3
% Long Term Debt of Capitalization	17.1	25.5	28.5	36.6	45.9	31.6	33.0	36.5	NM	62.8
% Return on Assets	15.5	13.8	10.3	4.1	0.6	6.0	9.3	0.5	NM	4.9
% Return on Equity	32.5	31.7	27.3	12.5	2.2	19.7	26.0	1.3	NM	10.0

Data as orig reptd.; bef. results of disc opers/spec. items. Per share data adj. for stk. divs.; EPS diluted. E-Estimated. NA-Not Available. NM-Not Meaningful. NR-Not Ranked. UR-Under Review.

Office: 1 Valero Way, San Antonio, TX 78249-1616.
Telephone: 210-345-2000.
Email: investorrelations@valero.com
Website: http://www.valero.com

Chrmn & CEO: W.R. Klesse
Pres: G.C. King
EVP & CFO: M.S. Ciskowski
EVP & Chief Admin Officer: K.D. Booke

SVP & Secy: J.D. Browning
Investor Contact: E. Fisher (210-345-2896)
Board Members: W. E. Bradford, R. K. Calgaard, J. D. Choate, I. F. Engelhardt, R. M. Escobedo, S. Kaufman Purcell, W. Klesse, B. Marbut, D. L. Nickles, R. A. Profusek

Founded: 1955
Domicile: Delaware
Employees: 21,836

Varian Medical Systems Inc

STANDARD &POOR'S

S&P Recommendation **HOLD** ★★★☆☆	Price	12-Mo. Target Price	Investment Style
	$49.22 (as of Nov 23, 2007)	$48.00	Large-Cap Growth

GICS Sector Health Care
Sub-Industry Health Care Equipment

Summary This leading maker of radiotherapy cancer systems also supplies X-ray tubes and flat-panel digital subsystems for imaging in medical, scientific, and industrial applications.

Key Stock Statistics (Source S&P, Vickers, company reports)

52-Wk Range	$50.80–37.30	S&P Oper. EPS 2008**E**	2.05	Market Capitalization(B)	$6.222	Beta	0.64
Trailing 12-Month EPS	$1.83	S&P Oper. EPS 2009**E**	2.30	Yield (%)	Nil	S&P 3-Yr. Proj. EPS CAGR(%)	13.00
Trailing 12-Month P/E	26.9	P/E on S&P Oper. EPS 2008**E**	24.0	Dividend Rate/Share	Nil	S&P Credit Rating	NA
$10K Invested 5 Yrs Ago	$20,297	Common Shares Outstg. (M)	126.4	Institutional Ownership (%)	84		

Price Performance

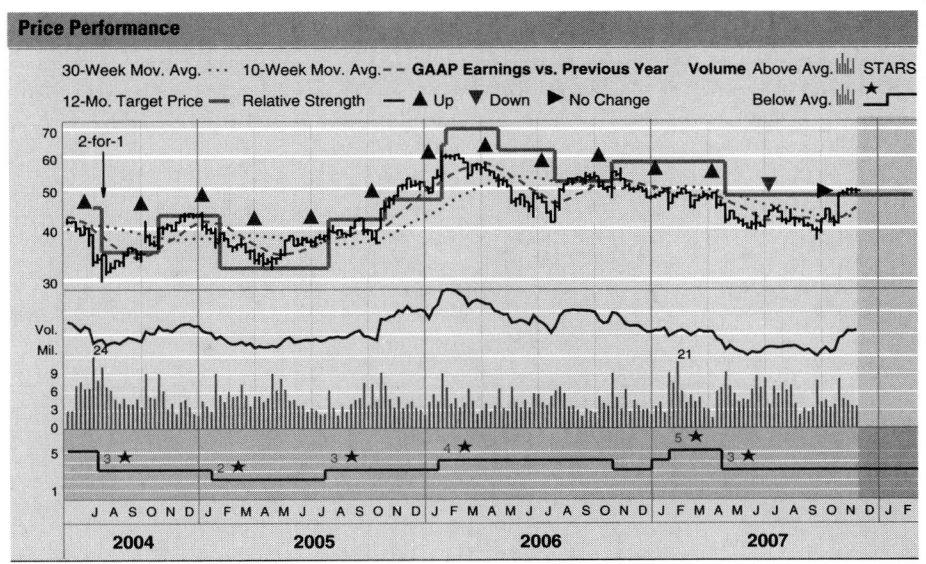

Legend: 30-Week Mov. Avg. · · · 10-Week Mov. Avg. - - GAAP Earnings vs. Previous Year — Volume Above Avg. / STARS; 12-Mo. Target Price — Relative Strength — ▲ Up ▼ Down ▶ No Change — Volume Below Avg.

2-for-1

Options: ASE

Analysis prepared by **Robert M. Gold** on November 05, 2007, when the stock traded at **$ 49.25.**

Highlights

➤ We expect that revenues in FY 08 (Sep.) will approach $2.0 billion, up from the $1.78 billion reported in FY 07, on rising Intensity Modulated Radiation Therapy sales, upgrades to image-guided radiation therapy technology, and accelerating growth for X-ray and brachytherapy products. We believe that efforts by the U.S. government to deploy automated cargo screening systems capable of detecting nuclear materials will help drive increased linear accelerator sales in the coming years.

➤ We see gross margins benefiting from a higher proportion of software revenues and rising contributions from the sale of flat panel displays: our FY 08 gross margin estimate is 41.5%, up from 41.3% in FY 07, and we think gross margins between 41.5% and 42.0% are sustainable. We expect to see some leverage on the SG&A line, and believe R&D spending will continue to absorb about 6.0% to 6.5% of sales over the coming three years. We think common share buybacks will continue to support EPS growth.

➤ Our FY 08 EPS forecast is $2.05, and we see FY 09 EPS reaching $2.30. Over the coming three years, we think EPS growth will average 13%.

Investment Rationale/Risk

➤ We believe that revenue growth in the coming quarters will continue to be bolstered by the clinical adoption of IMRT in North America and Europe, along with IGRT upgrades to the installed base. However, we think that the global radiation equipment market is competitive, and that an increasingly volatile oncology order pattern we are seeing in the U.S. reflected rising competition and a longer selling cycle into the U.S. hospital markets.

➤ Risks to our recommendation and target price include unfavorable changes in Medicare reimbursements, equipment pricing pressures, and an inability to continue to grow the oncology equipment order backlog in both U.S. and overseas markets.

➤ Our 12-month target price of $48 is about 21X our calendar 2008 EPS estimate of $2.33 and a PEG ratio of 1.6X, in line with our mid-cap device coverage universe, justified, in our opinion, by what we see as VAR's sustainable 13% long-term earnings growth rate and favorable product demand drivers.

Qualitative Risk Assessment

LOW	**MEDIUM**	HIGH

Our risk assessment reflects that while Varian offers some of the more technologically advanced products in the oncology equipment industry, the company operates in a competitive industry characterized by technological innovation and new product entrants. In addition, although we believe radiation therapy will continue to be an integral component of global cancer treatment protocols, the continued development of drug-based oncology treatments represents a substantial threat to the company's radiation therapy equipment business.

Quantitative Evaluations

S&P Quality Ranking B+

D	C	B-	B	**B+**	A-	A	A+

Relative Strength Rank STRONG 94

LOWEST = 1   HIGHEST = 99

Revenue/Earnings Data

Revenue (Million $)

	1Q	2Q	3Q	4Q	Year
2007	387.9	442.7	423.7	522.4	1,777
2006	334.2	413.9	395.7	454.0	1,598
2005	299.0	350.8	346.5	386.2	1,383
2004	267.0	320.6	303.1	344.8	1,236
2003	206.7	266.2	265.5	303.3	1,042
2002	175.1	220.5	216.1	261.4	873.1

Earnings Per Share ($)

2007	0.37	0.46	0.39	0.61	1.83
2006	0.30	0.41	0.49	0.61	1.80
2005	0.29	0.39	0.37	0.45	1.50
2004	0.21	0.30	0.30	0.37	1.18
2003	0.15	0.24	0.23	0.31	0.92
2002	0.10	0.17	0.16	0.24	0.66

Fiscal year ended Sep. 30. Next earnings report expected: Late January. EPS Estimates based on S&P Operating Earnings; historical GAAP earnings are as reported.

Dividend Data

Cash dividends were last paid in 1999.

Varian Medical Systems Inc

STANDARD
&POOR'S

Business Summary November 05, 2007

CORPORATE OVERVIEW. Varian is one of the largest manufacturers of oncology diagnostic products, X-ray tubes, and imaging subsystems. The company is focused primarily on capturing share in the global oncology radiation therapy markets. Cancer rates are expected to increase 50% by 2020.

MARKET PROFILE. Driven by an aging global population and improved diagnostic methods, the number of newly diagnosed cancer cases continues to increase. According to estimates published in February 2005 by the Annals of Oncology, nearly 2.9 million new cancer cases were diagnosed during 2004, and the U.S. National Cancer Institute estimates that cancer diagnoses will rise 1.6 million per year by 2010, a 23% increase from the 1.3 million cancers

per year seen in 2000. Radiation therapy is commonly used in the treatment of cancer, alone or in combination with surgery or chemotherapy. The most common type of radiotherapy uses X-rays delivered by external beams, and is administered using linear accelerators. In addition to external radiation, radioactive seeds, wires or ribbons are sometimes inserted into a tumor or into a body cavity (brachytherapy), a modality that does not require radiation to pass through healthy tissues.

Company Financials Fiscal Year Ended Sep. 30

Per Share Data ($)	2007	2006	2005	2004	2003	2002	2001	2000	1999	1998
Tangible Book Value	NA	5.21	4.11	3.74	3.71	3.05	2.93	2.13	1.51	4.69
Cash Flow	NA	2.02	1.70	1.32	1.06	0.81	0.64	0.55	0.38	0.96
Earnings	1.83	1.80	1.50	1.18	0.92	0.66	0.50	0.41	0.07	0.61
S&P Core Earnings	NA	1.80	1.34	1.04	0.78	0.54	0.40	NA	NA	NA
Dividends	Nil	Nil	Nil	Nil	Nil	Nil	Nil	Nil	0.03	0.10
Payout Ratio	Nil	Nil	Nil	Nil	Nil	Nil	Nil	Nil	37%	16%
Prices:High	50.21	61.70	52.92	46.49	35.65	25.66	19.31	17.75	10.75	14.59
Prices:Low	37.30	41.10	31.65	29.63	23.70	15.80	13.50	6.88	4.06	7.89
P/E Ratio:High	27	34	35	39	39	39	39	43	NM	24
P/E Ratio:Low	20	23	21	25	26	24	27	17	NM	13

Income Statement Analysis (Million $)										
Revenue	NA	1,598	1,383	1,236	1,042	873	774	690	590	1,422
Operating Income	NA	339	332	277	219	165	129	108	91.4	158
Depreciation	NA	29.6	27.1	20.8	20.3	20.4	19.3	17.8	37.4	42.7
Interest Expense	NA	4.65	4.70	4.67	4.38	4.49	4.13	5.16	10.0	8.84
Pretax Income	NA	319	308	257	201	146	107	84.9	18.2	113
Effective Tax Rate	NA	23.6%	33.0%	35.0%	35.0%	36.0%	36.5%	37.5%	55.0%	34.5%
Net Income	NA	244	207	167	131	93.6	68.0	53.0	8.20	73.8
S&P Core Earnings	NA	245	184	148	111	75.9	54.2	NA	NA	NA

Balance Sheet & Other Financial Data (Million $)										
Cash	NA	366	378	352	323	299	219	83.3	25.1	150
Current Assets	NA	1,156	1,017	885	806	651	620	451	382	840
Total Assets	NA	1,512	1,317	1,170	1,053	910	759	603	539	1,218
Current Liabilities	NA	644	544	461	409	358	285	250	270	505
Long Term Debt	NA	49.4	57.3	53.3	58.5	58.5	58.5	58.5	58.5	111
Common Equity	NA	797	659	614	564	504	418	270	185	558
Total Capital	NA	847	716	667	622	562	477	329	244	669
Capital Expenditures	NA	41.4	43.9	24.2	18.9	25.9	16.5	19.2	39.4	47.0
Cash Flow	NA	273	234	188	151	114	87.3	70.8	45.6	117
Current Ratio	NA	1.8	1.9	1.9	2.0	1.8	2.2	1.8	1.4	1.7
% Long Term Debt of Capitalization	NA	5.8	8.0	8.0	9.4	10.4	12.3	17.8	24.0	16.5
% Net Income of Revenue	NA	15.2	14.9	13.5	12.6	10.7	8.8	7.7	1.4	5.2
% Return on Assets	NA	17.2	16.5	15.0	13.3	11.2	10.0	9.3	0.1	6.4
% Return on Equity	NA	33.4	32.2	28.4	25.3	20.3	19.2	23.3	2.2	13.6

Data as orig reptd.; bef. results of disc opers/spec. items. Per share data adj. for stk. divs.; EPS diluted. E-Estimated. NA-Not Available. NM-Not Meaningful. NR-Not Ranked. UR-Under Review.

Office: 3100 Hansen Way, Palo Alto, CA 94304-1030.
Telephone: 650-493-4000.
Website: http://www.varian.com
Chrmn: R.M. Levy

Pres & CEO: T.E. Guertin
SVP & CFO: E.W. Finney
VP & General Counsel: J.W. Kuo
VP & Cntlr: T. Chen

Investor Contact: S. Sias (650-424-5782)
Board Members: S. L. Bostrom, J. S. Brown, R. A. Eckert, T. E. Guertin, M. R. Laret, R. M. Levy, A. S. Lichter, D. W. Martin, Jr., R. Naumann-Etienne, K. J. Thiry

Founded: 1976
Domicile: Delaware
Employees: 4,200

The McGraw-Hill Companies

VeriSign Inc

STANDARD &POOR'S

S&P Recommendation `HOLD` ★★★☆☆	Price $36.75 (as of Nov 23, 2007)	12-Mo. Target Price $34.00	Investment Style Large-Cap Blend

GICS Sector Information Technology
Sub-Industry Internet Software & Services

Summary This company is a leading provider of infrastructure services that enable secure digital communications and commerce.

Key Stock Statistics (Source S&P, Vickers, company reports)

52-Wk Range	$37.37– 22.77	S&P Oper. EPS 2007E	0.86	Market Capitalization(B)	$8.961	Beta	3.61
Trailing 12-Month EPS	$0.19	S&P Oper. EPS 2008E	1.14	Yield (%)	Nil	S&P 3-Yr. Proj. EPS CAGR(%)	21.00
Trailing 12-Month P/E	NM	P/E on S&P Oper. EPS 2007E	42.7	Dividend Rate/Share	Nil	S&P Credit Rating	NA
$10K Invested 5 Yrs Ago	$35,456	Common Shares Outstg. (M)	243.8	Institutional Ownership (%)	95		

Price Performance

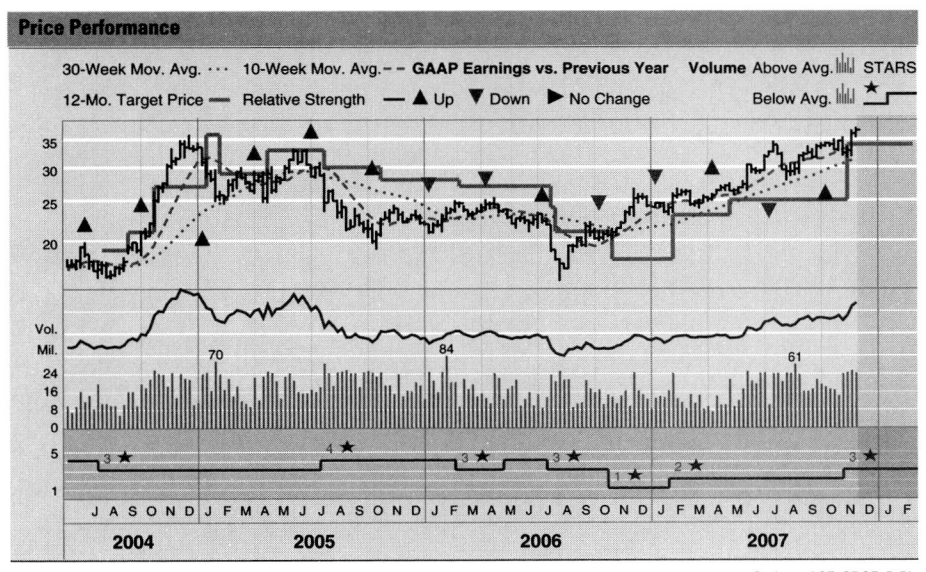

30-Week Mov. Avg. ···   10-Week Mov. Avg. - -   **GAAP Earnings vs. Previous Year**   Volume Above Avg. ▊▊▊ STARS
12-Mo. Target Price —   Relative Strength —   ▲ Up ▼ Down ► No Change   Below Avg. ▪▪▪ ★

Options: ASE, CBOE, P, Ph

Analysis prepared by **Scott H. Kessler** on November 05, 2007, when the stock traded at **$ 32.40**.

Highlights

▶ We believe VRSN stands to benefit from increasing spending on Internet security, online naming services, and certain wireless offerings. However, we expect 2007 revenues to decline 2%, reflecting the January 2007 divestiture of a majority stake in Jamba. Excluding the impact of this transaction, we estimate growth of 15%. We see 2008 growth at 14%, owing in part to higher domain-name prices.

▶ VRSN announced a $1 billion stock repurchase program in May 2006, but was unable buy back shares due to options-related issues. In mid-2007, VRSN largely resolved these matters. In August 2007, the company issued $1.25 billion in convertible notes, to be used predominantly for accelerated repurchases.

▶ VRSN has pursued notable divestitures in recent years, and we expect more such activity. In November 2005, VRSN sold its security gateway business to eBay (EBAY: strong buy, $34) for $370 million. In January 2007, the company combined its Jamba wireless content business with two of News Corp.'s (NWS: buy, $22) mobile businesses. VRSN received $188 million, and retained a 49% stake in the venture.

Investment Rationale/Risk

▶ VRSN is a diversified play on the continuing secular growth in Internet and wireless users and usage. However, we believe transactional efforts since mid-2004 have been excessive, detracting from VRSN's focus, transparency and balance sheet. VRSN announced a corporate and management reorganization in January 2007, to promote more effective sales practices. Although we are positive on ongoing consolidation efforts, we have concerns about significant management changes that started in late 2006.

▶ Risks to our opinion and target price include unexpected weakness in technology and telecommunications spending, and less aggressive actions intended to generate shareholder value than we foresee.

▶ VRSN's 2008 P/E and P/E-to-growth ratios were recently below those of the S&P 500 Internet Software & Services sub-industry, and related analyses lead to a value of $38. However, similar comparisons to the S&P 500 Technology sector, to which VRSN trades at a premium, yield a value of $25. Weighting these considerations results in our 12-month target price of $34.

Qualitative Risk Assessment

LOW	MEDIUM	**HIGH**

Our risk assessment reflects what we consider the emerging nature of, and notable competition in, many of the company's businesses, substantial corporate transactional activity since 2004, and numerous one-time items appearing in the company's recent financials.

Quantitative Evaluations

S&P Quality Ranking B-

D	C	**B-**	B	B+	A-	A	A+

Relative Strength Rank STRONG

`95`

LOWEST = 1   HIGHEST = 99

Revenue/Earnings Data

Revenue (Million $)

	1Q	2Q	3Q	4Q	Year
2007	373.1	363.2	373.6	--	--
2006	372.8	390.7	399.5	412.2	1,575
2005	401.0	444.8	414.8	392.1	1,609
2004	229.1	256.1	325.3	356.0	1,166
2003	269.8	265.3	268.1	251.6	1,055
2002	327.8	317.4	301.4	275.0	1,222

Earnings Per Share ($)

	1Q	2Q	3Q	4Q	Year
2007	0.24	-0.02	0.07	E0.28	E0.86
2006	0.06	1.52	0.06	-0.12	1.53
2005	0.17	0.14	0.17	0.07	0.53
2004	0.04	0.09	0.16	0.43	0.72
2003	-0.22	-0.60	-0.13	-0.13	-1.08
2002	-0.17	-20.31	-0.34	-0.17	-20.97

Fiscal year ended Dec. 31. Next earnings report expected: NA. EPS Estimates based on S&P Operating Earnings; historical GAAP earnings are as reported.

Dividend Data

No cash dividends have been paid.

Please read the **Required Disclosures and Analyst Certification** on the last page of this report.

The McGraw-Hill Companies

VeriSign Inc

Business Summary November 05, 2007

CORPORATE OVERVIEW. VeriSign provides infrastructure services intended to enable secure digital communications and commerce. Core offerings include security services, naming and directory services, and telecommunications services. The company has two primary operating units: the Internet Services Group (39% and 48% of revenues in 2006 and 2005, respectively), and the Communications Services Group (61%, 52%).

The Internet Services Group consists of two businesses: Security Services, and Information Services. Security Services includes network and applications security services (including managed security and global security consulting services), authentication services, commerce site services, and digital certificate services. Information Services (largely associated with VRSN being the exclusive registry of the .com and .net domain names) includes domain name registry services (VRSN owns and maintains the shared registration system for second-level domains), intelligent supply chain services, real-time publisher services, and digital brand management services. The Communications Services Group provides communications services to wireline, broadband and mobile operators, and enterprise customers. They include network connectivity and interoperability services, intelligent database services, con-

tent and application services, messaging services, clearing and settlement services, and billing and payment services.

CORPORATE STRATEGY. We believe VRSN has effectively diversified itself with multiple primary businesses. Although we see its business segments as largely independent of one another, they offer an unusual potential for cross-selling and shared research and development efforts, in our view. With its areas of focus established, VRSN has been expanding via regular acquisitions. The companies that VRSN purchases generally have proprietary offerings and technology that the company leverages with its expansive geographic footprint, customer base, and corporate alliances. We believe this is a sound strategy, particularly because many of the applications and areas that VRSN has been emphasizing are significantly fragmented, in our view. The company's challenge is to purchase the best companies at attractive valuations, and to integrate them successfully.

Company Financials Fiscal Year Ended Dec. 31

Per Share Data ($)	2006	2005	2004	2003	2002	2001	2000	1999	1998	1997
Tangible Book Value	2.44	2.98	2.92	3.16	1.89	3.50	4.15	2.88	0.88	NA
Cash Flow	2.47	1.25	1.05	-0.61	0.16	1.63	0.64	0.08	-0.38	-0.58
Earnings	1.53	0.53	0.72	-1.08	-20.97	-65.64	-19.57	0.03	-0.24	NA
S&P Core Earnings	1.45	NA	0.01	-1.75	-8.79	-35.05	NA	NA	NA	NA
Dividends	Nil	Nil	Nil	Nil	Nil	Nil	Nil	Nil	Nil	NA
Payout Ratio	Nil	Nil	Nil	Nil	Nil	Nil	Nil	Nil	Nil	NA
Prices:High	26.77	33.67	36.09	17.55	39.23	97.75	258.50	212.00	19.38	NA
Prices:Low	15.95	19.01	14.94	6.55	3.92	26.25	65.38	13.50	3.50	NA
P/E Ratio:High	17	64	50	NM	NM	NM	NM	NM	NM	NA
P/E Ratio:Low	10	36	21	NM	NM	NM	NM	NM	NM	NA

Income Statement Analysis (Million $)	2006	2005	2004	2003	2002	2001	2000	1999	1998	1997
Revenue	1,575	1,609	1,166	1,055	1,222	984	475	84.8	38.9	9.38
Operating Income	340	416	242	304	287	277	70.0	2.09	-15.6	-16.5
Depreciation	232	191	85.6	114	5,000	13,687	3,217	5.40	3.95	2.61
Interest Expense	Nil	Nil	Nil	Nil	149	20.7	Nil	Nil	Nil	NA
Pretax Income	140	248	214	-237	-4,951	-13,433	-3,114	3.12	-21.0	-20.7
Effective Tax Rate	NM	42.2%	12.9%	NM	NM	NM	NM	NM	NM	NA
Net Income	378	139	186	-260	-4,961	-13,356	-3,115	3.96	-19.7	-19.2
S&P Core Earnings	359	-1.39	2.76	-421	-2,080	-7,134	NA	NA	NA	NA

Balance Sheet & Other Financial Data (Million $)	2006	2005	2004	2003	2002	2001	2000	1999	1998	1997
Cash	501	477	331	394	282	306	460	70.4	22.8	3.94
Current Assets	1,332	1,228	1,006	880	604	1,091	1,186	183	53.7	14.9
Total Assets	3,974	3,173	2,593	2,100	2,391	7,538	19,195	341	64.3	24.4
Current Liabilities	1,359	938	700	555	665	834	665	42.7	22.6	9.69
Long Term Debt	Nil	Nil	Nil	Nil	Nil	Nil	Nil	Nil	Nil	NA
Common Equity	2,377	2,032	1,692	1,414	1,579	6,506	18,471	299	40.7	12.5
Total Capital	2,449	2,092	1,728	1,443	1,579	6,533	18,471	299	41.7	NA
Capital Expenditures	182	140	92.5	108	176	380	58.8	6.02	4.41	NA
Cash Flow	609	330	272	-145	38.9	331	101	9.36	-15.8	-16.6
Current Ratio	1.0	1.3	1.4	1.6	0.9	1.3	1.8	4.3	2.4	1.5
% Long Term Debt of Capitalization	Nil	Nil	Nil	Nil	Nil	Nil	Nil	Nil	Nil	NA
% Net Income of Revenue	24.0	8.6	16.0	NM	NM	NM	NM	4.7	NM	NA
% Return on Assets	10.6	4.8	7.9	NM	NM	NM	NM	2.0	NM	NA
% Return on Equity	17.1	7.4	12.1	NM	NM	NM	NM	2.3	NM	NA

Data as orig reptd.; bef. results of disc opers/spec. items. Per share data adj. for stk. divs.; EPS diluted. E-Estimated. NA-Not Available. NM-Not Meaningful. NR-Not Ranked. UR-Under Review.

Office: 487 East Middlefield Road, Mountain View, CA 94043.
Telephone: 650-961-7500.
Website: http://www.verisign.com
Chrmn: E. Mueller

Pres & CEO: W. Roper Jr.
Vice Chrmn: D.J. Bidzos
Investor Contact: A.L. Clement (866-447-8776)
EVP & CFO: A.L. Clement

Board Members: D. J. Bidzos, W. L. Chenevich, M. Guthrie, S. G. Kriens, R. H. Moore, E. A. Mueller, W. A. Roper, Jr., S. D. Sclavos, L. A. Simpson

Founded: 1995
Domicile: Delaware
Employees: 5,331

Verizon Communications Inc

STANDARD &POOR'S

S&P Recommendation	HOLD ★★★☆☆	Price $42.64 (as of Nov 23, 2007)	12-Mo. Target Price $44.00	Investment Style Large-Cap Value

GICS Sector Telecommunication Services
Sub-Industry Integrated Telecommunication Services

Summary VZ offers wireline, wireless and broadband services primarily in the northeastern part of the United States. In January 2006, VZ acquired MCI Inc., and during 2007 sold or spun off non-core assets.

Key Stock Statistics (Source S&P, Vickers, company reports)

52-Wk Range	$46.24–34.00	S&P Oper. EPS 2007E	2.40	Market Capitalization(B)	$123.244	Beta	0.96
Trailing 12-Month EPS	$1.93	S&P Oper. EPS 2008E	2.72	Yield (%)	4.03	S&P 3-Yr. Proj. EPS CAGR(%)	7.00
Trailing 12-Month P/E	22.1	P/E on S&P Oper. EPS 2007E	17.8	Dividend Rate/Share	$1.72	S&P Credit Rating	NR
$10K Invested 5 Yrs Ago	NA	Common Shares Outstg. (M)	2,890.3	Institutional Ownership (%)	65		

Price Performance

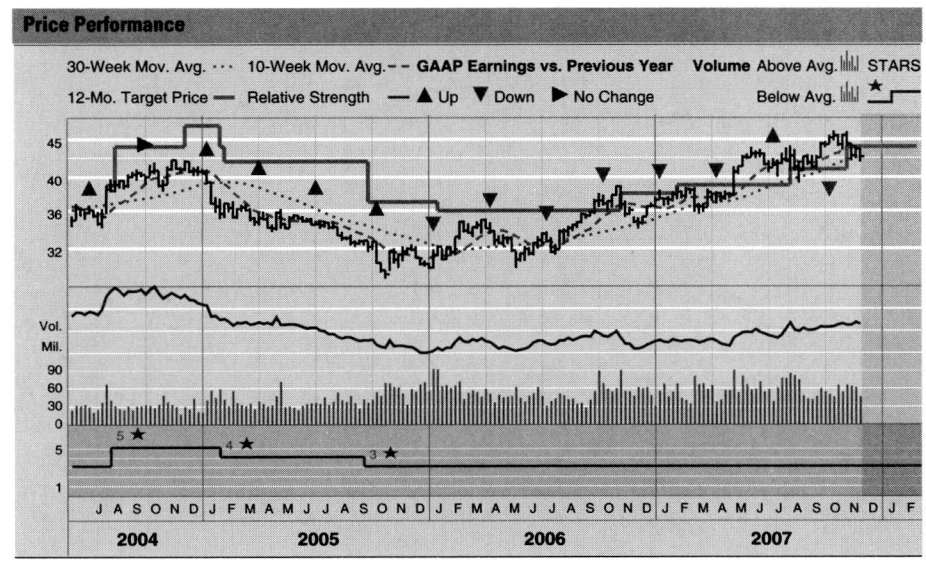

30-Week Mov. Avg. ··· 10-Week Mov. Avg. - - GAAP Earnings vs. Previous Year   Volume Above Avg. STARS
12-Mo. Target Price — Relative Strength — ▲ Up ▼ Down ► No Change   Below Avg.

Options: ASE, CBOE, P, Ph

Analysis prepared by **Todd Rosenbluth** on October 30, 2007, when the stock traded at **$ 45.51.**

Highlights

► We expect total revenues of $98.7 billion in 2008, up from a projected $94 billion in 2007, following the exclusion of sold discontinued directory and international operations. Strong wireless growth from data services and the penetration of FiOS broadband and video services should outweigh a decline in the domestic telecom unit's voice revenues. We believe the enterprise segment will improve from contract signings. Our estimates include revenues from the soon to be spun off access lines.

► We see an EBITDA margin expansion to 34% in 2008, up from a projected 33% in 2007. We forecast operational expense savings from the former MCI operations. In addition, we believe staff reductions and improved profitability at the wireless unit will be offset by the rollout of new fiber-based initiatives. We look for increased wireline efficiencies in 2008.

► We see net income being helped by our expectation of a low tax rate in 2008 and modest share repurchases. We estimate operating EPS of $2.40 in 2007 and $2.72 in 2008.

Investment Rationale/Risk

► We believe VZ's wireless segment continued to differentiate itself with market shares gains throughout 2007 and is well positioned to benefit from demand for data services. We also think that the MCI acquisition has helped VZ to compete in the enterprise market, although we believe further cost efficiencies are needed. While we see ongoing pressure from cable competition, we think VZ is having initial success with its fiber broadband and video offerings. The balance sheet is relatively strong, by our analysis, creating additional flexibility.

► Risks to our recommendation and target price include pricing pressures in the wireline and wireless segments, enterprise customer migration and wireless substitution, the rollout of fiber-based services, and a potential purchase of the outstanding stake in Verizon Wireless.

► Our blended 12-month target price of $44 is based on a forward P/E of 16X and an enterprise value/EBITDA multiple of 5.7X, in line with its peers based on our estimates. VZ's recent 3.7% dividend yield adds support, in our view.

Qualitative Risk Assessment

LOW	MEDIUM	HIGH

Our risk assessment reflects our view of VZ's strong cash flow generation and the pricing power it has over its suppliers, offset by the competitive landscape it faces offering telecom services.

Quantitative Evaluations

S&P Quality Ranking B

D	C	B-	B	B+	A-	A	A+

Relative Strength Rank MODERATE

67

LOWEST = 1   HIGHEST = 99

Revenue/Earnings Data

Revenue (Million $)

	1Q	2Q	3Q	4Q	Year
2007	22,584	23,273	23,772	--	--
2006	21,221	21,876	22,449	22,598	88,144
2005	18,179	18,569	19,038	19,326	75,112
2004	17,056	17,758	18,206	18,263	71,283
2003	16,490	16,829	17,155	17,278	67,752
2002	16,375	16,835	17,201	17,214	67,625

Earnings Per Share ($)

2007	0.51	0.58	0.44	E0.63	E2.40
2006	0.57	0.43	0.53	0.48	1.87
2005	0.63	0.75	0.67	0.59	2.65
2004	0.42	0.64	0.64	0.90	2.59
2003	0.63	0.46	0.64	-0.53	1.27
2002	Nil	-0.78	1.60	0.83	1.67

Fiscal year ended Dec. 31. Next earnings report expected: Late January. EPS Estimates based on S&P Operating Earnings; historical GAAP earnings are as reported.

Dividend Data (Dates: mm/dd Payment Date: mm/dd/yy)

Amount ($)	Date Decl.	Ex-Div. Date	Stk. of Record	Payment Date
0.405	12/07	01/08	01/10	02/01/07
0.405	03/01	04/05	04/10	05/01/07
0.405	06/07	07/06	07/10	08/01/07
0.430	09/06	10/05	10/10	11/01/07

Dividends have been paid since 1984. Source: Company reports.

Verizon Communications Inc

Business Summary October 30, 2007

CORPORATE OVERVIEW. As of September 2007, Verizon Communications (VZ) provided wireline service to 42.3 million access lines (down 8% from a year earlier), and, through its joint venture with the Vodafone Group, was the second-largest wireless carrier, with 63.7 million wireless customers (up 14%). About 65% of VZ's residential local service customers had also purchased DSL and/or long distance from VZ. In January 2006, VZ completed its $8.5 billion acquisition of MCI Inc. for cash and stock, adding consumer long distance operations and telecom services targeted to government and medium- and large-enterprise customers that combined with VZ's operations and have been renamed Verizon Business.

Verizon spun off its directory operations (4% of then projected 2006 revenues) into a separate entity, Idearc, in mid-November, and in December sold its Dominican Republic operations for $1.7 billion. In January 2007, VZ announced plans to spin out 1.5 million access lines in Maine, New Hampshire, and Vermont and merge the new entity with Fairpoint Communications (FRP), subject to necessary approvals. VZ shareholders would receive 1 share of FRP for every 55 VZ shares at the deal's closing, which we think is likely by the end of 2007.

MARKET PROFILE. In the third quarter of 2007, Verizon Wireless added 1.6 mil-

lion net subscribers and has what we estimate to be a more than 26% share of the market. Strong industrywide wireless rivalry has raised the level of competition, in our view, with new service plans and data services. As of September 2007, Verizon Wireless had a better-than-average 1.2% monthly churn rate, and 39.5 million customers were utilizing its data services. Wireless data average revenue per user rose 43% in the quarter and comprised 20% of service revenues. Our projected 2007 EBITDA margin of 45% for Verizon Wireless is the best in the industry, and we think it could further expand following the 2008 closing of a deal to acquire roaming partner Rural Cellular Corp, subject to necessary approvals.

Similar to its telecom peers, Verizon serves the Internet market through its broadband offerings (8 million connections) and has lowered prices and increased the speed of its connectivity in what we view as an effort to upgrade dial-up customers. As of the end of 2006, cable companies continued to lead the telecom providers, owning a 53% share of the residential broadband market.

Company Financials Fiscal Year Ended Dec. 31

Per Share Data ($)	2006	2005	2004	2003	2002	2001	2000	1999	1998	1997
Tangible Book Value	NM	NM	NM	NM	NM	NM	12.79	10.22	8.39	8.23
Cash Flow	1.87	7.61	7.67	6.14	6.56	5.22	8.43	6.59	5.62	5.29
Earnings	1.87	2.65	2.59	1.27	1.67	0.22	3.95	2.66	1.87	1.57
S&P Core Earnings	1.87	2.42	2.76	1.76	1.91	0.58	NA	NA	NA	NA
Dividends	1.62	1.60	1.54	1.54	1.54	1.54	1.54	1.54	1.54	1.49
Payout Ratio	86%	60%	60%	121%	92%	NM	39%	58%	82%	95%
Prices:High	38.95	41.06	42.27	44.31	51.09	57.40	66.00	69.50	61.19	45.88
Prices:Low	30.04	29.13	34.13	31.10	26.01	43.80	39.06	50.63	40.44	28.38
P/E Ratio:High	21	15	16	35	31	NM	17	26	33	29
P/E Ratio:Low	16	11	13	24	16	NM	10	19	22	18

Income Statement Analysis (Million $)										
Revenue	88,144	75,112	71,283	67,752	67,625	67,190	64,707	33,174	31,566	30,194
Depreciation	14,545	14,047	13,910	13,617	13,423	13,657	12,261	6,221	5,870	5,864
Maintenance	NA	NA	NA	NA	NA	NA	NA	NA	NA	NA
Construction Credits	NA	NA	NA	NA	NA	NA	NA	NA	NA	NA
Effective Tax Rate	21.9%	23.5%	22.8%	19.7%	21.7%	64.2%	38.9%	37.8%	40.2%	38.4%
Net Income	5,480	7,397	7,261	3,509	4,584	590	10,810	4,208	2,991	2,455
S&P Core Earnings	5,467	6,774	7,724	4,859	5,250	1,557	NA	NA	NA	NA

Balance Sheet & Other Financial Data (Million $)										
Gross Property	204,109	193,610	185,522	180,975	178,028	169,586	158,957	89,238	83,065	77,437
Net Property	82,356	75,305	74,124	75,316	74,496	74,419	69,504	39,299	36,816	35,039
Capital Expenditures	17,101	15,324	13,259	11,884	11,984	17,371	17,633	8,675	7,447	6,638
Total Capital	121,788	120,714	120,819	118,935	122,120	116,888	115,923	39,091	33,678	29,522
Fixed Charges Coverage	5.9	6.7	5.1	2.5	5.5	3.6	3.7	6.9	5.1	4.3
Capitalization:Long Term Debt	28,646	31,869	35,674	39,413	44,791	45,657	42,491	18,664	17,846	13,265
Capitalization:Preferred	Nil	Nil	Nil	Nil	Nil	Nil	Nil	Nil	Nil	200
Capitalization:Common	48,535	39,680	37,560	33,466	33,720	32,539	36,342	15,880	13,026	12,789
% Return on Revenue	6.2	9.8	10.2	5.2	6.8	0.9	16.7	12.7	9.5	8.1
% Return on Invested Capital	9.8	10.5	8.6	5.1	7.6	4.0	15.4	16.9	18.3	17.2
% Return on Common Equity	12.4	19.2	20.4	10.6	13.5	1.8	33.5	29.1	23.2	24.3
% Earned on Net Property	17.2	37.9	36.2	28.1	34.5	50.5	38.3	22.3	18.4	21.0
% Long Term Debt of Capitalization	37.1	44.5	48.7	54.1	36.6	58.4	53.9	54.0	57.8	50.5
Capital % Preferred	Nil	Nil	Nil	Nil	Nil	Nil	Nil	Nil	Nil	0.8
Capitalization:% Common	62.9	55.5	51.3	45.9	42.9	41.6	46.1	46.0	42.2	48.7

Data as orig reptd.; bef. results of disc opers/spec. items. Per share data adj. for stk. divs.; EPS diluted. E-Estimated. NA-Not Available. NM-Not Meaningful. NR-Not Ranked. UR-Under Review.

Office: 1095 Avenue of the Americas, New York, NY 10036.
Telephone: 212-395-2121.
Website: http://www.verizon.com
Chrmn & CEO: I.G. Seidenberg

Pres & COO: D.F. Strigl
EVP & CFO: D.A. Toben
EVP & General Counsel: W.P. Barr
EVP & CIO: S. Kheradpir

Investor Contact: C. Webster
Board Members: J. R. Barker, R. L. Carrion, F. Keeth, R. W. Lane, S. O. Moose, J. Neubauer, D. T. Nicolaisen, T. H. O'Brien, C. Otis Jr., H. B. Price, I. G. Seidenberg, W. V. Shipley, J. W. Snow, J. R. Stafford, R. D. Storey

Founded: 1983
Domicile: Delaware
Employees: 242,000

V.F. Corp

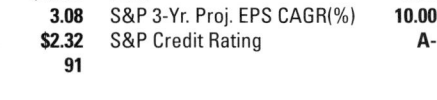

**STANDARD
&POOR'S**

S&P Recommendation BUY ★★★★☆	**Price** $75.25 (as of Nov 23, 2007)	**12-Mo. Target Price** $100.00	**Investment Style** Large-Cap Blend

GICS Sector Consumer Discretionary
Sub-Industry Apparel, Accessories & Luxury Goods

Summary This global apparel company with leading shares in denim and daypacks is transforming into a designer and marketer of lifestyle apparel brands.

Key Stock Statistics (Source S&P, Vickers, company reports)

52-Wk Range	$96.20–73.59	S&P Oper. EPS 2007**E**	5.35	Market Capitalization(B)	$8.359	Beta	0.70
Trailing 12-Month EPS	$4.71	S&P Oper. EPS 2008**E**	5.90	Yield (%)	3.08	S&P 3-Yr. Proj. EPS CAGR(%)	10.00
Trailing 12-Month P/E	16.0	P/E on S&P Oper. EPS 2007**E**	14.1	Dividend Rate/Share	$2.32	S&P Credit Rating	A-
$10K Invested 5 Yrs Ago	$21,993	Common Shares Outstg. (M)	111.1	Institutional Ownership (%)	91		

Price Performance

30-Week Mov. Avg. · · · 10-Week Mov. Avg. – – **GAAP Earnings vs. Previous Year** Volume Above Avg. STARS
12-Mo. Target Price — Relative Strength — ▲ Up ▼ Down ▶ No Change Below Avg. ★

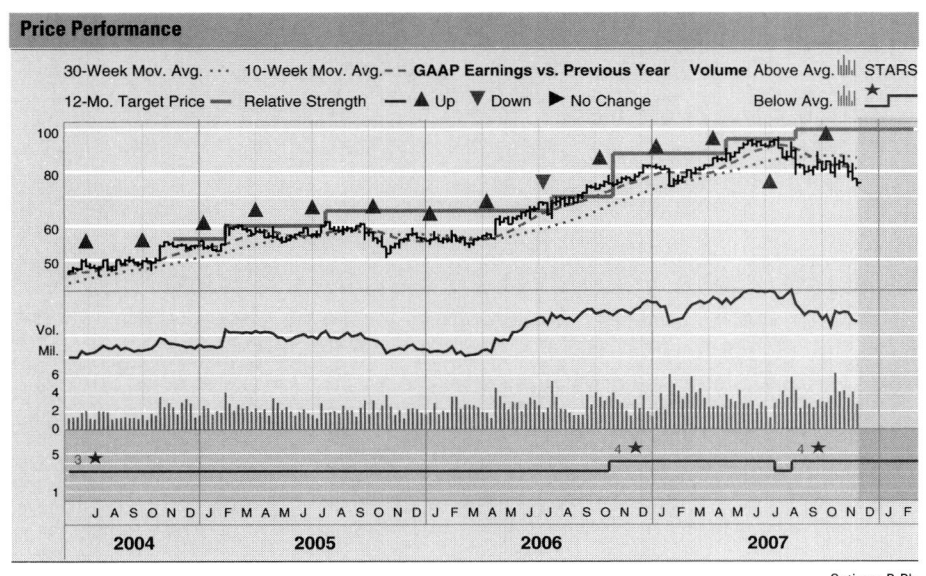

Options: P, Ph

Analysis prepared by **Marie Driscoll, CFA** on October 24, 2007, when the stock traded at **$81.12**.

Highlights

➤ We look for about 14% consolidated sales growth in 2007 and 9% in 2008, driven by double digit growth in VFC's lifestyle brands and low single digit increases in its denim and imagewear businesses. VFC ended 2006 with 538 owned retail locations, after opening 62 during the year, and we see a similar store opening schedule in 2007 generating a 15% sales gain in the retail division. We expect VFC's international jeanswear business to expand at a rate double the corporate average, in tandem with growing distribution and a strong order backlog. We see the Vans brand benefiting from further international market penetration.

➤ We project 40 basis point EBIT margin expansion reflecting a more favorable sales mix and early accretive results from new acquisitions in 2007, which are expected to add approximately $360 million to sales and $0.07 to EPS in 2007.

➤ We see continued increases in marketing spending to support its lifestyle brands, funded by sourcing savings. We see another 20 basis point increment EBIT margin expansion in 2008 to 13.9% of sales.

Investment Rationale/Risk

➤ We believe that a number of VFC's recent acquisitions have superior growth potential, as does further penetration of the international market. Given our view of the acumen of the company's management team, we anticipate market share gains and improving profitability. VFC continues to seek lifestyle brand acquisitions to add to its portfolio. Despite its maturity, we think that VFC's denim business provides steady low single digit growth while generating substantial cash flow and profits that VFC can employ at faster growing lifestyle brands with superior ROI opportunities.

➤ Risks to our recommendation and target price include fashion and inventory risk, and integration risk from recent acquisitions.

➤ Our 12-month target price of $100 is derived by incorporating a peer group forward P/E multiple of about 16.9X applied to our 2008 EPS estimate of $5.90. The dividend was recently increased 5.5% (following a 90% increment in early 2006) and recently yielded about 2.8%.

Qualitative Risk Assessment

LOW	MEDIUM	HIGH

Our risk assessment reflects our view of VFC's strong cash flow, offset by integration risk as VFC pursues growth via acquisitions.

Quantitative Evaluations

S&P Quality Ranking A-

D	C	B-	B	B+	A-	A	A+

Relative Strength Rank MODERATE

39

LOWEST = 1   HIGHEST = 99

Revenue/Earnings Data

Revenue (Million $)

	1Q	2Q	3Q	4Q	Year
2007	1,674	1,517	2,073	--	--
2006	1,456	1,351	1,810	1,599	6,216
2005	1,582	1,452	1,822	1,646	6,502
2004	1,433	1,270	1,793	1,560	6,055
2003	1,250	1,135	1,435	1,387	5,207
2002	1,212	1,160	1,400	1,311	5,084

Earnings Per Share ($)

2007	1.17	0.93	1.86	E1.40	E5.35
2006	1.05	0.80	1.64	1.24	4.73
2005	1.00	0.85	1.57	1.13	4.54
2004	0.93	0.80	1.38	1.10	4.21
2003	0.83	0.68	1.14	0.96	3.61
2002	0.67	0.79	1.15	0.69	3.24

Fiscal year ended Dec. 31. Next earnings report expected: Early February. EPS Estimates based on S&P Operating Earnings; historical GAAP earnings are as reported.

Dividend Data (Dates: mm/dd Payment Date: mm/dd/yy)

Amount ($)	Date Decl.	Ex-Div. Date	Stk. of Record	Payment Date
0.550	02/06	03/07	03/09	03/19/07
0.550	04/24	06/06	06/08	06/18/07
0.550	07/19	09/06	09/10	09/20/07
0.580	10/18	12/06	12/10	12/20/07

Dividends have been paid since 1941. Source: Company reports.

Please read the Required Disclosures and Analyst Certification on the last page of this report.

The **McGraw·Hill** Companies

V.F. Corp

STANDARD &POOR'S

Business Summary October 24, 2007

CORPORATE OVERVIEW. VF Corp. is the world's largest apparel manufacturer, and holds the leading position in several market categories, including jean-swear, workwear and daypacks. In early 2004, VFC developed a growth plan to support its long-term sales growth target of 8% annually, its 14% operating margin goal, and a 17% return on invested capital goal. The growth strategy consists of six drivers: building new, growing lifestyle brands; expanding share with successful retailers; growing internationally; leveraging supply chain and information technology; identifying, developing and recruiting qualified leaders; and expanding its direct to consumer business.

MARKET PROFILE. VFC participates in the broad apparel market, spanning product categories from women's intimate apparel to denim, as well as the outdoor market for apparel and accessories via its lifestyle brands. Apparel is a mature market, with demand mirroring population growth and a modicum related to fashion; it is fragmented, with national brands marketed by 20 companies accounting for about 30% of total apparel sales and the remaining 70% comprised of smaller and/or private label "store" brands. Deflationary pricing pressure is, we think, a function of channel competition and production steadily moving offshore to low-cost producers in Asia, especially India and

China. S&P forecasts a low single digit increase in 2007 and 2008 apparel sales, generally in line with GDP growth, versus a 5% advance in 2006 and a 4% gain in both 2004 and 2005.

The outdoor market is reaching a broader audience, in our view, as more Americans are attracted to a healthy lifestyle. According to the Outdoor Industry Foundation, during 2004 (latest available), more than 70% of Americans 16 and older, or 159 million people, participated in at least one outdoor sport (26% in the 16-24 year old age group), with a mean household income of $60,000. Hiking and biking are the most popular activities, with more than 75 million participants. The Outdoor Industry Association estimated retail sales of products (apparel, footwear and equipment) used in outdoor activities at $33 billion for the 12 months ended July 2005. Spurring growth is the increase in participants as well as enthusiasts.

Company Financials Fiscal Year Ended Dec. 31

Per Share Data ($)	2006	2005	2004	2003	2002	2001	2000	1999	1998	1997
Tangible Book Value	13.18	8.78	7.56	8.61	10.91	9.97	9.71	10.08	9.36	8.69
Cash Flow	5.74	5.56	5.53	4.64	4.35	0.00	3.73	5.71	4.39	3.87
Earnings	4.73	4.54	4.21	3.61	3.24	1.19	2.27	2.99	3.10	2.70
S&P Core Earnings	4.82	4.67	4.36	3.70	2.75	0.77	NA	NA	NA	NA
Dividends	1.94	1.10	1.05	1.01	0.97	0.93	0.89	0.85	0.81	0.77
Payout Ratio	41%	24%	25%	28%	30%	78%	39%	28%	26%	29%
Prices:High	83.10	61.61	55.61	44.08	45.64	42.70	36.90	55.00	54.69	48.25
Prices:Low	53.25	50.44	42.06	32.62	31.50	28.15	20.94	27.44	33.44	32.25
P/E Ratio:High	18	14	13	12	14	36	16	18	18	18
P/E Ratio:Low	11	11	10	9	10	24	9	9	11	12

Income Statement Analysis (Million $)										
Revenue	6,216	6,502	6,055	5,207	5,084	5,519	5,748	5,552	5,479	5,222
Operating Income	935	944	874	718	729	516	683	820	845	761
Depreciation	108	116	141	104	107	169	173	335	161	156
Interest Expense	57.3	70.6	76.1	61.4	71.3	93.4	88.7	71.4	62.0	50.0
Pretax Income	777	771	712	599	562	263	432	596	631	585
Effective Tax Rate	31.2%	32.7%	33.3%	33.5%	35.1%	47.6%	38.1%	38.5%	38.5%	40.0%
Net Income	535	519	475	398	364	138	267	366	388	351
S&P Core Earnings	544	532	490	406	303	84.6	NA	NA	NA	NA

Balance Sheet & Other Financial Data (Million $)										
Cash	343	297	486	515	496	332	119	79.9	63.0	124
Current Assets	2,578	2,365	2,379	2,209	2,075	2,031	2,110	1,877	1,848	1,601
Total Assets	5,466	5,171	5,004	4,246	3,503	4,103	4,358	4,027	3,837	3,323
Current Liabilities	1,015	1,152	1,372	872	875	814	1,006	1,113	1,033	766
Long Term Debt	635	648	557	956	602	904	905	518	522	516
Common Equity	3,265	2,808	2,513	1,951	1,658	2,113	2,192	2,164	2,046	1,841
Total Capital	3,901	3,479	3,096	2,938	2,297	3,062	3,145	2,733	2,622	2,439
Capital Expenditures	127	110	81.4	86.6	64.5	81.6	125	150	189	154
Cash Flow	643	635	615	502	472	304	437	698	549	503
Current Ratio	2.5	2.1	1.7	2.5	2.4	2.5	2.1	1.7	1.8	2.1
% Long Term Debt of Capitalization	16.3	18.6	18.0	32.6	26.2	29.5	28.8	18.9	19.9	21.1
% Net Income of Revenue	8.6	7.9	7.8	7.6	7.2	2.5	4.6	6.6	7.1	6.7
% Return on Assets	10.1	10.2	10.3	10.3	9.6	3.3	6.4	9.3	10.8	10.4
% Return on Equity	17.6	19.5	21.3	22.1	19.3	6.3	12.1	17.1	20.0	18.3

Data as orig reptd.; bef. results of disc opers/spec. items. Per share data adj. for stk. divs.; EPS diluted. E-Estimated. NA-Not Available. NM-Not Meaningful. NR-Not Ranked. UR-Under Review.

Office: 105 Corporate Center Boulevard , Greensboro, NC 27408.
Telephone: 336-424-6000.
Email: irrequest@vfc.com
Website: http://www.vfc.com

Chrmn & CEO: M.J. McDonald
Pres & COO: E.C. Wiseman
SVP & CFO: R.K. Shearer
VP & Treas: F. Pickard, III

VP, Secy & General Counsel: C.S. Cummings
Investor Contact: C. Knoebel (336-424-6189)
Board Members: E. E. Crutchfield, J. Ernesto de Bedout, U. F. Fairbairn, B. S. Feigin, G. Fellows, D. Hesse, R. J. Hurst, W. A. McCollough, M. J. McDonald, C. Otis, Jr., M. R. Sharp, R. G. Viault, E. C. Wiseman

Founded: 1899
Domicile: Pennsylvania
Employees: 45,500

The McGraw-Hill Companies

Viacom Inc

STANDARD &POOR'S

S&P Recommendation	**HOLD** ★★★☆☆	Price	12-Mo. Target Price	Investment Style
		$40.70 (as of Nov 23, 2007)	$45.00	Large-Cap Blend

GICS Sector Consumer Discretionary
Sub-Industry Movies & Entertainment

Summary Among the key brands of this entertainment content provider, one of the two companies that emerged after the January 2006 split of "old" Viacom into two companies, are MTV Networks and Paramount Pictures (which acquired DreamWorks studios).

Key Stock Statistics (Source S&P, Vickers, company reports)

52-Wk Range	$45.03– 33.74	S&P Oper. EPS 2007**E**	2.36	Market Capitalization(B)	$25.578	Beta		NA
Trailing 12-Month EPS	$2.55	S&P Oper. EPS 2008**E**	2.72	Yield (%)	Nil	S&P 3-Yr. Proj. EPS CAGR(%)		12.00
Trailing 12-Month P/E	16.0	P/E on S&P Oper. EPS 2007**E**	17.2	Dividend Rate/Share	Nil	S&P Credit Rating		NA
$10K Invested 5 Yrs Ago	NA	Common Shares Outstg. (M)	686.6	Institutional Ownership (%)	79			

Price Performance

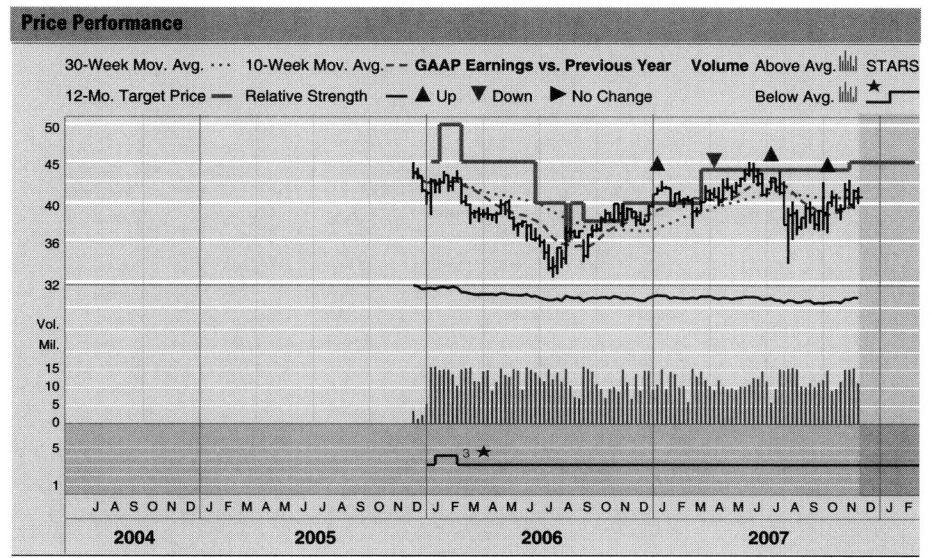

30-Week Mov. Avg. ··· 10-Week Mov. Avg. - - **GAAP Earnings vs. Previous Year** Volume Above Avg. ▮▮▮ STARS
12-Mo. Target Price — Relative Strength — ▲ Up ▼ Down ▶ No Change Below Avg. ▮▮▮ ★

J A S O N D | J F M A M J J A S O N D | J F M A M J J A S O N D | J F M A M J J A S O N D | J F
2004 | 2005 | 2006 | 2007

Options: ASE, CBOE, P, Ph

Analysis prepared by **Tuna N. Amobi, CFA, CPA** on November 05, 2007, when the stock traded at **$ 41.58**.

Highlights

➤ We estimate that total revenues will rise about 16% and 10% in 2007 and 2008, respectively, aided by worldwide advertising and affiliate revenue growth, on stronger overseas gains. After a seemingly spectacular 2007 for the film studio following the February 2006 acquisition of DreamWorks, we see relatively modest gains in 2008, from both the theatrical and home entertainment windows. However, strong growth in the consumer licensing business should remain on track, and nascent digital revenues should continue to ramp up nicely from a 2007 target of about $500 million.

➤ We project 2007 margins to be dampened by higher cable programming expenses, which combined with recent restructuring steps at the international networks, could lead to a significant margin expansion in 2008. Meanwhile, film margins should improve with a stronger slate.

➤ For 2007 and 2008, we project total EBITDA of about $3.3 billion and $3.7 billion, respectively. After interest expense and 38% effective taxes, we forecast EPS of $2.36 in 2007 and $2.72 in 2008, assuming continued modest buybacks under a current $4 billion plan.

Investment Rationale/Risk

➤ In early November, VIA.B reported what we view as relatively strong third quarter results, on continued gains in worldwide affiliate fees and advertising, combined with solid worldwide box office receipts for Transformers, and also Shrek 3, both likely set to reap strong DVD sales through the 2007 holidays and beyond. We note next year's strong summer film lineup anchored by the highly anticipated Indiana Jones 4, as well as Iron Man. Meanwhile, VIA.B expects a 10%-15% margin expansion at MTV international, on the heels of a restructuring that was recently substantially completed. We think the scatter ad trends at the MTV U.S. networks have recently improved, after a strong upfront market for the 2007/2008 season.

➤ Risks to our recommendation and target price include a sharp advertising slowdown, potential ratings weakness, increased competition for younger demographics, dilutive acquisitions, film volatility, and exchange exposure.

➤ Our 12-month target price of $45 blends sum-of-the-parts analysis, 11.2X total enterprise value to EBITDA, and a 1.1X 2008 P/E- to-growth ratio, in line with peers and the S&P 500.

Qualitative Risk Assessment

LOW	**MEDIUM**	HIGH

Our risk assessment of this pure content player reflects what we view as its leading demographically targeted brands, relatively strong growth prospects and ample financial flexibility, offset by its exposure to cyclical advertising and a highly volatile filmed entertainment business.

Quantitative Evaluations

S&P Quality Ranking NR

D	C	B-	B	B+	A-	A	A+

Relative Strength Rank STRONG
84
LOWEST = 1 HIGHEST = 99

Revenue/Earnings Data

Revenue (Million $)

	1Q	2Q	3Q	4Q	Year
2007	2,746	3,186	3,271	--	--
2006	2,368	2,847	2,660	3,593	11,467
2005	2,107	2,302	2,478	2,724	9,610
2004	--	--	--	--	8,132
2003	--	--	--	--	--
2002	--	--	--	--	--

Earnings Per Share ($)

2007	0.29	0.63	0.67	E0.84	E2.36
2006	0.43	0.58	0.50	0.69	2.19
2005	--	--	--	0.29	1.73
2004	--	--	--	--	1.48
2003	--	--	--	--	--
2002	--	--	--	--	--

Fiscal year ended Dec. 31. Next earnings report expected: Mid March. EPS Estimates based on S&P Operating Earnings; historical GAAP earnings are as reported.

Dividend Data

No cash dividends have been paid.

The McGraw·Hill Companies

Viacom Inc

STANDARD & POOR'S

Business Summary November 05, 2007

CORPORATE OVERVIEW. In its present form, the "new" Viacom is one of the two public companies created after the January 2006 separation of the "old" Viacom into two independent public entities (the "old" Viacom was renamed CBS Corp.). Each Class A and B shareholder of the "old" Viacom received 0.5 of a share of the corresponding A or B stock of each of the new entities. We believe that the company is the faster growing of the two companies resulting from the separation, and is specifically targeted to growth-oriented investors.

The company's cable networks segment (63% of 2006 revenues) is mainly comprised of MTV Networks (including MTV, Nickelodeon, VH1, Comedy Central, Country Music Television, Spike TV, TV Land, Logo, Neopets, Xfire and VIVA) and BET Networks. The entertainment segment (37%) includes Paramount Pictures film studio (and home entertainment) and Famous Music (publishing). About 37% of 2006 revenues were derived from ad sales, 18% from affiliate fees, 35% from feature films, and 10% from other ancillary sources (including merchandise licensing).

CORPORATE STRATEGY. We see CEO Philippe Dauman's management team focused on digital initiatives, aided by partnerships with Internet and technology companies, such as pacts with Yahoo! and online video site Joost. Since the start of 2006, the company has made selective digital acquisitions (mostly in online gaming and films), including Xfire, Y2M, Atom Entertainment, Harmonic Music and Quizilla. The company's global footprint traverses Europe and emerging markets (India and China), with nearly 125 channels (including over 95 MTV channels) across 169 territories in 28 languages, reaching nearly 450 million homes. The company recently had about 300 web sites, and launched a social networking site called Flux.

Company Financials Fiscal Year Ended Dec. 31

Per Share Data ($)	2006	2005	2004	2003	2002	2001	2000	1999	1998	1997
Tangible Book Value	NM	NM	NM	NA	NA	NA	NA	NA	NA	NA
Cash Flow	2.70	2.08	1.78	NA	NA	NA	NA	NA	NA	NA
Earnings	2.19	1.73	1.48	NA	NA	NA	NA	NA	NA	NA
S&P Core Earnings	2.22	1.46	1.47	NA	NA	NA	NA	NA	NA	NA
Dividends	Nil	Nil	NA	NA	NA	NA	NA	NA	NA	NA
Payout Ratio	Nil	Nil	NA	NA	NA	NA	NA	NA	NA	NA
Prices:High	43.90	44.95	NA	NA	NA	NA	NA	NA	NA	NA
Prices:Low	32.42	39.78	NA	NA	NA	NA	NA	NA	NA	NA
P/E Ratio:High	20	26	NA	NA	NA	NA	NA	NA	NA	NA
P/E Ratio:Low	15	23	NA	NA	NA	NA	NA	NA	NA	NA

Income Statement Analysis (Million $)	2006	2005	2004	2003	2002	2001	2000	1999	1998	1997
Revenue	11,467	9,610	8,132	NA	NA	NA	NA	NA	NA	NA
Operating Income	3,137	2,625	2,534	NA	NA	NA	NA	NA	NA	NA
Depreciation	366	259	2,522	NA	NA	NA	NA	NA	NA	NA
Interest Expense	472	23.0	20.0	NA	NA	NA	NA	NA	NA	NA
Pretax Income	2,322	2,328	2,017	NA	NA	NA	NA	NA	NA	NA
Effective Tax Rate	31.8%	43.8%	36.4%	NA	NA	NA	NA	NA	NA	NA
Net Income	1,570	1,304	1,281	NA	NA	NA	NA	NA	NA	NA
S&P Core Earnings	1,592	1,165	1,282	NA	NA	NA	NA	NA	NA	NA

Balance Sheet & Other Financial Data (Million $)	2006	2005	2004	2003	2002	2001	2000	1999	1998	1997
Cash	706	361	99.2	NA	NA	NA	NA	NA	NA	NA
Current Assets	4,211	3,513	2,384	NA	NA	NA	NA	NA	NA	NA
Total Assets	21,797	19,116	18,400	NA	NA	NA	NA	NA	NA	NA
Current Liabilities	4,617	3,269	2,617	NA	NA	NA	NA	NA	NA	NA
Long Term Debt	7,584	5,702	3,718	NA	NA	NA	NA	NA	NA	NA
Common Equity	7,166	7,788	9,905	NA	NA	NA	NA	NA	NA	NA
Total Capital	14,932	13,534	13,623	NA	NA	NA	NA	NA	NA	NA
Capital Expenditures	210	193	NA	NA	NA	NA	NA	NA	NA	NA
Cash Flow	1,936	1,563	1,533	NA	NA	NA	NA	NA	NA	NA
Current Ratio	0.9	1.1	0.9	NA	NA	NA	NA	NA	NA	NA
% Long Term Debt of Capitalization	50.8	42.1	27.3	NA	NA	NA	NA	NA	NA	NA
% Net Income of Revenue	13.7	13.6	15.8	NA	NA	NA	NA	NA	NA	NA
% Return on Assets	7.7	6.9	NA	NA	NA	NA	NA	NA	NA	NA
% Return on Equity	21.0	12.3	NA	NA	NA	NA	NA	NA	NA	NA

Data as orig reptd.; bef. results of disc opers/spec. items. Per share data adj. for stk. divs.; EPS diluted. E-Estimated. NA-Not Available. NM-Not Meaningful. NR-Not Ranked. UR-Under Review.

Office: 1515 Broadway , New York, NY 10036-5794.
Telephone: 212-258-6000.
Website: http://www.viacom.com
Exec Chrmn: S.M. Redstone

Pres & CEO: P. Dauman
Sr EVP, CFO & Chief Admin Officer: T.E. Dooley
EVP, Secy & General Counsel: M.D. Fricklas
SVP, Chief Acctg Officer & Cntlr: J. Tortoroli

Investor Contact: J. Bombassei (212-258-6000)
Board Members: G. S. Abrams, P. P. Dauman, T. E. Dooley, E. V. Futter, A. C. Greenberg, R. K. Kraft, C. E. Phillips, Jr., S. Redstone, S. M. Redstone, F. V. Salerno, W. Schwartz

Founded: 2005
Domicile: Delaware
Employees: 10,600

The McGraw-Hill Companies

STANDARD &POOR'S

Vornado Realty Trust

S&P Recommendation	HOLD ★★★☆☆	Price $90.83 (as of Nov 23, 2007)	12-Mo. Target Price $114.00	Investment Style Large-Cap Blend

GICS Sector Financials
Sub-Industry Diversified REITS

Summary This real estate investment trust owns a diverse group of properties, including Northeast retail properties, New York City office buildings, and other interests.

Key Stock Statistics (Source S&P, Vickers, company reports)

52-Wk Range	$136.55– 83.59	S&P FFO/Sh. 2007E	6.05	Market Capitalization(B)	$13.807	Beta	0.64
Trailing 12-Month FFO/Share	NA	S&P FFO/Sh. 2008E	6.40	Yield (%)	3.96	S&P 3-Yr. FFO/Sh. Proj. CAGR(%)	8.00
Trailing 12-Month P/FFO	NA	P/FFO on S&P FFO/Sh. 2007E	15.0	Dividend Rate/Share	$3.60	S&P Credit Rating	BBB+
$10K Invested 5 Yrs Ago	$31,121	Common Shares Outstg. (M)	152.0	Institutional Ownership (%)	90		

Price Performance

30-Week Mov. Avg. ··· 10-Week Mov. Avg. - - GAAP Earnings vs. Previous Year   Volume Above Avg. |l|l| STARS
12-Mo. Target Price — Relative Strength — ▲ Up ▼ Down ▶ No Change   Below Avg. |l|l|

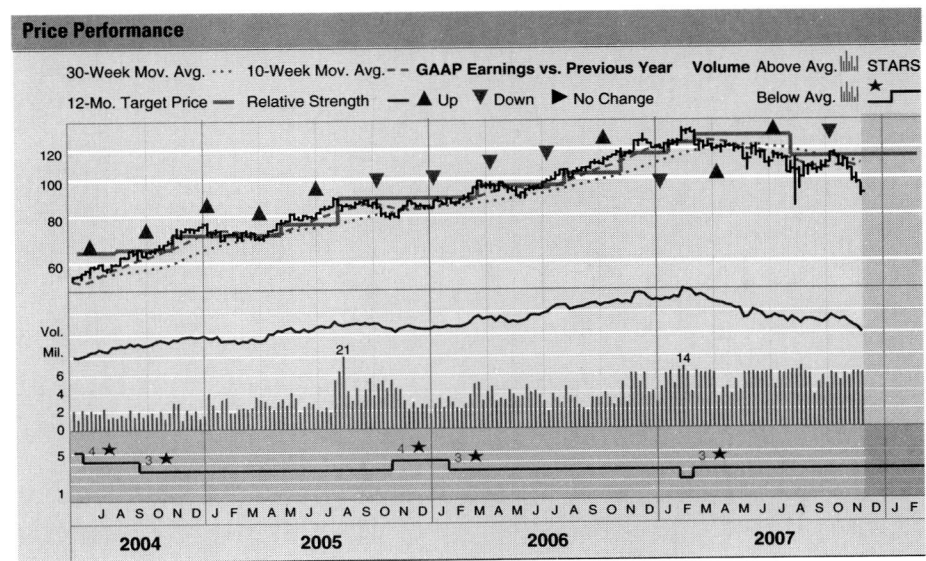

Analysis prepared by **Royal F. Shepard, CFA** on November 07, 2007, when the stock traded at **$ 101.50.**

Qualitative Risk Assessment

LOW	MEDIUM	HIGH

Our risk assessment of VNO reflects its large market capitalization, and what we see as its financial strength, diversified asset portfolio and low stock volatility.

Quantitative Evaluations

S&P Quality Ranking   A

D	C	B-	B	B+	A-	A	A+

Relative Strength Rank   WEAK

24

LOWEST = 1   HIGHEST = 99

Revenue/FFO Data

Revenue (Million $)

	1Q	2Q	3Q	4Q	Year
2007	737.1	793.5	--	--	853.0
2006	647.3	663.0	678.5	723.3	2,712
2005	598.7	594.8	657.0	697.2	2,548
2004	391.4	397.8	413.4	504.7	1,707
2003	365.0	371.1	380.2	386.8	1,503
2002	346.3	353.3	361.2	366.8	1,435

FFO Per Share ($)

2007	1.65	1.72	1.35	E1.34	E6.05
2006	1.37	1.49	1.31	1.34	5.51
2005	1.84	1.51	0.65	1.26	5.21
2004	1.01	1.22	1.18	2.22	5.63
2003	1.15	1.14	1.04	1.08	4.38
2002	1.06	1.03	0.98	0.79	3.62

Fiscal year ended Dec. 31. Next earnings report expected: Late February. FFO Estimates based on S&P Funds From Operations Est..

Dividend Data (Dates: mm/dd Payment Date: mm/dd/yy)

Amount ($)	Date Decl.	Ex-Div. Date	Stk. of Record	Payment Date
0.850	01/15	01/29	01/31	02/13/07
0.850	02/22	04/27	05/01	05/21/07
0.850	05/17	08/07	08/09	08/22/07
0.900	07/25	10/10	10/12	10/26/07

Dividends have been paid since 1990. Source: Company reports.

Highlights

➤ VNO's quarterly earnings are volatile due in part to accounting rules requiring the mark-to-market of its many equity investments. Even so, we view operating earnings as driven primarily by strong office and retail markets in New York City. We are somewhat less sanguine about the Washington DC, office market, where VNO has several properties under re-development, including two buildings at the large Crystal City project.

➤ We think 2008 earnings will benefit from increased office rents, particularly in New York, and a moderately higher contribution from VNO's equity investment in Toys R Us. However, VNO is likely to recognize lower gains on its equity in McDonald's Corp. (MCD: strong buy, $59), as a portion of this investment has been unwound. All told, we estimate EPS of $3.40, up from $3.20 in 2007. Our 2008 projection of per-share FFO is $6.40, 5.8% higher than an estimate $6.05 in 2007.

➤ VNO pays an annual dividend of $3.60. We project that the trust's cash flow, after capital expenditures and leasing commissions, will more than cover the new payout, and we look for a small increase in 2008.

Investment Rationale/Risk

➤ We think VNO has the financial resources to expand a strong portfolio of office and retail assets in supply-limited markets. Its pipeline of development opportunities in New York City is particularly attractive, in our view. Recent turmoil in the credit markets, though, may defer the trust's ability to unlock capital gains on some of its existing assets. Recently selling at about a 20% premium to diversified peers based on price to estimated 2008 FFO, however, we find the shares fairly reflect long-term growth prospects.

➤ Risks to our opinion and target price include a rise in interest rates, and regional economic declines in New York and/or Washington, DC. We also have corporate governance concerns related to anti-takeover defenses, including a classified board and blank check preferred stock.

➤ Our 12-month target price of $114 is based on our dividend discount model, which assumes a 9.7% discount rate, terminal growth of 4% and $0.50 of annual special dividends over the next five years. This implies a multiple of 18X estimated 2008 FFO, about in line with other office-oriented REITs.

Vornado Realty Trust

STANDARD
&POOR'S

Business Summary November 07, 2007

CORPORATE OVERVIEW. Vornado Realty Trust is a diversified REIT that has interests in a wide range of properties, including office buildings, retail properties, refrigerated warehouses, a hotel, and dry warehouses, among others, primarily in the Northeast. The company conducts its business through, was the sole general partner of, and, as of September 30, 2007, owned 90.0% of the limited partnership interests, in Vornado Realty L.P.

MARKET PROFILE. During 2006, VNO derived 42% of operating segment EBITDA from office properties. The market for office leases is inherently cyclical. The U.S. office market tends to track the overall economy on a lagged basis. At year-end 2006, we believe the national vacancy rate was approaching 13%, reflecting improvement since cyclical lows in 2002-2003.

Local economic conditions, particularly the employment level, play an important role in determining competitive dynamics. In our opinion, VNO's principal target markets, the New York City metropolitan area and Washington DC, have among the lowest vacancy rates in the nation at less than 10%. In addition, unlike many markets, rates on new or renewed leases are often at higher rates than those previously in place. At December 31, 2006, VNO owned or

had an interest in 116 office properties totaling 31.7 million sq. ft. The New York portfolio was 97.5% occupied at December 31, 2006; the Washington, DC, portfolio was 92.2% occupied.

In 2006, VNO derived about 16% of EBITDA from its retail segment. As of December 31, 2006, the retail portfolio included about 19.3 million sq. ft. in 21 states, Washington DC, and Puerto Rico. For VNO, as well as other retail oriented REITs, location and the financial health and growth of its retail tenants are among the most important factors affecting the success of its portfolio. Further, the companies in this industry enjoy relatively high barriers to entry, since developing new shopping centers requires large amounts of capital as well as time-consuming regulatory approvals which have been difficult to obtain in the recent past amid concerns about traffic and pollution. We expect VNO to focus on the re-development of recently acquired properties, including 1540 Broadway and the Manhattan Mall, both in New York City.

Company Financials Fiscal Year Ended Dec. 31

Per Share Data ($)	2006	2005	2004	2003	2002	2001	2000	1999	1998	1997
Tangible Book Value	35.22	31.38	26.86	24.15	21.68	21.15	18.31	18.14	17.55	14.19
Earnings	3.13	3.27	3.75	2.29	2.18	2.50	2.21	1.94	1.59	0.79
S&P Core Earnings	2.62	3.09	3.62	3.63	2.15	2.58	NA	NA	NA	NA
Dividends	3.25	3.85	2.89	2.91	2.97	2.31	1.97	1.81	1.64	1.36
Payout Ratio	104%	118%	77%	127%	136%	92%	89%	93%	103%	172%
Prices:High	131.35	89.70	76.99	55.84	47.20	42.03	40.75	40.00	49.81	47.38
Prices:Low	83.28	68.25	47.00	33.25	33.20	34.47	29.87	29.69	26.00	25.38
P/E Ratio:High	42	27	21	24	22	17	18	21	31	60
P/E Ratio:Low	27	21	13	15	15	14	14	15	16	32

Income Statement Analysis (Million $)										
Rental Income	1,568	1,397	1,345	1,261	1,249	842	695	591	426	168
Mortgage Income	Nil	Nil	Nil	Nil	Nil	Nil	Nil	Nil	Nil	Nil
Total Income	2,712	2,548	1,707	1,503	1,435	986	827	697	510	209
General Expenses	1,588	1,488	825	706	668	472	366	322	295	88.3
Interest Expense	478	341	242	230	240	173	170	142	115	42.9
Provision for Losses	Nil	Nil	Nil	Nil	Nil	Nil	Nil	Nil	Nil	Nil
Depreciation	397	335	243	215	206	124	99.8	83.6	59.2	45.9
Net Income	607	507	514	285	263	267	235	203	153	61.0
S&P Core Earnings	393	435	476	421	236	238	NA	NA	NA	NA

Balance Sheet & Other Financial Data (Million $)										
Cash	4,003	1,941	1,390	1,464	1,512	1,867	1,931	1,565	4,206	2,291
Total Assets	17,954	13,637	11,581	9,519	9,018	6,777	6,370	5,479	4,426	2,524
Real Estate Investment	13,553	11,449	9,757	7,748	7,560	4,690	4,295	3,922	3,316	1,564
Loss Reserve	Nil	Nil	Nil	Nil	Nil	Nil	Nil	Nil	Nil	Nil
Net Investment	11,585	9,776	8,349	6,879	6,822	4,184	3,901	3,613	3,089	1,391
Short Term Debt	778	398	Nil	Nil	Nil	Nil	425	681	268	120
Capitalization:Debt	9,056	5,857	4,937	3,768	3,622	1,643	2,232	1,368	1,783	957
Capitalization:Equity	5,322	4,260	3,301	2,827	2,362	2,101	1,597	1,577	1,782	1,025
Capitalization:Total	16,335	12,208	8,238	8,767	8,287	5,693	5,767	4,645	2,216	2,330
% Earnings & Depreciation/Assets	6.3	6.6	7.1	5.4	5.9	5.9	5.6	5.8	6.1	6.9
Price Times Book Value:High	3.7	2.9	2.9	2.3	2.2	2.0	2.2	2.2	2.8	3.3
Price Times Book Value:Low	2.4	2.2	1.7	1.4	1.5	1.6	1.6	1.6	1.5	1.8

Data as orig reptd.; bef. results of disc opers/spec. items. Per share data adj. for stk. divs.; EPS diluted. E-Estimated. NA-Not Available. NM-Not Meaningful. NR-Not Ranked. UR-Under Review.

Vulcan Materials Co

S&P Recommendation	HOLD ★★★☆☆	Price	12-Mo. Target Price	Investment Style
		$81.71 (as of Nov 23, 2007)	$95.00	Large-Cap Growth

GICS Sector Materials
Sub-Industry Construction Materials

Summary This major producer of construction materials has agreed to acquire Florida Rock Industries Inc. for cash and stock totaling about $4.6 billion.

Key Stock Statistics (Source S&P, Vickers, company reports)

52-Wk Range	$128.62– 77.36	S&P Oper. EPS 2007E	5.15	Market Capitalization(B)	$8.841	Beta	1.45
Trailing 12-Month EPS	$4.89	S&P Oper. EPS 2008E	5.60	Yield (%)	2.25	S&P 3-Yr. Proj. EPS CAGR(%)	9.00
Trailing 12-Month P/E	16.7	P/E on S&P Oper. EPS 2007E	15.9	Dividend Rate/Share	$1.84	S&P Credit Rating	A-
$10K Invested 5 Yrs Ago	$24,694	Common Shares Outstg. (M)	108.2	Institutional Ownership (%)	85		

Price Performance

30-Week Mov. Avg. · · · 10-Week Mov. Avg. - - - GAAP Earnings vs. Previous Year   Volume Above Avg. STARS
12-Mo. Target Price — Relative Strength — ▲ Up ▼ Down ► No Change   Below Avg.

Options: P

Analysis prepared by **Stuart J. Benway, CFA** on November 05, 2007, when the stock traded at **$ 81.28.**

Highlights

▶ On February 19, 2007, VMC announced an agreement to acquire Florida Rock Industries Inc. (FRK) for cash and stock totaling about $4.6 billion. The proposed acquisition is expected to close in the fourth quarter of 2007, subject to necessary approvals.

▶ For the company as presently constituted, we look for an 8% sales decline in 2007 and a 3%-5% increase in 2008. For this year, a projected drop in volume caused largely by the weakness in the residential housing sector should be offset by higher prices. These higher prices are based on our forecast for continued strength in nonresidential construction and in highway spending, as well as a tight supply of raw materials used in aggregate production. We think higher realizations will lead to modestly wider margins in 2008.

▶ Aided by higher prices, we project operating EPS of $5.15 in 2007, versus 2006's operating EPS of $4.63. For 2008, we look for further growth to $5.60 per share. Long term, we see EPS benefiting from tighter supplies of aggregates and increases in infrastructure spending.

Investment Rationale/Risk

▶ We see VMC as a beneficiary of generally tighter supplies of aggregates, implementation of the highway spending bill, an eventual recovery in residential construction, and continued expansion into high growth regions of the U.S. But, assuming that the company acquires FRK, we believe that the debt resulting from the proposed acquisition will limit VMC's ability to increase its dividend or buy back shares, given its stated intention to reduce its debt. In our view, this constraint, along with the increased debt, will limit the extent to which VMC's P/E can expand.

▶ Risks to our recommendation and target price include the possibility that aggregate demand is less robust than we project due to lower commercial construction activity, and that the proposed acquisition of Florida Rock does not occur.

▶ We look for VMC to trade at about 17X our 2008 EPS estimate. This is about in the middle of its historical range of the past 10 years. We believe improving return on capital and higher operating margins will support a 17X P/E. On that basis, our 12-month target price is $95.

Qualitative Risk Assessment

LOW	MEDIUM	HIGH

Our risk assessment reflects that while VMC's earnings are exposed to the construction industry, about 44% of the aggregates volume comes from public construction, which is more stable than commercial construction. In addition, we view VMC's balance sheet and free cash flow generation as strong.

Quantitative Evaluations

S&P Quality Ranking A-

D	C	B-	B	B+	A-	A	A+

Relative Strength Rank MODERATE

44

LOWEST = 1   HIGHEST = 99

Revenue/Earnings Data

Revenue (Million $)

	1Q	2Q	3Q	4Q	Year
2007	687.2	878.8	904.9	--	--
2006	708.7	888.2	929.3	816.3	3,342
2005	528.6	782.1	830.0	754.6	2,895
2004	617.5	816.3	891.2	608.7	2,454
2003	566.7	766.8	829.9	728.7	2,892
2002	587.1	681.4	785.8	676.0	2,797

Earnings Per Share ($)

2007	0.91	1.46	1.47	E1.29	E5.15
2006	0.70	1.47	1.45	1.19	4.79
2005	0.21	0.98	1.23	0.89	3.30
2004	0.14	0.85	0.96	0.62	2.52
2003	0.01	0.65	0.91	0.59	2.18
2002	0.11	0.64	0.75	0.36	1.86

Fiscal year ended Dec. 31. Next earnings report expected: Early February. EPS Estimates based on S&P Operating Earnings; historical GAAP earnings are as reported.

Dividend Data (Dates: mm/dd Payment Date: mm/dd/yy)

Amount ($)	Date Decl.	Ex-Div. Date	Stk. of Record	Payment Date
0.460	02/09	02/21	02/23	03/09/07
0.460	05/11	05/23	05/25	06/11/07
0.460	07/13	08/22	08/24	09/10/07
0.460	10/12	11/21	11/26	12/10/07

Dividends have been paid since 1934. Source: Company reports.

Please read the Required Disclosures and Analyst Certification on the last page of this report.

Business Summary November 05, 2007

CORPORATE OVERVIEW. Vulcan Materials is the largest U.S. producer of construction aggregates and a major producer of asphalt and ready-mixed concrete. Proven and probable reserves of aggregates were 11.4 billion tons at the end of 2006, representing a reserve life of 44.3 years based on current production rates. Third party shipments of aggregates totaled about 242.5 million tons in 2006, shipments of asphalt mix were 11.6 million tons and concrete shipments totaled 2.9 million cubic yards. Construction aggregates were 70% of 2006's sales, asphalt mix 16%, concrete 9% and other products, 5%. VMC estimates that 44% of its aggregates shipments in 2006 went to publicly funded construction projects. The remainder went into the construction of housing, nonresidential buildings, commercial and industrial facilities, or was used as railroad ballast, and in non-construction uses including agricultural and various industrial applications.

CORPORATE STRATEGY. VMC's main strategy is to achieve sales and EPS growth by expanding in metropolitan areas that demographers expect will experience the largest absolute growth in population in the future.

MARKET PROFILE. Construction aggregates include crushed stone, sand and gravel, rock asphalt and recrushed asphalt and concrete. According to the

U.S. Geological Survey (USGS), aggregates production in the U.S. in 2006 totaled 2.69 billion metric tons. Aggregates are employed in virtually all types of construction, including highway construction and maintenance, and in the production of asphaltic and portland cement concrete mixes. VMC's main competitors in the aggregates business are La Farge North America, Martin Marietta Materials, and Texas Industries. VMC estimates that the 10 largest aggregates producers in the nation supply approximately one-third of the total national market, resulting in highly fragmented markets in some areas. Because of the relatively high transportation costs inherent in the business, competition generally is limited to areas in proximity to production facilities. Barriers to enter the aggregates industry are high. Zoning and permitting regulations have made it increasingly difficult for the construction aggregates industry to expand existing quarries or to develop new quarries in some markets. Consequently, aggregates prices are less price constrained, particularly in markets where there are limited reserves.

Company Financials Fiscal Year Ended Dec. 31

Per Share Data ($)	2006	2005	2004	2003	2002	2001	2000	1999	1998	1997
Tangible Book Value	14.60	15.05	13.77	12.01	11.04	10.02	9.00	8.63	11.47	9.81
Cash Flow	7.04	5.43	4.88	4.87	4.47	4.89	4.43	4.37	3.86	3.21
Earnings	4.79	3.30	2.52	2.18	1.86	2.17	2.29	2.35	2.50	2.03
S&P Core Earnings	4.53	3.17	2.29	1.89	1.51	1.81	NA	NA	NA	NA
Dividends	1.48	1.16	1.04	0.97	0.94	0.90	0.84	0.78	0.69	0.63
Payout Ratio	31%	35%	41%	44%	51%	41%	37%	33%	28%	31%
Prices:High	93.85	76.31	55.53	48.60	49.95	55.30	48.88	51.25	44.67	34.65
Prices:Low	65.85	52.36	41.94	28.75	32.35	37.50	36.50	34.31	31.33	18.42
P/E Ratio:High	20	23	22	22	27	25	21	22	18	17
P/E Ratio:Low	14	16	17	13	17	17	16	15	13	9

Income Statement Analysis (Million $)										
Revenue	3,342	2,895	2,454	2,892	2,797	3,020	2,492	2,356	1,776	1,679
Operating Income	914	690	623	618	560	649	573	565	481	409
Depreciation	225	221	245	277	268	278	232	207	138	121
Interest Expense	26.3	37.1	40.3	54.1	55.0	61.3	48.1	48.6	7.23	6.91
Pretax Income	703	480	376	311	260	324	312	352	375	301
Effective Tax Rate	32.1%	28.4%	30.4%	28.3%	25.8%	31.3%	29.6%	31.8%	31.7%	30.4%
Net Income	477	344	261	223	190	223	220	240	256	209
S&P Core Earnings	452	328	236	194	155	186	NA	NA	NA	NA

Balance Sheet & Other Financial Data (Million $)										
Cash	55.2	275	271	417	171	101	55.3	52.8	181	129
Current Assets	731	1,165	1,418	1,050	790	730	695	625	576	487
Total Assets	3,424	3,589	3,665	3,637	3,448	3,398	3,229	2,839	1,659	1,449
Current Liabilities	494	579	427	543	298	344	572	387	211	208
Long Term Debt	322	323	605	339	858	906	685	699	76.5	81.9
Common Equity	2,001	2,127	2,014	1,803	1,697	1,604	1,471	1,324	1,154	1,025
Total Capital	2,611	2,725	2,967	2,573	2,993	2,829	2,426	2,273	1,329	1,162
Capital Expenditures	435	216	204	194	249	287	340	315	203	161
Cash Flow	702	565	506	501	458	501	452	447	394	330
Current Ratio	1.5	2.0	3.3	1.9	2.7	2.1	1.2	1.6	2.7	2.3
% Long Term Debt of Capitalization	12.3	11.9	20.4	13.2	28.7	32.0	28.3	30.7	5.8	7.0
% Net Income of Revenue	14.3	11.9	10.6	7.7	6.8	7.4	8.8	10.2	14.4	12.5
% Return on Assets	13.6	9.5	7.2	6.3	5.6	6.7	7.2	10.7	16.5	15.1
% Return on Equity	23.1	16.6	13.7	12.8	11.5	14.5	15.7	19.4	23.5	21.6

Data as orig reptd.; bef. results of disc opers/spec. items. Per share data adj. for stk. divs.; EPS diluted. E-Estimated. NA-Not Available. NM-Not Meaningful. NR-Not Ranked. UR-Under Review.

Office: 1200 Urban Center Drive, Birmingham, AL 35242.
Telephone: 205-298-3000.
Email: ir@vmcmail.com
Website: http://www.vulcanmaterials.com

Chrmn & CEO: D.M. James
SVP, CFO & Treas: D.F. Sansone
SVP, Secy & General Counsel: W.F. Denson, III
VP, Cntlr & CIO: E.A. Khan

Treas: P. Alford
Investor Contact: M. Warren (205-298-3220)
Board Members: P. J. Carroll, Jr., L. D. DeSimone, P. W. Farmer, H. A. Franklin, D. M. James, D. J. McGregor, J. V. Napier, D. B. Rice, O. R. Smith, V. J. Trosino

Founded: 1910
Domicile: New Jersey
Employees: 7,983

Wachovia Corp

STANDARD &POOR'S

S&P Recommendation **BUY** ★★★★☆	Price	12-Mo. Target Price	Investment Style
	$41.05 (as of Nov 23, 2007)	$47.00	Large-Cap Value

GICS Sector Financials
Sub-Industry Diversified Banks

Summary This bank holding company, the fourth largest in the U.S., operates banking offices in 21 states and Washington, DC.

Key Stock Statistics (Source S&P, Vickers, company reports)

52-Wk Range	$58.80– 36.69	S&P Oper. EPS 2007**E**	3.91	Market Capitalization(B)	$81.185	Beta	0.75
Trailing 12-Month EPS	$4.50	S&P Oper. EPS 2008**E**	4.63	Yield (%)	6.24	S&P 3-Yr. Proj. EPS CAGR(%)	10.00
Trailing 12-Month P/E	9.1	P/E on S&P Oper. EPS 2007**E**	10.5	Dividend Rate/Share	$2.56	S&P Credit Rating	AA-
$10K Invested 5 Yrs Ago	$13,686	Common Shares Outstg. (M)	1,977.7	Institutional Ownership (%)	57		

Price Performance

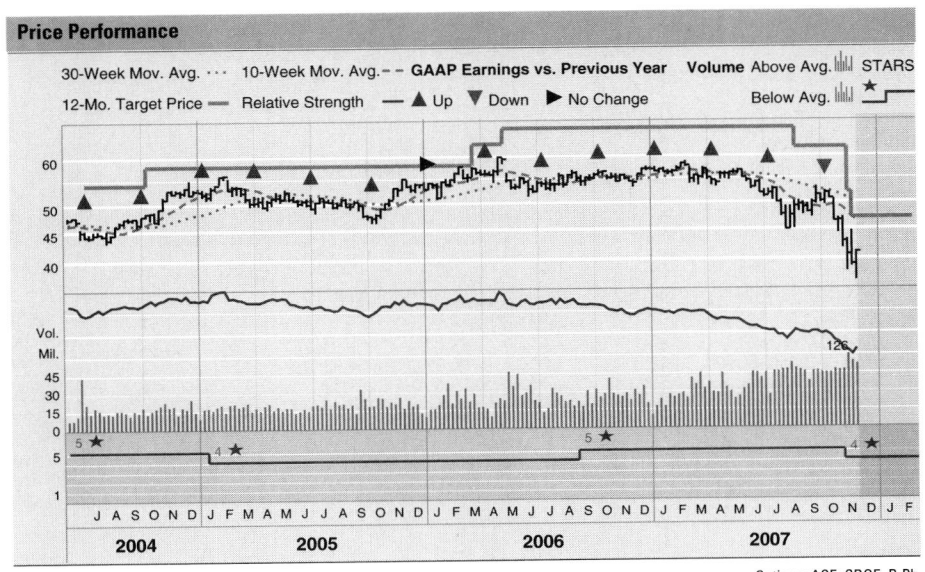

30-Week Mov. Avg. · · · 10-Week Mov. Avg. - - **GAAP Earnings vs. Previous Year** Volume Above Avg. STARS
12-Mo. Target Price — Relative Strength — ▲ Up ▼ Down ▶ No Change Below Avg. ★

Options: ASE, CBOE, P, Ph

Analysis prepared by **Frank Braden, CFA** on November 15, 2007, when the stock traded at **$ 41.93**.

Highlights

➤ After announcing a $1.1 billion pretax write-down of its ABS CDOs in October, WB has a remaining exposure of $676 million. While we expect additional writedowns if market conditions do not improve, we believe WB has been more conservative than its peers in loss estimations. We forecast strong gains in fee income in 2008, driven by the expansion of WB's private bank and the acquisition of A.G. Edwards. Net interest income should be hurt by some of the negative effects of a highly competitive pricing environment.

➤ We believe provisions are likely to increase at a faster pace as the size and longevity of the California housing downturn increases, despite the historical success of Golden West's option ARM portfolio. In our view, the company will continue to aggressively target planned expense reductions in its attempt to continue to post above-industry-average EPS growth with a strong efficiency ratio. We think near-term pressure on margins may result as WB sells more fixed rate loans through Golden West branches.

➤ We estimate operating EPS of $3.91 in 2007 and $4.63 in 2008.

Investment Rationale/Risk

➤ We view positively WB's focus on expense control, credit quality, and productivity improvements, which should allow for balanced above-peer-average long-term growth in a variety of economic and interest rate scenarios. Credit quality of the Golden West portfolio showed signs of weakening in the third quarter, and we expect continued upward pressure on delinquencies as adjustable rates continue to reset at higher levels. We believe the acquisition of A.G. Edwards and the expansion of WB's private bank enhance the company's exposure to the shifting needs of retiring baby boomers.

➤ Risks to our recommendation and target price include a severe economic downturn; greater credit losses than we expect; integration risk; and increased mortgage stress relating to its option arm portfolio.

➤ Our 12-month target price of $47 equates to about 10.2X our 2008 operating EPS estimate, a discount to WB's historical average, based on the difficult credit and mortgage environment.

Qualitative Risk Assessment

LOW	MEDIUM	HIGH

Our risk assessment reflects our view of Wachovia's solid fundamentals coupled with a diversity in business lines and geography. In our opinion, WB's benefits from its diversity and strong management will be partially offset by its exposure to the California mortgage market from the Golden West acquisition.

Quantitative Evaluations

S&P Quality Ranking A-

D	C	B-	B	B+	A-	A	A+

Relative Strength Rank MODERATE

31

LOWEST = 1 HIGHEST = 99

Revenue/Earnings Data

Revenue (Million $)

	1Q	2Q	3Q	4Q	Year
2007	13,889	14,595	13,592	--	--
2006	10,224	10,987	11,249	14,350	46,810
2005	8,448	8,679	9,302	9,479	35,908
2004	6,766	6,626	6,902	7,773	28,067
2003	5,776	5,841	6,315	6,542	24,474
2002	5,930	6,004	5,802	5,855	23,591

Earnings Per Share ($)

2007	1.20	1.24	0.89	E0.58	E3.91
2006	1.09	1.17	1.17	1.18	4.61
2005	1.01	1.04	1.06	0.95	4.05
2004	0.94	0.95	0.96	0.95	3.81
2003	0.76	0.77	0.82	0.83	3.17
2002	0.66	0.62	0.66	0.66	2.60

Fiscal year ended Dec. 31. Next earnings report expected: Late January. EPS Estimates based on S&P Operating Earnings; historical GAAP earnings are as reported.

Dividend Data (Dates: mm/dd Payment Date: mm/dd/yy)

Amount ($)	Date Decl.	Ex-Div. Date	Stk. of Record	Payment Date
0.560	02/20	02/26	02/28	03/15/07
0.560	04/17	05/29	05/31	06/15/07
0.640	08/21	08/29	08/31	09/17/07
0.640	10/16	11/28	11/30	12/17/07

Dividends have been paid since 1914. Source: Company reports.

Please read the Required Disclosures and Analyst Certification on the last page of this report.

The McGraw-Hill Companies

Wachovia Corp

STANDARD &POOR'S

Business Summary November 15, 2007

CORPORATE OVERVIEW. WB consists of several reporting segments: general bank (GB); capital management (CM); wealth management (WM); corporate and investment bank (CIB); and parent. GB provides a broad range of banking products and services to individuals, small businesses, commercial enterprises and governmental institutions in 21 states and Washington, D.C. It focuses on small business customers with annual revenues of up to $3 million; business banking customers with annual revenues between $3 million and $15 million; and commercial customers with revenues between $15 million and $250 million. CM leverages its multi-channel distribution to provide a full line of proprietary and nonproprietary investment and retirement products and services to retail and institutional clients. Retail brokerage services are offered through the 2,700 offices of Wachovia Securities in 49 states and Washington, D.C., and in Latin America. Evergreen Investments, a large and diversified asset management company, manages investments for a broad range of retail and institutional investors.

WM provides private banking, trust and investment management and financial

planning services to high net worth individuals, their families and businesses. Wachovia Insurance Services offers commercial insurance brokerage and risk management services, employee benefits, life insurance, executive benefits and personal insurance services to businesses and individuals. The CIB division serves domestic and global corporate and institutional clients typically with revenues in excess of $250 million, and primarily in these key industry sectors: health care; media and communications; technology and services; finance; real estate; consumer and retail; industrial growth; defense and aerospace; and energy and power. CIB includes corporate lending, investment banking, and treasury and international trade finance lines of business. CIB also serves an institutional client base of money managers, hedge funds, insurance companies, pension funds, banks and broker dealers.

Company Financials Fiscal Year Ended Dec. 31

Per Share Data ($)	2006	2005	2004	2003	2002	2001	2000	1999	1998	1997
Tangible Book Value	15.60	15.76	15.25	15.27	14.48	11.50	11.92	11.22	12.36	14.71
Earnings	4.61	4.05	3.81	3.17	2.60	1.45	0.12	3.33	2.95	2.99
S&P Core Earnings	4.61	4.02	3.75	3.09	2.32	1.14	NA	NA	NA	NA
Dividends	2.14	1.94	1.66	1.25	1.00	0.96	1.92	1.88	1.58	1.22
Payout Ratio	46%	48%	44%	39%	38%	66%	NM	56%	54%	41%
Prices:High	60.04	56.28	55.01	46.74	39.88	36.60	38.88	65.75	65.94	53.00
Prices:Low	50.85	46.30	43.05	32.12	28.57	25.22	23.50	32.00	40.94	36.31
P/E Ratio:High	13	14	14	15	15	25	NM	20	22	18
P/E Ratio:Low	11	11	11	10	11	17	NM	10	14	12

Income Statement Analysis (Million $)										
Net Interest Income	15,249	13,681	11,961	10,607	9,823	7,775	7,277	7,452	7,277	5,743
Tax Equivalent Adjustment	155	219	250	256	218	159	117	118	117	Nil
Non Interest Income	14,545	12,130	10,789	9,309	7,836	7,003	5,682	6,995	6,198	3,362
Loan Loss Provision	434	249	257	586	1,479	1,947	691	692	691	840
% Expense/Operating Revenue	60.5%	60.9%	63.8%	65.4%	65.3%	65.8%	89.6%	60.8%	67.5%	61.4%
Pretax Income	11,470	9,804	7,633	6,080	4,667	2,293	703	4,831	3,965	2,710
Effective Tax Rate	31.3%	30.9%	31.7%	30.1%	23.3%	29.4%	80.4%	33.3%	27.1%	30.0%
Net Income	7,745	6,429	5,214	4,247	3,579	1,619	138	3,223	2,891	1,896
% Net Interest Margin	3.12	3.24	3.41	3.72	3.92	3.57	3.81	3.79	3.81	4.36
S&P Core Earnings	7,740	6,386	5,141	4,144	3,187	1,255	NA	NA	NA	NA

Balance Sheet & Other Financial Data (Million $)										
Money Market Assets	62,452	65,257	72,809	61,747	45,827	46,180	36,109	27,542	12,675	13,907
Investment Securities	108,619	114,889	110,597	100,445	75,804	58,467	49,246	53,035	53,988	23,590
Commercial Loans	121,626	112,695	141,226	107,466	109,097	61,258	87,447	80,619	79,689	28,111
Other Loans	298,532	146,320	82,614	58,105	54,000	102,543	36,313	54,947	59,720	72,148
Total Assets	707,121	520,755	493,324	401,032	341,839	330,452	254,170	253,024	237,363	157,274
Demand Deposits	66,572	67,587	64,197	48,683	44,640	43,464	30,315	31,375	35,614	21,753
Time Deposits	340,886	257,407	230,856	172,542	146,878	143,989	112,353	109,672	106,853	81,136
Long Term Debt	138,594	48,971	46,759	36,730	39,662	41,733	35,809	31,975	22,949	8,042
Common Equity	69,716	47,561	47,317	32,428	32,078	28,438	15,347	16,709	17,173	12,032
% Return on Assets	1.2	1.3	1.2	1.1	1.1	0.6	0.1	1.3	1.5	1.3
% Return on Equity	13.2	13.6	13.1	13.2	11.8	7.4	0.9	19.2	19.8	17.2
% Loan Loss Reserve	1.0	1.0	1.2	1.5	1.7	-1.8	1.4	1.3	1.3	1.3
% Loans/Deposits	102.2	81.7	80.3	74.8	85.2	87.4	86.7	96.1	97.7	94.2
% Equity to Assets	10.5	9.4	8.9	8.7	9.0	7.5	6.3	6.9	7.4	7.4

Data as orig reptd.; bef. results of disc opers/spec. items. Per share data adj. for stk. divs.; EPS diluted. E-Estimated. NA-Not Available. NM-Not Meaningful. NR-Not Ranked. UR-Under Review.

Office: One Wachovia Center, Charlotte, NC 28288-0013.
Telephone: 704-374-6565.
Website: http://www.wachovia.com
Chrmn, Pres & CEO: G.K. Thompson

Vice Chrmn: B.P. Jenkins, III
Sr EVP: D.M. Carroll
Sr EVP: S.E. Cummings
Sr EVP: S.A. Kelly

Board Members: J. D. Baker, II, R. J. Brown, P. C. Browning, J. T. Casteen, III, J. A. Gitt, W. H. Goodwin, Jr., M. C. Herringer, R. A. Ingram, D. M. James, M. J. McDonald, J. Neubauer, T. D. Proctor, E. S. Rady, V. L. Richey, R. G. Shaw, L. L. Smith, G. K. Thompson, J. C. Whitaker, Jr., D. D. Young

Auditor: KPMG
Founded: 1879
Domicile: North Carolina
Employees: 108,238

The McGraw-Hill Companies

Walgreen Co

S&P Recommendation HOLD ★★★☆☆

Price	**12-Mo. Target Price**	**Investment Style**
$39.73 (as of Nov 23, 2007)	$45.00	Large-Cap Growth

GICS Sector Consumer Staples
Sub-Industry Drug Retail

Summary As the largest U.S. retail drug chain in terms of revenues, this company operates about 6,000 drug stores in 48 states and Puerto Rico.

Key Stock Statistics (Source S&P, Vickers, company reports)

52-Wk Range	$49.10–37.10	S&P Oper. EPS 2008**E**	2.25	Market Capitalization(B)	$39.397	Beta	0.07
Trailing 12-Month EPS	$2.03	S&P Oper. EPS 2009**E**	2.52	Yield (%)	0.96	S&P 3-Yr. Proj. EPS CAGR(%)	13.00
Trailing 12-Month P/E	19.6	P/E on S&P Oper. EPS 2008**E**	17.7	Dividend Rate/Share	$0.38	S&P Credit Rating	A+
$10K Invested 5 Yrs Ago	$13,738	Common Shares Outstg. (M)	991.6	Institutional Ownership (%)	66		

Price Performance

30-Week Mov. Avg. ···   10-Week Mov. Avg. - -   **GAAP Earnings vs. Previous Year**   Volume Above Avg. STARS
12-Mo. Target Price —   Relative Strength —   ▲ Up   ▼ Down   ▶ No Change   Below Avg.

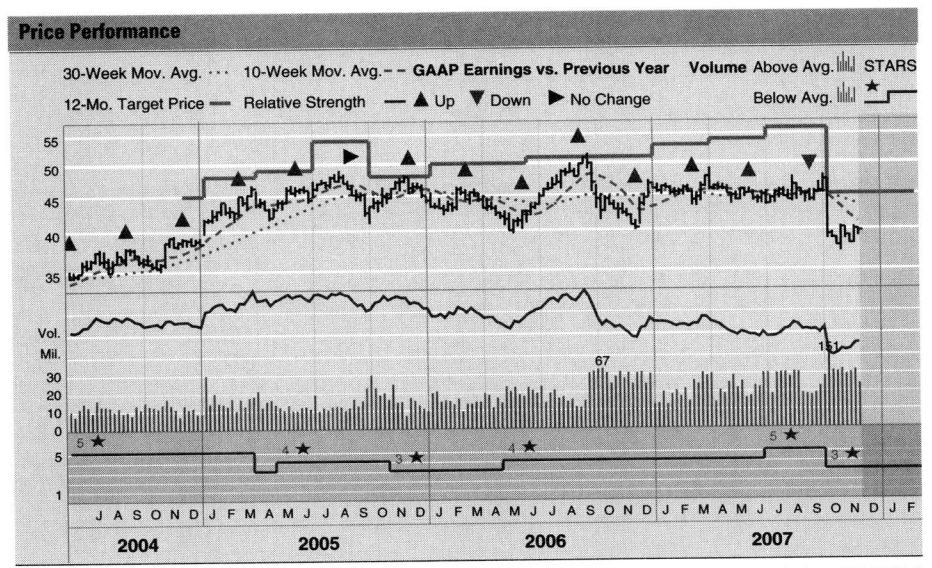

Options: ASE, CBOE, P

Analysis prepared by **Joseph Agnese** on October 02, 2007, when the stock traded at **$ 40.16**.

Highlights

➤ We see sales advancing about 10% in FY 08 (Aug.), fueled by the expected opening of about 550 new stores (at least 475 net new stores after closings and relocations), a pharmacy same-store sales gain of about 7%, and front-end same-store sales growth of about 5%. We see front-end growth benefiting from improved traffic trends and better convenience levels as the company expands store operating hours and the number of freestanding locations while improving the product assortment.

➤ We expect margins to be flat as benefits from increased sales of generic drugs, improved sales leverage from new stores, and better volumes from new Medicare Part D recipients, are offset by a shift in the mix as the pharmacy segment becomes a larger portion of the product mix. We think WAG's investment in in-store digital photo finishing labs will continue to benefit sales and gross margins by increasing traffic flow despite increased operating costs.

➤ We look for FY 08 operating EPS to increase about 10%, to $2.25, from operating EPS of $2.05 in FY 07.

Investment Rationale/Risk

➤ We believe the company is well positioned to benefit from increased generic drug sales, improved traffic trends due to new Medicare legislation, new store growth, and favorable demographics.

➤ Risks to our recommendation and target price include a weaker than expected economy, increased competition from peers and other retail formats, and legislative changes that may affect drug reimbursements.

➤ Our 12-month target price of $45 is based on our forward P/E analyses. The stock recently traded at about 20X FY 07 operating EPS of $2.05, around 1.4X our projected three-year EPS growth rate of 13%, and a slight premium to the shares of other drug chains we cover. We believe an above-average multiple is justified by what we see as WAG's long history of stable earnings growth, strong balance sheet, and leadership position in its industry. Applying a P/E of 20X, in line with its historical average of 1.5X projected growth, to our FY 08 EPS estimate of $2.25 results in a value of $45.

Qualitative Risk Assessment

LOW	**MEDIUM**	HIGH

Our risk assessment reflects the company's leadership position, resulting in what we see as strong market share positions, in a relatively stable U.S. retail drug industry, offset by growth of non-traditional competitors and potential legislation changes.

Quantitative Evaluations

S&P Quality Ranking   A+

D	C	B-	B	B+	A-	A	**A+**

Relative Strength Rank   MODERATE

64

LOWEST = 1   HIGHEST = 99

Revenue/Earnings Data

Revenue (Million $)

	1Q	2Q	3Q	4Q	Year
2007	12,709	13,934	13,698	13,422	53,762
2006	10,900	12,163	12,175	12,170	47,409
2005	9,889	10,987	10,831	10,495	42,202
2004	8,721	9,782	9,579	9,427	37,508
2003	7,485	8,446	8,328	8,246	32,505
2002	6,559	7,489	7,398	7,235	28,681

Earnings Per Share ($)

2007	0.43	0.65	0.56	0.40	2.03
2006	0.34	0.51	0.46	0.41	1.72
2005	0.32	0.48	0.40	0.32	1.52
2004	0.25	0.42	0.33	0.32	1.32
2003	0.22	0.36	0.29	0.27	1.14
2002	0.18	0.32	0.25	0.24	0.99

Fiscal year ended Aug. 31. Next earnings report expected: Late December. EPS Estimates based on S&P Operating Earnings; historical GAAP earnings are as reported.

Dividend Data (Dates: mm/dd Payment Date: mm/dd/yy)

Amount ($)	Date Decl.	Ex-Div. Date	Stk. of Record	Payment Date
0.078	01/10	02/14	02/16	03/12/07
0.078	04/10	05/16	05/18	06/12/07
0.095	07/11	08/16	08/20	09/12/07
0.095	10/10	11/07	11/12	12/12/07

Dividends have been paid since 1933. Source: Company reports.

Walgreen Co

STANDARD &POOR'S

Business Summary October 02, 2007

CORPORATE OVERVIEW. Walgreen Co. is one of the largest drug store chains in the U.S., based on sales and store count. In 1909, the company's founder, Charles Rudolph Walgreen Sr., purchased one of the busiest drug stores on Chicago's South Side, and transformed it by constructing an ice cream fountain that featured his own brand of ice cream. The ice cream fountain was the forerunner of the famous Walgreen's soda fountain, which became the main attraction for customers from the 1920s through the 1950s. People lined up to buy a product that WAG invented in the early 1920s: the milkshake. The company continued to be innovative by pioneering computerized pharmacies connected by satellite in 1981, completing chain wide point-of-sale scanning in 1991, and introducing freestanding stores with drive-thru pharmacies in 1992.

MARKET PROFILE. Walgreen operates the largest U.S. drugstore chain based on sales, generating $53.8 billion in sales in FY 07 (Aug.). According to our analysis, the company filled 583 million prescriptions in FY 07, and accounts for about 17% of the U.S. retail market. The company experienced an 5.7%

growth rate in prescription volume in FY 07, outpacing our estimate of a low single digit growth rate for the industry. On a dollar basis, WAG pharmacy sales rose 15% in FY 07, to $35 billion, versus our estimate of an upper single digit growth rate for the total industry, on comparable prescription sales growth of 9.5%. Sales of non-pharmacy items outperformed competitors, with the company increasing market share in 59 out of its top 60 core categories versus, drugstore, grocery and mass merchant competition. Based on store count, Walgreen is the second largest chain store operator in the U.S. As of August, 2007, the company operated 5,997 drug stores in 48 states and Puerto Rico, up 9.8% from 5,461 a year earlier. As of August 2007, the company believed it was on pace to exceed it's goal of operating at least 7,000 total stores by FY 10.

Company Financials Fiscal Year Ended Aug. 31

Per Share Data ($)	2007	2006	2005	2004	2003	2002	2001	2000	1999	1998
Tangible Book Value	NA	9.61	8.69	8.04	7.02	6.08	5.11	4.19	3.47	2.86
Cash Flow	NA	2.28	1.99	1.71	1.47	1.29	1.12	0.99	0.82	0.72
Earnings	2.03	1.72	1.52	1.32	1.14	0.99	0.86	0.76	0.62	0.54
S&P Core Earnings	2.03	1.71	1.44	1.27	1.07	0.93	0.80	NA	NA	NA
Dividends	0.33	0.27	0.22	0.18	0.16	0.15	0.14	0.14	0.13	0.13
Payout Ratio	16%	16%	15%	14%	14%	15%	16%	18%	21%	23%
Prices:High	49.10	51.60	49.01	39.51	37.42	40.70	45.29	45.75	33.94	30.22
Prices:Low	37.10	39.55	39.66	32.00	26.90	27.70	28.70	22.06	22.69	14.78
P/E Ratio:High	24	30	32	30	33	41	53	60	55	56
P/E Ratio:Low	18	23	26	24	24	28	33	29	37	28

Income Statement Analysis (Million $)										
Revenue	NA	47,409	42,202	37,508	32,505	28,681	24,623	21,207	17,839	15,307
Operating Income	NA	3,274	2,906	2,546	2,194	1,932	1,668	1,454	1,226	1,024
Depreciation	NA	572	482	403	346	307	269	230	210	189
Interest Expense	NA	Nil	Nil	Nil	Nil	Nil	3.10	0.40	0.40	1.00
Pretax Income	NA	2,754	2,456	2,176	1,889	1,637	1,423	1,263	1,027	877
Effective Tax Rate	NA	36.4%	36.5%	37.5%	37.8%	37.8%	37.8%	38.5%	39.2%	38.8%
Net Income	NA	1,751	1,560	1,360	1,176	1,019	886	777	624	537
S&P Core Earnings	2,042	1,754	1,478	1,302	1,104	955	820	NA	NA	NA

Balance Sheet & Other Financial Data (Million $)										
Cash	NA	920	577	1,696	1,017	450	16.9	12.8	142	144
Current Assets	NA	9,705	8,317	7,764	6,358	5,167	4,394	3,550	3,222	2,623
Total Assets	NA	17,131	14,609	13,342	11,406	9,879	8,834	7,104	5,907	4,902
Current Liabilities	NA	5,755	4,481	4,078	3,421	2,955	3,012	2,304	1,924	1,580
Long Term Debt	NA	Nil	Nil	Nil	Nil	Nil	Nil	Nil	Nil	Nil
Common Equity	NA	10,116	8,890	8,228	7,196	6,230	5,207	4,234	3,484	2,849
Total Capital	NA	10,257	9,130	8,556	7,424	6,407	5,344	4,336	3,559	2,938
Capital Expenditures	NA	1,338	1,238	940	795	934	1,237	1,119	696	641
Cash Flow	NA	2,323	2,042	1,763	1,522	1,327	1,155	1,007	834	726
Current Ratio	NA	1.7	1.9	1.9	1.9	1.7	1.5	1.5	1.7	1.7
% Long Term Debt of Capitalization	NA	Nil	Nil	Nil	Nil	Nil	Nil	Nil	Nil	Nil
% Net Income of Revenue	NA	3.7	3.7	3.6	3.6	3.6	3.6	3.7	3.5	3.5
% Return on Assets	NA	11.0	11.2	10.9	11.0	10.9	11.1	11.9	11.5	11.8
% Return on Equity	NA	18.4	18.3	17.6	17.5	17.8	18.8	20.1	19.7	20.6

Data as orig reptd.; bef. results of disc opers/spec. items. Per share data adj. for stk. divs.; EPS diluted. E-Estimated. NA-Not Available. NM-Not Meaningful. NR-Not Ranked. UR-Under Review.

Office: 200 Wilmot Road, Deerfield, IL 60015.
Telephone: 847-940-2500.
Email: investor.relations@walgreens.com
Website: http://www.walgreens.com

Chrmn & CEO: J.A. Rein
Pres & COO: G.D. Wasson
SVP & CFO: W. Rudolphsen
SVP, Secy & General Counsel: D. Green

VP & Treas: J.W. Spina
Investor Contact: R.J. Hans (847-940-2500)
Board Members: W. C. Foote, J. J. Howard, A. G. McNally, C. Reed, J. Rein, N. M. Schlichting, D. Y. Schwartz, J. A. Skinner, C. R. Walgreen, III, M. M. von Ferstel

Founded: 1901
Domicile: Illinois
Employees: 226,000

The McGraw-Hill Companies

Wal-Mart Stores Inc

STANDARD &POOR'S

S&P Recommendation **HOLD** ★★★☆☆	Price $45.73 (as of Nov 23, 2007)	12-Mo. Target Price $50.00	Investment Style Large-Cap Blend

GICS Sector Consumer Staples
Sub-Industry Hypermarkets & Super Centers

Summary WMT, the largest retailer in North America, operates a chain of discount department stores, wholesale clubs, and combination discount stores and supermarkets.

Key Stock Statistics (Source S&P, Vickers, company reports)

52-Wk Range	$51.44– 42.09	S&P Oper. EPS 2008**E**	3.16	Market Capitalization(B)	$186.040	Beta	0.51
Trailing 12-Month EPS	$3.06	S&P Oper. EPS 2009**E**	3.35	Yield (%)	1.92	S&P 3-Yr. Proj. EPS CAGR(%)	8.00
Trailing 12-Month P/E	14.9	P/E on S&P Oper. EPS 2008**E**	14.5	Dividend Rate/Share	$0.88	S&P Credit Rating	AA
$10K Invested 5 Yrs Ago	$9,023	Common Shares Outstg. (M)	4,068.2	Institutional Ownership (%)	39		

Price Performance

30-Week Mov. Avg. · · · 10-Week Mov. Avg. - - GAAP Earnings vs. Previous Year Volume Above Avg. STARS
12-Mo. Target Price — Relative Strength — ▲ Up ▼ Down ▶ No Change   Below Avg. ★

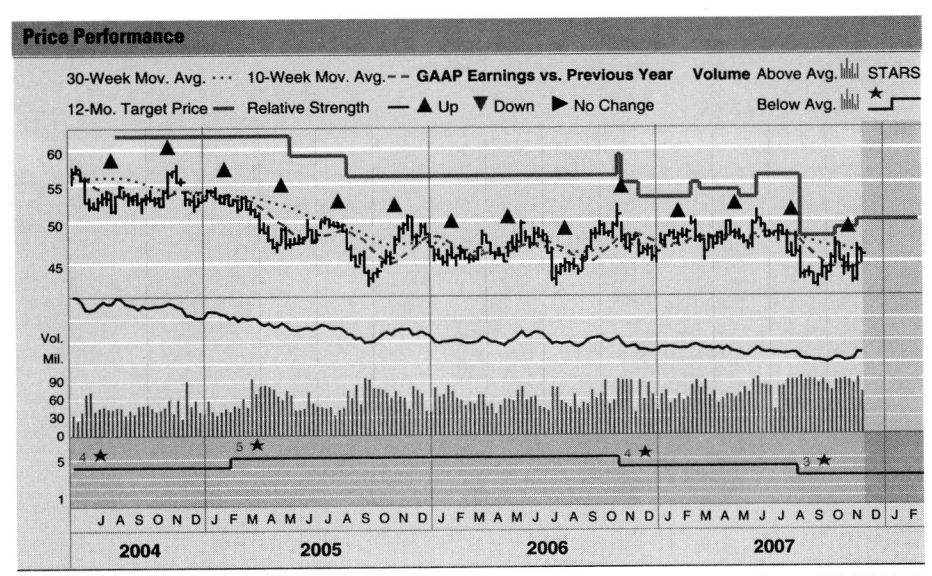

Options: ASE, CBOE, P, Ph

Analysis prepared by **Joseph Agnese** on November 16, 2007, when the stock traded at **$ 46.23**.

Highlights

➤ We expect FY 09 (Jan.) net sales to increase 6.9% to $405 billion from our estimate of $379 billion in FY 08, driven by 2% to 3% growth in same-store sales and the addition of around 6% square footage of new retail space, including 170 new U.S. supercenters (approximately 90 would be relocations or expansions of existing discount stores) and 25 million new international square footage. We look for comparable store sales to benefit from significant progress with store remodelings as the company continues to make inroads into international markets.

➤ We estimate that EBITDA margins will narrow slightly due to a shift in the product mix, reflecting higher sales of food, pharmacy and electronics products and sluggish first half sales in the apparel and home categories. We believe an increased focus on mid-price point merchandise and private label offerings should help the home and apparel categories in the second half of FY 09. Additionally, we see benefits from improved labor productivity due to the rollout of new scheduling software.

➤ We project operating EPS of $3.35 for FY 09, up 6.0% from our estimate of $3.16 for FY 08.

Investment Rationale/Risk

➤ We believe long-term earnings growth will be driven by international expansion and supported by efforts to significantly remodel the U.S. store base and increase volumes at existing locations while reducing cannibalization through a slowdown in square footage growth.

➤ Risks to our recommendation and target price include economic pressures such as rising unemployment or lower consumer confidence, which would negatively affect WMT's core customers and the company's results.

➤ Our 12-month target price of $50 is derived from a weighted blend of our analysis of relative P/E ratios as well as our discounted cash flow (DCF) model. Our DCF model suggests an intrinsic value of $53 per share and assumes a weighted average cost of capital of 9% and a terminal growth rate of 3%. However, we believe that until investors are confident that the company can gain market share at existing stores by producing comparable store sales growth in the low- to mid-single digits, the shares will trade below the S&P 500 on a P/E basis. Applying a P/E of 14X to our FY 09 EPS estimate of $3.35 implies a value of $47.

Qualitative Risk Assessment

LOW	MEDIUM	HIGH

Our risk assessment of Wal-Mart Stores reflects our view of the company's: high quality earnings, as reflected in its S&P Quality Ranking of A+; dominant market share positions; continued price leadership; and strong cash flow generation.

Quantitative Evaluations

S&P Quality Ranking   **A+**

D	C	B-	B	B+	A-	A	**A+**

Relative Strength Rank   **STRONG**

84

LOWEST = 1   HIGHEST = 99

Revenue/Earnings Data

Revenue (Million $)

	1Q	2Q	3Q	4Q	Year
2008	86,410	93,012	91,949	--	--
2007	79,613	85,430	84,467	99,078	344,992
2006	71,680	76,811	75,436	89,273	312,427
2005	64,763	69,722	68,520	82,216	285,222
2004	56,718	62,637	62,480	74,494	256,329
2003	54,960	59,694	58,797	71,073	244,524

Earnings Per Share ($)

	1Q	2Q	3Q	4Q	Year
2008	0.68	0.76	0.70	E1.03	E3.16
2007	0.64	0.72	0.62	0.95	2.92
2006	0.58	0.67	0.57	0.86	2.68
2005	0.50	0.62	0.54	0.75	2.41
2004	0.41	0.52	0.46	0.63	2.03
2003	0.37	0.46	0.41	0.57	1.81

Fiscal year ended Jan. 31. Next earnings report expected: Mid February. EPS Estimates based on S&P Operating Earnings; historical GAAP earnings are as reported.

Dividend Data (Dates: mm/dd Payment Date: mm/dd/yy)

Amount ($)	Date Decl.	Ex-Div. Date	Stk. of Record	Payment Date
0.220	03/08	03/14	03/16	04/02/07
0.220	03/08	05/16	05/18	06/04/07
0.220	03/08	08/15	08/17	09/04/07
0.220	03/08	12/12	12/14	01/02/08

Dividends have been paid since 1973. Source: Company reports.

Wal-Mart Stores Inc

STANDARD
&POOR'S

Business Summary November 16, 2007

CORPORATE OVERVIEW. Wal-Mart, the largest retailer in North America, has set its sights on other parts of the world. The company's operations are divided into three divisions: Wal-Mart, Sam's Club, and International. In FY 07 (Jan.), the Wal-Mart segment, comprised of discount stores, Supercenters and Neighborhood Markets, had sales of $226.3 billion, up 7.8% from the level of FY 06. Sam's Club sales totaled $41.6 billion, up 4.5%. In international markets, in which WMT operates a variety of formats, some via joint ventures, sales rose 30%, to $77.1 billion. Internationally, WMT operated 13 units in Argentina, 299 in Brazil, 289 in Canada, 73 in China (through joint ventures), 413 in Central America, 392 in Japan, 889 in Mexico, 54 in Puerto Rico, and 335 in the U.K.

MARKET PROFILE. With over 138 million people walking into Wal-Mart stores every week, the company is a dominant player in many of the markets in

which it competes. With FY 07 sales of about $109 billion within supermarket related categories (grocery, candy and tobacco; pharmaceuticals, health and beauty aids; photo processing), the Wal-Mart division is the largest supermarket operator in the U.S., commanding an estimated 22% market share of the $500 billion supermarket industry. Other major product categories within the Wal-Mart division include hardgoods ($41 billion in estimated sales in FY 07), softgoods ($34 billion), electronics ($23 billion) and sporting goods ($11 billion). Sam's Club is the second largest warehouse club in the U.S., with sales of $41.6 billion in FY 07.

Company Financials Fiscal Year Ended Jan. 31

Per Share Data ($)	2007	2006	2005	2004	2003	2002	2001	2000	1999	1998
Tangible Book Value	11.57	9.84	9.12	7.83	6.78	5.95	4.99	3.69	4.75	4.13
Cash Flow	4.23	3.81	3.44	2.91	2.58	2.22	2.04	1.78	1.41	1.15
Earnings	2.92	2.68	2.41	2.03	1.81	1.50	1.40	1.25	0.99	0.78
S&P Core Earnings	2.92	2.66	2.41	2.03	1.79	1.47	1.39	NA	NA	NA
Dividends	0.67	0.60	0.52	0.36	0.30	0.28	0.24	0.20	0.16	0.14
Payout Ratio	23%	22%	22%	18%	17%	19%	17%	16%	16%	17%
Calendar Year	2006	2005	2004	2003	2002	2001	2000	1999	1998	1997
Prices:High	52.15	54.60	61.31	60.20	63.94	58.75	69.00	70.25	41.38	20.97
Prices:Low	42.31	42.31	51.08	46.25	43.72	42.00	41.44	38.68	18.78	11.00
P/E Ratio:High	18	20	25	30	35	39	49	56	42	27
P/E Ratio:Low	14	16	21	23	24	28	30	31	19	14

Income Statement Analysis (Million $)

	2007	2006	2005	2004	2003	2002	2001	2000	1999	1998
Revenue	348,650	312,427	285,222	256,329	244,524	217,799	191,329	165,013	137,634	117,958
Operating Income	22,298	23,247	18,729	16,525	15,075	15,367	12,392	10,684	8,418	6,796
Depreciation	5,459	4,717	4,405	3,852	3,432	3,290	2,868	2,375	1,872	1,634
Interest Expense	1,809	1,420	1,187	996	1,063	1,326	1,374	1,022	797	784
Pretax Income	18,968	17,358	16,105	14,193	12,719	10,751	10,116	9,083	7,323	5,719
Effective Tax Rate	33.6%	33.4%	34.7%	36.1%	35.3%	36.2%	36.5%	36.8%	37.4%	37.0%
Net Income	12,178	11,231	10,267	8,861	8,039	6,671	6,295	5,575	4,430	3,526
S&P Core Earnings	12,178	11,134	10,267	8,861	7,955	6,592	6,235	NA	NA	NA

Balance Sheet & Other Financial Data (Million $)

	2007	2006	2005	2004	2003	2002	2001	2000	1999	1998
Cash	7,373	6,414	5,488	5,199	2,758	2,161	2,054	1,856	1,879	1,447
Current Assets	46,588	43,824	38,491	34,421	30,483	28,246	26,555	24,356	21,132	19,352
Total Assets	151,193	138,187	120,223	104,912	94,685	83,451	78,130	70,349	49,996	45,384
Current Liabilities	51,754	48,826	42,888	37,418	32,617	27,282	28,949	25,803	16,762	14,460
Long Term Debt	30,735	30,171	23,669	20,099	19,608	18,732	15,655	16,674	9,607	9,674
Common Equity	61,573	53,171	49,396	43,623	39,337	35,102	31,343	25,834	21,112	18,503
Total Capital	94,468	84,809	74,388	65,206	60,307	55,041	48,138	43,987	32,518	30,115
Capital Expenditures	15,666	14,563	12,893	10,308	9,355	8,383	8,042	6,183	3,734	2,636
Cash Flow	17,637	15,948	14,672	12,713	11,471	9,961	9,163	7,950	6,302	5,160
Current Ratio	0.9	0.9	0.9	0.9	0.9	1.0	0.9	0.9	1.3	1.3
% Long Term Debt of Capitalization	32.5	35.6	31.8	30.8	32.5	34.0	32.5	38.0	29.5	32.1
% Net Income of Revenue	3.5	3.5	3.6	3.5	3.3	3.1	3.3	3.4	3.2	3.0
% Return on Assets	8.4	8.7	9.1	8.9	9.0	8.3	8.5	9.3	9.3	8.3
% Return on Equity	21.2	21.9	22.1	21.3	21.6	20.1	22.0	23.8	22.4	19.8

Data as orig reptd.; bef. results of disc opers/spec. items. Per share data adj. for stk. divs.; EPS diluted. E-Estimated. NA-Not Available. NM-Not Meaningful. NR-Not Ranked. UR-Under Review.

Office: 702 S.W. 8th Street, Bentonville, AR 72716.
Telephone: 479-273-4000.
Website: http://www.walmartstores.com
Chrmn: S.R. Walton

Pres & CEO: H.L. Scott, Jr.
Vice Chrmn: M.T. Duke
Vice Chrmn & Chief Admin Officer: J. Menzer
Investor Contact: T.M. Schoewe (479-273-4000)

Board Members: A. Alvarez, J. Breyer, M. M. Burns, J. I. Cash, Jr., R. C. Corbett, D. N. Daft, D. Glass, R. A. Hernandez, H. L. Scott, Jr., J. C. Shewmaker, J. H. Villarreal, J. Walton, S. R. Walton, C. J. Williams, L. S. Wolf

Founded: 1945
Domicile: Delaware
Employees: 1,900,000

Washington Mutual Inc

STANDARD &POOR'S

S&P Recommendation SELL ★ ★ ☆ ☆ ☆

Price	12-Mo. Target Price	Investment Style
$18.21 (as of Nov 23, 2007)	$15.00	Large-Cap Blend

GICS Sector Financials
Sub-Industry Thrifts & Mortgage Finance

Summary Washington Mutual is the largest U.S. savings and loan company and the seventh biggest among all U.S.-based bank and thrift holding companies, based on assets.

Key Stock Statistics (Source S&P, Vickers, company reports)

52-Wk Range	$46.38–17.04	S&P Oper. EPS 2007E	2.35	Market Capitalization(B)	$15.947	Beta		0.68
Trailing 12-Month EPS	$3.12	S&P Oper. EPS 2008E	1.65	Yield (%)	12.30	S&P 3-Yr. Proj. EPS CAGR(%)		NA
Trailing 12-Month P/E	5.8	P/E on S&P Oper. EPS 2007E	7.7	Dividend Rate/Share	$2.24	S&P Credit Rating		A-
$10K Invested 5 Yrs Ago	$6,358	Common Shares Outstg. (M)	875.7	Institutional Ownership (%)	93			

Price Performance

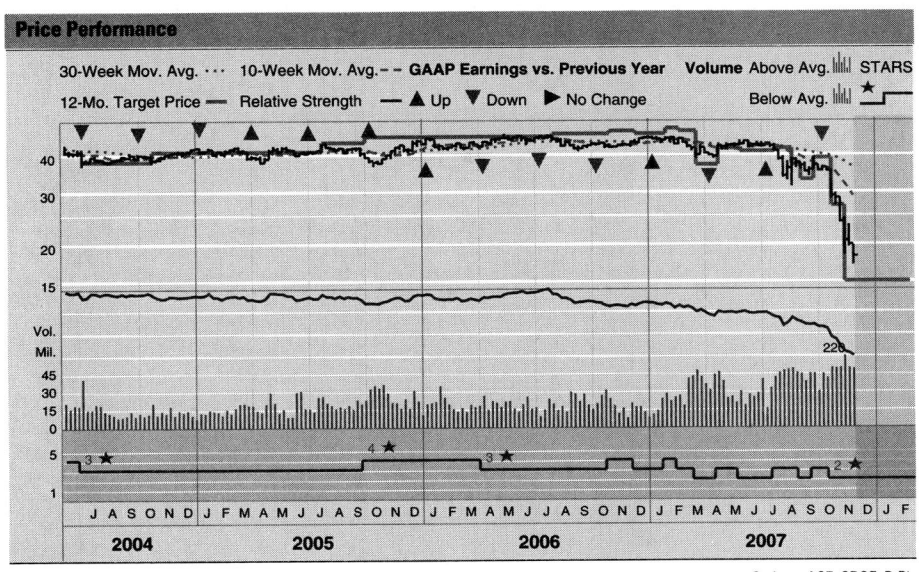

30-Week Mov. Avg. · · · 10-Week Mov. Avg. – – GAAP Earnings vs. Previous Year   Volume Above Avg. STARS
12-Mo. Target Price — Relative Strength — ▲ Up ▼ Down ▶ No Change   Below Avg. ★

Options: ASE, CBOE, P, Ph

Analysis prepared by **Stuart Plesser** on November 08, 2007, when the stock traded at **$ 18.70**.

Highlights

➤ We expect average earning assets to increase in the low-single digits in 2008, as loan expansion will likely be tempered by capital restraints. We look for an expansion in the net interest margin, from a balance sheet repositioning and modest fee growth, to result in a 10% increase in revenue from suppressed levels in 2007. Our assumptions include a net interest margin of 2.90% (up from projected 2.85% in 2007), an average earning asset increase of 3.0%, and a 15% increase in non-interest income, assuming no major writedown of securities.

➤ With WM's continued focus on expense control, we see non-interest expense increasing 2.5% in 2008, due to higher revenues. Our forecast for non-interest expense to total revenues is 54.0%, down from a projected 58.0% in 2007. Due to the addition of higher-risk credit card loans to its portfolio and a pickup in net charge-offs from its home loan division, we believe loan loss provisions will almost double in 2008, to $5.2 billion.

➤ Assuming an effective tax rate of 35%, we estimate operating EPS of $2.35 in 2007, down from 2006's $3.50. Our 2008 EPS estimate is $1.65.

Investment Rationale/Risk

➤ Despite $967 million of provisions in the third quarter, we think WM's allowance reserve is still too low. We note that its allowance comprises only 41% of nonperforming loans, well below peers. We see chargeoffs increasing at an accelerated rate as housing will likely decline roughly 10% through mid-2008. Although WM should benefit from the recent Fed rate cut of 50 basis points, and balance sheet repositioning, we believe that credit issues will outstrip net interest margin gains. Our negative outlook regarding WM's credit is supported by its heavy concentration of subprime loans, which comprise roughly 8.5% of its loan portfolio. Besides subprime loans, the company also has a heavy concentration of home equity loans and Option ARM loans. WM may also be hurt by claims that its home loans were based on over-inflated appraisal values.

➤ Risks to our recommendation and target price include a further steepening of the yield curve and better-than-projected credit quality.

➤ Our 12-month target price of $15 implies a P/E of 9.1X applied to our 2008 EPS estimate, below WM's historical average. We believe this discount is warranted in light of credit issues.

Qualitative Risk Assessment

LOW	MEDIUM	HIGH

Our risk assessment reflects WM's exposure to the cyclicality of the mortgage industry. However, we see this as being offset by an increasingly diversified balance sheet as well as earnings from the retail banking and card services businesses.

Quantitative Evaluations

S&P Quality Ranking A

D	C	B-	B	B+	A-	A	A+

Relative Strength Rank WEAK

4

LOWEST = 1   HIGHEST = 99

Revenue/Earnings Data

Revenue (Million $)

	1Q	2Q	3Q	4Q	Year
2007	6,549	6,506	--	--	--
2006	6,382	6,513	6,675	6,802	26,284
2005	4,768	4,973	5,314	6,174	21,820
2004	3,958	3,646	4,075	4,283	15,962
2003	4,523	4,664	4,562	4,264	18,013
2002	4,690	4,793	4,793	4,760	19,037

Earnings Per Share ($)

2007	0.86	0.92	0.23	E0.32	E2.35
2006	0.98	0.78	0.76	1.10	3.18
2005	1.01	0.95	0.92	0.85	3.73
2004	0.73	0.55	0.76	0.76	2.81
2003	1.05	1.10	1.09	0.91	4.12
2002	0.98	1.01	1.01	1.03	4.05

Fiscal year ended Dec. 31. Next earnings report expected: Mid January. EPS Estimates based on S&P Operating Earnings; historical GAAP earnings are as reported.

Dividend Data (Dates: mm/dd Payment Date: mm/dd/yy)

Amount ($)	Date Decl.	Ex-Div. Date	Stk. of Record	Payment Date
0.540	01/19	01/29	01/31	02/15/07
0.550	04/17	04/26	04/30	05/15/07
0.560	07/17	07/27	07/31	08/15/07
0.560	10/16	10/29	10/31	11/15/07

Dividends have been paid since 1986. Source: Company reports.

Please read the Required Disclosures and Analyst Certification on the last page of this report.

The **McGraw-Hill** Companies

Washington Mutual Inc

STANDARD &POOR'S

Business Summary November 08, 2007

CORPORATE OVERVIEW. Washington Mutual, Inc. is a retailer of financial services to consumers and small businesses. WM has four operating segments: Retail Banking and Financial Services, which provides non-mortgage consumer loans and other banking and investment products to individuals and small businesses; Home Loans, which originates, services, purchases and sells home loans and includes its subprime subsidiary, Long Beach Mortgage Co.; Commercial, which provides multi-family, commercial real estate and construction loans; and Card Services, which was formed following WM's acquisition of Providian Financial Corp. (PVN) on October 1, 2005. Effective January 1, 2006, WM reorganized its single-family residential mortgage lending operations by combining Long Beach and Mortgage Banker Finance, its warehouse lending unit, in the Home Loans group from the Commercial group. Due to the unpredictable nature of mortgage banking activities, we believe WM's earnings volatility is greater than that of a traditional thrift, but we see some of this mitigated by efforts to diversify its assets away from residential mortgages.

MARKET PROFILE. At the end of 2006, WM operated in 15 states: California (ranked fourth of all states WM has a presence, based on a deposit market share of approximately 9.6%), New York (eighth, 1.8%), Washington (second, 10.8%), Florida (sixth, 3.1%), Texas (sixth, 2.6%), Oregon (third, 9.9%), New Jersey (ninth, 1.3%), Nevada (first, 56.1%), Arizona (tenth, 1.2%), Illinois (14th, 0.3%), Utah (11th, 0.5%), Georgia (15th, 0.4%), Idaho (fifth, 3.1%), Colorado (12th, 0.5%) and Connecticut (15th, 0.1%). Based on current income levels and projected changes in population and household income, we believe the prospects for its markets are above average.

Company Financials Fiscal Year Ended Dec. 31

Per Share Data ($)	2006	2005	2004	2003	2002	2001	2000	1999	1998	1997
Tangible Book Value	18.43	19.43	17.20	15.38	14.36	13.44	11.21	9.16	9.37	9.09
Earnings	3.18	3.73	2.81	4.12	4.05	3.15	2.36	2.11	1.71	0.83
S&P Core Earnings	3.08	3.70	2.77	4.05	3.94	3.03	NA	NA	NA	NA
Dividends	2.06	1.90	1.74	1.40	1.06	0.90	0.76	0.65	0.55	0.47
Payout Ratio	65%	51%	62%	34%	26%	29%	32%	31%	37%	57%
Prices:High	47.01	45.06	45.47	46.85	39.98	42.99	37.29	30.50	34.44	32.28
Prices:Low	41.03	36.64	36.80	32.40	27.80	26.52	14.42	16.46	17.83	18.78
P/E Ratio:High	15	12	16	11	10	14	16	14	20	39
P/E Ratio:Low	13	10	13	8	7	8	6	8	10	23

Income Statement Analysis (Million $)	2006	2005	2004	2003	2002	2001	2000	1999	1998	1997
Net Interest Income	8,121	7,886	7,116	7,629	8,341	6,876	4,311	4,452	4,292	2,656
Loan Loss Provision	816	316	209	42.0	595	575	185	167	162	207
Non Interest Income	6,377	8,272	6,994	5,174	4,022	1,883	1,985	1,509	1,524	751
Non Interest Expenses	8,807	7,870	5,014	7,408	6,382	4,167	3,126	2,910	3,284	2,300
Pretax Income	4,875	5,438	3,984	6,029	6,154	4,311	2,984	2,884	2,369	901
Effective Tax Rate	34.0%	36.9%	37.8%	37.1%	36.7%	36.6%	36.4%	37.0%	37.2%	46.5%
Net Income	3,114	3,432	2,479	3,793	3,896	2,732	1,899	1,817	1,487	482
% Net Interest Margin	2.60	2.67	2.82	3.11	3.48	3.32	2.38	2.63	2.88	3.03
S&P Core Earnings	3,007	3,400	2,446	3,735	3,788	2,616	NA	NA	NA	NA

Balance Sheet & Other Financial Data (Million $)	2006	2005	2004	2003	2002	2001	2000	1999	1998	1997
Total Assets	346,288	343,839	307,918	275,178	268,298	242,506	194,716	186,514	165,493	96,981
Loans	223,330	227,937	205,770	174,394	145,875	131,587	118,612	113,497	108,371	67,140
Deposits	213,956	193,167	173,658	153,181	155,516	107,182	79,574	81,130	85,492	50,986
Capitalization:Debt	47,712	55,166	34,442	22,123	22,198	23,883	29,951	28,313	45,198	23,791
Capitalization:Equity	26,477	27,616	21,226	19,742	20,134	14,063	10,166	9,053	9,344	5,191
Capitalization:Total	77,129	82,782	21,226	41,865	42,332	38,048	40,117	37,366	54,542	29,100
% Return on Assets	0.9	1.1	0.9	1.4	1.5	1.2	1.0	1.0	1.0	0.5
% Return on Equity	11.6	14.1	12.1	19.1	22.8	22.5	19.8	19.8	20.2	9.3
% Loan Loss Reserve	0.6	0.6	0.5	0.6	0.9	0.9	-0.8	0.9	1.0	1.0
% Risk Based Capital	12.2	11.6	12.4	10.8	11.4	10.9	11.4	11.2	12.1	NA
Price Times Book Value:High	2.6	2.3	2.6	2.0	2.8	3.2	3.3	3.3	3.7	3.9
Price Times Book Value:Low	2.2	1.9	2.1	2.1	1.9	2.0	1.3	1.8	1.9	2.3

Data as orig reptd.; bef. results of disc opers/spec. items. Per share data adj. for stk. divs.; EPS diluted. E-Estimated. NA-Not Available. NM-Not Meaningful. NR-Not Ranked. UR-Under Review.

Office: 1301 2nd Ave, Seattle, WA 98101-2005.
Telephone: 206-461-2000.
Website: http://www.wamu.com
Chrmn & CEO: K.K. Killinger

Pres & COO: S. Rotella
Sr EVP & General Counsel: F.L. Chapman
EVP & CFO: T.W. Casey
SVP & Cntlr: J.F. Woods

Board Members: A. V. Farrell, S. E. Frank, K. K. Killinger, T. C. Leppert, C. M. Lillis, P. D. Matthews, R. Montaya, M. K. Murphy, M. Osmer-McQuade, M. E. Pugh, W. G. Reed, Jr., O. C. Smith, J. H. Stever

Founded: 1889
Domicile: Washington
Employees: 49,824

The McGraw-Hill Companies

Waste Management Inc.

STANDARD &POOR'S

S&P Recommendation	**BUY** ★★★★☆	Price $34.03 (as of Nov 23, 2007)	12-Mo. Target Price $42.00	Investment Style Large-Cap Blend

GICS Sector Industrials
Sub-Industry Environmental & Facilities Services

Summary This Houston-based company is the largest U.S. trash hauling/disposal concern.

Key Stock Statistics (Source S&P, Vickers, company reports)

52-Wk Range	$41.19– 32.40	S&P Oper. EPS 2007E	2.05	Market Capitalization(B)	$17.665	Beta	0.87
Trailing 12-Month EPS	$2.07	S&P Oper. EPS 2008E	2.30	Yield (%)	2.82	S&P 3-Yr. Proj. EPS CAGR(%)	11.00
Trailing 12-Month P/E	16.4	P/E on S&P Oper. EPS 2007E	16.6	Dividend Rate/Share	$0.96	S&P Credit Rating	BBB
$10K Invested 5 Yrs Ago	$15,703	Common Shares Outstg. (M)	519.1	Institutional Ownership (%)	83		

Price Performance

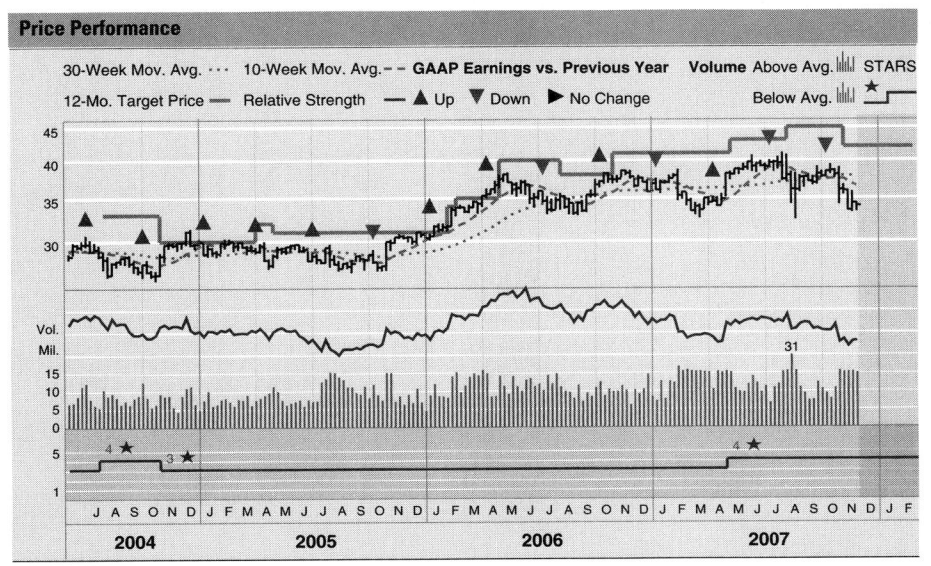

30-Week Mov. Avg. · · · 10-Week Mov. Avg. — **GAAP Earnings vs. Previous Year**   Volume Above Avg. ▮▮▮ STARS
12-Mo. Target Price — Relative Strength — ▲ Up ▼ Down ▶ No Change   Below Avg. ▮▮▮ ★

Options: ASE, CBOE, P, Ph

Analysis prepared by **Stewart Scharf** on October 31, 2007, when the stock traded at **$ 35.86**.

Highlights

➤ We project a gradual improvement in internal revenue growth during 2008 to about 3%, as collection and landfill price hikes offset soft volume. We expect WMI to continue to sacrifice collection volume in favor of maintaining its pricing strategy and margins.

➤ We project that gross margins (before depreciation and amortization (D&A)) will expand to about 37% in 2007, from 35.7% in 2006, and widen further in 2008, due to cost savings from routing initiatives and further pricing initiatives at landfills and transfer stations. We see the EBITDA margin widening by another 100 basis points in 2008 from our projected 26% in 2007, as WMI continues to divest underperforming assets, and improve productivity, maintenance and safety, which should reduce workers' compensation costs.

➤ We estimate an effective tax rate of 36.5% for 2007 and no longer expect a $0.04 energy-related tax credit in the second half due to the high price of crude oil. We see operating EPS of $2.05, before a $0.09 net gain, on 4% fewer shares. In 2008, we project a 12% rise in EPS to $2.30.

Investment Rationale/Risk

➤ We have a buy recommendation on the shares, primarily based on valuation, and the company's pricing and divestiture strategy, as WMI focuses on higher-margin customers.

➤ Risks to our recommendation and target price include a significant rise in fuel costs, a sharply weakening economy, further labor disputes, a decline in the customer retention rate, and a potential inability to raise prices enough to meet return on invested capital (ROIC) goals.

➤ We view the stock's recent dividend yield of about 2.6%, above the 1.8% yield of the S&P 500, as attractive. Correlating a projected P/E of 16X our 2008 EPS estimate with other relative metrics, including WMI's historical five-year average P/E, and forward peer and market multiples, we arrive at a value of about $39. Based on our discounted cash flow model, using an 8.5% weighted average cost of capital and 3% terminal growth, intrinsic value is $45. Blending these metrics, we derive our 12-month target price of $42, equal to what we consider a warranted forward P/E of 18.3X our 2008 EPS estimate.

Qualitative Risk Assessment

LOW	MEDIUM	HIGH

Our risk assessment reflects broad-based pricing initiatives and fuel surcharges geared to reducing volatile fuel costs, a favorable interest rate environment, and what we view as a strong balance sheet with declining debt levels and solid return on equity. In addition, we view corporate governance practices as sound.

Quantitative Evaluations

S&P Quality Ranking   B

D	C	B-	**B**	B+	A-	A	A+

Relative Strength Rank   MODERATE

45

LOWEST = 1   HIGHEST = 99

Revenue/Earnings Data

Revenue (Million $)

	1Q	2Q	3Q	4Q	Year
2007	3,188	3,358	3,403	--	--
2006	3,229	3,410	3,441	3,283	13,363
2005	3,038	3,289	3,375	3,372	13,074
2004	2,896	3,138	3,274	3,208	12,516
2003	2,716	2,915	2,975	2,968	11,574
2002	2,609	2,825	2,896	2,812	11,142

Earnings Per Share ($)

2007	0.42	0.64	0.54	E0.51	E2.05
2006	0.34	0.76	0.55	0.46	2.10
2005	0.26	0.92	0.38	0.52	2.09
2004	0.25	0.37	0.52	0.47	1.60
2003	0.18	0.30	0.35	0.39	1.21
2002	0.22	0.35	0.38	0.39	1.33

Fiscal year ended Dec. 31. Next earnings report expected: Early February. EPS Estimates based on S&P Operating Earnings; historical GAAP earnings are as reported.

Dividend Data (Dates: mm/dd Payment Date: mm/dd/yy)

Amount ($)	Date Decl.	Ex-Div. Date	Stk. of Record	Payment Date
0.240	03/01	03/08	03/12	03/23/07
0.240	05/11	05/31	06/04	06/22/07
0.240	08/24	08/30	09/04	09/21/07
0.240	11/13	11/29	12/03	12/19/07

Dividends have been paid since 1998. Source: Company reports.

Waste Management Inc.

STANDARD &POOR'S

Business Summary October 31, 2007

CORPORATE OVERVIEW. Waste Management, the largest U.S. waste disposal company in North America, provides collection, transfer, recycling and re-source recovery, as well as disposal services. It also owns U.S. waste-to-energy facilities. Recently, it had more than 430 collection operations, and owned or operated 277 landfills. In 2006, revenues from the North American solid waste (NASW) business were: 56% collection; 20% landfill; 5.7% waste-to-energy (Wheelabrator Technologies unit); 11% transfer; and 6.8% recycling and other. WMI's average remaining landfill life was recently about 28 years (35 years when considering remaining permitted capacity, probable expansion capacity at 62 landfills, and projected annual disposal volume). WMI's internalization rate was 66.5% at September 30, 2007, down slightly from 66.7% at year-end 2006.

We project free cash flow of about $1.5 billion for 2007, targeted mainly for

share buybacks and dividend payments. In 2006, WMI bought back $1.07 billion of stock (nearly 31 million shares). It plans to spend about $1.3 billion on buybacks in 2007 ($1.06 billion spent in the first nine months). We believe capital expenditures will be near $1.0 billion, and will be slated for buying land around landfills, a new computer system to be rolled out by early 2008, and fleet upgrades; we also expect WMI to invest in landfill gas-to-energy, medical waste projects, and other initiatives. We see some loss of market share in competitive pricing regions, such as the Midwest. The company continues to focus on improving its fleet maintenance and employee safety measures.

Company Financials Fiscal Year Ended Dec. 31

Per Share Data ($)	2006	2005	2004	2003	2002	2001	2000	1999	1998	1997
Tangible Book Value	1.52	1.10	0.91	0.24	0.21	0.43	NM	NM	NM	4.51
Cash Flow	4.66	4.50	3.90	3.44	5.29	2.97	2.14	1.99	1.25	2.47
Earnings	2.10	2.09	1.60	1.21	1.33	0.80	-0.16	-0.64	-1.31	1.26
S&P Core Earnings	2.05	1.90	1.48	1.09	1.17	1.04	NA	NA	NA	NA
Dividends	0.88	0.80	0.75	0.01	0.01	0.01	0.01	0.02	0.02	Nil
Payout Ratio	42%	38%	47%	1%	1%	1%	NM	NM	NM	Nil
Prices:High	38.64	31.03	31.42	29.72	31.25	32.50	28.31	60.00	58.19	44.13
Prices:Low	30.08	26.80	25.67	19.39	20.20	22.51	13.00	14.00	34.44	28.63
P/E Ratio:High	18	15	20	25	23	41	NM	NM	NM	35
P/E Ratio:Low	14	13	16	16	15	28	NM	NM	NM	23

Income Statement Analysis (Million $)	2006	2005	2004	2003	2002	2001	2000	1999	1998	1997
Revenue	13,363	13,074	12,516	11,574	11,142	11,322	12,492	13,127	12,703	2,614
Operating Income	3,388	3,167	3,021	2,841	2,870	3,034	3,216	2,154	4,010	983
Depreciation	1,334	1,361	1,336	1,265	2,444	1,371	1,429	1,614	1,499	303
Interest Expense	545	496	455	439	462	541	748	770	681	104
Pretax Income	1,518	1,140	1,214	1,129	1,240	792	344	-139	-676	463
Effective Tax Rate	21.4%	NM	20.3%	35.8%	34.2%	35.9%	NM	NM	NM	41.0%
Net Income	1,149	1,182	931	719	823	503	-97.0	-395	-767	273
S&P Core Earnings	1,121	1,072	864	643	725	653	NA	NA	NA	NA

Balance Sheet & Other Financial Data (Million $)	2006	2005	2004	2003	2002	2001	2000	1999	1998	1997
Cash	614	666	443	135	264	730	94.0	181	88.7	51.2
Current Assets	3,182	3,451	2,819	2,588	2,700	3,124	2,457	6,221	3,881	655
Total Assets	20,600	21,135	20,905	20,656	19,631	19,490	18,565	22,681	22,715	6,623
Current Liabilities	3,268	3,257	3,205	3,332	3,173	3,721	2,937	7,489	4,294	569
Long Term Debt	7,495	8,165	8,182	7,997	8,062	7,709	8,372	8,399	11,114	2,724
Common Equity	6,222	6,121	5,971	5,563	5,308	5,392	4,801	4,403	4,372	2,629
Total Capital	15,357	15,931	14,435	15,473	13,389	14,241	14,067	13,540	16,069	5,674
Capital Expenditures	1,329	1,180	1,258	1,200	1,287	1,328	1,313	1,327	1,651	436
Cash Flow	2,483	2,543	2,267	1,984	3,267	1,874	1,332	1,219	732	577
Current Ratio	1.0	1.1	0.9	0.8	0.9	0.8	0.8	0.8	0.9	1.2
% Long Term Debt of Capitalization	48.8	51.3	56.7	51.7	60.2	54.1	59.5	62.0	69.2	48.0
% Net Income of Revenue	8.6	9.0	7.4	6.2	7.4	4.4	NM	NM	NM	10.5
% Return on Assets	5.5	5.6	4.5	3.5	4.2	2.6	NM	NM	NM	4.1
% Return on Equity	18.6	19.6	16.1	13.2	15.4	9.9	NM	NM	NM	10.4

Data as orig reptd.; bef. results of disc opers/spec. items. Per share data adj. for stk. divs.; EPS diluted. E-Estimated. NA-Not Available. NM-Not Meaningful. NR-Not Ranked. UR-Under Review.

Office: 1001 Fannin Street, Houston, TX 77002.
Telephone: 713-512-6200.
Website: http://www.wm.com
Chrmn: J.C. Pope

Pres & COO: L. O'Donnell, III
CEO: D.P. Steiner
SVP & CFO: R.G. Simpson
SVP, General Counsel & CCO: R.L. Wittenbraker

Investor Contact: G. Nikkel (713-265-1358)
Board Members: P. S. Cafferty, F. M. Clark, P. W. Gross, T. I. Morgan, J. C. Pope, W. R. Reum, S. G. Rothmeier, D. P. Steiner, T. Weidemeyer

Founded: 1894
Domicile: Delaware
Employees: 48,000

The McGraw-Hill Companies

Waters Corp

STANDARD &POOR'S

S&P Recommendation BUY ★★★★☆

Price	$77.35 (as of Nov 23, 2007)
12-Mo. Target Price	$84.00
Investment Style	Large-Cap Growth

GICS Sector Health Care
Sub-Industry Life Sciences Tools & Services

Summary This company manufactures scientific and industrial analytical equipments such as liquid chromatography, thermal analysis and mass spectrometry products.

Key Stock Statistics (Source S&P, Vickers, company reports)

52-Wk Range	$77.98–48.35	S&P Oper. EPS 2007E	2.83	Market Capitalization(B)	$7.720
Trailing 12-Month EPS	$2.42	S&P Oper. EPS 2008E	3.30	Yield (%)	Nil
Trailing 12-Month P/E	32.0	P/E on S&P Oper. EPS 2007E	27.3	Dividend Rate/Share	Nil
$10K Invested 5 Yrs Ago	$28,385	Common Shares Outstg. (M)	99.8	Institutional Ownership (%)	90

Beta	1.68
S&P 3-Yr. Proj. EPS CAGR(%)	18.00
S&P Credit Rating	NA

Price Performance

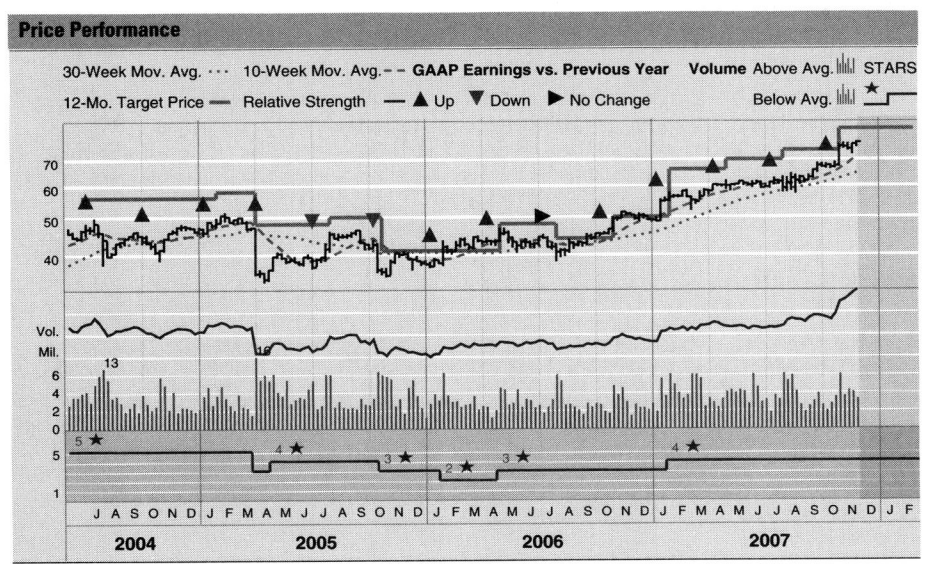

Analysis prepared by **Jeffrey Loo, CFA** on October 26, 2007, when the stock traded at **$75.67**.

Options: CBOE, Ph

Highlights

➤ We see 2007 and 2008 sales growing 15% and 9%, to $1.47 billion and $1.6 billion, respectively. We foresee solid growth throughout WAT's end-user market, and we believe small and midsize firms, including pharmaceutical services firms such as contract research organizations, are driving sales growth while demand from large U.S. pharmaceuticals is improving. We expect gross margins to decline 60 basis points (bps) in 2007 (in spite of increased manufacturing in Singapore), as new products have higher costs early in their lifecycles, but should rebound 80 bps in 2008 aided by higher sales of consumables. We see operating leverage lifting operating margins 130 bps and 140 bps in 2007 and 2008.

➤ We see continued improvements in the U.S. and Europe, while growth in India and China should remain strong albeit slower than the rapid pace experienced in the past two years.

➤ We estimate 2007 and 2008 operating EPS of $2.83 and $3.30, respectively, aided by a lower share count due to stock buybacks. But we believe WAT's buyback program leverages the company as it finances the program with debt and free cash flow.

Investment Rationale/Risk

➤ We think solid growth is sustainable over the next several quarters as we believe end-user demand is broad based and geographically diverse. We expect solid sales growth throughout WAT's product lines, in particular, mass spectrometry and in Thermal Analysis. We believe the mass spectrometry market is growing, and we see WAT gaining market share with its systems integration approach and with new products, such as the Synapt High Definition MS and tandem quadrupole devices. We also anticipate continued strength in industrial end markets, and we believe food safety applications will expand WAT's client base. Although we see competitive pressure on Acquity UPLC rising, we see strong demand for consumables.

➤ Risks to our recommendation and target price include soft equipment sales if pharmaceutical and research firms limit capital spending, and a softening in industrial end markets following several years of robust growth.

➤ Based on a blend of our DCF model, which assumes a WACC of 9.2% and a terminal growth rate of 3%, and our P/E-to-growth (PEG) analysis, using a PEG ratio of 1.4X, in line with peers, our 12-month target price is $84.

Qualitative Risk Assessment

LOW | **MEDIUM** | HIGH

Our risk assessment reflects WAT's strong market share in the liquid chromatography and mass spectrometry markets, offset by a highly competitive marketplace and a reliance on customer demand for expensive instruments.

Quantitative Evaluations

S&P Quality Ranking B+

D | C | B- | B | **B+** | A- | A | A+

Relative Strength Rank STRONG 95

LOWEST = 1   HIGHEST = 99

Revenue/Earnings Data

Revenue (Million $)

	1Q	2Q	3Q	4Q	Year
2007	330.8	352.6	352.6	--	--
2006	290.2	301.9	301.2	386.9	1,280
2005	268.3	284.6	273.0	332.3	1,158
2004	255.1	260.5	264.8	324.2	1,105
2003	221.0	231.8	230.4	275.1	958.2
2002	200.3	217.2	216.1	256.4	890.0

Earnings Per Share ($)

2007	0.54	0.59	0.52	E1.05	E2.83
2006	0.42	0.46	0.49	0.78	2.13
2005	0.38	0.46	0.22	0.71	1.74
2004	0.33	0.49	0.42	0.58	1.82
2003	0.26	0.33	0.29	0.47	1.34
2002	0.27	0.28	0.29	0.30	1.12

Fiscal year ended Dec. 31. Next earnings report expected: Late January. EPS Estimates based on S&P Operating Earnings; historical GAAP earnings are as reported.

Dividend Data

No cash dividends have been paid.

Waters Corp

STANDARD & POOR'S

Business Summary October 26, 2007

CORPORATE OVERVIEW. Waters manufactures, distributes, and services analytical instruments to the pharmaceutical, life sciences, biochemical, industrial, academic, and government end markets. Analytical instruments and components manufactured include high performance liquid chromatography (HPLC) instruments, columns and other consumables, mass spectrometry (MS) instruments that can be integrated with other analytical instruments, and thermal analysis (TA) and rheology instruments. HPLC is the standard technique to identify and analyze constituent components of various chemicals and materials. Its unique performance capabilities let it separate and identify 80% of known chemicals and materials. HPLC is used to analyze substances in a variety of industries for R&D, quality control, and process engineering applications. Pharmaceutical and life science industries use HPLC primarily to identify new drugs.

In March 2004, WAT introduced a novel technology that it describes as Ultra Performance Chromatography, the Acquity UPLC. WAT believes the Acquity UPLC provides more comprehensive chemical separation and faster analysis times compared to the HPLC. MS is an analytical technique used to identify unknown compounds, quantify known materials, and elucidate the structural and chemical properties of molecules by measuring the masses of individual molecules that have been converted into ions. These products serve diverse markets, including pharmaceutical and environmental industries. The TA In-

struments division makes and services thermal analysis and rheology instruments used for the physical characterization of polymers and related materials. Thermal analysis measures physical characteristics of materials as a function of temperature. Changes in temperature affect several characteristics of materials, such as their physical state, weight, dimension and mechanical and electrical properties, which may be measured using thermal analysis techniques. As a result, thermal analysis is widely used to develop, produce, and characterize materials in industries such as plastics, chemicals, and pharmaceuticals.

WAT has supplemented its internal growth with various strategic acquisitions. In March 2004, WAT acquired NuGenesis Technologies Corp. for about $43 million. NuGenesis and Creon Lab formed the company's new Lab Informatics market segment. In March 2006, WAT acquired VICAM, a provider of bioseparation and rapid detection instruments for food safety. In August 2006, WAT acquired Thermometric AB, and in November 2006, WAT acquired Environmental Resource Associates, a provider of environmental testing and services.

Company Financials Fiscal Year Ended Dec. 31

Per Share Data ($)	2006	2005	2004	2003	2002	2001	2000	1999	1998	1997
Tangible Book Value	NM	NM	3.05	2.67	NM	3.19	2.21	0.98	NM	NM
Cash Flow	2.57	2.12	2.16	1.60	1.40	1.08	1.36	1.14	0.78	0.09
Earnings	2.13	1.74	1.82	1.34	1.12	0.84	1.14	0.92	0.57	-0.08
S&P Core Earnings	2.18	1.57	1.45	1.18	0.99	1.07	NA	NA	NA	NA
Dividends	Nil	Nil	Nil	Nil	Nil	Nil	Nil	Nil	Nil	Nil
Payout Ratio	Nil	Nil	Nil	Nil	Nil	Nil	Nil	Nil	Nil	Nil
Prices:High	51.64	51.57	49.80	33.42	39.25	85.38	90.94	33.84	21.88	12.11
Prices:Low	37.06	33.99	33.10	19.79	17.86	22.33	21.97	18.13	9.13	5.78
P/E Ratio:High	24	30	27	25	35	NM	80	37	39	NM
P/E Ratio:Low	17	20	18	15	16	NM	19	20	16	NM

Income Statement Analysis (Million $)	2006	2005	2004	2003	2002	2001	2000	1999	1998	1997
Revenue	1,280	1,158	1,105	958	890	859	795	704	619	465
Operating Income	355	330	321	271	251	258	240	205	164	113
Depreciation	46.2	43.7	41.9	33.8	37.2	34.0	29.4	28.9	27.2	20.0
Interest Expense	51.7	24.7	10.1	2.37	2.48	1.26	Nil	8.95	18.3	13.7
Pretax Income	263	275	286	224	195	147	211	168	102	7.47
Effective Tax Rate	15.5%	26.4%	21.6%	23.6%	22.1%	22.3%	26.0%	27.0%	26.7%	211.0%
Net Income	222	202	224	171	152	115	156	122	74.4	-8.29
S&P Core Earnings	227	183	179	150	134	147	NA	NA	NA	NA

Balance Sheet & Other Financial Data (Million $)	2006	2005	2004	2003	2002	2001	2000	1999	1998	1997
Cash	514	494	539	357	313	227	75.5	3.80	5.50	3.11
Current Assets	1,000	913	974	715	636	523	344	247	252	213
Total Assets	1,617	1,429	1,460	1,131	1,011	887	692	584	578	552
Current Liabilities	686	604	493	379	320	281	221	198	186	171
Long Term Debt	500	500	250	125	Nil	Nil	Nil	81.1	218	305
Common Equity	362	284	679	590	665	582	452	292	150	62.3
Total Capital	862	784	929	715	665	582	452	373	377	376
Capital Expenditures	51.4	51.0	66.2	34.6	37.9	42.4	35.4	19.4	15.0	18.2
Cash Flow	268	246	266	205	189	148	186	151	101	10.8
Current Ratio	1.5	1.5	2.0	1.9	2.0	1.9	1.6	1.3	1.4	1.2
% Long Term Debt of Capitalization	58.0	63.8	26.9	17.5	Nil	Nil	Nil	21.7	57.8	81.1
% Net Income of Revenue	17.4	17.4	20.3	17.8	17.1	13.3	19.6	17.4	12.0	NM
% Return on Assets	14.6	14.0	17.3	15.9	16.0	14.5	24.4	21.1	13.2	NM
% Return on Equity	68.8	42.0	35.3	27.2	24.3	22.2	42.0	55.3	69.1	NM

Data as orig reptd.; bef. results of disc opers/spec. items. Per share data adj. for stk. divs.; EPS diluted. E-Estimated. NA-Not Available. NM-Not Meaningful. NR-Not Ranked. UR-Under Review.

Office: 34 Maple Street, Milford, MA 01757-3696.
Telephone: 508-478-2000.
Email: info@waters.com
Website: http://www.waters.com

Chrmn & CEO: D.A. Berthiaume
VP & CFO: J. Ornell
VP, Secy & General Counsel: M.T. Beaudouin

Board Members: J. Bekenstein, M. J. Berendt, D. A. Berthiaume, E. Conard, L. H. Glimcher, C. A. Kuebler, W. J. Miller, J. A. Reed, T. P. Salice

Founded: 1991
Domicile: Delaware
Employees: 4,687

The McGraw-Hill Companies

Watson Pharmaceuticals Inc.

STANDARD &POOR'S

S&P Recommendation HOLD ★★★☆☆	**Price** $27.87 (as of Nov 23, 2007)	**12-Mo. Target Price** $33.00	**Investment Style** Large-Cap Blend

GICS Sector Health Care
Sub-Industry Pharmaceuticals

Summary This company produces generic and branded drugs. In November 2006, Watson acquired rival generic drugmaker Andrx Corp. for $1.9 billion in cash.

Key Stock Statistics (Source S&P, Vickers, company reports)

52-Wk Range	$33.91– 24.89	S&P Oper. EPS 2007E	1.30	Market Capitalization(B)	$2.857
Trailing 12-Month EPS	$-3.87	S&P Oper. EPS 2008E	1.95	Yield (%)	Nil
Trailing 12-Month P/E	NM	P/E on S&P Oper. EPS 2007E	21.4	Dividend Rate/Share	Nil
$10K Invested 5 Yrs Ago	$9,123	Common Shares Outstg. (M)	102.5	Institutional Ownership (%)	96

Beta	1.26
S&P 3-Yr. Proj. EPS CAGR(%)	20.00
S&P Credit Rating	BBB-

Price Performance

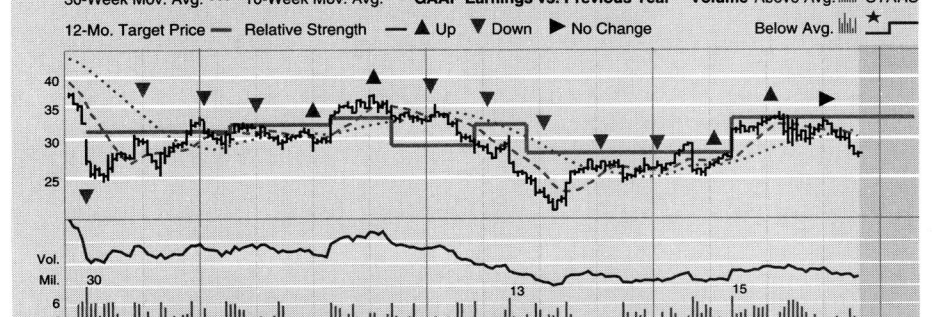

30-Week Mov. Avg. ···· 10-Week Mov. Avg. – – **GAAP Earnings vs. Previous Year** Volume Above Avg. STARS
12-Mo. Target Price — Relative Strength — ▲ Up ▼ Down ▶ No Change Below Avg.

Options: ASE, CBOE, Ph

Analysis prepared by **Herman B. Saftlas** on November 21, 2007, when the stock traded at **$ 27.58**.

Highlights

➤ We project 2008 revenue growth in the high single digits from an indicated $2.5 billion in 2007. The increase should be paced by gains in the principal generics division, boosted by new generic versions of Duragesic pain patch, Flonase allergy treatment and Concerta for AD-HD. We also see higher sales in the distribution division, boosted by a rise in new generic launches. However, branded product sales will probably fall short of the 2007 level, reflecting increased competitive pressures in nephrology and other specialty pharmaceutical lines.

➤ We expect gross margins to widen somewhat in 2008, helped by the projected higher volume, along with savings accruing from the closings of excess or inefficient manufacturing capacity. Cost controls are also expected to result in well controlled SG&A and R&D spending, while amortization of intangible assets is expected to drop sharply. Interest expense is also likely to be lower.

➤ We estimate operating EPS of $1.95 for 2008, up from the $1.30 that we forecast for 2007 (before $0.10 a share of nonrecurring charges).

Investment Rationale/Risk

➤ We believe the recent hiring of Paul Bisaro as CEO, succeeding retiring Allen Chao, is a positive development. Mr. Bisaro was formerly a highly regarded COO at rival generic drugmaker Barr Pharmaceuticals. Under Mr. Bisaro, we think WPI will be able to face the task of integrating the acquisition of Andrx Corp. and expanding the depth and geographic reach of WPI's drug businesses. WPI recently added generic versions of Duragesic, Wellbutrin XL and Toprol XL to its generic portfolio. WPI's generic pipeline consists of over 70 ANDAs. We also think WPI has a promising branded drug pipeline.

➤ Risks to our recommendation and target price include failure to resolve Andrx's FDA-cited manufacturing quality control issues, heavier than expected competitive pressures, and possible pipeline disappointments.

➤ Our 12-month target price of $33 is based on a peer level P/E multiple of 17X our 2008 EPS estimate. Our DCF model, which assumes decelerating cash flow growth over the next 10 years, a WACC of 7%, and perpetuity growth of 1%, also indicates intrinsic value of $33.

Qualitative Risk Assessment

LOW	**MEDIUM**	HIGH

Our risk assessment reflects risks common to the generic pharmaceutical business, which include the ability to successfully develop generic products, obtain regulatory approvals, and legally challenge branded patents. However, we believe these risks are offset by the company's wide and diverse generic portfolio and the balance afforded by WPI's branded drug business.

Quantitative Evaluations

S&P Quality Ranking B-

D	C	**B-**	B	B+	A-	A	A+

Relative Strength Rank MODERATE
44
LOWEST = 1 HIGHEST = 99

Revenue/Earnings Data

Revenue (Million $)

	1Q	2Q	3Q	4Q	Year
2007	671.6	603.0	594.7	--	--
2006	407.2	510.4	440.5	621.2	1,979
2005	400.8	416.3	410.3	418.8	1,646
2004	409.7	399.4	408.0	423.5	1,641
2003	336.9	355.9	358.8	406.2	1,458
2002	285.7	300.1	307.9	329.6	1,223

Earnings Per Share ($)

2007	0.29	0.33	0.31	E0.34	E1.30
2006	0.23	-0.15	0.31	-4.80	-4.37
2005	0.32	0.35	0.35	0.19	1.21
2004	0.39	0.29	0.13	0.46	1.27
2003	0.44	0.47	0.47	0.48	1.86
2002	0.30	0.56	0.38	0.40	1.64

Fiscal year ended Dec. 31. Next earnings report expected: Late February. EPS Estimates based on S&P Operating Earnings; historical GAAP earnings are as reported.

Dividend Data

No cash dividends have been paid.

Watson Pharmaceuticals Inc.

STANDARD &POOR'S

Business Summary November 21, 2007

CORPORATE PROFILE. Watson Pharmaceuticals is a leading maker of generic pharmaceuticals. WPI targets difficult to produce niche off-patent drugs. WPI significantly expanded its generic business with the acquisition of Andrx Corp. Watson also offers a line of specialty branded pharmaceuticals, largely in the areas of urology and nephrology.

Many WPI pharmaceuticals incorporate the company's novel proprietary drug delivery systems, such as transmucosal, vaginal and transdermal systems that allow for defined rates of drug release. Total revenues in 2006 were 77% from generic drugs, 18% from branded drugs, and 5% from distributed products.

WPI markets over 150 generic drug products, which comprise a broad cross section of therapeutic categories. Key segments include oral contraceptives, analgesics, antihypertensives, diuretics, antiulcers, antipsychotics, anti-inflammatories, analgesics, hormone replacements, antispasmodics and antidiarrheals.

During 2006, the company launched 13 generic products, and filed 27 Abbreviated New Drug Applications (ANDAs). WPI now has over 70 ANDAs on file at the FDA, including 17 tentative approvals. In April 2006, WPI launched a generic version of Pravachol, a cholesterol-lowering agent; and in September 2006, the company launched a generic version of Seasonale, an extended-regimen oral contraceptive. WPI also earned commission revenue in 2006 from the marketing of a generic version of Actiq, a potent painkiller.

Branded pharmaceuticals comprise specialty drugs and nephrology products. Specialty drugs includes urology; antihypertensive, psychiatry, pain management and dermatology products; and a genital warts treatment. Key products include Trelstar, a treatment for prostate cancer; Oxytrol, an oxybutynin transdermal patch to treat urinary incontinence; and Androderm, a testosterone transdermal patch.

The nephrology product line consists of products used to treat iron deficiency anemia. The primary product is Ferrlecit, which is indicated for patients undergoing hemodialysis in conjunction with erythropoietin therapy. Ferrlecit accounted for about 7% of revenues and 17% of gross profits in 2006. Branded products are marketed to urologists, primary care physicians, endocrinologists, obstetricians and gynecologists.

Company Financials Fiscal Year Ended Dec. 31

Per Share Data ($)	2006	2005	2004	2003	2002	2001	2000	1999	1998	1997
Tangible Book Value	0.09	8.81	7.97	5.54	4.33	3.79	0.98	5.00	3.08	3.14
Cash Flow	-2.23	2.87	2.07	2.78	2.45	2.01	2.34	2.28	1.66	1.17
Earnings	-4.37	1.21	1.27	1.86	1.64	1.07	1.65	1.83	1.32	1.01
S&P Core Earnings	-4.32	1.09	1.16	1.64	1.36	0.52	NA	NA	NA	NA
Dividends	Nil	Nil	Nil	Nil	Nil	Nil	Nil	Nil	Nil	Nil
Payout Ratio	Nil	Nil	Nil	Nil	Nil	Nil	Nil	Nil	Nil	Nil
Prices:High	35.27	36.93	49.19	50.12	33.25	66.39	71.50	62.94	63.00	34.13
Prices:Low	21.35	27.99	24.50	26.90	17.95	26.50	33.69	26.50	30.50	16.00
P/E Ratio:High	NM	31	39	27	20	62	43	34	48	34
P/E Ratio:Low	NM	23	19	14	11	25	20	14	23	16

Income Statement Analysis (Million $)										
Revenue	1,979	1,646	1,641	1,458	1,223	1,161	812	689	556	338
Operating Income	364	450	419	439	386	404	227	281	237	152
Depreciation	218	207	107	100	86.6	101	71.4	44.0	31.3	14.6
Interest Expense	22.1	14.5	13.3	25.8	22.1	27.8	24.3	11.1	7.06	NA
Pretax Income	-411	219	237	318	279	199	355	273	199	145
Effective Tax Rate	NM	37.0%	36.1%	36.2%	37.0%	41.5%	52.0%	34.4%	39.3%	37.6%
Net Income	-445	138	151	203	176	116	171	179	121	90.2
S&P Core Earnings	-441	123	137	178	146	56.3	NA	NA	NA	NA

Balance Sheet & Other Financial Data (Million $)										
Cash	161	630	680	574	273	329	238	116	72.7	82.8
Current Assets	1,262	1,360	1,370	1,323	921	890	831	435	293	247
Total Assets	3,761	3,080	3,244	3,283	2,663	2,528	2,580	1,439	1,070	755
Current Liabilities	690	246	256	339	375	245	280	129	94.8	99.8
Long Term Debt	1,124	588	588	723	332	416	438	150	150	2.39
Common Equity	1,680	2,104	2,243	2,057	1,798	1,672	1,548	1,055	750	565
Total Capital	3,008	2,692	2,831	2,924	2,282	2,274	2,242	1,292	955	604
Capital Expenditures	44.4	78.8	69.2	151	87.5	62.0	34.3	26.8	26.5	14.6
Cash Flow	-227	345	258	303	262	218	242	223	152	105
Current Ratio	1.8	5.5	5.4	3.9	2.5	3.6	3.0	3.4	3.1	2.5
% Long Term Debt of Capitalization	37.4	21.8	20.8	24.7	14.5	18.3	19.6	11.6	15.7	0.4
% Net Income of Revenue	NM	8.4	9.2	13.9	14.4	10.0	21.0	26.0	21.7	26.7
% Return on Assets	NM	4.4	4.6	6.8	6.8	4.6	8.4	13.9	13.2	15.4
% Return on Equity	NM	6.4	7.0	10.5	10.1	7.2	13.1	19.3	18.4	19.0

Data as orig reptd.; bef. results of disc opers/spec. items. Per share data adj. for stk. divs.; EPS diluted. E-Estimated. NA-Not Available. NM-Not Meaningful. NR-Not Ranked. UR-Under Review.

Office: 311 Bonnie Circle, Corona, CA 92880-2882.
Telephone: 951-493-5300.
Website: http://www.watson.com
Chrmn, Pres & CEO: A.Y. Chao

SVP, Secy & General Counsel: D.A. Buchen
SVP & CIO: T.R. Giordano
VP, CFO, Chief Acctg Officer & Cntlr: R.T. Joyce
Investor Contact: P. Eisenhaur (951-493-5300)

Board Members: A. Y. Chao, M. J. Fedida, M. J. Feldman, A. F. Hummel, C. M. Klema, J. Michelson, R. R. Taylor, A. L. Turner, F. G. Weiss
Founded: 1983
Domicile: Nevada
Employees: 5,300

Weatherford International Ltd.

STANDARD &POOR'S

S&P Recommendation HOLD ★★★☆☆	**Price** $62.29 (as of Nov 23, 2007)	**12-Mo. Target Price** $69.00	**Investment Style** Large-Cap Growth

GICS Sector Energy
Sub-Industry Oil & Gas Equipment & Services

Summary This company is one of the leading global providers of equipment and services used for the drilling, completion, and production of oil and natural gas wells.

Key Stock Statistics (Source S&P, Vickers, company reports)

52-Wk Range	$71.00–35.90	S&P Oper. EPS 2007E	3.44	Market Capitalization(B)	$20.991	Beta	0.83
Trailing 12-Month EPS	$2.91	S&P Oper. EPS 2008E	4.35	Yield (%)	Nil	S&P 3-Yr. Proj. EPS CAGR(%)	25.00
Trailing 12-Month P/E	21.4	P/E on S&P Oper. EPS 2007E	18.1	Dividend Rate/Share	Nil	S&P Credit Rating	BBB+
$10K Invested 5 Yrs Ago	$31,161	Common Shares Outstg. (M)	337.0	Institutional Ownership (%)	94		

Price Performance

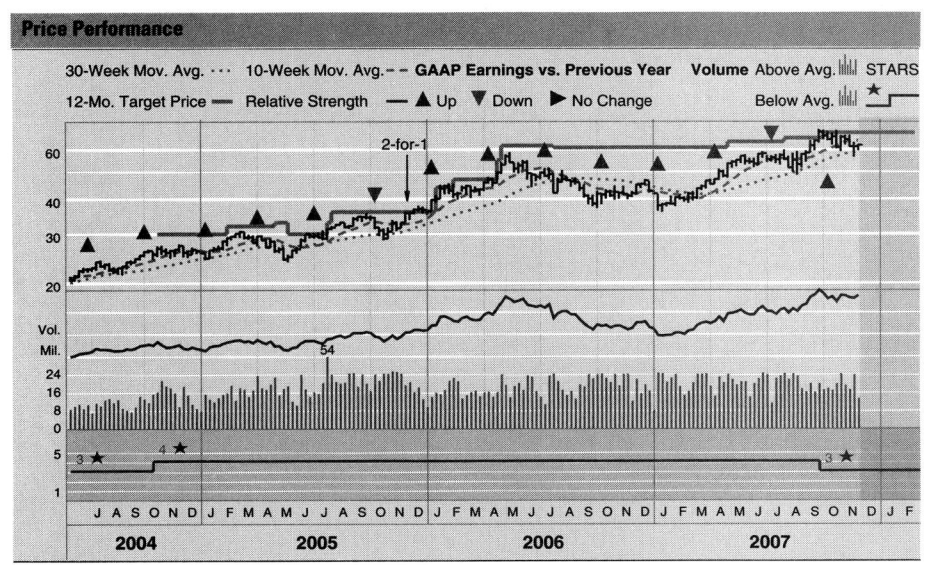

30-Week Mov. Avg. ··· 10-Week Mov. Avg. -- GAAP Earnings vs. Previous Year Volume Above Avg. STARS
12-Mo. Target Price — Relative Strength ▲ Up ▼ Down ▶ No Change Below Avg.

Options: CBOE

Analysis prepared by **Stewart Glickman, CFA** on September 25, 2007, when the stock traded at **$66.93**.

Highlights

► In July, the company said that it expected healthy single digit sales growth in the U.S. in the second half of 2007, and thought that the sharp downturn in Canada was unsustainable and likely to be a trough. Overall, we expect a fairly modest sales growth rate in North America; we think WFT's prospects will increasingly be driven by growth overseas, and, in particular, in the Eastern Hemisphere.

► The company has increased its presence in a number of frontier regions over the past few years, including the Caspian Sea, the Middle East, and North Africa. While we think such regions carry higher operational risks than those in mature areas, we believe that growth opportunities in such regions typically can benefit greatly from newer drilling and completion technologies. We expect well construction and wireline businesses to perform strongly in 2008.

► For 2007, we project total revenue growth of 17%, mainly via an expansion in international operations. We foresee operating margins in the low 20% area in 2007, compared to about 20% in 2006. Our 2007 and 2008 EPS estimates are $3.44 and $4.35, respectively.

Investment Rationale/Risk

► We think WFT's strategy of focusing its oilfield services growth opportunities in the Eastern Hemisphere is a sound one, given our view that frontier regions offer strong growth potential. We believe the Precision Drilling oilfield services segment, previously marketed mainly in North America, could be expanded to the Eastern Hemisphere as a result of WFT's greater breadth.

► Risks to our recommendation and target price include reduced drilling activity in key geographic markets; sharply lower oil and natural gas prices; and business risks associated with operating in frontier regions.

► Our DCF model, assuming a WACC of 10.2%, and terminal growth of 3%, indicates intrinsic value of $68. On a relative valuation basis, we think the shares merit a modest discount to peers in light of projected 2008 return on invested capital of 15%, below peers. Based on a 10X multiple applied to our 2008 EBITDA estimate, and about 16X our 2008 EPS estimate (slightly below peers), and our DCF model, we arrive at our 12-month target price of $69.

Qualitative Risk Assessment

LOW	MEDIUM	HIGH

Our risk assessment reflects this company's exposure to crude oil and natural gas prices, capital spending decisions made by oil and gas producers, and geographic risk associated with operating in frontier regions around the globe. This is offset by leading edge technology and its commitment to technological innovation in oilfield services.

Quantitative Evaluations

S&P Quality Ranking   B-

D	C	B-	B	B+	A-	A	A+

Relative Strength Rank   STRONG

77

LOWEST = 1   HIGHEST = 99

Revenue/Earnings Data

Revenue (Million $)

	1Q	2Q	3Q	4Q	Year
2007	1,852	1,816	1,972	--	--
2006	1,536	1,539	1,697	1,808	6,579
2005	857.7	937.3	1,077	1,461	4,333
2004	712.6	742.2	794.3	882.6	3,132
2003	589.3	617.7	660.5	723.9	2,591
2002	568.3	593.9	584.9	581.9	2,329

Earnings Per Share ($)

2007	0.81	0.51	0.85	E1.00	E3.44
2006	0.57	0.52	0.66	0.78	2.53
2005	0.28	0.32	0.15	0.69	1.47
2004	0.19	0.29	0.25	0.45	1.18
2003	0.14	0.11	0.12	0.18	0.55
2002	0.18	0.16	-0.51	0.13	-0.03

Fiscal year ended Dec. 31. Next earnings report expected: Late January. EPS Estimates based on S&P Operating Earnings; historical GAAP earnings are as reported.

Dividend Data

No cash dividends have been paid.

Weatherford International Ltd.

Business Summary September 25, 2007

CORPORATE OVERVIEW. Weatherford International is one of the world's leading providers of equipment and services for the drilling, completion and production of oil and natural gas wells. As of December 31, 2006, it had more than 800 manufacturing and service locations in over 100 countries. North America contributed 56% of 2006 revenues (U.S. 38% and Canada 18%), while International operations contributed 44%. Internationally, the Middle East and North Africa region added 14% of total revenues; Europe/CIS/West Africa region 13%; Latin America 11%; and Asia Pacific 6%.

CORPORATE STRATEGY. WFT has focused its long-term strategy on the geographic expansion of its products and services to the Eastern Hemisphere (Europe, Africa, the Middle East, Russia, and Asia), and on product and service expansion that assists in the drilling of new oilfields or efficiently producing oil and gas from existing oilfields. We view this strategy as consistent with ongoing secular trends in the energy industry, as oil and gas producers--including supermajors, large independents, and nationalized oil companies--seek low-cost, high-growth opportunities. Frequently, such opportunities tend to be located in such frontier regions, and/or are found in challenging ge-

ological conditions that demand improved technologies.

IMPACT OF MAJOR DEVELOPMENTS. Following the April 2000 spin-off of the Grant Prideco Drilling Products division and the February 2001 merger of the Compression Services division into a subsidiary of Universal Compression Holdings, Inc., WFT's business was divided into three principal operating divisions: Drilling and Intervention Services; Completion Systems; and Artificial Lift Systems. In April 2003, the company restructured its reporting divisions, and reported results in two segments: Drilling Services and Production Systems. In August 2005, WFT completed the acquisition of Precision Energy Services (PES) and Precision Drilling International (PDI). Following these acquisitions, the company reorganized into three operating segments: Evaluation, Drilling & Intervention Services (EDI); Completion & Production Services (CPS); and Other Operations.

Company Financials Fiscal Year Ended Dec. 31

Per Share Data ($)	2006	2005	2004	2003	2002	2001	2000	1999	1998	1997
Tangible Book Value	7.56	6.45	4.95	3.11	0.90	1.94	1.17	3.89	3.51	1.32
Cash Flow	3.89	2.48	1.99	1.43	0.87	1.59	0.73	0.89	1.20	1.24
Earnings	2.53	1.47	1.18	0.55	-0.03	0.88	-0.21	0.08	0.33	0.89
Dividends	Nil	Nil	Nil	Nil	Nil	Nil	Nil	Nil	Nil	Nil
Payout Ratio	Nil	Nil	Nil	Nil	Nil	Nil	Nil	Nil	Nil	Nil
Prices:High	58.73	37.94	27.62	23.85	27.13	30.18	31.00	21.06	29.22	36.50
Prices:Low	36.50	23.82	17.91	15.65	16.28	11.36	15.88	8.38	7.50	11.69
P/E Ratio:High	23	26	24	44	NM	34	NM	NM	89	41
P/E Ratio:Low	14	16	15	29	NM	13	NM	NM	23	13

Income Statement Analysis (Million $)										
Revenue	6,579	4,333	3,132	2,591	2,329	2,329	1,814	1,240	2,011	892
Operating Income	1,817	977	649	499	488	596	372	231	461	176
Depreciation, Depletion and Amortization	483	334	256	233	215	208	199	167	171	33.7
Interest Expense	110	80.3	63.6	76.7	85.5	74.0	59.3	44.9	54.5	23.1
Pretax Income	1,224	626	431	195	-9.84	339	71.3	28.4	99.4	129
Effective Tax Rate	25.9%	25.4%	21.5%	26.0%	NM	36.3%	NM	29.9%	34.8%	34.9%
Net Income	896	466	337	143	-6.03	215	-38.9	16.2	64.8	83.7

Balance Sheet & Other Financial Data (Million $)										
Cash	126	134	317	56.1	48.8	88.8	154	44.4	40.2	31.9
Current Assets	3,360	2,639	1,943	1,436	1,259	1,231	1,242	869	1,082	631
Total Assets	10,139	8,580	5,543	5,000	4,495	4,296	3,462	3,514	2,832	1,366
Current Liabilities	2,043	1,998	660	782	877	760	463	666	557	314
Long Term Debt	1,565	632	1,404	1,380	1,514	1,500	1,133	629	632	446
Common Equity	6,175	5,667	3,313	2,708	1,974	1,838	1,338	1,833	1,494	527
Total Capital	7,876	6,387	4,748	4,107	3,523	3,437	2,834	2,661	2,126	1,052
Capital Expenditures	1,071	527	311	303	269	339	267	174	206	62.6
Cash Flow	1,379	801	593	376	209	423	160	183	236	117
Current Ratio	1.6	1.3	2.9	1.8	1.4	1.6	2.7	1.3	1.9	2.0
% Long Term Debt of Capitalization	19.9	9.9	29.6	33.6	43.0	43.6	40.0	23.6	29.7	42.4
% Return on Assets	9.6	6.6	6.4	3.0	NM	5.5	NM	0.5	3.1	7.5
% Return on Equity	15.1	10.4	11.2	6.1	NM	13.5	NM	1.0	6.4	17.1

Data as orig reptd.; bef. results of disc opers/spec. items. Per share data adj. for stk. divs.; EPS diluted. E-Estimated. NA-Not Available. NM-Not Meaningful. NR-Not Ranked. UR-Under Review.

Office: 515 Post Oak Boulevard, Houston, TX 77027-3415.
Telephone: 713-693-4000.
Email: investor.relations@weatherford.com
Website: http://www.weatherford.com

Chrmn, Pres & CEO: B.J. Duroc-Danner
COO: E.L. Colley, III
Investor Contact: A.P. Becnel (713-693-4136)
SVP & CFO: A.P. Becnel

SVP & CTO: S.E. Ferguson
Board Members: N. F. Brady, D. J. Butters, B. J. Duroc-Danner, S. B. Lubar, W. E. Macaulay, R. B. Millard, R. K. Moses, Jr., R. A. Rayne

Founded: 1972
Domicile: Bermuda
Employees: 33,000

STANDARD &POOR'S

WellPoint Inc

| **S&P Recommendation** BUY ★★★★☆ | **Price** $81.76 (as of Nov 23, 2007) | **12-Mo. Target Price** $91.00 | **Investment Style** Large-Cap Growth |

GICS Sector Health Care
Sub-Industry Managed Health Care

Summary This Indiana-based Blue Cross and Blue Shield licensee is the largest managed health organization in the U.S., serving more than 34 million members in 14 states.

Key Stock Statistics (Source S&P, Vickers, company reports)

52-Wk Range	$86.25– 71.46	S&P Oper. EPS 2007**E**	5.55	Market Capitalization(B)	$46.712
Trailing 12-Month EPS	$5.34	S&P Oper. EPS 2008**E**	6.40	Yield (%)	Nil
Trailing 12-Month P/E	15.3	P/E on S&P Oper. EPS 2007**E**	14.7	Dividend Rate/Share	Nil
$10K Invested 5 Yrs Ago	$27,510	Common Shares Outstg. (M)	571.3	Institutional Ownership (%)	87

Beta	0.17
S&P 3-Yr. Proj. EPS CAGR(%)	15.00
S&P Credit Rating	A-

Price Performance

30-Week Mov. Avg. ··· 10-Week Mov. Avg.- - **GAAP Earnings vs. Previous Year** Volume Above Avg. STARS
12-Mo. Target Price — Relative Strength — ▲ Up ▼ Down ▶ No Change Below Avg. ★

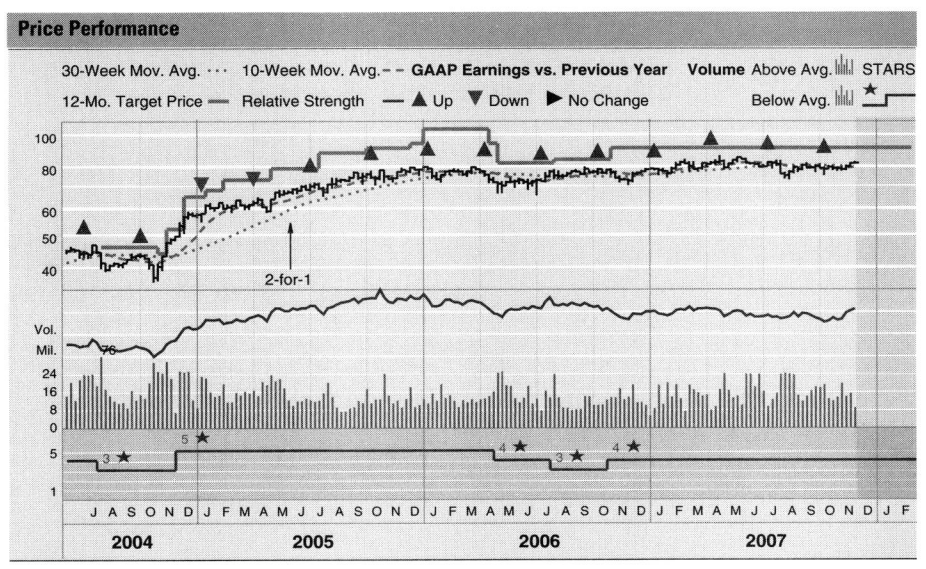

Options: ASE, CBOE, Ph

Analysis prepared by **Phillip M. Seligman** on October 30, 2007, when the stock traded at **$ 79.08**.

Highlights

➤ We look for 2008 operating revenues to rise by 7.5%, to $64.5 billion, from the $60 billion we see in 2007. Drivers include premium rate hikes in excess of medical and SG&A cost trends and WLP's view of 3% higher enrollment (one million net new members), led by healthy gains in national accounts, Medicaid and Medicare, and a small turnaround in individual and local group enrollment.

➤ We expect the firm-wide medical loss ratio (MLR) to be flat to down modestly, with premium price hikes above medical cost trends, which WLP pegs at slightly under 8%. In addition, WLP received Medicaid rate increases in eight of its 11 California counties and is currently finalizing the terms with the state. It plans to negotiate rate increases in two additional California counties that will be effective January 1, 2008. Elsewhere, we forecast that the SG&A cost ratio will decline by 10 basis points (bps), partly on the absence of late-2007 investments for 2008 growth opportunities.

➤ We look for operating EPS of $5.55 in 2007 and $6.40 in 2008, versus 2006's $4.79. We see share repurchases and higher investment income also aiding EPS growth.

Investment Rationale/Risk

➤ While WLP lowered its 2007 enrollment growth guidance twice, we are encouraged by its view of stronger overall membership growth in 2008. Thanks to recent large account wins, the company expects to add more new National Accounts members in 2008 than in 2007. Moreover, it sees such gains despite employee reductions it expects in the automobile, home building and mortgage industries. We see new products helping to revitalize UniCare, its non-Blues health plan business, while its pharmacy benefit management business benefits from the recent garnering of a major new customer. WLP's expanding market diversification and Blue Cross/Blue Shield tie are competitive advantages, in our view. We like its active medical cost control, and believe WLP has significant financial flexibility, given its strong cash flow.

➤ Risks to our recommendation and target price include enrollment losses, medical cost spikes, and unfavorable regulatory changes.

➤ Our 12-month target price of $91 reflects a peer-level P/E-to-earnings growth (PEG) ratio of 1.1X, assuming three-year growth of about 15%, and our 2007 EPS estimate.

Qualitative Risk Assessment

LOW	MEDIUM	HIGH

Our risk assessment reflects WLP's leadership in the highly fragmented managed care market, our view of its strong cash flow, and its history of improving financial performance. We believe that its geographic, market and product diversity will enable these trends to be sustainable in most economic conditions. However, we think that enrollment growth going forward will be limited by heightened competition that we see following consolidation in the managed care industry.

Quantitative Evaluations

S&P Quality Ranking   NR

D	C	B-	B	B+	A-	A	A+

Relative Strength Rank   STRONG

86

LOWEST = 1   HIGHEST = 99

Revenue/Earnings Data

Revenue (Million $)

	1Q	2Q	3Q	4Q	Year
2007	15,079	15,260	15,234	--	--
2006	13,820	14,152	14,426	14,556	56,953
2005	11,100	11,299	11,305	11,432	45,136
2004	4,574	4,608	4,807	6,826	20,815
2003	4,100	4,114	4,262	4,295	16,771
2002	2,812	2,900	3,579	3,900	13,282

Earnings Per Share ($)

2007	1.26	1.35	1.45	E1.50	E5.55
2006	1.09	1.17	1.29	1.28	4.82
2005	0.98	0.90	1.02	1.04	3.94
2004	1.04	0.83	0.85	0.46	3.05
2003	0.68	0.63	0.69	0.74	2.73
2002	0.48	0.51	0.65	0.60	2.26

Fiscal year ended Dec. 31. Next earnings report expected: Late January. EPS Estimates based on S&P Operating Earnings; historical GAAP earnings are as reported.

Dividend Data

No cash dividends have been paid.

Please read the Required Disclosures and Analyst Certification on the last page of this report.

The **McGraw-Hill** Companies

WellPoint Inc

STANDARD &POOR'S

Business Summary October 30, 2007

CORPORATE OVERVIEW. WellPoint, Inc. was formed by the merger consummated on November 30, 2004, between publicly traded managed care giants Anthem, Inc. and WellPoint Health Networks Inc. (WHN). Consequently, all historical data in this report are for Anthem. WLP is the largest publicly traded commercial health benefits company in the U.S., serving 34.8 million members as of September 30, 2007 (versus 34.1 million at December 31, 2006), and an independent licensee of the Blue Cross and Blue Shield Association. It serves members as the Blue Cross licensee for California and the Blue Cross or Blue Cross and Blue Shield (BCBS) licensee in all or parts of 13 other states. WLP also serves members in various parts of the U.S. as UniCare and conducts insurance operations in all 50 states and Puerto Rico through an affiliate.

WLP's network-based managed care plans include preferred provider organizations (PPOs), health maintenance organizations (HMOs), point-of-service plans (POS), traditional indemnity plans and other hybrid plans, including consumer-driven health plans (CDHPs), hospital only, and limited benefit products. It also provides managed care services to self-funded customers. In addition, WLP provides specialty and other products and services, including

pharmacy benefit management, group life and disability insurance, dental, vision, behavioral health, workers compensation and long-term care insurance. Approximately 92% of 2006 operating revenue was derived from premium income and 8% from administrative services and other revenues.

The customer base includes local group (16,649,000 members as of September 30, 2007, versus 16,766,000 as of December 31, 2006); individuals under age 65 (2,432,000 versus 2,488,000); National Accounts (multi-state employers primarily headquartered in WLP's service area with 1,000 or more eligible employees, with 5% or more located outside headquarters state, 6,388,000 versus 6,136,000); BlueCard (enrollees of non-owned BCBS plans who receive benefits in WLP's BCBS markets, 4,562,000 versus 4,279,000); Senior (1,250,000 versus 1,193,000); State Sponsored (2,141,000 versus 1,882,000); and Federal Employee Program (1,383,000 versus 1,357,000).

Company Financials Fiscal Year Ended Dec. 31

Per Share Data ($)	2006	2005	2004	2003	2002	2001	2000	1999	1998	1997
Tangible Book Value	2.92	2.78	2.03	8.44	5.76	7.71	7.66	NA	NA	NA
Cash Flow	4.82	3.94	2.05	3.59	2.90	2.23	1.55	NA	NA	NA
Earnings	4.82	3.94	3.05	2.73	2.26	1.65	1.05	NA	NA	NA
S&P Core Earnings	4.79	3.82	2.69	2.49	1.93	1.16	NA	NA	NA	NA
Dividends	Nil	Nil	Nil	Nil	Nil	Nil	NA	NA	NA	NA
Payout Ratio	Nil	Nil	Nil	Nil	Nil	Nil	NA	NA	NA	NA
Prices:High	80.37	80.40	58.88	41.45	37.75	25.95	NA	NA	NA	NA
Prices:Low	65.50	54.58	36.10	26.50	23.20	18.00	NA	NA	NA	NA
P/E Ratio:High	17	20	19	15	17	16	NA	NA	NA	NA
P/E Ratio:Low	14	14	12	10	10	11	NA	NA	NA	NA

Income Statement Analysis (Million $)

	2006	2005	2004	2003	2002	2001	2000	1999	1998	1997
Revenue	56,953	45,136	20,815	16,771	13,282	10,445	8,771	NA	NA	NA
Operating Income	5,748	4,750	2,072	1,595	1,093	733	487	NA	NA	NA
Depreciation	430	634	279	245	157	121	102	NA	NA	NA
Interest Expense	404	226	142	131	98.5	60.2	69.6	NA	NA	NA
Pretax Income	4,914	3,890	1,443	1,219	808	525	315	NA	NA	NA
Effective Tax Rate	37.0%	36.7%	33.5%	36.1%	31.6%	35.0%	30.8%	NA	NA	NA
Net Income	3,095	2,464	960	774	549	342	216	NA	NA	NA
S&P Core Earnings	3,077	2,402	842	708	467	240	NA	NA	NA	NA

Balance Sheet & Other Financial Data (Million $)

	2006	2005	2004	2003	2002	2001	2000	1999	1998	1997
Cash	2,602	2,897	1,457	523	744	406	421	NA	NA	NA
Current Assets	11,807	25,945	19,358	8,865	7,877	5,300	5,025	NA	NA	NA
Total Assets	51,760	51,405	39,738	13,439	12,293	6,277	6,021	NA	NA	NA
Current Liabilities	15,323	14,857	11,571	4,772	4,449	2,963	2,784	NA	NA	NA
Long Term Debt	6,493	6,325	4,277	1,663	1,659	818	789	NA	NA	NA
Common Equity	25,299	25,755	20,331	6,000	5,362	2,060	2,055	NA	NA	NA
Total Capital	35,142	35,386	27,204	8,188	7,412	2,878	2,844	NA	NA	NA
Capital Expenditures	194	162	137	111	123	70.4	NA	NA	NA	NA
Cash Flow	3,095	2,464	1,239	1,019	706	463	318	NA	NA	NA
Current Ratio	0.8	1.7	1.7	1.9	1.8	1.8	1.8	NA	NA	NA
% Long Term Debt of Capitalization	18.5	17.9	15.7	20.3	22.4	28.4	27.7	NA	NA	NA
% Net Income of Revenue	62.1	5.5	4.7	4.6	50.8	35.6	2.5	NA	NA	NA
% Return on Assets	6.0	5.4	3.6	6.0	5.9	5.7	NA	NA	NA	NA
% Return on Equity	12.1	10.7	7.2	13.6	14.8	17.2	NA	NA	NA	NA

Data as orig reptd.; bef. results of disc opers/spec. items. Per share data adj. for stk. divs.; EPS diluted. E-Estimated. NA-Not Available. NM-Not Meaningful. NR-Not Ranked. UR-Under Review.

Office: 120 Monument Circle, Indianapolis, IN 46204-4903.
Telephone: 317-488-6000.
Email: anthem.corporate.communications@anthem.com
Website: http://www.wellpoint.com

Chrmn: L.C. Glasscock
Pres & CEO: A.F. Braly
COO: M. Boxer
Investor Contact: W.S. DeVeydt (317-488-6390)

EVP & CFO: W.S. DeVeydt
Board Members: L. D. Baker, Jr., S. B. Bayh, A. F. Braly, S. P. Burke, W. H. Bush, L. C. Glasscock, J. A. Hill, W. Y. Jobe, V. S. Liss, W. G. Mays, R. G. Peru, J. G. Pisano, D. W. Riegle, Jr., W. J. Ryan, G. A. Schaefer, Jr., J. M. Ward, J. E. Zuccotti

Founded: 1944
Domicile: Indiana
Employees: 42,000

Wells Fargo & Co

STANDARD &POOR'S

S&P Recommendation HOLD ★★★☆☆	**Price** $30.54 (as of Nov 29, 2007)	**12-Mo. Target Price** $38.00	**Investment Style** Large-Cap Blend

GICS Sector Financials
Sub-Industry Diversified Banks

Summary This bank holding company provides banking, insurance, investment, mortgage and consumer finance services throughout North America.

Key Stock Statistics (Source S&P, Vickers, company reports)

52-Wk Range	$37.99–29.29	S&P Oper. EPS 2007E	2.43	Market Capitalization(B)	$102.682	Beta	0.31
Trailing 12-Month EPS	$2.65	S&P Oper. EPS 2008E	2.90	Yield (%)	4.06	S&P 3-Yr. Proj. EPS CAGR(%)	10.00
Trailing 12-Month P/E	11.5	P/E on S&P Oper. EPS 2007E	12.6	Dividend Rate/Share	$1.24	S&P Credit Rating	AA+
$10K Invested 5 Yrs Ago	$15,250	Common Shares Outstg. (M)	3,362.2	Institutional Ownership (%)	70		

Price Performance

30-Week Mov. Avg. · · ·   10-Week Mov. Avg. – –   **GAAP Earnings vs. Previous Year**   Volume Above Avg. ▮▮▮ STARS

12-Mo. Target Price —   Relative Strength —   ▲ Up   ▼ Down   ▶ No Change   Below Avg. ▮▮▮ ★

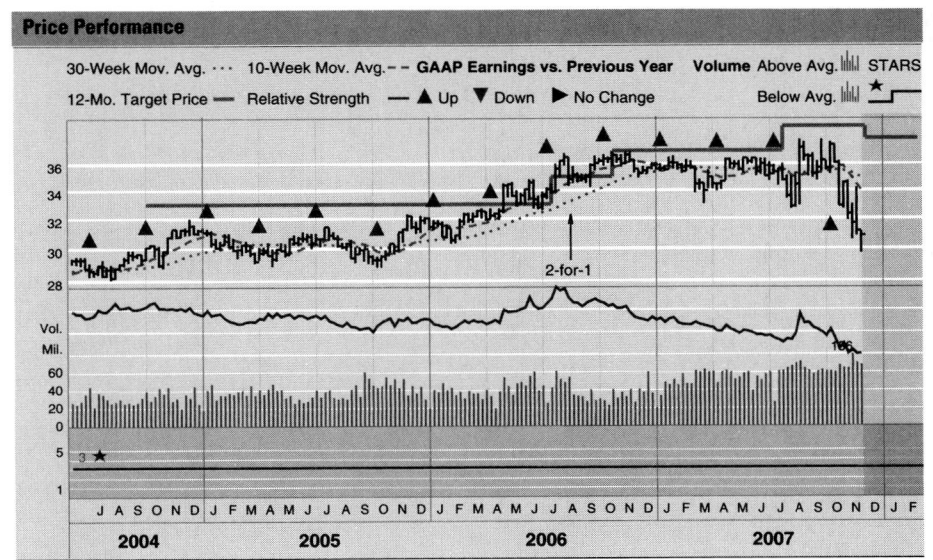

Options: ASE, CBOE, P, Ph

Highlights

➤ The 12-month target price for WFC has recently been changed to $38.00 from $39.00. The Highlights section of this Stock Report will be updated accordingly.

Investment Rationale/Risk

➤ The Investment Rationale/Risk section of this Stock Report will be updated shortly. For the latest News story on WFC from MarketScope, see below.

➤ 11/28/07 11:51 am EST... S&P REITERATES HOLD RECOMMENDATION ON SHARES OF WELLS FARGO (WFC 31.17***): WFC will take a $1.4B pretax charge in Q4, largely relating to higher losses it expects in its home equity loan portfolio. It is no longer acquiring these loans via correspondent relationships and certain other indirect channels, and has tightened its lending standards. However, WFC still has $71.5B in its home equity loan portfolio and a large exposure to the California housing market. We are lowering our '07 and '08 EPS estimates to $2.43 and $2.90 from $2.72 and $2.98, respectively, and reducing our 12-month target price by $1 to $38, 13X our '08 estimate. /F. Braden-CFA

Qualitative Risk Assessment

LOW	MEDIUM	HIGH

Our risk assessment reflects what we see as solid business fundamentals and a strong customer base. We view WFC as well diversified and able to withstand a major global or U.S. economic downturn.

Quantitative Evaluations

S&P Quality Ranking A

D	C	B-	B	B+	A-	A	A+

Relative Strength Rank MODERATE

33

LOWEST = 1   HIGHEST = 99

Revenue/Earnings Data

Revenue (Million $)

	1Q	2Q	3Q	4Q	Year
2007	12,570	13,268	13,796	--	--
2006	11,217	11,882	12,286	12,594	47,979
2005	9,509	9,529	10,427	10,897	40,407
2004	7,955	8,269	8,305	9,347	33,876
2003	7,561	7,637	8,170	8,257	31,800
2002	6,982	7,005	7,044	7,443	28,473

Earnings Per Share ($)

2007	0.66	0.67	0.68	E0.42	E2.43
2006	0.60	0.61	0.64	0.64	2.49
2005	0.54	0.56	0.58	0.57	2.25
2004	0.52	0.50	0.51	0.52	2.05
2003	0.44	0.45	0.46	0.48	1.83
2002	0.40	0.41	0.42	0.43	1.66

Fiscal year ended Dec. 31. Next earnings report expected: Mid January. EPS Estimates based on S&P Operating Earnings; historical GAAP earnings are as reported.

Dividend Data (Dates: mm/dd Payment Date: mm/dd/yy)

Amount ($)	Date Decl.	Ex-Div. Date	Stk. of Record	Payment Date
0.280	01/23	01/31	02/02	03/01/07
0.280	04/24	05/02	05/04	06/01/07
0.310	07/24	08/08	08/10	09/01/07
0.310	10/23	11/07	11/09	12/01/07

Dividends have been paid since 1939. Source: Company reports.

Wells Fargo & Co

STANDARD &POOR'S

Business Summary October 18, 2007

CORPORATE OVERVIEW. WFC has three lines of business for management reporting: community banking, wholesale banking, and Wells Fargo Financial. The community banking group offers a complete line of banking and diversified financial products and services to consumers and small businesses with annual sales generally up to $20 million, in which the owner generally is the financial decision maker. Community banking also offers investment management and other services to retail customers and high net worth individuals, insurance, securities brokerage through affiliates and venture capital financing.

Community banking serves customers through a wide range of channels, which include traditional banking stores, in-store banking centers, business centers and ATMs. In addition, Phone Bank centers and the National Business Banking Center provide 24-hour telephone service. Online banking services include a single sign-on to online banking, bill pay and brokerage, as well as online banking for small business.

The wholesale banking group serves businesses across the U.S. with annual sales generally in excess of $10 million. Wholesale banking provides a complete line of commercial, corporate and real estate banking products and services. These include traditional commercial loans and lines of credit, letters of credit, asset-based lending, equipment leasing, mezzanine financing, high-yield debt, international trade facilities, foreign exchange services, treasury management, investment management, institutional fixed income and equity sales, interest rate, commodity and equity risk management, online/electronic products, insurance brokerage services and investment banking services.

Wholesale banking manages and administers institutional investments, employee benefit trusts and mutual funds, including the Wells Fargo Advantage Funds. Wholesale banking includes the majority ownership interest in the Wells Fargo HSBC Trade Bank, which provides trade financing, letters of credit, and collection services, and is sometimes supported by the Export-Import Bank of the United States.

Company Financials Fiscal Year Ended Dec. 31

Per Share Data ($)	2006	2005	2004	2003	2002	2001	2000	1999	1998	1997
Tangible Book Value	10.13	8.76	7.95	7.04	6.11	4.90	4.59	3.96	3.39	4.51
Earnings	2.49	2.25	2.05	1.83	1.66	0.99	1.17	1.12	0.58	0.88
S&P Core Earnings	2.47	2.18	1.96	1.78	1.57	0.84	NA	NA	NA	NA
Dividends	1.08	1.00	0.93	0.75	0.55	0.50	0.45	0.39	0.35	0.31
Payout Ratio	43%	44%	45%	41%	33%	51%	39%	35%	60%	35%
Prices:High	36.99	32.35	32.02	29.59	26.72	27.41	28.19	24.97	21.94	19.75
Prices:Low	30.31	28.81	27.16	21.64	21.65	19.13	15.69	16.09	13.75	10.69
P/E Ratio:High	15	14	16	16	16	28	24	22	37	23
P/E Ratio:Low	12	13	13	12	13	19	13	14	24	12

Income Statement Analysis (Million $)										
Net Interest Income	19,951	18,504	17,150	16,007	14,855	12,460	10,865	9,355	8,990	4,033
Tax Equivalent Adjustment	116	110	104	NA	NA	NA	65.0	64.0	59.0	44.5
Non Interest Income	12,964	14,054	12,530	12,323	9,348	7,227	9,565	6,653	6,427	2,924
Loan Loss Provision	2,204	2,383	1,717	1,722	1,733	1,780	1,329	1,045	1,545	525
% Expense/Operating Revenue	69.0%	58.2%	64.8%	60.7%	52.2%	65.5%	57.7%	60.9%	68.4%	63.5%
Pretax Income	12,745	11,548	10,769	9,477	8,854	5,479	6,549	5,948	3,293	2,050
Effective Tax Rate	33.4%	33.6%	34.9%	34.6%	35.5%	37.5%	38.5%	37.0%	40.8%	34.1%
Net Income	8,482	7,671	7,014	6,202	5,710	3,423	4,026	3,747	1,950	1,351
% Net Interest Margin	4.83	4.86	4.89	5.08	5.57	5.36	5.35	5.66	5.79	5.74
S&P Core Earnings	8,401	7,423	6,722	6,055	5,374	2,894	NA	NA	NA	NA

Balance Sheet & Other Financial Data (Million $)										
Money Market Assets	11,685	16,211	14,020	2,745	3,174	2,530	1,598	1,554	1,517	1,501
Investment Securities	42,629	41,834	33,717	32,953	27,947	40,308	38,655	38,518	31,997	18,731
Commercial Loans	122,065	108,903	98,515	48,729	47,292	47,547	60,541	46,538	41,830	12,878
Other Loans	273,069	201,934	189,071	204,344	149,342	124,952	10,583	72,926	66,164	31,757
Total Assets	481,996	481,741	427,849	387,798	349,259	307,569	272,426	218,102	202,475	88,540
Demand Deposits	89,119	87,712	81,082	74,387	74,094	65,362	55,096	42,916	43,732	16,253
Time Deposits	221,124	226,738	193,776	173,140	142,822	121,904	114,463	89,792	90,056	39,204
Long Term Debt	72,404	79,668	73,580	63,642	50,205	38,530	32,981	24,160	19,709	12,767
Common Equity	45,492	40,335	37,596	34,255	30,107	26,996	26,103	21,860	20,296	6,755
% Return on Assets	1.8	1.7	1.7	1.7	1.7	1.2	1.6	1.8	1.0	1.6
% Return on Equity	19.8	19.7	19.5	19.3	20.0	12.8	16.2	17.6	14.2	21.2
% Loan Loss Reserve	1.1	1.1	1.2	1.3	1.5	1.8	2.1	2.5	2.9	2.9
% Loans/Deposits	113.8	111.9	118.6	117.0	117.3	110.9	104.7	93.8	79.0	76.7
% Equity to Assets	8.9	8.6	8.8	8.7	8.7	9.2	9.7	10.0	10.2	7.4

Data as orig reptd.; bef. results of disc opers/spec. items. Per share data adj. for stk. divs.; EPS diluted. E-Estimated. NA-Not Available. NM-Not Meaningful. NR-Not Ranked. UR-Under Review.

Office: 420 Montgomery St, San Francisco, CA 94163.
Telephone: 1-866-878-5865.
Website: http://www.wellsfargo.com
Chrmn & CEO: R.M. Kovacevich

Pres & COO: J.G. Stumpf
Sr EVP: M.C. Oman
Sr EVP: D.A. Hoyt
Sr EVP & CFO: H.I. Atkins

Board Members: J. S. Chen, L. H. Dean, S. E. Engel, E. Hernandez, Jr., R. L. Joss, R. M. Kovacevich, R. D. McCormick, C. H. Milligan, N. G. Moore, P. J. Quigley, D. B. Rice, J. M. Runstad, S. W. Sanger, J. G. Stumpf, S. G. Swenson, M. W. Wright

Founded: 1929
Domicile: Delaware
Employees: 158,000

The McGraw-Hill Companies

Wendy's International Inc.

S&P Recommendation **SELL** ★ ★ ☆ ☆ ☆	Price $28.10 (as of Nov 23, 2007)	12-Mo. Target Price $27.00	Investment Style Large-Cap Blend

GICS Sector Consumer Discretionary
Sub-Industry Restaurants

Summary This company operates or franchises over 6,300 Wendy's Old Fashioned Hamburgers restaurants in North America and about 325 international Wendy's restaurants.

Key Stock Statistics (Source S&P, Vickers, company reports)

52-Wk Range	$42.22– 27.24	S&P Oper. EPS 2007**E**	1.05	Market Capitalization(B)	$2.454	Beta	0.60
Trailing 12-Month EPS	$0.85	S&P Oper. EPS 2008**E**	1.20	Yield (%)	1.78	S&P 3-Yr. Proj. EPS CAGR(%)	10.00
Trailing 12-Month P/E	33.1	P/E on S&P Oper. EPS 2007**E**	26.8	Dividend Rate/Share	$0.50	S&P Credit Rating	BB-
$10K Invested 5 Yrs Ago	NA	Common Shares Outstg. (M)	87.3	Institutional Ownership (%)	93		

Price Performance

30-Week Mov. Avg. · · · 10-Week Mov. Avg. − − **GAAP Earnings vs. Previous Year** Volume Above Avg. ▮▮▮ STARS
12-Mo. Target Price — Relative Strength — ▲ Up ▼ Down ▶ No Change Below Avg. ▮▮▮ ★

Options: CBOE, P

Analysis prepared by **Mark S. Basham** on November 05, 2007, when the stock traded at **$ 32.23**.

Highlights

➤ In March 2007, a special committee of independent directors was formed to investigate further strategic options for the company, and on June 18, the committee decided to explore a possible sale of the company. We believe these actions were in response to pressure from major stockholders to boost shareholder value.

➤ Our view is that there is some justification for this pressure, as WEN has fallen short of its financial goals in 2007. As of June 18, it expected to report 2007 EBITDA of $295 million - $315 million and EPS of $1.09 - $1.23. At that time, WEN also said that in light of the ongoing activity of the special committee, it would no longer update its 2007 guidance, and it suspended all financial guidance for 2008 and beyond.

➤ Third-quarter same-store sales at company-owned units rose 0.2%, which we view as disappointing. We estimate 2007 EPS of $1.05, below the last company guidance given. For 2008, we forecast that EPS will increase 14%, to $1.20, reflecting margin gains from the closure of underperforming units and about 80 new store openings, as well as the absence of $0.11 of expenses incurred in 2007 related to the special board committee's activities.

Investment Rationale/Risk

➤ The shares were recently trading at a moderate premium to peers, which we attribute to speculation regarding the outcome of the special directors committee decision to explore a sale of the company. We have lowered our recommendation to sell, from hold, as we think recent weak results will lead to a bid below the current price.

➤ Risks to our opinion and target price include better than expected sales should the economy resume its momentum. It is possible that having multiple parties bid for the company could drive the price higher.

➤ Our 12-month target price of $27 reflects an enterprise value of 10X estimated 2007 EBITDA, which is down from our prior view that the company could fetch a price of as much as 11.5X EBITDA. This is in response to tighter credit conditions in general, and for leveraged M&A in particular.

Qualitative Risk Assessment

LOW	MEDIUM	HIGH

Wendy's competes in the relatively mature U.S. fast food industry, in which it has trailed competitors in introducing new menu and service innovations over the past several years. In faster growing international markets, it has only a limited presence.

Quantitative Evaluations

S&P Quality Ranking B+

D	C	B-	B	B+	A-	A	A+

Relative Strength Rank WEAK

23

LOWEST = 1   HIGHEST = 99

Revenue/Earnings Data

Revenue (Million $)

	1Q	2Q	3Q	4Q	Year
2007	590.2	632.9	631.2	--	--
2006	578.7	634.1	630.1	596.4	2,439
2005	894.2	951.0	960.6	977.3	3,783
2004	834.8	908.9	914.0	972.8	3,635
2003	694.0	786.0	806.5	862.4	3,149
2002	612.4	684.1	722.1	711.7	2,730

Earnings Per Share ($)

2007	0.15	0.33	0.33	E0.24	E1.05
2006	-0.05	0.08	0.20	0.09	0.32
2005	0.45	0.61	0.61	0.25	1.92
2004	0.45	0.62	0.60	-1.20	0.45
2003	0.38	0.53	0.58	0.56	2.05
2002	0.39	0.54	0.52	0.44	1.89

Fiscal year ended Dec. 31. Next earnings report expected: Early February. EPS Estimates based on S&P Operating Earnings; historical GAAP earnings are as reported.

Dividend Data (Dates: mm/dd Payment Date: mm/dd/yy)

Amount ($)	Date Decl.	Ex-Div. Date	Stk. of Record	Payment Date
0.085	02/02	02/08	02/12	02/27/07
0.125	04/25	05/03	05/07	05/21/07
0.125	07/30	08/02	08/06	08/20/07
0.125	10/25	11/01	11/05	11/19/07

Dividends have been paid since 1976. Source: Company reports.

The McGraw-Hill Companies

Wendy's International Inc.

**STANDARD
&POOR'S**

Business Summary November 05, 2007

COMPANY OVERVIEW. Wendy's International operates Wendy's Old Fashioned Hamburgers, the world's third largest quick service restaurant (QSR) chain. At September 30, 2007, the chain totaled 6,633 restaurants, concentrated in the U.S. and Canada. Of these restaurants, 1,431 were operated by the company and 5,202 by franchisees. Franchisees pay monthly royalty fees, typically 4% of sales.

MARKET PROFILE. According to the National Restaurant Association, sales at limited service restaurants totaled $143 billion in 2006. Wendy's main competitors in the hamburger segment of the fast-food industry are McDonald's (2006 domestic systemwide sales of $27.1 billion), and Burger King ($7.9 billion). Strong regional competitors include Sonic Drive-In ($3.3 billion) and Jack In The Box ($2.9 billion). Driven by new product development and higher menu prices, sales rose at an annual rate of 5.0% from 2004 to 2006. We expect growth rates to slow to 4.0% to 5.0% over the next several years, mainly due to increasing price competition, lower rates of expansion, and loss of U.S. market share.

CORPORATE STRATEGY. In 2006, WEN focused on improving shareholder returns by improving the operating performance of its core Wendy's concept. Concurrently, WEN sold and spun off to shareholders its ownership of other fast food concepts. In March 2006, WEN sold a 17.25% stake of Tim Hortons in an IPO. It spun off the remaining 82.25% stake to shareholders on September 30, 2006. The company used the proceeds from the Tim Hortons IPO primarily to finance the repurchase of 26.2 million common shares during 2006 for about $1 billion.

In November 2006, the company sold its Baja Fresh chain to outside investors for approximately $31 million. Finally, the company is currently looking to sell its Cafe Express concept, and, as of the fourth quarter of 2006, it classified the Cafe Express segment as discontinued operations.

Company Financials Fiscal Year Ended Dec. 31

Per Share Data ($)	2006	2005	2004	2003	2002	2001	2000	1999	1998	1997
Tangible Book Value	16.74	16.02	13.41	12.15	9.84	9.40	9.48	8.60	9.37	9.78
Cash Flow	1.39	3.63	2.02	3.51	3.10	2.62	2.31	2.06	1.63	1.68
Earnings	0.32	1.92	0.45	2.05	1.89	1.65	1.44	1.32	0.95	0.97
S&P Core Earnings	0.31	1.48	1.92	1.94	1.74	1.54	NA	NA	NA	NA
Dividends	0.60	0.75	0.48	0.24	0.24	0.24	0.24	0.24	0.24	0.24
Payout Ratio	186%	39%	107%	12%	13%	15%	17%	18%	25%	25%
Prices:High	67.19	56.40	42.75	41.55	41.60	30.50	27.13	31.69	25.19	27.94
Prices:Low	31.75	36.73	31.74	23.97	26.15	20.00	14.00	19.69	18.13	19.63
P/E Ratio:High	NM	29	95	20	22	18	19	24	27	29
P/E Ratio:Low	NM	19	71	12	14	12	10	15	19	20

Income Statement Analysis (Million $)										
Revenue	2,439	3,783	3,635	3,149	2,730	2,391	2,237	2,072	1,948	2,037
Operating Income	201	603	599	586	531	453	424	389	346	335
Depreciation	124	200	182	168	143	123	113	103	100	105
Interest Expense	35.7	46.4	47.0	45.8	41.5	30.2	28.9	10.2	19.8	18.9
Pretax Income	42.5	338	184	378	346	307	271	269	208	219
Effective Tax Rate	12.8%	33.7%	71.7%	37.5%	36.8%	37.0%	37.5%	38.0%	40.6%	40.5%
Net Income	37.0	224	52.0	236	219	194	170	167	123	131
S&P Core Earnings	36.0	173	222	221	200	181	NA	NA	NA	NA

Balance Sheet & Other Financial Data (Million $)										
Cash	231	393	177	171	172	111	170	211	161	234
Current Assets	757	757	459	463	331	266	319	350	314	382
Total Assets	3,440	3,440	3,198	3,164	2,667	2,076	1,958	1,884	1,838	1,942
Current Liabilities	583	583	688	528	360	297	296	284	249	213
Long Term Debt	540	616	594	693	682	651	448	449	446	250
Common Equity	2,059	2,059	1,716	1,980	1,449	1,030	1,126	1,065	1,068	1,184
Total Capital	2,671	2,753	2,419	2,805	2,239	1,763	1,647	1,584	1,575	1,715
Capital Expenditures	181	371	341	342	331	301	276	248	242	295
Cash Flow	161	424	234	404	362	317	283	270	224	236
Current Ratio	1.3	1.3	0.7	0.9	0.9	0.9	1.1	1.2	1.3	1.8
% Long Term Debt of Capitalization	20.2	22.4	24.5	24.7	30.4	36.9	27.2	28.3	28.3	14.6
% Net Income of Revenue	1.5	5.9	1.4	7.5	8.0	8.1	7.6	8.0	6.3	6.4
% Return on Assets	1.3	6.8	1.6	8.0	9.2	9.6	8.8	9.0	6.5	7.0
% Return on Equity	2.4	11.9	3.0	13.8	17.7	18.0	15.5	15.6	11.0	11.7

Data as orig reptd.; bef. results of disc opers/spec. items. Per share data adj. for stk. divs.; EPS diluted. E-Estimated. NA-Not Available. NM-Not Meaningful. NR-Not Ranked. UR-Under Review.

Office: 4288 West Dublin-Granville Road, Dublin, OH 43017-0256.
Telephone: 614-764-3100.
Email: investor_relations@wendys.com
Website: http://www.wendys-invest.com

Chrmn: J.V. Pickett
Pres & CEO: K.B. Anderson
COO: D.J. Near
EVP & CFO: J. Fitzsimmons

EVP & Treas: J.F. Catherwood
Investor Contact: J.D. Barker
Board Members: K. B. Anderson, A. B. Crane, J. Hill, T. F. Keller, W. E. Kirwan, D. P. Lauer, J. W. Levin, J. R. Lewis, J. F. Millar, S. I. Oran, J. V. Pickett, P. H. Rothschild, J. R. Thompson

Founded: 1969
Domicile: Ohio
Employees: 46,000

Western Union Co

STANDARD &POOR'S

S&P Recommendation **HOLD** ★★★☆☆	Price $21.68 (as of Nov 23, 2007)	12-Mo. Target Price $24.00	Investment Style Large-Cap Blend

GICS Sector Information Technology
Sub-Industry Data Processing & Outsourced Services

Summary Spun off from First Data Corp. in September 2006, Western Union is a leading independent provider of consumer money transfer services.

Key Stock Statistics (Source S&P, Vickers, company reports)

52-Wk Range	$24.14– 15.00	S&P Oper. EPS 2007**E**	1.11	Market Capitalization(B)	$16.751	Beta	NA
Trailing 12-Month EPS	$1.07	S&P Oper. EPS 2008**E**	1.25	Yield (%)	NA	S&P 3-Yr. Proj. EPS CAGR(%)	12.00
Trailing 12-Month P/E	20.3	P/E on S&P Oper. EPS 2007**E**	19.5	Dividend Rate/Share	NA	S&P Credit Rating	NA
$10K Invested 5 Yrs Ago	NA	Common Shares Outstg. (M)	772.7	Institutional Ownership (%)	85		

Price Performance

30-Week Mov. Avg. ··· 10-Week Mov. Avg. - - GAAP Earnings vs. Previous Year Volume Above Avg. STARS
12-Mo. Target Price — Relative Strength — ▲ Up ▼ Down ► No Change Below Avg. ★

Options: ASE, CBOE, P, Ph

Analysis prepared by **Zaineb Bokhari** on October 25, 2007, when the stock traded at **$ 21.69**.

Highlights

➤ We forecast that revenues will rise 10% in 2007, with growth paced by an 8% increase in transaction fees and an 18% advance in foreign exchange revenues. We expect the company's recently completed acquisition of SEPSA, will add 1% to overall revenue growth in 2007. We think revenue growth of 12% is achievable in 2008, supported by WU's rising international presence and growing agent network.

➤ We expect gross and operating margins to narrow modestly in 2007, reflecting our outlook for a competitive pricing environment for WU's core money transfer business. We also look for SG&A to rise in 2007, as a percentage of revenues, due to WU's ongoing investment in its brand as well as additional expenses related to its structure as a public company. We anticipate that gross and operating margins will widen modestly in 2008.

➤ After projected taxes at 30%, we estimate EPS of $1.11 in 2007 and $1.25 in 2008. We think WU will continue to repurchase shares under its remaining authorization, aiding EPS in both years.

Investment Rationale/Risk

➤ WU has experienced a slowing in its U.S. to Mexico business, possibly hurt by uncertainty with respect to U.S. immigration policy and, we believe, sluggish U.S. construction activity. We believe WU's market leadership and geographic diversity (beyond the U.S. and Mexico) will enable it to weather headwinds related to future immigration policy changes. However, we look for near-term financial results to be restrained by this slowdown and by price pressure from smaller competitors, which are attempting to gain market share.

➤ Risks to our recommendation and target price include accelerating consumer adoption of digital alternatives to WU's money transfer offerings, competition from traditional financial institutions and money transfer peers, and the potential for a negative impact from the U.S. government's anti-money-laundering and anti-terrorism measures.

➤ Our DCF model, which assumes a WACC of 10% and a perpetuity growth rate of 3%, leads to an intrinsic value of $24, which is our 12-month target price. At this level, the shares would trade at a P/E of about 19.2X our 2008 EPS estimate, modestly above peers at 18.1X.

Qualitative Risk Assessment

LOW	MEDIUM	HIGH

Our risk assessment reflects what we see as relatively high barriers to entry in WU's businesses and its market leadership, offset by risks related to consolidation in the financial services area, and the uncertainty related to the ongoing immigration debate in the U.S.

Quantitative Evaluations

S&P Quality Ranking — NR

D	C	B-	B	B+	A-	A	A+

Relative Strength Rank — STRONG

86

LOWEST = 1 HIGHEST = 99

Revenue/Earnings Data

Revenue (Million $)

	1Q	2Q	3Q	4Q	Year
2007	1,131	1,203	1,257	--	--
2006	1,043	1,114	1,140	1,173	4,470
2005	919.6	980.8	1,019	1,068	3,988
2004	--	--	--	--	--
2003	--	--	--	--	--
2002	--	--	--	--	--

Earnings Per Share ($)

	1Q	2Q	3Q	4Q	Year
2007	0.25	0.26	0.28	E0.32	E1.11
2006	0.29	0.29	0.34	0.28	1.19
2005	--	--	--	--	0.96
2004	--	--	--	--	--
2003	--	--	--	--	--
2002	--	--	--	--	--

Fiscal year ended Dec. 31. Next earnings report expected: Early February. EPS Estimates based on S&P Operating Earnings; historical GAAP earnings are as reported.

Dividend Data (Dates: mm/dd Payment Date: mm/dd/yy)

Amount ($)	Date Decl.	Ex-Div. Date	Stk. of Record	Payment Date
0.010	12/05	12/13	12/15	12/28/06

Dividends have been paid since 2006. Source: Company reports.

Please read the Required Disclosures and Analyst Certification on the last page of this report.

Western Union Co

STANDARD & POOR'S

Business Summary October 25, 2007

CORPORATE OVERVIEW. Spun off from First Data Corp. in September 2006, Western Union is a leading independent provider of consumer money transfer services. WU offers its services through a network of over 305,000 agent locations spanning more than 200 countries and territories. The company provides its services globally, mainly under the Western Union brand name and also under the Orlandi Valuta and Vigo brands. WU derives the majority of revenues from fees that consumers pay when they send money. The company's main segments include consumer-to-consumer (C2C; 84% of 2006 revenues) and consumer-to-business (C2B; 14%).

WU's core C2C services allow customers to transfer money to other individuals. The majority of these transfers are originated in cash at Western Union agent locations, although consumers can also send money via the Internet, telephone, credit or debit card and, in some cases, through bank debits. In 2006, C2C transactions increased 24%, to 147 million, while C2C transaction fees rose about 12%.

Through its C2B segment, consumers can make payments to businesses electronically, over the telephone, via the Internet, or at one of WU's agent locations. The company has long-standing relationships with billers such as utilities, auto finance companies, mortgage servicers, financial service providers

and government agencies who accept such payments. In 2006, WU's C2B transactions increased 16%, to over 249 million, while C2B transaction fees rose about 5%.

CORPORATE STRATEGY. The pursuit of growth through international expansion is a key tenet of Western Union's growth strategy. The company estimates that about 85% of its C2C transactions involve at least one non-U.S. location. The U.S. accounted for 14% of 2006 consolidated revenues while Mexico accounted for 8%. Outside of these two countries, WU's revenue base is well-diversified geographically. Building on and maintaining its well-recognized consumer brand is another key element to the company's strategy. WU has spent 7% of revenues on marketing, advertising and developing customer loyalty programs in each of 2004, 2005, and 2006. The company has also invested about 3% of annual revenues in selective price reductions on its C2C services in individual markets depending on the dynamics within those markets. We think the difference in growth between transaction fees and transaction volumes is evidence of this strategy.

Company Financials Fiscal Year Ended Dec. 31

Per Share Data ($)	2006	2005	2004	2003	2002	2001	2000	1999	1998	1997
Tangible Book Value	NM	NM	NA	NA	NA	NA	NA	NA	NA	NA
Cash Flow	1.32	NA	NA	NA	NA	NA	NA	NA	NA	NA
Earnings	1.19	0.96	NA	NA	NA	NA	NA	NA	NA	NA
S&P Core Earnings	1.18	1.10	0.95	NA	NA	NA	NA	NA	NA	NA
Dividends	0.01	NA	NA	NA	NA	NA	NA	NA	NA	NA
Payout Ratio	1%	NA	NA	NA	NA	NA	NA	NA	NA	NA
Prices:High	24.14	NA	NA	NA	NA	NA	NA	NA	NA	NA
Prices:Low	16.85	NA	NA	NA	NA	NA	NA	NA	NA	NA
P/E Ratio:High	20	NA	NA	NA	NA	NA	NA	NA	NA	NA
P/E Ratio:Low	14	NA	NA	NA	NA	NA	NA	NA	NA	NA

Income Statement Analysis (Million $)										
Revenue	4,470	3,988	NA	NA	NA	NA	NA	NA	NA	NA
Operating Income	1,415	NA	NA	NA	NA	NA	NA	NA	NA	NA
Depreciation	104	NA	NA	NA	NA	NA	NA	NA	NA	NA
Interest Expense	53.0	202	NA	NA	NA	NA	NA	NA	NA	NA
Pretax Income	1,335	1,063	NA	NA	NA	NA	NA	NA	NA	NA
Effective Tax Rate	31.5%	29.5%	NA	NA	NA	NA	NA	NA	NA	NA
Net Income	914	749	NA	NA	NA	NA	NA	NA	NA	NA
S&P Core Earnings	913	859	734	NA	NA	NA	NA	NA	NA	NA

Balance Sheet & Other Financial Data (Million $)										
Cash	1,422	1,186	NA	NA	NA	NA	NA	NA	NA	NA
Current Assets	NA	NA	NA	NA	NA	NA	NA	NA	NA	NA
Total Assets	5,321	4,659	NA	NA	NA	NA	NA	NA	NA	NA
Current Liabilities	NA	NA	NA	NA	NA	NA	NA	NA	NA	NA
Long Term Debt	2,996	3,500	NA	NA	NA	NA	NA	NA	NA	NA
Common Equity	-315	-687	NA	NA	NA	NA	NA	NA	NA	NA
Total Capital	2,681	2,183	NA	NA	NA	NA	NA	NA	NA	NA
Capital Expenditures	64.0	NA	NA	NA	NA	NA	NA	NA	NA	NA
Cash Flow	1,018	NA	NA	NA	NA	NA	NA	NA	NA	NA
Current Ratio	NA	NA	NA	NA	NA	NA	NA	NA	NA	NA
% Long Term Debt of Capitalization	112.0	160.3	NA	NA	NA	NA	NA	NA	NA	NA
% Net Income of Revenue	20.4	18.8	NA	NA	NA	NA	NA	NA	NA	NA
% Return on Assets	18.3	NA	NA	NA	NA	NA	NA	NA	NA	NA
% Return on Equity	NM	NA	NA	NA	NA	NA	NA	NA	NA	NA

Data as orig reptd.; bef. results of disc opers/spec. items. Per share data adj. for stk. divs.; EPS diluted. Pro forma data in 2005, balance sheet and book value as of Jun. 30, 2006. E-Estimated. NA-Not Available. NM-Not Meaningful. NR-Not Ranked. UR-Under Review.

Office: 12500 East Belford Avenue, Englewood, CO 80112.
Telephone: 866-405-5012.
Website: http://www.westernunion.com
Chrmn: J.M. Greenberg

Pres & CEO: C.A. Gold
EVP & CFO: S. Scheirman
EVP, Secy & General Counsel: D. Schlapbach
Investor Contact: G. Kohn (720-332-8276)

Board Members: D. S. Devitre, L. Fayne Levinson, C. A. Gold, J. M. Greenberg, B. D. Holden, A. J. Lacy, R. G. Mendoza, M. A. Miles, Jr., D. Stevenson

Founded: 1851
Domicile: Delaware
Employees: 5,900

Weyerhaeuser Co

STANDARD &POOR'S

S&P Recommendation **HOLD** ★★★☆☆	Price $68.71 (as of Nov 23, 2007)	12-Mo. Target Price $80.00	Investment Style Large-Cap Blend

GICS Sector Materials
Sub-Industry Forest Products

Summary One of the world's largest integrated forest products companies, WY grows timber; makes and sells forest products, pulp, and packaging; and engages in real estate construction and development.

Key Stock Statistics (Source S&P, Vickers, company reports)

52-Wk Range	$87.09– 59.67	S&P Oper. EPS 2007**E**	1.70	Market Capitalization(B)	$14.962	Beta	1.20
Trailing 12-Month EPS	$6.04	S&P Oper. EPS 2008**E**	2.50	Yield (%)	3.49	S&P 3-Yr. Proj. EPS CAGR(%)	5.00
Trailing 12-Month P/E	11.4	P/E on S&P Oper. EPS 2007**E**	40.4	Dividend Rate/Share	$2.40	S&P Credit Rating	BBB
$10K Invested 5 Yrs Ago	$16,500	Common Shares Outstg. (M)	217.8	Institutional Ownership (%)	81		

Price Performance

30-Week Mov. Avg. · · · 10-Week Mov. Avg. - - **GAAP Earnings vs. Previous Year** Volume Above Avg. STARS
12-Mo. Target Price — Relative Strength — ▲ Up ▼ Down ▶ No Change Below Avg.

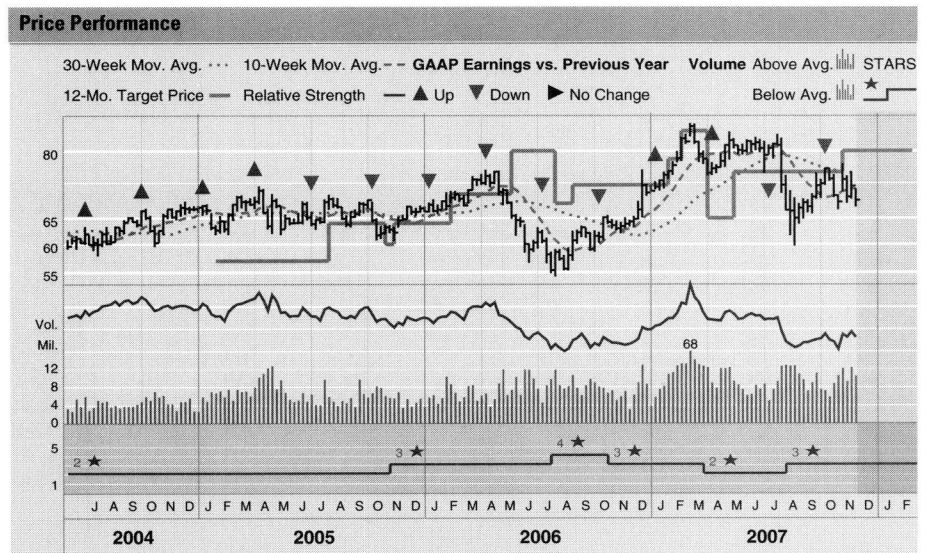

Analysis prepared by **Stuart J. Benway, CFA** on November 14, 2007, when the stock traded at **$ 73.99.**

Options: CBOE, P

Qualitative Risk Assessment

LOW	**MEDIUM**	HIGH

Our risk assessment reflects that Weyerhaeuser operates in a cyclical industry, with large capital requirements and significant variability in both costs and prices. However, the company is one of the largest companies in the industry, and we believe it has a major base of assets and modest debt levels.

Quantitative Evaluations

S&P Quality Ranking B

D	C	B-	**B**	B+	A-	A	A+

Relative Strength Rank MODERATE

59

LOWEST = 1   HIGHEST = 99

Revenue/Earnings Data

Revenue (Million $)

	1Q	2Q	3Q	4Q	Year
2007	3,891	4,334	4,146	--	--
2006	5,256	5,657	5,328	5,655	21,896
2005	5,404	5,838	5,604	5,868	22,629
2004	5,037	5,893	5,849	5,886	22,665
2003	4,614	4,930	5,184	5,145	19,873
2002	3,991	4,922	4,890	4,718	18,521

Earnings Per Share ($)

2007	-0.07	0.17	0.34	E0.47	E1.70
2006	-2.36	1.20	0.75	1.67	1.44
2005	0.98	1.22	1.16	-1.00	2.36
2004	0.54	1.57	2.45	0.82	5.43
2003	-0.19	0.71	0.37	0.41	1.30
2002	0.24	0.32	0.06	0.57	1.09

Fiscal year ended Dec. 31. Next earnings report expected: Early February. EPS Estimates based on S&P Operating Earnings; historical GAAP earnings are as reported.

Highlights

➤ We look for a 10%-12% decline in revenues from continuing operations in 2007, but reported sales could fall more than 20% with the fine paper divestiture. S&P projects a decline of 26% in housing starts in 2007, and we believe this projected downturn will prevent a recovery in prices for lumber and panels and lead to lower closings and sale prices in the home building segment. For 2008, we see little revenue growth, based primarily on our forecast for a further 13% decline in housing starts.

➤ We believe cost reductions in packaging will be more than offset by higher recycled fiber costs. In addition, an expected continuation of the housing market downturn is likely to lead to reduced profits at the wood products and home building businesses. However, higher prices and volume in fibers should be a partial offsetting factor. We estimate that operating margins will fall about 270 basis points in 2007, before recovering by 140 basis points in 2008.

➤ Our operating EPS estimate for 2007 is $1.70, down from EPS of $3.68 in 2006, and we forecast 2008 EPS of $2.50.

Investment Rationale/Risk

➤ WY has taken several steps to bolster its performance, either by cutting costs at underperforming businesses or divesting them, and investing in higher growth areas. However, we expect the housing downturn to hurt profits, although we think a combination of good cost control and steady conditions in the pulp and packaging segments will allow the company to maintain profitability in coming quarters.

➤ Risks to our recommendation and target price include a renewed downturn in wood product prices, continued contraction of the credit markets, a lack of recovery in the housing market, and a drop in prices in the packaging sector.

➤ Given the company's recent and potential corporate repositioning moves, we believe it is appropriate to value these shares on a sum-of-the-parts basis. Our model recognizes the cyclical characteristics of the wood products and real estate businesses, the relative stability of the fibers unit, and the significant value of the timberlands. Considering these factors, we value the shares at $80, which is our 12-month target price.

Dividend Data (Dates: mm/dd Payment Date: mm/dd/yy)

Amount ($)	Date Decl.	Ex-Div. Date	Stk. of Record	Payment Date
0.600	01/11	01/31	02/02	02/26/07
0.600	04/19	05/02	05/04	05/29/07
0.600	07/12	08/01	08/03	08/27/07
0.600	10/18	11/07	11/09	12/03/07

Dividends have been paid since 1933. Source: Company reports.

Weyerhaeuser Co

Business Summary November 14, 2007

CORPORATE OVERVIEW. Weyerhaeuser, one of the world's largest integrated forest products companies, is primarily engaged in growing and harvesting timber; the production, distribution and sale of wood and paper products; and real estate development. Through its timberlands segment (5% of 2006 sales), WY manages 5.7 million acres of company-owned timberlands and leases 700,000 acres of timberlands in eight states. The wood products businesses (36%) produce and sell softwood and hardwood lumber, plywood and veneer, composite panels, oriented strand board, and engineered lumber. Products made by the pulp and paper unit (21%) include paper grade, absorbent, dissolving and specialty pulp grades. Paper products include coated papers, which are used in the printing and publishing industries. The containerboard, packaging and recycling segment (22%) manufactures corrugating medium, linerboard and kraft paper. Through Weyerhaeuser Real Estate Company (15%), the company is involved in the development of single-family housing and residential lots, including the development of master-planned communities.

MARKET PROFILE. Weyerhaeuser operates in a highly cyclical and capital-intensive industry. Demand for the company's products is dependent on a number of factors, including industrial non-durable goods production, consumer spending, commercial printing and advertising activity, white collar employment levels, domestic and Japanese new home construction and repair and remodeling activity, and movements in currency exchange rates. Historical prices for paper and wood products have been volatile, and, despite its size, WY has had only a limited direct influence over the timing and extent of price changes for its products. Pricing is significantly affected by the relationship between supply and demand, and supply is influenced primarily by fluctuations in available manufacturing capacity.

Company Financials Fiscal Year Ended Dec. 31

Per Share Data ($)	2006	2005	2004	2003	2002	2001	2000	1999	1998	1997
Tangible Book Value	28.92	27.81	24.84	17.44	15.80	25.45	25.95	27.15	22.74	23.31
Cash Flow	6.88	7.80	10.76	7.23	6.63	5.94	7.52	6.07	4.55	4.85
Earnings	1.44	2.36	5.43	1.30	1.09	1.61	3.72	2.98	1.47	1.71
S&P Core Earnings	2.97	1.79	4.37	0.70	-0.75	NA	NA	NA	NA	NA
Dividends	2.20	1.90	1.60	1.60	1.60	1.60	1.60	1.60	1.60	1.60
Payout Ratio	182%	81%	29%	123%	147%	99%	43%	54%	109%	94%
Prices:High	75.50	71.85	68.59	64.70	68.09	63.50	74.50	73.94	62.00	63.94
Prices:Low	54.25	60.62	55.06	45.40	37.35	42.77	36.06	49.56	36.75	42.63
P/E Ratio:High	62	30	13	50	62	39	20	25	42	37
P/E Ratio:Low	45	26	10	35	34	27	10	17	25	25

Income Statement Analysis (Million $)										
Revenue	21,896	22,629	22,665	19,873	18,521	14,545	15,980	12,262	10,766	11,210
Operating Income	2,914	3,443	4,028	2,716	2,455	1,689	2,536	1,902	1,385	1,486
Depreciation	1,283	1,337	1,322	1,318	1,225	876	859	640	616	628
Interest Expense	531	730	829	796	771	344	351	277	273	297
Pretax Income	826	906	1,945	436	371	516	1,323	970	463	539
Effective Tax Rate	57.0%	35.8%	34.0%	33.9%	35.0%	31.4%	36.5%	36.5%	36.5%	36.5%
Net Income	355	582	1,283	288	241	354	840	616	294	342
S&P Core Earnings	728	444	1,029	156	-168	2.35	NA	NA	NA	NA

Balance Sheet & Other Financial Data (Million $)										
Cash	243	1,104	1,197	202	122	204	123	1,643	35.0	122
Current Assets	4,121	4,876	5,293	4,021	3,888	3,061	3,288	4,543	2,170	2,294
Total Assets	26,862	28,229	29,954	28,109	28,219	18,293	18,195	18,339	12,834	13,075
Current Liabilities	3,129	3,255	3,149	2,525	2,994	1,863	2,704	2,934	1,499	1,384
Long Term Debt	7,675	8,262	10,144	12,397	12,721	5,715	5,114	4,453	4,662	4,743
Common Equity	9,095	9,800	9,255	7,109	6,623	6,695	6,832	7,173	4,526	4,649
Total Capital	20,461	22,097	23,932	23,800	23,400	14,787	14,323	13,611	10,592	10,931
Capital Expenditures	837	861	492	608	930	660	848	487	615	656
Cash Flow	1,638	1,919	2,605	1,606	1,466	1,230	1,699	1,256	910	970
Current Ratio	1.3	1.5	1.7	1.6	1.3	1.6	1.2	1.5	1.4	1.7
% Long Term Debt of Capitalization	37.5	37.4	42.4	52.1	54.4	38.6	35.7	32.7	44.0	43.4
% Net Income of Revenue	1.6	2.6	5.7	1.4	1.3	2.4	5.3	5.0	2.7	3.1
% Return on Assets	1.3	2.0	4.4	1.0	1.0	1.9	4.6	4.0	2.3	2.6
% Return on Equity	3.8	6.1	15.7	4.2	3.6	5.2	12.0	10.5	6.4	7.4

Data as orig reptd.; bef. results of disc opers/spec. items. Per share data adj. for stk. divs.; EPS diluted. E-Estimated. NA-Not Available. NM-Not Meaningful. NR-Not Ranked. UR-Under Review.

Office: 33663 Weyerhaeuser Way South, Federal Way, WA 98003.
Telephone: 253-924-2345.
Email: invrelations@weyerhaeuser.com
Website: http://www.weyerhaeuser.com

Chrmn, Pres & CEO: S.R. Rogel
COO & EVP: R.E. Hanson
EVP & CFO: P.M. Bedient
SVP & CTO: M.P. Drake

SVP & General Counsel: S.D. McDade
Investor Contact: K.F. McAuley (253-924-2058)
Board Members: D. A. Cafaro, R. F. Haskayne, M. R. Ingram, J. I. Kieckhefer, A. G. Langbo, D. F. Mazankowski, N. W. Piasecki, S. R. Rogel, R. H. Sinkfield, D. M. Steuert, J. N. Sullivan, K. Williams, C. R. Williamson

Founded: 1900
Domicile: Washington
Employees: 46,737

STANDARD &POOR'S

Whirlpool Corp

S&P Recommendation	BUY ★★★★☆	Price	12-Mo. Target Price	Investment Style
		$77.88 (as of Nov 23, 2007)	$106.00	Large-Cap Blend

GICS Sector Consumer Discretionary
Sub-Industry Household Appliances

Summary Whirlpool, which acquired Maytag, is the world's largest manufacturer of home appliances. Sears, Roebuck is its biggest customer.

Key Stock Statistics (Source S&P, Vickers, company reports)

52-Wk Range	$118.00– 72.10	S&P Oper. EPS 2007**E**	8.30	Market Capitalization(B)	$6.075	Beta	1.44
Trailing 12-Month EPS	$7.00	S&P Oper. EPS 2008**E**	9.65	Yield (%)	2.21	S&P 3-Yr. Proj. EPS CAGR(%)	12.00
Trailing 12-Month P/E	11.1	P/E on S&P Oper. EPS 2007**E**	9.4	Dividend Rate/Share	$1.72	S&P Credit Rating	BBB
$10K Invested 5 Yrs Ago	$16,694	Common Shares Outstg. (M)	78.0	Institutional Ownership (%)	NM		

Price Performance

30-Week Mov. Avg. · · · 10-Week Mov. Avg. – – GAAP Earnings vs. Previous Year Volume Above Avg. STARS
12-Mo. Target Price — Relative Strength — ▲ Up ▼ Down ▶ No Change Below Avg.

Options: CBOE, P

Analysis prepared by **Kenneth M. Leon, CPA** on October 23, 2007, when the stock traded at **$ 83.82**.

Highlights

➤ We see sales rising 5.5% in 2007 and 5.0% in 2008, including revenues from the 2006 Maytag acquisition. While sales in the U.S. appliance market are down 2% to 3% year to date, we believe WHR is realizing double-digit sales growth from Europe and emerging markets, along with new product momentum from product brands acquired in the Maytag acquisition. WHR has a strong reputation for product innovation.

➤ During 2007, we expect WHR to realize in excess of $400 million in cost savings from the Maytag acquisition, offset by higher material- and oil-related costs -- expected to rise $570 million. With improved cost control initiatives in other areas, we believe operating margins will widen in the next two years.

➤ For 2007, we expect the operating margin to widen to 5.4%, from 5.0% in 2006, and then expand to 6.3% in 2008 unless raw material costs rise further. Longer term, we believe that WHR will benefit from its larger scale and purchasing power, which should translate into improved productivity. We see operating EPS of $8.30 for 2007, followed by EPS of $9.65 in 2008.

Investment Rationale/Risk

➤ From lower domestic revenues in 2007, we forecast a U.S. rebound in unit volumes and sales in 2008 and continued double digit sales growth overseas, especially in Asia and Latin America. We believe that the product revitalization of Maytag is going well and offers WHR an opportunity to enhance its competitive position. Excluding integration costs, we believe that WHR is doing a solid job of managing costs in a challenging U.S. appliance market, which we expect to improve in 2008.

➤ Risks to our recommendation and target price include unfavorable changes in business conditions or growth prospects in WHR's major markets, greater competition and/or loss of market share, further increases in raw material prices, and delays in realizing cost savings from the Maytag merger.

➤ Our 12-month target price of $106 is based on a target P/E of about 11X, near the middle of the five-year historical range for WHR and the peer average, applied to our forward 12-month EPS estimate of $9.65, plus consideration of dividends we project.

Qualitative Risk Assessment

LOW	MEDIUM	HIGH

Our risk assessment reflects WHR's leading market share across many brands, offset by intense industry rivalry and heightened competition from foreign companies. While WHR benefits from its scale advantages, raw material costs remain an uncontrollable variable for the company.

Quantitative Evaluations

S&P Quality Ranking B+

D	C	B-	B	B+	A-	A	A+

Relative Strength Rank MODERATE

34

LOWEST = 1   HIGHEST = 99

Revenue/Earnings Data

Revenue (Million $)

	1Q	2Q	3Q	4Q	Year
2007	4,389	4,854	4,840	--	--
2006	3,536	4,747	4,843	4,954	18,080
2005	3,208	3,556	3,599	3,954	14,317
2004	3,007	3,264	3,318	3,632	13,220
2003	2,716	2,988	3,113	3,359	12,176
2002	2,574	2,737	2,759	2,947	11,016

Earnings Per Share ($)

2007	1.55	2.00	2.20	E2.30	E8.30
2006	1.70	1.26	1.68	1.67	6.35
2005	1.26	1.42	1.66	1.83	6.19
2004	1.43	1.53	1.50	1.44	5.90
2003	1.32	1.35	1.48	1.76	5.91
2002	1.21	0.91	1.46	0.20	3.78

Fiscal year ended Dec. 31. Next earnings report expected: Early February. EPS Estimates based on S&P Operating Earnings; historical GAAP earnings are as reported.

Dividend Data (Dates: mm/dd Payment Date: mm/dd/yy)

Amount ($)	Date Decl.	Ex-Div. Date	Stk. of Record	Payment Date
0.430	02/20	02/28	03/02	03/15/07
0.430	04/17	05/16	05/18	06/15/07
0.430	08/21	08/29	08/31	09/15/07
0.430	10/15	11/14	11/16	12/15/07

Dividends have been paid since 1929. Source: Company reports.

Whirlpool Corp

STANDARD
&POOR'S

Business Summary October 23, 2007

CORPORATE OVERVIEW. Whirlpool manufactures and markets a full line of major appliances and related products, primarily for home use. Products are manufactured in 12 countries and marketed worldwide under 14 main brand names. The company's growth strategy over the past several years has been to introduce innovative new products, strengthen customer loyalty, expand its global footprint, enhance distribution channels, and make strategic acquisitions where appropriate.

MARKET PROFILE. Two thirds of WHR's total sales in 2006 were from North America. As the market leader, its major product brands in the U.S. include Whirlpool, Maytag, KitchenAid, Jenn-Air, Roper, Estate, Admiral, Magic Chef, Amana, and Inglis. In Europe, which generated 19% of sales, products are marketed under the Whirlpool, Maytag, Amana, Bauknecht, Ignis, Laden, Polar and KitchenAid brand names. Markets also include Latin America and Asia. About 13% of total sales in 2006 were in Latin America, where WHR distributes its major home appliances under the Whirlpool, Brastemp, Consul and Eslabon de Lugo brand names. About 2% of sales were in Asia.

COMPETITIVE LANDSCAPE. The company has been able to retain a number

one position in brand and market share in most global regions. Combined with high reliability, WHR has developed strong customer loyalty. Competitors in the appliance industry include long-time incumbents Electrolux and General Electric, as well as expanding foreign operations such as LG Electronics, Bosch Siemens, Samsung, Fisher & Paykel, and Haier.

Major product categories include home laundry appliances (30% of 2006 sales revenue); home refrigerators and freezers (30%); home cooking appliances (16%); and other appliances (24%). Other appliances include home dishwashers, room air-conditioning equipment, and mixers, among others. Net sales rose to $18.1 billion in 2006, from $14.3 billion in 2005 and $13.2 billion in 2004, reflecting the presence of the acquired Maytag businesses for most of 2006. In 2006, the company sold 54,881 units of major and minor appliances, up 16.5% from 47,096 units in 2005.

Company Financials Fiscal Year Ended Dec. 31

Per Share Data ($)	2006	2005	2004	2003	2002	2001	2000	1999	1998	1997
Tangible Book Value	NM	21.49	19.85	15.23	5.82	11.10	13.97	14.29	14.01	11.25
Cash Flow	13.54	12.65	12.35	12.00	9.62	6.32	10.39	9.64	9.71	4.13
Earnings	6.35	6.19	5.90	5.91	3.78	0.50	5.20	4.56	4.06	-0.62
S&P Core Earnings	6.33	5.99	5.58	5.71	2.12	-1.91	NA	NA	NA	NA
Dividends	2.15	1.72	1.72	1.36	1.36	1.02	1.36	1.36	1.36	1.36
Payout Ratio	34%	28%	29%	23%	36%	NM	26%	30%	33%	NM
Prices:High	96.00	86.52	80.00	73.35	79.80	74.20	68.31	78.25	75.25	69.50
Prices:Low	74.07	60.78	54.53	42.80	39.23	45.88	31.50	40.94	43.69	45.25
P/E Ratio:High	15	14	14	12	21	NM	13	17	19	NM
P/E Ratio:Low	12	10	9	7	10	NM	6	9	11	NM

Income Statement Analysis (Million $)										
Revenue	18,080	14,317	13,220	12,176	11,016	10,343	10,325	10,511	10,323	8,617
Operating Income	1,428	1,291	1,218	1,219	1,207	1,147	1,178	1,261	1,126	710
Depreciation	550	442	445	427	405	396	371	386	438	356
Interest Expense	202	130	128	137	143	162	180	166	260	168
Pretax Income	620	598	615	652	468	89.0	580	510	565	-104
Effective Tax Rate	20.3%	28.6%	34.0%	35.0%	41.2%	48.3%	34.5%	38.6%	37.0%	NM
Net Income	486	422	406	414	262	34.0	367	347	310	-46.0
S&P Core Earnings	484	408	384	401	147	-130	NA	NA	NA	NA

Balance Sheet & Other Financial Data (Million $)										
Cash	262	524	243	249	192	316	114	261	636	578
Current Assets	6,476	4,710	4,514	3,865	3,327	3,311	3,237	3,177	3,882	4,281
Total Assets	13,878	8,248	8,181	7,361	6,631	6,967	6,902	6,826	7,935	8,270
Current Liabilities	6,002	4,301	3,985	3,589	3,505	3,082	3,303	2,892	3,267	3,676
Long Term Debt	1,798	745	1,160	1,134	1,092	1,295	795	714	1,087	1,074
Common Equity	3,283	1,745	1,606	1,301	796	2,126	1,684	1,867	2,001	1,771
Total Capital	5,481	2,749	3,074	2,734	2,083	3,725	2,801	2,738	3,854	3,035
Capital Expenditures	576	484	511	423	430	378	375	437	523	378
Cash Flow	1,036	864	851	841	667	430	738	733	748	310
Current Ratio	1.1	1.1	1.1	1.1	0.9	1.1	1.0	1.1	1.2	1.2
% Long Term Debt of Capitalization	32.8	27.1	37.8	41.5	52.4	34.8	28.4	26.1	28.2	35.4
% Net Income of Revenue	2.7	2.9	3.1	3.4	2.4	0.3	3.6	3.3	3.0	NM
% Return on Assets	4.4	5.1	5.2	5.9	3.9	0.5	5.3	4.7	3.8	NM
% Return on Equity	19.3	25.2	27.9	40.6	22.8	1.5	20.7	17.9	16.4	NM

Data as orig reptd.; bef. results of disc opers/spec. items. Per share data adj. for stk. divs.; EPS diluted. E-Estimated. NA-Not Available. NM-Not Meaningful. NR-Not Ranked. UR-Under Review.

Office: 2000 N M 63, Benton Harbor, MI 49022-2692.
Telephone: 269-923-5000.
Email: info@whirlpool.com
Website: http://www.whirlpool.com

Chrmn & CEO: J.M. Fettig
EVP & CFO: R.W. Templin
EVP & CTO: M.D. Thieneman
Secy: R.T. Kenagy

Investor Contact: L. Venturelli (269-923-4678)
Board Members: H. Cain, G. T. DiCamillo, J. M. Fettig, A. D. Gilmour, K. J. Hempel, M. F. Johnston, W. T. Kerr, A. G. Langbo, M. L. Marsh, P. G. Stern, J. D. Stoney, M. A. Todman, M. D. White

Founded: 1906
Domicile: Delaware
Employees: 73,416

The **McGraw·Hill** Companies

STANDARD &POOR'S

Whole Foods Market Inc

S&P Recommendation `HOLD` ★★★☆☆

Price $40.54 (as of Nov 26, 2007)	**12-Mo. Target Price** $50.00	**Investment Style** Large-Cap Blend

GICS Sector Consumer Staples
Sub-Industry Food Retail

Summary This company owns and operates the largest U.S. chain of natural and organic foods supermarkets.

Key Stock Statistics (Source S&P, Vickers, company reports)

52-Wk Range	$53.65–36.00	S&P Oper. EPS 2008**E**	1.50	Market Capitalization(B)	$5.635	Beta	0.94
Trailing 12-Month EPS	$1.29	S&P Oper. EPS 2009**E**	1.85	Yield (%)	1.97	S&P 3-Yr. Proj. EPS CAGR(%)	10.00
Trailing 12-Month P/E	31.4	P/E on S&P Oper. EPS 2008**E**	27.0	Dividend Rate/Share	$0.80	S&P Credit Rating	BB+
$10K Invested 5 Yrs Ago	$16,610	Common Shares Outstg. (M)	139.0	Institutional Ownership (%)	93		

Price Performance

30-Week Mov. Avg. ··· 10-Week Mov. Avg. - - **GAAP Earnings vs. Previous Year** Volume Above Avg. STARS
12-Mo. Target Price — Relative Strength — ▲ Up ▼ Down ► No Change Below Avg. ★

Options: ASE

Analysis prepared by **Joseph Agnese** on November 26, 2007, when the stock traded at **$ 40.75**.

Highlights

➤ We expect FY 08 (Sep.) sales to grow to about $8.5 billion, up 28% from $6.6 billion in FY 07. We see growth fueled by the integration of Wild Oats Markets, 18% square footage growth, and projected comparable-store sales gains of 7.5% to 9.5%.

➤ We believe margins will narrow significantly as the company begins the integration of acquired Wild Oats Markets stores and from both an acceleration in new store growth and the lack of leverage within new stores. Additionally, we believe the company will continue to maintain pricing flexibility at legacy stores, partially offsetting an improved product mix and procurement. However, we think G&A expenses are likely to stabilize as a percentage of revenues, as improved sales leverage offsets increased costs of investment in marketing. We estimate that pre-opening and relocation expenses will increase significantly as square footage growth accelerates.

➤ We project that FY 08 operating EPS will increase 16%, to $1.50, from $1.29 in FY 07.

Investment Rationale/Risk

➤ In September 2007, WFMI acquired Wild Oats Markets for about $700 million in cash and debt. We view the acquisition favorably and believe it will eventually result in significant sales and margin benefits.

➤ Risks to our recommendation and target price include intensifying competition, particularly in the company's California markets, as conventional supermarkets promote aggressively to win back market share and as new competitors enter the market.

➤ Our 12-month target price of $50 is based on our P/E-to-growth analysis. As WFMI is the fastest growing public retail food chain in the U.S. under our coverage, we expect its shares to trade at a significant P/E premium to supermarket peers and the S&P 500. Although we see a slowdown in near-term earnings growth due to a significant rise in expenses related to expansion plans, we believe investments to accelerate square footage growth and the recent acquisition of Wild Oats will lead to faster earnings growth. Assuming the shares trade at 1.6X our long-term growth target of 17%, we apply a multiple of 27X to our FY 09 EPS estimate of $1.85 to derive our target price of $50.

Qualitative Risk Assessment

LOW	**MEDIUM**	HIGH

Our risk assessment incorporates our view of a strong balance sheet and growing natural and organic food industry sales momentum, offset by an intensely competitive environment in the retail food industry.

Quantitative Evaluations

S&P Quality Ranking B

D	C	B-	**B**	B+	A-	A	A+

Relative Strength Rank MODERATE

32

LOWEST = 1   HIGHEST = 99

Revenue/Earnings Data

Revenue (Million $)

	1Q	2Q	3Q	4Q	Year
2007	1,871	1,463	1,514	1,743	6,592
2006	1,667	1,312	1,338	1,291	5,607
2005	1,368	1,085	1,133	1,115	4,701
2004	1,118	902.1	917.4	927.3	3,865
2003	923.8	725.1	749.0	750.7	3,149
2002	780.8	622.8	648.8	638.1	2,690

Earnings Per Share ($)

	1Q	2Q	3Q	4Q	Year
2007	0.38	0.32	0.35	0.24	1.29
2006	0.40	0.36	0.37	0.28	1.41
2005	0.35	0.29	0.29	0.07	0.99
2004	0.30	0.27	0.25	0.23	1.05
2003	0.21	0.21	0.23	0.19	0.83
2002	0.17	0.17	0.18	0.18	0.70

Fiscal year ended Sep. 30. Next earnings report expected: Late February. EPS Estimates based on S&P Operating Earnings; historical GAAP earnings are as reported.

Dividend Data (Dates: mm/dd Payment Date: mm/dd/yy)

Amount ($)	Date Decl.	Ex-Div. Date	Stk. of Record	Payment Date
0.180	03/05	04/11	04/13	04/24/07
0.180	06/06	07/11	07/13	07/24/07
0.180	09/21	10/10	10/12	10/23/07
0.200	11/20	01/09	01/11	01/22/08

Dividends have been paid since 2004. Source: Company reports.

Whole Foods Market Inc

STANDARD &POOR'S

Business Summary November 26, 2007

Whole Foods Market, established in 1980, has grown into the largest U.S. retailer of natural and organic foods, with $5.6 billion in sales in FY 06 (Sep.). Reflecting a series of store openings and acquisitions, the company has expanded from a single Austin, TX, store in 1980 to a chain of more than 202 stores in 31 states plus Washington, DC, Canada and the United Kingdom. The company strives to differentiate its stores from those of its competitors by tailoring its product mix, customer service attitude, and store environment to appeal to health conscious and gourmet customers. By 2010, the company's goal is to have over $12 billion in sales.

Stores average about 37,200 sq. ft., and offer a selection of some 30,000 food and non-food products. Each store contributes an average of almost $34 million in annual sales, with sales per sq. ft. of $939. Products sold include natural and organic foods and beverages; dietary supplements; natural personal care products; natural household goods; and educational products. Natural foods can be defined as foods that are minimally processed, largely or completely free of artificial ingredients, preservatives and other non-naturally occurring chemicals, and as near as possible to their whole, natural state. Organic foods are based on the minimal use of off-farm inputs and on management practices that restore, maintain and enhance the ecology.

The company opens or acquires stores in existing regions, and in metropolitan areas in which it believes it can become the leading natural foods supermarket retailer. In developing new stores, WFMI seeks to open large format units of 50,000 sq. ft. to 80,000 sq. ft., located on premium sites, often in urban, highly populated areas. Although approximately 33% of its store base consists of acquired stores, the company expects more of its future growth to come from developing new stores. As of September 2007, WFMI had signed leases for 87 stores averaging approximately 51,200 square feet in size, which is about 48% larger than its existing store base average. As of September 2007, the company operated about 7.5 million square feet of retail space, with about 4.5 million square feet (48% of existing sq. ft.) of retail space that were under development at that time.

Company Financials Fiscal Year Ended Sep. 30

Per Share Data ($)	2007	2006	2005	2004	2003	2002	2001	2000	1999	1998
Tangible Book Value	NA	9.00	9.06	6.82	5.57	4.21	2.98	2.11	2.35	2.16
Cash Flow	NA	2.48	1.93	1.84	1.54	1.34	1.16	0.85	0.87	0.79
Earnings	1.29	1.41	0.99	1.05	0.83	0.70	0.61	0.26	0.39	0.41
S&P Core Earnings	NA	1.40	-0.21	0.85	0.70	0.58	0.38	NA	NA	NA
Dividends	0.69	0.88	0.42	0.23	Nil	Nil	Nil	Nil	Nil	Nil
Payout Ratio	53%	62%	42%	22%	Nil	Nil	Nil	Nil	Nil	Nil
Prices:High	53.65	78.27	79.90	48.74	33.81	27.30	23.25	15.94	12.41	17.53
Prices:Low	36.00	45.56	44.14	32.96	22.39	17.74	9.73	8.59	7.06	8.00
P/E Ratio:High	42	56	81	47	41	39	38	60	32	43
P/E Ratio:Low	28	32	45	32	27	25	16	32	18	20

Income Statement Analysis (Million $)										
Revenue	NA	5,607	4,701	3,865	3,149	2,690	2,272	1,839	1,568	1,390
Operating Income	NA	475	363	341	285	248	209	181	144	125
Depreciation	NA	156	134	112	98.0	85.9	78.8	63.9	53.3	42.3
Interest Expense	NA	0.03	2.22	7.25	8.11	10.4	17.9	15.1	8.25	7.69
Pretax Income	NA	340	237	229	173	141	89.8	63.5	69.1	72.1
Effective Tax Rate	NA	40.0%	42.5%	40.0%	40.0%	40.0%	42.5%	54.5%	39.0%	37.0%
Net Income	NA	204	136	137	104	84.5	51.6	28.9	42.2	45.4
S&P Core Earnings	NA	202	-28.0	109	85.0	70.4	43.0	NA	NA	NA

Balance Sheet & Other Financial Data (Million $)										
Cash	NA	2.25	309	198	166	12.6	1.84	0.40	9.02	36.7
Current Assets	NA	624	673	485	364	172	145	152	141	184
Total Assets	NA	2,043	1,889	1,520	1,197	943	829	760	660	545
Current Liabilities	NA	510	418	331	240	176	156	143	121	91.0
Long Term Debt	NA	8.61	12.9	165	163	162	251	298	209	159
Common Equity	NA	1,404	1,366	988	776	589	409	307	311	277
Total Capital	NA	1,413	1,379	1,173	942	751	660	605	525	439
Capital Expenditures	NA	132	116	110	84.1	61.4	49.0	111	75.0	41.2
Cash Flow	NA	360	270	249	202	170	130	92.8	95.5	87.7
Current Ratio	NA	1.2	1.6	1.5	1.5	1.0	0.9	1.1	1.2	2.0
% Long Term Debt of Capitalization	NA	0.6	0.9	14.0	17.3	21.6	38.0	49.2	39.8	36.2
% Net Income of Revenue	NA	3.6	2.9	3.5	3.3	3.1	2.3	1.6	2.7	3.3
% Return on Assets	NA	10.4	8.0	10.1	9.7	9.5	6.5	4.1	7.0	9.6
% Return on Equity	NA	14.7	11.8	15.5	15.2	16.9	14.4	9.4	14.3	18.8

Data as orig reptd.; bef. results of disc opers/spec. items. Per share data adj. for stk. divs.; EPS diluted. E-Estimated. NA-Not Available. NM-Not Meaningful. NR-Not Ranked. UR-Under Review.

Office: 550 Bowie St, Austin, TX 78703-4644.
Telephone: 512-477-4455.
Website: http://www.wholefoods.com
Chrmn & CEO: J.P. Mackey

COO & Co-Pres: A.C. Gallo
COO & Co-Pres: W. Robb
EVP & CFO: G.F. Chamberlain
Investor Contact: C. McCann (512-477-4455)

Board Members: D. W. Dupree, J. B. Elstrott, G. Greene, H. Hassan, J. Mackey, L. A. Mason, M. Siegel, R. Z. Sorenson

Founded: 1978
Domicile: Texas
Employees: 41,500

Williams Cos Inc. (The)

STANDARD &POOR'S

S&P Recommendation **BUY** ★★★★☆	Price $34.94 (as of Nov 23, 2007)	12-Mo. Target Price $43.00	Investment Style Large-Cap Blend

GICS Sector Energy
Sub-Industry Oil & Gas Storage & Transportation

Summary This Oklahoma-based company, which primarily finds, produces, gathers, processes and transports natural gas, also manages a wholesale power business.

Key Stock Statistics (Source S&P, Vickers, company reports)

52-Wk Range	$37.74– 25.17	S&P Oper. EPS 2007**E**	1.51	Market Capitalization(B)	$20.972	Beta	1.31
Trailing 12-Month EPS	$1.49	S&P Oper. EPS 2008**E**	1.78	Yield (%)	1.14	S&P 3-Yr. Proj. EPS CAGR(%)	15.00
Trailing 12-Month P/E	23.5	P/E on S&P Oper. EPS 2007**E**	23.1	Dividend Rate/Share	$0.40	S&P Credit Rating	BBB-
$10K Invested 5 Yrs Ago	$125,768	Common Shares Outstg. (M)	600.2	Institutional Ownership (%)	82		

Price Performance

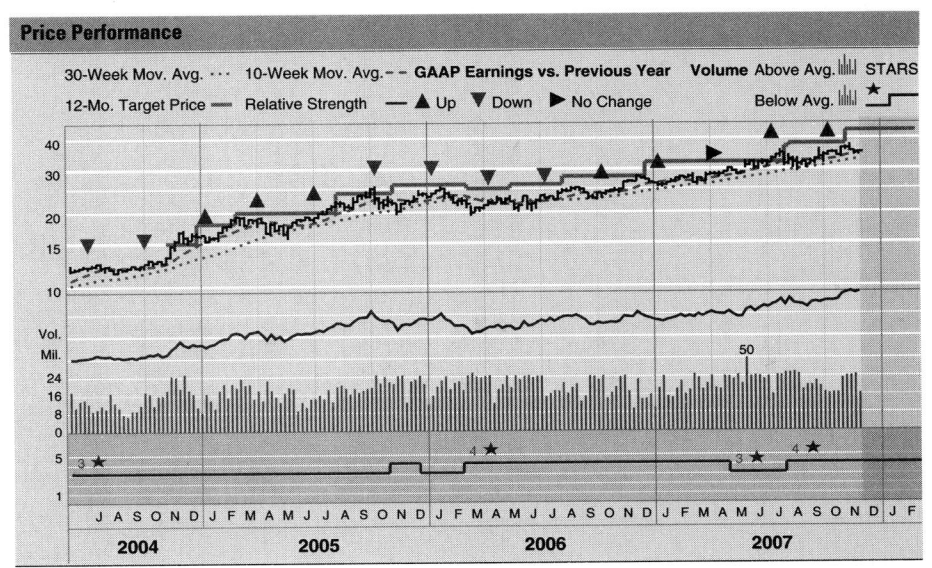

30-Week Mov. Avg. ··· 10-Week Mov. Avg. - - GAAP Earnings vs. Previous Year Volume Above Avg. STARS
12-Mo. Target Price — Relative Strength — ▲ Up ▼ Down ▶ No Change Below Avg.

Options: ASE, CBOE, P

Analysis prepared by **Michael Kay** on November 08, 2007, when the stock traded at **$ 35.43**.

Highlights

➤ We see expanding gas production, pipeline operations and midstream segment as the key earnings drivers over the next several years. Pipelines are seeing higher returns allowed in recent rate cases and capacity expansion in the Rockies. We expect E&P to benefit from the development of drilling prospects, and WMB plans to expand annual production volumes by 15%-20% per annum for the next three years. Third quarter EPS of $0.39, versus $0.28, surpassed our estimate of $0.36 as strong NGL margins boosted the midstream segment 35% and E&P volumes grew 15%.

➤ Over the next year, we expect WMB to place more assets into the master limited partnership (MLP), Williams Partners (WPZ). In July, WMB announced plans to form a new publicly traded MLP that will own interstate natural gas pipeline assets, with an initial stake in the Northwest Pipeline, a 3,900 mile system in the Pacific Northwest.

➤ For 2007, WMB expects to spend between $2.8 billion and $2.95 billion in capital expenditures, and for 2008, between $2.48 billion and $2.83 billion. In July, the company announced plans to repurchase up to $1 billion in stock.

Investment Rationale/Risk

➤ We expect WMB to continue to expand drilling in the highly active Piceance Basin. In our view, the company has a significant inventory of acreage that, if developed, could boost proven reserves by well over 50% in 2007. We view WMB as moderate risk, unlike several peers, given that it generates earnings and cash flow from stable fee-based or regulated assets and rising oil and gas reserves. We look for Rocky Mountain natural gas prices to improve from third quarter levels with the addition of pipeline capacity.

➤ Risks to our recommendation and target price include sharp reductions in power margins and natural gas prices, divestitures of power trading contracts, and lower rates for WMB's FERC regulated pipelines.

➤ We believe WMB, as a large pipeline firm with other operations experiencing visible organic growth, should trade at a premium to pipeline and multi-industry peers. Our 12-month target price of $43 reflects a price to tangible book value of 3.5X and an enterprise value to projected 2008 EBITDA multiple of 9X. We view positively WMB's plans to form a new MLP, noting the success it has had with past MLP spinoffs.

Qualitative Risk Assessment

LOW	MEDIUM	HIGH

Our risk assessment reflects our belief that although WMB has an E&P segment that can be very volatile, the company is involved in several complementary industries. Offsetting this volatility, its business portfolio is overweighted in regulated industries with largely fixed returns, in our opinion.

Quantitative Evaluations

S&P Quality Ranking   B

D	C	B-	B	B+	A-	A	A+

Relative Strength Rank   STRONG

85

LOWEST = 1   HIGHEST = 99

Revenue/Earnings Data

Revenue (Million $)

	1Q	2Q	3Q	4Q	Year
2007	2,852	2,823	2,860	--	--
2006	3,028	2,715	3,300	2,770	11,813
2005	2,954	2,871	3,082	3,676	12,584
2004	3,070	3,052	3,375	2,964	12,461
2003	4,833	3,657	4,795	3,549	16,834
2002	1,622	1,057	1,266	1,703	5,608

Earnings Per Share ($)

	1Q	2Q	3Q	4Q	Year
2007	0.22	0.40	0.38	E0.40	E1.51
2006	0.22	-0.11	0.19	0.25	0.55
2005	0.34	0.07	0.01	0.12	0.53
2004	Nil	-0.03	0.03	0.17	0.18
2003	-0.09	0.17	0.04	-0.16	-0.03
2002	0.05	-0.59	-0.35	-0.26	-1.14

Fiscal year ended Dec. 31. Next earnings report expected: NA. EPS Estimates based on S&P Operating Earnings; historical GAAP earnings are as reported.

Dividend Data (Dates: mm/dd Payment Date: mm/dd/yy)

Amount ($)	Date Decl.	Ex-Div. Date	Stk. of Record	Payment Date
0.090	01/29	03/07	03/09	03/26/07
0.100	04/10	05/23	05/25	06/11/07
0.100	07/19	08/22	08/24	09/10/07
0.100	11/15	12/12	12/14	12/31/07

Dividends have been paid since 1974. Source: Company reports.

Please read the Required Disclosures and Analyst Certification on the last page of this report.

The McGraw-Hill Companies

Williams Cos Inc. (The)

Business Summary November 08, 2007

CORPORATE OVERVIEW. WMB primarily finds, produces, gathers, and processes and transports natural gas. WMB also manages a wholesale power business. Operations are concentrated in the Pacific Northwest, Rocky Mountains, Gulf Coast, Southern California and Eastern Seaboard.

In February 2003, WMB announced a business strategy focused on migrating to an integrated natural gas business comprised of a smaller portfolio of natural gas businesses, reducing debt and increasing liquidity via asset sales, strategic levels of financing, and reductions in operating costs.

CORPORATE STRATEGY. WMB has transitioned its corporate strategy toward aggressively focusing on the market in the segments in which it perceives a sustainable competitive advantage, primarily its exploration and production (E&P) segment and its midstream segment. With about 3.9 Tcfe of proved reserves (99% natural gas, 53% proved developed), natural gas is produced from tight sands formations and coal bed methane reserves in the Piceance (67% of total reserves at December 31, 2006), San Juan (17%), Powder River (10%), Arkoma and other basins (6%).

The midstream division provides natural gas gathering, processing and treating, and natural gas liquid fractionation, storage and marketing, with primary service areas concentrated in the western states of Wyoming, Colorado, and

New Mexico, and the onshore and offshore shelf and deepwater areas in and around the Gulf Coast states of Texas, Louisiana, Mississippi and Alabama. Geographically, midstream natural gas assets are positioned to maximize commercial and operational synergies with other WMB assets (e.g., offshore gathering and processing assets attach and process or condition natural gas supplies delivered to the Transco pipeline; WMB gathering and processing facilities in the San Juan basin handle about 80% of the group's wellhead production in the basin).

The gas pipeline division has 14,400 miles of pipeline, with total annual throughput of 2,500 trillion BTUs, including the Transcontinental Gas Pipeline (Transco) and the Northwest Pipeline. Each pipeline system operates under Federal Energy Regulatory Commission (FERC) approved tariffs that establish rates, cost recovery mechanisms, and service terms and conditions. The established rates are a function of WMB's cost of providing services, including a "reasonable" return on invested capital (ROIC).

Company Financials Fiscal Year Ended Dec. 31

Per Share Data ($)	2006	2005	2004	2003	2002	2001	2000	1999	1998	1997
Tangible Book Value	8.48	7.70	7.06	5.96	7.15	9.43	13.26	11.69	8.34	9.35
Cash Flow	1.97	1.75	1.37	1.27	0.53	3.17	3.80	2.04	1.82	2.49
Earnings	0.55	0.53	0.18	-0.03	-1.14	1.67	1.95	0.36	0.32	1.04
S&P Core Earnings	0.78	0.64	0.05	-0.26	-1.34	1.40	NA	NA	NA	NA
Dividends	0.35	0.25	0.08	0.04	0.42	0.68	0.60	0.60	0.60	0.54
Payout Ratio	63%	47%	44%	NM	NM	41%	31%	167%	171%	52%
Prices:High	28.32	25.72	17.18	10.73	26.35	46.44	49.75	53.75	36.94	28.63
Prices:Low	19.35	15.18	8.49	2.51	0.78	20.80	29.50	28.00	20.00	18.13
P/E Ratio:High	51	49	95	NM	NM	28	26	NM	NM	28
P/E Ratio:Low	35	29	47	NM	NM	12	15	NM	NM	17

Income Statement Analysis (Million $)										
Revenue	11,813	12,584	12,461	16,834	5,608	11,035	10,398	8,593	7,658	4,410
Operating Income	2,124	1,972	1,903	1,849	1,566	3,389	2,602	1,591	1,372	1,414
Depreciation	866	740	668	671	775	798	832	742	646	500
Interest Expense	659	664	833	1,241	1,325	747	1,010	668	515	405
Pretax Income	579	557	246	71.0	-617	1,533	1,415	316	247	542
Effective Tax Rate	35.6%	38.4%	53.4%	51.3%	NM	41.1%	39.1%	51.0%	44.6%	32.8%
Net Income	333	317	93.2	15.2	-502	835	873	162	147	351
S&P Core Earnings	480	388	27.3	-144	-699	703	NA	NA	NA	NA

Balance Sheet & Other Financial Data (Million $)										
Cash	2,269	1,597	930	2,316	2,019	1,301	1,211	1,092	503	81.3
Current Assets	6,322	9,697	6,044	8,795	12,886	12,938	15,477	6,517	3,532	2,256
Total Assets	25,402	29,443	23,993	27,022	34,989	38,906	40,197	25,289	18,647	13,879
Current Liabilities	4,694	8,450	5,146	6,270	11,309	13,495	16,804	5,772	4,439	3,027
Long Term Debt	7,622	7,591	7,712	11,040	11,896	10,621	10,532	9,746	6,366	4,565
Common Equity	6,073	5,428	4,956	4,102	4,778	6,044	5,892	5,585	4,155	3,430
Total Capital	17,656	15,741	15,238	17,595	20,723	21,532	20,693	18,475	13,193	9,973
Capital Expenditures	-2,509	1,299	787	957	1,824	1,922	4,904	3,513	1,708	1,162
Cash Flow	1,198	1,057	762	657	274	1,633	1,705	901	786	840
Current Ratio	1.3	1.1	1.2	1.4	1.1	1.0	0.9	1.1	0.8	0.7
% Long Term Debt of Capitalization	43.2	48.2	50.6	62.7	57.4	49.3	50.9	52.8	48.3	45.8
% Net Income of Revenue	2.8	2.5	0.7	0.1	NM	7.6	8.4	1.9	1.9	7.9
% Return on Assets	1.2	1.2	0.4	0.0	NM	2.3	2.7	0.7	0.9	2.7
% Return on Equity	5.8	6.1	2.1	0.0	NM	14.0	15.2	3.3	3.7	10.2

Data as orig reptd.; bef. results of disc opers/spec. items. Per share data adj. for stk. divs.; EPS diluted. E-Estimated. NA-Not Available. NM-Not Meaningful. NR-Not Ranked. UR-Under Review.

Office: 1 Williams Ctr, Tulsa, OK 74172-0140.
Telephone: 918-573-2000.
Website: http://www.williams.com
Chrmn, Pres & CEO: S.J. Malcolm

SVP & CFO: D. Chappel
SVP & Chief Admin Officer: M.P. Johnson, Sr.
SVP & General Counsel: J.J. Bender
Investor Contact: R. George (918-573-3679)

Board Members: K. B. Cooper, I. F. Engelhardt, W. R. Granberry, W. E. Green, J. H. Hinshaw, W. R. Howell, C. M. Lillis, G. A. Lorch, W. G. Lowrie, F. T. MacInnis, S. J. Malcolm, J. D. Stoney

Founded: 1908
Domicile: Delaware
Employees: 4,313

STANDARD &POOR'S

Windstream Corp

S&P Recommendation **BUY** ★★★★☆	Price $13.03 (as of Nov 23, 2007)	12-Mo. Target Price $15.00	Investment Style Large-Cap Value

GICS Sector Telecommunication Services
Sub-Industry Integrated Telecommunication Services

Summary This company was formed through the combination of former Alltel wireline assets and Valor Communications in July 2006. It provides telephone service to more than 3 million lines in rural markets and expanded in August 2007 with the acquisition of CT Communications.

Key Stock Statistics (Source S&P, Vickers, company reports)

52-Wk Range	$15.63– 12.46	S&P Oper. EPS 2007**E**	0.95	Market Capitalization(B)	$6.220	Beta	NA
Trailing 12-Month EPS	$0.94	S&P Oper. EPS 2008**E**	1.00	Yield (%)	7.67	S&P 3-Yr. Proj. EPS CAGR(%)	3.00
Trailing 12-Month P/E	13.9	P/E on S&P Oper. EPS 2007**E**	13.7	Dividend Rate/Share	$1.00	S&P Credit Rating	NA
$10K Invested 5 Yrs Ago	NA	Common Shares Outstg. (M)	477.4	Institutional Ownership (%)	72		

Price Performance

30-Week Mov. Avg. · · · 10-Week Mov. Avg. — **GAAP Earnings vs. Previous Year** Volume Above Avg. ▕▍▍ STARS
12-Mo. Target Price — Relative Strength — ▲ Up ▼ Down ▶ No Change Below Avg. ▕▍▍

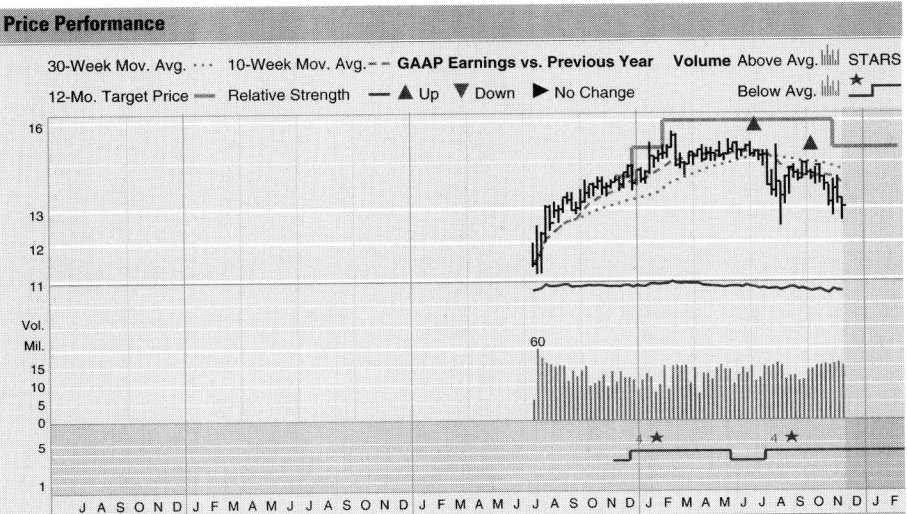

Options: CBOE, Ph

Analysis prepared by **Todd Rosenbluth** on November 09, 2007, when the stock traded at **$ 13.45**.

Highlights

➤ We project 2008 revenues of $3.34 billion, up from an expected $3.26 billion in 2007, aided by $190 million from assets acquired in the third quarter of 2007. We see broadband customer additions offsetting the impact of access line losses, although we believe broadband growth will slow from 2007 levels due to an above average penetration rate and increased competition. We expect that broadband and satellite offerings, plus modest price hikes, will help increase revenue per household.

➤ WIN has agreed to sell its directory operations, subject to necessary approvals, with a closing expected in the fourth quarter of 2007. We expect WIN's EBITDA margin to narrow to 50% in 2008, from 52% in 2007, due to the CT acquisition and increased sales and marketing costs. We see benefits from the integration of customer service and network service costs increasing throughout 2008.

➤ We forecast operating EPS of $0.95 in 2007, and we project $1.00 in 2008, aided by a modestly lower share count and lower interest costs.

Investment Rationale/Risk

➤ We think WIN will face less competition than most telecom carriers because of the rural nature of its access lines. We believe operating cash flow will be sufficient to support the dividend, and we see growth stemming from cost savings and increasing revenues per customer. We expect the proceeds from the planned asset sale to support its recent acquisition of CT Communications. While we see cost synergy opportunities, we believe operational risk adds challenges.

➤ Risks to our recommendation and target price include increased cable telephony competition, pressure on cash flow that puts dividend payments in jeopardy, challenges in integrating the acquired assets, and a delayed sale of its assets.

➤ Our 12-month target price is $15, representing a P/E of 15X our 2008 EPS estimate and an enterprise value/EBITDA multiple of 7.5X, a slight premium to rural telecom peers. On a total return basis, with its recent yield of about 7.8%, which is above the telecom services sector average, we view the shares as attractive.

Qualitative Risk Assessment

LOW	**MEDIUM**	HIGH

Our risk assessment reflects the stable rural markets that WIN serves and our view of its lower than peers debt leverage, offset by the risks we see in integrating acquisitions.

Quantitative Evaluations

S&P Quality Ranking NR

D	C	B-	B	B+	A-	A	A+

Relative Strength Rank MODERATE

53

LOWEST = 1   HIGHEST = 99

Revenue/Earnings Data

Revenue (Million $)

	1Q	2Q	3Q	4Q	Year
2007	783.7	826.7	822.6	--	--
2006	--	125.5	771.4	827.6	3,033
2005	--	--	--	--	3,414
2004	--	--	--	--	--
2003	--	--	--	--	--
2002	--	--	--	--	--

Earnings Per Share ($)

	1Q	2Q	3Q	4Q	Year
2007	0.21	0.24	0.25	E0.23	E0.95
2006	--	0.22	0.21	0.25	1.02
2005	--	--	--	--	0.83
2004	--	--	--	--	--
2003	--	--	--	--	--
2002	--	--	--	--	--

Fiscal year ended Dec. 31. Next earnings report expected: Early February. EPS Estimates based on S&P Operating Earnings; historical GAAP earnings are as reported.

Dividend Data (Dates: mm/dd Payment Date: mm/dd/yy)

Amount ($)	Date Decl.	Ex-Div. Date	Stk. of Record	Payment Date
0.250	02/07	03/28	03/30	04/16/07
0.250	05/09	06/27	06/29	07/16/07
0.250	08/07	09/26	09/28	10/15/07
0.250	11/07	12/26	12/28	01/15/08

Dividends have been paid since 2006. Source: Company reports.

Please read the Required Disclosures and Analyst Certification on the last page of this report.

The McGraw-Hill Companies

Windstream Corp

**STANDARD
&POOR'S**

Business Summary November 09, 2007

CORPORATE OVERVIEW. In July 2006, Alltel Corp spun out its wireline operations into a separate entity. Immediately after the consummation of the tax free spin-off, the entity merged with Valor Communications, and the resulting company was renamed Windstream Corporation. As of September 2007, WIN had 3.24 million access lines, including approximately 500,000 lines that were previously part of Valor and 132,000 that were part of the CT Communications operations that were acquired in August 2007. The company also had 830,000 broadband customers (26% of access lines). WIN operates primarily in rural markets in the southern U.S., such as Lexington, KY, and Lincoln NB, with an average of only 25 access lines per square mile. The company's offerings include local and long distance voice and data services, both for mostly residential customers. In addition to its wireline operations, WIN operates a directory publication business. In December 2006, WIN announced plans to split off and sell its directory operations to a private equity firm for $525 million in a tax-free transaction. The two-stage planned deal, which awaits necessary approvals and involves a debt exchange, should largely close in the fourth quarter of 2007. We believe 2007 revenues are being boosted by network asset sales to Alltel previously considered part of internal operations.

CORPORATE STRATEGY. In 2007, WIN is focused on integrating the operations of the former companies and completing another acquisition. In the third quarter of 2006, WIN consolidated call centers and IT systems and launched a new brand. The company is looking to grow by offering broadband and digital TV (through a wholesale satellite product with Echostar) to retain its wireline customers and improve revenue per customer. As of September 2007, WIN's average monthly revenue per household was $83, up 8% from a year earlier. In our view, this is a different approach than some rural telecom providers that have begun to feature a wholesale wireless offering. In 2007, WIN has been targeting customers who did not have a wireline phone and recommending its broadband product.

In August 2007, WIN completed its acquisition of CT Communications (CTCI), a telecom service provider in North Carolina, for $31.50 a share, or $585 million. CTCI had $179 million of revenue and $57 million of EBITDA in the 12 months ended March 2007. While we believe operational and capital spending synergies are attainable, we think that the above average enterprise value/EBITDA multiple adds operational risk.

Company Financials Fiscal Year Ended Dec. 31

Per Share Data ($)	2006	2005	2004	2003	2002	2001	2000	1999	1998	1997
Tangible Book Value	NM	NM	NA	NA	NA	NA	NA	NA	NA	NA
Cash Flow	1.88	2.08	NA	NA	NA	NA	NA	NA	NA	NA
Earnings	1.02	0.83	NA	NA	NA	NA	NA	NA	NA	NA
S&P Core Earnings	0.95	0.80	0.80	NA	NA	NA	NA	NA	NA	NA
Dividends	0.38	NA	NA	NA	NA	NA	NA	NA	NA	NA
Payout Ratio	37%	NA	NA	NA	NA	NA	NA	NA	NA	NA
Prices:High	14.43	NA	NA	NA	NA	NA	NA	NA	NA	NA
Prices:Low	11.13	NA	NA	NA	NA	NA	NA	NA	NA	NA
P/E Ratio:High	14	NA	NA	NA	NA	NA	NA	NA	NA	NA
P/E Ratio:Low	11	NA	NA	NA	NA	NA	NA	NA	NA	NA

Income Statement Analysis (Million $)	2006	2005	2004	2003	2002	2001	2000	1999	1998	1997
Revenue	3,033	3,414	NA	NA	NA	NA	NA	NA	NA	NA
Operating Income	1,398	1,617	NA	NA	NA	NA	NA	NA	NA	NA
Depreciation	450	593	NA	NA	NA	NA	NA	NA	NA	NA
Interest Expense	210	391	NA	NA	NA	NA	NA	NA	NA	NA
Pretax Income	722	662	NA	NA	NA	NA	NA	NA	NA	NA
Effective Tax Rate	38.3%	40.5%	NA	NA	NA	NA	NA	NA	NA	NA
Net Income	446	394	NA	NA	NA	NA	NA	NA	NA	NA
S&P Core Earnings	451	382	382	NA	NA	NA	NA	NA	NA	NA

Balance Sheet & Other Financial Data (Million $)	2006	2005	2004	2003	2002	2001	2000	1999	1998	1997
Cash	387	119	NA	NA	NA	NA	NA	NA	NA	NA
Current Assets	877	533	NA	NA	NA	NA	NA	NA	NA	NA
Total Assets	8,031	7,751	NA	NA	NA	NA	NA	NA	NA	NA
Current Liabilities	685	459	NA	NA	NA	NA	NA	NA	NA	NA
Long Term Debt	5,456	5,525	NA	NA	NA	NA	NA	NA	NA	NA
Common Equity	470	533	NA	NA	NA	NA	NA	NA	NA	NA
Total Capital	6,917	7,064	NA	NA	NA	NA	NA	NA	NA	NA
Capital Expenditures	374	NA	NA	NA	NA	NA	NA	NA	NA	NA
Cash Flow	895	987	NA	NA	NA	NA	NA	NA	NA	NA
Current Ratio	1.3	1.2	NA	NA	NA	NA	NA	NA	NA	NA
% Long Term Debt of Capitalization	78.9	78.2	NA	NA	NA	NA	NA	NA	NA	NA
% Net Income of Revenue	14.7	11.5	NA	NA	NA	NA	NA	NA	NA	NA
% Return on Assets	6.9	NA	NA	NA	NA	NA	NA	NA	NA	NA
% Return on Equity	22.5	NA	NA	NA	NA	NA	NA	NA	NA	NA

Data as orig reptd.; bef. results of disc opers/spec. items. Per share data adj. for stk. divs.; EPS diluted. E-Estimated. NA-Not Available. NM-Not Meaningful. NR-Not Ranked. UR-Under Review.

Office: 4001 N Rodney Parham Rd, Little Rock, AR 72212-2442.
Telephone: 501-748-7000.
Website: http://www.windstream.com
Chrmn: F.X. Frantz

Pres & CEO: J.R. Gardner
COO: K.D. Paglusch
EVP & CFO: B.K. Whittington
EVP & General Counsel: J.P. Fletcher

Investor Contact: M. Michaels (501-748-7578)
Board Members: S. E. Beall III, D. E. Foster, F. X. Frantz, J. R. Gardner, J. T. Hinson, J. K. Jones, W. A. Montgomery, F. E. Reed, A. J. de Nicola

Founded: 2000
Domicile: Delaware
Employees: 8,017

The McGraw-Hill Companies

WM. Wrigley Jr. Co

STANDARD &POOR'S

S&P Recommendation **SELL** ★★☆☆☆	Price $62.47 (as of Nov 23, 2007)	12-Mo. Target Price $60.00	Investment Style Large-Cap Growth

GICS Sector Consumer Staples
Sub-Industry Packaged Foods & Meats

Summary This company is the world's largest producer of chewing gum, with approximately 60% of the U.S. market. The Wrigley family controls 51% of the supervoting Class B stock.

Key Stock Statistics (Source S&P, Vickers, company reports)

52-Wk Range	$69.12– 48.52	S&P Oper. EPS 2007**E**	2.25	Market Capitalization(B)	$13.409
Trailing 12-Month EPS	$2.18	S&P Oper. EPS 2008**E**	2.48	Yield (%)	1.86
Trailing 12-Month P/E	28.7	P/E on S&P Oper. EPS 2007**E**	27.8	Dividend Rate/Share	$1.16
$10K Invested 5 Yrs Ago	$18,679	Common Shares Outstg. (M)	275.0	Institutional Ownership (%)	74

Beta	0.31
S&P 3-Yr. Proj. EPS CAGR(%)	10.00
S&P Credit Rating	NA

Price Performance

30-Week Mov. Avg. · · · 10-Week Mov. Avg. - - **GAAP Earnings vs. Previous Year** Volume Above Avg. STARS
12-Mo. Target Price — Relative Strength — ▲ Up ▼ Down ► No Change Below Avg. ★

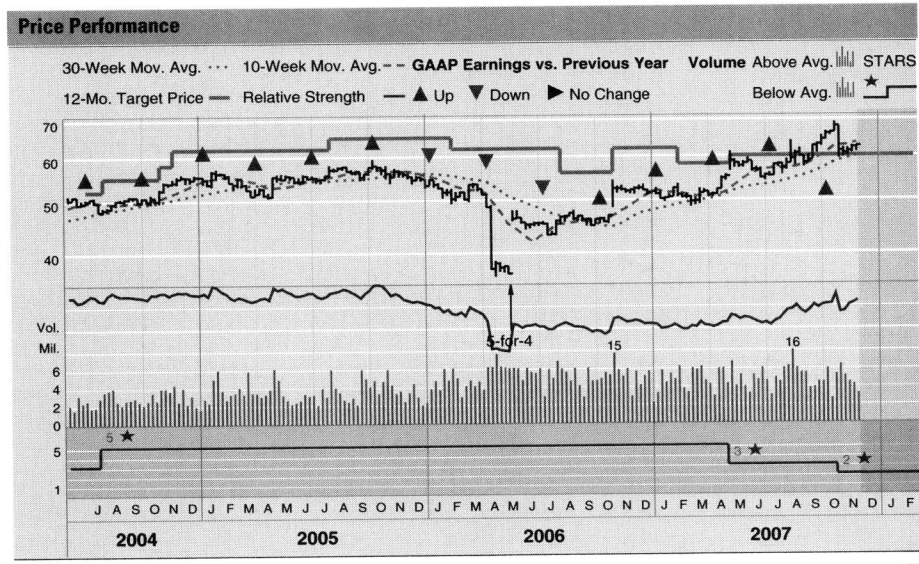

Options: ASE

Qualitative Risk Assessment

LOW	MEDIUM	HIGH

Our risk assessment for WM. Wrigley Jr. Company reflects the relatively stable nature of the company's end markets, our view of a strong balance sheet and cash flow, leading global market shares, and an S&P Quality Ranking of A+ that reflects above-average growth and stability in earnings and dividends.

Quantitative Evaluations

S&P Quality Ranking   A+

D	C	B-	B	B+	A-	A	A+

Relative Strength Rank   STRONG

81

LOWEST = 1   HIGHEST = 99

Revenue/Earnings Data

Revenue (Million $)

	1Q	2Q	3Q	4Q	Year
2007	1,256	1,378	1,333	--	--
2006	1,076	1,207	1,179	1,224	4,686
2005	950.4	1,040	1,062	1,106	4,159
2004	812.2	957.9	916.7	961.9	3,649
2003	672.4	792.6	782.9	821.2	3,069
2002	599.0	708.5	699.5	739.3	2,746

Earnings Per Share ($)

2007	0.52	0.61	0.59	E0.54	E2.25
2006	0.40	0.51	0.53	0.46	1.90
2005	0.46	0.58	0.46	0.34	1.83
2004	0.39	0.50	0.45	0.42	1.75
2003	0.34	0.45	0.40	0.39	1.58
2002	0.30	0.39	0.35	0.38	1.42

Fiscal year ended Dec. 31. Next earnings report expected: Early February. EPS Estimates based on S&P Operating Earnings; historical GAAP earnings are as reported.

Highlights

➤ The STARS recommendation for WWY has recently been changed to 2 (sell) from 3 (hold). The Highlights section of this Stock Report will be updated accordingly.

Investment Rationale/Risk

➤ The Investment Rationale/Risk section of this Stock Report will be updated shortly. For the latest News story on WWY from MarketScope, see below.

➤ 10/24/07 02:30 pm EDT... S&P DOWNGRADES WRIGLEY SHARES TO SELL FROM HOLD (WWY 62.28**): Before special items, $0.59 vs. $0.55 Q3 EPS matches our estimate. Sales growth of 13% includes contributions from currency fluctuation and acquisition. WWY appears pleased with launch of its new "5" gum, but we have some concern about overall 2% sales drop in North America, as trade inventory levels dropped. Flattish overall gross margin (before charges) is disappointing. We are keeping our '07 EPS estimate, before items, at $2.25, and 08's at $2.48. Our 12-month target price remains $60, leaving no upside from current level. Indicated dividend yield is about 1.9%. / T.Graves-CFA

Dividend Data (Dates: mm/dd Payment Date: mm/dd/yy)

Amount ($)	Date Decl.	Ex-Div. Date	Stk. of Record	Payment Date
0.290	02/06	04/11	04/13	05/01/07
0.290	05/24	07/11	07/13	08/01/07
0.290	08/15	10/11	10/15	11/01/07
0.290	10/24	01/11	01/15	02/01/08

Dividends have been paid since 1913. Source: Company reports.

WM. Wrigley Jr. Co

STANDARD &POOR'S

Business Summary August 27, 2007

CORPORATE OVERVIEW. Since 1891, this company has concentrated its operations largely on the manufacture and marketing of chewing gum. In June 2005, Wrigley diversified its business with the acquisition of the Life Savers, Altoids, Creme Savers and Sugus brands. In our view, a larger presence in the mints, hard candy and chewy candy categories has broadened the company's opportunities for the development of new products and increased efficiencies.

Principal WWY products include: Wrigley's Spearmint; Doublemint; Juicy Fruit; Big Red; Winterfresh; and Extra. Other products include: Airwaves; Freedent; Ice White; Orbit; P.K.; and Hubba Bubba (bubble gum).

By geographic area, sales contributions in 2006 were: North America, consisting of the U.S. and Canada, 37%; the EMEAI region, consisting of Europe, the

Middle East, Africa and India, 44%; Asia, 13%; and all other, 5.1%. In alphabetical order, WWY's 10 largest revenue producing countries outside of the U.S. in 2006 were Australia, Canada, China, France, Germany, Poland, Russia, Spain, Taiwan, and the United Kingdom. WWY brands are sold in more than 180 countries.

In October 2006, Wrigley announced the appointment of William Perez as president and CEO; former WWY president and CEO William Wrigley, Jr. remains chairman of the board.

Company Financials Fiscal Year Ended Dec. 31

Per Share Data ($)	2006	2005	2004	2003	2002	2001	2000	1999	1998	1997
Tangible Book Value	2.98	2.66	7.01	6.48	5.42	4.54	2.01	3.98	3.98	3.40
Cash Flow	2.62	2.49	2.26	2.01	1.73	1.53	1.36	1.27	1.24	1.11
Earnings	1.90	1.83	1.75	1.58	1.42	1.29	1.16	1.06	1.05	0.94
S&P Core Earnings	1.91	1.80	1.73	1.56	1.33	1.20	NA	NA	NA	NA
Dividends	1.06	0.86	0.74	0.69	0.64	0.60	0.56	0.53	0.52	0.47
Payout Ratio	56%	47%	42%	44%	45%	46%	48%	50%	49%	50%
Prices:High	54.71	59.48	55.99	47.12	47.12	42.64	38.65	40.25	41.72	32.82
Prices:Low	43.00	50.62	43.84	40.84	35.37	34.35	23.94	26.60	28.37	21.82
P/E Ratio:High	29	32	32	30	33	33	33	38	40	35
P/E Ratio:Low	23	28	25	26	25	27	21	25	27	23

Income Statement Analysis (Million $)	2006	2005	2004	2003	2002	2001	2000	1999	1998	1997
Revenue	4,686	4,159	3,649	3,069	2,746	2,430	2,146	2,062	2,005	1,937
Operating Income	1,067	952	862	769	671	582	521	489	468	432
Depreciation	200	175	142	120	85.6	68.3	57.9	61.3	55.8	50.4
Interest Expense	61.8	31.6	Nil	Nil	Nil	Nil	Nil	0.71	0.62	0.96
Pretax Income	769	755	720	652	583	527	479	444	441	394
Effective Tax Rate	31.2%	31.5%	31.6%	31.6%	31.2%	31.2%	31.4%	30.7%	30.9%	31.1%
Net Income	529	517	493	446	402	363	329	308	305	272
S&P Core Earnings	532	508	488	438	374	336	NA	NA	NA	NA

Balance Sheet & Other Financial Data (Million $)	2006	2005	2004	2003	2002	2001	2000	1999	1998	1997
Cash	254	258	629	505	279	308	301	288	215	207
Current Assets	1,481	1,306	1,506	1,291	1,006	914	829	804	843	798
Total Assets	4,662	4,460	3,167	2,520	2,108	1,766	1,575	1,548	1,521	1,343
Current Liabilities	1,027	981	718	465	386	332	288	252	219	226
Long Term Debt	1,000	1,000	Nil	Nil	Nil	Nil	Nil	Nil	Nil	Nil
Common Equity	2,388	2,214	2,179	1,821	1,523	1,276	1,133	1,139	1,157	985
Total Capital	3,388	3,325	2,267	1,904	1,593	1,319	1,173	1,184	1,197	1,016
Capital Expenditures	328	282	220	220	217	182	125	128	148	127
Cash Flow	729	693	635	566	487	431	387	369	360	322
Current Ratio	1.4	1.3	2.1	2.8	2.6	2.7	2.9	3.2	3.9	3.5
% Long Term Debt of Capitalization	29.5	30.1	Nil	Nil	Nil	Nil	Nil	Nil	Nil	Nil
% Net Income of Revenue	11.3	12.4	13.5	14.5	14.6	14.9	15.3	14.9	15.2	14.0
% Return on Assets	11.7	13.6	17.3	19.3	20.7	21.7	21.1	20.1	21.3	21.1
% Return on Equity	23.0	23.5	24.7	26.7	28.7	30.1	29.0	26.8	28.4	28.9

Data as orig reptd.; bef. results of disc opers/spec. items. Per share data adj. for stk. divs.; EPS diluted. E-Estimated. NA-Not Available. NM-Not Meaningful. NR-Not Ranked. UR-Under Review.

Office: 410 North Michigan Avenue, Chicago, IL, USA 60611.
Telephone: 312-644-2121.
Website: http://www.wrigley.com
Exec Chrmn: W. Wrigley, Jr.

Pres & CEO: W.D. Perez
SVP & CFO: R. Gamoran
SVP & Chief Admin Officer: D. Petrovich
VP & Treas: A.J. Schneider

Investor Contact: L. Macon (312-645-3993)
Board Members: J. F. Bard, H. B. Bernick, T. A. Knowlton, W. D. Perez, J. Rau, M. R. Rich, S. B. Sample, A. Shumate, R. K. Smucker, W. Wrigley, Jr.

Founded: 1910
Domicile: Delaware
Employees: 15,800

The McGraw·Hill Companies

Wyeth

STANDARD & POOR'S

S&P Recommendation	HOLD ★★★☆☆	Price $46.90 (as of Nov 23, 2007)	12-Mo. Target Price $52.00	Investment Style Large-Cap Growth

GICS Sector Health Care
Sub-Industry Pharmaceuticals

Summary Wyeth is a leading maker of prescription drugs and OTC medications.

Key Stock Statistics (Source S&P, Vickers, company reports)

52-Wk Range	$62.20–43.65	S&P Oper. EPS 2007 **E** 3.53	Market Capitalization(B) $63.064	Beta	0.85
Trailing 12-Month EPS	$3.26	S&P Oper. EPS 2008 **E** 3.85	Yield (%) 2.39	S&P 3-Yr. Proj. EPS CAGR(%)	10.00
Trailing 12-Month P/E	14.4	P/E on S&P Oper. EPS 2007 **E** 13.3	Dividend Rate/Share $1.12	S&P Credit Rating	A+
$10K Invested 5 Yrs Ago	$14,403	Common Shares Outstg. (M) 1,344.6	Institutional Ownership (%) 81		

Price Performance

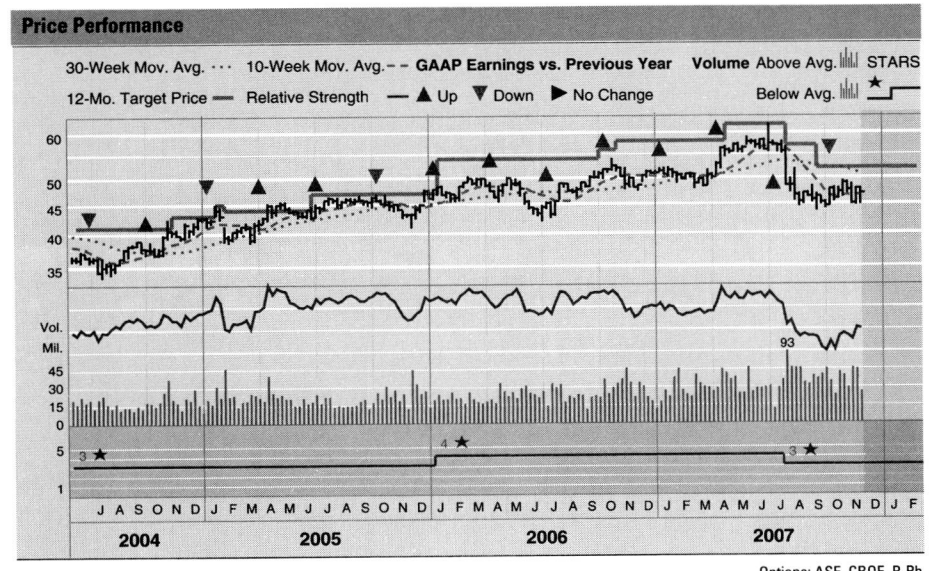

30-Week Mov. Avg. ··· 10-Week Mov. Avg. - - GAAP Earnings vs. Previous Year Volume Above Avg. STARS
12-Mo. Target Price — Relative Strength — ▲ Up ▼ Down ▶ No Change Below Avg.

Options: ASE, CBOE, P, Ph

Analysis prepared by **Herman B. Saftlas** on October 24, 2007, when the stock traded at **$ 47.56**.

Qualitative Risk Assessment

LOW | **MEDIUM** | HIGH

Our risk assessment reflects that Wyeth is subject to the inherent risks associated with the pharmaceuticals business, which include generic threats to branded drugs, as well as pipeline and regulatory risks. However, although the company still has significant potential diet drug liability risk, we believe it has made meaningful progress in resolving diet drug litigation, with planned agreements to settle most of its remaining outstanding cases.

Quantitative Evaluations

S&P Quality Ranking B

D | C | B- | **B** | B+ | A- | A | A+

Relative Strength Rank STRONG
72
LOWEST = 1   HIGHEST = 99

Highlights

➤ We project revenues will advance about 5% in 2008, driven largely by growth in Prevnar pediatric vaccine, and Enbrel, an anti-inflammatory agent. We think both products will continue to benefit from strong consumer demand and greater penetration of foreign markets. We also expect greater contributions from new products, which include Tygacil antibiotic, Pristiq antidepressant, and Torisel anticancer agent. However, we think sales of older products such as Effexor and Protonix will decline. We look for sales of animal health and consumer products to remain relatively flat.

➤ We expect 2008 gross margins to be roughly comparable with the 74% we forecast for 2007. Helped by ongoing cost controls, SG&A will likely account for a lower percentage of sales in 2008. However, we project higher R&D spending on pipeline drugs. We forecast that interest expense will increase, while we look for other income to decline.

➤ We expect the tax rate to remain near the 28.5% rate that we forecast for 2007. We project operating EPS of $3.85 for 2008, up from the $3.53 we estimate for 2007.

Investment Rationale/Risk

➤ Wyeth recently sustained a legal setback with a U.S. court that denied its motion for an injunction to prevent generic drugmaker Teva from launching a generic version of Protonix (we estimate 2007 sales of $1.9 billion). However, it remains unclear to us whether Teva will launch at-risk, given unresolved patent litigation. WYE had a few pipeline setbacks in recent months, but we think pipeline news flow may improve in 2008. We recommend holding the shares, which recently traded at 2.5X our 2008 sales forecast, and 12.4X our 2008 EPS estimate, both representing discounts to peer averages.

➤ Risks to our recommendation and target price include possible future pipeline setbacks, as well as earlier-than-expected losses of patent protection on key products.

➤ Our 12-month target price of $52 applies a modest discount to peers P/E of 13.5X to our 2008 EPS estimate. Our target price also approximates our calculation of WYE's intrinsic value based on our DCF model, which assumes decelerating free cash flow growth over 10 years and a WACC of 7.3%. The shares recently yielded about 2.4%.

Revenue/Earnings Data

Revenue (Million $)

	1Q	2Q	3Q	4Q	Year
2007	5,369	5,648	5,620	--	--
2006	4,838	5,157	5,136	5,220	20,351
2005	4,579	4,714	4,716	4,747	18,756
2004	4,015	4,223	4,472	4,648	17,358
2003	3,689	3,747	4,082	4,333	15,851
2002	3,644	3,503	3,624	3,814	14,584

Earnings Per Share ($)

2007	0.92	0.87	0.84	E0.86	E3.53
2006	0.82	0.78	0.85	0.63	3.08
2005	0.80	0.72	0.64	0.54	2.70
2004	0.56	0.62	1.06	-1.32	0.91
2003	0.96	0.65	-0.32	0.25	1.54
2002	0.65	0.45	1.05	1.18	3.33

Fiscal year ended Dec. 31. Next earnings report expected: Late January. EPS Estimates based on S&P Operating Earnings; historical GAAP earnings are as reported.

Dividend Data (Dates: mm/dd Payment Date: mm/dd/yy)

Amount ($)	Date Decl.	Ex-Div. Date	Stk. of Record	Payment Date
0.260	01/25	02/09	02/13	03/01/07
0.260	04/26	05/09	05/11	06/01/07
0.260	06/28	08/09	08/13	09/04/07
0.280	09/27	11/08	11/13	12/03/07

Dividends have been paid since 1919. Source: Company reports.

Wyeth

STANDARD &POOR'S

Business Summary October 24, 2007

CORPORATE OVERVIEW. Wyeth (formerly American Home Products) is a leading producer of prescription pharmaceuticals, as well as consumer medications and animal health products. WYE's corporate strategy in recent years has focused on higher-margin products, while divesting less profitable businesses. Human prescription pharmaceuticals accounted for 83% of total sales in 2006, consumer health care products 12%, and animal health products 5%. Foreign operations are significant, accounting for 46% of sales in 2006.

WYE's largest selling product is Effexor (sales of $3.7 billion in 2006), an antidepressant that works on both serotonin and norepinephrine. Other key products include Protonix ($1.8 billion), a treatment for heartburn caused by gastroesophageal erosive reflux disease; Prevnar ($2.0 billion), a broad-based pediatric vaccine; Enbrel ($1.5 billion), a treatment for rheumatoid arthritis that is marketed in conjunction with Amgen, Inc.; and Zosyn/Tazocin ($972 million), an injectable penicillin antibiotic. The company also offers Cordarone, Veralan and Ziac cardiovasculars; Lodine, Oruvail and Naprelan antiarthritics; Suprax, and Minocin anti-infectives; and Refacto, a factor VIII treatment for hemophilia A.

WYE remains a leader in women's drugs, with its line of Premarin estrogen and PremPro/Premphase estrogen/progestin hormone replacement therapy (HRT) products (sales of $1.1 billion in 2006), and oral contraceptives ($455 million) such as Triphasil, Lo/Ovral and Alesse. The HRT business was negatively affected by clinical studies released in mid-2002 that highlighted cardiovascular and cancer risks with HRT products.

A full line of pediatric and adult nutritional products (sales of $1.2 billion) is offered, including infant formulas and adult supplements. The Whitehall and A.H. Robins divisions offer a broad range of OTC medications such as Advil and Anacin analgesics, Dimetapp and Robitussin for coughs and colds, Primatene for asthma, Preparation H for hemorrhoids, and Centrum and Solgar vitamins.

Company Financials Fiscal Year Ended Dec. 31

Per Share Data ($)	2006	2005	2004	2003	2002	2001	2000	1999	1998	1997
Tangible Book Value	7.71	6.23	4.33	4.01	3.22	0.17	NM	NM	1.23	NM
Cash Flow	3.72	3.26	1.37	1.94	3.72	2.17	-0.28	-0.42	2.35	4.18
Earnings	3.08	2.70	0.91	1.54	3.33	1.72	-0.69	-0.94	1.85	1.56
S&P Core Earnings	3.11	2.49	2.62	1.78	1.73	1.92	NA	NA	NA	NA
Dividends	1.01	0.94	0.92	0.92	0.92	0.92	0.92	0.91	0.87	0.83
Payout Ratio	33%	35%	101%	60%	28%	53%	NM	NM	47%	53%
Prices:High	54.13	47.88	44.70	49.95	66.51	63.80	65.25	70.25	58.75	42.44
Prices:Low	41.91	38.48	33.50	32.75	28.25	52.00	39.38	36.50	37.75	28.50
P/E Ratio:High	18	18	49	32	20	37	NM	NM	32	27
P/E Ratio:Low	14	14	37	21	8	30	NM	NM	20	18

Income Statement Analysis (Million $)	2006	2005	2004	2003	2002	2001	2000	1999	1998	1997
Revenue	20,351	18,756	17,358	15,851	14,584	14,129	13,263	13,550	13,463	14,196
Operating Income	5,955	5,244	4,773	4,450	4,060	4,299	3,808	3,759	3,931	3,946
Depreciation	803	787	622	538	485	608	534	682	665	701
Interest Expense	499	357	110	103	202	146	239	343	323	462
Pretax Income	5,430	4,781	-130	2,362	6,097	2,869	-1,101	-1,926	3,585	2,815
Effective Tax Rate	22.7%	23.5%	NM	13.1%	27.1%	20.3%	NM	NM	31.0%	27.4%
Net Income	4,197	3,656	1,234	2,051	4,447	2,285	-901	-1,227	2,474	2,043
S&P Core Earnings	4,228	3,372	3,542	2,379	2,313	2,551	NA	NA	NA	NA

Balance Sheet & Other Financial Data (Million $)	2006	2005	2004	2003	2002	2001	2000	1999	1998	1997
Cash	8,727	8,235	6,489	7,180	3,947	3,027	2,985	2,413	1,301	1,051
Current Assets	17,514	18,045	14,438	14,962	11,596	9,767	10,181	9,738	7,956	7,361
Total Assets	36,479	35,841	33,630	31,032	25,995	22,968	21,092	23,906	21,079	20,825
Current Liabilities	7,222	9,948	8,536	8,430	5,476	7,257	9,742	7,110	4,211	4,327
Long Term Debt	9,097	9,231	7,792	8,076	7,546	7,357	2,395	3,669	3,859	5,032
Common Equity	14,653	11,994	9,848	9,294	8,156	4,073	2,818	6,216	9,615	8,176
Total Capital	23,749	21,226	17,640	17,371	15,702	11,430	5,213	9,885	13,695	13,415
Capital Expenditures	1,290	1,081	1,255	1,909	1,932	1,924	1,682	1,000	810	830
Cash Flow	5,000	4,443	1,856	2,589	4,932	2,893	-367	-545	3,139	2,744
Current Ratio	2.4	1.8	1.7	1.8	2.1	1.3	1.0	1.4	1.9	1.7
% Long Term Debt of Capitalization	38.3	43.5	44.2	46.5	48.1	64.4	45.9	37.1	28.2	37.5
% Net Income of Revenue	20.6	19.5	NM	12.9	30.5	16.2	NM	NM	18.4	14.4
% Return on Assets	11.6	10.5	NM	7.2	18.2	10.4	NM	NM	11.8	9.8
% Return on Equity	31.5	33.5	NM	23.5	72.7	66.3	NM	NM	27.8	27.0

Data as orig reptd.; bef. results of disc opers/spec. items. Per share data adj. for stk. divs.; EPS diluted. E-Estimated. NA-Not Available. NM-Not Meaningful. NR-Not Ranked. UR-Under Review.

Office: 5 Giralda Farms, Madison, NJ 07940-1021.
Telephone: 973-660-5000.
Website: http://www.wyeth.com
Chrmn & CEO: R. Essner

Pres, Vice Chrmn & COO: B.J. Poussot
Vice Chrmn & CFO: K.J. Martin
SVP & General Counsel: L.V. Stein
VP & Secy: E.M. Lach

Investor Contact: J.R. Victoria (973-660-5000)
Board Members: R. Essner, J. D. Feerick, F. D. Fergusson, V. F. Ganzi, R. S. Langer, J. P. Mascotte, R. J. McGuire, M. L. Polan, B. Poussot, G. L. Rogers, I. G. Seidenberg, W. V. Shipley, J. R. Torell, III

Founded: 1926
Domicile: Delaware
Employees: 50,060

Wyndham Worldwide Corp

STANDARD &POOR'S

S&P Recommendation `HOLD` ★ ★ ★ ☆ ☆

Price $28.28 (as of Nov 23, 2007)	**12-Mo. Target Price** $35.00	**Investment Style** Large-Cap Blend

GICS Sector Consumer Discretionary
Sub-Industry Hotels, Resorts & Cruise Lines

Summary This company's operations include the sale of interests in vacation ownership resorts; facilitating the exchange and rental of access to vacation properties; and the franchising of hotels.

Key Stock Statistics (Source S&P, Vickers, company reports)

52-Wk Range	$39.40– 26.73	S&P Oper. EPS 2007**E**	2.10	Market Capitalization(B)	$5.051	Beta	NA
Trailing 12-Month EPS	$2.10	S&P Oper. EPS 2008**E**	2.35	Yield (%)	0.57	S&P 3-Yr. Proj. EPS CAGR(%)	8.00
Trailing 12-Month P/E	13.5	P/E on S&P Oper. EPS 2007**E**	13.5	Dividend Rate/Share	$0.16	S&P Credit Rating	BBB
$10K Invested 5 Yrs Ago	NA	Common Shares Outstg. (M)	178.6	Institutional Ownership (%)	87		

Price Performance

30-Week Mov. Avg. ··· 10-Week Mov. Avg. -- **GAAP Earnings vs. Previous Year** Volume Above Avg. STARS
12-Mo. Target Price — Relative Strength — ▲ Up ▼ Down ▶ No Change Below Avg.

Options: CBOE, Ph

Analysis prepared by **Mark S. Basham** on November 02, 2007, when the stock traded at **$ 31.78**.

Highlights

➤ We project revenue of about $4.45 billion in 2007, up 16% from $3.84 billion in 2006. In the first nine months of 2007, sales of vacation ownership units and unit upgrades were up 22% year over year; we do not think this is sustainable. Vacation exchange and rental transactions increased 3.1%, while a 12% increase in average net price per rental included a 5 point favorable impact from foreign currency movements. Lodging revenues rose 8%, reflecting the 2006 acquisition of Baymont Inn & Suites and a 4% increase in RevPAR.

➤ Excluding the effect from adjustments in accrued liabilities for certain litigation in which WYN's former parent Cendant is named as the defendant, as well as other costs and changes in reserves established at the time WYN separated from Cendant, we estimate 2007 EPS of $2.10, vs. $1.70 on a similar basis in 2006.

➤ We estimate 2008 EPS of $2.35, on a 9% increase in revenues. We expect vacation rental and hotel operations to perform relatively well, but we think economic uncertainty and tighter credit conditions will lead in marginally higher vacation ownership sales.

Investment Rationale/Risk

➤ Our hold opinion reflects our increasing concern about the vacation ownership market, as we expect market conditions to force WYN to adopt tougher standards to qualify buyers. Our recommendation reflects our view that the shares are fairly valued at a discount on a P/E basis versus hotel peers, due to WYN's relatively greater exposure to the vacation market.

➤ Risks to our recommendation and target price include weaker than expected consumer confidence and a related negative impact on vacation spending by consumers. Also, future travel activity could be negatively affected by higher aviation fuel costs or fears of terrorism.

➤ We believe the stock should have lower P/E and enterprise value multiples than some lodging industry peers in our coverage universe. We think a target P/E of 15X applied to our 2008 EPS estimate is appropriate, given that lodging group valuations have contracted since mid-July. Our 12-month target price of $35 reflects a P/E multiple of about 15X applied to our 2008 EPS estimate of $2.35.

Qualitative Risk Assessment

LOW	**MEDIUM**	HIGH

Our risk assessment reflects our view that the company's business is likely to be sensitive to changes in consumer confidence and travel conditions (including threats of terrorism), offset by the company's ability to attract and retain affiliated properties.

Quantitative Evaluations

S&P Quality Ranking NR

D	C	B-	B	B+	A-	A	A+

Relative Strength Rank MODERATE

37

LOWEST = 1   HIGHEST = 99

Revenue/Earnings Data

Revenue (Million $)

	1Q	2Q	3Q	4Q	Year
2007	1,012	1,100	1,216	--	--
2006	870.0	955.0	1,047	970.0	3,842
2005	--	--	--	--	3,471
2004	--	--	--	--	--
2003	--	--	--	--	--
2002	--	--	--	--	--

Earnings Per Share ($)

2007	0.45	0.52	0.65	E0.44	E2.10
2006	0.46	0.37	0.45	0.48	1.77
2005	--	--	--	--	1.73
2004	--	--	--	--	--
2003	--	--	--	--	--
2002	--	--	--	--	--

Fiscal year ended Dec. 31. Next earnings report expected: Mid February. EPS Estimates based on S&P Operating Earnings; historical GAAP earnings are as reported.

Dividend Data (Dates: mm/dd Payment Date: mm/dd/yy)

Amount ($)	Date Decl.	Ex-Div. Date	Stk. of Record	Payment Date
0.040	08/01	08/09	08/13	09/04/07
0.040	10/25	11/08	11/13	12/04/07

Dividends have been paid since 2007. Source: Company reports.

The McGraw·Hill Companies

Wyndham Worldwide Corp

STANDARD
&POOR'S

Business Summary November 02, 2007

CORPORATE OVERVIEW. This company, which operates lodging, vacation exchange and rental and vacation ownership businesses, was previously part of Cendant Corp. On July 31, 2006, Cendant distributed one share of WYN common stock for every five shares of Cendant common stock outstanding as of the close of business July 21.

The Wyndham Hotel Group franchises hotels in various segments of the lodging industry and provides property management services to owners of upscale branded hotels. As of September 30, 2007, WYN's lodging business had 6,460 franchised hotels with approximately 541,000 rooms in operation. At that time, there were also about 940 hotels with over 104,000 rooms in the development pipeline, of which 45% represented new construction, as opposed to conversion from other property brands, and 30% were in international markets.

WYN's RCI Global Vacation Network provides vacation exchange products and services to developers, managers and owners of intervals of vacation ownership interests, and markets vacation rental properties. WYN's vacation exchange and rental business has access for specified periods, often on an exclusive basis, to over 60,000 vacation properties located in 100 countries. Membership as of September 30, 2007, was over 3.4 million.

WYN's vacation ownership segment includes marketing and sales of vacation ownership interests, consumer financing in connection with the purchase by individuals of vacation ownership interests, property management services for property owners' associations, and development and acquisition of vacation ownership resorts. WYN's vacation ownership business is now affiliated with the Wyndham brand in a deemphasis of the Fairfield and Trendwest brands. WYN has developed or acquired about 140 vacation ownership resorts in North America, the Caribbean and the South Pacific, that serve more than 800,000 owners of vacation ownership interests and other real estate interests.

CORPORATE STRATEGY. We expect WYN's growth strategy to include efforts to add more properties to its hotel systems, especially outside of North America and in the middle and upscale segments of the North American market; to add more vacation rental properties in North America; and to leverage the Wyndham name in the higher-end vacation ownership market.

Company Financials Fiscal Year Ended Dec. 31

Per Share Data ($)	2006	2005	2004	2003	2002	2001	2000	1999	1998	1997
Tangible Book Value	NM	NM	NA	NA	NA	NA	NA	NA	NA	NA
Cash Flow	2.63	2.37	NA	NA	NA	NA	NA	NA	NA	NA
Earnings	1.77	1.73	NA	NA	NA	NA	NA	NA	NA	NA
S&P Core Earnings	1.75	1.97	NA	NA	NA	NA	NA	NA	NA	NA
Dividends	Nil	Nil	NA	NA	NA	NA	NA	NA	NA	NA
Payout Ratio	Nil	Nil	NA	NA	NA	NA	NA	NA	NA	NA
Prices:High	34.87	NA	NA	NA	NA	NA	NA	NA	NA	NA
Prices:Low	25.48	NA	NA	NA	NA	NA	NA	NA	NA	NA
P/E Ratio:High	20	NA	NA	NA	NA	NA	NA	NA	NA	NA
P/E Ratio:Low	14	NA	NA	NA	NA	NA	NA	NA	NA	NA

Income Statement Analysis (Million $)	2006	2005	2004	2003	2002	2001	2000	1999	1998	1997
Revenue	3,842	3,471	NA	NA	NA	NA	NA	NA	NA	NA
Operating Income	824	699	NA	NA	NA	NA	NA	NA	NA	NA
Depreciation	148	135	NA	NA	NA	NA	NA	NA	NA	NA
Interest Expense	67.0	41.0	NA	NA	NA	NA	NA	NA	NA	NA
Pretax Income	542	523	NA	NA	NA	NA	NA	NA	NA	NA
Effective Tax Rate	35.1%	29.8%	NA	NA	NA	NA	NA	NA	NA	NA
Net Income	352	367	NA	NA	NA	NA	NA	NA	NA	NA
S&P Core Earnings	352	419	NA	NA	NA	NA	NA	NA	NA	NA

Balance Sheet & Other Financial Data (Million $)	2006	2005	2004	2003	2002	2001	2000	1999	1998	1997
Cash	269	106	NA	NA	NA	NA	NA	NA	NA	NA
Current Assets	2,052	1,874	NA	NA	NA	NA	NA	NA	NA	NA
Total Assets	9,520	8,590	NA	NA	NA	NA	NA	NA	NA	NA
Current Liabilities	1,977	2,212	NA	NA	NA	NA	NA	NA	NA	NA
Long Term Debt	1,322	1,733	NA	NA	NA	NA	NA	NA	NA	NA
Common Equity	3,559	3,464	NA	NA	NA	NA	NA	NA	NA	NA
Total Capital	5,663	5,987	NA	NA	NA	NA	NA	NA	NA	NA
Capital Expenditures	191	134	NA	NA	NA	NA	NA	NA	NA	NA
Cash Flow	500	502	NA	NA	NA	NA	NA	NA	NA	NA
Current Ratio	1.0	0.9	NA	NA	NA	NA	NA	NA	NA	NA
% Long Term Debt of Capitalization	23.3	28.9	NA	NA	NA	NA	NA	NA	NA	NA
% Net Income of Revenue	9.2	10.5	NA	NA	NA	NA	NA	NA	NA	NA
% Return on Assets	3.8	NA	NA	NA	NA	NA	NA	NA	NA	NA
% Return on Equity	8.2	NA	NA	NA	NA	NA	NA	NA	NA	NA

Data as orig reptd.; bef. results of disc opers/spec. items. Per share data adj. for stk. divs.; EPS diluted. E-Estimated. NA-Not Available. NM-Not Meaningful. NR-Not Ranked. UR-Under Review.

Office: Seven Sylvan Way, Parsippany, NJ 07054.
Telephone: 973-753-6000.
Website: http://www.wyndhamworldwide.com
Chrmn & CEO: S.P. Holmes

EVP & CFO: V.M. Wilson
EVP & General Counsel: S.G. McLester
SVP & Chief Acctg Officer: N. Rossi
SVP & Secy: L.A. Feldman

Investor Contact: M. Happer (973-753-5500)
Board Members: M. J. Biblowit, J. E. Buckman, G. Herrera, S. P. Holmes, B. Mulroney, P. D. Richards, M. H. Wargotz

Founded: 2003
Domicile: Delaware
Employees: 30,100

Xcel Energy Inc.

STANDARD &POOR'S

S&P Recommendation BUY ★★★★☆

Price	12-Mo. Target Price	Investment Style
$22.16 (as of Nov 23, 2007)	$24.00	Large-Cap Value

GICS Sector Utilities
Sub-Industry Multi-Utilities

Summary This energy holding company was created through the August 2000 merger of Minneapolis-based Northern States Power and Denver-based New Century Energies.

Key Stock Statistics (Source S&P, Vickers, company reports)

52-Wk Range	$25.03–19.59	S&P Oper. EPS 2007E	1.40	Market Capitalization(B)	$9.306	Beta	0.64
Trailing 12-Month EPS	$1.29	S&P Oper. EPS 2008E	1.50	Yield (%)	4.15	S&P 3-Yr. Proj. EPS CAGR(%)	6.00
Trailing 12-Month P/E	17.2	P/E on S&P Oper. EPS 2007E	15.8	Dividend Rate/Share	$0.92	S&P Credit Rating	BBB+
$10K Invested 5 Yrs Ago	$25,968	Common Shares Outstg. (M)	419.9	Institutional Ownership (%)	67		

Price Performance

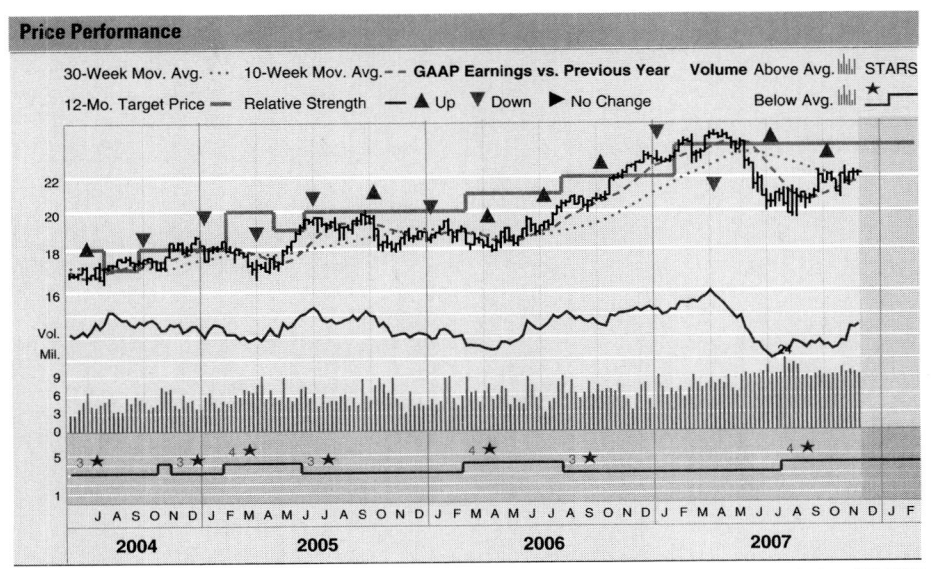

30-Week Mov. Avg. ··· 10-Week Mov. Avg. - - **GAAP Earnings vs. Previous Year** Volume Above Avg. STARS
12-Mo. Target Price — Relative Strength — ▲ Up ▼ Down ▶ No Change Below Avg.

Options: ASE, CBOE

Analysis prepared by **Justin McCann** on October 26, 2007, when the stock traded at **$21.86**.

Highlights

➤ We expect EPS from continuing operations in 2007 to increase about 2% from 2006 EPS from continuing operations of $1.35. After an effective tax rate of 24.2% in 2006, we expect an effective tax rate of about 33.5% in 2007. The $0.05 a share year-over-year increase in the first nine months of 2007 reflects rate increases, a decline in natural gas costs and relatively flat fuel and purchased power costs.

➤ We expect 2008 EPS from continuing operations to increase about 7% from the level anticipated for 2007. The projected advance would reflect expected electric and gas rate increases in Wisconsin, as well as a full year of gas rate hikes in Colorado, Minnesota and North Dakota. We expect the Public Service Commission of Wisconsin to rule on the requested rate increases in the fourth quarter of 2007 and for the new rates to be implemented in early 2008.

➤ On September 21, 2007, the U.S. government accepted the $64.4 million settlement agreement reached on June 19, 2007, with representatives of the Department of Justice and the IRS concerning a dispute over the tax deductibility of company-owned life insurance (COLI).

Investment Rationale/Risk

➤ With an above-peers yield from the dividend, we believe the stock remains attractive for above-average total return. Although the shares outperformed XEL's electric and gas utility peers in 2006 (up 24.1%), they have underperformed year to date (down around 6%). We believe the year-to-date underperformance reflected the much lower than previously expected results projected for 2007.

➤ Risks to our recommendation and target price include the possibility of an economic downturn in the company's service territory, unfavorable legislative or regulatory decisions, and a major decline in the average P/E of the group as a whole.

➤ With the dividend recently providing a yield of 4.3% (versus an average peer yield of 3.6%), we see the shares benefiting from the 15% tax rate on dividends. We expect the annual dividend to be increased at a rate of 2% to 4%, and to provide support for the shares. We see the shares trading at a discount-to-peers P/E of about 16X our 2008 EPS estimate of $1.50. Our 12-month target price is $24.

Qualitative Risk Assessment

LOW	MEDIUM	HIGH

Our risk assessment reflects the steady cash flow that we expect from the regulated electric and gas utility operations, which have a relatively low-cost power supply, our view of a generally healthy economy in most of the company's service territories, and a relatively supportive regulatory environment.

Quantitative Evaluations

S&P Quality Ranking B

D	C	B-	**B**	B+	A-	A	A+

Relative Strength Rank STRONG
85
LOWEST = 1 HIGHEST = 99

Revenue/Earnings Data

Revenue (Million $)

	1Q	2Q	3Q	4Q	Year
2007	2,764	2,267	2,400	--	--
2006	2,888	2,074	2,412	2,467	9,840
2005	2,381	2,074	2,289	2,882	9,625
2004	2,280	1,797	2,009	2,259	8,345
2003	2,086	1,722	2,020	2,110	7,938
2002	2,371	2,227	2,473	2,454	9,524

Earnings Per Share ($)

2007	0.28	0.29	0.57	E0.26	E1.40
2006	0.36	0.24	0.53	0.23	1.35
2005	0.31	0.18	0.47	0.24	1.20
2004	0.35	0.21	0.40	0.30	1.27
2003	0.31	0.14	0.43	0.36	1.23
2002	0.26	0.22	-4.10	-0.54	-4.36

Fiscal year ended Dec. 31. Next earnings report expected: Late January. EPS Estimates based on S&P Operating Earnings; historical GAAP earnings are as reported.

Dividend Data (Dates: mm/dd Payment Date: mm/dd/yy)

Amount ($)	Date Decl.	Ex-Div. Date	Stk. of Record	Payment Date
0.223	12/13	12/26	12/28	01/20/07
0.223	02/21	03/27	03/29	04/20/07
0.230	05/23	06/26	06/28	07/20/07
0.230	08/21	09/25	09/27	10/20/07

Dividends have been paid since 1910. Source: Company reports.

Xcel Energy Inc.

STANDARD &POOR'S

Business Summary October 26, 2007

CORPORATE OVERVIEW. Xcel Energy Inc. (XEL) is a holding company with a diverse portfolio of regulated and nonregulated subsidiaries. The company's utility subsidiaries are Northern States Power Company at Minnesota and Wisconsin (NSPM and NSPW respectively), Public Services Company of Colorado (PSCo), and Southwestern Public Service Co. (SPS), which provide electric and gas services in eight western and Midwestern states, and West-Gas Interstate Inc. (WGI), an interstate natural gas pipeline. XEL's nonregulated subsidiaries include Eloigne Co., which operates rental housing projects. The electric utility operations accounted for 77.3% of operating revenues in 2006; the natural gas utility operations, 21.9%; and non-regulated and other, 0.8%.

CORPORATE STRATEGY. XEL's strategy is to continue investing in the core utility business and to earn the authorized returns, and to divest those businesses not linked to the electric and natural gas operations. In its most significant transaction, the company divested its ownership interest in NRG Energy, which was involved in independent power projects in the U.S. and internation-

ally, in December 2003. XEL had divested its ownership interest in nearly all of its non-utility subsidiaries as of December 31, 2005. XEL's other remaining non-regulated non-utility business is Eloigne, which invests in projects qualifying for low income housing tax credits. XEL expects the demand for energy to increase in the future, especially in Colorado and Minnesota, and plans to invest around $8 billion over the next five years in its core operations. This would include the expansion of its wind power capacity from nearly 1,300 megawatts (mw) at the end of 2006 to at least 2,800 mw by the end of 2007. The company also has a strong focus on system reliability and continues to invest in transmission and distribution systems. To recover the cost without the delay caused by the filing of rate cases, XEL gets regulatory approval for rate riders. This ensures fair returns on the company's investment.

Company Financials Fiscal Year Ended Dec. 31

Per Share Data ($)	2006	2005	2004	2003	2002	2001	2000	1999	1998	1997
Tangible Book Value	14.28	13.11	12.99	12.95	11.44	17.91	15.79	15.67	15.58	15.23
Earnings	1.35	1.20	1.27	1.23	-4.36	2.27	1.54	1.43	1.84	1.70
S&P Core Earnings	1.35	1.15	1.21	1.03	-4.57	1.68	NA	NA	NA	NA
Dividends	0.88	0.85	0.81	0.75	1.13	1.50	1.47	1.44	1.42	1.40
Payout Ratio	65%	71%	64%	61%	NM	66%	96%	101%	77%	82%
Prices:High	23.63	20.19	18.78	17.40	28.49	31.85	30.00	27.94	30.81	29.44
Prices:Low	17.80	16.50	15.48	10.40	5.12	24.19	16.13	19.31	25.69	22.25
P/E Ratio:High	18	17	15	14	NM	14	19	20	17	17
P/E Ratio:Low	13	14	12	8	NM	11	10	14	14	13

Income Statement Analysis (Million $)										
Revenue	9,840	9,625	8,345	7,938	9,524	15,028	11,592	2,869	2,819	2,734
Depreciation	822	782	708	756	1,037	949	792	356	338	326
Maintenance	NA	NA	NA	NA	NA	NA	NA	179	181	165
Fixed Charges Coverage	2.43	2.43	2.36	2.50	1.54	2.37	2.54	1.86	2.64	7.80
Construction Credits	56.0	0.88	33.6	NA	NA	NA	NA	7.00	15.8	16.6
Effective Tax Rate	24.2%	25.8%	23.2%	23.7%	NM	28.2%	34.2%	22.8%	27.1%	29.0%
Net Income	569	499	527	510	-1,661	785	546	224	282	237
S&P Core Earnings	566	472	498	417	-1,745	579	NA	NA	NA	NA

Balance Sheet & Other Financial Data (Million $)										
Gross Property	25,219	24,054	23,160	22,371	29,119	31,770	25,000	13,478	11,049	10,460
Capital Expenditures	1,626	1,304	1,274	951	1,503	5,366	2,196	462	411	433
Net Property	15,549	14,696	14,096	13,667	18,816	21,165	15,273	8,146	6,020	5,759
Capitalization:Long Term Debt	6,450	5,898	6,493	6,519	7,044	12,612	8,060	3,653	2,051	1,879
Capitalization:% Long Term Debt	52.1	51.3	55.0	55.0	59.6	66.7	58.7	57.8	44.2	42.2
Capitalization:Preferred	105	105	105	105	105	105	105	104	105	200
Capitalization:% Preferred	0.85	0.91	0.89	0.89	0.89	0.56	0.76	1.65	2.26	4.50
Capitalization:Common	5,817	5,484	5,203	5,222	4,665	6,194	5,562	2,558	2,482	2,372
Capitalization:% Common	47.0	47.7	44.1	44.1	39.5	32.8	40.5	40.5	53.5	53.3
Total Capital	14,751	13,813	14,019	14,017	13,303	22,040	15,996	7,246	5,581	5,382
% Operating Ratio	89.9	98.6	88.8	88.1	78.0	87.1	87.0	85.9	85.6	85.0
% Earned on Net Property	7.8	13.0	7.8	8.0	13.0	10.7	11.2	4.8	6.2	NA
% Return on Revenue	5.8	5.2	6.3	6.4	NM	5.2	4.7	7.8	10.0	8.7
% Return on Invested Capital	7.4	6.9	7.0	7.3	12.4	10.9	10.3	7.5	11.5	9.2
% Return on Common Equity	10.1	9.2	10.1	10.1	NM	13.5	10.0	8.7	11.4	NA

Data as orig reptd.; bef. results of disc opers/spec. items. Per share data adj. for stk. divs.; EPS diluted. E-Estimated. NA-Not Available. NM-Not Meaningful. NR-Not Ranked. UR-Under Review.

Office: 414 Nicollet Mall, Minneapolis, MN 55401-4993.
Telephone: 612-330-5500.
Website: http://www.xcelenergy.com
Chrmn, Pres & CEO: R.C. Kelly

VP & CFO: B.G. Fowke, III
VP & Treas: G.E. Tyson, II
VP & Secy: C.J. Hart
VP & General Counsel: G.R. Johnson

Investor Contact: P. Johnson (612-215-4535)
Board Members: C. C. Burgess, F. W. Corrigan, R. K. Davis, R. R. Hemminghaus, A. B. Hirschfeld, R. C. Kelly, D. W. Leatherdale, A. F. Moreno, M. R. Preska, A. P. Sampson, R. H. Truly, D. A. Westerlund, T. V. Wolf

Founded: 1909
Domicile: Minnesota
Employees: 9,735

The McGraw-Hill Companies

Xerox Corp

STANDARD &POOR'S

S&P Recommendation	**BUY** ★★★★☆	Price $16.56 (as of Nov 23, 2007)	12-Mo. Target Price $20.00	Investment Style Large-Cap Blend

GICS Sector Information Technology
Sub-Industry Office Electronics

Summary This company serves the worldwide document processing market, offering a complete line of copiers, electronic printers, and other office and computer equipment.

Key Stock Statistics (Source S&P, Vickers, company reports)

52-Wk Range	$20.18–15.26	S&P Oper. EPS 2007E	1.19	Market Capitalization(B)	$15.308	Beta	1.88
Trailing 12-Month EPS	$1.02	S&P Oper. EPS 2008E	1.35	Yield (%)	1.03	S&P 3-Yr. Proj. EPS CAGR(%)	9.00
Trailing 12-Month P/E	16.2	P/E on S&P Oper. EPS 2007E	13.9	Dividend Rate/Share	$0.17	S&P Credit Rating	BBB-
$10K Invested 5 Yrs Ago	$20,195	Common Shares Outstg. (M)	924.4	Institutional Ownership (%)	90		

Price Performance

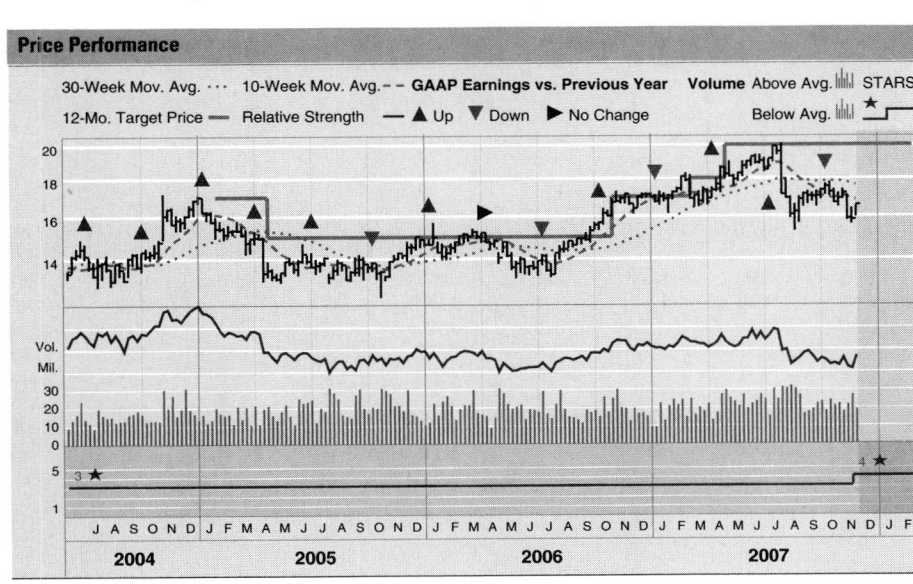

- 30-Week Mov. Avg. ···· 10-Week Mov. Avg. — **GAAP Earnings vs. Previous Year** Volume Above Avg. STARS
- 12-Mo. Target Price — Relative Strength — ▲ Up ▼ Down ▶ No Change Below Avg. ★

Options: ASE, CBOE, P, Ph

Analysis prepared by **Thomas W. Smith, CFA** on November 19, 2007, when the stock traded at **$16.08**.

Highlights

➤ We believe revenues will increase almost 9% in 2007 and 5% per year in 2008 and 2009. Acquisitions and currency effects are boosting the revenue pace for 2007. Prime drivers for growth in 2008, by our analysis, include many new digital and color offerings, plus continuing expansion in international markets. Tempering growth is the maturity of the U.S. market. On November 19, XRX declared a quarterly cash dividend for the first time since 2001, which we view as an indication of improving stability in sales and operations.

➤ We see gross margins remaining around 41% for the next few years, benefiting from higher volumes and new products, and offset by a more challenging pricing environment and a less-favorable business mix. We expect operating margins to trend slightly higher from 2007 to 2009, owing largely to ongoing cost-control initiatives.

➤ In May 2007, XRX acquired Global Imaging Systems in a debt-financed transaction valued at $1.5 billion to better pursue small- and medium-sized business opportunities. We anticipate that EPS will be aided by an active stock buyback program.

Investment Rationale/Risk

➤ We believe the company's turnaround efforts have delivered positive results, including a stronger balance sheet, reduced expenses, and more diverse and innovative product offerings. Despite many challenges that we see for XRX, including modest demand for office products and lively competition, we believe that the valuation is attractive based on our P/E analysis. The announcement of plans to resume dividends adds to the shares' attractiveness, in our view.

➤ Risks to our recommendation and target price include a more aggressive pricing environment, elongated sales cycles, and delays in the deployment of new products. Although XRX has significant recurring revenues, we view the potential for slower economic growth than we forecast as a risk.

➤ Our 12-month target price of $20 is based largely on our P/E analysis. Given the context of modest U.S. economic growth that we foresee for 2008, we apply a target P/E multiple of 15X, a bit below the 16X that we view as the middle of a three-year historical average for XRX, to our 12-month forward EPS estimate of $1.36.

Qualitative Risk Assessment

LOW	**MEDIUM**	HIGH

Our risk assessment reflects our view of XRX's efforts to spur growth and improve profitability, offset by what we see as lackluster organic revenue growth.

Quantitative Evaluations

S&P Quality Ranking   B

D	C	B-	**B**	B+	A-	A	A+

Relative Strength Rank   **MODERATE**

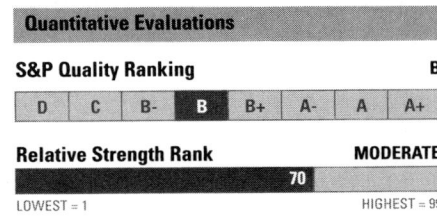

70

LOWEST = 1   HIGHEST = 99

Revenue/Earnings Data

Revenue (Million $)

	1Q	2Q	3Q	4Q	Year
2007	3,836	4,208	4,302	--	--
2006	3,695	3,977	3,844	4,379	15,895
2005	3,771	3,921	3,759	4,250	15,701
2004	3,827	3,853	3,716	4,326	15,722
2003	3,757	3,920	3,732	4,292	15,701
2002	3,858	3,952	3,793	4,246	15,849

Earnings Per Share ($)

2007	0.24	0.28	0.27	E0.41	E1.19
2006	0.20	0.26	0.54	0.22	1.22
2005	0.20	0.35	0.06	0.27	0.90
2004	0.17	0.21	0.17	0.24	0.78
2003	-0.10	0.09	0.11	0.22	0.36
2002	-0.07	0.12	0.04	0.01	0.10

Fiscal year ended Dec. 31. Next earnings report expected: Late January. EPS Estimates based on S&P Operating Earnings; historical GAAP earnings are as reported.

Dividend Data (Dates: mm/dd Payment Date: mm/dd/yy)

Amount ($)	Date Decl.	Ex-Div. Date	Stk. of Record	Payment Date
0.043	11/19	12/27	12/31	01/31/08

Dividends have been paid since 2008. Source: Company reports.

Xerox Corp

STANDARD &POOR'S

Business Summary November 19, 2007

CORPORATE OVERVIEW. XRX competes in the monochrome (black and white) and color segments, and believes it can differentiate itself versus peers by providing what it believes to be the industry's broadest range of document products, solutions and services. In addition, XRX also provides software and solutions intended to help businesses easily print books or create personalized documents for customers. The company's services include operating in-house production centers, developing on-line document repositories, and analyzing how customers can most efficiently create and share documents in the office.

In 2006, revenues from major segments were as follows: production 29% (29% in 2005), office 48% (49%), developing markets 12% (12%) and other 11% (11%).

The company has, and is likely to continue to have, a substantial amount of debt, partly because like other large technology hardware companies, it provides customer financing. At year-end 2006, XRX had more than $7 billion in total debt.

MARKET PROFILE. Xerox participates in an estimated $117 billion total market opportunity, which includes digital multifunction devices, as well as traditional copiers, printers, faxes, software, and supplies, and services. While the company has been experiencing what we view as lackluster revenue growth over the past several years, Xerox hopes to capitalize on a transition in the document industry away from older light lens devices to digital technology, a transition from black and white to color, and the management of publishing and printing jobs over the Internet. XRX has targeted key areas for growth, including color systems, the replacement of multiple single-function office devices with multifunction systems, and the transition of low-end offset printing to digital technology.

Company Financials Fiscal Year Ended Dec. 31

Per Share Data ($)	2006	2005	2004	2003	2002	2001	2000	1999	1998	1997
Tangible Book Value	5.04	4.68	4.29	1.57	NM	0.52	2.86	4.79	4.76	5.54
Cash Flow	1.95	1.62	1.45	1.25	1.38	1.72	0.96	3.13	2.00	2.96
Earnings	1.22	0.90	0.78	0.36	0.10	-0.17	-0.44	1.96	0.80	2.02
S&P Core Earnings	1.27	0.88	0.75	0.53	-0.17	-1.33	NA	NA	NA	NA
Dividends	Nil	Nil	Nil	Nil	Nil	0.05	0.65	0.78	0.70	0.64
Payout Ratio	Nil	Nil	Nil	Nil	Nil	NM	NM	40%	87%	32%
Prices:High	17.31	17.02	17.24	13.89	11.45	11.35	29.31	63.94	60.81	44.00
Prices:Low	13.16	12.40	12.55	7.90	4.20	4.69	3.75	19.00	33.09	25.75
P/E Ratio:High	14	19	22	39	NM	NM	NM	33	76	22
P/E Ratio:Low	11	14	16	22	NM	NM	NM	10	41	13

Income Statement Analysis (Million $)	2006	2005	2004	2003	2002	2001	2000	1999	1998	1997
Revenue	15,895	15,701	15,722	15,701	15,849	17,008	18,701	19,228	19,449	18,166
Operating Income	2,165	2,159	2,451	2,585	2,803	3,011	1,946	3,815	3,685	3,400
Depreciation	636	637	686	748	1,035	1,332	948	935	821	739
Interest Expense	305	231	708	362	401	457	605	547	570	520
Pretax Income	922	928	1,116	494	306	418	-323	2,104	837	2,268
Effective Tax Rate	NM	NM	30.5%	27.1%	19.6%	NM	NM	30.0%	24.7%	32.1%
Net Income	1,210	933	776	360	154	-109	-257	1,424	585	1,452
S&P Core Earnings	1,235	862	666	434	-128	-931	NA	NA	NA	NA

Balance Sheet & Other Financial Data (Million $)	2006	2005	2004	2003	2002	2001	2000	1999	1998	1997
Cash	1,399	1,322	3,218	2,477	2,887	3,990	1,741	126	79.0	75.0
Current Assets	8,754	8,736	10,928	10,335	11,019	12,600	13,022	11,985	12,475	10,766
Total Assets	21,709	21,953	24,884	24,591	25,458	27,689	29,475	28,814	30,024	27,732
Current Liabilities	4,698	4,346	6,300	7,569	7,787	10,260	6,268	7,950	8,507	7,692
Long Term Debt	6,284	6,765	7,767	8,739	11,485	11,815	16,042	11,632	11,505	9,416
Common Equity	7,080	6,319	6,244	3,291	1,893	1,820	3,493	4,911	4,857	4,985
Total Capital	13,364	13,973	14,900	13,418	14,001	14,313	20,323	17,339	17,173	15,233
Capital Expenditures	215	181	204	197	146	219	452	594	566	520
Cash Flow	1,846	1,512	1,389	1,037	1,116	1,209	638	2,305	1,350	2,134
Current Ratio	1.9	2.0	1.7	1.4	1.4	1.2	2.1	1.5	1.5	1.4
% Long Term Debt of Capitalization	47.0	48.4	52.1	65.1	82.0	82.5	78.9	67.1	67.0	61.8
% Net Income of Revenue	7.6	5.9	4.9	2.3	1.0	NM	NM	7.4	3.0	8.0
% Return on Assets	5.5	4.0	3.1	1.4	0.6	NM	NM	4.8	2.0	5.3
% Return on Equity	18.1	13.9	14.7	11.1	4.4	NM	NM	28.1	10.7	29.8

Data as orig reptd.; bef. results of disc opers/spec. items. Per share data adj. for stk. divs.; EPS diluted. E-Estimated. NA-Not Available. NM-Not Meaningful. NR-Not Ranked. UR-Under Review.

Office: 800 Long Ridge Road, Stamford, CT 06904-1600.
Telephone: 203-968-3000.
Website: http://www.xerox.com
Chrmn & CEO: A.M. Mulcahy

Pres: U.M. Burns
SVP & CFO: L.A. Zimmerman
SVP, Secy & General Counsel: D. Liu
VP & Chief Acctg Officer: G.R. Kabureck

Investor Contact: J.H. Lesco
Board Members: G. A. Britt, U. M. Burns, R. Harrington, W. Hunter, V. E. Jordan, Jr., H. Kopper, R. S. Larsen, R. A. McDonald, A. M. Mulcahy, N. J. Nicholas, Jr., A. Reese, S. Robert

Founded: 1906
Domicile: New York
Employees: 53,700

The McGraw-Hill Companies

Xilinx Inc

STANDARD &POOR'S

S&P Recommendation	HOLD ★★★☆☆	Price $21.69 (as of Nov 23, 2007)	12-Mo. Target Price $32.00	Investment Style Large-Cap Growth

GICS Sector Information Technology
Sub-Industry Semiconductors

Summary This California-based company is the world's largest supplier of programmable logic chips and related development system software.

Key Stock Statistics (Source S&P, Vickers, company reports)

52-Wk Range	$30.50–21.51	S&P Oper. EPS 2008E	1.24	Market Capitalization(B)	$6.418	Beta		2.30
Trailing 12-Month EPS	$1.08	S&P Oper. EPS 2009E	1.56	Yield (%)	2.21	S&P 3-Yr. Proj. EPS CAGR(%)		9.00
Trailing 12-Month P/E	20.1	P/E on S&P Oper. EPS 2008E	17.5	Dividend Rate/Share	$0.48	S&P Credit Rating		NA
$10K Invested 5 Yrs Ago	$9,388	Common Shares Outstg. (M)	295.9	Institutional Ownership (%)	96			

Price Performance

30-Week Mov. Avg. ···· 10-Week Mov. Avg. ‑ ‑ GAAP Earnings vs. Previous Year   Volume Above Avg. STARS
12-Mo. Target Price ── Relative Strength ── ▲ Up ▼ Down ► No Change   Below Avg. ★

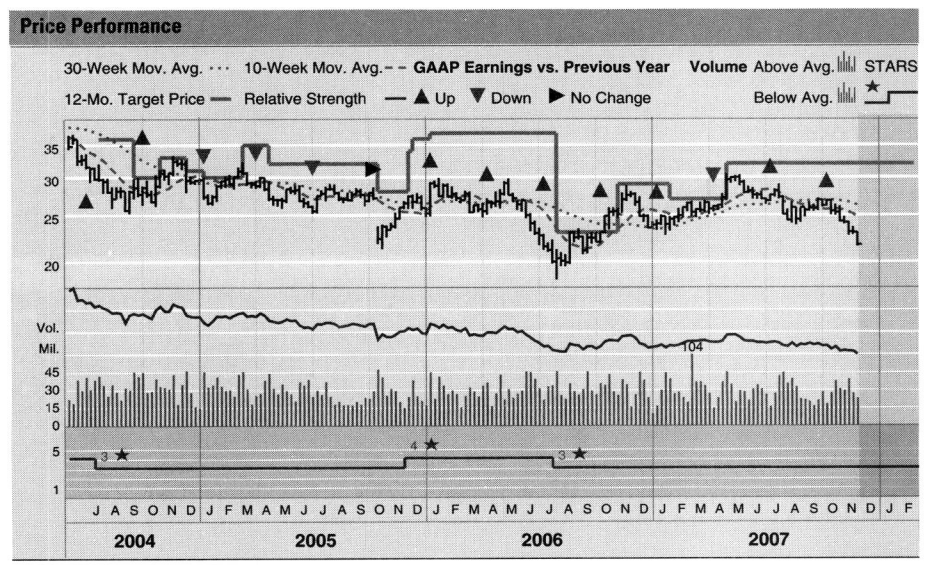

Options: ASE, CBOE, P

Analysis prepared by **Clyde Montevirgen** on October 22, 2007, when the stock traded at **$ 25.65.**

Highlights

➤ We project essentially flat revenues for FY 08 (Mar.), compared to 6.7% sales growth in FY 07. We have a guarded near-term outlook, based on XLNX's turns-based business expectations and uncertainty on wireline communication products, but we see industrial, consumer and wireless product sales growing faster in coming quarters. Although we view favorably the company's migration to 65 nanometer products, we are somewhat doubtful of market share gains, given strong positioning by main competitor Altera. In FY 09, we anticipate sales growth of 14%.

➤ We see gross margins widening to 62% in FY 08, slightly above FY 07 levels. The company generally maintains fairly steady gross margins at relatively high levels compared to most semiconductor peers, partly reflecting its effective management of fixed costs by partnering with chip foundries, in our opinion. We look for operating margins of about 23% in FY 08, reflecting moderate top-line growth and cost containment actions.

➤ We forecast EPS of $1.24 for FY 08 and $1.56 for FY 09.

Investment Rationale/Risk

➤ XLNX is the market share leader in a category of semiconductors, namely programmable chips, that we expect to expand faster than the overall semiconductor industry growth pace of 4% on a calendar 2007 basis. However, we see slower sales growth given recent inventory problems and formidable competition. Although we see XLNX effectively reducing operating costs to improve profitability, we think valuation multiples will likely be subdued near term until XLNX can exhibit better top-line growth.

➤ Risks to our recommendation and target price include industry cyclicality, dependence on chip foundry partners for production, fluctuation in chip inventories, and reliance on stock-based compensation that we view as moderately high versus peers.

➤ Our 12-month target price of $32 is based on a blend of our price-to-sales (P/S) and P/E analyses. We apply a P/S multiple of 5X, at the low end of the historical range, to our 12-month forward sales estimate, arriving at a value of $33. We also apply a P/E multiple of 20X, above the peer average, to our FY 09 EPS estimate to derive a value of $31.

Qualitative Risk Assessment

LOW	MEDIUM	HIGH

Our risk assessment reflects the cyclicality of the semiconductor industry, offset by the company's position as the largest competitor in a fast-growing niche, our view of its debt-free position, its diverse end markets, and its sharing of factory operations risk with chip foundry partners.

Quantitative Evaluations

S&P Quality Ranking   **B**

D	C	B-	B	B+	A-	A	A+

Relative Strength Rank   **WEAK**

27

LOWEST = 1   HIGHEST = 99

Revenue/Earnings Data

Revenue (Million $)

	1Q	2Q	3Q	4Q	Year
2008	445.9	444.9	--	--	--
2007	481.4	467.2	450.7	443.5	1,843
2006	405.4	398.9	449.6	472.3	1,726
2005	423.6	403.3	355.4	391.0	1,573
2004	313.3	315.6	365.6	403.4	1,398
2003	289.9	277.9	282.7	305.5	1,156

Earnings Per Share ($)

2008	0.28	0.30	E0.31	E0.35	E1.24
2007	0.24	0.27	0.26	0.27	1.02
2006	0.21	0.24	0.23	0.32	1.00
2005	0.26	0.24	0.18	0.19	0.87
2004	0.13	0.16	0.19	0.36	0.85
2003	0.12	0.11	-0.01	0.14	0.36

Fiscal year ended Mar. 31. Next earnings report expected: Mid January. EPS Estimates based on S&P Operating Earnings; historical GAAP earnings are as reported.

Dividend Data (Dates: mm/dd Payment Date: mm/dd/yy)

Amount ($)	Date Decl.	Ex-Div. Date	Stk. of Record	Payment Date
0.090	01/23	02/05	02/07	02/28/07
0.120	02/26	05/07	05/09	05/30/07
0.120	07/19	08/13	08/15	09/05/07
0.120	10/24	11/09	11/14	12/05/07

Dividends have been paid since 2004. Source: Company reports.

Please read the Required Disclosures and Analyst Certification on the last page of this report.

The McGraw-Hill Companies

Xilinx Inc

STANDARD &POOR'S

Business Summary October 22, 2007

CORPORATE OVERVIEW. Founded in 1984, Xilinx is the world's leading supplier of programmable logic devices (PLDs) based on market share. These devices include field programmable gate arrays (FPGAs) and complex programmable logic devices (CPLDs). They are standard integrated circuits (ICs) that are programmed by customers to perform desired logic operations. The company believes it provides high levels of integration and creates significant time and cost savings for electronic equipment manufacturers in the telecommunications, networking, computing and industrial markets.

Xilinx's FPGAs are proprietary ICs designed by the company; they provide a combination of the high logic density usually associated with custom gate arrays, the time-to-market advantages of programmable logic, and the availability of a standard product. The company has several product families, including the XC4000, Coolrunner, Spartan and Virtex lines. The Virtex-II Pro product line, introduced in March 2002, is a platform for programmable systems, enabling very high-bandwidth system-on-a-chip designs with the flexibility and low development cost of programmable logic. FPGAs account for the vast majority of sales, but the company also derives revenue from development and system software tools, and field engineering support.

Products are classified as new, mainstream, base and support. New products accounted for 23% of FY 07 (Mar.) sales (12% in FY 06), mainstream products 54% (61%), base products 17% (21%), and support products 6% (6%). Revenue by end market in FY 07 broke down as follows: 45% (55% in FY 06) communications, 45% (40%) consumer, automotive, industrial and other, and 10% (11%) data processing.

Xilinx sells its products globally to OEMs and to electronic components distributors who resell these products. Avnet distributes the majority of the company's products worldwide. Following the 2005 merger of Avnet and Memec, another of the company's distributors, the combined entity accounted for 86% of total FY 07 revenues. No end customer accounted for more than 10% of Xilinx's revenues.

Company Financials Fiscal Year Ended Mar. 31

Per Share Data ($)	2007	2006	2005	2004	2003	2002	2001	2000	1999	1998
Tangible Book Value	5.54	7.53	7.24	6.79	5.44	5.26	5.82	5.68	2.82	1.89
Cash Flow	1.24	1.19	1.05	1.05	0.57	-0.02	0.36	2.03	0.52	0.50
Earnings	1.02	1.00	0.87	0.85	0.36	-0.34	0.10	1.90	0.42	0.40
S&P Core Earnings	1.01	0.78	0.58	0.57	0.05	-0.31	0.35	NA	NA	NA
Dividends	0.28	0.28	0.20	Nil	Nil	Nil	Nil	Nil	Nil	Nil
Payout Ratio	27%	28%	23%	Nil	Nil	Nil	Nil	Nil	Nil	Nil
Calendar Year	2006	2005	2004	2003	2002	2001	2000	1999	1998	1997
Prices:High	29.98	32.30	45.40	39.20	47.15	59.25	98.31	48.56	16.75	14.63
Prices:Low	18.35	21.25	25.21	18.50	13.50	19.52	35.25	15.31	7.44	7.13
P/E Ratio:High	29	32	47	46	NM	NM	NM	26	40	37
P/E Ratio:Low	18	21	26	22	NM	NM	NM	8	18	18

Income Statement Analysis (Million $)

	2007	2006	2005	2004	2003	2002	2001	2000	1999	1998
Revenue	1,843	1,726	1,573	1,398	1,156	1,016	1,659	1,021	662	614
Operating Income	424	489	442	412	283	87.3	568	371	214	207
Depreciation	73.9	69.5	63.1	67.9	72.5	106	93.5	44.2	32.1	32.7
Interest Expense	Nil	Nil	Nil	Nil	Nil	0.06	0.17	Nil	11.9	13.9
Pretax Income	431	457	401	351	170	-193	61.1	1,030	184	183
Effective Tax Rate	18.7%	22.4%	21.9%	13.6%	26.0%	NM	42.3%	36.7%	29.8%	30.9%
Net Income	351	354	313	303	126	-114	35.3	652	129	127
S&P Core Earnings	348	277	205	204	18.1	-103	132	NA	NA	NA

Balance Sheet & Other Financial Data (Million $)

	2007	2006	2005	2004	2003	2002	2001	2000	1999	1998
Cash	636	783	449	337	214	230	209	85.5	53.6	167
Current Assets	1,700	1,648	1,466	1,302	1,175	999	1,102	1,041	658	600
Total Assets	3,179	3,174	3,039	2,937	2,422	2,335	2,502	2,349	1,070	941
Current Liabilities	303	345	298	381	314	196	350	245	167	126
Long Term Debt	1,000	Nil	Nil	Nil	Nil	Nil	Nil	Nil	Nil	250
Common Equity	1,773	2,729	2,674	2,483	1,951	1,904	1,918	1,777	879	550
Total Capital	2,875	2,821	2,741	2,556	2,108	2,140	2,152	2,104	903	816
Capital Expenditures	111	67.0	61.4	41.0	46.0	94.9	223	144	40.9	29.7
Cash Flow	425	424	376	371	198	-7.51	129	697	161	159
Current Ratio	5.6	4.8	4.9	3.4	3.7	5.1	3.1	4.3	3.9	4.8
% Long Term Debt of Capitalization	34.8	Nil	Nil	Nil	Nil	Nil	Nil	Nil	Nil	30.6
% Net Income of Revenue	19.0	20.5	19.8	21.7	10.9	NM	2.1	63.9	19.5	20.6
% Return on Assets	11.0	11.4	10.5	11.3	5.3	NM	1.5	38.2	12.9	14.2
% Return on Equity	15.6	13.1	12.1	13.7	6.5	NM	1.9	49.1	18.1	24.3

Data as orig reptd.; bef. results of disc opers/spec. items. Per share data adj. for stk. divs.; EPS diluted. E-Estimated. NA-Not Available. NM-Not Meaningful. NR-Not Ranked. UR-Under Review.

Office: 2100 Logic Drive, San Jose, CA, USA 95124-3400.
Telephone: 408-559-7778.
Email: ir@xilinx.com
Website: http://www.xilinx.com

Chrmn, Pres & CEO: W.P. Roelandts
Investor Contact: J.A. Olson (408-559-7778)
VP & CFO: J.A. Olson

Board Members: J. L. Doyle, J. G. Fishman, P. T. Gianos, W. G. Howard, Jr., J. M. Patterson, W. P. Roelandts, M. C. Turner, E. W. Vanderslice

Founded: 1984
Domicile: Delaware
Employees: 3,353

XL Capital Ltd

STANDARD &POOR'S

| **S&P Recommendation** STRONG SELL ★☆☆☆☆ | **Price** $49.78 (as of Nov 26, 2007) | **12-Mo. Target Price** $50.00 | **Investment Style** Large-Cap Blend |

GICS Sector Financials
Sub-Industry Property & Casualty Insurance

Summary Bermuda-based XL, which originally provided excess liability coverage, has expanded into providing a broad array of commercial lines insurance, reinsurance and other risk management services.

Key Stock Statistics (Source S&P, Vickers, company reports)

52-Wk Range	$85.67– 49.66	S&P Oper. EPS 2007E	11.40	Market Capitalization(B)	$8.873	Beta	0.98
Trailing 12-Month EPS	$10.51	S&P Oper. EPS 2008E	10.35	Yield (%)	3.05	S&P 3-Yr. Proj. EPS CAGR(%)	NA
Trailing 12-Month P/E	4.7	P/E on S&P Oper. EPS 2007E	4.4	Dividend Rate/Share	$1.52	S&P Credit Rating	NA
$10K Invested 5 Yrs Ago	$7,391	Common Shares Outstg. (M)	178.3	Institutional Ownership (%)	100		

Price Performance

30-Week Mov. Avg. · · · 10-Week Mov. Avg. - - **GAAP Earnings vs. Previous Year** Volume Above Avg. ▮▮▮ STARS
12-Mo. Target Price — Relative Strength — ▲ Up ▼ Down ► No Change Below Avg. ▮▮▮

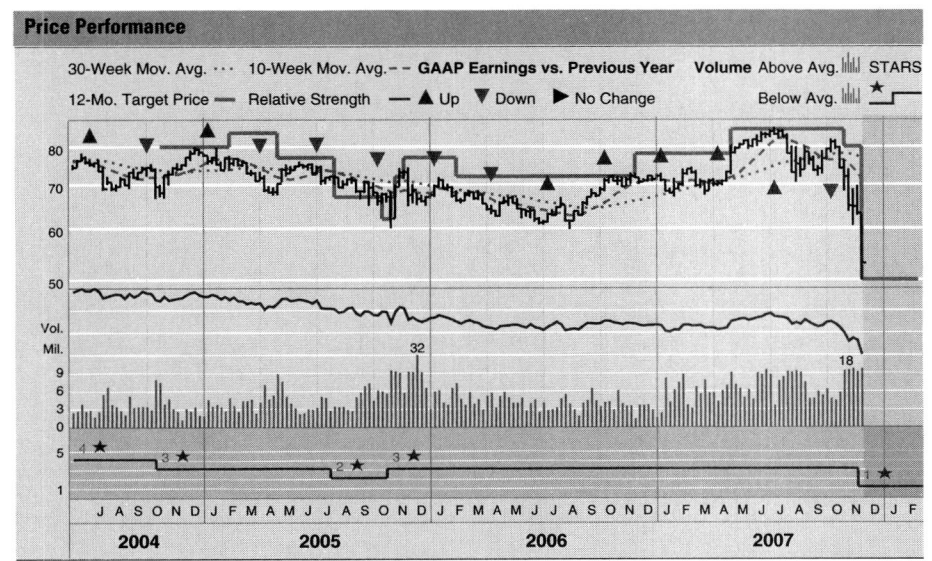

Options: CBOE, P, Ph

Analysis prepared by **Cathy A. Seifert** on November 26, 2007, when the stock traded at **$ 52.06**.

Highlights

➤ We expect earned premiums to decline 5% to 7% in 2008, versus a decline of 3% to 5% we anticipate for 2007, reflecting a more competitive pricing environment. Favorable prior year loss developments on certain casualty lines offset the impact of higher property loss costs and aided underwriting results in the first nine months of 2007, as evidenced by the combined ratio, which improved to 87.2% in the 2007 interim, from 89.8% in 2006. We expect underwriting margins to contract in 2008.

➤ Net investment income growth in 2007 and 2008 will likely not be as strong as the 34% rise in 2006, but should remain in the double digits.

➤ We estimate operating EPS of $11.40 in 2007 and $10.35 in 2008, versus $9.83 of operating EPS reported for 2006. XL incurred a $10.86 loss per share in 2005 amid after-tax catastrophe losses of nearly $1.9 billion, and an after-tax, fourth quarter charge of $834.2 million related to certain post-closing actuarial adjustments related to its 2001 acquisition of Winterthur International.

Investment Rationale/Risk

➤ Our strong sell recommendation reflects our view that the shares could come under additional pressure in coming periods, largely owing to XL's exposure to the financial guaranty market. We believe XL will have to write down its investment in 46%-owned SCA Capital (NYSE; SCA) by some $500 million. We are also concerned that XL may incur claims from its reinsurance agreements with SCA, but we cannot quantify the impact at this juncture.

➤ Risks to our recommendation and target price include a less than anticipated decline in premium rates and underwriting margins; a lesser deterioration in the credit quality of XL's investment portfolio; and a less than anticipated negative financial impact stemming from XL's relationship with SCA.

➤ Our 12-month target price of $50 assumes that the shares will trade at approximately 1.1X estimated 2007 tangible book value, reflecting our view of XL's higher risk mix of business versus many of its peers.

Qualitative Risk Assessment

| LOW | MEDIUM | HIGH |

Our risk assessment reflects our concerns about XL's exposure to catastrophe losses and financial guaranty reinsurance claims, the adequacy of its loss reserves in certain liability lines of business, and our view that XL could face writedowns of its fixed income investment portfolio and certain other investments. This is only partially offset by our view of XL as an opportunistic underwriter capable of leveraging opportunities for growth.

Quantitative Evaluations

S&P Quality Ranking B-

| D | C | **B-** | B | B+ | A- | A | A+ |

Relative Strength Rank WEAK

8

LOWEST = 1   HIGHEST = 99

Revenue/Earnings Data

Revenue (Million $)

	1Q	2Q	3Q	4Q	Year
2007	2,483	2,597	2,153	--	--
2006	2,473	2,499	2,364	2,496	9,833
2005	2,401	4,108	2,296	2,479	11,285
2004	2,157	3,179	2,370	2,390	10,028
2003	1,792	1,892	1,969	2,363	8,017
2002	1,165	1,168	2,340	1,942	6,578

Earnings Per Share ($)

2007	3.06	3.00	1.82	E2.37	E11.40
2006	2.56	2.10	2.32	2.62	9.60
2005	3.18	0.97	-7.53	-5.51	-9.14
2004	3.25	2.62	0.16	2.07	8.13
2003	1.74	2.51	0.71	-2.29	2.69
2002	0.65	-0.68	1.34	1.56	2.88

Fiscal year ended Dec. 31. Next earnings report expected: Early February. EPS Estimates based on S&P Operating Earnings; historical GAAP earnings are as reported.

Dividend Data (Dates: mm/dd Payment Date: mm/dd/yy)

Amount ($)	Date Decl.	Ex-Div. Date	Stk. of Record	Payment Date
0.380	01/26	03/13	03/15	03/30/07
0.380	04/30	06/07	06/11	06/29/07
0.380	07/27	09/06	09/10	09/28/07
0.380	11/02	12/06	12/10	12/28/07

Dividends have been paid since 1992. Source: Company reports.

Please read the Required Disclosures and Analyst Certification on the last page of this report.

The McGraw-Hill Companies

XL Capital Ltd

STANDARD &POOR'S

Business Summary November 26, 2007

Bermuda-based XL was formed in 1986 by a consortium of Fortune 500 companies to provide excess liability coverage. Since then, XL has expanded (mostly via acquisitions) to include insurance, reinsurance, and other financial services. Gross written premiums of nearly $9.8 billion in 2006 (down 17% from $11.8 billion of gross written premiums in 2005) were divided: insurance 57%, reinsurance 32%, life operations 6%, financial lines and other 5%.

Insurance business written includes general liability, as well as other specialized types of liability coverage, such as directors' and officers' liability and professional and employment practices liability coverage. An array of property coverage, as well as marine and aviation coverage, is also offered. Insurance net written premiums of $4.15 billion in 2006 were divided: professional liability 36%, casualty 19%, marine/energy/aviation/satellite 17%, property 14%, property catastrophe 2%, and other specialty lines 12%.

Reinsurance business written includes treaty and facultative reinsurance to primary insurers of casualty risk. Reinsurance net written premiums totaled $2.4 billion in 2006 and were divided: property 30%, casualty 26%, professional liability 12%, property catastrophe 10%, marine, energy aviation and satellite 6%, and other lines (which include political risk, surety, warranty, accident/ health) for 16%.

Life operations include reinsurance written from other life insurers, principally to help in managing mortality, morbidity, survivorship, investment, and lapse risks. Net written premiums totaled $558.5 million in 2006 and was divided: annuity risks 56%, traditional life insurance 44%. The financial services unit provides insurance and reinsurance solutions for complex financial risks.

In July 2001, the company acquired Winterthur International, for about $330.2 million in cash (as adjusted). As part of the transaction, XL received certain post-closing arrangements protecting it against (among other things) certain types of adverse loss development. XL valued the post-closing payment at $1.45 billion, and Winterthur Swiss Insurance Co. (the seller) believed the post-closing payment was $541 million. In December 2005, an independent actuarial review concluded that Winterthur's estimate was closer than the estimate submitted by XL. As a result of this difference, XL recorded a fourth quarter 2005 after-tax charge of $834.2 million.

Company Financials Fiscal Year Ended Dec. 31

Per Share Data ($)	2006	2005	2004	2003	2002	2001	2000	1999	1998	1997
Tangible Book Value	45.93	37.08	42.55	37.07	36.13	28.35	31.86	30.91	29.67	26.20
Operating Earnings	NA	NA	NA	NA	5.10	-3.67	4.52	3.63	4.36	3.95
Earnings	9.60	-9.14	8.13	2.69	2.88	-4.55	4.03	3.62	6.20	7.84
Dividends	1.52	2.00	1.96	1.92	1.88	1.84	1.80	1.76	1.64	1.36
Payout Ratio	16%	NM	24%	71%	65%	NM	45%	49%	26%	17%
Prices:High	72.90	79.80	82.00	88.87	98.48	96.50	89.25	75.75	84.00	65.19
Prices:Low	59.82	60.03	66.70	63.49	58.45	61.50	39.00	41.94	59.13	36.88
P/E Ratio:High	8	NM	10	33	34	NM	22	21	14	8
P/E Ratio:Low	6	NM	8	24	20	NM	10	12	10	5

Income Statement Analysis (Million $)	2006	2005	2004	2003	2002	2001	2000	1999	1998	1997
Premium Income	559	2,238	1,406	6,969	5,990	3,476	2,035	1,750	685	541
Net Investment Income	1,978	1,475	995	780	735	563	542	525	279	217
Other Revenue	8,904	8,864	7,426	268	-147	18.0	140	236	253	402
Total Revenue	9,833	11,285	10,028	8,017	6,578	4,057	2,717	2,511	1,218	1,159
Pretax Income	2,007	-1,194	1,260	451	442	-764	451	431	594	682
Net Operating Income	NA	NA	NA	NA	701	-465	NA	NA	NA	NA
Net Income	1,763	-1,252	1,167	412	406	-576	506	471	588	677

Balance Sheet & Other Financial Data (Million $)	2006	2005	2004	2003	2002	2001	2000	1999	1998	1997
Cash & Equivalent	2,656	4,085	2,631	2,698	3,785	2,044	1,074	669	503	395
Premiums Due	4,698	4,842	4,934	4,847	4,833	2,182	1,120	1,126	690	363
Investment Assets:Bonds	36,121	32,310	25,100	19,494	14,483	10,832	8,605	7,581	5,213	3,417
Investment Assets:Stocks	891	869	963	583	575	548	557	1,136	1,129	838
Investment Assets:Loans	Nil	Nil	Nil	Nil	Nil	Nil	Nil	Nil	Nil	Nil
Investment Assets:Total	42,137	38,171	30,066	22,821	17,956	13,741	10,472	9,768	6,616	4,255
Deferred Policy Costs	870	866	845	778	688	394	309	276	98.0	22.0
Total Assets	59,309	58,455	49,015	40,764	35,647	27,963	16,942	15,091	10,109	6,088
Debt	3,368	3,413	2,721	1,905	1,878	1,605	450	411	Nil	Nil
Common Equity	16,422	14,078	12,286	10,171	6,569	5,437	5,574	5,577	4,818	2,479
Property & Casualty:Loss Ratio	60.7	107.1	68.6	75.3	68.0	105.0	70.4	69.1	57.0	67.6
Property & Casualty:Expense Ratio	27.8	25.8	27.4	27.3	29.0	34.9	36.4	34.3	26.3	18.2
Property & Casualty Combined Ratio	88.5	132.9	96.0	102.6	97.0	139.9	106.8	103.4	83.3	85.8
% Return on Revenue	18.6	NM	11.9	5.2	6.0	NM	18.6	19.9	48.3	77.2
% Return on Equity	11.3	NM	10.0	3.9	6.6	NM	9.1	8.4	16.1	29.5

Data as orig reptd.; bef. results of disc opers/spec. items. Per share data adj. for stk. divs.; EPS diluted. E-Estimated. NA-Not Available. NM-Not Meaningful. NR-Not Ranked. UR-Under Review.

Office: XL House, 1 Bermudiana Rd, Hamilton, Bermuda HM 11.
Telephone: 441-292-8515.
Website: http://www.xlcapital.com
Chrmn: M.P. Esposito, Jr.

Pres & CEO: B.M. O'Hara
COO & EVP: H.C. Keeling
EVP & CFO: F.E. Luck
EVP & General Counsel: C.F. Barr

Investor Contact: D.R. Radulski (441-294-7460)
Board Members: D. Comey, M. P. Esposito, Jr., R. R. Glauber, H. Haag, J. Mauriello, E. M. McQuade, B. M. O'Hara, R. S. Parker, C. E. Rance, A. Z. Senter, J. T. Thornton, E. E. Thrower

Founded: 1986
Domicile: Cayman Islands
Employees: 3,500

XTO Energy Inc.

STANDARD &POOR'S

S&P Recommendation	HOLD ★★★☆☆	Price $63.65 (as of Nov 23, 2007)	12-Mo. Target Price $65.00	Investment Style Large-Cap Growth

GICS Sector Energy
Sub-Industry Oil & Gas Exploration & Production

Summary This independent oil and gas producer is highly leveraged to unconventional natural gas resources (such as tight gas, shale gas and coal bed methane) in the U.S.

Key Stock Statistics (Source S&P, Vickers, company reports)

52-Wk Range	$67.49– 43.86	S&P Oper. EPS 2007**E** 4.25	Market Capitalization(B) $23.444	Beta	0.83
Trailing 12-Month EPS	$4.38	S&P Oper. EPS 2008**E** 4.61	Yield (%) 0.94	S&P 3-Yr. Proj. EPS CAGR(%)	5.00
Trailing 12-Month P/E	14.5	P/E on S&P Oper. EPS 2007**E** 15.0	Dividend Rate/Share $0.60	S&P Credit Rating	BBB
$10K Invested 5 Yrs Ago	NA	Common Shares Outstg. (M) 368.3	Institutional Ownership (%) 86		

Price Performance

30-Week Mov. Avg. · · · 10-Week Mov. Avg. - - **GAAP Earnings vs. Previous Year** Volume Above Avg. STARS
12-Mo. Target Price — Relative Strength — ▲ Up ▼ Down ▶ No Change   Below Avg. ★

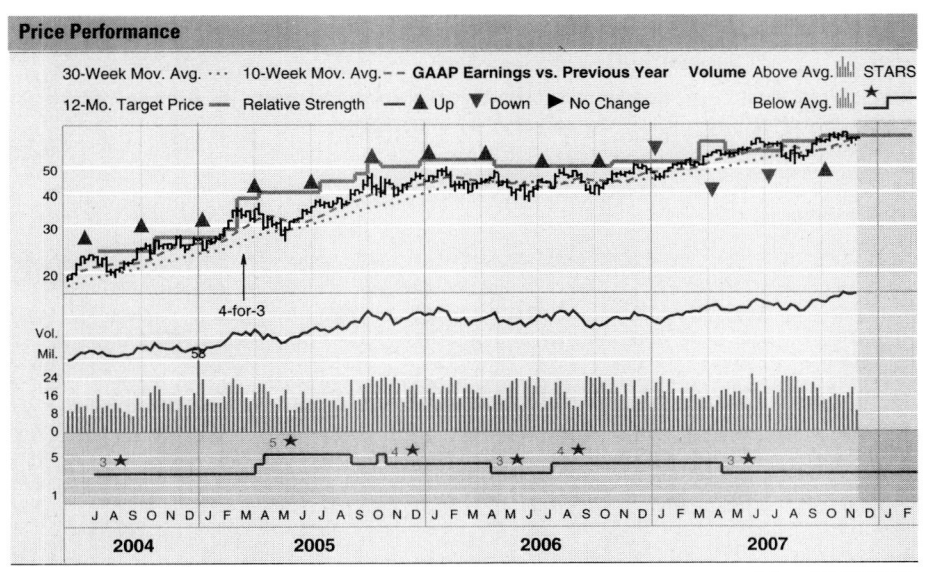

Options: ASE, CBOE, P, Ph

Analysis prepared by **Tina J. Vital** on October 24, 2007, when the stock traded at **$ 63.87**.

Highlights

➤ XTO has expanded on its strong positions in Texas and the Rockies. We expect development projects in the East Texas/Freestone Trend, the Barnett Shale and the San Juan Basin areas will drive oil and gas production growth of about 19% in 2007 and 15% in 2008 (compared to company guidance of 18% and 17%, respectively). As a result of efficiency gains in these plays, we project operating earnings will increase almost 3% in 2007 and 10% in 2008.

➤ XTO has ruled out an MLP involving midstream assets but has stated that it is reviewing options to form a $500 million exploration and production MLP, which, we believe, was solidified with the addition of acquired properties in the Rockies. We expect a final decision in early 2008.

➤ For the 2007 fourth quarter, about 980,000 Mcf of natural gas production is hedged at $8.97 per Mcf, and about 1,000,000 Mcf is hedged at $8.35 per Mcf for 2008. XTO has hedged about 37,500 barrels of its oil production for the remainder of 2007 at $74.40 per barrel and about 30,000 barrels of its 2008 oil production at $74.20.

Investment Rationale/Risk

➤ In July, XTO acquired properties from Dominion Resources for $2.5 billion (proved reserves of 1.06 Tcfe, and production of 200,000 Mcfe/d); we estimate XTO paid $2.36/Mcfe, a favorable price, in our view, given other recent deals. In October, XTO added 25,000 Mcfe/d of production in the Barnett Shale through $550 million in acquisitions. We believe XTO will continue to achieve low-risk production growth through organic investment and external acquisitions. We estimate its three-year (2004-2006) organic reserve replacement is above the peer average, its finding and development costs are below peers, and its proved acquisition costs are in line with peers.

➤ Risks to our recommendation and target price include changes to economic, industrial and operating conditions such as difficulties in replacing reserves, and aggressively priced and financed acquisitions.

➤ A blend of our discounted cash flow (assuming a WACC of 8.3%, and terminal growth of 3%) and relative valuations leads us to our 12-month target price of $65, representing an expected enterprise value of 6.5X our 2008 EBITDA estimate, a premium to peers.

Qualitative Risk Assessment

LOW	MEDIUM	HIGH

Our risk assessment for XTO reflects our view of its position as a large independent exploration and production company focused on unconventional natural gas resources with sizable acreage positions in low-risk drilling opportunities in the U.S. This is offset by our view of XTO's relatively high debt leverage, reflecting its aggressive growth through acquisition strategy.

Quantitative Evaluations

S&P Quality Ranking B+

D	C	B-	B	B+	A-	A	A+

Relative Strength Rank STRONG

85

LOWEST = 1   HIGHEST = 99

Revenue/Earnings Data

Revenue (Million $)

	1Q	2Q	3Q	4Q	Year
2007	1,169	1,329	1,421	--	--
2006	1,215	1,066	1,096	1,199	4,576
2005	628.9	748.7	964.2	1,177	3,519
2004	394.8	444.8	507.4	600.7	1,948
2003	253.5	282.2	322.1	331.9	1,190
2002	180.0	189.2	201.7	239.3	810.2

Earnings Per Share ($)

	1Q	2Q	3Q	4Q	Year
2007	1.03	1.14	1.05	E0.96	E4.25
2006	1.26	1.62	0.99	1.16	5.03
2005	0.47	0.60	0.85	1.22	3.15
2004	0.30	0.30	0.40	0.50	1.52
2003	0.23	0.19	0.33	0.20	0.95
2002	0.16	0.12	0.18	0.20	0.66

Fiscal year ended Dec. 31. Next earnings report expected: Mid February. EPS Estimates based on S&P Operating Earnings; historical GAAP earnings are as reported.

Dividend Data (Dates: mm/dd Payment Date: mm/dd/yy)

Amount ($)	Date Decl.	Ex-Div. Date	Stk. of Record	Payment Date
0.120	05/15	06/27	06/29	07/13/07
0.120	08/21	09/26	09/28	10/15/07
5-for-4	11/14	12/14	11/28	12/13/07
0.120	11/14	12/27	12/31	01/15/08

Dividends have been paid since 1993. Source: Company reports.

Please read the Required Disclosures and Analyst Certification on the last page of this report.

The McGraw-Hill Companies

XTO Energy Inc.

STANDARD &POOR'S

Business Summary October 24, 2007

CORPORATE OVERVIEW. XTO Energy (formerly Cross Timbers Oil Co.) produces and markets natural gas, natural gas liquids (NGLs) and crude oil predominantly from its southwestern and central U.S. properties, most of which XTO operates. The company has achieved production and proved reserve growth generally through producing property acquisitions, followed by development. Development activities are usually funded by cash flow from operating activities. Funding sources for acquisitions include proceeds from sales of public equity and debt, bank borrowings, cash flow from operating activities, or a combination of these sources.

As of December 31, 2006, the company's proved oil and gas reserves were up 12%, year to year, to 8.55 trillion cubic feet equivalent (Tcfe), for a reserve-to-production index of 15.3 years. During 2006, XTO replaced 265% of production via extensions, additions and discoveries. Proved natural gas reserves at year-end 2006 were up 14% from the level a year earlier, to 6.94 trillion cubic feet (Tcf). Proved crude oil reserves were 3% higher, at 214 million barrels (bbl). Proved developed reserves accounted for 67% of total proved reserves.

COMPETITIVE LANDSCAPE. XTO's addressable market is the North American

continent. As a large onshore natural gas producer, XTO competes in a fragmented market that is beginning to rationalize, in our view, into several large onshore players.

XTO has been one of the most active consolidators of onshore U.S. natural gas assets, having purchased 3.26 Tcfe of reserves for $4.8 billion over the past five years for a per proved acquisition cost of $1.48. We believe XTO has created value through acquisitions by employing "unconventional resource recovery techniques." Such unconventional plays include tight gas, coal-bed methane (CBM), and fractured shale formations, which are characterized by a low proportion of exploration capital expenditures resulting in relatively low risk resource acquisition capability. In our view, the main driver of value in these resource plays is the development of repeatable drilling techniques, increasing productivity organically, and moving reserves characterized as probable and possible to the proven category.

Company Financials Fiscal Year Ended Dec. 31

Per Share Data ($)	2006	2005	2004	2003	2002	2001	2000	1999	1998	1997
Tangible Book Value	15.25	11.01	5.62	4.70	3.22	2.98	1.82	1.02	0.67	0.72
Cash Flow	7.50	5.04	2.06	1.90	1.40	1.64	1.58	0.64	0.06	0.36
Earnings	5.03	3.15	1.52	0.95	0.66	1.06	0.46	0.19	-0.33	0.12
S&P Core Earnings	4.23	3.01	1.41	0.91	0.65	0.90	NA	NA	NA	NA
Dividends	0.32	0.24	0.09	0.02	0.02	0.02	0.01	0.01	0.02	0.03
Payout Ratio	6%	8%	6%	3%	3%	2%	2%	7%	NM	25%
Prices:High	51.24	47.61	27.66	17.58	11.88	9.78	8.70	3.03	4.23	3.83
Prices:Low	36.51	23.87	15.35	10.21	6.61	5.54	1.51	0.91	1.01	1.97
P/E Ratio:High	10	15	18	19	18	9	19	16	NM	32
P/E Ratio:Low	7	8	10	11	10	5	3	5	NM	17

Income Statement Analysis (Million $)										
Revenue	4,576	3,519	1,948	1,190	810	839	601	341	249	201
Operating Income	3,445	2,198	1,338	801	550	611	398	208	124	114
Depreciation, Depletion and Amortization	875	655	407	284	204	154	260	112	83.6	47.7
Interest Expense	180	153	93.7	63.8	53.6	55.6	78.9	64.2	52.1	26.7
Pretax Income	2,961	1,810	826	445	287	455	176	70.6	-106	39.2
Effective Tax Rate	37.2%	36.4%	38.5%	35.5%	35.1%	35.6%	33.7%	33.9%	NM	34.5%
Net Income	1,860	1,152	508	287	186	293	117	46.7	-69.8	25.7
S&P Core Earnings	1,565	1,098	476	275	183	249	NA	NA	NA	NA

Balance Sheet & Other Financial Data (Million $)										
Cash	5.00	2.00	9.70	7.00	15.0	6.81	7.44	5.73	12.3	3.82
Current Assets	1,585	943	437	261	245	239	193	113	138	52.2
Total Assets	12,885	9,857	6,110	3,611	2,648	2,132	1,592	1,477	1,208	788
Current Liabilities	1,240	884	501	321	286	202	219	74.2	99.6	54.9
Long Term Debt	3,451	3,109	2,043	1,252	1,118	856	769	991	921	539
Common Equity	5,865	4,209	2,599	1,466	908	821	470	249	149	142
Total Capital	11,294	7,318	5,398	3,144	2,312	1,876	1,349	1,395	1,105	730
Capital Expenditures	616	1,621	1,905	654	358	225	45.6	270	296	257
Cash Flow	2,735	1,807	915	571	390	448	375	157	12.0	71.6
Current Ratio	1.3	1.1	0.9	0.8	0.9	1.2	0.9	1.5	1.4	1.0
% Long Term Debt of Capitalization	30.6	42.5	37.8	39.8	48.4	45.6	57.0	71.1	83.3	73.8
% Return on Assets	16.4	14.4	10.4	9.2	7.8	15.8	7.6	3.5	NM	3.9
% Return on Equity	36.9	33.8	25.0	24.1	21.5	45.4	32.0	21.3	NM	18.7

Data as orig reptd.; bef. results of disc opers/spec. items. Per share data adj. for stk. divs.; EPS diluted. E-Estimated. NA-Not Available. NM-Not Meaningful. NR-Not Ranked. UR-Under Review.

Office: 810 Houston St, Fort Worth, TX 76102.
Telephone: 817-870-2800.
Email: investor_relations@xtoenergy.com
Website: http://www.xtoenergy.com

Chrmn & CEO: B.R. Simpson
Pres: K.A. Hutton
Sr EVP: V.O. Vennerberg, II
EVP & CFO: L.G. Baldwin

Investor Contact: G.D. Simpson (817-870-2800)
Board Members: W. H. Adams, III, L. G. Baldwin, L. G. Collins, K. A. Hutton, P. R. Kevil, T. L. Petrus, J. P. Randall, S. G. Sherman, H. D. Simons, B. R. Simpson, V. O. Vennerberg, II

Founded: 1986
Domicile: Delaware
Employees: 1,939

The McGraw-Hill Companies

Yahoo! Inc

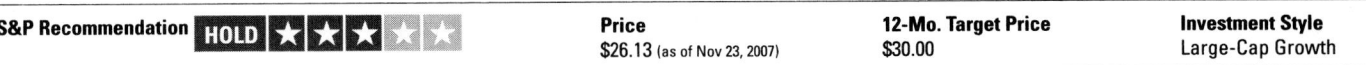

STANDARD &POOR'S

S&P Recommendation **HOLD** ★★★☆☆	Price $26.13 (as of Nov 23, 2007)	12-Mo. Target Price $30.00	Investment Style Large-Cap Growth

GICS Sector Information Technology
Sub-Industry Internet Software & Services

Summary This company is one of the world's largest providers of online content and services.

Key Stock Statistics (Source S&P, Vickers, company reports)

52-Wk Range	$34.08–22.27	S&P Oper. EPS 2007E	0.46	Market Capitalization(B)	$35.202	Beta	1.91
Trailing 12-Month EPS	$0.51	S&P Oper. EPS 2008E	0.60	Yield (%)	Nil	S&P 3-Yr. Proj. EPS CAGR(%)	17.00
Trailing 12-Month P/E	51.2	P/E on S&P Oper. EPS 2007E	56.8	Dividend Rate/Share	Nil	S&P Credit Rating	BBB-
$10K Invested 5 Yrs Ago	$28,402	Common Shares Outstg. (M)	1,347.2	Institutional Ownership (%)	72		

Price Performance

30-Week Mov. Avg. · · · 10-Week Mov. Avg. - - - **GAAP Earnings vs. Previous Year** Volume Above Avg. ▯▯▯▯ STARS
12-Mo. Target Price — Relative Strength — ▲ Up ▼ Down ▶ No Change Below Avg. ▯▯▯▯ ★

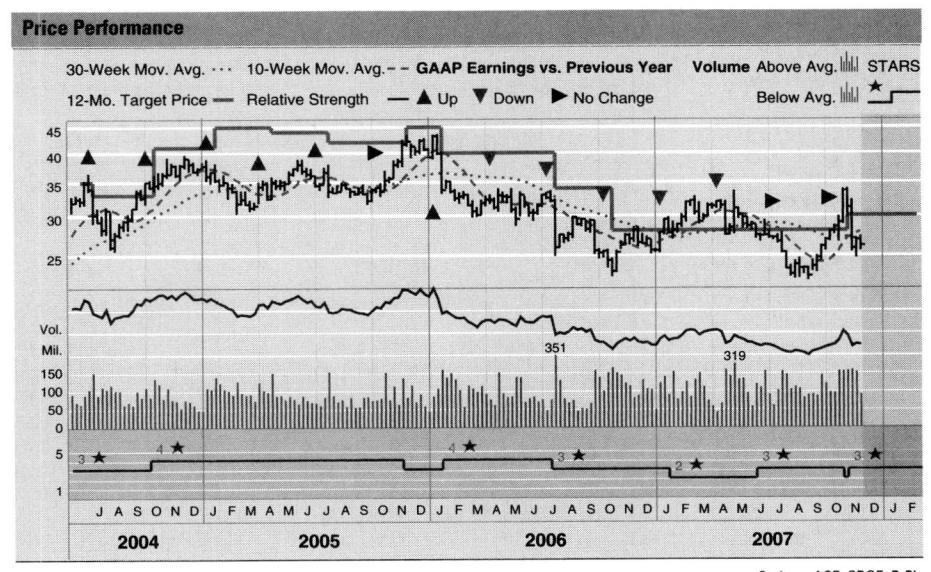

Options: ASE, CBOE, P, Ph

Analysis prepared by **Scott H. Kessler** on November 09, 2007, when the stock traded at **$ 25.48**.

Highlights

➤ We see revenues excluding traffic acquisition costs rising 13% in 2007 and 17% in 2008, reflecting the anticipated positive impact of Panama, YHOO's new search technology system. We expect that YHOO will increasingly focus on providing more holistic solutions, combining display and search advertising, premium and non-premium display offerings, and domestic and international options.

➤ We expect that revenues will continue to benefit from secular growth in online advertising. However, we would not be surprised if fee revenues or margins were hurt by revised terms related to YHOO's co-branded access services. We think operating margins bottomed in 2007, reflecting the benefits of Panama and YHOO's efforts to realign its operations.

➤ In July 2007, YHOO acquired the 20% of Right Media that it did not already own for $650 million. In September 2007, YHOO announced the proposed purchase of BlueLithium for about $300 million, and we expect consummation by December 2007, subject to approvals. We see these deals as aiding YHOO's non-premium display advertising initiative.

Investment Rationale/Risk

➤ We think an increasing percentage of advertising budgets are being spent online, and YHOO's global reach has appeal. However, we believe YHOO's failure to significantly capitalize on social networking and online video has negatively affected fundamentals, especially in display advertising. We think YHOO's increased awareness of its shortcomings and new emphasis on clear priorities are positives.

➤ Risks to our recommendation and target price include the possibility of increasing competition, material market share losses, and the value of YHOO's Alibaba investments appreciating less significantly than we expect.

➤ Our DCF model, which assumes a WACC of 11.6%, annual FCF growth averaging 23% from 2007 to 2011, and a terminal growth rate of 3%, yields an intrinsic value estimate of $17. Our relative P/E and P/E-to-growth analyses also lead to a price of $17, accounting for a modest premium to peer due to YHOO's strong brand and balance sheet, excluding the value of YHOO's minority stakes in four Asian businesses that we think are worth about $13. Given these considerations, our 12-month target price is $30.

Qualitative Risk Assessment

LOW	MEDIUM	**HIGH**

The company is a large and well-capitalized leader in a number of areas related to Internet content and services. However, in our view, the markets in which it participates change rapidly and have relatively low barriers to entry, which has contributed to the notable competition that we have observed.

Quantitative Evaluations

S&P Quality Ranking   **B**

D	C	B-	**B**	B+	A-	A	A+

Relative Strength Rank   **MODERATE**

57

LOWEST = 1   HIGHEST = 99

Revenue/Earnings Data

Revenue (Million $)

	1Q	2Q	3Q	4Q	Year
2007	1,672	1,015	1,768	--	--
2006	1,567	1,576	1,580	1,702	6,426
2005	1,174	1,253	1,330	1,501	5,258
2004	757.8	832.3	906.7	1,078	3,575
2003	283.0	321.4	356.8	663.9	1,625
2002	192.7	225.8	248.8	285.8	953.1

Earnings Per Share ($)

2007	0.10	0.11	0.11	E0.14	E0.46
2006	0.11	0.11	0.11	0.19	0.52
2005	0.14	0.51	0.17	0.46	1.28
2004	0.07	0.08	0.17	0.25	0.58
2003	0.04	0.04	0.05	0.06	0.19
2002	0.01	0.02	0.03	0.04	0.09

Fiscal year ended Dec. 31. Next earnings report expected: Late January. EPS Estimates based on S&P Operating Earnings; historical GAAP earnings are as reported.

Dividend Data

No cash dividends have been paid.

Yahoo! Inc

STANDARD &POOR'S

Business Summary November 09, 2007

CORPORATE OVERVIEW. Yahoo! is one of the world's largest Internet companies. Primary categories for its properties and services are Search and Marketplace (focused on areas including search, yellow pages, maps, real estate, shopping, auctions, travel, autos, HotJobs, and small business); Information and Content (including The Yahoo! Front Page; My Yahoo!; news and information related to finance, health, sports and entertainment; music; and games); and Communications and Consumer Services (premium Internet packages, e-mail, instant messaging, photo-sharing, community services, and dating services). YHOO's worldwide registered users (excluding the 34% stake in Yahoo! Japan as of December 2006, estimated 40% interest in Alibaba Group as of October 2007, estimated 30% holding in Alibaba.com as of October 2007, and 10% share of Gmarket as of March 2007) rose to 477 million as of September 2007, from 418 million a year earlier. Active registered users increased to 248 million, from 215 million.

In December 2006, YHOO announced a major business and management reorganization. The company was reconstituted in three groups: the Audience Group, the Advertiser & Publisher Group, and the Technology Group. Blake Jorgensen became CFO in June 2007. Soon thereafter, YHOO's new operating structure was tweaked somewhat, and co-founder and board member Jerry Yang replaced Terry Semel as CEO, and long-time CFO Sue Decker became President and COO. One-time COO Dan Rosensweig, CTO and Technology Group leader Farzad Nazem, and Chief Sales Officer Wenda Millard left the company in the first half of 2007. Other important executives have also left the company.

CORPORATE STRATEGY. In mid-2007, YHOO unveiled a new strategy intended in part to help the company deliver better financial performance. The company will be emphasizing three main areas of differentiation to strengthen and grow its ecosystem -- offering unique insights to its constituencies, promoting significant solution openness through its websites and platforms, and providing the most compelling options for partners. We believe these are reasonable priorities, and will enable the company to more effectively innovate and execute.

More importantly, in our view, YHOO also has set three primary multi-year objectives. First, the company wants to be the starting point for the most Internet consumers. Second, it wants to be a "must buy" for the most advertisers. Third, it wants to deliver industry-leading platforms that attract the most developers. We think this set of goals will enable the company to better streamline its operations and focus its investment.

Company Financials Fiscal Year Ended Dec. 31

Per Share Data ($)	2006	2005	2004	2003	2002	2001	2000	1999	1998	1997
Tangible Book Value	4.25	3.59	2.94	1.64	1.47	1.52	1.69	1.11	0.62	0.16
Cash Flow	0.89	1.54	0.79	0.31	0.18	0.03	0.11	0.09	0.04	-0.03
Earnings	0.52	1.28	0.58	0.19	0.09	-0.08	0.06	0.05	0.03	-0.03
S&P Core Earnings	0.51	0.56	0.24	0.03	-0.32	-0.85	NA	NA	NA	NA
Dividends	Nil	Nil	Nil	Nil	Nil	Nil	Nil	Nil	Nil	Nil
Payout Ratio	Nil	Nil	Nil	Nil	Nil	Nil	Nil	Nil	Nil	Nil
Prices:High	43.66	43.45	39.79	22.74	10.68	21.69	125.03	112.00	35.75	4.44
Prices:Low	22.65	30.30	20.57	8.25	4.47	4.01	12.53	27.50	3.60	0.70
P/E Ratio:High	84	34	69	NM	NM	NM	NM	NM	NM	NM
P/E Ratio:Low	44	24	35	NM	NM	NM	NM	NM	NM	NM

Income Statement Analysis (Million $)	2006	2005	2004	2003	2002	2001	2000	1999	1998	1997
Revenue	6,426	5,258	3,575	1,625	953	717	1,110	589	203	67.4
Operating Income	1,481	1,505	1,000	455	198	34.5	390	197	58.4	-0.95
Depreciation	540	397	311	160	109	131	69.1	42.3	10.2	2.55
Interest Expense	Nil	Nil	Nil	Nil	Nil	Nil	Nil	Nil	Nil	Nil
Pretax Income	293	2,672	1,280	391	180	-81.1	264	104	43.3	-23.6
Effective Tax Rate	NM	28.7%	34.2%	37.6%	39.7%	NM	71.2%	39.0%	41.1%	NM
Net Income	751	1,896	840	238	107	-92.8	70.8	61.1	25.6	-22.9
S&P Core Earnings	744	840	353	35.5	-377	-966	NA	NA	NA	NA

Balance Sheet & Other Financial Data (Million $)	2006	2005	2004	2003	2002	2001	2000	1999	1998	1997
Cash	2,601	2,561	3,512	1,310	774	926	1,120	872	433	156
Current Assets	3,750	3,450	4,090	1,722	970	1,052	1,291	946	467	107
Total Assets	11,514	10,832	9,178	5,932	2,790	2,379	2,270	1,470	622	142
Current Liabilities	1,474	1,204	1,181	708	412	359	311	192	80.0	23.5
Long Term Debt	750	750	750	750	Nil	Nil	Nil	Nil	Nil	Nil
Common Equity	9,161	8,566	7,101	4,363	2,262	1,967	1,897	1,261	536	118
Total Capital	9,919	9,316	7,896	5,151	2,294	1,997	1,926	1,265	540	118
Capital Expenditures	689	409	246	117	51.6	86.2	94.4	49.5	11.9	6.60
Cash Flow	1,291	2,293	1,151	398	216	37.8	140	103	35.8	-20.3
Current Ratio	2.5	2.9	3.5	2.4	2.4	2.9	4.1	4.9	5.8	4.6
% Long Term Debt of Capitalization	7.6	8.0	9.5	14.6	Nil	Nil	Nil	Nil	Nil	Nil
% Net Income of Revenue	11.7	36.0	23.5	14.6	11.2	NM	6.4	10.3	12.6	NM
% Return on Assets	6.7	18.9	11.1	5.5	4.1	NM	3.7	5.4	6.7	NM
% Return on Equity	8.5	24.2	14.6	7.2	5.1	NM	4.5	6.3	7.8	NM

Data as orig reptd.; bef. results of disc opers/spec. items. Per share data adj. for stk. divs.; EPS diluted. E-Estimated. NA-Not Available. NM-Not Meaningful. NR-Not Ranked. UR-Under Review.

Office: 701 First Avenue, Sunnyvale, CA 94089.
Telephone: 408-349-3300.
Email: investor_relations@yahoo-inc.com
Website: http://www.yahoo.com

Chrmn & CEO: J. Yang
Pres: S. Decker
CFO: B. Jorgensen
Chief Acctg Officer: M.J. Murray

Investor Contact: C. LaRocca (408-349-5188)
Board Members: R. Bostock, R. Burkle, E. Hippeau, V. Joshi, A. Kern, R. Kotick, E. Kozel, T. Semel, M. Wilderotter, G. Wilson, J. Yang

Founded: 1995
Domicile: Delaware
Employees: 11,400

The McGraw-Hill Companies

STANDARD &POOR'S

YUM! Brands Inc.

S&P Recommendation **BUY** ★★★★☆	Price $37.65 (as of Nov 23, 2007)	12-Mo. Target Price $45.00	Investment Style Large-Cap Growth

GICS Sector Consumer Discretionary
Sub-Industry Restaurants

Summary This company operates or franchises the largest number of fast food restaurants in the world, with nearly 35,000 units, including the KFC, Pizza Hut and Taco Bell chains.

Key Stock Statistics (Source S&P, Vickers, company reports)

52-Wk Range	$40.60–27.51	S&P Oper. EPS 2007E	1.66	Market Capitalization(B)	$19.149	Beta	0.92
Trailing 12-Month EPS	$1.65	S&P Oper. EPS 2008E	1.90	Yield (%)	1.59	S&P 3-Yr. Proj. EPS CAGR(%)	14.00
Trailing 12-Month P/E	22.8	P/E on S&P Oper. EPS 2007E	22.7	Dividend Rate/Share	$0.60	S&P Credit Rating	BBB-
$10K Invested 5 Yrs Ago	$33,009	Common Shares Outstg. (M)	508.6	Institutional Ownership (%)	85		

Price Performance

30-Week Mov. Avg. · · · 10-Week Mov. Avg. – – **GAAP Earnings vs. Previous Year** Volume Above Avg. STARS
12-Mo. Target Price — Relative Strength — ▲ Up ▼ Down ► No Change Below Avg. ★

2-for-1

Options: ASE, CBOE, Ph

Analysis prepared by **Mark S. Basham** on October 16, 2007, when the stock traded at **$37.32.**

Highlights

➤ YUM plans to open at least 1,000 restaurants annually, with a focus on international expansion. We expect 2007 systemwide sales to grow about 5%, paced by double digit international expansion and flat U.S. same-store sales. U.S. sales have been negatively affected by publicity regarding an E. coli outbreak and rat infestation that affected a number of restaurants. We see wider profit margins, primarily reflecting improving margins at international operations, with operating profit growth of 20% to 25% for the China division, and 12% to 14% for the Yum! Restaurants International division.

➤ We project 2007 EPS of $1.66, up 14% from $1.46 earned in 2006. Our estimate reflects expenses related to the E. coli outbreak at a number of mid-Atlantic Taco Bell restaurants of $0.02 and $0.03 in 2007 and 2006, respectively, as well as share buybacks in 2007 equal to 3.5% of the shares outstanding.

➤ For 2008, we forecast systemwide sales growth of about 7%, with China once again outpacing the International and U.S. divisions. Refranchising efforts, positive forex effects and further share buybacks will likely contribute to a 14% rise in EPS, to $1.90.

Investment Rationale/Risk

➤ We recently upgraded our opinion on the shares to buy, from hold, as we expect U.S. financial comparisons to be relatively stronger against weak second half results a year ago, which were hurt by negative fallout from food safety problems at a small number of locations. We think YUM can increase earnings per share by at least 10% annually over the next several years through global expansion, the refranchising of U.S. restaurants, and improvement in the profitability of its base global business.

➤ Risks to our recommendation and target price include potentially greater than expected increases in food and labor costs, currency exchange rate risk, and other political and operating risks associated with international expansion. In addition, effects from food safety issues may last longer and be worse than we expect.

➤ Our 12-month target price of $45 is based on our discounted cash flow analysis, which assumes a weighted average cost of capital of 8.6%, and free cash flow increases of 10% to 12% annually for the next five years, then gradually slowing to a terminal rate of 2%.

Qualitative Risk Assessment

LOW	MEDIUM	HIGH

YUM competes in the relatively stable fast food industry, in which its concepts possess a very strong brand name presence. However, operating margins can vary widely due to fluctuations in food costs. Furthermore, YUM's profits can be affected by changing currency exchange rates due to its large and fast growing international business.

Quantitative Evaluations

S&P Quality Ranking — B+

D	C	B-	B	**B+**	A-	A	A+

Relative Strength Rank — STRONG

88

LOWEST = 1   HIGHEST = 99

Revenue/Earnings Data

Revenue (Million $)

	1Q	2Q	3Q	4Q	Year
2007	2,223	2,367	2,564	--	--
2006	2,085	2,182	2,278	3,016	9,561
2005	2,054	2,153	2,243	2,899	9,349
2004	1,970	2,077	2,179	2,785	9,011
2003	1,802	1,936	1,989	2,653	8,380
2002	1,614	1,767	1,915	2,461	7,757

Earnings Per Share ($)

2007	0.35	0.39	0.50	E0.42	E1.66
2006	0.29	0.34	0.42	0.42	1.46
2005	0.25	0.29	0.35	0.39	1.28
2004	0.24	0.29	0.31	0.39	1.21
2003	0.20	0.20	0.26	0.35	1.01
2002	0.20	0.23	0.24	0.28	0.94

Fiscal year ended Dec. 31. Next earnings report expected: Mid February. EPS Estimates based on S&P Operating Earnings; historical GAAP earnings are as reported.

Dividend Data (Dates: mm/dd Payment Date: mm/dd/yy)

Amount ($)	Date Decl.	Ex-Div. Date	Stk. of Record	Payment Date
2-for-1	05/17	06/27	06/01	06/26/07
0.150	05/17	07/11	07/13	08/03/07
0.150	09/20	10/10	10/12	11/02/07
0.150	11/16	01/09	01/11	02/01/08

Dividends have been paid since 2004. Source: Company reports.

The **McGraw·Hill** Companies

YUM! Brands Inc.

STANDARD &POOR'S

Business Summary October 16, 2007

Yum! Brands has the world's largest quick service restaurant (QSR) system, with nearly 35,000 restaurants in more than 100 countries and territories. The company operates and franchises restaurants under the KFC, Pizza Hut, Taco Bell, Long John Silver's and A&W All American Food concepts. In 2006, the company's brands generated just over $30 billion in systemwide sales and $9.6 billion in worldwide revenues, up 2.3% from 2005.

KFC (originally Kentucky Fried Chicken) is the leader in the U.S. chicken QSR segment, with about a 46% market share during 2006 (45% in 2005). Systemwide sales totaled approximately $5.3 billion in the U.S. and $14.2 billion worldwide in 2006. At the end of 2006, KFC operated 5,394 units in the U.S. and 8,864 units internationally.

Pizza Hut is the world's largest restaurant chain specializing in ready-to-eat pizza products. In 2006, it led the U.S. pizza QSR segment with about a 15% market share (15% in 2005). Systemwide sales totaled $5.2 billion in the U.S. and $9.3 billion worldwide in 2006. As of December 2006, it operated 7,532 units in the U.S. and 5,153 units internationally.

Taco Bell is the leader in the U.S. Mexican food QSR segment, with about a

58% market share (65% in 2005). Systemwide sales totaled $6.3 billion in the U.S. and $6.5 billion worldwide in 2006. At the end of 2006, it operated 5,608 units in the U.S. and 236 units internationally.

In each concept, units are operated by the company as well as by independent franchisees, licensees, or unconsolidated affiliates. Over the past several years, YUM rebalanced its system toward increased franchisee ownership, to focus resources on growth opportunities. At the end of 2006, 22% of worldwide units were operated by YUM, 68% by franchisees, 6% by licensees, and 4% by unconsolidated affiliates. Company-owned units accounted for 87% of total revenues in 2006, compared to 88% in 2005..

The company intends to refranchise approximately 1,500 units by 2008, thereby reducing company ownership to about 17% of the U.S. system. During 2006, 452 company-owned U.S. restaurants were sold to franchisees.

Company Financials Fiscal Year Ended Dec. 31

Per Share Data ($)	2006	2005	2004	2003	2002	2001	2000	1999	1998	1997
Tangible Book Value	0.81	1.04	1.20	0.42	NM	NM	NM	NM	NM	NA
Cash Flow	2.46	2.07	1.95	1.67	1.54	1.39	1.29	1.58	1.38	0.70
Earnings	1.46	1.28	1.21	1.01	0.94	0.81	0.69	0.98	0.71	-0.18
S&P Core Earnings	1.51	1.26	1.15	1.04	0.80	0.68	NA	NA	NA	NA
Dividends	0.26	0.22	0.10	Nil	Nil	Nil	Nil	Nil	Nil	Nil
Payout Ratio	18%	17%	8%	Nil	Nil	Nil	Nil	Nil	Nil	Nil
Prices:High	31.84	26.90	23.74	17.71	16.58	13.33	9.64	18.47	12.72	9.06
Prices:Low	22.11	22.37	16.07	10.77	10.18	7.89	5.89	8.75	6.27	6.97
P/E Ratio:High	22	21	20	18	18	16	14	19	18	NM
P/E Ratio:Low	15	18	13	11	11	10	9	9	9	NM

Income Statement Analysis (Million $)	2006	2005	2004	2003	2002	2001	2000	1999	1998	1997
Revenue	9,561	9,349	9,011	8,380	7,757	6,953	7,093	7,822	8,468	9,681
Operating Income	1,724	1,538	1,518	1,471	1,375	1,220	1,217	1,280	1,185	1,198
Depreciation	479	469	448	401	370	354	354	386	417	536
Interest Expense	154	127	129	173	172	158	176	202	272	276
Pretax Income	1,108	1,026	1,026	886	858	733	684	1,038	756	-35.0
Effective Tax Rate	25.6%	25.7%	27.9%	30.2%	32.1%	32.9%	39.6%	39.6%	41.1%	NM
Net Income	824	762	740	618	583	492	413	627	445	-111
S&P Core Earnings	849	754	704	635	494	416	NA	NA	NA	NA

Balance Sheet & Other Financial Data (Million $)	2006	2005	2004	2003	2002	2001	2000	1999	1998	1997
Cash	319	158	62.0	192	130	110	133	89.0	121	268
Current Assets	901	837	747	806	730	547	688	486	625	683
Total Assets	6,353	5,698	5,696	5,620	5,400	4,388	4,149	3,961	4,531	5,098
Current Liabilities	1,724	1,605	1,376	1,461	1,520	1,805	1,216	1,298	1,473	1,579
Long Term Debt	2,045	1,649	1,731	2,056	2,299	1,552	2,397	2,391	3,436	4,551
Common Equity	1,437	1,449	1,595	1,120	594	104	-322	-560	-1,163	-1,620
Total Capital	3,482	3,098	3,326	3,176	2,893	1,656	2,085	1,838	2,338	2,964
Capital Expenditures	614	609	645	663	760	636	572	470	460	541
Cash Flow	1,303	1,231	1,188	1,019	953	846	767	1,013	862	425
Current Ratio	0.5	0.5	0.5	0.6	0.5	0.3	0.6	0.4	0.4	0.4
% Long Term Debt of Capitalization	58.7	53.2	52.0	64.7	79.5	93.7	115.0	130.1	147.0	153.5
% Net Income of Revenue	8.6	8.2	8.2	7.4	7.5	7.1	5.8	8.0	5.3	NM
% Return on Assets	13.6	13.4	13.1	11.2	11.9	11.5	10.2	14.8	9.2	NM
% Return on Equity	57.1	50.1	54.5	72.1	167.0	NM	NM	NM	NM	NM

Data as orig reptd.; bef. results of disc opers/spec. items. Per share data adj. for stk. divs.; EPS diluted. E-Estimated. NA-Not Available. NM-Not Meaningful. NR-Not Ranked. UR-Under Review.

Office: 1441 Gardiner Lane, Louisville, KY 40213.
Telephone: 502-874-8300.
Email: yum.investors@yum.com
Website: http://www.yum.com

Chrmn & CEO: D.C. Novak
COO: P. Hearl
SVP & CFO: R. Carucci
SVP, Secy & General Counsel: C.L. Campbell

SVP & Cntlr: T.F. Knopf
Investor Contact: Q. Nghe (502-874-8918)
Board Members: D. Dorman, M. Ferragamo, J. D. Grissom, B. G. Hill, R. Holland, Jr., K. G. Langone, J. Linen, T. C. Nelson, D. C. Novak, T. M. Ryan, J. Trujillo, R. J. Ulrich

Founded: 1997
Domicile: North Carolina
Employees: 280,000

The McGraw·Hill Companies

Zimmer Holdings Inc.

STANDARD &POOR'S

S&P Recommendation **BUY** ★★★★☆	Price $64.55 (as of Nov 23, 2007)	12-Mo. Target Price $77.00	Investment Style Large-Cap Growth

GICS Sector Health Care
Sub-Industry Health Care Equipment

Summary This company, spun off by Bristol-Myers Squibb in August 2001, manufactures orthopedic reconstructive implants, fracture management products and dental implants.

Key Stock Statistics (Source S&P, Vickers, company reports)

52-Wk Range	$94.38– 63.00	S&P Oper. EPS 2007 **E**	3.91	Market Capitalization(B)	$15.245	Beta	0.43
Trailing 12-Month EPS	$3.15	S&P Oper. EPS 2008 **E**	4.25	Yield (%)	Nil	S&P 3-Yr. Proj. EPS CAGR(%)	11.00
Trailing 12-Month P/E	20.5	P/E on S&P Oper. EPS 2007 **E**	16.5	Dividend Rate/Share	Nil	S&P Credit Rating	A-
$10K Invested 5 Yrs Ago	$16,577	Common Shares Outstg. (M)	236.2	Institutional Ownership (%)	78		

Price Performance

30-Week Mov. Avg. · · · 10-Week Mov. Avg. - - **GAAP Earnings vs. Previous Year** Volume Above Avg. |||| STARS
12-Mo. Target Price — Relative Strength — ▲ Up ▼ Down ► No Change Below Avg. |||| ★

Options: ASE, CBOE, P, Ph

Analysis prepared by **Robert M. Gold** on November 05, 2007, when the stock traded at **$ 68.25.**

Highlights

➤ We see 2008 revenues of $4.1 billion, up from an estimated $3.9 billion in 2007, which assumes reconstructive implant sales of about $3.5 billion (versus $3.3 billion in 2007), fracture management of $200 million ($205 million), spine of $190 million ($200 million) and other sales of $250 million ($230 million). We believe global pricing across the implant space will rise by about 1% in 2008.

➤ We believe competition in the hip business may impact unit pricing in this category during 2008, but we expect that gross margin pressures will be modest as new products are introduced and global pricing across the implant space rises modestly. However, we think operating margins in 2008 will be negatively impacted by higher R&D spending and costs associated with the recent settlement of a Department of Justice investigation on Zimmer and several of its peers which will include mandated federal oversight of its physician consulting practices. We think these costs will reduced 2008 earnings by about $0.12 a share.

➤ We see 2008 operating EPS of $4.25, up from a projected $3.91 in 2007, and believe Zimmer's long term growth rate will approximate 12%.

Investment Rationale/Risk

➤ Although we anticipate that the company will face challenges generating double digit sales and earnings growth in 2008, we think the long term demand drivers for its orthopedic implants remain in tact and believe unit pricing globally will remain favorable in 2008. In our view, the pace of new product rollouts in 2007 has been disappointing, especially in the hip and knee areas, but we think the pipeline remains among the best in our orthopedic device coverage universe.

➤ Risks to our recommendation and target price include unfavorable Medicare reimbursement changes and greater than expected device reimbursement cuts in key overseas markets, particularly Japan.

➤ Our 12-month target price is $77, or about 18X our 2008 EPS estimate and 1.5X on a forward P/E to growth basis, in line with peers. Although we believe competitive pressures, higher R&D spending, costs tied to the DoJ settlement and a higher tax rate will restrict EPS growth in 2008, we think low double-digit growth will be restored in 2009 as new products are introduced and costs associated with the DoJ settlement diminish.

Qualitative Risk Assessment

LOW	MEDIUM	HIGH

Our risk assessment reflects that Zimmer operates in a highly competitive industry characterized by relatively short product life cycles, thereby requiring a significant number of new product introductions to maintain market share and sustain gross profit margins. Many of the company's customers are reimbursed by the federal government through Medicare, and a more restrictive budgetary environment could, in our view, result in lower prices paid to medical device suppliers such as Zimmer. However, this is offset as we believe the company stands among the dominant manufacturers in the orthopedic device industry, with substantial global salesforce capabilities and an expansive product line.

Quantitative Evaluations

S&P Quality Ranking NR

D	C	B-	B	B+	A-	A	A+

Relative Strength Rank WEAK

24

LOWEST = 1   HIGHEST = 99

Revenue/Earnings Data

Revenue (Million $)

	1Q	2Q	3Q	4Q	Year
2007	950.2	970.6	903.2	--	--
2006	860.4	881.6	819.8	933.6	3,495
2005	828.5	846.8	762.5	848.3	3,286
2004	742.2	737.4	700.2	801.1	2,981
2003	390.1	411.1	398.2	701.6	1,901
2002	319.1	345.6	337.5	370.2	1,372

Earnings Per Share ($)

2007	0.98	0.97	0.19	E1.05	E3.91
2006	0.82	0.81	0.76	1.02	3.40
2005	0.70	0.76	0.67	0.80	2.93
2004	0.40	0.47	0.52	0.81	2.19
2003	0.41	0.45	0.43	0.15	1.38
2002	0.28	0.34	0.33	0.37	1.31

Fiscal year ended Dec. 31. Next earnings report expected: Late January. EPS Estimates based on S&P Operating Earnings; historical GAAP earnings are as reported.

Dividend Data

No cash dividends have been paid.

Zimmer Holdings Inc.

**STANDARD
&POOR'S**

Business Summary November 05, 2007

CORPORATE OVERVIEW. Zimmer Holdings primarily designs, develops, manufactures and markets orthopedic reconstructive implants and fracture management products. The former division of Bristol-Myers Squibb was spun off to BMY shareholders in August 2001.

Zimmer's reconstructive implants (83% of 2006 sales) are used to restore function lost due to disease or trauma in joints such as knees, hips, shoulders and elbows. The company offers a wide range of products for specialized knee procedures, including The NexGen Complete Knee Solution, NexGen Legacy, NexGen Revision Knee, Innex Total Knee System, M/G Unicompartmental Knee System, and Prolong Highly Crosslinked Polyethylene Articular Surface material. Hip replacement products include the VerSys Hip System, the ZMR Hip System, the Trilogy Acetabular System and a line of specialty hip products. The company also continues to develop a portfolio of minimally invasive hip replacement procedures. ZMH sells the Coonrad/Morrey product line of elbow replacement implant products, along with a line of restorative dental products.

In the spine/trauma area (11%), the company sells devices used to reattach or stabilize damaged bone and tissue to support the body's natural healing process. The most common stabilization of bone fractures concerns the internal fixation of bone fragments, which can involve the use of an assortment of plates, screws, rods, wires and pins. ZMH offers a line of products designed for use in fracture fixation.

ZMH makes and markets other orthopedic surgical products (6%) used by surgeons for orthopedic as well as non-orthopedic procedures. Products include tourniquets, blood management systems, wound debridgement products, powered surgical instruments, pain management devices, and orthopedic soft goods that provide support and/or heat retention and compression for trauma of the knee, ankle, back and upper extremities, including the shoulder, elbow, neck and wrist.

Company Financials Fiscal Year Ended Dec. 31

Per Share Data ($)	2006	2005	2004	2003	2002	2001	2000	1999	1998	1997
Tangible Book Value	7.15	7.94	2.52	0.38	1.88	0.41	NM	NA	NA	NA
Cash Flow	4.21	3.68	2.92	1.87	1.43	0.89	0.92	NA	NA	NA
Earnings	3.40	2.93	2.19	1.38	1.31	0.77	0.81	NA	NA	NA
S&P Core Earnings	3.36	2.73	2.08	1.31	1.24	0.70	NA	NA	NA	NA
Dividends	Nil	Nil	Nil	Nil	Nil	Nil	NA	NA	NA	NA
Payout Ratio	Nil	Nil	Nil	Nil	Nil	Nil	NA	NA	NA	NA
Prices:High	79.11	89.10	89.44	71.85	43.00	33.30	NA	NA	NA	NA
Prices:Low	52.20	60.19	64.40	38.02	28.00	24.70	NA	NA	NA	NA
P/E Ratio:High	23	30	41	52	33	43	NA	NA	NA	NA
P/E Ratio:Low	15	21	29	28	21	32	NA	NA	NA	NA

Income Statement Analysis (Million $)

	2006	2005	2004	2003	2002	2001	2000	1999	1998	1997
Revenue	3,495	3,286	2,981	1,901	1,372	1,179	1,041	NA	NA	NA
Operating Income	1,369	1,297	1,026	633	426	272	291	NA	NA	NA
Depreciation	197	186	181	103	25.0	23.4	23.0	NA	NA	NA
Interest Expense	4.00	14.0	32.0	13.0	12.0	7.40	29.0	NA	NA	NA
Pretax Income	1,169	1,040	732	438	389	241	239	NA	NA	NA
Effective Tax Rate	28.5%	29.5%	25.9%	33.6%	33.7%	37.8%	34.3%	NA	NA	NA
Net Income	835	733	542	291	258	150	157	NA	NA	NA
S&P Core Earnings	823	682	515	277	244	137	NA	NA	NA	NA

Balance Sheet & Other Financial Data (Million $)

	2006	2005	2004	2003	2002	2001	2000	1999	1998	1997
Cash	266	233	155	78.0	16.0	18.4	50.0	NA	NA	NA
Current Assets	1,746	1,576	1,561	1,339	612	509	487	NA	NA	NA
Total Assets	5,974	5,722	5,696	5,156	859	745	669	NA	NA	NA
Current Liabilities	628	607	701	645	401	373	217	NA	NA	NA
Long Term Debt	100	82.0	624	1,008	Nil	214	500	NA	NA	NA
Common Equity	4,921	4,683	3,943	3,143	366	78.7	-48.0	NA	NA	NA
Total Capital	5,024	4,767	4,574	4,158	366	293	452	NA	NA	NA
Capital Expenditures	142	105	101	45.0	34.0	54.7	NA	NA	NA	NA
Cash Flow	1,032	919	723	394	283	173	180	NA	NA	NA
Current Ratio	2.8	2.6	2.2	2.1	1.5	1.4	2.2	NA	NA	NA
% Long Term Debt of Capitalization	1.9	1.7	13.6	24.2	Nil	73.0	110.6	NA	NA	NA
% Net Income of Revenue	23.8	22.3	18.1	15.3	18.9	12.7	15.1	NA	NA	NA
% Return on Assets	14.2	12.8	9.9	9.7	32.1	22.4	NA	NA	NA	NA
% Return on Equity	17.3	16.9	15.2	10.6	115.0	NM	NA	NA	NA	NA

Data as orig reptd.; bef. results of disc opers/spec. items. Per share data adj. for stk. divs.; EPS diluted. E-Estimated. NA-Not Available. NM-Not Meaningful. NR-Not Ranked. UR-Under Review.

Office: 345 East Main Street, Warsaw, IN 46580.
Telephone: 574-267-6131.
Email: zimmer.infoperson@zimmer.com
Website: http://www.zimmer.com

Chrmn: J.R. Elliott
Pres & CEO: D.C. Dvorak
EVP & CFO: J.T. Crines
SVP & CSO: C.R. Blanchard

Secy: C.F. Phipps
Board Members: D. C. Dvorak, J. R. Elliott, S. M. Essig, L. C. Glasscock, A. J. Higgins, J. L. McGoldrick, A. A. White, III

Founded: 1927
Domicile: Delaware
Employees: 6,900

The McGraw-Hill Companies

Zions BanCorp

STANDARD &POOR'S

S&P Recommendation HOLD ★★★☆☆	**Price** $52.00 (as of Nov 23, 2007)	**12-Mo. Target Price** $70.00	**Investment Style** Large-Cap Blend

GICS Sector Financials
Sub-Industry Regional Banks

Summary ZION has more than 500 full-service banking offices in 10 western states. At September 30, 2007, it had assets of $50.1 billion and deposits of $35.8 billion.

Key Stock Statistics (Source S&P, Vickers, company reports)

52-Wk Range	$88.56– 48.51	S&P Oper. EPS 2007**E**	5.29	Market Capitalization(B)	$5.618	Beta	0.46
Trailing 12-Month EPS	$5.33	S&P Oper. EPS 2008**E**	5.45	Yield (%)	3.31	S&P 3-Yr. Proj. EPS CAGR(%)	2.70
Trailing 12-Month P/E	9.8	P/E on S&P Oper. EPS 2007**E**	9.8	Dividend Rate/Share	$1.72	S&P Credit Rating	BBB+
$10K Invested 5 Yrs Ago	$13,903	Common Shares Outstg. (M)	108.0	Institutional Ownership (%)	58		

Price Performance

30-Week Mov. Avg. · · · 10-Week Mov. Avg. - - GAAP Earnings vs. Previous Year   Volume Above Avg. STARS
12-Mo. Target Price — Relative Strength — ▲ Up ▼ Down ► No Change   Below Avg. ★

Options: CBOE, Ph

Analysis prepared by **Erik Oja** on November 14, 2007, when the stock traded at **$ 56.34**.

Highlights

➤ Our 2008 forecasts for ZION are: loan growth of about 5.5%, a 10 basis point reduction in net interest margin (NIM) to 4.34%, net interest income growth of 4.1%, and non-interest income growth of 3.1%, leading to revenue growth of 3.9%. For 2007, we expect ZION to record a NIM of 4.44%, among the highest in the industry, but down 19 basis points from 2006's 4.63%, due to our expectation that loan yields will begin to decline before funding costs will.

➤ Until the 2007 third quarter, ZION's credit quality was among the best in the regional banking industry. With the increase in non-performing loans to 0.49% of total loans at September 30, from 0.23% at June 30, we think ZION will take higher loan loss provisioning expenses in 2008 than we had previously expected. We now see loan loss provisions of $167 million in 2008, up 36% from our estimate of $123 million in 2007, and $72.5 million in 2006.

➤ We recently reduced our EPS estimates for 2007 and 2008, primarily due to our increased estimates of loan loss provisioning. We now project operating EPS of $5.29 in 2007, down 1.3% from 2006's $5.36, and forecast 2008 EPS of $5.45, an increase of 3.0%.

Investment Rationale/Risk

➤ We are cautious about ZION in the wake of third-quarter 2007 results, which included a large increase in non-performing loans and an accompanying increase in loan loss provisioning, plus the expense of purchasing asset-backed commercial paper from Lockhart Funding during the recent disruptions to the credit markets. ZION currently trades at 10.4X our 2008 EPS estimate of $5.45, down significantly from the 14.5X forward multiple the shares traded at earlier this year.

➤ Risks to our recommendation and target price include an economic slowdown adversely affecting loan growth, credit quality, and fee income growth.

➤ Our 12-month target price of $70 is based on a forward P/E multiple of 12.8X our 2008 EPS estimate of $5.45, above the 12.0X multiple at which we estimate ZION's mid-cap regional banking peers currently trade. We believe this premium valuation is warranted by our expectation that ZION's lending margins will remain among the highest in the industry in 2008, and that ZION has taken aggressive steps to restore credit quality.

Qualitative Risk Assessment

LOW	MEDIUM	HIGH

Our risk assessment reflects the strong credit quality of the company's loan portfolio, and its history of profitability. While the company operates in a highly competitive and fragmented industry, companies in the industry tend to produce relatively stable financial results.

Quantitative Evaluations

S&P Quality Ranking   A

D	C	B-	B	B+	A-	**A**	A+

Relative Strength Rank   WEAK

18

LOWEST = 1   HIGHEST = 99

Revenue/Earnings Data

Revenue (Million $)

	1Q	2Q	3Q	4Q	Year
2007	915.9	931.0	963.6	--	--
2006	767.1	824.1	876.9	901.2	3,369
2005	525.8	562.3	594.5	666.5	2,349
2004	457.4	469.8	492.6	503.3	1,923
2003	445.7	454.3	539.6	449.8	1,889
2002	460.8	472.7	441.4	462.2	1,833

Earnings Per Share ($)

2007	1.36	1.43	1.22	E1.34	E5.29
2006	1.28	1.35	1.42	1.32	5.36
2005	1.20	1.30	1.34	1.32	5.16
2004	1.10	1.09	1.13	1.15	4.47
2003	0.96	1.02	0.71	1.05	3.74
2002	0.89	0.92	0.71	0.92	3.44

Fiscal year ended Dec. 31. Next earnings report expected: Late January. EPS Estimates based on S&P Operating Earnings; historical GAAP earnings are as reported.

Dividend Data (Dates: mm/dd Payment Date: mm/dd/yy)

Amount ($)	Date Decl.	Ex-Div. Date	Stk. of Record	Payment Date
0.390	01/29	02/05	02/07	02/21/07
0.430	05/04	05/08	05/09	05/23/07
0.430	07/20	08/06	08/08	08/22/07
0.430	10/29	11/05	11/07	11/21/07

Dividends have been paid since 1966. Source: Company reports.

Please read the Required Disclosures and Analyst Certification on the last page of this report.

The McGraw-Hill Companies

Zions BanCorp

STANDARD &POOR'S

Business Summary November 14, 2007

CORPORATE OVERVIEW. ZION is a financial holding company that operates eight different banks in 10 western states, with each bank operating as an individual segment under a different name and management. In addition, the company's Other segment contains the parent company operations, certain nonbank subsidiaries and operating units, The Commerce Bank of Oregon, and eliminations of transactions between segments.

The company's largest bank, Zions First National Bank, serves Utah and Idaho and accounted for 31% of loans and 29% of deposits at year-end 2006. ZFNB also houses the company's capital markets and wealth management operations. California Bank & Trust (24% of loans and 23% of deposits) serves California and has loan production offices in Arizona, Colorado, Florida, Georgia, Illinois, Michigan, Missouri, Nevada, Ohio, Oregon and Washington. Amegy Corporation (18% of loans and 22% of deposits), acquired in December 2005, serves Houston and Dallas, Texas. National Bank of Arizona (12% of loans and

10% of deposits) serves the Phoenix and Tucson metropolitan areas. Nevada State Bank (9% of loans and 9% of deposits) serves the state of Nevada. Vectra Bank Colorado (5% of loans and 5% of deposits) serves Colorado. The Commerce Bank of Washington (1% of loans and 2% of deposits) has one office in the Seattle area serving businesses, executives, and professionals.

The company tries to control risks by maintaining formal loan policies and procedures, independent compliance examinations of adherence to the policies and procedures, performing portfolio risk analysis, using financial instruments to reduce interest rate risk, and by pursuing a loan portfolio diversification strategy.

Company Financials Fiscal Year Ended Dec. 31

Per Share Data ($)	2006	2005	2004	2003	2002	2001	2000	1999	1998	1997
Tangible Book Value	25.15	20.45	23.29	20.96	17.21	15.19	13.06	11.61	9.44	7.76
Earnings	5.36	5.16	4.47	3.74	3.44	3.15	1.86	2.26	1.91	1.89
S&P Core Earnings	5.36	5.04	4.33	4.42	3.17	2.42	NA	NA	NA	NA
Dividends	1.47	1.44	1.26	1.02	0.80	0.80	0.89	0.86	0.52	0.58
Payout Ratio	27%	28%	28%	27%	23%	25%	48%	38%	27%	30%
Prices:High	85.25	77.67	69.29	63.86	59.65	64.00	62.88	75.88	62.50	46.00
Prices:Low	75.13	63.33	54.08	39.31	34.14	42.30	32.00	48.25	37.88	25.44
P/E Ratio:High	16	15	16	17	17	20	34	34	33	24
P/E Ratio:Low	14	12	12	11	10	13	17	21	20	13

Income Statement Analysis (Million $)										
Net Interest Income	1,765	1,361	1,174	1,095	1,035	950	803	741	544	352
Tax Equivalent Adjustment	24.3	21.1	NA	NA	NA	NA	NA	16.2	8.84	6.90
Non Interest Income	527	439	425	426	402	388	274	270	199	143
Loan Loss Provision	72.6	43.0	44.1	69.9	71.9	73.2	31.8	18.0	12.2	6.18
% Expense/Operating Revenue	57.4%	56.4%	57.8%	63.7%	59.8%	63.9%	75.9%	66.4%	68.3%	60.9%
Pretax Income	913	742	624	546	481	440	243	309	218	188
Effective Tax Rate	34.8%	35.5%	35.3%	39.1%	34.9%	35.8%	32.8%	35.5%	32.5%	34.8%
Net Income	583	480	406	340	317	290	162	194	147	122
% Net Interest Margin	4.63	4.58	4.32	4.45	4.56	4.64	4.27	4.31	4.60	4.27
S&P Core Earnings	579	469	394	402	292	223	NA	NA	NA	NA

Balance Sheet & Other Financial Data (Million $)										
Money Market Assets	369	667	593	569	543	280	528	525	804	898
Investment Securities	6,790	6,996	5,786	5,402	4,238	3,463	4,188	4,437	3,488	2,629
Commercial Loans	27,559	23,122	16,337	10,404	13,648	4,110	3,615	3,311	2,905	1,393
Other Loans	7,260	7,131	6,395	9,613	5,195	13,304	10,843	9,133	7,777	3,521
Total Assets	46,970	42,780	31,470	28,558	26,566	24,304	21,939	20,281	16,649	9,522
Demand Deposits	25,869	9,954	6,822	5,883	5,117	4,481	3,586	3,277	3,170	1,783
Time Deposits	9,113	22,689	16,471	15,014	15,015	13,361	11,484	10,786	8,622	5,071
Long Term Debt	2,495	2,746	1,919	1,843	1,310	781	420	453	511	470
Common Equity	4,747	4,237	2,790	2,540	2,374	2,281	1,779	1,660	1,014	655
% Return on Assets	1.3	1.3	2.0	1.2	1.2	1.3	0.8	1.0	1.1	1.5
% Return on Equity	12.9	13.7	15.2	13.8	13.6	14.3	9.4	12.5	17.6	21.0
% Loan Loss Reserve	1.1	1.1	1.2	0.9	1.4	1.5	1.3	1.6	1.9	1.7
% Loans/Deposits	99.1	92.3	97.1	142.6	96.0	97.0	96.6	91.0	79.8	71.1
% Equity to Assets	10.0	9.5	13.3	8.9	9.2	8.8	8.1	8.1	6.4	7.3

Data as orig reptd.; bef. results of disc opers/spec. items. Per share data adj. for stk. divs.; EPS diluted. E-Estimated. NA-Not Available. NM-Not Meaningful. NR-Not Ranked. UR-Under Review.

Office: 1 S Main St 15th Fl, Salt Lake City, UT, USA 84111-1904.
Telephone: 801-524-4787.
Website: http://www.zionsbancorporation.com
Chrmn, Pres & CEO: H.H. Simmons

Vice Chrmn & CFO: D. Arnold
Investor Contact: C.B. Hinckley (801-524-4787)
SVP & Cntlr: N.X. Bellon
General Counsel: T. Laursen

Board Members: D. L. Arnold, J. C. Atkin, R. D. Cash, P. Frobes, J. D. Heaney, R. B. Porter, S. D. Quinn, H. H. Simmons, L. E. Simmons, S. C. Wheelbright, S. T. Williams

Founded: 1961
Domicile: Utah
Employees: 10,618

The McGraw-Hill Companies